O'Connor's California Practice Civil Pretrial

2015 Editors

David I. Levine
University of California Hastings College of the Law

Hon. Michol O'Connor (Ret.)
Jones McClure Publishing

William R. Slomanson
Thomas Jefferson School of Law

Jones McClure Publishing
Houston, Texas

O'Connor's California Litigation Series
Suggested cite form: *O'Connor's California Practice * Civil Pretrial* (2015)

Jones McClure Publishing
Product List

Mailing address:
P.O. Box 3348
Houston, TX 77253-3348

Shipping address:
2160 Taylor St.
Houston, TX 77007

Phone: (713) 335-8200
(800) OCONNOR (626-6667)
Fax: (713) 335-8201

www.JonesMcClure.com

Print date: March 13, 2015
Printed in the United States of America

ISBN 978-1-59839-212-8

This book is intended to provide attorneys with current information about selected California cases, rules, and statutes. The information in this book, however, may not be sufficient in dealing with a client's particular legal problem, and Jones McClure Publishing, David I. Levine, Michol O'Connor, and William R. Slomanson do not warrant or represent its suitability for this purpose. Attorneys using this book do so with the understanding that the information published in it should not be relied on as a substitute for independent research using original sources of authority.

Subscription Notice: This book is updated periodically to reflect current law. When you order this book, you can choose to be enrolled in our subscription program, which entitles you to a lower annual price. Before we send you an updated book, we send you a letter confirming that you want the new edition. You have the option at that time to change or cancel your order. If you do not change or cancel your order, the book will be shipped to you. If you decide to return the book, the return postage is your responsibility. If you did not purchase this book directly from Jones McClure Publishing, you are not registered as a subscriber and will not receive this update service. You can change your subscription status at any time in writing.

Introduction

If this is your first time using ***O'Connor's California Practice * Civil Pretrial***, let us start out by telling you how the book is organized. The first part of the book is the commentaries, which are organized around the development of a lawsuit, beginning with a general overview and the pleadings; progressing through pretrial motions, discovery, and subpoenas; and ending with nontrial dispositions. The commentaries contain thousands of citations to statutes, court rules, cases, and the most popular secondary sources, such as those by California Education for the Bar, Rutter Group, and Witkin Legal Institute.

The second part of the book is an annotated California Evidence Code that also includes all the California Law Revision Commission comments. In creating the headings for the Code, we tried to follow Bryan Garner's *Guidelines for Drafting & Editing Court Rules* to give you a better roadmap for locating the code provisions and understanding their scope. In almost all the case annotations, we directly quoted the court's opinion rather than paraphrasing it. So if the judge asks you, "What exactly did the court say in *Smith v. Jones*, counselor?," you can quote the court verbatim.

With each new edition of the book, we strive to improve the quality of the commentaries and code annotations and to make the book more useful overall. Here are some highlights from the 2015 edition:

- We updated the commentaries to incorporate amendments to statutes (including the Civil Code, Code of Civil Procedure, Evidence Code, and Government Code), the Rules of Court, Judicial Council Forms, and more. We marked discussions that incorporate legislative or rule changes with ⑮ in the margin to draw your attention to the change and to alert you to the year in which it took effect.
- We updated the Evidence Code to incorporate amendments from 2014 legislation. Amended sections are marked with Ⓐ, enacted sections are marked with Ⓔ, new text is underlined, and deleted text is ~~struck through~~.
- We updated the commentaries and the Evidence Code annotations with new case law from 2014 and the beginning of 2015.
- We revised and expanded the chart that lists common filing fees. See "Common Fees," chart 1-4, p. 58.
- We added a section on sanctions for bad-faith actions or tactics under CCP §128.5. Before January 1, 2015, §128.5 only applied to anti-SLAPP motions and proceedings initiated on or before December 31, 1994. Now, §128.5 sanctions are available in all civil actions. See "Bad-Faith Actions or Tactics – Frivolous or Intended to Cause Delay," ch. 5-K, §3, p. 576.
- We added a discussion of the recent U.S. Supreme Court decision in ***Daimler AG v. Bauman*** (2014) ___ U.S. ___, 134 S.Ct. 746, as it relates to the use of agency to acquire personal jurisdiction over a nonresident corporate defendant. See "Agency," ch. 3-G, §6.1.1(2), p. 289.
- We revised the discussion of the exhaustion-of-administrative-remedies doctrine and how it relates to a court's subject-matter jurisdiction over a case. See "Note," ch. 3-A , §2.3, p. 190; "Cases within exclusive administrative jurisdiction," ch. 3-E, §2.2.3, p. 249.
- We expanded and clarified the discussion of confidential intent for purposes of the marital-communications privilege. See "Made in confidence," ch. 6-D, §2.3.3, p. 660.
- We added timetables to help calculate deadlines for a defendant's time to answer a complaint and a defendant's motion to transfer venue. See Timetables, beginning on p. 1433.

We hope that ***O'Connor's California Practice*** will become your first source for pretrial procedure. To make sure that happens, we want to know what you think about the book. So please send us your comments early and often, and we will work hard to meet—and beat—your expectations.

CONVENTIONS

In writing this book, we have tried to produce a plain-English reference guide that is easy for attorneys and judges to use. To this end, we should point out a few things about the book. First, the Evidence Code is in double columns so it can be instantly distinguished from the commentaries. Second, we supply page headers and side-tabs for quick reference. Third, when other sections of this book are relevant, we cross-reference them. Fourth, we include practice tips and caution notes that are separate from the main text so they can be easily spotted. Fifth, the amendments to the Code of Civil Procedure, Evidence Code, and Rules of Court discussed in the commentaries are marked with ⓯ to draw the reader's attention to the change. In the Evidence Code, amended code sections are marked with Ⓐ, enacted code sections are marked with Ⓔ, new text is underlined, deleted text is ~~struck through~~, and code sections that are scheduled to sunset before the next edition of this book is published are marked with 💣.

To reduce gender-specific language, we refer to trial judges as the "trial court" and to most parties as "it" as if the parties were corporations, which they often are. When gender-specific language cannot be avoided, we use the feminine pronoun. In citing California cases, statutes, and rules, we follow the *California Style Manual* (4th ed. 2000) as closely as possible, but we vary from it occasionally to make reading easier. For example, we have added district numbering for court-of-appeals cases and omitted "supra" designations in short citations. We have also abbreviated code and rule titles. Most significantly, we have abbreviated the Code of Civil Procedure as "CCP," California Rules of Court as "CRC," and Federal Rules of Civil Procedure as "FRCP." When you cite cases, rules, and statutes in a motion or brief, we suggest you use the more traditional citation forms contained in the *California Style Manual*.

ABOUT THE 2015 EDITORS

David I. Levine is a Professor of Law at the University of California Hastings College of the Law in San Francisco, specializing in civil procedure and remedies. Before joining the faculty at Hastings, Professor Levine served as a law clerk to Judge Alvin B. Rubin of the Fifth Circuit United States Court of Appeals and was an associate in the litigation department of Morrison & Foerster LLP in San Francisco. He served as Associate Academic Dean from 1989 to 1991 and is the adviser for the Civil Litigation Concentration. He is coauthor or coeditor of seven books, including *Remedies: Public and Private* and *California Civil Procedure*, as well as the author of articles on civil procedure, torts, and institutional reform litigation. ***O'Connor's California Practice*** is his fourth work in the field of California civil procedure.

Justice Michol O'Connor began her legal career as an Assistant U.S. Attorney for the Southern District of Texas and then practiced trial and appellate law in the private sector. She was later elected to the First Court of Appeals in Houston, Texas, and served there for over a decade. While on the bench, Justice O'Connor recognized that practicing lawyers needed a dependable go-to resource for questions about procedure. The legal-reference market at the time was flooded with expensive multivolume treatises that were difficult to navigate and understand. Having already established herself as a respected author and lecturer through State Bar legal-education programs, Justice O'Connor focused her efforts on creating an entirely new kind of law book—an affordable one-volume reference manual that was reliable, written in plain English, and organized in the way lawyers actually practiced. With her first book, ***O'Connor's Texas Rules * Civil Trials***, she changed the way lawyers practice in Texas. Since her retirement from the bench, Justice O'Connor's publishing company has grown to produce over two dozen titles covering a variety of substantive and procedural topics—all of which continue to fill the need she recognized two decades ago. Today, lawyers across the country trust the ***O'Connor's*** series as their first source for the law.

William R. Slomanson is a Professor of Law at Thomas Jefferson School of Law (San Diego) and a Visiting Professor at Pristina University (Kosovo). He specializes in civil procedure and international law. He was an attorney for a Los Angeles insurance defense firm before joining the Thomas Jefferson School of Law faculty. He was appointed Editor of the American Society of International Law United Nations section (1992-2012), and served as section chair from 1995 to 2006. In 1999, he was appointed to the California Law Revision Commission's Civil Procedure Panel of Experts. He has published extensively in the fields of civil procedure and international law, having authored or coauthored 25 books for various legal publishers. His coauthored classroom text and individually authored *Califor-*

nia Civil Procedure in a Nutshell are used by numerous law schools in California. He has lectured at law schools or legal conferences in Armenia, Belgium, Canada, China, Cuba, England, France, Georgia, Greece, Hungary, Ireland, Kosovo, Mexico, Nagorno-Karabakh, the Netherlands, Russia, Spain, Turkey, Ukraine, and at various locations in the United States.

YOUR SUGGESTIONS

We welcome your comments. If you think we should have included (or excluded) something, or if you see anything that needs to be corrected, please let us know. Send your comments to the mailing address or fax number shown on the copyright page, or by e-mail to James Hancock, Assistant Managing Legal Editor, at jhancock@jonesmcclure.com.

CAVEAT

This book provides citations to important opinions that interpret the California Code of Civil Procedure, California Evidence Code, and California Rules of Court through February 20, 2015. All websites cited or referenced throughout the book are current through February 20, 2015. You may disagree with our explanations of the cases, statutes, and rules cited in this book. You should therefore use this book only as a research guide. Read the cases, statutes, and rules yourself and make your own evaluation of them.

EDITORIAL & PRODUCTION STAFF

As always, the staff of Jones McClure worked hard to prepare this publication, both in its substance and in its layout. The people who worked on this edition of ***O'Connor's California Practice * Civil Pretrial*** are listed below.

EXECUTIVE EDITOR
Jason E. Wilson, J.D.

MANAGING LEGAL EDITOR
Jessica Ryan Luna, J.D.

ASSITANT MANAGING LEGAL EDITOR
James Hancock, J.D.

SENIOR DEVELOPMENT EDITORS
Hoang Thi Dang, J.D.
Vincent Lorino, J.D.

LEGAL EDITORS
Courtney J. Drake, J.D.
Kristen N. Ellis, J.D.
Jessica Younger Field, J.D.
Sarah Arocha Ostriyznick, J.D.
John Passmore, J.D.
Kristen K. Sheils, J.D.

LEGAL EDITORIAL ASSISTANTS
Jessica Chomitzky, J.D.
Blake Freeny
Erin Gage, J.D.
Monica A. Garza, J.D.
Holly C. Gummert
Jordyn Johnson, J.D.
Lauren Males
Stephanie R. Marrone, J.D.

PRODUCTION MANAGER
Beverly B. Bellot

PRODUCTION EDITOR
Sara Y. Rhodes

PRODUCTION STAFF
Danielle E. Boss
Jessica Crisp
Abigail L. Endler
Nicole E. Hammond
Clare Jensen
Sara C. Rolater
Sarah M. Rutledge
Daniel Spence
Jenny Sulak
Donna E. Vass
Annabelle M. Wilde

COPYEDITORS
Danielle E. Boss
Annabelle M. Wilde

PROOFREADER
Sarah M. Rutledge

MICHOL O'CONNOR
Houston, Texas

Master Table of Contents

CONTENTS

CALIFORNIA CIVIL PRETRIAL
CHAPTER 1. GENERAL CONCEPTS
TABLE OF CONTENTS

CALIFORNIA CIVIL PRETRIAL
CHAPTER 1. GENERAL CONCEPTS
TABLE OF CONTENTS

CHAPTER 1. GENERAL CONCEPTS
TABLE OF CONTENTS

1. GENERAL CONCEPTS

A. INTRODUCTION TO CALIFORNIA CIVIL PROCEDURE

There are four main sources of authority for civil procedure in California: the Code of Civil Procedure, the Evidence Code, the California Rules of Court, and local rules adopted by individual superior courts.

§1. CODE OF CIVIL PROCEDURE

In 1872, the California Legislature enacted the Code of Civil Procedure. *See* CCP §2. The Code of Civil Procedure applies to all civil actions and civil special proceedings in California state courts. *See id.* §30 (definition of "civil action"), §31 (Penal Code governs criminal actions); *see, e.g.*, ***People v. Superior Ct.*** (2001) 25 Cal.4th 703, 727 (CCP §639 does not apply to special proceeding of criminal nature); ***Gonzales v. Superior Ct.*** (1935) 3 Cal.2d 260, 263 (CCP §473 applies only to civil cases); ***321 Henderson Receivables Origination LLC v. Tomahawk*** (5th Dist.2009) 172 Cal.App.4th 290, 301 (CCP §581 applies to special proceedings, which include proceedings for approval of structured-settlement payment transfers under Structured Settlement Transfer Act). The Legislature amends the Code of Civil Procedure based on the recommendation of the California Law Revision Commission. *See* Gov. C. §§8291, 8292. The Commission is charged with reviewing the Code of Civil Procedure and related case law and recommending revisions and amendments. Gov. C. §8289. California legislative sessions last two years and convene at noon on the first Monday in December of each even-numbered year and adjourn at midnight on November 30 of the following even-numbered year. Cal. Const., art. IV, §3(a). For a history of the development of the Code of Civil Procedure from 1872 to 1954, see Miller, *History of the California Code of Civil Procedure*, 23 West's Ann. Cal. Codes 1-44 (1955).

§2. EVIDENCE CODE

In 1965, the California Legislature enacted the Evidence Code. 7 Cal. Law Revision Comm'n Rep. (1965) p. 1007. The Evidence Code applies to all civil actions and proceedings. *See* Evid. C. §300 (Evidence Code applies to all actions except grand-jury proceedings); *see also id.* §105 (defining "action" to include both civil and criminal actions), §120 (defining "civil action" to include civil proceedings). Like the Code of Civil Procedure, the Evidence Code may be amended during a legislative session based on the recommendation of the California Law Revision Commission. *See* Gov. C. §§8291, 8292.

§3. CALIFORNIA RULES OF COURT

In 1962, the California Judicial Council, which is constitutionally authorized to adopt rules for court administration, practice, and procedure, adopted the California Rules of Court. *See* Cal. Const., art. VI, §6; 2 Witkin, *California Procedure* (5th ed. 2008 & Supp.2014) Courts, §187. The California Rules of Court are statewide rules covering pretrial, trial, and appellate procedures and are designed to augment the general provisions of the Code of Civil Procedure. *See* CCP §§575, 901. The California Rules of Court preempt all local rules relating to pleadings, demurrers, ex parte applications, motions, discovery, provisional remedies, and the form and format of papers. CRC 3.20(a). The California Rules of Court have the force and effect of law as long as they are not inconsistent with any statute. ***Cantillon v. Superior Ct.*** (2d Dist.1957) 150 Cal.App.2d 184, 187. A rule of court can go beyond the provisions of a statute as long as it furthers the statutory purpose. But a rule of court cannot change statutory requirements. ***People v. Hall*** (1994) 8 Cal.4th 950, 960; *see* ***California Ct. Reporters Ass'n v. Judicial Council*** (1st Dist.1997) 59 Cal.App.4th 959, 964; ***California Ct. Reporters Ass'n v. Judicial Council*** (1st Dist.1995) 39 Cal.App.4th 15, 33-34. The Judicial Council has also adopted official forms to be used for certain types of motions and proceedings. Rules, forms, and standards of judicial administration are circulated for comment twice a year for adoption effective January 1 and July 1. The rules and official forms are available at www.courts.ca.gov. For a brief overview of the history, function, and rulemaking process of the Judicial Council, see *Profile: Judicial Council of California, Administrative Office of the Courts*, Judicial Council of California, www.courts.ca.gov/documents/profilejc.pdf.

§4. LOCAL RULES

A superior court can adopt a local rule if (1) the court is permitted to by statute or the California Rules of Court or (2) the rule is not inconsistent with a statute, the California Rules of Court, or case law. *See* CCP §575.1; Gov. C. §68070(a); CRC 3.20(a); *see, e.g.*, ***Pacific Trends Lamp & Lighting Prods. v. J. White, Inc.*** (4th Dist.1998) 65 Cal.App.4th 1131, 1134-35 (local rule that imposed meet-and-confer requirement on motion for new trial conflicted with Code of Civil Procedure).

NOTE

Some courts adopt what they call "local policies" as opposed to "local rules." However, these policies are treated as local rules, and the same requirements apply. See Weil & Brown, California Practice Guide: Civil Procedure Before Trial (CD-ROM ed. 2014), ¶9:10 (referred to as Weil, Civil Procedure Before Trial); see, e.g., ***Lokeijak v. City of Irvine*** *(4th Dist.1998) 65 Cal.App.4th 341, 342 n.1 (court's "local policy" was a local rule and subject to requirements of CCP §575.1(c)).*

§4.1 Scope of local rules. A "local rule" is any rule, regulation, order, policy, form, or standard of general application adopted by a court to govern practice or procedure in that court or by a judge of the court to govern practice or procedure in that judge's courtroom. CRC 10.613(a)(2); *see* ***Volkswagen v. Superior Ct.*** (1st Dist.2001) 94 Cal.App.4th 695, 703. For a rule to be of "general application," it does not have to apply to all citizens of the state, but it should apply to all members of a class, kind, or order. *E.g.*, ***Volkswagen***, 94 Cal.App.4th at 704 (general order was rule of general application because it applied to all asbestos cases filed).

§4.2 Types of local rules.

1. Superior-court local rules. Most counties have local rules that apply to cases and proceedings in the superior courts within that county. *See* CCP §575.1(a), (b); *see, e.g.*, Super. Ct. Los Angeles Cty. Loc. R. (www.lacourt.org/courtrules/ui). The rules are usually published by local legal newspapers and are available on each court's website, the links to which can be accessed through www.courts.ca.gov.

2. Courtroom local rules. Most courts have courtroom local rules, also known as "local, local rules," that apply only to the cases and proceedings in the courtroom of the judge that adopted them. *See* CCP §575.1(c); ***Kalivas v. Barry Controls Corp.*** (2d Dist.1996) 49 Cal.App.4th 1152, 1158; Weil, *Civil Procedure Before Trial*, ¶9:12.

PRACTICE TIP

Always check with the court clerk during the case-management conference for local, local rules, which can affect trial dates, motion-in-limine deadlines, and other courtroom procedures.

§4.3 Procedures for adopting local rules. CCP §575.1 and CRC 10.613 prescribe the procedures for enacting and adopting local rules. *See* ***Hall v. Superior Ct.*** (2d Dist.2005) 133 Cal.App.4th 908, 915 & n.11 (discussing former CRC 981, now CRC 10.613). If a rule does not comply with these procedures, it is invalid and unenforceable. *See id.* at 916; ***Kalivas v. Barry Controls Corp.*** (2d Dist.1996) 49 Cal.App.4th 1152, 1159-60; Weil, *Civil Procedure Before Trial*, ¶¶9:7-9:12.

§4.4 Force of local rules. Local rules have the force and effect of law if they were formally adopted and published by the court and they are not inconsistent with state statutes, the California Rules of Court, or case law. *See* CCP §575.1(c); Gov. C. §68070(a); ***Mann v. Cracchiolo*** (1985) 38 Cal.3d 18, 29; ***Thatcher v. Lucky Stores*** (4thDist.2000) 79 Cal.App.4th 1081, 1084-85; ***Sierra Craft, Inc. v. Magnum Enters.*** (4th Dist.1998) 64 Cal.App.4th 1252, 1255; ***Kalivas v. Barry Controls Corp.*** (2d Dist.1996) 49 Cal.App.4th 1152, 1158; *see, e.g.*, ***Hall v. Superior***

Ct. (2d Dist.2005) 133 Cal.App.4th 908, 916 (court's local policy, which was in essence a local rule, was invalid because it was not properly adopted). Generally, a superior court's interpretation of its own rules is binding on other courts, unless the interpretation violates due process. *See* ***Villacampa v. Russell*** (1st Dist.1986) 178 Cal.App.3d 906, 911.

§4.5 Preempted local rules. For some areas of practice, local rules are specifically preempted by the California Rules of Court.

1. Matters preempted. The California Rules of Court preempt local rules on the following:

(1) Motions. CRC 3.20(a); *see, e.g.*, ***Kalivas v. Barry Controls Corp.*** (2d Dist.1996) 49 Cal.App.4th 1152, 1158 (local rule requiring joint statement of disputed and undisputed facts with MSJ violated CCP §437c(b) requirement that parties file separate statements).

(2) Demurrers. CRC 3.20(a).

(3) Discovery. *Id.*

(4) Pleadings. *Id. But see* ***Volkswagen v. Superior Ct.*** (1st Dist.2001) 94 Cal.App.4th 695, 704-05 (general order in complex asbestos litigation allowing master complaint and answer was implicitly authorized by former CRC 1800, now 3.400).

(5) Ex parte applications. CRC 3.20(a).

(6) Provisional remedies. *Id.*

(7) Form and format of papers. *Id.*

2. Matters not preempted. The California Rules of Court do not preempt local rules on the following:

(1) Trial and post-trial proceedings, including motions in limine. CRC 3.20(b)(1); *see* CRC 3.1112(f) (timing and place of filing and service of motion in limine are at discretion of trial judge).

(2) Injunction proceedings for harassment, group violence, or workplace violence, as authorized by CCP §§527.6, 527.7, and 527.8. CRC 3.20(b)(2).

(3) Proceedings under any of the following codes: Family Code, Penal Code, Probate Code, and Welfare and Institutions Code. CRC 3.20(b)(2).

(4) Criminal proceedings. *Id.*

(5) Eminent-domain proceedings. CRC 3.20(b)(3).

(6) Rules adopted under the Trial Court Delay Reduction Act. CRC 3.20(b)(4); *see* Gov. C. §68612; CRC 3.711.

(7) Other court business, such as internal management. *See* CRC 10.613(j); *see, e.g.*, Super. Ct. Santa Barbara Cty. Loc. R., rule 1003 (counsel must provide accurate estimates of time required for hearing when scheduling all matters on court calendars).

§4.6 Sanctions for violating local rules. If an attorney, a party represented by an attorney, or a party appearing in propria persona ("pro per") violates a local rule, the court can award sanctions against the attorney, the party,or both. *See* CCP §575.2. See "Party in propria persona," ch. 1-G, §3.1.2, p. 65; "Violation of Local Rule of Court," ch. 5-K, §6, p. 588.

1. Types of sanctions. If a local rule is violated, the court on its own or on a party's motion can make an order imposing any of the sanctions listed below. *See* ***Carlson v. State of Cal. Dept. of Fish & Game*** (2d Dist.1998) 68 Cal.App.4th 1268, 1279-80 (sanctions for violating local rule are available under CCP §575.2 even if local rule does not provide for sanctions).

(1) Striking all or part of any pleading of the party. CCP §575.2(a); *e.g.*, ***Del Junco v. Hufnagel*** (2d Dist.2007) 150 Cal.App.4th 789, 799-800 (superior court had jurisdiction to strike D's answer based on conduct of both D and D's attorney).

(2) Dismissing all or part of the action or proceeding. CCP §575.2(a). Dismissal for violating the court's fast-track rules is appropriate only when (1) the violation was caused by the party, not the attorney, and (2) no less severe sanction would be effective. ***Tliche v. Van Quathem*** (2d Dist.1998) 66 Cal.App.4th 1054, 1061-62; *see* CCP §575.2(b); Gov. C. §68608(b). See "Violation of Fast-Track Rules," ch. 10-F, §11, p. 1182.

(3) Entering a default judgment against the party. CCP §575.2(a); *e.g.*, ***Del Junco***, 150 Cal.App.4th at 799-800 (superior court had jurisdiction to strike D's answer and enter default judgment based on conduct of both D and D's attorney).

(4) Requiring the party or its attorney to pay reasonable expenses, including attorney fees, to the party who filed the motion for sanctions. CCP §575.2(a).

(5) Imposing lesser penalties as otherwise provided by law. CCP §575.2(a); *e.g.*, ***Rietveld v. Rosebud Storage Partners*** (3d Dist.2004) 121 Cal.App.4th 250, 257 (monetary sanctions were allowable because they were lesser sanctions than dismissal).

2. Innocent party. If a party did not participate in its attorney's violation of a local rule, the court cannot impose sanctions that adversely affect the party's case. CCP §575.2(b); ***Franklin Capital Corp. v. Wilson*** (4th Dist.2007) 148 Cal.App.4th 187, 212.

§4.7 Effective date. If a local rule is properly adopted, it becomes effective on the first January 1 or July 1 following the 45th day after the rule was filed with the Judicial Council and the court clerk and was made available for public examination. Gov. C. §68071.

B. PAPERS, FORMS, DECLARATIONS & AFFIDAVITS

§1. GENERAL

§1.1 Purpose. Before filing any document with the court, a party should check the appropriate statutes and rules to determine if there are any requirements for the form or format of the document. There are general requirements for papers filed in the superior court that apply to most filings, and there are requirements about the use of preprinted forms. There are also requirements for declarations and affidavits, which can sometimes be used as substitutes for sworn oral testimony.

§1.2 Primary authority. CCP §§128.7, 421, 422.30, 422.40, 2009, 2015.5; CRC 2.3, 2.100 et seq., 2.130 et seq.

§1.3 Secondary authority. The following secondary sources are cited as authority in this subchapter:

- *California Civil Procedure Before Trial* (CEB Online ed. 2014) (referred to as *CEB Procedure Before Trial*).
- Weil & Brown, *California Practice Guide: Civil Procedure Before Trial* (CD-ROM ed. 2014) (referred to as Weil, *Civil Procedure Before Trial*).
- Witkin, *California Procedure* (5th ed. 2008 & Supp.2014) (referred to as Witkin, *Cal. Procedure*).

§1.4 Judicial Council forms. The Judicial Council has adopted a number of forms for use in pleading and motion practice. *See, e.g.*, Judicial Council Forms, form CM-010 (civil case cover sheet), form MC-051 (notice of motion and motion to be relieved as counsel), form PLD-C-001 (complaint for breach of contract), form PLD-050 (general denial). For information about the Judicial Council forms, see the forms page on the California Courts website at www.courts.ca.gov/forms.htm.

§2. GENERAL REQUIREMENTS FOR PAPERS

The California Rules of Court specify the form and format of papers filed in the superior courts. CRC 2.100(b).

§2.1 Papers defined. The term "papers" includes any document offered for filing in any case, unless the document is (1) an exhibit, (2) a copy of an exhibit, (3) a Judicial Council form, (4) a local-court form, (5) certain forms for juvenile-dependency proceedings, (6) a record on appeal in a limited civil case, or (7) a brief filed in an appellate division. *See* CRC 2.3(2), 2.119. Because the California Rules of Court preempt local rules, the superior courts cannot enact or enforce local rules on the form or format of papers. CRC 2.100(a).

NOTE

Many types of papers, including certain discovery and pretrial documents, are served in a lawsuit but not filed with the court. See "Documents not filed," ch. 1-F, §2.2, p. 46. Because these documents are not filed, they do not have to comply with the general requirements for papers discussed in this section unless otherwise noted. See CRC 2.3(2) ("papers" includes only documents offered for filing).

---

§2.2 Type of paper. A party must use opaque, unglazed paper that is white or unbleached, of standard quality, and at least 20-pound weight. CRC 2.103. The paper must measure 8½ by 11 inches. *Id.*

§2.3 Font, type size & color.

1. Font. A paper must be printed in a font essentially equivalent to Courier, Times New Roman, or Arial. CRC 2.105.

2. **Type size.**

(1) **Original papers.**

(a) **Main text.** For original papers, the main text must be in at least 12-point type. CRC 2.104; *see* CCP §1019.

(b) **Footer text.** For original papers, the title of the paper must appear in the footer. CRC 2.110(b). The footer text must be in at least 10-point type. CRC 2.110(c); *see* CCP §1019. See "Footers," §2.5.1(5), p. 12.

(2) **Copies.** A party must have copies prepared by photocopying or another duplication process that produces clear and permanent copies as legible as printing in at least 12-point type. CRC 2.104.

3. **Print color.** A paper must be printed in black or blue-black. CRC 2.106.

§2.4 Binding & hole punches.

1. **All papers.** A party must ensure that each paper consists entirely of original pages without riders, is firmly bound together at the top, and contains two prepunched normal-sized holes that are centered 2½ inches apart and 5/8 inch from the top of the page. *See* CRC 2.113, 2.115.

2. **Motions.** For motions, a party must also ensure that all pages of each document and exhibit are attached together at the top by a method that permits pages to be easily turned and each page's entire content to be read. CRC 3.1110(e).

§2.5 Layout.

1. **All pages.** All pages in a paper must be in the following form:

(1) **Single-sided vs. double-sided.** Papers filed with the court must be printed on only one side of a page. CRC 2.102; *see* CRC 2.117. Papers served on a party, however, can be printed on both sides of the page if the party agrees. CRC 2.117.

(2) **Margins.** Each page must have margins at least one inch from the left edge and at least one-half inch from the right edge. CRC 2.107.

(3) **Line spacing & numbering.** A party must space and number the lines on each page as follows:

(a) The lines on each page must be 1½-spaced or double-spaced. CRC 2.108(1).

(b) The lines on each page must be numbered consecutively, beginning with the number 1 on each page. CRC 2.108(1), (4). Line numbers must be placed at the left margin and separated from the text of the paper by a vertical column of space at least one-fifth inch wide or by a single or double vertical line. CRC 2.108(4). Each line number must be aligned with a line of type, or the line numbers must be evenly spaced vertically on the page. *Id.* There must be at least three line numbers for every vertical inch on the page. *Id.* See "Complaint Sample," ❶, below.

(c) Lines that describe real property can be single-spaced. CRC 2.108(2).

(d) Footnotes, quotations, and printed forms of corporate surety bonds and undertakings can be single-spaced and have unnumbered lines if they comply generally with the space requirements of CRC 2.111. CRC 2.108(3).

COMPLAINT SAMPLE

JOHNSON, JONES & SMITH, LLP ❹
JANE JOHNSON
State Bar No. 456789
2121 Market Street
Los Angeles, California 99999 ❺
Telephone: (456) 789-1011
Fax: (456) 789-1010
E-mail: jjohnson@lawyer.com

Attorney for Plaintiffs

SUPERIOR COURT OF CALIFORNIA ❻
COUNTY OF SACRAMENTO

JOHN SMITH & ROBERT JONES, on ❼ behalf of themselves and the general public, Plaintiffs, vs. DEF, INC., BENJAMIN FRANKLIN, DAN DICKERSON, Defendants.	Case No. ________ ❽ COMPLAINT FOR UNFAIR, ❾ UNLAWFUL, AND DECEPTIVE BUSINESS PRACTICES; REQUESTS FOR INJUNCTION AND OTHER EQUITABLE RELIEF

❶

INTRODUCTION

Plaintiffs, John Smith and Robert Jones, on behalf of themselves and the general public, bring this action to challenge the Defendants' unlawful and unfair practice of seizing consumers' tax refunds to repay debts owed to other third-party lenders without consent, permission, or authorization. In the alternative, Plaintiffs challenge the Defendants' practice of misleading consumers into entering into loan agreements that permit the Defendants to seize tax refunds for debt-collection purposes. Plaintiffs seek compensatory and punitive damages, injunctive relief, and attorneys' fees, costs, and expenses.

1 ❷

Complaint for Unfair, Unlawful & Deceptive Business Practices ❸

(4) Page numbering. A party must number each page consecutively at the bottom unless otherwise provided by another rule. CRC 2.109; *see also* CRC 3.1110(c) (for motions, documents bound together must be consecutively paginated). See "Complaint Sample," ❷, above.

(5) Footers. A party must include a footer in the bottom margin of each page, placed below the page number and divided from the rest of the page by a printed line. *See* CRC 2.110(a). The footer must contain the title of the paper or some clear and concise abbreviation. CRC 2.110(b). For example, the footer might state "Complaint" or "XYZ Corp.'s Motion for Summary Judgment." *Id.* The footer text must be in at least 10-point type. CRC 2.110(c). See "Complaint Sample," ❸, above.

2. **First page.** The first page of every paper must include the following:

(1) Attorney or party information. A party must include information about the attorney for the party who is filing the paper or about the party who is representing herself. See "Complaint Sample," ❹, above. Specifically, a party must include the following information in the space starting one inch from the top and to the left of the center of the page (i.e., line 1):

NOTE

If a single paper is filed on behalf of several parties with different attorneys, the information in (a)-(d) below must be provided for each attorney, followed in each instance with a statement identifying the attorney's client. CEB Procedure Before Trial, §11.19.

(a) The name of either the attorney for the party who is filing the paper or the party herself if she is appearing in person. CRC 2.111(1). If the party is representing herself, she is "in propria persona" and should indicate her status on the complaint. *CEB Procedure Before Trial*, §11.17. See "Party in propria persona," ch. 1-G, §3.1.2, p. 65. If the attorney's law-firm name is included, the court may permit any attorney from that firm to appear for the named client without any additional filings or formalities. ***Ellis Law Grp. v. Nevada City Sugar Loaf Props.*** (3d Dist.2014) 230 Cal.App.4th 244, 258; *CEB Procedure Before Trial*, §11.18. If there are several attorneys from different offices representing the party, each of their names can be listed, and each attorney listed can appear for the party, but the first attorney listed should be the one who can receive service and answer inquiries about the case. *CEB Procedure Before Trial*, §11.19.

(b) The office address of the party's attorney or the party. CRC 2.111(1). If there is no office address, the attorney or party should use her residence address or mailing address. *Id.*

(c) The telephone number, fax number, and e-mail address of the party's attorney or the party. *Id.*

NOTE

By including a fax number or e-mail address, the attorney or the party is not consenting to service by fax or e-mail. CRC 2.111(1).

(d) The State Bar membership number of the party's attorney. CRC 2.111(1).

(2) Clerk's space. A party must leave blank the space to the right of the center of the page and between lines 1 and 7. CRC 2.111(2). This space is for the clerk's use. *Id.* See "Complaint Sample," ❺, above.

(3) Title of court. A party must include the title of the court on line 8, which must be at least 3 1/3 inches from the top of the paper. CRC 2.111(3). See "Complaint Sample," ❻, above.

(4) Title of case. A party must include the title of the case below the title of the court in the space to the left of the center of the page. CRC 2.111(4).

(a) Initial complaint or cross-complaint. For each initial complaint or cross-complaint, the name of each party must appear on a separate line beginning at the left margin of the page. CRC 2.111(4); *see* CCP §422.40. Each party named should also be designated by party type (i.e., plaintiff, defendant, cross-complainant, or cross-defendant). *See* 4 Witkin, *Cal. Procedure*, Pleading, §473; *see, e.g.*, Judicial Council Forms, form PLD-C-001 (complaint for breach of contract), form PLD-PI-001 (complaint for personal injury, property damage, or wrongful death). See "Complaint Sample," ❼, above.

(b) Later pleadings & papers. For each later pleading or paper, a party need only include a short title of the case stating (1) the name of the first party on each side and an appropriate indication of other parties (e.g., "et al." or "and others") and (2) whether one or more cross-actions are involved (e.g., "and Related Cross-Action"). CRC 2.111(4); *see* CCP §422.40.

(5) Case number. A party must include the case number in the space to the right of and opposite the title of the case. CRC 2.111(5). See "Complaint Sample," ❽, above.

(6) Nature of paper. A party must include, in the space below the case number, the nature of the paper (e.g., complaint, answer, response, opposition, stipulation). CRC 2.111(6).

(a) Complaints. For complaints, the party must also identify the nature of the action or proceeding (e.g., "Complaint for Damages—Breach of Contract," "Complaint for Damages—Personal Injury"). CRC 2.111(6); *CEB Procedure Before Trial*, §11.24.

[1] Correct title. The parties should title their pleadings in a manner that is useful to the court, the clerk, and the attorneys. The title should always identify the type of pleading (e.g., "Complaint for ..."). See "Complaint Sample," ❾, above.

[2] Incorrect title. If the party makes an error in the title of the pleading, the court will usually treat the pleading as if it had been properly named. *See* ***Shahvar v. Superior Ct.*** (6th Dist.1994) 25 Cal.App.4th 653, 659 n.1 (trivial defect does not affect nature of document); *see also* CCP §475 (court must disregard any pleading error or defect that does not affect substantial rights). The court will look to the substance of the pleading to determine its nature. ***Hutchason v. Marks*** (2d Dist.1942) 54 Cal.App.2d 113, 114; *see* ***Estate of Lewy*** (2d Dist.1974) 39 Cal.App.3d 729, 734.

(b) Answers, responses, or oppositions. For answers, responses, or oppositions filed in cases with multiple parties, the party must specifically identify the complaining, propounding, or moving party and the complaint, motion, or other matter being answered or opposed. CRC 2.111(6).

(c) Motions. For motions, the party must include (1) the date, time, and location of any scheduled hearing and the name of the judge hearing the motion, if known, (2) the nature or title of any attached document other than an exhibit, (3) the date the action was filed, and (4) the trial date, if one has been set. CRC 3.1110(b). See "Motion Sample," ❶, below. If the party chooses to appear by telephone at a hearing on the motion, the party can include the phrase "Telephone Appearance" below the title of the motion, opposition, or reply. CRC 3.670(h)(1)(A). See "By telephone," ch. 1-H, §5.4.2, p. 85.

MOTION SAMPLE

JOHNSON, JONES & SMITH, LLP
JANE JOHNSON
State Bar No. 456789
2121 Market Street
Los Angeles, California 99999
Telephone: (456) 789-1011
Fax: (456) 789-1010
E-mail: jjohnson@lawyer.com

Attorney for Plaintiffs

SUPERIOR COURT OF CALIFORNIA
COUNTY OF SACRAMENTO

JOHN SMITH & ROBERT JONES, on behalf of themselves and the general public,	Case No. 01AB0000001
Plaintiffs,	NOTICE OF MOTION FOR SUMMARY JUDGMENT; MEMORANDUM OF POINTS AND AUTHORITIES IN SUPPORT; ORDER
vs.	
DEF, INC., BENJAMIN FRANKLIN, DAN DICKERSON,	Date: July 1, 2015 ❶ Time: 9:00 a.m. Judge: Hon. Jack Miller ❷ Location: Dept. 15 Suit filed: Jan. 2, 2015 Trial date: Dec. 10, 2015
Defendants.	

(7) Judge & department. A party must include, in the space below the nature of the paper, the name of the judge and the department to which the case is assigned, once both are known. CRC 2.111(7). See "Motion Sample," ❷, above.

(8) Referee. A party must include, in the space below the nature of the paper, the word "Referee" and the name of the referee for any paper filed in a case pending before a referee appointed under CCP §638 or §639. CRC 2.111(8).

(9) Limited civil cases. For the following papers in limited civil cases, a party must provide additional information on the first page. For a discussion of limited civil cases, see "Limited cases," ch. 3-E, §4.2.2, p. 258.

(a) Complaint, petition, or application. In a complaint, petition, or application filed in a limited civil case, the party must include, in the space below the nature of the paper, the amount demanded, which should be stated as either "Amount demanded exceeds $10,000" or "Amount demanded does not exceed $10,000." CRC 2.111(9); *see* Gov. C. §70613(b).

(b) Pleadings & other papers. In the caption of every pleading and other paper filed in a limited civil case, the party must include the words "Limited Civil Case." CRC 2.111(10); *see* CCP §422.30(b). The "caption" is the part of the pleading or paper that sets forth (1) the name of the court, (2) the name of the county where the action is brought, and (3) the title of the action. CCP §422.30(a).

(10) Reclassified cases. If a case is reclassified, a party must state in the caption or title that the case is either a limited civil case reclassified as an unlimited civil case or an unlimited civil case reclassified as a limited civil case. CRC 2.111(11); *see also* CCP §422.30 (definition of "caption"). See "Reclassification," ch. 3-E, §4.5, p. 266.

(a) By amendment. If the case is reclassified by an amended complaint, a cross-complaint, an amended cross-complaint, or another pleading, the caption must also indicate that the action or proceeding is reclassified by the pleading. CRC 2.111(11); *see* CCP §§403.020, 403.030.

(b) By stipulation. If the case is reclassified by stipulation, the title of the stipulation must state that the action or proceeding is reclassified by the stipulation. CRC 2.111(11); *see* CCP §403.050.

(c) By motion. If the case is reclassified by motion, the court can allow or require the pleadings to be amended to ensure that the action or proceeding is properly presented and determined. CCP §403.070(b); *see id.* §403.040. See "Motion to Reclassify," ch. 5-D, p. 492.

§2.6 Social Security & financial-account information.

1. Excluded. In most cases, a party must exclude Social Security and financial-account numbers from all pleadings and other papers that are to be filed in the court's public file. CRC 1.20(b)(2).

2. Redacted. If Social Security or financial-account numbers are required by law or court order to be included in filed papers, only the last four digits of the number may be used. CRC 1.20(b)(2). On a showing of good cause, the court may order the party filing the redacted document to also file a confidential reference list that contains the redacted numbers. CRC 1.20(b)(4). The confidential list must identify each redacted number, specify a reference that corresponds to each number, and identify the documents where each reference appears. *See id.*; Judicial Council Forms, form MC-120. If a confidential reference list is ordered, it must be completed on Judicial Council Form MC-120. CRC 1.20(b)(4).

3. Exception. A party does not have to exclude or redact Social Security and financial-account numbers from documents or records that are filed in their entirety either confidentially or under seal. CRC 1.20(b)(1).

§2.7 Signature.

1. Who must sign. Every pleading, petition, written notice of motion, or other similar paper must be signed by at least one attorney of record or by the party if not represented by an attorney. CCP §128.7(a). The paper must include the signer's address and telephone number, if any. *Id.* An unsigned paper will be struck unless the attorney or party corrects the omission promptly after being notified of it. *Id.*; *see* ***Vaccaro v. Kaiman*** (2d Dist.1998) 63 Cal.App.4th 761, 768 (unsigned pleading can be struck under CCP §436(b), but attorney should first be given opportunity to cure defect).

(1) Attorney of record. When signed by an attorney, the paper must identify the attorney by name, address, telephone number, fax number, e-mail address, and State Bar number. *See* CCP §128.7(a); CRC 2.111(1). The attorney who signs the first pleading in an action is the party's attorney of record until written notice of another attorney's substitution as attorney of record is filed with the court and served on opposing counsel. *See* CCP §§284, 285; ***Baker v. Boxx*** (2d Dist.1991) 226 Cal.App.3d 1303, 1310; *see, e.g.*, ***Parkside Rlty. Co. v. MacDonald*** (1914)

167 Cal. 342, 344 (counsel who signed complaint was attorney of record for P). Only the attorney of record, or an attorney associated with her, is entitled to recognition by the courts. *See* ***In re Marriage of Park*** (1980) 27 Cal.3d 337, 343; ***Drummond v. West*** (1931) 212 Cal. 766, 769; ***Streit v. Covington & Crowe*** (4th Dist.2000) 82 Cal.App.4th 441, 445. *But see* ***Carrara v. Carrara*** (1st Dist.1953) 121 Cal.App.2d 59, 62-63 (although formal substitution requirements were not met, court recognized attorney substituting for attorney of record when no one was prejudiced).

(2) Party. When signed by a party acting in propria persona, the paper must identify the party by name, address, telephone number, fax number, and e-mail address. *See* CCP §128.7(a); CRC 2.111(1). But if the party is represented by an attorney, the party cannot sign and file her own papers. *See* ***In re Barnett*** (2003) 31 Cal.4th 466, 471 (criminal case; parties represented in court by attorney of record are required to act through attorney); ***Electric Utils. Co. v. Smallpage*** (3d Dist.1934) 137 Cal.App. 640, 642 (while litigant has attorney of record, that attorney retains exclusive right to appear and control court proceedings). A party's action taken without the consent of its attorney of record does not have to be recognized by the court. ***In re Estate of Cowell*** (1914) 167 Cal. 228, 232.

2. Certification. The signature of an attorney or party on a paper certifies that, to the best of the signer's knowledge, information, and belief, formed after a reasonable inquiry, all of the following are true:

(1) The paper is not being presented primarily for an improper purpose, such as to harass, to cause unnecessary delay, or to cause needless increase in the cost of litigation. CCP §128.7(b)(1).

(2) The claims, defenses, or other legal contentions are warranted by existing law or by a nonfrivolous argument for the extension, modification, or reversal of existing law or the establishment of new law. *Id.* §128.7(b)(2).

(3) The allegations and other factual contentions have evidentiary support or, if specifically identified, are likely to have evidentiary support after a reasonable opportunity for further investigation or discovery. *Id.* §128.7(b)(3).

(4) The denials of factual contentions are warranted on the evidence or, if specifically identified, are reasonably based on a lack of information or belief. *Id.* §128.7(b)(4).

NOTE

A court may award sanctions for violation of any of the statutory conditions listed in CCP §128.7(b). CCP §128.7(c). *See "Motion for Sanctions," ch. 5-K, p. 561.*

§2.8 Attachments.

1. Civil case cover sheet. A party must attach Judicial Council Form CM-010 ("Civil Case Cover Sheet") to the first paper filed in an action or proceeding, other than one filed in small-claims court or under the Probate Code, Family Code, or Welfare and Institutions Code. CRC 3.220(a), (b). For a copy of Form CM-010, see www.courts.ca.gov/documents/cm010.pdf.

(1) Contents. For a discussion of the contents of a civil case cover sheet, see "Civil case cover sheet," ch. 3-C, §3.1, p. 211.

(2) Service. The cover sheet does not need to be served on opposing parties unless the plaintiff indicates that the case is (1) a complex case under CRC 3.400 through 3.403 or (2) a collections case under CRC 3.740. *See* CRC 3.220(a). If the plaintiff checks the box on the cover sheet indicating that the case is a complex or collections case, a copy of the cover sheet must be served with the complaint. *Id.*

(3) Purpose. The cover sheet is used for statistical purposes. CRC 3.220(a); ***Maginn v. City of Glendale*** (2d Dist.1999) 72 Cal.App.4th 1102, 1106. It may also affect the assignment of a complex case. CRC 3.220(a).

(4) Sanctions. If a party does not file a cover sheet or files a defective or incomplete cover sheet, the court can impose sanctions against the party, her attorney, or both under CRC 2.30. CRC 3.220(c).

2. Other cover sheets. Other cover sheets must be filed in addition to Form CM-010 if required by local rule. CRC 3.220(a); *see, e.g.*, ***Carlson v. State of Cal. Dept. of Fish & Game*** (2d Dist.1998) 68 Cal.App.4th 1268, 1273 n.3 (local rule required certificate of assignment to be filed with complaint); ***Rojas v. Cutsforth*** (2d Dist.1998) 67 Cal.App.4th 774, 776 (local rule required first-filed document to include Declaration for Court Assignment form).

3. ADR information package. In all general civil cases, the plaintiff must serve on each defendant a copy of an ADR information package provided by the court with the complaint. CRC 3.221(c). Cross-complainants must also serve a copy of the ADR information package on any new parties along with the cross-complaint. *Id.*

4. Exhibits.

(1) All papers. When any exhibit is prepared by a machine copying process, the party must ensure that the exhibit is equal to typewritten material in legibility and permanency of image. CRC 2.114. A party can attach exhibits to pages of the specified size. *Id.*; *see* CRC 2.103 (papers must be 8½ by 11 inches); *see also* CRC 2.302 (exhibits that are larger than 8½ by 11 inches must be reduced to no more than 8½ by 11 inches before being sent by fax).

(2) Motions. For exhibits to motions, a party must also do the following:

(a) Dividers. The party must separate each exhibit by a hard 8½-by-11-inch sheet with hard paper or plastic tabs extending below the bottom of the page that bear the exhibit designation. CRC 3.1110(f).

(b) Binding. The party must ensure that all pages in each exhibit are attached together at the top so that the pages can be easily turned and the entire content of each page can be read. CRC 3.1110(e).

(c) Index. The party must provide an index to the exhibits. CRC 3.1110(f).

NOTE

When a party makes or opposes a motion for summary judgment or summary adjudication, it does not need to provide an index if the exhibits are 25 pages or less. See CRC 3.1350(g). Whether this exception applies to other types of motions is unclear.

(d) Grouping exhibits. The party must group pages from a single deposition and associated exhibits into a single exhibit. CRC 3.1110(f).

PRACTICE TIP

When preparing pages from a deposition, be sure to highlight the relevant part of the testimony. See CRC 3.1116(c).

(e) Translation. The party must attach an English translation, certified under oath by a qualified interpreter, of any exhibit written in a foreign language. CRC 3.1110(g).

§2.9 Incorporation by reference.

1. What can be incorporated.

(1) Documents. A party can incorporate documents by reference into a pleading or motion by attaching them as exhibits, setting forth a distinct and definite reference to the attachment, and explaining the purpose of the reference. *See* ***Holly Sugar Corp. v. Johnson*** (1941) 18 Cal.2d 218, 225-26; *see, e.g.*, ***Del Mar Beach Club Owners Ass'n v. Imperial Contracting Co.*** (4th Dist.1981) 123 Cal.App.3d 898, 908 (incorporation of exhibit was proper when P directly referred to exhibit in its entirety for purpose of establishing standing); ***Byrne v. Harvey*** (1st Dist.1962) 211 Cal.App.2d 92, 103 (contract can be pleaded "in haec verba"—that is, in its own words—by attaching copy as exhibit and incorporating terms by reference in pleading). For motions, if the reference is to a paper filed before the motion (e.g., a declaration filed in connection with an earlier motion), the reference must also include the date the paper was signed and its title. CRC 3.1110(d).

(2) Allegations. The party can incorporate allegations by reference from the same document or from other documents included in the court's file of the same case. *See* ***Turney v. Collins*** (2d Dist.1941) 48 Cal.App.2d 381, 388; 4 Witkin, *Cal. Procedure*, Pleading, §436; *see, e.g.*, ***Cornelison v. Kornbluth*** (1975) 15 Cal.3d 590, 594 (second cause of action incorporated material allegations supporting first cause of action); ***Reid v. Merrill*** (1935) 4 Cal.2d 693, 695 (cross-complaint incorporated affirmative defense included in answer).

2. What cannot be incorporated. A party cannot incorporate by reference allegations or documents filed in another case without attaching them as exhibits. *See* ***People v. De La Guerra*** (1864) 24 Cal. 73, 78, *overruled on other grounds*, ***Flores v. Arroyo*** (1961) 56 Cal.2d 492; 4 Witkin, *Cal. Procedure*, Pleading, §436; *see, e.g.*, ***Legg v. Ford*** (2d Dist.1960) 185 Cal.App.2d 534, 540-41 (pleadings included in record of former proceeding could not be made part of P's complaint without attaching papers or otherwise making them part of the record).

§2.10 Marks on face of paper. A party must ensure that any additions, deletions, or interlineations to the face of a paper are initialed by either the clerk or the judge at the time of filing. CRC 2.116.

§3. GENERAL REQUIREMENTS FOR FORMS

The Judicial Council specifies the format for many forms filed in the superior court. CRC 2.100(b). The term "forms" includes Judicial Council forms, local court forms, and all other official forms filed in the superior courts. CRC 2.130; *see* CRC 2.140, 2.141. Judicial Council forms are governed by CRC 1.30 through 1.45, and local court forms are governed by CRC 10.613 and 10.614. The purpose of these rules is threefold: (1) to establish a list of mandatory-use and optional-use forms, (2) to restrict the ability of courts and publishers reprinting the forms to modify them, and (3) to provide other guidance to the courts and parties who are using the forms. *See, e.g.*, CRC 1.31(e) (courts generally cannot require use of altered mandatory Judicial Council form in place of original Judicial Council form), CRC 1.42 (listing situations where court cannot reject Judicial Council form), CRC 10.614(6) (local court form must be designed so no typing is required in margin).

§3.1 All forms.

1. Binding & hole punches. A party must ensure that each form (1) contains two prepunched normal-sized holes that are centered 2½ inches apart and 5/8 inch from the top of the form and (2) is firmly bound at the top if the form is longer than one page. CRC 2.133 (hole punching), CRC 2.134(c) (binding). See "Binding & hole punches," §2.4, p. 10.

2. Layout. See "Layout," §2.5, p. 10.

(1) Single-sided. A party can use one side of a page for a form longer than one page, even if the original form is printed on two sides. CRC 2.134(a), 10.614(8).

(2) Double-sided. A party can use both sides of a page for a form longer than one page. *See* CRC 2.134(b), 10.614(8). When printing on both sides, the party must "tumble" the form—that is, the reverse side must be rotated 180 degrees so the form is printed head to foot. *See* CRC 2.134(b), 10.614(8).

§3.2 Judicial Council forms – additional requirements.

1. Electronic duplication. A party or attorney can file a duplicate of a Judicial Council form produced by a computer and a printer or similar device with a resolution of at least 300 dots per inch. CRC 1.44.

2. True copy. A party using a Judicial Council form must file a true copy of the original form, and the filing must be as legible as a printed form. CRC 1.43.

3. Pleadings.

(1) Approved cause-of-action forms. A party using an approved cause-of-action form can attach it to any approved form of complaint or cross-complaint. CRC 1.45(b).

(2) Unapproved cause-of-action forms. A party pleading a cause of action for which no form has been approved can prepare a form following the general format for papers and, if necessary, attach the form to any

other approved form of complaint or cross-complaint. CRC 1.45(c). See "General Requirements for Papers," §2, p. 9. The party must number each paragraph consecutively. CRC 1.45(c). The paragraph number should be preceded by one or more identifying letters from the cause of action's title (e.g., "Aslt-1" for an assault cause of action). *Id.*

§3.3 Local court forms – additional requirements. A party must print local forms on paper measuring no more than 8½ by 11 inches and no less than 8½ by 5 inches. CRC 10.614(1).

§3.4 Signature. The declarant or affiant must sign with her true name, except when a party files suit under a fictitious name, in which case the affiant can sign under the fictitious name. *See* ***Doe v. Superior Ct.*** (2d Dist.2011) 194 Cal.App.4th 750, 754-55; ***Doe v. Lincoln Unified Sch. Dist.*** (1st Dist.2010) 188 Cal.App.4th 758, 767. See "Doe plaintiffs," ch. 3-C, §2.3.1(7)(a), p. 209.

§4. GENERAL REQUIREMENTS FOR DECLARATIONS & AFFIDAVITS

§4.1 Declaration vs. affidavit. Declarations and affidavits are frequently used as a substitute for sworn oral testimony. *See* CCP §§2009, 2015.5; Weil, *Civil Procedure Before Trial*, ¶9:46; *see, e.g.*, Prob. C. §1022 (affidavits can be used as evidence in uncontested will proceedings); *see also* CRC 3.1306(a) (evidence at law-and-motion hearing must be by declaration or request for judicial notice without testimony unless ordered otherwise for good cause). Declarations are used more often than affidavits because they are easier to prepare. Weil, *Civil Procedure Before Trial*, ¶9:47.

PRACTICE TIP

If the declaration or affidavit is in a foreign language, the party must attach an English translation certified under oath by a qualified interpreter. See CRC 3.1110(g).

---

1. Declaration. A declaration is an unsworn, written statement made under penalty of perjury whenever state law requires or permits facts to be proved by affidavits or other sworn statements (e.g., verifications, certificates, oaths). *See* CCP §2015.5; ***Kulshrestha v. First Un. Commercial Corp.*** (2004) 33 Cal.4th 601, 610; *see also* ***Blum v. Superior Ct.*** (2d Dist.2006) 141 Cal.App.4th 418, 427 (reason for permitting declaration under penalty of perjury is to ensure it contains truthful factual representations and is made in good faith).

(1) Elements. The declaration must include three elements: (1) a certification "under penalty of perjury" that the declaration is true and correct, (2) the declarant's signature, and (3) a statement of the date of execution. CCP §2015.5; *see* ***Blum***, 141 Cal.App.4th at 427 (under CCP §2015.5, "subscribe" means to sign with one's own hand); *see, e.g.*, ***In re Marriage of Reese*** (4th Dist.1999) 73 Cal.App.4th 1214, 1222-23 (declaration signed by attorney on declarant's behalf was invalid).

(a) Executed inside California. If the declaration is executed inside California, it must include a statement of the location of execution. CCP §2015.5. An in-state declaration that does not state a place of execution and that it is "true" under penalty of perjury is still valid if it includes the declarant's address and was made "under penalty of perjury." *See* ***People v. Pacific Land Research Co.*** (1977) 20 Cal.3d 10, 21 n.11.

(b) Executed outside California. If the declaration is executed outside California, the certification must be made "under penalty of perjury under the laws of the State of California." CCP §2015.5; *see* ***Kulshrestha***, 33 Cal.4th at 618.

(2) Facts only. The declaration must be limited to facts and should not contain legal arguments. *See* ***In re Marriage of Heggie*** (4th Dist.2002) 99 Cal.App.4th 28, 30 n.3.

2. Affidavit. An affidavit is a written declaration made under oath and without notice to the adverse party. CCP §2003.

15 **(1) Form.** An affidavit must contain a jurat, which is a certificate proving that the affidavit was made before an officer authorized to administer oaths. *See* CCP §2012; Gov. C. §8202; ***People v. Egan*** (3d Dist.1983) 141 Cal.App.3d 798, 801 & n.3; *see also* ***Bank of Venice v. de Luna*** (2d Dist.1912) 19 Cal.App. 219, 222 (primary purpose

of officer's signature on jurat is to witness affiant's signature on affidavit). The jurat must contain a notice at the top in an enclosed box that states: "A notary public or other officer completing this certificate verifies only the identity of the individual who signed the document to which this certificate is attached, and not the truthfulness, accuracy, or validity of that document." Gov. C. §8202(b). For the mandatory form of the jurat, see Gov. C. §8202(d).

(2) Deposition as affidavit. Because a deposition is a written declaration made under oath, it can be used instead of an affidavit with an evidentiary motion as long as the deposition was taken in the same action. *See* ***Gatton v. A.P. Green Servs.*** (1st Dist.1998) 64 Cal.App.4th 688, 695-96. A deposition taken in a different action can also be used instead of an affidavit, but the deposition may be ruled inadmissible based on a hearsay objection by an opposing party. *See, e.g.*, ***L&B Real Estate v. Superior Ct.*** (2d Dist.1998) 67 Cal.App.4th 1342, 1348 (deposition was hearsay); ***Gatton***, 64 Cal.App.4th at 696 (same).

§4.2 Who can testify. Any person is "competent" or qualified to make a declaration or affidavit if she has personal knowledge of, or is qualified as an expert to give testimony on, the matters set forth in the declaration or affidavit. *See* Evid. C. §§702, 720; ***Slusher v. Durrer*** (3d Dist.1977) 69 Cal.App.3d 747, 753; *see, e.g.*, ***Hayman v. Block*** (2d Dist.1986) 176 Cal.App.3d 629, 638 (in summary-judgment proceedings, personal knowledge and competency must be shown in supporting and opposing declarations and affidavits); ***Bowden v. Robinson*** (4th Dist.1977) 67 Cal.App.3d 705, 719-20 (facts stated in declaration did not show declarant was competent to testify); *see also* ***Cowles Mags. & Broad., Inc. v. Elysium, Inc.*** (2d Dist.1967) 255 Cal.App.2d 731, 734 (statements in declarations or affidavits are disregarded if they cannot withstand the tests to which oral testimony is subjected). Statements in declarations and affidavits are presumed to be made on personal knowledge unless either of the following applies:

1. The statements could not have been made on personal knowledge. ***Weathers v. Kaiser Found. Hosps.*** (1971) 5 Cal.3d 98, 106.

2. The declaration or affidavit states it is based on "information and belief." *Id.* Declarations or affidavits based on information and belief—which indicates that the declarant or affiant, in good faith, believes the allegations to be true—are usually disregarded as hearsay. *See* ***City of Santa Cruz v. Municipal Ct.*** (1989) 49 Cal.3d 74, 93 n.9; *see, e.g.*, ***Franklin v. Nat C. Goldstone Agency*** (1949) 33 Cal.2d 628, 631 (affidavit based on information and belief was hearsay); ***Burger v. Superior Ct.*** (1st Dist.1984) 151 Cal.App.3d 1013, 1019 (third party's information-and-belief verification was not evidence). *But see* ***North Beverly Park Homeowners Ass'n v. Bisno*** (2d Dist.2007) 147 Cal.App.4th 762, 778-79 (dicta; CCP §2009 creates hearsay exception for declarations and affidavits in support of party's motion). Statements such as "to the best of my knowledge" are treated the same as information-and-belief statements. *See* ***Bowden***, 67 Cal.App.3d at 719-20.

§4.3 Permitted uses. Declarations and affidavits can be used in any case as expressly permitted by statute. CCP §2009. Specifically, declarations and affidavits can be used to do any of the following:

1. Verify a pleading or paper in a special proceeding. *Id.*
2. Prove the service of a summons, notice, or other paper in an action or special proceeding. *Id.*
3. Obtain a provisional remedy. *Id.*
4. Obtain the examination of a witness. *Id.*
5. Obtain a stay of proceedings. *Id.*
6. Establish a record of birth in uncontested proceedings. *Id.*
7. Support a motion. *Id.*; ***McDonald v. Superior Ct.*** (4th Dist.1994) 22 Cal.App.4th 364, 370.

C. PLEADING PRACTICE

§1. GENERAL

§1.1 Purpose. Pleadings are the parties' formal allegations of their claims and defenses. CCP §420. Pleadings initiate and communicate the nature of the lawsuit, define and shape the issues, furnish a basis for the evidence, and provide a foundation for res judicata. *See* ***Lewis v. Fahn*** (3d Dist.1952) 113 Cal.App.2d 95, 100-01; ***Crown Prods. v. California Food Prods.*** (1st Dist.1947) 77 Cal.App.2d 543, 550.

§1.2 Primary authority. CCP §§85, 420, 422.10, 430.10, 464, 472.

§1.3 Secondary authority. The following secondary sources are cited as authority in this subchapter:

- *California Civil Procedure Before Trial* (CEB Online ed. 2014) (referred to as *CEB Procedure Before Trial*).
- Witkin, *California Evidence* (5th ed. 2012 & Supp.2014) (referred to as Witkin, *Cal. Evidence*).
- Witkin, *California Procedure* (5th ed. 2008 & Supp.2014) (referred to as Witkin, *Cal. Procedure*).

§1.4 Judicial Council forms. The Judicial Council has adopted a number of forms for use in pleading practice. *See, e.g.*, Judicial Council Forms, form PLD-C-001 (complaint for breach of contract), form PLD-050 (general denial). For information about the Judicial Council forms, see the forms page on the California Courts website at www.courts.ca.gov/forms.htm.

§2. TYPES OF PLEADINGS

The only pleadings that are permitted in civil actions are the complaint, the answer, the cross-complaint, and the demurrer. CCP §92(a) (limited civil cases), §422.10 (unlimited civil cases); *see, e.g.*, ***Barragan v. Banco BCH*** (4th Dist.1986) 188 Cal.App.3d 283, 299 (MSJ is not a pleading).

§2.1 Complaint. A civil complaint is a pleading that sets out the formal allegations and claims of a party. ***County of Santa Clara v. Perry*** (1998) 18 Cal.4th 435, 442; *see* CCP §§420, 422.10. The purpose of the complaint is to frame and limit the issues and to apprise the defendant of the basis on which the plaintiff is seeking to recover. ***Committee on Children's TV, Inc. v. General Foods Corp.*** (1983) 35 Cal.3d 197, 211-12. See "Plaintiff's Original Complaint," ch. 3-C, p. 203.

§2.2 Answer. An answer is a pleading that denies the allegations in the plaintiff's complaint, identifies any defenses, and prevents a default judgment. *See* CCP §422.10 (answer is a pleading), §431.20(a) (material allegations in complaint not denied in answer are taken as true), §585 (court can enter default judgment if D does not file answer), §590 (issue of fact arises when answer controverts material allegation in complaint). See "Answer," ch. 4-B, p. 332.

§2.3 Cross-complaint. A cross-complaint is a pleading that sets out the formal allegations and claims of the defendant against the plaintiff, a codefendant, or a person who is not yet a party to the action. *See* CCP §§422.10, 428.10; *see also* ***Bertero v. National Gen. Corp.*** (1974) 13 Cal.3d 43, 52 n.2 (in 1971, California Legislature eliminated cross-action and counterclaim practice by enacting CCP §428.80). See "Cross-Complaint," ch. 4-C, p. 349.

§2.4 Demurrer. A demurrer is a pleading that informs the plaintiff of defects in its complaint by challenging the legal sufficiency of the plaintiff's claims for relief. *See* CCP §422.10; ***Roman v. County of L.A.*** (2d Dist.2000) 85 Cal.App.4th 316, 321; ***Marina Tenants Ass'n v. Deauville Marina Dev. Co.*** (2d Dist.1986) 181 Cal.App.3d 122, 127. A demurrer cannot be used to resolve factual issues. ***Ramsden v. Western Un.*** (2d Dist.1977) 71 Cal.App.3d 873, 879. Although a demurrer is considered a pleading, it is treated procedurally as a motion. *See* CRC 3.1103(c). See "Law & Motion Practice," ch. 1-D, p. 26; "Demurrer," ch. 4-H, p. 396.

§3. FILING & SERVING PLEADINGS

All pleadings must be filed with the court and served on the parties. See "Filing Documents," ch. 1-F, p. 45; "Serving Documents," ch. 1-G, p. 63; "Joining the Defendant—Service of Process," ch. 3-H, p. 295.

§4. PLEADINGS & PROCEDURAL CLASSIFICATIONS

§4.1 Initial classification. A civil case is initially classified as either "limited" or "unlimited" based on the relief requested in the complaint or cross-complaint. *See* ***Ytuarte v. Superior Ct.*** (2d Dist.2005) 129 Cal.App.4th 266, 274; *see also* CCP §85 (conditions for determining when civil case is limited). A case that is not limited is referred to as unlimited. CCP §88. Once a case is classified, that classification generally continues throughout the litigation. ***Ytuarte***, 129 Cal.App.4th at 274. These classifications are important because the procedures and available relief are different for each. *Id.* For a discussion of these classifications, see "Procedural Classifications of Civil Cases," ch. 3-E, §4, p. 255.

§4.2 Reclassification. If a case is improperly classified, either a party or the court can file a motion to reclassify. CCP §403.040(a); ***Garau v. Torrance Unified Sch. Dist.*** (2d Dist.2006) 137 Cal.App.4th 192, 199. See "Motion to Reclassify," ch. 5-D, p. 492.

§5. CHANGING PLEADINGS

The parties can change the relevant issues in a proceeding by amending and supplementing the pleadings. *See* CCP §§464(a), 472.

§5.1 Amended pleadings. An amended pleading corrects or changes a previous pleading by adding or deleting information. An amended pleading supersedes the previous pleading, which becomes ineffective. ***Meyer v. State Bd. of Equalization*** (1954) 42 Cal.2d 376, 384; ***Lee v. Bank of Am. Nat'l Trust & Sav. Ass'n*** (4th Dist.1994) 27 Cal.App.4th 197, 215; ***Puchta v. Rothman*** (1st Dist.1950) 99 Cal.App.2d 285, 291; 5 Witkin, *Cal. Procedure*, Pleading, §1187. See "Amending the Complaint," ch. 3-C, §6, p. 228; "Amending the Answer," ch. 4-B, §9, p. 347.

§5.2 Supplemental pleadings. A supplemental pleading sets out transactions, occurrences, or events that have happened since the filing date of the previous pleading. *See* CCP §464(a); ***Hebert v. Los Angeles Raiders, Ltd.*** (2d Dist.1991) 23 Cal.App.4th 414, 426. A supplemental pleading adds to—but does not replace or supersede—the previous pleading. In other words, it cannot allege facts that constitute an entirely new cause of action or defense. *See* ***Flood v. Simpson*** (2d Dist.1975) 45 Cal.App.3d 644, 647. Before filing a supplemental pleading, the party must file a motion to supplement with the court. *See* CCP §464(a); ***Hebert***, 23 Cal.App.4th at 426; ***Earp v. Nobmann*** (3d Dist.1981) 122 Cal.App.3d 270, 287, *disapproved on other grounds*, ***Silberg v. Anderson*** (1990) 50 Cal.3d 205; 5 Witkin, *Cal. Procedure*, Pleading, §1247. The court can grant the motion and allow a supplemental pleading only after reasonable notice to the other party. *See* ***Hebert***, 23 Cal.App.4th at 426; ***Earp***, 122 Cal.App.3d at 287. See "Supplementing the Complaint," ch. 3-C, §7, p. 238; "Supplementing the Answer," ch. 4-B, §10, p. 348.

§6. RESPONDING TO PLEADINGS

Parties should always respond to pleadings. The failure to respond can often result in the loss of substantive rights, such as by a default judgment or waiver of defenses. *See, e.g.*, CCP §585 (default judgment after failure to answer); ***Bogue v. Roeth*** (3d Dist.1929) 98 Cal.App. 257, 262 (court sustained objections to D's cross-examination of witness on subject of whether P's tender of payment was sufficient because D did not specifically deny tender in its answer). See "Default Judgment," ch. 10-A, p. 1089. For a discussion of how to respond to pleadings, see "Defendant's Responses & Pleadings," ch. 4, p. 325.

§7. CHALLENGING PLEADINGS

§7.1 Defective pleadings.

1. **Types of defects.** Pleading defects can be challenged as defects in form or defects in substance.

(1) Defect in form. A defect in form relates to how a claim is pleaded, such as the failure to include a signature on the complaint. *See* ***Merritt v. Glidden*** (1870) 39 Cal. 559, 564.

(2) Defect in substance. A defect in substance relates to the merits of the claim, such as an absolute defense being disclosed by the allegations in the complaint. *See* ***Koch v. Rodlin Enters.*** (1st Dist.1990) 223 Cal.App.3d 1591, 1597.

2. Challenging defect.

(1) Timely object. A party should object to any defect in form or substance as soon as it becomes apparent. *See, e.g.*, ***Ghirardo v. Antonioli*** (1996) 14 Cal.4th 39, 48 (P waived objection based on D's failure to plead affirmative defense by not objecting when D raised defense in post-trial brief); ***Knapp v. Doherty*** (6th Dist.2004) 123 Cal.App.4th 76, 90 (D waived objection to P's reliance on unpleaded theory in opposition to MSJ); ***People v. Ciancio*** (2d Dist.2003) 109 Cal.App.4th 175, 193 (D waived objection that petition for writ of habeas corpus was mislabeled as a motion by not raising defect with superior court); ***FPI Dev., Inc. v. Nakashima*** (3d Dist.1991) 231 Cal.App.3d 367, 385 (P waived challenge to sufficiency of pleadings); *see also* ***Fleischmann v. Lotito*** (1936) 6 Cal.2d 365, 367 (party cannot raise formal pleading defects for first time on appeal); ***Abner Doble Co. v. Keystone Consol. Mining Co.*** (1904) 145 Cal. 490, 495-96 (when there is defect in form or substance and opposing party did not object before verdict, verdict is assumed to have cured defect).

(2) Use proper procedural device. The primary method for challenging pleading defects is a demurrer. *See* CCP §430.10. See "Demurrer," ch. 4-H, p. 396. But to challenge defects that are not susceptible to demurrer, a party can use these procedural devices:

(a) A motion to strike. ***City of King City v. Community Bank*** (6th Dist.2005) 131 Cal.App.4th 913, 923 n.3; *e.g.*, ***CLD Constr., Inc. v. City of San Ramon*** (1st Dist.2004) 120 Cal.App.4th 1141, 1146 (D filed motion to strike complaint that was signed by P-corporation's president, not its attorney); *see* ***Zavala v. Board of Trs. of the Leland Stanford, Jr., Univ.*** (6th Dist.1993) 16 Cal.App.4th 1755, 1761 (proper procedure for objecting to unverified pleading is to file motion to strike). See "Motion to Strike," ch. 4-J, p. 418.

(b) A motion for judgment on the pleadings. *See* ***Smiley v. Citibank*** (1995) 11 Cal.4th 138, 146 (motion for judgment on pleadings has same purpose as general demurrer), *aff'd*, (1996) 517 U.S. 735. See "Motion for Judgment on the Pleadings," ch. 4-I, p. 411.

(c) A motion for summary judgment. *See, e.g.*, ***Woo v. Superior Ct.*** (4th Dist.1999) 75 Cal.App.4th 169, 174-75 (D filed MSJ on limitations grounds because amended complaint adding D did not relate back to original complaint). See "Motion for Summary Judgment," ch. 10-B, p. 1117.

(d) A motion for sanctions. *See, e.g.*, ***Eichenbaum v. Alon*** (2d Dist.2003) 106 Cal.App.4th 967, 972-73 (P sanctioned under CCP §§128.7 and 177.5 for repeatedly filing complaints naming deceased person as D despite contrary court orders). See "Motion for Sanctions," ch. 5-K, p. 561.

(e) A motion to dismiss. *See, e.g.*, ***Carlson v. State of Cal. Dept. of Fish & Game*** (2d Dist.1998) 68 Cal.App.4th 1268, 1280 (dicta; under CCP §575.2, court could dismiss complaint for failure to attach certificate of assignment as required by local rule). See "Involuntary Dismissal—Delay in Prosecution," ch. 10-E, p. 1160; "Involuntary Dismissal—Other Grounds," ch. 10-F, p. 1180.

(f) An answer. *See* CCP §430.30(b) (when grounds for objection do not appear on face of complaint, D can raise objection in answer). See "Answer," ch. 4-B, p. 332.

3. Curing defect. Once a party challenges a defective pleading, the opposing party should be given an opportunity to correct the defect unless no amendment could change the result. *See* ***Fox v. Ethicon Endo-Surgery, Inc.*** (2005) 35 Cal.4th 797, 810; ***Scott v. City of Indian Wells*** (1972) 6 Cal.3d 541, 549. In some cases, however, the party must seek leave to amend. *See, e.g.*, ***Law Offices of Dixon R. Howell v. Valley*** (6th Dist.2005) 129 Cal.App.4th 1076, 1104 n.22 (party must move to amend pleading if it wants to rely on unpleaded theories or defenses to defeat MSJ); ***Leibert v. Transworld Sys.*** (1st Dist.1995) 32 Cal.App.4th 1693, 1699 (same). See "Amending the Complaint," ch. 3-C, §6, p. 228; "Amending the Answer," ch. 4-B, §9, p. 347.

§7.2 Groundless pleadings. An attorney or party who violates the certification requirements for pleadings under CCP §128.7 can be sanctioned. *See* ***Bockrath v. Aldrich Chem. Co.*** (1999) 21 Cal.4th 71, 82; ***Peake v. Underwood*** (4th Dist.2014) 227 Cal.App.4th 428, 440-41; ***Burkle v. Burkle*** (2d Dist.2006) 144 Cal.App.4th 387, 399. See "Certification," ch. 1-B, §2.7.2, p. 16; "Motion for Sanctions," ch. 5-K, p. 561.

§8. USING PLEADINGS

§8.1 Current pleadings – judicial-admissions doctrine. An assertion of fact or a failure to deny an assertion of fact in a party's current pleading can be used against the party as a judicial admission. ***Castillo v. Barrera*** (2d Dist.2007) 146 Cal.App.4th 1317, 1324 (assertion of fact); ***St. Paul Mercury Ins. v. Frontier Pac. Ins.*** (4th Dist.2003) 111 Cal.App.4th 1234, 1248 (same); ***Rodriguez v. Municipal Ct.*** (5th Dist.1972) 25 Cal.App.3d 521, 526-27 (failure to deny); ***Reich v. Yow*** (2d Dist.1967) 249 Cal.App.2d 12, 14-15 (same); *see* ***Oliver v. Swiss Club Tell*** (1st Dist.1963) 222 Cal.App.2d 528, 539 (inadequate denial on information and belief constitutes admission); *see, e.g.*, ***Valerio v. Andrew Youngquist Constr.*** (1st Dist.2002) 103 Cal.App.4th 1264, 1271 (D admitted to contract in answer to cross-complaint). Legal conclusions or assertions involving a mixed question of law and fact in a party's current pleading are not judicial admissions. ***Stroud v. Tunzi*** (2d Dist.2008) 160 Cal.App.4th 377, 384. To be a judicial admission, a statement in a pleading must be well pleaded and material. *See* ***Valerio***, 103 Cal.App.4th at 1271; 4 Witkin, *Cal. Procedure*, Pleading, §452.

1. Applicability of doctrine.

(1) Verified & unverified pleadings. The judicial-admissions doctrine has been applied to both verified and unverified pleadings. *See* ***Reichert v. General Ins.*** (1968) 68 Cal.2d 822, 836 (unverified complaint); ***California Nat'l Bank v. Woodbridge Plaza LLC*** (4th Dist.2008) 164 Cal.App.4th 137, 146 (verified complaint); ***DeCamp v. First Kensington Corp.*** (2d Dist.1978) 83 Cal.App.3d 268, 282 (unverified answer). A "verified pleading" is one that is supported by an affidavit verifying the truth of the allegations. *See* ***Star Motor Imps., Inc. v. Superior Ct.*** (1st Dist.1979) 88 Cal.App.3d 201, 204.

(2) Alternative theories. A party can plead alternative theories without judicially admitting facts if the theories do not contain contradictory facts. 1 Witkin, *Cal. Evidence*, Hearsay, §98; *see* ***Faulkner v. California Toll Bridge Auth.*** (1953) 40 Cal.2d 317, 328; *see, e.g.*, ***Farmers Ins. Exch. v. Superior Ct.*** (4th Dist.2000) 79 Cal.App.4th 1400, 1404 n.3 (D could defend action by denying defect in tire and reserve option of seeking indemnity from third persons on theory that D was responsible for defect, if there was one); ***Lewis Ave. Parent Teachers' Ass'n v. Hussey*** (1st Dist.1967) 250 Cal.App.2d 232, 236-37 (D could both deny existence of agency relationship and claim indemnity in event relationship was established). If the pleading contains two directly contradictory allegations, the allegation that bears most strongly against the pleader will be regarded as a judicial admission. ***Manti v. Gunari*** (1st Dist.1970) 5 Cal.App.3d 442, 450; ***Beatty v. Pacific States S&L Co.*** (2d Dist.1935) 4 Cal.App.2d 692, 697. If the pleading contains a specific allegation under one theory and a more general contradictory allegation under another theory, the more specific affirmative allegation will be regarded as a judicial admission. *See* ***Faulkner***, 40 Cal.2d at 328-29; ***Alfaro v. Community Hous. Imprv. Sys. & Planning Ass'n*** (6th Dist.2009) 171 Cal.App.4th 1356, 1381-82.

2. Effect of doctrine. A judicial admission about a dispositive fact (i.e., a fact that definitively resolves a legal issue) is conclusive against the party making it, bars the party from disputing it, and relieves the opposing party of the burden of proving the admitted fact. *See* ***St. Paul Mercury***, 111 Cal.App.4th at 1248 (in summary-judgment or summary-adjudication proceedings, admissions in pleading are conclusive and incontrovertible); ***Gates v. Bank of Am. Nat'l Trust & Sav. Ass'n*** (2d Dist.1953) 120 Cal.App.2d 571, 575 (party cannot dispute allegation made in its pleading); *Black's Law Dictionary* 709 (10th ed. 2014) (definition of "dispositive fact"); *see, e.g.*, ***Malone v. Roy*** (1897) 118 Cal. 512, 514 (superior court erred by allowing P to introduce evidence contradicting his complaint's allegations about rental value of property). Once a dispositive fact is conclusively established by judicial admission, it is deemed admitted and removed from the issues to be tried. *See* ***Castillo***, 146 Cal.App.4th at 1324; ***St. Paul Mercury***, 111 Cal.App.4th at 1248; ***Uram v. Abex Corp.*** (1st Dist.1990) 217 Cal.App.3d 1425, 1433. However, if the fact is not dispositive of an ultimate issue, the pleader can introduce other evidence on that issue. ***Electronic Equip. Express, Inc. v. Donald H. Seiler & Co.*** (1st Dist.1981) 122 Cal.App.3d 834, 850.

§8.2 Superseded pleadings. Once a pleading is amended, the previous pleading becomes ineffective and no longer functions as a pleading. ***Meyer v. State Bd. of Equalization*** (1954) 42 Cal.2d 376, 384.

1. Evidentiary effect. An assertion of fact or a failure to deny an assertion of fact in a party's superseded pleading, whether verified or unverified, can be used against the party for impeachment purposes. *See* ***Meyer***, 42

Cal.2d at 385; ***Schuh v. R.H. Herron Co.*** (1917) 177 Cal. 13, 17; ***Staples v. Hoefke*** (2d Dist.1987) 189 Cal.App.3d 1397, 1412. It is unclear whether a superseded pleading can be used under the Evidence Code as substantive evidence to establish a fact. *Compare* ***Meyer***, 42 Cal.2d at 384 (superseded pleading cannot be used as direct evidence to establish fact), *and* ***Staples***, 189 Cal.App.3d at 1412 (same), *with* ***Deveny v. Entropin, Inc.*** (4th Dist.2006) 139 Cal.App.4th 408, 426 (superseded pleading can be used as declaration against interest), ***City of Pleasant Hill v. First Baptist Church*** (1st Dist.1969) 1 Cal.App.3d 384, 419 (urging that rule in ***Meyer*** be revisited in light of adoption of Evid. Code), *and* 1 Witkin, *Cal. Evidence*, Hearsay, §98 (rule in ***Meyer*** has lost significance since adoption of Evid. C. §1235, which provides hearsay exception for prior inconsistent statements).

2. No sham amendment. A party cannot attempt to avoid the adverse effects of an original pleading by filing an amended pleading that omits, corrects, or substitutes new facts for the facts in the original pleading. See "Amendment is sham," ch. 3-C, §6.2.4(4)(e), p. 234. A party can, however, amend the pleading if the party can sufficiently explain the reason for the omission or contradiction. *See* ***Reichert v. General Ins.*** (1968) 68 Cal.2d 822, 836 (party should be allowed to correct pleading if it was made as result of mistake or inadvertence); ***Macomber v. State*** (1st Dist.1967) 250 Cal.App.2d 391, 399 (rule against sham pleadings does not prevent party from correcting ambiguous statements of fact); *see, e.g.*, ***Deveny***, 139 Cal.App.4th at 426 (sham-pleading doctrine did not apply because Ps showed that mistake was made in drafting original complaint).

§8.3 Earlier pleadings.

1. Evidentiary admission. An assertion of fact or a failure to deny an assertion of fact in a party's pleading in an earlier case can be used against the party as an evidentiary admission for substantive evidence or for impeachment. *See* Evid. C. §§1220, 1235; ***Minish v. Hanuman Fellowship*** (6th Dist.2013) 214 Cal.App.4th 437, 457-58; ***Jogani v. Jogani*** (2d Dist.2006) 141 Cal.App.4th 158, 175; ***Dolinar v. Pedone*** (3d Dist.1944) 63 Cal.App.2d 169, 176-77. This rule has been applied to both verified and unverified pleadings. *See, e.g.*, ***Magnolia Square Homeowners Ass'n v. Safeco Ins.*** (6th Dist.1990) 221 Cal.App.3d 1049, 1060-61 (unverified amended complaint); ***Dolinar***, 63 Cal.App.2d at 176-77 (answer verified by attorney). Unlike judicial admissions, evidentiary admissions are not conclusive and can be controverted. *See* ***Minish***, 214 Cal.App.4th at 457-58 (party against whom pleading is offered can show that statements were mistakenly or inadvertently made or not authorized).

2. Judicial admission. All material allegations in a complaint on which a default judgment was entered in an earlier case can be used against the defaulting party as judicial admissions. ***Bohn v. Watson*** (2d Dist.1954) 130 Cal.App.2d 24, 33; ***Fitzgerald v. Herzer*** (2d Dist.1947) 78 Cal.App.2d 127, 131. See "Current pleadings – judicial-admissions doctrine," §8.1, p. 24.

§9. APPELLATE REVIEW

§9.1 Generally. The adequacy of pleadings is determined in light of CCP §452, which provides that all pleadings must be liberally construed to do substantial justice. ***In re Estate of Wickersham*** (1908) 153 Cal. 603, 608; ***Je Ho Lim v. The.TV Corp.*** (2d Dist.2002) 99 Cal.App.4th 684, 689-90; *see* ***Alliance Mortg. Co. v. Rothwell*** (1995) 10 Cal.4th 1226, 1232.

1. De novo. When a superior court sustains a demurrer or grants a motion for judgment on the pleadings, an appellate court will review the ruling de novo. ***Gerawan Farming, Inc. v. Lyons*** (2000) 24 Cal.4th 468, 515 (motion for judgment on pleadings); ***Rappaport-Scott v. Interinsurance Exch. of the Auto. Club*** (2d Dist.2007) 146 Cal.App.4th 831, 835 (demurrer); ***Aron v. U-Haul Co.*** (2d Dist.2006) 143 Cal.App.4th 796, 802 (motion for judgment on pleadings).

2. Abuse of discretion. If the superior court dismissed the case without first giving the party an opportunity to amend, an appellate court will review the superior court's ruling to dismiss for abuse of discretion. *See* ***Aubry v. Tri-City Hosp. Dist.*** (1992) 2 Cal.4th 962, 967 (abuse of discretion to sustain demurrer without leave to amend if there is reasonable possibility that defect could be cured by amendment); ***Blank v. Kirwan*** (1985) 39 Cal.3d 311, 318 (same). If the superior court dismissed the case after giving the party an opportunity to amend, but the party

did not timely do so, an appellate court will also review the superior court's ruling to dismiss for abuse of discretion. *See, e.g.*, ***Gitmed v. General Motors Corp.*** (2d Dist.1994) 26 Cal.App.4th 824, 827 (dismissal after demurrer under CCP §581(f)(2)).

§9.2 Leave to amend. Generally, the superior court's ruling granting or denying leave to amend is reviewed for abuse of discretion. ***Emerald Bay Cmty. Ass'n v. Golden Eagle Ins.*** (4th Dist.2005) 130 Cal.App.4th 1078, 1097; ***Bedolla v. Logan & Frazer*** (1st Dist.1975) 52 Cal.App.3d 118, 135. But when the superior court bases its decision to deny leave to amend on a legal conclusion, that decision is reviewed de novo. *See, e.g.*, ***Fuller v. Tucker*** (2d Dist.2000) 84 Cal.App.4th 1163, 1169 (superior court's denial of amendment rested on interpretation of CCP §474).

D. LAW & MOTION PRACTICE

Law-and-motion practice in California generally refers to the rules of procedure that apply to making, filing, serving, and opposing motions. A motion is simply an application for a court order. CCP §1003. Motions are distinguishable from complaints and formal petitions because they do not involve an independent right or remedy; instead, motions relate to some issue that is ancillary to an ongoing action or proceeding. ***Hospital Sys. v. Office of Statewide Health Planning & Dev.*** (3d Dist.1994) 25 Cal.App.4th 1686, 1691. Although most motion practice occurs before trial, motions can also be made during trial (e.g., motion for nonsuit), after trial (e.g., motion to set aside a judgment), and during appeal (e.g., motion to strike). *See* CRC 3.1103(a), 8.204(e)(2)(B).

Generally, there are three ways in which a motion can be brought—orally, by ex parte application, and by noticed motion. Kiesel et al., *Matthew Bender Practice Guide: California Pretrial Civil Procedure* (2014), §26.04. Oral motions are generally reserved for open court when both sides are present, and ex parte applications are typically used when there is no time for formal notice. *Id.* §§26.04, 26.05[1], [2]. The majority of pretrial motion practice in California is by noticed motion. *Id.* §§26.04, 26.05[3].

This subchapter discusses the law-and-motion rules that apply generally to most pretrial noticed motions. The rules discussed in this subchapter do not apply, however, to pretrial motion practice in actions under the Family Code, the Probate Code, the Welfare and Institutions Code, or CCP §§527.6 through 527.85. Because some noticed motions have specific requirements that differ from the general law-and-motion rules discussed in this subchapter (e.g., noticed motions for summary judgment have different format and evidentiary requirements), each subchapter that discusses a particular motion should be read. For a discussion of the law-and-motion rules that apply to ex parte applications, see "Ex Parte Practice," ch. 1-E, p. 39.

§1. GENERAL

§1.1 Purpose. A motion is used to obtain a court order in an action or proceeding. *See* CCP §1003; ***Hospital Sys. v. Office of Statewide Health Planning & Dev.*** (3d Dist.1994) 25 Cal.App.4th 1686, 1691.

§1.2 Primary authority. CCP §§1003-1008; CRC 3.1100 et seq.; *see also* CCP §§1010-1020 (rules on notice, filing, and service of papers).

§1.3 Secondary authority. The following secondary sources are cited as authority in this subchapter:

- *California Civil Procedure Before Trial* (CEB Online ed. 2014) (referred to as *CEB Procedure Before Trial*).
- Kiesel et al., *Matthew Bender Practice Guide: California Pretrial Civil Procedure* (2014) (referred to as Kiesel, *Cal. Pretrial Civil Procedure*).
- State Bar of California, *Attorney Guidelines of Civility & Professionalism (Civility Toolbox)* (2009), ethics.calbar.ca.gov/Ethics/AttorneyCivilityandProfessionalism.aspx (referred to as *Cal. Attorney Guidelines*).
- Weil & Brown, *California Practice Guide: Civil Procedure Before Trial* (CD-ROM ed. 2014) (referred to as Weil, *Civil Procedure Before Trial*).

§1.4 Judicial Council forms. The Judicial Council has adopted a number of forms for use in law and motion practice. *See, e.g.*, Judicial Council Forms, form MC-051 (notice of motion and motion to be relieved as counsel). For information about the Judicial Council forms, see the forms page on the California Courts website at www.courts.ca.gov/forms.htm.

§2. LAW GOVERNING MOTION PRACTICE

Generally, motion practice is governed by the Code of Civil Procedure and the California Rules of Court. All local rules relating to motion practice, including those relating to the form and format of papers, are null and void unless otherwise permitted or required by a statute or a California Rule of Court. CRC 3.20(a); *see, e.g.*, CRC 3.1308 (permitting courts to adopt by local rule procedures for tentative rulings). Thus, to the extent that a local rule relating to motion practice conflicts with a statute or a California Rule of Court, the local rule is preempted. *See, e.g.*, Super. Ct. Contra Costa Cty. Loc. R., rule 3.46 (noting that local rule on time to plead or respond after hearing is subject to preemption by California Rules of Court). See "Local Rules," ch. 1-A, §4, p. 6. This does not mean that all local rules relating to motion practice are preempted. For example, courts are not prohibited from specifying by local rule the days on which motions will be heard on their calendar. *See* CRC 3.1304(a); *see, e.g.*, Super. Ct. Santa Clara Cty. Loc. R. (civil), rule 7.A & 7.B (motions will be heard on Tuesdays and Thursdays).

§3. NOTICED MOTION DEFINED

A noticed motion is a written motion that is accompanied by a written notice to the opposing party that identifies the time, date, and place of the hearing, the nature of the relief sought, the grounds for the motion, and any papers that support the motion. *CEB Procedure Before Trial*, §12.19; *see* CCP §1010; CRC 3.1110(a). The noticed motion is the most common motion made in California. Kiesel, *Cal. Pretrial Civil Procedure*, §26.04.

§4. WHEN NOTICED MOTION REQUIRED

§4.1 Expressly required. Generally, a noticed motion must be given whenever a statute or rule expressly requires it. *See, e.g.*, CCP §418.10(a)(2) (D may file and serve notice of motion to stay or dismiss for forum non conveniens), §1005(a)(1)-(a)(12) (list of motions that require written notice); CRC 3.1320(i) (order striking amended pleading must be obtained by noticed motion), CRC 3.1342(a) (party seeking discretionary dismissal for delay in prosecution must file and serve notice of motion). A noticed motion is also required for any proceeding under the Code of Civil Procedure that requires notice, as long as no other time or method is prescribed by law or by the court or judge. CCP §1005(a)(13).

§4.2 Implicitly required. A noticed motion may be required even when a statute does not expressly require one. As a general rule, a noticed motion must be given whenever the order sought may affect the opposing party's rights. ***McDonald v. Severy*** (1936) 6 Cal.2d 629, 631.

§5. MOTION PAPERS

"Motion papers" for a noticed motion generally include a notice of motion, the motion itself, and a memorandum of points and authorities in support of the motion. CRC 3.1112(a), 3.1113(a); ***Luri v. Greenwald*** (2d Dist.2003) 107 Cal.App.4th 1119, 1126. These components can be filed separately, or they can be combined into a single document if the caption specifies each component separately. CRC 3.1112(c); ***Luri***, 107 Cal.App.4th at 1126. Motion papers can also include papers filed in support of the motion, such as declarations, exhibits, appendixes, and other documents or pleadings. CRC 3.1112(b).

NOTE

Some noticed motions require additional papers in support. For example, motions for summary judgment require a separate statement of undisputed facts to be filed and served with the motion papers. CCP §437c(b)(1); CRC 3.1350(c)(2). To determine if a particular motion requires additional support, see the relevant subchapter in this book.

§5.1 Notice of motion & motion. The purpose of the notice of motion and the motion is to (1) ask the court for an order and (2) give the opposing party adequate time to prepare an opposition. *See* CCP §1003; ***Arambula v. Union Carbide Corp.*** (2d Dist.2005) 128 Cal.App.4th 333, 343. Although they are separate components, the notice of motion (also referred to as a "notice of hearing") and the motion itself are usually combined into a single document referred to as a "notice of motion and motion." *See* ***Luri v. Greenwald*** (2d Dist.2003) 107 Cal.App.4th 1119, 1127. The notice of motion and the motion must be in writing and meet the following requirements:

PRACTICE TIP

Some motions require special information to be included in the notice of motion and motion. Review the relevant subchapter in this book to see if a particular type of motion requires additional information.

1. General requirements for papers. The notice of motion and motion must meet the general requirements for papers. See "General Requirements for Papers," ch. 1-B, §2, p. 9.

2. First-page requirements. The notice of motion and motion must meet the general requirements for the first page of every paper and the specific requirements for the first page of a motion. See "First page," ch. 1-B, §2.5.2, p. 12.

3. Other requirements. The notice of motion and motion must include the following information:

(1) The name of the movant. CRC 3.1112(d)(1).

(2) The names of the parties to whom the motion is addressed. CRC 3.1112(d)(2).

(3) The grounds for the motion and the nature of the order sought. CCP §1010; CRC 3.1110(a), 3.1112(d)(3); ***Sole Energy Co. v. Hodges*** (4th Dist.2005) 128 Cal.App.4th 199, 207; ***Luri***, 107 Cal.App.4th at 1125; ***Josephson v. Superior Ct.*** (2d Dist.1963) 219 Cal.App.2d 354, 362; *see* ***Hernandez v. National Dairy Prods. Co.*** (2d Dist.1954) 126 Cal.App.2d 490, 493 (notice must sufficiently define issues for information and attention of opposing party and court). This information must be included in the first paragraph. CRC 3.1110(a). If the motion challenges a pleading, it must identify the specific part of the pleading being challenged. CRC 3.1112(d)(4). The court can overlook any omission in the notice if the supporting papers clearly identify the grounds for the motion. ***Luri***, 107 Cal.App.4th at 1125; ***366-386 Geary St., L.P. v. Superior Ct.*** (1st Dist.1990) 219 Cal.App.3d 1186, 1200; ***Carrasco v. Craft*** (5th Dist.1985) 164 Cal.App.3d 796, 808. *But see* ***Hernandez***, 126 Cal.App.2d at 493 (grounds must be stated in notice; otherwise, purpose of notice of motion would be limited to advising of time and place of hearing).

PRACTICE TIP

It is common for the notice to use boilerplate language such as the following: "This motion is based on this Notice of Motion and Motion, the supporting Memorandum of Points and Authorities, any supporting papers, all other pleadings, records, and files in this action, and the arguments and evidence that may be presented to the Court at the hearing." E.g., ***Carrasco****, 164 Cal.App.3d at 808. When the motion is based on evidence, it is better to refer specifically to each document supporting the motion or opposition (e.g., "declaration of John Smith"). If the notice refers to a paper that the opposing party has not yet received, the paper must accompany the notice. CCP §1010.*

§5.2 Memorandum of points & authorities.

1. When required. A supporting memorandum is required for most motions. *See* CRC 3.1113(a). If the movant does not attach a memorandum, the court can deny the motion or can find that all grounds not supported are waived. *Id.*; *cf.* ***Jermstad v. McNelis*** (3d Dist.1989) 210 Cal.App.3d 528, 538 (special demurrer).

2. When not required. For motions that do not require a memorandum, a party can submit one or the court can order one when it would further the interests of justice. CRC 3.1114(b). A memorandum is not required for the following applications, motions, or petitions if filed on a Judicial Council form:

(1) Application for appointment of a guardian ad litem in a civil case. CRC 3.1114(a)(1).

(2) Application for an order extending time to serve a pleading. CRC 3.1114(a)(2).

(3) Motion to be relieved as counsel. CRC 3.1114(a)(3).

(4) Motion filed in a small-claims case. CRC 3.1114(a)(4).

(5) Petition for change of name or gender. CRC 3.1114(a)(5).

(6) Petition for declaration of emancipation of a minor. CRC 3.1114(a)(6).

(7) Petition for an injunction prohibiting harassment. CRC 3.1114(a)(7).

(8) Petition for a protective order to prevent elder or dependent-adult abuse. CRC 3.1114(a)(8).

(9) Petition for order to prevent postsecondary school violence. CRC 3.1114(a)(9).

(10) Petition of an employer for an injunction prohibiting workplace violence. CRC 3.1114(a)(10).

(11) Petition for an order prohibiting abuse (transitional housing). CRC 3.1114(a)(11).

(12) Petition to approve the compromise of a claim of a minor or a person with a disability. CRC 3.1114(a)(12).

(13) Petition for withdrawal of funds from a blocked account. CRC 3.1114(a)(13).

3. Format. The format of the memorandum must meet the requirements of papers generally. See "General Requirements for Papers," ch. 1-B, §2, p. 9.

(1) Length. For most motions, the "opening" or "first" memorandum cannot exceed 15 pages. CRC 3.1113(d). For summary-judgment or summary-adjudication motions, the memorandum cannot exceed 20 pages. *Id.* This page limit does not include exhibits, declarations, attachments, the table of contents, the table of authorities, or the proof of service. *Id.* The party can ask the court for permission to file a longer memorandum by filing an ex parte application, with written notice to the other parties at least one day before the memorandum is due, explaining why the argument cannot be made within the page limit. CRC 3.1113(e); *see* ***Collins v. Hertz Corp.*** (2d Dist.2006) 144 Cal.App.4th 64, 71. If the memorandum exceeds the page limit and the party has not obtained permission from the court to file a longer one, the memorandum will be deemed to have been filed late at the time of filing and can be struck from the files. *See* CRC 3.1113(g).

PRACTICE TIP

The court may allow the parties to stipulate to a memorandum that exceeds the page limits.

(2) Contents.

(a) Tables of contents & authorities. The memorandum must include a table of contents and a table of authorities if it exceeds ten pages. CRC 3.1113(f). If the memorandum includes a table of contents and a table of authorities, it must be paginated as follows:

[1] The caption page or pages must not be numbered. CRC 3.1113(h)(1).

[2] The pages of the tables must be numbered consecutively using lowercase Roman numerals starting on the first page of the tables. CRC 3.1113(h)(2).

[3] The pages of the text must be numbered consecutively using Arabic numerals starting on the first page of the text. CRC 3.1113(h)(3).

(b) Statement of facts. The memorandum must include a statement of facts. CRC 3.1113(b). The party should ensure that each stated fact is supported by admissible evidence and followed by a reference to the evidence accompanying the motion or opposition. *See* ***Smith, Smith & Kring v. Superior Ct.*** (4th Dist.1997) 60 Cal.App.4th 573, 577-78; *see also* ***Calcor Space Facility, Inc. v. Superior Ct.*** (4th Dist.1997) 53 Cal.App.4th 216, 224 (in law-and-motion practice, factual evidence is supplied to court through declarations).

(c) Summary of argument. The memorandum must include an opening summary of argument if it exceeds 15 pages. CRC 3.1113(f). Unless the memorandum is in support of a summary-judgment or summary-adjudication motion, the party must ask the court for permission to file a memorandum that exceeds 15 pages. *See* CRC 3.1113(d). See "Length," §5.2.3(1), p. 29.

(d) Statement of law, arguments & evidence. The memorandum must include a concise statement of the law, arguments, and evidence relied on and a discussion of the statutes, cases, and textbooks cited in support of the movant's position. CRC 3.1113(b); *see* ***People v. Williams*** (1999) 20 Cal.4th 119, 129 (movant bears burden of informing opponent and court of specific basis for its motion); *see, e.g.*, ***Black v. Financial Freedom Senior Funding Corp.*** (1st Dist.2001) 92 Cal.App.4th 917, 925 n.9 (movant waived argument on merits of nonmovant's claims because movant did not address claims in memorandum); *see also* ***Hope Int'l Univ. v. Superior Ct.*** (4th Dist.2004) 119 Cal.App.4th 719, 731-32 (for MSJ, movant is not required to organize points and authorities by each cause of action).

(3) Citations & references.

(a) Style manual. Citations to cases and authorities in the memorandum must follow the style stated in either the *California Style Manual* or *The Bluebook: A Uniform System of Citation*. CRC 1.200. Once the movant chooses a style manual, it must use the style prescribed in that manual throughout the memorandum. *Id.*

(b) Case citations. Case citations must include the official reporter volume and page number and the year of decision. CRC 3.1113(c). The court cannot require any other cite form. *Id.* For case citation form, see *California Style Manual* (4th ed. 2000) §§1:12-1:37.

(c) Exhibit references. If the memorandum refers to exhibits in supporting or opposing papers, the reference must indicate the number or letter of the exhibit, the specific page, and if applicable, the paragraph or line number (e.g., "Exhibit A, page 3, line 2"). CRC 3.1113(k).

(d) References to filed papers. If the memorandum refers to any paper already in the court's file, the paper must be referred to by date of execution and title. CRC 3.1110(d).

§5.3 Supporting evidence. Some motions cannot be supported by extrinsic evidence other than judicially noticed facts (e.g., demurrers, motions for judgment on the pleadings), but most motions can be supported by evidence in the form of declarations, deposition transcripts, discovery responses, and other documents. Weil, *Civil Procedure Before Trial*, ¶9:43; *see, e.g.*, CCP §437c(b)(1) (MSJ must be supported by affidavits, declarations, admissions, interrogatory answers, depositions, and matters subject to judicial notice); ***Vahle v. Barwick*** (1st Dist.2001) 93 Cal.App.4th 1323, 1329 (D supported MSJ with series of letters); ***Olson Prtshp. v. Gaylord Plating Lab*** (2d Dist.1990) 226 Cal.App.3d 235, 242 n.7 (verified supplemental answers to interrogatories were competent evidence to defeat MSJ). See "Demurrer," ch. 4-H, p. 396; "Motion for Judgment on the Pleadings," ch. 4-I, p. 411. If the memorandum is supported by evidence that is not already in the court's file, the evidence should be attached to the notice of motion if possible and filed and served with the motion papers. *See* CCP §§1005(b), 1010; CRC 3.1113(j). See "Filing & Serving Noticed Motions," §7, p. 33. For a discussion of how exhibits should be presented to the court, see "Exhibits," ch. 1-B, §2.8.4, p. 17.

NOTE

Some local rules do not allow oral testimony at the hearing on a motion unless the party explains why the evidence cannot be presented by declaration or affidavit. E.g., Super. Ct. Calaveras Cty. Loc. R., rule 3.3(b); Super. Ct. Los Angeles Cty. Loc. R., rule 3.7; Super. Ct. Merced Cty. Loc. R., rule 3.d; see also Super. Ct. Butte Cty. Loc. R., rule 2.12 (at default-judgment hearing, evidence is usually presented by declarations rather than oral testimony, although witnesses may need to be present).

1. Declarations. If the motion papers include a declaration, the declaration's caption must state the name of the declarant and must specifically identify the motion it supports. CRC 3.1115. See "Declaration," ch. 1-B, §4.1.1, p. 19. If the declaration incorporates materials by reference, the materials must be provided and must conform to the rules of evidence. *See* ***Angelus Chevrolet v. State*** (2d Dist.1981) 115 Cal.App.3d 995, 1001.

2. Deposition testimony. If the motion papers include deposition testimony as an exhibit, the testimony excerpts must be accompanied by a title page, which must state the name of the deponent and the date of the deposition (usually the deposition transcript's title page). CRC 3.1116(a). After the title page, the exhibit must contain only the relevant pages of the transcript and the court reporter's certification page (located at the back of the transcript). *See* CRC 3.1116(b). The original page number of any deposition page must be clearly visible. *Id.* The relevant part of any deposition testimony must be marked in a way that calls attention to the testimony. CRC 3.1116(c). See "Using Depositions in Court Proceedings," ch. 7-B, §13, p. 810.

3. Documents.

(1) Authenticity. If the motion papers include discovery responses, business records, or other writings, the party should include declarations laying a proper foundation for authenticity. *See* Evid. C. §250 (definition of "writing"), §1400 et seq. (authentication rules); Weil, *Civil Procedure Before Trial*, ¶9:50a (to authenticate discovery responses, attach declaration from attorney or court reporter confirming that responses were actually given); *see, e.g.*, ***Claudio v. Regents of the Univ. of Cal.*** (3d Dist.2005) 134 Cal.App.4th 224, 244 (letter was not authenticated because it was not referenced in declaration). Authentication simply requires a party to establish that the writing is what the party claims it is. Evid. C. §1400; *see* ***Interinsurance Exch. of the Auto. Club v. Velji*** (2d Dist.1975) 44 Cal.App.3d 310, 318. Authentication does not overcome any admissibility problems, such as hearsay. ***Stockinger v. Feather River Cmty. Coll.*** (3d Dist.2003) 111 Cal.App.4th 1014, 1027-28.

(2) Admissibility. If the motion papers include business records or other writings, the party may need to include declarations laying a proper foundation for admissibility. *See* Evid. C. §250 (definition of "writing"). A writing is admissible if it can be entered into evidence. *See Black's Law Dictionary* 56 (10th ed. 2014) (definition of "admissible"); *see, e.g.*, ***Sanchez v. Hillerich & Bradsby Co.*** (2d Dist.2002) 104 Cal.App.4th 703, 720 (declaration did not provide foundation for admissibility because it did not state how reports were prepared or what sources of information they were based on). For example, if the movant relies on business records or other writings for the truth of what is contained in them, the movant may need to establish an exception to the hearsay rule. *See, e.g.*, ***Ampex Corp. v. Cargle*** (1st Dist.2005) 128 Cal.App.4th 1569, 1573 n.2 (computer printouts from website were not hearsay because they were offered to show their existence, not for truth of their contents); ***Pajaro Valley Water Mgmt. Agency v. McGrath*** (6th Dist.2005) 128 Cal.App.4th 1093, 1107-08 (D's declaration that was based in part on water bills was hearsay because it did not establish hearsay exception for bills).

4. Pleadings.

(1) Party's own verified pleadings. Generally, a party can rely on its own verified pleading to support or oppose a motion if the pleading can be treated as an affidavit or declaration. *See* CCP §446(a); ***Mission Imps., Inc. v. Superior Ct.*** (1982) 31 Cal.3d 921, 929 n.7 (verified complaint can be considered in ruling on motion to change venue); ***Mosby v. Superior Ct.*** (3d Dist.1974) 43 Cal.App.3d 219, 227 (same). *But see* CCP §437c(p) (party's own pleading cannot be used as evidence for or against MSJ); ***Hecimovich v. Encinal Sch. Parent Teacher Org.*** (1st

Dist.2012) 203 Cal.App.4th 450, 474 n.8 (verified pleading cannot be used as evidence for anti-SLAPP motion). A verified pleading cannot be treated as an affidavit or declaration if the pleading is verified by an attorney on behalf of a party or by an officer on behalf of a corporation or public agency. CCP §446(a); *see* ***Mission Imps.***, 31 Cal.3d at 929 n.7. Opposition to many types of motions can be supported by verified pleadings. *See* ***Burger v. Superior Ct.*** (1st Dist.1984) 151 Cal.App.3d 1013, 1019 (verified complaint can be considered as counteraffidavit to motion to expunge lis pendens); ***Atkins, Kroll & Co. v. Broadway Lumber Co.*** (1st Dist.1963) 222 Cal.App.2d 646, 654 (verified complaint can be considered as counteraffidavit to motion for change of venue); ***Quick v. Corsaro*** (1st Dist.1960) 180 Cal.App.2d 831, 835 (same); *see, e.g.*, ***Wolfe v. City of Alexandria*** (1st Dist.1990) 217 Cal.App.3d 541, 546 (verified complaint treated as declaration in opposition to motion to quash service of process).

(2) Opposing party's pleadings. A party can rely on its opponent's pleading, whether verified or unverified, if the pleading contains judicial admissions. See "Using Pleadings," ch. 1-C, §8, p. 24.

5. Judicially noticed matters. If the motion papers include matters subject to judicial notice, the party should make a separate request for judicial notice of those matters. See "Request for Judicial Notice," ch. 5-J, p. 547.

6. Supporting authority.

(1) California cases. If a California case is cited before it is published in the Official Reports advance sheets, the party must include the title, case number, date of decision, and appellate-district number for cases from the courts of appeals. CRC 3.1113(i)(2). If required by the judge, a copy of the opinion must be lodged with the papers that cite it and must be tabbed like an exhibit under CRC 3.1110(f). CRC 3.1113(i)(2). See "Documents lodged," ch. 1-F, §2.3, p. 47. If an opinion is only available electronically, a copy of the opinion must be included with the papers that cite it. CRC 8.1115(c). If the opinion is not certified for publication or ordered published, it cannot be cited or relied on by a party or the court unless the opinion is relevant (1) under the doctrines of law of the case, res judicata, or collateral estoppel or (2) to a criminal or disciplinary action because it states reasons for a decision affecting the same defendant or respondent in a similar action. CRC 8.1115(a), (b). *But see* ***Mangini v. J.G. Durand Int'l*** (1st Dist.1994) 31 Cal.App.4th 214, 219 (court cited its prior, depublished opinions to show that same issue was presented to California Supreme Court in those cases and that issue remained unresolved); ***Conrad v. Ball Corp.*** (1st Dist.1994) 24 Cal.App.4th 439, 443 n.2 (stating that California Supreme Court has suggested that unpublished opinions may be cited if they are not "relied on").

(2) Other authority. If required by the judge, a copy of any authority other than California cases, statutes, constitutional provisions, or state or local rules must be lodged with the papers that cite it and must be tabbed like an exhibit under CRC 3.1110(f). CRC 3.1113(i)(1). See "Documents lodged," ch. 1-F, §2.3, p. 47. The party must promptly provide a copy of such authority to any other party requesting a copy. CRC 3.1113(i)(3). If the authority is an unpublished federal case, the party may be able to cite it. *See* ***Bowen v. Ziasun Techs.*** (4th Dist.2004) 116 Cal.App.4th 777, 787 n.6 (former CRC 977(a), now CRC 8.1115(a), does not explicitly prohibit party from citing unpublished federal cases).

NOTE

The attached, tabbed copies of "other authority" form what is commonly referred to as the "Appendix of Foreign Authorities."

---

§5.4 Request for judicial notice. The motion papers can be accompanied by a separate request for judicial notice under CRC 3.1306(c). CRC 3.1113(*l*); *see* ***Stevenson Real Estate Servs. v. CB Richard Ellis Real Estate Servs.*** (2d Dist.2006) 138 Cal.App.4th 1215, 1221. See "Request for Judicial Notice," ch. 5-J, p. 547.

§5.5 Proposed order. The motion papers can be accompanied by a proposed order, which must be lodged and served with the papers but not attached to them. CRC 3.1113(m); *see, e.g.*, Super. Ct. San Francisco Cty. Loc. R., rule 8.7.B (party moving for or opposing MSJ or MSA must bring to hearing proposed order that complies with CCP §437c(g)). See "Documents lodged," ch. 1-F, §2.3, p. 47.

§5.6 Proof of service. The motion papers should include a proof of service. *See* CRC 3.1300(c); *CEB Procedure Before Trial*, §12.82; *see, e.g.*, ***Ovitz v. Schulman*** (2d Dist.2005) 133 Cal.App.4th 830, 837 n.3 (court disregarded motion to vacate because it was filed without proof of service). See "Attach proof of service," ch. 1-G, §7.1.1(2), p. 74. If a proof of service is not filed with the motion papers, it must be filed at least five court days before the hearing. CRC 3.1300(c).

§6. DUTY TO MEET & CONFER

Before filing a noticed motion, an attorney should contact the opposing attorney to attempt to informally resolve the dispute. *See* Super. Ct. Los Angeles Cty. Loc. R., appendix 3.A(h)(1); *Cal. Attorney Guidelines*, §10; Weil, *Civil Procedure Before Trial*, ¶9:13.10. If the opposing attorney has no objection to the motion, the attorney can file an unopposed motion or avoid filing the motion completely. *Cal. Attorney Guidelines*, §10. For certain motions, a party may be required to "meet and confer" before the motion can be filed—that is, make a reasonable and good-faith attempt to informally resolve each issue presented in the motion. *See* CCP §2016.040 (requirements for meet-and-confer declaration); *see, e.g., id.* §2025.480(b) (motion to compel answers or production at deposition must be accompanied by meet-and-confer declaration). For a discussion of the meet-and-confer requirement in case-management conferences and discovery proceedings, see "Meet-and-Confer Requirement," ch. 5-A, §6, p. 466, and "Meet-and-Confer Obligation," ch. 7-A, §10, p. 761.

§7. FILING & SERVING NOTICED MOTIONS

§7.1 Filing.

1. Where to file. Unless otherwise provided by local rule, all motion papers are filed with the court clerk. CRC 3.1302(a).

NOTE

Some courts, by local rule, require the moving party to deliver a courtesy copy of the motion to the judge before the hearing. E.g., Super. Ct. San Francisco Cty. Loc. R., rule 3.4 (requires file-endorsed courtesy copy on day paper is filed for Department 610 cases); Super. Ct. Sonoma Cty. Loc. R., rule 5.1.C (recommends hand-delivering courtesy copy of any motion filed within 21 days before hearing).

---

2. What to file. For a general discussion of what to file and what not to file, see "What to File," ch. 1-F, §2, p. 45.

(1) Notice of motion, motion & memorandum. The notice of motion, the motion, and the memorandum must be filed with the court. *See* CCP §1005(b); CRC 3.1300(a), 3.1302(a).

(2) Supporting evidence.

(a) Generally. In most cases, if the motion is supported by evidence that is not already in the court's file, the originals must be filed with the court. *See* CCP §1005(b) (supporting papers must be filed); Kiesel, *Cal. Pretrial Civil Procedure*, §26.43[5][e] (supporting evidence not before court must accompany motion). See "Original & copy," ch. 1-F, §2.1.2, p. 46.

(b) Discovery documents. If the motion is being supported by discovery documents, copies of the relevant questions and answers should be filed with the motion, but not the originals. Weil, *Civil Procedure Before Trial*, ¶9:50; *see* CCP §§2025.550(a), 2030.280(a), 2033.270(a).

(3) Request for judicial notice. See "Request for Judicial Notice," ch. 5-J, p. 547.

(4) Proof of service. See "Proof of service," §5.6, this page.

NOTE

Proposed orders as well as authority cited in the memorandum that is not from California or has not been published yet in the Official Reports are "lodged" with the court, not filed. See "Documents lodged," ch. 1-F, §2.3, p. 47.

3. How to file. See "How to File," ch. 1-F, §4, p. 47.

4. Deadline to file. The deadline to file a pretrial noticed motion generally depends on two things: (1) the type of relief that is requested and (2) the amount of notice that is required before the motion is heard.

(1) Deadline for relief. Generally, pretrial noticed motions can be filed anytime before trial as long as the action is pending. *See* Kiesel, *Cal. Pretrial Civil Procedure*, §26.07. For some motions, however, the deadline to file is defined specifically by statute. For example, some motions must be requested before the defendant makes a general appearance (e.g., motion to quash service) or within a certain time after a complaint has been served (e.g., motion to transfer venue, demurrer, motion to strike). Some motions can also be considered untimely if they are filed too early (e.g., motion for summary judgment, motion to dismiss for delay in prosecution). For a discussion of the deadlines that apply to a specific motion, see the relevant subchapter in this book.

(2) Deadline for notice. Generally, a noticed motion must be filed at least 16 court days before the hearing date. CCP §1005(b); *see* CRC 3.1300(a). See "Court days," ch. 1-F, §5.1.3(1)(b), p. 54. The 16-court-day requirement under CCP §1005 applies unless the period is shortened by court order or a different period is specifically required by law. CCP §1005(b); CRC 3.1300(a); *see* ***People v. American Contractors Indem.*** (2d Dist.1999) 74 Cal.App.4th 1037, 1049 (applying former CCP §1005; statute applies unless another statute specifically provides for different period). See "Shortening Time," ch. 5-E, p. 497. For example, a motion to dismiss for delay in prosecution must be filed 45 days before the hearing. CRC 3.1342(a). For a discussion of the filing requirements that apply to a specific motion, see the relevant subchapter in this book. For a discussion of how to calculate the deadline to file a document, see "Retrospective deadlines," ch. 1-F, §5.2, p. 56.

5. Filing fees. Generally, filing fees must be paid when the motion is filed unless the party asks the court to waive fees. See "Filing Fees," ch. 1-F, §7, p. 58. The filing fee for a noticed motion will depend on a number of factors (e.g., type of motion, the case's classification, whether the motion requires a hearing, whether the motion is the first paper filed in an action). For a discussion of the filing fees that apply to a specific motion, see "Common Fees," chart 1-4, p. 58.

§7.2 Serving.

1. Whom to serve. Motion papers must be served on all parties who have appeared in the action and who have not defaulted regardless of whether the motion seeks relief against that party. *See* CCP §1010; Weil, *Civil Procedure Before Trial*, ¶9:82.5.

2. What to serve. See "What to Serve," ch. 1-G, §2, p. 63.

(1) Notice of motion, motion & memorandum. The notice of motion, the motion, and the memorandum must be served. *See* CCP §1005(b).

(2) Supporting evidence. If the motion is supported by evidence that has not already been served on the party, copies of the supporting papers must be served. *See* CCP §1005(b) (supporting papers must be filed and copies must be served), §1010 (copy of supporting papers must be served on party if not previously served).

(3) Request for judicial notice. See "Request for Judicial Notice," ch. 5-J, p. 547.

(4) Proposed order. See "Proposed order," §5.5, p. 32.

3. How to serve. See "How to Serve," ch. 1-G, §5, p. 66.

4. Deadline to serve. Generally, the deadline for serving the motion papers is the same as the deadline for filing them. See "Deadline to file," §7.1.4, this page. For most noticed motions, the motion papers must be served at least 16 court days before the hearing on the motion. CCP §1005(b); *see* CRC 3.1300(a). See "Court days," ch. 1-F, §5.1.3(1)(b), p. 54. The 16-court-day requirement under CCP §1005 applies unless the notice period is shortened by court order or a different notice period is specifically required by law. CCP §1005(b); CRC 3.1300(a); *see, e.g.*, CCP §437c(a) (MSJ must be served 75 days before hearing if motion is served by personal delivery). See "Shortening

Time," ch. 5-E, p. 497. For example, the 16-court-day requirement can be increased based on how the notice of motion was served (e.g., 16-court-day requirement increased by 5 calendar days if notice of motion served by mail to California address). CCP §1005(b). For a discussion of the service requirements for a specific motion, see the relevant subchapter in this book. For a discussion of how to calculate the deadline to serve a document, see "Retrospective deadlines," ch. 1-G, §6.2, p. 71.

§7.3 Effect of filing & serving. A motion is "made" (i.e., becomes effective) when the notice of motion is both filed and served. CCP §1005.5; *see* ***Arambula v. Union Carbide Corp.*** (2d Dist.2005) 128 Cal.App.4th 333, 341 (although motion for relief under CCP §473(b) was timely filed, it was not served on adverse party, so court had no authority to grant relief); *cf.* ***People v. Dianda*** (1st Dist.1986) 178 Cal.App.3d 174, 177 (prosecutor's motion to reinstate under Pen. C. §871.5 is "made" at time of filing and service of motion).

§8. OPPOSITION PAPERS

If a party chooses to oppose a motion, it should file and serve "opposition papers," which include a memorandum of points and authorities and any supporting papers such as declarations or other evidence. The nonmovant can leave the motion unopposed or negotiate a resolution instead of filing an opposition. *See CEB Procedure Before Trial*, §§12.91-12.96; Weil, *Civil Procedure Before Trial*, ¶¶9:101-9:101.1. But choosing not to file an opposition can have several adverse consequences, such as waiver of objections or denial of oral argument. *See* CRC 3.1342(b) (failure to file and serve written opposition to motion to dismiss can be construed as admission that motion has merit); ***Carlton v. Quint*** (2d Dist.2000) 77 Cal.App.4th 690, 697 (failure to complain about defective service waives issue on appeal); ***Sexton v. Superior Ct.*** (2d Dist.1997) 58 Cal.App.4th 1403, 1410 (under local rules, if party does not file opposition papers, court can refuse to hear oral argument); ***Annex British Cars, Inc. v. Parker-Rhodes*** (1st Dist.1988) 198 Cal.App.3d 788, 792 (local rule prohibited oral argument on motion when opposition papers were not filed). *But see* ***Thomson v. Continental Ins.*** (1967) 66 Cal.2d 738, 745-46 (P's failure to file affidavit opposing motion to dismiss for forum non conveniens did not prevent him from obtaining reversal on appeal because venue motion must stand on its own grounds rather than on weakness of opposition).

NOTE

The party can file a notice of nonopposition if it does not want to oppose the motion. See, e.g., ***Profit Concepts Mgmt. v. Griffith*** *(4th Dist.2008) 162 Cal.App.4th 950, 953 (after D moved to quash service of summons, P filed notice of nonopposition). By doing this, the party concedes that the motion is valid. See, e.g.,* ***Stuart v. Lilves*** *(1st Dist.1989) 210 Cal.App.3d 1215, 1219 n.1 (P conceded that his claim was invalid when he filed nonopposition to D's MSJ). But see* ***Chinese Yellow Pages Co. v. Chinese Overseas Mktg. Serv.*** *(2d Dist.2008) 170 Cal.App.4th 868, 876 (creditor filed conditional nonopposition to dismissal motion that conceded nothing unless certain technical issues were resolved). The moving party can also file a notice of nonopposition to inform the court that no opposition was filed.*

§8.1 Memorandum of points & authorities. The memorandum in opposition should be in the same format as the memorandum in support. *See CEB Procedure Before Trial*, §12.100; Weil, *Civil Procedure Before Trial*, ¶9:103. See "Memorandum of points & authorities," §5.2, p. 28.

NOTE

For a good discussion of tips on drafting a memorandum in opposition, see CEB Procedure Before Trial, §12.101; Weil, Civil Procedure Before Trial, ¶¶9:101-9:103.3.

1. Length. The memorandum in opposition is subject to the same page limits as the memorandum in support (i.e., it generally cannot exceed 15 pages). CRC 3.1113(d). See "Length," §5.2.3(1), p. 29.

2. Contents. The memorandum in opposition should include the same contents as required for the memorandum in support. See "Contents," §5.2.3(2), p. 29. When attacking the motion, the nonmovant can raise three types of challenges: procedural, evidentiary, and substantive. *See CEB Procedure Before Trial*, §§12.97-12.99; Weil, *Civil Procedure Before Trial*, ¶¶9:102-9:102.10.

(1) Procedural challenge. The nonmovant can challenge a defect in procedure. *See CEB Procedure Before Trial*, §12.97; Weil, *Civil Procedure Before Trial*, ¶9:102.1; *see, e.g.*, ***Bohn v. Bohn*** (1913) 164 Cal. 532, 538 (P objected to motion to transfer because of insufficiency of notice). If the objection is based on a defect or irregularity in the notice of motion, the nonmovant will need to decide to either (1) make the objection and seek a continuance to file an opposition on the merits if the objection is overruled or (2) waive the objection and address the merits of the motion. *See* ***Eliceche v. Federal Land Bank Ass'n*** (5th Dist.2002) 103 Cal.App.4th 1349, 1375; ***Carlton v. Quint*** (2d Dist.2000) 77 Cal.App.4th 690, 697-98; *see, e.g.*, ***Karlsson v. Ford Motor Co.*** (2d Dist.2006) 140 Cal.App.4th 1202, 1224 (D waived objection to defect in notice by attending court hearing and arguing on merits). A party does not waive an objection to a defect in the notice when its appearance at a hearing is for the limited purpose of challenging the defect. ***Bohn***, 164 Cal. at 538-39.

(2) Evidentiary challenge. The nonmovant can challenge the evidence supporting the motion. *See CEB Procedure Before Trial*, §12.98; Weil, *Civil Procedure Before Trial*, ¶9:102.5. If the nonmovant does not raise an evidentiary objection, the objection is waived. *See* Evid. C. §353(a); ***Broden v. Marin Humane Soc'y*** (1st Dist.1999) 70 Cal.App.4th 1212, 1227. The objection can be filed separately or as part of the memorandum. *CEB Procedure Before Trial*, §12.98; *see* Weil, *Civil Procedure Before Trial*, ¶9:102.6.

PRACTICE TIP

Evidentiary objections can be filed and served with the memorandum or they can be raised at the hearing. Weil, Civil Procedure Before Trial, ¶9:102.7. If the nonmovant waits until the hearing to raise them, it must ensure that a court reporter will be there to make a record of the court's ruling. Id.

---

(3) Substantive challenge. The nonmovant can challenge the motion on the merits (i.e., its legal sufficiency). *See CEB Procedure Before Trial*, §12.99; Weil, *Civil Procedure Before Trial*, ¶9:102.10; *see, e.g.*, ***Rus, Miliband & Smith v. Conkle & Olesten*** (4th Dist.2003) 113 Cal.App.4th 656, 667 (opposition to attorney's motion to withdraw was based on merits); ***Silva v. Superior Ct.*** (2d Dist.1981) 119 Cal.App.3d 301, 304-05 (real party in interest's opposition challenged sufficiency of petitioner's motion to change venue under CCP §397).

§8.2 Supporting evidence. Evidence that can be used to support a motion can also be used to support an opposition. See "Supporting evidence," §5.3, p. 30.

§8.3 Request for judicial notice. Opposition papers can also be accompanied by a separate request for judicial notice. *See* CRC 3.1113(*l*). See "Request for Judicial Notice," ch. 5-J, p. 547.

NOTE

Oppositions to some motions require additional attachments. See, e.g., CCP §437c(b)(3) (opposition to MSJ must include separate statement). See the relevant subchapter in this book to determine if an opposition to a particular type of motion requires additional attachments.

---

§8.4 Proof of service. See "Proof of service," §5.6, p. 33.

§8.5 Filing & serving opposition.

1. What to file & serve. All opposition papers (e.g., memorandum, supporting evidence) must be filed with the court, and a copy must be served on each party. CCP §1005(b). For a general discussion of what to file and serve in motion practice, see "What to file," §7.1.2, p. 33; "What to serve," §7.2.2, p. 34.

2. How to file & serve.

(1) Filing. See "How to File," ch. 1-F, §4, p. 47.

(2) Serving. Opposition papers must be served by personal delivery, fax, express mail, or other means consistent with CCP §§1010-1013. CCP §1005(c). See "How to Serve," ch. 1-G, §5, p. 66.

3. Deadline to file & serve.

(1) Generally. In most cases, opposition papers must be filed and served at least nine court days before the hearing. CCP §1005(b). See "Court days," ch. 1-F, §5.1.3(1)(b), p. 54. The nine-court-day requirement under CCP §1005 applies unless the period is shortened by court order or a different period is specifically required by law. *See* CCP §1005(b); CRC 3.1300(b); *see, e.g.*, CCP §437c(b)(2) (opposition papers to MSJ must be filed and served 14 days before hearing unless court orders otherwise for good cause). See "Shortening Time," ch. 5-E, p. 497. The method of service used must be reasonably calculated to ensure delivery of the opposition to the other party no later than the close of the next business day after the opposition has been filed with the court clerk. CCP §1005(c). For a discussion of the deadlines that apply to a specific motion, see the relevant subchapter in this book. For a discussion of how to calculate the deadline to file and serve, see "Retrospective deadlines," ch. 1-F, §5.2, p. 56 (filing), and "Retrospective deadlines," ch. 1-G, §6.2, p. 71 (serving).

(2) No extension based on method of service. Unlike with other papers, the deadline to respond to a noticed motion is not extended based on how the noticed motion was served (e.g., by mail, by fax). *See* CCP §1005(b) (§1013, which extends the time to respond, does not apply to opposition or reply papers). Thus, if a noticed motion is served by mail, the deadline to file and serve the opposition papers is still nine court days before the hearing; the deadline is not extended by five calendar days. Weil, *Civil Procedure Before Trial*, ¶9:105.

§9. REPLY PAPERS

The movant can file reply papers to rebut arguments or evidence introduced in the opposition papers. *See, e.g.*, CCP §437c(b)(4) (deadline for filing and serving reply to opposition to MSJ); ***Jimenez v. County of L.A.*** (2d Dist.2005) 130 Cal.App.4th 133, 138-39 (in response to new issue raised in opposition to MSJ, D's reply papers included rebuttal testimony and request for judicial notice).

§9.1 Memorandum of points & authorities.

1. Length. A reply memorandum cannot exceed ten pages. CRC 3.1113(d).

2. Contents. A reply memorandum should not raise new issues but instead only address issues raised in the opposition. *CEB Procedure Before Trial*, §12.110.

§9.2 Supporting evidence. Generally, evidence that can be used to support a motion can be used to support a reply. See "Supporting evidence," §5.3, p. 30. But courts are unlikely to consider new evidence (i.e., evidence that was not previously raised) except in rare cases. ***Plenger v. Alza Corp.*** (4th Dist.1992) 11 Cal.App.4th 349, 362 n.8.

§9.3 Request for judicial notice. The reply papers can be accompanied by a separate request for judicial notice. *See* CRC 3.1113(*l*); *see, e.g.*, ***Jimenez v. County of L.A.*** (2d Dist.2005) 130 Cal.App.4th 133, 138-39 (in response to new issue raised in opposition to MSJ, D's reply papers included rebuttal testimony and request for judicial notice). See "Request for Judicial Notice," ch. 5-J, p. 547.

§9.4 Proposed order. See "Proposed order," §5.5, p. 32.

§9.5 Proof of service. See "Proof of service," §5.6, p. 33.

§9.6 Filing & serving reply papers.

1. What to file & serve. All reply papers (e.g., memorandum, supporting evidence) must be filed with the court, and a copy must be served on each party. CCP §1005(b). For a general discussion of what to file and serve in motion practice, see "What to file," §7.1.2, p. 33; "What to serve," §7.2.2, p. 34.

2. How to file & serve.

(1) Filing. See "How to File," ch. 1-F, §4, p. 47.

(2) Serving. Reply papers must be served by personal delivery, fax, express mail, or other means consistent with CCP §§1010-1013. CCP §1005(c). See "How to Serve," ch. 1-G, §5, p. 66.

3. Deadline to file & serve.

(1) Generally. In most cases, reply papers must be filed and served at least five court days before the hearing. CCP §1005(b). See "Court days," ch. 1-F, §5.1.3(1)(b), p. 54. The five-court-day requirement under CCP §1005 applies unless the period is shortened by court order or a different period is specifically required by law. *See* CCP §1005(b); CRC 3.1300(b); *see, e.g.*, CCP §437c(b)(4) (reply papers to opposition to MSJ must be filed and served five days before hearing unless court orders otherwise for good cause). See "Shortening Time," ch. 5-E, p. 497. The method of service used must be reasonably calculated to ensure delivery of the reply papers to the other party no later than the close of the next business day after the reply has been filed with the court clerk. CCP §1005(c). For a discussion of the deadlines that apply to a specific motion, see the relevant subchapter in this book. For a discussion of how to calculate the deadline to file and serve, see "Retrospective deadlines," ch. 1-F, §5.2, p. 56 (filing), and "Retrospective deadlines," ch. 1-G, §6.2, p. 71 (serving).

(2) No extension based on method of service. As with opposition papers, the deadline to file and serve a reply is not extended based on how the opposition was served (e.g., by mail, by fax). *See* CCP §1005(b) (§1013, which extends the time within which to respond, does not apply to opposition or reply papers). See "No extension based on method of service," §8.5.3(2), p. 37.

NOTE

Unless excused by the court for good cause, written objections to the evidence used by a party opposing a motion for summary judgment or summary adjudication must be filed and served at the same time as the reply papers are filed and served. CRC 3.1354(a).

---

§10. JOINING MOTION

A party can join another party's motion by filing a notice of joinder. To be effective, the joinder must (1) be timely, (2) establish the necessary factual foundation to support the motion, and (3) request affirmative relief on behalf of the joining party. *See, e.g.*, ***Barak v. Quisenberry Law Firm*** (2d Dist.2006) 135 Cal.App.4th 654, 661 (D's joinder in co-D's special motion to strike was effective because it established requisite factual foundation and requested affirmative relief); ***Commonwealth Energy Corp. v. Investor Data Exch., Inc.*** (4th Dist.2003) 110 Cal.App.4th 26, 31 n.3 (D's joinder in co-D's motion to dismiss was effective because it requested relief for D himself); ***Frazee v. Seely*** (4th Dist.2002) 95 Cal.App.4th 627, 636-37 (D's joinder in co-D's MSJ was ineffective because it was untimely and was not supported by separate statement of undisputed facts).

§11. HEARING

For a discussion of hearings on motions, see "Hearings," ch. 1-H, p. 79.

§12. RULING & ORDER

A court acts on a motion by granting or denying the relief requested. ***Kaneko Ford Design v. Citipark, Inc.*** (2d Dist.1988) 202 Cal.App.3d 1220, 1227. When making a ruling, the court usually considers only the grounds specified in the notice of motion. ***Luri v. Greenwald*** (2d Dist.2003) 107 Cal.App.4th 1119, 1126-27; ***366-386 Geary St., L.P. v. Superior Ct.*** (1st Dist.1990) 219 Cal.App.3d 1186, 1199. The court can consider a ground not stated in the notice if that ground is discussed in and supported by the motion papers and if the movant is clearly seeking relief on that ground. ***Luri***, 107 Cal.App.4th at 1126-27; *e.g.*, ***366-386 Geary St., L.P.***, 219 Cal.App.3d at 1200 (notice of motion failed to refer to statute as ground for relief, and motion papers did not cure defect); *see* ***Carrasco v. Craft*** (5th Dist.1985)

164 Cal.App.3d 796, 807-08. For a discussion of a court's ruling and order on a specific motion, see the relevant subchapter in this book. For a general discussion of rulings and orders, see "Rulings & Orders," ch. 1-I, p. 89.

§13. APPELLATE REVIEW

The appellate court reviews the superior court's ruling on a motion according to the law applicable to the type of motion. *See, e.g.*, ***Bono v. David*** (1st Dist.2007) 147 Cal.App.4th 1055, 1061-62 (order on motion to compel arbitration reviewed de novo); ***Britts v. Superior Ct.*** (6th Dist.2006) 145 Cal.App.4th 1112, 1123 (order on motion to compel discovery reviewed for abuse of discretion). For a discussion of the standard of review that applies to a specific motion, see the relevant subchapter in this book. For a general discussion of standards of review, see "Standards of review," ch. 1-I, §7.2, p. 95.

E. EX PARTE PRACTICE

§1. GENERAL

§1.1 Purpose. Ex parte practice involves any application for relief sought by one party without giving notice or an opportunity to respond to any other party or person interested in the outcome. *See Black's Law Dictionary* 697 (10th ed. 2014). The use of "ex parte" in this context, however, is something of a misnomer because the California Rules of Court require the party requesting relief to give some form of notice to all parties. *See* CRC 3.1203. *But see* Weil & Brown, *California Practice Guide: Civil Procedure Before Trial* (CD-ROM ed. 2014) ¶9:354.5 (arguing that CRC 3.1203 does not apply when statute authorizes court order without notice to opposing party). Still, because notice can be given a very short time before the hearing, the ex parte process can help a party obtain expedited relief.

§1.2 Primary authority. CRC 3.1200 et seq.

§1.3 Secondary authority. The following secondary sources are cited as authority in this subchapter:

- *California Civil Procedure Before Trial* (CEB Online ed. 2014) (referred to as *CEB Procedure Before Trial*).
- Weil & Brown, *California Practice Guide: Civil Procedure Before Trial* (CD-ROM ed. 2014) (referred to as Weil, *Civil Procedure Before Trial*).
- Witkin, *California Procedure* (5th ed. 2008 & Supp.2014) (referred to as Witkin, *Cal. Procedure*).
- Younger & Bradley, *Younger on California Motions* (2014-15) (referred to as Younger, *Cal. Motions*).

§1.4 Judicial Council forms. The Judicial Council has adopted a number of forms for use in ex parte practice. *See, e.g.*, Judicial Council Forms, form CM-020 (ex parte application for extension of time to serve pleading). For information about the Judicial Council forms, see the forms page on the California Courts website at www.courts.ca.gov/forms.htm.

§2. LAW GOVERNING EX PARTE PRACTICE

Generally, ex parte practice is governed by the Code of Civil Procedure and the California Rules of Court. All local rules relating to ex parte practice, including those relating to the form and format of papers, are null and void unless otherwise permitted or required by a statute or a California Rule of Court. CRC 3.20(a). Thus, to the extent that a local rule relating to ex parte practice conflicts with a statute or a California Rule of Court, the local rule is preempted. See "Local Rules," ch. 1-A, §4, p. 6.

§3. AVAILABILITY OF RELIEF

Because of the potential one-sidedness of an ex parte application and the obvious due-process concerns raised by such a request, only limited forms of relief are available ex parte. *See* Weil, *Civil Procedure Before Trial*, ¶¶9:345-9:347; 6 Witkin, *Cal. Procedure*, Proceedings Without Trial, §58. Ex parte relief can be granted only when a statute or rule either provides for it or does not explicitly require notice or motion. *See* ***Sole Energy Co. v. Hodges*** (4th Dist.2005) 128 Cal.App.4th 199, 207; ***St. Paul Fire & Mar. Ins. v. Superior Ct.*** (1st Dist.1984) 156 Cal.App.3d 82,

86; *see, e.g.*, ***Lang v. Superior Ct.*** (1st Dist.1984) 153 Cal.App.3d 510, 516 (local rule requiring application for wage assignment for child support to be on noticed motion violated Civ. C. §4701, which allowed applications to be made ex parte).

§3.1 When available.

1. **Explicitly authorized.** Ex parte relief is available if a statute or rule explicitly provides for it. Some examples of ex parte relief include orders for the following:

- To extend time to serve pleadings. CRC 3.110(e).
- To shorten or extend time for scheduling a deposition. CCP §2025.270(d); *see, e.g.*, ***McMillan v. Superior Ct.*** (4th Dist.1983) 146 Cal.App.3d 1014, 1017 (Ds sought ex parte order to shorten time to take expert's deposition).
- To continue a motion for summary judgment to obtain discovery. CCP §437c(h); *see id.* §425.18(e) (continuance of MSJ by party opposing special motion to strike SLAPPback).
- To shorten time to respond to a complaint for libel or slander to 20 days after service of summons. *Id.* §460.5(a).
- To dismiss for failure to amend a complaint after the court sustained a demurrer with leave to amend. CRC 3.1320(h); *see* CCP §581(f)(2); ***Datig v. Dove Books, Inc.*** (2d Dist.1999) 73 Cal.App.4th 964, 977-78.
- To appoint a receiver. CRC 3.1175.
- To allow for the filing of a longer memorandum in support of a motion. CRC 3.1113(e).
- To revoke or set aside a renewed application for an order. CCP §1008(b).

2. **Implicitly authorized.** Ex parte relief may also be available if a statute or rule does not explicitly deny a party's right to seek it or does not require the relief to be sought on notice or motion. *See* ***Sole Energy Co. v. Hodges*** (4th Dist.2005) 128 Cal.App.4th 199, 207; ***Titmas v. Superior Ct.*** (4th Dist.2001) 87 Cal.App.4th 738, 743; ***St. Paul Fire & Mar. Ins. v. Superior Ct.*** (1st Dist.1984) 156 Cal.App.3d 82, 86; *see, e.g.*, ***Parker v. Wolters Kluwer U.S., Inc.*** (2d Dist.2007) 149 Cal.App.4th 285, 296 (superior court could not award discovery sanctions ex parte because CCP §2023.030 explicitly requires notice). See "When not available," §3.2, p. 41. For example, CCP §373 has been interpreted to allow a plaintiff to file an ex parte application to have a guardian ad litem appointed because the statute does not require the party to give notice. ***Granger v. Sherriff*** (1901) 133 Cal. 416, 418; *see* ***Sarracino v. Superior Ct.*** (1974) 13 Cal.3d 1, 12; ***In re Sara D.*** (5th Dist.2001) 87 Cal.App.4th 661, 670-71. Although no statutes or cases explain when ex parte relief is implicitly authorized, there are the following general guidelines:

(1) **Does relief affect opposing party's rights?** If the relief sought would affect the opposing party's rights, the party cannot seek it ex parte. Weil, *Civil Procedure Before Trial*, ¶9:349; *see* ***McDonald v. Severy*** (1936) 6 Cal.2d 629, 631 (notice of motion required when order sought may affect rights of opposing party); *see, e.g.*, ***Miller v. Foremost Motors, Inc.*** (4th Dist.1993) 16 Cal.App.4th 1271, 1275-76 (court's ex parte order granting motion to vacate dismissal and entering judgment against D was error because D should have been given notice of motion).

(2) **Is relief for emergency or noncontroversial issues?** If the relief sought is for either an emergency or a noncontroversial issue, the party may be able to obtain ex parte relief. Younger, *Cal. Motions*, §§31:1, 31:6.

(a) **Emergency relief.** Ex parte relief may be available for emergencies when there is no time for formal notice. *See* Younger, *Cal. Motions*, §§31:1, 31:6, 31:22; *see, e.g.*, ***Datig***, 73 Cal.App.4th at 981 (D violated local rules by making ex parte application without bona fide emergency). Some situations in which emergency relief may be sought ex parte include scheduling conflicts, when witnesses are omitted from a mandated witness list, and when a stay of execution is necessary. *See* Younger, *Cal. Motions*, §§31:8, 31:9, 31:13; *see, e.g.*, ***Phipps v. Fike*** (4th Dist.2003) No. D041080 (unpub.; 10-22-03) (P's attorney's declaration that D was not timely served with opposition before scheduled hearing date satisfied "immediate danger" requirements of former CRC 379(g), now CRC 3.1202(c)).

(b) Noncontroversial relief. Ex parte relief may be available for noncontroversial issues (i.e., minor, nonsubstantive ones) when formal notice would serve no useful purpose. *See* Younger, *Cal. Motions*, §§31:1, 31:6. The most common example is an ex parte application to shorten the length of time to serve a notice of motion. *Id.* §31:12; *see, e.g.*, ***Campanella v. Takaoka*** (2d Dist.1984) 160 Cal.App.3d 504, 508 (Ps sought ex parte order to shorten time to serve notice of motion to specially set case for trial), *disapproved on other grounds*, ***Salas v. Sears, Roebuck & Co.*** (1986) 42 Cal.3d 342.

§3.2 When not available. Ex parte relief is not available if a statute or rule explicitly denies a party's right to seek it or requires the relief to be sought on notice or motion. *See, e.g.*, Super. Ct. Santa Cruz Cty. Loc. R., rule 1.3.02(b) (ex parte applications not allowed for stipulated orders, orders after hearings, judgments after trial, or default judgments); ***Leader v. Health Indus.*** (2d Dist.2001) 89 Cal.App.4th 603, 612-13 (under CCP §473(a)(1), P is required to file noticed motion for leave to amend complaint after D's demurrer is heard); ***Alliance Bank v. Murray*** (2d Dist.1984) 161 Cal.App.3d 1, 6 (court's minute order conditionally authorizing ex parte application on shortened notice for sanctions for D's failure to appear at deposition violated express terms of former CCP §2034(d), which required both notice and motion).

§4. NOTICE OF APPLICATION

§4.1 When required. A notice of ex parte application is required for all ex parte applications, unless the party can show notice should not be given because of "exceptional circumstances." CRC 3.1203(a); *see, e.g.*, ***McWethy v. Elansari*** (4th Dist.2007) No. D047317 (unpub.; 3-14-07) (notice of ex parte application to appoint postjudgment receiver not required when it would alert judgment debtor, who was known to have secret assets, of receiver's attempt to collect judgment).

CAUTION

The notice requirement for ex parte applications should not be confused with the notice requirement for motions generally. For noticed motions, see "Notice of motion & motion," ch. 1-D, §5.1, p. 28.

---

§4.2 Notice to all parties. When notice of an ex parte application is required, it must be given to all parties. CRC 3.1203(a).

§4.3 Form. The notice of the ex parte application can be given orally or in writing. *See* CRC 3.1204(b)(1), (b)(2) (declaration of notice must state manner of actual or attempted notice); *see, e.g.*, ***Datig v. Dove Books, Inc.*** (2d Dist.1999) 73 Cal.App.4th 964, 977 (declaration did not state what attorney said on phone messages and did not state when messages were left). Regardless of how notice is given, the person giving it must do all of the following:

1. Specify the nature of the relief that will be requested. CRC 3.1204(a)(1).

2. State the date, time, and place of the hearing. *Id.*

3. Attempt to determine whether the notified party will appear at the hearing to oppose the application. CRC 3.1204(a)(2).

4. Comply with any additional local rules on notice. For example, under Appendix 3.A(j)(2) of the Superior Court of Los Angeles County local rules, the attorney should make a diligent effort to notify the opposing party or the attorney known or likely to represent the opposing party and should make reasonable efforts to accommodate the schedule of the opposing party or its attorney. *See, e.g.*, ***Datig***, 73 Cal.App.4th at 981 (attorney's efforts to notify opposing counsel by calling and leaving message to call back was not notice of anything).

§4.4 Deadline.

1. One court day's notice. In most cases, notice of the ex parte application must be given to all parties by 10:00 a.m. on the court day before the ex parte hearing. CRC 3.1203(a); *see* ***In re Sara D.*** (5th Dist.2001) 87 Cal.App.4th 661, 670; *see, e.g.*, CRC 3.1113(e) (notice of ex parte application to file a memorandum longer than 15

pages must be given to other parties at least 24 hours before the memorandum is due); ***Datig v. Dove Books, Inc.*** (2d Dist.1999) 73 Cal.App.4th 964, 977 (court erred by granting ex parte application for dismissal without proper notice to P). See "Court days," ch. 1-F, §5.1.3(1)(b), p. 54.

2. Shorter notice. An ex parte application can be made on shorter notice if (1) exceptional circumstances justify it or (2) the application is made in an unlawful-detainer proceeding and the notice given is reasonable. CRC 3.1203; *see* Super. Ct. Napa Cty. Loc. R., rule 2.5.A (court can waive notice for good cause); ***Western Steel & Ship Repair, Inc. v. RMI, Inc.*** (4th Dist.1986) 176 Cal.App.3d 1108, 1117 (court can waive notice under appropriate circumstances).

§5. APPLICATION PAPERS

"Application papers" for ex parte relief include an application, a memorandum in support, a declaration of notice, a declaration in support, a proposed order, and if necessary, the underlying motion. CRC 3.1201; *see* Younger, *Cal. Motions*, §31:37. Application papers are submitted instead of ordinary notice of motion and motion papers, but they serve the same function.

§5.1 Application. The party seeking ex parte relief must file an application. CRC 3.1201(1).

1. Format. The format of the ex parte application must meet the requirements of papers generally. *See* CRC 3.1201 (request must be in writing). See "General Requirements for Papers," ch. 1-B, §2, p. 9. The application must contain a case caption, which includes the name of the court and county where the action is brought and the title of the action. *See* CRC 3.1201(1); *cf.* CCP §422.30(a) (caption for pleadings). It should also contain a title that identifies the nature of the paper, such as "Ex Parte Application for …" or "Ex Parte Motion for Order …." Younger, *Cal. Motions*, §31:37; *see, e.g.*, Judicial Council Forms, form CM-020 (ex parte application for extension of time to serve pleading).

2. Contents.

(1) Mandatory. The application must state all of the following:

(a) The relief requested. CRC 3.1201(1).

(b) The name, address, and telephone number of any attorney known to represent any other party or, if no such attorney is known, the name, address, and telephone number of the other party, if known. CRC 3.1202(a).

(c) A list of all earlier ex parte applications and the court's action taken on them if the current application seeks the same relief and the earlier ex parte applications were refused in whole or in part. CRC 3.1202(b).

(2) Discretionary. The application should state the facts that support why ex parte relief should be granted. *See* CRC 3.1202(c); Younger, *Cal. Motions*, §31:37. The party should explain that ex parte relief is appropriate because (1) it is explicitly authorized by statute, (2) it is implicitly authorized by statute, or (3) there is a threat of irreparable harm or immediate danger. *See* CRC 3.1202(c). If possible, the party should show that the opposing party will not be prejudiced and state that it is willing to compensate the opposing party for any detrimental effect of the proposed order. *See* Younger, *Cal. Motions*, §31:39.

§5.2 Memorandum of points & authorities.

1. When required. A supporting memorandum is required for most ex parte applications. CRC 3.1201(4). The memorandum should follow the format of memorandums in normal motion practice. *See* Younger, *Cal. Motions*, §31:39. See "Format," ch. 1-D, §5.2.3, p. 29.

2. When not required. For applications that do not require a memorandum, a party can submit one or the court can order one when it would further the interests of justice. CRC 3.1114(b). A memorandum is not required for the following applications if the application is filed on a Judicial Council form:

(1) Application for appointment of a guardian ad litem in a civil case. CRC 3.1114(a)(1).

(2) Application for an order extending time to serve a pleading. CRC 3.1114(a)(2).

§5.3 Declarations. The party seeking ex parte relief must file a declaration of notice and a declaration in support of the application. CRC 3.1201(2), (3).

1. Declaration of notice. The declaration of notice must be in writing, be based on personal knowledge, and describe the notice given to the other parties. *See* CRC 3.1201(3), 3.1204(b). Local rules may require more specific information in the declaration. *See, e.g.*, Super. Ct. Sonoma Cty. Loc. R., rule 5.6.B & 5.6.C (listing additional information to include in declaration).

CAUTION

When providing a declaration of notice, make sure the declarant is the person who gave or attempted to give notice; otherwise, the declaration may be inadmissible hearsay. See Younger, Cal. Motions, §31:38.

The declaration must do one of the following:

(1) Provide a detailed description of the notice given. CRC 3.1204(b)(1). When describing the notice given, the party seeking ex parte relief should state all of the following:

(a) The date, time, and manner of the notice, including whether the notice was given to the other parties by 10:00 a.m. on the court day before the hearing. *See* CRC 3.1203(a), 3.1204(b)(1). If the notice was given after this time, the declaration must explain the exceptional circumstances justifying the shorter notice period. CRC 3.1204(c)(1); *see, e.g.*, Super. Ct. El Dorado Cty. Loc. R., rule 7.10.10.B(2) (in construing "exceptional circumstances," court requires at least four hours' notice in case of ex parte application for TRO for harassment). In unlawful-detainer proceedings, the declaration does not have to demonstrate exceptional circumstances, but it must demonstrate that the amount of notice is reasonable. CRC 3.1204(c)(2).

(b) The name of the party who was notified. CRC 3.1204(b)(1).

(c) What the notified party was told of the relief sought. *Id.*

(d) The notified party's response, including whether the party is expected to oppose the application. *Id.*

(2) State that the party seeking ex parte relief attempted in good faith to give notice but was unable to do so, and describe the effort made to inform the other parties. CRC 3.1204(b)(2); *see, e.g.*, ***Datig v. Dove Books, Inc.*** (2d Dist.1999) 73 Cal.App.4th 964, 977 (declaration was insufficient because it did not state contents or times of phone messages); *see also* Super. Ct. Solano Cty. Forms, form 1070-G, at www.solanocourts.com/LocalForms.html (sample declaration of notice for probate guardianship matters).

(3) State one or more specific reasons why the party seeking ex parte relief should not be required to give notice to the other parties. CRC 3.1204(b)(3); *see, e.g.*, ***Wilburn v. Oakland Hosp.*** (1st Dist.1989) 213 Cal.App.3d 1107, 1111 (D cited case in its ex parte motion to dismiss as supporting authority for granting dismissal without notice).

2. Declaration in support. The declaration in support of the application must be in writing, be based on personal knowledge, and describe the irreparable harm, immediate danger, or other statutory basis for granting ex parte relief. *See* CRC 3.1201(2), 3.1202(c).

PRACTICE TIP

The declaration in support and the declaration of notice are usually combined into a single document.

§5.4 Proposed order. The party seeking ex parte relief must include a proposed order. CRC 3.1201(5). The proposed order must be lodged and served with the application papers but not attached to them. CRC 3.1113(m); *CEB Procedure Before Trial*, §13.19. See "Documents lodged," ch. 1-F, §2.3, p. 47.

§5.5 Underlying motion. If the party is seeking ex parte relief to shorten the time to serve a motion or to exceed the page limit for a motion, the party should file the underlying motion with the other application papers. Younger, *Cal. Motions*, §31:41.

§6. FILING, SERVING & PROVIDING COURT FILE

§6.1 Filing. The filing procedures for ex parte applications differ by court, and sometimes by judge. Before filing an application, check the court's local and courtroom rules.

1. **File with clerk.** Some courts require the party seeking ex parte relief to file the application papers with the clerk before the hearing. *E.g.*, Super. Ct. San Francisco Cty. Loc. R., rule 9.0.B (file-endorsed copies of papers must be submitted to clerk at least two hours before hearing); Super. Ct. Santa Barbara Cty. Loc. R., rule 1009 (ex parte applications must be filed in clerk's office of the appropriate court division where case is pending); Super. Ct. Tuolumne Cty. Loc. R., rule 1.13 (applicant must submit motion papers before hearing).

2. **Present to judge.** Some courts require the party seeking ex parte relief to present the papers to the judge immediately before the hearing. *E.g.*, Super. Ct. Santa Clara Cty. Loc. R. (civil), rule 7.F (ex parte applications must be brought to case-management judge's department); Super. Ct. Sonoma Cty. Loc. R., rule 5.6.A (civil ex parte applications must be presented to assigned judge at times and locations designated by court); *see* Younger, *Cal. Motions*, §31:36.

§6.2 Serving. The party seeking ex parte relief must, at the first reasonable opportunity, serve the application papers on any other party who will appear at the hearing. CRC 3.1206; ***Datig v. Dove Books, Inc.*** (2d Dist.1999) 73 Cal.App.4th 964, 976-77; *e.g.*, ***Doe v. Independent Consultant Pharmacist Servs.*** (2d Dist.2004) No. B171398 (unpub.; 12-22-04) (opposing party was properly served with application papers when he appeared at ex parte hearing). The party can usually serve the papers at the hearing, but it should serve them sooner if the application was filed well before the hearing. *CEB Procedure Before Trial*, §13.12. If the papers have not been served on an appearing party either before or at the hearing, the court cannot hold a hearing on the ex parte application unless the party seeking relief shows exceptional circumstances. CRC 3.1206; ***Datig***, 73 Cal.App.4th at 976-77.

§6.3 Providing court file. Some courts require the party seeking ex parte relief to ensure that the court file is available to the judge when she hears the application. *See* Younger, *Cal. Motions*, §31:36.

§7. OPPOSING EX PARTE APPLICATION

The party opposing the ex parte application can challenge the requested relief either in writing or orally at the hearing. *See* Younger, *Cal. Motions*, §§31:42, 31:43. If the party chooses to oppose the application in writing, it must serve the opposition papers on any other party who will appear at the hearing at the first reasonable opportunity. CRC 3.1206.

PRACTICE TIP

It is best to oppose the ex parte application in writing. The judge may not take the bench when considering an application, which means there may not be an opportunity to make an oral opposition.

§8. HEARING

§8.1 Appearance required. In most cases, the party seeking ex parte relief must appear either in person or by telephone to present its application to the court. *See* CRC 3.1207; ***Eliceche v. Federal Land Bank Ass'n*** (5th Dist.2002) 103 Cal.App.4th 1349, 1369. See "Party's appearance," ch. 1-H, §5.4, p. 84. If the party does not appear, the court will not grant the relief. *See* CRC 3.1207.

NOTE

Some courts require ex parte hearings to be scheduled in advance. E.g., Super. Ct. San Francisco Cty. Loc. R., rule 9.0.B (ex parte hearings must be scheduled at least 24 hours in advance).

§8.2 Appearance not required. The court can consider the following ex parte applications without the party's appearance:

1. An application to file a memorandum in excess of the applicable page limit. CRC 3.1207(1).

2. An application for an extension of time to serve pleadings. CRC 3.1207(2).

3. An application setting a hearing date on an alternative writ (i.e., a writ commanding someone to do a specific thing) or an order to show cause. *See* CRC 3.1207(3); *Black's Law Dictionary* 1845 (10th ed. 2014).

4. A stipulated application for an ex parte order. CRC 3.1207(4).

NOTE

A party's appearance at the ex parte hearing is not considered a general appearance that waives its right to quash service of summons for lack of personal jurisdiction under CCP §418.10. CCP §418.11.

§9. RULING & ORDER

See "Rulings & Orders," ch. 1-I, p. 89.

F. FILING DOCUMENTS

§1. GENERAL

§1.1 Purpose. The purpose of filing documents is to place them in the court's record of the lawsuit. *See **In re Marriage of Cueva*** (4th Dist.1978) 86 Cal.App.3d 290, 301 (record includes every document filed in superior court). Filing documents should not be confused with serving them. Documents are *filed* with the clerk, but they are *served* on the other parties in the lawsuit. CRC 1.21(b). See "Serving Documents," ch. 1-G, p. 63.

§1.2 Primary authority. CCP §§12-13b, 135, 411.10, 415.10, 465, 1005, 1010.5, 1010.6, 1054; Gov. C. §§6700, 6803, 6804, 69846.5; CRC 1.20, 1.31, 1.42, 2.100, 2.117, 2.118, 2.130-2.141, 2.200-2.305, 2.400(b), 2.551-2.571, 3.50-3.58, 3.100, 3.250, 3.1100, 3.1103(a), 3.1300, 3.1302.

§1.3 Secondary authority. The following secondary source is cited as authority in this subchapter:

- Witkin, *California Procedure* (5th ed. 2008 & Supp.2014) (referred to as Witkin, *Cal. Procedure*).

§1.4 Judicial Council forms.

- CM-010 (mandatory), civil case cover sheet.
- MC-005 (mandatory), facsimile transmission cover sheet.
- MC-040 (optional), notice of change of address or other contact information.
- FW-001 (mandatory), request to waive court fees.
- FW-002 (optional), request to waive additional court fees.

§2. WHAT TO FILE

§2.1 Documents filed. Most documents (e.g., pleadings, motions, supporting evidence) must be filed with the court clerk. *E.g.*, CCP §465 (except with leave of court, all pleadings after complaint must be filed), §1005(b) (except with leave of court, all motion and supporting papers must be filed 16 court days before hearing). For a discussion of the form and format of documents filed with the court, see "General Requirements for Papers," ch. 1-B, §2, p. 9.

1. Cover sheet. The first document filed in an action or proceeding must be accompanied by a cover sheet. CRC 3.220(a). Judicial Council Form CM-010 must be used in all civil actions, except those filed in small-claims court or filed under the Probate Code, Family Code, or Welfare and Institutions Code. CRC 3.220(b)(1). See

"Civil case cover sheet," ch. 1-B, §2.8.1, p. 16. If the first document does not include a cover sheet, the filing party, the party's attorney, or both can be sanctioned. CRC 3.220(c).

2. Original & copy. Generally, original documents are filed, and copies are served on the parties. *See* CCP §1005(b); CRC 2.400(b); *see also* CCP §415.10 (copy of summons and complaint is served). When a document such as a discovery request is not filed with the court but is served on the parties, the serving party must keep the original with a proof of service. CRC 3.250(b). See "Proving Service," ch. 1-G, §7, p. 74. The rules for filing original documents and copies vary from court to court. Some courts require a party to file only the original document. *E.g.*, Super. Ct. Placer Cty. Loc. R., rule 10.9.E (copies can be received by court, but only originals will be filed). Other courts require a party to file a copy with the original. *E.g.*, Super. Ct. Marin Cty. Loc. R., rule 1.4.A (original must be filed with one copy); Super. Ct. San Francisco Cty. Loc. R., rule 2.6.B (certain documents must be filed with file-stamped courtesy copy).

NOTE

A party can, and sometimes must, file an electronic document instead of a hard copy if the court has an electronic-filing program. See "Electronic filing," §4.4, p. 49.

---

§2.2 Documents not filed. Some documents should not be filed unless they are relevant to determining a motion or are ordered to be filed by the court. *See* CRC 3.250(a). These include the following:

1. Deposition documents.

(1) A deposition notice and the response to it. CRC 3.250(a)(3).

(2) A notice of intention to record testimony by audiotape or videotape. CRC 3.250(a)(5).

(3) A notice of intention to take oral depositions by telephone, videoconference, or other remote electronic means. CRC 3.250(a)(6).

(4) An agreement or notice of agreement to set or extend time for depositions or responses to discovery requests. CRC 3.250(a)(7).

2. Expert-discovery documents.

(1) A demand for exchange of expert witnesses. CRC 3.250(a)(13).

(2) A demand for production of discoverable reports and writings of expert witnesses. CRC 3.250(a)(14).

(3) A list of expert witnesses whose opinion a party intends to offer in evidence at trial or by declaration. CRC 3.250(a)(15).

(4) A statement that a party does not presently intend to offer the testimony of any expert witness. CRC 3.250(a)(16).

3. Other discovery documents.

(1) A subpoena or subpoena duces tecum. CRC 3.250(a)(1), (a)(2).

(2) Interrogatories and the responses or objections to them. CRC 3.250(a)(8).

(3) A demand for production or inspection of documents, things, and places, and the response or objections to the demand. CRC 3.250(a)(9).

(4) A request for admission and the response or objections to it. CRC 3.250(a)(10).

(5) An agreement for physical and mental examinations. CRC 3.250(a)(11).

(6) A demand for delivery of medical reports and the response to it. CRC 3.250(a)(12).

(7) A declaration for additional discovery. CRC 3.250(a)(17).

(8) A stipulation to increase the number of discovery requests from what is specified by statute and a notice of the stipulation. CRC 3.250(a)(18).

4. Other pretrial documents.

(1) A notice of privacy rights to a consumer or employee whose personal records are sought and the objections to the notice. *See* CRC 3.250(a)(4).

(2) A demand for a bill of particulars or an accounting and the response to it. CRC 3.250(a)(19).

(3) A request for a statement of damages and the response to it, unless the request is accompanied by a request to enter default and is the notice of special and general damages. CRC 3.250(a)(20).

(4) A notice of deposit of jury fees. CRC 3.250(a)(21).

(5) A notice to produce a party, agent, or tangible thing before a court, and the response to the notice. CRC 3.250(a)(22).

(6) An offer to compromise, unless the offer is accompanied by an original proof of acceptance and a written judgment for the court's signature and entry of judgment. CRC 3.250(a)(23).

§2.3 Documents lodged. Some documents can be (or must be) lodged with the court rather than filed. A lodged document is temporarily deposited with the court but not filed. *See* CRC 2.550(b)(3), 2.575(a)(3). For example, proposed orders and judgments must be lodged with the court, and so must any cited authority required by the judge to be lodged, such as authority that is not from California or has not been published yet in the Official Reports. *See* CRC 3.1113(i)(1), (i)(2), (m). Discovery documents and other large or bulky items can also be lodged rather than filed when they are used to support a motion. *See, e.g.*, Super. Ct. Los Angeles Cty. Loc. R., rule 3.4(b) (all exhibits not attached to motion papers must be lodged with court). To lodge a document, the party depositing the material must usually provide the court clerk with a self-addressed, stamped envelope so the material can be mailed back once the court is done reviewing it. CRC 3.1302(b). Some courts, however, may permit the party to simply pick up the lodged documents after the hearing rather than having them mailed back. *E.g.*, Super. Ct. Los Angeles Cty. Loc. R., rule 3.4(b).

§3. WHERE TO FILE

Generally, all documents must be filed in the court clerk's office unless otherwise provided by law. *See* CRC 3.1302(a) (except as provided by local rule, all law-and-motion papers must be filed in clerk's office); ***United Farm Workers v. Agricultural Labor Relations Bd.*** (1985) 37 Cal.3d 912, 918 (filing means actual delivery to clerk's office during office hours). The county clerk's office is the court clerk's office for purposes of filing documents unless a separate clerk of the court or superior-court executive officer has been appointed. *See* ***Zumwalt v. Superior Ct.*** (1989) 49 Cal.3d 167, 179-80; Gov. C. §§26803, 69840(a), 71620(b).

§4. HOW TO FILE

§4.1 Mail. A party can file a document by mailing it to the clerk's office. *See* CRC 3.1302(a). A document is not considered filed when mailed; it is considered filed only when the clerk receives it. CRC 1.20(a). When filing a document by mail, the party should send it early enough to make sure it reaches the clerk's office by the deadline. See "When to File," §5, p. 52.

§4.2 Delivery. A party can file a document by delivering it to the clerk's office. *See* CRC 3.1302(a). The specific requirements for filing by delivery are generally found in the local rules.

1. Hand-delivery. A party can file a document by hand-delivery at the clerk's filing counter during the clerk's normal business hours. *See* CRC 1.20(a) (document is filed on day clerk receives it). Some local rules have specific procedures or restrictions on the delivery of documents. *E.g.*, Super. Ct. Los Angeles Cty. Loc. R., rule 3.4(a) (public cannot enter clerk's office to file documents after 4:30 p.m.); Super. Ct. Sonoma Cty. Loc. R., rule 18.11 (listing documents that can be filed over-the-counter and stating that all others must be left in processing basket).

2. Drop-box delivery. If the clerk's filing counter is closed anytime between 8:30 a.m. and 4:00 p.m. on a court day, a drop box must be available to deposit documents for filing. CRC 2.210(a). See "Court days," §5.1.3(1)(b), p. 54. A party can deliver documents to a drop box after hours. *See* CRC 2.210(c). The clerk must be able to determine whether a document was deposited in the drop box before or after the deadline for same-day filing. CRC 2.210(d).

(1) Deposited by 4:00 p.m. A document deposited in the court's drop box by 4:00 p.m. on a court day is considered filed on that day. CRC 2.210(b).

(2) Deposited after 4:00 p.m. A document deposited in the clerk's drop box after 4:00 p.m. on a court day is considered filed on the next court day unless the local rules extend the deadline for same-day filing. CRC 2.210(c)(1); *see, e.g.*, Super. Ct. Tulare Cty. Loc. R., rule 100 (filings placed in drop box by 5:00 p.m. will be file-stamped that day).

(3) Deposited on holiday. A document deposited in the clerk's drop box on a judicial holiday is considered filed on the next court day. CRC 2.210(c)(2). For a discussion of judicial holidays, see "Determine last day," §5.1.5, p. 55.

§4.3 Fax. A party can file any document with the clerk's office by fax, except for a will, codicil, bond, or undertaking (e.g., a surety). CRC 2.300(b); *see also* CCP §995.140 (definition of "bond"), §995.190 (definition of "undertaking").

1. Through agency or by party. A party can file a document by faxing it to a fax-filing agency or by faxing it directly to the clerk. CRC 2.303(a), 2.304(a).

(1) Fax-filing agency. The clerk must accept filings made by a fax-filing agency. CRC 2.304(a). A "fax-filing agency" is an entity that receives documents by fax, prepares them for filing, and then physically transports and files them with the clerk. CRC 2.301(7), 2.303(a), (b).

(a) Party's agent. A fax-filing agency acts as an agent of the party, not of the court. CRC 2.303(a).

(b) Certification. When a fax-filing agency files a document with the court, it certifies that it has complied with the California Rules of Court and that the document filed is the full and unaltered document received by fax from the filing party. CRC 2.303(e).

(c) Notation. Each document filed by a fax-filing agency must contain the phrase "By fax" immediately below the document's title. CRC 2.303(f).

(2) Direct fax filing. The clerk must accept documents faxed by a party to the clerk's office if the local rules permit direct fax filing. CRC 2.304(a); *see, e.g.*, Super. Ct. San Diego Cty. Loc. R., rule 2.5.2.B (in limited civil cases, documents not required to be accompanied by fee can be directly faxed); Super. Ct. San Francisco Cty. Loc. R., rule 2.6.C (court does not accept filings faxed directly to its fax machines).

(a) Cover sheet. The party faxing a document directly to the clerk must use Judicial Council Form MC-005 as the cover sheet. CRC 2.304(b).

(b) Handling instructions. The cover sheet must be followed by any special handling instructions needed to ensure that the document will comply with local rules. CRC 2.304(b); *e.g.*, ***Fry v. Superior Ct.*** (2d Dist.2013) 222 Cal.App.4th 475, 482-83 (party's peremptory challenge was properly denied because it did not include handling instructions indicating to whom the challenge should be directed; by failing to include instructions, party did not comply with requirement that challenge be "made to" assigned or presiding judge).

(c) Notation. Each document filed by direct fax filing must contain the phrase "By fax" immediately below the document's title. CRC 2.304(c).

(d) Transmission record. The party faxing a document directly to the clerk must print a transmission record of the fax. CRC 2.304(d); *see also* CRC 2.301(6) (definition of "transmission record"). The party can use the transmission record as the basis for a motion to file the document nunc pro tunc (i.e., retroactively) if the document was not received by the clerk because of a transmission error or if the document was not processed by the clerk after receipt. CRC 2.304(d).

2. Format. All documents faxed to the clerk must comply with CRC 2.100 through 2.119. CRC 2.302. See "General Requirements for Papers," ch. 1-B, §2, p. 9.

3. Signature. A signature on a faxed document is considered an original signature. CRC 2.305(d). By filing a signed document by fax, the party represents that it has the original signed document in its possession. CRC 2.305(a). If a demand for production of the original document is made, the parties must arrange a meeting to examine the original document. CRC 2.305(c). See "Signature," ch. 1-B, §2.7, p. 15.

4. Fee payment. The fees for fax filing are paid either by the fax-filing agency or by the party.

(1) Fax-filing agency. The fax-filing agency is responsible for paying the fee to file a document on behalf of a party. CRC 2.303(b)(3). The agency is not required to accept documents for filing if the party sending the documents has not arranged ahead of time to pay the agency's fees. CRC 2.303(c). If the agency receives documents from a party who has not made such arrangements, the agency can discard the documents without notifying the party. *Id.* See "Filing Fees," §7, p. 58.

(2) Direct fax filing. For documents faxed directly to the clerk, the court can permit a party to pay filing fees by credit card, debit card, electronic fund transfer, or debit account. CRC 2.304(e)(1). See "Form of payment," §7.2, p. 58.

§4.4 Electronic filing. A party can, and in some cases must, electronically file (e-file) a document if the court has an e-filing program. *See* CCP §1010.6(b); CRC 2.252(a). Each court that permits or mandates e-filing must publish its rules in electronic and print formats. CRC 2.254(a). The court's local rules must meet the conditions under CCP §1010.6(b) and comply with the California Rules of Court (CRC 2.250 et seq.). *See* CCP §1010.6(b); CRC 3.20(a).

1. Party's responsibilities.

(1) Before filing. Before e-filing a document, the party must do the following:

(a) Determine if court permits or mandates e-filing. The party must determine if the court has adopted an e-filing program. *See* CCP §1010.6(b); *see, e.g.*, Super. Ct. Orange Cty. Loc. R., rule 352; Super. Ct. Sacramento Cty. Loc. R., rule 1.20; Super. Ct. San Bernardino Cty. Loc. R., rule 1800; Super. Ct. San Joaquin Cty. Loc. R., rule 9-100; Super. Ct. Ventura Cty. Loc. R., rule 4.05. If the court has an e-filing program, the party must determine if e-filing is permissive or mandatory for its case. Generally, a court can make e-filing permissive in any civil case by local rule. CRC 2.253(a). The court can make e-filing mandatory by local rule or court order. CRC 2.251(c)(1).

[1] Mandatory by local rule. A court, by local rule, can require a party to e-file documents in the following types of cases:

[a] Civil cases generally. CRC 2.253(b)(1)(A).

[b] Civil cases of a specific category, such as limited or unlimited civil cases. CRC 2.253(b)(1)(B).

[c] Civil cases of a specific case type, such as contract, collections, personal injury, or employment. CRC 2.253(b)(1)(C).

[d] Civil cases assigned to a judge for all purposes. CRC 2.253(b)(1)(D).

[e] Civil cases assigned to a specific department, courtroom, or courthouse. CRC 2.253(b)(1)(E).

[f] Class claims, consolidated claims, groups of actions, coordinated actions, or complex actions. CRC 2.253(b)(1)(F).

[g] Any combination of the above. CRC 2.253(b)(1)(G).

[2] Mandatory by court order.

[a] Generally. A court, on a party's motion or on its own, can order the parties to e-file documents in a class action, a consolidated action, a group of actions, a coordinated action, or an action that is declared complex under CRC 3.403, provided that (1) it has adopted local rules conforming with the requirements of CCP §1010.6 and (2) the order would not cause undue hardship or significant prejudice to any party. *See* CCP §1010.6(b), (c); CRC 2.251(c)(1), 2.253(c)(1).

[b] **Notice.** If the court proposes to make the order on its own motion, the court must give the parties an opportunity to respond by mailing them a notice of the proposed order at least ten days before the order takes effect. CRC 2.253(c)(2). If the court later determines that a new party should also be ordered to e-file, the court should either (1) give the parties at least ten days' notice that it plans to order the new party to e-file or (2) order the new party to e-file documents and in its order state that the new party may object within ten days after service of the order or by a later time that the court may specify. CRC 2.253(c)(3).

[c] **Additional provisions.** The court's order can provide that (1) documents previously filed in paper form may be resubmitted in electronic form and (2) when the court sends confirmation of filing to all parties, receipt of the confirmation constitutes service of the filing if the filed document is available electronically. CRC 2.253(c)(4).

(b) **Determine if exception to mandatory e-filing applies.** If the court requires e-filing for a particular case, the party should determine whether an exception to mandatory e-filing applies.

[1] **Pro per party.** Mandatory e-filing requirements do not apply to a party appearing pro per. CRC 2.253(b)(2). See "Party in propria persona," ch. 1-G, §3.1.2, p. 65. In cases involving both represented and self-represented parties, represented parties may be required to e-file, but self-represented parties must affirmatively agree to e-file. CRC 2.253(b)(3).

[2] **Undue hardship or significant prejudice.** Mandatory e-filing requirements do not apply if a court excuses a party from the requirement because the party has shown undue hardship or significant prejudice. CRC 2.253(b)(4); *see* Judicial Council forms, form EFS-007 (request for exemption from mandatory electronic filing and service), form EFS-008 (order of exemption from electronic filing and service).

[3] **Not feasible.** Mandatory e-filing requirements do not apply if it is not feasible for a party to convert a document to an electronic form and the court allows the party to file the document in paper form. CRC 2.252(d).

(c) **Comply with court rules.** The party must read and comply with the court's local e-filing rules. *See* CRC 2.256(a)(1). Some courts require the e-filer to have an online filing account or to use a particular electronic-filing service provider (EFSP). *See* CRC 2.250(b)(8) (EFSP is person or entity that receives filing from party and transmits it to court as party's agent), CRC 2.252(b) (court can require e-filing through EFSP, directly, or both). For example, the Orange County Superior Court requires filings in all limited, unlimited, and complex cases to be made electronically unless the party has been specifically excused from doing so by the court. Super. Ct. Orange Cty. Loc. R., rule 352.

(d) **Provide electronic-service address.** The e-filer must provide the court and the EFSP, if one is used, one or more electronic-service addresses (i.e., e-mail addresses) at which it agrees to accept service. CRC 2.256(a)(4), (a)(6). If the e-filer's electronic-service address changes, the e-filer must immediately provide the court, the EFSP (if one is used), and all parties with the new address. CRC 2.256(a)(5), (a)(6); *see* Judicial Council Forms, form MC-040.

(2) **When filing.** When e-filing a document, the e-filer must do the following:

(a) **Provide case information.** The e-filer must furnish any information the court needs to process the case. CRC 2.256(a)(2).

(b) **Check for viruses.** The e-filer must take all reasonable steps to ensure that the filing does not contain harmful computer code, such as a virus. CRC 2.256(a)(3).

(c) **Pay fees or e-file application to waive fees.** The e-filer must submit filing fees or e-file an application to waive fees and costs. *See* CCP §1010.6(b)(6) (court must permit party to e-file application to waive fees and costs); CRC 2.252(f) (court may permit party to e-file application to waive fees and costs), CRC 2.258(b) (eligible persons may seek waiver of fees and costs), CRC 2.259(b) (filing can be rejected if fees are not paid). See

"Filing Fees," §7, p. 58. The court can permit the fees to be paid by credit card, debit card, electronic fund transfer, debit account, or some other method of payment. CRC 2.258(a). See "Form of payment," §7.2, p. 58. If the court has contracted with an EFSP, the court can also authorize the EFSP to charge the e-filer a reasonable fee for the EFSP's services. CRC 2.255(b).

(3) After filing. After e-filing a document, the e-filer should verify that the document was received and accepted for filing by the court. CRC 2.259(a)(4). There is no presumption that the court received and filed the document unless the e-filer receives a confirmation from the court. *Id.*

2. Court's responsibilities.

(1) Generally. The court must promptly provide notice of any known problem that interferes with e-filing during the court's regular filing hours. CRC 2.254(b).

(2) After filing. After a paper has been e-filed, the court must do the following:

(a) Confirm receipt. The court—or the EFSP if one has been contracted with—must send confirmation to the e-filer that the document was received. *See* CCP §1010.6(b)(4); CRC 2.255(d)(1), 2.259(a)(1). The confirmation must indicate the date and time of receipt and must be sent to the e-filer's electronic-service address. CRC 2.255(d)(2), 2.259(a)(1), (a)(3). The court must maintain a record of receipt confirmations sent to the e-filer. CRC 2.259(a)(3).

(b) Confirm or reject filing. After receiving electronically submitted documents, the court must review the documents and either confirm or reject the filing. CRC 2.255(d)(3), 2.259(a)(2), (b).

[1] Confirm. If the documents comply with the filing requirements and all required fees have been paid, the court must promptly send confirmation of the filing to the e-filer's electronic-service address (and to the EFSP if applicable). CRC 2.255(d)(3), 2.259(a)(2), (a)(3). The confirmation must indicate the date and time of filing, any transaction number associated with the filing, the titles of the filed documents, and the filing fees assessed. CRC 2.259(a)(2). The confirmation is proof of the date and time of filing. *Id.*

[2] Reject. If the documents do not comply with the filing requirements or all the required fees have not been paid, the court must promptly send notice of rejection to the e-filer's electronic-service address (and to the EFSP if applicable). CRC 2.255(d)(3), 2.259(a)(3), (b). The notice must state the reasons for rejection. CRC 2.259(b).

(c) Allow access to documents. The court must allow public access to an e-filed document unless (1) access is limited under CRC 2.250-2.259 or 2.500-2.506, (2) the document is sealed under CRC 2.551(b), or (3) the document is made confidential by law. CRC 2.254(c); *see* CRC 2.503(a).

3. Document format.

(1) Generally. An e-filed document must be in a format specified by the court unless the document cannot be created in that format. CRC 2.256(b). The format adopted by the court must meet the following requirements: (1) the software required to create and read documents in the specified format must be in the public domain or available at reasonable cost, and (2) the printing of documents must not result in the loss of document text, format, or appearance. *Id.* The formatting rules adopted by the court for e-filed documents prevail over other formatting rules under the California Rules of Court. *Id.*

(2) When original required. When an original, printed document must be filed, the e-filer can file an electronic copy if it files the original hard copy within ten calendar days. CRC 2.252(e).

4. Signatures. A digital signature does not have to be included in an e-filed document. CRC 2.257(d).

(1) Sworn documents. When an e-filed document must be signed under penalty of perjury, the declarant must sign a printed copy of the document before or on the same day as it is e-filed. CCP §1010.6(b)(2)(B);

CRC 2.257(a)(1). See "Signature," ch. 1-B, §2.7, p. 15. The e-filer must keep the signed copy. CCP §1010.6(b)(2)(B); *see* CRC 2.257(a)(2). The court or any party can demand production of the signed copy anytime after the document is filed. CCP §1010.6(b)(2)(B); CRC 2.257(a)(3), (a)(5).

(2) Unsworn documents. When an e-filed document does not have to be signed under penalty of perjury, the document is considered signed when it is filed. CCP §1010.6(b)(2)(A); CRC 2.257(b).

(3) Other party's signature. When an e-filed document must be signed by an opposing party (e.g., a stipulation), the e-filer must get the opposing party's signature on a printed copy of the document before e-filing it. CRC 2.257(c)(1), (c)(3). The e-filer must keep the signed copy of the document. CRC 2.257(c)(2). The court or any party can demand production of the signed copy anytime after the document is filed. *Id.*

(4) Judicial signature. If a document requires a signature by a court or judicial officer, the document can be signed in any manner allowed by law. CRC 2.257(e).

5. Effect of e-filing.

(1) Generally. Filing a document electronically has the same legal effect as filing an original paper document. CCP §1010.6(b)(1); *see* CRC 2.252(c)(1) (same legal effect as document in paper form). Despite this, if the action or proceeding requires an original document to be filed, the e-filer must file the original with the court within ten calendar days after it is e-filed. CRC 2.252(e).

(2) On filing deadlines. Filing a document electronically does not alter any filing deadline. CRC 2.252(c)(2). A document that is received electronically by the court after the close of business is generally considered received on the next court day. CRC 2.259(c). However, a court may provide by local rule that documents required by local rule to be e-filed are deemed filed (1) on the same court day if they are received electronically before midnight on a court day and (2) on the next court day if received after midnight. CRC 2.253(b)(7), 2.259(c). See "Mandatory by local rule," §4.4.1(1)(a)[1], p. 49. If the e-filer can show that a technical problem with the court's e-filing system prevented the e-filer from filing a document on a particular day, the document—other than a complaint or other initial pleading—will be considered filed on that day. CRC 2.259(d).

(3) On electronic service. A represented party who e-files a document with the court automatically agrees to accept electronic service. CRC 2.251(b)(1)(B). However, a party that is appearing pro per must affirmatively consent to electronic service. *Id.* See "Electronic service," ch. 1-G, §5.1.5, p. 68.

(4) On summons. If an e-filed document requires service of summons (e.g., complaint), the court can transmit a summons electronically to the e-filer. CCP §1010.6(b)(5); CRC 2.259(f)(1). If the court plans to transmit the summons electronically, it must notify the e-filer immediately after receiving the document. CCP §1010.6(b)(5). The electronically transmitted summons must contain the court's seal and the assigned case number and can be printed and served like an original summons. *Id.*; CRC 2.259(f)(2), (f)(3).

§5. WHEN TO FILE

A party should file a document before the filing deadline established by the Code of Civil Procedure, another statute, the California Rules of Court, or a court order. To calculate a particular deadline, the party must first determine whether the deadline is prospective (i.e., calculated forward from a past event, such as the date discovery was served) or retrospective (i.e., calculated backward from a future event, such as the date of trial). The party must then calculate the deadline by (1) counting from the first day the time period for filing a document begins, (2) counting all intervening days, months, or years in the time period, and (3) determining when certain days, such as judicial holidays, should be excluded from the time period.

§5.1 Prospective deadlines. If the party is required to act *after* some event has occurred, the deadline is prospective. A prospective deadline usually uses a phrase such as "within 60 days after" or "no later than 60 days after." *See, e.g.*, CCP §585.5(b) (motion to set aside default judgment must be filed within 60 days after D first receives notice of levy under writ of execution), §2025.480(b) (motion to compel answers to deposition must be made

no later than 60 days after deposition record is completed); CRC 3.110(b) (proof of service of summons and complaint must be filed within 60 days after complaint is filed). To calculate a prospective deadline, the party must do the following:

1-1. CALCULATING PROSPECTIVE FILING DEADLINES

Step	Action	Section	Deadline
1	Determine date of triggering event	§5.1.1, this page	
2	Count forward to end of deadline	§5.1.2, this page, §5.1.3, this page	Step 1 + number of days, months, or years in deadline
3	Add extra time based on method of service if applicable	§5.1.4, p. 54	If by personal delivery, Step 2 If by intrastate mail, Step 2 + 5 calendar days If by interstate mail, Step 2 + 10 calendar days If by international mail, Step 2 + 20 calendar days If by express mail, Step 2 + 2 court days If by fax, Step 2 + 2 court days If by electronic service, Step 2 + 2 court days
4	Determine last day	§5.1.5, p. 55	Last day of Step 3, or count forward to next court day if last day is Saturday, Sunday, or judicial holiday

1. Determine date of triggering event.

(1) First day triggered by filing. The deadline for filing a document can be triggered by the date another document was filed with the court. *See, e.g.*, CCP §659a (ten-day deadline to file affidavits supporting motion for new trial triggered by date notice of motion was filed); CRC 3.1600(a) (ten-day deadline to file memorandum in support of motion for new trial triggered by date notice of intent to move for new trial was filed).

(2) First day triggered by service. The deadline for filing a document can be triggered by the date another document was served on the party. *See, e.g.*, CRC 3.1342(b) (15-day deadline to file written opposition to motion to dismiss for failure to prosecute triggered by date notice of motion was served). Usually, the method of service (e.g., mail, electronic service) determines the date when service is considered complete. *See, e.g.*, CCP §1013(a) (service by mail considered complete when document is deposited in mail); CRC 2.251(h)(1) (electronic service considered complete at time of transmission by e-filer or EFSP or when notification of service is sent). See "How to Serve," ch. 1-G, §5, p. 66. In some cases, however, the date a document was served may not be the triggering date. For example, if a document was served by the court clerk and the date of the postage cancellation or postage-meter imprint, as shown on the envelope, is more than one day after the date the clerk stated in the proof of service that she deposited the document for mailing, the first day is the date of the cancellation or imprint. *See* CCP §1013a(4); *see, e.g.*, ***Staten v. Heale*** (3d Dist.1997) 57 Cal.App.4th 1084, 1088 (postage cancellation could not be deemed date of service because clerk's proof of service stated date of deposit was July 25 and postage cancellation date was July 26—only one day after).

2. Count forward. The party should begin counting forward from the day the time period for filing the document starts—that is, the date of the triggering event—making sure to skip that day. *See* Civ. C. §10; CCP §12; CRC 1.10(a). For example, if a defendant has 30 days to file a motion after some event, and that event occurs on a Monday (i.e., the day of the triggering event), Monday is "day 0," Tuesday is "day 1," Wednesday is "day 2," and so on.

3. Count intervening time. The party should count the total number of days, months, or years in the time period for filing the document.

(1) Days. If the party must file a document within a stated number of days, when the period ends depends on whether the days are calendar days or court days.

(a) Calendar days. If the days to be counted are "days" or "calendar days," count every day after the first day—including Saturdays, Sundays, and other judicial holidays—until the last day of the deadline. *See* Civ. C. §10; CCP §12; CRC 1.10(a); *see also* ***Iverson v. Superior Ct.*** (4th Dist.1985) 167 Cal.App.3d 544, 548 ("days" means calendar days, not court days).

(b) Court days. If the days to be counted are "court days" or "judicial days," count every day after the first day that is not a weekend day or other judicial holiday. *See* CCP §12; ***In re Maurice E.*** (1st Dist.2005) 132 Cal.App.4th 474, 478; ***People v. Pickens*** (4th Dist.1981) 124 Cal.App.3d 800, 804 & n.2. For a discussion of judicial holidays, see "Determine last day," §5.1.5, p. 55. A "court day" or "judicial day" is any day the court is open for business. *See* ***In re Maurice E.***, 132 Cal.App.4th at 478; ***Pickens***, 124 Cal.App.3d at 804.

(2) Months. If the party must file a document within a stated number of months, the period usually ends on the same numerical day in the concluding month as in the beginning month. *See* Civ. C. §14 ("month" means calendar month); CCP §17(b)(4) (same). However, if the deadline is for a six-month period, the deadline is either six calendar months or 182 calendar days, whichever is longer. *See* Gov. C. §6803; ***Gonzales v. County of L.A.*** (2d Dist.1988) 199 Cal.App.3d 601, 604; *see, e.g.*, ***Marchuk v. Ralphs Grocery Co.*** (4th Dist.1990) 226 Cal.App.3d 1273, 1275-76 (six-month period starting on Friday, January 20, 1989, ended 182 days later, on Friday, July 21, 1989, or six months and one calendar day later).

(3) Years. If the party must file a document within a stated number of years, the period ends on the 365th calendar day of the concluding year. *See* Gov. C. §6803; ***Overby v. Overby*** (1st Dist.1957) 154 Cal.App.2d 813, 816-17. If the year is a leap year, February 28 and 29 are counted as a single day. Gov. C. §6803.

4. Add time for method of service.

(1) Generally. If the deadline to file a document is triggered by the service of another document, the party may get to add extra time to the deadline based on how the party was served. *See, e.g.*, ***Lam v. Ngo*** (4th Dist.2001) 91 Cal.App.4th 832, 842 (service of amended complaint by mail extended D's time to file anti-SLAPP motion by five days). Generally, under CCP §§1010.6(a)(4) and 1013, a party's duty to act or respond is extended if the duty is triggered by the service of another document and the document is served by mail, express mail, overnight delivery, fax, or electronic service. For a discussion of how much time is added to the deadline based on the method of service, see "Add time for method of service," ch. 1-G, §6.1.4, p. 70.

CAUTION

Extra time is added only when the deadline is triggered by service, not filing. See ***Camper v. Workers' Comp. Appeals Bd.*** *(1992) 3 Cal.4th 679, 684-85 (when prescribed time period is commenced by some circumstance, act, or occurrence other than service, CCP §1013 does not apply);* ***People v. $20,000 U.S. Currency*** *(3d Dist.1991) 235 Cal.App.3d 682, 689 (statutes and rules invoking extensions under CCP §1013 usually provide that allotted time runs from service of document); see also CCP §1010.6(a)(4) (any right or duty to act after service by electronic transmission must be extended), §1013 (any right or duty to act after service by mail, express mail, overnight delivery, or fax must be extended).*

(2) Exceptions. The extensions under §§1010.6(a)(4) and 1013 do not apply if a specific exception is provided by law. CCP §§1010.6(a)(4), 1013. For example, if a judgment is served by mail, express mail, overnight delivery, fax, or electronic service, it does not extend a party's deadline to file (1) a notice of intention to move for new trial, (2) a notice of intention to move to vacate a judgment under CCP §633a, or (3) a notice of appeal. *See id.* §§1010.6(a)(4), 1013; *see also* ***Division of Labor Stds. Enforcement v. Atlantic Baking Co.*** (2d Dist.2001) 89 Cal.App.4th 891, 895 (extensions allowed under CCP §1013 do not apply to jurisdictional deadlines). The extensions also do not apply to a summons for a complaint that is served by mail. CCP §413.20. Thus, the deadline to file an answer to a complaint is 30 days after service of summons, regardless of whether the summons was served by mail. *See id.* §§412.20(a)(3), 413.20.

CAUTION

There is no clear authority on when you add the extra time for method of service—before you determine the last day to act or after. See "Determine last day," §5.1.5, this page. In 2010, the California Legislature added CCP §12c. Under §12c, to calculate a retrospective deadline that is based on a hearing date (e.g., 16 court days before a hearing), any time added to the deadline for the method of service is added "after" you have determined the last day to act. CCP §12c(b). Until there is clear guidance on how the days should be added in calculating a prospective deadline, the best approach is to add the extra time before you calculate the last day to act so you file your response sooner rather than later.

5. Determine last day. The party should count the last day unless it is a Saturday, Sunday, or other judicial holiday. CRC 1.10(a); *see* Civ. C. §10; CCP §§12, 12a. If the last day falls on a Saturday, Sunday, or other judicial holiday, the deadline is the next court day. CRC 1.10(b); *see* Civ. C. §10; CCP §§12, 12a; ***Concerned Citizens Coalition v. City of Stockton*** (3d Dist.2005) 128 Cal.App.4th 70, 75 n.4. Judicial holidays include the following:

(1) Official holidays. A holiday, as used in Civ. C. §10 and CCP §§12 and 12a, includes all days when state offices are officially closed except Admission Day (September 9). CCP §§12a(a), 12b, 135; Gov. C. §6700; *see* ***Los Angeles City Empls. Un. v. City of El Monte*** (2d Dist.1985) 177 Cal.App.3d 615, 620-21; *see also* CCP §134(d) (fact that court is open on judicial holiday does not make day a nonholiday). If a holiday falls on a Saturday, the court will observe it on the preceding Friday. CRC 1.11. If a holiday falls on a Sunday, the court will observe it on the following Monday. *Id.*

1-2. JUDICIAL HOLIDAYS

	Name of holiday	Date of holiday	Authority
1	New Year's Day	January 1	Gov. C. §6700(a)(2)
2	Dr. Martin Luther King, Jr. Day*	Third Monday in January	Gov. C. §6700(a)(3)
3	Lincoln Day	February 12	Gov. C. §6700(a)(4)
4	Washington's Birthday	Third Monday in February	Gov. C. §6700(a)(5)
5	Cesar Chavez Day*	March 31	Gov. C. §6700(a)(6)
6	Good Friday (12 p.m. to 3 p.m.)	Friday before Easter	Gov. C. §6700(a)(15)
7	Memorial Day	Last Monday in May	Gov. C. §6700(a)(7)
8	Independence Day	July 4	Gov. C. §6700(a)(8)
9	Labor Day	First Monday in September	Gov. C. §6700(a)(9)
 10	Native American Day	Fourth Friday in September	Gov. C. §6700(a)(11)
11	Columbus Day	Second Monday in October	Gov. C. §6700(a)(12)
12	Veterans Day	November 11	Gov. C. §6700(a)(13)
13	Thanksgiving Day	Fourth Thursday in November	CCP §135; Gov. C. §6700(a)(16)
14	Day after Thanksgiving	Fourth Friday in November	CCP §135
15	Christmas Day	December 25	Gov. C. §6700(a)(14)

* Not required holidays unless designated by city or county.

(2) Appointed days. A holiday includes any day appointed by the U.S. President or Governor of California as a day for a public fast, thanksgiving, or holiday. CCP §135; Gov. C. §6700(a)(16).

(3) Weekends. A holiday includes any Saturday or Sunday. CCP §§12a(a), 135; Gov. C. §6700(a)(1); CRC 1.10(b).

(4) Emergencies. A holiday includes any day a court clerk's office is closed for business for the entire day because of an emergency. *See* CCP §12b.

§5.2 Retrospective deadlines. If the party is required to act *before* some event will occur, the deadline is retrospective. A retrospective deadline usually uses a phrase such as "at least 75 days before" or "not less than five days before." *See, e.g.*, CCP §437c(b)(2) (opposition to MSJ must be filed not less than 14 days before hearing), §484.070(e) (claim of exemption from attachment must be filed not less than five days before hearing), §1005(b) (all motion and supporting papers must be filed at least 16 court days before hearing). To calculate a retrospective deadline, the party must do the following:

1-3. CALCULATING RETROSPECTIVE FILING DEADLINES

Step	Action	Section	Deadline
1	Determine date of triggering event	§5.2.1, this page	
2	Count backward to beginning of deadline	§5.2.2, p. 57, §5.2.3, p. 57	Step 1 + number of days, months, or years in deadline
3	Determine last day	§5.2.4, p. 57	Last day of Step 2, or count backward to next court day if last day is Saturday, Sunday, or judicial holiday

1. Determine date of triggering event. The most common retrospective deadlines are those relating to discovery, hearings, and trials.

(1) Discovery. Retrospective deadlines relating to discovery generally involve deadlines that set the last day to conduct a hearing on a discovery-related motion before the discovery cutoff date as specified in the Discovery Act. *See* CCP §2024.020(a) (discovery proceedings and motions generally), §2024.030 (discovery proceedings involving experts).

(a) Discovery cutoff date. Discovery cutoff dates are linked to the initial trial date. ***Beverly Hosp. v. Superior Ct.*** (2d Dist.1993) 19 Cal.App.4th 1289, 1292. The "initial trial date" is the first date the court assigns for the start of trial. ***Fairmont Ins. v. Superior Ct.*** (2000) 22 Cal.4th 245, 250.

PRACTICE TIP

A continuance or resetting of the initial trial date does not automatically reopen or extend the period for discovery. CCP §2024.020(b); ***Fairmont Ins.****, 22 Cal.4th at 250-51;* ***Beverly Hosp.****, 19 Cal.App.4th at 1295. If more time is needed, ask the court to link the discovery cutoff date and the deadline for discovery motions to the new trial date. See "Modifying discovery cutoffs," ch. 7-A, §5.2.3, p. 748.*

(b) Discovery motions. Discovery motions must be heard by the 15th day before the initial trial date. CCP §2024.020(a). Discovery motions relating to experts must be heard by the tenth day before the initial trial date. *Id.* §2024.030. For example, if a party wants to file notice of a hearing on a motion to compel discovery by personal delivery, the last day to file the notice would be 37 calendar days before the initial trial date. This is calculated by adding 15 calendar days for the discovery cutoff under CCP §2024.020(a) and 16 court days for the notice of motion under CCP §1005, and also by skipping six weekend days.

(2) Hearings. Retrospective deadlines relating to hearings generally involve deadlines that set the last day to file certain documents before the date of the hearing. *See, e.g.*, CCP §437c(b)(2) (opposition to MSJ must be filed not less than 14 days before hearing), §484.070(f) (notice of opposition to claim that personal property is

exempt from attachment must be filed not less than two days before hearing). The most common hearing deadlines involve motion practice—that is, the deadlines for filing (and serving) a notice of motion, a motion and any supporting papers, an opposition, or a reply.

(a) Motion papers. Under CCP §1005, most notices of motions, motions, and supporting papers presented to the court for an order (unless presented during a hearing or trial) must be filed at least 16 court days before the hearing (i.e., the "motion cutoff date"). CCP §1005(b); CRC 3.1300(a); *see* ***People v. American Contractors Indem.*** (2d Dist.1999) 74 Cal.App.4th 1037, 1049 (applying former CCP §1005; statute applies unless another statute specifically provides for different notice period). See "Court days," §5.1.3(1)(b), p. 54; "Deadline to file," ch. 1-D, §7.1.4, p. 34.

(b) Opposition papers. Most papers opposing a motion must be filed at least nine court days before the hearing. CCP §1005(b). See "Court days," §5.1.3(1)(b), p. 54; "Deadline to file & serve," ch. 1-D, §8.5.3, p. 37.

(c) Reply papers. Most papers replying to an opposition must be filed at least five court days before the hearing. CCP §1005(b). See "Court days," §5.1.3(1)(b), p. 54; "Deadline to file & serve," ch. 1-D, §9.6.3, p. 38.

(3) Trials. Retrospective deadlines relating to trials generally involve deadlines that set the last day to file certain documents before the date of trial. *See, e.g.*, CRC 3.891(a)(2) (stipulation to mediate case must be filed "not later than 90 days before trial").

2. Count backward. The party should begin counting backward from the date of the triggering event, making sure to skip that day. CCP §12c(a); *see* Civ. C. §10; CCP §12; CRC 1.10(a); *see, e.g.*, ***Pamela H. v. Superior Ct.*** (1st Dist.1977) 68 Cal.App.3d 916, 919 (motion to disqualify had to be filed on June 25, counting back five days from hearing date of June 30 and excluding day of hearing itself). For example, if a party has 16 days to file a motion before a hearing, and the hearing is scheduled for a Friday, Friday is "day 0," the preceding Thursday is "day 1," the preceding Wednesday is "day 2," and so on.

3. Count intervening time. The party should count the intervening days, months, or years. See "Count intervening time," §5.1.3, p. 53.

4. Determine last day. The party should count the last day unless it is a Saturday, Sunday, or other judicial holiday. CRC 1.10(a); *see* Civ. C. §10; CCP §§12, 12c(a); *see, e.g.*, ***Pamela H.***, 68 Cal.App.3d at 919 (motion to disqualify had to be filed on June 25, counting back five days from hearing date of June 30, and including the last day). If the last day falls on a Saturday, Sunday, or other judicial holiday, continue to count backward until the next day that is not a Saturday, Sunday, or other judicial holiday. See "Determine last day," §5.1.5, p. 55.

CAUTION

The California Supreme Court has held that if a statute requires an act to occur "not less than" or "not later than" a certain time period before an event (e.g., 31st day before election), the last day is counted—even if it is a Saturday, Sunday, or other judicial holiday. See, e.g., ***Steele v. Bartlett*** *(1941) 18 Cal.2d 573, 574 (Election Code required nominating papers to be filed not later than 31st day before election; because 31st day fell on Sunday, papers filed on following Monday were late). In 2010, however, the California Legislature added CCP §12c. Under §12c, if any law requires an act to be performed no later than a specified number of days before a "hearing date," the party should count the last day unless it is excluded under §12—that is, unless it is a Saturday, Sunday, or other judicial holiday. CCP §12c(a). It is unclear whether §12c(a) is meant to apply only to hearing dates and not to other events.*

§6. EXTENDING TIME TO FILE

§6.1 Motion to extend time. A motion to extend time is a request for more time to do some required act, such as filing a document. *See* CRC 1.10(c); *see, e.g.*, CCP §437c(h) (court can extend time to file additional affidavits in support of MSJ), §659a (court can extend time to file affidavits in support of motion for new trial), §1054(a) (court

can extend time to file pleading, bill of exception, or amendment to bill of exception); ***Erikson v. Weiner*** (3d Dist.1996) 48 Cal.App.4th 1663, 1672 (court could extend deadline to file affidavit in support of motion for new trial, but not beyond 20 days under CCP §659a). A motion to extend time should be filed as soon as the party realizes that more time is needed. A party filing a motion to extend must disclose in writing the nature of the case and what extensions, if any, have already been granted by court order or agreement of the parties. CRC 2.20(b). See "Extending Time," ch. 5-F, p. 501.

§6.2 Agreement to extend time. The parties can agree to extend a filing deadline. *See, e.g.*, ***Olinick v. BMG Entm't*** (2d Dist.2006) 138 Cal.App.4th 1286, 1295 (agreement to 15-day extension to answer or respond to complaint); ***Lincolnshire Condo., Ltd. v. Superior Ct.*** (4th Dist.1984) 158 Cal.App.3d 524, 526 (agreement to extend time to file motion to compel further responses to interrogatories). The agreement should be in writing and be signed by both parties. *See* ***Lincolnshire Condo.***, 158 Cal.App.3d at 526. *But see* ***Olinick***, 138 Cal.App.4th at 1295 (D's letter to P confirming that P agreed to 15-day extension to respond to complaint established parties' agreement to extend time). The agreement, however, cannot extend a deadline that is mandatory and jurisdictional. *See* ***Lincolnshire Condo.***, 158 Cal.App.3d at 525-26. For example, the deadline to file a motion for new trial or to set aside a default judgment is mandatory and jurisdictional. *See* ***Arambula v. Union Carbide Corp.*** (2d Dist.2005) 128 Cal.App.4th 333, 344-45 (dicta).

§7. FILING FEES

Generally, the party filing a document must either pay filing fees or file an application to waive fees. See "Application to waive fees," §7.3, p. 60. Chart 1-4, below, summarizes common civil filing fees for superior courts.

1-4. COMMON FEES

	Action	Fee	Authority
1	Filing first paper in unlimited civil case	$435*	Gov. C. §§70602.5(a), 70602.6(a), (b), 70611, 70612; *see also id.* §70602.6(d) ($40 fee in §70602.6 sunsets 7-1-15)
2	Filing first paper in limited civil case	$225-$370	Gov. C. §§70602.5(b), (c), 70613, 70614
3	Party designation or court determination that case is complex	$1,000**	Gov. C. §70616(e); *see also id.* §70616(i) ($1,000 fee sunsets and $550 fee returns 7-1-15)
4	Filing motion that requires hearing, generally	$60	Gov. C. §70617(a); *see also id.* §70617(g) ($60 fee sunsets and $40 fee returns 7-1-15)
5	Transmission of case file to new venue	$50	Gov. C. §70618
6	Reclassifying case from limited to unlimited	$140	Gov. C. §70619

* Because fees are subject to change, the filing party should check with the clerk or the Judicial Council's Statewide Civil Fee Schedule, available at www.courts.ca.gov.

** This fee is in addition to the first-paper filing fee required for all civil cases. Gov. C. §70616(a), (b). The total complex fees collected from the defendants, intervenors, respondents, or other adverse parties cannot exceed $18,000. *Id.* §70616(b); *see also id.* §70616(i) ($18,000 maximum fee sunsets and $10,000 maximum fee returns 7-1-15).

§7.1 Due when filed. The filing fees are usually due when the document is filed. *See* CCP §§411.20, 411.21. *But see* Gov. C. §70616(a), (b) (if case is not designated or counterdesignated as complex when first paper is filed, complex-case fee is due within ten calendar days of court's order designating case as complex).

§7.2 Form of payment.

1. **Check.** The clerk can accept a check for payment of the filing fee. *See* CCP §§411.20(a), 411.21(a).

(1) Check returned. If the check for filing a complaint, first paper, or any later filing is returned without payment, the clerk can accept the filing but must notify the filing party (and the party who tendered the check,

if different from the filing party) that the filing will be voided unless payment is received. CCP §411.20(a), (b), (d). Until payment is received by the clerk, the court can suspend proceedings involving the filing party. *Id.* §411.20(f). These procedures apply to both plaintiffs and defendants. *Id.* §411.20(d).

(a) Notice. The clerk's notice must be sent by mail and must state (1) the check was returned, (2) an administrative charge has been imposed for the cost of processing the returned check and notifying the filing party, and (3) the amount of time the party has to pay the filing fee and administrative charge. CCP §411.20(a); *see also id.* §411.20(d) (returned check for adverse party's document), §411.20(f) (notice of suspended proceedings), §411.20(g) (amount of administrative charge).

(b) Deadline. The filing party or the party who tendered the check usually has 20 days after the notice is mailed to make the required payment. CCP §411.20(a), (b). If a hearing or trial is scheduled before the end of the 20-day period, the payment must be made before the hearing or trial. *Id.* §411.20(e).

(c) Method of payment. The party must pay the filing fee in cash, by certified check, or by other means specified by the court. CCP §411.20(a). Payment cannot be made by personal check or traveler's check. *Id.* If the court suspended the proceedings, the party must pay by cashier's check or other means as ordered by the court. *Id.* §411.20(f).

(d) Void filing. If the filing party or the party who tendered the check does not make the required payment before the deadline, the clerk must void the filing. CCP §411.20(b); ***Hu v. Silgan Containers Corp.*** (3d Dist.1999) 70 Cal.App.4th 1261, 1267. The clerk must also void any documents filed by an adverse party in response to the original filing. CCP §411.20(c). The adverse party must be notified that the documents have been voided. *Id.* The clerk is not required to preserve a copy of a voided document and can dispose of the document immediately after the payment deadline. *Id.* §411.20(b).

(e) Refund – adverse party. If the clerk voids the filing, the clerk must refund the fee paid by an adverse party to file a document in response to the original filing if (1) the adverse party requests a refund within 20 days after the required notice to the adverse party is mailed and (2) the document filed by the adverse party is not a cross-complaint or other first paper seeking affirmative relief. CCP §411.20(c).

(2) Check for less than full amount – complaint or first paper. If the check for filing a complaint or other first paper is for less than the required fee, the clerk must accept the document for filing and notify the filing party (and the party who tendered the check, if different from the filing party) that the filing will be voided unless the outstanding balance is paid. CCP §411.21(a), (b). These procedures apply to both plaintiffs and defendants. *Id.* §411.21(e).

(a) Notice. The clerk's notice must be sent by mail and must state (1) the check was for an amount less than the required filing fee, (2) an administrative charge has been imposed for the cost of processing the returned check and notifying the filing party, and (3) the amount of time the party has to pay the filing fee and administrative charge. CCP §411.21(a); *see also id.* §411.21(g) (amount of administrative charge).

(b) Deadline. The filing party or the party who tendered the check usually has 20 days after the notice is mailed to make the additional required payment. CCP §411.21(a), (b). If a hearing or trial is scheduled before the end of the 20-day period, the payment must be made before the hearing or trial. *Id.* §411.21(f).

(c) Void filing. If the filing party or the party who tendered the check does not make the required payment before the deadline, the clerk must void the filing. CCP §411.21(b). The clerk must also void any documents filed by an adverse party in response to the original filing. *Id.* §411.21(d). The adverse party must be notified that the documents have been voided. *Id.* The clerk is not required to preserve a copy of a voided document and can dispose of the document immediately after the payment deadline. *Id.* §411.21(b).

[1] Refund – filing party. If the clerk voids the filing and the filing party requests a refund, the clerk must refund the payment of the filing fee, minus the court's administrative charge. CCP §411.21(c); *see also id.* §411.21(g) (amount of administrative charge).

[2] **Refund – adverse party.** If the clerk voids the filing, the clerk must refund the fee paid by an adverse party to file a document in response to the original filing if (1) the adverse party requests a refund within 20 days after the required notice to the adverse party is mailed and (2) the document filed by the adverse party is not a cross-complaint or other first paper seeking affirmative relief. CCP §411.21(d).

(3) Check for less than full amount – other documents. If the check for filing a document other than a complaint or first paper is for less than the required fee, the clerk cannot accept the document for filing. *See* Gov. C. §§6100, 26820; ***Mirvis v. Crowder*** (1st Dist.1995) 32 Cal.App.4th 1684, 1686-87; ***Kientz v. Harris*** (3d Dist.1953) 117 Cal.App.2d 787, 790.

2. Credit or debit card. The clerk can accept a credit or debit card for payment of filing fees if the court has been given approval by the Judicial Council. *See* Gov. C. §6159(b)(2), (c); CRC 3.100.

(1) Direct fax filing – credit or debit card. If the party is filing by fax directly and paying by credit or debit card, the cover sheet must include (1) the card account number, (2) the cardholder's signature, and (3) the card's expiration date. CRC 2.304(e)(1). If the charge is rejected, the court must follow the same procedure for returned checks. CRC 2.304(e)(2). See "Check returned," §7.2.1(1), p. 58.

(2) Direct fax filing – debit account. If the party is filing by fax directly, the court can allow an attorney or party to establish an account with the court for payment of direct-fax-filing fees. CRC 2.304(f). The court can require an advance deposit in the account of up to $1,000, or the court can agree to bill the attorney or party. *Id.* The court cannot bill the attorney or party more than once a month. *Id.*

3. Electronic fund transfer. The clerk can accept electronic fund transfers for payment of filing fees if the court has been given approval by the Judicial Council. *See* Gov. C. §6159(b)(2), (c).

§7.3 Application to waive fees. A party who cannot afford to pay the fees and costs associated with filing suit can ask the court to waive certain fees and costs by filing an application for initial-fee waiver. *See* CRC 3.50. The fees and costs that can be waived are listed in CRC 3.55 and 3.56. The party must use Judicial Council Form FW-001 for the initial-fee waiver and Judicial Council Form FW-002 for waiver of additional fees and costs. CRC 3.51. The court has five court days to consider and act on the application. Gov. C. §68634.5(f); CRC 3.53. If the court does not act within five court days, the application is deemed granted and the court clerk must prepare and serve Judicial Council Form FW-005. CRC 3.53. The court can later withdraw the waiver and order the party to pay the previously waived fees and costs if the conditions of Gov. C. §§68636 and 68637 are met. Gov. C. §68631; CRC 3.50(a). For more on waiving court fees, see 3 Witkin, *Cal. Procedure*, Actions, §§416-429.

§8. ACCEPTING FILED DOCUMENTS

§8.1 Deemed filed. A document is deemed filed when it is received by the court clerk. CRC 1.20.

§8.2 Noncomplying documents.

1. Acceptance by clerk.

(1) CRC 2.100-2.117 defects. Generally, the clerk cannot accept for filing documents that do not comply with CRC 2.100 through 2.117. CRC 2.118(a). See "General Requirements for Papers," ch. 1-B, §2, p. 9. However, the clerk's refusal to accept a document cannot be based solely on any of the following reasons:

(a) The document is handwritten. CRC 2.118(a)(1), 2.135(1).

(b) The document is handwritten in an ink color other than black or blue-black. CRC 2.118(a)(2), 2.135(2).

(c) The first page of the document does not include the attorney's or party's fax number or e-mail address. CRC 2.118(b).

(d) The document does not comply with the court's local rules. ***Carlson v. State of Cal. Dept. of Fish & Game*** (2d Dist.1998) 68 Cal.App.4th 1268, 1281; *see also* CCP §402(a)(3) (clerk cannot reject case for filing because local rule requires filing in another location).

(e) The document is untimely. CRC 3.1300(d).

(2) Other defects. The clerk should accept for filing documents that do not comply with other minor form requirements if the defect does not significantly impede the fulfillment of the requirement's purpose. *E.g.*, ***Rojas v. Cutsforth*** (2d Dist.1998) 67 Cal.App.4th 774, 777 (clerk should have accepted filed documents despite lack of signature on court-assignment form; lack of signature did not impede clerk's ability to determine which division case should be assigned to); *see* ***Voit v. Superior Ct.*** (6th Dist.2011) 201 Cal.App.4th 1285, 1287.

2. Acceptance by court. The court can accept for filing documents that do not comply with CRC 2.100 through 2.117 as long as the filing party shows good cause for doing so. CRC 2.118(c).

§8.3 Endorsing document. When a document is filed, the clerk must endorse it with the day, month, and year it was filed. Gov. C. §69846.5. The endorsement, or file stamp, creates a rebuttable presumption that the clerk endorsed the document on the day it was presented for filing. *See* ***Estate of Crabtree*** (4th Dist.1992) 4 Cal.App.4th 1119, 1125. To rebut this presumption, a party challenging the clerk's endorsement must offer affirmative evidence that the document was filed on a different date. *See, e.g.*, *id.* at 1125-26 (insufficient evidence was presented to overcome presumption of clerk's endorsement).

§9. PROVING DATE OF FILING

When a dispute arises about when a document was filed, the date the document was presented to the clerk controls, even over the file-stamp date on the document. *See* ***Carlson v. State of Cal. Dept. of Fish & Game*** (2d Dist.1998) 68 Cal.App.4th 1268, 1281; *see, e.g.*, ***Berger v. California Ins. Guar. Ass'n*** (2d Dist.2005) 128 Cal.App.4th 989, 996 n.5 (complaint was file-stamped February 13, 2002, but record clearly showed and parties agreed that complaint was filed February 13, 2003); ***Lozoya v. Superior Ct.*** (2d Dist.1987) 189 Cal.App.3d 1332, 1338 n.4 (motion was file-stamped August 6 but was actually presented for filing August 5). Methods for proving the date a document was presented include the following:

§9.1 Clerk's records. To prove the date a document was filed by mail, delivery, fax, or e-filing, a party can present a certified copy of the clerk's filing records. *See, e.g.*, ***Horsford v. Board of Trs.*** (5th Dist.2005) 132 Cal.App.4th 359, 382 (party's request for judicial notice included certified copy of superior court's docket).

§9.2 Fax-transmission record. To prove the date a document was filed by fax, a party can present an authenticated transmission verification record. *See* CRC 2.301(6), 2.304(d); *see also* Evid. C. §1401(a) (writing must be authenticated before it is received as evidence). See "Transmission record," §4.3.1(2)(d), p. 48.

§9.3 E-filing confirmation. To prove the date a document was e-filed, a party can present the court's confirmation that the document was filed. *See* CRC 2.259(a)(2). See "Confirm," §4.4.2(2)(b)[1], p. 51.

§9.4 Testimony of delivery service. To prove the date a document was filed, a party can present sworn testimony from the delivery service employed to file the document. This testimony alone, however, may not be enough to overcome the file-stamped date. *See, e.g.*, ***Estate of Crabtree*** (4th Dist.1992) 4 Cal.App.4th 1119, 1125-26 (sworn testimony of delivery service's supervisor was insufficient to overcome presumption of clerk's file stamp).

§9.5 Conformed copy. To prove the date a document was filed by mail or delivery, a party can present a conformed copy of the filed document. *See, e.g.*, ***People v. Brar*** (4th Dist.2005) 134 Cal.App.4th 659, 664 (lack of conformed copy supported reasonable inference that document was not filed); ***Datig v. Dove Books, Inc.*** (2d Dist.1999) 73 Cal.App.4th 964, 978-79 (party could have opposed motion to dismiss by presenting conformed copy of amended complaint); *see also* ***Pinkerton's, Inc. v. Superior Ct.*** (4th Dist.1996) 49 Cal.App.4th 1342, 1347 (dicta; noting that superior court denied motion to set aside default because no responsive pleading was filed with it, and despite D's statement that proposed demurrer had been part of motion, D could not produce conformed copy). A conformed copy is an exact copy of an endorsed document that can be used to confirm the date that the original document was received and filed. *See* CRC 2.117; *Black's Law Dictionary* 410 (10th ed. 2014); *cf.* ***Tri-County Elevator Co. v. Superior Ct.*** (2d Dist.1982) 135 Cal.App.3d 271, 276 (conformed copy of judgment can function as notice of entry of judgment). See "Endorsing document," §8.3, this page.

§10. LOST DOCUMENTS

§10.1 Fire or public calamity. CCP §§1953-1953.06 establish the procedure for dealing with the loss, damage, or destruction of filed documents by fire or public calamity.

1. Certified copy available. An interested person can apply by verified petition for an order authorizing the use of a certified copy of a document shown to be lost, damaged, or destroyed. CCP §1953.01; *see also id.* §1953.05 (in rem proceedings). The court can order the certified copy to have the same effect as the original. *Id.* §1953.02; *see also id.* §1953.05 (in rem proceedings).

2. Certified copy unavailable. If a certified copy is not available, an interested person who is not at fault for the loss and who could be harmed if a copy of the document is not supplied can submit a verified application for an order reciting the substance and effect of the document. CCP §§1953.03, 1953.04. After notice of the application has been given, the court can order the recitation to have the same effect as the original. *Id.* §§1953.03, 1953.04.

3. Record on appeal. If an action has been appealed, an interested party can obtain a certified copy of the transcript filed with the court of appeal and file it in the superior court from which the appeal was taken. CCP §1953.06. The certified copy can be used in the same way as the superior court's original record. *Id.*

§10.2 Other reason. When a document is lost, damaged, or destroyed for any other reason, the court has the inherent power to restore the record with a certified copy of the missing document. *See, e.g.*, ***Wilson v. Nichols*** (1st Dist.1942) 55 Cal.App.2d 678, 681 (certified copy took place of original, which had become detached from files and lost). If a certified copy is not available, the court can restore the record by admitting other evidence of the missing document's contents. *See, e.g.*, ***Creditors' Un. v. Lundy*** (1st Dist.1911) 16 Cal.App. 567, 570-71 (recital of contents of authentic document by witness's testimony was admissible).

§11. COURT INDEXES, REGISTER OF ACTIONS & MINUTES

§11.1 Court indexes. The clerk must keep indexes of all actions and proceedings filed in the court. Gov. C. §69842. The clerk must keep separate indexes of plaintiffs' and defendants' names, and every entry must include the case number and the names of all adverse parties. *Id.*

§11.2 Court register of actions. The clerk must keep a register of actions for all filed documents. The clerk can do so in either of the following ways:

1. List of filings. The clerk can keep a register of actions by maintaining a list of all documents filed in an action and the dates when the documents were filed. Gov. C. §69845; *see, e.g.*, ***Mesler v. Bragg Mgmt. Co.*** (2d Dist.1990) 219 Cal.App.3d 983, 988-89 & n.6 (register entry that remittitur was filed); ***Alvarado v. City of Port Hueneme*** (2d Dist.1982) 133 Cal.App.3d 695, 707 (clerk made appropriate entry in register of filed arbitration award).

PRACTICE TIP

Although not always reliable, most courts maintain lists of filed documents on their websites.

2. Preserving documents. The clerk can keep a register of actions by preserving all documents filed, lodged, or maintained in connection with an action. Gov. C. §69845.5.

§11.3 Court minutes. The clerk must keep minutes of the court containing entries for all the court's orders, judgments, and decrees. Gov. C. §69844. The clerk may include other information in the court's minutes. ***Copley Press, Inc. v. Superior Ct.*** (4th Dist.1992) 6 Cal.App.4th 106, 110. See "Oral ruling," ch. 1-I, §3.2, p. 90.

G. SERVING DOCUMENTS

§1. GENERAL

§1.1 Purpose. The purpose of serving documents is to give the other parties a copy of what is being filed with the court. Serving documents should not be confused with filing them. Documents are *filed* with the clerk, and copies are *served* on other parties. *See* CRC 1.21(b). This subchapter applies only to serving documents after the complaint has been filed and the court has acquired jurisdiction over the parties. It does not apply to service of process, which has more complicated requirements. For information about service of process, see "Joining the Defendant—Service of Process," ch. 3-H, p. 295.

§1.2 Primary authority. CCP §§422.10, 465, 1005-1006, 1010-1020; CRC 1.21, 1.41, 2.20, 2.251, 2.252, 2.256, 2.305, 2.306, 3.400, 3.510, 3.1300, 3.1312.

§1.3 Judicial Council forms.

- MC-040 (optional), notice of change of address or other contact information.
- EFS-005 (optional), consent to electronic service and notice of electronic-service address.
- EFS-010 (optional), notice of change of electronic-service address.
- POS-020 (optional), proof of personal service.
- POS-030 (optional), proof of service by first-class mail.
- POS-040 (optional), proof of service—civil.
- POS-050/EFS-050 (optional), proof of electronic service.

§2. WHAT TO SERVE

Generally, all documents filed with the court should be served on all parties who have appeared in the action. *See* CCP §1014. A filing about the merits of a case that is not served on opposing counsel is an improper ex parte communication, unless there is a specific exception. *See* Rules Prof. Conduct, rule 5-300(B).

NOTE

CRC 2.117 allows a party to serve the opposing party with papers printed on both sides of the page if the opposing party agrees. CRC 2.117. The party should file in the court a copy that is printed on only one side of the page. See id.

§2.1 Most documents.

1. Pleadings. All pleadings after the complaint must be served, unless the court directs otherwise. CCP §465. Pleadings include answers, cross-complaints, and demurrers. *Id.* §422.10.

2. Motion, opposition & reply papers.

(1) Motion papers. A notice of the motion, the memorandum in support, and any supporting papers, such as affidavits and discovery responses, must be served. *See* CCP §§1005(b), 1010; CRC 3.1300(a).

(2) Opposition papers. An opposition to a motion and any supporting papers must be served. *See* CCP §1005(b), (c).

(3) Reply papers. A reply to an opposition and any supporting papers must be served. *See* CCP §1005(c).

3. Proposed orders. A proposed order must be served on all parties for approval. CRC 3.1312(a). A proposed order should be served with motion papers, but it should not be attached to a motion. CRC 3.1113(m).

4. **Discovery.** Discovery requests and responses must be served on all parties who have appeared. *See, e.g.*, CCP §2025.240 (deposition notice), §2030.080(b) (interrogatories), §2031.040 (demand to produce), §2033.070 (request for admission). But when service would be unduly expensive or burdensome, the court can relax the requirement of service of all discovery on all parties. *See, e.g.*, *id.* §2030.080(b) (court can order that service of interrogatories on all parties is unnecessary); *see also* CRC 3.510(b) (court can order service on single, designated counsel in complex case).

5. **Other documents.** The Code of Civil Procedure, the California Rules of Court, or local rules may require service of other types of documents. *See, e.g.*, CCP §170.3(c)(1) (verified statement objecting to hearing or trial before disqualified judge must be served); CRC 3.221(c) (ADR information package must be served), CRC 3.300(b) (Notice of Related Case must be served), CRC 3.1380(c) (settlement-conference statement must be served); Super. Ct. Los Angeles Cty. Loc. R., rule 3.25(e) (same); Super. Ct. San Diego Cty. Loc. R., rule 2.2.3 (same).

§2.2 Documents not required to be served.

1. **Notice of appeal.** A party is not required to serve a notice of appeal or cross-appeal on the other parties in a limited civil case. *See* CRC 8.100(a)(1), (f). The court clerk is required to notify the other parties of the filing of the notice of appeal. CRC 8.100(e)(1).

2. **Documents to defaulting party.** A party is not required to serve documents on another party who has not appeared or against whom a default judgment has been entered. CCP §§1010, 1014. But a defaulting party is still entitled to receive amended pleadings or other documents that affect its rights. *See id.* §1010; ***Thompson v. Cook*** (1942) 20 Cal.2d 564, 568.

§3. WHOM TO SERVE

§3.1 Attorney or party? If a party is represented by an attorney, most documents must be served on the attorney. CCP §1015; CRC 1.21(a). The Rules of Professional Conduct prohibit an attorney from communicating directly with a party who is represented by counsel, so an attorney who serves documents on a party rather than the party's attorney may be disciplined. *See* Rules Prof. Conduct, rules 1-100(A), 2-100. If a party who has appeared resides outside the state and has no attorney or is without representation, the court clerk or judge may be served instead. *See* CCP §§167, 1015.

1. **Represented party.**

(1) **Service on party's attorney.** When a party is represented by an attorney, most documents must be served on the attorney instead of the party. CCP §1015; CRC 1.21(a); *see also* ***Allied Grape Growers v. Bronco Wine Co.*** (5th Dist.1988) 203 Cal.App.3d 432, 448 n.12 (notice of motion served on party's attorney is imputed to party).

(2) **Service on party directly.** Some documents can be served directly on a represented party instead of its attorney.

(a) **Process.** Process can be served directly on a represented party. *See* CCP §1015; ***Miranda v. 21st Century Ins.*** (4th Dist.2004) 117 Cal.App.4th 913, 927. See "Joining the Defendant—Service of Process," ch. 3-H, p. 295.

(b) **Complaint.** A copy of the complaint can be served directly on a represented party. *See* CCP §413.10. See "Joining the Defendant—Service of Process," ch. 3-H, p. 295.

(c) **Subpoena.** A trial subpoena can be served directly on a represented party. CCP §1015; ***Miranda***, 117 Cal.App.4th at 927. See "Parties – trial subpoenas," ch. 8-A, §4.1.1(1)(c), p. 938.

(d) **Writ.** A writ can be served directly on a represented party. CCP §1015; *see, e.g.*, *id.* §§512.030 & 512.050 (possession of personal property), §699.545 (execution), §1073 (review), §1088 (mandate), §1105 (prohibition served same as mandate), §1166a(b) (possession of real property).

(e) Contempt paper. A contempt paper (i.e., an affidavit and show-cause order) must be served directly on a represented party, unless the party attempts to avoid service. ***Cedars-Sinai Imaging Med. Grp. v. Superior Ct.*** (2d Dist.2000) 83 Cal.App.4th 1281, 1286-87; *see* CCP §1015; ***Golden Gate Consol. Hydraulic Mining Co. v. Superior Ct.*** (1884) 65 Cal. 187, 191-92; ***Johnson v. Superior Ct.*** (1883) 63 Cal. 578, 580. See "Contempt," ch. 8-E, §3.4, p. 999; "Contempt sanctions," ch. 9-A, §4.3, p. 1007. When a defendant attempts to avoid service of a show-cause order, service on the defendant's attorney is sufficient. ***Golden Gate Consol.***, 65 Cal. at 192.

(f) Other documents. Other documents can be served directly on a represented party if a statute authorizes the service. For example, in probate litigation, conservatorship investigation reports must be served on the recommended conservator, not the recommended conservator's attorney. Welfare & Inst. C. §5354(a); ***Conservatorship of Ivey*** (4th Dist.1986) 186 Cal.App.3d 1559, 1565.

(3) Service on clerk or judge. Documents can be served on the court clerk, or on the judge if there is no clerk, when the attorney for the party to be served has no known California address. *See* CCP §§167, 1015.

PRACTICE TIP

Attorneys without a California office can file a notice of address with the court to receive service. CCP §1015. Judicial Council Form MC-040 can be used for this purpose.

2. Party in propria persona. A party in propria persona represents herself in court. *See Black's Law Dictionary* 1416 (10th ed. 2014) (definition of "pro se"); *see also* ***Merco Constr. Eng'rs, Inc. v. Municipal Ct.*** (1978) 21 Cal.3d 724, 731 (corporation cannot act in propria persona). A party may use an attorney but still act in propria persona if the attorney is not made the attorney of record. *See* ***Mix v. Tumanjan Dev. Corp.*** (2d Dist.2002) 102 Cal.App.4th 1318, 1324. But a party cannot claim to be acting in propria persona if the attorney does all the substantive work and makes appearances on the party's behalf. *See* ***Quaglino v. Quaglino*** (2d Dist.1979) 88 Cal.App.3d 542, 548. If a party's only attorney is removed or suspended from practice during the suit, the party is considered to be acting in propria persona. CCP §1015. A person cannot appear in propria persona for another person. ***Drake v. Superior Ct.*** (4th Dist.1994) 21 Cal.App.4th 1826, 1830.

(1) California resident. A party in propria persona who resides in California can be served with all documents. *See* CCP §1010.

(2) Nonresident. A party in propria persona who resides outside California can be served with documents by delivering them to the court clerk or to the judge, if there is no clerk. *See* CCP §§167, 1010, 1015; *see, e.g.*, ***Leverett v. Superior Ct.*** (1st Dist.1963) 222 Cal.App.2d 126, 128 & n.2 (service on clerk valid for party that left state). Service in this manner is permitted only when the party has appeared in the suit. *See* CCP §§1014, 1015.

§3.2 Which attorney? Documents must be served on the party's attorney of record. ***Macri v. Carson Tahoe Hosp., Inc.*** (5th Dist.1966) 247 Cal.App.2d 63, 65; *see* CCP §1015; ***Lyydikainen v. Industrial Acc. Comm'n*** (1st Dist.1939) 36 Cal.App.2d 298, 303. See "Attorney of record," ch. 1-B, §2.7.1(1), p. 15.

1. Attorney of record. The attorney of record is named by the client as her agent for service of documents. ***Reynolds v. Reynolds*** (1943) 21 Cal.2d 580, 584; ***In re Marriage of Armato*** (2d Dist.2001) 88 Cal.App.4th 1030, 1043. The authority of an attorney of record to act on the party's behalf is presumed when the attorney's name appears on the pleadings. *See* ***Epley v. Califro*** (1958) 49 Cal.2d 849, 853-54; ***Turner v. Caruthers*** (1861) 17 Cal. 431, 432-33; ***Baker v. Boxx*** (2d Dist.1991) 226 Cal.App.3d 1303, 1310; *see also* ***Sowden v. Idaho Quartz Mining Co.*** (1880) 55 Cal. 443, 452-53 (P's attorney could not claim his associate attorney had no authority to accept service of notice of motion for new trial because associate's name appeared on briefs).

2. Other attorneys. It is not unusual for a party to be represented by more than one attorney. ***Mix v. Tumanjan Dev. Corp.*** (2d Dist.2002) 102 Cal.App.4th 1318, 1324. If there are several attorneys of record, documents should be served on each of them. *See* ***Straw v. Pacific Tel. & Tel. Co.*** (2d Dist.1961) 189 Cal.App.2d 270, 273. *But see* Super. Ct. Fresno Cty. Loc. R., rule 2.1.16 (when law firm is attorney of record, attorney who signed initial pleading is designated to receive notices in case).

§3.3 Which parties? Generally, documents should be served on all parties in the suit.

1. Complex cases. If there are multiple parties and the case meets certain requirements, the court can designate the case as "complex." CRC 3.400. See "Complex case," ch. 3-C, §3.1.2(2), p. 211. In complex cases, a liaison attorney can be designated for each side to accept service and distribute documents to the appropriate parties. *See* CRC 3.506, 3.510(b).

2. Other cases. If a case is not complex, documents should be served on each party's attorney of record. CCP §1015.

PRACTICE TIP

The plaintiff should always keep a current copy of the service list (i.e., a list of the parties and their addresses for service) and make sure it accurately reflects the plaintiff's own service information and the information of the other plaintiffs. See CRC 3.254(a)(1). If more than two plaintiffs have appeared in a case and they are represented by different attorneys, the first-named plaintiff in the complaint must maintain the service list for the court or any party who requests it. CRC 3.254(a).

---

§4. WHO CAN SERVE

Generally, anyone who is over 18 and not a party to a suit can serve documents. CCP §1013a; *see, e.g.*, ***Silver v. McNamee*** (4th Dist.1999) 69 Cal.App.4th 269, 280 (service valid when attorney's paralegal mailed notice of motion to begin professional-negligence suit); ***Conservatorship of Wyatt*** (4th Dist.1987) 195 Cal.App.3d 391, 397 (service valid when employee of petitioner, county department of social services, prepared documents and delivered them to person who regularly deposits mail); *see also* ***Dobrick v. Hathaway*** (2d Dist.1984) 160 Cal.App.3d 913, 922 (service invalid because attorney's secretary did not allege in proof of service that she was over 18 and not party to suit).

§5. HOW TO SERVE

§5.1 Methods of service.

1. Personal delivery. Documents can be served by personal delivery. CCP §1011. The party can use a clerk, messenger, or delivery agency to personally serve documents. ***Heinlen v. Heilbron*** (1892) 94 Cal. 636, 640. Service is complete at the time of personal delivery. ***Arambula v. Union Carbide Corp.*** (2d Dist.2005) 128 Cal.App.4th 333, 341 n.7. The following are the specific methods for service by personal delivery:

(1) Hand to attorney or party. A document can be served by handing it to the attorney or party. CCP §1011.

(2) Deliver to attorney's office. A document can be served by delivering it to the attorney's office. CCP §1011(a). The document must be in an envelope labeled to identify the attorney being served. *Id.*

(a) Leave with receptionist. A document can be served by leaving the envelope with a receptionist or other person in charge of the office. CCP §1011(a); *see, e.g.*, ***King v. Wilson*** (2d Dist.1950) 101 Cal.App.2d 242, 244 (service on switchboard operator valid; she was considered in charge of office despite affidavit by attorney that she was not his secretary or agent to accept service).

(b) Leave in conspicuous place. If no one is available to accept service, the envelope can be left in a conspicuous place in the attorney's office between 9:00 a.m. and 5:00 p.m. CCP §1011(a); *see, e.g.*, ***People v. Perris Irrigation Dist.*** (1904) 142 Cal. 601, 603-04 (document left on attorney's desk while person in charge of office watched was service in conspicuous place); ***Dalzell v. Superior Ct.*** (1885) 67 Cal. 453, 454 (affidavit of service stating that no one was in front room of attorney's office was insufficient to prove that attorney was not in office when notice of appeal was left on his desk).

(3) Deliver to attorney's residence. A document can be served by leaving it in a labeled envelope at the attorney's residence with someone who is at least 18 years old. CCP §1011(a). Service at an attorney's residence is proper only when the attorney's office is closed and when the office and residence are in the same county. *Id.*

(4) Deliver to party's residence. A document can be served by leaving it between 8:00 a.m. and 6:00 p.m. at the party's residence with a person who is at least 18 years old. CCP §1011(b). Service at a party's residence is proper only if the document is a subpoena, writ, process issued in the suit, or contempt paper or if the party being served is acting in propria persona. *See id.* §1015.

(5) Leave with court clerk. A document can be served by leaving it with the court clerk or, if there is no clerk, with the judge. *See* CCP §§167, 1011, 1015. Service on the clerk or judge is proper only if (1) the recipient's address is unknown, (2) the party's attorney has no office in California, or (3) the party has appeared in the suit in propria persona and is not a California resident. *See id.* §§167, 1011, 1015. If service is made on a party with an unknown address, the document must be in an envelope addressed to the recipient in care of the clerk or judge. CRC 3.252(a). The back of the envelope must contain the name of the party, the case name and number, and the following statement: "Service is being made under CCP section 1011(b) on a party whose residence address is unknown." CRC 3.252(b).

2. Regular mail. Documents can be served by mail. CCP §1012. To be served by regular mail, a document must be sent in a sealed envelope addressed to the recipient at the last office address given by the recipient in a filing with the court. *Id.* §1013(a). If the office address is not known, the envelope must be sent to the recipient's residence. *Id.* The date and general location of mailing should be noted on the face of the document or recited in an unsigned declaration of service attached to a copy of the document served. *Id.* §1013(b). See "Proving service by mail or express mail," §7.1.3, p. 75. Service by mail is complete upon deposit in a U.S. Postal Service (USPS) post office, subpost office, substation, mailbox, mail chute, or similar USPS facility. CCP §1013(a); ***Berg v. Darden*** (2d Dist.2004) 120 Cal.App.4th 721, 733.

3. Express mail or overnight delivery. Documents can be served by express mail using the USPS or by overnight delivery using an express-service carrier (e.g., FedEx, UPS). CCP §1013(c). To be served by express mail, a document must be placed in a sealed envelope and deposited in a USPS post office, subpost office, substation, mailbox, mail chute, or similar USPS facility. *Id.* To be served by overnight delivery, the document must be placed in an envelope or package provided by the express-service carrier and deposited in a place maintained by the carrier or given to an authorized express courier. *Id.* With either method, the envelope must be addressed to the recipient at the last office address given by the recipient in a filing with the court. *Id.* If the office address is not known, the envelope must be sent to the recipient's residence. *Id.* The postage or fee for delivery must be paid. *Id.* The date and general location of mailing should be noted on the face of the document or recited in an unsigned declaration of service attached to a copy of the document served. *Id.* §1013(d). See "Proving service by mail or express mail," §7.1.3, p. 75. Service is complete upon deposit. CCP §1013(c).

4. Fax. By agreement, documents can be served by fax transmission. CCP §1013(e); CRC 2.306(a)(1). The document should be sent to the last fax number given by the recipient in a filing with the court. CCP §1013(e); CRC 2.306(a)(2). Service is complete when the entire document is transmitted. CCP §1013(e); CRC 2.306(g). Service after 5:00 p.m. is deemed to occur the next court day. CRC 2.306(g).

(1) By agreement only. The parties must agree in writing to receive service by fax. CCP §1013(e); CRC 2.306(a)(1); *see, e.g.*, ***Berg***, 120 Cal.App.4th at 732 (fax service improper without written agreement). *But see* ***Jones v. Catholic Healthcare W.*** (3d Dist.2007) 147 Cal.App.4th 300, 309 (attorney could rely on past experience with D that it would accept notice of intent to sue transmitted by fax). A party or attorney who agrees to accept fax service must make its fax machine available between 9:00 a.m. and 5:00 p.m. on days that are not court holidays. CRC 2.306(f).

(2) Include transmission information. The serving party must include with the fax its name, fax number, the date and time of the transmission, and the name and fax number of the recipient. CRC 2.306(h)(1), (h)(2); *see* CCP §1013(a).

(3) Keep original. When a signed document is served by fax, the serving party must keep the original document in its files. *See* CRC 2.305(a). The party must produce the original document if another party demands an examination. *See* CRC 2.305(b), (c). The demand must be served on all parties but is not filed with the court. CRC 2.305(b). A signature transmitted by fax is deemed to be an original. CRC 2.305(d); *see* CCP §1010.5.

(4) Keep copy for proof of service. For proof of service, the serving party should keep a copy of the served document that either (1) bears a notation of the date and place of transmission and the fax number to which the document was transmitted or (2) is attached to an unsigned copy of the declaration of service containing the fax number to which the document was transmitted. CCP §1013(f). See "Proving service by fax," §7.1.6, p. 78.

5. Electronic service. Documents can be served electronically if electronic service is mandatory or the parties agree to it. *See* CCP §§1010.6(a)(2), (c), 1013(g); CRC 2.251(b), (c), 2.253(c).

(1) Methods. Electronic service can be made by electronic transmission or electronic notification. CCP §1010.6(a)(1)(A); CRC 2.250(b)(2).

(a) Electronic transmission. Electronic transmission means the transmission of a document by electronic means to the electronic-service address at or through which a party or other person has authorized electronic service. CCP §1010.6(a)(1)(B); CRC 2.250(b)(3).

(b) Electronic notification. Electronic notification means the notification of a party or other person that a document is served by sending an electronic message to the electronic-service address at or through which the party or other person has authorized electronic service, specifying the exact name of the document served and providing a hyperlink at which the served document can be viewed and downloaded. CCP §1010.6(a)(1)(C); CRC 2.250(b)(4). A party that serves a document by electronic notification must do the following:

[1] Ensure that the document can be viewed and downloaded using the hyperlink provided. CRC 2.251(g)(1).

[2] Preserve the document without any change, alteration, or modification from the time the document is posted until the time the hyperlink is terminated. CRC 2.251(g)(2).

[3] Maintain the hyperlink until either (1) all parties in the case have settled or the case has ended and the time for appeals has expired, or (2) if the party is no longer in the case, 60 days after the party gave notice to all other parties that it is no longer in the case and that they have 60 days to download any documents. CRC 2.251(g)(3).

NOTE

The court can electronically serve notices, orders, judgments, and other documents the same way the parties do when serving documents on each other. CRC 2.251(j).

---

(2) When allowed.

(a) Mandatory. Documents can be served electronically if electronic service is mandatory. Electronic service is mandatory if it is required by local rule or court order or if electronic filing (e-filing) is mandatory. However, a pro per party is exempt from any mandatory electronic-service requirements, and a represented party must be excused from the requirement if it can show undue hardship or significant prejudice. *See* CRC 2.253(b)(2), (b)(4); *see, e.g.*, Judicial Council forms, form EFS-007 (request for exemption from mandatory electronic filing and service), form EFS-008 (order of exemption from mandatory electronic filing and service).

[1] Mandatory by local rule. A court, by local rule, can require a party to electronically serve documents in certain types of cases. CRC 2.251(c)(1), 2.253(b)(1). For a list of those cases, see "Mandatory by local rule," ch. 1-F, §4.4.1(1)(a)[1], p. 49.

[2] Mandatory by court order. Except when personal service is required by statute or rule, a court can order a party to electronically serve documents in any class action, consolidated action, group of actions, coordinated action, or complex action if the order would not cause undue hardship or significant prejudice to any party. CRC 2.253(c)(1); *see* CRC 2.251(c)(1). See "Mandatory by court order," ch. 1-F, §4.4.1(1)(a)[2], p. 49.

[3] Mandatory due to mandatory e-filing. Except when personal service is required by statute or rule or the court orders otherwise, a party that is required to e-file documents in an action must also serve documents electronically to, and accept service of documents electronically from, all other parties. CRC 2.251(c)(2). For a discussion of when e-filing is required, see "Electronic filing," ch. 1-F, §4.4, p. 49.

(b) Permissive. Documents can be served electronically if the parties consent to electronic service. CCP §1010.6(a)(2); CRC 2.251(b). A party can consent to electronic service either expressly or impliedly.

[1] Express consent. A party expressly consents to electronic service by serving notice of its consent on all parties and filing the notice with the court. CRC 2.251(b)(1)(A). This notice can be given on Judicial Council Form EFS-005. The notice must include the electronic-service address at which the party agrees to accept electronic service. CRC 2.251(b)(1)(A); *see* Judicial Council Forms, form EFS-005.

[2] Implied consent. A represented party impliedly consents to electronic service when it e-files any document with the court. CRC 2.251(b)(1)(B). A pro per party must expressly consent to electronic service; the party cannot impliedly consent. *Id.* The electronic-service address the party gave to the court under CRC 2.256(a)(4) is the address other parties should use to serve papers on that party. CRC 2.251(b)(1)(B); *see* CRC 2.251(f)(3) (address is presumed valid if party has filed from that address and has not filed and served notice that address is not valid); *see also* CRC 2.256 (general responsibilities of e-filers). For a discussion of how to e-file, see "Electronic filing," ch. 1-F, §4.4, p. 49.

NOTE

A nonparty cannot be served electronically unless the nonparty consents to it, the law provides for it, or the court orders it. CRC 2.251(e)(2).

---

(3) When complete. If electronic service is performed directly by a party, service is complete at the time of the electronic transmission of the document or at the time that the electronic notification of service of the document is sent. CCP §1010.6(a)(4); CRC 2.251(h)(1). If an electronic-filing service provider (EFSP) is used, service is complete at the time the EFSP electronically transmits the document or sends electronic notification of service. CRC 2.251(h)(1). Service after 5:00 p.m. is deemed to occur the next court day. *See* CRC 2.251(h)(4); *cf.* CCP §1010.6(b)(3) (documents filed with court after close of business are deemed filed next day; close of business means earlier of 5:00 p.m. or time that court's filing counter closes).

(4) Change of electronic-service address. A party whose electronic-service address changes while the suit is pending must file a notice of change of address electronically with the court and serve it electronically on all parties. CRC 2.251(c)(3), (f)(1). Judicial Council Form EFS-010 can be used for this purpose.

§5.2 Service in complex cases. Special service rules apply to cases designated by the court as complex. For example, the court, on a party's motion or on its own, can order the parties to serve all documents electronically. CRC 2.253(c)(1); *see* CRC 3.512. The court can also create a central electronic depository for documents and order that all parties with access to the depository are deemed served with the documents filed in the depository. CRC 3.750(b)(10), 3.751. See "Complex case," ch. 3-C, §3.1.2(2), p. 211.

§6. WHEN TO SERVE

A party should serve a document before the deadline established by statute or court order. The deadline to serve is calculated in the same way as the deadline to file. See "When to File," ch. 1-F, §5, p. 52. To calculate a particular deadline, the party must first determine whether the deadline is prospective (i.e., calculated forward from a past event,

such as the date discovery was served) or retrospective (i.e., calculated backward from a future event, such as the date of trial). The party must then calculate the deadline by (1) counting from the first day the time period for serving a document begins, (2) counting all intervening days, months, or years in the time period, (3) adding any extra days to the time period based on the method of service used, and (4) determining when certain days, such as judicial holidays, should be excluded from the time period.

§6.1 Prospective deadlines. If the party is required to act *after* some event has occurred, the deadline is prospective. A prospective deadline usually uses a phrase such as "within 30 days after" or "no later than 60 days after." *See, e.g.*, CCP §1987(c) (objections to notice requesting witness to produce books and records at hearing or trial can be made within five days after service of notice), §2030.260(a) (responses to interrogatories must be served within 30 days after service), §2032.230(b) (response to demand for physical examination must be served within 20 days after service of demand). To calculate a prospective deadline, the party must do the following:

1-5. CALCULATING PROSPECTIVE SERVICE DEADLINES

Step	Action	Section	Deadline
1	Determine date of triggering event	§6.1.1, this page	
2	Count forward to end of deadline	§6.1.2, this page, §6.1.3, this page	Step 1 + number of days, months, or years in deadline
3	Add extra time based on original method of service if applicable	§6.1.4, this page	If by personal delivery, Step 2 If by intrastate mail, Step 2 + 5 calendar days If by interstate mail, Step 2 + 10 calendar days If by international mail, Step 2 + 20 calendar days If by express mail, Step 2 + 2 court days If by fax, Step 2 + 2 court days If by electronic service, Step 2 + 2 court days
4	Determine last day	§6.1.5, p. 71	Last day of Step 3, or count forward to next court day if last day is Saturday, Sunday, or judicial holiday

1. Determine date of triggering event. Most prospective deadlines are triggered by the filing or serving of some other document, such as a motion or a discovery request. See "Determine date of triggering event," ch. 1-F, §5.1.1, p. 53.

2. Count forward. The party should begin counting forward from the day the time period for serving the document starts—that is, the date of the triggering event—making sure to skip that day. *See* Civ. C. §10; CCP §12; CRC 1.10(a). For example, if the plaintiff has 30 days to serve answers to the defendant's interrogatories, which were served on Monday (i.e., the day of the triggering event), Monday is "day 0," Tuesday is "day 1," Wednesday is "day 2," and so on.

3. Count intervening time. The party should count the total number of days, months, or years in the time period for serving the document. *See, e.g.*, CCP §2033.250(a) (response to requests for admission must be served within 30 days after service of requests). For a discussion of how to calculate days, months, and years, see "Count intervening time," ch. 1-F, §5.1.3, p. 53.

4. Add time for method of service. If the deadline to serve a document is triggered by the service of another document (e.g., deadline to respond to interrogatories is triggered by service of interrogatory requests), the party may get to add extra time to the deadline based on the original method of service used, as required by CCP §§1010.6(a)(4) and 1013.

(1) Personal delivery. If the deadline to serve is triggered by a document that was served by personal delivery, the party cannot add any extra time to the deadline. See "Personal delivery," §5.1.1, p. 66.

(2) Mail. If the deadline to serve is triggered by a document that was served by mail, the party must add extra time to the deadline based on whether the mailing was intrastate, interstate, or international. *See* CCP §1013(a). See "Regular mail," §5.1.2, p. 67.

(a) Intrastate. If the mailing was within California, the party must add five calendar days to its deadline to serve. CCP §1013(a); *see* ***Deyo v. Kilbourne*** (2d Dist.1978) 84 Cal.App.3d 771, 788 & n.18 (deadline to file and serve motion to compel further discovery responses is extended when answers are served by mail); *see, e.g.,* ***Kroupa v. Sunrise Ford*** (2d Dist.1999) 77 Cal.App.4th 835, 841 n.6 (under CCP §§632 and 1013(a), D had 15 days to file and serve request for statement of decision after court clerk mailed statement of intended decision); ***California Bus. Council for Equal Opportunity v. Superior Ct.*** (3d Dist.1997) 52 Cal.App.4th 1100, 1106 (because written order assigning judge was mailed to petitioner in California, petitioner had 15 days to file and serve challenge under CCP §§170.6(2) and 1013); ***Shell Oil Co. v. Superior Ct.*** (2d Dist.1975) 50 Cal.App.3d 489, 491 (deadline to file and serve objection to written request to produce records under former CCP §1987(c) was extended by five days when request was served by mail).

(b) Interstate. If the mailing was outside California but within the United States, the party must add ten calendar days to its deadline to serve. CCP §1013(a).

(c) International. If the mailing was outside the United States, the party must add 20 calendar days to its deadline to serve. CCP §1013(a).

(3) Express mail or overnight delivery. If the deadline to serve is triggered by a document that was served by express mail or overnight delivery, the party must add two court days to the deadline. CCP §1013(c). See "Express mail or overnight delivery," §5.1.3, p. 67.

(4) Fax. If the deadline to serve is triggered by a document that was served by fax, the party must add two court days to the deadline. CCP §1013(e). See "Fax," §5.1.4, p. 67.

(5) Electronic service. If the deadline to serve is triggered by a document that was served by electronic transmission, the party must add two court days to the deadline. CCP §1010.6(a)(4); CRC 2.251(h)(2). See "Electronic service," §5.1.5, p. 68.

CAUTION

There is no clear authority on when you add the extra time for method of service—before you determine the last day to act or after. See "Determine last day," ch. 1-F, §5.1.5, p. 55. In 2010, the California Legislature added CCP §12c. Under §12c, to calculate a retrospective deadline that is based on a hearing date (e.g., 16 court days before a hearing), any time added to the deadline for the method of service is added "after" you have determined the last day to act. CCP §12c(b). Until there is clear guidance on how the days should be added in calculating a prospective deadline, the best approach is to add the extra time before you calculate the last day to act so you serve your response sooner rather than later.

5. Determine last day. The party should count the last day unless it is a Saturday, Sunday, or other judicial holiday. CCP §§12, 12a; CRC 1.10(a). For a discussion of how to calculate the last day, see "Determine last day," ch. 1-F, §5.1.5, p. 55.

§6.2 Retrospective deadlines. If the party is required to act before some event will occur, the deadline is retrospective. A retrospective deadline usually uses a phrase such as "at least 75 days before" or "no less than five days before." *See, e.g.,* CCP §437c(a) (notice of MSJ and supporting papers must be served at least 75 days before hearing date), §1005(b) (all motion and supporting papers must be served at least 16 court days before hearing), §1282.2(a)(1) (arbitrator must serve notice of arbitration hearing on parties no less than seven days before hearing); CRC 3.725(a) (parties must serve case-management statement on all other parties no later than 15 calendar days before date of conference), CRC 3.894(b)(1) (parties must serve list of mediation participants on mediator and

other parties at least five court days before first mediation session). To calculate a retrospective deadline, the party must determine if the triggering event—that is, the event in the future that determines the party's deadline to serve—is a hearing date or some other event.

1. Triggering event – hearing date. If the triggering event that determines the party's deadline to serve is a hearing date (e.g., serve 16 court days before the hearing), the party must do the following:

1-6. CALCULATING RETROSPECTIVE SERVICE DEADLINES

Step	Action	Section	Deadline
1	Determine date of triggering event	§6.2.1(1), this page	
2	Count backward to beginning of deadline	§6.2.1(2), this page, §6.2.1(3), this page	Step 1 + number of days, months, or years in deadline
3	Determine last day	§6.2.1(4), this page	Last day of Step 2, or count backward to next court day if last day is Saturday, Sunday, or judicial holiday
4	Add extra time based on method of service if applicable	§6.2.1(5), this page	If by personal delivery, Step 3 If by intrastate mail, Step 3 + 5 calendar days If by interstate mail, Step 3 + 10 calendar days If by international mail, Step 3 + 20 calendar days If by express mail and documents are motion papers, Step 3 + 2 calendar days If by express mail and documents are not motion papers, Step 3 + 2 court days If by fax and documents are motion papers, Step 3 + 2 calendar days If by fax and documents are not motion papers, Step 3 + 2 court days If by electronic service, Step 3 + 2 court days
5	Determine last day	§6.2.1(6), p. 74	Last day of Step 4, or count backward to next court day if last day is Saturday, Sunday, or judicial holiday

(1) Determine date of triggering event. The party must first determine the date of the hearing.

(2) Count backward. After determining the hearing date, the party must begin counting backward starting with the day before the hearing (thus, skipping the hearing date) for the required time to serve. CCP §§12, 12c(a). For example, if a party has 16 court days to serve a motion before a hearing, and the hearing is scheduled for Friday, Friday is "day 0," the preceding Thursday is "day 1," the preceding Wednesday is "day 2," and so on. *See, e.g.*, ***Dahms v. Downtown Pomona Prop. & Bus. Imprv. Dist.*** (2d Dist.2009) 174 Cal.App.4th 708, 715 n.3 (motion must be served on 16th court day counting back from hearing date and excluding hearing date itself).

(3) Count intervening time. The party should count the intervening days, months, or years. See "Count intervening time," ch. 1-F, §5.1.3, p. 53.

(4) Determine last day. The party should count the last day unless it is a Saturday, Sunday, or other judicial holiday. *See* CCP §§12, 12a, 12c(a); CRC 1.10(a). If the last day falls on a Saturday, Sunday, or other judicial holiday, continue to count backward until the next day that is not a Saturday, Sunday, or other judicial holiday. *See* CCP §§12, 12a, 12c. For a discussion of judicial holidays, see "Determine last day," ch. 1-F, §5.1.5, p. 55.

(5) Add time for method of service. After determining the last day, the party should count backward from that day for any extra days that are added based on the method of service. *See* CCP §12c(b). The amount of time added will generally depend on the method of service and the type of document to be served before the hearing.

NOTE

Not all deadlines to serve are extended by the method of service. For example, the deadlines to serve opposition and reply papers to a noticed motion (i.e., nine court days before the hearing and five court days before the hearing) are not extended by the method of service. See CCP §1005(b) (extensions under §1013 do not apply to opposition or reply papers). Also, some statutes have specific extension provisions for certain motions. See, e.g., id. §437c(a) (extension of time for service of MSJ). Before adding extra time to serve a paper, check the relevant discussion in this book.

(a) Personal delivery. If the document will be served by personal delivery, the party cannot add any extra time to its deadline to serve. See "Personal delivery," §5.1.1, p. 66.

(b) Mail. If the document will be served by mail, the party must add extra time to its deadline to serve based on whether the mailing is intrastate, interstate, or international. *See* CCP §1005(b) (noticed motions), §1013(a) (papers generally). See "Regular mail," §5.1.2, p. 67.

[1] Intrastate. If the mailing is within California, the party must add five calendar days to its deadline to serve. CCP §1005(b) (extension of time for noticed motion), §1013(a) (extension of time for service by mail generally); *e.g.*, ***Lecuyer v. Sunset Trails Apts.*** (4th Dist.2004) 120 Cal.App.4th 920, 927 (when offer of judgment is served by mail to address in California, notice period is extended by five days, so party must count backward 15 days).

[2] Interstate. If the mailing is outside California but within the United States, the party must add ten calendar days to its deadline to serve. CCP §1005(b) (extension of time for noticed motion), §1013(a) (extension of time for service by mail generally).

[3] International. If the mailing is outside the United States, the party must add 20 calendar days to its deadline to serve. CCP §1005(b) (extension of time for noticed motion), §1013(a) (extension of time for service by mail generally).

(c) Express mail or overnight delivery. If the document will be served by express mail or overnight delivery, the party must add extra time to its deadline to serve based on the type of document being served. See "Express mail or overnight delivery," §5.1.3, p. 67.

[1] Noticed motion. For noticed motions, the party must add two calendar days to its deadline to serve. CCP §1005(b).

[2] Other documents. For other documents, the party must add two court days to its deadline to serve. CCP §1013(c).

(d) Fax. If the document will be served by fax, the party must add extra time to its deadline to serve based on the type of document being served. See "Fax," §5.1.4, p. 67.

[1] Noticed motions. For noticed motions, the party must add two calendar days to its deadline to serve. CCP §1005(b).

[2] Other documents. For other documents, the party must add two court days to its deadline to serve. CCP §1013(e); CRC 2.306(d).

NOTE

Under CRC 2.306(d), the notice period for papers served by fax is extended by two court days, not calendar days. However, CCP §1005(b) trumps this rule. See ***California Ct. Reporters Ass'n v. Judicial Council*** *(1st Dist.1995) 39 Cal.App.4th 15, 22 (Judicial Council cannot adopt rules of court that are inconsistent with statutes).*

(e) Electronic service. If the document will be served by electronic transmission, the party must add two court days to its deadline to serve. CCP §1010.6(a)(4). See "Electronic service," §5.1.5, p. 68.

(6) Determine last day. After adding any extra days for method of service, the party should determine the last day. If the last day falls on a Saturday, Sunday or judicial holiday, the party should continue to count backward until the next day that is not a Saturday, Sunday, or other judicial holiday. *See* CCP §§12, 12a, 12c. For a discussion of judicial holidays, see "Determine last day," ch. 1-F, §5.1.5, p. 55.

2. Triggering event – event other than hearing date. If the triggering event that determines the party's deadline to serve a document is an event other than a hearing date (e.g., trial date, discovery cutoff date), the party should calculate its deadline in almost the same way as calculating the deadline to serve a document before a hearing. See "Triggering event – hearing date," §6.2.1, p. 72. The only difference is when you add the extra time for method of service—before you determine the last day to act or after. For hearing dates, it is clear that the extra time for service is added after you determine the last day to act. CCP §12c(b). But it is unclear whether the California Legislature in enacting §12c(b) made an exception for hearing dates or instead stated a general preference for how all deadlines should be calculated. Until this issue is resolved, the best approach is to follow the calculation for hearing dates so more notice is given rather than less.

§7. PROVING SERVICE

A properly served document is presumed to have been received by the addressee. *See* Evid. C. §641 (correctly addressed and properly mailed document is presumed to have been received by addressee); ***Jones v. Catholic Healthcare W.*** (3d Dist.2007) 147 Cal.App.4th 300, 308 (service is presumed if serving party satisfied requirements of CCP §1013); ***Colleen M. v. Fertility & Surgical Assocs.*** (2d Dist.2005) 132 Cal.App.4th 1466, 1479-80 (proof of service creates rebuttable presumption that documents were received). A party can rebut the presumption by introducing evidence that the document was not received. *See* ***Phay Him v. City & Cty. of S.F.*** (1st Dist.2005) 133 Cal.App.4th 437, 445; ***Bonzer v. City of Huntington Park*** (2d Dist.1993) 20 Cal.App.4th 1474, 1481; *cf.* ***Craig v. Brown & Root, Inc.*** (2d Dist.2000) 84 Cal.App.4th 416, 421-22 (party introduced evidence to rebut presumption that she had received memorandum and brochure describing her employer's dispute-resolution program).

§7.1 Establishing presumption of proper service.

1. Methods of proving service. The presumption that a document was properly served can be established by one of two methods:

(1) Add notation. To prove service by regular mail, express or overnight mail, or fax, a party can add a notation to the served document indicating the date and place of mailing, deposit, or transmission. *See* CCP §1013(b), (d), (f). The notation raises the presumption that the document was properly served. *See* ***Berg v. Darden*** (2d Dist.2004) 120 Cal.App.4th 721, 733.

(2) Attach proof of service. To prove service by personal delivery, regular mail, express or overnight mail, fax, or electronic service, a party can attach an unsigned proof of service to the document. *See* CCP §1013(b), (d), (f) (regular mail, express or overnight mail, and fax); CRC 2.251(i)(1) (additional requirements for electronic service), CRC 2.306(h) (additional requirements for fax). Once service is completed, the person who served the document should sign the proof of service. *See, e.g.*, CCP §594(b) (to prove service of notice of trial, party may introduce affidavit or certificate). A "proof of service" can be a certificate of service, an affidavit of service, or a declaration of service.

(a) Certificate of service. A certificate of service is a written statement of the facts surrounding service, signed by an active member of the State Bar of California. CCP §1013a(2); *see also* ***Forslund v. Forslund*** (1st Dist.1964) 225 Cal.App.2d 476, 486 (certificate of service by mail, which was attached to show-cause order, met requirements of CCP §1013a(2)).

(b) Affidavit of service. An affidavit of service is a written declaration of the facts surrounding service, made under oath (i.e., notarized) by the person who deposited the document for service. *See* CCP §1013a(1) & (3) (affidavits used to prove service), §2003 (definition of "affidavit"), §2009 (when affidavit can be

used); *see, e.g.*, ***Dalzell v. Superior Ct.*** (1885) 67 Cal. 453, 454 (affidavit of service stating that no one was in front room of attorney's office was insufficient to prove that attorney was not in office when notice of appeal was left on his desk); ***Daiki Otsuka v. Balangue*** (2d Dist.1949) 92 Cal.App.2d 788, 790-91 (D's affidavit of service properly recited that documents were deposited in mail and addressed to P's attorneys at their offices).

(c) Declaration of service. A declaration of service is a written statement of the facts surrounding service signed under penalty of perjury by the person serving the document. *See* CCP §2015.5. A declaration of service can be used instead of an affidavit or certificate. *See id.* The person making the declaration of service must include a statement that (1) the contents of the declaration are true and correct and (2) the declaration is made under penalty of perjury under California law. *Id.* All proofs of service approved by the Judicial Council are declarations of service, which are easier to prepare and execute than affidavits.

2. Proving service by personal delivery. To prove service by personal delivery, a party can file and introduce a proof of service containing the following:

NOTE

The proof of service should be filed only if the served document is filed. See CRC 3.250(a), (b); see, e.g., CRC 3.110(b) (proof of service of complaint must be filed within 60 days after complaint filed). If the document cannot be filed, the proof of service should also not be filed. See CRC 3.250(a), (b).

---

(1) The name, address, and telephone number of the person serving the document. *See, e.g.*, Judicial Council Forms, form POS-020, form POS-040. If a messenger served the document, the messenger must sign the proof of service. *See, e.g., id.* form POS-040.

(2) A statement that the person serving the document is over 18 and is not a party to the suit. *See, e.g., id.*

(3) The exact title of the document served. *See, e.g., id.*

(4) The name of the person served. *See, e.g., id.*

(5) The address at which service occurred. *See, e.g., id.*

(6) The date and time of service. *See, e.g., id.*

(7) The manner of service. *See, e.g., id.* For example, if the person serving the document delivered it to a party, the proof of service should state that delivery was made by handing the document to the party or by leaving it at the party's residence between 8:00 a.m. and 6:00 p.m. with someone who is 18 or older. *See* CCP §1011(b).

3. Proving service by mail or express mail. To prove service by regular mail or express mail, a party can file and introduce an affidavit or certificate as proof of service, the contents of which will depend on whether the person serving the document has personal knowledge of the mailing. *See* CCP §1013a(1) (affidavit if person has personal knowledge), §1013a(2) (certificate if attorney has personal knowledge), §1013a(3) (affidavit if person has no personal knowledge). If the court clerk mailed the document, service is proved with a certificate signed by the clerk. *Id.* §1013a(4).

(1) Mailing based on personal knowledge. When the person signing the declaration has personal knowledge of the mailing, the proof of service must contain the following:

(a) The name, address, and telephone number of the person serving the document. *See* CCP §1013a(1), (2); *see, e.g.*, Judicial Council Forms, form POS-030, form POS-040.

(b) A statement that the person serving the document is not a party to the suit. CCP §1013a(1), (2); *see, e.g.*, Judicial Council Forms, form POS-030, form POS-040.

(c) A statement that the person serving the document either (1) is over 18 and is a resident of or works in the county where the mailing took place or (2) is an active member of the State Bar of California. CCP §1013a(1), (2); *see, e.g.*, Judicial Council Forms, form POS-030, form POS-040.

(d) The exact title of the document served. CCP §1013a(1), (2); *see, e.g.*, Judicial Council Forms, form POS-030, form POS-040.

(e) The date the document was mailed. CCP §1013a(1), (2); *see, e.g.*, Judicial Council Forms, form POS-030, form POS-040.

(f) The place where the document was put in the mail. CCP §1013a(1), (2); *see id.* §1013(d) (service by express mail through USPS); *see, e.g.*, Judicial Council Forms, form POS-030, form POS-040. Courts have consistently held that listing the city and state where the document was put in the mail is sufficient to satisfy the requirements of CCP §1013a. ***Phay Him v. City & Cty. of S.F.*** (1st Dist.2005) 133 Cal.App.4th 437, 443-44.

(g) A statement that the document was placed in a sealed envelope and deposited in the mail with the postage fully paid. CCP §1013a(1), (2); *see* ***Katelaris v. County of Orange*** (4th Dist.2001) 92 Cal.App.4th 1211, 1215 (declaration must establish declarant's firsthand knowledge that document was mailed); *see, e.g.*, Judicial Council Forms, form POS-030, form POS-040.

(h) The name and address of the person served, as shown on the envelope. CCP §1013a(1), (2); *see* ***Preis v. American Indem. Co.*** (2d Dist.1990) 220 Cal.App.3d 752, 759-60; *see, e.g.*, Judicial Council Forms, form POS-030, form POS-040.

(2) Mailing not based on personal knowledge. When the person signing the proof of service does not have personal knowledge of the mailing, but can testify about her business's practices for collecting and processing mail with the USPS, the proof of service must be by affidavit or declaration and contain the following:

(a) The name, address, and telephone number of the person serving the document. *See* CCP §1013a(3); *see, e.g.*, Judicial Council Forms, form POS-030, form POS-040.

(b) A statement that the person serving the document is over 18, is a resident of or works in the county where the mailing took place, and is not a party to the suit. CCP §1013a(3); *see, e.g.*, Judicial Council Forms, form POS-030, form POS-040.

(c) A statement that the person serving the document is readily familiar with her business's practices for collecting and processing mail with the USPS. CCP §1013a(3); *see* ***Bonzer v. City of Huntington Park*** (2d Dist.1993) 20 Cal.App.4th 1474, 1478 & n.4; *see, e.g.*, Judicial Council Forms, form POS-030, form POS-040; *see also* ***Conservatorship of Wyatt*** (4th Dist.1987) 195 Cal.App.3d 391, 397 (by preparing documents and delivering them to person who regularly deposits mail, county employee substantially complied with CCP §1013a).

(d) A statement that the same day the document is placed for collection and processing, it is deposited in the ordinary course of business with the USPS in a sealed envelope with postage fully paid. *See* CCP §1013a(3); *see, e.g.*, Judicial Council Forms, form POS-030, form POS-040. *But see* ***Glasser v. Glasser*** (2d Dist.1998) 64 Cal.App.4th 1004, 1011 (although proof of service did not expressly state that envelope was sealed and placed for collection and mailing following ordinary business practices, evidence proved that notice was served in "substantial compliance" with CCP §1013a).

(e) The exact title of the document served. CCP §1013a(3); *see, e.g.*, Judicial Council Forms, form POS-030, form POS-040.

(f) The date the document was mailed. CCP §1013a(3); *see, e.g.*, Judicial Council Forms, form POS-030, form POS-040.

(g) The address of the business where the document was placed for deposit in the mail. *See* CCP §1013a(3); *see, e.g.*, Judicial Council Forms, form POS-030, form POS-040.

(h) The name and address of the person served, as shown on the envelope. CCP §1013a(3); *see, e.g.*, Judicial Council Forms, form POS-030, form POS-040.

(3) Mailing by court clerk. When the court clerk mails the document and signs the proof of service, the proof of service must contain the following:

(a) The name of the clerk and the clerk's court. CCP §1013a(4).

(b) A statement that the clerk is not a party to the suit. *Id.*

(c) The exact title of the document served. *Id.*

(d) The date and place where the document was mailed. *Id.*

(e) A statement that the document was placed in a sealed envelope and deposited in the mail with the postage fully paid. *Id.*

(f) The name and address of the person served, as shown on the envelope. *Id.*; *see, e.g.*, ***American Contractors Indem. Co. v. County of Orange*** (4th Dist.2005) 130 Cal.App.4th 579, 583 (clerk's declaration of service under CCP §1013a(4) was defective because it did not include recipient's address).

4. Proving service by overnight mail. To prove service by overnight mail, a party can file and introduce a proof of service, by affidavit or certificate, containing the following:

(1) The name, address, and telephone number of the person serving the document. *See* CCP §1013a(1), (2); *see, e.g.*, Judicial Council Forms, form POS-040.

(2) A statement that the person serving the document is not a party to the suit. CCP §1013a(1), (2); *see, e.g.*, Judicial Council Forms, form POS-040.

(3) A statement that the person serving the document either (1) is over 18 and is a resident of or works in the county where the mailing took place or (2) is an active member of the State Bar of California. CCP §1013a(1), (2); *see, e.g.*, Judicial Council Forms, form POS-040.

(4) The exact title of the document served. CCP §1013a(1), (2); *see, e.g.*, Judicial Council Forms, form POS-040.

(5) The date the document was mailed. CCP §1013a(1), (2); *see, e.g.*, Judicial Council Forms, form POS-040.

(6) A statement that the document was placed in an envelope or package provided by an overnight-delivery carrier with delivery fees paid or provided for. *See* CCP §1013(c); *see, e.g.*, Judicial Council Forms, form POS-040.

(7) A statement that the envelope or package was either (1) placed for collection and delivery at an office or a regularly used drop box of the carrier or (2) delivered to a courier or driver authorized by the carrier to receive documents. *See* CCP §1013(c); *see, e.g.*, Judicial Council Forms, form POS-040.

(8) The name and address of the person served, as shown on the envelope. CCP §1013a(1), (2); *see id.* §1013(c); ***Preis***, 220 Cal.App.3d at 759-60; *see, e.g.*, Judicial Council Forms, form POS-040.

5. Proving service by registered mail. To prove service by registered mail, a party can introduce a return receipt. *See* CCP §1020 (proof of service by registered mail); *see also* ***Bear Creek Master Ass'n v. Edwards*** (4th Dist.2005) 130 Cal.App.4th 1470, 1486 (notice that must be sent by mail can be sent by registered mail).

(1) Return receipt. A return receipt signed by the addressee creates a presumption that service was received. CCP §1020. The addressee cannot claim she was not served by refusing to sign the return receipt. ***Bear Creek***, 130 Cal.App.4th at 1487. The return receipt can be in the form of a postcard, fax, or e-mail. USPS Form 3811. If the receipt is lost or not returned, a party can request an after-mailing return receipt from the USPS that establishes the date of delivery and identifies the person who received delivery based on USPS records. *Id.* Form 3811-A.

(2) Use of registered mail. Service by registered mail can be used only for notices that are required by law and that are not (1) notices required to be given to a party or its attorney and (2) notices whose service is governed by any other section of CCP, title 14, chapter 5, or otherwise specifically provided for by other law. CCP §1020.

6. Proving service by fax. To prove service by fax, a party can file and introduce a proof of service containing the following:

(1) The name, address, telephone number, and fax number of the person serving the document. *See* CCP §1013a(1), (2); CRC 2.306(h)(1); *see, e.g.*, Judicial Council Forms, form POS-040.

(2) A statement that the person serving the document is not a party to the suit. *See* CCP §1013a(1), (2); *see, e.g.*, Judicial Council Forms, form POS-040.

(3) A statement that the person serving the document either (1) is over 18 and is a resident of or works in the county where the faxing took place or (2) is an active member of the State Bar of California. *See* CCP §1013a(1), (2); *see, e.g.*, Judicial Council Forms, form POS-040.

(4) The exact title of the document served. *See* CCP §1013a(1), (2); *see, e.g.*, Judicial Council Forms, form POS-040.

(5) The date and time the document was served. CRC 2.306(h)(1); *see, e.g.*, Judicial Council Forms, form POS-040.

(6) The name and fax number of the person served. CRC 2.306(h)(2); *see, e.g.*, Judicial Council Forms, form POS-040.

(7) A statement that the document was sent by fax based on the parties' agreement to accept service by fax and that the fax was reported as complete and without error. *See* CRC 2.306(a)(1), (h)(3); *see, e.g.*, Judicial Council Forms, form POS-040.

(8) A statement that the transmission report was properly issued by the sending fax machine. CRC 2.306(h)(4); *see, e.g.*, Judicial Council Forms, form POS-040. A copy of the transmission report must be attached to the proof of service. CRC 2.306(h)(4); *see, e.g.*, Judicial Council Forms, form POS-040.

7. Proving electronic service. To prove electronic service, a party can file and introduce a proof of service containing the following:

(1) The name, address, telephone number, and electronic-service address of the person serving the document. *See* CCP §1013a(1), (2); CRC 2.251(i)(1)(A); *see, e.g.*, Judicial Council Forms, form POS-050/EFS-050.

(2) A statement that the person serving the document either (1) is over 18 and is a resident of or works in the county where the electronic service took place or (2) is an active member of the State Bar of California. *See* CCP §1013a(1), (2); CRC 2.251(i)(1); *see, e.g.*, Judicial Council Forms, form POS-050/EFS-050.

(3) The exact title of the document served. *See* CCP §1013a(1), (2); CRC 2.251(i)(1); *see, e.g.*, Judicial Council Forms, form POS-050/EFS-050.

(4) The date and time the document was served. CRC 2.251(i)(1)(B); *see, e.g.*, Judicial Council Forms, form POS-050/EFS-050.

(5) The name and electronic-service address of the person served. CRC 2.251(i)(1)(C); *see, e.g.*, Judicial Council Forms, form POS-050/EFS-050.

(6) A statement that the document was served electronically. CRC 2.251(i)(1)(D); *see, e.g.*, Judicial Council Forms, form POS-050/EFS-050.

NOTE

CCP §1013a requires that the person who served the document state in the proof of service that she is not a party to the suit. See CRC 2.251(i)(1) (proof of electronic service may be made under §1013a). However, CCP §1010.6(a)(1)(A) allows a party to directly perform electronic service. Thus, the optional form for proof of electronic service, Judicial Council Form POS-050/EFS-050, was recently amended to remove the statement that the person filing the proof of service is not a party to the suit. See Report to the Judicial Council, Rules & Forms: Miscellaneous Technical Changes (Oct. 28, 2014).

§7.2 Rebutting presumption of proper service. The presumption of proper service can be rebutted by introducing evidence that the document was not received. ***Bonzer v. City of Huntington Park*** (2d Dist.1993) 20 Cal.App.4th 1474, 1481; *see* ***Phay Him v. City & Cty. of S.F.*** (1st Dist.2005) 133 Cal.App.4th 437, 445; ***Craig v. Brown & Root, Inc.*** (2d Dist.2000) 84 Cal.App.4th 416, 421. To rebut the presumption, the party should file an opposition complaining of the defective service. *See* ***Carlton v. Quint*** (2d Dist.2000) 77 Cal.App.4th 690, 698 (failure to file opposition complaining of defective service waives issue on appeal). The opposition should be supported by sworn testimony that neither the attorney of record nor the party received the document. *See, e.g.*, ***Bonzer***, 20 Cal.App.4th at 1479-80 (D presented declarations from six people about mail-handling procedures and stating that no one in office had received P's notice). The sworn testimony should also include evidence of the mail-handling procedures in the attorney's office or party's business. *See, e.g.*, ***Phay Him***, 133 Cal.App.4th at 444 (secretary declared she was in charge of mail and never received notice); ***Colleen M. v. Fertility & Surgical Assocs.*** (2d Dist.2005) 132 Cal.App.4th 1466, 1480 (attorney testified he was never "made aware" of documents; testimony insufficient to overcome presumption of valid service).

§8. SANCTIONS FOR FAILURE TO SERVE PLEADINGS

If a party has not served copies of pleadings it has filed with the court and has not obtained an order extending the time to serve the pleadings, the court can issue an order to show cause why sanctions should not be imposed. CRC 3.110(f); *see* CCP §128(a)(4) (power of court to order obedience to its rules), §128.7(d) (sanctions court can impose). For a discussion of sanctions, see "Motion for Sanctions," ch. 5-K, p. 561.

H. HEARINGS

This subchapter covers hearings on pretrial motions and applications. It does not cover administrative hearings, certain evidentiary hearings, or hearings on other proceedings such as small claims.

§1. GENERAL

§1.1 Purpose. Many statutes in the Code of Civil Procedure use terms such as "hearing," "hear," or "must determine" when describing a court's obligation to resolve a disputed matter. *See* ***Titmas v. Superior Ct.*** (4th Dist.2001) 87 Cal.App.4th 738, 743. In the context of civil practice—specifically, motion practice—a hearing serves the purpose of bringing the parties together before the court to argue and sometimes to present evidence. *See* ***Lewis v. Superior Ct.*** (1999) 19 Cal.4th 1232, 1247. The right to a hearing, however, does not necessarily entitle a party to argue the matter in open court. See "Right to oral argument," §5.2, p. 81. Thus, the term "hearing" can mean either the court's consideration of a matter on written submission or an oral hearing for presentation of argument, evidence, or both. *See* CRC 3.1207, 3.1304(c).

§1.2 Primary authority. CCP §§124, 166, 595.2, 1005, 1010; CRC 1.150, 2.550, 2.585, 2.950, 2.952, 2.956, 3.514, 3.670, 3.1100, 3.1110, 3.1112, 3.1152, 3.1200-3.1207, 3.1300, 3.1304, 3.1306, 3.1308, 3.1310.

§1.3 Secondary authority. The following secondary source is cited as authority in this subchapter:

- Witkin, *California Procedure* (5th ed. 2008 & Supp.2014) (referred to as Witkin, *Cal. Procedure*).

§2. HEARING REQUIRED

A hearing is required anytime a statute or rule provides for one. *See, e.g.*, CCP §575.2(a) (sanctions for violating local rules can be imposed only if party to be sanctioned is given opportunity to be heard). When a statute provides for an order to be made by "motion," the statute is usually interpreted to impose both notice and hearing requirements. ***St. Paul Fire & Mar. Ins. v. Superior Ct.*** (1st Dist.1984) 156 Cal.App.3d 82, 86; *e.g.*, ***Titmas v. Superior Ct.*** (4th Dist.2001) 87 Cal.App.4th 738, 743 (use of term "motion" in CCP §1987.1, rather than "ex parte application," imposed both notice and hearing requirements). When the statutory language is not clear, the court can examine it to determine whether a right to a hearing is implied. *See, e.g.*, ***Bravo v. Ismaj*** (4th Dist.2002) 99 Cal.App.4th 211, 225 (right to hearing implied under CCP §391.7, even though statute is silent on whether P is entitled to hearing after D moves for prefiling order on ground that P is "vexatious litigant"). If there is a right to a hearing, the court must hold one before deciding the matter unless (1) a statute or rule expressly states that the court can rule on the mater without a hearing or (2) the parties agree to submit the matter for determination without a hearing. *See* CRC 3.1207(4), 3.1304(c); ***Titmas***, 87 Cal.App.4th at 743 & n.3.

§3. SCHEDULING HEARING

In most cases, the party seeking relief from the court will schedule the hearing date. However, some statutes require the court clerk to set the date automatically. *See, e.g.*, CCP §425.16(f) (clerk must schedule hearing on special motion to strike in anti-SLAPP action within 30 days after motion is served); ***Chitsazzadeh v. Kramer & Kaslow*** (2d Dist.2011) 199 Cal.App.4th 676, 685 n.7 (same). If the party is required to set the hearing date, it should determine when the court hears motions and other applications and call the court clerk to schedule a date that will provide the proper amount of notice.

§3.1 Determine hearing days. Usually, the court clerk posts a general hearing schedule showing which days and in which departments certain types of hearings are held. CRC 3.1304(a). The hearing schedule is often listed in the local rules, displayed at the clerk's office, or posted on the court's website. *See, e.g.*, Super. Ct. San Francisco Cty. Loc. R., rule 8.2.A.1 (all limited and unlimited jurisdiction matters are heard in Department 302 at 9:30 a.m. Monday through Friday); Super. Ct. Santa Cruz Cty. Loc. R., rule 1.1.06 (hearing schedule posted on court's website).

§3.2 Schedule hearing date. To schedule a hearing, the party should call the court clerk to request a hearing date. *See, e.g.*, Super. Ct. Fresno Cty. Loc. R., rule 2.2.1 (before filing motion, date and time for hearing must be reserved with clerk); Super. Ct. San Bernardino Cty. Loc. R., rule 520 (no motion can be noticed for hearing without first requesting date from clerk); *see also* 6 Witkin, *Cal. Procedure*, Proceedings Without Trial, §36 (noticed motions are usually heard on a "law and motion session" fixed by the court's local rules). Before requesting a hearing date, the party's attorney may contact opposing counsel and attempt to agree on a date. The requesting party should ask for a date far enough in the future to ensure it has enough time to give any required notice of the hearing.

PRACTICE TIP

Reserve your desired hearing date (especially for motions for summary judgment) as soon as possible before it becomes unavailable.

---

§4. NOTICING HEARING

A court has a duty to hear a timely motion or application. ***Fair Political Practices Comm'n v. American Civil Rights Coalition, Inc.*** (3d Dist.2004) 121 Cal.App.4th 1171, 1177; *see also* ***McDonald v. Severy*** (1936) 6 Cal.2d 629, 631 (motion can be granted only after party has given statutorily required notice providing opportunity to respond). Whether a motion or application is "timely" usually depends on whether the requesting party has given the required notice before the date set for hearing. *See* ***Titmas v. Superior Ct.*** (4th Dist.2001) 87 Cal.App.4th 738, 743 (notice requirements tied to time set for hearing); *see, e.g.*, CCP §1005(b) (all motion papers must be filed and served at least 16 court days before hearing). For most hearings in civil suits, the notice procedure depends on whether the hearing is for a noticed motion or an ex parte application.

§4.1 Noticed motion. A "noticed motion" is a motion that must be served and filed in the manner required by CCP §1005. *See* CRC 3.1300(a). Section 1005 requires, among other things, that the motion be accompanied by a notice of the hearing date. *See* CCP §1005(b); CRC 3.1112(a)(1).

1. Form of notice. The notice of hearing usually appears in a party's "notice of motion and motion." The terms "notice of hearing" and "notice of motion" are interchangeable—they both refer to the notice a moving party gives to other parties that a motion will be heard on a particular date. *See* CCP §1010 (notice of motion must state when it will be heard); CRC 3.1112(a)(1) (filed papers must include notice of hearing); *see also* ***Arambula v. Union Carbide Corp.*** (2d Dist.2005) 128 Cal.App.4th 333, 343 (purpose of notice of motion is to provide adequate time to prepare opposition). For a discussion of the form of the notice, see "Notice of motion & motion," ch. 1-D, §5.1, p. 28.

2. Deadline for serving notice. The notice of hearing must be served within the time period required by the applicable statute or court order. *See* CCP §1005(b); CRC 3.1300(a). For motions generally, that time period is at least 16 court days before the hearing date. CCP §1005(b). Because other motions may have different deadlines for serving notice, see the specific chapter in this book covering the motion. To determine how to calculate the deadline for serving a noticed motion, see "When to Serve," ch. 1-G, §6, p. 69.

§4.2 Ex parte application. By definition, an "ex parte application" is a request to the court for an order or relief made for the benefit of one party without notice to or argument by any other interested party or person. *Black's Law Dictionary* 1168 (10th ed. 2014) (definition of "ex parte motion"). The use of "ex parte" in this context, however, is something of a misnomer because the California Rules of Court require the party requesting relief to give some form of notice to all parties. *See* CRC 3.1203(a). See "Ex Parte Practice," ch. 1-E, p. 39.

1. Form of notice. The notice of ex parte application is not the same kind of notice that is given for noticed motions. Although it can be provided in writing, the notice of ex parte application can also be given orally. *See* CRC 3.1204(b)(1) & (b)(2) (declaration of notice must state manner of given or attempted notice). For a discussion of the form of the notice, see "Form," ch. 1-E, §4.3, p. 41.

2. Deadline for giving notice. The notice of ex parte application usually must be given to all parties by 10:00 a.m. one court day before the ex parte hearing. CRC 3.1203. For a discussion of the deadline for giving notice, see "Deadline," ch. 1-E, §4.4, p. 41.

§5. CONDUCTING HEARING

§5.1 Type of hearing.

1. Argument. Most hearings on motions or applications are for argument only. *See* CRC 3.1306(a) (evidence received at motion hearing must be by declaration or request for judicial notice without testimony or cross-examination); ***Mediterranean Constr. Co. v. State Farm Fire & Cas. Co.*** (4th Dist.1998) 66 Cal.App.4th 257, 263 (litigants are not given right to present testimony at hearings).

2. Taking of evidence. A party may give oral testimony at a hearing with the court's permission. *See* CRC 3.1306(a) (court can allow testimony for good cause); *see, e.g.*, CRC 3.514 (oral testimony not permitted at hearing involving coordination of complex actions unless assigned judge allows it); *see also* ***American Fed'n of State, Cty. & Mun. Empls. v. Metropolitan Water Dist.*** (2d Dist.2005) 126 Cal.App.4th 247, 263 (in writ-of-mandate hearing, court has broad discretion to decide case based on declarations and other documents rather than live, oral testimony). To get permission, the party must (1) show good cause for the testimony and (2) file a written statement describing the nature and extent of the testimony and giving a reasonable time estimate for the hearing. *See* CRC 3.1306(a), (b). See "Live testimony," §6.2, p. 88.

§5.2 Right to oral argument.

1. No absolute right. A party does not have an absolute right to present oral argument on every matter brought before the court. *See* ***Golden Gate Lumber Co. v. Sahrbacher*** (1894) 105 Cal. 114, 118. Simply because a statute or rule provides for a "hearing" does not give a party the right to orally argue the matter. ***Lewis v. Superior***

Ct. (1999) 19 Cal.4th 1232, 1247; ***Harbour Vista, LLC v. HSBC Mortg. Servs.*** (4th Dist.2011) 201 Cal.App.4th 1496, 1507. A general concern about fairness and the quality of jurisprudence has led the courts to develop general standards for determining whether oral argument on a given matter is mandated. *See* Cal. Law Revision Comm'n, *Oral Argument in Civil Procedure (Draft of Report)*, pp. 6-8 (2006), www.clrc.ca.gov/pub/2006/MM06-15.pdf. To determine whether a party has a right to present oral argument on a matter, the courts will consider whether the right is impliedly provided by statute or rule.

NOTE

*For a good discussion of the public policy behind the need for allowing oral argument, see **Mediterranean Constr. Co. v. State Farm Fire & Cas. Co.** (4th Dist.1998) 66 Cal.App.4th 257, 264-65.*

2. Implied right. A party is entitled to present oral argument if the context of the statute or rule authorizing the hearing indicates that oral argument is expected and the nature of the dispute indicates that argument would help resolve an actual controversy. *See* ***Harbour Vista***, 201 Cal.App.4th at 1507; *see, e.g.*, ***Lewis***, 19 Cal.4th at 1247 (context of statute did not indicate oral argument was intended); ***In re Marriage of Dunn*** (4th Dist.2002) 103 Cal.App.4th 345, 348 (context of postjudgment motion to modify child-custody order contemplated oral hearing).

(1) Context of statute. In determining whether a statute or rule authorizes oral argument, the court should address the following questions:

(a) Does the judge act as a fact-finder or adjudicate any issues at the hearing? ***Harbour Vista***, 201 Cal.App.4th at 1507.

(b) Can the litigants rely on any procedural remedies (e.g., making evidentiary objections, orally moving for a continuance) at the hearing? *Id.*

(c) Does the hearing involve a critical pretrial matter of considerable significance to the parties? *Id.*; *e.g.*, ***Titmas v. Superior Ct.*** (4th Dist.2001) 87 Cal.App.4th 738, 742 (protection of attorney-client privilege was critical matter).

(2) Nature of dispute. In determining whether a statute or rule authorizes oral argument, the court should consider whether there is an authentic dispute or whether the issues are so obvious or well settled that oral argument would amount to an "empty gesture." ***TJX Cos. v. Superior Ct.*** (4th Dist.2001) 87 Cal.App.4th 747, 751; *see* ***Lewis***, 19 Cal.4th at 1258-59.

(3) Right to argument.

(a) Recognized. The courts have recognized the right to oral argument in the following matters:

[1] Demurrer. ***Medix Ambulance Serv. v. Superior Ct.*** (4th Dist.2002) 97 Cal.App.4th 109, 115.

[2] Summary judgment. ***Brannon v. Superior Ct.*** (4th Dist.2004) 114 Cal.App.4th 1203, 1211; ***Mediterranean Constr.***, 66 Cal.App.4th at 262.

[3] Motion to quash. *See* ***Titmas***, 87 Cal.App.4th at 742-43.

[4] Motion to dismiss. *See* ***Cordova v. Vons Grocery Co.*** (2d Dist.1987) 196 Cal.App.3d 1526, 1531 (hearing on motion to dismiss can be held with hearing on other motion). If the opposing party has already had an opportunity to avoid dismissal, a hearing is not required. *See, e.g.*, ***Oppenheimer v. Deutchman*** (Los Angeles Cty. Superior Ct. Appellate Dept. 1955) 132 Cal.App.2d Supp. 875, 879 (notice of motion to dismiss was not required after demurrer sustained).

[5] Motion to appoint a receiver. *See* ***Cal-Am. Income Prop. Fund VII v. Brown Dev. Corp.*** (4th Dist.1982) 138 Cal.App.3d 268, 273 n.3.

[6] Action to quiet title. ***Harbour Vista***, 201 Cal.App.4th at 1507.

NOTE

Some local rules limit the time for oral argument. E.g., Super. Ct. Napa Cty. Loc. R., rule 6.10 (court can continue hearing to different date if argument exceeds 15 minutes); Super. Ct. Santa Cruz Cty. Loc. R., rule 2.4.03(a) (10 minutes per side); Super. Ct. Sonoma Cty. Loc. R., rule 5.5.B (20 minutes for entire hearing).

(b) Not recognized. The courts have not recognized the right to oral argument in the following matters:

[1] Motion to dismiss for failure to timely amend. *See* ***Wilburn v. Oakland Hosp.*** (1st Dist.1989) 213 Cal.App.3d 1107, 1111.

[2] Motion to withdraw motion to vacate default judgment. *See* ***Muller v. Muller*** (1st Dist.1956) 141 Cal.App.2d 722, 731.

[3] Motion to reopen for additional evidence. *See* ***Ensher, Alexander & Barsoom, Inc. v. Ensher*** (3d Dist.1964) 225 Cal.App.2d 318, 324-26.

[4] Motion for new trial. ***Kimmel v. Keefe*** (1st Dist.1970) 9 Cal.App.3d 402, 408; *see* ***Collins v. Nelson*** (2d Dist.1940) 41 Cal.App.2d 107, 113 (court can also decline to receive or read briefs on motion for new trial).

§5.3 Place of hearing.

1. Hearing in open court. Most hearings are held in open court. *See* CCP §1004; ***McDowell v. Orsini*** (2d Dist.1976) 54 Cal.App.3d 951, 959. In some cases, the court is required to hear a matter in open court. For example, most substantive hearings must be conducted in open court because civil proceedings are "presumptively open" to the public. *See* CCP §124; ***NBC Subsidiary (KNBC-TV), Inc. v. Superior Ct.*** (1999) 20 Cal.4th 1178, 1217. A substantive hearing can be closed only after notice to the public is given, a hearing is held, and the court makes certain express findings. *See* ***NBC Subsidiary***, 20 Cal.4th at 1217-18.

2. Hearing in chambers. Some hearings can be held in chambers. *See* CCP §166(a).

(1) What can be heard. The court can do all of the following in chambers:

(a) Hear and dispose of orders or writs usually decided on an ex parte application. CCP §166(a)(1).

(b) Approve bonds and undertakings. *Id.* §166(a)(5).

(c) Appoint a referee. *Id.* §166(a)(1).

(d) Require and receive inventories and accounts that must be filed. *Id.*

(e) Order notice of settlement of supplemental accounts. *Id.*

(f) Suspend the powers of personal representatives, guardians, and conservators. *Id.*

(g) Appoint special administrators. *Id.*

(h) Grant letters of temporary guardianship or conservatorship. *Id.*; *see* ***In re Joshua G.*** (4th Dist.2005) 129 Cal.App.4th 189, 201 (evidence of child's wishes in child-dependency hearing can be presented in chambers).

(i) Approve or reject claims. CCP §166(a)(1).

(j) Issue all writs and processes necessary for probate matters. *Id.*

(k) Hear and dispose of all motions for new trial under CCP §657. *Id.* §166(a)(2).

(*l*) Hear and dispose of all motions to modify or vacate a judgment under CCP §663. *Id.* §166(a)(2).

(m) Decide motions to tax costs of enforcing a judgment. *Id.* §166(a)(4).

(n) Decide uncontested actions, proceedings, demurrers, motions, petitions, applications, and other matters. *Id.* §166(a)(3).

(o) Determine whether a claim of Fifth Amendment privilege is valid. ***Warford v. Medeiros*** (1st Dist.1984) 160 Cal.App.3d 1035, 1048.

(2) What cannot be heard. The court cannot hear any of the following matters in chambers:

(a) Action for dissolution of marriage. CCP §166(a)(3); *see also* ***In re Marriage of Dunn*** (4th Dist.2002) 103 Cal.App.4th 345, 348-49 (reversing postdissolution modification order issued in chambers).

(b) Action for legal separation. CCP §166(a)(3).

(c) Action for judgment of nullity of marriage. *Id.*; ***Maduro v. Maduro*** (1st Dist.1944) 62 Cal.App.2d 776, 779.

(d) Application for confirmation of the sale of real property in a probate proceeding. CCP §166(a)(3).

§5.4 Party's appearance.

NOTE

In this section, the term "party" includes the attorney who appears and speaks for the party. The party can also appear, but only the attorney can speak.

---

1. In person. A party can appear in person at most hearings. Of course, no personal appearance is possible if the court denies oral argument and decides the matter on the briefs.

(1) Noticed motion. For noticed motions, the moving party is usually not required to appear in person at the hearing. *See* CRC 3.1304(c). If the party is not going to appear, it should give written notice of nonappearance. *Id.* The motion can then be submitted for the court's decision without the party's appearance unless the court orders otherwise. *Id.* If the notice of nonappearance is not given and the moving party does not appear at the hearing, the court can either (1) take the matter off the calendar, to be reset only on the party's motion, or (2) decide the motion. CRC 3.1304(d).

(2) Ex parte application. For ex parte applications, the moving party is usually required to appear either in person or by telephone at the hearing. *See* CRC 3.1207 (ex parte application will be considered without personal or telephone appearance in only four circumstances); *see, e.g.*, Super. Ct. Napa Cty. Loc. R., rule 7.7.E (family-law court; if applicant does not appear at scheduled hearing time, application will be denied). *But see* ***Eliceche v. Federal Land Bank Ass'n*** (5th Dist.2002) 103 Cal.App.4th 1349, 1357, 1373 (granting ex parte application without applicant's appearance was not error because opposing party was not prejudiced). The following are the only ex parte orders that can be granted without the moving party's appearance:

(a) Orders that allow a party to file a memorandum exceeding the page limit. CRC 3.1207(1).

(b) Orders that allow for an extension of time to serve pleadings. CRC 3.1207(2).

(c) Orders that set hearing dates on alternative writs and show-cause orders. CRC 3.1207(3).

(d) Orders that are stipulated by the parties. CRC 3.1207(4).

2. By telephone. A party can appear by telephone at most nonevidentiary hearings. *See* CCP §367.5(a); CRC 3.670(c), (e); *see also* CRC 3.670(f)(1) (when exercising discretion in deciding whether to allow telephone appearance, courts should consider general policy favoring telephone appearances).

PRACTICE TIP

Check the local rules for any specific procedures for appearing by telephone. See, e.g., Super. Ct. Santa Cruz Cty. Loc. R., rule 2.6.04(b), (c) (attorney must call five minutes before hearing and state name each time she speaks).

(1) Party's appearance.

(a) When allowed. In all general civil cases, a party that has given notice can appear by telephone in any hearing unless a personal appearance is required. *See* CRC 3.670(c), (d).

(b) When not allowed.

[1] Types of hearings. A party cannot appear by telephone at the following hearings unless the court allows it:

[a] A hearing where witnesses are expected to testify. CRC 3.670(e)(1)(A).

[b] A hearing on a temporary restraining order. CRC 3.670(e)(1)(B).

[c] A hearing on a motion in limine. CCP §367.5(b)(3); CRC 3.670(e)(1)(E).

[d] A hearing on a petition to confirm the sale of property under the Probate Code. CRC 3.670(e)(1)(F).

[e] Any hearing in which the court orders a party to appear in person based on a determination that a personal appearance would materially assist in the determination of the hearing or the effective management or resolution of the case. CCP §367.5(c); CRC 3.670(f)(2). If a hearing is already underway, the court can issue a continuance of the proceeding and order a personal appearance. CRC 3.670(g).

[2] Persons. The following persons cannot appear by telephone unless the court allows it:

[a] A person ordered to appear to show cause why sanctions should not be imposed for violating a court order or rule. CRC 3.670(e)(2)(A).

[b] A person ordered to appear in an order or citation issued under the Probate Code. CRC 3.670(e)(2)(B).

(2) Giving notice of appearance. A party that wants to appear by telephone must give notice. *See* CCP §367.5(b); CRC 3.670(h).

(a) Noticed motion.

[1] Include notice in papers. For noticed motions, a party that wants to appear by telephone can give notice by including the phrase "Telephone Appearance" below the title of the motion, opposition, or reply papers filed by the party. CRC 3.670(h)(1)(A).

[2] Provide separate notice. For noticed motions, a party that wants to appear by telephone can give notice by notifying the court and all other parties at least two court days before the hearing of the party's intent to appear by telephone. CRC 3.670(h)(1)(B).

[a] Oral notice. The party can give oral notice either in person or by telephone of its intent to appear by telephone. CRC 3.670(h)(1)(B).

[b] Written notice. The party can give written notice of its intent to appear by telephone by filing a "Notice of Intent to Appear by Telephone." CRC 3.670(h)(1)(B). The written notice must be filed with the court at least two court days before the hearing and served on the other parties by personal delivery, fax, express mail, e-mail, or another method reasonably calculated to ensure delivery by the end of the next business day. *Id.*

NOTE

If a party that has not given notice of a telephone appearance receives notice of a telephone appearance from another party under the procedures for noticed motions, it can decide to appear by telephone and must notify the court and all other parties of its intent to appear by telephone. CRC 3.670(h)(2). This notice must be given no later than noon on the court day before the appearance. Id.

(b) Ex parte application.

[1] Applicant's notice. For ex parte applications, an applicant that wants to appear by telephone must give notice of its intent by doing all of the following:

[a] The applicant must include the phrase "Telephone Appearance" below the title of the application papers. CRC 3.670(h)(3)(A). See "Application Papers," ch. 1-E, §5, p. 42.

[b] The applicant must file and serve the application papers so they will be received by the court and all parties by 10:00 a.m. at least two court days before the ex parte appearance. CRC 3.670(d)(1), (h)(3)(B).

[c] If required by local rule, the applicant must ensure that copies of the application papers have been received by the department conducting the hearing. CRC 3.670(d)(1), (h)(3)(C).

[2] Notice by any other party. For ex parte applications, any party that wants to appear by telephone other than an applicant must give either oral or written notice of its intent to the court and all other parties by 2:00 p.m. on the court day before the appearance. CRC 3.670(h)(4).

[a] Oral notice. The party can give oral notice either in person or by telephone. CRC 3.670(h)(4).

[b] Written notice. The party can give written notice by filing a "Notice of Intent to Appear by Telephone." CRC 3.670(h)(4). The written notice must be filed with the court and served on the other parties by any means reasonably calculated to ensure delivery by the close of business on the court day before the appearance. *Id.*

(3) Requiring personal appearance. After a party has given notice of its intent to appear by telephone, the court can determine whether the party's personal appearance is required. *See* CRC 3.670(i). If the court requires personal appearance, it must give reasonable notice to all parties before the hearing and can continue the hearing if necessary to accommodate the personal appearance. *Id.* The court can direct the court clerk, a court-appointed vendor, a party, or an attorney to give the notice. *Id.* If the court uses a telephonic tentative-ruling system for motion matters (i.e., a telephone system through which a party can find out how the judge intends to rule on a motion), the court's notice that the party or parties must appear in person can be given as part of the tentative ruling if the notice is given one court day before the hearing. *Id.*; *see* CRC 3.1308 (tentative rulings).

(4) Rescinding notice of appearance. If a party who gave notice to appear by telephone under the procedures for noticed motions decides instead to appear in person, the party can appear in person. CRC 3.670(h)(5).

(5) Waiving notice of appearance. The court should, on a showing of good cause or unforeseen circumstances, allow a party to appear by telephone even if that party has not given notice. CRC 3.670(h)(6).

(6) Conducting hearing.

(a) Speaker's statements & identity. The court must ensure that all participants can (1) hear every statement made and (2) identify the person making the statement. CRC 3.670(n).

(b) Making record. Hearings attended by telephone must be recorded to the same extent and in the same manner as hearings attended in person. CRC 3.670(o). See "Who makes record," §5.6, this page.

(c) Teleconferencing services. The court can directly provide or contract with a private vendor for teleconferencing services, and the court or vendor can charge parties attending by telephone a fee for its services. *See* CRC 3.670(j), (k).

(d) Conference-call provider. A court, by local rule, can designate a particular conference-call provider that must be used for telephone appearances. CRC 3.670(p).

PRACTICE TIP

Some courts prohibit callers from using cellular phones when appearing by telephone. E.g., Super. Ct. Santa Cruz Cty. Loc. R., rule 2.6.04(a)(3).

§5.5 Who conducts hearing. A hearing is usually conducted by the trial judge. *See* CCP §170 (judge has duty to decide any proceeding she is not disqualified from); ***Case v. Lazben Fin. Co.*** (2d Dist.2002) 99 Cal.App.4th 172, 184 (essential power of judicial branch is to resolve controversies between parties). The court, on a party's motion or on its own, can refer the hearing to a referee to decide the matter. CCP §638 (reference by agreement), §639 (reference without agreement). See "Stipulation or Motion for Reference," ch. 2-E, p. 163. The court can appoint a temporary judge (i.e., a judge pro tempore) to decide the matter if the parties stipulate to it. Cal. Const., art. VI, §21; *see* ***In re Courtney H.*** (1st Dist.1995) 38 Cal.App.4th 1221, 1227 (parties may impliedly stipulate, through their conduct, to appointment of temporary judge); *see also* CCP §259 (commissioner can be appointed to conduct hearings in case).

§5.6 Who makes record. The official reporter attends court sessions and creates a verbatim record of the proceedings. *See* CRC 2.956(e)(2).

1. Who can report. An official reporter can report on civil proceedings. *See* CCP §269(a)(1); Gov. C. §69941. An official reporter is a court-appointed reporter whose fee for attending and reporting is paid for by the court or the county and who was not employed by a party to report specific causes. *See* Gov. C. §§69941, 69947; CRC 2.956(e)(2). The term "official reporter" includes the following:

(1) An "official court reporter" or "official reporter," as those terms are used in CCP §269 and Gov. C. §69941. CRC 2.956(e)(2).

(2) An "official reporter pro tempore," as that term is used in Gov. C. §70044 and other statutes. *See* CRC 2.956(e)(2); *see also* Stats. 2002, ch. 784, §330 (repealed Gov. C. §69945 and replaced with §70044); Gov. C. §70044 (right of pro tem reporters to serve without court order or stipulations). When an official court reporter is not available for a hearing or trial, any party can arrange for a certified shorthand reporter to serve as an official reporter pro tempore. CRC 2.956(c).

2. Duties of reporter.

(1) Make record. An official reporter must make a full record of the proceedings. *See* CCP §269(a). This includes taking down in shorthand all testimony, objections, rulings, exceptions, attorneys' arguments, and judge's statements, remarks, and oral instructions. *Id.*

(2) Preserve notes. An official reporter must preserve the reporting notes from a proceeding. *See* Gov. C. §69955(a). The notes must be kept either by the reporter in a place designated by the court or by the court clerk. *Id.* Reporting notes are considered official records of the court and can be destroyed only on court order issued at least five years after the notes were taken. *Id.* §69955(a), (e).

3. Burden to secure reporter.

(1) Generally. In civil proceedings, an official reporter functions on a demand basis—that is, a party is usually responsible for ensuring that a reporter is present to create a record of what is said during the proceeding. ***In re Christina P.*** (3d Dist.1985) 175 Cal.App.3d 115, 129; *see* CCP §269(a)(1) (official reporter must take down civil proceedings on court order or at party's request). For example, a party who wants to make objections to evidence supporting a motion for summary judgment must arrange for a court reporter to be present at the hearing. CRC 3.1352(2); ***Mediterranean Constr. Co. v. State Farm Fire & Cas. Co.*** (4th Dist.1998) 66 Cal.App.4th 257, 263-64. In many cases, the party's failure to request an official reporter can amount to a waiver of the right to appeal. *See* ***Mediterranean Constr.***, 66 Cal.App.4th at 263-64. However, the absence of an official shorthand record does not prohibit the parties from establishing a relevant event by other means, such as by admission or independent testimony. ***Los Angeles Cty. Ct. Reporters Ass'n v. Superior Ct.*** (5th Dist.1995) 31 Cal.App.4th 403, 410.

(2) Notice of availability of services. The court must give notice in its local rules if it does not regularly provide for the reporting or electronic recording of motion hearings. CRC 3.1310; *see also* CRC 2.952-2.954 (rules for electronic recording of proceedings), CRC 2.956(b)(1) (local policy must be posted in clerk's office), CRC 2.956(b)(2) (local policy must be published in newspaper or copy must be given to parties at least ten days before any hearing). When the court does not regularly provide these services, the local rules must provide a procedure for a party to obtain court reporting or recording services. CRC 3.1310; *see* CRC 2.956(c) (party can arrange for certified shorthand reporter when official reporter not available).

4. Evidentiary presumption. CCP §273(a) creates an evidentiary presumption that an official reporter's report, when transcribed and certified, is prima facie evidence of the testimony and proceedings. ***Los Angeles Cty. Ct. Reporters***, 31 Cal.App.4th at 409. If a transcribed and certified report is not available because the party did not request one under CCP §269, the evidentiary presumption is not available, and the party will have to establish the relevant events through other means, such as by requests for admission or through independent testimony. ***Los Angeles Cty. Ct. Reporters***, 31 Cal.App.4th at 410.

§6. PRESENTING EVIDENCE

§6.1 Written evidence. In most cases, the evidence at a hearing is limited to written evidence, which includes declarations and supporting papers filed by the parties. *See* CCP §1005(b) (supporting papers must be filed and served), §2009 (use of affidavits); CRC 3.1116 (deposition testimony used as exhibit for motion), CRC 3.1306(a) (limiting use of testimony at motion hearing).

§6.2 Live testimony. A party must request permission to present live testimony at a motion hearing. CRC 3.1306(a). The court can allow live testimony only on a showing of good cause. *Id.*

1. Written request. A party seeking permission to present live testimony must file a written statement that (1) describes the nature and extent of the testimony and (2) gives a reasonable time estimate for the hearing. CRC 3.1306(b). If the party needs to secure the attendance of a witness at the hearing, it can obtain a subpoena for appearance. *See* CCP §1985. See "Trial & Hearing Subpoenas," ch. 8-C, p. 970.

2. Deadline. The written request must be filed at least three court days before the hearing. CRC 3.1306(b). If the request is filed less than five court days before the hearing, the request must be served on the other parties in a way that ensures they will receive it at least two days before the hearing. *Id.*

3. Exception for rebuttal. A request is not required if a party wants to present live testimony to rebut another party's live testimony. CRC 3.1306(b).

§6.3 Judicial notice. A party can request that the court take judicial notice of laws, regulations, governmental acts, court records, court rules, international and foreign laws, facts that are common knowledge, and undisputed facts and propositions. Evid. C. §§452, 453; *see* CRC 3.1306(a), (c). See "Request for Judicial Notice," ch. 5-J, p. 547.

§7. CONTINUANCE

For a discussion of obtaining a continuance of a hearing, see "Requests for Continuance or Stay," ch. 5-I, p. 534.

I. RULINGS & ORDERS

§1. GENERAL

This subchapter discusses rulings and orders generally. This subchapter does not discuss rulings on evidentiary or other types of objections. For a discussion of rulings on objections to summary-judgment evidence, see "Ruling on objections," ch. 10-B, §10.3, p. 1135.

§1.1 Purpose. The purpose of a ruling and order is to announce and record the court's decision on a pending matter.

§1.2 Primary authority. CRC 3.1109, 3.1312; *see also* CRC 3.670(i) (telephonic tentative-ruling systems), CRC 3.1308 (tentative rulings).

§1.3 Secondary authority. The following secondary sources are cited as authority in this subchapter:

- Weil & Brown, *California Practice Guide: Civil Procedure Before Trial* (CD-ROM ed. 2014) (referred to as Weil, *Civil Procedure Before Trial*).
- Witkin, *California Procedure* (5th ed. 2008 & Supp.2014) (referred to as Witkin, *Cal. Procedure*).
- Younger & Bradley, *Younger on California Motions* (2014-15) (referred to as Younger, *Cal. Motions*).

§1.4 Judicial Council form.

- EFS-020 (mandatory), proposed order cover sheet for electronic filing.

§2. JUDGMENT VS. ORDER

A judgment is the court's final written ruling that determines the parties' rights in the lawsuit. *See* CCP §§577, 1064; ***Griset v. Fair Political Practices Comm'n*** (2001) 25 Cal.4th 688, 697. An order is any ruling by the court not included in a judgment (e.g., a ruling on a motion). CCP §1003; ***Passavanti v. Williams*** (4th Dist.1990) 225 Cal.App.3d 1602, 1605. There can be many orders issued while the suit is pending, but there can be only one judgment. ***Passavanti***, 225 Cal.App.3d at 1605.

§3. TYPES OF RULINGS

The court can make two types of rulings: tentative and oral. A ruling is final only when it is made on the record and becomes an order. See "Record of Ruling," §4, p. 90.

§3.1 Tentative ruling. A tentative ruling is a statement issued by the court indicating how it is inclined to rule on a motion noticed for hearing based on the papers and evidence submitted. *See, e.g.*, ***Baker-Hoey v. Lockheed Martin Corp.*** (4th Dist.2003) 111 Cal.App.4th 592, 596 (court issued tentative rulings on recovery and apportionment of discovery costs). The purpose of a tentative ruling is to (1) shorten the time for the hearing by focusing the discussion or (2) eliminate the need for the parties or attorneys to appear for oral argument. Younger, *Cal. Motions*, §4:53.

1. Necessity & availability. A court is not required to issue a tentative ruling. CRC 3.1308(e). But if it does issue one, it must make the tentative ruling available by a specified time and method. *E.g.*, CRC 3.1308(a)(1) (if notice of intent to appear is required, tentative ruling must be made available by telephone).

2. Types.

(1) Ruling before hearing date. A court can issue a tentative ruling before a scheduled hearing date, but the timing and effect of the ruling will depend on whether the court requires a party to give notice of intent to appear at the hearing. *See* CRC 3.1308(a), (b).

(a) Notice of intent to appear required. If the court requires a party to give notice of intent to appear at the hearing, the tentative ruling automatically becomes the court's final ruling unless the court requests oral argument or a party gives the required notice. CRC 3.1308(a)(1); *see* ***Brannon v. Superior Ct.*** (4th Dist.2004) 114 Cal.App.4th 1203, 1209-10.

[1] **Method & deadline.** The court's tentative ruling must be made available by telephone and can be made by any other method (e.g., on the Internet) designated by the court by 3:00 p.m. on the court day before the hearing date. CRC 3.1308(a)(1); *see, e.g.*, Super. Ct. San Francisco Cty. Loc. R., rule 8.3.A.

[2] **Notice of intent.** The notice of intent to appear must be given to the other parties in person or by telephone. CRC 3.1308(a)(1). Notice to the court must be accepted by telephone and may be accepted by any other method designated by the court. *Id.* The notice must be given to the other parties and the court by 4:00 p.m. on the court day before the hearing date. *Id.*

(b) Notice of intent to appear not required. If the court does not require a party to give notice of intent to appear at the hearing, the tentative ruling does not become the court's final ruling until the hearing takes place. CRC 3.1308(a)(2); ***Brannon***, 114 Cal.App.4th at 1210.

[1] **Method & deadline.** The court's tentative ruling must be made available by telephone and can be made by any other method designated by the court. CRC 3.1308(a)(2). The tentative ruling must be available by a specific time designated by the court. *Id.*

[2] **Notice of intent.** Because the court does not require notice of intent to appear, the parties can simply appear on the scheduled hearing date to present oral argument without providing additional notice. *See* CRC 3.1308(a)(2).

(2) Ruling on hearing date. A court can issue a tentative ruling on the scheduled hearing date regardless of whether the court requires a party to give notice of intent to appear at the hearing. *See* CRC 3.1308(b). Like tentative rulings issued before the hearing when no notice of intent to appear is required, the court's ruling will not become the final ruling until after the hearing. A tentative ruling issued on the hearing date must be issued in one of the following ways:

(a) By posting a calendar note containing the tentative ruling. CRC 3.1308(b)(1).

(b) By announcing the tentative ruling at the time of oral argument. CRC 3.1308(b)(2). Some courts issue tentative rulings during in-chambers hearings held before the scheduled hearing. *See, e.g.*, ***Elnekave v. Via Dolce Homeowners Ass'n*** (2d Dist.2006) 142 Cal.App.4th 1193, 1197 (court issued tentative ruling on settlement).

NOTE

Any party to a motion can agree to "submit on the ruling"—which means the party agrees to the tentative ruling—although the prevailing party is usually the one who submits. A party can submit on the ruling either before or during the hearing, depending on when the tentative ruling comes down. For a complete discussion of submitting on a tentative ruling, see Younger, Cal. Motions, §§4:58-4:67.

---

3. Effect. A tentative ruling is not binding on the court. ***Jespersen v. Zubiate-Beauchamp*** (2d Dist.2003) 114 Cal.App.4th 624, 633; ***In re Marriage of Hafferkamp*** (1st Dist.1998) 61 Cal.App.4th 789, 794.

4. Additional briefing. In a tentative ruling, the court can ask the parties to provide further argument on issues the court is interested in. CRC 3.1308(a).

§3.2 Oral ruling. An oral ruling is a ruling stated by the judge in open court during or at the conclusion of a hearing. An oral ruling does not become an effective order until it is entered in the permanent minutes or filed in writing with the clerk. ***In re Marriage of Drake*** (2d Dist.1997) 53 Cal.App.4th 1139, 1170; *see, e.g.*, ***Jablon v. Henneberger*** (1949) 33 Cal.2d 773, 774-75 (time to appeal action began when court's denial of motion for new trial was entered into permanent minutes, not when oral ruling was announced in open court).

§4. RECORD OF RULING

To be effective, a ruling must be made on the record. A ruling on the record is a final order, and it must be recorded by either (1) a minute order entered by the clerk in the court's official minutes or (2) a written order submitted by a

party or issued by the court. *See* CCP §1003 (order is any direction of court made or entered in writing and not included in judgment); ***In re Marcus*** (6th Dist.2006) 138 Cal.App.4th 1009, 1015-16 (record of ruling can be written order or detailed entry in court's minutes); ***In re Marriage of Drake*** (2d Dist.1997) 53 Cal.App.4th 1139, 1170 (oral ruling not effective until filed in writing or entered in minutes); ***County of Nev. v. Superior Ct.*** (3d Dist.1986) 183 Cal.App.3d 806, 808-09 (ruling can be either formal written order or minute order entered by clerk).

§4.1 Minute order. A minute order is an entry made by the clerk in the court's official minutes indicating the date and substance of the court's ruling on an issue. *See* CRC 8.104(c)(2); ***Mandjik v. Eden Township Hosp. Dist.*** (1st Dist.1992) 4 Cal.App.4th 1488, 1497. A minute order can be entered after a tentative or oral ruling or after a matter was decided on submission. If the court's ruling is entered in the minutes, the ruling is preserved for appeal if the minute order does not direct the parties to prepare a written order. ***In re Marriage of Dupre*** (3d Dist.2005) 127 Cal.App.4th 1517, 1523; ***In re Marriage of Lechowick*** (1st Dist.1998) 65 Cal.App.4th 1406, 1410. A minute order that directs the parties to prepare a written order is not a final order and does not start the running of any deadlines. *See* ***Annette F. v. Sharon S.*** (4th Dist.2005) 130 Cal.App.4th 1448, 1455.

NOTE

For certain matters, the court cannot issue a minute order but must instead reduce its ruling to a written order. See "Required by rule," §4.2.4, p. 93.

1. Types of minutes.

(1) Rough minutes. The court clerk's "rough" minutes are notes taken during court sessions and are not the official minutes of the court. ***Copley Press, Inc. v. Superior Ct.*** (4th Dist.1992) 6 Cal.App.4th 106, 115. The clerk's rough minutes are not minute orders, and they do not start the running of any deadlines. ***Mandjik***, 4 Cal.App.4th at 1497. Until the clerk enters the court's ruling in the permanent minutes, the court is free to change its ruling. ***People v. Surety Ins.*** (5th Dist.1983) 148 Cal.App.3d 351, 357.

(2) Permanent minutes. The court clerk's "permanent" minutes—sometimes referred to as "smooth" minutes—are the official entries made by the clerk in the court's record. *See* ***Mandjik***, 4 Cal.App.4th at 1497-98. The clerk's permanent minutes are minute orders, and they start the running of applicable deadlines. *See id.* To clearly identify an entry as part of the permanent minutes, the clerk should include the case number and should sign and date the entry and place it in the case's court file. *See id.*; *see also* Gov. C. §69844 (clerk must date entries in court's minutes).

2. Contradicts oral ruling. When a minute order contradicts the court's oral ruling, the terms of the minute order are controlling. *See* ***In re Marriage of Drake*** (2d Dist.1997) 53 Cal.App.4th 1139, 1170.

§4.2 Written order. A written order is a court ruling that is put in writing. A written order is not legally effective until it is signed and filed. ***Maxwell v. Perkins*** (2d Dist.1953) 116 Cal.App.2d 752, 756; *see* ***In re Marriage of Hafferkamp*** (1st Dist.1998) 61 Cal.App.4th 789, 793. Until the written order is signed and filed, the court can change its ruling. *See* ***In re Marcus*** (6th Dist.2006) 138 Cal.App.4th 1009, 1016. See "Changing Ruling," §6, p. 94. A ruling is made into a written order in the following ways:

1. Submitted by party.

(1) Discretionary. A party can submit a proposed order with its motion papers. CRC 3.1113(m); *see, e.g.*, ***Maughan v. Google Tech.*** (2d Dist.2006) 143 Cal.App.4th 1242, 1245 n.2 (court did not sign party's proposed order on anti-SLAPP motion). A party can also submit a proposed order with its opposition to a motion. Weil, *Civil Procedure Before Trial*, ¶9:103.13. See "Proposed order," ch. 1-D, §5.5, p. 32.

(2) Mandatory. A party who prevails on a motion must submit a proposed order for the court's signature, regardless of whether the court issued an earlier minute order. *See* CRC 3.1312(a); ***Hughey v. City of Hayward*** (1st Dist.1994) 24 Cal.App.4th 206, 209. However, if the prevailing party submitted a proposed order with its motion papers and the motion was unopposed, the party does not have to resubmit the order. CRC 3.1312(e).

CAUTION

If the court issued an earlier minute order and did not specifically direct that a written order be prepared, the order's entry date for purposes of appeal is the date the minute order was entered in the permanent minutes. See CRC 8.104(c)(2). An order prepared under CRC 3.1312(a) is not considered an order prepared by direction of the court, and thus does not start the running of the clock for purposes of appeal. CRC 8.104(c)(2). One court has noted that these rules create "a trap for the unwary" and has called on the Judicial Council to clarify them. See ***Hughey****, 24 Cal.App.4th at 209-10.*

(a) Prevailing party's notice of proposed order. If the motion is opposed, the prevailing party must serve a proposed order that conforms with the ruling on the other parties for their approval. CRC 3.1312(a). The proposed order must be served within five days after the court's ruling by any method authorized by law that is reasonably calculated to ensure delivery no later than the close of the next business day. *Id.* See "Methods of service," ch. 1-G, §5.1, p. 66. The prevailing party is not required to send the proposed order if the parties waived notice or if the court ordered that the proposed order should not be sent. CRC 3.1312(a).

(b) Losing party's notice of approval. The losing party must notify the prevailing party of whether it approves the order within five days after being served. CRC 3.1312(a). The losing party's deadline to respond is not extended by the prevailing party's method of service. *See id.* (extensions for method of service under any rule or statute do not apply). If the losing party does not approve the order, the losing party must state all its reasons for disapproval, and the court may conduct a hearing to resolve the issue. *See id.*; *see, e.g.*, ***Conservatorship of McElroy*** (4th Dist.2002) 104 Cal.App.4th 536, 542 (court conducted several hearings on extensive objections to proposed order). If the losing party does not provide timely notice of its approval or disapproval, the proposed order is deemed approved. CRC 3.1312(a).

(c) Submission of proposed order. The prevailing party must submit the proposed order to the court with a summary of any other party's responses or a statement that no responses were received. CRC 3.1312(b). The proposed order must be submitted promptly after the five-day approval period for the losing party expires. *Id.* If the proposed order is submitted to the court electronically (in a case allowing for electronic filing), the following versions of the proposed order must be submitted:

[1] A PDF version that includes the proposed order attached to a completed Judicial Council Form EFS-020 (proposed order cover sheet). CRC 3.1312(c)(1).

[2] An editable word-processing version of the proposed order. CRC 3.1312(c)(2). The e-mail sent to the court must copy all parties in the action. *Id.*

NOTE

Courts that permit electronic filing of proposed orders must provide an electronic address to which the editable versions of proposed orders are to be sent and must specify any particular requirements for the word-processing format of the orders. CRC 3.1312(c).

(d) Failure to timely submit order. If the prevailing party does not prepare and submit a proposed order in a timely manner, any other party can submit its own proposed order. CRC 3.1312(d).

2. Prepared by court. The court can prepare its own formal written order, which becomes effective when it is signed and filed. *See* ***Ketscher v. Superior Ct.*** (5th Dist.1970) 9 Cal.App.3d 601, 604; ***Lee v. Cranford*** (2d Dist.1951) 107 Cal.App.2d 677, 680; ***Lind v. Baker*** (4th Dist.1941) 48 Cal.App.2d 234, 244.

3. Requested by court. The court can delegate the task of preparing a formal written order to the prevailing party for the court's approval. This directive can be expressly stated in the court's minute order, or it can be made orally at the hearing as long as the court's ruling has not been entered in the minutes. *See* ***Cohen v. Superior***

Ct. (1st Dist.1966) 244 Cal.App.2d 650, 653 n.3 (unless court's minute order expressly directs that written order be prepared, signed, and filed, minute order is court's final decision; later formal written order has no effect).

4. Required by rule. Some rulings must be put in writing.

(1) Dismissal. An order dismissing an action must be in writing. CCP §581d. See "Voluntary Dismissal," ch. 10-D, p. 1150; "Involuntary Dismissal—Delay in Prosecution," ch. 10-E, p. 1160; "Involuntary Dismissal—Other Grounds," ch. 10-F, p. 1180.

(2) Summary judgment. An order denying or granting a motion for summary judgment must be recorded on the record by a court reporter or by written order. CCP §437c(g); *see, e.g.*, ***Beatrice Cos. v. Superior Ct.*** (5th Dist.1986) 182 Cal.App.3d 525, 527 (written order denying MSJ did not comply with requirements of CCP §437c(g)). See "Motion for Summary Judgment," ch. 10-B, p. 1117.

(3) Sanctions. An order imposing sanctions must be in writing and recite the conduct justifying the order. CRC 2.30(e); *see also* CCP §128.5(c) (written order required for party to pay reasonable expenses for bad-faith actions). See "Motion for Sanctions," ch. 5-K, p. 561; "Discovery Sanctions," ch. 9-A, p. 1003.

§5. NOTICE OF ORDER

§5.1 Notice by clerk. The clerk must immediately notify parties of the court's order on a motion taken under submission. CRC 3.1109(a); ***Kalenian v. Insen*** (2d Dist.2014) 225 Cal.App.4th 569, 579.

1. Method of notice. The clerk can serve notice of the court's order by mail. CRC 3.1109(a). If the order is appealable, the clerk's notice must comply with CCP §1013(a). *See* ***Triumph Precision Prods. v. Insurance Co. of N. Am.*** (2d Dist.1979) 91 Cal.App.3d 362, 365 (CCP §1013(a) applies to mailing of clerk's notice announcing entry of appealable order). See "Regular mail," ch. 1-G, §5.1.2, p. 67.

2. Form of notice. The notice must specifically identify the matter ruled on, and if there are more than two parties, the notice must also name the moving party and the party against whom relief was requested. CRC 3.1109(b).

3. Effect of no notice. The clerk's failure to give notice does not extend the time for performing any act, except the time to appeal. CRC 3.1109(c).

§5.2 Notice by party. The prevailing party must serve the other parties with notice of the court's order, unless the court orders otherwise or all other parties waived the right to notice in open court and their waiver was recorded in the court's minutes. CCP §1019.5(a).

1. Method of notice. The prevailing party can serve notice of the court's order by personal delivery, regular mail, or express mail or by fax or electronic service when the parties have agreed to it. *See* CCP §1019.5(a); *see, e.g.*, ***Forrest v. Department of Corps.*** (2d Dist.2007) 150 Cal.App.4th 183, 193 (prevailing party served notice of order by express mail), *disapproved on other grounds*, ***Shalant v. Girardi*** (2011) 51 Cal.4th 1164; *see also* CCP §§1010.6-1013 (rules for service by personal delivery, mail, fax, and electronic delivery). See "Methods of service," ch. 1-G, §5.1, p. 66.

2. Form of notice. The prevailing party should provide notice of the court's order by drafting a notice and attaching a copy of the order. *See* CCP §1010 (notice must be in writing, and copy of paper should accompany notice if paper was not previously served on or filed by party receiving it); *see, e.g.*, ***People v. $20,000 U.S. Currency*** (3d Dist.1991) 235 Cal.App.3d 682, 686 (prevailing party served notice of order by mailing copy to opposing counsel and including notice recounting court's ruling).

§5.3 Notice by court. The court must serve the parties with notice of an order made on the court's own motion—that is, any order not issued in response to a party's motion or application. CCP §1019.5(b); ***California Bus. Council for Equal Opportunity v. Superior Ct.*** (3d Dist.1997) 52 Cal.App.4th 1100, 1106. Notice by the court is not required if all parties waived the right to notice in open court and their waiver was entered in the minutes. CCP §1019.5(b); ***California Bus. Council***, 52 Cal.App.4th at 1106.

1. **Method of notice.** The court can serve notice of its order by personal delivery or mail. *See* CCP §§1011, 1012, 1019.5(b); ***California Bus. Council***, 52 Cal.App.4th at 1106.

2. **Manner of notice.** The court should provide notice of its order by drafting a notice of entry and attaching a copy of the order. *See* CCP §1010 (notice must be in writing, and copy of paper should accompany notice if paper was not previously served on or filed by party receiving it).

§6. CHANGING RULING

Until an order is entered on the record, the court can change its ruling for any reason. *See* ***Darling, Hall & Rae v. Kritt*** (2d Dist.1999) 75 Cal.App.4th 1148, 1156. Once an order is entered, however, the court can change its ruling only in the following ways:

§6.1 Court's inherent power. A court retains the inherent authority to change its ruling at any time before the entry of judgment. ***Darling, Hall & Rae v. Kritt*** (2d Dist.1999) 75 Cal.App.4th 1148, 1156. A court must act on its own motion to initiate this process, and a party's motion asking the court to reconsider on this basis is improper. *See* ***Le Francois v. Goel*** (2005) 35 Cal.4th 1094, 1108. But a party can informally ask the court (e.g., at a status conference) to reconsider an earlier ruling as long as opposing counsel is present. *Id.*; Weil, *Civil Procedure Before Trial*, ¶9:327.6. If the court intends to reconsider an earlier ruling, it must notify the parties of its intention, solicit briefing, and hold a hearing. ***Le Francois***, 35 Cal.4th at 1108.

§6.2 Motion for reconsideration. A party can ask the court to reconsider and enter a different ruling on an issue by filing a motion for reconsideration. See "Motion for Reconsideration," ch. 5-G, §3, p. 508.

§6.3 Motion for renewal. When a motion has been denied in whole or in part, the movant can request the same relief at a later time by filing a motion for renewal. See "Motion for Renewal," ch. 5-G, §4, p. 516.

§7. REVIEW

§7.1 Challenging ruling. There are three ways to challenge a superior court's ruling:

1. **Appeal after final judgment.** Generally, a party can challenge a ruling only by appeal after the superior court renders a final judgment. *See* CCP §904.1(a); ***Angell v. Superior Ct.*** (4th Dist.1999) 73 Cal.App.4th 691, 697.

2. **Interlocutory appeal.** Some interlocutory orders can be challenged before the rendition of a final judgment. Examples of these appealable orders include the following:

(1) An interlocutory order for an accounting in an action to redeem real or personal property from a mortgage or lien. CCP §904.1(a)(8).

(2) An interlocutory order directing that partition be made in an action for partition. *Id.* §904.1(a)(9); *see* ***Williams v. Wells Fargo Bank & Un. Trust Co.*** (1941) 17 Cal.2d 104, 106.

(3) An interlocutory order for sanctions exceeding $5,000. CCP §904.1(a)(11).

(4) A final collateral order. ***Malek v. Koshak*** (2d Dist.2011) 200 Cal.App.4th 1540, 1545. See "Final collateral order," ch. 7-A, §17.1.2(3), p. 777.

NOTE

For an in-depth discussion of appealable judgments and orders, see 9 Witkin, Cal. Procedure, Appeal, §§85-94.

3. **Extraordinary writ.** The term "extraordinary writ" refers to writs of mandamus, prohibition, certiorari, habeas corpus, and other similar actions. ***Gales v. Superior Ct.*** (2d Dist.1996) 47 Cal.App.4th 1596, 1602. Extraordinary writs are usually used by a party to obtain relief from a nonappealable order.

(1) Mandamus. A party can seek a writ of mandamus (or mandate) to obtain relief from a nonappealable order. ***City of Hanford v. Superior Ct.*** (5th Dist.1989) 208 Cal.App.3d 580, 586; *see* CCP §1085; *see also id.* §1084 (mandamus also called mandate).

(2) Prohibition. A party can seek a writ of prohibition to obtain relief from a nonappealable order issued by a court acting outside its jurisdiction. ***Citizens Utils. Co. v. Superior Ct.*** (1963) 59 Cal.2d 805, 813; *see* CCP §§1102, 1103. Even if an order is appealable, a party can seek a writ of prohibition when the remedy by appeal is inadequate. 9 Witkin, *Cal. Procedure*, Appeal, §91.

(3) Certiorari. A party can seek a writ of certiorari (or review) to obtain relief from a nonappealable order issued by a court acting outside its jurisdiction. *See* CCP §1068; ***Kramer v. Superior Court*** (1950) 36 Cal.2d 159, 161-62; *see also* CCP §1067 (writ of certiorari also called writ of review). Unlike a writ of prohibition, certiorari is not an available remedy if an appeal is possible. *See* CCP §1068(a). The scope of this review is limited to defects in jurisdiction; insufficiency of evidence and errors of law within jurisdiction are not reviewable. 9 Witkin, *Cal. Procedure*, Appeal, §91; *see* ***Kramer***, 36 Cal.2d at 162.

§7.2 Standards of review.

1. Legal issues. Questions of law are reviewed de novo, without any deference to the superior court's decision. ***Young v. McCoy*** (2d Dist.2007) 147 Cal.App.4th 1078, 1083 (questions of law reviewed de novo); ***Wagner v. Columbia Pictures Indus.*** (2d Dist.2007) 146 Cal.App.4th 586, 589 (no deference to superior court's findings when reviewing de novo). For example, interpretation of a statute is a question of law. ***Young***, 147 Cal.App.4th at 1083.

2. Fact issues. Appellate courts will defer to the superior court's rulings when reviewing issues of fact. ***Ghirardo v. Antonioli*** (1994) 8 Cal.4th 791, 800. The appellate court will overturn the superior court's ruling on a fact issue only if there is no substantial evidence to support the court's findings. ***Road Sprinkler Fitters Local Un. v. G&G Fire Sprinklers, Inc.*** (3d Dist.2002) 102 Cal.App.4th 765, 782.

3. Court's discretion. When a matter falls within the sound discretion of the superior court (e.g., a discovery dispute), the appropriate standard of review is abuse of discretion. ***Britts v. Superior Ct.*** (6th Dist.2006) 145 Cal.App.4th 1112, 1123. Under this standard, the appellate court must defer to the superior court's ruling unless it is arbitrary, capricious, entirely lacking in evidentiary support, or inconsistent with proper procedure. ***D.H. Williams Constr., Inc. v. Clovis Unified Sch. Dist.*** (5th Dist.2007) 146 Cal.App.4th 757, 763.

California Civil Pretrial

Chapter 2. Attorneys & Judges

Table of Contents

TABLE OF CONTENTS

2. ATTORNEYS & JUDGES

A. APPLICATION TO APPEAR PRO HAC VICE

This subchapter discusses applications to appear pro hac vice in California superior courts. This subchapter does not discuss pro hac vice applications in the California Supreme Court or courts of appeals, nor does it discuss other methods that nonlicensed attorneys can use to appear in California courts. For the rules on these topics, see CRC 9.40-9.48.

§1. GENERAL

§1.1 Purpose. An application to appear pro hac vice allows an out-of-state attorney to handle a specific case in a California court. CRC 9.40(a); *see Black's Law Dictionary* 1405 (10th ed. 2014).

§1.2 Primary authority. CRC 9.40.

§1.3 Secondary authority. The following secondary source is cited as authority in this subchapter:

- Younger & Bradley, *Younger on California Motions* (2014-15) (referred to as Younger, *Cal. Motions*).

§2. APPLICATION

§2.1 Who can file. An application to appear pro hac vice can be made by an eligible out-of-state attorney. CRC 9.40(a). To be eligible, the attorney must meet the following requirements:

1. Be a member in good standing of, and be eligible to practice before, the bar of any federal court or the highest court in any U.S. state or territory other than California. *Id.*

2. Have already been retained in a particular case pending in a California court. *Id.*

3. Be associated with an attorney of record who is an active member of the California State Bar. *Id.*

4. Not be a California resident. CRC 9.40(a)(1).

5. Not be regularly employed in California. CRC 9.40(a)(2).

6. Not be regularly engaged in substantial business, professional, or other activities in California. CRC 9.40(a)(3). Trial courts have broad discretion in deciding what are substantial activities. *See* ***Walter E. Heller W., Inc. v. Superior Ct.*** (2d Dist.1980) 111 Cal.App.3d 706, 711. For example, one court has held that an out-of-state attorney's three-year representation of a California client by telephone and written correspondence did not qualify as substantial activity in California. *Id.* at 710-11.

§2.2 Filing & serving.

1. **Filing.** The applicant must file a verified application and proof of service with the court in which she is requesting permission to appear pro hac vice. CRC 9.40(c)(1). See "Proving service by mail or express mail," ch. 1-G, §7.1.3, p. 75.

2. **Serving.**

(1) **Parties.** The applicant must serve a copy of the application and a notice of hearing on all parties who have appeared in the case. CRC 9.40(c)(1). The notice of hearing must be served at least 16 court days before the hearing, unless the court requires a shorter period. *See* CCP §1005(b); CRC 9.40(c)(1).

NOTE

Although CRC 9.40(c)(1) states that the proof of service must be made by mail under CCP §1013a, it is unlikely that a court will refuse to hear an application if the opposing party is personally served. See Younger, Cal. Motions, §19:14.

(2) State Bar of California. The applicant must serve a copy of the application, a copy of the notice of hearing, and a $50 application fee on the State Bar of California at its San Francisco office. *See* CRC 9.40(c)(1), (e). A credit-card payment form can be obtained from the State Bar's website at admissions.calbar.ca.gov/Requirements/ProHacVice.aspx.

§2.3 Form. An application to appear pro hac vice should be in writing and in the same form as other motion papers. State Bar of California, *Pro Hac Vice*, admissions.calbar.ca.gov/Requirements/ProHacVice.aspx; *see* CRC 9.40(a), (c)(1). See "Motion Papers," ch. 1-D, §5, p. 27. The application must contain a notice of hearing. CRC 9.40(c)(1). See "Motions," ch. 1-B, §2.5.2(6)(c), p. 13.

§2.4 Contents.

1. Application.

(1) Generally. An application to appear pro hac vice must state the following:

(a) The applicant's residential and office addresses. CRC 9.40(d)(1).

(b) The courts to which the applicant has been admitted to practice and the dates of admission. CRC 9.40(d)(2).

(c) That the applicant is a member in good standing in those courts. CRC 9.40(d)(3).

(d) That the applicant is not currently suspended or disbarred in any court. CRC 9.40(d)(4).

(e) Whether the applicant has filed an application to appear pro hac vice in California within the past two years and, if so, the titles of the courts and cases in which the applicant filed an earlier application, the date of each application, and whether the applications were granted. CRC 9.40(d)(5).

(f) The name, address, and telephone number of the active member of the State Bar of California who is the attorney of record. CRC 9.40(d)(6).

(2) Verified. The application must be verified under penalty of perjury under California law. *See* CCP §2015.5; CRC 9.40(c)(1).

2. Memorandum of points & authorities. No memorandum of law is required for an application to appear pro hac vice.

3. Supporting evidence. No additional evidence is required to support an application to appear pro hac vice.

PRACTICE TIP

The applicant should call the court clerk to ask if the court has additional requirements for the application. admissions.calbar.ca.gov/Requirements/ProHacVice.aspx.

---

§2.5 Filing fees. An applicant seeking permission to appear pro hac vice in a superior court must pay a $500 filing fee. Gov. C. §70617(e)(1). See "Filing Fees," ch. 1-F, §7, p. 58.

NOTE

The filing fee under Gov. C. §70617(e)(1) is in addition to the $50 application fee the attorney must pay to the State Bar of California under CRC 9.40(e).

---

§3. OPPOSITION

A party can file an opposition to an application to appear pro hac vice. *See, e.g.*, ***Ross v. Kish*** (2d Dist.2006) 145 Cal.App.4th 188, 193 (P opposed D's attorney's pro hac vice appearance); ***Walter E. Heller W., Inc. v. Superior Ct.*** (2d Dist.1980) 111 Cal.App.3d 706, 709 (D opposed Ps' attorney's pro hac vice appearance). The party can oppose the

application on the grounds that the applicant is not eligible to appear or has appeared pro hac vice too many times in California. *See* CRC 9.40(b) (repeated pro hac vice appearances are cause for denial of application); *see, e.g.*, ***Ross***, 145 Cal.App.4th at 193 (applicant's request for pro hac vice admission was denied because he did not associate with member of State Bar of California, his registration with New York State Bar Association was delinquent, and his notice of hearing was defective); ***Walter E. Heller W., Inc.***, 111 Cal.App.3d at 710-11 (D unsuccessfully opposed Ps' attorney's pro hac vice appearance on ground that attorney made several trips to California and did significant work for California clients). See "Who can file," §2.1, p. 99. Whether an applicant has appeared pro hac vice too many times to appear again is in the court's discretion. *See, e.g.*, ***Walter E. Heller W., Inc.***, 111 Cal.App.3d at 710 (one previous pro hac vice appearance was not cause to deny pro hac vice application). For a discussion of filing an opposition, see "Opposition Papers," ch. 1-D, §8, p. 35.

NOTE

Courts usually grant an application to appear pro hac vice, so oppositions should be filed only in exceptional circumstances. Younger, Cal. Motions, §19.17.

§4. HEARING

Hearings on applications to appear pro hac vice are conducted in the same manner as civil hearings generally. See "Hearings," ch. 1-H, p. 79.

PRACTICE TIP

The applicant should call the court clerk to see if the California attorney of record needs to attend the hearing.

§5. RULING

The court's ruling on an application to appear pro hac vice is discretionary. CRC 9.40(a); *see* ***U.S. Golf Ass'n v. Arroyo Software Corp.*** (1st Dist.1999) 69 Cal.App.4th 607, 624; ***Walter E. Heller W., Inc. v. Superior Ct.*** (2d Dist.1980) 111 Cal.App.3d 706, 711.

§6. ORDER

§6.1 Form. The court's ruling on an application to appear pro hac vice should be recorded either in writing or by minute order. See "Record of Ruling," ch. 1-I, §4, p. 90.

§6.2 Effect of ruling. If the court grants the application to appear pro hac vice, the pro hac vice attorney's conduct is subject to the jurisdiction of the California courts and the State Bar of California to the same extent as members of the State Bar of California. CRC 9.40(f). The court can revoke the attorney's pro hac vice status or impose sanctions against the attorney for misconduct. ***Sheller v. Superior Ct.*** (2d Dist.2008) 158 Cal.App.4th 1697, 1716-17.

§6.3 Maintaining status. To maintain pro hac vice status in a case that extends beyond a year, the attorney must pay a renewal fee of $500 by the anniversary of the date the application to appear pro hac vice was granted. Gov. C. §70617(e)(2). The renewal fee must be paid for each year the attorney wants to maintain pro hac vice status in the case. *Id.*

§7. MOTION FOR RECONSIDERATION

A party who unsuccessfully made or opposed an application to appear pro hac vice can file a motion for reconsideration. CCP §1008(a). See "Motion for Reconsideration," ch. 5-G, §3, p. 508.

§8. MOTION FOR RENEWAL

A party who unsuccessfully made an application to appear pro hac vice can file a motion for renewal. CCP §1008(b). See "Motion for Renewal," ch. 5-G, §4, p. 516.

§9. APPELLATE REVIEW

§9.1 Writ of mandate. An order granting or denying an application to appear pro hac vice can be reviewed by writ of mandate. Younger, *Cal. Motions*, §19:19; *see* ***Walter E. Heller W., Inc. v. Superior Ct.*** (2d Dist.1980) 111 Cal.App.3d 706, 708. The trial court's ruling on the application to appear pro hac vice is reviewed for abuse of discretion. *See* CRC 9.40(a); ***Walter E. Heller W., Inc.***, 111 Cal.App.3d at 711.

§9.2 No direct appeal. An order granting or denying an application to appear pro hac vice cannot by reviewed by direct appeal. Younger, *Cal. Motions*, §19:19; *see* CCP §§904.1(a), 904.2.

B. ATTORNEY'S WITHDRAWAL OR REMOVAL

This subchapter discusses how an attorney of record can withdraw or be removed under CCP §§284 and 285 and CRC 3.36 and 3.1362. This subchapter does not discuss an attorney's withdrawal in a domestic-relations proceeding under CCP §285.1 or the procedures that apply when an attorney dies, resigns, or is disbarred or suspended from practice. For the statutes and rules on these topics, see CCP §286 and CRC 9.20.

§1. GENERAL

§1.1 Purpose. The purpose of an attorney's withdrawal or removal is to end the relationship between the attorney and the client. *See* CCP §§284, 285; CRC 3.36.

§1.2 Primary authority. CCP §§284, 285; CRC 3.36, 3.1362; Rules Prof. Conduct, rule 3-700.

§1.3 Secondary authority. The following secondary sources are cited as authority in this subchapter:

- *California Civil Procedure Before Trial* (CEB Online ed. 2014) (referred to as *CEB Procedure Before Trial*).
- Weil & Brown, *California Practice Guide: Civil Procedure Before Trial* (CD-ROM ed. 2014) (referred to as Weil, *Civil Procedure Before Trial*).
- Witkin, *California Procedure* (5th ed. 2008 & Supp.2014) (referred to as Witkin, *Cal. Procedure*).
- Younger & Bradley, *Younger on California Motions* (2014-15) (referred to as Younger, *Cal. Motions*).

§1.4 Judicial Council forms.

- MC-050 (mandatory), substitution of attorney without court order.
- MC-051 (mandatory), notice of motion and motion to be relieved as counsel.
- MC-052 (mandatory), declaration in support of attorney's motion to be relieved as counsel.
- MC-053 (mandatory), order granting attorney's motion to be relieved as counsel.
- MC-950 (mandatory), notice of limited-scope representation.
- MC-955 (optional), application to be relieved as attorney on completion of limited-scope representation.
- MC-956 (optional), objection to application to be relieved as attorney on completion of limited-scope representation.
- MC-958 (optional), order on application to be relieved as attorney on completion of limited-scope representation.

§2. OVERVIEW

§2.1 Methods of withdrawal or removal. An attorney of record can withdraw or be removed in the following ways:

1. **Consent.** The attorney and the client can consent to the attorney's withdrawal. CCP §284(1). See "Withdrawal by Consent," §3, p. 104.

2. Client's motion. If the attorney does not consent to the withdrawal, the client can file a motion to remove the attorney. CCP §284(2). See "Client's Motion to Remove Attorney," §4, p. 105.

3. Attorney's motion. If the client does not consent to the withdrawal, the attorney can file a motion to be relieved as counsel. CCP §284(2); CRC 3.1362; *see* CRC 3.36(c), (d). The motion can be brought during the attorney's representation or after the attorney has completed a limited-scope representation. See "Attorney's Motion to Withdraw – Generally," §5, p. 108; "Attorney's Application to Withdraw After Completion of LSR," §6, p. 113.

§2.2 Continuance to hire new attorney. After the withdrawal or removal of an attorney, a client can ask the court for a continuance under CRC 3.1332(c)(4) to hire a new attorney if one has not already been chosen. *See, e.g.*, ***Gottlieb v. Kest*** (2d Dist.2006) 141 Cal.App.4th 110, 129 (client requested and court granted continuance to hire new attorney after consensual withdrawal). See "Requests for Continuance or Stay," ch. 5-I, p. 534. If a continuance is not granted, the client may have to appear pro per (i.e., represent itself) or face a dismissal for lack of representation. See "Pro per substitution," §3.2.2, p. 104.

1. Required showing – interest of justice. Under CRC 3.1332(c)(4), a continuance can be granted if the client can affirmatively show that the attorney's substitution was required in the interest of justice.

2. Court's discretion. The granting of a continuance under CRC 3.1332(c)(4) is discretionary; a client does not have an absolute right to a continuance when an attorney withdraws or is removed. ***County of San Bernardino v. Doria Mining & Eng'g*** (4th Dist.1977) 72 Cal.App.3d 776, 783-84 (discussing Standards of Judicial Administration §9(4), now CRC 3.1332(c)(4)). This is true even when the attorney withdraws right before trial. *See, e.g., id.* at 784 (court did not abuse its discretion by denying continuance requested on day of trial); ***Slaughter v. Zimman*** (2d Dist.1951) 105 Cal.App.2d 623, 625 (court did not abuse its discretion by denying continuance after attorney withdrew eight days before trial).

3. Factors. Some of the factors courts will consider in determining whether to grant a continuance to hire a new attorney include the following:

(1) The client's diligence in seeking a new attorney. ***County of San Bernardino***, 72 Cal.App.3d at 783.

(2) Whether the client had advance notice of the attorney's intent to withdraw. *See, e.g.*, ***Vann v. Shilleh*** (2d Dist.1975) 54 Cal.App.3d 192, 197 (court abused discretion by not granting continuance when attorney withdrew Friday before Monday of trial and client did not have advance warning).

(3) Who requested the substitution. *See, e.g., id.* (court considered that it was attorney who sought withdrawal, not client).

(4) Whether the substitution was necessary—that is, was the attorney of record unable or unwilling to represent the party. ***County of San Bernardino***, 72 Cal.App.3d at 783.

NOTE

For a discussion of other factors courts can consider in ruling on a motion for continuance, see "Requests for Continuance or Stay," ch. 5-I, p. 534.

§2.3 Ethical duties of attorney.

1. Before withdrawal. An attorney who is withdrawing must take reasonable steps to avoid reasonably foreseeable prejudice to the client's rights. Rules Prof. Conduct, rule 3-700(A)(2). Whether an attorney has taken reasonable steps before withdrawing depends on the circumstances of the case, but an attorney should, at the very least, do the following before withdrawing:

(1) Give notice to the client of the attorney's withdrawal. *Id.*

(2) Allow the client time to hire another attorney. *Id.*; ***Kirsch v. Duryea*** (1978) 21 Cal.3d 303, 310.

(3) Notify the client of upcoming deadlines and court dates. *See* CRC 3.1362(e) (court may delay effective date of order relieving attorney until client has received copy of signed order stating all scheduled hearing dates); *see, e.g.*, ***Miller v. Metzinger*** (2d Dist.1979) 91 Cal.App.3d 31, 42 (attorney had duty to notify client of applicable statute of limitations).

2. After representation ends. After an attorney's representation of a client ends, the attorney has the following duties:

(1) Return client property. The attorney must promptly release to the client all client papers and property if the client requests them, unless a protective order or nondisclosure agreement prevents the release. Rules Prof. Conduct, rule 3-700(D)(1). Client papers and property include all correspondence, pleadings, deposition transcripts, exhibits, physical evidence, expert reports, and other items reasonably necessary for the client's representation. *Id.* The property must be returned regardless of whether the client paid for it. *Id.*

NOTE

The attorney can make and retain copies of the client's papers at the attorney's own expense. Rules Prof. Conduct, rule 3-700, discussion ¶3.

(2) Refund unearned fees. The attorney must promptly refund any fee paid to the attorney that has not been earned. Rules Prof. Conduct, rule 3-700(D)(2). The attorney is not required to refund a retainer fee that was paid solely to ensure that the attorney was available to represent the client. *Id.*

§3. WITHDRAWAL BY CONSENT

Under CCP §284(1), the client and the attorney can consent to the attorney's withdrawal. Normally, when a client asks her attorney to withdraw, the attorney should agree to it. If the attorney does not agree, the client will be forced to file a motion to remove the attorney, and the attorney may be subject to disciplinary action if she does not explain her reasons for not executing the consensual withdrawal. *See* ***Conroy v. State Bar*** (1991) 53 Cal.3d 495, 505 & n.7. See "Client's Motion to Remove Attorney," §4, p. 105. For a discussion of the possible reasons an attorney can give for not agreeing to a consensual withdrawal, see "Opposition," §4.2, p. 106.

§3.1 How to withdraw by consent. A consensual withdrawal under §284(1) can be accomplished in either of the following ways:

1. Form MC-050. The client and the attorney can agree to the withdrawal by filing mandatory Judicial Council Form MC-050 with the court clerk. *See* CCP §284(1). The form must list the name of the former attorney and either list the name and contact information of the new attorney or indicate that the party will appear pro per (i.e., represent itself). Judicial Council Forms, form MC-050. If a new attorney has been chosen, the client, former attorney, and new attorney must sign the form acknowledging their consent to the substitution. *Id.* If the client is appearing pro per, the client and former attorney must sign the form. *Id.*

2. Oral stipulation. The client and the attorney can agree to the withdrawal by an oral stipulation entered in the court minutes. CCP §284(1). The oral stipulation should cover the same matters as in Judicial Council Form MC-050.

§3.2 Court approval.

1. New-attorney substitution. If the client is substituting a new attorney, no court approval is required. *See* ***Hock v. Superior Ct.*** (4th Dist.1990) 221 Cal.App.3d 670, 673-74 (court has no discretion to refuse consensual substitution); Judicial Council Forms, form MC-050 ("Substitution of Attorney—Civil (Without Court Order)").

2. Pro per substitution. If the client elects to appear pro per, court approval may be required if the client cannot appear in that capacity. In most cases, the following parties cannot appear in the capacity of a pro per litigant: guardians, conservators, trustees, personal representatives, probate fiduciaries, corporations, guardians ad litem, and unincorporated associations. Judicial Council Forms, form MC-050. Depending on the circumstances of the case, the court may do the following:

(1) Require court approval before the pro per substitution is effective. *See, e.g.*, Super. Ct. Monterey Cty. Loc. R., rule 4.11.B (court approval required for pro per substitution of attorneys in certain proceedings); Super. Ct. San Diego Cty. Loc. R., rule 4.21.1.B (same).

(2) Require the attorney to remain in the case until a new attorney is substituted. *See, e.g.*, ***Torres v. Friedman*** (2d Dist.1985) 169 Cal.App.3d 880, 887-88 (substitution of guardian ad litem was ineffective and original attorney was never removed as attorney of record).

(3) Accept the pro per substitution, grant the client a continuance to find a new attorney (if a continuance was requested), and dismiss the case for lack of representation if a new attorney is not substituted. *Cf.* ***Ferruzzo v. Superior Ct.*** (4th Dist.1980) 104 Cal.App.3d 501, 504 (court granted attorney's motion to withdraw as attorney for corporation even though corporation was unable to appear pro per and did not have another attorney).

§3.3 Service.

1. Generally. Notice of the substitution of an attorney must be served on all parties to the case. *See* CCP §§284(1), 285; Judicial Council Forms, form MC-050.

2. By mail. If service is made by mail, an unsigned, completed copy of proof of service by mail must be served with the notice of substitution. Judicial Council Forms, form MC-050. After all parties are served, the person who served them must complete and sign the proof of service and give it to the court clerk for filing. *Id.* If the client is substituting itself pro per, someone else must complete service and sign the proof of service by mail. *Id.* See "Proving service by mail or express mail," ch. 1-G, §7.1.3, p. 75.

§3.4 Effective date of substitution. The substitution of an attorney is effective when the adverse party receives written notice of the substitution. *See* CCP §285. Until written notice is received, the adverse party must recognize the former attorney as the attorney of record. *Id.*

§4. CLIENT'S MOTION TO REMOVE ATTORNEY

If the attorney does not consent to the withdrawal, the client can file a motion to remove the attorney. CCP §284(2).

§4.1 Motion.

1. Who can file. The client can file a motion to remove the attorney. CCP §284(2); *see, e.g.*, ***Redevelopment Agency v. Superior Ct.*** (1st Dist.1961) 195 Cal.App.2d 591, 592 (P filed motion to remove attorney after attorney did not consent to substitution).

2. Deadline to file & serve. The motion must be filed and served at least 16 court days before the hearing. CCP §1005(b). See "Retrospective deadlines," ch. 1-G, §6.2, p. 71. If the motion is served by a method other than personal delivery, the client will have to add more time to the 16-day period. CCP §1005(b). See "Add time for method of service," ch. 1-G, §6.2.1(5), p. 72.

3. Contents.

(1) Notice of motion & motion.

(a) Generally. The motion must be requested in writing by noticed motion. ***In re Marriage of Erickson*** (4th Dist.2006) 141 Cal.App.4th 707, 712 n.1; *see* CCP §§284(2), 1005(a)(13). See "Notice of motion & motion," ch. 1-D, §5.1, p. 28.

(b) Relief. The notice of motion and motion must briefly state the relief sought. CRC 3.1110(a) (notice of motion must state nature of order being sought), CRC 3.1112(d)(3) (motion must briefly state relief sought). The notice of motion and motion should ask the court to remove the attorney of record and either substitute a new attorney or permit the client to appear pro per. *See, e.g.*, ***Estate of McManus*** (1st Dist.1963) 214 Cal.App.2d 390, 392 (motion requested substitution of attorney); *cf.* Judicial Council Forms, form MC-050 (client can elect to appear pro per after consensual withdrawal).

NOTE

Before requesting permission to appear pro per, the client should determine whether it is the type of party that can appear in that capacity. See "Pro per substitution," §3.2.2, p. 104.

(c) Grounds. The notice of motion and motion must briefly state the grounds for the attorney's removal. CRC 3.1110(a) (notice of motion must state grounds for issuance of order), CRC 3.1112(d)(3) (motion must briefly state basis for motion). In most situations, a client can remove an attorney with or without cause. ***Fracasse v. Brent*** (1972) 6 Cal.3d 784, 790; ***Redevelopment Agency***, 195 Cal.App.2d at 593. For a discussion of when a client may have to establish cause for removing an attorney, see "Interest in subject matter," §4.2.2(1), this page.

(2) No memorandum of points & authorities. The motion does not have to include a memorandum in support. *Cf.* CRC 3.1114(a)(3) (no memorandum required for attorney's motion to withdraw), CRC 3.1362(b) (same).

(3) Declaration.

(a) Client's declaration. The motion should be supported by a declaration from the client. *See CEB Procedure Before Trial*, §4.58. The client's declaration should state (1) the name of the former attorney, (2) that the former attorney has declined or is unable to sign a consensual withdrawal, and (3) either the name and contact information of the new attorney or that the party will appear pro per. *See id.*

(b) New attorney's declaration. If the client is substituting the former attorney with a new attorney, the motion should be supported by a declaration from the new attorney. *See CEB Procedure Before Trial*, §4.59. The new attorney's declaration should state that the attorney has agreed to act as the client's attorney of record in the case. *See id.*

(4) Proposed order. The client can submit a proposed order with the motion. *See* CRC 3.1113(m). If a proposed order is submitted, it must be lodged and served with the motion papers, not attached to them. *Id.*

4. Filing fees. When the motion is filed, the client must pay a filing fee to the court clerk or request a waiver of the fee. See "Filing Fees," ch. 1-F, §7, p. 58.

§4.2 Opposition. The attorney can respond to a motion to remove by filing an opposition.

1. Deadline to file & serve. See "Deadline to file & serve," ch. 1-D, §8.5.3, p. 37.

2. Grounds. The attorney can file an opposition on the following grounds:

(1) Interest in subject matter. The attorney can oppose the motion on the ground that she has a "power coupled with an interest" in the subject matter of the suit that prevents the client from discharging her without cause. ***Todd v. Superior Ct.*** (1919) 181 Cal. 406, 413; ***Fivey v. Chambers*** (1st Dist.1962) 199 Cal.App.2d 457, 462-63; ***Redevelopment Agency v. Superior Ct.*** (1st Dist.1961) 195 Cal.App.2d 591, 593. Under agency law, when a principal gives an agent a "power coupled with an interest," the agency relationship is considered irrevocable—that is, it is no longer within the power of the principal to terminate the agency at will. ***Becket v. Welton Becket & Assocs.*** (2d Dist.1974) 39 Cal.App.3d 815, 820. This rule of agency law also applies to the attorney-client relationship. *See* ***Isrin v. Superior Ct.*** (1965) 63 Cal.2d 153, 159. If a client gives an attorney the power to act as its attorney and that power is coupled with an interest, the client cannot terminate the relationship without cause. A power is coupled with an interest when one of the following is true:

(a) The attorney has a beneficial interest in the subject matter of the litigation—other than an interest in recovering fees from the litigation—and that interest is enforceable in the attorney's own name. ***Isrin***, 63 Cal.2d at 159-60; ***Todd***, 181 Cal. at 417; *see, e.g.*, ***O'Connell v. Superior Ct.*** (1935) 2 Cal.2d 418, 423-24 (attorney could be discharged without cause because employment contract did not give attorney interest in subject matter of litigation; it only gave attorney interest in recovering fees to compensate for attorney's services); ***Redevelopment***

Agency, 195 Cal.App.2d at 594-95 (city's attorney could not be discharged without cause because city agency contracted with city to litigate all issues involving condemnation of city property and city had social and economic interest in condemned property).

(b) The power is given as security for the payment of money other than for the attorney's services. ***Todd***, 181 Cal. at 417; *see, e.g.*, ***Norton v. Whitehead*** (1890) 84 Cal. 263, 268 (P loaned money to contractor to complete work on contract, and in return, contractor gave P power of attorney to collect money due on contract; power of attorney was not revoked by contractor's death because power was coupled with interest).

(c) The power is given as security for the performance of any act that is deemed valuable. ***Todd***, 181 Cal. at 417.

(2) Improper notice. The attorney can oppose the motion on the ground that she was not given proper notice of the motion. *See, e.g.*, ***Rundberg v. Belcher*** (1897) 118 Cal. 589, 590-91 (court denied motion when timely notice was not given to attorney).

(3) Client cannot represent itself. The attorney can oppose the motion on the ground that the client has elected to appear pro per but cannot appear in that capacity. See "Pro per substitution," §3.2.2, p. 104.

3. Contents. For a general discussion of the contents of an opposition, see "Opposition Papers," ch. 1-D, §8, p. 35.

§4.3 Reply. The movant can file and serve a reply to the opposition. The reply must be filed and served at least five court days before the hearing. CCP §1005(b). See "Reply Papers," ch. 1-D, §9, p. 37.

§4.4 Hearing. Hearings on a motion to remove are conducted in the same manner as civil hearings generally. See "Hearings," ch. 1-H, p. 79.

§4.5 Ruling. Under most circumstances, the court must grant a client's motion to remove its attorney because a client has an absolute right to discharge its attorney for any reason. *See* ***Fracasse v. Brent*** (1972) 6 Cal.3d 784, 790; ***Redevelopment Agency v. Superior Ct.*** (1st Dist.1961) 195 Cal.App.2d 591, 593; *see, e.g.*, ***In re Estate of Hardenberg*** (1936) 6 Cal.2d 371, 371-72 (court granted motion to remove attorney even when opposition argued that client was bribed or blackmailed into substituting attorneys). For a discussion of the limited circumstances in which a court can deny a motion to remove an attorney, see "Grounds," §4.2.2, p. 106.

§4.6 Order.

1. Form. The court's ruling on the motion to remove the attorney must be recorded either in writing or by minute order. See "Record of Ruling," ch. 1-I, §4, p. 90.

2. Contents. If the court grants the order, the order should state the name of the person being substituted for the former attorney (i.e., either the name of the new attorney or the client's name if the client is going to appear pro per). *See CEB Procedure Before Trial*, §4.60.

3. Effective date of substitution. See "Effective date of substitution," §3.4, p. 105.

§4.7 Motion for reconsideration. A party who is adversely affected by a court's order on a motion to remove an attorney can file a motion for reconsideration. CCP §1008(a). See "Motion for Reconsideration," ch. 5-G, §3, p. 508.

§4.8 Motion for renewal. A party whose motion to remove an attorney is denied can file a motion for renewal. CCP §1008(b). See "Motion for Renewal," ch. 5-G, §4, p. 516.

§4.9 Appellate review. The court's ruling on a motion to remove an attorney cannot be challenged on appeal until the court renders a final judgment in the case. *See* CCP §904.1(a). A party or the attorney can challenge the court's ruling before a final judgment, however, by filing a petition for a writ of mandate. *See* ***Todd v. Superior Ct.*** (1919) 181 Cal. 406, 408; ***Rundberg v. Belcher*** (1897) 118 Cal. 589, 590; ***Redevelopment Agency v. Superior Ct.*** (1st Dist.1961) 195 Cal.App.2d 591, 592.

§5. ATTORNEY'S MOTION TO WITHDRAW – GENERALLY

If the client does not consent to the attorney's withdrawal, the attorney can file a motion to withdraw (also known as a motion to be relieved as counsel). *See* CCP §284(2); CRC 3.1362.

§5.1 Grounds. An attorney can file a motion to withdraw if (1) the basis for her withdrawal is either mandatory or permissive under the Rules of Professional Conduct and (2) the withdrawal would not prejudice the interests of the client or another party.

1. Basis for withdrawal.

(1) Mandatory. Under the Rules of Professional Conduct, an attorney must file a motion to withdraw if any of the following is true:

(a) Action brought to harass or injure. The attorney knows or should know that her client is bringing an action, conducting a defense, asserting a position in litigation, or taking an appeal without probable cause and for the purpose of harassing or maliciously injuring any person. Rules Prof. Conduct, rule 3-700(B)(1).

(b) Unreasonably difficult to continue representation. The attorney's mental or physical condition makes it unreasonably difficult to carry out her employment effectively. Rules Prof. Conduct, rule 3-700(B)(3).

(c) Definite rule violation. The attorney knows or should know that continued employment will result in a violation of the Rules of Professional Conduct or the State Bar Act (i.e., Bus. & Prof. C. §§6000-6243). Rules Prof. Conduct, rule 3-700(B)(2).

CAUTION

If there is a mandatory basis for withdrawal and the attorney does not request a withdrawal, the attorney may be subject to disciplinary sanctions, a motion to disqualify, civil damages, and the forfeiture of attorney fees. See, e.g., ***Jeffry v. Pounds*** *(3d Dist.1977) 67 Cal.App.3d 6, 12 (firm not entitled to fees for services rendered after violation of rule of professional conduct);* ***Ishmael v. Millington*** *(3d Dist.1966) 241 Cal.App.2d 520, 526-27 (former client sued attorney for loss of property caused by attorney's lack of full disclosure in dual representation).* *See "Motion to Disqualify Attorney," ch. 2-C, p. 118.*

---

(2) Permissive. Under the Rules of Professional Conduct, an attorney can request a withdrawal if any of the following is true:

(a) Client problems. The client does any of the following:

[1] Insists on presenting a claim or defense that is not warranted under existing law and cannot be supported by a good-faith argument for an extension, a modification, or a reversal of existing law. Rules Prof. Conduct, rule 3-700(C)(1)(a).

[2] Seeks to pursue an illegal course of conduct or insists that the attorney pursue a course of conduct that is illegal or prohibited by the Rules of Professional Conduct or the State Bar Act. Rules Prof. Conduct, rule 3-700(C)(1)(b), (C)(1)(c).

[3] Makes it unreasonably difficult for the attorney to carry out her employment effectively. *Id.* rule 3-700(C)(1)(d); *see, e.g.,* ***Loeb v. Record*** (5th Dist.2008) 162 Cal.App.4th 431, 439 (attorney-client relationship had eroded substantially, and client refused to execute documents leading to resolution of case or substitution of attorney); ***Steven M. Garber & Assocs. v. Eskandarian*** (2d Dist.2007) 150 Cal.App.4th 813, 818 (motion to be relieved as counsel granted when attorney lost contact with client); ***Rus, Miliband & Smith v. Conkle & Olesten*** (4th Dist.2003) 113 Cal.App.4th 656, 667 (firm filed motion to be relieved as counsel because of breakdown in communications with client).

[4] Insists, in a matter not pending before a tribunal, that the attorney engage in conduct that is contrary to her judgment and advice but is not prohibited by the Rules of Professional Conduct or the State Bar Act. Rules Prof. Conduct, rule 3-700(C)(1)(e).

[5] Breaches an agreement or obligation to the attorney involving expenses or fees. *Id.* rule 3-700(C)(1)(f); *see, e.g.*, ***Ferruzzo v. Superior Ct.*** (4th Dist.1980) 104 Cal.App.3d 501, 502 (motion to withdraw filed for noncooperation and nonpayment of attorney fees).

(b) Possible rule violation. The attorney's continued employment is likely to result in a violation of the Rules of Professional Conduct or the State Bar Act. Rules Prof. Conduct, rule 3-700(C)(2).

(c) Inability to work with co-counsel. The attorney's inability to work with co-counsel indicates that the client's best interests will likely be served by withdrawal. Rules Prof. Conduct, rule 3-700(C)(3).

(d) Difficulty of representation. The attorney's mental or physical condition makes it difficult for her to carry out her employment effectively. Rules Prof. Conduct, rule 3-700(C)(4).

(e) Good cause for withdrawal. The attorney believes in good faith, in a proceeding pending before a tribunal, that the tribunal will find other good cause for withdrawal. Rules Prof. Conduct, rule 3-700(C)(6).

2. No prejudice to client or other parties. An attorney can request a withdrawal as long as the withdrawal would not prejudice the interests of the client or another party. *See* Rules Prof. Conduct, rule 3-700(A)(2) (client's interests); ***Ramirez v. Sturdevant*** (1st Dist.1994) 21 Cal.App.4th 904, 915 (same); ***Hodcarriers, Bldg. & Common Laborers Local Un. v. Miller*** (4th Dist.1966) 243 Cal.App.2d 391, 395 (third party's interests); ***Linn v. Superior Ct.*** (2d Dist.1926) 79 Cal.App. 721, 725 (same). Because prejudice is often asserted as a ground for opposing the withdrawal, the attorney should try to address any prejudicial concerns in her declaration. See "Declaration," §5.2.3(3), this page. For example, if an attorney seeks a withdrawal on the eve of trial, it is likely to be considered both prejudicial and an ethical violation. *See* ***Vann v. Shilleh*** (2d Dist.1975) 54 Cal.App.3d 192, 197. Under Rule of Professional Conduct 3-700(A)(2), an attorney has an ethical duty to give her client sufficient notice and time to hire a new attorney before withdrawing. See "Ethical duties of attorney," §2.3, p. 103. The violation of this ethical duty may be unavoidable, however, if the attorney discovers on the eve of trial that she has a mandatory duty to withdraw under the Rules of Professional Conduct. *See* Rules Prof. Conduct, rule 3-700(B). See "Mandatory," §5.1.1(1), p. 108. In this instance, the attorney should explain the emergency nature of the late motion. For a discussion of other factors an attorney might want to address to counter a claim of prejudice, see "Grounds – prejudice," §5.3.2, p. 111.

§5.2 Motion.

1. Who can file. The attorney can file a motion to withdraw. CCP §284(2); *see* CRC 3.1362.

2. Deadline to file & serve. The motion must be filed with the court and served on the client and all parties who have appeared in the case at least 16 court days before the hearing. *See* CCP §1005(b); CRC 3.1362(d). See "Retrospective deadlines," ch. 1-G, §6.2, p. 71. If the motion is served by a method other than personal delivery, the attorney will have to add more time to the 16-day period. CCP §1005(b). See "Add time for method of service," ch. 1-G, §6.2.1(5), p. 72.

3. Contents.

(1) Notice of motion & motion. The notice of motion and motion must be made using Judicial Council Form MC-051. CRC 3.1362(a).

(2) No memorandum of points & authorities. The motion does not have to include a memorandum in support. CRC 3.1114(a)(3), 3.1362(b).

(3) Declaration. The motion must be supported by a declaration from the attorney. CRC 3.1362(c). The declaration must be made using Judicial Council Form MC-052. CRC 3.1362(c). The declaration must address the following:

(a) Reasons for withdrawal.

[1] Generally. The declaration must state, in general terms, why a motion to withdraw was brought instead of filing a consensual withdrawal under CCP §284(1). CRC 3.1362(c); Judicial Council Forms, form MC-052.

[2] Withdrawal based on confidential information. If the reason for withdrawal is based on confidential information, the declaration should state, in general terms, the basis for the withdrawal without compromising the confidentiality of the attorney-client relationship. CRC 3.1362(c). When the duty of confidentiality prevents the attorney from disclosing the underlying basis for the withdrawal, the court cannot force the attorney to disclose the protected information. ***Aceves v. Superior Ct.*** (4th Dist.1996) 51 Cal.App.4th 584, 596. But this does not mean that the court is obligated to accept a blanket statement that confidential information requires the attorney's withdrawal. *E.g.*, ***Manfredi & Levine v. Superior Ct.*** (2d Dist.1998) 66 Cal.App.4th 1128, 1134 (court did not abuse its discretion by denying motion to withdraw when court asked attorney to explain conflict and attorney replied that he could not and would not explain it). The court has a duty to explore the basis for the withdrawal, and the attorney has a corresponding duty to respond and describe the general nature of the conflict as fully as possible within the confines of the duty of confidentiality. *Id.*; ***Aceves***, 51 Cal.App.4th at 592-93. For example, if an attorney claims that she has a conflict of interest but the attorney-client privilege prevents her from disclosing the basis of the withdrawal, the attorney should (1) give meaningful information about the general nature of the conflict, (2) make clear that the attorney evaluated exceptions to the privilege, and (3) state whether a conflict is likely to occur if a new attorney is hired. *See* ***Manfredi & Levine***, 66 Cal.App.4th at 1135-36. If there is no question about the attorney's good faith or sincerity, the court should accept the attorney's explanation. ***Leversen v. Superior Ct.*** (1983) 34 Cal.3d 530, 539; *see* ***Aceves***, 51 Cal.App.4th at 593-94 (it is proper for court to rely solely on attorney's explanation because attorney is in best position to determine if conflict would affect quality of representation); *see, e.g.*, ***Manfredi & Levine***, 66 Cal.App.4th at 1133-34 (court questioned attorney's good faith and sincerity because attorney used several delay tactics and refused to give general description of conflict).

PRACTICE TIP

If the attorney's withdrawal is based on confidential information, the attorney can avoid the risk of accidentally disclosing that information in the declaration by simply asking the court for an in camera hearing. Younger, Cal. Motions, §17:19; see ***Manfredi & Levine****, 66 Cal.App.4th at 1136; see, e.g.,* ***Forrest v. Department of Corps.*** *(2d Dist.2007) 150 Cal.App.4th 183, 194 (after attorney filed conclusory declaration that continued representation would require him to violate ethical rules, court held in camera hearing), disapproved on other grounds,* ***Shalant v. Girardi*** *(2011) 51 Cal.4th 1164. See "In camera," §5.5.2, p. 111.*

(b) Service. The attorney's declaration must state how the notice of motion and motion, the declaration, and the proposed order were served on the client. Judicial Council Forms, form MC-052; *see* CRC 3.1362(d). If the attorney has been unable to serve the client, the attorney's declaration should state why the motion should still be granted. Judicial Council Forms, form MC-052.

(4) Supporting evidence. For a discussion of the types of evidence that can be used to support a motion, see "Supporting evidence," ch. 1-D, §5.3, p. 30.

(5) Request for judicial notice. If the motion to withdraw is based on matters the court can take judicial notice of, the attorney can ask the court to take judicial notice of the matters. *See* CRC 3.1113(*l*). A request for judicial notice must be made in a separate document. *Id.* See "Request for Judicial Notice," ch. 5-J, p. 547.

(6) Proposed order. The motion must be accompanied by a proposed order in the form of Judicial Council Form MC-053. CRC 3.1362(e). The proposed order must be served on the client and all other parties who have appeared in the case. CRC 3.1362(d). The order must specify all hearing dates scheduled in the case, including the day of trial, if known. CRC 3.1362(e). If no hearing date is scheduled, the court can set one and specify that in the order. *Id.*

4. Filing fees. When the motion is filed, the attorney must pay a filing fee to the court clerk. See "Filing Fees," ch. 1-F, §7, p. 58.

§5.3 Opposition. The client or another party can respond to a motion to withdraw by filing an opposition. Younger, *Cal. Motions*, §17:32 (client or another party), §17.33 (another party); *see, e.g.*, ***Manfredi & Levine v. Superior Ct.*** (2d Dist.1998) 66 Cal.App.4th 1128, 1131 (Ds filed opposition to P's attorney's motion to withdraw).

1. Deadline to file & serve. See "Deadline to file & serve," ch. 1-D, §8.5.3, p. 37.

2. Grounds – prejudice. A party can oppose the motion on the ground that it would prejudice the client's or another party's interests. *See* Rules Prof. Conduct, rule 3-700(A)(2) (client's interests); ***Ramirez v. Sturdevant*** (1st Dist.1994) 21 Cal.App.4th 904, 915 (same); ***Hodcarriers, Bldg. & Common Laborers Local Un. v. Miller*** (4th Dist.1966) 243 Cal.App.2d 391, 395 (another party's interests); ***Linn v. Superior Ct.*** (2d Dist.1926) 79 Cal.App. 721, 725 (same). In determining whether the interests of a client or another party would be prejudiced by an attorney's withdrawal, courts have considered the following factors:

(1) The amount of notice given to the client. ***Linn***, 79 Cal.App. at 725.

(2) The amount of time already committed to the representation. *See, e.g.*, *id.* (attorney spent over two years representing client on legal matter).

(3) The costs that have already been incurred and the cost of hiring a new attorney. *See id.*; *see, e.g.*, ***Moore v. U.S.*** (E.D.Cal.2008) No. CIV S-04-423 FCD JFM (slip op.; 4-28-08) (client would not be financially prejudiced because case was taken on contingency basis and, by asserting contractual right to withdraw, attorney abandoned right to fees).

(4) Whether the withdrawal would delay a pending trial or hearing. ***Mandell v. Superior Ct.*** (2d Dist.1977) 67 Cal.App.3d 1, 4; *see* Younger, *Cal. Motions*, §17:30 (closer motion is brought to trial, more likely court is to deny it); *see, e.g.*, ***Hodcarriers, Bldg. & Common Laborers***, 243 Cal.App.2d at 395 (motion denied in part because it was requested during recess in trial); ***Linn***, 79 Cal.App. at 725 (motion brought on day before trial could have led to continuance and possible injury to another party).

NOTE

Prejudice is the only ground that can be asserted in opposition to a motion to withdraw. Younger, Cal. Motions, §17:33.

---

3. Contents. For a general discussion of the contents of an opposition, see "Opposition Papers," ch. 1-D, §8, p. 35.

§5.4 Reply. The attorney can file a reply to the opposition. *See, e.g.*, ***Rus, Miliband & Smith v. Conkle & Olesten*** (4th Dist.2003) 113 Cal.App.4th 656, 667 (attorneys filed reply to clients' opposition). The reply must be filed and served at least five court days before the hearing. CCP §1005(b). See "Reply Papers," ch. 1-D, §9, p. 37.

§5.5 Hearing.

1. Generally. Hearings on a motion to withdraw are conducted in the same manner as civil hearings generally. See "Hearings," ch. 1-H, p. 79.

2. In camera. The attorney can ask the court for an in camera hearing if the withdrawal is based on confidential matters. *See* ***Manfredi & Levine v. Superior Ct.*** (2d Dist.1998) 66 Cal.App.4th 1128, 1136; *see, e.g.*, ***Forrest v. Department of Corps.*** (2d Dist.2007) 150 Cal.App.4th 183, 194 (court conducted in camera hearing when attorney requested withdrawal based on privileged matters), *disapproved on other grounds*, ***Shalant v. Girardi*** (2011) 51 Cal.4th 1164. At the in camera hearing, the attorney can reveal some information to help the court determine whether a conflict exists, but the court cannot require the attorney to disclose the very communication that is claimed to be protected by the attorney-client privilege. ***Costco Wholesale Corp. v. Superior Ct.*** (2009) 47 Cal.4th 725, 737.

§5.6 Ruling. The grant or denial of an attorney's motion to withdraw is discretionary; an attorney does not have an absolute right to withdraw. ***Linn v. Superior Ct.*** (2d Dist.1926) 79 Cal.App. 721, 723-26; *see* ***Manfredi & Levine v. Superior Ct.*** (2d Dist.1998) 66 Cal.App.4th 1128, 1133. Although the Rules of Professional Conduct list circumstances in which an attorney "must" withdraw, no court has held that a court loses its discretion to deny a motion in these circumstances. Presumably, a court could still deny a mandatory motion to withdraw if the withdrawal would prejudice the interests of the client or another party. *See, e.g.*, ***Moore v. U.S.*** (E.D.Cal.2008) No. CIV S-04-423 FCD JFM (slip op.; 4-28-08) (after court found actual conflict of interest that triggered mandatory withdrawal under Rule Prof. Conduct 3-700(B)(2), court considered whether withdrawal would prejudice client or other party). If the attorney's withdrawal would not be prejudicial, however, the court should grant the motion rather than force an unwilling attorney to work for a client. *See* ***Rus, Miliband & Smith v. Conkle & Olesten*** (4th Dist.2003) 113 Cal.App.4th 656, 673 (no reason to force unwilling attorney-client relationship); ***Ramirez v. Sturdevant*** (1st Dist.1994) 21 Cal.App.4th 904, 915 (no reason for court to deny motion when no prejudice is found); ***Linn***, 79 Cal.App. at 725 (in great majority of instances, attorney should be permitted to withdraw unless prejudice is found).

NOTE

One court has held that a trial court abuses its discretion if it denies a motion to withdraw solely on the ground that the client cannot appear pro per. E.g., **Ferruzzo v. Superior Ct.** *(4th Dist.1980) 104 Cal.App.3d 501, 503-04 (trial court abused its discretion by determining it did not have authority to grant attorney's motion to withdraw as counsel for uncooperative corporate client because withdrawal would violate rule against corporate self-representation). If the granting of a motion to withdraw will result in a violation of the rule against self-representation, the court should inform the client of its need to find a substitute attorney or face the possibility of a dismissal for lack of representation.* See **Gamet v. Blanchard** *(4th Dist.2001) 91 Cal.App.4th 1276, 1284 n.5 (court has duty to inform corporate client of need for representation); cf.* **Torres v. Friedman** *(2d Dist.1985) 169 Cal.App.3d 880, 888 (court should inform guardian ad litem of need to find replacement counsel).*

§5.7 Order.

1. Form. The court's ruling on the motion to withdraw must be recorded either in writing or by minute order. See "Record of Ruling," ch. 1-I, §4, p. 90.

2. Contents. If the court grants the motion, the court should sign the attorney's proposed order and state whether the withdrawal was mandatory or permissive if alternative grounds for withdrawal were asserted. See "Proposed order," §5.2.3(6), p. 110.

3. Effective date of withdrawal. If the court grants the motion, the attorney is withdrawn as the attorney of record on the date the order is signed. *See* Judicial Council Forms, form MC-053. A copy of the signed order must be served on the client and all parties who have appeared in the case, and the court can delay the effective date of the order until proof of service has been filed with the court. CRC 3.1362(e).

NOTE

Under CCP §286, when an attorney "ceases to act as such," the attorney's client is entitled to appoint another attorney or appear pro per before any further proceedings are conducted against the client. Section 286 does not apply, however, when an attorney files a motion to withdraw. **Gion v. Stroud** *(1st Dist.1961) 191 Cal.App.2d 277, 279.*

§5.8 Motion for reconsideration. A party who is adversely affected by a court's order on an attorney's motion to withdraw can file a motion for reconsideration. CCP §1008(a). See "Motion for Reconsideration," ch. 5-G, §3, p. 508.

§5.9 Motion for renewal. An attorney whose motion to withdraw has been denied can file a motion for renewal. CCP §1008(b). See "Motion for Renewal," ch. 5-G, §4, p. 516.

§5.10 Appellate review. The court's ruling on an attorney's motion to withdraw cannot be challenged on appeal until the court renders a final judgment in the case. *See* CCP §904.1(a). A party or the attorney can challenge the court's ruling before a final judgment, however, by filing a petition for a writ of mandate. *See, e.g.*, ***Manfredi & Levine v. Superior Ct.*** (2d Dist.1998) 66 Cal.App.4th 1128, 1131 (law firm sought relief through petition for writ of mandate after court denied motion to withdraw). The trial court's ruling is reviewed for abuse of discretion. *Id.* at 1133.

§6. ATTORNEY'S APPLICATION TO WITHDRAW AFTER COMPLETION OF LSR

An attorney can be retained for a limited-scope representation (LSR). CRC 3.35(a). An LSR is a relationship between an attorney and a client in which they agree that the scope of the legal services will be limited to specific tasks. *Id.* For example, an attorney may agree to represent a client only at a particular hearing, a particular deposition, or trial. Weil, *Civil Procedure Before Trial*, ¶1:192; *see* Judicial Council Forms, form MC-950.

§6.1 Notice of LSR. If the attorney and client enter into an LSR and the attorney will be making an appearance in the case (e.g., at a hearing, deposition, or trial), a notice of LSR should be filed with the court and served on all parties. *See* CRC 3.35(c), 3.37(a). If the LSR only involves preparing legal documents, a notice is not required. *See* CRC 3.37(a).

1. Who can file. The attorney or the client can file a notice of LSR. CRC 3.36(a).

2. Deadline to file & serve. There is no deadline to file or serve the notice. *See* CRC 3.36. The notice should be filed and served on all parties, however, as soon as possible so the attorney is entitled to receive copies of the papers in the case. *See* CRC 3.36(b).

3. Contents. The notice of LSR must be made using Judicial Council Form MC-950. CRC 3.36(a). By signing the notice, the client agrees to sign Judicial Council Form MC-050 ("Substitution of Attorney—Civil (Without Court Order)") at the completion of the LSR. Judicial Council Forms, form MC-950. See "Withdrawal by Consent," §3, p. 104.

§6.2 Withdrawal from LSR.

1. Client signed Form MC-050. If the client signed Judicial Council Form MC-050 at the completion of the LSR, no other steps need to be taken for the attorney to withdraw. *See* CRC 3.36(c); Judicial Council Forms, form MC-050. See "Withdrawal by Consent," §3, p. 104.

2. Client did not sign Form MC-050. If the client did not sign Judicial Council Form MC-050 at the completion of the LSR, the attorney must file and serve an application to withdraw (also known as an application to be relieved as counsel). *See* CRC 3.36(c), (d).

(1) Application to withdraw.

(a) Who can file. The attorney providing the LSR can file an application to withdraw. *See* CRC 3.36(c), (d).

(b) Deadline to file & serve. There is no deadline to file or serve the application. *See* CRC 3.36. The application should be filed and served, however, as soon as possible to relieve the attorney providing the LSR from any further obligations.

(c) Who to serve. The application must be served on the client and all other parties or attorneys for parties in the case. CRC 3.36(e).

(d) Contents.

[1] Form. The application must be made using Judicial Council Form MC-955. CRC 3.36(d).

[2] Supporting evidence. The application should be supported by the notice of LSR. *See* Judicial Council Forms, form MC-950, form MC-955. See "Notice of LSR," §6.1, p. 113.

[3] Form MC-956. The application that is served on the client must include a blank copy of Judicial Council Form MC-956. CRC 3.36(e); *see* Judicial Council Forms, form MC-956 (form for objecting to application).

(e) Filing fees. When the application is filed, the attorney must pay a filing fee to the court clerk. See "Filing Fees," ch. 1-F, §7, p. 58.

(2) Client's response to application.

(a) Objection. The client can oppose the application by filing an objection.

[1] Deadline to file & serve. An objection must be filed with the court and served on the attorney providing the LSR and all other parties within 15 days after the application was personally served on the client (or within 20 days if service was by mail). *See* CRC 3.36(f), (g); Judicial Council Forms, form MC-956.

[2] Contents. The objection can be made using Judicial Council Form MC-956. CRC 3.36(g). If the client chooses to draft her own objection, it should contain the information from Form MC-956, including an explanation of what services from the LSR remain to be completed and why the services should be completed by the attorney providing the LSR. *See* Judicial Council Forms, form MC-956.

[3] Hearing. If an objection is timely made, the clerk must set a hearing date no later than 25 days after the objection is filed and send notice of the hearing to the attorney providing the LSR, the client, and the other parties. CRC 3.36(g). The hearing should be conducted in the same manner as civil hearings generally. See "Hearings," ch. 1-H, p. 79.

(b) No objection. If the client does not file an objection, the attorney must file with the court (1) an updated Judicial Council Form MC-955 marked to indicate that no objection was made and (2) a proposed order on the application. CRC 3.36(f); *see* Judicial Council Forms, form MC-955 (attorney can check box to indicate that no objection has been served), form MC-958 (optional form for order on application). The clerk will then forward the order for the judge's signature. CRC 3.36(f).

(3) Ruling. The court should grant the application to withdraw as long as the attorney has completed the services required under the LSR. *See* CRC 3.36(c).

(4) Order.

(a) Form. The court's ruling on the application to withdraw must be recorded either in writing or by minute order. See "Record of Ruling," ch. 1-I, §4, p. 90. If in writing, the order can be made using Judicial Council Form MC-958.

(b) Effect of ruling.

[1] Application denied. If the court denies the application, the attorney must complete the services that the court finds are still outstanding under the LSR. *See* Judicial Council Forms, form MC-958.

[2] Application granted.

[a] Opposed application. If the court grants an opposed application, the attorney is relieved as the attorney of record in the case. *See* Judicial Council Forms, form MC-958.

[b] Unopposed application. If the court grants an unopposed application, the attorney must serve a copy of the signed order on the client and all parties who have appeared in the case or their attorneys. CRC 3.36(h). The court can delay the effective date of the order until proof of service has been filed with the court. *Id.*

(5) **Motion for reconsideration.** A party who is adversely affected by a court's order on the application to withdraw can file a motion for reconsideration. CCP §1008(a). See "Motion for Reconsideration," ch. 5-G, §3, p. 508.

(6) **Motion for renewal.** An attorney whose application to withdraw is denied can file a motion for renewal. CCP §1008(b). See "Motion for Renewal," ch. 5-G, §4, p. 516.

(7) **Appellate review.** The ruling on the application to withdraw is not appealable until the court renders a final judgment in the case. *See* CCP §904.1(a). A party or the attorney can challenge the court's ruling before a final judgment, however, by filing a petition for a writ of mandate. *Cf.* ***Manfredi & Levine v. Superior Ct.*** (2d Dist.1998) 66 Cal.App.4th 1128, 1131 (law firm filed writ of mandate when its motion to withdraw from non-LSR representation was denied).

§7. RECOVERING FEES & COSTS AFTER REMOVAL OR WITHDRAWAL

An attorney who is removed or who withdraws from representation may be able to recover attorney fees and costs advanced on the client's behalf. In most cases, an attorney must file an independent action to recover fees and costs. *See* ***Carroll v. Interstate Brands Corp.*** (1st Dist.2002) 99 Cal.App.4th 1168, 1177; ***Hansen v. Jacobsen*** (1st Dist.1986) 186 Cal.App.3d 350, 356. An attorney cannot seek a recovery by intervening in the case from which she was removed or withdrawn unless authorized by statute. 1 Witkin, *Cal. Procedure*, Attorneys, §208; *see* ***Carroll***, 99 Cal.App.4th at 1177; ***Hansen***, 186 Cal.App.3d at 356.

§7.1 Recovering attorney fees – hourly-fee case.

An attorney's right to recover attorney fees for work the attorney performed in an hourly-fee case before being removed by a client or withdrawing from representation is generally governed by contract law. *See* ***Oliver v. Campbell*** (1954) 43 Cal.2d 298, 302 (attorney who is removed by client can seek damages under contract or treat contract as rescinded and recover reasonable value of attorney's services based on quantum meruit); *CEB Procedure Before Trial*, §5.43 (attorney's right to enforce fee agreement is similar to enforcement of contract). However, an attorney cannot seek damages for breach of contract based solely on the client's discharge of the attorney because a client has the absolute right to remove an attorney. ***Fracasse v. Brent*** (1972) 6 Cal.3d 784, 790-91. Instead, the attorney is limited to recovering the reasonable value of the attorney's services on the basis of quantum meruit. *Id.* at 791.

§7.2 Recovering attorney fees – contingent-fee case.

1. When permissible.

(1) **After attorney is removed.** An attorney who is removed by a client from a contingent-fee case with or without cause can recover attorney fees for work the attorney performed before being removed. ***Fracasse v. Brent*** (1972) 6 Cal.3d 784, 791.

(2) **After attorney withdraws – justifiable cause.** An attorney can recover attorney fees for work the attorney performed before withdrawing from a contingent-fee case if the attorney withdrew for justifiable cause. ***Rus, Miliband & Smith v. Conkle & Olesten*** (4th Dist.2003) 113 Cal.App.4th 656, 672; ***Estate of Falco*** (2d Dist.1987) 188 Cal.App.3d 1004, 1013-14. Justifiable cause is not necessarily established by an order granting a withdrawal. ***Estate of Falco***, 188 Cal.App.3d at 1014. The cause required to withdraw from a case is not the same as the cause required to recover attorney fees. *Id.*

(a) **What is justifiable cause.**

[1] **Mandatory withdrawal.** The attorney's withdrawal may be for justifiable cause if withdrawal was mandatory under the Rules of Professional Conduct. ***Estate of Falco***, 188 Cal.App.3d at 1016. See "Mandatory," §5.1.1(1), p. 108. To demonstrate that the mandatory withdrawal was for justifiable cause, the attorney has the burden of proving the following:

[a] **Withdrawal required.** The attorney must prove that she was truly obligated to withdraw to comply with an ethical duty under the Rules of Professional Conduct. ***Duchrow v. Forrest*** (2d Dist.2013) 215 Cal.App.4th 1359, 1383; ***Rus, Miliband & Smith***, 113 Cal.App.4th at 674; *see* Rules Prof. Conduct, rule 3-700(B).

WITHDRAWAL OR REMOVAL

[b] Motivated by ethical obligation. The attorney must prove that her overwhelming and primary motivation to withdraw was to comply with the ethical duty. ***Duchrow***, 215 Cal.App.4th at 1383. If the attorney withdraws primarily because of some other motive, the attorney cannot recover fees even though the attorney was ethically required to withdraw. *See* ***Rus, Miliband & Smith***, 113 Cal.App.4th at 674.

[c] Good faith. The attorney must prove that she commenced the action on behalf of the client in good faith. ***Duchrow***, 215 Cal.App.4th at 1383; ***Estate of Falco***, 188 Cal.App.3d at 1016.

[d] Client obtained recovery. The attorney must prove that the client obtained a recovery after the attorney withdrew. ***Duchrow***, 215 Cal.App.4th at 1383; ***Estate of Falco***, 188 Cal.App.3d at 1016.

[e] Attorney contributed towards client's recovery. The attorney must prove that the attorney's work contributed in some measurable degree toward the client's ultimate recovery. ***Duchrow***, 215 Cal.App.4th at 1383; ***Estate of Falco***, 188 Cal.App.3d at 1016.

CAUTION

Division Two of the Second District Court of Appeal, in an unpublished opinion, refused to expand the rule in contingent-fee cases—that an attorney's withdrawal must generally be mandatory to recover attorney fees—to hourly-fee cases. ***Risner v. Freid & Goldsman*** *(2d Dist.2007) No. B188211 (unpub.; 11-13-07).*

---

[2] Permissive withdrawal. The attorney's withdrawal may be for justifiable cause if withdrawal is permitted but not required under the Rules of Professional Conduct. ***Rus, Miliband & Smith***, 113 Cal.App.4th at 675; ***Estate of Falco***, 188 Cal.App.3d at 1016 n.12; *see* Rules Prof. Conduct, rule 3-700(C). See "Permissive," §5.1.1(2), p. 108. For a permissive withdrawal to be for justifiable cause, the attorney must assert compelling reasons for the withdrawal—reasons that withstand heightened scrutiny. ***Rus, Miliband & Smith***, 113 Cal.App.4th at 675; ***Estate of Falco***, 188 Cal.App.3d at 1016 n.12.

(b) What is not justifiable cause.

[1] Client's refusal to settle. An attorney who withdraws from a contingent-fee case because the client refuses to settle does not withdraw for justifiable cause. ***Estate of Falco***, 188 Cal.App.3d at 1018.

[2] Meritless case. An attorney who withdraws from a contingent-fee case on the basis that the case is meritless does not withdraw for justifiable cause. *See* ***Hensel v. Cohen*** (2d Dist.1984) 155 Cal.App.3d 563, 567-68.

(3) After attorney withdraws – client settles on similar terms. An attorney can recover attorney fees for work the attorney performed before withdrawing from a contingent-fee case if the attorney withdrew because the client refused to settle and the client later settles on substantially the same terms as those negotiated by the attorney. ***Estate of Falco***, 188 Cal.App.3d at 1019. Because a client has an absolute right to refuse to settle, the attorney cannot recover fees under this circumstance on the basis that she withdrew for justifiable cause. *Id.* at 1018-19. Instead, the attorney can recover fees only on the basis of unjust enrichment. *Id.* at 1019.

2. Amount recoverable.

(1) Most cases – reasonable value. In most cases, the amount of fees an attorney can recover after being removed or withdrawing for justifiable cause from a contingent-fee case is the reasonable value of the attorney's services on the basis of quantum meruit. *See* ***Fracasse***, 6 Cal.3d at 791 (attorney's removal); ***Duchrow***, 215 Cal.App.4th at 1382 (attorney's withdrawal). The rationale for using quantum meruit as the basis for recovery rather than breach of contract is that a client has an absolute right to remove an attorney. ***Fracasse***, 6 Cal.3d at 791. Thus, the client's right to remove is considered an implied term of the contract, and exercising that right is not considered a breach. *Id.*

(a) Burden of proof. An attorney seeking to recover attorney fees under quantum meruit has the burden of proving what services were performed and the reasonable value of the services. *See* ***Mardirossian & Assocs. v. Ersoff*** (2d Dist.2007) 153 Cal.App.4th 257, 272.

(b) Determining reasonable value. Generally, the reasonable value of the attorney's services is the number of hours spent multiplied by a reasonable rate. ***Mardirossian & Assocs.***, 153 Cal.App.4th at 272; *see* ***Cazares v. Saenz*** (4th Dist.1989) 208 Cal.App.3d 279, 286-87 (in contingent-fee cases, formula is overly narrow view of quantum meruit standard). The factors a court can consider in making this calculation include the following:

[1] The nature of the litigation. ***Duchrow***, 215 Cal.App.4th at 1383.

[2] The novelty and difficulty of the issues involved in the litigation. ***Fergus v. Songer*** (2d Dist.2007) 150 Cal.App.4th 552, 561; *see* ***Duchrow***, 215 Cal.App.4th at 1383.

[3] The amount in controversy. ***Fracasse***, 6 Cal.3d at 792; ***Duchrow***, 215 Cal.App.4th at 1383.

[4] The degree of skill required. ***Duchrow***, 215 Cal.App.4th at 1383; ***Fergus***, 150 Cal.App.4th at 561.

[5] The amount of skill and attention the attorney devoted to the litigation and the likelihood that this prevented the attorney from accepting other employment. *See* ***Mardirossian & Assocs.***, 153 Cal.App.4th at 272; ***Fergus***, 150 Cal.App.4th at 567-68.

[6] The fee customarily charged by others in the legal community with similar experience. ***Cazares***, 208 Cal.App.3d at 287.

[7] Whether the fees were fixed or contingent. *See id.* (attorney may be entitled to enhanced fee in contingent-fee case).

NOTE

In contingent-fee cases, if the contingent fee is insufficient to meet the quantum meruit claims of the removed attorney and the existing attorney, the contingent fee should be distributed among all attorneys in proportion to the time spent on the case by each. ***Spires v. American Bus Lines*** *(1st Dist.1984) 158 Cal.App.3d 211, 216.*

[8] Time limitations imposed by the client or the circumstances. ***Fergus***, 150 Cal.App.4th at 561.

[9] The attorney's education, age, skill, reputation, and experience. *See* ***Duchrow***, 215 Cal.App.4th at 1383; ***Fergus***, 150 Cal.App.4th at 561.

[10] The nature and length of the attorney's professional relationship with the client. ***Fergus***, 150 Cal.App.4th at 561.

[11] The fee amount that the client originally agreed to pay. ***Oliver v. Campbell*** (1954) 43 Cal.2d 298, 305; *see* ***Fergus***, 150 Cal.App.4th at 561.

[12] The attorney's success or failure in handling particular issues in the litigation and the amount of fees in proportion to the results obtained. *See* ***Duchrow***, 215 Cal.App.4th at 1383; ***Fergus***, 150 Cal.App.4th at 561.

[13] The stage of the litigation at which the attorney was removed or withdrawn. *See* ***Fracasse***, 6 Cal.3d at 791 (reasonable value may be entire amount that would have been due as contingent fee if discharge of attorney was "on the courthouse steps"); *see, e.g.*, ***Joseph E. Di Loreto, Inc. v. O'Neill*** (2d Dist.1991) 1 Cal.App.4th 149, 157-58 (attorney who performed all obligations under contract at time of discharge was entitled to full contract price).

[14] The results achieved by the attorney for the client. ***Fracasse***, 6 Cal.3d at 792; *see, e.g.*, ***Fergus***, 150 Cal.App.4th at 567-68 (attorney ultimately recovered $4.8 million for client based on original $308,000 judgment).

(2) Client settles on similar terms – unjust enrichment. If an attorney withdraws from a contingent-fee case because of a client's refusal to settle, the attorney can recover fees as restitution to prevent the client's unjust enrichment if the client later settles on substantially the same terms as those negotiated by the attorney before she withdrew. ***Estate of Falco***, 188 Cal.App.3d at 1019.

§7.3 Recovering costs. Few courts have addressed whether an attorney can recover costs that were paid before the attorney was removed or withdrawn. The courts that have addressed the issue have done so in the context of a contingent-fee agreement. If the contingent-fee agreement states that costs will be paid from the client's gross recovery, the removed or withdrawn attorney can recover costs advanced on behalf of the client only after the client recovers in the suit by settlement or judgment. ***Kroff v. Larson*** (6th Dist.1985) 167 Cal.App.3d 857, 860-61; *see, e.g.*, ***Hensel v. Cohen*** (2d Dist.1984) 155 Cal.App.3d 563, 565 n.1 (parties agreed that attorney was entitled to costs if client eventually recovered).

PRACTICE TIP

To recover costs before the client recovers in a contingent-fee case, the attorney should include a provision in the retainer agreement stating that costs advanced by the attorney are payable "on demand." See Weil, Civil Procedure Before Trial, ¶1:425.

C. MOTION TO DISQUALIFY ATTORNEY

This subchapter discusses how to bring a motion to disqualify another party's attorney. For a discussion of how a party can remove its own attorney or how an attorney can remove herself, see "Attorney's Withdrawal or Removal," ch. 2-B, p. 102.

§1. GENERAL

§1.1 Purpose. A motion to disqualify an attorney (also known as a motion to recuse) is used to involuntarily end an attorney's representation of another party. Younger & Bradley, *Younger on California Motions* (2014-15), §18:1; *see also* ***Gong v. RFG Oil, Inc.*** (4th Dist.2008) 166 Cal.App.4th 209, 214 (disqualification involves conflict between client's right to counsel of own choosing and need to maintain ethical standards of legal profession). The motion is generally brought on the ground that the attorney acted unethically in some way, but it can also be brought because another person's action caused the attorney to be vicariously disqualified. *See* ***In re Complex Asbestos Litig.*** (1st Dist.1991) 232 Cal.App.3d 572, 592. The purpose of disqualification is preventative, not punitive—that is, an attorney should not be disqualified purely as a punitive or disciplinary matter. ***Neal v. Health Net, Inc.*** (2d Dist.2002) 100 Cal.App.4th 831, 844. Instead, a disqualification motion should be used to preserve the public's trust in the administration of justice and the integrity of the judicial system. ***People v. SpeeDee Oil Change Sys.*** (1999) 20 Cal.4th 1135, 1145.

§1.2 Primary authority. CCP §128(a)(5); Rules Prof. Conduct, rules 2-100, 3-310, 3-600, 5-210.

NOTE

While the court's ability to disqualify an attorney stems from its power under CCP §128(a)(5) to control the conduct of persons involved in a judicial proceeding, case law dictates how the motion should be made and evaluated. See ***Zador Corp. v. Kwan*** *(6th Dist.1995) 31 Cal.App.4th 1285, 1292-93;* ***In re Complex Asbestos Litig.*** *(1st Dist.1991) 232 Cal.App.3d 572, 585; Younger, Cal. Motions, §§18:2, 18:3.*

§1.3 Secondary authority. The following secondary sources are cited as authority in this subchapter:

- *California Civil Procedure Before Trial* (CEB Online ed. 2014) (referred to as *CEB Procedure Before Trial*).
- Witkin, *California Procedure* (5th ed. 2008 & Supp.2014) (referred to as Witkin, *Cal. Procedure*).
- Younger & Bradley, *Younger on California Motions* (2014-15) (referred to as Younger, *Cal. Motions*).

§2. GROUNDS

The most common grounds for a motion to disqualify an attorney are the following: (1) concurrent representation, (2) successive representation, (3) confidential information obtained from an expert, a consultant, or an employee, (4) prohibited communication with a represented party, or (5) dual role as a witness and an advocate. For a discussion of other ethical rules that can form the basis of a motion to disqualify, see 1 Witkin, *Cal. Procedure*, Attorneys, §§407-465.

§2.1 Concurrent representation. A motion to disqualify can be made on the ground that the attorney is concurrently representing two or more clients whose interests actually or potentially conflict. *See* Rules Prof. Conduct, rule 3-310(C). To bring a motion to disqualify on this ground, the movant must establish that (1) the attorney owes the movant a duty of loyalty, (2) the attorney is concurrently representing the movant and another client, (3) the movant's and the other client's interests actually or potentially conflict, and (4) the attorney has not obtained consent from both the movant and the other client. *See id.*

NOTE

To avoid disqualification for engaging in the concurrent representation of two or more clients, the attorney cannot simply drop one client before the hearing on the motion to disqualify. ***American Airlines, Inc. v. Sheppard, Mullin, Richter & Hampton*** *(2d Dist.2002) 96 Cal.App.4th 1017, 1037;* ***State Farm Mut. Auto. Ins. v. Federal Ins.*** *(5th Dist.1999) 72 Cal.App.4th 1422, 1431;* ***Truck Ins. Exch. v. Fireman's Fund Ins.*** *(1st Dist.1992) 6 Cal.App.4th 1050, 1057. But an attorney may be able to avoid disqualification if the attorney immediately withdraws after learning about the concurrent representation and the concurrent representation either (1) was unforeseen and occurred by mere happenstance or (2) was not caused by the attorney (e.g., when a corporate client is acquired by another company that the attorney had a relationship with). See* ***Truck Ins. Exch.***, *6 Cal.App.4th at 1058-59. In these cases, the attorney may avoid disqualification for concurrent representation but may be subject to disqualification for successive representation.* *See "Successive representation," §2.2, p. 124.*

1. Duty of loyalty. To disqualify an attorney based on concurrent representation, the movant must show that the attorney owes it a duty of loyalty. *See* ***In re Charlisse C.*** (2008) 45 Cal.4th 145, 160. The purpose of the rule prohibiting concurrent representations is to protect the duty of loyalty. *Id.*

(1) Attorney-client relationship. A duty of loyalty generally arises from an attorney-client relationship. ***Responsible Citizens v. Superior Ct.*** (5th Dist.1993) 16 Cal.App.4th 1717, 1733.

(a) Generally.

[1] How it is created. The attorney-client relationship can be created only by an express or implied contract; it cannot be created by the unilateral declaration of one party to the relationship. ***Koo v. Rubio's Rests., Inc.*** (4th Dist.2003) 109 Cal.App.4th 719, 729. An express contract is generally established by proof of a written engagement letter. *See* ***Goldberg v. Warner/Chappell Music, Inc.*** (2d Dist.2005) 125 Cal.App.4th 752, 757; ***In re Jaeger*** (Bankr.C.D.Cal.1997) 213 B.R. 578, 586-87. An implied contract is established by examining the totality of the circumstances of the attorney and purported client's relationship. *See* ***Responsible Citizens***, 16 Cal.App.4th at 1733. If the totality of the circumstances implies that the attorney agreed not to accept other representations adverse

to the purported client's personal interest, then an implied attorney-client relationship will be established. *See id.* Some of the factors courts consider in determining whether an implied contract has been created are the following:

[a] Whether the purported client divulged confidential information to the attorney. ***People v. SpeeDee Oil Change Sys.*** (1999) 20 Cal.4th 1135, 1148. The disclosure of confidential information is considered the primary factor in determining whether an implied attorney-client relationship has been established. *Id.*; *see* ***Med-Trans Corp. v. City of Cal. City*** (5th Dist.2007) 156 Cal.App.4th 655, 668 (movant must show, directly or by reasonable inference, that attorney acquired confidential information); ***Abubakar v. County of Solano*** (E.D.Cal.2008) No. Civ. S-06-2268 LKK/EFB (slip op.; 2-4-08) (attorney-client relationship is formed whenever confidential information is disclosed); *see, e.g.*, ***In re Marriage of Zimmerman*** (1st Dist.1993) 16 Cal.App.4th 556, 565 (no confidential disclosures were claimed, and it was unlikely that confidential information would have been given in 20-minute phone conversation when purported client simply outlined case).

[b] The nature and extent of the contacts between the attorney and the purported client. ***In re Marriage of Zimmerman***, 16 Cal.App.4th at 564; *see* ***SpeeDee Oil Change***, 20 Cal.4th at 1149; ***Responsible Citizens***, 16 Cal.App.4th at 1733; ***Fox v. Pollack*** (1st Dist.1986) 181 Cal.App.3d 954, 959. Even the briefest conversation between an attorney and a potential client can result in establishment of an attorney-client relationship if confidential information has been exchanged. ***SpeeDee Oil Change***, 20 Cal.4th at 1148.

[c] Whether the attorney provided the purported client with legal advice. *Id.*; *see* ***Fox***, 181 Cal.App.3d at 959.

[d] Whether the purported client sought or paid for the attorney's services. *See* ***Fox***, 181 Cal.App.3d at 959. The payment or nonpayment of attorney fees alone, however, does not determine the existence of an attorney-client relationship—it is merely a factor. *See* ***SpeeDee Oil Change***, 20 Cal.4th at 1148 (lack of fee agreement does not prevent relationship from arising); ***Lasky, Haas, Cohler & Munter v. Superior Ct.*** (2d Dist.1985) 172 Cal.App.3d 264, 285 (payment of attorney fees does not establish attorney-client relationship).

[2] Who it applies to. When an attorney-client relationship is established, it may extend to others outside the immediate relationship.

[a] Attorneys in firm. When a client retains a single attorney, the client also establishes an attorney-client relationship with any attorney who is a partner of or employed by the retained attorney. ***Streit v. Covington & Crowe*** (4th Dist.2000) 82 Cal.App.4th 441, 445. Thus, when a movant establishes that an attorney is disqualified for an ethical violation, the disqualification will generally extend to the attorney's entire firm. *See* ***City & Cty. of S.F. v. Cobra Solutions, Inc.*** (2006) 38 Cal.4th 839, 847-48; ***SpeeDee Oil Change***, 20 Cal.4th at 1139. See "Vicarious disqualification," §3.3.1(2)(b), p. 131.

[b] Associated attorneys. When a client retains an attorney and the attorney associates with another attorney on a particular case, the attorney-client relationship also extends to the associated attorney. ***Streit***, 82 Cal.App.4th at 445; *see also* ***Raskin v. Superior Ct.*** (2d Dist.1934) 138 Cal.App. 668, 670 (customary for attorneys of record to employ outside attorneys to assist in representation). The associated attorney owes the client the same duties the attorney of record owes, regardless of the duties that were assigned to the associated attorney. *See* ***Streit***, 82 Cal.App.4th at 447 (associated attorney and attorney of record owe same duty of loyalty to client); ***Pollack v. Lytle*** (2d Dist.1981) 120 Cal.App.3d 931, 942 (same), *disapproved on other grounds*, ***Beck v. Wecht*** (2002) 28 Cal.4th 289. This is true even if the associated attorney is being paid by the attorney of record or is not being paid at all. ***Streit***, 82 Cal.App.4th at 447.

(b) Corporation as client.

[1] Generally. An attorney who represents a corporation has an attorney-client relationship with the corporation itself; the attorney does not also represent the corporation's parent company, subsidiaries, directors, officers, employees, members, shareholders, or other constituents. *See* Rules Prof. Conduct, rule 3-600(A), (D); ***Morrison Knudsen Corp. v. Hancock, Rothert & Bunshoft, LLP*** (1st Dist.1999) 69 Cal.App.4th 223, 240; State

Bar Formal Opinion No. 1989-113. An attorney can, however, represent an individual director, officer, employee, member, shareholder, or other constituent separately from the corporation as long as the attorney's representation does not violate the rule against concurrent or successive representations. *See* Rules Prof. Conduct, rules 3-310, 3-600(E). See "Concurrent representation," §2.1, p. 119; "Successive representation," §2.2, p. 124.

[2] Single-entity exception. An attorney who represents a corporation has an attorney-client relationship with both the corporation and the corporation's parent company or subsidiary if the two corporations are alter egos or have such a unity of interest that they should be treated as a single entity. *See* State Bar Formal Opinion No. 1989-113. If the two corporations are treated as a single entity, the attorney must follow the rules on concurrent and successive representations. *See* ***Brooklyn Navy Yard Cogeneration Partners v. Superior Ct.*** (4th Dist.1997) 60 Cal.App.4th 248, 258. See "Concurrent representation," §2.1, p. 119; "Successive representation," §2.2, p. 124.

[a] Alter-ego test. Under the alter-ego test, two corporations will be treated as a single entity if (1) there is such a unity of interest that the two corporations no longer have separate "personalities" and (2) inequitable results will follow if the corporations are not treated as a single entity. ***Brooklyn Navy Yard***, 60 Cal.App.4th at 257-58.

[b] Unity-of-interest test. Under the unity-of-interest test, two entities will be treated as a single entity if there is a sufficient unity of interest between the two. ***Morrison Knudsen Corp.***, 69 Cal.App.4th at 241. In determining whether there is a unity of interest, courts consider the following: (1) the separateness of the entities involved, (2) whether corporate formalities are observed, (3) the extent to which each entity has a distinct and independent management and board of directors, and (4) whether one entity could be considered the alter ego of the other. *Id.*

NOTE

Courts are split on whether the alter-ego test or unity-of-interest test should be used to determine when two corporations should be treated as a single entity for disqualification purposes. See ***Faughn v. Perez*** *(5th Dist.2006) 145 Cal.App.4th 592, 611 (recognizing court split but declining to decide appropriate test). The court in* ***Faughn*** *suggested that the conflicting court opinions may be reconciled by the different factual situations presented in each case. Id. Compare* ***Morrison Knudsen Corp.****, 69 Cal.App.4th at 252-53 (applying unity-of-interest test when representations were successive), with* ***Brooklyn Navy Yard****, 60 Cal.App.4th at 257-58 (applying alter-ego test when representations were concurrent).*

(c) Partnership as client. An attorney who represents a partnership has an attorney-client relationship with the partnership itself; the attorney does not also represent the individual partners unless there is an express or implied agreement. *See* ***Responsible Citizens***, 16 Cal.App.4th at 1732. If there is an express or implied agreement to also represent an individual partner, the attorney must follow the rules on concurrent and successive representations. See "Concurrent representation," §2.1, p. 119; "Successive representation," §2.2, p. 124. In determining whether an implied agreement exists, courts consider the following:

[1] The size of the partnership. ***Johnson v. Superior Ct.*** (4th Dist.1995) 38 Cal.App.4th 463, 476; ***Responsible Citizens***, 16 Cal.App.4th at 1733. If the partnership has only a few members, that may suggest individual representation of the members. ***Johnson***, 38 Cal.App.4th at 476.

[2] The nature and scope of the attorney's engagement (i.e., whether the nature and scope of the engagement go beyond routine partnership business and relate to the individual partners' interests). *Id.* at 476-77; ***Responsible Citizens***, 16 Cal.App.4th at 1733.

[3] The kind and extent of contacts between the attorney and the individual partners. ***Johnson***, 38 Cal.App.4th at 477; ***Responsible Citizens***, 16 Cal.App.4th at 1733.

[4] The attorney's access to financial information about the individual partners' interests. ***Johnson***, 38 Cal.App.4th at 477; ***Responsible Citizens***, 16 Cal.App.4th at 1733.

[5] Whether there is an implied agreement by the attorney not to accept representations adverse to the individual partners' interests. ***Johnson***, 38 Cal.App.4th at 477; ***Responsible Citizens***, 16 Cal.App.4th at 1733.

(d) Insurance company as client. An attorney who is hired by an insurance company to defend an insured against a claim covered under an insurance policy represents both the insurer and the insured. ***State Farm***, 72 Cal.App.4th at 1428-29. Thus, the attorney must follow the rules on concurrent and successive representations. See "Concurrent representation," §2.1, p. 119; "Successive representation," §2.2, p. 124. If a conflict between the insured and insurer arises and the insured does not consent in writing to waive the conflict, the insured has a right to independent counsel at the insurer's expense. Civ. C. §2860(a). For more on representing an insured and insurer, see 1 Witkin, *Cal. Procedure*, Attorneys, §§117-125.

(e) Shareholder as client. An attorney who represents a shareholder in a derivative action has an attorney-client relationship with only the shareholder; the attorney does not also represent the corporation simply by filing the derivative action. *See* ***Shen v. Miller*** (2d Dist.2012) 212 Cal.App.4th 48, 57-58.

(2) Nonclients. A duty of loyalty can arise outside the attorney-client relationship if a person has some other type of confidential or fiduciary relationship with the attorney. *See* ***American Airlines***, 96 Cal.App.4th at 1032-34 (Rule Prof. Conduct 3-310(C) does not require representation of both clients as an attorney); *see, e.g.*, ***William H. Raley Co. v. Superior Ct.*** (4th Dist.1983) 149 Cal.App.3d 1042, 1047-48 (firm was disqualified from representing P in suit against D-corporation because firm's senior partner served as director of bank that held 100% of D-corporation's stock as trustee).

CAUTION

Based on former Rule of Professional Conduct 5-102(B), the court in ***William H. Raley Co.*** *held that a movant who has no attorney-client relationship but who has a confidential or fiduciary relationship with the attorney can bring a motion to disqualify based on the attorney's representation of parties with conflicting interests.* ***William H. Raley Co.****, 149 Cal.App.3d at 1046-47. Former rule 5-102(B) stated that an attorney could not represent "conflicting interests" without the written consent of all parties concerned. Effective May 27, 1989, former rule 5-102(B) became part of rule 3-310. Rule 3-310(C) states that an attorney cannot represent more than one "client" if their interests conflict without the written consent of each "client." Based on the amendment, one court has held that rule 3-310 applies only when there is an attorney-client relationship and that* ***William H. Raley Co.*** *has been superseded by the amendment.* ***Oaks Mgmt. v. Superior Ct.*** *(4th Dist.2006) 145 Cal.App.4th 453, 465. Other courts, however, continue to follow the holding in* ***William H. Raley Co.*** *E.g.,* ***Morrison Knudsen Corp.****, 69 Cal.App.4th at 232;* ***Allen v. Academic Games Leagues*** *(C.D.Cal.1993) 831 F.Supp. 785, 789, aff'd, (9th Cir.1996) 89 F.3d 614.*

2. Engaged in concurrent representation. To disqualify an attorney based on concurrent representation, the movant must show that the attorney is simultaneously representing two or more clients in the same matter or in unrelated matters. *See* Rules Prof. Conduct, rule 3-310(C); ***Flatt v. Superior Ct.*** (1994) 9 Cal.4th 275, 284; ***Sharp v. Next Entm't, Inc.*** (2d Dist.2008) 163 Cal.App.4th 410, 428; ***Cal W. Nurseries, Inc. v. Superior Ct.*** (4th Dist.2005) 129 Cal.App.4th 1170, 1175.

(1) Same matter. The rule against concurrently representing two or more clients in the same matter applies to all types of legal employment, including litigation and transactional matters or other common enterprises or legal relationships. Rules Prof. Conduct, rule 3-310, discussion ¶7.

(2) Unrelated matters. The rule against concurrently representing two or more clients in unrelated matters applies to litigation and transactional matters. Rules Prof. Conduct, rule 3-310, discussion ¶8; *see* ***Fremont Indem. Co. v. Fremont Gen. Corp.*** (2d Dist.2006) 143 Cal.App.4th 50, 64 (conflict occurs when attorney represents clients with adverse interests in unrelated matters even if there is no risk that confidences obtained in one matter could be used in other matter). Some examples of an attorney's representation of multiple clients in unrelated matters include the following:

- Attorney could not represent plaintiff in cross-complaint because attorney was currently representing defendant in another, unrelated action. ***Cal W. Nurseries***, 129 Cal.App.4th at 1176.
- Attorney could not represent wife in dissolution of marriage because attorney was currently representing husband in personal-injury action. ***Jeffry v. Pounds*** (3d Dist.1977) 67 Cal.App.3d 6, 8.
- Attorney could not cross-examine expert witness in medical-malpractice action because attorney's firm was currently representing witness in ongoing disciplinary proceedings. ***Hernandez v. Paicius*** (4th Dist.2003) 109 Cal.App.4th 452, 466, *disapproved on other grounds*, ***People v. Freeman*** (2010) 47 Cal.4th 993.

3. Interests conflict. To disqualify an attorney based on concurrent representation, the movant must show that the clients' interests actually or potentially conflict in matters in which the attorney is involved; it is insufficient to show that the clients' interests conflict in a third matter in which the attorney is not involved. *See* Rules Prof. Conduct, rule 3-310(C); ***Fremont Indem.***, 143 Cal.App.4th at 66.

(1) Actual conflict. Clients' interests actually conflict when the attorney's representation of one client is less effective because she represents the other client. ***Gilbert v. National Corp. for Hous. Prtshps.*** (1st Dist.1999) 71 Cal.App.4th 1240, 1253; ***Spindle v. Chubb/Pac. Indem. Grp.*** (2d Dist.1979) 89 Cal.App.3d 706, 713; *see, e.g.*, ***Gong v. RFG Oil, Inc.*** (4th Dist.2008) 166 Cal.App.4th 209, 216 (actual conflict was present when attorney could not promote closely held corporation's interests without negatively affecting shareholder's interests).

(2) Potential conflict. Clients' interests potentially conflict when there is no present actual conflict of interest but there is a possibility that an actual conflict might arise in the future from developments that have not yet occurred or facts that have not yet become known. ***In re Jaeger***, 213 B.R. at 584; *see, e.g.*, ***Klemm v. Superior Ct.*** (5th Dist.1977) 75 Cal.App.3d 893, 899 (attorney's representation of husband and wife in uncontested dissolution of marriage created potential conflict). To establish a potential conflict, the movant must show more than a remote possibility of a conflict. ***In re Jaeger***, 213 B.R. at 584; *see* ***Baker Manock & Jensen v. Superior Ct.*** (5th Dist.2009) 175 Cal.App.4th 1414, 1424 (hypothetical possibility of conflict of interest cannot result in attorney disqualification). The movant must show that there is a likelihood that a conflict will occur and that it would materially interfere with the attorney's independent professional judgment in representing her client. ***In re Jaeger***, 213 B.R. at 584-85.

4. No consent. To disqualify an attorney based on concurrent representation, the movant must establish that the attorney did not obtain informed written consent from both the movant and the other client. *See* Rules Prof. Conduct, rule 3-310(C) (must have written consent from each client). Informed written consent is a client's written agreement to the concurrent representation after the attorney has provided written disclosure of the conflict. *Id.* rule 3-310(A)(2). The written disclosure must inform the client of (1) the relevant circumstances of the actual or potential conflict and (2) the actual and reasonably foreseeable consequences of the conflict. *Id.* rule 3-310(A)(1); *see* ***Zador Corp. v. Kwan*** (6th Dist.1995) 31 Cal.App.4th 1285, 1301 (every possible consequence of conflict does not have to be disclosed for waiver to be valid). For consent to be valid, the clients must indicate that they know of, understand, and acknowledge the conflict of interest. ***Sharp***, 163 Cal.App.4th at 429.

NOTE

In some situations, Rule of Professional Conduct 3-310(C) may require the attorney to get informed written consent twice: once when a potential conflict arises and again if an actual conflict arises. ***In re Marriage of Friedman*** *(2d Dist.2002) 100 Cal.App.4th 65, 70.*

DISQUALIFY ATTORNEY

(1) No implied consent. A client cannot impliedly consent to a concurrent representation. ***Blecher & Collins, P.C. v. Northwest Airlines, Inc.*** (C.D.Cal.1994) 858 F.Supp. 1442, 1455; *see* ***State Farm***, 72 Cal.App.4th at 1435.

(2) No consent at trial or hearing. A client cannot consent to a concurrent representation at a trial or contested hearing when there is an actual conflict. ***Klemm***, 75 Cal.App.3d at 898.

§2.2 Successive representation. A motion to disqualify can be made on the ground that the attorney is successively representing clients with adverse interests. *See* Rules Prof. Conduct, rule 3-310(E). To bring a motion to disqualify on this ground, the movant (e.g., a former client) must establish that (1) the attorney owes the movant a duty of confidentiality, (2) the attorney has the movant's confidential information and is currently representing a new client whose interests are adverse to the movant's, and (3) the attorney has not obtained consent from the movant and the new client. *See id.*

1. Duty of confidentiality. To disqualify an attorney based on successive representation, the movant must establish that the attorney owes her a duty of confidentiality. *See* ***Civil Serv. Comm'n v. Superior Ct.*** (4th Dist.1984) 163 Cal.App.3d 70, 79. The purpose of the rule prohibiting successive representations is to protect the duty of confidentiality. ***In re Charlisse C.*** (2008) 45 Cal.4th 145, 159-60.

(1) Attorney-client relationship. A duty of confidentiality generally arises from an attorney-client relationship. *See* Bus. & Prof. C. §6068(e)(1); ***Commercial Std. Title Co. v. Superior Ct.*** (4th Dist.1979) 92 Cal.App.3d 934, 945. The duty to preserve a client's confidential information applies to both present and former clients. ***Commercial Std. Title***, 92 Cal.App.3d at 945. For a discussion of how an attorney-client relationship is established, see "Attorney-client relationship," §2.1.1(1), p. 119.

(2) Nonclients. In some instances, an attorney may owe a duty of confidentiality to a movant who was not a former client (i.e., a nonclient). *See* ***DCH Health Servs. v. Waite*** (4th Dist.2002) 95 Cal.App.4th 829, 832-33 (duty of confidentiality can extend beyond attorney-client relationship); *see, e.g.*, ***Kennedy v. Eldridge*** (3d Dist.2011) 201 Cal.App.4th 1197, 1208 (although there was no attorney-client relationship, movant could bring motion to disqualify attorney who acquired movant's confidential information during representation of movant's father in earlier family-law matter); ***Meza v. H. Muehlstein & Co.*** (2d Dist.2009) 176 Cal.App.4th 969, 980-81 (although there was no attorney-client relationship, movant could bring motion to disqualify attorney who acquired movant's confidential information during joint-defense representation).

2. Attorney has confidential information. To disqualify an attorney based on successive representation, the movant must show that the attorney obtained the movant's confidential information and that the information is material to the new client's representation. *See* Rules Prof. Conduct, rule 3-310(E); ***Knight v. Ferguson*** (2d Dist.2007) 149 Cal.App.4th 1207, 1213. In conflict analysis, the term "confidential information" is broader than the communications protected by the attorney-client privilege. ***Knight***, 149 Cal.App.4th at 1215. The term includes a client's attitudes, practices, business customs, litigation philosophy, strengths, weaknesses, and strategy. *Id.*; *see* ***Morrison Knudsen Corp. v. Hancock, Rothert & Bunshoft, LLP*** (1st Dist.1999) 69 Cal.App.4th 223, 236 (confidential information includes identity of key decision makers, organizational structure, litigation philosophy, and financial impact of pending and existing claims). The movant can prove that the attorney is in possession of the movant's confidential information in either of the following ways:

(1) Actual possession. The movant can prove that the attorney actually has confidential information that is material to the attorney's representation of the new client. ***Faughn v. Perez*** (5th Dist.2006) 145 Cal.App.4th 592, 603. While the movant does not need to disclose the actual confidential information that the attorney has, the movant must at least explain the nature of the information and how it is material to the current representation. ***Elliott v. McFarland Unified Sch. Dist.*** (5th Dist.1985) 165 Cal.App.3d 562, 572; *see, e.g.*, ***H.F. Ahmanson & Co. v. Salomon Bros.*** (2d Dist.1991) 229 Cal.App.3d 1445, 1459 (declarations from former client were

not sufficient to prove that attorney actually had confidential information, or if attorney did, how it would be material to current litigation). Confidential information obtained from the first representation is material if it is directly at issue or of critical importance in the second representation. ***Farris v. Fireman's Fund Ins.*** (5th Dist.2004) 119 Cal.App.4th 671, 680.

(2) Presumed possession. The movant can prove that the attorney is presumed to have confidential information that is material to the attorney's representation of the new client. ***Faughn***, 145 Cal.App.4th at 603; *see* ***In re Marriage of Zimmerman*** (1st Dist.1993) 16 Cal.App.4th 556, 563 (no requirement that movant establish actual possession of confidential information). The attorney's possession of confidential information will be presumed if the movant can prove that (1) there is a substantial relationship between the attorney's former representation of the movant and her current representation of the new client and (2) the movant's confidential information would normally have been imparted to the attorney based on the former representation or relationship. ***Khani v. Ford Motor Co.*** (2d Dist.2013) 215 Cal.App.4th 916, 920.

(a) Substantially related representations. To prove that the former and current representations are substantially related, the movant must show that the information material to the evaluation, prosecution, settlement, or accomplishment of the former representation is also material to the evaluation, prosecution, settlement, or accomplishment of the new representation. ***Faughn***, 145 Cal.App.4th at 604-05; ***Jessen v. Hartford Cas. Ins.*** (5th Dist.2003) 111 Cal.App.4th 698, 713. The movant can do this by showing the similarities between the factual situations and the legal questions posed by the two representations. ***Morrison Knudsen Corp.***, 69 Cal.App.4th at 234; *e.g.*, ***Knight***, 149 Cal.App.4th at 1213 (movant established that representations were substantially related when attorney consulted former client on lease and partnership agreement that was subject of current litigation); ***H.F. Ahmanson & Co.***, 229 Cal.App.3d at 1455 (movant did not establish any factual or legal similarities between former and current representations).

(b) Attorney was in position to obtain confidential information.

[1] Attorney personally represented movant. If the attorney personally represented the movant, it is conclusively presumed that the attorney obtained the movant's confidential information; no other evidence is required. ***City & Cty. of S.F. v. Cobra Solutions, Inc.*** (2006) 38 Cal.4th 839, 847; ***Jessen***, 111 Cal.App.4th at 709; ***H.F. Ahmanson & Co.***, 229 Cal.App.3d at 1452 & n.2; ***Civil Serv. Comm'n***, 163 Cal.App.3d at 79. Because the presumption is conclusive, the court will not delve into the specifics of the communications between the attorney and the movant in an effort to determine whether the attorney actually received confidential information. ***Jessen***, 111 Cal.App.4th at 709; ***Civil Serv. Comm'n***, 163 Cal.App.3d at 79; *see* ***City Nat'l Bank v. Adams*** (2d Dist.2002) 96 Cal.App.4th 315, 330 (there is no exception to conclusive-presumption rule when attorney personally represented former client).

[2] Attorney did not personally represent movant. If the attorney did not personally represent the movant in the former matter, the movant must show that the attorney's relationship with the movant made it likely that the attorney acquired confidential information material to the current representation. ***Jessen***, 111 Cal.App.4th at 710. A common situation that justifies the disqualification of an attorney who did not personally represent a former client is when another attorney had a personal relationship with the former client and that attorney's knowledge of the client's confidential information is imputed to the attorney. ***Fremont Indem. Co. v. Fremont Gen. Corp.*** (2d Dist.2006) 143 Cal.App.4th 50, 68 n.6; *see, e.g.*, ***Faughn***, 145 Cal.App.4th at 610-11 (evidence did not establish that confidential information was imputed to attorney solely because attorney's former firm handled 220 other cases on movant's behalf). Whether the former client's confidential information will be imputed to an attorney who did not personally represent the client depends on the following:

[a] Member of former firm represented movant. If a member of the attorney's former firm represented the movant, confidential information will not automatically be imputed to the attorney. ***Adams v. Aerojet-Gen. Corp.*** (3d Dist.2001) 86 Cal.App.4th 1324, 1335; *see* ***Faughn***, 145 Cal.App.4th at 610-11. Instead, whether confidential information will be imputed depends on whether the attorney was reasonably likely to have obtained the movant's confidential information before she left the firm. ***Aerojet-Gen.***, 86 Cal.App.4th at 1335; *see*

Faughn, 145 Cal.App.4th at 610. In making this determination, a court can consider the following: (1) the time the attorney spent working on the movant's behalf, (2) the attorney's exposure to formulation of policy or strategy in matters relating to the current dispute, (3) whether the attorney worked out of the same branch office that handled the former litigation, and (4) whether the attorney's administrative or management duties placed her in a position where she would have been exposed to matters relevant to the current dispute. ***Aerojet-Gen.***, 86 Cal.App.4th at 1340; *see* ***Ochoa v. Fordel, Inc.*** (5th Dist.2007) 146 Cal.App.4th 898, 908. If it was reasonably likely that the attorney obtained confidential information, the burden shifts to the attorney to prove that she had no exposure to confidential information while she was a member of the former firm. *See* ***Ochoa***, 146 Cal.App.4th at 908-09; ***Aerojet-Gen.***, 86 Cal.App.4th at 1340-41. To meet this burden, the attorney must affirmatively prove that she had no exposure to confidential information; a cursory denial is not sufficient. ***Ochoa***, 146 Cal.App.4th at 908-09; ***Aerojet-Gen.***, 86 Cal.App.4th at 1340-41.

[b] Member of current firm represented movant. If a member or former member of the attorney's current firm represented the movant, whether confidential information will be imputed to the attorney depends on whether the member who represented the movant has left the firm or is still working at the firm.

- **Member is still with firm.** If the member who represented the movant is still working at the firm, then it will be presumed that the entire firm has been exposed to confidential information. *See* ***Kirk v. First Am. Title Ins.*** (2d Dist.2010) 183 Cal.App.4th 776, 809-10; ***Goldberg v. Warner/Chappell Music, Inc.*** (2d Dist.2005) 125 Cal.App.4th 752, 759-60. In certain situations, the presumption may be rebutted by evidence that the firm's ethical walls were sufficient to protect against the dissemination of confidential information. *See* ***Kirk***, 183 Cal.App.4th at 814. See "Ethical wall," §4.2.4, p. 133.

- **Member has left firm.** If the member who represented the movant is no longer working at the firm, then in most cases, confidential information will not automatically be imputed to the attorneys who remain at the firm. *See* ***Goldberg***, 125 Cal.App.4th at 755. In these situations, it must be established that the attorneys who remained at the firm were actually exposed to confidential information before the former member left the firm. ***Kirk***, 183 Cal.App.4th at 815-16; *see* ***Goldberg***, 125 Cal.App.4th at 762. To determine if the remaining attorneys were exposed to confidential information, the firm's use of ethical walls to protect against the dissemination of confidential information may be considered. ***Kirk***, 183 Cal.App.4th at 816. See "Ethical wall," §4.2.4, p. 133.

3. No consent. To disqualify an attorney based on successive representation, the movant must establish that the attorney did not obtain unqualified, informed written consent from both the movant and the other client. *See* Rules Prof. Conduct, rule 3-310(E); *see, e.g.*, ***Montgomery v. Superior Ct.*** (4th Dist.2010) 186 Cal.App.4th 1051, 1056-57 (former client could not waive attorney-client privilege only for relevant information presented in case). Unlike consent to concurrent representations, consent to successive representations can be implied from conduct. *See* ***Blecher & Collins, P.C. v. Northwest Airlines, Inc.*** (C.D.Cal.1994) 858 F.Supp. 1442, 1455; *see, e.g.*, ***Health Maint. Network v. Blue Cross*** (2d Dist.1988) 202 Cal.App.3d 1043, 1063-64 (former client impliedly consented to adverse representation because it provided new client with attorney); ***River W., Inc. v. Nickel*** (5th Dist.1987) 188 Cal.App.3d 1297, 1312-13 (former client impliedly consented to adverse representation because it delayed in filing motion to disqualify by 39 months).

§2.3 Confidential information from expert, consultant, or employee. A motion to disqualify can be made on the ground that the attorney obtained the movant's confidential information from the movant's attorney's former expert, consultant, or employee (e.g., paralegal, investigator, secretary). *See* ***Western Digital Corp. v. Superior Ct.*** (4th Dist.1998) 60 Cal.App.4th 1471, 1479-80 (expert); ***Toyota Motor Sales, U.S.A., Inc. v. Superior Ct.*** (2d Dist.1996) 46 Cal.App.4th 778, 782 (consultant and employee); ***Shadow Traffic Network v. Superior Ct.*** (2d Dist.1994) 24 Cal.App.4th 1067, 1078-79 (expert). To bring a motion to disqualify on this ground, the movant must establish the following:

1. Actually had confidential information. The movant must establish that its present or past attorney's former expert, consultant, or employee actually had the movant's confidential information. *See* ***Western Digital***, 60 Cal.App.4th at 1487; ***In re Complex Asbestos Litig.*** (1st Dist.1991) 232 Cal.App.3d 572, 596. Disqualification

cannot be based on an adverse party's possession and disclosure of the movant's confidential information. ***Neal v. Health Net, Inc.*** (2d Dist.2002) 100 Cal.App.4th 831, 843-44.

(1) Actual possession. The movant can establish that the former expert, consultant, or employee actually had the movant's confidential information by showing that the information was actually disclosed to or accessed by the individual. *See, e.g.*, ***Collins v. State*** (3d Dist.2004) 121 Cal.App.4th 1112, 1128 (declaration from movant's attorney showed that attorney discussed movant's lawsuit with expert and disclosed confidential work-product information); ***In re Complex Asbestos Litig.***, 232 Cal.App.3d at 597-98 (computer access log showed that paralegal viewed movant's case files containing settlement evaluations). While the movant does not have to specify the actual confidential information possessed, the movant must explain the nature of the confidential information that the former expert, consultant, or employee was exposed to. ***Collins***, 121 Cal.App.4th at 1127. It is insufficient for the movant to show that the individual's access to the information was merely potential or hypothetical. ***Western Digital***, 60 Cal.App.4th at 1487; ***In re Complex Asbestos Litig.***, 232 Cal.App.3d at 596 n.13.

NOTE

*The court in **In re Complex Asbestos Litig.** rejected the argument that the substantial-relationship test, which is used to presume that an attorney has confidential information in successive-representation cases, applies to an attorney's former expert, consultant, or employee. **In re Complex Asbestos Litig.**, 232 Cal.App.3d at 595. See "Substantially related representations," §2.2.2(2)(a), p. 125.*

(2) Confidential information. The movant must establish that the information that the former expert, consultant, or employee has was confidential and that its confidentiality has not been waived. ***Roush v. Seagate Tech.*** (6th Dist.2007) 150 Cal.App.4th 210, 220-21. Under this ground of disqualification, courts have defined the term "confidential information" to mean information that would be protected by the attorney-client or work-product privilege. *See id.* at 225 (attorney-client and work-product privileges); ***Shandralina G. v. Homonchuk*** (4th Dist.2007) 147 Cal.App.4th 395, 406-07 (same); ***In re Complex Asbestos Litig.***, 232 Cal.App.3d at 592 & n.8 (attorney-client privilege); ***County of L.A. v. Superior Ct.*** (2d Dist.1990) 222 Cal.App.3d 647, 657-58 (work-product privilege). For a discussion of these privileges and how they can be waived, see "Attorney-Related Privileges," ch. 6-B, p. 613.

NOTE

*The term "confidential information" is given a broader meaning when a motion for disqualification is based on successive representation. See **Knight v. Ferguson** (2d Dist.2007) 149 Cal.App.4th 1207, 1215. See "Attorney has confidential information," §2.2.2, p. 124.*

2. Material to current litigation. The movant must establish that the movant's confidential information is material to the current litigation. ***Western Digital***, 60 Cal.App.4th at 1487; ***In re Complex Asbestos Litig.***, 232 Cal.App.3d at 596. The following confidential information was held to be materially related to current litigation:

(1) Law firm's settlement evaluations of movant's asbestos cases were materially related to the current asbestos litigation. *See* ***In re Complex Asbestos Litig.***, 232 Cal.App.3d at 597-98.

(2) Attorney's litigation and trial strategies were materially related to the current litigation. *See* ***Shadow Traffic Network***, 24 Cal.App.4th at 1082.

3. Confidential information disclosed. The movant must establish that the former expert, consultant, or employee disclosed the movant's confidential information to the opposing attorney. *See* ***Shadow Traffic Network***, 24 Cal.App.4th at 1084; ***In re Complex Asbestos Litig.***, 232 Cal.App.3d at 596.

(1) Presumption. A presumption that the movant's confidential information was disclosed applies if the opposing attorney hired the former expert, consultant, or employee. *See* ***Toyota Motor Sales***, 46 Cal.App.4th

at 782; ***In re Complex Asbestos Litig.***, 232 Cal.App.3d at 596. The presumption is necessary because the movant no longer has access to the former expert, consultant, or employee to determine whether confidential information was disclosed to the opposing attorney. ***In re Complex Asbestos Litig.***, 232 Cal.App.3d at 596. The presumption can be rebutted by evidence that the former expert, consultant, or employee (1) did not disclose the movant's confidential information to the opposing attorney or (2) was screened from any involvement with the current litigation. *See* ***Western Digital***, 60 Cal.App.4th at 1485, 1488; ***Shadow Traffic Network***, 24 Cal.App.4th at 1087 & n.13; ***In re Complex Asbestos Litig.***, 232 Cal.App.3d at 593-94. For a discussion of screening procedures, see "Ethical wall," §4.2.4, p. 133.

(2) No presumption. No presumption of disclosure applies if (1) the expert hired by the opposing attorney is still retained and controlled by the movant, (2) the opposing attorney did not knowingly hire the movant's expert, and (3) the expert did not intentionally advise both sides. *See* ***Shandralina G.***, 147 Cal.App.4th at 412-13; ***Collins***, 121 Cal.App.4th at 1129. In that situation, the presumption is unnecessary because the movant can satisfy its burden of proving that confidential information was disclosed by simply speaking with its own expert. *See* ***Collins***, 121 Cal.App.4th at 1129.

4. No consent. The movant must establish that the opposing attorney did not obtain informed written consent from the movant's attorney to hire the former expert, consultant, or employee. *See* ***Shadow Traffic Network***, 24 Cal.App.4th at 1084; ***In re Complex Asbestos Litig.***, 232 Cal.App.3d at 592-93 & n.9. See "No consent," §2.1.4, p. 123.

§2.4 Communication with represented party. A motion to disqualify can be made on the ground that the attorney interfered with an attorney-client relationship by communicating with a represented party. *See* Rules Prof. Conduct, rule 2-100(A); ***Jackson v. Ingersoll-Rand Co.*** (1st Dist.1996) 42 Cal.App.4th 1163, 1167. To disqualify an attorney based on the attorney's communication with a represented party, the movant must establish the following:

1. Communicated with represented party. The movant must establish that the attorney, while representing a client, communicated with a represented party on the opposing side of the legal matter. *See* Rules Prof. Conduct, rule 2-100(A).

(1) Communication. The attorney's communication with the represented party can be direct or indirect but must relate to the legal matter that is the subject of the client's representation. *See* Rules Prof. Conduct, rule 2-100(A); *see, e.g.*, ***Truitt v. Superior Ct.*** (2d Dist.1997) 59 Cal.App.4th 1183, 1187-88 (attorney indirectly communicated with opposing party through attorney's investigator). The legal matter can relate to a litigation, prelitigation, or transactional matter. *See* Rules Prof. Conduct, rule 2-100, discussion ¶4 ("subject of the representation" not limited to litigation context); ***Jorgensen v. Taco Bell Corp.*** (1st Dist.1996) 50 Cal.App.4th 1398, 1401 (rule 2-100 might be violated if attorney sought to interview opposing party about matters not yet in litigation). The following communications, however, are not prohibited:

(a) Communications with a public officer, board, committee, or body. Rules Prof. Conduct, rule 2-100(C)(1).

(b) Communications initiated by a party seeking advice or representation from an independent attorney of the party's choice. *Id.* rule 2-100(C)(2); *see id.* rule 2-100, discussion ¶3 (attorney cannot give legal advice to opposing party because she is not an independent attorney).

(c) Communications with the opposing party if the attorney is a party to the legal matter. *Id.* rule 2-100, discussion ¶2.

(d) Communications otherwise authorized by law. *Id.* rule 2-100(C)(3); *see id.* rule 2-100, discussion ¶1.

(2) Represented party. The party that the attorney communicated with must be represented by an attorney on the opposing side of the legal matter. *See* Rules Prof. Conduct, rule 2-100(A); *see, e.g.*, ***Jorgensen***, 50 Cal.App.4th at 1401 (attorney could conduct prelitigation interview of corporation's employees because corporation was not involved in any legal matter); ***Jackson***, 42 Cal.App.4th at 1167 (attorney could communicate with P's ex-wife

because law firm no longer represented her after her only cause of action was dismissed). Generally, a party is represented when it has an attorney of record. ***Abeles v. State Bar*** (1973) 9 Cal.3d 603, 609; *see, e.g.*, ***McMillan v. Shadow Ridge at Oak Park Homeowner's Ass'n*** (2d Dist.2008) 165 Cal.App.4th 960, 966-67 (attorney could communicate with P when court record showed that P was representing herself and attorney assisting her was never substituted as attorney of record). The representation lasts only as long as there is an ongoing attorney-client relationship. *See* ***Jackson***, 42 Cal.App.4th at 1167-68 (Rule Prof. Conduct 2-100 is designed to preserve existing attorney-client relationships; after ex-wife's suit was dismissed, she was no longer represented). If a corporation, association, or partnership is represented by an attorney in a legal matter, certain current employees are also considered to be represented. *See* Rules Prof. Conduct, rule 2-100, discussion ¶5. These employees include the following:

(a) An officer, director, or managing agent of a corporation or association. Rules Prof. Conduct, rule 2-100(B)(1). Managing agents are employees who exercise substantial discretionary authority over decisions that determine policy for the organization. ***Snider v. Superior Ct.*** (4th Dist.2003) 113 Cal.App.4th 1187, 1209.

(b) A partner or managing agent of a partnership. Rules Prof. Conduct, rule 2-100(B)(1).

(c) An association member or employee of an association, corporation, or partnership if the subject of the communication is any act of or omission by the person in connection with the matter that may be binding on or imputed to the organization for purposes of civil or criminal liability. *Id.* rule 2-100(B)(2).

(d) An association member or employee of an association, corporation, or partnership whose statement may amount to an admission by the organization. *Id.*

NOTE

Rule of Professional Conduct 2-100(B) does not prohibit an attorney from contacting former employees of a corporation who are not represented. ***Triple A Mach. Shop, Inc. v. State*** *(1st Dist.1989) 213 Cal.App.3d 131, 140.*

2. Actual knowledge of representation. The movant must establish that the attorney had actual knowledge that the party was represented by an attorney. Rules Prof. Conduct, rule 2-100(A); *see* ***Snider***, 113 Cal.App.4th at 1215 (attorney should not be disqualified because she "should have known" that opposing party was represented). The mere fact that the attorney knows that a corporation employs in-house counsel is insufficient to establish the attorney's actual knowledge. *See, e.g.*, ***Truitt***, 59 Cal.App.4th at 1189 (no evidence that attorney knew corporation was represented when attorney did not receive any oral or written communication from corporation about being represented and attorney directed all prelitigation communications to corporation's claims department).

3. Prejudice to movant. The movant must establish that the attorney's communication with the represented party will have a continuing effect on the current litigation that is prejudicial to the movant. *See* ***Baugh v. Garl*** (2d Dist.2006) 137 Cal.App.4th 737, 744-45. For example, the movant can show that the communication resulted in the movant's confidential information being disclosed to the opposing attorney. *See, e.g.*, ***La Jolla Cove Motel & Hotel Apts., Inc. v. Superior Ct.*** (4th Dist.2004) 121 Cal.App.4th 773, 790 (motion to disqualify was properly denied when there was no evidence that attorneys obtained confidential information from represented party).

4. No consent. The movant must establish that the attorney did not obtain consent from the represented party's attorney before communicating with the represented party. *See* Rules Prof. Conduct, rule 2-100(A). Rule 2-100(A) does not require consent to be in writing. See "No consent," §2.1.4, p. 123.

NOTE

If an officer or director of a corporation is represented by an independent attorney (i.e., a different attorney from the one that represents the corporation), consent from the employee's attorney is sufficient to permit communication with the employee; consent from the corporation's attorney is not also required. ***La Jolla Cove Motel****, 121 Cal.App.4th at 784.*

§2.5 Attorney as witness. A motion to disqualify can be made on the ground that the attorney should be disqualified because she will be called as a witness by her own client or by the opposing party in a jury trial. *See* Rules Prof. Conduct, rule 5-210; ***Smith, Smith & Kring v. Superior Ct.*** (4th Dist.1997) 60 Cal.App.4th 573, 578-79. To disqualify an attorney because she will be a witness in a jury trial, the movant must establish the following:

1. Advocate + witness before jury. The movant must establish that the attorney will be acting as both an advocate and a testifying witness before a jury. *See* Rules Prof. Conduct, rule 5-210; *see also id.* rule 5-210, discussion (attorney from advocate's firm is not prohibited from testifying before jury). The advocating attorney or an attorney from the advocating attorney's firm can testify as a witness in an adversarial proceeding before a judge. *Id.* rule 5-210, discussion. One court has argued that the prohibition against an attorney being a witness should extend to bench trials. ***Kennedy v. Eldridge*** (3d Dist.2011) 201 Cal.App.4th 1197, 1210-11. In ***Kennedy***, the Third District Court of Appeal asserted that the difficulties arising from an attorney acting as both advocate and witness are present regardless of whether the attorney's testimony is given in front of a jury or a judge. *Id.* at 1210. Specifically, an advocate must be partisan, while a witness must be factual. *Id.* Noting that the prohibitions in the California Rules of Professional Conduct are not exclusive, the Third District relied on the ABA Model Rules' general prohibition against an attorney being both an advocate and a witness. ***Kennedy***, 201 Cal.App.4th at 1210.

2. Contested matter. The movant must establish that the attorney's testimony will concern a contested matter other than the nature and value of legal services rendered in the case. *See* Rules Prof. Conduct, rule 5-210(A), (B).

3. Testimony necessary. The movant must establish that the attorney's testimony is necessary. ***Smith, Smith & Kring***, 60 Cal.App.4th at 581. Some of the factors courts consider in determining whether an attorney's testimony is necessary are (1) the significance of the matters that she will testify about, (2) the weight of her testimony, and (3) the availability of other witnesses or documentary evidence to independently establish the matters. ***People v. Dunkle*** (2005) 36 Cal.4th 861, 915, *disapproved on other grounds*, ***People v. Doolin*** (2009) 45 Cal.4th 390; ***Smith, Smith & Kring***, 60 Cal.App.4th at 581.

4. No consent or consent + detriment. The movant must (1) allege that the attorney did not obtain informed written consent or (2) if consent was obtained, establish that permitting the attorney to testify would be detrimental to the movant or harmful to the integrity of the judicial process. *See* Rules Prof. Conduct, rule 5-210(C); ***Smith, Smith & Kring***, 60 Cal.App.4th at 579. *But see* ***People v. Roldan*** (2005) 35 Cal.4th 646, 727-28 (permitted client to give oral consent in open court), *disapproved on other grounds*, ***People v. Doolin*** (2009) 45 Cal.4th 390. See "No consent," §2.1.4, p. 123.

(1) Detrimental to movant. To prove that the attorney's dual role as witness and advocate would be detrimental to the movant, the movant can show that the attorney has the movant's confidential information. *See* ***Smith, Smith & Kring***, 60 Cal.App.4th at 579.

(2) Harmful to judicial process. To prove that the attorney's dual role as witness and advocate would be harmful to the judicial process, the movant must establish that any harm to the judicial process would outweigh a client's right to the counsel of her choice and the expense of replacing counsel. ***Smith, Smith & Kring***, 60 Cal.App.4th at 580. Close calls should be resolved in favor of the client's right to be represented by the counsel of her choice. *Id.*

§3. MOTION

§3.1 Who can file. A motion to disqualify an attorney can be made by a party or on the court's own motion. *See* ***Asbestos Claims Facility v. Berry & Berry*** (1st Dist.1990) 219 Cal.App.3d 9, 27 n.6 (court can disqualify attorney on its own motion), *disapproved on other grounds*, ***Kowis v. Howard*** (1992) 3 Cal.4th 888; *see, e.g.*, ***Gregori v. Bank of Am.*** (1st Dist.1989) 207 Cal.App.3d 291, 295 (Ds moved to disqualify Ps' attorneys). The party does not have to be a client or former client of the attorney to make the motion. ***Kennedy v. Eldridge*** (3d Dist.2011) 201 Cal.App.4th 1197, 1204-05 (nonclient can bring motion to disqualify when ethical breach is "manifest and glaring" and affects

nonclient's interest in litigation). Generally, a nonparty cannot bring a motion to disqualify a party's attorney and should instead file a separate action to enjoin the attorney from continuing to represent the party. ***Machado v. Superior Ct.*** (3d Dist.2007) 148 Cal.App.4th 875, 880-81. One court, however, has allowed a nonparty to bring a motion to disqualify when the nonparty should have been a named party but the plaintiff excluded the nonparty from the suit to avoid an earlier disqualification order. *See id.* at 881-82.

§3.2 Deadline to file & serve. The motion to disqualify must be filed and served at least 16 court days before the hearing and within a reasonable time after the grounds for disqualification become apparent. *See* CCP §1005(b); ***River W., Inc. v. Nickel*** (5th Dist.1987) 188 Cal.App.3d 1297, 1309. See "Delay tactic," §4.2.2, p. 132; "Retrospective deadlines," ch. 1-G, §6.2, p. 71.

§3.3 Contents.

1. Notice of motion & motion. The motion to disqualify should be requested in writing by noticed motion. Younger, *Cal. Motions*, §18:30; *see, e.g.*, ***Western Cont'l Oper. Co. v. Natural Gas Corp.*** (1st Dist.1989) 212 Cal.App.3d 752, 764 (D served Ps with notice of motion and motion to disqualify). See "Notice of motion & motion," ch. 1-D, §5.1, p. 28.

(1) Grounds. The motion should briefly state the grounds for the disqualification. CRC 3.1112(d)(3). See "Grounds," §2, p. 119.

(2) Relief.

(a) Generally. The motion should briefly state the relief sought. CRC 3.1112(d)(3).

(b) Vicarious disqualification. The motion can seek the vicarious disqualification of the attorney's entire firm. *See* ***In re Charlisse C.*** (2008) 45 Cal.4th 145, 161. The vicarious-disqualification rule is based on the presumption that attorneys who practice together share access to privileged and confidential information. ***City & Cty. of S.F. v. Cobra Solutions, Inc.*** (2006) 38 Cal.4th 839, 847-48; ***People v. SpeeDee Oil Change Sys.*** (1999) 20 Cal.4th 1135, 1153-54. Thus, if one attorney is disqualified for obtaining confidential information, all attorneys who work with that attorney should be similarly disqualified. ***In re Charlisse C.***, 45 Cal.4th at 161; *see, e.g.*, ***Shadow Traffic Network v. Superior Ct.*** (2d Dist.1994) 24 Cal.App.4th 1067, 1087-88 (entire firm disqualified because it hired expert previously consulted by opposing counsel). Because the vicarious-disqualification rule is intended to safeguard a client's legitimate expectation that its confidential information will be protected, the rule generally does not apply if the attorney is being disqualified for an ethical violation that does not involve confidential information. *See CEB Procedure Before Trial*, §2.66; *see, e.g.*, Rules Prof. Conduct, rule 5-210, discussion ¶2 (attorney should not be disqualified for serving dual role when another attorney in firm is serving as witness); ***Mills Land & Water Co. v. Golden W. Ref. Co.*** (4th Dist.1986) 186 Cal.App.3d 116, 136 (because confidential information was not divulged, disqualification for communicating with represented party was limited to individual attorney and not entire firm). For a discussion of how a firm can avoid the vicarious-disqualification rule by using ethical walls, see "Ethical wall," §4.2.4, p. 133.

NOTE

Courts refuse to apply vicarious disqualification that involves "double imputation"—that is, when it would require confidential information to first be imputed to an attorney in the disqualified attorney's office and then from that attorney to a third attorney in an entirely separate office. ***Frazier v. Superior Ct.*** *(4th Dist.2002) 97 Cal.App.4th 23, 26-27; see, e.g.,* ***Derivi Constr. & Architecture, Inc. v. Wong*** *(3d Dist.2004) 118 Cal.App.4th 1268, 1270 (court refused to extend vicarious disqualification to attorney whose wife's firm was disqualified).*

2. Memorandum of points & authorities. The motion to disqualify must include a memorandum in support. CRC 3.1112(a)(3), 3.1113(a). See "Memorandum of points & authorities," ch. 1-D, §5.2, p. 28.

3. Supporting evidence.

(1) Generally. For a discussion of the types of evidence that can be used to support a motion, see "Supporting evidence," ch. 1-D, §5.3, p. 30.

(2) Confidential information. If the disclosure of confidential information is necessary to support a motion to disqualify, the movant should file the information under court seal for an in camera review. ***Faughn v. Perez*** (5th Dist.2006) 145 Cal.App.4th 592, 602.

4. Request for judicial notice. If the motion to disqualify is based on matters the court can take judicial notice of, the movant can ask the court to take judicial notice of the matters. *See* CRC 3.1113(*l*). A request for judicial notice must be made in a separate document. *Id.* See "Request for Judicial Notice," ch. 5-J, p. 547.

5. Proposed order. The movant can submit a proposed order with the motion to disqualify. *See* CRC 3.1113(m). If a proposed order is submitted, it must be lodged and served with the motion papers, not attached to them. *Id.*

§3.4 Filing fees. When the motion is filed, the movant must pay a filing fee to the court clerk or request a waiver of the fee. See "Filing Fees," ch. 1-F, §7, p. 58.

§4. OPPOSITION

The nonmovant can respond to a motion to disqualify by filing an opposition.

§4.1 Deadline to file & serve. See "Deadline to file & serve," ch. 1-D, §8.5.3, p. 37.

§4.2 Grounds. The nonmovant can oppose the motion on the following grounds:

1. Consent. The nonmovant can oppose the motion on the ground that the attorney received consent for the alleged ethical violation. For a discussion of the type of consent required for each ground of disqualification, see "Grounds," §2, p. 119.

2. Delay tactic. The nonmovant can oppose the motion on the ground that it was brought as a delay tactic. *E.g.*, ***In re Complex Asbestos Litig.*** (1st Dist.1991) 232 Cal.App.3d 572, 599 (disqualification based on hiring former employee); ***River W., Inc. v. Nickel*** (5th Dist.1987) 188 Cal.App.3d 1297, 1309 (disqualification based on successive representation). A mere delay in bringing the motion, however, is not dispositive; the delay must be extreme in terms of time and consequence. ***Gong v. RFG Oil, Inc.*** (4th Dist.2008) 166 Cal.App.4th 209, 217; *e.g.*, ***River W.***, 188 Cal.App.3d at 1311 (39-month delay in making motion, after opponent spent $387,000 in litigation costs, was unreasonable and prejudicial). To succeed on this ground, the nonmovant must make a prima facie showing that (1) there was unreasonable delay in bringing the motion and (2) the delay will cause prejudice to the nonmovant. ***Fiduciary Trust Int'l v. Superior Ct.*** (2d Dist.2013) 218 Cal.App.4th 465, 490; ***In re Complex Asbestos Litig.***, 232 Cal.App.3d at 599; ***River W.***, 188 Cal.App.3d at 1309. If a prima facie showing is made, the burden shifts back to the movant to prove that the delay was justified. ***Gong***, 166 Cal.App.4th at 217; ***In re Complex Asbestos Litig.***, 232 Cal.App.3d at 599; ***River W.***, 188 Cal.App.3d at 1309. To prove that the delay was justified, the movant should show (1) when it discovered the ground for disqualification, (2) how quickly the motion was made after discovery, (3) whether it was represented by an attorney after the ground for disqualification was discovered, (4) whether anyone prevented the movant from making the motion earlier, and if so, under what circumstances, and (5) whether an earlier motion would have been inappropriate or futile and why. *See* ***River W.***, 188 Cal.App.3d at 1309.

NOTE

It is unclear whether the nonmovant can oppose the motion on the ground that it was a delay tactic when the motion is based on the attorney's concurrent representation of clients with conflicting interests. The Fourth District Court of Appeal has suggested that delay may be an exception to the general rule that an attorney is automatically disqualified in this situation. See ***Gong****, 166 Cal.App.4th at 216-17. But the Second District Court of Appeal has indicated that automatic disqualification is proper, regardless of whether the motion was brought for delay.* ***Blue Water Sunset, LLC v. Markowitz*** *(2d Dist.2011) 192 Cal.App.4th 477, 490.*

3. Harassment tactic. The nonmovant can oppose the motion on the ground that it was brought as a harassment tactic. *See* ***Gregori v. Bank of Am.*** (1st Dist.1989) 207 Cal.App.3d 291, 301. For example, courts are skeptical of motions to disqualify made by litigation adversaries who are not affected by an alleged conflict of interest, particularly when the affected persons do not object. ***McPhearson v. Michaels Co.*** (3d Dist.2002) 96 Cal.App.4th 843, 849-50.

4. Ethical wall. If the motion to disqualify seeks to vicariously disqualify the attorney's entire firm, the attorney can oppose the motion on the ground that an ethical wall was in place to screen attorneys from confidential information. *See* ***In re Charlisse C.*** (2008) 45 Cal.4th 145, 166 (burden is on attorney resisting disqualification to show appropriate screening methods were used to protect confidential information). See "Vicarious disqualification," §3.3.1(2)(b), p. 131. An ethical wall is a set of policies and procedures designed to prevent attorneys within a firm from sharing or being exposed to confidential information. *See* ***Henriksen v. Great Am. S&L*** (1st Dist.1992) 11 Cal.App.4th 109, 116 n.6. Some typical components of an ethical wall include (1) the physical, geographical, and departmental separation of attorneys, (2) prohibitions against and sanctions for discussing confidential matters, (3) established rules and procedures preventing access to confidential information and files, (4) procedures preventing a disqualified attorney from sharing in the profits from the representation, and (5) continuing education in professional responsibility. ***Kirk v. First Am. Title Ins.*** (2d Dist.2010) 183 Cal.App.4th 776, 810-11; ***Henriksen***, 11 Cal.App.4th at 116 n.6. The effectiveness of an ethical wall, however, is not determined by whether a prescribed list of components is present but by whether the wall meets its ultimate goal: does the wall support a reasonable inference that confidential information was not or will not be disclosed by the tainted attorney to any other member of the firm. ***Kirk***, 183 Cal.App.4th at 814. Whether an ethical wall will be effective to prevent the vicarious disqualification of an entire firm depends on the ground of disqualification asserted and whether the attorney is in private practice or government practice.

(1) Concurrent representation. Few cases have addressed whether ethical walls are effective to prevent the vicarious disqualification of an attorney's office for a concurrent representation. See "Concurrent representation," §2.1, p. 119. One court that has addressed the issue has held that ethical walls can be effective in a government office. *See* ***Castro v. Los Angeles Cty Bd. of Supervisors*** (2d Dist.1991) 232 Cal.App.3d 1432, 1444-45. In ***Castro***, the Los Angeles County Board of Supervisors formed a nonprofit public corporation—Dependency Court Legal Services, Inc. (DCLS). *See id.* at 1436. The purpose of DCLS was to represent parents and children in a dependency proceeding, even when the parties had conflicting interests. *Id.* DCLS argued that no conflict of interest would arise because (1) the organization was divided into three separate law groups, each group representing a different party in the dependency proceeding (mother, father, and child), (2) each law group had an independent supervisor who was the attorney of record, (3) all decisions about the handling of a case by a law group were made only by attorneys within that group, (4) staff attorneys reported only to the head of their respective law group, (5) no one outside a law group had access to confidential information, (6) only the head of a law group could recommend firing and salary adjustments of the staff attorneys, (7) each law group was physically separate from the others and had independent files, computers, office space, and clerical help, and (8) the governmental unit that had administrative responsibilities over the DCLS played no role in handling individual cases and had no access to confidential information. *Id.* at 1437-38. The court concluded that the organizational structure of DCLS and the fact that government attorneys do not have a financial interest in the matters they work on were sufficient to prevent the vicarious disqualification of the entire government office. *Id.* at 1441-42; *see also* ***In re Charlisse C.***, 45 Cal.4th at 160 (noting that stringent disqualification standard in ***Castro*** applies to concurrent representations and not successive representations).

(2) Successive representation.

(a) Private practice. In successive-representation cases, courts have generally held that the use of ethical walls is not effective for preventing the vicarious disqualification of an attorney's entire office when an attorney moves from one private law office to another. *E.g.*, ***Meza v. H. Muehlstein & Co.*** (2d Dist.2009) 176 Cal.App.4th 969, 978-79; ***Henriksen***, 11 Cal.App.4th at 117; ***Hitachi, Ltd. v. Tatung Co.*** (N.D.Cal.2006) 419 F.Supp.2d

1158, 1164. See "Successive representation," §2.2, p. 124. The Second District Court of Appeal has held that such a conclusive rule should not apply unless the attorney switches sides in the same legal matter (e.g., attorney who formerly represented D against P moves to new firm that represents P against D in same legal matter). ***Kirk***, 183 Cal.App.4th at 814. The court held that in all other cases, when an attorney moves from one private law office to another, the use of ethical walls should be considered to determine whether vicarious disqualification is required. *Id.*

(b) Government practice. In successive-representation cases, courts have permitted the use of ethical walls to prevent the vicarious disqualification of an attorney's entire office when an attorney leaves private practice for government employment, leaves government employment for private practice, or switches from one government office to another. *See* ***In re Charlisse C.***, 45 Cal.4th at 163; ***City of Santa Barbara v. Superior Ct.*** (2d Dist.2004) 122 Cal.App.4th 17, 25, 27; ***Chambers v. Superior Ct.*** (3d Dist.1981) 121 Cal.App.3d 893, 902-03. Courts have cited several reasons for the government-practice exception, including that government attorneys do not have a financial interest in the matters they work on and that the government would have a harder time recruiting qualified attorneys if they knew their future prospects in the private sector would be limited. ***City of Santa Barbara***, 122 Cal.App.4th at 24. Ethical walls may be ineffective, however, when the attorney with the actual conflict has managerial, supervisory, or policymaking responsibilities within the government office. ***In re Charlisse C.***, 45 Cal.4th at 163. In deciding whether vicarious disqualification should apply in these situations, the court should (1) make a factual inquiry into the attorney's actual duties and responsibilities to determine what effect they might have on the subordinate attorneys' handling of the litigation and (2) consider whether public awareness of the case, the conflicted attorney's role in the litigation, or another circumstance is likely to cast doubt on the integrity of the government office's continued participation in the matter. *Id.* at 165.

(3) Confidential information from expert, consultant, or employee. In cases involving the hiring of a former expert, consultant, or employee, courts have permitted the use of ethical walls to prevent the vicarious disqualification of an attorney's entire office. *See* ***Western Digital Corp. v. Superior Ct.*** (4th Dist.1998) 60 Cal.App.4th 1471, 1488 (showing formal screening process is one way, but not only way, to prove that confidential information was not disclosed or used); ***In re Complex Asbestos Litig.***, 232 Cal.App.3d at 593 (presumption of shared confidences is rebuttable when confidential information is obtained by nonattorneys; most likely means of rebutting presumption is to implement screening procedures). See "Confidential information from expert, consultant, or employee," §2.3, p. 126.

§4.3 Contents. For a general discussion of the contents of an opposition, see "Opposition Papers," ch. 1-D, §8, p. 35.

§5. REPLY

The movant can file and serve a reply to the opposition. The reply must be filed and served at least five court days before the hearing. CCP §1005(b). See "Reply Papers," ch. 1-D, §9, p. 37.

§6. HEARING

Hearings on a motion to disqualify are conducted in the same manner as civil hearings generally. See "Hearings," ch. 1-H, p. 79.

§7. RULING

§7.1 Generally.

1. Discretionary. In most cases, the court's decision to grant or deny a motion to disqualify an attorney is within the court's discretion. In exercising its discretion, the court must balance two competing interests: (1) the combined weight of a party's right to chosen counsel, the attorney's interest in representing the client, the financial burden in replacing counsel, and any tactical abuse underlying the motion, and (2) the need to maintain ethical standards of professional responsibility. ***Med-Trans Corp. v. City of Cal. City*** (5th Dist.2007) 156 Cal.App.4th 655, 663-64; *see* ***Shen v. Miller*** (2d Dist.2012) 212 Cal.App.4th 48, 55; ***In re Marriage of Zimmerman*** (1st Dist.1993) 16

Cal.App.4th 556, 562-63. The client's right to chosen counsel must yield, however, to ethical considerations that affect the "fundamental principles" of the judicial system. ***People v. SpeeDee Oil Change Sys.*** (1999) 20 Cal.4th 1135, 1145. The California Supreme Court noted that there are two ethical considerations that fundamentally affect the judicial system: (1) the duty of loyalty (concurrent representations) and (2) the duty of confidentiality (successive representations). *Id.* at 1146. Thus, a party's right to chosen counsel should not be weighed against a motion for disqualification that is based on concurrent or successive representation. *See* ***H.F. Ahmanson & Co. v. Salomon Bros.*** (2d Dist.1991) 229 Cal.App.3d 1445, 1451 (successive representation; after finding ethical violation, court does not balance parties' competing interests); ***River W., Inc. v. Nickel*** (5th Dist.1987) 188 Cal.App.3d 1297, 1308 (same). In fact, the only factor that has been successfully asserted against a motion to disqualify when concurrent or successive representation has been found is tactical abuse. *See, e.g.*, ***River W.***, 188 Cal.App.3d at 1313 (successive representation; disqualification order reversed because of D's unreasonable delay in bringing motion and resulting prejudice to P).

2. Mandatory. Generally, the granting of a motion to disqualify an attorney is mandatory when the attorney concurrently represents adversaries in the same legal matter at a contested hearing or trial. *See* ***Blue Water Sunset, LLC v. Markowitz*** (2d Dist.2011) 192 Cal.App.4th 477, 490; ***Klemm v. Superior Ct.*** (5th Dist.1977) 75 Cal.App.3d 893, 898. In these situations, even a client's consent to the representation will not be sufficient to avoid disqualification. ***Klemm***, 75 Cal.App.3d at 898. However, courts have left open the possibility that automatic disqualification is not mandatory in certain situations. *See* ***Blue Water Sunset***, 192 Cal.App.4th at 487 (automatic disqualification is rule "in all but a few instances"); ***Gong v. RFG Oil, Inc.*** (4th Dist.2008) 166 Cal.App.4th 209, 216-17 (suggesting that delay may be exception to automatic disqualification if impact is sufficiently extreme); ***State Farm Mut. Auto. Ins. v. Federal Ins.*** (5th Dist.1999) 72 Cal.App.4th 1422, 1432 (suggesting that attorney can avoid automatic disqualification by immediately withdrawing from concurrent adverse representation that occurred by mere happenstance); ***Truck Ins. Exch. v. Fireman's Fund Ins.*** (1st Dist.1992) 6 Cal.App.4th 1050, 1058-59 (same).

§7.2 Effect of consent. Generally, the court will not disqualify an attorney if the attorney has obtained consent for the ethical violation. For a discussion of the different types of consent required, see "Grounds," §2, p. 119. Even if consent is obtained, it does not eliminate the court's discretion in deciding whether to disqualify the attorney. The court can still disqualify the attorney if, despite obtaining consent, it is not reasonably likely that the attorney will be able to provide adequate representation to one or more clients. ***Sharp v. Next Entm't, Inc.*** (2d Dist.2008) 163 Cal.App.4th 410, 436; *see* ***Klemm v. Superior Ct.*** (5th Dist.1977) 75 Cal.App.3d 893, 898 (client cannot consent to concurrent representation at trial or contested hearing when there is an actual conflict); *see, e.g.*, ***In re A.C.*** (4th Dist.2000) 80 Cal.App.4th 994, 1002 (consent not sufficient to avoid disqualification when attorney, who pleaded no contest to sexually abusing his own daughters, tried to represent daughters in petition to destroy their juvenile-dependency files).

§8. ORDER

§8.1 Form. The court's ruling on the motion to disqualify must be recorded either in writing or by minute order. *See, e.g.*, ***Fremont Indem. Co. v. Fremont Gen. Corp.*** (2d Dist.2006) 143 Cal.App.4th 50, 60 (minute order); *see also* ***Responsible Citizens v. Superior Ct.*** (5th Dist.1993) 16 Cal.App.4th 1717, 1734 n.6 (statement of decision not required for disqualification motions). See "Record of Ruling," ch. 1-I, §4, p. 90.

§8.2 Contents. The order should state the basis of the court's ruling. *See, e.g.*, ***Rosenfeld Constr. Co. v. Superior Ct.*** (5th Dist.1991) 235 Cal.App.3d 566, 572 (order stated that motion was denied because no attorney at firm had knowledge of earlier representation and there was no actual or potential conflict). One court has held that if the court balances the competing interests in deciding whether to grant or deny the motion, the court must indicate on the record what factors it considered and make specific findings of fact about the factors. ***Smith, Smith & Kring v. Superior Ct.*** (4th Dist.1997) 60 Cal.App.4th 573, 582. For a discussion of the factors the court can consider, see "Discretionary," §7.1.1, p. 134.

§8.3 Notice. See "Notice of Order," ch. 1-I, §5, p. 93.

§8.4 Effect of disqualification. If the court grants the motion to disqualify, the attorney is entitled to recover attorney fees for work done before the ethical violation occurred. *E.g.*, ***Jeffry v. Pounds*** (3d Dist.1977) 67 Cal.App.3d 6, 12 (attorney was barred from recovering attorney fees from time conflict of interest arose). Whether the attorney can recover fees for work done after the violation occurred may depend on the egregiousness of the ethical violation. *See* ***Mardirossian & Assocs. v. Ersoff*** (2d Dist.2007) 153 Cal.App.4th 257, 278; ***Pringle v. La Chapelle*** (2d Dist.1999) 73 Cal.App.4th 1000, 1006. For a discussion of recovering attorney fees after an attorney is removed, see "Recovering Fees & Costs After Removal or Withdrawal," ch. 2-B, §7, p. 115.

§9. MOTION FOR RECONSIDERATION

A party who is adversely affected by a court's order on a motion to disqualify can file a motion for reconsideration. *See* CCP §1008(a). See "Motion for Reconsideration," ch. 5-G, §3, p. 508.

§10. MOTION FOR RENEWAL

A party whose motion to disqualify is denied can file a motion for renewal. *See* CCP §1008(b). See "Motion for Renewal," ch. 5-G, §4, p. 516.

§11. APPELLATE REVIEW

§11.1 Appealability.

1. Writ of mandate. A ruling on a motion to disqualify can be challenged by filing a petition for a writ of mandate. *See* ***Reed v. Superior Ct.*** (2d Dist.2001) 92 Cal.App.4th 448, 455-56; *see, e.g.*, ***Dill v. Superior Ct.*** (3d Dist.1984) 158 Cal.App.3d 301, 302 (P filed petition for writ of mandate challenging order denying motion to disqualify). A petition for a writ of mandate accompanied by a request for an immediate stay is the preferred method for challenging a ruling on a motion to disqualify. ***Apple Computer, Inc. v. Superior Ct.*** (2d Dist.2005) 126 Cal.App.4th 1253, 1263-64.

2. Direct appeal. A ruling on a motion to disqualify is an appealable order subject to immediate appellate review. ***Machado v. Superior Ct.*** (3d Dist.2007) 148 Cal.App.4th 875, 882; ***Reed***, 92 Cal.App.4th at 452; *see also* ***Meehan v. Hopps*** (1955) 45 Cal.2d 213, 215-16 (order denying motion to disqualify and to enjoin counsel from disclosing confidential information about case was appealable because denial of motions for injunctive relief is appealable).

NOTE

Courts disagree on whether a ruling on a motion to disqualify is reviewable on appeal from the final judgment. Compare ***Machado****, 148 Cal.App.4th at 884 (not reviewable on appeal from final judgment because CCP §906 does not allow court to review any decision or order from which an appeal might have been taken), with* ***Pour Le Bebe, Inc. v. Guess? Inc.*** *(2d Dist.2003) 112 Cal.App.4th 810, 837 (reviewable on appeal from final judgment if complaining party can show that ruling affected outcome of proceeding and prejudiced party), and* ***In re Sophia B.*** *(4th Dist.1988) 203 Cal.App.3d 1436, 1439 (same).*

---

§11.2 Standard of review. The trial court's ruling on a motion to disqualify is reviewed for abuse of discretion. ***In re Charlisse C.*** (2008) 45 Cal.4th 145, 159. The court's factual findings are accepted as correct if supported by substantial evidence, while its legal conclusions are reviewed de novo. *Id.*; *see* ***Shen v. Miller*** (2d Dist.2012) 212 Cal.App.4th 48, 55 (when there are no material fact issues in dispute, court's ruling is question of law).

D. MOTION & STATEMENT TO DISQUALIFY JUDGE

This subchapter discusses how to disqualify a superior-court judge, court commissioner, or referee from a hearing or trial. This subchapter does not discuss how to disqualify arbitrators or temporary judges. For the statutes and rules on these topics, see CCP §1141.18(d) (judicial arbitrators) and §1281.91 (arbitrators in contractual arbitration proceedings) and CRC 2.818(f) (temporary judges appointed by court), CRC 2.831(e) (temporary judges requested by parties), and CRC 3.816 (judicial arbitrators).

§1. GENERAL

§1.1 Purpose. Motions and statements to disqualify a judge are used to remove a superior-court judge, court commissioner, or referee from a hearing or trial. *See* CCP §§170.3(c)(1), 170.5(a), 170.6(a)(1), (a)(2). The ability to disqualify a judge safeguards each party's right to a fair and impartial hearing or trial and preserves the public's confidence in the judicial system. *See* ***Curle v. Superior Ct.*** (2001) 24 Cal.4th 1057, 1070 (statement of disqualification); ***Hemingway v. Superior Ct.*** (4th Dist.2004) 122 Cal.App.4th 1148, 1154 (motion to disqualify).

§1.2 Primary authority. CCP §§170.1-170.8.

§1.3 Secondary authority. The following secondary sources are cited as authority in this subchapter:

- *California Civil Procedure Before Trial* (CEB Online ed. 2014) (referred to as *CEB Procedure Before Trial*).
- *California Judges Benchguides: Disqualification of Judge* (CJER 2010) (referred to as *Cal. Judges Benchguides*).
- *California Trial Practice: Civil Procedure During Trial* (CEB Online ed. 2014) (referred to as *CEB Procedure During Trial*).
- Kiesel et al., *Matthew Bender Practice Guide: California Pretrial Civil Procedure* (2014) (referred to as Kiesel, *Cal. Pretrial Civil Procedure*).
- Witkin, *California Procedure* (5th ed. 2008 & Supp.2014) (referred to as Witkin, *Cal. Procedure*).

§2. WHO CAN BE DISQUALIFIED

Motions to disqualify and statements of disqualification can be used to disqualify superior-court judges, court commissioners, and referees from a hearing or trial. *See* CCP §§170.3(c)(1), 170.5(a), 170.6(a)(1), (a)(2).

NOTE

For ease of reference, the term "judge" will be used throughout this subchapter to refer to superior-court judges, court commissioners, and referees.

§3. METHODS OF DISQUALIFICATION

A party can disqualify a judge by filing either a motion to disqualify (also known as a peremptory challenge) or a statement of disqualification (also known as a challenge for cause). The methods of disqualification are cumulative, not mutually exclusive. CCP §170.6(b); *see* ***Pacific & Sw. Annual Conf. of the United Methodist Ch. v. Superior Ct.*** (4th Dist.1978) 82 Cal.App.3d 72, 80 (motion to disqualify and statement of disqualification are separate and distinct methods of disqualification).

There are several important differences between the two methods of disqualification. A motion to disqualify can be filed only once but does not require factual proof of the judge's prejudice to be successful. ***Home Ins. v. Superior Ct.*** (2005) 34 Cal.4th 1025, 1032. A statement of disqualification, on the other hand, can be filed multiple times as long as each new statement alleges facts suggesting new grounds for the disqualification. CCP §170.4(c)(3).

Although no statutory rules require one method to be asserted before another, sometimes there is a practical reason for a party to assert one method before another. *See* ***Pacific & Sw. Annual Conf.***, 82 Cal.App.3d at 80. If there is

cause for disqualification, a party should save its motion to disqualify and file a statement of disqualification. *CEB Procedure During Trial*, §6.31. If a party is unsure whether cause exists, a motion to disqualify should be filed instead or requested in the alternative. *See* ***Pacific & Sw. Annual Conf.***, 82 Cal.App.3d at 80 (motion to disqualify is "ace in the hole"). Chart 2-1, below, summarizes some of the differences between the two methods of disqualification.

2-1. MOTION TO DISQUALIFY VS. STATEMENT OF DISQUALIFICATION			
		Motion to disqualify	**Statement of disqualification**
1	How many can be made	One motion per party or side. See §4.2.7(2), p. 144.	No limit if facts establishing new grounds for disqualification are discovered or arise after initial statement was filed. See §5.4.6, p. 159.
2	Proof required	No factual proof of prejudice required. See §4.1.2, this page.	Must state facts showing cause for disqualification. See §5.4.5(1)(a), p. 159.
3	Deadline to file	Before hearing or trial commences unless exception requires earlier deadline. See §4.2.6, p. 141.	Earliest practicable opportunity. See §5.4.2(1), p. 157.

§4. MOTION TO DISQUALIFY – PEREMPTORY CHALLENGE

§4.1 Movant's burden. To prevail on a motion to disqualify, the movant must do the following:

1. Hearing, trial, or all-purpose assignment. The movant must establish that there is (1) a pending hearing involving a contested issue of fact or law, (2) a pending trial, or (3) an all-purpose assignment. ***Grant v. Superior Ct.*** (6th Dist.2001) 90 Cal.App.4th 518, 526; *see* CCP §170.6(a)(1), (a)(2).

(1) Pending hearing. A pending hearing involving a contested issue of fact or law is a hearing that (1) has been placed on the court's calendar and (2) requires the court to rule on some disputed issue of fact or law based on legal argument, evidence, or both. *See* ***Grant***, 90 Cal.App.4th at 525-26. Case-management conferences, pretrial conferences, and settlement conferences do not qualify as pending hearings because they do not require the judge to rule on any contested issue of fact or law. *See id.* at 526.

(2) Pending trial. A pending trial is a trial that has been placed on the court's calendar. *See* ***Grant***, 90 Cal.App.4th at 525.

(3) All-purpose assignment. An all-purpose assignment occurs when (1) the method of assigning cases instantly pinpoints the judge the parties can expect to preside at trial, and (2) that judge has been assigned to the case for all purposes (i.e., the judge is expected to preside over all aspects of the case, including motions and trial). ***People v. Superior Ct. (Lavi)*** (1993) 4 Cal.4th 1164, 1180; ***Grant***, 90 Cal.App.4th at 524. There is no requirement that a hearing or trial be pending before a party files a motion to disqualify a judge who has been assigned to a case for all purposes. *See* ***Grant***, 90 Cal.App.4th at 525 (trial date does not have to be set). For a discussion of all-purpose assignments, see "All-purpose assignment," §4.2.5(2)(b), p. 140.

2. Judge is prejudiced. The movant must assert that the judge is prejudiced against a party, an attorney, or the interests of a party or an attorney. CCP §170.6(a)(1). The movant does not have to prove actual prejudice; a good-faith belief that the judge is prejudiced is sufficient. ***Solberg v. Superior Ct.*** (1977) 19 Cal.3d 182, 193; ***Entente Design, Inc. v. Superior Ct.*** (4th Dist.2013) 214 Cal.App.4th 385, 389. *But see* ***School Dist. of Okaloosa Cty. v. Superior Ct.*** (2d Dist. 1997) 58 Cal.App.4th 1126, 1136-37 (motion to disqualify cannot be opposed on ground that it was made in bad faith). To assert that the judge is prejudiced, the movant must allege that the judge is prejudiced against a party, an attorney, or the interests of a party or an attorney so that the party or attorney cannot, or believes she cannot, have a fair and impartial hearing or trial before the judge. CCP §170.6(a)(2).

§4.2 Motion.

1. Who can file. A party to, or an attorney appearing in, an action or proceeding can file a motion to disqualify a judge. CCP §170.6(a)(2). The motion cannot be made by a nonparty. *See* ***Avelar v. Superior Ct.*** (4th

Dist.1992) 7 Cal.App.4th 1270, 1277 (nonparty witness cannot make motion to disqualify); *see, e.g.*, ***Frisk v. Superior Ct.*** (4th Dist.2011) 200 Cal.App.4th 402, 410-11 (D's motion to disqualify was deemed moot because D was dismissed from suit before court ruled on motion).

2. Form.

(1) Generally. In most cases, the motion can be made either orally or in writing. *See* CCP §170.6(a)(2).

(2) Exception. A motion to disqualify a judge in a coordination proceeding must be in writing. CRC 3.516. For a discussion of coordination of complex cases, see *CEB Procedure Before Trial*, §§44.14-44.41.

3. Contents.

(1) Generally. A written motion to disqualify a judge should comply with the general requirements for the first page of a paper that is filed with the court. See "First page," ch. 1-B, §2.5.2, p. 12. The paper does not have to be labeled a "motion"; it just needs to contain an express request for relief. *See* ***Fry v. Superior Ct.*** (2d Dist.2013) 222 Cal.App.4th 475, 482; ***Louisiana-Pac. Corp. v. Philo Lumber Co.*** (1st Dist.1985) 163 Cal.App.3d 1212, 1223; *see, e.g.*, Super. Ct. Los Angeles Cty., Form LACIV 015 (form captioned "Peremptory Challenge to Judicial Officer"); Super. Ct. San Diego Cty., Form CIV-249 (form captioned "Peremptory Challenge").

(a) Request disqualification & reassignment. The motion should request the disqualification of the judge and a reassignment of the hearing or trial to a different judge. *See* CCP §170.6(a)(4); *see, e.g.*, Super. Ct. San Diego Cty., Form CIV-249 (form requests reassignment); ***Louisiana-Pac.***, 163 Cal.App.3d at 1223 (D's motion requested judge's disqualification). One court recently held that a request for relief contained in the motion's caption, without any additional language requesting relief in the motion, is sufficient. ***Fry***, 222 Cal.App.4th at 482 (upholding Super. Ct. Los Angeles Cty., Form LACIV 015 because caption including "Peremptory Challenge to Judicial Officer" indicated request for relief).

(b) Court's order. The motion can provide a place for the court to grant or deny the request for disqualification and reassignment. *See* Super. Ct. San Diego Cty., Form CIV-249.

(2) Supporting evidence. The motion must be supported by one of the following: an oral statement made under oath, an affidavit, or a declaration. CCP §170.6(a)(2); *see, e.g.*, ***People v. St. Andrew*** (1st Dist.1980) 101 Cal.App.3d 450, 456 (oral motion to disqualify was defective because attorney's statement was not oral statement under oath, affidavit, or declaration). The supporting evidence must state that the judge before whom the hearing or trial is pending or to whom the case is assigned is prejudiced against a party, an attorney, or the interests of a party or an attorney so that the party or attorney cannot, or believes she cannot, have a fair and impartial hearing or trial. CCP §170.6(a)(2), (a)(6), (a)(7). If the movant submits an affidavit, it must be in substantially the same form as the sample affidavit provided by CCP §170.6(a)(6). If the movant makes an oral statement under oath or a declaration, it must contain substantially the same information as the sample affidavit in CCP §170.6(a)(6). *Id.* §170.6(a)(7). The supporting evidence can be incorporated in the motion or filed separately. *See, e.g.*, Super. Ct. San Diego Cty., Form CIV-249 (declaration included in form for motion); ***Fry***, 222 Cal.App.4th at 482 (Super. Ct. Los Angeles Cty., Form LACIV 015 satisfied affidavit and motion requirements for peremptory challenge; movant was not required to file separate documents).

NOTE

The movant is not required to state specific facts or reasons why she believes the judge is prejudiced. ***Solberg v. Superior Ct.*** *(1977) 19 Cal.3d 182, 199. A simple statement that she believes the judge is prejudiced is all that is required. See id.*

4. Notice.

(1) Before motion filed. The movant is not required to serve notice on all parties before the motion is filed. *See* CCP §170.6(a)(2) ("party ... may establish this prejudice by an oral or written motion without prior notice").

(2) After motion filed. The movant is required to serve notice on all parties within five days after the motion is filed. CCP §170.6(a)(3).

5. Where to file. The motion must be filed with the proper judge. *See* CCP §170.6(a)(2); ***Fry***, 222 Cal.App.4th at 482-83.

CAUTION

Although CCP §170.6(a)(2) requires the motion to be "made to" the proper judge, the movant can file the motion with the court clerk instead of handing it to the judge personally. See CCP §170.6(a)(2); ***Fry****, 222 Cal.App.4th at 484. If the movant files the motion with the court clerk, the movant must provide instructions directing the motion to the proper judge. See, e.g.,* ***Fry****, 222 Cal.App.4th at 483 (court properly denied peremptory challenge because movant fax-filed motion with clerk but did not specifically direct motion to assigned or presiding judge).*

(1) When disqualifying judge from hearing.

(a) Most actions or proceedings. In most actions or proceedings, the movant should file its motion to disqualify a judge from a hearing with either the assigned judge (i.e., the judge who is being challenged) or the supervising judge of the court (also known as the presiding judge). *See CEB Procedure During Trial*, §6.59.

(b) Coordination proceeding. In a coordination proceeding, the motion must be filed with the assigned judge. CRC 3.516.

(2) When disqualifying judge from trial. A motion to disqualify a judge from a trial must be filed with one of the following, depending on the type of assignment that was made: the assigned judge, the supervising judge, or the master-calendar judge (i.e., the judge supervising the master calendar). *See Cal. Judges Benchguides*, §2.42. Labels used by the court may be viewed as prima facie evidence of what type of assignment occurred (e.g., "master-calendar court" would be prima facie evidence of a master-calendar assignment), but it is the function and purpose of the court, not the label, that determines what type of assignment occurred. ***Daniel V. v. Superior Ct.*** (3d Dist.2006) 139 Cal.App.4th 28, 40; *see, e.g.*, ***People v. Superior Ct. (Lavi)*** (1993) 4 Cal.4th 1164, 1174-75 (fact that judge's department was labeled as master-calendar court was not conclusive). The party contesting the label has the burden to prove that the label does not fit the court. ***Daniel V.***, 139 Cal.App.4th at 40; *e.g.*, ***D.M. v. Superior Ct.*** (2d Dist.2011) 196 Cal.App.4th 879, 887-88 (although court labeled assignment as all-purpose assignment, referee could not handle entire juvenile-court matter without stipulation of parties).

(a) Master-calendar assignment. When a trial has been assigned to a judge from a master-calendar court, the motion must be filed with the master-calendar judge. CCP §170.6(a)(2). A trial assignment from a master-calendar court occurs when (1) the parties have advance notice that a court is a master-calendar court, (2) the parties personally appear before the master-calendar judge when the assignment is made, (3) the master-calendar judge assigns a trial-ready case to a trial-ready courtroom—that is, a courtroom that is available on the same day as the assignment or the following morning—and (4) the identity of the assigned judge is known. *See* ***Lavi***, 4 Cal.4th at 1176-77 & n.8 (element 3); ***Entente Design, Inc. v. Superior Ct.*** (4th Dist.2013) 214 Cal.App.4th 385, 391-92 (element 1); ***People v. Bonds*** (1st Dist.1988) 200 Cal.App.3d 1018, 1024 (element 4); ***People v. Montalvo*** (2d Dist.1981) 117 Cal.App.3d 790, 794 (element 2). For a discussion of master-calendar courts, see "Master-calendar system," ch. 3-E, §3.3.1(2)(a), p. 253.

(b) All-purpose assignment. When a trial has been assigned to a judge for all purposes (also known as direct calendaring), the motion must be filed with either the assigned judge or the presiding judge of the court. CCP §170.6(a)(2). An all-purpose assignment occurs when (1) the method of assigning cases instantly pinpoints the judge whom the parties can expect to preside at trial and (2) the assigned judge is expected to handle the case in its entirety from the time of the assignment. ***Lavi***, 4 Cal.4th at 1180; ***Daniel V.***, 139 Cal.App.4th at 39. One court has held that an assignment is an all-purpose assignment only if it derives from a court order or written local

rule. *E.g.*, ***Daniel V.***, 139 Cal.App.4th at 40-41 (purported all-purpose assignment was not effective because it was made in notice of petition by deputy county clerk according to informal court practice). Although the court's opinion in ***Daniel V.*** was limited to all-purpose assignments in juvenile cases under the Welfare and Institutions Code, the court's reasoning would seem to have broader application. *See* ***Daniel V.***, 139 Cal.App.4th at 46 (peremptory challenge is important due-process right, and courts must refrain from any tactic or maneuver that has practical effect of diminishing right). For a discussion of all-purpose assignments, see "Direct-calendar system," ch. 3-E, §3.3.1(2)(b), p. 253.

(c) Single-judge-court assignment. When a trial has been assigned to a judge in a court that is authorized to have only one judge, the motion must be filed with that judge. *Cal. Judges Benchguides*, §2.42.

(d) Coordination-proceeding assignment. When a trial has been assigned to a judge in a coordination proceeding, the motion must be filed with the assigned judge. CRC 3.516.

(e) New-trial assignment. When a judge whose decision or final judgment was reversed after a successful appeal or writ proceeding has been assigned to the new trial on remand, the motion must be filed with the assigned judge. *Cal. Judges Benchguides*, §2.42. For a discussion of what qualifies as a new trial, see "Remand for new trial," §4.2.7(2)(b)[2][b], p. 146.

(f) Assignment to other identifiable judge. When a trial has been assigned to a judge whose identity is reasonably certain at least ten days before the trial and no other type of assignment applies, the motion must be filed with either the assigned judge or the supervising judge. *Cal. Judges Benchguides*, §2.42. The identity of the judge is reasonably certain if a party can determine the judge assigned or scheduled to conduct the trial through investigation or inquiry. *See* ***Lavi***, 4 Cal.4th at 1183; ***Lawrence v. Superior Ct.*** (2d Dist.1988) 206 Cal.App.3d 611, 617.

6. Deadline to file.

(1) Generally. Generally, a motion to disqualify a judge must be filed before the hearing or trial has commenced. ***Lavi***, 4 Cal.4th at 1171; ***Entente Design***, 214 Cal.App.4th at 389. If the general deadline is met, the motion to disqualify is timely unless an exception to the general rule requires the motion to be filed earlier. ***Lavi***, 4 Cal.4th at 1171; ***Shipp v. Superior Ct.*** (2d Dist.1992) 5 Cal.App.4th 147, 150; *see* CCP §170.6(a)(2) (exceptions to general rule). See "Exceptions," §4.2.6(2), p. 143.

NOTE

In most cases, an exception to the general deadline will apply.

(a) Before hearing commences.

[1] Generally. For purposes of bringing a timely motion to disqualify, a hearing commences when the court convenes the parties. *See, e.g.*, ***Schorr v. Superior Ct.*** (2d Dist.1980) 105 Cal.App.3d 568, 570 (conference in chambers commenced hearing on orders to show cause).

[2] Effect of earlier hearing. If the judge has already presided over a hearing in the case, a party is generally not barred from bringing a motion to disqualify the judge from a later hearing. CCP §170.6(a)(2). This rule does not apply, however, if the judge at the earlier hearing determined a contested fact issue that related to the merits of the case. ***Swift v. Superior Ct.*** (6th Dist.2009) 172 Cal.App.4th 878, 883; *see* CCP §170.6(a)(2). If the judge has already made such a determination, a party can no longer bring a motion to disqualify. *See* CCP §170.6(a)(2); ***Swift***, 172 Cal.App.4th at 883. The only way to disqualify a judge after that point is to bring a statement of disqualification. See "Statement of Disqualification – Challenge for Cause," §5, p. 150.

[a] Rulings that resolve facts relating to merits. Rulings on the following pretrial motions determine contested fact issues related to the merits of a case:

- Motions for preliminary injunctions that assess the likelihood of success at trial. ***Pacific & Sw. Annual Conf. of the United Methodist Ch. v. Superior Ct.*** (4th Dist.1978) 82 Cal.App.3d 72, 80. *But see* ***Guardado v. Superior Ct.*** (2d Dist.2008) 163 Cal.App.4th 91, 98-99 (preliminary determination under Civ. C. §3295(c) that P has demonstrated substantial probability that it will prevail on claim for punitive damages is not determination of contested fact issue).

- Motions for summary adjudication of "make or break" issues involving contract interpretation. ***California Fed. S&L Ass'n v. Superior Ct.*** (2d Dist.1987) 189 Cal.App.3d 267, 271. *But see* ***Fight for the Rams v. Superior Ct.*** (4th Dist.1996) 41 Cal.App.4th 953, 959-60 (court in ***California Fed. S&L*** ignored requirement that ruling determine contested fact issues).

- Motions to suppress in criminal proceedings. ***In re Abdul Y.*** (3d Dist.1982) 130 Cal.App.3d 847, 859-60.

[b] Rulings that do not resolve facts relating to merits. Rulings on most pretrial motions do not determine contested fact issues related to the merits of a case. ***Swift***, 172 Cal.App.4th at 883; ***School Dist. of Okaloosa Cty. v. Superior Ct.*** (2d Dist.1997) 58 Cal.App.4th 1126, 1133. Rulings on the following pretrial motions do not determine contested fact issues related to the merits of a case:

- Demurrers. *See* ***Fight for the Rams***, 41 Cal.App.4th at 958.

- Motions for judgment on the pleadings. *See* ***Hospital Council of N. Cal. v. Superior Ct.*** (1st Dist.1973) 30 Cal.App.3d 331, 337.

- Motions for summary judgment. ***Bambula v. Superior Ct.*** (3d Dist.1985) 174 Cal.App.3d 653, 657.

- Motions for summary adjudication. ***Zilog, Inc. v. Superior Ct.*** (6th Dist.2001) 86 Cal.App.4th 1309, 1322. *But see* ***California Fed. S&L***, 189 Cal.App.3d at 271 (ruling on summary adjudication of "make or break" issue involving contract interpretation was considered to have resolved contested fact issue that was related to merits).

- Ex parte motions for temporary restraining orders. ***Landmark Holding Grp. v. Superior Ct.*** (2d Dist.1987) 193 Cal.App.3d 525, 528.

- Motions for continuance. ***Los Angeles Cty. Dept. of Pub. Soc. Servs. v. Superior Ct.*** (2d Dist.1977) 69 Cal.App.3d 407, 417.

- Motions to transfer. *Id.*

- Motions to quash for lack of personal jurisdiction. ***School Dist. of Okaloosa Cty.***, 58 Cal.App.4th at 1133-34.

- Motions to compel discovery. *See* ***Swift***, 172 Cal.App.4th at 884.

(b) Before trial commences.

[1] Generally. For purposes of bringing a timely motion to disqualify, a jury trial commences when the name of the first juror is drawn, and a bench trial commences when the plaintiff's attorney makes an opening statement. CCP §170.6(a)(2). If the plaintiff's attorney does not make an opening statement, a bench trial commences when the first witness is sworn, other evidence is presented, or the trial otherwise commences. *Id.*

[2] Effect of earlier hearing. If the judge has already presided over a hearing in the case, a party is generally not barred from bringing a motion to disqualify the judge from the trial. CCP §170.6(a)(2). This rule does not apply, however, if the judge at the earlier hearing determined a contested fact issue that related to the merits of the case. ***Swift***, 172 Cal.App.4th at 883; *see* CCP §170.6(a)(2). If the judge has already made such a determination, a party can no longer bring a motion to disqualify. *See* CCP §170.6(a)(2); ***Swift***, 172 Cal.App.4th at 883. The only way to disqualify a judge after that point is to bring a statement of disqualification. See "Statement of Disqualification – Challenge for Cause," §5, p. 150.

(2) Exceptions. The general deadline for filing a motion to disqualify does not apply if an exception requires the motion to be filed earlier. The deadline to file most motions to disqualify will depend on the type of assignment that was made. Chart 2-2, below, summarizes how the type of assignment affects the deadline to file the motion.

2-2. EXCEPTIONS TO GENERAL DEADLINE

	Type of assignment	Deadline
1	Master-calendar assignment	When case is assigned for trial. See §4.2.6(2)(a), this page.
2	All-purpose assignment	Within 15 days after service of notice of assignment or, if movant has not generally appeared, within 15 days after general appearance. See §4.2.6(2)(b), this page.
3	Single-judge-court assignment	Within 30 days after movant's general appearance. See §4.2.6(2)(c), this page.
4	Coordination-proceeding assignment	Within 20 days after service of order assigning judge. See §4.2.6(2)(d), this page.
5	New-trial assignment	Within 60 days after receipt of notice of assignment. See §4.2.6(2)(e), this page.
6	Assignment to other identifiable judge	No later than 5 days before hearing or trial. See §4.2.6(2)(f), p. 144.

(a) Master-calendar assignment. If a trial has been assigned to a judge from a master-calendar court, the motion must be made no later than the time the case is assigned to the judge for trial. CCP §170.6(a)(2); ***Grant v. Superior Ct.*** (6th Dist.2001) 90 Cal.App.4th 518, 524. For a discussion of when a trial assignment occurs, see "Master-calendar assignment," §4.2.5(2)(a), p. 140.

(b) All-purpose assignment. If a case has been assigned to a judge for all purposes, the motion must be filed within 15 days after service of the notice of the assignment. CCP §170.6(a)(2). The movant has additional time to file the motion if the notice of the assignment is served by mail. *See id.* §1013(a); *see, e.g.*, ***California Bus. Council v. Superior Ct.*** (3d Dist.1997) 52 Cal.App.4th 1100, 1106 (deadline for filing motion to disqualify in all-purpose assignment extended five days because notice of assignment mailed to California address). If the movant has not made a general appearance when notice is given, the motion must be filed within 15 days after the movant's general appearance. *See* CCP §170.6(a)(2); ***National Fin. Lending, LLC v. Superior Ct.*** (4th Dist.2013) 222 Cal.App.4th 262, 270; *see also* ***La Seigneurie U.S. Holdings, Inc. v. Superior Ct.*** (2d Dist.1994) 29 Cal.App.4th 1500, 1504 ("appearance" under CCP §170.6 is interpreted to mean "general appearance"). For a discussion of when a trial assignment occurs, see "All-purpose assignment," §4.2.5(2)(b), p. 140.

(c) Single-judge-court assignment. If a hearing or trial has been assigned to a judge in a court that is authorized to have only one judge, the motion must be made within 30 days after the movant's general appearance. *See* CCP §170.6(a)(2) (motion must be made within 30 days after party's "first appearance"); ***Brown v. Swickard*** (3d Dist.1985) 163 Cal.App.3d 820, 826 (party makes "first appearance" when it submits itself to court's jurisdiction). For examples of acts constituting a general appearance, see "Examples – general appearance," ch. 3-G, §5.1.1(2)(a), p. 285.

(d) Coordination-proceeding assignment. If a hearing or trial has been assigned to a judge in a coordination proceeding, the motion must be filed within 20 days after service of the order assigning the judge to the coordination proceeding. CRC 3.516. The movant has additional time after the 20-day deadline to file the motion if the order is served by mail. *See* CCP §1013(a); *see, e.g.*, ***Citicorp N. Am., Inc. v. Superior Ct.*** (2d Dist.1989) 213 Cal.App.3d 563, 571 (deadline for filing motion to disqualify judge in coordination proceeding extended five days because notice of assignment mailed to California address).

(e) New-trial assignment. If a judge whose decision or final judgment was reversed after a successful appeal or writ proceeding has been assigned to the new trial on remand, the successful party must file its motion within 60 days after the party or party's attorney receives notice of the assignment. *See* CCP §170.6(a)(2) (stating deadline for filing motion to disqualify after reversal on appeal of trial court's decision or final judgment);

Overton v. Superior Ct. (4th Dist.1994) 22 Cal.App.4th 112, 116 (interpreting term "appeal" under §170.6(a)(2) to include writ proceeding resulting in new trial); *see, e.g.*, ***Hendershot v. Superior Ct.*** (2d Dist.1993) 20 Cal.App.4th 860, 863 (motion to disqualify filed within 60 days after D knew of assignment was timely). The issuance of a remittitur does not qualify as notice of the assignment. ***Ghaffarpour v. Superior Ct.*** (2d Dist.2012) 202 Cal.App.4th 1463, 1466. For a discussion of what qualifies as a new trial, see "Remand for new trial," §4.2.7(2)(b)[2][b], p. 146.

(f) Assignment to other identifiable judge. If a hearing or trial has been assigned to a judge whose identity is reasonably certain at least ten days before the hearing or trial and no other type of assignment applies, the motion must be filed at least five days before the hearing or trial. ***Lavi***, 4 Cal.4th at 1183, 1185; *see*, CCP §170.6(a)(2). The identity of the judge is reasonably certain if a party can determine the judge assigned or scheduled to conduct the hearing or trial through investigation or inquiry. *See* ***Lavi***, 4 Cal.4th at 1183; ***Lawrence***, 206 Cal.App.3d at 617.

[1] Assignment to department. If a hearing or trial is assigned to a particular department rather than a particular judge but one judge regularly conducts hearings or trials in that department, the identity of the judge is reasonably certain unless other information indicates it is unlikely that the regularly assigned judge will conduct the hearing or trial. *See* ***Lavi***, 4 Cal.4th at 1183; *see, e.g.*, ***Kaiser Found. Hosps. v. Superior Ct.*** (1st Dist.1987) 190 Cal.App.3d 721, 725 (ten-day/five-day rule applied in court with tentative-ruling procedure in which motions are assigned to department with regularly assigned judge).

[2] Effect of continuances. If a hearing or trial is assigned to a particular department and the original date for the hearing or trial is continued, the motion is timely if it is filed at least five days before the continued date. ***In re Abdul Y.***, 130 Cal.App.3d at 857 n.7; ***In re Jose S.*** (4th Dist.1978) 78 Cal.App.3d 619, 627. The continued date, however, must have been sought in good faith and for good cause. ***People v. Richard*** (2d Dist.1978) 85 Cal.App.3d 292, 298.

NOTE

Two courts have stated a contrary rule—that is, the motion must be filed at least five days before the original hearing or trial date rather than the continued date. See ***Hospital Council****, 30 Cal.App.3d at 338-39;* ***People v. Kennedy*** *(4th Dist.1967) 256 Cal.App.2d 755, 762-63. Other courts, however, have distinguished the discussion in these cases as dicta. See* ***In re Jose S.****, 78 Cal.App.3d at 627 (distinguishing* ***Hospital Council*** *because motion would have been untimely even based on continued date);* ***Zdonek v. Superior Ct.*** *(2d Dist.1974) 38 Cal.App.3d 849, 854-55 & n.6 (distinguishing* ***Kennedy*** *because it was decided based on master-calendar rule and not ten-day/five-day rule).*

7. Limitations on motion.

(1) No right to withdraw motion. A motion to disqualify a judge cannot be withdrawn. ***Stebbins v. White*** (3d Dist.1987) 190 Cal.App.3d 769, 780-81. But if the judge proceeds with the hearing or trial despite the motion, the movant waives the judge's disqualification by participating in the hearing or trial without objection. *See* ***Andrisani v. Saugus Colony Ltd.*** (2d Dist.1992) 8 Cal.App.4th 517, 526 (party who files peremptory challenge but does not bring issue to court's attention waives right to assert issue on appeal); ***Stebbins***, 190 Cal.App.3d at 782 (same).

(2) Only one motion allowed.

(a) Generally. Generally, only one motion to disqualify a judge is allowed for each party or side in a case. CCP §170.6(a)(4); ***Home Ins. v. Superior Ct.*** (2005) 34 Cal.4th 1025, 1032.

[1] Per party. If there are only two parties in the case (e.g., plaintiff and defendant), then one motion can be made by each party. CCP §170.6(a)(4).

[2] **Per side.** If there is more than one party on a side (e.g., codefendants), then only one motion can be made by each side. CCP §170.6(a)(4); ***Home Ins.***, 34 Cal.4th at 1032. The limitation of one motion per side applies even if the moving party is dismissed from the case or another party is added after the motion is filed. ***Home Ins.***, 34 Cal.4th at 1033. Normally, all plaintiffs constitute a side and all defendants constitute a side. ***Pappa v. Superior Ct.*** (1960) 54 Cal.2d 350, 353-54; *see* CRC 3.516 (all Ps or similar parties in coordinated actions constitute a side and all Ds or similar parties constitute a side). But there can be more than two sides to a case if the interests of coplaintiffs or codefendants are substantially adverse. ***Pappa***, 54 Cal.2d at 353-54. The burden is on the party claiming it is on a different side than a coplaintiff or codefendant to present evidence of an actual conflict so the court can determine if the interests of the joined parties are substantially adverse. ***Home Ins.***, 34 Cal.4th at 1037; *e.g.*, ***Orion Comms. v. Superior Ct.*** (4th Dist.2014) 226 Cal.App.4th 152, 164-65 (dicta; fact that co-Ds were represented by separate counsel or may have been jointly liable did not establish actual conflict of interest). For example, an actual conflict that makes the interests of codefendants substantially adverse can occur if part of a defendant's litigation strategy is to shift responsibility to a codefendant. *See* ***Johnson v. Superior Ct.*** (1958) 50 Cal.2d 693, 700 (dicta; two Ds whose automobiles collide and injure P may have substantially adverse interests); ***Avital v. Superior Ct.*** (2d Dist.1981) 114 Cal.App.3d 297, 302 (criminal D attempting to shift responsibility to another D is "classic example" of substantially adverse interest).

DISQUALIFY JUDGE

[3] **Continuation of proceeding.** Each party or side is limited to one motion throughout all stages of a proceeding, including any later proceedings that are a continuation of the proceeding. ***Home Ins.***, 34 Cal.4th at 1033 n.4; *see* ***National Fin. Lending***, 222 Cal.App.4th at 277. A later proceeding is a continuation of an earlier proceeding if it (1) involves the same parties, (2) represents a later stage of the parties' litigation with each other or arises from conduct in or orders made during the earlier proceeding, and (3) involves substantially the same issues—that is, the later proceeding presents matters that are necessarily relevant and material to the issues in the earlier proceeding. *See* ***McClenny v. Superior Ct.*** (1964) 60 Cal.2d 677, 684; ***National Fin. Lending***, 222 Cal.App.4th at 277-78; ***Pickett v. Superior Ct.*** (2d Dist.2012) 203 Cal.App.4th 887, 893; *see, e.g.*, ***Pappa***, 54 Cal.2d at 353 (retrial after mistrial was continuation of earlier trial); ***Nissan Motor Corp. v. Superior Ct.*** (4th Dist.1992) 6 Cal.App.4th 150, 155 (consolidated actions arising from different injuries and damages and under different fact patterns were separate and distinct actions). For example, a proceeding to modify custody is considered a continuation of the original proceeding that determined custody. ***Jacobs v. Superior Ct.*** (1959) 53 Cal.2d 187, 190.

(b) **Exceptions.**

[1] **Untimely or defective motion.** A party or side can make a second motion to disqualify if the first motion was denied because it was untimely or not properly made. *E.g.*, ***Truck Ins. Exch. v. Superior Ct.*** (2d Dist.1998) 67 Cal.App.4th 142, 147-48 (peremptory challenge is exhausted when change of judge occurs, not when party files motion). See "Contents," §4.2.3, p. 139; "Deadline to file," §4.2.6, p. 141.

[2] **After appeal or writ.** A party can make a second motion to disqualify if the party successfully challenged the trial court's decision or final judgment by an appeal or a writ proceeding and the same judge who issued the decision or final judgment is assigned to conduct the new trial on remand. CCP §170.6(a)(2); *see* ***Overton***, 22 Cal.App.4th at 115-16 (interpreting term "appeal" under §170.6(a)(2) to include writ proceeding resulting in new trial).

[a] **Original trial.** The trial court's decision or final judgment must have been in conjunction with a trial. ***State Farm Mut. Auto. Ins. v. Superior Ct.*** (2d Dist.2004) 121 Cal.App.4th 490, 499; *see* CCP §656 (defining "new trial" for motions for new trial). A trial includes motions that decide the case on the merits or otherwise terminate the case. *See* ***State Farm***, 121 Cal.App.4th at 501; *see, e.g.*, ***Burdusis v. Superior Ct.*** (2d Dist.2005) 133 Cal.App.4th 88, 93 (P could not file motion to disqualify after reversal of order denying class certification because order did not address merits of case or terminate case); ***Stubblefield Constr. Co. v. Superior Ct.*** (4th Dist.2000) 81 Cal.App.4th 762, 765-66 (Ps could file second motion to disqualify after partial reversal of order granting summary judgment).

[b] **Remand for new trial.** The case must be remanded to the same judge for a new trial. CCP §170.6(a)(2); ***Geddes v. Superior Ct.*** (2d Dist.2005) 126 Cal.App.4th 417, 423-24. A new trial is a reexamination of one or more factual or legal issues that was in controversy in the earlier proceeding. ***Geddes***, 126 Cal.App.4th at 424; *see, e.g.*, ***Stubblefield Constr.***, 81 Cal.App.4th at 765-66 (remand to reexamine issue of law from summary-judgment proceeding was remand for new trial); ***Stegs Invs. v. Superior Ct.*** (2d Dist.1991) 233 Cal.App.3d 572, 576 (remand for evidentiary hearing to determine single issue of fact from earlier trial was remand for new trial). A remand with instructions for the court to complete a task that was not performed in the earlier proceeding or to perform a purely ministerial task (e.g., recalculating interest) is insufficient. *E.g.*, ***Geddes***, 126 Cal.App.4th at 423-24 & n.4 (P could not file motion to disqualify when remand only instructed trial court to state factual and legal basis for order granting summary judgment); *see* ***Stegs Invs.***, 233 Cal.App.3d at 576.

DISQUALIFY JUDGE

PRACTICE TIP

Instead of making a second motion to disqualify after a successful appeal, a party can ask the appellate court, in the interest of justice, to direct that any proceedings after remand be heard before a judge other than the one whose decision or final judgment was reversed. CCP §170.1(c).

§4.3 Opposition.

1. **Who can file.** The party to the action or proceeding can oppose a motion to disqualify. *See, e.g.*, ***Guardado v. Superior Ct.*** (2d Dist.2008) 163 Cal.App.4th 91, 94 (party opposed motion); ***Bravo v. Superior Ct.*** (2d Dist.2007) 149 Cal.App.4th 1489, 1493 (same).

2. **When to file.** Because a motion to disqualify is generally determined on an expedited basis without notice and a hearing, any opposition should be filed as soon as possible. *See* CCP §170.6(a)(4) (motion should be granted without any further act or proof if motion is duly presented with proper supporting evidence); ***Truck Ins. Exch. v. Superior Ct.*** (2d Dist.1998) 67 Cal.App.4th 142, 147 (notice and hearing are not required before motion to disqualify is granted); *see, e.g.*, ***People v. Superior Ct. (Lavi)*** (1993) 4 Cal.4th 1164, 1170-71 (motion was determined one day after being filed); ***Davcon, Inc. v. Roberts & Morgan*** (4th Dist.2003) 110 Cal.App.4th 1355, 1357 (motion was determined on same day it was filed); ***School Dist. of Okaloosa Cty. v. Superior Ct.*** (2d Dist.1997) 58 Cal.App.4th 1126, 1130 (opposition was filed four days after motion was filed and five days before motion was heard); ***Stevens v. Superior Ct.*** (4th Dist.1997) 52 Cal.App.4th 55, 58 (motion was determined four days after being filed).

3. **Form.** Depending on how much time is available and how the motion was brought, the opposition can be asserted in writing or orally in court. *See, e.g.*, ***Bravo***, 149 Cal.App.4th at 1493 (opposing party filed written memorandum); ***Zilog, Inc. v. Superior Ct.*** (6th Dist.2001) 86 Cal.App.4th 1309, 1313 (opposing party filed written opposition). For a general discussion of the contents of an opposition, see "Opposition Papers," ch. 1-D, §8, p. 35.

4. **Grounds.** A motion to disqualify can be opposed on any of the following grounds:

(1) **Not filed with proper judge.** The motion can be opposed on the ground that it was not filed with the proper judge. *See* CCP §170.6(a)(2); ***Fry v. Superior Ct.*** (2d Dist.2013) 222 Cal.App.4th 475, 482-83. See "Where to file," §4.2.5, p. 140.

(2) **Untimely motion.** The motion can be opposed on the ground that it is untimely. *See* ***Shipp v. Superior Ct.*** (2d Dist.1992) 5 Cal.App.4th 147, 151-52. The motion is untimely if it is filed too early or too late. *See, e.g.*, ***Grant v. Superior Ct.*** (6th Dist.2001) 90 Cal.App.4th 518, 527-28 (court properly denied motion to disqualify because motion was filed before there was pending hearing or trial). See "Deadline to file," §4.2.6, p. 141.

(3) **Second motion.** The motion can be opposed on the ground that an earlier motion was filed by the movant or movant's side and none of the exceptions that would allow the movant to file a second motion apply. See "Only one motion allowed," §4.2.7(2), p. 144.

(4) Defective motion. The motion can be opposed on the ground that it is defective in form—that is, it is not supported by a proper sworn statement, affidavit, or declaration. *See* CCP §170.6(a)(2), (a)(6), (a)(7); *see, e.g.*, ***People v. St. Andrew*** (1st Dist.1980) 101 Cal.App.3d 450, 456 (motion to disqualify denied because attorney's oral statement did not qualify as statement under oath). See "Supporting evidence," §4.2.3(2), p. 139. Before the motion is denied, however, the movant will likely be given the opportunity to correct the defect. *See* ***St. Andrew***, 101 Cal.App.3d at 457 (judge has duty to call attention to omissions in evidence or defects in pleadings that are likely to result in decision not on merits of case); *see, e.g.*, ***Retes v. Superior Ct.*** (1st Dist.1981) 122 Cal.App.3d 799, 807 (court should have allowed attorney to correct defective motion by allowing attorney to sign declaration in open court).

(5) Bad faith.

(a) Generally – not a defense. In most instances, a motion to disqualify cannot be opposed on the ground that it was made in bad faith. ***Swift v. Superior Ct.*** (6th Dist.2009) 172 Cal.App.4th 878, 884 n.2; ***School Dist. of Okaloosa Cty.***, 58 Cal.App.4th at 1136-37. The law assumes that a party who disqualifies a judge under CCP §170.6 does so in good faith. ***Brown v. Superior Ct.*** (2d Dist.1981) 124 Cal.App.3d 1059, 1061.

(b) Exception – racial discrimination. A motion to disqualify can be opposed on the ground that it was used to disqualify a judge solely on the basis of race. ***People v. Superior Ct. (Williams)*** (3d Dist.1992) 8 Cal.App.4th 688, 707. To oppose a motion on the basis of racial discrimination, the party opposing the motion has the initial burden of establishing a prima facie case of invidious discrimination. *Id.* at 708 & n.2 (noting that it may be more appropriate to require higher standard than prima facie showing before inquiring into motion's good faith). To meet this burden, the party must (1) establish that the judge is a member of a cognizable racial group and (2) show facts and any other relevant circumstances that would raise an inference that the party bringing the motion to disqualify excluded the judge because of race. *E.g., id.* at 709-10 (record showing movant used peremptory challenge in earlier trial to exclude black females from jury was insufficient to establish likelihood of discrimination in new trial when nonmovant did not present transcript from earlier trial). If a prima facie showing is made, the burden shifts to the party who brought the motion to disqualify to provide a race-neutral explanation for the motion. *Id.* at 708. If a race-neutral explanation is provided, the trial court must then decide whether the party opposing the motion has established purposeful discrimination. *Id.*

§4.4 Reply. The movant can file a reply to the opposition. *See* ***Guardado v. Superior Ct.*** (2d Dist.2008) 163 Cal.App.4th 91, 94. Any reply should be filed before a hearing is conducted on the motion. See "Reply Papers," ch. 1-D, §9, p. 37.

§4.5 Hearing. Generally, hearings are not required for a motion to disqualify. ***Frisk v. Superior Ct.*** (4th Dist.2011) 200 Cal.App.4th 402, 408; ***Truck Ins. Exch. v. Superior Ct.*** (2d Dist.1998) 67 Cal.App.4th 142, 147; *see* CCP §170.6(a)(4) (motion should be granted without any further act or proof if motion is duly presented with proper supporting evidence). A court should hold a hearing, however, if there are any fact questions about the propriety of the motion. *See* ***Shipp v. Superior Ct.*** (2d Dist.1992) 5 Cal.App.4th 147, 151 (if determination of timeliness involves fact questions, court should hold hearing). See "Hearings," ch. 1-H, p. 79.

NOTE

If a motion's timeliness is being contested, the following evidence should be presented at the hearing: (1) the original record of the case's assignment, (2) the trial court's policy about case assignments, and (3) the circumstances of the case's specific assignment. ***Shipp****, 5 Cal.App.4th at 151.*

§4.6 Ruling. When a peremptory challenge is filed, the court may inquire into the timeliness and form of the motion. ***McCartney v. Commission on Judicial Disqualifications*** (1974) 12 Cal.3d 512, 531-32, *disapproved on other grounds*, ***Spruance v. Commission on Judicial Qualifications*** (1975) 13 Cal.3d 778, *and* ***Doan v. Commission on Judicial Performance*** (1995) 11 Cal.4th 294; ***Frisk v. Superior Ct.*** (4th Dist.2011) (Div. 3) 200 Cal.App.4th

402, 406. Generally, if the motion is timely and properly made, the court must grant the disqualification without any further act or proof. CCP §170.6(a)(4); ***Home Ins. v. Superior Ct.*** (2005) 34 Cal.4th 1025, 1032; *see* ***Truck Ins. Exch. v. Superior Ct.*** (2d Dist.1998) 67 Cal.App.4th 142, 147-48 ("duly" under CCP §170.6(a)(3), now §170.6(a)(4), means proper in both form and substance). The only time a timely and properly made motion can be denied is when the motion is brought to disqualify a judge solely on the basis of race. *See* ***People v. Superior Ct. (Williams)*** (3d Dist.1992) 8 Cal.App.4th 688, 699, 707. See "Exception – racial discrimination," §4.3.4(5)(b), p. 147.

CAUTION

Courts disagree on when a peremptory challenge is effective. Some courts have held that the challenge is effective immediately upon filing if the motion is timely and in the proper form. E.g., ***Davcon, Inc. v. Roberts & Morgan*** *(4th Dist.2003) (Div. 2) 110 Cal.App.4th 1355, 1360;* ***Louisiana-Pac. Corp. v. Philo Lumber Co.*** *(1st Dist.1985) 163 Cal.App.3d 1212, 1219; see* ***Jane Doe 8015 v. Superior Ct.*** *(6th Dist.2007) 148 Cal.App.4th 489, 494 (dicta; disqualification is instantaneous on filing). Another court has held that the challenge is not effective until the court actually rules on it, regardless of whether the motion was timely and properly made at the time it was filed. E.g.,* ***Frisk****, 200 Cal.App.4th at 406, 410-11 (trial court properly deemed peremptory challenge moot because co-D who filed challenge was dismissed before court had opportunity to review it; disqualification does not occur until court has opportunity to assess timeliness and form of peremptory challenge).*

§4.7 Order.

1. Form. The court's ruling on a motion to disqualify must be recorded either in writing or by minute order. *See, e.g.,* ***Davcon, Inc. v. Roberts & Morgan*** (4th Dist.2003) 110 Cal.App.4th 1355, 1357 (minute order). See "Record of Ruling," ch. 1-I, §4, p. 90.

2. Contents. The order should state whether the motion was granted or denied. *See* Super. Ct. San Diego Cty., Form CIV-249.

3. Notice. See "Notice of Order," ch. 1-I, §5, p. 93.

4. Effect of disqualification.

(1) On hearing or trial. If the motion is granted, the hearing or trial must be assigned or transferred to another judge as soon as possible. *See* CCP §170.6(a)(4), (a)(5). The assignment must be made by the master-calendar judge if there is one. *Id.* §170.6(a)(4). If there is no other judge in the court where the hearing or trial is pending, the assignment must be made by the Chair of the Judicial Council. *Id.*; *see id.* §170.8.

(2) On right to continuance. If the motion is granted, a party can ask the newly assigned judge to continue the hearing or trial. *See, e.g.,* ***People v. Courts*** (1985) 37 Cal.3d 784, 788 (D renewed motion for continuance before newly assigned judge). See "Requests for Continuance or Stay," ch. 5-I, p. 534. The disqualification of a judge does not entitle a party to a continuance, but the court can grant a continuance if (1) it is required for the court's convenience or (2) the movant shows good cause. CCP §170.6(a)(5). If a continuance is granted, the hearing or trial must be continued from day to day or for other limited periods. *Id.*

(3) On judge's power to act. If the motion is granted, the disqualification takes effect immediately, and the judge has no power to conduct any trials or hearings involving a contested issue of fact or law or to make any further rulings in the case. ***Geddes v. Superior Ct.*** (2d Dist.2005) 126 Cal.App.4th 417, 425; *e.g.,* ***Mezzetti v. Superior Ct.*** (1st Dist.1979) 94 Cal.App.3d 987, 990-91 (judge could conduct settlement conference after motion to disqualify was filed because settlement conference was not hearing involving contested issue of fact or law); *see* CCP §170.6(a)(1). The judge can make rulings, however, on matters that were heard before the motion was filed. *See* ***Stevens v. Superior Ct.*** (2d Dist.1988) 198 Cal.App.3d 932, 939.

(4) On judge's rulings.

(a) Past rulings. Rulings made by a judge before she is disqualified remain valid. See "On judge's power to act," §4.7.4(3), p. 148.

(b) Future rulings. Courts disagree on whether rulings made by a judge after she is disqualified are void or voidable.

[1] Void. Some courts hold that a ruling made by a disqualified judge is void for lack of subject-matter jurisdiction. *See **Ziesmer v. Superior Ct.*** (2d Dist.2003) (Div. 6) 107 Cal.App.4th 360, 363-64; ***Zilog, Inc. v. Superior Ct.*** (6th Dist.2001) 86 Cal.App.4th 1309, 1323; ***Louisiana-Pac. Corp. v. Philo Lumber Co.*** (1st Dist.1985) 163 Cal.App.3d 1212, 1219.

[2] Voidable. Some courts hold that a ruling made by a disqualified judge is only voidable. *See **Frisk v. Superior Ct.*** (4th Dist.2011) 200 Cal.App.4th 402, 412; ***Andrisani v. Saugus Colony Ltd.*** (2d Dist.1992) (Div. 5) 8 Cal.App.4th 517, 525; ***In re Steven O.*** (5th Dist.1991) 229 Cal.App.3d 46, 54; ***Stebbins v. White*** (3d Dist.1987) 190 Cal.App.3d 769, 781-82; ***In re Christian J.*** (3d Dist.1984) 155 Cal.App.3d 276, 280.

§4.8 Motion for reconsideration. A party who is adversely affected by a court's order on a motion to disqualify can file a motion for reconsideration. CCP §1008(a); ***Stephens v. Superior Ct.*** (4th Dist.2002) 96 Cal.App.4th 54, 64-65. *But see **Davcon, Inc. v. Roberts & Morgan*** (4th Dist.2003) 110 Cal.App.4th 1355, 1364 n.9 (dicta; court cannot reconsider and correct erroneous granting of motion to disqualify). See "Motion for Reconsideration," ch. 5-G, §3, p. 508.

1. Motion denied. A motion to reconsider the denial of a motion to disqualify must be filed with the judge who denied the motion. *See **Bambula v. Superior Ct.*** (3d Dist.1985) 174 Cal.App.3d 653, 655-56; ***Micro/Vest Corp. v. Superior Ct.*** (1st Dist.1984) 150 Cal.App.3d 1085, 1090.

2. Motion granted. A motion to reconsider the granting of a motion to disqualify must be filed with the judge who granted the motion unless that judge is disqualified, in which case the motion must be filed with the newly assigned judge. *See, e.g.*, ***Geddes v. Superior Ct.*** (2d Dist.2005) 126 Cal.App.4th 417, 426-27 (disqualified judge could not reconsider his own order granting motion to disqualify); ***Stephens***, 96 Cal.App.4th at 64-65 (judge who was not disqualified reconsidered his own order granting motion to disqualify original judge). If the order granting the motion to disqualify is vacated, the challenged judge is considered to have never been disqualified. *See **Stephens***, 96 Cal.App.4th at 65.

§4.9 Motion for renewal. A party whose motion to disqualify is denied can file a motion for renewal. *See, e.g.*, ***Micro/Vest Corp. v. Superior Ct.*** (1st Dist.1984) 150 Cal.App.3d 1085, 1088 (Ds filed second motion to disqualify after first motion was denied as untimely). See "Motion for Renewal," ch. 5-G, §4, p. 516.

§4.10 Appellate review.

1. Appealability.

(1) Writ of mandate. A party can challenge an order granting or denying a motion to disqualify by filing a petition for a writ of mandate. CCP §170.3(d); *see **People v. Hull*** (1991) 1 Cal.4th 266, 271-72 (CCP §170.3(d) applies whether issue of disqualification is raised by peremptory challenge or challenge for cause).

(a) Who can bring petition. Only parties to the proceeding can file a petition for a writ of mandate; the disqualified judge cannot seek review of her own disqualification. CCP §170.3(d); ***Curle v. Superior Ct.*** (2001) 24 Cal.4th 1057, 1071.

(b) Deadline to file & serve. The petition must be filed and served within ten days after the service of a written notice of entry of the court's order; oral notice of the court's order is not sufficient. *See* CCP §170.3(d); *see, e.g.*, ***D.M. v. Superior Ct.*** (2d Dist.2011) 196 Cal.App.4th 879, 885-86 (oral notice of denial at hearing was not sufficient to trigger deadline to file writ). See "Prospective deadlines," ch. 1-F, §5.1, p. 52. If notice is

served by mail, the time to file and serve the petition is extended according to the rules for service by mail. CCP §170.3(d); *see id.* §1013(a). See "Add time for method of service," ch. 1-G, §6.2.1(5), p. 72.

(2) Direct appeal. An order granting or denying a motion to disqualify is not directly appealable. CCP §170.3(d); ***Hull***, 1 Cal.4th at 276.

2. Standard of review.

(1) Generally. Courts are split on what the proper standard of review is for a ruling on a motion to disqualify. Some courts hold that the standard of review is abuse of discretion. *E.g.*, ***Fry v. Superior Ct.*** (2d Dist.2013) (Div. 1) 222 Cal.App.4th 475, 480-81; ***Entente Design, Inc. v. Superior Ct.*** (4th Dist.2013) 214 Cal.App.4th 385, 389; ***Jonathon M. v. Superior Ct.*** (3d Dist.2006) 141 Cal.App.4th 1093, 1098; ***People v. Superior Ct. (Maloy)*** (5th Dist.2001) 91 Cal.App.4th 391, 395. Other courts hold that the standard of review is de novo because the trial court has no discretion when deciding a motion to disqualify, which involves application of the law to undisputed facts. *E.g.*, ***Jane Doe 8015 v. Superior Ct.*** (6th Dist.2007) 148 Cal.App.4th 489, 493; ***Ziesmer v. Superior Ct.*** (2d Dist.2003) (Div. 6) 107 Cal.App.4th 360, 363.

(2) Racial discrimination. If the court's ruling on a motion to disqualify included a finding that the motion was or was not made because of racial discrimination, that finding is normally entitled to "considerable deference." *See* ***People v. Superior Ct. (Williams)*** (3d Dist.1992) 8 Cal.App.4th 688, 709 (trial judges are in best position to make determination on purposeful discrimination because of their knowledge of local conditions, familiarity with attorneys, powers of observation, understanding of trial techniques, and judicial experience). See "Exception – racial discrimination," §4.3.4(5)(b), p. 147.

§5. STATEMENT OF DISQUALIFICATION – CHALLENGE FOR CAUSE

§5.1 Generally.

1. Judge's duty to disqualify herself. A judge has an independent duty to disqualify herself from any proceeding (i.e., action, case, cause, motion, or special proceeding) when disqualification is required by law. Code Jud. Ethics, canon 3E(1); *see* CCP §§170.3(a)(1), 170.5(f); *see, e.g.*, ***People v. Freeman*** (2010) 47 Cal.4th 993, 997 (judge recused himself from hearing bail motion because of accusations that D was stalking judge's friend). See "Grounds for disqualification," §5.2, p. 151. Thus, a judge must make reasonable efforts to keep herself informed of her personal and financial interests, as well as the interests of her spouse and children living in the household. CCP §170.1(a)(3)(C). Once a judge determines that she should disqualify herself from a proceeding, the judge should do the following:

(1) Disclose basis for disqualification. The judge should disclose the basis for her disqualification on the record. CCP §170.3(b)(1); *see also* Cal. Cmte. Jud. Ethics Ops., CJEO Formal Op. No. 2013-002 (12-11-13) pp. 7-9 (providing guidance on how to make disclosure part of record when proceeding is not reported or electronically recorded).

NOTE

Even if a judge believes there are no actual grounds for disqualification, the Code of Judicial Ethics requires a judge to disclose on the record any information known to her that is reasonably relevant to whether or not she should be disqualified under CCP §170.1. Code Jud. Ethics, canon 3E(2)(a); see also **Brown v. American Bicycle Grp.** *(4th Dist.2014) 224 Cal.App.4th 665, 672-73 (Code Jud. Ethics, canon 3E(2) requires judge to disclose information relevant to disqualification for cause under CCP §170.1, not information that would enable party to file peremptory challenge under CCP §170.6). A judge also has a mandatory duty to disclose any campaign contribution that she received from a party or an attorney in a matter that is before the court if the cumulative amount of the contribution is $100 or more. See CCP §170.1(a)(9)(C); Gov. C. §84211(f); Code Jud. Ethics, canon 3E(2)(b).*

(2) Ask for waiver. The judge can ask the parties and their attorneys if they want to waive the grounds for her disqualification. CCP §170.3(b)(1). In asking for a waiver, the judge cannot attempt to induce the waiver or learn which parties or attorneys favored or opposed it. *Id.* §170.3(b)(3).

(a) Grounds that can be waived. Generally, all grounds for disqualification can be waived except when any of the following is true:

[1] The judge has been a material witness in the matter. CCP §170.3(b)(2)(B); *see id.* §170.1(a)(9)(D). See "Personal knowledge of disputed facts," §5.2.1, this page.

[2] The judge has served as an attorney in the matter. CCP §170.3(b)(2)(B); *see id.* §170.1(a)(9)(D). See "Served as attorney in current proceeding," §5.2.2, p. 152.

[3] The judge has a personal bias or prejudice against a party. CCP §170.3(b)(2)(A); *see id.* §170.1(a)(9)(D). See "Reasonable doubt of impartiality," §5.2.9, p. 154.

(b) Requirements of waiver.

[1] Most waivers. For most waivers to be effective, they must (1) be in writing, (2) state a waivable ground for disqualification, (3) be signed by all parties and their attorneys, and (4) be filed in the record. *See* CCP §170.3(b)(1).

[2] Campaign-contribution waiver. To waive a judge's disqualification based on her receipt of a campaign contribution that exceeds $1,500 by a party or an attorney in the proceeding, only the party who did not make the contribution needs to give the waiver. CCP §170.1(a)(9)(D). By requiring only the noncontributing party's consent to the waiver of disqualification, the contributing party cannot unilaterally seek the disqualification of a judge she dislikes by simply contributing to the judge's campaign. Assem. Com. on Judiciary, Analysis of Assem. Bill No. 2487 (2009-2010 Reg. Sess.) as amended April 20, 2010, p. 9.

(3) Notify presiding judge or another person. If the grounds for disqualification are not or cannot be waived, the judge must give notice of her disqualification to (1) the supervising judge of the court or (2) the person authorized to appoint her replacement if the disqualified judge is the only judge or the supervising judge of the court. *See* CCP §170.3(a)(1), (a)(2); *see also id.* §170.8 (Chairman of Judicial Council can appoint replacement judge when no judge of court is qualified to preside in proceeding).

2. Party's right to seek disqualification. If a judge should disqualify herself but does not do so, a party to the proceeding can disqualify the judge by filing a statement of disqualification. CCP §170.3(c)(1). See "Statement," §5.4, p. 157.

3. Rule of necessity. The "rule of necessity" allows a judge who would otherwise be disqualified to decide an issue in a proceeding if no other judge is available to decide the issue. ***Olson v. Cory*** (1980) 27 Cal.3d 532, 537; *see* Code Jud. Ethics, canon 3E, advisory committee's cmt. (rule of necessity may override rule of disqualification).

§5.2 Grounds for disqualification. A judge must be disqualified in the following situations:

1. Personal knowledge of disputed facts. A judge must be disqualified if she has personal knowledge of disputed evidentiary facts relating to the proceeding. CCP §170.1(a)(1)(A). A judge is deemed to have personal knowledge of such facts if the judge knows that one of the following individuals is likely to be a material witness in the proceeding: (1) the judge, (2) the judge's spouse, (3) a person within the third degree of relationship to the judge or the judge's spouse, or (4) the spouse of a person within the third degree of relationship to the judge or the judge's spouse. *Id.* §170.1(a)(1)(B). See "Consanguinity," ch. 2-E, §4.2.4(1), p. 166 (discussing persons within third degree of relationship). A material witness is a person who can give testimony that no one else or only a few other people can provide and that is significant to determining the proceeding. *See* ***People v. Williams*** (1997) 16 Cal.4th 635, 653 (testimony must be important, more or less necessary, go to merits of case, or have some likelihood of affecting outcome of case).

2. Served as attorney in current proceeding. A judge must be disqualified if she served as an attorney in the current proceeding. CCP §170.1(a)(2)(A). A judge is deemed to have served as an attorney in the current proceeding in the following circumstances:

(1) Judge represented party in past two years. A judge is deemed to have served as an attorney in the current proceeding if, within the past two years, a party to the proceeding or an officer, director, or trustee of a party was either (1) the judge's client while the judge was in private practice or (2) the client of an attorney associated with the judge. CCP §170.1(a)(2)(B)(i). Private practice includes a fee-for-service, retainer, or salaried representation of private clients or public agencies. *Id.* §170.5(e). It does not include either (1) serving as a full-time employee of a public agency or (2) working exclusively for legal-aid offices, public-defender offices, or similar nonprofit entities whose clientele is by law restricted to the indigent. *Id.*

(2) Judge associated with attorney in past two years. A judge is deemed to have served as an attorney in the current proceeding if, within the past two years, the judge and an attorney in the proceeding were associated in private practice together. CCP §170.1(a)(2)(B)(ii); *see also id.* §170.5(e) (definition of "private practice").

(3) Judge was attorney or officer of public agency. A judge is deemed to have served as an attorney in the current proceeding if she (1) served as an attorney for, or an officer of, a public agency that is a party to the current proceeding and (2) personally advised or in any way represented the public agency on the factual or legal issues involved in the current proceeding. CCP §170.1(a)(2)(C). The judge does not act as an officer of a public agency by being a member of the Legislature or a state or local-agency official acting in a legislative capacity. *Id.* §170.5(c).

3. Served as attorney in other proceeding. A judge must be disqualified if she served as an attorney for a party in an earlier proceeding that involved the same issues as the current proceeding. CCP §170.1(a)(2)(A). For a judge to be disqualified, the issues that were common to both proceedings must have been disputed. *See, e.g.*, ***In re Arthur S.*** (5th Dist.1991) 228 Cal.App.3d 814, 821 (no disqualification when party admitted common fact issue in earlier proceeding); ***Muller v. Muller*** (1st Dist.1965) 235 Cal.App.2d 341, 344 (no disqualification when later proceeding ended in default judgment).

4. Gave legal advice in current proceeding. A judge must be disqualified if she gave legal advice to a party in the current proceeding on any matter involved in the current proceeding. CCP §170.1(a)(2)(A).

5. Financial interest. A judge must be disqualified if she has a financial interest in the subject matter of the proceeding or in a party to the proceeding. CCP §170.1(a)(3)(A). A judge is deemed to have a financial interest if (1) the judge or the judge's spouse is a fiduciary who has a financial interest or (2) the judge's spouse or minor child living in the judge's household has a financial interest. *Id.* §170.1(a)(3)(B). A fiduciary includes an executor, trustee, guardian, or administrator. *Id.* §170.5(g).

(1) Defined. A financial interest is defined as any of the following:

(a) Ownership of more than a 1% legal or equitable interest in a party. CCP §170.5(b).

(b) A legal or equitable interest in a party that has a fair market value in excess of $1,500. *Id.*

(c) Ownership of a corporate bond issued by a party to the proceeding that has a fair market value in excess of $1,500. Code Jud. Ethics, canon 3E(3).

(d) Ownership of a government bond issued by a party to the proceeding if the outcome of the proceeding could substantially affect the value of the bond. *Id.*

(e) A position as a director, adviser, or other active participant in the affairs of a party to the proceeding. CCP §170.5(b).

(2) Exceptions.

(a) Owning securities in mutual or common fund. An ownership interest in a mutual or common investment fund that holds securities is not a financial interest in the securities held by the fund unless the judge participates in the management of the fund. CCP §170.5(b)(1).

(b) Owning bonds in mutual or common fund. An ownership interest in a mutual or common investment fund that holds bonds is not a financial interest in the bonds held by the fund. Code Jud. Ethics, canon 3E(3).

(c) Holding office in certain organizations. The holding of an office in an educational, religious, charitable, fraternal, or civic organization is not a financial interest in any securities held by the organization. CCP §170.5(b)(2).

(d) Proprietary interest. A proprietary interest as a policyholder in a mutual-insurance company, a depositor in a mutual savings association, or a similar proprietary interest is not a financial interest in the organization unless the outcome of the proceeding could substantially affect the value of the interest. CCP §170.5(b)(3).

NOTE

CCP §170.5(b) defines a judge's financial interest only in relation to a party; it does not define a judge's financial interest in relation to the subject matter of a proceeding. Before the enactment of §170.5(b), a judge was disqualified from any action or proceeding in which she was "interested." Stats. 1984, ch. 193, §9, p. 577. A judge was considered "interested" if she had an interest in the subject matter of the proceeding (e.g., a pecuniary or proprietary interest) that was direct, proximate, substantial, and certain—that is, the judge or her property would be directly affected by the judgment in the proceeding. See ***Lindsay-Strathmore Irrigation Dist. v. Superior Ct.*** *(1920) 182 Cal. 315, 329-30;* ***Central & W. Basin Water Replenishment Dist. v. Wong*** *(3d Dist.1976) 55 Cal.App.3d 191, 194. An interest that was remote, indirect, contingent, or uncertain would not disqualify the judge. E.g.,* ***Central & W. Basin***, *55 Cal.App.3d at 194-95 (judge who owned home within water district was not disqualified from suit that might result in lower tax or water rates; impact on judge's property was contingent on water district's decision to reduce tax rate).*

6. Interest in estate-administration proceeding. A judge must be disqualified if she is (1) presiding over an estate-administration proceeding for purposes other than to transfer the proceeding to another court and (2) interested in the proceeding because any of the following is true:

(1) The judge is a beneficiary or creditor of the estate. Prob. C. §7060(a)(1).

(2) The judge is named as an executor or a trustee in the will. *Id.* §7060(a)(2).

(3) The judge participated in the drafting or execution of the will, including acting as a witness to the will, and the judge is presiding over a proceeding (1) that occurs before the admission of the will to probate, (2) to admit the will to probate, or (3) involving the validity or interpretation of the will. *Id.* §7060(b).

(4) The judge is otherwise interested. *Id.* §7060(a)(3).

7. Relationship with party to proceeding. A judge must be disqualified if any of the following individuals is a party to the proceeding or an officer, a director, or a trustee of a party: (1) the judge, (2) the judge's spouse, (3) a person within the third degree of relationship to the judge or the judge's spouse, or (4) the spouse of a person within the third degree of relationship to the judge or the judge's spouse. CCP §170.1(a)(4). See "Consanguinity," ch. 2-E, §4.2.4(1), p. 166 (discussing persons within third degree of relationship).

(1) Must be real party. For disqualification to apply, the judge or person related to the judge must be a real party to the proceeding. *See* ***Younger v. Superior Ct.*** (1902) 136 Cal. 682, 685. A real party is a party that has an actual and substantial interest in the subject matter of the proceeding and would be benefited or harmed by a judgment. ***County of Alameda v. State Bd. of Control*** (1st Dist.1993) 14 Cal.App.4th 1096, 1103; *see* ***Redevelopment Agency v. Commission on State Mandates*** (4th Dist.1996) 43 Cal.App.4th 1188, 1197 (real party in interest is person whose interest will be directly affected by proceeding). See "Real party in interest," ch. 3-C, §2.1.1, p. 204.

DISQUALIFY JUDGE

(2) Must be joined in good faith. For disqualification to apply, the judge or person related to the judge must have been joined in the proceeding by a party acting in good faith. *See* ***Younger***, 136 Cal. at 684-85. The judge or person related to the judge cannot be made a party to the proceeding for the sole purpose of disqualifying the judge. *See id.* at 684. See "Joinder of Parties," ch. 3-B, §3, p. 193.

8. Relationship with attorney in proceeding. A judge must be disqualified if either of the following is true:

(1) An attorney or an attorney's spouse in the current proceeding is the spouse, former spouse, child, sibling, or parent of the judge or the judge's spouse. CCP §170.1(a)(5).

(2) An attorney in the current proceeding is associated in private practice with the spouse, former spouse, child, sibling, or parent of the judge or the judge's spouse. *Id.*; *see also id.* §170.5(e) (definition of "private practice").

9. Reasonable doubt of impartiality. A judge must be disqualified if there is a reasonable doubt that she can be impartial. CCP §170.1(a)(6)(A)(iii). The standard for disqualification under CCP §170.1(a)(6)(A)(iii) is an objective one; the judge's personal view of her own impartiality is not a factor. ***Flier v. Superior Ct.*** (1st Dist.1994) 23 Cal.App.4th 165, 170 (discussing former CCP §170.1(a)(6)(C), now §170.1(a)(6)(A)(iii)). The standard is whether a reasonable member of the public, aware of all the facts and circumstances when the statement of disqualification was made, would fairly entertain doubts about the judge's impartiality. ***Wechsler v. Superior Ct.*** (4th Dist.2014) 224 Cal.App.4th 384, 391; ***Flier***, 23 Cal.App.4th at 170. Proof of actual bias or prejudice is not required—the appearance of either is sufficient. *See* ***People v. Freeman*** (2010) 47 Cal.4th 993, 1000-01; ***Wechsler***, 224 Cal.App.4th at 390.

(1) Appearance of bias toward party. The appearance of bias or prejudice toward a party is sufficient to support a judge's disqualification. *See* CCP §170.3(b)(2)(A); ***Freeman***, 47 Cal.4th at 1000-01; ***Flier***, 23 Cal.App.4th at 170.

(a) Examples of bias. Bias was found in the following situations:

[1] The judge stated in an affidavit that he believed the defendant was guilty of a crime. ***Calhoun v. Superior Ct.*** (1958) 51 Cal.2d 257, 259-60.

[2] The judge stated that he considered sexual-harassment cases to be a misuse of the judicial system and suggested that the plaintiff was at fault for putting herself in harm's way and not resisting the defendant's advances. *Cf.* ***Catchpole v. Brannon*** (1st Dist.1995) 36 Cal.App.4th 237, 249, 253 (judge's bias was sufficient to set aside judgment for due-process violation), *disapproved on other grounds*, ***People v. Freeman*** (2010) 47 Cal.4th 993.

[3] The judge's statements indicated he would not permit deaf-mutes, regardless of their competence or qualifications, to become adoptive parents. ***Adoption of Richardson*** (2d Dist.1967) 251 Cal.App.2d 222, 232.

[4] The judge referred to the wife in a divorce proceeding as a "lovely girl" who had "nothing going for her except for her physical attractiveness." *Cf.* ***In re Marriage of Iverson*** (4th Dist.1992) 11 Cal.App.4th 1495, 1498 (judge's bias was sufficient to set aside judgment for due-process violation), *disapproved on other grounds*, ***People v. Freeman*** (2010) 47 Cal.4th 993.

[5] The judge repeatedly made unsubstantiated rulings and comments, giving the appearance that he had become too personally and emotionally involved in the case. ***In re Marriage of Tharp*** (5th Dist.2010) 188 Cal.App.4th 1295, 1327-28.

(b) Examples of no bias. Bias was not found in the following situations:

[1] The judge made an erroneous ruling against a party. *See* ***McEwen v. Occidental Life Ins.*** (1916) 172 Cal. 6, 11 (erroneous rulings against litigant, even when numerous and continuous, are not considered bias or prejudice).

[2] The judge expressed an opinion in the discharge of her official duties. *Id.*; *e.g.*, ***Garcia v. Estate of Norton*** (1st Dist.1986) 183 Cal.App.3d 413, 422-23 (judge told D in chambers that he ought to settle lawsuit because there appeared to be clear liability; statement was made in context of trying to settle case).

[3] The judge referred to the defendant, who was a black male, as a "boy." ***Flier***, 23 Cal.App.4th at 171-72.

(2) Appearance of bias toward attorney. The appearance of bias or prejudice toward an attorney is sufficient to support a judge's disqualification. *See* CCP §170.1(a)(6)(B); *see, e.g.*, ***Adams v. Commission on Judicial Performance*** (1995) 10 Cal.4th 866, 903-04 (judge's receipt of gifts from attorneys was sufficient to create reasonable doubt that judge would be impartial); ***Hernandez v. Vitamin Shoppe Indus.*** (1st Dist.2009) 174 Cal.App.4th 1441, 1450 (judge's comments toward attorney were sufficient to create reasonable doubt that judge would be impartial); *see also* ***Wechsler***, 224 Cal.App.4th at 396 (judge's agreement to officiate at attorney's wedding, combined with social connection or receipt of benefits, would create reasonable doubt that judge would be impartial).

NOTE

Before amendments were enacted in 2005, CCP §170.1(a)(6) was divided into three subparts: (A), (B), and (C). Stats. 2002, ch. 1094, §1. Subsection (C) stated that a judge must be disqualified if "a person aware of the facts might reasonably entertain a doubt that the judge would be able to be impartial. Bias or prejudice towards a lawyer in the proceeding may be grounds for disqualification." Id. Under this version of the statute, courts applied the reasonable-doubt standard to claims of bias or prejudice toward an attorney. See, e.g., ***Adams****, 10 Cal.4th at 904 (court applied reasonable-doubt standard against judge who had accepted gifts and favors from several attorneys). In 2005, subsection (C) was deleted, and its content was divided into two separate subsections: the part on reasonable doubt became §170.1(a)(6)(A)(iii), and the part on attorney bias or prejudice became §170.1(a)(6)(B). Stats. 2005, ch. 332, §1. It is unclear whether the Legislature intended to remove the reasonable-doubt standard from claims of bias or prejudice toward an attorney, or whether the change was intended to be nonsubstantive. Although no court has directly addressed the issue, some commentators and at least one court suggest the reasonable-doubt standard still applies to claims of bias toward attorneys. See Kiesel, Cal. Pretrial Civil Procedure, §22.18[7][b] (test for bias under CCP §170.1(a)(6)(B) is whether reasonable member of public, aware of all facts, would fairly entertain doubts about judge's impartiality); see, e.g.,* ***Hernandez****, 174 Cal.App.4th at 1448 (post-2005 amendment, court applied reasonable-doubt standard to claim of bias toward attorney); see also Cal. Judges Benchguides, §2.15 (bias toward attorney under CCP §170.1(a)(6)(B) is example of disqualifying bias under §170.1(a)(6)(A)(iii)).*

(3) Appearance of bias toward witness. The appearance of bias or prejudice toward a witness is sufficient to support a judge's disqualification. ***In re Henry C.*** (5th Dist.1984) 161 Cal.App.3d 646, 653; *Cal. Judges Benchguides*, §2.15. *Contra* ***Evans v. Superior Ct.*** (2d Dist.1930) 107 Cal.App. 372, 379.

10. Physical impairment. A judge must be disqualified if she has a temporary or permanent physical impairment that prevents her from being able to properly perceive the evidence or conduct the proceeding. CCP §170.1(a)(7); *see, e.g.*, ***People v. Pratt*** (1st Dist.1962) 205 Cal.App.2d 838, 846 (fact that judge was blind, without more, did not show that judge was unable to properly perceive evidence or conduct proceeding).

11. Employment as DRN. A judge must be disqualified if (1) she is employed or prospectively employed as a dispute-resolution neutral (DRN) and (2) her employment or prospective employment is at issue in the proceeding. *See* CCP §170.1(a)(8)(A).

(1) Employed or prospectively employed as DRN.

(a) DRN defined. A DRN is an arbitrator, mediator, temporary judge appointed under California Constitution article VI, §21, referee appointed under CCP §638 or 639, special master, neutral evaluator, settlement officer, or settlement facilitator. CCP §170.1(a)(8)(B)(iii).

(b) Employed or prospectively employed. A judge is employed or prospectively employed as a DRN if any of the following is true:

[1] The judge has been employed or engaged in other compensated service as a DRN in the past. CCP §170.1(a)(8)(A).

[2] The judge has a current arrangement concerning prospective employment or other compensated service as a DRN. *Id.*

[3] The judge is currently participating in, or within the past two years has participated in, discussions about prospective employment or service as a DRN. *Id.* A judge participates in discussions if she either (1) solicits or otherwise indicates an interest in accepting or negotiating possible employment or service or (2) responds to an unsolicited statement about, or an offer of, possible employment or service by expressing an interest in, inquiring about, or encouraging the person making the statement or offer to provide additional information about the possible employment or service. *Id.* §170.1(a)(8)(B)(i). A judge does not participate in discussions if her response to an unsolicited statement or question about, or an offer of, future employment or service is limited to (1) responding negatively, (2) declining the offer, or (3) declining to discuss the employment or service. *Id.*

(2) Employment as DRN is at issue. If a judge is employed or prospectively employed as a DRN, the judge must be disqualified if any of the following is true:

(a) The judge's current arrangement as a DRN is with a party to the proceeding. CCP §170.1(a)(8)(A)(i).

(b) The judge was previously employed as a DRN with a party to the proceeding. *Id.*

(c) The judge's past discussions about prospective employment as a DRN were with a party to the proceeding. *Id.*

(d) The judge must resolve issues relating to the enforcement of an agreement to submit a dispute to alternative dispute resolution (ADR). *Id.* §170.1(a)(8)(A)(ii).

(e) The judge must resolve issues relating to the enforcement of an award or other final decision by a DRN. *Id.*

(f) The judge directs the parties to participate in ADR, and the DRN will be an individual or entity with whom the judge has a current arrangement, has previously been employed or served, or is discussing or has discussed employment or service. *Id.* §170.1(a)(8)(A)(iii).

(g) The judge will select a DRN or an entity to conduct ADR in the matter before the judge, and among those available for selection is an individual or entity with whom the judge has a current arrangement, has previously been employed or served, or is discussing or has discussed employment or service. *Id.* §170.1(a)(8)(A)(iv).

NOTE

Under CCP §170.1(a)(8), the term "party" includes the parent, subsidiary, or other legal affiliate of any entity that is a party to the proceeding and is involved in the transaction, contract, or facts that give rise to the issues subject to the proceeding. CCP §170.1(a)(8)(B)(ii).

---

12. Campaign contribution. A judge must be disqualified if she has received a contribution that exceeds $1,500 from a party or an attorney in the proceeding and if either of the following applies:

(1) The contribution was received in support of the judge's last election, if the last election was within the last six years. CCP §170.1(a)(9)(A)(i).

(2) The contribution was received in anticipation of an upcoming election. *Id.* §170.1(a)(9)(A)(ii).

NOTE

The California Supreme Court Committee on Judicial Ethics has advised that CCP §170.1(a)(9) does not require disqualification when an attorney in the proceeding practices law with other attorneys and (1) the attorney's private firm contributes more than $1,500 or (2) the combined contributions from the other attorneys exceed $1,500. See Cal. Cmte. Jud. Ethics Ops., CJEO Formal Op. No. 2013-003 (12-11-13) pp. 1-2. However, the judge must still consider whether these contributions raise questions about the judge's impartiality under CCP §170.1(a)(6)(A)(iii). See CCP §170.1(a)(9)(B); Cal. Cmte. Jud. Ethics Ops., CJEO Formal Op. No. 2013-003 (12-11-13) pp. 1-2.

§5.3 Invalid grounds for disqualification. The following are not valid grounds for disqualification:

1. Group affiliation. A judge cannot be disqualified because (1) the judge belongs or does not belong to a particular racial, ethnic, religious, sexual, or similar group and (2) the proceeding involves the rights of that group. CCP §170.2(a).

2. Expressed view. A judge cannot be disqualified for expressing in any capacity a view on a legal or factual issue presented in the proceeding, except as provided in CCP §170.1(a)(2), (b), or (c). CCP §170.2(b). See "Served as attorney in current proceeding," §5.2.2, p. 152; "Served as attorney in other proceeding," §5.2.3, p. 152; "Gave legal advice in current proceeding," §5.2.4, p. 152.

3. Participation in lawmaking. A judge cannot be disqualified for having participated as an attorney or a public official in the drafting of laws or in the effort to pass or defeat laws when the meaning, effect, or application of the law is at issue in the proceeding, unless the judge believes her involvement was so well known that the public would reasonably doubt the judge's impartiality. CCP §170.2(c).

§5.4 Statement.

1. Who can file. Any party to the proceeding can file a statement of disqualification. CCP §170.3(c)(1).

2. Deadline to file.

(1) At earliest practicable opportunity. The statement must be filed with the court clerk at the earliest "practicable" opportunity after the party (1) knows the identity of the judge assigned to the hearing or trial and (2) discovers facts constituting the grounds for disqualification. *See* CCP §170.3(c)(1); ***Hollingsworth v. Superior Ct.*** (4th Dist.1987) 191 Cal.App.3d 22, 28. The purpose of the expedited deadline is to prevent a party from waiting for an unfavorable ruling before filing a statement to disqualify. ***Tri Cty. Bank v. Superior Ct.*** (5th Dist.2008) 167 Cal.App.4th 1332, 1337-38. Typically, a statement filed the same day or a few days after a party discovers facts supporting a ground for disqualification will be timely. *See, e.g.*, ***People v. Panah*** (2005) 35 Cal.4th 395, 446 (statement filed 53 days later was untimely); ***Tri Cty. Bank***, 167 Cal.App.4th at 1338 (statement filed seven months later was untimely); ***Fine v. Superior Ct.*** (2d Dist.2002) 97 Cal.App.4th 651, 658, 667 (statement filed same day was timely; statement struck for other reasons); ***Sincavage v. Superior Ct.*** (1st Dist.1996) 42 Cal.App.4th 224, 228 (statement filed eight days later was timely). If a party discovers facts and then waits until the judge enters an unfavorable ruling before filing the statement, the statement will not be timely. ***Urias v. Harris Farms, Inc.*** (5th Dist.1991) 234 Cal.App.3d 415, 424-25; *see, e.g.*, ***Alhusainy v. Superior Ct.*** (4th Dist.2006) 143 Cal.App.4th 385, 394 (statement filed after D lost motion to withdraw guilty plea was untimely because D knew all facts relied on in statement 16 days before D lost motion).

NOTE

*A party does not have a duty to investigate a judge's background or relationships to determine whether there are grounds for disqualification. See **Urias**, 234 Cal.App.3d at 425. Rather, it is the judge's responsibility to disclose to the parties any information that is reasonably relevant to whether or not she should be disqualified. Code Jud. Ethics, canon 3E(2); **Urias**, 234 Cal.App.3d at 425. Thus, a party will not be charged with knowing information about a judge that is available in the public domain but not otherwise disclosed. See, e.g., **Urias**, 234 Cal.App.3d at 425 (statement was not untimely even though ground for disqualification could have been discovered earlier if party would have looked in online attorney database).*

(a) Grounds discovered before appeal. If grounds for disqualification are discovered after an entry of judgment but before an appeal is taken, a statement of disqualification can still be filed with the trial court. *See, e.g.*, ***Urias***, 234 Cal.App.3d at 423 (P discovered grounds for disqualification after summary judgment was granted; judge was disqualified after judgment was entered).

(b) Grounds discovered during or after appeal. If grounds for disqualification are discovered during or after an appeal, a statement of disqualification can no longer be filed. *See* ***North Beverly Park Homeowners Ass'n v. Bisno*** (2d Dist.2007) 147 Cal.App.4th 762, 774 (after appeals are exhausted); ***Betz v. Pankow*** (1st Dist.1993) 16 Cal.App.4th 931, 940 (while appeal is pending). Different methods are used to raise the issue of disqualification during and after an appeal.

[1] During appeal. To raise the issue of disqualification during an appeal, a party can file a petition for a writ of error with the appellate court. *See* ***Betz***, 16 Cal.App.4th at 941.

[2] After appeal. To raise the issue of disqualification after an appeal, a party can file a motion to vacate the judgment with the trial court if jurisdiction is returned to the trial court. *See* ***Betz***, 16 Cal.App.4th at 941 (after appellate court orders remittitur, trial court has jurisdiction to hear motion to vacate). If jurisdiction is not returned to the trial court and the judgment is no longer subject to a direct attack (i.e., when the trial and appellate courts no longer have the power to change the judgment), a party may be able to raise the issue of disqualification by filing an independent action to void the judgment. *See* ***North Beverly Park***, 147 Cal.App.4th at 776 (assuming without deciding that party can raise disqualification after judgment is no longer subject to direct attack). This remedy is only available, however, if the court views the judgment of a disqualified judge as being void and not voidable. *See id.* at 769. Voidable judgments are not subject to a collateral attack. *See id.* See "Grounds discovered after judgment entered," §5.6.2(3), p. 162.

(2) Waiver by untimely statement. In most cases, a party who does not timely file a statement of disqualification impliedly waives the right to have the judge disqualified for cause. ***Tri Cty. Bank***, 167 Cal.App.4th at 1337. But the waiver is not automatic; the challenged judge must still respond to the statement. *See* ***Urias***, 234 Cal.App.3d at 421. See "Judge's response," §5.5, p. 159. If the judge does not timely answer or strike the statement, the judge is deemed to consent to disqualification and is automatically disqualified. ***Urias***, 234 Cal.App.3d at 421; *see* CCP §170.3(c)(4) (judge who does not timely file consent or answer is deemed to consent to disqualification).

3. Service. Copies of the statement must be (1) served on each party or party's attorney who has appeared in the proceeding and (2) personally served on either the challenged judge or, if the judge is in the courthouse or in chambers, the judge's clerk. CCP §170.3(c)(1).

4. Form. The statement must be in writing. CCP §170.3(c)(1).

5. Contents.

(1) Generally. The statement must comply with the general requirements for a paper that is filed with the court. *See* CCP §170.3(c)(1). See "General Requirements for Papers," ch. 1-B, §2, p. 9. The statement is not a motion, so the requirements for motions do not apply. ***Urias***, 234 Cal.App.3d at 422.

(a) Grounds for disqualification. The statement must object to the judge's participation in the hearing or trial and set out facts constituting the grounds for disqualification. CCP §170.3(c)(1); ***Hollingsworth***, 191 Cal.App.3d at 25. Conclusory allegations are not sufficient. ***Urias***, 234 Cal.App.3d at 426. See "Grounds for disqualification," §5.2, p. 151.

(b) Verification. The statement must be verified. CCP §170.3(c)(1); *see id.* §446. A statement in the form of a declaration or an affidavit satisfies the verification requirement. *See, e.g.*, ***Hollingsworth***, 191 Cal.App.3d at 25-26 (declaration stating grounds for disqualification was sufficient to satisfy verification requirement). A statement containing allegations on information and belief is not sufficient. *See* ***Urias***, 234 Cal.App.3d at 426. See "General Requirements for Declarations & Affidavits," ch. 1-B, §4, p. 19.

(2) Supporting evidence. See "Supporting evidence," ch. 1-D, §5.3, p. 30.

6. Limitation. A party can file only one statement of disqualification against the same judge unless facts suggesting new grounds for disqualification arise or are first discovered after the first statement was filed. CCP §170.4(c)(3). See "Motion for renewal," §5.8, p. 162.

7. Effect of filing statement. The filing of a statement of disqualification divests the judge of most of her powers to act until the statement is decided. CCP §170.4(d); *see* ***Urias***, 234 Cal.App.3d at 420-21. Until the statement is decided, the judge can only do the following:

(1) Maintain jurisdiction. The judge can take any action or issue any order necessary to maintain the court's jurisdiction pending the assignment of a judge that is not disqualified. CCP §170.4(a)(1); *see, e.g.*, ***Fine***, 97 Cal.App.4th at 669 (court issued stay of proceedings pending resolution of statement to maintain jurisdiction).

(2) Request another judge. The judge can ask another judge to act in the judge's place if the parties agree. CCP §170.4(a)(2). By asking another judge to act in her place, the challenged judge does not concede that she should be disqualified. CCP §170.3(c)(2).

(3) Hear default matters. The judge can hear and determine default matters. CCP §170.4(a)(3).

(4) Issue possession order. The judge can issue an order for possession before judgment in eminent-domain proceedings. CCP §170.4(a)(4).

(5) Set hearing or trial. The judge can set proceedings for hearing or trial. CCP §170.4(a)(5).

(6) Conduct settlement conferences. The judge can conduct settlement conferences. CCP §170.4(a)(6).

(7) Proceed with hearing or trial. If the statement is filed after a hearing or trial has commenced, the judge can proceed with the hearing or trial. CCP §170.4(c)(1). But if the judge is later determined to be disqualified, all the judge's rulings and orders made after the statement is filed must be vacated. *Id.* See "Effect of disqualification," §5.6, p. 161.

(a) Commencement – generally. For most proceedings, a hearing or trial commences when (1) voir dire begins, (2) the first witness is sworn, or (3) a motion is submitted for decision, whichever occurs first. CCP §170.4(c)(1); *e.g.*, ***Eckert v. Superior Ct.*** (4th Dist.1999) 69 Cal.App.4th 262, 266 (trial commenced when motions in limine were submitted for decision).

(b) Commencement in single-judge or all-purpose assignment. If the proceeding has been assigned to a single-judge court or an all-purpose judge and the hearing or trial has been set 30 or more days in advance before a judge whose name was known at the time, the hearing or trial is deemed to have commenced ten days before the scheduled hearing or trial date if the grounds for disqualification were known before that time. CCP §170.4(c)(2).

§5.5 Judge's response. The challenged judge may respond to a statement of disqualification in one of three ways: (1) by striking the statement, (2) by consenting to the disqualification, or (3) by filing an answer.

1. Strike defective statement. The challenged judge can respond to the statement by entering an order striking it. CCP §170.4(b); *see, e.g.*, ***PBA, LLC v. KPOD, Ltd.*** (2d Dist.2003) 112 Cal.App.4th 965, 973 (order striking statement of disqualification was recorded by minute order).

(1) Deadline. An order striking the statement must be made within ten days after the statement is filed or served, whichever is later. ***Lewis v. Superior Ct.*** (2d Dist.1988) 198 Cal.App.3d 1101, 1103-04.

(2) Grounds. The challenged judge can strike the statement for any of the following reasons:

(a) Untimely. The statement can be struck because it was not timely filed. CCP §170.4(b). See "At earliest practicable opportunity," §5.4.2(1), p. 157.

(b) No legal grounds. The statement can be struck because the statement, on its face, did not disclose any legal grounds for disqualification. CCP §170.4(b). See "Grounds for disqualification," §5.2, p. 151.

(c) No new grounds. The statement can be struck because the party filed an earlier statement, and the new statement does not allege facts constituting new grounds for disqualification. CCP §170.4(c)(3). See "Limitation," §5.4.6, p. 159.

2. Consent to disqualification. The challenged judge can respond to the statement by consenting to it. CCP §170.3(c)(3). The judge can consent to the disqualification in the following ways:

(1) No response. The judge can consent to the disqualification by not making a timely response. CCP §170.3(c)(4). If the judge does not timely respond to the statement by either striking it or filing an answer, the judge is deemed to have consented to the disqualification. *Id.*; ***Urias v. Harris Farms, Inc.*** (5th Dist.1991) 234 Cal.App.3d 415, 421. If no timely response is made, the clerk will notify the supervising judge of the court (also known as the presiding judge) or the person authorized to appoint a replacement that the judge has disqualified herself. CCP §170.3(c)(4).

(2) File consent. The judge can consent to the disqualification by filing a written consent. *See* CCP §170.3(c)(3). Consent must be filed within ten days after the statement is filed or served, whichever is later. *Id.* If the judge files a consent, the judge must notify the supervising judge of the court (also known as the presiding judge) or the person authorized to appoint a replacement that she has disqualified herself. *Id.*

3. File answer. The challenged judge can respond to the statement by filing an answer. CCP §170.3(c)(3).

(1) Deadline to file. The answer must be filed (1) before an order striking the statement is entered and (2) within ten days after the statement is filed or served, whichever is later. *See* CCP §170.3(c)(3) (establishing ten-day deadline for filing answer); ***PBA, LLC***, 112 Cal.App.4th at 973 (judge cannot file consent or answer after striking statement because statement no longer exists).

NOTE

Although an answer cannot be filed after a court enters an order to strike, the filing of an answer does not prevent the judge from later striking the statement. ***PBA, LLC****, 112 Cal.App.4th at 973.*

(2) Service. The clerk must send a copy of the answer to each party or party's attorney who has appeared in the proceeding. CCP §170.3(c)(3).

(3) Form. The answer must be in writing. CCP §170.3(c)(3).

(4) Contents.

(a) Response to allegations. The answer can admit or deny any or all of the statement's allegations and set out additional facts that are material or relevant to the issue of disqualification. CCP §170.3(c)(3).

(b) Verification. The answer must be verified. CCP §170.3(c)(3); *see id.* §446. An answer in the form of a declaration or an affidavit satisfies the verification requirement. *See, e.g.*, ***People v. Mayfield*** (1997) 14 Cal.4th 668, 811 (judge's declaration was sufficient to satisfy verification requirement).

(5) Effect of filing answer.

(a) Judge selected to determine disqualification. If the challenged judge files an answer to the statement, another judge must be selected to rule on the statement of disqualification. *See* CCP §170.3(c)(5).

[1] Selected by parties. The statement will be heard and determined by a judge selected by the parties if the parties can agree on a judge within five days after receiving notice of the challenged judge's answer. CCP §170.3(c)(5).

CAUTION

If the parties agree on a judge but the statement is inadvertently referred to another judge, the parties must immediately object. See ***Mayfield****, 14 Cal.4th at 811. If no objection is made, the parties' consent will be implied. See id.*

[2] Selected by Judicial Council. If the parties are unable to agree on another judge within five days after receiving notice of the challenged judge's answer, the clerk must notify the executive officer of the Judicial Council. CCP §170.3(c)(5). The chair of the Judicial Council must then select a judge as soon as possible. *Id.* If the chair is unable to select a judge, the judge must then be selected by the vice chair of the Judicial Council. *Id.*

NOTE

A party cannot file a motion or statement to disqualify the judge selected to decide the statement. CCP §170.3(c)(5).

(b) Procedure for decision. The judge selected to rule on the statement can decide the issue of disqualification based on the statement, the judge's answer, and any other written arguments asked for by the judge, or the judge can set the matter for a hearing at the earliest practicable time. CCP §170.3(c)(6); *see* ***Urias***, 234 Cal.App.3d at 422. If the judge chooses to conduct a hearing, the judge must allow the parties and the challenged judge to present oral argument and, if good cause is shown, to present evidence on any disputed fact issue. CCP §170.3(c)(6).

(c) Notice of ruling. If the judge grants the disqualification, the judge must notify the supervising judge of the court (also known as the presiding judge) or the person with the authority to appoint a replacement that the challenged judge has been disqualified. CCP §170.3(c)(6).

§5.6 Effect of disqualification.

1. On judge's power to act. If the statement of disqualification is granted, the disqualified judge may continue to act only as permitted under CCP §170.4(a). See "Effect of filing statement," §5.4.7, p. 159.

2. On judge's rulings. The effect of disqualification on the judge's rulings depends on when the grounds for disqualification were discovered and when the statement of disqualification was filed.

(1) Grounds discovered after ruling. If grounds for disqualification are discovered after a judge made a ruling but before the judge completed judicial action in the case (i.e., entered judgment), the judge's ruling is valid and should not be set aside by the replacement judge unless good cause is shown. CCP §170.3(b)(4); ***Urias v. Harris Farms, Inc.*** (5th Dist.1991) 234 Cal.App.3d 415, 423; *e.g.*, ***People v. Williams*** (2d Dist.2007) 156 Cal.App.4th 949, 956 (judge's ruling remained valid because it was made before judge was disqualified and D did not show good cause for setting aside ruling).

(2) Statement filed during hearing or trial. If the statement of disqualification is filed after the hearing or trial has commenced, the rulings that the disqualified judge made after the statement was filed must be vacated. CCP §170.4(c)(1); ***North Beverly Park Homeowners Ass'n v. Bisno*** (2d Dist.2007) 147 Cal.App.4th 762, 771. For a discussion of when a hearing or trial commences, see "Proceed with hearing or trial," §5.4.7(7), p. 159.

(3) Grounds discovered after judgment entered. If grounds for disqualification are discovered after an entry of judgment, courts disagree on whether the court's judgment is void or voidable. *See* ***Betz v. Pankow*** (1st Dist.1993) 16 Cal.App.4th 931, 938-39 (CCP §§170-170.5 do not discuss validity of judgment entered by disqualified judge); ***Urias***, 234 Cal.App.3d at 423 (noting conflict); ***North Beverly Park***, 147 Cal.App.4th at 768-69 (same); *see generally* 2 Witkin, *Cal. Procedure*, Courts, §§94, 95 (discussing conflict).

(a) Ruling void. Some courts hold that a judgment entered by a disqualified judge is void for lack of subject-matter jurisdiction. *See* ***Giometti v. Etienne*** (1934) 219 Cal. 687, 689; ***Rossco Holdings, Inc. v. Bank of Am.*** (2d Dist.2007) 149 Cal.App.4th 1353, 1362-63; ***Christie v. City of El Centro*** (4th Dist.2006) 135 Cal.App.4th 767, 779-80.

(b) Ruling voidable. Some courts hold that a judgment entered by a disqualified judge is only voidable. *See* ***Betz***, 16 Cal.App.4th at 940; ***Urias***, 234 Cal.App.3d at 423-24.

§5.7 Motion for reconsideration. A party who is adversely affected by a court's order on a statement of disqualification can file a motion for reconsideration. CCP §1008(a); *see, e.g.*, ***Lavine v. Hospital of the Good Samaritan*** (2d Dist.1985) 169 Cal.App.3d 1019, 1025 (P filed motion for reconsideration of order denying statement of disqualification). See "Motion for Reconsideration," ch. 5-G, §3, p. 508.

§5.8 Motion for renewal. It is unclear whether a party whose statement of disqualification is denied can file a motion for renewal under CCP §1008(b). See "Motion for Renewal," ch. 5-G, §4, p. 516. Under §1008(b), a party can renew an application for the same order if new or different facts, circumstances, or law come to light. But under CCP §170.4(c)(3), a party cannot file more than one statement of disqualification against the same judge unless "facts suggesting new grounds" for disqualification arise or are discovered after the first statement was filed. Under a plain reading of §170.4(c)(3), not only must new or different facts come to light, but these facts must support a new ground for disqualification; a party cannot renew a statement on the same ground for disqualification that was denied earlier.

§5.9 Appellate review.

1. Appealability.

(1) Writ of mandate. An order granting, denying, or striking a statement of disqualification can be challenged by filing a petition for a writ of mandate. *See* CCP §170.3(d); ***People v. Lucas*** (2014) 60 Cal.4th 153, 304; *see, e.g.*, ***Hollingsworth v. Superior Ct.*** (4th Dist.1987) 191 Cal.App.3d 22, 25 (order to strike reviewed by writ of mandate). See "Writ of mandate," §4.10.1(1), p. 149.

(2) Direct appeal. Generally, an order granting, denying, or striking a statement of disqualification is not directly appealable. *See* CCP §170.3(d); ***Lucas***, 60 Cal.4th at 304. But an order denying a statement of disqualification is appealable if a party claims that the judge's bias or prejudice denied the party its constitutional due-process right to an impartial judge. ***People v. Chatman*** (2006) 38 Cal.4th 344, 362-63.

2. Standard of review. Generally, the ruling on a statement of disqualification is reviewed for abuse of discretion. ***People v. Alvarez*** (1996) 14 Cal.4th 155, 237. But if the facts supporting the statement are undisputed, the issue of disqualification becomes a question of law and the standard of review is de novo. ***Wechsler v. Superior Ct.*** (4th Dist.2014) 224 Cal.App.4th 384, 391-92.

E. STIPULATION OR MOTION FOR REFERENCE

This subchapter discusses the procedures for appointing a referee under CCP §§638 and 639. The act of appointing a referee is called a "reference." This subchapter does not discuss the procedures for appointing a referee in proceedings not covered under §§638 and 639, such as proceedings to enforce money judgments (CCP §§708.110-708.140), partition proceedings (CCP §§873.010-873.060), or suits to determine water rights (Water C. §§2000, 2001).

§1. GENERAL

§1.1 Purpose. The purpose of appointing a referee in an action or proceeding is to expedite the review and determination of issues, especially those that are complex, contentious, or require the examination of large amounts of information. *See **Jovine v. FHP, Inc.*** (2d Dist.1998) 64 Cal.App.4th 1506, 1521 (referee is commonly used when complicated accounts can more conveniently be taken or examined outside court); ***DeBlase v. Superior Ct.*** (2d Dist.1996) 41 Cal.App.4th 1279, 1284 (referee is especially appropriate for ongoing discovery disputes). A referee can be appointed to (1) conduct hearings, (2) resolve discovery disputes, (3) render decisions on factual or legal issues, or (4) make recommendations to the court on how it should decide particular factual or legal issues. *See* CCP §§638(a), (b), 639(a), 643-645; ***Sy First Family L.P. v. Cheung*** (4th Dist.1999) 70 Cal.App.4th 1334, 1341; ***Jovine***, 64 Cal.App.4th at 1521.

NOTE

The court can appoint up to three referees to hear and determine issues in an action or proceeding. CCP §640(a), (b). For simplicity's sake, most of the discussion in this subchapter only refers to a single referee, but the discussion applies equally to situations involving multiple referees.

§1.2 Primary authority. CCP §§638-645.1; CRC 3.900-3.932.

§1.3 Secondary authority. The following secondary sources are cited as authority in this subchapter:

- *California Civil Discovery Practice* (CEB Online ed. 2014) (referred to as *CEB Discovery Practice*).
- *California Civil Procedure Before Trial* (CEB Online ed. 2014) (referred to as *CEB Procedure Before Trial*).
- Kiesel et al., *Matthew Bender Practice Guide: California Pretrial Civil Procedure* (2014) (referred to as Kiesel, *Cal. Pretrial Civil Procedure*).
- Lee, *Appointing a Discovery Referee in California State Court*, 27 Los Angeles Lawyer 10 (Dec. 2004) (referred to as Lee, *Appointing a Discovery Referee*).
- Witkin, *California Procedure* (5th ed. 2008 & Supp.2014) (referred to as Witkin, *Cal. Procedure*).

§1.4 Judicial Council forms.

- ADR-109 (optional), stipulation or motion for order appointing referee.
- ADR-110 (optional), order appointing referee.
- ADR-111 (optional), report of referee.

§2. CONSIDERATIONS BEFORE APPOINTING REFEREE

In deciding whether to seek the appointment of a referee, the following advantages and disadvantages should be considered:

§2.1 Advantages.

1. **Time.** A referee can usually dedicate more time and effort than a judge to becoming familiar with and analyzing a complex issue. *See **DeBlase v. Superior Ct.*** (2d Dist.1996) 41 Cal.App.4th 1279, 1284 (referees are especially appropriate for determining privilege claims that require sifting through many documents).

2. **Expertise.** A referee with specialized knowledge, training, or experience can be selected to determine sophisticated, technical, or complex issues. *See CEB Procedure Before Trial*, §§45.59, 45.60; *cf.* CCP §641.2 (party can object to referee who has inadequate technical knowledge in certain environmental-law actions).

3. **Convenience.** Proceedings before a referee can be scheduled at convenient times and held at convenient locations to reduce travel distances and the time, effort, and expense of transporting large quantities of documents or other evidence. *See* ***Jovine v. FHP, Inc.*** (2d Dist.1998) 64 Cal.App.4th 1506, 1521 (referees most commonly used when complicated accounts can more conveniently be taken or examined outside court); *CEB Procedure Before Trial*, §45.60 (parties can set trial at mutually convenient time).

§2.2 Disadvantages.

1. **Costs.** Referee services can be very expensive, especially when the referee must examine a large number of documents to determine an issue or dispute. Lee, *Appointing a Discovery Referee*, 27 Los Angeles Lawyer at 10; *see* ***Solorzano v. Superior Ct.*** (2d Dist.1993) 18 Cal.App.4th 603, 614 (privately compensated referees can cost between $200 and $300 per hour).

2. **No contempt power.** A referee does not have the power to punish for contempt. *CEB Procedure Before Trial*, §45.60; *see* ***Marcus v. Workmen's Comp. Appeals Bd.*** (1st Dist.1973) 35 Cal.App.3d 598, 603-04 (nonjudicial officers have no power to punish for contempt unless specially authorized by law; CCP §1211 appears to require contempts of subordinate officers to be reported to the court rather than directly adjudicated). A referee can only present a statement of facts describing a party's offending conduct and recommend that the court hold the party in contempt. *See* CCP §1211(a) (contempt committed outside immediate presence of court requires statement of facts from referee); *see also* ***Sauer v. Superior Ct.*** (4th Dist.1987) 195 Cal.App.3d 213, 224-25 (discovery referee can recommend that court impose discovery sanctions).

§3. TYPES OF REFERENCES

Under CCP §§638 and 639, a reference can be either general or special.

§3.1 General reference. A general reference is a referral of all factual and legal issues in an action or proceeding for hearing and determination by a referee. ***Ellsworth v. Ellsworth*** (1954) 42 Cal.2d 719, 722; ***O'Donoghue v. Superior Ct.*** (1st Dist.2013) 219 Cal.App.4th 245, 255.

1. **Consent required.** A general reference can be made only if all parties consent. CCP §638; ***Holt v. Kelly*** (1978) 20 Cal.3d 560, 562; ***Murphy v. Padilla*** (6th Dist.1996) 42 Cal.App.4th 707, 714. See "Appointing Referee – Consensual," §5, p. 167.

2. **Referee's decision final.** The referee's decision under a general reference stands as the decision of the court. CCP §644(a). It is reviewed in the same manner as a trial-court judgment. *See id.* §645. See "Court's review of statement of decision," §12.1, p. 186.

§3.2 Special reference. A special reference is a referral of only certain issues in an action or proceeding for hearing and determination by a referee. *See* CCP §§638(b), 639(a).

1. **Consent optional.** A special reference can be made with or without the consent of the parties. *See* CCP §638(b) (consensual special reference), §639 (nonconsensual special reference). See "Appointing Referee – Consensual," §5, p. 167; "Appointing Referee – Nonconsensual," §6, p. 175.

2. **Scope of reference.**

(1) **Consensual.** If all parties consent to the special reference, the court can appoint a referee to ascertain a fact that is necessary for the court to determine the action or proceeding. CCP §638(b); *see* ***Murphy v. Padilla*** (6th Dist.1996) 42 Cal.App.4th 707, 713.

(2) **Nonconsensual.** If all parties do not consent to the special reference, the court can appoint a referee to hear and determine only issues that are explicitly authorized by CCP §639. ***In re Marriage of Galis*** (2d

Dist.1983) 149 Cal.App.3d 147, 150-51; *see* ***Aetna Life Ins. v. Superior Ct.*** (4th Dist.1986) 182 Cal.App.3d 431, 435. Issues that can be heard and determined by a referee under §639 are the following:

(a) Accounting. The court can appoint a referee to do the following:

[1] Resolve a fact issue that requires examination of a long account. CCP §639(a)(1).

[2] Report on any specific fact question that requires examination of a long account. *Id.*

[3] Conduct an accounting that is necessary for the court's information before judgment. *Id.* §639(a)(2).

[4] Conduct an accounting that is necessary for carrying a judgment or order into effect. *Id.*

(b) Fact issue not raised in pleadings. The court can appoint a referee to hear and determine a fact issue that was not raised in the pleadings. CCP §639(a)(3). A fact issue arises from the pleadings when a material fact is alleged in the complaint and controverted in the answer. *See id.* §§588, 590.

(c) Information in special proceeding. The court can appoint a referee to obtain information in a special proceeding. CCP §639(a)(4); *see* ***Jeld-Wen, Inc. v. Superior Ct.*** (4th Dist.2007) 146 Cal.App.4th 536, 542 (referee can be appointed to "obtain information" for court). A special proceeding is generally defined as a case that was not, under common law or equity practice, either an action at law or a suit in equity. ***People v. Superior Ct. (Laff)*** (2001) 25 Cal.4th 703, 725; *see* CCP §§22, 23; *see, e.g.*, ***Holt v. Kelly*** (1978) 20 Cal.3d 560, 562 (referee appointed in mandamus proceeding concerning confiscation of petitioner's property); ***In re Reed*** (1928) 204 Cal. 119, 121 (referee appointed to take evidence and report conclusions in action to quiet title). For a special reference to be authorized under §639(a)(4), the special proceeding in question must be civil, not criminal. ***Laff***, 25 Cal.4th at 731-32.

(d) Discovery motions & disputes. The court can appoint a referee to hear and determine some or all discovery motions and disputes in an action if exceptional circumstances make it necessary. CCP §639(a)(5), (d)(2); CRC 3.920(c), 3.922(c)(2); *see* CCP §639(c) (order appointing discovery referee must state whether referee is being appointed for all discovery purposes). The following are examples of exceptional circumstances that may justify the appointment of a discovery referee:

[1] The discovery motion or dispute involves multiple issues. ***Taggares v. Superior Ct.*** (4th Dist.1998) 62 Cal.App.4th 94, 105.

[2] There are multiple discovery motions to be heard. *Id.*

[3] The number of documents to be reviewed would make resolving the discovery dispute time-consuming. *Id.*; *see* ***DeBlase v. Superior Ct.*** (2d Dist.1996) 41 Cal.App.4th 1279, 1284 (appointment of discovery referee is especially appropriate for determining privilege claims that require sifting through many documents).

[4] A party is requesting a voluminous amount of records to be placed under seal. CRC 2.550(e)(2).

[5] The obstructive behavior of an attorney or witness is causing excessive delays in the discovery process. *See* ***DeBlase***, 41 Cal.App.4th at 1284 (appointment of discovery referee is especially appropriate when deposition requires presence of neutral presiding officer or when case involves ongoing discovery disputes); *CEB Discovery Practice*, §2.68 (discovery referee can stop obstructive behavior and avoid unnecessary motions to compel).

NOTE

In 2000, CCP §639(d)(2) was added, which allowed courts to appoint a discovery referee only in "exceptional circumstances." Stats. 2000, ch. 644, §2.5. The amendment was intended to be consistent with the decision in ***Taggares****, which listed certain factors that would allow the court to appoint a discovery referee. Sen. Com. on Judiciary, Analysis of Assem. Bill No. 2912 (1999-2000 Reg. Sess.).*

3. **Referee's decision advisory.** The referee's decision under a special reference is only advisory. CCP §644(b). The court must independently review the referee's decision before either adopting it in whole or in part or entering its own findings of fact and conclusions of law. *See id.*; ***Yeboah v. Progeny Ventures, Inc.*** (2d Dist.2005) 128 Cal.App.4th 443, 450.

§4. WHO CAN SERVE AS REFEREE

§4.1 Qualified juror. Generally, a person can serve as a referee if she meets all the requirements for serving as a juror, except for the requirement of residence within a particular county. *See* CCP §641(a). To serve as a referee, the person must meet the following requirements:

1. The person must be a citizen of the United States. *Id.* §203(a)(1).
2. The person must be 18 or older. *Id.* §203(a)(2).
3. The person must be a resident of California. *Id.* §203(a)(3).
4. The person must not have been convicted of malfeasance in office or of a felony, or if convicted, the person must have had her civil rights restored. *Id.* §203(a)(5).
5. The person must have sufficient knowledge of the English language. *Id.* §203(a)(6).
6. The person cannot currently be a juror in a trial or grand-jury proceeding in the state. *Id.* §203(a)(7).
7. The person cannot be the subject of a conservatorship. *Id.* §203(a)(8).

§4.2 Exceptions. Certain persons cannot serve as a referee even if they are qualified to be a juror.

1. **Former judicial officer who is no longer Bar member.** A person cannot serve as a referee if she is a former judicial officer who is not an active or inactive member of the State Bar. CRC 3.903, 3.923.

2. **Not technically qualified.** A person cannot serve as a referee in certain environmental actions brought under the Government Code if she is not technically qualified in the subject matter of the proceeding. CCP §641.2; *see* Gov. C. §§12600-12612.

3. **Served as juror or witness.** A person cannot serve as a referee if she has served as a juror or witness in any trial between the parties. CCP §641(d).

4. **Related to party or judge.**

(1) **Consanguinity.** A person cannot serve as a referee if she is related by consanguinity within the third degree to any party, to an officer of a corporation that is a party, or to any judge of the court making the appointment. CCP §641(b). Individuals within the third degree of consanguinity are (1) a parent and child, (2) siblings, (3) aunts, uncles, nieces, and nephews, (4) grandparents and grandchildren, and (5) great-grandparents and great-grandchildren. *See **People v. Williams*** (1997) 16 Cal.4th 635, 653; ***Robinson v. Southern Pac. Co.*** (1895) 105 Cal. 526, 557.

(2) **Affinity.** A person cannot serve as a referee if she is related by affinity (i.e., by marriage) within the third degree to any party, to an officer of a corporation that is a party, or to any judge of the court making the appointment. CCP §641(b). Spouses are related to each other by affinity, and they are related to each other's relatives by affinity in the same manner that each spouse is related to their relatives by consanguinity. ***People v. Meza*** (6th Dist.1987) 188 Cal.App.3d 1631, 1643; *see* CCP §17(b)(9).

5. **Connected with party.** A person cannot serve as a referee if she has any of the following relationships with a party:

(1) Guardian and ward. CCP §641(c).

(2) Conservator and conservatee. *Id.*

(3) Master and servant. *Id.*; *see also* ***Townsend v. State*** (2d Dist.1987) 191 Cal.App.3d 1530, 1535 (discussing difficulty in defining master and servant relationship).

(4) Employer and clerk. CCP §641(c).

(5) Principal and agent. *Id.*

(6) Members of the same family. *Id.*

(7) Business partners. *Id.*

(8) Security on any bond or obligation of a party. *Id.*

6. Biased or interested.

(1) Interest in case. A person cannot serve as a referee if she has an interest in (1) the outcome of the action or proceeding or (2) one of the main issues in the action or proceeding. CCP §641(e).

(2) Opinion or belief. A person cannot serve as a referee if she has formed or expressed an unqualified opinion or belief about the merits of the action or proceeding. CCP §641(f).

(3) Enmity or bias. A person cannot serve as a referee if she demonstrates enmity or bias toward a party appearing in the action or proceeding. CCP §641(g).

§5. APPOINTING REFEREE – CONSENSUAL

If all parties consent to the reference, the court can appoint a referee on the parties' stipulation or on a party's motion. CCP §638; CRC 3.901.

§5.1 Stipulation.

1. Who can file. The parties can stipulate to a consensual reference either directly or through their attorneys. *See* CCP §§283(1), 638.

2. Deadline to file. There is no specified deadline for filing the stipulation. *See* CCP §638; CRC 3.901.

3. Form.

(1) Oral. The stipulation can be made orally. *See* CCP §638 (referee may be appointed on agreement of parties entered in court's minutes). An oral stipulation must be made in open court and entered in the court's minutes. ***Jovine v. FHP, Inc.*** (2d Dist.1998) 64 Cal.App.4th 1506, 1527; *see* CCP §638. Consent to the reference must be explicit and not implied from silence. *See, e.g.*, ***Smith v. Polack*** (1852) 2 Cal. 92, 94 (when appointment of referee would have waived D's right to jury trial, consent to appointment could not be implied from attorney's silence).

(2) Written. The stipulation can be made in writing. CRC 3.901. A written stipulation can be made using Judicial Council Form ADR-109.

4. Where to file.

(1) Oral stipulation. An oral stipulation must be made in open court and recorded in the court's minutes. *See* CCP §638.

(2) Written stipulation. A written stipulation must be filed with the clerk or judge. CCP §638.

5. Contents.

(1) Stipulation. The stipulation should contain the following information:

(a) Scope of reference. The stipulation must state whether the parties are asking for a general or special reference. CRC 3.901(b)(1); *see* CCP §638. See "General reference," §3.1, p. 164; "Special reference," §3.2, p. 164. If the stipulation is for a special reference, the stipulation must specify the issues to be determined by the referee. CRC 3.901(b)(1); *see* CCP §638(b). See "Consensual," §3.2.2(1), p. 164.

(b) Compensation. The stipulation must state whether the referee will be privately compensated or serve at no cost to the parties. CRC 3.901(b)(2).

[1] Agreed compensation. If the parties agree on how to apportion responsibility for payment of referee fees, the stipulation should state the terms of the agreement. *See* CCP §645.1(a).

[2] No agreement on compensation. If the parties do not agree on how to apportion responsibility for payment of referee fees, the stipulation should ask the court to divide responsibility for payment between the parties in a fair and reasonable manner. *See* CCP §645.1.

(c) Use of court facilities or personnel. The stipulation must state whether the use of court facilities or personnel is requested. CRC 3.901(b)(3). If the use of court facilities or personnel is requested, the stipulation must (1) describe the use sought (e.g., using a courtroom to conduct hearings) and (2) state why permitting the use of court facilities or personnel would further the interest of justice. *Id.*; *see* CRC 3.907.

(d) Identity of referee.

[1] Agreed appointment. If the parties agree to use a particular referee, the stipulation should identify the person by name, business address, telephone number, and if applicable, State Bar number and membership status (e.g., active, inactive). *See* CRC 3.902(1) (requirements for order appointing referee); *see, e.g.*, Judicial Council Forms, form ADR-109, item 3 (sample motion). See "Who Can Serve as Referee," §4, p. 166.

[2] Nominations. If the parties do not agree to use a particular referee, the stipulation should nominate up to three persons per party for appointment as referee. CCP §640(b). The stipulation should identify each nominated person by name, business address, telephone number, and if applicable, State Bar number and membership status (e.g., active, inactive). *See* CRC 3.902(1) (requirements for order appointing referee); Judicial Council Forms, form ADR-109, item 3 (sample motion). See "Who Can Serve as Referee," §4, p. 166.

(e) Referee's report & recommendation or statement of decision.

[1] Deadline to submit. The stipulation should request a specific deadline for submitting the referee's report and recommendation or statement of decision to the court if a deadline other than the standard 20-day deadline is needed. *See* CCP §643(a), (b). See "Deadline to file," §10.1.1, p. 183.

[2] Manner of delivery. The stipulation should designate how the referee's report and recommendation or statement of decision will be delivered to the court and the parties. *See* CCP §643(b).

(2) Proposed order. If the stipulation is in writing, it must be accompanied by a proposed order. CRC 3.901(b)(5). See "Order," §5.7, p. 173.

(3) Referee's certification. If the stipulation is in writing and the parties have agreed to use a particular referee, the stipulation must be accompanied by the proposed referee's certification. CRC 3.901(b)(4); Kiesel, *Cal. Pretrial Civil Procedure*, §25.05[1]. If the stipulation is made orally or the parties have not agreed to use a particular referee, the certification must be filed with the court before the referee begins referee services. CRC 3.904(a). The referee's certification must be in writing and contain the following:

(a) A statement that the person consents to serve as referee as provided in the order of appointment if and when she is appointed. CRC 3.904(a)(1); *see* Kiesel, *Cal. Pretrial Civil Procedure*, §25.26.

(b) A statement certifying that the person is aware of and will comply with the applicable provisions of the California Rules of Court and Canon 6 of the Code of Judicial Ethics. CRC 3.904(a)(1); Kiesel, *Cal. Pretrial Civil Procedure*, §25.26.

(c) The signature of the proposed referee. Kiesel, *Cal. Pretrial Civil Procedure*, §25.26.

(4) Cover letter. If the parties have agreed to the appointment of a particular referee, the stipulation should be accompanied by a cover letter asking the clerk to present the stipulation and proposed order to the

assigned judge for her signature. Kiesel, *Cal. Pretrial Civil Procedure*, §25.03; *see* CRC 3.901(a). If no judge has been assigned, the cover letter should ask the clerk to present the stipulation and proposed order to the presiding judge or the law-and-motion judge. *See* CRC 3.901(a).

§5.2 Motion.

1. Who can file. A motion for a consensual reference can be made by any party to the action or proceeding that has agreed in a written contract or lease that any controversy arising from the contract or lease must be heard by a referee. CCP §638.

2. Deadline to file & serve. The motion must be filed and served at least 16 court days before the hearing. CCP §1005(b). See "Retrospective deadlines," ch. 1-G, §6.2, p. 71. If the motion is served by a method other than personal delivery, the movant will have to add more time to the 16-day period. CCP §1005(b). See "Add time for method of service," ch. 1-G, §6.2.1(5), p. 72.

3. Contents.

(1) Notice of motion & motion. The motion should be made in writing by noticed motion. *See* Kiesel, *Cal. Pretrial Civil Procedure*, §25.03. See "Notice of motion & motion," ch. 1-D, §5.1, p. 28. The motion must contain the same information required in the stipulation. CRC 3.901(b). See "Stipulation," §5.1.5(1), p. 167. If a party chooses, it can submit a motion for a consensual reference by using Judicial Council Form ADR-109.

(2) Memorandum of points & authorities. The motion must include a memorandum in support. CRC 3.1112(a)(3). See "Memorandum of points & authorities," ch. 1-D, §5.2, p. 28.

(3) Contract or lease. The motion should be accompanied by the contract or lease that supports the appointment of the referee. Kiesel, *Cal. Pretrial Civil Procedure*, §25.03; *see* CRC 3.1112(b).

(4) Proposed order. The motion must be accompanied by a proposed order. CRC 3.901(b)(5). See "Order," §5.7, p. 173.

(5) Referee's certification. If the parties have agreed to the appointment of a particular referee, the motion must be accompanied by the proposed referee's certification. CRC 3.901(b)(4); Kiesel, *Cal. Pretrial Civil Procedure*, §25.05[1]. See "Referee's certification," §5.1.5(3), p. 168.

§5.3 Response.

1. Nomination of referee. If the parties have not agreed to the appointment of a particular referee, a party can respond to a motion for a consensual reference by submitting to the court up to three persons that the party nominates to serve as referee. CCP §640(b). The party should identify each nominated person by name, business address, telephone number, and if applicable, State Bar number and membership status (e.g., active, inactive). *See* CRC 3.902(1) (requirements of order); Judicial Council Forms, form ADR-109, item 3 (sample motion).

2. Motion to withdraw stipulation. A party can respond to a stipulation for a consensual reference by filing a motion to withdraw the stipulation. *See* CRC 3.906.

(1) Deadline to file & serve. The motion must be filed with the court and served on all parties and the referee at least 16 court days before the hearing. *See* CCP §1005(b); CRC 3.906(b). See "Retrospective deadlines," ch. 1-G, §6.2, p. 71. If the motion is served by a method other than personal delivery, the movant will have to add more time to the 16-day period. CCP §1005(b). See "Add time for method of service," ch. 1-G, §6.2.1(5), p. 72.

NOTE

Other than the general deadline for filing noticed motions, there is no specific deadline for filing a motion to withdraw a stipulation for a consensual reference. CRC 3.906(a)(1) does seem to suggest, however, that a motion to withdraw a stipulation could be filed after a referee is appointed and makes a ruling. CRC 3.906(a)(1) prohibits a party from bringing a motion to withdraw because of factual or legal error in a referee's ruling. By prohibiting motions only in these limited circumstances, CRC 3.906(a)(1) suggests that a motion to withdraw could be filed after a referee makes a ruling if other good cause exists.

(2) Contents.

(a) Notice of motion & motion. The motion should be made in writing by noticed motion. CRC 3.906(b). See "Notice of motion & motion," ch. 1-D, §5.1, p. 28.

(b) Declaration. The motion must be supported by a declaration of facts establishing good cause for withdrawing the stipulation. CRC 3.906(a). See "Declaration," ch. 1-B, §4.1.1, p. 19.

[1] Facts considered good cause. No court has addressed what facts will be considered good cause for withdrawing a stipulation for a consensual reference. Most courts have held that a party may be relieved from a stipulation in other contexts, however, if it can show any of the following:

[a] The party entered into the stipulation because of inadvertence, excusable neglect, fraud, or a mistake of fact or law. ***Los Angeles City Sch. Dist. v. Landier Inv.*** (2d Dist.1960) 177 Cal.App.2d 744, 750.

[b] A change in the underlying conditions that prompted the stipulation has occurred, and this change of conditions could not have been anticipated by the movant. *Id.*

[c] Special circumstances make it unjust to enforce the stipulation. *Id.*

[2] Facts not considered good cause. The movant cannot establish good cause based on either of the following:

[a] A declaration that the referee's ruling is based on an error of fact or law. CRC 3.906(a)(1).

[b] The issuance of an order requiring that hearings before the referee be conducted at a site that is easily accessible to the public and appropriate for seating people who have notified the court of their intention to attend the hearings. CRC 3.906(a)(2); *see* CRC 3.931(c) (formerly CRC 3.910). See "Location," §9.1.3, p. 182.

(c) Proposed order. The movant can submit a proposed order with the motion. CRC 3.1113(m). The proposed order must be lodged and served with the motion papers, not attached to them. *Id.*

3. Opposition – objecting to nominated referee. A party can oppose a stipulation or motion for a consensual reference by filing a written objection to the appointment of a particular person nominated as a referee. CRC 3.905.

(1) Deadline to file & serve. The objection must be filed with the court with reasonable diligence and served on all parties and the nominated referee. CRC 3.905. Although CRC 3.905 does not provide a specific deadline for filing a written objection to a nominated referee, courts and commentators have suggested that the objection should be filed before the referee is appointed. *See* Kiesel, *Cal. Pretrial Civil Procedure*, §25.15[1]; *see, e.g.*, ***Bonner v. Lehfeldt*** (1st Dist.1919) 39 Cal.App. 649, 652 (party waived right to object by appearing before court-appointed commissioner). Once a referee has been appointed, a party can object to the referee by filing a motion to disqualify (also known as a peremptory challenge) or a statement of disqualification. See "Disqualifying Appointed Referee," §8, p. 181.

(2) Form. The objection must be in writing and should comply with the general requirements for opposition papers. *See* CRC 3.905. See "Opposition Papers," ch. 1-D, §8, p. 35.

(3) Grounds for objection. The objection should state the reasons why the person is not qualified to serve as a referee. *See* CCP §641. See "Who Can Serve as Referee," §4, p. 166.

(4) No waiver. A party does not waive its right to object to the appointment of a particular person as a referee by stipulating to or making a motion for a consensual reference or by submitting nominations for appointment. CCP §640(c); CRC 3.905. See "Nomination of referee," §5.3.1, p. 169.

4. Opposition – objecting to contractual reference. A party can oppose a motion for a consensual reference by filing an objection to the motion.

(1) Deadline to file & serve. The objection must be filed and served on all parties at least nine court days before the hearing. CCP §1005(b).

(2) Form. The objection must be in writing and should comply with the general requirements for opposition papers. *See* CCP §642. See "Opposition Papers," ch. 1-D, §8, p. 35.

(3) Grounds for objection. A party can object to a motion for a consensual reference on the following grounds:

(a) Waiver. A party can object on the ground that the right to enforce a contractual reference provision has been waived. *See* ***O'Donoghue v. Superior Ct.*** (1st Dist.2013) 219 Cal.App.4th 245, 261-62. The First District Court of Appeal recently addressed the issue and considered authority concerning waiver of a contractual right to arbitration to determine whether the plaintiff waived its contractual right to a reference. *Id.* No other court has addressed this issue.

(b) No written contract or lease. A party can object on the ground that there is no written contract or lease that requires all disputes arising from the contract or lease to be heard by a referee. *See* CCP §638; *see, e.g.*, ***Treo @ Kettner Homeowners Ass'n v. Superior Ct.*** (4th Dist.2008) 166 Cal.App.4th 1055, 1060 (P opposed motion for reference on ground that document containing reference provision was not contract).

(c) Unenforceable contract or lease. A party can object on the ground that the reference provision in the written contract or lease is unconscionable and therefore unenforceable. *See* Civ. C. §1670.5; ***Pardee Constr. Co. v. Superior Ct.*** (4th Dist.2002) 100 Cal.App.4th 1081, 1085. To be unenforceable, the reference provision must have been procedurally and substantively unconscionable when the parties executed the contract or lease. ***Greenbriar Homes Cmty., Inc. v. Superior Ct.*** (3d Dist.2004) 117 Cal.App.4th 337, 343-44, *disapproved on other grounds*, ***Tarrant Bell Prop., LLC v. Superior Ct.*** (2011) 51 Cal.4th 538; ***Pardee Constr.***, 100 Cal.App.4th at 1088. Whether a reference provision is unconscionable is determined by the court on a case-by-case basis. *See* ***Trend Homes, Inc. v. Superior Ct.*** (5th Dist.2005) 131 Cal.App.4th 950, 956, *disapproved on other grounds*, ***Tarrant Bell Prop., LLC v. Superior Ct.*** (2011) 51 Cal.4th 538.

NOTE

Procedural unconscionability and substantive unconscionability do not need to be present in the same degree to render a reference provision in a written contract or lease unenforceable. ***Pardee Constr.****, 100 Cal.App.4th at 1088. The more substantively unconscionable the provision is, the less evidence of procedural unconscionability is required to prove that the provision is unenforceable, and vice versa.* ***O'Donoghue****, 219 Cal.App.4th at 258;* ***Greenbriar Homes Cmty.****, 117 Cal.App.4th at 344;* ***Pardee Constr.****, 100 Cal.App.4th at 1088.*

[1] Procedural unconscionability. A reference provision is procedurally unconscionable if its inclusion in the contract or lease is oppressive or surprising. ***Pardee Constr.***, 100 Cal.App.4th at 1089. The issue of whether the provision is oppressive or surprising is determined by examining the circumstances of the parties' contract negotiations. *Id.* at 1088.

[a] Oppression. A reference provision is oppressive if the nonobjecting party was able to include the provision because of unequal bargaining power between the parties. ***Pardee Constr.***, 100 Cal.App.4th at 1089. The following factors can support a finding that a reference provision is oppressive:

- **No negotiation.** The provision was included without any real negotiation between the parties (e.g., in a standard adhesion contract). *See* ***O'Donoghue***, 219 Cal.App.4th at 258-59; ***Trend Homes***, 131 Cal.App.4th at 957-58; ***Pardee Constr.***, 100 Cal.App.4th at 1089.

• **No choice.** The objecting party had no real choice but to agree to the reference provision. *See **O'Donoghue***, 219 Cal.App.4th at 258-59; ***Pardee Constr.***, 100 Cal.App.4th at 1089. For example, a party who is in a significantly weaker economic position may have to agree to a reference provision because the party has no bargaining power and the provision is presented as part of a "take it or leave it" contract. *Compare **Pardee Constr.***, 100 Cal.App.4th at 1087 (finding that home buyers were unlikely to have significant bargaining power with developer), *with **Trend Homes***, 131 Cal.App.4th at 958 (reference provision was negotiable because it had to be initialed by home buyer and seller).

• **Could not understand or appreciate.** The objecting party did not have sufficient education, experience, or sophistication to understand or appreciate the significance of the reference provision. *See **Trend Homes***, 131 Cal.App.4th at 959.

• **Pressure.** The objecting party was pressured to sign the contract or lease without reading it carefully. *See **Trend Homes***, 131 Cal.App.4th at 959.

• **No consultation.** The objecting party was not given an opportunity to consult another person, such as an attorney, before signing the contract or lease. *See **Trend Homes***, 131 Cal.App.4th at 959.

[b] **Surprise.** A reference provision is surprising if it is drafted or included in the contract or lease in a way that is misleading or makes it difficult to locate, read, or understand. *See **Pardee Constr.***, 100 Cal.App.4th at 1089-90. The following factors can support a finding that a reference provision is surprising:

• **Hidden provision.** The reference provision is included in the contract or lease in a place where a party would not expect to find it or where it is unlikely to be read carefully. *See **Greenbriar Homes Cmty.***, 117 Cal.App.4th at 345 (provision buried in agreement may be unconscionable); *see, e.g.*, ***O'Donoghue***, 219 Cal.App.4th at 259 (reference provision was not surprising when it was placed immediately above signature line at end of short contract). But a reference provision is not considered hidden in the contract or lease if it is specifically brought to the objecting party's attention before the party signs the contract or lease. *See, e.g.*, ***Trend Homes***, 131 Cal.App.4th at 959 (reference provision was not surprising because it had to be initialed by both parties); ***Woodside Homes v. Superior Ct.*** (4th Dist.2003) 107 Cal.App.4th 723, 729 (same).

• **Misleading caption.** The caption used to introduce the provision is misleading because it does not correctly or meaningfully describe the provision's significance. *See, e.g.*, ***Pardee Constr.***, 100 Cal.App.4th at 1090 (caption using terms "Judicial Reference" and "Trial by Judge in Court of Competent Jurisdiction" was misleading because trial provision applied only if reference provision was not enforced).

• **Difficult to read.** The typeface or formatting of the provision makes it difficult to read. *See, e.g.*, ***Greenbriar Homes Cmty.***, 117 Cal.App.4th at 345 (provision that was written clearly in same font size as rest of contract was not unconscionable); ***Pardee Constr.***, 100 Cal.App.4th at 1089-90 (provision that was difficult to read because it was printed in dense, single-spaced capital letters was unconscionable).

• **Difficult to understand.** The provision is worded in a way that makes it difficult to understand. *See, e.g.*, ***Greenbriar Homes Cmty.***, 117 Cal.App.4th at 345 (easily understood reference provision was not unconscionable).

[2] **Substantive unconscionability.** A reference provision is substantively unconscionable if the terms of the provision are harsh, oppressive, or so one-sided that they "shock the conscience." ***Pardee Constr.***, 100 Cal.App.4th at 1090. The following factors can support a finding that a reference provision is substantively unconscionable:

[a] **Sole benefit.** The provision includes terms that solely benefit the party who included the provision in the contract or lease. *See **Pardee Constr.***, 100 Cal.App.4th at 1091; *see also **Greenbriar Homes Cmty.***, 117 Cal.App.4th at 345 (reference provision that did not limit relief available to party was not unconscionable). For example, a general reference provision in a home-purchase contract can be substantively unconscionable if it

waives the buyer's right to seek punitive damages. *See, e.g.*, ***Pardee Constr.***, 100 Cal.App.4th at 1091. But a reference provision that benefits only the party who included it in the contract or lease may not be substantively unconscionable if the objecting party received some other benefit in return for agreeing to the provision. *See, e.g.*, *id.* at 1092 (nothing in record indicated that party opposing reference received benefit in return for waiving right to jury trial).

[b] More expensive. The referee fees would be greater than the costs the party would have to pay to proceed in litigation before the court. ***Woodside Homes***, 107 Cal.App.4th at 733.

(d) Multiplicity of suits. A party may be able to object on the ground that the reference provision should not be enforced because granting the reference would result in the case being divided between the trial court and a referee (i.e., some Ps signed reference agreement while others did not). A court has discretion to refuse to enforce a reference provision in a written contract or lease when the possibility of multiple suits would result in inconsistent rulings and would not promote judicial economy. ***Tarrant Bell Prop., LLC v. Superior Ct.*** (2011) 51 Cal.4th 538, 544-45.

(4) Invalid grounds for objection. A party cannot object to a motion for a consensual reference on the ground that the reference provision does not contain explicit language waiving the right to a jury trial. ***O'Donoghue***, 219 Cal.App.4th at 256-57.

§5.4 Reply. A party can file and serve a reply to opposition papers. The reply must be filed and served at least five court days before the hearing. CCP §1005(b). See "Reply Papers," ch. 1-D, §9, p. 37.

§5.5 Hearing.

1. When required. Generally, a hearing is not required for a consensual reference if the parties have agreed on the particular person who will serve as the referee. *See* Kiesel, *Cal. Pretrial Civil Procedure*, §25.03 (if parties agree on individual to be appointed, proposed order should be presented to judge). A hearing is required, however, if the parties have not agreed on the person who will serve as the referee or have contested the consensual reference in some way. *See* Civ. C. §1670.5(b) (parties must have opportunity to present evidence of unconscionability of contract provision); CCP §642 (objection to referee must be heard by judge); CRC 3.906(b) (motion to withdraw stipulation must be heard by judge).

2. Who hears & decides. The hearing must be held before the judge assigned to the case. *See* CCP §642; CRC 3.901(a), 3.906(b). If the case has not been assigned, the matter must be heard and decided by either the presiding judge or the law-and-motion judge. *See* CRC 3.901(a), 3.906(b).

§5.6 Ruling.

1. Discretionary. A court has discretion to deny a consensual reference that is contractually agreed to by the parties. ***Tarrant Bell Prop., LLC v. Superior Ct.*** (2011) 51 Cal.4th 538, 544.

2. Referee selection. If the court grants the consensual reference, it must appoint the person (or persons) agreed on by the parties to serve as referee. CCP §640(a). If the parties do not agree, the court must appoint one to three persons nominated by the parties against whom there is no valid legal objection. *Id.* §640(b). If the parties do not submit any nominations, the court can either (1) make its own selection of one to three referees against whom there is no valid legal objection or (2) appoint a court commissioner of the county where the action or proceeding is pending to serve as referee. *Id.*

§5.7 Order.

1. Form. The court's ruling on a stipulation or motion for a consensual reference must be recorded either in writing or by minute order. *See* CRC 3.902; *see, e.g.*, ***Pardee Constr. Co. v. Superior Ct.*** (4th Dist.2002) 100 Cal.App.4th 1081, 1092 (court denied motion for appointment of referee by minute order). See "Record of Ruling," ch. 1-I, §4, p. 90. An order appointing a consensual referee can be made using Judicial Council Form ADR-110.

2. Contents. If the court grants the consensual reference, the order appointing a referee should contain the following information:

(1) Grounds for reference. The order should state whether the reference is based on a stipulation between the parties or a reference provision in a written contract or lease. *See* CCP §638; *see, e.g.*, Judicial Council Forms, form ADR-110, item 1.

(2) Identity of referee. The order must identify the person or persons (no more than three) appointed to serve as referee. *See* CCP §640(a), (b); CRC 3.902(1). See "Referee selection," §5.6.2, p. 173. Each referee must be identified by name, business address, telephone number, and State Bar number if applicable. CRC 3.902(1); *see, e.g.*, Judicial Council Forms, form ADR-110, item 3 (requiring that order also identify each referee's State Bar membership status, e.g., active, inactive).

(3) Scope of reference. The order must state whether the reference is a general or special reference. *See* CRC 3.902(2); *see, e.g.*, Judicial Council Forms, form ADR-110, item 4. If the order is for a special reference, the order must state the issues to be heard and determined by the referee. CRC 3.902(2); *see, e.g.*, Judicial Council Forms, form ADR-110, item 4.

(4) Compensation. The order must state whether the referee will be privately compensated. CRC 3.902(3); *see, e.g.*, Judicial Council Forms, form ADR-110, item 5. The court cannot order private compensation for any referee who is a court employee or officer at the time of appointment. CCP §645.1(b).

(a) By agreement. If the parties agree on the manner and amount of compensation, the order should state that the referee will be compensated according to the terms of the agreement. CCP §§645.1(a), 1023; *see, e.g.*, Judicial Council Forms, form ADR-110, item 5. The court cannot order private compensation in a manner that conflicts with the express terms of the agreement. *E.g.*, ***Carr Bus. Enters. v. City of Chowchilla*** (5th Dist.2008) 166 Cal.App.4th 25, 29-30 (parties' stipulation to split fees prevailed over court's award of fees as costs); *see* CCP §§645.1(a), 1023.

(b) Determined by court. If the parties request that the court determine the terms of referee compensation, the order should state the following:

[1] The maximum hourly rate that the referee can charge for referee services. *See* CCP §§645.1, 1023.

[2] The portion of referee fees for which each party is responsible that the court determines to be fair and reasonable. *See id.* §645.1.

(5) Use of court facilities or personnel. The order must state whether the use of court facilities or personnel is authorized for reference proceedings. CRC 3.902(4); *see, e.g.*, Judicial Council Forms, form ADR-110, item 6. See "Use of court facilities or personnel," §5.1.5(1)(c), p. 168. The order cannot authorize use of court facilities, court personnel, or summoned jurors for reference proceedings unless the presiding judge or her designee makes a finding that their use will further the interest of justice. CRC 3.907.

(6) Referee's report & recommendation or statement of decision. The order should state the deadline and manner for submitting the referee's report and recommendation or statement of decision to the court and the parties. *See* CCP §643(a), (b); *see, e.g.*, Judicial Council Forms, form ADR-110, item 8.

3. Effect of order.

(1) Reference granted. If the court grants the stipulation or motion for a consensual reference and appoints a referee, the issues referred in the order are heard and determined by the referee in a separate proceeding. See "Proceedings Before Referee," §9, p. 182.

(2) Reference denied. If the court denies the stipulation or motion for a consensual reference, the case remains with the court.

§5.8 Review.

1. Appealability. The ruling on a stipulation or motion for a consensual reference is not appealable until the court enters a final judgment in the case. *See* CCP §904.1(a)(1) (no appeal from interlocutory judgment); ***Providence Baptist Ch. v. Superior Ct.*** (1952) 40 Cal.2d 55, 59 (order appointing referee is interlocutory and not appealable until after final judgment). A party can challenge the ruling before entry of judgment, however, by filing a

petition for writ of mandate. *See, e.g.*, ***Greenbriar Homes Cmty., Inc. v. Superior Ct.*** (3d Dist.2004) 117 Cal.App.4th 337, 348 (writ of mandate issued to vacate order denying request for consensual reference), *disapproved on other grounds*, ***Tarrant Bell Prop., LLC v. Superior Ct.*** (2011) 51 Cal.4th 538; *cf.* ***Taggares v. Superior Ct.*** (4th Dist.1998) 62 Cal.App.4th 94, 106-07 (writ of mandate issued to vacate order appointing discovery referee).

2. Standard of review. The ruling on a stipulation or motion for a consensual reference is reviewed for abuse of discretion. *See* ***Greenbriar Homes Cmty.***, 117 Cal.App.4th at 346; *cf.* ***Taggares***, 62 Cal.App.4th at 106 (special reference).

§6. APPOINTING REFEREE – NONCONSENSUAL

If consent cannot be obtained from all parties to the action or proceeding, the court's authority is limited to making a nonconsensual special reference. CCP §639(a). See "Special reference," §3.2, p. 164.

§6.1 Motion. A motion is required for a nonconsensual reference. CCP §639(a).

1. Who can file. A party or the court on its own motion can make a motion for a nonconsensual reference. CCP §639(a).

2. Deadline to file & serve. The motion must be filed and served at least 16 court days before the hearing. CCP §1005(b); *see* CRC 3.921(a) (motion under CCP §639 must be filed and served). See "Retrospective deadlines," ch. 1-G, §6.2, p. 71. If the motion is served by a method other than personal delivery, the movant will have to add more time to the 16-day period. CCP §1005(b). See "Add time for method of service," ch. 1-G, §6.2.1(5), p. 72.

3. Contents.

(1) Notice of motion & motion. The motion should be made in writing by noticed motion. Kiesel, *Cal. Pretrial Civil Procedure*, §25.03; *see* CRC 3.921(a) (motion must be filed and served); *see, e.g.*, ***U.S. Fid. & Guar. Co. v. Superior Ct.*** (4th Dist.1988) 204 Cal.App.3d 1513, 1519 (party filed noticed motion for appointment of referee under CCP §639). See "Notice of motion & motion," ch. 1-D, §5.1, p. 28. The motion should contain the following information:

(a) Grounds for reference. The motion should state the reasons that a special reference is needed and identify the specific statutory provisions that authorize the reference. *See* CCP §639(d)(1) (requirements of order); *see, e.g.*, Judicial Council Forms, form ADR-109, item 2b. See "Nonconsensual," §3.2.2(2), p. 164. If the motion requests appointment of a discovery referee, the motion should describe the exceptional circumstances that require the reference. *See* CCP §639(d)(2) (requirements of order). See "Discovery motions & disputes," §3.2.2(2)(d), p. 165.

(b) Identity of referee. The motion should identify up to three persons nominated by the movant to serve as referee. *See* CCP §640(b). The motion should identify each nominated person by name, business address, telephone number, and if applicable, State Bar number and membership status (e.g., active, inactive). *See* CRC 3.922(b) (requirements of order); *see, e.g.*, Judicial Council Forms, form ADR-109, item 3.

(c) Scope of reference. The motion must state the specific matters to be heard and determined by the referee. CRC 3.921(a); *see, e.g.*, Judicial Council Forms, form ADR-109, item 4b. See "Nonconsensual," §3.2.2(2), p. 164.

(d) Compensation. The motion should specifically request appointment of either a privately compensated referee or a referee who will serve at no cost to the parties. *See* CRC 3.922(f) (requirements of order); *see, e.g.*, Judicial Council Forms, form ADR-109, item 5. If a privately compensated referee is requested, the motion can ask the court to specify the maximum number of hours the referee can charge. *See* CCP §639(d)(5) (requirements of order); CRC 3.922(f)(1) (same).

(e) Use of court facilities or personnel. The motion should state whether use of court facilities or personnel is requested for reference proceedings. *See* CRC 3.922(g) (requirements of order), CRC 3.926 (same); *see, e.g.*, Judicial Council Forms, form ADR-109, item 6. If the use of court facilities or personnel is requested, the motion should describe the use sought. *See* CRC 3.922(g) (requirements of order); *see, e.g.*, Judicial Council Forms, form ADR-109, item 6.

(f) Referee's report & recommendation. The motion should request a specific deadline for submitting the referee's report and recommendation to the court if a deadline other than the standard 20-day deadline is needed. *See* CCP §643(a), (b). See "Special reference – report & recommendation," §10.2, p. 184.

(2) Memorandum of points & authorities. The motion must include a memorandum in support. CRC 3.1112(a)(3); Kiesel, *Cal. Pretrial Civil Procedure*, §25.03. See "Memorandum of points & authorities," ch. 1-D, §5.2, p. 28.

(3) Proposed order. The motion can be accompanied by a proposed order. CRC 3.1113(m). The proposed order must be lodged and served with the motion papers, not attached to them. *Id.*

(4) Referee's certification. If the movant is requesting the appointment of a particular referee, the motion must be accompanied by a proposed certificate from the person nominated as the referee. CRC 3.921(a); *see* CRC 3.924(a). See "Referee's certification," §5.1.5(3), p. 168.

§6.2 Response.

1. Nomination of referee. A party can respond to a motion for a nonconsensual reference by submitting to the court up to three persons that the party nominates to serve as referee. *See* CCP §640(b). The party should identify each nominated person by name, business address, telephone number, and if applicable, State Bar number and membership status (e.g., active, inactive). *See* CRC 3.922(b) (requirements of order); Judicial Council Forms, form ADR-109, item 3 (sample motion).

2. Limitation on charged hours. A party can respond to a motion for a nonconsensual reference by asking the court to specify the maximum number of hours the referee can charge if the referee is going to be privately compensated. *See* CCP §639(d)(5) (requirements of order); CRC 3.922(f)(1) (same).

3. Opposition – objecting to nominated referee. A party can oppose a motion for a nonconsensual reference by filing a written objection to the appointment of a particular person nominated as a referee. CCP §641; CRC 3.925.

(1) Deadline to file & serve. The objection must be filed with the court with reasonable diligence and served on all parties and the nominated referee. *See* CRC 3.925; Kiesel, *Cal. Pretrial Civil Procedure*, §25.17[1][a]; *cf.* CRC 3.905 (objection to appointment of particular person as referee under consensual reference must be served on all parties and referee). The objection should be filed before the referee is appointed. See "Deadline to file & serve," §5.3.3(1), p. 170.

(2) Form. The objection must be in writing and should comply with the general requirements for opposition papers. *See* CRC 3.925. See "Opposition Papers," ch. 1-D, §8, p. 35.

(3) Grounds for objection. The objection should state the reasons why the person is not qualified to serve as a referee. *See* CCP §641. See "Who Can Serve as Referee," §4, p. 166.

(4) No waiver. A party does not waive its right to object to the appointment of a particular person as a referee by making a motion for a nonconsensual reference or by submitting nominees for appointment. CCP §640(c); CRC 3.925. See "Nomination of referee," §6.2.1, this page.

4. Opposition – objecting to nonconsensual reference. A party can oppose a motion for a nonconsensual reference by filing an opposition to the motion.

(1) Deadline to file & serve. The objection must be filed and served at least nine court days before the hearing. CCP §1005(b).

(2) Form. The objection must be in writing and should comply with the general requirements for opposition papers. *See* CCP §642. See "Opposition Papers," ch. 1-D, §8, p. 35.

(3) Grounds.

(a) Not authorized. A party can object to the motion on the ground that the nonconsensual reference is not authorized. *See* ***In re Marriage of Galis*** (2d Dist.1983) 149 Cal.App.3d 147, 149-50. A nonconsensual referee can be appointed to hear and determine only issues that are explicitly authorized by CCP §639. ***Jovine***

v. ***FHP, Inc.*** (2d Dist.1998) 64 Cal.App.4th 1506, 1523; ***In re Marriage of Galis***, 149 Cal.App.3d at 150-51; *see* ***Aetna Life Ins. v. Superior Ct.*** (4th Dist.1986) 182 Cal.App.3d 431, 435. Any matter outside of §639 that is referred to a nonconsensual referee is considered to be in excess of the court's jurisdiction. *See* ***Jovine***, 64 Cal.App.4th at 1531-32; ***Aetna Life Ins.***, 182 Cal.App.3d at 435.

(b) Inappropriate discovery referral. A party can object to the motion on the ground that the discovery referral, although authorized by statute, is inappropriate for either of the following reasons:

[1] Affects other parties' rights. The discovery referral is inappropriate because it will affect the rights of other parties to the action or proceeding who are not involved in the discovery disputes. ***Taggares v. Superior Ct.*** (4th Dist.1998) 62 Cal.App.4th 94, 106.

[2] Involves new, complex, or unsettled legal issues. The discovery referral is inappropriate because the referee will be required to determine new, complex, or unsettled legal issues. ***Taggares***, 62 Cal.App.4th at 106.

(c) Inability to pay. A party can object to the motion on the ground that it seeks the appointment of a privately compensated referee and the objecting party is economically unable to pay a pro rata share of the fees. *See* CCP §639(d)(6)(A); CRC 3.922(f)(2). A court cannot appoint a privately compensated referee if a party is economically unable to pay its pro rata share and the other party does not voluntarily agree to pay that additional share. CCP §639(d)(6)(A). For a discussion of how a court determines whether a party is unable to pay referee fees, see "Appointing privately compensated referee," §6.5.2(2), this page.

§6.3 Reply. The movant can file and serve a reply to opposition papers. The reply must be filed and served at least five court days before the hearing. CCP §1005(b). See "Reply Papers," ch. 1-D, §9, p. 37.

§6.4 Hearing.

1. Required. A hearing on a motion for a nonconsensual reference is required. CRC 3.921(b); *see* CCP §642 (objections must be heard by court). See "Hearings," ch. 1-H, p. 79.

2. Who hears & decides. The hearing must be held before the judge assigned to the case. CCP §642; CRC 3.921(b). If the case has not been assigned, the matter must be heard and decided by either the presiding judge or the law-and-motion judge. CRC 3.921(b). The motion cannot be heard and decided by a referee. CCP §642.

§6.5 Ruling.

1. Discretionary. The court's ruling on a motion for a nonconsensual reference is discretionary. ***Mashon v. Haddock*** (2d Dist.1961) 190 Cal.App.2d 151, 169; *see* CCP §639(a) (referee "may" be appointed).

2. Referee selection.

(1) Generally. For a discussion of the referee selection process, see "Referee selection," §5.6.2, p. 173.

(2) Appointing privately compensated referee. If a privately compensated referee is requested for a nonconsensual reference, the court must do the following before appointing the referee:

(a) Determine if parties are able to pay. The first step the court must take is to determine whether the parties are economically able to pay referee fees. *See* CCP §§639(d)(6), 645.1(b). If the parties are unable to pay referee fees, the court cannot appoint a privately compensated referee. *Id.* §639(d)(6)(A). The burden to show an inability to pay is on the parties; the court does not have a duty to evaluate a party's ability to pay if the issue is not raised. *See id.*

[1] Factors to be considered.

[a] Generally. If a party has claimed an inability to pay its pro rata share of referee fees, the court must consider only the party's ability to pay, not the ability of the party's attorney to advance payment of referee fees. CCP §639(d)(6)(B); *see* ***Taggares v. Superior Ct.*** (4th Dist.1998) 62 Cal.App.4th 94, 103 (imposing

MOTION FOR REFERENCE

referee fees on party's attorney would raise concerns of equal protection, due process, and fundamental fairness). The factors the court must consider in making its determination are the following:

• The estimated cost of the referral. CCP §639(d)(6)(B). Any amount proposed by the court must be reasonable. *Id.* §1023.

NOTE

Any party can object to the court's proposed fees for the referee. See CCP §639(d)(5); CRC 3.925. A party does not waive its right to object simply because it filed the motion for reference. CRC 3.925.

• The impact of the proposed fees on the party's ability to proceed with the litigation. CCP §639(d)(6)(B).

• Any other relevant circumstances that affect the party's ability to pay referee fees. *See id.*; *see, e.g.*, ***Hood v. Superior Ct.*** (2d Dist.1999) 72 Cal.App.4th 446, 449-50 (party submitted sworn statement of income and expenses).

[b] In forma pauperis. A party who is proceeding in forma pauperis is automatically deemed to be economically unable to pay referee fees. CCP §639(d)(6)(B); *see* ***Solorzano v. Superior Ct.*** (2d Dist.1993) 18 Cal.App.4th 603, 615 (order imposing referee fees on party proceeding in forma pauperis is never fair and reasonable).

[2] Effect of court's finding.

[a] Parties able to pay. If the court finds that no party has established an inability to pay its pro rata share of referee fees, the court must then determine how the fees will apportioned. CCP §639(d)(6)(A); *see id.* §645.1(b). See "Apportion fees," §6.5.2(2)(b), this page.

[b] One or more parties unable to pay. If the court finds that one or more parties have established an inability to pay its pro rata share of referee fees, the court cannot appoint a privately compensated referee unless another party who is able to pay voluntarily agrees to pay the additional share. CCP §639(d)(6)(A); *see id.* §645.1(b).

(b) Apportion fees. If the court has determined that the parties are economically able to pay referee fees, the court must determine how the fees will be apportioned. CCP §645.1(b); *see* CRC 3.922(f)(3); *see also* ***DeBlase v. Superior Ct.*** (2d Dist.1996) 41 Cal.App.4th 1279, 1285-86 (court cannot defer issue of allocating referee fees until after referee makes recommendation when party claims indigence). The court must apportion the fees in a fair and reasonable manner. CCP §645.1(b); CRC 3.922(f)(3). Any party can object to the court's proposed apportionment; a party does not waive its right to object simply because it filed the motion for reference. *See* CRC 3.925.

§6.6 Order.

1. Form. The court's ruling on a motion for a nonconsensual reference must be recorded in writing or by minute order. See "Record of Ruling," ch. 1-I, §4, p. 90. If the court appoints a referee, the order must be in writing and can be made using Judicial Council Form ADR-110. *See* CCP §639(d); CRC 3.922(a).

2. Contents. An order appointing a referee should contain the following information:

(1) Grounds for reference.

(a) Statutory basis. The order must state the specific statutory provision under which the reference is made. CRC 3.922(c). See "Nonconsensual," §3.2.2(2), p. 164.

(b) Discovery referral. If the order refers discovery motions or disputes, the order must describe the exceptional circumstances that require the reference. CCP §639(d)(2); CRC 3.922(c)(2); *see, e.g.*, Judicial Council Forms, form ADR-110, item 2a.

(c) All other referrals. For all referrals other than discovery referrals, the order must state the reasons for the reference. CCP §639(d)(1); CRC 3.922(c)(1); *see, e.g.*, Judicial Council Forms, form ADR-110, item 2b.

(2) Identity of referee. The order must identify the person or persons (no more than three) appointed to serve as referee. *See* CCP §640(a), (b); CRC 3.923. See "Referee selection," §5.6.2, p. 173. Each referee must be identified by name, business address, telephone number, and State Bar number if applicable. CRC 3.922(b); *see* CCP §639(d)(4); *see, e.g.*, Judicial Council Forms, form ADR-110, item 3 (suggesting that order also identify each referee's State Bar membership status, e.g., active, inactive).

(3) Scope of reference.

(a) Discovery referral. An order that appoints a discovery referee must state whether the court is referring all discovery matters or only specific discovery motions or disputes. CRC 3.922(d)(2); *see, e.g.*, Judicial Council Forms, form ADR-110, item 4b(2). If only specific discovery motions or disputes are being referred, the order must identify them. *See* CRC 3.922(d)(1); *see, e.g.*, Judicial Council Forms, form ADR-110, item 4b.

(b) All other referrals. For all referrals other than discovery referrals, the order must state the specific issue or issues to be heard and determined by the referee or referees. *See* CCP §639(d)(3); CRC 3.922(d)(1).

(4) Authority of discovery referee. An order that refers discovery matters must state that the referee is authorized to do all the following:

(a) Set the date, time, and place for all hearings. CRC 3.922(e).

(b) Direct the issuance of subpoenas. *Id.*

(c) Preside over hearings. *Id.*

(d) Take evidence. *Id.*

(e) Rule on objections, motions, and other requests made during the hearings. *Id.*

(5) Compensation. The order must state whether the referee will be privately compensated. *See* CCP §639(d)(5); CRC 3.922(f). The court cannot order private compensation for any referee who is a court employee or officer at the time of appointment. CCP §645.1(b).

(a) Privately compensated. If the order states that the referee will be privately compensated, the order must include the following:

[1] Finding on ability to pay. The order must include one of the following findings:

[a] No party has established an economic inability to pay a pro rata share of referee fees. CCP §639(d)(6)(A); CRC 3.922(f)(2)(A); *see, e.g.*, Judicial Council Forms, form ADR-110, item 2c(1).

[b] One or more parties have established an inability to pay a pro rata share of referee fees, but another party has voluntarily agreed to pay the amount that those parties cannot pay themselves. CCP §639(d)(6)(A); *see* ***Taggares v. Superior Ct.*** (4th Dist.1998) 62 Cal.App.4th 94, 104 (court cannot impose entire cost of reference on objecting party); *see, e.g.*, Judicial Council Forms, form ADR-110, item 2c(2). The order should state the name of the party or parties who are unable to pay and the name of the party or parties who have voluntarily agreed to pay the additional share. *See, e.g.*, Judicial Council Forms, form ADR-110, item 2c(2).

[2] Maximum hourly rate. The order must state the maximum hourly rate the referee can charge for services. CCP §639(d)(5); CRC 3.922(f)(1); *see, e.g.*, Judicial Council Forms, form ADR-110, item 5c(1).

[3] Maximum hours. If requested by a party, the order must state the maximum number of hours the referee can charge for services. CCP §639(d)(5); CRC 3.922(f)(1); *see, e.g.*, Judicial Council Forms, form ADR-110, item 5c(2).

[4] Apportionment of fees. The order should state how the referee fees will be apportioned. *See* CCP §645.1(b); CRC 3.922(f)(3); *see, e.g.*, Judicial Council Forms, form ADR-110, item 5c(3). See "Apportion fees," §6.5.2(2)(b), p. 178.

NOTE

After the order of appointment has been entered, the court can readjust the apportionment of fees if a party later establishes an inability to pay or if the referee recommends a different apportionment in its report. See CCP §643(c); CRC 3.922(f)(3); ***DeBlase v. Superior Ct.*** *(2d Dist.1996) 41 Cal.App.4th 1279, 1286.*

(b) Uncompensated. If the referee will not be compensated, the order should state that the referee will be appointed at no cost to the parties. *See* CCP §639(d)(6)(A); *see, e.g.*, Judicial Council Forms, form ADR-110, items 2c(3), 5a.

(6) Use of court facilities or personnel. The order must state what use, if any, of court facilities and personnel is authorized in connection with the reference. CRC 3.922(g); *see, e.g.*, Judicial Council Forms, form ADR-110, item 6. The use of court facilities and personnel for nonconsensual reference proceedings is authorized only to the extent stated in the reference order. CRC 3.926.

(7) Referee's report & recommendation. The order should state the deadline for submitting the referee's report and recommendation to the court. *See* CCP §643(a), (b); *see, e.g.*, Judicial Council Forms, form ADR-110, item 8a. See "Special reference – report & recommendation," §10.2, p. 184.

§6.7 Modifying order. The court can change the terms of appointment at any time on a party's or the court's own motion. CCP §643(c). A party's motion must be supported by good cause. *Id.*

§6.8 Review. See "Review," §5.8, p. 174.

§7. DUTIES OF APPOINTED REFEREE

§7.1 Certification. The appointed referee must complete the referee's certification before beginning service if it has not already been filed with the court. CRC 3.904(a), 3.924(a). See "Referee's certification," §5.1.5(3), p. 168.

§7.2 Statement identifying contact person. The appointed referee must file with the court a statement providing the name, telephone number, and mailing address of a person who may be contacted to obtain information about (1) the date, time, location, and general nature of all proceedings pending before the referee that would be open to the public if held before a judge and (2) how to access documents or exhibits submitted to the referee that would be open to the public if filed or lodged with a court. *See* CRC 2.400(d)(2), 3.931(b)(1). See "Public access," §9.1.2, p. 182. In addition, the statement may also provide the address of a publicly accessible website where the same information can be obtained. *See* CRC 3.931(b)(2).

1. Deadline to file. The statement must be filed at the same time the referee files her certification. CRC 2.400(d)(2), 3.931(b)(1). See "Certification," §7.1, this page.

2. Posting statement. The clerk must post the information from the statement in the court facility. CRC 3.931(b)(3).

3. Amending statement. The appointed referee must promptly file an amended statement with the court if there is a change in the statement's information. CRC 2.400(d)(2), 3.931(b)(1).

§7.3 Disclosure. The appointed referee must disclose certain information to the parties that may be relevant to a motion to disqualify the referee under CCP §170.6. CRC 3.904(b), 3.924(b). See "Motion to Disqualify – Peremptory Challenge," ch. 2-D, §4, p. 138.

1. Required information. The referee's disclosure must include the following information:

(1) Any information reasonably relevant to the issue of disqualification under Canon 6D(3) of the Code of Judicial Ethics, including any past or present personal or professional relationship between the referee or the referee's law firm and a party, attorney, or law firm involved in the current case. *See* CRC 3.904(b), 3.924(b); Code Jud. Ethics, canon 6D(5)(a).

(2) Membership in any organization that practices invidious discrimination on the basis of race, sex, religion, national origin, or sexual orientation. CRC 3.904(b)(1), 3.924(b)(1); Code Jud. Ethics, canon 6D(5)(b). The referee does not have to disclose membership in a religious organization, an official U.S. military organization, or a nonprofit youth organization as long as the referee's membership does not violate the rules governing conduct of extrajudicial activities. Code Jud. Ethics, canon 6D(5)(b).

(3) The number and nature of any other proceedings in the past 24 months in which the referee has been privately compensated by a party, attorney, law firm, or insurance company involved in the current case. CRC 3.904(b)(2), 3.924(b)(2). Privately compensated service includes service as an attorney, expert witness, consultant, judge, referee, arbitrator, mediator, settlement facilitator, or other dispute-resolution neutral. CRC 3.904(b)(2), 3.924(b)(2).

2. Deadline.

(1) Before motion to disqualify. The referee's disclosure must normally be made no later than five days before the deadline to file a motion to disqualify the referee. CRC 3.904(b), 3.924(b). See "Deadline," §8.1.2, this page.

(2) After motion to disqualify. The referee's disclosure can be made after the deadline to file a motion to disqualify under the following circumstances:

(a) Not aware of appointment. If the referee was not aware of her appointment before the deadline, the referee's disclosure must be made as soon as practicable after the referee learns of her appointment. CRC 3.904(b), 3.924(b).

(b) Not aware of information. If the referee was not aware of information that must be disclosed before the deadline, the referee's disclosure must be made as soon as practicable after the referee becomes aware of the information. CRC 3.904(b), 3.924(b).

§8. DISQUALIFYING APPOINTED REFEREE

§8.1 Motion to disqualify. A party can disqualify an appointed referee by filing a motion to disqualify (also known as a peremptory challenge) on the ground that the referee is prejudiced against a party, an attorney, or the interests of a party or an attorney appearing in the action or proceeding. CCP §170.6(a)(1); *see **Pedus Servs. v. Superior Ct.*** (2d Dist.1999) 72 Cal.App.4th 140, 143-44 (discovery referee can be removed by motion to disqualify).

1. General requirements. See "Motion to Disqualify – Peremptory Challenge," ch. 2-D, §4, p. 138.

2. Deadline.

(1) Motion to disqualify discovery referee.

(a) All-purpose discovery referee. A motion to disqualify a referee appointed to hear and determine all discovery matters must be filed within ten days after notice of the referee's appointment. CCP §639(b)(A). If a party has not yet appeared in the action or proceeding, the party can file a motion to disqualify the referee within ten days after making an appearance. *Id.*

(b) Limited-purpose discovery referee. A motion to disqualify a referee appointed to hear and determine specific discovery motions or disputes must be filed at least five days before the date the referee is scheduled to hear the discovery motion or dispute if the referee's identity is known at least ten days before the hearing date. CCP §639(b)(B). If the referee's identity is not known at least ten days before the hearing date, the specific deadline does not apply and the general requirements for a motion to disqualify must be followed. See "Deadline to file," ch. 2-D, §4.2.6, p. 141.

(2) Motion to disqualify all other referees. A motion to disqualify a referee other than a discovery referee must comply with the same deadline requirements that apply to other motions to disqualify. See "Deadline to file," ch. 2-D, §4.2.6, p. 141.

§8.2 Statement of disqualification. A party can disqualify an appointed referee by filing a statement of disqualification based on any of the grounds for disqualifying a judge. *See* CCP §170.1 (listing grounds for disqualifying judge), §170.5(a) (definition of "judge" includes referee). See "Statement of Disqualification – Challenge for Cause," ch. 2-D, §5, p. 150.

§9. PROCEEDINGS BEFORE REFEREE

§9.1 Generally.

1. Conducting proceeding. Proceedings before a referee are conducted in the same manner as proceedings before a court. ***Phelps v. Peabody*** (1857) 7 Cal. 53; ***Sy First Family L.P. v. Cheung*** (4th Dist.1999) 70 Cal.App.4th 1334, 1341; *see* ***Goodrich v. Mayor & Common Council of Marysville*** (1855) 5 Cal. 430, 431 (trial by referee must be conducted in same manner as trial by court). Thus, parties must comply with the rules of evidence and make any objections to the referee's rulings just as they would before a court. *See* Evid. C. §300; ***Phelps***, 7 Cal. at 52.

2. Public access.

(1) To proceedings. Proceedings before a referee that would be open to the public if held before a court must be open to the public regardless of whether they are held in a court facility or another location. CRC 3.931(a); *see* CRC 2.400(e).

(2) To documents & exhibits. Documents and exhibits in the referee's possession that would be open to the public if filed or lodged with a court must be made available during business hours for inspection by any person within a reasonable time after request and under reasonable conditions. CRC 2.400(d)(1).

3. Location.

(1) Easily accessible to public. The presiding judge or her designee, on the application of any person or on the judge's own motion, can order that hearings before the referee that will be open to the public must be conducted at a site that is easily accessible to the public and appropriate for seating people who have notified the court of their intention to attend the hearings. CRC 3.931(c)(1). The application must be filed with the court, be served on all parties and the referee, and state facts showing good cause for granting the application. *Id.* The proceeding before the referee is not stayed while the application is pending unless ordered by the judge or her designee. *Id.*

(2) 15 minutes from court's staff worksite. If a court staff mediator or evaluator is required to attend a hearing before a referee, the hearing must take place at a location requiring no more than 15 minutes' travel time from the mediator's or evaluator's worksite unless otherwise ordered by the presiding judge or her designee. CRC 3.931(c)(2).

§9.2 Filing documents.

1. Generally.

(1) Originals filed with clerk. All original documents in a case pending before a referee must be filed with the court clerk in the same manner as if the case were being heard by a judge, including filing within any specified time limits and paying any required fees. CRC 2.400(b)(1); *see* CRC 3.930. See "Original & copy," ch. 1-F, §2.1.2, p. 46.

(2) File-stamped copy for referee. The filing party must provide to the referee a file-stamped copy of each document relevant to the issues before the referee. CRC 2.400(b)(1).

(3) Notice of nonacceptance or cancellation. If a party has submitted a document to the referee that is not accepted for filing or for which the filing is later canceled, the party must immediately notify the referee. CRC 2.400(b)(4).

2. Documents considered only after filing. If a document must be filed with the court before it can be considered by a judge, the referee must not accept or consider any copy of that document unless it is file-stamped or accompanied by a declaration stating that the original document has been submitted to the court for filing. CRC 2.400(b)(2); *see* CRC 3.930.

3. Documents considered before filing. If a document can be considered by a judge before it is filed with the court or if a party submits an ex parte application, the party that submits the document or application to the referee must (1) file the original with the court no later than the next court day after the document or application was submitted to the referee and (2) promptly provide a file-stamped copy to the referee. CRC 2.400(b)(3); *see* CRC 3.930.

§9.3 Delivering exhibits.

1. To referee on request. On request of a referee, the clerk must deliver exhibits filed or lodged with the court to the referee. CRC 2.400(c)(2); *see* CRC 3.930. The referee must not release the exhibits to any person other than the clerk unless the court orders otherwise. CRC 2.400(c)(2).

2. To clerk at end of proceeding. If proceedings are conducted by a referee outside court facilities, the exhibits will be kept by the referee and delivered to the clerk at the conclusion of the proceedings unless the parties file, and the court approves, a written stipulation providing for a different disposition of the exhibits. CRC 2.400(c)(2); *see* CRC 3.930.

§9.4 Motions or applications to be heard by court.

1. To seal records. A motion or application to seal records must be heard by the judge assigned to the case and not the referee. CRC 3.932(a). If no judge has been assigned, the motion or application must be heard by the presiding judge or her designee. *Id.* The motion or application must be filed with the court and served on all parties and the referee. *Id.*

2. For leave to file complaint in intervention. A motion for leave to file a complaint in intervention must be heard by the judge assigned to the case and not the referee. CRC 3.932(b). If no judge has been assigned, the motion must be heard by the presiding judge or her designee. *Id.* The motion must be filed with the court and served on all parties and the referee. *Id.* If intervention is allowed, the case must be returned to the trial-court docket unless all parties stipulate to proceed before the referee under a consensual reference. *Id.* See "Stipulation," §5.1, p. 167; "Intervention," ch. 5-C, p. 483.

§10. REFEREE'S DETERMINATION

§10.1 General reference – statement of decision. The referee's determination under a general reference is called the referee's statement of decision. *See* CCP §§638(a), 644(a); ***Treo @ Kettner Homeowners Ass'n v. Superior Ct.*** (4th Dist.2008) 166 Cal.App.4th 1055, 1061.

1. Deadline to file. The statement of decision must be filed with the court within 20 days after proceedings before the referee have ended and the issues are submitted for decision unless the court ordered otherwise. *See* CCP §643(a), (b); *see, e.g.*, Judicial Council Forms, form ADR-110, item 8a.

2. Form. The statement of decision must be in writing unless the court ordered otherwise. CCP §643(a); *see id.* §643(b); *see, e.g.*, Judicial Council Forms, form ADR-110, item 8a.

3. Contents.

(1) Generally. The statement of decision must contain the referee's determination on the issues stated in the order of appointment. *See* CCP §643(b); *see, e.g.*, Judicial Council Forms, form ADR-110, items 4a, 8b(1).

(2) Objections. The statement of decision should state any objections that were raised by a party during the proceeding. *See* ***Phelps v. Peabody*** (1857) 7 Cal. 53.

4. Effect of determination. The statement of decision stands as the decision of the court, and the court may enter judgment on it as if the action had been tried by the court. CCP §644(a).

§10.2 Special reference – report & recommendation. The referee's determination under a consensual or nonconsensual special reference is called the referee's report and recommendation. *See* CCP §§643(c), 644(b); *see, e.g.*, ***Doppes v. Bentley Motors, Inc.*** (4th Dist.2009) 174 Cal.App.4th 967, 971 (court referred to discovery referee's decision as report and recommendation). *But see* CCP §643(a) (referring to referee determinations generally as statements of decision); ***Estate of Beard*** (1st Dist.1999) 71 Cal.App.4th 753, 766 (court referred to referee's decision under special reference as statement of decision).

1. Consensual special reference. The following rules apply to a report and recommendation for a consensual special reference (i.e., a special reference under CCP §638(b)):

(1) Deadline to file. The report and recommendation must be filed with the court within 20 days after proceedings before the referee have ended and the issues are submitted for decision unless the court ordered otherwise. *See* CCP §643(a), (c); *see, e.g.*, Judicial Council Forms, form ADR-110, item 8a.

(2) Form & contents.

(a) Generally. The referee should report in the manner agreed to by the parties and approved by the court. CCP §643(b).

(b) Objections. The report and recommendation should state any objections that were raised by a party during the proceeding. *See* ***Branger v. Chevalier*** (1858) 9 Cal. 353, 362 (party should verify that objections are stated in referee's report).

(3) Effect of report & recommendation. The referee's report and recommendation is only advisory and must be independently considered by the court before it can be adopted in whole or in part. CCP §644(b).

2. Nonconsensual special reference. The following rules apply to a report and recommendation for a nonconsensual special reference (i.e., a special reference under CCP §639):

(1) Deadline to file. The report and recommendation must be filed with the court within 20 days after proceedings before the referee have ended and the issues are submitted for decision unless the court ordered otherwise. *See* CCP §643(a), (c); *see, e.g.*, Judicial Council Forms, form ADR-110, item 8a.

(2) Form. The report and recommendation must be in writing. *See* CCP §643(c) (must file and serve report and recommendation).

(3) Contents.

(a) Generally. The report and recommendation must contain the following:

[1] A recommendation on the merits for any disputed issue. CCP §643(c).

[2] A statement of the total hours spent and total fees charged by the referee. *Id.*

[3] A recommendation on how referee fees should be apportioned among the parties. *Id.*

(b) Objections. See "Objections," §10.2.1(2)(b), this page.

(4) Service. The report and recommendation must be served on all parties. CCP §643(c).

(5) Effect of report & recommendation. See "Effect of report & recommendation," §10.2.1(3), this page.

§11. CHALLENGING REFEREE'S DETERMINATION

§11.1 Challenging statement of decision. The referee's statement of decision under a general reference stands as the court's decision, and the court can enter judgment once the statement is filed with the clerk. CCP §644(a); *see id.* §645. The entry of judgment is a matter of course; thus, any objection to the referee's statement of

decision must be asserted before it is filed with the clerk. *See* ***Peabody v. Phelps*** (1858) 9 Cal. 213, 224-25. Once judgment is entered, a party can challenge the judgment just as if it were made by the court. CCP §645. See "Court's review of statement of decision," §12.1, p. 186.

§11.2 Challenging report & recommendation.

1. By objection. A party can challenge a referee's report and recommendation under a special reference before it is adopted by the court by filing an objection. CCP §643(c). A party that does not file an objection waives the right to challenge the referee's findings on appeal. ***Martino v. Denevi*** (1st Dist.1986) 182 Cal.App.3d 553, 557; *see, e.g.*, ***Hoeft v. Hotchkiss*** (3d Dist.1926) 76 Cal.App. 670, 671 (party could not raise lack of notice on appeal because she did not file objection on that basis before court adopted referee's report).

NOTE

It is unclear whether a party can file an objection to a consensual special reference under CCP §638(b). CCP §643(c), which authorizes the filing of objections to a report from a special referee, only refers to special referees appointed under CCP §639 (i.e., for a nonconsensual special reference).

(1) Deadline to file. The objection must be filed with the court within ten days after the referee files and serves the report and recommendation unless the court orders otherwise. CCP §643(c).

(2) Form. The objection must be in writing. *See* CCP §643(c) (objection must be filed and served).

(3) Service. The objection must be served on all parties and the referee. CCP §643(c).

(4) Grounds. A party can object to the referee's report and recommendation on the following nonexclusive grounds:

(a) The referee committed an act that materially affects the rights of a party, such as improperly admitting or excluding evidence. ***Branger v. Chevalier*** (1858) 9 Cal. 353, 362; ***Martino***, 182 Cal.App.3d at 557.

(b) The referee's findings are not supported by the evidence. *See* ***Martino***, 182 Cal.App.3d at 557; ***Hoeft***, 76 Cal.App. at 671.

(c) The referee did not timely file the report and recommendation with the court and this prejudiced the objecting party. *See* ***In re Marriage of Michaely*** (2d Dist.2007) 150 Cal.App.4th 802, 807-08.

(d) The referee's recommendation for apportioning responsibility for paying referee fees was not fair and reasonable. *See* CCP §§643(c), 645.1(b); CRC 3.925.

(5) Response. Responses to the objections must be in writing and must be filed and served on the referee and all parties within ten days after the objections are served. CCP §643(c).

2. By motion to modify or disregard. The court can modify or disregard (i.e., set aside) the referee's report and recommendation on a party's or the court's own motion.

(1) Deadline. The motion can be brought at any time. *See* CCP §643(c) (court can exercise its power to modify or disregard referee's report and recommendation at any time).

(2) Grounds. If the motion is brought by a party, the party must establish good cause for modifying or disregarding the report and recommendation. CCP §643(c).

NOTE

Before amendments to CCP §643 were enacted in 2000, courts recognized two methods for challenging a special referee's findings: filing objections and filing a motion to set aside. See ***Martino****, 182 Cal.App.3d at 557 (party can object to or move to set aside referee's report and recommendation). The motion to set aside was required to be made by noticed motion and filed promptly after the report and recommendation was filed with the court. See id. In 2000, subsections (b) and (c) were added to §643. Stats. 2000, ch. 644, §8. Subsection (c) specifies the procedure for filing an objection to a referee's report and recommendation and permits the court*

to modify or disregard the referee's report and recommendation at "any time" on a party's or its own motion. CCP §643(c). It is unclear whether the right to modify or disregard under subsection (c) was meant to replace the former practice of filing a motion to set aside promptly after the report and recommendation was filed. Since its enactment in 2000, there have been no reported cases involving a motion to set aside under this former practice. Despite this development, commentators contend that a motion to set aside under pre-2000 law is still available. E.g., 6 Witkin, Cal. Procedure, Proceedings Without Trial, §76.

§12. REVIEWING REFEREE'S DETERMINATION

§12.1 Court's review of statement of decision. Once the referee's statement of decision in a general reference is filed with the court, the court can enter judgment on the statement. CCP §§644(a), 645; ***Ellsworth v. Ellsworth*** (1954) 42 Cal.2d 719, 722. The entry of judgment is a matter of course; if the court does not enter judgment, a party can file a writ of mandate to compel entry. *See* ***Peabody v. Phelps*** (1858) 9 Cal. 213, 224-25; ***Russell v. Elliott*** (1852) 2 Cal. 245, 248. In entering judgment, the court is not permitted to modify the referee's findings. *See* ***Lewis v. Grunberg*** (1928) 205 Cal. 158, 162. After judgment has been entered, a party can seek review of the judgment by filing a motion for new trial, a motion to vacate the judgment, or an appeal. *See* CCP §645 (referee's decision under §638 reviewed in same manner as court's decision); ***SFPP, L.P. v. Burlington N. & Santa Fe Ry.*** (5th Dist.2004) 121 Cal.App.4th 452, 466 (referee's decision can be reviewed by motion to vacate judgment); ***Clark v. Rancho Santa Fe Ass'n*** (4th Dist.1989) 216 Cal.App.3d 606, 624 (referee's decision can be reviewed by motion for new trial). If a party files a motion for new trial, the motion should be decided by the referee unless the parties' agreement or court's order states otherwise. ***Clark***, 216 Cal.App.3d at 625.

§12.2 Court's review of report & recommendation. The referee's report and recommendation under a special reference is only advisory and must be independently considered by the court. CCP §644(b); *see* ***Yeboah v. Progeny Ventures, Inc.*** (2d Dist.2005) 128 Cal.App.4th 443, 450. The court can adopt the report and recommendation in whole or in part, modify it, or set it aside. *See* CCP §§643(c), 644(b). In determining what action to take, the court must consider any objections and responses to the report and recommendation. *Id.* §644(b). See "By objection," §11.2.1, p. 185. In making its determination, the court does not have to conduct a hearing. ***Marathon Nat'l Bank v. Superior Ct.*** (2d Dist.1993) 19 Cal.App.4th 1256, 1261.

1. Report adopted. If the court adopts a special referee's findings, the findings are treated as a special verdict. CCP §645; ***Bird v. Superior Ct.*** (2d Dist.1980) 112 Cal.App.3d 595, 600. As a special verdict, the special referee's findings are not appealable until after final judgment. ***Yeboah***, 128 Cal.App.4th at 450.

2. Report set aside. If the court sets aside the referee's report and recommendation, the order vacating the report and recommendation is interlocutory and not subject to appeal until after final judgment. ***Ellsworth v. Ellsworth*** (1954) 42 Cal.2d 719, 723; ***Johnston v. Dopkins*** (1856) 6 Cal. 83, 84. After the report and recommendation is set aside, the court can either refer the issue back to the referee or proceed on its own. ***McHenry v. Moore*** (1855) 5 Cal. 90, 92.

CALIFORNIA CIVIL PRETRIAL
CHAPTER 3. PLAINTIFF'S LAWSUIT
TABLE OF CONTENTS

TABLE OF CONTENTS

3. PLAINTIFF'S LAWSUIT

A. BEFORE SUIT

§1. GENERAL

§1.1 Purpose. The plaintiff should check applicable statutes and any documents the suit is based on to determine if any action should be taken before filing suit.

§1.2 Secondary authority. The following secondary sources are cited as authority in this subchapter:

- Ball, *The Perfect Preservation Letter*, www.craigball.com/ppl.pdf (referred to as Ball, *The Perfect Preservation Letter*).
- *California Civil Procedure Before Trial* (CEB Online ed. 2014) (referred to as *CEB Procedure Before Trial*).
- Weil & Brown, *California Practice Guide: Civil Procedure Before Trial* (CD-ROM ed. 2014) (referred to as Weil, *Civil Procedure Before Trial*).
- ***O'Connor's Federal Rules * Civil Trials*** (2015) (referred to as ***O'Connor's Federal Rules***).

§2. PREFILING CONSIDERATIONS

Before filing suit, the plaintiff should determine whether to (1) send a preservation letter, (2) send the potential defendant a written notice or demand, (3) exhaust administrative remedies, or (4) submit the dispute to some form of alternative dispute resolution.

§2.1 Send preservation letter. The plaintiff may need to send a preservation letter to anyone who likely possesses relevant information. A preservation letter usually (1) describes the potential litigation and the parties involved, (2) asks the recipient to suspend any document-destruction policy, (3) reminds the recipient of the duty to preserve information relevant to the suit, (4) identifies the specific documents, electronically stored information, and tangible things that should be preserved, and (5) provides instructions on how to preserve those items. *See* Ball, *The Perfect Preservation Letter*, at 6-7; Weil, *Civil Procedure Before Trial*, ¶1:569; *see also* ***Temple Cmty. Hosp. v. Superior Ct.*** (1999) 20 Cal.4th 464, 476-77 (discussing remedies available to punish and deter conduct resulting in destruction of evidence); ***Cedars-Sinai Med. Ctr. v. Superior Ct.*** (1998) 18 Cal.4th 1, 11-13 (same).

§2.2 Send notice or demand. The plaintiff may need to send a presuit notice or demand. Provisions requiring a presuit notice or demand are often included in contracts and statutes. *See generally* Weil, *Civil Procedure Before Trial*, ¶¶1:646-1:872.40 (discussing various claims requiring presuit notice or demand). Many contracts contain provisions that impose conditions precedent to filing suit, such as giving potential defendants notice of the claim and notice of the intent to sue. *See, e.g.*, ***1231 Euclid Homeowners Ass'n v. State Farm Fire & Cas. Co.*** (2d Dist.2006) 135 Cal.App.4th 1008, 1020-21 (insured's failure to provide timely notice of claim and proof of loss as required by insurance policy was complete defense to breach-of-contract claim against insurer). Similarly, some statutes require that a plaintiff, before filing suit, send the defendant a demand letter stating the extent of the plaintiff's damages, attorney fees, and costs. *See, e.g.*, CCP §364(a), (b) (notice of intent to sue for medical malpractice); Gov. C. §910 (presentation of claim against public entity).

§2.3 Exhaust administrative remedies. The plaintiff must exhaust all administrative remedies and submit necessary administrative claims whenever required by statute or administrative rule. *See* ***Abelleira v. District Ct.*** (1941) 17 Cal.2d 280, 292; ***Lopez v. Civil Serv. Comm'n of S.F.*** (1st Dist.1991) 232 Cal.App.3d 307, 314. If the plaintiff does not file a required administrative claim and wait for either the agency to rule on the claim or a prescribed time to pass, a trial court generally cannot hear the dispute. *See* ***Johnson v. City of Loma Linda*** (2000) 24 Cal.4th 61, 70 (exhaustion of administrative remedies is jurisdictional prerequisite to filing suit); ***Abelleira***, 17 Cal.2d at 293 (same).

NOTE

Courts often refer to exhaustion of administrative remedies as a jurisdictional prerequisite to filing suit. E.g., ***Abelleira****, 17 Cal.2d at 293. In this context, the term "jurisdictional prerequisite" does not mean it is a prerequisite for subject-matter jurisdiction; it only means that a court's failure to apply the administrative-exhaustion requirement is judicial error that can be corrected by issuance of a writ of prohibition.* ***Kim v. Konad USA Distrib.*** *(4th Dist.2014) 226 Cal.App.4th 1336, 1347;* ***Mokler v. County of Orange*** *(4th Dist.2007) 157 Cal.App.4th 121, 134. Failure to exhaust administrative remedies can deprive a court of subject-matter jurisdiction, however, if a statute specifically makes it a jurisdictional requirement. See "Cases with statutory prerequisites," ch. 3-E, §2.2.1, p. 249. If the failure to exhaust administrative remedies does not deprive a court of subject-matter jurisdiction, the defense can be waived if it is not timely asserted.* ***Kim****, 226 Cal.App.4th at 1347-48.*

§2.4 Submit dispute to ADR. The plaintiff may be required to submit the dispute to some form of alternative dispute resolution (ADR) (e.g., arbitration or mediation) before filing suit—or instead of litigation altogether. *See, e.g.,* ***Lange v. Schilling*** (3d Dist.2008) 163 Cal.App.4th 1412, 1416-17 (P could not recover attorney fees because contract stated no party could recover attorney fees unless dispute was first submitted to mediation).

§3. JURISDICTIONAL CONSIDERATIONS

Before filing suit, the plaintiff should determine which court has proper jurisdiction over the matter.

§3.1 State or federal court. Some cases must be filed in federal court (e.g., patent and copyright), some must be filed in state court (e.g., suits with no federal question or diversity), and others can be filed in either state or federal court. In the last situation, the plaintiff should decide where it has an advantage and file in that jurisdiction. If the plaintiff wants to avoid removal to federal court, it should include a local defendant if possible. For information about federal jurisdiction and removal to federal court, see ***O'Connor's Federal Rules***, "Choosing the Court—Jurisdiction," ch. 2-F, p. 121; "Defendant's Notice of Removal," ch. 4-A, p. 267.

§3.2 California or sister state. The plaintiff must determine whether there is a valid forum-selection clause. If a suit involves a contract containing a forum-selection clause, the clause may limit the plaintiff's choice of forum. *See, e.g.,* ***Smith, Valentino & Smith, Inc. v. Superior Ct.*** (1976) 17 Cal.3d 491, 495-96 (forum-selection clause requiring California corporation to bring suit in Pennsylvania was enforced).

§3.3 California. Before filing suit in California, the plaintiff must determine the following:

1. Subject-matter jurisdiction. The plaintiff must determine which court has subject-matter jurisdiction. See "Choosing the Court—Subject-Matter Jurisdiction," ch. 3-E, p. 248.

2. Venue. If the plaintiff determines that a California court has jurisdiction over the subject matter of the suit, it must decide which specific California court is the proper venue for the suit. See "Choosing the Court—Venue," ch. 3-F, p. 270.

3. Personal jurisdiction. After the plaintiff determines which particular court the suit can be filed in, it must determine whether the court can exercise personal jurisdiction over the defendant. For a discussion of how a court exercises personal jurisdiction, see "Joining the Defendant—Personal Jurisdiction," ch. 3-G, p. 283.

§4. OTHER CONSIDERATIONS

Before filing suit, the plaintiff should consider various other matters.

§4.1 Internet research. Information about a defendant can be found on the Internet. For example, to find information about a business entity (e.g., registered agent, officers, directors), go to the website of the California Secretary of State, kepler.sos.ca.gov. To find information about property appraisal in California, go to www.boe.ca.gov/proptaxes/assessors.htm. To find a person's address and telephone number, go to www.anywho.com. Other Internet

companies can, for a fee, provide comprehensive information about individuals, including location, family members, nearest neighbors with listed telephone numbers, judgments, and bankruptcies. See, for example, www.ussearch.com.

§4.2 Presuit discovery. A plaintiff can secure discovery before filing suit by filing a verified petition and obtaining an order authorizing the taking of discovery before suit. *See* CCP §§2035.010(a), 2035.030; ***Orr v. City of Stockton*** (3d Dist.2007) 150 Cal.App.4th 622, 630-31. Presuit discovery is useful to preserve evidence or obtain testimony when a critical witness is old, ill, or about to leave the jurisdiction. See "Presuit Discovery," ch. 7-J, p. 923.

§4.3 Appointment of legal representative. When a party is a minor or a person who lacks the legal capacity to make decisions, the attorney should determine if the party has a legal representative with the capacity to file or defend the suit. *See* CCP §372(a). *See generally CEB Procedure Before Trial*, §§9.52-9.75 (discussing how to appoint guardians ad litem).

B. PARTIES & CLAIMS

§1. GENERAL

§1.1 Purpose. Multiple parties and claims are often joined in a single suit to ensure judicial economy and to avoid the risk of inconsistent judgments. *See* ***Joerger v. Pacific Gas & Elec. Co.*** (1929) 207 Cal. 8, 20; ***Deltakeeper v. Oakdale Irrigation Dist.*** (3d Dist.2001) 94 Cal.App.4th 1092, 1100-01; *see also Black's Law Dictionary* 965 (10th ed. 2014) (definition of "joinder").

§1.2 Primary authority. CCP §§378-379.5, 386, 389, 426.10, 426.30, 427.10, 428.10-428.80, 430.10, 1048; CRC 3.350.

§1.3 Secondary authority. The following secondary sources are cited as authority in this subchapter:

- *California Civil Procedure Before Trial* (CEB Online ed. 2014) (referred to as *CEB Procedure Before Trial*).
- Witkin, *California Procedure* (5th ed. 2008 & Supp.2014) (referred to as Witkin, *Cal. Procedure*).
- ***O'Connor's Federal Rules * Civil Trials*** (2015) (referred to as ***O'Connor's Federal Rules***).

§2. JOINING PARTIES & CLAIMS

Parties and claims can be joined in a suit using any of the following methods:

§2.1 Complaint. Parties and claims are typically joined in a suit through a complaint, which is initiated by the plaintiff. *See* CCP §350 (complaint initiates suit), §411.10 (same). See "Plaintiff's Original Complaint," ch. 3-C, p. 203. The plaintiff is not required to join all potential defendants. *See* ***Countrywide Home Loans, Inc. v. Superior Ct.*** (2d Dist.1999) 69 Cal.App.4th 785, 796. However, the plaintiff is required to bring all claims it has against the defendants arising out of the transaction or occurrence that is the basis of the suit. *See* ***Hulsey v. Koehler*** (3d Dist.1990) 218 Cal.App.3d 1150, 1157.

§2.2 Cross-complaint. Parties and claims can be joined in a suit through a cross-complaint. A cross-complaint is an affirmative claim for relief that is treated as an action separate from the complaint. *See* ***K.R.L. Prtshp. v. Superior Ct.*** (3d Dist.2004) 120 Cal.App.4th 490, 503. A cross-complaint is most commonly brought by a defendant against the plaintiff, a codefendant, or a third party. If a cross-complaint has been filed against a codefendant or a third party, the codefendant or third party can in turn file a cross-complaint against any of the other parties to the suit. *See* CCP §428.10. For a complete discussion of joining parties and claims by cross-complaint, see "Cross-Complaint," ch. 4-C, p. 349.

§2.3 Demurrer. Necessary and indispensable parties can be joined by amending the complaint after a demurrer has been sustained. *See* CCP §430.10(d); CRC 3.1320(g). A demurrer is a procedure used to attack defects that appear on the face of the plaintiff's complaint. *See* CCP §430.10(d); ***Union Carbide Corp. v. Superior Ct.*** (1984) 36

Cal.3d 15, 22; ***Harboring Villas Homeowners Ass'n v. Superior Ct.*** (4th Dist.1998) 63 Cal.App.4th 426, 429; *see, e.g.*, ***Jermstad v. McNelis*** (3d Dist.1989) 210 Cal.App.3d 528, 538 (special demurrer, supported by memorandum of points and authorities, must be used to establish nonjoinder of necessary party). The demurrer is filed at the outset of the case, before or along with the defendant's answer. *See* CCP §§430.30(c), 430.40(a); ***Roy v. Superior Ct.*** (4th Dist.2005) 127 Cal.App.4th 337, 344. Because of this timing, the evidence available to substantiate a defendant's joinder claim in a demurrer is usually limited to the plaintiff's complaint. *See, e.g.*, ***Union Carbide***, 36 Cal.3d at 22 (information in P's complaint insufficient to support D's demurrer for joinder); ***Harboring Villas***, 63 Cal.App.4th at 429-30 (same). Thus, a demurrer is not very useful for joining a necessary or indispensable party, with one possible exception. *See* 5 Witkin, *Cal. Procedure*, Pleading, §972. A demurrer may be the best option for a defendant seeking joinder if there is a statute governing the cause of action that expressly identifies the necessary or indispensable parties to the suit. *See, e.g.*, Gov. C. §12591 (statute governing actions to modify charitable trusts requires joinder of attorney general). In this situation, the plaintiff's complaint alone may be sufficient evidence to establish joinder. *See, e.g.*, ***Abbot Kinney Co. v. City of L.A.*** (1959) 53 Cal.2d 52, 58 (statute governing actions involving title to tidelands requires joinder of the state); ***Watkins v. Nutting*** (1941) 17 Cal.2d 490, 498 (wrongful-death act requires joinder of all heirs). If a defendant's demurrer establishes that an absent party is necessary and indispensable to the suit, the court can sustain the demurrer with leave to amend the complaint. *See* CCP §389; CRC 3.1320(g); ***Tuller v. Superior Ct.*** (1932) 215 Cal. 352, 355; ***Conrad v. Unemployment Ins. Appeals Bd.*** (1st Dist.1975) 47 Cal.App.3d 237, 241. If the complaint is not amended, the complaint can be dismissed. CCP §581(f)(2). For a complete discussion of filing a demurrer, see "Demurrer," ch. 4-H, p. 396.

NOTE

A demurrer cannot be used to join a permissive party. ***Jermstad****, 210 Cal.App.3d at 538.*

§2.4 Motion. Necessary and indispensable parties can be joined in a suit through a party's or a court's own motion. CCP §389; 4 Witkin, *Cal. Procedure*, Pleading, §§191-192. The plaintiff can request that the court order joinder, with permission to amend the complaint if necessary. 4 Witkin, *Cal. Procedure*, Pleading, §191. The defendant can raise the issue by a motion for joinder. *See, e.g.*, ***Citizens Task Force on Sohio v. Board of Harbor Comm'rs*** (1979) 23 Cal.3d 812, 814 (D's motion to join necessary party granted); ***Community Redev. Agency v. Force Elecs.*** (2d Dist.1997) 55 Cal.App.4th 622, 627 (same). The court must raise the issue on its own motion, even if the parties do not, and must order joinder if an absent party is necessary and indispensable to the suit. CCP §389; ***Gabriel P. v. Suedi D.*** (2d Dist.2006) 141 Cal.App.4th 850, 865; ***Solomon v. Redona*** (2d Dist.1921) 52 Cal.App. 300, 306; *see also* ***Miracle Adhesives Corp. v. Peninsula Tile Contractors' Ass'n*** (1st Dist.1958) 157 Cal.App.2d 591, 595 (appellate court raised nonjoinder issue, reversed judgment, and ordered trial court to join indispensable party).

§2.5 Intervention. Parties and claims can be joined in a suit through a complaint in intervention. A complaint in intervention is a procedure for a person to join a suit already in progress. CCP §387. A party who qualifies and enters a suit as an intervenor is vested with all the procedural remedies and rights of the original parties. ***Savaglio v. Wal-Mart Stores*** (1st Dist.2007) 149 Cal.App.4th 588, 602. For a complete discussion of joining parties and claims by a complaint in intervention, see "Intervention," ch. 5-C, p. 483.

§2.6 Interpleader. Parties and claims can be joined in a suit through an interpleader action. Interpleader is a procedure for a person in possession of property claimed by others to transfer the property and the dispute to the court. *See* CCP §386; ***Fidelity & Deposit Co. v. Santa Monica Fin. Co.*** (2d Dist.1960) 182 Cal.App.2d 211, 216-17. An interpleader action is usually viewed as two suits: one between the plaintiff (i.e., the stakeholder) and the defendants (i.e., the claimants) to determine the plaintiff's right to interplead the property, and another between the defendants to determine who should receive the interpleaded property. ***State Farm Fire & Cas. Co. v. Pietak*** (3d Dist.2001) 90 Cal.App.4th 600, 612. For a complete discussion of joining parties and claims by a complaint in interpleader, see "Interpleader," ch. 3-D, p. 239.

§2.7 Consolidation. Parties and claims can be joined in a suit through a motion to consolidate. A motion to consolidate asks the court to combine two or more suits that have a common question of law or fact. *See* CCP §1048(a);

Hamilton v. Asbestos Corp. (2000) 22 Cal.4th 1127, 1148-49; *see also* CRC 3.350(a) (requirements for motion). Suits can be completely consolidated, which means that the pleadings are merged, one set of findings is made, and one judgment is rendered. ***Sanchez v. Superior Ct.*** (6th Dist.1988) 203 Cal.App.3d 1391, 1396; *see* CCP §1048(a). Or suits can be consolidated only for trial, which means that the pleadings, findings, and judgments are kept separate. ***Sanchez***, 203 Cal.App.3d at 1396; *see* CCP §1048(a). For a discussion of joining parties and claims by a motion to consolidate, see "Consolidating Cases," ch. 5-H, §4, p. 522.

§3. JOINDER OF PARTIES

§3.1 Compulsory joinder – §389. CCP §389 sets out separate tests for determining whether a party is either "necessary" or "indispensable" to the suit. *See* CCP §389(a), (b). All indispensable parties are necessary, but not all necessary parties are indispensable. *See* ***Thomson v. Talbert Drainage Dist.*** (4th Dist.1959) 168 Cal.App.2d 687, 689; *cf.* ***Schlumberger Indus. v. National Sur. Corp.*** (4th Cir.1994) 36 F.3d 1274, 1285-86 (interpreting FRCP 19). Because the plaintiff must identify in the complaint (or cross-complaint) all necessary parties who are not joined in the suit and state why they are not joined, the plaintiff must assess whether (1) the absent party is necessary to the suit, (2) the absent party can be joined, and (3) the absent party is indispensable to the resolution of the suit. *See* CCP §389.

NOTE

CCP §389 was revised in 1971 to conform substantially to FRCP 19. 10 Cal. Law Revision Comm'n Rep. (1971) p. 535. Thus, cases addressing FRCP 19 can be used as a guide for interpreting §389. ***Countrywide Home Loans, Inc. v. Superior Ct.*** *(2d Dist.1999) 69 Cal.App.4th 785, 791-92;* ***People v. Community Redev. Agency*** *(4th Dist.1997) 56 Cal.App.4th 868, 874-75.*

1. Absent party is necessary. An absent party is necessary to the suit in the following instances:

(1) Complete relief is not possible among the existing parties. CCP §389(a); ***Countrywide Home Loans***, 69 Cal.App.4th at 793-94. Complete relief is all the relief the parties have asked for. *See, e.g.*, ***Deltakeeper v. Oakdale Irrigation Dist.*** (3d Dist.2001) 94 Cal.App.4th 1092, 1101 (court could give parties complete relief in proceeding challenging environmental-impact report because court could resolve adequacy of report). The focus is only on whether complete relief can be given to the parties named in the suit, not to other potential, unnamed parties. *Id.*; ***Countrywide Home Loans***, 69 Cal.App.4th at 794; *e.g.*, ***Arabia v. BAC Home Loans Servicing, L.P.*** (4th Dist.2012) 208 Cal.App.4th 462, 481 (in judicial-foreclosure suit, relief could be given to parties without joining junior lienholder who was not involved in loan); *see, e.g.*, ***Citizens Ass'n for Sensible Dev. v. County of Inyo*** (4th Dist.1985) 172 Cal.App.3d 151, 161 (in suit to challenge approval to develop property, complete relief could be granted without current property owner as party).

(2) The absent party claims an interest relating to the subject of the litigation. CCP §389(a); *e.g.*, ***Van Zant v. Apple Inc.*** (6th Dist.2014) 229 Cal.App.4th 965, 974-75 (party claimed interest in subject of litigation by litigating it in federal court). The absent party must actually make a claim and not merely have an interest in the litigation; an existing party cannot make the claim on the absent party's behalf. *See* ***Hartenstine v. Superior Ct.*** (4th Dist.1987) 196 Cal.App.3d 206, 222. The disposition of the case without the absent party must also do one of the following:

(a) Impair or impede, as a practical matter, the absent party's ability to protect its interest in the litigation. CCP §389(a); *see* ***Olszewski v. Scripps Health*** (2003) 30 Cal.4th 798, 808 (person is necessary party if judgment will affect her rights); ***Sierra Club, Inc. v. California Coastal Comm'n*** (1st Dist.1979) 95 Cal.App.3d 495, 501 (person is necessary party if requested relief would injure or affect her interest). An absent party's ability to protect its interest is not considered impaired or impeded if another party to the suit has the same interest in the litigation. ***Deltakeeper***, 94 Cal.App.4th at 1102; *see, e.g.*, ***Las Virgenes Educators Ass'n v. Las Virgenes Unified Sch. Dist.*** (2d Dist.2001) 86 Cal.App.4th 1, 9 (parents' interest in changing children's citizenship grades was represented by school district); ***Community Redev. Agency***, 56 Cal.App.4th at 877 (Native American tribe's interest in

defending legality of contract was adequately represented by other party to contract); ***Citizens Ass'n for Sensible Dev.***, 172 Cal.App.3d at 161 (property owner's interest in challenging approval to develop property was adequately represented by party who was in process of purchasing property).

(b) Leave any of the existing parties subject to a substantial risk of incurring multiple or inconsistent obligations because of the claimed interest. CCP §389(a). For there to be a "substantial risk" of multiple or inconsistent obligations, the risk must be more than a theoretical possibility. ***Union Carbide Corp. v. Superior Ct.*** (1984) 36 Cal.3d 15, 21. The plaintiff should consider the following factors in assessing the risk:

[1] Whether the absent party has threatened to file or has already filed a related suit. *See, e.g.*, *id.* at 23-24 (in price-fixing action, no evidence that intermediate purchasers in chain of distribution had filed their own suits); ***Las Virgenes Educators***, 86 Cal.App.4th at 9 (school district never claimed that parents had threatened to file suit over children's citizenship grades).

[2] Whether the absent party may be waiting to file suit until after a judgment in the pending suit. *See, e.g.*, ***Harboring Villas Homeowners Ass'n v. Superior Ct.*** (4th Dist.1998) 63 Cal.App.4th 426, 430 (waiting for judgment in pending suit was impractical for Ps because statute of limitations had almost expired).

[3] Whether the absent party's rights overlap with the rights of the parties to the pending suit. *See, e.g.*, ***Las Virgenes Educators***, 86 Cal.App.4th at 9 (school district's authority to change grades only incidentally affected interests of students and their parents); ***Harboring Villas***, 63 Cal.App.4th at 431 (rights of secured lenders for condominium units did not overlap with rights of condominium homeowners' association). When all parties' interests are clearly defined and do not appear to be in competition with one another (i.e., the recovery by each person or party of the entire amount of her claim does not affect the ability of the others to recover on their own claims), there is no substantial risk of multiple or inconsistent liability. *See, e.g.*, ***Niederer v. Ferreira*** (2d Dist.1987) 189 Cal.App.3d 1485, 1495 (P's and absent parties' interest in promissory note was clearly allocated).

[4] Whether the absent party's interest in the subject matter is moot. *See, e.g.*, ***Las Virgenes Educators***, 86 Cal.App.4th at 9 (parents' interest in suit affecting children's citizenship grades was moot because membership in honor society and eligibility for field trip had not been affected and grades would not have lasting impact in future).

2. Absent party can be joined. If the absent party is necessary to the suit, it must be capable of being joined in the litigation. *See* CCP §389(a). Joinder is allowed in most circumstances, but there are a few common reasons why an absent party cannot be joined:

(1) The court would lose subject-matter jurisdiction. CCP §389(a); 10 Cal. Law Revision Comm'n Rep. (1971) p. 535. For example, federal courts have exclusive jurisdiction over certain parties (e.g., foreign consuls) and claims (e.g., Federal Tort Claims Act). 10 Cal. Law Revision Comm'n Rep. (1971) p. 535; *see, e.g.*, ***Linear Tech. v. Applied Materials, Inc.*** (6th Dist.2007) 152 Cal.App.4th 115, 123-24 (analyzing whether contract claims were subject to federal-question jurisdiction because they arose under patent law); *see also* ***Citizens Task Force on Sohio v. Board of Harbor Comm'rs*** (1979) 23 Cal.3d 812, 814 (D could not join Public Utilities Commission in superior-court proceeding because only California Supreme Court has subject-matter jurisdiction to review Commission's actions).

(2) The court cannot obtain personal jurisdiction over the absent party. 10 Cal. Law Revision Comm'n Rep. (1971) p. 535. See "Joining the Defendant—Personal Jurisdiction," ch. 3-G, p. 283.

(3) The absent party cannot be served with process. *See* CCP §389(a). See "Joining the Defendant—Service of Process," ch. 3-H, p. 295.

3. Absent party is indispensable. If the absent party is necessary but not capable of being joined, the plaintiff should assess whether the party is indispensable to the suit. *See* CCP §389(b); ***County of San Joaquin v. State Water Res. Control Bd.*** (3d Dist.1997) 54 Cal.App.4th 1144, 1149. If the absent party is indispensable, the court must dismiss the case. CCP §389(b); ***Deltakeeper***, 94 Cal.App.4th at 1099-1100. A party is indispensable when

equity and good conscience require the party's presence. *See* CCP §389(b). The plaintiff should consider the following factors in assessing whether the absent party is indispensable:

(1) Whether a judgment rendered in the party's absence would be prejudicial to that party or to others who are already parties. CCP §389(b); 10 Cal. Law Revision Comm'n Rep. (1971) p. 535. The analysis of this factor is substantially the same as that under §389(a)—namely, whether the judgment would (1) impair or impede the absent party's ability to protect its interest in the litigation or (2) subject existing parties to multiple or inconsistent obligations. ***Deltakeeper***, 94 Cal.App.4th at 1107; *see, e.g.*, ***Citizens Ass'n for Sensible Dev.***, 172 Cal.App.3d at 162 (property owner was not indispensable party to suit challenging approval to develop property because party in process of buying property adequately represented property owner's interests).

(2) Whether the prejudice to the absent party could be lessened or avoided by including protective provisions in the judgment, by shaping the relief, or by taking other measures. CCP §389(b); *see, e.g.*, ***Save Our Bay, Inc. v. San Diego Unified Port Dist.*** (4th Dist.1996) 42 Cal.App.4th 686, 699 (no shaping of judgment required because effect on absent party's interest was "merely incidental"). The court may be able to avoid prejudice by doing the following:

(a) Awarding money damages instead of specific relief. *Cf.* ***Miller & Lux, Inc. v. Nickel*** (N.D.Cal.1956) 141 F.Supp. 41, 46 (interpreting federal case law).

(b) Requiring a party to indemnify the absent party or another party if damages are recovered in a related suit. *Cf.* ***Inmobiliaria Axial, S.A. de C.V. v. Robles Int'l Servs.*** (W.D.Tex.2007) No. EP-07-CA-00269-KC (slip op.; 10-11-07) (applying FRCP 19).

(c) Conditioning the payment of damages on the outcome of a related suit. *Cf.* ***Provident Tradesmens Bank & Trust Co. v. Patterson*** (1968) 390 U.S. 102, 115 (suggesting 3d Circuit could have withheld payment pending later suits).

(d) Capping the amount of damages awarded. *Cf. id.* at 115-16 (suggesting 3d Circuit could have accepted Ps' agreement to limit claims to amount of insurance policy).

(3) Whether a judgment rendered in the party's absence would be adequate. CCP §389(b); 10 Cal. Law Revision Comm'n Rep. (1971) p. 535. A judgment is not adequate if it is vulnerable to collateral attack or if it will not be binding on the person who cannot be joined. *See* ***Hayes v. State Dept. of Developmental Servs.*** (3d Dist.2006) 138 Cal.App.4th 1523, 1533-34; ***Kaczorowski v. Board of Supervisors for the Cty. of Mendocino*** (1st Dist.2001) 88 Cal.App.4th 564, 570; ***Save Our Bay***, 42 Cal.App.4th at 699. A judgment is adequate, however, when the party's absence would not have a direct impact on resolving the issues. *See* ***Community Redev. Agency***, 56 Cal.App.4th at 883; *see, e.g.*, ***Deltakeeper***, 94 Cal.App.4th at 1108 (judgment was adequate because absent parties would have been limited to same legal arguments as joined parties, and D was bound by collective litigation agreement involving nonjoined parties).

(4) Whether the plaintiff would have an adequate remedy if the case is dismissed for nonjoinder. CCP §389(b); *see, e.g.*, ***Deltakeeper***, 94 Cal.App.4th at 1108 (Ps would not have adequate remedy because statute of limitations had run); ***County of San Joaquin***, 54 Cal.App.4th at 1155 (parties had adequate remedy in pending federal suit); ***Save Our Bay***, 42 Cal.App.4th at 699 (even though P had no adequate remedy, other factors still required dismissal).

CAUTION

Some courts have held that the controlling test for determining whether an absent party is indispensable is whether the "plaintiff seeks some type of affirmative relief which, if granted, would injure or affect the interest of a third person not joined." E.g., ***In re Marriage of Ramirez*** *(4th Dist.2011) 198 Cal.App.4th 336, 344;* ***Tracy Press, Inc. v. Superior Ct.*** *(3d Dist.2008) 164 Cal.App.4th 1290, 1298;* ***Bradley v. Department of Corr. & Rehab.*** *(5th Dist.2008) 158 Cal.App.4th 1612, 1628;* ***Liang v. San Francisco Residential Rent Stabilization & Arbitration Bd.*** *(1st Dist.2004) 124 Cal.App.4th 775, 778. When §389(b) was revised*

PARTIES & CLAIMS

in 1971 to conform to FRCP 19, the Law Revision Commission noted that the factors provided in the statute were substantially the same as those that had guided the courts for years before its revision. 10 Cal. Law Revision Comm'n Rep. (1971) p. 536. There was no suggestion, however, that certain factors were more important than others, or that there was a "controlling test." In fact, some courts have made the point that the §389(b) factors are not hierarchical and that no one factor is determinative. E.g., ***TG Oceanside, L.P. v. City of Oceanside*** *(4th Dist.2007) 156 Cal.App.4th 1355, 1365;* ***County of Imperial v. Superior Ct.*** *(3d Dist.2007) 152 Cal.App.4th 13, 35;* ***Deltakeeper****, 94 Cal.App.4th at 1106-07;* ***Silver v. Los Angeles Cty. Metro. Transp. Auth.*** *(2d Dist.2000) 79 Cal.App.4th 338, 349.*

§3.2 Compulsory joinder – other statutes. Other statutes may require the joinder of specific persons as parties in certain types of suits. *See* 4 Witkin, *Cal. Procedure*, Pleading, §193; *see, e.g.*, CCP §376(a) (parents must be joined in suit for personal injury to child); Fam. C. §7635(a) (child age 12 or older must be joined in suit to establish paternity); Veh. C. §17152 (operator of vehicle must be joined in suit against vehicle owner if personal jurisdiction over operator can be secured).

§3.3 Permissive joinder.

1. Plaintiffs.

(1) Multiple plaintiffs. CCP §378 sets out the tests for determining whether multiple plaintiffs can choose to join together in the same suit.

NOTE

CCP §378(a)(1) and (b) were revised to conform substantially to former FRCP 20(a), now FRCP 20(a)(1) and (a)(3). 10 Cal. Law Revision Comm'n Rep. (1971) p. 528. Thus, cases addressing FRCP 20 can be used as a guide for interpreting §378. Cf. ***Countrywide Home Loans, Inc. v. Superior Ct.*** *(2d Dist.1999) 69 Cal.App.4th 785, 791-92 (court can look to federal case law on FRCP 19 when interpreting CCP §389).*

(a) Same transaction + common question. Multiple plaintiffs can join together in the same suit when they assert claims—severally, jointly, or alternatively—that relate to or arise from the same transaction or occurrence and involve any common question of law or fact. CCP §378(a)(1).

[1] Severally, jointly, or alternatively. The plaintiffs' claims can be asserted severally, jointly, or alternatively. CCP §378(a)(1); *see id.* §378(b) (judgment can be given for one or more Ps according to their respective right to relief). Although the claims are joined in a single suit, each claim retains its separate character as if it were pleaded in a separate suit. ***Brennan v. Superior Ct.*** (3d Dist.1994) 30 Cal.App.4th 454, 461-62. In other words, joinder under CCP §378(a)(1) simply reflects the plaintiffs' election to consolidate several causes of action at the beginning, rather than bringing several actions and consolidating them later. ***Brennan***, 30 Cal.App.4th at 462.

[2] Same transaction or occurrence. The plaintiffs' claims can be asserted in the same suit if they relate to or arise from the same transaction, occurrence, or series of transactions or occurrences. CCP §378(a)(1). The courts have construed this requirement broadly and determine on a case-by-case basis whether the plaintiffs' factual allegations constitute the same transaction or occurrence. *See* ***State Farm Fire & Cas. Co. v. Superior Ct.*** (2d Dist.1996) 45 Cal.App.4th 1093, 1113; *cf.* ***Coughlin v. Rogers*** (9th Cir.1997) 130 F.3d 1348, 1350 ("same transaction" requirement under FRCP 20(a) focuses on similarities between factual backgrounds of each claim).

[a] Factual relationship sufficient. The following are examples of when courts have found the factual relationship between the plaintiffs' claims sufficient to support joinder: • Patients who were sexually assaulted by a doctor sued the doctor's employer for negligent hiring and supervision. ***Moe v. Anderson*** (3d Dist.2012) 207 Cal.App.4th 826, 835-36. • Manufacturer's employees and the employees' family members sued

PARTIES & CLAIMS

for exposure to hazardous chemical at various times over 20 to 30 years. ***Anaya v. Superior Ct.*** (1st Dist.1984) 160 Cal.App.3d 228, 230-31. These claims satisfied the test even though the type of exposure varied (inhalation, drinking water, and physical contact) and the plaintiffs were not all exposed at the same time. *Id.* at 233. • Homeowner's insurance purchasers sued their insurance company for systematically deceiving them by reducing the scope of their coverage without adequate notice while charging the same premiums. ***State Farm Fire & Cas.***, 45 Cal.App.4th at 1113. • Drivers and passengers asserted claims for personal injuries sustained in a single automobile accident. ***Colla v. Carmichael U-Drive Autos, Inc.*** (San Francisco Cty. Superior Ct. Appellate Dept. 1930) 111 Cal.App.Supp. 784, 787. • Home purchasers sued contractor, original owner of subdivision, real-estate agents, and mortgage lender for conspiracy to sell homes at inflated prices. ***Adams v. Albany*** (4th Dist.1954) 124 Cal.App.2d 639, 646.

[b] Factual relationship insufficient. The following are examples of when courts have found the factual relationship between the plaintiffs' claims insufficient to support joinder: • Patients who were sexually assaulted by a doctor sued the doctor for various causes of action related to the assaults, but the claims involved separate and distinct sexual assaults during separate and distinct periods of time. ***Moe***, 207 Cal.App.4th at 833. • Chiropractors sued state employees and newspaper for trespass in their offices and conversion of personal property, but the only thing the chiropractors' claims had in common was that these incidents took place on the same day. ***Coleman v. Twin Coast Newspaper, Inc.*** (2d Dist.1959) 175 Cal.App.2d 650, 654. • Homeowners filed insurance claims for real and personal property damage that resulted from a single large storm, but the claims involved many different types of property, the damage occurred at widely separated locations, and the damage was caused in a variety of ways under various conditions. *Cf.* ***Farmers Ins. Exch. v. Adams*** (1st Dist.1985) 170 Cal.App.3d 712, 722-23 (interpreting test for joinder of Ds under CCP §379), *disapproved on other grounds*, ***Garvey v. State Farm Fire & Cas. Co.*** (1989) 48 Cal.3d 395.

[3] Common question. The plaintiffs' claims can be asserted in the same suit if they involve any common question of law or fact. CCP §378(a)(1). This requirement is satisfied if there is at least one question of law or fact shared by each plaintiff's claim, no matter how many other questions of law or fact are involved. ***Anaya***, 160 Cal.App.3d at 233.

[4] Interest in action or relief. The plaintiffs' claims can be asserted in the same suit even if all the plaintiffs are not interested in every cause of action asserted or claim for relief requested. CCP §378(b).

(b) Same property or controversy. Multiple plaintiffs can join together in the same suit when they assert claims, rights, or interests in the same property or controversy at issue. CCP §378(a)(2); *see, e.g.*, ***Parker v. Walker*** (3d Dist.1992) 5 Cal.App.4th 1173, 1182-83 (joinder of Ps was proper because suit was based on common interest in money judgment). Joinder under this provision is proper even if the plaintiffs are not interested in every cause of action asserted or claim for relief requested. CCP §378(b).

NOTE

CCP §378(a)(2) is a remnant of the pre-1971 version of §378, and it does not expand the scope of joinder under §378(a)(1). 10 Cal. Law Revision Comm'n Rep. (1971) p. 528. The provision was left in to make clear that any person who could have been joined as a plaintiff under former CCP §378 can still be joined under the current version. 10 Cal. Law Revision Comm'n Rep. (1971) p. 528.

(2) Involuntary plaintiff. A person who should be joined as a plaintiff but will not consent to joinder can instead be joined as a defendant. CCP §382; *see, e.g.*, ***Hall v. Southern Pac. Co.*** (1st Dist.1919) 40 Cal.App. 39, 43 (Ps, deceased employee's heirs, joined employer as D in suit to recover damages). This person is sometimes referred to as an "involuntary plaintiff." *See* ***Harboring Villas Homeowners Ass'n v. Superior Ct.*** (4th Dist.1998) 63 Cal.App.4th 426, 431. To designate a person as an involuntary plaintiff, the plaintiff should do the following:

(a) Determine whether joinder is proper. The plaintiff should determine whether the person's joinder would be proper.

PARTIES & CLAIMS

NOTE

A person can be joined as an involuntary plaintiff even after the statute of limitations has expired. ***Worthington v. Kaiser Found. Health Plan, Inc.*** *(2d Dist.1970) 8 Cal.App.3d 435, 447.*

[1] **Interested person.** A person can be joined as an involuntary plaintiff when that person has an interest in the underlying suit similar to that of the plaintiff. *See* 4 Witkin, *Cal. Procedure*, Pleading, §§193, 209. For example, a corporation can be an involuntary plaintiff in a shareholder's derivative suit because the interests of the corporation in the underlying suit can be similar, if not identical, to the interests of the shareholder. *See* ***Patrick v. Alacer Corp.*** (4th Dist.2008) 167 Cal.App.4th 995, 1006.

[2] **Indivisible claims.** A person can be joined as an involuntary plaintiff when the suit is to recover damages for an indivisible claim—that is, a claim that cannot be made in separate suits. *See, e.g.*, ***Watkins v. Nutting*** (1941) 17 Cal.2d 490, 498 (claims of heirs for wrongful death of decedent); ***Nightingale v. Scannell*** (1856) 6 Cal. 506, 509 (claims of partners for damage to partnership property).

[3] **Indirect claims.** A person can be joined as an involuntary plaintiff when the suit is for claims the plaintiff does not have standing to pursue directly. *See, e.g.*, ***In re Estate of Clark*** (1923) 190 Cal. 354, 358-59 (dicta; heirs can file suit to collect debts owed to estate by joining administrator who refuses to collect); ***Patrick***, 167 Cal.App.4th at 1003-04 (shareholder can bring derivative suit on corporation's behalf when directors refuse to act).

(b) Ask person to join. The plaintiff should ask the person to join the suit voluntarily before adding the person as an involuntary plaintiff. *See* ***Martin v. Howe*** (1922) 190 Cal. 187, 196.

(c) Designate & explain. If the person refuses to join the suit, the plaintiff should designate the person as a defendant. CCP §382. This designation, however, does not change the relationship between the parties—that is, the involuntary plaintiff should be treated like any other plaintiff. ***Watkins***, 17 Cal.2d at 498; ***Ferraro v. Camarlinghi*** (6th Dist.2008) 161 Cal.App.4th 509, 534; ***Estate of Kuebler v. Superior Ct.*** (4th Dist.1978) 81 Cal.App.3d 500, 503. For example, a default judgment cannot be entered against an involuntary plaintiff. ***Watkins***, 17 Cal.2d at 498-99; ***Estate of Kuebler***, 81 Cal.App.3d at 504; *see* ***Gilmore v. Los Angeles Ry.*** (1930) 211 Cal. 192, 198-99. Once designated, the plaintiff must explain in the complaint the reason for joining the person as an involuntary plaintiff. CCP §382.

2. Defendants. CCP §379 sets out the tests for determining whether multiple defendants can be joined together in the same suit.

NOTE

In 1971, §379 was revised to provide grounds for the joinder of defendants similar to those for the joinder of plaintiffs under §378, which was modeled after FRCP 20(a). 10 Cal. Law Revision Comm'n Rep. (1971) p. 529.

(1) Same transaction + common question. Multiple defendants can be joined together in the same suit when the plaintiff or plaintiffs assert claims—severally, jointly, or alternatively—against the defendants that relate to or arise from the same transaction or occurrence and involve any common question of law or fact. CCP §379(a)(1).

(a) Severally, jointly, or alternatively. Multiple defendants can be joined together in the same suit even though the plaintiffs' claims are asserted severally, jointly, or alternatively. CCP §379(a)(1); *see id.* §379(b) (judgment can be given against one or more Ds according to their respective liabilities); *see, e.g.*, ***Kraft v. Smith*** (1944) 24 Cal.2d 124, 128-30 (P could join two doctors who operated on P's leg at different times); ***Service***

Employees Int'l Un. v. Hollywood Park, Inc. (2d Dist.1983) 149 Cal.App.3d 745, 758 (P could join D even though D was alleged to have been liable on only one count). See "Severally, jointly, or alternatively," §3.3.1(1)(a)[1], p. 196.

(b) Same transaction or occurrence. Multiple defendants can be joined together in the same suit if the plaintiffs' claims relate to or arise from the same transaction, occurrence, or series of transactions or occurrences. CCP §379(a)(1); ***Colusa Air Pollution Control Dist. v. Superior Ct.*** (2d Dist.1991) 226 Cal.App.3d 880, 885-86; *e.g.*, ***Farmers Ins. Exch.***, 170 Cal.App.3d at 722-23 (D-insureds could not be joined under §379(a)(1) in P-insurer's declaratory-judgment action simply because Ds suffered property damage during same storm). See "Same transaction or occurrence," §3.3.1(1)(a)[2], p. 196.

(c) Common question. Multiple defendants can be joined together in the same suit if the plaintiffs' claims involve any common question of law or fact. CCP §379(a)(1); *e.g.*, ***Colusa Air Pollution Control Dist.***, 226 Cal.App.3d at 885-86 (Ds were properly joined under §379(a)(1) because Ps' claims involved common issues of law and fact). See "Common question," §3.3.1(1)(a)[3], p. 197.

(d) Interest in action or relief. Multiple defendants can be joined together in the same suit even if all the defendants are not interested in every cause of action asserted or claim for relief requested. CCP §379(b).

(2) Same property or controversy. Multiple defendants can be joined together in the same suit when an adverse claim, right, or interest in the same property or controversy at issue is asserted against them. CCP §379(a)(2).

NOTE

CCP §379(a)(2) is a remnant of the pre-1971 version of §379, and it was left in to make clear that any person who could have been joined as a defendant under former §379 can still be joined under the current version. 10 Cal. Law Revision Comm'n Rep. (1971) p. 529.

(3) D's liability uncertain. Multiple defendants can be joined together in the same suit when the plaintiff is uncertain which defendant or how much each defendant is liable to the plaintiff. CCP §379(c); *see* ***Landau v. Salam*** (1971) 4 Cal.3d 901, 906-07.

3. Third parties. A third party can be joined in a suit by cross-complaint when the cause of action asserted against the third party (1) arises out of the same transaction, occurrence, or series of transactions or occurrences that are asserted against the cross-plaintiff or (2) asserts a claim, right, or interest in the property or controversy that is the subject of the action asserted against the cross-plaintiff. CCP §428.10(b); *see id.* §428.20. This test is the same as that for permissive joinder of plaintiffs and defendants under CCP §§378 and 379, and it requires, at a minimum, a subject-matter connection between the cause of action pleaded against the third-party plaintiff and the cause of action pleaded against the third-party defendant. *See* 10 Cal. Law Revision Comm'n Rep. (1971) p. 552; *see, e.g.*, ***Platt v. Coldwell Banker Residential Real Estate Servs.*** (4th Dist.1990) 217 Cal.App.3d 1439, 1444 (under §428.10(b), D can usually file cross-complaint against any person from whom D seeks equitable indemnity); ***Daon Corp. v. Place Homeowners Ass'n*** (1st Dist.1989) 207 Cal.App.3d 1449, 1455 (under §428.10(b), D can file cross-complaint against any person from whom D seeks total or partial indemnity based on comparative fault). See "Same transaction or occurrence," §3.3.1(1)(a)[2], p. 196. For a discussion of joining third parties by cross-complaint, see "Cross-Complaint," ch. 4-C, p. 349.

NOTE

A third-party cross-complaint is the California equivalent of federal impleader. ***Countrywide Home Loans****, 69 Cal.App.4th at 797. See* ***O'Connor's Federal Rules****, "Third-party claim," ch. 3-L, §5.3, p. 263.*

PARTIES & CLAIMS

4. Orders. When plaintiffs or defendants have been joined under CCP §378 or 379, the court can issue orders to protect the parties and ensure the orderly disposition of the case.

(1) Protect parties. When plaintiffs or defendants are permissively joined, the court can issue orders to protect any party from embarrassment, delay, or undue expense. CCP §379.5; ***Anaya***, 160 Cal.App.3d at 233-34.

(2) Case management. When plaintiffs or defendants are permissively joined, the court can order separate trials or issue other orders to address any case-management concerns. CCP §379.5; ***Anaya***, 160 Cal.App.3d at 233-34.

§4. JOINDER OF CLAIMS

The parties can bring as many claims as they have against each other or against third parties. Claims are joined by the complaint and the cross-complaint. *See* CCP §427.10.

§4.1 Compulsory joinder of claims. A defendant must assert in a cross-complaint all related causes of action it has against the plaintiff. CCP §426.30(a); *see also* ***Banerian v. O'Malley*** (1st Dist.1974) 42 Cal.App.3d 604, 612 (compulsory joinder of claims applies only between Ps and Ds). The purpose of this compulsory-cross-claim rule is to prevent parties from splitting a cause of action into a series of suits in piecemeal litigation and to avoid conflicting judgments. *See* ***Carroll v. Import Motors, Inc.*** (1st Dist.1995) 33 Cal.App.4th 1429, 1435; ***Hulsey v. Koehler*** (3d Dist.1990) 218 Cal.App.3d 1150, 1157-58; ***Saunders v. New Capital for Small Businesses, Inc.*** (1st Dist.1964) 231 Cal.App.2d 324, 334.

PARTIES & CLAIMS

CAUTION

The compulsory-cross-claim rule also applies to plaintiffs. Although the plaintiff may initially choose the claims it wants to bring against the defendant, if the defendant asserts claims against the plaintiff by cross-claim, the plaintiff must then assert all of its compulsory cross-claims or they will be barred in a later suit. See, e.g., ***Carroll****, 33 Cal.App.4th at 1435-36 (P's claims were barred under CCP §426.30 because they arose from same transaction that served as basis for D's cross-complaint in first suit).*

1. Claim is compulsory. For the defendant's claim to be compulsory, the following criteria must be met:

(1) Claim is related. The defendant's claim must be a "related cause of action." CCP §426.30(a). A related cause of action is a claim that arises out of the same transaction, occurrence, or series of transactions or occurrences that form the basis for the plaintiff's claims against the defendant. *Id.* §426.10(c); ***Align Tech. v. Tran*** (6th Dist.2009) 179 Cal.App.4th 949, 960. The term "transaction" is liberally construed to mean a series of acts or occurrences that are logically related. ***Align Tech.***, 179 Cal.App.4th at 960; ***Currie Med. Specialties, Inc. v. Bowen*** (4th Dist.1982) 136 Cal.App.3d 774, 777; ***Ranchers Bank v. Pressman*** (2d Dist.1971) 19 Cal.App.3d 612, 620; ***Saunders***, 231 Cal.App.2d at 336. The primary test for "logical relatedness" is a question about duplication of time and effort—namely, are any factual or legal issues relevant to the claims? ***Align Tech.***, 179 Cal.App.4th at 960.

(2) Claim exists at time of answer. The compulsory-cross-claim rule applies only to the related causes of action the defendant has when it serves its answer. CCP §426.30(a); ***Align Tech.***, 179 Cal.App.4th at 970; *see* ***Crocker Nat'l Bank v. Emerald*** (3d Dist.1990) 221 Cal.App.3d 852, 864. The rule does not apply to related causes of action that arise after service. CCP §426.30(a); *see* ***Align Tech.***, 179 Cal.App.4th at 970; ***Crocker Nat'l Bank***, 221 Cal.App.3d at 864.

(3) Claim asserted in civil action. The claim must be asserted in a civil action. CCP §426.60(a). A civil action includes almost all civil proceedings but does not include the following:

(a) Special proceedings, except eminent-domain proceedings. *See* CCP §§426.60(a), 426.70(a); *see, e.g.,* ***Superior Motels, Inc. v. Rinn Motor Hotels, Inc.*** (1st Dist.1987) 195 Cal.App.3d 1032, 1066 (no cross-complaint in unlawful-detainer actions).

(b) Actions in small-claims court. CCP §426.60(b). The defendant in a small-claims suit may file a claim in the same suit if the amount sought does not exceed the jurisdictional limit of the court. CCP §116.360(a); ***Davis v. Superior Ct.*** (1st Dist.1980) 102 Cal.App.3d 164, 170.

(c) Actions for declaratory relief when the only relief sought is a declaration of the rights and duties of the respective parties. CCP §426.60(c); *see* ***California State Auto. Ass'n v. Superior Ct.*** (3d Dist.1986) 184 Cal.App.3d 1428, 1433 n.6 (no obligation to assert related claims by way of cross-complaint in declaratory-judgment proceeding).

CAUTION

The statute governing a particular special proceeding may provide its own compulsory-joinder rules for that proceeding. 10 Cal. Law Revision Comm'n Rep. (1971) p. 1133 (comment to §426.60). For example, one court has stated that CCP §386 might allow a claimant in an interpleader action to bring a compulsory claim against the stakeholder in a separate proceeding. See ***State Farm Fire & Cas. Co. v. Pietak*** *(3d Dist.2001) 90 Cal.App.4th 600, 615. But see* ***Cheiker v. Prudential Ins.*** *(9th Cir.1987) 820 F.2d 334, 336 (applying California compulsory-cross-complaint statute to interpleader action).*

---

(4) Claim not pending. The claim must not be pending in a suit in another court. CCP §426.40(c).

(5) Court has jurisdiction.

(a) Over defendant. The court must have jurisdiction to render a personal judgment against the defendant. CCP §426.30(b)(1); *see* ***Thompson Pac. Constr., Inc. v. City of Sunnyvale*** (6th Dist.2007) 155 Cal.App.4th 525, 538 (court cannot render personal judgment if no service of process). See "Joining the Defendant—Personal Jurisdiction," ch. 3-G, p. 283.

(b) Over additional parties. The court must have personal jurisdiction over any additional parties that are necessary for the claim to be adjudicated. CCP §426.40(a). See "Joining the Defendant—Personal Jurisdiction," ch. 3-G, p. 283.

(c) Over claim. The court, and any other court the claim could be transferred to under CCP §396, cannot be prohibited by the U.S. or California Constitution or by statute from hearing the claim. CCP §426.40(b). If the claim falls under the exclusive jurisdiction of the federal courts, the claim cannot be subject to compulsory joinder. 10 Cal. Law Revision Comm'n Rep. (1971) p. 548.

2. Waiver. If the defendant does not assert a compulsory claim before the plaintiff's case goes to trial, the defendant is barred from asserting the claim in a later suit. *See* CCP §426.30(a); ***City of Hanford v. Superior Ct.*** (5th Dist.1989) 208 Cal.App.3d 580, 587. This bar can be raised by demurrer in any later suit. *See, e.g.,* ***AL Holding Co. v. O'Brien & Hicks, Inc.*** (1st Dist.1999) 75 Cal.App.4th 1310, 1312 & n.1 (D demurred to P's complaint on ground that P's cause of action was barred because issue was never raised by compulsory cross-complaint in earlier suit). The claim is not waived, however, if the defendant did not file an answer in the original suit. CCP §426.30(b)(2); ***Morris v. Blank*** (2d Dist.2001) 94 Cal.App.4th 823, 831.

§4.2 Permissive joinder of claims. Parties can assert in a cross-complaint as many causes of action as they have against other parties and third parties who have not yet been brought into the suit.

1. P's claims. One or more plaintiffs can assert in the complaint any causes of action they may have against one or more defendants. CCP §427.10(a). The causes of action do not have to be related. *See id.* If the unrelated causes of action would be difficult to try together, they can be severed for trial purposes under CCP §1048(b). 10 Cal. Law Revision Comm'n Rep. (1971) p. 551; *CEB Procedure Before Trial*, §15.24.

CAUTION

If the unrelated claims are severed for trial, the plaintiff must bring each claim to trial within five years after the suit was commenced to avoid dismissal of the claim. See CCP §583.310; ***Sagi Plumbing v. Chartered Constr. Corp.*** *(2d Dist.2004) 123 Cal.App.4th 443, 450. See "No trial after action commenced," ch. 10-E, §4.3, p. 1165.*

2. D's claims.

(1) Against P. A defendant can assert in a cross-complaint most causes of action it has against the plaintiff or a third-party plaintiff. CCP §§428.10(a), 428.30; *see also* ***Nomellini Constr. Co. v. Harris*** (5th Dist.1969) 272 Cal.App.2d 352, 357 (permissive cross-complaints help parties avoid multiplicity of suits by enabling court to render final and binding judgment on all matters in dispute). The defendant's claims do not need to be factually related to the plaintiff's claims. 10 Cal. Law Revision Comm'n Rep. (1971) p. 1143; *CEB Procedure Before Trial*, §26.16; *see* ***Kajima Eng'g & Constr., Inc. v. City of L.A.*** (2d Dist.2002) 95 Cal.App.4th 921, 934 (party can file cross-complaint against another party for any existing cause of action regardless of its nature and origin).

(a) Eminent-domain proceedings. The defendant cannot assert a permissive claim by cross-complaint against the plaintiff in an eminent-domain proceeding. *See* CCP §§426.70, 428.10(a), 428.30.

(b) Unlawful-detainer actions. The defendant cannot assert a permissive claim by cross-complaint against the plaintiff in an unlawful-detainer action. ***Superior Motels, Inc. v. Rinn Motor Hotels, Inc.*** (1st Dist.1987) 195 Cal.App.3d 1032, 1066. This prohibition does not apply, however, if the tenant has voluntarily surrendered possession of the property before the issues of fact are finally joined. ***Union Oil Co. v. Chandler*** (1st Dist.1970) 4 Cal.App.3d 716, 722.

(2) Against codefendant or third party.

(a) Related claims. A defendant can assert in a cross-complaint a claim against a codefendant or third party who is alleged to be liable on the plaintiff's claim against the defendant. CCP §428.10(b); *see, e.g.*, ***Insurance Co. of N. Am. v. Liberty Mut. Ins.*** (3d Dist.1982) 128 Cal.App.3d 297, 303 (P, who was D in underlying suit, could have filed permissive cross-complaint against D in first suit, thus bringing D into that suit as third-party D, but P did not have to and could instead pursue its claims against D in later suit). For a discussion of the standard for joining a third party on a related claim, see "Third parties," §3.3.3, p. 199.

(b) Unrelated claims. A defendant can assert in its cross-complaint under §428.10(b) any claims it may have against a codefendant or third party joined under §428.10(b), even if those claims are unrelated to the plaintiff's claim against the defendant. *See* CCP §428.30. In other words, a defendant can join all claims it may have against a cross-defendant if just one claim arises out of the same transaction or occurrence as the underlying suit. *See id.* §§428.10(b), 428.30. If the unrelated claims would be difficult to try together, they can be severed for trial purposes under CCP §1048(b). 10 Cal. Law Revision Comm'n Rep. (1971) p. 1144.

§5. REMEDIES

§5.1 For misjoinder. To raise the issue of misjoinder of claims or parties, the complaining party should file a demurrer or state the issue in its answer. CCP §430.10(d); *see* ***Time for Living, Inc. v. Guy Hatfield Homes/All Am. Dev. Co.*** (4th Dist.1991) 230 Cal.App.3d 30, 41. See "Answer," ch. 4-B, p. 332; "Demurrer," ch. 4-H, p. 396. The court should drop parties and sever claims that are improperly joined. *See* CCP §379.5 (court may order separate trials or make other orders in the interest of justice); ***Landau v. Salam*** (1971) 4 Cal.3d 901, 908 (preferred remedies for misjoinder are severance or protective order); ***Geraci v. United Servs. Auto. Ass'n*** (2d Dist.1987) 188 Cal.App.3d 1245, 1252 n.4 (same).

§5.2 For nonjoinder. To raise the issue of nonjoinder of a necessary or indispensable party, the complaining party should file either (1) a demurrer, if all the facts necessary to establish compulsory joinder appear on the face of the complaint, or (2) a motion for joinder. *See* ***Union Carbide Corp. v. Superior Ct.*** (1984) 36 Cal.3d 15, 22 (demurrer); ***Citizens Task Force on Sohio v. Board of Harbor Comm'rs*** (1979) 23 Cal.3d 812, 814 (motion); ***Jermstad v. McNelis*** (3d Dist.1989) 210 Cal.App.3d 528, 538 (demurrer). See "Demurrer," ch. 4-H, p. 396. The court can

PARTIES & CLAIMS

also order the joinder of a necessary or indispensable party on its own motion. ***Gabriel P. v. Suedi D.*** (2d Dist.2006) 141 Cal.App.4th 850, 865. An objection to the absence of an indispensable party can be raised at any time. ***Kraus v. Willow Park Pub. Golf Course*** (1st Dist.1977) 73 Cal.App.3d 354, 369 n.11. But a claim of error for not joining an absent party is waived on appeal unless it is appropriately raised at trial or there is a compelling reason of equity or policy warranting the delay. ***Jermstad***, 210 Cal.App.3d at 538; 4 Witkin, *Cal. Procedure*, Pleading, §184; *see* ***Kraus***, 73 Cal.App.3d at 370 n.11.

§5.3 For barred claims. To raise the issue of whether a claim is barred by res judicata because it was subject to compulsory joinder in an earlier suit, the complaining party should either (1) file a demurrer, if all the facts necessary to establish res judicata appear on the face of the complaint, or (2) specifically plead res judicata as an affirmative defense in its answer. *See* ***Brosterhous v. State Bar*** (1995) 12 Cal.4th 315, 324 (res judicata is usually raised in answer but can be raised by demurrer); ***Hulsey v. Koehler*** (3d Dist.1990) 218 Cal.App.3d 1150, 1158 (must specifically plead res judicata as affirmative defense in answer); *see, e.g.*, ***Sylvester v. Soulsberg*** (5th Dist.1967) 252 Cal.App.2d 185, 187-88 (Ds pleaded dismissal with prejudice to earlier suit). If the claim is subject to compulsory joinder in a suit that is in progress, the complaining party can raise the issue by a plea in abatement. *See* ***Kittle Mfg. v. Davis*** (2d Dist.1935) 8 Cal.App.2d 504, 509. See "Compulsory joinder of claims," §4.1, p. 200; "Affirmative Defenses," ch. 4-B, §5, p. 343.

C. PLAINTIFF'S ORIGINAL COMPLAINT

§1. GENERAL

§1.1 Purpose. The plaintiff begins its lawsuit by filing the complaint. CCP §§350, 411.10. Filing a complaint is mandatory to invoke the jurisdiction of the trial court, and any judgment obtained when no complaint has been filed is void. ***Tinn v. U.S. Dist. Atty.*** (1906) 148 Cal. 773, 776. The plaintiff's complaint frames and limits the issues for trial. ***Committee on Children's TV, Inc. v. General Foods Corp.*** (1983) 35 Cal.3d 197, 211-12; ***Fuentes v. Tucker*** (1947) 31 Cal.2d 1, 4. The complaint gives the defendant fair notice of the basis of the plaintiff's claims, thus enabling the defendant to prepare a defense. *See* ***Perkins v. Superior Ct.*** (2d Dist.1981) 117 Cal.App.3d 1, 6.

§1.2 Primary authority. CCP §§350, 411.10-411.35, 422.10-422.40.

§1.3 Secondary authority. The following secondary sources are cited as authority in this subchapter:

- *California Civil Procedure Before Trial* (CEB Online ed. 2014) (referred to as *CEB Procedure Before Trial*).
- Weil & Brown, *California Practice Guide: Civil Procedure Before Trial* (CD-ROM ed. 2014) (referred to as Weil, *Civil Procedure Before Trial*).
- Witkin, *California Procedure* (5th ed. 2008 & Supp.2014) (referred to as Witkin, *Cal. Procedure*).

§1.4 Judicial Council forms.

- CIV-050 (mandatory), statement of damages.
- CM-010 (mandatory), civil case cover sheet.
- PLD-C-001 through PLD-C-001(3) (optional), contract claims.
- PLD-PI-001 through PLD-PI-001(6) (optional), claims for personal injury, property damage, or wrongful death.
- UD-100 (optional), unlawful detainer.

§2. STANDING & CAPACITY

§2.1 Standing. Standing is a person's right to sue for relief on the alleged cause of action. ***American Alt. Energy Partners II v. Windridge, Inc.*** (5th Dist.1996) 42 Cal.App.4th 551, 559. Standing derives from the principle that the court's jurisdiction can be invoked only by a proper plaintiff. *See* ***City of Santa Monica v. Stewart*** (2d

ORIGINAL COMPLAINT

Dist.2005) 126 Cal.App.4th 43, 59. A plaintiff's standing is a threshold issue to be resolved by the court, because without it there is no actual controversy for the court to determine. ***CashCall, Inc. v. Superior Ct.*** (4th Dist.2008) 159 Cal.App.4th 273, 286; *see* ***Apartment Ass'n v. City of L.A.*** (2d Dist.2006) 136 Cal.App.4th 119, 128; ***Clifford S. v. Superior Ct.*** (4th Dist.1995) 38 Cal.App.4th 747, 751. In other words, standing is a jurisdictional prerequisite to maintaining a cause of action or obtaining affirmative relief of any kind. *See* ***Common Cause v. Board of Supervisors*** (1989) 49 Cal.3d 432, 438. The standing requirement ensures that any judgment rendered by the court will protect the defendant from later having to defend against other claimants to the same claim. ***Keru Invs. v. Cube Co.*** (2d Dist.1998) 63 Cal.App.4th 1412, 1424. An objection to standing cannot be waived and can be raised for the first time on appeal. ***Associated Builders & Contractors, Inc. v. San Francisco Airports Comm'n*** (1999) 21 Cal.4th 352, 361.

1. Real party in interest. A plaintiff has standing if it is a "real party in interest." *See* CCP §367; ***Windham at Carmel Mountain Ranch Ass'n v. Superior Ct.*** (4th Dist.2003) 109 Cal.App.4th 1162, 1172-73; ***O'Flaherty v. Belgum*** (2d Dist.2004) 115 Cal.App.4th 1044, 1094 (Grignon, P.J., dissenting). A real party in interest is one who has an actual and substantial interest in the subject matter of the action and who stands to benefit from or be injured by a judgment. ***County of Alameda v. State Bd. of Control*** (1st Dist.1993) 14 Cal.App.4th 1096, 1103; *see* ***Zubarau v. City of Palmdale*** (2d Dist.2011) 192 Cal.App.4th 289, 300; *see also* ***B.C. Cotton, Inc. v. Voss*** (3d Dist.1995) 33 Cal.App.4th 929, 948 (person objecting to statute or regulatory measure must show actual or threatened injury from enactment). For example, a real party in interest includes any person who owns or holds title to the claim or property that is the subject of the action. *See, e.g.*, ***Saks v. Damon Raike & Co.*** (1st Dist.1992) 7 Cal.App.4th 419, 427 (in action brought on behalf of express trust, real party in interest is trustee because it has legal title to action); ***Vaughn v. Dame Constr. Co.*** (4th Dist.1990) 223 Cal.App.3d 144, 148-49 (in action for injury to real property, P had standing to seek damages because she owned property at time of injury and did not assign action when she sold property after suit was filed); ***Tomlin v. Walt Disney Prods.*** (2d Dist.1971) 18 Cal.App.3d 226, 238-39 (in action for unfair competition, songwriter did not have standing to sue because his publisher owned title to song that was basis for suit). Some of the types of plaintiffs that are often faced with standing challenges include the following:

(1) Minors. A minor has standing to enforce her rights. Fam. C. §6601; *see, e.g.*, ***Reliance Life Ins. v. Jaffe*** (2d Dist.1953) 121 Cal.App.2d 241, 244 (child could enforce provisions of property settlement agreement made for his benefit). Although the minor is the real party in interest, the action must be brought by a guardian or conservator of the estate or a guardian ad litem appointed by the court. CCP §372(a); *see* ***Westphal v. Arnoux*** (1st Dist.1921) 51 Cal.App. 532, 536; *see also* ***J.W. v. Superior Ct.*** (2d Dist.1993) 17 Cal.App.4th 958, 967-68 (nonattorney guardian ad litem cannot appear in pro per on behalf of minor).

(2) Corporations. A corporation has standing to enforce its rights. *See* ***PacLink Comms. Int'l v. Superior Ct.*** (2d Dist.2001) 90 Cal.App.4th 958, 965; Weil, *Civil Procedure Before Trial*, ¶2:14. If the corporation refuses to act, an individual stockholder has standing to assert the corporation's right though a shareholder derivative action. ***Jones v. H.F. Ahmanson & Co.*** (1969) 1 Cal.3d 93, 106-07; ***PacLink***, 90 Cal.App.4th at 965; Weil, *Civil Procedure Before Trial*, ¶2.15; *see* 5 Witkin, *Cal. Procedure*, Pleading, §912.

(3) Partnerships. A partnership has standing to enforce its rights. *See* ***Mayer v. C.W. Driver*** (2d Dist.2002) 98 Cal.App.4th 48, 60; Weil, *Civil Procedure Before Trial*, ¶2:15.5. Individual partners do not have standing to sue for damage to the partnership or to their beneficial interest in the partnership's property because the partnership itself holds title to all claims and assets. *See* ***Mayer***, 98 Cal.App.4th at 60.

(4) Associations. An association has standing to enforce its members' rights when (1) its members have standing to sue in their own right, (2) the interests it seeks to protect are relevant to the organization's purpose, and (3) the members' individual participation in the suit is not required. ***Airline Pilots Ass'n v. United Airlines, Inc.*** (1st Dist.2014) 223 Cal.App.4th 706, 726; ***Property Owners of Whispering Palms, Inc. v. Newport Pac., Inc.*** (4th Dist.2005) 132 Cal.App.4th 666, 673; *see, e.g.*, ***Market Lofts Cmty. Ass'n v. 9th St. Mkt. Lofts, LLC*** (2d Dist.2014) 222 Cal.App.4th 924, 932-33 (homeowners' association had standing to sue as representative of individual homeowners). An association also has standing to enforce its own rights. Weil, *Civil Procedure Before Trial*,

¶2:15.10. For example, a property association has standing to enforce its own rights in matters related to (1) the enforcement of governing documents, (2) damage to the common area, (3) damage to a separate interest that the association is required to maintain or repair, or (4) damage to a separate interest that arises out of damage to the common area or to a separate interest that the association is required to maintain or repair. Civ. C. §6858.

(5) Personal representatives & heirs. A personal representative has standing to enforce the rights of the decedent's estate. *See* CCP §369(a)(1); ***Olson v. Toy*** (3d Dist.1996) 46 Cal.App.4th 818, 823-24; 4 Witkin, *Cal. Procedure*, Pleading, §134; *see also* ***Roes v. Wong*** (4th Dist.1999) 69 Cal.App.4th 375, 378 (executor of deceased borrower's estate has standing to assert usury). A "personal representative" ordinarily is (1) an executor named in the will, (2) a successor to that executor, called an "administrator-with-the-will-annexed," or (3) an administrator when the decedent died without naming an executor. ***Estate of Hilton*** (2d Dist.1996) 44 Cal.App.4th 890, 894 n.1; *see* Prob. C. §58(a). Generally, an heir does not have standing to sue on behalf of the estate. ***Holland v. McCarthy*** (1918) 177 Cal. 507, 510; ***Olson***, 46 Cal.App.4th at 823-24. For a discussion of when an heir does have standing to sue, see 4 Witkin, *Cal. Procedure*, Pleading, §§135-136.

(6) Trustees & beneficiaries. A trustee has standing to enforce the rights of an express trust. CCP §369(a)(2); ***Saks***, 7 Cal.App.4th at 427; ***Powers v. Ashton*** (2d Dist.1975) 45 Cal.App.3d 783, 787; *see* Weil, *Civil Procedure Before Trial*, ¶2:6; 4 Witkin, *Cal. Procedure*, Pleading, §137. Generally, the action must be brought in the name of the trustee only. ***King v. Johnston*** (4th Dist.2009) 178 Cal.App.4th 1488, 1499-1500; *see* Prob. C. §17200(a); ***Tilton v. Reclamation Dist.*** (1st Dist.2006) 142 Cal.App.4th 848, 851 n.1. In some circumstances, however, the beneficiary of a trust has standing to sue another beneficiary, a third party, or the trustee on behalf of the trust. *See* Prob. C. §16420; ***King***, 178 Cal.App.4th at 1500; ***Wolf v. Mitchell, Silberberg & Knupp*** (2d Dist.1999) 76 Cal.App.4th 1030, 1036-37; ***Saks***, 7 Cal.App.4th at 427-28; Weil, *Civil Procedure Before Trial*, ¶¶2:6.6-2:6.7; 4 Witkin, *Cal. Procedure*, Pleading, §138; *see, e.g.*, ***Estate of Giraldin*** (2012) 55 Cal.4th 1058, 1062 (Ps, as remainder beneficiaries of decedent's revocable inter vivos trust, had standing to sue trustee for breach of fiduciary duty committed against settlor while settlor was alive and trust was revocable); ***Estate of Lowrie*** (2d Dist.2004) 118 Cal.App.4th 220, 231 (P, as beneficiary of decedent's trust, had standing to sue trustee for elder-abuse claim).

(7) Promisees & third-party beneficiaries. A promisee of a third-party beneficiary contract—that is, a person in whose name a contract is made for the benefit of another—has standing to enforce the contract. CCP §369(a)(3); 4 Witkin, *Cal. Procedure*, Pleading, §142; *see, e.g.*, ***Tandy v. Waesch*** (1908) 154 Cal. 108, 110 (P had standing to sue for recovery of purchase price for property when he entered into contract in his own name on behalf of third party). The third-party beneficiary also has standing to enforce the contract. Civ. C. §1559; Weil, *Civil Procedure Before Trial*, ¶2:34; 4 Witkin, *Cal. Procedure*, Pleading, §143; *see, e.g.*, ***Reliance Life Ins.***, 121 Cal.App.2d at 244 (child can enforce provisions of property settlement agreement made for his benefit in same manner as party to agreement).

(8) Assignees & assignors. An assignee of a cause of action has standing to sue on it. ***Reios v. Mardis*** (1st Dist.1912) 18 Cal.App. 276, 280; Weil, *Civil Procedure Before Trial*, ¶2:16; 4 Witkin, *Cal. Procedure*, Pleading, §127; *see, e.g.*, ***Timed Out, LLC v. Youabian, Inc.*** (2d Dist.2014) 229 Cal.App.4th 1001, 1009-10 (assignee of action for misappropriation of likeness had standing to sue when nonparties' images were used without their consent). If the assignee has received an assignment for collection purposes only, it has standing to sue on the assigned claim. ***Harrison v. Adams*** (1942) 20 Cal.2d 646, 650; ***Royal Co. Auctioneers, Inc. v. Coast Printing Equip. Co.*** (1st Dist.1987) 193 Cal.App.3d 868, 873. An assignment of a cause of action can be express or implied. *See* ***California Bank & Trust v. Piedmont Oper. Prtshp.*** (4th Dist.2013) 218 Cal.App.4th 1322, 1347 (assignment vests in assignee the assigned item and all related rights and remedies). If the assignee has received only a partial assignment, it has standing to sue on the assigned claim if it joins the assignor in the action. ***Cain v. State Farm Mut. Auto. Ins.*** (1st Dist.1975) 47 Cal.App.3d 783, 794-95. Likewise, if the assignor has assigned only a part of the claim, it has standing to sue on the claim if it joins the assignee in the action. *Id.* Once the assignor assigns the entire claim, it is no longer a real party in interest and does not have standing to sue. ***Johnson v. County of Fresno*** (5th Dist.2003) 111 Cal.App.4th 1087, 1096.

NOTE

Not all causes of action are assignable. A cause of action arising out of a right to recover money or property (e.g., a breach of contract) is generally assignable whereas a cause of action arising out of an injury of a purely personal nature (e.g., a personal-injury tort) is generally not assignable. See Civ. C. §§953, 954; ***Goodley v. Wank & Wank, Inc.*** *(2d Dist.1976) 62 Cal.App.3d 389, 393-94; see, e.g.,* ***White Mountains Reinsurance Co. v. Borton Petrini, LLP*** *(3d Dist.2013) 221 Cal.App.4th 890, 909 (P-insurance company had standing despite rule against assignment of legal-malpractice claims because assignment was part of larger commercial transfer between companies).*

(9) Subrogees & subrogors. A subrogee has standing to enforce the rights of the subrogor. *See* Weil, *Civil Procedure Before Trial*, ¶¶2:28-2:31.2; 4 Witkin, *Cal. Procedure*, Pleading, §132; *see, e.g.*, ***Offer v. Superior Ct.*** (1924) 194 Cal. 114, 121 (in personal-injury action involving insured, real party in interest includes insurer-subrogee who has paid insured for its loss). For a discussion of the problems associated with a subrogee's and subrogor's right to sue when the subrogation is only partial, see ***Hodge v. Kirkpatrick Dev., Inc.*** (4th Dist.2005) 130 Cal.App.4th 540, 550-51, and 4 Witkin, *Cal. Procedure*, Pleading, §133.

2. Persons authorized by statute. A plaintiff has standing if its right to sue is authorized by statute. *See* CCP §§367, 369(a)(4); 4 Witkin, *Cal. Procedure*, Pleading, §144; *see, e.g.*, CCP §376(a) (in action for personal injury to child, parents have standing to sue), §377.60 (in action for wrongful death, surviving spouse, domestic partner, children, grandchildren, and other dependents have standing to sue); ***Kwikset Corp. v. Superior Ct.*** (2011) 51 Cal.4th 310, 320-21 (in unfair-competition and false-advertising actions, standing is limited by statute to those who have lost money or property as result of alleged misconduct). *See generally* 4 Witkin, *Cal. Procedure*, Pleading, §§145-172 (discussing types of plaintiffs authorized by statute to sue). Whether the plaintiff is also a real party in interest is not relevant to the question of statutory standing. ***IBM Pers. Pension Plan v. City & Cty. of S.F.*** (1st Dist.2005) 131 Cal.App.4th 1291, 1301-02; ***Black Rock Placer Mining Dist. v. Summit Water & Irrigation Co.*** (3d Dist.1943) 56 Cal.App.2d 513, 517.

§2.2 Capacity. Capacity is a person's ability to file (or defend) a suit. *See* ***Color-Vue, Inc. v. Abrams*** (2d Dist.1996) 44 Cal.App.4th 1599, 1604; ***American Alt. Energy Partners II v. Windridge, Inc.*** (5th Dist.1996) 42 Cal.App.4th 551, 559; *see, e.g.*, 11 U.S.C. §323(b) (trustee of bankrupt's estate has capacity to sue and be sued). In general, any person or entity, including "artificial persons" such as corporations, partnerships, and associations, has capacity to file suit. ***American Alt. Energy***, 42 Cal.App.4th at 559. A party lacks capacity to sue if it suffers from a general disability, such as infancy, insanity, or some defect in how it has sued. ***Klopstock v. Superior Ct.*** (1941) 17 Cal.2d 13, 18; ***Hudis v. Crawford*** (6th Dist.2005) 125 Cal.App.4th 1586, 1592; *see, e.g.*, ***Color-Vue, Inc.***, 44 Cal.App.4th at 1603-04 (corporation whose powers have been suspended for nonpayment of taxes lacks capacity to sue); ***O'Flaherty v. Belgum*** (2d Dist.2004) 115 Cal.App.4th 1044, 1095 (Grignon, P.J., dissenting) (estate or trust is not legal entity and thus has no capacity to sue). Unlike an objection to standing, an objection to capacity can be waived. *See* ***American Alt. Energy***, 42 Cal.App.4th at 559.

NOTE

Distinguishing between standing and capacity is sometimes difficult. See, e.g., ***American Alt. Energy***, *42 Cal.App.4th at 559 (parties incorrectly stated issue in terms of standing instead of capacity);* ***Pillsbury v. Karmgard*** *(4th Dist.1994) 22 Cal.App.4th 743, 757 (P characterized issue in terms of capacity instead of standing). A person has standing if she is personally aggrieved, regardless of whether she has legal authority to act; a person has capacity if she has the authority to file suit, regardless of whether she has a beneficial interest in the suit. See*

***Pillsbury**, 22 Cal.App.4th at 757 n.15. Another way of looking at the distinction is this: when a party has an interest in a suit but needs a surrogate to bring or defend it, the party does not have capacity. For example, capacity is a problem for a minor who attempts to file suit. Even though the minor has an interest in the suit, it must be filed by a proper representative. See CCP §372(a); **Westphal v. Arnoux** (1st Dist.1921) 51 Cal.App. 532, 536.*

§2.3 Pleading. The complaint must establish both (1) the plaintiff's standing and capacity to sue and (2) the defendant's capacity to be sued. *See* 5 Witkin, *Cal. Procedure*, Pleading, §§907, 908. The complaint's caption and allegations of fact determine the identities of the parties. ***Plumlee v. Poag*** (2d Dist.1984) 150 Cal.App.3d 541, 547; ***Miller v. Superior Ct.*** (2d Dist.1914) 26 Cal.App. 41, 44.

1. Caption. In the caption, the plaintiff should indicate both the capacity in which it is suing and the capacity in which the defendant is being sued. *See* 5 Witkin, *Cal. Procedure*, Pleading, §907 (capacity is usually established by correct designation of party in caption). For example, if the plaintiff is a corporation, the caption should state "ABC Company, a corporation." If the plaintiff is suing in a representative capacity, the caption should also include the word "as," or else the terms used after the party's name may be treated as merely descriptive of the person rather than the capacity in which she is suing (i.e., "descriptio personae"). ***Burling v. Thompkins*** (1888) 77 Cal. 257, 258. For example, if the plaintiff is an heir to a decedent and is suing for wrongful death, the plaintiff should identify herself as "{*name of plaintiff*}, as heir-at-law." *See* ***Peterson v. John Crane, Inc.*** (1st Dist.2007) 154 Cal.App.4th 498, 507. However, a mistake in the caption is not fatal to the suit if the body of the complaint alleges facts showing the party's capacity. ***Owens v. Dudley*** (1912) 162 Cal. 422, 425; *e.g.*, ***Carr v. Carr*** (3d Dist.1911) 15 Cal.App. 480, 482-83 (P's omission of "as" in caption was not defective because allegations in complaint showed P was suing as administrator of estate). The following are designations of some of the most common types of parties:

(1) Individual. A party suing or being sued in an individual capacity should be identified by name only. *See* CCP §422.40. When the party is suing or being sued in more than one capacity, her capacity as an individual should be designated as follows: "{*name of party*}, individually and {*other capacity, e.g., as trustee*}." *See, e.g.*, ***Alexander v. Superior Ct.*** (6th Dist.2003) 114 Cal.App.4th 723, 725 (Ds were sued in individual capacities and as d/b/a's); *see also* ***Holman v. County of Santa Cruz*** (1st Dist.1949) 91 Cal.App.2d 502, 513 (if judgment is sought against official in individual capacity, she should be designated as such).

(2) Minor or incompetent. A minor or person who lacks the legal capacity to make decisions should be designated as follows: "{*name of party*}, a {*minor/person who lacks the legal capacity to make decisions*}, by {*name of guardian*}, {*his/her*} {*guardian/guardian ad litem*}." *See* CCP §372(a); ***Siegal v. Superior Ct.*** (2d Dist.1962) 203 Cal.App.2d 22, 24-25; 4 Witkin, *Cal. Procedure*, Pleading, §72; *see also* ***Loock v. Pioneer Title Ins. & Trust Co.*** (4th Dist.1935) 4 Cal.App.2d 245, 248 (action brought on behalf of minor who has general guardian must be brought in name of minor by guardian). If the guardian is unknown (e.g., when the minor is being sued), the designation should simply be "{*name of party*}, a {*minor/person who lacks the legal capacity to make decisions*}." *See CEB Procedure Before Trial*, §14.6; 4 Witkin, *Cal. Procedure*, Pleading, §72. The body of the complaint should allege facts showing the guardian's ability to conduct the litigation on the ward's behalf. *See, e.g.*, ***Campbell v. Jewish Cmte. for Personal Serv.*** (1st Dist.1954) 125 Cal.App.2d 771, 774 (complaint was defective on face because P did not allege he had been appointed guardian or had authority to sue on behalf of brother, who was real party in interest).

(3) Corporation. A corporation suing or being sued can be identified by name only. *CEB Procedure Before Trial*, §14.20; *see* ***Craig v. San Fernando Furniture Co.*** (2d Dist.1928) 89 Cal.App. 167, 171; *see, e.g.*, ***Meller & Snyder v. R&T Props., Inc.*** (2d Dist.1998) 62 Cal.App.4th 1303, 1310-11 (complaint against "Robert Tieger, individually and doing business as R&T Properties" did not assert claim against R&T Properties, Inc.); *see also* Corp. C. §207 (corporation has all powers of natural person). It is not necessary to allege facts in the body of the complaint demonstrating the corporation's capacity. ***Craig***, 89 Cal.App. at 171; *see* ***Los Angeles Ry. v. Davis*** (1905) 146 Cal. 179, 180-81; 5 Witkin, *Cal. Procedure*, Pleading, §899. However, there are several practical considerations that should be taken into account before omitting both the designation in the caption and the allegations in the body of the

complaint. *See generally* Weil, *Civil Procedure Before Trial*, ¶¶6:49-6:64 (discussing arguments for identifying corporation's capacity). For example, if there is a possibility that a default judgment against a corporate defendant could be entered, the plaintiff will have to designate the party's capacity and make the appropriate allegations. *See* ***Earl W. Schott, Inc. v. Kalar*** (5th Dist.1993) 20 Cal.App.4th 943, 946; Weil, *Civil Procedure Before Trial*, ¶¶6:55, 6:59.

NOTE

Although corporations have standing to sue or be sued, they must usually appear in court through an attorney. ***Merco Constr. Eng'rs, Inc. v. Municipal Ct.*** *(1978) 21 Cal.3d 724, 729-30;* ***Gamet v. Blanchard*** *(4th Dist.2001) 91 Cal.App.4th 1276, 1284 n.5. For small-claims cases, however, a corporation can appear through an officer, director, or employee. CCP §116.540(b); see* ***Merco Constr. Eng'rs****, 21 Cal.3d at 730.*

(4) Partnership or unincorporated association. A partnership or unincorporated association suing or being sued should be identified by the name it has assumed or the name by which it is known. CCP §369.5(a); ***American Alt. Energy Partners II v. Windridge, Inc.*** (5th Dist.1996) 42 Cal.App.4th 551, 559; *see* 5 Witkin, *Cal. Procedure*, Pleading, §901; *see also* Bus. & Prof. C. §17918 (partnership or association operating under fictitious business name must file statement of fictitious business name before it can maintain suit on account or contract); ***Barr v. United Methodist Ch.*** (4th Dist.1979) 90 Cal.App.3d 259, 266 (unincorporated associations include many groups, such as labor unions, political parties, social clubs, religious organizations, environmental societies, athletic organizations, condominium owners, lodges, stock exchanges, and veterans). If desired, the plaintiff can indicate in the caption that it is "a partnership" or "an unincorporated association," but it should refrain from adding such a designation for a defendant-partnership or association. *See CEB Procedure Before Trial*, §§14.18, 14.19. *But see* Weil, *Civil Procedure Before Trial*, ¶¶6:60, 6:68.3 (suggesting that when status of business entity is unknown, P should sue D in every plausible capacity). The partnership or unincorporated association is not considered a defendant to the suit if only the members are named as defendants or if they are individually named as "copartners doing business under the firm name of" or given a similar designation. 4 Witkin, *Cal. Procedure*, Pleading, §99; *see* ***Hildebrand v. Stonecrest Corp.*** (1st Dist.1959) 174 Cal.App.2d 158, 169; ***Ferry v. North Pac. Stages*** (3d Dist.1931) 112 Cal.App. 348, 351; *CEB Procedure Before Trial*, §14.19. For a partnership or association to be made a party, it must be specifically named. ***Ferry***, 112 Cal.App. at 351. To sue both the partnership or association and its individual members, the plaintiff should designate each defendant's capacity separately. *See* 4 Witkin, *Cal. Procedure*, Pleading, §99; *see, e.g.*, ***Nelson v. East Side Grocery Co.*** (1st Dist.1915) 26 Cal.App. 344, 347 (even though caption only named association as defendant, body of complaint and prayer clearly indicated individual members were also defendants); *see also* CCP §369.5(b) (member of partnership or unincorporated association may be joined as party in action against partnership or association).

NOTE

Although unincorporated associations have standing to sue or be sued, they must usually appear in court through an attorney. ***Clean Air Transp. Sys. v. San Mateo Cty. Transit Dist.*** *(1st Dist.1988) 198 Cal.App.3d 576, 578-79.*

(5) Representative.

(a) Personal. A person suing or being sued as a personal representative must be identified by its representative capacity: "{*name of party*}, as {*executor/administrator*} of the {*will/estate*} of {*name of decedent*}, deceased." *See* 5 Witkin, *Cal. Procedure*, Pleading, §902. Although it is not necessary to allege facts in the body of the complaint showing the party's capacity, the common practice is to do so. *See* ***Grisingher v. Shaeffer*** (2d Dist.1938) 25 Cal.App.2d 5, 9 (in action against personal representative, P does not have to allege facts showing how D obtained representative capacity, only that D is executor or administrator); *see, e.g.*, ***Plumlee***, 150 Cal.App.3d at 546-47 (although caption seemed to indicate Ds were being sued as individuals, body of complaint established that D1 and D2 were sued as executors and D3 was sued as administrator-with-will-annexed).

(b) Other. A person suing or being sued in a representative capacity (e.g., as a receiver) must be identified by that capacity: "{*name of party*}, as {*identify capacity, e.g.*, Receiver for Jones Bros., a partnership *or* Trustee of the Jones Family Trust}." *See* Weil, *Civil Procedure Before Trial*, ¶6:75. The body of the complaint should allege facts sufficient to show the party's representative capacity. ***Sealite, Inc. v. Finster*** (1st Dist.1957) 149 Cal.App.2d 612, 618.

(6) Public official. A person suing or being sued in her capacity as a public official must be identified by that capacity: "{*name of public official*}, as {*official designation, e.g.*, Director of Agriculture of the State of California}." *See* ***Boland v. Cecil*** (Los Angeles Cty. Superior Ct. Appellate Dept. 1944) 65 Cal.App.2d Supp. 832, 840; *see also* Gov. C. §11180 (authorizing head of Department of State to bring suit). The plaintiff should allege in the body of the complaint a cause of action against the defendant in her official capacity. *See* ***Owens***, 162 Cal. at 425; ***Reed v. Molony*** (3d Dist.1940) 38 Cal.App.2d 405, 411.

(7) Fictitious name.

15 **(a) Doe plaintiffs.** A plaintiff may be able to sue under a fictitious name when the plaintiff's need for anonymity outweighs both the prejudice to the opposing party and the public's interest in knowing the plaintiff's identity. ***Doe v. Lincoln Unified Sch. Dist.*** (1st Dist.2010) 188 Cal.App.4th 758, 766-67; ***Starbucks Corp. v. Superior Ct.*** (4th Dist.2008) 168 Cal.App.4th 1436, 1452 n.7; *see, e.g.*, Civ. C. §1708.85(f)(1) (P can sue under fictitious name in suit for wrongful distribution of private sexual material); ***Doe v. Roe*** (1st Dist.1990) 218 Cal.App.3d 1538, 1541 n.1 (parties with herpes allowed to proceed anonymously by stipulation and court order). For example, a plaintiff might need to remain anonymous when (1) identification would create a risk of retaliatory physical or mental harm, (2) anonymity is necessary to protect privacy in a sensitive and highly personal matter, or (3) the plaintiff is compelled to admit an intention to engage in illegal conduct. ***Lincoln Unified Sch. Dist.***, 188 Cal.App.4th at 767; *see, e.g.*, ***Doe v. Superior Ct.*** (2d Dist.2011) 194 Cal.App.4th 750, 752-53 (rape victim allowed to proceed anonymously in her civil suit).

(b) Doe defendants. A plaintiff can sue a defendant under a fictitious name (e.g., "John Doe") when the plaintiff is unaware of either the defendant's name or the defendant's connection to the case. *See* CCP §474. When the plaintiff is suing a fictitious defendant, it should designate the defendant simply as "Doe One." *See* ***Dieckmann v. Superior Ct.*** (2d Dist.1985) 175 Cal.App.3d 345, 354 (use of "Doe" to indicate D is fictitiously named has become uniform practice). If there is more than one fictitious defendant, the plaintiff should designate them as, for example, "Does One through Five, inclusive." *See* ***Carol Gilbert, Inc. v. Haller*** (6th Dist.2009) 179 Cal.App.4th 852, 855. The plaintiff should allege in the body of the complaint that "Defendants Doe One through Five, inclusive, are sued according to California CCP §474," and that one or more of the defendants are liable to the plaintiff. *See* ***Winding Creek v. McGlashan*** (1st Dist.1996) 44 Cal.App.4th 933, 941; ***Motor City Sales v. Superior Ct.*** (5th Dist.1973) 31 Cal.App.3d 342, 347.

NOTE

*A plaintiff may choose to sue a defendant under a fictitious name for several reasons, most commonly to file suit within the limitations period for bringing a cause of action against the unknown defendant. See **Fuller v. Tucker** (2d Dist.2000) 84 Cal.App.4th 1163, 1171-72.*

[1] When permitted. The plaintiff can use a fictitious name for one or more defendants in the complaint in either of the following situations:

[a] Identity unknown. The plaintiff can sue a defendant under a fictitious name if the plaintiff is actually unaware of the defendant's real name. CCP §474; ***Fuller***, 84 Cal.App.4th at 1170. The plaintiff can rely on §474 even if it did not use reasonable diligence to discover the defendant's real name. ***Fuller***, 84 Cal.App.4th at 1170.

CAUTION

It is not clear whether a plaintiff can use a fictitious name for a public entity sued under the Government Claims Act. One court, in dicta, has stated that a plaintiff cannot because if the plaintiff did not know the identity of the public entity being sued, the plaintiff could not have timely presented the claim to the entity, and thus the action would be barred. See ***Olden v. Hatchell*** *(1st Dist.1984) 154 Cal.App.3d 1032, 1036-37. Another court, however, disagreed with* ***Olden****, finding that a plaintiff could use a fictitious name when the plaintiff "fortuitously" presents her claim to the appropriate entity and is otherwise ignorant of the defendant's true identity when she does so. See* ***Carlino v. Los Angeles Cty. Flood Control Dist.*** *(2d Dist.1992) 10 Cal.App.4th 1526, 1536.*

[b] Connection unknown. The plaintiff can sue a defendant under a fictitious name if the plaintiff does not know how the defendant is connected to the facts giving rise to the plaintiff's cause of action. ***General Motors Corp. v. Superior Ct.*** (2d Dist.1996) 48 Cal.App.4th 580, 593-94; ***Wallis v. Southern Pac. Transp.*** (1st Dist.1976) 61 Cal.App.3d 782, 786. Whether the plaintiff can sue a defendant by a fictitious name under this theory is based solely on what the plaintiff actually knew when the suit was filed, not what the plaintiff could have discovered before filing the suit. ***McOwen v. Grossman*** (2d Dist.2007) 153 Cal.App.4th 937, 942; ***Fuller***, 84 Cal.App.4th at 1170. Because the plaintiff is still required to state a cause of action against each Doe defendant named in the complaint, the fictitious name is essentially used as a placeholder for defendants whose actual identities or whose connection to the cause of action will be discovered later. *See* ***Fireman's Fund Ins. v. Sparks Constr., Inc.*** (4th Dist.2004) 114 Cal.App.4th 1135, 1143; ***General Motors***, 48 Cal.App.4th at 594-95; *see, e.g.*, ***Parker v. Robert E. McKee, Inc.*** (2d Dist.1992) 3 Cal.App.4th 512, 518 (P knew D's identity when complaint was filed for personal injury during construction project, but did not know of D's legal capacity as general contractor).

[2] Identifying defendant. Once a defendant has been sued under a fictitious name, the plaintiff has three years from the date of filing to identify and serve that defendant. *See* CCP §§474, 583.210. When the defendant has been identified, the plaintiff must amend the complaint (and any later pleadings) to include the defendant's actual name. CCP §474; *see* ***Carol Gilbert, Inc.***, 179 Cal.App.4th at 856. The amended complaint must specifically state that the named defendant is being substituted for the fictitious Doe defendant. *See* ***Woo v. Superior Ct.*** (4th Dist.1999) 75 Cal.App.4th 169, 176. See "Naming Doe defendant," §6.4, p. 236. After the complaint has been amended, it must be served on the defendant with a summons that contains a §474 notice. *See* CCP §471.5; ***Carol Gilbert, Inc.***, 179 Cal.App.4th at 859. See "Joining the Defendant—Service of Process," ch. 3-H, p. 295.

2. Body of complaint. In the body of the complaint, the plaintiff must allege a cause of action establishing that the plaintiff either is entitled to relief itself or has a right to bring suit on behalf of someone who is. *See* 5 Witkin, *Cal. Procedure*, Pleading, §908; *see, e.g.*, ***Aron v. U-Haul Co.*** (2d Dist.2006) 143 Cal.App.4th 796, 802-03 (P had standing to sue for unfair competition because he alleged facts supporting each element of claim under Bus. & Prof. C. §17204); ***Armijo v. Miles*** (2d Dist.2005) 127 Cal.App.4th 1405, 1421-22 (P had standing to sue for wrongful death because she alleged facts supporting each element of standing under former Fam. C. §297(b)); ***County of L.A. v. Ferguson*** (2d Dist.1979) 94 Cal.App.3d 549, 557-58 (county did not have standing to sue for child support on behalf of minor child because county did not allege it was providing public assistance to child); ***Black Rock Placer Mining Dist. v. Summit Water & Irrigation Co.*** (3d Dist.1943) 56 Cal.App.2d 513, 516-17 (P did not have standing to seek condemnation of property through eminent domain because P did not allege facts showing suit was brought by person authorized by statute).

§3. CONTENTS & FORMAT OF COMPLAINT

The complaint must comply with the content and formatting requirements of the California Rules of Court. *See* CRC 2.100-2.141. See "General Requirements for Papers," ch. 1-B, §2, p. 9.

§3.1 Civil case cover sheet. Judicial Council Form CM-010 ("Civil Case Cover Sheet") must be filed with every complaint except complaints filed in small-claims court or filed under the Probate Code, Family Law Code, or Welfare and Institutions Code. CRC 3.220(b)(1).

1. Unlimited or limited. The plaintiff must designate on the cover sheet whether the case is unlimited or limited. Judicial Council Forms, form CM-010. See "Unlimited cases," ch. 3-E, §4.2.1, p. 257; "Limited cases," ch. 3-E, §4.2.2, p. 258.

2. Type of case. The plaintiff must designate on the cover sheet the type of case involved. Judicial Council Forms, form CM-010.

(1) Collections case. If the plaintiff checks the box on the cover sheet indicating that the case is a collections case, the cover sheet must be served on the defendant with the initial complaint. CRC 3.220(a), 3.740(b). A collections case is an action to recover money owed in a sum certain of not more than $25,000 that arises from a transaction in which property, services, or money was acquired on credit. CRC 3.740(a).

(2) Complex case. If the plaintiff checks the box on the cover sheet indicating that the case is a complex case, a copy of the cover sheet must be served on the defendant with the initial complaint. CRC 3.220(a). A complex case is an action requiring exceptional judicial management to (1) avoid putting unnecessary burdens on the court or parties and (2) expedite the case, keep costs reasonable, and promote effective decision-making. CRC 3.400(a).

(a) General factors. In deciding whether a case is complex, the plaintiff should consider if the case is likely to involve any of the following:

[1] Numerous pretrial motions raising difficult or novel legal issues that will be time consuming to resolve. CRC 3.400(b)(1).

[2] Management of a large number of witnesses or a substantial amount of documentary evidence. CRC 3.400(b)(2).

[3] Management of a large number of separately represented parties. CRC 3.400(b)(3).

[4] Coordination with related actions pending in one or more courts in other counties, states, or countries, or in a federal court. CRC 3.400(b)(4).

[5] Substantial postjudgment judicial supervision. CRC 3.400(b)(5).

(b) Cases provisionally designated as complex. In some cases, the plaintiff must check the box on the cover sheet indicating that the case is complex because the case has been predetermined to be complex. In this situation, the case is only provisionally complex; the court will make a final determination of whether the case is complex after the complaint is filed. See "Assignment to Case-Management Plan," ch. 5-A, §5, p. 464.

[1] California Rules of Court. Under the California Rules of Court, the following cases are provisionally complex unless the court declares otherwise under CRC 3.400(d):

[a] Antitrust or trade-regulation claims. CRC 3.400(c)(1).

[b] Construction-defect claims involving many parties or structures. CRC 3.400(c)(2).

[c] Securities claims or investment losses involving many parties. CRC 3.400(c)(3).

[d] Environmental or toxic-tort claims involving many parties. CRC 3.400(c)(4).

[e] Claims involving mass torts. CRC 3.400(c)(5).

[f] Claims involving class actions. CRC 3.400(c)(6).

[g] Insurance-coverage claims arising from any of the claims listed in [a] through [f] above. CRC 3.400(c)(7).

ORIGINAL COMPLAINT

[2] **Local rules.** The court can declare types of cases provisionally complex or not provisionally complex by local rule. CRC 3.400(d).

3. **Remedies sought.** The plaintiff must designate on the cover sheet the remedies it is seeking. Judicial Council Forms, form CM-010.

4. **Number of causes of action.** The plaintiff must designate on the cover sheet the number of causes of action being asserted. Judicial Council Forms, form CM-010. See "Determining cause of action," §3.6.1, p. 215.

5. **Class action.** The plaintiff must designate on the cover sheet whether the case is a class action. Judicial Council Forms, form CM-010.

6. **Related cases.** The cover sheet includes an instruction to plaintiffs who know of any related cases to file and serve a notice of related case. Judicial Council Forms, form CM-010; *see* CRC 3.300(b) (if party knows of related case, party has duty to file and serve notice of related case). The plaintiff can use Judicial Council Form CM-015 to do so. Judicial Council Forms, form CM-010. See "Relating Cases," ch. 5-H, §3, p. 520.

§3.2 First page.

1. **Attorney information.** The first page of the complaint must include information about the plaintiff's attorney or the plaintiff herself, if she is appearing in propria persona. See "Attorney or party information," ch. 1-B, §2.5.2(1), p. 12.

2. **Clerk's space.** The first page of the complaint must leave a blank space for the clerk's use. See "Clerk's space," ch. 1-B, §2.5.2(2), p. 12.

3. **Caption.** The first page of the complaint must include a caption. *See* CCP §422.30.

(1) **Court & county.** The caption must identify the court and county where the action is filed. CCP §422.30(a)(1). See "Title of court," ch. 1-B, §2.5.2(3), p. 12.

(2) **Title of action.** The caption must include a title of the action. CCP §422.30(a)(2). See "Title of case," ch. 1-B, §2.5.2(4), p. 12.

(a) **Parties' names.** The title of the action must include each party's full name. CCP §422.40; ***Elling Corp. v. Superior Ct.*** (2d Dist.1975) 48 Cal.App.3d 89, 94.

NOTE

Simply identifying the defendant in the caption is not enough. The plaintiff must ensure that the defendant or defendants against whom each theory of liability is alleged are specifically named in the body of the complaint. See ***Davaloo v. State Farm Ins.*** *(2d Dist.2005) 135 Cal.App.4th 409, 418-19 (allegations in complaint, not caption, state cause of action against D);* ***Falahati v. Shinji Kondo*** *(2d Dist.2005) 127 Cal.App.4th 823, 829 (boilerplate allegation against all Ds is not effective against particular D because caption is not part of statement of cause of action). But see* ***Hawley Bros. Hardware Co. v. Brownstone*** *(1899) 123 Cal. 643, 646 (allegation against Ds named in caption as group would be sufficient identification). See "Body of complaint," §2.3.2, p. 210.*

[1] **Assumed name.** A party can sue and be sued under its assumed name—that is, any name by which it is known or recognized. ***Emery v. Kipp*** (1908) 154 Cal. 83, 86; ***Cabrera v. McMullen*** (3d Dist.1988) 204 Cal.App.3d 1, 4; *see* CCP §369.5(a); ***Hurt v. Haering*** (1922) 190 Cal. 198, 201; ***American Alt. Energy Partners II v. Windridge, Inc.*** (5th Dist.1996) 42 Cal.App.4th 551, 559.

[2] **Omitted name.** A defendant whose name is omitted from the title of the action is a party when the complaint is filed if the body of the complaint specifically alleges the defendant to be liable to the plain-

tiff in some way. *See* ***Bell v. Tri-City Hosp. Dist.*** (4th Dist.1987) 196 Cal.App.3d 438, 445-46, *disapproved on other grounds*, ***State v. Superior Ct.*** (2004) 32 Cal.4th 1234; *see, e.g.*, ***Nelson v. East Side Grocery Co.*** (1st Dist.1915) 26 Cal.App. 344, 347 (even though caption only named association as D, body of complaint and prayer clearly indicated individual members were also Ds). If the complaint does not allege that the defendant is liable, the defendant becomes a party when it is properly designated in an amended complaint. *See, e.g.*, ***Ard v. County of Contra Costa*** (1st Dist.2001) 93 Cal.App.4th 339, 346 (trial court dismissed P's suit because D-county, which was not designated in caption or body of initial complaint, did not become party until it was added by amended complaint filed after Government Claims Act deadline).

[3] Misspelled name. A misspelled name is sufficient identification of a party if the party's identity can be ascertained. For example, under the rule of idem sonans (Latin for "sounding the same"), a misspelled name is sufficient identification if it sounds practically the same as the correct name. *See, e.g.*, ***Galliano v. Kilfoy*** (1892) 94 Cal. 86, 88-89 (under idem sonans, default judgment against "Rosa Kilfoy" was valid although return of service was made on "Rose Kilfoy"); ***Seaver v. Fitzgerald*** (1863) 23 Cal. 86, 92 (default judgment against "D.C. Seaver" based on publication of summons designating D as "D.C. Seavers" was valid because names were substantially the same).

[4] Misnomer. If a plaintiff sues and serves the correct defendant but misnames the defendant, the error is misnomer. *See* ***Brookview Condo. Owners' Ass'n v. Heltzer Enters.-Brookview*** (4th Dist.1990) 218 Cal.App.3d 502, 511 n.7; *see, e.g.*, ***Billings v. Edwards*** (2d Dist.1979) 91 Cal.App.3d 826, 830-31 (misnomer when P served "John Edwards Pest Control" rather than "Edwards and Son Pest Control" and "Bryant Exterminators" rather than "Bryant Exterminating Co." because correct corporate officers of entities were timely served); ***Canifax v. Hercules Powder Co.*** (3d Dist.1965) 237 Cal.App.2d 44, 56-57 (misnomer when correct D, "Coast Manufacturing and Supply Company," was served, but P identified D as "Coast Equipment Company" in complaint); ***Thompson v. Palmer Corp.*** (2d Dist.1956) 138 Cal.App.2d 387, 396 (original complaint designating "R.C. Tucker, Jr., D.D. Rohrbaugh, R.C. Tucker, Sr., David Ritchie, and Jack Alber as individuals doing business as Bob 'N Del" was not misnomer of "Bob 'N Del, a corporation"). The plaintiff has the burden of pleading misnomer and seeking leave to file an amended complaint. *See* CCP §473; ***Thompson***, 138 Cal.App.2d at 390. See "Amending the Complaint," §6, p. 228. A misnomer can be corrected by amendment even after the statute of limitations expires. ***Mayberry v. Coca Cola Bottling Co.*** (3d Dist.1966) 244 Cal.App.2d 350, 352; *see* CCP §473(a)(1); ***Hawkins v. Pacific Coast Bldg. Prods.*** (3d Dist.2004) 124 Cal.App.4th 1497, 1504.

[5] Misidentification. If the plaintiff sues and serves a party that does not have an interest in the suit, the error is misidentification. *See* ***Stephens v. Berry*** (1st Dist.1967) 249 Cal.App.2d 474, 478-79. Misidentification occurs when there are two separate individuals or legal entities with similar names, and the plaintiff sues the wrong one. *See, e.g.*, ***Mayberry***, 244 Cal.App.2d at 351 (P sued "Coca Cola Bottling Company of Sacramento, Ltd." when it should have sued "Coca Cola Bottling Company of Sacramento, a partnership"). Once the limitations period has run, a misidentification can be corrected if the plaintiff shows (1) there were two separate entities, (2) the attorney for the incorrect entity either represented or knew who the correct entity was, (3) the attorney's conduct in some way concealed the limitations problem, and (4) the correct entity was not misled or disadvantaged (i.e., prejudiced) by the mistake. *See* ***Kleinecke v. Montecito Water Dist.*** (2d Dist.1983) 147 Cal.App.3d 240, 245-47; ***Mayberry***, 244 Cal.App.2d at 352-53. *But see* ***Wright v. Redwood Theatres, Inc.*** (3d Dist.1942) 49 Cal.App.2d 403, 408-09 (equitable-estoppel defense based on claim that D's attorney "allowed" P to believe she sued correct party was denied because attorney is under no obligation to inform P that it has sued wrong party).

(b) Party's capacity. The title of the action should identify the capacity in which each party is suing or being sued. If a party's capacity is not properly designated, the allegations contained in the body of the complaint can be reviewed to determine the proper capacity. *See, e.g.*, ***St. Mary's Hosp. v. Perry*** (1907) 152 Cal. 338, 340 (title of action indicated D was sued "as executrix," but allegations in body of complaint showed suit was brought

against D as individual); ***Carr v. Carr*** (3d Dist.1911) 15 Cal.App. 480, 482-83 (title of action did not indicate P was suing "as administrator" of decedent's estate, but allegations in body of complaint showed suit was brought in that capacity); *see also* ***Reed v. Molony*** (3d Dist.1940) 38 Cal.App.2d 405, 411 (whether D is sued in individual or official capacity is determined from allegations in pleadings). For a discussion of capacity designations, see "Caption," §2.3.1, p. 207.

(c) Nature of paper & character of action. The title of the action should identify the nature of the paper and the character of the action being filed—that is, some indication of the primary right at issue and the form of relief sought. *See* CRC 2.111(6); *see, e.g.*, ***Sacramento & San Joaquin Drainage Dist. v. Superior Ct.*** (1925) 196 Cal. 414, 421 (complaint titled "Complaint to quiet title and for injunction"); ***United Food & Commercial Workers Un. v. Superior Ct.*** (2d Dist.2000) 83 Cal.App.4th 566, 571 n.4 (complaint titled "Verified Complaint for Temporary Restraining Order and Preliminary and Permanent Injunctions and Damages"). Even though the title is not part of the plaintiff's allegations in support of a cause of action, the title is helpful to the court in understanding the basis of the plaintiff's suit. ***United Food***, 83 Cal.App.4th at 571 n.4.

[1] Limited civil case. If the action is a limited civil case, the title must specifically say so. CCP §422.30(b).

[2] Defective title. A defective title will not invalidate the complaint if it intelligibly refers to the action or proceeding. CCP §1046; *e.g.*, ***In re McGrew*** (1920) 183 Cal. 177, 181-82 (pleading was sufficient when complaint in independent action to invalidate adoption was titled as if it were petition for relief from default judgment under CCP §473).

§3.3 Statement of venue. The complaint does not have to include a separate statement of facts supporting venue unless the action is for unlawful detainer, based on certain installment sales, or for a limited civil case for goods or services. *See* Civ. C. §§1812.10, 2984.4; CCP §§395(b), 396(a); *see also* ***Saito v. Policy Holders Life Ins.*** (3d Dist.1933) 132 Cal.App. 412, 414-15 (P need only plead cause of action in ordinary and concise language, not evidentiary or jurisdictional facts); Weil, *Civil Procedure Before Trial*, ¶6:98 (venue allegations are not required). Instead, venue will be determined based on the facts alleged in the body of the complaint because proper venue is determined based on the "main relief" requested. See "Determine essential character of each cause of action," ch. 3-F, §2.2, p. 271 (discussing main-relief rule). Thus, the plaintiff must ensure that the allegations supporting each cause of action are carefully drafted. *See, e.g.*, ***M.H. Golden Constr. Co. v. Superior Ct.*** (4th Dist.1950) 98 Cal.App.2d 811, 814 (P pleaded facts in complaint sufficient to show that main relief was transitory in character, and P was entitled to retain action in county where it was commenced).

§3.4 Statement of jurisdiction. The complaint does not have to include a separate statement of facts supporting subject-matter jurisdiction. *See* ***Cheney v. Trauzettel*** (1937) 9 Cal.2d 158, 160. Instead, jurisdiction will be determined based on the facts alleged in the body of the complaint because subject-matter jurisdiction is determined based on the sufficiency of the cause of action pleaded or relief requested. *See* CCP §430.10(a). See "Defect appears on face of complaint," ch. 4-D, §3.1, p. 356. If the plaintiff was required to perform certain conditions precedent to bringing the suit, such as exhausting all administrative remedies, it should specifically plead facts showing those conditions were met. *See, e.g.*, ***Hood v. Hacienda La Puente Unified Sch. Dist.*** (2d Dist.1998) 65 Cal.App.4th 435, 439-40 (in whistleblower suit under Gov. C. §8547.8, P must allege it pursued administrative remedies as prerequisite to commencing action); ***Richmond v. Frederick*** (1st Dist.1953) 116 Cal.App.2d 541, 543 (in suit on open account, complaint alleged jurisdictional facts including filing and rejection of claim).

§3.5 Statement of personal jurisdiction. If the defendant is a nonresident, the plaintiff must allege facts establishing that the defendant is subject to personal jurisdiction in California. *See* ***In re Automobile Antitrust Cases I & II*** (1st Dist.2005) 135 Cal.App.4th 100, 110. See "Joining the Defendant—Personal Jurisdiction," ch. 3-G, p. 283.

§3.6 Body of complaint. The complaint must include a statement of facts constituting one or more causes of action. CCP §425.10(a)(1). This is usually referred to as the "body of the complaint." *See, e.g.*, ***Davaloo v. State Farm Ins.*** (2d Dist.2005) 135 Cal.App.4th 409, 418 (allegations in body of complaint, not caption, constitute cause of action against D).

1. Determining cause of action.

(1) Primary-right theory. Whether a given set of facts constitutes a cause of action is determined by the "primary-right theory." *See* ***Slater v. Blackwood*** (1975) 15 Cal.3d 791, 795; 4 Witkin, *Cal. Procedure*, Pleading, §34. Under this theory, a cause of action consists of (1) a primary right of the plaintiff, (2) a corresponding primary duty of the defendant, and (3) a wrongful act by the defendant that constitutes a breach of the defendant's duty. ***Grisham v. Philip Morris U.S.A., Inc.*** (2007) 40 Cal.4th 623, 641; ***Mycogen Corp. v. Monsanto Co.*** (2002) 28 Cal.4th 888, 904; ***Crowley v. Katleman*** (1994) 8 Cal.4th 666, 681. A plaintiff's primary right is usually expressed as the right to be free from the particular harm suffered. ***Crowley***, 8 Cal.4th at 681. Examples of primary rights include the right to be free from personal injury, the right to possess property, and the right to have a contract performed. ***Olsen v. Breeze, Inc.*** (3d Dist.1996) 48 Cal.App.4th 608, 625. For pleading purposes, the plaintiff has only one cause of action for each primary right that has been violated. *See* ***Boeken v. Philip Morris USA, Inc.*** (2010) 48 Cal.4th 788, 798; ***Grisham***, 40 Cal.4th at 641.

(2) Compared to "count." The phrase "cause of action" is commonly confused with the term "count," which refers to a legal theory (e.g., negligence) or remedy (e.g., rescission) that compensates the plaintiff for a violation of its primary right. *See* ***McDowell v. Watson*** (4th Dist.1997) 59 Cal.App.4th 1155, 1160; ***Lilienthal & Fowler v. Superior Ct.*** (1st Dist.1993) 12 Cal.App.4th 1848, 1853; *see, e.g.*, ***Slater***, 15 Cal.3d at 795-96 (P's legal theories were counts, not causes of action); *see also* 4 Witkin, *Cal. Procedure*, Pleading, §35 (discussing meaning of phrase). Multiple counts, for example, are merely ways of stating the same cause of action differently. ***Crowley***, 8 Cal.4th at 683 n.11. Thus, to avoid confusion, attorneys should avoid using one term for the other. *See* ***Bay Cities Paving & Grading, Inc. v. Lawyers' Mut. Ins.*** (1993) 5 Cal.4th 854, 860 ("cause of action" must be distinguished from "remedy" and "relief" sought).

2. Pleading cause of action. In the complaint, a cause of action is expressed in terms of a legal theory of the defendant's liability and a remedy sought.

(1) Legal theory. For each cause of action, the plaintiff can plead one or more legal theories. ***Eichler Homes v. Superior Ct.*** (1961) 55 Cal.2d 845, 847-48; ***Lilienthal***, 12 Cal.App.4th at 1853; *see* ***Crowley***, 8 Cal.4th at 681-82; *see also* 4 Witkin, *Cal. Procedure*, Pleading, §§36-39 (discussing legal theory of wrong). The pleaded theories can be inconsistent. *See* ***Berman v. Bromberg*** (2d Dist.1997) 56 Cal.App.4th 936, 944-45; ***Beatty v. Pacific States S&L Co.*** (2d Dist.1935) 4 Cal.App.2d 692, 696; 4 Witkin, *Cal. Procedure*, Pleading, §§402-406; *see, e.g.*, ***Cameron v. Ah Quong*** (1917) 175 Cal. 377, 381-82 (court allowed intervenor to plead ownership in fee and by adverse possession). This is referred to as "pleading in the alternative." ***Mendoza v. Continental Sales Co.*** (5th Dist.2006) 140 Cal.App.4th 1395, 1402; *see, e.g.*, ***Landeros v. Flood*** (1976) 17 Cal.3d 399, 413 (alternative theories of common-law negligence and statutory liability can be pleaded in separate counts).

(2) Remedy. For each cause of action, the plaintiff can seek one or more legal or equitable remedies. *See* ***Crowley***, 8 Cal.4th at 682; ***Hutchinson v. Ainsworth*** (1887) 73 Cal. 452, 455; 4 Witkin, *Cal. Procedure*, Pleading, §§40, 41; *see, e.g.*, ***Wulfjen v. Dolton*** (1944) 24 Cal.2d 891, 895-96 (in earlier action against Ds for rescission of contract, P could have also pleaded in the alternative damages resulting from fraud). Like legal theories, the remedies can be inconsistent. ***Mackenzie v. Voelker*** (1st Dist.1954) 123 Cal.App.2d 538, 541; *see* ***Akin v. Certain Underwriters at Lloyd's London*** (4th Dist.2006) 140 Cal.App.4th 291, 296 (action for rescission and action for breach of contract are alternative remedies); *see, e.g.*, ***BGJ Assocs. v. Superior Ct.*** (2d Dist.1999) 75 Cal.App.4th 952, 971-72 (in dispute over sale of real property, P sought either money damages based on tort and fraud theories or imposition of constructive trust).

3. Form of pleading. Each cause of action must be organized by a heading and supported by allegations of fact.

(1) Heading. The body of the complaint must contain a heading for each cause of action stating the following:

(a) The number for each cause of action (e.g., "First Cause of Action"). CRC 2.112(1).

(b) The nature of each count of the cause of action (e.g., "First Cause of Action for Negligence," "First Cause of Action for Fraud"). CRC 2.112(2).

(c) The name of the plaintiff asserting the cause of action, if there is more than one plaintiff named in the complaint (e.g., "First Cause of Action for Negligence by Plaintiff Jones"). CRC 2.112(3).

(d) The name of the defendant or defendants against whom the cause of action is asserted (e.g., "First Cause of Action for Negligence by Plaintiff Jones against Defendant Smith"). CRC 2.112(4).

(2) Allegations of fact. The body of the complaint must contain allegations of fact in ordinary and concise language. CCP §425.10(a)(1).

(a) What to plead – ultimate facts. The allegations of fact that must be pleaded in the complaint are the "ultimate facts." *See* ***Committee on Children's TV, Inc. v. General Foods Corp.*** (1983) 35 Cal.3d 197, 212; ***Green v. Palmer*** (1860) 15 Cal. 411, 415-16; ***Knox v. Dean*** (4th Dist.2012) 205 Cal.App.4th 417, 431. Ultimate facts are the facts needed to establish each element of the legal theory pleaded. *See* ***Committee on Children's TV***, 35 Cal.3d at 212; ***Green***, 15 Cal. at 416; ***Kamen v. Lindly*** (6th Dist.2001) 94 Cal.App.4th 197, 201; *see, e.g.*, ***Sinai Temple v. Kaplan*** (2d Dist.1976) 54 Cal.App.3d 1103, 1113 (complaint was not sufficient to assert cause of action because it did not allege injury or damages suffered). Only the facts that support the elements of the cause of action need to be asserted; the plaintiff does not need to plead the evidence it will use to prove the facts. ***Committee on Children's TV***, 35 Cal.3d at 212. If the complaint sets out the evidence that the ultimate facts are based on, and the evidence actually negates rather than supports the ultimate facts, the evidentiary facts will control and the plaintiff's complaint will be insufficient to assert a cause of action. ***Stafford v. Ballinger*** (2d Dist.1962) 199 Cal.App.2d 289, 292.

ORIGINAL COMPLAINT

CAUTION

The California Judicial Council may prescribe by rule the format and content of the forms used in the California courts. Gov. C. §68511; see CCP §425.12; see, e.g., Judicial Council Forms, form PLD-C-001 (Complaint – Contract), form PLD-PI-001 (Complaint – Personal Injury, Property Damage, Wrongful Death). But a party who uses the Judicial Council forms is still required to plead the ultimate facts in the complaint. E.g., ***People v. Superior Ct.*** *(2d Dist.1992) 5 Cal.App.4th 1480, 1484 (demurrer to Judicial Council form was sustained for not asserting cause of action).*

[1] Conclusory facts. Courts have struggled with distinguishing ultimate facts from conclusions of law. *See* ***Burks v. Poppy Constr. Co.*** (1962) 57 Cal.2d 463, 473 (difference between ultimate facts and conclusions of law is "matter of degree"). Conclusions of law are generally treated as surplusage and cannot be considered in determining whether the pleading is sufficient to assert a cause of action. ***Krug v. Meeham*** (2d Dist.1952) 109 Cal.App.2d 274, 277. See "Conclusions of law," §3.6.3(2)(d)[1], p. 219. But the California Supreme Court has recognized that, in certain situations, conclusory facts—which seem like conclusions of law—can be pleaded as ultimate facts. Some of the allegations that can be pleaded in a conclusory manner include the following:

[a] Ownership of property. *E.g.*, ***In re Estate of Bixler*** (1924) 194 Cal. 585, 589 (conclusory allegation that party is owner of property is sufficient).

[b] Negligence. *E.g.*, ***McMillan v. Western Pac. R.R.*** (1960) 54 Cal.2d 841, 845 (conclusory allegation that particular act was "negligently done" is sufficient without stating particular omission that made it negligent); ***Rannard v. Lockheed Aircraft Corp.*** (1945) 26 Cal.2d 149, 155 (same).

[c] Proximate cause. *E.g.*, ***Rannard***, 26 Cal.2d at 156 (conclusory allegation that negligent act was "direct and proximate consequence and result" of P's injury was sufficient).

NOTE

When the pleaded facts of negligence and injury do not naturally give rise to an inference of causation, the plaintiff cannot plead proximate cause in a conclusory manner, but must plead the specific facts explaining how the conduct caused or contributed to the injury. ***Bockrath v. Aldrich Chem. Co.*** *(1999) 21 Cal.4th 71, 78.*

[d] Course and scope of employment. *E.g.*, ***May v. Farrell*** (1st Dist.1928) 94 Cal.App. 703, 707-08 (conclusory allegation that D was acting within course and scope of employment is sufficient unless D's act is ordinarily outside scope of employment, such as assault); *see* ***Burks***, 57 Cal.2d at 473-74 (citing ***May*** with approval).

[e] Agency. *E.g.*, ***Skopp v. Weaver*** (1976) 16 Cal.3d 432, 439 (conclusory allegation that person is an "agent" of another is sufficient without stating particular facts that explain how agency relationship arose).

[f] Riparian character of land. *E.g.*, ***Hudson v. West*** (1957) 47 Cal.2d 823, 828-29 (conclusory, general allegation that "land is riparian" is sufficient without stating particular facts that establish land as riparian).

[2] Common counts. The requirement that ultimate facts be pleaded in the complaint does not apply to "common counts." *See* 4 Witkin, *Cal. Procedure*, Pleading, §553. A common count does not assert a specific cause action, but rather pleads, in a simplified form, the existence of a monetary indebtedness (e.g., money had and received). ***McBride v. Boughton*** (1st Dist.2004) 123 Cal.App.4th 379, 394. A common count is generally stated as a conclusion of law, without any of the facts that support it. ***Western Title Ins. & Guar. Co. v. Bartolacelli*** (1st Dist.1954) 124 Cal.App.2d 690, 694. To sufficiently plead a common count, the complaint need only allege the following: (1) a statement of indebtedness in a sum certain, (2) the consideration given, and (3) nonpayment. ***Farmers Ins. Exch. v. Zerin*** (3d Dist.1997) 53 Cal.App.4th 445, 460. For example, a cause of action for money had and received is sufficiently pleaded if the complaint alleges that the defendant "is indebted to the plaintiff in a certain sum for money had and received by the defendant for the use of the plaintiff." *Id.*

(b) How to plead.

[1] In ordinary & concise language. Each ultimate fact must be stated in ordinary and concise language. CCP §425.10(a)(1); *see* ***Green***, 15 Cal. at 417. The facts should be alleged directly, not inferentially. Weil, *Civil Procedure Before Trial*, ¶6:224; *see* ***Pennie v. Hildreth*** (1889) 81 Cal. 127, 131.

[2] With specificity. Generally, the ultimate facts must be pleaded with enough specificity so that the defendant will know the nature, source, and extent of the plaintiff's cause of action. ***Youngman v. Nevada Irrigation Dist.*** (1969) 70 Cal.2d 240, 245. The degree of specificity required in pleading facts depends on the extent to which the defendant, in fairness, needs detailed information that can be conveniently provided by the plaintiff; less specificity is required when the defendant may be assumed to have knowledge of the facts equal to that possessed by the plaintiff. ***Jackson v. Pasadena City Sch. Dist.*** (1963) 59 Cal.2d 876, 879. This general rule of specificity is defined more precisely for certain causes of action, including the following:

[a] Statutory causes of action. In an action to recover under a statute, the complaint must plead every fact essential to impose liability under the statute and every fact specifically required by the statute to be pleaded. *See* ***Lopez v. Southern Cal. Rapid Transit Dist.*** (1985) 40 Cal.3d 780, 795; *see, e.g.*, CCP §425.50(a) (listing pleading requirements for construction-related accessibility claim). For example, if an action for negligence is based on a statutory duty, the complaint must identify, at the very least, the statute or enactment that establishes the duty. ***Searcy v. Hemet Unified Sch. Dist.*** (4th Dist.1986) 177 Cal.App.3d 792, 802.

NOTE

If a cause of action is based on a private statute or ordinance, the complaint is sufficient if it refers to the statute or ordinance by its title and day of passage. CCP §459; e.g., ***City of Tulare v. Hevren*** *(1899) 126 Cal. 226, 229 (pleading city ordinance by simply referring to it as "that certain ordinance of said city of Tulare known as ordinance No. 66" was insufficient);* ***Agnew v. City of L.A.*** *(2d Dist.1950) 99 Cal.App.2d 105, 106 (referring to ordinance only by number, and not attempting to plead it in any other manner, was insufficient); see* ***Taliaferro v. Wampler*** *(1st Dist.1954) 127 Cal.App.2d 306, 308 (if P chooses not to allege adoption and effect of ordinance in detail, it must at least allege ordinance's title and date of passage). A private statute is one that concerns only certain designated individuals and affects only their private rights. CCP §1898.*

[b] Action supporting punitive damages. To support a recovery of punitive damages, the plaintiff must plead in its complaint (1) a cause of action that supports a claim for punitive damages and (2) ultimate facts proving that the defendant acted with malice, oppression, or fraud. *See* Civ. C. §3294(a). See "Punitive damages," ch. 7-G, §2.1, p. 869. In negligence suits against a health-care provider or suits against a religious corporation, the plaintiff cannot seek punitive damages until the court grants the plaintiff's motion for leave to amend the complaint to include a claim for punitive damages. *See* CCP §§425.13(a), 425.14; ***College Hosp., Inc. v. Superior Ct.*** (1994) 8 Cal.4th 704, 713. See "Noticed motion for leave to amend," §6.2.4, p. 232.

[c] Breach of contract.

- **Form & terms.** In an action for breach of contract, the complaint must allege whether the contract is written, oral, or implied by conduct. ***Otworth v. Southern Pac. Transp.*** (2d Dist.1985) 166 Cal.App.3d 452, 458-59. If the action is based on a written contract, the contractual terms must be set out verbatim in the body of the complaint or a copy of the contract must be attached and incorporated by reference. *Id.* at 459. If the action is based on an oral contract, the terms must be alleged in the body of the complaint. ***Gautier v. General Tel. Co.*** (2d Dist.1965) 234 Cal.App.2d 302, 305.

- **Performance of condition.** In an action for breach of contract, the complaint can allege the satisfaction of a condition precedent generally if the condition to be performed is an act (e.g., "plaintiff duly performed all the conditions on his part"). CCP §457; ***Careau & Co. v. Security Pac. Bus. Credit, Inc.*** (2d Dist.1990) 222 Cal.App.3d 1371, 1389; *see also* CCP §459 (same rules of pleading apply to performance of conditions precedent under statute or ordinance). If the condition precedent is an event rather than an act, the complaint must contain specific allegations of the happening of the event. ***Careau & Co.***, 222 Cal.App.3d at 1389.

[d] Fraud. In an action for fraud, the complaint must plead facts demonstrating how, when, where, to whom, and by what means fraudulent representations were made. ***Lazar v. Superior Ct.*** (1996) 12 Cal.4th 631, 645. If the defendant is a corporation, the complaint must further allege the names of the persons who made the representations, their authority to speak, to whom they spoke, what they said or wrote, and when it was said or written. *Id.* Less specificity is required, however, when the allegations indicate that the defendant necessarily possesses full information about the facts or controversy. ***Committee on Children's TV***, 35 Cal.3d at 217.

[e] Libel & slander. In an action for libel or slander, the complaint can allege generally that a defamatory matter concerning the plaintiff was published or spoken. CCP §460.

[f] Action to recover real property. In an action to recover real property, the complaint must describe the real property at issue with sufficient certainty so that an officer can identify the property on execution of the judgment. CCP §455.

[3] On information & belief. If the ultimate facts are not matters within the plaintiff's personal knowledge, the facts can be based on "information and belief" when the plaintiff has information leading her to believe that the allegations are true. ***Pridonoff v. Balokovich*** (1951) 36 Cal.2d 788, 792; *see, e.g.*, ***Searcy***, 177

Cal.App.3d at 802 (P could not include allegation based on information and belief in complaint because fact could be determined by examining public laws); ***Thompson v. Sutton*** (3d Dist.1942) 50 Cal.App.2d 272, 279 (D could not include allegation based on information and belief in answer because facts were peculiarly within its knowledge).

(c) How to organize.

[1] Use numbered paragraphs. The facts can be stated in separate paragraphs or, if closely related, grouped together in a single paragraph. *CEB Procedure Before Trial*, §15.5.1. Although not required, it is good practice to number each paragraph consecutively throughout the complaint. Weil, *Civil Procedure Before Trial*, ¶¶6:114-6:116.

[2] Use separate counts. For each cause of action, the plaintiff should organize its facts according to the legal theory of the defendant's liability (e.g., fraud). *See* Weil, *Civil Procedure Before Trial*, ¶6:244; *see, e.g.*, ***Samuels v. Superior Ct.*** (2d Dist.1969) 276 Cal.App.2d 264, 268 n.3 (complaint was "hodgepodge" that confused counts with separate causes of action); ***Pagett v. Indemnity Ins. Co.*** (1st Dist.1942) 54 Cal.App.2d 646, 651 (theory of P's complaint was nearly impossible to determine because of "jumble of allegations" and confusion resulting from "promiscuous incorporation by reference" of allegations from one count to another); *see also* ***Perry v. Robertson*** (3d Dist.1988) 201 Cal.App.3d 333, 339 (legal theory provides "organizing principle" and identifies kinds of facts material to case). Although not required, this practice promotes clear and understandable pleadings and may help the plaintiff avoid a special demurrer on the grounds of uncertainty. *See* CCP §430.10(f); ***Williams v. Beechnut Nutrition Corp.*** (2d Dist.1986) 185 Cal.App.3d 135, 139 & n.2. The practice is also consistent with many of the Judicial Council forms that require the plaintiff to identify its legal theories. *E.g.*, Judicial Council Forms, form PLD-C-001 (complaint for contract claims), form PLD-PI-001 (complaint for personal-injury claims). If a group of facts is common to multiple counts, the plaintiff can state those under a separate heading before pleading each count.

ORIGINAL COMPLAINT

[3] Avoid repetition. The plaintiff is not required to restate the same facts for every count. It is common practice to incorporate by reference allegations from causes of action or counts previously pleaded. Weil, *Civil Procedure Before Trial*, ¶6:236; *see, e.g.*, ***Segal v. Silberstein*** (2d Dist.2007) 156 Cal.App.4th 627, 630-31 & n.2 (complaint alleged 18 "causes of action," 17 of which incorporated allegations pleaded in first cause of action). But the incorporated facts should be germane to the alleged count to avoid problems such as ambiguity and redundancy. *See* ***Kelly v. General Tel. Co.*** (2d Dist.1982) 136 Cal.App.3d 278, 285 ("chain letter" pleading, or wholesale incorporation of allegations by reference, should be avoided); *see, e.g.*, ***Philipson & Simon v. Gulsvig*** (4th Dist.2007) 154 Cal.App.4th 347, 362 (for each count, P incorporated by reference all preceding allegations, which required court to sort through complaint to find allegations supporting each count).

CAUTION

While many courts have no problem with the practice of incorporating allegations by reference, some courts disfavor it. E.g., ***N.T. Hill Inc. v. City of Fresno*** *(5th Dist.1999) 72 Cal.App.4th 977, 981 n.2 (condemning "unnecessary, confusing, repetitive, and utterly irritating practice of incorporating all prior allegations into each succeeding separately numbered count").*

[4] Incorporate exhibits. The plaintiff can incorporate an exhibit by reference when the exhibit's contents are needed to support a cause of action or count. *See* ***Otworth***, 166 Cal.App.3d at 459 (in breach-of-contract action, complaint must include contract terms verbatim or copy of contract must be attached and incorporated by reference). See "Exhibits," §3.9, p. 223.

(d) What not to plead.

[1] Conclusions of law. The plaintiff should not state a legal inference or conclusion of law in the complaint. ***Green***, 15 Cal. at 414; *see also* ***Krug***, 109 Cal.App.2d at 277 (allegation of conclusion of law is considered surplusage and will be disregarded in considering sufficiency of pleading). Unfortunately, there is no clear test for determining whether an allegation is a conclusion of law or an ultimate fact. *See* ***Burks***, 57 Cal.2d at 473. For

example, the allegation "defendant ran its train in a negligent manner and at a negligent rate of speed" includes a conclusion of law, but it is considered a proper allegation of an ultimate fact. ***Ellis v. Central Cal. Traction Co.*** (3d Dist.1918) 37 Cal.App. 390, 395-96; *see also* ***Peninsula Props. Co. v. County of Santa Cruz*** (1950) 34 Cal.2d 626, 629 (cross-complainant properly alleged it was "owner" of real property); ***May***, 94 Cal.App. at 707-08 (complaint properly alleged employee was "acting within the scope of his employment"). One suggested test looks at whether the plaintiff would need to plead additional facts to provide the defendant with sufficient notice of the claim. *See* ***Burks***, 57 Cal.2d at 474; ***Perry***, 201 Cal.App.3d at 339 n.3; ***Semole v. Sansoucie*** (2d Dist.1972) 28 Cal.App.3d 714, 721. If so, the allegation is a conclusion of law. *See, e.g.*, ***McAllister v. County of Monterey*** (6th Dist.2007) 147 Cal.App.4th 253, 291 (allegation that D's action was "null and void" was conclusion of law because phrase was not defined and did not have accepted legal meaning); ***Logan v. Southern Cal. Rapid Transit Dist.*** (2d Dist.1982) 136 Cal.App.3d 116, 126 (allegation that D-agency did not give P due process was conclusion of law because complaint did not show how due-process rights were violated).

[2] Evidence of ultimate facts. The plaintiff should not state evidence of ultimate facts in the complaint. ***Green***, 15 Cal. at 415; *see, e.g.*, ***Skopp***, 16 Cal.3d at 439 (allegation that Ds acted as agents was sufficient; P did not have to allege additional facts explaining how agency relationship arose).

[3] Contradictory facts. The plaintiff should not state contradictory facts in a verified complaint. *See* ***Steiner v. Rowley*** (1950) 35 Cal.2d 713, 718-19; *see, e.g.*, ***Faulkner v. California Toll Bridge Auth.*** (1953) 40 Cal.2d 317, 328-29 (verified complaint made contradictory assertions about whether D-agency gave Ps opportunity to voice objections to bridge construction); *see also* ***Manti v. Gunari*** (1st Dist.1970) 5 Cal.App.3d 442, 449 (dicta; rule against pleading contradictory facts applies to unverified pleadings as well). See "Verification," §3.10, p. 224.

ORIGINAL COMPLAINT

[4] Arguments. The plaintiff should not make arguments in the complaint. ***Green***, 15 Cal. at 414; *see, e.g.*, ***Roberts v. Roberts*** (2d Dist.1947) 81 Cal.App.2d 871, 886 (allegations that settlement agreement was unfair and against public policy were inferential and argumentative statements, not direct statements of material facts), *disapproved on other grounds*, ***Spellens v. Spellens*** (1957) 49 Cal.2d 210.

[5] Hypothetical statements. The plaintiff should not make hypothetical statements in the complaint. ***Green***, 15 Cal. at 414; *see, e.g.*, ***Parnell v. Smart*** (3d Dist.1977) 66 Cal.App.3d 833, 836-37 (P's cause of action against Ds could not be conditioned on what might happen in suit against insurance company).

§3.7 Prayer. The complaint must include a demand for judgment—usually called a "prayer"—for the relief that the plaintiff claims to be entitled to receive. CCP §425.10(a)(2); *see also* ***Ytuarte v. Superior Ct.*** (2d Dist.2005) 129 Cal.App.4th 266, 274 (prayer initially determines whether action is limited or unlimited). The prayer should be a separate paragraph at the end of the complaint. *CEB Procedure Before Trial*, §15.7. The prayer usually tracks the relief or remedies requested in the body of the complaint.

1. Contents.

(1) Damages.

(a) Actual. If the plaintiff is seeking money damages, the amount must usually be stated in the prayer. CCP §425.10(a)(2); ***Matera v. McLeod*** (2d Dist.2006) 145 Cal.App.4th 44, 60. The purpose of a prayer for damages is to put the defendant on notice of its potential liability for actual damages in the event of a default. *See* ***Schwab v. Rondel Homes, Inc.*** (1991) 53 Cal.3d 428, 433 (default judgment is limited to damages of which D has notice). See "Default Judgment," ch. 10-A, p. 1089.

NOTE

Giving notice of the defendant's potential liability is important because it sets the ceiling on the plaintiff's recovery if the defendant defaults. ***Janssen v. Luu*** *(2d Dist.1997) 57 Cal.App.4th 272, 274-75; see* ***Becker v. S.P.V. Constr. Co.*** *(1980) 27 Cal.3d 489, 494. A default judgment in*

excess of that amount is void. ***Heidary v. Yadollahi*** *(4th Dist.2002) 99 Cal.App.4th 857, 864;* ***Janssen****, 57 Cal.App.4th at 275. For a discussion of the prayer for damages and its effect on the ceiling for limited and unlimited civil cases, see "Sets maximum award," ch. 10-A, §4.3.2, p. 1096.*

[1] Personal-injury or wrongful-death actions. In actions for personal injury or wrongful death, no amount can be stated in the prayer. CCP §425.10(b); *see also* ***Candelaria v. Avitia*** (6th Dist.1990) 219 Cal.App.3d 1436, 1441 (purpose of §425.10(b) is to protect Ds from negative publicity caused by greatly inflated damages claims). The amount can be provided to the defendant in a separate statement of damages. *See* CCP §425.11. See "Statement of Damages," §5, p. 226.

[2] Other actions. In actions other than those for personal injury or wrongful death, the prayer must allege a specific dollar amount. CCP §425.10(a)(2); ***Becker***, 27 Cal.3d at 494. A prayer that merely seeks damages "according to proof" or "in excess of the jurisdictional amount" is insufficient to put the defendant on notice and will not support a default judgment. *See* ***Becker***, 27 Cal.3d at 494; ***Van Sickle v. Gilbert*** (3d Dist.2011) 196 Cal.App.4th 1495, 1528-29. A defective prayer can be cured if the plaintiff alleged a specific amount of damages in the body of the complaint. ***Becker***, 27 Cal.3d at 494; *see* ***Heidary***, 99 Cal.App.4th at 865-66. Allegations specifying the amount of damages should not be confused with allegations of fact that include numbers; the latter cannot be used to cure a defective prayer. *See* ***Heidary***, 99 Cal.App.4th at 866.

CAUTION

If the action is not for personal injury or wrongful death, the plaintiff cannot use a statement of damages as a substitute for notifying a defendant of its potential liability. ***Levine v. Smith*** *(2d Dist.2006) 145 Cal.App.4th 1131, 1136-37;* ***Electronic Funds Solutions, LLC v. Murphy*** *(4th Dist.2005) 134 Cal.App.4th 1161, 1176. If a default judgment is taken, the plaintiff will be limited to the amount of damages specified in the complaint.* ***Levine****, 145 Cal.App.4th at 1136-37.*

(b) Punitive. If the plaintiff is seeking punitive damages, no amount can be stated in the prayer. Civ. C. §3295(e); ***Matera***, 145 Cal.App.4th at 60; *see* CCP §425.10(b). This applies to all cases seeking punitive damages. ***Electronic Funds Solutions***, 134 Cal.App.4th at 1178. The amount can be provided to the defendant in a separate statement of damages. *See* CCP §425.11. See "Statement of Damages," §5, p. 226.

(c) Treble. If the plaintiff is seeking treble damages, the amount sought and the statute authorizing the award should be stated in the prayer. *See* ***Ostling v. Loring*** (3d Dist.1994) 27 Cal.App.4th 1731, 1741-42; *see also* ***Paul A. Mosesian & Sons, Inc. v. Danielian*** (4th Dist.1942) 52 Cal.App.2d 387, 389 (D's answer and evidence introduced at trial indicated she was defending an action for treble damages; on appeal, D could not challenge sufficiency of complaint to support award of treble damages).

(2) Equitable relief. If the plaintiff is seeking equitable relief, the remedy sought should be stated in the prayer. When equitable relief is demanded in the prayer, the court cannot order the parties to judicial arbitration unless the relief is deemed "frivolous or insubstantial." CCP §1141.13.

(3) Prejudgment interest. If the plaintiff is seeking prejudgment interest, the prayer should request it. *See* ***North Oakland Med. Clinic v. Rogers*** (1st Dist.1998) 65 Cal.App.4th 824, 829. However, in a contested case, prejudgment interest can be awarded without a prayer. ***Newby v. Vroman*** (1st Dist.1992) 11 Cal.App.4th 283, 286.

(4) Attorney fees. If the plaintiff is seeking attorney fees, the prayer should request them. Weil, *Civil Procedure Before Trial*, ¶6:275; *see, e.g.,* ***Wiley v. Rhodes*** (4th Dist.1990) 223 Cal.App.3d 1470, 1474 (default judgment cannot include award for attorney fees unless it was demanded in complaint and included in prayer). The body of the complaint must allege facts showing the statutory or contractual basis for the award. ***Wiley***, 223 Cal.App.3d

at 1474; *see, e.g.*, ***Hasler v. Howard*** (2d Dist.2004) 120 Cal.App.4th 1023, 1027 (complaint prayed for attorney fees but contained no allegations of basis for award); ***Garamendi v. Golden Eagle Ins.*** (1st Dist.2004) 116 Cal.App.4th 694, 708-09 (complaint neither prayed for attorney fees nor alleged facts showing existence of agreement that would allow P to recover fees).

(5) Costs. If the plaintiff is seeking costs that are not otherwise recoverable as a matter of law, the prayer should request them and identify the basis for the award. *See* ***Hsu v. Semiconductor Sys.*** (1st Dist.2005) 126 Cal.App.4th 1330, 1341 (recovery of costs provided by contract must be specifically pleaded).

(6) Other relief. As a catchall for any relief or remedy not specifically pleaded in the body of the complaint or the prayer, the plaintiff should include a request for "such other and further relief as the court may deem proper." *E.g.*, ***Slovensky v. Friedman*** (3d Dist.2006) 142 Cal.App.4th 1518, 1536 (general prayer was sufficient to plead disgorgement as remedy); ***North Oakland Med. Clinic***, 65 Cal.App.4th at 829 (general prayer allowed court to award prejudgment interest).

2. Effect.

(1) Classification. The prayer is relevant to determining whether the action qualifies as an unlimited civil case, a limited civil case, or a small-claims case. *See* ***Ytuarte***, 129 Cal.App.4th at 274; *see, e.g.*, ***Wolitarsky v. Blue Cross*** (2d Dist.1997) 53 Cal.App.4th 338, 348-49 (P's action was not small-claims case because prayer sought treble damages, which pushed claim for $2,000 over $5,000 jurisdictional threshold as set by contract).

(2) Nature of action. The prayer is relevant to determining the nature of the cause of action—that is, whether it is legal, equitable, or both. *See* ***Hails v. Martz*** (1946) 28 Cal.2d 775, 777-78; ***Williams v. Southern Pac. R.R.*** (1907) 150 Cal. 624, 628. But the prayer is not conclusive of this determination. ***C&K Eng'g Contractors v. Amber Steel Co.*** (1978) 23 Cal.3d 1, 9; ***DiPirro v. Bondo Corp.*** (1st Dist.2007) 153 Cal.App.4th 150, 179.

(3) Available relief.

(a) In contested cases. In contested cases (i.e., when the defendant has answered), the plaintiff is entitled to any relief "consistent with the case made by the complaint and embraced within the issue[s]." CCP §580(a); *see, e.g.*, ***Britz, Inc. v. Alfa-Laval Food & Dairy Co.*** (5th Dist.1995) 34 Cal.App.4th 1085, 1106 (in contested action on money claim, prejudgment interest is "embraced within the issue" and can be awarded even if not in prayer). In other words, the plaintiff can be awarded relief even though the specific relief is not prayed for in the complaint. ***Estate of Kalal*** (1st Dist.1981) 121 Cal.App.3d 841, 845 n.3; ***Barber v. LeRoy*** (2d Dist.1974) 40 Cal.App.3d 336, 345-46; *see* ***Furia v. Helm*** (1st Dist.2003) 111 Cal.App.4th 945, 957 (absence of prayer for specific amount is not fatal if pleaded facts entitle P to relief). When specific relief is prayed for, the plaintiff can be awarded greater relief in any of the following instances:

[1] The body of the complaint requested a greater amount than what was prayed for. ***Castaic Clay Mfg. v. Dedes*** (2d Dist.1987) 195 Cal.App.3d 444, 449; *see, e.g.*, ***Garamendi***, 116 Cal.App.4th at 706 (complaint and discovery made clear Ps were seeking to recover more than $125,000).

[2] The plaintiff asked for leave to amend the complaint to conform it to the proof after trial. ***Damele v. Mack Trucks, Inc.*** (1st Dist.1990) 219 Cal.App.3d 29, 39; ***Castaic Clay***, 195 Cal.App.3d at 449.

[3] The amount of damages was greater than what was indicated in the body of the complaint or prayed for, but was tried by consent without surprise or prejudice to the defendant. ***Damele***, 219 Cal.App.3d at 39; ***Castaic Clay***, 195 Cal.App.3d at 449-50; *e.g.*, ***Wozniak v. Lucutz*** (2d Dist.2002) 102 Cal.App.4th 1031, 1045 (P not entitled to greater award because there was no evidence D tried issue by consent or waived remittance clause in complaint), *disapproved on other grounds*, ***Le Francois v. Goel*** (2005) 35 Cal.4th 1094.

(b) In uncontested cases. In uncontested cases (i.e., when the defendant has not answered or its answer has been struck as a discovery sanction), the plaintiff's relief is generally limited to the dollar amount demanded in the prayer or, in cases of personal injury or wrongful death, the dollar amount set forth in the statement of damages. ***Simke, Chodos, Silberfeld & Anteau, Inc. v. Athans*** (2d Dist.2011) 195 Cal.App.4th 1275, 1278;

see CCP §§425.11, 580(a); ***Greenup v. Rodman*** (1986) 42 Cal.3d 822, 826; ***In re Marriage of Wells*** (5th Dist.1989) 206 Cal.App.3d 1434, 1437; *see, e.g.*, ***Barragan v. Banco BCH*** (4th Dist.1986) 188 Cal.App.3d 283, 305 (P's default judgment of $1 million in actual damages was reduced to amount requested in prayer, which was $500,000). The limit placed on the plaintiff's recovery applies only to damages; the plaintiff is not required to request a specific amount of attorney fees in its prayer or statement of damages in order to recover its fees. *See* ***Athans***, 195 Cal.App.4th at 1278. A defective prayer for damages can be cured if a specific amount of damages is alleged in the body of the complaint. ***Becker***, 27 Cal.3d at 494.

NOTE

Before the plaintiff can take a default in an action seeking damages for personal injury or wrongful death or in an action seeking punitive damages, the plaintiff must serve the defendant with a statement of damages. See CCP §§425.11, 425.115; ***Wiley****, 223 Cal.App.3d at 1473. See "Statement of Damages," §5, p. 226.*

§3.8 Signature. The complaint must include a signature. See "Signature," ch. 1-B, §2.7, p. 15.

§3.9 Exhibits. A document can be pleaded in haec verba (i.e., verbatim) by attaching it as an exhibit and incorporating the text by reference. ***Holly Sugar Corp. v. Johnson*** (1941) 18 Cal.2d 218, 225; ***Silvers v. Grossman*** (1920) 183 Cal. 696, 700.

PRACTICE TIP

The plaintiff can also plead a document in haec verba by copying the text into the body of the complaint, or it can simply plead the document's legal effect. ***Holly Sugar****, 18 Cal.2d at 225; e.g.,* ***Construction Prot. Servs. v. TIG Specialty Ins.*** *(2002) 29 Cal.4th 189, 198-99 (P alleged legal effect of insurance policy).*

1. Required. Some causes of action require certain documents or things to be attached to the complaint.

(1) Action involving literary, artistic, or intellectual productions. When the plaintiff brings a cause of action, whether in tort or contract, for infringement of her rights in a literary, artistic, or intellectual production, the original and infringing productions must be attached to the complaint unless they are too bulky or their nature makes them impractical to attach. CCP §429.30(b); *see* ***Edgar Rice Burroughs, Inc. v. Metro-Goldwyn-Mayer, Inc.*** (2d Dist.1962) 205 Cal.App.2d 441, 445-46; *see, e.g.*, ***Palmer v. Metro-Goldwyn-Mayer Pictures*** (2d Dist.1953) 119 Cal.App.2d 456, 457 (D's motion picture was not attached to complaint as exhibit because of its nature, bulk, and unavailability).

(2) Action challenging state agency action. When the plaintiff brings suit to challenge an action being taken by a state agency, a complete transcript of all the evidence the agency relied on must be attached to the complaint. ***Faulkner v. California Toll Bridge Auth.*** (1953) 40 Cal.2d 317, 330. If the plaintiff does not attach the transcript, it must allege in the body of the complaint the substance of all the evidence the agency received before making its decision. *Id.* at 331.

2. Substitute for allegations. The recitals in a document can serve as a substitute for material allegations in the body of the complaint. ***Byrne v. Harvey*** (1st Dist.1962) 211 Cal.App.2d 92, 103; 4 Witkin, *Cal. Procedure*, Pleading, §430. When the document is the foundation for a cause of action, the plaintiff only needs to plead it in haec verba. ***Silvers***, 183 Cal. at 700. When the document is not the foundation for a cause of action but is needed to supply factual allegations to support the claim, the plaintiff should plead it in haec verba and specifically state the document's purpose in the body of the complaint. *See* ***Holly Sugar***, 18 Cal.2d at 226.

(1) Ambiguous terms. If any of the relevant terms in the document are ambiguous, the plaintiff must explain in the body of the complaint how the terms should be interpreted. ***Silvers***, 183 Cal. at 700; ***Durkee v.***

Cota (1887) 74 Cal. 313, 315; *see* ***Beck v. American Health Grp. Int'l*** (2d Dist.1989) 211 Cal.App.3d 1555, 1561. If the plaintiff does not provide an explanation, the cause of action can be dismissed. *See, e.g.*, ***Durkee***, 74 Cal. at 315 (complaint did not state cause of action because it did not explain covenant to convey "full and abundant water right" for purchased land). If the plaintiff provides a reasonable explanation, its interpretation will be accepted for the purpose of avoiding a demurrer. ***Connell v. Zaid*** (4th Dist.1969) 268 Cal.App.2d 788, 794-95. If the explanation is not reasonable, however, the plaintiff's interpretation can be ignored and the terms can be interpreted according to their plain meaning within the context of the entire document. *See* ***Beck***, 211 Cal.App.3d at 1561.

(2) Implied facts. Only facts appearing directly on the face of the document will serve as a substitute for material allegations. *See* ***Silvers***, 183 Cal. at 700; ***Durkee***, 74 Cal. at 315. The document cannot establish facts by implication, such as preliminary or collateral matters. *See* ***Silvers***, 183 Cal. at 700; ***Lambert v. Haskell*** (1889) 80 Cal. 611, 613.

(3) Contradictory facts. The unambiguous terms of an exhibit will control over conflicting allegations in the body of the complaint. *See* ***Stoddard v. Treadwell*** (1864) 26 Cal. 294, 303; ***Burnett v. Chimney Sweep, LLC*** (2d Dist.2004) 123 Cal.App.4th 1057, 1064; ***Freeman v. San Diego Ass'n of Realtors*** (4th Dist.1999) 77 Cal.App.4th 171, 178 n.3; ***Alphonzo E. Bell Corp. v. Bell View Oil Syndicate*** (1st Dist.1941) 46 Cal.App.2d 684, 691.

§3.10 Verification. A verification is a declaration or affidavit that swears to the truth of the allegations in the body of the complaint. *See* CCP §§446(a), 2009, 2015.5; ***Star Motor Imports, Inc. v. Superior Ct.*** (1st Dist.1979) 88 Cal.App.3d 201, 204. The purpose of verification is to ensure that the allegations in the complaint are made in good faith. ***Patterson & Frisbie v. Ely*** (1861) 19 Cal. 28, 39; ***Frio v. Superior Ct.*** (2d Dist.1988) 203 Cal.App.3d 1480, 1498.

1. When to verify. A complaint must be verified only when required by statute. CCP §128.7(a); ***Murrieta Valley Unified Sch. Dist. v. County of Riverside*** (4th Dist.1991) 228 Cal.App.3d 1212, 1222. But in some cases, the plaintiff may choose to verify the complaint.

(1) Mandatory. The following are some of the more common pleadings that are required by statute to be verified:

(a) Petitions for a writ of mandate. CCP §1086.

(b) Petitions for a writ of prohibition. *Id.* §1103(a).

(c) Petitions relating to probate matters. Prob. C. §1021.

(d) Petitions filed under the Family Code. Fam. C. §212.

(e) Complaints requesting a preliminary injunction. CCP §527(a).

(f) Complaints alleging forcible entry or forcible or unlawful detainer. *Id.* §1166(a).

(g) Complaints for actions relating to consumer installment contracts. *See* Civ. C. §1812.10(c); CCP §396a(a).

(h) Complaints for actions relating to retail car sales. *See* Civ. C. §2984.4(c); CCP §396a(a).

(i) Actions to quiet title to a piece of property. CCP §761.020.

(j) Actions for the involuntary dissolution of a corporation. Corp. C. §1800(a).

(2) Voluntary. A plaintiff may choose to verify the complaint even though verification is not required. ***People v. Godines*** (2d Dist.1936) 17 Cal.App.2d 721, 725; *see* ***Parke & Lacy Co. v. Inter Nos Oil & Dev. Co.*** (1905) 147 Cal. 490, 493-94. Before choosing to do so, the plaintiff should consider the advantages and disadvantages of verification.

NOTE

Commentators agree that complaints are rarely verified unless required by statute. See CEB Procedure Before Trial, §15.17; Weil, Civil Procedure Before Trial, ¶6:319.

(a) **Advantages.** The following are some of the advantages of verifying the complaint:

[1] When a complaint is verified, the defendant's answer must also be verified. CCP §446(a).

[2] When a complaint is verified, the defendant cannot answer with a general denial but must specifically deny each material allegation in the complaint under penalty of perjury; all material allegations that are not specifically denied are deemed admitted. *See* CCP §§431.20(a), 431.30(d), 446(a); ***DeCamp v. First Kensington Corp.*** (2d Dist.1978) 83 Cal.App.3d 268, 276; ***Godines***, 17 Cal.App.2d at 725-26; *see, e.g.*, ***Racouillat v. Rene*** (1867) 32 Cal. 450, 453-54 (D's denial of notice of mortgage was sufficient).

(b) **Disadvantages.** The following are some of the disadvantages of verifying the complaint:

[1] The plaintiff cannot plead inconsistent facts. ***Steiner v. Rowley*** (1950) 35 Cal.2d 713, 718-19; ***Berman v. Bromberg*** (2d Dist.1997) 56 Cal.App.4th 936, 944-45.

[2] The plaintiff may be exposed to impeachment or a perjury charge if the proof at trial contradicts the complaint. *CEB Procedure Before Trial*, §15.17; Weil, *Civil Procedure Before Trial*, ¶6.318(b).

[3] The plaintiff may be stuck with the allegations because once alleged, the facts cannot be withdrawn from consideration by merely filing an amended pleading omitting them without explanation. ***Wennerholm v. Stanford Univ. Sch. of Med.*** (1942) 20 Cal.2d 713, 716; ***Appl v. Lee Swett Livestock Co.*** (1st Dist.1987) 192 Cal.App.3d 466, 470; *see, e.g.*, ***Williamson v. Joyce*** (1902) 137 Cal. 151, 153 (court considered allegation in verified original complaint when deciding demurrer to amended complaint, which simply omitted the allegation).

[4] The plaintiff may be deemed to have waived the attorney-client privilege for the matter alleged in the pleading if its attorney verifies the complaint. Weil, *Civil Procedure Before Trial*, ¶6.318(d).

2. How to verify. A complaint is verified by attaching a declaration or affidavit stating that the verifying party knows the facts alleged in the complaint to be true or believes those facts alleged on information and belief to be true. CCP §446(a); *see id.* §2015.5; *see, e.g.*, ***Conservatorship of Isaac O.*** (4th Dist.1987) 190 Cal.App.3d 50, 54-55 (P used declaration). For the requirements of a declaration or affidavit, see "General Requirements for Declarations & Affidavits," ch. 1-B, §4, p. 19. The plaintiff only needs to substantially comply with a statutory verification requirement. *See* ***Sheeley v. City of Santa Clara*** (1st Dist.1963) 215 Cal.App.2d 83, 85. "Substantial compliance" means the verification must be clear and certain enough to sustain an indictment for perjury against the verifying party if the verification is shown to be false. *Id.*

3. Who can verify.

(1) Plaintiff. Complaints are generally verified by the plaintiff. *See* CCP §446(a).

(2) Attorney or nonparty. An attorney or nonparty can verify a complaint in certain situations, but should avoid doing so. *See* CCP §446(a); ***DeCamp***, 83 Cal.App.3d at 275. The declaration or affidavit must explain why the party itself did not verify the complaint. CCP §446(a); ***Conservatorship of Isaac O.***, 190 Cal.App.3d at 54. *But see* ***Soltani-Rastegar v. Superior Ct.*** (1st Dist.1989) 208 Cal.App.3d 424, 428 (court upheld nonparty verification that lacked explanation). An attorney or nonparty can verify the complaint in the following instances:

(a) The party is absent from the county where the attorney has her office and obtaining the party's signature is impractical. *See* CCP §446(a); ***Zavala v. Board of Trs.*** (6th Dist.1993) 16 Cal.App.4th 1755, 1760; ***DeCamp***, 83 Cal.App.3d at 274-75. The attorney's or nonparty's declaration or affidavit must state that she read the complaint and that the matters stated in it are true based on her information and belief. CCP §446(a).

(b) The party is unable to verify the complaint for some reason. CCP §446(a). The attorney's or nonparty's declaration or affidavit must state that she read the complaint and that the matters stated in it are true based on her information and belief. *Id.*

(c) The facts are within the knowledge of the party's attorney or some other person verifying the complaint. CCP §446(a); *see, e.g.*, ***Conservatorship of Isaac O.***, 190 Cal.App.3d at 54-55 (employee of party verified petition because he was more familiar with alleged facts).

(3) Corporation. When a corporation is a party, the complaint can be verified by any officer of the corporation. CCP §446(a); *see, e.g.*, ***Alpha Beta Co. v. Superior Ct.*** (5th Dist.1984) 157 Cal.App.3d 818, 823-24 (answer to complaint was verified by officer serving as vice president and general counsel). The officer's declaration or affidavit must state that she read the complaint and that the matters stated in it are true based on her information and belief. CCP §446(a).

(4) Public entities & officers. The State of California and each of its counties, cities, districts, school districts, public agencies, public corporations, and public officers acting in their official capacity are exempt from having to verify a complaint. CCP §446(a); *see* ***Murrieta Valley***, 228 Cal.App.3d at 1222-23.

4. Challenging unverified complaint. A party can file a motion to strike an unverified complaint when verification is required. ***Zavala***, 16 Cal.App.4th at 1761. An objection to lack of verification must be raised before trial or else it is waived. *Id.*; *see* ***In re Marriage of Melton*** (6th Dist.1994) 28 Cal.App.4th 931, 939.

§4. FILING & SERVING COMPLAINT

§4.1 Filing.

1. When to file. The complaint must be filed within the limitations period for each claim that has accrued. *See* CCP §312; ***Fox v. Ethicon Endo-Surgery, Inc.*** (2005) 35 Cal.4th 797, 806; *see, e.g.*, CCP §335.1 (two years for personal injury), §337 (four years for breach of contract), §338 (three years for property damage).

2. Where to file. For a discussion of how to choose the proper venue for filing suit, see "Choosing the Court—Venue," ch. 3-F, p. 270.

3. How to file. See "How to File," ch. 1-F, §4, p. 47.

4. Filing fees. When the initial complaint is filed, the plaintiff must pay a filing fee to the court clerk or request a waiver of the fee. See "Filing Fees," ch. 1-F, §7, p. 58.

§4.2 Serving. For a discussion of how to serve an original complaint and summons, see "Joining the Defendant—Service of Process," ch. 3-H, p. 295.

§5. STATEMENT OF DAMAGES

§5.1 Actual damages. In personal-injury or wrongful-death actions, the defendant is notified of the amount of actual (i.e., general and special) damages sought by the plaintiff through a statement of damages. *See* CCP §425.11. The purpose of the statement of damages is to give the defendant "one last clear chance" to respond to the complaint by providing it with actual notice of its potential liability. ***Garamendi v. Golden Eagle Ins.*** (1st Dist.2004) 116 Cal.App.4th 694, 704.

1. When required. The plaintiff must serve the defendant with a statement of damages if (1) the action involves a personal-injury or wrongful-death claim and (2) either the defendant asks for the statement or the plaintiff intends to seek a default against the defendant. CCP §425.11.

(1) Personal-injury or wrongful-death action. A statement of damages is required in a personal-injury action, a wrongful-death action, or an action in which claims for personal injury or death are closely intertwined with other claims, such as those for economic damages. *See* CCP §425.11; *see, e.g.*, ***Barragan v. Banco BCH*** (4th Dist.1986) 188 Cal.App.3d 283, 303-04 (statement not required because P's personal-injury claims were not intertwined with economic-loss claims); ***Jones v. Interstate Recovery Serv.*** (4th Dist.1984) 160 Cal.App.3d 925, 929-30 (statement required because Ps' personal-injury claims were closely tied to their non-personal-injury claims). A statement of damages is not required, however, if the plaintiff has requested relief for emotional distress but the request is merely incidental to the cause of action. *See* ***Schwab v. Rondel Homes, Inc.*** (1991) 53 Cal.3d 428, 432.

(2) After request or before default.

(a) After D's request. A statement of damages must be served within 15 days after the plaintiff has received a written request from the defendant. CCP §425.11(b). If the statement of damages is not timely served, the defendant can ask the court to order the plaintiff to serve the statement. *Id.*; ***Argame v. Werasophon***

(4th Dist.1997) 57 Cal.App.4th 616, 618. If the defendant does not make a motion to compel the plaintiff to serve the statement, the defendant waives any right to later exclude evidence of damages at trial. ***Argame***, 57 Cal.App.4th at 618.

(b) Before default. A statement of damages must be served before the plaintiff can request entry of a default against the defendant. CCP §425.11(c); ***Garamendi***, 116 Cal.App.4th at 704. *But see* ***Weakly-Hoyt v. Foster*** (5th Dist.2014) 230 Cal.App.4th 928, 932-33 (P was prohibited from serving statement of damages on D before requesting entry of default because D's bankruptcy proceeding automatically stayed P's suit; relief from automatic stay allowed P to recover damages only from D's insurer). This requirement applies even when the default is entered as a discovery sanction. ***Greenup v. Rodman*** (1986) 42 Cal.3d 822, 827-28; ***Van Sickle v. Gilbert*** (3d Dist.2011) 196 Cal.App.4th 1495, 1521. A statement served after a default is entered by the clerk is invalid, even if served before a default judgment is rendered. ***Hamm v. Elkin*** (1st Dist.1987) 196 Cal.App.3d 1343, 1345-46. Courts disagree on how far in advance the statement of damages must be served before requesting entry of default. Some courts require the statement to be served 30 days before requesting entry of default. *E.g.*, ***Twine v. Compton Supermkt.*** (2d Dist.1986) (Div. 7) 179 Cal.App.3d 514, 517; ***Plotitsa v. Superior Ct.*** (2d Dist.1983) (Div. 4) 140 Cal.App.3d 755, 761. Other courts require the statement to be served within a reasonable amount of time. *See, e.g.*, ***Matera v. McLeod*** (2d Dist.2006) (Div. 3) 145 Cal.App.4th 44, 62 (2 days not reasonable); ***Schwab v. Southern Cal. Gas Co.*** (4th Dist.2004) (Div. 2) 114 Cal.App.4th 1308, 1322-23 (15 days reasonable); ***California Novelties, Inc. v. Sokoloff*** (4th Dist.1992) (Div. 3) 6 Cal.App.4th 936, 944-45 (17 days reasonable); *see also* ***Rondel Homes***, 53 Cal.3d at 435 (dicta; defendant entitled to notice within reasonable period of time); ***Connelly v. Castillo*** (2d Dist.1987) (Div. 6) 190 Cal.App.3d 1583, 1589-90 (whether 27 days was reasonable could only have been determined by timely motion under CCP §473).

PRACTICE TIP

If the action requires a defendant to be served with a statement of damages before default can be entered, you should serve the defendant with the statement of damages at the same time as the complaint. This will ensure that default can be entered as soon as the deadline to respond expires.

2. Form. The plaintiff must use Judicial Council Form CIV-050, which requires the plaintiff to separately state the amounts of general and special damages. *See* CCP §425.12(b); ***Southern Cal. Gas***, 114 Cal.App.4th at 1322. The statement can be combined with a statement of punitive damages under CCP §425.115. CCP §425.11(e). See "Punitive damages," §5.2, p. 228.

3. Service. The statement of damages must be served as follows:

(1) D has not appeared. If the defendant has not appeared, the statement must be served in the same manner as a summons. CCP §425.11(d)(1); *e.g.*, ***Anastos v. Lee*** (4th Dist.2004) 118 Cal.App.4th 1314, 1318 (statement of damages properly served by publication after court authorized P to serve summons and complaint by publication). See "Joining the Defendant—Service of Process," ch. 3-H, p. 295.

(2) D has appeared. If the defendant has appeared, the statement can be served in the same manner as a summons or in the manner provided for papers generally. CCP §425.11(d)(2); *see, e.g.*, ***Beeman v. Burling*** (1st Dist.1990) 216 Cal.App.3d 1586, 1594 (D appeared by filing demurrer and motion to strike; default was proper when P served statement of damages by mail). See "Serving Documents," ch. 1-G, p. 63; "Joining the Defendant—Service of Process," ch. 3-H, p. 295. The statement must be served on the party's attorney or on the party herself if she has filed suit in propria persona. CCP §425.11(d)(2).

4. Filing. The statement of damages (or request for statement and response) does not need to be filed with the court. CRC 3.250(a)(20); ***Scognamillo v. Herrick*** (2d Dist.2003) 106 Cal.App.4th 1139, 1147. However, the statement and proofs of service should be filed if the statement is part of the papers requesting the entry of default. CRC 3.250(a)(20).

5. Effect.

(1) D has not appeared. If the defendant has not appeared, the statement limits the amount of actual damages the plaintiff can recover in a default judgment. *See* CCP §§580(a), 585(a)-(c); ***Matera***, 145 Cal.App.4th at 60. See "Before default," §5.1.1(2)(b), p. 227.

(2) D has appeared. If the defendant has appeared, the statement does not limit the amount of damages the plaintiff can recover. *See* ***Damele v. Mack Trucks, Inc.*** (1st Dist.1990) 219 Cal.App.3d 29, 41.

§5.2 Punitive damages. In any action seeking punitive damages, the defendant is notified of the amount of punitive damages sought by the plaintiff through a statement of punitive damages.

1. When required. A statement of punitive damages must be served before the plaintiff can take a default against the defendant if the motion for default includes a request for punitive damages. CCP §425.115(f); *see* ***Electronic Funds Solutions, LLC v. Murphy*** (4th Dist.2005) 134 Cal.App.4th 1161, 1178; *see, e.g.*, ***Heidary v. Yadollahi*** (4th Dist.2002) 99 Cal.App.4th 857, 867 (trial court could not award punitive damages after default when statement was filed after default was entered and was never served on cross-Ds). This requirement applies even when the default is entered as a discovery sanction. ***Van Sickle v. Gilbert*** (3d Dist.2011) 196 Cal.App.4th 1495, 1521. The statement preserves the plaintiff's right to seek punitive damages as authorized by Civ. C. §3294. CCP §425.115(b).

2. Form. The plaintiff must use Judicial Council Form CIV-050. *See* CCP §425.12(b). The statement can be combined with a statement of damages under CCP §425.11. CCP §425.115(e).

3. Service. The statement of damages must be served as follows:

(1) D has not appeared. If the defendant has not appeared, the statement must be served in the same manner as a summons. CCP §425.115(g)(1). See "Joining the Defendant—Service of Process," ch. 3-H, p. 295.

(2) D has appeared. If the defendant has appeared, the statement can be served in the same manner as a summons or in the manner provided for papers generally. CCP §425.115(g)(2). See "Serving Documents," ch. 1-G, p. 63; "Joining the Defendant—Service of Process," ch. 3-H, p. 295. The statement must be served on the party's attorney or on the party herself if she has filed suit in propria persona. CCP §425.115(g)(2).

4. Filing. The statement of damages (or request for statement and response) does not need to be filed with the court. CRC 3.250(a)(20). However, the statement and proofs of service should be filed if the statement is part of the papers requesting the entry of default. *Id.*

5. Effect.

(1) D has not appeared. If the defendant has not appeared, the statement limits the amount of punitive damages the plaintiff can recover in a default judgment. *See* CCP §§580(a), 585(a)-(c); ***Matera v. McLeod*** (2d Dist.2006) 145 Cal.App.4th 44, 60.

(2) D has appeared. If the defendant has appeared, the statement does not limit the amount of punitive damages the plaintiff can recover. CCP §425.115(c).

§6. AMENDING THE COMPLAINT

After the suit has commenced, the plaintiff may need to amend the complaint to correct errors or defects or to add or remove parties or claims.

§6.1 Ways to amend. The plaintiff can amend the complaint in the following three ways:

1. Marked-up complaint. The plaintiff can amend the complaint by marking on the face of it. *See* CRC 3.1324(d); ***Smith v. Kessler*** (2d Dist.1974) 43 Cal.App.3d 26, 31. Any alterations must be initialed by the judge or the court clerk to be effective. CRC 3.1324(d). This amendment procedure is rarely allowed; the court will usually require the plaintiff to file a separate document. Weil, *Civil Procedure Before Trial*, ¶6:621.

2. Separate amendment. The plaintiff can amend the complaint by filing a separate amendment to it. *See* CCP §471.5(a); CRC 3.1324(a)(1); *see, e.g.*, ***Ford v. Superior Ct.*** (4th Dist.1973) 34 Cal.App.3d 338, 343 (P filed two amendments to original complaint). This is referred to as an "amendment to the complaint," and its purpose is to add, substitute, or change a part of the complaint. *See* ***Cohen v. Superior Ct.*** (1st Dist.1966) 244 Cal.App.2d 650, 657. The amendment should list the changes to be made and identify the page, paragraph, and line number where each change applies. Weil, *Civil Procedure Before Trial*, ¶6:622. This amendment procedure should only be used to make relatively simple changes to the complaint. *Id.*

3. Amended complaint. The plaintiff can amend the complaint by filing a complete, revised complaint. *See* CCP §471.5(a); ***Cohen***, 244 Cal.App.2d at 657; *CEB Procedure Before Trial*, §16.7; Weil, *Civil Procedure Before Trial*, ¶6:623. This is referred to as an "amended complaint," and its purpose is to provide a rewritten complaint that supersedes the original. ***Cohen***, 244 Cal.App.2d at 657; *see* CRC 3.1324(a)(1). This amendment procedure is usually preferred by the court (and may be required) because judges tend to dislike working with two separate pleadings. *See CEB Procedure Before Trial*, §16.7; Weil, *Civil Procedure Before Trial*, ¶6:624.

CAUTION

*In some situations, the plaintiff must file an amended complaint instead of an amendment to the complaint. See, e.g., **Stoiber v. Honeychuck** (5th Dist.1980) 101 Cal.App.3d 903, 931 (P must file amended complaint when D's demurrer to complaint is sustained).*

ORIGINAL COMPLAINT

§6.2 Procedure for amending.

1. Filing & serving amended complaint. The plaintiff can amend the complaint simply by filing and serving an amendment in two instances:

(1) Without leave of court – before answer or hearing on demurrer. The plaintiff can amend the complaint "of course"—that is, anytime (1) before the answer or a demurrer is filed or (2) after a demurrer is filed but before the hearing. CCP §472; ***Leader v. Health Indus.*** (2d Dist.2001) 89 Cal.App.4th 603, 612; *see* ***Dowling v. Comerford*** (1893) 99 Cal. 204, 205-06; ***Elder v. Spinks*** (1878) 53 Cal. 293, 294. If the plaintiff has sued two or more defendants, one defendant's answer does not prohibit the plaintiff from filing an amended complaint concerning any other defendant who has not answered or demurred or whose demurrer has not been heard by the court. *See* ***Barton v. Khan*** (2d Dist.2007) 157 Cal.App.4th 1216, 1221.

(a) Types of changes. The plaintiff can make any type of change to the complaint, including adding new parties. ***Gross v. DOT*** (1st Dist.1986) 180 Cal.App.3d 1102, 1105; Weil, *Civil Procedure Before Trial*, ¶6:606.

(b) No fees or leave required. The plaintiff is not required to pay a fee or seek leave of court to file the amendment. CCP §472.

(c) Notice not required. The plaintiff is not required to notify the defendant before filing the amendment. *See* CCP §472.

(d) Form of amendment. The amendment can be in the form of an amendment to the complaint or an amended complaint. *See* CCP §472; Weil, *Civil Procedure Before Trial*, ¶6:607; *see also* ***Lee v. Bank of Am. Nat'l Trust & Sav. Ass'n*** (4th Dist.1994) 27 Cal.App.4th 197, 215 (amendment to complaint under §472 operates as "amended complaint," not "supplemental complaint").

(e) Service. The plaintiff must serve a copy of the amendment or amended complaint on the defendant. CCP §472. If the defendant is in default, the amended complaint will "open the default." See "Opening default," §6.5.4, p. 237.

(2) With leave of court – after hearing on demurrer or motion to strike. The plaintiff can amend the complaint after the court has sustained the defendant's demurrer or granted the defendant's motion to

strike with leave to amend. *See* CCP §472a(c), (d); ***Velez v. Smith*** (1st Dist.2006) 142 Cal.App.4th 1154, 1174-75; ***McGettigan v. Bay Area Rapid Transit Dist.*** (1st Dist.1997) 57 Cal.App.4th 1011, 1023-24. See "Demurrer," ch. 4-H, p. 396; "Motion to Strike," ch. 4-J, p. 418.

(a) Types of changes. The plaintiff should amend only the part of the complaint that was affected by the court's order. Weil, *Civil Procedure Before Trial*, ¶6:635.5; *see* ***People v. Clausen*** (1st Dist.1967) 248 Cal.App.2d 770, 785-86. If the plaintiff needs to add additional parties to cure the defect, it must seek additional leave of court under CCP §473. *See* ***Taliaferro v. Davis*** (1st Dist.1963) 220 Cal.App.2d 793, 795; ***Schaefer v. Berinstein*** (2d Dist.1956) 140 Cal.App.2d 278, 299. See "Noticed motion for leave to amend," §6.2.4, p. 232.

(b) Leave required. The plaintiff must obtain leave of court to file the amendment. *See* ***Velez***, 142 Cal.App.4th at 1174-75. To obtain leave, the plaintiff should show the court how it would amend the complaint to cure the defects. ***Vaccaro v. Kaiman*** (2d Dist.1998) 63 Cal.App.4th 761, 768 (motion to strike); ***McGettigan***, 57 Cal.App.4th at 1023-24 (demurrer). If there is a reasonable possibility that the defect can be cured by amendment, the court should grant leave to amend. ***Vaccaro***, 63 Cal.App.4th at 768 (motion to strike); ***McGettigan***, 57 Cal.App.4th at 1023 (demurrer).

(c) Notice not required. The plaintiff is not required to notify the defendant before filing the amendment because the defendant has notice of the court's ruling. *See* ***Harlan v. DOT*** (5th Dist.2005) 132 Cal.App.4th 868, 873-75.

(d) Form of amendment. The amendment should be in the form of an amended complaint. ***Stoiber v. Honeychuck*** (5th Dist.1980) 101 Cal.App.3d 903, 931.

(e) Deadline to file. The plaintiff must file the amended complaint by the deadline stated in the court's order. *See* CCP §472a(c), (d). Generally, if no deadline is stated in an order sustaining a demurrer, the plaintiff must file the amended complaint within ten days after being served with notice of the order, unless notice is waived, in which case the plaintiff must file the amended complaint within ten days of the hearing on the demurrer. *See id.* §472b; CRC 3.1320(g); ***People v. $20,000 U.S. Currency*** (3d Dist.1991) 235 Cal.App.3d 682, 691. If the plaintiff files the amended complaint after the deadline, the court can either accept the late filing or require the plaintiff to file a noticed motion for leave. ***Harlan***, 132 Cal.App.4th at 873.

(f) Service. The plaintiff must serve a copy of the amended complaint on all parties, including parties that did not challenge the original complaint. *See* CCP §471.5(a); ***Cohen v. Superior Ct.*** (1st Dist.1966) 244 Cal.App.2d 650, 656.

2. Stipulation. The plaintiff can amend the complaint by obtaining the defendant's stipulation to allow the amendment. *See, e.g.*, ***Rosales v. Battle*** (4th Dist.2003) 113 Cal.App.4th 1178, 1181 (parties stipulated to first amended complaint). A defendant should stipulate to nonprejudicial amendments to avoid unnecessary costs and delay. *See* Weil, *Civil Procedure Before Trial*, ¶6:668.

3. Ex parte application for leave to amend. The plaintiff can amend the complaint by filing an ex parte application for leave to amend. *See* CCP §473(a)(1); *CEB Procedure Before Trial*, §16.13; Weil, *Civil Procedure Before Trial*, ¶6:618.

NOTE

Although ex parte relief is not explicitly authorized by CCP §473(a)(1), it does appear to be implicitly authorized. For the steps to determine whether a statute implicitly authorizes ex parte relief, see "Implicitly authorized," ch. 1-E, §3.1.2, p. 40.

(1) Types of changes. The plaintiff is limited in the types of changes it can make. The changes are usually limited to adding or deleting a party, correcting a mistake in a party's name, or fixing other small mistakes, such as attaching missing exhibits or correcting the form of the verification. *See* CCP §473(a)(1); *CEB Procedure*

Before Trial, §16.13; Weil, *Civil Procedure Before Trial*, ¶6:619; *see, e.g.*, ***Kuperman v. Great Republic Life Ins.*** (2d Dist.1987) 195 Cal.App.3d 943, 946-47 (trial court granted Ps' ex parte application for order permitting them to file third amended complaint reinstating D as party-D). See "Parties' names," §3.2.3(2)(a), p. 212 (discussing common problems in naming parties). If the change is substantive, the plaintiff will be required to file a noticed motion for leave to amend. *See, e.g.*, ***Board of Trs. v. Superior Ct.*** (6th Dist.2007) 149 Cal.App.4th 1154, 1159 (P ordered to file noticed motion for leave to amend after he first filed ex parte application, which sought to amend complaint by making several substantive changes). See "Noticed motion for leave to amend," §6.2.4, p. 232.

(2) Formal notice not required. The plaintiff is not required to give formal notice of the ex parte application; however, the plaintiff must follow proper ex parte practice, which does require the plaintiff to give a limited form of notice. See "Notice of Application," ch. 1-E, §4, p. 41.

(3) Deadline to file. There is no deadline for filing an ex parte application for leave to amend the complaint.

(4) Application.

(a) General requirements. The application must meet the general requirements for applications for ex parte relief. See "Application Papers," ch. 1-E, §5, p. 42.

(b) Grounds. The application must do the following:

[1] Identify the grounds supporting the plaintiff's right to amend (e.g., the amendment is correcting a mistake in a party's name). *See CEB Procedure Before Trial*, §16.21.

[2] Identify the changes to be made in the current complaint. CRC 3.1324(a).

(c) Declaration. The motion must include a separate declaration stating (1) the effect of the amendment, (2) why the amendment is necessary and proper, (3) when the facts giving rise to the amendment were discovered, and (4) the reasons why the request for amendment was not made earlier. CRC 3.1324(b).

(d) Proposed amendment. The motion must include a copy of the proposed amendment or amended complaint. CRC 3.1324(a)(1).

NOTE

Some courts provide their own forms for amending a complaint to correct a party's name. See, e.g., Super. Ct. Los Angeles Cty., Form LACIV 105; Super. Ct. San Diego Cty., Form CIV-012.

(5) Filing & serving application. If the court grants the application, the plaintiff must file the amendment or amended complaint and serve a copy on all affected defendants. CCP §471.5(a). If the defendant has appeared in the action, the plaintiff is probably not required to file a new or amended summons with an amended complaint. *See* ***Engebretson & Co. v. Harrison*** (4th Dist.1981) 125 Cal.App.3d 436, 441 n.3 (§471.5 does not contain provision requiring new or amended summons, which implies there is no such requirement). However, if the defendant has not appeared and the amended complaint "opens the default," the plaintiff must file a new or amended summons. *See* ***In re Marriage of Rhoades*** (4th Dist.1984) 157 Cal.App.3d 169, 172; ***Engebretson & Co.***, 125 Cal.App.3d at 442-43. See "Opening default," §6.5.4, p. 237; "Joining the Defendant—Service of Process," ch. 3-H, p. 295.

NOTE

If the amendment is adding a defendant to the action, the plaintiff must give the newly added defendant an opportunity to file an answer before seeking a default judgment. See ***Falahati v. Shinji Kondo*** *(2d Dist.2005) 127 Cal.App.4th 823, 832. See "Defendant's answer," §6.5.1, p. 236.*

(6) Nonconforming amendment. If the amendment does not conform to the court's order granting leave to amend, the court may strike the nonconforming portion of the amendment or amended complaint. CCP §436(b); *see* ***Quiroz v. Seventh Ave. Ctr.*** (6th Dist.2006) 140 Cal.App.4th 1256, 1281. The nonconforming portion can be struck on a party's or the court's own motion. CCP §436. See "Motion to Strike," ch. 4-J, p. 418.

4. Noticed motion for leave to amend. The plaintiff can amend the complaint by filing and serving a noticed motion for leave to amend. *See* CCP §§473(a)(1), 576.

(1) Types of changes. The plaintiff can make any type of change to the complaint. *See* CCP §473(a)(1) (court may allow amendment to any pleading on any just terms); Weil, *Civil Procedure Before Trial*, ¶6:640 (court has discretion to permit any sort of amendment).

(2) Deadline. The plaintiff can file a motion for leave at any stage of the action—even after an answer has been filed, a demurrer hearing has been held, or the complaint has already been amended one or more times. *See* CCP §473(a)(1); ***Leader***, 89 Cal.App.4th at 613. The plaintiff risks, however, having the motion denied if the proposed amendment is made after a long, unexplained delay. *E.g.*, ***Melican v. Regents of the Univ. of Cal.*** (4th Dist.2007) 151 Cal.App.4th 168, 175-76 (P's request to amend five years after claim should have been added was unreasonable). *But see* ***Kittredge Sports Co. v. Superior Ct.*** (4th Dist.1989) 213 Cal.App.3d 1045, 1048 (court cannot deny amendment after unreasonable delay if amendment would not prejudice D).

(3) Motion. A motion for leave must satisfy the following requirements:

(a) General requirements. The motion must meet the general requirements for motions, including notice to the defendant. *See* CCP §473(a)(1). See "Motion Papers," ch. 1-D, §5, p. 27.

(b) Grounds. The motion must do the following:

[1] Identify the grounds supporting the plaintiff's right to amend.

[2] Identify any allegations in the current complaint that will be deleted. CRC 3.1324(a)(2). The motion must specify the allegations by page, paragraph, and line number. *Id.*

[3] Identify any allegations that will be added to the complaint. CRC 3.1324(a)(3). The motion must specify where the allegations will be inserted by page, paragraph, and line number. *Id.*

[4] State that the motion is timely—that is, the motion was filed soon after it became apparent an amendment was necessary. *See* ***Morgan v. Superior Ct.*** (2d Dist.1959) 172 Cal.App.2d 527, 530. See "Deadline," §6.2.4(2), this page.

[5] Explain how the amendment will not prejudice the opposing party. *See* ***Morgan***, 172 Cal.App.2d at 530.

[6] Explain how the amendment will allow the plaintiff to assert a meritorious cause of action. *See id.*

[7] Request that the proposed amended complaint be deemed filed and served on the date the court grants the motion for leave. Weil, *Civil Procedure Before Trial*, ¶6:670; *see, e.g.*, ***Wiener v. Superior Ct.*** (2d Dist.1976) 58 Cal.App.3d 525, 528 (court's minute order reflected that motion for leave to amend complaint was deemed filed on date motion was granted); ***Scruggs v. Haynes*** (1st Dist.1967) 252 Cal.App.2d 256, 260 (court's minute order reflected that proposed amended complaint was deemed to have been served and filed as of order date).

(c) Declaration. The motion must include a separate declaration stating the following:

[1] The effect of the amendment. CRC 3.1324(b)(1).

[2] Why the amendment is necessary and proper. CRC 3.1324(b)(2).

[3] When the facts supporting the amendment were discovered. CRC 3.1324(b)(3); *see, e.g.*, ***Huff v. Wilkins*** (4th Dist.2006) 138 Cal.App.4th 732, 746 (court did not abuse discretion in denying motion because P conceded he had no new facts to support proposed claim).

[4] Why the amendment was not requested earlier. CRC 3.1324(b)(4); *see, e.g.*, ***Record v. Reason*** (2d Dist.1999) 73 Cal.App.4th 472, 486-87 (trial court did not abuse discretion in denying motion because of delay when facts supporting amendment were known to P before suit was filed); ***Honig v. Financial Corp.*** (2d Dist.1992) 6 Cal.App.4th 960, 966 (trial court abused discretion in denying motion when facts supporting amendment occurred after suit was filed).

[5] Any additional facts showing that justice will be served by granting the motion. *See* ***Plummer v. Superior Ct.*** (2d Dist.1963) 212 Cal.App.2d 841, 844.

(d) Proposed amendment. The motion must include a copy of the proposed amendment or amended complaint. CRC 3.1324(a)(1). The proposed amendment or amended complaint must be serially numbered to distinguish it from earlier versions of the complaint or previous amendments. *Id.*

(4) Response. The defendant should file a response to the plaintiff's motion only if necessary. Otherwise, the defendant can leave the motion unopposed or stipulate to the amendment. See "Stipulation," §6.2.2, p. 230. When challenging a motion to amend, the defendant can argue that the motion should be denied for any of the following reasons:

(a) Delay. The defendant can argue that the motion should be denied because the plaintiff waited too long to request the amendment and offered no excuse for the delay. *See* ***Bedolla v. Logan & Frazer*** (1st Dist.1975) 52 Cal.App.3d 118, 136. To support its argument, the defendant should show that (1) the plaintiff had knowledge of the facts and delayed making the amendment and (2) the defendant will be prejudiced by the amendment. *See* ***Roemer v. Retail Credit Co.*** (1st Dist.1975) 44 Cal.App.3d 926, 939-40; *cf.* ***Moss Estate Co. v. Adler*** (1953) 41 Cal.2d 581, 586 (D's motion for leave to amend answer was properly denied because amendment, which was made 12 days before trial and one year after D had knowledge of facts, would have required continuance for additional discovery).

(b) Prejudice. The defendant can argue that the motion should be denied because the defendant will be prejudiced by the amendment. *See* ***Higgins v. Del Faro*** (2d Dist.1981) 123 Cal.App.3d 558, 564; ***Hirsa v. Superior Ct.*** (1st Dist.1981) 118 Cal.App.3d 486, 490. Prejudice can occur when the amendment would delay the trial, result in a loss of critical evidence, or add to the defendant's trial preparation costs. ***Solit v. Tokai Bank*** (2d Dist.1999) 68 Cal.App.4th 1435, 1448; ***Kolani v. Gluska*** (2d Dist.1998) 64 Cal.App.4th 402, 412; *see, e.g.*, ***Vogel v. Thrifty Drug Co.*** (1954) 43 Cal.2d 184, 189 (motion to amend was properly denied when it was made the day of trial, added cause of action for breach of warranty that injected new issues of law and fact, and did not plead essential element supporting theory of liability); ***Estate of Murphy*** (2d Dist.1978) 82 Cal.App.3d 304, 311 (motion for leave to amend was properly denied because motion, which was made at start of trial, sought to add issue P was in no position to prove). An amendment is not prejudicial simply because it would make admissible otherwise relevant evidence that is damaging to the defendant. *See, e.g.*, ***Hirsa***, 118 Cal.App.3d at 490 (addition of count for negligent entrustment, which related back to original complaint, was not prejudicial simply because count would make D's motor-vehicle violations and accidents material and admissible).

(c) No cause of action. The defendant can argue that the motion should be denied because the amendment does not state a valid cause of action. ***Soderberg v. McKinney*** (2d Dist.1996) 44 Cal.App.4th 1760, 1773; ***Foxborough v. Van Atta*** (1st Dist.1994) 26 Cal.App.4th 217, 230; *see* ***Huff***, 138 Cal.App.4th at 746 (leave to amend is properly denied when facts are undisputed and there is no liability under P's amended theory); *see, e.g.*, ***Lopez v. City of San Diego*** (4th Dist.1987) 190 Cal.App.3d 678, 683 (leave to amend was properly denied because proposed amendment did not explain how city police did not act reasonably to protect Ps). However, if the proposed cause of action is a novel one, the court should permit the amendment and allow the parties to test the action's legal sufficiency by demurrer, motion for judgment on the pleadings, or other proceedings. ***Kittredge Sports***, 213 Cal.App.3d at 1048; ***California Cas. Gen. Ins. v. Superior Ct.*** (4th Dist.1985) 173 Cal.App.3d 274, 281, *disapproved on other grounds*, ***Kransco v. American Empire Surplus Lines Ins.*** (2000) 23 Cal.4th 390.

(d) Barred by limitations. The defendant can argue that the motion should be denied because the amendment does not "relate back" to the original complaint and the statute of limitations for the cause of action

has expired. *See* ***Cloud v. Northrop Grumman Corp.*** (2d Dist.1998) 67 Cal.App.4th 995, 1011 (leave to amend is properly denied if any possible amendment would inevitably be barred by limitations); *see, e.g.*, ***Quiroz***, 140 Cal.App.4th at 1281 (proposed amendment was barred by limitations, and no further amendment could have cured defect). See "Avoiding limitations – relation back," §6.3, this page.

(e) Amendment is sham. The defendant can argue that the motion should be denied because the amendment is a "sham." *See* ***Vallejo Dev. Co. v. Beck Dev. Co.*** (1st Dist.1994) 24 Cal.App.4th 929, 946. A sham amendment occurs when the plaintiff attempts to avoid a defect in the original complaint by filing an amended complaint that omits, corrects, or substitutes new facts for the facts creating the defect. *See* ***Reichert v. General Ins.*** (1968) 68 Cal.2d 822, 836; ***Vallejo Dev.***, 24 Cal.App.4th at 946; ***Lee v. Hensley*** (4th Dist.1951) 103 Cal.App.2d 697, 709. To support its argument, the defendant should show that the plaintiff (1) omitted, corrected, or substituted new facts that contradict allegations in the original complaint or exhibits to the complaint and (2) did not sufficiently explain the reason for the contradiction. *See* ***Banis Rest. Design, Inc. v. Serrano*** (3d Dist.2005) 134 Cal.App.4th 1035, 1044-45; ***Vallejo Dev.***, 24 Cal.App.4th at 946; *see, e.g.*, ***Dang v. Smith*** (6th Dist.2010) 190 Cal.App.4th 646, 658 (Ds did not show P's substitution of word "perfect" for word "record" was contradictory allegation).

CAUTION

Unless the plaintiff can explain the reason for the contradiction, the court will read the omitted or inconsistent facts into the amended complaint, thus subjecting it to demurrer. ***Hendy v. Losse*** *(1991) 54 Cal.3d 723, 742-43;* ***Banis Rest. Design****, 134 Cal.App.4th at 1044.*

ORIGINAL COMPLAINT

(f) Noncompliance with rule of court. The defendant can argue that the motion should be denied because the plaintiff did not comply with the requirements of CRC 3.1324 for motions for leave to amend. *See* ***Bank of Am. Nat'l Trust***, 27 Cal.App.4th at 217 n.15.

(5) Ruling. The court should liberally allow amendments to ensure that the case is disposed of on the merits. ***Douglas v. Superior Ct.*** (4th Dist.1989) 215 Cal.App.3d 155, 158.

(a) Grants motion. If the court grants the motion, it can impose conditions when necessary. *See* CCP §§473(a)(1), 576; ***Armenta v. Mueller Co.*** (2d Dist.2006) 142 Cal.App.4th 636, 642. The conditions should be limited, however, to what will compensate the defendant for any inconvenience caused by the late amendment. ***Williams v. Myer*** (1907) 150 Cal. 714, 718; ***Armenta***, 142 Cal.App.4th at 642. The conditions can include continuing the trial date (if the defendant requests it) or ordering the plaintiff to pay costs and fees incurred by the defendant as a result of the amendment. *See* CCP §473(a)(2); *see, e.g.*, ***Williams***, 150 Cal. at 718-19 (P required to pay attorney fees and costs for jurors and witnesses).

(b) Denies motion. If the court denies the motion, it cannot do so solely because the plaintiff has already amended the complaint one or more times. *See* ***Douglas***, 215 Cal.App.3d at 158.

(6) Filing & serving amendment. If the motion for leave is granted, the plaintiff must file the amended complaint with the court and serve a copy on all defendants affected by the amendment. CCP §471.5(a). See "Filing & serving application," §6.2.3(5), p. 231.

(7) Nonconforming amendment. If the amendment does not conform to the court's order granting leave to amend, the court may strike the nonconforming portion of the amendment or amended complaint. CCP §436(b); *see* ***Quiroz***, 140 Cal.App.4th at 1281. See "Nonconforming amendment," §6.2.3(6), p. 232.

§6.3 Avoiding limitations – relation back. The plaintiff's right to amend the complaint may be denied if the amendment would be barred by any applicable statute of limitations. ***Cloud v. Northrop Grumman Corp.*** (2d Dist.1998) 67 Cal.App.4th 995, 1011; *see, e.g.*, ***San Diego Gas & Elec. Co. v. Superior Ct.*** (4th Dist.2007) 146 Cal.App.4th 1545, 1553 (court erred in allowing P to amend complaint to add party as additional heir because limitations period had expired on wrongful-death claim). However, an amended complaint is not barred by limitations if it

"relates back"—that is, if the amended complaint is deemed filed on the date the original complaint was filed. ***Bjorndal v. Superior Ct.*** (1st Dist.2012) 211 Cal.App.4th 1100, 1113; ***Quiroz v. Seventh Ave. Ctr.*** (6th Dist.2006) 140 Cal.App.4th 1256, 1278. For the amended complaint to relate back, it must be based on the same general set of facts as the original complaint. ***Branick v. Downey S&L Ass'n*** (2006) 39 Cal.4th 235, 244; ***Austin v. Massachusetts Bonding & Ins.*** (1961) 56 Cal.2d 596, 600; *see also* ***Goldman v. Wilsey Foods, Inc.*** (2d Dist.1989) 216 Cal.App.3d 1085, 1094 (relation-back doctrine focuses on factual similarity, not rights or obligations arising from facts). An amended complaint is based on the same general set of facts when it involves the same injury and the same instrumentality. ***Dudley v. DOT*** (3d Dist.2001) 90 Cal.App.4th 255, 266; *see* ***Hirsa v. Superior Ct.*** (1st Dist.1981) 118 Cal.App.3d 486, 489.

NOTE

One court of appeal summarizes the "same general set of facts" requirement like this: different acts leading to distinct injuries are not part of the same general set of facts even though they may be part of the same "story." ***McCauley v. Howard Jarvis Taxpayers Ass'n*** *(4th Dist.1998) 68 Cal.App.4th 1255, 1262; see* ***Lee v. Bank of Am. Nat'l Trust & Sav. Ass'n*** *(4th Dist.1994) 27 Cal.App.4th 197, 207-09 (discussing cases relying on "story" analysis for same general set of facts).*

1. Same injury. The amended complaint must involve the same injury as the original complaint. ***Branick***, 39 Cal.4th at 244; ***Norgart v. Upjohn Co.*** (1999) 21 Cal.4th 383, 408-09. An amended complaint involves the same injury when it seeks recovery for violation of the same primary right alleged in the original complaint. ***Rowland v. Superior Ct.*** (4th Dist.1985) 171 Cal.App.3d 1214, 1217; *e.g.*, ***Weinstock v. Eissler*** (1st Dist.1964) 224 Cal.App.2d 212, 234-35 (amended complaint alleging fraud count related back because it sought recovery for same primary right—wrongful invasion of P's body—alleged in original complaint). See "Primary-right theory," §3.6.1(1), p. 215. If the amended complaint seeks to enforce an independent right or to impose greater liability on the defendant, the amendment will not relate back to the original complaint. ***Quiroz***, 140 Cal.App.4th at 1278; *see* ***American W. Banker v. Price Waterhouse*** (5th Dist.1993) 12 Cal.App.4th 39, 48; *see, e.g.*, ***Bartalo v. Superior Ct.*** (2d Dist.1975) 51 Cal.App.3d 526, 533-34 (amended complaint adding husband as P and claim for loss of consortium did not relate back to wife's original complaint for personal injuries).

(1) Adding plaintiffs. An amended complaint will relate back if it merely seeks to make a technical change in the capacity in which the plaintiff sued on the same cause of action or to substitute a plaintiff (real party in interest) who has standing to sue for one who lacks standing. ***San Diego Gas***, 146 Cal.App.4th at 1550; *see* ***Branick***, 39 Cal.4th at 243; ***O'Flaherty v. Belgum*** (2d Dist.2004) 115 Cal.App.4th 1044, 1095-96 (Grignon, P.J., dissenting). See "Misnomer," §3.2.3(2)(a)[4], p. 213. An amended pleading that adds a new plaintiff will relate back unless the new party seeks to enforce an independent right or to impose greater liability against the defendants. ***Brumley v. FDCC Cal., Inc.*** (1st Dist.2007) 156 Cal.App.4th 312, 324; ***San Diego Gas***, 146 Cal.App.4th at 1550; *see, e.g.*, ***Bartalo***, 51 Cal.App.3d at 533-34 (amended complaint adding husband as P and claim for loss of consortium did not relate back to wife's original complaint for personal injuries).

(2) Adding defendants. An amended complaint will relate back if it merely seeks to substitute the true name of a fictitiously named defendant or corrects a misnomer. *See* ***Hawkins v. Pacific Coast Bldg. Prods.*** (3d Dist.2004) 124 Cal.App.4th 1497, 1504; ***Woo v. Superior Ct.*** (4th Dist.1999) 75 Cal.App.4th 169, 176. See "Misnomer," §3.2.3(2)(a)[4], p. 213; "Naming Doe defendant," §6.4, p. 236. An amended complaint that seeks to add a new defendant will not relate back. ***Hawkins***, 124 Cal.App.4th at 1503; ***Woo***, 75 Cal.App.4th at 176.

2. Same instrumentality. The amended complaint must involve the same "instrumentality" as the original complaint—that is, the injury must be caused by the same thing. *See* ***Branick***, 39 Cal.4th at 244; ***Norgart***, 21 Cal.4th at 408-09; *see, e.g.*, ***Olson v. Volkswagen of Am.*** (2d Dist.1988) 201 Cal.App.3d 1437, 1442-43 (amended complaint relates back when original complaint is against driver of vehicle and amended complaint seeks to bring in other

ORIGINAL COMPLAINT

Ds, originally named as Doe-Ds, on warranty and product-liability theories). For example, an allegation that the plaintiff was electrocuted by a defective lamp is based on a different instrumentality than an allegation that the plaintiff was injured by a defective hair dryer. ***Coronet Mfg. Co. v. Superior Ct.*** (2d Dist.1979) 90 Cal.App.3d 342, 347.

§6.4 Naming Doe defendant. The plaintiff must amend the complaint when she discovers the true name of a defendant who was fictitiously named in the complaint as a Doe defendant. CCP §474. See "Doe defendants," §2.3.1(7)(b), p. 209. Until the plaintiff amends the complaint to reflect the Doe defendant's true name, the court cannot enter a judgment against that defendant. ***Meller & Snyder v. R&T Props., Inc.*** (2d Dist.1998) 62 Cal.App.4th 1303, 1311.

1. Request. The plaintiff should submit a written request for leave to amend. *See* Weil, *Civil Procedure Before Trial*, ¶6:613; *see, e.g.*, ***Barrows v. American Motors Corp.*** (2d Dist.1983) 144 Cal.App.3d 1, 6 (Ps filed motion for leave to amend). Some courts provide their own forms for amending the complaint to identify Doe defendants. *See, e.g.*, Super. Ct. Los Angeles Cty., Form LACIV 105; Super. Ct. San Diego Cty., Form CIV-012. To avoid an argument over whether the plaintiff's claims against the Doe defendant are barred by limitations, the request should state the following:

(1) The now-identified defendant is being substituted for the Doe defendant. *See* ***Austin v. Massachusetts Bonding & Ins.*** (1961) 56 Cal.2d 596, 599; ***Woo v. Superior Ct.*** (4th Dist.1999) 75 Cal.App.4th 169, 176.

(2) The plaintiff was truly ignorant of the Doe defendant's identity or liability when the original complaint was filed. *See* CCP §474; ***Hazel v. Hewlett*** (2d Dist.1988) 201 Cal.App.3d 1458, 1464-65; ***Miller v. Thomas*** (2d Dist.1981) 121 Cal.App.3d 440, 444-45. The plaintiff's ignorance must be real and not feigned. ***Balon v. Drost*** (1st Dist.1993) 20 Cal.App.4th 483, 488; ***Munoz v. Purdy*** (4th Dist.1979) 91 Cal.App.3d 942, 947. The plaintiff's ignorance can be the result of negligence because §474 does not require a duty of reasonable diligence to discover the defendant's true name. ***Irving v. Carpentier*** (1886) 70 Cal. 23, 26; ***Balon***, 20 Cal.App.4th at 488-89. One court has held, however, that if the plaintiff knew the defendant's name but forgot it when the complaint was filed, the plaintiff has the burden to review readily available information to determine the defendant's identity. ***Woo***, 75 Cal.App.4th at 180.

(3) The amended complaint "relates back" to the original complaint. See "Avoiding limitations – relation back," §6.3, p. 234.

2. Proposed amended complaint. The proposed amended complaint must state that the now-identified defendant is being substituted for the Doe defendant. ***Woo***, 75 Cal.App.4th at 176.

3. Serving amended complaint. The plaintiff is not required to serve the amended complaint on the defendant or other parties. Weil, *Civil Procedure Before Trial*, ¶6:615; *see* ***Drotleff v. Renshaw*** (1949) 34 Cal.2d 176, 181-82.

§6.5 Effect of amendment.

1. Defendant's answer. When an amendment or amended complaint is filed, the defendant must file a new or amended answer within 30 days after the amendment or amended complaint was served. CCP §471.5(a). Under §471.5, an "answer" also includes a demurrer. *See* ***McAllister v. County of Monterey*** (6th Dist.2007) 147 Cal.App.4th 253, 281; Weil, *Civil Procedure Before Trial*, ¶6:689.

(1) Answer required. When the amended complaint contains material changes (e.g., changing or adding a cause of action) affecting the defendant, the defendant cannot stand on its original answer but must file a new or amended answer to avoid a default judgment. ***Gray v. Hall*** (1928) 203 Cal. 306, 310-11; ***Carrasco v. Craft*** (5th Dist.1985) 164 Cal.App.3d 796, 808-09; *see* CCP §471.5.

(2) Answer not required. Although CCP §471.5 makes an answer to an amendment or amended complaint mandatory, there are specific instances when the defendant can choose to stand on its current answer.

(a) Minor corrections. When the amended complaint contains only minor corrections (e.g., corrections of typographical errors), the defendant can stand on its original answer and does not need to file a new or amended answer. *See* ***Gray***, 203 Cal. at 310-11; ***Carrasco***, 164 Cal.App.3d at 808-09. However, any new allegations in the amended complaint that are not put in issue by the answer will be admitted. ***Carrasco***, 164 Cal.App.3d at 809.

(b) Defendant unaffected. When the amended complaint contains substantive changes that only affect a codefendant, the defendant unaffected by the amendment can stand on its original answer. *See* ***Carrasco***, 164 Cal.App.3d at 811.

2. Original complaint superseded. When an amended complaint makes substantive changes to the original complaint, the amendment usually supersedes the original and becomes the sole basis for the cause of action. ***Anmaco, Inc. v. Bohlken*** (1st Dist.1993) 13 Cal.App.4th 891, 901; *see, e.g.*, ***JKC3H8 v. Colton*** (3d Dist.2013) 221 Cal.App.4th 468, 477 (amended complaint filed before anti-SLAPP motion was filed made anti-SLAPP motion directed at original complaint moot). In other words, the original complaint no longer has any effect as a pleading or as a basis for judgment. ***Anmaco, Inc.***, 13 Cal.App.4th at 901. In some cases, however, the original complaint will still be effective.

(1) Minor corrections. An amendment that makes minor corrections to the original complaint (e.g., corrections of typographical errors) does not supersede the original complaint. *See* ***Cole v. Roebling Constr. Co.*** (1909) 156 Cal. 443, 446; ***Beeman v. Burling*** (1st Dist.1990) 216 Cal.App.3d 1586, 1594-95; ***Ford v. Superior Ct.*** (4th Dist.1973) 34 Cal.App.3d 338, 342.

(2) Contradictions & omissions. An amendment that omits, corrects, or substitutes new facts for facts stated in the original complaint in an attempt to avoid a material defect in the complaint does not supersede the original complaint if the plaintiff does not adequately explain the reason for the omission, correction, or substitution. *See* ***Vallejo Dev. Co. v. Beck Dev. Co.*** (1st Dist.1994) 24 Cal.App.4th 929, 946; ***Billings v. Rexford Park Apts.*** (2d Dist.1966) 244 Cal.App.2d 317, 320; ***Mock v. Santa Monica Hosp.*** (2d Dist.1960) 187 Cal.App.2d 57, 60. See "Amendment is sham," §6.2.4(4)(e), p. 234.

3. Omitted defendants. When an amended complaint omits a defendant who was named in the original complaint, the omitted defendant is considered dismissed from the action. ***Fireman's Fund Ins. v. Sparks Constr., Inc.*** (4th Dist.2004) 114 Cal.App.4th 1135, 1142; *see* ***Lamoreux v. San Diego & Ariz. E. Ry.*** (1957) 48 Cal.2d 617, 627, *overruled on other grounds*, ***Leung v. Verdugo Hills Hosp.*** (2012) 55 Cal.4th 291. However, the defendant can be rejoined in a later amendment if the statute of limitations has not run on the cause of action asserted against it. ***Kuperman v. Great Republic Life Ins.*** (2d Dist.1987) 195 Cal.App.3d 943, 947; *see, e.g.*, ***Fireman's Fund***, 114 Cal.App.4th at 1143 (D1 and D2 could not be added by amended complaint because earlier amended complaint omitted all Doe Ds and statute of limitations had run against them).

4. Opening default. When an amended complaint makes material changes to the original complaint that affect a defendant in default, the amendment "opens the default." ***Cole***, 156 Cal. at 446; ***Ostling v. Loring*** (3d Dist.1994) 27 Cal.App.4th 1731, 1743. In other words, the default judgment against the defendant is set aside and the defendant can file an answer to the amended complaint. ***Beeman***, 216 Cal.App.3d at 1594-95. See "Default Judgment," ch. 10-A, p. 1089.

(1) Material change. A change is "material" if it would affect the defendant's decision not to contest the action. ***Ostling***, 27 Cal.App.4th at 1744; *see* ***Engebretson & Co. v. Harrison*** (4th Dist.1981) 125 Cal.App.3d 436, 442. For example, a new or different theory of liability or a change that subjects the defendant to increased liability for damages is a material change that opens the default. *See* ***Ostling***, 27 Cal.App.4th at 1744; ***Ford***, 34 Cal.App.3d at 343.

(2) Minor corrections. A change that merely corrects the form of the complaint (e.g., corrections of typographical errors) is not material and does not open the default. *See* ***Cole***, 156 Cal. at 446; ***People v. Mendocino Cty. Assessor's Parcel No. 056-500-09*** (1st Dist.1997) 58 Cal.App.4th 120, 126; ***Beeman***, 216 Cal.App.3d at 1594-95.

5. Changing classification. When an amended complaint changes the jurisdictional classification from limited to unlimited, the plaintiff must pay the reclassification fee specified in CCP §403.060 when it files the amendment, and the clerk must reclassify the case promptly after receiving payment. CCP §403.020(a). If the amendment

changes the jurisdictional classification from unlimited to limited, the plaintiff does not have to pay a fee, and the clerk must reclassify the case promptly after the amendment is filed. *Id.*

§7. SUPPLEMENTING THE COMPLAINT

After the complaint has been filed, the plaintiff may need to supplement it with facts that occur after the filing.

§7.1 Scope. A supplemental complaint adds facts that have occurred since the last live complaint. CCP §464(a); *e.g.*, ***Erickson v. Boothe*** (3d Dist.1954) 127 Cal.App.2d 644, 647-48 (trial court correctly denied permission to supplement complaint because facts about waste during D's possession of property happened before suit was filed). These "occurring after" facts must be material to the cause of action pleaded in the original complaint. CCP §464(a); *see* ***Flood v. Simpson*** (2d Dist.1975) 45 Cal.App.3d 644, 647. Facts that are not consistent with or in aid of the original action cannot be added by a supplemental complaint. *See, e.g.*, ***Imperial Land Co. v. Imperial Irrigation Dist.*** (1916) 173 Cal. 668, 673 (supplemental complaint properly denied when Ps had no cause of action when original complaint was filed).

1. Relief. A supplemental complaint can allege facts supporting a claim for different or additional relief, such as a new element of damages suffered after the original complaint was filed. *See, e.g.*, ***Jarchow v. Transamerica Title Ins.*** (4th Dist.1975) 48 Cal.App.3d 917, 948-49 (P filed supplemental complaint alleging mental distress occurring after suit was filed but caused by D's acts committed before suit was filed), *overruled on other grounds*, ***Soto v. Royal Globe Ins.*** (4th Dist.1986) 184 Cal.App.3d 420.

2. Cause of action. A supplemental complaint cannot allege facts supporting a new cause of action. ***Jacob v. Lorenz*** (1893) 98 Cal. 332, 337; *see* ***Hebert v. Los Angeles Raiders, Ltd.*** (2d Dist.1991) 23 Cal.App.4th 414, 426; ***Flood***, 45 Cal.App.3d at 647; *see also* ***Hutnick v. U.S. Fid. & Guar. Co.*** (1988) 47 Cal.3d 456, 464 (supplemental complaint that does not introduce new cause of action is not subject to statute of limitations).

§7.2 Procedure for supplementing. In most cases, the plaintiff must ask the court for permission to file a supplemental complaint. *See* CCP §464(a); ***Hebert v. Los Angeles Raiders, Ltd.*** (2d Dist.1991) 23 Cal.App.4th 414, 426. The same liberal policy of allowing amendments to the complaint also applies to supplemental complaints. *See* ***Louie Queriolo Trucking, Inc. v. Superior Ct.*** (5th Dist.1967) 252 Cal.App.2d 194, 197-98.

1. Noticed motion. To obtain the court's permission to file a supplemental complaint, the plaintiff must file a noticed motion for leave to file. ***Hebert***, 23 Cal.App.4th at 426; *see* CCP §464(a). See "Motion Papers," ch. 1-D, §5, p. 27. However, a noticed motion for leave to file is not required in a child-support or paternity action. CCP §464(b).

2. Filing & serving. If the court grants permission to file a supplemental complaint, the plaintiff must file the supplemental complaint with the court. *See* CCP §464(c); ***Stephani v. Abbott*** (3d Dist.1934) 137 Cal.App. 510, 516. Once the supplemental complaint is filed, the clerk must issue an amended or supplemental summons under CCP §412.10. CCP §464(c). Service of the supplemental summons and complaint must be made in the same manner as that for the initial summons. *Id.*

§7.3 Effect on original complaint.

1. Does not supersede. A supplemental complaint does not supersede the original complaint. ***Macmorris Sales Corp. v. Kozak*** (2d Dist.1968) 263 Cal.App.2d 430, 439. Both the original and the supplemental complaint are considered separate pleadings, and the supplemental complaint simply adds new allegations to be considered in conjunction with the original. *See* ***Stack v. Welder*** (1935) 3 Cal.2d 71, 76; ***ITT Gilfillan, Inc. v. City of L.A.*** (2d Dist.1982) 136 Cal.App.3d 581, 589; ***Macmorris Sales***, 263 Cal.App.2d at 439.

2. Does not cure.

(1) Defective complaint. A supplemental complaint cannot cure an original complaint that did not state a cause of action when it was filed. ***Imperial Land Co. v. Imperial Irrigation Dist.*** (1916) 173 Cal. 668, 673; ***Wittenbrock v. Bellmer*** (1880) 57 Cal. 12, 13.

(2) **Premature complaint.** A supplemental complaint cannot cure an original complaint that was filed before the plaintiff's cause of action against the defendant accrued. ***Virgin v. State Farm Fire & Cas. Co.*** (4th Dist.1990) 218 Cal.App.3d 1372, 1375 n.4. For example, a supplemental complaint cannot cure a complaint in a breach-of-contract action that was filed before the breach occurred. *Cf.* ***Lee v. Bank of Am. Nat'l Trust & Sav. Ass'n*** (4th Dist.1994) 27 Cal.App.4th 197, 207 (amended complaint).

D. INTERPLEADER

This subchapter discusses interpleader actions under the California Code of Civil Procedure. For federal interpleader actions, see ***O'Connor's Federal Rules * Civil Trials*** (2015), "Interpleader," ch. 2-C, p. 94.

§1. GENERAL

§1.1 Purpose. Interpleader allows a party exposed to multiple claims on a single obligation (the stakeholder) to settle the claims in one proceeding. *See* CCP §386; ***Dial 800 v. Fesbinder*** (2d Dist.2004) 118 Cal.App.4th 32, 43. An interpleader action is often viewed as two lawsuits in one: the first being between the stakeholder and the claimants to determine the right to interplead, and the second being between the claimants themselves to determine whose claim is superior. *See* ***Dial 800***, 118 Cal.App.4th at 43; ***State Farm Fire & Cas. Co. v. Pietak*** (3d Dist.2001) 90 Cal.App.4th 600, 612. Interpleader protects the stakeholder from multiple lawsuits and the possibility of double vexation. ***Hancock Oil Co. v. Hopkins*** (1944) 24 Cal.2d 497, 508; ***Farmers New World Life Ins. v. Rees*** (2d Dist.2013) 219 Cal.App.4th 307, 315; ***City of Morgan Hill v. Brown*** (6th Dist.1999) 71 Cal.App.4th 1114, 1122. Interpleader is commonly used to determine the right to insurance proceeds, property in escrow, and bank deposits. ***Pacific Loan Mgmt. v. Superior Ct.*** (6th Dist.1987) 196 Cal.App.3d 1485, 1490; *see California Civil Procedure Before Trial* (CEB Online ed. 2014) §§28.8-28.10.

§1.2 Primary authority. CCP §§386-386.6.

§1.3 Secondary authority. The following secondary sources are cited as authority in this subchapter:

- *California Civil Procedure Before Trial* (CEB Online ed. 2014) (referred to as *CEB Procedure Before Trial*).
- Weil & Brown, *California Practice Guide: Civil Procedure Before Trial* (CD-ROM ed. 2014) (referred to as Weil, *Civil Procedure Before Trial*).
- Witkin, *California Procedure* (5th ed. 2008 & Supp.2014) (referred to as Witkin, *Cal. Procedure*).

§2. PARTIES

§2.1 Stakeholder. A "stakeholder" is any person, firm, corporation, association, or other entity who holds money or property (i.e., the "stake") and who is or may be subject to inconsistent claims to that property. *See* CCP §386(a), (b). The stakeholder may be (1) a plaintiff who initiates the interpleader action or (2) a defendant who institutes the interpleader proceeding in an ongoing suit by filing a cross-claim. *See id.* §386(a), (b). The stakeholder may be either "disinterested" or "interested."

1. **Disinterested stakeholder.** A disinterested stakeholder puts the stake into the possession of the court, is dismissed from the proceeding, and leaves the competing claimants to litigate among themselves for ownership of the stake. *See* CCP §§386, 386.5; ***Virtanen v. O'Connell*** (4th Dist.2006) 140 Cal.App.4th 688, 698; *see, e.g.*, ***Hustead v. Superior Ct.*** (1st Dist.1969) 2 Cal.App.3d 780, 784 (garnishee subject to conflicting claims for rent due).

2. **Interested stakeholder.** An interested stakeholder claims an interest in the stake, puts the stake into the possession of the court, and litigates with the claimants for ownership of the stake. *See* CCP §386; *CEB Procedure Before Trial*, §28.1. When an interested stakeholder is involved, the proceeding is usually referred to as "partial interpleader." *See* ***City of Morgan Hill v. Brown*** (6th Dist.1999) 71 Cal.App.4th 1114, 1123.

§2.2 Claimant. A "claimant" is a person or entity who asserts an interest in the stake. *See* ***City of Morgan Hill v. Brown*** (6th Dist.1999) 71 Cal.App.4th 1114, 1123. The various claimants must assert a claim to the same stake and be adverse to one another. *See* CCP §386(b); ***City of Morgan Hill***, 71 Cal.App.4th at 1123.

§3. INITIATING INTERPLEADER ACTION

An interpleader action can be initiated by a pleading (i.e., complaint or verified cross-complaint) or by a motion (i.e., motion for substitution and discharge or motion for discharge and dismissal).

§3.1 Pleading.

1. Complaint in interpleader. To bring an interpleader action, an interested or disinterested stakeholder can file a complaint in interpleader. *See* CCP §386(a), (b).

(1) Form. The complaint in interpleader should be in the same form as complaints in general. See "Contents & Format of Complaint," ch. 3-C, §3, p. 210. Although the stakeholder is usually named as "plaintiff" and the claimants as "defendants," no affirmative relief is actually sought. *See* ***Cantu v. Resolution Trust Corp.*** (2d Dist.1992) 4 Cal.App.4th 857, 875. The claimant is merely being offered the opportunity to assert a right to the stake. *Id.*

(2) Grounds. The complaint in interpleader should allege all of the following to support the stakeholder's right to interpleader:

(a) Claims to same stake. The stakeholder must allege facts showing that the claimants have claimed, or might claim, some right, title, or interest in the same stake. *See* CCP §386(a), (b); ***Hancock Oil Co. v. Hopkins*** (1944) 24 Cal.2d 497, 504; ***Fidelity S&L Ass'n v. Rodgers*** (1919) 180 Cal. 683, 684-85; ***City of Morgan Hill v. Brown*** (6th Dist.1999) 71 Cal.App.4th 1114, 1123; *see, e.g.*, ***Williams v. Gilmore*** (3d Dist.1942) 51 Cal.App.2d 684, 687 (Ds made conflicting claims against P relating to payment of judgments).

(b) Claims conflict. The stakeholder must allege facts showing that the claims are adverse to and independent of one another. *See* CCP §386(a), (b); ***Fidelity S&L***, 180 Cal. at 684-85. The claims do not need to be identical or have the same origin. CCP §386(a), (b); *see* ***Hancock Oil***, 24 Cal.2d at 504. For example, if the claimants both assert an interest in money held by the stakeholder, one claimant can assert a right to half of the money, while the other can assert a right to all of it. ***City of Morgan Hill***, 71 Cal.App.4th at 1123.

(c) Rightful claim unapparent. The stakeholder must allege facts showing why it cannot safely determine which claim is valid. *E.g.*, ***Westamerica Bank v. City of Berkley*** (1st Dist.2011) 201 Cal.App.4th 598, 607-08 (bank could not interplead funds when escrow agreement controlled by Pub. Contract C. §22300 required bank to turn over funds to city); *see* ***Fidelity S&L***, 180 Cal. at 684-85. The stakeholder does not need to evaluate the validity of the claims or attempt to resolve the dispute; it must simply show that it does not, in good faith, know which party has the rightful claim. *See* ***Fidelity S&L***, 180 Cal. at 684-85; ***Cantu***, 4 Cal.App.4th at 876; ***Bank of Am. Nat'l Trust & Sav. Ass'n v. Carr*** (1st Dist.1956) 138 Cal.App.2d 727, 738; *CEB Procedure Before Trial*, §28.37.

(d) Reasonable probability or valid threat of double vexation. The stakeholder must allege facts showing a reasonable probability or valid threat of double vexation. ***Farmers New World Life Ins. v. Rees*** (2d Dist.2013) 219 Cal.App.4th 307, 315; ***Westamerica Bank***, 201 Cal.App.4th at 608; *see* CCP §386(a), (b); ***Hancock Oil***, 24 Cal.2d at 510; *see, e.g.*, ***City of Morgan Hill***, 71 Cal.App.4th at 1125-26 (stakeholder did not show valid threat of double vexation on its obligation to pay attorney fees). An interpleader action cannot be maintained on the mere pretext or suspicion of double vexation. *E.g.*, ***Westamerica Bank***, 201 Cal.App.4th at 608 (hypothetical possibility that bank would be held financially responsible if claimant responsible for holding stakeholder harmless was insolvent was too speculative to support interpleader).

(e) Stake disclaimed. The stakeholder must disclaim either all or part of its interest in the stake. CCP §386(a), (b); *see, e.g.*, ***Fox v. Sutton*** (1900) 127 Cal. 515, 517 (P alleged it had no interest in stake).

(f) Stake deposited. The stakeholder should state whether it will deposit the stake with the court clerk when the complaint is filed. *See* CCP §386(c). If the stake is not deposited, the stakeholder must request a court order stating to whom the stakeholder should deliver the money or property. *See* CCP §386(a), (b); ***Weingetz v. Cheverton*** (1st Dist.1951) 102 Cal.App.2d 67, 80.

(3) Request for costs & attorney fees. The stakeholder can request an award of costs and attorney fees from the amount deposited with the court if it has incurred costs and fees in the proceedings. CCP §386.6(a); ***Canal Ins. v. Tackett*** (3d Dist.2004) 117 Cal.App.4th 239, 243. The fees requested must be attributable solely to the work performed on the interpleader action. ***Sweeney v. McClaran*** (3d Dist.1976) 58 Cal.App.3d 824, 830-31. Fees for work performed on such things as negotiations, investigations, and claims for affirmative relief are not recoverable under CCP §386.6. ***Sweeney***, 58 Cal.App.3d at 830.

CAUTION

If the stakeholder does not deposit the stake with the court clerk, it is not entitled to an award of costs and attorney fees under CCP §386.6. ***Wells Fargo Bank v. Zinnel*** *(3d Dist.2004) 125 Cal.App.4th 393, 400-01; CEB Procedure Before Trial, §28.22.*

(4) Prayer. The prayer should include a request for the following relief:

(a) That the claimants be ordered to interplead and litigate their claims. CCP §386(a), (b); *see* ***Fox***, 127 Cal. at 517.

(b) That the claimants be enjoined from bringing any other actions against the stakeholder concerning the stake. *See* CCP §386(f).

(c) That the stakeholder be discharged from all liability to the claimants. *See id.* §386(a); ***Fox***, 127 Cal. at 517.

(d) That the stakeholder be awarded costs and reasonable attorney fees. CCP §386.6(a).

(e) That the stakeholder be granted any other relief the court deems proper. See "Other relief," ch. 3-C, §3.7.1(6), p. 222.

(5) Verification. There is no requirement that the complaint in interpleader be verified. Weil, *Civil Procedure Before Trial*, ¶2:487; *see* CCP §386(a), (b) (stating that cross-complaint must be verified, but silent on complaint in interpleader). *But see* ***Pacific Loan Mgmt. v. Superior Ct.*** (6th Dist.1987) 196 Cal.App.3d 1485, 1489 (dicta; stating CCP §386(b) simply requires stakeholder to file verified pleading disclaiming interest in money or property claimed); *CEB Procedure Before Trial*, §28.37 (because good faith is issue in interpleader, stakeholder should verify complaint).

(6) Service. The stakeholder must serve the claimants with summons and the complaint in interpleader as in other civil suits. See "Joining the Defendant—Service of Process," ch. 3-H, p. 295.

2. Cross-complaint in interpleader. To bring an interpleader action, an interested or disinterested stakeholder who has been sued on a claim to the stake can file a cross-complaint in interpleader. *See* CCP §386(a), (b).

CAUTION

The stakeholder-defendant should remember to also file an answer to the complaint. See CEB Procedure Before Trial, §28.35. See "Answer," ch. 4-B, p. 332. The answer can be served with the cross-complaint.

(1) Form. The cross-complaint in interpleader should be in the same form as cross-complaints in general. See "Format & Contents," ch. 4-C, §4, p. 351.

(2) Grounds. The cross-complaint in interpleader should allege the same grounds as a complaint in interpleader would. *CEB Procedure Before Trial*, §28.35. See "Grounds," §3.1.1(2), p. 240.

(3) Prayer. The prayer should include the same requested relief as in a complaint in interpleader and an additional request that the court dismiss the claimant-plaintiff's complaint with prejudice. *CEB Procedure Before Trial*, §28.35. See "Prayer," §3.1.1(4), this page.

(4) Verification. The cross-complaint must be verified. CCP §386(a), (b).

(5) Service. The stakeholder-defendant must timely serve the claimant-plaintiff with the answer and cross-complaint in interpleader as in other civil suits. See "Answer," ch. 4-B, p. 332; "Cross-Complaint," ch. 4-C, p. 349. Any other claimants named as cross-defendants must also be served with summons and the cross-complaint.

§3.2 Motion.

1. Motion for substitution & discharge. To bring an interpleader action, a disinterested stakeholder who has been sued on a claim to the stake does not have to file a cross-claim but can instead file a noticed motion for substitution and discharge. *See* CCP §386(a); Weil, *Civil Procedure Before Trial*, ¶2:489.

CAUTION

The stakeholder-defendant should remember to also file an answer to the complaint. See "Answer," ch. 4-B, p. 332. The answer can be served with the motion.

---

(1) Deadline to file. The stakeholder-defendant must make the motion before filing an answer. CCP §386(a). However, the court can allow the stakeholder-defendant to withdraw an answer that has already been filed and then make the motion. ***Israel v. Bryan*** (2d Dist.1921) 52 Cal.App. 66, 71-72.

(2) General requirements. The motion must meet the general requirements for motions, including notice to the plaintiff and other nonparty claimants. *See* CCP §386(a). For the requirements for noticed motions, see "Motion Papers," ch. 1-D, §5, p. 27. For the requirements for filing and serving, see "Filing Documents," ch. 1-F, p. 45; "Serving Documents," ch. 1-G, p. 63.

(3) Grounds. The motion must do the following to establish the stakeholder-defendant's right to interpleader:

(a) State that the plaintiff has brought suit against the stakeholder-defendant on a contract or for the recovery of specific personal property. CCP §386(a).

(b) Explain that another person, who is not a party to the suit, has made a claim against the stakeholder-defendant on the same contract or for the same personal property. *Id.*

(c) State that the stakeholder-defendant has not colluded with the nonparty in making the conflicting claim. *Id.*

(d) Explain that the stakeholder-defendant is a mere stakeholder and has no interest in the contract or property that is the subject matter of the suit. *See* ***Hellman Commercial Trust & Sav. Bank v. Alden*** (1929) 206 Cal. 592, 600.

(e) Explain how the plaintiff's and nonparty's claims are adverse to and independent of one another. CCP §386(a); *see* 4 Witkin, *Cal. Procedure*, Pleading, §245.

(f) State that the stakeholder-defendant is ready, willing, and able to deposit the amount claimed on the contract or deliver the money or property to a person designated by the court. *See* CCP §386(a); *see, e.g.*, ***DeCoe v. Johnson*** (3d Dist.1921) 54 Cal.App. 592, 595 (in affidavit, D stated it was "ready, willing, and able to make payment").

(g) Request the following relief:

[1] That the nonparty-claimant be substituted in place of the stakeholder-defendant, and the stakeholder-defendant be dismissed from the action. CCP §386(a).

[2] That the stakeholder-defendant be discharged from all liability to the claimants. *Id.*

[3] That the stakeholder-defendant be awarded costs and reasonable attorney fees. *Id.* §386.6(a).

(4) Declaration. The motion should include a separate declaration supporting each ground stated in the motion. *CEB Procedure Before Trial*, §28.34. The declaration should at least state the following:

(a) Another person, who is not a party to the suit, has made a claim against the stakeholder-defendant on the same contract or for the same personal property. CCP §386(a).

(b) The stakeholder-defendant has not colluded with the nonparty in making the conflicting claim. *Id.*

(5) Proposed order. The stakeholder-defendant should submit with the motion a proposed order that substitutes the third party in its place, discharges it of all liability, awards its costs and attorney fees, and dismisses it from the case.

(6) Service. The stakeholder-defendant must timely serve the claimant-plaintiff and nonparty claimants with the motion as in other civil suits. See "Serving Documents," ch. 1-G, p. 63.

2. Motion for discharge & dismissal. To bring an interpleader action, a disinterested stakeholder who has been sued for a specific amount of money alleged to be wrongfully withheld can file a noticed motion for discharge and dismissal. CCP §386.5.

(1) Deadline to file. The stakeholder-defendant can make the motion at any time. *See* CCP §386.5.

(2) General requirements. The motion must meet the general requirements for motions, including notice to the party-claimants. *See* CCP §386.5; *CEB Procedure Before Trial*, §28.34. For the requirements for noticed motions, see "Motion Papers," ch. 1-D, §5, p. 27. For the requirements for filing and serving, see "Filing Documents," ch. 1-F, p. 45; "Serving Documents," ch. 1-G, p. 63.

(3) Grounds. The motion must do the following to establish the stakeholder-defendant's right to interpleader:

(a) State that the plaintiff has brought suit against the stakeholder-defendant for the recovery of a specific amount of money alleged to be wrongfully withheld. CCP §386.5.

(b) Explain that another party has made a claim against the stakeholder-defendant for the same money. *Id.*

(c) Explain that the stakeholder-defendant is a mere stakeholder and has no interest in the money. *Id.*

(d) Explain how the plaintiff's and other parties' claims conflict. *See id.*; 4 Witkin, *Cal. Procedure*, Pleading, §248.

(e) State that the stakeholder-defendant is ready, willing, and able to deposit the money with the court clerk. *See* CCP §386.5 (dismissal is contingent on stakeholder-D depositing funds).

(f) Request the following relief:

[1] That the stakeholder-defendant be discharged from all liability to the claimants and be dismissed from the suit. *Id.*

[2] That the stakeholder-defendant be awarded costs and reasonable attorney fees. *Id.* §386.6(a). The stakeholder-defendant should itemize its costs and give a basis for the attorney fees incurred. *CEB Procedure Before Trial*, §28.34.

(4) Declaration. The motion should include a separate declaration supporting each ground stated in the motion. *CEB Procedure Before Trial*, §28.34. The declaration should at least state the following:

(a) Two or more parties have made conflicting demands on a specific amount of money. CCP §386.5.

(b) The stakeholder-defendant is a mere stakeholder and has no interest in all or part of the money. *Id.*

(5) Proposed order. The stakeholder-defendant should submit with the motion a proposed order that discharges it of all liability, awards its costs and attorney fees, and dismisses it from the case.

(6) Service. The stakeholder-defendant must timely serve the claimant-plaintiff and nonparty claimants with the motion as in other civil suits. See "Serving Documents," ch. 1-G, p. 63.

§4. DEPOSIT OF STAKE

When the complaint or motion is filed, the stakeholder can deposit the stake with the court clerk. CCP §386(c); *see also* ***Fox v. Sutton*** (1900) 127 Cal. 515, 519 (paying money into court registry is not prerequisite to maintaining suit).

§4.1 Type of deposit.

1. Money. Money that is interest-bearing can be deposited if both the principal and the interest can be definitely ascertained at the time of the deposit. *See* ***Williams v. Gilmore*** (3d Dist.1942) 51 Cal.App.2d 684, 688.

2. Other property. If the stake is real or personal property, the stakeholder can deposit the deed or value of the property with the court clerk. *See, e.g.*, ***Business Title Corp. v. U.S.*** (1978) 21 Cal.3d 710, 716 n.8 (in escrow holder's interpleader action, P-stakeholder deposited cash, promissory note, and security agreement); ***Richardson v. Richardson*** (2d Dist.1986) 180 Cal.App.3d 91, 93-94 (in wife's suit to compel compliance with marital settlement agreement, D-partnership filed cross-complaint in interpleader and deposited liquidated value of D-husband's partnership interest).

§4.2 Timing of deposit. The stakeholder can voluntarily deposit the stake anytime without the need for a court order directing the stakeholder to make the deposit. ***Wells Fargo Bank v. Zinnel*** (3d Dist.2004) 125 Cal.App.4th 393, 403; *see, e.g.*, ***Jang v. State Farm Fire & Cas. Co.*** (1st Dist.2000) 80 Cal.App.4th 1291, 1294-95 (D-insurer filed cross-complaint in interpleader and deposited settlement funds with court clerk).

§4.3 Partial deposit. If the amount claimed by one or more of the claimants is greater than the amount of the stake (i.e., the amount the stakeholder admits it owes), the stakeholder can deposit the lesser amount. CCP §386(c). This is called a "partial deposit." *See* ***Crocker-Anglo Nat'l Bank v. American Trust Co.*** (1st Dist.1959) 170 Cal.App.2d 289, 300.

§4.4 Effect of deposit. Any interest on the amount deposited and any damages for retaining the property (or its value) stop accruing after the date of the deposit or delivery. CCP §386(c).

§4.5 Investment of deposit. When a deposit has been made, any party can ask the court to invest the deposit in an insured interest-bearing account. CCP §386.1. Any accrued interest must be allocated to the parties in the same proportion as the original funds are allocated. *Id.*

§5. RESPONSE

§5.1 To stakeholder.

1. Type of response. The type of response the claimant can use depends on which procedural mechanism the stakeholder used to initiate the interpleader action. If the interpleader action is initiated by a complaint or cross-complaint, the claimant can oppose the action by demurrer, answer, or motion. *See* CCP §386(d); ***Continental Nat'l Bank v. Stoltz*** (1st Dist.1920) 46 Cal.App. 532, 535-36; *CEB Procedure Before Trial*, §28.39. If the interpleader action is initiated by a motion, the claimant can simply file a response to the motion. *CEB Procedure Before Trial*, §28.39. For the general requirements for each type of response, see "Opposition Papers," ch. 1-D, §8, p. 35; "Answer," ch. 4-B, p. 332; "Demurrer," ch. 4-H, p. 396; "Motion to Strike," ch. 4-J, p. 418.

2. Deadline to respond. The deadline to respond depends on the type of response made—that is, whether the claimant files a demurrer, answer, motion, or response to the stakeholder's motion. If the claimant does not timely respond, however, it waives any objections it may have had to the interpleader action. *See* ***Farmers New World Life Ins. v. Rees*** (2d Dist.2013) 219 Cal.App.4th 307, 317; ***O'Connell v. Zimmerman*** (3d Dist.1958) 157 Cal.App.2d 330, 337. To determine when to respond, see "Opposition papers," ch. 1-F, §5.2.1(2)(b), p. 57; "Retrospective deadlines," ch. 1-G, §6.2, p. 71; "Deadline to Answer," ch. 4-B, §2, p. 333; "Deadline to file & serve," ch. 4-H, §4.2, p. 403 (demurrer); "Deadline to file & serve," ch. 4-J, §3.2, p. 420 (motion to strike).

3. Challenges to interpleader. When the stakeholder files a complaint in interpleader, the claimant's response is limited to challenging the stakeholder's right to interplead—that is, whether the requirements for interpleader have been met. ***State Farm Fire & Cas. Co. v. Pietak*** (3d Dist.2001) 90 Cal.App.4th 600, 612. The following are some of the challenges the claimant can make:

(1) No conflicting claims. The claimant can argue that the stakeholder is not subject to and has no reason to anticipate conflicting claims to the same stake. *See* CCP §386(a), (b); ***Fidelity S&L Ass'n v. Rodgers*** (1919) 180 Cal. 683, 684-85; *see also CEB Procedure Before Trial*, §28.39 (D can argue that claims do not conflict because total amount of claims does not exceed stake).

(2) No interest in stake. The claimant can argue that it is not asserting an interest in the same stake as the other claimant. *See* ***Hancock Oil Co. v. Hopkins*** (1944) 24 Cal.2d 497, 504; ***Fidelity S&L***, 180 Cal. at 684-85; ***City of Morgan Hill v. Brown*** (6th Dist.1999) 71 Cal.App.4th 1114, 1123.

(3) Claim by collusion. The claimant can argue that the conflicting claim to the stake is the result of collusion between the other claimant and the stakeholder. *See* CCP §386(a); ***Sullivan v. Lusk*** (3d Dist.1907) 7 Cal.App. 186, 187, *disapproved on other grounds*, ***Monogram Co. v. Kingsley*** (1951) 38 Cal.2d 28.

(4) Stakeholder is wrongdoer. The claimant can argue that the stakeholder came into the disputed money or property by actively participating in a wrongful act. *See* ***Young v. Colyear*** (2d Dist.1921) 54 Cal.App. 232, 234; *see also* ***Williams v. Gilmore*** (3d Dist.1942) 51 Cal.App.2d 684, 689 (interpleader is equitable proceeding); *CEB Procedure Before Trial*, §28.39 (because interpleader is equitable action, equitable defenses, such as estoppel, waiver, laches, and unclean hands, should apply).

(5) Right to funds in jeopardy. The claimant can argue that the interpleader action is inadequate to preserve its rights to the stake or that it would be damaged if the court issued an injunction. *See* ***Department of Educ. v. Superior Ct.*** (2d Dist.1979) 97 Cal.App.3d 977, 979.

(6) No right to discharge. The claimant can argue that the stakeholder is not entitled to be discharged from liability to the claimant. *See, e.g.*, ***San Francisco Sav. Un. v. Long*** (1898) 123 Cal. 107, 110 (Ds waived any objections to discharge and dismissal of P-stakeholder, who was not mere stakeholder but was interested party to contract).

(7) No right to costs or fees. The claimant can argue that the stakeholder is not entitled to an award of costs or attorney fees. *See CEB Procedure Before Trial*, §28.39; *see, e.g.*, ***Wells Fargo Bank v. Zinnel*** (3d Dist.2004) 125 Cal.App.4th 393, 400-01 (stakeholder not entitled to costs or fees because it did not deposit funds into court registry).

4. Related claims. When the stakeholder files a complaint in interpleader, the claimant cannot seek affirmative relief by cross-complaint and is limited to having the action dismissed. ***Conner v. Bank of Bakersfield*** (1917) 174 Cal. 400, 403; ***City of L.A. v. Amidor*** (1903) 140 Cal. 400, 401. However, there is some doubt about whether the claimant must assert compulsory cross-complaints under CCP §426.30.

(1) Required. One court has held that CCP §426.30 applies to interpleader actions. ***Cheiker v. Prudential Ins.*** (9th Cir.1987) 820 F.2d 334, 336. Thus, all claims arising out of the same transaction as the interpleader action must be brought in the form of a cross-complaint. *Id.* at 337.

(2) Not required. One court has stated that CCP §386 might allow a claimant in an interpleader action to bring a compulsory claim against the stakeholder in a separate proceeding. *See **State Farm Fire & Cas.***, 90 Cal.App.4th at 615. The court suggests that the claimant is not required to assert its compulsory claims because interpleader actions may fit within the "[e]xcept as otherwise provided by statute" language of CCP §426.30. ***State Farm Fire & Cas.***, 90 Cal.App.4th at 615.

PRACTICE TIP

One commentator has suggested that claimants should simply file a cross-complaint to avoid the issue of whether it is necessary to bring related claims in an interpleader action. Weil, Civil Procedure Before Trial, ¶2:491.5.

§5.2 To other claimant. The claimant should file a cross-complaint against the other claimant or claimants asserting its right to the stake. *See CEB Procedure Before Trial*, §28.39. See "Cross-Complaint," ch. 4-C, p. 349.

§6. STAKEHOLDER LIABILITY

When a disinterested stakeholder properly files an interpleader action, the stakeholder is protected from tort liability if there are valid, competing claims to the stake. ***Cantu v. Resolution Trust Corp.*** (2d Dist.1992) 4 Cal.App.4th 857, 873-74; *see* ***Shopoff & Cavallo LLP v. Hyon*** (1st Dist.2008) 167 Cal.App.4th 1489, 1508; ***Pacific Loan Mgmt. v. Superior Ct.*** (6th Dist.1987) 196 Cal.App.3d 1485, 1492. However, a stakeholder may be subject to liability if it is clear beyond dispute that a claimant has an immediate right to the stake. *See, e.g.*, ***Lehto v. Allstate Ins.*** (2d Dist.1994) 31 Cal.App.4th 60, 69 (interpleader will not absolve insurer of liability if it refuses in bad faith to offer policy limits); ***Pacific Loan***, 196 Cal.App.3d at 1491 (interpleader can be abuse of process when claimant has immediate right to funds); ***National Life & Acc. Ins. v. Edwards*** (2d Dist.1981) 119 Cal.App.3d 326, 340 (bad-faith action can be permitted on showing that claims of interpleading parties were not asserted in good faith).

CAUTION

*One court has suggested that it may be possible for a disinterested stakeholder to waive its protection from liability in an interpleader action if it does not object to an independent claim raised by the claimant in the same action. See **State Farm Fire & Cas. Co. v. Pietak** (3d Dist.2001) 90 Cal.App.4th 600, 614.*

§7. HEARING & TRIAL

An interpleader action is a two-step procedure. ***Principal Life Ins. v. Peterson*** (5th Dist.2007) 156 Cal.App.4th 676, 682; ***Dial 800 v. Fesbinder*** (2d Dist.2004) 118 Cal.App.4th 32, 43.

§7.1 Step one – hearing on right to interpleader. In the first step of an interpleader action, the court must determine whether the stakeholder can maintain an interpleader action and force the claimants to interplead. ***Farmers New World Life Ins. v. Rees*** (2d Dist.2013) 219 Cal.App.4th 307, 315; ***City of Morgan Hill v. Brown*** (6th Dist.1999) 71 Cal.App.4th 1114, 1126-27. Unless the parties stipulate to the stakeholder's right to interplead, the court must conduct a hearing, take evidence, and determine whether there are valid objections to the interpleader. *See* ***Lincoln Nat'l Life Ins. v. Mitchell*** (2d Dist.1974) 41 Cal.App.3d 16, 19.

PRACTICE TIP

*To obtain a determination on an interpleader action initiated by a complaint or cross-complaint, a disinterested stakeholder should file a noticed motion for discharge and dismissal. See, e.g., **Sweeney v. McClaran** (3d Dist.1976) 58 Cal.App.3d 824, 827 (after serving cross-complaint for interpleader, disinterested D-stakeholder filed motion for discharge and dismissal); **Lincoln Nat'l**, 41 Cal.App.3d at 18 (after serving complaint for interpleader, disinterested P-stakeholder*

filed motion for "judgment of interpleader" requesting that it be discharged from further liability). The motion should also request an award of costs and attorney fees under CCP §386.6. See ***Canal Ins. v. Tackett*** *(3d Dist.2004) 117 Cal.App.4th 239, 244 (request for costs and fees was waived because P-stakeholder retracted request until after judgment).*

1. Interpleader appropriate. If the court determines that interpleader is appropriate, it can make the following interlocutory orders:

(1) Require the stakeholder to deposit the funds or property owed into the court's registry (if it has not already done so). ***Lincoln Nat'l***, 41 Cal.App.3d at 19; *see, e.g.*, ***Durkin v. Durkin*** (1st Dist.1955) 133 Cal.App.2d 283, 293 (based on cross-complaint in interpleader, court ordered D-stakeholder to deposit funds at issue with court clerk).

(2) Discharge the stakeholder from liability. *See* ***Dial 800 v. Fesbinder*** (2d Dist.2004) 118 Cal.App.4th 32, 43; ***City of Morgan Hill***, 71 Cal.App.4th at 1126-27; *see, e.g.*, ***Durkin***, 133 Cal.App.2d at 293 (court discharged D-stakeholder from liability after it deposited funds at issue with court clerk). If the stakeholder is interested, it can be discharged from liability only up to the amount deposited or to the extent of the property delivered into the court's registry. 4 Witkin, *Cal. Procedure*, Pleading, §252. *But see CEB Procedure Before Trial*, §28.8 (interested stakeholder cannot be discharged).

(3) Substitute the appropriate nonparty claimant (if necessary) and dismiss the stakeholder from the action after the stake is deposited into the court's registry. *See* CCP §§386(a), 386.5; *CEB Procedure Before Trial*, §28.31. If the stakeholder is interested, it cannot be dismissed and must remain a party to the action. *CEB Procedure Before Trial*, §28.42.

(4) Enjoin the rival claimants from taking any action against the stakeholder. CCP §386(f). The court may even restrain the enforcement of a judgment. ***Surety Co. of the Pac. v. Piver*** (Sonoma Cty. Superior Ct. Appellate Dept. 1983) 149 Cal.App.3d Supp. 29, 31-32.

(5) Award costs and attorney fees to the stakeholder. CCP §386.6(a); ***Farmers New World***, 219 Cal.App.4th at 315-16; ***Sweeney***, 58 Cal.App.3d at 828. If the court discharges and dismisses the stakeholder and agrees to award costs and attorney fees, it should specify in the order the amount of costs and fees to be paid from the funds on deposit. *See* ***Great-W. Life Assur. Co. v. Superior Ct.*** (2d Dist.1969) 271 Cal.App.2d 124, 128. The court can reserve for a later determination which of the claimants, if any, will assume the burden for the costs and fees awarded. CCP §386.6(a); ***Great-W. Life***, 271 Cal.App.2d at 128.

2. Interpleader not appropriate. If the suit is not properly brought as an interpleader action, the court will dismiss it.

§7.2 Step two – trial on merits. In the second step of an interpleader action, the court will hold a trial on the merits to determine the rights of the various claimants to the property in the court's custody. ***Lincoln Nat'l Life Ins. v. Mitchell*** (2d Dist.1974) 41 Cal.App.3d 16, 19; ***Weingetz v. Cheverton*** (1st Dist.1951) 102 Cal.App.2d 67, 80; *see* CCP §386(e). For a discussion of the parties' rights to a jury trial, see *CEB Procedure Before Trial*, §28.43; 4 Witkin, *Cal. Procedure*, Pleading, §256.

§8. REVIEW

An order granting interpleader is interlocutory and nonappealable until a final judgment is entered disposing of the claims of the remaining claimants. ***Lincoln Nat'l Life Ins. v. Mitchell*** (2d Dist.1974) 41 Cal.App.3d 16, 19; *see* ***Camp v. Oakland Mortg. & Fin. Co.*** (1928) 205 Cal. 380, 382-83 (order of substitution under §386 is interlocutory); 4 Witkin, *Cal. Procedure*, Pleading, §251 (same); *see, e.g.*, ***City of Morgan Hill v. Brown*** (6th Dist.1999) 71 Cal.App.4th 1114, 1118 (appeal taken on complaint in interpleader after court granted summary judgment on claimants' claims). However, some courts of appeal have held that if the trial court awards costs and attorney fees from the funds deposited in the court's registry, the order is immediately appealable. *E.g.*, ***Southern Cal. Gas Co. v. Flannery*** (2d Dist.2014) 232 Cal.App.4th 477, 490 & n.7; ***Sweeney v. McClaran*** (3d Dist.1976) 58 Cal.App.3d 824, 827-28.

E. CHOOSING THE COURT—SUBJECT-MATTER JURISDICTION

§1. GENERAL

§1.1 Purpose. Before filing suit, the plaintiff must decide in which of the California trial courts the suit should be filed. That decision is made by choosing a court with subject-matter jurisdiction and in which venue is proper. Subject-matter jurisdiction addresses the court's power to hear and resolve a particular dispute or cause of action; venue addresses the issue of whether the court is located in a county that can hear the suit. *See* ***Donaldson v. National Mar., Inc.*** (2005) 35 Cal.4th 503, 512; ***California State Parks Found. v. Superior Ct.*** (4th Dist.2007) 150 Cal.App.4th 826, 833; ***Estate of Buckley*** (5th Dist.1982) 132 Cal.App.3d 434, 448. For a discussion of venue, see "Choosing the Court—Venue," ch. 3-F, p. 270. Subject-matter jurisdiction cannot be conferred, expanded, or waived by the parties, and an order entered by a court without subject-matter jurisdiction is void and subject to collateral attack. ***In re Marriage of Jensen*** (4th Dist.2003) 114 Cal.App.4th 587, 593; *see* ***Housing Grp. v. United Nat'l Ins.*** (1st Dist.2001) 90 Cal.App.4th 1106, 1113, 1115; ***Chromy v. Lawrance*** (2d Dist.1991) 233 Cal.App.3d 1521, 1524. A court always has the power to hear and determine whether it has subject-matter jurisdiction in a particular case. ***Abelleira v. District Ct.*** (1941) 17 Cal.2d 280, 302-03.

NOTE

For a discussion of how to challenge a court's subject-matter jurisdiction, see "Challenging Subject-Matter Jurisdiction," ch. 4-D, p. 355.

SUBJECT-MATTER JURISDICTION

§1.2 Primary authority. Cal. Const., art. VI, §§1-11; CCP §§32.5, 85-100, 116.220-116.225, 116.390, 116.770-116.780, 396, 403.010-403.090, 410.50, 575.1-575.2, 580, 904-912, 1032-1033; Gov. C. §§68070, 68603; CRC 8.100, 8.486, 8.500, 8.552, 8.821, 8.1002, 8.1005, 8.1008.

§1.3 Secondary authority. The following secondary sources are cited as authority in this subchapter:

- *California Civil Procedure Before Trial* (CEB Online ed. 2014) (referred to as *CEB Procedure Before Trial*).
- Weil & Brown, *California Practice Guide: Civil Procedure Before Trial* (CD-ROM ed. 2014) (referred to as Weil, *Civil Procedure Before Trial*).
- Weller et al., *Report on the California Three Track Civil Litigation Study* (2002), www.clrc.ca.gov/pub/BKST/BKST-3TrackCivJur.pdf (referred to as Weller et al., *Three Track Civil Litigation Study*).
- Witkin, *California Procedure* (5th ed. 2008 & Supp.2014) (referred to as Witkin, *Cal. Procedure*).
- ***O'Connor's Federal Rules * Civil Trials*** (2015) (referred to as ***O'Connor's Federal Rules***).

§1.4 Judicial Council forms.

- CM-010 (mandatory), civil case cover sheet.
- DISC-010 (mandatory), case questionnaire – limited civil cases.
- DISC-015 (mandatory), request for statement of witnesses and evidence – limited civil cases.
- SC-100 (mandatory), plaintiff's claim and order to go to small-claims court.
- SC-100A (mandatory), attachment for listing additional plaintiffs or defendants to go to small-claims court.
- SC-100-INFO (mandatory), information for small-claims plaintiff.
- SC-107 (mandatory), small-claims subpoena.
- SC-120 (mandatory), defendant's claim and order to go to small-claims court.

§2. SUBJECT-MATTER JURISDICTION OF SUPERIOR COURTS

§2.1 Scope of jurisdiction. The California Constitution gives superior courts original jurisdiction in all cases, including habeas corpus proceedings and proceedings for extraordinary relief (e.g., mandamus, prohibition, and

certiorari). Cal. Const., art. VI, §10; *see* ***People v. Robertson*** (1989) 48 Cal.3d 18, 34 (criminal case); *see also* ***Berry v. Pacific Sportfishing, Inc.*** (9th Cir.1967) 372 F.2d 213, 215 (California superior court has general rather than limited jurisdiction); Weil, *Civil Procedure Before Trial*, ¶3:3 (each superior court has general jurisdiction, which means it can adjudicate any case brought before it). Unless otherwise specified by statute or rule, a superior court can adopt any suitable method of practice or procedure to exercise its subject-matter jurisdiction. *See* CCP §187; ***People v. Picklesimer*** (2010) 48 Cal.4th 330, 338; ***Tide Water Associated Oil Co. v. Superior Ct.*** (1955) 43 Cal.2d 815, 825.

§2.2 Limits on jurisdiction. A superior court's ability to exercise its broad subject-matter jurisdiction can be limited in certain instances, such as the following:

1. Cases with statutory prerequisites. A superior court cannot exercise subject-matter jurisdiction if the plaintiff did not satisfy a statutory jurisdictional requirement. *See, e.g.*, Fam. C. §3421(a) (under Uniform Child Custody Jurisdiction & Enforcement Act, court has jurisdiction to make initial child-custody determination only when certain conditions are met); ***Hu v. Silgan Containers Corp.*** (3d Dist.1999) 70 Cal.App.4th 1261, 1265-66 (under CCP §411.20, court lost jurisdiction over case because P did not pay filing fee within 20 days after notification that initial check was returned without payment).

2. Cases within exclusive federal jurisdiction. A superior court cannot exercise subject-matter jurisdiction over cases that fall within the exclusive jurisdiction of the federal courts. *See, e.g.*, 29 U.S.C. §1132(e)(1) (claims for injunctive or other equitable relief under Employee Retirement Income Security Act); *see also* ***Totten v. Hill*** (1st Dist.2007) 154 Cal.App.4th 40, 51-52 (under complete-preemption doctrine, case can be removed to federal court when suit is completely preempted by federal law, even if claim is pleaded in terms of state law). For a list of claims subject to the federal courts' exclusive jurisdiction, see ***O'Connor's Federal Rules***, "Exclusive federal jurisdiction," ch. 2-F, §2.3.1(2), p. 123.

3. Cases within exclusive administrative jurisdiction. A superior court cannot exercise subject-matter jurisdiction over proceedings that must be filed and adjudicated in an administrative court designated by statute to hear the particular matter. *See* ***Larson v. State Pers. Bd.*** (5th Dist.1994) 28 Cal.App.4th 265, 273 (California Constitution confers quasi-judicial powers on statewide administrative agencies). For example, a plaintiff's failure to exhaust administrative remedies can deprive a court of subject-matter jurisdiction if a statute specifically makes exhaustion of administrative remedies a jurisdictional requirement. *See* ***Saffer v. JP Morgan Chase Bank*** (2d Dist.2014) 225 Cal.App.4th 1239, 1250-51 (distinguishing cases holding that failure to exhaust administrative remedies does not deprive court of subject-matter jurisdiction because those cases did not involve statute making administrative exhaustion a jurisdictional requirement). Examples of proceedings that must be adjudicated by an administrative court include the following:

(1) Workers' compensation. Workers' compensation matters are under the exclusive jurisdiction of the Workers' Compensation Appeals Board. *See* Lab. C. §3601; ***Appl v. Lee Swett Livestock Co.*** (1st Dist.1987) 192 Cal.App.3d 466, 473. Superior courts have no jurisdiction to review or interfere with the decisions of the Board. Lab. C. §5955.

(2) Public employment relations. Public employment relations cases are under the exclusive jurisdiction of the Public Employment Relations Board (PERB), even if other claims are alleged in the complaint. *See, e.g.*, ***Personnel Comm'n v. Barstow Unified Sch. Dist.*** (4th Dist.1996) 43 Cal.App.4th 871, 885-86 (public-school transportation workers). *See generally* ***Coachella Valley Mosquito & Vector Control Dist. v. California Pub. Empl. Relations Bd.*** (2005) 35 Cal.4th 1072, 1085-86 (history of PERB jurisdiction).

(3) Public utilities. Public utility matters are under the exclusive jurisdiction of the Public Utilities Commission (PUC). ***Anchor Lighting v. Southern Cal. Edison Co.*** (2d Dist.2006) 142 Cal.App.4th 541, 547-48. *See generally* Cal. Const., art. XII, §§1-6 (authority and duties of PUC). Superior courts have no jurisdiction to review or interfere with the decisions of the PUC. Pub. Util. C. §1759(a); *see also* ***Mata v. Pacific Gas & Elec. Co.*** (1st Dist.2014) 224 Cal.App.4th 309, 315 (explaining three-part test used to determine whether action is barred by Pub. Util. C. §1759 because it interferes with PUC's regulatory authority). The California Supreme Court has exclusive jurisdiction to review PUC decisions relating solely to water corporations. Pub. Util. C. §1756(f).

(4) Attorney admission & discipline. Attorney admission decisions and attorney discipline matters are within the jurisdiction of the California State Bar and the California Supreme Court. *See* CRC 9.10, 9.20; ***In re Rose*** (2000) 22 Cal.4th 430, 442; ***Smith v. State Bar*** (2d Dist.1989) 212 Cal.App.3d 971, 978. The State Bar is not an ordinary administrative court; it has an internal review department and its decisions are recommendations to the Supreme Court. *See* CRC 9.10(a), (g), 9.12; ***In re Rose***, 22 Cal.4th at 439. If a petition for review of a decision is filed, the Supreme Court undertakes an independent examination of the matter. *See* ***In re Rose***, 22 Cal.4th at 442-43. If no petition is filed, a State Bar decision becomes a final order of the Supreme Court. CRC 9.18(b).

4. Cases subject to concurrent jurisdiction. A superior court sometimes cannot (or will not) exercise subject-matter jurisdiction over a case if a court with concurrent jurisdiction becomes involved. Concurrent jurisdiction means that more than one court has jurisdiction over a matter. *See Black's Law Dictionary* 980-81 (10th ed. 2014). An action can be brought in any court with concurrent jurisdiction. *See, e.g.*, ***In re Marriage of Perry*** (4th Dist.1997) 58 Cal.App.4th 1104, 1111 (family and probate court had concurrent jurisdiction over child-support claim against trust created by deceased father). A superior court can have concurrent jurisdiction with another California court, with another state's court, or with a federal court.

(1) Another California court. When two or more California courts have concurrent jurisdiction, the first court to exercise jurisdiction over the matter acquires exclusive jurisdiction. ***Advanced Bionics Corp. v. Medtronic, Inc.*** (2002) 29 Cal.4th 697, 707; ***County of Siskiyou v. Superior Ct.*** (3d Dist.2013) 217 Cal.App.4th 83, 89; ***Levine v. Smith*** (2d Dist.2006) 145 Cal.App.4th 1131, 1135. This is referred to as the "first-filed" or "exclusive concurrent jurisdiction" rule. *See* ***Advanced Bionics***, 29 Cal.4th at 707; ***County of Siskiyou***, 217 Cal.App.4th at 89; ***Franklin & Franklin v. 7-Eleven Owners for Fair Franchising*** (1st Dist.2000) 85 Cal.App.4th 1168, 1175. The rule requires the second action to be stayed when an appropriate pleading (i.e., a demurrer or answer) is filed. *See* ***People v. American Autoplan, Inc.*** (2d Dist.1993) 20 Cal.App.4th 760, 774 (application for preliminary injunction was not appropriate pleading; thus, court did not have power to stay or transfer second action). Once a matter is pending in one court or department, another court or department cannot interfere. ***Browne v. Superior Ct.*** (1940) 16 Cal.2d 593, 597 (court); ***Elsea v. Saberi*** (1st Dist.1992) 4 Cal.App.4th 625, 631 (department). For a discussion of departments and the organization of superior courts, see "Organization of Superior Courts – Departments," §3, p. 252. If a judgment in the first court becomes final, it can be set aside by another court only if it is void. *E.g.*, ***Levine***, 145 Cal.App.4th at 1135-36 (default judgment in one county was void and could not support separate collection action brought in another county).

SUBJECT-MATTER JURISDICTION

NOTE

While the first-filed rule is mandatory, noncompliance with the rule does not make a court's ruling void. ***American Autoplan****, 20 Cal.App.4th at 772. Error in applying the rule is reversible only when the error results in a miscarriage of justice or prejudice to the party asserting the rule. Id.*

(a) Identical cases not required. The first-filed rule does not require that the parties, causes of action, or remedies sought be identical. ***County of Siskiyou***, 217 Cal.App.4th at 89; ***Plant Insulation Co. v. Fibreboard Corp.*** (1st Dist.1990) 224 Cal.App.3d 781, 788. It is sufficient that the issue in both actions is the same and arises from the same transaction, and that the court exercising original jurisdiction has the power to bring before it all the necessary parties, litigate all the issues, and grant all the relief any of the parties might be entitled to under the pleadings. *See* ***County of Siskiyou***, 217 Cal.App.4th at 89; ***Plant Insulation***, 224 Cal.App.3d at 788.

(b) Waiver. A party can waive the first court's exclusive concurrent jurisdiction by not properly raising the issue in the second court. *See* ***American Autoplan***, 20 Cal.App.4th at 774. A party should raise the issue of exclusive concurrent jurisdiction in its answer or by filing a demurrer or a motion to dismiss, stay, or transfer. *See id.*

(2) Another state's court. When a California court has concurrent jurisdiction with a court of another state, a party can ask for a stay of one of the proceedings.

(a) **Court's discretion.** The first-filed rule does not apply between courts of different states; the decision to grant or refuse the stay is left to the court's discretion and is a matter of judicial restraint and comity. *See* ***Advanced Bionics***, 29 Cal.4th at 707; ***Simmons v. Superior Ct.*** (2d Dist.1950) 96 Cal.App.2d 119, 123-24.

(b) **Statutory limitations on parallel proceedings.** Some statutes do not allow parallel proceedings and require that only one court exercise jurisdiction over certain matters. *See, e.g.*, ***In re Stephanie M.*** (1994) 7 Cal.4th 295, 315 (child custody); ***Plas v. Superior Ct.*** (3d Dist.1984) 155 Cal.App.3d 1008, 1021 & n.9 (same).

(3) **Federal court.** When a California court has concurrent jurisdiction with a federal court (e.g., diversity case with amount in controversy over $75,000), the California court usually cannot obtain exclusive jurisdiction over the matter. *See* 28 U.S.C. §1332(a); ***Gregg v. Superior Ct.*** (1st Dist.1987) 194 Cal.App.3d 134, 137. Usually, if both a state court and a federal court obtain jurisdiction over a case, each can proceed until one or the other reaches a final judgment that becomes res judicata on the issue. ***Gregg***, 194 Cal.App.3d at 137; *see* ***Donovan v. City of Dallas*** (1964) 377 U.S. 408, 412 (federal and state courts should not interfere with each other's proceedings). If a proceeding involves property, however, the state or federal court with custody of the property at issue has exclusive jurisdiction to proceed. ***Donovan***, 377 U.S. at 412. To avoid res judicata issues, a party can ask for a stay of one of the proceedings if neither court has exclusive jurisdiction. *See* ***Benitez v. Williams*** (2d Dist.2013) 219 Cal.App.4th 270, 276. A stay in this situation is discretionary, rather than mandatory. *Id.* For a list of claims over which state courts have concurrent jurisdiction with federal courts, see ***O'Connor's Federal Rules***, "Nonexclusive federal jurisdiction," ch. 2-F, §2.3.1(1), p. 123.

PRACTICE TIP

Before filing, consider whether federal court would be a better forum for your case. A federal court abides by more restrictive procedural rules, has different voir dire procedures and jury verdict requirements, and might have a different trend of decisions. Other considerations include the location of the federal court in relation to the parties, witnesses, and counsel.

5. **Cases involving change of venue.** A superior court cannot exercise subject-matter jurisdiction over a case after it grants an order changing venue. *See, e.g.*, ***Cody v. Justice Ct.*** (1st Dist.1965) 238 Cal.App.2d 275, 286 n.8 (order changing venue divested original court of jurisdiction to proceed further in case).

6. **Cases involving governmental immunity.** A superior court cannot exercise subject-matter jurisdiction over claims for money damages against public entities or employees protected by a governmental immunity. *See* ***Gates v. Superior Ct.*** (2d Dist.1995) 32 Cal.App.4th 481, 509; *CEB Procedure Before Trial*, §6.11.

7. **Cases dismissed voluntarily.** A superior court generally cannot exercise subject-matter jurisdiction over a case after the plaintiff voluntarily dismisses the case. ***Roski v. Superior Ct.*** (2d Dist.1971) 17 Cal.App.3d 841, 845; *see* CCP §581(b)(1). The court can, however, exercise its jurisdiction if a voluntary dismissal is not allowed. For a discussion of when a voluntary dismissal is not allowed, see "Voluntary Dismissal Before Trial Commences," ch. 10-D, §3, p. 1151.

8. **Cases involving religious matters.** A superior court cannot exercise subject-matter jurisdiction over cases involving religious matters. For example, superior courts have no jurisdiction in disputes relating to the hiring, firing, discipline, or administration of clergy. ***Higgins v. Maher*** (4th Dist.1989) 210 Cal.App.3d 1168, 1175. A superior court can, however, decide church property disputes that are severable from controversies over religious doctrine. *See* ***Singh v. Singh*** (1st Dist.2004) 114 Cal.App.4th 1264, 1281; ***Protestant Episcopal Ch. v. Barker*** (2d Dist.1981) 115 Cal.App.3d 599, 615.

9. **Cases involving foreign state.** A superior court cannot exercise subject-matter jurisdiction over foreign states except as provided by federal law because a foreign state is generally immune from a federal or state court's jurisdiction. *See* 28 U.S.C. §§1604, 1605, 1607; Weil, *Civil Procedure Before Trial*, ¶3:123.40.

10. Cases involving Indian tribes. A superior court generally cannot exercise subject-matter jurisdiction over actions against Indian tribes because, as a matter of federal law, an Indian tribe is subject to suit only when Congress has authorized the suit or the tribe has waived its immunity. ***Kiowa Tribe v. Manufacturing Techs.*** (1998) 523 U.S. 751, 754.

§3. ORGANIZATION OF SUPERIOR COURTS – DEPARTMENTS

There are 58 counties in California, with each having just one superior court. *See* Cal. Const., art. VI, §4. To provide for the efficient administration of justice, each superior court consists of departments that handle both general and special duties of the court. *See* ***Elsea v. Saberi*** (1st Dist.1992) 4 Cal.App.4th 625, 631. Although often referred to as a type of court (e.g., "probate court"), a department is not a court separate and distinct from the superior court. *See* ***Schlyen v. Schlyen*** (1954) 43 Cal.2d 361, 375; *see, e.g.*, 28 Cal. Law Revision Comm'n Rep. (1998) p. 148 (statute authorizes continued use of "small-claims court" even though small-claims division is not separate court). Instead, a department is merely a designation that a judge or judges have been assigned to handle one of the superior court's general or special duties. *See, e.g.*, ***In re Chantal S.*** (1996) 13 Cal.4th 196, 201 ("family court" is not separate court with special jurisdiction but instead is superior court performing one of its general duties).

§3.1 Establishment of departments.

1. By presiding judge. Many departments are established by the presiding judge of the superior court—usually under the authority of the superior court's local rules—to distribute the court's business. *See* ***Schlyen v. Schlyen*** (1954) 43 Cal.2d 361, 371; ***White v. Superior Ct.*** (1895) 110 Cal. 60, 67; ***People v. Grace*** (2d Dist.1926) 77 Cal.App. 752, 759; *see also* Gov. C. §69508(a) (presiding judge of superior court having three or more judges must distribute business of court among judges and prescribe order of business).

2. By statute. Some departments are required by statute to handle special proceedings, such as proceedings for extraordinary relief, small claims, or juvenile cases. *See, e.g.*, Cal. Const., art. VI, §10 (appellate division of superior court has original jurisdiction over proceedings for extraordinary relief); CCP §116.210 (superior court has separate division to hear small claims); Welfare & Inst. C. §246 (presiding judge must designate one or more judges to hear all juvenile cases).

§3.2 Jurisdiction of departments.

1. Subject-matter jurisdiction. Subject-matter jurisdiction is vested in the superior court for a county, not in any particular department. ***B.F. v. Superior Ct.*** (2d Dist.2012) 207 Cal.App.4th 621, 628; ***Glade v. Glade*** (2d Dist.1995) 38 Cal.App.4th 1441, 1449. A department shares the superior court's subject-matter jurisdiction—that is, each department of the superior court has subject-matter jurisdiction over all cases. ***B.F.***, 207 Cal.App.4th at 628; *see* ***In re Harris*** (1993) 5 Cal.4th 813, 837 (criminal case). But a department's ability to exercise all of its subject-matter jurisdiction is usually limited to certain types (e.g., family), classes (e.g., small claims), or aspects (e.g., discovery disputes) of cases. *See* ***People v. Malveaux*** (2d Dist.1996) 50 Cal.App.4th 1425, 1439 (criminal case); 2 Witkin, *Cal. Procedure*, Courts, §218 (division of superior court into departments), §222 (under proper circumstances, any judge of superior court may exercise any of its subject-matter jurisdiction, even specialized jurisdiction such as juvenile or probate), §223 (special courts, such as juvenile and probate courts, exercise specialized statutory jurisdiction and follow specialized statutory procedure). If the department exceeds these limitations, it acts in "excess of jurisdiction." *See* ***In re Harris***, 5 Cal.4th at 837-38 & n.12 (felony proceedings against minor should be heard by juvenile court, not criminal court); 2 Witkin, *Cal. Procedure*, Courts, §223 (when distinct subject-matter jurisdiction is given to special court, that court should exercise that jurisdiction). An act taken in excess of jurisdiction is voidable if the objecting party is not barred from challenging the act by waiver, laches, or estoppel. *See* ***In re Michael R.*** (4th Dist.2006) 137 Cal.App.4th 126, 146; ***Conservatorship of O'Connor*** (1st Dist.1996) 48 Cal.App.4th 1076, 1088.

2. Priority of jurisdiction. Once a department has been assigned a case for hearing and determination, that department has "priority of jurisdiction" over the case, meaning no other department can interfere with its proceedings until the case is disposed of or removed from the department. ***Williams v. Superior Ct.*** (1939) 14

Cal.2d 656, 662; *see, e.g.*, ***In re Marriage of Schenck*** (3d Dist.1991) 228 Cal.App.3d 1474, 1482-84 & n.4 (family-law department had priority of jurisdiction over community property, so wife could not ask law-and-motion department to order sale of house to satisfy child and spousal support). When the department renders a judgment on the matter before it, the judgment is binding on all other departments unless it is overturned by the court of appeal or the Supreme Court. ***Ford v. Superior Ct.*** (2d Dist.1986) 188 Cal.App.3d 737, 742. A department can, however, hear a habeas corpus petition based on another department's judgment. *See* ***In re Ramirez*** (2d Dist.2001) 89 Cal.App.4th 1312, 1318.

§3.3 Types of departments.

1. General civil. The term "civil department" is a broad designation for the departments within a superior court that have general jurisdiction over civil cases. These departments are usually referred to by number (e.g., Department 1), but some are referred to by the procedural classifications of the cases they hear (e.g., small-claims court). The jurisdiction of a department that presides over a civil case (or some aspect of it) depends primarily on two things: (1) the case's procedural classification and (2) the case-management system used by the superior court.

(1) Procedural classification. Civil cases are handled by a three-track procedural system divided according to the case's amount in controversy. Weller et al., *Three Track Civil Litigation Study*, at 1. Under this system, a case is classified as an unlimited civil case, a limited case, or a small-claims case when filed. The department's jurisdiction is limited by the rules of practice and procedure applicable to that class of case. *See* ***Wozniak v. Lucutz*** (2d Dist.2002) 102 Cal.App.4th 1031, 1039 (limited civil cases are governed by economic litigation procedures and other procedural distinctions), *disapproved on other grounds*, ***LeFrancois v. Goel*** (2005) 35 Cal.4th 1094. For a complete discussion of these procedural classifications and a summary of their rules of practice and procedure, see "Procedural Classifications of Civil Cases," §4, p. 255.

(2) Case-management system. Once a case has been classified, the superior court's case-management system determines whether one or several departments will be involved in the disposition of the suit.

(a) Master-calendar system. Some superior courts use a master-calendar system in which cases are assigned to one department for "trial purposes" and other departments for case management, pretrial matters, and settlement. Weil, *Civil Procedure Before Trial*, ¶12:35. This is called a master-calendar system because parts of a case are assigned to different departments from a single master calendar. *See id.* Under a master-calendar system, each department's jurisdiction is limited (1) to resolving the part of the case assigned to that department and (2) by the case's procedural classification. See "Effect of classification," §4.3, p. 261.

(b) Direct-calendar system. Some superior courts use a direct-calendar system in which cases are randomly assigned to a single judge for "all purposes." Weil, *Civil Procedure Before Trial*, ¶12:36; *see* CCP §170.6(a)(2); CRC 3.734. Under this all-purpose assignment system, the judge of the department is directly responsible for maintaining her own calendar, setting and handling all motions and other proceedings, and conducting trial. Weil, *Civil Procedure Before Trial*, ¶12:36. Because the department is responsible for the entire case, its jurisdiction is limited only by the case's procedural classification. See "Effect of classification," §4.3, p. 261.

(c) Mixed system. Some superior courts use a combination of master-calendar and direct-calendar systems. *See, e.g.*, Super. Ct. San Diego Cty. Loc. R., rule 2.1.3 (new cases are assigned either to master calendar or to judge for all purposes); ***Hypertouch, Inc. v. Superior Ct.*** (1st Dist.2005) 128 Cal.App.4th 1527, 1554 n.15 (dicta; presiding judge of San Mateo Superior Court should have assigned class-action suit to one judge for all purposes rather than distributing judicial responsibility among many judges).

2. Appellate. The appellate department, now known as the "appellate division," has original jurisdiction over proceedings for extraordinary relief and appellate jurisdiction over limited civil cases. *See* Cal. Const., art. VI, §§10, 11(b).

(1) Original jurisdiction. The appellate division has original jurisdiction over proceedings for extraordinary relief (e.g., mandamus, certiorari, prohibition) in cases that are subject to the superior court's appellate jurisdiction. Cal. Const., art. VI, §10; *e.g.*, ***Kernes v. Superior Ct.*** (4th Dist.2000) 77 Cal.App.4th 525, 528-29 (appellate division had jurisdiction to issue writ of mandate about order recusing city attorney because division had appellate jurisdiction over underlying misdemeanor case). The appellate division does not have original jurisdiction in habeas corpus proceedings; that jurisdiction is vested with the superior court. ***In re Ramirez*** (2d Dist.2001) 89 Cal.App.4th 1312, 1319.

(2) Appellate jurisdiction. The appellate division has appellate jurisdiction over limited civil cases. CCP §904.2; CRC 8.821(a)(1); ***General Elec. Capital Auto Fin. Servs. v. Appellate Div.*** (2d Dist.2001) 88 Cal.App.4th 136, 143; *see* Cal. Const., art. VI, §11(b). Matters that can be appealed from limited civil cases include the following:

(a) Judgments, except interlocutory judgments or judgments of contempt that are made final and conclusive by CCP §1222. CCP §904.2(a); ***General Elec.***, 88 Cal.App.4th at 143.

(b) Postjudgment orders. CCP §904.2(b). One court of appeal has held that the appellate division has jurisdiction to review a postjudgment enforcement order of a small-claims court. ***General Elec.***, 88 Cal.App.4th at 144-45.

(c) Orders changing or refusing to change the place of trial. CCP §904.2(c).

(d) Orders granting a motion to quash service of summons. *Id.* §904.2(d).

(e) Orders granting a motion to stay or written orders to dismiss the action under CCP §581d on the ground of inconvenient forum. *Id.* §904.2(d).

(f) Orders granting a new trial. *Id.* §904.2(e).

(g) Orders denying a motion for judgment notwithstanding the verdict. *Id.*

(h) Orders discharging or refusing to discharge an attachment or granting a right-to-attach order. *Id.* §904.2(f).

(i) Orders granting or dissolving an injunction or refusing to grant or dissolve an injunction. *Id.* §904.2(g).

(j) Orders appointing a receiver. *Id.* §904.2(h).

3. Family. The family department, also called the "family court," has jurisdiction over family matters, which include support actions, marital dissolutions, actions under the Uniform Interstate Family Support Act, and proceedings under the Family Conciliation Court Law. *See* Fam. C. §§200, 1810, 1830, 4902, 4905, 4909, 4914; *see, e.g.*, ***Glade v. Glade*** (2d Dist.1995) 38 Cal.App.4th 1441, 1450 (family court had jurisdiction over trust involved in disposition of marital property); *see also* ***In re Michael R.*** (4th Dist.2006) 137 Cal.App.4th 126, 146 (although probate court has exclusive jurisdiction over guardianships, family court acquired jurisdiction over custody determination when temporary guardianship lapsed). Like other departments, the family court has limited jurisdiction; it can exercise jurisdiction only over the subject matter authorized by the Family Code and can acquire jurisdiction over that subject matter only in the manner prescribed by the Code. *See* ***In re Marriage of Davis*** (5th Dist.1977) 68 Cal.App.3d 294, 300.

4. Probate. The probate department, also called the "probate court," has jurisdiction over probate matters, which include proceedings involving probate, guardianship, trusts, powers of attorney, and advanced health-care directives. *See* Prob. C. §2200 (guardianship & conservatorship), §4520 (powers of attorney), §4760 (advanced health-care directives), §7050 (probate), §17000 (trusts); *see, e.g.*, ***Conservatorship of Coffey*** (1st Dist.1986) 186 Cal.App.3d 1431, 1439 (probate court has jurisdiction over suit to surcharge conservator). Like other departments,

the probate court has limited jurisdiction; it can exercise jurisdiction only over the subject matter authorized by the Probate Code and can acquire jurisdiction over that subject matter only in the manner prescribed by the Code. *See* ***Conservatorship of Coffey***, 186 Cal.App.3d at 1439. When presiding over probate matters, however, the court acts as a court of general jurisdiction and has all the powers of the superior court. Prob. C. §800; *e.g.*, *id.* §4520 (court handling proceedings involving powers of attorney is court of general jurisdiction and has same powers as superior court).

(1) Definitions.

(a) Probate. Probate issues involve the passage of title to the decedent's property by will or intestate succession. *See* Prob. C. §7000; *see, e.g.*, ***Estate of Jimenez*** (2d Dist.1997) 56 Cal.App.4th 733, 740 (disposition of decedent's remains could not be decided in probate court; remains are not estate property and will made no provision for disposition of decedent's remains).

(b) Internal affairs of trusts. Internal affairs of trusts include modifying the terms of a trust, changing a designated successor trustee, deviating from trust provisions, exercising authority over a trustee's acts, and administering a trust's financial arrangements. ***Harnedy v. Whitty*** (1st Dist.2003) 110 Cal.App.4th 1333, 1345; ***Estate of Mullins*** (2d Dist.1988) 206 Cal.App.3d 924, 931; *see, e.g.*, ***Patton v. Sherwood*** (2d Dist.2007) 152 Cal.App.4th 339, 341 (suit for accounting).

(2) Jurisdiction over trusts – exclusive & concurrent. If the probate department exercises jurisdiction over a trust, it has the following jurisdiction:

(a) Exclusive jurisdiction over proceedings about the internal affairs of that trust. Prob. C. §17000(a).

(b) Concurrent jurisdiction over actions to determine the existence of the trust, actions by or against creditors or debtors of the trust, and other actions involving the trustees and third persons. *Id.* §17000(b).

(3) Transfer of separate civil actions. The Probate Code provides that separate civil actions can be severed and transferred to the appropriate department. Prob. C. §801.

SUBJECT-MATTER JURISDICTION

5. Juvenile. The juvenile department, also called the "juvenile court," has jurisdiction over juvenile matters, which include dependency, custody wardship, delinquency, and criminal matters. Welfare & Inst. C. §245; *see id.* §300 (dependency), §304 (custody), §388 (wardship), §601 (delinquency), §602 (juvenile crime); *see also* ***In re Shirley K.*** (4th Dist.2006) 140 Cal.App.4th 65, 72-73 (juvenile court reviews adoption determinations by Health & Human Services Agency); ***In re Joshua G.*** (4th Dist.2005) 129 Cal.App.4th 189, 202 (in dependency proceedings, court has jurisdiction over children, not parents). The presiding judge of the superior court must designate one or more judges to hear all juvenile cases. Welfare & Inst. C. §246. When presiding over juvenile matters, the superior court must be referred to as the "juvenile court." *Id.* §245. Like other departments, the juvenile court has limited jurisdiction; it can exercise jurisdiction only over the subject matter authorized by the Welfare & Institutions Code and can acquire jurisdiction over that subject matter only in the manner prescribed by the Code. *See* ***In re Chantal S.*** (1996) 13 Cal.4th 196, 200.

6. Small claims. Each superior court must have a small-claims division, usually referred to as the "small-claims court." CCP §116.210. Like all other departments, the small-claims court is not a separate court from the superior court. 28 Cal. Law Revision Comm'n Rep. (1998) p. 148. Generally, the small-claims court has jurisdiction over limited civil cases with amounts in controversy up to $5,000. ***General Elec.***, 88 Cal.App.4th at 142; *see* CCP §§87, 116.210, 116.220(a)(1). See "Small claims," §4.2.3, p. 260. The small-claims court is designed to resolve minor civil disputes expeditiously, inexpensively, and fairly. ***General Elec.***, 88 Cal.App.4th at 142; *see* CCP §116.120(b), (c).

§4. PROCEDURAL CLASSIFICATIONS OF CIVIL CASES

Cases filed in superior court are initially classified as unlimited, limited, or small-claims cases. The basis for classification mainly depends on the amount in controversy and the relief requested. *See* CCP §§85-88. The classification

of a case is important because it dictates how cases are adjudicated and what relief is available to the parties. *See* ***Pajaro Valley Water Mgmt. Agency v. McGrath*** (6th Dist.2005) 128 Cal.App.4th 1093, 1103; *see, e.g.*, CCP §580(b)(1) (monetary damages over $25,000 cannot be awarded in limited civil case). See "Effect of classification," §4.3, p. 261. Depending on the size of the county, classification can also determine the superior-court department to which a case is assigned. *See, e.g.*, CCP §116.220(a) (listing actions over which small-claims court has jurisdiction).

§4.1 Calculating amount in controversy. The classification of a case usually depends on the amount in controversy. *See* Weller et al., *Three Track Civil Litigation Study*, at 1. The amount in controversy is the amount of the demand, the value of the property, or the amount of the lien in dispute. CCP §85(a).

NOTE

Although the 1998 unification of the municipal and superior courts in each county eliminated municipal courts and created the jurisdictional labels of unlimited and limited jurisdiction, the analysis for determining the amount in controversy remains the same. ***Ytuarte v. Superior Ct.*** *(2d Dist.2005) 129 Cal.App.4th 266, 274; see* ***Stern v. Superior Ct.*** *(2d Dist.2003) 105 Cal.App.4th 223, 230-31 & n.2. Thus, cases from before 1998 that discuss jurisdiction based on the amount in controversy still apply.*

SUBJECT-MATTER JURISDICTION

1. Determined by complaint. The amount in controversy is generally established by the prayer or demand of the complaint. ***Security Pac. Nat'l Bank v. Lyon*** (Los Angeles Cty. Superior Ct. Appellate Dept. 1980) 105 Cal.App.3d Supp. 8, 14; *see* ***Minor v. Municipal Ct.*** (1st Dist.1990) 219 Cal.App.3d 1541, 1547; ***People v. Argonaut Ins.*** (3d Dist.1977) 71 Cal.App.3d 994, 996. The court may examine the rest of the complaint to determine whether the alleged facts support the amount indicated in the prayer or demand. *See, e.g.*, ***Security Pac. Nat'l***, 105 Cal.App.3d Supp. at 14 (court determined allegations did not support demand in cross-complaint because they were made in bad faith); ***Williams v. Rosinsky Motor Co.*** (Los Angeles Cty. Superior Ct. Appellate Dept. 1955) 133 Cal.App.2d Supp. 798, 802-03 (facts alleged in complaint exceeded court's jurisdiction despite demand for amount within jurisdictional limits). The court will ignore bad-faith, frivolous, or vexatious demands when calculating the amount in controversy. *See* ***Security Pac. Nat'l***, 105 Cal.App.3d Supp. at 12.

2. What is included. The amount in controversy includes actual, special, punitive, and treble damages. *See, e.g.*, ***Williams v. Superior Ct.*** (2d Dist.1990) 219 Cal.App.3d 171, 179-80 (allegations of special damages allowed case to remain in superior court); ***Block v. Tobin*** (1st Dist.1975) 45 Cal.App.3d 214, 222 (prayer for punitive damages brought amount in controversy within jurisdiction of superior court). While the complaint cannot always state the exact amount of damages sought, all damages are considered when determining the amount in controversy. *See* ***Schwartz v. California Claim Serv.*** (2d Dist.1942) 52 Cal.App.2d 47, 56; *see also* Civ. C. §3295(e) (amount of punitive damages cannot be stated in complaint); CCP §425.10(b) (amount of actual or punitive damages for personal injury or wrongful death cannot be stated in complaint). For example, if the suit seeks damages based on the value of property, the complaint should indicate the reasonable value of the property, or at least its approximate value. *See* ***Holm v. Davis*** (2d Dist.1935) 8 Cal.App.2d 328, 329. A nonspecific demand (e.g., demand for damages "in excess of $25,000") can be sufficient to establish the amount in controversy for jurisdictional purposes. *See* ***Engebretson & Co. v. Harrison*** (4th Dist.1981) 125 Cal.App.3d 436, 444. See "Prayer," ch. 3-C, §3.7, p. 220.

3. What is excluded.

(1) Attorney fees. The amount in controversy does not usually include attorney fees. CCP §85(a); ***Charnay v. Cobert*** (2d Dist.2006) 145 Cal.App.4th 170, 180 n.10. Attorney fees are costs incidental to the judgment, not part of the damages. ***Lozada v. City & Cty. of S.F.*** (1st Dist.2006) 145 Cal.App.4th 1139, 1160; *see* CCP

§1033.5(a)(10); *see also* ***Combs v. State Farm Fire & Cas. Co.*** (1st Dist.2006) 143 Cal.App.4th 1338, 1345 (attorney fees are rarely considered damages because they do not compensate for injury); ***Stokus v. Marsh*** (1st Dist. 1990) 217 Cal.App.3d 647, 653 (court can award attorney fees exceeding maximum jurisdiction of court). Attorney fees can be considered in determining the amount in controversy only when a statute or contract specifies that attorney fees are damages separate from costs. *See, e.g.*, ***Cirimele v. Shinazy*** (1st Dist.1954) 124 Cal.App.2d 46, 52-53 (attorney fees authorized by promissory note were special damages, not costs); ***Garcia v. Ebeling Motor Co.*** (2d Dist.1949) 89 Cal.App.2d 688, 694-95 (Price Control Act allowed attorney fees as part of penalty separate from costs).

(2) Interest. The amount in controversy does not include prejudgment or postjudgment interest. CCP §85(a).

(3) Costs. The amount in controversy does not include court costs. CCP §85(a).

4. Multiple claims & parties.

(1) Multiple claims.

(a) P's claims. All the plaintiff's claims against a single defendant are added together to determine the amount in controversy. *See* ***Hammell v. Superior Ct.*** (1932) 217 Cal. 5, 7; ***Perry v. Farley Bros. Moving & Storage, Inc.*** (2d Dist.1970) 6 Cal.App.3d 884, 888. Each claim represents a single amount of damages, no matter how many different theories of recovery are asserted in support of the claim. *See* ***Perry***, 6 Cal.App.3d at 888.

(b) D's claims. If the defendant files a cross-complaint, the defendant's claims are added to the amount in controversy. *See* CCP §403.030. By increasing the amount in controversy, a cross-complaint may change the jurisdictional classification of a case. *See id.* See "Cross-complaint," §4.5.1(2), p. 267.

SUBJECT-MATTER JURISDICTION

(2) Multiple parties.

(a) Multiple Ps. If multiple plaintiffs have claims against a single defendant, the amount in controversy depends on whether those claims are related or unrelated.

[1] Related claims. If multiple plaintiffs bring related claims against one defendant, the claims can be joined and added together to determine the amount in controversy. *See* ***Frost v. Mighetto*** (4th Dist.1937) 22 Cal.App.2d 612, 615; Weil, *Civil Procedure Before Trial*, ¶3:105.

[2] Unrelated claims. If multiple plaintiffs bring unrelated claims against one defendant and each claim is less than the jurisdictional minimum of the court, the claims cannot be joined and added together to determine the amount in controversy. *See* ***Hammell***, 217 Cal. at 7; ***Winrod v. Wolters*** (1903) 141 Cal. 399, 402-03; Weil, *Civil Procedure Before Trial*, ¶3:106. However, if multiple plaintiffs bring unrelated claims against one defendant and at least one of the claims is within the jurisdictional limit of the court, the court acquires jurisdiction over all the claims. *See* ***Emery v. Pacific Empls. Ins.*** (1937) 8 Cal.2d 663, 668-69; Weil, *Civil Procedure Before Trial*, ¶3:107.

(b) Multiple Ds. If a single plaintiff has separate claims against several defendants, each claim is treated separately in determining the amount in controversy. *See* ***Emery***, 8 Cal.2d at 666.

§4.2 Classifying civil cases.

1. Unlimited cases. A civil action or proceeding is classified as an unlimited case if either of the following applies:

(1) Not a limited case. The case is not classified as a limited case. CCP §88; *see also id.* §86 (defining "limited cases"); ***Ytuarte v. Superior Ct.*** (2d Dist.2005) 129 Cal.App.4th 266, 275 (unlimited is "catchall" designation). See "Limited cases," §4.2.2, p. 258. The amount in controversy for a limited case cannot exceed $25,000,

although some statutes provide that certain cases are not limited even if the amount in controversy is less than $25,000. *See* CCP §85(a); *see, e.g.*, *id.* §871.3(a) (actions relating to good-faith improvements to real property owned by another are unlimited, regardless of amount in controversy).

(2) Involves the legality of a tax, impost, assessment, toll, or municipal fine. The case involves the legality of a tax, impost, assessment, toll, or municipal fine. *See* CCP §86(a)(1); *see, e.g.*, ***Pajaro Valley Water Mgmt. Agency v. McGrath*** (6th Dist.2005) 128 Cal.App.4th 1093, 1102-03 (D's challenge of tax-like charges provided basis for reclassification of case as unlimited).

2. Limited cases. A civil action or proceeding is classified as a limited case if all the following conditions are met:

(1) $25,000 or less. The amount in controversy does not exceed $25,000, excluding attorney fees, interest, and costs. CCP §85(a); *see id.* §86(a)(1); ***Stern v. Superior Ct.*** (2d Dist.2003) 105 Cal.App.4th 223, 230.

(2) Appropriate relief. The relief sought is a type that can be granted in a limited civil case. CCP §85(b). This requirement was designed to preserve the limitations on the types of equitable relief awardable in the former municipal court. 28 Cal. Law Revision Comm'n Rep. (1998) p. 139. Most types of relief can be granted in a limited civil case, but the following cannot:

(a) Damages exceeding $25,000, excluding attorney fees, interest, and costs. CCP §580(b)(1); *see* ***Ytuarte***, 129 Cal.App.4th at 274-75.

(b) A permanent injunction, unless authorized by another statute. CCP §580(b)(2).

(c) A determination of title to real property. *Id.* §580(b)(3).

(d) Declaratory relief, except as authorized by CCP §86. *Id.* §580(b)(4).

(3) Action classified as limited case. The relief sought is exclusively a type described in a statute that either classifies the action or proceeding as a limited civil case or provides that the action or proceeding is within the original jurisdiction of the former municipal court. CCP §85(c). The types of actions specifically classified as limited cases by statute include the following:

(a) Cases at law in which the demand (excluding interest) or the value of the property in controversy amounts to $25,000 or less. *Id.* §86(a)(1).

(b) Actions for dissolution of a partnership if the total assets of the partnership do not exceed $25,000. *Id.* §86(a)(2).

(c) Actions of interpleader if the amount of money or property involved does not exceed $25,000. *Id.*

(d) Actions to cancel, rescind, or revise a contract when the relief is sought in connection with an action to recover money not exceeding $25,000 or property of a value not exceeding $25,000. *Id.* §86(a)(3).

(e) Proceedings in forcible entry or unlawful detainer if the amount of damages claimed does not exceed $25,000. *Id.* §86(a)(4).

(f) Actions to enforce or foreclose liens on personal property if the liens do not exceed $25,000. *Id.* §86(a)(5).

(g) Actions to enforce, foreclose, or release liens of mechanics, materialmen, artisans, and laborers. *Id.* §86(a)(6). The action is not a limited civil case if (1) it seeks to enforce a lien involving property affected by a separate unlimited case or (2) all the liens sought to be foreclosed on the same property total more than $25,000. *Id.*

(h) Actions to enforce or foreclose an assessment lien on a common-interest development, as defined by Civ. C. §4100 or 6534. CCP §86(a)(6); *see* Civ. C. §§4100, 6534. The action is not a limited civil case if

(1) it seeks to enforce a lien involving property affected by a separate unlimited case or (2) all the liens sought to be foreclosed on the same property total more than $25,000. CCP §86(a)(6).

(i) Actions for declaratory relief brought:

[1] By a cross-complaint claiming an indemnity right to the relief demanded in the complaint. *Id.* §86(a)(7)(A).

[2] By a cross-complaint in an otherwise limited case. *Id.*

[3] To conduct a trial after a nonbinding fee arbitration between an attorney and a client if the amount in controversy does not exceed $25,000. *Id.* §86(a)(7)(B).

(j) Actions to issue temporary restraining orders and preliminary injunctions. *Id.* §86(a)(8).

(k) Actions to take accounts when necessary to preserve the property rights of a party to a limited civil case. *Id.*

(*l*) Actions to appoint a receiver or to determine title to personal property seized in a limited civil case. *Id.*

(m) Actions to enforce judgments. *Id.*

(n) Actions by a judgment creditor to reach personal property of a judgment debtor held by a third party if the judgment debtor's interest in the property does not exceed $25,000. *Id.* §86(a)(9); *see id.* §708.210.

(o) Actions to enforce a debt owed to a judgment debtor if the debt does not exceed $25,000. *Id.* §86(a)(9).

(p) Certain arbitration-related petitions if the matter to be resolved by arbitration is a limited civil case or the award does not exceed $25,000. *Id.* §86(a)(10).

(q) Actions brought under the Long-Term Care, Health, Safety and Security Act of 1973 if civil penalties are not sought or they do not exceed $25,000. CCP §86.1.

(r) The following cases in equity:

[1] To try title to personal property up to $25,000 in value. *Id.* §86(b)(1).

[2] When equity is pleaded as a defense in a limited case. *Id.* §86(b)(2).

[3] To vacate a judgment or order obtained in a limited civil case through fraud, mistake, inadvertence, or excusable neglect. *Id.* §86(b)(3).

(s) Actions or proceedings that were formerly under the jurisdiction of the municipal courts. *See id.* §85(c). CCP §85 lists various provisions formerly under municipal-court jurisdiction, including the following:

[1] Civ. C. §§798.61, 798.88. CCP §85(c)(1) (inclusion of §798.88 sunsets 1-1-16).

[2] Civ. C. §§1719, 3342.5. CCP §85(c)(2), (c)(3).

[3] CCP §§86, 86.1, 1710.20. CCP §85(c)(4)-(c)(6).

[4] Food & Agr. C. §§7581, 12647, 27601, 31503, 31621, 52514, 53564. CCP §85(c)(7)-(c)(13).

[5] Gov. C. §§53069.4, 53075.6, 53075.61. CCP §85(c)(14)-(c)(16).

[6] Pub. Util. C. §5411.5. CCP §85(c)(17).

[7] Veh. C. §§9872.1, 10751, 14607.6, 40230, 40256. CCP §85(c)(18)-(c)(22).

(t) Actions by a mobile-home park's management to obtain a judicial declaration that a particular mobile home has been abandoned, regardless of value. Civ. C. §798.61(c); Weil, *Civil Procedure Before Trial*, ¶3:29.2.

SUBJECT-MATTER JURISDICTION

PRACTICE TIP

If the plaintiff is filing a limited civil case, the caption of the complaint must state that the case is a limited civil case. CCP §422.30(b); CRC 2.111(10). See "Pleadings & other papers," ch. 1-B, §2.5.2(9)(b), p. 15.

3. Small claims. Generally, small claims are limited civil cases with amounts in controversy up to $5,000. ***General Elec. Capital Auto Fin. Servs. v. Appellate Div.*** (2d Dist.2001) 88 Cal.App.4th 136, 142; *see* CCP §§87, 116.210, 116.220(a)(1). See "Limited cases," §4.2.2, p. 258. Certain actions have lower or higher limits. *See, e.g.*, CCP §116.220(c) ($2,500-$6,500 for certain actions against guarantors), §116.221 ($10,000 for actions brought by natural person). The specific actions and proceedings designated as small claims include the following:

(1) Recovery of money if the amount demanded does not exceed $5,000. CCP §116.220(a)(1).

(2) Enforcement of payment of delinquent unsecured personal-property taxes up to $5,000, unless the legality of the tax is challenged by the defendant. *Id.* §116.220(a)(2).

(3) Issuance of a writ of possession if the amount demanded does not exceed $5,000. *Id.* §116.220(a)(3); *see* Civ. C. §§1861.5, 1861.10.

(4) Confirmation, correction, or vacation of a binding arbitration award of attorney fees, not exceeding $5,000, between an attorney and a client. CCP §116.220(a)(4).

(5) Hearing de novo between an attorney and a client after a nonbinding arbitration of a fee dispute not exceeding $5,000. *Id. See generally* Bus. & Prof. C. §§6200-6206 (rules governing arbitration of attorney fees).

(6) Actions for an injunction or other equitable relief when a statute expressly authorizes a small-claims court to award that relief. CCP §116.220(a)(5).

(7) Recovery up to $2,500 in any action against a defendant guarantor that does not charge a fee for its guarantor or surety services. *Id.* §116.220(c)(2).

(8) Recovery up to $6,500 in any action against a defendant guarantor that charges a fee for its guarantor or surety services. *Id.* §116.220(c)(3).

(9) Recovery up to $4,000 in any action by an entity other than a natural person against the Registrar of the Contractors' State License Board as guarantor. *Id.* §116.220(c)(4).

(10) Recovery up to $10,000 in any action brought by a natural person against the Registrar of the Contractors' State License Board as guarantor. *See id.* §§116.220(c)(1), 116.221.

(11) Actions brought by a natural person if the amount demanded does not exceed $10,000. *Id.* §116.221. However, if the action is brought by a natural person for damages for bodily injury from an automobile accident and the defendant is covered by an insurance policy that includes a duty to defend, the action is designated as a small claim only if the amount demanded does not exceed $7,500. *Id.* §116.224.

PRACTICE TIP

If the defendant has a cross-claim over the jurisdictional limit, the defendant can file a separate action in superior court and ask the small-claims court to transfer the plaintiff's small-claims action to the superior court. CCP §116.390(a).

§4.3 Effect of classification. The classification of a case as unlimited, limited, or small-claims does not affect the fundamental subject-matter jurisdiction of the superior court. *See* ***Pajaro Valley Water Mgmt. Agency v. McGrath*** (6th Dist.2005) 128 Cal.App.4th 1093, 1103; *see also* ***Wozniak v. Lucutz*** (2d Dist.2002) 102 Cal.App.4th 1031, 1036 n.1 (parties' references to "limited jurisdiction court" and "unlimited jurisdiction court" were misleading because after unification there is only one superior court), *disapproved on other grounds*, ***LeFrancois v. Goel*** (2005) 35 Cal.4th 1094. Classification does, however, determine which procedures apply, what type of relief can be granted, and how the case is appealed. *See* ***Pajaro Valley***, 128 Cal.App.4th at 1103. Chart 3-1, below, summarizes the important differences between unlimited, limited, and small-claims cases.

3-1. EFFECT OF CLASSIFICATION

		Unlimited	Limited	Small-claims
Procedures				
1	Pleadings	All pleadings allowed.	Only complaints, answers, cross-complaints, answers to cross-complaints, and general demurrers allowed. CCP §92(a).	No formal pleading required. CCP §116.310(a); *see id.* §§116.320, 116.360. Only JCF SC-100 and SC-120 allowed. *See* CCP §116.320.
2	Discovery	Civil Discovery Act applies. *See* CCP §§2016.010-2036.050.	Limited discovery. CCP §§94, 95. JCF DISC-010 and DISC-015 can be used. *See* CCP §§93(a), 96, 97.	Regular pretrial discovery not allowed. CCP §116.310(b). Only JCF SC-107 allowed.
3	Motions	No limitations.	No limitations, except motion to strike can only challenge alleged damages. CCP §92(d), (e).	No limitations. *See, e.g.*, JCF SC-105 (general), SC-108 (correct or cancel judgment), SC-114 (amend party names), SC-135 (vacate judgment), SC-150 (postpone trial).
4	Scheduling	75% of trials should occur within 12 months of filing. CRC 3.714(b)(1)(A).*	90% of trials should occur within 12 months of filing. CRC 3.714(b)(2)(A).*	Hearing held within 70 days of order setting hearing. CCP §116.330(a). Hearing can be held during day or night, Monday through Saturday. *Id.* §116.250.
5	Trial	Normal trial.	Trial limited by economic litigation rules. *See* CCP §§90-100.	Informal hearing without jury. CCP §116.510; *see id.* §116.520.
6	Evidence	Rules of Evidence apply.	Rules of Evidence apply. Direct testimony of witnesses and experts can be presented by affidavit, declaration, or deposition transcript. CCP §98.	Rules of Evidence do not apply. ***Houghtaling*** (4th Dist.1993) 17 Cal.App.4th 1128, 1139. Experts can testify only on personal knowledge. CCP §116.531.
7	Representation by attorney	Allowed.	Allowed.	Not allowed. CCP §116.530(a).
8	Service requirements	CCP §§413.10-417.40; JCF POS-010, POS-015.	CCP §§413.10-417.40; JCF POS-010, POS-015.	CCP §116.340; JCF SC-104, SC-104B.
9	Filing fees	$435. *See* Gov. C. §§70602.5(a), 70602.6(a), (b), 70611.	$225 or $370. *See* Gov. C. §§70602.5(b), (c), 70613(a), (b).	$30-$100. CCP §116.230.

SUBJECT-MATTER JURISDICTION

3-1. EFFECT OF CLASSIFICATION (CONTINUED)				
		Unlimited	Limited	Small-claims
Relief				
10	Monetary relief	Unlimited.	Up to $25,000. CCP §§86, 580(b)(1).	Generally up to $5,000 unless statute states otherwise. *See* CCP §§116.220, 116.221, 116.224.
11	Equitable relief	All types of equitable relief available.	Equitable relief available except for permanent injunctions and real-property determinations. CCP §580(b)(2), (b)(3). Limited declaratory relief. *See id.* §§86(a)(7), 580(b)(4).	Limited to rescission, restitution, reformation, and specific performance. CCP §116.220(b).
12	Award of costs	Costs generally awarded to prevailing party. CCP §1032(b). Award discretionary if case could have been brought in court of limited jurisdiction. *Id.* §1033(a).	Costs generally awarded to prevailing party. CCP §1032(b). If recovery is less than $5,000: (1) award discretionary if case could have been small claim, (2) if case could not have been small claim, award requires notification to D and is limited to filing and service costs and attorney fees. *Id.* §1033(b).	Costs awarded to prevailing party. CCP §116.820(c).
Appeal				
13	Right of appeal	Parties can appeal.	Parties can appeal.	P cannot appeal its own complaint. CCP §116.710(a). D cannot appeal its countercomplaint. *See id.* §116.710(b).
14	Court of appeal	Appeal is made to court of appeal. CCP §904.1(a); *see* Cal. Const., art. VI, §11. California Supreme Court can review any decision of court of appeal. Cal. Const., art. VI, §12(b); CRC 8.500(a)(1).	Appeal is made to appellate division of superior court. CCP §904.2. Appealable rulings are listed in CCP §904.2.	Appeal is made to superior court by trial de novo. *See* CCP §§116.710(b), 116.770(a). Trial de novo judgment is final and not appealable. *Id.* §116.780(a).

* The case-management order setting the trial date depends on the individual merits of the case. *See* CRC 3.714(a), 3.715(a), 3.727.
JCF = Judicial Council Form

1. Unlimited cases.

(1) No procedural limitations. Unlimited cases are not subject to the restrictive economic litigation procedures that apply to limited cases. *See* CCP §91; ***Pajaro Valley***, 128 Cal.App.4th at 1103.

(2) No limitations on relief. All types of relief can be granted in unlimited cases. *See* CCP §580(b).

(a) Monetary relief. For monetary relief, the amount in controversy must exceed $25,000, but the court can enter a judgment for less than that amount. *See* CCP §403.040(e); ***Ytuarte v. Superior Ct.*** (2d Dist.2005) 129 Cal.App.4th 266, 275.

(b) Costs.

[1] General rule. The prevailing party in an unlimited case is entitled to recover its costs. *See* CCP §1032(b); ***Steele v. Jensen Instr. Co.*** (2d Dist.1997) 59 Cal.App.4th 326, 330; *see also* ***Goodman v. Lozano*** (2010) 47 Cal.4th 1327, 1338-39 (despite judgment in Ps' favor, Ds were prevailing parties under CCP §1032 because settlement offsets reduced Ps' recovery to zero; Ds awarded costs and attorney fees).

[2] Exception. When the prevailing party in an unlimited civil case recovers less than $25,000, the court has discretion to determine costs. CCP §1033(a); ***Chavez v. City of L.A.*** (2010) 47 Cal.4th 970, 975-76 & n.1.

NOTE

Section 1033 is a cost-shifting statute designed to encourage a plaintiff to file suit in the appropriate court. ***Steele****, 59 Cal.App.4th at 330-31. The rule gives courts discretion to deny costs to a plaintiff who files a suit as an unlimited case but recovers a judgment in an amount that could have been rendered in a court of limited jurisdiction. See id.*

(3) Appeal. In unlimited cases, appeals are made to the court of appeal. CCP §904.1(a); *see* Cal. Const., art. VI, §11. The California Supreme Court can review any decision made by the court of appeal. Cal. Const., art. VI, §12(b); CRC 8.500(a)(1). See "Appeal of unlimited cases," §7.1, p. 268.

2. Limited cases.

(1) Procedural limitations. Limited cases must be conducted under the rules for economic litigation. *See* CCP §91(a). These rules impose certain procedural limitations on limited cases, including the following:

(a) Limited pleadings. The only pleadings allowed in a limited case are complaints, answers, cross-complaints, answers to cross-complaints, and general demurrers. CCP §92(a). Special demurrers are not allowed. *Id.* §92(c).

(b) Unverified answers. In a limited case the answer can be unverified, even if the complaint or cross-complaint is verified. CCP §92(b).

(c) Motion to strike – limited grounds. Motions to strike are allowed only on the grounds that the damages or relief sought are not supported by the allegations in the complaint. CCP §92(d). All other motions are permitted in limited cases. *Id.* §92(e). See "Motion to Strike," ch. 4-J, p. 418.

(d) Limited discovery.

[1] Traditional methods. Discovery is permitted only to the extent provided by CCP §§94 and 95. CCP §94. Parties are allowed a combination of 35 interrogatories, demands to produce documents or things, and requests for admission. *Id.* §94(a). Parties are allowed one oral or written deposition. *Id.* §94(b). Parties can serve a subpoena duces tecum, ask for physical and mental examinations, and ask for the identity of expert witnesses. *Id.* §94(c)-(e).

[2] Questionnaire. The plaintiff can serve with its complaint a case questionnaire using Judicial Council Form DISC-010. *See* CCP §93(a). This case questionnaire elicits the basic information about each party's case. *Id.* §93(c). The defendant must completely and timely respond to the questionnaire or be subject to an order compelling responses or sanctions. *Id.* §93(e). The defendant's completed questionnaire must be served with its answer, but is not filed with the court. *See id.* §93(b).

[3] Witness request. Any party can serve a request for statement of witnesses and evidence, which must be used to call any witness or introduce any evidence at trial. *See* CCP §§96, 97; Judicial Council Forms, form DISC-015. This request is not filed with the court. CCP §96(e).

(2) Limited relief.

(a) Monetary relief. Monetary damages over $25,000 cannot be awarded in a limited civil case. CCP §580(b)(1); ***Ytuarte***, 129 Cal.App.4th at 274-75; *see* CCP §86. If a limited case is misclassified because of an extra amount in the demand, the plaintiff may give up the extra amount and the suit may continue as a limited case. CCP §403.040(f).

(b) Equitable relief.

[1] No permanent injunctions. Most permanent injunctions cannot be granted in a limited case. CCP §580(b)(2); ***Ytuarte***, 129 Cal.App.4th at 275. Temporary restraining orders and preliminary injunctions, however, can be granted. *See* CCP §86(a)(8).

[2] No real-property title determinations. Determinations of title to real property cannot be made in a limited case. CCP §580(b)(3). Only title to personal property worth up to $25,000 can be determined in a limited case. *Id.* §86(b)(1).

[3] Limited declaratory relief. Only certain types of declaratory relief can be granted in a limited case. *See* CCP §§86(a)(7), 580(b)(4). See "Action classified as limited case," §4.2.2(3)(i), p. 259.

(c) Costs. The prevailing party in a limited case is usually entitled to recover its costs. *See* CCP §1032(b); ***Steele***, 59 Cal.App.4th at 330. However, when the prevailing plaintiff in a limited case recovers less than $5,000, the following rules apply:

[1] If the party could have brought the suit in small-claims court (i.e., the claim was for less than $5,000) but did not do so, the court may either fully allow, partially allow, or deny costs to the prevailing party. CCP §1033(b)(1).

[2] If the party could not have brought the suit in small-claims court (i.e., the claim was between $5,000 and $25,000), the recovery of costs is limited to the actual costs of filing, service, and if otherwise allowed by law, attorney fees. *Id.* §1033(b)(2). These costs will be awarded only if the plaintiff shows it notified the defendant in writing before filing suit that costs could be awarded with judgment. *Id.*

SUBJECT-MATTER JURISDICTION

NOTE

Section 1033 is a cost-shifting statute designed to encourage a plaintiff to file suit in the appropriate court. ***Steele****, 59 Cal.App.4th at 330-31. The rule gives trial courts discretion to deny costs to a plaintiff who files suit in a court of limited jurisdiction but recovers a judgment in an amount that could have been rendered in a small-claims court. See id.*

(3) Limited right of appeal. A limited case is appealed to the appellate division of the superior court rather than the court of appeal. CCP §904.2; ***Ytuarte***, 129 Cal.App.4th at 275; *see* CCP §100.

(4) Lower fees. The initial filing fee is lower in a limited case than in an unlimited case. See "Filing fees," ch. 3-C, §4.1.4, p. 226.

(5) Prepared testimony. A party can offer the prepared testimony of relevant witnesses in the form of an affidavit, declaration, or deposition transcript instead of presenting direct testimony. CCP §98. This includes expert testimony and testimony to authenticate documents. *Id.*

(6) Conclusiveness of judgment. A judgment or final order in a limited case is conclusive between the parties (and their successors in interest), but it does not collaterally estop a party (or a successor in interest) in other litigation with a nonparty. CCP §99; Weil, *Civil Procedure Before Trial*, ¶3:40.5.

3. Small-claims cases. Small claims must be conducted under the rules of the Small Claims Act. *See* CCP §§116.110, 116.120. To save time and money, a small-claims case is resolved at a simple, informal hearing rather than a trial. *Id.* §116.510. For general information on bringing a small claim, see Judicial Council Form SC-100-INFO.

(1) Procedural limitations. Small-claims cases are subject to certain procedural limitations, including the following:

(a) No attorney. An attorney cannot take part in the conduct or defense of a small-claims case except as a litigant. CCP §116.530(a), (b); *see id.* §116.320(c). An attorney can, however, give advice to a party, testify about facts within her knowledge, and represent a party in an appeal to the general superior court or in connection with the enforcement of a small-claims judgment. *Id.* §116.530(c); *see id.* §116.770(c).

(b) Lenient service rules. The requirements for service on the defendant in a small-claims case are more lenient than the service of summons in a limited or unlimited case in superior court. *See* CCP §116.340; *see also* Judicial Council Forms, form SC-104B (explaining small-claims proof of service). See "Small claims," ch. 3-H, §5.4.1, p. 310.

(c) Expedited scheduling. The clerk schedules the case for hearing within 70 days after the order setting the hearing. CCP §116.330(a). The court can set a new date if a party asks for the hearing to be postponed. *See id.* §116.570(a)(4)(A), (c). Hearings can be held at any time, day or night, Monday through Saturday. *Id.* §116.250.

(d) No formal pleadings. No formal pleadings other than the Judicial Council's claim forms are necessary in a small-claims case. CCP §116.310(a); *see id.* §§116.320(b), 116.360; *see, e.g.*, Judicial Council Forms, form SC-100 (plaintiff's claim), form SC-120 (defendant's claim).

(e) Limits on discovery. The pretrial discovery procedures described in CCP §2019.010 are not allowed. CCP §116.310(b); ***Rosenberg v. Superior Ct.*** (6th Dist.1998) 67 Cal.App.4th 860, 865. A small-claims subpoena for personal appearance and production of documents and things at the hearing or trial de novo can be issued by the parties using Judicial Council Form SC-107.

(f) Informal hearing without jury. The hearing and disposition of a small-claims case is informal. CCP §116.510; ***Sanderson v. Niemann*** (1941) 17 Cal.2d 563, 573; *see* CCP §116.520. A jury is not present, even when the judgment is appealed by a trial de novo to the general superior court. CCP §116.770(b); ***Crouchman v. Superior Ct.*** (1988) 45 Cal.3d 1167, 1172.

(g) No rules of evidence. The rules of evidence do not apply in small-claims cases. *E.g.*, ***Houghtaling v. Superior Ct.*** (4th Dist.1993) 17 Cal.App.4th 1128, 1139 (affidavit containing hearsay admissible). Experts can testify only about facts based on personal knowledge. CCP §116.531.

(h) Limited number of suits. A person can file up to two small-claims suits in a year with demands over $2,500. CCP §116.231(a); *see also id.* §116.231(b) (claims for more than $2,500 must be accompanied by declaration that no more than two small claims have been filed in past year). This limitation does not apply to small claims filed by a city, county, school district, local district, or any other local public entity. *Id.* §116.231(a), (d).

(i) No assigned claims. No claim can be filed or maintained in small-claims court by the assignee of a claim. CCP §116.420(a).

(2) Limited relief.

(a) Monetary relief. A small-claims court can award monetary relief only up to its jurisdictional limits. *See* ***Jellinek v. Superior Ct.*** (6th Dist.1991) 228 Cal.App.3d 652, 656. See "Small claims," §4.2.3, p. 260. By filing a suit in small-claims court, a plaintiff waives any damages exceeding the court's jurisdictional limit. ***Jellinek***, 228 Cal.App.3d at 656; *see* CCP §116.220(d). If the plaintiff decides to seek more damages, it must dismiss the small-claims suit and file a separate suit in superior court. *See* ***Jellinek***, 228 Cal.App.3d at 659. The plaintiff cannot split one cause of action into multiple claims to stay in small-claims court. *See, e.g.*, ***Lekse v. Municipal Ct.*** (2d Dist.1982) 138 Cal.App.3d 188, 194-95 (cause of action for rent could not be split into separate claims by month for rent past due).

(b) Equitable relief. Instead of or in addition to money damages, the court can grant equitable relief in the form of rescission, restitution, reformation, or specific performance. CCP §116.220(b). But injunctions and other forms of equitable relief are not allowed unless a statute expressly authorizes the small-claims court to grant that relief. *Id.* §116.220(a)(5).

(c) Costs & interest. The prevailing party in a small-claims case is entitled to the costs of enforcing the judgment and to accrued interest. CCP §116.820(c).

(3) Limited right of appeal. The plaintiff in a small-claims case cannot appeal the judgment on its own claim, nor can the defendant appeal the judgment on its counterclaim. *See* CCP §§116.320(c), 116.710(a), (b);

Pitzen v. Superior Ct. (4th Dist.2004) 120 Cal.App.4th 1374, 1380; ***Acuna v. Gunderson Chevrolet, Inc.*** (2d Dist.1993) 19 Cal.App.4th 1467, 1471. Each party can, however, appeal the judgment on the other's claim. CCP §116.710(b); ***Linton v. Superior Ct.*** (1st Dist.1997) 53 Cal.App.4th 1097, 1105-06. A judgment is appealed to the superior court by a trial de novo before a different judicial officer. *See* CCP §§116.710(b), 116.770(a); CRC 8.952(2). See "Appeal of small claims," §7.3, p. 269.

(4) Sliding-scale fees. The fees for filing small claims depend on the amount of the claim and whether the claimant has filed more than 12 other small claims in the past year. *See* CCP §116.230.

(5) Challenging venue or location. The defendant can challenge the venue or court location by writing to the court and mailing a copy of the challenge to each of the other parties to the action; a personal appearance at the hearing is not required. CCP §116.370(b).

§4.4 Fast-track scheduling. Under the authority of the Trial Court Delay Reduction Act, the Judicial Council sets goals for the resolution of civil cases based on their classification. *See* Gov. C. §68603; CRC 3.714(b). While no deadlines are imposed by statute, courts must make local rules and case-management orders to meet these goals. *See* CRC 3.711, 3.727(4). These are commonly called fast-track rules. Weil, *Civil Procedure Before Trial*, ¶12:48.

PRACTICE TIP

Be aware of the fast-track rules where the suit is filed, because they vary from court to court and can affect important procedural deadlines. See Gov. C. §68616. Unlike most local rules, fast-track rules are not preempted by the California Rules of Court or other statutes. See "Overview of Case-Management Process," ch. 5-A, §2, p. 461.

SUBJECT-MATTER JURISDICTION

1. Disposition time goals.

(1) Unlimited cases. The court's goal is to manage unlimited cases after filing so that 75% are disposed of within 12 months, 85% are disposed of within 18 months, and 100% are disposed of within 24 months. CRC 3.714(b)(1).

(2) Limited cases. The court's goal is to manage limited cases after filing so that 90% are disposed of within 12 months, 98% are disposed of within 18 months, and 100% are disposed of within 24 months. CRC 3.714(b)(2).

(3) Small-claims cases. The court's goal is to manage small-claims cases after filing so that 90% are disposed of within 75 days and 100% are disposed of within 95 days. Cal. Stds. Jud. Admin. 2.2(h). Although the Judicial Council sets these goals, small-claims cases are excluded from all delay-reduction programs. *See* Gov. C. §68620(b). However, a hearing must be held within 70 days after the order setting the hearing. CCP §116.330(a). Hearings can be held at any time, day or night, Monday through Saturday. *Id.* §116.250.

2. Exceptions. Certain cases are exempt from fast-track rules. For a discussion of these cases, see "Applicability of Case-Management Rules," ch. 5-A, §3, p. 462.

§4.5 Reclassification. Once classified, a case can later be reclassified. *See* CCP §§403.020(a), 403.030, 403.040(a), 403.050(a); ***Ytuarte v. Superior Ct.*** (2d Dist.2005) 129 Cal.App.4th 266, 275-76. Reclassification does not change the jurisdiction of the court but affects the procedures governing how the case is litigated. ***Pajaro Valley Water Mgmt. Agency v. McGrath*** (6th Dist.2005) 128 Cal.App.4th 1093, 1103. See "Effect of classification," §4.3, p. 261. When a case is reclassified, it is considered filed when the initial complaint was filed, not when the reclassification occurred. CCP §403.070(a).

1. How to reclassify.

(1) Amended complaint. The plaintiff can change the jurisdictional classification of the case by amending the complaint. CCP §403.020(a); *see* ***Pajaro Valley***, 128 Cal.App.4th at 1103. The caption must indicate

that the case is being reclassified by the amended complaint. CRC 2.111(11). The clerk will reclassify the case when the plaintiff files the amended complaint and pays any applicable reclassification fee. See "Reclassification fee," §4.5.3, this page.

(2) Cross-complaint. The defendant can change the jurisdictional classification of the case by filing or amending a cross-complaint. *See* CCP §§403.020(a), 403.030. The caption must indicate that the case is being reclassified by the cross-complaint. *Id.* §403.030; CRC 2.111(11). When filing the cross-complaint, the defendant must pay any applicable reclassification fee. See "Reclassification fee," §4.5.3, this page.

(3) Motion to reclassify. A party can file a motion for reclassification if the case was classified incorrectly. CCP §403.040(a). See "Motion to Reclassify," ch. 5-D, p. 492. The court, on its own motion, can reclassify a case at any time. CCP §403.040(a).

(4) Stipulation. The parties can stipulate to reclassification of the case within the time allowed to respond to the initial pleading (i.e., within 30 days after the complaint is served). *See* CCP §§403.050(a), 412.20(a)(3). The title of the stipulation must state that the case is reclassified by the stipulation. CRC 2.111(11). Applicable reclassification fees must be paid when the stipulation is filed.

2. Evaluating amount in controversy. When basing a reclassification decision on the amount in controversy, the court looks at the possibility of a jurisdictionally appropriate verdict, not the merits of the claim. ***Stern v. Superior Ct.*** (2d Dist.2003) 105 Cal.App.4th 223, 233. For a limited case to be reclassified as unlimited, the evidence presented need only show a possibility of damages over $25,000. *See* ***Ytuarte***, 129 Cal.App.4th at 279. For an unlimited case to be reclassified as limited, the court must reasonably determine that the matter will necessarily result in a verdict below $25,001. ***Stern***, 105 Cal.App.4th at 233; *see* ***Walker v. Superior Ct.*** (1991) 53 Cal.3d 257, 270 (preunification transfer under CCP §396). Evidence the court can consider includes the prayer or demand in the complaint, an arbitration award, or the amount of a settlement proposal. ***Stern***, 105 Cal.App.4th at 233. Courts exercise caution when deciding whether to reclassify an unlimited case as limited because the reclassification will limit both the relief available and the parties' procedural rights. *See* ***Walker***, 53 Cal.3d at 271; ***Ytuarte***, 129 Cal.App.4th at 274-75.

3. Reclassification fee. Reclassifying a limited case as unlimited requires the payment of a reclassification fee. *See* CCP §§403.020(a), 403.030, 403.040(c)(1), 403.050(b), 403.060(a); *see also* Gov. C. §70619 (currently $140). If the fee is not paid, the case will not be reclassified and it will continue as a limited case. CCP §§403.040(d)(3), 403.060(b). There is no fee for reclassifying an unlimited case as limited. *Id.* §§403.020(a), 403.040(c)(2), 403.060(c). Parties are not entitled to a refund of the fees paid when the case was originally classified as unlimited. *Id.* §403.060(c).

4. Pleading deadlines unchanged. A motion for reclassification does not extend the moving party's time to amend, answer, or otherwise respond to a pleading. CCP §403.040(a). See "Motion to Reclassify," ch. 5-D, p. 492.

5. Review. An order reclassifying a case is not a final, appealable order. ***Garau v. Torrance Unified Sch. Dist.*** (2d Dist.2006) 137 Cal.App.4th 192, 199. A party must file a petition for writ of mandate to obtain review of a reclassification order. CCP §403.080; ***Garau***, 137 Cal.App.4th at 198. The trial court's decision to reclassify is reviewed for abuse of discretion. *See* ***Walker***, 53 Cal.3d at 272 (preunification transfer under CCP §396).

§5. TRANSFER

A case can be transferred from one court to another. Transfers were more common before unification; jurisdictional issues are now mostly resolved by reclassification, not by transfer. *See* ***Pajaro Valley Water Mgmt. Agency v. McGrath*** (6th Dist.2005) 128 Cal.App.4th 1093, 1104 n.4.

§5.1 From general civil division to appellate courts. If it becomes apparent that a court does not have subject-matter jurisdiction over a case, the case can be transferred to a court with jurisdiction on a party's motion or on the court's own motion. *See* CCP §396(b). While CCP §396 lost most of its significance after municipal courts and

superior courts were unified, the provision arguably empowers the superior court to transfer cases within the original jurisdiction of the appellate courts to the court of appeal or Supreme Court. *See* ***Pajaro Valley Water Mgmt. Agency v. McGrath*** (6th Dist.2005) 128 Cal.App.4th 1093, 1104 n.4; ***Padilla v. Department of Alcoholic Bev. Control*** (5th Dist.1996) 43 Cal.App.4th 1151, 1157. *Contra* ***TrafficSchoolOnline, Inc. v. Superior Ct.*** (2d Dist.2001) 89 Cal.App.4th 222, 234-35 (CCP §396 does not allow superior court to transfer case to court of appeal or Supreme Court).

§5.2 From appellate division to court of appeal. The appellate division can certify a case to be transferred to the court of appeal on its own motion or on a party's motion. CRC 8.1005(a); *see* CCP §911; CRC 8.1002, 8.1008(a). A case can be transferred when it is necessary to ensure uniformity of decision or to settle an important question of law. CCP §911; CRC 8.1005(a)(1); ***Anchor Mar. Repair Co. v. Magnan*** (4th Dist.2001) 93 Cal.App.4th 525, 528-29. If a motion for certification and transfer is denied, the decision can be reviewed by the court of appeal through a petition for writ of mandate. ***Anchor Mar.***, 93 Cal.App.4th at 529.

§5.3 From court of appeal to Supreme Court. The Supreme Court can, before decision, transfer a case pending in the court of appeal to itself. Cal. Const., art. VI, §12(a); CRC 8.552(a). The Supreme Court can also transfer a case from itself to a court of appeal, or from one court of appeal or appellate division to another. Cal. Const., art. VI, §12(a); *see* CRC 8.500(b)(4).

§6. CHALLENGING SUBJECT-MATTER JURISDICTION

For a discussion of how to challenge subject-matter jurisdiction, see "Challenging Subject-Matter Jurisdiction," ch. 4-D, p. 355.

§7. APPEAL

Appellate jurisdiction is conferred by the California Constitution. ***Leone v. Medical Bd.*** (2000) 22 Cal.4th 660, 668; ***In re Establishment of Perris City News*** (4th Dist.2002) 96 Cal.App.4th 1194, 1199; *see* Cal. Const., art. VI, §11. But statutes determine the right to appeal and in which court a claim can be appealed. *See* CCP §904; ***Leone***, 22 Cal.4th at 668; ***Anchor Mar. Repair Co. v. Magnan*** (4th Dist.2001) 93 Cal.App.4th 525, 528. Where an appeal is made depends on the classification of the case.

§7.1 Appeal of unlimited cases. An appeal of a judgment or order in an unlimited case is made to the intermediate court of appeal. CCP §904.1(a); *see* Cal. Const., art. VI, §11. There are six district courts of appeal that hear cases from the counties within their jurisdiction. For information on the courts of appeal, see www.courts.ca.gov/courts/courtsofappeal.htm. The notice of appeal filed by an appellant does not need to specify the district to which the appeal will be taken; the appeal will be treated as taken to the court of appeal for the district in which the superior court is located. CRC 8.100(a)(2).

1. **Appealable orders.** The following orders are appealable:

(1) Postjudgment orders. CCP §904.1(a)(2).

(2) Orders granting a motion to quash service of summons. *Id.* §904.1(a)(3).

(3) Orders granting a motion to stay or written orders to dismiss the case under CCP §581d on the ground of inconvenient forum. *Id.* §904.1(a)(3).

(4) Orders granting a new trial. *Id.* §904.1(a)(4).

(5) Orders denying a motion for judgment notwithstanding the verdict. *Id.*

(6) Orders discharging or refusing to discharge an attachment or granting a right-to-attach order. *Id.* §904.1(a)(5).

(7) Orders granting or dissolving an injunction, or refusing to grant or dissolve an injunction. *Id.* §904.1(a)(6).

SUBJECT-MATTER JURISDICTION

(8) Orders appointing a receiver. *Id.* §904.1(a)(7).

(9) Orders appealable under the Family Code or Probate Code. CCP §904.1(a)(10).

(10) Orders directing payment of monetary sanctions over $5,000 by a party or an attorney. *Id.* §904.1(a)(12).

(11) Orders granting or denying a special motion to strike in an anti-SLAPP action under CCP §425.16. *Id.* §904.1(a)(13).

2. Appealable interlocutory orders. Most interlocutory orders and final contempt judgments are not appealable. *See* CCP §§904.1(a)(1), 1222. However, the following interlocutory orders are appealable:

(1) Interlocutory judgments, orders, or decrees made to redeem real or personal property from a mortgage or lien, or determining the right to redeem and directing an accounting. *Id.* §904.1(a)(8).

(2) Interlocutory judgments in a suit for partition determining the rights and interests of the respective parties and directing the partition to be made. *Id.* §904.1(a)(9).

(3) Interlocutory judgments directing payment of monetary sanctions over $5,000 by a party or an attorney. *Id.* §904.1(a)(11).

§7.2 Appeal of limited cases. An appeal of a judgment or order in a limited case is made to the appellate division of the superior court rather than the court of appeal. CCP §904.2; ***Ytuarte v. Superior Ct.*** (2d Dist.2005) 129 Cal.App.4th 266, 275; *see* CCP §100.

1. Appealable orders. The following orders are appealable:

(1) Postjudgment orders. CCP §904.2(b).

(2) Orders granting or denying a motion to transfer venue. *Id.* §904.2(c).

(3) Orders granting a motion to stay or written orders to dismiss the case under CCP §581d on the ground of inconvenient forum. *Id.* §904.2(d).

(4) Orders granting a new trial. *Id.* §904.2(e).

(5) Orders denying a motion for judgment notwithstanding the verdict. *Id.*

(6) Orders discharging or refusing to discharge an attachment or granting a right-to-attach order. *Id.* §904.2(f).

(7) Orders granting or dissolving an injunction or refusing to grant or dissolve an injunction. *Id.* §904.2(g).

(8) Orders appointing a receiver. *Id.* §904.2(h).

2. Nonappealable orders. Interlocutory orders and final contempt judgments are not appealable. CCP §904.2(b).

§7.3 Appeal of small claims. An appeal of a small-claims judgment is made to the general superior court, not the appellate division of the superior court. *See* CCP §§77(e), 116.770(a), 904.5; ***General Elec. Capital Auto Fin. Servs. v. Appellate Div.*** (2d Dist.2001) 88 Cal.App.4th 136, 144 (appellate division of superior court has no jurisdiction over appeals from small-claims judgments). All the parties' claims are considered at a de novo hearing. CCP §116.770(a), (d); ***Universal City Nissan, Inc. v. Superior Ct.*** (2d Dist.1998) 65 Cal.App.4th 203, 205-06. After the de novo hearing, a judgment is entered, which is final and not appealable. CCP §116.780(a); ***Acuna v. Gunderson Chevrolet, Inc.*** (2d Dist.1993) 19 Cal.App.4th 1467, 1471; *see* ***Pitzen v. Superior Ct.*** (4th Dist.2004) 120 Cal.App.4th 1374, 1386 (P forfeits right of appellate review by bringing small-claims suit). One court of appeal has held that an appeal of a postjudgment enforcement order issued by either the small-claims court or the superior court is made to the appellate division of the superior court. *See* ***General Elec.***, 88 Cal.App.4th at 144-45 (small-claims enforcement orders are reviewed in same manner as postjudgment enforcement orders in limited cases).

§7.4 Appeal of administrative decisions. Generally, an appeal of an administrative tribunal's order or decision is made by writ of review to the court of appeal or the Supreme Court. *See, e.g.*, ***Department of Rehab. v. Workers' Comp. Appeals Bd.*** (2003) 30 Cal.4th 1281, 1288-90 (Workers' Compensation Appeals Board decision); ***Southern Cal. Edison Co. v. Public Utils. Comm'n*** (2d Dist.2006) 140 Cal.App.4th 1085, 1095-96 (Public Utilities Commission decision). The reviewing court defers to the factual findings of the administrative tribunal and only considers questions of law. *See* ***State Pers. Bd. v. Department of Pers. Admin.*** (2005) 37 Cal.4th 512, 522; *see also* ***Larson v. State Pers. Bd.*** (5th Dist.1994) 28 Cal.App.4th 265, 273 (factual findings must be supported by substantial evidence, and agency must have acted within its jurisdiction).

§7.5 Courts of appeal. The jurisdiction of the courts of appeal is conferred by the California Constitution. *See* Cal. Const., art. VI, §§10, 11. Courts of appeal have both original and appellate jurisdiction.

1. Original jurisdiction. Courts of appeal have original jurisdiction to issue extraordinary writs of mandate, certiorari, and prohibition. Cal. Const., art. VI, §10.

2. Appellate jurisdiction. Courts of appeal generally have appellate jurisdiction over matters within the original jurisdiction of superior courts. *See* Cal. Const., art. VI, §11(a). Courts of appeal do not, however, have appellate jurisdiction when a judgment of death has been pronounced. *Id.*

§7.6 Supreme Court. The California Supreme Court's jurisdiction is conferred by the California Constitution. *See* Cal. Const., art. VI, §§1, 2, 10-12. The Supreme Court has both original and appellate jurisdiction.

1. Original jurisdiction. The Supreme Court has original jurisdiction to issue extraordinary writs of mandate, certiorari, and prohibition. Cal. Const., art. VI, §10. However, a petition for an extraordinary writ should first be filed in a lower court unless a showing is made to justify the original application to the Supreme Court. *See* CRC 8.486(a)(1).

2. Appellate jurisdiction. The Supreme Court has appellate jurisdiction over any case from a court of appeal. Cal. Const., art. VI, §12(b). The Supreme Court has exclusive jurisdiction to review final decisions of the Public Utilities Commission and disciplinary recommendations of the State Bar. See "Public utilities," §2.2.3(3), p. 249; "Attorney admission & discipline," §2.2.3(4), p. 250.

F. CHOOSING THE COURT—VENUE

§1. GENERAL

§1.1 Purpose. Once the plaintiff determines that a California court has jurisdiction over the subject matter of the suit, it must decide the proper venue for the suit—that is, in which of the 58 California counties will the suit be filed. Unlike subject-matter or personal jurisdiction, both of which address a court's power to adjudicate a suit, venue only addresses the issue of whether the court is located in a county that can hear the suit. *See* ***California State Parks Found. v. Superior Ct.*** (4th Dist.2007) 150 Cal.App.4th 826, 833 (term "venue" denotes particular county within state where case is to be heard); ***Milliken v. Gray*** (2d Dist.1969) 276 Cal.App.2d 595, 600 (term "venue" denotes geographical location and political subdivision within which the court that will hear suit is situated). Which county is the proper venue for a particular suit is determined according to the venue statutes and common law. *See* ***California State Parks***, 150 Cal.App.4th at 833; *see also* CCP §§392-403 (venue statutes). The statutes governing venue selection are designed to protect the defendant and the witnesses against a plaintiff's choice of an unfair or inconvenient forum. *See* ***Smith v. Smith*** (1891) 88 Cal. 572, 576; *see also* ***Lebastchi v. Superior Ct.*** (4th Dist.1995) 33 Cal.App.4th 1465, 1469 (law favors right of trial at D's residence).

§1.2 Primary authority. CCP §§392-395.5, 396b; Gov. C. §§955, 955.2, 955.3.

NOTE

For a discussion of how to challenge venue, see "Motion to Transfer or Change Venue," ch. 4-E, p. 359.

§1.3 Secondary authority. The following secondary sources are cited as authority in this subchapter:

- *California Civil Procedure Before Trial* (CEB Online ed. 2014) (referred to as *CEB Procedure Before Trial*).
- Weil & Brown, *California Practice Guide: Civil Procedure Before Trial* (CD-ROM ed. 2014) (referred to as Weil, *Civil Procedure Before Trial*).
- Witkin, *California Procedure* (5th ed. 2008 & Supp.2014) (referred to as Witkin, *Cal. Procedure*).

§2. DETERMINING VENUE

CAUTION

Choosing the wrong venue can expose a plaintiff's attorney to sanctions. See CCP §396b(b).

The California venue scheme is a mixture of statutory and common-law rules that create a hierarchical structure for determining proper venue. All lawsuits should be brought according to the following venue scheme:

§2.1 Apply any venue-selection clause. To establish proper venue, the plaintiff must determine whether the suit is subject to an enforceable venue-selection clause. A venue-selection clause will be enforced if it is negotiated by sophisticated parties as part of an arm's-length transaction and the place fixed for trial is consistent with a location allowed by statute. ***Battaglia Enters. v. Superior Ct.*** (4th Dist.2013) 215 Cal.App.4th 309, 318; *see* ***Arntz Builders v. Superior Ct.*** (1st Dist.2004) 122 Cal.App.4th 1195, 1201; ***Alexander v. Superior Ct.*** (6th Dist.2003) 114 Cal.App.4th 723, 731-32.

CAUTION

A venue-selection clause is not the same as a forum-selection clause. ***Alexander****, 114 Cal.App.4th at 726-27. A venue-selection clause determines the county of the court that will hear a suit. Id. at 727. A forum-selection clause determines the state or nation of the court that will hear a suit. Id. Forum-selection clauses are more often the subject of litigation than venue-selection clauses. See, e.g.,* ***Smith, Valentino & Smith, Inc. v. Superior Ct. (1976) 17 Cal.3d*** *491, 495-96 (forum-selection clause requiring California corporation to bring suit in Pennsylvania was enforced). For a discussion of enforcing forum-selection clauses, see* *"Forum-selection clause," ch. 3-G, §5.1.2(1), p. 287.*

§2.2 Determine essential character of each cause of action. To establish proper venue, the plaintiff must determine (1) the number of causes of action pleaded and (2) the essential character of each separate action. *See* ***Lebastchi v. Superior Ct.*** (4th Dist.1995) 33 Cal.App.4th 1465, 1469; ***Massae v. Superior Ct.*** (1st Dist.1981) 118 Cal.App.3d 527, 535-36; 3 Witkin, *Cal. Procedure*, Actions, §§787, 788. For a discussion of what constitutes a cause of action, see "Determining cause of action," ch. 3-C, §3.6.1, p. 215. The action's character is determined by applying the "main-relief rule," which determines character based on the relief primarily sought or the principal object of the action. *See* ***California State Parks Found. v. Superior Ct.*** (4th Dist.2007) 150 Cal.App.4th 826, 833; ***Foundation Eng'rs, Inc. v. Superior Ct.*** (6th Dist.1993) 19 Cal.App.4th 104, 109; ***Massae***, 118 Cal.App.3d at 535; 3 Witkin, *Cal. Procedure*, Actions, §788. An action's main relief is determined by the allegations of the complaint, assuming they are true, and the nature of a default judgment that could be rendered for the plaintiff. ***Peiser v. Mettler*** (1958) 50 Cal.2d 594, 601; *see* ***Neet v. Holmes*** (1942) 19 Cal.2d 605, 607.

1. Main relief involves real-property rights. Under the main-relief rule, if the action seeks relief that primarily involves rights in ownership or use of real property, the action is characterized as "local." ***Brown v. Superior Ct.*** (1984) 37 Cal.3d 477, 482 n.5. This characterization does not change even if the plaintiff also asked for incidental relief involving personal rights (e.g., money damages). 3 Witkin, *Cal. Procedure*, Actions, §788; *see* ***Massae***, 118 Cal.App.3d at 535-36; *see, e.g.,* ***State v. Royal Consol. Mining Co.*** (1921) 187 Cal. 343, 351 (demand for rents

VENUE

was incidental to main relief, which sought possession of land); ***Foundation Eng'rs***, 19 Cal.App.4th at 112 (demand for declaratory relief and damages resulting from breach of implied warranty did not affect characterization of action as one for injuries to real property). Local actions should generally be tried in the county where the real property is located. *See* CCP §392(a). For a discussion of local actions, see "Local Actions," §3, this page.

2. **Main relief involves personal rights.** Under the main-relief rule, if the action seeks relief that primarily involves rights that are personal, the action is characterized as "transitory." ***Brown***, 37 Cal.3d at 482 n.5. This characterization does not change even if the plaintiff also asked for incidental relief involving title to or possession of real property. 3 Witkin, *Cal. Procedure*, Actions, §788; *e.g.*, ***Central Bank v. Superior Ct.*** (5th Dist.1973) 30 Cal.App.3d 913, 917 (action to foreclose mechanic's lien was incidental to main relief, which sought money judgment for labor and material P furnished for Ds). Transitory actions should generally be tried in the county of the defendant's residence. *See* CCP §395(a). For a discussion of transitory actions, see "Transitory Actions," §4, p. 273.

§2.3 Determine whether conflicting venue rules apply. To establish proper venue when two or more causes of action have been pleaded or two or more defendants have been sued, the plaintiff must apply the "mixed-action rules." See "Mixed-Action Rules," §5, p. 281.

§2.4 Find location within county to file suit. Once the proper county of venue has been determined, the plaintiff must determine whether the local rules require the action to be filed in a specific location within the county to avoid processing delays and possible sanctions. *See* CCP §402(a). The action cannot be rejected by the clerk or dismissed by the court if the plaintiff files or tries to file the action in the wrong location, but the action can be transferred to the proper location. CCP §402(a)(3). *But see* Weil, *Civil Procedure Before Trial*, ¶3:602 (branch-court clerks have been known to violate statute by refusing to file complaints presented in wrong branch).

§3. LOCAL ACTIONS

§3.1 Types of local actions. If the action seeks relief that primarily involves rights in ownership or use of real property, the action is characterized as "local." ***Brown v. Superior Ct.*** (1984) 37 Cal.3d 477, 482 n.5. The following are examples of local actions:

1. Actions for the recovery of real property or any interest in real property. CCP §392(a)(1); *see* ***Etter v. Vollmer*** (3d Dist.1956) 139 Cal.App.2d 718, 720. Examples include actions for unlawful detainer and setting aside fraudulent conveyances. *See* ***Sloss v. De Toro*** (1888) 77 Cal. 129, 132 (fraudulent conveyance); ***Childs v. Eltinge*** (4th Dist.1973) 29 Cal.App.3d 843, 851 (unlawful detainer); ***Etter***, 139 Cal.App.2d at 720 (fraudulent conveyance).

2. Actions to determine any right or interest in real property. CCP §392(a)(1); *e.g.*, ***Sloss***, 77 Cal. at 131-32 (action to set aside sale of land was local because it involved determination of right or interest in real property); ***Rice v. Schubert*** (4th Dist.1951) 101 Cal.App.2d 638, 640 (action to set aside conveyance of real property was local because judgment on complaint would result in determination of interest in real property); *see CEB Procedure Before Trial*, §8.34 (listing examples). Examples include actions to do the following:

(1) Quiet title. ***Wood v. Emig*** (1st Dist.1943) 58 Cal.App.2d 851, 856-57.

(2) Cancel a deed or other instrument that affects title. *See, e.g.*, ***Eckstrand v. Wilshusen*** (1933) 217 Cal. 380, 382-83 (action sought to have fraudulently obtained deed canceled and to have title reconveyed to P).

(3) Reform a contract for the sale of real property. ***Franklin v. Dutton*** (1889) 79 Cal. 605, 606.

(4) Reform a deed of trust on real property. ***Massae v. Superior Ct.*** (1st Dist.1981) 118 Cal.App.3d 527, 539.

(5) Obtain real property through the specific performance of a contract. ***Foundation Eng'rs, Inc. v. Superior Ct.*** (6th Dist.1993) 19 Cal.App.4th 104, 111.

3. Actions for injuries to real property. CCP §392(a)(1); *e.g.*, ***Wolfe v. Wallace*** (3d Dist.1957) 154 Cal.App.2d 523, 527 (destruction of trees was injury to real property); *see CEB Procedure Before Trial*, §8.35 (listing examples). Examples include actions involving the following:

(1) Indirect or consequential injuries to real property, such as slander of title and malicious prosecution of a claim to real property. *See* ***Coley v. Hecker*** (1928) 206 Cal. 22, 26, 28 (slander of title); ***Wick v. Mattison*** (1st Dist.1962) 207 Cal.App.2d 608, 610 (malicious prosecution).

(2) Injury to a building or improvement if the structure was intended to be permanently attached to the ground. *See* ***Gosliner v. Briones*** (1921) 187 Cal. 557, 562.

(3) Injury to growing crops. ***Stauffer Chem. Co. v. Superior Ct.*** (3d Dist.1968) 265 Cal.App.2d 1, 3-4.

4. Foreclosures of liens and mortgages on real property. CCP §392(a)(2); *see* ***Appel v. Hubbard*** (4th Dist.1957) 155 Cal.App.2d 639, 642-43. Even if the plaintiff seeks to recover the debt secured by the lien, foreclosure actions remain local in nature. *See* ***Case v. Kirkwood*** (4th Dist.1931) 119 Cal.App. 207, 210-11. Foreclosure of a mechanic's lien, like a mortgage foreclosure, is an in rem action and is local in nature. ***Central Bank v. Superior Ct.*** (5th Dist.1973) 30 Cal.App.3d 913, 917.

5. Actions to partition real property. CCP §872.110(b)(1); ***Hecker v. Ross*** (4th Dist.1960) 183 Cal.App.2d 30, 32; *see* CCP §392(a)(1).

6. Eminent-domain or condemnation actions, including inverse-condemnation actions. ***Williams v. Merced Irrigation Dist.*** (1935) 4 Cal.2d 238, 241; *see* CCP §1250.020(a); Gov. C. §955.

§3.2 General venue rule. Local actions should be tried in the county where the real property is located. *See* CCP §392(a).

1. Single property located in multiple counties. If the real property is located in more than one county, venue is proper in any of the counties where the real property is located. *See* CCP §392(a); ***Pacific Gas & Elec. Co. v. Scott*** (1938) 10 Cal.2d 581, 586.

2. Multiple properties located in multiple counties. If the local action involves two or more properties located in multiple counties (e.g., suit on a debt secured by multiple mortgages), venue is proper in any of the counties where any of the properties or any part of them is located. *See* ***Appel v. Hubbard*** (4th Dist.1957) 155 Cal.App.2d 639, 643.

3. Unlawful-detainer actions. If the local action is an unlawful-detainer action as defined by CCP §1161, venue is proper in the county where the real property, or some part of it, is located. CCP §392. Within that county, the proper court location for trial of an unlawful-detainer proceeding is the court that tries unlawful-detainer proceedings nearest or most accessible to where the real property is located. *Id.* §392(b).

§4. TRANSITORY ACTIONS

§4.1 Types of transitory actions. If the action seeks relief that primarily involves rights that are personal, the action is characterized as "transitory." ***Brown v. Superior Ct.*** (1984) 37 Cal.3d 477, 482 n.5. Transitory actions include claims that could have arisen anywhere, such as personal-injury torts or breaches of contract. *See* ***Peiser v. Mettler*** (1958) 50 Cal.2d 594, 601 (breach of contract is clearly transitory); ***McManus v. Red Salmon Canning Co.*** (1st Dist.1918) 37 Cal.App. 133, 136-37 (action for wrongful death, like other torts, is transitory action); *see, e.g.*, ***Holstein v. Superior Ct.*** (4th Dist.1969) 275 Cal.App.2d 708, 710 (equitable action by judgment creditor).

§4.2 General venue rule. Transitory actions should be tried in the county where the defendant resides at the commencement of the action, unless a specific venue statute provides for a different venue. *See* CCP §395(a); ***Brown v. Superior Ct.*** (1984) 37 Cal.3d 477, 482-83. The continued enactment of specific venue statutes has reduced the number of transitory actions that are subject to this general rule. ***Forster v. Superior Ct.*** (2d Dist.1992) 11 Cal.App.4th 782, 791. For a discussion of specific venue statutes, see "Specific venue statutes," §4.3, p. 275.

NOTE

When multiple defendants have been sued, the plaintiff can pick any defendant's county of residence, and no other defendant will have the right to transfer the suit even if the resident defendant joins the motion to change venue. See ***Monogram Co. v. Kingsley*** *(1951) 38 Cal.2d 28, 33-34;* ***K.R.L. Prtshp. v. Superior Ct.*** *(3d Dist.2004) 120 Cal.App.4th 490, 504.*

VENUE

1. D's residence. The defendant's residence depends on its status—that is, whether the defendant is an individual, a corporation, a partnership or association, or a governmental entity.

(1) D is individual. An individual resides in the county where she lives if her intent is to remain in that place. *See* ***Burt v. Scarborough*** (1961) 56 Cal.2d 817, 820 (residence is fixed home of party as understood by party and her neighbors and friends); ***Younger v. Spreckels*** (1st Dist.1909) 12 Cal.App. 175, 177-78 (same).

(a) Multiple residences. The fact that an individual might reside in another location during certain seasons or times of the year (e.g., a summer house) does not make the individual a resident of that county for venue purposes. ***Burt***, 56 Cal.2d at 820. Thus, an individual may have several residences at the same time and for different purposes, but she can have only one "residence," or domicile, under CCP §395. ***Burt***, 56 Cal.2d at 820-21.

(b) Military service. The fact that an individual enlists in the U.S. military or naval service does not mean that she has abandoned or lost the domicile she had before entering the service or that she has acquired a new domicile at the place where she serves. ***Johnston v. Benton*** (1st Dist.1925) 73 Cal.App. 565, 569. The servicemember's residence is the location where she intended to establish residence. *Id.*

(2) D is corporation.

(a) Domestic corporation. A domestic corporation resides in the county where its principal place of business is located. ***Gallup v. Sacramento & San Joaquin Drainage Dist.*** (1915) 171 Cal. 71, 74-75 (public corporation); ***All-Cool Aluminum Awning Co. v. Superior Ct.*** (5th Dist.1964) 224 Cal.App.2d 660, 666 (private corporation). A corporation's principal place of business is the place designated in its organizational documents filed with the Secretary of State. ***Rosas v. Superior Ct.*** (2d Dist.1994) 25 Cal.App.4th 671, 673-74. *But see* ***Partch v. Adams*** (1st Dist.1942) 55 Cal.App.2d 1, 6 (while articles of incorporation usually govern residence issue, sometimes residence is county where corporation conducts its operations).

(b) Foreign corporation. A foreign corporation's residence is determined in the same manner as that of a domestic corporation if it is qualified to do business in California. *See* ***Easton v. Superior Ct.*** (4th Dist.1970) 12 Cal.App.3d 243, 246; *see also* Corp. C. §2105 (requirements for obtaining certificate of qualification). See "Domestic corporation," §4.2.1(2)(a), this page. If it is not qualified to do business in California, the foreign corporation has no residence in the state for venue purposes. *See* ***Hale v. Bohannon*** (1952) 38 Cal.2d 458, 473-75. See "D is foreign corporation," §4.3.1(2), p. 276.

(3) D is partnership or association. A partnership or an unincorporated association resides in the county named in its statement that designates a principal office address and that is filed with the Secretary of State under Corp. C. §18200 (for unincorporated associations) or §15800 (for partnerships). *See* CCP §395.2; ***Mosby v. Superior Ct.*** (3d Dist.1974) 43 Cal.App.3d 219, 225 & n.4; *see, e.g.*, ***Buran Equip. Co. v. Superior Ct.*** (6th Dist.1987) 190 Cal.App.3d 1662, 1665-66 (partnership not entitled to change of venue to county designated in statement because venue was proper for individual co-Ds). The statement establishes an unincorporated association's right to be treated for venue purposes as if it were a corporation having its principal place of business in the county of its principal office. ***San Francisco Found. v. Superior Ct.*** (1984) 37 Cal.3d 285, 296; ***Rosas***, 25 Cal.App.4th at 676-77. If the unincorporated association has not filed a statement, it resides in any county where a member of the association resides. *See* ***Carruth v. Superior Ct.*** (4th Dist.1978) 80 Cal.App.3d 215, 222-23 & n.2.

NOTE

The unincorporated association's statement can be filed before or when venue is challenged by a motion to transfer. ***San Francisco Found.****, 37 Cal.3d at 296-97.*

(4) D is governmental entity.

(a) State. The State, which includes the State of California and any office, officer, department, division, bureau, board, commission, or agency of the State, resides in many counties for venue purposes. *See* Gov. C. §940.6 (defining "State"). The official residence of many state agencies and officers is fixed by statute in Sacramento County, and even when not fixed by statute, the residence of some state agencies and officers is assumed to

be Sacramento County. ***Regents of the Univ. of Cal. v. Superior Ct.*** (1970) 3 Cal.3d 529, 535 n.6. Venue for suits brought against the State, however, is usually governed by specific venue rules. *See id.* at 534. The venue rules for general civil actions will apply to actions against the State when no other statute applies. *Id.*

(b) County, city, or local agency. A county, city, city and county, or local agency resides in the county where the entity is situated. *See* CCP §394(a); ***County of Orange v. Superior Ct.*** (1st Dist.1999) 73 Cal.App.4th 1189, 1191. For venue purposes, "local agency" means any governmental district, board, or agency, or any other local governmental body or corporation, but does not include the State of California or any of its agencies, departments, commissions, or boards. CCP §394(b).

(c) Public officer. A public officer does not reside in a particular county for venue purposes. *See* ***California State Parks Found. v. Superior Ct.*** (4th Dist.2007) 150 Cal.App.4th 826, 844-845. Instead, venue for suits against public officers is governed by specific venue rules. *See, e.g., id.* at 845 (under CCP §393(b), venue in suits against public officials is in county where injury occurred, not where public official resides). See "D is public officer," §4.3.1(5), p. 277.

(5) D is Doe defendant. A Doe defendant's residence is not relevant for venue purposes until the defendant is actually named in the complaint and served with summons. *See* ***Liera v. Los Angeles Fin. Co.*** (4th Dist.1950) 99 Cal.App.2d 254, 257; ***Warren v. Ritter*** (4th Dist.1943) 61 Cal.App.2d 403, 405; ***Kallen v. Serretto*** (1st Dist.1932) 126 Cal.App. 548, 549. Once a Doe defendant is named and served, its residence can support a motion to change venue. ***Gutierrez v. Superior Ct.*** (1st Dist.1966) 243 Cal.App.2d 710, 721-22. See "Motion to Transfer or Change Venue," ch. 4-E, p. 359.

2. Residency problems. In some cases, the action cannot be tried in the county where the defendant resides.

(1) D resides out of state. If all the defendants reside outside the state, the action can be tried in any county the plaintiff designates in the complaint. CCP §395(a). But the plaintiff must show that it was diligent in trying to determine the defendant's residence before suit. ***Thurber v. Thurber*** (1896) 113 Cal. 607, 610-11; ***Mahler v. Drummer Boy Gold Mining Co.*** (3d Dist.1907) 7 Cal.App. 190, 193.

(2) D is leaving state. If the defendant is about to depart from the state with no intent to return or if there is no reasonable likelihood of an early return, the action can be tried in any county where either party resides or where service is made. *See* CCP §395(a); ***Polk v. Bradbury*** (1st Dist.1932) 127 Cal.App. 383, 384-85.

(3) D has no known address. If the defendant resides in the state but the county of residence is unknown to the plaintiff, the action can be tried in any county the plaintiff designates in the complaint. CCP §395(a). But the plaintiff must show that it was diligent in trying to determine the defendant's residence before filing suit. ***Thurber***, 113 Cal. at 610-11; ***Mahler***, 7 Cal.App. at 193.

(4) D was improperly joined. If the defendant was improperly joined or was joined solely for the purpose of having the action tried in the county where it resides, the defendant's residence must be disregarded when determining venue. CCP §395(a); *see* ***Peiser v. Mettler*** (1958) 50 Cal.2d 594, 603; ***Buran Equip.***, 190 Cal.App.3d at 1666; ***California Collection Agency, Inc. v. Fontana*** (1st Dist.1943) 61 Cal.App.2d 648, 653-654; *CEB Procedure Before Trial*, §8.14 (listing examples). A defendant is properly joined if the plaintiff has a good-faith, reasonable belief that it has a cause of action against that defendant. ***Peiser***, 50 Cal.2d at 603. If the plaintiff selects a venue in bad faith, the plaintiff's attorney may be held personally liable for the defendant's reasonable expenses and attorney fees incurred in making a motion to transfer. *See* CCP §396b(b).

§4.3 Specific venue statutes. The general venue rule for transitory actions is subject to many statutory exceptions that provide expanded venue options depending on the type of defendant sued or the type of action brought.

1. Type of D.

(1) D is private domestic corporation. An action against a private domestic corporation can be brought in the following counties:

VENUE

(a) Place of business. The action can be brought in the county where the corporation's principal place of business is situated. CCP §395.5. To determine the corporation's principal place of business, the plaintiff can rely on corporate filings with the Secretary of State's office. *See, e.g.*, ***Rosas v. Superior Ct.*** (2d Dist.1994) 25 Cal.App.4th 671, 677 (domestic corporation identified Los Angeles as its principal office in its articles of incorporation and annual statements; corporation could not defeat venue selection by showing principal place of business was located elsewhere).

(b) Obligation or liability. The action can be brought in the county where the alleged obligation or liability arose. CCP §395.5; *see, e.g.*, ***United Pac. Ins. v. Superior Ct.*** (3d Dist.1967) 254 Cal.App.2d 897, 899 (discussing former Cal. Const., art. XII, §16, now CCP §395.5; in wrongful-attachment action, corporate D could be sued in county where levy was made that deprived owner of use of property). A liability "arises" where the injury occurs. ***Black Diamond Asphalt, Inc. v. Superior Ct.*** (3d Dist.2003) 109 Cal.App.4th 166, 172. This option applies to obligations or liabilities created by tort, contract, or statute. *See* ***Mission Imports, Inc. v. Superior Ct.*** (1982) 31 Cal.3d 921, 928; ***Black Diamond Asphalt***, 109 Cal.App.4th at 171-72.

(c) Contract. The action can be brought in the county where the contract being sued on was made, to be performed, or breached. CCP §395.5; *e.g.*, ***Karson Indus. v. Superior Ct.*** (1st Dist.1969) 273 Cal.App.2d 7, 8 (breach occurred in county where D mailed letter canceling orders).

[1] Made. The place where a contract is "made" is where the last act necessary to making the contract valid—usually the act constituting acceptance—is performed. ***Jhirmack Enters. v. Superior Ct.*** (2d Dist.1979) 96 Cal.App.3d 715, 723.

[2] To be performed. The place where a contract is "to be performed" does not have to be designated in the contract and is determined by the specific obligation on which the plaintiff is suing. *See, e.g.*, ***Anaheim Extrusion Co. v. Superior Ct.*** (4th Dist.1985) 170 Cal.App.3d 1201, 1203 (obligation alleged to have been breached was payment for goods; thus, contract was to be performed at place where payments were to be made, not where goods were to be delivered). Under CCP §395.5, the plaintiff can choose the county where either it or the defendant was to perform. *See* ***Mosby v. Superior Ct.*** (3d Dist.1974) 43 Cal.App.3d 219, 225 (dicta; §395.5 applies equally to performance by P or D).

[3] Breached. The place where a contract is "breached" depends on the nature of the breach alleged to have occurred. *See, e.g.*, ***Jhirmack Enters.***, 96 Cal.App.3d at 724 (P alleged D breached contract by mailing notice of cancellation; breach occurred in county where D mailed notice, not in county where P read it).

NOTE

CCP §395.5 applies only to private corporations, not public ones. See ***Regents of the Univ. of Cal. v. Superior Ct.*** *(1970) 3 Cal.3d 529, 534 (discussing former Cal. Const., art. XII, §16, now CCP §395.5);* ***Yedor v. Ocean Acc. & Guar. Corp.*** *(2d Dist.1948) 85 Cal.App.2d 698, 702 (same). Its purpose is to permit a wider choice of venue options for suits against corporations or associations than for suits against individuals.* ***Mission Imports***, *31 Cal.3d at 928;* ***Black Diamond Asphalt***, *109 Cal.App.4th at 171.*

(2) D is foreign corporation. An action against a foreign corporation that is qualified to do business in California can be brought in the same manner as an action against a domestic corporation. *See* ***Easton v. Superior Ct.*** (4th Dist.1970) 12 Cal.App.3d 243, 246. See "D is private domestic corporation," §4.3.1(1), p. 275. If the foreign corporation is not qualified to do business in California, the action can be brought in any county in the state. *See* ***Easton***, 12 Cal.App.3d at 246-47.

(3) D is partnership or association. An action against a partnership or association can be brought in the following counties:

(a) Principal place of business. The action can be brought in the county where the partnership or association's principal place of business is situated. *See* CCP §§395.2, 395.5. The partnership or association's "principal place of business" is its principal in-state office, which is designated in the partnership or association's

statement filed with the Secretary of State. *See* CCP §§395.2, 395.5; ***Black Diamond Asphalt***, 109 Cal.App.4th at 170. If the partnership or association has not filed the statement, the action can be brought in any county where a member of the partnership or association resides. *See* ***Carruth v. Superior Ct.*** (4th Dist.1978) 80 Cal.App.3d 215, 222-23 & n.2; ***Mosby***, 43 Cal.App.3d at 229-30 & n.7.

(b) Obligation or liability. The action can be brought in the county where the alleged obligation or liability arose. CCP §395.5; ***Juneau Spruce Corp. v. International Longshoremen's & Warehousemen's Un.*** (1951) 37 Cal.2d 760, 763 (discussing former Cal. Const., art. XII, §16, now CCP §395.5). See "Obligation or liability," §4.3.1(1)(b), p. 276.

(c) Contract. The action can be brought in the county where the contract being sued on was made, to be performed, or breached. CCP §395.5; ***Juneau Spruce***, 37 Cal.2d at 763. See "Contract," §4.3.1(1)(c), p. 276.

(4) D is State. An action against the State can be brought in any of several counties depending on what type of transitory action it is.

(a) Claim for money or damages. For actions against the State alleging a claim for money or damages, venue is proper in either Sacramento County or in any city or county where the Attorney General has an office. *See* CCP §401(1); Gov. C. §955; *see also* ***Tharp v. Superior Ct.*** (1982) 32 Cal.3d 496, 499-501 (under Gov. C. §955, Attorney General can change venue to Sacramento County). A claim for money or damages is an action (1) for which the filing of a claim is a statutory prerequisite to filing suit or (2) that is specifically exempted from this prerequisite. *See* ***Tharp***, 32 Cal.3d at 500-01; *see also* Gov. C. §905 (listing claims exempted from filing requirement), §905.2 (listing certain claims that must be filed).

(b) Action for injury to person or property. For actions against the State alleging injury or death to a person or injury to personal property, venue is proper in the county where the injury or injury causing death occurred. Gov. C. §955.2. It is not clear whether Gov. C. §955.2 governs *all* tort actions against the State. *Compare* ***State v. Superior Ct.*** (2d Dist.1967) 252 Cal.App.2d 637, 639 (dicta; stating that Legislature intended Gov. C. §955.2 to govern all tort cases in which State is D), *with* ***Hatcher v. California State Univ.*** (Los Angeles Cty. Superior Ct. Appellate Dept. 1983) 146 Cal.App.3d Supp. 1, 4-5 & n.1 (holding that Gov. C. §955.2 does not control actions brought under Information Practices Act of 1977, which includes its own venue provisions in Civ. C. §1798.49).

(c) Action for inverse condemnation. For actions against the State for taking or damaging private property for public use, venue is proper in the county where the property is situated. Gov. C. §955.

(d) Action by city, county, city & county, or local agency. For actions against the State brought by a city, county, city and county, or local agency, venue is proper in (1) the city, county, or city and county where the plaintiff is situated, (2) Sacramento County, or (3) any city or county where the Attorney General has an office. *See* CCP §401(1); Gov. C. §955.3.

(5) D is public officer. An action against a public officer, or a person specially appointed to perform the duties of a public officer, for an act done by the officer or person in her official capacity can be brought in the county where all or part of the cause of action arose. CCP §393(b); ***California State Parks Found. v. Superior Ct.*** (4th Dist.2007) 150 Cal.App.4th 826, 833. The same rule applies to actions against a person who, by a public officer's command or in the public officer's aid, does anything relating to the officer's duties. CCP §393(b).

(a) Public officer. The term "public officer" is broadly defined. A public officer can include a state agency, department, institution, board, or other public entity if there is no statutorily designated administrative or enforcement officer. ***Regents of Univ. of Cal.***, 3 Cal.3d at 537-38.

(b) Action arises. A cause of action "arises" in the county where the effects of the public officer's administrative action are felt—that is, where the plaintiff is injured—and not where the public officer is situated or where the challenged action was taken. ***California State Parks***, 150 Cal.App.4th at 834.

(c) Affirmative acts only. CCP §393 applies only to the public officer's affirmative acts that interfere with either private or public rights; it does not apply to the public officer's mere omissions, neglect of official duty, or threatened future acts. *See* ***California State Parks***, 150 Cal.App.4th at 834.

2. Type of action.

(1) Action for personal injury. An action for personal injury can be brought in either the county where the injury occurred or the county where some or all of the defendants reside at the beginning of the action. CCP §395(a). For purposes of CCP §395(a), an action for "injury to person" includes only those actions alleging an actual physical injury or death from a wrongful act or negligence. *See* ***Cubic Corp. v. Superior Ct.*** (1st Dist.1986) 186 Cal.App.3d 622, 625. Actions not involving physical injury or death, such as those seeking damages for injury to character or reputation, severe humiliation, mental anguish, or emotional distress, are not included under the statute. *See id.*; *see, e.g.*, ***Graham v. Mixon*** (1917) 177 Cal. 88, 91 (libel and slander are not injury to person); ***Cacciaguidi v. Superior Ct.*** (2d Dist.1990) 226 Cal.App.3d 181, 185-87 (abuse of process is not injury to person); ***Carruth***, 80 Cal.App.3d at 220 (malicious prosecution is not injury to person). Actions that are not considered an injury to person under CCP §395(a) are subject to the general venue rule. See "General venue rule," §4.2, p. 273.

(2) Action for personal-property damage. An action for injury to personal property can be brought in either the county where the injury occurred or the county where some or all of the defendants reside at the beginning of the action. CCP §395(a). For purposes of CCP §395(a), an action for "injury to personal property" includes only those actions alleging an actual physical injury to the property. ***Mason v. Buck*** (1st Dist.1929) 99 Cal.App. 219, 221. Actions not involving physical injury to property, such as those seeking damages for conversion, specific recovery, or interference with business relations, are not included under the statute. *See, e.g.*, ***Johnson v. Superior Ct.*** (5th Dist.1965) 232 Cal.App.2d 212, 218-20 (interference with business relations); ***Mason***, 99 Cal.App. at 221 (conversion). Actions that are not considered an injury to personal property under CCP §395(a) are subject to the general venue rule. *E.g.*, ***Mason***, 99 Cal.App. at 221 (conversion actions must be brought in county where D resides). See "General venue rule," §4.2, p. 273.

VENUE

(3) Action on contract.

(a) Generally. If a defendant has contracted to perform an obligation in a particular county, an action for breach of that obligation can be brought in the county where (1) the contract was in fact entered into, (2) the defendant is to perform the obligation as specified by a special written contract, or (3) the defendant or any other defendant resides at the beginning of the action. CCP §395(a); ***Armstrong v. Smith*** (1st Dist.1942) 49 Cal.App.2d 528, 531-32.

[1] Where contract was entered into. A contract is "entered into" in the place where the final act needed to make it a valid and binding agreement occurs. ***Mitchell v. Superior Ct.*** (2d Dist.1986) 186 Cal.App.3d 1040, 1045; *see* ***Bank of Yolo v. Sperry Flour Co.*** (1903) 141 Cal. 314, 315. This final act is usually the acceptance of the offer. ***Mitchell***, 186 Cal.App.3d at 1045-46; *see CEB Procedure Before Trial*, §8.21 (listing examples); *see, e.g.*, ***Wilson v. Scannavino*** (3d Dist.1958) 159 Cal.App.2d 369, 371 (contract made by phone was entered into where recipient of call accepted offer); ***Young v. John Haar Pickle Co.*** (3d Dist.1956) 139 Cal.App.2d 534, 535 (contract was entered into where parties signed it). If the contract designates the place where the contract was executed, the designation is prima facie evidence of the location where the contract was entered into. ***Braunstein v. Superior Ct.*** (1st Dist.1964) 225 Cal.App.2d 691, 697. However, this proof can be rebutted by parol evidence showing a different location. *Id.*; *e.g.*, ***Taylor v. Lundblade*** (3d Dist.1941) 43 Cal.App.2d 638, 639-40 (contract designated Humboldt County, but parol evidence established Del Norte County as actual location).

[2] Where obligation is to be performed. An obligation is "to be performed" in the county where the defendant incurred the obligation, unless the parties have a special written contract to the contrary. CCP §395(a); ***Caffrey v. Tilton*** (1952) 38 Cal.2d 371, 373; *see* ***Mosby***, 43 Cal.App.3d at 224-25 (dicta; §395 is limited to performance by D); *see also* ***Barquis v. Merchants Collection Ass'n*** (1972) 7 Cal.3d 94, 114 n.15 (purpose of special-contract requirement is to protect D's venue rights from being destroyed by P's unilateral assignment of

obligation to distant assignee). Usually, a defendant incurs an obligation at the location where the contract was entered into. *See* ***Armstrong***, 49 Cal.App.2d at 533-34. Under CCP §395(a), this location can be changed by a special written contract, which can be a separate agreement or an express stipulation but cannot be implied or established by parol evidence. *See* ***Caffrey***, 38 Cal.2d at 374; ***Mitchell***, 186 Cal.App.3d at 1047; ***Armstrong***, 49 Cal.App.2d at 536-37. To establish venue outside the county where the obligation was incurred, the special written contract must specify a geographic location for performance. ***Mitchell***, 186 Cal.App.3d at 1050; *see* ***Armstrong***, 49 Cal.App.2d at 536; *see also CEB Procedure Before Trial*, §8.24 (listing examples); 3 Witkin, *Cal. Procedure*, Actions, §843 (listing examples).

NOTE

The "special written contract" limitation applies only to individuals, not businesses. See CCP §395(a) (contains special-written-contract limitation), §395.5 (no mention of special-written-contract limitation); ***Mosby****, 43 Cal.App.3d at 223-25 (venue for transitory action against natural person is generally governed by CCP §395; venue for action against unincorporated business association is governed by CCP §§395.2, 395.5). For breach-of-contract actions against businesses, see "Contract," §4.3.1(1)(c), p. 276; "Contract," §4.3.1(3)(c), p. 277.*

[3] Where D resides. For a discussion of how to determine a defendant's residence, see "D's residence," §4.2.1, p. 274.

(b) Consumer contracts. Under CCP §395(b), an action arising from certain consumer contracts must be brought in a specific county and judicial district within that county.

[1] Types of contracts. CCP §395(b) applies to an action arising from either (1) an offer or provision of goods, services, loans, or extensions of credit intended primarily for personal, family, or household use, other than actions arising from retail installment contracts or motor-vehicle installment sales, or (2) a transaction consummated as a proximate result of either an unsolicited telephone call made by a seller engaged in the business of consummating transactions of that kind or a telephone call or electronic transmission made by the buyer or lessee in response to a solicitation by the seller. CCP §395(b); *see also* Civ. C. §1812.10 (special venue provision for retail installment contracts), §2984.4 (special venue provision for installment sales of motor vehicles); *CEB Procedure Before Trial*, §§8.26, 8.27 (discussing venue for installment contracts).

NOTE

A provision in any type of consumer contract described in CCP §395(b) that attempts to waive the venue statute is void and unenforceable. CCP §395(c).

[2] Proper county. The action must be brought in the county where the buyer or lessee (1) signed the contract, (2) resided when the contract was entered into, or (3) resides at the beginning of the action. CCP §395(b).

[3] Proper judicial district in county. Within the proper county, the action must be brought in the location where the superior court of the county tries the same type of case that is nearest or most accessible to (1) where the buyer or lessee resides, (2) where the buyer or lessee in fact signed the contract, (3) where the buyer or lessee resided when the contract was entered into, or (4) where the buyer or lessee resides at the beginning of the action. CCP §395(b). If none of these apply, the action can be tried anywhere in the county. *Id.* The superior court can specify by local rule the nearest or most accessible court location where such cases will be tried. *Id.*

(4) Action for marriage dissolution. An action to dissolve a marriage must be brought in the county where either the petitioner or the respondent has been a resident for three months before the start of the proceeding. CCP §395(a).

(5) Action to nullify marriage or obtain legal separation. An action to nullify a marriage or obtain a legal separation must be brought in the county where either party resides at the start of the proceeding. CCP §395(a).

(6) Action to change name. A petition for a name change must be brought in the county where the person whose name is proposed to be changed resides. CCP §1276(a). When a court-appointed guardian petitions to change the name of a minor, the petition must be brought in the court that appointed the guardian. *Id.* §1276(e).

(7) Action relating to minor.

(a) Child-support proceeding. An action to enforce a child-support obligation under Fam. C. §3900 or to establish and enforce a foreign judgment or order for a child-support obligation must be brought in the county where the child resides. CCP §395(a).

(b) Guardianship & conservatorship proceeding. A proceeding seeking to establish guardianship or conservatorship over a proposed ward or conservatee who is a California resident must be brought in the county (1) where the proposed ward or conservatee resides or (2) that may be in the proposed ward's or conservatee's best interest. Prob. C. §2201. If the proposed ward or conservatee is a nonresident, the proceeding must be brought in the county (1) where the proposed ward or conservatee is temporarily living or (2) that may be in the proposed ward's or conservatee's best interest. *Id.* §2202(a).

(c) Uniform Parentage Act proceeding. A proceeding under the Uniform Parentage Act must be brought in the county (1) where the child resides or is found, (2) where a licensed California adoption agency to which the child has been relinquished or is proposed to be relinquished maintains an office, (3) where the office of the Department of Social Services or a public adoption agency investigating a pending or proposed adoption petition is located, or (4) where the parent's estate was (or could be) probated, if the parent is deceased. Fam. C. §7620(b).

(d) Adoption proceeding. A standard adoption proceeding must be brought in the county where the proposed adoptive parent lives or in any other county authorized by Fam. C. §8609.5. Fam. C. §8714(a); *see also id.* §8912(a) (intercountry adoptions), §9000(a) (stepparent adoptions).

(e) Uniform Transfers to Minors Act proceeding. A proceeding under the Uniform Transfers to Minors Act must be brought in the county where either the custodian or the minor resides if the minor resides in California. Prob. C. §3921(a). If the minor does not reside in California, the proceeding must be brought in the county where the transferor, the custodian, or a parent resides, or the county where the estate of the deceased or incapacitated custodian is being administered. *Id.* §3921(b).

(8) Action against D representing estate. An action on a claim for the payment of money or for the recovery of personal property against a defendant in its official or representative capacity as executor, administrator, guardian, conservator, or trustee must be brought in the county with jurisdiction over the estate that the defendant represents. CCP §395.1. Different venue rules apply to actions against trustees of living and testamentary trusts. *See id.*; Prob. C. §17005.

(a) Living trusts. An action against a trustee of a living trust must be brought in the county where the principal place of the trust's administration is located. Prob. C. §17005(a)(1). If a living trust has no trustee, a proceeding to appoint a trustee must be brought in the county where the trust property or some part of it is located. *Id.* §17005(b).

(b) Testamentary trusts. An action against a trustee of a testamentary trust must be brought in either the county where the decedent's estate is administered or the county where the principal place of the trust's administration is located. Prob. C. §17005(a)(2).

(9) Action to dissolve corporation. An action to dissolve a corporation can be brought in the county where the principal executive office of the corporation is located. *See* Corp. C. §§177, 1800(a), 1904. If the corporation does not have a principal executive office in the state, the action can be brought in Sacramento County. *See* Corp. C. §§177, 1800(a), 1904.

(10) Action to recover penalty or forfeiture. An action to recover a penalty or forfeiture imposed by statute can be brought in the county where the cause of action or some part of it arose. CCP §393(a); *see* ***County of Riverside v. Superior Ct.*** (1968) 69 Cal.2d 828, 830. But if the penalty or forfeiture was imposed for an offense on a lake, river, or other stream of water situated in two or more counties, the action can be brought in any county bordering on the lake, river, or stream and opposite to the place where the offense was committed. CCP §393(a).

(11) Action to establish nonresident tax status. An action by an individual to establish that she is a nonresident for personal income-tax purposes must be brought in Sacramento County, Los Angeles County, or in the City and County of San Francisco. CCP §1060.5.

(12) Action under Fair Employment & Housing Act. An action for violation of the Fair Employment and Housing Act can be brought in any county where (1) the unlawful practice was committed, (2) the relevant records are maintained and administered, or (3) the aggrieved person would have worked or had access to the public accommodation but for the unlawful practice. Gov. C. §12965(b). If the defendant is not found in any of these counties, the action can be brought in the county where the defendant resides or maintains its principal office. *Id.*

§5. MIXED-ACTION RULES

A "mixed action" is an action in which a plaintiff alleges two or more causes of action that are each governed by a different venue statute, or joins two or more defendants who are subject to different venue standards. ***Brown v. Superior Ct.*** (1984) 37 Cal.3d 477, 488; *see* ***State v. Superior Ct.*** (2d Dist.1967) 252 Cal.App.2d 637, 640; 3 Witkin, *Cal. Procedure*, Actions, §883. Under either scenario, two or more inconsistent venue provisions would apply in the same case. ***Brown***, 37 Cal.3d at 488. To resolve this conflict, the plaintiff must apply what courts and commentators call the "mixed-action rules." *See id.* at 487.

§5.1 Two or more causes of action pleaded.

If two or more causes of action are pleaded, venue is determined by the character of all the actions.

1. Local vs. local. If two or more causes of action are pleaded, all of which are characterized as local but involve properties located in different counties, the entire action is subject to the general rule that venue is proper in any county where some part of a relevant property is situated. *See* CCP §392(a); ***Appel v. Hubbard*** (4th Dist.1957) 155 Cal.App.2d 639, 643.

2. Local vs. transitory. If two or more causes of action are pleaded, one of which is characterized as local and another as transitory, the entire action is subject to the general rule that the transitory action governs venue. ***Hays v. Cowles*** (1st Dist.1943) 60 Cal.App.2d 514, 516; *see* ***Central Bank v. Superior Ct.*** (5th Dist.1973) 30 Cal.App.3d 913, 918 (P cannot deprive D of right to have transitory action tried in county of residence by joining local action); *see, e.g.*, ***Bybee v. Fairchild*** (1st Dist.1946) 75 Cal.App.2d 35, 43 (D entitled to change of venue to county of residence when P alleged separate causes of action, one local and another transitory). Thus, if the proper venues for the local action and the transitory action are different, the plaintiff may be forced to try the entire case in the defendant's county of residence. *See, e.g.*, ***Padron v. Superior Ct.*** (3d Dist.2006) No. C053412 (unpub.; 11-21-06) (trial court should have granted D's motion to transfer venue to county of residence when P alleged separate local and transitory actions and filed suit in county where property was located).

3. Transitory vs. transitory. If two or more causes of action are pleaded, all of which are characterized as transitory, and if venue is not proper for all the causes of action, the entire action is subject to the general rule that the defendant can seek a change of venue, usually to the county where it resides. *See* ***Brown v. Superior Ct.*** (1984) 37 Cal.3d 477, 488 & n.10; ***Jhirmack Enters. v. Superior Ct.*** (2d Dist.1979) 96 Cal.App.3d 715, 720; *see, e.g.*, ***Mission Imports, Inc. v. Superior Ct.*** (1982) 31 Cal.3d 921, 927-28 (D not entitled to change of venue to principal place of business because P established proper venue for all causes of action); ***Goossen v. Clifton*** (1st Dist.1946) 75 Cal.App.2d 44, 49-50 (D entitled to change of venue to county of residence because P established proper venue only for one of two causes of action).

4. Effect of special venue statute. If two or more causes of action are pleaded, one of which is governed by a special venue statute, the entire action is subject to the general rule that the special venue statute controls if it would promote an important public policy. *See, e.g.*, ***Brown***, 37 Cal.3d at 488 (venue for mixed action that

VENUE

includes cause of action arising under Fair Employment and Housing Act is governed by special venue provisions of FEHA). However, this general rule does not apply when (1) the plaintiff files suit in a county different from that specified in the special venue provision or (2) the special venue provision does not promote an important public policy sufficient to preempt the general venue rules. *See* ***Ford Motor Credit Co. v. Superior Ct.*** (2d Dist.1996) 50 Cal.App.4th 306, 310 (if P relies on venue provisions of FEHA, it must file suit in proper county according to FEHA, and if it does not, D can force change to county of D's residence); ***Gallin v. Superior Ct.*** (4th Dist.1991) 230 Cal.App.3d 541, 545-46 (Consumers Legal Remedies Act does not preempt general venue rules because it does not protect a fundamental right).

§5.2 Two or more Ds joined. If two or more defendants are joined in an action but the defendants are subject to different venue standards, venue is usually proper for all defendants if it is proper for one of them. *See* ***State v. Superior Ct.*** (2d Dist.1967) 252 Cal.App.2d 637, 640; Weil, *Civil Procedure Before Trial*, ¶3:496 (when venue is proper in several counties, D cannot force transfer to county of residence); *see, e.g.*, ***Dreher v. Fidelity & Cas. Co.*** (1st Dist.1957) 148 Cal.App.2d 695, 700 (venue proper for individual D when action brought in corporate co-D's county of residence). However, this general rule has several exceptions:

VENUE

1. **Individual & private corporation or association.** If an individual and a private corporation or unincorporated association are joined as defendants in the same action, the individual defendant can transfer the entire action to any defendant's county of residence if the plaintiff filed the action in a county that is proper for suing a corporation or association under CCP §395.5 but is not a county where the defendants reside or have a principal place of business. ***Brown v. Superior Ct.*** (1984) 37 Cal.3d 477, 482 n.6; ***Carruth v. Superior Ct.*** (4th Dist.1978) 80 Cal.App.3d 215, 220-21; ***State***, 252 Cal.App.2d at 640-41. The plaintiff can defeat the individual defendant's right to choose venue by (1) filing suit in the corporation's or association's county of residence, (2) specifically alleging that the individual defendant is liable for the corporation's act on the ground of alter ego, or (3) specifically alleging that the individual defendant, who is a member of an association, is personally liable to the plaintiff. *See* ***Lebastchi v. Superior Ct.*** (4th Dist.1995) 33 Cal.App.4th 1465, 1470-71 (alter ego alleged); ***Buran Equip. Co. v. Superior Ct.*** (6th Dist.1987) 190 Cal.App.3d 1662, 1667-68 (individual association member sued); ***Mosby v. Superior Ct.*** (3d Dist.1974) 43 Cal.App.3d 219, 226 (suit filed in association's county of residence).

2. **Individual or private corporation & State.** If an individual, private corporation, or association and the State are joined as defendants in the same action, the State (through the Attorney General) can transfer the entire action to Sacramento County if the action alleges the State is liable on an express contract or for negligence that does not result in injury or death to a person or injury to personal property. *See* Gov. C. §§955, 955.2; ***Tharp v. Superior Ct.*** (1982) 32 Cal.3d 496, 499-501. The State's right to transfer the case trumps the plaintiff's venue selection, unless the plaintiff filed suit in a county where the Attorney General has an office. *See* CCP §401(1) (suit against State that can be removed to Sacramento County can be filed in any county where the AG has an office). But if the action is for injury or death to a person or injury to personal property, the State can transfer the entire action to the county where the injury or the injury causing death occurred. Gov. C. §955.2; *see* ***State v. Superior Ct.*** (3d Dist.1965) 238 Cal.App.2d 691, 694. If the plaintiff is a county, city, or local agency, the State is treated like any other private party and can seek a transfer only under the grounds listed in CCP §397. Gov. C. §955.3. See "Motion to Transfer or Change Venue," ch. 4-E, p. 359.

3. **Individual or private corporation & local governmental entity.** If an individual, private corporation, or association and a county, city, city and county, or local agency are joined as defendants in the same action for negligent injury to a person or property, the county, city, city and county, or local agency can ask for a transfer of the entire action to its home county if the injury occurred there. *See* CCP §394(a); ***Tutor-Saliba-Perini Jt.V. v. Superior Ct.*** (2d Dist.1991) 233 Cal.App.3d 736, 743; ***Delgado v. Superior Ct.*** (3d Dist.1977) 74 Cal.App.3d 560, 563-64. This is true even if there is an individual codefendant who resides in a different county; venue would not be proper in the individual codefendant's county of residence. ***County of Orange v. Superior Ct.*** (1st Dist.1999) 73 Cal.App.4th 1189, 1191-92; *see* CCP §394(a); ***Ventura Unified Sch. Dist. v. Superior Ct.*** (2d Dist.2001) 92 Cal.App.4th 811, 814. This "home county" rule applies only to negligence actions. *See* CCP §394(a). For nonnegligence actions, general

venue rules apply; venue is proper in any county where at least one defendant resides. *Id.* §395(a); *see, e.g.*, ***Tutor-Saliba-Perini Jt.V.***, 233 Cal.App.3d at 743-44 (action against local agency was proper in co-D's county of residence because suit against agency was for breach of contract, indemnity, and contribution, not negligent injury).

G. JOINING THE DEFENDANT—PERSONAL JURISDICTION

§1. GENERAL

§1.1 Purpose. Before filing suit, the plaintiff must determine whether the court has personal jurisdiction over the defendant—that is, whether the court has the power to bind the defendant with a judgment. *See* ***World-Wide Volkswagen Corp. v. Woodson*** (1980) 444 U.S. 286, 291; ***Donaldson v. National Mar., Inc.*** (2005) 35 Cal.4th 503, 512; ***Strathvale Holdings v. E.B.H.*** (2d Dist.2005) 126 Cal.App.4th 1241, 1249. The court's power to exercise personal jurisdiction comes from (1) the defendant's presence in, contacts with, or conduct in California and (2) valid service. *See* ***World-Wide Volkswagen***, 444 U.S. at 291; ***Donaldson***, 35 Cal.4th at 512; ***Greener v. Workers' Comp. Appeals Bd.*** (1993) 6 Cal.4th 1028, 1034-35; ***Ziller Elecs. Lab GmbH v. Superior Ct.*** (2d Dist.1988) 206 Cal.App.3d 1222, 1229. See "Joining the Defendant—Service of Process," ch. 3-H, p. 295. The plaintiff must establish personal jurisdiction because a judgment entered by a court lacking personal jurisdiction is void. *See* ***Burnham v. Superior Ct.*** (1990) 495 U.S. 604, 608-09; ***Strathvale Holdings***, 126 Cal.App.4th at 1249.

§1.2 Primary authority. CCP §410.10.

§1.3 Secondary authority. The following secondary sources are cited as authority in this subchapter:

- Weil & Brown, *California Practice Guide: Civil Procedure Before Trial* (CD-ROM ed. 2014) (referred to as Weil, *Civil Procedure Before Trial*).
- Witkin, *California Procedure* (5th ed. 2008 & Supp.2014) (referred to as Witkin, *Cal. Procedure*).

§2. LONG-ARM STATUTE

CCP §410.10 operates as California's general long-arm statute, authorizing California courts to exercise personal jurisdiction over nonresidents to the fullest extent permitted by due process. ***F. Hoffman-La Roche, Ltd. v. Superior Ct.*** (6th Dist.2005) 130 Cal.App.4th 782, 795; ***Muckle v. Superior Ct.*** (4th Dist.2002) 102 Cal.App.4th 218, 226 n.6; *see* CCP §410.10; ***Snowney v. Harrah's Entm't, Inc.*** (2005) 35 Cal.4th 1054, 1061; ***Vons Cos. v. Seabest Foods, Inc.*** (1996) 14 Cal.4th 434, 444. Due process protects defendants from being subject to the judgments of a California court when they have not established any meaningful contacts, ties, or relations with the state. *See* ***Vons Cos.***, 14 Cal.4th at 445. Personal jurisdiction must be based on either a defendant's presence in California or other conduct allowing the court to exercise personal jurisdiction over the defendant. ***Greener v. Workers' Comp. Appeals Bd.*** (1993) 6 Cal.4th 1028, 1034-35. Courts have articulated four grounds for exercising personal jurisdiction over a defendant: (1) domicile, (2) physical presence, (3) consent, and (4) minimum contacts. *See* ***Muckle***, 102 Cal.App.4th at 226.

§3. DOMICILE

A California court can exercise personal jurisdiction over a defendant who is domiciled in California. ***Milliken v. Meyer*** (1940) 311 U.S. 457, 462; ***F. Hoffman-La Roche, Ltd. v. Superior Ct.*** (6th Dist.2005) 130 Cal.App.4th 782, 796; ***Muckle v. Superior Ct.*** (4th Dist.2002) 102 Cal.App.4th 218, 226; *see* ***Smith v. Smith*** (1955) 45 Cal.2d 235, 243. A defendant's "domicile" is the place where it resides with the intent to remain indefinitely. *See* ***Noble v. Franchise Tax Bd.*** (2d Dist.2004) 118 Cal.App.4th 560, 568. If a defendant is residing in another state but was domiciled in California when the suit was initiated, the exercise of personal jurisdiction in California is proper if the defendant was served with process. ***Milliken***, 311 U.S. at 462-63; ***Allen v. Superior Ct.*** (1953) 41 Cal.2d 306, 312-13.

§4. PHYSICAL PRESENCE

A California court can exercise personal jurisdiction over a defendant who is personally served with process while physically present in California. ***Burnham v. Superior Ct.*** (1990) 495 U.S. 604, 610-11; ***Muckle v. Superior Ct.*** (4th

PERSONAL JURISDICTION

Dist.2002) 102 Cal.App.4th 218, 226; ***In re Marriage of Fitzgerald & King*** (6th Dist.1995) 39 Cal.App.4th 1419, 1425-26. In some cases, however, a defendant's physical presence in California is insufficient to establish personal jurisdiction.

§4.1 Immunity from jurisdiction. A person who is physically present in California is not subject to personal jurisdiction based solely on the person's physical presence in the state to participate as a party in a child-custody proceeding or as a petitioner in a child-support proceeding. *See* Fam. C. §§3409(a), 4928(a); ***In re Marriage of Fitzgerald & King*** (6th Dist.1995) 39 Cal.App.4th 1419, 1428. This immunity from personal jurisdiction does not apply, however, to any acts the person commits in the state that are unrelated to the person's participation in the proceeding. *See* Fam. C. §§3409(c), 4928(c).

§4.2 Immunity from service. A person who is physically present in California is not subject to personal jurisdiction if the person is immune from service of process. *See* 2 Witkin, *Cal. Procedure*, Jurisdiction, §126.

1. Common-law immunities. At common law, certain people were granted immunity from service of process because the state had an interest in securing their presence and these people might not otherwise come to the state. *See* ***Severn v. Adidas Sportschuhfabriken*** (1st Dist.1973) 33 Cal.App.3d 754, 758-59. These people included (1) witnesses, parties, and attorneys who voluntarily entered the state to participate in a legal proceeding, (2) extradited criminal defendants, (3) legislators, (4) diplomatic officers, and (5) nonresidents performing a public duty. *See* 3 Witkin, *Cal. Procedure*, Actions, §§971-980. The common-law immunity for witnesses and parties who voluntarily entered the state to participate in a legal proceeding has been eliminated. *See* ***Silverman v. Superior Ct.*** (2d Dist.1988) 203 Cal.App.3d 145, 149 (eliminating immunity from service of process for parties present in state to participate in unrelated legal proceeding); ***Severn***, 33 Cal.App.3d at 762 (eliminating immunity from service of process for witnesses voluntarily present in state to participate in unrelated legal proceeding). But the common-law immunity has not been eliminated for other people traditionally immune from service of process. *See* 3 Witkin, *Cal. Procedure*, Actions, §977 (issue left open whether nonresident attorney coming into state to participate in litigation was still immune from service of process).

2. Constitutional immunity. The California Constitution grants immunity from service of process to state legislators during a legislative session and for five days before and after a legislative session. Cal. Const., art. IV, §14; *see* ***Harmer v. Superior Ct.*** (3d Dist.1969) 275 Cal.App.2d 345, 348 (constitutional immunity from service of process for state legislators applies to any kind of lawsuit).

3. Statutory immunities.

(1) Criminal proceeding.

(a) Witness in California. A person who is physically present in California to comply with a subpoena to testify in California in a criminal proceeding is immune from service of process in any civil or criminal action based on matters that occurred before the person entered California under the subpoena. Pen. C. §1334.4.

(b) Witness in another state. A person who is physically present in California while going to or returning from another state in compliance with a subpoena to testify in the other state in a criminal proceeding is immune from service of process in any civil or criminal action based on matters that occurred before the person entered California under the subpoena. Pen. C. §1334.5.

(c) Extradited criminal defendant. A person who is physically present in California because she was extradited or waived extradition on a criminal charge is immune from service of process in a civil action arising from the same facts as the criminal proceeding, until the person has been convicted in the criminal proceeding or, if acquitted, until the person has had a reasonable opportunity to return to the state from which she was extradited. Pen. C. §1555.

(2) Child-custody proceeding. A person who is physically present in California is immune from service of process while participating as a party in a child-custody proceeding if the sole basis for exercising jurisdiction is the party's physical presence. *See* Fam. C. §3409(b).

(3) Child-support proceeding. A person who is physically present in California is immune from service of process while participating as a petitioner in a child-support proceeding. Fam. C. §4928(b). Immunity from service of process does not apply, however, for any acts the person commits while present in the state to participate in the proceeding that are unrelated to the person's participation in the proceeding. *Id.* §4928(c).

(4) Conciliation proceeding. A person who is a conciliator, a party to a conciliation proceeding, or a representative of a party to a conciliation proceeding is immune from service of process while physically present in the state to arrange for or participate in a conciliation proceeding involving an international commercial dispute. CCP §1297.431.

§4.3 Involuntarily present in state. A court can refuse to exercise jurisdiction over a person if her physical presence in California was obtained by unlawful force or fraud. ***Titus v. Superior Ct.*** (1st Dist.1972) 23 Cal.App.3d 792, 798; *see, e.g.*, ***People v. Williams*** (6th Dist.1999) 77 Cal.App.4th 436, 458 (court did not refuse to exercise jurisdiction even though D claimed he was being held unlawfully in civil commitment proceeding); ***Forbes v. Cameron Pet., Inc.*** (2d Dist.1978) 83 Cal.App.3d 257, 261 (court refused to exercise jurisdiction after D claimed P fraudulently induced him to enter state in order to serve him with complaint). It is unclear, however, whether a defendant's involuntary presence in California in other situations (e.g., airport stopover, medical emergency) would preclude the court from exercising personal jurisdiction. *See* ***Burnham v. Superior Ct.*** (1990) 495 U.S. 604, 637 n.11 (Brennan, Marshall, Blackmun, O'Connor, JJ., concurring) (declining to address when D's involuntary presence in state would preclude court's exercise of personal jurisdiction); Weil, *Civil Procedure Before Trial*, ¶3:144 (unclear whether exercise of personal jurisdiction is permitted over nonresidents whose presence in state is involuntary).

§5. CONSENT

A California court can exercise personal jurisdiction over a defendant who has either expressly or impliedly consented to the jurisdiction. ***Insurance Corp. v. Compagnie des Bauxites*** (1982) 456 U.S. 694, 703; ***Nobel Farms, Inc. v. Pasero*** (4th Dist.2003) 106 Cal.App.4th 654, 658; *see* ***Muckle v. Superior Ct.*** (4th Dist.2002) 102 Cal.App.4th 218, 226.

§5.1 Express consent. A defendant expressly consents to the court's jurisdiction by making a general appearance or by agreeing to jurisdiction in a contract. ***Nobel Farms, Inc. v. Pasero*** (4th Dist.2003) 106 Cal.App.4th 654, 658.

1. General appearance. A defendant can consent to the exercise of personal jurisdiction by making a general appearance in the action. ***Nobel Farms***, 106 Cal.App.4th at 658. When a defendant generally appears, any objections to personal jurisdiction are waived, including defects in service. *See* CCP §410.50(a); ***Dial 800 v. Fesbinder*** (2d Dist.2004) 118 Cal.App.4th 32, 52; ***Fireman's Fund Ins. v. Sparks Constr., Inc.*** (4th Dist.2004) 114 Cal.App.4th 1135, 1147. Determining if a defendant has made a general appearance depends on whether the defendant has challenged the court's personal jurisdiction with a motion to quash service of summons. See "Motion to Quash Service of Summons," ch. 4-G, p. 389.

(1) Actions taken with or after motion to quash. If a defendant makes a motion to quash, the defendant can take any simultaneous or later action—including filing an answer, a demurrer, or a motion to strike—without making a general appearance. CCP §418.10(e)(1); *see* ***Factor Health Mgmt. v. Superior Ct.*** (2d Dist.2005) 132 Cal.App.4th 246, 251-52; ***Roy v. Superior Ct.*** (4th Dist.2005) 127 Cal.App.4th 337, 345. The defendant will only be deemed to have generally appeared if the court denies the motion to quash. CCP §418.10(e)(1). If the court denies the motion, the defendant is not deemed to have appeared until the court enters the order or, if the defendant petitions for a writ of mandate, at the conclusion of the writ proceedings. *Id.* §418.10(e)(1), (e)(2).

(2) Actions taken before motion to quash. If a defendant has not made a motion to quash, the defendant generally appears by filing an answer or seeking other types of affirmative relief, whether in person or by an attorney. *See* CCP §§418.10(e), 1014; ***Mansour v. Superior Ct.*** (4th Dist.1995) 38 Cal.App.4th 1750, 1756.

(a) Examples – general appearance. If the defendant has not made a motion to quash, the defendant generally appears by doing any of the following:

[1] Answering the complaint. CCP §1014; ***Fireman's Fund***, 114 Cal.App.4th at 1145; *e.g.*, ***Kriebel v. City Council of San Diego*** (4th Dist.1980) 112 Cal.App.3d 693, 699-700 (Ds generally appeared by filing answer, even though it contained objections to personal jurisdiction).

[2] Filing any of the following:

[a] A demurrer. CCP §1014.

[b] A notice of motion to strike. *Id.*

[c] A notice of motion to transfer based on improper venue. *Id.*; *see id.* §396b.

[d] A motion for reclassification. *Id.* §1014; *see id.* §403.040.

[3] Giving the plaintiff a written notice of appearance either personally or through an attorney. *Id.* §1014; ***Davenport v. Superior Ct.*** (1920) 183 Cal. 506, 509; *see* ***Farmers & Merchs. Nat'l Bank v. Superior Ct.*** (1945) 25 Cal.2d 842, 846.

[4] Expressing an intent to submit to the court's jurisdiction by doing either of the following:

[a] Stipulating to accept service of process. *See* ***General Ins. v. Superior Ct.*** (1975) 15 Cal.3d 449, 453.

[b] Stipulating to an extension of time to appear, answer, demur, or plead. ***Sprague v. County of San Diego*** (4th Dist.2003) 106 Cal.App.4th 119, 131; ***Kriebel***, 112 Cal.App.3d at 699; *see* ***RCA Corp. v. Superior Ct.*** (1st Dist.1975) 47 Cal.App.3d 1007, 1009-10.

[5] Participating in the action in a way that recognizes the court's jurisdiction. ***Factor Health***, 132 Cal.App.4th at 250; *e.g.*, ***Hamilton v. Asbestos Corp.*** (2000) 22 Cal.4th 1127, 1147 (D generally appeared by participating in action from beginning to end).

[6] Seeking any affirmative relief other than a motion to quash for lack of personal jurisdiction. ***Dial 800***, 118 Cal.App.4th at 52; *see* ***Lacey v. Bertone*** (1949) 33 Cal.2d 649, 651 (D submits to court's jurisdiction if she requests any relief that assumes she is properly before the court); ***Factor Health***, 132 Cal.App.4th at 250 (D makes general appearance by seeking relief that is available only if court has jurisdiction). For example, a defendant can generally appear by doing any of the following:

[a] Challenging the merits of the action. ***Fireman's Fund***, 114 Cal.App.4th at 1145 (general appearance when party contests merits of case or raises nonjurisdictional objections); *see* ***Davenport***, 183 Cal. at 511 (general appearance when D seeks ruling or order on merits of case); *see, e.g.*, ***Alioto Fish Co. v. Alioto*** (1st Dist.1994) 27 Cal.App.4th 1669, 1689 (D generally appeared by filing oppositions on merits to fee, receiver, and sanctions orders).

[b] Seeking a continuance. ***City of Riverside v. Horspool*** (4th Dist.2014) 223 Cal.App.4th 670, 679-80; *see* ***366-386 Geary St., L.P. v. Superior Ct.*** (1st Dist.1990) 219 Cal.App.3d 1186, 1194 n.2.

[c] Initiating discovery. ***Factor Health***, 132 Cal.App.4th at 250; *see* ***Mansour***, 38 Cal.App.4th at 1757; ***Creed v. Schultz*** (1st Dist.1983) 148 Cal.App.3d 733, 740. However, requesting discovery for the limited purpose of challenging the court's exercise of personal jurisdiction does not constitute a general appearance. ***Factor Health***, 132 Cal.App.4th at 250; *see* ***Harding v. Harding*** (2d Dist.2002) 99 Cal.App.4th 626, 636.

[d] Answering discovery. *See* ***Estate of Heil*** (6th Dist.1989) 210 Cal.App.3d 1503, 1512 (participating in discovery subjects party to court's jurisdiction); ***Chitwood v. County of L.A.*** (2d Dist.1971) 14 Cal.App.3d 522, 527-28 (answering interrogatories subjects party to court's jurisdiction).

NOTE

A nonparty that is not named in the pleadings makes a general appearance and submits to the court's personal jurisdiction if the nonparty seeks affirmative relief or opposes a motion on the merits. E.g., ***People v. Ciancio*** *(2d Dist.2003) 109 Cal.App.4th 175, 192-93 (nonparty generally appeared when it filed response to order to show cause and argued merits of motion).*

(b) Examples – no general appearance. Even if the defendant has not made a motion to quash, the defendant does not generally appear by doing any of the following:

[1] Stipulating to extend the time for service of process under CCP §583.230. CCP §583.220(a).

[2] Filing a motion to dismiss for failure to timely prosecute the action. *Id.* §583.220(b).

[3] Stipulating to an extension of time to plead after filing a motion to dismiss for failure to timely prosecute the action. *Id.* §583.220(c).

[4] Appearing at a hearing for ex parte relief or an ex parte provisional remedy, such as a preliminary injunction. *Id.* §418.11; ***Factor Health***, 132 Cal.App.4th at 250.

[5] Participating in a cross-action. *See* ***Botsford v. Pascoe*** (1st Dist.1979) 94 Cal.App.3d 62, 67-68 (complaint and cross-complaint are separate and independent actions; general appearance in one does not necessarily constitute general appearance in the other); *see, e.g.*, ***Glenwood Homeowners Ass'n v. Prosher Dev. Ltd.*** (2d Dist.1980) 111 Cal.App.3d 1002, 1005 (D did not make general appearance in original suit by filing answer to cross-complaint).

2. Contract. A defendant can consent to the exercise of personal jurisdiction by agreeing to the jurisdiction in a contract. ***Berard Constr. Co. v. Municipal Ct.*** (2d Dist.1975) 49 Cal.App.3d 710, 721. Examples of consent by contract include the following:

(1) Forum-selection clause.

(a) Mandatory clause. A defendant expressly consents to personal jurisdiction by signing a contract that contains a mandatory forum-selection clause exclusively requiring litigation in California. *See* ***National Equip. Rental, Ltd. v. Szukhent*** (1964) 375 U.S. 311, 315-16; ***Berard Constr.***, 49 Cal.App.3d at 721. If the contract was voluntarily entered into and negotiated between parties of equal bargaining strength, the clause will be enforced unless it is unfair or unreasonable. *See* ***Smith, Valentino & Smith, Inc. v. Superior Ct.*** (1976) 17 Cal.3d 491, 495-96; ***Berg v. MTC Elecs. Techs.*** (2d Dist.1998) 61 Cal.App.4th 349, 358; ***Cal-State Bus. Prods. & Servs. v. Ricoh*** (3d Dist.1993) 12 Cal.App.4th 1666, 1678-79; *see, e.g.*, ***Aral v. Earthlink, Inc.*** (2d Dist.2005) 134 Cal.App.4th 544, 561 (forum-selection clause requiring P-consumers to travel 2,000 miles to recover small sum was unreasonable and unenforceable).

(b) Permissive clause. The defendant does not necessarily consent to jurisdiction if the forum-selection clause does not specify an exclusive forum; in such a case, the clause is "permissive," and the court applies the general principles of forum non conveniens. ***Berg***, 61 Cal.App.4th at 359. See "Forum Non Conveniens," ch. 4-F, p. 375.

(2) Arbitration clause. A defendant expressly consents to personal jurisdiction for suits to compel arbitration or to enforce arbitration awards by signing a contract that contains an arbitration clause providing for arbitration to be held in California. *See* CCP §1293; ***Boghos v. Certain Underwriters at Lloyd's of London*** (2005) 36 Cal.4th 495, 503. The enforceability of this type of arbitration clause is analyzed in the same manner as the enforceability of a forum-selection clause. ***Aral***, 134 Cal.App.4th at 553-54. See "Forum-selection clause," §5.1.2(1), this page.

(3) Cognovit clause. A defendant expressly consents to personal jurisdiction by signing a contract that contains a "cognovit clause" waiving service of process. *See* ***D.H. Overmyer Co. v. Frick Co.*** (1972) 405 U.S. 174, 187. The cognovit agreement must be negotiated by parties with equal bargaining power to establish a voluntary, knowing, and intelligent waiver of due-process rights. *See* ***Isbell v. County of Sonoma*** (1978) 21 Cal.3d 61, 70; *see, e.g.*, ***Commercial Nat'l Bank v. Kermeen*** (1st Dist.1990) 225 Cal.App.3d 396, 400-01 (cognovit clause in preprinted form, without more, did not waive notice and hearing; thus, court lacked jurisdiction).

§5.2 Implied consent. A defendant can impliedly consent to the court's jurisdiction by its conduct. ***Sea Foods Co. v. O.M. Foods Co.*** (2d Dist.2007) 150 Cal.App.4th 769, 786. If a party brings suit in a California court, the party

impliedly consents to jurisdiction in any action related to the action it brought. *Id.*; *e.g.*, ***Nobel Farms, Inc. v. Pasero*** (4th Dist.2003) 106 Cal.App.4th 654, 659 (by suing client for fees in California, Mexican attorney impliedly consented to California jurisdiction for client's later malpractice suit).

NOTE

A nonresident defendant's appointment of an agent for service of process in California is not consent to the exercise of jurisdiction in the state. See ***DVI, Inc. v. Superior Ct.*** *(4th Dist.2002) 104 Cal.App.4th 1080, 1095;* ***Gray Line Tours v. Reynolds Elec. & Eng'g Co.*** *(2d Dist.1987) 193 Cal.App.3d 190, 194-95. Similarly, a service-of-process statute designating an agent for service does not result in consent to the exercise of jurisdiction in the state. See, e.g.,* ***Thomson v. Anderson*** *(4th Dist.2003) 113 Cal.App.4th 258, 270 (Franchise Investment Law designating service on Commissioner of Corporations);* ***In re Marriage of Martin*** *(5th Dist.1989) 207 Cal.App.3d 1426, 1433 (Insurance Code designating service on Insurance Commissioner).*

§6. MINIMUM CONTACTS

A California court can exercise personal jurisdiction over a nonresident defendant who has "minimum contacts" with the state. ***Pavlovich v. Superior Ct.*** (2002) 29 Cal.4th 262, 268; ***Virtualmagic Asia, Inc. v. Fil-Cartoons, Inc.*** (4th Dist.2002) 99 Cal.App.4th 228, 238. A defendant has minimum contacts if the quality and nature of its activity in the forum state (referred to as "contacts") is such that it is reasonable and fair to require the defendant to conduct a defense in that state. ***Pavlovich***, 29 Cal.4th at 268. Depending on the extent of a defendant's contacts with California, it may be subject to either general jurisdiction or specific jurisdiction. ***Elkman v. National States Ins.*** (2d Dist.2009) 173 Cal.App.4th 1305, 1314; *see* ***Pavlovich***, 29 Cal.4th at 268-69; ***Vons Cos. v. Seabest Foods, Inc.*** (1996) 14 Cal.4th 434, 445-46.

§6.1 General jurisdiction. A court can exercise general jurisdiction over a nonresident defendant when the defendant's in-state contacts are substantial, continuous, and systematic. ***Vons Cos. v. Seabest Foods, Inc.*** (1996) 14 Cal.4th 434, 445; ***Elkman v. National States Ins.*** (2d Dist.2009) 173 Cal.App.4th 1305, 1314; ***Luberski, Inc. v. Oleificio F.LLI Amato S.R.L.*** (4th Dist.2009) 171 Cal.App.4th 409, 413-14; ***Shisler v. Sanfer Sports Cars, Inc.*** (6th Dist.2006) 146 Cal.App.4th 1254, 1258-59. This standard is difficult to meet. *See* ***Bancroft & Masters, Inc. v. Augusta Nat'l Inc.*** (9th Cir.2000) 223 F.3d 1082, 1086; ***Paneno v. Centres for Academic Programmes Abroad Ltd.*** (2d Dist.2004) 118 Cal.App.4th 1447, 1455. When it is met, though, the court can exercise jurisdiction over the defendant even if the cause of action is unrelated to the defendant's in-state activities. ***Vons Cos.***, 14 Cal.4th at 445.

1. D's contacts. To establish minimum contacts for general jurisdiction, the plaintiff must itemize the defendant's contacts with California. Only the defendant's contacts are relevant to establishing general jurisdiction. ***Young v. Daimler AG*** (1st Dist.2014) 228 Cal.App.4th 855, 866; *see* ***Rush v. Savchuk*** (1980) 444 U.S. 320, 331-32 (requirements of due process must be satisfied for each D over whom court exercises jurisdiction). However, some courts have held or suggested that, under the principles of alter ego or agency, another entity's or person's contacts can be attributed to the defendant to establish general jurisdiction. ***Healthmarkets, Inc. v. Superior Ct.*** (2d Dist.2009) 171 Cal.App.4th 1160, 1169 (listing cases).

(1) Alter ego. An entity's contacts with California can be attributed to its parent company when evidence establishes that the parent and subsidiary are alter egos. *See* ***F. Hoffman-La Roche, Ltd. v. Superior Ct.*** (6th Dist.2005) 130 Cal.App.4th 782, 796; ***Sonora Diamond Corp. v. Superior Ct.*** (5th Dist.2000) 83 Cal.App.4th 523, 538; *see also* ***DVI, Inc. v. Superior Ct.*** (4th Dist.2002) 104 Cal.App.4th 1080, 1094 (adopting ***Sonora Diamond***). *But see* ***Healthmarkets, Inc.***, 171 Cal.App.4th at 1170 (courts cannot rely on state substantive law of agency and alter ego to determine constitutional limits of personal jurisdiction). The alter-ego doctrine is used to establish jurisdiction when an abuse of the corporate privilege justifies disregarding the corporate identity to hold the equitable owners of a corporation liable for the corporation's actions. *See* ***Sonora Diamond***, 83 Cal.App.4th at 538 (when corporate entity is used to perpetrate fraud, circumvent statute, or accomplish wrongful or inequitable purpose, acts are

treated as those of parent); *see also F. Hoffman-La Roche*, 130 Cal.App.4th at 797 (when alter ego is shown, court pierces corporate veil). To invoke the alter-ego doctrine, the plaintiff must establish (1) a unity of interest and ownership between the parent and subsidiary such that they do not have separate identities, and (2) an unfair result if the acts at issue are treated as the subsidiary's alone. ***Sonora Diamond***, 83 Cal.App.4th at 538. The factors considered in this determination include the following:

(a) Commingling of funds and assets. *Id.*

(b) The representation by one entity that it is liable for the debts of the other. *Id.*

(c) Identical equitable ownership of the two entities. *Id.*

(d) Use of the same offices and employees. *Id.* at 538-39.

(e) Inadequate capitalization. *Id.* at 539.

(f) Use of one entity as a mere shell or conduit for the affairs of the other. *Id.*

(2) Agency.

CAUTION

It is unclear under what circumstances a court can exercise general jurisdiction over a defendant based solely on its agent's contacts with California in light of the U.S. Supreme Court's decision in ***Daimler AG v. Bauman*** *(2014) ___ U.S. ___, 134 S.Ct. 746.* ***Bauman*** *involved a nonresident corporate defendant whose indirect subsidiary did substantial business in California.* ***Bauman***, *___ U.S. at ___, 134 S.Ct. at 752. The Court held that the defendant's contacts with California were not sufficient to justify the exercise of general jurisdiction over it even if its subsidiary were subject to general jurisdiction in California (i.e., the subsidiary was "at home" in California) and the subsidiary's contacts with California could be imputed to the defendant through an agency relationship. Id. at ___, 134 S.Ct. at 761-62. Following* ***Bauman***, *it will be extremely difficult—if not impossible—to establish minimum contacts for general jurisdiction over a defendant based solely on its agent's contacts with California. See, e.g.,* ***Young v. Daimler AG*** *(1st Dist.2014) 228 Cal.App.4th 855, 867 (affirming trial court's determination that it could not exercise general jurisdiction over D based on U.S. Supreme Court's unrelated decision in* ***Bauman****); see also Monestier, Where is Home Depot "At Home"?: Daimler v. Bauman and the End of Doing Business Jurisdiction, 66 Hastings L.J. 233, 287-93 (analyzing decision in* ***Bauman*** *and its effect on court's use of agency principles to exercise general jurisdiction).*

(a) Generally. An entity's contacts with California can be attributed to its parent company when evidence establishes that the parent has the right to control the activities of the alleged agent. *See* ***Aquila, Inc. v. Superior Ct.*** (4th Dist.2007) 148 Cal.App.4th 556, 577; ***F. Hoffman-La Roche***, 130 Cal.App.4th at 797; ***Sonora Diamond***, 83 Cal.App.4th at 540-41. *But see* ***Healthmarkets, Inc.***, 171 Cal.App.4th at 1170 (courts cannot rely on state substantive law of agency and alter ego to determine constitutional limits of personal jurisdiction). Control is the key characteristic of an agency relationship. ***Sonora Diamond***, 83 Cal.App.4th at 541. Therefore, when the parent exercises such a degree of control over its subsidiary that the subsidiary is only a means through which the parent acts, or is merely an incorporated department of the parent, the subsidiary will be regarded as the parent's agent. *Id.* The nature of the control must reflect the parent's purposeful disregard of the subsidiary's independent corporate existence. ***Virtualmagic Asia, Inc. v. Fil-Cartoons, Inc.*** (4th Dist.2002) 99 Cal.App.4th 228, 245; ***Sonora Diamond***, 83 Cal.App.4th at 542.

(b) Representative-services doctrine. The representative-services doctrine involves a type of agency relationship that supports the exercise of general jurisdiction when a subsidiary performs a function that is compatible with and assists the parent in the pursuit of the parent's own business. ***F. Hoffman-La Roche***, 130

PERSONAL JURISDICTION

Cal.App.4th at 798; ***Sonora Diamond***, 83 Cal.App.4th at 543; *cf.* ***Paneno***, 118 Cal.App.4th at 1456-57 (general jurisdiction was exercised even though companies were merely affiliates rather than parent-subsidiary). *But see* ***Healthmarkets, Inc.***, 171 Cal.App.4th at 1170 (courts cannot rely on state substantive law of agency and alter ego to determine constitutional limits of personal jurisdiction). To invoke the representative-services doctrine, the plaintiff must demonstrate strong evidence of the parent's pervasive control of the subsidiary (i.e., the control veers into management and day-to-day operations). ***Aquila, Inc.***, 148 Cal.App.4th at 577; *e.g.*, ***In re Automobile Antitrust Cases I & II*** (1st Dist.2005) 135 Cal.App.4th 100, 120-21 (parent automobile manufacturers exerted no day-to-day control over subsidiary distributors); *see, e.g.*, ***F. Hoffman-La Roche***, 130 Cal.App.4th at 797 (representative-services doctrine did not apply when parent was merely a holding company passively investing in subsidiaries). To do so, the plaintiff must show both an agency relationship and that the purposes and functions of the parent and the subsidiary are the same. *See* ***Aquila, Inc.***, 148 Cal.App.4th at 578.

2. Contacts are substantial, continuous & systematic. To establish minimum contacts for general jurisdiction, the plaintiff must show that the defendant's contacts are substantial, continuous, and systematic. *See* ***Vons Cos.***, 14 Cal.4th at 445. The defendant's contacts with the forum must be so continuous and systematic that the defendant is essentially "at home" in the forum. ***Bauman***, ___ U.S. at ___, 134 S.Ct. at 761. Generally, a defendant who is an individual is "at home" where she is domiciled while a corporate defendant is "at home" where it is incorporated and where it has its principal place of business. *Id.* at ___, 134 S.Ct. at 760. In exceptional cases, a corporate defendant's contacts with a forum may be so substantial as to render it "at home" even when the forum is not where it is incorporated or where it has its principal place of business. *Id.* at ___, 134 S.Ct. at 761 n.19. Factors that courts can consider to determine if a case is "exceptional" include whether the defendant makes sales, solicits business, or engages in business in the state; has offices, property, employees, or bank accounts in the state; or pays taxes, designates an agent for service of process, or holds a license in the state. *See* ***Shisler***, 146 Cal.App.4th at 1259; ***F. Hoffman-La Roche***, 130 Cal.App.4th at 796; ***Bancroft & Masters***, 223 F.3d at 1086; ***Metro-Goldwyn-Mayer Studios Inc. v. Grokster, Ltd.*** (C.D.Cal.2003) 243 F.Supp.2d 1073, 1083-84.

PERSONAL JURISDICTION

§6.2 Specific jurisdiction. A court can exercise specific jurisdiction over a nonresident defendant if (1) the defendant has purposefully availed itself of the forum's benefits and protections, (2) the cause of action relates to or arises out of the defendant's contacts with the forum, and (3) the exercise of personal jurisdiction would comport with fair play and substantial justice. ***Pavlovich v. Superior Ct.*** (2002) 29 Cal.4th 262, 269; ***Bombardier Recreational Prods. v. Dow Chem. Can. ULC*** (3d Dist.2013) 216 Cal.App.4th 591, 598.

1. Purposeful availment. To establish minimum contacts for specific jurisdiction, the plaintiff must show that the defendant has purposefully availed itself of the privileges of conducting business in California. *See* ***Bancroft & Masters, Inc. v. Augusta Nat'l Inc.*** (9th Cir.2000) 223 F.3d 1082, 1086; ***Muckle v. Superior Ct.*** (4th Dist.2002) 102 Cal.App.4th 218, 227. In this analysis, (1) only the defendant's contacts with California are considered, not the defendant's contacts with persons who reside there, (2) the defendant's contacts must have been purposeful rather than random, fortuitous, or attenuated, and (3) the defendant must have sought some benefit by availing itself of the jurisdiction. *See* ***Walden v. Fiore*** (2014) ___ U.S. ___, 134 S.Ct. 1115, 1122-23; ***Burger King Corp. v. Rudzewicz*** (1985) 471 U.S. 462, 474-75; ***Vons Cos. v. Seabest Foods, Inc.*** (1996) 14 Cal.4th 434, 446, 458. Some courts have relaxed this analysis by allowing the plaintiff to rely on the contacts of another entity or person and attribute those contacts to the defendant under the principles of alter ego or agency. *E.g.*, ***Virtualmagic Asia, Inc. v. Fil-Cartoons, Inc.*** (4th Dist.2002) 99 Cal.App.4th 228, 244; ***Northern Nat. Gas Co. v. Superior Ct.*** (5th Dist.1976) 64 Cal.App.3d 983, 994-95. *But see* ***Healthmarkets, Inc. v. Superior Ct.*** (2d Dist.2009) 171 Cal.App.4th 1160, 1170 (courts cannot rely on state substantive law of agency and alter ego to determine constitutional limits of personal jurisdiction). See "D's contacts," §6.1.1, p. 288. Regardless of the contacts being considered, the courts have developed several tests for determining whether the contacts satisfy the purposeful-availment analysis.

(1) Effects test. Under the "effects test," a defendant purposefully avails itself of the California forum when it engages in tortious conduct expressly aimed at or targeting California knowing that the conduct would cause harm there. ***Pavlovich***, 29 Cal.4th at 272-73; *e.g.*, ***Archdiocese v. Superior Ct.*** (4th Dist.2003) 112 Cal.App.4th

423, 436 (Milwaukee Archdiocese targeted California by sending known pedophile-priest there, where he continued to molest boys); *see, e.g.*, ***Calder v. Jones*** (1984) 465 U.S. 783, 789-90 (Ds wrote magazine story about California resident knowing resident's career would be damaged and magazine's highest circulation was in California). California must have been the focal point of the conduct. ***In re Automobile Antitrust Cases I & II*** (1st Dist.2005) 135 Cal.App.4th 100, 122; *see* ***Gilmore Bank v. AsiaTrust N.Z. Ltd.*** (4th Dist.2014) 223 Cal.App.4th 1558, 1569-70 (effects test requires only that D expressly aim conduct at California, not at particular person in California). Asserting only that a defendant knew or should have known that her conduct would cause harm in California is not enough. ***Pavlovich***, 29 Cal.4th at 270-73.

(2) Contract. A defendant can purposefully avail itself of the California forum by entering into a contractual relationship with a California party. ***Vons Cos.***, 14 Cal.4th at 449-50; *see* ***Goehring v. Superior Ct.*** (4th Dist.1998) 62 Cal.App.4th 894, 907 (contract does not automatically show purposeful availment, especially if contract is governed by another state's law). To determine whether the defendant purposefully availed itself, the court must evaluate the contract terms and the surrounding circumstances. ***Goehring***, 62 Cal.App.4th at 907; *see* ***Burger King***, 471 U.S. at 479. Relevant factors include negotiations, contemplated future consequences, the parties' course of dealing, and the contract's choice-of-law provision. *E.g.*, ***Burger King***, 471 U.S. at 479-82 (D purposefully availed himself of benefits of doing business in Florida when contract was governed by Florida law, course of dealings emphasized Florida as headquarters, and all negotiations and communications were directed to Florida office); ***Goehring***, 62 Cal.App.4th at 907 (no purposeful availment of California forum when sales, security, and escrow agreements were negotiated in, prepared in, executed in, and governed by Texas law).

(3) Stream-of-commerce doctrine. Under the stream-of-commerce doctrine, a defendant purposefully avails itself of the California forum when (1) it places products in the stream of commerce with an expectation that they will be purchased or used by consumers in California and (2) the conduct creates a substantial connection with the state (i.e., the income earned from the sale or use of the products in California is substantial). ***People v. Native Wholesale Sup.*** (3d Dist.2011) 196 Cal.App.4th 357, 364; *see* ***World-Wide Volkswagen Corp. v. Woodson*** (1980) 444 U.S. 286, 297-98; ***Bridgestone Corp. v. Superior Ct.*** (2d Dist.2002) 99 Cal.App.4th 767, 777. The defendant's expectation must be established by something more than proof that the defendant placed a product into the stream of commerce—even if it was aware the product would reach California. ***Felix v. Bomoro Kommanditgesellschaft*** (2d Dist.1987) 196 Cal.App.3d 106, 114-15; *see* ***J. McIntyre Mach., Ltd. v. Nicastro*** (2011) ___ U.S. ___, 131 S.Ct. 2780, 2788 (plurality op.); ***Dow Chem. Can. ULC v. Superior Ct.*** (2d Dist.2011) 202 Cal.App.4th 170, 179. The plaintiff must show that the defendant's conduct indicated an intent or purpose to serve the California market. *See* ***Felix***, 196 Cal.App.3d at 116; *see, e.g.*, ***Carretti v. Italpast*** (4th Dist.2002) 101 Cal.App.4th 1236, 1248 (manufacturer's random sales of product in Italy to distributor for resale anywhere in the U.S. were not sufficient to establish personal jurisdiction even though it was foreseeable products could reach California); *see* ***Dow Chem.***, 202 Cal.App.4th at 179. Such conduct could include: mail campaigns, telemarketing, use of the Internet, designing a product for the market, advertising, providing customer help channels in California, or marketing the product through a distributor for sale in California. *See* ***West Corp. v. Superior Ct.*** (4th Dist.2004) 116 Cal.App.4th 1167, 1174; ***Carretti***, 101 Cal.App.4th at 1248; *see, e.g.*, ***Bridgestone Corp.***, 99 Cal.App.4th at 777 (D indirectly served market by selling thousands of products to distributor for delivery and sale to consumers in California). Even a product sold only once can subject a defendant to jurisdiction if the sale is accompanied by additional conduct constituting an effort to serve the market. *See, e.g.*, ***Secrest Mach. Corp. v. Superior Ct.*** (1983) 33 Cal.3d 664, 670-71 (D sold machine directly to California user, which generated substantial income, sent employee to California to assist in installation, provided spare parts, gave maintenance advice, and advertised other products for sale).

(4) Internet activity. A defendant can purposefully avail itself of the California forum by operating an interactive website that is accessible to California residents. *See* ***Cybersell, Inc. v. Cybersell, Inc.*** (9th Cir.1997) 130 F.3d 414, 419. To determine whether a website is used to purposefully avail oneself of the benefits of doing business in California, the courts use a sliding-scale analysis. *See* ***Snowney v. Harrah's Entm't, Inc.*** (2005) 35 Cal.4th 1054, 1063 (applying sliding-scale analysis adopted in ***Pavlovich***); ***Pavlovich***, 29 Cal.4th at 274 (adopting sliding-scale analysis used in ***Zippo Mfg. v. Zippo Dot Com, Inc.*** (W.D.Pa.1997) 952 F.Supp. 1119). At one end of the scale

are passive websites on which the defendant has merely posted information; at the other end are websites that the defendant clearly uses to do business over the Internet. ***Snowney***, 35 Cal.4th at 1063; ***Pavlovich***, 29 Cal.4th at 274. In the middle of the scale are interactive websites where a user can exchange information with the host computer. ***Snowney***, 35 Cal.4th at 1063.

(a) Passive website. A defendant does not purposefully avail itself of the California forum by simply making information available on a website that is accessible to users in California. *See, e.g.*, ***Pavlovich***, 29 Cal.4th at 274 (website posted information and had no interactive features); ***Cybersell, Inc.***, 130 F.3d at 419-20 (website advertised e-mail sign-up for its product but did not have sign-up feature on website and no money changed hands through Internet).

(b) Interactive website. A defendant can purposefully avail itself of the California forum by operating an interactive website, depending on (1) the level of interactivity and (2) the commercial nature of the exchange of information that occurs on the website. ***Snowney***, 35 Cal.4th at 1063; ***Pavlovich***, 29 Cal.4th at 274. The greater the interactivity and commercial nature, the more likely that the defendant has purposefully availed itself of the California forum. *See* ***Metro-Goldwyn-Mayer Studios Inc. v. Grokster, Ltd.*** (C.D.Cal. 2003) 243 F.Supp.2d 1073, 1087. For a defendant to purposefully avail itself of the California forum, the website must purposefully direct activity toward California. *See* ***Shisler v. Sanfer Sports Cars, Inc.*** (6th Dist.2006) 146 Cal.App.4th 1254, 1261 (even when effect of website is felt in California, no personal jurisdiction unless act is purposefully directed at California); ***Millennium Enters. v. Millennium Music, LP*** (D.Or.1999) 33 F.Supp.2d 907, 921-22 (even when website is interactive, D must have targeted forum state); *see, e.g.*, ***Online Partners.com, Inc. v. Atlanticnet Media Corp.*** (N.D.Cal.2000) No. C 98-4146 SI ENE (slip op.; 1-20-00) (jurisdiction found when D engaged in conduct with intent to harm California P).

[1] Test.

[a] Level of interactivity. To determine a website's level of interactivity, the court must examine (1) the extent of interactive features on the website and (2) whether California residents have used those features. *See* ***Cybersell, Inc.***, 130 F.3d at 419 (some courts consider number of hits website has received from forum state); ***Advanced Software, Inc. v. Datapharm, Inc.*** (C.D.Cal.1998) No. CV 98-5943 DDP (RZx) (slip op.; 11-6-98) (level of interactivity is not implicated unless California resident has actually taken advantage of interactive part of website).

[b] Commercial nature of exchange. The more commercial the nature of the exchange of information, the more likely that the defendant has purposefully availed itself of the California forum. ***Jewish Def. Org. v. Superior Ct.*** (2d Dist.1999) 72 Cal.App.4th 1045, 1060; *see* ***Snowney***, 35 Cal.4th at 1063. The nature of the commercial activity must be substantial enough that it approximates physical presence. *See* ***New Tech Stainless Steel Prods. v. Sun Mfg.*** (C.D.Cal.2004) No. CV 04-1181-RGK (FMOx) (slip op.; 7-20-04).

[2] Examples. Chart 3-2, below, gives examples of how courts have evaluated different kinds of websites.

3-2. PERSONAL JURISDICTION – INTERACTIVE WEBSITES

	Facts	Personal jurisdiction?	Case
1	Website advertised cars and provided credit application; no files exchanged, and no other business conducted over Internet	No	***Shisler*** (6th Dist.2006) 146 Cal.App.4th 1254, 1261
2	Website charged subscription fee for access to its chat room, but there was no evidence that a California resident had visited the website	No	***Asser*** (1st Dist.2004) No. A102812 (unpub.; 1-29-04)

3-2. PERSONAL JURISDICTION – INTERACTIVE WEBSITES (CONTINUED)

	Facts	Personal jurisdiction?	Case
3	Website allowed customers to submit purchase orders and credit-card payments for products, but there was no evidence that any transactions were actually completed through the website or that the defendants conducted business with any California residents through the website	No	***Amini Innovation*** (C.D.Cal.2007) 497 F.Supp.2d 1093, 1104
4	Website allowed customers to view products and submit orders; customer obtained company's phone number from website, then negotiated the contract by phone and e-mail	No	***Giles*** (2d Dist.2007) No. B196756 (unpub.; 12-19-07)
5	Website allowed consumers to download free software; consumers who downloaded the software were required to accept a licensing agreement; website operators admitted that nearly two million of its users were California residents	Yes	***Metro-Goldwyn-Mayer Studios*** (C.D.Cal.2003) 243 F.Supp.2d 1073, 1087
6	Website allowed customers to e-mail the company by clicking on the e-mail address	No	***Directed Elecs.*** (4th Dist.2004) No. D041533 (unpub.; 2-17-04)
7	Website allowed customers to purchase compact discs, join a discount club, and request franchising information	No	***Millennium Enters.*** (D.Or.1999) 33 F.Supp.2d 907, 920-21 (applying ***Zippo***)
8	Website advertised its services and offered and provided a subscription to those services, and at least one California resident used its interactive features	Yes	***Online Partners.com*** (N.D.Cal.2000) No. C 98-4146 SI ENE (slip op.; 1-20-00)
9	Website actively encouraged and received resumes and solicited people seeking training and help with Internet-related projects; level of interactivity was so high, jurisdiction was proper even though D had only made contact with one forum resident	Yes	***Tech Heads*** (D.Or.2000) 105 F.Supp.2d 1142, 1150-51 (applying ***Zippo***)
10	Website allowed users to contact the company for information and to access other websites; no products were sold on the website; no online gaming was available on the website	No	***Mullally*** (D.Nev.2007) No. 2:05-cv-00154-BES-GWF (slip op.; 2-28-07) (applying ***Zippo***)

(c) Internet business. A defendant purposefully avails itself of the California forum when it clearly does business over the Internet. ***Snowney***, 35 Cal.4th at 1063; ***Pavlovich***, 29 Cal.4th at 274. A defendant clearly does business over the Internet when it enters into contracts with California residents and those contracts involve the knowing and repeated transmission of computer files over the Internet. ***Snowney***, 35 Cal.4th at 1063; ***Pavlovich***, 29 Cal.4th at 274.

2. Relatedness. To establish minimum contacts for specific jurisdiction, the plaintiff must show that its claim relates to or arises from the defendant's contacts with the forum. ***Pavlovich***, 29 Cal.4th at 269. This is referred to as the "relatedness" requirement. ***Snowney***, 35 Cal.4th at 1067. This requirement is satisfied if there is a substantial nexus or connection between the defendant's California contacts and the plaintiff's claim. *Id.* at 1068; ***Vons Cos.***, 14 Cal.4th at 456; *see* ***McGee v. International Life Ins.*** (1957) 355 U.S. 220, 223 (single contract can support jurisdiction if it creates a substantial connection with forum). If the plaintiff's claim bears a substantial connection to the defendant's contacts, the exercise of jurisdiction is warranted even if (1) the claim does not arise directly from the defendant's contacts or (2) the defendant's contacts are not directed at the plaintiff. ***Snowney***, 35 Cal.4th at 1068; ***Vons Cos.***, 14 Cal.4th at 452, 457. Thus, the only time a plaintiff's claim does not arise from the defendant's contacts with the state is when the operative facts of the controversy are unrelated to the defendant's contacts. ***Snowney***, 35 Cal.4th at 1068; ***Vons Cos.***, 14 Cal.4th at 455.

3. Fair play & substantial justice. If the plaintiff establishes that the defendant's contacts are sufficient to invoke specific jurisdiction, the burden shifts to the defendant to establish that exercising jurisdiction would

be unreasonable—that is, it would offend traditional notions of fair play and substantial justice. *See* ***Vons Cos.***, 14 Cal.4th at 449. Generally, exercising personal jurisdiction over a nonresident defendant is presumptively reasonable if the defendant has purposefully availed itself of the forum state. ***Caruth v. International Psychoanalytical Ass'n*** (9th Cir.1995) 59 F.3d 126, 128. The presumption of reasonableness can be overcome, however, by a compelling argument that the presence of some other consideration would render jurisdiction unreasonable. *Id.*; *see* ***Burger King***, 471 U.S. at 477. To determine whether the exercise of jurisdiction would be reasonable, the court must balance seven factors, none of which is dispositive by itself. ***Core-Vent Corp. v. Nobel Indus. AB*** (9th Cir.1993) 11 F.3d 1482, 1487-88. The factors the court must balance are the following:

(1) The extent of the defendant's interjection into the forum state's affairs. ***Core-Vent Corp.***, 11 F.3d at 1487; *see* ***Cornelison v. Chaney*** (1976) 16 Cal.3d 143, 151 (extent to which cause of action arose out of D's local activities); ***Integral Dev. Corp. v. Weissenbach*** (6th Dist.2002) 99 Cal.App.4th 576, 591 (same).

(2) The burden to the defendant in defending the action in the forum. ***Core-Vent Corp.***, 11 F.3d at 1487; ***Vons Cos.***, 14 Cal.4th at 448. Because modern transportation and communications have made the ability of nonresidents to litigate in foreign courts much less burdensome, this factor will not overcome a clear justification for exercising jurisdiction unless the inconvenience is so great that it constitutes a deprivation of due process. ***Integral Dev.***, 99 Cal.App.4th at 592.

(3) The forum state's interest in adjudicating the dispute. ***Core-Vent Corp.***, 11 F.3d at 1487; ***Vons Cos.***, 14 Cal.4th at 448; *e.g.*, ***Epic Comms. v. Richwave Tech.*** (6th Dist.2009) 179 Cal.App.4th 314, 336 (although state's interest in suit is diminished if parties are not residents, state retains interest in securing remedy for wrongs occurring in state).

(4) The most efficient judicial resolution of the controversy. ***Core-Vent Corp.***, 11 F.3d at 1487; *see* ***Vons Cos.***, 14 Cal.4th at 448 (judicial economy). With this factor, courts look primarily at where the witnesses and evidence are located. ***Core-Vent Corp.***, 11 F.3d at 1489; *see* ***Cornelison***, 16 Cal.3d at 151 (availability of evidence in one place rather than another). If the plaintiff would be forced to bring one action against some defendants in the forum state and another action elsewhere, the desire to avoid multiple lawsuits with possibly conflicting results will weigh against the forum state. *See* ***Rowe v. Dorrough*** (1st Dist.1984) 150 Cal.App.3d 901, 906.

(5) The extent of conflict with the sovereignty of the defendant's state or nation. ***Core-Vent Corp.***, 11 F.3d at 1487; *see* ***Vons Cos.***, 14 Cal.4th at 448 (shared interest of states in furthering fundamental substantive social policies). With this factor, when the defendant is from a foreign nation, the barrier to exercising jurisdiction is higher than when the defendant is from a sister state. ***Core-Vent Corp.***, 11 F.3d at 1489.

(6) The importance of the forum to the plaintiff's interest in convenient and effective relief. *Id.* at 1487-88; ***Vons Cos.***, 14 Cal.4th at 448. Because a plaintiff will usually prefer to try a case where she lives, this factor is given little weight. *See* ***Caruth***, 59 F.3d at 129; ***Core-Vent Corp.***, 11 F.3d at 1490.

(7) The existence of an alternative forum. ***Core-Vent Corp.***, 11 F.3d at 1488; *see* ***Cornelison***, 16 Cal.3d at 151 (ease of access to alternative forum). For this factor, the plaintiff bears the burden to prove the unavailability of an alternative forum. ***Core-Vent Corp.***, 11 F.3d at 1490.

H. JOINING THE DEFENDANT—SERVICE OF PROCESS

§1. GENERAL

§1.1 Purpose. Service of both the summons (also known as "process") and a copy of the complaint is the official method by which a plaintiff notifies a defendant that it is being sued. *See* CCP §17(b)(6) (defining "process"); Gov. C. §22 (same), §26660(a) (same). The purposes of service of process are (1) to give the court jurisdiction over the defendant, (2) to satisfy due-process requirements by giving the defendant notice of the suit, and (3) to give the defendant the opportunity to defend itself. *See* ***Kappel v. Bartlett*** (2d Dist.1988) 200 Cal.App.3d 1457, 1464; ***Mannesmann DeMag, Ltd. v. Superior Ct.*** (5th Dist.1985) 172 Cal.App.3d 1118, 1122; ***Kriebel v. City Council of San Diego*** (4th Dist.1980) 112 Cal.App.3d 693, 699; ***Nellis v. Justices' Ct.*** (2d Dist.1912) 20 Cal.App. 394, 397. Without valid service of process, the court does not obtain personal jurisdiction over the defendant unless the defendant has waived process by making a general appearance. *See* ***MJS Enters. v. Superior Ct.*** (5th Dist.1984) 153 Cal.App.3d 555, 557. Judgment cannot be rendered against a defendant unless the court obtains personal jurisdiction over the defendant. *See* CCP §1917 (jurisdiction over both case and parties needed to support judgment); ***Northington v. Industrial Acc. Comm'n*** (4th Dist.1937) 23 Cal.App.2d 255, 259-60 (jurisdiction over party can be obtained if party makes general appearance); *see, e.g.*, ***General Ins. v. Superior Ct.*** (1975) 15 Cal.3d 449, 452-53 (D submitted to court's jurisdiction by sending letter accepting service and confirming extension of time to file answer); *see also* CCP §410.30(b) (D waives challenge to court's exercise of personal jurisdiction if it makes general appearance); ***Donaldson v. National Mar., Inc.*** (2005) 35 Cal.4th 503, 512 (dicta; D waived objection to court's lack of personal jurisdiction by accepting service and making general appearance).

NOTE

In this subchapter, service of the summons and the complaint or cross-complaint is referred to as "service of process."

§1.2 Primary authority. CCP §§17(b)(6), 412.10-417.40, 474, 583.210-583.250; CRC 3.110.

§1.3 Secondary authority. The following secondary sources are cited as authority in this subchapter:

- Weil & Brown, *California Practice Guide: Civil Procedure Before Trial* (CD-ROM ed. 2014) (referred to as Weil, *Civil Procedure Before Trial*).
- ***O'Connor's Federal Rules * Civil Trials*** (2015) (referred to as ***O'Connor's Federal Rules***).

§1.4 Judicial Council forms.

- SUM-100 through SUM-145 (mandatory), summonses.
- SUM-200(A) (mandatory), additional parties attachment.
- SUM-300 (mandatory), declaration of lost summons after service.
- POS-010 (mandatory), proof of service of summons.
- POS-015 (mandatory), notice and acknowledgment of receipt.

§2. COMPLIANCE WITH STATUTORY REQUIREMENTS

To avoid challenges to service of process, a plaintiff should strictly comply with the statutory requirements for service of process. See "Improper service," ch. 4-G, §2.2, p. 390; "No service or improper service of process," ch. 10-A, §9.1.4(1)(c), p. 1112. Strict compliance with the statutory requirements is generally not necessary, however, if the defendant receives actual notice of the suit and the plaintiff substantially complies with all the statutory requirements. *See* ***Trackman v. Kenney*** (3d Dist.2010) 187 Cal.App.4th 175, 184 (minor deficiencies cannot be used to defeat service); ***Dill v. Berquist Constr. Co.*** (4th Dist.1994) 24 Cal.App.4th 1426, 1436-37 (statutory provisions regarding service of process should be liberally construed to effectuate service). *But see* ***American Express Centurion Bank v.***

Zara (6th Dist.2011) 199 Cal.App.4th 383, 390-91 (court questioned whether substantial-compliance standard should be used to uphold default judgment). Substantial compliance means actual compliance with "every reasonable objective of the statute." ***Southern Pac. Transp. v. State Bd. of Equalization*** (3d Dist.1985) 175 Cal.App.3d 438, 442; *see, e.g.*, ***Carol Gilbert, Inc. v. Haller*** (6th Dist.2009) 179 Cal.App.4th 852, 865-66 (summons that did not indicate D was sued under fictitious name did not substantially comply with statute); ***Summers v. McClanahan*** (2d Dist.2006) 140 Cal.App.4th 403, 414-15 (service on individual who was not authorized to accept service did not substantially comply with statute); ***MJS Enters. v. Superior Ct.*** (5th Dist.1984) 153 Cal.App.3d 555, 557-58 (summons that did not contain mandatory notice did not substantially comply with statute). Courts have recognized, however, that strict compliance with statutory service requirements is required when service is by publication. *E.g.*, ***County of Riverside v. Superior Ct.*** (4th Dist.1997) 54 Cal.App.4th 443, 450.

§3. OBTAINING THE SUMMONS

§3.1 Requirements for summons. For most civil actions, Judicial Council Form SUM-100, which is a mandatory-use form, must be used for the summons. *See* CRC 1.31(a) (forms adopted by Judicial Council for mandatory use must, wherever applicable, be used by all parties and must be accepted for filing by all courts); *see also* CCP §412.20(c) (form approved by Judicial Council deemed to comply with requirements for summons).

NOTE

This subchapter addresses the requirements for summonses in civil actions generally. For certain actions, however, there may be additional or different requirements for the summons. Judicial Council of Cal. Ann. Rep. (1969) p. 39; see, e.g., CCP §751.05 (in action to reestablish destroyed land records, summons must include description of real property involved and be directed to all persons claiming interest in property), §861.1 (in validation actions, summons must provide detailed summary of matter public agency or person seeks to validate); Fam. C. §2040(a) (in certain family-law proceedings, summons must contain temporary restraining order). The Judicial Council has adopted a number of other mandatory-use forms for summonses. See, e.g., Judicial Council Forms, form DE-125 (probate), form FL-110 (family law generally), form SUM-120 (joint debtor), form SUM-130 (unlawful detainer), form SUM-140 (storage-lien enforcement).

1. Information about plaintiff. The summons must contain the following information about the plaintiff:

(1) Identification of plaintiff. The summons must contain each plaintiff's name. CCP §412.20(a)(2). If additional space is needed to identify all the plaintiffs, the plaintiff should use the additional-parties attachment, Judicial Council Form SUM-200(A).

(2) Identification of plaintiff's attorney. The summons must contain the name, address, and telephone number of the plaintiff's attorney or the plaintiff herself, if she is acting in pro per. Judicial Council Form SUM-100.

2. Information about defendant. The summons must contain the following information about the defendant:

(1) Identification of defendant. The summons must contain each defendant's name. CCP §412.20(a)(2); *see, e.g.*, ***General Motors Corp. v. Superior Ct.*** (2d Dist.1971) 15 Cal.App.3d 81, 86-87 (summons was defective because it designated person other than D). If additional space is needed to identify all the defendants, the plaintiff should use the additional-parties attachment, Judicial Council Form SUM-200(A).

(2) Identification of status of person served. The summons must identify the status of the person being served. *See* Judicial Council Form SUM-100 (referred to as "Notice to the Person Served"). If the person is being served in more than one capacity, the summons should indicate each status (e.g., as an individual and a corporate agent). *See* CCP §412.30.

CAUTION

Be sure to fill out every part of the summons once it has been issued by the clerk. If the summons is incomplete, the court may find that it does not have personal jurisdiction over the defendant. Compare ***Mannesmann DeMag, Ltd. v. Superior Ct.*** *(5th Dist.1985) 172 Cal.App.3d 1118, 1122-23 (court did not acquire personal jurisdiction over D-corporation because summons did not include D's name or indicate that person who received service was being served as agent of D-corporation), with* ***Cory v. Crocker Nat'l Bank*** *(1st Dist.1981) 123 Cal.App.3d 665, 670 (court acquired personal jurisdiction over D-corporation even though summons did not indicate status of person served because D-corporation was only named D and summons explicitly indicated that service was under CCP §416.10).*

(a) Individual. The plaintiff must identify, by placing a check mark in the appropriate box, whether the person is being served as an individual defendant. *See* Judicial Council Forms, form SUM-100.

(b) Fictitious name. The plaintiff must identify, by placing a check mark in the appropriate box, whether the person is being served as a person sued under a fictitious name (i.e., a Doe defendant), and if so, the plaintiff must specify the fictitious name. *See* Judicial Council Forms, form SUM-100. See "Doe defendants," ch. 3-C, §2.3.1(7)(b), p. 209. The summons must contain—"in substance"—the following notice under CCP §474:

> To the person served: You are hereby served in the within {*action/proceedings*} {*as/on behalf of*} the person sued under the fictitious name of {*state name of fictitious party*}.

See ***Carol Gilbert, Inc. v. Haller*** (6th Dist.2009) 179 Cal.App.4th 852, 858-59. This notice requirement is satisfied by Judicial Council Form SUM-100. The plaintiff must also identify, by placing a check mark in the appropriate box, whether the Doe defendant is a corporation or association. *See* Judicial Council Forms, form SUM-100; *see, e.g.*, ***Schering Corp. v. Superior Ct.*** (2d Dist.1975) 52 Cal.App.3d 737, 742 (summons incomplete because assistant manager was served as or on behalf of "Doe 1," who according to complaint was a physician, and summons did not indicate assistant manager was served on behalf of corporation, the intended Doe defendant). Without this notice, the plaintiff cannot take a default judgment against the defendant. CCP §474.

(c) Corporation or association. The plaintiff must identify, by placing a check mark in the appropriate box, whether the person is being served on behalf of (1) a corporation, (2) a defunct corporation, or (3) an association or partnership. *See* Judicial Council Forms, form SUM-100. The plaintiff must state the name of the person or entity on whose behalf the person served is accepting service. *See* Judicial Council of Cal. Ann. Rep. (1969) p. 40 (service on corporation or unincorporated association can be accomplished only by serving some individual as its representative); *see, e.g.*, ***Schering Corp.***, 52 Cal.App.3d at 742 (summons did not comply with CCP §412.30 because it did not state that person was served on behalf of D-corporation); ***Snyder Trust Enters. v. WorldPoint Interactive, Inc.*** (1st Dist.2004) No. A105407 (unpub.; 9-30-04) (summons defective because it did not state that summons was served on behalf of cross-D-corporation). The summons must contain the following notice (in substance) under CCP §412.30:

> To the person served: You are hereby served in the within {*action/special proceeding*} on behalf of {*state name of corporation or unincorporated association*} as a person upon whom a copy of the summons and of the complaint may be delivered to effect service on said party under the provisions of {*state appropriate provisions of CCP ch. 4, starting with §413.10*}.

Courts have held that this notice requirement is satisfied by Judicial Council Form SUM-100. *See, e.g.*, ***Cory***, 123 Cal.App.3d at 669 (because P is only required to substantially comply with CCP §412.30 to render service of summons on corporation effective, Judicial Council form satisfied statutory notice requirements). Without this notice, the plaintiff cannot take a default judgment against the defendant. CCP §412.30.

(d) Limited-liability company. Judicial Council Form SUM-100 does not provide a specific box for the plaintiff to check if the person is being served on behalf of a limited-liability company. One commentator suggests that the plaintiff should mark the box for "other" and write in "Corp. Code §17061" next to it. Weil, *Civil Procedure Before Trial*, ¶4:93.

(e) Minors, conservatees, authorized persons & others. The plaintiff must identify, by placing a check mark in the appropriate box, whether the person is being served on behalf of (1) a minor, (2) a conservatee, (3) another person who has authorized the person served to receive process, or (4) another person or entity. *See* Judicial Council Forms, form SUM-100. The plaintiff must specify the name of the person or entity on whose behalf the person served is accepting service. *See id.*

3. Information about court. The summons must identify the court where the suit is pending. CCP §412.20(a)(1).

4. Notices. The summons must contain the following notices:

(1) Notice of suit. The summons must include the following statement in boldface type, at the top of the summons, above all other matter, in both English and Spanish:

> "Notice! You have been sued. The court may decide against you without your being heard unless you respond within 30 days. Read information below."
>
> "¡Aviso! Lo han demandado. Si no responde dentro de 30 días, la corte puede decidir en su contra sin escuchar su versión. Lea la información a continuación."

See CCP §412.20(a)(6). Counties may, by ordinance, require that this notice be stated in additional languages. *Id.* §412.20(b).

(2) Deadline to file response. The summons must direct the defendant to file with the court a written pleading in response to the complaint within 30 days after the summons is served on the defendant. CCP §412.20(a)(3).

(3) Default judgment. The summons must notify the defendant that unless it responds, (1) the court will enter a default judgment after the plaintiff files an application for one, and (2) in that application, the plaintiff can request that all the relief demanded in the complaint be granted, which could result in the court ordering defendant's wages to be garnished, money or other property taken, or other relief. CCP §412.20(a)(4).

(4) Seek advice of attorney. The summons must include the following statement in boldface type: "You may seek the advice of an attorney in any matter connected with the complaint or this summons. Such attorney should be consulted promptly so that your pleading may be filed or entered within the time required by this summons." CCP §412.20(a)(5).

5. Date of service. The summons should contain the date it was issued or personally delivered to the person being served. *See* CCP §415.10. CCP §412.20 (contents of summons), however, does not require the summons to be dated, and §415.10 (requirements for personal delivery) specifically states that the lack of a date does not render the summons defective. Thus, a summons without a date or with an incorrect date is still valid and effective. *Id.* §415.10; *see* ***Hibernia S&L Soc'y v. Churchill*** (1900) 128 Cal. 633, 634-35.

6. Signature & seal. The summons must be signed by the court clerk and stamped with the seal of the court where the suit is pending. CCP §412.20(a); *see id.* §153(b). The lack of a signature and seal, however, does not automatically render the summons defective if it otherwise substantially complies with §412.20. *See, e.g.*, ***Ystrom v. Handel*** (2d Dist.1988) 205 Cal.App.3d 144, 151-52 (summons missing signature and seal that was served with "Declaration of Lost Original Summons" was not substantially defective).

§3.2 Issuance of summons. After the plaintiff files the complaint and pays all applicable fees, the clerk will issue either (1) a single summons for service on all the defendants or (2) separate summonses for service on one or more defendants. *See* CCP §412.10; ***Maginn v. City of Glendale*** (2d Dist.1999) 72 Cal.App.4th 1102, 1104; Judicial Council of Cal. Ann. Rep. (1969) p. 37. When the clerk issues the summons, the clerk will assign a case number,

sign the summons, and affix the seal to it. *See* CCP §412.20(a). The clerk must keep the original summons in the court records and provide to the plaintiff a copy of each summons issued. *Id.* §412.10.

1. Electronically transmitted summons. If local rules allow for electronic filing and the plaintiff files the complaint electronically and pays all applicable fees, the clerk will issue either (1) a single summons for service on all the defendants or (2) separate summonses for service on one or more defendants. *See* CCP §1010.6(b)(5); Judicial Council of Cal. Ann. Rep. (1969) p. 37. The clerk must keep the original summons in the court records and can transmit the summons electronically to the plaintiff. CCP §1010.6(b)(5); *see* CRC 2.259(f)(1). The electronically transmitted summons must contain an image of the court's seal and the assigned case number. CCP §1010.6(b)(5); CRC 2.259(f)(2). The plaintiff can then print the electronically transmitted summons and have it personally served, which has the same legal effect as personally serving a copy of an original summons. CCP §1010.6(b)(5); CRC 2.259(f)(3).

2. New or amended summons. If the court has obtained jurisdiction over a defendant through service of a copy of the original summons and the complaint, the plaintiff does not need to obtain a new or amended summons for that defendant if it amends the complaint. ***Engebretson & Co. v. Harrison*** (4th Dist.1981) 125 Cal.App.3d 436, 441 & n.3; Judicial Council of Cal. Ann. Rep. (1969) p. 37; *see* ***Gillette v. Burbank Cmty. Hosp.*** (2d Dist.1976) 56 Cal.App.3d 430, 433. However, the plaintiff may need to obtain an amended or additional summons if the complaint is amended before service of process is made or if a new defendant is added. See "Amending summons," §11.1, p. 324.

§3.3 Papers served.

1. Service papers.

(1) Most cases. For most civil actions, the plaintiff must serve the "service papers" on the defendant, which include the following:

(a) The summons. *See, e.g.*, CCP §415.10 (personal delivery), §415.30 (service by mail); *see also* Judicial Council Forms, form POS-010.

(b) The complaint. *See, e.g.*, CCP §415.10 (personal delivery), §415.30 (service by mail); *see also* Judicial Council Forms, form POS-010.

(c) The ADR information package supplied by the court. CRC 3.221(c); *see* Judicial Council Forms, form POS-010.

(2) Small-claims actions. For small-claims actions, the plaintiff must serve on the defendant a copy of the claim and the order setting a hearing on the claim, instead of the service papers. *See* CCP §116.340(a). See "Claim & order – small-claims action," §3.4, p. 300.

2. Other papers. For some methods of service or some types of civil actions, the plaintiff may need to serve additional papers on the defendant.

(1) Methods of service.

(a) By mail. When the defendant is served by mail, the plaintiff must serve two copies of a notice and acknowledgment of receipt with the service papers. CCP §415.30(a). See "Most cases," §3.3.1(1), this page; "Service by U.S. mail," §5.1.2, p. 302. If the defendant is a person who is out of state and the plaintiff serves her under CCP §415.40, the plaintiff only needs to serve her with the service papers. *See* CCP §415.40. If the plaintiff completes service under any other statutory provision that allows for service by mail, the plaintiff must comply with the requirements specified by that statute. *See, e.g.*, Veh. C. §17455 (auto-accident cases). See "Service under other California statute," §5.2.2(3), p. 308.

(b) By publication. When the defendant is served by publication, the plaintiff must mail a copy of the court's order authorizing service by publication with the service papers if the plaintiff locates the defendant before the end of the publication period. CCP §415.50(b). See "Service by publication," §5.1.4, p. 304.

(2) **Types of actions.**

(a) **Complex cases.** In complex cases, the plaintiff must serve the case cover sheet with the service papers. CRC 3.220(a).

(b) **Personal-injury or wrongful-death actions.** In personal-injury or wrongful-death actions, the plaintiff can serve a statement of actual damages with the service papers. *See* CCP §425.11(b), (c); *see, e.g.*, ***Anastos v. Lee*** (4th Dist.2004) 118 Cal.App.4th 1314, 1318 (P served summons, complaint, and statement of damages by publication). See "Actual damages," ch. 3-C, §5.1, p. 226. Although the plaintiff is not required to serve the statement with the service papers, it may want to do so to save time, reduce costs, and allow for a default judgment as soon as the defendant's time to answer expires.

(c) **Actions seeking punitive damages.** In actions seeking punitive damages, the plaintiff can serve a statement of punitive damages with the service papers. *See* CCP §425.115. See "Punitive damages," ch. 3-C, §5.2, p. 228. Although the plaintiff is not required to serve the statement with the service papers, it may want to do so to save time, reduce costs, and allow for a default judgment as soon as the defendant's time to answer expires.

(d) **Unlawful-detainer actions.** In unlawful-detainer actions, the plaintiff can serve a form for a prejudgment claim of right to possession with the service papers. CCP §415.46(a); *see* Judicial Council Forms, form CP 10.5. This form requires occupants who are not named in the summons and complaint to join the suit (by returning the completed form) within ten days after service or be evicted without a hearing. Judicial Council Forms, form CP 10.5; *see* CCP §1174.25. Although the plaintiff is not required to serve the form with the service papers, it may want to do so to avoid a delay of eviction if an unknown occupant files a claim of right to possession. See "Prejudgment claim for possession," §5.4.2(2), p. 311.

SERVICE OF PROCESS

§3.4 Claim & order – small-claims action. A summons is not issued for small-claims actions. Instead, the plaintiff files a claim with the court clerk, who then issues an order setting the claim for a hearing. *See* CCP §§116.320(a), 116.330. The hearing in a small-claims action is equivalent to trial in a limited or unlimited civil case—that is, the parties are directed to appear with the witnesses and documents needed to prove their claim or defense. *See id.* §116.330(a).

1. **Claim.** The plaintiff must use Judicial Council Form SC-100 to file the claim. *See* CCP §116.320(b).

2. **Order.**

(1) **When issued.** The clerk must issue the order setting the small-claims action for hearing after either of the following:

(a) The claim is filed. CCP §116.330(a).

(b) The clerk has mailed a copy of the claim to the defendant by any method that provides a return receipt and has received the defendant's return receipt. *Id.* §116.330(b).

(2) **Contents.** The order issued by the clerk must do all the following:

(a) Schedule the hearing for the action at least 20 days, but no more than 70 days, after the date the order is issued. CCP §116.330(a).

(b) Direct the parties to appear at the time set for the hearing. *Id.*

(c) Direct the parties to secure the attendance of witnesses and bring the documents needed to prove their claim or defense. *Id.*

§4. WHO CAN SERVE PROCESS

Process can be served by any person who is at least 18 and is not a party to the action. CCP §414.10; *see, e.g.*, ***Caldwell v. Coppola*** (4th Dist.1990) 219 Cal.App.3d 859, 865 ("named person" who is protected under domestic-violence injunction cannot serve process); ***In re Marriage of Smith*** (1st Dist.1982) 135 Cal.App.3d 543, 545 (service invalid when wife served husband with petition to dissolve marriage and wife's mother executed return of service and filed

it with clerk). For example, an attorney can serve process. ***Caldwell***, 219 Cal.App.3d at 865; ***Sheehan v. All Persons*** (1st Dist.1926) 80 Cal.App. 393, 398. Process can also be served by any duly qualified and acting marshal or sheriff of any county in California. Gov. C. §26665.

NOTE

Anyone who makes more than ten services of process a year must comply with the registration and bond requirements for process servers. See Bus. & Prof. C. §§22350-22360. However, the failure to comply with these requirements will not render service invalid or ineffective if the process server has otherwise complied with the general requirements for serving summons under CCP ch. 4. CCP §413.40. Attorneys and their employees are exempt from these requirements if they are serving process in cases for which the attorney is providing legal services. Bus. & Prof. C. §22350(b)(2); see ***Kappel v. Bartlett*** *(2d Dist.1988) 200 Cal.App.3d 1457, 1464.*

§5. METHODS OF SERVICE

Service of process is accomplished by providing the person or entity to be served with the service papers. If a defendant cannot be served by one of the methods below and does not waive service, it cannot be subject to the court's jurisdiction regardless of its minimum contacts with the forum. See "Minimum Contacts," ch. 3-G, §6, p. 288. The method of service usually depends on where the defendant is located, but in some cases it can be based on the type of action brought.

§5.1 Defendant in California. If the service papers are to be served on a person located in California, the following methods of service can be used. *See* CCP §413.10(a).

1. Service by personal delivery. Process can be served by personal delivery, which is the preferred method of service. *See* CCP §415.10; ***Kott v. Superior Ct.*** (2d Dist.1996) 45 Cal.App.4th 1126, 1137. To serve by personal delivery, the person serving process usually hands the service papers to the person being served. *See* ***Sternbeck v. Buck*** (2d Dist.1957) 148 Cal.App.2d 829, 832 ("personal service" means actual delivery of papers to D in person); *see, e.g.*, ***Tsakos Shipping & Trading, S.A. v. Juniper Garden Town Homes, Ltd.*** (4th Dist.1993) 12 Cal.App.4th 74, 84 (D was not "personally served" under CCP §415.10 when process server left copy of notice of sister-state judgment with receptionist at D's attorney's office).

(1) Defendant refuses to accept service. A defendant cannot defeat service by making physical service impossible. *Cf.* ***Khourie, Crew & Jaeger v. Sabek, Inc.*** (1st Dist.1990) 220 Cal.App.3d 1009, 1013 (substitute-service case). If the defendant refuses to take the service papers, personal service can be completed if the process server identifies herself, tells the person being served that she or the person on whose behalf she is being served is being served with process, and leaves the service papers as close as possible to the person being served. *See, e.g.*, ***Trujillo v. Trujillo*** (3d Dist.1945) 71 Cal.App.2d 257, 259-60 (service sufficient when process server clearly identified documents being served and placed them between wiper and windshield of D's car while D sat locked inside); ***In re Ball*** (2d Dist.1934) 2 Cal.App.2d 578, 578-79 (service sufficient when process server was within 12 feet of D, indicated that he had papers for D, and tossed papers toward D after D stated "you have nothing for me" and began to walk away); *see also* ***Sternbeck***, 148 Cal.App.2d at 833 (strict requirements for manual delivery of service papers are relaxed when D attempts to flee approaching process server).

15 **(2) Defendant lives in gated community.** If the person to be served lives in a gated community, the process server must be given access to the community for a reasonable period of time to deliver the service papers. CCP §415.21(a). The process server must complete the steps below if there is a guard or other security person assigned to control access to the community. *See id.* §415.21(b).

(a) Show the guard a current driver's license or other identification. *Id.* §415.21(a).

(b) Show the guard either of the following:

[1] A badge or other confirmation that the person serving process is acting in her capacity as a representative of a county sheriff or marshal. *Id.* §415.21(a)(1).

[2] Evidence that the person serving process is currently registered as a process server or licensed as a private investigator. *Id.* §415.21(a)(2).

(3) When completed. Service by personal delivery is completed at the time of delivery. CCP §415.10.

2. Service by U.S. mail. Process can be served by mail. CCP §415.30(a). To serve process by mail to a person located in California, the plaintiff must mail by first-class mail or airmail, postage prepaid, (1) a copy of the summons and the complaint, (2) two copies of a "Notice and Acknowledgment of Receipt of Summons," and (3) a return envelope, postage prepaid, addressed to the sender. CCP §415.30(a).

(1) Envelope.

(a) Addressee. The envelope containing the summons, complaint, notice, and return envelope should be addressed to the proper person to be served. *Cf.* ***Dill v. Berquist Constr. Co.*** (4th Dist.1994) 24 Cal.App.4th 1426, 1436-37 (service on out-of-state D defective because P did not address envelopes to any individual authorized to accept service on behalf of corporation and no other evidence showed that proper person received summons). See "Who May Be Served," §6, p. 313.

(b) Address. The envelope containing the summons, complaint, notice, and return envelope should be addressed to a location where letters would most likely reach the person being served. *See* ***Transamerica Title Ins. v. Hendrix*** (2d Dist.1995) 34 Cal.App.4th 740, 745-46; *cf.* ***Bolkiah v. Superior Ct.*** (2d Dist.1999) 74 Cal.App.4th 984, 1001 (service on out-of-state D; P established that Ds could be reached or had received correspondence at various addresses listed on correspondence from Ds to P). The most common examples are the defendant's residence, place of business, and post-office box. *See* ***Transamerica Title***, 34 Cal.App.4th at 745-46.

(2) Notice & acknowledgment of receipt.

(a) Form. The form of the notice and acknowledgment is specified in CCP §415.30(b), but the form requirements are also satisfied by Judicial Council Form POS-015. *See* CCP §415.30(e).

(b) Not timely returned. If the person to whom the summons, complaint, and notice are mailed does not complete and return the acknowledgment form within 20 days after the date of mailing, the defendant is liable for all reasonable expenses the plaintiff incurs in serving or attempting to serve the defendant by another method. CCP §415.30(d). This deadline is not extended by CCP §1013, which operates to extend time when documents are served by mail. *Id.* §413.20. The court must award the expenses if the plaintiff files a motion, with or without notice, requesting them and the defendant does not show good cause for denying the request. *Id.* §415.30(d). The plaintiff is entitled to recover the expenses even if it is not entitled to recover its costs in the action. *Id.*

(3) When completed. If the person being served returns the notice to the plaintiff, service by mail is completed on the date the person signed the notice. CCP §415.30(c); *see* ***Bolkiah***, 74 Cal.App.4th at 1000. If the person does not timely return a signed notice, service is not complete and another method must be used. Weil, *Civil Procedure Before Trial*, ¶¶4:225, 4:238; *see, e.g.*, ***Tandy Corp. v. Superior Ct.*** (3d Dist.1981) 117 Cal.App.3d 911, 913 (service by mail was not completed because D's agent did not execute and return acknowledgment of receipt of summons). A postal-service return receipt cannot be used as a substitute for an executed acknowledgment of receipt of summons. ***Tandy Corp.***, 117 Cal.App.3d at 913.

3. Substitute service. A summons can be served by a combination of personal delivery and mail. *See* CCP §415.20. Service of process under §415.20 is known as "substitute service." *See* ***Ellard v. Conway*** (4th Dist.2001) 94 Cal.App.4th 540, 544 (CCP §415.20 authorizes substitute service of process instead of personal delivery). Substitute service can be used for service of process on the following entities: (1) corporations, (2) forfeited or dissolved corporations, (3) joint-stock companies or associations, (4) unincorporated associations, and (5) public entities. *See* CCP §§415.20(a), 416.10-416.50. Substitute service can be used for service of process on the following individuals: (1) minors, (2) wards and conservatees, (3) political candidates, and (4) persons not otherwise specified in CCP art. 4. *See id.* §§415.20(b), 416.60-416.90.

(1) How to serve – entity.

(a) Leave service papers at office or mailing address. To serve an entity by substitute service, the process server must do the following:

[1] Leave a copy of the service papers (1) at the office of the person being served during usual office hours or (2) at the mailing address, other than a U.S. Postal Service post-office box, of the person being served if no physical address is known. CCP §415.20(a); *see, e.g.*, ***Khourie, Crew & Jaeger***, 220 Cal.App.3d at 1012-13 (substitute service proper when process server attempted to leave service papers during usual office hours, but had to leave papers on other side of locked door when woman at D's office would not open the door). For purposes of substitute service, a "mailing address" can include a private or commercial post-office box. *Cf.* ***Ellard***, 94 Cal.App.4th at 546 (service under §415.20(b) for individuals).

[2] Leave the service papers with a person who is apparently in charge. CCP §415.20(a); *e.g.*, ***Khourie, Crew & Jaeger***, 220 Cal.App.3d at 1013 (substitute service proper when papers were left with only person who responded to process server's attempts to enter D's locked office). If the service papers are being left at a mailing address, the person being given the papers must be at least 18 and told the nature of what is being given to her. CCP §415.20(a).

(b) Mail service papers to place where papers were left. To serve an entity by substitute service, the process server must also mail a copy of the service papers by first-class mail, postage prepaid, to the person being served at the place where the service papers were left. CCP §415.20(a); *see* ***Tsakos Shipping***, 12 Cal.App.4th at 85.

(2) How to serve – individual.

(a) Determine personal service cannot be completed. To serve an individual by substitute service, the process server must determine that the service papers cannot, with reasonable diligence, be personally served. CCP §415.20(b); *see also* ***Earl W. Schott, Inc. v. Kalar*** (5th Dist.1993) 20 Cal.App.4th 943, 945 (P tried to avoid §415.20(b)'s reasonable-diligence requirement by referring to D as a "corporation" without proof that D was in fact a corporation). Whether the process server was reasonably diligent is usually determined on a case-by-case basis; however, two or three attempts of personal service at a proper place will usually satisfy the requirement. *See* ***Bein v. Brechtel-Jochim Grp.*** (4th Dist.1992) 6 Cal.App.4th 1387, 1391-92; *see, e.g.*, ***Ellard***, 94 Cal.App.4th at 545 (one attempt at personal service was sufficient to show reasonable diligence because Ds' gate guard told process server that Ds had moved and forwarding address was commercial post-office box); ***Burchett v. City of Newport Beach*** (4th Dist.1995) 33 Cal.App.4th 1472, 1477-78 (zero attempts to personally serve D were not sufficient to show reasonable diligence); ***Espindola v. Nunez*** (4th Dist.1988) 199 Cal.App.3d 1389, 1391-92 (three attempts to serve Ds at their home were sufficient to show reasonable diligence when process server, on fourth attempt, left copy of husband's summons with co-D wife). The burden is on the plaintiff to show reasonable diligence. ***American Express Centurion Bank v. Zara*** (6th Dist.2011) 199 Cal.App.4th 383, 389.

(b) Leave service papers at house, business, or mailing address. To serve an individual by substitute service, the process server must do the following:

[1] Leave the service papers at the individual's residence, usual place of abode, usual place of business, or usual mailing address other than a U.S. Postal Service post-office box. CCP §415.20(b); *see, e.g.*, ***Zirbes v. Stratton*** (2d Dist.1986) 187 Cal.App.3d 1407, 1415-16 & n.2 (substitute service at D's parents' home was ineffective because D did not reside there). For purposes of substitute service, a "mailing address" can include a private or commercial post-office box. ***Hearn v. Howard*** (2d Dist.2009) 177 Cal.App.4th 1193, 1203; ***Ellard***, 94 Cal.App.4th at 546.

[2] Leave the service papers in the presence of a competent member of the individual's household or a person apparently in charge of the individual's office, place of business, or usual mailing address other than a U.S. Postal Service post-office box. CCP §415.20(b); *e.g.*, ***Hearn***, 177 Cal.App.4th at 1201-02 (papers left with

"person apparently in charge"; service on clerk at private post-office-box business was sufficient even though clerk was not manager and refused to confirm whether D rented post-office box at location); ***Ellard***, 94 Cal.App.4th at 545-47 (papers left with "person apparently in charge"; manager of commercial post-office-box business, whose job was to deliver mail to lessees of post-office boxes, knew Ds and told process server that Ds received mail at post-office box). A "competent member of the household" does not mean the person must be a member of the family that resides there. *See* ***Bein***, 6 Cal.App.4th at 1393 & n.4 ("household" to be liberally construed). The person being given the papers must be at least 18 and told the nature of what is being given to her. CCP §415.20(b); *e.g.*, ***Ellard***, 94 Cal.App.4th at 545 (process server informed manager of commercial post-office-box business of contents of papers).

(c) Mail service papers to place where papers were left. To serve an individual by substitute service, the process server must also mail a copy of the service papers by first-class mail, postage prepaid, to the person being served at the place where the service papers were left. CCP §415.20(b); *see, e.g.*, ***Ellard***, 94 Cal.App.4th at 545 (after leaving service papers with manager of commercial post-office-box business, process server mailed copy to Ds).

(3) When completed. Substitute service is completed ten days after a copy of the service papers is mailed. CCP §415.20. For purposes of a motion to dismiss under CCP §583.210 for delay in service of summons, service is considered effective on the last day the service papers are mailed and the proof of service is filed in the court. *See* ***Ginns v. Shumate*** (2d Dist.1977) 65 Cal.App.3d 802, 805 (interpreting predecessor to §583.210). See "No service of summons & complaint," ch. 10-E, §4.1, p. 1162.

4. Service by publication. Process can be served by publication. CCP §415.50(a). Service by publication is usually requested through an ex parte application. *See, e.g.*, ***Watts v. Crawford*** (1995) 10 Cal.4th 743, 746 (ex parte application filed after repeated attempts to determine D's address and locate Ds failed). See "Ex Parte Practice," ch. 1-E, p. 39.

(1) When allowed. Publication can only be used as a last resort for service of process. ***Watts***, 10 Cal.4th at 749 n.5. The court can order service by publication only when the defendant's whereabouts are unknown and she cannot be served personally, by mail, or by substitute service through the exercise of reasonable diligence. CCP §415.50(a); Judicial Council of Cal. Ann. Rep. (1969) p. 48; *see* ***Watts***, 10 Cal.4th at 749 n.5 (no service by publication if D's address can be determined); ***David B. v. Superior Ct.*** (1st Dist.1994) 21 Cal.App.4th 1010, 1016 (service by publication sufficient only when D's whereabouts remain unknown after reasonably diligent inquiry).

(2) Affidavit. The plaintiff must prove the requirements for service by publication by affidavit. CCP §415.50(a). The plaintiff can use an affidavit from any person with personal knowledge of relevant facts, and affidavits from more than one person can be used if necessary. Judicial Council of Cal. Ann. Rep. (1969) p. 49; *see* ***Rue v. Quinn*** (1902) 137 Cal. 651, 655; ***Olvera v. Olvera*** (4th Dist.1991) 232 Cal.App.3d 32, 42.

PRACTICE TIP

If the plaintiff is going to rely on multiple affidavits to support service by publication, the affidavits should all be made as close in time to one another as possible. See Judicial Council of Cal. Ann. Rep. (1969) p. 49. If the affidavits are not made at roughly the same time, the court may reject the plaintiff's request for service by publication on the ground that circumstances may have changed since the earlier affidavits were made. See id. For example, the court might reject the plaintiff's request because new information has been discovered on the defendant's whereabouts, rendering earlier searches for the defendant in another location no longer adequate. See ***Kott****, 45 Cal.App.4th at 1138.*

(a) Reasonable diligence. The affidavit must establish that the plaintiff has exercised reasonable diligence, meaning that she or her representative has conducted a thorough, systematic investigation and inquiry in good faith to locate and serve the defendant. ***Watts***, 10 Cal.4th at 749 n.5; *see* CCP §415.50(a); Judicial Council of Cal. Ann. Rep. (1969) p. 49.

[1] Attempts to locate. The affidavit must give a detailed description of the attempts to locate the defendant. Judicial Council of Cal. Ann. Rep. (1969) p. 49; *see* ***Watts***, 10 Cal.4th at 749 n.5 (courts require showing of exhaustive attempts to locate D). The plaintiff's attempts to locate the defendant must exhaust all likely sources of information and cannot ignore obvious methods for determining the defendant's whereabouts. *See* ***Watts***, 10 Cal.4th at 749 n.5; *see, e.g.*, ***Kott***, 45 Cal.App.4th at 1138-39 (P did not seek D's address from D's attorney or through interrogatories to other Ds who had been served); ***David B.***, 21 Cal.App.4th at 1016 (no reasonable diligence because Marine Corps was not contacted, even though D-father was identified as Marine on minor's birth certificate).

[a] Mandatory sources. Sources of information that must always be consulted unless they are unavailable or clearly will not provide useful information are the following:

- The defendant's relatives, friends, acquaintances, and employer. Judicial Council of Cal. Ann. Rep. (1969) p. 49; *see* ***Watts***, 10 Cal.4th at 749 n.5; *see, e.g.*, ***Vorburg v. Vorburg*** (1941) 18 Cal.2d 794, 796 (P could not consult relatives or friends because they were unknown to her).
- City directories. ***Watts***, 10 Cal.4th at 749 n.5; Judicial Council of Cal. Ann. Rep. (1969) p. 49; *see, e.g.*, ***Vorburg***, 18 Cal.2d at 796 (P did not have to consult city directory because D had probably left California).
- Telephone directories. ***Watts***, 10 Cal.4th at 749 n.5; Judicial Council of Cal. Ann. Rep. (1969) p. 49; *see, e.g.*, ***Vorburg***, 18 Cal.2d at 796 (P did not have to consult telephone directory because D had probably left California).
- The voter registry. ***Watts***, 10 Cal.4th at 749 n.5; Judicial Council of Cal. Ann. Rep. (1969) p. 49. *But see* CCP §415.50(e) (P not required to search voter-registration rolls when prohibited by law or published agency policy).
- Real-property and personal-property records near the defendant's last known location. ***Watts***, 10 Cal.4th at 749 n.5; Judicial Council of Cal. Ann. Rep. (1969) p. 49.

[b] Unused sources. If the plaintiff does not consult one of the mandatory sources listed above or other seemingly likely sources of information, an explanation for why these sources were not used must be included in the plaintiff's affidavit. *See, e.g.*, ***Olvera***, 232 Cal.App.3d at 42 (affidavit did not explain why return address on letter sent by D would not be helpful in locating D).

[2] Attempts to serve. The affidavit must describe any attempts the plaintiff made to serve the defendant by one of the other methods of service. Judicial Council of Cal. Ann. Rep. (1969) p. 49.

(b) D's status. The affidavit must establish the defendant's relationship to the action by showing either of the following:

[1] D is proper party. The affidavit must establish that either (1) the plaintiff has a cause of action against the defendant or (2) the defendant is a necessary or proper party to the action. CCP §415.50(a)(1); *see, e.g.*, ***Islamic Republic of Iran v. Pahlavi*** (2d Dist.1984) 160 Cal.App.3d 620, 627 (affidavit that was "a medley of conclusions and political declamation" did not establish that P had cause of action against D). See "Joinder of Parties," ch. 3-B, §3, p. 193.

[2] D has or claims interest in property. The affidavit must establish that (1) the defendant has or claims an interest in real property or personal property located in California that is subject to the court's jurisdiction or (2) the relief demanded in the action will exclude the defendant entirely or in part from any interest it has in the property. CCP §415.50(a)(2).

(3) Court's order. The court's order must direct the plaintiff to publish a copy of the summons in the newspaper named in the order. CCP §415.50(b).

(a) California newspaper. The court's order must name a newspaper that is published in California and most likely to give actual notice of the suit to the defendant. CCP §415.50(b).

(b) How long to publish. The court's order must direct the plaintiff to have the summons published once a week for four consecutive weeks in the newspaper named in the order, unless the court in its discretion orders the plaintiff to publish the summons a different number of times or for a longer period of time. *See* CCP §415.50(b); Gov. C. §6064. The four-week period includes the first day the summons is published and ends 28 days later. Gov. C. §6064.

(c) How often to publish. The newspaper must be published at least once a week, and there must be at least five intervening days between each day the summons is published. Gov. C. §6064. For example, if the plaintiff has the summons published on a Friday, the earliest day the plaintiff can have the summons published again is the following Thursday.

(d) Mail to located defendant. The court's order must direct the plaintiff to mail to the defendant a copy of the summons, complaint, and order for publication as soon as reasonably possible if the plaintiff locates the defendant before the end of the publication period. *See* CCP §415.50(b) (copies must be mailed "forthwith"); *see also* ***Anderson v. Goff*** (1887) 72 Cal. 65, 73 (defining "forthwith" to mean "as soon as by reasonable exertion").

(4) When completed. Service of process is completed once the publication period expires.

CAUTION

Be sure to request service by publication far enough in advance so the publication period will be complete before the deadline for service has expired. If the publication period does not end until after the absolute three-year deadline for service of process, the plaintiff's suit must be dismissed. See CCP §§583.210(a), 583.250; ***Perez v. Smith*** *(1st Dist.1993) 19 Cal.App.4th 1595, 1597.* *See "Deadlines for prosecution," ch. 10-E, §2.2, p. 1160.*

(5) Other service methods still valid. The plaintiff can still serve the defendant by personal delivery, mail, or substitute service after service by publication is ordered. *See* CCP §415.50(d).

5. Service by posting. Process can be served by posting. CCP §415.45(a).

(1) When allowed. Posting can only be used as a last resort for service of process in unlawful-detainer actions. *See* CCP §415.45(a). The court can order service by posting only when the defendant cannot be served personally, by mail, or by substitute service through the exercise of reasonable diligence. *See id.*

(2) Affidavit. The plaintiff must prove by affidavit the requirements for service by posting. CCP §415.45(a).

(a) Reasonable diligence. The affidavit must establish that the plaintiff has exercised reasonable diligence in trying to locate and serve the defendant personally, by mail, and by substitute service. *See* CCP §415.45(a). To determine if the plaintiff has exercised reasonable diligence under CCP §415.45, the court must evaluate each case on its own facts. ***Board of Trs. v. Ham*** (6th Dist.2013) 216 Cal.App.4th 330, 339. Unlike service by publication, the plaintiff is not required to conduct an extensive investigation into all possible whereabouts of the defendant before requesting service by posting. *Id.* at 338.

(b) D's status. The affidavit must establish the defendant's relationship to the action by showing either of the following:

[1] D is proper party. The affidavit must establish that either (1) the plaintiff has a cause of action against the defendant or (2) the defendant is a necessary or proper party to the action. CCP §415.45(a)(1). See "Joinder of Parties," ch. 3-B, §3, p. 193.

[2] D has or claims interest in property. The affidavit must establish that (1) the defendant has or claims an interest in real property located in California that is subject to the court's jurisdiction or (2) the relief demanded in the action will exclude the defendant entirely or in part from any interest it has in the property. CCP §415.45(a)(2).

(3) Court's order. The court's order must direct the plaintiff to do all the following:

(a) Post the summons on the premises in a way most likely to give actual notice of the unlawful-detainer action. CCP §415.45(b).

(b) Send by certified mail a copy of the summons and complaint to the defendant at her last known address. *Id.*

(4) When completed. Service of process is completed on the tenth day after the summons is posted and deposited in the mail. CCP §415.45(c).

(5) Other service methods still valid. The plaintiff can still serve the defendant by personal delivery, mail, or substitute service after service by posting is ordered. *See* CCP §415.45(d) (regardless of order allowing for service of process by posting, P can serve in any manner other than publication).

§5.2 Defendant outside California but in U.S. If the service papers are to be served on a person located outside California but in the United States, the methods of service listed below can be used. *See* CCP §413.10(b).

1. Service by personal delivery. Process can be served by personal delivery, which is the preferred method of service. See "Service by personal delivery," §5.1.1, p. 301.

2. Service by U.S. mail. Process can be served by mail. CCP §§415.30, 415.40. To serve process by mail to a person located outside California but in the United States, the plaintiff can complete service under any of the statutes listed below. *See* ***Watts v. Crawford*** (1995) 10 Cal.4th 743, 748.

(1) Service under §415.30. The plaintiff can complete service by mail under CCP §415.30. See "Service by U.S. mail," §5.1.2, p. 302. But the nonresident defendant's acknowledgment of receipt of service does not subject it to the jurisdiction of the California courts. *See* ***In re Marriage of Merideth*** (1st Dist.1982) 129 Cal.App.3d 356, 361-62. The plaintiff must also ensure that the defendant has minimum contacts with California sufficient to support the court's exercise of personal jurisdiction. Weil, *Civil Procedure Before Trial*, ¶4:237; *see, e.g.*, ***In re Marriage of Merideth***, 129 Cal.App.3d at 363 (wife admitted husband's contacts with California were insufficient to establish personal jurisdiction). See "Minimum Contacts," ch. 3-G, §6, p. 288.

(2) Service under §415.40. The plaintiff can complete service by mailing a copy of the summons and complaint by first-class mail, postage prepaid, return receipt requested. CCP §415.40.

(a) Envelope. The envelope containing the summons and complaint should be correctly addressed to the proper person to be served. *See* ***Cruz v. Fagor Am., Inc.*** (4th Dist.2007) 146 Cal.App.4th 488, 497-98; *see, e.g.*, ***Dill v. Berquist Constr. Co.*** (4th Dist.1994) 24 Cal.App.4th 1426, 1436-37 (service defective because P did not address envelopes to any individual authorized to accept service on behalf of D-corporation and no other evidence showed that proper person received summons); ***Taylor-Rush v. Multitech Corp.*** (1st Dist.1990) 217 Cal.App.3d 103, 110-11 (service defective because envelope was addressed to D at wrong address and P did not show that persons who signed return receipt were authorized to accept mail on D's behalf or that D actually received summons).

(b) Return receipt. The return receipt does not have to be signed by the defendant as long as it is signed by someone authorized to accept mail on the defendant's behalf. ***Cruz***, 146 Cal.App.4th at 498; ***Neadeau v. Foster*** (3d Dist.1982) 129 Cal.App.3d 234, 236-37. When establishing proof of service, the plaintiff may have to support the record by an affidavit showing that the person who signed the return receipt was authorized to accept the defendant's mail. *See* ***Taylor-Rush***, 217 Cal.App.3d at 110; *see, e.g.*, ***Cruz***, 146 Cal.App.4th at 498-99 (P's attorney stated in affidavit that he confirmed with U.S. Postal Service that person who accepted mail regularly received mail on D's behalf at address on envelope); ***Dill***, 24 Cal.App.4th at 1437-38 (P did not present evidence that person who signed receipt was authorized to accept service of process); ***Neadeau***, 129 Cal.App.3d at 237 (P's employee stated in affidavit that person who signed return receipt was D's employee and was authorized to sign for and accept mail on D's behalf); *see also* CCP §417.20(a) (proof of out-of-state service).

NOTE

When attempting service by mail under §415.40, the plaintiff does not need to serve and obtain an executed acknowledgment of receipt of summons. ***Bolkiah v. Superior Ct.*** *(2d Dist.1999) 74 Cal.App.4th 984, 1000. The plaintiff is only required to obtain a signed return receipt. See CCP §415.40;* ***Bolkiah****, 74 Cal.App.4th at 1000.*

(c) When completed. Service by mail under §415.40 is completed ten days after a copy of the summons and complaint is mailed. CCP §415.40. For purposes of a motion to dismiss under CCP §583.210 for delay in service of summons, service is considered effective on the day the service papers are mailed and the proof of service is made. *See* ***Johnson & Johnson v. Superior Ct.*** (1985) 38 Cal.3d 243, 250 (interpreting predecessor to §583.210). See "No service of summons & complaint," ch. 10-E, §4.1, p. 1162.

(3) Service under other California statute. The plaintiff can complete service by mail under any other California statute authorizing service of process by mail. *See* ***Anderson v. Sherman*** (2d Dist.1981) 125 Cal.App.3d 228, 236-37. For example, if a nonresident defendant gets into an auto accident in California and at the time has a California driver's license, the plaintiff in a suit arising from the accident can complete service of process by sending the defendant the notice of service and a copy of the summons and complaint by registered mail. *See* Veh. C. §§17455, 17460, 17461; ***Ostrus v. Price*** (2d Dist.1978) 82 Cal.App.3d 518, 524.

(4) Service under other state's law. The plaintiff can complete service by mail under the law of the state where the person is served. CCP §413.10(b).

3. Substitute service. Process can be served by a combination of personal delivery and mail—known as "substitute service"—on an out-of-state defendant in the same manner as for an in-state defendant. *See* ***Watts***, 10 Cal.4th at 748 (out-of-state defendant can be served by personal delivery, mail, or substitute service); *see also* CCP §415.20 (describing process for substitute service). See "Substitute service," §5.1.3, p. 302.

4. Service by publication. Process can be served by publication on an out-of-state defendant in the same manner as for an in-state defendant. *See* CCP §415.50(b). See "Service by publication," §5.1.4, p. 304. In addition to ordering publication in a California newspaper, the court may also order the plaintiff to publish the summons in a specified newspaper that is published outside California and is most likely to give the defendant actual notice of the suit. CCP §415.50(b).

5. Service by posting. Process can be served on an out-of-state defendant by posting in the same manner as for an in-state defendant. *See* CCP §415.45. See "Service by posting," §5.1.5, p. 306.

§5.3 Defendant outside U.S. To serve a foreign defendant, the plaintiff may need to comply with the Hague Convention on the Service Abroad of Judicial and Extrajudicial Documents ("Hague Convention on Service") or any other applicable treaty. *See* U.S. Const., art. VI, cl. 2. If there are no mandatory treaty requirements, the plaintiff can serve the foreign defendant (1) under the foreign jurisdiction's laws for service of process, (2) in the manner designated by the foreign jurisdiction in response to a letter rogatory, or (3) under California law for service of process if there is no other mandatory method of service. *See* CCP §413.10(c).

1. Hague Convention. For a discussion of service of process under the Hague Convention, see ***O'Connor's Federal Rules***, "Service under Hague Convention," ch. 2-H, §6.3.2, p. 172.

(1) Convention applies. The plaintiff must use the Hague Convention's service methods if judicial documents must be transmitted to the defendant in a country that has signed the Hague Convention. *See* ***Volkswagenwerk A.G. v. Shlunk*** (1988) 486 U.S. 694, 698-99; ***In re Alyssa F.*** (4th Dist.2003) 112 Cal.App.4th 846, 852; ***Honda Motor Co. v. Superior Ct.*** (6th Dist.1992) 10 Cal.App.4th 1043, 1045. Service by any other method is void, even if the method used gives the defendant actual notice of the lawsuit. ***Floveyor Int'l v. Superior Ct.*** (2d Dist.1997) 59 Cal.App.4th 789, 794. The plaintiff can also choose to use Hague Convention methods even though they are not required in a particular case. ***Volkswagenwerk***, 486 U.S. at 706.

NOTE

*Article 10 of the Hague Convention provides for alternative methods of service as long as the foreign jurisdiction does not object. See Hague Convention on Service, art. 10. California courts are divided on whether service of process by mail is permitted under Article 10(a) when the foreign jurisdiction has not objected to service under that section of the Convention. Compare **Denlinger v. Chinadotcom Corp.** (6th Dist.2003) 110 Cal.App.4th 1396, 1405 (service by mail allowed), and **Shoei Kako Co. v. Superior Ct.** (1st Dist.1973) 33 Cal.App.3d 808, 822 (same), with **Honda Motor**, 10 Cal.App.4th at 1047-49 (service by mail not allowed), and **Suzuki Motor Co. v. Superior Ct.** (4th Dist.1988) 200 Cal.App.3d 1476, 1484 (same). See **O'Connor's Federal Rules**, "Alternative service," ch. 2-H, §6.3.2(2), p. 173.*

(2) Convention does not apply.

(a) Service in U.S. The Hague Convention does not apply when the plaintiff can serve the defendant without transmitting documents outside the United States. *See* ***Volkswagenwerk***, 486 U.S. at 707-08. For example, a foreign defendant can be served without transmitting documents outside the United States when the defendant has, or is required or deemed to have, a local agent for service of process. *See id.* at 707; ***Kott v. Superior Ct.*** (2d Dist.1996) 45 Cal.App.4th 1126, 1133-34; *see, e.g.*, ***Yamaha Motor Co. v. Superior Ct.*** (4th Dist.2009) 174 Cal.App.4th 264, 267 (service on foreign company's American subsidiary was valid as service on foreign company).

(b) Address unknown. The Hague Convention does not apply when the plaintiff does not know the foreign defendant's address and the address cannot be determined through reasonable diligence. ***Kott***, 45 Cal.App.4th at 1136; *see* Hague Convention on Service, art. 1.

2. Other treaty. The plaintiff must comply with any other treaty governing service in the country where the defendant is to be served. *See* U.S. Const., art. VI, cl. 2 (treaties are binding on state courts); ***Shoei Kako***, 33 Cal.App.3d at 819 (court cannot exercise jurisdiction in violation of international treaty). See ***O'Connor's Federal Rules***, "Preference for service according to international agreements," ch. 2-H, §6.3.1, p. 171.

3. Foreign jurisdiction's law. The plaintiff can serve the defendant in any way allowed by the foreign jurisdiction's own laws on service of process, but only if the court finds that service under the foreign jurisdiction's laws is reasonably calculated to give actual notice to the defendant. CCP §413.10(c).

4. Letter rogatory. The plaintiff can serve the defendant in the way directed by the foreign jurisdiction in response to a letter rogatory if the court finds that service is reasonably calculated to give actual notice to the defendant. CCP §413.10(c). A letter rogatory is a formal request from a court in one country to another country's judicial authorities for assistance with service of process. ***Magness v. Russian Fed'n*** (5th Cir.2001) 247 F.3d 609, 614 n.10.

5. California law. The California Code of Civil Procedure specifically allows for service of process on a party outside the United States in the same manner as service on a party in California. *See* CCP §§413.10(c), 415.40. The plaintiff can serve the defendant under California law only when there is no other mandatory method for service. *See id.* §413.10(c).

(1) Service by personal delivery. Process can be served by personal delivery. CCP §415.10. Personal delivery is the preferred method of service. ***Kott***, 45 Cal.App.4th at 1137. See "Service by personal delivery," §5.1.1, p. 301.

(2) Service by mail. Process can be served by mail. CCP §415.40. To serve by mail, the plaintiff must send a copy of the summons and the complaint by first-class mail, postage prepaid, return receipt requested. *Id.* See "Service by U.S. mail," §5.1.2, p. 302.

(3) Substitute service. Process can be served by substitute service. *See* CCP §415.20; ***Volkswagenwerk***, 486 U.S. at 705 (dicta). See "Substitute service," §5.1.3, p. 302.

(4) Service by court order. Process can be served by any other method directed by the court. CCP §413.10(c); *see id.* §415.40.

§5.4 Type of action.

1. Small claims. Service of process in a small-claims action is subject to more lenient requirements than those in a limited or unlimited civil case. In a small-claims action, service can be completed by the court clerk or the plaintiff.

(1) Service by clerk. The court clerk can serve the claim and order (see "Claim & order – small-claims action," §3.4, p. 300) by either of the following methods:

(a) Mail claim & order. The court clerk can mail copies of the claim and order to the defendant. CCP §116.340(a)(1); ***Cabrini Villas Homeowners Ass'n v. Haghverdian*** (2d Dist.2003) 111 Cal.App.4th 683, 690. Any form of mail service can be used if it provides for a return receipt. CCP §116.340(a)(1); ***Cabrini Villas***, 111 Cal.App.4th at 690. The clerk does not need to mail a copy of the order to the plaintiff, presumably because the order is issued when the claim is filed and the plaintiff is given a copy. *See* CCP §§116.330(a), 116.340(a)(1).

(b) Mail claim, then order. The court clerk can mail a copy of the claim to the defendant, wait to receive the return receipt for delivery, and then issue and mail to the parties the order setting the hearing on the claim. CCP §§116.330(b), 116.340(a)(4). Any form of mail service can be used if it provides for a return receipt. *Id.* §116.330(b)(1), (b)(3).

(2) Service by plaintiff. The plaintiff can serve the claim and order by either of the following methods:

(a) Personal service. The plaintiff can personally deliver copies of the claim and order to the defendant. CCP §116.340(a)(2); ***Cabrini Villas***, 111 Cal.App.4th at 690.

(b) Substitute service. The plaintiff can serve copies of the claim and order by substitute service. CCP §116.340(a)(3); ***Cabrini Villas***, 111 Cal.App.4th at 690. When serving an entity described in CCP §§416.10-416.50 or an individual described in CCP §§416.60-416.90, the following rules apply in small-claims actions:

[1] The plaintiff is not required to attempt personal delivery before using substitute service. CCP §116.340(a)(3); ***Cabrini Villas***, 111 Cal.App.4th at 690; *see also* CCP §415.20(b) (for substitute service in limited and unlimited civil cases, P must attempt personal service first). See "Determine personal service cannot be completed," §5.1.3(2)(a), p. 303.

[2] The plaintiff can (1) give copies of the claim and order to the sheriff or marshal who will deliver the papers to any person authorized by the defendant to receive service of process, and (2) mail a copy of the papers to the defendant's usual mailing address. CCP §116.340(a)(3).

(3) In state only. In most small-claims actions, service of process must be made within California. CCP §116.340(e). However, there are two exceptions:

(a) Real-property actions. In a small-claims action relating to real property in California, a nonresident owner of record who has no lawfully designated agent in California for service of process can be served by any method listed under §116.340(a). CCP §116.340(f). See "Service by clerk," §5.4.1(1), this page; "Service by plaintiff," §5.4.1(2), this page.

(b) Motor-vehicle actions. In a small-claims action relating to a motor-vehicle accident occurring in California, a nonresident owner or operator of a motor vehicle can be served in any of the following ways:

[1] By constructive service authorized by Veh. C. §§17450-17461 regardless of whether the defendant was a nonresident when the accident occurred or when the claim was filed. CCP §116.340(g).

SERVICE OF PROCESS

[2] By registered mail as authorized by Veh. C. §17454 or §17455 and sent to the Director of the California Department of Motor Vehicles and the defendant. CCP §116.340(g).

[3] By any method authorized by CCP chapter 5.5 and sent to the Director of the California Department of Motor Vehicles and the defendant. CCP §116.340(g).

(4) When completed. Service is completed on any of the following dates:

(a) The date the defendant signs the return receipt. CCP §116.340(d).

(b) The date the defendant is personally served. *Id.*

(c) Ten days after the papers are mailed, when the plaintiff uses substitute service. *See id.* §§116.340(d), 415.20.

(d) The date of service as established by any other competent evidence. *Id.* §116.340(d).

2. Unlawful detainer. Service of process in most unlawful-detainer actions differs from service of process in unlawful-detainer actions involving either a prejudgment claim for possession or a claim for abandoned property.

(1) Most actions.

(a) Whom to serve. Service of process is made on the tenant and any subtenant. CCP §415.46(a).

(b) How to serve. Service of process in most unlawful-detainer actions can be made in the same manner as service in civil suits generally.

[1] Personal delivery. Service of process can be made by personal delivery. *See* CCP §§415.10, 415.45(d). See "Service by personal delivery," §5.1.1, p. 301.

[2] Mail. Service of process can be made by mail. *See* CCP §§415.30, 415.45(d). See "Service by U.S. mail," §5.1.2, p. 302.

[3] Substitute service. Service of process can be made by substitute service. *See* CCP §§415.20, 415.45(d). See "Substitute service," §5.1.3, p. 302.

[4] Posting. Service of process can be made by posting only if the plaintiff is unable to complete service by any method other than publication. CCP §415.45(a). See "Service by posting," §5.1.5, p. 306.

NOTE

Service of process in unlawful-detainer actions cannot be made by publication. See CCP §415.45(d) (regardless of order allowing for service of process by posting, P can serve in any manner other than publication).

(2) Prejudgment claim for possession. When the unlawful-detainer action involves a prejudgment claim for possession, service of process must be made in the following manner.

(a) Whom to serve. Service of process must be made on all occupants of the premises. *See* CCP §415.46(a). An "occupant" is any person other than the tenant or subtenant (i.e., a person not named in the summons and complaint) who appears to occupy the premises or who may claim to have occupied the premises when the unlawful-detainer action is filed. *See id.* The process server must make a reasonably diligent effort to determine whether there are adult occupants of the premises and their identities. *Id.* §415.46(c)(1). The identities of the occupants can be determined by asking the defendant, at the time of personal service, or any person of suitable age and discretion who appears to reside at the premises. *Id.*

(b) Who can serve. Service of process must be made by a marshal, sheriff, or registered process server. CCP §415.46(b).

(c) What to serve. The process server must serve a copy of a prejudgment claim of right to possession attached to the summons and complaint for the unlawful-detainer action (the "service papers"). CCP §415.46(a). The process server must use the statutory form for this claim. *Id.* §415.46(a), (f); *see* Judicial Council Forms, form CP-10.5.

(d) How to serve.

[1] Personal delivery + notice by posting & mail. If the occupant's identity is disclosed, the process server must first attempt to personally serve the occupant (if she is present at the premises) with the service papers (i.e., claim form, summons, and complaint). CCP §415.46(c)(2). If the occupant cannot be personally served, the process server can complete service by doing the following:

[a] State the date of service on the form for the prejudgment claim of right to possession and all copies of the form. *Id.* §415.46(c)(4). The claim is valid even if the process server does not put the date of service on the form. *Id.*

[b] Leave a copy of the service papers, addressed to the occupant, with a person of suitable age and discretion who is at the premises. *Id.* §415.46(c)(2).

[c] Affix a copy of the service papers in a conspicuous place on the premises in a manner most likely to give actual notice to the occupant. *Id.* The papers must be attached so that they cannot be easily removed. *Id.*

[d] Send a copy of the service papers by first-class mail. *Id.*

[2] Drop delivery + notice by posting & mail. If any occupant's identity is undisclosed or if substitute service under CCP §415.20 is made on the tenant and subtenant, the process server must complete service by doing the following:

[a] State the date of service on the form for the prejudgment claim of right to possession and all copies of the form. CCP §415.46(c)(4). The claim is valid even if the process server does not put the date of service on the form. *Id.*

[b] Leave a copy of the service papers at the premises at the same time service is made on the tenant and subtenant. *Id.* §415.46(c)(3).

[c] Affix a copy of the service papers in a conspicuous place on the premises in a manner most likely to give actual notice to an occupant. *Id.* The papers must be attached so that they cannot be easily removed. *Id.*

[d] Send a copy of the service papers addressed to "all occupants in care of the named tenant" to the premises by first-class mail. *Id.*

(3) Abandoned property. When the unlawful-detainer action involves a claim that the lessee abandoned the premises, service of process must be made in the following manner.

(a) Whom to serve. Service of process must be made on the lessee of the real property that is the subject of the unlawful-detainer action. *See* CCP §415.47.

(b) When to serve. Service of process under CCP §415.47 can be made after (1) the lessor has given the lessee written notice under Civ. C. §1951.3 of its belief that the lessee has abandoned the leased premises and (2) the lessee has given notice of its intent not to abandon the leased property ("notice of intent") under Civ. C. §1951.3. *See* CCP §415.47(a), (b).

(c) How to serve.

[1] Address provided. If the lessee provided in the notice of intent an address at which she could be served by certified mail in an unlawful-detainer action, the lessor can serve process by mailing the summons and complaint by certified mail, postage prepaid, to the lessee at that address within 60 days after the lessor receives the lessee's notice of intent. CCP §415.47(a).

[2] Address not provided. If the lessee did not provide in the notice of intent an address at which she could be served by certified mail in an unlawful-detainer action, the lessor can serve process by mailing the summons and complaint by certified mail, postage prepaid, to the lessee within 60 days after the lessor received the lessee's notice of intent. CCP §415.47(b). The summons and complaint can be mailed to either of the following addresses:

[a] The same address to which the lessor's notice of belief of abandonment was addressed if the notice was given by mail. *Id.*

[b] The address of the real property if the lessor's notice of belief of abandonment was personally served on the lessee. *Id.*

[3] Other service methods still valid. The plaintiff can still serve the defendant by personal delivery, mail, substitute service, or posting. *See* CCP §415.47(c).

(d) When completed. Service is completed on the tenth day after the summons is deposited in the mail. CCP §415.47(a), (b).

§6. WHO MAY BE SERVED

There are two issues regarding the proper person to serve. First, when the defendant is not an individual, who is authorized to receive service of process for the defendant? Second, when service on the defendant is not possible, who can be served as a proxy for the defendant? Chart 3-3, below, should help answer both of these questions.

3-3. PROPER PERSON TO SERVE

	If defendant is	Personal service is made on	Substitute or constructive service may be made on
1	Administrative Office of the Courts	Secretariat of the Judicial Council. Gov. C. §955.9(d).	
2	Bank corporation	• Agent for service of process. CCP §416.10(a), (c). • President, chief executive officer, other head of the corporation, vice president, secretary, assistant secretary, treasurer, assistant treasurer, controller, chief financial officer, general manager, or person authorized by corporation to accept service. *Id.* §416.10(b), (c). • Cashier or assistant cashier. *Id.* §416.10(c); Corp. C. §2110.	• Person who is apparently in charge of office of person authorized to be served. CCP §415.20(a). • Person who is apparently in charge of usual mailing address of person authorized to be served (other than a U.S. post-office box) and is at least 18. *Id.* • Secretary of State. *Id.* §416.10(d); Corp. C. §1702(a).
3	City	Clerk, secretary, president, presiding officer, or other head of city's governing body. CCP §416.50(a); *see, e.g.*, ***Wagner*** (2d Dist.2000) 78 Cal.App.4th 943, 949 (summons mailed to city clerk); ***Abrahamson*** (3d Dist.1949) 90 Cal.App.2d 523, 527-28 (mayor served with complaint), *disapproved on other grounds*, ***Ansell*** (1950) 35 Cal.2d 76.	• Person who is apparently in charge of office of person authorized to be served. CCP §415.20(a). • Person who is apparently in charge of usual mailing address of person authorized to be served (other than a U.S. post-office box) and is at least 18. *Id.*

3-3. PROPER PERSON TO SERVE (CONTINUED)

	If defendant is	Personal service is made on	Substitute or constructive service may be made on
4	Corporation, domestic	• Natural person designated as agent for service of process in statement or designation filed with Secretary of State. CCP §416.10(a), (c); Corp. C. §§1502(b), 1701. • Domestic or foreign corporation designated as agent for service of process in statement or certificate filed with Secretary of State. Corp. C. §§1502(b), 1505(a), 1701. • President, chief executive officer, other head of the corporation, vice president, secretary, assistant secretary, treasurer, assistant treasurer, controller, chief financial officer, general manager, or person authorized by corporation to accept service. CCP §416.10(b).	• Person who is apparently in charge of office, place of business, or usual mailing address of person authorized to be served (other than a U.S. post-office box) and is at least 18. CCP §415.20(a). • Secretary of State. *Id.* §416.10(d); Corp. C. §1702(a).
5	Corporation, foreign	• Natural person designated as agent for service of process in statement or designation filed with Secretary of State. CCP §416.10(a); Corp. C. §§1502(b), 2105(a)(4). • Domestic or foreign corporation designated as agent for service of process in statement or certificate filed with Secretary of State. Corp. C. §§1502(b), 1505(a), 2105(a)(4).	• Person who is apparently in charge of office, place of business, or usual mailing address of person authorized to be served (other than a U.S. post-office box) and is at least 18. CCP §415.20(a). • Secretary of State. *Id.* §416.10(d); Corp. C. §§1702(a), 2105(a)(6)(A), 2111(a).
6	Corporation, forfeited or dissolved	• Trustee for corporation and its stockholders or members. CCP §416.20(a). • Officer, director, or person in charge of corporation's assets. *Id.* §416.20(b); Corp. C. §2011(b). • Any person who could have been served as corporation's agent at the time of dissolution, if no officer, director, or person in charge of corporation's assets can be found with reasonable diligence. CCP §416.20(b); Corp. C. §2011(b).	• Person who is apparently in charge of office, place of business, or usual mailing address of person authorized to be served (other than a U.S. post-office box) and is at least 18. CCP §415.20(a). • Secretary of State. *Id.* §416.10(d); Corp. C. §§2011(b), 2105(a)(6)(A), 2111(a).
7	County	Clerk, secretary, president, presiding officer, or other head of county's governing body. CCP §416.50(a).	Person who is apparently in charge of office, place of business, or usual mailing address of person authorized to be served (other than a U.S. post-office box) and is at least 18. CCP §415.20(a).
8	Court of appeal	Clerk or administrator of the court. Gov. C. §955.9(b).	
9	Deceased person	• Personal representative of estate, heirs, and devisees in proceeding to revoke probate of will. Prob. C. §8271(a). • Personal representative of estate for claim against estate. *See id.* §9354(b). • Insurer, or person designated in writing by insurer, in action to establish deceased person's liability covered by insurance. *Id.* §552(a).	

3-3. PROPER PERSON TO SERVE (CONTINUED)

	If defendant is	Personal service is made on	Substitute or constructive service may be made on
10	Department of Transportation	Director of Transportation or Attorney General, in action for taking or damage of private property arising from work done by Department of Transportation. Gov. C. §955.6(a).	
11	Department of Water Resources	Director of Water Resources or Attorney General, in action for taking or damage of private property arising from work done by Department of Water Resources. Gov. C. §955.8(a).	
12	Individual	• The defendant. CCP §416.90. • Person authorized by defendant to receive service of process. *Id.* Authorization to receive service of process can be explicit or implicit. *See* ***Estate of Moss*** (2d Dist.2012) 204 Cal.App.4th 521, 532; ***Warner Bros. Records*** (2d Dist.1974) 36 Cal.App.3d 1012, 1018-19; *see, e.g.*, ***Summers*** (2d Dist.2006) 140 Cal.App.4th 403, 414 (no evidence personal manager was D's ostensible agent for service).	• Person who is competent member of defendant's household and is at least 18. CCP §415.20(b). • Person who is apparently in charge of defendant's office, place of business, or usual mailing address (other than a U.S. post-office box) and is at least 18. *Id.*
13	Insurance company, foreign	Agent named in written designation filed with Insurance Commissioner. Ins. C. §1600.	Insurance Commissioner, if foreign insurance company no longer conducts business in state or does not have agent for service of process in state. Ins. C. §1604.
14	Joint-stock company or association	Same as permitted for a corporation. *See* CCP §416.30. See Corporation, rows 4-6, above.	Same as permitted for a corporation. *See* CCP §416.30. See Corporation, rows 4-6, above.
15	Judge, court of appeal	Clerk or administrator of court of appeal. Gov. C. §955.9(b).	
16	Judge, superior court	Court executive officer. Gov. C. §955.9(a).	
17	Judge, Supreme Court of California	Clerk of the Supreme Court of California. Gov. C. §955.9(c).	
18	Judicial Council	Secretariat of the Judicial Council. Gov. C. §955.9(d).	
19	Limited-liability company, domestic	Agent for service of process designated in statement filed with Secretary of State. Corp. C. §17060(a)(2).	Secretary of State, Assistant Secretary of State, or Deputy Secretary of State, if agent has resigned or cannot be served with reasonable diligence. Corp. C. §17061(c)(1).
20	Limited-liability company, foreign	• Agent for service of process designated in statement filed with Secretary of State. Corp. C. §17060(a)(2). • Secretary of State, if foreign limited-liability company conducts business in state without registering. *Id.* §§17061(b), 17456(d).	Secretary of State, Assistant Secretary of State, or Deputy Secretary of State, if agent has resigned or cannot be served with reasonable diligence. Corp. C. §17061(c)(1).
21	Lottery Commission	Director of California State Lottery Commission or her designated representative at Commission headquarters in Sacramento. Gov. C. §8880.72.	

3-3. PROPER PERSON TO SERVE (CONTINUED)

	If defendant is	Personal service is made on	Substitute or constructive service may be made on
22	Minor	Parent, guardian, conservator, or similar fiduciary. CCP §416.60. If none of these individuals can be found with reasonable diligence, then (1) any person having the minor's care or control, (2) any person with whom the minor resides, or (3) any person who employs the minor. *Id.* A copy must also be personally delivered to the minor if she is at least 12. *Id.*	• Person who is competent member of defendant's household and is at least 18. CCP §415.20(b). • Person who is apparently in charge of defendant's office, place of business, or usual mailing address (other than a U.S. post-office box) and is at least 18. *Id.*
23	Nonresident defendant – auto accident	The defendant or her agent for service of process. CCP §416.90.	Director of Motor Vehicles. Veh. C. §17451.
24	Partnership, general	• Agent for service of process designated in statement filed with Secretary of State. CCP §416.40(a). • General partner. *Id.* • General manager of partnership. *Id.*	Person who is apparently in charge of office, place of business, or usual mailing address of person authorized to be served (other than a U.S. post-office box) and is at least 18. CCP §415.20(a).
25	Partnership, foreign	Agent named in written designation filed with Secretary of State. Corp. C. §15800(a).	Secretary of State, Assistant Secretary of State, or Deputy Secretary of State if no agent designated, agent cannot be served with due diligence, or agent no longer authorized to receive service of process. Corp. C. §15800(b).
26	Partnership, limited	• Agent for service of process designated in statement filed with Secretary of State. CCP §416.40(a). • General manager of partnership. *Id.*	Person who is apparently in charge of office, place of business, or usual mailing address of person authorized to be served (other than a U.S. post-office box) and is at least 18. CCP §415.20(a).
27	Political candidate	• The candidate. CCP §416.90. • If action relates to candidacy, Secretary of State or county elections official with whom declaration of candidacy was filed. *Id.* §416.80; Elec. C. §12.	• Person who is competent member of defendant's household and is at least 18. CCP §415.20(b). • Person who is apparently in charge of defendant's office, place of business, or usual mailing address (other than a U.S. post-office box) and is at least 18. *Id.*
28	Public entity (e.g., state agency, county, city)	Clerk, secretary, president, presiding officer, or other head of governing body. CCP §416.50(a).	• Person who is apparently in charge of office, place of business, or usual mailing address of person authorized to be served (other than a U.S. post-office box) and is at least 18. CCP §415.20(a). • Secretary of State if the defendant has filed an inaccurate or incomplete statement in the Roster of Public Agencies or has not filed a statement at all. Gov. C. §§960.2, 960.3; *see id.* §53051.
29	State of California	Attorney General. Gov. C. §955.4(a).	
30	Superior court	Court executive officer. Gov. C. §955.9(a).	
31	Supreme Court of California	Clerk of the Supreme Court of California. Gov. C. §955.9(c).	

3-3. PROPER PERSON TO SERVE (CONTINUED)			
	If defendant is	Personal service is made on	Substitute or constructive service may be made on
32	Unincorporated association	• Person designated as agent for service of process in statement filed with Secretary of State. CCP §416.40(b); Corp. C. §18200(a)(2)(B). • President or other head of association, vice president, secretary or assistant secretary, treasurer or assistant treasurer, general manager, or person authorized by association to receive service of process. CCP §416.40(b).	• Person who is apparently in charge of office, place of business, or usual mailing address of person authorized to be served (other than a U.S. post-office box) and is at least 18. CCP §415.20(a). • Members of association designated by court order if the defendant has not designated agent or agent cannot be served with reasonable diligence. Corp. C. §18220.
33	Ward or conservatee (incompetent adult)	• The ward or conservatee. CCP §416.70. • Guardian, conservator, or similar fiduciary. *Id.*	• Person who is competent member of defendant's household and is at least 18. CCP §415.20(b). • Person who is apparently in charge of defendant's office, place of business, or usual mailing address (other than a U.S. post-office box) and is at least 18. *Id.*

§7. DEADLINE FOR SERVICE

For a discussion of how to calculate deadlines, see "When to Serve," ch. 1-G, §6, p. 69.

NOTE

For a discussion of the effect of fast-track rules on dismissals for delay in prosecution under CCP §583.210 et seq., see "Effect of Fast-Track Rules," ch. 10-E, §3, p. 1161.

§7.1 Limited & unlimited civil cases.

1. Timely service. In most civil cases (except unlawful-detainer actions, Family Code cases, or proceedings governed by other law), the plaintiff must complete service of process by the following deadlines:

(1) Original complaint. The summons and complaint must be served on all defendants named in the original complaint within 60 days after the complaint is filed, except in collections cases. CRC 3.110(a)-(b); *see* Gov. C. §68603(a) (requiring Judicial Council to adopt standards for timely disposition of civil actions). In collections cases, the summons and complaint must be served on all defendants named in the original complaint within 180 days after the complaint is filed. CRC 3.740(d). See "Collections case," ch. 3-C, §3.1.2(1), p. 211.

(2) Amended complaint. When a complaint is amended to add a new defendant, the summons and a copy of the amended complaint must be served on the new defendant within 30 days after the amended complaint is filed. CRC 3.110(b).

(3) Cross-complaint. When a cross-complaint adds a new party, the summons and a copy of the cross-complaint must be served on the new party within 30 days after the cross-complaint is filed. CRC 3.110(c). A copy of the cross-complaint must also be served on all other parties by the same deadline. *Id.*

2. Extension of time to serve. If the plaintiff cannot timely complete service of the original, amended, or cross complaint, it may be able to get an extension of time by filing an ex parte application. To get an extension, the plaintiff must do the following:

(1) File the application before the applicable deadline has passed. CRC 3.110(e).

(2) Attach a declaration to the application that (1) explains why service has not been completed, (2) documents the party's attempts to complete service, and (3) proposes a new deadline for the party to complete service. CRC 3.110(e). If the plaintiff is using Judicial Council Form CM-020, a separate declaration is unnecessary.

PRACTICE TIP

Be sure to check your local rules to determine if the court has a different procedure for getting an extension of time to file the original complaint. See Gov. C. §68616(a) (by local rule, court can authorize extension of 60-day period for filing original complaint); see, e.g., Super. Ct. Fresno Cty. Loc. R., rule 2.1.6.A (P may file noticed motion or ex parte application to extend time based on good cause).

3. Effect of untimely service. If the summons and complaint are not timely served, and if the plaintiff has not obtained an order extending the time to serve, the court can issue an order to show cause why sanctions should not be imposed or why the action against the defendant should not be dismissed. CRC 3.110(f); *see* CCP §583.150. See "Involuntary Dismissal—Delay in Prosecution," ch. 10-E, p. 1160.

§7.2 Small-claims cases. The deadline for service of the claim and order in a small-claims action depends on where the defendant resides.

1. Defendant in county. If the defendant resides in the county where the small-claims action is filed, copies of the claim and order must be served at least 15 days before the hearing date. CCP §116.340(b).

2. Defendant outside county. If the defendant does not reside in the county where the small-claims action is filed, copies of the claim and order must be served at least 20 days before the hearing date. CCP §116.340(b).

§8. WAIVER OF SERVICE

A defendant can waive service of process by entering a general appearance in the action. *See* CCP §410.50(a). For a discussion of when a defendant makes a general appearance, see "General appearance," ch. 3-G, §5.1.1, p. 285.

§9. PROOF OF SERVICE

A properly executed proof of service informs the court that the plaintiff has completed all acts necessary to serve process on the defendant. *See, e.g.*, ***Dill v. Berquist Constr. Co.*** (4th Dist.1994) 24 Cal.App.4th 1426, 1442 & n.15 (proofs of service were not properly executed and thus did not show that all necessary acts were completed). If the proof of service complies with all relevant statutory requirements, a rebuttable presumption that service was proper will arise when the proof is filed. ***Floveyor Int'l v. Superior Ct.*** (2d Dist.1997) 59 Cal.App.4th 789, 795; ***Dill***, 24 Cal.App.4th at 1441-42.

§9.1 Establishing proof of service. Proof of service is usually established by filing a form with the court. However, proof of service can also be established when the person being served does either of the following:

1. Executes a written admission acknowledging receipt of the summons and complaint. CCP §§417.10(d), 417.20(d). If the person is being served by mail, the serving party can have the person execute Judicial Council Form POS-015 to admit service. *See* CCP §415.30(e).

2. Makes a general appearance before the deadline to file the proof of service. CCP §417.30; *see* CCP §583.220; *see, e.g.*, ***Biss v. Bohr*** (4th Dist.1995) 40 Cal.App.4th 1246, 1251 (answer before deadline made filing return of summons unnecessary); ***Wong v. Armstrong World Indus.*** (1st Dist.1991) 232 Cal.App.3d 1032, 1034-35 (same). See "General appearance," ch. 3-G, §5.1.1, p. 285.

§9.2 Forms.

1. Service under California law. When service of process is made under California law, the proof of service must be based on the following forms.

(1) Judicial Council forms. The forms for proof of service created by the Judicial Council are mandatory. *See* CCP §417.10(f) (Judicial Council form is mandatory for personal service). The forms can be downloaded or filled out online and printed from the California Courts' website, www.courts.ca.gov/forms.htm. The following forms are necessary for proof of service of process:

(a) Judicial Council Form POS-010, proof of service of summons.

(b) Judicial Council Form POS-015, notice and acknowledgment of receipt.

(2) User-generated forms. A plaintiff is allowed to use its own form for proof of service instead of Judicial Council Form POS-010 if the plaintiff's form (1) is prepared entirely by word processor, typewriter, or similar process and (2) complies with the detailed formatting, font, and content requirements listed under CRC 2.150(a). *See* CRC 2.150(a). The form prepared by the plaintiff must copy the contents of Form POS-010 word-for-word except for the instructions. CRC 2.150(a)(3).

2. Service under foreign law. When service of process is made under foreign law, the proof of service must comply with the form used in the foreign jurisdiction. *See* CCP §417.20(c); Judicial Council of Cal. Ann. Rep. (1969) p. 59. If necessary, the California court can impose additional requirements for the proof of service for due-process reasons. *See* CCP §417.20(c); Judicial Council of Cal. Ann. Rep. (1969) p. 59. For example, the court may require the plaintiff to include a statement with the proof of service that explains the foreign law governing service of process and proof of service. Judicial Council of Cal. Ann. Rep. (1969) p. 59. See "Service under foreign law," §9.4.2(3), p. 322.

§9.3 Who completes form. The proof-of-service form must be completed by the person who served the papers. CCP §417.10(a), (e). See "Who Can Serve Process," §4, p. 300. If the defendant is served by publication, the proof-of-service form must be completed by the publisher or printer, or the publisher's or printer's foreperson or principal clerk. CCP §417.10(b). See "Service by publication," §9.4.1(5)(d)[1], p. 321.

SERVICE OF PROCESS

§9.4 Contents of form.

1. Service made in California. In most civil actions, Judicial Council Form POS-010 must be used to prove service of process made in California. The person serving the summons and complaint (referred to as the "serving person") must complete the following items on Judicial Council Form POS-010:

(1) Heading. In the heading of Form POS-010, the serving person must identify (1) who is causing the proof of service to be filed (the attorney or a pro per party), that person's address, telephone number, fax number (optional), and e-mail address (optional), the attorney's state bar number (if not pro per), and the name of the party represented by the attorney (if not pro per), (2) the court name, address, and branch name, and (3) the case name and number.

(2) Papers served. Item 2 of Form POS-010 requires the serving person to designate which papers were served on the defendant. See "Papers served," §3.3, p. 299.

(3) Person served. Item 3 of Form POS-010 requires the serving person to identify the defendant and, if necessary, the person accepting service on the defendant's behalf (e.g., an agent for service of process). See "Identification of defendant," §3.1.2(1), p. 296.

(a) Party served. Item 3a requires the serving person to identify the name of the defendant, as stated in the service papers. *See* CCP §417.10(a).

(b) Person served for party. Item 3b requires the serving person to identify the name of the person served for the defendant and her relationship to the defendant—that is, whether the person has been served on behalf of an entity (e.g., corporation) or as an authorized agent for service of process. *See* CCP §417.10(a); *see, e.g.*, ***Dill v. Berquist Constr. Co.*** (4th Dist.1994) 24 Cal.App.4th 1426, 1441-42 (proof of service showing that summons was addressed only to corporations and not specific persons to be served did not raise presumption of proper service). See "Identification of status of person served," §3.1.2(2), p. 296. Item 3b of Form POS-010 does not require the serving person to identify the name of the person on whom substitute service was made.

(4) Address. Item 4 of Form POS-010 requires the serving person to state the address where the process was served. *See* CCP §417.10(a).

(5) Method of service. Item 5 of Form POS-010 requires the serving person to identify which method of service was used. *See* CCP §417.10(a). See "Methods of Service," §5, p. 301.

CAUTION

When the action is brought against a corporation or an unincorporated association and process is served by personal delivery, mail, or substitute service, the proof of service must show that the notice required under CCP §412.30 appeared on the copy of the summons served, if in fact it did. See CCP §417.10(a); see also id. §412.30 (no default judgment against corporation or association if notice not included on summons). See "Corporation or association," §3.1.2(2)(c), p. 297. However, nothing in Form POS-010 suggests that the serving person needs to make this certification. If the plaintiff wants to make the certification required by CCP §417.10(a), it should include a declaration from the serving person stating that the notice appeared on the summons.

(a) Personal service. If the defendant was personally served, Item 5a requires the serving person to state the date and time that service was completed. *See* CCP §§415.10, 417.10(a). See "Service by personal delivery," §5.1.1, p. 301.

(b) Substitute service. If the defendant is served by substitute service, Item 5b requires the serving person to do all the following:

[1] State the date and time the papers were served. *See* CCP §417.10(a). See "Substitute service," §5.1.3, p. 302.

[2] Identify the person with whom the papers were left. *See* CCP §§415.20, 417.10(a). See "Substitute service," §5.1.3, p. 302.

[3] Indicate the location where the papers were left (i.e., business, home, or mailing address). *See* CCP §§415.20, 417.10(a). See "Leave service papers at office or mailing address," §5.1.3(1)(a), p. 303; "Leave service papers at house, business, or mailing address," §5.1.3(2)(b), p. 303.

[4] Indicate the service papers were mailed to the person served at the place where copies of the papers were left. *See* CCP §415.20. See "Mail service papers to place where papers were left," §5.1.3(1)(b), p. 303; "Mail service papers to place where papers were left," §5.1.3(2)(c), p. 304. Item 5b(4) allows the plaintiff to either (1) state in the proof of service the date the copies were mailed and the city they were mailed from or (2) attach a declaration of mailing.

[5] If the defendant is a person, attach a declaration of diligence that describes the serving person's attempts to personally serve the defendant before resorting to substitute service. *See* CCP §415.20(b). See "Determine personal service cannot be completed," §5.1.3(2)(a), p. 303.

(c) Service by mail. If the defendant is served by mail, Item 5c requires the serving person to do all the following:

[1] State the date the service papers were mailed and the city they were mailed from. *See* CCP §417.10(a). See "Service by U.S. mail," §5.1.2, p. 302.

[2] Indicate whether the service papers were:

[a] Mailed with two copies of the notice and acknowledgment of receipt and a postage-paid return envelope addressed to the plaintiff. CCP §§415.30(a), 417.10(a); *see* ***Shoei Kako Co. v. Superior Ct.*** (1st Dist.1973) 33 Cal.App.3d 808, 816 n.2 (service by mail not effective until written acknowledgment received). See "Service by U.S. mail," §5.1.2, p. 302. If the service papers were mailed with the notice, Item 5c(3) requires the serving person to attach a completed notice to the proof of service.

[b] Mailed to an out-of-state address with return receipt requested. *See* CCP §415.40.

(d) Other method. If the defendant is served by another method, Item 5d requires the serving person to (1) specify the method used, (2) indicate the statute allowing service by this method, and (3) if necessary, attach an additional page to the proof of service describing how service was made. *See* CCP §417.10(c). If the statute does not include proof-of-service requirements, the proof of service must satisfy the requirements for a similar manner of service under CCP §417.10. *See id.* §417.10(c); *see also id.* §413.30 (court can impose requirements for proof of service when not specified by other law). Some of the more common methods include the following:

[1] Service by publication. If the defendant is served by publication, the proof of service must include (1) an affidavit from the publisher or printer, or the publisher's or printer's foreperson or principal clerk, stating the time and place of publication, and (2) an affidavit stating the time and place that copies of the summons and complaint were mailed to the defendant, if copies were in fact mailed. CCP §417.10(b). See "Service by publication," §5.1.4, p. 304.

[2] Service by posting. If the defendant is served in an unlawful-detainer action by posting the summons on the property, the proof of service must include (1) an affidavit from the person who posted the summons stating the time and place of posting, and (2) an affidavit stating the time and place that copies of the summons and complaint were mailed to the defendant, if copies were in fact mailed. CCP §417.10(e). See "Service by posting," §5.1.5, p. 306. If the unlawful-detainer action involves a prejudgment claim for possession of the property, the proof of service must also include a statement that service of process was completed according to CCP §415.46. *See* CCP §415.46(d). See "Prejudgment claim for possession," §5.4.2(2), p. 311.

(6) Capacity of party served. Item 6 of Form POS-010 requires the serving person to indicate in what capacity the defendant is receiving the service papers (e.g., as defendant, as agent for corporate defendant). See "Identification of status of person served," §3.1.2(2), p. 296. If the defendant is being served under a fictitious name, Item 6b of Form POS-010 requires the serving person to state the fictitious name. *See* CCP §474; ***Pelayo v. J.J. Lee Mgmt. Co.*** (2d Dist.2009) 174 Cal.App.4th 484, 496. The serving person should also state that notice of identity was given by endorsement on the copy of the summons or complaint. CCP §474; *see* ***Armstrong v. Superior Ct.*** (2d Dist.1956) 144 Cal.App.2d 420, 424 (notice under CCP §474 is mandatory for court to have jurisdiction over person sued under fictitious name). See "Fictitious name," §3.1.2(2)(b), p. 297.

(7) Server's identity. Item 7 of Form POS-010 requires the serving person to identify herself. *See* CCP §417.40; *see also* Bus. & Prof. C. §22351(a) (registration of process servers).

(a) Name, address, telephone number. Items 7a, 7b, and 7c require the serving person to state her name, address, and telephone number.

(b) Fee for service. Item 7d requires the serving person to state the fee for service, if any.

(c) Status as process server. Item 7e requires the serving person to state whether she is either a registered California process server or exempt from registration. *See* Bus. & Prof. C. §22350. If the person is a registered process server, Item 7e(3) requires her to state (1) whether she is an owner, employee, or independent contractor, (2) her registration number, and (3) her county of registration. *See* CCP §417.40.

(8) Declaration or certification. Items 8 and 9 of Form POS-010 require the serving person to either (1) declare under penalty of perjury that the contents of the proof of service are true and correct or (2) identify herself as a California sheriff or marshal and certify that the contents of the proof of service are true and correct. *See* CCP §417.10(a), (b) & (e) (proof of service in California by affidavit), §417.20(e) (proof of service on nonresident by posting must include affidavit), §2009 (affidavit can be used to prove service in action or special proceeding).

2. Service outside California. There is no Judicial Council form for proof of service made outside California. The form of the proof of service will depend on how the serving person serves the summons and complaint.

(1) Service under California statute. If the defendant is served under a California statute, the proof of service must include the information required by CCP §417.10. *See* CCP §417.20(a). Because Judicial Council Form POS-010 satisfies the requirements of CCP §417.10, the serving person should follow that form when completing the proof of service. *See, e.g.*, ***Cruz v. Fagor Am., Inc.*** (4th Dist.2007) 146 Cal.App.4th 488, 497 (P completed and signed Judicial Council proof-of-service form for service on nonresident D).

(a) Return receipt or other evidence. If the summons and complaint are served by mail under CCP §415.40, the proof of service must also include a return receipt or other evidence to satisfy the court that the copies of the summons and complaint were actually delivered to the defendant. CCP §417.20(a); *see, e.g.*, ***Cruz***, 146 Cal.App.4th at 498 (to establish actual delivery, P attached signed return receipt to proof-of-service form); ***Bolkiah v. Superior Ct.*** (2d Dist.1999) 74 Cal.App.4th 984, 1001 (to establish actual delivery, P introduced evidence that it mailed copies of summons and complaint to multiple addresses listed by Ds on regular correspondence with P and that P had been directed by Ds to send all correspondence to one of those addresses); ***In re Marriage of Tusinger*** (2d Dist.1985) 170 Cal.App.3d 80, 82-83 (to establish actual delivery, court took judicial notice of letter sent by D's attorney to P's attorney acknowledging that D had received divorce petition days earlier); ***Stamps v. Superior Ct.*** (3d Dist.1971) 14 Cal.App.3d 108, 110 (return receipt that was not signed but returned marked "unclaimed" was not proof of actual delivery). See "Service by U.S. mail," §5.2.2, p. 307.

(b) Authority to receive mail. If the summons and complaint are served by mail and the serving person includes a signed return receipt that is not signed by the defendant, the serving person may need to submit additional evidence establishing that the person who signed the receipt was authorized to receive mail on the defendant's behalf. *See* ***Neadeau v. Foster*** (3d Dist.1982) 129 Cal.App.3d 234, 237-38; *see, e.g.*, ***Cruz***, 146 Cal.App.4th at 498-99 (P's attorney submitted declaration that he confirmed with U.S. Postal Service that person who signed receipt regularly received mail on D's behalf); ***Dill***, 24 Cal.App.4th at 1441 (validity of service was not established when only evidence was proof of service showing that summons was addressed to corporate Ds and not specific persons to be served). See "Return receipt," §5.2.2(2)(b), p. 307.

(2) Service under court order. If the defendant is served under a court order, the proof of service must include any information required by the order. CCP §417.20(b).

(3) Service under foreign law. If the defendant is served under the law of a foreign jurisdiction where she is located, the proof of service must include any information required for an action in the courts of general jurisdiction of the place where the defendant is served. CCP §417.20(c); *e.g.*, ***Floveyor Int'l v. Superior Ct.*** (2d Dist.1997) 59 Cal.App.4th 789, 795-96 (D served in England under Hague Convention). See "Defendant outside U.S.," §5.3, p. 308. The court can impose additional requirements for proof of service to satisfy due process. *See* CCP §417.20(c).

(4) Service by posting. If the defendant is served in an unlawful-detainer action by posting the summons on the property, the proof of service must include (1) an affidavit from the person who posted the summons stating the time and place of posting and (2) an affidavit stating the time and place that copies of the summons and complaint were mailed to the defendant, if copies were in fact mailed. CCP §417.20(e). See "Service by posting," §5.1.5, p. 306.

§9.5 Deadline to file. The plaintiff must file a proof of service with the court by the applicable deadline listed below.

PRACTICE TIP

File your proof of service as soon as possible. If the proof of service is not timely filed, the delay may cast doubt about whether the defendant was properly served. See, e.g., ***Graf v. Gaslight*** *(2d Dist.1990) 225 Cal.App.3d 291, 295 (delay of nearly seven months between time summons and complaint were served and time proof of service was filed created doubt about veracity of alleged service of process), disapproved on other grounds,* ***Watts v. Crawford*** *(1995) 10 Cal.4th 743.*

---

1. Limited & unlimited civil actions.

(1) Determining deadline.

(a) Original complaint. Proof of service of the original complaint must be filed within 60 days after the complaint is filed, unless the court modifies the deadline. CRC 3.110(b), (e).

(b) **Amended complaint.** Proof of service of an amended complaint that adds a new defendant must be served on the new defendant within 30 days after the amended complaint is filed. CRC 3.110(b).

(c) **Cross-complaint.**

[1] **Party has appeared.** Proof of service of a cross-complaint against a party who has appeared in the action must be filed when the cross-complaint is filed. CRC 3.110(c).

[2] **New party.** Proof of service of a cross-complaint against a new party to the action must be filed within 30 days after the cross-complaint is filed. CRC 3.110(c).

(2) Modifying deadline. The court, on its own or a party's motion, can shorten or extend the deadline to file the proof of service. CRC 3.110(e). If a party files a motion to extend time, the motion must be:

(a) Filed by the serving party before the original deadline for proof of service. *Id.*

(b) Accompanied by a declaration that explains why service has not been completed, documents the party's attempts to complete service, and proposes a new deadline for the party to complete service. *Id.*

(3) Effect of untimely filing. Neither the Code of Civil Procedure nor the California Rules of Court authorize dismissal of an action if proof of service is not timely filed. Dismissal is authorized only when actual service of the summons and complaint is not completed by the appropriate deadline. *See* CCP §583.250(a)(2). For a discussion of dismissal for untimely service, see "No service of summons & complaint," ch. 10-E, §4.1, p. 1162.

2. Small-claims actions. Proof of service of the claim and order must be filed at least five days before the hearing. CCP §116.340(c).

§9.6 Default judgment. Proof of service should be filed before a default judgment is entered, but a default judgment is not invalid simply because proof of service has not been filed. *See* ***Herman v. Santee*** (1894) 103 Cal. 519, 523-25; ***National Diversified Servs. v. Bernstein*** (6th Dist.1985) 168 Cal.App.3d 410, 416. *But see* CCP §1169 (proof of service must be filed before default judgment in unlawful-detainer proceeding). The court acquires jurisdiction to enter judgment against a defendant when the defendant is served with process, not when the proof of service is filed. ***Herman***, 103 Cal. at 523; ***Courtney v. Abex Corp.*** (1st Dist.1986) 176 Cal.App.3d 343, 346-47. If proof of service is not filed before entry of a default judgment, the court can allow the plaintiff to file proof of service nunc pro tunc, which is deemed filed on the date the default judgment was entered. *See* ***Herman***, 103 Cal. at 523-24.

SERVICE OF PROCESS

§10. FEES FOR SERVICE

The fee for service of process depends on who served the process.

15 **§10.1 Public officer.** If process is served by a public officer, the plaintiff pays the fee authorized by law at the time of service. *See* CCP §1033.5(a)(4)(A). The current statutory fee is $40. Gov. C. §26720.9; *see id.* §26721.

§10.2 Registered process server. If process is served by a registered process server, the plaintiff pays the amount actually incurred in making service or some other negotiated fee. *See* CCP §1033.5(a)(4)(B). This fee may include costs for a stakeout or other means used to locate the defendant. *See id.*

§10.3 Publisher. If process is served by publication, the plaintiff pays the amount actually incurred in making service. *See* CCP §1033.5(a)(4)(C).

§10.4 Other person. If process is served by any person other than a public officer, registered process server, or publisher, the plaintiff pays either the amount actually incurred in making service or the amount allowed to a public officer, whichever is less. *See* CCP §1033.5(a)(4)(D). See "Public officer," §10.1, this page.

NOTE

All expenses for service of process can be recovered as costs if the plaintiff prevails in the action. See CCP §1033.5(a)(4).

§11. AMENDING SUMMONS & PROOF OF SERVICE

§11.1 Amending summons. If the plaintiff amends the complaint, it is not required to obtain an amended or additional summons to serve the amended complaint on a defendant subject to the court's jurisdiction. ***Engebretson & Co. v. Harrison*** (4th Dist.1981) 125 Cal.App.3d 436, 441 & n.3; Judicial Council of Cal. Ann. Rep. (1969) pp. 37-38. However, the plaintiff may need to obtain an amended or additional summons in the following circumstances.

1. **Amendment before service.** If the complaint is substantively amended before any service of process is made, the plaintiff should secure from the court clerk an amended summons that refers to the amended complaint. ***Gillette v. Burbank Cmty. Hosp.*** (2d Dist.1976) 56 Cal.App.3d 430, 433; Judicial Council of Cal. Ann. Rep. (1969) p. 37; *see, e.g.*, ***Levin v. Ligon*** (1st Dist.2006) 140 Cal.App.4th 1456, 1461 (plaintiff filed amended summons withdrawing claim). *But see* ***Engebretson & Co.***, 125 Cal.App.3d at 441 n.3 (absence of statutory provision requiring service of new or amended summons with amended complaint strongly implies there is no such requirement). If the amended complaint makes only technical or other nonsubstantive changes, an amended summons is not necessary. *See* ***Gillette***, 56 Cal.App.3d at 433-34.

2. **Added defendant.** If the complaint is amended to add a new defendant, the plaintiff must secure from the court clerk an amended summons that refers to the new defendant and amended complaint. ***Gillette***, 56 Cal.App.3d at 433; Judicial Council of Cal. Ann. Rep. (1969) pp. 37-38.

§11.2 Amending proof of service. The proof of service can be amended at any time to reflect the actual facts of service on the defendant. *See, e.g.*, ***City of Salinas v. Lee*** (1933) 217 Cal. 252, 254-55 (amended affidavit of service entered several years after judgment); ***Herman v. Santee*** (1894) 103 Cal. 519, 523-25 (amended proof of service filed after default judgment); ***McGinn v. Rees*** (1st Dist.1917) 33 Cal.App. 291, 295 (proposed amended proof of service should have been allowed because it conformed to facts and supported default judgment); *see also* ***Drinnon v. Oliver*** (1st Dist.1972) 24 Cal.App.3d 571, 585 (defective affidavit of service is not fatal to court's jurisdiction and can be amended), *disapproved on other grounds*, ***Johnson & Johnson v. Superior Ct.*** (1985) 38 Cal.3d 243.

California Civil Pretrial

Chapter 4. Defendant's Responses & Pleadings

Table of Contents

CHAPTER 4. DEFENDANT'S RESPONSES & PLEADINGS
TABLE OF CONTENTS

CHAPTER 4. DEFENDANT'S RESPONSES & PLEADINGS
TABLE OF CONTENTS

Table of Contents

4. DEFENDANT'S RESPONSES & PLEADINGS

A. OVERVIEW

§1. GENERAL

§1.1 Purpose. After service of process, the defendant must respond to the complaint with a responsive pleading or other motion to avoid default. *See* CCP §585(a)-(c), (e) (clerk must enter default on request unless D files answer, demurrer, or other designated motion within time specified in summons or allowed by court); ***Barragan v. Banco BCH*** (4th Dist.1986) 188 Cal.App.3d 283, 297 (same).

§1.2 Primary authority. CCP §§418.10, 410.30.

§1.3 Secondary authority. The following secondary sources are cited as authority in this subchapter:

- *California Civil Procedure Before Trial* (CEB Online ed. 2014) (referred to as *CEB Procedure Before Trial*).
- ***O'Connor's Federal Rules * Civil Trials*** (2015) (referred to as ***O'Connor's Federal Rules***).

§2. PREANSWER CONSIDERATIONS

Before answering a complaint (or cross-complaint), a defendant should consider (1) its obligations under any applicable insurance policy, (2) the possibility and desirability of avoiding litigation through settlement or alternative dispute resolution, (3) whether its response will constitute a general appearance, and (4) whether the plaintiff complied with any applicable prefiling notice requirements.

§2.1 Obligations to insurer. If the claim is covered by insurance, the defendant should read its policy and give its insurance carrier all the proper notices required under the policy. If notice is not given, the insurer is usually relieved of liability for any covered claims if the insurer can show it was prejudiced by the lack of notice. *See* ***Billington v. Interinsurance Exch.*** (1969) 71 Cal.2d 728, 737 (insurer protected from liability only when lack of compliance with policy results in substantial prejudice to insurer); ***Campbell v. Allstate Ins.*** (1963) 60 Cal.2d 303, 305-06 (even without notice, insurer still liable if it does not show substantial prejudice).

§2.2 Avoiding litigation.

1. Settlement. After suit is filed and the defendant has had a reasonable time to evaluate the merits of the plaintiff's claim, the defendant should consider making a reasonable offer to settle. *See CEB Procedure Before Trial*, §46.3. If the defendant makes a good-faith offer of judgment in writing under CCP §998 that the plaintiff rejects and the plaintiff does not obtain a more favorable judgment, the plaintiff (1) cannot recover its postoffer costs, (2) must pay the defendant's costs from the time of the offer, and (3) may be required to pay the defendant's reasonable expert-witness fees. CCP §998(b), (c)(1); ***Adams v. Ford Motor Co.*** (2d Dist.2011) 199 Cal.App.4th 1475, 1482-83 & n.8.

2. Alternative dispute resolution. If the parties are required by contract or statute to submit a dispute to a form of alternative dispute resolution (ADR), the defendant should determine whether and how to ask the court to compel ADR and stay the proceeding. *See, e.g.*, CCP §1281.7 (petition to compel arbitration based on written agreement under CCP §1281.2 can be filed instead of answer); ***Compulink Mgmt. Ctr., Inc. v. St. Paul Fire & Mar. Ins.*** (2d Dist.2008) 169 Cal.App.4th 289, 296 (D-insurer petitioned court under Civ. C. §2860(c) to compel arbitration on amount of attorney fees allegedly owed for defense provided by P-insured's independent counsel).

§2.3 Type of appearance.

1. General appearance. A defendant subjects itself to the jurisdiction of the court by making a general appearance. ***Fireman's Fund Ins. v. Sparks Constr., Inc.*** (4th Dist.2004) 114 Cal.App.4th 1135, 1145; ***Titus v. Superior Ct.*** (1st Dist.1972) 23 Cal.App.3d 792, 800-01; *see* CCP §410.50(a) (general appearance is equivalent to personal service of summons). A general appearance includes an answer, a demurrer, a notice of motion to strike, a notice of motion to transfer under CCP §396b, a motion for reclassification under CCP §403.040, and a notice of

OVERVIEW

appearance (made in writing or orally through the defendant's attorney as noted in court records). CCP §1014; *see, e.g.*, ***Fireman's Fund***, 114 Cal.App.4th at 1145 (although complaint was ineffectively served, Ds were subject to court's jurisdiction after filing answers). Actions other than those listed in CCP §1014 can subject a defendant to the court's jurisdiction. ***Hamilton v. Asbestos Corp.*** (2000) 22 Cal.4th 1127, 1147. For a list of other actions that have been held to constitute a general appearance, see ***Dial 800 v. Fesbinder*** (2d Dist.2004) 118 Cal.App.4th 32, 53-54.

2. Special appearance. A defendant does not subject itself to the jurisdiction of the court by making a special appearance. CCP §418.10(e)(1); ***Air Mach. Com SRL v. Superior Ct.*** (4th Dist.2010) 186 Cal.App.4th 414, 426. A special appearance is a motion under CCP §418.10 to (1) quash service for lack of jurisdiction, (2) dismiss or stay the action because of inconvenient forum, or (3) dismiss the action for failure to prosecute. *See* CCP §418.10(a), (e)(1), (e)(3). When a defendant successfully makes a special appearance, no motion or other action of the defendant will constitute a general appearance until the entry of the court's order denying the §418.10 motion. CCP §418.10(e)(1).

NOTE

Even though federal courts abolished the distinction between the common-law general and special appearances in 1937, California continues to recognize it. ***Air Mach. Com****, 186 Cal.App.4th at 427.*

§2.4 Prefiling requirements. See "Before Suit," ch. 3-A, p. 189.

§3. ORDER OF DEFENDANT'S RESPONSES

§3.1 Removal. The purpose of a notice of removal is to allow a defendant to remove a case from state court to federal court when the federal court would have original jurisdiction over the subject matter. *See* 28 U.S.C. §§1441-1455; ***City of Chi. v. International Coll. of Surgeons*** (1997) 522 U.S. 156, 163. The reasons a defendant might choose to remove a case to federal court are varied, and include trying to avoid local prejudice or having the case tried before a judge who may be more familiar with the law at issue. For a discussion of the procedure for notice of removal, and the plaintiff's motion for remand, see ***O'Connor's Federal Rules***, "Removal & Remand," ch. 4, p. 265. For a discussion of the motions a defendant can file if the removal is denied and the suit is remanded back to the state superior court, see "Deadline to answer after remand," ch. 4-B, §2.1.2(3), p. 336.

§3.2 Preanswer motions & pleadings. The purpose of a preanswer motion is to eliminate unnecessary delay at the pleading stage. *See, e.g.*, ***Roy v. Superior Ct.*** (4th Dist.2005) 127 Cal.App.4th 337, 344 (CCP §418.10(e)(3) requires D to file motion to quash challenging personal jurisdiction at first possible instance, thus promoting judicial economy). Most preanswer motions must be filed before or simultaneously with the answer; otherwise, the issue challenged by the preanswer motion will be waived. *See* ***Roy***, 127 Cal.App.4th at 344 (motion to quash must be filed simultaneously with other preanswer motions). Some preanswer motions, however, must be filed before or simultaneously with other preanswer motions—namely, before or with a demurrer or motion to strike—to avoid waiver. CCP §418.10(e)(3). The types of preanswer motions that can be filed include the following:

1. Motion to quash service of summons. CCP §418.10(a)(1). A motion to quash is used to challenge the court's exercise of personal jurisdiction over the defendant. See "Motion to Quash Service of Summons," ch. 4-G, p. 389. A motion to quash must be filed before or simultaneously with a motion to strike or a demurrer or the defendant will waive its right to contest personal jurisdiction. *See* CCP §418.10(e)(3); ***Roy***, 127 Cal.App.4th at 344.

2. Motion to dismiss or stay for forum non conveniens (FNC). CCP §418.10(a)(2); *see id.* §410.30. A motion to dismiss or stay for FNC is used to ask the court to dismiss or stay the action because a court outside California would have jurisdiction over the dispute and is a more appropriate forum for hearing the action. See "Forum Non Conveniens," ch. 4-F, p. 375. A motion for FNC can be filed before or after the defendant has made a general appearance, but it cannot be filed after the defendant files a motion to strike or demurrer. ***Britton v. Dallas Airmotive,***

Inc. (1st Dist.2007) 153 Cal.App.4th 127, 133-34. If the motion is not filed before or simultaneously with a motion to strike or demurrer, the defendant will waive its right to contest the forum on the basis of FNC. CCP §418.10(e)(3); ***Britton***, 153 Cal.App.4th at 133.

3. Motion to dismiss under CCP §§583.110-583.430. CCP §418.10(a)(3). A motion to dismiss under §583.110 et seq. is used to ask the court to dismiss the action because the plaintiff has not timely prosecuted it. See "Involuntary Dismissal—Delay in Prosecution," ch. 10-E, p. 1160. For certain motions for delay in prosecution, the defendant must file the motion before or simultaneously with a motion to strike or a demurrer or it is waived. CCP §418.10(e)(3).

4. General demurrer. *See* CCP §422.10. A general demurrer is used to challenge defects that appear on the face of the complaint or that can be established by judicially noticed facts. The defects that can be challenged by a general demurrer are a court's lack of subject-matter jurisdiction and a complaint that is legally insufficient to support a cause of action. See "General demurrer," ch. 4-H, §3.1, p. 398.

5. Special demurrer. *See* CCP §§422.10, 430.10. A special demurrer is used to challenge defects that appear on the face of the complaint or that can be established by judicially noticed facts. The defects that can be challenged by a special demurrer include the following: lack of capacity to bring suit; concurrent jurisdiction; nonjoinder or misjoinder of a party; and an uncertain, ambiguous, or unintelligible complaint. See "Special demurrer," ch. 4-H, §3.2, p. 400.

6. Motion to strike. CCP §435. A motion to strike is used to challenge the legal sufficiency of all or part of a complaint. Possible challenges include (1) the complaint alleges irrelevant, false, or improper matters and (2) the complaint is drafted or filed in violation of the laws of California, a court rule, or a court order. See "Motion to Strike," ch. 4-J, p. 418.

NOTE

Although a defendant usually makes a general appearance when it files an answer, a motion to strike, or a demurrer, a general appearance is not made if those responses are filed simultaneously with a successful motion to quash, motion to dismiss or stay for forum non conveniens, or motion to dismiss for delay in prosecution. CCP §418.10(e)(1). See "Preanswer motions & pleadings," §3.2, p. 330.

---

7. Motion to transfer to proper court. CCP §396b; *see id.* §396b(a) (motion can be filed by itself). A motion to transfer to the proper court is used to challenge the plaintiff's choice of venue on the grounds that the case was filed in an improper court. *See id.* §396b(a). See "Motion to Transfer to Proper Court," ch. 4-E, §3, p. 360.

8. Petition to compel arbitration. CCP §§1281.2, 1281.7. A petition to compel arbitration is filed in lieu of an answer to enforce a written agreement to arbitrate the controversy. *Id.* §1281.7; *see id.* §1281.2. A motion to stay the suit pending arbitration can be filed with the petition. *Id.* §1281.4. See "Pending arbitration," ch. 5-I, §3.6, p. 546.

§3.3 Answer, denial & cross-complaint. The purpose of the answer (or denial) and cross-complaint is to either challenge matters alleged in the plaintiff's complaint, assert affirmative relief, or both.

1. Answer. CCP §422.10. An answer is generally used to deny material allegations in the complaint that the defendant believes are untrue, to assert affirmative defenses, and to challenge defects that do not appear on the face of the complaint or cannot be established by judicially noticed facts. *See id.* §431.20(a) (allegations not controverted by answer can be taken as true). See "Answer," ch. 4-B, p. 332.

2. General denial. CCP §431.40. For cases in which the amount in controversy is no more than $1,000, a general denial can be filed instead of an answer. *Id.* See "General denials," ch. 4-B, §4.1, p. 340.

3. Cross-complaint. CCP §428.10. A cross-complaint is used to join other related claims and parties and certain unrelated claims to ensure a complete determination of the controversy among the parties to the action. See "Cross-Complaint," ch. 4-C, p. 349.

§3.4 Postanswer motions. The defendant can file several postanswer motions that serve similar purposes to preanswer motions and responsive pleadings and motions—namely, to promote justice or to eliminate unnecessary delay or the need for trial. The types of postanswer motions that can be filed include the following:

1. Motion to dismiss or stay for FNC under CCP §410.30(b). ***Britton v. Dallas Airmotive, Inc.*** (1st Dist.2007) 153 Cal.App.4th 127, 133-34. See "Preanswer motions & pleadings," §3.2.2, p. 330.

2. Motion to change venue. *See* CCP §§396b, 397. A motion to change venue is used to challenge the plaintiff's choice of venue on the ground that the case should be transferred to another California court even though the county of suit is otherwise proper. For example, the defendant can file a motion to change venue to another county that would be more convenient for the witnesses. CCP §397(c); *see, e.g.*, ***Thomas v. Placerville Gold Quartz Mining Co.*** (1884) 65 Cal. 600, 601 (neither P nor D can move for change of venue because of convenience of witnesses until after answer). See "Motion to Change Venue," ch. 4-E, §4, p. 365.

3. Motion for judgment on the pleadings. *See* CCP §438; ***Cordova v. 21st Century Ins.*** (2d Dist.2005) 129 Cal.App.4th 89, 109. A motion for judgment on the pleadings is used to challenge the complaint in the same manner as a general demurrer. See "Motion for Judgment on the Pleadings," ch. 4-I, p. 411.

4. Special motion to strike. CCP §§425.16-425.18. A special motion to strike is used to challenge two types of actions relating to strategic lawsuits against public participation (SLAPP). First, a special motion to strike can be used to challenge a cause of action arising from a defendant's exercise of its constitutional right of free speech or petition for the redress of grievances in connection with a public issue. *See id.* §425.16(b)(1). These motions are referred to as "anti-SLAPP motions." See "Special Motion to Strike—Anti-SLAPP Motion," ch. 4-K, p. 425. Second, a special motion to strike can be used to challenge a SLAPPback suit, which is a special action for malicious prosecution or abuse of process that arises from the dismissal of an earlier SLAPP suit (i.e., as a result of the granting of an anti-SLAPP motion). *See* CCP §425.18(a). This motion allows the defendant to seek an early dismissal of the SLAPPback based on the constitutional protections of the right to petition. See "Special Motion to Strike—Anti-SLAPPback Motion," ch. 4-L, p. 450.

B. ANSWER

§1. GENERAL

§1.1 Purpose. A party can file an answer when named as a defendant in a complaint or cross-complaint. *See* CCP §§92(a), 422.10. The defendant can use the answer to deny or admit allegations made in the complaint and to set out any defenses it may have. *Id.* §431.30(b). In most cases, an answer cannot set out a claim for affirmative relief. *See id.* §431.30(c). See "Affirmative Relief," §6, p. 346. To make a claim for affirmative relief, the defendant must file a cross-complaint. *See* CCP §428.10. See "Cross-Complaint," ch. 4-C, p. 349. Filing an answer qualifies as a general appearance (unless it is filed simultaneously with a preanswer motion) and prevents the plaintiff from seeking a default judgment. *See* CCP §§412.20(a)(4), 418.10(e)(1), 585, 1014; ***A&B Metal Prods. v. MacArthur Props., Inc.*** (1st Dist.1970) 11 Cal.App.3d 642, 647. See "Preanswer motions & pleadings," ch. 4-A, §3.2, p. 330. The answer raises fact issues for trial when it controverts the material allegations of the complaint or asserts new matters (e.g., defenses). CCP §590.

NOTE

Answers to complaints and answers to cross-complaints are largely governed by the same rules. See CCP §431.30(a)(1) ("complaint" includes cross-complaint). Third-party defendants, however, are subject to some unique rules and procedures when asserting affirmative defenses to a cross-complaint. See "Special answer," ch. 4-C, §7.1.3, p. 352.

§1.2 Primary authority. CCP §§92, 412.20, 422.10, 431.30.

§1.3 Secondary authority. The following secondary sources are cited as authority in this subchapter:

- *California Civil Procedure Before Trial* (CEB Online ed. 2014) (referred to as *CEB Procedure Before Trial*).
- Judicial Council of Cal., Civil & Small Claims Advisory Cmte., *Civil Practice & Procedure: Response to Amended Complaint* (Aug. 13, 2010), www.courts.ca.gov/documents/20101029itema12.pdf (referred to as *Report on Civil Practice & Procedure*).
- Weil & Brown, *California Practice Guide: Civil Procedure Before Trial* (CD-ROM ed. 2014) (referred to as Weil, *Civil Procedure Before Trial*).
- Witkin, *California Procedure* (5th ed. 2008 & Supp.2014) (referred to as Witkin, *Cal. Procedure*).
- Younger & Bradley, *Younger on California Motions* (2014-15) (referred to as Younger, *Cal. Motions*).
- ***O'Connor's Federal Rules * Civil Trials*** (2015) (referred to as ***O'Connor's Federal Rules***).

§1.4 Judicial Council forms. The Judicial Council has adopted form answers for cases based on breach of contract, personal injury, property damage, unlawful detainer, and wrongful death. *See* Judicial Council Forms, form PLD-C-010 (contract), form PLD-PI-003 (personal injury, property damage, and wrongful death), form UD-105 (unlawful detainer). The use of these forms is optional. *See* CRC 1.35 & Appendix A.

§2. DEADLINE TO ANSWER

§2.1 Determining deadline. The specific deadline for filing an answer depends on whether a preanswer motion was filed and ruled on first.

1. Preanswer motion filed. Filing a preanswer motion extends the deadline for filing the answer until the court rules on the motion.

(1) Court denies motion. If the court denies the preanswer motion, the defendant must serve its answer by the following deadlines:

(a) Motion to quash service. If the court denies the defendant's motion to quash service, the defendant has 15 days from the date it is served with written notice that the motion was denied to file an answer. CCP §418.10(b). The court may extend the deadline for up to 20 days when good cause is shown. *Id.* If the defendant seeks a writ of mandate for appellate review of the denial, the deadline is extended to ten days after the defendant receives notice of final judgment in the mandate proceeding. *Id.* §418.10(c). This ten-day period can be extended for up to 20 days when good cause is shown. *Id.*

(b) Motion to stay or dismiss for inconvenient forum. If the court denies the defendant's motion to stay or dismiss for inconvenient forum, the defendant has 15 days from the date it is served with written notice that the motion was denied to file an answer. CCP §418.10(b). As with quashing service, the deadline can be extended for good cause or when a writ of mandate is sought. See "Motion to quash service," §2.1.1(1)(a), this page.

(c) Motion to dismiss for delay in prosecution. If the court denies the defendant's motion to dismiss for delay in prosecution, the defendant has 15 days from the date it is served with written notice that the motion was denied to file an answer. CCP §418.10(b). As with quashing service, the deadline can be extended for good cause or when a writ of mandate is sought. See "Motion to quash service," §2.1.1(1)(a), this page.

(d) Demurrer. If the court overrules the defendant's demurrer to the complaint and an answer was not filed with the demurrer, the defendant has ten days from service of the ruling to file an answer unless the court orders otherwise. *See* CCP §§472a(b), 472b; CRC 3.1320(g); ***Skrbina v. Fleming Cos.*** (3d Dist.1996) 45 Cal.App.4th 1353, 1364. In forcible-entry, forcible-detainer, and unlawful-detainer actions, the defendant has five days to answer. CRC 3.1320(g).

(e) Motion to strike. If the court denies the defendant's motion to strike, the defendant must file an answer by the deadline set by the court. *See* CCP §472a(d) (court must allow D to file answer if it denies D's motion to strike), §1054(a) (court can extend deadline to file answer up to 30 days). See "Denies motion," ch. 4-J, §7.2.1, p. 423. Courts usually require the defendant to file an answer within ten days after the ruling. *See* Weil, *Civil Procedure Before Trial*, ¶¶7:133, 7:206.

(f) Motion to transfer venue. If the court denies the defendant's motion to transfer venue, the defendant has 30 days from the ruling to file an answer unless the court orders otherwise. CRC 3.1326; *see* CCP §396b(e).

(g) Petition to compel arbitration. If the court denies the defendant's petition to compel arbitration, the defendant has 15 days from the ruling to file an answer. CCP §1281.7.

(2) Court grants motion. If the court grants the preanswer motion, whether and when the defendant must serve its answer depend on the type of motion granted:

(a) Motion to quash service. If the court grants the defendant's motion to quash service, the suit is dismissed and no answer is filed unless the plaintiff successfully challenges the dismissal. *See* ***APRI Ins. Co. v. Superior Ct.*** (2d Dist.1999) 76 Cal.App.4th 176, 181.

(b) Motion to stay or dismiss for inconvenient forum. If the court grants the defendant's motion to stay or dismiss for inconvenient forum and the plaintiff files suit in the alternative forum, the alternative forum's laws determine if and when the defendant must file an answer.

(c) Motion to dismiss for delay in prosecution. If the court grants the defendant's motion to dismiss for delay in prosecution, the suit is dismissed and no answer is filed. *See* CCP §583.250(a)(2).

(d) Demurrer.

[1] Without leave to amend. If the court sustains a demurrer to the entire complaint without leave to amend, the suit is dismissed and no answer is filed. *See* CCP §581(f)(1); *see, e.g.*, ***Banks v. Hathaway*** (2d Dist.2002) 97 Cal.App.4th 949, 952 (court granted dismissal on its own motion based on order sustaining demurrer without leave to amend); *see also* Younger, *Cal. Motions*, §6:43 (if demurrer is sustained without leave to amend, court should do so early in case). See "Demurrer – Without Leave to Amend," ch. 10-F, §2, p. 1180. If the court sustains a partial demurrer without leave to amend, the defendant has ten days to file an answer to the remaining causes of action. CRC 3.1320(j)(3).

[2] With leave to amend.

[a] Plaintiff amends complaint. If the court sustains a demurrer with leave to amend and the plaintiff amends the complaint, the defendant must file an answer to the amended complaint within 30 days after service of the copy of amendments or the amended complaint. CCP §471.5(a); *see Report on Civil Practice & Procedure* at 2-3 (discussing how amendment to CRC 3.1320(j)(2) resolves conflict with deadline to answer under CCP §471.5).

[b] Plaintiff does not amend complaint. If the court sustains a demurrer with leave to amend and the plaintiff does not timely amend the complaint, the defendant—

- Has 10 days after the time to amend has expired to answer to the remaining causes of action that were not subject to the demurrer. CRC 3.1320(j)(2); *Report on Civil Practice & Procedure* at 3.

- Can make a motion to dismiss the entire complaint after the time to amend has expired if the demurrer was sustained as to the entire complaint. CCP §581(f)(2); *Report on Civil Practice & Procedure* at 3. The motion to dismiss the entire action and for entry of judgment is made by ex parte application. CRC 3.1320(h).

(e) Motion to strike.

[1] Without leave to amend. If the court grants a motion to strike the entire complaint without leave to amend, the suit can be dismissed (and thus no answer is necessary) if either party moves for dismissal. CCP §581(f)(3); *see* ***Vaccaro v. Kaiman*** (2d Dist.1998) 63 Cal.App.4th 761, 769. If the court grants the

defendant's motion to strike part of the complaint without leave to amend, the defendant must file an answer to the remaining parts of the complaint within the time allowed by the court. *See* CCP §586(a)(3).

[2] With leave to amend.

[a] Plaintiff amends complaint. If the court grants a motion to strike with leave to amend and the plaintiff amends the complaint, the defendant must file an answer to the amended complaint within 30 days after service of the copy of the amendments or the amended complaint. *See* CCP §471.5(a).

[b] Plaintiff does not amend complaint. If the court grants a motion to strike with leave to amend and the plaintiff does not timely amend the complaint, the defendant—

- Must answer the remaining causes of action that were not subject to the motion to strike within the time allowed by the court. *See* CCP §586(a)(3).
- Can make a motion to dismiss the entire complaint after the time to amend has expired if the motion to strike was sustained as to the entire complaint. CCP §581(f)(4).

(f) Motion to transfer venue. If the court grants the defendant's motion to transfer venue, the defendant must file an answer in the new court within 30 days after the new court mails notice of receipt and the new case number. CRC 3.1326.

(g) Petition to compel arbitration. If the court grants the defendant's petition to compel arbitration and motion to stay, the suit is stayed and the parties will proceed to arbitration. *See* CCP §§1281.2, 1281.4, 1281.7. Whether an answer is due in the arbitration proceeding is determined by the rules adopted by the arbitration agreement. *See, e.g.*, ***Villinger/Nicholls Dev. Co. v. Meleyco*** (3d Dist.1995) 31 Cal.App.4th 321, 323-24 & n.1 (arbitration agreement adopted Construction Industry Arbitration Rules).

2. No preanswer motion filed. If no preanswer motion was filed, the answer must be filed by the following deadlines:

(1) Deadline to answer after service.

(a) Answer to complaint. The answer to a complaint must be filed within 30 days after service of the summons and complaint on the defendant. *See* CCP §412.20(a)(3). To determine when service of summons is complete, see "Methods of Service," ch. 3-H, §5, p. 301.

NOTE

Under CCP §1013, a party's deadline to act can be extended if papers were served on the party by mail. The extensions in §1013, however, do not apply to the filing of an answer. CCP §413.20. Thus, if a summons was served by mail, the deadline to file an answer is still 30 days after service is complete. See CCP §412.20(a)(3).

[1] Unlawful-detainer, forcible-detainer & forcible-entry suits. In unlawful-detainer, forcible-detainer, and forcible-entry suits, the answer to a complaint must be filed within five days (including Saturdays and Sundays, but excluding all other judicial holidays) after service of the summons and complaint on the defendant. *See* CCP §§1167, 1167.3. If the last day for filing the answer falls on a Saturday or Sunday, the response period extends to the next court day. *Id.* §1167. See "Determine last day," ch. 1-F, §5.1.5, p. 55.

[2] Libel & slander suits. In libel and slander suits, the 30-day deadline to file the answer can be shortened to 20 days after the summons and complaint are served on the defendant. *See* CCP §460.5(a). To shorten the deadline, the plaintiff must file an ex parte application. *Id.* If the court grants the application, the clerk must endorse the summons to reflect that the deadline to answer has been shortened. *Id.*

(b) Answer to amended complaint. The answer to an amended complaint must be filed within 30 days after service of the copy of the amendments or the amended complaint unless the court orders otherwise. CCP §471.5(a); *see id.* §586(a)(1). When an amended complaint is served in a libel and slander suit involving a public-office election campaign, the answer is due within ten days unless the court orders otherwise. *Id.* §460.7(b). The

defendant should check the local rules to see if the court has adopted the Trial Court Delay Reduction Act, which can affect the response period. *See* Gov. C. §§68600-68620; CRC 3.720.

(c) Answer to cross-complaint. The answer to a cross-complaint must be filed within 30 days after receiving service of the cross-complaint. *See* CCP §432.10.

(2) Deadline to answer if removal occurs. When the defendant has removed the action to federal court without filing a response in the state court, the defendant must file an answer in federal court by the latest of the following: (1) within 21 days after receiving a copy of the initial pleading stating the claim, (2) within 21 days after service of summons for the initial pleading on file at the time of service, or (3) within 7 days after the filing of the notice of removal. FRCP 81(c)(2). For a further discussion of the deadline to answer after removal, see ***O'Connor's Federal Rules***, "Deadline to answer after removal," ch. 3-A, §5.2.2(3), p. 189.

(3) Deadline to answer after remand. When the defendant has removed the action to federal court without filing a response in the state court and the federal court remands for improper removal, the defendant has 30 days from the day the state court receives the case on remand to file certain preanswer motions or other responsive pleadings. *See* CCP §430.90(a). The type of responsive pleading the defendant may file after remand depends on whether it has made a general appearance in the case and what previous motions it has filed. *See id.* A motion to dismiss for failure to timely serve, motion to quash summons, or motion to stay or dismiss for inconvenient forum can only be filed if (1) the defendant has not made a general appearance in state or federal court and (2) the state court did not previously rule on a similar motion before removal. *Id.* §430.90(a)(1). A demurrer or motion to strike can only be filed if (1) an answer was not filed in federal court and (2) a demurrer or motion to strike raising similar issues was not filed and ruled on in state or federal court. *Id.* §430.90(a)(2)(B). If the demurrer or motion to strike is denied by the court, the defendant must file an answer within 30 days after the ruling unless an answer was filed with the demurrer or motion to strike. *Id.*

§2.2 Calculating deadline. To calculate the deadline, count forward from the date the response period starts by the total number of days for the response period. *See* CCP §12. The first day (e.g., the date service of summons is complete) is not counted, but the last day (i.e., the date the answer must be filed) is. *Id.* For example, if the defendant is personally served with summons and a copy of the complaint on day 0 and does not file a preanswer motion, the 30-day deadline to file the answer begins on day 1. If the last day is a weekend or holiday, the due date is the next court day. *See id.* §§12, 12a, 12b. See "Determine last day," ch. 1-F, §5.1.5, p. 55.

§2.3 Extending deadline.

ANSWER

1. By stipulation. The parties can stipulate to one 15-day extension beyond the normal 30-day time period without the court's permission. CRC 3.110(d). The parties can stipulate to a longer extension period or multiple extensions only with the court's permission. *See* CCP §1054; ***McAllister v. County of Monterey*** (6th Dist.2007) 147 Cal.App.4th 253, 281; *see, e.g.*, ***Lopez v. Fancelli*** (3d Dist.1990) 221 Cal.App.3d 1305, 1308 (parties stipulated to open extension of time, subject to 30-day written notice, for answering complaint). The parties should check the local rules to see if the court has adopted the Trial Court Delay Reduction Act, which can affect these stipulations. *See* Gov. C. §§68600-68620; CRC 3.720.

2. By court order. The court can issue an order extending the response time.

(1) Sua sponte. The court can extend the response time based on its own motion. CRC 3.110(e); *see* CCP §§473(a)(1), 1054(a).

(2) By application. The defendant can ask the court to extend the response time. CRC 3.110(e); *see* CCP §1054. The defendant must file an application, accompanied by a declaration, before the initial response period has elapsed. CRC 3.110(e). The extension cannot exceed 30 days without the plaintiff's consent. CCP §1054(a).

(a) Application. The defendant may use the Judicial Council's ex parte application form. *See* Judicial Council Forms, form CM-020.

(b) Declaration. The defendant's declaration must do the following:

[1] Show why service has not been completed. CRC 3.110(e).

[2] Document the efforts made to complete service. *Id.*

[3] Specify the date by which service is proposed to be completed. *Id.*

§3. FORMAT OF ANSWER

The answer must comply with the formatting and content requirements of the California Rules of Court. *See* CRC 2.100-2.119, 2.130-2.141. See "General Requirements for Papers," ch. 1-B, §2, p. 9.

§3.1 Civil case cover sheet.

1. Generally. In most cases, the defendant is not required to file a civil case cover sheet when it files an answer or any other response. See "Civil case cover sheet," ch. 1-B, §2.8.1, p. 16.

2. Complex case designation.

(1) Countering plaintiff's designation. If the defendant disagrees with the plaintiff's designation of the case as complex or not complex on the civil case cover sheet, the defendant can counter the plaintiff's designation by filing and serving its own civil case cover sheet with the proper designation. *See* CRC 3.402(a), (b); Judicial Council Forms, form CM-010. For the definition of a complex case, see "Complexity," ch. 5-A, §5.2.2, p. 465. The defendant's cover sheet must be filed and served no later than the defendant's first appearance. CRC 3.402(a), (b).

(2) Joining plaintiff's designation. If the defendant agrees with the plaintiff's designation of the case as complex on the civil case cover sheet, the defendant can join the plaintiff's designation by filing and serving its own civil case cover sheet and indicating so. *See* CRC 3.402(c) (D can join P in designating case as complex); Judicial Council Forms, form CM-010 (containing box for D to check if joint designation). For the definition of a complex case, see "Complexity," ch. 5-A, §5.2.2, p. 465.

§3.2 First page.

1. Attorney information. The first page of the answer must include information about the defendant's attorney, or the defendant herself if she is appearing in propria persona. See "Attorney or party information," ch. 1-B, §2.5.2(1), p. 12.

2. Clerk's space. The first page must have a blank space to the right of the center of the page for the clerk's use. See "Clerk's space," ch. 1-B, §2.5.2(2), p. 12.

3. Caption. The first page of the answer must include a caption. *See* CCP §422.30(a).

(1) Court & county. The caption must identify the court and county where the action is filed. CCP §422.30(a)(1). See "Title of court," ch. 1-B, §2.5.2(3), p. 12.

(2) Title. The caption must include a title. CCP §422.30(a)(2).

(a) Parties' names. The title of the answer must state the name of the first party on each side with an appropriate indication of any other parties (e.g., "et al."). CCP §422.40; CRC 2.111(4).

(b) Case number. The title of the answer must identify the number of the case. CRC 2.111(5).

(c) Nature of paper. The title of the answer must identify the nature of the paper and, if more than one defendant has been named, must state the name of each defendant on whose behalf the answer is filed (e.g., "Answer of ABC Corp."). CRC 2.111(6).

PRACTICE TIP

Although the title of the answer does not have to state the name of each party, common practice is to restate the title exactly as it appears on the complaint.

4. Introduction. The first page customarily has a brief introduction that identifies the answering defendant. *E.g.*, *CEB Procedure Before Trial*, §25.16 (if multiple Ds are sued, introductory language should identify each answering D).

§3.3 Body. The body of the answer consists of headings, answers, and defenses. *See* CCP §431.30(b); *CEB Procedure Before Trial*, §25.17.

1. Headings. The body of the answer should contain a heading for each answer and defense. *See* CRC 2.112.

(1) Answer. An answer consists of general or specific denials.

(a) General denial. If the answer is a general denial only (i.e., a blanket denial of all material allegations in the complaint), the heading can simply state "General Denial." See "General denials," §4.1, p. 340.

(b) Specific denials. If the answer is a series of specific denials (i.e., a denial of one or more allegations in the complaint), the heading should refer to the cause of action it is intended to answer (e.g., "Answer to First Cause of Action for Negligence"). If the complaint contains more than one cause of action that incorporates common allegations by reference, the answer can also include a heading for those allegations (e.g., "Answer to Common Allegations"). See "Specific denials," §4.2, p. 342.

(2) Defense. A heading for a defense should state the following:

(a) The number of the defense (e.g., "First Affirmative Defense"). CRC 2.112(1).

(b) The nature of each defense (e.g., "First Affirmative Defense (Statute of Limitations)"). CRC 2.112(2).

(c) The name of the defendant asserting the defense if there is more than one (e.g., "First Affirmative Defense (Statute of Limitations) by Defendant Smith"). CRC 2.112(3).

(d) The name of the plaintiff or plaintiffs against whom the defense is asserted (e.g., "First Affirmative Defense (Statute of Limitations) by Defendant Smith against Plaintiff Jones"). CRC 2.112(4).

(e) The cause of action challenged by the affirmative defense, unless the defense is raised to all causes of action (e.g., "First Affirmative Defense (Rescission) by Defendant Smith against Plaintiff Jones to Second Cause of Action"). *See CEB Procedure Before Trial*, §25.19.

2. Answers. The body of the answer should contain any denials of the material allegations in the complaint. See "Denials," §4, p. 340.

3. Defenses. The body of the answer should contain any defenses to the complaint. See "Affirmative Defenses," §5, p. 343.

§3.4 Demand for relief. The answer does not have to include a demand for relief—usually called a "prayer"—specifying the relief the defendant claims to be entitled to receive. *CEB Procedure Before Trial*, §25.20. Most attorneys include one, though, using language similar to the following: "For these reasons, defendant asks the court to render judgment that plaintiff take nothing, assess costs against plaintiff, and award all other relief to which defendant is entitled." *See id.*; Weil, *Civil Procedure Before Trial*, ¶6:482.

1. No affirmative relief. In most cases, the defendant cannot ask for affirmative relief in the prayer; to request affirmative relief, the defendant must file a separate cross-complaint in the action. *See* CCP §431.30(c). See "Affirmative Relief," §6, p. 346; "Cross-Complaint," ch. 4-C, p. 349.

2. Attorney fees. If the defendant could be entitled to an award of attorney fees, it can ask for them in the prayer. Weil, *Civil Procedure Before Trial*, ¶6:485; *see* ***North Assocs. v. Bell*** (1st Dist.1986) 184 Cal.App.3d 860, 865 n.2; *see also* Civ. C. §1717(a) (prevailing party in contract action is entitled to reasonable attorney fees in addition to other costs if contract provides for recovery of fees and costs). The defendant may be required to take other

procedural steps before it can recover attorney fees. *See, e.g.*, Civ. C. §1717(b)(1) (party must make noticed motion for court to determine who is prevailing party entitled to award of fees).

§3.5 Signature. The same rules governing the signature on the complaint apply to the signature on the answer. See "Signature," ch. 1-B, §2.7, p. 15.

§3.6 Filing fees. When the answer is filed, the defendant must pay a filing fee to the court clerk or request a waiver of the fee. See "Filing Fees," ch. 1-F, §7, p. 58.

§3.7 Verification. A verification is an affidavit or declaration that swears to the truth of the matters stated in the answer. *See* ***Christopher v. Condogeorge*** (1900) 128 Cal. 581, 584-85.

1. When to verify. When the complaint is verified, the answer must also be verified. CCP §446(a). However, there are exceptions to this general rule.

(1) Limited civil cases. In limited civil cases, the answer does not need to be verified. CCP §92(b).

(2) Public entities or officers.

(a) As defendant. In cases brought against public entities or officers sued in their official capacity, the answer does not need to be verified. *See* CCP §446(a); ***Murrieta Valley Unified Sch. Dist. v. County of Riverside*** (4th Dist.1991) 228 Cal.App.3d 1212, 1223.

(b) As plaintiff. In cases brought by public entities or officers in their official capacity, the defendant must verify its answer unless (1) an admission of the truth of the complaint might subject the defendant to a criminal prosecution or (2) the defendant is itself a public entity or officer. CCP §446(a).

2. How to verify. Answers are verified in the same manner as complaints. See "How to verify," ch. 3-C, §3.10.2, p. 225.

3. Who can verify.

(1) Defendant. Answers are generally verified by the defendant. *See* CCP §446(a).

(2) Attorney or nonparty. An attorney or other nonparty can verify the answer in certain situations. *See* CCP §446(a); ***DeCamp v. First Kensington Corp.*** (2d Dist.1978) 83 Cal.App.3d 268, 275. The affidavit or declaration must explain why the party did not verify the answer. CCP §446(a); *see* ***Conservatorship of Isaac O.*** (4th Dist.1987) 190 Cal.App.3d 50, 54. *But see* ***Soltani-Rastegar v. Superior Ct.*** (1st Dist.1989) 208 Cal.App.3d 424, 428 (court upheld attorney's verification that lacked explanation). An attorney or other nonparty can verify the answer in any of the following situations:

(a) The party is absent from the county where the attorney has her office, and obtaining the party's signature is impractical. *See* CCP §446(a); ***DeCamp***, 83 Cal.App.3d at 274-75. In this situation, the attorney's affidavit or declaration must state that she read the answer and that the matters stated in it are true based on her information and belief. CCP §446(a).

(b) The party is unable to verify the answer for some reason. *Id.* In this situation, the attorney's affidavit or declaration must state that she read the answer and that the matters stated in it are true based on her information and belief. *Id.*

(c) The facts are within the knowledge of the party's attorney or some other person verifying the answer. *Id.*; *see, e.g.*, ***Conservatorship of Isaac O.***, 190 Cal.App.3d at 55 (employee of party verified petition because he was more familiar with alleged facts).

CAUTION

Verification of the answer by the attorney is discouraged. CEB Procedure Before Trial, §25.28; Weil, Civil Procedure Before Trial, ¶6:493.

(3) Corporation. When a corporation is a party, the answer can be verified by any officer of the corporation. CCP §446(a). The officer's affidavit or declaration must state that she read the answer and that the matters stated in it are true based on her information and belief. *Id.*

4. Challenging unverified answer. A party can file a motion to strike an unverified answer when verification is required. ***Zavala v. Board of Trs.*** (6th Dist.1993) 16 Cal.App.4th 1755, 1761. An objection to lack of verification must be raised at the trial-court level before trial or else it is waived. *See* ***In re Marriage of Melton*** (6th Dist.1994) 28 Cal.App.4th 931, 939; ***Zavala***, 16 Cal.App.4th at 1760-61.

5. Effect of verification.

(1) On attorney-client privilege. When an attorney prepares the answer and the defendant verifies it "on information and belief," the verification is not deemed to have disclosed a "significant portion" of an attorney-client communication, and thus does not constitute a waiver of the privilege under Evid. C. §912(a). *See* ***Alpha Beta Co. v. Superior Ct.*** (5th Dist.1984) 157 Cal.App.3d 818, 830-31; *CEB Procedure Before Trial*, §25.28; Weil, *Civil Procedure Before Trial*, ¶6:497.

(2) On right against self-incrimination. A defendant cannot refuse to verify her answer on the basis of the right against self-incrimination unless the plaintiff is a public entity or officer. *See* CCP §446(a). But by verifying the answer, the defendant does not waive her right against self-incrimination. ***Alvarez v. Sanchez*** (1st Dist.1984) 158 Cal.App.3d 709, 715. That is, the information in the verified answer cannot be used against the defendant in a criminal case. *See* ***DeCamp***, 83 Cal.App.3d at 280. Because a corporate defendant does not have a right against self-incrimination, its verified answer can be used against it in a later criminal proceeding. *See id.* at 281-82. See "Privilege Against Self-Incrimination," ch. 6-F, §2, p. 687.

§4. DENIALS

The defendant must deny any material allegations in the complaint that it believes are untrue. *See* CCP §§431.30(b)(1), 590. Material allegations are those that are essential to the claim and that could not be struck from the complaint without leaving it insufficient. *Id.* §431.10(a); *see also id.* §431.10(b) (definition of "immaterial allegation"). The answer raises a fact issue for trial when it controverts a material allegation in the complaint. *Id.* §590. Every material allegation in the complaint that is not controverted by the answer will be taken as true. *Id.* §431.20(a); ***Hennefer v. Butcher*** (2d Dist.1986) 182 Cal.App.3d 492, 504. A denial can be general or specific. *See* CCP §431.30(b)(1).

§4.1 General denials. A general denial is a denial of each and every allegation in the complaint. *See* ***Edger v. Foster*** (2d Dist.1941) 48 Cal.App.2d 580, 583.

1. When to use. The defendant's ability to make an effective general denial depends primarily on the classification of the case (i.e., unlimited or limited) and whether the complaint was verified. See "Procedural Classifications of Civil Cases," ch. 3-E, §4, p. 255.

(1) Unlimited civil cases.

(a) Unverified complaint. In unlimited civil cases, the defendant can make a general denial in response to an unverified complaint. *See* CCP §431.30(d); *see, e.g.*, ***Mission Hous. Dev. Co. v. City & Cty. of S.F.*** (1st Dist.1997) 59 Cal.App.4th 55, 67-68 (D's general denial put in issue all material allegations in unverified complaint).

(b) Verified complaint. In unlimited civil cases, the defendant cannot make a general denial in response to a verified complaint; when the complaint is verified, the denial of the allegations must be made positively or according to the information and belief of the defendant. *See* CCP §431.30(d). If the defendant makes a general denial to a verified complaint, the material allegations in the complaint are deemed admitted. *See id.* §431.20(a). However, the denial is not a judicial admission of the legal effect of the complaint's allegations. *See* ***Stroud v. Tunzi*** (2d Dist.2008) 160 Cal.App.4th 377, 383-84.

(2) Limited civil cases. A defendant in a limited civil case under CCP §§90-100 can, in most cases, make a general denial regardless of whether the complaint is verified. *See* CCP §431.30(d).

(a) Matters over $1,000. If the demand or the value of the property at issue exceeds $1,000, the defendant cannot make a general denial to a verified complaint if the claim has been assigned to a third party for collection. *See* CCP §§431.30(d), 431.40(a). Instead of a general denial, the defendant must deny the allegations positively or according to the defendant's information and belief. *Id.* §431.30(d).

(b) Matters $1,000 or less. If the demand or the value of the property at issue does not exceed $1,000, the defendant can make a general denial to a verified complaint even if the claim has been assigned to a third party for collection. *See* CCP §§431.30(d), 431.40(a); Weil, *Civil Procedure Before Trial*, ¶6:410.

2. Form of denial. The general denial should be set out in a separate paragraph and, if defenses or other matters are stated in the answer, numbered. *See* CCP §431.30(g); CRC 2.112(1); *CEB Procedure Before Trial*, §25.18.

(1) Traditional general denial. The general denial usually denies all the allegations in the complaint. For example, a traditional general denial might state the following: "Under California Code of Civil Procedure §431.30(d), the defendant denies each and every allegation contained in the complaint, and denies that the plaintiff sustained damages in the sum or sums alleged or in any other sum, or at all." *See CEB Procedure Before Trial*, §25.31; Weil, *Civil Procedure Before Trial*, ¶6:403.

(2) Judicial Council form. The Judicial Council has adopted a general-denial form that the defendant may file instead of an answer. *See* Judicial Council Forms, form PLD-050. Use of the form is mandatory if the defendant chooses to make a general denial and the amount asked for in the complaint or the value of the property involved is $1,000 or less. *Id.*; *see* Gov. C. §68511; CRC 1.31(a).

3. Effect of denial. When effective, a general denial puts in issue all of the complaint's material allegations. CCP §431.30(d); ***Mentone Irrigation Co. v. Redlands Elec. Light & Power Co.*** (1909) 155 Cal. 323, 325. The following are examples of matters put in issue in certain actions.

CAUTION

In an action involving a negotiable instrument, the validity of the signatures is admitted unless specifically denied by the defendant. Cal. U.C.C. §3308(a). In other words, a general denial will not put in issue a defense of forgery. See "Affirmative Defenses," §5, p. 343.

(1) Action on promissory note. In an action based on a promissory note, a general denial will put the following in issue:

(a) The purported contract is wholly void. ***FPI Dev., Inc. v. Nakashima*** (3d Dist.1991) 231 Cal.App.3d 367, 383-84.

(b) The copy of the note is false. *Id.*

(c) The defendant already paid the note in accordance with its terms. *Id.*

(d) The note was not signed. *Id.* at 384.

(2) Action for breach of contract. In an action based on a breach of contract, a general denial will put the following in issue:

(a) The existence of the contract. ***Walsh v. West Valley Mission Cmty. Coll. Dist.*** (6th Dist.1998) 66 Cal.App.4th 1532, 1545.

(b) The plaintiff's performance under the contract. *Id.*

(c) The plaintiff's excuses for nonperformance. *Id.*

(d) The defendant's nonperformance under the contract. *Id.*

(e) The plaintiff's damages. *Id.*

§4.2 Specific denials. A specific denial is a denial of one or more particular allegations in the complaint. *Black's Law Dictionary* 527 (10th ed. 2014); *see* CCP §431.30(f).

1. When to use. The defendant must make specific denials to raise fact issues when the complaint is verified, unless it is a limited civil case. *See* CCP §431.30(d).

2. Form of denial. The specific denial should be set out in separate paragraphs and numbered. *CEB Procedure Before Trial*, §25.18; *see* CCP §431.30(g); CRC 2.112(1). There are five main ways to specifically deny allegations in a complaint:

(1) Deny allegations verbatim. The defendant can make a specific denial by restating and denying each particular allegation. *See CEB Procedure Before Trial*, §25.37; *see, e.g.*, ***Racouillat v. Rene*** (1867) 32 Cal. 450, 453-54 (D's answer specifically denied allegation that D had knowledge of P's mortgage by stating that D had no notice of P's mortgage at or before time of property purchase). Restating and denying each allegation is labor-intensive and exposes the defendant to possible "negative-pregnant" issues. 5 Witkin, *Cal. Procedure*, Pleading, §1063. See "Negative-pregnant denials," §4.3, p. 343.

(2) Deny paragraphs or parts. The defendant can make a specific denial by denying specific paragraphs or parts of the complaint. CCP §431.30(f). For example, the answer may state that "Defendant denies generally and specifically each and every allegation contained in paragraphs 6, 7, 8, 9, and 10." *See* ***Conley v. Lieber*** (4th Dist.1979) 97 Cal.App.3d 646, 655; ***Edger v. Foster*** (2d Dist.1941) 48 Cal.App.2d 580, 583; *CEB Procedure Before Trial*, §25.38.

(3) Expressly admit allegations + general denial. The defendant can make a specific denial by expressly admitting certain allegations and generally denying all the remaining allegations. CCP §431.30(f); *see CEB Procedure Before Trial*, §25.40; *see, e.g.*, ***Whiteside v. United Theatres*** (3d Dist.1951) 106 Cal.App.2d 471, 473 (Ds admitted company was California corporation and certain other allegations but denied each and every allegation of paragraphs in complaint not specifically admitted).

(4) Deny allegations on information & belief + general denial. The defendant can make a specific denial by denying an allegation based on "information and belief" or for "lack of sufficient information or belief," and, if necessary, by either generally denying all the remaining allegations or expressly admitting any truthful allegation and generally denying the remaining allegations. CCP §431.30(f); *see* ***Dobbins v. Hardister*** (1st Dist.1966) 242 Cal.App.2d 787, 791; *CEB Procedure Before Trial*, §25.48; 5 Witkin, *Cal. Procedure*, Pleading, §1065. A denial based on information and belief (or lack of either) will be disregarded or struck in the following instances:

(a) D lacks information only. If the defendant denies an allegation because the defendant lacks sufficient knowledge or information to form a belief, but does not also state that it lacks belief about the allegation, the denial will be disregarded. *See* ***May v. Board of Dirs. of El Camino Irrigation Dist.*** (1949) 34 Cal.2d 125, 127; ***Aronson & Co. v. Pearson*** (1926) 199 Cal. 295, 297-98.

(b) D has actual knowledge. If the defendant has actual knowledge of the facts that would allow it to admit or deny the allegation, or if the facts are presumed to be within its knowledge, the denial will be deemed a sham and evasive and either disregarded or struck. *See* ***Dobbins***, 242 Cal.App.2d at 791; *CEB Procedure Before Trial*, §25.45; *see, e.g.*, ***Goldwater v. Oltman*** (1930) 210 Cal. 408, 424-25 (whether Ds delivered note was presumably within their knowledge); ***Oliver v. Swiss Club Tell*** (1st Dist.1963) 222 Cal.App.2d 528, 540 (whether D was unincorporated association was presumably within its knowledge); ***Zany v. Rawhide Gold Mining Co.*** (3d Dist.1911) 15 Cal.App. 373, 375-76 (whether D entered into contract and performed contractual obligations was presumably within its knowledge). If for some reason the defendant does not know something it should know, the answer should explain why. *See* ***Zany***, 15 Cal.App. at 375-76.

(c) D has constructive knowledge. If the defendant has the means of determining the facts that would allow it to admit or deny the allegation, the denial will be deemed a sham and evasive and either disregarded or struck. ***Dobbins***, 242 Cal.App.2d at 791. For example, a defendant cannot deny a matter of public record based on information and belief. *See* ***Taylor v. Newton*** (3d Dist.1953) 117 Cal.App.2d 752, 760; Weil, *Civil Procedure Before Trial*, ¶6:429; *see, e.g.*, ***Art Metal Constr. Co. v. A.F. Anderson Co.*** (1920) 182 Cal. 29, 33 (D could have ascertained whether foreign corporation was qualified to do business in California by examining public records).

(5) Make affirmative contradiction. Although discouraged, the defendant can specifically deny an allegation by making a contradictory or inconsistent statement in its answer that shows the allegation to be untrue. *See* ***Perkins v. Brock*** (1889) 80 Cal. 320, 322; *CEB Procedure Before Trial*, §25.41; *see, e.g.*, ***Elliott v. Bertsch*** (3d Dist.1943) 59 Cal.App.2d 543, 546-47 (D effectively denied allegation that P owned water rights by stating that D owned rights).

3. Effect of denial. When effective, a specific denial will put in issue only the material allegations that are controverted; any allegation that is not controverted will be taken as true. *See* CCP §431.20(a).

§4.3 Negative-pregnant denials. As a practical matter, the defendant should avoid making a negative-pregnant denial—that is, a denial of a statement's literal truth but not its substance. *See* ***Vogel v. Felice*** (6th Dist.2005) 127 Cal.App.4th 1006, 1021. *See generally* ***Johndrow v. Thomas*** (1947) 31 Cal.2d 202, 209 (the rule against negatives pregnant is not an absolute rule but a rule of construction; sufficiency of findings turns on the particular case). For example, if a defendant denies an allegation that he "owes his wife and kids thousands" ("thousands" meaning $2,000 or more) by asserting "I do not owe my wife and kids thousands," the denial is open to an interpretation that the allegation is substantially true (e.g., the defendant owes his wife and kids $1,999). ***Vogel***, 127 Cal.App.4th at 1021-22. This example also demonstrates the danger of "conjunctive" denials; the use of the conjunction "and" in the denial could mean (1) the combined debt to his wife and children is less than $2,000, (2) the debt to his children is less than $2,000, but the debt to his wife may be greater, or (3) the debt to his wife is less than $2,000, but the debt to his children may be greater. *Id.* at 1022. The defendant can avoid a negative-pregnant denial by doing the following:

1. Denying in the disjunctive (i.e., using "or" instead of "and"). *See id.*

2. Making a general denial, if appropriate. *See* CCP §431.30(d). See "General denials," §4.1, p. 340.

3. Making denials by referencing paragraph numbers. *See* CCP §431.30(f). See "Deny paragraphs or parts," §4.2.2(2), p. 342.

4. If using factual denials (e.g., "I do not owe my wife or kids thousands"), broadening the scope of the denial to eliminate any possible uncertainties (e.g., "I do not owe my wife or kids thousands or any other amount"). *See* ***Vogel***, 127 Cal.App.4th at 1021-22.

5. Ending the answer with a broad, catchall denial (e.g., "Except as otherwise admitted or denied in this answer, defendant denies each and every allegation contained in the complaint"). Weil, *Civil Procedure Before Trial*, ¶6:422.

§5. AFFIRMATIVE DEFENSES

The answer may contain a statement of any new matter constituting a defense. CCP §431.30(b)(2). The phrase "new matter" means something relied on by the defendant that is not put in issue by the plaintiff. ***Quantification Settlement Agreement Cases*** (3d Dist.2011) 201 Cal.App.4th 758, 812. Thus, matters that are not responsive to essential allegations of the complaint must be raised in the answer as "new matter" or they will be waived. *Id.* at 812-13. The phrase "new matter" is also commonly known as an affirmative defense. *Id.* at 812. Unlike a denial, which controverts the essential allegations of the complaint, an affirmative defense sets out new facts showing that the plaintiff cannot succeed regardless of whether the allegations in the complaint are true. *See id.* at 812-13; ***Walsh v. West Valley Mission Cmty. Coll. Dist.*** (6th Dist.1998) 66 Cal.App.4th 1532, 1546. By asserting an affirmative defense, the defendant raises a fact issue to be resolved. *See* CCP §590.

§5.1 Form of defense. The answer must state each defense separately. CCP §431.30(g). For a discussion of how to draft a heading for a defense, see "Defense," §3.3.1(2), p. 338.

1. Allegations of fact. The answer must contain allegations of fact in ordinary and concise language to support each defense pleaded. *See* CCP §431.30(b)(2) (answer must contain statement of any new matter constituting defense); ***Quantification Settlement Agreement Cases*** (3d Dist.2011) 201 Cal.App.4th 758, 812-13 (affirmative defenses must be pleaded with as much detail as causes of action). The facts to be stated must be "ultimate facts," not legal conclusions. *CEB Procedure Before Trial*, §25.58; *see* ***Quantification Settlement***, 201 Cal.App.4th at 812-13; *see, e.g.*, ***FPI Dev., Inc. v. Nakashima*** (3d Dist.1991) 231 Cal.App.3d 367, 384 (D's affirmative defenses inappropriately consisted of legal conclusions that would not have survived P's demurrer). Thus, when drafting an affirmative defense, the defendant should follow the same fact-pleading requirements for allegations of fact in a complaint. *See* ***Quantification Settlement***, 201 Cal.App.4th at 812-13; *CEB Procedure Before Trial*, §25.58. See "Allegations of fact," ch. 3-C, §3.6.3(2), p. 216.

NOTE

Not all affirmative defenses require specific allegations of fact. For example, the defense of statute of limitations can be stated generally: "the cause of action is barred by {identify specific code, section, and subsection}." CCP §458; Weil, Civil Procedure Before Trial, ¶¶6:462-6:464.

2. Inconsistent defenses. The defendant may plead inconsistent defenses in its answer. ***South Santa Clara Valley Water Conserv. Dist. v. Johnson*** (1st Dist.1964) 231 Cal.App.2d 388, 403; *e.g.*, ***Edger v. Foster*** (2d Dist.1941) 48 Cal.App.2d 580, 583 (D's answer denied certain material allegations, but D's affirmative defense alleged same material allegations as true). However, each defense must be kept separate and be internally consistent. *See* ***Banta v. Siller*** (1898) 121 Cal. 414, 417-18; ***People v. Tulare Packing Co.*** (4th Dist.1938) 25 Cal.App.2d 717, 730; *CEB Procedure Before Trial*, §25.53; *see, e.g.*, ***Poe v. Francis*** (2d Dist.1933) 132 Cal.App. 330, 335 (D could not admit and deny material allegation in same defense).

§5.2 Types of defenses. The following are some of the affirmative defenses a defendant can raise in its answer:

1. Contract defenses.

(1) Lack of consideration. ***Elster's Sales v. Longo*** (2d Dist.1970) 4 Cal.App.3d 216, 221-22.

(2) Mistake. *See* ***Behm v. Fireside Thrift Co.*** (5th Dist.1969) 272 Cal.App.2d 15, 22.

(3) Fraud. *See* ***Pacific State Bank v. Greene*** (3d Dist.2003) 110 Cal.App.4th 375, 382.

(4) Duress. *See* ***Crowley v. Katleman*** (1994) 8 Cal.4th 666, 677.

(5) Undue influence. *See id.*

(6) Minority. *See* ***Merry v. Garibaldi*** (3d Dist.1941) 48 Cal.App.2d 397, 403.

(7) Incompetency. *See* ***Singh v. Burkhart*** (2d Dist.1963) 218 Cal.App.2d 285, 290; ***San Francisco Credit Clearing-House v. MacDonald*** (1st Dist.1912) 18 Cal.App. 212, 215.

(8) Excuse. ***Jacobs v. Tenneco W., Inc.*** (5th Dist.1986) 186 Cal.App.3d 1413, 1418-19; *see* ***San Mateo Cmty. Coll. Dist. v. Half Moon Bay L.P.*** (1st Dist.1998) 65 Cal.App.4th 401, 414.

(9) Rescission. *See* Civ. C. §1692; ***Donovan v. RRL Corp.*** (2001) 26 Cal.4th 261, 278 n.5; ***Harris v. Rudin, Richman & Appel*** (2d Dist.2002) 95 Cal.App.4th 1332, 1337.

(10) Novation. *See* ***Alexander v. Angel*** (1951) 37 Cal.2d 856, 858; ***Douillard v. Woodd*** (1942) 20 Cal.2d 665, 666-67.

(11) Account stated. *See* ***Trafton v. Youngblood*** (1968) 69 Cal.2d 17, 22-23 & n.2.

(12) Accord and satisfaction. ***Owens v. Noble*** (3d Dist.1946) 77 Cal.App.2d 209, 215.

(13) Discharge in bankruptcy. *See* 11 U.S.C. §524(a); ***Martin v. Martin*** (1970) 2 Cal.3d 752, 759.

(14) Illegality. *See* ***Yoo v. Robi*** (2d Dist.2005) 126 Cal.App.4th 1089, 1103.

(15) Failure of condition. *See* ***Bank of Santa Ana v. Molina*** (4th Dist.1969) 1 Cal.App.3d 607, 620-21; ***McDonald v. Filice*** (5th Dist.1967) 252 Cal.App.2d 613, 625 n.2; ***Standard Oil Co. v. Houser*** (2d Dist.1950) 101 Cal.App.2d 480, 488. In most cases, asserting a failure of condition or lack of performance is not a new matter and is put in issue by a denial of the plaintiff's allegation of performance in the complaint. Weil, *Civil Procedure Before Trial*, ¶6:440; *see* ***Eucalyptus Growers Ass'n v. Orange Cty. Nursery & Land Co.*** (1917) 174 Cal. 330, 332-34.

(16) Statute of frauds. *See* ***Howard v. Adams*** (1940) 16 Cal.2d 253, 257.

(17) Ultra vires (i.e., contract is beyond scope of authority). *See* ***Quantification Settlement Agreement Cases*** (3d Dist.2011) 201 Cal.App.4th 758, 812-13. *See generally* ***Allen v. Hussey*** (2d Dist.1950) 101 Cal.App.2d 457, 472-73 (contract entered into by public agency beyond its authority was void).

(18) Insurance contract – exemption from liability. *See* CCP §431.50. If an insurer claims exemption from liability on the ground that the loss was remotely caused by or would not have occurred but for a peril excluded in the insurance contract, the insurer must set out and specify in its answer the following:

(a) The peril that was the proximate cause of the loss. *Id.*

(b) How the excluded peril contributed to the loss or caused the covered peril. *Id.*

(c) If the insured claims that the excluded peril caused the covered peril, on what premises or at what place the excluded peril caused the covered peril. *Id.*

2. Tort defenses.

(1) Self-defense. ***Dutro v. Castoro*** (1st Dist.1936) 16 Cal.App.2d 116, 117.

(2) Comparative negligence. *See* ***Lu v. Grewal*** (2d Dist.2005) 130 Cal.App.4th 841, 847.

(3) Assumption of risk. *See* ***Peart v. Ferro*** (1st Dist.2004) 119 Cal.App.4th 60, 68.

(4) Workers' compensation – exclusive-remedy rule. *See* Lab. C. §3600(a); ***Gibbs v. American Airlines, Inc.*** (1st Dist.1999) 74 Cal.App.4th 1, 12. When injured on the job, workers' compensation is often the employee's exclusive remedy against the employer. *See* Lab. C. §3600(a). When a complaint alleges facts indicating that the Workers' Compensation Act applies, the complaint is subject to demurrer unless it states additional facts showing otherwise. ***Gibbs***, 74 Cal.App.4th at 12. If the complaint does not allege the existence of an employer-employee relationship or that the injury occurred in the course of employment, the defendant must plead and prove that workers' compensation is the plaintiff's exclusive remedy. *See id.* at 13.

3. Plea in abatement. A plea in abatement is a technical objection to the place, time, or method of asserting the plaintiff's claim without disputing the claim's merits. *Black's Law Dictionary* 1338 (10th ed. 2014); *see* ***Color-Vue, Inc. v. Abrams*** (2d Dist.1996) 44 Cal.App.4th 1599, 1604. If the grounds for the objection appear on the face of the complaint, the plea can be raised by demurrer (or, under the modern trend, as a defense in the answer); if the grounds do not appear on the face of the complaint, the plea must be raised in the answer. ***Tingley v. Times Mirror Co.*** (1907) 151 Cal. 1, 13; *see* CCP §430.30; ***Color-Vue***, 44 Cal.App.4th at 1604; *see, e.g.*, ***Martin v. Pacific Sw. Royalties, Inc.*** (2d Dist.1940) 41 Cal.App.2d 161, 171 (D waived plea in abatement based on pendency of another action between same parties because it did not raise objection by demurrer or answer); *see also CEB Procedure Before Trial*, §25.56 (noting modern trend of allowing Ds to use answers to raise objections to matters appearing on face of complaint). See "Demurrer," ch. 4-H, p. 396. If the plea is successful, the court will delay the case until the defect is resolved. *See* CCP §597; ***Shuffer v. Board of Trs.*** (2d Dist.1977) 67 Cal.App.3d 208, 217; ***Bank of Am. Nat'l Trust & Sav. Ass'n v. Cohen*** (2d Dist.1937) 21 Cal.App.2d 510, 512-13.

4. **Other defenses.**

(1) Statute of limitations. *See* ***County of L.A. v. Commission on State Mandates*** (2d Dist.2007) 150 Cal.App.4th 898, 912. The answer should cite the applicable provision and subdivision of the statute on which the defense relies. *See* CCP §458. *But see* ***Hydro-Mill Co. v. Hayward, Tilton & Rolapp Ins. Assocs.*** (2d Dist.2004) 115 Cal.App.4th 1145, 1164-65 (not pleading subdivision of statute does not nullify defense when no other subdivision could possibly apply).

(2) Waiver. *See* ***Central Bldg., LLC v. Cooper*** (1st Dist.2005) 127 Cal.App.4th 1053, 1064 n.11.

(3) Unclean hands. ***Kendall-Jackson Winery, Ltd. v. Superior Ct.*** (5th Dist.1999) 76 Cal.App.4th 970, 978.

(4) Res judicata. *See* ***Griset v. Fair Political Practices Comm'n*** (2001) 25 Cal.4th 688, 694; ***Bernhard v. Bank of Am. Nat'l Trust & Sav. Ass'n*** (1942) 19 Cal.2d 807, 810.

(5) Estoppel. ***Fair Oaks Bank v. Johnson*** (1926) 198 Cal. 196, 201.

(6) Laches. ***In re Marriage of Dancy*** (4th Dist.2000) 82 Cal.App.4th 1142, 1158.

(7) Release. *See* ***Hildebrand v. Stonecrest Corp.*** (1st Dist.1959) 174 Cal.App.2d 158, 165.

(8) Setoff. CCP §431.70; ***Interstate Grp. Adm'rs, Inc. v. Cravens, Dargan & Co.*** (1st Dist.1985) 174 Cal.App.3d 700, 706.

(9) Privilege. ***Cruey v. Gannett Co.*** (1st Dist.1998) 64 Cal.App.4th 356, 367. See "Discovery & Privileges," ch. 6, p. 599.

(10) Right to arbitration. ***Ross v. Blanchard*** (2d Dist.1967) 251 Cal.App.2d 739, 742; *see* ***Guess?, Inc. v. Superior Ct.*** (2d Dist.2000) 79 Cal.App.4th 553, 557-58. See "Alternative dispute resolution," ch. 4-A, §2.2.2, p. 329.

(11) Immunity. *See generally* Gov. C. §§810-867 (immunity statutes).

§5.3 Waiving defense. An affirmative defense is usually waived if the defendant does not plead it in the answer. CCP §430.80(a); ***California Acad. of Sci. v. County of Fresno*** (5th Dist.1987) 192 Cal.App.3d 1436, 1442; *see* CCP §431.20(a); ***Carranza v. Noroian*** (5th Dist.1966) 240 Cal.App.2d 481, 487-88. The following defenses, however, can be raised after the answer has been filed:

1. The complaint does not state facts sufficient to constitute a cause of action. CCP §430.80(a); ***Fried v. Municipal Ct.*** (2d Dist.1949) 94 Cal.App.2d 376, 378.

2. Illegality based on public policy. ***Lewis & Queen v. N.M. Ball Sons*** (1957) 48 Cal.2d 141, 147-48; ***Yoo v. Robi*** (2d Dist.2005) 126 Cal.App.4th 1089, 1103.

3. Lack of subject-matter jurisdiction. CCP §430.80(a). See "Limits on jurisdiction," ch. 3-E, §2.2, p. 249.

§6. AFFIRMATIVE RELIEF

In most cases, the defendant cannot claim affirmative relief in the answer but must instead file a cross-complaint. *See* CCP §431.30(c); ***City of Stockton v. Superior Ct.*** (2007) 42 Cal.4th 730, 745-46 & n.12. *But see* CCP §872.430 (in suit for partition of real property, D can plead for contribution or other compensation in answer); ***In re Marriage of Tamraz*** (2d Dist.1994) 24 Cal.App.4th 1740, 1747 (in marriage-dissolution proceeding, D can seek affirmative relief in answer because cross-complaints are not allowed); ***Jay v. Dollarhide*** (5th Dist.1970) 3 Cal.App.3d 1001, 1031 (in quiet-title actions, D does not have to seek affirmative relief by cross-complaint), *disapproved on other grounds*, ***Morris v. Thogmartin*** (5th Dist.1973) 29 Cal.App.3d 922. See "Cross-Complaint," ch. 4-C, p. 349. This is true even for matters that can be pleaded as both an affirmative defense in the answer and a cause of action in a separate cross-complaint (e.g., claim of fraud in the inducement of the signature of a contract). *CEB Procedure Before Trial*, §25.78.

NOTE

CCP §431.70, which allows for a setoff (i.e., the "defense of payment"), contains language suggesting that the defense could result in an award of affirmative relief in violation of §431.30(c) if the defendant's claim for payment is (1) greater than the plaintiff's and (2) not barred by limitations. See ***Construction Prot. Servs. v. TIG Specialty Ins.*** *(2002) 29 Cal.4th 189, 197. But the Supreme Court has made clear that §431.70 can only be used defensively—that is, to defeat the plaintiff's claim. Id. at 197-98. If the defendant wants to seek affirmative relief on its claim, it must do so by cross-complaint. Id. at 198.*

§7. JOINT ANSWERS

Defendants may choose to file a joint answer. *See, e.g.,* ***Consulting Eng'rs & Land Survs. v. Professional Eng'rs in Cal. Gov't*** (2007) 42 Cal.4th 578, 584 (two Ds filed joint answer). Joint answers are only appropriate for defendants who plan on making identical responses to the complaint. *See CEB Procedure Before Trial*, §25.16.

CAUTION

A defendant who is a prevailing party under CCP §1032 may be denied an award of costs if it filed a joint answer with a losing defendant. See ***Wakefield v. Bohlin*** *(6th Dist.2006) 145 Cal.App.4th 963, 984 (when Ds are united in interest or join in making same defenses in same answer, "prevailing party" definition in §1032(a)(4) does not apply and D against whom P does not recover is not entitled to costs as matter of right), disapproved on other grounds,* ***Goodman v. Lozano*** *(2010) 47 Cal.4th 1327.*

§8. RESPONDING TO THE ANSWER

In California, the plaintiff has no obligation to file a reply to the answer. *See* 4 Witkin, *Cal. Procedure*, Pleading, §4(4). By statute, any affirmative defense asserted by the defendant is automatically deemed to be controverted by the plaintiff. *See* CCP §431.20(b); 4 Witkin, *Cal. Procedure*, Pleading, §4(3).

§9. AMENDING THE ANSWER

After the answer has been filed, the defendant may need to amend it to correct errors or defects or to add new matters.

§9.1 Form of amendment. The defendant can amend the answer in one of three ways:

1. Marked-up answer. The defendant can amend the answer by marking on the face of it. CRC 3.1324(d). Any alterations must be initialed by the judge or the court clerk to be effective. *Id.* This type of amendment is rarely allowed; the court will usually require the defendant to file a separate document.

2. Separate amendment to answer. The defendant can amend the answer by filing a separate amendment to it. *See* CRC 3.1324(a)(1); ***Cohen v. Superior Ct.*** (1st Dist.1966) 244 Cal.App.2d 650, 657; *CEB Procedure Before Trial*, §25.99; Weil, *Civil Procedure Before Trial*, ¶6:622. This amendment is referred to as an "amendment to the original answer," and its purpose is to add, substitute, or change a part of the answer. *See* ***Cohen***, 244 Cal.App.2d at 657. The amendment should list the changes to be made and identify the page, paragraph, and line number where each change applies. Weil, *Civil Procedure Before Trial*, ¶6:622. This type of amendment should only be used to make relatively simple changes to the answer. *Id.*

3. Amended answer. The defendant can amend the answer by filing a complete, revised answer. *See* CRC 3.1324(a)(1), (c); ***Cohen***, 244 Cal.App.2d at 657; *CEB Procedure Before Trial*, §25.98; Weil, *Civil Procedure Before Trial*, ¶6.623. This amendment is referred to as an "amended answer," and its purpose is to provide a rewritten answer that supersedes the original. *See* ***Cohen***, 244 Cal.App.2d at 657; *CEB Procedure Before Trial*, §25.98. This type

of amendment is usually preferred by the court (and may be required) because judges tend to dislike working with two separate pleadings. Weil, *Civil Procedure Before Trial*, ¶6:624; *cf. CEB Procedure Before Trial*, §16.7 (discussing amended complaints).

§9.2 Procedure for amending. The procedures for amending an answer are the same as those for amending a complaint. See "Procedure for amending," ch. 3-C, §6.2, p. 229.

1. By filing & serving amended answer. The defendant can amend the answer by simply filing and serving an amendment in two instances:

(1) Without leave of court – before demurrer or hearing on demurrer. The defendant can amend the answer once at any time without leave of court (i.e., an amendment "of course") either before a demurrer is filed or after a demurrer is filed but before the hearing. CCP §472. See "Without leave of court – before answer or hearing on demurrer," ch. 3-C, §6.2.1(1), p. 229.

(2) With leave of court – after hearing on demurrer or motion to strike. The defendant can amend the answer after the court has granted the plaintiff's demurrer with leave to amend or granted the plaintiff's motion to strike with leave to amend. *See* CCP §472a(c), (d). See "With leave of court – after hearing on demurrer or motion to strike," ch. 3-C, §6.2.1(2), p. 229.

2. By stipulation. The defendant can amend the answer by obtaining the plaintiff's stipulation to allow the amendment. *See CEB Procedure Before Trial*, §25.105; *see, e.g.*, ***U.S. Nat'l Bank v. Bank of Am. Nat'l Trust & Sav. Ass'n*** (2d Dist.1963) 214 Cal.App.2d 74, 75 (dicta; parties took demurrer off calendar and stipulated to amended answer).

3. By ex parte application to amend. The defendant can amend the answer by filing an ex parte application for leave to amend. *See* CCP §473(a)(1); Weil, *Civil Procedure Before Trial*, ¶6:618. See "Ex parte application for leave to amend," ch. 3-C, §6.2.3, p. 230.

4. By noticed motion for leave to amend. The defendant can amend the answer by filing and serving a noticed motion for leave to amend at any time. *See* CCP §473(a)(1); Weil, *Civil Procedure Before Trial*, ¶6:636. The courts are usually very liberal when considering whether to grant leave to amend an answer because a defendant who is denied leave to amend may be permanently deprived of a defense to the action. ***Hulsey v. Koehler*** (3d Dist.1990) 218 Cal.App.3d 1150, 1159; ***Ramos v. City of Santa Clara*** (1st Dist.1973) 35 Cal.App.3d 93, 95-96; Weil, *Civil Procedure Before Trial*, ¶6:643. But this does not mean that an amendment will be *freely* allowed. *See* ***Hulsey***, 218 Cal.App.3d at 1159 (courts are more critical of proposed amendments to answers when offered after long unexplained delay or on day before trial); *see, e.g.*, ***Silica Brick Co. v. Winsor*** (1915) 171 Cal. 18, 22 (trial court did not abuse discretion in refusing amended answer because it was a sham and not made in good faith); ***Fisher v. Larsen*** (4th Dist.1982) 138 Cal.App.3d 627, 649 (trial court did not abuse discretion in denying leave to amend because P knew of defects in complaint for five months). See "Noticed motion for leave to amend," ch. 3-C, §6.2.4, p. 232.

§9.3 Effect of amendment. When an amended answer makes substantive changes to the original (or previous) answer, the amendment supersedes the original. *See* ***Jackson v. Pacific Gas & Elec. Co.*** (3d Dist.1949) 95 Cal.App.2d 204, 211 (former pleadings that have been substituted by amended pleadings filed with leave of court are considered abandoned and may be considered only for limited purposes). See "Original complaint superseded," ch. 3-C, §6.5.2, p. 237. There are instances, however, when an original verified answer could be used against the defendant, such as for impeachment at trial. *See* ***Kambourian v. Gray*** (2d Dist.1947) 81 Cal.App.2d 783, 789.

§10. SUPPLEMENTING THE ANSWER

When relevant events occur after the answer has been filed, the defendant may be allowed to file a supplemental answer. CCP §464(a); *see* ***Security-First Nat'l Bank v. Hauer*** (2d Dist.1941) 47 Cal.App.2d 302, 307. For example, a supplemental answer may be necessary when events giving rise to a new defense occur after the original answer has been filed. ***People v. Douglas*** (2d Dist.1971) 15 Cal.App.3d 814, 818-19. The courts are usually very liberal when considering whether to grant leave to supplement an answer when the after-occurring facts are pertinent. *Id.* at 820.

If the facts are not pertinent, leave to supplement can be denied. *See* ***Louie Queriolo Trucking, Inc. v. Superior Ct.*** (5th Dist.1967) 252 Cal.App.2d 194, 198 (trial court may deny right to file supplemental pleading if new matter does not, as matter of law, constitute defense).

§10.1 Effect on live answer. Unlike an amended answer, a supplemental answer does not supersede the original answer; it simply adds new allegations to be considered in conjunction with the original. *See* Weil, *Civil Procedure Before Trial*, ¶6:795.

§10.2 Procedure. The procedure for supplementing an answer is the same as that for supplementing the complaint. See "Procedure for supplementing," ch. 3-C, §7.2, p. 238.

C. CROSS-COMPLAINT

§1. GENERAL

§1.1 Purpose. The purpose of a cross-complaint is to ensure a complete determination of the entire controversy among the parties in a single proceeding. ***Valley Circle Estates v. VTN Consol., Inc.*** (1983) 33 Cal.3d 604, 614; ***Bewley v. Riggs*** (5th Dist.1968) 262 Cal.App.2d 188, 192. A defendant may file a separate pleading (i.e., apart from the answer) for affirmative relief against the plaintiff, a codefendant, or a third party. *See* CCP §428.10; ***McLarand, Vasquez & Partners v. Downey S&L Ass'n*** (4th Dist.1991) 231 Cal.App.3d 1450, 1454. A cross-complaint is considered to be a separate action from the complaint and thus is completely severable from the original complaint and answer. ***Coachella Valley Mosquito & Vector Control Dist. v. City of Indio*** (4th Dist.2002) 101 Cal.App.4th 12, 16; ***Security Pac. Nat'l Bank v. Adamo*** (2d Dist.1983) 142 Cal.App.3d 492, 496; *see* ***Tomales Bay Oyster Corp. v. Superior Ct.*** (1950) 35 Cal.2d 389, 394; ***Metropolitan Transit Sys. v. Superior Ct.*** (4th Dist.2007) 153 Cal.App.4th 293, 300. Because a cross-complaint is treated as a separate action, when a defendant files a cross-complaint against a plaintiff, each party is simultaneously a plaintiff and a defendant. ***Pacific Fin. Corp. v. Superior Ct.*** (1933) 219 Cal. 179, 182; ***Douglas v. Superior Ct.*** (2d Dist.1949) 94 Cal.App.2d 395, 398; *see also* ***Metropolitan Transit***, 153 Cal.App.4th at 301 (common understanding of "plaintiff" necessarily includes "cross-complainant," and "defendant" includes "cross-defendant").

§1.2 Primary authority. CCP §426.10 et seq. (compulsory cross-complaints), §428.10 et seq. (permissive cross-complaints).

§1.3 Secondary authority. The following secondary sources are cited as authority in this subchapter:

- *California Civil Procedure Before Trial* (CEB Online ed. 2014) (referred to as *CEB Procedure Before Trial*).
- Weil & Brown, *California Practice Guide: Civil Procedure Before Trial* (CD-ROM ed. 2014) (referred to as Weil, *Civil Procedure Before Trial*).
- Witkin, *California Procedure* (5th ed. 2008 & Supp.2014) (referred to as Witkin, *Cal. Procedure*).

§1.4 Judicial Council forms.

- PLD-C-001 (optional), cross-complaint (contract).
- PLD-PI-002 (optional), cross-complaint (personal injury, property damage, and wrongful death).
- SC-120 (mandatory), defendant's claim and order to go to small-claims court.

§2. TYPES OF CROSS-COMPLAINTS

§2.1 Against plaintiff. A defendant can, and in some cases must, assert claims against the plaintiff by filing a cross-complaint. *See* CCP §§426.30, 428.10(a), 428.50(a). The term "plaintiff" includes a person who files either a complaint or a cross-complaint. *Id.* §426.10(b); *see id.* §428.10.

1. Compulsory cross-complaint. A defendant must file a cross-complaint against the plaintiff asserting any related causes of action existing when the defendant serves its answer to avoid waiving those claims. CCP

§426.30(a). The purpose of a compulsory cross-complaint is similar to that of res judicata—namely, to prevent parties from splitting a cause of action into a series of suits in piecemeal litigation. ***Hulsey v. Koehler*** (3d Dist.1990) 218 Cal.App.3d 1150, 1157-58. To determine whether a claim is compulsory, see "Compulsory joinder of claims," ch. 3-B, §4.1, p. 200.

2. Permissive cross-complaint. A defendant can file a cross-complaint against the plaintiff for any related cause of action arising after the defendant serves its answer or for any cause of action unrelated to the plaintiff's suit. *See* CCP §428.10(a); ***Crocker Nat'l Bank v. Emerald*** (3d Dist.1990) 221 Cal.App.3d 852, 864; 10 Cal. Law Revision Comm'n Rep. (1970) pp. 551-52; Weil, *Civil Procedure Before Trial*, ¶6:516. If the defendant files a cross-complaint under §428.10(a), it can join with that claim any other causes of action it has against the plaintiff. *See* CCP §428.30. A permissive cross-complaint enables the court to render a final and binding judgment on all the matters in dispute between the parties. ***Nomellini Constr. Co. v. Harris*** (5th Dist.1969) 272 Cal.App.2d 352, 357. To determine whether a claim is permissive, see "Against P," ch. 3-B, §4.2.2(1), p. 202.

§2.2 Against codefendant or third party. A defendant can file a cross-complaint against a codefendant or third party if the defendant's cause of action (1) arises from the same transaction, occurrence, or series of transactions or occurrences as the action brought against the defendant, or (2) asserts a claim, right, or interest in the property or controversy that is the subject of the action brought against the defendant. CCP §428.10(b); *see, e.g.*, ***Paragon Real Estate Grp. v. Hansen*** (1st Dist.2009) 178 Cal.App.4th 177, 186-87 (D's cross-complaint against unrelated co-D for equitable indemnity was proper under CCP §428.10). A cross-complaint against a codefendant or third party is always permissive. *See* CCP §428.10(b); ***Insurance Co. of N. Am. v. Liberty Mut. Ins.*** (3d Dist.1982) 128 Cal.App.3d 297, 303. If the defendant files a cross-complaint under §428.10(b), it can join with that claim any other causes of action it has against that party. *See* CCP §428.30. Thus, the defendant can join all claims it may have against a cross-defendant if just one claim arises from the same subject matter as the underlying suit. *See id.* §§428.10(b), 428.30. To determine how to assert a cause of action against a codefendant or third party, see "Against codefendant or third party," ch. 3-B, §4.2.2(2), p. 202.

NOTE

When the defendant files a cross-complaint under CCP §428.10, it can join any person as a cross-complainant or cross-defendant if, had the cross-complaint been filed as an independent action, the joinder of that party would have been permitted by the statutes governing joinder of parties. CCP §428.20; see id. §§378, 379. This statement is consistent with the general principle that a cross-complaint is treated like a complaint in an independent action. 10 Cal. Law Revision Comm'n Rep. (1970) pp. 552-53. For the requirements for joining parties, see "Joinder of Parties," ch. 3-B, §3, p. 193.

§3. DEADLINE TO FILE

§3.1 Against plaintiff. The defendant can file the cross-complaint as a matter of right anytime before or at the time the answer is due, if the cross-complaint is brought against the plaintiff (i.e., a party who files either a complaint or a cross-complaint). *See* CCP §§426.30(a), 428.50(a); ***Nels E. Nelson, Inc. v. Tarman*** (1st Dist.1958) 163 Cal.App.2d 714, 730; Weil, *Civil Procedure Before Trial*, ¶6:552. The defendant must obtain leave to file a cross-complaint anytime after that date. CCP §428.50(c); *see id.* §426.50. See "Motion for Leave to File," §6, p. 351. The defendant cannot file a cross-complaint after judgment is entered on the complaint. *See* ***City of Hanford v. Superior Ct.*** (5th Dist.1989) 208 Cal.App.3d 580, 587.

§3.2 Against codefendant or third party. The defendant can file the cross-complaint as a matter of right anytime before the court sets a date for trial, if the cross-complaint is brought against a codefendant or third party. CCP §428.50(b); Weil, *Civil Procedure Before Trial*, ¶6:553. The defendant must obtain leave to file a cross-complaint anytime after that date, even if the court later changes or vacates the trial date. *See* CCP §428.50(c); ***Loney v. Superior***

Ct. (3d Dist.1984) 160 Cal.App.3d 719, 722-23. See "Motion for Leave to File," §6, this page. The defendant cannot file a cross-complaint after judgment is entered on the complaint. *See* ***City of Hanford v. Superior Ct.*** (5th Dist.1989) 208 Cal.App.3d 580, 587.

§4. FORMAT & CONTENTS

§4.1 Generally. The cross-complaint must comply with the formatting and content requirements of the California Rules of Court. *See* CRC 2.100-2.119, 2.130-2.141. See "General Requirements for Papers," ch. 1-B, §2, p. 9. The rules governing the format of the cross-complaint are nearly identical to those for the complaint. *See* CCP §425.10 (complaint and cross-complaint must contain statement of facts and demand for judgment). See "Contents & Format of Complaint," ch. 3-C, §3, p. 210. The caption of the cross-complaint, however, should identify both the original parties (i.e., plaintiff and defendant) and the parties to the cross-complaint, known as the "cross-complainant" and the "cross-defendant." *See CEB Procedure Before Trial*, §26.31; Weil, *Civil Procedure Before Trial*, ¶6:547.

§4.2 Reclassifying limited cases. If the defendant's cross-complaint causes the action to exceed the maximum amount in controversy for a limited civil case (or otherwise changes the limited nature of the action), the defendant must do the following:

1. Include language in the caption of the cross-complaint indicating that the action is a limited civil case to be reclassified by the filing of a cross-complaint. CCP §403.030.

2. Pay the reclassification fees provided in CCP §403.060. *Id.* §403.030.

§5. SERVING & FILING

§5.1 Serving. The defendant must serve the cross-complaint on each party in the action. CCP §428.60; *see* CRC 3.110(c) (if cross-complaint adds new parties, it must be served on all parties).

1. Parties. If a party has appeared in the action, the cross-complaint is normally served on its attorney. CCP §428.60(2). It can also be served on the party, if she has appeared without an attorney, in the same manner as service of papers. *Id.* See "Serving Documents," ch. 1-G, p. 63.

2. Nonparties. To serve a nonparty that has not appeared in the action, the defendant must serve a summons for the cross-complaint on the nonparty in the same manner as a complaint. CCP §428.60(1); *e.g.*, ***Fox Woodsum Lumber Co. v. Janes*** (2d Dist.1946) 76 Cal.App.2d 748, 751 (cross-P was required to serve summons on cross-Ds who had not appeared, but not on P and co-D, who were already parties to suit). The cross-defendant must be served with the summons, a copy of the cross-complaint (or the most recently amended cross-complaint), and any answers that have been filed. CRC 3.222. See "Joining the Defendant—Service of Process," ch. 3-H, p. 295.

§5.2 Filing. The defendant must file the cross-complaint and proof of service. *See* CRC 3.110(c).

1. Parties. If the cross-complaint was served on a party, the defendant must file the cross-complaint and proof of service at the same time. CRC 3.110(c).

2. Nonparties. If the cross-complaint was served on a nonparty, the defendant must file the cross-complaint and, within 30 days after the date of filing, proof of service. CRC 3.110(c).

§6. MOTION FOR LEAVE TO FILE

§6.1 Deadline to file. See "Deadline to File," §3, p. 350.

§6.2 Grounds for relief. The defendant can seek leave to file a cross-complaint on the following grounds:

1. Compulsory cross-complaint. If the cross-complaint is compulsory, the defendant must allege that its failure to timely plead the claim was in good faith. CCP §426.50. "Good faith" is established by proving a negative—namely, there is no substantial evidence that the defendant acted in bad faith. *See* ***Silver Orgs. v. Frank*** (1st Dist.1990) 217 Cal.App.3d 94, 100; *see, e.g.*, ***Gherman v. Colburn*** (2d Dist.1977) 72 Cal.App.3d 544, 559 (bad faith established because D knew of claims for over 30 days and waited to file cross-complaint until first day of trial and

because of long history of litigation between parties). A finding of bad faith requires evidence of "dishonest purpose, moral obliquity, sinister motive, furtive design or ill will." ***Silver Orgs.***, 217 Cal.App.3d at 100. Evidence of oversight, inadvertence, neglect, or mistake is, by itself, insufficient to establish bad faith. *Id.* at 99; *see* CCP §426.50.

2. Permissive cross-complaint. If the cross-complaint is permissive, the defendant must show that leave to file should be granted in the interest of justice. *See* CCP §428.50(c). The defendant should argue that it was not dilatory in seeking leave. *See, e.g.*, ***Crocker Nat'l Bank v. Emerald*** (3d Dist.1990) 221 Cal.App.3d 852, 864 (cross-P provided no explanation for delay in seeking permission to file proposed cross-complaint); Weil, *Civil Procedure Before Trial*, ¶6:562 (motion should explain delay, such as recent discovery of new facts).

§6.3 Form. A motion for leave to file a cross-complaint should be in writing and in the same form as noticed motions generally. See "Motion Papers," ch. 1-D, §5, p. 27.

§6.4 Setting the hearing. The hearing for a motion for leave to file is set according to the general rules for a noticed motion. See "Noticed motion," ch. 1-H, §4.1, p. 81.

§6.5 Court's ruling.

1. Compulsory cross-complaint. If the cross-complaint is compulsory and the defendant establishes good faith, the court must grant leave to file. CCP §426.50. Section 426.50 is liberally construed to prevent parties from forfeiting their causes of action. *Id.*; ***Silver Orgs. v. Frank*** (1st Dist.1990) 217 Cal.App.3d 94, 98-99. To prevent injustice, however, the court can impose terms and conditions (e.g., postponement, payment of costs) when granting leave. ***Silver Orgs.***, 217 Cal.App.3d at 101; 10 Cal. Law Revision Comm'n Rep. (1971) p. 1133; *see* CCP §426.50.

2. Permissive cross-complaint. If the cross-complaint is permissive, the decision to grant leave is solely within the court's discretion. ***Crocker Nat'l Bank v. Emerald*** (3d Dist.1990) 221 Cal.App.3d 852, 864.

§7. RESPONDING TO CROSS-COMPLAINT

The cross-defendant must file a response to the cross-complaint or else risk a default judgment. *See* ***Saum v. Reppert*** (3d Dist.1995) 35 Cal.App.4th 1766, 1773.

§7.1 Types of responses.

1. Preanswer motion. The cross-defendant can respond by filing a preanswer motion. CCP §432.10. See "Preanswer motions & pleadings," ch. 4-A, §3.2, p. 330.

2. Demurrer. The cross-defendant can respond by filing a demurrer. CCP §432.10. See "Demurrer," ch. 4-H, p. 396.

3. Special answer. A cross-defendant who is a codefendant or third party can respond by filing a special answer. CCP §428.70(b). A special answer allows the cross-defendant to allege any defenses the original defendant may have against the original plaintiff. *See id.*; 10 Cal. Law Revision Comm'n Rep. (1970) p. 555. This lets the cross-defendant protect itself from the original defendant's neglect in asserting a proper defense to the original plaintiff's action. 10 Cal. Law Revision Comm'n Rep. (1970) p. 555. The special answer gives the cross-defendant the right to participate in the action directly against the original plaintiff. ***Administrative Mgmt. Servs. v. Fidelity & Deposit Co.*** (2d Dist.1982) 129 Cal.App.3d 484, 489.

(1) When to file. A special answer can be filed only when (1) the defendant cross-complains against a codefendant or third party and (2) the cross-complaint alleges the codefendant or third party is liable to the defendant for any amounts it may have to pay the plaintiff. *See* CCP §428.70; 10 Cal. Law Revision Comm'n Rep. (1970) p. 555. The codefendant or third party should file the special answer when it files its answer to the defendant's cross-complaint. CCP §428.70(b).

(2) What to file. A special answer is a separate document from the codefendant's or third party's answer to the cross-complaint and contains any defenses the original defendant could assert against the original plaintiff. *See* CCP §428.70(b); 10 Cal. Law Revision Comm'n Rep. (1970) p. 555.

(3) Whom to serve. A special answer must be served on both the original defendant and the original plaintiff. *See* CCP §428.70(b).

4. Other pleading. The cross-defendant can respond by filing another pleading, such as an answer or a cross-complaint. *See* CCP §§428.10, 432.10. See "Answer, denial & cross-complaint," ch. 4-A, §3.3, p. 331.

§7.2 Deadline to respond. The cross-defendant has 30 days after service of the cross-complaint to file and serve a response. CCP §432.10. The deadline to file and serve may be extended by one of the following:

1. Method of service. The deadline is extended if the cross-defendant has appeared in the action and the cross-complaint is served by mail, express mail, fax, or electronic transmission. *See* CCP §§428.60(2), 1013; 3 Witkin, *Cal. Procedure*, Actions, §1020. See "Add time for method of service," ch. 1-G, §6.1.4, p. 70.

2. Stipulation. The parties can stipulate to one 15-day extension without leave of court. CRC 3.110(d).

3. Court order. The court, on its own motion or the cross-defendant's application, can extend the 30-day response period. CRC 3.110(e). If the cross-defendant seeks the extension, its application must be filed before the time for service has passed. *Id.* The application must be supported by a declaration containing the following:

(1) An explanation showing why service has not been completed. *Id.*

(2) Documentation of the efforts made to complete service. *Id.*

(3) The date by which service is proposed to be completed. *Id.*

§8. AMENDING CROSS-COMPLAINT

The procedures for amending a cross-complaint are generally the same as those for amending a complaint. *See* CCP §§472, 472a, 473; ***People v. Clausen*** (1st Dist.1967) 248 Cal.App.2d 770, 782. See "Amending the Complaint," ch. 3-C, §6, p. 228. One notable exception, however, is that the statute of limitations will not bar the defendant from amending its compulsory cross-complaint to include a claim based on an injury that is different from the injury alleged in the original cross-complaint as long as (1) the injuries arose from the same occurrence and (2) the limitations period for the new claim did not expire before the plaintiff filed its original complaint. *See* ***Sidney v. Superior Ct.*** (2d Dist.1988) 198 Cal.App.3d 710, 714, 717.

§9. SUPPLEMENTING CROSS-COMPLAINT

The rules for supplementing a complaint also apply to a cross-complaint. See "Supplementing the Complaint," ch. 3-C, §7, p. 238.

§10. OTHER ISSUES

§10.1 Limitations. In most cases, the statute of limitations will bar a cross-complaint if the limitations period expires before the cross-complaint is filed. *See* ***Luna Records Corp. v. Alvarado*** (1st Dist.1991) 232 Cal.App.3d 1023, 1026; ***Sidney v. Superior Ct.*** (2d Dist.1988) 198 Cal.App.3d 710, 714. However, there are some exceptions.

1. Defendant vs. plaintiff. When the defendant files a cross-complaint against the plaintiff, the statute of limitations will not bar the cross-complaint if all of the following are true:

(1) The defendant's cross-complaint asserts a cause of action against the plaintiff. *See* ***Sidney***, 198 Cal.App.3d at 714-15. This exception does not apply to cross-complaints against codefendants or third parties. ***Trindade v. Superior Ct.*** (1st Dist.1973) 29 Cal.App.3d 857, 859.

(2) The defendant's cause of action arises from the same transaction or occurrence as the cause of action asserted in the complaint. ***Sidney***, 198 Cal.App.3d at 714. In other words, the claim must be compulsory. Weil, *Civil Procedure Before Trial*, ¶6:595.

(3) The limitations period for the defendant's cause of action had not expired before the plaintiff filed the original complaint. *See* ***Sidney***, 198 Cal.App.3d at 714.

CAUTION

If the defendant voluntarily dismisses, and does not renew, a compulsory cross-complaint before the action is final, the defendant will be barred from asserting the claims in a later action. ***Hill v. City of Clovis*** *(5th Dist.1998) 63 Cal.App.4th 434, 445;* ***Carroll v. Import Motors, Inc.*** *(1st Dist.1995) 33 Cal.App.4th 1429, 1435-36.*

2. Contractor vs. subcontractor. When a contractor files a cross-complaint against a subcontractor, the statute of limitations will not bar the cross-complaint if all of the following are true:

(1) A property owner filed an action against the contractor to recover damages for latent construction defects or for property damage arising from the latent defects within ten years after the construction was substantially completed. *See* CCP §337.15(a); *see, e.g.*, ***Grange Debris Box & Wrecking Co. v. Superior Ct.*** (1st Dist.1993) 16 Cal.App.4th 1349, 1355 (contractor's cross-complaint barred because original action not brought until after ten years from date of substantial completion of construction), *disapproved on other grounds*, ***Lantzy v. Centex Homes*** (2003) 31 Cal.4th 363. If the action is filed after ten years, the property owner must allege the contractor engaged in willful misconduct or fraudulently concealed the defects. *See* CCP §337.15(f); ***Pine Terrace Apts., L.P. v. Windscape, LLC*** (5th Dist.2009) 170 Cal.App.4th 1, 15.

(2) The contractor is seeking equitable indemnity from the subcontractor. ***Valley Circle Estates v. VTN Consol., Inc.*** (1983) 33 Cal.3d 604, 609; *see* CCP §337.15(c).

NOTE

While the statute of limitations may bar a defendant's cross-complaint for monetary relief, the defendant may still be able to assert the right of setoff as an affirmative defense in its answer. See CCP §431.70; ***Construction Prot. Servs. v. TIG Specialty Ins.*** *(2002) 29 Cal.4th 189, 195.* *See "Affirmative Defenses," ch. 4-B, §5, p. 343.*

§10.2 Exceeding court's jurisdiction – small claims. In certain small-claims cases, the defendant can file its cross-complaint as an original complaint in a court of competent jurisdiction (i.e., in superior court as a limited or unlimited civil case).

1. Grounds. The defendant can initiate a separate action in the superior court if the following requirements are met:

(1) The plaintiff sued the defendant in small-claims court. *See* CCP §116.390(a).

(2) The defendant has a claim against the plaintiff that exceeds the jurisdictional limits of the small-claims court. *Id.*

(3) The defendant's claim relates to the contract, transaction, matter, or event that is the subject of the plaintiff's claim. *Id.*

2. What to file. The defendant must file the following in the small-claims court:

(1) A request to transfer the plaintiff's claim to the superior court. CCP §116.390(a).

(2) A declaration stating facts about the defendant's claim against the plaintiff. *Id.* §116.390(b).

(3) A copy of the defendant's complaint against the plaintiff. *Id.*

3. Deadline to file. The defendant must file the request and a copy of the complaint at or before the time set for the hearing on the small-claims action. CCP §116.390(b).

4. Service. The defendant must have a copy of the declaration and complaint personally served on the plaintiff at or before the time set for the hearing on the small-claims action. CCP §116.390(b).

5. Ruling. In ruling on a motion to transfer, the small-claims court can do the following:

(1) Render judgment on the small-claims action before transferring. CCP §116.390(c).

(2) Not render judgment and transfer the small-claims action. *Id.*

(3) Refuse to transfer the small-claims action on the ground that justice would not be served. *Id.*

6. Files & papers. If the court transfers the small-claims action, it must transmit all files and papers to the appropriate department of the superior court. CCP §116.390(d).

7. Fees & costs.

(1) Plaintiff appears. If the court transfers the small-claims action, the plaintiff does not need to pay any fees to the superior-court clerk unless it makes an appearance in that court. CCP §116.390(e). If the plaintiff makes an appearance, it must pay the filing fee and any other fee required of a defendant in the superior court. *Id.*

(2) Plaintiff does not prevail. If the superior court rules against the plaintiff, the defendant can be awarded costs incurred as a result of transferring the small-claims action, including attorney fees and filing fees. CCP §116.390(e).

§10.3 Separate trials. After the defendant files its cross-complaint, the court can, on its own motion, order separate trials for the sake of convenience, the avoidance of prejudice, or expediency and economy. CCP §1048(b). Determining whether to order separate trials is within the court's discretion. ***McLellan v. McLellan*** (2d Dist.1972) 23 Cal.App.3d 343, 353; ***Vegetable Oil Prods. Co. v. Superior Ct.*** (2d Dist.1963) 213 Cal.App.2d 252, 259.

D. CHALLENGING SUBJECT-MATTER JURISDICTION

§1. GENERAL

§1.1 Purpose. Subject-matter jurisdiction is a court's power to hear or determine a particular case. ***Donaldson v. National Mar., Inc.*** (2005) 35 Cal.4th 503, 512; *see* ***Abelleira v. District Ct. of Appeal*** (1941) 17 Cal.2d 280, 288; ***Totten v. Hill*** (1st Dist.2007) 154 Cal.App.4th 40, 46. The purpose of challenging subject-matter jurisdiction is to prevent the court from acting in a matter over which it has no authority. For more on the subject-matter jurisdiction of California courts, see "Choosing the Court—Subject-Matter Jurisdiction," ch. 3-E, p. 248.

§1.2 Primary authority. *See* CCP §430.10(a) (demurrer or answer), §436(b) (motion to strike), §437c(a) (motion for summary judgment), §437c(f) (motion for summary adjudication), §438(c)(1)(B)(i) (motion for judgment on the pleadings).

§1.3 Secondary authority. The following secondary sources are cited as authority in this subchapter:

- *California Civil Procedure Before Trial* (CEB Online ed. 2014) (referred to as *CEB Procedure Before Trial*).
- Weil & Brown, *California Practice Guide: Civil Procedure Before Trial* (CD-ROM ed. 2014) (referred to as Weil, *Civil Procedure Before Trial*).
- Younger & Bradley, *Younger on California Motions* (2014-15) (referred to as Younger, *Cal. Motions*).
- ***O'Connor's Federal Rules * Civil Trials*** (2015) (referred to as ***O'Connor's Federal Rules***).

§2. GROUNDS FOR CHALLENGING

For a discussion of the grounds that can be raised to challenge a court's subject-matter jurisdiction, see "Choosing the Court—Subject-Matter Jurisdiction," ch. 3-E, p. 248.

§3. PROCEDURES FOR CHALLENGING

A court's subject-matter jurisdiction can be challenged at any time—even for the first time on appeal—because the issue of a court's subject-matter jurisdiction cannot be waived. *See* CCP §430.80(a); ***Great W. Casinos, Inc. v. Morongo Band of Mission Indians*** (2d Dist.1999) 74 Cal.App.4th 1407, 1417-18; ***Keiffer v. Bechtel Corp.*** (1st

Dist.1998) 65 Cal.App.4th 893, 896. A number of procedural devices can be used to bring the matter to the court's attention. *See* ***Barnick v. Longs Drug Stores*** (4th Dist.1988) 203 Cal.App.3d 377, 379 (defect in subject-matter jurisdiction is so basic that it can be raised at any time by any available procedure). These include the following: (1) a demurrer, (2) a motion to strike, (3) a motion for judgment on the pleadings, (4) a notice of removal to federal court, (5) a motion for summary judgment, (6) a motion for summary adjudication, and (7) an affirmative defense in the answer. Choosing the right procedure depends on whether the defect appears on the face of the complaint.

4-1. OVERVIEW OF PROCEDURES

	Procedure	Time to file	What is challenged
		Defect on face of complaint	
1	Demurrer	Within 30 days after service of summons	Entire complaint or cause of action
2	Motion to strike	Within 30 days after service of summons	All or part of complaint or cause of action
3	Motion for judgment on the pleadings	After answer filed and time to demur has passed, but not after pretrial-conference order entered or within 30 days of initial trial date, whichever is later	Entire complaint or cause of action
4	Removal	Within 30 days after D receives summons and initial complaint	One or more removable claims
		Defect not on face of complaint	
5	Motion for summary judgment	At least 60 days after general appearance, but not within 105-125 days of trial date (deadline varies depending on method of service)	Entire complaint
6	Motion for summary adjudication	At least 60 days after general appearance, but not within 105-125 days of trial date (deadline varies depending on method of service)	One or more causes of action
7	Answer – affirmative defense	Within 30 days after service of complaint	All or part of complaint or cause of action
8	Removal	Within 30 days after D receives paper indicating removable claim	One or more removable claims

§3.1 Defect appears on face of complaint. Certain procedures can be used when the court's lack of subject-matter jurisdiction is apparent on the face of the complaint or from any matter that is judicially noticeable. *See* CCP §430.30(a) (demurrer), §436(b) (motion to strike), §438(d) (motion for judgment on pleadings); *see, e.g.*, ***Ansley v. Ameriquest Mortg. Co.*** (9th Cir.2003) 340 F.3d 858, 861 (in federal-question cases, suit removable when federal question appears on face of properly pleaded complaint). In other words, the defect cannot be established by extrinsic evidence. This evidentiary limitation makes these procedures of limited value because (1) the court is presumed to have jurisdiction over the action, (2) the plaintiff is not required to plead facts in its complaint establishing the court's subject-matter jurisdiction, and (3) the defendant must affirmatively show lack of jurisdiction. *See* ***Cheney v. Trauzettel*** (1937) 9 Cal.2d 158, 160; Younger, *Cal. Motions*, §6:11. These procedures include the following:

1. Demurrer. A defendant normally challenges the court's subject-matter jurisdiction by demurrer. *See* CCP §§430.10(a), 430.30(a); ***Greener v. Workers' Comp. Appeals Bd.*** (1993) 6 Cal.4th 1028, 1036. See "Demurrer," ch. 4-H, p. 396.

(1) Timing. A demurrer must be served and filed within 30 days after service of summons. *See* CCP §§412.20(a)(3), 430.40(a), 432.10. This deadline makes the demurrer an attractive method for challenging subject-matter jurisdiction because it could resolve the issue before much money has been spent. *See* Younger, *Cal. Motions*, §6:11.

(2) Scope. A demurrer can challenge the entire complaint or a specific cause of action. CCP §430.50(a); *see* ***PH II, Inc. v. Superior Ct.*** (1st Dist.1995) 33 Cal.App.4th 1680, 1682-83 (demurrer cannot be used to challenge part of cause of action; to challenge less than entire cause of action, D must use motion to strike). If a demurrer challenges an entire complaint, it will be overruled if a single cause of action in the complaint is not vulnerable to challenge. ***Lord v. Garland*** (1946) 27 Cal.2d 840, 850; *CEB Procedure Before Trial*, §23.21. For a discussion of counts and causes of action, see "Determining cause of action," ch. 3-C, §3.6.1, p. 215.

2. Motion to strike. A defendant can challenge the court's subject-matter jurisdiction with a motion to strike. ***Greener***, 6 Cal.4th at 1036; *see* ***Velez v. Smith*** (1st Dist.2006) 142 Cal.App.4th 1154, 1160. See "Motion to Strike," ch. 4-J, p. 418.

(1) Timing. A motion to strike must be served and filed within 30 days after service of summons. *See* CCP §§412.20(a)(3), 435(b)(1); CRC 3.1322(b). This deadline makes the motion to strike an attractive method for challenging subject-matter jurisdiction because it could resolve the issue before much money has been spent. *Cf.* Younger, *Cal. Motions*, §6:11 (discussing demurrers).

(2) Scope. A motion to strike can challenge all or any part of the complaint. *See* CCP §436(b). Thus, a defendant can use a motion to strike to knock out a single count in a cause of action, which is something most of the other procedural devices cannot do. Motions to strike are rarely used to challenge the court's jurisdiction over an entire action. For a discussion of counts and causes of action, see "Determining cause of action," ch. 3-C, §3.6.1, p. 215.

3. Motion for judgment on the pleadings. A defendant can challenge the court's subject-matter jurisdiction with a motion for judgment on the pleadings. CCP §438(c)(1)(B)(i); *see* ***Saks v. Parilla, Hubbard & Militzok*** (4th Dist.1998) 67 Cal.App.4th 565, 567. See "Motion for Judgment on the Pleadings," ch. 4-I, p. 411.

(1) Timing. A motion for judgment on the pleadings can be made only after an answer is filed and the time to demur has passed (i.e., more than 30 days after service of summons). *See* CCP §§412.20(a)(3), 432.10, 438(f)(2). This may make the motion more attractive than a demurrer because it gives the defendant some additional time to determine whether the court has subject-matter jurisdiction, while allowing the motion to still be filed relatively early in the action. However, the time to file the motion is not unlimited; it cannot be filed after a pretrial-conference order has been entered or within 30 days of the initial trial date, whichever is later, unless the court grants leave. *Id.* §438(e); *see* Weil, *Civil Procedure Before Trial*, ¶7:280.

(2) Scope. A motion for judgment on the pleadings is comparable to a demurrer. ***Evans v. California Trailer Ct., Inc.*** (5th Dist.1994) 28 Cal.App.4th 540, 548. Thus, the motion can challenge the entire complaint or a specific cause of action, but not individual counts. *See* ***Fire Ins. Exch. v. Superior Ct.*** (2d Dist.2004) 116 Cal.App.4th 446, 452. *But see* Weil, *Civil Procedure Before Trial*, ¶7:295 (in complex litigation, court can use motion to eliminate improper counts). See "Compared to 'count'," ch. 3-C, §3.6.1(2), p. 215 (discussing difference between cause of action and count).

4. Removal. A defendant can challenge the court's subject-matter jurisdiction with a notice of removal to federal court. *See* 28 U.S.C. §§1441, 1446. The notice must be filed within 30 days after the defendant receives both the summons and a copy of the initial complaint that indicates a removable claim. *See id.* §1446(b)(1); ***Murphy Bros. v. Michetti Pipe Stringing, Inc.*** (1999) 526 U.S. 344, 354. For a discussion of the jurisdiction of federal courts, see ***O'Connor's Federal Rules***, "Choosing the Court—Jurisdiction," ch. 2-F, p. 121. For a discussion of removal to federal court, see ***O'Connor's Federal Rules***, "Defendant's Notice of Removal," ch. 4-A, p. 267.

§3.2 Defect does not appear on face of complaint. Certain procedures must be used when the court's lack of subject-matter jurisdiction does not appear on the face of the complaint or from any matter that is judicially noticeable but instead can only be established by extrinsic evidence. *See* CCP §430.30(b) (answer), §437c(b)(1) (motion for summary judgment), §437c(f) (motion for summary adjudication); *see, e.g.*, ***Harris v. Bankers Life & Cas. Co.*** (9th Cir.2005) 425 F.3d 689, 695-96 (although suit was not removable when initial complaint was filed, suit later became removable). These procedures include the following:

CHALLENGING JURISDICTION

1. Motion for summary judgment. A defendant can challenge the court's subject-matter jurisdiction with a motion for summary judgment. ***Greener v. Workers' Comp. Appeals Bd.*** (1993) 6 Cal.4th 1028, 1036; ***Garofalo v. Princess Cruises, Inc.*** (2d Dist.2000) 85 Cal.App.4th 1060, 1068; *see* CCP §437c(a). See "Motion for Summary Judgment," ch. 10-B, p. 1117.

(1) Timing. A motion for summary judgment can be made after 60 days have passed from the general appearance of the parties. CCP §437c(a). See "General appearance," ch. 3-G, §5.1.1, p. 285. The deadline for serving a motion for summary judgment depends on the method of service. See "Generally," ch. 10-B, §6.2.2(1), p. 1122; "Date," ch. 10-B, §11.2, p. 1136.

(2) Scope. A motion for summary judgment challenges the entire action. *See* CCP §437c(a); ***Aguilar v. Atlantic Richfield Co.*** (2001) 25 Cal.4th 826, 843; Younger, *Cal. Motions*, §16:2. Thus, if the motion is successful, it ends the case. Younger, *Cal. Motions*, §16:2.

2. Motion for summary adjudication. A defendant can challenge the court's subject-matter jurisdiction with a motion for summary adjudication. Weil, *Civil Procedure Before Trial*, ¶10:230.5; *see* CCP §437c(f)(1); *see also* ***Grant-Burton v. Covenant Care, Inc.*** (2d Dist.2002) 99 Cal.App.4th 1361, 1370 (principles governing summary judgment also apply to summary adjudication). See "Motion for Summary Adjudication," ch. 10-C, p. 1145.

(1) Timing. A motion for summary adjudication is subject to the same timing and deadlines as a motion for summary judgment. *See* CCP §437c(f)(2). See "Timing," §3.2.1(1), this page.

(2) Scope. A motion for summary adjudication can be used to argue that the court does not have subject-matter jurisdiction over one or more causes of action. *See* CCP §437c(f)(1).

3. Answer – affirmative defense. A defendant can challenge the court's subject-matter jurisdiction with an affirmative defense in its answer. *See* ***Warburton/Buttner v. Superior Ct.*** (4th Dist.2002) 103 Cal.App.4th 1170, 1176 & n.2. Unlike other procedural devices, an affirmative defense only puts the alleged defect in issue; it does not resolve whether the court lacks subject-matter jurisdiction. Because an affirmative defense requires proof of facts beyond those stated in the complaint, the defendant will have to establish the defense through another procedural device, such as a motion for summary judgment, or at trial. *See, e.g.*, ***Masi v. Nagle*** (3d Dist.1992) 5 Cal.App.4th 608, 611 (D filed motion for summary judgment on ground that court lacked subject-matter jurisdiction because Ps had not met preconditions to suit and had not exhausted administrative remedies); *see also* ***City of Stockton v. Superior Ct.*** (2007) 42 Cal.4th 730, 746 n.12 (affirmative defense depends on facts beyond those put at issue by P). See "Affirmative Defenses," ch. 4-B, §5, p. 343.

4. Removal. A defendant can challenge the court's subject-matter jurisdiction with a notice of removal to federal court when the suit is not removable at the time of filing but later becomes removable. *See* 28 U.S.C. §1446(b)(3). The notice must be filed within 30 days after the defendant receives a copy of an amended pleading, motion, order, or other paper that indicates a removable claim. *Id.*; *see* ***Harris***, 425 F.3d at 697 (30-day window to file notice of removal runs from time D is on notice of removability). For a discussion of the jurisdiction of federal courts, see ***O'Connor's Federal Rules***, "Choosing the Court—Jurisdiction," ch. 2-F, p. 121. For a discussion of removal to federal court, see ***O'Connor's Federal Rules***, "Defendant's Notice of Removal," ch. 4-A, p. 267.

E. MOTION TO TRANSFER OR CHANGE VENUE

This subchapter discusses motions to transfer or change venue in ordinary civil actions. It does not cover the specialized transfer procedures in small-claims actions (CCP §116.370) or in actions brought under the Labor Code, the Public Utilities Code, or the Probate Code. Nor does it cover motions to transfer for the purpose of coordinating actions involving common questions of fact or law. For a discussion of that type of motion, see "Coordinating Noncomplex Cases," ch. 5-H, §5, p. 529.

§1. GENERAL

§1.1 Purpose. There are several different types of motions to transfer or change venue, but they are all used for the same purpose—to move a case from one county to another. *See* CCP §§394(a), 396a(b), 396b(a), 397, 397.5, 401(2); ***Olinick v. BMG Entm't*** (2d Dist.2006) 138 Cal.App.4th 1286, 1291 n.4; *see, e.g.*, ***Cubic Corp. v. Superior Ct.*** (1st Dist.1986) 186 Cal.App.3d 622, 623-24 (D moved to change venue from Alameda County to San Diego County).

§1.2 Primary authority. CCP §§394, 396a, 396b, 397, 397.5, 398, 399, 400, 401.

§1.3 Secondary authority. The following secondary sources are cited as authority in this subchapter:

- *California Civil Procedure Before Trial* (CEB Online ed. 2014) (referred to as *CEB Procedure Before Trial*).
- Weil & Brown, *California Practice Guide: Civil Procedure Before Trial* (CD-ROM ed. 2014) (referred to as Weil, *Civil Procedure Before Trial*).
- Witkin, *California Procedure* (5th ed. 2008 & Supp.2014) (referred to as Witkin, *Cal. Procedure*).

§2. OVERVIEW

Choosing the right venue motion depends primarily on the movant's grounds for the transfer or change. Other important factors include whether the movant is a plaintiff or a defendant and whether any of the parties is a governmental entity. For a brief overview of the different kinds of motions, see "Types of Venue Motions," chart 4-2, this page.

NOTE

A motion to "transfer" venue is different from a motion to "change" venue. The former is used to challenge venue when it is improper. The latter is used to challenge venue when it is proper but the case should be tried elsewhere for other reasons.

4-2. TYPES OF VENUE MOTIONS

	Type of motion	Grounds	Who can file	Authority
1	Transfer to proper court	County of suit is improper.	• Defendant • Court in unlawful-detainer and certain consumer actions	CCP §§396a(b), 396b(a), 397(a)
2	Change venue	(1) No impartial trial, (2) convenience of witnesses, (3) no qualified judge, or (4) ends of justice in marital-dissolution proceeding.	Any party	CCP §§397(b)-(e), 397.5

4-2. TYPES OF VENUE MOTIONS (CONTINUED)

Type of motion		Grounds	Who can file	Authority
3	Transfer to neutral county	(1) Plaintiff is a local governmental entity and suit was not filed in neutral county, or (2) defendant is a local governmental entity and (a) suit was not filed in neutral county or (b) suit alleges entity negligently injured plaintiff, plaintiff's property, or both and was not filed in entity-county or county where entity is situated.	• For (1), any party • For (2), defendant that is local governmental entity	CCP §394(a)
4	Remove action from Sacramento County	Plaintiff is a state governmental entity, suit was filed in Sacramento County, action is not a proceeding involving unclaimed property in possession of federal entity or officers, and defendant resides or has principal office in different county.	Defendant	CCP §§401(2), 1609

§3. MOTION TO TRANSFER TO PROPER COURT

The venue where the plaintiff's original complaint is filed is presumed to be the proper place for trial. ***Mission Imps., Inc. v. Superior Ct.*** (1982) 31 Cal.3d 921, 929; ***Black Diamond Asphalt, Inc. v. Superior Ct.*** (3d Dist.2003) 109 Cal.App.4th 166, 170. If the venue is improper, the defendant bears the burden of bringing this defect to the court's attention. *See* ***Mission Imps.***, 31 Cal.3d at 929. The defendant can raise the issue of improper venue by making a motion to transfer the action to the proper court. *See* CCP §§396a(b), 396b(a), 397(a). To determine whether an action has been filed in the proper court, see "Choosing the Court—Venue," ch. 3-F, p. 270.

§3.1 Who can file.

1. Defendant. The defendant can file a motion to transfer. CCP §§396a(b), 396b(a). If there are multiple defendants, one defendant can file a motion to transfer without having to join or obtain the consent of the other defendants. *See* ***Goossen v. Clifton*** (1st Dist.1946) 75 Cal.App.2d 44, 50. If the motion is granted, the court will transfer the action to the county desired by the moving defendant, even though any of the other defendants' county of residence would also be proper. *See* ***Cubic Corp. v. Superior Ct.*** (1st Dist.1986) 186 Cal.App.3d 622, 625. The following types of defendants cannot file a motion to transfer for improper venue:

(1) Person appearing for fictitiously named defendant. A person who voluntarily appears in place of a fictitiously named defendant cannot file a motion to transfer. *See* ***Liera v. Los Angeles Fin. Co.*** (4th Dist.1950) 99 Cal.App.2d 254, 257 (person not named as party to suit and not served as one sued by fictitious name has no right to appear in action).

(2) Cross-defendant. A cross-defendant named in a compulsory cross-complaint cannot file a motion to transfer for improper venue under CCP §396b. *See* ***K.R.L. Prtshp. v. Superior Ct.*** (3d Dist.2004) 120 Cal.App.4th 490, 503-04. However, a cross-defendant can file a motion to transfer to a neutral county when a local governmental entity is a party. *See* ***Metropolitan Transit Sys. v. Superior Ct.*** (4th Dist.2007) 153 Cal.App.4th 293, 302-03. See "Transfer to neutral county – local governmental entity is party," §5.1, p. 369.

2. Plaintiff. The plaintiff cannot file a motion to transfer. *See* CCP §§396a(b), 396b(a); ***Cook v. Pendergast*** (1882) 61 Cal. 72, 79.

3. Court. In most cases, the court cannot transfer venue on its own motion. *See* CCP §§396b(a), 397(a); ***Hamilton v. Superior Ct.*** (1st Dist.1974) 37 Cal.App.3d 418, 423 & n.3. But it can transfer venue on its own motion in the following actions:

(1) Consumer actions. The court can transfer venue on its own motion if the action arises from any of the following:

(a) A retail installment contract. *See* Civ. C. §1812.10; CCP §396a(b).

(b) An automobile sales contract. *See* Civ. C. §2984.4; CCP §396a(b).

(c) An offer or provision of goods, services, loans, or extensions of credit intended primarily for personal, family, or household use. *See* CCP §§395(b), 396a(b).

(d) A transaction consummated as a proximate result of either (1) an unsolicited telephone call made by a seller engaged in the business of consummating transactions of that kind or (2) a telephone call or electronic transmission made by a buyer or lessee in response to a solicitation by a seller. *See id.* §§395(b), 396a(b).

(2) Unlawful-detainer actions. The court can transfer venue on its own motion when the action is for unlawful detainer. CCP §396a(b); *see also id.* §1161 (definition of "unlawful detainer action").

NOTE

A superior court can specify by local rule the location where certain actions should be filed, heard, or tried within a given county. CCP §402(a)(1), (a)(2). Although the court cannot dismiss a case filed at a different location, it can transfer the case on its own motion to the proper location. Id. §402(a)(3).

§3.2 Grounds for transfer. A motion to transfer must be granted if the defendant establishes that the county where the plaintiff filed suit is not the proper venue for the action. CCP §§396a(b), 396b(a); *see id.* §397(a). To prevail on the motion to transfer, the defendant must show one of the following:

1. Local action. The local nature of the action requires transfer to the county where the real property at issue (or some part of that real property) is located. See "Local Actions," ch. 3-F, §3, p. 272.

2. Transitory action, no specific venue statute. The action must be transferred to the county where the defendant resided when the action began because the action is transitory in nature and no specific venue statute applies. See "General venue rule," ch. 3-F, §4.2, p. 273.

3. Specific venue statute. A specific venue statute requires transfer to one of the counties described in the statute. See "Specific venue statutes," ch. 3-F, §4.3, p. 275.

4. Mixed action. A mixed-action rule requires transfer to a county other than the county of suit. A "mixed action" is when a plaintiff alleges two or more causes of action that are governed by different venue rules or joins two or more defendants who are subject to different venue standards. See "Mixed-Action Rules," ch. 3-F, §5, p. 281.

§3.3 Grounds for sanctions.

1. Against plaintiff. The defendant can ask the court to order the plaintiff's attorney to pay the reasonable expenses and attorney fees incurred by the defendant in making the motion to transfer. CCP §396b(b). To prevail on its request, the defendant should show that the plaintiff (1) rejected the defendant's offer to stipulate to a change of venue that was reasonably made and (2) did not select the venue in good faith, given the facts and the law the plaintiff knew or should have known when it filed the complaint. *Id.*

2. Against defendant. The plaintiff can ask the court to order the defendant's attorney to pay the reasonable expenses and attorney fees incurred by the plaintiff in opposing the motion to transfer. CCP §396b(b). To prevail on its request, the plaintiff should show that the defendant (1) did not reasonably make an offer to stipulate to a change of venue and (2) brought the motion to transfer in bad faith, given the facts and the law the defendant knew or should have known when it filed the motion. *Id.*

§3.4 Motion papers.

1. Deadline to file & serve.

(1) Filing. A motion to transfer must be filed within the time permitted to respond to the complaint (i.e., within 30 calendar days after service of summons). *See* CCP §§396a(e), 396b(a), 412.20(a)(3). See "Deadline to Answer," ch. 4-B, §2, p. 333. If the defendant does not timely file the motion, its right to have the action transferred to the proper court is waived in most cases. *See* CCP §396b(a); ***Dugar v. Happy Tiger Records, Inc.*** (2d Dist.1974) 41 Cal.App.3d 811, 819-20. But in unlawful-detainer and certain consumer actions, the defendant waives the right to transfer only if it consents in writing or in open court to try the case in the county where the suit was filed. *See* CCP §396a(b); ***Barquis v. Merchants Collection Ass'n*** (1972) 7 Cal.3d 94, 117-18. For a description of the consumer actions covered by this exception, see "Consumer actions," §3.1.3(1), p. 361.

(2) Serving. A motion to transfer must be served at least 16 court days before the hearing on the motion. *See* CCP §1005(b). See "Deadline to serve," ch. 1-D, §7.2.4, p. 34; "Retrospective deadlines," ch. 1-G, §6.2, p. 71.

2. Form of motion. A motion to transfer should be in writing and in the same form as noticed motions generally. See "Motion Papers," ch. 1-D, §5, p. 27. Specific issues relevant to motions to transfer include the following:

(1) Deny P's venue facts. The motion must specifically deny the venue facts in the plaintiff's complaint; if not, they are taken as true. *See* ***Smith v. Stanford Research Inst.*** (1st Dist.1963) 212 Cal.App.2d 750, 754. If there is more than one defendant, the motion must specifically deny that the county of suit is proper for each defendant. *See* ***Sequoia Pine Mills, Inc. v. Superior Ct.*** (5th Dist.1968) 258 Cal.App.2d 65, 67-68.

(2) Allege county of proper venue. The motion must ask the court to transfer the case to a specific county and provide facts showing why venue is proper in that county. *See* ***Sequoia Pine Mills***, 258 Cal.App.2d at 68. *But see* CCP §398 (D can designate transferee court either in notice of motion or in open court, entered in minutes or docket, when transfer order is made).

(3) Request expenses & attorney fees. The motion can ask the court to order the plaintiff's attorney to pay for the reasonable expenses and attorney fees incurred by the defendant in making the motion. CCP §396b(b). See "Against plaintiff," §3.3.1, p. 361.

(4) Attach proof of service. The motion must include a proof of service showing that the plaintiff was served with a copy of the motion papers. CCP §396b(a). See "Proof of service," ch. 1-D, §5.6, p. 33.

(5) File before or with responsive pleading. The motion can be filed before or simultaneously with an answer or other responsive pleading. *See* CCP §396b(a); *see, e.g.*, ***Karson Indus. v. Superior Ct.*** (1st Dist.1969) 273 Cal.App.2d 7, 8 (D filed motion to transfer with demurrer).

TRANSFER OR CHANGE VENUE

PRACTICE TIP

There is a tactical advantage to making the motion before filing an answer. If there is no answer on file and the defendant establishes that venue is improper, the court must grant the motion. ***Scribner v. Superior Ct.*** *(1st Dist.1971) 19 Cal.App.3d 764, 766; see CCP §396b(a), (d). But if an answer is on file, the court can retain the action if the plaintiff can show that doing so would promote the convenience of witnesses or the ends of justice. CCP §396b(d);* ***Scribner***, *19 Cal.App.3d at 766. See "Convenience of witnesses," §4.2.2, p. 366.*

(6) Supporting evidence. The following types of evidence can be used to support a motion to transfer:

(a) Declarations & affidavits. A motion to transfer is typically supported by declarations and affidavits. *CEB Procedure Before Trial*, §20.13; *see* CRC 3.1306(a); *see, e.g.*, ***Fletcher v. Nordesta Homes, Inc.*** (2d Dist.1961) 192 Cal.App.2d 33, 36-37 (D filed affidavit in support of motion to transfer venue). See "General Requirements for Declarations & Affidavits," ch. 1-B, §4, p. 19; "Supporting evidence," ch. 1-D, §5.3, p. 30.

(b) Verified complaint. A motion to transfer can be supported by uncontroverted allegations stated in a verified complaint. ***Mission Imps., Inc. v. Superior Ct.*** (1982) 31 Cal.3d 921, 929 n.7; *CEB Procedure Before Trial*, §20.13; *see* ***Mosby v. Superior Ct.*** (3d Dist.1974) 43 Cal.App.3d 219, 227.

(c) Judicial notice. A motion to transfer can be supported by matters noticed by the court. *See* CRC 3.1306(a). See "Request for Judicial Notice," ch. 5-J, p. 547.

(d) Oral testimony. The court may allow oral testimony for a motion to transfer if good cause is shown. *See* CRC 3.1306(a); ***Haldane v. Haldane*** (2d Dist.1962) 210 Cal.App.2d 587, 593; *CEB Procedure Before Trial*, §20.13.

3. Effect of motion.

(1) On defendant. A defendant who files a motion to transfer usually makes a general appearance in the action. CCP §1014; *cf.* CRC 5.62(a)(3) (family and juvenile rules). For a discussion of the exception to this rule, see "Actions taken with or after motion to quash," ch. 3-G, §5.1.1(1), p. 285.

(2) On court. A motion to transfer automatically stays the proceedings and suspends the court's power to rule on most issues until the motion has been determined. ***Mission Imps.***, 31 Cal.3d at 926 n.3; ***Thompson v. Thames*** (2d Dist.1997) 57 Cal.App.4th 1296, 1303-04; ***Moore v. Powell*** (4th Dist.1977) 70 Cal.App.3d 583, 587; *CEB Procedure Before Trial*, §20.18; *see, e.g.*, CCP §581(i) (action cannot be dismissed while motion to transfer is pending); ***River W., Inc. v. Nickel*** (5th Dist.1987) 188 Cal.App.3d 1297, 1312 (trial court could not hear disqualification motion while venue motion was pending). But the court can take the following actions while a motion to transfer is pending:

(a) Marital-dissolution & legal-separation proceedings. In a marital-dissolution or legal-separation proceeding, the court can consider and determine the following:

[1] Motions for allowance of temporary spousal support, child support, and attorney fees and costs. CCP §396b(c).

[2] Motions to determine child custody and visitation. *Id.*

(b) Child support. The court can consider and determine child-support matters. ***Thompson***, 57 Cal.App.4th at 1305.

(3) On time to plead. A motion to transfer automatically extends the defendant's time to demur, move to strike, or otherwise plead. *See* CCP §396b(e). See "Order," §3.7, p. 364.

(4) On default judgment. A motion to transfer prevents the entry of a default judgment against the moving party while the motion is pending or within the time period granted by the court to answer. *See* CCP §586(a)(6).

§3.5 Opposition papers. The opposing party should file a response to the motion to transfer venue. For a discussion of opposition papers generally, see "Opposition Papers," ch. 1-D, §8, p. 35.

1. Documents to file.

(1) Answer on file. If there is an answer on file, the plaintiff can oppose the motion by filing a counterdeclaration, counteraffidavit, or motion to retain the action in the plaintiff's chosen forum on the grounds that the convenience of witnesses or the ends of justice would be promoted. *CEB Procedure Before Trial*, §20.19; *see* CCP §396b(d); ***Braunstein v. Superior Ct.*** (1st Dist.1964) 225 Cal.App.2d 691, 697. See "Convenience of witnesses," §4.2.2, p. 366.

(2) No answer on file. If there is no answer on file, the plaintiff can oppose the motion by filing a counterdeclaration or counteraffidavit. *CEB Procedure Before Trial*, §20.19; *see* ***Hall v. Superior Ct.*** (1st Dist.1963) 211 Cal.App.2d 634, 638; ***Mills v. Dickson*** (3d Dist.1933) 129 Cal.App. 728, 732. The plaintiff cannot file a motion to retain the action. *See* CCP §396b(d); ***Gordon v. Perkins*** (1928) 203 Cal. 183, 185; *CEB Procedure Before Trial*, §20.19.

A verified complaint is treated as a counteraffidavit to the extent it contradicts the defendant's motion. ***Hall***, 211 Cal.App.2d at 638. Additional counterdeclarations or counteraffidavits to support the plaintiff's venue choice may be necessary if the complaint does not address all the factual issues raised in the defendant's motion. *Id.*

NOTE

If the defendant's motion to transfer is successful, the plaintiff can, after the answer is filed in the transferee court, make a motion to have the case transferred back to the transferor court on the grounds that the convenience of witnesses or the ends of justice would be promoted. ***Scribner v. Superior Ct.*** *(1st Dist.1971) 19 Cal.App.3d 764, 766; see CEB Procedure Before Trial, §20.19; 3 Witkin, Cal. Procedure, Actions, §947.*

2. Request for expenses & attorney fees. The plaintiff can ask the court to order the defendant's attorney to pay for the reasonable expenses and attorney fees incurred by the plaintiff in opposing the motion. CCP §396b(b). See "Against defendant," §3.3.2, p. 361.

§3.6 Hearing. Hearings on a motion to transfer are conducted in the same manner as civil hearings generally. See "Hearings," ch. 1-H, p. 79.

§3.7 Order.

1. Grants motion. If the defendant has not answered when it makes the motion to transfer, the court must grant the motion if the defendant establishes that venue is improper. CCP §396b(a); *see* ***Johnson v. Superior Ct.*** (5th Dist.1965) 232 Cal.App.2d 212, 214.

(1) Transferee court. If the motion is granted, the parties can agree to have the action transferred to any proper court. CCP §398; ***Cubic Corp. v. Superior Ct.*** (1st Dist.1986) 186 Cal.App.3d 622, 625. The agreement can be made by written stipulation or in open court and entered in the minutes. CCP §398; *see* Gov. C. §69844. If the parties cannot agree on a new court, the action will be transferred to any proper court designated by the defendant in the notice of motion or in open court and entered in the minutes when the transfer order is made. *See* CCP §398. If the defendant does not designate a new court, the court will select one. *Id.* See "Transfer of Action," §7, p. 373.

NOTE

If the court orders a transfer on its own motion, the court will select the new court. CCP §398.

(2) Expenses & attorney fees. If the motion is granted, the court can order the plaintiff's attorney to pay the reasonable expenses and attorney fees incurred by the defendant in making the motion. CCP §396b(b). See "Against plaintiff," §3.3.1, p. 361.

(3) Time to plead. If the motion is granted and the defendant has not already filed a response, the defendant has 30 calendar days to move to strike, demur, or otherwise plead in the transferee court. *See* CRC 3.1326. The 30 days are counted from the date the transferee court mails notice of receipt of the case and its new case number. *Id.*; *see* CCP §586(a)(6)(B).

2. Denies motion. If the defendant has not answered when it makes the motion to transfer, the court can deny the motion if the defendant has not established that venue is improper. *See* CCP §396b(a). If the defendant has answered when it makes the motion to transfer, the court can deny the motion and retain the action if it finds that doing so would promote the convenience of witnesses or the ends of justice. *Id.* §396b(d); ***Johnson***, 232 Cal.App.2d at 214.

(1) Expenses & attorney fees. If the motion is denied, the court can order the defendant's attorney to pay the reasonable expenses and attorney fees incurred by the plaintiff in opposing the motion. CCP §396b(b). See "Against defendant," §3.3.2, p. 361.

(2) **Time to plead.** If the motion is denied, the defendant has 30 calendar days to move to strike, demur, or otherwise plead if it has not already filed a response. CRC 3.1326.

§4. MOTION TO CHANGE VENUE

If the venue designated in the plaintiff's complaint is proper, a party can still attempt to change the venue for the action to a different county by filing a motion to change venue. *See* CCP §§397(b)-(e), 397.5; ***Paesano v. Superior Ct.*** (3d Dist.1988) 204 Cal.App.3d 17, 20-21.

§4.1 Who can file.

1. **Defendant.** The defendant can file a motion to change venue. *See* CCP §397; *see, e.g.*, ***Lieberman v. Superior Ct.*** (2d Dist.1987) 194 Cal.App.3d 396, 399 (D made motion to change venue on grounds that convenience of witnesses and ends of justice would be promoted); ***Hecker v. Ross*** (4th Dist.1960) 183 Cal.App.2d 30, 31 (same).

2. **Plaintiff.** The plaintiff can file a motion to change venue. ***Cook v. Pendergast*** (1882) 61 Cal. 72, 79; *see* CCP §397; ***People v. Ocean Shore R.R.*** (1st Dist.1938) 24 Cal.App.2d 420, 423; *see, e.g.*, ***Carruthers v. Crown Prods.*** (2d Dist.1948) 89 Cal.App.2d 326, 326-27 (P made motion to change venue on grounds that convenience of witnesses and ends of justice would be promoted). If there are multiple plaintiffs, one plaintiff can file a motion to change venue without having to join or obtain the consent of the other plaintiffs. *See* ***Ocean Shore***, 24 Cal.App.2d at 424-25.

3. **Court.** The court cannot change venue on its own motion. *See* CCP §397; ***Hamilton v. Superior Ct.*** (1st Dist.1974) 37 Cal.App.3d 418, 423 & n.3.

§4.2 Grounds. A party can file a motion to change venue on the grounds that (1) an impartial trial cannot be had in the county of suit, (2) the convenience of witnesses and the ends of justice would be promoted by the change, (3) there is no qualified judge in the county of suit, or (4) in a proceeding to end a marriage in which one or both of the parties reside outside the county of suit, the ends of justice would be promoted by the change. *See* CCP §§397(b)-(e), 397.5.

1. **No impartial trial.** Venue can be changed if an impartial trial cannot be had in the county of suit. CCP §397(b); ***Paesano v. Superior Ct.*** (3d Dist.1988) 204 Cal.App.3d 17, 20. To prevail on this ground, the movant must show that it is subject to actual, widespread prejudice in the county. *See* ***Ohio Cas. Ins. v. Superior Ct.*** (3d Dist.1994) 30 Cal.App.4th 444, 452; ***People v. Ocean Shore R.R.*** (1st Dist.1938) 24 Cal.App.2d 420, 427-28. Although there is no single set of factors the movant can address to establish the lack of impartiality, courts have considered the factors listed below when determining whether to grant a motion to change venue.

TRANSFER OR CHANGE VENUE

(1) **Pervasiveness.** The pervasiveness of the prejudice throughout the county. *See, e.g.*, ***Ocean Shore***, 24 Cal.App.2d at 427-28 (nearly 200 affidavits showed widespread prejudice). To be compelling, the evidence should demonstrate the prejudice is widespread and not limited to an isolated part of the county. *See, e.g.*, ***Riverside Cty. Flood Control & Water Conserv. Dist. v. Joseph W. Wolfskill Co.*** (4th Dist.1957) 147 Cal.App.2d 714, 716-17 (no widespread prejudice shown when only 1/10 of county was subject to tax that might cause prejudice against movant); ***Ross v. Kalin*** (2d Dist.1921) 53 Cal.App. 616, 617-19 (although movant was tarred and feathered by angry mob of up to 300, no widespread prejudice shown when county had 8,000-12,000 potential jurors).

(2) **Longevity.** The length of time the prejudice has been present. *See, e.g.*, ***Ocean Shore***, 24 Cal.App.2d at 427-28 (prejudice extended over many years).

(3) **Intensity.** The intensity of the prejudice. *See* ***Ocean Shore***, 24 Cal.App.2d at 426; *see, e.g.*, ***J.I. Case Threshing Co. v. Copren Bros.*** (3d Dist.1917) 35 Cal.App. 70, 79 (fact that nonmovants were "well and favorably known" in county of suit was not sufficient to establish prejudice).

(4) **Publicity.** Any publicity concerning the subject matter of the action. *See* ***J.I. Case Threshing***, 35 Cal.App. at 79; *see, e.g.*, ***Nguyen v. Superior Ct.*** (1st Dist.1996) 49 Cal.App.4th 1781, 1791 (two newspaper articles

reporting on incident did not demonstrate sufficient prejudice); ***Ocean Shore***, 24 Cal.App.2d at 427-28 (civic meetings and newspaper editorials and articles demonstrated sufficient prejudice); ***Ross***, 53 Cal.App. at 617 (newspaper editorials approving of mob attack against movant did not demonstrate sufficient prejudice).

(5) Inability to impanel jury. The difficulty of impaneling a jury. *See, e.g.*, ***People v. Probate Ct.*** (1873) 46 Cal. 245, 246 (three previous juries had been unable to reach decision). The court may postpone its decision on the motion because the movant often cannot make an adequate showing of prejudice before it unsuccessfully makes an attempt to select a jury. *See* ***Cook v. Pendergast*** (1882) 61 Cal. 72, 79-80; ***Ocean Shore***, 24 Cal.App.2d at 426-27; ***J.I. Case Threshing***, 35 Cal.App. at 79; *CEB Procedure Before Trial*, §20.10.

NOTE

Although the statute is silent on this point, a motion to change venue based on the inability to obtain an impartial trial is often only available in jury trials, not bench trials. See ***Nguyen***, *49 Cal.App.4th at 1791 (prospect of jury trial is crucial in determining whether impartial trial can be had). If a motion to change venue based on lack of impartiality is available in a bench trial, the movant would have to show that the judge lacks impartiality, rather than the community in general. See id.; see also* ***Stuart v. Everly*** *(1st Dist.1920) 50 Cal.App. 551, 552 (P's motion to change venue based on lack of impartiality of judge is controlled by CCP §397, not §170 et seq.).*

2. Convenience of witnesses. Venue can be changed if the convenience of witnesses and the ends of justice would be promoted by the change. CCP §397(c); *see* ***Harden v. Skinner & Hammond*** (1st Dist.1955) 130 Cal.App.2d 750, 754. To prevail on this ground, the movant must (1) provide the names of the witnesses, (2) describe the nature of their testimony, (3) explain how the county of suit would be inconvenient for them, and (4) show how the ends of justice would be promoted by a change in venue.

(1) Witness names. The movant must provide the names of all the witnesses expected to testify for the movant. ***Peiser v. Mettler*** (1958) 50 Cal.2d 594, 607; ***Corfee v. Southern Cal. Edison Co.*** (2d Dist.1962) 202 Cal.App.2d 473, 477; *see* ***Loehr v. Latham*** (1860) 15 Cal. 418, 419; *see, e.g.*, ***First-Trust Joint Stock Land Bank v. Meredith*** (2d Dist.1936) 16 Cal.App.2d 504, 507 (movant named her own witnesses).

(2) Testimony. The movant must describe the substance of each witness's expected testimony and explain why that testimony is material, relevant, and admissible. *See* ***Peiser***, 50 Cal.2d at 607; ***J.C. Millett Co. v. Latchford-Marble Glass Co.*** (2d Dist.1959) 167 Cal.App.2d 218, 225-26. Although the movant does not need to specifically describe the expected testimony, the court must have enough information to evaluate its materiality. *See* ***Edwards v. Pierson*** (2d Dist.1957) 156 Cal.App.2d 72, 75; ***Juneau v. Juneau*** (4th Dist.1941) 45 Cal.App.2d 14, 16-17.

(3) Inconvenience. The movant must make a detailed, factual showing of why it would be inconvenient for the witnesses to appear in the court where the action is currently pending. *See* ***Union Trust Life Ins. v. Superior Ct.*** (2d Dist.1968) 259 Cal.App.2d 23, 28-29; ***Stute v. Burinda*** (Los Angeles Cty. Superior Ct. Appellate Dept. 1981) 123 Cal.App.3d Supp. 11, 17.

(a) Types of inconvenience. The county of suit may be inconvenient for a witness for any of the following reasons:

[1] The witness resides in a different county. *See* ***Harden***, 130 Cal.App.2d at 754. While not dispositive, the court will consider whether the majority of witnesses reside in or near a different county. *See* ***Scott v. Stuart*** (1923) 190 Cal. 526, 529; ***Harden***, 130 Cal.App.2d at 754; *see, e.g.*, ***Figley v. California Arrow Airlines*** (3d Dist.1952) 111 Cal.App.2d 285, 287 (motion to change venue based on inconvenience of eight witnesses was defeated by opposition based on inconvenience of one litigant).

[2] The witness's poor health makes travel to the county of suit difficult. *See* ***Figley***, 111 Cal.App.2d at 287.

[3] Forcing the witness to travel to the county of suit would cause economic hardship. *See id.*

(b) Types of witnesses. The court will consider the inconvenience of only certain witnesses.

[1] Nonparty nonexperts. The court will consider the inconvenience of nonparty, nonexpert witnesses. *See **Wrin v. Ohlandt*** (1931) 213 Cal. 158, 160; ***Harden***, 130 Cal.App.2d at 754-55.

[2] Parties. The court will usually not consider the inconvenience of parties. ***Wrin***, 213 Cal. at 160; ***Harden***, 130 Cal.App.2d at 755; ***Rios v. Lacey Trucking Co.*** (2d Dist.1954) 123 Cal.App.2d 865, 868. However, the court will consider a party's inconvenience if a serious illness prevents the party from traveling to a distant county to testify. ***Lieberman v. Superior Ct.*** (2d Dist.1987) 194 Cal.App.3d 396, 401; ***Simonian v. Simonian*** (1st Dist.1950) 97 Cal.App.2d 68, 69.

[3] Employees. The court will usually not consider the inconvenience of a party's employee. ***Security Inv. v. Gifford*** (1918) 179 Cal. 277, 278; ***Harden***, 130 Cal.App.2d at 757; ***Stute***, 123 Cal.App.3d Supp. at 17. However, the court will consider an employee's inconvenience when the employee is to be called as a witness for the opposing party. ***Harden***, 130 Cal.App.2d at 757.

[4] Attorneys. The court will not consider the inconvenience of the attorneys. ***Lieppman v. Lieber*** (2d Dist.1986) 180 Cal.App.3d 914, 920.

[5] Expert witnesses. The court will usually not consider the inconvenience of expert witnesses. ***Wrin***, 213 Cal. at 160; ***Security Inv.***, 179 Cal. at 278. However, the court will consider an expert's inconvenience when the expert has personal knowledge of relevant facts. ***Security Inv.***, 179 Cal. at 278; *see **Wrin***, 213 Cal. at 160.

(4) Ends of justice. The movant must show that the ends of justice would be promoted by the change. CCP §397(c); ***Pearson v. Superior Ct.*** (1st Dist.1962) 199 Cal.App.2d 69, 77. A change in venue may promote the ends of justice if it does any of the following:

(a) Avoids delay and expense in court proceedings. ***Pearson***, 199 Cal.App.2d at 77.

(b) Allows the witnesses to give testimony to the jury (or court) firsthand instead of through depositions. ***J.C. Millett***, 167 Cal.App.2d at 228.

(c) Saves the witnesses time and expense. *Id.*

(d) Makes the witnesses more readily accessible for immediate recall if further testimony is desired. *Id.*

3. No qualified judge. Venue can be changed if there is no judge of the court qualified to act. CCP §397(d).

NOTE

CCP §397(d) is effectively obsolete. 3 Witkin, Cal. Procedure, Actions, §957. Now, if there is no qualified judge of the court, the chief justice will simply assign an outside judge to hear the matter instead of transferring the entire case. See CCP §170.8; ***People v. Spring Valley Co.*** *(1st Dist.1952) 109 Cal.App.2d 656, 672; 3 Witkin, Cal. Procedure, Actions, §957.*

---

4. Ends of justice in marital-dissolution proceeding. Venue can be changed in a proceeding to end a marriage if one or both of the parties reside in a different county. *See* CCP §§397(e), 397.5.

NOTE

CCP §397(e) (out-of-county respondent) only applies to proceedings for marital dissolution, but CCP §397.5 (out-of-county petitioner and respondent) applies to proceedings for marital dissolution, nullification, and legal separation.

(1) Out-of-county respondent. A respondent who resides outside the county of suit can move to change the venue of the action to her county of residence. CCP §397(e). To prevail, the respondent must show the following:

(a) The petitioner has resided in the county of suit for at least three months before the beginning of the proceeding. *Id.*

(b) The respondent, at the beginning of the proceeding, lived in a different county. *Id.*

(c) The ends of justice would be promoted by the change. *Id.*; *see, e.g.*, ***Silva v. Superior Ct.*** (2d Dist.1981) 119 Cal.App.3d 301, 306-07 (justice promoted by changing venue to respondent's home county because he was gainfully employed and fully responsible for young children). In determining whether a change in venue would promote the ends of justice under §397(e), the court may consider (1) the factors under §397(c), (2) the expense and hardship of the respondent and any children, and (3) the children's residence if the children need to be accessible for the court's examination. ***Pearson***, 199 Cal.App.2d at 81. See "Ends of justice," §4.2.2(4), p. 367.

(2) Out-of-county petitioner & respondent. If both the petitioner and the respondent have moved from the county of suit, either party can move to change the venue of the action to his or her county of residence. CCP §397.5. To prevail, the moving party must show the following:

(a) Both the petitioner and the respondent have moved from the county of suit. *Id.*

(b) The ends of justice would be promoted by the change. *Id.* See "Ends of justice," §4.2.2(4), p. 367.

(c) The convenience of the parties would be promoted by the change. CCP §397.5; *see, e.g.*, ***In re Marriage of Straeck*** (2d Dist.1984) 156 Cal.App.3d 617, 625 (convenience of parties would be promoted by change of venue because change would prevent inconsistent child-support orders from different counties). For examples of inconvenience, see "Types of inconvenience," §4.2.2(3)(a), p. 366.

§4.3 Motion papers.

1. Deadline to file & serve.

(1) Filing. A motion to change venue must be filed within a reasonable time after the answer is filed. *See* ***Cooney v. Cooney*** (1944) 25 Cal.2d 202, 208 (convenience of witnesses); ***Cook v. Pendergast*** (1882) 61 Cal. 72, 79-80 (impartial trial); ***Buran Equip. Co. v. Superior Ct.*** (6th Dist.1987) 190 Cal.App.3d 1662, 1665 (convenience of witness); ***Delgado v. Superior Ct.*** (3d Dist.1977) 74 Cal.App.3d 560, 562-63 (same); *cf.* ***Newman v. County of Sonoma*** (1961) 56 Cal.2d 625, 628 (motion to transfer under CCP §394 must be made within reasonable time). Although there is no bright-line rule for determining what is a "reasonable" time, the court is likely to allow a motion if (1) it does not appear that the motion was made for dilatory purposes and (2) doing so would not cause the other side substantial prejudice. *See CEB Procedure Before Trial*, §20.9; *see, e.g.*, ***Willingham v. Pecora*** (4th Dist.1941) 44 Cal.App.2d 289, 295 (movants waited four months before making motion to change venue shortly before trial; appellate court affirmed denial of motion because granting motion would result in unjust delay); *cf.* ***Marin Cmty. Coll. Dist. v. Superior Ct.*** (1st Dist.1977) 72 Cal.App.3d 719, 723 (same factors considered by court for motion to transfer).

(2) Serving. A motion to change venue must be served at least 16 court days before the hearing on the motion. CCP §1005(b). See "Deadline to serve," ch. 1-D, §7.2.4, p. 34; "Retrospective deadlines," ch. 1-G, §6.2, p. 71.

2. Form of motion. A motion to change venue should be in writing and in the same form as noticed motions generally. See "Motion Papers," ch. 1-D, §5, p. 27.

3. Supporting evidence. A motion to change venue can be supported by the same types of evidence used to support a motion to transfer. See "Supporting evidence," §3.4.2(6), p. 362. Like motions to transfer, motions to change venue are typically supported by declarations and affidavits. *CEB Procedure Before Trial*, §20.13; *see* CRC

TRANSFER OR CHANGE VENUE

3.1306(a); ***Dillman v. Superior Ct.*** (2d Dist.1962) 205 Cal.App.2d 769, 773. See "General Requirements for Declarations & Affidavits," ch. 1-B, §4, p. 19; "Supporting evidence," ch. 1-D, §5.3, p. 30.

4. Transfer fees. The motion must be filed with all the applicable transfer fees. *See* CCP §399(a). See "Payment of transfer fees," §7.2, p. 373.

§4.4 Opposition papers. The opposing party should file a response to the motion to change venue. For a discussion of opposition papers generally, see "Opposition Papers," ch. 1-D, §8, p. 35. When a motion to change venue is based on the convenience of witnesses, the opposing party can do the following:

1. Argue inconvenience. The opposing party can argue that the proposed venue change will inconvenience its own witnesses. ***Scott v. Stuart*** (1923) 190 Cal. 526, 529.

2. Show evidence is cumulative. The opposing party can argue that the expected testimony of an inconvenienced witness is cumulative—that is, the witness's testimony will be the same as that of another witness and is therefore unnecessary. *See* ***Harden v. Skinner & Hammond*** (1st Dist.1955) 130 Cal.App.2d 750, 756; ***Figley v. California Arrow Airlines*** (3d Dist.1952) 111 Cal.App.2d 285, 287.

3. Stipulate to testimony. The opposing party can state that it is willing to stipulate to the expected testimony of the inconvenienced witnesses, and thus those witnesses are unnecessary. *See, e.g.*, ***Churchill v. White*** (4th Dist.1953) 119 Cal.App.2d 503, 505 (Ds were willing to stipulate to extent and value of services rendered by P's nurse).

§4.5 Hearing. Hearings on a motion to change venue are conducted in the same manner as civil hearings generally. See "Hearings," ch. 1-H, p. 79.

§4.6 Order.

1. Grants motion.

(1) Inconvenience, lack of impartiality, or no qualified judge. If the motion is granted because of the inconvenience of witnesses or because there is a lack of impartiality or a qualified judge, the parties can agree to have the action transferred to a court with subject-matter jurisdiction. CCP §398. See "Choosing the Court—Subject-Matter Jurisdiction," ch. 3-E, p. 248. The agreement can be made by written stipulation or in open court and entered in the minutes. CCP §398; *see* Gov. C. §69844. If the parties cannot agree on a new venue, the court will transfer the action to the nearest or most accessible court where the grounds for the motion (e.g., inconvenience of witnesses) do not apply. CCP §398. See "Transfer of Action," §7, p. 373.

(2) Ends of justice.

(a) Marital-dissolution proceedings only. If the motion is granted under CCP §397(e), the court must transfer the proceeding to the movant's county of residence if it finds that the ends of justice would be promoted by the change. See "Out-of-county respondent," §4.2.4(1), p. 368.

(b) Marital-dissolution, nullification, or legal-separation proceedings. If the motion is granted under CCP §397.5, the court may transfer the proceeding to either party's county of residence if it finds that the convenience of the parties and the ends of justice would be promoted by the change. See "Out-of-county petitioner & respondent," §4.2.4(2), p. 368.

2. Denies motion. If the motion is denied, the action stays in that court.

§5. MOTIONS TO TRANSFER IN ACTIONS INVOLVING GOVERNMENTAL ENTITIES

When one of the parties is a governmental entity, two additional types of transfer motions may be available: (1) a motion to transfer to a neutral county and (2) a motion to remove the action from Sacramento County.

§5.1 Transfer to neutral county – local governmental entity is party. A motion to transfer an action to a neutral county is available when a county, city and county, city, or local agency (collectively referred to as "local governmental entity") is a party. *See* CCP §394(a). A "local agency" is any governmental district, board, or agency, or

any other local governmental body or corporation, but it does not include the State of California or any of its agencies, departments, commissions, or boards. *Id.* §394(b). The purpose of this motion is to protect the parties from local bias. ***City of Oakland v. Darbee*** (1st Dist.1951) 102 Cal.App.2d 493, 498.

NOTE

A motion to transfer to a "neutral county" is something of a misnomer. One of the grounds under §394(a) provides that a local governmental entity can have certain cases (i.e., actions alleging the entity negligently caused injury to P, P's property, or both) transferred to it, if the entity is a county and the injury occurred there, or to the county where the entity is situated.

1. **Who can file.** For a discussion of who can file, see "Grounds," §5.1.2, this page.

2. **Grounds.**

(1) P is local governmental entity. If the plaintiff is a local governmental entity and the defendant is not, either the plaintiff or the defendant can seek a transfer. CCP §394(a). To prevail on the motion, the movant must show the following:

(a) The plaintiff is a local governmental entity. *See id.*

(b) The plaintiff is not a local child-support agency suing under Fam. C. §17400, 17402, 17404, or 17416. CCP §394(a).

(c) The name of the plaintiff-county, if the plaintiff is a county or city and county, or the name of the county where the plaintiff is situated, if the plaintiff is a city or local agency. *See id.*; ***City of Oakland***, 102 Cal.App.2d at 497.

(d) The name of the county where the defendant resides, does business, or is situated. *See* CCP §394(a); ***County of Nevada v. Phillips*** (3d Dist.1952) 111 Cal.App.2d 428, 429-30.

(e) The county of suit is not a neutral venue—that is, the county of suit is the plaintiff-county, a county where the plaintiff is situated, or a county where the defendant resides, does business, or is situated. *See* CCP §394(a); ***City of Oakland***, 102 Cal.App.2d at 497; *see also* ***City of Stockton v. Wilson*** (3d Dist.1926) 79 Cal.App. 422, 424-25 (no purpose served by transferring from one neutral county to another).

(f) The action must be transferred to a neutral county. CCP §394(a). The motion does not have to designate a neutral county for transfer. ***City of Oakland***, 102 Cal.App.2d at 497.

(2) D is local governmental entity. If the defendant is a local governmental entity, it can seek a transfer. CCP §394(a). To prevail on the motion, the defendant must show the following:

(a) The defendant is a local governmental entity. *See id.*

(b) The county of suit is not the defendant-county, if the defendant is a county or city and county, or a county where the defendant is situated, if the defendant is a city or local agency. *See id.*

(c) The action must be transferred to either of the following:

[1] A neutral county. *See id.*

[2] The defendant-county, if the defendant is a county or city and county, or the county where the defendant is situated, if the defendant is a city or local agency. *Id.* If the defendant asks for a transfer to either of these counties, the defendant must also show the following:

[a] The complaint alleges the defendant or its agents or employees negligently caused an injury to the plaintiff, the plaintiff's property, or both. *Id.*

[b] The alleged injury occurred within the defendant-county, if the defendant is a county or city and county, or the county where the defendant is situated, if the defendant is a city or local agency. *Id.*

NOTE

If the defendant's motion to transfer is successful, the plaintiff can, after the answer is filed in the transferee court, make a motion to have the case transferred back to the transferor court under any ground specified in CCP §397. See ***Paesano v. Superior Ct.*** *(3d Dist.1988) 204 Cal.App.3d 17, 20-21.*

3. Motion papers.

(1) Deadline to file & serve.

(a) Filing. A motion to transfer to a neutral county must be filed within a reasonable time. ***Newman v. County of Sonoma*** (1961) 56 Cal.2d 625, 628; ***Adams v. Superior Ct.*** (4th Dist.1964) 226 Cal.App.2d 365, 367.

(b) Serving. A motion to transfer to a neutral county must be served at least 16 court days before the hearing on the motion. CCP §1005(b). See "Deadline to serve," ch. 1-D, §7.2.4, p. 34; "Retrospective deadlines," ch. 1-G, §6.2, p. 71.

(2) Form of motion. A motion to transfer to a neutral county should be in writing and in the same form as noticed motions generally. See "Motion Papers," ch. 1-D, §5, p. 27.

(3) Supporting evidence. A motion to transfer to a neutral county can be supported by the same types of evidence used to support a motion to transfer venue. See "Supporting evidence," §3.4.2(6), p. 362.

4. Opposition papers. The opposing party should file a response to the motion to transfer. For a discussion of opposition papers generally, see "Opposition Papers," ch. 1-D, §8, p. 35.

5. Hearing. Hearings on a motion to transfer to a neutral county are conducted in the same manner as civil hearings generally. See "Hearings," ch. 1-H, p. 79.

6. Order.

(1) Grants motion. If the movant makes the required showing, the court must grant the motion. *See* CCP §394(a). See "Transfer of Action," §7, p. 373.

(a) Determining neutral venue. If the motion is granted, the parties can agree on the neutral county by written stipulation or orally in open court and entered in the minutes. CCP §394(a). Otherwise, the court will select a neutral county. *See* ***Adams***, 226 Cal.App.2d at 369; ***County of Nevada***, 111 Cal.App.2d at 429.

(b) Bench trial. If the action is one in which there is no right to a jury trial or a jury trial has been waived, the court can retain the action and ask the chairperson of the Judicial Council to assign a disinterested judge from a neutral county to hear the case. CCP §394(a).

(2) Denies motion. If the motion is denied, the action stays in that court.

7. Effect of transfer.

(1) Subpoenaed witnesses. When the action is transferred to a neutral county, any witness served with a trial subpoena to attend and give testimony at a hearing in the court within the original county must attend hearings in the transferee county. CCP §394(a).

(2) Additional costs incurred. When the action is transferred to a neutral county and the opposing party did not consent to the transfer, the nonconsenting party is entitled to recover the following additional costs regardless of the outcome of the action:

(a) The living and traveling expenses of the nonconsenting party. CCP §394(a).

(b) The living and traveling expenses of the nonconsenting party's witnesses that the court determines to be material. *Id.*; *see also* ***City of Burbank v. Nordahl*** (4th Dist.1962) 199 Cal.App.2d 311, 329-30 (additional expenses incurred by party's attorney not recoverable under CCP §394). For each witness, the nonconsenting party is limited to $5 per day in excess of the witness fees and mileage allowed by law. CCP §394(a).

(c) Any other costs "occasioned by the transfer" of the action. *Id.*

§5.2 Remove action from Sacramento County – state governmental entity is party. A motion to remove an action from Sacramento County to a more convenient venue is available when the State of California or one of its departments, institutions, boards, commissions, bureaus, officers, or agencies (collectively referred to as "state governmental entity") brings an action in Sacramento County. *See* CCP §401(2).

1. Who can file. A defendant can file a motion to remove an action brought by a state governmental entity in Sacramento County. *See* CCP §401(2).

2. Grounds. To prevail on a motion to remove the action, the defendant must show the following:

(1) The plaintiff is the State of California or a state governmental entity. *See* CCP §401(2).

(2) The action was commenced in Sacramento County under California law. *Id.*

(3) The action is not a proceeding involving unclaimed property in the possession of federal officers, agencies, or employees. *See id.* §1609; *see also id.* §1601(a) (definition of "unclaimed property").

(4) The defendant resides or has its principal office in a different county. *See id.* §401(2).

3. Motion papers.

(1) Deadline to file & serve.

(a) Filing. A motion to remove an action brought by a state governmental entity in Sacramento County should be made within a reasonable time. *Cf.* ***Newman v. County of Sonoma*** (1961) 56 Cal.2d 625, 628 (motion to transfer in action involving local governmental entity); ***Adams v. Superior Ct.*** (4th Dist.1964) 226 Cal.App.2d 365, 367 (same).

(b) Serving. A motion to remove an action brought by a state governmental entity in Sacramento County must be served at least 16 court days before the hearing on the motion. CCP §1005(b). See "Deadline to serve," ch. 1-D, §7.2.4, p. 34; "Retrospective deadlines," ch. 1-G, §6.2, p. 71.

(2) Form of motion. A motion to remove an action brought by a state governmental entity in Sacramento County should be in writing and in the same form as noticed motions generally. See "Motion Papers," ch. 1-D, §5, p. 27.

(3) Supporting evidence. A motion to remove an action brought by a state governmental entity in Sacramento County can be supported by the same types of evidence used to support a motion to transfer venue. See "Supporting evidence," §3.4.2(6), p. 362.

4. Opposition papers. The opposing party should file a response to the motion to remove. For a discussion of opposition papers generally, see "Opposition Papers," ch. 1-D, §8, p. 35.

5. Hearing. Hearings on a motion to remove are conducted in the same manner as civil hearings generally. See "Hearings," ch. 1-H, p. 79.

6. Order.

(1) Grants motion. If the defendant makes the required showing, the court must grant the motion. *See* CCP §401(2). If the court grants the motion, it will transfer the action to the county where the Attorney General has an office nearest to the county where the defendant resides or has its principal office. *Id.* See "Transfer of Action," §7, p. 373.

(2) Denies motion. If the motion is denied, the action stays in that court.

§6. STIPULATION TO TRANSFER

Changing venue does not have to be an adversarial process. Parties are free to stipulate to a transfer. Weil, *Civil Procedure Before Trial*, ¶3:549; *see* ***Brock v. Superior Ct.*** (1947) 29 Cal.2d 629, 634; ***Bechtel Corp. v. Superior Ct.*** (5th Dist.1973) 33 Cal.App.3d 405, 410. However, the transfer must be to a court that has subject-matter jurisdiction over the case. CCP §398. See "Choosing the Court—Subject-Matter Jurisdiction," ch. 3-E, p. 248.

§7. TRANSFER OF ACTION

When a motion to transfer or change venue is granted, the transferee court takes jurisdiction over the action and all matters and proceedings related to it. *See* CCP §399(c); ***London v. Morrison*** (2d Dist.1950) 99 Cal.App.2d 876, 879. However, jurisdiction does not actually vest in the transferee court until (1) the transferor court's file is transmitted to the transferee court and (2) the transfer fees are paid. *See* ***London***, 99 Cal.App.2d at 879.

NOTE

A plaintiff cannot prevent a transfer by voluntarily dismissing its action and then refiling it at a later time. See ***Plum v. Forgay Lumber Co.*** *(3d Dist.1931) 118 Cal.App. 76, 79. But the plaintiff can, after the answer is filed in the transferee court, make a motion to have the case transferred back to the transferor court on the grounds that the convenience of witnesses or the ends of justice would be promoted.* ***Scribner v. Superior Ct.*** *(1st Dist.1971) 19 Cal.App.3d 764, 766; see CEB Procedure Before Trial, §20.19; 3 Witkin, Cal. Procedure, Actions, §947.*

§7.1 Transmission of court file. When the court orders an action to be transferred, the clerk of the transferor court must transmit the court's file (which includes all of the pleadings, papers, and transcripts) to the clerk of the transferee court after the time to file a petition expires or after the judgment denying a petition for a writ of mandate becomes final. CCP §399(a); *CEB Procedure Before Trial*, §20.27.

§7.2 Payment of transfer fees.

1. What fees must be paid. When the court orders an action to be transferred, the following fees must be paid before the transfer can occur:

(1) The fee for transmitting the court's file, which is $50. Gov. C. §70618.

(2) The transferee court's uniform filing fee. *Id.* The transferor court's clerk will transmit the uniform filing fee with the court's file to the clerk or judge of the transferee court. *Id.*

(3) Any additional fees required by law.

2. Who pays fees.

(1) Motion to transfer venue – improper venue. If a motion to transfer is granted on grounds that venue was not proper, the transfer costs and fees must be paid by the plaintiff before the transfer is made. CCP §399(a).

(a) Additional fees. The transfer costs and fees include any expenses and attorney fees awarded to the defendant as sanctions under CCP §396b(b). CCP §399(a). See "Against plaintiff," §3.3.1, p. 361.

(b) Reimbursement for D. If the defendant paid the transfer costs and fees when it filed the motion, it is entitled to reimbursement when the transfer order is made. CCP §399(a).

(c) If P does not pay. If the plaintiff does not pay the costs and fees within five days after service of notice of the transfer order, any other interested party (whether named in the complaint as a party or not) can pay them. CCP §399(a). This payment will either (1) be recoverable as a cost if the defendant prevails in the action or (2) be offset against and deducted from the amount awarded to the plaintiff if the plaintiff prevails. *Id.*

(2) **Motion to change venue.** If a motion to change venue is granted under CCP §397(b), (c), (d), or (e), the transfer costs and fees must be paid by the movant when the notice of motion is filed. CCP §399(a); *CEB Procedure Before Trial*, §20.29.

(3) **Motion to transfer or remove – actions involving governmental entities.** If a motion to transfer or remove an action involving a governmental entity is granted under CCP §394(a) (transfer to neutral county) or §401(2) (removal from Sacramento County), the transfer costs and fees must be paid before the case can be transferred. *See* CCP §399(a). Section 399(a) does not specify who should pay the costs and fees, but presumably they should be paid by the movant. *Cf. id.* (movant must pay costs and fees when motion is based on CCP §397(b), (c), (d), or (e)). However, if the movant is a governmental entity, it may be exempt from paying any costs or fees. *See* Gov. C. §6103.

3. **When to pay fees.** The transfer costs and fees must be paid within (1) 30 days after service of notice of the transfer order, (2) 30 days after notice of finality of the transfer order if a petition for a writ of mandate was filed or an appeal was taken and a stay of proceedings was issued, or (3) 60 days after service of notice of the transfer order if a petition for a writ of mandate was filed or an appeal was taken and no stay of proceedings was issued. *See* CCP §399(a). If the party responsible for paying the transfer costs and fees does not timely pay them, the following apply:

(1) The action cannot be prosecuted in any court until the costs and fees are paid. *Id.*

(2) Any party can file a noticed motion to dismiss the action without prejudice on the condition that no other action can be started in another court before the costs and fees are paid. *Id.*

§7.3 Notice of transmission.

1. **By clerk of transferor court.** The clerk of the transferor court must give all parties that have appeared in the action notice by mail of the date the court's file was transmitted. CCP §399(b). The notice should be mailed when the court's file is transmitted. *Id.*

2. **By clerk of transferee court.** The clerk of the transferee court must give all parties that have appeared in the action notice by mail of the date the action was filed and the assigned case number. CCP §399(b). The notice should be mailed promptly after receiving the court's file. *Id.*

§8. RENEWAL OF MOTION

Parties are discouraged from making renewed motions to transfer or change venue unless they can show new or different facts, circumstances, or law. *See* CCP §1008(b); ***Smith v. Pelton Water Wheel Co.*** (1907) 151 Cal. 399, 400-01; ***Seybert v. County of Imperial*** (2d Dist.1956) 139 Cal.App.2d 221, 228; ***Yellow Mfg. Acceptance Corp. v. Stoddard*** (1st Dist.1949) 93 Cal.App.2d 301, 305. The denial of a venue challenge on one ground, however, may not prevent the filing of a second motion on a different ground. *Compare* ***Seybert***, 139 Cal.App.2d at 228-30 (court considered renewed motion to change venue based on different ground from first motion), *with* ***Yellow Mfg.***, 93 Cal.App.2d at 305 (court denied second motion to change venue because ground for second motion could have been brought in first motion). For a discussion of the renewal of motions, see "Motion for Renewal," ch. 5-G, §4, p. 516.

§9. APPELLATE REVIEW

A party can request appellate review of a motion to transfer or change venue either by filing a petition for a writ of mandate or by direct appeal, depending on whether the case is limited or unlimited. For a discussion of case classification, see "Procedural Classifications of Civil Cases," ch. 3-E, §4, p. 255.

§9.1 Writ of mandate.

1. **Unlimited civil case.** In an unlimited civil case, an order granting or denying a motion to transfer or change venue can be reviewed by a petition for a writ of mandate. *See* CCP §400; *see, e.g.*, ***Adams v. Superior Ct.*** (4th Dist.1964) 226 Cal.App.2d 365, 369 (appellate court issued writ of mandate directing trial court to transfer case to neutral county under CCP §394).

(1) **Deadline to file.** A party must file a petition for a writ of mandate within 20 days after service of written notice of the order granting or denying the motion. CCP §400. The trial court can, for good cause, extend the time for up to ten more days if the original deadline has not yet passed. *Id.*

(2) **Copy to trial court.** The petitioning party must file a copy of the petition in the trial court immediately after the petition is filed in the appellate court. CCP §400.

(3) **Stay of proceedings.** The appellate court can stay all proceedings in the case until judgment on the petition becomes final. CCP §400.

2. **Limited civil case.** In a limited civil case, an order granting or denying a motion to transfer or change venue cannot be reviewed by a petition for a writ of mandate; instead, a party should file a direct appeal. *See* CCP §§904.2(c), 1086. See "Direct appeal," §9.2, this page.

§9.2 Direct appeal.

1. **Limited civil case.** In a limited civil case, a ruling on a motion to transfer or change venue can be appealed to the appellate division of the superior court. CCP §904.2(c). Generally, a party must file the notice of appeal within 30 days after being served with a file-stamped copy of the order. CRC 8.822(a)(1). If an opposing party files a motion to reconsider the order, the time to appeal is extended. CRC 8.823(e); *see* CRC 8.822(a)(1).

2. **Unlimited civil case.** In an unlimited civil case, a ruling on a motion to transfer or change venue is not appealable; instead, a party should file a petition for a writ of mandate. *See* CCP §904.2(c); ***Calhoun v. Vallejo City Unified Sch. Dist.*** (1st Dist.1993) 20 Cal.App.4th 39, 41. See "Writ of mandate," §9.1, p. 374.

§9.3 Standard of review. Generally, the standard of review for an order granting or denying a motion to transfer or change venue is abuse of discretion. *See* ***State Bd. of Equalization v. Superior Ct.*** (6th Dist.2006) 138 Cal.App.4th 951, 954 (court abuses discretion when venue is mandatory in another county). In cases in which the court's decision on a motion to transfer is predominantly legal, a de novo standard of review will apply. ***County of Siskiyou v. Superior Ct.*** (3d Dist.2013) 217 Cal.App.4th 83, 92; ***Kennedy/Jenks Consultants, Inc. v. Superior Ct.*** (1st Dist.2000) 80 Cal.App.4th 948, 959 & n.6.

F. FORUM NON CONVENIENS

§1. GENERAL

§1.1 Purpose. Forum non conveniens (FNC) is an equitable doctrine that gives the court discretion to decline its jurisdiction over a transitory cause of action to avoid imposing an inconvenient forum on a litigant. ***Stangvik v. Shiley Inc.*** (1991) 54 Cal.3d 744, 751; ***Price v. Atchison, Topeka & Santa Fe Ry.*** (1954) 42 Cal.2d 577, 580; ***Boaz v. Boyle & Co.*** (2d Dist.1995) 40 Cal.App.4th 700, 706-07. See "Transitory Actions," ch. 3-F, §4, p. 273. The doctrine can be applied in two ways: a motion to stay or dismiss for FNC or a motion to stay or dismiss based on a forum-selection clause (FSC). A motion to stay or dismiss for FNC asks the court to decline jurisdiction because a court outside California has jurisdiction over the dispute and is a more appropriate forum. *See* CCP §§410.30, 418.10(a)(2); ***Stangvik***, 54 Cal.3d at 751. See "Motion to Stay or Dismiss – Forum Non Conveniens," §2, p. 376. A motion to stay or dismiss based on an FSC asks the court to decline jurisdiction because the parties chose a forum outside California as the proper place to hear the action. ***Smith, Valentino & Smith, Inc. v. Superior Ct.*** (1976) 17 Cal.3d 491, 495. See "Motion to Stay or Dismiss – Forum-Selection Clause," §3, p. 383.

§1.2 Primary authority. CCP §§410.30, 418.10, 904.1(a)(3), 904.2(d).

§1.3 Secondary authority. The following secondary sources are cited as authority in this subchapter:

- *California Civil Procedure Before Trial* (CEB Online ed. 2014) (referred to as *CEB Procedure Before Trial*).
- Kiesel et al., *Matthew Bender Practice Guide: California Pretrial Civil Procedure* (2014) (referred to as Kiesel, *Cal. Pretrial Civil Procedure*).
- Schwing, *California Affirmative Defenses* (2008) (referred to as Schwing, *Cal. Affirmative Defenses*).

§2. MOTION TO STAY OR DISMISS – FORUM NON CONVENIENS

§2.1 Grounds. To prevail on a motion to stay or dismiss for forum non conveniens (FNC), the defendant must establish that (1) the proposed alternative forum is "suitable" and (2) the interest of substantial justice would be served by having the action heard in the alternative forum. *See* CCP §410.30(a); ***Stangvik v. Shiley Inc.*** (1991) 54 Cal.3d 744, 751.

1. Suitability of alternative forum. The defendant must show that the alternative forum is a suitable place for trial. ***Stangvik***, 54 Cal.3d at 751. Suitability is a threshold issue on which the court has no discretion; if the court finds that the alternative forum is not suitable, it must deny the motion. *See id.* at 752 & n.3; ***Boaz v. Boyle & Co.*** (2d Dist.1995) 40 Cal.App.4th 700, 711; ***Shiley Inc. v. Superior Ct.*** (4th Dist.1992) 4 Cal.App.4th 126, 131-32. An alternative forum is suitable only if the defendant establishes all the following:

(1) Alternative forum has jurisdiction over Ds. The alternative forum must be able to exercise jurisdiction over all defendants. *See* ***Stangvik***, 54 Cal.3d at 752; ***American Cemwood Corp. v. American Home Assur. Co.*** (1st Dist.2001) 87 Cal.App.4th 431, 440. In other words, the plaintiff must be able to sue all the defendants in the alternative forum. ***American Cemwood***, 87 Cal.App.4th at 437-38. This jurisdictional requirement can be established by proof that the defendants have consented to the alternative forum's jurisdiction. ***Hahn v. Diaz-Barba*** (4th Dist.2011) 194 Cal.App.4th 1177, 1190; *see, e.g.*, ***Stangvik***, 54 Cal.3d at 752 (all Ds stipulated they would submit to jurisdiction in foreign forum). In some cases, however, requiring the defendant to prove the alternative forum's jurisdictional reach over all defendants may be unreasonable, such as actions in which a large number of defendants are sued. *See, e.g.*, ***American Cemwood***, 87 Cal.App.4th at 439-40 (not unreasonable to require Ds to prove that three other Ds were subject to jurisdiction in alternative forum); ***Hansen v. Owens-Corning Fiberglas Corp.*** (1st Dist.1996) 51 Cal.App.4th 753, 759 (unreasonable to require D to prove that 200 other Ds were subject to jurisdiction in alternative forum). In those cases, the movant should ask the court to stay the action pending a determination in the alternative forum that all defendants are subject to that court's jurisdiction. *See* ***Hansen***, 51 Cal.App.4th at 759.

(2) No procedural bar. There must be no procedural bar to the ability of the alternative forum to hear the plaintiff's claim on the merits. ***Boaz***, 40 Cal.App.4th at 711; *see* ***Stangvik***, 54 Cal.3d at 752 (statute of limitations cannot bar suit). If there is a procedural bar, the defendant should stipulate that it will waive the bar. *See* ***Stangvik***, 54 Cal.3d at 752; ***Roman v. Liberty Univ., Inc.*** (4th Dist.2008) 162 Cal.App.4th 670, 682-83; ***Boaz***, 40 Cal.App.4th at 711.

(3) Adequate remedy. The remedy provided by the alternative forum cannot be so inadequate as to amount to no remedy at all. *See* ***Stangvik***, 54 Cal.3d at 753 & n.5; ***Shiley Inc.***, 4 Cal.App.4th at 133-34; *cf.* ***Piper Aircraft Co. v. Reyno*** (1981) 454 U.S. 235, 254 & n.22 (interpreting FNC under federal common law). Circumstances establishing the inadequacy of an alternative forum are rare. ***Boaz***, 40 Cal.App.4th at 711.

(a) Remedy is adequate. A forum's remedy is adequate if the suit can be brought in the alternative forum, even if the suit cannot necessarily be won there. ***Guimei v. General Elec. Co.*** (2d Dist.2009) 172 Cal.App.4th 689, 696; ***Roman***, 162 Cal.App.4th at 683; ***Chong v. Superior Ct.*** (2d Dist.1997) 58 Cal.App.4th 1032, 1037. The fact that the alternative forum's law is less favorable to the plaintiff or that recovery would be more difficult if not impossible is irrelevant to whether the forum is suitable. ***Stangvik***, 54 Cal.3d at 753 n.5; ***Guimei***, 172 Cal.App.4th at 696; ***Boaz***, 40 Cal.App.4th at 711; *see, e.g.*, ***Roman***, 162 Cal.App.4th at 683 (although Virginia's comparative-negligence law could completely bar P's recovery for negligence, Virginia was suitable forum because P was not prevented from filing negligence suit).

(b) Remedy is inadequate. A forum's remedy is inadequate if there is "no independent judiciary or due process of law." ***Investors Equity Life Holding Co. v. Schmidt*** (4th Dist.2011) 195 Cal.App.4th 1519, 1530; ***Guimei***, 172 Cal.App.4th at 697; ***Boaz***, 40 Cal.App.4th at 711. To establish a forum's inadequacy, the party opposing the motion must do more than make general allegations of corruption, lack of due process, or other factors making the forum unsuitable. ***Guimei***, 172 Cal.App.4th at 697. For example, an alternative forum would be inadequate if the opposing party shows that the movant could dictate the outcome of the dispute through control over

the alternative forum's courts. *Cf.* ***Daventree Ltd. v. Republic of Azerbaijan*** (S.D.N.Y.2004) 349 F.Supp.2d 736, 756 (interpreting FNC under federal common law; possibility that D1, a foreign government, could dictate outcome of legal dispute because of its control over country's courts would effectively foreclose Ps' right to pursue their claims in that country).

NOTE

No court has ever found that a U.S. forum provides an inadequate remedy. See ***Shiley Inc.****, 4 Cal.App.4th at 133-34.*

2. Interest of substantial justice. The defendant must show that it would be in the interest of substantial justice to have the action heard in the alternative forum. CCP §410.30(a). To prove that the action should be heard in the alternative forum, the movant must show that the balance of certain private and public interests points strongly toward the alternative forum. *See* ***Stangvik***, 54 Cal.3d at 751; ***Morris v. AGFA Corp.*** (1st Dist.2006) 144 Cal.App.4th 1452, 1463-64; *see, e.g.*, ***Hansen***, 51 Cal.App.4th at 761 (because Montana was suitable forum and factors weighed heavily in its favor, court did not abuse discretion in staying action); *cf.* ***Piper Aircraft***, 454 U.S. at 255 (interpreting FNC under federal common law; strong presumption favoring P's choice of forum can be overcome only when factors clearly point toward alternate forum). The balancing test is flexible, and no undue emphasis should be given to any single factor. ***Stangvik***, 54 Cal.3d at 753. The factors fit into three broad categories: (1) the relationship of the case and the parties to each forum, (2) concerns of judicial administration, and (3) the convenience of the parties and witnesses. ***Ford Motor Co. v. Insurance Co. of N. Am.*** (2d Dist.1995) 35 Cal.App.4th 604, 611.

(1) Relationship of case & parties to forums. The defendant should address the following factors that relate to the relationship of the case and the parties to each forum:

(a) Plaintiff's residence. The plaintiff's residence is an important factor to consider in determining whether to stay or dismiss a case for FNC.

[1] In California. If the plaintiff is a resident of California—including a resident corporation—the plaintiff's choice of forum is given substantial deference and should not be disturbed unless the balance of private and public factors strongly favors the defendant. *See* ***Stangvik***, 54 Cal.3d at 754-55. When a dismissal is sought in such cases, the defendant has the heightened burden to prove that California is a "seriously inconvenient" forum. ***National Football League v. Fireman's Fund Ins.*** (2d Dist.2013) (Div. 5) 216 Cal.App.4th 902, 931-32. When a stay is sought in such cases, courts disagree on the burden that should be placed on the defendant. *Compare* ***Morris***, 144 Cal.App.4th at 1464 (D has burden to prove that California is seriously inconvenient forum), *and* ***In re Marriage of Taschen*** (2d Dist.2005) (Div. 1) 134 Cal.App.4th 681, 691 (same), *with* ***National Football League***, 216 Cal.App.4th at 933 (disagreeing that D has burden to prove seriously inconvenient forum when D is seeking stay rather than dismissal), *and* ***Century Indem. Co. v. Bank of Am.*** (1st Dist.1997) 58 Cal.App.4th 408, 412-13 (same).

[2] In another state. If the plaintiff is a resident of another state, courts disagree on what level of deference should be attributed to the plaintiff's choice of forum. Most courts have held that when a plaintiff is from another state, the plaintiff's choice of forum should be given substantial deference like a California resident, and should not be disturbed unless the balance of private and public factors strongly favors the defendant. ***Morris***, 144 Cal.App.4th at 1465 & n.6; ***Ford Motor***, 35 Cal.App.4th at 610-11; *cf.* ***Lueck v. Sundstrand Corp.*** (9th Cir.2001) 236 F.3d 1137, 1143 (interpreting FNC under federal common law; when P is U.S. citizen, D must satisfy heavy burden of proof). One court recently held, however, that when a plaintiff is from another state, the plaintiff's choice of forum should be given due deference but not a strong presumption. ***National Football League***, 216 Cal.App.4th at 929.

[3] In foreign country. If the plaintiff is a resident of a foreign country, the plaintiff's choice of forum is given less deference. *See* ***Stangvik***, 54 Cal.3d at 755 & n.7; ***Campbell v. Parker-Hannifin Corp.*** (1st Dist.1999) 69 Cal.App.4th 1534, 1543; *cf.* ***Piper Aircraft***, 454 U.S. at 256 (interpreting FNC under federal common law).

(b) Defendant's residence. The defendant's residence is a factor to be considered in determining whether to stay or dismiss a case for FNC. ***Stangvik***, 54 Cal.3d at 755-56; *see* ***Ford Motor***, 35 Cal.App.4th at 612; ***Great N. Ry. v. Superior Ct.*** (1st Dist.1970) 12 Cal.App.3d 105, 113. For example, if a defendant is a corporation, the corporation's place of business and state of incorporation are presumptively convenient forums. ***Stangvik***, 54 Cal.3d at 755; ***Morris***, 144 Cal.App.4th at 1465. If the defendant's residence or principal place of business is in California, courts are less likely to dismiss or stay an action for FNC. Schwing, *Cal. Affirmative Defenses*, §6:5. *But see* ***Stangvik***, 54 Cal.3d at 761 (simply because D has principal place of business in California and tort was committed there does not mean court should ignore other relevant court-congestion factors in determining whether California is convenient forum).

(c) Other factors. Other factors to be considered in determining whether to stay or dismiss a case for FNC include the following:

[1] The defendant's amenability to personal jurisdiction in the alternative forum. ***Archibald v. Cinerama Hotels*** (1976) 15 Cal.3d 853, 860; ***Ford Motor***, 35 Cal.App.4th at 612; ***Great N. Ry.***, 12 Cal.App.3d at 113. See "Alternative forum has jurisdiction over Ds," §2.1.1(1), p. 376.

[2] California's ability to exercise personal jurisdiction over all indispensable parties. Schwing, *Cal. Affirmative Defenses*, §6:4. If one or more indispensable parties cannot be joined, the court may be required to dismiss the case under CCP §389(b) even if other grounds supporting the motion to stay or dismiss for FNC are not present. *See* Schwing, *Cal. Affirmative Defenses*, §6:4; *see, e.g.*, ***Atlantic Richfield Co. v. Superior Ct.*** (2d Dist.1975) 51 Cal.App.3d 168, 175-76 (California could not acquire jurisdiction over 57 nonresidents claiming an interest in oil royalties at issue). See "Absent party is indispensable," ch. 3-B, §3.1.3, p. 194.

[3] California's interest in providing a forum for some or all of the parties. ***Ford Motor***, 35 Cal.App.4th at 612; ***Great N. Ry.***, 12 Cal.App.3d at 114.

[4] Whether the parties have a relationship to California that requires them to participate in judicial proceedings in California. ***Ford Motor***, 35 Cal.App.4th at 612; ***Great N. Ry.***, 12 Cal.App.3d at 114.

[5] Whether the situation, transaction, or events from which the action arose exist in, occurred in, or had a substantial relationship to California. ***Great N. Ry.***, 12 Cal.App.3d at 113; *see* ***Ford Motor***, 35 Cal.App.4th at 612.

[6] California's interest in regulating the situation or conduct involved. ***Ford Motor***, 35 Cal.App.4th at 612; ***Great N. Ry.***, 12 Cal.App.3d at 114.

[7] The public interest in the case. ***Ford Motor***, 35 Cal.App.4th at 612; ***Great N. Ry.***, 12 Cal.App.3d at 114.

[8] Whether prosecution of the action may place a burden on California courts that is unfair, inequitable, or disproportionate in view of the relationship of the parties or the cause of action to California. ***Great N. Ry.***, 12 Cal.App.3d at 113-14; *see* ***Ford Motor***, 35 Cal.App.4th at 612.

(2) Concerns of judicial administration. The defendant should address the following factors that relate to concerns of judicial administration:

(a) The differences in conflict-of-laws rules applicable in California and the alternative forum. ***Ford Motor***, 35 Cal.App.4th at 614; ***Great N. Ry.***, 12 Cal.App.3d at 113.

(b) Whether any judgment entered in the action would be enforceable in California. ***Ford Motor***, 35 Cal.App.4th at 614; ***Great N. Ry.***, 12 Cal.App.3d at 113.

(c) The avoidance of a multiplicity of actions and inconsistent adjudications. ***Ford Motor***, 35 Cal.App.4th at 614; ***Great N. Ry.***, 12 Cal.App.3d at 114.

(d) The relative probability of administrative difficulties and other inconveniences from crowded calendars and congested courts between California and the alternative forum. ***Ford Motor***, 35 Cal.App.4th at 614; ***Great N. Ry.***, 12 Cal.App.3d at 114; *e.g.*, ***Stangvik***, 54 Cal.3d at 757-58 (court would be overburdened by trying hundreds of complex product-liability suits for Ps from foreign countries).

(e) Whether jury duty will be imposed on a community having no relation to the litigation. ***Ford Motor***, 35 Cal.App.4th at 614; ***Great N. Ry.***, 12 Cal.App.3d at 114; *see* ***Stangvik***, 54 Cal.3d at 751; *see, e.g.*, ***Hansen***, 51 Cal.App.4th at 760 (unduly burdensome for California residents to sit on jury for injury that occurred outside California to nonresident).

(f) The injustice to and burden on local courts and taxpayers. ***Ford Motor***, 35 Cal.App.4th at 614; ***Great N. Ry.***, 12 Cal.App.3d at 114.

(g) The availability of the alternative forum. ***Ford Motor***, 35 Cal.App.4th at 614; ***Great N. Ry.***, 12 Cal.App.3d at 114.

(3) Convenience of parties & witnesses. The defendant should address the following factors that relate to the convenience of the parties and witnesses:

(a) The relative convenience to the parties and witnesses of trial in the alternative forum. ***Great N. Ry.***, 12 Cal.App.3d at 113; *see* ***Ford Motor***, 35 Cal.App.4th at 616. The convenience to the attorneys cannot be considered. *See* ***Jagger v. Superior Ct.*** (2d Dist.1979) 96 Cal.App.3d 579, 589.

(b) Whether any party would be substantially disadvantaged by having to try the action in California or the alternative forum. ***Ford Motor***, 35 Cal.App.4th at 616; ***Great N. Ry.***, 12 Cal.App.3d at 113.

(c) Whether the witnesses would be inconvenienced if the action were tried in California or the alternative forum. ***Ford Motor***, 35 Cal.App.4th at 616; ***Great N. Ry.***, 12 Cal.App.3d at 113; *see* ***Archibald***, 15 Cal.3d at 860.

(d) The relative expense to the parties of maintaining the action in California or the alternative forum. ***Stangvik***, 54 Cal.3d at 751; ***Archibald***, 15 Cal.3d at 860; ***Ford Motor***, 35 Cal.App.4th at 616; ***Great N. Ry.***, 12 Cal.App.3d at 113; *see* Schwing, *Cal. Affirmative Defenses*, §6:10 (court should consider expenses relative to financial condition of each party).

(e) Whether viewing the premises where the incident occurred or physical evidence that cannot be easily moved will benefit the trier of fact in deciding the case. *See* ***Ford Motor***, 35 Cal.App.4th at 616; ***Great N. Ry.***, 12 Cal.App.3d at 113.

(f) The relative ease of access to sources of proof. ***Stangvik***, 54 Cal.3d at 751; ***Ford Motor***, 35 Cal.App.4th at 616; ***Great N. Ry.***, 12 Cal.App.3d at 114.

(g) The availability of compulsory process for attendance of witnesses. ***Stangvik***, 54 Cal.3d at 751; ***Ford Motor***, 35 Cal.App.4th at 616; ***Great N. Ry.***, 12 Cal.App.3d at 114.

(h) The relative advantages and obstacles to a fair trial. ***Ford Motor***, 35 Cal.App.4th at 616; ***Great N. Ry.***, 12 Cal.App.3d at 114.

(i) The inconvenience of presenting testimony by deposition. ***Ford Motor***, 35 Cal.App.4th at 616; ***Great N. Ry.***, 12 Cal.App.3d at 114. The fact that evidence must be presented by deposition testimony is not dispositive. The focus of the inquiry is on potential witnesses—namely, whether a party will have to use deposition testimony or videotape for witnesses whose credibility is critical or whose physical presence in front of a jury is necessary. *See* Schwing, *Cal. Affirmative Defenses*, §6:8.

(j) Other practical considerations that make trial of the case convenient, expeditious, and inexpensive. ***Ford Motor***, 35 Cal.App.4th at 616; ***Great N. Ry.***, 12 Cal.App.3d at 115.

§2.2 Motion.

1. Who can file.

(1) Defendant has not appeared – §418.10 motion. If the defendant has not generally appeared (e.g., by filing an answer), the defendant must file a motion to stay or dismiss for FNC under CCP §418.10. ***Britton***

FORUM NON CONVENIENS

v. ***Dallas Airmotive, Inc.*** (1st Dist.2007) 153 Cal.App.4th 127, 134; *see* CCP §§410.30(b), 418.10(a)(2). A motion under §418.10 does not constitute a general appearance. CCP §418.10(d).

(2) Defendant has appeared – §410.30 motion. If the defendant has generally appeared, any party (usually the defendant) can file a motion to stay or dismiss for FNC under CCP §410.30, or the court can stay or dismiss the action on its own motion. ***In re Marriage of Taschen*** (2d Dist.2005) 134 Cal.App.4th 681, 687-88; *see* ***Britton***, 153 Cal.App.4th at 134.

2. Deadline to file & serve.

(1) Section 418.10 motion. Generally, a motion to stay or dismiss for FNC under §418.10 must be filed and served before the defendant generally appears. *See* CCP §§410.30(b), 418.10(a), (e)(3); ***Britton***, 153 Cal.App.4th at 134; Kiesel, *Cal. Pretrial Civil Procedure*, §9.26[1][a]; *see, e.g.*, ***Olinick v. BMG Entm't*** (2d Dist.2006) 138 Cal.App.4th 1286, 1295 (D timely filed motion under §418.10 when it filed motion during 15-day extension to respond to complaint). But the motion can be filed simultaneously with an answer, a demurrer, or a motion strike. CCP §418.10(e). If the motion is not filed before or simultaneously with a motion to strike or demurrer, the defendant will waive its right to contest the forum on the basis of FNC. CCP §418.10(e)(3); ***Britton***, 153 Cal.App.4th at 134. For a discussion of what constitutes a general appearance, see "General appearance," ch. 3-G, §5.1.1, p. 285.

NOTE

A motion to stay or dismiss under §418.10 prevents the court from entering a default judgment against the defendant until the motion is denied and the defendant's time to plead has expired. CCP §418.10(d); see id. §585(a).

(2) Section 410.30 motion.

(a) No demurrer or motion to strike filed. If the defendant has generally appeared but has not filed a demurrer or a motion to strike, a motion to stay or dismiss for FNC under §410.30 can be filed and served at any time. *See* ***Britton***, 153 Cal.App.4th at 133; ***Morris v. AGFA Corp.*** (1st Dist.2006) 144 Cal.App.4th 1452, 1461. But an unreasonable delay in bringing the motion will weigh against the movant when the court considers the motion. *See* ***Britton***, 153 Cal.App.4th at 135; *see, e.g.*, ***Morris***, 144 Cal.App.4th at 1461 (motion to stay was properly granted because Ps were not prejudiced by delayed filing).

CAUTION

A motion to stay or dismiss for FNC under §410.30 should be used when it is necessary to conduct discovery before filing the motion. See ***Britton***, *153 Cal.App.4th at 134-35. If the attorney thinks that FNC may be an issue in the case, any discovery that is requested should not go beyond the scope of establishing the grounds for the FNC motion.* ***Martinez v. Ford Motor Co.*** *(2d Dist.2010) 185 Cal.App.4th 9, 18. If the requested discovery goes beyond the scope, the attorney may be estopped from asserting an FNC motion. See, e.g., id. at 21 (because exhibits attached to complaint identified Ps as Mexican citizens, Ds should have known that FNC might be issue in case; Ds could not complain that California was inconvenient forum after propounding 1,400 pages of discovery that went beyond scope of establishing grounds for FNC).*

(b) Demurrer or motion to strike filed. If the defendant has generally appeared by filing a demurrer or a motion to strike, the defendant cannot bring a motion to stay or dismiss for FNC under §410.30. ***Britton***, 153 Cal.App.4th at 133.

3. Contents.

(1) Notice of motion & motion.

(a) Generally. A motion to stay or dismiss for FNC should be requested in writing by noticed motion. CCP §418.10(a); *see id.* §410.30. See "Notice of motion & motion," ch. 1-D, §5.1, p. 28. A noticed motion under §418.10 should designate a hearing date no later than 30 days after the notice is filed. CCP §418.10(b). A noticed motion under §410.30 can designate a hearing date in the same manner as other noticed motions. See "Noticed motion," ch. 1-H, §4.1, p. 81. For a discussion of how far in advance of the hearing the notice of motion and motion must be filed and served, see "Motion papers," ch. 1-F, §5.2.1(2)(a), p. 57; "Retrospective deadlines," ch. 1-G, §6.2, p. 71.

(b) Relief. The notice of motion and motion must describe the relief sought. *See* CRC 3.1110(a) (notice of motion must state nature of order being sought), CRC 3.1112(d)(3) (motion must briefly state relief sought).

[1] Dismissal vs. stay. In most cases, the defendant can ask the court to dismiss the action if it grants the motion. However, when the plaintiff is a California resident, the suit should be stayed, not dismissed, unless it is an extraordinary case. ***Archibald v. Cinerama Hotels*** (1976) 15 Cal.3d 853, 858; Schwing, *Cal. Affirmative Defenses*, §6:3. Some examples of "extraordinary cases" include actions involving a California resident who is a nominal party suing for a beneficiary or creditor (e.g., a will administrator who is a California resident suing on behalf of a nonresident beneficiary) and actions in which California cannot obtain jurisdiction over an indispensable party. ***Archibald***, 15 Cal.3d at 859 & n.6.

[2] Attorney fees. The defendant can ask for attorney fees if the suit is based on a contract that contains a provision allowing a prevailing party to recover attorney fees. ***PNEC Corp. v. Meyer*** (4th Dist.2010) 190 Cal.App.4th 66, 71.

PRACTICE TIP

*When making a motion for FNC requesting a dismissal, the defendant should request a stay as an alternative. CEB Procedure Before Trial, §21.13. A court is more willing to grant a stay because it can resume the California suit if the plaintiff is unable to obtain relief in the alternative forum. See **Archibald**, 15 Cal.3d at 857-58; CEB Procedure Before Trial, §§21.13, 21.21.*

(c) Grounds. The notice of motion and motion must briefly state the grounds for the relief (e.g., "the motion is made on the ground that California is an inconvenient forum and, in the interest of substantial justice, the case should be heard in a forum outside this state"). *See* CRC 3.1110(a) (notice of motion must state grounds for issuance of order), CRC 3.1112(d)(3) (motion must briefly state basis for motion). See "Grounds," §2.1, p. 376.

(2) Memorandum of points & authorities.

The motion must include a memorandum in support of the motion. CRC 3.1112(a)(3), 3.1113(a). See "Memorandum of points & authorities," ch. 1-D, §5.2, p. 28.

(3) Supporting evidence.

A motion to stay or dismiss for FNC can be supported by the following types of evidence:

(a) Verified pleadings. A motion for FNC can be supported by the plaintiff's verified pleadings. See "Using Pleadings," ch. 1-C, §8, p. 24.

(b) Affidavits & declarations. A motion for FNC can be supported by affidavits and declarations. *See* ***Morris***, 144 Cal.App.4th at 1458, 1462 (affidavits and declarations); ***Cal-State Bus. Prods. & Servs. v. Ricoh*** (3d Dist.1993) 12 Cal.App.4th 1666, 1671 (declarations); *CEB Procedure Before Trial*, §21.19 (same). See "General Requirements for Declarations & Affidavits," ch. 1-B, §4, p. 19.

(c) Discovery. A motion for FNC can be supported by discovery such as deposition testimony, interrogatory answers, and admissions. *See* ***Britton***, 153 Cal.App.4th at 134-35 (general discovery); ***Morris***, 144 Cal.App.4th at 1462 (discovery responses).

(d) Stipulations. A motion for FNC can be supported by the defendant's sworn stipulations. *See, e.g.*, ***Stangvik v. Shiley Inc.*** (1991) 54 Cal.3d 744, 752 (Ds stipulated they would submit to jurisdiction in foreign forum).

(4) Request for judicial notice. The motion can be accompanied by a request for judicial notice. *See* CRC 3.1113(*l*) (requirements for request); *CEB Procedure Before Trial*, §21.19 (D should ask court to take judicial notice of law in alternative forum to demonstrate alternative forum's suitability). The request must be made in a separate document and must list the specific items for which notice is requested. CRC 3.1113(*l*). See "Request for Judicial Notice," ch. 5-J, p. 547.

(5) Proposed order. The motion can include a proposed order. *See* CRC 3.1113(m). If a proposed order is submitted, it must be lodged and served with the motion papers, not attached to them. *Id.* See "Documents lodged," ch. 1-F, §2.3, p. 47.

4. Filing fees. When the motion is filed, the defendant must pay a filing fee to the court clerk or request a waiver of the fee. See "Filing Fees," ch. 1-F, §7, p. 58.

5. Motion filed with other challenges. A motion to stay or dismiss for FNC can be filed simultaneously with an answer, a demurrer, or a motion to strike. CCP §418.10(e).

§2.3 Opposition. A party can respond to a motion to stay or dismiss for FNC by filing and serving an opposition. See "Opposition Papers," ch. 1-D, §8, p. 35.

1. Deadline to file & serve. The opposition papers must be filed and served at least nine court days before the hearing. CCP §1005(b). See "Filing & serving opposition," ch. 1-D, §8.5, p. 36.

2. Grounds. A motion to stay or dismiss for FNC can be opposed on the following nonexclusive grounds:

(1) FSC. The motion can be opposed on the ground that a forum-selection clause (FSC) requires the dispute to be resolved in California. If the FSC is mandatory, the burden will shift to the party moving for FNC to prove that the FSC is invalid or unreasonable. ***Intershop Comms., AG v. Superior Ct.*** (1st Dist.2002) 104 Cal.App.4th 191, 198. See "Mandatory FSC," §3.1.1, p. 383; "Movant's burden," §3.2, p. 384. If the FSC is permissive, the court can consider it as a factor in deciding to grant or deny a motion based on FNC. ***Berg v. MTC Elecs. Techs. Co.*** (2d Dist.1998) 61 Cal.App.4th 349, 359. See "Permissive FSC," §3.1.2, p. 384.

(2) Waiver. The motion can be opposed on the ground that the party waived its right to argue that California is an inconvenient forum. For a discussion of when a party waives its right to bring a motion for FNC, see "Deadline to file & serve," §2.2.2, p. 380.

3. Contents. For a general discussion of the contents of an opposition, see "Opposition Papers," ch. 1-D, §8, p. 35.

§2.4 Reply. The defendant can file and serve a reply to opposition papers. The reply must be filed and served at least five court days before the hearing. *See* CCP §1005(b). See "Reply Papers," ch. 1-D, §9, p. 37.

§2.5 Hearing.

1. Generally. For a discussion of hearings generally, see "Hearings," ch. 1-H, p. 79.

2. Date of hearing. The hearing on the motion to stay or dismiss for FNC should be heard within 30 days after the notice of motion is filed. *See* CCP §418.10(b).

§2.6 Ruling. In ruling on a motion to stay or dismiss for FNC, the court must first determine if the alternative forum is suitable. ***Stangvik v. Shiley Inc.*** (1991) 54 Cal.3d 744, 751. See "Suitability of alternative forum," §2.1.1, p. 376. If the alternative forum is not suitable, the court must deny the motion; suitability is a threshold issue on which the court has no discretion. *See* ***Stangvik***, 54 Cal.3d at 752 & n.3; ***Boaz v. Boyle & Co.*** (2d Dist.1995) 40 Cal.App.4th 700, 711; ***Shiley Inc. v. Superior Ct.*** (4th Dist.1992) 4 Cal.App.4th 126, 131-32. If the alternative forum is suitable, the court must balance the private and public interests to determine whether the motion should be granted

or denied. ***Stangvik***, 54 Cal.3d at 751. If the plaintiff is a resident of California or another state, the plaintiff's choice of forum should not be disturbed unless the balance of private and public factors strongly favors the defendant. ***Morris v. AGFA Corp.*** (1st Dist.2006) 144 Cal.App.4th 1452, 1465 & n.6. If the plaintiff is a resident of a foreign country, the plaintiff's choice of forum is given less deference. ***Stangvik***, 54 Cal.3d at 755 & n.7; ***Campbell v. Parker-Hannifin Corp.*** (1st Dist.1999) 69 Cal.App.4th 1534, 1543.

§2.7 Order. The court is not required to explain its reasons for granting or denying a motion to stay or dismiss for FNC. ***Campbell v. Parker-Hannifin Corp.*** (1st Dist.1999) 69 Cal.App.4th 1534, 1542; ***Cal-State Bus. Prods. & Servs. v. Ricoh*** (3d Dist.1993) 12 Cal.App.4th 1666, 1676.

1. Grants motion.

(1) Stay. An order staying the action can be made orally and entered in the minutes. *See, e.g.*, ***Campbell***, 69 Cal.App.4th at 1540 (court issued minute order granting motion to stay). When a suit is stayed, the court retains jurisdiction and can resume the suit when certain conditions are met. ***Archibald v. Cinerama Hotels*** (1976) 15 Cal.3d 853, 857; *see* ***Morris v. AGFA Corp.*** (1st Dist.2006) 144 Cal.App.4th 1452, 1460.

(a) Conditions. The court can require the defendant to agree to certain conditions before it will stay the suit in favor of an alternative forum. CCP §410.30(a); *see* ***Stangvik v. Shiley Inc.*** (1991) 54 Cal.3d 744, 750 & n.2; ***Morris***, 144 Cal.App.4th at 1460. The court can impose any condition it finds just. CCP §410.30(a). Some of the conditions the court can impose include the following: (1) the defendant will submit to the alternative forum's jurisdiction, (2) the defendant will send any necessary documents to the alternative jurisdiction, (3) the defendant will not raise a limitations defense in the alternative forum, and (4) the defendant will pay any final judgment rendered in the alternative forum. *See* ***Stangvik***, 54 Cal.3d at 750 & n.2.

(b) Lifting stay. If the defendant does not abide by the required conditions, the court can protect the plaintiff's interest by ordering the stay lifted and continuing the suit in California. *See* ***Archibald***, 15 Cal.3d at 857; ***Morris***, 144 Cal.App.4th at 1460. The court can also lift the stay if the alternative forum unreasonably delays the suit or fails to reach a resolution on the merits. ***Archibald***, 15 Cal.3d at 857.

(2) Dismiss. An order dismissing the action must be a written order signed by the judge and filed in the action. CCP §581d. When a suit is dismissed, the court does not retain any jurisdiction and cannot resume the suit. ***Archibald***, 15 Cal.3d at 857-58.

2. Denies motion. If the defendant filed a motion under §418.10 and did not include an answer or other responsive pleading with it, the defendant has 15 days after receiving written notice denying the motion to file a pleading. CCP §418.10(b). On a showing of good cause, the defendant can ask the court for an additional 20 days to file. *Id.*

§3. MOTION TO STAY OR DISMISS – FORUM-SELECTION CLAUSE

Parties can contractually agree to have their legal disputes resolved in a specific forum. *See* ***Smith, Valentino & Smith, Inc. v. Superior Ct.*** (1976) 17 Cal.3d 491, 495. These forum-selection clauses (FSCs) are valid and enforceable in California. *Id.* at 496. To enforce an FSC, a party can file a motion to stay or dismiss under CCP §410.30 or 418.10. *See* ***Berg v. MTC Elecs. Techs. Co.*** (2d Dist.1998) 61 Cal.App.4th 349, 358; *see also* ***Smith, Valentino & Smith***, 17 Cal.3d at 495 (motion to dismiss under §410.30; court may decline to exercise jurisdiction in recognition of parties' free and voluntary choice of different forum).

§3.1 Types of FSCs. There are two types of FSCs: mandatory and permissive.

1. Mandatory FSC. A mandatory FSC expressly requires that litigation be heard exclusively in a particular forum. ***Intershop Comms., AG v. Superior Ct.*** (1st Dist.2002) 104 Cal.App.4th 191, 196; *see, e.g.*, ***Cal-State Bus. Prods. & Servs. v. Ricoh*** (3d Dist.1993) 12 Cal.App.4th 1666, 1672 n.4 ("any appropriate state or federal district court located in the Borough of Manhattan, New York City, New York shall have exclusive jurisdiction over any case [or] controversy arising under or in connection with this Agreement"); ***Lu v. Dryclean-U.S.A.*** (1st Dist.1992) 11

Cal.App.4th 1490, 1492 ("[a]ny and all litigation that may arise as a result of this Agreement shall be litigated in Dade County, Florida"). A mandatory FSC is generally enforced unless the party opposing it (usually the plaintiff) establishes that the FSC is invalid or unreasonable. *See* ***Intershop Comms.***, 104 Cal.App.4th at 196, 198; ***Berg v. MTC Elecs. Techs. Co.*** (2d Dist.1998) 61 Cal.App.4th 349, 358. See "Opposition," §3.4, p. 385.

2. Permissive FSC. A permissive FSC authorizes jurisdiction in a particular forum, but it does not require the litigation to occur only there. ***Intershop Comms.***, 104 Cal.App.4th at 196; *see, e.g.*, ***Berg***, 61 Cal.App.4th at 357 ("[t]he company has expressly submitted to the jurisdiction of the State of California"). It does not rule out other jurisdictions by making only one forum the exclusive place of jurisdiction. *See* ***Intershop Comms.***, 104 Cal.App.4th at 197. If the FSC is permissive, then traditional FNC analysis applies—the party enforcing it (usually the defendant) has the burden to prove that the other forum is suitable and that it would be in the interest of substantial justice to hear the case there. *See id.* at 196; ***Berg***, 61 Cal.App.4th at 359. The existence of a permissive FSC is one factor considered along with the other FNC factors. ***Animal Film, LLC v. D.E.J. Prods.*** (2d Dist.2011) 193 Cal.App.4th 466, 471. See "Motion to Stay or Dismiss – Forum Non Conveniens," §2, p. 376.

§3.2 Movant's burden. A mandatory FSC is presumed valid and enforceable. ***Intershop Comms., AG v. Superior Ct.*** (1st Dist.2002) 104 Cal.App.4th 191, 198. See "Mandatory FSC," §3.1.1, p. 383. Thus, the movant meets its burden on a motion to stay or dismiss by simply showing the existence of an FSC. ***Benefit Ass'n Int'l v. Superior Ct.*** (1st Dist.1996) 46 Cal.App.4th 827, 835. The party opposing the enforcement of the FSC generally has the burden to establish that it is invalid or unreasonable. *See* ***Intershop Comms.***, 104 Cal.App.4th at 198; *cf.* ***Bremen v. Zapata Off-Shore Co.*** (1972) 407 U.S. 1, 15 (interpreting federal common law; FSC should be enforced unless opposing party shows that enforcement would be unreasonable or that clause was invalid for reasons such as fraud or overreaching). The only time the movant has the initial burden to prove that the FSC is enforceable is when the FSC threatens to undermine a party's nonwaivable statutory rights in California. *See* ***America Online, Inc. v. Superior Ct.*** (1st Dist.2001) 90 Cal.App.4th 1, 10-11; ***Wimsatt v. Beverly Hills Weight Loss Clinics Int'l*** (4th Dist.1995) 32 Cal.App.4th 1511, 1522; *see also* Civ. C. §3513 (law established for public reason cannot be contravened by private agreement); ***Bickel v. City of Piedmont*** (1997) 16 Cal.4th 1040, 1048 (rights conferred by statute can be waived unless specific statutory provisions prohibit waiver). In that case, the movant has the burden to prove that enforcement of the FSC will not result in a significant diminution of rights. *See* ***America Online***, 90 Cal.App.4th at 10-11; ***Wimsatt***, 32 Cal.App.4th at 1522. This may be accomplished by comparing the rights waived in California to the rights available to the party in the alternative forum. *See* ***America Online***, 90 Cal.App.4th at 15-18 (suggesting that this may be appropriate analysis, but concluding that FSC was not enforceable because it violated statute's antiwaiver provision).

PRACTICE TIP

Although the movant generally does not have the initial burden to prove that an FSC is valid or reasonable, the movant may want to preemptively address those issues in its motion. See, e.g., ***America Online****, 90 Cal.App.4th at 6 (in support of its motion, D argued that FSC was presumptively valid, rational, voluntary, and conscionable and did not violate public policy). For a discussion of the issues the movant may want to address, see "Grounds," §3.4.2, p. 385.*

FORUM NON CONVENIENS

§3.3 Motion.

1. Who can file. Generally, a motion to stay or dismiss based on an FSC can be filed by any party to the contract. *See* ***Intershop Comms., AG v. Superior Ct.*** (1st Dist.2002) 104 Cal.App.4th 191, 195; *see, e.g.*, ***Lifeco Servs. v. Superior Ct.*** (6th Dist.1990) 222 Cal.App.3d 331, 337 (P could seek to stay based on FSC after first seeking injunctive relief in California because relief was requested in good faith and in response to perceived emergency). But an FSC can also be enforced by a third-party beneficiary or a person who is closely related to the contractual relationship. *See* ***Berclain Am. Latina, S.A. de C.V. v. Baan Co.*** (1st Dist.1999) 74 Cal.App.4th 401, 405, 407-08; *see also* Civ. C. §1559 (contract may be enforced by third-party beneficiary). To be closely related to the contractual relationship, the person must show by specific conduct or express agreement that (1) the person agreed to be bound by

the terms of the contract, (2) the contracting parties intended for the person to benefit from the contract, or (3) there is sufficient evidence of a defined and intertwining business relationship between the person and the contracting parties. ***Bancomer, S.A. v. Superior Ct.*** (2d Dist.1996) 44 Cal.App.4th 1450, 1461; *see, e.g.*, ***Lu v. Dryclean-U.S.A.*** (1st Dist.1992) 11 Cal.App.4th 1490, 1494 (Ds could assert FSC because they allegedly participated in fraudulent representations that caused P to enter into contract and they were allegedly alter ego of another D who signed contract).

2. Deadline to file & serve.

(1) Section 418.10 motion. The deadline to file and serve a motion to stay or dismiss based on an FSC under §418.10 is the same as that for an ordinary FNC motion. *See, e.g.*, ***Olinick v. BMG Entm't*** (2d Dist.2006) 138 Cal.App.4th 1286, 1295 (court applied CCP §418.10 deadlines to D's motion to enforce FSC). See "Section 418.10 motion," §2.2.2(1), p. 380.

NOTE

Under §418.10(e)(3), a party waives its right to argue that California is an inconvenient forum if the party files a demurrer or motion to strike before contesting the California forum. One court has held that if a party demurs to claims that are not within the scope of the FSC (i.e., noncontract claims), the party does not waive its right to later contest the forum for claims that are within the FSC's scope. ***Intershop Comms.**, 104 Cal.App.4th at 202.*

(2) Section 410.30 motion. A motion to stay or dismiss based on an FSC under §410.30 must be filed and served within a reasonable time. *E.g.*, ***Trident Labs, Inc. v. Merrill Lynch Commercial Fin. Corp.*** (2d Dist.2011) 200 Cal.App.4th 147, 155 (19-month delay in bringing motion after D extensively litigated in current forum, without any justification offered, was not reasonable time).

3. Contents.

(1) Generally. A motion to stay or dismiss based on an FSC should be requested in the same manner as an FNC motion. *See* ***Cal-State Bus. Prods. & Servs. v. Ricoh*** (3d Dist.1993) 12 Cal.App.4th 1666, 1680 (D can enforce FSC by bringing motion under §410.30 or 418.10). For the general requirements for an FNC motion, see "Contents," §2.2.3, p. 381.

(2) Supporting evidence. A motion based on an FSC should include an attached copy of the contract containing the FSC. *See* ***Cal-State Bus.***, 12 Cal.App.4th at 1671-72. The motion can also be supported by the same type of evidence that supports a traditional motion. See "Supporting evidence," §2.2.3(3), p. 381.

§3.4 Opposition. A party can respond to a motion to stay or dismiss based on an FSC by filing and serving opposition papers. See "Opposition Papers," ch. 1-D, §8, p. 35. Because a mandatory FSC is presumed valid and enforceable, if a party does not file an opposition to the motion, the court may grant the motion simply on the showing of the FSC. *See* ***Benefit Ass'n Int'l v. Superior Ct.*** (1st Dist.1996) 46 Cal.App.4th 827, 835. The burden to prove that the FSC is unenforceable is on the party opposing the motion. ***Intershop Comms., AG v. Superior Ct.*** (1st Dist.2002) 104 Cal.App.4th 191, 198.

1. Deadline to file & serve. The opposition must be filed and served at least nine court days before the hearing. *See* CCP §1005(b). See "Filing & serving opposition," ch. 1-D, §8.5, p. 36.

2. Grounds. A motion to stay or dismiss based on an FSC can be opposed on the following nonexclusive grounds:

(1) No standing to enforce FSC. The motion can be opposed on the ground that the movant does not have standing to enforce the FSC. *See, e.g.*, ***Bancomer, S.A. v. Superior Ct.*** (2d Dist.1996) 44 Cal.App.4th 1450, 1454 (D could not enforce FSC because it was not party to contract, third-party beneficiary, or person closely related to contractual relationship). See "Who can file," §3.3.1, p. 384.

(2) Action outside scope of FSC. The motion can be opposed on the ground that the plaintiff's causes of action do not fall within the scope of the FSC. *See, e.g.*, ***Bancomer, S.A.***, 44 Cal.App.4th at 1461-62 (P's tort claims did not relate to FSC and were outside its scope). For example, if the FSC only covers suits over contract disputes, most tort actions will not be subject to the FSC. *See id.* But torts that are related to breach of contract (e.g., intentional interference with advantageous business relationships) may be included. ***Smith, Valentino & Smith, Inc. v. Superior Ct.*** (1976) 17 Cal.3d 491, 497.

(3) FSC permissive. The motion can be opposed on the ground that the FSC is permissive, not mandatory. See "Types of FSCs," §3.1, p. 383. If the FSC is permissive, the movant has the burden to prove that the other forum is suitable and that it would be in the interest of substantial justice to hear the case there. *See **Intershop Comms.***, 104 Cal.App.4th at 196. See "Motion to Stay or Dismiss – Forum Non Conveniens," §2, p. 376.

(4) FSC invalid. The motion can be opposed on the ground that the FSC is invalid. *See **Wimsatt v. Beverly Hills Weight Loss Clinics Int'l*** (4th Dist.1995) 32 Cal.App.4th 1511, 1519-20; ***Cal-State Bus. Prods. & Servs. v. Ricoh*** (3d Dist.1993) 12 Cal.App.4th 1666, 1679; *cf.* ***Bremen v. Zapata Off-Shore Co.*** (1972) 407 U.S. 1, 15 (interpreting federal common law; FSC should be enforced unless opposing party shows that enforcement would be unreasonable or that clause was invalid for reasons such as fraud or overreaching). The question of invalidity goes to the FSC, not to the contract as a whole. *Cf.* ***Bremen***, 407 U.S. at 15 (interpreting federal common law; FSC should be enforced specifically unless clause is clearly shown to be invalid). Some of the arguments that can be made to contest the validity of an FSC include the following:

(a) P did not freely & voluntarily agree to FSC. The validity of an FSC can be contested on the ground that the plaintiff did not freely and voluntarily agree to the FSC. *See **Smith, Valentino & Smith***, 17 Cal.3d at 495-96; ***America Online, Inc. v. Superior Ct.*** (1st Dist.2001) 90 Cal.App.4th 1, 11; ***CQL Original Prods. v. National Hockey League Players' Ass'n*** (4th Dist.1995) 39 Cal.App.4th 1347, 1355; *see also* Civ. C. §1565 (consent to contract must be free, mutual, and communicated by each party to the other).

[1] Arm's length contract. Generally, if the FSC was negotiated at arm's length, courts will find that the contract was freely and voluntarily entered into. *See **Smith, Valentino & Smith***, 17 Cal.3d at 495-96; ***CQL Original***, 39 Cal.App.4th at 1353.

[2] Adhesion contract. If the FSC was in an adhesion contract, the clause will not be enforceable unless it provided adequate notice to the party that it was agreeing to the jurisdiction stated in the clause. ***Aral v. Earthlink, Inc.*** (2d Dist.2005) 134 Cal.App.4th 544, 560, *abrogated on other grounds*, ***AT&T Mobility LLC v. Concepcion*** (2011) ___ U.S. ___, 131 S.Ct. 1740; ***Intershop Comms.***, 104 Cal.App.4th at 201-02; *e.g.*, ***Hunt v. Superior Ct.*** (4th Dist.2000) 81 Cal.App.4th 901, 908 (parties' consent to "applicable jurisdiction" did not provide sufficient notice of forum); *see also* ***CQL Original***, 39 Cal.App.4th at 1355 (even if party cannot negotiate to alter terms of contract, party has power to walk away). It is not a defense to an FSC, however, that the party did not read the clause. *See **Aral***, 134 Cal.App.4th at 560.

(b) FSC is unconscionable. The validity of an FSC can be contested on the ground that the clause itself is unconscionable. *See* Civ. C. §1670.5 (court may refuse to enforce clause in contract that is unconscionable); ***Nagrampa v. Mailcoups, Inc.*** (9th Cir.2006) 469 F.3d 1257, 1287 (discussing California law); *see, e.g.*, ***America Online***, 90 Cal.App.4th at 18 n.17 (trial court held that FSC was part of unconscionable adhesion contract); ***Bolter v. Superior Ct.*** (4th Dist.2001) 87 Cal.App.4th 900, 911 (FSC was unconscionable and struck from contract); *see also* ***Parada v. Superior Ct.*** (4th Dist.2009) 176 Cal.App.4th 1554, 1569 (unconscionability applies to both adhesion and arm's length contracts). To be unenforceable, the clause must be both procedurally and substantively unconscionable. ***Armendariz v. Foundation Health Psychcare Servs.*** (2000) 24 Cal.4th 83, 114. Both elements must be present, but not necessarily in the same degree. *Id.* For example, the more substantively oppressive a clause is, the less evidence of procedural unconscionability is required, and vice versa. *Id.*

[1] Procedural unconscionability. Procedural unconscionability concerns the manner in which the clause was negotiated and the circumstances of the parties at that time. *See **Kinney v. United Healthcare Servs.*** (4th Dist.1999) 70 Cal.App.4th 1322, 1329. The analysis focuses on two factors: oppression and surprise.

Id. Oppression arises from the inequality of bargaining power, which results in no real negotiation or meaningful choice. *Id.* Surprise involves the extent to which the supposedly agreed-upon terms are hidden in the contract. *Id.*

[2] **Substantive unconscionability.** Substantive unconscionability focuses on the terms of the clause and whether those terms are so one-sided as to shock the conscience. *See* ***Kinney***, 70 Cal.App.4th at 1330. The primary consideration is whether the agreement contains a "modicum of bilaterality." *Cf.* ***Armendariz***, 24 Cal.4th at 117 (arbitration clause). An FSC can be substantively unconscionable if the place and manner restrictions would impose such a financial hardship that the FSC would effectively prevent a party from pursuing its claims. *See* ***Nagrampa***, 469 F.3d at 1288-89 (although inconvenience and additional expense generally cannot be used to determine if FSC is unreasonable, they can be considered in determining whether FSC is substantively unconscionable); *see, e.g.*, ***Bolter***, 87 Cal.App.4th at 909-10 (clause required franchisees wanting to resolve any disputes to close down their shops, fly to Utah, and pay for local counsel).

(5) **FSC unreasonable.** The motion can be opposed on the ground that the FSC is unreasonable. ***Smith, Valentino & Smith***, 17 Cal.3d at 496. Even if the FSC is valid, the court can refuse to enforce it if it is unreasonable. *Id.* An FSC can be unreasonable for the following reasons:

(a) **Not available.** An FSC is unreasonable if the alternative forum is unavailable. ***CQL Original***, 39 Cal.App.4th at 1354; ***Cal-State Bus.***, 12 Cal.App.4th at 1679. A forum is unavailable if it does not recognize the plaintiff's cause of action. *See, e.g.*, ***America Online***, 90 Cal.App.4th at 5 (FSC unenforceable because Virginia courts did not allow consumer lawsuits to be brought as class actions).

(b) **No substantial justice.** An FSC is unreasonable if the alternative forum is unable to accomplish substantial justice. ***CQL Original***, 39 Cal.App.4th at 1354; ***Cal-State Bus.***, 12 Cal.App.4th at 1679.

(c) **No rational basis.** An FSC is unreasonable if there is no rational basis for the alternative forum. ***CQL Original***, 39 Cal.App.4th at 1354; ***Cal-State Bus.***, 12 Cal.App.4th at 1679. A forum can have a rational basis even if it is unrelated to the domiciles of the parties or the transactions involved. *E.g.*, ***Cal-State Bus.***, 12 Cal.App.4th at 1682 (choice of New York forum was not irrational despite lack of "nexus" to New York; it was reasonable for parties to avail themselves of New York courts' expertise in commercial litigation).

(d) **Inconvenient & expensive.** Generally, an FSC is not considered unreasonable simply because it would be inconvenient and expensive to conduct the litigation in the alternative forum. ***Smith, Valentino & Smith***, 17 Cal.3d at 496; ***Intershop Comms.***, 104 Cal.App.4th at 199-200; ***CQL Original***, 39 Cal.App.4th at 1354; ***Cal-State Bus.***, 12 Cal.App.4th at 1679. This is especially true when the contract was freely negotiated and the inconvenience or expense was contemplated at the time of contracting. *See* ***Smith, Valentino & Smith***, 17 Cal.3d at 496; *cf.* ***Bremen***, 407 U.S. at 17-18 (interpreting federal common law). Inconvenience and expense may be considered, however, when the FSC is in an adhesion contract and the FSC would require the plaintiff to travel a far distance to recover a small sum. *See, e.g.*, ***Aral***, 134 Cal.App.4th at 561 (FSC in adhesion contract was unreasonable as matter of law because it would require P to travel 2,000 miles to recover $40 to $50).

(6) **FSC violates public policy.** The motion can be opposed on the ground that the FSC violates public policy. *See* ***CQL Original***, 39 Cal.App.4th at 1354; ***Cal-State Bus.***, 12 Cal.App.4th at 1680 (dicta). A court will refuse to defer to the parties' alternative forum if enforcing the FSC would bring about a result contrary to the forum's public policy. ***CQL Original***, 39 Cal.App.4th at 1354; *see* ***Cal-State Bus.***, 12 Cal.App.4th at 1680 (dicta). Courts have held that an FSC violates public policy when it would cause a party to lose a nonwaivable statutory right. *See, e.g.*, ***America Online***, 90 Cal.App.4th at 15 (FSC unenforceable because it violated antiwaiver provisions of Consumers Legal Remedies Act); *see also* Civ. C. §3513 (law established for public reason cannot be contravened by private agreement); ***Bickel v. City of Piedmont*** (1997) 16 Cal.4th 1040, 1048 & n.4 (rights conferred by statute can be waived unless specific statutory provisions prohibit waiver).

(7) **FSC void by statute.** The motion can be opposed on the ground that the FSC is void by statute. For example, the following statutes make FSCs void and unenforceable in certain situations:

(a) Construction contracts – CCP §410.42. An FSC that specifies a forum other than California is void and unenforceable in a construction contract between a contractor and a subcontractor if (1) the contractor and the subcontractor have principal offices in California and (2) the work of improvement is to be performed in California. CCP §410.42(a)(1); *see also* Civ. C. §3106 (defining "work of improvement").

(b) Claims relating to certain goods & services – CCP §116.225. An FSC that specifies a forum other than California is void and unenforceable if (1) the action arises from an offer or provision of goods, services, property, or credit primarily for personal, family, or household purposes and (2) the action falls within the jurisdiction of a California small-claims court. CCP §116.225. This applies only to agreements entered into or renewed on or after January 1, 2003. *Id.*

(8) Waiver. The motion can be opposed on the ground that the party waived its right to argue that California is an inconvenient forum. For a discussion of when a party waives its right to bring a motion based on an FSC, see "Deadline to file & serve," §3.3.2, p. 385.

3. Contents. For a general discussion of the contents of an opposition, see "Opposition Papers," ch. 1-D, §8, p. 35.

§3.5 Reply. See "Reply," §2.4, p. 382.

§3.6 Hearing. See "Hearing," §2.5, p. 382.

§3.7 Ruling. If the FSC is mandatory, the court will likely grant the motion unless the nonmovant can establish that the FSC is unenforceable. *See* ***Smith, Valentino & Smith, Inc. v. Superior Ct.*** (1976) 17 Cal.3d 491, 495-96 (although decision remains in court's discretion, modern trend is to grant motion to enforce mandatory FSC). See "Opposition," §3.4, p. 385. If the FSC is permissive, the court can treat the motion as a traditional motion to stay or dismiss for FNC. *See* ***Intershop Comms., AG v. Superior Ct.*** (1st Dist.2002) 104 Cal.App.4th 191, 196; ***Berg v. MTC Elecs. Techs. Co.*** (2d Dist.1998) 61 Cal.App.4th 349, 359. See "Grounds," §2.1, p. 376. In making its determination, the court can consider the FSC as a factor in deciding to grant or deny the motion. ***Berg***, 61 Cal.App.4th at 359.

§3.8 Order. See "Order," §2.7, p. 383.

§4. MOTION FOR RECONSIDERATION

A party who is adversely affected by a court's order on a motion to stay or dismiss for FNC or based on an FSC can file a motion for reconsideration. *See* CCP §1008(a). See "Motion for Reconsideration," ch. 5-G, §3, p. 508.

§5. MOTION FOR RENEWAL

§5.1 Section 418.10 motion. A party whose §418.10 motion to stay or dismiss for FNC or based on an FSC is denied can file a motion for renewal. *See* CCP §1008(b). See "Motion for Renewal," ch. 5-G, §4, p. 516.

§5.2 Section 410.30 motion. A party whose §410.30 motion to stay or dismiss for FNC or based on an FSC is denied can file a motion for renewal. *See* CCP §1008(b). See "Motion for Renewal," ch. 5-G, §4, p. 516. Because the court can bring its own motion to stay or dismiss under §410.30, it may overlook deficiencies in the party's renewal motion. *See, e.g.*, ***Williamson v. Mazda Motor*** (4th Dist.2012) 212 Cal.App.4th 449, 454-55 (although court found that near completion of discovery and development of Ds' causation defense qualified as changed circumstances, court suggested that trial court could grant motion for renewal even if motion did not satisfy requirements of CCP §1008). *But see* ***Kerns v. CSE Ins.*** (1st Dist.2003) 106 Cal.App.4th 368, 394 n.22 (court is jurisdictionally barred from considering renewed motion that is not in compliance with §1008). A judge can consider a renewed motion and overrule an order issued by a predecessor judge if the predecessor judge is unavailable. ***Williamson***, 212 Cal.App.4th at 454-55.

§6. APPELLATE REVIEW

§6.1 Appealability.

1. Motion granted. A trial court's ruling granting a motion to stay or dismiss for FNC or based on an FSC can be appealed. CCP §904.1(a)(3) (FNC; unlimited civil case), §904.2(d) (FNC; limited civil case); *see, e.g.*, ***Olinick v. BMG Entm't*** (2d Dist.2006) 138 Cal.App.4th 1286, 1293 n.6 (order granting motion to dismiss based on FSC was appealable under §904.1); ***Lu v. Dryclean-U.S.A.*** (1st Dist.1992) 11 Cal.App.4th 1490, 1492-93 (same).

2. Motion denied. A trial court's denial of a motion to stay or dismiss for FNC or based on an FSC cannot be appealed. *See* CCP §904.1(a)(3). However, a defendant can challenge the denial by filing a petition for a writ of mandate. *Id.* §418.10(c); *see, e.g.*, ***Bancomer, S.A. v. Superior Ct.*** (2d Dist.1996) 44 Cal.App.4th 1450, 1456 (D petitioned for writ of mandate after denial of its motion under CCP §410.30); ***Lifeco Servs. v. Superior Ct.*** (6th Dist.1990) 222 Cal.App.3d 331, 333 (Ds petitioned for writ of mandate under §418.10(c) after court denied motion to dismiss based on FSC).

§6.2 Standard of review.

1. Motion to stay or dismiss for FNC. The appellate review process for a traditional motion is a two-step process that mirrors the trial court's review. First, a trial court's ruling on whether the alternative forum is suitable is reviewed de novo. ***Morris v. AGFA Corp.*** (1st Dist.2006) 144 Cal.App.4th 1452, 1464. *Contra* ***Guimei v. General Elec. Co.*** (2d Dist.2009) 172 Cal.App.4th 689, 696 (reviewing court's finding of suitable alternative forum under substantial-evidence standard). Second, a trial court's weighing of the private and public factors is reviewed for abuse of discretion. ***Roman v. Liberty Univ., Inc.*** (4th Dist.2008) 162 Cal.App.4th 670, 682; ***Morris***, 144 Cal.App.4th at 1464. An appellate court is less likely to find an abuse of discretion if the trial court stayed the action rather than dismissing it. *See* ***Investors Equity Life Holding Co. v. Schmidt*** (4th Dist.2011) 195 Cal.App.4th 1519, 1534.

2. Motion to stay or dismiss based on FSC. The courts are split on the appropriate standard of review for a motion to dismiss based on an FSC. Some courts hold that the trial court's ruling is reviewed under a substantial-evidence standard. *See* ***CQL Original Prods. v. National Hockey League Players' Ass'n*** (4th Dist.1995) 39 Cal.App.4th 1347, 1354; ***Cal-State Bus. Prods. & Servs. v. Ricoh*** (3d Dist.1993) 12 Cal.App.4th 1666, 1680. The substantial-evidence standard requires the reviewing court to assess whether the ultimate issues were established by a solid, reasonable, and credible showing. ***CQL Original***, 39 Cal.App.4th at 1354 n.4; ***Cal-State Bus.***, 12 Cal.App.4th at 1680. Other courts hold that the trial court's ruling is reviewed for abuse of discretion. *See* ***America Online, Inc. v. Superior Ct.*** (1st Dist.2001) 90 Cal.App.4th 1, 9 (abuse-of-discretion standard applies to FSC cases); ***Bancomer, S.A. v. Superior Ct.*** (2d Dist.1996) 44 Cal.App.4th 1450, 1457 (same).

G. MOTION TO QUASH SERVICE OF SUMMONS

§1. GENERAL

§1.1 Purpose. A motion to quash service of summons is used to challenge a court's exercise of personal jurisdiction over a defendant. CCP §418.10(a)(1); ***Greener v. Workers' Comp. Appeals Bd.*** (1993) 6 Cal.4th 1028, 1036. For a court to have personal jurisdiction over a defendant, two elements are required: (1) there must be some basis for exercising jurisdiction (i.e., defendant's consent, physical presence, domicile, or minimum contacts) and (2) service of summons must be proper. ***Ziller Elecs. Lab GmbH v. Superior Ct.*** (2d Dist.1988) 206 Cal.App.3d 1222, 1229. A motion to quash service of summons can be used to challenge one or both elements of personal jurisdiction. *See id.* (if D files motion to quash service of summons, P has burden to establish both elements of personal jurisdiction).

§1.2 Primary authority. CCP §§410.10, 412.10-417.40, 418.10, 583.210, 1014.

§1.3 Secondary authority. The following secondary sources are cited as authority in this subchapter:

- Weil & Brown, *California Practice Guide: Civil Procedure Before Trial* (CD-ROM ed. 2014) (referred to as Weil, *Civil Procedure Before Trial*).
- Younger & Bradley, *Younger on California Motions* (2014-15) (referred to as Younger, *Cal. Motions*).

§2. GROUNDS

A motion to quash can be brought for one or both of the following reasons:

§2.1 No basis for personal jurisdiction. A motion to quash can be brought on the ground that the court lacks personal jurisdiction over the defendant because there is no basis for jurisdiction—that is, the defendant (1) did not consent to jurisdiction in California, (2) was not personally served while physically present in California, (3) is

not domiciled in California, and (4) does not have minimum contacts with California. *See, e.g.*, ***Szynalski v. Superior Ct.*** (2d Dist.2009) 172 Cal.App.4th 1, 8 (D filed motion to quash on grounds that he did not have sufficient minimum contacts and did not consent to jurisdiction); ***Centerpoint Energy, Inc. v. Superior Ct.*** (4th Dist.2007) 157 Cal.App.4th 1101, 1110 (D filed motion to quash on ground that it did not have sufficient minimum contacts); ***In re Marriage of Fitzgerald*** (6th Dist.1995) 39 Cal.App.4th 1419, 1427 (D filed motion to quash on ground that she was not served while physically present in California); ***In re Marriage of Thornton*** (5th Dist.1982) 135 Cal.App.3d 500, 507 (D filed motion to quash on ground that he was not domiciled in California). For a discussion of the basis for personal jurisdiction, see "Joining the Defendant—Personal Jurisdiction," ch. 3-G, p. 283.

§2.2 Improper service. A motion to quash can be brought on the ground that the court lacks personal jurisdiction over the defendant because service was improper. *E.g.*, ***Tresway Aero, Inc. v. Superior Ct.*** (1971) 5 Cal.3d 431, 433 (D filed motion to quash on ground that service on corporation was defective because it did not comply with CCP §410, now §412.30); *see, e.g.*, ***County of Riverside v. Superior Ct.*** (4th Dist.1997) 54 Cal.App.4th 443, 446 (D filed motion to quash on ground that service was defective because summons did not specify date for answering and appearing). For a discussion of service of summons, see "Joining the Defendant—Service of Process," ch. 3-H, p. 295.

NOTE

In many cases, motions to quash for improper service are a waste of time and money because the result of granting the motion is that the plaintiff can cure the defect by re-serving the defendant. Younger, Cal. Motions, §5:21; see ***Roberts v. Home Ins. Indem. Co.*** *(1st Dist.1975) 48 Cal.App.3d 313, 317. If service can be cured by simply re-serving the defendant, the defendant should agree to be re-served. Younger, Cal. Motions, §5:22. But motions to quash for improper service should be brought when the defect in service cannot be cured by being re-served. The two most common situations in which service cannot be cured are when the defendant is immune from service and when the time to serve has expired. If the time to serve has expired, a defendant should bring a motion to dismiss instead of a motion to quash service. See* ***Tandy Corp. v. Superior Ct.*** *(3d Dist.1982) 129 Cal.App.3d 734, 741 n.5. For a discussion of motions to dismiss for lack of service, see "No service of summons & complaint," ch. 10-E, §4.1, p. 1162. For a discussion of immunity from service, see "Immunity from service," ch. 3-G, §4.2, p. 284.*

MOTION TO QUASH

§3. MOTION

§3.1 Who can file. A defendant can file a motion to quash service of summons. CCP §418.10(a)(1).

§3.2 Deadline to file & serve. Generally, a motion to quash must be filed and served before the defendant makes a general appearance and at least 16 court days before the hearing. *See* CCP §418.10(a) (must be filed and served on or before D's time to plead unless extended by good cause), §418.10(b) (notice must be served in same manner and at same time as required by CCP §1005(b)), §418.10(e)(3) (D waives right to challenge personal jurisdiction if it does not file motion to quash when it files demurrer or motion to strike), §1005(b) (moving and supporting papers must be filed at least 16 court days before hearing); ***Dial 800 v. Fesbinder*** (2d Dist.2004) 118 Cal.App.4th 32, 52 (D waives right to object to personal jurisdiction if it seeks relief on any basis other than motion to quash for lack of personal jurisdiction). But the motion can be filed simultaneously with an answer, a demurrer, or a motion to strike. CCP §418.10(e); ***Roy v. Superior Ct.*** (4th Dist.2005) 127 Cal.App.4th 337, 344. See "Filing & Serving Noticed Motions," ch. 1-D, §7, p. 33; "General appearance," ch. 3-G, §5.1.1, p. 285.

NOTE

After a motion to quash has been filed and served, any act that occurs afterward does not result in a general appearance unless the motion to quash is denied. See CCP §418.10(e)(1) (no act constitutes general appearance until motion denied); ***Air Mach. Com SRL v. Superior Ct.*** *(4th*

Dist.2010) 186 Cal.App.4th 414, 427-28 (Legislature intended word "act" to be interpreted broadly; it is not limited to acts that are defensive in nature); Younger, Cal. Motions, §5:4 (no act constitutes general appearance until motion denied).

§3.3 Contents.

1. Notice of motion & motion.

(1) Generally. The motion to quash must be requested in writing by noticed motion. CCP §1005(a)(4). The notice of motion should designate a hearing date no later than 30 days after the notice is filed. *Id.* §418.10(b); Weil, *Civil Procedure Before Trial*, ¶3:381. See "Notice of motion & motion," ch. 1-D, §5.1, p. 28.

NOTE

The 30-day hearing deadline has been held to be permissive rather than mandatory. See ***Olinick v. BMG Entm't*** *(2d Dist.2006) 138 Cal.App.4th 1286, 1296 (late hearing date on motion to quash does not deprive court of jurisdiction to consider merits of motion).*

(2) Relief. The notice of motion and motion must describe the relief sought. *See* CRC 3.1110(a) (notice of motion must state nature of order being sought), CRC 3.1112(d)(3) (motion must briefly state relief sought). If the motion to quash is brought on the ground that there is no basis for personal jurisdiction, the defendant can ask the court to dismiss the complaint without prejudice. *See* CCP §581(h). If the motion to quash is brought on the ground that service was improper, the defendant can ask the court to quash service.

(3) Grounds. The notice of motion and motion must briefly state the grounds for the relief (e.g., "the motion is made on the ground that the court lacks personal jurisdiction over the defendant"). *See* CRC 3.1110(a) (notice of motion must state grounds for issuance of order), CRC 3.1112(d)(3) (motion must briefly state basis for motion). See "Grounds," §2, p. 389.

2. Memorandum of points & authorities. The motion to quash must include a memorandum in support of the motion. CRC 3.1112(a)(3), 3.1113(a). See "Memorandum of points & authorities," ch. 1-D, §5.2, p. 28.

3. Supporting evidence. The defendant should attach evidence to support its motion. *See* ***School Dist. of Okaloosa Cty. v. Superior Ct.*** (2d Dist.1997) 58 Cal.App.4th 1126, 1131 (D must present some admissible evidence in form of affidavits or declarations to place issue of lack of jurisdiction before court); *see, e.g.*, ***Aquila, Inc. v. Superior Ct.*** (4th Dist.2007) 148 Cal.App.4th 556, 563 (D supported motion to quash with declarations). The defendant does not have to provide supporting evidence, however, until the plaintiff shows that the court has personal jurisdiction over the defendant. *See* ***Floveyor Int'l v. Superior Ct.*** (2d Dist.1997) 59 Cal.App.4th 789, 793-94. In other words, the defendant can file a motion to quash without supporting evidence and then do nothing until the plaintiff has provided evidence that the court has personal jurisdiction. *See id.* at 794. For a discussion of the types of supporting evidence that can be used, see "Supporting evidence," ch. 1-D, §5.3, p. 30.

4. Request for judicial notice. If the motion to quash is based on matters the court can take judicial notice of, the defendant can ask the court to take judicial notice of those matters. *See* CRC 3.1113(*l*). A request for judicial notice must be made in a separate document. *Id.* See "Request for Judicial Notice," ch. 5-J, p. 547.

5. Proposed order. The defendant can submit a proposed order with the motion to quash. *See* CRC 3.1113(m). If a proposed order is submitted, it must be lodged and served with the motion papers, not attached to them. *Id.* See "Documents lodged," ch. 1-F, §2.3, p. 47.

§3.4 Filing fees. When the motion is filed, the defendant must pay a filing fee to the court clerk or request a waiver of the fee. See "Filing Fees," ch. 1-F, §7, p. 58.

§4. RESPONSE

§4.1 Motion for continuance. The plaintiff can respond to a motion to quash by filing a motion for a continuance to conduct discovery. *See* ***In re Automobile Antitrust Cases I & II*** (1st Dist.2005) 135 Cal.App.4th 100, 127. To prevail on a motion for continuance, the plaintiff must demonstrate how the discovery is likely to lead to the production of facts that would establish jurisdiction. *Id.* The motion for continuance should be made before the hearing

on the motion to quash. *See* ***Thomson v. Anderson*** (4th Dist.2003) 113 Cal.App.4th 258, 271. The court's ruling on a motion for continuance is discretionary. ***HealthMarkets, Inc. v. Superior Ct.*** (2d Dist.2009) 171 Cal.App.4th 1160, 1173; ***Thomson***, 113 Cal.App.4th at 271. See "Requests for Continuance or Stay," ch. 5-I, p. 534.

§4.2 Opposition. The plaintiff can respond to a motion to quash by filing an opposition. When the defendant makes a motion to quash, the burden is placed on the plaintiff to prove, by a preponderance of the evidence, facts justifying the exercise of jurisdiction over the defendant. ***Anglo Irish Bank Corp. v. Superior Ct.*** (2d Dist.2008) 165 Cal.App.4th 969, 980; ***School Dist. of Okaloosa Cty. v. Superior Ct.*** (2d Dist.1997) 58 Cal.App.4th 1126, 1131; *see* ***Vons Cos. v. Seabest Foods, Inc.*** (1996) 14 Cal.4th 434, 449. Thus, a plaintiff must file an opposition to defeat a motion to quash. *See* ***Floveyor Int'l v. Superior Ct.*** (2d Dist.1997) 59 Cal.App.4th 789, 794 (D does not have to act on motion until P makes prima facie showing of jurisdiction); *see, e.g.*, ***Profit Concepts Mgmt. v. Griffith*** (4th Dist.2008) 162 Cal.App.4th 950, 953 (motion to quash granted when P filed notice of nonopposition). To meet its burden, the plaintiff's opposition must be supported by evidence sufficient to justify a finding that the court can properly exercise jurisdiction over the defendant; mere allegations of fact or allegations in an unverified complaint are not sufficient. ***In re Automobile Antitrust Cases I & II*** (1st Dist.2005) 135 Cal.App.4th 100, 110.

PRACTICE TIP

If the motion to quash is based on defective service and the service can be cured (i.e., the time to serve has not expired and the defendant is not immune from service), the plaintiff should simply re-serve the defendant rather than oppose the motion. See Younger, Cal. Motions, §5:23. See "Improper service," §2.2, p. 390.

---

1. Deadline to file & serve. The opposition papers must be filed and served at least nine court days before the hearing. *See* CCP §1005(b). See "Filing & serving opposition," ch. 1-D, §8.5, p. 36.

2. Grounds.

(1) Generally. To meet its burden, the plaintiff must establish personal jurisdiction on any grounds challenged by the defendant—if the defendant alleges that there is no basis for personal jurisdiction and that service was improper, the plaintiff must establish both a basis for personal jurisdiction and proper service. *See* ***Ziller Elecs. Lab GmbH v. Superior Ct.*** (2d Dist.1988) 206 Cal.App.3d 1222, 1229; *see, e.g.*, ***Summers v. McClanahan*** (2d Dist.2006) 140 Cal.App.4th 403, 413 (when D challenged court's jurisdiction on ground of improper service, P had burden to prove effective service). If multiple defendants challenge jurisdiction, the plaintiff must offer jurisdictional facts supporting personal jurisdiction over each individual defendant. ***In re Automobile Antitrust***, 135 Cal.App.4th at 118.

(2) Personal jurisdiction. If the defendant's motion to quash alleges that there is no basis for exercising personal jurisdiction, the plaintiff's opposition should establish one of the following grounds for jurisdiction:

(a) Consent. See "Consent," ch. 3-G, §5, p. 285.

(b) Physical presence. See "Physical Presence," ch. 3-G, §4, p. 283.

(c) Domicile. See "Domicile," ch. 3-G, §3, p. 283.

(d) Minimum contacts. See "Minimum Contacts," ch. 3-G, §6, p. 288.

NOTE

If the plaintiff asserts in its opposition that the defendant has sufficient contacts with California to support specific jurisdiction, the plaintiff's opposition should also argue that exercising jurisdiction over the defendant is reasonable (i.e., comports with fair play and substantial justice). See "Fair play & substantial justice," ch. 3-G, §6.2.3, p. 293.

(3) Service. If the defendant's motion to quash alleges that service of summons was improper, the plaintiff's opposition should establish that service was proper. See "Joining the Defendant—Service of Process," ch. 3-H, p. 295.

(4) Waiver. The motion can be opposed on the ground that the party waived its right to contest personal jurisdiction. See "Deadline to file & serve," §3.2, p. 390.

3. Contents. For a general discussion of the contents of an opposition, see "Opposition Papers," ch. 1-D, §8, p. 35.

§5. REPLY

The defendant can file and serve a reply to opposition papers. The reply must be filed and served at least five court days before the hearing. *See* CCP §1005(b). See "Reply Papers," ch. 1-D, §9, p. 37.

NOTE

If the plaintiff argues in its opposition that the court has specific jurisdiction over the defendant, the defendant's reply should argue that the exercise of jurisdiction would be unreasonable. ***Vons Cos. v. Seabest Foods, Inc.*** *(1996) 14 Cal.4th 434, 449; see* ***Aquila, Inc. v. Superior Ct.*** *(4th Dist.2007) 148 Cal.App.4th 556, 570 (D must make compelling case demonstrating that exercise of jurisdiction would be unreasonable); see, e.g.,* ***Steinberg v. International Comm'n on Holocaust Era Ins. Claims*** *(2d Dist.2005) 133 Cal.App.4th 689, 694 n.8 (D showed that exercise of personal jurisdiction would be unreasonable because of competing foreign-relations interests implicated by action). For a discussion of the factors the court can consider when determining whether the exercise of specific jurisdiction would be reasonable, see "Fair play & substantial justice," ch. 3-G, §6.2.3, p. 293.*

§6. HEARING

§6.1 Generally. For a discussion of hearings generally, see "Hearings," ch. 1-H, p. 79.

§6.2 Date of hearing. The hearing on the motion to quash should be heard within 30 days after the notice of motion is filed. *See* CCP §418.10(b).

§7. RULING

§7.1 Standard for granting motion. A motion to quash must be granted if the court finds that either (1) there is no basis for exercising personal jurisdiction over the defendant or (2) service on the defendant was improper. *See* ***Ziller Elecs. Lab GmbH v. Superior Ct.*** (2d Dist.1988) 206 Cal.App.3d 1222, 1229.

§7.2 Court's determination.

1. Generally. The burden is on the plaintiff to prove by a preponderance of the evidence that a basis for jurisdiction exists. See "Opposition," §4.2, p. 392. If the plaintiff does not meet its burden, the court must grant the motion to quash. *See, e.g.,* ***Shisler v. Sanfer Sports Cars, Inc.*** (6th Dist.2006) 146 Cal.App.4th 1254, 1261-62 (motion granted because P was unable to establish sufficient minimum contacts for general or specific jurisdiction).

2. Allegation of specific jurisdiction. If the plaintiff proves by a preponderance of the evidence that the defendant has sufficient contacts for specific jurisdiction, the burden shifts to the defendant to prove that the exercise of jurisdiction would be unreasonable (i.e., does not comport with fair play and substantial justice). ***Vons Cos. v. Seabest Foods, Inc.*** (1996) 14 Cal.4th 434, 449; ***Anglo Irish Bank Corp. v. Superior Ct.*** (2d Dist.2008) 165 Cal.App.4th 969, 980; ***Aquila, Inc. v. Superior Ct.*** (4th Dist.2007) 148 Cal.App.4th 556, 570; *see also* ***Burger King Corp. v. Rudzewicz*** (1985) 471 U.S. 462, 476 (once D's minimum contacts are established, contacts can be considered with other factors to determine if personal jurisdiction would comport with fair play and substantial justice). If

the defendant does not meet its burden, the court must deny the motion to quash. For a discussion of the factors of fair play and substantial justice, see "Fair play & substantial justice," ch. 3-G, §6.2.3, p. 293.

§7.3 Court's role. Generally, in determining a motion to quash, the court should only consider jurisdictional facts; it should not consider the merits of the plaintiff's claim. *See* ***In re Automobile Antitrust Cases I & II*** (1st Dist.2005) 135 Cal.App.4th 100, 110. But when personal jurisdiction depends on the merits of a claim and the motion to quash negates that claim, the court can consider the merits in determining the motion to quash. *See* ***In re Automobile Antitrust***, 135 Cal.App.4th at 110; ***Regents of the Univ. of N.M. v. Superior Ct.*** (2d Dist.1975) 52 Cal.App.3d 964, 970 n.7; *see, e.g.*, ***Delta Imps., Inc. v. Municipal Ct.*** (2d Dist.1983) 146 Cal.App.3d 1033, 1035 (court had to examine whether complaint stated cause of action for unlawful detainer to determine whether five-day summons was proper).

§8. ORDER

§8.1 Form. The court's ruling on the motion to quash must be recorded either in writing or by minute order. *See, e.g.*, ***Luberski, Inc. v. Oleificio F.LLI Amato S.R.L.*** (4th Dist.2009) 171 Cal.App.4th 409, 413 (court granted motion to quash by minute order). See "Record of Ruling," ch. 1-I, §4, p. 90.

§8.2 Contents. The order should state the basis of the court's decision. *See, e.g.*, ***Luberski, Inc. v. Oleificio F.LLI Amato S.R.L.*** (4th Dist.2009) 171 Cal.App.4th 409, 413 (order stated that motion was granted on grounds that court had neither specific nor general jurisdiction over D because D did not have requisite minimum contacts and did not direct activity toward California); ***Anglo Irish Bank Corp. v. Superior Ct.*** (2d Dist.2008) 165 Cal.App.4th 969, 977 (order stated that motion was denied on grounds that court had personal jurisdiction over D based on agency and representative-services doctrines). *But see* ***F. Hoffman-La Roche, Ltd. v. Superior Ct.*** (6th Dist.2005) 130 Cal.App.4th 782, 793 (order did not state basis for denial).

§8.3 Effect of order.

1. Motion denied. If a motion to quash is denied, the defendant must file either a pleading or a writ of mandate.

(1) Pleading. If the defendant wants to file a pleading, it must do so within 15 days after being served with written notice that an order denying the motion to quash has been entered. CCP §418.10(b); *see also id.* §418.10(d) (court cannot enter default against D until time to plead has passed). The court can extend the time to plead for up to 20 more days on a showing of good cause. *Id.* §418.10(b).

NOTE

If the defendant makes a general appearance (i.e., files an answer or otherwise generally appears) after its motion to quash is denied, it waives any error on appeal. See ***McCorkle v. City of L.A.*** *(1969) 70 Cal.2d 252, 258.*

(2) Writ of mandate. If the defendant wants to file a writ of mandate, it must do so before pleading and within 10 days after being served with written notice that an order denying the motion to quash has been entered (or within 20 days if the court extends the deadline on a showing of good cause). CCP §418.10(c). Serving and filing notice of a petition for a writ of mandate extends the defendant's deadline to file a responsive pleading to 10 days after the defendant is served with written notice that the writ of mandate was denied (or to 20 days if the court extends the time to plead on a showing of good cause). *Id.* A defendant who challenges a motion to quash by writ of mandate does not make a general appearance. *Id.* §418.10(e)(2).

2. Motion granted.

(1) No basis for personal jurisdiction. If a motion to quash is granted because there was no basis for personal jurisdiction, the court can dismiss the complaint without prejudice, either in whole or as to the moving defendant if there are any remaining defendants in the action. CCP §581(h). Although the dismissal without

prejudice is not res judicata on the merits of the action, it is res judicata on the court's jurisdictional ruling. *See* ***MIB, Inc. v. Superior Ct.*** (2d Dist.1980) 106 Cal.App.3d 228, 234-35; *see, e.g.*, ***Sabek, Inc. v. Engelhard Corp.*** (6th Dist.1998) 65 Cal.App.4th 992, 998-99 (earlier finding of no minimum contacts prevented P from filing later complaint based on same claim).

(2) Improper service. If a motion to quash is granted for improper service, the service of the summons is quashed and the defendant is dismissed from the action. ***Ziller Elecs. Lab GmbH v. Superior Ct.*** (2d Dist.1988) 206 Cal.App.3d 1222, 1231. The plaintiff can attempt to cure the defective service by re-serving the defendant. ***Roberts v. Home Ins. Indem. Co.*** (1st Dist.1975) 48 Cal.App.3d 313, 317.

NOTE

If the defendant moves to quash service of summons on both jurisdictional grounds (i.e., no basis for personal jurisdiction and improper service) and the court grants the motion for improper service but finds a basis for jurisdiction, the court's finding of jurisdiction is binding; the defendant cannot file a second motion to quash for lack of jurisdiction after being re-served. ***Ziller Elecs.****, 206 Cal.App.3d at 1226. But an earlier finding of jurisdiction does not prevent a court from reconsidering its ruling. Id. at 1230.*

(3) Motion for attorney fees & costs. After a motion to quash is granted, the defendant can file a motion for attorney fees and costs. ***Shisler v. Sanfer Sports Cars, Inc.*** (6th Dist.2008) 167 Cal.App.4th 1, 8-9. A defendant does not make a general appearance by filing a motion for attorney fees and costs after a motion to quash is granted. *Id.* at 8.

§9. MOTION FOR RECONSIDERATION

A party adversely affected by a court's order on a motion to quash can file a motion for reconsideration if the court has not entered a judgment (e.g., entered a written order of dismissal of the defendant). *See* ***APRI Ins. Co. v. Superior Ct.*** (2d Dist.1999) 76 Cal.App.4th 176, 180-81. A defendant's motion for reconsideration filed after the court denies its motion to quash is not a general appearance. ***Josephson v. Superior Ct.*** (2d Dist.1963) 219 Cal.App.2d 354, 362 n.4. See "Motion for Reconsideration," ch. 5-G, §3, p. 508.

§10. MOTION FOR RENEWAL

A party whose motion to quash is denied can file a motion for renewal. *See* CCP §1008(b). See "Motion for Renewal," ch. 5-G, §4, p. 516.

§11. APPELLATE REVIEW

§11.1 Writ of mandate.

See "Writ of mandate," §8.3.1(2), p. 394.

§11.2 Direct appeal.

1. When applicable.

(1) Motion denied. An order denying a motion to quash is not appealable but can be reviewed by a petition for writ of mandate. *See* CCP §418.10(c); ***Parsons v. Superior Ct.*** (Marin Cty. Superior Ct. Appellate Div. 2007) 149 Cal.App.4th Supp. 1, 6. See "Writ of mandate," §8.3.1(2), p. 394.

(2) Motion granted. An order granting a motion to quash is appealable. CCP §904.1(a)(3); ***League to Save Lake Tahoe v. Tahoe Reg'l Planning Agency*** (3d Dist.1980) 105 Cal.App.3d 394, 399.

2. Standard of review.

(1) De novo. When there is no conflicting evidence, the trial court's ruling is reviewed de novo. ***Vons Cos. v. Seabest Foods, Inc.*** (1996) 14 Cal.4th 434, 449; ***As You Sow v. Crawford Labs.*** (1st Dist.1996) 50 Cal.App.4th 1859, 1866.

(2) **Substantial evidence.** When there is conflicting evidence, the trial court's ruling will not be disturbed if supported by substantial evidence. ***Vons Cos.***, 14 Cal.4th at 449. *But see* ***As You Sow***, 50 Cal.App.4th at 1866 (abuse-of-discretion standard).

H. DEMURRER

This subchapter discusses a demurrer under CCP §430.10. Demurrers are available in all civil proceedings except Family Code proceedings. *See* CRC 5.74(b)(2); *California Civil Procedure Before Trial* (CEB Online ed. 2014), §23.5.

§1. GENERAL

§1.1 Purpose. A demurrer is used to challenge a defect in the pleadings that can be resolved as a matter of law—most commonly the legal sufficiency of the factual allegations in the complaint (i.e., the complaint does not state facts sufficient to constitute a cause of action). *See* CCP §§430.10(e), 589(a); Younger & Bradley, *Younger on California Motions* (2014-15), §6:1. Because a demurrer challenges only the pleadings and not the evidence, a demurrer is available only when a defect appears on the face of the pleading or when the defect can be judicially noticed. ***Hahn v. Mirda*** (1st Dist.2007) 147 Cal.App.4th 740, 747; *see* CCP §430.30(a).

§1.2 Primary authority. CCP §§430.10-430.80; CRC 3.1320.

§1.3 Secondary authority. The following secondary sources are cited as authority in this subchapter:

- *California Civil Procedure Before Trial* (CEB Online ed. 2014) (referred to as *CEB Procedure Before Trial*).
- Judicial Council of Cal., Civil & Small Claims Advisory Cmte., *Civil Practice & Procedure: Response to Amended Complaint* (Aug. 13, 2010), www.courts.ca.gov/documents/20101029itema12.pdf (referred to as *Report on Civil Practice & Procedure*).
- Kiesel et al., *Matthew Bender Practice Guide: California Pretrial Civil Procedure* (2014) (referred to as Kiesel, *Cal. Pretrial Civil Procedure*).
- Schwing, *California Affirmative Defenses* (2008) (referred to as Schwing, *Cal. Affirmative Defenses*).
- Thomas, *California Civil Courtroom Handbook* (2014) (referred to as Thomas, *Courtroom Handbook*).
- Weil & Brown, *California Practice Guide: Civil Procedure Before Trial* (CD-ROM ed. 2014) (referred to as Weil, *Civil Procedure Before Trial*).
- Witkin, *California Procedure* (5th ed. 2008 & Supp.2014) (referred to as Witkin, *Cal. Procedure*).
- Younger & Bradley, *Younger on California Motions* (2014-15) (referred to as Younger, *Cal. Motions*).

§2. OVERVIEW

§2.1 What can a demurrer challenge?

1. Entire pleading. A demurrer can be used to challenge an entire pleading—that is, a complaint, a cross-complaint, a complaint in intervention, or an answer. CCP §387(a) (complaint in intervention), §430.50 (complaint, cross-complaint, or answer).

NOTE

For ease of reference, the term "complaint" will be used throughout this subchapter to refer to complaints, cross-complaints, and complaints in intervention.

---

2. Particular cause of action or defense. A demurrer can be used to challenge a particular cause of action or defense in a pleading. CCP §430.50; *see* CRC 3.1320(b) (demurrer can be directed at one cause of action without answering other causes of action). If directed at a particular cause of action, the demurrer must dispose of

the entire cause of action; it cannot be used to challenge part of a cause of action or a particular damage or remedy. *See* ***Kong v. City of Hawaiian Gardens Redev. Agency*** (2d Dist.2002) 108 Cal.App.4th 1028, 1047; *see, e.g.*, ***Grieves v. Superior Ct.*** (4th Dist.1984) 157 Cal.App.3d 159, 163 (punitive-damages allegations not subject to demurrer); *see also* ***Caldera Pharms. v. Regents of the Univ. of Cal.*** (1st Dist.2012) 205 Cal.App.4th 338, 368 (prayer of complaint not subject to demurrer). For purposes of a demurrer, a cause of action is defined as the plaintiff's primary right. ***Skrbina v. Fleming Cos.*** (3d Dist.1996) 45 Cal.App.4th 1353, 1364. For a discussion of the primary-right theory, see "Determining cause of action," ch. 3-C, §3.6.1, p. 215.

PRACTICE TIP

If only part of a cause of action is defective, a party should file a motion to strike instead of a demurrer. ***Caliber Bodyworks, Inc. v. Superior Ct.*** *(2d Dist.2005) 134 Cal.App.4th 365, 385. See "Motion to Strike," ch. 4-J, p. 418.*

§2.2 What type of evidence will support a demurrer? A demurrer must be based on a defect that appears on the face of the challenged pleading or that is subject to judicial notice. ***County of Fresno v. Shelton*** (5th Dist.1998) 66 Cal.App.4th 996, 1008-09; *see* CCP §430.30(a), (b); ***Holiday Matinee, Inc. v. Rambus, Inc.*** (6th Dist.2004) 118 Cal.App.4th 1413, 1420-21.

1. Face of pleading. A defect appears on the "face" of a pleading if it is clearly and affirmatively evident from the pleading itself without consideration of any extrinsic evidence. *See* ***Sheehan v. San Francisco 49ers, Ltd.*** (2009) 45 Cal.4th 992, 998; ***Geneva Towers L.P. v. City & Cty. of S.F.*** (2003) 29 Cal.4th 769, 781; ***Hydrotech Sys. v. Oasis Waterpark*** (1991) 52 Cal.3d 988, 994 n.4. Thus, a demurring party is prohibited from relying on evidentiary material outside the challenged pleading or making factual allegations in the demurrer that are not also raised in the challenged pleading. *See, e.g.*, ***Harboring Villas Homeowners Ass'n v. Superior Ct.*** (4th Dist.1998) 63 Cal.App.4th 426, 429 (D made allegation in demurrer that none of trust deed holders were made parties to action; allegation was improper because complaint did not suggest that units were subject to trust deeds); ***Cravens v. Coghlan*** (1st Dist.1957) 154 Cal.App.2d 215, 217 (D made allegation in demurrer that P did not have capacity to sue because P was in prison or on parole; allegation was improper because P did not address his capacity in complaint); ***Tyree v. Epstein*** (2d Dist.1950) 99 Cal.App.2d 361, 362-63 (D attached affidavit and hospital record to support demurrer; court erred in considering evidence outside complaint to rule on demurrer).

PRACTICE TIP

If the defect does not appear on the face of the complaint, consider raising the issue in the answer or in a motion for summary judgment. See "Answer," ch. 4-B, p. 332; "Motion for Summary Judgment," ch. 10-B, p. 1117.

2. Judicially noticed facts. A demurrer can be based on judicially noticed facts. CCP §§430.30(a), 430.70; ***State v. CCC Info. Servs.*** (2d Dist.2007) 149 Cal.App.4th 402, 412; *see, e.g.*, ***Bistawros v. Greenberg*** (2d Dist.1987) 189 Cal.App.3d 189, 192 (court took judicial notice of other actions filed by P). For example, factual allegations in a complaint can be disregarded if they conflict with judicially noticed discovery responses given by the plaintiff. ***Bockrath v. Aldrich Chem. Co.*** (1999) 21 Cal.4th 71, 83; *see also* ***Swahn Grp. v. Segal*** (3d Dist.2010) 183 Cal.App.4th 831, 844 (court can sustain a demurrer on ground of judicial estoppel).

(1) Matters that can be judicially noticed. For a discussion of the matters that can be judicially noticed, see "Request for Judicial Notice," ch. 5-J, p. 547.

(2) Effect of judicial notice. For a discussion of how the court can use judicially noticed facts to rule on a demurrer, see "Judicially noticed documents," §8.2.5, p. 407.

§2.3 What type of demurrer should be filed – general or special? There are two types of demurrers—general and special. *See* ***Buss v. J.O. Martin Co.*** (1st Dist.1966) 241 Cal.App.2d 123, 133. Whether a party files a general or special demurrer depends on the grounds for the demurrer and the classification of the case.

1. Grounds. For the grounds a general demurrer can be based on, see "General demurrer," §3.1, this page. For the grounds a special demurrer can be based on, see "Special demurrer," §3.2, p. 400.

2. Classification of case.

(1) Unlimited cases. In unlimited civil cases, both general and special demurrers are available. *See* CCP §422.10. See "Classifying civil cases," ch. 3-E, §4.2, p. 257.

(2) Limited cases. In limited civil cases, general demurrers are available but special demurrers are not. *See* CCP §92(a), (c). See "Classifying civil cases," ch. 3-E, §4.2, p. 257.

§2.4 What is the effect of filing a demurrer?

1. General appearance. A party who files a demurrer makes a general appearance in the action. CCP §1014. See "General appearance," ch. 3-G, §5.1.1, p. 285. To preserve challenges that can be waived by making a general appearance, the party should file the demurrer with those challenges. *See* CCP §418.10(e). See "With challenges waived by general appearance," §4.5.3, p. 405.

2. No default judgment. By timely filing a demurrer, a defendant prevents the plaintiff from taking a default judgment while the demurrer is pending. *See* CCP §585.

§2.5 What if a demurrer is not filed – is the objection waived? Objections that can be brought by general demurrer cannot be waived—that is, a party can still challenge a pleading for lack of subject-matter jurisdiction or for not stating facts sufficient to constitute a cause of action after the time to demur has passed. *See* CCP §430.80; ***Great W. Casinos, Inc. v. Morongo Band of Mission Indians*** (2d Dist.1999) 74 Cal.App.4th 1407, 1417; ***Buford v. State*** (5th Dist.1980) 104 Cal.App.3d 811, 826; ***Bowden v. Robinson*** (4th Dist.1977) 67 Cal.App.3d 705, 710. See "General demurrer," §3.1, this page. Objections that can be brought by special demurrer, however, are waived if not asserted by special demurrer or in the answer. *See* CCP §430.80. See "Special demurrer," §3.2, p. 400.

§3. GROUNDS

§3.1 General demurrer.

1. To complaint. A general demurrer to a complaint can be based on any of the following grounds:

(1) No subject-matter jurisdiction. A defendant can file a general demurrer to a complaint on the ground that the court lacks subject-matter jurisdiction over the alleged cause of action. ***Buss v. J.O. Martin Co.*** (1st Dist.1966) 241 Cal.App.2d 123, 133; Younger, *Cal. Motions*, §6:4; *see* CCP §430.10(a). A court may lack subject-matter jurisdiction over a cause of action for any of the following reasons:

(a) A statutory prerequisite to bringing suit has not been satisfied. See "Cases with statutory prerequisites," ch. 3-E, §2.2.1, p. 249.

(b) The action falls within the exclusive jurisdiction of federal courts. See "Cases within exclusive federal jurisdiction," ch. 3-E, §2.2.2, p. 249.

(c) Required administrative proceedings have not taken place. See "Cases within exclusive administrative jurisdiction," ch. 3-E, §2.2.3, p. 249.

(d) Another court has acquired exclusive jurisdiction over the matter. See "Cases subject to concurrent jurisdiction," ch. 3-E, §2.2.4, p. 250.

(e) The court has ordered a change of venue. See "Cases involving change of venue," ch. 3-E, §2.2.5, p. 251.

(f) The parties are protected by governmental immunity. See "Cases involving governmental immunity," ch. 3-E, §2.2.6, p. 251.

(g) The case was voluntarily dismissed. See "Cases dismissed voluntarily," ch. 3-E, §2.2.7, p. 251.

(h) The case involves an ecclesiastical controversy. See "Cases involving religious matters," ch. 3-E, §2.2.8, p. 251.

(i) The case involves a foreign state. See "Cases involving foreign state," ch. 3-E, §2.2.9, p. 251.

(j) The case involves an Indian tribe. See "Cases involving Indian tribes," ch. 3-E, §2.2.10, p. 252.

(2) Facts do not state cause of action.

(a) Generally. A defendant can file a general demurrer to a complaint on the ground that it does not state facts sufficient to constitute a cause of action. CCP §430.10(e); ***Holiday Matinee, Inc. v. Rambus, Inc.*** (6th Dist.2004) 118 Cal.App.4th 1413, 1420; *see* ***Sheehan v. San Francisco 49ers, Ltd.*** (2009) 45 Cal.4th 992, 997. To sufficiently allege a cause of action, a complaint must allege all the ultimate facts—that is, the facts needed to establish each element of the cause of action pleaded. *See* ***Committee on Children's TV, Inc. v. General Foods Corp.*** (1983) 35 Cal.3d 197, 212; ***Kamen v. Lindly*** (6th Dist.2001) 94 Cal.App.4th 197, 201; ***Buss***, 241 Cal.App.2d at 133-34. See "What to plead – ultimate facts," ch. 3-C, §3.6.3(2)(a), p. 216. A pleading does not sufficiently state a cause of action when the facts in the pleading establish any of the following:

[1] An essential element of a cause of action is missing. *See* ***Baldwin v. Marina City Props., Inc.*** (2d Dist.1978) 79 Cal.App.3d 393, 410; *see, e.g.*, ***Johnson v. Ralphs Grocery Co.*** (4th Dist.2012) 204 Cal.App.4th 1097, 1108 (in intentional-infliction-of-emotional-distress claim, P did not show that D's conduct was outrageous).

[2] The cause of action is not recognized in California. Schwing, *Cal. Affirmative Defenses*, §9.1.

[3] The plaintiff lacks standing to sue. ***Parker v. Bowron*** (1953) 40 Cal.2d 344, 351. See "Standing," ch. 3-C, §2.1, p. 203.

[4] The statute of limitations bars the claim. *See* ***Aryeh v. Canon Bus. Solutions, Inc.*** (2013) 55 Cal.4th 1185, 1190; ***Czajkowski v. Haskell & White, LLP*** (4th Dist.2012) 208 Cal.App.4th 166, 169; ***Van De Kamps Coalition v. Board of Trs.*** (2d Dist.2012) 206 Cal.App.4th 1036, 1044.

[5] An affirmative defense bars the claim. ***McKenney v. Purepac Pharm.*** (5th Dist.2008) 167 Cal.App.4th 72, 78-79. See "Affirmative Defenses," ch. 4-B, §5, p. 343.

[6] The injury complained of has not yet occurred. ***Harvey v. Chilton*** (1858) 11 Cal. 114, 119-20.

[7] A condition precedent to liability has not occurred. *See* ***Happe v. Stout*** (1852) 2 Cal. 460, 462.

[8] The contract sued on is within the statute of frauds but does not comply with its requirements. ***Parker v. Solomon*** (2d Dist.1959) 171 Cal.App.2d 125, 136.

NOTE

Form pleadings approved by California's Judicial Council are not immune from a demurrer. See, e.g., ***People v. Superior Ct.*** *(2d Dist.1992) 5 Cal.App.4th 1480, 1486 (demurrer to Judicial Council form should have been sustained for inadequately stating cause of action).*

(b) Common counts. Generally, a complaint that pleads a common count is not subject to demurrer for not alleging sufficient facts to state a cause of action. ***Farmers Ins. Exch. v. Zerin*** (3d Dist.1997) 53 Cal.App.4th 445, 460; Schwing, *Cal. Affirmative Defenses*, §9:2. This general rule does not apply, however, if the common count is based on the same facts asserted in a specific cause of action, and the specific cause of action is

defective. ***Draper v. Patterson*** (3d Dist.1958) 156 Cal.App.2d 606, 609. In that situation, the specific count and the common count are both subject to demurrer. *Id.* For a discussion of common counts, see "Common counts," ch. 3-C, §3.6.3(2)(a)[2], p. 217.

(3) Declaratory relief not proper or necessary. In a declaratory-relief action, the defendant can file a general demurrer on the ground that declaratory relief is not necessary or proper at the time under all the circumstances. *See, e.g.,* ***State v. Superior Ct.*** (1974) 12 Cal.3d 237, 249 (demurrer should have been sustained because declaratory-relief action is not appropriate to review administrative decisions); ***Osseous Techs. v. DiscoveryOrtho Partners*** (4th Dist.2010) 191 Cal.App.4th 357, 375-76 (court properly sustained demurrer when parties had no ongoing contractual relationship and it appeared declaratory-relief request was filed as litigation strategy).

2. To answer. A general demurrer to an answer can be based on the ground that the answer does not state facts sufficient to constitute a defense. CCP §430.20(a); ***Timberidge Enters. v. City of Santa Rosa*** (1st Dist.1978) 86 Cal.App.3d 873, 880; *see, e.g.,* ***Richard B. Levine, Inc. v. Higashi*** (4th Dist.2005) 131 Cal.App.4th 566, 573 n.4 (answer that pleaded statute of limitations as defense but did not comply with pleading requirement under CCP §458 was subject to demurrer). For example, an answer containing a defense that is barred by the statute of limitations or laches is vulnerable to a general demurrer. *See* ***Universal Land Co. v. All Persons*** (1st Dist.1959) 172 Cal.App.2d 739, 741-43. See "Answer," ch. 4-B, p. 332.

§3.2 Special demurrer.

1. To complaint. A special demurrer to a complaint can be based on any of the following grounds:

(1) No capacity to sue. A defendant can file a special demurrer to a complaint on the ground that the person who filed the complaint does not have the legal capacity to sue. Younger, *Cal. Motions*, §6:5; *see* CCP §430.10(b). See "Capacity," ch. 3-C, §2.2, p. 206.

NOTE

Capacity to sue is different from standing to sue. ***Friendly Vill. Cmty. Ass'n v. Silva & Hill Constr. Co.*** *(2d Dist.1973) 31 Cal.App.3d 220, 224. The issue of standing is raised through a general demurrer, but the issue of capacity must be raised through a special demurrer. See id. See "Standing & Capacity," ch. 3-C, §2, p. 203.*

(2) Another pending action. A defendant can file a special demurrer to a complaint on the ground that there is another action pending between the parties over the same issues. This type of demurrer can be based on either the statutory rule or the exclusive-concurrent-jurisdiction rule.

(a) Statutory rule. A defendant can file a special demurrer to a complaint under CCP §430.10(c) on the ground that there is another action pending between the same parties on the same cause of action. Younger, *Cal. Motions*, §6:5; *see* ***Bescos v. Bank of Am.*** (2d Dist.2003) 105 Cal.App.4th 378, 396-97; ***Bistawros v. Greenberg*** (2d Dist.1987) 189 Cal.App.3d 189, 191-92. A demurrer filed on this ground is sometimes referred to as a plea in abatement. Younger, *Cal. Motions*, §6:20. If a demurrer is sustained on this ground, the second action should be stayed—not dismissed—until the first action is terminated. *Id.* For a demurrer to be sustained on this ground, the defendant must show the following:

[1] Multiple actions pending in California. The defendant must show that there are multiple actions pending in California courts. ***Leadford v. Leadford*** (1st Dist.1992) 6 Cal.App.4th 571, 574. If one action is pending in California and another action is pending in a foreign jurisdiction, the defendant should file a motion to stay, not a demurrer. *Id.*

[2] Same parties. The defendant must show that the parties in both actions are the same and stand in the same relative position as plaintiff and defendant. *See* ***Plant Insulation Co. v. Fibreboard Corp.*** (1st Dist.1990) 224 Cal.App.3d 781, 787; *CEB Procedure Before Trial*, §23.32.

[3] Same cause of action. The defendant must show that both actions are based on substantially the same cause of action. ***Lord v. Garland*** (1946) 27 Cal.2d 840, 848; ***Bescos***, 105 Cal.App.4th at 397; ***Plant Insulation***, 224 Cal.App.3d at 787; ***Bistawros***, 189 Cal.App.3d at 192. To do this, the defendant must show that a judgment in the first action would be a complete bar to recovery in the second action. ***Lord***, 27 Cal.2d at 848.

(b) Rule of exclusive, concurrent jurisdiction. A defendant can file a special demurrer to a complaint based on the rule of exclusive, concurrent jurisdiction. *See* ***People v. American Autoplan, Inc.*** (2d Dist.1993) 20 Cal.App.4th 760, 771; ***Plant Insulation***, 224 Cal.App.3d at 787-88. Under this rule, when two superior courts have concurrent jurisdiction over the same subject matter and all parties involved, the first court to assume jurisdiction has exclusive and continuing jurisdiction over the case. ***American Autoplan***, 20 Cal.App.4th at 769-70; ***Plant Insulation***, 224 Cal.App.3d at 786-87. See "Cases subject to concurrent jurisdiction," ch. 3-E, §2.2.4, p. 250. If a demurrer is sustained on this ground, the second action should be stayed—not dismissed—until the first action is terminated. ***Plant Insulation***, 224 Cal.App.3d at 791-92.

PRACTICE TIP

Although the rule of exclusive, concurrent jurisdiction is similar in effect to a statutory plea in abatement, it has been interpreted and applied more broadly. ***Plant Insulation****, 224 Cal.App.3d at 788. Thus, a demurrer based on this rule might succeed when the grounds for a statutory plea in abatement prove to be too narrow. Id.*

---

[1] Same parties not required. The rule of exclusive, concurrent jurisdiction does not require absolute identity of parties. ***Plant Insulation***, 224 Cal.App.3d at 788. The rule will apply if the court exercising original jurisdiction has the power to bring before it all the necessary parties. *Id.* See "Cases subject to concurrent jurisdiction," ch. 3-E, §2.2.4, p. 250; "Absent party is necessary," ch. 3-B, §3.1.1, p. 193.

[2] Same cause of action not required. The rule of exclusive, concurrent jurisdiction does not require absolute identity of the causes of action. ***Plant Insulation***, 224 Cal.App.3d at 788. The rule will apply if the issue in both actions is the same or arises from the same transaction. *Id.* at 789.

[3] Same remedies not required. The rule of exclusive, concurrent jurisdiction does not require absolute identity of the remedies sought. ***Plant Insulation***, 224 Cal.App.3d at 788. The rule will apply if the court exercising original jurisdiction has the power to litigate all the issues and grant all the relief that any of the parties might be entitled to under the pleadings. *Id.*

(3) Nonjoinder or misjoinder of parties. A defendant can file a special demurrer to a complaint on the ground that there is a defect or misjoinder of parties. *See* CCP §430.10(d); Younger, *Cal. Motions*, §6:5.

(a) Nonjoinder. A defect of parties means that there is a person or entity that should be a party to the action but is not—that is, a necessary or indispensable party. Thomas, *Courtroom Handbook*, §11:12; *see, e.g.*, ***Union Carbide Corp. v. Superior Ct.*** (1984) 36 Cal.3d 15, 19 (demurrer brought for nonjoinder of indispensable parties). To determine who should be a party to the action, see "Absent party is necessary," ch. 3-B, §3.1.1, p. 193; "Absent party is indispensable," ch. 3-B, §3.1.3, p. 194.

NOTE

A demurrer is not the best procedure for joining a necessary or indispensable party. See 5 Witkin, Cal. Procedure, Pleading, §972. Under CCP §389, the court is required to join a necessary or indispensable party by court order. The court's determination to join a necessary or indispensable party can be made on a party's motion or on the court's own initiative, and can be made at any stage of the proceeding. ***Union Carbide****, 36 Cal.3d at 22. Because the court may not have sufficient information when the demurrer is brought to determine who is a necessary or indispensable party, it may be beneficial to bring a motion to join a party at a later stage (e.g., after discovery has been conducted). See id. at 24.*

DEMURRER

(b) Misjoinder. A misjoinder of parties means that one or more parties (defendant or plaintiff) should not have been joined in the action. See "Joinder of Parties," ch. 3-B, §3, p. 193. Some courts have held that a defendant can prevail on this ground only when she shows some prejudice suffered or interests affected by the misjoinder. *See* ***Anaya v. Superior Ct.*** (1st Dist.1984) 160 Cal.App.3d 228, 231 n.1; *see also* ***Royal Surplus Lines Ins. v. Ranger Ins.*** (2d Dist.2002) 100 Cal.App.4th 193, 203 (most issues alleged against joined parties were inextricably intertwined; thus, possible prejudice was not sufficient reason to find misjoinder). Other courts have suggested that a defendant can prevail if she establishes that the party was not properly joined under the technical rules of compulsory or permissive joinder. *See, e.g.,* ***Moe v. Anderson*** (3d Dist.2012) 207 Cal.App.4th 826, 834 (properly joined D successfully demurred against improperly joined Ps because assault claims did not relate to or arise from same transaction or occurrence).

(4) Uncertainty.

(a) Generally. A defendant can file a special demurrer to a complaint on the ground that it is uncertain, ambiguous, or unintelligible. *See* CCP §430.10(f); ***Johnson v. Mead*** (1st Dist.1987) 191 Cal.App.3d 156, 160; ***Ankeny v. Lockheed Missiles & Space Co.*** (1st Dist.1979) 88 Cal.App.3d 531, 537; Younger, *Cal. Motions*, §6:5. A demurrer for uncertainty can only be directed at the ultimate facts pleaded; it cannot be brought on the basis that an immaterial allegation in the pleading is uncertain. *See* ***Rannard v. Lockheed Aircraft Corp.*** (1945) 26 Cal.2d 149, 156-57; ***Gonzales v. State*** (1st Dist.1977) 68 Cal.App.3d 621, 631, *disapproved on other grounds*, ***City of Stockton v. Superior Ct.*** (2007) 42 Cal.4th 730. If a demurrer is brought for uncertainty, the demurrer must specify the uncertain, ambiguous, or unintelligible parts of the complaint. ***Johnson v. Clark*** (1936) 7 Cal.2d 529, 536. For a discussion of the specificity requirements for pleading certain causes of action, see "With specificity," ch. 3-C, §3.6.3(2)(b)[2], p. 217.

NOTE

Ambiguities that are within the defendant's knowledge or that can be resolved through discovery are not appropriate for demurrer. See ***Khoury v. Maly's of Cal., Inc.*** *(2d Dist.1993) 14 Cal.App.4th 612, 616;* ***A.F. Arnold & Co. v. Pacific Prof'l Ins.*** *(2d Dist.1972) 27 Cal.App.3d 710, 718;* ***Gressley v. Williams*** *(2d Dist.1961) 193 Cal.App.2d 636, 644; Weil, Civil Procedure Before Trial, ¶7:86.*

(b) Common counts. A demurrer for uncertainty cannot be brought against a common count. ***Weitzenkorn v. Lesser*** (1953) 40 Cal.2d 778, 792-93; *see* CCP §454. If the defendant wants to know the items of an account, the defendant can demand a copy of the account from the plaintiff. CCP §454; *see* 4 Witkin, *Cal. Procedure*, Pleading, §503. See "Common counts," ch. 3-C, §3.6.3(2)(a)[2], p. 217.

(5) Type of contract not specified. In a contract action, a defendant can file a special demurrer to a complaint on the ground that it cannot be determined from the pleadings whether the contract is written, oral, or implied by conduct. CCP §430.10(g); *see* ***Holcomb v. Wells Fargo Bank*** (4th Dist.2007) 155 Cal.App.4th 490, 500-01.

(6) No certificate of merit filed. In a professional-negligence action against architects, engineers, or land surveyors, the defendant can file a special demurrer to the complaint on the ground that the certificate of merit was not filed as required by CCP §411.35. *See* CCP §430.10(h); ***Price v. Dames & Moore*** (1st Dist.2001) 92 Cal.App.4th 355, 360-61.

NOTE

The Code of Civil Procedure provides that a defendant can demur against a complaint on the ground that no certificate was filed as required by CCP §411.36. CCP §430.10(i). Section 411.36, however, was repealed in 1997 by a sunsetting provision in §411.36(i). Stats. 1993, ch. 151, §4.

2. To answer. A special demurrer to an answer can be based on any of the following grounds:

(1) Answer is uncertain. A plaintiff can file a special demurrer to an answer on the ground that it is uncertain, ambiguous, or unintelligible. CCP §430.20(b). The demurrer must specify the uncertain, ambiguous, or unintelligible parts of the answer. ***Coons v. Thompson*** (2d Dist.1946) 75 Cal.App.2d 687, 690.

(2) Type of contract is not specified. When an answer pleads a contract, the plaintiff can file a special demurrer on the ground that it cannot be determined from the answer whether the contract is written or oral. CCP §430.20(c).

§4. MOTION

Although a demurrer is considered a pleading under the Code of Civil Procedure, it is treated procedurally as a motion. *See* CCP §422.10; CRC 3.1103(c).

§4.1 Who can file.

1. Generally. Any party against whom a complaint, cross-complaint, complaint in intervention, or answer was filed can file a demurrer. CCP §§387(a), 430.10, 430.20.

2. Multiple Ds. If there are multiple defendants, the defendants can file a joint demurrer. *See, e.g.*, ***Weinstock v. Eissler*** (1st Dist.1964) 224 Cal.App.2d 212, 222-23 & n.11 (three Ds filed demurrers separately and three other Ds filed joint demurrer). If a joint demurrer is filed, a special demurrer can be overruled if the complaint is sufficient against any defendant. ***Majestic Rlty. Co. v. Pacific Lighting Corp.*** (2d Dist.1974) 37 Cal.App.3d 641, 642-43 (rule applies only to special demurrers). To avoid this outcome, the joint demurrer should indicate that the grounds for demurrer are asserted separately for each defendant. *CEB Procedure Before Trial*, §23.19.

§4.2 Deadline to file & serve.

1. In response to complaint or cross-complaint.

(1) Original. In most cases, a demurrer to an original complaint or cross-complaint should be filed and served within 30 days after service of the pleading. Kiesel, *Cal. Pretrial Civil Procedure*, §11.12[1]; *see* CCP §§430.40(a), 432.10. If a case was originally removed to federal court and then remanded back to state court, a demurrer to the complaint should be made within 30 days after remand if (1) no answer was filed in federal court and (2) no demurrer raising the same or similar issues was filed and ruled on in federal court before remand. CCP §430.90(a)(2)(B). The court has discretion to consider an untimely demurrer. *See* ***Jackson v. Doe*** (1st Dist.2011) 192 Cal.App.4th 742, 749.

(2) Amended. There is no statutory deadline for filing and serving a demurrer to an amended complaint or cross-complaint. *See* ***McAllister v. County of Monterey*** (6th Dist.2007) 147 Cal.App.4th 253, 280. Presumably, the same deadlines that apply to demurring to an original complaint apply to an amended complaint or cross-complaint. *See* CCP §471.5(a); *CEB Procedure Before Trial*, §23.41; Weil, *Civil Procedure Before Trial*, ¶7:139. See "Original," §4.2.1(1), this page.

NOTE

A party is not prohibited from filing a demurrer to an amended complaint on the same grounds that were unsuccessfully brought against the original complaint. ***Pavicich v. Santucci*** *(6th Dist.2000) 85 Cal.App.4th 382, 389 n.3;* ***Pacific States Enters. v. City of Coachella*** *(4th Dist.1993) 13 Cal.App.4th 1414, 1420 n.3; see* ***Clausing v. San Francisco Unified Sch. Dist.*** *(1st Dist.1990) 221 Cal.App.3d 1224, 1232.*

2. In response to answer.

(1) Original. A demurrer to an original answer should be filed and served within ten days after service of the answer. Kiesel, *Cal. Pretrial Civil Procedure*, §11.12[2]; *see* CCP §430.40(b).

(2) Amended. A demurrer to an amended answer can be filed and served within ten days after service of the amended answer, unless the court orders otherwise. *See* CCP §471.5(b).

> **NOTE**
>
> *The deadlines to file a demurrer have been held to be permissive rather than mandatory. See **Jackson**, 192 Cal.App.4th at 750; **McAllister**, 147 Cal.App.4th at 280. A court can, in its discretion, extend the time for demurrer. See **Jackson**, 192 Cal.App.4th at 750; **McAllister**, 147 Cal.App.4th at 281-82. If the time to file a general demurrer against a complaint has passed, consider filing a motion for judgment on the pleadings. See "Motion for Judgment on the Pleadings," ch. 4-I, p. 411.*

§4.3 Contents.

1. Notice of motion & motion. The demurrer should be requested in writing by noticed motion. *See* CRC 3.1103(c), 3.1320(c); ***McClure v. Donovan*** (1949) 33 Cal.2d 717, 724; ***Redondo Imprv. Co. v. City of Redondo Beach*** (3d Dist.1934) 3 Cal.App.2d 299, 302. The notice of motion must designate a hearing date no later than 35 days after the demurrer is filed or on the next available day—unless good cause for a later or earlier hearing date is shown. CRC 3.1320(d). See "Notice of motion & motion," ch. 1-D, §5.1, p. 28.

(1) Caption. The caption of the demurrer must state, on the first page immediately below the number of the case, the name of the party making the demurrer and the name of the party whose pleading is being challenged. *See* CRC 3.1320(e).

(2) Relief. The notice of motion and motion must describe the relief sought. *See* CRC 3.1110(a) (notice of motion must state nature of order being sought), CRC 3.1112(d)(3) (motion must briefly state relief sought).

(3) Grounds. The notice of motion and motion must briefly state the grounds for the relief. *See* CRC 3.1110(a) (notice of motion must state grounds for issuance of order), CRC 3.1112(d)(3) (motion must briefly state basis for motion). See "Grounds," §3, p. 398. Each ground of the demurrer must be distinctly specified and separately stated in its own paragraph. *See* CCP §430.60; CRC 3.1320(a). In describing a ground, the demurrer must state whether it applies to the entire challenged pleading or only to specific causes of action. CRC 3.1320(a); *see* 5 Witkin, *Cal. Procedure*, Pleading, §954 (demurrer that refers to whole complaint will be sustained only if all counts in complaint are defective).

> **NOTE**
>
> *If the ground for the demurrer is that the alleged cause of action is barred by the statute of limitations, the demurrer does not have to comply with the pleading requirements of CCP §458. **Bainbridge v. Stoner** (1940) 16 Cal.2d 423, 431. Under §458, when pleading the statute of limitations as a defense, the answer should cite the appropriate code section and subdivision if applicable. For purposes of a demurrer, it is sufficient if the appropriate code section is cited without a subdivision or if the demurrer simply states that the "cause of action is barred by the statute of limitations." See **Bainbridge**, 16 Cal.2d at 431.*

2. Memorandum of points & authorities. The demurrer, whether general or special, must include a memorandum in support of the motion. CRC 3.1112(a)(3), 3.1113(a). If a memorandum is not included, the court can construe it as an admission that a special demurrer is not meritorious, in which case the court will overrule the demurrer and consider the grounds for the demurrer waived. CRC 3.1113(a); *see* 5 Witkin, *Cal. Procedure*, Pleading, §980(1). The grounds for a general demurrer cannot be waived. *See* CCP §430.80(a); 5 Witkin, *Cal. Procedure*, Pleading, §§969, 980(1). If the demurrer is based on matters the court can take judicial notice of, the memorandum must specify those matters. CCP §430.70. See "Memorandum of points & authorities," ch. 1-D, §5.2, p. 28.

3. Request for judicial notice. If the movant's memorandum specifies matters that the court should take judicial notice of, the movant must also file a separate document asking the court to take judicial notice of those matters. Kiesel, *Cal. Pretrial Civil Procedure*, §11.16[3][c].

4. Proposed order. The movant can submit a proposed order with the demurrer. CRC 3.1113(m). If a proposed order is submitted, it must be lodged and served with the motion papers, not attached to them. *Id.* See "Documents lodged," ch. 1-F, §2.3, p. 47.

§4.4 Filing fees. When the demurrer is filed, the movant must pay a filing fee to the court clerk or request a waiver of the fee. See "Filing Fees," ch. 1-F, §7, p. 58.

§4.5 Demurrer filed with other challenges.

1. With answer. A demurrer can be filed simultaneously with an answer. CCP §430.30(c).

2. With motion to strike. A demurrer can be filed simultaneously with a motion to strike. Kiesel, *Cal. Pretrial Civil Procedure*, §12.07; *see* CRC 3.1322(b) (if demurrer and motion to strike are filed simultaneously, both must be noticed for hearing and heard at same time). If a pleading is susceptible to both a motion to strike and a demurrer, both must be filed at the same time. 5 Witkin, *Cal. Procedure*, Pleading, §1015; *see Report on Civil Practice & Procedure* at 3 (Judicial Council amended CRC 3.1320(j) to remove party's ability to file motion to strike after demurrer has been sustained or overruled). For a discussion of motions to strike, see "Motion to Strike," ch. 4-J, p. 418.

3. With challenges waived by general appearance. A demurrer can be filed simultaneously with a motion to quash, a motion to dismiss for forum non conveniens, or a motion to dismiss for delay in prosecution. *See* CCP §418.10(e). If a party files a demurrer before filing these motions, the party will have made a general appearance and waived its right to raise the issues of lack of personal jurisdiction, inadequacy of process, inadequacy of service of process, forum non conveniens, and delay in prosecution. *See id.* §§418.10(e)(3), 1014.

§5. RESPONSE

§5.1 Amend pleadings. A party can respond to a demurrer by amending the challenged pleading before the hearing. CCP §472. A party can amend its pleading once before the hearing without requesting leave of court. *Id.* See "Amending the Complaint," ch. 3-C, §6, p. 228; "Amending the Answer," ch. 4-B, §9, p. 347.

§5.2 Motion to strike. A party can respond to a demurrer by filing a motion to strike. *See* CCP §437. If a motion to strike the demurrer is filed, the hearing on the motion will be heard at the same time as the hearing on the demurrer. *Id.* §435(b)(3). See "Motion to Strike," ch. 4-J, p. 418.

NOTE

If a demurrer is filed late, the plaintiff should move to strike the demurrer rather than seek to have it overruled. See ***City of King City v. Community Bank*** *(6th Dist.2005) 131 Cal.App.4th 913, 923 n.4.*

§5.3 Voluntary dismissal. A party can respond to a demurrer by voluntarily dismissing the suit without prejudice before the court rules on the demurrer. *See* ***Wells v. Marina City Props., Inc.*** (1981) 29 Cal.3d 781, 785-86. See "Voluntary Dismissal," ch. 10-D, p. 1150.

§5.4 Opposition. A party can respond to a demurrer by filing opposition papers. *See, e.g.*, ***Fremont Indem. Co. v. Fremont Gen. Corp.*** (2d Dist.2007) 148 Cal.App.4th 97, 125-26 (P opposed demurrer by showing that complaint stated sufficient cause of action); ***Barrows v. American Motors Corp.*** (2d Dist.1983) 144 Cal.App.3d 1, 9 (P opposed demurrer by showing how demurrer relied on extrinsic declaration and exhibit). Opposition papers must be filed and served at least nine court days before the hearing. *See* CCP §1005(b); CRC 3.1300(a). See "Opposition Papers," ch. 1-D, §8, p. 35.

§6. REPLY

The movant can file and serve a reply to opposition papers. The reply must be filed and served at least five court days before the hearing. *See* CCP §1005(b). See "Reply Papers," ch. 1-D, §9, p. 37.

§7. HEARING

§7.1 Generally. For a discussion of hearings generally, see "Hearings," ch. 1-H, p. 79.

§7.2 Date of hearing. The hearing on the demurrer must be conducted within 35 days after the demurrer is filed or on the next available day. CRC 3.1320(d). For good cause shown, the court can hold the hearing at an earlier or later time. *Id.* If the demurrer is never scheduled for a hearing, the court can consider the demurrer abandoned. *See* ***Barragan v. Banco BCH*** (4th Dist.1986) 188 Cal.App.3d 283, 298-99.

NOTE

The parties can stipulate to the demurrer going off calendar and to the filing of an amended complaint. ***Harding v. Collazo*** *(2d Dist.1986) 177 Cal.App.3d 1044, 1053. This would be the functional equivalent of an order sustaining the demurrer with leave to amend, in that the action can be dismissed if the plaintiff does not amend within the stipulated time. Id.*

---

§7.3 Oral argument. In a complicated case or a case in which the facts are in dispute, the parties may be entitled to oral argument. *See* ***Medix Ambulance Serv. v. Superior Ct.*** (4th Dist.2002) 97 Cal.App.4th 109, 114-15; *see, e.g.*, ***TJX Cos. v. Superior Ct.*** (4th Dist.2001) 87 Cal.App.4th 747, 751 (oral argument necessary to determine demurrer on class-action allegations).

§7.4 Appearance.

1. **Nonmovant does not appear.** If the nonmovant does not appear at the hearing, the movant can have the court dispose of the demurrer unless the hearing is continued for good cause. CRC 3.1320(f).

2. **Movant does not appear.** Generally, if the movant does not appear at the hearing, the nonmovant can have the court dispose of the demurrer unless the hearing is continued for good cause. CRC 3.1320(f). But if the movant does not appear in support of a special demurrer, the court can consider the nonappearance to be (1) an admission that the demurrer is not meritorious and (2) a waiver of all grounds described in the demurrer. *Id.*

3. **Neither party appears.** If neither party appears for the hearing, the court can do the following:

(1) Dispose of the demurrer. CRC 3.1320(f).

(2) Drop the demurrer from the court calendar. *Id.* The court can have the hearing restored on notice or on terms it deems proper. *Id.*

(3) Order the hearing to be continued to a future date. *Id.*

PRACTICE TIP

If you cannot attend the hearing, give the court notice of nonappearance and ask that the judge rule on the demurrer based on the papers on file. CEB Procedure Before Trial, §23.53; see CRC 3.1304(c).

---

§8. RULING

§8.1 Standard for sustaining demurrer.

1. **Demurrer to entire pleading.** A demurrer that attacks an entire pleading will be sustained if the court finds that no count in the pleading entitles the pleading party to relief. *See* ***Western Title Ins. & Guar. Co. v. Bartolacelli*** (1st Dist.1954) 124 Cal.App.2d 690, 694 (error to sustain demurrer to entire multicount complaint when

one count stated cause of action). If the court finds that the pleading party is entitled to relief on any count in the pleading, it must overrule the demurrer. ***Buss v. J.O. Martin Co.*** (1st Dist.1966) 241 Cal.App.2d 123, 133-34; *see* ***South Shore Land Co. v. Petersen*** (1st Dist.1964) 226 Cal.App.2d 725, 733-34 (court must consider each count separately and must overrule demurrer if any count stands).

2. Demurrer to particular count. A demurrer that attacks a particular count in a pleading will be sustained if the court finds a defect in that count. 5 Witkin, *Cal. Procedure*, Pleading, §956.

§8.2 Court's guidelines. In ruling on a demurrer, courts apply the following guidelines:

1. Material facts taken as true. The court must take all the material facts pleaded as true. ***Sheehan v. San Francisco 49ers, Ltd.*** (2009) 45 Cal.4th 992, 998; ***Zelig v. County of L.A.*** (2002) 27 Cal.4th 1112, 1126. The court will also take as true any facts essential to a cause of action that can be inferred from the alleged facts. ***Harvey v. City of Holtville*** (4th Dist.1969) 271 Cal.App.2d 816, 819; *CEB Procedure Before Trial*, §23.54. But the court will not take as true contentions, deductions, conclusions of fact or law, or allegations that are contrary to matters that the court has taken judicial notice of. *See* ***Zelig***, 27 Cal.4th at 1126; ***Gentry v. eBay, Inc.*** (4th Dist.2002) 99 Cal.App.4th 816, 824; *CEB Procedure Before Trial*, §23.54.

2. Liberally construed. The court must liberally construe the allegations in the pleading with the goal of attaining substantial justice among the parties. CCP §452; ***King v. Central Bank*** (1977) 18 Cal.3d 840, 843. The court attains substantial justice by upholding a pleading if the facts alleged are adequate to state a cause of action under any theory. *See* ***Sheehan***, 45 Cal.4th at 998; ***Berkley v. Dowds*** (2d Dist.2007) 152 Cal.App.4th 518, 525; ***Buss v. J.O. Martin Co.*** (1st Dist.1966) 241 Cal.App.2d 123, 133-34. Even if the facts are not clearly stated, a pleading showing some right to relief will withstand a demurrer. *See* ***Gressley v. Williams*** (2d Dist.1961) 193 Cal.App.2d 636, 643-44.

3. Doubts resolved against pleader. The court will presume that a party's case is stated as favorably as possible in that party's pleadings, and any doubts about the pleading will be resolved against the pleading party. ***Feldesman v. McGovern*** (1st Dist.1941) 44 Cal.App.2d 566, 571. For example, if a fact necessary to the plaintiff's cause of action is not alleged in the complaint, the court must construe the omission to mean that the fact does not exist. *Id.*

4. Specific allegations control. The court will follow the rule that specific allegations in the pleading control over general allegations. *E.g.*, ***Gentry***, 99 Cal.App.4th at 827-28 (specific allegations in complaint showing that sale did not occur controlled over general allegations stating that sale did occur).

5. Judicially noticed documents. If the court has agreed to take judicial notice of a document, the court does not have to accept the truth of the document's contents or a party's proposed interpretation of the document. ***Joslin v. H.A.S. Ins. Brokerage*** (4th Dist.1986) 184 Cal.App.3d 369, 374. The court may accept the truth of the document's contents or a party's interpretation, however, when one of the following is true:

(1) When the document is an order, statement of decision, or judgment from a court. *Id.*; ***Garcia v. Sterling*** (2d Dist.1985) 176 Cal.App.3d 17, 22.

(2) When the party whose pleadings are being challenged made a statement in the document and that statement contradicts allegations in the party's pleading. *See* ***Joslin***, 184 Cal.App.3d at 375; ***Del E. Webb Corp. v. Structural Materials Co.*** (2d Dist.1981) 123 Cal.App.3d 593, 604-05; ***Able v. Van Der Zee*** (2d Dist.1967) 256 Cal.App.2d 728, 734.

(3) When the document's contents are not or cannot be factually disputed. ***Joslin***, 184 Cal.App.3d at 375; *see* ***C.R. v. Tenet Healthcare Corp.*** (2d Dist.2009) 169 Cal.App.4th 1094, 1103-04 (general rule is that truthfulness and interpretation of document's contents are disputable).

§9. ORDER

§9.1 Form. The court's ruling on the demurrer must be recorded either in writing or by minute order. *See, e.g.*, ***Payne v. Rader*** (3d Dist.2008) 167 Cal.App.4th 1569, 1572 (court sustained demurrer by minute order). See "Record of Ruling," ch. 1-I, §4, p. 90.

§9.2 Contents.

1. **Demurrer overruled.** If the court overrules a demurrer, the court does not have to state the grounds for its decision. *Cf.* CCP §472d (grounds for decision must be stated when court sustains demurrer). For a discussion of the effects of overruling a demurrer, see "Demurrer overruled," §9.4.1, p. 409.

NOTE

Although CCP §472d does not require the court to state the grounds for its decision when overruling a demurrer, the better practice is to state the grounds. Grounds that are overruled in a demurrer cannot be asserted in a later filed motion for a judgment on the pleadings unless a material change in the law has occurred since the ruling. CCP §438(g); see, e.g., ***Farber v. Bay View Terrace Homeowners Ass'n*** *(4th Dist.2006) 141 Cal.App.4th 1007, 1013 (because court stated in its order that it was not considering lack of standing in overruling demurrer, ground could be asserted in motion for judgment on the pleadings without proof of material change in law).*

2. **Demurrer sustained.** If the court sustains a demurrer, the court must specify the grounds for its decision and state whether the demurrer is sustained with or without leave to amend. For a discussion of the effects of sustaining a demurrer, see "Demurrer sustained," §9.4.2, p. 409.

(1) **Grounds.** When a court sustains a demurrer, the court must include in its ruling a statement of the specific grounds on which the ruling is based. CCP §472d. The statement can refer to the grounds stated in the demurrer by page and paragraph number. *Id.*; *see* ***Mautner v. Peralta*** (1st Dist.1989) 215 Cal.App.3d 796, 801-02 (detailed statement not required, but court must specify relevant parts of demurrer).

NOTE

If the court does not state any grounds, it will be considered harmless error unless the party against whom the demurrer has been sustained can demonstrate prejudice. ***Brown v. State*** *(4th Dist.1993) 21 Cal.App.4th 1500, 1506, disapproved on other grounds,* ***Massingill v. Department of Food & Agric.*** *(4th Dist.2002) 102 Cal.App.4th 498; see* ***Wheeler v. County of San Bernardino*** *(4th Dist.1978) 76 Cal.App.3d 841, 846 n.3 (demurrer order will be upheld on any sufficient ground, regardless of whether trial court relied on ground or not). If the party does not object to the lack of stated grounds, the issue is waived.* ***E.F. Hutton & Co. v. City Nat'l Bank*** *(2d Dist.1983) 149 Cal.App.3d 60, 65 n.1; see CCP §472d;* ***Krawitz v. Rusch*** *(4th Dist.1989) 209 Cal.App.3d 957, 962.*

(2) **Leave to amend.** When a court sustains a demurrer, the court should specify whether it is sustained with or without leave to amend. *See* ***Martin v. Bridgeport Cmty. Ass'n*** (2d Dist.2009) 173 Cal.App.4th 1024, 1031 (court has discretion to sustain demurrer with or without leave); *see, e.g.,* ***Meyer v. Sprint Spectrum L.P.*** (2009) 45 Cal.4th 634, 638-39 (court sustained one demurrer with leave to amend and later demurrer without leave to amend). Generally, leave to amend should be granted unless there is no reasonable possibility that the defect can be cured by amendment. ***Maxton v. Western States Metals*** (2d Dist.2012) 203 Cal.App.4th 81, 95; ***Association of Cmty. Orgs. for Reform Now v. Department of Indus. Relations*** (1st Dist.1995) 41 Cal.App.4th 298, 302; *see, e.g.,* ***Vernon v. State*** (1st Dist.2004) 116 Cal.App.4th 114, 133 (demurrer without leave to amend upheld because there was no liability under statutes that formed basis of P's claims); ***Moore v. Anderson Zeigler Disharoon Gallagher & Gray, P.C.*** (1st Dist.2003) 109 Cal.App.4th 1287, 1307 (demurrer without leave to amend upheld because Ds had no duty to nonclient to investigate testator's capacity); ***Friendly Vill. Cmty. Ass'n v. Silva & Hill Constr. Co.*** (2d Dist.1973) 31 Cal.App.3d 220, 225-26 (demurrer without leave to amend upheld because complaint showed Ps had no standing to sue). *But see* ***Guardian N. Bay, Inc. v. Superior Ct.*** (6th Dist.2001) 94 Cal.App.4th 963, 971 (court

can deny leave to amend if P does nothing to oppose demurrer). The burden is on the plaintiff to show that there is a reasonable possibility that the defect can be cured by amendment. ***Maxton***, 203 Cal.App.4th at 95; ***Association of Cmty. Orgs.***, 41 Cal.App.4th at 302. If the court grants leave to amend, it can set any conditions or terms that may be just. CCP §472a(c). See "Amending the Complaint," ch. 3-C, §6, p. 228.

§9.3 Notice of order. For a discussion of giving notice of the order, see "Notice of Order," ch. 1-I, §5, p. 93.

§9.4 Effect of demurrer.

1. Demurrer overruled.

(1) To complaint. If a demurrer to a complaint is overruled, the defendant has ten days to answer or otherwise plead to the complaint or the remaining causes of action, unless the court orders otherwise. CRC 3.1320(g), (j)(1). In an action involving forcible entry, forcible detainer, or unlawful detainer, the period to respond is shortened to five days. CRC 3.1320(g). The period begins to run from service of the signed decision or order, unless notice was waived in open court and the waiver was entered in the minutes. CCP §472b.

(2) To answer. If a demurrer to an answer is overruled, the action continues as if no demurrer had been made, and the facts alleged in the answer are considered denied by the plaintiff. CCP §472a(b); *see id.* §431.20(b).

2. Demurrer sustained.

(1) With leave to amend.

(a) Deadline to amend. Generally, if a demurrer is sustained with leave to amend, the nonmovant has ten days to amend the pleading unless the court orders otherwise. CRC 3.1320(g). In an action involving forcible entry, forcible detainer, or unlawful detainer, the period to amend is shortened to five days. *Id.* The period begins to run from service of the signed decision or order, unless notice was waived in open court and the waiver was entered in the minutes. CCP §472b.

NOTE

If the nonmovant elects to amend the pleading, the nonmovant waives any error in the court's order sustaining the demurrer. ***Sheehy v. Roman Catholic Archbishop*** *(1st Dist.1942) 49 Cal.App.2d 537, 541.*

(b) Stay discovery. The court can stay discovery pending the filing of an amended complaint, particularly when the plaintiff has had significant opportunity for discovery and has not shown how any additional discovery would help in stating a viable cause of action. *See* ***Terminals Equip. Co. v. City & Cty. of S.F.*** (1st Dist.1990) 221 Cal.App.3d 234, 246-47.

(c) Effect of no amendment.

[1] No amendment to entire complaint. If a demurrer is sustained for an entire complaint and the complaint is not amended within the specified time, either party, or the court on its own, can file a motion to dismiss. *See* CCP §581(f)(2) (either party); CRC 3.1320(h) (ex parte application to dismiss); *see, e.g.*, ***Ziegler v. Nickel*** (2d Dist.1998) 64 Cal.App.4th 545, 547 n.2 (court granted dismissal on its own motion). For a discussion of how to dismiss an action when no amendment has been made after a demurrer was sustained, see "Demurrer – No Amendment," ch. 10-F, §3, p. 1180.

[2] No amendment to entire answer. If a demurrer is sustained for an entire answer and the answer is not amended within the specified time, the plaintiff can seek a default judgment against the defendant. CCP §586(a)(5). See "Default Judgment," ch. 10-A, p. 1089.

[3] No amendment to specific cause of action or defense. If a demurrer is sustained for a specific cause of action or defense and the pleading is not amended within the specified time, the demurring party can file a motion to dismiss the specific cause of action or defense. *See* CCP §581(f)(2).

(2) **Without leave to amend.**

(a) **Entire complaint.** If a demurrer is sustained for an entire complaint without leave to amend, either party, or the court on its own, can file a motion to dismiss. *See* CCP §581(f)(1) (either party); *see, e.g.*, ***Kirkpatrick v. City of Oceanside*** (4th Dist.1991) 232 Cal.App.3d 267, 272-73 (court granted dismissal on its own motion). For a discussion of how to dismiss an action when leave to amend is not granted, see "Demurrer – Without Leave to Amend," ch. 10-F, §2, p. 1180.

(b) **Entire answer.** If a demurrer is sustained for an entire answer without leave to amend, the plaintiff should ask the court to enter judgment on the pleadings. *See* ***Bank of Am. Nat'l Trust & Sav. Ass'n v. Vannini*** (1st Dist.1956) 140 Cal.App.2d 120, 124. See "Motion for Judgment on the Pleadings," ch. 4-I, p. 411.

§10. MOTION FOR RECONSIDERATION

A party adversely affected by a court's order on a demurrer can file a motion for reconsideration. CCP §1008(a), (e). See "Motion for Reconsideration," ch. 5-G, §3, p. 508.

§11. MOTION FOR RENEWAL

A party whose demurrer is overruled can file a motion for renewal. CCP §1008(b). See "Motion for Renewal," ch. 5-G, §4, p. 516.

§12. APPELLATE REVIEW

§12.1 Writ of mandate. A party adversely affected by a court's order on a demurrer can file a writ of mandate. ***Coulter v. Superior Ct.*** (1978) 21 Cal.3d 144, 148; ***Babb v. Superior Ct.*** (1971) 3 Cal.3d 841, 851. Courts are reluctant to grant extraordinary relief at the pleading stage, but a writ of mandate will be granted when it appears that the trial court has deprived a party of its opportunity to plead its cause of action or defense and when extraordinary relief may prevent a needless and expensive trial and reversal. ***Coulter***, 21 Cal.3d at 148.

§12.2 Writ of prohibition. If a court overrules a demurrer made on the ground that the court has no subject-matter jurisdiction, the movant can file a petition for a writ of prohibition. *See* ***Tide Water Associated Oil Co. v. Superior Ct.*** (1955) 43 Cal.2d 815, 820; ***County of Santa Barbara v. Superior Ct.*** (2d Dist.1971) 15 Cal.App.3d 751, 754-55; *CEB Procedure Before Trial*, §23.63.

§12.3 Direct appeal.

1. **When applicable.**

(1) **Demurrer overruled.** An order overruling a demurrer is not an appealable order but can be reviewed on direct appeal after a final judgment has been entered in the action. ***San Diego Gas & Elec. Co. v. Superior Ct.*** (1996) 13 Cal.4th 893, 912-13.

(2) **Demurrer sustained.**

(a) **Without leave to amend.**

[1] **To entire pleading.** An order sustaining a demurrer to an entire pleading without leave to amend is not an appealable order but can be reviewed on direct appeal after a final judgment of dismissal is granted. ***Berri v. Superior Ct.*** (1955) 43 Cal.2d 856, 860; *see* CCP §472c(a), (c).

[2] **To particular cause of action or defense.** An order sustaining a demurrer to less than the entire pleading without leave to amend is not an appealable order, but the nonmovant can seek from the reviewing court a writ of mandate directing the trial court to overrule the demurrer. *See* ***Coulter v. Superior Ct.*** (1978) 21 Cal.3d 144, 148. See "Writ of mandate," §12.1, this page.

(b) **With leave to amend.**

[1] **To entire pleading.** An order sustaining a demurrer to an entire pleading with leave to amend is not an appealable order but can be reviewed on direct appeal if the nonmovant does not amend within the time allowed and a final judgment of dismissal is entered in the action. *See* ***Dye v. Caterpillar, Inc.*** (1st Dist.2011)

195 Cal.App.4th 1366, 1381; ***Jeffers v. Screen Extras Guild, Inc.*** (2d Dist.1951) 107 Cal.App.2d 253, 254. If the nonmovant elects to amend the pleading, the nonmovant waives any error in the court's order sustaining the demurrer. ***County of Santa Clara v. Atlantic Richfield Co.*** (6th Dist.2006) 137 Cal.App.4th 292, 312; ***Sheehy v. Roman Catholic Archbishop*** (1st Dist.1942) 49 Cal.App.2d 537, 540-41.

[2] To particular cause of action or defense. An order sustaining a demurrer to less than the entire pleading with leave to amend is not an appealable order until a final judgment has been entered on the rest of the pleading. *CEB Procedure Before Trial*, §23.67; *see* CCP §472c(b)(1), (b)(2), (c).

2. Standard of review.

(1) De novo. The court's ruling on a demurrer is reviewed de novo. ***San Diego City Firefighters, Local 145 v. Board of Admin.*** (4th Dist.2012) 206 Cal.App.4th 594, 605; ***Berkley v. Dowds*** (2d Dist.2007) 152 Cal.App.4th 518, 525; ***Sisemore v. Master Fin., Inc.*** (6th Dist.2007) 151 Cal.App.4th 1386, 1396; ***Flying Dutchman Park, Inc. v. City & Cty. of S.F.*** (1st Dist.2001) 93 Cal.App.4th 1129, 1134. The appellate court must affirm the order if it is correct on any ground stated in the demurrer, regardless of the trial court's stated reasons. ***Cedar Fair, L.P. v. City of Santa Clara*** (6th Dist.2011) 194 Cal.App.4th 1150, 1159; ***Mexia v. Rinker Boat Co.*** (4th Dist.2009) 174 Cal.App.4th 1297, 1303; *see* ***Weinstock v. Eissler*** (1st Dist.1964) 224 Cal.App.2d 212, 225 (CCP §472d does not limit appellate court's power to affirm only on grounds asserted in order; appellate court can affirm on any grounds requested in demurrer).

(2) Abuse of discretion. The court's ruling on whether to sustain the demurrer with or without leave to amend is reviewed for abuse of discretion. ***Van De Kamps Coalition v. Board of Trs.*** (2d Dist.2012) 206 Cal.App.4th 1036, 1044; ***Sisemore***, 151 Cal.App.4th at 1397. It is an abuse of discretion to deny leave to amend if there is a reasonable probability that the defect could be cured by amendment. ***San Diego City Firefighters***, 206 Cal.App.4th at 606; ***Sisemore***, 151 Cal.App.4th at 1397. The question whether the denial of leave was an abuse of discretion is reviewable on appeal regardless of whether a request to amend the pleading was made. CCP §472c(a); *see* ***San Diego City Firefighters***, 206 Cal.App.4th at 606 (reasonable probability that defect can be cured can be shown for first time on appeal); ***Dudley v. DOT*** (3d Dist.2001) 90 Cal.App.4th 255, 259 (appellant can argue new legal theory to cure pleading for first time on appeal).

§12.4 Time for amending complaint after remand. If the appellate court reverses and remands an order sustaining a demurrer to a complaint without leave to amend and directs the trial court to give leave, the plaintiff has 30 days from the time the clerk mails notice of the remittitur to file an amended complaint. *See* CCP §472b; ***Dye v. Caterpillar, Inc.*** (1st Dist.2011) 195 Cal.App.4th 1366, 1383 (appellate court reversed order sustaining demurrer to complaints without leave to amend, but did not direct trial court to give leave; 30-day time limit in §472b did not apply).

I. MOTION FOR JUDGMENT ON THE PLEADINGS

This subchapter discusses a motion for judgment on the pleadings (JOP) under CCP §438 and under common law.

§1. GENERAL

§1.1 Purpose. A motion for JOP is used to challenge a pleading in the same manner as a general demurrer—that is, the challenged pleading (1) establishes that the court does not have subject-matter jurisdiction or (2) does not allege facts sufficient to support a cause of action or defense. CCP §438(c)(1); *see* ***International Ass'n of Firefighters v. City of San Jose*** (6th Dist.2011) 195 Cal.App.4th 1179, 1196; ***Bufil v. Dollar Fin. Grp.*** (1st Dist.2008) 162 Cal.App.4th 1193, 1202. See "General demurrer," ch. 4-H, §3.1, p. 398. Like a demurrer, the grounds for a motion for JOP must appear on the face of the pleading or be based on facts capable of judicial notice. ***Bufil***, 162 Cal.App.4th at 1202. The only significant difference between the two motions is that a motion for JOP is brought after the time to file a general demurrer has expired. CCP §438(f); ***Caldera Pharms. v. Regents of the Univ. of Cal.*** (1st Dist.2012) 205 Cal.App.4th 338, 350; ***International Ass'n***, 195 Cal.App.4th at 1196.

§1.2 Primary authority. CCP §438; CRC 3.1103, 3.1112, 3.1113.

§1.3 Secondary authority. The following secondary sources are cited as authority in this subchapter:

- *California Civil Procedure Before Trial* (CEB Online ed. 2014) (referred to as *CEB Procedure Before Trial*).
- Kiesel et al., *Matthew Bender Practice Guide: California Pretrial Civil Procedure* (2014) (referred to as Kiesel, *Cal. Pretrial Civil Procedure*).
- Thomas, *California Civil Courtroom Handbook* (2014) (referred to as Thomas, *Courtroom Handbook*).
- Weil & Brown, *California Practice Guide: Civil Procedure Before Trial* (CD-ROM ed. 2014) (referred to as Weil, *Civil Procedure Before Trial*).

§2. STATUTORY & COMMON-LAW MOTIONS

Before 1994, a motion for JOP was recognized only at common law. ***Gerawan Farming, Inc. v. Lyons*** (2000) 24 Cal.4th 468, 482 n.2; *see* Sen. Com. on Judiciary, Analysis of Assem. Bill No. 58 (1993-1994 Reg. Sess.) August 16, 1993, p. 1. In 1993, the California Legislature codified the motion for JOP by enacting CCP §438. Stats. 1993, ch. 456, §5. The statutory motion contains a number of restrictions that did not exist at common law. The most significant are that the statutory motion cannot be (1) filed after a pretrial conference order has been entered or within 30 days before trial (whichever is later) unless the court grants leave or (2) asserted on the same grounds that were overruled in an earlier demurrer unless a material change in the law occurred. *See* CCP §438(e), (g).

Despite these differences—and the apparent codification of the common-law motion—most courts continue to recognize the common-law motion. *E.g.*, ***Gerawan Farming***, 24 Cal.4th at 482 n.2; ***Cordova v. 21st Century Ins.*** (2d Dist.2005) 129 Cal.App.4th 89, 109; ***Shea Homes L.P. v. County of Alameda*** (1st Dist.2003) 110 Cal.App.4th 1246, 1266; ***Saltarelli & Steponovich v. Douglas*** (4th Dist.1995) 40 Cal.App.4th 1, 5; ***Nettles v. Cummings*** (6th Dist.2005) No. H027821 (unpub.; 9-28-05); ***Carlson v. Young*** (5th Dist.2003) No. F038633 (unpub.; 3-3-03) (footnote 10); *see* Weil, *Civil Procedure Before Trial*, ¶7:277. The most common argument for why the common-law motion is still viable is that the grounds for a motion for JOP—which are the same for a general demurrer—can be raised at any time. *See* CCP §430.80 (grounds for general demurrer cannot be waived); *CEB Procedure Before Trial*, §27.4 (same). Thus, if the deadline to bring a statutory JOP has passed, a party should still be able to bring a common-law JOP. Only one unpublished opinion has interpreted §438 as replacing the common-law motion. ***Pourzia v. St. Mary Med. Ctr.*** (2d Dist.2006) No. B178159 (unpub.; 8-30-06) (footnote 6); *see also* ***Sarinana v. Soria*** (4th Dist.2007) No. G037930 (unpub.; 8-28-07) (questioning, but not deciding, whether common-law motion can still be brought).

Because most courts continue to recognize common-law motions for JOP, this subchapter will discuss both motions and note the differences where applicable.

PRACTICE TIP

Although most courts continue to recognize the common-law motion, the best practice is to comply with the statutory requirements whenever possible. Thomas, Courtroom Handbook, §11:37.

§3. GROUNDS

§3.1 Generally.

1. Against complaint. A motion for JOP can be used to challenge the entire complaint or any one of the causes of action in the complaint on the same grounds as a general demurrer—that is, (1) the court lacks subject-matter jurisdiction over the case or (2) the complaint does not state facts sufficient to constitute a cause of action. *See* CCP §438(c)(1)(B), (c)(2)(A); ***Smiley v. Citibank (S.D.)*** (1995) 11 Cal.4th 138, 145-46, *aff'd*, (1996) 517 U.S. 735; ***Mendoza v. Continental Sales Co.*** (5th Dist.2006) 140 Cal.App.4th 1395, 1401; ***City of Hawthorne v. H&C***

Disposal Co. (2d Dist.2003) 109 Cal.App.4th 1668, 1678; ***Heredia v. Farmers Ins. Exch.*** (6th Dist.1991) 228 Cal.App.3d 1345, 1358. For a discussion of these grounds, see "To complaint," ch. 4-H, §3.1.1, p. 398.

2. Against answer. A motion for JOP can be used to challenge the entire answer or any one of the affirmative defenses in the answer on the ground that (1) the complaint states facts sufficient to constitute a cause of action and (2) the answer does not state facts sufficient to constitute a defense to the complaint. *See* CCP §438(c)(1)(A), (c)(2)(B); *see, e.g.*, ***Hardy v. Admiral Oil Co.*** (1961) 56 Cal.2d 836, 839-41 (verified pleadings showed D admitted or was deemed to have admitted all facts necessary to entitle P to judgment as prayed for in complaint). For a discussion of what does and does not constitute facts sufficient to state a cause of action, see "Facts do not state cause of action," ch. 4-H, §3.1.1(2), p. 399.

§3.2 After demurrer overruled.

1. Statutory motion. If a party is filing a statutory motion for JOP on the same grounds that were overruled in an earlier demurrer, the party must show that a material change in the law has occurred since the demurrer was overruled. CCP §438(g)(1); *see* ***In re Alberto*** (2d Dist.2002) 102 Cal.App.4th 421, 430 n.4. The requirement that a party show a material change in law under §438(g) does not apply, however, if the statutory motion is brought on different grounds. CCP §438(g)(2).

2. Common-law motion. If a party is filing a common-law motion for JOP on the same grounds that were overruled in an earlier demurrer, the party does not have to show that a material change in the law has occurred. ***Rand-Luby v. Aaron's Envtl. Serv.*** (4th Dist.2009) No. G040376 (unpub.; 6-22-09) (footnote 3).

§4. MOTION

§4.1 Who can file.

1. Generally. A motion for JOP can be made by any party (plaintiff, cross-defendant, defendant, cross-complainant) or the court. *See* CCP §438(a), (b); *see, e.g.*, ***More v. Del Valle*** (1865) 28 Cal. 170, 172 (plaintiff); ***Columbia Cas. Co. v. Northwestern Nat'l Ins.*** (4th Dist.1991) 231 Cal.App.3d 457, 461 (cross-defendant); ***Moore v. California Minerals Prods.*** (2d Dist.1953) 115 Cal.App.2d 834, 836 (court); ***Smith v. Beauchamp*** (2d Dist.1945) 71 Cal.App.2d 250, 251 (defendant).

2. Multiple Ds. If there are multiple defendants, they can file a joint motion for JOP. *See* ***Waller v. Truck Ins. Exch., Inc.*** (1995) 11 Cal.4th 1, 14; ***Caldera Pharms. v. Regents of the Univ. of Cal.*** (1st Dist.2012) 205 Cal.App.4th 338, 349.

§4.2 Deadline to file & serve.

1. Statutory motion.

(1) Earliest date. A statutory motion for JOP must be filed and served after the time to demur has expired. CCP §438(f). For a discussion of the deadline to file and serve a demurrer, see "Deadline to file & serve," ch. 4-H, §4.2, p. 403.

(2) Latest date.

(a) Generally. A statutory motion for JOP cannot be filed and served (1) after a pretrial conference order under CCP §575 has been entered or (2) within 30 days of the date the action is initially set for trial, whichever is later. CCP §438(e).

(b) Exception. A statutory motion for JOP can be filed and served late with leave of court. ***Sutherland v. City of Fort Bragg*** (1st Dist.2000) 86 Cal.App.4th 13, 25 n.4; *see* CCP §438(e) ("unless the court otherwise permits"). Whether to allow late filing is solely in the court's discretion; no finding of good cause is required. ***Burnett v. Chimney Sweep, LLC*** (2d Dist.2004) 123 Cal.App.4th 1057, 1063; *see* ***Sutherland***, 86 Cal.App.4th at 25 n.4 (CCP §438(e) does not specify any grounds that might limit court's power to grant leave).

2. Common-law motion. A common-law motion for JOP can be filed and served at any time before final judgment, even during trial. *See* ***Stoops v. Abbassi*** (2d Dist.2002) 100 Cal.App.4th 644, 650; ***People v. $20,000 U.S. Currency*** (3d Dist.1991) 235 Cal.App.3d 682, 691. Because it can be filed at any time, a common-law motion can be brought without notice. Weil, *Civil Procedure Before Trial*, ¶7:321; *see* ***Kortmeyer v. California Ins. Guar. Ass'n*** (2d Dist.1992) 9 Cal.App.4th 1285, 1293 (motion for JOP can be made orally).

§4.3 Contents.

1. Statutory motion.

(1) Notice of motion & motion.

(a) Generally. A statutory motion for JOP should be requested in writing by noticed motion. Kiesel, *Cal. Pretrial Civil Procedure*, §11.45[4]; *see* CCP §§438(i)(2), 1010; *see also CEB Procedure Before Trial*, §27.28 (form for notice of motion for JOP). See "Notice of motion & motion," ch. 1-D, §5.1, p. 28. The notice of motion should designate a hearing date in the same manner as other noticed motions. See "Noticed motion," ch. 1-H, §4.1, p. 81. For a discussion of how far in advance of the hearing the notice of motion and motion must be filed and served, see "Motion papers," ch. 1-F, §5.2.1(2)(a), p. 57; "Retrospective deadlines," ch. 1-G, §6.2, p. 71.

(b) Relief. The notice of motion and motion must describe the relief sought. *See* CRC 3.1110(a) (notice of motion must state nature of order being sought), CRC 3.1112(d)(3) (motion must briefly state relief sought).

(c) Grounds. The notice of motion and motion must briefly state the grounds for the relief. *See* CRC 3.1110(a) (notice of motion must state grounds for issuance of order), CRC 3.1112(d)(3) (motion must briefly state basis for motion). See "Grounds," §3, p. 412.

(2) Memorandum of points & authorities. The motion must include a memorandum in support of the motion. CRC 3.1112(a)(3), 3.1113(a); *see also CEB Procedure Before Trial*, §27.31 (form for memorandum supporting motion for JOP). If the motion is based on matters the court can take judicial notice of, the notice of motion or memorandum of points and authorities must specify those matters. CCP §438(d). For the general contents of a memorandum, see "Memorandum of points & authorities," ch. 1-D, §5.2, p. 28.

(3) Request for judicial notice. If the motion is based on matters the court can take judicial notice of, the movant can ask for judicial notice. CRC 3.1113(*l*). A request for judicial notice must be made in a separate document. *Id.* See "Request for Judicial Notice," ch. 5-J, p. 547.

(4) Proposed order. The movant can submit a proposed order with the motion. CRC 3.1113(m). If a proposed order is submitted, it must be lodged and served with the motion papers, not attached to them. *Id.* See "Documents lodged," ch. 1-F, §2.3, p. 47.

2. Common-law motion. A common-law motion can be made orally or in writing. *See* ***Kortmeyer v. California Ins. Guar. Ass'n*** (2d Dist.1992) 9 Cal.App.4th 1285, 1293. When made in writing, a common-law motion should generally include the same contents as a statutory motion.

§4.4 Filing fees. When the motion is filed, the movant must pay a filing fee to the court clerk or request a waiver of the fee. See "Filing Fees," ch. 1-F, §7, p. 58.

§5. RESPONSE

§5.1 Amend pleadings. The nonmovant can respond to a motion for JOP by asking the court for leave to amend the challenged pleading before the hearing. *CEB Procedure Before Trial*, §27.14; *see* ***Foundation for Taxpayer & Consumer Rights v. Nextel Comms.*** (2d Dist.2006) 143 Cal.App.4th 131, 134.

§5.2 Opposition. The nonmovant can respond to a motion for JOP by filing opposition papers. *CEB Procedure Before Trial*, §27.14; *see, e.g.,* ***Fireside Bank v. Superior Ct.*** (2007) 40 Cal.4th 1069, 1076 (P opposed motion for JOP on merits and procedural grounds); ***Foundation for Taxpayer & Consumer Rights v. Nextel Comms.*** (2d

Dist.2006) 143 Cal.App.4th 131, 134 (P opposed motion and, alternatively, requested leave to amend pleadings); ***Sutherland v. City of Fort Bragg*** (1st Dist.2000) 86 Cal.App.4th 13, 17 (P opposed motion). Opposition papers must be filed and served at least nine court days before the hearing. *See* CCP §1005(b); CRC 3.1300(a). For a discussion of opposition papers, see "Opposition Papers," ch. 1-D, §8, p. 35.

§5.3 Cross-motion. The nonmovant can respond to a motion for JOP by filing a cross-motion for JOP. *See, e.g.*, ***County of L.A. v. Commission on State Mandates*** (2d Dist.2007) 150 Cal.App.4th 898, 910 (parties filed cross-motions for JOP); ***Consolidated Music Co. v. Morrison*** (1st Dist.1916) 30 Cal.App. 303, 304 (P filed motion for JOP and D responded by filing cross-motion).

§6. REPLY

The movant can file and serve a reply to the opposition papers. The reply must be filed and served at least five court days before the hearing. *See* CCP §1005(b). For a discussion of reply papers, see "Reply Papers," ch. 1-D, §9, p. 37.

§7. HEARING

§7.1 Generally. For a discussion of hearings generally, see "Hearings," ch. 1-H, p. 79.

§7.2 Appearance. If the nonmovant does not attend the hearing, the court will still rule on the motion. ***Dobbins v. Hardister*** (1st Dist.1966) 242 Cal.App.2d 787, 797. By not attending the hearing, the nonmovant does not waive (1) the challenged cause of action or defense or (2) the right to amend its pleading if it can be amended. *See* ***Pylon, Inc. v. Olympic Ins.*** (4th Dist.1969) 271 Cal.App.2d 643, 655-56; ***Dobbins***, 242 Cal.App.2d at 797; *CEB Procedure Before Trial*, §27.16.

§8. RULING

Courts follow the same guidelines for ruling on a motion for JOP as they do for ruling on a demurrer. *See* ***Smiley v. Citibank (S.D.)*** (1995) 11 Cal.4th 138, 145-46, *aff'd*, (1996) 517 U.S. 735; ***Camacho v. Automobile Club*** (2d Dist.2006) 142 Cal.App.4th 1394, 1398 n.4. See "Ruling," ch. 4-H, §8, p. 406.

§9. ORDER

§9.1 Form. The court's ruling on the motion for JOP must be recorded either in writing or by minute order. *See CEB Procedure Before Trial*, §27.21; *see, e.g.*, ***Mack v. State Bar of Cal.*** (2d Dist.2001) 92 Cal.App.4th 957, 960 (minute order); ***Golden Day Sch., Inc. v. California Dept. of Educ.*** (3d Dist.1999) 69 Cal.App.4th 681, 687 (same); ***Old Town Dev. Corp. v. Urban Renewal Agency*** (1st Dist.1967) 249 Cal.App.2d 313, 317 (same); *see also CEB Procedure Before Trial*, §27.29 (form for order for JOP). See "Record of Ruling," ch. 1-I, §4, p. 90.

§9.2 Contents. If the court grants the motion, the order should specify whether it is granted with or without leave to amend. *See* CCP §438(h)(1). Leave to amend should be granted if there is any reasonable possibility that the defect can be cured by amendment. ***Maxton v. Western States Metals*** (2d Dist.2012) 203 Cal.App.4th 81, 95; *see* ***Bettencourt v. Hennessy Indus.*** (1st Dist.2012) 205 Cal.App.4th 1103, 1111. The burden is on the plaintiff to show that there is a reasonable possibility that the defect can be cured by amendment. ***Maxton***, 203 Cal.App.4th at 95.

§9.3 Notice of order. For a discussion of giving notice of the order, see "Notice of Order," ch. 1-I, §5, p. 93.

§9.4 Effect of order.

1. Granted with leave to amend.

(1) Deadline to amend. Generally, if a motion for JOP is granted with leave to amend, the nonmovant has 30 days to amend. CCP §438(h)(2). Time begins to run from service of the notice of the court's ruling. ***People v. $20,000 U.S. Currency*** (3d Dist.1991) 235 Cal.App.3d 682, 691-92.

NOTE

If the nonmovant elects to amend the pleading, it waives any error in the order. ***Anmaco, Inc. v. Bohlken*** *(1st Dist.1993) 13 Cal.App.4th 891, 900.*

(2) Effect of no amendment.

(a) Entire pleading. If a motion for JOP is granted against an entire pleading with leave to amend, the court can enter judgment on the pleading after a hearing in the following circumstances:

[1] An amended pleading is filed late or does not comply with the court's previous ruling and the movant files a motion to strike the pleading and enter judgment. CCP §438(i)(1)(A); *see id.* §438(h)(4)(A), (h)(4)(B). See "Judgment," §12, this page.

[2] No amended pleading is filed and the movant files for entry of judgment. CCP §438(h)(4)(C), (i)(1)(B). See "Judgment," §12, this page.

(b) Specific cause of action or defense. If a motion for JOP is granted against a specific cause of action or defense with leave to amend and the pleading is not amended within the specified time, the movant can file a motion to strike the specific cause of action or defense. See "Motion to Strike," ch. 4-J, p. 418.

2. Granted without leave to amend. If a motion for JOP is granted against an entire pleading without leave to amend, the court will immediately enter judgment in favor of the movant. *See* CCP §438(h)(3) ("judgment shall be entered forthwith"). See "Judgment," §12, this page.

§10. MOTION FOR RECONSIDERATION

A party adversely affected by a court's order on a motion for JOP can file a motion for reconsideration. *See* CCP §1008(a), (e). See "Motion for Reconsideration," ch. 5-G, §3, p. 508.

§11. MOTION FOR RENEWAL

A party whose motion for JOP is denied can file a motion for renewal. *See* CCP §1008(b), (e). See "Motion for Renewal," ch. 5-G, §4, p. 516.

§12. JUDGMENT

If a JOP is entered, it is considered a final judgment on the merits. ***Molski v. Arciero Wine Grp.*** (2d Dist.2008) 164 Cal.App.4th 786, 791; ***O'Moore v. Driscoll*** (1st Dist.1933) 135 Cal.App. 770, 772. For a discussion of when a judgment is proper, see "Effect of order," §9.4, p. 415.

§12.1 Preparation. The prevailing party should prepare a proposed judgment and submit it to the court to sign and enter. *CEB Procedure Before Trial*, §27.21; *see also id.* §27.30 (form for JOP).

§12.2 Contents.

1. Generally. The judgment must comply with the general rules that apply to all papers filed with the court. *See* CRC 2.3 (with some exceptions, all documents offered for filing in any case must comply with rules).

2. Date granted. The judgment should state the date the order for JOP was granted. *See, e.g., CEB Procedure Before Trial*, §27.30 (form for JOP).

3. Grounds. The judgment should the state reasons for its issuance (e.g., complaint does not state facts sufficient to constitute cause of action). *See, e.g., CEB Procedure Before Trial*, §27.30 (form for JOP).

4. Relief. The judgment should state the relief awarded.

(1) Damages. The judgment should contain one of the following if the plaintiff sought monetary damages:

(a) P granted JOP. If a JOP is granted in favor of the plaintiff, the judgment should state the amount of monetary damages the plaintiff will recover from the defendant in dollars and cents (no fractions). *See* CCP §577.5; *see, e.g.*, *CEB Procedure Before Trial*, §27.30 (form for JOP); *see also* ***Kittle v. Lang*** (4th Dist.1951) 107 Cal.App.2d 604, 612 (judgment for money should be stated with certainty and specify amount awarded).

(b) D granted JOP. If a JOP is granted in favor of the defendant, the judgment should state that the plaintiff take nothing. *See, e.g.*, *CEB Procedure Before Trial*, §27.30 (form for JOP).

(2) Prejudgment interest. The judgment must state the amount of any prejudgment interest awarded. *See* CRC 3.1802.

(3) Attorney fees. The judgment should specify the amount of attorney fees awarded or be left blank so the fees can be determined at a later time. *See* ***Bankes v. Lucas*** (2d Dist.1992) 9 Cal.App.4th 365, 369; *see also* CRC 3.1702(b)(1) (serving and filing motion to claim attorney fees after judgment). Attorney fees are recoverable in a JOP if the fees are otherwise recoverable by law (i.e., by statute, by contract, or in equity). *See, e.g.*, ***Farber v. Bay View Terrace Homeowners Ass'n*** (4th Dist.2006) 141 Cal.App.4th 1007, 1011 (movant awarded attorney fees in JOP as prevailing party under Civ. C. §1354).

(4) Costs. The judgment should specify the amount of costs awarded or be left blank so the costs can be determined at a later time. *See* ***Bankes***, 9 Cal.App.4th at 369; *see, e.g.*, *CEB Procedure Before Trial*, §27.30 (form for JOP); *see also* CRC 3.1700(a)(1) (serving and filing memorandum of costs after judgment). Costs are recoverable in a JOP if the costs are otherwise recoverable by law. *See* CCP §1032(b) (prevailing party entitled to costs except as otherwise provided by statute); *see, e.g.*, ***Farber***, 141 Cal.App.4th at 1011 (prevailing party recovered costs in JOP under Civ. C. §1354); *see also* CCP §1033 (describing recoverable costs).

5. Date signed. The judgment should include the date the judgment is signed. *See, e.g.*, *CEB Procedure Before Trial*, §27.30 (form for JOP).

6. Signature line. The judgment should include a signature line for the judge. *See, e.g.*, *CEB Procedure Before Trial*, §27.30 (form for JOP).

§12.3 Entry of judgment. A judgment is not effective for any purpose until it is entered by the clerk. CCP §664. In most courts, a judgment is entered when the original judgment, signed by the judge, is filed with the clerk. ***Dodge v. Superior Ct.*** (4th Dist.2000) 77 Cal.App.4th 513, 518 n.5; *see* CCP §668.5. In courts that still use judgment books, a judgment is entered by the clerk when it is copied into the judgment book. ***Dodge***, 77 Cal.App.4th at 518 n.5; *see* CCP §668.

§12.4 Notice of entry. After the judgment is entered, a notice of entry must be served on all parties who appeared in the action. CCP §664.5. Failure to serve notice does not make a judgment void, but it does extend the time to file postjudgment motions. *E.g.*, ***Avenue v. Franco*** (4th Dist.2008) 162 Cal.App.4th 1224, 1228 (extending time to file notice of appeal).

1. Form of notice. There is no required form for the notice of entry; any written notice that conveys to the losing party that judgment has been entered is sufficient. ***Dodge v. Superior Ct.*** (4th Dist.2000) 77 Cal.App.4th 513, 518. Serving the losing party with a copy of the judgment showing the date of entry is sufficient for notice purposes. *Id.*

2. Who serves notice.

(1) Clerk. The court clerk must mail the notice of entry to all parties who have appeared in the action and execute a certificate that the notice was mailed if (1) the clerk was ordered to send notice or (2) the prevailing party was not represented by counsel. *See* CCP §664.5(b), (d).

(2) Party. The party who submitted the judgment for entry must prepare and mail a copy of the notice of entry to all parties who have appeared in the action and file with the court the original notice of entry along with proof of service if (1) the clerk was not ordered to send notice and (2) the prevailing party was represented by counsel. *See* CCP §664.5(a), (d).

§13. REVIEW

§13.1 By trial court. A party can ask the trial court to review a JOP by filing a motion for new trial. ***Carney v. Simmonds*** (1957) 49 Cal.2d 84, 90-91. For a discussion of other methods that can be used to challenge a judgment at the trial-court level, see "By trial court," ch. 10-B, §17.1, p. 1142.

§13.2 By appellate court. Appellate review of a trial court's ruling on a motion for JOP is conducted in the same manner as appellate review of a demurrer. ***Camacho v. Automobile Club*** (2d Dist.2006) 142 Cal.App.4th 1394, 1398 n.4; *see* ***Smiley v. Citibank (S.D.)*** (1995) 11 Cal.4th 138, 145-46 (court independently reviews JOP), *aff'd*, (1996) 517 U.S. 735. See "Appellate Review," ch. 4-H, §12, p. 410.

J. MOTION TO STRIKE

This subchapter covers general motions to strike. This subchapter does not cover special motions to strike SLAPP suits under CCP §425.16. For a discussion of those motions, see "Special Motion to Strike—Anti-SLAPP Motion," ch. 4-K, p. 425; "Special Motion to Strike—Anti-SLAPPback Motion," ch. 4-L, p. 450. For other ways to challenge pleadings, see "Demurrer," ch. 4-H, p. 396; "Motion for Judgment on the Pleadings," ch. 4-I, p. 411.

§1. GENERAL

§1.1 Purpose. A motion to strike is used to challenge the legal sufficiency of all or part of a pleading (i.e., a complaint, cross-complaint, answer, or demurrer). *See* CCP §§435(a), (b)(1), 436, 589(b). Motions to strike are often used to challenge pleading defects that cannot be challenged by demurrer. ***CLD Constr., Inc. v. City of San Ramon*** (1st Dist.2004) 120 Cal.App.4th 1141, 1146; ***Pierson v. Sharp Mem'l Hosp., Inc.*** (4th Dist.1989) 216 Cal.App.3d 340, 342; *see* ***Caliber Bodyworks, Inc. v. Superior Ct.*** (2d Dist.2005) 134 Cal.App.4th 365, 384-85 (motion to strike, not demurrer, should be used to challenge request for improper damages or remedy); ***PH II, Inc. v. Superior Ct.*** (1st Dist.1995) 33 Cal.App.4th 1680, 1682-83 (party must file motion to strike to challenge part of cause of action because demurrer can only challenge whole cause of action).

§1.2 Primary authority. CCP §§431.10, 435-437, 472a(d), 472c(b)(3); CRC 3.1322.

§1.3 Secondary authority. The following secondary sources are cited as authority in this subchapter:

- *California Civil Procedure Before Trial* (CEB Online ed. 2014) (referred to as *CEB Procedure Before Trial*).
- Kiesel et al., *Matthew Bender Practice Guide: California Pretrial Civil Procedure* (2014) (referred to as Kiesel, *Cal. Pretrial Civil Procedure*).
- Thomas, *California Civil Courtroom Handbook* (2014) (referred to as Thomas, *Courtroom Handbook*).
- Weil & Brown, *California Practice Guide: Civil Procedure Before Trial* (CD-ROM ed. 2014) (referred to as Weil, *Civil Procedure Before Trial*).

MOTION TO STRIKE

§2. GROUNDS

§2.1 Limited civil cases. To prevail on a motion to strike in a limited civil case, the movant must establish that the damages or relief sought is not supported by the complaint. CCP §92(d); *see CEB Procedure Before Trial*, §24.5. To determine whether a case is limited or unlimited, see "Classifying civil cases," ch. 3-E, §4.2, p. 257.

§2.2 Unlimited civil cases. To prevail on a motion to strike in an unlimited civil case, the movant must establish one of the following:

1. **Irrelevant, false, or improper matter.** The movant can show that the pleading contains irrelevant, false, or improper matter. CCP §436(a). Section 436(a) can only be used to strike unnecessary or abusive allegations from a pleading, not entire causes of action or entire pleadings. ***Ferraro v. Camarlinghi*** (6th Dist.2008) 161 Cal.App.4th 509, 528.

(1) Irrelevant matter. The movant can show that the pleading contains irrelevant matter. CCP §436(a). Examples of irrelevant matter include the following:

(a) An allegation that is not essential to the statement of a claim or defense. *See id.* §431.10(b)(1), (c); ***Stafford v. Shultz*** (1954) 42 Cal.2d 767, 782.

(b) An allegation that is neither pertinent to nor supported by an otherwise sufficient claim or defense. *See* CCP §431.10(b)(2), (c).

(c) A demand for relief that is not supported by the allegations of the complaint or cross-complaint. *See id.* §431.10(b)(3), (c); *see, e.g.*, ***Greshko v. County of L.A.*** (2d Dist.1987) 194 Cal.App.3d 822, 830 (cross-complaint for indemnity against settling D was struck because issue was irrelevant after court determined settlement was made in good faith).

(d) A legal conclusion that is not supported by facts. *See* Weil, *Civil Procedure Before Trial*, ¶7:179; *see, e.g.*, ***Perkins v. Superior Ct.*** (2d Dist.1981) 117 Cal.App.3d 1, 6-7 (court did not strike words "wrongfully and intentionally," "retaliation," and "oppression, fraud, and malice" when those words were used to plead the statutes and were supported by sufficient facts).

NOTE

A claim or defense that appears to be redundant of another claim or defense is not an "irrelevant matter" for purposes of a motion to strike. See, e.g., ***Blickman Turkus, LP v. MF Downtown Sunnyvale, LLC*** *(6th Dist.2008) 162 Cal.App.4th 858, 889-90 (P could not challenge causes of action it believed were redundant because redundancy is no longer proper subject for motions to strike).*

(2) False matter. The movant can show that the pleading contains false matter. CCP §436(a); ***Garcia v. Sterling*** (2d Dist.1985) 176 Cal.App.3d 17, 21. Because extrinsic evidence cannot be used to prove falsity, motions to strike generally only challenge facts contrary to judicially noticed facts (i.e., facts that cannot be reasonably disputed). *See* CCP §437(a); ***Garcia***, 176 Cal.App.3d at 21. See "Request for Judicial Notice," ch. 5-J, p. 547.

NOTE

Section 436(a) should not be used if the movant believes the entire cause of action or pleading was a sham. For example, a complaint is a sham when it is filed to circumvent a previous court ruling. See ***Ricard v. Grobstein, Goldman, Stevenson, Siegel, LeVine & Mangel*** *(2d Dist.1992) 6 Cal.App.4th 157, 162. Instead, the movant should file a demurrer or a motion to strike under §436(b). See, e.g.,* ***Janis v. California State Lottery Comm'n*** *(2d Dist.1998) 68 Cal.App.4th 824, 829 (court could strike entire complaint when amended complaint stated same causes of action that court dismissed in previous order).*

(3) Improper matter. The movant can show that improper matter was inserted into the pleading. CCP §436(a); *see, e.g.*, ***Mercury Interactive Corp. v. Klein*** (6th Dist.2007) 158 Cal.App.4th 60, 104 n.35 (dicta; improper matter included 48 pages of exhibits and quotes and references to exhibits in body of complaint). For example, the movant can show that improper damages were requested in a complaint. *See, e.g.*, ***Pacific Gas & Elec. Co. v. Superior Ct.*** (3d Dist.2006) 144 Cal.App.4th 19, 22 (improper demand for recovery of deductible); ***Caliber Bodyworks, Inc. v. Superior Ct.*** (2d Dist.2005) 134 Cal.App.4th 365, 384-85 (improper demand for civil penalties); ***Grieves v. Superior Ct.*** (4th Dist.1984) 157 Cal.App.3d 159, 166-68 (improper demand for punitive damages).

2. Nonconformance with law, rule, or order. The movant can show that all or part of the pleading was not drafted or filed in conformity with the laws of California, a court rule, or a court order. CCP §436(b). For example, a motion to strike can be used to challenge the following:

(1) An unverified pleading that is required to be verified. ***Perlman v. Municipal Ct.*** (2d Dist.1979) 99 Cal.App.3d 568, 575; *see* Weil, *Civil Procedure Before Trial*, ¶7:174.

(2) New claims that should have been brought by compulsory cross-complaint. *See* ***Carroll v. Import Motors, Inc.*** (1st Dist.1995) 33 Cal.App.4th 1429, 1433.

(3) Claims that violate the applicable statute of limitations. ***PH II, Inc. v. Superior Ct.*** (1st Dist.1995) 33 Cal.App.4th 1680, 1682-83; *CEB Procedure Before Trial*, §24.6.

(4) An improperly filed complaint. *See* Weil, *Civil Procedure Before Trial*, ¶7:174; *see, e.g.*, ***CLD Constr., Inc. v. City of San Ramon*** (1st Dist.2004) 120 Cal.App.4th 1141, 1145 (motion to strike based on ground that corporation cannot file pleading in propria persona).

(5) Lack of subject-matter jurisdiction. ***Greener v. Workers' Comp. Appeals Bd.*** (1993) 6 Cal.4th 1028, 1036; *see* ***Velez v. Smith*** (1st Dist.2006) 142 Cal.App.4th 1154, 1160. See "Choosing the Court—Subject-Matter Jurisdiction," ch. 3-E, p. 248.

(6) A pleading filed without obtaining the required leave of court. *See* Weil, *Civil Procedure Before Trial*, ¶7:174; *see, e.g.*, ***Loney v. Superior Ct.*** (3d Dist.1984) 160 Cal.App.3d 719, 721-22 (cross-complaint filed without leave); ***Schaefer v. Berinstein*** (2d Dist.1956) 140 Cal.App.2d 278, 299 (amended complaint filed without leave). *But see* ***Lohnes v. Astron Computer Prods.*** (4th Dist.2001) 94 Cal.App.4th 1150, 1153-54 (trial court erred in striking complaint in intervention that was filed without leave because intervenor had relied on court clerk's accepted practice for complaints in intervention).

(7) An untimely pleading. ***Tuck v. Thuesen*** (5th Dist.1970) 10 Cal.App.3d 193, 196, *overruled on other grounds*, ***Neel v. Magana, Olney, Levy, Cathcart & Gelfand*** (1971) 6 Cal.3d 176; *see* Weil, *Civil Procedure Before Trial*, ¶7:174.

(8) An untimely amended pleading after a demurrer is sustained with leave to amend. CRC 3.1320(i); ***Leader v. Health Indus.*** (2d Dist.2001) 89 Cal.App.4th 603, 613.

(9) An amended pleading filed late or that otherwise violates the court's earlier ruling granting a motion for judgment on the pleadings (JOP) with leave to amend. CCP §438(i)(1)(A); *see id.* §435(e).

(10) A pleading filed without the required certificate of merit. Thomas, *Courtroom Handbook*, §11:51; *see* CCP §340.1(g) (certificate of merit required in civil actions based on childhood sexual abuse), §411.35(g) (certificate of merit required in actions for professional negligence against architects, engineers, and land surveyors).

MOTION TO STRIKE

CAUTION

Some courts of appeals disagree over the reach of §436(b). The First and Third Districts have held that a motion to strike can challenge a complaint that fails to state facts sufficient to constitute a cause of action on the ground that it is not "drawn in conformity" with the laws of California. See ***Velez****, 142 Cal.App.4th at 1161;* ***Lodi v. Lodi*** *(3d Dist.1985) 173 Cal.App.3d 628, 631; see also CEB Procedure Before Trial, §24.18 (court can strike all or part of pleading on ground that would also be basis for demurrer). The Sixth District has held that §436(b) cannot be used to challenge such defects because it only authorizes a pleading to be struck for defects in form or the procedures under which the pleading was filed. See* ***Ferraro****, 161 Cal.App.4th at 528. Until this split is reconciled, the better practice is to file a demurrer when the motion is based on failure to state a cause of action.*

§3. MOTION

§3.1 Who can file. A motion to strike can be made by a party or by the court. *See* CCP §§435(b)(1), 436.

§3.2 Deadline to file & serve.

1. Court's motion. If the court strikes all or part of a pleading on its own motion, it can do so at any time and without notice. *See* CCP §436; ***Hale v. Laden*** (2d Dist.1986) 178 Cal.App.3d 668, 673.

2. Party's motion.

(1) In response to complaint or cross-complaint. If a party files a motion to strike a complaint or cross-complaint, the motion must be filed and served before the deadline to respond to the complaint or cross-complaint—usually within 30 days after service of summons. *See* CCP §435(a), (b)(1); CRC 3.1322(b); *see also* CCP §412.20(a)(3) (written response to complaint must be filed within 30 days after service of summons).

(2) In response to answer. If a party files a motion to strike an answer, the motion must be filed and served before the deadline to respond to the answer—within ten days after service of the answer. Weil, *Civil Procedure Before Trial*, ¶7:166.1; *see* CCP §435(a)(2), (b)(1); CRC 3.1322(b); *see also* CCP §430.40(b) (demurrer to answer must be filed within ten days after service of answer).

(3) In response to demurrer. If a party files a motion to strike a demurrer, the motion must be filed and served before the deadline to respond to the demurrer—at least nine court days before the hearing on the demurrer. *See* CCP §§435(a)(2), (b)(1), 1005(b); *see also id.* §435(b)(3) (motion to strike demurrer must be heard at same time as demurrer); CRC 3.1322(b) (same).

(4) In response to amended pleading after JOP granted. If a party files a motion to strike an amended pleading and asks the court to enter judgment in its favor because the amended pleading is filed late or otherwise violates the court's earlier ruling granting a motion for JOP with leave to amend, the deadlines for filing a motion to strike do not apply. CCP §435(b)(1); *see id.* §435(e) (motion to strike can be made as part of motion to enter judgment), §438(i)(1)(A) (party can move to strike amended pleading and enter judgment).

§3.3 Contents.

1. Notice of motion & motion.

(1) Generally. A motion to strike should be requested in writing by noticed motion. *See* CRC 3.1112(a). See "Notice of motion & motion," ch. 1-D, §5.1, p. 28. In most cases, the notice of motion should designate a hearing date in the same manner as other noticed motions. *See* CCP §435(b)(2). See "Noticed motion," ch. 1-H, §4.1, p. 81. However, if the motion to strike is filed with or in response to a demurrer, the hearing on the motion must be set to coincide with the hearing on the demurrer. CCP §435(b)(3); CRC 3.1322(b). For a discussion of how far in advance of the hearing the notice of motion and motion must be filed and served, see "Motion papers," ch. 1-F, §5.2.1(2)(a), p. 57; "Retrospective deadlines," ch. 1-G, §6.2, p. 71.

(2) Relief. The notice of motion and motion must describe the relief sought. *See* CRC 3.1110(a) (notice of motion must state nature of order being sought), CRC 3.1112(d)(3) (motion must briefly state relief sought). The notice of motion should specify the matters to be struck and number them consecutively. CRC 3.1322(a); Thomas, *Courtroom Handbook*, §11:53; *see also* Kiesel, *Cal. Pretrial Civil Procedure*, §12.24 (sample notice of motion to strike). The notice of motion must quote in full the portions sought to be struck, unless the motion seeks to strike an entire paragraph, cause of action, count, or defense. CRC 3.1322(a). An entire paragraph should be referenced by its number and page within the cause of action. *CEB Procedure Before Trial*, §24.14.

(3) Grounds. The notice of motion and motion must briefly state the grounds for the relief. *See* CRC 3.1110(a) (notice of motion must state grounds for issuance of order), CRC 3.1112(d)(3) (motion must briefly state basis for motion). See "Grounds," §2, p. 418.

2. Memorandum of points & authorities. The motion must include a memorandum in support of the motion. CRC 3.1112(a)(3), 3.1113(a). See "Memorandum of points & authorities," ch. 1-D, §5.2, p. 28.

3. Supporting evidence. A court can only consider evidence that either appears on the face of the challenged pleading or is judicially noticeable. CCP §437(a); ***City & Cty. of S.F. v. Strahlendorf*** (1st Dist.1992) 7 Cal.App.4th 1911, 1913; *e.g.*, ***Velez v. Smith*** (1st Dist.2006) 142 Cal.App.4th 1154, 1161-62 (court did not err when it refused to hear testimony). See "Request for Judicial Notice," ch. 5-J, p. 547. In other words, a movant cannot support its motion with extrinsic evidence (i.e., evidence that is not already part of the record). Weil, *Civil Procedure*

Before Trial, ¶7:169; *see* ***Velez***, 142 Cal.App.4th at 1161-62; *see, e.g.*, ***Circle Star Ctr. Assocs. v. Liberate Techs.*** (1st Dist.2007) 147 Cal.App.4th 1203, 1211 (court erred in striking allegations supporting claim for attorney fees because court would have to consult extrinsic evidence to determine challenge); ***City & Cty. of S.F.***, 7 Cal.App.4th at 1913 (court could not grant motion to strike based on evidence in particular affidavit). If the movant attempts to use extrinsic evidence, the court can either dismiss the motion or treat it as a motion for summary judgment. ***City & Cty. of S.F.***, 7 Cal.App.4th at 1913-14.

4. Request for judicial notice. A motion to strike based on a judicially noticed matter must specify that matter in either the notice of motion or the memorandum of points and authorities, unless the court allows otherwise. CCP §437(b). A separate request for judicial notice must also be filed. CRC 3.1113(*l*). See "Request for Judicial Notice," ch. 5-J, p. 547.

5. Proposed order. The movant can submit a proposed order with the motion. *See* CRC 3.1113(m). If a proposed order is submitted, it must be lodged and served with the motion papers, not attached to them. *Id.* See "Documents lodged," ch. 1-F, §2.3, p. 47.

§3.4 Filing fees. When the motion is filed, the movant must pay a filing fee to the court clerk or request a waiver of the fee. See "Filing Fees," ch. 1-F, §7, p. 58.

§3.5 Motion to strike filed with other challenges.

1. With answer. A motion to strike can be filed simultaneously with an answer. Kiesel, *Cal. Pretrial Civil Procedure*, §12.07. Filing a motion to strike with an answer may be appropriate when the motion to strike is only targeting part of the complaint. *Id.*

NOTE

If a party does not file an answer with its motion to strike, the court must give the party time to file an answer if the motion to strike is denied. CCP §472a(d).

---

2. With demurrer. A motion to strike can be filed simultaneously with a demurrer. Kiesel, *Cal. Pretrial Civil Procedure*, §12.07. See "With motion to strike," ch. 4-H, §4.5.2, p. 405.

3. With challenges waived by general appearance. A motion to strike can be filed simultaneously with a motion to quash, a motion to dismiss for forum non conveniens, or a motion to dismiss for delay in prosecution. *See* CCP §418.10(e). If a party files a general motion to strike before filing these motions, the party will have made a general appearance and waived its right to raise the issues of lack of personal jurisdiction, inadequacy of process, inadequacy of service of process, forum non conveniens, and delay in prosecution. *See id.* §§418.10(e)(3), 1014.

§3.6 Effect of motion.

1. On making general appearance. A party who files a motion to strike makes a general appearance in the action. CCP §1014. See "General appearance," ch. 3-G, §5.1.1, p. 285. To preserve challenges that can be waived by making a general appearance, the motion to strike should be filed simultaneously with those challenges. *See* CCP §418.10(e). See "With challenges waived by general appearance," §3.5.3, this page.

2. On time to demur. Making a motion to strike all or part of a complaint, cross-complaint, or answer does not extend the moving party's time to demur. CCP §435(d).

3. On time to answer. Making a motion to strike all or part of a complaint or cross-complaint without demurring automatically extends the moving party's time to answer. CCP §435(c).

4. On default judgment. Making a motion to strike all or part of a complaint or cross-complaint prevents the entry of a default against the moving party while the motion is pending, except as allowed by CCP §§585 and 586. CCP §435(c). See "Default Judgment," ch. 10-A, p. 1089.

§4. RESPONSE

§4.1 Amend pleadings. If the opposing party agrees with the motion to strike, it should respond to the motion by amending the challenged pleading. See "Procedure for amending," ch. 3-C, §6.2, p. 229.

§4.2 Opposition. If the opposing party does not agree with the motion to strike, it should file opposition papers, including a memorandum in opposition to the motion, to negate the movant's grounds for relief. *See* ***Velez v. Smith*** (1st Dist.2006) 142 Cal.App.4th 1154, 1160; ***Garcia v. Sterling*** (2d Dist.1985) 176 Cal.App.3d 17, 20. Opposition papers must be filed and served at least nine court days before the hearing. *See* CCP §1005(b). See "Opposition Papers," ch. 1-D, §8, p. 35.

§5. HEARING

Hearings on a motion to strike are conducted in the same manner as civil hearings generally. *See* ***Velez v. Smith*** (1st Dist.2006) 142 Cal.App.4th 1154, 1162 (court not required to grant leave to present oral testimony). For a discussion of hearings generally, see "Hearings," ch. 1-H, p. 79.

§6. RULING

The court has broad discretion in ruling on a motion to strike. ***Clements v. T.R. Bechtel Co.*** (1954) 43 Cal.2d 227, 242. When making its ruling, the court should (1) read the allegations of the challenged pleading as a whole, (2) read each allegation in context, and (3) assume the allegations are true. ***Clauson v. Superior Ct.*** (2d Dist.1998) 67 Cal.App.4th 1253, 1255; *see also* CCP §452 (allegations in pleadings should be liberally construed).

NOTE

If the movant files a motion to strike when it should have filed another motion (such as a demurrer), the court may overlook the defect and treat the motion as if it were properly designated. See Weil, Civil Procedure Before Trial, ¶7:158.2; see, e.g., ***Ferraro v. Camarlinghi*** *(6th Dist.2008) 161 Cal.App.4th 509, 529 (court treated motion to strike as general demurrer because motion was brought for failure to state cause of action);* ***City & Cty. of S.F. v. Strahlendorf*** *(1st Dist.1992) 7 Cal.App.4th 1911, 1913-14 (court treated motion to strike as motion for summary judgment because it was brought on grounds outside pleadings).*

---

§7. ORDER

§7.1 Form. The court's ruling on the motion to strike must be recorded either in writing or by minute order. See "Record of Ruling," ch. 1-I, §4, p. 90.

§7.2 Contents.

1. Denies motion. If the court denies a motion to strike a complaint or cross-complaint and no answer has been filed, the court should specify a deadline for filing and serving an answer. *See* CCP §472a(d) (court must permit party to file answer if motion denied); *see also* Kiesel, *Cal. Pretrial Civil Procedure*, §12.25 (sample order denying motion to strike).

2. Grants motion.

(1) Generally. If the court grants the motion, it should specify what has been struck (i.e., the entire pleading or specific parts of the pleading), whether leave to amend is granted, and the deadline for the amendment if leave is granted. *See* Kiesel, *Cal. Pretrial Civil Procedure*, §12.25 (sample order granting motion to strike); *see, e.g.,* ***Chinn v. KMR Prop. Mgmt.*** (2d Dist.2008) 166 Cal.App.4th 175, 180 (court allowed ten days to amend complaint).

(a) Leave to amend granted. Leave to amend should be granted if the defect is reasonably capable of being cured. ***CLD Constr., Inc. v. City of San Ramon*** (1st Dist.2004) 120 Cal.App.4th 1141, 1146; ***Vaccaro v. Kaiman*** (2d Dist.1998) 63 Cal.App.4th 761, 768. As a condition of granting leave, the court can impose any

terms it deems proper on the opposing party. CCP §472a(d). For example, the court can order the opposing party to pay the moving party's expenses in bringing the motion to strike. ***Vaccaro***, 63 Cal.App.4th at 769.

NOTE

Depending on how much material is struck, the court may mark the pleading with interlineations and initial the changes rather than have the party file an amended pleading. Thomas, Courtroom Handbook, §11:56.

(b) Leave to amend denied. Leave to amend should be denied only when the defect is not reasonably capable of being cured. *See **CLD Constr.***, 120 Cal.App.4th at 1146; *see, e.g.*, ***Greshko v. County of L.A.*** (2d Dist.1987) 194 Cal.App.3d 822, 830 (court properly struck one D's cross-complaint for indemnity against another D without leave to amend when indemnity was not available).

(2) When demurrer struck. If the court grants a motion to strike a demurrer and no answer has been filed, the court should specify a deadline for filing and serving an answer. *See* CCP §472a(c) (court must permit party to file answer if motion striking demurrer is granted); *see also* Kiesel, *Cal. Pretrial Civil Procedure*, §12.25 (sample order granting motion to strike). The court can impose terms that are just on the filing of the answer. CCP §472a(c).

§7.3 Notice of order. For a discussion of giving notice of the order, see "Notice of Order," ch. 1-I, §5, p. 93.

§7.4 Effect of order.

1. Granted with leave to amend.

(1) Complaint or cross-complaint. When a court grants a motion to strike all of a complaint or cross-complaint with leave to amend and the plaintiff does not timely amend, the court can dismiss the action after the defendant has filed a motion to dismiss. CCP §581(f)(4).

(2) Answer. When a court grants a motion to strike all or part of an answer with leave to amend, the plaintiff can seek a default judgment if the defendant does not timely amend. *See* CCP §586(a)(7). See "Default Judgment," ch. 10-A, p. 1089.

2. Granted without leave to amend.

(1) Complaint or cross-complaint. When a court grants a motion to strike all of a complaint or cross-complaint without leave to amend, the court can dismiss the action after the defendant has filed a motion to dismiss. CCP §581(f)(3). See "Motion to Strike – Without Leave to Amend," ch. 10-F, §4, p. 1181.

(2) Answer. When a court grants a motion to strike all of an answer without leave to amend, the plaintiff can seek a default judgment. *See* CCP §586(a)(7). See "Default Judgment," ch. 10-A, p. 1089.

§8. APPELLATE REVIEW

§8.1 Writ of mandate. An order granting or denying a motion to strike can be reviewed by writ of mandate. *See, e.g.*, ***Evans v. Superior Ct.*** (2d Dist.1977) 67 Cal.App.3d 162, 171-72 (writ issued ordering court to strike cross-complaint); ***Ford Motor Co. v. Superior Ct.*** (2d Dist.1971) 16 Cal.App.3d 442, 449 (writ issued ordering court to reinstate affirmative defenses that were struck).

§8.2 Direct appeal.

1. When appealable.

(1) Order denying motion. An order denying a motion to strike is not subject to appellate review until a final judgment is entered. *See* CCP §904.1 (listing orders that are directly appealable in unlimited civil cases), §904.2 (listing orders that are directly appealable in limited civil cases), §906 (discussing court's power to review interlocutory orders that are not otherwise appealable).

(2) Order granting motion. An order granting a motion to strike is not subject to appellate review until a final judgment is entered unless it leaves no issue to be determined for one party (e.g., strikes the entire complaint, strikes intervenor's complaint in intervention). ***Timberidge Enters. v. City of Santa Rosa*** (1st Dist.1978) 86 Cal.App.3d 873, 878; *see* ***Wilson v. Sharp*** (1954) 42 Cal.2d 675, 677 (order on motion to strike is appealable if it leaves no issue to be determined for one party); ***Watts v. Valley Med. Ctr.*** (5th Dist.1992) 8 Cal.App.4th 1050, 1057 (order on motion to strike affirmative defense is not appealable until final judgment); *see, e.g.*, ***Herrscher v. Herrscher*** (1953) 41 Cal.2d 300, 303-04 (order striking entire cross-complaint in which parties were not identical to those in original action was directly appealable); ***Kuperman v. Great Republic Life Ins.*** (2d Dist.1987) 195 Cal.App.3d 943, 946-47 (order striking entire complaint was appealable); *see also* CCP §904.1 (listing orders that are directly appealable in unlimited civil cases), §904.2 (listing orders that are directly appealable in limited civil cases).

NOTE

A party does not waive its right to challenge an order striking part of its pleading by filing an amended pleading. See CCP §472c(b)(3), (c).

2. Standard of review. Generally, a trial court's ruling on a motion to strike is reviewed for abuse of discretion. ***Price v. Starbucks Corp.*** (2d Dist.2011) 192 Cal.App.4th 1136, 1141; ***Pacific Gas & Elec. Co. v. Superior Ct.*** (3d Dist.2006) 144 Cal.App.4th 19, 23; ***Quiroz v. Seventh Ave. Ctr.*** (6th Dist.2006) 140 Cal.App.4th 1256, 1282; *see* CCP §436. A ruling striking a request for punitive damages, however, is reviewed de novo. ***Clauson v. Superior Ct.*** (2d Dist.1998) 67 Cal.App.4th 1253, 1255; ***Angie M. v. Superior Ct.*** (4th Dist.1995) 37 Cal.App.4th 1217, 1223.

K. SPECIAL MOTION TO STRIKE—ANTI-SLAPP MOTION

§1. GENERAL

§1.1 Purpose. A special motion to strike under CCP §425.16 is used to strike a meritless cause of action that seeks to chill a defendant's exercise of its constitutional right of free speech or petition for the redress of grievances in connection with a public issue. *See* CCP §425.16(a), (b)(1); ***Club Members for an Honest Election v. Sierra Club*** (2008) 45 Cal.4th 309, 315; ***Rusheen v. Cohen*** (2006) 37 Cal.4th 1048, 1055-56. A cause of action that seeks to chill these constitutional rights is referred to as a "SLAPP" action (strategic lawsuit against public participation), and the motion used to strike such an action is referred to as an "anti-SLAPP motion." Kiesel et al., *Matthew Bender Practice Guide: California Pretrial Civil Procedure* (2014), §13.02. Anti-SLAPP motions allow defendants to seek early dismissals of meritless SLAPPs. ***Club Members***, 45 Cal.4th at 315; Kiesel, *Cal. Pretrial Civil Procedure*, §13.02; *see* Weil & Brown, *California Practice Guide: Civil Procedure Before Trial* (CD-ROM ed. 2014), ¶7:500.

NOTE

Anti-SLAPP motions under CCP §425.16 can also be asserted to strike state-law claims in federal court that qualify as SLAPP actions. See ***Makaeff v. Trump Univ., LLC*** *(9th Cir.2013) 736 F.3d 1180, 1187; see, e.g.,* ***New.net, Inc. v. Lavasoft*** *(C.D.Cal.2004) 356 F.Supp.2d 1090, 1099-1100 (D properly directed its anti-SLAPP motion only at pendant state-law claims). Anti-SLAPP motions cannot, however, be used in a manner that conflicts with the Federal Rules.* ***Rogers v. Home Shopping Network, Inc.*** *(C.D.Cal.1999) 57 F.Supp.2d 973, 983. For example, the discovery-limiting aspects of CCP §425.16(f) and (g) do not apply in federal court if the anti-SLAPP motion is similar to a motion for summary judgment under FRCP 56 (e.g., motion alleges P lacks evidence) because FRCP 56 encourages discovery.* ***Rogers****, 57 F.Supp.2d at 982-83.*

§1.2 Primary authority. CCP §§425.16-425.18.

§1.3 Secondary authority. The following secondary sources are cited as authority in this subchapter:

- *Action Guide: Making & Opposing Special Motions to Strike Under the California Anti-SLAPP Statute* (CEB 2014) (referred to as *CEB Action Guide: Making & Opposing Special Motions to Strike*).
- Kiesel et al., *Matthew Bender Practice Guide: California Pretrial Civil Procedure* (2014) (referred to as Kiesel, *Cal. Pretrial Civil Procedure*).
- Weil & Brown, *California Practice Guide: Civil Procedure Before Trial* (CD-ROM ed. 2014) (referred to as Weil, *Civil Procedure Before Trial*).

§2. DEFENDANT'S BURDEN

To prevail on an anti-SLAPP motion, the defendant must make a prima facie showing that a cause of action asserted by the plaintiff arises from an act in furtherance of the defendant's constitutional right of free speech or petition as defined by CCP §425.16—the anti-SLAPP statute. *See* CCP §425.16(b)(1), (e); ***Rusheen v. Cohen*** (2006) 37 Cal.4th 1048, 1056; ***Navellier v. Sletten*** (2002) 29 Cal.4th 82, 87-88. To meet its burden, the defendant must show that (1) the plaintiff's complaint alleges activity that is constitutionally protected under the anti-SLAPP statute and (2) the plaintiff's cause of action arises from that protected activity. *See* ***Haight Ashbury Free Clinics, Inc. v. Happening House Ventures*** (1st Dist.2010) 184 Cal.App.4th 1539, 1547. Once the defendant has made the required showing, the burden shifts to the plaintiff to establish that it has a probability of prevailing on its cause of action. *Id.*; ***Cohen v. Brown*** (2d Dist.2009) 173 Cal.App.4th 302, 315; *see* CCP §425.16(b)(1). See "P can probably prevail," §4.4.2(4), p. 440.

NOTE

Unlike a general motion to strike, an anti-SLAPP motion can only be brought by the defendant. Compare CCP §425.16 (anti-SLAPP motion) with id. §435 (general motion to strike). See "Motion to Strike," ch. 4-J, p. 418.

§2.1 Protected acts. To meet its burden under the anti-SLAPP statute, the defendant must show that the plaintiff's complaint alleges acts that were performed in furtherance of the defendant's constitutional right of free speech or petition in connection with a public issue. ***Coretronic Corp. v. O'Connor*** (2d Dist.2011) 192 Cal.App.4th 1381, 1388; ***Haight Ashbury Free Clinics, Inc. v. Happening House Ventures*** (1st Dist.2010) 184 Cal.App.4th 1539, 1547; *see* CCP §425.16(b)(1); ***Flatley v. Mauro*** (2006) 39 Cal.4th 299, 311-12. Under this threshold determination, the defendant does not need to prove that the activity targeted by the plaintiff's cause of action is in fact constitutionally protected. ***Navellier v. Sletten*** (2002) 29 Cal.4th 82, 94-95; ***Haight Ashbury***, 184 Cal.App.4th at 1548. *Contra* ***D.C. v. R.R.*** (2d Dist.2010) 182 Cal.App.4th 1190, 1217-18 (if D's statement or writing threatens bodily harm, D must establish as threshold issue that speech was constitutionally protected). The defendant need only establish that the activity falls within the scope of constitutional activity protected by the anti-SLAPP statute. ***Haight Ashbury***, 184 Cal.App.4th at 1549; *see* ***Navellier***, 29 Cal.4th at 95. The act performed, however, must have been legal; if the defendant concedes that its act was illegal or the evidence conclusively establishes that the act was illegal as a matter of law, the defendant will not meet its burden. ***Flatley***, 39 Cal.4th at 320. See "D's act illegal," §4.4.2(3)(a)[2], p. 440. The acts that fall within the protection of the anti-SLAPP statute are the following:

1. Statement or writing made in official proceeding. A written or oral statement or a writing is a protected act if it is made by the defendant before any of the official proceedings listed below. *See* CCP §425.16(b)(1), (e)(1). The term "before" requires that the statement or writing be submitted to or presented in the proceeding at issue. ***Xi Zhao v. Wong*** (1st Dist.1996) 48 Cal.App.4th 1114, 1125, *disapproved on other grounds*, ***Briggs v. Eden Council for Hope & Opportunity*** (1999) 19 Cal.4th 1106; *see, e.g.*, ***Hansen v. Dept. of Corr. & Rehab.*** (5th

Dist.2008) 171 Cal.App.4th 1537, 1544 (affidavit submitted to court in support of search warrant was protected under anti-SLAPP statute). The defendant is not required to show that the statement or writing concerns an issue of public interest; it is presumed that any matter before an official proceeding has some public significance. *See* ***Briggs v. Eden Council for Hope & Opportunity*** (1999) 19 Cal.4th 1106, 1117-18. The official proceedings that the statement or writing must be made before are the following:

(1) Judicial proceeding. A statement or writing is a protected act if it is made before a judicial proceeding. *See* CCP §425.16(b)(1), (e)(1). For example, written documents filed with a court, such as a complaint, answer, motion, declaration, or affidavit, are protected. *See, e.g.*, ***Navellier***, 29 Cal.4th at 90 (counterclaim filed in federal court was statement or writing made before judicial proceeding); ***Hansen***, 171 Cal.App.4th at 1544 (search-warrant affidavit was writing made before judicial proceeding); ***Jespersen v. Zubiate-Beauchamp*** (2d Dist.2003) 114 Cal.App.4th 624, 629 (declaration filed in court was written statement made before judicial proceeding). A court filing that results in a claim for attorney malpractice, however, may not be protected. See "Attorney-malpractice action," §2.2.3, p. 434.

NOTE

Courts often look to the litigation privilege as an aid in determining the scope of protection under the anti-SLAPP statute. ***Flatley****, 39 Cal.4th at 322-23. The litigation privilege provides immunity from tort liability for communications made in a judicial proceeding or other official proceeding. See Civ. C. §47(b);* ***Rusheen v. Cohen*** *(2006) 37 Cal.4th 1048, 1057. But the litigation privilege and the anti-SLAPP statute are not identical, and they may not offer the same protections.* ***Flatley****, 39 Cal.4th at 323-24; e.g.,* ***Jarrow Formulas, Inc. v. LaMarche*** *(2003) 31 Cal.4th 728, 736-37 (although malicious-prosecution claims are exempt from litigation privilege, they are not exempt from anti-SLAPP statute);* ***Lefebvre v. Lefebvre*** *(2d Dist.2011) 199 Cal.App.4th 696, 704-05 (although some illegal acts may be privileged under litigation privilege, illegal acts are not protected under anti-SLAPP statute).*

(2) Legislative or executive proceeding. A statement or writing is a protected act if it is made before a legislative or executive proceeding. *See* CCP §425.16(b)(1), (e)(1); *see, e.g.*, ***Vargas v. City of Salinas*** (2009) 46 Cal.4th 1, 19 (slide presentations, reports, and flyer presented in local legislative proceeding of city council were protected).

(3) Other official proceeding. A statement or writing is a protected act if it is made before other official proceedings authorized by law. *See* CCP §425.16(b)(1), (e)(1). These proceedings are limited to (1) quasi-judicial proceedings that are part of a comprehensive statutory licensing scheme and subject to judicial review by administrative mandate and (2) proceedings established by statute to address a particular type of dispute. ***Century 21 Chamberlain & Assocs. v. Haberman*** (4th Dist.2009) 173 Cal.App.4th 1, 9.

(a) Official proceeding. Courts have found that the following are "other official proceedings" under the anti-SLAPP statute:

[1] Hospital peer-review proceedings. ***Kibler v. Northern Inyo Cty. Local Hosp. Dist.*** (2006) 39 Cal.4th 192, 199.

[2] Internal investigation conducted by the California Department of Corrections and Rehabilitation. ***Hansen***, 171 Cal.App.4th at 1544.

[3] State Bar-sponsored fee-arbitration proceeding. ***Philipson & Simon v. Gulsvig*** (4th Dist.2007) 154 Cal.App.4th 347, 358.

[4] State Board of Podiatric Medicine proceedings. ***Carver v. Bonds*** (1st Dist.2005) 135 Cal.App.4th 328, 350.

ANTI-SLAPP MOTION

(b) Not official proceeding. Courts have found that the following are not "other official proceedings" under the anti-SLAPP statute:

[1] Private, contractual arbitration. ***Century 21 Chamberlain***, 173 Cal.App.4th at 8-9.

[2] Nonjudicial foreclosure. *See* ***Garretson v. Post*** (4th Dist.2007) 156 Cal.App.4th 1508, 1520-21.

[3] Board-of-directors meeting by a nonprofit charity. ***Donovan v. Dan Murphy Found.*** (2d Dist.2012) 204 Cal.App.4th 1500, 1508.

[4] Homeowners' association meetings. ***Talega Maint. Corp. v. Standard Pac. Corp.*** (4th Dist.2014) 225 Cal.App.4th 722, 732.

2. Statement or writing made in connection with official proceeding. A written or oral statement or a writing is a protected act if it is made by the defendant in connection with an issue under consideration or review by a legislative, executive, or judicial body or any other official proceeding authorized by law. *See* CCP §425.16(b)(1), (e)(2); *see, e.g.*, ***GeneThera, Inc. v. Troy & Gould P.C.*** (2d Dist.2009) 171 Cal.App.4th 901, 907-08 (letter to opposing counsel extending settlement offer was protected under anti-SLAPP statute). The defendant is not required to show that the statement or writing concerns an issue of public interest; it is presumed that any matter before an official proceeding has some public significance. *See* ***Briggs***, 19 Cal.4th at 1117-18.

(1) In connection with. Statements or writings are made "in connection with" an issue under consideration or review if they are reasonably related to the issue. *See* ***Neville v. Chudacoff*** (2d Dist.2008) 160 Cal.App.4th 1255, 1266 ("reasonable relevancy" requirement under litigation privilege is analogous to "in connection" requirement). The statement or writing must be related to the substantive issues in the pending or anticipated litigation and must be directed to a person having some interest in the litigation. *See* ***City of Costa Mesa v. D'Alessio Invs.*** (4th Dist.2013) 214 Cal.App.4th 358, 373; ***Seltzer v. Barnes*** (1st Dist.2010) 182 Cal.App.4th 953, 962; ***Neville***, 160 Cal.App.4th at 1266.

(a) Pending litigation. Statements or writings made in connection with the issues in pending litigation are protected. ***Neville***, 160 Cal.App.4th at 1268; *see, e.g.*, ***GeneThera, Inc.***, 171 Cal.App.4th at 907-08 (letter to opposing counsel extending settlement offer was protected under anti-SLAPP statute).

(b) Anticipated litigation. Statements or writings made in preparation for anticipated litigation are protected if they concern the subject of the dispute and are made in anticipation of litigation contemplated in good faith and under serious consideration. ***Neville***, 160 Cal.App.4th at 1268; *see* ***Briggs***, 19 Cal.4th at 1115; *see, e.g.*, ***Lunada Biomedical v. Nunez*** (2d Dist.2014) 230 Cal.App.4th 459, 472 (notice and demand under California Legal Remedies Act and letter sent by D's attorney to propose settlement of anticipated litigation were protected under anti-SLAPP statute); ***Hansen***, 171 Cal.App.4th at 1544 (investigative reports by Department of Corrections were protected under anti-SLAPP statute even though criminal proceeding was never commenced). For example, submission of an insurance claim—although generally not protected—can be protected if the claim was submitted because it was a prerequisite to expected litigation or the equivalent of a prelitigation demand letter. ***People v. Anapol*** (2d Dist.2012) 211 Cal.App.4th 809, 827.

(2) Under consideration or review. An issue is "under consideration or review" if it is (1) kept before the mind, (2) given attentive thought, reflection, or meditation, or (3) subject to an inspection or examination. ***City of Costa Mesa***, 214 Cal.App.4th at 373; ***Maranatha Corr., LLC v. Department of Corr. & Rehab.*** (3d Dist.2008) 158 Cal.App.4th 1075, 1085; ***Braun v. Chronicle Publ'g*** (1st Dist.1997) 52 Cal.App.4th 1036, 1049. Statements or writings that are related to the proceeding itself and not the issues under consideration or review are not protected. *See, e.g.*, ***Blackburn v. Brady*** (4th Dist.2004) 116 Cal.App.4th 670, 677 (written bid and oral statements about bid at sheriff's auction were not protected; although auction stemmed from conclusion of litigation, auction itself was not under consideration or review); ***Paul v. Friedman*** (2d Dist.2002) 95 Cal.App.4th 853, 868 (attorney's disclosures to P's clients of P's personal information that was unrelated to claims in arbitration proceeding were not protected).

3. Statement or writing made in public forum. A written or oral statement or a writing is a protected act if it is made by the defendant in a place open to the public or a public forum and if it is in connection with an issue of public interest. *See* CCP §425.16(b)(1), (e)(3); *see, e.g.*, ***Maranatha Corr.***, 158 Cal.App.4th at 1086 (letter sent to newspaper accusing private prison contractor of misappropriating funds was protected); ***Seelig v. Infinity Broad. Corp.*** (1st Dist.2002) 97 Cal.App.4th 798, 807-08 (oral statements made during radio program about participant in reality television show were protected).

(1) Open to public or public forum. The statement or writing must be made in a place open to the public or a public forum. CCP §425.16(e)(3). A "public forum" is a place open to the use of the general public for purposes of assembly, communicating thoughts between citizens, and discussing public questions. ***Kurwa v. Harrington, Foxx, Dubrow & Canter, LLP*** (2d Dist.2007) 146 Cal.App.4th 841, 846; ***Weinberg v. Feisel*** (3d Dist.2003) 110 Cal.App.4th 1122, 1130. For example, public streets, sidewalks, and parks have traditionally been considered public forums. ***Xi Zhao***, 48 Cal.App.4th at 1126; *see* ***Huntingdon Life Sci., Inc. v. Stop Huntingdon Animal Cruelty USA, Inc.*** (4th Dist.2005) 129 Cal.App.4th 1228, 1247. But a public forum is not limited to a specific physical setting. ***Maranatha Corr.***, 158 Cal.App.4th at 1086. A public forum can also include means of communication, such as websites, newspapers, and magazines. *See* ***Nygård, Inc. v. Uusi-Kerttula*** (2d Dist.2008) 159 Cal.App.4th 1027, 1038. Courts disagree on the factors that determine whether a particular means of communication will be considered a public forum. *See id.* at 1037. Some courts have focused on whether a sufficient size of the public has a right to access the communication, while other courts have focused on whether the public has a right to access and comment on the communication. Means of communication that courts have addressed include the following:

(a) Websites. *See* ***Barrett v. Rosenthal*** (2006) 40 Cal.4th 33, 41 n.4 (websites accessible to general public are public forums); ***Kronemyer v. Internet Movie Database, Inc.*** (2d Dist.2007) 150 Cal.App.4th 941, 950 (same); ***Vogel v. Felice*** (6th Dist.2005) 127 Cal.App.4th 1006, 1015 (same); *see, e.g.*, ***Huntingdon Life Sci.***, 129 Cal.App.4th at 1247 (website that was accessible to general public was public forum); ***Wilbanks v. Wolk*** (1st Dist.2004) 121 Cal.App.4th 883, 896-97 (website that was accessible to general public but did not permit public comment was public forum).

(b) Internet chat rooms. *See, e.g.*, ***ComputerXpress, Inc. v. Jackson*** (4th Dist.2001) 93 Cal.App.4th 993, 1007 (Internet chat room that was accessible to general public free of charge and permitted public to read and post information freely was public forum).

(c) Newspapers. *See* ***Nygård, Inc.***, 159 Cal.App.4th at 1038-39 (newspaper that can be purchased and read by members of public but does not permit public comment is public forum); *see, e.g.*, ***Maranatha Corr.***, 158 Cal.App.4th at 1086 (local newspapers—Sacramento Bee and Victor Valley Daily Press—were public forums); ***Annette F. v. Sharon S.*** (4th Dist.2004) 119 Cal.App.4th 1146, 1161 (local newspaper—Gay and Lesbian Times of San Diego—was public forum; news publication that is vehicle for discussion of public issues and distributed to large and interested community is public forum); ***Xi Zhao***, 48 Cal.App.4th at 1131 (local newspaper—San Jose Mercury News—was not public forum); ***Lafayette Morehouse, Inc. v. Chronicle Publ'g*** (1st Dist.1995) 37 Cal.App.4th 855, 863 n.5 (dicta; newspapers in which content is controlled are not public forums).

(d) Magazines. *See* ***Nygård, Inc.***, 159 Cal.App.4th at 1039 (magazine that can be purchased and read by members of public is public forum regardless of whether magazine permits public comment).

(e) Newsletters. *See, e.g.*, ***Weinberg***, 110 Cal.App.4th at 1131 & n.4 (private newsletter that reached 700 members of collectors' association was not public forum); ***Damon v. Ocean Hills Journalism Club*** (4th Dist.2000) 85 Cal.App.4th 468, 476-77 (homeowners' association newsletter that reached 3,000 residents was public forum).

(f) Television broadcasts. *See, e.g.*, ***Metabolife Int'l v. Wornick*** (S.D.Cal.1999) 72 F.Supp.2d 1160, 1165 (widely disseminated television broadcast was public forum), *rev'd in part on other grounds*, (2001) 264 F.3d 832.

(g) Homeowners' association board meetings. *See, e.g.*, ***Cabrera v. Alam*** (4th Dist.2011) 197 Cal.App.4th 1077, 1087-88 (homeowners' association board meeting that was open to all homeowners and authorized representatives of homeowners was public forum).

(2) Issue of public interest. The statement or writing must be in connection with an issue of public interest. CCP §425.16(e)(3). Section 425.16 does not define the term "public interest." ***D.C.***, 182 Cal.App.4th at 1214. The courts of appeal have developed two approaches for determining whether a statement or writing is in connection with an issue of public interest.

(a) Principles of public interest. Several courts of appeal have applied First Amendment principles to determine if a statement or writing concerns a public interest under the anti-SLAPP statute. The principles are the same ones used by the U.S. Supreme Court to determine if speech concerns a public issue under the First Amendment. *See* ***Weinberg***, 110 Cal.App.4th at 1132-33 (citing U.S. Supreme Court opinions as support for each principle). The principles are as follows:

[1] A public interest must be more than a mere curiosity. ***Hailstone v. Martinez*** (5th Dist.2008) 169 Cal.App.4th 728, 736; ***Weinberg***, 110 Cal.App.4th at 1132.

CAUTION

The court in ***Weinberg*** *cited* ***Time, Inc. v. Firestone*** *(1976) 424 U.S. 448, 454-55, for the proposition that a public interest has to be something more than a mere curiosity.* ***Weinberg****, 110 Cal.App.4th at 1132. The U.S. Supreme Court in* ***Firestone*** *held that a divorce action involving a wealthy industrial family may have piqued the public's interest but it was not a public controversy under the First Amendment.* ***Firestone****, 424 U.S. at 454. A recent opinion from the Ninth Circuit Court of Appeals speculated that* ***Weinberg****'s adoption of* ***Firestone****'s holding suggests that a private controversy, even between famous individuals, is not enough to place the controversy within the public's interest.* ***Hilton v. Hallmark Cards*** *(9th Cir.2010) 599 F.3d 894, 907. The Ninth Circuit recognized that this particular viewpoint is in conflict with* ***Nygård, Inc. v. Uusi-Kerttula*** *(2d Dist.2008) 159 Cal.App.4th 1027, which held that an issue of public interest is "any issue" in which the public is interested.* ***Hilton****, 599 F.3d at 907 n.10; see* ***Nygård, Inc.****, 159 Cal.App.4th at 1042.*

[2] A matter of public interest should be something of concern to a substantial number of people. ***Rivera v. First DataBank, Inc.*** (4th Dist.2010) 187 Cal.App.4th 709, 716; ***Hailstone***, 169 Cal.App.4th at 736; ***Weinberg***, 110 Cal.App.4th at 1132. A matter of concern to only the speaker and a relatively small, specific audience is not a matter of public interest. ***Rivera***, 187 Cal.App.4th at 716; ***Hailstone***, 169 Cal.App.4th at 736; ***Weinberg***, 110 Cal.App.4th at 1132.

[3] A matter of public interest is not limited to political or community issues. ***Nygård, Inc.***, 159 Cal.App.4th at 1044; *see* ***Navellier***, 29 Cal.4th at 91 (noting its rejection of interpretation that anti-SLAPP statute only protects speech that pertains to heart of self-government); ***Church of Scientology v. Wollersheim*** (2d Dist.1996) 42 Cal.App.4th 628, 650 (matters of public interest include not just legislative and governmental activities, but activities that involve private persons and entities, especially when it can affect lives of many individuals), *disapproved on other grounds*, ***Equilon Enters. v. Consumer Cause, Inc.*** (2002) 29 Cal.4th 53; ***Hilton***, 599 F.3d at 905 (D's activity need not involve questions of civic concern; social or even lowbrow topics may suffice).

[4] There should be a degree of closeness between the challenged statement and the asserted public interest; the assertion of a broad and amorphous public interest is not sufficient. ***Rivera***, 187 Cal.App.4th at 716; ***Hailstone***, 169 Cal.App.4th at 736; ***Weinberg***, 110 Cal.App.4th at 1132; *see* ***D.C.***, 182 Cal.App.4th at 1216. For example, in ***World Fin. Grp. v. HBW Ins. & Fin. Servs.*** (2d Dist.2009) 172 Cal.App.4th 1561, 1569, the defendants argued that their efforts in trying to lure employees away from a competitor were protected activity because the pursuit of lawful employment, workforce mobility, and free competition are matters of public interest and protected public policy. The court held that focusing on society's general interest in the subject matter of the conduct instead of

the specific conduct in dispute was not sufficient to establish a public interest. ***World Fin.***, 172 Cal.App.4th at 1570 (one could identify strong public interest in vindication of any legal right); *see also* ***Dyer v. Childress*** (2d Dist.2007) 147 Cal.App.4th 1273, 1279-80 (Ds argued that speech in movie was protected because it addressed issues facing Generation X; court held speech in question was not protected because it was limited to portrayal of P's persona); ***Mann v. Quality Old Time Serv.*** (4th Dist.2004) 120 Cal.App.4th 90, 111 (Ds argued that speech was protected because pollution is matter of public interest; court held speech in question was not protected because it did not concern pollution or public health in general, but only P's specific business practices); ***Consumer Justice Ctr. v. Trimedica Int'l*** (4th Dist.2003) 107 Cal.App.4th 595, 601 (Ds argued that speech was protected because herbal dietary supplements are matter of public interest; court held speech in question was not protected because it only concerned effectiveness of one product).

[5] The focus of the speaker's conduct should be the public interest rather than a mere effort to gather ammunition for another round of private controversy. ***Weinberg***, 110 Cal.App.4th at 1132-33; *see* ***Rivera***, 187 Cal.App.4th at 716; ***Hailstone***, 169 Cal.App.4th at 736.

[6] A defendant cannot turn private information into a matter of public interest simply by communicating it to a large number of people. ***Hailstone***, 169 Cal.App.4th at 736; ***Weinberg***, 110 Cal.App.4th at 1133.

(b) Categories of public interest. Several courts of appeal have taken a more relaxed approach in determining whether a statement or writing concerns a public interest under the anti-SLAPP statute. ***Hilton***, 599 F.3d at 906. Generally, if a statement or writing falls within one of three categories, it will be considered to be in connection with an issue of public interest. *Id.* But the categories should not be considered mutually exclusive of the First Amendment principles. Many of the courts that apply the categorical approach also apply some of the First Amendment principles. *See, e.g.*, ***D.C.***, 182 Cal.App.4th at 1216 (applying principle that focus is on specific nature of speech rather than broad and amorphous generalities that might be abstracted from it); *see also* ***Hailstone***, 169 Cal.App.4th at 736-37 (listing all First Amendment principles but applying categorical approach). The categories are the following:

[1] Person or entity in public eye. Statements or writings that concern a person or entity in the public eye have been held to be in connection with an issue of public interest. *See* ***D.C.***, 182 Cal.App.4th at 1226; *see, e.g.*, ***Stewart v. Rolling Stone LLC*** (1st Dist.2010) 181 Cal.App.4th 664, 677-78 (magazine article discussing indie rock bands was in connection with issue of public interest); ***Seelig***, 97 Cal.App.4th at 807-08 (comments made during radio program about participant in reality television show were in connection with issue of public interest); ***Sipple v. Foundation for Nat'l Progress*** (2d Dist.1999) 71 Cal.App.4th 226, 238 (magazine article discussing allegations of domestic violence against nationally known political consultant was in connection with issue of public interest); ***Hilton***, 599 F.3d at 907 (Hallmark card that used Paris Hilton's image and catchphrase was in connection with issue of public interest).

[a] Person in public eye. The courts have not provided clear guidance on what is required for a person to be in the "public eye" or to what extent a statement or writing concerning such a person is in the public's interest. Some defendants have suggested that First Amendment principles should be used to guide the courts in making these determinations. *See, e.g.*, ***D.C.***, 182 Cal.App.4th at 1230 (Ds argued that P was public figure or limited public figure and that anything said about P involved public issue). Under the First Amendment, there are two types of public figures: limited-purpose public figures and all-purpose public figures. ***Gertz v. Robert Welch, Inc.*** (1974) 418 U.S. 323, 351. A limited-purpose public figure is a person who injects herself or is drawn by others into a public controversy. *Id.* Speech or writing concerning a limited-purpose public figure only receive heightened First Amendment protection if the speech or writing is related to the person's participation in the public controversy. *See* ***Ampex Corp. v. Cargle*** (1st Dist.2005) 128 Cal.App.4th 1569, 1577. Thus, not everything said or written about a limited-purpose public figure would be considered a matter of public interest for purposes of anti-SLAPP protection. *See* ***D.C.***, 182 Cal.App.4th at 1226. An all-purpose public figure, on the other hand, is a person who has achieved such pervasive fame or notoriety that she has become a public figure for all purposes and in all contexts. ***Gertz***, 418 U.S. at 351. It is unclear whether courts would consider all speech and writings concerning an all-purpose public figure

to be a matter of public interest under the anti-SLAPP statute. One federal district court stated in dicta that just because "a celebrity might be a public figure for purposes of the First Amendment should not mean that all speech about that celebrity is necessarily a public issue or an issue of public interest for purposes of §425.16(e)." ***Rogers v. Home Shopping Network, Inc.*** (C.D.Cal.1999) 57 F.Supp.2d 973, 985 n.7. Several appellate courts, however, have suggested that such fame or notoriety might be sufficient to make all statements concerning that person matters of public interest. *See, e.g.*, ***Stewart***, 181 Cal.App.4th at 677-78 (noting that public interest attaches to people who, by their accomplishments, mode of living, and professional standing or calling, create a legitimate and widespread attention to their activities); ***Nygård, Inc.***, 159 Cal.App.4th at 1044 (disagreeing with ***Rogers*** and other courts that have suggested §425.16 is limited to protecting speech involving only political or community issues).

[b] Entity in public eye. Factors the courts have considered to determine if an entity is in the public eye are (1) whether the entity is publicly traded, (2) the number of investors it has, and (3) whether the entity has promoted itself through numerous press releases. *See* ***Ampex Corp.***, 128 Cal.App.4th at 1576.

[2] Topic of widespread interest. Statements or writings that concern a topic of widespread public interest and contribute in some manner to a public discussion of the topic have been held to be in connection with an issue of public interest. *E.g.*, ***Rivera***, 187 Cal.App.4th at 716 (monograph discussing how to take antidepressant drug Paxil concerned topic of widespread public interest because of public's interest in depression); ***Hall v. Time Warner, Inc.*** (2d Dist.2007) 153 Cal.App.4th 1337, 1347 (television interview with beneficiary of Marlon Brando's estate concerned topic of widespread public interest because of public's fascination with Brando's personal life); ***Kronemyer***, 150 Cal.App.4th at 949 (website database containing information about movie "My Big Fat Greek Wedding" concerned topic of widespread public interest because it was successful independent film); *see* ***Wilbanks***, 121 Cal.App.4th at 898; *see, e.g.*, ***Integrated Healthcare Holdings, Inc. v. Fitzgibbons*** (4th Dist.2006) 140 Cal.App.4th 515, 524 (e-mail discussing financial survival of four hospitals within one county concerned topic of widespread public interest); ***M.G. v. Time Warner Inc.*** (4th Dist.2001) 89 Cal.App.4th 623, 629 (*Sports Illustrated* cover story on incidents of child molestation in youth sports concerned topic that was significant and of public importance). *But see* ***Cross v. Cooper*** (6th Dist.2011) 197 Cal.App.4th 357, 381 n.15 (disagreeing with courts that require statement of widespread public interest to also contribute in some manner to public discussion).

[3] Large impact. Statements or writings that could directly affect large numbers of people beyond the direct participants have been held to be in connection with an issue of public interest. *See* ***D.C.***, 182 Cal.App.4th at 1215; *see, e.g.*, ***Damon***, 85 Cal.App.4th at 479-80 (Ds' articles in newsletter questioning P's competence to manage homeowners' association presented issue of public interest because 3,000 homeowners were affected and statements concerned how group would be governed). If interest in the topic is limited to a small but definable portion of the public, such as a private group, organization, or community, the statement or writing must be in connection with an ongoing controversy, dispute, or discussion within the group. *E.g.*, ***Hailstone***, 169 Cal.App.4th at 738 (D's letter and conversation with other people alleging P was "double dipping" into union funds was issue of public interest because it affected 10,000 union members and P was part of ongoing investigation into misappropriation of funds); ***Du Charme v. International Bhd. of Elec. Workers*** (1st Dist.2003) 110 Cal.App.4th 107, 118-19 (D's written statement on website that union's manager was removed for financial mismanagement was not issue of public interest because there was no ongoing controversy, dispute, or discussion).

4. Other conduct involving public issue. Any other conduct is a protected act if it is performed by the defendant in furtherance of its constitutional right of free speech or petition in connection with a public issue or an issue of public interest. *See* CCP §425.16(b)(1), (e)(4). Unlike CCP §425.16(e)(3), which requires a statement or writing to be made in a place open to the public or a public forum, §425.16(e)(4) protects private communications as long as they concern a public issue. ***Wilbanks***, 121 Cal.App.4th at 897.

(1) Conduct. The defendant's qualifying conduct may include written or oral statements, writings, and other acts that do not fall into any other category of protected acts. *See, e.g.*, ***City of L.A. v. Animal Def. League*** (2d Dist.2006) 135 Cal.App.4th 606, 620 (demonstration in front of private home, leafleting, and publication of Internet articles protesting mistreatment of animals were protected under anti-SLAPP statute); ***Ruiz v. Harbor View***

Cmty. Ass'n (4th Dist.2005) 134 Cal.App.4th 1456, 1467-68 (letters exchanged between private persons concerning issue of public interest were protected under anti-SLAPP statute). The defendant's characterization of its conduct is irrelevant; the focus is on the actual conduct and its connection with an issue of public interest. *See, e.g.*, ***World Fin.***, 172 Cal.App.4th at 1569-70 (no connection with issue of public interest shown; Ds' claimed protected conduct was pursuit of lawful employment, but actual conduct was solicitation of business through personal conversations, flyers, and PowerPoint presentation); ***Dyer***, 147 Cal.App.4th at 1279-80 (no connection with issue of public interest shown; Ds' claimed protected conduct was making of movie that addressed issues of public interest, but actual conduct was alleged false portrayal of P's persona).

(2) In furtherance of. The conduct must be in furtherance of the defendant's exercise of its constitutional right of free speech or petition. CCP §425.16(e)(4). Conduct is in furtherance of the right of free speech or petition if it helps to advance it. ***Hunter v. CBS Broad., Inc.*** (2d Dist.2013) 221 Cal.App.4th 1510, 1521. For example, a news station's act of choosing a weather anchor is in furtherance of the right of free speech because it is done to help with news reporting. *Id.*

(3) Issue of public interest. The conduct must be in connection with an issue of public interest. CCP §425.16(e)(4). See "Issue of public interest," §2.1.3(2), p. 430.

NOTE

Although CCP §425.16(e)(4) refers to both a "public issue" and an "issue of public interest," there appears to be no difference between the two terms. Weil, Civil Procedure Before Trial, ¶7:780.

§2.2 Action arises from protected act. To meet its burden under the anti-SLAPP statute, the defendant must show that the challenged cause of action arises from the defendant's protected act. ***Haight Ashbury Free Clinics, Inc. v. Happening House Ventures*** (1st Dist.2010) 184 Cal.App.4th 1539, 1547; *see* CCP §425.16(b)(1).

1. Generally. To show that the challenged cause of action arises from the defendant's protected act, the focus is on the substance and not the form of the plaintiff's cause of action; the critical point is whether the cause of action was "based on" a protected act. ***Navellier v. Sletten*** (2002) 29 Cal.4th 82, 89, 92; ***All One God Faith, Inc. v. Organic & Sustainable Indus. Stds., Inc.*** (1st Dist.2010) 183 Cal.App.4th 1186, 1200; *see also* ***S.A. v. Maiden*** (4th Dist.2014) 229 Cal.App.4th 27, 35 (finding that all malicious-prosecution claims arise from protected activity because they depend on statements made in earlier judicial proceedings). An action does not arise from a protected act simply because it was triggered by the act or filed after the act took place. ***Navellier***, 29 Cal.4th at 89; *see* ***City of Cotati v. Cashman*** (2002) 29 Cal.4th 69, 78. To meet its burden, the defendant does not have to show the action was filed with the intent to chill or had the effect of chilling its right of free speech or petition. ***City of Cotati***, 29 Cal.4th at 75-76 (effect of chilling); ***Equilon Enters. v. Consumer Cause, Inc.*** (2002) 29 Cal.4th 53, 58-59 (intent to chill).

NOTE

*In **Navellier**, the California Supreme Court held that the anti-SLAPP statute does not categorically exclude any particular cause of action (e.g., fraud, breach of contract) from its operation. **Navellier**, 29 Cal.4th at 92. As long as the plaintiff's cause of action arises from the defendant's protected act, the anti-SLAPP statute will apply. See id. at 89. Despite this observation, most courts agree that the anti-SLAPP statute does not apply to a garden-variety attorney-malpractice action (i.e., when client sues former attorney based on attorney's representation of client).* *See "Attorney-malpractice action," §2.2.3, p. 434.*

2. Mixed cause of action. When a pleading alleges a cause of action that is supported by both protected and unprotected activity, it is the "gravamen or principal thrust" of the cause of action that determines whether the anti-SLAPP statute applies. ***City of Colton v. Singletary*** (4th Dist.2012) 206 Cal.App.4th 751, 767; ***Prediwave Corp.***

v. Simpson Thacher & Bartlett LLP (6th Dist.2009) 179 Cal.App.4th 1204, 1219; *see* ***Club Members for an Honest Election v. Sierra Club*** (2008) 45 Cal.4th 309, 319 (recognizing that gravamen-or-principal-thrust test has been applied to mixed causes of action). *Contra* ***Salma v. Capon*** (1st Dist.2008) 161 Cal.App.4th 1275, 1287-88 & n.5 (court applied merely-incidental test for mixed causes of action and refused to adopt gravamen-or-principal-thrust test). If the allegations concerning protected activity are only incidental to the gravamen or principal thrust of a cause of action, the cause of action is not subject to an anti-SLAPP motion. ***City of Colton***, 206 Cal.App.4th at 767; ***Digerati Holdings, LLC v. Young Money Entm't, LLC*** (2d Dist.2011) 194 Cal.App.4th 873, 884; ***Haight Ashbury***, 184 Cal.App.4th at 1551 & n.7; ***Robles v. Chalilpoyil*** (6th Dist.2010) 181 Cal.App.4th 566, 575.

(1) Incidental. A protected act is incidental to a cause of action when the act is merely evidence surrounding a dispute (e.g., evidence explaining why or how a dispute arose) or evidence that the unprotected activity has taken place; the act itself does not give rise to liability. *See* ***Hylton v. Frank E. Rogozienski, Inc.*** (4th Dist.2009) 177 Cal.App.4th 1264, 1272 (if protected activity is not core injury-producing conduct on which P's claim is based, protected activity is incidental); *see, e.g.*, ***Episcopal Church Cases*** (2009) 45 Cal.4th 467, 477-78 (principal thrust of action was to determine ownership of property; allegations concerning why D decided to disaffiliate with church had no bearing on who owned property and was simply background information); ***Martinez v. Metabolife Int'l*** (4th Dist.2003) 113 Cal.App.4th 181, 187-88 (principal thrust of action was to recover for injuries caused by defective product; allegations concerning D's commercial speech to market product had no bearing on D's liability for manufacturing defective product); ***Gallimore v. State Farm Fire & Cas. Ins.*** (2d Dist.2002) 102 Cal.App.4th 1388, 1399 (principal thrust of action was mishandling of insurance claims; allegations concerning Ds' written reports to Department of Insurance were only evidence that wrongful, unprotected activity took place, and P did not allege that reports were wrongful or caused injury).

(2) Not incidental. A protected act is not incidental to a cause of action when the act itself would independently support liability under the cause of action. *See* ***Haight Ashbury***, 184 Cal.App.4th at 1551; *see, e.g.*, ***Mann v. Quality Old Time Serv.*** (4th Dist.2004) 120 Cal.App.4th 90, 104 (because alleged protected activity formed "substantial part" of factual basis for liability, cause of action was subject to anti-SLAPP statute). The fact that the complaint makes far fewer allegations of protected acts than unprotected acts is irrelevant for determining whether the allegations are incidental. ***Haight Ashbury***, 184 Cal.App.4th at 1552-53. As long as one allegation of protected activity would support liability, the cause of action is subject to the anti-SLAPP statute. *See, e.g.*, *id.* (Ds met their burden even though only 2 out of 16 allegations supporting breach of fiduciary duty were considered protected activity).

3. Attorney-malpractice action. Most courts agree that the anti-SLAPP statute does not apply to a garden-variety attorney-malpractice action—that is, one against an attorney by a former client based on the attorney's representation of the client. *E.g.*, ***Thayer v. Kabateck Brown Kellner LLP*** (1st Dist.2012) 207 Cal.App.4th 141, 158; ***Prediwave Corp.***, 179 Cal.App.4th at 1227-28; ***Kolar v. Donahue, McIntosh & Hammerton*** (4th Dist.2006) 145 Cal.App.4th 1532, 1539-40; *see also* ***Chodos v. Cole*** (2d Dist.2012) 210 Cal.App.4th 692, 705 (attorney's claim against other attorneys for equitable indemnity in connection with claim of attorney malpractice should not be treated differently under anti-SLAPP statute than garden-variety malpractice claims). *But see* ***Jespersen v. Zubiate-Beauchamp*** (2d Dist.2003) 114 Cal.App.4th 624, 629-30 (anti-SLAPP statute may apply to attorney-malpractice action if action was based on attorney's acts in judicial proceeding or in connection with issue under review by court); ***Mindys Cosmetics, Inc. v. Dakar*** (9th Cir.2010) 611 F.3d 590, 597-98 (there is no categorical exclusion of attorney-malpractice claims from anti-SLAPP statute). An attorney-malpractice action is usually excluded from the anti-SLAPP statute because it does not arise from any petitioning activity but rather from the attorney's failure to competently represent the client. ***Kolar***, 145 Cal.App.4th at 1540. Instead of chilling the petitioning activity, the threat of malpractice encourages the attorney to petition competently and zealously. *Id.* Unlike an attorney-malpractice action, an action by a third party against an attorney for petitioning activity is not excluded from the anti-SLAPP statute because it could have a chilling effect on petitioning activity. *Id.*; *see* ***Prediwave Corp.***, 179 Cal.App.4th at 1227-28 (client's action against attorney based on attorney's acts on behalf of different client and nonclient's action against attorney

still fall within anti-SLAPP statute); *see, e.g.*, ***Thayer***, 207 Cal.App.4th at 157-58 (anti-SLAPP statute applied to non-client's action against attorney for fraud and breach of fiduciary duty).

§3. MOTION

§3.1 What to strike. The defendant can move to strike all causes of action or some of them. ***Doe v. Luster*** (2d Dist.2006) 145 Cal.App.4th 139, 143; *see* CCP §425.16(b)(1). The cause of action can appear in a complaint, cross-complaint, petition, amended complaint, or amended cross-complaint. *CEB Action Guide: Making & Opposing Special Motions to Strike*, Step 6, p. 13; *see* CCP §425.16(h); *see, e.g.*, ***City of L.A. v. Animal Def. League*** (2d Dist.2006) 135 Cal.App.4th 606, 617 (anti-SLAPP motion can be filed against petition for injunctive relief); ***Thomas v. Quintero*** (1st Dist.2005) 126 Cal.App.4th 635, 652 (anti-SLAPP motion cannot be filed against request for temporary restraining order).

NOTE

The term "complaint" is used throughout §3 of this subchapter to refer to a complaint, cross-complaint, or petition. See CCP §425.16(h).

§3.2 Who can file. Any person against whom a claim was filed can file an anti-SLAPP motion. *See* CCP §425.16(b)(1); Weil, *Civil Procedure Before Trial*, ¶7:595; *see, e.g.*, ***Foundation for Taxpayer & Consumer Rights v. Garamendi*** (2d Dist.2005) 132 Cal.App.4th 1375, 1392 (intervenor did not have standing to bring anti-SLAPP motion because no claim was brought against it). A defendant is not required to demonstrate that its protected act was made on its own behalf; it can be made on behalf of a client or the general public. ***Briggs v. Eden Council for Hope & Opportunity*** (1999) 19 Cal.4th 1106, 1116. For purposes of an anti-SLAPP motion, the term "person" includes all the following:

1. Individuals. *See* ***Schoendorf v. U.D. Registry, Inc.*** (2d Dist.2002) 97 Cal.App.4th 227, 235-36.

2. Corporations. *See* ***Navarro v. IHOP Props., Inc.*** (4th Dist.2005) 134 Cal.App.4th 834, 843.

3. Nonprofit organizations. *See, e.g.*, ***Governor Gray Davis Cmte. v. American Taxpayers Alliance*** (1st Dist.2002) 102 Cal.App.4th 449, 454-55 (nonprofit corporation filed anti-SLAPP motion).

4. Public officials and governmental entities. ***Vargas v. City of Salinas*** (2009) 46 Cal.4th 1, 17.

5. Successor entities. ***Daniell v. Riverside Partners I, L.P.*** (4th Dist.2012) 206 Cal.App.4th 1292, 1302.

§3.3 Deadline to file & serve.

1. Deadline to file. The anti-SLAPP motion must be filed within 60 days after service of the complaint. CCP §425.16(f). See "Prospective deadlines," ch. 1-F, §5.1, p. 52.

(1) Amended complaint. If a complaint is amended, the defendant has 60 days from service of the amended complaint to file an anti-SLAPP motion. *See* ***Country Side Villas Homeowners Ass'n v. Ivie*** (6th Dist.2011) 193 Cal.App.4th 1110, 1115-16; ***Yu v. Signet Bank/Va.*** (1st Dist.2002) 103 Cal.App.4th 298, 314-15. But the amendment must be substantive; if the amendment merely corrects an error in form, the motion must be filed within 60 days from the service of the original complaint. *See* ***Country Side Villas***, 193 Cal.App.4th at 1115-16. See "Joining the Defendant—Service of Process," ch. 3-H, p. 295.

NOTE

Depending on how the original or amended complaint was served, the defendant's deadline to file an anti-SLAPP motion may be extended as provided by CCP §1013. See, e.g., ***Lam v. Ky Ngo*** *(4th Dist.2001) 91 Cal.App.4th 832, 842 (service of amended complaint by mail extended D's time to file anti-SLAPP motion by five days).*

(2) Remanded from federal court. If an action was removed to federal court and then remanded back to state court, the defendant has 60 days from service of the notice of remand to file an anti-SLAPP motion (including any extra days if service was by mail). ***Morin v. Rosenthal*** (2d Dist.2004) 122 Cal.App.4th 673, 679.

(3) Late-filed motion. If the 60-day deadline has expired, the defendant should obtain leave of court to file an anti-SLAPP motion. *See* CCP §425.16(f); ***Kunysz v. Sandler*** (4th Dist.2007) 146 Cal.App.4th 1540, 1542-43; *see, e.g.*, ***Platypus Wear, Inc. v. Goldberg*** (4th Dist.2008) 166 Cal.App.4th 772, 777 (D filed ex parte application asking permission to file anti-SLAPP motion after 60-day deadline had expired). The defendant should give reasons for the delay in bringing the motion and explain how allowing the late filing would serve the purpose of the anti-SLAPP statute. *See, e.g.*, ***Platypus Wear***, 166 Cal.App.4th at 787-88 (order granting application to file anti-SLAPP motion reversed; delay in bringing motion was extreme, D's reasons for delay were weak, reasons for granting motion were unrelated to purpose of anti-SLAPP statute, and potential prejudice to P was great). If the defendant does not obtain leave to file an untimely motion, the motion will be denied unless the court exercises its discretion to consider it. ***Chitsazzadeh v. Kramer & Kaslow*** (2d Dist.2011) 199 Cal.App.4th 676, 684.

2. Deadline to serve. The anti-SLAPP motion must be served at least 16 court days before the hearing. *See* CCP §1005(b). If the motion is served by a method other than personal delivery, extra time is added to the 16-day period (e.g., five calendar days are added when notice is mailed in California to a California address). *See id.* See "Add time for method of service," ch. 1-G, §6.2.1(5), p. 72.

§3.4 Deadline for hearing. The hearing on the anti-SLAPP motion must be set by the court clerk within 30 days after service of the motion unless the court's docket conditions require a later hearing. CCP §425.16(f). But the anti-SLAPP motion cannot be denied solely because the defendant was unable to obtain a hearing within the 30-day deadline. *See* ***Hall v. Time Warner, Inc.*** (2d Dist.2007) 153 Cal.App.4th 1337, 1349 (after §425.16(f) was amended in 2005, D is no longer required to make sure hearing is timely scheduled).

§3.5 Contents.

1. Notice of motion & motion.

(1) Generally. An anti-SLAPP motion should be requested in writing by noticed motion. *CEB Action Guide: Making & Opposing Special Motions to Strike*, Step 16, p. 31. See "Notice of motion & motion," ch. 1-D, §5.1, p. 28.

(2) Relief. The notice of motion and motion must describe the relief sought. *See* CRC 3.1110(a) (notice of motion must state nature of order being sought), CRC 3.1112(d)(3) (motion must briefly state relief sought). The notice of motion should specify the matters to be struck (e.g., complaint, second cause of action). *See, e.g.*, Kiesel, *Cal. Pretrial Civil Procedure*, §13.24 (sample anti-SLAPP motion).

(3) Grounds. The notice of motion and motion must briefly state the grounds for the relief (e.g., "the motion will be made on the ground that the cause of action alleged against the defendant arises from an act in furtherance of defendant's right of free speech in connection with a public issue"). *See* CRC 3.1110(a) (notice of motion must state grounds for issuance of order), CRC 3.1112(d)(3) (motion must briefly state basis for motion); *see, e.g.*, Kiesel, *Cal. Pretrial Civil Procedure*, §13.24 (sample anti-SLAPP motion). See "Defendant's Burden," §2, p. 426.

2. Memorandum of points & authorities. The motion must include a memorandum in support of the motion. CRC 3.1112(a)(3), 3.1113(a). See "Memorandum of points & authorities," ch. 1-D, §5.2, p. 28.

3. Supporting evidence. The motion should be supported by admissible evidence in the form of pleadings, declarations, affidavits, or matters that can be judicially noticed. *See* CCP §425.16(b)(2); *see, e.g.*, ***Brill Media Co. v. TWC Grp.*** (2d Dist.2005) 132 Cal.App.4th 324, 329 (Ds filed judicial-notice request in support of anti-SLAPP motion), *disapproved on other grounds*, ***Simpson Strong-Tie Co. v. Gore*** (2010) 49 Cal.4th 12. See "Supporting evidence," ch. 1-D, §5.3, p. 30.

(1) Request for judicial notice. A request for judicial notice must be made in a separate document. CRC 3.1113(*l*). See "Request for Judicial Notice," ch. 5-J, p. 547.

(2) **Declaration.** If the first available hearing date is more than 30 days from service of the anti-SLAPP motion, the defendant should include a declaration from its attorney stating that the attorney contacted the court clerk and, because of the court's docket conditions, the first date the court had available was the hearing date stated in the motion papers. *CEB Action Guide: Making & Opposing Special Motions to Strike*, Step 17, p. 33. See "Deadline for hearing," §3.4, p. 436.

NOTE

This declaration might be unnecessary because a court can no longer deny an anti-SLAPP motion based on an untimely hearing. See ***Hall v. Time Warner, Inc.*** *(2d Dist.2007) 153 Cal.App.4th 1337, 1349. But the safest practice is to file the declaration anyway. CEB Action Guide: Making & Opposing Special Motions to Strike, Step 17, p. 33.*

4. **Request for attorney fees & costs.** The defendant can request attorney fees and costs for bringing the anti-SLAPP motion. *See* CCP §425.16(c)(1); ***Christian Research Inst. v. Alnor*** (4th Dist.2008) 165 Cal.App.4th 1315, 1320. The defendant can request attorney fees and costs in its anti-SLAPP motion, in a later filed memorandum of costs, or in a noticed motion. ***Melbostad v. Fisher*** (1st Dist.2008) 165 Cal.App.4th 987, 992; *see* ***Christian Research***, 165 Cal.App.4th at 1320. The defendant should support its request with sufficient evidence establishing the amount of attorney fees and costs incurred in making the motion. *CEB Action Guide: Making & Opposing Special Motions to Strike*, Step 24, p. 46. See "Supporting evidence," §3.5.3, p. 436. To recover attorney fees and costs, the defendant must establish any of the following:

(1) For most actions, the defendant need only show that it was the prevailing party. *See* CCP §425.16(c)(1).

(2) For an action against a public agency to obtain public records, the public agency must also show that the action was clearly frivolous. *See id.* §425.16(c)(2); Gov. C. §6259(d).

(3) For an action against a state body or a legislative body of a local agency to stop or prevent a violation of certain open-meeting requirements, the state or legislative body must also show that the action was clearly frivolous and totally lacking in merit. *See* CCP §425.16(c)(2); Gov. C. §§11130.5, 54960.5.

(4) For an action to obtain a judicial determination that an act by a state body or a legislative body of a local agency is null and void, the state or legislative body must also show that the action was clearly frivolous and totally lacking in merit. *See* CCP §425.16(c)(2); Gov. C. §§11130.5, 54960.5.

NOTE

If the defendant decides to request attorney fees and costs in a later-filed memorandum of costs or noticed motion, the defendant should notify the court in its anti-SLAPP memorandum that it plans to seek the recovery of attorney fees and costs. CEB Action Guide: Making & Opposing Special Motions to Strike, Step 24, p. 46.

5. **Proposed order.** The defendant can submit a proposed order with the motion. CRC 3.1113(m). If a proposed order is submitted, it must be lodged and served with the motion papers, not attached to them. *Id.* See "Documents lodged," ch. 1-F, §2.3, p. 47.

§3.6 Filing fees. When the motion is filed, the defendant must pay a filing fee to the court clerk or request a waiver of the fee. See "Filing Fees," ch. 1-F, §7, p. 58.

§3.7 Copy to Judicial Council. After filing the anti-SLAPP motion, the defendant must promptly send a copy of the endorsed, filed caption page of the motion to the Judicial Council by e-mail or fax. CCP §425.16(j)(1).

NOTE

The defendant must also send other documents related to the anti-SLAPP motion "promptly" to the Judicial Council. See CCP §425.16(j)(1). It is unclear whether this means the defendant can wait and send the caption page of the anti-SLAPP motion when it sends the other documents.

§3.8 Effect of motion on discovery. Generally, the filing of an anti-SLAPP motion stays all discovery proceedings. CCP §425.16(g). This includes any discovery motions that are pending when the anti-SLAPP motion is filed. ***Britts v. Superior Ct.*** (6th Dist.2006) 145 Cal.App.4th 1112, 1128. The discovery stay remains in effect until notice of entry of the order granting or denying the anti-SLAPP motion. CCP §425.16(g). The court, on noticed motion and for good cause shown, can order that specified discovery be conducted during the stay. *Id.* See "Motion to conduct discovery," §4.1, this page.

NOTE

The mandatory stay of discovery does not apply in federal court. ***Metabolife Int'l v. Wornick*** *(9th Cir.2001) 264 F.3d 832, 846. In federal court, a plaintiff is entitled to seek limited discovery to oppose an anti-SLAPP motion. See id.*

§4. RESPONSE

§4.1 Motion to conduct discovery. The plaintiff can respond to the anti-SLAPP motion by filing a noticed motion asking the court to allow it to conduct discovery if discovery is necessary to oppose the anti-SLAPP motion. *See* CCP §425.16(g) (filing anti-SLAPP motion stays all discovery proceedings, unless on party's noticed motion showing good cause, court orders that discovery be conducted); ***Britts v. Superior Ct.*** (6th Dist.2006) 145 Cal.App.4th 1112, 1129 (court does not have inherent power to allow discovery in absence of noticed motion); ***Ruiz v. Harbor View Cmty. Ass'n*** (4th Dist.2005) 134 Cal.App.4th 1456, 1475 (court can allow discovery limited to issues raised in anti-SLAPP motion). See "Notice of motion & motion," ch. 1-D, §5.1, p. 28. The plaintiff cannot simply ask the court to deny the anti-SLAPP motion on the ground that it did not have an opportunity to obtain relevant evidence. *CEB Action Guide: Making & Opposing Special Motions to Strike*, Step 30, pp. 49-50; *see, e.g.*, ***Lafayette Morehouse, Inc. v. Chronicle Publ'g*** (1st Dist.1995) 37 Cal.App.4th 855, 867 (court rejected P's argument that it was unable to adequately defend anti-SLAPP motion because P never sought any discovery in case).

1. Deadline to file & serve. A motion to conduct discovery must be filed and served at least 16 court days before the hearing on the discovery motion. *See* CCP §§425.16(g), 1005(b). See "Filing & Serving Noticed Motions," ch. 1-D, §7, p. 33.

2. Grounds. The plaintiff must show good cause to conduct discovery. CCP §425.16(g). There is good cause if discovery is necessary to oppose the anti-SLAPP motion and is tailored to that end. ***Britts***, 145 Cal.App.4th at 1125; *see* ***1-800 Contacts, Inc. v. Steinberg*** (2d Dist.2003) 107 Cal.App.4th 568, 593 (court will not allow discovery just to test D's declarations). To determine if there is good cause, the court can consider the following factors:

(1) Whether evidence necessary to establish the plaintiff's burden of proof is in the possession of the defendant or a third party. ***Garment Workers Ctr. v. Superior Ct.*** (2d Dist.2004) 117 Cal.App.4th 1156, 1162.

(2) Whether the information the plaintiff seeks to obtain is readily available from other sources or can be obtained through informal discovery. *Id.*

(3) Whether the information the plaintiff seeks is necessary to respond to the issues raised in the anti-SLAPP motion. *See id.* For example, if the defendant claims that the plaintiff does not have a probability of prevailing on the merits because its complaint is legally deficient, no amount of discovery can cure that defect. *Id.*

3. Accompanying motions.

(1) Motion for continuance. If discovery cannot be completed before the hearing on the anti-SLAPP motion, the plaintiff should file a motion to continue the hearing. *See, e.g.*, ***Paul v. Friedman*** (2d Dist.2002) 95 Cal.App.4th 853, 860 (while D's anti-SLAPP motion was pending, P filed motion to conduct discovery and to continue anti-SLAPP hearing). See "Requests for Continuance or Stay," ch. 5-I, p. 534.

(2) Motion to shorten time. If the plaintiff cannot give 16 court days' notice on the discovery motion, the plaintiff should file a motion to shorten the deadline for filing and serving the motion. *See* CRC 3.1300(b); *CEB Action Guide: Making & Opposing Special Motions to Strike*, Step 32, p. 54. See "Deadline to file & serve," §4.1.1, this page; "Shortening Time," ch. 5-E, p. 497.

§4.2 Amending complaint. The plaintiff can respond to an anti-SLAPP motion by filing an amended complaint. Filing an amended complaint before the hearing, however, does not make the anti-SLAPP motion moot; the court can still award attorney fees and costs to the defendant based on the allegations in the original complaint. *E.g.*, ***Sylmar Air Conditioning v. Pueblo Contracting Servs.*** (2d Dist.2004) (Div. 4) 122 Cal.App.4th 1049, 1055-56 (filing amended complaint under CCP §472 before hearing on anti-SLAPP motion did not render motion to strike moot; D can still recover fees and costs); *see, e.g.*, ***Prediwave Corp. v. Simpson Thacher & Bartlett LLP*** (6th Dist.2009) 179 Cal.App.4th 1204, 1209 (court did not consider amended complaint in ruling on anti-SLAPP motion). *But see* ***Law Offices of Andrew L. Ellis v. Yang*** (2d Dist.2009) (Div. 3) 178 Cal.App.4th 869, 881 (contending that ***Sylmar*** overstated rule; P should not be prevented from avoiding liability by amending complaint before hearing unless court has already made adverse tentative or definitive ruling on anti-SLAPP motion). To avoid liability on an anti-SLAPP motion after amending the complaint, the plaintiff must obtain a voluntary waiver of fees and costs from the defendant. *See* Kiesel, *Cal. Pretrial Civil Procedure*, §13.13[5][c].

NOTE

In federal court, the plaintiff can avoid liability under the anti-SLAPP statute by amending its complaint before the hearing. See ***Verizon Del., Inc. v. Covad Comms.*** *(9th Cir.2004) 377 F.3d 1081, 1091 (granting anti-SLAPP motion without granting P leave to amend would directly conflict with FRCP 15(a)).*

§4.3 Voluntary dismissal. The plaintiff can respond to an anti-SLAPP motion by filing a voluntary dismissal. If a voluntary dismissal is filed before trial, the dismissal is usually without prejudice (i.e., the plaintiff can refile the complaint), and the court will lose jurisdiction to strike the complaint or a cause of action. *E.g.*, ***Law Offices of Andrew L. Ellis v. Yang*** (2d Dist.2009) 178 Cal.App.4th 869, 881 (court lacked jurisdiction to rule on anti-SLAPP motion when P voluntarily dismissed case before hearing and before court made any adverse ruling on merits); *see* ***Kyle v. Carmon*** (3d Dist.1999) 71 Cal.App.4th 901, 908. See "Without prejudice," ch. 10-D, §2.2.2, p. 1150. The court will retain jurisdiction, however, to decide the merits of the motion for purposes of deciding whether the defendant is a prevailing party who is entitled to recover attorney fees and costs. ***Liu v. Moore*** (2d Dist.1999) 69 Cal.App.4th 745, 751; *see* ***Law Offices of Andrew L. Ellis***, 178 Cal.App.4th at 881; *see also* ***Pfeiffer Venice Props. v. Bernard*** (2d Dist.2002) 101 Cal.App.4th 211, 218 (court's ability to retain jurisdiction to determine fees and costs on anti-SLAPP motion after voluntary dismissal applies equally to involuntary dismissal). See "After voluntary dismissal," §8.2.2(3)(a)[2], p. 447 (discussing tests for determining prevailing party after voluntary dismissal). To avoid liability on an anti-SLAPP motion after a voluntary dismissal, the plaintiff must obtain a voluntary waiver of fees and costs from the defendant. *See* Kiesel, *Cal. Pretrial Civil Procedure*, §13.13[5][a].

§4.4 Opposition. The plaintiff can respond to an anti-SLAPP motion by filing an opposition.

1. Deadline to file & serve. The opposition papers must be filed and served at least nine court days before the hearing. CCP §1005(b). See "Filing & serving opposition," ch. 1-D, §8.5, p. 36.

2. Grounds.

(1) Procedural defect. The plaintiff can oppose the anti-SLAPP motion on the ground that the motion was not timely filed and served. *CEB Action Guide: Making & Opposing Special Motions to Strike*, Step 31, p. 51. See "Deadline to file & serve," §3.3, p. 435.

(2) Evidentiary objection. The plaintiff can oppose the anti-SLAPP motion on the ground that the evidence submitted in support of the motion contained inadmissible evidence, such as hearsay. *CEB Action Guide: Making & Opposing Special Motions to Strike*, Step 31, p. 51.

(3) No prima facie showing. The plaintiff can oppose the anti-SLAPP motion on the ground that the defendant did not make the required prima facie showing. See "Defendant's Burden," §2, p. 426.

(a) D's act not protected. The plaintiff can argue that the defendant has not shown that its act is protected under the anti-SLAPP statute. See "Protected acts," §2.1, p. 426.

[1] D's act was not exercise of free speech or petition. The plaintiff can argue that the defendant's act was not protected because it did not involve the exercise of free speech or petition. *See, e.g.*, ***Castillo v. Pacheco*** (2d Dist.2007) 150 Cal.App.4th 242, 251 (anti-SLAPP statute did not apply to cause of action arising from Ds' right of free exercise of religion).

[2] D's act illegal. The plaintiff can argue that the defendant's act was not protected because it was illegal as a matter of law. *See* ***Flatley v. Mauro*** (2006) 39 Cal.4th 299, 320. An act is illegal as a matter of law if either (1) the defendant conceded that its act was illegal or (2) the uncontroverted evidence conclusively establishes that the act was illegal. *Id.*; *see, e.g.*, ***Summit Bank v. Rogers*** (1st Dist.2012) 206 Cal.App.4th 669, 692 (D's defamatory comments that violated Fin. C. §1327 could not be deemed illegal as matter of law because statute was unconstitutional restriction on free speech); ***Lefebvre v. Lefebvre*** (2d Dist.2011) 199 Cal.App.4th 696, 705 (D could not show act was protected after conceding that she submitted false criminal report); ***Paul for Council v. Hanyecz*** (2d Dist.2001) 85 Cal.App.4th 1356, 1366-67 (Ds could not show act was protected after conceding that act involved was illegal money laundering), *disapproved on other grounds*, ***Equilon Enters. v. Consumer Cause, Inc.*** (2002) 29 Cal.4th 53. In this context, the term "illegal" means criminal, not merely in violation of a statute. ***Price v. Operating Eng'rs Local Un.*** (3d Dist.2011) 195 Cal.App.4th 962, 971; *e.g.*, ***Fremont Reorganizing Corp. v. Faigin*** (2d Dist.2011) 198 Cal.App.4th 1153, 1169 (attorney's violation of duty of confidentiality and loyalty to former client is not illegal as matter of law); *see* ***G.R. v. Intelligator*** (4th Dist.2010) 185 Cal.App.4th 606, 616 (violation of California Rule of Court does not trigger illegal-activity exception).

(b) P's cause of action does not arise from protected act. The plaintiff can argue that the defendant has not shown that the challenged cause of action arose from a protected act. See "Action arises from protected act," §2.2, p. 433.

(4) P can probably prevail. The plaintiff can oppose the anti-SLAPP motion on the ground that, even if the defendant has met its initial burden (i.e., made a prima facie showing that a cause of action asserted by the plaintiff arises from an act in furtherance of defendant's protected rights), the plaintiff has a probability of prevailing on its cause of action. CCP §425.16(b)(1); ***Oasis W. Rlty., LLC v. Goldman*** (2011) 51 Cal.4th 811, 819-20; ***Wallace v. McCubbin*** (1st Dist.2011) 196 Cal.App.4th 1169, 1181; ***Cohen v. Brown*** (2d Dist.2009) 173 Cal.App.4th 302, 315. Although the plaintiff is not obligated to demonstrate a probability of success if the defendant does not meet its initial burden, the plaintiff should at least brief the issue for the court. *See* ***Gallimore v. State Farm Fire & Cas. Ins.*** (2d Dist.2002) 102 Cal.App.4th 1388, 1396. If the issue is not briefed, the plaintiff may waive its right to argue the issue on appeal. *See, e.g.*, ***Haight Ashbury Free Clinics, Inc. v. Happening House Ventures*** (1st Dist.2010) 184 Cal.App.4th 1539, 1554 & n.9 (trial court erred in denying anti-SLAPP motion because D met its initial burden; because P did not brief issue of whether it had probability of prevailing, trial court was ordered to vacate denial and grant anti-SLAPP motion). To establish a probability of prevailing on the merits, the plaintiff must show the following:

(a) Legally sufficient. The plaintiff must show that it stated a legally sufficient cause of action in its complaint. ***Oasis W. Rlty.***, 51 Cal.4th at 820; ***Vargas v. City of Salinas*** (2009) 46 Cal.4th 1, 19-20. A legally sufficient cause of action is stated if the complaint alleges all the ultimate facts—that is, the facts needed to establish each element of the cause of action pleaded. *See* ***Drummond v. Desmarais*** (6th Dist.2009) 176 Cal.App.4th 439, 449; *see, e.g.*, ***Philipson & Simon v. Gulsvig*** (4th Dist.2007) 154 Cal.App.4th 347, 362-63 (P's complaint was insufficient to state cause of action for fraud). *But see* ***Nguyen-Lam v. Cao*** (4th Dist.2009) 171 Cal.App.4th 858, 865-66 (court granted P leave to amend complaint to allege required element after P presented evidence of element at hearing). See "What to plead – ultimate facts," ch. 3-C, §3.6.3(2)(a), p. 216.

(b) Factually sufficient.

[1] Generally. The plaintiff must show that the evidence submitted is prima facie sufficient to prove each element of the cause of action under the applicable burden of proof. *See* ***Oasis W. Rlty.***, 51 Cal. 4th at 820 (P must demonstrate that complaint is supported by sufficient prima facie showing of facts to

sustain favorable judgment if evidence submitted by P is credited); ***Wilson v. Parker, Covert & Chidester*** (2002) 28 Cal.4th 811, 821 (same); ***Ampex Corp. v. Cargle*** (1st Dist.2005) 128 Cal.App.4th 1569, 1578 (courts must consider pertinent burden of proof when determining whether P has shown probability of prevailing on merits). Under this standard, the plaintiff is only required to establish that her claim has minimal merit; the plaintiff is not required to prove the claim to the court. *See* ***Soukup v. Law Offices of Herbert Hafif*** (2006) 39 Cal.4th 260, 291; ***Mann v. Quality Old Time Serv.*** (4th Dist.2004) 120 Cal.App.4th 90, 105; *see also* ***Kyle v. Carmon*** (3d Dist.1999) 71 Cal.App.4th 901, 907 (P's burden is similar to standard used in determining nonsuit, directed verdict, or summary judgment). To meet its burden, the plaintiff must submit admissible evidence. ***Gilbert v. Sykes*** (3d Dist.2007) 147 Cal.App.4th 13, 26; ***Fashion 21 v. Coalition for Humane Immigrant Rights*** (2d Dist.2004) 117 Cal.App.4th 1138, 1147; *see, e.g.*, ***Manhattan Loft, LLC v. Mercury Liquors, Inc.*** (2d Dist.2009) 173 Cal.App.4th 1040, 1050-51 (P was required to establish, through competent, admissible evidence, all four elements of slander of title to show it had probability of prevailing on merits). Thus, statements made on information and belief are insufficient to establish a probability of prevailing on the merits unless the facts to be established are incapable of positive averment. ***Evans v. Unkow*** (1st Dist.1995) 38 Cal.App.4th 1490, 1497-98. Courts disagree, however, on whether verified pleadings are sufficient evidence to establish a probability of prevailing. *Compare* ***Salma v. Capon*** (1st Dist.2008) (Div. 5) 161 Cal.App.4th 1275, 1289-90 (verified pleadings are sufficient evidence; unlike summary-judgment statute, anti-SLAPP statute expressly permits rather than restricts use of such evidence), *with* ***Hecimovich v. Encinal Sch. Parent Teacher Org.*** (1st Dist.2012) (Div. 2) 203 Cal.App.4th 450, 474 & n.8 (verified pleading cannot be used as evidence for anti-SLAPP motion), *and* ***Hailstone v. Martinez*** (5th Dist.2008) 169 Cal.App.4th 728, 735 (same).

NOTE

The court can consider inadmissible evidence submitted by the plaintiff if the defendant does not properly object to that evidence. ***Gallagher v. Connell*** *(2d Dist.2004) 123 Cal.App.4th 1260, 1268-69.*

[2] Mixed cause of action. Courts disagree on the requirements for establishing a probability of prevailing on a mixed cause of action (i.e., a cause of action that is based on multiple acts, some of which are protected and some that are not). See "Mixed cause of action," §2.2.2, p. 433. Most courts adopt an all-or-nothing approach—that is, if the plaintiff shows a probability of prevailing on any part of the cause of action, the cause of action will not be struck, even if the only part that has merit is based on unprotected activity; if the plaintiff cannot establish a probability of prevailing on any part of the cause of action, the entire cause of action will be struck. *See* ***Burrill v. Nair*** (3d Dist.2013) 217 Cal.App.4th 357, 382; ***Wallace***, 196 Cal.App.4th at 1212; ***Mann***, 120 Cal.App.4th at 106. Two other courts have adopted a piecemeal approach—that is, the plaintiff must show a probability of prevailing on each allegation of protected activity within a cause of action, and a court can strike allegations of protected activity that the plaintiff has not shown a probability of prevailing on while allowing allegations of unprotected activity to remain. *See* ***Cho v. Chang*** (2d Dist.2013) 219 Cal.App.4th 521, 527; ***City of Colton v. Singletary*** (4th Dist.2012) (Div. 2) 206 Cal.App.4th 751, 772-73. It is unclear under the piecemeal approach whether the plaintiff must also show a probability of prevailing on allegations of unprotected activity. One court has stated in dicta that the plaintiff is not required to show a probability of prevailing on unprotected claims. *See* ***Cho***, 219 Cal.App.4th at 523 n.2.

NOTE

The courts are split on whether the plaintiff must show a probability of prevailing against the defendant's affirmative defenses. ***No Doubt v. Activision Publ'g*** *(2d Dist.2011) 192 Cal.App.4th 1018, 1029 n.4. Some courts hold that the plaintiff must demonstrate that the defenses are not applicable as a matter of law or make a prima facie showing of facts negating the defenses. E.g.,* ***Birkner v. Lam*** *(1st Dist.2007) (Div. 3) 156 Cal.App.4th 275, 285;* ***Paul for Council****, 85*

ANTI-SLAPP MOTION

Cal.App.4th at 1367; see, e.g., ***Dwight R. v. Christy B.*** *(4th Dist.2013) 212 Cal.App.4th 697, 715-16. Other courts hold that the defendant retains the burden of proof on its affirmative defenses. E.g.,* ***Seltzer v. Barnes*** *(1st Dist.2010) (Div. 5) 182 Cal.App.4th 953, 969;* ***Premier Med. Mgmt. Sys. v. California Ins. Guarantee Ass'n*** *(2d Dist.2006) (Div. 4) 136 Cal.App.4th 464, 477.*

(5) D waived anti-SLAPP protection. The plaintiff can oppose the anti-SLAPP motion on the ground that the defendant waived its right to anti-SLAPP protection. *See* ***Navellier v. Sletten*** (2002) 29 Cal.4th 82, 94. For example, a defendant can waive its right by contractually agreeing not to speak on or petition an issue. *Id.*

(6) Action is exempt. The plaintiff can oppose the anti-SLAPP motion on the ground that the challenged cause of action is exempt from the anti-SLAPP statute. The burden is on the plaintiff to establish that a cause of action is exempt. *See* ***Simpson Strong-Tie Co. v. Gore*** (2010) 49 Cal.4th 12, 26. The exempt causes of action are the following:

(a) Enforcement action. An enforcement action brought in the name of the people of the State of California by the Attorney General, district attorney, or city attorney, acting as a public prosecutor, is exempt from the anti-SLAPP statute. CCP §425.16(d); *see also* ***City of L.A. v. Animal Def. League*** (2d Dist.2006) 135 Cal.App.4th 606, 618 (enforcement-action exemption applies to both civil and criminal enforcement actions). To be exempt, the action must be brought to enforce laws aimed generally at public protection. *E.g.,* ***Animal Def. League***, 135 Cal.App.4th at 618-19 (action brought by city on behalf of individual public employees seeking injunctive relief against particular workplace violence was not enforcement action to protect public at large).

NOTE

Courts disagree on whether an otherwise exempt enforcement action will lose its exemption because it is brought in the name of the city or county instead of in the name of "the People." Compare ***City of Colton***, *206 Cal.App.4th at 776-77 (action must be brought in name of "the People"), with* ***Animal Def. League***, *135 Cal.App.4th at 618 (action can brought in name of city or county).*

(b) Public-interest action. An action brought solely in the public interest or on behalf of the general public is exempt from the anti-SLAPP statute. CCP §425.17(b); *e.g.,* ***People v. Acacia Research Corp.*** (4th Dist.2012) 210 Cal.App.4th 487, 491-92 (public-interest action includes qui tam action brought by private person on behalf of general public under Ins. C. §1871.7); ***Ingels v. Westwood One Broad. Servs.*** (2d Dist.2005) 129 Cal.App.4th 1050, 1066 (public-interest action includes class actions and similar suits by Ps acting as private attorneys general under CCP §1021.5). Actions brought solely in the public interest or on behalf of the general public are actions brought for the public good and not just about topics that the public might find interesting. ***Club Members for an Honest Election v. Sierra Club*** (2008) 45 Cal.4th 309, 318. For a public-interest action to be exempt, all the following must be true:

[1] Defendant. The defendant is not one of the following persons or organizations:

[a] Newspaper or magazine personnel. The defendant is not (1) a publisher, (2) an editor, (3) a reporter, or (4) a person who is or has been connected with or employed by a newspaper, magazine, or other periodical publication or by a press association or wire service. *See* CCP §425.17(d)(1); *see also* Cal. Const., art. I, §2(b) (listing newspaper and magazine personnel); Evid. C. §1070(a) (same).

[b] Radio or television personnel. The defendant is not (1) a radio or television news reporter or (2) a person who is or has been connected with or employed by a radio or television station. *See* CCP §425.17(d)(1); *see also* Cal. Const., art. I, §2(b) (listing radio and television personnel); Evid. C. §1070(b) (same).

[c] Book or journal publisher. The defendant is not a person engaged in the dissemination of ideas or expression in any book or academic journal while gathering, receiving, or processing information for communication to the public. CCP §425.17(d)(1); Weil, *Civil Procedure Before Trial*, ¶7:582.

[d] Nonprofit organization. The defendant is not a nonprofit organization that receives more than 50% of its annual revenues from federal, state, or local government grants, awards, programs, or reimbursements for services rendered. CCP §425.17(d)(3).

[2] Not based on expressive work. The action is not based on the creation, dissemination, exhibition, advertisement, or other similar promotion of any dramatic, literary, musical, political, or artistic work. CCP §425.17(d)(2); *see, e.g.*, ***Major v. Silna*** (2d Dist.2005) 134 Cal.App.4th 1485, 1494 (exemption for public-interest action did not apply because action was based on mailing of letters supporting political candidates). This includes but is not limited to a motion picture or television program or an article published in a newspaper or magazine of general circulation. CCP §425.17(d)(2); *see, e.g.*, ***Ingels***, 129 Cal.App.4th at 1068 (radio show was included under CCP §425.17(d)(2)).

[3] No greater relief sought. The plaintiff does not seek any relief greater than or different from the relief sought for the general public or a class of which the plaintiff is a member, other than attorney fees, costs, or penalties. CCP §425.17(b)(1); *see* ***Club Members***, 45 Cal.4th at 316; *see, e.g.*, ***Acacia Research***, 210 Cal.App.4th at 503 (qui tam action under Ins. C. §1871.7 was exempt as public-interest action; P asked for percentage of government's recovery as bounty for bringing action and not for personal damages); ***Ingels***, 129 Cal.App.4th at 1066-67 (age-discrimination action was not exempt as public-interest action; P asked for personal damages for loss of dignity, hurt feelings, and emotional distress). The entire action must have been brought in the public interest or on behalf of the general public; the action is not exempt if any part of the complaint seeks relief greater than or different from the relief sought for the general public. ***Club Members***, 45 Cal.4th at 312.

[4] Benefit to public. The action, if successful, would enforce an important right affecting the public interest and would confer a significant benefit, whether pecuniary or nonpecuniary, on the general public or a large class of persons. CCP §425.17(b)(2); *e.g.*, ***Northern Cal. Carpenters Reg'l Council v. Warmington Hercules Assocs.*** (1st Dist.2004) 124 Cal.App.4th 296, 300 (action by labor organization seeking to enforce city's wage policy for all nonunion workers was exempt as public-interest action).

[5] Private enforcement necessary. Private enforcement is necessary and places a disproportionate financial burden on the plaintiff in relation to the plaintiff's stake in the matter. CCP §425.17(b)(3); *e.g.*, ***City of Colton***, 206 Cal.App.4th at 778-79 (city's action was not exempt as public-interest action when city's financial burden was in direct proportion to its stake in matter). Private enforcement is necessary if no public entity has sought to enforce the rights that the plaintiff seeks to enforce; the possibility that a public entity might bring a lawsuit does not make private enforcement unnecessary. *See* ***Tourgeman v. Nelson & Kennard*** (4th Dist.2014) 222 Cal.App.4th 1447, 1464-65.

(c) Commercial-speech action. An action involving commercial speech is exempt from the anti-SLAPP statute if all the following are true:

[1] D engaged in business. The action is against a defendant primarily engaged in the business of selling or leasing goods or services, including but not limited to insurance, securities, or financial instruments. CCP §425.17(c); ***Simpson Strong-Tie***, 49 Cal.4th at 22; *e.g.*, ***All One God Faith, Inc. v. Organic & Sustainable Indus. Stds., Inc.*** (1st Dist.2010) 183 Cal.App.4th 1186, 1211-12 (trade association acting on behalf of its members was not primarily in business of selling or leasing goods or services); ***Brill Media Co. v. TCW Grp.*** (2d Dist.2005) 132 Cal.App.4th 324, 340-41 (Ds engaged in purchase and sale of financial instruments were primarily in business of selling or leasing goods or services), *disapproved on other grounds*, ***Simpson Strong-Tie Co. v. Gore*** (2010) 49 Cal.4th 12. But the defendant cannot be one of the persons or organizations described under the definition of "public interest" action. *See* CCP §425.17(d). See "Defendant," §4.4.2(6)(b)[1], p. 442.

[2] Not based on expressive work. The action is not based on an expressive work. *See* CCP §425.17(d)(2). See "Not based on expressive work," §4.4.2(6)(b)[2], this page.

[3] Statement or conduct. The action arises from the defendant's statement or conduct. CCP §425.17(c). See "Action arises from protected act," §2.2, p. 433. The statement can be an oral statement, such as a television broadcast, or a written statement, such as an e-mail. *See, e.g.*, ***Contemporary Servs. v. Staff Pro Inc.***

(4th Dist.2007) 152 Cal.App.4th 1043, 1055 (action based on statement made in e-mail); ***Physicians Cmte. for Responsible Med. v. Tyson Foods, Inc.*** (1st Dist.2004) 119 Cal.App.4th 120, 123 (action based on statements published in magazine and broadcast on television).

[a] Representations of fact. The statement or conduct must consist of representations of fact about the defendant's or a business competitor's business operations, goods, or services. CCP §425.17(c)(1); ***Simpson Strong-Tie***, 49 Cal.4th at 30. For example, a promise to take action in the future or a statement that is mere puffery or opinion is not commercial speech because it is not a representation of fact. *See* ***Demetriades v. Yelp, Inc.*** (2d Dist.2014) 228 Cal.App.4th 294, 311-12; ***Navarro v. IHOP Props., Inc.*** (4th Dist.2005) 134 Cal.App.4th 834, 840-41.

[b] Business purpose. The statement or conduct must be made for one of the following purposes:

- The statement or conduct was made to obtain approval for, promote, or secure the sales or leases of, or commercial transactions in, the defendant's goods or services. CCP §425.17(c)(1); ***Simpson Strong-Tie***, 49 Cal.4th at 30; *e.g.*, ***Contemporary Servs.***, 152 Cal.App.4th at 1053-54 (e-mail sent to "set the record straight" about lawsuit was not intended to obtain approval for, promote, or secure business for Ds' event-staffing services); ***Physicians Cmte.***, 119 Cal.App.4th at 128 (allegedly misleading oral and written statements in advertisement about chicken products were made for purpose of promoting sale of those products).

- The statement or conduct was made in the course of delivering the defendant's goods or services. CCP §425.17(c)(1); ***Simpson Strong-Tie***, 49 Cal.4th at 30; *e.g.*, ***Navarro***, 134 Cal.App.4th at 840-41 (allegedly false statements made to induce settlement of lawsuit were not made in course of delivering goods or services).

NOTE

An attorney's legal advice to a prospective client about pending litigation does not constitute commercial speech, even when that advice occurs at the same time the attorney is soliciting the prospective client. ***Taheri Law Grp. v. Evans*** *(2d Dist.2008) 160 Cal.App.4th 482, 492. Attorneys are not, however, completely excluded from the commercial-speech exemption. Id. at 491. For example, the exemption may apply to an attorney's conduct related to an advertising campaign. Id. at 492.*

[c] Intended audience. The statement or conduct must be made under one of the following circumstances:

- The statement or conduct was intended to reach an actual or potential buyer or customer, or a person likely to repeat the statement to or otherwise influence an actual or potential buyer or customer. CCP §425.17(c)(2); *e.g.*, ***Demetriades***, 228 Cal.App.4th at 312 (D's statement about accuracy and performance of its review filter was designed to attract users, and ultimately advertisers, to its website). There is no requirement that the buyer or customer be a buyer or customer of the defendant. *E.g.*, ***Brill Media***, 132 Cal.App.4th at 342 (Ds' statements to Ps' potential customers fell within commercial-speech exemption).

- The statement or conduct arose from or within the context of a regulatory approval process, proceeding, or investigation. CCP §425.17(c)(2). This does not include a statement or conduct by a telephone corporation—even if the statement or conduct concerns an important public issue—that was made in the course of a proceeding before the California Public Utilities Commission and that is the subject of a lawsuit brought by a competitor of the telephone corporation. *Id.*

3. Contents. For a general discussion of the contents of an opposition, see "Opposition Papers," ch. 1-D, §8, p. 35.

(1) Memorandum of points & authorities. See "Memorandum of points & authorities," ch. 1-D, §8.1, p. 35.

(2) Request for costs & reasonable attorney fees. The plaintiff can argue that the anti-SLAPP motion is frivolous or solely intended to cause unnecessary delay, and request that it be awarded costs and reasonable attorney fees under CCP §128.5 for opposing the motion. *See* CCP §425.16(c)(1); *see also* ***Carpenter v. Jack in the Box Corp.*** (2d Dist.2007) 151 Cal.App.4th 454, 469 (§128.5's legal requirements do not change or replace legal requirements stated in §425.16). A motion is frivolous when it is completely without merit or when its sole purpose is to harass the opposing party. CCP §128.5(b)(2); *e.g.*, ***Chitsazzadeh v. Kramer & Kaslow*** (2d Dist.2011) 199 Cal.App.4th 676, 683-84 (untimely anti-SLAPP motion is not frivolous or solely intended to cause unnecessary delay simply because it is filed without leave of court). The request should include enough information about the hours spent defending the motion for the court to calculate reasonable attorney fees. *CEB Action Guide: Making & Opposing Special Motions to Strike*, Step 41, p. 64. For a complete discussion of motions under CCP §128.5, see "Bad-Faith Actions or Tactics—Frivolous or Intended to Cause Delay," ch. 5-K, §3, p. 576.

(3) Supporting evidence. If the plaintiff opposes the anti-SLAPP motion on the ground that it has a probability of prevailing on its cause of action, the opposition papers must be supported by admissible evidence. ***Fashion 21***, 117 Cal.App.4th at 1147. See "Factually sufficient," §4.4.2(4)(b), p. 440. The evidence can be in the form of declarations, affidavits, or matters that can be judicially noticed. *See* CCP §425.16(b)(2); ***Nguyen-Lam***, 171 Cal.App.4th at 871; *see, e.g.*, ***Brill Media***, 132 Cal.App.4th at 339 (Ps filed declarations in opposition to anti-SLAPP motion). See "Request for Judicial Notice," ch. 5-J, p. 547.

4. Copy to Judicial Council. After filing the opposition, the plaintiff must promptly send a copy of the endorsed, filed caption page of the opposition to the Judicial Council by e-mail or fax. CCP §425.16(j)(1).

§5. REPLY

The defendant can file a reply to the opposition.

§5.1 Deadline to file & serve. The reply must be filed and served at least five court days before the hearing. CCP §1005(b). See "Filing & serving reply papers," ch. 1-D, §9.6, p. 37.

§5.2 Grounds.

1. Procedural challenge. The defendant can argue that the opposition was not timely filed and served or lacked the proper supporting evidence. See "Deadline to file & serve," §4.4.1, p. 439; "Supporting evidence," §4.4.3(3), this page.

2. Evidentiary challenge. The defendant can argue that the evidence submitted in support of the opposition contained inadmissible evidence, such as hearsay evidence. *See* ***Gilbert v. Sykes*** (3d Dist.2007) 147 Cal.App.4th 13, 26; *CEB Action Guide: Making & Opposing Special Motions to Strike*, Step 35, pp. 55-56.

3. No probability of prevailing. If the plaintiff has argued that it has a probability of prevailing on its cause of action, the defendant can argue that there is no probability the plaintiff will prevail. *See* CCP §425.16(b)(1). The defendant must support this argument with admissible evidence showing that either the plaintiff cannot establish an element of its cause of action or there is a complete defense to the cause of action. ***Peregrine Funding, Inc. v. Sheppard Mullin Richter & Hampton LLP*** (1st Dist.2005) 133 Cal.App.4th 658, 676; *see* ***Premier Med. Mgmt. Sys. v. California Ins. Guarantee Ass'n*** (2d Dist.2006) 136 Cal.App.4th 464, 477. See "Supporting evidence," §3.5.3, p. 436.

4. Action is not exempt. If the plaintiff has argued that the challenged cause of action is exempt from the anti-SLAPP statute, the defendant can argue that the action is not exempt or the defendant is one of the persons or organizations to which the exemption does not apply. See "Action is exempt," §4.4.2(6), p. 442.

§5.3 Contents. For a general discussion of the contents of a reply, see "Reply Papers," ch. 1-D, §9, p. 37.

§6. HEARING

Hearings on anti-SLAPP motions are conducted in the same manner as civil hearings generally. See "Hearings," ch. 1-H, p. 79.

§7. RULING

§7.1 Standard for granting. An anti-SLAPP motion must be granted if (1) the defendant makes a prima facie showing that the plaintiff's cause of action arises from an act by the defendant in furtherance of its right of free speech or petition in connection with a public issue and (2) the plaintiff cannot establish a probability of prevailing on its claim. *See* CCP §425.16(b)(1); ***Simpson Strong-Tie Co. v. Gore*** (2010) 49 Cal.4th 12, 21.

§7.2 Court's determination. In ruling on an anti-SLAPP motion, the court applies a two-step analysis. ***Simpson Strong-Tie Co. v. Gore*** (2010) 49 Cal.4th 12, 21.

1. Determine if D has met its burden. The court first determines whether the defendant has made a prima facie showing that the plaintiff's cause of action arises from an act by the defendant in furtherance of its right of free speech or petition in connection with a public issue. ***Simpson Strong-Tie***, 49 Cal.4th at 21. See "Defendant's Burden," §2, p. 426. If the defendant has not met its burden, the court must deny the motion; the court is not obligated to determine whether the plaintiff has demonstrated a probability of success. *See* ***Gallimore v. State Farm Fire & Cas. Ins.*** (2d Dist.2002) 102 Cal.App.4th 1388, 1396.

2. Determine if P has met its burden. If the defendant has met its burden, the court must then determine whether the plaintiff has established a probability of prevailing on its claim. ***Simpson Strong-Tie***, 49 Cal.4th at 21. The court can consider the evidentiary submissions of both the plaintiff and the defendant, but it cannot weigh the credibility or comparative probative strength of the competing evidence. ***Wilson v. Parker, Covert & Chidester*** (2002) 28 Cal.4th 811, 821; *see* CCP §425.16(b)(2). If the plaintiff has not met its burden or if the evidence submitted by the defendant defeats the plaintiff's prima facie showing as a matter of law, the court should grant the motion. *See* ***Simpson Strong-Tie***, 49 Cal.4th at 21; ***Soukup v. Law Offices of Herbert Hafif*** (2006) 39 Cal.4th 260, 291. In making this assessment, the court must accept as true the evidence that is favorable to the plaintiff. ***Soukup***, 39 Cal.4th at 291.

§7.3 Effect of ruling. If the court determines that the plaintiff has shown it has a probability of prevailing on its cause of action, that determination or the fact that there was a determination will not be admissible in evidence, nor will any burden of proof or degree of proof change at any later stage of the action or in any later action. CCP §425.16(b)(3).

§8. ORDER

§8.1 Form. The court's ruling on the anti-SLAPP motion must be recorded either in writing or by minute order. *See, e.g.*, ***Mendoza v. ADP Screening & Selection Servs.*** (2d Dist.2010) 182 Cal.App.4th 1644, 1651 (court entered minute order granting anti-SLAPP motion). See "Record of Ruling," ch. 1-I, §4, p. 90.

§8.2 Contents.

1. Motion denied. If the court denies the motion, the order should state the reasons for the denial. If the court finds that the anti-SLAPP motion was frivolous or solely intended to cause unnecessary delay, it must award the plaintiff costs and reasonable attorney fees under CCP §128.5 for defending the motion. CCP §425.16(c)(1). See "Request for costs & reasonable attorney fees," §4.4.3(2), p. 445. The order must recite in detail the conduct or circumstances justifying the award. CCP §128.5(c); *see, e.g.*, ***Carpenter v. Jack in the Box Corp.*** (2d Dist.2007) 151 Cal.App.4th 454, 470 (court's statement of reasons that incorporated motion papers and previous opinion was sufficient).

2. Motion granted.

(1) Generally.

(a) Strike entire complaint. If the court grants the anti-SLAPP motion for all causes of action, the order should strike the entire complaint with prejudice and enter a final judgment. *See CEB Action Guide: Making & Opposing Special Motions to Strike*, Step 40, p. 61; *see, e.g.*, ***Melbostad v. Fisher*** (1st Dist.2008) 165 Cal.App.4th 987, 994 (court's order dismissing entire complaint with prejudice was effective as judgment; no separate judgment was needed).

(b) Strike cause of action. If the court grants the anti-SLAPP motion for some but not all causes of action, the order should strike from the complaint the causes of action that violate CCP §425.16. *See* ***A.F. Brown Elec. Contractor, Inc. v. Rhino Elec. Sup.*** (4th Dist.2006) 137 Cal.App.4th 1118, 1124 (court must strike entire cause of action, not just particular allegations within cause of action); *see, e.g.*, ***Delois v. Barrett Block Partners*** (1st Dist.2009) 177 Cal.App.4th 940, 943 (court's order struck six of ten causes of action). *But see* ***Cho v. Chang*** (2d Dist.2013) 219 Cal.App.4th 521, 527 (court can strike offending portion of mixed cause of action and allow remaining portion to proceed); ***City of Colton v. Singletary*** (4th Dist.2012) 206 Cal.App.4th 751, 772-73 (same).

(2) No leave to amend. If the court grants the anti-SLAPP motion, the court cannot grant the plaintiff leave to amend its complaint. ***Schaffer v. City & Cty. of S.F.*** (1st Dist.2008) 168 Cal.App.4th 992, 1005; ***Simmons v. Allstate Ins.*** (3d Dist.2001) 92 Cal.App.4th 1068, 1073-74; *e.g.*, ***Martin v. Inland Empire Utils. Agency*** (4th Dist.2011) 198 Cal.App.4th 611, 629 (order granting anti-SLAPP motion with leave to amend is functional equivalent of denial).

(3) Attorney fees & costs.

(a) Who can recover. In most cases, a prevailing defendant on an anti-SLAPP motion is entitled to attorney fees and costs. CCP §425.16(c)(1); *see* ***Ketchum v. Moses*** (2001) 24 Cal.4th 1122, 1141-42 (award of fees and costs mandatory when D prevails). *But see* CCP §425.16(c)(2) (listing circumstances when prevailing D is not entitled to attorney fees if initial cause of action is brought under Gov. C. §6259, 11130, 11130.3, 54960, or 54960.1). See "Request for attorney fees & costs," §3.5.4, p. 437. To recover fees and costs, the defendant does not have to be liable for the fees and costs. *See, e.g.*, ***Rosenaur v. Scherer*** (3d Dist.2001) 88 Cal.App.4th 260, 287 (fees and costs recoverable even though attorney represented Ds pro bono). But it is necessary for the defendant to have been represented by separate counsel. *See* ***Witte v. Kaufman*** (3d Dist.2006) 141 Cal.App.4th 1201, 1211 (law firm that was represented by its own attorneys could not recover); *see also* ***Ellis Law Grp. v. Nevada City Sugar Loaf Props., LLC*** (3d Dist.2014) 230 Cal.App.4th 244, 256-57 (of-counsel attorneys who represent their law firms are not entitled to attorney fees; independent contractors may recover only if relationship with firm is not close, continuous, and personal). Thus, an attorney acting as a pro se defendant is not entitled to fees and costs under the anti-SLAPP statute unless the fees were incurred by consulting with an outside attorney. *See* ***Witte***, 141 Cal.App.4th at 1211-12.

[1] Prevailing D – generally. A defendant will be considered a prevailing party if the granting of the anti-SLAPP motion reduces the amount of litigation necessary to resolve the suit. *See, e.g.*, ***Moran v. Endres*** (2d Dist.2006) 135 Cal.App.4th 952, 955 (D was not prevailing party when order striking one cause of action out of ten did not change possible recovery, factual allegations, or work involved in trying case). If the effect of granting the motion is so insignificant that the defendant did not achieve any practical benefit, the defendant will not be a prevailing party. ***Fremont Reorganizing Corp. v. Faigin*** (2d Dist.2011) 198 Cal.App.4th 1153, 1177; ***Mann v. Quality Old Time Serv.*** (4th Dist.2006) 139 Cal.App.4th 328, 340.

[2] After voluntary dismissal. Courts disagree on how to determine if a defendant prevailed on an anti-SLAPP motion when the plaintiff voluntarily dismisses the suit before the hearing on the motion. See "Voluntary dismissal," §4.3, p. 439.

[a] Second District. The Second District Court of Appeal has held that the court must consider the merits of the anti-SLAPP motion to determine if the defendant prevailed. ***Liu v. Moore*** (2d Dist.1999) 69 Cal.App.4th 745, 751; *see also* ***Pfeiffer Venice Props. v. Bernard*** (2d Dist.2002) 101 Cal.App.4th 211, 218 (same standard applies if P's suit is involuntarily dismissed). If the anti-SLAPP motion has merit (i.e., the defendant meets its burden and the plaintiff does not), the defendant is the prevailing party. ***Liu***, 69 Cal.App.4th at 752.

[b] Fourth District. The divisions of the Fourth District Court of Appeal are split on the issue. Division Two has held that the court must look at which party realized its objectives in the litigation to determine the prevailing party. ***Coltrain v. Shewalter*** (4th Dist.1998) (Div. 2) 66 Cal.App.4th 94, 107. Because the defendant's goal is to make the plaintiff go away, ordinarily the defendant will be the prevailing party after a voluntary dismissal. *Id.* But if the plaintiff can show that its objectives were met for reasons unrelated to the merits of the

motion (e.g., it achieved its goals by reaching a settlement because the defendant was insolvent), the plaintiff may be the prevailing party. *Id.* Division One recently issued an opinion disagreeing with ***Coltrain*** to the extent ***Coltrain*** allows an award of attorney fees and costs without first addressing the merits of a defendant's anti-SLAPP motion. ***Tourgeman v. Nelson & Kennard*** (4th Dist.2014) (Div. 1) 222 Cal.App.4th 1447, 1457. The ***Tourgeman*** court instead agreed with the Second District Court of Appeal's decision in ***Liu*** and held that the trial court must first determine that the defendant would have prevailed on its anti-SLAPP motion before awarding attorney fees and costs. ***Tourgeman***, 222 Cal.App.4th at 1457.

(b) Amount recoverable. A prevailing defendant is entitled to recover fees and costs incurred for bringing the anti-SLAPP motion and for litigating the award of attorney fees. ***Ketchum***, 24 Cal.4th at 1141; *see* ***Christian Research Inst. v. Alnor*** (4th Dist.2008) 165 Cal.App.4th 1315, 1320 (D can recover fees and costs only for anti-SLAPP motion, not for entire litigation).

(c) Calculating fees.

[1] Lodestar method. Attorney fees under the anti-SLAPP statute are calculated using the lodestar method (i.e., multiplying a reasonable number of hours worked by the prevailing hourly rate in the community for similar work). ***Ketchum***, 24 Cal.4th at 1131-32; *see Black's Law Dictionary* 1084 (10th ed. 2014) (definition of "lodestar").

[2] Prevailing on only part of motion. If the defendant prevailed on only part of its anti-SLAPP motion, the court should subtract from the award the amount of fees and costs incurred in bringing the unsuccessful part of the motion. *See* ***Mann***, 139 Cal.App.4th at 344-45. To make this reduction, the court can (1) subtract the value of the hours worked on the unsuccessful part of the motion, or (2) if the hours worked on the successful and unsuccessful parts of the motion overlap, determine the percentage of litigation that is eliminated by the successful part of the motion and award only that percentage of attorney fees and costs. *E.g., id.* (court awarded only 50% of requested fees and costs when motion restricted factual allegations, reduced potential recovery, and limited work involved but did not affect three other causes of action, two of which were not even governed by §425.16).

NOTE

For a discussion of how to request attorney fees and costs in a later filed memorandum of costs or noticed motion, see "Procedure for claiming costs," ch. 10-D, §5.3.2, p. 1158.

---

§8.3 Copy to Judicial Council. Any party who files an anti-SLAPP motion or files an opposition to the motion must promptly send a conformed copy of any order issued under CCP §425.16, including any order granting or denying the anti-SLAPP motion or a request for discovery or attorney fees, to the Judicial Council by e-mail or fax. CCP §425.16(j)(1).

§9. APPELLATE REVIEW

§9.1 Appealability.

1. Anti-SLAPP motion.

(1) Immediately appealable. The orders listed below are immediately appealable. The appellate court reviews the order de novo. ***Flatley v. Mauro*** (2006) 39 Cal.4th 299, 325; ***Maranatha Corr., LLC v. Department of Corr. & Rehab.*** (3d Dist.2008) 158 Cal.App.4th 1075, 1084.

(a) Unlimited civil case – order granting motion. An order granting an anti-SLAPP motion in an unlimited civil case is immediately appealable. *See* CCP §§425.16(i), 904.1(a)(13).

(b) Unlimited civil case – order denying motion. Generally, an order denying an anti-SLAPP motion in an unlimited civil case is immediately appealable. *See* CCP §§425.16(i), 904.1(a)(13); *see also* ***Old Republic Constr. Program Grp. v. Boccardo Law Firm, Inc.*** (6th Dist.2014) 230 Cal.App.4th 859, 866 n.4 (order denying anti-SLAPP motion for some causes of action and granting it for others is immediately appealable by moving

party); ***White v. Lieberman*** (2d Dist.2002) 103 Cal.App.4th 210, 220 (order declaring anti-SLAPP motion moot is equivalent to denial and thus appealable). However, an order denying an anti-SLAPP motion on the ground that the action is exempt from the anti-SLAPP statute is not immediately appealable. See "Unlimited civil case – exempt action," §9.1.1(2)(b), this page.

(2) Not immediately appealable. The orders listed below are not immediately appealable. If an order is not immediately appealable, the defendant can either file a petition for a writ of mandate or appeal the order after the court renders a final judgment in the action. *See* CCP §§904.1(a)(1), 904.2(a); ***Goldstein v. Ralphs Grocery Co.*** (2d Dist.2004) 122 Cal.App.4th 229, 233-34; *see, e.g.*, ***Averill v. Superior Ct.*** (4th Dist.1996) 42 Cal.App.4th 1170, 1172 (D filed petition for writ of mandate after anti-SLAPP motion was denied).

(a) Limited civil case. An order either granting or denying an anti-SLAPP motion in a limited civil case is not immediately appealable. ***Citibank v. Tabalon*** (Los Angeles Cty. Superior Ct. Appellate Div. 2012) 209 Cal.App.4th Supp. 16, 20.

(b) Unlimited civil case – exempt action. An order denying an anti-SLAPP motion in an unlimited civil case on the ground that the action is exempt from the anti-SLAPP statute is not immediately appealable. *See* CCP §§425.16(i), 425.17(e), 904.1(a)(13); ***People v. McGraw-Hill Cos.*** (1st Dist.2014) 228 Cal.App.4th 1382, 1389. See "Action is exempt," §4.4.2(6), p. 442. Although an order denying an anti-SLAPP motion in an unlimited civil case is usually immediately appealable, CCP §425.17(e) excludes from the general rule an order denying an anti-SLAPP motion on the ground that the action is an exempt public-interest or commercial-speech action. See "Public-interest action," §4.4.2(6)(b), p. 442; "Commercial-speech action," §4.4.2(6)(c), p. 443. CCP §425.17(e) does not apply to exempt enforcement actions, but one court recently held that an order denying an anti-SLAPP motion on the ground that the action is an exempt enforcement action is also not immediately appealable. *See* ***McGraw-Hill Cos.***, 228 Cal.App.4th at 1389.

2. Application for leave to file late motion. An order granting or denying an application for leave to file a late anti-SLAPP motion is not appealable until the court renders a final judgment in the action. *See* CCP §904.1(a)(1). But if an immediate appeal is taken from an order granting or denying an anti-SLAPP motion, the plaintiff can, as part of its argument on appeal or in its response, seek review of an order granting an application to file a late motion. *See* CCP §906 (appellate court can review any previous rulings that affect order being appealed under §904.1); *see, e.g.*, ***Platypus Wear, Inc. v. Goldberg*** (4th Dist.2008) 166 Cal.App.4th 772, 781 (in responding to appeal, P sought review of order granting application to file late anti-SLAPP motion). The appellate court reviews the ruling on the application for abuse of discretion. ***Platypus Wear***, 166 Cal.App.4th at 782.

3. Motion to conduct discovery. An order granting or denying a motion to conduct discovery is not appealable until the court renders a final judgment in the action. *See* CCP §904.1(a)(1). A party can, however, file a petition for a writ of mandate to challenge the ruling on the motion to conduct discovery. *See, e.g.*, ***Garment Workers Ctr. v. Superior Ct.*** (2d Dist.2004) 117 Cal.App.4th 1156, 1159 (D filed petition for writ of mandate arguing that court should not have permitted P to conduct discovery after anti-SLAPP motion was filed). The appellate court reviews the discovery ruling for abuse of discretion. ***1-800 Contacts, Inc. v. Steinberg*** (2d Dist.2003) 107 Cal.App.4th 568, 593; *see* ***Garment Workers Ctr.***, 117 Cal.App.4th at 1159.

4. Request for attorney fees & costs.

(1) Plaintiff's request. If the ruling on the anti-SLAPP motion is appealed, an order granting or denying a plaintiff's request for attorney fees and costs under CCP §128.5 can be immediately appealed along with the motion. ***Baharian-Mehr v. Smith*** (4th Dist.2010) 189 Cal.App.4th 265, 274-75. *Contra* ***Doe v. Luster*** (2d Dist.2006) 145 Cal.App.4th 139, 150 (dicta). If the ruling on the anti-SLAPP motion is not appealed, an order granting or denying a plaintiff's request for attorney fees and costs cannot be appealed until after final judgment unless the award exceeds $5,000. *See* CCP §904.1(a)(12); ***Baharian-Mehr***, 189 Cal.App.4th at 274 & n.5; *see, e.g.*, ***Doe***, 145 Cal.App.4th at 150 (order on P's motion for recovery of fees filed after court denied anti-SLAPP motion was not appealable); *see also* ***Melbostad v. Fisher*** (1st Dist.2008) 165 Cal.App.4th 987, 994-95 (granting of anti-SLAPP motion that results in complete dismissal of case is final judgment for purposes of appeal).

(2) Defendant's request. An order granting or denying a defendant's request for attorney fees and costs can be immediately appealed as a final collateral order. ***City of Colton v. Singletary*** (4th Dist.2012) 206 Cal.App.4th 751, 781-82. See "Final collateral order," ch. 7-A, §17.1.2(3), p. 777.

§9.2 Copy to Judicial Council. Any party who files an anti-SLAPP motion or files an opposition to the motion must promptly send a copy of any related notice of appeal or petition for a writ of mandate to the Judicial Council by e-mail or fax. CCP §425.16(j)(1).

§9.3 Effect of appeal. The perfecting of an appeal from the denial an anti-SLAPP motion automatically stays all trial-court proceedings that involve the merits of the challenged cause of action. ***Varian Med. Sys. v. Delfino*** (2005) 35 Cal.4th 180, 191; *see* CCP §916(a). For example, the trial court cannot hold a trial on the challenged cause of action while the appeal is pending. *See* ***Varian Med.***, 35 Cal.4th at 196. But the trial court can entertain a motion for attorney fees while the appeal is pending. ***Doe v. Luster*** (2d Dist.2006) 145 Cal.App.4th 139, 144.

L. SPECIAL MOTION TO STRIKE—ANTI-SLAPPBACK MOTION

§1. GENERAL

§1.1 Purpose. When a plaintiff files a cause of action that arises from a defendant's exercise of its constitutional right of free speech or petition, the action is referred to as a SLAPP action (strategic lawsuit against public participation). ***Rusheen v. Cohen*** (2006) 37 Cal.4th 1048, 1055; *see* CCP §425.16. When a SLAPP action is filed, the defendant can have the action dismissed by filing a motion to strike and can recover attorney fees and costs (see "Suit 1" in Example, below). See "Special Motion to Strike—Anti-SLAPP Motion," ch. 4-K, p. 425. In an effort to recover more from the plaintiff, the defendant can file a separate action against the plaintiff for malicious prosecution or abuse of process (see "Suit 2" in Example, below). *See* ***Soukup v. Law Offices of Herbert Hafif*** (2006) 39 Cal.4th 260, 279-80. When such an action is filed, it is referred to as a "SLAPPback." CCP §425.18(b)(1). A SLAPPback is treated more favorably than ordinary actions for malicious prosecution and abuse of process. *See id.* §425.18(a). To defend against a SLAPPback, the plaintiff in the original SLAPP action—now the defendant in the action for malicious prosecution or abuse of process—can file its own motion to strike the SLAPPback, but must follow different procedures than a defendant filing an anti-SLAPP motion. *See id.* §425.18(d)(1); ***Soukup***, 39 Cal.4th at 281-82. A motion to strike a SLAPPback is referred to as an "anti-SLAPPback motion." *See* Kiesel et al., *Matthew Bender Practice Guide: California Pretrial Civil Procedure* (2014), §13.22A; Weil & Brown, *California Practice Guide: Civil Procedure Before Trial* (CD-ROM ed. 2014), ¶¶7:1205, 7:1206. The example below illustrates how the SLAPP and SLAPPback actions arise.

EXAMPLE
Suit 1: X sues Y for defamation → Y strikes defamation action as a SLAPP.
Suit 2: Y sues X for abuse of process → X strikes abuse-of-process action as a SLAPPback.

§1.2 Primary authority. CCP §§425.16-425.18.

§1.3 Secondary authority. The following secondary sources are cited as authority in this subchapter:

- *CEB Action Guide: Making & Opposing Special Motions to Strike Under the California Anti-SLAPP Statute* (CEB 2014) (referred to as *CEB Action Guide: Making & Opposing Special Motions to Strike*).
- Kiesel et al., *Matthew Bender Practice Guide: California Pretrial Civil Procedure* (2014) (referred to as Kiesel, *Cal. Pretrial Civil Procedure*).
- Weil & Brown, *California Practice Guide: Civil Procedure Before Trial* (CD-ROM ed. 2014) (referred to as Weil, *Civil Procedure Before Trial*).

§2. DEFENDANT'S BURDEN

To prevail on an anti-SLAPPback motion, the defendant must make a threshold showing that the plaintiff's action for malicious prosecution or abuse of process arises from the defendant's earlier filing or maintenance of a SLAPP action. *See* ***Soukup v. Law Offices of Herbert Hafif*** (2006) 39 Cal.4th 260, 290-91. Once the defendant has made this required showing, the burden shifts to the plaintiff to establish that it has a probability of prevailing on its cause of action. *Id.* at 291. See "P can probably prevail," §4.2.2(5), p. 453. To meet its burden, the defendant should show all the following:

§2.1 D filed earlier SLAPP action. The defendant should show that it filed an earlier action against the plaintiff that was dismissed as a SLAPP (see "Suit 1" in Example, above). *See* CCP §425.18(b)(1); Kiesel, *Cal. Pretrial Civil Procedure*, §13.22A[1].

§2.2 P has sued D for malicious prosecution or abuse of process. The defendant should show that the plaintiff in the current suit has filed an action against the defendant for malicious prosecution or abuse of process (see "Suit 2" in Example, above). *See* CCP §425.18(b)(1); Kiesel, *Cal. Pretrial Civil Procedure*, §13.22A[1].

§2.3 P's action is a SLAPPback. The defendant should show that the plaintiff's action against the defendant is a SLAPPback because it arises from the defendant's protected activity—that is, the filing or maintenance of the defendant's earlier SLAPP action. *See* CCP §425.18(b)(1); ***Soukup v. Law Offices of Herbert Hafif*** (2006) 39 Cal.4th 260, 291; Kiesel, *Cal. Pretrial Civil Procedure*, §13.22A[1]; *see also* ***Jarrow Formulas, Inc. v. LaMarche*** (2003) 31 Cal.4th 728, 734-35 (malicious-prosecution action falls under anti-SLAPP statute because it arises from protected activity of filing and prosecuting underlying suit).

§3. MOTION

§3.1 What to strike. The defendant can move to strike the entire complaint or one or more causes of action in the complaint. *See* CCP §425.18(g).

§3.2 Who can file. The defendant can file an anti-SLAPPback motion. CCP §425.18(b); ***Soukup v. Law Offices of Herbert Hafif*** (2006) 39 Cal.4th 260, 280.

§3.3 Deadline to file & serve.

1. Deadline to file. An anti-SLAPPback motion must be filed within one of the following deadlines:

(1) Within 120 days after service of the complaint. CCP §425.18(d)(1)(A).

(2) At the court's discretion, within six months after service of the complaint. *Id.* §425.18(d)(1)(B).

(3) At the court's discretion, at any later time if (1) the case is extraordinary, (2) the delay was not the defendant's fault, and (3) the court makes written findings stating the nature of the extraordinary case and the delay. *Id.* §425.18(d)(1)(C).

2. Deadline to serve. The anti-SLAPPback motion must be served at least 16 court days before the hearing date. CCP §1005(b). If the motion is served by means other than personal delivery, the defendant will have to add extra time to the 16-day period (e.g., five calendar days are added when notice is mailed in California to a California address). *Id.* See "Retrospective deadlines," ch. 1-G, §6.2, p. 71.

§3.4 Deadline for hearing. The hearing on the anti-SLAPPback motion must be set by the court clerk within 30 days after service of the motion unless the court's docket conditions require a later hearing. CCP §425.18(d)(2). But the motion cannot be denied solely because the defendant was unable to obtain a hearing within the 30-day deadline. *Cf.* ***Hall v. Time Warner, Inc.*** (2d Dist.2007) 153 Cal.App.4th 1337, 1349 (explaining identical deadline under CCP §425.16).

§3.5 Contents.

1. Notice of motion & motion.

(1) Generally. An anti-SLAPPback motion should be made by a noticed motion. *See* CRC 3.1112(a). See "Notice of motion & motion," ch. 1-D, §5.1, p. 28.

(2) Relief. The notice of motion and motion must describe the relief sought. *See* CRC 3.1110(a) (notice of motion must state nature of order being sought), CRC 3.1112(d)(3) (motion must briefly state relief sought). The notice of motion should specify the matters to be struck (e.g., complaint, second cause of action). *See* CRC 3.1112(d)(4).

(3) Grounds. The notice of motion and motion must briefly state the grounds for the relief (e.g., "the motion will be made on the ground that the cause of action alleged against the defendant arises from defendant's filing of an earlier cause of action against the plaintiff that was dismissed as a SLAPP action"). *See* CRC 3.1110(a) (notice of motion must state grounds for issuance of order), CRC 3.1112(d)(3) (motion must briefly state basis for motion). See "Defendant's Burden," §2, p. 451.

2. Memorandum of points & authorities. The motion must include a memorandum in support of the motion. CRC 3.1112(a)(3), 3.1113(a). See "Memorandum of points & authorities," ch. 1-D, §5.2, p. 28.

3. Supporting evidence. The defendant should attach evidence to support its motion. *See, e.g.,* ***Soukup v. Law Offices of Herbert Hafif*** (2006) 39 Cal.4th 260, 276 (Ds attached several exhibits, including declaration and pages from diary). See "Supporting evidence," ch. 4-K, §3.5.3, p. 436.

4. Request for judicial notice. The defendant can submit a request for judicial notice. *See* CRC 3.1113(*l*). The request must be made in a separate document. *Id.* See "Request for Judicial Notice," ch. 5-J, p. 547.

5. Proposed order. The defendant can submit a proposed order with the motion. *See* CRC 3.1113(m). If a proposed order is submitted, it must be lodged and served with the motion papers, not attached to them. *Id.* See "Documents lodged," ch. 1-F, §2.3, p. 47.

§3.6 Filing fees. When the motion is filed, the defendant must pay a filing fee to the court clerk or request a waiver of the fee. See "Filing Fees," ch. 1-F, §7, p. 58.

§3.7 Copy to Judicial Council. After filing the anti-SLAPPback motion, the defendant must promptly send a copy of the endorsed, filed caption page of the motion to the Judicial Council by e-mail or fax. *See* CCP §§425.16(j)(1), 425.18(b)(2), (c).

NOTE

The defendant must also send other documents related to the special motion to strike "promptly" to the Judicial Council. See CCP §§425.16(j)(1), 425.18(b)(2). It is unclear whether this means the defendant can wait and send the caption page of the special motion to strike when it sends the other documents.

---

§3.8 Effect of motion on discovery. The filing of an anti-SLAPPback motion does not stay discovery. *See* CCP §425.18(c) (§425.16(g) not applicable to anti-SLAPPback motions).

§4. RESPONSE

§4.1 Ex parte application for continuance. The plaintiff can respond to an anti-SLAPPback motion by filing an ex parte application for a continuance to conduct discovery. CCP §425.18(e). The court must grant the application if it appears there are facts supporting the opposition that cannot be presented until discovery is conducted. *Id.* See "Ex Parte Practice," ch. 1-E, p. 39.

§4.2 Opposition. The plaintiff can respond to an anti-SLAPPback motion by filing an opposition. *See* CCP §425.16(j)(1); ***Soukup v. Law Offices of Herbert Hafif*** (2006) 39 Cal.4th 260, 286-87.

1. Deadline to file & serve. The opposition papers must be filed and served nine court days before the hearing. CCP §1005(b). See "Filing & serving opposition," ch. 1-D, §8.5, p. 36.

2. Grounds. To defeat an anti-SLAPPback motion, the plaintiff must establish one of the following:

(1) Procedural defect. The plaintiff can oppose the anti-SLAPPback motion on the ground that the motion was not timely filed and served. See "Deadline to file & serve," §3.3, p. 451.

(2) Evidentiary objection. The plaintiff can oppose the anti-SLAPPback motion on the ground that the evidence submitted in support of the motion contained inadmissible evidence, such as hearsay. *Cf. CEB Action Guide: Making & Opposing Special Motions to Strike*, Step 31, p. 51 (discussing anti-SLAPP motion).

(3) P is public entity. The plaintiff can oppose the anti-SLAPPback motion on the ground that the motion is unavailable because the plaintiff is a public entity. CCP §425.18(i).

(4) D's SLAPP action was illegal. The plaintiff can oppose the anti-SLAPPback motion on the ground that the defendant's SLAPP action, which is the basis for plaintiff's current action against the defendant, was illegal as a matter of law. CCP §425.18(h). To show that the defendant's earlier SLAPP action was illegal as a matter of law, the plaintiff must establish that the illegality was conceded by the defendant or is conclusively established by the evidence presented in connection with the motion. ***Soukup***, 39 Cal.4th at 286-87. The plaintiff must identify with particularity the statute allegedly violated by the filing of the SLAPP action and must show the specific manner in which the statute was violated with reference to the statutory elements. *Id.* at 287. The mere fact that the SLAPP action was dismissed is not sufficient to establish illegality. *See id.* at 283.

(5) P can probably prevail. The plaintiff can oppose the anti-SLAPPback motion on the ground that even if the defendant has met its initial burden, the plaintiff has a probability of prevailing on its cause of action. ***Soukup***, 39 Cal.4th at 291. The plaintiff can show there is a probability it will prevail on its claim by demonstrating that its complaint is both legally sufficient and supported by a sufficient prima facie showing of facts, which, if proved at trial, will support a favorable judgment. *Id.* The plaintiff has to produce only enough facts to show minimal merit. *Id.*

(a) Malicious prosecution. To show it has a probability of prevailing on a malicious-prosecution claim, the plaintiff must make a prima facie showing that the underlying cause of action (1) was commenced by or at the direction of the defendant and ended with a judgment for the plaintiff, (2) was brought without probable cause, and (3) was initiated with malice. ***Soukup***, 39 Cal.4th at 292.

(b) Abuse of process. To show it has a probability of prevailing on an abuse-of-process claim, the plaintiff must make a prima facie showing that the defendant (1) contemplated an ulterior motive in using the court's process and (2) committed a willful act in using the court's process that was not proper in the regular conduct of the proceedings. ***Rusheen v. Cohen*** (2006) 37 Cal.4th 1048, 1057.

3. Contents. For a general discussion of the contents of an opposition, see "Opposition Papers," ch. 1-D, §8, p. 35.

(1) Memorandum of points & authorities. See "Memorandum of points & authorities," ch. 1-D, §8.1, p. 35.

(2) Request for costs & reasonable attorney fees. The plaintiff can allege that the anti-SLAPPback motion is frivolous and solely intended to cause unnecessary delay and request that it be awarded costs and reasonable attorney fees under CCP §128.5 for opposing the motion. CCP §425.18(f). A motion is frivolous when it is completely without merit or when its sole purpose is to harass the opposing party. *Id.* §128.5(b)(2). The request should include enough information about the hours spent defending the motion for the court to calculate reasonable attorney fees. *Cf. CEB Action Guide: Making & Opposing Special Motions to Strike*, Step 41, p. 64 (discussing P's request for attorney fees in anti-SLAPP motion). For a complete discussion of motions under CCP §128.5, see "Bad-Faith Actions or Tactics—Frivolous or Intended to Cause Delay," ch. 5-K, §3, p. 576.

NOTE

If the plaintiff does not request attorney fees and costs under CCP §128.5 in its response, and if it successfully opposes the motion, the plaintiff should file a separate motion for attorney fees and costs. Cf. ***Carpenter v. Jack in the Box Corp.*** *(2d Dist.2007) 151 Cal.App.4th 454, 459 (P filed motion for attorney fees and costs after denial of anti-SLAPP motion).*

(3) Supporting evidence. The opposition can be supported by the same type of evidence used to support the motion. See "Supporting evidence," ch. 1-D, §5.3, p. 30.

4. Copy to Judicial Council. After filing the opposition, the plaintiff must promptly send a copy of the endorsed, filed caption page of the opposition to the Judicial Council by e-mail or fax. *See* CCP §§425.16(j)(1), 425.18(b)(2), (c).

§5. REPLY

The defendant can file a reply to the opposition. See "Reply Papers," ch. 1-D, §9, p. 37.

§6. HEARING

Hearings on a special motion to strike a SLAPPback are conducted in the same manner as civil hearings generally. See "Hearings," ch. 1-H, p. 79.

§7. RULING

The court's ruling on an anti-SLAPPback motion is determined in the same way as a ruling on an anti-SLAPP motion. See "Ruling," ch. 4-K, §7, p. 446.

§8. ORDER

§8.1 Form. The court's ruling on the motion must be recorded either in writing or by minute order. See "Record of Ruling," ch. 1-I, §4, p. 90.

§8.2 Contents.

1. Motion denied. If the court denies the anti-SLAPPback motion and finds that the motion was frivolous or solely intended to cause unnecessary delay, it must award the plaintiff costs and reasonable attorney fees under CCP §128.5 for defending the motion. CCP §425.18(f). See "Request for costs & reasonable attorney fees," §4.2.3(2), p. 453. The order must be in writing and recite in detail the conduct or circumstances justifying the award. CCP §128.5(c); *cf. **Carpenter v. Jack in the Box Corp.*** (2d Dist.2007) 151 Cal.App.4th 454, 469-70 (court's statement of reasons for imposing fees and costs after denial of anti-SLAPP motion incorporated motion papers and previous opinion affirming denial of motion).

2. Motion granted.

(1) Generally.

(a) Strike entire complaint. If the court grants the motion for all causes of action, the order should strike the entire complaint with prejudice and enter a final judgment. *Cf. **Melbostad v. Fisher*** (1st Dist.2008) 165 Cal.App.4th 987, 994 (court's order granting anti-SLAPP motion for entire complaint was effective as order of dismissal, even if order did not use dismissal language); *CEB Action Guide: Making & Opposing Special Motions to Strike*, Step 40, p. 61 (D should prepare proposed judgment striking complaint if anti-SLAPP motion is granted for all causes of action).

(b) Strike cause of action. If the court grants the anti-SLAPPback motion for some but not all causes of action, the order should strike from the complaint the causes of action that violate CCP §425.18. *See* CCP §425.18(g) (court can strike particular causes of action and allow others to remain); *cf. **Delois v. Barrett Block Partners*** (1st Dist.2009) 177 Cal.App.4th 940, 943 (applying §425.16; court's order struck six of ten causes of action); ***A.F. Brown Elec. Contractor, Inc. v. Rhino Elec. Sup.*** (4th Dist.2006) 137 Cal.App.4th 1118, 1124 (applying §425.16; court must strike entire cause of action, not just particular allegations within cause of action).

(2) No attorney fees or costs. The defendant is not entitled to recover attorney fees or costs for prevailing on the anti-SLAPPback motion. *See* CCP §425.18(c) (§425.16(c) not applicable to anti-SLAPPback motions), §425.18(f) (no mention of attorney fees and costs for D, only for P).

§9. APPELLATE REVIEW

§9.1 Writ of mandate. Within 20 days after service of a written notice of the entry of the order, an aggrieved party can file a petition for a peremptory writ from the following:

1. An order denying the special motion to strike a SLAPPback. CCP §425.18(g).

2. An order granting the special motion to strike a SLAPPback for some but not all causes of action alleged in the complaint. *Id.*

§9.2 Direct appeal. An order granting or denying an anti-SLAPPback motion is not appealable until the court renders a final judgment in the action (e.g., grants the motion for all causes of action and dismisses the entire complaint). *See* CCP §425.18(c) (§425.16(i) not applicable to anti-SLAPPback motions).

§9.3 Copy to Judicial Council. Any party who files an anti-SLAPPback motion or files an opposition to the motion must promptly send a copy of any related notice of appeal or petition for a writ to the Judicial Council by e-mail or fax. *See* CCP §§425.16(j)(1), 425.18(b)(2), (c).

California Civil Pretrial

Chapter 5. Pretrial Motions

Table of Contents

TABLE OF CONTENTS

CHAPTER 5. PRETRIAL MOTIONS
TABLE OF CONTENTS

TABLE OF CONTENTS

5. PRETRIAL MOTIONS

A. CIVIL CASE MANAGEMENT

This subchapter discusses the case-management rules for general civil cases under the Trial Court Delay Reduction Act (TCDRA). This subchapter does not discuss the case-management rules for family-law, probate, juvenile-court, small-claims, unlawful-detainer, civil-petition, and class-action cases.

In 1990, the TCDRA was adopted to streamline court operations in an effort to cut down on the average time to trial in civil cases. *See generally* Gov. C. §§68600-68620 (TCDRA). To accomplish the goals of the TCDRA, the Judicial Council was directed to adopt standards for processing litigation more quickly. *See id.* §68603. The standards were enacted as the civil case-management rules, otherwise known as the "delay reduction" or "fast track" rules. *See* CRC 3.700, 3.713(a), 3.720(a). To ensure the efficient processing and resolution of civil cases, the rules created a framework within which the court, not the parties, would control the pace of the litigation. *See* CRC 3.713, 3.720(a).

Under the fast-track framework, the court is responsible for assuming and maintaining control of the pace of general civil litigation, and as part of that duty, the court must require the parties and their attorneys to prepare and resolve litigation without delay from the filing of the first document invoking the court's jurisdiction to the case's final disposition. Gov. C. §68607; Weil & Brown, *California Practice Guide: Civil Procedure Before Trial* (CD-ROM ed. 2014) ¶12:6. Each case is evaluated on its own merits under the case-management rules to determine its estimated time to disposition and its relative complexity. *See* Gov. C. §68603(c); CRC 3.714(a). This evaluation (also called a "case differential plan") determines what case-management plan, if any, should be assigned to control the pace of litigation, the details of which are determined at the initial case-management conference and recorded in the court's case-management order. *See* CRC 3.714(a), 3.728.

§1. GENERAL

§1.1 Purpose. The purpose of the civil case-management system is to secure a fair, timely, and efficient disposition of civil suits. CRC 3.700; *see* ***Lu v. Superior Ct.*** (4th Dist.1997) 55 Cal.App.4th 1264, 1267-68 (case-management orders lay out clear path and timetable for completion of all tasks necessary to ready case for trial); ***Stadish v. Superior Ct.*** (2d Dist.1999) 71 Cal.App.4th 1130, 1146 (Zebrowski, J., concurring) (case-management orders are designed to streamline case processing, to control delay and expense, and to promote just results).

§1.2 Primary authority. Gov. C. §§68600-68620; CRC 3.700-3.735, 3.750.

§1.3 Secondary authority. The following secondary sources are cited as authority in this subchapter:

- *California Civil Procedure Before Trial* (CEB Online ed. 2014) (referred to as *CEB Procedure Before Trial*).
- Kiesel et al., *Matthew Bender Practice Guide: California Pretrial Civil Procedure* (2014) (referred to as Kiesel, *Cal. Pretrial Civil Procedure*).
- Weil & Brown, *California Practice Guide: Civil Procedure Before Trial* (CD-ROM ed. 2014) (referred to as Weil, *Civil Procedure Before Trial*).

§1.4 Judicial Council forms.

- CM-010 (mandatory), civil-case cover sheet.
- CM-110 (mandatory), case-management statement.

§2. OVERVIEW OF CASE-MANAGEMENT PROCESS

Chart 5-1, below, outlines the general steps and timing of the case-management process under the Trial Court Delay Reduction Act (TCDRA). The steps and timing outlined below may be altered, however, by local rule. The TCDRA explicitly gives each court the power to adopt its own case-management rules. Gov. C. §68612; *see, e.g.*, CRC 3.711 (each court must adopt rules on differential case management). The local rules that are adopted to implement the TCDRA

are not preempted by the California Rules of Court or other statutes. *See* CRC 3.20(a), (b)(4). Thus, it is imperative that a party familiarize itself with a court's local rules on case management before proceeding with a case in superior court. *CEB Procedure Before Trial*, §40.4; *see* ***Moyal v. Lanphear*** (4th Dist.1989) 208 Cal.App.3d 491, 499 (attorneys have professional responsibility to be aware of local case-management rules).

5-1. OVERVIEW OF CASE-MANAGEMENT PROCESS UNDER TCDRA

	Step	Timing	Discussion
1	Plaintiff determines applicability of TCDRA's case-management rules	Before complaint is filed	§3, this page
2	Court sets date of initial case-management conference (CMC)	Typically when complaint is filed	§4.1, p. 463
3	Plaintiff or court sends notice of initial CMC	Typically when complaint is served, but no later than 45 days before initial CMC unless court orders otherwise	§4.2, p. 463
4	Court reviews case and either assigns it to or exempts it from case-management plan	No later than 180 days after complaint is filed	§5, p. 464
5	Parties meet and confer	No later than 30 calendar days before initial CMC	§6, p. 466
6	Parties file and serve case-management statement	No later than 15 calendar days before initial CMC	§7, p. 467
7	Initial CMC held	No later than 180 days after complaint is filed	§8, p. 468
8	Court issues case-management order	At or after CMC	§9, p. 472

§3. APPLICABILITY OF CASE-MANAGEMENT RULES

Before a plaintiff files a complaint, the plaintiff should determine if its case will be subject to the case-management rules under the TCDRA. If the case is subject to the rules, it may need to be disposed of within 12 to 24 months after the complaint is filed. Thus, if the plaintiff's case is not sufficiently prepared to meet the TCDRA's disposition time goals, the plaintiff should consider delaying the filing of its complaint. If the complaint must be filed to prevent the statute of limitations from running, the plaintiff can ask the defendant if it will agree to waive the statute of limitations. Weil, *Civil Procedure Before Trial*, ¶12:5; *see also* CCP §360.5 (requirements for waiver).

§3.1 General civil cases. The case-management rules under the TCDRA apply to most general civil cases. *See* CRC 3.712(a), 3.721. "General civil cases" include all civil cases except the following:

1. Probate, guardianship, conservatorship, juvenile, and family-law proceedings. CRC 1.6(4); *see* Gov. C. §68608(a).

2. Small-claims proceedings. CRC 1.6(4); *see* Gov. C. §68620(b).

3. Unlawful-detainer proceedings (i.e., actions based on forcible entry, forcible detainer, or unlawful detainer). CRC 1.6(4); *see* Gov. C. §68620(b). *See generally* CCP §§1159-1179a (summary proceedings for obtaining possession of real property in certain cases).

4. Certain civil petitions, including petitions to prevent civil harassment, elder abuse, and workplace violence, petitions for name change, election-contest petitions, and petitions for relief from late claims. *See* CRC 1.6(4), (5).

§3.2 Exceptions.

1. Cases exempted. The following general civil cases are exempt from the TCDRA's case-management rules:

(1) Cases exempted by local rule. CRC 3.720(b); *see, e.g.*, Super. Ct. Sacramento Cty. Loc. R., rule 2.46(E) (court can exempt certain civil cases from case-management rules in interest of justice). In response to the

current fiscal crisis in California, CRC 3.720 was amended to permit courts, by local rule, to exempt specified types or categories of general civil cases that are filed before January 1, 2016, from the case-management rules. *See* CRC 3.720(b) & advisory committee's cmt., www.courts.ca.gov/rules.htm. The exemptions are permissible as long as the court has in place alternative procedures and trial settings for the actions that are exempted and the court posts the alternative procedures on its website. CRC 3.720(b).

(2) Cases brought under the False Claims Act. CRC 2.573(e)(2). *See generally* Gov. C. §§12650-12656 (False Claims Act).

(3) Cases assigned to a judge for all purposes based on subject matter (e.g., asbestos cases). *See* Gov. C. §68608(a) (cases assigned to judge for all purposes based on subject matter need not be assigned to delay-reduction program), §68609(b) (cases assigned to judge for all purposes based on subject matter need not be assigned to exemplary delay-reduction program).

2. Cases conditionally exempted. The following general civil cases are exempt from the TCDRA's case-management rules until or unless a condition is met:

(1) Cases designated by the court as uninsured-motorist cases are exempt from the case-management rules until 180 days after the designation. CRC 3.712(b); *see* Gov. C. §68609.5; CRC 3.721.

(2) Cases included in a petition for coordination are exempt from the case-management rules unless the petition is granted and the coordination trial judge elects to establish a case-progression plan. CRC 3.712(c).

(3) Collections cases are exempt from the case-management rules unless the defendant files a responsive pleading. CRC 3.712(d), 3.740(c)(2). See "Collections case," ch. 3-C, §3.1.2(1), p. 211.

§4. DATE & NOTICE OF INITIAL CASE-MANAGEMENT CONFERENCE

§4.1 Date of initial CMC.

1. Most cases. In most cases, the court will set a date for an initial case-management conference (CMC) when the complaint is filed. *See* CRC 3.722(a); *see, e.g.*, Super. Ct. Contra Costa Cty. Loc. R., rule 3.8(a)(2) (clerk sets date when complaint is filed); Super. Ct. San Francisco Cty. Loc. R., rule 3.2.A (same); Super. Ct. San Mateo Cty. Loc. R., rule 2.3.E(1) (same). The initial CMC should be set for no later than 180 days after the complaint is filed. *See* CRC 3.721; *see, e.g.*, Super. Ct. Contra Costa Cty. Loc. R., rule 3.8(a)(2) (CMC will be set within 140 days after complaint is filed); Super. Ct. San Diego Cty. Loc. R., rule 2.1.9.A (CMC will be set approximately 150 days after complaint is filed). See "Scheduling," §8.1.1, p. 468.

2. Collections cases. In collections cases, the court will not set a date for the initial CMC until a responsive pleading is filed. *See* CRC 3.712(d), 3.721, 3.740(c)(2); *see, e.g.*, Super. Ct. Solano Cty. Loc. R., rule 4.6.c (date is set in limited collections cases after response is filed). See "Collections case," ch. 3-C, §3.1.2(1), p. 211.

3. Uninsured-motorist cases. In uninsured-motorist cases, the court will not set a date for the initial CMC until 180 days after the case is designated as such. *See* Gov. C. §68609.5; CRC 3.712(b), 3.721.

4. Complex cases. In complex cases, the court will set a date for the initial CMC at the earliest practical date. CRC 3.750(a). See "Complex case," ch. 3-C, §3.1.2(2), p. 211.

NOTE

Some courts' local rules do not require a CMC in certain cases. E.g., Super. Ct. Los Angeles Cty. Loc. R., rule 3.24(b) (CMC not held in limited civil cases); Super. Ct. Sacramento Cty. Loc. R., rule 2.50(C) (same).

§4.2 Notice of initial CMC.

Notice of the initial CMC must be given to all parties who are not in default. *See* CRC 3.722(b); ***Sporn v. Home Depot USA, Inc.*** (4th Dist.2005) 126 Cal.App.4th 1294, 1301-02.

1. Deadline. Notice must be given no later than 45 days before the initial CMC unless the court orders otherwise. CRC 3.722(b); *see, e.g.*, Super. Ct. San Mateo Cty. Loc. R., rule 2.3.E(3) (must serve notice at least 30 calendar days before CMC).

2. Manner. The manner in which notice is given is generally set by local rule. *See* CRC 3.722(b). For example, some courts require the clerk to serve notice when the complaint is filed. *E.g.*, Super. Ct. Sacramento Cty. Loc. R., rule 2.50(A). Other courts require the clerk to give notice to the plaintiff to be served with the complaint and the summons. *E.g.*, Super. Ct. San Francisco Cty. Loc. R., rule 3.2.A; Super. Ct. Sierra Cty. Loc. R., rule 3.1; Super. Ct. Solano Cty. Loc. R., rule 4.6.a, 4.6.d(1).

§5. ASSIGNMENT TO CASE-MANAGEMENT PLAN

Shortly after the complaint is filed, the court will evaluate the case to determine its estimated time to disposition and its complexity. *See* Gov. C. §68603(c); CRC 3.714(a); Kiesel, *Cal. Pretrial Civil Procedure*, §23.04[1][a]. The court's evaluation will determine what case-management plan, if any, should be assigned to control the pace of litigation.

§5.1 Deadline to conduct case evaluation.

1. Most cases. For most cases, the case evaluation must be completed within 180 days after the complaint is filed. CRC 3.721. The court is not required to conduct the evaluation in the presence of counsel. *See* Weil, *Civil Procedure Before Trial*, ¶12:77; *see also* CRC 3.714(a) (stating only that court must evaluate each case on its own merits).

2. Uninsured-motorist cases. For a case designated by the court as an uninsured-motorist case, the 180-day deadline to evaluate the case is tolled for 180 days after the designation. *See* Gov. C. §68609.5; CRC 3.712(b), 3.721.

3. Complex cases.

(1) Generally – earliest practical time. If the plaintiff has filed a civil-case cover sheet designating the case as complex or provisionally complex and the defendant has not filed its own cover sheet opposing the plaintiff's designation, the court must decide if the case is complex at the earliest practical time. CRC 3.403(a). See "Complex case," ch. 3-C, §3.1.2(2), p. 211; "Countering plaintiff's designation," ch. 4-B, §3.1.2(1), p. 337. The court can make this determination with or without a hearing. CRC 3.403(a).

(2) 30 days after counterdesignation. If the defendant has filed its own civil-case cover sheet opposing the plaintiff's designation of the case as complex or not complex, the court must decide if the case is complex within 30 days after the counterdesignation is filed. CRC 3.402(a), (b). See "Complex case," ch. 3-C, §3.1.2(2), p. 211; "Countering plaintiff's designation," ch. 4-B, §3.1.2(1), p. 337. The court can make this determination with or without a hearing. CRC 3.402(a) (noncomplex counterdesignation), CRC 3.402(b) (complex counterdesignation).

NOTE

The court on its own motion or on a party's noticed motion can determine, with or without a hearing, that a case is complex or that a case previously declared complex is not. CRC 3.403(b). If the court determines that a case is complex and the parties did not pay the complex-case fee ($550) when they filed their pleadings, the parties will have ten calendar days to pay the fee from the date the court files its order determining the case to be complex. See Gov. C. §70616(a), (b), (e).

---

4. Short-cause cases. For short-cause cases, the court on its own motion or by the parties' stipulation can exempt the case from any case-management review and set the case for trial. CRC 3.735(b). A short-cause case is one in which the time estimated for trial by all parties and the court is five hours or less. CRC 3.735(a). If a short-cause case is not completed within five hours, the judge can complete the trial or declare a mistrial. CRC 3.735(c). If the court declares a mistrial, the case is no longer a short-cause case and must be set either for a new trial or for a CMC under the appropriate case-management plan. *Id.*

§5.2 Evaluation factors.

1. Time for disposition. The court must determine the maximum time reasonably required to justly and effectively dispose of the case. CRC 3.715(a). To do this, the court must consider the following factors:

(1) Type and subject matter of the case. CRC 3.715(a)(1).

(2) Number of causes of action or affirmative defenses alleged. CRC 3.715(a)(2).

(3) Number of parties with separate interests. CRC 3.715(a)(3).

(4) Number of cross-complaints and the subject matter. CRC 3.715(a)(4).

(5) Complexity of issues, including issues of first impression. CRC 3.715(a)(5).

(6) Difficulty in identifying, locating, and serving parties. CRC 3.715(a)(6).

(7) Nature and extent of anticipated discovery. CRC 3.715(a)(7).

(8) Number and location of percipient witnesses and expert witnesses. CRC 3.715(a)(8).

(9) Estimated length of trial. CRC 3.715(a)(9).

(10) Whether some or all issues can be arbitrated or resolved through other ADR processes. CRC 3.715(a)(10).

(11) Statutory priority for the issue. CRC 3.715(a)(11).

(12) Likelihood of review by writ or appeal. CRC 3.715(a)(12).

(13) Amount in controversy and type of remedy sought, including measures of damages. CRC 3.715(a)(13).

(14) Pendency of other actions and proceedings that may affect the case. CRC 3.715(a)(14).

(15) Nature and extent of law-and-motion proceedings anticipated. CRC 3.715(a)(15).

(16) Nature and extent of injuries and damages. CRC 3.715(a)(16).

(17) Pendency of underinsured claims. CRC 3.715(a)(17).

(18) Any other factor that would affect the time for disposition of the case. CRC 3.715(a)(18).

2. Complexity. The court must evaluate whether the case is complex. *See* CRC 3.402(a), (b), 3.403. A complex case is one that requires exceptional judicial management (1) to avoid placing unnecessary burdens on the court or the litigants, (2) to expedite the case, (3) to keep costs reasonable, and (4) to promote efficient decision-making by the court, the parties, and counsel. CRC 3.400(a). In deciding whether a case is complex, the court must consider if the case is likely to involve any of the following:

(1) Numerous pretrial motions raising difficult or novel legal issues that will be time-consuming to resolve. CRC 3.400(b)(1).

(2) Management of a large number of witnesses or a substantial amount of documentary evidence. CRC 3.400(b)(2).

(3) Management of a large number of separately represented parties. CRC 3.400(b)(3).

(4) Coordination with related actions pending in one or more courts in other counties, states, or countries, or in federal court. CRC 3.400(b)(4).

(5) Substantial postjudgment judicial supervision. CRC 3.400(b)(5).

§5.3 Case-management assignment. After the court has evaluated the case, it must (1) assign it to a local case-management plan for expedited disposition if one has been adopted, (2) exempt the case as an exceptional case, or (3) assign it to a case-management plan for review under the disposition time goals in CRC 3.714(b). *See* CRC 3.714(a), (d).

1. Assignment to local case-management plan (uncomplicated cases). If the court determines that the case is uncomplicated, can be disposed of quickly, and does not need a CMC or review or similar event to guide the case to early resolution, the court can assign the case to a local case-management plan for disposition within six to nine months if such a plan has been adopted by local rule. CRC 3.714(d); *see* CRC 3.714(a)(3); *see, e.g.*, Super. Ct. Sonoma Cty. Loc. R., rule 4.1.C (local case-management plan).

2. Exemption as exceptional case. If the court determines that the case involves exceptional circumstances that will prevent the court and the parties from meeting the goals and deadlines imposed by the case-management rules, the court can, in the interest of justice, exempt the case from the disposition time goals in CRC 3.714(b). CRC 3.714(c)(1); *see* Cal. Stds. Jud. Admin. 2.2(g) (if case meets criteria in CRC 3.400 and 3.715 and involves exceptional circumstances or will require continuing review, case is exempt). If the case is exempted, the court must establish a case-progression plan and monitor the case to ensure timely disposition consistent with the exceptional circumstances, with the goal of disposing of the case within three years. CRC 3.714(c)(2); *see* CRC 3.714(a)(2).

3. Assignment to case-management plan for review. If the court determines that the case is neither uncomplicated nor exempt, the court should assign the case to a case-management plan for review under the case-management rules and disposition time goals in the California Rules of Court. *See* CRC 3.714(a)(1). These cases should be managed to meet the following case-disposition goals:

(1) **Unlimited civil cases.** Unlimited civil cases should be managed to meet the following goals:

(a) 75% are disposed of within 12 months after filing. CRC 3.714(b)(1)(A).

(b) 85% are disposed of within 18 months after filing. CRC 3.714(b)(1)(B).

(c) 100% are disposed of within 24 months after filing. CRC 3.714(b)(1)(C).

(2) **Limited civil cases.** Limited civil cases should be managed to meet the following goals:

(a) 90% are disposed of within 12 months after filing. CRC 3.714(b)(2)(A).

(b) 98% are disposed of within 18 months after filing. CRC 3.714(b)(2)(B).

(c) 100% are disposed of within 24 months after filing. CRC 3.714(b)(2)(C).

NOTE

The disposition goals in CRC 3.714(b) are merely guidelines; they are not meant to create deadlines for individual cases. CEB Procedure Before Trial, §40.9. The court must consider each case on its own merits and establish a plan that ensures that the case is set for trial as soon as appropriate for the particular case. CRC 3.714(b)(3).

---

§6. MEET-AND-CONFER REQUIREMENT

§6.1 Most cases. In most cases, the parties must meet and confer no later than 30 calendar days before the date set for the initial CMC unless the court sets a different deadline. CRC 3.724. The parties can meet and confer in person or by telephone. *Id.* When the parties meet and confer, they should do the following:

1. Consider each issue that must be addressed at the initial CMC. *Id.*; *see* CRC 3.727. See "Subjects to be addressed," §8.1.4, p. 468.

2. Resolve any discovery disputes and set a discovery schedule. CRC 3.724(1).

3. Identify and, if possible, informally resolve any anticipated motions. CRC 3.724(2).

4. Identify the uncontested facts and issues that may be the subject of stipulation. CRC 3.724(3).

5. Identify the facts and issues that are in dispute. CRC 3.724(4).

6. Determine whether the issues can be narrowed by eliminating any claims or defenses by motion or some other manner. CRC 3.724(5).

7. Determine whether settlement is possible. CRC 3.724(6).

8. Identify the dates when all parties and their attorneys are available for trial, including the reasons for any unavailability. CRC 3.724(7).

9. Consider any issues relating to the discovery of electronically stored information, including the development of a proposed plan for discovery. CRC 3.724(8). For the e-discovery issues that should be addressed at the initial CMC, see "Meet & Confer About Electronic Discovery," ch. 7-H, §6, p. 885.

10. Consider any other relevant matters. CRC 3.724(9).

§6.2 Complex cases. In complex cases, the court can order the parties' attorneys to meet and confer privately before the initial CMC. CRC 3.750(d). When the attorneys meet and confer, they should do the following:

1. Consider each issue that must be addressed at the initial CMC. *Id.* See "Subjects to be addressed," §8.2.3, p. 471.

2. Prepare a joint statement of matters agreed on and matters the court must rule on at the CMC, and a description of the major legal and factual issues involved in the litigation. CRC 3.750(d).

§7. CASE-MANAGEMENT STATEMENT

Each party must file and serve a case-management statement before the initial CMC. CRC 3.725(a). The purpose of a case-management statement is to inform the court about the issues to be addressed at the initial CMC. For a discussion of the issues to be addressed, see "Subjects to be addressed," §8.1.4, p. 468 (most cases); "Subjects to be addressed," §8.2.3, p. 471 (complex cases).

CAUTION

The filing of a case-management statement constitutes a general appearance in a case. See ***Mansour v. Superior Ct.*** *(4th Dist.1995) 38 Cal.App.4th 1750, 1757. See "General appearance," ch. 3-G, §5.1.1, p. 285.*

§7.1 Deadline to file & serve statement. Each party must file a case-management statement and serve it on all other parties no later than 15 calendar days before the date set for the initial CMC. CRC 3.725(a). See "Calendar days," ch. 1-F, §5.1.3(1)(a), p. 54; "Retrospective deadlines," ch. 1-F, §5.2, p. 56. Two or more parties can file a joint statement instead of filing separate statements. CRC 3.725(b); *see, e.g.*, ***Mansour v. Superior Ct.*** (4th Dist.1995) 38 Cal.App.4th 1750, 1757 (parties filed joint case-management statement).

§7.2 Form & content of statement. The case-management statement must be made on Judicial Council Form CM-110. CRC 3.725(c).

NOTE

If a party wants a jury trial, it should make the request in its case-management statement. CEB Procedure Before Trial, §40.64. If it does not, the party risks waiving the right to a jury trial. See CCP §631(f)(2); CEB Procedure Before Trial, §40.64.

§7.3 Responding to statement. There are no procedures for responding to a case-management statement. *See* CRC 3.700-3.735; *CEB Procedure Before Trial*, §40.65. If a party wants to challenge another party's case-management statement, the objections can be raised at the initial CMC. *See CEB Procedure Before Trial*, §40.65.

§8. INITIAL CASE-MANAGEMENT CONFERENCE

§8.1 Most cases. In most cases, the purpose of the initial CMC is to allow the court to comprehensively review the case and decide whether to assign the case to an ADR process, whether to set the case for trial, and whether to take any other action on the issues addressed at the conference. CRC 3.722(a); *see* ***Mansour v. Superior Ct.*** (4th Dist.1995) 38 Cal.App.4th 1750, 1757.

1. Scheduling. The initial CMC is generally the first case-management event conducted by court order, except for orders to show cause. CRC 3.722(a).

(1) Earliest date. The initial CMC must be set at least 30 days after service of the first responsive pleading or, if the parties have entered into a stipulated continuance under Gov. C. §68616(d), at least 30 days after expiration of the continuance. Gov. C. §68616(e).

(2) Latest date. The initial CMC must occur no later than 180 days after the initial complaint is filed unless the case is exempt. *See* CRC 3.721; *see, e.g.*, Super. Ct. Contra Costa Cty. Loc. R., rule 3.8(a)(2) (CMC will be set within 140 days after complaint is filed); Super. Ct. San Diego Cty. Loc. R., rule 2.1.9.A (CMC will be set approximately 150 days after complaint is filed).

2. Appearance. Each self-represented party or each party's attorney must usually appear in person or by telephone at the initial CMC and be familiar with the case and be prepared to discuss and commit to the party's position on each issue to be addressed. CRC 3.722(c); *see* CRC 3.670 (appearance by telephone). See "By telephone," ch. 1-H, §5.4.2, p. 85. But the parties' or their attorneys' appearance can be excused in the following instances:

(1) Not necessary. The court can excuse the parties' appearance if it determines that no appearance is necessary based on the parties' written submissions and other available information. CRC 3.722(d). If an appearance is not necessary, the court must notify the parties that their appearance is not required and issue a case-management order. *Id.* See "Case-Management Order," §9, p. 472.

(2) Limited civil cases. The court can, by local rule, provide that the parties in a limited civil case are not required to appear unless ordered to do so. CRC 3.722(e).

CAUTION

The court can impose sanctions against a party who does not appear at a CMC if the party received notice of the CMC and notice of possible sanctions for not appearing. See ***Lee v. An*** *(2d Dist.2008) 168 Cal.App.4th 558, 564-65. See "Violation of Court Order," ch. 5-K, §4, p. 581; "Violation of Local Rule of Court," ch. 5-K, §6, p. 588.*

---

3. Conducting. The initial CMC must be conducted in the manner provided by the court's local rules. CRC 3.728; *see, e.g.*, Super. Ct. Orange Cty. Loc. R., rule 317 (local rule detailing what must happen at CMC).

4. Subjects to be addressed. The parties must address, and the court may take action on, any of the following issues that apply:

(1) Whether there are any related cases. CRC 3.727(1); *see* CRC 3.300(b), (f) (any party that knows about related case has continuing duty to serve and file notice of related case unless another party has already done so). See "Relating Cases," ch. 5-H, §3, p. 520.

(2) Whether all parties named in the complaint or cross-complaint have been served, have appeared, or have been dismissed. CRC 3.727(2); *see also* CRC 3.728(8) (court can dismiss or sever from case any unserved or nonappearing Ds).

(3) Whether any parties might be added or any pleadings might be amended. CRC 3.727(3); *see, e.g.*, ***Castaneda v. Department of Corr. & Rehab.*** (2d Dist.2013) 212 Cal.App.4th 1051, 1064 n.4 (State's case-management statement informed court of possibility that P would amend complaint to include additional parties); ***Garau v. Torrance Unified Sch. Dist.*** (2d Dist.2006) 137 Cal.App.4th 192, 196 (Ps' attorney informed court at CMC of intent to amend complaint to raise additional issues).

(4) If the case is a limited civil case, whether the economic litigation procedures under CCP §90 et seq. will apply or whether a party intends to bring a motion to exempt the case from those procedures. CRC 3.727(4).

(5) Whether any other matters (e.g., a party's bankruptcy) may affect the court's jurisdiction or processing of the case. CRC 3.727(5).

(6) Whether the parties have stipulated to, or the case should be referred to, judicial arbitration (if the court has a judicial-arbitration program) or to any other ADR process, and if so, the date by which the judicial arbitration or other ADR process must be completed. CRC 3.727(6); *see* CRC 3.726 (parties can agree to use ADR by jointly completing ADR stipulation form and filing it with court); *see, e.g.*, ***O'Donoghue v. Superior Ct.*** (1st Dist.2013) 219 Cal.App.4th 245, 251 n.3 (P's case-management statement notified court that P would seek appointment of referee if Ds did not agree to one); ***De Santiago v. D&G Plumbing, Inc.*** (4th Dist.2007) 155 Cal.App.4th 365, 370 (court ordered parties to arbitration).

(7) Whether an early settlement conference should be scheduled, and if so, the date of the conference. CRC 3.727(7).

(8) Whether discovery has been completed, and if not, the date by which it will be completed. CRC 3.727(8); *see, e.g.*, ***Paduano v. American Honda Motor Co.*** (4th Dist.2009) 169 Cal.App.4th 1453, 1461 (D's case-management statement notified court of date depositions would be complete).

(9) The anticipated discovery issues. CRC 3.727(9); *see, e.g.*, ***St. Vincent's Sch. for Boys, Catholic Charities CYO v. City of San Rafael*** (1st Dist.2008) 161 Cal.App.4th 989, 1018 (P's case-management statement addressed disagreement with D over whether discovery was complete).

(10) Whether the case should be bifurcated or a hearing should be set for a motion to bifurcate under CCP §598. CRC 3.727(10); *see, e.g.*, ***First Presbyterian Ch. v. City of Berkeley*** (1st Dist.1997) 59 Cal.App.4th 1241, 1246 (court bifurcated issues in petition for writ of mandate from issues in complaint).

(11) Whether there are any cross-complaints that are not ready to be set for trial, and if so, whether they should be severed. CRC 3.727(11).

(12) Whether the case is entitled to any statutory preference, and if so, the statute granting the preference. CRC 3.727(12); *see, e.g.*, ***Landry v. Berryessa Un. Sch. Dist.*** (6th Dist.1995) 39 Cal.App.4th 691, 695 (Ps asked that CMC date be moved up because they were entitled to mandatory trial preference under CCP §36).

(13) Whether a jury trial is demanded, and if so, the identity of each party requesting a jury trial. CRC 3.727(13).

(14) If the trial date has not already been set, the date by which the case will be ready for trial and the available trial dates. CRC 3.727(14).

(15) The estimated length of the trial. CRC 3.727(15).

(16) The nature of the injuries. CRC 3.727(16).

(17) The amount of damages, including any special or punitive damages. CRC 3.727(17).

(18) Any additional relief sought. CRC 3.727(18); *see, e.g.*, ***Abouab v. City & Cty. of S.F.*** (1st Dist.2006) 141 Cal.App.4th 643, 657 (P advised court of intent to file motion for attorney fees).

(19) Whether there are any insurance-coverage issues that might affect the resolution of the case. CRC 3.727(19).

(20) Any other matters that should be considered by the court or addressed in its case-management order. CRC 3.727(20); *see, e.g.*, ***Fair v. Bakhtiari*** (2006) 40 Cal.4th 189, 193 (D's attorney asked for continuance at CMC).

5. Ruling on motions. The court can rule on motions set to be heard at the initial CMC. *See, e.g.*, ***Lopez v. State*** (4th Dist.1996) 49 Cal.App.4th 1292, 1296 (motion to dismiss set for hearing at CMC).

6. Setting case for trial. The court can set the case for trial at the initial CMC or another proceeding. *See* CRC 3.729. In setting a case for trial, the court must consider all the relevant facts and circumstances, which can include any of the following:

(1) The type and subject matter of the case to be tried. CRC 3.729(1).

(2) Whether the case has statutory priority. CRC 3.729(2); *see, e.g.*, CCP §36 (listing circumstances under which case is entitled to trial preference).

(3) The number of causes of action, cross-actions, and affirmative defenses that will be tried. CRC 3.729(3).

(4) Whether any significant amendments to the pleadings have been recently made or are likely to be made before trial. CRC 3.729(4).

(5) Whether the plaintiff intends to bring a motion to amend the complaint to seek punitive damages under CCP §425.13. CRC 3.729(5).

(6) The number of parties with separate interests who will be involved in the trial. CRC 3.729(6).

(7) The complexity of the issues to be tried, including issues of first impression. CRC 3.729(7).

(8) Any difficulties in identifying, locating, or serving parties. CRC 3.729(8).

(9) Whether all parties have been served, and if so, the date by which they were served. CRC 3.729(9).

(10) Whether all parties have appeared in the case, and if so, the date by which they appeared. CRC 3.729(10).

(11) How long the attorneys who will try the case have been involved in the case. CRC 3.729(11).

(12) The trial dates or the dates proposed by the parties and their attorneys. CRC 3.729(12).

(13) The professional and personal schedules of the parties and their attorneys, including any conflicts with previously assigned trial dates or other significant events. CRC 3.729(13).

(14) The amount of discovery, if any, that remains to be conducted in the case. CRC 3.729(14).

(15) The nature and extent of anticipated law-and-motion proceedings, including whether any motions for summary judgment will be filed. CRC 3.729(15).

(16) Whether any other pending actions or proceedings might affect the case. CRC 3.729(16).

(17) The amount in controversy and the type of remedy sought. CRC 3.729(17).

(18) The nature and extent of the injuries or damages, including whether these are ready for determination. CRC 3.729(18).

(19) The court's trial calendar, including the pendency of other trial dates. CRC 3.729(19).

(20) Whether the trial will be a jury or nonjury trial. CRC 3.729(20).

(21) The anticipated length of trial. CRC 3.729(21).

(22) The number, availability, and locations of witnesses, including witnesses who reside outside the county, state, or country. CRC 3.729(22).

(23) Whether there have been any previous continuances of the trial or delays in setting the case for trial. CRC 3.729(23).

(24) The achievement of a fair, timely, and efficient disposition of the case. CRC 3.729(24).

(25) Any other factor that would significantly affect the determination of the appropriate trial date. CRC 3.729(25).

§8.2 Complex cases. In complex cases, the purpose of the initial CMC is to expose essential issues early on and to avoid unnecessary and burdensome discovery procedures. CRC 3.750(c).

1. Scheduling. The initial CMC should be scheduled at the earliest practical date. CRC 3.750(a).

2. Appearance. All parties should be represented at the initial CMC. CRC 3.750(a).

3. Subjects to be addressed. The court should consider the following subjects at the initial CMC:

(1) Whether all parties named in the complaint or cross-complaint have been served, have appeared, or have been dismissed. CRC 3.750(b)(1).

(2) Whether any additional parties might be added or any pleadings might be amended. CRC 3.750(b)(2).

(3) The deadline for filing any remaining pleadings and serving any additional parties. CRC 3.750(b)(3); *cf.* ***Basurco v. 21st Century Ins.*** (2d Dist.2003) 108 Cal.App.4th 110, 122 (in consolidated cases, case-management order set deadlines for serving pleadings).

(4) Whether severance, consolidation, or coordination with other actions or the early trial of separate issues is appropriate. ***Lu v. Superior Ct.*** (4th Dist.1997) 55 Cal.App.4th 1264, 1268; *see* CRC 3.750(b)(4); *see, e.g.*, ***In re Groundwater Cases*** (1st Dist.2007) 154 Cal.App.4th 659, 669 (case-management order coordinated three cases).

(5) The schedule for discovery proceedings to avoid duplication and whether discovery should be stayed until all parties have been brought into the case. CRC 3.750(b)(5); *see, e.g.*, ***Cohn v. Corinthian Colls., Inc.*** (4th Dist.2008) 169 Cal.App.4th 523, 526 (court ordered that discovery be completed before motions for summary judgment were made).

(6) The schedule for settlement conferences or ADR. CRC 3.750(b)(6); *see* ***Lu***, 55 Cal.App.4th at 1268.

(7) Whether to appoint liaison or lead counsel to facilitate communication between the court and counsel and between individual attorneys. *See* CRC 3.750(b)(7); ***Lu***, 55 Cal.App.4th at 1268.

(8) Whether the court should implement a schedule for motions, including the deadline for filing any dispositive motions. *See* CRC 3.750(b)(8); *see, e.g.*, ***First State Ins. v. Superior Ct.*** (2d Dist.2000) 79 Cal.App.4th 324, 336 (although case-management order was invalid to extent that it prohibited filing of motions for summary judgment under CCP §437c, court could establish procedure for resolving motions after they were filed).

(9) The creation of preliminary and updated lists of the persons to be deposed and the subjects to be addressed in each deposition. CRC 3.750(b)(9).

(10) The exchange of documents and whether to establish an electronic-document depository that would eliminate the need for formal requests to produce. *See* CRC 3.750(b)(10); ***Lu***, 55 Cal.App.4th at 1268.

(11) Whether a special master should be appointed and the purposes of the appointment. CRC 3.750(b)(11); *see, e.g.*, ***Lu***, 55 Cal.App.4th at 1267 (referee appointed to manage discovery and conduct settlement conferences).

(12) Whether to establish a case-based website and other means to provide a current master list of addresses and telephone numbers of attorneys. CRC 3.750(b)(12); *see* ***Lu***, 55 Cal.App.4th at 1268.

(13) The schedule for further conferences. CRC 3.750(b)(13).

§9. CASE-MANAGEMENT ORDER

The court must enter a case-management order (CMO) setting a schedule for later proceedings and providing for the management of the case. CRC 3.728. The CMO lays out a clear path and timetable for the completion of all tasks necessary to ready the case for trial. ***Lu v. Superior Ct.*** (4th Dist.1997) 55 Cal.App.4th 1264, 1268. In complex cases, the court has broad authority to issue an appropriate CMO. *See* ***Fire Ins. Exch. v. Superior Ct.*** (2d Dist.2004) 116 Cal.App.4th 446, 452 (courts have broad discretion to fashion suitable methods of practice to manage complex litigation); ***Lu***, 55 Cal.App.4th at 1268 (detailed CMO satisfies requirement that court establish case-progression plan and monitor case); ***Cottle v. Superior Ct.*** (2d Dist.1992) 3 Cal.App.4th 1367, 1380 (courts have power to establish new procedure to manage and control complex cases).

§9.1 Contents.

1. What can be included.

(1) All cases. In all cases, the court can do any of the following in the CMO:

(a) Refer the case to judicial arbitration or other ADR process. CRC 3.728(1).

(b) Specify a date for completing the judicial arbitration or other ADR process if the case has been referred to ADR. CRC 3.728(2).

(c) Specify a trial date if the case is ready to be set for trial and a trial date has not already been set. CRC 3.728(3). See "Setting case for trial," §8.1.6, p. 470.

(d) Specify whether the trial will be a jury or nonjury trial. CRC 3.728(4).

(e) Identify each party demanding a jury trial. CRC 3.728(5).

(f) Estimate the length of trial. CRC 3.728(6).

(g) State whether all parties necessary to the disposition of the case have been served or have appeared. CRC 3.728(7).

(h) Dismiss or sever unserved or nonappearing defendants from the case. CRC 3.728(8).

(i) Specify the names and addresses of the attorneys who will try the case. CRC 3.728(9).

(j) Specify the date, time, and place for a mandatory settlement conference as provided in CRC 3.1380. CRC 3.728(10).

(k) Specify the date, time, and place for the final CMC if one is required by the court or the judge assigned to the case. CRC 3.728(11).

(*l*) Specify the date, time, and place of any additional CMCs or review. CRC 3.728(12).

(m) Make any additional orders that may be appropriate, including orders on issues to be addressed at a CMC and issues on which the parties must confer. CRC 3.728(13). See "Meet-and-Confer Requirement," §6, p. 466; "Subjects to be addressed," §8.1.4, p. 468; "Subjects to be addressed," §8.2.3, p. 471.

(2) Complex cases. In complex cases, the court can also include the following in the CMO:

(a) Time limits to expedite major phases of the litigation. *See* Cal. Stds. Jud. Admin. 3.10(d).

(b) Provisions for protective orders. ***Lu v. Superior Ct.*** (4th Dist.1997) 55 Cal.App.4th 1264, 1268. See "Relief," ch. 9-B, §3.3.1(1)(a), p. 1029.

(c) Provisions for specially prepared interrogatories or other procedures requiring all parties to disclose certain information, such as insurance coverage, damages claimed by the plaintiffs, and damages acknowledged by the defendants. ***Lu***, 55 Cal.App.4th at 1268.

(d) Rulings on issues raised by the pleadings. *See id.*; *see, e.g.*, ***Fire Ins. Exch. v. Superior Ct.*** (2d Dist.2004) 116 Cal.App.4th 446, 451 (on its own motion, court decided disputed insurance-coverage issues raised in pleadings).

(e) Provisions permitting alternatives to formal pleadings. ***Lu***, 55 Cal.App.4th at 1268. For example, when there are many defendants and cross-defendants seeking contribution and indemnity from each other, the court can provide that each defendant is deemed to have cross-complained against each of the other cross-defendants for contribution and indemnity. *Id.*; Weil, *Civil Procedure Before Trial*, ¶12:47.11.

(f) The date the case should be ready for trial. *Lu*, 55 Cal.App.4th at 1268.

(g) Rules on the use of a central electronic depository, such as providing that documents filed electronically in a central depository available to all parties are deemed served on all parties. CRC 3.751; *cf.* ***Landale-Cameron Ct., Inc. v. Ahonen*** (2d Dist.2007) 155 Cal.App.4th 1401, 1406 (in noncomplex case, court ordered that documents deposited in judicially sanctioned depository would be treated same as if party produced documents in response to formal request for production).

(h) A list of evidence to be excluded. *See* ***Cottle v. Superior Ct.*** (2d Dist.1992) 3 Cal.App.4th 1367, 1381.

(i) Any additional orders that may be appropriate. *See id.* at 1380 (courts have power to fashion new procedure to manage and control complex cases).

2. What cannot be included. The court cannot include in the CMO provisions that impose requirements or conditions greater than or inconsistent with any statute or Judicial Council rule. ***Bank of Am. v. Superior Ct.*** (4th Dist.2013) 212 Cal.App.4th 1076, 1098; *see* ***Hernandez v. Superior Ct.*** (2d Dist.2003) 112 Cal.App.4th 285, 295 (CMO in complex case is not preempted as long as it does not conflict with any statute or Judicial Council rule); *see, e.g.*, ***Jeld-Wen, Inc. v. Superior Ct.*** (4th Dist.2007) 146 Cal.App.4th 536, 543 (CMO requiring parties to attend and pay for mediation conflicted with statutory scheme for mediation and thus was improper); ***First State Ins. v. Superior Ct.*** (2d Dist.2000) 79 Cal.App.4th 324, 330 (CMO was invalid to extent it prevented parties from filing MSJs under CCP §437c); *cf.* ***McCarthy v. CB Richard Ellis, Inc.*** (2d Dist.2009) 174 Cal.App.4th 106, 121-22 (neither statute nor CRC on procedure for summary judgment can be changed by general court order).

§9.2 Effect of order. The CMO controls the course of the action or proceeding unless it is modified by a later order. CRC 3.730; *see also* CCP §576 (CMO can be amended).

§9.3 Sanctions. The court can impose sanctions against a party for not complying with the CMO. Gov. C. §68608(b); *see CEB Procedure Before Trial*, §40.89; *see, e.g.*, Super. Ct. Los Angeles Cty. Loc. R., rule 3.10 (court can impose sanctions for not complying with local rules or any order made under local rules). Due process requires that the sanctioned party receive notice of the possibility of sanctions. *See* ***Lee v. An*** (2d Dist.2008) 168 Cal.App.4th 558, 564-65. See "Violation of Court Order," ch. 5-K, §4, p. 581; "Violation of California Rule of Court," ch. 5-K, §5, p. 585; "Violation of Local Rule of Court," ch. 5-K, §6, p. 588.

§9.4 Appellate review. The CMO is not appealable until the court renders a final judgment in the case. *See* CCP §904.1(a)(2). A party can, however, file a petition for a writ of mandate to review the order. ***Fire Ins. Exch. v. Superior Ct.*** (2d Dist.2004) 116 Cal.App.4th 446, 452; *see* ***Lu v. Superior Ct.*** (4th Dist.1997) 55 Cal.App.4th 1264, 1267. The appellate court reviews the order for abuse of discretion. *See* ***Hernandez v. Superior Ct.*** (2d Dist.2003) 112 Cal.App.4th 285, 295.

§10. ADDITIONAL CASE-MANAGEMENT CONFERENCES (OPTIONAL)

Most cases will only require one initial and one final CMC. CRC 3.723, advisory committee's cmt., www.courts.ca.gov /rules.htm. Complex cases, however, usually require additional CMCs. *See id.*; *see also* CRC 3.750(b)(13) (at initial CMC, court should consider schedule for further conferences). In all general civil cases, the court, on its own motion or on a party's request, can order that one or more additional CMCs take place. CRC 3.723; *see, e.g.*, ***Shaw v.***

County of Santa Cruz (6th Dist.2008) 170 Cal.App.4th 229, 248-49 (P asked for CMC to set trial date before five-year deadline for prosecuting case expired); ***Bernardi v. County of Monterey*** (6th Dist.2008) 167 Cal.App.4th 1379, 1386 (D asked for CMC to clarify scope of discovery). An additional CMC can be ordered at any time. CRC 3.723. In deciding whether to order an additional CMC, the court must consider each case on its own merits. *Id.* A self-represented party or a party's attorney must appear at an additional CMC only if the appearance is necessary for the effective management of the case. *See id.*

§11. FINAL CASE-MANAGEMENT CONFERENCE

By local rule, the court will usually hold a final CMC (also called the "final-status conference," "trial-readiness conference," or "issue conference") a few days before the trial to narrow the issues and organize the case for trial. *See CEB Procedure Before Trial*, §40.88; Weil, *Civil Procedure Before Trial*, ¶12:85.5; *see, e.g.*, Super. Ct. Los Angeles Cty. Loc. R., rule 3.25(f) (final-status conference must be held no more than ten days before trial date). If a final CMC is required, its date, time, and place will be stated in the original CMO. *See* CRC 3.728(11); Weil, *Civil Procedure Before Trial*, ¶12:85.5. See "Case-Management Order," §9, p. 472.

B. MOTION FOR PREFERENCE

§1. GENERAL

§1.1 Purpose. The purpose of a motion for preference is to give precedence on the calendar to cases or issues that need to be resolved quickly. *See* CCP §36(f); CRC 3.1335(b). A case given "preference" is prioritized over other cases on the court's calendar, whether for a hearing or for trial. *See, e.g.*, CCP §36(f) (court must set trial within 120 days after preference is granted), §460.5(c) (court must give certain libel or slander actions preference in setting case for hearing or trial, and in hearing case).

§1.2 Primary authority. CCP §§36, 36.5, 37, 460.5, 527(e), 1062.3, 1141.20(b), 1179a, 1260.010, 1291.2; CRC 3.725(c), 3.727(12), 3.1335.

§1.3 Secondary authority. The following secondary sources are cited as authority in this subchapter:

- *California Civil Procedure Before Trial* (CEB Online ed. 2014) (referred to as *CEB Procedure Before Trial*).
- Kiesel et al., *Matthew Bender Practice Guide: California Pretrial Civil Procedure* (2014) (referred to as Kiesel, *Cal. Pretrial Civil Procedure*).
- Thomas, *California Civil Courtroom Handbook* (2014) (referred to as Thomas, *Courtroom Handbook*).
- Weil & Brown, *California Practice Guide: Civil Procedure Before Trial* (CD-ROM ed. 2014) (referred to as Weil, *Civil Procedure Before Trial*).
- Witkin, *California Procedure* (5th ed. 2008 & Supp.2014) (referred to as Witkin, *Cal. Procedure*).
- Younger & Bradley, *Younger on California Motions* (2014-15) (referred to as Younger, *Cal. Motions*).

§2. CONSIDERATIONS BEFORE REQUESTING PREFERENCE

§2.1 Is preference available? A party should determine early in the case whether preference is available. Kiesel, *Cal. Pretrial Civil Procedure*, §23.27. Preference can be obtained if (1) a specific cause of action is entitled to preference, (2) a party's status makes preference necessary, or (3) granting preference would serve the interests of justice. See "Grounds," §3, p. 475.

§2.2 Should preference be requested? A party should request preference if an earlier hearing or trial date is necessary to safeguard a party's substantive rights or would be otherwise advantageous. *See* ***Rice v. Superior Ct.*** (2d Dist.1982) 136 Cal.App.3d 81, 88-89 (CCP §36(a) safeguards rights and remedies of parties who might die or become incapacitated before case goes to trial because of their advanced age or serious medical condition); Kiesel, *Cal. Pretrial Civil Procedure*, §23.27 (counsel should determine whether an earlier trial date is advantageous); *see, e.g.*,

De Santiago v. D&G Plumbing, Inc. (4th Dist.2007) 155 Cal.App.4th 365, 374 (P's attorney had duty to take whatever measures were available to accelerate trial of case before expiration of five-year deadline, including bringing motion to advance trial). See "Grounds," §3, this page. But if an earlier hearing or trial date would leave the party with inadequate time to conduct discovery or to make certain pretrial motions, the party may not want to seek preference. Kiesel, *Cal. Pretrial Civil Procedure*, §23.27.

§2.3 When should preference be requested? A party should request preference at the earliest opportunity once the facts supporting the request become known. *See, e.g.*, ***Sanchez v. City of L.A.*** (2d Dist.2003) 109 Cal.App.4th 1262, 1273-74 (P's attorney had ample time after court set trial date to file motion to advance trial date to avoid dismissal). For trial settings, the earliest opportunity will usually be at the case-management conference. *See* CRC 3.727(12) (parties must address preference at case-management conference); Judicial Council Forms, form CM-110, item 9 (party must indicate if case is entitled to preference on case-management statement). See "Case-Management Statement," ch. 5-A, §7, p. 467; "Initial Case-Management Conference," ch. 5-A, §8, p. 468. If a party does not request preference at the case-management conference, the party can request preference at a later time during the proceedings, usually by noticed motion.

NOTE

Although there is no express deadline for requesting a preferential setting of a trial, there is an implied one: the request should be made within two years after the case has commenced. See CCP §583.420(a)(2)(B); CRC 3.1340(a). If the request is made after two years, the court has discretion to dismiss the case for delay in prosecution even if the plaintiff was originally entitled to a preferential setting. See ***Landry v. Berryessa Un. Sch. Dist.*** *(6th Dist.1995) 39 Cal.App.4th 691, 696-97 (mandatory preference under CCP §36 does not trump requirement for diligent prosecution in CCP §§583.410 and 583.420). See "Grounds – Discretionary Dismissal," ch. 10-E, §5, p. 1171.*

§3. GROUNDS

Preference can be obtained if (1) a specific cause of action is entitled to preference, (2) a party's status makes preference necessary, or (3) granting preference would serve the interests of justice.

§3.1 Cause of action entitled to preference. A party can request preference if the cause of action has been granted preference by statute. *See, e.g.*, ***Cohen v. Superior Ct.*** (1st Dist.1967) 248 Cal.App.2d 551, 553-54 (P filed motion to advance trial date based on unlawful-detainer statute). Statutes can grant preference for setting hearing and trial dates as well as other types of preference (e.g., the actual hearing or trial of the matter on the date set). The following are some of the more common actions or proceedings that are entitled to preference. For other types of actions or proceedings that are entitled to preference, see Weil, *Civil Procedure Before Trial*, ¶12:255, and 7 Witkin, *Cal. Procedure*, Trial, §72.

1. Declaratory-judgment action.

(1) Declaratory judgment only. An action for a declaratory judgment is entitled to preference if a declaratory judgment is the only relief requested. *See* CCP §1062.3. The declaratory-judgment action must be given the earliest trial date possible and takes precedence over all other actions, except older declaratory-judgment actions or other actions given preference by law. *Id.* §1062.3(a).

(2) Declaratory judgment with additional relief. An action for a declaratory judgment that requests additional relief beyond the declaratory judgment is entitled to preference only if a party makes a noticed motion showing that the action requires a speedy trial. CCP §1062.3(b).

NOTE

*The court has the power to refuse to hear a declaratory-judgment action that is not necessary or proper. CCP §1061. This power can be used to stay declaratory-judgment actions that are filed separately from related actions in an attempt to gain a preferential setting. See, e.g., **California Ins. Guarantee Ass'n v. Superior Ct.** (2d Dist.1991) 231 Cal.App.3d 1617, 1624 (insurance-coverage action requesting declaratory relief was stayed pending resolution of underlying action).*

2. Unlawful-detainer action. An unlawful-detainer action is entitled to preference over all other civil actions except other actions given special preference by law. *See* CCP §1179a. The preference must be given for hearing and trial settings and the actual hearing or trial of the matter on the date set. *Id.* If the request is to specially set a trial date, the court must set the date for trial within 20 days after the request is made. *Id.* §1170.5(a). However, a different date can be set when either of the following occurs:

(1) All the parties agree to an extension. *Id.* §1170.5(b).

(2) On its own motion or on the motion of any party, the court does both of the following:

(a) Holds a hearing and finds there is a reasonable probability that the plaintiff will prevail in the action and determines the amount of damages the plaintiff will suffer due to the extension beyond 20 days. *See id.* §1170.5(b), (c).

(b) Issues an order requiring the defendant to pay the amount into the court as the rent would have become due and payable or into an escrow designated by the court for as long as the defendant remains in possession while the action is pending. *See id.* §1170.5(b), (c).

3. Eminent-domain action. An eminent-domain action is entitled to preference over all other civil actions. CCP §1260.010. This preference must be given for hearing and trial settings. *Id.*

4. Action in which preliminary injunction granted. An action in which a preliminary injunction has been granted is entitled to preference. CCP §527(e). When the action is ready for trial, it must be given the earliest trial date possible, and the trial takes precedence over all other actions, except older actions given preference. *Id.*

NOTE

It is unclear whether preference can be granted in an action in which a preliminary injunction was sought but denied. Weil, Civil Procedure Before Trial, ¶12:242.1.

5. Action in which TRO granted. If a temporary restraining order (TRO) was issued without notice to the opposing party, a hearing on the order to show cause why a preliminary injunction should not be granted takes precedence over all other matters on the calendar that day, except older matters of a similar character and those given special preference by law. *See* CCP §527(d), (e).

6. Libel or slander action. An action for libel or slander in which the allegedly defamatory matter has been continuously published and is reasonably likely to continue to be published is entitled to preference over all other civil actions, except actions given special preference by law. *See* CCP §460.5(a), (c). The preference must be given for hearing and trial settings and the actual hearing or trial of the matter on the date set. *Id.* §460.5(c).

7. Action to be tried de novo after judicial arbitration. An action in which a party has elected to have a de novo trial after judicial arbitration has been completed is entitled to either (1) be given the same place on the active list as it had before arbitration or (2) receive civil priority on the next setting calendar. CCP §1141.20(b); *see* ***Howard v. Thrifty Drug & Disc. Stores*** (1995) 10 Cal.4th 424, 441-42. The purpose of §1141.20 is to allow plaintiffs who have engaged in arbitration to keep their place in line for trial eligibility. ***Howard***, 10 Cal.4th at 442.

CAUTION

The court can deny a motion to specially set a trial under §1141.20 when the plaintiff does not promptly make the request and the action is subject to discretionary dismissal for failure to timely prosecute under CCP §583.410. ***Howard****, 10 Cal.4th at 442. See "Grounds – Discretionary Dismissal," ch. 10-E, §5, p. 1171.*

8. Contractual-arbitration proceeding. A proceeding brought on a petition to enforce an arbitration agreement or confirm, correct, or vacate an arbitration award is entitled to preference over all other civil actions or proceedings, except older matters of the same character or those given special preference by law. CCP §1291.2; *see id.* §§1281.2, 1285. The preference must be given to the hearing setting and the actual hearing of the matter on the date set. *Id.* §1291.2.

§3.2 Party's status. A party's status may allow the party to obtain preference in the trial setting.

1. Party is 70 or older. A party can request a preferential trial setting if (1) she is 70 or older, (2) she has a substantial interest in the action as a whole, and (3) her health makes preference necessary to avoid prejudicing her interest in the litigation. *See* CCP §36(a), (c)(2); ***Laswell v. AG Seal Beach, LLC*** (2d Dist.2010) 189 Cal.App.4th 1399, 1403; *see, e.g.*, ***In re Marriage of Greenway*** (4th Dist.2013) 217 Cal.App.4th 628, 631-32 (court granted preferential trial setting to 76-year-old chemotherapy patient who feared his failing health would impede his ability to protect his substantial interest in his divorce case). Although CCP §36(a) states the party must be "over" 70, §36(c)(2) allows a party who is 70 to bring the motion. *See* CCP §36(a), (c)(2).

CAUTION

An attorney can be sued for malpractice if she does not request a preferential trial date for an elderly client who qualifies under CCP §36(a) and the client dies before the case is resolved. See, e.g., ***Granquist v. Sandberg*** *(3d Dist.1990) 219 Cal.App.3d 181, 187-88 (decedent's personal representative could pursue malpractice action against attorney who was aware of decedent's age and failing health but did not file motion for preference).*

2. Party is under 14. A party can request a preferential trial setting if she (1) is under 14, (2) is suing to recover damages for personal injury or wrongful death, and (3) has a substantial interest in the action as a whole. CCP §36(b).

3. Party is terminally ill. A party can request a preferential trial setting if (1) one of the parties suffers from an illness or condition that raises substantial medical doubt about the party's survival beyond six months and (2) the interests of justice will be served by granting the preference. CCP §36(d); ***Heda v. Superior Ct.*** (1st Dist.1990) 225 Cal.App.3d 525, 527-28; *see* ***Laswell***, 189 Cal.App.4th at 1403.

4. Plaintiff suffered damages caused during felony. A plaintiff can request a preferential trial setting if it is seeking damages allegedly caused by the defendant during the commission of a felony offense for which the defendant has been convicted. CCP §37(a).

§3.3 Interests of justice. A party can request a preferential trial setting if the interests of justice would be served by granting the preference. CCP §36(e). A motion for preference based on the interests of justice is sometimes referred to as a "motion to advance" or a "motion to specially set." *See* ***Howard v. Thrifty Drug & Disc. Stores*** (1995) 10 Cal.4th 424, 440; *CEB Procedure Before Trial*, §42.3. Circumstances that may justify granting the preference include the following:

1. Case is approaching mandatory-dismissal deadline. A plaintiff must request preference if its case is approaching a mandatory-dismissal deadline for delay in prosecution. *See* ***Howard***, 10 Cal.4th at 434 (P has duty to call court's attention to need for setting trial within five-year deadline); Younger, *Cal. Motions*, §24:13 (cases seem to assume that five-year statute problems are reason why CCP §36(e) exists); *see, e.g.*, ***Mesler v. Bragg Mgmt. Co.***

(2d Dist.1990) 219 Cal.App.3d 983, 989 (P filed motion to specially set case for trial on ground that three-year deadline for retrial after reversal by appellate court was about to expire); *see also* CCP §583.310 (five-year deadline to prosecute), §583.360 (dismissal for failure to timely prosecute). To obtain preference, the plaintiff should show the following:

(1) Mandatory dismissal is upcoming. The plaintiff must show that the case is approaching a mandatory-dismissal deadline for delay in prosecution. *See, e.g.*, ***Parlen v. Golden State Sanwa Bank*** (2d Dist.1987) 194 Cal.App.3d 906, 909 (P filed motion to specially set case for trial on ground that five-year period for bringing case to trial would expire in four months). The mandatory-dismissal deadlines applicable to a request for preference are (1) the five-year deadline for bringing a case to trial after the action is commenced and (2) the three-year deadline for retrial when a new trial has been granted. *See* CCP §§583.310, 583.320, 583.360; *see, e.g.*, ***Mesler***, 219 Cal.App.3d at 989 (three-year deadline); ***Parlen***, 194 Cal.App.3d at 909 (five-year deadline). See "Grounds – Mandatory Dismissal," ch. 10-E, §4, p. 1162.

(2) Plaintiff has excuse for delay. The plaintiff must show excusable delay (i.e., good cause for the delay in bringing the case to trial). ***Howard***, 10 Cal.4th at 440-41; *e.g.*, ***Nye v. 20th Century Ins.*** (2d Dist.1990) 225 Cal.App.3d 1041, 1045 (no excusable delay shown when attorney waited until 41 days before expiration of five-year deadline to inquire about status of case); ***Parlen***, 194 Cal.App.3d at 911-12 (no excusable delay or good cause established because P did not show she proceeded with reasonable diligence and did not explain why she had been unable to proceed toward trial in a more timely fashion); *see* CRC 3.1335(b) (request to advance or specially set must be supported by good cause). One court has held that the plaintiff's burden of showing excusable delay for bringing the case to trial is increased if the plaintiff is facing a shorter deadline for mandatory dismissal (i.e., three-year deadline after remittitur rather than five-year deadline) because a plaintiff facing a shorter deadline must be more diligent in monitoring the case's status. ***Mesler***, 219 Cal.App.3d at 994. See "Excuse for delay," ch. 10-E, §5.2.1(10)(b), p. 1173.

(3) Factors favor preference. The plaintiff should show that the factors the court must consider when ruling on a motion for discretionary dismissal for delay in prosecution favor the granting of preference. *See* ***Howard***, 10 Cal.4th at 441; ***Eliceche v. Federal Land Bank Ass'n*** (5th Dist.2002) 103 Cal.App.4th 1349, 1363-64; *see also* CCP §583.130 (public-policy factors); CRC 3.1342(e) (general factors). When addressing the factors, the plaintiff should be sure to (1) address the condition of the court calendar, (2) explain its dilatory conduct, if any, (3) show that the defendant will not be prejudiced by an accelerated trial date, and (4) show the likelihood of mandatory dismissal if the early trial date is denied. *See* ***Howard***, 10 Cal.4th at 441. See "Factors favoring dismissal," ch. 10-E, §5.2, p. 1172.

NOTE

Implementation of the Trial Court Delay Reduction Act, which set goals and established rules for the early disposition of cases, has had the practical effect of disposing of most cases before the deadlines in the dismissal statutes are triggered. See "Effect of Fast-Track Rules," ch. 10-E, §3, p. 1161. As a result, a party will rarely need to seek preference based on the impending expiration of a mandatory-dismissal deadline for delay in prosecution.

2. Plaintiff's requested relief will be moot. A party can request preference when the plaintiff's requested relief will be moot without it. *See, e.g.*, ***Giraldo v. Department of Corr. & Rehab.*** (1st Dist.2008) 168 Cal.App.4th 231, 240-41 (court granted P's motion for preference because request for injunctive and declaratory relief against prison officials would be moot after P was released from prison).

3. Party will not be able to assist in case. A party can request preference when she is about to lose the ability to assist in the preparation of her claims or defenses (e.g., the party is suffering from debilitating mental or physical disease). Thomas, *Courtroom Handbook*, §26:12.

4. Party will be absent for trial. A party can request preference when she is about to leave and will not be able to return for the trial (e.g., the party is entering military service or permanently moving abroad). Thomas, *Courtroom Handbook*, §26:12.

5. Party will be deprived of witness testimony. A party can request preference when she will be deprived of essential witness testimony if preference is not granted (e.g., a key witness is terminally ill or about to move out of state and it would be prejudicial for party to have to rely on witness's deposition testimony). Thomas, *Courtroom Handbook*, §26:12.

§4. MOTION

§4.1 Who can make. Whether a party can request preference will depend on the grounds alleged for the preferential or special setting. *See, e.g.*, CCP §36(a) & (c)(2) (any party 70 or older), §36(b) (any party under 14 in wrongful-death or personal-injury action), §37 (P who suffered damages caused by commission of felony). See "Grounds," §3, p. 475.

§4.2 How to make.

1. Most motions. Most motions for preference can be made in the following ways:

(1) At the case-management conference after the party files a case-management statement. *See* CRC 3.727(12); Thomas, *Courtroom Handbook*, §§26:7-26:10; Weil, *Civil Procedure Before Trial*, ¶12:270. See "Case-Management Statement," ch. 5-A, §7, p. 467; "Initial Case-Management Conference," ch. 5-A, §8, p. 468.

(2) By noticed motion. Thomas, *Courtroom Handbook*, §§26:7-26:9; Weil, *Civil Procedure Before Trial*, ¶12:271; *see* CCP §36(c)(1). See "Motion Papers," ch. 1-D, §5, p. 27.

2. Motions based on interests of justice. Motions for preference based on the interests of justice (also known as motions to advance or specially set) can be made in the following ways:

(1) At the case-management conference after the party files a case-management statement. *See* CRC 3.727(12); Thomas, *Courtroom Handbook*, §26:12; Weil, *Civil Procedure Before Trial*, ¶12:270. See "Case-Management Statement," ch. 5-A, §7, p. 467; "Initial Case-Management Conference," ch. 5-A, §8, p. 468.

(2) By ex parte application. Thomas, *Courtroom Handbook*, §26:12; *see* CRC 3.1335(a); Weil, *Civil Procedure Before Trial*, ¶12:271. See "Application Papers," ch. 1-E, §5, p. 42.

(3) By noticed motion. Thomas, *Courtroom Handbook*, §26:12; *see* CRC 3.1335(a); Weil, *Civil Procedure Before Trial*, ¶12:271. See "Motion Papers," ch. 1-D, §5, p. 27.

§4.3 When to make. A party should request preference at the earliest opportunity once the facts supporting the request become known. See "When should preference be requested?," §2.3, p. 475. However, once those facts are known, the specific deadlines for making the request will depend on the form of the request.

1. Case-management conference. For a discussion of when to raise preference issues at the case-management conference, see "Deadline to file & serve statement," ch. 5-A, §7.1, p. 467.

2. Ex parte application. For a discussion of the deadlines to file and serve ex parte applications, see "Deadline," ch. 1-E, §4.4, p. 41; "Filing, Serving & Providing Court File," ch. 1-E, §6, p. 44.

3. Noticed motion. For a discussion of the deadlines to file and serve noticed motions, see "Filing & Serving Noticed Motions," ch. 1-D, §7, p. 33.

§4.4 Contents. The contents of the motion depend on its form.

1. Case-management conference. The mandatory case-management statement simply requires the party requesting preference to check the box indicating the case is entitled to preference and to identify the statutory grounds for the preference. Judicial Council Forms, form CM-110, item 9. Depending on the grounds for relief, the party may need to provide supporting evidence at the initial case-management conference. *See, e.g.*, CCP §36(d)

(court may grant motion for preference accompanied by medical documentation showing that party suffers from illness or condition raising substantial medical doubt about survival beyond six months).

2. Ex parte application. For a discussion of the contents of ex parte applications generally, see "Application Papers," ch. 1-E, §5, p. 42. An ex parte application must include a declaration supporting good cause for the request. CRC 3.1335(b).

3. Noticed motion. For a discussion of the contents of noticed motions generally, see "Motion Papers," ch. 1-D, §5, p. 27. A noticed motion may need to be supported by the following evidence:

(1) Declaration – all parties served. A motion for preference based on a party's age or illness or in the interests of justice should be supported by a declaration that all essential parties have been served with process or have appeared, unless the court orders otherwise. CCP §36(c)(1).

(2) Declaration – party's age. A motion for preference based on a party's age must be supported by a certified copy of the party's birth certificate or by the party's declaration. *See* Kiesel, *Cal. Pretrial Civil Procedure*, §23.66; Weil, *Civil Procedure Before Trial*, ¶12:247.3. If a party is claiming preference because she is 70 or older and her health makes preference necessary, her health condition can be supported by her attorney's declaration about her medical diagnosis and prognosis based on information and belief. CCP §36.5; *see* Weil, *Civil Procedure Before Trial*, ¶12:247.1 (attorney's declaration allowed to have hearsay and conclusions). See "Party is 70 or older," §3.2.1, p. 477.

(3) Documents – party is terminally ill. A motion for preference based on a party being terminally ill must be supported by clear and convincing medical documentation concluding that the party suffers from an illness or condition that raises substantial medical doubt about the party's survival beyond six months. CCP §36(d).

§4.5 Filing fees. When filing a motion or application for preference, the movant must pay a filing fee to the court clerk or request a waiver of the fee. See "Filing Fees," ch. 1-F, §7, p. 58. There is no filing fee for a case-management statement. Gov. C. §70617(b)(3).

§5. RESPONSE

§5.1 Motion for discretionary dismissal. When appropriate, the nonmovant can respond to an ex parte application or noticed motion for preference by filing a motion for discretionary dismissal for delay in prosecution. *See* ***Landry v. Berryessa Un. Sch. Dist.*** (6th Dist.1995) 39 Cal.App.4th 691, 696-97 (court retains discretion to dismiss case for delay in prosecution even if P would normally be entitled to preference). The court can hear the motion to dismiss even if the motion does not comply with the 45-day notice requirement for a motion for discretionary dismissal because the movant, by requesting preference, is deemed to have waived the requirement. *See* ***Eliceche v. Federal Land Bank Ass'n*** (5th Dist.2002) 103 Cal.App.4th 1349, 1367; *see also* CRC 3.1342(a) (45-day notice requirement). See "Grounds – Discretionary Dismissal," ch. 10-E, §5, p. 1171.

§5.2 Opposition to application or motion. The nonmovant can respond to an ex parte application or noticed motion for preference by filing an opposition. See "Opposition Papers," ch. 1-D, §8, p. 35; "Opposing Ex Parte Application," ch. 1-E, §7, p. 44.

1. Grounds. The nonmovant can oppose the ex parte application or noticed motion based on any of the following grounds:

(1) Negate grounds for relief. The nonmovant can negate the movant's grounds for relief. See "Grounds," §3, p. 475.

(2) Preference will violate right to due process. If granting preference will leave the nonmovant with inadequate time to prepare for trial, the nonmovant can argue that granting preference will violate its right to due process. *See* ***In re Marriage of Greenway*** (4th Dist.2013) 217 Cal.App.4th 628, 633; ***Roe v. Superior Ct.*** (4th Dist.1990) 224 Cal.App.3d 642, 643 n.2; *see, e.g.*, ***Peters v. Superior Ct.*** (2d Dist.1989) 212 Cal.App.3d 218, 227 (court would not consider Ds' due-process argument because Ds did not claim that granting P's motion for preference would

leave them with inadequate time to prepare for trial). But no court has ruled yet on whether shortening a party's time to prepare for trial by granting preference (e.g., setting trial before the discovery period has ended) actually violates a party's due-process rights.

(3) Movant not diligent in bringing case to trial. If the motion is based on the ground that the case is approaching a mandatory-dismissal deadline for delay in prosecution, the nonmovant can argue that (1) the movant has not diligently moved the case toward trial and (2) the nonmovant will be prejudiced if preference is granted. *See* ***Howard v. Thrifty Drug & Disc. Stores*** (1995) 10 Cal.4th 424, 440-41 (P must make some showing of excusable delay for not bringing case to trial within five years); *see, e.g.*, ***Parlen v. Golden State Sanwa Bank*** (2d Dist.1987) 194 Cal.App.3d 906, 913 (D stated in its opposition that it would be unduly prejudiced if preference was granted because it would not have enough time to prepare for trial). The nonmovant should address the same factors in CRC 3.1342(e) that the court must consider when ruling on a motion for discretionary dismissal for delay in prosecution. *See* ***Howard***, 10 Cal.4th at 441; ***Eliceche v. Federal Land Bank Ass'n*** (5th Dist.2002) 103 Cal.App.4th 1349, 1363. See "Factors favor preference," §3.3.1(3), p. 478.

2. Supporting evidence – party is 70 or older. If the ex parte application or noticed motion is based on a party being 70 or older and in poor health, the opposition must be supported by competent evidence—not a declaration based on information and belief—challenging the movant's medical diagnosis and prognosis. *See* Weil, *Civil Procedure Before Trial*, ¶12:247.4. See "Declaration – party's age," §4.4.3(2), p. 480.

§6. HEARING

Hearings on an ex parte application or noticed motion for preference are conducted in the same manner as civil hearings generally. See "Hearings," ch. 1-H, p. 79.

§7. RULING

§7.1 Delay in prosecution. If delay in prosecution is an issue in the case, the court can determine whether the case should be dismissed, either on an opposing party's motion or on its own motion, even if the movant would normally be entitled to preference. *See* CCP §583.410; ***Landry v. Berryessa Un. Sch. Dist.*** (6th Dist.1995) 39 Cal.App.4th 691, 696-97. If the case is subject to dismissal for delay in prosecution, the court must first determine whether the movant has shown "excusable delay." *See* ***Howard v. Thrifty Drug & Disc. Stores*** (1995) 10 Cal.4th 424, 440-41. See "Plaintiff has excuse for delay," §3.3.1(2), p. 478. If the court determines that the movant made this showing, the court must then consider whether the factors relied on to rule on a motion to dismiss for delay in prosecution would favor granting the preference. ***Howard***, 10 Cal.4th at 441; ***Eliceche v. Federal Land Bank Ass'n*** (5th Dist.2002) 103 Cal.App.4th 1349, 1363; *see also* CCP §583.130 (public-policy factors); CRC 3.1342(e) (general factors). See "Factors favor preference," §3.3.1(3), p. 478.

§7.2 No delay in prosecution.

1. Mandatory preference.

(1) Party's age. If delay in prosecution is not an issue in the case, the court usually must grant a motion for preference made by a person entitled to preference for being 70 or older or under 14 if all the grounds are met. *See* CCP §36(a), (b); ***Landry v. Berryessa Un. Sch. Dist.*** (6th Dist.1995) 39 Cal.App.4th 691, 696; ***Kline v. Superior Ct.*** (2d Dist.1991) 227 Cal.App.3d 512, 515-16. See "Party is 70 or older," §3.2.1, p. 477; "Party is under 14," §3.2.2, p. 477.

(a) Effect on judicial arbitration. The right to a preferential trial date for a party who is 70 or older is mandatory even if the suit would normally be submitted to judicial arbitration under CCP §1141.11. *E.g.*, ***Vinokur v. Superior Ct.*** (2d Dist.1988) 198 Cal.App.3d 500, 503 (court could not order P to attend arbitration after she requested preferential trial date). Section 1141.11 directs courts to send certain cases to arbitration, based primarily on the amount in controversy and case classification.

(b) **Effect on contractual arbitration.** The right to a preferential trial date for a party who is 70 or older is not mandatory if an arbitration agreement requires that the suit be referred to arbitration. ***Laswell v. AG Seal Beach, LLC*** (2d Dist.2010) 189 Cal.App.4th 1399, 1409-10. Although a party's advanced age has no effect on contractual arbitration, the court should still consider the party's advanced age in scheduling the arbitration proceedings. *Id.*

(2) **Party seeks damages caused during felony.** If delay in prosecution is not an issue in the case, the court must grant a motion for preference made by a person seeking damages allegedly caused by the defendant during the commission of a felony offense if all the grounds are met. CCP §37(a). See "Plaintiff suffered damages caused during felony," §3.2.4, p. 477.

(3) **Specific cause of action entitled to preference.** If delay in prosecution is not an issue in the case, the court must grant a motion for preference in which the specific cause of action is entitled to preference. See "Cause of action entitled to preference," §3.1, p. 475.

2. **Discretionary preference.** If delay in prosecution is not an issue in the case, the decision to grant or deny a motion for preference based on a party being terminally ill or on the interests of justice is within the court's discretion. *See* CCP §36(d) & (e) (court may grant motion for preference in its discretion); ***Salas v. Sears, Roebuck & Co.*** (1986) 42 Cal.3d 342, 344 (ruling under former CCP §36(d), now §36(e), rests in sound discretion of court).

§8. ORDER

§8.1 Form. The court's ruling on the motion for preference must be recorded either in writing or by minute order. See "Record of Ruling," ch. 1-I, §4, p. 90.

§8.2 Contents. If preference is granted, the court should set the hearing or trial date.

1. **CCP §36.** If preference is granted under CCP §36, the court must usually set the trial date within 120 days after the motion is granted. CCP §36(f); *see, e.g.*, ***In re Marriage of Greenway*** (4th Dist.2013) 217 Cal.App.4th 628, 634 (order granting motion for preference on September 17, 2010, set trial for January 11, 2011). If the case is approaching a mandatory-dismissal deadline, the court may be willing to set the trial date before the deadline expires, but it is the plaintiff's responsibility to ensure that the case goes to trial before the deadline. *See* ***De Santiago v. D&G Plumbing, Inc.*** (4th Dist.2007) 155 Cal.App.4th 365, 374; ***Lee v. Park*** (2d Dist.1996) 43 Cal.App.4th 305, 309.

2. **When damages resulted from commission of felony.** If preference is granted because the plaintiff is seeking damages allegedly caused by the defendant during the commission of a felony offense, the court must "endeavor to try the action within 120 days of the grant of preference." CCP §37(b); Thomas, *Courtroom Handbook*, §26:10.

3. **Cause of action entitled to preference.** If preference is granted because the cause of action is entitled to preference, the court must set the hearing or trial date according to the statute governing the particular cause of action. See "Cause of action entitled to preference," §3.1, p. 475.

§9. EFFECT OF PREFERENCE

§9.1 Court's calendar. A case given preference is prioritized over other cases on the court's calendar, whether for a hearing or trial. *See, e.g.*, CCP §36(f) (court must set trial within 120 days after preference is granted). Some types of preferred cases are given preference over others. *See, e.g.*, *id.* §36(b) (case entitled to preference under CCP §36(a) is given preference over case entitled to preference under CCP §36(b)).

§9.2 Continuances.

1. **CCP §36.** If preference is granted under CCP §36, the court cannot grant a continuance after 120 days from the date the motion is granted except (1) for the physical disability of a party or party's attorney or (2) on a showing of good cause stated in the record. CCP §36(f). Any continuance that is granted cannot exceed 15 days, and only one continuance for physical disability can be granted to any party. *Id.*

PRACTICE TIP

If a party is too ill to proceed with the trial after being granted preference and a one-time continuance, the party can file a motion to have the case taken off the trial calendar. ***Greenblatt v. Kaplan's Rest.*** *(4th Dist.1985) 171 Cal.App.3d 991, 995-96.*

2. Libel or slander action. If preference is granted in a libel or slander action, any continuance granted cannot exceed ten days without the consent of the adverse party, unless good cause is shown by the party requesting the continuance. CCP §460.5(c).

§10. MOTION FOR RECONSIDERATION

A party adversely affected by a court's order on a motion for preference can file a motion for reconsideration. CCP §1008(a). See "Motion for Reconsideration," ch. 5-G, §3, p. 508.

§11. MOTION FOR RENEWAL

A party whose motion for preference is denied can file a motion for renewal. *See* CCP §1008(b). See "Motion for Renewal," ch. 5-G, §4, p. 516.

§12. APPELLATE REVIEW

§12.1 Writ of mandate. A party can challenge the ruling on a motion for preference by filing a petition for a writ of mandate. *See, e.g.,* ***Vinokur v. Superior Ct.*** (2d Dist.1988) 198 Cal.App.3d 500, 501 (P filed petition for writ of mandate after court denied motion for preference). The trial court's ruling is reviewed for abuse of discretion. *See, e.g.,* ***Koch-Ash v. Superior Ct.*** (2d Dist.1986) 180 Cal.App.3d 689, 698 (court abused its discretion by ignoring unquestionably controlling authority of §36(a) and (e)).

§12.2 Direct appeal. A party can challenge the ruling on a motion for preference by raising the issue on appeal after the entry of a final judgment. *See* CCP §§904.1(a), 904.2; ***Salas v. Sears, Roebuck & Co.*** (1986) 42 Cal.3d 342, 345 n.3; ***Salinas v. Atchison, Topeka & Santa Fe Ry.*** (5th Dist.1992) 5 Cal.App.4th 1, 9. Generally, the trial court's ruling is reviewed for abuse of discretion. ***Salas***, 42 Cal.3d at 349-50. If the facts supporting the motion are undisputed, however, the issue of preference becomes a question of law and the standard of review is de novo. *See* ***Goodstein v. Superior Ct.*** (2d Dist.1996) 42 Cal.App.4th 1635, 1641.

C. INTERVENTION

This subchapter discusses complaints in intervention under CCP §387. This subchapter does not discuss how to intervene in a probate suit or in a proceeding to validate a district redevelopment plan brought by a public agency, nor does it discuss intervention orders arising from arbitration agreements. For more on these topics, see CCP §§860-870.5 (validating proceedings), §1281.2 (intervention orders), and Prob. C. §48 (defining "interested person" in probate suits).

§1. GENERAL

§1.1 Purpose. Intervention is a procedure used to allow a nonparty to become a party to an action. CCP §387(a). Intervention protects the interests of nonparties who will be affected by a judgment in the action, reduces delay, and prevents multiple lawsuits involving the same issues. ***People v. Superior Ct.*** (1976) 17 Cal.3d 732, 736.

§1.2 Primary authority. CCP §387.

§1.3 Secondary authority. The following secondary sources are cited as authority in this subchapter:

- *California Civil Procedure Before Trial* (CEB Online ed. 2014) (referred to as *CEB Procedure Before Trial*).
- Thomas, *California Civil Courtroom Handbook* (2014) (referred to as Thomas, *Courtroom Handbook*).
- Weil & Brown, *California Practice Guide: Civil Procedure Before Trial* (CD-ROM ed. 2014) (referred to as Weil, *Civil Procedure Before Trial*).

§2. TYPES OF INTERVENTION

Intervention can be mandatory (i.e., as a matter of right) or permissive. ***Hodge v. Kirkpatrick Dev., Inc.*** (4th Dist.2005) 130 Cal.App.4th 540, 547; *see* CCP §387.

§2.1 Mandatory intervention. A nonparty has a right to intervene when (1) a statute gives it an unconditional right to intervene or (2) it has an interest in the property or transaction that is the subject matter of the action and, without intervention, the interest will not be adequately protected. CCP §387(b).

PRACTICE TIP

Mandatory intervention and compulsory joinder have similar requirements, so a nonparty may qualify to join the suit under both. See CCP §387(b) (mandatory intervention), §389(a) (compulsory joinder); ***Hodge v. Kirkpatrick Dev., Inc.*** *(4th Dist.2005) 130 Cal.App.4th 540, 556 (noting similarity); see, e.g.,* ***Marken v. Santa Monica-Malibu Unified Sch. Dist.*** *(2d Dist.2012) 202 Cal.App.4th 1250, 1258 (nonparty filed ex parte application requesting mandatory intervention and compulsory joinder in the alternative). Mandatory intervention is usually the preferred method, unless the request to intervene could be considered untimely, because (1) the test is less strict and (2) the party can file a pleading (i.e., the complaint in intervention) defining its own interest in the suit. CEB Procedure Before Trial, §31.8; see CCP §387(b) (requiring timely application), §389 (no time limit for compulsory joinder);* ***Fireman's Fund Ins. v. Gerlach*** *(1st Dist.1976) 56 Cal.App.3d 299, 302 (test for compulsory joinder is stricter than test for mandatory intervention). See "When to make," §3.1.4, p. 488; "Compulsory joinder – §389," ch. 3-B, §3.1, p. 193.*

1. Statute confers right. The nonparty can show that a statute gives it an unconditional right to intervene. CCP §387(b). The following are examples of statutes that give nonparties the right to intervene:

(1) Any shareholder or creditor of a corporation has a right to intervene in involuntary dissolution proceedings against the corporation. Corp. C. §1800(c); *CEB Procedure Before Trial*, §31.6.

(2) All creditors of a corporation have a right to intervene in an action against a shareholder to enforce subscription agreements. Corp. C. §414(b); *CEB Procedure Before Trial*, §31.6.

(3) Any person claiming a legal or equitable interest in real property that is the subject of a condemnation proceeding has a right to intervene. CCP §1250.230; *CEB Procedure Before Trial*, §31.6.

(4) A dissenting shareholder demanding the purchase of its shares as a result of a corporate reorganization, or any interested corporation, has a right to intervene in an action to determine whether the shareholder's shares are dissenting shares or to determine the fair market value of dissenting shares. Corp. C. §1304(a); *CEB Procedure Before Trial*, §31.6.

(5) Either an employer or an employee has a right to intervene in an industrial-injury suit commenced by the other against a third party. Lab. C. §3853; *see* ***Mar v. Sakti Int'l*** (1st Dist.1992) 9 Cal.App.4th 1780, 1782.

(6) The Labor Commissioner has the right to intervene in compensation-claim proceedings arising under Lab. C. §98.2 when questions of interpretation of statutes or administrative regulations are present. Lab. C. §98.5.

(7) Any member of a consumer class action has a right to intervene in the action. *See* Civ. C. §1781(e)(3); *CEB Procedure Before Trial*, §31.6.

(8) An Indian child's tribe and Indian custodian have the right to intervene in child-custody proceedings involving the Indian child. 25 U.S.C. §1911(c); CRC 5.482(e); *see* ***In re W.B.*** (2012) 55 Cal.4th 30, 48; *see, e.g.,* ***Guardianship of D.W.*** (1st Dist.2013) 221 Cal.App.4th 242, 249-50 (guardianship order was vacated when tribe was not given proper notice to intervene).

(9) A political subdivision has the right to intervene in claims brought on its behalf under the False Claims Act that allege violations involving political-subdivision funds. Gov. C. §12652(a)(3), (c)(7)(B); *e.g.*, ***Laraway v. Sutro & Co.*** (2d Dist.2002) 96 Cal.App.4th 266, 272 (school district intervened in action brought on its behalf by private person who alleged school-district employees conspired to obtain payment from school district on false travel claims); *see, e.g.*, ***San Francisco Unified Sch. Dist. v. First Student, Inc.*** (1st Dist.2013) 213 Cal.App.4th 1212, 1216 (school district declined to intervene in action brought on its behalf by private persons who alleged transit company failed to maintain company's buses as required by contract with school district).

2. Necessary to protect interest in property or transaction. The nonparty can show that it has an interest in the matter that requires the court to grant mandatory intervention. To show this, the nonparty must prove that (1) it has an interest in the property or transaction that is the subject matter of the action, (2) the disposition of the action might impair or impede its ability to protect that interest, and (3) its interest is not adequately represented by the current parties to the action. CCP §387(b); ***Hodge***, 130 Cal.App.4th at 547.

(1) Interest in property or transaction. The nonparty must show that it has an interest relating to the property or transaction that is the subject matter of the action. CCP §387(b); *see, e.g.*, ***Marken***, 202 Cal.App.4th at 1276 (dicta; nonparty who filed request to disclose public records had sufficient interest to intervene in separate suit seeking to enjoin their disclosure); ***Mylan Labs. v. Soon-Shiong*** (2d Dist.1999) 76 Cal.App.4th 71, 78-79 (nonparty could not intervene in breach-of-fiduciary-duty suit to prevent disclosure of its privileged documents because documents were not subject matter of suit). Generally, to meet the requirements for mandatory intervention, the nonparty must have a direct pecuniary interest in the property or transaction. *See* ***Coalition for Fair Rent v. Abdelnour*** (4th Dist.1980) 107 Cal.App.3d 97, 115; *see, e.g.*, ***Hodge***, 130 Cal.App.4th at 548-49 (insurer with subrogation rights can intervene in insured's negligence suit). A nonparty's interest in the outcome of a tort action is not considered a property interest under §387(b). ***California Physicians' Serv. v. Superior Ct.*** (2d Dist.1980) 102 Cal.App.3d 91, 96.

(2) Ability to protect interest impaired. The nonparty must show that the disposition of the action might impair or impede its ability to protect its interest. CCP §387(b); ***Marken***, 202 Cal.App.4th at 1269; ***Hodge***, 130 Cal.App.4th at 554. A nonparty's ability to protect its interest is impaired or impeded when the alternative methods of protecting the interest are not reasonable. *See, e.g.*, ***Siena Ct. Homeowners Ass'n v. Green Valley Corp.*** (6th Dist.2008) 164 Cal.App.4th 1416, 1425-26 (reasonable for third party to bring separate suit because its legal issues were independent of those in underlying suit); ***Hodge***, 130 Cal.App.4th at 551-52 (unreasonable to expect subrogated insurer to bring separate suit because it would hinder subrogation rights).

(3) Interest not adequately represented. The nonparty must show that its interest is not adequately represented by the current parties. CCP §387(b); *see* ***Redevelopment Agency of San Marcos v. Commission on State Mandates*** (4th Dist.1996) 43 Cal.App.4th 1188, 1198; *see, e.g.*, ***Marken***, 202 Cal.App.4th at 1276 (dicta; nonparty's interest in obtaining public records was not adequately represented by school district's delay in producing public records and tepid arguments in support of their disclosure); ***Hodge***, 130 Cal.App.4th at 555 (insurer's interests were not adequately represented when insurer's and insured's interests in outcome were in conflict); ***Coalition for Fair Rent***, 107 Cal.App.3d at 114-15 (intervention denied when there was no difference between position of party to suit and that of nonparty requesting intervention).

§2.2 Permissive intervention. A nonparty may intervene when (1) it follows the proper procedures for intervention, (2) it has a direct and immediate interest in the action, (3) intervention will not enlarge the issues in the action, and (4) the reasons for intervention outweigh any opposition presented by the parties currently in the action. ***Siena Ct. Homeowners Ass'n v. Green Valley Corp.*** (6th Dist.2008) 164 Cal.App.4th 1416, 1428; ***Royal Indem. Co. v. United Enters.*** (4th Dist.2008) 162 Cal.App.4th 194, 203.

1. Proper procedures. The nonparty must show that the proper procedures for intervention were followed. ***Siena Ct. Homeowners Ass'n***, 164 Cal.App.4th at 1428; ***Royal Indem.***, 162 Cal.App.4th at 203. For a discussion of these procedures, see "Motion for Leave to Intervene," §3, p. 488.

2. **Adequate interest.**

(1) Direct & immediate. The nonparty must show that it has a direct and immediate interest in the outcome of the suit. ***Siena Ct. Homeowners Ass'n***, 164 Cal.App.4th at 1428. The interest must be direct, not consequential. ***Hinton v. Beck*** (3d Dist.2009) 176 Cal.App.4th 1378, 1383. A nonparty has a direct interest when a judgment in the action would directly benefit or harm it. ***City & Cty. of S.F. v. State*** (1st Dist.2005) 128 Cal.App.4th 1030, 1037; *see* ***Continental Vinyl Prods. v. Mead Corp.*** (2d Dist.1972) 27 Cal.App.3d 543, 549. The benefit-or-harm analysis does not depend on the outcome of issues that would have to be litigated in a separate suit. *See* ***Hinton***, 176 Cal.App.4th at 1383 (describing analysis as "without reference to rights and duties not involved in the litigation"); ***Continental Vinyl***, 27 Cal.App.3d at 549 (same); *see, e.g.*, ***Royal Indem.***, 162 Cal.App.4th at 211-12 (intervention denied; nonparty would have to litigate completely separate negligence action before it could establish legal right to insurance proceeds from tortfeasor's insurer). If a separate suit would be necessary, the nonparty merely has a consequential interest—that is, one that indirectly benefits or harms it. *See* ***Hinton***, 176 Cal.App.4th at 1383; ***Continental Vinyl***, 27 Cal.App.3d at 550. An interest that is merely speculative is no interest at all. *See, e.g.*, ***City of Malibu v. California Coastal Comm'n*** (2d Dist.2005) 128 Cal.App.4th 897, 905 (nonparties' speculation that members of public might trespass on their property if public-access ways were opened did not justify intervention).

(a) Examples – direct interest. In the following examples, the court found a direct interest that justified intervention:

[1] An attorney entitled by statute to receive attorney fees in an action was allowed to intervene. ***Lindelli v. Town of San Anselmo*** (1st Dist.2006) 139 Cal.App.4th 1499, 1512.

[2] A school district was allowed to intervene in an action to defend a city resolution requiring a school-impact fee for new building permits that was designed to alleviate overcrowding in the district's schools caused by new subdivisions. ***Timberidge Enters. v. City of Santa Rosa*** (1st Dist.1978) 86 Cal.App.3d 873, 882.

[3] An insurer was allowed to intervene in a negligence suit against its insured when the insured had no answer on file and the insurer would have to directly pay for the impending default judgment. ***Reliance Ins. v. Superior Ct.*** (6th Dist.2000) 84 Cal.App.4th 383, 387-88.

[4] A joint tortfeasor who settled in an action was allowed to intervene for indemnity against another nonsettling joint tortfeasor in the action. ***Bolamperti v. Larco Mfg.*** (4th Dist.1985) 164 Cal.App.3d 249, 255.

[5] Official proponents of an initiative measure could intervene to defend the proposed initiative in a pre-election challenge in order to protect their constitutional and statutory rights under California law to have their proposed measure put to a vote of the people. ***Perry v. Brown*** (2011) 52 Cal.4th 1116, 1146.

NOTE

*In **Perry**, the California Supreme Court, at the request of the Ninth Circuit, addressed the question of whether official proponents of an initiative measure possess a particularized interest in the validity of the initiative. **Perry**, 52 Cal.4th at 1124. **Perry** held that official proponents who intervene in a pre-election challenge to the validity of an initiative measure possess a distinct interest in defending the proposed initiative because they are acting to protect their personal constitutional and statutory rights under California law to have their proposed measure put to a vote of the people. Id. at 1146; see **Mission Springs Water Dist. v. Verjil** (4th Dist.2013) 218 Cal.App.4th 892, 905-06. The **Perry** court did not determine whether official proponents possess a particularized interest in the initiative's validity once the measure has been approved by the voters. **Perry**, 52 Cal.4th at 1139. In a postelection challenge, however, when the public officials who ordinarily defend a challenged measure decline to do so, official proponents of an*

*initiative measure are authorized under state law to intervene in a judicial proceeding to assert the State's interest in the initiative's validity and to appeal a judgment invalidating the measure. Id. at 1152. In addressing **Perry**, the U.S. Supreme Court recently held that while official proponents have authority to assert the State's interests in defending voter-approved initiatives in California courts, that authority does not confer standing to similarly assert the State's interest in federal court. See **Hollingsworth v. Perry (2013)** ___ U.S. ___, 133 S.Ct. 2652, 2667.*

(b) Examples – no direct interest. In the following examples, the court did not find a direct interest that justified intervention:

[1] An attorney was not allowed to intervene to recover his attorney fees when the statute awarded attorney fees to the client, not to the attorney directly. ***Meadow v. Superior Ct.*** (1963) 59 Cal.2d 610, 615-16; ***Marshank v. Superior Ct.*** (2d Dist.1960) 180 Cal.App.2d 602, 605-06.

[2] An organization was not allowed to intervene in an action to defend the legality of an initiative banning same-sex marriage when it could not show that overturning the initiative would harm its members' marriages or future marriages or diminish members' legal rights, property rights, or freedoms. ***City & Cty. of S.F.***, 128 Cal.App.4th at 1038-39.

[3] A nonparty, who was a potential judgment creditor, was not allowed to intervene in an action between an insurer and its insured because the nonparty had no current judgment against the insured. ***Royal Indem.***, 162 Cal.App.4th at 211-12.

(2) Consequential interest becomes direct. Although a consequential interest is not sufficient to support intervention, the courts have recognized that the following circumstances may change a consequential interest into a direct interest:

(a) A party to the suit is pursuing or defending it in bad faith. ***Continental Vinyl***, 27 Cal.App.3d at 551; *see, e.g.*, ***Shively v. Eureka Tellurium Gold Mining Co.*** (1900) 129 Cal. 293, 295 (shareholders without direct interest were allowed to intervene in suit against corporation when directors and officers did not defend suit in good faith).

(b) The parties to the suit are acting in collusion against the nonparty. ***Continental Vinyl***, 27 Cal.App.3d at 551; *see, e.g.*, ***Linder v. Vogue Invs.*** (2d Dist.1966) 239 Cal.App.2d 338, 340-41 (limited partner allowed to intervene and defend suit when general partner agreed not to defend suit and let P execute default judgment against limited partnership).

(c) Only the nonparty can assert a position that should be litigated in the suit. ***Continental Vinyl***, 27 Cal.App.3d at 551; *see, e.g.*, ***County of San Bernardino v. Harsh Cal. Corp.*** (1959) 52 Cal.2d 341, 345-46 (U.S. was only entity that could argue and defend federal government's fiscal policy).

(3) No pecuniary or subject-matter requirements. The nonparty does not have to show a pecuniary or specific interest in the subject matter of the suit. *See* ***Simpson Redwood Co. v. State*** (1st Dist.1987) 196 Cal.App.3d 1192, 1201; *see, e.g.*, ***Bustop v. Superior Ct.*** (2d Dist.1977) 69 Cal.App.3d 66, 71 (nonparty's interest in social, educational, and economic impact of reassignment of students to other schools was sufficient to allow nonparty to intervene in litigation over school integration).

3. No enlargement of issues. The nonparty must show that the intervention will not enlarge the issues in the case. *E.g.*, ***Siena Ct. Homeowners Ass'n***, 164 Cal.App.4th at 1429 (nonparty could not intervene and add joint-use and maintenance-contract issues to construction-defect suit); ***Kuperstein v. Superior Ct.*** (4th Dist.1988) 204 Cal.App.3d 598, 600-01 (insurer could not intervene and add insurance-coverage issues to product-liability suit); ***People v. County of Trinity*** (3d Dist.1983) 147 Cal.App.3d 655, 661 (nonparty could intervene when its claims raised no new factual or legal issues). A nonparty can add a new cause of action without enlarging the issues if the facts of the new cause of action are the same as the facts currently in the suit. *See* ***Simpson Redwood Co.***, 196 Cal.App.3d at 1202.

4. Reasons for intervention outweigh opposition. The nonparty must show that its need to intervene in the case outweighs any reasons the parties may have to resist its intervention. ***County of Trinity***, 147 Cal.App.3d at 661; *see, e.g.*, ***Truck Ins. Exch. v. Superior Ct.*** (2d Dist.1997) 60 Cal.App.4th 342, 350-51 (P could not stop intervention on basis that it would no longer be able to take default judgment). For example, if a defendant is resisting the intervention simply because it might have to pay damages to the nonparty if intervention is permitted, the nonparty can argue that reason alone is insufficient to deny intervention. *See* ***Lindelli***, 139 Cal.App.4th at 1512.

§3. MOTION FOR LEAVE TO INTERVENE

Leave of court is required before a complaint in intervention can be filed. ***Lohnes v. Astron Computer Prods.*** (4th Dist.2001) 94 Cal.App.4th 1150, 1153; ***Beshara v. Goldberg*** (2d Dist.1963) 221 Cal.App.2d 392, 395; *see* ***Tokio Mar. & Fire Ins. v. Western Pac. Roofing Corp.*** (2d Dist.1999) 75 Cal.App.4th 110, 120 (nonparty cannot become intervenor in action through stipulation with current party).

§3.1 Motion.

1. Grounds. A motion for leave to intervene must be based on the grounds for either mandatory intervention or permissive intervention. *See* CCP §387. If the nonparty requests mandatory intervention, it should also ask for permissive intervention in the alternative. *See, e.g.*, ***Siena Ct. Homeowners Ass'n v. Green Valley Corp.*** (6th Dist.2008) 164 Cal.App.4th 1416, 1421 (motion for leave to intervene based on mandatory intervention and permissive intervention). See "Types of Intervention," §2, p. 484.

2. Who can make. Any nonparty can request leave to intervene. *See* CCP §387(a); ***Noya v. A.W. Coulter Trucking*** (2d Dist.2006) 143 Cal.App.4th 838, 842. There can be more than one intervenor. *See, e.g.*, ***Smith v. Parks Manor*** (2d Dist.1987) 197 Cal.App.3d 872, 877 (nonparty intervened as D after another nonparty intervened as P).

3. How to make.

(1) Ex parte application. The motion for leave to intervene can be made by an ex parte application. ***Adoption of Lenn E.*** (5th Dist.1986) 182 Cal.App.3d 210, 217; *see* ***Marken v. Santa Monica-Malibu Unified Sch. Dist.*** (2d Dist.2012) 202 Cal.App.4th 1250, 1258. See "Application Papers," ch. 1-E, §5, p. 42. A nonparty should seek leave to intervene ex parte when it believes that the parties would attempt to settle and dismiss the action before a noticed motion for leave to intervene could be heard by the court. *See* Weil, *Civil Procedure Before Trial*, ¶2:442; *see, e.g.*, ***Egly v. Superior Ct.*** (2d Dist.1970) 6 Cal.App.3d 476, 482-83 (P had absolute right to dismiss case before complaint in intervention was filed). See "Before dismissal," §3.1.4(2), p. 489. The nonparty should attach a declaration to the application stating any facts and reasons supporting its belief that the parties may attempt to settle and dismiss the suit before it can intervene. *See CEB Procedure Before Trial*, §31.43. If the court sets a hearing for the application, the nonparty should ask the court to stay all proceedings in the action, including dismissal. *Id.*

(2) Noticed motion. The motion for leave to intervene can be made by a noticed motion. *See* ***City & Cty. of S.F. v. State*** (1st Dist.2005) 128 Cal.App.4th 1030, 1034. See "Motion Papers," ch. 1-D, §5, p. 27.

(3) Oral motion. The motion for leave to intervene can be made orally if it is made in front of the parties and adequately informs the court and the other parties of the basis for the motion. *See* ***Simac Design, Inc. v. Alciati*** (1st Dist.1979) 92 Cal.App.3d 146, 157.

4. When to make. The motion for leave to intervene must be timely. CCP §387. Timeliness will depend on the facts of each case and the manner in which the motion is brought (i.e., orally, by ex parte application, or by noticed motion). *See* ***Mallick v. Superior Ct.*** (1st Dist.1979) 89 Cal.App.3d 434, 437 (if otherwise appropriate, intervention is possible even after judgment); *see, e.g.*, ***Marken***, 202 Cal.App.4th at 1277-78 (ex parte request for leave to intervene was untimely when nonparty was aware of action but waited to file request three days before scheduled hearing); ***Chavez v. Netflix, Inc.*** (1st Dist.2008) 162 Cal.App.4th 43, 51 (request for leave to intervene was untimely when filed after date specified by court in class notice). For example, a request made after an unreasonable delay that prejudices one of the parties to the action may be deemed untimely. *See* ***Truck Ins. Exch. v. Superior Ct.*** (2d

Dist.1997) 60 Cal.App.4th 342, 350-51; *see, e.g.*, ***Noya***, 143 Cal.App.4th at 842 (request for leave to intervene was untimely when filed several years into litigation and after parties had reached settlement agreement). At a minimum, a motion for leave must be filed before the following deadlines:

(1) Before statutory deadline. A motion based on an unconditional statutory right to intervene must be made within the time allowed by the statute, if specified. *See, e.g.*, ***Mar v. Sakti Int'l*** (1st Dist.1992) 9 Cal.App.4th 1780, 1784-85 (request for leave to intervene timely when filed after settlement but before trial on remaining issues; statute allowed intervention anytime before trial).

(2) Before dismissal. A motion for leave to intervene must be made before the suit is voluntarily dismissed. *See* ***Lohnes v. Astron Computer Prods.*** (4th Dist.2001) 94 Cal.App.4th 1150, 1153-54; ***Egly***, 6 Cal.App.3d at 482-83.

(3) Before statute of limitations runs.

(a) Most cases. For most cases, a motion for leave to intervene must be made before the statute of limitations runs on any new cause of action asserted in the complaint in intervention. *See* ***Basin Constr. Corp. v. Department of Water & Power of L.A.*** (2d Dist.1988) 199 Cal.App.3d 819, 824-25; ***Andersen v. Barton Mem'l Hosp., Inc.*** (3d Dist.1985) 166 Cal.App.3d 678, 682. If there are no new causes of action asserted, the motion is timely if the original complaint was filed within the applicable statute of limitations. *See CEB Procedure Before Trial*, §31.42.

(b) Cases under Lab. C. §3853. Under Lab. C. §3853, if an employee or employer (or its insurer) has timely filed an action against a third party for injuries to the employee, the party who did not file the action (i.e., the employee or employer) may be able to intervene in the suit even after the statute of limitations for bringing the original complaint has run. *Compare* ***O'Dell v. Freightliner Corp.*** (2d Dist.1992) 10 Cal.App.4th 645, 654 (employer or employee has unconditional right to intervene before trial on facts even after limitations period expires), *and* ***Jordan v. Superior Ct.*** (4th Dist.1981) 116 Cal.App.3d 202, 207-08 (same), *with* ***Fairmont Ins. v. Frank*** (4th Dist.1996) 42 Cal.App.4th 457, 460 (right to intervene after limitations period expires is not unconditional; intervenor must pursue its claim diligently), *and* ***Bishop v. Silva*** (6th Dist.1991) 234 Cal.App.3d 1317, 1327 (same).

PRACTICE TIP

If it is too late for a nonparty to request leave to intervene, the nonparty should consider asking the court to join it as a party to the action under the compulsory-joinder statute, CCP §389. See CEB Procedure Before Trial, §31.37. See "Compulsory joinder – §389," ch. 3-B, §3.1, p. 193.

---

5. Contents.

(1) Generally. For a discussion of the contents of noticed motions and ex parte applications generally, see "Motion Papers," ch. 1-D, §5, p. 27, and "Application Papers," ch. 1-E, §5, p. 42.

(2) Memorandum of points & authorities. The motion or ex parte application for leave to intervene should include a memorandum of points and authorities. See "Memorandum of points & authorities," ch. 1-D, §5.2, p. 28 (noticed motion); "Memorandum of points & authorities," ch. 1-E, §5.2, p. 42 (ex parte application).

(3) Supporting evidence. The nonparty should attach a declaration stating the facts that support intervention. Thomas, *Courtroom Handbook*, §8:14.

(4) Proposed complaint in intervention. The motion or ex parte application for leave to intervene should be accompanied by a proposed complaint in intervention. *See* CCP §387(a); ***Sutter Health Uninsured Pricing Cases*** (3d Dist.2009) 171 Cal.App.4th 495, 513; ***Jun v. Myers*** (2d Dist.2001) 88 Cal.App.4th 117, 120. See "Complaint in Intervention," §4, p. 491.

6. Filing fees. When the motion or application is filed, the movant must pay a filing fee to the court clerk or request a waiver of the fee. See "Filing Fees," ch. 1-F, §7, p. 58.

§3.2 Opposition.

1. Opposing ex parte application. If the nonparty files an ex parte application for leave to intervene, an opposing party may have an opportunity to challenge the application in writing or orally at the hearing. See "Opposing Ex Parte Application," ch. 1-E, §7, p. 44. If not, an opposing party can file a challenge to the complaint in intervention. See "Challenging the complaint," §4.3, p. 492.

2. Opposing noticed motion. If the nonparty files a noticed motion for leave to intervene, an opposing party can file opposition papers. If a party does not file opposition papers, the court can still deny the motion. But if the court grants the motion, any party who did not file an opposition waives any objection to the intervention on appeal. *See CEB Procedure Before Trial*, §31.48; Weil, *Civil Procedure Before Trial*, ¶2:446; *see, e.g.*, ***Bloom v. Waxman*** (2d Dist.1941) 48 Cal.App.2d 646, 647 (party who did not file any opposition to motion to intervene could not raise objection for first time on appeal).

(1) Deadline to file & serve. Opposition papers must be filed and served at least nine court days before the hearing. CCP §1005(b). See "Deadline to file & serve," ch. 1-D, §8.5.3, p. 37.

(2) Grounds. A party opposing the motion for leave to intervene should challenge the grounds for intervention. See "Types of Intervention," §2, p. 484.

(3) Contents. See "Opposition Papers," ch. 1-D, §8, p. 35.

§3.3 Hearing. Hearings on a motion for leave to intervene are conducted in the same manner as civil hearings generally. See "Hearings," ch. 1-H, p. 79.

§3.4 Ruling.

1. Standard for granting.

(1) Mandatory intervention. When the nonparty meets the requirements for mandatory intervention, the court must allow the nonparty to intervene even if doing so would add to the complexity of the action, create delay, or adversely affect the original parties to the action. *See* CCP §387(b); ***California Physicians' Serv. v. Superior Ct.*** (2d Dist.1980) 102 Cal.App.3d 91, 96.

(2) Permissive intervention. When the nonparty requests permissive intervention, the court has broad discretion to allow a nonparty to intervene. ***County of Alameda v. Carleson*** (1971) 5 Cal.3d 730, 736 n.4; ***City of Malibu v. California Coastal Comm'n*** (2d Dist.2005) 128 Cal.App.4th 897, 902.

2. Court's guidelines. CCP §387 should be construed liberally to allow for intervention. ***Simpson Redwood Co. v. State*** (1st Dist.1987) 196 Cal.App.3d 1192, 1200.

§3.5 Order. If the court grants the motion for leave to intervene, the order should allow the nonparty to file its complaint in intervention and can specify the deadline for doing so. See "Complaint in Intervention," §4, p. 491. Because the parties to the action can still dismiss the action even after the motion is granted, the party should file the complaint in intervention as soon as possible. *See* ***Klinghoffer v. Barasch*** (2d Dist.1970) 4 Cal.App.3d 258, 261-62.

§3.6 Motion for reconsideration. A party adversely affected by a court's ruling on a motion for leave to intervene can file a motion for reconsideration. *See* ***In re Baby Girl A.*** (4th Dist.1991) 230 Cal.App.3d 1611, 1616. See "Motion for Reconsideration," ch. 5-G, §3, p. 508.

§3.7 Motion for renewal. A party whose motion for leave to intervene is denied can file a motion for renewal. *See* CCP §1008(b). See "Motion for Renewal," ch. 5-G, §4, p. 516.

§3.8 Appellate review.

1. Direct appeal.

(1) Order denying intervention. An order denying a motion to intervene is appealable when it finally and adversely determines the rights of the moving party to proceed in the action. ***Marken v. Santa Monica-Malibu Unified Sch. Dist.*** (2d Dist.2012) 202 Cal.App.4th 1250, 1277; ***Hodge v. Kirkpatrick Dev., Inc.*** (4th

Dist.2005) 130 Cal.App.4th 540, 547. Thus, a motion that is denied based on a procedural error, such as being untimely filed, is not appealable. *E.g.*, ***Marken***, 202 Cal.App.4th at 1277 (denial of untimely ex parte application to intervene was not appealable). To timely appeal from a denial of a motion to intervene, the party must file the appeal within 180 days after the order denying intervention was entered, not after the judgment was rendered. *E.g.*, ***Quantification Settlement Agreement Cases*** (3d Dist.2011) 201 Cal.App.4th 758, 837 (appeal of denial from motion to intervene was untimely when party appealed from judgment instead of from order denying intervention).

(2) Order granting intervention. A party cannot directly appeal an order granting intervention but instead must wait until final judgment to appeal the court's ruling. ***Estate of Edwards*** (3d Dist.1978) 82 Cal.App.3d 885, 892.

2. Standard of review.

(1) Mandatory intervention. A ruling on mandatory intervention is reviewed de novo. *See* ***Redevelopment Agency of San Marcos v. Commission on State Mandates*** (4th Dist.1996) 43 Cal.App.4th 1188, 1198; ***California Physicians' Serv. v. Superior Ct.*** (2d Dist.1980) 102 Cal.App.3d 91, 96.

(2) Permissive intervention. A ruling on permissive intervention is reviewed for abuse of discretion. ***Dobbas v. Vitas*** (3d Dist.2011) 191 Cal.App.4th 1442, 1449; ***Noya v. A.W. Coulter Trucking*** (2d Dist.2006) 143 Cal.App.4th 838, 842; *see* ***Perry v. Brown*** (2011) 52 Cal.4th 1116, 1126.

§4. COMPLAINT IN INTERVENTION

§4.1 Filing & serving.

1. Filing. The nonparty must file a complaint in intervention to become a party to the action. *See* CCP §387; ***Klinghoffer v. Barasch*** (2d Dist.1970) 4 Cal.App.3d 258, 261. After filing the complaint in intervention, an intervenor has the same rights as an original party. *See* ***Perry v. Brown*** (2011) 52 Cal.4th 1116, 1131 n.7 (intervenor can appeal adverse judgment even if original D does not); ***City of San Diego v. Andrews*** (1924) 195 Cal. 111, 118 (intervenor can demand jury trial even if not demanded by original parties); ***Montgomery v. Bio-Med Specialties, Inc.*** (4th Dist.1986) 183 Cal.App.3d 1292, 1296 (intervening party is entitled to attorney fees as prevailing party in same manner as original party); ***Rhode v. National Med. Hosp.*** (2d Dist.1979) 93 Cal.App.3d 528, 537 (intervention treated as part of original action, not as separate action).

2. Serving.

(1) Parties who have not appeared. The nonparty must serve its complaint in intervention on all parties to the action who have not appeared as if it were serving an original complaint. CCP §387(a); Weil, *Civil Procedure Before Trial*, ¶2:444. See "General appearance," ch. 3-G, §5.1.1, p. 285; "Joining the Defendant—Service of Process," ch. 3-H, p. 295.

(2) Parties who have appeared. The nonparty must serve its complaint in intervention on the parties who have appeared in the same manner as service of documents or service of summons. CCP §387(a); *see* Weil, *Civil Procedure Before Trial*, ¶2:444. See "Serving Documents," ch. 1-G, p. 63; "General appearance," ch. 3-G, §5.1.1, p. 285; "Joining the Defendant—Service of Process," ch. 3-H, p. 295.

§4.2 Form. The complaint in intervention should be in the same form as an original pleading. See "Plaintiff's Original Complaint," ch. 3-C, p. 203; "Answer," ch. 4-B, p. 332.

1. Grounds for intervention. The complaint in intervention must state the grounds for intervention. See "Types of Intervention," §2, p. 484.

2. Demand relief. The complaint in intervention must do one of the following:

(1) Join with P. The complaint in intervention can join the nonparty with the plaintiff in claiming what is sought by the original complaint. CCP §387(a). When the nonparty is joining as a plaintiff, the complaint in intervention must state facts sufficient to constitute a cause of action. *CEB Procedure Before Trial*, §31.51. See "Body of complaint," ch. 3-C, §3.6, p. 215.

(2) Unite with D. The complaint in intervention can unite the nonparty with the defendant in resisting the claims of the plaintiff. CCP §387(a). When the nonparty is entering as a defendant, the complaint in intervention must state facts sufficient to constitute a defense. *See* ***Timberidge Enters. v. City of Santa Rosa*** (1st Dist.1978) 86 Cal.App.3d 873, 879-80; *CEB Procedure Before Trial*, §31.51. See "Answer," ch. 4-B, p. 332.

(3) Against P & D. The complaint in intervention can demand relief that is adverse to both the plaintiff and the defendant. CCP §387(a); *see, e.g.*, ***Belt Cas. Co. v. Furman*** (1933) 218 Cal. 359, 362 (each intervenor had separate cause of action against P and separate cause of action arising out of same transaction against D); ***Sobeck & Assocs. v. B&R Invs.*** (6th Dist.1989) 215 Cal.App.3d 861, 865 (nonparty filed motion to intervene based on interest in action that was adverse to both P and Ds).

NOTE

An intervenor cannot bring a new party into an action through a complaint in intervention. CEB Procedure Before Trial, §31.53.

---

§4.3 Challenging the complaint. If the nonparty filed an ex parte application, challenging the complaint may be the first opportunity the parties have to challenge intervention. *CEB Procedure Before Trial*, §31.46. But if the court granted a noticed motion for leave despite the parties' opposition, the parties may have a second chance to challenge intervention. *See, e.g.*, ***Timberidge Enters. v. City of Santa Rosa*** (1st Dist.1978) 86 Cal.App.3d 873, 879-80 (Ps filed demurrer to complaint challenging intervenors' standing to appear in action).

1. Deadline. A party served with a complaint in intervention can file a response within 30 days after service of the complaint in intervention. CCP §387(a).

2. Methods. A party served with a complaint in intervention can file a motion to strike, a demurrer, or another opposition to the complaint in intervention as if it were an original pleading. CCP §387(a); *see* ***Mar v. Sakti Int'l*** (1st Dist.1992) 9 Cal.App.4th 1780, 1785 (complaint in intervention subject to defenses and procedural objections); *see, e.g.*, ***De Santiago v. D&G Plumbing, Inc.*** (4th Dist.2007) 155 Cal.App.4th 365, 370 (motion to dismiss); ***Timberidge Enters.***, 86 Cal.App.3d at 880 (demurrer); ***Socialist Workers 1974 Cal. Campaign Cmte. v. Brown*** (2d Dist.1975) 53 Cal.App.3d 879, 886 (motion to strike). See "Defendant's Responses & Pleadings," ch. 4, p. 325; "Disposition Without Trial," ch. 10, p. 1087. But a party cannot move to dismiss the intervenor's complaint on the ground that the plaintiff's original complaint was dismissed. *See* ***Lohnes v. Astron Computer Prods.*** (4th Dist.2001) 94 Cal.App.4th 1150, 1153-54 (complaint in intervention survives voluntary dismissal of original complaint); ***Sanabria v. Embrey*** (2d Dist.2001) 92 Cal.App.4th 422, 425 (P can voluntarily dismiss her complaint but cannot dismiss entire action if complaint in intervention is pending); ***Personnel Comm'n of the Barstow Unified Sch. Dist. v. Barstow Unified Sch. Dist.*** (4th Dist.1996) 43 Cal.App.4th 871, 884 (complaint in intervention survives dismissal of main action).

D. MOTION TO RECLASSIFY

This subchapter discusses the procedure for changing the procedural classification of a civil action by a noticed motion to reclassify. See "Procedural Classifications of Civil Cases," ch. 3-E, §4, p. 255. This subchapter does not discuss any other method of changing a case's procedural classification. For a discussion of alternative methods of reclassification, see "Reclassification," ch. 3-E, §4.5, p. 266.

§1. GENERAL

§1.1 Purpose. A motion to reclassify asks the court to change the classification of a civil case from limited to unlimited or vice versa. CCP §403.040. Reclassification does not affect the subject-matter jurisdiction of the court, but it does affect how the case is litigated, the type of relief that can be granted, and how the case is appealed. *See* ***Pajaro Valley Water Mgmt. Agency v. McGrath*** (6th Dist.2005) 128 Cal.App.4th 1093, 1103. See "Effect of classification," ch. 3-E, §4.3, p. 261; "Reclassification," ch. 3-E, §4.5, p. 266.

§1.2 Primary authority. CCP §§85, 86, 403.010-403.090; Gov. C. §70619.

§1.3 Secondary authority. The following secondary sources are cited as authority in this subchapter:

- *California Civil Procedure Before Trial* (CEB Online ed. 2014) (referred to as *CEB Procedure Before Trial*).
- Weil & Brown, *California Practice Guide: Civil Procedure Before Trial* (CD-ROM ed. 2014) (referred to as Weil, *Civil Procedure Before Trial*).
- Younger & Bradley, *Younger on California Motions* (2014-15) (referred to as Younger, *Cal. Motions*).

§2. GROUNDS

The grounds for a motion to reclassify depend on whether the movant is trying to change the classification from limited to unlimited or from unlimited to limited.

§2.1 Limited to unlimited. To prevail on a motion to reclassify a case as unlimited, the movant must establish one of the following:

1. Case is not limited. The movant can show that the case is incorrectly classified as a limited civil case. See "Limited cases," ch. 3-E, §4.2.2, p. 258. If the movant seeks a reclassification because the amount in controversy exceeds $25,000, it need only show there is a possibility, not a probability, that the damages award will exceed $25,000. *See* ***Ytuarte v. Superior Ct.*** (2d Dist.2005) 129 Cal.App.4th 266, 279. See "Calculating amount in controversy," ch. 3-E, §4.1, p. 256.

2. Legality of tax at issue. The movant can show that the case involves the legality of a tax, impost, assessment, toll, or municipal fine. *See* CCP §86(a)(1); *see, e.g.*, ***Pajaro Valley Water Mgmt. Agency v. McGrath*** (6th Dist.2005) 128 Cal.App.4th 1093, 1102-03 (D's challenge of tax-like charges provided basis for reclassification of case as unlimited).

§2.2 Unlimited to limited. To prevail on a motion to reclassify a case as limited, the movant must show that the case is incorrectly classified as an unlimited civil case—that is, the case meets all the conditions for classification as a limited civil case. See "Limited cases," ch. 3-E, §4.2.2, p. 258. If the movant seeks a reclassification because the amount in controversy is $25,000 or less, it must show a legal certainty that the damages award will not exceed $25,000. ***Ytuarte v. Superior Ct.*** (2d Dist.2005) 129 Cal.App.4th 266, 277; *see also* ***Walker v. Superior Ct.*** (1991) 53 Cal.3d 257, 270-71 (courts should be cautious about changing case from unlimited to limited because it deprives P of chance to prove higher damages). See "Calculating amount in controversy," ch. 3-E, §4.1, p. 256.

§3. MOTION

§3.1 Who can file. A motion to reclassify can be made by a party or by the court on its own motion. CCP §403.040(a); ***Ytuarte v. Superior Ct.*** (2d Dist.2005) 129 Cal.App.4th 266, 275-76 & n.4; *see, e.g.*, ***Food Safety Net Servs. v. Eco Safe Sys. USA, Inc.*** (2d Dist.2012) 209 Cal.App.4th 1118, 1135-36 (court reclassified case after entering judgment on cross-complaint because judgment lowered value of remaining litigation). If the court acts on its own motion, it must give the parties notice and a sufficient opportunity to respond with reasons why classification should or should not be ordered. ***Stern v. Superior Ct.*** (2d Dist.2003) 105 Cal.App.4th 223, 230; *see* ***Walker v. Superior Ct.*** (1991) 53 Cal.3d 257, 271-72; *CEB Procedure Before Trial*, §6.32.

PRACTICE TIP

Instead of filing its own motion, a party can suggest to the court at a status conference or some other event where opposing counsel is present that the court reclassify the case on its own motion. See Younger, Cal. Motions, §21:21.

---

§3.2 Deadline to file & serve. The deadline to file and serve a motion to reclassify depends on whether the movant is (1) a plaintiff, cross-complainant, or petitioner or (2) a defendant or cross-defendant. The court can reclassify the case on its own motion at any time. CCP §403.040(a).

1. Movant is plaintiff, cross-complainant, or petitioner.

(1) Before time to amend. If the movant is a plaintiff, cross-complainant, or petitioner, it should file and serve the motion within the time it has to amend its initial pleading and at least 16 court days before the hearing. *See* CCP §§403.040(a), 1005(b). See "Retrospective deadlines," ch. 1-G, §6.2, p. 71 (rules for calculating deadlines to serve); "Procedure for amending," ch. 3-C, §6.2, p. 229 (deadlines for filing amended complaint). If the motion is served by a method other than personal delivery, the movant will have to add more time to the 16-day period. CCP §1005(b). See "Add time for method of service," ch. 1-G, §6.2.1(5), p. 72.

(2) After time to amend. If the movant is a plaintiff, cross-complainant, or petitioner and the time to amend its initial pleading has expired, the movant can still file a motion to reclassify but will have to show good cause for not seeking reclassification earlier. CCP §403.040(b).

2. Movant is defendant or cross-defendant.

(1) Before time to respond. If the movant is a defendant or cross-defendant, it should file and serve the motion within the time it has to respond to the initial pleading and at least 16 court days before the hearing. *See* CCP §§403.040(a), 1005(b); *see also id.* §412.20(a)(3) (deadline to answer complaint), §432.10 (deadline to answer cross-complaint), §471.5(a) (deadline to answer amended complaint). See "Retrospective deadlines," ch. 1-G, §6.2, p. 71 (rules for calculating deadlines to serve). If the motion is served by a method other than personal delivery, the movant will have to add more time to the 16-day period. CCP §1005(b). See "Add time for method of service," ch. 1-G, §6.2.1(5), p. 72.

(2) After time to respond. If the movant is a defendant or cross-defendant and the time to respond to the pleading has expired, the movant can still file a motion to reclassify but will have to show good cause for not seeking reclassification earlier. CCP §403.040(b).

§3.3 Contents.

1. Notice of motion & motion. The motion to reclassify should be made in writing by noticed motion. ***Stern v. Superior Ct.*** (2d Dist.2003) 105 Cal.App.4th 223, 230; *see* Weil, *Civil Procedure Before Trial*, ¶3:116 (usual noticed-motion procedures apply); Younger, *Cal. Motions*, §21.25 (Cal. Rules of Court on format and filing of papers apply). See "Motion Papers," ch. 1-D, §5, p. 27.

2. Memorandum of points & authorities. The motion to reclassify must include a memorandum in support of the motion. CRC 3.1112(a)(3), 3.1113(a). See "Memorandum of points & authorities," ch. 1-D, §5.2, p. 28.

3. Supporting evidence. The motion to reclassify can be supported by the same types of evidence as other noticed motions. See "Supporting evidence," ch. 1-D, §5.3, p. 30.

4. Judicial notice. The motion to reclassify can be based on matters the court can take judicial notice of. *See* CRC 3.1113(*l*). A request for judicial notice must be made in a separate document. *Id.* See "Request for Judicial Notice," ch. 5-J, p. 547.

5. Proposed order. The motion to reclassify can be accompanied by a proposed order. *See* CRC 3.1113(m). If a proposed order is submitted, it must be lodged and served with the motion papers, not attached to them. *Id.* See "Documents lodged," ch. 1-F, §2.3, p. 47.

§3.4 Filing fees. When the motion is filed, the movant must pay a filing fee to the court clerk or request a waiver of the fee. See "Filing Fees," ch. 1-F, §7, p. 58.

§3.5 Effect of filing. Filing a motion to reclassify does not extend the movant's time to amend, answer, or otherwise respond to a pleading. CCP §403.040(a).

§4. RESPONSE

§4.1 Opposition. The nonmovant can respond to the motion to reclassify by filing an opposition.

1. Deadline to file & serve. If a hearing has been granted on the motion to reclassify, the opposition must be filed and served at least nine court days before the hearing. CCP §1005(b). See "Filing & serving opposition," ch. 1-D, §8.5, p. 36.

2. Grounds. A motion to reclassify can be opposed by negating the grounds for relief. See "Grounds," §2, p. 493.

3. Contents. See "Opposition Papers," ch. 1-D, §8, p. 35.

§4.2 Amend complaint – remove excess. If the motion seeks to reclassify a case from limited to unlimited on the ground that the complaint demands an amount in excess of $25,000, the nonmovant can oppose the motion by amending its complaint to remove the amount in excess of $25,000. *See* CCP §403.040(f).

§5. REPLY

The movant can file and serve a reply to the opposition papers. If a hearing has been granted on the motion to reclassify, the reply must be filed and served at least five court days before the hearing. CCP §1005(b). See "Reply Papers," ch. 1-D, §9, p. 37.

§6. HEARING

The court may hold a hearing. *See* ***Stern v. Superior Ct.*** (2d Dist.2003) 105 Cal.App.4th 223, 230; *CEB Procedure Before Trial*, §6.34. If a hearing is not held, the court must at least ensure that the parties had notice and an opportunity to respond. ***Stern***, 105 Cal.App.4th at 230; *see* ***Walker v. Superior Ct.*** (1991) 53 Cal.3d 257, 272. Hearings on a motion to reclassify are conducted in the same manner as civil hearings generally. See "Hearings," ch. 1-H, p. 79.

§7. RULING

§7.1 Timely motions. A timely filed motion to reclassify must be granted if the grounds for relief are satisfied. CCP §403.040(a). See "Grounds," §2, p. 493.

NOTE

In ruling on motions to reclassify based on the amount in controversy, courts may look to case law addressing transfers from superior to municipal court and vice versa under former CCP §396. See Weil, Civil Procedure Before Trial, ¶¶3:118-3:120.6.

§7.2 Untimely motions. An untimely motion to reclassify must be granted if (1) the grounds for relief are satisfied and (2) the movant shows good cause for not seeking reclassification earlier. CCP §403.040(b). If the movant is unable to show good cause for the delay, the ruling on the motion is left to the court's discretion. ***Pajaro Valley Water Mgmt. Agency v. McGrath*** (6th Dist.2005) 128 Cal.App.4th 1093, 1104.

§8. ORDER

§8.1 Form. The court's ruling on the motion to reclassify must be recorded either in writing or by minute order. See "Record of Ruling," ch. 1-I, §4, p. 90.

§8.2 Contents. If the motion is granted, the court will determine whether a reclassification fee must be paid. *See* CCP §403.040(c). Whether a fee must be paid depends on how the case is reclassified.

1. Limited to unlimited. A reclassification fee must be paid to reclassify a case from limited to unlimited, unless the court orders otherwise. CCP §403.040(c)(1); *see id.* §403.060(a). The case will not be reclassified until the fee is paid. *Id.* §403.040(d)(2).

(1) Who pays. The fee must be paid by the party whose pleading causes the case to no longer satisfy the requirements of a limited case. CCP §403.040(c)(1). If the fee is not paid within five days after service of notice of the order granting the motion, any interested party can pay the fee and recover the expense at the case's conclusion as an item of cost in the damages award or as an offset deducted from the damages award. *Id.* §403.040(d)(2).

(2) Amount of fee. The fee is $140. Gov. C. §70619. This fee is in addition to any other fee due for the filing in a limited civil case. CCP §403.060(a); *CEB Procedure Before Trial*, §6.35.

(3) Deadline to pay. The fee must be paid within 30 days after service of notice of the reclassification order. CCP §403.040(d)(3). If it is not, the court can, on its own motion or on the motion of any party, do any of the following:

(a) Order the case to proceed as a limited case. *Id.*

(b) Dismiss the case without prejudice on the condition that no other action on the same matters can be initiated in any other court until the fee is paid. *Id.*

(c) Take any other action the court deems appropriate. *Id.*

2. Unlimited to limited. A reclassification fee is not required to reclassify a case from unlimited to limited, unless the court orders otherwise. CCP §403.040(c)(2); *see id.* §403.060(c). If no fee is required, the case should be promptly reclassified. *Id.* §403.040(d)(1).

NOTE

The plaintiff is not entitled to a refund of the difference between the unlimited-case filing fees and the limited-case filing fees when the court orders a case reclassified as limited. CCP §403.060(c).

§8.3 Effect of reclassification.

1. Filing date. If the case is reclassified, the initial filing date is used to calculate the deadline to avoid dismissal for delay in prosecution. *See* CCP §403.070(a) (reclassification does not change filing date); ***Giorgianni v. Crowley*** (6th Dist.2011) 197 Cal.App.4th 1462, 1483 (action is deemed commenced when complaint is initially filed, not at time of reclassification). See "Involuntary Dismissal—Delay in Prosecution," ch. 10-E, p. 1160.

2. Additional action. If the case is reclassified, the court may allow or require any appropriate action necessary for the proper presentation and determination of the reclassified proceeding (e.g., amending pleadings). CCP §403.070(b).

3. Appealable final judgment. If an original complaint is reclassified as a result of the entry of judgment on a cross-complaint, the entry of judgment on the cross-complaint may constitute an appealable final judgment. *See **Food Safety Net Servs. v. Eco Safe Sys. USA, Inc.*** (2d Dist.2012) 209 Cal.App.4th 1118, 1135-36.

§9. MOTION FOR RECONSIDERATION

A party adversely affected by a court's order on a motion to reclassify can file a motion for reconsideration. CCP §1008(a). See "Motion for Reconsideration," ch. 5-G, §3, p. 508.

§10. MOTION FOR RENEWAL

A party whose motion to reclassify is denied can file a motion for renewal. CCP §1008(b). See "Motion for Renewal," ch. 5-G, §4, p. 516.

§11. APPELLATE REVIEW

§11.1 Writ of mandate. A party can challenge the ruling on a motion to reclassify by seeking a writ of mandate. CCP §403.080; ***Garau v. Torrance Unified Sch. Dist.*** (2d Dist.2006) 137 Cal.App.4th 192, 198; ***Ytuarte v. Superior Ct.*** (2d Dist.2005) 129 Cal.App.4th 266, 272 n.1. A petition for a writ of mandate must be filed in the appellate court within 20 days after service of written notice of the order granting or denying reclassification, and a copy must be filed immediately afterward in the superior court. CCP §403.080; *CEB Procedure Before Trial*, §6.38; *see* ***Ytuarte***, 129 Cal.App.4th at 273. The superior court may, before the expiration of the 20-day deadline, extend the deadline up to an additional 10 days for good cause. CCP §403.080. The appellate court can stay proceedings in the trial court pending resolution of the writ. *Id.*

§11.2 No direct appeal. A party cannot challenge the ruling on a motion to reclassify by raising the issue on appeal. ***Garau v. Torrance Unified Sch. Dist.*** (2d Dist.2006) 137 Cal.App.4th 192, 199; Weil, *Civil Procedure Before Trial*, ¶3:122.

E. SHORTENING TIME

This subchapter discusses stipulations and applications to shorten time to perform certain pretrial procedures. This subchapter does not discuss how to shorten time periods for discovery. For a discussion of that topic, see "Modifying Discovery Procedures," ch. 7-A, §4, p. 743.

§1. GENERAL

§1.1 Purpose. A stipulation or application to shorten time is used to shorten the time a party has to move or act. *See* CRC 1.10(c) (shorten time to perform any act under Cal. Rules of Court), CRC 3.1300(b) (shorten time to file and serve papers). For example, an application is frequently used to shorten the notice period between the filing and serving of some motion and the ensuing hearing. *See, e.g.*, ***Salas v. Sears, Roebuck & Co.*** (1986) 42 Cal.3d 342, 344 (ex parte application to shorten notice period for motion for trial preference); ***Dailey v. Sears, Roebuck & Co.*** (4th Dist.2013) 214 Cal.App.4th 974, 981-82 (ex parte application to shorten notice period for motion for leave to file second amended complaint); ***Cardiff Equities, Inc. v. Superior Ct.*** (2d Dist.2008) 166 Cal.App.4th 1541, 1546 (ex parte application to shorten notice period for motion to lift stay); ***Eliceche v. Federal Land Bank Ass'n*** (5th Dist.2002) 103 Cal.App.4th 1349, 1355-56 (ex parte application to shorten notice period for motion for discretionary dismissal). An application for an order to shorten time is usually made to avoid prejudice or harm that would be caused by adherence to the normal time period. *See California Civil Procedure Before Trial* (CEB Online ed. 2014) §12.13.

§1.2 Primary authority. CCP §1005(b); CRC 1.10(c), 3.1300(b).

§1.3 Secondary authority. The following secondary sources are cited as authority in this subchapter:

- Kiesel et al., *Matthew Bender Practice Guide: California Pretrial Civil Procedure* (2014) (referred to as Kiesel, *Cal. Pretrial Civil Procedure*).
- Weil & Brown, *California Practice Guide: Civil Procedure Before Trial* (CD-ROM ed. 2014) (referred to as Weil, *Civil Procedure Before Trial*).
- Younger & Bradley, *Younger on California Motions* (2014-15) (referred to as Younger, *Cal. Motions*).

§2. MOVANT'S BURDEN

To prevail on an application to shorten time, the movant must establish that the time period at issue can be shortened and show good cause for the request.

§2.1 Time can be shortened.

1. Yes. Time periods that can be shortened by the court include the following:

(1) The time to file and serve papers under CCP §1005. CRC 3.1300(b).

(2) The time to serve the defendant a request for injunctive relief. CCP §§527(d)(2), 527.6(m), 527.8(m), 527.85(m).

(3) The time to file a responsive pleading in an action for libel or slander when it is likely that the defamatory matter will continue to be published. *Id.* §460.5(a).

(4) The time to make a motion for summary judgment. *Id.* §437c(a).

(5) The time between the hearing on a motion for summary judgment and the trial date. *See id.*

(6) The time to perform any act required under the California Rules of Court. CRC 1.10(c).

2. No. Time periods that cannot be shortened by the court include the following:

(1) The time to serve the complaint (i.e., cannot require shorter period than 60 days after filing). *See* Gov. C. §68616(a).

(2) The time to file a responsive pleading (i.e., in most cases, cannot require shorter period than 30 days after service of complaint). *See id.* §68616(b). *But see* CCP §460.5(a) (court can shorten period to respond to complaint alleging libel or slander when it is likely that defamatory matter will continue to be published), §460.7 (court must shorten period to respond when complaint alleges that libel or slander occurred during election campaign between candidates and holders of elective public office).

(3) The time to give notice of a motion for summary judgment (i.e., cannot give less than 75 days' notice). ***Cuff v. Grossmont Un. High Sch. Dist.*** (4th Dist.2013) 221 Cal.App.4th 582, 596; *see* Kiesel, *Cal. Pretrial Civil Procedure*, §27.09[2] (although court cannot shorten this deadline, parties can stipulate to shorter deadline).

(4) The time to appeal a judgment or an appealable order. ***Estate of Hanley*** (1943) 23 Cal.2d 120, 123; ***Annette F. v. Sharon S.*** (4th Dist.2005) 130 Cal.App.4th 1448, 1454.

(5) The time to request a trial de novo after an arbitration award. ***Karamzai v. Digitcom*** (2d Dist.1996) 51 Cal.App.4th 547, 550-51.

(6) The time to give notice of a trial date before an issue of fact can be tried without a party. *See* ***Au-Yang v. Barton*** (1999) 21 Cal.4th 958, 963-64 (although court cannot shorten deadline to give notice of trial date under CCP §594(a), parties can stipulate to shorter deadline).

§2.2 Good cause. For most requests to shorten time, the movant must show good cause. *E.g.*, CCP §§437c(a), 460.5(a), 527(d)(2), 527.6(m), 527.8(m), 527.85(m); CRC 3.1300(b). To show good cause, the movant should establish that shortening the time will prevent some harm, loss of right, or injury. *See, e.g.*, ***In re Marriage of Seagondollar*** (4th Dist.2006) 139 Cal.App.4th 1116, 1130 (court abused its discretion in denying application to shorten notice period for motion to quash service because it made motion moot). A mere lack of time for giving full notice does not constitute good cause. Weil, *Civil Procedure Before Trial*, ¶9:364.

§3. HOW TO REQUEST

A request to shorten time is typically made to the court in the form of either a stipulation or an ex parte application. Kiesel, *Cal. Pretrial Civil Procedure*, §27.09[2].

NOTE

A party can make a noticed motion to shorten time, but this is uncommon; time is usually of the essence in these situations. Kiesel, Cal. Pretrial Civil Procedure, §27.10.

§3.1 Stipulation. In most cases, the parties can stipulate to a shortening of time. *See* Kiesel, *Cal. Pretrial Civil Procedure*, §§27.09[2], 27.10. Some time periods that cannot be shortened by court order can be shortened by stipulation. *E.g.*, ***Au-Yang v. Barton*** (1999) 21 Cal.4th 958, 963-64 (although court cannot shorten deadline to give notice of trial date under CCP §594(a), parties can stipulate to shorter deadline); Kiesel, *Cal. Pretrial Civil Procedure*, §27.09[2] (although court cannot shorten deadline to give notice of MSJ under CCP §437c(a), parties can stipulate to shorter deadline). The stipulation should be (1) written, (2) agreed to by all attorneys of record for parties who have appeared in the action, and (3) filed in the court. *See* Kiesel, *Cal. Pretrial Civil Procedure*, §27.12 (because of due-process concerns, written stipulations are preferred over oral stipulations). If it is unclear whether a court will accept a written stipulation, the stipulation should be submitted as part of an ex parte application. *Id.*

CAUTION

Before presenting a stipulation to shorten time, check the court's local rules. Some local rules may prohibit the parties from stipulating to a shorter period of time. E.g., Super. Ct. Tuolumne Cty. Loc. R., rule 3.04 (stipulation to shorten time is not effective).

§3.2 Ex parte application.

1. Who can file. An application for an order to shorten time can be made by a party or by the court on its own motion. CRC 3.1300(b).

2. Deadline to file & serve.

(1) Notice of ex parte application. See "Deadline," ch. 1-E, §4.4, p. 41.

(2) Ex parte application. See "Filing, Serving & Providing Court File," ch. 1-E, §6, p. 44.

3. Contents.

(1) Application.

(a) Generally. See "Application Papers," ch. 1-E, §5, p. 42.

(b) Description of shortened time. The application should specify the time period that is being shortened and the new deadline to perform the act.

CAUTION

Before requesting a new deadline to perform a specified act, check the court's local rules. Some courts require that an opposing party be given a minimum amount of time to perform an act related to a matter that is placed on shortened time. E.g., Super. Ct. Sacramento Cty. Loc. R., rule 1.07(B) (must provide sufficient time for opposition papers to be filed and served five court days before new hearing date).

---

(2) Memorandum of points & authorities. The application for an order to shorten time must include a memorandum in support. CRC 3.1201(4). See "Memorandum of points & authorities," ch. 1-E, §5.2, p. 42.

(3) Declarations. The application must be supported by the following declarations:

(a) Declaration of notice. See "Declaration of notice," ch. 1-E, §5.3.1, p. 43.

(b) Declaration in support. The declaration in support of the application must show good cause. *See* CRC 3.1300(b). See "Good cause," §2.2, p. 498; "Declaration in support," ch. 1-E, §5.3.2, p. 43.

(4) Copy of stipulation. If the application is supported by a stipulation, a copy of the stipulation can be filed with the application. *See* Kiesel, *Cal. Pretrial Civil Procedure*, §27.12. See "Stipulation," §3.1, p. 498.

(5) Proposed order. The application must include a proposed order. CRC 3.1201(5).

(6) Underlying motion. If applicable, the movant should file the underlying motion (i.e., the motion for which the movant seeks a shortened notice period) with the application. *See* Younger, *Cal. Motions*, §31:41; *see, e.g.*, ***Eliceche v. Federal Land Bank Ass'n*** (5th Dist.2002) 103 Cal.App.4th 1349, 1355 (D filed both motion for discretionary dismissal and ex parte application for order shortening time to hear motion).

§4. OPPOSITION

§4.1 Form. The nonmovant can respond to an application to shorten time by opposing the application either in writing or orally at the hearing. See "Opposing Ex Parte Application," ch. 1-E, §7, p. 44.

§4.2 Deadline to serve. If the nonmovant chooses to oppose the application in writing, the opposition must be served on every party that will appear at the hearing at the first reasonable opportunity. CRC 3.1206.

§4.3 Grounds. The nonmovant can challenge the application for an order to shorten time on the following grounds:

1. Time cannot be shortened. The application can be opposed on the ground that the time period in question cannot be shortened. See "Time can be shortened," §2.1, p. 497.

2. No good cause. The application can be opposed on the ground that the movant lacks good cause. See "Good cause," §2.2, p. 498.

3. Violates due process. The application can be opposed on the ground that shortening time would be prejudicial and violate the nonmovant's right to due process. *See, e.g.*, ***Eliceche v. Federal Land Bank Ass'n*** (5th Dist.2002) 103 Cal.App.4th 1349, 1373 (P challenged order shortening time on ground that order denied him adequate opportunity to challenge dismissal motion and thus violated his right to due process).

§5. HEARING

Hearings on ex parte applications for orders to shorten time are conducted in the same manner as ex parte proceedings generally. See "Hearing," ch. 1-E, §8, p. 44. If the application is based on the parties' stipulation, the application can be considered without the movant's appearance. CRC 3.1207(4).

§6. RULING

The court has discretion in ruling on an application for an order to shorten time. *See* CRC 3.1300(b); ***In re Marriage of Seagondollar*** (4th Dist.2006) 139 Cal.App.4th 1116, 1130.

§7. ORDER

§7.1 Form. The court's ruling on the application for an order to shorten time must be recorded either in writing or by minute order. See "Record of Ruling," ch. 1-I, §4, p. 90.

§7.2 Contents. If the application is granted, the order should include a description of the shortened time period (e.g., the time for the hearing for which notice was shortened). Weil, *Civil Procedure Before Trial*, ¶9:366. If the order shortens the notice period for a motion, the order should include a deadline for (1) the movant to serve the motion and the order shortening time, (2) the movant to file proof of service, and (3) the opposing party to file and serve opposition papers to the motion. *Id.*

§8. MOTION FOR RECONSIDERATION

A party adversely affected by a court's order on an application to shorten time can file a motion for reconsideration. *See* CCP §1008(a). See "Motion for Reconsideration," ch. 5-G, §3, p. 508.

§9. MOTION FOR RENEWAL

A party whose application to shorten time is denied can file a motion for renewal. *See* CCP §1008(b). See "Motion for Renewal," ch. 5-G, §4, p. 516.

§10. APPELLATE REVIEW

§10.1 Writ of mandate. A party can challenge the ruling on an application for an order to shorten time by filing a petition for a writ of mandate. *See, e.g.*, ***McMahon v. Superior Ct.*** (2d Dist.2003) 106 Cal.App.4th 112, 114 (Ps challenged shortened notice period for summary-judgment hearing with petition for writ of mandate).

§10.2 Direct appeal. A party can challenge the ruling on an application for an order to shorten time by raising the issue on appeal after the entry of a final judgment. *See* CCP §904.1(a)(1); *see, e.g.*, ***Eliceche v. Federal Land Bank Ass'n*** (5th Dist.2002) 103 Cal.App.4th 1349, 1353 (after court granted dismissal motion, P appealed order shortening time for notice of dismissal hearing). The trial court's ruling is reviewed for abuse of discretion. *See* ***Campanella v. Takaoka*** (2d Dist.1984) 160 Cal.App.3d 504, 514, *disapproved on other grounds*, ***Salas v. Sears, Roebuck & Co.*** (1986) 42 Cal.3d 342; *see, e.g.*, ***In re Marriage of Seagondollar*** (4th Dist.2006) 139 Cal.App.4th 1116, 1130 (court abused its discretion by denying application to shorten time because denial made motion to quash service moot).

F. EXTENDING TIME

This subchapter discusses stipulations and applications to extend time to perform certain pretrial procedures. This subchapter does not discuss how to extend time periods for discovery. For a discussion of that topic, see "Modifying Discovery Procedures," ch. 7-A, §4, p. 743. For a discussion of extending the time to bring a case to trial, see "Effect of agreed extension," ch. 10-E, §4.3.2(3)(a), p. 1169.

§1. GENERAL

§1.1 Purpose. A stipulation or application to extend time is used to extend the time a party has to perform certain acts. *See* CCP §1054(a) (party can obtain extension of time for acts to be done that relate to pleadings or notices); CRC 3.110(d), (e) (parties can stipulate or file application to extend time to serve pleadings or responses).

§1.2 Primary authority. CCP §§1054, 1054.1; CRC 1.10(c), 2.20, 3.110(d), (e).

§1.3 Secondary authority. The following secondary sources are cited as authority in this subchapter:

- *California Civil Procedure Before Trial* (CEB Online ed. 2014) (referred to as *CEB Procedure Before Trial*).
- Kiesel et al., *Matthew Bender Practice Guide: California Pretrial Civil Procedure* (2014) (referred to as Kiesel, *Cal. Pretrial Civil Procedure*).
- Weil & Brown, *California Practice Guide: Civil Procedure Before Trial* (CD-ROM ed. 2014) (referred to as Weil, *Civil Procedure Before Trial*).
- Younger & Bradley, *Younger on California Motions* (2014-15) (referred to as Younger, *Cal. Motions*).

§1.4 Judicial Council forms.

- CM-020 (optional), ex parte application for extension of time to serve pleading.

§2. MOVANT'S BURDEN

To prevail on a request to extend time, the movant must establish that the time period at issue can be extended and establish the proper grounds for the request.

§2.1 Time can be extended.

1. Yes. Time periods that can be extended include the following:

(1) The time to file, serve, respond to, or amend pleadings. *See* CCP §§1054(a), 1054.1(a); CRC 3.110(e); *see, e.g.*, CCP §583.230 (parties may stipulate to extension of time to serve summons and complaint).

(2) The time to answer or file a demurrer. CCP §473(a)(1).

(3) The time to file a responsive pleading after the defendant's motion to quash or dismiss under CCP §418.10(a) is denied. *Id.* §418.10(b).

(4) The time to file a responsive pleading after the defendant's motion to quash or dismiss under CCP §418.10(a) is denied in a summary proceeding to obtain possession of real property. *Id.* §1167.4.

(5) The time to file a responsive pleading after the defendant receives written notice of a judgment in a mandate proceeding concerning the defendant's motion to quash or dismiss under CCP §418.10(a). *Id.* §418.10(c).

(6) The time to file and serve a notice. *See id.* §§1054(a), 1054.1(a); ***Burton v. Todd*** (1886) 68 Cal. 485, 488-89. For exceptions, see "Certain notice periods," §2.1.2(1), p. 502.

(7) The time to file a petition for writ of mandate after receiving written notice of one of the following orders:

(a) An order to transfer or change venue. CCP §400.

(b) An order reclassifying the case. *Id.* §403.080.

(c) An order coordinating cases. *Id.* §404.6.

(d) An order denying a motion to quash or dismiss under CCP §418.10(a). *Id.* §418.10(c).

(e) An order denying a motion for summary judgment. *See id.* §437c(m)(1) (peremptory writ).

(8) The time to prepare bills of exceptions or amendments to bills of exceptions. *Id.* §§1054(a), 1054.1(a).

(9) The time to file a motion for attorney fees. CRC 3.1702(b)(2), (c)(2), (d); ***Lewow v. Surfside III Condo. Owners Ass'n*** (2d Dist.2012) 203 Cal.App.4th 128, 134-35.

(10) The time to perform any act required under the California Rules of Court. CRC 1.10(c).

2. No. Time periods that cannot be extended include the following:

(1) Certain notice periods. The following notice periods cannot be extended:

(a) The time to serve notice of an appeal. CCP §§1054(a), 1054.1(a); ***Land v. Johnston*** (1909) 156 Cal. 253, 254-55; ***Annette F. v. Sharon S.*** (4th Dist.2005) 130 Cal.App.4th 1448, 1454.

(b) The time to serve notice of an intention to move for a new trial. CCP §§1054(a), 1054.1(a); *see* ***Union Collection Co. v. Oliver*** (1912) 162 Cal. 755, 756.

(2) Time periods specified in §1054.1. When an application for an order to extend time is based on an attorney's membership in the State Legislature, the following additional time periods cannot be extended:

(a) The time to serve notice of an intention to move to vacate a judgment. CCP §1054.1(a).

(b) The time to move for a judgment notwithstanding the verdict. *Id.*

§2.2 Grounds for extension. If the time period in question can be extended, the movant must establish the grounds for the extension.

1. Good cause. For most requests to extend time, the movant must show good cause. *E.g.*, CCP §§400, 403.080, 404.6, 418.10(b), (c), 437c(m)(1), 995.050, 1054(a), 1167.4(b); CRC 3.1702(d). *But see* CCP §473(a)(1) (must be in furtherance of justice). The threshold for good cause is usually low for the first extension (e.g., a statement about the attorney's busy workload and the other side's unwillingness to stipulate would probably suffice), but after that, it becomes increasingly difficult. Weil, *Civil Procedure Before Trial*, ¶9:361.

PRACTICE TIP

Before requesting an extension of time to respond to a complaint, the defendant should ask the plaintiff to stipulate to a 15-day extension. The parties can stipulate to one 15-day extension of the time to respond to the initial complaint without leave of court. CRC 3.110(d). This automatic extension is not available in unlawful-detainer actions, proceedings under the Family Code, collections cases under CRC 3.740(a), or other proceedings for which different service requirements are prescribed by law. CRC 3.110(a). For additional or longer extensions, the defendant must obtain leave of court.

---

2. Member of Legislature. For an extension of time under CCP §1054.1, the movant must show that its attorney of record is a member of the State Legislature and that one of the following is true:

(1) The Legislature is either in session or in a recess that will not exceed 40 days. CCP §1054.1(a).

(2) The attorney is a duly appointed member of a legislative committee that is meeting or is scheduled to meet at a time that the court finds will not give the member enough time to travel by ordinary means from the hearing, trial, or other proceeding to the meeting. *Id.*

§3. HOW TO REQUEST

A request to extend time is typically made to the court in the form of either a stipulation or an ex parte application. Kiesel, *Cal. Pretrial Civil Procedure*, §27.15[2].

NOTE

A party can make a noticed motion to extend time, but this is uncommon; time is usually of the essence in these situations. Kiesel, Cal. Pretrial Civil Procedure, §27.20.

§3.1 Stipulation. In most cases, the parties can stipulate to an extension of time. *See* CCP §1054(b); CRC 3.110(d); *see also* Super. Ct. Los Angeles Cty. Loc. R., appendix 3.A(a)(1) (initial requests for reasonable extensions of time should be agreed to as matter of courtesy unless time is of the essence); Super. Ct. Santa Barbara Cty. Loc. R., appendix 5, E.1 (attorney should not refuse reasonable requests for permissible extensions of time). The stipulation should be (1) written, (2) agreed to by all attorneys of record for parties who have appeared in the action, and (3) filed in the court. *See* CCP §1054(b); *see also* Younger, *Cal. Motions*, §31.23 (although rare, some courts require stipulations to be presented by ex parte application).

CAUTION

Before presenting a stipulation to extend time, check the court's local rules. Some local rules may limit the parties' ability to stipulate to time extensions that affect the court's case-disposition time goals. E.g., Super. Ct. Sacramento Cty. Loc. R., rule 2.53 (parties cannot extend time periods set out in court's case-management program); see Gov. C. §68616(d) (stipulations for extensions of time should not detract from court's case-disposition goals).

§3.2 Ex parte application.

1. Who can file. An application for an order to extend time can be made by a party or by the court on its own motion. *See* CCP §1054; CRC 1.10(c), 2.20, 3.110(d).

2. Deadline to file & serve.

(1) Notice of ex parte application. See "Deadline," ch. 1-E, §4.4, p. 41.

(2) Ex parte application.

(a) Filing. An ex parte application for an order to extend time must be filed before the time period in question has expired. *See* ***Coast Elec. Serv. v. Jensen*** (1st Dist.1931) 111 Cal.App. 124, 126; Weil, *Civil Procedure Before Trial*, ¶9:363; *see, e.g.*, CRC 3.110(e) (application to extend time to serve pleading must be filed before time for service has expired). An order based on an untimely application is void. ***Coast Elec.***, 111 Cal.App. at 126; *see, e.g.*, ***Manning v. Gavin*** (1939) 14 Cal.2d 44, 45 (order extending time to file bill of exceptions was set aside because it was entered after time to file had expired).

(b) Serving. See "Serving," ch. 1-E, §6.2, p. 44.

3. Contents.

(1) Application.

(a) Generally. See "Application Papers," ch. 1-E, §5, p. 42.

(b) Description of extension. The application should specify the length of the extension. Most statutes that authorize an extension also specify the permissible length of the extension. *E.g.*, CCP §400 (up to 10 days), §403.080 (same), §404.6 (same), §418.10(b) & (c) (up to 20 days), §437c(m)(1) (up to 10 days), §1054 (up to 30 days unless adverse party consents to longer period). Statutes that are silent on the length of the extension have been interpreted to be subject to the 30-day limit under CCP §1054(a). *See* ***Lewith v. Rehmke*** (1933) 217 Cal. 563, 565.

(c) **Disclosure of previous extensions.** The application must disclose in writing (1) the nature of the case and (2) what extensions, if any, have previously been granted or stipulated to. CRC 2.20(b).

PRACTICE TIP

If a party wants to extend the time to serve a pleading, it can use optional Judicial Council Form CM-020.

---

(2) **Memorandum of points & authorities.** Generally, the application must include a memorandum in support. CRC 3.1201(4). But if the movant uses Judicial Council Form CM-020 to request an extension of time to serve a pleading, no memorandum is required. CRC 3.1114(a)(2). See "Memorandum of points & authorities," ch. 1-E, §5.2, p. 42.

(3) **Declarations.** The application must be supported by the following declarations:

(a) **Declaration of notice.** See "Declaration of notice," ch. 1-E, §5.3.1, p. 43.

(b) **Declaration in support.**

[1] **Generally.** The declaration in support of the application must establish the grounds for the extension. See "Grounds for extension," §2.2, p. 502; "Declaration in support," ch. 1-E, §5.3.2, p. 43.

[2] **Declaration for extending time to serve pleading.** If the movant seeks to extend the time to serve a pleading, it must file a declaration that includes the following:

[a] An explanation for why service has not been completed. CRC 3.110(e).

[b] A description of the efforts that have been made to complete service. *Id.*

[c] The date by which service is proposed to be completed. *Id.*

(4) **Copy of stipulation.** If the application is supported by a stipulation, a copy of the stipulation can be filed with the application. *See* Younger, *Cal. Motions*, §31.23 (although rare, some courts require stipulations to be presented by ex parte application). See "Stipulation," §3.1, p. 503.

(5) **Proposed order.** The application must include a proposed order. CRC 3.1201(5). The proposed order must be lodged and served with the application, not attached to it. See "Documents lodged," ch. 1-F, §2.3, p. 47.

§4. OPPOSITION

§4.1 Form. The nonmovant can respond to an application for an order to extend time by opposing the application either in writing or orally at the hearing. *See* Younger, *Cal. Motions*, §§31:42, 31:43. See "Opposing Ex Parte Application," ch. 1-E, §7, p. 44.

§4.2 Deadline to serve. If the nonmovant chooses to oppose the application in writing, the opposition must be served at the first reasonable opportunity on every party that will appear at the hearing. CRC 3.1206.

§4.3 Grounds. Some of the grounds that can be raised include the following:

1. **Time cannot be extended.** The application can be opposed on the ground that the time period in question cannot be extended. See "Time can be extended," §2.1, p. 501.

2. **No good cause.** The application can be opposed on the ground that the movant lacks good cause. See "Good cause," §2.2.1, p. 502.

3. **Diminish right to pendente lite relief or provisional remedy.** If the application is based on the movant's attorney's membership in the State Legislature, the application can be opposed on the ground that an extension would diminish either of the following rights:

(1) The nonmovant's right to pendente lite relief (i.e., relief during the proceeding) in a paternity action. CCP §1054.1(b).

(2) The nonmovant's right to invoke a provisional remedy (e.g., pendente lite support in a domestic-relations controversy, the attachment and sale of perishable goods, a receivership for a failing business, a temporary restraining order, or a preliminary injunction). *Id.*

§5. HEARING

Hearings on ex parte applications to extend time are conducted in the same manner as ex parte proceedings generally. See "Hearing," ch. 1-E, §8, p. 44. Specific issues relevant to applications to extend time include the following:

§5.1 Judge. An application for an order to extend time must be heard and determined by the judge before whom the matter is pending. CRC 2.20(a). If that judge is dead, absent, or unable to conduct a hearing, the hearing can be held by another judge in the same court. *Id.*; *see, e.g.*, ***Johnson v. German Am. Ins.*** (1907) 150 Cal. 336, 339 (disqualified judge cannot conduct hearing on motion for extension of time).

§5.2 Appearance not required. An application for an order to extend time to serve pleadings or to extend time based on the parties' stipulation will be considered without an appearance by the movant. CRC 3.1207(2), (4).

§6. RULING

When making its ruling, the court's level of discretion depends on (1) the grounds for the extension and (2) whether the extension is opposed or agreed to.

§6.1 Good cause.

1. Stipulation. Generally, the court must grant a stipulated extension if (1) the time is extendable and (2) good cause is shown. *See* CCP §1054; Kiesel, *Cal. Pretrial Civil Procedure*, §27.22[1]. But some local rules may prohibit stipulated extensions of time that would affect the court's case-disposition time goals. *E.g.*, Super. Ct. Sacramento Cty. Loc. R., rule 2.53 (parties cannot extend time periods set out in court's case-management program).

2. Ex parte application. The court has discretion in ruling on an ex parte application for an order to extend time based on good cause. CCP §1054(a); ***Lucci v. United Credit & Collection Co.*** (1934) 220 Cal. 492, 495. See "Good cause," §2.2.1, p. 502. The court will likely grant the first application to extend, but additional applications will be granted more reluctantly. Weil, *Civil Procedure Before Trial*, ¶9:361; *see* ***Dobbins v. Hardister*** (1st Dist.1966) 242 Cal.App.2d 787, 795.

§6.2 Member of Legislature. The court must usually grant an application for an order to extend time if the movant's attorney of record is a member of the State Legislature and the other requirements of CCP §1054.1(a) are met. *See* CCP §1054.1. See "Member of Legislature," §2.2.2, p. 502. The ruling is left to the court's discretion, however, if the court determines that an extension would diminish a party's right to pendente lite relief or a provisional remedy. See "Diminish right to pendente lite relief or provisional remedy," §4.3.3, p. 504.

§7. ORDER

§7.1 Form. The court's ruling on an ex parte application for an order to extend time must be recorded either in writing or by minute order. See "Record of Ruling," ch. 1-I, §4, p. 90.

§7.2 Contents. If the application is granted, the order should specify the length of the extension.

1. Generally. Most statutes that authorize an extension also specify the permissible length of the extension. See "Description of extension," §3.2.3(1)(b), p. 503.

2. Requests under §1054 – good cause. When the application is based on good cause under CCP §1054, the court cannot grant an extension of time over 30 days unless the adverse party consents to it. CCP §1054(a); ***Lewith v. Rehmke*** (1933) 217 Cal. 563, 565; *see also* ***Keating v. Keating*** (2d Dist.1913) 23 Cal.App. 384, 385-86 (court cannot order second extension when it already ordered 30-day extension). This 30-day limit does not include any extension of time previously stipulated to by the parties. CCP §1054(b).

CAUTION

Many courts have enacted local fast-track rules that further limit the length or number of extensions available. CEB Procedure Before Trial, §25.91.

3. Requests under §1054.1 – member of Legislature. When the application is based on the attorney's membership in the State Legislature, the length of the extension depends on whether (1) the Legislature is in session or in recess or (2) a legislative committee that the attorney is a duly appointed member of is meeting or scheduled to meet. CCP §1054.1(a).

(1) Legislative session or recess. If time is being extended because the Legislature is in session or in recess, the court must grant an extension to a date that is at least 30 days after either of the following, whichever comes first:

(a) The final adjournment of the Legislature. CCP §1054.1(a).

(b) The beginning of a recess of more than 40 days. *Id.*

(2) Legislative-committee meeting. If time is being extended because a legislative committee that the attorney is a duly appointed member of is meeting or scheduled to meet, the court must grant an extension for a period that the court finds will be reasonably necessary to enable the attorney to participate in the action or proceeding. CCP §1054.1(a). If the extension would expire when the Legislature is to be in session, the court must grant an extension to a date that is at least 30 days after either of the following, whichever comes first:

(a) The final adjournment of the Legislature. *Id.*

(b) The beginning of a recess of more than 40 days. *Id.*

§7.3 Filing & service of order. An order extending time must be filed immediately, and copies must be served within 24 hours after the order is made or within another time that the court decides is appropriate. CRC 2.20(c).

§8. MOTION FOR RECONSIDERATION

A party adversely affected by a court's order on an application to extend time can file a motion for reconsideration. CCP §1008(a). See "Motion for Reconsideration," ch. 5-G, §3, p. 508.

§9. MOTION FOR RENEWAL

A party whose application to extend time is denied can file a motion for renewal. CCP §1008(b). See "Motion for Renewal," ch. 5-G, §4, p. 516.

§10. APPELLATE REVIEW

§10.1 Writ of mandate. A party can challenge the ruling on an ex parte application for an order to extend time by filing a petition for a writ of mandate. *Cf.* ***McMahon v. Superior Ct.*** (2d Dist.2003) 106 Cal.App.4th 112, 114 (Ps filed petition for writ of mandate challenging order shortening time).

§10.2 Direct appeal. A party can challenge the ruling on an ex parte application for an order to extend time by raising the issue on appeal after the entry of a final judgment. *See* CCP §904.1(a)(1). The trial court's ruling is reviewed for abuse of discretion. *See* ***Lucci v. United Credit & Collection Co.*** (1934) 220 Cal. 492, 495.

G. MOTION FOR RECONSIDERATION OR RENEWAL

This subchapter discusses motions to reconsider and motions to renew pretrial motions under CCP §1008. This subchapter does not discuss in detail the reconsideration or renewal of postjudgment motions.

§1. GENERAL

§1.1 Purpose. A motion for reconsideration is used to ask the court to modify, amend, or revoke its earlier order on a prior motion to the court because of new or different facts, circumstances, or law. CCP §1008(a). A motion for renewal is used when a party wants to refile an earlier motion for relief that was previously denied or conditionally granted because of new or different facts, circumstances, or law. *See id.* §1008(b).

§1.2 Primary authority. CCP §1008.

§1.3 Secondary authority. The following secondary sources are cited as authority in this subchapter:

- *California Civil Procedure Before Trial* (CEB Online ed. 2014) (referred to as *CEB Procedure Before Trial*).
- Kiesel et al., *Matthew Bender Practice Guide: California Pretrial Civil Procedure* (2014) (referred to as Kiesel, *Cal. Pretrial Civil Procedure*).
- Weil & Brown, *California Practice Guide: Civil Procedure Before Trial* (CD-ROM ed. 2014) (referred to as Weil, *Civil Procedure Before Trial*).
- Witkin, *California Procedure* (5th ed. 2008 & Supp.2014) (referred to as Witkin, *Cal. Procedure*).
- Younger & Bradley, *Younger on California Motions* (2014-15) (referred to as Younger, *Cal. Motions*).

§2. DISTINGUISHING RECONSIDERATION & RENEWAL

Motions for reconsideration and motions for renewal are based on the same grounds—that is, a party wants the court to consider new or different facts, circumstances, or law. CCP §1008(a) (reconsideration), §1008(b) (renewal). Although the grounds are the same, the motions serve two distinct purposes: a motion for reconsideration asks the court to reconsider an earlier order it made, while a motion for renewal asks the court to reconsider an earlier motion the party made unsuccessfully. Chart 5-2, below, illustrates the similarities and differences between the two motions.

5-2. RECONSIDERATION VS. RENEWAL

		Motion for reconsideration	Motion for renewal
1	Who can file	Party affected by order or court on its own motion. See §3.2, p. 511.	Party whose original motion was denied or conditionally granted. See §4.2.1, p. 517.
2	Grounds	• Party's motion – new or different facts, circumstances, or law. See §3.1.1, p. 508. • Court's motion – change in law or erroneous order. See §3.1.2, p. 510.	New or different facts, circumstances, or law. See §4.1, p. 516.
3	Deadline to file	• Party's motion – within ten days after service of written notice of entry of order and before entry of judgment. See §3.2.2(1), p. 512. • Court's motion – before entry of judgment. See §3.2.2(2), p. 512.	Same deadline as original motion. See §4.2.2, p. 517.

5-2. RECONSIDERATION VS. RENEWAL (CONTINUED)			
		Motion for reconsideration	Motion for renewal
4	Where to file	With same judge who issued order. See §3.2.3, p. 513.	With same judge who issued order or with any judge in court where action is pending. See §4.2.3, p. 517.
5	Relief	Modify, amend, or revoke earlier order. See §3.2.4(1)(a), p. 513.	Same relief requested in earlier motion. See §4.2.4(2), p. 517.

§3. MOTION FOR RECONSIDERATION

A motion for reconsideration can be made for any order, either interim or final, issued by the court in response to a party's motion in an action or proceeding. *See* CCP §1008(a), (e). An interim order is an intermediate ruling of some kind that requires further proceedings before the suit can be resolved. *See* ***People v. DeLouize*** (2004) 32 Cal.4th 1223, 1231; 7 Witkin, *Cal. Procedure*, Judgment, §8. A final order is an order that finally disposes of the suit. *See* ***DeLouize***, 32 Cal.4th at 1231.

§3.1 Grounds. A motion for reconsideration can be brought by a party or by the court on its own motion. *See* CCP §1008(a), (c). The grounds for the motion are different depending on if it is made by a party or the court.

1. Party's grounds.

(1) Valid grounds. A party can move for reconsideration of an interim or final order on the following grounds:

(a) New or different fact. A party can move for reconsideration based on a new or different fact. CCP §1008(a); *e.g.*, ***In re Marriage of La Moure*** (4th Dist.2013) 221 Cal.App.4th 1463, 1473 (in divorce case, court properly granted motion for reconsideration based on new evidence that husband illicitly removed $250,000 from pension plan). A new or different fact is one that was not available to the party when the underlying motion was presented to the court. *See* ***New York Times Co. v. Superior Ct.*** (2d Dist.2005) 135 Cal.App.4th 206, 212-13. A fact is not new or different if it was available to the party and simply not presented to the court. *See id.* at 213 (it is not enough that fact is new to court); *see, e.g.*, ***Brandwein v. Butler*** (4th Dist.2013) 218 Cal.App.4th 1485, 1503 (P's inability to anticipate that court would deny P leave to amend complaint to include previously known facts was insufficient to support motion for reconsideration); ***Foothills Townhome Ass'n v. Christiansen*** (4th Dist.1998) 65 Cal.App.4th 688, 692 n.6 (D's belief that certain evidence was not necessary at hearing was insufficient to support motion for reconsideration), *disapproved on other grounds*, ***Equilon Enters. v. Consumer Cause, Inc.*** (2002) 29 Cal.4th 53.

[1] Reason for delay. When moving for reconsideration based on a new or different fact, the party must explain why the fact was not presented earlier. ***In re Marriage of Herr*** (3d Dist.2009) 174 Cal.App.4th 1463, 1468; ***New York Times***, 135 Cal.App.4th at 212; *see* ***Garcia v. Hejmadi*** (1st Dist.1997) 58 Cal.App.4th 674, 690 (1992 amendments to CCP §1008 did not dispose of court-made diligence requirement). *Contra* ***Standard Microsystems Corp. v. Winbond Elecs. Corp.*** (6th Dist.2009) 179 Cal.App.4th 868, 895-96. A satisfactory explanation is given if the party shows that, despite its reasonable diligence in gathering and presenting all the relevant facts to the court, it could not have discovered or produced the fact earlier. ***New York Times***, 135 Cal.App.4th at 212-13; *see* ***Garcia***, 58 Cal.App.4th at 690. For example, a satisfactory explanation is given if the party timely made a discovery request but the opposing party did not respond with the fact until after the underlying motion was decided. *See, e.g.*, ***Hollister v. Benzl*** (4th Dist.1999) 71 Cal.App.4th 582, 585 (documents were not produced until after court decided petition to compel arbitration). A satisfactory explanation is not given if the fact could have been obtained earlier by a simple discovery request but was not. *See* ***New York Times***, 135 Cal.App.4th at 213.

[2] Affects merits. When moving for reconsideration based on a new or different fact, the party should explain how the fact affects the merits of the case. *See* ***Gilberd v. AC Transit*** (1st Dist.1995) 32 Cal.App.4th 1494, 1500; *see, e.g.*, ***Sakiyama v. AMF Bowling Ctrs., Inc.*** (2d Dist.2003) 110 Cal.App.4th 398, 402 (new

facts were not sufficient to support motion for reconsideration because they would not alter court's conclusion that D did not owe duty to Ps). A fact that will only have a collateral effect on the court's ruling is not sufficient to support a motion for reconsideration. *E.g.*, ***Gilberd***, 32 Cal.App.4th at 1500 (fact that party did not have chance to make oral argument was collateral to merits of motion).

(b) New or different circumstance. A party can move for reconsideration based on a new or different circumstance. CCP §1008(a). When moving for reconsideration based on a new or different circumstance, the party should explain how the circumstance affects the merits of the case. *See* ***Scott Co. v. U.S. Fid. & Guar. Ins.*** (6th Dist.2003) 107 Cal.App.4th 197, 206 n.8, *disapproved on other grounds*, ***Le Francois v. Goel*** (2005) 35 Cal.4th 1094; ***Gilberd***, 32 Cal.App.4th at 1500. The following are new or different circumstances that were sufficient to support a motion for reconsideration:

[1] The court reversed its order denying a motion to compel arbitration without giving the parties notice or an opportunity to be heard. ***Gravillis v. Coldwell Banker Residential Brokerage Co.*** (2d Dist.2006) 143 Cal.App.4th 761, 772.

[2] The court did not consider the cross-defendants' timely filed memorandum of points and authorities before it ruled on the application. ***Johnston v. Corrigan*** (2d Dist.2005) 127 Cal.App.4th 553, 556.

[3] The court did not allow a party to reply to new arguments raised in the opposing party's response. ***Kollander Constr., Inc. v. Superior Ct.*** (2d Dist.2002) 98 Cal.App.4th 304, 314, *disapproved on other grounds*, ***Le Francois v. Goel*** (2005) 35 Cal.4th 1094.

[4] After the court's ruling on a forum non conveniens motion, a codefendant submitted to the court's jurisdiction and waived all limitations defenses. ***Roulier v. Cannondale*** (2d Dist.2002) 101 Cal.App.4th 1180, 1185.

NOTE

A party's compliance with a court order is not considered a new or different fact or circumstance if the party complied only after the court dismissed the case for noncompliance. See ***Forrest v. Department of Corps.*** *(2d Dist.2007) 150 Cal.App.4th 183, 203-04, disapproved on other grounds,* ***Shalant v. Girardi*** *(2011) 51 Cal.4th 1164.*

(c) New or different law. A party can move for reconsideration based on new or different law. CCP §1008(a); ***Baldwin v. Home Sav. of Am.*** (1st Dist.1997) 59 Cal.App.4th 1192, 1196.

[1] New law. New law is case law that was decided, or statutory law that was enacted, after the court took the underlying motion under submission. *See, e.g.*, ***In re Marriage of Oropallo*** (2d Dist.1998) 68 Cal.App.4th 997, 1001-02 (case law that was published days after hearing and before court's ruling was new law); ***Baldwin***, 59 Cal.App.4th at 1196 (two-year-old case law was not new law because it could have been provided to court before ruling).

[a] Case law. For case law to be considered "new law," the following must be true: (1) the case must contain a new holding—that is, a holding different from case law that existed when the court took the motion under submission—and (2) the new holding must affect the court's ruling on the underlying motion. *See, e.g.*, ***Ovitz v. Schulman*** (2d Dist.2005) 133 Cal.App.4th 830, 848 (decision from Ninth Circuit was not new law because it relied on decisions from other circuits that existed at time of court's ruling; decisions from Ninth Circuit have no greater persuasive force on California courts than decisions from other circuits); ***In re Marriage of Oropallo***, 68 Cal.App.4th at 1002 (although decision contained new holding, it was not relevant to underlying motion).

[b] Statutory law. For a later-enacted statute to be considered "new law," it must have retroactive application. CCP §1008(f).

[2] Different law. Different law is case law or statutory law that was in existence when the court took the underlying motion under submission but was not asserted by the parties. *See, e.g.*, ***Scott Co.***, 107 Cal.App.4th at 205-06 (case law and statute that were cited during hearing could not support motion for reconsideration as different or new law); ***Baldwin***, 59 Cal.App.4th at 1196-97 (case law that was published before hearing

but not asserted by either party could support motion for reconsideration because it was different from authority originally asserted by parties). To establish this ground, the movant must show that it exercised reasonable diligence in researching and presenting all relevant legal arguments and persuasive authority in the underlying motion. *See* ***Ovitz***, 133 Cal.App.4th at 847 (party must provide satisfactory explanation for not providing law earlier); ***Baldwin***, 59 Cal.App.4th at 1200 (diligence requirement that applies to motions based on different facts applies to motions based on different law). *Contra* ***Standard Microsystems***, 179 Cal.App.4th at 895-96. See "Reason for delay," §3.1.1(1)(a)[1], p. 508.

(2) Invalid grounds. The following are invalid grounds for a party's motion for reconsideration:

(a) Mistake. A party cannot move for reconsideration based on the movant's ignorance of the law or imprecision in drafting. ***Pazderka v. Caballeros Dimas Alang, Inc.*** (1st Dist.1998) 62 Cal.App.4th 658, 670.

(b) Erroneous order. A party cannot move for reconsideration based on the court's erroneous order (i.e., the court's misinterpretation of facts or law). *See* ***Jones v. P.S. Dev. Co.*** (2d Dist.2008) 166 Cal.App.4th 707, 724, *disapproved on other grounds*, ***Reid v. Google, Inc.*** (2010) 50 Cal.4th 512; ***Gilberd***, 32 Cal.App.4th at 1500. A party can suggest to the court that it should reconsider its erroneous order on its own motion as long as the suggestion is not made ex parte. ***Le Francois v. Goel*** (2005) 35 Cal.4th 1094, 1108. See "Constitutional authority – erroneous interim order," §3.1.2(2), p. 511.

2. Court's grounds. The court has statutory authority to reconsider both interim and final orders and inherent constitutional authority to reconsider interim orders. *See* CCP §1008(c) (statutory authority to reconsider earlier order), §1008(e) (statutory authority applies to both interim and final orders); ***Brown, Winfield & Canzoneri, Inc. v. Superior Ct.*** (2010) 47 Cal.4th 1233, 1248 (constitutional authority to reconsider interim orders); ***Le Francois***, 35 Cal.4th at 1105 & n.4 (same).

(1) Statutory authority – change in law. The court has statutory authority to reconsider an interim or final order on its own motion if it determines that a change in law warrants reconsideration. *See* CCP §1008(c), (e). A court may consider a number of factors in determining whether to reconsider a prior order, including the importance of the change in law, the timing of the motion to reconsider, and the circumstances of the case. ***Farmers Ins. Exch. v. Superior Ct.*** (2d Dist.2013) 218 Cal.App.4th 96, 107; *see* ***Phillips v. Sprint PCS*** (1st Dist.2012) 209 Cal.App.4th 758, 769. The court has to find only that a change in law makes reconsideration of the earlier order appropriate, not that it makes the earlier order unjust. *See* ***International Ins. v. Superior Ct.*** (2d Dist.1998) 62 Cal.App.4th 784, 788. The following are examples of changes in law that can support the court's motion:

(a) Depublished opinion. A change in law can occur when an opinion that the court's earlier order was based on is depublished. ***Farmers***, 218 Cal.App.4th at 109; *see* CRC 8.1115(a) (court cannot rely on unpublished opinion); *cf.* ***People v. DeLouize*** (2004) 32 Cal.4th 1223, 1233 (criminal case; court reconsidered order granting motion for new trial when opinion that supported new trial was depublished and new opinion reached opposite conclusion).

(b) Overruled opinion. A change in law can occur when an opinion that the court's earlier order was based on is overruled. *See, e.g.*, ***Phillips***, 209 Cal.App.4th at 764-65 (court reconsidered order compelling arbitration when opinion that supported order was ruled to be preempted by federal law); ***Malek v. Blue Cross*** (2d Dist.2004) 121 Cal.App.4th 44, 54 (court reconsidered order compelling arbitration when opinion from Fourth District that supported order was overturned by opinion from Second District); ***Blake v. Ecker*** (2d Dist.2001) 93 Cal.App.4th 728, 739 (court was bound to reconsider order when opinion that supported order was overturned by Supreme Court), *disapproved on other grounds*, ***Le Francois v. Goel*** (2005) 35 Cal.4th 1094.

(c) New opinion. A change in law can occur when a new opinion is published that affects the court's order. *See, e.g.*, ***Valdez v. Himmelfarb*** (2d Dist.2006) 144 Cal.App.4th 1261, 1275 (appellate court held that trial court would abuse its discretion if it did not reconsider its sanction order after appellate court decided issue of first impression and remanded case).

(d) New or amended statute. A change in law can occur when a new or amended statute applies retroactively and affects the court's order. *See* CCP §1008(f).

(2) Constitutional authority – erroneous interim order. The court has inherent constitutional power to reconsider an erroneous interim order. ***Le Francois***, 35 Cal.4th at 1107; *see* ***Farmers***, 218 Cal.App.4th at 106 n.17 (CCP §1008 does not limit court's inherent power to reconsider its own rulings); ***In re Marriage of Barthold*** (1st Dist.2008) 158 Cal.App.4th 1301, 1303-04 (court's inherent authority applies even when court is prompted to reconsider its earlier ruling by party's faulty motion under CCP §1008).

NOTE

*In **Le Francois**, the Supreme Court stated that a court's constitutional authority "to reconsider interim orders does not necessarily apply to final orders, which present quite different concerns." **Le Francois**, 35 Cal.4th at 1105 n.4. One appellate court has interpreted the **Le Francois** cautionary statement to mean only that a court may not have the authority to reconsider "all" final orders, and that some final orders are available for reconsideration. **In re Marriage of Barthold**, 158 Cal.App.4th at 1312. The final order that was reconsidered in **In re Marriage of Barthold** denied an ex-wife's postjudgment motion to recover funds under a marital settlement agreement. Id. at 1304-05. The appellate court noted that although the order being reconsidered was final in one sense—there were no other issues to be resolved in the suit—it was not final in the sense that the time to appeal it had not yet expired. See id. at 1313 & n.9. If the time to appeal had expired, the concerns that the Court in **Le Francois** alluded to about permitting the reconsideration of a final order may have been applicable. **In re Marriage of Barthold**, 158 Cal.App.4th at 1313 n.9.*

§3.2 Motion.

1. Who can file.

(1) Party. Any party affected by a court's order can file a motion for reconsideration of that order. CCP §1008(a).

NOTE

*In limited circumstances, a nonparty can file a motion for reconsideration. For example, a nonparty can file a motion to reconsider an order sealing court records. **Wilson v. Science Applications Int'l** (4th Dist.1997) 52 Cal.App.4th 1025, 1032. The right to reconsider such orders is extended to nonparties to protect the public's interest in accessing court records. See id. at 1031. A nonparty who brings a motion for reconsideration on this basis must comply with the requirements of CCP §1008(a). E.g., **Wilson**, 52 Cal.App.4th at 1032-33 (nonparty must file motion within ten days after being served with order; because nonparty was not served with order, nonparty could file motion six years after order was entered).*

(2) Court. The court can reconsider its order on its own motion. CCP §1008(c); *see* ***Le Francois v. Goel*** (2005) 35 Cal.4th 1094, 1107; ***Phillips v. Sprint PCS*** (1st Dist.2012) 209 Cal.App.4th 758, 765. See "Court's grounds," §3.1.2, p. 510. If the court grants reconsideration on its own motion, the court must give the parties notice and an opportunity to submit written responses. ***Brown, Winfield & Canzoneri, Inc. v. Superior Ct.*** (2010) 47 Cal.4th 1233, 1250; ***Le Francois***, 35 Cal.4th at 1108; ***Montegani v. Johnson*** (5th Dist.2008) 162 Cal.App.4th 1231, 1238. If the court granted the motion to reconsider based on an erroneous ruling, the court cannot ask the parties to submit any new or additional evidence. ***In re Marriage of Herr*** (3d Dist.2009) 174 Cal.App.4th 1463, 1469-70; ***In re Marriage of Barthold*** (1st Dist.2008) 158 Cal.App.4th 1301, 1314. See "Constitutional authority – erroneous interim order," §3.1.2(2), this page.

2. **Deadline to file.**

(1) **Party's motion.**

(a) **Within ten days after service.** A party must file a motion for reconsideration within ten days after it is served with written notice of entry of the order. CCP §1008(a); ***Farmers Ins. Exch. v. Superior Ct.*** (2d Dist.2013) 218 Cal.App.4th 96, 102; *see, e.g.*, ***Wiz Tech. v. Coopers & Lybrand LLP*** (2d Dist.2003) 106 Cal.App.4th 1, 16 (court did not abuse discretion by denying motion filed one day after ten-day deadline). The ten-day time period begins after service of written notice of the order's entry, not after service of the order itself. *See* ***Forrest v. Department of Corps.*** (2d Dist.2007) 150 Cal.App.4th 183, 202-03, *disapproved on other grounds*, ***Shalant v. Girardi*** (2011) 51 Cal.4th 1164. The deadline is extended for service by mail. Weil, *Civil Procedure Before Trial*, ¶9:326.1; *see* CCP §1008(e) (§1008 sets out court's jurisdiction over applications for reconsideration), §1013(a) (requires extension for service by mail unless there is specific exception); ***Poster v. Southern Cal. Rapid Transit Dist.*** (1990) 52 Cal.3d 266, 274 (§1013 does not apply to statutes that set jurisdictional deadlines).

PRACTICE TIP

If the ten-day deadline for filing a motion for reconsideration has expired, ask the court to reconsider its ruling on its own motion. See ***Le Francois****, 35 Cal.4th at 1108;* ***Farmers****, 218 Cal.App.4th at 102 & n.10. See "Court's motion," §3.2.2(2), this page. Filing a late motion for reconsideration can be punished as a contempt and with sanctions. CCP §1008(d). When asking the court to reconsider its ruling on its own motion, make sure the opposing party is present.* ***Le Francois****, 35 Cal.4th at 1108.*

(b) **Before judgment entered.** A party must file a motion for reconsideration before a final judgment is entered. *See* ***Aguilar v. Atlantic Richfield Co.*** (2001) 25 Cal.4th 826, 859 n.29 (trial court loses jurisdiction to rule on motion for reconsideration after entry of judgment); ***Sole Energy Co. v. Petrominerals Corp.*** (4th Dist.2005) 128 Cal.App.4th 187, 192 (same); Weil, *Civil Procedure Before Trial*, ¶9:332.1 (same). A final judgment is entered when it is filed with the clerk or entered into the court's judgment book. ***Dodge v. Superior Ct.*** (4th Dist.2000) 77 Cal.App.4th 513, 518 n.5. After the entry of a final judgment, the court no longer has jurisdiction to rule on the motion. ***20th Century Ins. v. Superior Ct.*** (2d Dist.2001) 90 Cal.App.4th 1247, 1259; ***APRI Ins. Co. S.A. v. Superior Ct.*** (2d Dist.1999) 76 Cal.App.4th 176, 182. If final judgment has been entered, the party should instead file a motion for new trial, a motion to vacate the judgment, or an appeal. *See* ***Sole Energy***, 128 Cal.App.4th at 192 (court may treat motion for reconsideration filed after entry of judgment as motion for new trial); ***20th Century Ins.***, 90 Cal.App.4th at 1259 (after entry of judgment, court can correct error only through certain limited procedures such as motions for new trial and motions to vacate); Weil, *Civil Procedure Before Trial*, ¶9:332.3 (party should file motion for new trial to challenge order after entry of judgment).

NOTE

After entry of judgment, the court loses jurisdiction to reconsider the judgment and any interim orders that have been subsumed within that judgment. See ***D.R.S. Trading Co. v. Barnes*** *(4th Dist.2009) 180 Cal.App.4th 815, 817. The court does not lose jurisdiction, however, to reconsider orders on postjudgment motions. E.g., id. (court could reconsider order on postjudgment motion for relief from default judgment);* ***In re Marriage of Barthold****, 158 Cal.App.4th at 1312-13 (court could reconsider order on postjudgment motion to establish rights under divorce decree).*

---

(2) **Court's motion.** The court can reconsider its order anytime before entering a final judgment. ***Blake v. Ecker*** (2d Dist.2001) 93 Cal.App.4th 728, 739 n.10, *disapproved on other grounds*, ***Le Francois v. Goel*** (2005) 35 Cal.4th 1094; *e.g.*, ***Phillips***, 209 Cal.App.4th at 768 (court reconsidered its order over four years later); *see* ***Kerns v. CSE Ins.*** (1st Dist.2003) 106 Cal.App.4th 368, 388. See "Before judgment entered," §3.2.2(1)(b), this page.

3. Where to file. The motion for reconsideration must be filed with the same judge who issued the order. CCP §1008(a); *see* ***Geddes v. Superior Ct.*** (2d Dist.2005) 126 Cal.App.4th 417, 425-26. If the judge is unavailable, another judge in the same court can hear the motion. ***Geddes***, 126 Cal.App.4th at 426; *see* CCP §1008(a) (party must present motion to same judge or court that made order).

4. Contents.

(1) Notice of motion & motion. The motion for reconsideration should be made in writing by noticed motion. *See, e.g.*, ***Coast S&L Ass'n v. Black*** (2d Dist.1986) 187 Cal.App.3d 1494, 1499 (Ds filed noticed motion for reconsideration); *CEB Procedure Before Trial*, §36.226 (sample form for noticed motion for reconsideration of order granting MSJ). See "Notice of motion & motion," ch. 1-D, §5.1, p. 28.

(a) Relief. The motion should briefly state the relief sought. CRC 3.1112(d)(3). A motion for reconsideration can ask the court to modify, amend, or revoke its earlier order. CCP §1008(a).

(b) Grounds. The motion should briefly state the grounds for the motion. CRC 3.1112(d)(3). See "Valid grounds," §3.1.1(1), p. 508.

(2) Memorandum of points & authorities. The motion must include a memorandum in support of the motion. CRC 3.1112(a)(3), 3.1113(a). See "Memorandum of points & authorities," ch. 1-D, §5.2, p. 28.

(3) Movant's declaration or affidavit. The motion must include a declaration or affidavit in support of the motion. *See* CCP §1008(a) (motion must include affidavit), §2015.5 (motion may use declaration instead of affidavit); Weil, *Civil Procedure Before Trial*, ¶9:331 (motion must be accompanied by affidavit or declaration); *see, e.g.*, ***Branner v. Regents of the Univ. of Cal.*** (3d Dist.2009) 175 Cal.App.4th 1043, 1048 (motion was invalid because it did not include affidavit or declaration). The declaration or affidavit must state the following:

(a) The type of application that was originally made to the court (e.g., "Plaintiff's Motion for Summary Judgment"). CCP §1008(a).

(b) The date the application was made. *Id.*

(c) The judge to whom the application was made. *Id.*

(d) The order or decisions that were made on the application. *Id.*

(e) The new or different facts, circumstances, or law that the motion for reconsideration is based on. *Id.*

(4) Other supporting evidence. The motion can include other supporting evidence. *See, e.g.*, ***Gaillard v. Natomas Co.*** (1st Dist.1989) 208 Cal.App.3d 1250, 1270 n.10 (Ps filed deposition transcript in support of motion). See "Supporting evidence," ch. 1-D, §5.3, p. 30.

(5) Request for judicial notice. If a party's motion is based on matters the court can take judicial notice of, the party can ask the court to take judicial notice of those matters. *See* CRC 3.1113(*l*). A request for judicial notice must be made in a separate document. *Id.* See "Request for Judicial Notice," ch. 5-J, p. 547.

(6) Proposed order. The motion can be accompanied by a proposed order. *See* CRC 3.1113(m). If a proposed order is submitted, it must be lodged and served with the motion papers, not attached to them. *Id.* See "Documents lodged," ch. 1-F, §2.3, p. 47.

5. Effect of filing. The filing of a valid motion to reconsider an appealable order extends the time to appeal from that order until (1) 30 days after the clerk or a party serves an order denying the motion or a notice of entry of the order, (2) 90 days after the first motion to reconsider is filed, or (3) 180 days after entry of the appealable order, whichever is earliest. CRC 8.108(e); *see* CRC 8.104(a) (normal time to appeal); ***Lister v. Bowen*** (1st Dist.2013) 215 Cal.App.4th 319, 329 & n.3 (filing of motion for reconsideration extends time to appeal to earliest of three circumstances); *see also* CRC 8.108(e), advisory committee's cmt., www.courts.ca.gov/rules.htm (CRC 8.108(e) applies

only when party makes motion; it does not apply when court makes its own motion). A valid motion for reconsideration is one that complies with the procedural requirements of CCP §1008(a). CRC 8.108(e), advisory committee's cmt., www.courts.ca.gov/rules.htm; *see, e.g.*, ***Branner***, 175 Cal.App.4th at 1047-48 (motion for reconsideration that did not include affidavit or declaration did not extend appeal period).

§3.3 Response.

1. Opposition. The nonmovant can respond to a motion for reconsideration by filing an opposition.

(1) Deadline to file & serve. If a hearing has been granted on the motion, the opposition must be filed and served at least nine court days before the hearing. CCP §1005(b). See "Filing & serving opposition," ch. 1-D, §8.5, p. 36.

(2) Grounds. A motion for reconsideration can be opposed on any of the following grounds:

(a) No change in facts, circumstances, or law. The motion can be opposed on the ground that there are no new or different facts, circumstances, or law that require reconsideration of the court's order. *See* CCP §1008(a). See "Valid grounds," §3.1.1(1), p. 508.

(b) No explanation for late presentation. The motion can be opposed on the ground that it does not explain why the new or different facts, circumstances, or law were not previously presented to the court. *See, e.g.*, ***Brandwein v. Butler*** (4th Dist.2013) 218 Cal.App.4th 1485, 1503 (trial court denied motion for reconsideration because movant did not provide adequate explanation for not producing information earlier); ***In re Marriage of Turkanis*** (2d Dist.2013) 213 Cal.App.4th 332, 342 (same). See "Reason for delay," §3.1.1(1)(a)[1], p. 508.

(c) No effect on order. The motion can be opposed on the ground that the new or different facts, circumstances, or law have no effect on the merits of the order. *See* ***Gilberd v. AC Transit*** (1st Dist.1995) 32 Cal.App.4th 1494, 1500. See "Affects merits," §3.1.1(1)(a)[2], p. 508.

(d) Not timely filed. The motion can be opposed on the ground that it was not timely filed. *See, e.g.*, ***In re Marriage of Herr*** (3d Dist.2009) 174 Cal.App.4th 1463, 1467 (wife opposed motion on ground that it was filed outside ten-day deadline); ***Sole Energy Co. v. Petrominerals Corp.*** (4th Dist.2005) 128 Cal.App.4th 187, 191 (Ds opposed motion on ground that court had no jurisdiction to rule on motion because judgment had been entered). See "Deadline to file," §3.2.2, p. 512.

(e) Prejudice. The motion can be opposed on the ground that it will prejudice a party. *See, e.g.*, ***Phillips v. Sprint PCS*** (1st Dist.2012) 209 Cal.App.4th 758, 769 (court did not abuse its discretion in reconsidering order issued over four years earlier when P had done little to advance case to trial and no prejudice was shown).

(f) Not filed with same judge. The motion can be opposed on the ground that it was not filed with the same judge or court that issued the order. *See* CCP §1008(a) (motion must be filed with same judge or court). See "Where to file," §3.2.3, p. 513.

(g) No proper supporting declaration. The motion can be opposed on the ground that it is not supported by a declaration that meets the statutory requirements. *See* ***Branner v. Regents of the Univ. of Cal.*** (3d Dist.2009) 175 Cal.App.4th 1043, 1048. See "Movant's declaration or affidavit," §3.2.4(3), p. 513.

(3) Contents. See "Opposition Papers," ch. 1-D, §8, p. 35.

2. Motion for sanctions. The nonmovant can respond to a motion for reconsideration by filing a motion for sanctions if the movant violated the requirements of CCP §1008. CCP §1008(d); *see id.* §128.7; *cf.* ***Taylor v. Varga*** (2d Dist.1995) 37 Cal.App.4th 750, 761-62 (court granted motion for sanctions against party under CCP §128.5 for filing late motion that misstated facts and law and was frivolous, in bad faith, and intended to cause unnecessary delay). See "Papers—Frivolous or Improper," ch. 5-K, §2, p. 561.

§3.4 Reply. The movant can file and serve a reply to the opposition papers. If a hearing has been granted on the motion, the reply must be filed and served at least five court days before the hearing. CCP §1005(b). See "Reply Papers," ch. 1-D, §9, p. 37.

§3.5 Hearing.

1. Party's motion. The court should hold a hearing on a party's motion for reconsideration. *See* CCP §1005.5 (although noticed motion that is filed and served is deemed to be pending before court, it does not deprive party of hearing if party is otherwise entitled to one); *see, e.g.*, ***Gravillis v. Coldwell Banker Residential Brokerage Co.*** (2d Dist.2006) 143 Cal.App.4th 761, 772 (court's granting of motion without notice or hearing established new circumstances that justified second motion for reconsideration). *But see* ***Muller v. Tanner*** (1st Dist.1969) 2 Cal.App.3d 445, 462 (if record before trial court does not establish merits of motion, court does not commit prejudicial error by not conducting hearing on motion). See "Hearings," ch. 1-H, p. 79.

2. Court's motion. The court must hold a hearing if the court grants reconsideration on its own motion. ***Brown, Winfield & Canzoneri, Inc. v. Superior Ct.*** (2010) 47 Cal.4th 1233, 1250; ***Le Francois v. Goel*** (2005) 35 Cal.4th 1094, 1108; ***Montegani v. Johnson*** (5th Dist.2008) 162 Cal.App.4th 1231, 1238.

§3.6 Ruling.

1. Deadline. The court must rule on a motion for reconsideration before a final judgment is entered. ***Aguilar v. Atlantic Richfield Co.*** (2001) 25 Cal.4th 826, 859 n.29; ***Sole Energy Co. v. Petrominerals Corp.*** (4th Dist.2005) 128 Cal.App.4th 187, 192. After the entry of a final judgment, the court no longer has jurisdiction to rule on the motion. ***20th Century Ins. v. Superior Ct.*** (2d Dist.2001) 90 Cal.App.4th 1247, 1259; ***APRI Ins. Co. S.A. v. Superior Ct.*** (2d Dist.1999) 76 Cal.App.4th 176, 182. See "Before judgment entered," §3.2.2(1)(b), p. 512.

2. Party's motion.

(1) Deny. If a party's motion does not comply with the requirements of CCP §1008(a) (e.g., untimely, no new evidence or law), the court must deny the motion. *See* CCP §1008(d) (court can revoke or vacate order that is made contrary to §1008); ***Kerns v. CSE Ins.*** (1st Dist.2003) 106 Cal.App.4th 368, 394 n.22 (court is jurisdictionally barred from considering motion for reconsideration that does not comply with §1008).

(2) Grant. If a party's motion complies with the requirements of CCP §1008(a), the court should grant the motion and then reexamine the merits of its earlier order. *See* ***Standard Microsystems Corp. v. Winbond Elecs. Corp.*** (6th Dist.2009) 179 Cal.App.4th 868, 890 (after court grants motion, it should then determine merits of earlier order).

3. Court's motion. If the court decides on its own motion to reconsider an earlier erroneous order, the court must consider only the evidence that was initially filed with the underlying motion in making its ruling; the court cannot ask for or consider additional evidence. ***In re Marriage of Herr*** (3d Dist.2009) 174 Cal.App.4th 1463, 1469-70; ***In re Marriage of Barthold*** (1st Dist.2008) 158 Cal.App.4th 1301, 1314. See "Constitutional authority – erroneous interim order," §3.1.2(2), p. 511.

§3.7 Order.

1. Form. The court's ruling on the motion for reconsideration should be recorded either in writing or by minute order. *See, e.g.*, Kiesel, *Cal. Pretrial Civil Procedure*, §29.32 (written order). *But see* ***Ramon v. Aerospace Corp.*** (2d Dist.1996) 50 Cal.App.4th 1233, 1238 (court can impliedly deny reconsideration by entering judgment based on court's original order); ***Nave v. Taggart*** (5th Dist.1995) 34 Cal.App.4th 1173, 1176-77 (same). See "Record of Ruling," ch. 1-I, §4, p. 90.

2. Contents.

(1) Action on earlier order. If the court grants reconsideration, the court can modify, amend, revoke, or affirm its earlier order. *See* CCP §1008(a), (c); ***Mink v. Superior Ct.*** (4th Dist.1992) 2 Cal.App.4th 1338, 1342.

(2) Sanctions or contempt. If the court determines that a party violated the requirements of CCP §1008, the court can punish the party with contempt and sanctions as permitted by CCP §128.7. CCP §1008(d). See "Papers—Frivolous or Improper," ch. 5-K, §2, p. 561.

§3.8 Review.

1. By trial court. If an order of reconsideration is made contrary to the requirements of CCP §1008, the order can be revoked by the judge who made it or be vacated by a judge of the court where the action or proceeding is pending. CCP §1008(d).

2. By appellate court.

(1) Writ of mandate or prohibition. An order granting or denying a motion for reconsideration can be reviewed by writ of mandate or prohibition. *See* Younger, *Cal. Motions*, §27:36; *see, e.g.*, ***City & Cty. of S.F. v. Superior Ct.*** (1959) 53 Cal.2d 236, 243 (writ of prohibition is proper when court exceeds its jurisdiction); ***Farmers Ins. Exch. v. Superior Ct.*** (2d Dist.2013) 218 Cal.App.4th 96, 108 (writ of mandate was appropriate when court's decision not to reconsider its prior order on its own motion was based on misinterpretation of law); ***New York Times Co. v. Superior Ct.*** (2d Dist.2005) 135 Cal.App.4th 206, 215-16 (writ of mandate issued to vacate order granting motion for reconsideration that violated requirements of CCP §1008).

(2) Direct appeal.

(a) Grant. Generally, an order granting a motion for reconsideration is not an appealable order. *See* CCP §§904.1, 904.2; Younger, *Cal. Motions*, §27:33. The grant is generally an interlocutory order that can be reviewed only after an appealable order or judgment has been entered. *See* CCP §906. The order arising from the grant of reconsideration may be appealable, however, if the order itself is an appealable order. *See* Younger, *Cal. Motions*, §27:33; *see, e.g.*, CCP §904.1(a)(13) (grant of special motion to strike is appealable order); ***Johnston v. Corrigan*** (2d Dist.2005) 127 Cal.App.4th 553, 555-56 (order awarding attorney fees under CCP §425.16 that arose from grant of motion for reconsideration was appealable).

(b) Denial. An order denying a motion for reconsideration is an appealable order if it is part of the appeal from the underlying order or from the judgment. CCP §1008(g); *see id.* §906; ***Fleur Du Lac Estates Ass'n v. Mansouri*** (3d Dist.2012) 205 Cal.App.4th 249, 255-56; *see, e.g.*, ***Kalivas v. Barry Controls Corp.*** (2d Dist.1996) 49 Cal.App.4th 1152, 1160-61 (court reviewed denial of reconsideration of MSJ after summary judgment was entered).

(c) Standard of review. A trial court's ruling on a motion for reconsideration is reviewed for abuse of discretion. ***Farmers***, 218 Cal.App.4th at 106; *see, e.g.*, ***Phillips v. Sprint PCS*** (1st Dist.2012) 209 Cal.App.4th 758, 769 (court did not abuse its discretion in reconsidering order issued over four years earlier when P had done little to advance case to trial and no prejudice was shown).

§4. MOTION FOR RENEWAL

If a party files a motion that is denied in whole or in part, or granted conditionally or on terms, the party can file a new motion seeking the same order. CCP §1008(b). A motion for renewal is simply the refiling of the earlier motion that was denied or conditionally granted.

§4.1 Grounds. A party can file a motion for renewal of an interim or final order if there are new or different facts, circumstances, or law that would support the unconditional granting of the motion. *See* CCP §1008(b), (e); ***Phillips v. Sprint PCS*** (1st Dist.2012) 209 Cal.App.4th 758, 768. The diligence requirements that apply to motions for reconsideration also apply to motions for renewal. ***California Corr. Peace Officers Ass'n v. Virga*** (1st Dist.2010) 181 Cal.App.4th 30, 46 n.14. For a discussion of what constitutes new or different facts, circumstances, or law, see "Party's grounds," §3.1.1, p. 508.

NOTE

It is unclear whether a party filing a motion for renewal is relieved from having to show new facts, circumstances, or law if the court denies the party's original motion without prejudice. See Weil, Civil Procedure Before Trial, ¶9:338 (effect of denial without prejudice is unclear

*because CCP §1008 is jurisdictional and creates no exception for denial of motion without prejudice). Two courts have suggested that a denial of a motion without prejudice impliedly invites a party to renew the motion after correcting any deficiency in the motion so that the court can reconsider its original order under its inherent authority. See **Sanai v. Saltz** (2d Dist.2009) 170 Cal.App.4th 746, 782 (court directed party to file motion for renewal); **Farber v. Bay View Terrace Homeowners Ass'n** (4th Dist.2006) 141 Cal.App.4th 1007, 1015 (court indicated it wanted to reconsider motion for attorney fees when it denied motion without prejudice).*

§4.2 Motion.

1. Who can file. Any party can file a motion for renewal if its original motion was either (1) denied in whole or in part or (2) granted with conditions or terms. CCP §1008(b).

2. Deadline to file. The motion for renewal must be filed within the deadline for filing the original motion. *See, e.g.,* ***Kunysz v. Sandler*** (4th Dist.2007) 146 Cal.App.4th 1540, 1543 (motion for renewal filed after deadline for filing anti-SLAPP motion was untimely); ***Northridge Fin. Corp. v. Hamblin*** (2d Dist.1975) 48 Cal.App.3d 819, 825-26 (motion for renewal filed after deadline for filing motion for relief from judgment was untimely). No additional deadline for filing the motion is imposed under CCP §1008(b). ***Stephen v. Enterprise Rent-A-Car*** (1st Dist.1991) 235 Cal.App.3d 806, 816.

CAUTION

*Although there is no additional deadline imposed under CCP §1008(b), there may be practical time limitations for filing a motion for renewal. For example, a second motion for class certification is ineffective once the order denying the first motion becomes final (i.e., the period for immediate appeal has expired). **Safaie v. Jacuzzi Whirlpool Bath, Inc.** (4th Dist.2011) 192 Cal.App.4th 1160, 1169-70; **Stephen**, 235 Cal.App.3d at 817-18.*

3. Where to file. The motion for renewal can be filed with the same judge who issued the order on the original motion or with another judge in the court where the action or proceeding is pending. *See* ***Deauville Rest., Inc. v. Superior Ct.*** (2d Dist.2001) 90 Cal.App.4th 843, 850 (unlike motion for reconsideration, motion for renewal does not have to be filed with same judge who issued order on original motion).

4. Contents.

(1) Generally. The motion for renewal should be filed in the same manner as the original motion (e.g., if the original motion was noticed, the motion for renewal should be noticed). *CEB Procedure Before Trial*, §38.117.

(2) Same order. The motion for renewal must seek the same order that was previously denied or conditionally granted. CCP §1008(b). A motion for renewal seeks the same order if it seeks relief identical to what was requested in the original motion. *See* ***California Corr. Peace Officers Ass'n v. Virga*** (1st Dist.2010) 181 Cal.App.4th 30, 43. It is not necessary, however, that the recovery of identical relief in the motion for renewal be based on the same grounds that were raised in the original motion. *See id. But see* ***Standard Microsystems Corp. v. Winbond Elecs. Corp.*** (6th Dist.2009) 179 Cal.App.4th 868, 892 (questioning whether two motions seeking same relief on different grounds should be viewed as motions seeking same order).

(3) Movant's declaration. The motion for renewal must include a declaration in support of the motion that contains the same information required for a motion for reconsideration. *See* CCP §1008(b). See "Movant's declaration or affidavit," §3.2.4(3), p. 513.

§4.3 Response.

1. Opposition. The nonmovant can respond to a motion for renewal by filing an opposition.

(1) Deadline to file & serve. The opposition must be filed and served within the deadline for filing an opposition to the original motion (e.g., for renewed noticed motion, nine court days before hearing). See "Filing & serving opposition," ch. 1-D, §8.5, p. 36.

(2) **Grounds.**

(a) **Contesting renewal.**

[1] **Generally.** For the most part, a motion for renewal can be opposed on the same grounds as a motion for reconsideration. See "Grounds," §3.3.1(2), p. 514. But a motion for renewal cannot be opposed on the ground that the motion was (1) not filed with the same judge who issued the original order or (2) not filed within ten days after notice of entry of order. *Compare* CCP §1008(a) (motion for reconsideration must be filed with same judge within ten days after service of notice of entry) *with id.* §1008(b) (no such requirements for motion for renewal).

[2] **Not same order.** A motion for renewal can be opposed on the ground that the motion is not seeking the same order that was sought in the original motion. *See* CCP §1008(b); *see, e.g.*, ***Sorenson v. Superior Ct.*** (6th Dist.2013) 219 Cal.App.4th 409, 420-21 & n.13 (motion seeking substantially broader relief than original request did not seek renewal of same order). See "Same order," §4.2.4(2), p. 517.

(b) **Contesting underlying motion.** A party can oppose a motion for renewal on the merits of the motion.

(3) **Contents.** See "Opposition Papers," ch. 1-D, §8, p. 35.

2. **Motion for sanctions.** The nonmovant can respond to a motion for renewal by filing a motion for sanctions if the movant violated the requirements of CCP §1008. CCP §1008(d); *see id.* §128.7. See "Papers—Frivolous or Improper," ch. 5-K, §2, p. 561.

§4.4 Reply. The movant can file and serve a reply to the opposition papers. The reply must be filed and served in the same manner as a reply to the original motion. See "Reply Papers," ch. 1-D, §9, p. 37.

§4.5 Hearing. Hearings on a motion for renewal are conducted in the same manner as hearings on the original motion. See "Hearings," ch. 1-H, p. 79.

§4.6 Ruling. If a party's motion for renewal does not comply with the requirements of CCP §1008 (e.g., no new or different facts, circumstances, or law), the court must deny the motion. *See* CCP §1008(b) (any order made in violation of §1008(b) can be revoked or set aside by ex parte motion); ***Kerns v. CSE Ins.*** (1st Dist.2003) 106 Cal.App.4th 368, 394 n.22 (court is jurisdictionally barred from considering renewed motion that is not in compliance with §1008).

§4.7 Order.

1. **Form.** The court's ruling on the motion for renewal should be recorded either in writing or by minute order. See "Record of Ruling," ch. 1-I, §4, p. 90.

2. **Contents.**

(1) **Renewed motion.** If the court grants the motion for renewal, the order on the motion should comply with the requirements for the original motion. The order on the motion for renewal will replace the court's original order. *See* CCP §1008(b).

(2) **Sanctions or contempt.** If the court determines that a party violated the requirements of CCP §1008, the court can punish the party with contempt and sanctions as permitted by CCP §128.7. CCP §1008(d). See "Papers—Frivolous or Improper," ch. 5-K, §2, p. 561.

§4.8 Review.

1. **By trial court.** The trial court can revoke or set aside an order arising from the granting of a motion for renewal, either on its own motion or on a party's ex parte motion, if it determines that the requirements of CCP §1008(b) were not followed. CCP §1008(b).

2. **By appellate court.**

(1) **Writ of mandate or prohibition.** An order granting or denying a motion for renewal can be reviewed by writ of mandate or prohibition. Younger, *Cal. Motions*, §27:36; *see* ***City & Cty. of S.F. v. Superior Ct.*** (1959)

53 Cal.2d 236, 243 (writ of prohibition proper when court exceeds its jurisdiction); *see, e.g.*, ***Roulier v. Cannondale*** (2d Dist.2002) 101 Cal.App.4th 1180, 1185-86 (writ of mandate issued to compel consideration of motion for renewal); *cf.* ***New York Times Co. v. Superior Ct.*** (2d Dist.2005) 135 Cal.App.4th 206, 215-16 (writ of mandate issued to vacate order granting motion for reconsideration that violated requirements of CCP §1008).

(2) Direct appeal.

(a) Generally – not appealable. Generally, an order granting or denying a motion for renewal is not an appealable order. *See* CCP §§904.1, 904.2. The grant or denial is generally an interlocutory order that can be reviewed only after an appealable order or judgment has been entered. *See id.* §906; *see, e.g.*, ***California Corr. Peace Officers Ass'n v. Virga*** (1st Dist.2010) 181 Cal.App.4th 30, 41-42 (court reviewed denial of motion for renewal after summary judgment was entered). The grant or denial of a motion for renewal may be directly appealable, however, if the order arising from the grant or denial is itself an appealable order. *See, e.g.*, ***Kunysz v. Sandler*** (4th Dist.2007) 146 Cal.App.4th 1540, 1541 (party appealed denial of renewed special motion to strike); ***Sunset Millennium Assocs. v. LHO Grafton Hotel, L.P.*** (2d Dist.2006) 146 Cal.App.4th 300, 302 (party appealed grant of renewed special motion to strike).

(b) Standard of review. A trial court's ruling on a motion for renewal is reviewed for abuse of discretion. ***California Corr. Peace Officers***, 181 Cal.App.4th at 42.

H. RELATING, CONSOLIDATING & COORDINATING CASES

This subchapter discusses the procedures for relating, consolidating, and coordinating cases. This subchapter discusses consolidation only under CCP §1048(a); it does not discuss the procedures for consolidating actions involving an employee or employer against a third party (Lab. C. §3853), actions challenging the validity of public-agency acts (CCP §865), or contractual arbitration proceedings (CCP §1281.3). This subchapter also does not discuss coordination of complex cases. For a discussion of that topic, see *California Civil Procedure Before Trial* (CEB Online ed. 2014) §§44.14-44.41 and the Judicial Council Civil Case Coordination FAQs at www.courts.ca.gov/courts/27922.htm.

§1. GENERAL

§1.1 Purpose. Relating, consolidating, and coordinating cases are all methods used to promote judicial economy either by assigning similarly related cases to the same judge or department (relating cases) or by combining case proceedings (e.g., trial, discovery) when cases share a common question of law or fact (consolidating and coordinating cases). *See* CCP §403 (coordinating cases), §1048(a) (consolidating cases); CRC 3.300(h) (relating cases).

§1.2 Primary authority. CCP §§403, 1048(a); CRC 3.300, 3.350, 3.500.

§1.3 Secondary authority. The following secondary sources are cited as authority in this subchapter:

- *California Civil Procedure Before Trial* (CEB Online ed. 2014) (referred to as *CEB Procedure Before Trial*).
- Kiesel et al., *Matthew Bender Practice Guide: California Pretrial Civil Procedure* (2014) (referred to as Kiesel, *Cal. Pretrial Civil Procedure*).
- Thomas, *California Civil Courtroom Handbook* (2014) (referred to as Thomas, *Courtroom Handbook*).
- Weil & Brown, *California Practice Guide: Civil Procedure Before Trial* (CD-ROM ed. 2014) (referred to as Weil, *Civil Procedure Before Trial*).
- Witkin, *California Procedure* (5th ed. 2008 & Supp.2014) (referred to as Witkin, *Cal. Procedure*).
- Younger & Bradley, *Younger on California Motions* (2014-15) (referred to as Younger, *Cal. Motions*).
- ***O'Connor's Federal Rules * Civil Trials*** (2015) (referred to as ***O'Connor's Federal Rules***).

§1.4 Judicial Council forms.

- CM-015 (optional), notice of related case.

§2. DISTINGUISHING RELATION, CONSOLIDATION & COORDINATION

Chart 5-3, below, distinguishes between the relation, consolidation, and coordination of pending cases.

5-3. RELATING, CONSOLIDATING & COORDINATING CASES					
		When applicable	Effect	Procedure	Deadline
1	Relating cases. See §3, this page.	When a pending case and another pending, dismissed, or disposed-of case in a state or federal court in California: (1) involve the same parties and claims, (2) arise from a similar transaction or incident requiring determination of a similar question of law or fact, (3) involve the same property, or (4) would require duplication of judicial resources if heard by different judges.	• Noncomplex cases pending in the same state court can be assigned to the same judge or department. • Cases pending in different state courts can be informally or formally coordinated.	Party files and serves notice of related case.	No later than 15 days after party knows or learns that cases are related.
2	Consolidating cases. See §4, p. 522.	When cases pending in the same state court involve a common question of law or fact.	Cases can be consolidated for all purposes, for trial, or for other limited purposes.	Party files and serves motion to consolidate or court consolidates on its own motion.	None.
3	Coordinating cases. See §5, p. 529.	When noncomplex cases pending in different state courts involve a common question of law or fact.	Cases can be transferred to one superior court so they can be formally consolidated.	Party files and serves motion to transfer for purposes of coordination.	None.

§3. RELATING CASES

Under CRC 3.300, parties have a duty to notify the court when they know or learn that a pending case is related to another case in California. CRC 3.300(b). If all the related cases have been filed in one superior court, the court can order the cases related and assign them to a single judge or department. CRC 3.300(h)(1). If the related cases are pending in different superior courts, the judges and the parties in the related cases can decide whether to coordinate the proceedings informally or formally by a motion to coordinate under CCP §403 (noncomplex cases) or §§404-404.9 (complex cases). CRC 3.300(h)(2). See "Coordinating Noncomplex Cases," §5, p. 529.

§3.1 When cases are related. A pending case is related to another case if (1) the other case is pending or has been dismissed or disposed of by judgment in a state or federal court in California and (2) the cases meet one of the requirements listed below. *See* CRC 3.300(a)(1), (b).

1. The cases involve the same parties and are based on the same or similar claims. CRC 3.300(a)(1).

2. The cases arise from the same or substantially identical transactions, incidents, or events requiring the determination of the same or substantially identical questions of law or fact. CRC 3.300(a)(2); *see, e.g.*, ***Nutragenetics, LLC v. Superior Ct.*** (2d Dist.2009) 179 Cal.App.4th 243, 250 (court granted Ds' application to relate cases that involved substantially same acts of misconduct and that required interpretation and application of same document between same parties).

3. The cases involve claims against, title to, possession of, or damages to the same property. CRC 3.300(a)(3).

4. The cases are likely to require substantial duplication of judicial resources if heard by different judges. CRC 3.300(a)(4); *see, e.g.*, ***Nutragenetics***, 179 Cal.App.4th at 250 (court granted Ds' application to relate cases that would involve substantial duplication of labor if heard by different judges).

§3.2 Notice of related case.

1. Who must file. Any party who knows or learns that a pending case is related to another case must file a notice of related case unless another party has already filed and served the notice. *See* CRC 3.300(b), (k).

2. Deadline to file & serve. The notice of related case must be filed in all pending cases and served on all parties in each pending case as soon as possible, but no later than 15 days after the party learns that the cases are related. *See* CRC 3.300(d), (e). If a party knows at the time of filing suit that the case is related to another case, the party should file and serve the notice when it files suit. *See* CRC 3.300(f) (duty to file notice applies when party files suit with knowledge of related suit); *see, e.g.*, ***Nutragenetics, LLC v. Superior Ct.*** (2d Dist.2009) 179 Cal.App.4th 243, 248 (party filed suit and notice of related case on same day). See "Filing Documents," ch. 1-F, p. 45; "Serving Documents," ch. 1-G, p. 63.

3. Form. The notice of related case must be in writing and can be made on Judicial Council Form CM-015. *See* CRC 3.300(b) (notice must be filed and served).

4. Contents. The notice of related case must include a list of all related civil cases. CRC 3.300(c)(1). The cases should be listed in chronological order according to the date of filing. Judicial Council Forms, form CM-015. For each case listed, the following information must be included:

(1) Case name. CRC 3.300(c)(1).

(2) Case number. *Id.*

(3) Court name. *Id.*

(4) Department. CRC 3.300(c)(2).

(5) Case type (e.g., limited civil, unlimited civil, probate, family law). *See* Judicial Council Forms, form CM-015.

(6) Filing date. CRC 3.300(c)(1).

(7) Whether the case is complex. *See* Judicial Council Forms, form CM-015.

(8) Case status (i.e., pending, dismissed with prejudice, dismissed without prejudice, disposed of by judgment). *See id.*

(9) Description of how the case is related. CRC 3.300(c)(3); *see* Judicial Council Forms, form CM-015.

§3.3 Response. A party can support or oppose the notice of related case. CRC 3.300(g).

1. Deadline to file & serve. The response must be filed in all pending cases and served on all parties in each pending case within five days after the party is served with the notice. CRC 3.300(g).

2. Contents.

(1) Response supporting notice. A response supporting the notice of related case should state why the party agrees that the cases are related. *See* CRC 3.300(g) (party may file and serve response supporting notice).

(2) Response opposing notice. A response opposing the notice of related case must state one of the following:

(a) Why one or more of the listed cases are not related. CRC 3.300(g).

(b) Why there is good cause for the court to not transfer the cases to or from a particular court or department. *Id.*

§3.4 Ruling.

1. Cases pending in same court. If all the cases that are alleged to be related have been filed in the same superior court, the cases can be ordered related—including probate and family-law cases—and can be assigned to a single judge or department. CRC 3.300(h)(1). Cases cannot be ordered related, however, if one of the

RELATING, CONSOLIDATING & COORDINATING

cases is complex. *See* CRC 3.300(h)(3) (CRC 3.300(h)(1) does not apply to complex cases). See "Complex case," ch. 3-C, §3.1.2(2), p. 211. If a case is complex, a party must use the procedure for consolidating cases. *See* CRC 3.300(h)(1)(E) (if procedure to relate cases under CRC 3.300(h)(1) does not apply, party must use procedure to consolidate cases). See "Consolidating Cases," §4, this page. How cases are assigned in a particular superior court affects who can order the cases related.

(1) Master calendar. In a superior court where there is a master calendar, the presiding judge rules on the notice. CRC 3.300(h)(1). A presiding judge is the judge chosen to manage the court. *See* Gov. C. §69508 (selecting presiding judge in court with three or more judges), §69508.5 (selecting presiding judge in court with two judges); CRC 10.602(a) (selecting presiding judge), CRC 10.603(a) (duties of presiding judge). See "Master-calendar system," ch. 3-E, §3.3.1(2)(a), p. 253.

(2) Cases assigned to single judge or department. In a superior court that assigns cases to a single judge or department, the following rules apply:

(a) Limited or unlimited cases. If all the cases listed in the notice are either limited or unlimited civil cases (but not both), the judge who has the earliest filed case rules on the notice. CRC 3.300(h)(1)(A).

(b) Limited & unlimited cases. If the cases listed in the notice include both limited and unlimited civil cases, the judge who has the earliest filed unlimited case rules on the notice. CRC 3.300(h)(1)(B).

(c) Probate or family-law cases. If the cases listed in the notice include a probate or family-law case, the presiding judge (or a judge designated by the presiding judge) rules on the notice. CRC 3.300(h)(1)(C).

2. Cases pending in different superior courts. If the cases that are alleged to be related have been filed in different superior courts, the judge assigned to the earliest filed case can informally confer with the parties and with the other judges to determine the feasibility and desirability of joint discovery orders and other informal or formal means of coordinating the cases. CRC 3.300(h)(2)(A). If it is determined that the cases should be formally coordinated, the parties must use the procedure for coordinating cases under CCP §403 (noncomplex cases) or §§404-404.9 (complex cases). CRC 3.300(h)(2)(B). See "Coordinating Noncomplex Cases," §5, p. 529.

§3.5 Order.

1. Notice. If the court orders the cases related under CRC 3.300(h)(1) (i.e., when all related cases have been filed in the same superior court), the court must either (1) file a notice of the order in all pending cases and serve a copy of the notice on all parties listed in the notice or (2) direct a party to file the notice in all pending cases and serve a copy on all parties. CRC 3.300(i).

2. Effect of order.

(1) Cases related. If the court rules that the cases are related, they can be assigned to the same judge or department. *See* CRC 3.300(h)(1)(A)-(h)(1)(C).

(2) Cases not related. If the court rules that the cases are not related, they remain assigned to the court, judge, or department where they were pending when the notice of related case was filed and served. CRC 3.300(j). Any party in any of the cases listed in the notice can then file a motion to have the cases related. CRC 3.300(h)(1)(D). This motion must be filed with the presiding judge (or a judge designated by the presiding judge to hear the motion). *Id.*

§4. CONSOLIDATING CASES

When cases involving a common question of law or fact are pending in the same superior court (i.e., the same county), the cases can be consolidated on a party's motion or on the court's own motion under CCP §1048(a). The cases can be consolidated for all purposes, only for trial, or for other limited purposes (e.g., discovery). See "Relief," §4.2.4(1)(a), p. 525.

NOTE

Consolidation is also authorized under other statutes for specific types of actions. See, e.g., Civ. C. §3065a (logger's and lumbermen's lien-foreclosure action), §3149 (mechanic's lien-foreclosure action), §3175 (stop-notice action against owner or construction lender), §3214 (stop-notice action against contractor and public entity); CCP §376(h) (injury-to-child action), §377.62(b) (wrongful-death action); Corp. C. §1304(b) (dissenting-shareholder action); Food & Agr. C. §55653 (food producer's lien-foreclosure action); Sts. & Hy. C. §5414 (assessment-recovery action). Generally, these statutes do not eliminate a party's requirement to comply with CCP §1048(a); they simply serve as reminders that consolidation is available. See Younger, Cal. Motions, §22:3; see, e.g., CCP §376(h) (injury-to-child and wrongful-death actions can be consolidated for trial as provided under §1048), §377.62(b) (wrongful-death actions can be consolidated as provided under §1048).

§4.1 Movant's burden. To prevail on a motion to consolidate, the movant must establish that (1) the cases are pending before the same court, (2) the cases share a common question of law or fact, and (3) the benefits of consolidation outweigh the burdens.

NOTE

CCP §1048(a) is modeled after FRCP 42. ***Rodriguez v. Bethlehem Steel Corp.*** *(1974) 12 Cal.3d 382, 407 n.28; Weil, Civil Procedure Before Trial, ¶12:348. Thus, cases interpreting the federal rule can be used as persuasive authority when there is no controlling state law on an issue. See Weil, Civil Procedure Before Trial, ¶12:348; Younger, Cal. Motions, §22.2. For a discussion of consolidation under the federal rule, see* ***O'Connor's Federal Rules****, "Motion to Consolidate," ch. 5-K, p. 396.*

1. Cases pending in same court. The movant must establish that the cases sought to be consolidated are pending in the same superior court—that is, in the same county. *See* CCP §1048(a); Weil, *Civil Procedure Before Trial*, ¶12:350; *see also* CRC 3.300(h)(1)(E) (if procedure for relating cases does not apply, party must use procedure under §1048 to consolidate cases in same superior court); 4 Witkin, *Cal. Procedure*, Pleading, §352 (consolidation occurs when cases are filed in single court, and coordination occurs when cases are filed in different courts). Cases are pending in the same superior court even if they are pending in different departments. *See CEB Procedure Before Trial*, §§43.27, 43.28; *see, e.g.*, ***Estate of Bliss*** (2d Dist.1962) 199 Cal.App.2d 630, 640-41 (court consolidated probate case with case in equity to set aside inter vivos gift). *But see* Super. Ct. Los Angeles Cty. Loc. R., rule 3.3(g)(1) (cases cannot be consolidated until they are in same department). A case is considered to be pending from the time it is filed until its final determination on appeal or until the time for appeal has passed (unless the judgment is satisfied sooner). CCP §1049; *see, e.g.*, ***Sosnick v. Sosnick*** (1st Dist.1999) 71 Cal.App.4th 1335, 1339-40 (court exceeded its jurisdiction when it consolidated pending tort action with dissolution action because dissolution action was no longer pending).

NOTE

CCP §1048(a) does not limit the types of cases that can be consolidated. Thus, under §1048(a), a court can consolidate a complex case with a noncomplex case and a limited civil case with an unlimited civil case. See CRC 3.300(h)(1)(E) (if procedure for relating cases does not apply, party must use procedure under §1048 to consolidate cases in same superior court), CRC 3.300(h)(3) (procedure for relating cases under CRC 3.300(h)(1) does not apply to complex cases); Super. Ct. Los Angeles Cty. Loc. R., rule 3.3(g)(3) (consolidation of limited case with unlimited case).

2. Cases have common question of law or fact. The movant must establish that the cases sought to be consolidated involve a common question of law or fact. *See* CCP §1048(a). Common questions of law or fact can arise in cases that share common parties and involve a common transaction (e.g., contract) or incident (e.g., automobile accident). *See, e.g., id.* §377.62(b) (wrongful-death action and survivor action can be consolidated under §1048 when actions arise from same wrongful act or neglect); ***Martin-Bragg v. Moore*** (2d Dist.2013) 219 Cal.App.4th 367, 385 (trial court has power to consolidate unlawful-detainer proceeding with quiet-title action involving same property because successful claim of title by tenant would defeat landlord's right to possession); ***Sanchez v. Superior Ct.*** (6th Dist.1988) 203 Cal.App.3d 1391, 1395 (cases arising from same car accident were ordered consolidated for trial). The more predominant and significant the common questions are to the litigation, the more likely the motion will be granted. *See CEB Procedure Before Trial*, §43.36 (coordination factors can be persuasive in arguing for consolidation); Thomas, *Courtroom Handbook*, §14.47 (same); *cf.* CCP §404.1 (factors considered for coordination). Common questions of fact generally present a more compelling case for consolidation than common questions of law. *CEB Procedure Before Trial*, §43.33.

3. Consolidation beneficial. The movant should establish that the benefits of consolidation outweigh the burdens. *See CEB Procedure Before Trial*, §43.32; *cf.* ***Hendrix v. Raybestos-Manhattan, Inc.*** (11th Cir.1985) 776 F.2d 1492, 1495 (interpreting basis for consolidation under FRCP 42(a)); ***Arnold v. Eastern Air Lines, Inc.*** (4th Cir.1982) 681 F.2d 186, 193 (same). To establish this, the movant should argue that consolidation will do one or more of the following:

(1) Save time (i.e., the length of time to conclude one suit versus multiple suits). *See* CCP §1048(a); *CEB Procedure Before Trial*, §43.33.

(2) Save money. *See* CCP §1048(a); *CEB Procedure Before Trial*, §43.33.

(3) Help prevent the inconsistent adjudication of common factual and legal issues. *See CEB Procedure Before Trial*, §43.36 (coordination factors can be persuasive in arguing for consolidation); Thomas, *Courtroom Handbook*, §14.47 (same); *cf.* CCP §404.1 (factors considered for coordination).

(4) Lessen the burden on judicial resources. *See CEB Procedure Before Trial*, §43.36 (coordination factors can be persuasive in arguing for consolidation); Thomas, *Courtroom Handbook*, §14.47 (same); *cf.* CCP §404.1 (factors considered for coordination).

(5) Promote the convenience of the parties, witnesses, and attorneys. *See CEB Procedure Before Trial*, §43.36 (coordination factors can be persuasive in arguing for consolidation); Thomas, *Courtroom Handbook*, §14.47 (same); *cf.* CCP §404.1 (factors considered for coordination).

(6) Encourage settlement. *See CEB Procedure Before Trial*, §43.36 (coordination factors can be persuasive in arguing for consolidation); Thomas, *Courtroom Handbook*, §14.47 (same); *cf.* CCP §404.1 (factors considered for coordination).

(7) Avoid prejudice. *See, e.g.,* ***Martin-Bragg***, 219 Cal.App.4th at 370-71 (trial court's refusal to consolidate cases prejudiced D by denying opportunity for discovery and forcing litigation of complex issue in summary proceeding).

§4.2 Motion.

1. Who can file. A party or the court on its own motion can make a motion to consolidate. *See* CCP §1048(a); *see, e.g.,* ***Nissan Motor Corp. v. Superior Ct.*** (4th Dist.1992) 6 Cal.App.4th 150, 153 (court ordered consolidation of three actions on its own motion); ***Sanchez v. Superior Ct.*** (6th Dist.1988) 203 Cal.App.3d 1391, 1395 (Ps filed noticed motion to consolidate two actions).

PRACTICE TIP

Instead of filing a motion to consolidate, a party can submit to the court a stipulation to consolidate if all parties consent to the consolidation either orally or in writing. CEB Procedure Before Trial, §43.48; see ***Sutter Health Uninsured Pricing Cases*** *(3d Dist.2009) 171 Cal.App.4th*

495, 514 (if there is no stipulation, party must file noticed motion); Kiesel, Cal. Pretrial Civil Procedure, §32.27 (sample form for written stipulation to consolidate for all purposes), §32.30 (sample form for written stipulation to consolidate for trial); see, e.g., ***Phillips v. Beilsten*** *(2d Dist.1958) 164 Cal.App.2d 450, 454 (attorneys for parties presented judge with written stipulation proposing consolidation of two actions for trial).*

2. Deadline to file & serve. The notice of motion and motion must be filed in the court and served on all parties in each case sought to be consolidated at least 16 court days before the hearing on the motion. *See* CCP §1005(b); CRC 3.350(a)(2)(B). See "Retrospective deadlines," ch. 1-G, §6.2, p. 71. If the motion is served by means other than personal delivery, the movant will need to add more time to the 16-day period (e.g., five calendar days are added when notice is mailed to California address). CCP §1005(b). See "Add time for method of service," ch. 1-G, §6.2.1(5), p. 72.

NOTE

Other than the general deadline for noticed motions, there is no deadline for filing a motion to consolidate. See CCP §1048(a); Younger, Cal. Motions, §§22:27, 22:30. But a delay in making the motion can undermine the argument that consolidation would promote judicial economy. See Thomas, Courtroom Handbook, §14:45. See "Consolidation beneficial," §4.1.3, p. 524.

3. Where to file. The notice of motion and motion must be filed in the court where each case sought to be consolidated is pending. *See* CRC 3.350(a)(1)(C), 3.350(a)(2)(C). But memorandums, declarations, and other supporting papers must be filed only in the lowest-numbered case. CRC 3.350(a)(2)(A).

4. Contents.

(1) Notice of motion & motion. The motion should be made in writing by noticed motion. ***Sutter Health Uninsured***, 171 Cal.App.4th at 514; *see* CRC 3.350; *see, e.g.*, ***Sanchez***, 203 Cal.App.3d at 1395 (Ps filed noticed motion to consolidate two actions). See "Notice of motion & motion," ch. 1-D, §5.1, p. 28. The motion should contain the following information:

(a) Relief. The notice of motion and motion should briefly state the relief sought (e.g., "Defendant asks the Court for an order consolidating Case No. 1234 with Case No. 1236 for all purposes as permitted under Code of Civil Procedure Section 1048(a)"). *See* CRC 3.1110(a), 3.1112(d)(3); *see, e.g.*, ***Stubblefield Constr. Co. v. City of San Bernardino*** (4th Dist.1995) 32 Cal.App.4th 687, 702 (P's motion asked court to consolidate cases for trial). The motion can request the following types of consolidation:

[1] Consolidation for all purposes. The motion can ask the court to consolidate cases for all purposes. ***Hamilton v. Asbestos Corp.*** (2000) 22 Cal.4th 1127, 1147; *see* CCP §1048(a). If the cases are consolidated for all purposes, (1) the cases are merged into a single proceeding under one case number, (2) all the allegations in the various complaints are taken together and treated as one pleading, and (3) there is only one verdict or set of findings and one judgment. *See* ***Hamilton***, 22 Cal.4th at 1147; ***Syngenta Crop Prot., Inc. v. Helliker*** (2d Dist.2006) 138 Cal.App.4th 1135, 1150 n.3.

[2] Consolidation for trial. The motion can ask the court to consolidate cases for purposes of trial. ***Stubblefield Constr.***, 32 Cal.App.4th at 701; *see* CCP §1048(a). If the cases are consolidated for trial, each case retains its separate identity—that is, the pleadings, verdicts, findings, and judgments are kept separate. *See* ***Sanchez***, 203 Cal.App.3d at 1396; ***Mueller v. J.C. Penney Co.*** (4th Dist.1985) 173 Cal.App.3d 713, 722. The cases are simply tried together, and the evidence presented in one case will be applied to the other case, if relevant. ***Stubblefield Constr.***, 32 Cal.App.4th at 701; *see* ***Mueller***, 173 Cal.App.3d at 722 (party does not lose right to examine witnesses just because actions are consolidated for trial).

[3] Consolidation for discovery or pretrial matters. The motion can ask the court to consolidate cases for purposes of discovery or for specific pretrial matters. *See* CCP §1048(a) (can order joint hearings of any matters in issue in the actions); *CEB Procedure Before Trial*, §43.54 (can consolidate selected pretrial

proceedings); Younger, *Cal. Motions*, §22:4 (can consolidate for purpose of trial preparation); *see, e.g.*, ***State v. Altus Fin., S.A.*** (2005) 36 Cal.4th 1284, 1293 (cases consolidated for discovery and pretrial matters); ***Austin B. v. Escondido Un. Sch. Dist.*** (4th Dist.2007) 149 Cal.App.4th 860, 870 (cases consolidated for discovery and trial); ***Frieman v. San Rafael Rock Quarry, Inc.*** (1st Dist.2004) 116 Cal.App.4th 29, 33 (cases consolidated for discovery and pretrial determinations).

(b) Grounds. The notice of motion and motion should briefly state the grounds for the motion (e.g., "the motion will be made on the grounds that the cases are pending before this Court, the cases involve a common question of fact, and consolidation will avoid unnecessary costs and delay"). *See* CRC 3.1110(a), 3.1112(d)(3). See "Movant's burden," §4.1, p. 523.

(c) Case information. For each case sought to be consolidated, the motion must contain the following information:

[1] The caption (i.e., the case's title, the court's name, and the county where the case is pending) and case number. *See* CRC 3.350(a)(1)(B); *see also* CCP §422.30 (information included in caption). The lowest-numbered case must be listed first. CRC 3.350(a)(1)(B).

[2] The named parties. CRC 3.350(a)(1)(A).

[3] The parties that have appeared. *Id.*

[4] The attorneys of record. *Id.*

(2) Memorandum of points & authorities. The motion must include a memorandum in support of the motion. CRC 3.1112(a)(3). See "Memorandum of points & authorities," ch. 1-D, §5.2, p. 28.

(3) Supporting evidence. The motion can include supporting evidence. CRC 3.1112(b). See "Supporting evidence," ch. 1-D, §5.3, p. 30.

(4) Proof of service. The motion must include proof of service. CRC 3.350(a)(2)(C). See "Proof of service," ch. 1-D, §5.6, p. 33.

(5) Proposed order. The motion can include a proposed order. *See* CRC 3.1113(m). If a proposed order is submitted, it must be lodged and served with the motion papers, not attached to them. *Id.* See "Documents lodged," ch. 1-F, §2.3, p. 47.

5. Filing fees. When the motion is filed, the movant must pay a filing fee to the court clerk or request a waiver of the fee. See "Filing Fees," ch. 1-F, §7, p. 58. Although a motion to consolidate is filed in each case sought to be consolidated, it is deemed a single motion for the purpose of determining the appropriate filing fee. CRC 3.350(a)(2)(A).

NOTE

If the motion to consolidate seeks to consolidate a limited case with an unlimited case, local rules may require the limited case to be reclassified as unlimited before the cases can be consolidated, along with payment of a reclassification fee. E.g., Super. Ct. Los Angeles Cty. Loc. R., rule 3.3(g)(3). See "Procedural Classifications of Civil Cases," ch. 3-E, §4, p. 255.

---

§4.3 Opposition. The nonmovant can respond to a motion to consolidate by filing an opposition.

1. Deadline to file & serve. The opposition must be filed and served at least nine court days before the hearing. CCP §1005(b). See "Filing & serving opposition," ch. 1-D, §8.5, p. 36.

2. Grounds. The nonmovant can oppose the motion to consolidate on any of the following grounds:

(1) Cases pending in different courts. The motion can be opposed on the ground that the cases sought to be consolidated are pending in different superior courts (i.e., different counties). See "Cases pending in same court," §4.1.1, p. 523.

(2) No common question of law or fact. The motion can be opposed on the ground that the cases sought to be consolidated do not involve a common question of law or fact. *See* ***Sosnick v. Sosnick*** (1st Dist.1999) 71 Cal.App.4th 1335, 1339-40 (court exceeded jurisdiction by granting husband's motion to consolidate tort action with divorce proceeding when no question of law or fact was pending in divorce proceeding). See "Cases have common question of law or fact," §4.1.2, p. 524.

(3) Consolidation burdensome. The motion can be opposed on the ground that the burdens of consolidation outweigh any benefits. Possible arguments include the following:

(a) Unconstitutionally complex. The nonmovant can argue that consolidation will violate its right to due process by creating an overly complex case that would be too difficult and confusing for the jury to comprehend. *See CEB Procedure Before Trial*, §43.21; *see, e.g.*, ***Todd-Stenberg v. Dalkon Shield Claimants Trust*** (1st Dist.1996) 48 Cal.App.4th 976, 978-79 (D argued on appeal that consolidation caused jury confusion and thus violated its right to due process).

(b) Prejudice. The nonmovant can argue that consolidation will prejudice the nonmovant in one or more of the following ways:

[1] Inconsistent arguments. Consolidation will force the nonmovant to make inconsistent arguments. *See, e.g.*, ***State Farm Mut. Auto. Ins. v. Superior Ct.*** (1956) 47 Cal.2d 428, 430-31 (order consolidating declaratory-relief action and personal-injury action would have forced insurance company to make inconsistent arguments about status of passengers in car accident).

[2] Undesirable coparty. Consolidation will force the nonmovant to share a side with an undesirable coparty. Younger, *Cal. Motions*, §22:37; *cf.* ***People v. Massie*** (1967) 66 Cal.2d 899, 916-17 (prejudicial association with co-D is factor court should consider when deciding whether to order separate trials of co-Ds under Pen. C. §1098).

[3] Inordinate expense. Consolidation will cause a party with a relatively small case to incur a substantial increase in discovery or trial expenses. Younger, *Cal. Motions*, §22:37.

[4] Cases in different stages of preparedness. Consolidation will combine cases that are at different stages of trial preparedness. *CEB Procedure Before Trial*, §43.34; *cf.* CRC 3.521(d) (imminence of trial in case otherwise appropriate for coordination can be ground for denial of coordination motion). This could be prejudicial to a party in a case that was ready for trial because consolidation with a new case would likely cause delay and an inequitable discrepancy in work product. *See* Younger, *Cal. Motions*, §22:6; *cf.* CCP §404.1 (court considers relative development of cases and work product when ruling on coordination motion). It could also be prejudicial to a party in a relatively new case because the party might be rushed into trial. *See* Younger, *Cal. Motions*, §22:6.

[5] Undesirable evidence. Consolidation will result in the admission of evidence that would not otherwise be admissible. *CEB Procedure Before Trial*, §43.34; *see, e.g.*, ***Johnson v. Western Air Express Corp.*** (2d Dist.1941) 45 Cal.App.2d 614, 621-22 (Ps argued that evidence of earning capacity presented during consolidated trials, admissible only in personal-injury action, prejudiced their wrongful-death action).

NOTE

The court can minimize the prejudicial effect of undesirable evidence with a carefully crafted jury instruction. See, e.g., ***Johnson****, 45 Cal.App.2d at 623-24 (jury instruction told jurors to disregard evidence of earning potential when assessing damages for wrongful-death action).*

[6] Loss of summary procedures. Consolidation will deny a party's right to summary procedures. *See, e.g.*, ***Martin-Bragg v. Moore*** (2d Dist.2013) 219 Cal.App.4th 367, 389 (court denied tenant's motion to consolidate unlawful-detainer proceeding with quiet-title action because consolidation would deny landlord's right to expedited summary procedures of unlawful-detainer law).

3. Contents. See "Opposition Papers," ch. 1-D, §8, p. 35.

§4.4 Reply. The movant can file and serve a reply to opposition papers. The reply must be filed and served at least five court days before the hearing. CCP §1005(b). See "Reply Papers," ch. 1-D, §9, p. 37.

§4.5 Hearing. Hearings on a motion to consolidate are conducted in the same manner as civil hearings generally. See "Hearings," ch. 1-H, p. 79.

§4.6 Ruling.

1. Standard for granting. The court's decision to grant or deny a motion to consolidate is within the court's discretion. ***Hamilton v. Asbestos Corp.*** (2000) 22 Cal.4th 1127, 1149; *see* CCP §1048(a) (court "may" order consolidation); ***Todd-Stenberg v. Dalkon Shield Claimants Trust*** (1st Dist.1996) 48 Cal.App.4th 976, 978-79 (ruling not disturbed on appeal unless clear abuse of discretion).

2. Court's guidelines.

(1) Common issue of law or fact. The court must find that the cases involve a common question of law or fact before it can consolidate them. *CEB Procedure Before Trial*, §43.31; *see* CCP §1048(a); *see, e.g.*, ***Martin-Bragg v. Moore*** (2d Dist.2013) 219 Cal.App.4th 367, 385 (trial court has power to consolidate unlawful-detainer proceeding with quiet-title action involving same property because successful claim of title by tenant would defeat landlord's right to possession); ***Todd-Stenberg***, 48 Cal.App.4th at 979 (trial court correctly ruled that there were common questions of fact between product-liability cases when all cases would require substantial time explaining how disease occurs, whether product can cause disease, and other factors that can cause disease). See "Cases have common question of law or fact," §4.1.2, p. 524.

(2) Balancing test. If the court finds that there are common issues of law or fact, the court must then determine if the benefits of consolidation outweigh the burdens. *CEB Procedure Before Trial*, §43.32. See "Consolidation beneficial," §4.1.3, p. 524; "Consolidation burdensome," §4.3.2(3), p. 527. If the court finds that a party would be unduly prejudiced or that the jury would be unduly confused, it must deny the motion unless it can order conditions or protections to prevent the prejudice or confusion. *See, e.g.*, ***State Farm Mut. Auto. Ins. v. Superior Ct.*** (1956) 47 Cal.2d 428, 430-31 (trial court abused discretion when consolidation forced P to make inconsistent arguments, alerted jury that insurance coverage was available in personal-injury action, and unduly confused jury with different tests for similar determination); ***Martin-Bragg***, 219 Cal.App.4th at 389 (trial court had discretion to fashion conditions and limitations to protect party's interest in preserving summary procedures); ***Todd-Stenberg***, 48 Cal.App.4th at 980 (trial court correctly found that there was no undue prejudice or confusion from consolidation when there were only three Ps, evidence for each P was carefully presented, and different verdict amounts showed that jury distinguished between Ps).

§4.7 Order.

1. Form. The court's ruling on the motion to consolidate must be recorded in writing. *See* CRC 3.350(c) (order must be filed in all cases). See "Written order," ch. 1-I, §4.2, p. 91.

2. Contents. If the motion for consolidation is granted, the order should specify (1) the lead case, (2) the cases being consolidated into the lead case, and (3) the type of consolidation granted. *See* CRC 3.350(b) (lowest-numbered case is lead case unless order provides otherwise); Kiesel, *Cal. Pretrial Civil Procedure*, §32.29 (sample order consolidating cases for all purposes), §32.32 (sample order consolidating cases for trial). See "Relief," §4.2.4(1)(a), p. 525. The order can also include conditions or protections to prevent costs, delay, or prejudice. *See* CCP §1048(a) (court can make orders to avoid unnecessary costs or delay); *CEB Procedure Before Trial*, §43.58 (court can protect parties from prejudice by making rulings ancillary to consolidation).

3. Filing. The order granting or denying all or part of the motion must be filed in each case sought to be consolidated. CRC 3.350(c).

4. Effect of order.

(1) Generally.

(a) Lead case. If the motion is granted, the lowest-numbered case among the consolidated cases becomes the lead case unless the order provides otherwise. CRC 3.350(b).

(b) Caption & case numbers. If the motion is granted, all filed documents must include the caption and case number of the lead case, followed by the case numbers of all the other consolidated cases. CRC 3.350(d).

(2) Consolidation for all purposes.

(a) Filing documents. If a motion to consolidate for all purposes is granted, all later documents must be filed only in the lead case. CRC 3.350(c). See "Consolidation for all purposes," §4.2.4(1)(a)[1], p. 525; "Lead case," §4.7.4(1)(a), p. 528.

(b) General appearance. If a motion to consolidate for all purposes is granted, a general appearance in one consolidated case constitutes a general appearance in all consolidated cases. *See, e.g.*, ***Hamilton v. Asbestos Corp.*** (2000) 22 Cal.4th 1127, 1148-49 (D's general appearance in one case was general appearance in all consolidated cases because cases were consolidated for all purposes); ***Sanchez v. Superior Ct.*** (6th Dist.1988) 203 Cal.App.3d 1391, 1395-96 (D's general appearance in first case was not general appearance in second case because cases were consolidated for trial only). See "Examples – general appearance," ch. 3-G, §5.1.1(2)(a), p. 285.

(c) Pleadings & judgments. See "Consolidation for all purposes," §4.2.4(1)(a)[1], p. 525.

(3) Consolidation for trial. See "Consolidation for trial," §4.2.4(1)(a)[2], p. 525.

(4) Consolidation for discovery or pretrial matters. See "Consolidation for discovery or pretrial matters," §4.2.4(1)(a)[3], p. 525.

§4.8 Motion for reconsideration. A party adversely affected by a court's order on a motion to consolidate can file a motion for reconsideration. CCP §1008(a). See "Motion for Reconsideration," ch. 5-G, §3, p. 508.

§4.9 Motion for renewal. A party whose motion to consolidate is denied can file a motion for renewal. *See* CCP §1008(b). See "Motion for Renewal," ch. 5-G, §4, p. 516.

§4.10 Appellate review.

1. Writ of mandate. An order on a motion to consolidate can be reviewed by writ of mandate. *See* ***State Farm Mut. Auto. Ins. v. Superior Ct.*** (1956) 47 Cal.2d 428, 432 (party was entitled to writ of mandate to sever improperly consolidated cases).

2. Direct appeal. An order on a motion to consolidate is not appealable until the court enters a final judgment in the case. ***State Farm***, 47 Cal.2d at 432; *see* CCP §§904.1(a), 904.2. A trial court's ruling on a motion to consolidate is reviewed for abuse of discretion. ***Todd-Stenberg v. Dalkon Shield Claimants Trust*** (1st Dist.1996) 48 Cal.App.4th 976, 978-79.

§5. COORDINATING NONCOMPLEX CASES

When noncomplex cases involving a common question of law or fact are pending in different superior courts (i.e., different counties), a judge in one court can transfer the cases to her court on a party's motion to transfer for coordination. *See* CCP §403. Once the cases are transferred, the judge can consolidate the cases for trial as permitted under CCP §1048. *Id.* §403.

NOTE

The procedure for coordinating noncomplex cases is very different from the procedure for coordinating complex cases. To coordinate complex cases, a party must file a petition for coordination with the Chairperson of the Judicial Council ("Chief Justice"). CCP §404. The coordination of complex cases is governed by CCP §§404-404.9 and CRC 3.501-3.550.

§5.1 Movant's burden. To prevail on a motion to transfer for coordination, the movant must establish the following:

1. Cases pending in different courts. The movant must establish that the cases sought to be coordinated are pending in different superior courts. *See* CCP §403; *CEB Procedure Before Trial*, §44.7.

2. Cases not complex. The movant must establish that the cases sought to be coordinated are not complex. CCP §403; CRC 3.500(c)(1); *see CEB Procedure Before Trial*, §44.42 (sample motion to transfer case for coordination); *see also* CRC 3.400(a) (definition of "complex case"), CRC 3.400(b) (factors used to determine if case is complex). See "Complexity," ch. 5-A, §5.2.2, p. 465.

3. Cases have common question of law or fact. The movant must establish that the cases sought to be coordinated share a common question of law or fact. *See* CCP §§403, 404. Common questions of law or fact can arise in cases that share common parties and involve a common transaction (e.g., contract) or incident (e.g., automobile accident). *Cf. id.* §377.62(b) (wrongful-death action and survivor action can be consolidated under CCP §1048 when actions arise from same wrongful act or neglect).

4. Coordination just. The movant must establish that coordination will promote the interests of justice. *See* CCP §§403, 404.1. To establish this, the movant should argue one or more of the following:

(1) The common question of law or fact is predominant and significant to the litigation. *See* CCP §§403, 404.1; *cf.* ***McGhan Med. Corp. v. Superior Ct.*** (4th Dist.1992) 11 Cal.App.4th 804, 814 (complex case; coordination was proper when all complaints alleged damages as result of same product defect related to breast-implant devices and most complaints alleged that causes of action were similar).

(2) Coordination is convenient for the parties, witnesses, and attorneys. *See* CCP §§403, 404.1.

(3) The cases are at approximately the same stage of development and the work product of the attorneys is about equal. *See* CCP §§403, 404.1; *cf.* ***Farmers Ins. Exch. v. Superior Ct.*** (1st Dist.1992) 10 Cal.App.4th 1509, 1511 (complex case; "relative development" of case, including nature and extent of pretrial rulings, is factor to be considered).

(4) Coordination will lessen the burden on judicial resources. *See* CCP §§403, 404.1.

(5) Coordination will reduce the risk of duplicative and inconsistent rulings, orders, or judgments. *See id.* §§403, 404.1.

(6) If coordination is denied, the likelihood of settlement without further litigation is low. *See id.* §§403, 404.1.

5. Good-faith effort to obtain agreement. The movant must establish that it made a good-faith effort to get all parties from each case to agree to the transfer. CCP §403; CRC 3.500(b), 3.500(c)(2).

6. Notice of duty to disclose. The movant must establish that it informed the parties of their duty to disclose to the court any information they may have about any other motions to transfer that would be affected if the court granted its motion. CRC 3.500(c)(3).

CAUTION

If the court determines that a party did not disclose information to the court about other pending transfer requests, the court may, after providing notice and a hearing, find the party in criminal contempt for unlawful interference with the processes of the court. CEB Procedure Before Trial, §44.13; see CCP §1209(a)(9); CRC 3.500(g).

§5.2 Motion.

1. Who can file. Any party can file a motion to transfer for coordination. *See* CCP §403. The court cannot make a motion to transfer for coordination on its own initiative. Weil, *Civil Procedure Before Trial*, ¶12:405.5; *see* CCP §403.

2. Deadline to file & serve. The notice of motion and motion must be filed in the court and served on all parties in each case sought to be coordinated and on each court where the cases are pending at least 16 court days before the hearing on the motion. *See* CCP §§403, 1005(b); CRC 3.500(c). See "Retrospective deadlines," ch. 1-G,

§6.2, p. 71. If the motion is served by means other than personal delivery, the movant will need to add more time to the 16-day period (e.g., five calendar days are added when notice is mailed to California address). CCP §1005(b). See "Add time for method of service," ch. 1-G, §6.2.1(5), p. 72.

3. Contents.

(1) Notice of motion & motion. The motion must be made in writing by noticed motion. *See* CCP §403; CRC 3.500(c). See "Notice of motion & motion," ch. 1-D, §5.1, p. 28.

(a) Relief. The notice of motion and motion should briefly state the relief sought (e.g., "Plaintiff asks the Court for an order transferring Smith v. Jones, Case No. 1234, Alameda County Superior Court, to this Court for coordination with cases listed in the attached declaration as permitted under Code of Civil Procedure Section 403"). *See* CCP §403; CRC 3.1110(a), 3.1112(d)(3); *see, e.g.*, *CEB Procedure Before Trial*, §44.42 (sample notice of motion).

(b) Grounds. The notice of motion and motion should briefly state the grounds for the motion (e.g., "the motion will be made on the grounds that the cases involve a common question of law or fact, the cases are not complex and are pending in different courts of this state, the movant has made a good-faith effort to have the parties agree to the transfer, and coordination will promote the interests of justice"). *See* CCP §§403, 404, 404.1; CRC 3.1110(a), 3.1112(d)(3); *see, e.g.*, Kiesel, *Cal. Pretrial Civil Procedure*, §32.33 (sample notice of motion). See "Movant's burden," §5.1, p. 529.

(2) Memorandum of points & authorities. The motion must include a memorandum in support of the motion. CRC 3.1112(a)(3). See "Memorandum of points & authorities," ch. 1-D, §5.2, p. 28.

(3) Movant's declaration. The motion must include a declaration in support of the motion. CCP §403; CRC 3.500(c). See "Declarations," ch. 1-D, §5.3.1, p. 31.

(a) Court & party information. For each case sought to be transferred, the declaration should include the following information:

[1] The caption (i.e., the case's title, the court's name, and the county where the case is pending) and case number. *See, e.g.*, *CEB Procedure Before Trial*, §44.43 (sample declaration); Kiesel, *Cal. Pretrial Civil Procedure*, §32.33 (same); *cf.* CRC 3.521(a)(4) (petition for coordination in complex cases).

[2] The named parties. *See, e.g.*, *CEB Procedure Before Trial*, §44.43 (sample declaration); Kiesel, *Cal. Pretrial Civil Procedure*, §32.33 (same); *cf.* CRC 3.521(a)(2) (petition for coordination in complex cases).

[3] The name and address of each party's attorney of record. *See, e.g.*, *CEB Procedure Before Trial*, §44.43 (sample declaration); Kiesel, *Cal. Pretrial Civil Procedure*, §32.33 (same); *cf.* CRC 3.521(a)(2) (petition for coordination in complex cases).

[4] The status of the case, including the status of any pretrial or discovery motions or orders that are known to the declarant. *See, e.g.*, *CEB Procedure Before Trial*, §44.43 (sample declaration); Kiesel, *Cal. Pretrial Civil Procedure*, §32.33 (same); *cf.* CRC 3.521(a)(6) (petition for coordination in complex cases).

(b) Declaration about other pending cases. The declaration should include a statement by the declarant that she either (1) knows of no other cases pending in California that share a common question of law or fact with the case or (2) knows of another case pending in California that shares a common question of law or fact but is not included in the motion for specified reasons. *See, e.g.*, *CEB Procedure Before Trial*, §44.43 (sample declaration); Kiesel, *Cal. Pretrial Civil Procedure*, §32.33 (same); *cf.* CRC 3.521(a)(5) (petition for coordination in complex cases).

(c) Facts supporting motion. The declaration must include facts that show the following:

[1] The cases meet the standards for coordination under CCP §404.1. CCP §403; *see, e.g.*, *CEB Procedure Before Trial*, §44.43 (sample declaration); Kiesel, *Cal. Pretrial Civil Procedure*, §32.33 (same). See "Coordination just," §5.1.4, p. 530.

[2] The cases are not complex. CCP §403; CRC 3.500(c)(1); *see, e.g.*, *CEB Procedure Before Trial*, §44.43 (sample declaration); Kiesel, *Cal. Pretrial Civil Procedure*, §32.33 (same). See "Cases not complex," §5.1.2, p. 530.

[3] The movant has made a good-faith effort to obtain agreement to the transfer and consolidation from all parties to each case. CCP §403; CRC 3.500(c)(2); *see, e.g.*, *CEB Procedure Before Trial*, §44.43 (sample declaration); Kiesel, *Cal. Pretrial Civil Procedure*, §32.33 (same).

[4] The movant has notified all parties to each case of their obligation to disclose to the court any information they may have about any other motions requesting transfer of any case that would be affected by the granting of the motion. CRC 3.500(c)(3); *see, e.g.*, *CEB Procedure Before Trial*, §44.43 (sample declaration); Kiesel, *Cal. Pretrial Civil Procedure*, §32.33 (same).

(4) Other supporting evidence. The motion can include other supporting evidence. See "Supporting evidence," ch. 1-D, §5.3, p. 30.

(5) Proposed order. The motion can include a proposed order. *See* CRC 3.1113(m). If a proposed order is submitted, it must be lodged and served with the motion papers, not attached to them. *Id.* See "Documents lodged," ch. 1-F, §2.3, p. 47.

4. Filing fees. When the motion is filed, the movant must pay a filing fee to the court clerk or request a waiver of the fee. See "Filing Fees," ch. 1-F, §7, p. 58.

§5.3 Opposition. A party can respond to a motion to transfer for coordination by filing an opposition. CCP §403. The opposition must be filed and served at least nine court days before the hearing. *Id.* §1005(b). See "Opposition Papers," ch. 1-D, §8, p. 35.

§5.4 Reply. The movant can file and serve a reply to opposition papers. The reply must be filed and served at least five court days before the hearing. CCP §1005(b). See "Reply Papers," ch. 1-D, §9, p. 37.

§5.5 Hearing. Hearings on a motion to transfer for coordination are conducted in the same manner as civil hearings generally. *See* CRC 3.500(c) (motion to transfer under CCP §403 must conform to requirements generally applicable to motions). See "Hearings," ch. 1-H, p. 79.

§5.6 Ruling. The court's decision to grant or deny a motion to transfer for coordination is within the court's discretion. *See* CCP §403 (court "may" transfer action for coordination).

§5.7 Order.

1. Form. The court's ruling on a motion to transfer for coordination must be recorded either in writing or by minute order. See "Record of Ruling," ch. 1-I, §4, p. 90.

2. Contents.

(1) Motion denied. If the motion is denied, the court can order the parties to prepare, serve, and file a motion to have the cases transferred to another, more appropriate court for consolidation. CRC 3.500(h).

(2) Motion granted. If the court grants the motion, the order should include the following:

(a) Reasons coordination just. The order must state the reasons supporting the finding that the transfer will promote the interests of justice. CRC 3.500(d). The reasons must refer to the factors specified under CCP §404.1 and the fact that the cases are not complex. *See* CCP §404.1; CRC 3.500(d). See "Coordination just," §5.1.4, p. 530.

(b) Identify coordinated actions. The order should identify the cases transferred by title, case number, and court. *See, e.g.*, Kiesel, *Cal. Pretrial Civil Procedure*, §32.34 (sample order).

3. Service. If the court grants the motion, the movant must serve a copy of the order on the following:

(1) All the parties to each case. CRC 3.500(e).

(2) The Judicial Council. *Id.*

(3) The presiding judge of the court where each case to be transferred is pending. *Id.*

4. Effect of order.

(1) On consolidation. If the motion is granted, the court can consolidate the cases under CCP §1048(a). CCP §403. The court can consolidate the cases without any further motion or hearing. *Id.* The movant has the responsibility, however, to take all appropriate action necessary to ensure that (1) the transfer takes place and (2) proceedings are initiated to complete the consolidation. CRC 3.500(f). See "Consolidating Cases," §4, p. 522.

NOTE

It is unclear under CCP §399(a) whether fees and costs have to be paid when cases are transferred for purposes of coordination and, if so, who pays them. Although §399(a) states that fees and costs have to be paid when an order transferring a case is made under "any of the provisions of this title," §399(a) does not discuss who is liable for fees and costs when a transfer is made for purposes of coordination.

(2) On conflicting orders. If the motion is granted but the transfer order conflicts with another transfer order for coordination from a different court, the Administrative Office of the Courts will notify the presiding judges of the courts that issued the conflicting orders. CRC 3.500(g). The presiding judges of those courts must then confer with each other and with the judges who issued the conflicting orders to resolve the conflict. *Id.*

§5.8 Motion for reconsideration. A party adversely affected by a court's order on a motion to transfer for coordination can file a motion for reconsideration. CCP §1008(a). See "Motion for Reconsideration," ch. 5-G, §3, p. 508.

§5.9 Motion for renewal. A party whose motion to transfer for coordination is denied can file a motion for renewal. *See* CCP §1008(b). See "Motion for Renewal," ch. 5-G, §4, p. 516.

§5.10 Appellate review.

1. Writ of mandate. An order on a motion to transfer for coordination can be reviewed by a petition for a writ of mandate. *See* CCP §1085; *cf. id.* §404.6 (complex cases; writ of mandate available to review order on petition to coordinate); ***Lautrup, Inc. v. Trans-W. Disc. Corp.*** (2d Dist.1976) 64 Cal.App.3d 316, 317 (complex case; mandate is appropriate way to seek review of order denying coordination).

2. Direct appeal. An order on a motion to transfer for coordination is not appealable until the court enters a final judgment in the case. *See* CCP §904.1(a); *cf.* ***Lautrup, Inc.***, 64 Cal.App.3d at 317 (complex case).

3. Standard of review. A trial court's ruling on a motion to transfer for coordination is reviewed under two different standards. *Cf.* ***McGhan Med. Corp. v. Superior Ct.*** (4th Dist.1992) 11 Cal.App.4th 804, 809 (complex case). The court's identification of the common questions of law or fact is a question of fact that will be reviewed for abuse of discretion. *Cf. id.* at 809-10 (complex case). The court's selection of the appropriate law to apply and whether coordination would promote the interests of justice are questions of law that are reviewed de novo. *Cf. id.* at 809-10 (complex case).

I. REQUESTS FOR CONTINUANCE OR STAY

This subchapter discusses requests for continuance or stay in civil actions generally. For a list of special statutes providing for continuances in particular actions or proceedings, see 7 Witkin, *California Procedure* (5th ed. 2008 & Supp.2014) Trial, §31.

§1. GENERAL

§1.1 Purpose. The purpose of a request for continuance or stay is to postpone or suspend proceedings in a civil action. *See* CRC 3.1332(b); *see, e.g.*, ***Firestone v. Hoffman*** (2d Dist.2006) 140 Cal.App.4th 1408, 1413 (request for continuance of trial date); ***Lerma v. County of Orange*** (4th Dist.2004) 120 Cal.App.4th 709, 713 (request for continuance of hearing date); ***Pacers, Inc. v. Superior Ct.*** (4th Dist.1984) 162 Cal.App.3d 686, 690-91 (motion to stay discovery pending criminal proceeding).

§1.2 Primary authority. CCP §§437c(h), 473, 594a, 595, 595.2, 595.4; Mil. & Vet. C. §403; CRC 3.1332; 50 U.S.C. app. §522; ***Smith v. Jones*** (1900) 128 Cal. 14, 15.

§1.3 Secondary authority. The following secondary sources are cited as authority in this subchapter:

- Kiesel et al., *Matthew Bender Practice Guide: California Pretrial Civil Procedure* (2014) (referred to as Kiesel, *Cal. Pretrial Civil Procedure*).
- Sullivan, *A Judge's Guide to the Servicemembers Civil Relief Act* (2007), www.oregon.gov/OMD/JAG/docs/SCRA_ENCL_4_Judges_Guide.pdf?ga=t.
- Weil & Brown, *California Practice Guide: Civil Procedure Before Trial* (CD-ROM ed. 2014) (referred to as Weil, *Civil Procedure Before Trial*).
- Witkin, *California Procedure* (5th ed. 2008 & Supp.2014) (referred to as Witkin, *Cal. Procedure*).

§2. CONTINUANCE

Some statutes provide specific grounds for a continuance, but as one commentator has noted, "there is no comprehensive statutory coverage of the subject." 7 Witkin, *Cal. Procedure*, Trial, §8; *see also* Weil, *Civil Procedure Before Trial*, ¶9:116.1 (procedures for obtaining continuance of hearing varies among courts). The following are some of the most common grounds for requesting a continuance of a hearing or a trial date.

§2.1 Agreement.

1. Continuing hearing date. Under most courts' local rules and CCP §595.2, a party can request a continuance of a hearing by agreement.

(1) Movant's burden. To continue a hearing based on the parties' agreement, the movant (i.e., the party seeking the continuance) should consult the court's local rules. Although CCP §595.2 permits parties to agree to continue a hearing, some courts may require additional support for the continuance such as good cause. *Compare* Super. Ct. Butte Cty. Loc. R., rule 2.8(a) (good cause not required if stipulated continuance is requested before close of business on third court day before hearing) *with* Super. Ct. Monterey Cty. Loc. R., rule 7.04 (continuance will not be granted without showing of good cause), Super. Ct. Sacramento Cty. Loc. R., rule 2.30(C) (same), *and* Super. Ct. Santa Barbara Cty. Loc. R., rule 1001 (continuances will not be granted solely on basis of stipulation). See "Good cause," §2.2, p. 536. Some courts may also restrict the number of agreed continuances or impose a greater burden when more than one agreed continuance is requested. *E.g.*, Super. Ct. Butte Cty. Loc. R., rule 2.8(b) (after second stipulated continuance, parties must obtain court order for additional continuances); Super. Ct. El Dorado Cty. Loc. R., rule 7.10.04.A (only one continuance allowed); Super. Ct. Sonoma Cty. Loc. R., rule 5.3 (only one stipulated continuance allowed).

(2) Form of request. Because CCP §595.2 does not specify the procedure for requesting an agreed continuance, the movant should contact the court clerk or consult the court's local rules to determine the proper procedure. Some of the ways in which an agreed continuance can be brought to the court's attention include the following:

(a) Orally by telephone. Some courts allow the movant to inform the court of the parties' agreement by simply telephoning the court a reasonable time before the hearing. *E.g.*, Super. Ct. Butte Cty. Loc. R., rule 2.8(a) (party can call clerk's office if request is made before close of business on third court day before hearing); Super. Ct. El Dorado Cty. Loc. R., rule 7.10.04.B (party can call calendar clerk no later than 26 hours before hearing or 2 hours before tentative decision is published, whichever is earlier); *see* Weil, *Civil Procedure Before Trial*, ¶9:116.1.

(b) Written stipulation. Some courts allow the movant to inform the court of the parties' agreement by filing a written stipulation a reasonable time before the hearing. Weil, *Civil Procedure Before Trial*, ¶9:116.1; *e.g.*, Super. Ct. Contra Costa Cty. Loc. R., rule 3.49 (written stipulation must be filed by 12:00 p.m. one court day before scheduled hearing); Super. Ct. Riverside Cty. Loc. R., rule 3320.2 (written stipulation must be filed as soon as reasonably possible); Super. Ct. Yolo Cty. Loc. R., rule 11.3(e) (law-and-motion matters may be continued once by clerk at least five court days before hearing).

(c) Ex parte application. Some courts allow the movant to inform the court of the parties' agreement by filing an ex parte application. Weil, *Civil Procedure Before Trial*, ¶9:116.1; *e.g.*, Super. Ct. Amador Cty. Loc. R., rule 4.06 (continuance of hearing on summary judgment or summary adjudication may be by ex parte application); Super. Ct. Ventura Cty. Loc. R., rule 8.04.C (continuance must be brought by written stipulation or ex parte application).

(3) Filing fees. Depending on how the request is made (e.g., by stipulation, by ex parte application) and whether the court requires an order or a hearing, a filing fee may be required, unless a waiver is granted. *See* Gov. C. §70617(a) (filing fee for paper requiring hearing), §70617(b)(5) (no fee for stipulation that does not require order), §70617(c)(1), (c)(2) (filing fee when party files request, application, motion, or stipulation requiring order, and no hearing is required). See "Filing Fees," ch. 1-F, §7, p. 58.

(4) Ruling.

(a) CCP §595.2. Although CCP §595.2 states that the court "shall" postpone a hearing if the parties agree to a continuance, courts have interpreted the statute to be discretionary rather than mandatory. ***Lorraine v. McComb*** (1934) 220 Cal. 753, 757; ***Pham v. Nguyen*** (4th Dist.1997) 54 Cal.App.4th 11, 14-15; ***County of San Bernardino v. Doria Mining & Eng'g*** (4th Dist.1977) 72 Cal.App.3d 776, 784.

(b) Local rules. Some local rules may specify whether the court has discretion to grant an agreed continuance or whether the continuance will be granted automatically. *E.g.*, Super. Ct. El Dorado Cty. Loc. R., rule 7.10.04.C (all continuances, other than stipulated continuances, are discretionary); Super. Ct. San Francisco Cty. Loc. R., rule 8.2.B.1 (court has discretion to grant continuances despite parties' agreement to the contrary). As a general rule, however, courts have discretion to grant or deny a continuance.

2. Continuing trial date. CCP §595.2 states that the court "shall" postpone a trial date if all attorneys of record for the parties who have appeared in the action agree to the continuance. CCP §595.2. *But see* Super. Ct. Sacramento Cty. Loc. R., rule 2.11(1) (trial continuances under §595.2 are discretionary). Despite this statutory authority, most courts require a movant to meet the standards for a trial continuance under CRC 3.1332 by showing good cause. *E.g.*, Super. Ct. Napa Cty. Loc. R., rule 6.7 (trial continuances must be supported by good cause); Super. Ct. San Francisco Cty. Loc. R., rule 6.0.B (stipulated trial continuances must be supported by ex parte application showing good cause); Super. Ct. Santa Cruz Cty. Loc. R., rule 2.2.07(b)(1) (stipulated trial continuances must be supported by declaration showing good cause); Super. Ct. Yolo Cty. Loc. R., rule 11.14 (all continuances of long-cause matters must meet requirements under CRC 3.1332); *see also* CRC 3.1332(c) (all requests for trial continuances—whether contested, uncontested, or stipulated—must be supported by good cause); Super. Ct. Humboldt Cty. Loc. R., rule 2.3 (stipulation by parties is not sufficient basis for trial continuance). Courts that have interpreted §595.2 have also found the statute to be discretionary rather than mandatory. See "CCP §595.2," §2.1.1(4)(a), this page. For a discussion of what is required to establish good cause for a trial continuance, see "Good cause," §2.2.2(1)(a), p. 536.

§2.2 Good cause.

1. Continuing hearing date. No statute or California Rule of Court permits a continuance of hearings generally for good cause. Despite this, most courts—either by local rule or through their inherent power—permit a party to request a continuance of a hearing for good cause. *See* ***Rapid Transit Advocates, Inc. v. Southern Cal. Rapid Transit Dist.*** (2d Dist.1986) 185 Cal.App.3d 996, 1003 (courts, under their inherent power to control litigation, can grant continuances for good cause at any stage of proceedings); Kiesel, *Cal. Pretrial Civil Procedure*, §30.05 (same); *see, e.g.*, Super. Ct. Lake Cty. Loc. R., rule 3.5.A (continuance of hearing without notice must be supported by showing of good cause); Super. Ct. Monterey Cty. Loc. R., rule 7.04 (continuance of hearing will not be granted without showing of good cause); Super. Ct. Sacramento Cty. Loc. R., rule 2.30(C) (continuance of hearing by stipulation will not be granted without showing of good cause); *see also* CCP §128(a)(3) (courts have power to provide for orderly conduct of proceedings). Some appellate courts have even suggested that a court may abuse its discretion if it denies a timely request to continue a hearing that is supported by good cause. *See, e.g.*, ***Cotton v. Starcare Med. Grp.*** (4th Dist.2010) 183 Cal.App.4th 437, 444-45 (court abused its discretion when it rejected parties' stipulation to continue hearing on demurrers and motions to strike because parties established good cause); ***Lerma v. County of Orange*** (4th Dist.2004) 120 Cal.App.4th 709, 716 (court abused its discretion when it denied motion for continuance of summary-judgment hearing because movant established good cause); ***Mahoney v. Southland Mental Health Assocs.*** (2d Dist.1990) 223 Cal.App.3d 167, 170, 172 (motion for continuance of summary-judgment hearing was properly denied because motion was untimely and movant did not establish good cause).

(1) Movant's burden. Most local rules that permit a continuance of a hearing for good cause do not provide any guidance on what is required to establish good cause. One court has suggested that the standards for determining whether good cause has been established to continue a trial date are instructive. ***Mahoney***, 223 Cal.App.3d at 170. For a discussion of what is considered good cause to continue a trial date, see "Good cause," §2.2.2(1)(a), this page.

(2) Form of request. Because no statute or California Rule of Court governs continuances of hearings generally for good cause, the movant should contact the court clerk or consult the court's local rules to determine the proper procedure. *See, e.g.*, Super. Ct. Lake Cty. Loc. R., rule 3.5.A (continuance of hearing without notice for good cause must be supported by declaration).

(3) Filing fees. See "Filing fees," §2.1.1(3), p. 535.

(4) Ruling. Unless made mandatory by local rule, the court's decision to grant or deny a request to continue a hearing for good cause is within the court's discretion. *See* ***Mahoney***, 223 Cal.App.3d at 170. See "Local rules," §2.1.1(4)(b), p. 535.

2. Continuing trial date. A party can make a motion for continuance of a trial date for good cause. CRC 3.1332(c).

(1) Movant's burden. To prevail on a motion for continuance of a trial date for good cause, the movant (1) must show good cause for the continuance and (2) should show that other relevant factors favor a continuance. *See* CRC 3.1332(c), (d); ***Thurman v. Bayshore Transit Mgmt.*** (4th Dist.2012) 203 Cal.App.4th 1112, 1127.

(a) Good cause. CRC 3.1332 contains a nonexclusive list of circumstances that may show good cause. *See* CRC 3.1332(c); *see, e.g.*, ***Thurman***, 203 Cal.App.4th at 1123-24 (trial court granted multiple continuances based on stipulated agreement to permit Supreme Court to issue opinion that would fundamentally affect suit). These circumstances include the following:

[1] Unavailable for trial.

[a] Party. The movant can show that (1) it is unavailable for trial because of death, illness, or other excusable circumstances and (2) its presence at the trial is necessary. *See* CRC 3.1332(c)(2); *see, e.g.*, ***Lewis v. Neptune Soc'y Corp.*** (1st Dist.1987) 195 Cal.App.3d 427, 429-30 (D-representative's illness was not

good cause for continuance because it did not prevent him from attending trial); ***Young v. Redman*** (2d Dist.1976) 55 Cal.App.3d 827, 832 (D's absence from country was not good cause for continuance because there was no showing of any emergency requiring D's absence); ***Hurley v. Kazantzis*** (1st Dist.1947) 82 Cal.App.2d 378, 379 (D's inability to attend trial was not good cause for continuance because there was no showing that D's presence was necessary).

[b] Party's trial attorney. The movant can show that its trial attorney is unavailable for trial because of death, illness, or other excusable circumstances. CRC 3.1332(c)(3); *see* ***Hernandez v. Superior Ct.*** (2d Dist.2004) 115 Cal.App.4th 1242, 1247-48 (death or serious illness of party or party's trial attorney is normally considered good cause for continuance); *see, e.g.*, ***Oliveros v. County of L.A.*** (2d Dist.2004) 120 Cal.App.4th 1389, 1400 (D's attorney's unexpected trial in another case created scheduling conflict that constituted good cause for continuance).

[c] Essential witness. The movant can show that an essential lay or expert witness is unavailable for trial because of death, illness, or other excusable circumstances. CRC 3.1332(c)(1). The witness's expected testimony at trial must (1) be material to the proceedings, (2) be necessary (i.e., it cannot otherwise be proved), and (3) have been diligently obtained. *See* CCP §595.4; ***Oak Knoll Broad. Corp. v. Hudgings*** (2d Dist.1969) 275 Cal.App.2d 563, 566; *see, e.g.*, ***Jurado v. Toys "R" Us, Inc.*** (2d Dist.1993) 12 Cal.App.4th 1615, 1617-18 (court abused discretion by denying motion for continuance based on unavailability of witnesses when attorney exercised due diligence in subpoenaing witnesses and following up on subpoenas); ***Lewis***, 195 Cal.App.3d at 429-30 (court did not abuse discretion by denying motion for continuance based on unavailability of witness when declaration did not state what witness's testimony would be and attorney admitted that witness's testimony would have been cumulative).

[2] Substitution of attorney. The movant can show that its trial attorney must be substituted in the interests of justice. CRC 3.1332(c)(4). The substitution must be necessary (i.e., the attorney is unable or unwilling to represent the movant), and the movant must have used due diligence in trying to obtain a new attorney. ***County of San Bernardino v. Doria Mining & Eng'g*** (4th Dist.1977) 72 Cal.App.3d 776, 783; *see, e.g.*, ***Forrest v. Department of Corps.*** (2d Dist.2007) 150 Cal.App.4th 183, 201-02 (court did not abuse discretion in denying further continuances for P, who did not obtain new attorney after being given several opportunities to do so), *disapproved on other grounds*, ***Shalant v. Girardi*** (2011) 51 Cal.4th 1164; ***Vann v. Shilleh*** (2d Dist.1975) 54 Cal.App.3d 192, 197-98 (court abused discretion by denying Ds' motion for continuance when Ds' attorney withdrew on eve of trial and Ds did not have time to obtain new attorney).

[3] Newly added party.

[a] Movant is newly added party. The movant can show that it has been newly added to the case and has not had a reasonable opportunity to conduct discovery and prepare for trial. CRC 3.1332(c)(5)(A).

[b] Movant is existing party. The movant can show that a new party has been added to the case and the movant has not had a reasonable opportunity to conduct discovery and prepare for trial regarding the new party's involvement in the case. CRC 3.1332(c)(5)(B).

[4] Unable to obtain evidence. The movant can show that there is essential testimonial, documentary, or other material evidence that the movant has been unable to obtain despite its diligent efforts. CRC 3.1332(c)(6); *see* CCP §595.4; *see, e.g.*, ***Advantec Grp. v. Edwin's Plumbing Co.*** (2d Dist.2007) 153 Cal.App.4th 621, 630-31 (court did not abuse discretion in denying D's motion for continuance to obtain certificate of licensure that should have been obtained before trial began); ***Lea v. Shank*** (4th Dist.1970) 5 Cal.App.3d 964, 977 (court did not abuse discretion in denying Ds' motion for continuance for an indefinite time to obtain evidence of unknown content).

[5] Unanticipated change in case status. The movant can show that there has been a significant, unanticipated change in the status of the case and, as a result, the case is not ready for trial. CRC 3.1332(c)(7). For example, a continuance may be granted when a party has been surprised at trial by unexpected

testimony and needs more time to respond to the testimony. ***In re Marriage of Hoffmeister*** (1st Dist.1984) 161 Cal.App.3d 1163, 1169; *see, e.g.*, ***Crosby v. Martinez*** (2d Dist.1958) 159 Cal.App.2d 534, 541 (Ps were entitled to short continuance of trial to produce witness to rebut unexpected admission of hearsay evidence).

(b) Other relevant factors. The movant should show that other relevant factors favor a continuance. *See* CRC 3.1332(d) (court must consider all relevant facts and circumstances in ruling on motion for continuance). Factors relevant to a motion for continuance of a trial date for good cause include the following:

[1] The proximity of the trial date. CRC 3.1332(d)(1).

[2] Whether there was any previous continuance, extension of time, or delay of trial due to any party. CRC 3.1332(d)(2).

[3] The length of the continuance requested. CRC 3.1332(d)(3).

[4] The availability of alternative means to address the basis for the continuance. CRC 3.1332(d)(4).

[5] The prejudice that parties or witnesses will suffer as a result of the continuance. CRC 3.1332(d)(5).

[6] If the case is entitled to a preferential trial setting, the reasons for that status and whether the need for a continuance outweighs the need to avoid delay. CRC 3.1332(d)(6). See "Motion for Preference," ch. 5-B, p. 474.

[7] The court's calendar and the impact of granting a continuance on other pending trials. CRC 3.1332(d)(7).

[8] Whether trial counsel is engaged in another trial. CRC 3.1332(d)(8).

[9] Whether all parties have stipulated to a continuance. CRC 3.1332(d)(9).

[10] Whether the interests of justice are best served by a continuance, imposing conditions on a continuance, or the trial of the matter. CRC 3.1332(d)(10).

[11] Any other relevant fact or circumstance. CRC 3.1332(d)(11).

(2) Motion.

(a) Who can file. A party can file a motion for continuance of a trial date for good cause. CRC 3.1332(b).

(b) Deadline to file & serve. The motion must be filed and served as soon as reasonably practical after the need for the continuance is discovered. CRC 3.1332(b); *see, e.g.*, ***County of San Bernardino***, 72 Cal.App.3d at 783 (D's motion for continuance made on day of trial was untimely because need for continuance was discovered over one week before trial).

(c) Form. The motion must be requested in writing by noticed motion or ex parte application (even if the continuance is uncontested or stipulated). CRC 3.1332(b).

PRACTICE TIP

In an emergency situation, the court may be able to grant an oral motion for continuance under its inherent power. Kiesel, Cal. Pretrial Civil Procedure, §30.09[5][a]; see, e.g., ***Jurado****, 12 Cal.App.4th at 1617-18 (court erred in denying P's oral motion for continuance made on day of trial when P had just learned that subpoenaed witness would not be appearing for trial);* ***Crosby****, 159 Cal.App.2d at 541 (court erred in denying Ps' oral motion for continuance made during trial to produce witness to rebut unexpected admission of hearsay evidence). But if time permits, it is best to file an ex parte application. Kiesel, Cal. Pretrial Civil Procedure, §30.09[5][a]; see id. §30.09[4][a] (ex parte applications can be filed in urgent circumstances).*

(d) Contents.

[1] Noticed motion. For a discussion of the contents of noticed motions generally, see "Motion Papers," ch. 1-D, §5, p. 27. A noticed motion must be supported by the following evidence:

[a] Declaration – good cause. The motion must be supported by a declaration showing good cause for the continuance. *See* CRC 3.1332(b), (c). See "Good cause," §2.2.2(1)(a), p. 536.

[b] Declaration – evidence needed. If the motion is based on an absence of evidence, the declaration must show (1) how the evidence is material and (2) that due diligence has been used in trying to obtain the evidence. CCP §595.4. If the motion is based on the absence of a material witness, the court may also require that the declaration state what testimony the witness is expected to give. *Id.*; *see, e.g.*, ***Lewis***, 195 Cal.App.3d at 430 (court did not abuse discretion in denying continuance when declaration did not state what witness's testimony would be). See "Unable to obtain evidence," §2.2.2(1)(a)[4], p. 537.

[2] Ex parte application. For a discussion of the contents of ex parte applications generally, see "Application Papers," ch. 1-E, §5, p. 42. The application must be supported by the same declarations needed to support a noticed motion for continuance. See "Noticed motion," §2.2.2(2)(d)[1], this page.

(e) Filing fee. When the motion or application is filed, the movant must pay a filing fee to the court clerk or request a waiver of the fee. See "Filing Fees," ch. 1-F, §7, p. 58.

(3) Response.

(a) Opposition. The nonmovant can respond to a noticed motion or ex parte application for continuance by filing an opposition. For a discussion of opposing a noticed motion, see "Opposition Papers," ch. 1-D, §8, p. 35. For a discussion of opposing an ex parte application, see "Opposing Ex Parte Application," ch. 1-E, §7, p. 44. The nonmovant can oppose the motion or application based on any of the following grounds:

[1] Procedural defects. The motion or application can be opposed on the ground that it is procedurally defective. *See, e.g.*, ***Vesco v. Superior Ct.*** (2d Dist.2013) 221 Cal.App.4th 275, 277 (court erred in granting ex parte motion for continuance based on CRC 1.100 without providing P notice and opportunity to view documents on which motion was based); ***Lewis***, 195 Cal.App.3d at 430 (court did not abuse discretion in denying D's motion for continuance when declaration did not state what unavailable witness's testimony would be); ***County of San Bernardino***, 72 Cal.App.3d at 783-84 (court did not abuse discretion in denying D's motion for continuance that was neither noticed nor timely made).

[2] No good cause. The motion or application can be opposed on the ground that there is no good cause for a continuance. *See, e.g.*, ***Everts v. Will S. Fawcett Co.*** (4th Dist.1934) 3 Cal.App.2d 261, 266-67 (P opposed continuance on ground that allegedly sick, bedridden witness was seen in public and appeared to be in good health). See "Good cause," §2.2.2(1)(a), p. 536.

[3] Other relevant factors do not favor continuance. The motion or application can be opposed on the ground that other relevant factors do not favor a continuance. *See* CRC 3.1332(d) (court must consider all relevant facts and circumstances in ruling on motion for continuance). See "Other relevant factors," §2.2.2(1)(b), p. 538. For example, the nonmovant can show that it would be prejudiced by a continuance. *See* CRC 3.1332(d)(5); *see, e.g.*, ***Vesco***, 221 Cal.App.4th at 278-79 (P opposed continuance on ground that P would be prejudiced by continuing to pay mortgage and maintenance costs on house in which movant lived rent-free); ***Forrest***, 150 Cal.App.4th at 200 (D opposed continuance on ground that it would be prejudiced by continuance because its trial witness had serious illness and might be unavailable for continued trial date).

(b) Admit to evidence. If the motion or application for continuance of the trial date for good cause is based on the absence of a material witness, the nonmovant can defeat the motion or application by admitting that the evidence set out in the movant's declaration would (1) be the same as that given at trial and (2) be considered as actually given at trial or offered and overruled as improper. CCP §595.4. See "Declaration – evidence needed," §2.2.2(2)(d)[1][b], this page.

(4) Hearing. Hearings on a motion for continuance of the trial date for good cause are conducted in the same manner as civil hearings generally. See "Hearings," ch. 1-H, p. 79.

(5) Ruling.

(a) Discretionary. The decision to grant or deny a motion for continuance of the trial date for good cause is within the court's discretion. ***Oliveros***, 120 Cal.App.4th at 1395.

(b) Court's determination.

[1] Does motion comply with procedural requirements? The court must determine whether the motion for continuance of the trial date for good cause complies with the procedural requirements. *See* CRC 3.1332(b). The court can deny a procedurally defective motion or excuse the noncompliance. *See* ***Jurado***, 12 Cal.App.4th at 1618 (court can excuse noncompliance with affidavit requirement by accepting attorney's oral representations in open court); ***Mahoney***, 223 Cal.App.3d at 172 (court can excuse noncompliance with declaration requirement but is not required to do so); *see, e.g.*, ***County of San Bernardino***, 72 Cal.App.3d at 783-84 (court did not abuse discretion in denying D's motion for continuance that was neither noticed nor timely made).

[2] Does motion show good cause? If the motion complies with the procedural requirements or the court has excused the noncompliance, the court must determine whether the motion shows good cause for a continuance. *See* CRC 3.1332(c). See "Good cause," §2.2.2(1)(a), p. 536. The court must deny the motion if no good cause is shown. *See* CRC 3.1332(c).

[3] Balancing test. If good cause is shown, the court must consider and balance the relevant factors listed in CRC 3.1332(d), keeping in mind that the strong public policy in favor of deciding cases on the merits outweighs the competing policy favoring judicial efficiency. *See* CRC 3.1332(d); ***Oliveros***, 120 Cal.App.4th at 1395; *see also* Gov. C. §68607(g) (court must adopt and use firm, consistent policy against continuances, to maximum extent possible and reasonable and in all stages of litigation); CRC 3.1332(c) (although continuances of trials are disfavored, each request for continuance must be considered on its own merits). See "Other relevant factors," §2.2.2(1)(b), p. 538. Thus, when good cause is shown, the court should usually grant the continuance unless other circumstances suggest a lack of diligence or other abusive conduct by the movant. ***Hernandez***, 115 Cal.App.4th at 1246-47; *see, e.g.*, ***Forrest***, 150 Cal.App.4th at 200-01 (court did not abuse discretion in denying continuance when D showed it would be prejudiced by continuance and P was not diligent in obtaining new attorney).

(6) Order.

(a) Form. The court's ruling on the motion for continuance of the trial date for good cause must be recorded either in writing or by minute order. See "Record of Ruling," ch. 1-I, §4, p. 90.

(b) Contents.

[1] New trial date. If the motion is granted, the order should specify a new trial date. *See* Kiesel, *Cal. Pretrial Civil Procedure*, §30.28 (sample order).

[2] Payment of nonmovant's fees. If the motion is granted, the court can order as a condition of granting the continuance that the movant pay the nonmovant's reasonable expenses incurred as a result of the continuance. CCP §1024; ***Rosen v. Superior Ct.*** (2d Dist.1966) 244 Cal.App.2d 586, 593. The expenses are not limited to items taxable as costs after trial and may include travel expenses and fees for court reporters, witnesses, and jurors. ***Rosen***, 244 Cal.App.2d at 593; ***Wilkin v. Tadlock*** (3d Dist.1952) 110 Cal.App.2d 156, 158; 7 Witkin, *Cal. Procedure*, Trial, §34. The expenses cannot include attorney fees. ***Levine v. Pollack*** (2d Dist.1995) 37 Cal.App.4th 129, 139; ***DeCesare v. Lembert*** (5th Dist.1983) 144 Cal.App.3d 20, 25.

§2.3 Member of Legislature. If a member of the State Legislature is a party, attorney of record, or principal witness in the case, a party, the legislative member, or the court on its own motion can ask the court for a continuance of a hearing or trial date or any other proceeding. *See* CCP §595.

1. Movant's burden. To prevail on a motion for continuance based on membership in the State Legislature, the movant must show the following:

(1) A member of the State Legislature is a party, an attorney of record, or a principal witness in the case. CCP §595. The legislative member can become an attorney of record in the case at any time, whether before or after the commencement of a legislative session or before or after being appointed to a legislative interim committee. *Id.*

(2) The legislative member is unavailable for a hearing, trial, or other proceeding because of one of the following:

(a) The Legislature is in session or in recess (not exceeding 40 days). *Id.*

(b) The legislative member is a duly appointed member of a legislative interim committee and the committee (1) is meeting or (2) is scheduled to meet at a time that the court finds will not give the member enough time to travel from the hearing, trial, or other proceeding to the meeting. *Id.*

2. Form of request. CCP §595 does not specify the procedures for requesting a continuance (i.e., orally or in writing by noticed motion or ex parte application). Presumably, a party, attorney of record, or principal witness in the case can request a continuance by noticed motion or ex parte application. *See* CCP §595 (hearing or trial must be postponed when grounds for continuance appear to court); *see, e.g.*, ***Thurmond v. Superior Ct.*** (1967) 66 Cal.2d 836, 838 (attorney of record requested continuance of hearing by ex parte application). See "Motion Papers," ch. 1-D, §5, p. 27; "Application Papers," ch. 1-E, §5, p. 42.

3. Opposition.

(1) Generally. The form of the nonmovant's response will depend on whether the movant sought relief by noticed motion or ex parte application. See "Opposition Papers," ch. 1-D, §8, p. 35; "Opposing Ex Parte Application," ch. 1-E, §7, p. 44.

(2) Grounds. The motion can be opposed on the ground that a continuance would defeat or diminish either of the following rights:

(a) The nonmovant's right to pendente lite relief (i.e., relief during the proceeding) in a paternity action. CCP §595.

(b) The nonmovant's right to invoke a provisional remedy (e.g., pendente lite support in a domestic-relations controversy, the attachment and sale of perishable goods, a receivership for a failing business, a temporary restraining order, or a preliminary injunction). *Id.*

4. Ruling. The court must usually grant the motion if the movant has met the requirements of CCP §595. CCP §595. See "Movant's burden," §2.3.1, this page. The court's ruling is discretionary, however, if the court determines that a continuance would defeat or diminish the nonmovant's right (1) to pendente lite relief or (2) to invoke a provisional remedy. CCP §595. See "Grounds," §2.3.3(2), this page.

5. Order.

(1) Form. The court's ruling on the motion for continuance must be recorded either in writing or by minute order. See "Record of Ruling," ch. 1-I, §4, p. 90.

(2) Contents. If the motion is granted, the order should specify the length of the continuance.

(a) Date certain. The court must continue the hearing, trial, or other proceeding to a specific date. CCP §595.

(b) Earliest date without attorney's consent. The court cannot continue the hearing, trial, or other proceeding to the following dates without the consent of the attorney of record:

[1] **Legislative session or recess.** If a continuance is granted because the Legislature is in session or in recess, the hearing, trial, or other proceeding cannot be scheduled within 30 days after final adjournment of the Legislature or the commencement of a recess of more than 40 days unless the attorney of record consents. CCP §595; 7 Witkin, *Cal. Procedure*, Trial, §28(2). If the Legislature is still in recess following this period and a date for the hearing, trial, or other proceeding is available, the hearing, trial, or other proceeding must be scheduled on that date, if possible. CCP §595; 7 Witkin, *Cal. Procedure*, Trial, §28(2).

[2] **Legislative-committee meeting.** If a continuance is granted because a legislative interim committee is meeting or scheduled to meet, the hearing, trial, or other proceeding cannot be scheduled after the meeting is adjourned or recessed without giving the legislative member a reasonable period of time to travel from the place of the meeting to the place of the hearing, trial, or other proceeding unless the attorney of record consents. CCP §595; 7 Witkin, *Cal. Procedure*, Trial, §28(3). But if the Legislature is in session after the meeting is adjourned or recessed, the date restrictions for when the Legislature is in session apply. CCP §595; 7 Witkin, *Cal. Procedure*, Trial, §28(4). See "Legislative session or recess," §2.3.5(2)(b)[1], this page.

6. Effect of order. If the court grants a continuance and postpones a hearing or trial date, the order will also suspend—for the same time period as the continuance—the running of the time period for any court ruling or proceeding or the performance of any act by a party that is affected by the continuance. CCP §595.

§2.4 Additional discovery.

1. To oppose summary judgment. A party can ask the court for a continuance of a summary-judgment hearing on the ground that additional discovery is needed to oppose the motion. CCP §437c(h); ***Rodriguez v. Oto*** (6th Dist.2013) 212 Cal.App.4th 1020, 1037-38. For a discussion of filing motions for continuance in response to motions for summary judgment, see "Motion for continuance," ch. 10-B, §7.1, p. 1126.

2. To oppose anti-SLAPPback motion. A party can ask the court for a continuance of a hearing on an anti-SLAPPback motion on the ground that additional discovery is needed to oppose the motion. *See* CCP §425.18(e). For a discussion of filing motions for continuance in response to an anti-SLAPPback motion, see "Ex parte application for continuance," ch. 4-L, §4.1, p. 452.

§2.5 Similar proceeding pending. If another pending action or proceeding involving the same parties and substantially the same issues would decide one or more issues in the case, a party can ask the court for a continuance of the trial date or the court on its own motion can continue the trial date based on principles of comity and judicial economy. *See* ***Thomson v. Continental Ins.*** (1967) 66 Cal.2d 738, 746; ***Simmons v. Superior Ct.*** (2d Dist.1950) 96 Cal.App.2d 119, 123-24; 7 Witkin, *Cal. Procedure*, Trial, §§22, 23; *see, e.g.*, ***Anthony v. General Motors Corp.*** (2d Dist.1973) 33 Cal.App.3d 699, 708 (court should have continued rather than dismissed action based on pending federal action involving similar issue). The decision to grant or deny a motion for continuance based on another pending action is within the court's discretion. ***Thomson***, 66 Cal.2d at 746; *see* ***Christensen v. Superior Ct.*** (2d Dist.1973) 32 Cal.App.3d 749, 754-55.

§2.6 Opposing application for preliminary injunction. A party can ask the court for a continuance of a hearing on an application for a preliminary injunction on the ground that a temporary restraining order was granted without notice to the party and a continuance is needed to oppose the application for a preliminary injunction. CCP §527(d)(4). The party is entitled to one continuance for a reasonable period of not less than 15 days or any shorter period requested by the party. *Id.*; *see also* ***Freeman v. Sullivant*** (2d Dist.2011) 192 Cal.App.4th 523, 529 (mandatory continuance under CCP §527 does not apply to civil harassment restraining orders under CCP §527.6).

§2.7 Court engaged in another trial. The court can continue a trial on its own motion if it is engaged in another trial. CCP §594a; *see, e.g.*, ***De Santiago v. D&G Plumbing, Inc.*** (4th Dist.2007) 155 Cal.App.4th 365, 369 (court continued trial on its own motion based on its unavailability).

§2.8 Leave to amend pleading. The court can continue a trial on its own motion if the granting of a motion for leave to amend a pleading makes postponement necessary. CCP §§473(a)(2), 594a. See "Grants motion," ch. 3-C, §6.2.4(5)(a), p. 234.

§3. STAY

A motion to stay asks the court to temporarily suspend a proceeding. *See Black's Law Dictionary* 1639 (10th ed. 2014) (defining "stay"). The following are some of the most common grounds for requesting a stay of an action or proceeding.

§3.1 Inherent power. A party can ask the court to stay an action or proceeding based on the court's inherent power to stay in the interest of justice and to promote judicial efficiency. *See* Cal. Const., art. VI, §1 (vesting courts with judicial power); CCP §128 (giving court power in proceedings before it); ***Adams v. Paul*** (1995) 11 Cal.4th 583, 593 (court has inherent power to stay related actions); ***Smith v. Jones*** (1900) 128 Cal. 14, 15 (court has right to postpone case); ***Koch-Ash v. Superior Ct.*** (2d Dist.1986) 180 Cal.App.3d 689, 696 (court has inherent authority to stay trial); *see also* ***Walker v. Superior Ct.*** (1991) 53 Cal.3d 257, 266-67 (California Supreme Court has repeatedly recognized inherent power of courts, derived from both statute and Constitution, to ensure orderly administration of justice).

1. Grounds. The court's inherent power is most commonly exercised in suits in which a related proceeding is pending in another court. *See* ***Jordache Enters. v. Brobeck, Phleger & Harrison*** (1998) 18 Cal.4th 739, 758 (a court can avoid problems of simultaneous litigation by exercising its inherent power to stay an action); ***Adams***, 11 Cal.4th at 592-93 (courts have authority to stay malpractice suits until underlying litigation is resolved to avoid inconsistent pleadings and judgments).

(1) Underlying action would be res judicata. The court can stay an action when the resolution of an earlier related action would be res judicata of some or all of the issues in the case. ***Houghton v. Superior Ct.*** (1922) 187 Cal. 661, 666.

(a) Criminal malpractice. If a plaintiff timely files suit against her attorney for malpractice that resulted in the plaintiff's criminal conviction, the court can stay the malpractice action until the plaintiff has exhausted her postconviction remedies for the underlying criminal case. ***Coscia v. McKenna & Cuneo*** (2001) 25 Cal.4th 1194, 1210-11.

(b) Insurance coverage. If an insurer files a declaratory-judgment action disputing coverage in an underlying civil action, the court can stay the declaratory-judgment action when the coverage question turns on facts to be litigated in the underlying action. ***Montrose Chem. Corp. v. Superior Ct.*** (1993) 6 Cal.4th 287, 301; ***United Enters. v. Superior Ct.*** (4th Dist.2010) 183 Cal.App.4th 1004, 1011-12; ***Great Am. Ins. v. Superior Ct.*** (2d Dist.2009) 178 Cal.App.4th 221, 235. But if the coverage question is logically unrelated to the issues in the underlying action or can be resolved based on undisputed facts or law, the court can allow the declaratory-judgment action to proceed to judgment. ***Great Am. Ins.***, 178 Cal.App.4th at 235-36; *see* ***Montrose Chem.***, 6 Cal.4th at 302.

(c) Unlawful detainer. When an unlawful-detainer proceeding and unlimited civil action concerning title on the same property are simultaneously pending, the court can stay the unlawful-detainer proceeding until the issue of title is resolved. ***Martin-Bragg v. Moore*** (2d Dist.2013) 219 Cal.App.4th 367, 385.

(2) Concurrent civil & criminal proceedings. The court can stay a civil action (or discovery in a civil action) when the party seeking the stay is a defendant in concurrent and related civil and criminal proceedings. *See* ***People v. Coleman*** (1975) 13 Cal.3d 867, 884-85; ***People v. Rizzo*** (2d Dist.2013) 214 Cal.App.4th 921, 951-52; ***Avant! Corp. v. Superior Ct.*** (6th Dist.2000) 79 Cal.App.4th 876, 882; ***Pacers, Inc. v. Superior Ct.*** (4th Dist.1984) 162 Cal.App.3d 686, 690.

2. Form of request.

(1) Generally. Presumably, a party can request a stay based on the court's inherent power by noticed motion or, when appropriate, by ex parte application. For a discussion of noticed motions and ex parte applications, see "Motion Papers," ch. 1-D, §5, p. 27; "Application Papers," ch. 1-E, §5, p. 42.

(2) Stipulation. The parties can stipulate to a stay. ***Thurman v. Bayshore Transit Mgmt.*** (4th Dist.2012) 203 Cal.App.4th 1112, 1123.

3. Opposition.

(1) Generally. The form of the nonmovant's response will depend on whether the movant sought relief by noticed motion or ex parte application. See "Opposition Papers," ch. 1-D, §8, p. 35; "Opposing Ex Parte Application," ch. 1-E, §7, p. 44.

(2) Grounds. The motion can be opposed on the ground that the court cannot grant a stay under its inherent power because (1) the suit qualifies for a mandatory preferential trial setting or (2) the court lacks jurisdiction over the suit. *See* ***Frieberg v. City of Mission Viejo*** (4th Dist.1995) 33 Cal.App.4th 1484, 1489 (court must have jurisdiction over case to stay proceedings under its inherent power); ***Koch-Ash***, 180 Cal.App.3d at 696-97 (court cannot stay case under its inherent power if statute expressly provides for mandatory preferential trial setting); *see, e.g.*, ***Martin-Bragg***, 219 Cal.App.4th at 379 (court declined to stay unlawful-detainer proceeding because it was entitled to preference under CCP §1179a). See "Mandatory preference," ch. 5-B, §7.2.1, p. 481.

§3.2 Armed forces. If a party is in military service with the armed forces, the party can ask the court to stay the action or proceeding or the court on its own motion can order a stay under the Servicemembers Civil Relief Act (SCRA). 50 U.S.C. app. §522(b)(1); *see* ***In re A.R.*** (4th Dist.2009) 170 Cal.App.4th 733, 741 (SCRA must be construed to prevent any disadvantage to servicemember litigant resulting from military service).

1. Movant's burden. To prevail on an application for a stay under the SCRA, the party must show the following:

(1) The party is in military service or has been released from military service within the last 90 days. 50 U.S.C. app. §522(a)(1). Military service means (1) active duty in the Army, Navy, Air Force, Marine Corps, or Coast Guard, (2) active service in the National Guard for more than 30 consecutive days authorized by the President or Secretary of Defense to respond to a national emergency, (3) active service as a commissioned officer of the Public Health Service or the National Oceanic and Atmospheric Administration, or (4) any period in which a party in military service is absent from duty because of sickness, wounds, leave, or other lawful cause. *Id.* §511(2).

(2) The party has received notice of the action or proceeding. *Id.* §522(a)(2).

(3) The party's ability to participate in the action or proceeding is materially affected by the party's military duty. ***George P. v. Superior Ct.*** (2d Dist.2005) 127 Cal.App.4th 216, 223-24; *see* 50 U.S.C. app. §522(b)(2), (d)(1).

2. Application.

(1) Form. The form of the party's application is not specified in §522. Presumably, a party can request a stay by noticed motion or ex parte application, but a less formal request may also be sufficient. *See* Sullivan, *A Judge's Guide to the Servicemembers Civil Relief Act*, at 3; *see, e.g.*, ***In re Marriage of E.U.*** (4th Dist.2012) 212 Cal.App.4th 1377, 1380-81 (in child-custody case, father filed applications for stay under SCRA); ***In re A.R.***, 170 Cal.App.4th at 738 (in juvenile-dependency case, father filed written motion to stay under SCRA). See "Motion Papers," ch. 1-D, §5, p. 27; "Application Papers," ch. 1-E, §5, p. 42.

(2) Contents. The application for a stay must include the following:

(a) A letter or other communication stating how the party's current military duty materially affects her ability to appear and a date when she will be available to appear. 50 U.S.C. app. §522(b)(2)(A); *see* ***In re Marriage of E.U.***, 212 Cal.App.4th at 1380-81 & n.4.

(b) A letter or other communication from the party's commanding officer stating that the party's current military duty prevents appearance and that military leave is not authorized. 50 U.S.C. app. §522(b)(2)(B); *see* ***In re Marriage of E.U.***, 212 Cal.App.4th at 1380-81 & n.4.

(3) Additional application. A servicemember can file an application for an additional stay if the servicemember's military duty continues to materially affect her ability to appear. 50 U.S.C. app. §522(d)(1). The request for an additional stay can be made in the initial application or in a later application. *Id.* The same information is required for both applications. *Id.* See "Contents," §3.2.2(2), this page.

(4) Effect of application. An application for a stay does not constitute an appearance for jurisdictional purposes or a waiver of any substantive or procedural defense (including a defense relating to lack of personal jurisdiction). 50 U.S.C. app. §522(c).

3. Opposition.

(1) Generally. The form of the nonmovant's response will depend on whether the movant sought relief by noticed motion or ex parte application. See "Opposition Papers," ch. 1-D, §8, p. 35; "Opposing Ex Parte Application," ch. 1-E, §7, p. 44.

(2) Grounds. The application for a stay (initial or additional) can be opposed on the grounds that the application does not include the letters or other communications required by the statute or that the letters or communications provided do not establish that the movant's military duty materially affects her ability to participate in the litigation. *See* 50 U.S.C. app. §522(b)(2), (d)(1); *see, e.g.*, ***George P.***, 127 Cal.App.4th at 225-26 (father's ability to defend against dependency case was not adversely affected by his military duty when he was able to participate in case before his deployment and was able to provide testimony and communicate with his attorney during his service); *see also* Sullivan, *A Judge's Guide to the Servicemembers Civil Relief Act*, at 6 (listing questions that court or party can ask movant to inquire about movant's ability to appear in court). See "Contents," §3.2.2(2), p. 544.

4. Ruling.

(1) Court's motion. The ruling on the court's own motion for a stay is within the court's discretion. *See* 50 U.S.C. app. §522(b)(1) (court can stay action on its own motion).

(2) Party's application. The court must grant the party's initial application for a stay if the party has provided the appropriate letters or communications required by the statute. 50 U.S.C. app. §522(b)(1); ***In re A.R.***, 170 Cal.App.4th at 741-42 & n.5. See "Contents," §3.2.2(2), p. 544. But the granting of additional applications for a stay is discretionary, and the court can deny the application if it finds the party's ability to prosecute or defend the action is not materially affected by the party's military duty. *See* 50 U.S.C. app. §522(d)(1); *see, e.g.*, ***George P.***, 127 Cal.App.4th at 225-26 (court properly denied request for additional stay because father's military service did not adversely affect his ability to defend against dependency case).

5. Order.

(1) Form. The court's ruling on the application for a stay must be recorded either in writing or by minute order. See "Record of Ruling," ch. 1-I, §4, p. 90.

(2) Contents.

(a) Application granted. If the application is granted, the court should specify the length of the stay. For a party's initial application, the court must stay the action or proceeding for at least 90 days. 50 U.S.C. app. §522(b)(1).

(b) Application denied. If the application for an additional stay is denied, the court must appoint an attorney to represent the servicemember in the action or proceeding. 50 U.S.C. app. §522(d)(2).

§3.3 National Guard or U.S. Military Reserve. If a party is in military service with the National Guard or U.S. Military Reserve or has been released from military service within the last 60 days, the party can ask the court to stay the action or proceeding or the court on its own motion can order a stay. *See* Mil. & Vet. C. §§400(a), 403(a). Military service means (1) full-time active federal or state service in the National Guard for more than 7 days in any 14-day period authorized by the President or the Governor or (2) full-time active duty in the U.S. Military Reserve for more than 7 days in any 14-day period. *Id.* §400. Section 403 does not specify the form of a party's application. Presumably, a party can request a stay by noticed motion or ex parte application. See "Motion Papers," ch. 1-D, §5, p. 27; "Application Papers," ch. 1-E, §5, p. 42. The court's ruling is discretionary, and the court can deny the application if it finds that the party's ability to prosecute or defend the action is not materially affected by the party's

military service. Mil. & Vet. C. §403(a). If the court grants the application, the court can stay the action or proceeding for the period of military service plus an additional three months. *Id.* §403(d).

§3.4 Forum non conveniens. The court can stay an action for forum non conveniens. CCP §410.30(a). See "Forum Non Conveniens," ch. 4-F, p. 375.

§3.5 Pending motion on deposition. The court can stay a deposition until the determination of a motion for protective order or motion to quash. CCP §2025.270(d) (protective order). See "Request stay," ch. 9-C, §3.1.3(2)(b), p. 1040; "Request stay," ch. 9-C, §4.1.3(2)(b), p. 1043.

§3.6 Pending arbitration.

1. Arbitration ordered. The court must stay an action on a party's motion if a court of competent jurisdiction (whether in California or not) has ordered arbitration of an issue that is also at issue in the action pending before the court. CCP §1281.4 ¶1. A single overlapping issue is sufficient to mandate a stay under CCP §1281.4. ***Heritage Provider Network, Inc. v. Superior Ct.*** (2d Dist.2008) 158 Cal.App.4th 1146, 1152-53. Any party to the judicial proceeding is entitled to the stay; it is irrelevant that the party seeking the stay is not a party to the arbitration agreement. *Id.* at 1152. The stay should last until the arbitration is complete or until an earlier time that the court specifies. CCP §1281.4 ¶1; *see* ***MKJA, Inc. v. 123 Fit Franchising, LLC*** (4th Dist.2011) 191 Cal.App.4th 643, 660-61 (court can lift stay before completion of arbitration only if lifting stay will not frustrate arbitrator's jurisdiction; lifting stay because party could not afford arbitration was not permissible ground).

2. Application for arbitration. The court must stay an action on a party's motion when an application has been made to a court of competent jurisdiction (whether in California or not) for arbitration of an issue that is also at issue in the action pending before the court. CCP §1281.4 ¶2; *see* ***MKJA***, 191 Cal.App.4th at 647. The stay should last until the application is determined. CCP §1281.4 ¶2. If the application is granted, the court must stay the action until the arbitration is complete or until an earlier time that the court specifies. *Id.* See "Arbitration ordered," §3.6.1, this page.

3. Severance. If the issue that is subject to arbitration is severable, the stay can be granted for that issue only. CCP §1281.4 ¶3; ***Cruz v. PacifiCare Health Sys.*** (2003) 30 Cal.4th 303, 320.

§4. EFFECT OF TRIAL CONTINUANCE ON DISCOVERY

A continuance of a trial date will not automatically extend the initial discovery deadline (e.g., 30 days before initial trial date) or reopen discovery after the deadline has passed. *See* CCP §2024.020; ***Fairmont Ins. v. Superior Ct.*** (2000) 22 Cal.4th 245, 251. See "Modifying discovery cutoffs," ch. 7-A, §5.2.3, p. 748 (discussing motions to reopen discovery after new trial date has been set). But a continuance of a trial date does require the party requesting the continuance, if asked by an opposing party, to consent to the taking of the deposition of any witness of the opposing party who is in attendance. CCP §596. The witness's deposition testimony can be (1) taken before a judge or clerk of the court in which the case is pending or any notary public as directed by the court and (2) read at trial with the same effect and subject to the same objections as if the witness were present at trial. *Id.*

§5. MOTION FOR RECONSIDERATION

A party adversely affected by the court's order of continuance or stay can file a motion for reconsideration. CCP §1008(a). See "Motion for Reconsideration," ch. 5-G, §3, p. 508.

§6. MOTION FOR RENEWAL

A party whose application or motion for continuance or stay is denied can file a motion for renewal. CCP §1008(b). See "Motion for Renewal," ch. 5-G, §4, p. 516.

§7. APPELLATE REVIEW

§7.1 Writ of mandate. A party can challenge the ruling on a request for continuance or stay by filing a petition for a writ of mandate. *See* ***Whalen v. Superior Ct.*** (2d Dist.1960) 184 Cal.App.2d 598, 601-02 (motion for continuance); *see, e.g.*, ***Smith v. Jones*** (1900) 128 Cal. 14, 15 (Ps sought writ of mandate to compel trial court to vacate

stay and render judgment; petition denied); ***Vesco v. Superior Ct.*** (2d Dist.2013) 221 Cal.App.4th 275, 280-81 (court granted P's petition for writ of mandate to compel trial court to vacate order granting trial continuance); ***Avant! Corp. v. Superior Ct.*** (6th Dist.2000) 79 Cal.App.4th 876, 878 (D sought writ of mandate to compel trial court to vacate order denying motion to stay discovery; petition denied).

§7.2 Direct appeal. A party can challenge the court's ruling on a request for continuance or stay by raising the issue on appeal after the entry of a final judgment. *See* CCP §904.1(a)(1) (appealable order in unlimited civil cases), §904.2(a) (appealable order in limited civil cases); *see, e.g.*, ***Thurman v. Bayshore Transit Mgmt.*** (4th Dist.2012) 203 Cal.App.4th 1112, 1119 (P appealed denial of motion for continuance); ***Bains v. Moores*** (4th Dist.2009) 172 Cal.App.4th 445, 450 (Ps appealed denial of motion to stay).

§7.3 Standard of review. Generally, the trial court's ruling is reviewed for abuse of discretion. ***Dailey v. Sears, Roebuck & Co.*** (4th Dist.2013) 214 Cal.App.4th 974, 1004 (continuance of hearing); ***Bains v. Moores*** (4th Dist.2009) 172 Cal.App.4th 445, 480 (stay of all proceedings); ***Forrest v. Department of Corps.*** (2d Dist.2007) 150 Cal.App.4th 183, 200 (continuance of trial), *disapproved on other grounds*, ***Shalant v. Girardi*** (2011) 51 Cal.4th 1164; *see, e.g.*, ***Cotton v. Starcare Med. Grp.*** (4th Dist.2010) 183 Cal.App.4th 437, 445 (denial of continuance that has practical effect of denying applicant fair hearing is often reversible error). But if the facts supporting the motion are undisputed, the issue of continuance or stay becomes a question of law, and the standard of review is de novo. *See* ***In re A.R.*** (4th Dist.2009) 170 Cal.App.4th 733, 740.

J. REQUEST FOR JUDICIAL NOTICE

§1. GENERAL

§1.1 Purpose. A request for judicial notice asks the court to recognize and accept facts or legal matters that cannot reasonably be disputed. ***Unruh-Haxton v. Regents of the Univ. of Cal.*** (4th Dist.2008) 162 Cal.App.4th 343, 364; *see* Evid. C. §§451-452.5; ***Scott v. JPMorgan Chase Bank*** (1st Dist.2013) 214 Cal.App.4th 743, 759; ***Fremont Indem. Co. v. Fremont Gen. Corp.*** (2d Dist.2007) 148 Cal.App.4th 97, 113. Judicial notice saves time and reduces costs by eliminating the need for formal proof. *See* ***Unruh-Haxton***, 162 Cal.App.4th at 364 (judicial notice eliminates need for formal proof of matter of law or fact); ***Mozzetti v. City of Brisbane*** (1st Dist.1977) 67 Cal.App.3d 565, 578 (judicial notice expedites production and introduction of evidence); 1 Witkin, *California Evidence* (5th ed. 2012 & Supp.2014), Judicial Notice, §1 (judicial notice is highly desirable means for saving time and money).

§1.2 Primary authority. Evid. C. §§450-460; CRC 3.1113(*l*), 3.1306(c).

§1.3 Secondary authority. The following secondary sources are cited as authority in this subchapter:

- Wegner, *California Practice Guide: Civil Trials & Evidence* (CD-ROM ed. 2014) (referred to as Wegner, *Civil Trials & Evidence*).
- Witkin, *California Evidence* (5th ed. 2012 & Supp.2014) (referred to as Witkin, *Cal. Evidence*).

§2. GROUNDS

To prevail on a request for judicial notice, the requesting party must establish that the matter is relevant and that the court is required or authorized to take judicial notice of the matter.

§2.1 Relevance. The requesting party must establish that the matter is relevant to a material issue in the action or proceeding. ***People v. Shamrock Foods Co.*** (2000) 24 Cal.4th 415, 422 n.2; ***Deveny v. Entropin, Inc.*** (4th Dist.2006) 139 Cal.App.4th 408, 418; *see* Evid. C. §351; *see, e.g.*, ***Ketchum v. Moses*** (2001) 24 Cal.4th 1122, 1135 n.1 (court denied request for judicial notice of items concerning unrelated proposed legislation because items had little relevance to material issue); ***Jordache Enters. v. Brobeck, Phleger & Harrison*** (1998) 18 Cal.4th 739, 748 n.6 (court denied request for judicial notice of irrelevant legislative materials and court decisions); ***Valley Med. Transp. v. Apple Valley Fire Prot. Dist.*** (1998) 17 Cal.4th 747, 761 n.4 (court denied request for judicial notice of irrelevant declarations from similar cases). To be relevant, the matter must help prove or disprove an important, disputed fact.

Evid. C. §210; *see* ***Golden Gate Land Holdings LLC v. East Bay Reg'l Park Dist.*** (1st Dist.2013) 215 Cal.App.4th 353, 366-67; ***People v. Broderick Boys*** (3d Dist.2007) 149 Cal.App.4th 1506, 1524; ***Heppler v. J.M. Peters Co.*** (4th Dist.1999) 73 Cal.App.4th 1265, 1286 (court properly refused to take judicial notice of its ruling that settlement was made in good faith because it was irrelevant and would be confusing and misleading).

§2.2 Required or authorized by law. The requesting party must establish that the court is required or authorized to take judicial notice of the matter. Evid. C. §450. These grounds for judicial notice are commonly referred to as "mandatory," "conditional mandatory," and "permissive" notice.

1. Mandatory notice. The court must take judicial notice of the following matters, regardless of whether a party requests it:

(1) California authority.

(a) California law. The court must take judicial notice of the law in the Constitution, statutes, and cases of California. Evid. C. §451(a); *e.g.*, ***Kasem v. Dion-Kindem*** (2d Dist.2014) 230 Cal.App.4th 1395, 1400 (trial court erred in not taking judicial notice of California statutes establishing that sewage is hazardous material). Unpublished cases may be judicially noticed only if they are relevant to the current action or proceeding under the doctrine of law of the case, res judicata, or collateral estoppel. ***Alvarez v. May Dept. Stores*** (2d Dist.2006) 143 Cal.App.4th 1223, 1240; *see* CRC 8.1115(b) (listing exceptions to rule against citing or relying on unpublished opinions).

(b) County or city charters. The court must take judicial notice of the provisions of county or city charters described under Section 3, 4, or 5 of Article XI of the California Constitution. Evid. C. §451(a); *see, e.g.*, ***Edgerly v. City of Oakland*** (1st Dist.2012) 211 Cal.App.4th 1191, 1194 n.1 (city charter).

(c) Court rules. The court must take judicial notice of the California Rules of Court adopted by the Judicial Council. Evid. C. §451(c).

(d) Agency regulations. The court must take judicial notice of the contents of a regulation or repeal of a regulation by a California state agency if (1) a certified copy is filed with the Secretary of State or (2) it is published or incorporated by reference in the California Code of Regulations or the California Code of Regulations Supplement. *See* Evid. C. §451(b); Gov. C. §§11343.6, 11344.6.

(e) State Bar rules. The court must take judicial notice of the Rules of Professional Conduct adopted by the California State Bar. Evid. C. §451(c); *see* Bus. & Prof. C. §6076.

(f) State Personnel Board rules. The court must take judicial notice of the rules, regulations, and amendments adopted by the State Personnel Board. Gov. C. §18576; *see* Evid. C. §451(b).

(g) Department of Human Resources rules. The court must take judicial notice of the rules, regulations, and amendments adopted by the Department of Human Resources. Gov. C. §18576; *see* Evid. C. §451(b).

(2) Federal authority.

(a) Federal law. The court must take judicial notice of the law in the U.S. Constitution, federal statutes, and federal cases. Evid. C. §451(a); *e.g.*, ***Kasem***, 230 Cal.App.4th at 1400 (trial court erred in not taking judicial notice of federal statutes establishing that sewage is hazardous material).

(b) Federal rules. The court must take judicial notice of rules of pleading, practice, and procedure adopted by the U.S. Supreme Court, including the Rules of the U.S. Supreme Court, the Federal Rules of Civil Procedure, the Federal Rules of Criminal Procedure, the Admiralty Rules, the Rules of the Court of Claims, the Rules of the Customs Court, and the General Orders and Forms in Bankruptcy. Evid. C. §451(d).

(c) Federal Register. The court must take judicial notice of information published in the Federal Register (e.g., notices of proposed rulemaking and agency regulations). 44 U.S.C. §1507; *see* Evid. C. §451(b); ***Southern Cal. Reg'l Rail Auth. v. Superior Ct.*** (2d Dist.2008) 163 Cal.App.4th 712, 728 n.8.

(3) Words & phrases. The court must take judicial notice of the ordinary and popular meaning of all English words and phrases. *See* Evid. C. §451(e); ***Clarke v. Fitch*** (1871) 41 Cal. 472, 477; ***Golden Sec. Thrift & Loan Ass'n v. First Am. Title Ins.*** (4th Dist.1997) 53 Cal.App.4th 250, 256; *see, e.g.*, ***Sierra Club v. Superior Ct.*** (2013) 57 Cal.4th 157, 171 (court took judicial notice of dictionary definition of "program"); ***Castro v. State*** (1970) 2 Cal.3d 223, 238-39 & n.28 (court took judicial notice of dictionary definition of "newspaper"); ***Colgan v. Leatherman Tool Grp.*** (2d Dist.2006) 135 Cal.App.4th 663, 685 n.18 (court would not take judicial notice of industry association's specialized definition of "manufacturing" because it was not relevant to determination of term's ordinary and popular meaning); ***California Sch. of Culinary Arts v. Lujan*** (2d Dist.2003) 112 Cal.App.4th 16, 28 (court denied request for judicial notice of encyclopedia definition of "college" because term did not have common meaning). However, §451(e) does not authorize the court to resort to a dictionary to resolve factual questions that do not turn on conventional linguistic usage. ***Parker v. Twentieth Century-Fox Film Corp.*** (1970) 3 Cal.3d 176, 189 (Sullivan, C.J., dissenting).

(4) Legal expressions. The court must take judicial notice of the true meaning of all legal expressions, including the meaning of terms used in the California Constitution and statutes. Evid. C. §451(e); ***Hom v. Clark*** (1st Dist.1963) 221 Cal.App.2d 622, 637; *e.g.*, ***Sheehy v. Shinn*** (1894) 103 Cal. 325, 329-30 (court could take judicial notice of meaning of "on margin" in California Constitution); *see, e.g.*, ***In re Estate of Minor*** (2d Dist.1922) 59 Cal.App. 616, 619 (court gave "their heirs and assigns" its usual legal meaning).

(5) Universally known facts. The court must take judicial notice of facts and propositions of generalized knowledge that are so universally known they cannot reasonably be disputed. Evid. C. §451(f); *see* 7 Cal. Law Revision Comm'n Rep. (1965) p. 1066 (information must be widely known, not just known to judge). The facts and propositions must be generally known by people of average intelligence and knowledge. 7 Cal. Law Revision Comm'n Rep. (1965) pp. 1065-66. The following are examples of universally known facts and propositions that can be judicially noticed:

(a) Streetlights make streets and sidewalks safer. *See* ***Howard Jarvis Taxpayers Ass'n v. City of Riverside*** (4th Dist.1999) 73 Cal.App.4th 679, 685-86 & n.4.

(b) Street gangs engage in violent acts. *See* ***Medina v. Hillshore Partners*** (2d Dist.1995) 40 Cal.App.4th 477, 481.

(c) Baseballs are thrown toward batters at baseball games. *See* ***Avila v. Citrus Cmty. Coll. Dist.*** (2006) 38 Cal.4th 148, 165 n.12.

(d) Radar is a valid method of measuring speed. *See* ***People v. MacLaird*** (1st Dist.1968) 264 Cal.App.2d 972, 975.

(e) There are many kinds of copying machines using different processes. *See* ***Barreiro v. State Bar*** (1970) 2 Cal.3d 912, 925.

(6) Matters listed under other law. The court must take judicial notice of matters required to be judicially noticed under other statutes outside the Evidence Code. 7 Cal. Law Revision Comm'n Rep. (1965) p. 1063; *see* Evid. C. §450. For example, the court must take judicial notice of the seal affixed or imprinted on an order, certificate, or other instrument issued by the Director of the Department of Managed Health Care. Health & Saf. C. §1341.3.

2. Conditional mandatory notice. Under certain circumstances, the court must take judicial notice of permissive matters listed under Evid. C. §452. Evid. C. §453. See "Permissive notice," §2.2.3, p. 550. For a court to be compelled to take judicial notice of permissive matters, the party requesting judicial notice must satisfy the following conditions:

(1) Party gives sufficient notice. The requesting party must give each adverse party sufficient notice of the request, through the pleadings or otherwise. Evid. C. §453(a); 7 Cal. Law Revision Comm'n Rep. (1965) p. 1071; *see, e.g.*, ***Pacific Lumber Co. v. State Water Res. Control Bd.*** (2006) 37 Cal.4th 921, 936 n.4 (court denied

request to judicially notice legislative and executive reports when it was made only five days before oral argument). How much time is enough varies depending on the case. 7 Cal. Law Revision Comm'n Rep. (1965) p. 1071.

(2) Party gives sufficient information. The requesting party must give the court sufficient information to take judicial notice of the matter. Evid. C. §453(b); *see* ***People v. Moore*** (5th Dist.1997) 59 Cal.App.4th 168, 177 (court is not required to research information on its own); ***Whispering Pines Mobile Home Park, Ltd. v. City of Scotts Valley*** (6th Dist.1986) 180 Cal.App.3d 152, 162 (court can deny judicial notice if sufficient information is not provided by party); *see, e.g.*, ***Barker v. Garza*** (2d Dist.2013) 218 Cal.App.4th 1449, 1452 n.1 (court denied P's request for judicial notice of law-review article and article on model-code website when P did not provide sufficient information for court to determine if judicial notice was proper); ***Center for Biological Diversity v. Fish & Game Comm'n*** (3d Dist.2008) 166 Cal.App.4th 597, 605 n.11 (court denied request for judicial notice of orders when copies of orders were not supplied). Information must come from sources that are reliable, trustworthy, and accurate. ***Moore***, 59 Cal.App.4th at 177. What constitutes a sufficient source of information varies depending on the matter. *Id.*; 7 Cal. Law Revision Comm'n Rep. (1965) p. 1072. For example, the court may require expert testimony for difficult matters. 7 Cal. Law Revision Comm'n Rep. (1965) p. 1072.

3. Permissive notice. The court can take judicial notice of the following matters, regardless of whether a party requests it:

(1) Law of other jurisdictions.

(a) Other states. The court can take judicial notice of the law in the constitution, statutes, and cases of other U.S. states. Evid. C. §452(a); *see, e.g.*, ***Barker***, 218 Cal.App.4th at 1452 n.1 (court granted judicial notice of Michigan Drug Dealer Liability Act); *see also* Evid. C. §220 ("state" includes any state, district, commonwealth, territory, or insular possession).

(b) Foreign jurisdictions. The court can take judicial notice of the laws of an organization of nations, foreign nations, and public entities in foreign nations. Evid. C. §452(f); 7 Cal. Law Revision Comm'n Rep. (1965) p. 1069.

(2) Resolutions & private acts. The court can take judicial notice of resolutions and private acts passed by the U.S. Congress and the California Legislature. Evid. C. §452(a). Private acts are bills that affect only specific individuals, not the general public (e.g., bills that benefit veterans). *See Black's Law Dictionary* 1635 (10th ed. 2014) (definition of "special statute").

(3) Regulations & legislative enactments. The court can take judicial notice of regulations or legislative enactments issued by or under the authority of the United States or any public entity in the United States. Evid. C. §452(b); *see* 7 Cal. Law Revision Comm'n Rep. (1965) p. 1068 (Evid. C. §452(b) allows for judicial notice of regulations not covered under §451(b) and regulations of other U.S. states, territories, and possessions). A public entity includes a nation, state, county, city and county, city, district, public authority, public agency, or any other political subdivision or public corporation, whether foreign or domestic. Evid. C. §200. Examples of regulations and legislative enactments by a public entity that can be judicially noticed include the following:

(a) Public notices issued by the California Department of Food and Agriculture. *See* ***Pacific Merch. Shipping Ass'n v. Voss*** (1995) 12 Cal.4th 503, 512 n.5.

(b) Public Health Service Guidelines issued by the U.S. Department of Health and Human Services. *See* ***Love v. Superior Ct.*** (1st Dist.1990) 226 Cal.App.3d 736, 743 n.5.

(c) County resolutions. *See* ***Cooke v. Superior Ct.*** (3d Dist.1989) 213 Cal.App.3d 401, 416, *disapproved on other grounds*, ***County of San Diego v. State*** (1997) 15 Cal.4th 68.

(d) City or county ordinances. 7 Cal. Law Revision Comm'n Rep. (1965) p. 1068; *see* ***City of Ontario v. Superior Ct.*** (4th Dist.1993) 12 Cal.App.4th 894, 899 n.5; *see, e.g.*, ***Calguns Found. v. County of San Mateo*** (1st Dist.2013) 218 Cal.App.4th 661, 666 n.6 (court granted judicial notice of city and county ordinances).

(e) City-council resolutions. *See* ***May v. City of Milpitas*** (6th Dist.2013) 217 Cal.App.4th 1307, 1318-19.

(f) School-district resolutions. *See* ***Warmington Old Town Assocs. v. Tustin Unified Sch. Dist.*** (4th Dist.2002) 101 Cal.App.4th 840, 858 n.3.

(g) Safety standards in an advisory circular issued by the Federal Aviation Administration. ***Sierra Pac. Holdings, Inc. v. County of Ventura*** (2d Dist. 2012) 204 Cal.App.4th 509, 512 n.1.

(4) Official acts. The court can take judicial notice of official acts of federal and state legislative, executive, and judicial departments. Evid. C. §452(c); *e.g.*, ***Scott v. JPMorgan Chase Bank*** (1st Dist.2013) 214 Cal.App.4th 743, 752-53 (FDIC's official acts of seizing assets, publishing purchase-and-assumption agreement, and transferring assets but not liabilities were judicially noticeable). A common official act that can be noticed is the creation of an official document. *See, e.g.*, ***Town of Atherton v. California High-Speed Rail Auth.*** (3d Dist.2014) 228 Cal.App.4th 314, 338 (court took judicial notice of state senator's letter contained in Senate Daily Journal). Although the court can take judicial notice of the existence, contents, and authenticity of an official document, the court cannot take judicial notice of the truth of factual matters or a particular interpretation of a document. *See* ***Glaski v. Bank of Am.*** (5th Dist.2013) 218 Cal.App.4th 1079, 1090; ***Scott***, 214 Cal.App.4th at 754; ***Herrera v. Deutsche Bank Nat'l Trust Co.*** (3d Dist.2011) 196 Cal.App.4th 1366, 1375; *see, e.g.*, ***Mangini v. R.J. Reynolds Tobacco Co.*** (1994) 7 Cal.4th 1057, 1063-64 (court took judicial notice of materials relating to legislative history of statute at issue, but denied request to notice letter from state attorneys general to U.S. senator urging repeal of statute), *overruled on other grounds*, ***In re Tobacco Cases II*** (2007) 41 Cal.4th 1257. Examples of official documents that can be judicially noticed include the following:

(a) Cognizable legislative history of bills. *See* ***Kaufman & Broad Cmty., Inc. v. Performance Plastering, Inc.*** (3d Dist.2005) 133 Cal.App.4th 26, 29. To be cognizable, the legislative history must show the view of the whole legislature, not of individual members. *Id.* at 30. *See generally id.* at 31-39 (detailed list of legislative history that is and is not cognizable).

PRACTICE TIP

When requesting judicial notice of legislative history, the movant should specify each separate document it wants judicially noticed and state why each document is cognizable. ***Kaufman & Broad Cmty.****, 133 Cal.App.4th at 31.*

(b) Reports issued by government entities. *See, e.g.*, ***People v. Rodriguez*** (2012) 55 Cal.4th 1125, 1129 n.4 (California Legislative Counsel report); ***Aguilar v. Atlantic Richfield Co.*** (2001) 25 Cal.4th 826, 842 n.3 (California Attorney General's report); ***Mitsubishi Materials Corp. v. Superior Ct.*** (4th Dist.2003) 113 Cal.App.4th 55, 63 n.5 (U.S. Senate report); ***League for Prot. of Oakland's Architectural & Historic Res. v. City of Oakland*** (1st Dist.1997) 52 Cal.App.4th 896, 900 n.2 (city's technical report on historic preservation).

(c) State budget acts and summaries. *See* ***Carmel Valley Fire Prot. Dist. v. State*** (2001) 25 Cal.4th 287, 293 n.2.

(d) Public Utilities Commission decisions. *See* ***Wise v. Pacific Gas & Elec. Co.*** (1st Dist.1999) 77 Cal.App.4th 287, 297.

(e) Official documents prepared by state administrative boards. *See, e.g.*, ***Harris v. Alcoholic Bev. Control Appeals Bd.*** (1965) 62 Cal.2d 589, 595-96 (court took judicial notice of bulletin that was prepared by director of Department of Alcoholic Beverages and sent to area administrators); ***Fowler v. Howell*** (2d Dist.1996) 42 Cal.App.4th 1746, 1750 (court took judicial notice of California State Personnel Board decision); *see also* ***Stevens v. Superior Ct.*** (2d Dist.1999) 75 Cal.App.4th 594, 607-08 (court cannot take judicial notice of documents prepared by private parties and merely on file with state agency).

(f) Recorded documents. *See* ***Ragland v. U.S. Bank Nat'l Ass'n*** (4th Dist.2012) 209 Cal.App.4th 182, 194 (recorded deed is official act of executive branch, of which court may take judicial notice); ***Fontenot v. Wells Fargo Bank*** (1st Dist.2011) 198 Cal.App.4th 256, 264-65 (courts have taken judicial notice of existence and recordation of recorded documents). In addition to taking judicial notice of the existence, contents, and authenticity of the document, if the document is a legally operative document that is not reasonably subject to dispute, the court can take judicial notice of facts that derive from the legally operative effect of the document. *See* ***Scott***, 214 Cal.App.4th at 754-55 (court does not abuse its discretion in taking judicial notice of facts that derive from legal effect of documents); ***Fontenot***, 198 Cal.App.4th at 265 (court may deduce and rely on legal effect of recorded document when effect is clear from face of document; permissible for court to take judicial notice of document's recordation, date document was recorded and executed, parties to transaction, and document's legally operative effect). Whether the fact to be judicially noticed is the document or record itself, the legal effect of the document, a fact asserted within the document, or an act by a government agency, the essential question is whether the fact to be judicially noticed is not reasonably subject to dispute. ***Scott***, 214 Cal.App.4th at 759.

(g) Contracts. *See, e.g.*, ***Scott***, 214 Cal.App.4th at 753 (trial court's judicial notice of government contract with savings bank was proper because official acts evinced in contract were judicially noticeable and contract was not reasonably subject to dispute). In addition to taking judicial notice of the existence and contents of the contract, the court can take judicial notice of facts that derive from the legally operative effect of the contract if those facts are not reasonably subject to dispute. *Id.* at 754-55. For a discussion of judicial notice of legally operative documents, see "Official acts," §2.2.3(4)(f), this page.

(5) Court records. The court can take judicial notice of the records of any California court or other state or federal court. Evid. C. §452(d); *e.g.*, ***In re Marquez*** (2003) 30 Cal.4th 14, 18 n.2 (court took judicial notice of court records in two underlying appeals); *see* CRC 3.1306(c) (listing requirements for judicial notice of court's own records); *see also* ***Thayer v. Kabateck Brown Kellner LLP*** (1st Dist.2012) 207 Cal.App.4th 141, 155-56 (court records do not have to be sworn or certified for court to take judicial notice of them).

(a) Existence. The court can take judicial notice of the existence of court records. *See* ***Laabs v. City of Victorville*** (4th Dist.2008) 163 Cal.App.4th 1242, 1266; ***North Beverly Park Homeowners Ass'n v. Bisno*** (2d Dist.2007) 147 Cal.App.4th 762, 778. For example, courts can take judicial notice of the following records:

[1] Pleadings. *See, e.g.*, ***Sustainable Transp. Advocates v. Santa Barbara Cty. Ass'n of Gov'ts*** (2d Dist.2009) 179 Cal.App.4th 113, 119 n.2 (court took judicial notice of petition for writ of mandate filed in trial court); ***Gbur v. Cohen*** (2d Dist.1979) 93 Cal.App.3d 296, 301 (court took judicial notice of pertinent allegations in first amended cross-complaint).

[2] Discovery. *See, e.g.*, ***Williams v. Southern Cal. Gas Co.*** (2d Dist.2009) 176 Cal.App.4th 591, 600 (court could take judicial notice of discovery responses but could not make any factual inferences from them).

[3] Orders, judgments, and findings of fact and conclusions of law. ***Kilroy v. State*** (3d Dist.2004) 119 Cal.App.4th 140, 145; ***Lockley v. Law Office of Cantrell, Green, Pekich, Cruz & McCort*** (2d Dist.2001) 91 Cal.App.4th 875, 882; *see* ***Deveny v. Entropin, Inc.*** (4th Dist.2006) 139 Cal.App.4th 408, 418 (court can take judicial notice of unpublished orders and decisions in related federal proceeding); *see, e.g.*, ***Burrill v. Nair*** (3d Dist.2013) 217 Cal.App.4th 357, 364 & n.1 (court took judicial notice of unpublished opinions in previous appeals in same custody dispute); ***In re C.C.*** (2d Dist.2009) 172 Cal.App.4th 1481, 1487 n.3 (court took judicial notice of minute order).

[4] Settlement agreements. *See* ***City of Atascadero v. Merrill Lynch, Pierce, Fenner & Smith, Inc.*** (1st Dist.1998) 68 Cal.App.4th 445, 459 n.12.

[5] Computer-generated official court records specified by the Judicial Council that are (1) related to criminal convictions and (2) certified by a superior-court clerk under Gov. C. §69844.5 when they are entered. *See* Evid. C. §452.5(a).

[6] A party's plea in an earlier criminal proceeding. *See* ***City of Bell v. Superior Ct.*** (2d Dist.2013) 220 Cal.App.4th 236, 243 n.7.

(b) Facts. The court can take judicial notice of the truth of the results reached in court records (e.g., court's denial of relief), but it cannot take judicial notice of the truth of the factual matters asserted in those documents, including the factual findings or hearsay statements made in them. ***Steed v. Department of Consumer Affairs*** (2d Dist.2012) 204 Cal.App.4th 112, 120-121; *see* ***Kilroy***, 119 Cal.App.4th at 145; ***Lockley***, 91 Cal.App.4th at 882; ***Williams v. Wraxall*** (1st Dist.1995) 33 Cal.App.4th 120, 130 n.7; 1 Witkin, *Cal. Evidence*, Judicial Notice, §26; *see, e.g.*, ***Rialto Police Benefit Ass'n v. City of Rialto*** (4th Dist.2007) 155 Cal.App.4th 1295, 1299 n.2 (court denied request to judicially notice facts asserted in declaration filed in support of petition for writ of mandate). For example, a trial judge's findings of fact can be judicially noticed to prove that certain findings were made but not to establish that one party's testimony must necessarily have been true. ***Plumley v. Mockett*** (2d Dist.2008) 164 Cal.App.4th 1031, 1050; *see* ***Steed***, 204 Cal.App.4th at 120-121; *see also* ***Magnolia Square Homeowners Ass'n v. Safeco Ins.*** (6th Dist.1990) 221 Cal.App.3d 1049, 1056-57 (court could take judicial notice of court records because they were offered to prove notice, not truth of factual allegations contained in them). Likewise, an appellate court's description of facts in an opinion is the hearsay assertion of the justices who delivered it, so it can only be judicially noticed to prove that an opinion was delivered and that the court made certain orders, factual findings, judgments, and conclusions of law. ***Lockley***, 91 Cal.App.4th at 885. *But see* ***Weiner v. Mitchell, Silberg & Knupp*** (2d Dist.1980) 114 Cal.App.3d 39, 46 (court could take judicial notice of truth of facts stated in appellate opinion). A court can, however, take judicial notice of a factual finding in a prior judicial opinion if it has a res judicata or collateral-estoppel effect in a subsequent action. ***Kilroy***, 119 Cal.App.4th at 148.

NOTE

Although the courts in ***Scott*** *and* ***Fontenot*** *did not specify whether their analysis of judicial notice of legally operative documents applies to court documents, it is possible that the reasoning in* ***Scott*** *and* ***Fontenot*** *could extend to judicial notice of facts that derive from the legally operative effect of court orders and judgments. See* ***Fontenot****, 198 Cal.App.4th at 266 n.6 (rejecting* ***Abernathy Valley, Inc. v. County of Solano*** *(1st Dist.2009) 173 Cal.App.4th 42, 54 n.6, which declined to take judicial notice of deeds, judgments, and indentures as evidence of actual conveyances because such use would require accepting truth of facts stated therein); cf.* ***Scott****, 214 Cal.App.4th at 755 (no abuse of discretion in taking judicial notice of legal effect of order issued by federal government's former Office of Thrift Supervision);* ***Kilroy****, 119 Cal.App.4th at 148 (even though factual finding in prior judicial decision may not establish truth of fact for purposes of judicial notice, finding itself may be proper subject of judicial notice if it has res judicata or collateral-estoppel effect in subsequent action). For a discussion of judicial notice of legally operative documents, see "Official acts," §2.2.3(4)(f), p. 552.*

(6) Court rules. The court can take judicial notice of the procedural rules of any U.S., California, or other state court. Evid. C. §452(e); *see, e.g.*, ***State v. Bragg*** (2d Dist.1986) 183 Cal.App.3d 1018, 1027 & n.9 (court took judicial notice of Los Angeles Superior Court local rule).

(7) Common knowledge. The court can take judicial notice of facts and matters that are common knowledge in the court's territorial jurisdiction (i.e., the county where the court sits) and that cannot reasonably be disputed. Evid. C. §452(g); 7 Cal. Law Revision Comm'n Rep. (1965) pp. 1069-70. Judicial notice can be taken of information about matters located outside the court's territorial jurisdiction as long as that information is common knowledge among residents within the court's territorial jurisdiction. 7 Cal. Law Revision Comm'n Rep. (1965) p. 1070. Examples of common knowledge in a court's territorial jurisdiction that can be judicially noticed include the following:

(a) The identity of a public official. *See, e.g.*, ***People v. Rhodes*** (1974) 12 Cal.3d 180, 182 n.1 (D's counsel was city attorney).

(b) A local highway is heavily traveled at a particular time. *See* ***People v. Tobin*** (1st Dist.1990) 219 Cal.App.3d 634, 639.

(c) A curfew was imposed in the area on a particular date because of rioting. *See* ***In re Juan C.*** (2d Dist.1994) 28 Cal.App.4th 1093, 1098-99.

(d) Certain companies are private entities that provide retail or commercial services. ***Pacific Gas & Elec. Co. v. City & Cty. of San Francisco*** (1st Dist.2012) 206 Cal.App.4th 897, 903 n.7.

(e) There is no city of "Idaho" in California. ***In re Suhey G.*** (2d Dist.2013) 221 Cal.App.4th 732, 735 n.7.

(8) Immediately & accurately verifiable information. The court can take judicial notice of facts and matters that (1) can be immediately and accurately verified by consulting sources of reasonably indisputable accuracy (e.g., treatises, encyclopedias, almanacs, and information provided by experts) and (2) cannot reasonably be disputed. Evid. C. §452(h); ***People v. Archerd*** (1970) 3 Cal.3d 615, 638. Examples of immediately and accurately verifiable information that can be judicially noticed include the following:

(a) Recorded documents. *See* ***West v. JPMorgan Chase Bank*** (4th Dist.2013) 214 Cal.App.4th 780, 803 (recorded deed); ***Poseidon Dev., Inc. v. Woodland Lane Estates, LLC*** (3d Dist.2007) 152 Cal.App.4th 1106, 1117 (same); *see also* ***B&P Dev. Corp. v. City of Saratoga*** (6th Dist.1986) 185 Cal.App.3d 949, 960 (recorded subdivision map). In addition to taking judicial notice of the existence, contents, and authenticity of the document, if the document is legally operative, the court can take judicial notice of facts that derive from the legally operative effect of the document if those facts are not reasonably subject to dispute. *See* ***Scott***, 214 Cal.App.4th at 754-55. For a discussion of judicial notice of legally operative documents, see "Official acts," §2.2.3(4)(f), p. 552.

(b) Contracts. *See* ***Scott***, 214 Cal.App.4th at 753 (trial court's judicial notice of government contract with savings bank was proper because contract was not reasonably subject to dispute). In addition to taking judicial notice of the existence and contents of the contract, the court can take judicial notice of facts that derive from the legally operative effect of the contract if those facts are not reasonably subject to dispute. *Id.* at 754-55. For a discussion of judicial notice of legally operative documents, see "Official acts," §2.2.3(4)(g), p. 552.

(c) Geographic information. *See, e.g.*, ***People v. Danielson*** (1992) 3 Cal.4th 691, 704-05 (standard map of county), *overruled on other grounds*, ***Price v. Superior Ct.*** (2001) 25 Cal.4th 1046; ***People v. Chavarria*** (2d Dist.2013) 213 Cal.App.4th 1364, 1367 n.2 (location of city within county and county within area code); ***In re Alice M.*** (6th Dist.2008) 161 Cal.App.4th 1189, 1201 n.7 (geographic size of town); ***City of Anaheim v. Workers' Comp. Appeals Bd.*** (4th Dist.1981) 116 Cal.App.3d 248, 261 n.17 (distance and travel time between locations).

(d) Historical information. *See, e.g.*, ***Estate of Rudolph*** (1st Dist.1980) 112 Cal.App.3d 81, 83 (June was only month in 1978 in which 26th day fell on Monday).

(e) Natural events. *See, e.g.*, ***People v. Mai*** (2013) 57 Cal.4th 986, 1016 n.8 (sunset occurred in Fullerton at 8:04 p.m. on July 13, 1996).

(f) Published rules or procedures followed by an entity or organization. *See, e.g.*, ***Boghos v. Certain Underwriters at Lloyd's of London*** (2005) 36 Cal.4th 495, 505 n.6 (American Arbitration Association rules); ***Gentry v. Ebay, Inc.*** (4th Dist.2002) 99 Cal.App.4th 816, 823-24 (procedure for listing item on eBay).

(g) Facts widely accepted as true by experts and specialists in the natural, physical, and social sciences. *See* ***Gould v. Maryland Sound Indus.*** (2d Dist.1995) 31 Cal.App.4th 1137, 1145.

(h) Foreign court records. *See, e.g.*, ***In re Marriage of Taschen*** (2d Dist.2005) 134 Cal.App.4th 681, 688 n.3 (judgment of German court).

(i) Demographics and other statistical information. *See, e.g.*, ***Mission Springs Water Dist. v. Verjil*** (4th Dist.2013) 218 Cal.App.4th 892, 915 & n.5 (Bureau of Labor Statistics Consumer Price Index); ***In re Alice M.***, 161 Cal.App.4th at 1201 n.7 (population of town); ***Moehring v. Thomas*** (3d Dist.2005) 126 Cal.App.4th 1515, 1523 n.4 (U.S. Census information).

(9) Matters listed under other law. The court can take judicial notice of matters that can be judicially noticed under other statutes outside the Evidence Code. 7 Cal. Law Revision Comm'n Rep. (1965) p. 1062; *see* Evid. C. §450. For example, Civ. C. §53 allows the court to take judicial notice of a recorded real-property instrument in a civil-rights suit to void a discriminatory clause in the instrument. Civ. C. §53(c).

NOTE

The same information can often be judicially noticed under both Evid. C. §451 (mandatory) and §452 (permissive). See, e.g., ***Wells Fargo Bank v. Goldzband*** *(5th Dist.1997) 53 Cal.App.4th 596, 624 n.12 (passage and approval of Senate bill and its provisions qualified for judicial notice under Evid. C. §§451 and 452). When information is judicially noticeable under both sections, the court must first determine whether it must judicially notice the information under §451. See Evid. C. §452 (court can take judicial notice under §452 to extent not covered by §451).*

§3. REQUEST

§3.1 Who can make. Any party can ask the court to take judicial notice. *See* Evid. C. §453. The court can—and in some cases must—take judicial notice of matters on its own motion. *See id.* §§451, 452; 7 Cal. Law Revision Comm'n Rep. (1965) pp. 1063, 1067; *see, e.g.*, ***City of San Diego v. Shapiro*** (4th Dist.2014) 228 Cal.App.4th 756, 776 n.17 (court took judicial notice of ballot-pamphlet materials on its own motion).

§3.2 How to make.

1. Mandatory notice. The court must take judicial notice of a matter under Evid. C. §451 regardless of whether a party makes a formal request to do so. 7 Cal. Law Revision Comm'n Rep. (1965) p. 1063; Wegner, *Civil Trials & Evidence*, §8:906; *see, e.g.*, ***Day v. Rosenthal*** (2d Dist.1985) 170 Cal.App.3d 1125, 1147 (court was compelled to take judicial notice of standards established by Rules of Professional Conduct when considering attorney's alleged breach of standard of care). For example, a party does not have to formally request judicial notice of the law that applies to a case; instead, the party should simply provide the court with citations to the pertinent authority. *See* ***People v. Rodriguez*** (2012) 55 Cal.4th 1125, 1129 n.4 (request for judicial notice of published material is unnecessary; citation to material is sufficient); ***Quelimane Co. v. Stewart Title Guar. Co.*** (1998) 19 Cal.4th 26, 45 n.9 (same); ***Stop Youth Addiction, Inc. v. Lucky Stores*** (1998) 17 Cal.4th 553, 571 n.9 (same). Even if no citations are provided, the court should still, within reason, research and apply the applicable law. 7 Cal. Law Revision Comm'n Rep. (1965) p. 1064. But this does not mean that a party should never make a formal request. A formal request may be beneficial if the matter to be judicially noticed is unpublished (and thus cannot be cited) or is a disputed fact. *See, e.g.*, ***California Sch. of Culinary Arts v. Lujan*** (2d Dist.2003) 112 Cal.App.4th 16, 26 (D formally requested judicial notice of meaning of several words and phrases, including "college," which was disputed by parties). Regardless of whether a formal request is made, as a practical matter, a party should always provide helpful supporting information to the court. *See* Wegner, *Civil Trials & Evidence*, §8:907. When referencing information the court may not have easy access to (e.g., federal regulations, state ordinances, secondary sources), the party should go a step further and provide copies of the information to the court. *Id.* §8:915.

2. Permissive notice. The court can take judicial notice of a matter under Evid. C. §452 regardless of whether a party makes a formal request to do so. 7 Cal. Law Revision Comm'n Rep. (1965) p. 1067. But the court can be compelled to take notice of a matter if a party makes a formal request and complies with the requirements of Evid. C. §453. 7 Cal. Law Revision Comm'n Rep. (1965) p. 1067; *see* ***People v. Maxwell*** (2d Dist.1978) 78 Cal.App.3d 124, 130 (court must take judicial notice if oral request complies with Evid. C. §453). See "Conditional mandatory notice," §2.2.2, p. 549.

§3.3 Deadline. There is no deadline for the court to act on its own motion or for a party to make a request for judicial notice of most matters under Evid. C. §451 or §452. But for certain matters, the court or party must give notice before the court takes judicial notice.

1. Matter is of substantial consequence. If the court takes or a party requests judicial notice of a universally known fact under Evid. C. §451(f) or of any permissive matter listed in §452 that is of substantial consequence to the determination of the action, the court must give each party a reasonable opportunity to respond before the matter is judicially noticed. Evid. C. §455(a); *see* ***Estate of Nicholas*** (3d Dist.1986) 177 Cal.App.3d 1071, 1090 (court cannot judicially notice matter of substantial consequence without notice to parties); *see, e.g.*, ***Carroll v. State*** (4th Dist.1990) 217 Cal.App.3d 134, 144 (court did not give opposing party opportunity to present information on judicial notice of statements made by judge in another case because statements were not of substantial consequence).

(1) Substantial consequence. A matter is of substantial consequence if it is significant to the determination of a material issue. *See, e.g.*, ***California Sch. Bds. Ass'n v. State*** (3d Dist.2009) 171 Cal.App.4th 1183, 1205 & n.8 (newly filed complaint in another action was not of substantial consequence because issues in complaint were moot in current action); ***Sole Energy Co. v. Hodges*** (4th Dist.2005) 128 Cal.App.4th 199, 205 n.2 (confirmation of service of order was not of substantial consequence in appeal from default judgment).

(2) Reasonable opportunity to respond. The parties who may oppose judicial notice must be given a reasonable opportunity to respond to the propriety of taking judicial notice before the jury is instructed or the case is submitted for the court's decision. Evid. C. §455(a). What constitutes a reasonable opportunity to respond will depend on the complexity of the matter and its importance to the case. 7 Cal. Law Revision Comm'n Rep. (1965) p. 1074 (discussing examples of important and unimportant matters). For example, a complex question about the applicability of foreign law may require the court to hold a hearing. *Id.*

2. Matter depends on information not received in open court. If the court considers information from any source that is not received in open court, including expert advice, the court must give each party a reasonable opportunity to respond to the information before the court takes judicial notice. Evid. C. §455(b). See "Ruling," §6, p. 558.

3. Matter must be noticed. If a party makes a request under Evid. C. §453 for the court to take judicial notice of a permissive matter listed in §452, the court is required to notice the matter if certain conditions, including notice to the adverse parties, are satisfied. See "Conditional mandatory notice," §2.2.2, p. 549.

§3.4 Form.

1. Pretrial motion. When the request is made in connection with a pretrial motion, the request should be made in a separately filed motion, not in the supporting memorandum. CRC 3.1113(*l*); *see* Wegner, *Civil Trials & Evidence*, §8:911.

2. At hearing or trial. When the request is made orally at a hearing (or during trial), the request should be made on the record. Wegner, *Civil Trials & Evidence*, §8:911; *see also* ***People v. Maxwell*** (2d Dist.1978) 78 Cal.App.3d 124, 130 (court must take judicial notice if oral request complies with Evid. C. §453).

3. In preparation for trial. When the request is made in preparation for issues that will come up at trial, the request should be made in the same manner as a motion in limine. Wegner, *Civil Trials & Evidence*, §8:911.

§3.5 Supporting materials. To support the request for judicial notice, the requesting party can provide any source of pertinent information, including the advice of experts. Evid. C. §454(a)(1). See "Party gives sufficient information," §2.2.2(2), p. 550. The requesting party must provide the court and parties with a copy of the material to be judicially noticed. CRC 3.1306(c). The material to be judicially noticed should be properly authenticated. *See, e.g.*, ***People v. Rodriguez*** (2012) 55 Cal.4th 1125, 1129 n.4 (court denied judicial notice of uncertified legislative materials); ***Leibert v. Transworld Sys.*** (1st Dist.1995) 32 Cal.App.4th 1693, 1700 (secondhand reports of conversations and unauthenticated documents were insufficient to require judicial notice).

1. Material in court's file. If the information to be noticed is part of the court's file, the requesting party must (1) specify in writing the part of the court's file to be noticed and (2) make arrangements with the clerk to have the file in the courtroom when the request for judicial notice is heard. CRC 3.1306(c). If the material is part of another court's file, the requesting party will need to get certified copies of the material or subpoena the file. ***Ross v.***

Creel Printing & Publ'g Co. (1st Dist.2002) 100 Cal.App.4th 736, 743. If certified copies are not provided, the requesting party has the burden to demonstrate why they are not available. *Id.*

2. Criminal conviction. If the material to be noticed is a record of a criminal conviction, the requesting party must provide a certified copy of the conviction record in paper or electronic form. *See* Evid. C. §§452.5(b)(1), 1530. The copy of the conviction record can only be used to establish the following:

(1) The commission, attempted commission, or solicitation of a crime. *Id.* §452.5(b)(1).

(2) An earlier conviction of a crime. *Id.*

(3) The fact that a person served time in prison. *Id.*

(4) Any other act, condition, or event recorded in the conviction record. *Id.*

§3.6 Expert advice. To support the request for judicial notice, the requesting party (or the court on its own motion) can ask the court to appoint one or more experts to provide advice on taking judicial notice of a matter. Evid. C. §460. If the court appoints an expert, the expert must be appointed and compensated according to the rules in Evid. C. §730 et seq. *Id.* §460.

§4. RESPONSE

§4.1 Deadline to challenge. There is no deadline for a party to challenge a request for judicial notice or the court's announcement that it either has or will take judicial notice of a matter. Practically speaking, however, if a request is made as part of a pretrial motion, the challenge should be made in the opposition papers. Likewise, if the request is made in open court or the court announces its intent to take judicial notice, the challenge should be made before the court rules on the matter. For certain matters, the responding party must be given an opportunity to respond before the court can make a ruling.

1. Matter is of substantial consequence. For matters of substantial consequence under Evid. C. §455, the responding party must be given a reasonable opportunity to present to the court information relevant to (1) the propriety of taking judicial notice of the matter and (2) the "tenor" (i.e., meaning) of the matter to be noticed. Evid. C. §455(a); *see Black's Law Dictionary* 1697 (10th ed. 2014) (defining "tenor"). See "Matter is of substantial consequence," §3.3.1, p. 556.

2. Matter depends on information not received in open court. For matters that depend on information that was not received in open court, including expert advice, the court must give each party a reasonable opportunity to respond to the information. Evid. C. §455(b).

3. Matter must be noticed. For matters subject to conditional mandatory notice under Evid. C. §453, the responding party must be given sufficient notice to enable the court to meet the request. Evid. C. §453(a); *see* 7 Cal. Law Revision Comm'n Rep. (1965) p. 1071 (when notice given is not sufficient, court can decline to take judicial notice). See "Party gives sufficient notice," §2.2.2(1), p. 549.

§4.2 Challenges. A party can challenge the propriety of taking judicial notice of a matter on any of the following grounds:

1. Evidentiary objections. A party can challenge the taking of judicial notice on any of the following evidentiary grounds:

(1) Authentication. The matter to be noticed is not properly authenticated. *See* ***Wolf v. CDS Devco*** (4th Dist.2010) 185 Cal.App.4th 903, 915.

(2) Hearsay. The matter to be noticed is hearsay. *See* ***Herrera v. Deutsche Bank Nat'l Trust Co.*** (3d Dist.2011) 196 Cal.App.4th 1366, 1375; ***Williams v. Wraxall*** (1st Dist.1995) 33 Cal.App.4th 120, 130 n.7. See "Facts," §2.2.3(5)(b), p. 553.

(3) Privilege. The matter to be noticed is privileged. *See* Evid. C. §454(a)(2).

(4) **Probative value outweighed.** The probative value of the matter to be noticed is substantially outweighed by the probability that its admission will either waste time or create substantial danger of undue prejudice, confusing the issues, or misleading the jury. *See* Evid. C. §§352, 454(a)(2); *see, e.g.*, ***Mitroff v. United Servs. Auto. Ass'n*** (1st Dist.1999) 72 Cal.App.4th 1230, 1243 (court was not required to take judicial notice of court records in unrelated actions because it would have required detailed inquiry into facts and contentions of parties); ***Mozzetti v. City of Brisbane*** (1st Dist.1977) 67 Cal.App.3d 565, 578 (court denied request for judicial notice of proclamation published in Federal Register declaring that county was loan disaster area based on lack of relevance and Evid. C. §352).

2. **Procedural objections.** A party can challenge the taking of judicial notice on procedural grounds. For example, a party can object that notice of the request was not given soon enough to allow it to prepare an adequate response. *See* Evid. C. §§453(a), 455; ***Estate of Nicholas*** (3d Dist.1986) 177 Cal.App.3d 1071, 1090.

3. **Substantive objections.** A party can challenge the taking of judicial notice on any of the following substantive grounds:

(1) **Not authorized by law.** Judicial notice of the matter is not authorized by statute or case law. *See* Evid. C. §450; *see, e.g.*, ***County of Orange v. Smith*** (4th Dist.2005) 132 Cal.App.4th 1434, 1450 (no authority for judicial notice of law-review articles). See "Required or authorized by law," §2.2, p. 548.

(2) **Not relevant.** The matter is not relevant to the issues in the action or proceeding. *See* ***People v. Shamrock Foods Co.*** (2000) 24 Cal.4th 415, 422 n.2; ***Mangini v. R.J. Reynolds Tobacco Co.*** (1994) 7 Cal.4th 1057, 1063, *overruled on other grounds*, ***In re Tobacco Cases II*** (2007) 41 Cal.4th 1257.

(3) **Reasonably disputed matters.** The matter is reasonably disputed by the parties. *See* Evid. C. §§451(f), 452(g), (h); ***Unruh-Haxton v. Regents of the Univ. of Cal.*** (4th Dist.2008) 162 Cal.App.4th 343, 364. The following are examples of ways to establish that a matter is reasonably disputed:

(a) **Disputed accuracy.** The accuracy of sources used to establish the matter is questionable. *See* Evid. C. §452(h); *see, e.g.*, ***Whispering Pines Mobile Home Park, Ltd. v. City of Scotts Valley*** (6th Dist.1986) 180 Cal.App.3d 152, 162 (court had no way of knowing whether sources were indisputably accurate); ***San Luis Obispo Bay Props., Inc. v. Pacific Gas & Elec. Co.*** (2d Dist.1972) 28 Cal.App.3d 556, 563 (court questioned whether statement of property value in Public Utilities Commission's opinion was finding by Commission or mere recital of contract provisions).

(b) **Disputed interpretation.** The matter to be noticed is based on a particular interpretation of certain facts, and the objecting party can offer a different reasonable interpretation of those facts. *See* ***Unruh-Haxton***, 162 Cal.App.4th at 365 (taking judicial notice of document is different from accepting particular interpretation of its contents). For example, judicial notice that there was a valid contract between the parties can be reasonably disputed by contentions that the contract was signed under fraud or duress. *See* ***Fremont Indem. Co. v. Fremont Gen. Corp.*** (2d Dist.2007) 148 Cal.App.4th 97, 115.

§5. HEARING

A request for judicial notice does not always result in a hearing. For example, in a case in which there is no dispute about the existence and validity of a city ordinance, no hearing would be needed. 7 Cal. Law Revision Comm'n Rep. (1965) p. 1074. But a party would be entitled to a hearing when the matter to be judicially noticed is complex and important to the case. *See id.* See "Hearings," ch. 1-H, p. 79.

§6. RULING

§6.1 Sources considered. The court has discretion in deciding what sources of information are reliable enough to prove particular matters. 7 Cal. Law Revision Comm'n Rep. (1965) p. 1073. The court can consider any information provided to it by the parties and evidence from any other source that is not received in open court. Evid. C. §454(a). If the court considers evidence from a source that is not received in open court, including expert advice,

the information must be made part of the record. *Id.* §455(b). For example, if the court considers expert advice on the law of an organization of nations, a foreign nation, or a public entity in a foreign nation and that advice is not received in open court, the advice must be in writing. *Id.* §454(b).

§6.2 Discretion on ruling.

1. No discretion. The court must take judicial notice of the following:

(1) Mandatory matters under Evid. C. §451.

(2) Permissive matters under Evid. C. §452 if the requesting party provided sufficient notice to the parties and sufficient information to the court. *Id.* §453. See "Conditional mandatory notice," §2.2.2, p. 549.

2. Discretion. The court may take judicial notice of permissive matters under Evid. C. §452.

§7. ORDER

§7.1 Form. The court's ruling on the request must be recorded either in writing or by minute order. See "Record of Ruling," ch. 1-I, §4, p. 90.

§7.2 Effect of ruling.

1. Request granted.

(1) Contradictory evidence excluded. If the court grants the request, any evidence that contradicts the judicially noticed matter is inadmissible. *See* Evid. C. §457; ***People v. Moore*** (5th Dist.1997) 59 Cal.App.4th 168, 185; 7 Cal. Law Revision Comm'n Rep. (1965) p. 1075.

(2) Jury instruction. If the court grants the request and judicially notices a fact that the jury would normally determine, it should (and when requested, must) instruct the jury to accept as true the judicially noticed fact. Evid. C. §457; 7 Cal. Law Revision Comm'n Rep. (1965) p. 1075; 1 Witkin, *Cal. Evidence*, Judicial Notice, §44.

2. Request denied.

(1) Prompt notice of denial. If the court denies the request for judicial notice, it must notify the parties as soon as possible to give the parties an opportunity to submit evidence on the matter the court refused to notice. 7 Cal. Law Revision Comm'n Rep. (1965) p. 1075; *see* Evid. C. §456.

(2) Can notice at later time. If the court denies the request, it can still judicially notice the matter in a later proceeding. Evid. C. §458; 7 Cal. Law Revision Comm'n Rep. (1965) p. 1075. For example, the court's refusal to take judicial notice of a fact at trial does not bar it from taking judicial notice of the fact at a hearing on a motion for new trial. ***Ponce v. Tractor Sup.*** (1st Dist.1972) 29 Cal.App.3d 500, 509; 7 Cal. Law Revision Comm'n Rep. (1965) p. 1075.

§8. MOTION FOR RECONSIDERATION

A party adversely affected by the court's order on a request for judicial notice can file a motion for reconsideration. CCP §1008(a). See "Motion for Reconsideration," ch. 5-G, §3, p. 508.

§9. MOTION FOR RENEWAL

A party whose request for judicial notice is denied can file a motion for renewal. CCP §1008(b). See "Motion for Renewal," ch. 5-G, §4, p. 516.

§10. APPELLATE REVIEW

§10.1 Writ of mandate. An order on a request for judicial notice can be reviewed by a petition for a writ of mandate. *See, e.g.*, ***Aquila v. Superior Ct.*** (4th Dist.2007) 148 Cal.App.4th 556, 569 (D challenged judicial notice of certain contracts, PUC decisions, and SEC filings through writ proceeding).

§10.2 Direct appeal. An order on a request for judicial notice is not appealable until the court enters a final judgment in the action. *See* CCP §§904.1(a), 904.2.

§10.3 Standard of review.

1. Under §451. No case has addressed the standard of review for a court's ruling on whether to take judicial notice of a matter under Evid. C. §451. Unless the court refused to take judicial notice because the matter was not relevant under Evid. C. §351, the standard of review is probably de novo because the court has no discretion under §451. *Cf.* ***Jane Doe 8015 v. Superior Ct.*** (6th Dist.2007) 148 Cal.App.4th 489, 493 (court has no discretion to deny motion to disqualify judge under CCP §170.6, so review is de novo).

2. Under §452. The court's ruling on whether to take judicial notice of a matter under Evid. C. §452 is reviewed for abuse of discretion. *See* ***Jenkins v. JPMorgan Chase Bank*** (4th Dist.2013) 216 Cal.App.4th 497, 536; ***Washington v. County of Contra Costa*** (1st Dist.1995) 38 Cal.App.4th 890, 901.

3. Under §453. If the court denies judicial notice of a matter under Evid. C. §453, the court's decision must be upheld unless the information provided about the matter was so persuasive that no reasonable judge would have refused to take judicial notice. ***Willis v. State*** (3d Dist.1994) 22 Cal.App.4th 287, 291. See "Conditional mandatory notice," §2.2.2, p. 549.

4. Under §351 or §352. If the court excludes a judicially noticeable matter under Evid. C. §351 because the matter is not relevant or under §352 because the matter's probative value is substantially outweighed by its prejudicial effect, the court's ruling should not be disturbed unless the objecting party shows an abuse of discretion. *See* ***People v. Benavides*** (2005) 35 Cal.4th 69, 90; ***Mozzetti v. City of Brisbane*** (1st Dist.1977) 67 Cal.App.3d 565, 578. See "Probative value outweighed," §4.2.1(4), p. 558.

§10.4 Ruling on error. A trial court's improper ruling on a request for judicial notice is subject to harmless-error analysis. ***Aquila v. Superior Ct.*** (4th Dist.2007) 148 Cal.App.4th 556, 569; 1 Witkin, *Cal. Evidence*, Judicial Notice, §46; *see* 7 Cal. Law Revision Comm'n Rep. (1965) p. 1063. In other words, the appellate court will remand the case only if the improper denial or improper grant was a harmful error. *See* ***Aquila***, 148 Cal.App.4th at 569.

§11. JUDICIAL NOTICE BY APPELLATE COURT

§11.1 When required.

1. Proper notice by trial court. The appellate court must take judicial notice of any matter that was properly noticed by the trial court. Evid. C. §459(a); 7 Cal. Law Revision Comm'n Rep. (1965) p. 1076.

2. Mandatory notice. The appellate court must take judicial notice when it is mandatory under Evid. C. §451 or §453, even if the trial court did not judicially notice the matter. Evid. C. §459(a); 7 Cal. Law Revision Comm'n Rep. (1965) p. 1076. See "Mandatory notice," §2.2.1, p. 548; "Conditional mandatory notice," §2.2.2, p. 549.

§11.2 When permitted. The appellate court can take judicial notice of any matter listed under Evid. C. §452. Evid. C. §459(a); *see* ***Varcoe v. Lee*** (1919) 180 Cal. 338, 343 (appellate court can properly take judicial notice of any matter of which court of original jurisdiction could properly take notice). But judicial notice of a matter under §452 is rarely appropriate if judicial notice was not first requested by the parties from the trial court. *See* ***Long Truong v. Cu Van Nguyen*** (6th Dist.2007) 156 Cal.App.4th 865, 882; ***Coy v. County of L.A.*** (2d Dist.1991) 235 Cal.App.3d 1077, 1083 n.3; *see also* ***Brosterhous v. State Bar*** (1995) 12 Cal.4th 315, 325 (appellate court can take judicial notice of matters not before trial court, but it is not required to do so).

§11.3 How used. The appellate court can give the judicially noticed matter a different "tenor" (i.e., meaning) than the one given by the trial court. Evid. C. §459(a); *see Black's Law Dictionary* 1697 (10th ed. 2014) (defining "tenor").

K. MOTION FOR SANCTIONS

15 This subchapter discusses five different motions for sanctions: (1) motions based on the presentation of frivolous papers or papers brought for an improper purpose (CCP §128.7), (2) motions based on bad-faith actions or tactics that are frivolous or solely intended to cause unnecessary delay (CCP §128.5), (3) motions based on a violation of a court order (CCP §177.5), (4) motions based on a violation of the California Rules of Court (CRC 2.30), and (5) motions based on a violation of a local rule of court (CCP §575.2). This subchapter does not discuss either the court's inherent power to sanction or sanctions under CCP §1038 (sanctions for an unfounded tort action against government entities or for an unfounded indemnity or contribution claim in a civil action). For a discussion of sanctions for improper venue, discovery sanctions, and sanctions for presenting declarations in bad faith or for purposes of delay under CCP §437c(j), see "Grounds for sanctions," ch. 4-E, §3.3, p. 361; "Discovery Sanctions," ch. 9-A, p. 1003; "Bad faith," ch. 10-B, §9.2.2(3), p. 1132.

§1. GENERAL

§1.1 Purpose. The purpose of sanctions is to deter improper conduct and to encourage compliance with court orders and rules. *See* CCP §128.7(d) (sanctions for filing frivolous paper should only be severe enough to deter improper conduct), §177.5 (court can impose sanctions for violating court order), §575.2 (court can impose sanctions for not complying with local rules); CRC 2.30 (court can impose sanctions for not complying with rules of court).

§1.2 Primary authority. CCP §§128.5, 128.7, 177.5, 575.2; CRC 2.30.

§1.3 Secondary authority. The following secondary sources are cited as authority in this subchapter:

- *California Trial Practice: Civil Procedure During Trial* (CEB Online ed. 2014) (referred to as *CEB Procedure During Trial*).
- Kiesel et al., *Matthew Bender Practice Guide: California Pretrial Civil Procedure* (2014) (referred to as Kiesel, *Cal. Pretrial Civil Procedure*).
- Weil & Brown, *California Practice Guide: Civil Procedure Before Trial* (CD-ROM ed. 2014) (referred to as Weil, *Civil Procedure Before Trial*).
- Witkin, *California Procedure* (5th ed. 2008 & Supp.2014) (referred to as Witkin, *Cal. Procedure*).

15 §2. PAPERS—FRIVOLOUS OR IMPROPER

Under CCP §128.7, a motion for sanctions can be brought against an attorney or a party appearing pro per for presenting to the court a frivolous paper or a paper for an improper purpose.

NOTE

The Code of Civil Procedure has two statutes—CCP §§128.5 and 128.7—that authorize sanctions for presenting frivolous papers or papers for an improper purpose. As recently amended, §128.5 allows an award of reasonable expenses incurred by a party as a result of another party's bad-faith actions or tactics that are frivolous or solely intended to cause unnecessary delay. "Actions or tactics" is broadly defined and includes the filing of papers. See CCP §128.5(b)(1). However, the movant's burden under §128.5 is more onerous than it is under §128.7. See Assem. Com. on Judiciary, Analysis of Assem. Bill No. 2494 (2013-2014 Reg. Sess.) as amended April 10, 2014, p. 4 (§128.5 requires that conduct be subjectively in bad faith and objectively without merit; §128.7 requires objective standard only). Thus, it is easier to obtain sanctions for frivolous or improper papers by bringing the motion under §128.7. For a complete discussion of §128.5, see "Bad-Faith Actions or Tactics—Frivolous or Intended to Cause Delay," §3, p. 576.

§2.1 Movant's burden. To prevail on a motion for sanctions under §128.7, the movant must establish that a challengeable paper was presented to the court and the paper was frivolous (i.e., without legal or factual merit) or brought for an improper purpose. *See* CCP §128.7(b), (c).

NOTE

Section 128.7 is modeled after, and nearly identical to, the 1993 amended version of FRCP 11. ***Guillemin v. Stein*** *(3d Dist.2002) 104 Cal.App.4th 156, 167. When the California Legislature enacted §128.7, it also adopted the Advisory Committee's notes to Rule 11 as a statement of legislative intent.* ***Barnes v. Department of Corr.*** *(5th Dist.1999) 74 Cal.App.4th 126, 132. Thus, cases interpreting amended FRCP 11 and the Advisory Committee's notes to Rule 11 can be used as persuasive authority. See* ***Day v. Collingwood*** *(4th Dist.2006) 144 Cal.App.4th 1116, 1125 n.3; see, e.g.,* ***Barnes****, 74 Cal.App.4th at 136 (court relied on Advisory Committee's notes to conclude that formal, rather than informal, notice is required under §128.7).*

1. Paper challengeable. The movant must establish that the offending paper is challengeable under §128.7. *See* CCP §128.7(b) (list of challengeable papers).

(1) Papers that can be challenged. Pleadings (i.e., complaints, cross-complaints, answers, and demurrers), petitions, written notices of motions, and other similar papers can be challenged under §128.7. *See* CCP §§128.7(b), (c), 435(a). See "Types of Pleadings," ch. 1-C, §2, p. 21. The phrase "other similar papers" presumably includes papers attached to motions (e.g., memorandums of points and authorities and declarations), oppositions, and reply papers. *See* Weil, *Civil Procedure Before Trial*, ¶¶9:1154, 9:1155.

(2) Papers that cannot be challenged. Discovery papers—including disclosures, requests, responses, objections, and discovery motions—cannot be challenged under §128.7. CCP §128.7(g). For a discussion of challenging discovery papers, see "Discovery Sanctions," ch. 9-A, p. 1003.

2. Paper presented to court. The movant must establish that the challengeable paper was presented to the court. *See* CCP §128.7(b), (c). A paper is "presented" to the court when it is signed, filed, submitted, or later advocated. *Id.* §128.7(b); *e.g.*, ***Optimal Mkts., Inc. v. Salant*** (6th Dist.2013) 221 Cal.App.4th 912, 922-23 (P's attorneys did not present frivolous paper to court when they advocated claims to arbitrator based on complaint that had been filed by P's previous attorneys). The phrase "later advocated" means that an attorney or a person appearing pro per can be sanctioned for arguing a position in a paper that was not frivolous when it was originally signed, filed, or submitted but was frivolous when it was argued. *See* ***Peake v. Underwood*** (4th Dist.2014) 227 Cal.App.4th 428, 441; Weil, *Civil Procedure Before Trial*, ¶9:1161; *see, e.g.*, ***Clark v. Optical Coating Lab.*** (1st Dist.2008) 165 Cal.App.4th 150, 178 (D argued that P's later advocacy of petition, after court excluded P's evidence supporting petition, violated §128.7). By later advocating a position in an earlier-filed paper, the attorney or person appearing pro per is reaffirming that the paper is not frivolous or brought for an improper purpose. *Cf.* FRCP 11, advisory committee's notes (1993). For example, if an attorney during a pretrial conference insists on a position contained in an earlier-filed pleading that she knows no longer has any merit, the attorney can be sanctioned for presenting a frivolous paper. *Cf. id.* Thus, an attorney has a continuing duty under §128.7 to ensure that arguments contained in papers are not frivolous or brought for an improper purpose when they are argued to the court. *See* Weil, *Civil Procedure Before Trial*, ¶¶9:1160, 9:1161. In cases in which an attorney has withdrawn and been replaced by another, this continuing duty may require the substitute attorney to reevaluate the papers that were signed, filed, or submitted by the original attorney. *See id.* ¶9:1161.5.

NOTE

A frivolous oral argument cannot be the basis for sanctions under §128.7 if the argument was not previously included in a filed, signed, or submitted paper. See Weil, Civil Procedure Before Trial, ¶9:1160; cf. FRCP 11, advisory committee's notes (1993); ***In re Bees*** *(4th Cir.2009) 562 F.3d 284, 289 (interpreting FRCP 11).*

3. Paper frivolous or brought for improper purpose. The movant must establish that when the challengeable paper was presented to the court, it was frivolous or brought for an improper purpose under an objective standard. *See* CCP §128.7(b), (c).

(1) Frivolous.

(a) Legally frivolous. Sanctions can be imposed if the paper was legally frivolous. ***Guillemin***, 104 Cal.App.4th at 167; *see* CCP §128.7(b)(2), (c). A paper is legally frivolous if it makes claims or defenses that are not warranted by (1) existing law or (2) a nonfrivolous argument for extending, modifying, or reversing existing law or for establishing new law. *See* CCP §128.7(b)(2), (c).

[1] Not warranted by existing law. Legal contentions are generally not warranted by existing law if they have been foreclosed by well-settled law or previously rejected by the court. *See, e.g.*, ***Burkle v. Burkle*** (2d Dist.2006) 144 Cal.App.4th 387, 399-400 (P made frivolous claim when well-settled law clearly rejected her position); *cf.* ***Simon Debartolo Grp. v. Richard E. Jacobs Grp.*** (2d Cir.1999) 186 F.3d 157, 167 (interpreting FRCP 11; legal position is frivolous if it is clear under existing precedent that there is no chance of success); ***Roundtree v. U.S.*** (9th Cir.1994) 40 F.3d 1036, 1040 (interpreting FRCP 11; claim was frivolous because it had been previously rejected by court).

[2] Not warranted by nonfrivolous argument for change in law. Arguments for a change in the law are considered frivolous when they are not objectively reasonable. *Cf.* FRCP 11, advisory committee's notes (1993). This standard is intended to eliminate any "empty-head, pure-heart" justification for patently frivolous arguments. *Cf. id.* In applying this standard, courts should not construe it in a way that chills an attorney's enthusiasm or creativity in pursuing legal theories. *Cf.* FRCP 11, advisory committee's notes (1983). An attorney should be permitted to pursue legal arguments in an innovative and sensible way. *E.g.*, ***Guillemin***, 104 Cal.App.4th at 168 (attorney's argument that term "public agency" in statute did not include individuals was reasonable). In determining whether an argument is reasonable, courts should consider whether the argument has support in court opinions, in law-review articles, or from other attorneys. *Cf.* FRCP 11, advisory committee's notes (1993); ***Pierce v. F.R. Tripler & Co.*** (2d Cir.1992) 955 F.2d 820, 830-31 (interpreting FRCP 11; D's argument was not frivolous because it was supported by opinion of state supreme court).

NOTE

Generally, a party will not be sanctioned if she does not cite case law or statutory law that is contrary to her position. Cf. ***U.S. v. Stringfellow*** *(9th Cir.1990) 911 F.2d 225, 226 (interpreting FRCP 11). But if the omission would make the party's argument frivolous, or if the party deliberately misstates law that is unfavorable to her position, then sanctions can be imposed. Cf. id.;* ***Teamsters Local No. 579 v. B&M Transit, Inc.*** *(7th Cir.1989) 882 F.2d 274, 280 (interpreting FRCP 11).*

(b) Factually frivolous. Sanctions can be imposed if the paper was factually frivolous. ***Hopkins & Carley v. Gens*** (6th Dist.2011) 200 Cal.App.4th 1401, 1420; ***Guillemin***, 104 Cal.App.4th at 167; *see* CCP §128.7(b)(3), (b)(4), (c).

[1] Frivolous contentions. A paper is factually frivolous if factual contentions in the paper (1) lack evidentiary support or (2) are unlikely to have evidentiary support after a reasonable opportunity for investigation or discovery. *See* CCP §128.7(b)(3), (c); ***Hopkins & Carley***, 200 Cal.App.4th at 1420 (motion contained factual inaccuracies); *see also* ***Bockrath v. Aldrich Chem. Co.*** (1999) 21 Cal.4th 71, 81-82 (P cannot sue based purely on speculation and then try to use discovery process to determine if speculation is correct; §128.7 provides remedy for improperly speculative pleading). If a party knows that a factual contention lacks evidentiary support but she reasonably believes that evidentiary support will be discovered after further investigation, the party must specifically identify that contention in her paper. *See* CCP §128.7(b)(3); Weil, *Civil Procedure Before Trial*, ¶9:1171. But a party does not shield herself from sanctions by merely identifying unsupported factual contentions in her paper. If the circumstances when the paper was presented suggest that the party could not have had a reasonable belief that evidentiary support could be found, then the party can still be subject to sanctions.

NOTE

When a person certifies under §128.7(b)(3) that there is or likely will be evidentiary support for the factual contentions in her paper, she is not certifying that she will prevail on her factual contentions. Cf. FRCP 11, advisory committee's notes (1993). Thus, a person is not subject to sanctions simply because a summary judgment is rendered against her. ***Peake****, 227 Cal.App.4th at 448; Weil, Civil Procedure Before Trial, ¶9:1168; cf. FRCP 11, advisory committee's notes (1993). On the other hand, if a person has sufficient evidence to defeat a motion for summary judgment, she also has sufficient evidence to defeat a motion for sanctions under §128.7(b)(3). Weil, Civil Procedure Before Trial, ¶9:1168; cf. FRCP 11, advisory committee's notes (1993).*

[2] Frivolous denials. A paper is factually frivolous if denials of factual contentions in the paper are neither warranted by the evidence nor based on belief or a lack of information. *See* CCP §128.7(b)(4), (c). Under this provision, a person should not deny allegations that she knows to be true; she should only deny allegations that she reasonably believes are not true. *Cf.* FRCP 11, advisory committee's notes (1993). A person can have a reasonable belief that a factual contention is not true when (1) there is evidence that contradicts the contention, (2) there is no evidence to support the contention, or (3) the person has a reasonable basis for doubting the credibility of the only evidence that supports the contention. *Cf. id.*

(2) Improper purpose. Sanctions can be imposed if the paper was presented primarily for an improper purpose, such as to harass or to cause unnecessary delay or expense. *See* CCP §128.7(b)(1), (c); ***Hopkins & Carley***, 200 Cal.App.4th at 1420; ***Guillemin***, 104 Cal.App.4th at 167; *see, e.g.*, ***Musaelian v. Adams*** (2009) 45 Cal.4th 512, 515-16 (P filed retaliatory suit for improper purpose by trying to gain better bargaining position in ongoing litigation).

(a) Must be primary purpose. Under CCP §128.7(b)(1), the movant must establish that the improper purpose was the "primary" reason for presenting the paper to the court.

NOTE

The standard for proving that a paper is brought for an improper purpose under CCP §128.7 is different from the standard that applies under FRCP 11. Under FRCP 11, a party can be sanctioned if a paper is brought for "any" improper purpose.

(b) Can apply to nonfrivolous paper. In some cases, a person can be sanctioned for presenting a nonfrivolous paper for an improper purpose. *Cf.* ***Whitehead v. Food Max*** (5th Cir.2003) 332 F.3d 796, 805 (interpreting FRCP 11); ***Senese v. Chicago Area I.B. of T. Pension Fund*** (7th Cir.2001) 237 F.3d 819, 826 (same).

[1] Complaints. A person cannot be sanctioned for presenting a nonfrivolous complaint for an improper purpose. *Cf.* ***Townsend v. Holman Consulting Corp.*** (9th Cir.1990) 929 F.2d 1358, 1362 (interpreting FRCP 11; courts do not want to hinder how people exercise their substantive legal rights); ***Zaldivar v. City of L.A.*** (9th Cir.1986) 780 F.2d 823, 832 (interpreting FRCP 11; signing of nonfrivolous complaint that initiates suit cannot be considered improper).

[2] Other papers. A person can be sanctioned for presenting other nonfrivolous papers (besides complaints) for an improper purpose. *Cf.* ***Whitehead***, 332 F.3d at 805 (interpreting FRCP 11); ***Zaldivar***, 780 F.2d at 832 & n.10 (same). Nonfrivolous papers can be brought for an improper purpose when (1) they are filed excessively, (2) they contain abusive language, (3) the person has no sincere intent of pursuing them, or (4) their primary purpose is to generate publicity in order to embarrass the opposing party. *Cf.* ***Whitehead***, 332 F.3d at 805-06 (interpreting FRCP 11).

(3) Objective standard. Whether a paper is frivolous or brought for an improper purpose is determined by an objective standard—that is, was it reasonable under the circumstances for the person to believe that

the paper was neither frivolous nor brought for an improper purpose when it was presented to the court. *See* CCP §128.7(b). Although presenting a paper for an "improper purpose" suggests that the person's subjective intent is in issue, the objective standard applies to both claims. *Cf.* ***Townsend***, 929 F.2d at 1362 (interpreting FRCP 11). Under this objective standard, a person has an affirmative duty to make a reasonable inquiry into the facts and law before presenting a paper to the court. *See* CCP §128.7(b); *cf.* ***Business Guides, Inc. v. Chromatic Comms. Enters.*** (1991) 498 U.S. 533, 550-51 (interpreting FRCP 11; duty to make reasonable inquiry into facts applies to represented party); ***Bhambra v. True*** (N.D.Cal.2010) No. C 09-4685 CRB (slip op.; 4-29-10) (order interpreting FRCP 11; duty to make reasonable inquiry applies to pro per litigants). What is reasonable, however, is determined by the circumstances of the case. *See* CCP §128.7(b).

(a) Factors for determining reasonableness of inquiry. The movant should argue that the following factors establish that the person's inquiry into the facts and law was not reasonable:

[1] General factors.

[a] The person's status. *Cf.* ***Warren v. Guelker*** (9th Cir.1994) 29 F.3d 1386, 1390 (interpreting FRCP 11). An attorney will be held to a higher standard of inquiry than a person appearing pro per. *Cf.* ***Business Guides, Inc. v. Chromatic Comms. Enters.*** (9th Cir.1989) 892 F.2d 802, 811-12 (interpreting FRCP 11; what is objectively reasonable for party appearing pro per and for attorney may differ), *aff'd*, (1991) 498 U.S. 533; ***Kurkowski v. Volcker*** (8th Cir.1987) 819 F.2d 201, 204 (interpreting FRCP 11; pro per complaints should be read liberally). The reasonableness of an attorney's inquiry will be tested against the conduct of a competent attorney. *Cf.* ***Zaldivar***, 780 F.2d at 830 (interpreting FRCP 11).

[b] The time available for investigation. *Cf.* ***Cooter & Gell v. Hartmarx Corp.*** (1990) 496 U.S. 384, 401-02 (interpreting FRCP 11; inquiry that is unreasonable when attorney has months to prepare complaint may be reasonable when attorney has only days before statute of limitations runs); ***Townsend***, 929 F.2d at 1364 (interpreting FRCP 11; cursory inquiry will be tolerated more if there was not enough time to investigate). An attorney with ample time to present a paper may be expected to (1) interview witnesses and any attorneys who represented the client in an earlier proceeding, (2) examine available documents, (3) check available public records when appropriate, (4) determine whether any obvious affirmative defenses apply, and (5) verify information obtained from sources. *Cf.* 2 *Moore's Federal Practice 3d* §11.11[2][b] (2014) (discussing FRCP 11).

[c] Whether the case was accepted from another member of the bar or a referring attorney. *Cf.* ***Childs v. State Farm Mut. Auto. Ins.*** (5th Cir.1994) 29 F.3d 1018, 1026 (interpreting FRCP 11). To some extent, an attorney may satisfy the duty of a reasonable inquiry by relying on a referring attorney's work. *Cf.* ***Unioil, Inc. v. E.F. Hutton & Co.*** (9th Cir.1986) 809 F.2d 548, 558 (interpreting FRCP 11). But an attorney has some duty to gain personal knowledge of the case; she cannot entirely delegate her duty to make a reasonable inquiry to a referring attorney. *Cf.* ***Garr v. U.S. Healthcare, Inc.*** (3d Cir.1994) 22 F.3d 1274, 1280 (interpreting FRCP 11); ***Unioil***, 809 F.2d at 558 (same).

[d] The cost of conducting a prefiling investigation. *Cf.* ***Thomas v. Capital Sec. Servs.*** (5th Cir.1988) 836 F.2d 866, 875 (interpreting FRCP 11).

[e] The likelihood that further investigation would produce more evidence. *Cf.* ***Thornton v. General Motors Corp.*** (5th Cir.1998) 136 F.3d 450, 454 (interpreting FRCP 11; court should consider need for discovery); ***Szabo Food Serv. v. Canteen Corp.*** (7th Cir.1987) 823 F.2d 1073, 1083 (interpreting FRCP 11; further investigation is not required if it is not likely to produce more evidence).

[2] Factors for determining if paper was legally frivolous.

[a] The person's familiarity with the law. *Cf.* ***Huettig & Schromm, Inc. v. Landscape Contractors Council*** (9th Cir.1986) 790 F.2d 1421, 1426-27 (interpreting FRCP 11; experienced labor-law attorneys knew or should have known that client had no cause of action).

[b] The complexity of the legal issues. *Cf.* ***Lichtenstein v. Consolidated Servs. Grp.*** (1st Cir.1999) 173 F.3d 17, 23 (interpreting FRCP 11).

[c] Whether the law is settled. *See, e.g.*, ***Burkle***, 144 Cal.App.4th at 399-400 (claim was frivolous because well-settled law clearly precluded claim); *cf.* ***Westlake N. Prop. Owners Ass'n v. City of Thousand Oaks*** (9th Cir.1990) 915 F.2d 1301, 1307 (interpreting FRCP 11; claim was not frivolous because law was not settled on whether individuals and groups were bound by judgments entered into by municipalities).

[d] Whether the legal contention has been previously rejected by the court. *Cf.* ***Roundtree***, 40 F.3d at 1040 (interpreting FRCP 11; claim was frivolous because it had been previously rejected by court).

[e] Whether the argument for extending, modifying, or reversing existing law or establishing new law is supported in court opinions, in law-review articles, or by other attorneys. *Cf.* FRCP 11, advisory committee's notes (1993); ***Pierce***, 955 F.2d at 830-31 (interpreting FRCP 11; D's argument was not frivolous because it was supported by opinion of state supreme court).

[3] Factors for determining if paper was factually frivolous.

[a] The extent to which the attorney relied on the client for factual support. *Cf.* ***Business Guides***, 498 U.S. at 549-50 (interpreting FRCP 11; court may sanction client instead of attorney when attorney had to rely on client who misrepresented facts). An attorney may rely on objectively reasonable representations made by her client. *Cf.* ***Hadges v. Yonkers Racing Corp.*** (2d Cir.1995) 48 F.3d 1320, 1329-30 (interpreting FRCP 11). But an attorney cannot blindly accept a client's representations without further investigation or corroboration. Weil, *Civil Procedure Before Trial*, ¶9:1165; *cf.* ***Childs***, 29 F.3d at 1026 (interpreting FRCP 11; attorney's reliance on client's representation that he did not stage accident and on alleged conspirator's representation that there was no fraud was not reasonable).

[b] The extent to which the person relied on an expert's opinion. *Cf.* ***Coffey v. Healthtrust, Inc.*** (10th Cir.1993) 1 F.3d 1101, 1104 (interpreting FRCP 11). A person can rely on an expert's opinion as long as the reliance is reasonable under the circumstances. *Cf. id.* The existence of a contrary expert opinion does not, by itself, make a person's reliance unreasonable. *Cf. id.* (attorney's reliance on expert's opinion was reasonable because of expert's unwavering belief in his findings even after reviewing contrary opinions, his level of expertise, and court's acceptance of him as expert).

[c] Whether the opposing party controls the relevant facts. *Cf.* ***Townsend***, 929 F.2d at 1364 (interpreting FRCP 11). A party should be given more leeway in early stages of litigation to make allegations that are not well grounded when the opposing party is in control of the relevant facts. *Cf. id.*

[d] Whether the factual allegations relate to an opposing party's knowledge, purpose, intent, or state of mind. *Cf. id.* A party should be given more leeway to make allegations about the opposing party's knowledge, purpose, intent, or state of mind. *Cf. id.*

[e] The complexity of the factual issues. *Cf.* ***Brown v. Federation of State Med. Bds.*** (7th Cir.1987) 830 F.2d 1429, 1435 (interpreting FRCP 11).

(b) Reasonableness tested at time of presentation. The reasonableness of the inquiry is tested at the time the paper was presented—that is, when it was signed, filed, submitted, or later advocated. *See* Weil, *Civil Procedure Before Trial*, ¶¶9:1160, 9:1161; *cf.* FRCP 11, advisory committee's notes (1983) (court should avoid using hindsight to test whether inquiry was reasonable). Thus, a person is not subject to sanctions if a paper that was not frivolous when it was presented to the court turns out to be frivolous later. *Cf.* ***Garr***, 22 F.3d at 1279 (interpreting FRCP 11). Likewise, a person does not avoid sanctions if, by a stroke of luck, a paper that was frivolous when it was presented is later discovered to have legal or factual merit. *Cf. id. But cf.* ***In re Keegan Mgmt. Co., Secs. Litig.*** (9th Cir.1996) 78 F.3d 431, 434 (interpreting FRCP 11; court erred in not considering after-acquired factual evidence that supported complaint).

PRACTICE TIP

If a client insists on presenting a paper that the attorney knows is frivolous, the attorney should withdraw. Weil, Civil Procedure Before Trial, ¶9:1074. See "Attorney's Withdrawal or Removal," ch. 2-B, p. 102. An attorney can be sanctioned for presenting a frivolous paper even if she is only carrying out her client's wishes. Weil, Civil Procedure Before Trial, ¶9:1074; cf. ***Young v. Rosenthal*** *(2d Dist.1989) 212 Cal.App.3d 96, 127-28 (interpreting CCP §128.5).*

4. Conduct justifies sanctions. The movant should establish that the person's conduct justifies the imposition of sanctions. Even if a challenged paper is frivolous or brought for an improper purpose, the court can decide not to impose sanctions. ***Peake***, 227 Cal.App.4th at 448; *see* CCP §128.7(c) (court "may" impose sanctions); *cf.* FRCP 11, advisory committee's notes (1993) (court has significant discretion to determine what sanctions, if any, should be imposed). To convince the court that sanctions are justified, the movant should argue the following:

(1) The person's conduct was willful or negligent. *Cf.* FRCP 11, advisory committee's notes (1993).

(2) The person's conduct was part of a pattern of activity, not an isolated event. *Cf. id.*

(3) The person has engaged in similar conduct in other litigation. *Cf. id.*

(4) The conduct was intended to injure. *Cf. id.*

(5) The conduct infected the entire paper or a significant aspect of the paper. *Cf. id.* If a paper contains both frivolous and nonfrivolous allegations, the court should consider the significance of the frivolous allegations to determine whether to impose sanctions. *Cf.* ***Holgate v. Baldwin*** (9th Cir.2005) 425 F.3d 671, 677 (interpreting FRCP 11; existence of one nonfrivolous claim does not immunize complaint from sanctions); ***Townsend***, 929 F.2d at 1364 (interpreting FRCP 11; court must consider significance of claim in pleading as a whole). A minor or insignificant allegation should not result in sanctions. *Cf.* ***Townsend***, 929 F.2d at 1364-65 & n.4 (interpreting FRCP 11).

(6) The conduct affected the time or expense in litigating the suit. *Cf.* FRCP 11, advisory committee's notes (1993).

(7) The person was trained in the law. *Cf. id.* In deciding whether to impose sanctions, the court can consider whether the person appeared pro per, but the court cannot decline to impose sanctions simply for that reason. *Cf.* ***Warren***, 29 F.3d at 1390 (interpreting FRCP 11).

§2.2 Motion.

1. Who can file.

(1) Party. A party can file a motion for sanctions under CCP §128.7. CCP §128.7(c)(1).

(2) Court. The court can impose sanctions on its own motion under §128.7. CCP §128.7(c)(2). To impose sanctions on its own motion, the court must enter an order to show cause. *Id.* The order to show cause must describe the specific conduct that violated §128.7(b) and direct the person to be sanctioned to either (1) show cause why she has not violated §128.7(b) or (2) correct or withdraw the challenged paper within 21 days after service of the order. *Id.* §128.7(c)(2). If the paper is corrected or withdrawn within the 21-day period, sanctions cannot be imposed. See "Generally – after safe-harbor period ends," §2.2.2(2)(a), p. 568.

CAUTION

Be careful when using federal cases as persuasive authority on how a California court brings its own motion. FRCP 11 does not require the court to give a person 21 days to correct or withdraw a paper. ***Malovec v. Hamrell*** *(2d Dist.1999) 70 Cal.App.4th 434, 440.*

2. Deadline to serve & file.

(1) Deadline to serve.

(a) Generally. The movant should promptly serve the notice of motion and motion on the person to be sanctioned after the challenged paper is presented to the court. *See* CCP §128.7(c) (court must consider whether party seeking sanctions exercised due diligence); ***Hart v. Hart*** (4th Dist.2002) 95 Cal.App.4th 410, 414 (rule requires service of notice of motion and motion); *CEB Procedure During Trial*, §26.42 (motion should be served promptly, but if discovery is critical to determining motion, it should not be served until opposing party has reasonable time for discovery).

(b) Before disposition of paper or suit. The notice of motion and motion must be served on the person being sanctioned before the challenged paper or suit is disposed of. *See* ***Barnes v. Department of Corr.*** (5th Dist.1999) 74 Cal.App.4th 126, 135 (motion must be served before conclusion of case).

(2) Deadline to file.

(a) Generally – after safe-harbor period ends. The motion must be filed in the court no earlier than 21 days after the notice of motion and motion were served on the person being sanctioned, and at least 16 court days before the hearing on the motion (more time must be added to the 16-day period if served by means other than personal delivery). *See* CCP §128.7(c)(1) (motion cannot be filed until 21 days after service), §1005(b) (motion must be served and filed at least 16 court days before hearing). The 21-day period is intended to give the person being sanctioned a "safe-harbor" opportunity to avoid sanctions by correcting or withdrawing the challenged paper. *See id.* §128.7(c)(1); ***Martorana v. Marlin & Saltzman*** (2d Dist.2009) 175 Cal.App.4th 685, 699. Courts have not decided whether a person is entitled to additional time to correct or withdraw the paper when the person is served by mail. *See* ***In re Marriage of Falcone*** (6th Dist.2008) 164 Cal.App.4th 814, 826 (issue raised but not decided); *see also* CCP §1013(a) ("any right or duty to do any act or make any response within any period … shall be extended … upon service by mail").

CAUTION

Make sure the motion filed in the court is identical to the motion served on the party. ***In re Marriage of Falcone****, 164 Cal.App.4th at 827. If the motions are different, the 21-day safe-harbor period will restart. See, e.g.,* ***Hart****, 95 Cal.App.4th at 414 (filed motion restarted safe-harbor period because it contained additional declarations and supplemental points and authorities that were not present in motion served on party).*

(b) Effect of correction or disposition before safe-harbor period ends. The movant can no longer file the motion for sanctions if one of the following occurs before the safe-harbor period ends:

[1] The paper is corrected or withdrawn. CCP §128.7(c)(1); ***Li v. Majestic Indus. Hills*** (1st Dist.2009) 177 Cal.App.4th 585, 591.

[2] The paper is disposed of by the court. ***Li***, 177 Cal.App.4th at 594.

PRACTICE TIP

If a hearing on the paper is scheduled to be conducted before the safe-harbor period ends, the party moving for sanctions should ask the court to either (1) shorten the safe-harbor period so the motion for sanctions can be heard on the same day as the challenged paper or (2) continue the hearing date of the challenged paper until a date after the safe-harbor period ends. ***Li****, 177 Cal.App.4th at 595.*

[3] The entire suit is disposed of. *Cf.* ***Li***, 177 Cal.App.4th at 595 (FRCP 11 motion must be served at least 21 days before entry of final judgment).

(c) Effect of disposition after safe-harbor period ends. If the challenged paper is not corrected, withdrawn, or disposed of before the safe-harbor period ends, the motion for sanctions can be filed anytime thereafter, even after the court disposes of the paper or the entire suit. ***Li***, 177 Cal.App.4th at 592; *see* ***Day v. Collingwood*** (4th Dist.2006) 144 Cal.App.4th 1116, 1127-28; *see, e.g.*, ***Eichenbaum v. Alon*** (2d Dist.2003) 106 Cal.App.4th 967, 974-75 (D could file motion for sanctions after P voluntarily dismissed suit because voluntary dismissal did not occur until after 21-day period ended). A court is neither jurisdictionally nor statutorily barred from hearing a motion for sanctions that is filed after a judgment has been entered as long as the party was given the full 21 days to correct or withdraw the paper before the judgment was entered. ***Li***, 177 Cal.App.4th at 592; *see* ***Day***, 144 Cal.App.4th at 1128.

3. Form. The motion must be in writing and filed separately from other motions. *See* CCP §128.7(c)(1). See "Motion Papers," ch. 1-D, §5, p. 27.

4. Contents.

(1) Notice of motion & motion.

(a) Generally. The notice of motion must comply with the requirements of CCP §1010. CCP §128.7(c)(1); *e.g.*, ***Galleria Plus, Inc. v. Hanmi Bank*** (2d Dist.2009) 179 Cal.App.4th 535, 538 (notice that did not specify date and time of hearing was defective); *see* ***Barnes***, 74 Cal.App.4th at 136. See "Notice of motion & motion," ch. 1-D, §5.1, p. 28.

NOTE

When requesting a hearing date on the motion, make sure to request a date far enough in advance to meet the 21-day safe-harbor period and the 16-court-day notice period.

(b) Relief.

[1] Sanctions. The notice of motion and motion must describe the sanctions sought. *See* CRC 3.1110(a) (notice of motion must state nature of order sought), CRC 3.1112(d)(3) (motion must briefly state relief sought). The movant can seek both nonmonetary and monetary sanctions. *See* CCP §128.7(d).

[a] Nonmonetary sanctions. The movant can ask the court to impose nonmonetary sanctions, such as striking the offending paper or enjoining the person from presenting papers in the future. *Cf.* FRCP 11, advisory committee's notes (1993) (court can strike offending paper); ***Tropf v. Fidelity Nat'l Title Ins.*** (6th Cir.2002) 289 F.3d 929, 940 (interpreting FRCP 11; Ps were permanently enjoined from filing new suit asserting claims arising from same factual or legal claims alleged in current suit without permission from district court).

[b] Monetary sanctions. The movant can ask the court to award the following monetary sanctions:

- **Fees & expenses – sanctionable conduct.** The movant can ask the court to award the reasonable attorney fees and expenses it incurred as a result of the sanctionable conduct. CCP §128.7(d).
- **Fees & expenses – presenting motion.** The movant can ask the court to award the reasonable attorney fees and expenses it incurred in presenting the motion. *See* CCP §128.7(c)(1).

NOTE

If the movant is appearing pro per, attorney fees and expenses are not recoverable—even if the movant is an attorney. ***Musaelian v. Adams*** *(2009) 45 Cal.4th 512, 520.*

- **Punitive damages.** The movant can ask the court to award punitive damages if the person being sanctioned (1) is the plaintiff in the suit, (2) has been convicted of a felony, (3) is suing

MOTION FOR SANCTIONS

the victim or the victim's heir, relative, estate, or personal representative for alleged injuries that arose from the person's felonious act, and (4) is guilty of fraud, oppression, or malice in maintaining the suit. CCP §128.7(f).

[2] **Person to be sanctioned.** If the movant is seeking monetary damages, the notice of motion must identify the person against whom sanctions are sought. ***Cromwell v. Cummings*** (Orange Cty. Superior Ct. Appellate Dept. 1998) 65 Cal.App.4th Supp. 10, 13. Generally, the person who signed, filed, submitted, or advocated the paper should be the person who is sanctioned. *Cf.* FRCP 11, advisory committee's notes (1993). The court can decide to impose sanctions, however, on any person the court determines is responsible for violating §128.7(b), including the attorney, members of the attorney's firm, co-counsel, other law firms, and the client. *Cf.* FRCP 11, advisory committee's notes (1993). But the court cannot impose monetary sanctions on a client for presenting a legally frivolous allegation. *See* CCP §128.7(d)(1). See "Legally frivolous," §2.1.3(1)(a), p. 563.

(c) **Grounds.** The notice of motion and motion must briefly state the grounds for the motion and describe the specific conduct that violated §128.7(b). *See* CCP §128.7(c)(1) (motion must describe specific conduct that violated §128.7(b)); CRC 3.1110(a) (notice of motion must state grounds for issuance of order), CRC 3.1112(d)(3) (motion must briefly state basis for motion); *see, e.g.*, ***Musaelian v. Adams*** (1st Dist.2011) 197 Cal.App.4th 1251, 1257 (memorandum of costs seeking attorney fees for opposing motion for sanctions was insufficient to support award because it did not state that §128.7 was basis for award or meet other procedural requirements). See "Movant's burden," §2.1, p. 561. In describing the specific conduct, the motion cannot merely state that the paper is frivolous or brought for an improper purpose. *See* ***Barnes***, 74 Cal.App.4th at 135. Instead, the motion should explain how or why the paper is frivolous or brought for an improper purpose. *See id.*

(2) **Memorandum of points & authorities.** The motion must include a memorandum in support of the motion. CRC 3.1112(a)(3), 3.1113(a). See "Memorandum of points & authorities," ch. 1-D, §5.2, p. 28.

(3) **Supporting evidence.** See "Supporting evidence," ch. 1-D, §5.3, p. 30.

(4) **Request for judicial notice.** The motion can be accompanied by a request for judicial notice. *See* CRC 3.1113(*l*). The request must be filed and served separately from the motion and must list the specific items for which notice is requested. *Id.*

(5) **Proposed order.** The motion can include a proposed order. *See* CRC 3.1113(m). If a proposed order is submitted, it must be lodged and served with the motion papers, not attached to them. *Id.* See "Documents lodged," ch. 1-F, §2.3, p. 47.

§2.3 Response. The nonmovant can respond to a motion for sanctions by (1) asking the court to extend the safe-harbor period, (2) correcting or withdrawing the challenged paper, or (3) filing an opposition.

1. **Extension of safe-harbor period.** The nonmovant can respond to a motion for sanctions by asking the court to extend the safe-harbor period so additional investigation or discovery can be conducted. *CEB Procedure During Trial*, §26.44.

2. **Correction or withdrawal.** The nonmovant can avoid sanctions by correcting or withdrawing the challenged paper within the safe-harbor period (i.e., within 21 days after being served with the notice of motion and motion or the order to show cause). *See* CCP §128.7(c)(1), (c)(2); ***Interstate Specialty Mktg., Inc. v. ICRA Sapphire, Inc.*** (4th Dist.2013) 217 Cal.App.4th 708, 710.

(1) **How to correct or withdraw.** To avoid sanctions under CCP §128.7(c)(1), the paper must be appropriately corrected or withdrawn. Although the statute does not require a formal amendment to avoid sanctions, the better practice is to correct the paper by filing an amendment, filing a dismissal or written stipulation of withdrawal, or making a written correction on the paper itself. Weil, *Civil Procedure Before Trial*, ¶¶9:1204, 9:1205; *cf.* FRCP 11, advisory committee's notes (1993) (while sometimes helpful, formal amendment is not required).

(2) **Notice of correction or withdrawal.** If the nonmovant corrects or withdraws the paper, it must give notice to the movant before the safe-harbor period ends to avoid sanctions. ***Liberty Mut. Fire Ins. v. McKenzie*** (2d Dist.2001) 88 Cal.App.4th 681, 692; Weil, *Civil Procedure Before Trial*, ¶9:1205.5.

3. Opposition. The nonmovant can respond to a motion for sanctions by filing an opposition.

(1) Deadline to file & serve. The nonmovant must file and serve the opposition at least nine court days before the hearing. CCP §1005(b). See "Filing & serving opposition," ch. 1-D, §8.5, p. 36.

(2) Grounds.

(a) Procedural. The nonmovant can oppose a motion for sanctions under §128.7 on the following procedural grounds:

[1] The motion was not timely served and filed. *See* CCP §128.7(c)(1); *see, e.g.*, ***Martorana v. Marlin & Saltzman*** (2d Dist.2009) 175 Cal.App.4th 685, 698 (P argued movant did not serve separate motion 21 days before filing it with court).

[2] The motion was not filed separately. *See* CCP §128.7(c)(1).

[3] The motion did not meet the requirements of CCP §1010. *See, e.g.*, ***Galleria Plus, Inc. v. Hanmi Bank*** (2d Dist.2009) 179 Cal.App.4th 535, 538 (notice that did not specify date and time of hearing was defective); ***Barnes v. Department of Corr.*** (5th Dist.1999) 74 Cal.App.4th 126, 136 (informal written notice was defective).

[4] The motion does not identify the person against whom the movant is seeking monetary sanctions. *See* ***Cromwell v. Cummings*** (Orange Cty. Superior Ct. Appellate Dept. 1998) 65 Cal.App.4th Supp. 10, 13 (identifying person who is subject to monetary sanctions is constitutionally required by due process). See "Person to be sanctioned," §2.2.4(1)(b)[2], p. 570.

(b) Substantive. The nonmovant can oppose a motion for sanctions under §128.7 on the following substantive grounds:

[1] The challenged paper was neither frivolous nor brought for an improper purpose. *See, e.g.*, ***Interstate Specialty Mktg.***, 217 Cal.App.4th at 717 (mistaken attachment of wrong draft of contract to verified pleading was not sanctionable because it was not done for improper purpose); ***Clark v. Optical Coating Lab.*** (1st Dist.2008) 165 Cal.App.4th 150, 178-79 (action that was supported by enough evidence to sustain favorable jury verdict was not sanctionable for lack of evidentiary support); ***Guillemin v. Stein*** (3d Dist.2002) 104 Cal.App.4th 156, 168 (attorney's interpretation of statute was reasonable). In arguing that a paper did not violate §128.7(b), the nonmovant should show the circumstances that existed when the paper was presented to establish that it was reasonable for the nonmovant to believe that the paper was neither frivolous nor brought for an improper purpose. *See* ***Interstate Specialty Mktg.***, 217 Cal.App.4th at 717. See "Objective standard," §2.1.3(3), p. 564.

[2] The nonmovant cannot be sanctioned for presenting a nonfrivolous complaint for an improper purpose. *Cf.* ***Townsend v. Holman Consulting Corp.*** (9th Cir.1990) 929 F.2d 1358, 1362 (interpreting FRCP 11; courts do not want to hinder how people exercise their substantive legal rights).

[3] The paper cannot be challenged under §128.7. *See, e.g.*, CCP §128.7(g) (discovery requests, disclosures, responses, objections, and motions are not sanctionable under §128.7). See "Paper challengeable," §2.1.1, p. 562.

[4] The nonmovant is not subject to monetary sanctions for a violation of §128.7(b)(2) because it was represented by an attorney. *See* CCP §128.7(d)(1).

[5] The requested sanctions exceed what is sufficient to deter the conduct from being repeated. *See id.*

[6] The nonmovant's conduct does not justify the imposition of sanctions. See "Conduct justifies sanctions," §2.1.4, p. 567.

(3) Sanctions. The nonmovant can ask the court to impose sanctions under §128.7 against the movant because the motion for sanctions was made for an improper purpose (e.g., to harass, delay, or increase expense).

CCP §128.7(h). Although §128.7(h) does not state whether a counter-request for sanctions must be filed in a separate motion, one federal court has held that a counter-request for sanctions does not have to meet the separate-motion requirement or the safe-harbor period. ***Patelco Credit Un. v. Sahni*** (9th Cir.2001) 262 F.3d 897, 913 (interpreting FRCP 11).

(4) Attorney fees & expenses incurred in opposing motion. The nonmovant can ask the court to award the attorney fees and expenses it incurred in opposing the motion. *See* CCP §128.7(c)(1). Attorney fees and expenses incurred in opposing the motion will usually not be warranted unless the motion itself was frivolous. ***Musaelian v. Adams*** (1st Dist.2011) 197 Cal.App.4th 1251, 1258.

(5) Contents. See "Opposition Papers," ch. 1-D, §8, p. 35.

§2.4 Hearing. The court must hold a hearing if the challenged paper is not corrected or withdrawn during the safe-harbor period. *See* CCP §128.7(c) (requiring notice and opportunity to respond); ***Levy v. Blum*** (5th Dist.2001) 92 Cal.App.4th 625, 637 (dicta; discussing procedure for bringing motion for sanctions); *cf.* ***In re Marriage of Flaherty*** (1982) 31 Cal.3d 637, 651-52 (sanctions for frivolous appeal; due process requires some type of hearing before depriving a person of property). The scope of the hearing is within the court's discretion (i.e., a party is not entitled to an evidentiary hearing). *Cf.* ***Seykora v. Superior Ct.*** (2d Dist.1991) 232 Cal.App.3d 1075, 1081-82 (CCP §177.5 sanctions); ***Lavine v. Hospital of the Good Samaritan*** (2d Dist.1985) 169 Cal.App.3d 1019, 1028 (CCP §128.5 sanctions). See "Hearings," ch. 1-H, p. 79.

§2.5 Ruling.

1. Generally – discretionary. The court has discretion to grant or deny a motion for sanctions that meets the grounds of §128.7. *See* CCP §128.7(c) (court "may" impose sanctions); *cf.* FRCP 11, advisory committee's notes (1993) (court has significant discretion to determine what sanctions, if any, should be imposed).

2. Court's considerations.

(1) Determining whether paper violated §128.7(b). In determining whether a challenged paper violated §128.7(b), the court should determine if it was reasonable—under the circumstances that existed when the paper was presented—for a person to believe that the paper was neither frivolous nor brought for an improper purpose. *See* CCP §128.7(b). See "Objective standard," §2.1.3(3), p. 564.

(2) Determining whether to impose sanctions. In determining whether to impose sanctions, the court should consider the person's conduct and status (e.g., attorney, person appearing pro per, client, law firm). *Cf.* FRCP 11, advisory committee's notes (1993). See "Conduct justifies sanctions," §2.1.4, p. 567.

(3) Determining what sanctions to impose.

(a) Generally – reasonably necessary to deter repetition. In determining what sanctions to impose, the court should not impose sanctions any more severe than reasonably necessary to deter repetition of the improper conduct by the offending person or comparable conduct by a similarly situated person. CCP §128.7(d); *see, e.g.*, ***Eichenbaum v. Alon*** (2d Dist.2003) 106 Cal.App.4th 967, 973 (court limited sanctions to awarding movant reasonable attorney fees and costs).

(b) Monetary sanctions. In determining the amount of any monetary sanctions to impose, the court should consider the financial resources of the person being sanctioned. *Cf.* FRCP 11, advisory committee's notes (1993).

§2.6 Order.

1. Form. The court's ruling on the motion for sanctions under §128.7 must be recorded either in writing or by minute order. *See* Weil, *Civil Procedure Before Trial*, ¶9:1236 (written order or oral statement on record is sufficient); *see, e.g.*, Kiesel, *Cal. Pretrial Civil Procedure*, §35.17 (sample order on motion for sanctions). See "Record of Ruling," ch. 1-I, §4, p. 90.

2. Contents.

(1) Motion denied. If the court denies the motion, it should state whether the challenged paper violated §128.7(b), and if so, why sanctions are not being imposed. *Cf.* ***Warren v. Guelker*** (9th Cir.1994) 29 F.3d 1386, 1389-90 (interpreting FRCP 11).

(2) Motion granted. If the court grants the motion, the order must contain the following information:

(a) Describe sanctionable conduct. The order must describe the conduct that violated §128.7(b). CCP §128.7(e); *see, e.g.*, ***Hopkins & Carley v. Gens*** (6th Dist.2011) 200 Cal.App.4th 1401, 1417-18 (order was sufficient when it tracked statutory language and stated that motion was filed without legal support and for improper purpose); Kiesel, *Cal. Pretrial Civil Procedure*, §35.17 (sample order on motion for sanctions).

(b) Specify basis for sanctions. The order must specify the basis for the sanctions imposed. CCP §128.7(e); *see, e.g.*, ***Hopkins & Carley***, 200 Cal.App.4th at 1418 (order was sufficient when it stated that amount was awarded in part to deter repetition and to compensate party for costs incurred in opposing motion).

[1] Nonmonetary sanctions. Some of the nonmonetary sanctions the court can impose include the following:

[a] Striking the challenged paper. *Cf.* FRCP 11, advisory committee's notes (1993).

[b] Enjoining the person from presenting future papers without court approval. *Cf.* ***Tropf v. Fidelity Nat'l Title Ins.*** (6th Cir.2002) 289 F.3d 929, 940 (interpreting FRCP 11).

[c] Admonishing, reprimanding, or censuring the person. *Cf.* FRCP 11, advisory committee's notes (1993).

[d] Requiring the attorney to participate in continuing-legal-education programs. *Cf. id.*

[e] Referring the matter to disciplinary authorities. *Cf. id.*

[2] Monetary sanctions. The court can impose the following monetary sanctions:

[a] Fine. The court can order the person to pay a fine to the court. CCP §128.7(d).

NOTE

If the court imposes sanctions on its own motion, the only monetary sanction it can impose is a fine payable to the court. ***Malovec v. Hamrell*** *(2d Dist.1999) 70 Cal.App.4th 434, 443-44. The court cannot award monetary sanctions that are payable to a party.* ***Interstate Specialty Mktg., Inc. v. ICRA Sapphire, Inc.*** *(4th Dist.2013) 217 Cal.App.4th 708, 717;* ***Malovec****, 70 Cal.App.4th at 443-44.*

---

[b] Attorney fees & expenses caused by sanctionable conduct. The court can order the person to pay the movant's reasonable attorney fees and expenses incurred as a result of the sanctionable conduct. CCP §128.7(d).

[c] Attorney fees & expenses incurred in presenting motion. The court can order the person to pay the movant's reasonable attorney fees and expenses incurred in presenting the motion. *See* CCP §128.7(c)(1).

NOTE

The court cannot award attorney fees and expenses to a movant appearing pro per—even if the movant is an attorney. See ***Musaelian v. Adams*** *(2009) 45 Cal.4th 512, 520.*

[d] Punitive damages. The court can order the person to pay punitive damages under §128.7(f). See "Monetary sanctions," §2.2.4(1)(b)[1][b], p. 569.

(c) Identify person sanctions are imposed against.

[1] Generally. The order must identify the person against whom sanctions are imposed. *See, e.g.*, Kiesel, *Cal. Pretrial Civil Procedure*, §35.17 (sample order on motion for sanctions).

[2] Monetary sanctions.

[a] Attorney & client.

- **Generally.** The court can apportion monetary sanctions between the attorney and the client based on their relative responsibility. Weil, *Civil Procedure Before Trial*, ¶9:1226; *cf.* ***Business Guides, Inc. v. Chromatic Comms. Enters.*** (1991) 498 U.S. 533, 550 (interpreting FRCP 11; court has power to sanction client in addition to, or instead of, attorney). When appropriate, the court can hold the attorney and the client jointly and severally liable for the sanctions. *See, e.g.*, ***Liberty Mut. Fire Ins. v. McKenzie*** (2d Dist.2001) 88 Cal.App.4th 681, 691 (court imposed monetary sanctions against cross-P and his attorney, jointly and severally); *cf.* ***Estate of Calloway v. Marvel Entm't Grp.*** (2d Cir.1993) 9 F.3d 237, 239 (interpreting FRCP 11; joint and several liability appropriate when sanctionable conduct was coordinated effort of attorney and client); ***Kendrick v. Zanides*** (N.D.Cal.1985) 609 F.Supp. 1162, 1173 (interpreting FRCP 11; joint and several liability appropriate when attorney and client were equally responsible for sanctionable conduct).

- **Exception – frivolous legal contention.** The court cannot impose monetary sanctions against a client for a frivolous legal contention under CCP §128.7(b)(2). CCP §128.7(d)(1).

[b] Law firm. If the court imposes monetary sanctions on a law firm's partner, associate, or employee, the court must hold the law firm jointly responsible unless there are exceptional circumstances. CCP §128.7(c)(1).

(d) Identify person sanctions are payable to. If the court imposes monetary sanctions, the order must identify the person to whom the sanctions are payable. *See, e.g.*, ***Liberty Mut. Fire Ins.***, 88 Cal.App.4th at 691 (cross-P and his attorney were ordered to pay monetary sanctions to cross-D's attorneys); Kiesel, *Cal. Pretrial Civil Procedure*, §35.17 (sample order on motion for sanctions). See "Note," §2.6.2(2)(b)[2][a], p. 573.

3. Effect of order – notice to State Bar. If the court imposes monetary sanctions of $1,000 or more against an attorney, the following must be done:

(1) The court must notify the State Bar that sanctions were imposed and notify the sanctioned attorney of the referral to the State Bar. Bus. & Prof. C. §6086.7(a)(3), (b); *see* CRC 10.609(a), (c).

(2) The attorney must send written notice to the State Bar within 30 days after she has knowledge of the sanctions. *See id.* §6068(o)(3).

4. Enforcing order. Some of the ways in which an order for sanctions can be enforced include the following:

(1) Additional sanctions. The movant can ask the court to impose further sanctions. *See* CCP §177.5 (authorizing court to impose sanctions for violation of court order); *see, e.g.*, ***Twentieth Century Ins. v. Choong*** (2d Dist.2000) 79 Cal.App.4th 1274, 1278-79 (court did not abuse its discretion when it assessed further sanctions for not paying sanctions awarded in original order).

(2) Writ of execution. The movant can ask the court to issue a writ of execution and levy on the person's property. *See* ***Newland v. Superior Ct.*** (2d Dist.1995) 40 Cal.App.4th 608, 615; Weil, *Civil Procedure Before Trial*, ¶9:1285. For a discussion of writs of execution, see 8 Witkin, *Cal. Procedure*, Enforcement of Judgment, §§107-114.

(3) Judgment. The movant can ask the court to enter a judgment on the sanctions order. Weil, *Civil Procedure Before Trial*, ¶9:1285. Once a judgment is entered, the movant can record an abstract of judgment, which creates a judgment lien on the sanctioned person's home or other assets. *Id.* For a discussion of abstracts of judgments, see 7 Witkin, *Cal. Procedure*, Judgment, §64.

§2.7 Motion for reconsideration. A party adversely affected by a court's order on a motion for sanctions can file a motion for reconsideration. CCP §1008(a). See "Motion for Reconsideration," ch. 5-G, §3, p. 508.

§2.8 Motion for renewal. A party whose motion for sanctions is denied can file a motion for renewal. CCP §1008(b). See "Motion for Renewal," ch. 5-G, §4, p. 516.

§2.9 Appellate review.

1. Writ of mandate. A party can file a petition for a writ of mandate to challenge a sanctions order that is not immediately appealable. *See, e.g.*, CCP §904.1(b) (sanctions of $5,000 or less can be reviewed by petition for extraordinary writ); ***Wells Props. v. Popkin*** (4th Dist.1992) 9 Cal.App.4th 1053, 1055 (court declined to construe party's appeal of order denying sanctions as petition for writ of mandate).

2. Direct appeal.

(1) Order granting sanctions. The appealability of an order granting sanctions varies, depending on (1) whether the case is classified as limited or unlimited, (2) the person against whom the sanctions are imposed, and (3) the dollar amount of the sanctions imposed. See "Procedural Classifications of Civil Cases," ch. 3-E, §4, p. 255.

(a) Unlimited civil cases.

[1] Sanctions against party or party's attorney.

[a] Sanctions of over $5,000. In an unlimited civil case, an order imposing monetary sanctions of over $5,000 against a party or party's attorney is immediately appealable. CCP §904.1(a)(11), (a)(12). This threshold amount cannot be met by aggregating two or more sanctions awards that are based on separate conduct, even if they are payable to the same person and awarded at the same time. Weil, *Civil Procedure Before Trial*, ¶9:1290; *see* ***Champion/L.B.S. Assocs. Dev. Co. v. E-Z Serve Pet. Mktg., Inc.*** (4th Dist.1993) 15 Cal.App.4th 56, 59-60. But courts disagree on whether sanctions awards based on the same conduct can be aggregated to meet the appealability threshold. *Compare* ***Calhoun v. Vallejo City Unified Sch. Dist.*** (1st Dist.1993) 20 Cal.App.4th 39, 45 (establishing bright-line rule that sanctions awards cannot, under any circumstances, be aggregated to meet appealability threshold), *with* ***Champion/L.B.S. Assocs.***, 15 Cal.App.4th at 59-60 (dicta; aggregation of sanctions awards based on same conduct would be proper).

CAUTION

A party should not wait until the entry of a final judgment to appeal an award of sanctions in excess of $5,000. Weil, Civil Procedure Before Trial, ¶9:1289. The right to appeal the award is waived unless a notice of appeal is filed within 180 days after entry of the order or within 60 days after service of notice of the entry, whichever comes first. See CRC 8.104(a); ***Imuta v. Nakano*** *(2d Dist.1991) 233 Cal.App.3d 1570, 1578 & n.9; Weil, Civil Procedure Before Trial, ¶9:1289.*

[b] Sanctions of $5,000 or less. In an unlimited civil case, an order imposing monetary sanctions of $5,000 or less against a party or party's attorney is generally not appealable until the entry of a final judgment. CCP §904.1(b). But the appellate court, in its discretion, may permit review by extraordinary writ. *Id.*

[c] Nonmonetary sanctions. In an unlimited civil case, an order imposing nonmonetary sanctions against a party or party's attorney is not appealable until the entry of a final judgment. Kiesel, *Cal. Pretrial Civil Procedure*, §35.15; *see* CCP §904.1(a)(1) (appeal can be taken from judgment); ***Mileikowsky v. Tenet Healthsystem*** (2d Dist.2005) 128 Cal.App.4th 262, 264 (order granting motion for terminating sanctions is not appealable until entry of order of dismissal).

[2] Sanctions against nonparty. In an unlimited civil case, an order imposing monetary sanctions or ordering the performance of an act against a person or entity that is neither a party nor a party's attorney is immediately appealable as a final order on a collateral matter. Weil, *Civil Procedure Before Trial*, ¶9:1291; *see, e.g.*, ***Diepenbrock v. Brown*** (1st Dist.2012) 208 Cal.App.4th 743, 746 (because nonparty's appeal did not affect underlying litigation, it was appropriate to apply collateral-order exception); ***Barton v. Ahmanson Devs., Inc.*** (2d Dist.1993) 17 Cal.App.4th 1358, 1362 (monetary sanctions against attorney who no longer represented party was immediately appealable); *see also* ***Marsh v. Mountain Zephyr, Inc.*** (4th Dist.1996) 43 Cal.App.4th 289, 297-98 (explaining collateral-order exception).

(b) Limited civil cases. Courts disagree on whether an order imposing sanctions in a limited civil case is immediately appealable. *Compare* ***Drum v. Superior Ct.*** (4th Dist.2006) 139 Cal.App.4th 845, 851 (monetary sanctions in limited civil cases not involving discovery are immediately appealable under collateral-order exception), *with* ***Lim v. Silverton*** (Los Angeles Cty. Superior Ct. Appellate Dept. 1997) 61 Cal.App.4th Supp. 1, 4 (Legislature did not intend for any sanctions in limited civil cases to be immediately appealable); *see also* ***Marsh***, 43 Cal.App.4th at 297-98 (explaining collateral-order exception).

(2) Order denying sanctions. Generally, an order denying sanctions is not appealable until the entry of a final judgment. ***Wells Props.***, 9 Cal.App.4th at 1056 (Sonenshine, J., dissenting); *see* CCP §904.1(a)(1) (unlimited civil case), §904.2(a) (limited civil case). But in some circumstances, an order denying sanctions is immediately appealable as a final order on a collateral matter. *See* ***Muller v. Fresno Cmty. Hosp. & Med. Ctr.*** (2d Dist.2009) 172 Cal.App.4th 887, 904-05 (possibility that sanctions order could not be reviewed as part of judgment made it appropriate to apply collateral-order exception). *But see* ***Wells Props.***, 9 Cal.App.4th at 1055 (court held that order denying sanctions was not appealable even though there was no judgment to appeal from once default judgment was vacated).

3. Standard of review. Generally, the ruling on a motion for sanctions is reviewed for abuse of discretion. ***Vidrio v. Hernandez*** (2d Dist.2009) 172 Cal.App.4th 1443, 1452; ***Day v. Collingwood*** (4th Dist.2006) 144 Cal.App.4th 1116, 1130. But if the facts supporting the motion are undisputed, the issue of sanctions becomes a question of law and the standard of review is de novo. ***Galleria Plus, Inc. v. Hanmi Bank*** (2d Dist.2009) 179 Cal.App.4th 535, 538; *see* ***Collins v. Department of Transp.*** (3d Dist.2003) 114 Cal.App.4th 859, 865.

15 §3. BAD-FAITH ACTIONS OR TACTICS—FRIVOLOUS OR INTENDED TO CAUSE DELAY

Under CCP §128.5, a motion for sanctions can be brought against an attorney, a party, or both for bad-faith actions or tactics. CCP §128.5(a). If the bad-faith actions or tactics include the presentation of frivolous or improper papers, a party filing a motion under §128.5 should consider also filing a motion under §128.7, because §128.7 sanctions are easier to obtain. See "Papers—Frivolous or Improper," §2, p. 561.

NOTE

Before January 1, 2015, CCP §128.5 applied only to (1) SLAPP motions (i.e., special motions to strike) and (2) any proceeding initiated on or before December 31, 1994, that a court still had continuing jurisdiction over. See CCP §425.16(c)(1) (anti-SLAPP motions), §425.18(f) (anti-SLAPPback motions); see, e.g., ***Levy v. Blum*** *(5th Dist.2001) 92 Cal.App.4th 625, 641 (sanctions could be recovered under §128.5 in enforcement action when probate court still had continuing jurisdiction over administration of disputed trust admitted to probate in 1974). The California Legislature recently amended §128.5 to allow its use in proceedings initiated after December 31, 1994. See Assem. Bill No. 2494 (2013-2014 Reg. Sess.). The amendments to §128.5 sunset on January 1, 2018, unless the Legislature makes further amendments to extend its effective dates. CCP §128.5(i).*

§3.1 Movant's burden. To prevail on a motion for sanctions under §128.5, the movant must establish that an opposing party's bad-faith actions or tactics were frivolous or solely intended to cause unnecessary delay. *See* CCP §128.5(a).

1. Actions or tactics that can be challenged. The movant must establish that the nonmovant engaged in actions or tactics that are challengeable under §128.5. *See* CCP §128.5(a), (b)(1).

(1) Defined. "Actions or tactics" is broadly defined to include many types of litigation strategies. *See* CCP §128.5(b)(1); *see also* Assem. Com. on Judiciary, Analysis of Assem. Bill No. 2494 (2013-2014 Reg. Sess.) as amended April 10, 2014, p. 5 (§128.5 applies to acts beyond frivolous filings). Actions or tactics that are challengeable include, but are not limited to, the following:

(a) Making a motion. CCP §128.5(b)(1).

(b) Opposing a motion. *Id.*

(c) Filing and serving a complaint. *Id.*

(d) Filing and serving a cross-complaint. *Id.*

(e) Filing and serving an answer. *Id.*

(f) Filing and serving a responsive pleading. *Id.*

(2) Excluded actions or tactics. The following acts are not challengeable under §128.5:

(a) Filing a complaint without serving it on an opposing party. CCP §128.5(b)(1).

(b) Making disclosures. *Id.* §128.5(e).

(c) Making discovery requests, responses, objections, or motions. *Id.*

2. Frivolous or intended to cause delay. The movant must establish that the nonmovant's actions or tactics were frivolous or solely intended to cause unnecessary delay. *See* CCP §128.5(a).

(1) Frivolous. "Frivolous" means that the action or tactic is totally and completely without merit or for the sole purpose of harassing an opposing party. CCP §128.5(b)(2). Whether an action or tactic is totally and completely without merit is determined by an objective standard—that is, whether a reasonable attorney would have found the action or tactic totally and completely without merit. *See* ***Bach v. McNelis*** (3d Dist.1989) 207 Cal.App.3d 852, 876. Whether an action or tactic is solely intended to harass is determined by a subjective standard—that is, whether the nonmovant intended to harass the movant. *See id.*

(2) Delay. Whether an action or tactic is solely intended to delay is determined by a subjective standard—that is, whether the nonmovant intended to delay the movant. *See* ***Bach***, 207 Cal.App.3d at 876.

3. Bad faith. The movant may have to establish that the nonmovant acted in bad faith, depending on whether the nonmovant's actions or tactics were completely without merit or were solely intended to harass or cause unnecessary delay.

(1) Acts without merit. If an action or tactic is objectively without merit, courts are divided about whether the movant must separately establish the nonmovant's bad faith. *See* Weil, *Civil Procedure Before Trial*, ¶9:1020. Some courts have concluded that the movant must separately establish the nonmovant's bad faith. *See* ***In re Marriage of Reese*** (4th Dist.1999) 73 Cal.App.4th 1214, 1220-21; ***Javor v. Dellinger*** (2d Dist.1992) 2 Cal.App.4th 1258, 1260-61. Other courts have held that if the conduct is objectively without merit, there is no need to prove the nonmovant's bad faith. *See* ***On v. Cow Hollow Props.*** (1st Dist.1990) 222 Cal.App.3d 1568, 1575; ***Bach***, 207 Cal.App.3d at 876.

(2) Acts intended to harass or delay. If an action or tactic was solely intended to harass or cause unnecessary delay, then the nonmovant's bad faith is established as a matter of law. *See* ***Javor***, 2 Cal.App.4th at 1261; ***Llamas v. Diaz*** (4th Dist.1990) 218 Cal.App.3d 1043, 1047-48 & n.9.

4. Conduct justifies sanctions. The movant should establish that the nonmovant's conduct justifies the imposition of sanctions. Even if an action or tactic is frivolous or solely intended to cause delay, the court can decline to impose sanctions. *See* CCP §128.5(a) (court "may" impose sanctions). Thus, the movant should explain

why the nonmovant's conduct is particularly egregious. *See* ***Weisman v. Bower*** (2d Dist.1987) 193 Cal.App.3d 1231, 1236 (whether sanctions are warranted depends on evaluation of all circumstances surrounding questioned action or tactic); *see, e.g.*, ***Abandonato v. Coldren*** (4th Dist.1995) 41 Cal.App.4th 264, 267 (court awarded sanctions under §128.5 based on party's pattern of conduct over course of litigation), *disapproved on other grounds*, ***Musaelian v. Adams*** (2009) 45 Cal.4th 512.

§3.2 Motion.

1. Who can file.

(1) Party. A party can file a motion for sanctions under §128.5. *See* CCP §128.5(c), (h)(1).

(2) Court. The court can impose sanctions on its own motion under §128.5. *See* CCP §128.5(c). To impose sanctions on its own motion, the court must enter an order to show cause. *See id.* §§128.5(c), (f), 128.7(c)(2). See "Court," §2.2.1(2), p. 567.

2. Deadline to serve & file. The deadlines to serve and file a motion under §128.5 are the same as those under §128.7(c). CCP §128.5(f). See "Deadline to serve & file," §2.2.2, p. 568.

NOTE

A party making a motion for sanctions under §128.5 must follow the service and filing procedures in §128.7, including the 21-day safe-harbor period that allows the other party to correct or withdraw a challenged paper. See CCP §§128.5(f), 128.7(c)(1). However, the safe-harbor period makes little sense when the movant challenges actions or tactics under §128.5 that cannot be corrected or withdrawn—that is, something other than the presentation of a paper. See "Generally – after safe-harbor period ends," §2.2.2(2)(a), p. 568.

---

3. Form. The motion must be in writing and filed separately from other motions. *See* CCP §§128.5(f), 128.7(c)(1). See "Motion Papers," ch. 1-D, §5, p. 27.

4. Contents.

(1) Notice of motion & motion.

(a) Generally. The notice of motion must comply with the requirements of CCP §1010. *See* CCP §§128.5(f), 128.7(c)(1). See "Notice of motion & motion," ch. 1-D, §5.1, p. 28.

(b) Relief. The notice of motion and motion must describe the sanctions sought. *See* CRC 3.1110(a) (notice of motion must state nature of order sought), CRC 3.1112(d)(3) (motion must briefly state relief sought). The movant can seek reasonable expenses and punitive damages. *See* CCP §128.5(a), (d).

[1] Reasonable expenses. The movant can ask the court to award the reasonable expenses it incurred as a result of the nonmovant's actions or tactics. *See* CCP §128.5(a). Reasonable expenses can include attorney fees. *Id.*

[2] Punitive damages. The movant can ask the court to award punitive damages if the nonmovant being sanctioned (1) is the plaintiff in the suit, (2) has been convicted of a felony, (3) is suing the victim or the victim's heir, relative, estate, or personal representative for alleged injuries that arose from the person's felonious act, and (4) is guilty of fraud, oppression, or malice in maintaining the suit. *See* CCP §128.5(d).

(c) Grounds. The notice of motion and motion must briefly state the grounds for the motion and describe the specific conduct that violated §128.5. *See* CCP §128.5(f) (§128.5 sanctions must be imposed consistently with standards in §128.7(c)), §128.7(c)(1) (motion under §128.7 must describe specific conduct that violated §128.7(b)); CRC 3.1110(a) (notice of motion must state grounds for issuance of order), CRC 3.1112(d)(3) (motion must briefly state basis for motion); *cf.* ***Musaelian v. Adams*** (1st Dist.2011) 197 Cal.App.4th 1251, 1257 (§128.7

sanctions; memorandum of costs seeking attorney fees for opposing motion for sanctions was insufficient to support award because it did not state that §128.7 was basis for award or meet other procedural requirements). See "Movant's burden," §3.1, p. 576. In describing the specific conduct, the motion cannot merely state that the action or tactic was frivolous or used solely to harass the movant. *See* ***In re Marriage of Quinlan*** (1st Dist.1989) 209 Cal.App.3d 1417, 1421-22. Instead, the motion should explain how or why the action or tactic was frivolous or solely intended to cause delay. *See id.*

(2) Memorandum of points & authorities. The motion must include a memorandum in support of the motion. CRC 3.1112(a)(3), 3.1113(a). See "Memorandum of points & authorities," ch. 1-D, §5.2, p. 28.

(3) Supporting evidence. See "Supporting evidence," ch. 1-D, §5.3, p. 30.

(4) Request for judicial notice. The motion can be accompanied by a request for judicial notice. *See* CRC 3.1113(*l*). The request must be filed and served separately from the motion and must list the specific items for which notice is requested. *Id.*

(5) Proposed order. The motion can include a proposed order. *See* CRC 3.1113(m). If a proposed order is submitted, it must be lodged and served with the motion papers, not attached to them. *Id.* See "Documents lodged," ch. 1-F, §2.3, p. 47.

5. Copy to California Research Bureau. The movant must e-mail a copy of the endorsed, filed caption page of the motion to the California Research Bureau of the California State Library promptly after filing the motion. CCP §128.5(h)(1). The movant must indicate whether a motion for sanctions was also made under §128.7. *Id.* §128.5(h)(1).

§3.3 Response. The nonmovant can respond to a motion for sanctions by (1) asking the court to extend the safe-harbor period, (2) correcting or withdrawing the challenged action or tactic, or (3) filing an opposition.

1. Extension of safe-harbor period. The nonmovant can respond to a motion for sanctions by asking the court to extend the safe-harbor period so additional investigation or discovery can be conducted. *CEB Procedure During Trial*, §26.44. See "Deadline to serve & file," §3.2.2, p. 578.

2. Correction or withdrawal. If the action or tactic can be corrected or withdrawn, the nonmovant can correct or withdraw the action or tactic using the procedures applicable to §128.7(c). *See* CCP §128.5(f). See "Correction or withdrawal," §2.3.2, p. 570.

3. Opposition. The nonmovant can respond to a motion for sanctions by filing an opposition.

(1) Deadline to file & serve. The nonmovant must file and serve the opposition at least nine court days before the hearing. CCP §1005(b). See "Filing & serving opposition," ch. 1-D, §8.5, p. 36.

(2) Grounds.

(a) Procedural. The nonmovant can oppose a motion for sanctions under §128.5 on the same procedural grounds as a §128.7 motion. *See* CCP §128.5(f). See "Procedural," §2.3.3(2)(a), p. 571.

(b) Substantive. The nonmovant can oppose a motion for sanctions under §128.5 on the following substantive grounds:

[1] The nonmovant's conduct cannot be challenged under §128.5. See "Excluded actions or tactics," §3.1.1(2), p. 577.

[2] The action or tactic was neither frivolous nor solely intended to cause unnecessary delay. See "Frivolous or intended to cause delay," §3.1.2, p. 577.

[3] The nonmovant did not act in bad faith. See "Bad faith," §3.1.3, p. 577.

[4] The nonmovant's conduct does not justify the imposition of sanctions. See "Conduct justifies sanctions," §3.1.4, p. 577.

(3) Sanctions. The nonmovant can ask the court to impose sanctions under §128.7 against the movant because the motion for sanctions was made for an improper purpose (e.g., to harass, delay, or increase expense). *See* CCP §§128.5(f), 128.7(h). Although §128.7(h) does not state whether a counter-request for sanctions must be filed in a separate motion, one federal court has held that a counter-request for sanctions does not have to meet the separate-motion requirement or the safe-harbor period. ***Patelco Credit Un. v. Sahni*** (9th Cir.2001) 262 F.3d 897, 913 (interpreting FRCP 11).

(4) Attorney fees & expenses incurred in opposing motion. The nonmovant can ask the court to award the attorney fees and expenses it incurred in opposing the motion. *See* CCP §§128.5(f), 128.7(c)(1). Attorney fees and expenses incurred in opposing the motion will usually not be warranted unless the motion itself was frivolous. *Cf.* ***Musaelian v. Adams*** (1st Dist.2011) 197 Cal.App.4th 1251, 1257-58 (discussing sanctions under §128.7).

(5) Contents. See "Opposition Papers," ch. 1-D, §8, p. 35.

§3.4 Hearing. The court must hold a hearing before awarding sanctions. CCP §128.5(c); *see id.* §128.5(f) (sanctions must be imposed consistently with procedures for §128.7), §128.7(c) (requiring notice and opportunity to respond); *cf.* ***In re Marriage of Flaherty*** (1982) 31 Cal.3d 637, 651-52 (sanctions for frivolous appeal; due process requires some type of hearing before depriving a person of property). The scope of the hearing is within the court's discretion (i.e., a party is not entitled to an evidentiary hearing). ***Lavine v. Hospital of the Good Samaritan*** (2d Dist.1985) 169 Cal.App.3d 1019, 1028 (CCP §128.5 sanctions); *cf.* ***Seykora v. Superior Ct.*** (2d Dist.1991) 232 Cal.App.3d 1075, 1081-82 (CCP §177.5 sanctions). See "Hearings," ch. 1-H, p. 79.

§3.5 Ruling.

1. Generally – discretionary. The court has discretion to grant or deny a motion for sanctions that meets the grounds of §128.5. *See* CCP §128.5(a) (court "may" impose sanctions).

2. Court's considerations.

(1) Determining whether action or tactic violated §128.5. In determining whether a challenged action or tactic violated §128.5, the court should determine (1) whether the nonmovant's conduct was frivolous or solely intended to cause delay and (2) whether the nonmovant acted in bad faith. See "Frivolous or intended to cause delay," §3.1.2, p. 577; "Bad faith," §3.1.3, p. 577.

(2) Determining whether to impose sanctions. In determining whether to impose sanctions, the court should consider the seriousness of the challenged action or tactic, the nonmovant's conduct over the course of the litigation, and all the circumstances surrounding the challenged action or tactic. *See* ***Weisman v. Bower*** (2d Dist.1987) 193 Cal.App.3d 1231, 1236 (whether sanctions are warranted depends on evaluation of all circumstances surrounding questioned action or tactic); *see, e.g.,* ***Abandonato v. Coldren*** (4th Dist.1995) 41 Cal.App.4th 264, 267 (court awarded sanctions under §128.5 based on party's pattern of conduct over course of litigation), *disapproved on other grounds,* ***Musaelian v. Adams*** (2009) 45 Cal.4th 512. See "Conduct justifies sanctions," §3.1.4, p. 577.

(3) Determining what sanctions to impose.

(a) Generally – reasonably necessary to deter repetition. In determining what sanctions to impose, the court should not impose sanctions any more severe than reasonably necessary to deter repetition of the improper conduct by the offending person or comparable conduct by a similarly situated person. *See* CCP §§128.5(f), 128.7(d).

NOTE

It is not clear whether the limit under §128.7(d) that sanctions cannot exceed an amount reasonably necessary to deter similar conduct could result in an award under §128.5(a) that is less than the movant's reasonable expenses.

(b) Expenses. In determining the amount of sanctions to impose for expenses and attorney fees, the court should consider whether the expenses and fees incurred by the movant were reasonable. *See* CCP §128.5(a).

§3.6 Order.

1. Form.

(1) Motion denied. The court's order denying the motion for sanctions must be recorded either in writing or by minute order. See "Record of Ruling," ch. 1-I, §4, p. 90.

(2) Motion granted. The court's order granting the motion for sanctions must be in writing. CCP §128.5(c).

2. Contents.

(1) Motion denied. If the court denies the motion, it should state whether the challenged action or tactic violated §128.5, and if so, why sanctions are not being imposed. *Cf. **Warren v. Guelker*** (9th Cir.1994) 29 F.3d 1386, 1389-90 (interpreting FRCP 11).

(2) Motion granted. If the court grants the motion, the order must contain the following information:

(a) Describe circumstances justifying sanctions. If the court grants the motion, the order must recite in detail the conduct or circumstances justifying the order. CCP §128.5(c). No particular form is required—a trial court's minute order addressing the facts and law supporting the sanctions is sufficient. Weil, *Civil Procedure Before Trial*, ¶9:1120.

(b) Identify person sanctions are imposed against. If the court grants the motion, the order must identify the person against whom sanctions are imposed. *Cf.* Kiesel, *Cal. Pretrial Civil Procedure*, §35.17 (sample order on motion for §128.7 sanctions). The court can impose sanctions against an attorney, a party, or both. CCP §128.5(a). When appropriate, the court can hold the attorney and the client jointly and severally liable for the sanctions. *See* Weil, *Civil Procedure Before Trial*, ¶9:1075.

3. Effect of order – notice to State Bar. See "Effect of order – notice to State Bar," §2.6.3, p. 574.

4. Copy to California Research Bureau. The movant must e-mail a conformed copy of the order to the California Research Bureau of the California State Library. CCP §128.5(h)(1).

5. Enforcing order. See "Enforcing order," §2.6.4, p. 574.

§3.7 Motion for reconsideration. A party adversely affected by a court's order on a motion for sanctions can file a motion for reconsideration. CCP §1008(a). See "Motion for Reconsideration," ch. 5-G, §3, p. 508.

§3.8 Motion for renewal. A party whose motion for sanctions is denied can file a motion for renewal. CCP §1008(b). See "Motion for Renewal," ch. 5-G, §4, p. 516.

§3.9 Appellate review. See "Appellate review," §2.9, p. 575.

NOTE

The party who filed the motion must e-mail a copy of any related notice of appeal or petition for a writ to the California Research Bureau of the California State Library. CCP §128.5(h)(1).

§4. VIOLATION OF COURT ORDER

Under CCP §177.5, monetary sanctions can be imposed against a witness, a party, or a party's attorney for violating a court order. Monetary sanctions under §177.5 can be imposed in addition to any other sanctions permitted by law.

See CCP §177.5. Although a request for monetary sanctions under §177.5 can be made by a party, sanctions are usually imposed by the court on its own motion because they are payable only to the court. Weil, *Civil Procedure Before Trial*, ¶9.1271; *see* CCP §177.5.

§4.1 Movant's burden. To prevail on a motion for sanctions under CCP §177.5, the movant must establish the following:

1. Knowing violation. The movant must establish that a witness, a party, or a party's attorney knowingly violated a court order. ***In re Woodham*** (4th Dist.2001) 95 Cal.App.4th 438, 445; *see* CCP §177.5; *see, e.g.*, ***Winikow v. Superior Ct.*** (2d Dist.2000) 82 Cal.App.4th 719, 727 (court abused discretion by imposing sanctions against party who did not violate order); ***Twentieth Century Ins. v. Choong*** (2d Dist.2000) 79 Cal.App.4th 1274, 1276 (court acted within discretion in sanctioning attorney for failing to pay original sanction; attorney had knowledge of original sanction order when he was present in courtroom at time order was issued and minute order clearly reflected that order was imposed on him personally). A violation does not have to be willful to be sanctionable. ***In re Woodham***, 95 Cal.App.4th at 446.

2. Lawful court order. The movant must establish that the order violated was a lawful court order. CCP §177.5.

(1) Lawful. A court order is lawful if it was within the court's power to make it. *See, e.g.*, ***People v. Ward*** (2d Dist.2009) 173 Cal.App.4th 1518, 1528 (court's order prohibiting attorney from using phrase "prosecutorial misconduct" in front of jury was within court's power to control proceedings before it).

(2) Court order. The violation must be of a preexisting court order; violation of a rule of professional conduct, a rule of court, or a legal tenet is not sufficient to support sanctions under §177.5. *See* ***Bryan v. Bank of Am.*** (1st Dist.2001) 86 Cal.App.4th 185, 197 (§177.5 does not authorize sanctions for violation of court rules); *see, e.g.*, ***Conservatorship of Becerra*** (4th Dist.2009) 175 Cal.App.4th 1474, 1484 (violation of rule of professional conduct was not violation of court order); ***Vidrio v. Hernandez*** (2d Dist.2009) 172 Cal.App.4th 1443, 1455 (violation of insurer's duty to negotiate in good faith was not violation of court order); ***People v. Muhammad*** (2d Dist.2003) 108 Cal.App.4th 313, 316 (improper peremptory challenge was not violation of court order). *But see* ***People v. Tabb*** (4th Dist.1991) 228 Cal.App.3d 1300, 1311 (violation of attorney's professional duty to appear at scheduled hearing for client is sufficient to support sanctions; no separate order commanding attorney to appear is required). The court's order can be oral or written. *See, e.g.*, ***In re Woodham***, 95 Cal.App.4th at 440 & n.3 (written order to timely respond to administrative appeals by inmates was sufficient); ***Seykora v. Superior Ct.*** (2d Dist.1991) 232 Cal.App.3d 1075, 1078 (oral order not to leave courtroom was sufficient).

§4.2 Motion.

1. Who can file.

(1) Party. A party can ask the court to impose sanctions under §177.5 in its moving or responding papers (e.g., opposition, reply). CCP §177.5.

(2) Court. The court can impose sanctions on its own motion under §177.5. CCP §177.5. Before imposing sanctions on its own motion, the court must give notice to the person being sanctioned. *Id.* The adequacy of the court's notice is determined on a case-by-case basis. ***Seykora v. Superior Ct.*** (2d Dist.1991) 232 Cal.App.3d 1075, 1081. Generally, notice will be adequate if the court advises the party that sanctions are being considered and the party has an opportunity to prepare for the hearing. *See id.*; *see, e.g.*, ***People v. Hundal*** (3d Dist.2008) 168 Cal.App.4th 965, 970 (court's oral statement, "I don't know what to do about this; I am going to think about it," was not sufficient notice that court was considering imposition of sanctions). Notice does not have to be given formally in writing; notice in open court can be sufficient. *See, e.g.*, ***Seykora***, 232 Cal.App.3d at 1081 (one day's notice was sufficient when it was given in open court); ***Caldwell v. Samuels Jewelers*** (6th Dist.1990) 222 Cal.App.3d 970, 976-77 (notice given at same time as hearing was sufficient when parties stipulated that court could hear sanctions issue).

NOTE

A party can file papers in support of a court's motion to impose sanctions. See, e.g., ***Vidrio v. Hernandez*** *(2d Dist.2009) 172 Cal.App.4th 1443, 1450 (after court issued order for party's attorney to show cause why sanctions should not be imposed, opposing party filed declaration in support of sanctions).*

2. Deadline to file & serve. A motion for sanctions must be filed in the court and served on all parties who have appeared in the case at least 16 court days before the hearing on the motion. *See* CCP §1005(b). See "Retrospective deadlines," ch. 1-G, §6.2, p. 71. If the motion is served by a method other than personal delivery, the movant will have to add more time to the 16-day period. *See* CCP §1005(b). See "Add time for method of service," ch. 1-G, §6.2.1(5), p. 72.

3. Contents.

(1) Notice of motion & motion.

(a) Generally. If the motion is requested in a party's motion papers, it should be requested by noticed motion. *See* CCP §177.5 (person to be sanctioned must be given notice). See "Notice of motion & motion," ch. 1-D, §5.1, p. 28.

(b) Relief.

[1] Sanctions. The notice of motion and motion must describe the sanctions sought. *See* CRC 3.1110(a) (notice of motion must state nature of order sought), CRC 3.1112(d)(3) (motion must briefly state relief sought). The movant can seek reasonable monetary sanctions of up to $1,500. CCP §177.5.

[2] Person to be sanctioned. The notice of motion and motion must identify the person against whom sanctions are sought. *See* ***Cromwell v. Cummings*** (Orange Cty. Superior Ct. Appellate Dept. 1998) 65 Cal.App.4th Supp. 10, 13. Sanctions under §177.5 can only be sought against a witness, a party, or a party's attorney. *See* CCP §177.5; *see, e.g.,* ***Vidrio***, 172 Cal.App.4th at 1455 (nonparty could not be sanctioned under §177.5).

(c) Grounds. The notice of motion and motion must briefly state the grounds for the motion. *See* CRC 3.1110(a) (notice of motion must state grounds for issuance of order), CRC 3.1112(d)(3) (motion must briefly state basis for motion). See "Movant's burden," §3.1, p. 576.

(2) Memorandum of points & authorities. The motion must include a memorandum in support of the motion. CRC 3.1112(a)(3), 3.1113(a). See "Memorandum of points & authorities," ch. 1-D, §5.2, p. 28.

(3) Supporting evidence. See "Supporting evidence," ch. 1-D, §5.3, p. 30.

(4) Request for judicial notice. The motion can be accompanied by a request for judicial notice. *See* CRC 3.1113(*l*). The request must be filed and served separately from the motion and must list the specific items for which notice is requested. *Id.*

(5) Proposed order. The motion can be accompanied by a proposed order. *See* CRC 3.1113(m). If a proposed order is submitted, it must be lodged and served with the motion papers, not attached to them. *Id.* See "Documents lodged," ch. 1-F, §2.3, p. 47.

§4.3 Opposition. The nonmovant can respond to a motion for sanctions by filing an opposition.

1. Deadline to file & serve. The nonmovant must file and serve the opposition at least nine court days before the hearing. CCP §1005(b). See "Filing & serving opposition," ch. 1-D, §8.5, p. 36.

2. Grounds.

(1) Procedural. The nonmovant can oppose a motion for sanctions under CCP §177.5 on the following procedural grounds:

(a) The nonmovant did not receive adequate notice. *See* ***Seykora v. Superior Ct.*** (2d Dist.1991) 232 Cal.App.3d 1075, 1081. See "Court," §4.2.1(2), p. 582 (discussing adequacy of court's notice).

(b) The motion does not identify the person against whom monetary sanctions are sought. *See* ***Cromwell v. Cummings*** (Orange Cty. Superior Ct. Appellate Dept. 1998) 65 Cal.App.4th Supp. 10, 13.

(2) Substantive. The nonmovant can oppose a motion for sanctions under §177.5 on the following substantive grounds:

(a) The nonmovant is not a sanctionable person under §177.5—that is, the nonmovant is not a witness, a party, or a party's attorney. *See* CCP §177.5; *see, e.g.*, ***Vidrio v. Hernandez*** (2d Dist.2009) 172 Cal.App.4th 1443, 1455 (nonparty could not be sanctioned under §177.5).

(b) The court order was not lawful. *See* CCP §177.5. See "Lawful," §4.1.2(1), p. 582.

(c) The nonmovant did not knowingly violate the court order. *See, e.g.*, ***Scott C. Moody, Inc. v. Staar Surgical Co.*** (4th Dist.2011) 195 Cal.App.4th 1043, 1049 (nonmovant claimed he did not clearly understand court order). See "Knowing violation," §4.1.1, p. 582.

(d) The nonmovant did not violate the court order. *See* CCP §177.5.

(e) The alleged violation is not subject to sanctions because it constitutes advocacy before the court. *Id.*; *see, e.g.*, ***Trans-Action Commercial Investors, Ltd. v. Firmaterr, Inc.*** (1st Dist.1997) 60 Cal.App.4th 352, 370 (court did not impose sanctions under §177.5 because improper questioning of witnesses could be considered advocacy). Advocacy is the act of pleading, arguing, supporting, or recommending a particular position or idea. ***Scott C. Moody, Inc.***, 195 Cal.App.4th at 1049; ***People v. Ward*** (2d Dist.2009) 173 Cal.App.4th 1518, 1529. To be exempt from sanctions, the advocacy must be proper and on behalf of a party. ***Ward***, 173 Cal.App.4th at 1529. Once a court rules that a particular argument can no longer be made, however, the act of arguing that position is no longer considered advocacy but instead a violation of a court order. *See id.* at 1530.

(f) The nonmovant had good cause or substantial justification for violating the court order. *See* CCP §177.5; *see, e.g.*, ***In re Woodham*** (4th Dist.2001) 95 Cal.App.4th 438, 446-47 (party unsuccessfully opposed court's motion on ground that increase in workload and administrative error were valid excuses for violating court order).

3. Contents. See "Opposition Papers," ch. 1-D, §8, p. 35.

§4.4 Reply. The movant can file and serve a reply to the opposition papers. The reply must be filed and served at least five court days before the hearing. CCP §1005(b). See "Reply Papers," ch. 1-D, §9, p. 37.

§4.5 Hearing. The court must hold a hearing before imposing sanctions. ***People v. Hundal*** (3d Dist.2008) 168 Cal.App.4th 965, 970; *see* CCP §177.5; ***Seykora v. Superior Ct.*** (2d Dist.1991) 232 Cal.App.3d 1075, 1081-82. At the hearing, the court must give the person to be sanctioned an opportunity to address why sanctions should not be imposed. *See* ***Hundal***, 168 Cal.App.4th at 970 (court must allow person being sanctioned to address lawfulness of order, existence of violation, and good cause or substantial justification for violation); ***Seykora***, 232 Cal.App.3d at 1082 (when violation occurs in court's presence, due process is served if party is given opportunity to appear and offer excuse for her behavior). The person being sanctioned is not entitled, however, to an evidentiary hearing in which oral testimony is presented. ***Seykora***, 232 Cal.App.3d at 1082. The scope of the hearing is within the court's discretion. *Id.* See "Hearings," ch. 1-H, p. 79.

§4.6 Ruling. The decision to grant or deny a motion for sanctions is within the court's discretion. ***Winikow v. Superior Ct.*** (2d Dist.2000) 82 Cal.App.4th 719, 726; *see* ***Conservatorship of Becerra*** (4th Dist.2009) 175 Cal.App.4th 1474, 1482. The court's discretion must be exercised in a reasonable manner with the statute's purpose in mind. ***Winikow***, 82 Cal.App.4th at 726. CCP §177.5 has two purposes: to compensate public agencies for the cost of unnecessary hearings and to broaden the type of conduct the court can punish. ***In re Woodham*** (4th Dist.2001) 95 Cal.App.4th 438, 443-44. Thus, sanctions under §177.5 can be imposed for either a compensatory or a punitive purpose. ***In re Woodham***, 95 Cal.App.4th at 444. Sanctions cannot be imposed, however, to coerce a party to settle a case. ***Barrientos v. City of L.A.*** (2d Dist.1994) 30 Cal.App.4th 63, 72.

§4.7 Order.

1. Form.

(1) Motion denied. The court's order denying the motion for sanctions must be recorded either in writing or by minute order. See "Record of Ruling," ch. 1-I, §4, p. 90.

(2) Motion granted. The court's order granting the motion for sanctions must be in writing. CCP §177.5; *see, e.g.*, ***People v. Hundal*** (3d Dist.2008) 168 Cal.App.4th 965, 970 (oral order for sanctions was improper).

2. Contents. If the court imposes sanctions, the order must contain the following information:

(1) Describe sanctionable conduct. The order must describe in detail the conduct or circumstances justifying the order. CCP §177.5; ***People v. Ward*** (2d Dist.2009) 173 Cal.App.4th 1518, 1531; ***Caldwell v. Samuels Jewelers*** (6th Dist.1990) 222 Cal.App.3d 970, 977.

(2) Specify sanctions. The order must specify the amount of monetary sanctions being imposed. The court can impose reasonable monetary sanctions of up to $1,500. CCP §177.5; ***Sino Century Dev. Ltd. v. Farley*** (2d Dist.2012) 211 Cal.App.4th 688, 700. The dollar amount does not have to be based on what the misconduct actually cost the court; it merely has to be reasonable and within the statutory limit. *E.g.*, ***Twentieth Century Ins. v. Choong*** (2d Dist.2000) 79 Cal.App.4th 1274, 1278-79 (sanction of $250 for not paying original sanction was reasonable, within statutory limit, and not abuse of discretion); *see* ***In re Woodham*** (4th Dist.2001) 95 Cal.App.4th 438, 444 (sanctions can be either compensatory or punitive).

(3) Identify person sanctions are imposed against. The order must identify the person against whom sanctions are imposed. *See* CCP §177.5; *see, e.g.*, ***Choong***, 79 Cal.App.4th at 1276 (minute order showed sanctions were imposed on attorney personally).

(4) Make sanctions payable to court. The order must make the monetary sanctions payable to the court. *See* CCP §177.5.

3. Effect of order – notice to State Bar. See "Effect of order – notice to State Bar," §2.6.3, p. 574.

4. Enforcing order. See "Enforcing order," §2.6.4, p. 574.

§4.8 Motion for reconsideration. A party adversely affected by a court's order on a motion for sanctions can file a motion for reconsideration. CCP §1008(a). See "Motion for Reconsideration," ch. 5-G, §3, p. 508.

§4.9 Motion for renewal. A party whose motion for sanctions is denied can file a motion for renewal. *See* CCP §1008(b). See "Motion for Renewal," ch. 5-G, §4, p. 516.

§4.10 Appellate review. See "Appellate review," §2.9, p. 575.

§5. VIOLATION OF CALIFORNIA RULE OF COURT

Under CRC 2.30, monetary sanctions can be imposed against a person for not complying with the California Rules of Court. Sanctions under CRC 2.30 can be imposed in addition to any other sanctions permitted by law, and a motion for CRC 2.30 sanctions can be made by a party or the court. *See* CRC 2.30(b), (c). Unlike monetary sanctions under CCP §177.5, monetary sanctions under CRC 2.30 can be payable to the court, an aggrieved person, or both. CRC 2.30(b).

§5.1 Movant's burden. To prevail on a motion for sanctions under CRC 2.30, the movant must establish that a witness, a party, a party's attorney, an insurer, or any other individual or entity whose consent is necessary for the disposition of the case violated the California Rules of Court. *See* CRC 2.30(b); *see, e.g.*, ***Vidrio v. Hernandez*** (2d Dist.2009) 172 Cal.App.4th 1443, 1460 (insurer's failure to participate in good faith at settlement conference did not violate any California Rule of Court and thus was not sanctionable). The rule of court violated must be a rule relating to general civil cases, unlawful-detainer cases, probate proceedings, civil proceedings in the appellate division of the superior court, or small-claims cases. CRC 2.30(a); *see, e.g.*, ***In re Marriage of Bianco*** (4th Dist.2013) 221

Cal.App.4th 826, 829 (attorney's negligent hiring of ineligible co-counsel to assist in divorce case was not sanctionable because family-law proceedings are not general civil cases).

§5.2 Motion.

1. Who can file.

(1) Party. A party can file a motion for sanctions under CRC 2.30. CRC 2.30(c).

(2) Court. The court can impose sanctions on its own motion under CRC 2.30. CRC 2.30(c). Before imposing sanctions on its own motion, the court must give the person to be sanctioned notice. *Id.* The court can give notice by issuing an order to show cause that (1) states the rule that has been violated, (2) describes the specific conduct that appears to have violated the rule, and (3) directs the person to be sanctioned to show cause why sanctions should not be imposed for violating the rule. *Id.*

2. Deadline to file & serve. See "Deadline to file & serve," §4.2.2, p. 583.

3. Contents.

(1) Notice of motion & motion.

(a) Generally. The motion for sanctions must be requested in writing by noticed motion. CRC 2.30(c). See "Notice of motion & motion," ch. 1-D, §5.1, p. 28.

(b) Relief. The notice of motion and motion must describe the relief sought. *See* CRC 3.1110(a) (notice of motion must state nature of order sought), CRC 3.1112(d)(3) (motion must briefly state relief sought).

[1] Sanctions. The movant can ask the court to order the person being sanctioned to pay a reasonable amount of monetary sanctions. CRC 2.30(b); ***Sino Century Dev. Ltd. v. Farley*** (2d Dist.2012) 211 Cal.App.4th 688, 691. There is no limit on the amount the court can impose as long as it is reasonable. *See* CRC 2.30(b).

[2] Attorney fees & expenses. The movant can ask the court to order the person being sanctioned to pay the aggrieved party's reasonable expenses, including the reasonable attorney fees and costs incurred in connection with the party's motion for sanctions or the order to show cause. CRC 2.30(d). CRC 2.30(d) does not, however, authorize the recovery of attorney fees that were incurred as a result of the rule violation. ***Sino Century Dev.***, 211 Cal.App.4th at 698.

NOTE

*"Reasonable monetary sanctions" under CRC 2.30(b) cannot include attorney fees as sanctions. See **Sino Century Dev.**, 211 Cal.App.4th at 697-98. In **Sino Century Dev.**, the Second District Court of Appeal reversed a trial court's order imposing full compensation of all attorney fees incurred as a result of a rules violation. Id. at 691. The appellate court reasoned that because CRC 2.30(b) did not specifically authorize attorney fees as sanctions, and CRC 2.30(d) limited recoverable attorney fees to those incurred in connection with the motion for sanctions or order to show cause, the trial court had no authority to award attorney fees as sanctions for violating a rule of court. See **Sino Century Dev.**, 211 Cal.App.4th at 697-98.*

(c) Person to be sanctioned. The notice of motion and motion must identify the person against whom sanctions are sought. CRC 2.30(c); *see* ***Cromwell v. Cummings*** (Orange Cty. Superior Ct. Appellate Dept. 1998) 65 Cal.App.4th Supp. 10, 13. Sanctions under CRC 2.30 can be sought against only a witness, a party, a party's attorney, an insurer, or any other individual or entity whose consent is necessary for the disposition of the case. CRC 2.30(b).

(d) Grounds. The notice of motion and motion must briefly state the grounds for the motion. *See* CRC 3.1110(a) (notice of motion must state grounds for issuance of order), CRC 3.1112(d)(3) (motion must briefly state basis for motion). See "Movant's burden," §4.1, p. 582. The notice of motion and motion must state the rule that was violated and describe the specific conduct that violated the rule. CRC 2.30(c).

(2) Memorandum of points & authorities. The motion must include a memorandum in support of the motion. CRC 3.1112(a)(3), 3.1113(a). See "Memorandum of points & authorities," ch. 1-D, §5.2, p. 28.

(3) Supporting evidence. See "Supporting evidence," ch. 1-D, §5.3, p. 30.

(4) Request for judicial notice. The motion can be accompanied by a request for judicial notice. *See* CRC 3.1113(*l*). The request must be filed and served separately from the motion and must list the specific items for which notice is requested. *Id.*

(5) Proposed order. The motion can be accompanied by a proposed order. *See* CRC 3.1113(m). If a proposed order is submitted, it must be lodged and served with the motion papers, not attached to them. *Id.* See "Documents lodged," ch. 1-F, §2.3, p. 47.

§5.3 Opposition. The nonmovant can respond to a motion for sanctions by filing an opposition.

1. Deadline to file & serve. The nonmovant must file and serve the opposition at least nine court days before the hearing. CCP §1005(b). See "Filing & serving opposition," ch. 1-D, §8.5, p. 36.

2. Grounds.

(1) Procedural. The nonmovant can oppose a motion for sanctions under CRC 2.30 on the following procedural grounds:

(a) The nonmovant did not receive proper notice. *See* CRC 2.30(c).

(b) The motion does not identify the party against whom monetary sanctions are sought. *See id.*

(c) The motion did not specify the rule violated or describe the conduct that violated the rule. *See id.*

(2) Substantive. The nonmovant can oppose a motion for sanctions under CRC 2.30 on the following substantive grounds:

(a) The nonmovant is not a sanctionable person under CRC 2.30—that is, the nonmovant is not a witness, a party, a party's attorney, an insurer, or any other individual or entity whose consent is necessary for the disposition of the case. *See* CRC 2.30(b).

(b) The nonmovant did not violate the rule of court. *See id.*

(c) The nonmovant had good cause for violating the rule of court. *See id.*

(d) The rule of court is invalid. *See, e.g.*, ***Trans-Action Commercial Investors, Ltd. v. Firmaterr, Inc.*** (1st Dist.1997) 60 Cal.App.4th 352, 354-55 (sanctions could not be imposed under former CRC 227, now CRC 2.30, because former rule conflicted with legislative scheme for imposing sanctions). A state rule of court is invalid if it directly or indirectly conflicts with a state statute. *See* ***Trans-Action Commercial Investors***, 60 Cal.App.4th at 363-64 (state rule of court must not conflict with statutory intent).

3. Contents. See "Opposition Papers," ch. 1-D, §8, p. 35.

§5.4 Reply. The movant can file and serve a reply to the opposition papers. The reply must be filed and served at least five court days before the hearing. CCP §1005(b). See "Reply Papers," ch. 1-D, §9, p. 37.

§5.5 Hearing. The court must hold a hearing before imposing sanctions. *See* CRC 2.30(b) (requiring opportunity to be heard). See "Hearing," §4.5, p. 584.

§5.6 Ruling. The decision to grant or deny a motion for sanctions is within the court's discretion. ***Winikow v. Superior Ct.*** (2d Dist.2000) 82 Cal.App.4th 719, 726.

§5.7 Order.

1. Form.

(1) Motion denied. The court's order denying the motion for sanctions must be recorded either in writing or by minute order. See "Record of Ruling," ch. 1-I, §4, p. 90.

(2) Motion granted. The court's order granting the motion for sanctions must be in writing. CRC 2.30(e).

2. Contents. If the court grants the motion, the order must contain the following information:

(1) Describe sanctionable conduct. The order must describe in detail the conduct or circumstances justifying the order. CRC 2.30(e); *see* ***Caldwell v. Samuels Jewelers*** (6th Dist.1990) 222 Cal.App.3d 970, 978.

(2) Specify sanctions. The order must specify the amount of monetary sanctions being imposed. See "Monetary sanctions," §2.2.4(1)(b)[1][b], p. 569.

(3) Identify person sanctions are imposed against. The order must identify the person against whom sanctions are imposed. *See* CRC 2.30(b); *see, e.g.*, ***Ellerbee v. County of L.A.*** (2d Dist.2010) 187 Cal.App.4th 1206, 1212 (order imposed sanctions against Ds and Ds' attorney). If the person responsible for the rule violation is an attorney and not a party, the court can only impose sanctions against the attorney. CRC 2.30(b); *e.g.*, ***Levitz v. The Warlocks*** (2d Dist.2007) 148 Cal.App.4th 531, 535-36 (P's attorney, not P, should have been sanctioned for inadequate declarations).

(4) Identify person sanctions are payable to. The order must identify the person to whom sanctions are payable. *See* CRC 2.30(b); *see, e.g.*, ***Ellerbee***, 187 Cal.App.4th at 1212 (Ds and Ds' attorney were ordered to pay $6,194 to P's attorney). The court can order monetary sanctions payable to the court, an aggrieved person, or both. CRC 2.30(b).

3. Effect of order – notice to State Bar. See "Effect of order – notice to State Bar," §2.6.3, p. 574.

4. Enforcing order. See "Enforcing order," §2.6.4, p. 574.

§5.8 Motion for reconsideration. A party adversely affected by a court's order on a motion for sanctions can file a motion for reconsideration. CCP §1008(a). See "Motion for Reconsideration," ch. 5-G, §3, p. 508.

§5.9 Motion for renewal. A party whose motion for sanctions is denied can file a motion for renewal. *See* CCP §1008(b). See "Motion for Renewal," ch. 5-G, §4, p. 516.

§5.10 Appellate review. See "Appellate review," §2.9, p. 575.

§6. VIOLATION OF LOCAL RULE OF COURT

Under CCP §575.2, a court can impose sanctions against an attorney, a represented party, or a person appearing pro per who does not comply with a local rule of court that authorizes the imposition of sanctions. CCP §575.2(a); *see, e.g.*, Super. Ct. Solano Cty. Loc. R., rule 4.13(a) (noncompliance with local rules can result in sanctions).

NOTE

Gov. C. §68608(b) encourages courts to impose sanctions for violating local fast-track rules. Section 68608(b) does not, however, independently authorize sanctions; the authority to sanction must be found in other provisions of law, such as CCP §575.2. See Gov. C. §68608(b); see, e.g., ***Garcia v. McCutchen*** *(1997) 16 Cal.4th 469, 475-76 (sanctions for violation of local fast-track rules is subject to limitation in §575.2(b)).*

§6.1 Movant's burden. To prevail on a motion for sanctions under CCP §575.2, the movant must show that (1) an attorney, a represented party, or a person appearing pro per violated a local rule of court and (2) the court's local rules authorize sanctions. *See* CCP §575.2(a); *see, e.g.*, ***Carlson v. State of Cal. Dept. of Fish & Game*** (2d Dist.1998) 68 Cal.App.4th 1268, 1279-80 (neither §575.2 nor local rules authorized clerk to sanction party by refusing to file complaint for lack of certificate of assignment).

§6.2 Motion.

1. Who can file.

(1) Party. A party can file a motion for sanctions under §575.2. CCP §575.2(a).

(2) Court. The court can impose sanctions on its own motion under §575.2. CCP §575.2(a). Before imposing sanctions on its own motion, the court must give the person to be sanctioned notice. *Id.* Section 575.2 does not specify whether the court's notice must be in writing.

2. Deadline to file & serve. See "Deadline to file & serve," §4.2.2, p. 583.

3. Contents.

(1) Notice of motion & motion.

(a) Generally. The motion for sanctions must be requested in writing by noticed motion. *See* CCP §575.2(a) (party to be sanctioned is entitled to notice). See "Notice of motion & motion," ch. 1-D, §5.1, p. 28.

(b) Relief.

[1] Sanctions. The notice of motion and motion must describe the sanctions sought. *See* CRC 3.1110(a) (notice of motion must state nature of order sought), CRC 3.1112(d)(3) (motion must briefly state relief sought).

[a] Generally. The movant can ask the court to order the following sanctions:

- Strike all or part of the party's pleading. CCP §575.2(a).
- Dismiss all or part of the proceeding. *Id.*
- Enter a judgment of default. *Id.*
- Impose penalties of a lesser nature as otherwise provided by law. *Id.*; *e.g.*, ***Rietveld v. Rosebud Storage Partners*** (3d Dist.2004) 121 Cal.App.4th 250, 257 (sanctions of $2,380, which represented fees and costs party incurred in arbitration and in making motion for sanctions, were not excessive); *see, e.g.*, Super. Ct. Solano Cty. Loc. R., rule 4.13(a) (noncompliance with local rules can result in monetary sanctions, evidentiary sanctions, other sanctions, and contempt).

[b] Attorney fees & expenses. The movant can ask the court to order the person being sanctioned to pay the movant's reasonable expenses in making the motion, including the movant's reasonable attorney fees. CCP §575.2(a); ***Sino Century Dev. Ltd. v. Farley*** (2d Dist.2012) 211 Cal.App.4th 688, 699.

[2] Person to be sanctioned. If monetary sanctions are being sought, the notice of motion and motion must identify the person against whom sanctions are sought. *See* ***Cromwell v. Cummings*** (Orange Cty. Superior Ct. Appellate Dept. 1998) 65 Cal.App.4th Supp. 10, 13. Sanctions under §575.2 can only be sought against an attorney, a represented party, or a person appearing pro per. CCP §575.2(a).

(c) Grounds. The notice of motion and motion must briefly state the grounds for the motion. *See* CRC 3.1110(a) (notice of motion must state grounds for issuance of order), CRC 3.1112(d)(3) (motion must briefly state basis for motion). See "Movant's burden," §5.1, p. 585. The notice of motion and motion should state the rule that was violated and describe the specific conduct that violated the rule. *Cf.* CRC 2.30(c) (requirement for violation of California Rules of Court).

(2) Memorandum of points & authorities. The motion must include a memorandum in support of the motion. CRC 3.1112(a)(3), 3.1113(a). See "Memorandum of points & authorities," ch. 1-D, §5.2, p. 28.

(3) Supporting evidence. See "Supporting evidence," ch. 1-D, §5.3, p. 30.

(4) Request for judicial notice. The motion can be accompanied by a request for judicial notice. *See* CRC 3.1113(*l*). The request must be filed and served separately from the motion and must list the specific items for which notice is requested. *Id.*

(5) Proposed order. The motion can be accompanied by a proposed order. *See* CRC 3.1113(m). If a proposed order is submitted, it must be lodged and served with the motion papers, not attached to them. CRC 3.1113(m). See "Documents lodged," ch. 1-F, §2.3, p. 47.

§6.3 Opposition. The nonmovant can respond to a motion for sanctions by filing an opposition.

1. Deadline to file & serve. The nonmovant must file and serve the opposition at least nine court days before the hearing. CCP §1005(b). See "Filing & serving opposition," ch. 1-D, §8.5, p. 36.

2. Grounds.

(1) Procedural. The nonmovant can oppose a motion for sanctions under §575.2 on the following procedural grounds:

(a) The nonmovant did not receive proper notice. *See* CCP §575.2(a).

(b) The motion does not identify the person against whom monetary sanctions are sought. *See* ***Cromwell v. Cummings*** (Orange Cty. Superior Ct. Appellate Dept. 1998) 65 Cal.App.4th Supp. 10, 13.

(c) The motion did not specify the rule violated or describe the conduct that violated the rule. *Cf.* CRC 2.30(c) (requirement for violation of California Rules of Court).

(2) Substantive. The nonmovant can oppose a motion for sanctions under §575.2 on the following substantive grounds:

(a) The nonmovant is not a sanctionable person under §575.2—that is, the nonmovant is not an attorney, a represented party, or a person appearing pro per. *See* CCP §575.2(a).

(b) The nonmovant did not violate the local rule. *See id.*

(c) The local rule is invalid. A local rule is invalid if it conflicts with a California statute or rule of court. ***Carlson v. State of Cal. Dept. of Fish & Game*** (2d Dist.1998) 68 Cal.App.4th 1268, 1279; *see, e.g.*, ***Rietveld v. Rosebud Storage Partners*** (3d Dist.2004) 121 Cal.App.4th 250, 256 (attorney opposed motion for sanctions on ground that local rule conflicted with state rules).

3. Contents. See "Opposition Papers," ch. 1-D, §8, p. 35.

§6.4 Reply. The movant can file and serve a reply to the opposition papers. The reply must be filed and served at least five court days before the hearing. CCP §1005(b). See "Reply Papers," ch. 1-D, §9, p. 37.

§6.5 Hearing. The court must hold a hearing before imposing sanctions. *See* CCP §575.2(a) (party to be sanctioned is entitled to notice and opportunity to be heard); *see, e.g.*, ***Annex British Cars, Inc. v. Parker-Rhodes*** (1st Dist.1988) 198 Cal.App.3d 788, 792-93 (order denying reconsideration of sanctions order was reversed with directions for court to hold hearing). See "Hearing," §4.5, p. 584.

§6.6 Ruling. The decision to grant or deny a motion for sanctions is within the court's discretion. *See* ***Cooks v. Superior Ct.*** (2d Dist.1990) 224 Cal.App.3d 723, 725.

§6.7 Order.

1. Form.

(1) Motion denied. The court's order denying the motion for sanctions must be recorded either in writing or by minute order. See "Record of Ruling," ch. 1-I, §4, p. 90.

(2) Motion granted. The court's order granting the motion for sanctions should be in writing. *See* ***Caldwell v. Samuels Jewelers*** (6th Dist.1990) 222 Cal.App.3d 970, 978 (due process requires that any order imposing sanctions state with particularity the basis for sanctions); *cf.* CCP §177.5 (sanctions order for violation of court order must be in writing); CRC 2.30(e) (sanctions order for failure to comply with Cal. Rules of Court must be in writing).

2. **Contents.** If the court grants the motion, the order must contain the following information:

(1) **Describe sanctionable conduct.** The order must describe in detail the conduct or circumstances justifying the order. *See* ***Caldwell***, 222 Cal.App.3d at 978 (due process requires that any order imposing sanctions state with particularity the basis for sanctions); *cf.* CCP §177.5 (sanctions order for violation of court order must describe conduct justifying order); CRC 2.30(e) (sanctions order for failure to comply with Cal. Rules of Court must describe conduct justifying order).

(2) **Specify sanctions.** The order must specify the sanctions being imposed. See "Relief," §5.2.3(1)(b), p. 586.

(3) **Identify person sanctions are imposed against.** The order must identify the person against whom sanctions are imposed. *See* CCP §575.2(a); *see, e.g.*, ***Ellerbee v. County of L.A.*** (2d Dist.2010) 187 Cal.App.4th 1206, 1212 (order imposed sanctions against Ds and Ds' attorney). If the person responsible for the rule violation is an attorney and not a party, any penalty should be imposed against the attorney and should not adversely affect the party's cause of action or defense. CCP §575.2(b).

(4) **Identify person sanctions are payable to.** If the court imposes monetary sanctions, the order must identify the person to whom sanctions are payable. *See* CCP §575.2(a); *see, e.g.*, ***Ellerbee***, 187 Cal.App.4th at 1212 (Ds and Ds' attorney were ordered to pay $6,194 to P's attorney).

3. **Effect of order – notice to State Bar.** See "Effect of order – notice to State Bar," §2.6.3, p. 574.

4. **Enforcing order.** See "Enforcing order," §2.6.4, p. 574.

§6.8 Motion for reconsideration. A party adversely affected by a court's order on a motion for sanctions can file a motion for reconsideration. CCP §1008(a). See "Motion for Reconsideration," ch. 5-G, §3, p. 508.

§6.9 Motion for renewal. A party whose motion for sanctions is denied can file a motion for renewal. *See* CCP §1008(b). See "Motion for Renewal," ch. 5-G, §4, p. 516.

§6.10 Appellate review. See "Appellate review," §2.9, p. 575.

L. EXCLUDING EXPERT TESTIMONY

§1. GENERAL

§1.1 Purpose. The court has a gatekeeping responsibility to determine the admissibility of expert testimony. *See* Evid. C. §402(b) (court may hear and determine the question of the admissibility of evidence outside the presence or hearing of the jury); ***Sargon Enters. v. University of S. Cal.*** (2012) 55 Cal.4th 747, 770 (court must act as gatekeeper to exclude speculative or irrelevant expert opinions from jury's consideration). But the court is not required to exercise this responsibility without a party's valid objection. ***In re Powell*** (1988) 45 Cal.3d 894, 905-06.

§1.2 Primary authority. Evid. C. §§350, 352, 402, 720, 800-805; CRC 3.1112.

§1.3 Secondary authority. The following secondary sources are cited as authority in this subchapter:

- *California Trial Practice: Civil Procedure During Trial* (CEB Online ed. 2014) (referred to as *CEB Procedure During Trial*).

- Wegner, *California Practice Guide: Civil Trials & Evidence* (CD-ROM ed. 2014) (referred to as Wegner, *Civil Trials & Evidence*).

§2. PRETRIAL DISCLOSURE

Disclosure of expert information, including qualifications and anticipated testimony, is governed primarily by CCP §2034. See "Expert Discovery," ch. 7-I, p. 898. Parties should review this information and determine whether a motion in limine to exclude expert testimony is appropriate.

§3. GROUNDS

To object to an expert or the expert's opinion testimony, a party can file a motion in limine to exclude or limit the expert's testimony. The following factors determine whether an expert's opinion is admissible:

§3.1 Qualifications & competency. The expert must be qualified to give an opinion by "special knowledge, skill, experience, training, or education," and the qualifications must be related to the particular subject on which the witness is giving expert testimony. Evid. C. §720(a); ***Jackson v. Deft, Inc.*** (1st Dist.1990) 223 Cal.App.3d 1305, 1319; *e.g.*, ***Garrett v. Howmedica Osteonics Corp.*** (2d Dist.2013) 214 Cal.App.4th 173, 190 (metallurgist with over 30 years of experience in materials analysis was qualified to test nature and hardness of materials used in prosthetic device); *see* ***People v. Kelly*** (1976) 17 Cal.3d 24, 39 (competency of expert is in relation to topic and fields of knowledge about which witness is asked to testify). An expert's special knowledge, skill, experience, training, or education may be shown by any otherwise admissible evidence, including the expert's own testimony. Evid. C. §702(b). Whether an expert is qualified depends on the facts of each case, the expert's specific qualifications, and the issues on which the expert is asked to give an opinion. *See* ***People v. Davis*** (1965) 62 Cal.2d 791, 801. In deciding whether an expert is qualified, trial courts have looked at such factors as education and experience working in the field related to the opinion given, specific classes or seminars attended, familiarity with relevant literature, and familiarity with the subject matter and the specific facts of the case. *See* ***People v. Clark*** (1993) 5 Cal.4th 950, 1018-19; ***Miller v. Los Angeles Cty. Flood Control Dist.*** (1973) 8 Cal.3d 689, 701; *see, e.g.*, ***People v. Montes*** (2014) 58 Cal.4th 809, 861 (police officer was qualified to testify on D's social affiliation with street gang based on six years' experience as officer, familiarity with gangs in area, and 20-30 hours of formal training on gangs); ***People v. Cook*** (2007) 40 Cal.4th 1334, 1346 (criminalist was qualified to perform electrophoretic testing and to relate results, based on ten years' experience in crime lab, courses taken, thesis on electrophoresis, and qualification as expert on subject in approximately seven cases). An expert is not required to have a formal education or professional degree and can still be qualified to give an opinion in a particular field even if she has not worked in that field. *See* ***Osborn v. Irwin Mem'l Blood Bank*** (1st Dist.1992) 5 Cal.App.4th 234, 274-75; ***People v. King*** (2d Dist.1968) 266 Cal.App.2d 437, 443; *see, e.g.*, ***Ammon v. Superior Ct.*** (1st Dist.1988) 205 Cal.App.3d 783, 791 (physician may be competent based on education or observation to give opinion outside of specialty); ***Mann v. Cracchiolo*** (1985) 38 Cal.3d 18, 38-39 (surgeon qualified to testify about X-rays even though he was not a radiologist). The level of an expert's expertise goes to the weight of the expert's testimony, not its admissibility. ***Chavez v. Glock, Inc.*** (2d Dist.2012) 207 Cal.App.4th 1283, 1319.

§3.2 Helpfulness. The expert's opinion must be "sufficiently beyond common experience that [it will] assist the trier of fact." Evid. C. §801(a); *see, e.g.*, ***Pedeferri v. Seidner Enters.*** (2d Dist.2013) 216 Cal.App.4th 359, 374 (probable effect of intoxicants other than alcohol is topic sufficiently beyond common knowledge of most jurors; thus, expert testimony is required). If the subject of the expert testimony is one of such common knowledge that people of ordinary education could reach a conclusion as intelligently as the expert witness, the testimony is improper. ***People v. Jones*** (2012) 54 Cal.4th 1, 60; *see, e.g.*, ***Burton v. Sanner*** (4th Dist.2012) 207 Cal.App.4th 12, 19 (court erred in allowing retired police officer to testify about reasonableness of D's self-defense claim because jury was capable of determining whether D acted reasonably under circumstances at issue). But this standard does not require a finding that the jury is completely ignorant about the subject matter of the expert's opinion before the testimony can be admitted. ***Jones***, 54 Cal.4th at 60. Rather, the expert's opinion testimony is improper only when it would add nothing at all to the jury's "common fund of information." *Id.*

§3.3 Foundational matter.

1. Most opinion testimony. For expert-opinion testimony to be admissible, the matter relied on by the expert in forming her opinion and the reasons for that opinion must be reliable. *See* Evid. C. §§801(b), 802; ***Sargon Enters. v. University of S. Cal.*** (2012) 55 Cal.4th 747, 770-71; ***Garrett v. Howmedica Osteonics Corp.*** (2d Dist.2013) 214 Cal.App.4th 173, 186-87.

(1) Matter is reliable. To be reliable, the matter relied on by the expert must satisfy the following three tests:

(a) Perceived, personally known, or made known. The matter relied on by the expert in forming her opinion must be perceived by, personally known to, or made known to the expert before or at the hearing in which the opinion is given. Evid. C. §801(b); 7 Cal. Law Revision Comm'n Rep. (1965) p. 1139.

(b) Relied on by experts. The matter must be of a type that can reasonably be relied on by experts in forming an opinion. Evid. C. §801(b); ***Sargon Enters.***, 55 Cal.4th at 769-70; ***Lockheed Litigation Cases*** (2d Dist.2004) 115 Cal.App.4th 558, 564; 7 Cal. Law Revision Comm'n Rep. (1965) p. 1139. The reasonableness of an expert's reliance is a question of degree and can vary with the circumstances of each case. ***People v. Clauser/Wells Prtshp.*** (4th Dist.2002) 95 Cal.App.4th 1066, 1085. For example, in some fields of expert knowledge, an expert can rely on statements made by and information received from other persons; in other fields of expert knowledge, an expert cannot do so. 7 Cal. Law Revision Comm'n Rep. (1965) p. 1137. In determining whether the matter is of a type that can be reasonably relied on, the court should give strong consideration to factors of necessity and relative reliability, and should not weigh the probative value of the expert's opinion, substitute its own opinion for the expert's, or presume to be an expert. *See* ***Garrett***, 214 Cal.App.4th at 186-87; ***Howard Entm't, Inc. v. Kudrow*** (2d Dist.2012) 208 Cal.App.4th 1102, 1115.

[1] Speculative, irrelevant, or unsupported matter. An expert cannot reasonably rely on speculative, irrelevant, or unsupported assertions. *See* ***Sargon Enters.***, 55 Cal.4th at 770; ***Mitchell v. United Nat'l Ins.*** (2d Dist.2005) 127 Cal.App.4th 457, 478; ***Lockheed Litigation Cases***, 115 Cal.App.4th at 563-64; *see, e.g.*, ***Pedeferri v. Seidner Enters.*** (2d Dist.2013) 216 Cal.App.4th 359, 375 (toxicologist's testimony that D was chronic marijuana user and therefore likely to have been unimpaired while driving was improperly admitted because underlying assumptions that D was longtime user of marijuana and had repeatedly driven while using marijuana lacked evidentiary basis); ***Garrett***, 214 Cal.App.4th at 187 (expert testimony on testing of prosthetic device was improperly excluded when expert stated multiple specific tests he ran on product; it was not necessary to describe each particular testing process in declarations opposing MSJ); ***P&D Consultants, Inc. v. City of Carlsbad*** (4th Dist.2010) 190 Cal.App.4th 1332, 1349 (conclusory testimony by damages expert, for which party offered no basis, was properly excluded); ***Stephen v. Ford Motor Co.*** (2d Dist.2005) 134 Cal.App.4th 1363, 1371 (expert testimony about alleged tire defect, when expert relied only on amateur photographs and unrelated tire incidents, was speculative and properly excluded); ***Roscoe Moss Co. v. Jenkins*** (2d Dist.1942) 55 Cal.App.2d 369, 379-80 (expert testimony based on comparison of two wells was improperly admitted because there was no support for assumption that two wells were comparable).

[2] Inadmissible evidence. An expert can rely on material not admitted into evidence or inadmissible evidence, such as hearsay, as long as the material is reliable and of a type reasonably relied on by experts in that particular field. ***People v. Gardeley*** (1996) 14 Cal.4th 605, 618; *see* ***People v. Catlin*** (2001) 26 Cal.4th 81, 137; ***Korsak v. Atlas Hotels, Inc.*** (4th Dist.1992) 2 Cal.App.4th 1516, 1524-25; *see, e.g.*, ***Miranda v. Bomel Constr. Co.*** (4th Dist.2010) 187 Cal.App.4th 1326, 1343 (expert could rely on scientific facts contained in scientific articles and reports; opponent did not challenge facts as being unreliable); *see also* Evid. C. §804 (expert can rely on opinion or statement of another).

PRACTICE TIP

On direct examination, an expert can testify about the basis for her opinion, including the inadmissible evidence that she relied on. See Evid. C. §802; ***Catlin****, 26 Cal.4th at 137. Although an expert can state on direct examination the matters she relied on in forming her opinion, prejudice can arise if the details of those matters are revealed to the jury and the matters are otherwise inadmissible.* ***People v. Montiel*** *(1993) 5 Cal.4th 877, 919. Under Evid. C. §352, courts have considerable discretion to exclude or limit the introduction of such evidence or control how the expert is questioned to prevent the jury from learning of the evidence if its probative value is outweighed by its prejudicial effect. See* ***Gardeley****, 14 Cal.4th at 619;* ***Montiel****, 5 Cal.4th at 919; see, e.g.,* ***People v. McWhorter*** *(2009) 47 Cal.4th 318, 362 (court properly excluded expert opinion based solely on report containing inadmissible witness statements);* ***Grimshaw v.***

***Ford Motor Co.** (4th Dist.1981) 119 Cal.App.3d 757, 788-89 (expert was not permitted to read reports or relate their contents in detail to jury, and jury was given limiting instruction that any hearsay matters were only to show basis of expert's opinion and not for truth of matter asserted). In making this decision, the court should balance the expert's need to consider the inadmissible evidence, the jury's need for information sufficient to evaluate the expert's opinion, and the opponent's interest in avoiding the jury's substantive use of the inadmissible evidence. **Montiel**, 5 Cal.4th at 919. See "Motion denied in part," §7.3, p. 597.*

(c) Not prohibited by law. An expert cannot rely on a matter that has been declared to be an improper basis for an expert opinion by California constitutional, statutory, or decisional law. Evid. C. §§160, 801(b); 7 Cal. Law Revision Comm'n Rep. (1965) p. 1139; *see, e.g.*, Evid. C. §822 (listing evidence that cannot be used as bases for opinion on value of property in eminent-domain proceeding). For example, expert testimony that is based on a new scientific technique must satisfy the reliability standards set out in ***People v. Kelly*** (1976) 17 Cal.3d 24. See "Opinion testimony based on new scientific technique," §3.3.2, this page.

(2) Reasoning or methodology is reliable. To be reliable, an expert's opinion must be based on reasons that are (1) supported by the matter the expert relies on and not speculative and (2) not prohibited by law. Evid. C. §802; *see* ***Sargon Enters.***, 55 Cal.4th at 771-72.

(a) Supported & not speculative. An expert's opinion is reliable if the matter relied on to form the opinion provides a reasonable basis for the opinion and the reasons for the opinion are not speculative. *See* ***Sargon Enters.***, 55 Cal.4th at 771-72. The reasonableness of the expert's opinion can be measured by the "analytical gap" between the basis and the conclusions; if the gap between the data and the opinion is too great, the opinion is unreliable. *E.g.*, *id.* at 771 (although expert's methodology would have been appropriate in proper case, expert did not base conclusions on any objective evidence or other provable data relevant to P's business, so expert's opinion was speculative); *see, e.g.*, ***Parlour Enters. v. Kirin Grp.*** (4th Dist.2007) 152 Cal.App.4th 281, 290-91 (expert testimony based on comparison of P's company to publicly traded company was too speculative when companies were not comparable).

(b) Not prohibited by law. An expert's opinion is not reliable if the expert is precluded by California constitutional, statutory, or decisional law from relying on the reasons that serve as the basis for the opinion. Evid. C. §§160, 802; *see* ***Sargon Enters.***, 55 Cal.4th at 771-72.

2. Opinion testimony based on new scientific technique. For expert-opinion testimony based on a new scientific technique to be admissible, it must satisfy the standards for both general admissibility of expert testimony and admissibility of scientific testimony set out in ***People v. Kelly*** (1976) 17 Cal.3d 24 (the "***Kelly*** rule"). *See* ***People v. Stoll*** (1989) 49 Cal.3d 1136, 1155. See "Most opinion testimony," §3.3.1, p. 592. The opponent of the expert-opinion testimony bears the initial burden of showing that the ***Kelly*** rule applies. *See* ***People v. Eubanks*** (2011) 53 Cal.4th 110, 140; *see also* ***People v. Hill*** (1st Dist.2011) 191 Cal.App.4th 1104, 1123-24 (nonoffering party provided no authority for its claim that ***Kelly*** should apply). If the ***Kelly*** rule does apply, the burden shifts to the proponent of the testimony to show that it is admissible under ***Kelly***. *See* ***People v. Pizarro*** (5th Dist.2003) 110 Cal.App.4th 530, 554-55, *disapproved on other grounds*, ***People v. Wilson*** (2006) 38 Cal.4th 1237; ***People v. John W.*** (1st Dist.1986) 185 Cal.App.3d 801, 805, *disapproved on other grounds*, ***People v. Stoll*** (1989) 49 Cal.3d 1136.

CAUTION

*In **Kelly**, the California Supreme Court adopted expert admissibility standards set out in **Frye v. U.S.**, 293 F. 1013 (D.C.Cir.1923). Although the U.S. Supreme Court has since held in **Daubert v. Merrell Dow Pharms.** (1993) 509 U.S. 579, 587, that FRE 702 abrogated **Frye**, the California Supreme Court has declined to follow **Daubert**. See **People v. Leahy** (1994) 8 Cal.4th 587, 591.*

(1) Does *Kelly* rule apply? Most expert-opinion testimony is not subject to the *Kelly* rule. For example, the *Kelly* rule usually does not apply to expert medical testimony. *See* ***People v. McDonald*** (1984) 37 Cal.3d 351, 373, *overruled on other grounds*, ***People v. Mendoza*** (2000) 23 Cal.4th 896; *see, e.g.*, ***Roberti v. Andy's Termite & Pest Control, Inc.*** (2d Dist.2003) 113 Cal.App.4th 893, 903 (***Kelly*** did not apply to expert medical opinion on causation). For the *Kelly* rule to apply, the expert's opinion must be based, in whole or in part, on a technique, process, or theory that is new to science and the law. ***Stoll***, 49 Cal.3d at 1156. There is no clear test for newness, but the courts have considered the following when determining whether the *Kelly* rule applies:

(a) Does technique convey misleading aura of certainty? The *Kelly* rule may apply if expert-opinion testimony is based on a new, novel, or experimental technique that conveys to the jury a "misleading aura of certainty." ***Stoll***, 49 Cal.3d at 1155-56. Testimony conveys a misleading aura of certainty when it is based on an unproven technique or procedure but will appear to the jury to provide some definitive truth. *Id.* at 1156. If the testimony effectively blindsides the jury in this way, it will probably be subject to the *Kelly* rule. *See* ***Eubanks***, 53 Cal.4th at 140; ***People v. Venegas*** (1998) 18 Cal.4th 47, 80; ***Stoll***, 49 Cal.3d at 1157.

(b) Is technique difficult for laypersons to evaluate? The *Kelly* rule may apply if expert-opinion testimony is based on a technique so foreign to everyday experience that it would be unusually difficult for laypersons to evaluate. ***People v. Cowan*** (2010) 50 Cal.4th 401, 470.

(c) Does technique combine existing techniques? The *Kelly* rule may not apply if expert-opinion testimony is simply based on a new combination of existing techniques. *See* ***Cowan***, 50 Cal.4th at 470.

(d) Does technique simply isolate physical evidence? The *Kelly* rule may not apply if expert-opinion testimony is based on a new procedure that simply isolates physical evidence whose existence, appearance, nature, and meaning are obvious to the senses of a layperson. *E.g.*, ***Cowan***, 50 Cal.4th at 470-71 (expert's novel combination of two methods relating to ascertaining pattern created when bullet was fired from particular gun merely isolated physical evidence); ***People v. Webb*** (1993) 6 Cal.4th 494, 524 (laser procedure used to identify fingerprints was not new scientific technique subject to ***Kelly*** rule); ***People v. Ayala*** (2000) 24 Cal.4th 243, 281 (radiologist's testimony about likely size of bullet lodged in victim was not subject to ***Kelly*** rule).

(2) Has *Kelly* rule been satisfied? If the court determines that the *Kelly* rule applies, an expert's opinion testimony cannot be admitted unless the following are established:

(a) Technique is generally accepted as reliable. The technique relied on by the expert must be generally accepted as reliable in the relevant scientific community. ***People v. Bolden*** (2002) 29 Cal.4th 515, 544; *see* ***People v. Soto*** (1999) 21 Cal.4th 512, 518-519; ***Leahy***, 8 Cal.4th at 594; ***Kelly***, 17 Cal.3d at 30. General acceptance can be established in either of the following ways:

[1] Evidence of acceptance. The proponent of the testimony can show a consensus drawn from a typical cross-section of the relevant, qualified scientific community. ***Soto***, 21 Cal.4th at 519; *see* ***Venegas***, 18 Cal.4th at 85 (***Kelly*** rule does not require absolute unanimity, but it does require support by clear majority of relevant scientific community). When evaluating whether there is a consensus, the court will consider both the quality and quantity of the evidence supporting or opposing the reliability of the new scientific technique. ***Venegas***, 18 Cal.4th at 85. For example, majority support or opposition by minimally qualified individuals is considered to be of little value. *Id.* The court does not need to be convinced that the technique is scientifically reliable or valid, but only that the relevant scientific community has generally accepted the technique as reliable. ***Bolden***, 29 Cal.4th at 546.

[2] Recognized by published appellate decision. The proponent of the testimony can show that a published appellate decision has affirmed a trial-court ruling admitting evidence obtained by the scientific technique under ***Kelly***. ***Bolden***, 29 Cal.4th at 545. This includes published out-of-state precedent. ***People v. Allen*** (2d Dist.1999) 72 Cal.App.4th 1093, 1099. However, the opponent of the testimony can challenge this proof by showing that the attitude of the community has changed since the opinion was published. ***Bolden***, 29 Cal.4th at 545.

(b) Witness is properly qualified expert. The witness testifying about the technique and its application must be a properly qualified expert on the subject. ***Bolden***, 29 Cal.4th at 544-545; *see* ***Soto***, 21 Cal.4th at 518-519; ***Leahy***, 8 Cal.4th at 594; ***Kelly***, 17 Cal.3d at 30.

(c) **Correct scientific procedures were used.** The scientific procedures used must correctly comply with the methodology of the technique. *See* ***Bolden***, 29 Cal.4th at 545; ***Soto***, 21 Cal.4th at 519; ***Leahy***, 8 Cal.4th at 594; ***Kelly***, 17 Cal.3d at 30. The procedures may be performed by the expert or by others with the expert relying on the results. *See* ***Venegas***, 18 Cal.4th at 81. Regardless of who performed the procedures, the expert must be familiar with what was done and be able to testify that correct scientific procedures were used. *Id.*; *see also* ***Soto***, 21 Cal.4th at 529-30 (additional experts may also testify to support claim that correct scientific procedures were used).

§4. MOTION

§4.1 Who can make. Any party can make a motion in limine to exclude expert testimony.

§4.2 How to make. There is no express statutory authority for motions in limine, but they are well recognized in practice and by case law. ***Clemens v. American Warranty Corp.*** (2d Dist.1987) 193 Cal.App.3d 444, 451; Wegner, *Civil Trials & Evidence*, §4:225; *see, e.g.*, CRC 3.1112(f) (recognizing notice-of-hearing exception for motions in limine); ***People v. Morris*** (1991) 53 Cal.3d 152, 188 (motions in limine are commonly used); ***Kelly v. New W. Fed. Sav.*** (2d Dist.1996) 49 Cal.App.4th 659, 669-71 (discussing proper and improper uses of motions in limine). For more on making, filing, and serving motions, see "Papers, Forms, Declarations & Affidavits," ch. 1-B, p. 9; "Law & Motion Practice," ch. 1-D, p. 26.

1. Notice. A motion in limine does not need to be accompanied by a notice of hearing. CRC 3.1112(f); *CEB Procedure During Trial*, §7.23. No notice is required because the court will usually rule on any motions in limine at the pretrial conference or during trial. *See* Wegner, *Civil Trials & Evidence*, §§4:234-4:236, 4:285.

2. Local rules & judge's procedures. Motions in limine may be governed by particular local rules and judge's procedures. *See, e.g.*, Super. Ct. Los Angeles Cty. Loc. R., rule 3.57(a) (requiring special evidentiary support for motions in limine). The movant should check these sources to determine whether there are additional requirements for the motion.

§4.3 Deadline. Motions in limine can be made at any time before trial, or during trial but before the evidence that is the subject of the motion is admitted, unless a time and place for filing and service of the motion is set by court order or local rule. *See* CRC 3.1112(f) (time for filing is at court's discretion); ***Godfrey v. Steinpress*** (5th Cir.1982) 128 Cal.App.3d 154, 168 (after pretrial conference); *see, e.g.*, CRC 3.1548(b)(10) (for expedited trials, motion must be served on all parties 25 days before trial); Super. Ct. San Francisco Cty. Loc. R., rule 6.1 (motion must be served by mail at least ten days or personally served at least five days before trial). If no deadline is set, a party should usually file the motion early enough before trial to give the court time to consider all the legal issues.

§4.4 Contents.

1. Format. A motion in limine should be in writing and in the same form as noticed motions generally. See "Motion Papers," ch. 1-D, §5, p. 27. A court can consider an oral motion, but issues related to expert-opinion testimony are frequently complex, which makes written motions preferable. *See* Wegner, *Civil Trials & Evidence*, §4:291; *see also CEB Procedure During Trial*, §7.17 (written motion ensures that legal issues are thoroughly covered).

2. Supporting evidence. A motion in limine can be accompanied by supporting declarations or deposition excerpts. *See* CRC 3.1115, 3.1116.

§5. OPPOSITION

The party offering the expert testimony ("responding party") should respond to the motion in limine by filing an opposition.

§5.1 Deadline to respond. The responding party should file the opposition either as soon as possible before the court will consider the matter—usually at the final-status conference—or before the deadline set by court order or local rule. *See, e.g.*, Super. Ct. Orange Loc. R., rule 317 (opposition to motion in limine due by noon on Friday before trial).

§5.2 Grounds. The responding party should oppose the motion in limine by negating the grounds for relief. See "Grounds," §3, p. 592.

§5.3 Contents. See "Opposition Papers," ch. 1-D, §8, p. 35.

§6. HEARING

A motion in limine is usually not set for a separate hearing but rather is taken up by the court at a pretrial conference (e.g., a final-status conference) or during trial. *See* Wegner, *Civil Trials & Evidence*, §§4:234-4:236, 4:285. If the court is uncertain whether the expert's opinion is admissible, the court can hold a hearing to determine whether the opinion should be excluded. *See, e.g.*, ***Sargon Enters. v. University of S. Cal.*** (2012) 55 Cal.4th 747, 776 (trial court did not abuse its discretion in excluding expert following lengthy evidentiary hearing). See "Hearings," ch. 1-H, p. 79.

§7. RULING

A trial court has broad discretion to admit or exclude expert testimony, but the discretion is not absolute. *See* ***Sargon Enters. v. University of S. Cal.*** (2012) 55 Cal.4th 747, 772 (court should be cautious in excluding expert testimony); ***Burton v. Sanner*** (4th Dist.2012) 207 Cal.App.4th 12, 18 (court cannot exceed bounds of reason). The court must decide whether the opinion is admissible but must not weigh the opinion's probative value or substitute its own opinion for the expert's opinion. *See* ***Sargon Enters.***, 55 Cal.4th at 772.

§7.1 Motion granted. The court can grant the motion and exclude the expert or expert's opinion testimony. If the court excludes the expert, the party offering the expert should request the right to seek reconsideration, a continuance to apply for writ review, and a continuance to substitute the excluded expert. *See* Wegner, *Civil Trials & Evidence*, §§4:306-4.307.3. At trial, the party should make an offer of proof on the record. *See* Evid. C. §354(a); Wegner, *Civil Trials & Evidence*, §4:306. The offer should include evidence about the qualifications of the expert, the opinion that the expert would give if permitted to testify at trial, evidence of the relevance and reliability of the opinion, and a statement of how and why the exclusion of the opinion affected a substantial right of the party. *See, e.g.*, ***Gordon v. Nissan Motor Co.*** (2d Dist.2009) 170 Cal.App.4th 1103, 1113-14 (P's written offer of proof containing details of what experts' testimony would establish about automobile defect was sufficient). A verdict or finding will not be set aside due to the erroneous exclusion of an expert's testimony unless the exclusion resulted in a miscarriage of justice and the trial court was made aware of the substance, purpose, and relevance of the excluded evidence. *See* Evid. C. §354; *see also* ***Gordon***, 170 Cal.App.4th at 1113-14 (P's supplemental expert-witness disclosure statement and argument in opposition to motion to strike expert gave court sufficient notice of substance, purpose, and relevance of proposed expert testimony).

§7.2 Motion denied. If the expert is admitted, the party who objected to the expert should object again when the expert is offered at trial and make clear the specific grounds for the objection. *See* Evid. C. §353. The party who objected to the expert can refer to the record of the pretrial hearing if one exists to preserve error on appeal. *See* ***People v. Morris*** (1991) 53 Cal.3d 152, 189.

§7.3 Motion denied in part. The court may exclude only certain objectionable portions of an expert's opinion. *See, e.g.*, ***People v. Sims*** (1993) 5 Cal.4th 405, 435 n.5 (court denied motion to exclude but ruled that any reference to certain testimony was inadmissible). If the court partially excludes the expert's testimony, the offering party should make an offer of proof for the excluded testimony. See "Motion granted," §7.1, this page. The party objecting to the expert's testimony should clearly state the specific grounds for objection to any of the testimony that is admitted. See "Motion denied," §7.2, this page.

§8. APPELLATE REVIEW

§8.1 Standard of review.

1. Abuse of discretion. The trial court's ruling on a motion in limine to exclude expert testimony is reviewed for abuse of discretion. ***Sargon Enters. v. University of S. Cal.*** (2012) 55 Cal.4th 747, 773; ***Garrett v. Howmedica Osteonics Corp.*** (2d Dist.2013) 214 Cal.App.4th 173, 187.

2. De novo. If a trial court's ruling on a motion in limine to exclude expert testimony depends on an interpretation of a statute, the court's statutory interpretation is reviewed de novo. ***Sargon Enters.***, 55 Cal.4th at 773; ***Garrett***, 214 Cal.App.4th at 187.

§8.2 Direct appeal. An order on a motion in limine to exclude expert testimony is usually not appealable until the trial court enters a final judgment in the case. *See* CCP §§904.1, 904.2. But if the court's ruling excluding expert testimony would effectively prevent a party from advancing its claim, the ruling can be treated as the functional equivalent of a nonsuit and can be appealed directly by writ. *See* ***Aas v. Superior Ct.*** (2000) 24 Cal.4th 627, 634-35; ***R&B Auto Ctr. Inc. v. Farmers Grp.*** (4th Dist.2006) 140 Cal.App.4th 327, 358.

CALIFORNIA CIVIL PRETRIAL

CHAPTER 6. DISCOVERY & PRIVILEGES

TABLE OF CONTENTS

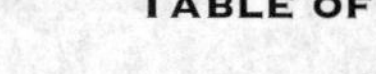

CALIFORNIA CIVIL PRETRIAL

CHAPTER 6. DISCOVERY & PRIVILEGES

TABLE OF CONTENTS

Table of Contents

6. DISCOVERY & PRIVILEGES

A. SCOPE OF DISCOVERY

§1. GENERAL

This subchapter discusses the scope of discovery—that is, which information and things are discoverable and which are not. This chapter does not discuss the procedures for obtaining discoverable information (e.g., depositions, interrogatories). For that topic, see "Types of Discovery," ch. 7-A, §2, p. 739.

§1.1 Purpose. The scope of discovery, which is defined by the Civil Discovery Act (CDA), is expansive. CCP §§2017.010-2017.320. The purpose of allowing expansive discovery is to avoid surprise at trial. ***Emerson Elec. Co. v. Superior Ct.*** (1997) 16 Cal.4th 1101, 1107; ***Greyhound Corp. v. Superior Ct.*** (1961) 56 Cal.2d 355, 376.

§1.2 Primary authority. CCP §§2016.010-2018.080; Evid. C. §210 (relevant evidence).

§1.3 Secondary authority. The following secondary sources are cited as authority in this subchapter:

- *California Civil Discovery Practice* (CEB Online ed. 2014) (referred to as *CEB Discovery Practice*).
- Nelson & Rosenberg, *A Duty Everlasting: The Perils of Applying Traditional Doctrines of Spoliation to Electronic Discovery*, 12 Rich. J.L. & Tech. 14 (2006) (referred to as Nelson & Rosenberg, *A Duty Everlasting*, 12 Rich. J.L. & Tech.).
- Wegner, *California Practice Guide: Civil Trials & Evidence* (CD-ROM ed. 2014) (referred to as Wegner, *Civil Trials & Evidence*).

§2. WHAT IS DISCOVERABLE

§2.1 Scope of discovery. Chapter 2 of the CDA sets out the scope of discovery for civil cases. CCP §§2017.010-2017.320. The scope of discovery is intended to be very broad. ***Emerson Elec. Co. v. Superior Ct.*** (1997) 16 Cal.4th 1101, 1108; ***Puerto v. Superior Ct.*** (2d Dist.2008) 158 Cal.App.4th 1242, 1249; ***Juarez v. Arcadia Fin., Ltd.*** (4th Dist.2007) 152 Cal.App.4th 889, 912. Because of this broad scope, discovery statutes are interpreted liberally in favor of discovery. ***Gonzalez v. Superior Ct.*** (2d Dist.1995) 33 Cal.App.4th 1539, 1546; *see* ***Colonial Life & Acc. Ins. v. Superior Ct.*** (1982) 31 Cal.3d 785, 790. Generally, a party can discover any nonprivileged information relevant to the claim or defense of any other party. CCP §2017.010; *e.g.*, ***Stewart v. Colonial W. Agency, Inc.*** (2d Dist.2001) 87 Cal.App.4th 1006, 1013-14 (in wrongful-termination suit, deposition questions about how manager treated other employees were relevant and should have been answered). There are five principal questions relating to the scope of discovery:

1. *Is the information relevant to the subject matter of the case?* Information is within the scope of discovery if it is relevant to the claims and defenses asserted in the case or to the determination of any motion made in the case. CCP §2017.010; *see* Evid. C. §210 (definition of "relevant evidence"). Information is relevant if it might reasonably help a party evaluate a case, prepare for trial, or facilitate a settlement. ***TBG Ins. Servs. v. Superior Ct.*** (2d Dist.2002) 96 Cal.App.4th 443, 448.

2. *Is the information admissible or reasonably calculated to lead to the discovery of admissible evidence?* Information is within the scope of discovery if it is either admissible evidence or reasonably calculated to lead to the discovery of admissible evidence. CCP §2017.010; ***Catholic Mut. Relief Soc. v. Superior Ct.*** (2007) 42 Cal.4th 358, 366. In other words, the requested information does not have to be admissible at trial to be discoverable. ***Greyhound Corp. v. Superior Ct.*** (1961) 56 Cal.2d 355, 391; ***Volkswagen v. Superior Ct.*** (1st Dist.2006) 139 Cal.App.4th 1481, 1490-91. There is no precise test for determining whether information is reasonably calculated to lead to the discovery of admissible evidence, but one key factor is whether the information will aid in a party's preparation for trial. *See* ***Pacific Tel. & Tel. Co. v. Superior Ct.*** (1970) 2 Cal.3d 161, 172.

3. *Is there an exemption that prevents the discovery of the information?* Information is not within the scope of discovery if it is exempt from discovery. *See* CCP §2017.010. See "What Is Not Discoverable," §3, p. 610.

4. *Do the discovery rules permit the type of discovery method necessary to secure the information?* Information is not within the scope of discovery if it cannot be obtained through a method approved by the CDA. *See* CCP §2019.010 (list of approved discovery methods); *see, e.g.*, ***Browne v. Superior Ct.*** (1st Dist.1979) 98 Cal.App.3d 610, 615 (CDA requires licensed physician to perform physical examinations, so P in personal-injury suit could not be required to submit to examination by nonphysician). But parties can agree to modify the discovery procedures for any method approved by the CDA. CCP §2016.030. See "Modifying discovery by stipulation," ch. 7-A, §4.1, p. 743.

5. *Did the court limit discovery?* Information is not discoverable if a court order limits discovery. CCP §2017.010. The court can limit discovery if the burden, expense, or intrusiveness of discovery clearly outweighs the likelihood that the information will lead to the discovery of admissible evidence. *Id.* §2017.020(a). See "Motion for Protective Order," ch. 9-B, p. 1024.

§2.2 Types of discoverable information. The following matters are discoverable:

1. Party's identity.

(1) Unknown defendant. A plaintiff can initiate an action against an unknown defendant by filing a complaint naming the unknown defendant using a fictitious name (e.g., John Doe), conducting discovery to obtain the defendant's real name, and amending the complaint once the defendant's identity is known. CCP §474; *see* ***Bernson v. Browning-Ferris Indus.*** (1994) 7 Cal.4th 926, 937 (P can file "Doe complaint" to extend statute of limitations against unknown D); *see also* CCP §2035.010(b) (P cannot file petition for presuit discovery to identify potential Ds in unfiled suit). See "Doe defendants," ch. 3-C, §2.3.1(7)(b), p. 209.

(2) Potential class members. A party can discover the identities of potential members of a class action. ***Pioneer Elecs. (USA), Inc. v. Superior Ct.*** (2007) 40 Cal.4th 360, 373; *see* ***Parris v. Superior Ct.*** (2d Dist.2003) 109 Cal.App.4th 285, 300-01 (court can compel D to provide names and addresses of potential class members if it determines that rights of potential Ps outweigh danger of potential abuse).

2. Party's factual conclusions. A party can discover another party's factual conclusions or assertions and the basis for and information about a factual conclusion or assertion. *See* CCP §2030.010(b) (interrogatories), §2033.010 (requests for admission); ***Rifkind v. Superior Ct.*** (2d Dist.1994) 22 Cal.App.4th 1255, 1259 (depositions). A party can discover whether the other party admits that certain facts are true by making a request for admission. CCP §2033.010.

3. Party's legal contentions. A party can discover another party's legal contentions, including the facts, witnesses, and writings on which the party's legal contentions are based, by interrogatory or request for admission. *See* CCP §2030.010(b) (interrogatories), §2033.010 (requests for admission). An example of a legal-contention interrogatory is one that asks a defendant to state all facts, list all witnesses, and identify all documents that support the affirmative defenses asserted in the answer to the complaint. *See* ***Burke v. Superior Ct.*** (1969) 71 Cal.2d 276, 280-81; ***Rifkind***, 22 Cal.App.4th at 1256. See "Legal contentions," ch. 7-C, §3.1.5(2), p. 818. By comparison, a party cannot ask for another party's legal contentions during a deposition. ***Rifkind***, 22 Cal.App.4th at 1262-63. A deponent cannot be expected to sort through the facts during a deposition and apply the law to those facts; that is the attorney's job. *Id.*

4. Party's opinions. A party can discover another party's opinions that relate to a fact or the application of the law to a fact. *See* CCP §2030.010(b) (interrogatories), §2033.010 (requests for admission).

5. Party's statements.

(1) Other party's statement. A party can discover any relevant statements made by another party or by a person authorized by the other party to make the statements. ***Volkswagen v. Superior Ct.*** (1st Dist.2006) 139 Cal.App.4th 1481, 1492; *cf.* Evid. C. §1220 (party's statements), §1221 (party's adoptive statements), §1222(a) (party's authorized statements).

(2) **Party's own statement.** A party can discover from another party its own statements about the event that gave rise to the lawsuit. ***Hartbrodt v. Burke*** (2d Dist.1996) 42 Cal.App.4th 168, 173; *see* CCP §2031.010 (inspection demand); *see, e.g.*, ***Dowell v. Superior Ct.*** (1956) 47 Cal.2d 483, 488-89 (party could obtain own statement given in hospital).

6. Tangible things. A party can discover the existence, description, nature, custody, condition, and location of any relevant thing that is not privileged and is in the possession, custody, or control of another party or a nonparty. CCP §2017.010; *see also id.* §1985 (subpoena), §2017.210 (contents of insurance), §2025.280 (notice of deposition), §2031.010 (inspection demand). The following things, when relevant, not privileged, and in the possession of the other party or a nonparty, are discoverable:

(1) Documents. *Id.* §1985(a) (subpoena), §2020.510(a) (deposition subpoena to produce). For the definition of "documents," see "Documents," ch. 7-E, §3.1.1, p. 846.

(2) Books. CCP §1985(a).

(3) Business records. *Id.* §§1987.3, 2020.410, 2020.510(a)(2). For the definition of "business records," see "Business records," ch. 8-B, §5.1.4(1), p. 965.

(4) Electronically stored information. CCP §§1985(a), 1985.8(a), 2017.010, 2020.510(a), 2025.280(a). This includes (1) voice-mail messages and files, (2) e-mail messages and files, (3) deleted files, programs, or e-mails, (4) data files, (5) program files, (6) backup and archival tapes, (7) temporary files, (8) portable electronic devices (e.g., flash drives, laptop computers, cell phones), (9) system history files, (10) website information stored in textual, graphical, or audio format, (11) website log files, (12) cache files, and (13) cookies. *See* ***Super Film v. UCB Films, Inc.*** (D.Kan.2004) 219 F.R.D. 649, 657; Nelson & Rosenberg, *A Duty Everlasting*, 12 Rich. J.L. & Tech. at 3. See "Scope of Electronic Discovery," ch. 7-H, §4, p. 881.

(5) Computer hard drives. A party's computer hard drive is discoverable to allow the requesting party to search for electronic documents. *See* ***Dodge, Warren & Peters Ins. Servs. v. Riley*** (4th Dist.2003) 105 Cal.App.4th 1414, 1420-21. See "Mirror imaging," ch. 7-H, §2.2.11, p. 877.

(6) Photographs. *See, e.g.*, ***Smith v. Superior Ct.*** (3d Dist.1961) 189 Cal.App.2d 6, 12-13 (P was entitled to interrogate opponents about existence, identity, and location of photographs of accident scene).

(7) Other tangible things. CCP §§1985, 2017.010, 2020.510(a). Other discoverable tangible things include drawings, graphs, charts, sound recordings, images, and other data or data compilations from which information can be obtained. *See* ***Toshiba Am. Elec. Components, Inc. v. Superior Ct.*** (6th Dist.2004) 124 Cal.App.4th 762, 770 (dicta).

7. Insurance. A party can discover the following information about an insurance or indemnity agreement:

(1) Defendant's insurance. A party can discover the information about any agreement under which an insurance carrier may be liable to (1) satisfy in whole or in part a judgment that may be entered in the case or (2) indemnify or reimburse for payments made to satisfy the judgment. CCP §2017.210. That information includes the following:

(a) Existence. A party can discover the existence of relevant insurance policies. CCP §2017.210.

(b) Contents. A party can discover the contents of relevant insurance policies. CCP §§2017.210, 2030.010.

(c) Carrier & limits. A party can discover the identity of an insurance carrier and the nature and limits of a policy's coverage. CCP §2017.210.

(d) Disputed coverage. A party can discover whether an insurance carrier is disputing an agreement's coverage of the claim involved in a case, but the party cannot discover the nature and substance of the dispute. CCP §2017.210.

(2) **Nonparty's insurance.** A party can discover the existence and contents of a nonparty's insurance agreement if the insurance is at issue in the case. *See, e.g.*, ***Hecht, Solberg, Robinson, Goldberg & Bagley LLP v. Superior Ct.*** (4th Dist.2006) 137 Cal.App.4th 579, 598 (nonparty's insurance agreement was necessary to prove P's claim in legal-malpractice suit).

8. Settlement agreements. In some situations, a party may be able to discover a settlement agreement. *Compare* ***Norton v. Superior Ct.*** (2d Dist.1994) 24 Cal.App.4th 1750, 1761-62 (in legal-malpractice suit, terms and conditions of P's settlement agreement with insurer could lead to discovery of admissible evidence, such as P's bias and credibility), *with* ***Hinshaw, Winkler, Draa, Marsh & Still v. Superior Ct.*** (6th Dist.1996) 51 Cal.App.4th 233, 241-42 (in legal-malpractice suit, settlement agreement negotiated by D on behalf of third parties could not be discovered because agreement was entitled to privacy protection).

9. Financial information. A party can discover financial information that is relevant to damages.

(1) **Punitive damages.** In a suit seeking punitive damages, the plaintiff may be able to discover the defendant's profits and financial condition. Civ. C. §3295(c). See "Motion to Discover Financial Information," ch. 7-G, p. 868.

(2) **Personal-injury damages.** In a personal-injury or wrongful-death suit, the defendant can discover the nature and amount of damages the plaintiff seeks. CCP §425.11(b); *see also id.* §425.10(b) (personal-injury complaint cannot state amount of damages sought). See "Statement of Damages," ch. 3-C, §5, p. 226.

10. Entry on land. A party can discover information about land by entering and inspecting it. See "Land," ch. 7-E, §3.1.3, p. 846.

11. Medical condition. A party can discover information about a person's physical or mental condition if that condition is in controversy. CCP §2032.020(a). The person must be a party, an agent of a party, or in a party's custody or legal control. *Id.* See "Medical Examinations," ch. 7-F, p. 855.

12. Witness information.

(1) **Expert witnesses.** A party can discover the identities of, opinions of, and other information about the experts that the other party intends to call as witnesses at trial. CCP §§2034.210-2034.240, 2034.260-2034.270; *see* ***Kalaba v. Gray*** (2d Dist.2002) 95 Cal.App.4th 1416, 1423. See "Expert Discovery," ch. 7-I, p. 898.

(2) **Percipient witnesses.** A party can discover information about percipient witnesses. A percipient witness testifies about facts within her personal knowledge—that is, facts she personally observed. *See Black's Law Dictionary* 1839 (10th ed. 2014). For a discussion of percipient expert witnesses, see "Percipient expert," ch. 7-I, §2.5, p. 899.

(a) **Witness identity.** A party can discover the identities and locations of people who have knowledge of any discoverable matter. *See* CCP §§2017.010, 2030.010(b); ***Rico v. Mitsubishi Motors Corp.*** (2007) 42 Cal.4th 807, 816; ***Davies v. Superior Ct.*** (1984) 36 Cal.3d 291, 295 n.2. Witnesses include all people with knowledge of relevant information that either is admissible or appears to be reasonably calculated to lead to the discovery of admissible evidence. *See* ***Tien v. Superior Ct.*** (2d Dist.2006) 139 Cal.App.4th 528, 535; *see also* Judicial Council Forms, form DISC-001, interrogatory 12.1 (asking for name, address, and telephone number of each person who witnessed the accident, made statements, or heard statements, or who the party claims has knowledge). The identities of witnesses are not subject to the attorney-client or work-product privilege. ***Huffy Corp. v. Superior Ct.*** (2d Dist.2003) 112 Cal.App.4th 97, 109. "Location" refers to the witnesses' contact information, which includes addresses and telephone numbers. *See* ***Puerto v. Superior Ct.*** (2d Dist.2008) 158 Cal.App.4th 1242, 1248-49.

(b) **Witness statements.** A party can discover witness statements if they do not contain privileged information (e.g., attorney notes reflecting opinions about the statements). See "Witness statements," ch. 6-B, §3.5.1(3), p. 632; "Independently prepared witness statements," ch. 6-B, §3.6.1, p. 634.

13. Exceptions to privilege. A party can discover information that is normally protected by a discovery privilege or exemption if an exception to the privilege or exemption applies. *See, e.g.*, Evid. C. §§996-1007 (exceptions to physician-patient privilege). To determine whether information alleged to be privileged or exempt from discovery can be discovered, see the relevant discussion in subchapters 6-B through 6-I.

14. Waiver of privilege. A party can discover information that is normally protected by a discovery privilege or exemption if the privilege or exemption has been waived. *See, e.g.*, ***City of L.A. v. Superior Ct.*** (2d Dist.1985) 170 Cal.App.3d 744, 754 (Ds could discover statements made to P-city attorney because privilege had been waived by disclosure). A waiver is the intentional relinquishment of a known right. ***BP Alaska Expl., Inc. v. Superior Ct.*** (5th Dist.1988) 199 Cal.App.3d 1240, 1252; *see also* Civ. C. §3513 (person can waive any advantage of law intended solely for that person's benefit). The waiver of a privilege must be a voluntary and knowing act done with sufficient awareness of the relevant circumstances and likely consequences. ***Roberts v. Superior Ct.*** (1973) 9 Cal.3d 330, 343. Only a privilege holder, or a person authorized by the holder, can waive the privilege. *See* Evid. C. §912(a); ***California Consumer Health Care Council v. California Dept. of Managed Health Care*** (3d Dist.2008) 161 Cal.App.4th 684, 694. Once a privilege is waived, no one can assert it. Evid. C. §912(a). To prevent waiver of a privilege, the privilege holder must take "reasonable steps" to protect the privileged information. ***Regents of the Univ. of Cal. v. Superior Ct.*** (4th Dist.2008) 165 Cal.App.4th 672, 675.

15 **(1) Waiver under Evid. C. §912(a).** Evid. C. §912 governs the waiver of the confidential-communication privileges listed in §912(a). The waivers outlined in Evid. C. §912(a) are expressly limited to the following privileges: (a) attorney-client, (b) lawyer-referral-service–client, (c) marital communications, (d) physician-patient, (e) psychotherapist-patient, (f) clergy-penitent, (g) sexual-assault-counselor–victim, (h) domestic-violence-counselor–victim, and (i) human-trafficking-caseworker–victim. However, the courts have held that the work-product privilege is also waived under the same circumstances as the attorney-client privilege. ***Wells Fargo Bank v. Superior Ct.*** (2000) 22 Cal.4th 201, 214. A confidential-communication privilege can be waived in any of the following ways:

(a) Waiver by disclosure. The holder of a confidential-communication privilege waives the privilege by disclosing a significant part of the communication without coercion. Evid. C. §912(a); *see, e.g.*, ***Coito v. Superior Ct.*** (2012) 54 Cal.4th 480, 501 (use of protected witness statement during deposition waived work-product privilege for that statement); ***Calvert v. State Bar*** (1991) 54 Cal.3d 765, 780 (client's testimony about her confidential communications with attorney waived attorney-client privilege); ***Regents of the Univ. of Cal. v. Workers' Comp. Appeals Bd.*** (4th Dist.2014) 226 Cal.App.4th 1530, 1536 (production of attorney-related privileged information in response to administrative judge's order did not waive privileges); ***Regents of the Univ. of Cal.***, 165 Cal.App.4th at 675 (disclosures of attorney-related privileged information to governmental agencies under threat of regulatory action and indictment did not waive privileges). A "significant part" means enough information to reveal the specific content of the communication. *See* ***Southern Cal. Gas Co. v. Public Utils. Comm'n*** (1990) 50 Cal.3d 31, 49. Disclosure of the existence of a privileged relationship does not amount to disclosure of the content of a privileged communication and is not a waiver of the privilege. *Id.*; ***Mitchell v. Superior Ct.*** (1984) 37 Cal.3d 591, 602. Waiver is limited to the privileged communications actually revealed by the holder's disclosure, not other confidential communications. ***Jones v. Superior Ct.*** (1st Dist.1981) 119 Cal.App.3d 534, 546-47. For exceptions to waiver by disclosure, see "Privilege not waived," §3.3.2, p. 612.

(b) Waiver by consent to disclosure. The holder of a confidential-communication privilege waives the privilege by consenting to the disclosure of the confidential communication to a third party who has no interest in maintaining the confidentiality of a significant part of the communication. Evid. C. §912(a); *see, e.g.*, ***Roberts***, 9 Cal.3d at 341 (privilege was not waived when physician exchanged records with other treating physicians who were also subject to privilege); ***Klang v. Shell Oil Co.*** (2d Dist.1971) 17 Cal.App.3d 933, 938 (attorney-client privilege was lost when disclosure was made to police officer). For marital communications, both spouses must consent. ***People v. Dorsey*** (2d Dist.1975) 46 Cal.App.3d 706, 717. A privilege holder can consent to disclosure either expressly or impliedly.

[1] Express consent. The privilege holder can consent to disclosure by making a written or oral statement that indicates consent to the disclosure. *See* Evid. C. §912(a); ***Jones***, 119 Cal.App.3d at 546; *see, e.g.*, ***Hiott v. Superior Ct.*** (2d Dist.1993) 16 Cal.App.4th 712, 719-20 (waiver by signature on interrogatory answers stating that video would be produced); ***Torbensen v. Family Life Ins.*** (3d Dist.1958) 163 Cal.App.2d 401, 404 (waiver by written release).

[2] Implied consent. The privilege holder can consent to disclosure by implication. ***Eisendrath v. Superior Ct.*** (2d Dist.2003) 109 Cal.App.4th 351, 363. But if the statute authorizing the privilege requires express consent to disclosure, the privilege holder cannot consent by implication. *See, e.g., id.* (because mediation privilege requires express consent, it cannot be waived by implication).

[a] By conduct. The privilege holder impliedly consents to disclosure by conduct that indicates consent to disclosure. Evid. C. §912(a). Conduct that indicates consent includes the failure to claim the privilege in any proceeding in which the holder has the legal standing and opportunity to claim it. *Id.*; ***Calvert***, 54 Cal.3d at 780; ***Kerner v. Superior Ct.*** (2d Dist.2012) 206 Cal.App.4th 84, 112; *see, e.g.*, ***Hiott***, 16 Cal.App.4th at 719-20 (P waived privilege protecting videotape when, in her response to request for production, she acknowledged videotape and offered D a copy). For example, an equivocal statement by the holder's attorney can support a finding of waiver if the holder, through its attorney, fails to claim the privilege knowing that privileged information is sought and if the holder is given an opportunity to object. ***Kerner***, 206 Cal.App.4th at 114.

[b] By use. The privilege holder impliedly consents to disclosure by allowing a deponent to rely on a privileged document for her testimony. *See* Evid. C. §912(a); *see, e.g.*, ***Kerns Constr. Co. v. Superior Ct.*** (4th Dist.1968) 266 Cal.App.2d 405, 413-14 (work-product privilege for accident reports was waived when deponent had to review reports to give testimony). A witness cannot testify about material contained in a document and then prevent disclosure of the document. ***Kerns Constr.***, 266 Cal.App.2d at 414.

[c] By raising issue. The privilege holder impliedly consents to disclosure by tendering an issue involving the substance or content of a protected communication. *See* ***Eisendrath***, 109 Cal.App.4th at 363; ***Rockwell Int'l v. Superior Ct.*** (2d Dist.1994) 26 Cal.App.4th 1255, 1268; *see also* Evid. C. §958 (client claims attorney breached legal duty), §984 (proceedings between spouses), §996 (litigant places her medical condition in issue), §1001 (patient claims physician breached legal duty), §1016 (litigant places her mental or emotional condition in issue), §1020 (litigant claims psychotherapist breached legal duty). This is referred to as the "in-issue doctrine." ***Eisendrath***, 109 Cal.App.4th at 363. To establish this waiver, the party opposing the privilege must show the following:

- **In issue.** The privilege holder put the confidential information in issue. ***Southern Cal. Gas***, 50 Cal.3d at 40. For example, a client can waive the attorney-client privilege by filing a legal-malpractice suit against the attorney or by asserting reliance on an attorney's advice as an affirmative defense. ***Merritt v. Superior Ct.*** (2d Dist.1970) 9 Cal.App.3d 721, 730; *see also* ***Vesco v. Superior Ct.*** (2d Dist.2013) 221 Cal.App.4th 275, 279 (physician-patient privilege waived by filing motion for continuance of trial based on medical necessity); ***California Consumer Health Care Council v. Kaiser Found. Health Plan, Inc.*** (1st Dist.2006) 142 Cal.App.4th 21, 33 (physician-patient privilege waived by filing medical-malpractice suit).

- **Fairness.** The fair adjudication of the suit requires the disclosure of the communication. ***Southern Cal. Gas***, 50 Cal.3d at 40; ***Mitchell***, 37 Cal.3d at 604 (dicta); *see* ***Vesco***, 221 Cal.App.4th at 279.

(2) Waiver under Evid. C. §912(d). The holders of some confidential-communication privileges can waive the privilege if a disclosure is not "reasonably necessary" to accomplish the purpose for which the holder consulted the professional. *See* Evid. C. §912(d) (reasonably necessary disclosures are not waivers of privilege); ***Roush v. Seagate Tech.*** (6th Dist.2007) 150 Cal.App.4th 210, 225 (party must prove disclosure was reasonably necessary). An example of an unnecessary disclosure is a corporation's dissemination of privileged attorney-client communications to all its employees, including those without a need to know. *See, e.g.*, ***Zurich Am. Ins. v. Superior Ct.*** (2d Dist.2007) 155 Cal.App.4th 1485, 1503-04 (trial court must determine if corporation waived privilege by distributing information to unnecessary employees). To show that a disclosure of attorney-client or work-product information to a third person did not waive the privilege, the holder must establish that (1) the holder had a reasonable expectation that the third person would keep the information confidential and (2) the disclosure was reasonably necessary for the attorney's representation of the client. *See* ***OXY Res. Cal. LLC v. Superior Ct.*** (1st Dist.2004) 115

Cal.App.4th 874, 891 (work product). An attorney's disclosure of work product to a client does not waive the work-product privilege. See "Disclosure to client," ch. 6-B, §3.5.1(8), p. 632.

15 **(a) Privileges to which waiver applies.** Evid. C. §912(d) lists the following confidential-communication privileges to which the reasonably-necessary-disclosure language applies: (1) attorney-client, (2) lawyer-referral-service–client, (3) physician-patient, (4) psychotherapist-patient, (5) sexual-assault-counselor–victim, (6) domestic-violence-counselor–victim, and (7) human-trafficking-caseworker–victim. Each section of the Evidence Code defining these privileges includes the same reasonably-necessary-disclosure language that appears in §912(d). *See* Evid. C. §952 (attorney and client), §965(b) (lawyer-referral service and client), §992 (physician and patient), §1012 (psychotherapist and patient), §1035.4 (sexual-assault counselor and victim), §1037.2(a) (domestic-violence counselor and victim), §1038.2(c) (human-trafficking caseworker and victim). The reasonably-necessary-disclosure provision also applies to the work-product privilege. *See, e.g.*, ***Wells Fargo***, 22 Cal.4th at 214 (disclosure by one attorney to another attorney for same client did not waive work-product privilege); ***Roush***, 150 Cal.App.4th at 225 (provision applied to both attorney-client and work-product privileges).

(b) Privileges to which waiver does not apply. Evid. C. §912(d) does not list the marital-communications privilege or the clergy-penitent privilege, and the Evidence Code does not define these two privileges with the reasonably-necessary-disclosure language; thus, waiver by reasonably necessary disclosure does not apply to them. *See* Evid. C. §980 (marital-communications privilege), §1033 (clergy-penitent privilege).

(3) Waiver by discovery default. The holder of a discovery privilege waives the privilege if she does not make a specific and timely objection to the disclosure of confidential information during discovery. CCP §2025.460(a) (depositions), §2030.290(a) (interrogatories), §2031.300(a) (inspection demands), §2033.280(a) (requests for admission). The court can, on motion, relieve the party from waiver if certain conditions are satisfied. *See id.* §2030.290(a) (interrogatories), §2031.300(a) (inspection demands), §2033.280(a) (requests for admission); ***Stadish v. Superior Ct.*** (2d Dist.1999) 71 Cal.App.4th 1130, 1141 (waiver of trade-secret privilege). See "Motion for Relief from Waiver of Objections," ch. 9-H, p. 1082. Timely objections, even if boilerplate, prevent waiver. ***Best Prods. v. Superior Ct.*** (2d Dist.2004) 119 Cal.App.4th 1181, 1188. See "Grounds for Discovery Objections," ch. 7-A, §11, p. 765.

(4) Waiver by demanding medical report. By demanding a copy of a report from a physical or mental examination (or by taking the deposition of the person who conducted the examination), a party who submitted to the examination or produced another person for the examination waives all discovery privileges and work-product protection relating to all reports, writings, and testimony of any physician, psychologist, or licensed health-care practitioner who has examined the party (or person produced by the party) regarding the same physical or mental condition at issue. CCP §2032.630.

(5) Waiver by contract. The privilege holder can contractually consent in advance to the disclosure of privileged information. *See* ***Maas v. Municipal Ct.*** (1st Dist.1985) 175 Cal.App.3d 601, 606. Contractual consent must be clear and unambiguous. *See id.* at 607; ***Torbensen***, 163 Cal.App.2d at 404; Wegner, *Civil Trials & Evidence* ¶8:1892. For example, by signing a release of medical records as part of an insurance-coverage application, a person waives the medical privileges relating to those medical records. ***Torbensen***, 163 Cal.App.2d at 404.

15. Information not protected by privilege. The following theories of privilege are not recognized by California courts and do not protect information from discovery:

(1) Accountant-client.

(a) Generally. California courts do not recognize an accountant-client privilege. *CEB Discovery Practice*, §3.38; *see* ***Strasbourger Pearson Tulcin Wolff Inc. v. Wiz Tech.*** (4th Dist.1999) 69 Cal.App.4th 1399, 1409. But a client does have a constitutional right to keep financial information private, which must be balanced against a party's right to discover relevant facts. *See* ***Pioneer Elecs.***, 40 Cal.4th at 368. When a party serves an accountant with a subpoena for a client's financial information, the client must also be served with a copy of the subpoena and given an opportunity to object. See "Subpoenas for Personal Records," ch. 8-D, p. 977.

(b) Attorney acting as accountant. When an attorney prepares a client's tax return, the attorney-client privilege does not shield the communications from discovery if the same information would have been communicated to an accountant. ***U.S. v. Ackert***, 169 F.3d 136, 139 (2d Cir.1999); *see* 26 U.S.C. §7525(a)(1) (in non-criminal tax matters, tax advice between taxpayer and tax practitioner is covered by attorney-client privilege to extent that communication would be privileged if it were between taxpayer and attorney).

(2) Bank-customer. California courts do not recognize a bank-customer privilege. ***Pioneer Elecs.***, 40 Cal.4th at 368; *see* ***Fortunato v. Superior Ct.*** (2d Dist.2003) 114 Cal.App.4th 475, 480. But a bank customer does have a constitutional right to keep financial information private, which must be balanced against a party's right to discover relevant facts. ***Pioneer Elecs.***, 40 Cal.4th at 368. When a party serves a bank with a subpoena for a customer's financial information, the customer must also be served with a copy of the subpoena and given an opportunity to object. See "Subpoenas for Personal Records," ch. 8-D, p. 977.

(3) Insurance adjusters. California courts do not recognize an insured-insurer privilege. *CEB Discovery Practice*, §3.18. But statements given by an insured to agents of her insurance company may be protected under the attorney-client privilege if the dominant purpose of the communication is for litigation. *See* ***Soltani-Rastegar v. Superior Ct.*** (1st Dist.1989) 208 Cal.App.3d 424, 427-28.

(4) Ombudsman. California courts do not recognize an ombudsman privilege. ***Ombudsman Servs. v. Superior Ct.*** (3d Dist.2007) 154 Cal.App.4th 1233, 1243; ***Garstang v. Superior Ct.*** (2d Dist.1995) 39 Cal.App.4th 526, 532. But a person may have a constitutional right to keep communications made to an ombudsman private, which must be balanced against a party's right to discover relevant facts. ***Garstang***, 39 Cal.App.4th at 535.

(5) Parent-child. California courts do not recognize a parent-child privilege. ***De Los Santos v. Superior Ct.*** (1980) 27 Cal.3d 677, 683.

(6) Self-evaluation. California courts do not recognize a self-evaluation privilege, also known as the self-critical-analysis privilege, which is a privilege against disclosing any critique by a person or entity of its own operations, policies, or processes. ***Cloud v. Superior Ct.*** (2d Dist.1996) 50 Cal.App.4th 1552, 1554; *CEB Discovery Practice*, §3.142.

(7) Union representative. California courts do not recognize a privilege for communications between a union representative and a union member. *E.g.*, ***American Airlines, Inc. v. Superior Ct.*** (2d Dist.2003) 114 Cal.App.4th 881, 890.

§3. WHAT IS NOT DISCOVERABLE

Some matters are not discoverable because they are beyond the scope of discovery, are privileged, or are exempt from discovery for some other reason.

§3.1 Not relevant. Information is not discoverable if it is not relevant and will not lead to the discovery of admissible evidence. See "*Is the information relevant to the subject matter of the case?*," under "Scope of discovery," §2.1.1, p. 603. For example, the mental processes used by a member of a government agency in reaching an administrative decision, including any evidence relied on and reasoning used in making that decision, are irrelevant and beyond the scope of discovery. *See* ***City of Fairfield v. Superior Ct.*** (1975) 14 Cal.3d 768, 772; ***State v. Superior Ct.*** (1974) 12 Cal.3d 237, 257-58.

§3.2 Not obtainable by discovery procedure. Information is not discoverable if it cannot be obtained by one of the discovery procedures provided by the CDA. See "*Do the discovery rules permit the type of discovery method necessary to secure the information?*," under "Scope of discovery," §2.1.4, p. 604. The only way to secure information that is not discoverable through CDA discovery procedures is by agreement of the parties. *See* CCP §2016.030 (parties can agree to modify discovery).

§3.3 Privileged & exempt information. Information is not discoverable if it is privileged or otherwise exempt from disclosure. For information that is not discoverable because of a particular discovery privilege or exemption, see the relevant discussion in subchapters 6-B through 6-I.

1. Statutory privileges. The only privileges, immunities, and exemptions from discovery that are recognized under California law are those created by statute. Evid. C. §911; ***Roberts v. City of Palmdale*** (1993) 5 Cal.4th 363, 373; ***OXY Res. Cal. LLC v. Superior Ct.*** (1st Dist.2004) 115 Cal.App.4th 874, 888-89. The Evidence Code defines "statute" broadly to include all California statutes, as well as federal statutes, treaties, and any constitutional provisions. Evid. C. §230; ***Union Bank v. Superior Ct.*** (1st Dist.2005) 130 Cal.App.4th 378, 388-89; *see* ***People v. Corona*** (1st Dist.1989) 211 Cal.App.3d 529, 540 (treaty-based privilege is created by statute); *see also* Evid. C. §920 (Evidence Code provisions do not repeal privileges established by other statutes).

PRACTICE TIP

There are major differences between federal and state discovery privileges. ***Cloud v. Superior Ct.*** *(2d Dist.1996) 50 Cal.App.4th 1552, 1558. Under federal law, privileges are governed by the common law as limited by the Constitution, statutes, and Supreme Court rules.* ***Jaffee v. Redmond*** *(1996) 518 U.S. 1, 8-9. Under state law, privileges are governed by statutes, not the common law.* ***Cloud****, 50 Cal.App.4th at 1558-59; see Evid. C. §911.*

---

(1) Evidence Code privileges. The Evidence Code establishes the following privileges, immunities, and exemptions from discovery in civil cases:

15 **(a) Confidential-communication privileges.** The following privileges are governed by Evid. C. §912 (waiver of confidentiality of communication) and §917 (presumption of confidentiality of communication):

[1] Attorney-client privilege. Evid. C. §§912(a), 917(a), 954. See "Attorney-Related Privileges," ch. 6-B, p. 613.

[2] Lawyer-referral-service–client privilege. Evid. C. §§912(a), 917(a), 965-968. See "LRS-Client Privilege," ch. 6-B, §4, p. 639.

[3] Marital-communications privilege. Evid. C. §§912(a), 917(a), 980. See "Marital-Communications Privilege," ch. 6-D, §2, p. 659.

[4] Physician-patient privilege. Evid. C. §§912(a), 917(a), 994. See "Physician-Patient Privilege," ch. 6-E, §1, p. 665.

[5] Psychotherapist-patient privilege. Evid. C. §§912(a), 917(a), 1014. See "Psychotherapist-Patient Privilege," ch. 6-E, §2, p. 672.

[6] Clergy-penitent privilege. Evid. C. §§912(a), 917(a), 1033-1034. See "Clergy-Penitent Privilege," ch. 6-F, §4, p. 700.

[7] Sexual-assault-counselor–victim privilege. Evid. C. §§912(a), 917(a), 1035.8. This privilege is not covered in this book.

[8] Domestic-violence-counselor–victim privilege. *Id.* §§912(a), 917(a), 1037.5. This privilege is not covered in this book.

[9] Human-trafficking-caseworker–victim privilege. *Id.* §§912(a), 917(a), 1038. This privilege is not covered in this book.

(b) Other Evidence Code privileges. The following privileges, exemptions, and immunities are governed by other Evidence Code provisions:

[1] Privilege against self-incrimination. Evid. C. §940. See "Privilege Against Self-Incrimination," ch. 6-F, §2, p. 687.

[2] Spousal-testimonial privileges. Evid. C. §971. See "Spousal-Testimonial Privileges," ch. 6-D, §1, p. 651.

[3] Official-information privilege. Evid. C. §1040. See "Official-Information Privilege," ch. 6-H, §1, p. 712.

[4] Voter privilege. Evid. C. §1050. See "Voter Privilege," ch. 6-F, §5, p. 704.

[5] Trade-secret privilege. Evid. C. §1060. See "Trade-Secret Privilege," ch. 6-C, §1, p. 642.

[6] Journalist's shield-law immunity. Evid. C. §1070. See "Journalist's Shield-Law Immunity," ch. 6-G, §1, p. 706.

[7] Mediation exemption. Evid. C. §1119. See "Mediation Exemption," ch. 6-I, p. 726.

[8] Medical peer-review privilege. Evid. C. §1157. See "Medical Peer-Review Privilege," ch. 6-E, §3, p. 677.

(2) Privileges under other laws. The following privileges and immunities created by other statutes are recognized in civil cases:

(a) Work-product privilege. CCP §2018.030. See "Work-Product Privilege," ch. 6-B, §3, p. 628.

(b) Private-investigator privilege. *See* Bus. & Prof. C. §7539(a). See "Private-Investigator Privilege," ch. 6-C, §2, p. 649.

(c) Reporter's privilege. Cal. Const., art. I, §2, subd. (b); ***Mitchell v. Superior Ct.*** (1984) 37 Cal.3d 268, 279. See "Reporter's Privilege," ch. 6-G, §2, p. 710.

(d) Peace-officer and custodial-officer personnel-records privilege. Evid. C. §§1043, 1045-1047. See "Officer-Records Privilege," ch. 6-H, §4, p. 721.

(e) Tax-return privilege. Rev. & Tax. C. §19542. See "Tax-Return Privilege," ch. 6-F, §3, p. 697.

2. Privilege not waived. Privileged information that has been disclosed is not discoverable (i.e., the privilege is not waived) if the disclosure was made under any of the following conditions:

(1) Inadvertent disclosure. An inadvertent disclosure of privileged information is not a waiver of the privilege. *See* ***Rico v. Mitsubishi Motors Corp.*** (2007) 42 Cal.4th 807, 817-18 (work-product privilege); ***State Comp. Ins. Fund v. WPS, Inc.*** (2d Dist.1999) 70 Cal.App.4th 644, 654 (attorney-client privilege); ***O'Mary v. Mitsubishi Elecs. Am., Inc.*** (4th Dist.1997) 59 Cal.App.4th 563, 577 (same). An attorney who receives privileged attorney-client or work-product information that was inadvertently produced must protect that privileged information. *See* ***Rico***, 42 Cal.4th at 817; ***Wallis v. PHL Assocs.*** (3d Dist.2008) 168 Cal.App.4th 882, 889. To protect the privileged information, the receiving attorney (1) should refrain from examining the materials any more than necessary to determine that they are privileged and (2) must immediately notify the sender that she has the privileged materials. ***Clark v. Superior Ct.*** (4th Dist.2011) 196 Cal.App.4th 37, 53 (dicta); ***State Comp. Ins. Fund***, 70 Cal.App.4th at 656.

(2) Coerced disclosure. A coerced disclosure of privileged information is not a waiver of the privilege. *See* Evid. C. §912(a) (consent must be given freely); *see, e.g.*, ***Regents of the Univ. of Cal. v. Superior Ct.*** (4th Dist.2008) 165 Cal.App.4th 672, 684 (because corporations were forced to waive privileges in government investigation, they did not waive privileges in other proceedings).

(3) Erroneously compelled disclosure. A disclosure made after a claim of privilege was erroneously overruled is not admissible against the privilege holder. Evid. C. §919.

(4) Erroneously admitted disclosure. A disclosure made after a judge refused to exclude the privileged information as required by Evid. C. §916 is not admissible against the privilege holder. Evid. C. §919(a). Section 916 requires the judge to exclude privileged information if the person from whom the information is sought is not authorized to claim the privilege and no party to the suit is authorized to claim the privilege.

15 **(5) Joint-holder disclosure.** When a privilege is held jointly, the disclosure of confidential information by one of the privilege holders does not affect the other holders' right to claim the privilege. Evid. C. §912(b);

Bank of Am. v. Superior Ct. (4th Dist.2013) 212 Cal.App.4th 1076, 1096; ***Roush v. Seagate Tech.*** (6th Dist.2007) 150 Cal.App.4th 210, 223; *see also* Evid. C. §962 (defining "joint clients" of attorney). *But see* ***Palay v. Superior Ct.*** (2d Dist.1993) 18 Cal.App.4th 919, 927 (mother's joint privilege with infant for prenatal records was overcome by litigation exception for infant's personal-injury claim). Each joint holder has an independent right to protect the privilege, and one holder cannot waive the privilege without the consent of the other holders. ***Roush***, 150 Cal.App.4th at 223; ***Armenta v. Superior Ct.*** (2d Dist.2002) 101 Cal.App.4th 525, 533. This exception applies to the following communication privileges: (1) attorney-client, (2) lawyer-referral-service–client, (3) physician-patient, (4) psychotherapist-patient, (5) sexual-assault-counselor–victim, (6) domestic-violence-counselor–victim, and (7) human-trafficking-caseworker–victim. Evid. C. §912(b).

(6) Privileged disclosure. A disclosure that is itself privileged is not a waiver of the privilege. Evid. C. §912(c). For example, a wife does not waive the attorney-client privilege by telling her husband in confidence what she told her attorney. *See id.* §980.

(7) Necessary disclosure. A disclosure of information protected by a confidential-communication privilege is not a waiver of the privilege if the disclosure was "reasonably necessary" to accomplish the purpose for which the professional was consulted. Evid. C. §912(d). Examples of reasonably necessary disclosures include a patient's presentation of a prescription to a pharmacist and an attorney's consultation with another attorney. *See id.*; 7 Cal. Law Revision Comm'n Rep. (1965) p. 1155. An unnecessary disclosure is a waiver of the privilege. See "Waiver under Evid. C. §912(d)," §2.2.14(2), p. 608.

15 **(8) Unauthorized disclosure.** A disclosure of privileged information is not a waiver of a privilege if the disclosure is not made by the privilege holder or a person authorized by the holder to disclose the privileged information. *See* Evid. C. §912(a); *see also id.* §954 (attorney's client has a "privilege to ... prevent another from disclosing" confidential information), §966 (lawyer-referral-service–client), §980 (marital communications), §994 (physician-patient), §1014 (psychotherapist-patient), §1033 (clergy-penitent), §1035.8 (victim of sexual assault), §1037.5 (victim of domestic violence), §1038 (victim of human trafficking). Thus, when a privileged conversation is overheard, the privilege holder can prevent the eavesdropper from disclosing the conversation to any other person. *See* ***Menendez v. Superior Ct.*** (1992) 3 Cal.4th 435, 448. This "privilege to prevent" effectively repudiates the old eavesdropper rule, under which the privilege was defeated if a privileged conversation was overheard by an eavesdropper. *Id.*

B. ATTORNEY-RELATED PRIVILEGES

This subchapter covers the attorney-client, work-product, and lawyer-referral-service–client (LRS-client) privileges. Although the work-product privilege is not included in the Evidence Code, it is identified as a privilege (or as a doctrine) by the courts. *See, e.g.*, ***People v. Bennett*** (2009) 45 Cal.4th 577, 595 (referring to work product as privilege); ***Rico v. Mitsubishi Motors Corp.*** (2007) 42 Cal.4th 807, 814 (discussing work product as doctrine).

NOTE

For ease of reference, the term "work-product privilege" will be used throughout this subchapter.

§1. GENERAL

The attorney-client (and similar LRS-client) and work-product privileges differ in purpose and scope. *See* ***Wellpoint Health Networks, Inc. v. Superior Ct.*** (2d Dist.1997) 59 Cal.App.4th 110, 119-20; ***BP Alaska Expl., Inc. v. Superior Ct.*** (5th Dist.1988) 199 Cal.App.3d 1240, 1255-56. The protection provided by the work-product privilege is distinct from and broader than the attorney-client and LRS-client privileges. *See* ***U.S. v. Nobles*** (1975) 422 U.S. 225, 238 n.11. For example, the attorney-client privilege covers only communications between the attorney and the client, while the work-product privilege protects all material generated by the attorney, even material that is never communicated to the client. ***Aetna Cas. & Sur. Co. v. Superior Ct.*** (1st Dist.1984) 153 Cal.App.3d 467, 478 n.4.

6-1. ATTORNEY-CLIENT VS. LRS-CLIENT VS. WORK-PRODUCT PRIVILEGES

		Attorney-client privilege	LRS-client privilege	Work-product privilege
1	Authority	Evid. C. §950 et seq.	Evid. C. §965 et seq.	CCP §2018.010 et seq.
2	What is covered by privilege	• Confidential communications between attorney and client to obtain legal advice; includes communications through attorney's staff and client's representatives • Communications between attorney and consulting experts • Communications with an accountant that are necessary or highly useful for obtaining legal advice	• Confidential communications between LRS and client for purpose of retaining attorney or obtaining legal services or advice from attorney; includes communications with LRS staff members	• All work generated in legal capacity by attorney or attorney's employees, including work not shared with client • Work generated by consulting experts for attorney
3	Duration of privilege	As long as someone remains to claim privilege	As long as someone remains to claim privilege	As long as someone remains to claim privilege
4	Nature of privilege	Absolute	Absolute	• Absolute, for core work product • Qualified, for noncore work product
5	Who owns privilege ("holder")	Client	Client	Attorney
6	Who can assert privilege	• Client • Attorney, on client's behalf • Person authorized by client to assert privilege	• Client • LRS or LRS staff member, on client's behalf • Person authorized by client to assert privilege	• Attorney • Client, on attorney's behalf • Party in propria persona
7	In camera inspection to determine privilege	No	No	Yes
8	Crime-fraud exception	Exception applies; information is discoverable	Exception applies; information is discoverable	Exception does not apply in civil cases; information is not discoverable

§2. ATTORNEY-CLIENT PRIVILEGE

§2.1 General. The attorney-client privilege protects confidential communications between attorneys and their clients. Evid. C. §954.

1. Purpose. The purpose of the attorney-client privilege is to encourage full and frank communication between attorneys and their clients. ***People v. Meredith*** (1981) 29 Cal.3d 682, 690; ***Greyhound Corp. v. Superior Ct.*** (1961) 56 Cal.2d 355, 396.

2. Primary authority. Evid. C. §§950-962; ***D.I. Chadbourne, Inc. v. Superior Ct.*** (1964) 60 Cal.2d 723; ***2,022 Ranch, L.L.C. v. Superior Ct.*** (4th Dist.2003) 113 Cal.App.4th 1377, *disapproved on other grounds*, ***Costco Wholesale Corp. v. Superior Ct.*** (2009) 47 Cal.4th 725; ***Insurance Co. of N. Am. v. Superior Ct.*** (2d Dist.1980) 108 Cal.App.3d 758.

3. Secondary authority. The following secondary sources are cited as authority in this section:

- *California Civil Discovery Practice* (CEB Online ed. 2014) (referred to as *CEB Discovery Practice*).
- *California Trial Objections* (CEB Online ed. 2014) (referred to as *CEB Trial Objections*).

• Jefferson, *California Evidence Benchbook* (CEB Online ed. 2014) (referred to as *Jefferson's Evid. Benchbook*).

• Wegner, *California Practice Guide: Civil Trials & Evidence* (CD-ROM ed. 2014) (referred to as Wegner, *Civil Trials & Evidence*).

§2.2 Nature of attorney-client privilege.

1. Absolute. The attorney-client privilege is absolute, which means the court cannot order disclosure of information protected by the privilege. ***Costco Wholesale Corp. v. Superior Ct.*** (2009) 47 Cal.4th 725, 732; ***Chubb & Son v. Superior Ct.*** (1st Dist.2014) 228 Cal.App.4th 1094, 1103; ***Gordon v. Superior Ct.*** (2d Dist.1997) 55 Cal.App.4th 1546, 1557; Wegner, *Civil Trials & Evidence*, ¶8:1988; *see, e.g.*, ***Venture Law Grp. v. Superior Ct.*** (6th Dist.2004) 118 Cal.App.4th 96, 102 (discovery order compelling answers in violation of attorney-client privilege was abuse of discretion). Although the attorney-client privilege does prevent discovery of relevant evidence, this concern is outweighed by the importance of preserving the confidential relationship between attorneys and their clients. ***Mitchell v. Superior Ct.*** (1984) 37 Cal.3d 591, 599-600; *see, e.g.*, ***Wells Fargo Bank v. Superior Ct.*** (2000) 22 Cal.4th 201, 206 (court refused to recognize fiduciary exception to attorney-client privilege).

2. Duration. The attorney-client privilege lasts as long as the privilege holder asserts it. *See* Evid. C. §954; ***Venture Law***, 118 Cal.App.4th at 103; 7 Cal. Law Revision Comm'n Rep. (1965) p. 1167. See "Holder," §2.5.1, p. 620. The holder can continue to assert the privilege after the attorney-client relationship has ended. *See* Wegner, *Civil Trials & Evidence*, ¶8:1993 (right to claim attorney-client privilege survives termination of litigation); *see also* ***City & Cty. of S.F. v. Cobra Solutions, Inc.*** (2006) 38 Cal.4th 839, 846 (attorney's duty of confidentiality survives termination of attorney's representation). The attorney-client privilege terminates when there is no holder to assert the privilege after the client's death or dissolution. See "Dead or defunct client," §2.5.1(2), p. 621. The death of the attorney does not affect the privilege. Wegner, *Civil Trials & Evidence*, ¶8:1992.

3. Discovery & evidentiary. The attorney-client privilege is both a discovery privilege and an evidentiary privilege because the information protected by the privilege is not subject to either discovery or disclosure at trial. *See* Evid. C. §954 (client has privilege to refuse to disclose and to prevent others from disclosing).

§2.3 Elements of attorney-client privilege. To establish the attorney-client privilege, the person asserting the privilege must show the following:

1. Attorney & client formed relationship. The attorney and the client established an attorney-client relationship. *See* Evid. C. §§950, 951; ***Sullivan v. Superior Ct.*** (1st Dist.1972) 29 Cal.App.3d 64, 69; *see, e.g.*, ***Hiott v. Superior Ct.*** (2d Dist.1993) 16 Cal.App.4th 712, 718 (court found there was attorney-client relationship because P considered herself to be client when her brother, an attorney, recorded their conversation in hospital). An attorney-client relationship is established when the relationship includes (1) an attorney, (2) a client, and (3) a consultation for some legal purpose. *See* ***Perkins v. West Coast Lumber Co.*** (1900) 129 Cal. 427, 429 (attorney-client relationship is established when party seeking legal advice consults attorney and secures that advice); ***Gulf Ins. v. Berger, Kahn, Shafton, Moss, Figler, Simon & Gladstone*** (2d Dist.2000) 79 Cal.App.4th 114, 126 (same); *see also* ***Bank of Am. v. Superior Ct.*** (4th Dist.2013) 212 Cal.App.4th 1076, 1090-91 (absent conflict of interest, tripartite attorney-client relationship can exist between insurer, insured, and counsel selected for insured by insurer; no formal retainer agreement between insurer and counsel is necessary to create relationship).

(1) Attorney. For a discussion of who is an "attorney" for purposes of the privilege, see "Attorney," §2.4.1, p. 617.

(2) Client. For a discussion of who is a "client" for purposes of the privilege, see "Client," §2.4.2, p. 617.

(3) Consultation. The client must have consulted the attorney for the purpose of (1) retaining the attorney, (2) obtaining legal services, or (3) obtaining legal advice. Evid. C. §951. A consultation to retain an attorney is protected even if the client does not hire the attorney. See "Client," §2.4.2, p. 617.

(a) Sole purpose – legal services or advice. The attorney-client privilege protects communications made to retain the attorney or to obtain legal services or advice. Evid. C. §951; *see* ***City & Cty. of S.F. v. Superior Ct.*** (1951) 37 Cal.2d 227, 234-35 (communication in course of professional employment). The privilege applies whether the legal services were sought for litigation or nonlitigation purposes. ***Wellpoint Health Networks, Inc. v. Superior Ct.*** (2d Dist.1997) 59 Cal.App.4th 110, 119-20.

(b) Dual purpose – legal & nonlegal services or advice. The attorney-client privilege protects some dual-purpose communications, which are those made for both legal and nonlegal purposes. ***2,022 Ranch, L.L.C. v. Superior Ct.*** (4th Dist.2003) 113 Cal.App.4th 1377, 1390, *disapproved on other grounds*, ***Costco Wholesale Corp. v. Superior Ct.*** (2009) 47 Cal.4th 725; *see* ***Aetna Cas. & Sur. Co. v. Superior Ct.*** (1st Dist.1984) 153 Cal.App.3d 467, 475. For the privilege to apply, the dominant purpose of the communication must have been to obtain legal services or advice. ***Travelers Ins. v. Superior Ct.*** (1st Dist.1983) 143 Cal.App.3d 436, 452; ***Montebello Rose Co. v. Agricultural Labor Relations Bd.*** (5th Dist.1981) 119 Cal.App.3d 1, 32; *see* ***Wellpoint Health Networks***, 59 Cal.App.4th at 123. The dominant-purpose test looks at the purpose of the relationship between the parties to the communication and not at the content of the communication; that is, the test asks whether the relationship was principally an attorney-client one. ***Costco Wholesale Corp. v. Superior Ct.*** (2009) 47 Cal.4th 725, 739-40; ***Clark v. Superior Ct.*** (4th Dist.2011) 196 Cal.App.4th 37, 51. See "Nonlegal work," §2.7.4, p. 623. If the party claiming the privilege shows that the dominant purpose of the relationship was an attorney-client one, the communication is protected. ***Costco Wholesale***, 47 Cal.4th at 739-40; ***Clark***, 196 Cal.App.4th at 51.

2. Attorney & client communicated. The attorney and client communicated (i.e., transmitted information between them) in the course of their relationship. Evid. C. §952; ***Martin v. Workers' Comp. Appeals Bd.*** (2d Dist.1997) 59 Cal.App.4th 333, 345, *disapproved on other grounds*, ***Costco Wholesale Corp. v. Superior Ct.*** (2009) 47 Cal.4th 725; ***Sullivan***, 29 Cal.App.3d at 69.

3. Communication made confidentially. The attorney and client communicated confidentially. ***Insurance Co. of N. Am. v. Superior Ct.*** (2d Dist.1980) 108 Cal.App.3d 758, 765; ***Sullivan***, 29 Cal.App.3d at 69. For a communication to be confidential, the client must have intended for it to be confidential and must not have disclosed it to an unnecessary third person.

(1) Presumption of confidentiality. If the communication was made in the course of the attorney-client relationship, it is presumed to be confidential. Evid. C. §917(a); *CEB Discovery Practice*, §3.12; *Jefferson's Evid. Benchbook*, §42.14. In other words, the person claiming the privilege does not need to show that the communication was made in confidence. *See* 7 Cal. Law Revision Comm'n Rep. (1965) p. 1160. The person opposing the privilege can rebut the presumption by showing that the communication was not confidential. Evid. C. §917(a); 7 Cal. Law Revision Comm'n Rep. (1965) pp. 1160-61.

(2) Client intended confidentiality. Communications are privileged only when the client intends for them to be confidential. ***McKnew v. Superior Ct.*** (1943) 23 Cal.2d 58, 66; ***Benge v. Superior Ct.*** (5th Dist.1982) 131 Cal.App.3d 336, 346; ***Insurance Co. of N. Am.***, 108 Cal.App.3d at 765. The client's intent, not the attorney's, controls whether a communication was intended to be confidential. *See, e.g.*, ***Hiott***, 16 Cal.App.4th at 718 (P considered herself a client, and her conversation with attorney confidential, when conversation was recorded). If the client is a legal entity and the client's employee makes a statement related to the purpose for which the client has consulted the attorney, the following rules govern whether the communication was intended to be confidential:

(a) Client did not ask employee to make statement. A corporate client's intent that an employee communication be confidential does not control when (1) its employee makes a statement, (2) the employer did not expressly direct the employee to make the statement, and (3) the employee either does not know that the statement is sought on a confidential basis or does know but does not intend for the statement to be confidential. ***D.I. Chadbourne, Inc. v. Superior Ct.*** (1964) 60 Cal.2d 723, 737-38. In other words, the employee's intent controls. *Id.*

(b) Client's carrier asked employee to make statement. A corporate client's intent that an employee communication be confidential does not control when (1) its employee makes a statement, (2) the employer, at the request of its insurance carrier, directed the employee to make the statement, and (3) the carrier did not advise the employer that the statement was to be a confidential communication. ***D.I. Chadbourne, Inc.***, 60 Cal.2d at 738. In this situation, the corporate employer is prevented from claiming that it intended for the statement to be made as a confidential communication. *See id.* However, if the insurance carrier tells the corporate employer that the report is intended to be a confidential communication for the employer's attorney, the employer's intent would control. *See* ***Payless Drug Stores v. Superior Ct.*** (1st Dist.1976) 54 Cal.App.3d 988, 991; *Jefferson's Evid. Benchbook*, §§42.36, 42.44, 42.46; *see, e.g.*, ***Sierra Vista Hosp. v. Superior Ct.*** (2d Dist.1967) 248 Cal.App.2d 359, 368-69 (incident report prepared by hospital administrator was privileged).

(3) Communication shared with third persons.

(a) Necessary third persons. An attorney-client communication made in the presence of a third person is confidential only if the disclosure was necessary to (1) further the client's interest or (2) transmit the information or accomplish the purpose for which the attorney was consulted. Evid. C. §§912(d), 952. For a discussion of third persons to whom confidential communications can be disclosed, see "Necessary third persons," §2.4.3, p. 618.

(b) Unnecessary third persons. An attorney-client communication made in the presence of an unnecessary third person is not confidential. ***Zurich Am. Ins. v. Superior Ct.*** (2d Dist.2007) 155 Cal.App.4th 1485, 1503; ***Insurance Co. of N. Am.***, 108 Cal.App.3d at 765; *see* Evid. C. §§912(d), 952; ***D.I. Chadbourne, Inc.***, 60 Cal.2d at 735; ***McKnew***, 23 Cal.2d at 66. For example, a third-party witness who has no interest in the matter could destroy the attorney-client privilege. ***D.I. Chadbourne, Inc.***, 60 Cal.2d at 735; *see* ***McKnew***, 23 Cal.2d at 66; *see, e.g.*, ***Zurich Am.***, 155 Cal.App.4th at 1503-04 (privilege is destroyed if corporate employee who has no need to know information is given access to document protected by privilege).

§2.4 Communicants to attorney-client privilege. Communicants to the attorney-client privilege include the attorney, the client, and any necessary third persons.

1. Attorney. An attorney includes any of the following:

(1) Any person who is authorized, or who the client reasonably believed is authorized, to practice law in any state or nation. Evid. C. §950. This includes an employer's in-house counsel. Wegner, *Civil Trials & Evidence*, ¶8:1997; *see, e.g.*, ***Alpha Beta Co. v. Superior Ct.*** (5th Dist.1984) 157 Cal.App.3d 818, 826 (communications between D's president and in-house counsel about defense to lawsuit were privileged). However, the communications are not covered by the privilege if the attorney was acting as a business agent for the employer (e.g., negotiations, business advice) when she made or received them. *See* ***Chicago Title Ins. v. Superior Ct.*** (1st Dist.1985) 174 Cal.App.3d 1142, 1151.

(2) A law corporation or a member of the California State Bar who is employed by a law corporation. Evid. C. §954 (last paragraph); *CEB Trial Objections*, §34.8; *see* Corp. C. §13406(b) (law corporation can be nonprofit public-benefit corporation); ***Frye v. Tenderloin Hous. Clinic, Inc.*** (2006) 38 Cal.4th 23, 35 (law corporation includes nonprofit corporations and for-profit corporations); *see, e.g.*, ***In re Brown*** (1995) 12 Cal.4th 205, 209 (private law firm was law corporation).

2. Client. A client is a person who, directly or through an authorized representative, consults an attorney to retain the attorney or to obtain professional legal services or advice. Evid. C. §951; ***HLC Props., Ltd. v. Superior Ct.*** (2005) 35 Cal.4th 54, 61; *see* ***Sullivan v. Superior Ct.*** (1st Dist.1972) 29 Cal.App.3d 64, 69; *see, e.g.*, ***Benge v. Superior Ct.*** (5th Dist.1982) 131 Cal.App.3d 336, 347-48 (attorney-client relationship covered meeting of union attorneys and union members to discuss possible personal-injury actions). A person who consults with an attorney is a client even if the person decides not to hire the attorney or if the attorney decides not to represent the person. ***Benge***, 131 Cal.App.3d at 347; ***Sullivan***, 29 Cal.App.3d at 69. A person is not a client if she consults an attorney for

nonlegal services or advice in the attorney's capacity as a friend rather than in her professional capacity as an attorney. ***Kerner v. Superior Ct.*** (2d Dist.2012) 206 Cal.App.4th 84, 117; *see* ***People v. Gionis*** (1995) 9 Cal.4th 1196, 1212.

(1) Natural person. A client can be a natural person. *See* ***Insurance Co. of N. Am. v. Superior Ct.*** (2d Dist.1980) 108 Cal.App.3d 758, 763 (natural and artificial persons are entitled to full benefit of attorney-client privilege); *see, e.g.*, ***HLC Props.***, 35 Cal.4th at 62-63 (because client consulted attorney personally, privilege did not belong to his unincorporated business organization). The person can be a minor or an incompetent. *See* Evid. C. §951 ("client" includes person who consults attorney through representative); *see, e.g.*, ***De Los Santos v. Superior Ct.*** (1980) 27 Cal.3d 677, 682 (minor's disclosure to parent for transmission to attorney was privileged).

(2) Legal entity. A client can be a legal entity that consults an attorney through its representative. ***Costco Wholesale Corp. v. Superior Ct.*** (2009) 47 Cal.4th 725, 733; *Jefferson's Evid. Benchbook*, §42.11. This includes corporations, limited-liability companies, nonprofit corporations, public entities, and unincorporated associations (e.g., labor unions, social clubs, and fraternal societies). *See* Evid. C. §175 ("person" includes firm, association, organization, partnership, business trust, corporation, limited-liability company, and public entity), §954 ("persons" includes partnerships, corporations, limited-liability companies, associations, and other groups and entities); ***D.I. Chadbourne, Inc. v. Superior Ct.*** (1964) 60 Cal.2d 723, 732 (corporation); ***Citizens for Ceres v. Superior Ct.*** (5th Dist.2013) 217 Cal.App.4th 889, 913 (city council); ***Tritek Telecom, Inc. v. Superior Ct.*** (4th Dist.2009) 169 Cal.App.4th 1385, 1389 (corporation).

3. Necessary third persons. A necessary third person is any person to whom a confidential communication is disclosed in any of the following circumstances: (1) the disclosure was reasonably necessary to transmit the information between the attorney and the client, (2) the disclosure was reasonably necessary to accomplish the purpose for which the attorney was consulted, or (3) the person was present during the disclosure to further the client's interest in the consultation. Evid. C. §952. This includes the following persons:

(1) Agents.

(a) Of attorney. Confidential communications can be disclosed to and transmitted by an attorney's agent. *See* ***City & Cty. of S.F. v. Superior Ct.*** (1951) 37 Cal.2d 227, 236-37; ***Insurance Co. of N. Am.***, 108 Cal.App.3d at 771; 7 Cal. Law Revision Comm'n Rep. (1965) p. 1164. The following are examples of agents who can be communicants to the privilege:

[1] Legal secretary, paralegal, receptionist, or clerk. ***People v. Meredith*** (1981) 29 Cal.3d 682, 690 n.3 (legal secretary, paralegal, receptionist); ***City & Cty. of S.F.***, 37 Cal.2d at 236 (secretary or clerk); ***Insurance Co. of N. Am.***, 108 Cal.App.3d at 771 (same); 7 Cal. Law Revision Comm'n Rep. (1965) p. 1164.

[2] Investigator. ***Meredith***, 29 Cal.3d at 690 & n.3.

[3] Stenographer. ***City & Cty. of S.F.***, 37 Cal.2d at 236.

(b) Of client. Confidential communications can be disclosed to and transmitted by a client's agent when (1) the agent must communicate something from the client because the client is unable to make the communication or (2) the communication can be better transmitted through a specialist. ***Suezaki v. Superior Ct.*** (1962) 58 Cal.2d 166, 177; *see* ***City & Cty. of S.F.***, 37 Cal.2d at 236-37; *Jefferson's Evid. Benchbook*, §42.19. For a communication through an agent to be protected, it must be (1) about the client (e.g., a medical report) or (2) information passed from the client to the agent for transmission to the attorney. ***Suezaki***, 58 Cal.2d at 177; *Jefferson's Evid. Benchbook*, §42.19. The following are examples of agents who can be communicants to the privilege:

[1] Interpreter. *See* ***City & Cty. of S.F.***, 37 Cal.2d at 236-37; *see also* Cal. Stds. Jud. Admin. 2.11(a)(2) (court-appointed interpreters must be instructed not to disclose communications between attorney and client).

[2] Minor's parent. *See* Evid. C. §951 ("client" includes person who consults attorney through representative); *see, e.g.*, ***De Los Santos***, 27 Cal.3d at 682 (minor's disclosure to parent for transmission to attorney was privileged).

[3] Nontestifying expert consultant. 7 Cal. Law Revision Comm'n Rep. (1965) pp. 1164-65; *Jefferson's Evid. Benchbook*, §42.19; *see* ***San Diego P.A. v. Superior Ct.*** (1962) 58 Cal.2d 194, 202 (privilege applies to expert's communications with attorney that are in the nature of confidential communication from client); ***Elijah W. v. Superior Ct.*** (2d Dist.2013) 216 Cal.App.4th 140, 151-52 (privilege applies to expert's communications with client). See "Consulting expert," ch. 7-I, §2.1, p. 898. For example, if an attorney hires a physician to examine a client's injuries from a car accident, the physician's communications with the attorney are privileged. *See* ***City & Cty. of S.F.***, 37 Cal.2d at 234-35; *Jefferson's Evid. Benchbook*, §42.19. If the attorney decides to use the consultant as a trial witness, the communications with the consultant do not retain their confidentiality. ***People v. Ledesma*** (2006) 39 Cal.4th 641, 695. See "Loss of confidential status," ch. 7-I, §4.1.2(2), p. 901.

CAUTION

If the client sees a physician before consulting an attorney, the physician-patient privilege—not the attorney-client privilege—controls the discoverability of the client's communications. See ***City & Cty. of S.F.***, *37 Cal.2d at 237-38. See "Physician-Patient Privilege," ch. 6-E, §1, p. 665.*

(2) Employees of legal entity. Confidential information can be disclosed to and transmitted by a legal-entity client's employee if the disclosure is reasonably necessary to further the interest of the client's legal consultation. *See* Evid. C. §952; ***Zurich Am. Ins. v. Superior Ct.*** (2d Dist.2007) 155 Cal.App.4th 1485, 1495-96; ***Insurance Co. of N. Am.***, 108 Cal.App.3d at 771. In other words, not all employees fall within the category of "necessary third persons." *See, e.g.*, ***Zurich Am.***, 155 Cal.App.4th at 1503 (case remanded to trial court to determine whether insurer's employees were necessary third persons). The following are some common issues involving employees as necessary third persons to an employer's confidential communications:

(a) Company spokesperson. An employee who speaks to the attorney on the employer's behalf is a necessary third person if the employee is a person who would ordinarily be used to communicate with the employer's attorney and the communication transmits information emanating from the employer, not from the employee. ***D.I. Chadbourne, Inc.***, 60 Cal.2d at 736-37; *CEB Trial Objections*, §34.5. A legal entity can speak only through an officer, an employee, or some other natural person. ***D.I. Chadbourne, Inc.***, 60 Cal.2d at 732.

(b) Reporting employee. An employee who is not a defendant or would not be charged with liability and who makes a report or statement is a necessary third person for purposes of the report or statement if (1) the employee's connection with the matter arises from her employment, (2) the report or statement was required by standing rule or in the employer's ordinary course of business (e.g., accident report), and (3) the employer directed the making of the report or statement for confidential transmission to its attorney. ***D.I. Chadbourne, Inc.***, 60 Cal.2d at 737; *Jefferson's Evid. Benchbook*, §42.32; *see, e.g.*, ***O'Mary v. Mitsubishi Elecs. Am., Inc.*** (4th Dist.1997) 59 Cal.App.4th 563, 577 (list of employees to be terminated, prepared by human-resources manager to send to attorneys for legal advice, was protected).

[1] Report taken by agent. The report or statement can be given to the employer's agent, such as the employer's insurance company. ***D.I. Chadbourne, Inc.***, 60 Cal.2d at 737.

[2] Report has dual purpose. If the entity had more than one purpose in directing the employee to make the report or statement, the report or statement remains privileged if the dominant purpose was to obtain legal advice. ***D.I. Chadbourne, Inc.***, 60 Cal.2d at 737; *see Jefferson's Evid. Benchbook*, §42.43; Wegner, *Civil Trials & Evidence*, ¶8:2041. However, if a secondary use of the report involves a waiver of the privilege, the privilege is lost. ***D.I. Chadbourne, Inc.***, 60 Cal.2d at 737; *see, e.g.*, ***Kerns Constr. Co. v. Superior Ct.*** (4th Dist.1968) 266 Cal.App.2d 405, 413-14 (report prepared by employee was privileged until employee used report to refresh memory during deposition).

(c) "Need to know" employee. An employee who receives a confidential communication is a necessary third person if the employee was on a need-to-know basis. ***Zurich Am.***, 155 Cal.App.4th at 1503; ***Insurance Co. of N. Am.***, 108 Cal.App.3d at 765; *see CEB Trial Objections*, §34.5 (confidential communications of legal strategy between corporate employees on need-to-know basis presumptively fall within attorney-client privilege).

(d) Codefendant employee. An employee who is or may be a defendant and who gives a statement revealing knowledge of facts for which the employee or her defendant-employer may be charged is a necessary third person if the statement is (1) given to a representative of the defendant-employer and (2) delivered to the attorney who represents (or will represent) the employee, the defendant-employer, or both. ***D.I. Chadbourne, Inc.***, 60 Cal.2d at 736; *Jefferson's Evid. Benchbook*, §42.29.

(e) Holding company's officers or employees. A holding company's officers or employees who communicate with the attorney for a wholly owned subsidiary or affiliate are necessary third persons if the communications are necessary for the officers or employees to properly perform their duties. ***Insurance Co. of N. Am.***, 108 Cal.App.3d at 771. The communications are not covered by the privilege if there is a conflict of interest or some other antagonistic relationship between the holding company and its subsidiary. *Id.* at 769-70.

(3) Other persons. Confidential information can be disclosed to other persons with whom the attorney or client must communicate to further the client's interest in obtaining legal advice. *See* ***Benge***, 131 Cal.App.3d at 346 (necessary persons may include spouse, parent, business associate, joint client, or any other person who may meet with client and attorney about matter of joint concern); 7 Cal. Law Revision Comm'n Rep. (1965) p. 1165 (same); *see, e.g.*, ***Seahaus La Jolla Owners Ass'n v. Superior Ct.*** (4th Dist.2014) 224 Cal.App.4th 754, 776 (disclosures at litigation-update meetings to individual homeowners of P-client association were "reasonably necessary" to accomplish purpose for which association's lawyers were consulted).

§2.5 Who can assert attorney-client privilege. The attorney-client privilege belongs to the client, not to the attorney. Evid. C. §953. The following persons can assert the privilege for the client:

1. Holder. The client—including joint clients—is the holder of the privilege. Evid. C. §953; ***Bank of Am. v. Superior Ct.*** (4th Dist.2013) 212 Cal.App.4th 1076, 1096; ***Kerner v. Superior Ct.*** (2d Dist.2012) 206 Cal.App.4th 84, 111; ***OXY Res. Cal. LLC v. Superior Ct.*** (1st Dist.2004) 115 Cal.App.4th 874, 901. The holder can assert the privilege to prevent disclosure of protected information. Evid. C. §954(a); ***HLC Props., Ltd. v. Superior Ct.*** (2005) 35 Cal.4th 54, 61. The identity of the privilege holder depends on whether the client is alive or functioning or dead or defunct. It does not depend on who pays the attorney's fee. ***Wells Fargo Bank v. Superior Ct.*** (2000) 22 Cal.4th 201, 213.

(1) Alive or functioning client.

(a) Client is natural person. A natural person can be the holder of the attorney-client privilege. *See* Evid. C. §951 ("client" defined as "person"). When the client is a natural person, the identity of the privilege holder depends on whether the client has a guardian or conservator. *See id.* §953.

[1] No guardian or conservator. If the client has no guardian or conservator, the client is the privilege holder. Evid. C. §953(a). See "Client," §2.4.2, p. 617.

[2] Guardian or conservator. If the client has a guardian or conservator, the guardian or conservator is the privilege holder. Evid. C. §953(b); Wegner, *Civil Trials & Evidence*, ¶8:2049; *see, e.g.*, ***De Los Santos v. Superior Ct.*** (1980) 27 Cal.3d 677, 682 (minor P's mother, in her capacity as guardian ad litem, was privilege holder).

(b) Client is legal entity. An entity that is not a natural person can be the holder of the attorney-client privilege. *See* Evid. C. §175 ("person" includes firm, association, organization, partnership, business trust, corporation, limited-liability company, or public entity), §951 ("client" defined as "person").

[1] Corporation. A corporation can be the holder of the attorney-client privilege. ***McDermott, Will & Emery v. Superior Ct.*** (2d Dist.2000) 83 Cal.App.4th 378, 383; ***National Football League Props., Inc. v. Superior Ct.*** (6th Dist.1998) 65 Cal.App.4th 100, 109. A corporation's officers can assert the attorney-client privilege on the corporation's behalf. *See* ***National Football League***, 65 Cal.App.4th at 111. A corporation's shareholders cannot assert the attorney-client privilege on the corporation's behalf, even in a derivative action and even

if the corporation is in dissolution proceedings. ***Reilly v. Greenwald & Hoffman, LLP*** (4th Dist.2011) 196 Cal.App.4th 891, 901-02; *see* ***McDermott, Will & Emery***, 83 Cal.App.4th at 385 (shareholders are not holders of attorney-client privilege).

[2] Association. An association can be the holder of the attorney-client privilege. *See* ***Smith v. Laguna Sur Villas Cmty. Ass'n*** (4th Dist.2000) 79 Cal.App.4th 639, 643. The individual members of the association are not privilege holders. *See id.*

[3] Unincorporated organization. An unincorporated organization, such as a union, social club, or fraternal organization, can be the holder of the attorney-client privilege. ***HLC Props.***, 35 Cal.4th at 62. The individual members of the unincorporated organization are not privilege holders. *Id.*

[4] Public entity. A public entity can be the holder of the attorney-client privilege. ***Roberts v. City of Palmdale*** (1993) 5 Cal.4th 363, 370 & 371 n.3; *see* ***St. Croix v. Superior Ct.*** (1st Dist.2014) 228 Cal.App.4th 434, 443.

(2) Dead or defunct client. When the client no longer exists (i.e., is dead or defunct), the identity of the privilege holder can vary.

(a) Dead person. If the client is dead, the holder of the attorney-client privilege is the client's personal representative, including one appointed under Prob. C. §12252. Evid. C. §953(c). Only a personal representative can claim the attorney-client privilege of a dead client. *Id.*; ***HLC Props.***, 35 Cal.4th at 65. The privilege transfers to the personal representative (i.e., the executor of the estate) after the client's death. ***HLC Props.***, 35 Cal.4th at 65-66. The privilege terminates when the estate is fully distributed and the personal representative is discharged. *Id.* at 66; 7 Cal. Law Revision Comm'n Rep. (1965) p. 1167; Wegner, *Civil Trials & Evidence*, ¶¶8:1990, 8:2050.

(b) Defunct legal entity. If a firm, association, organization, partnership, business trust, corporation, or public entity no longer exists, the holder of the attorney-client privilege is the entity's successor, assignee, trustee in dissolution, or similar representative. Evid. C. §953(d); *see, e.g.*, ***Venture Law Grp. v. Superior Ct.*** (6th Dist.2004) 118 Cal.App.4th 96, 103 (privilege belongs to successor corporation after merger); *see also* ***HLC Props.***, 35 Cal.4th at 66-67 (deceased client's estate does not qualify as "organization"). As long as there is a holder for the defunct entity, the privilege survives. Wegner, *Civil Trials & Evidence*, ¶¶8:1991, 8:2051; *see* ***Venture Law***, 118 Cal.App.4th at 103.

2. Authorized person. A person authorized by the privilege holder can assert the privilege. Evid. C. §954(b); ***HLC Props.***, 35 Cal.4th at 61; *CEB Discovery Practice*, §3.44; *Jefferson's Evid. Benchbook*, §42.23.

3. Attorney. The attorney who represented the client at the time of the communication can assert the privilege on the client's behalf. Evid. C. §§954(c), 955. The attorney must claim the privilege for the client whenever information protected by the attorney-client privilege is sought. *Id.* §955; ***Kerner***, 206 Cal.App.4th at 111-12; ***Venture Law***, 118 Cal.App.4th at 103. The attorney cannot claim the privilege if (1) there is no longer anyone who holds the privilege or (2) a person authorized to allow disclosure (i.e., the holder) instructs the attorney to disclose the communication. Evid. C. §954(c); *see* ***Dickerson v. Superior Ct.*** (1st Dist.1982) 135 Cal.App.3d 93, 98 (as long as there is a holder, attorney must claim privilege unless instructed not to do so). See "Waiver by disclosure," ch. 6-A, §2.2.14(1)(a), p. 607.

§2.6 What attorney-client privilege protects. The attorney-client privilege protects many types of communications between the attorney and the client.

1. Confidential communications. The attorney-client privilege protects from discovery confidential communications between an attorney and a client made to obtain legal services or advice. *See* Evid. C. §§951, 952, 954.

(1) Form of communication. The privilege protects any means of communicating information—such as orally, in writing, by electronic mail, or by actions, signs, photographs, X-rays, or other images that transmit

confidential information—by or on behalf of the client to the client's attorney. *See **Mitchell v. Superior Ct.*** (1984) 37 Cal.3d 591, 600; ***City & Cty. of S.F. v. Superior Ct.*** (1951) 37 Cal.2d 227, 235-36; ***Bank of Am. v. Superior Ct.*** (4th Dist.2013) 212 Cal.App.4th 1076, 1099; ***Wellpoint Health Networks, Inc. v. Superior Ct.*** (2d Dist.1997) 59 Cal.App.4th 110, 119; Wegner, *Civil Trials & Evidence*, ¶8:2021; *see, e.g.*, ***Hiott v. Superior Ct.*** (2d Dist.1993) 16 Cal.App.4th 712, 718 (P's videotaped conversation with attorney was protected); *see also* ***Suezaki v. Superior Ct.*** (1962) 58 Cal.2d 166, 177 (film taken of P by Ds' investigator in personal-injury suit did not convey confidential information from Ds to Ds' attorney).

(2) Content of communication. The privilege protects the following types of content:

(a) Legal advice. All types of legal advice, including transactional advice and advice in contemplation of threatened litigation. ***Costco Wholesale Corp. v. Superior Ct.*** (2009) 47 Cal.4th 725, 733; ***Roberts v. City of Palmdale*** (1993) 5 Cal.4th 363, 371; ***Titmas v. Superior Ct.*** (4th Dist.2001) 87 Cal.App.4th 738, 744.

(b) Legal opinions. The attorney's legal opinions formed as a result of the attorney-client relationship. Evid. C. §952; ***Lohman v. Superior Ct.*** (1st Dist.1978) 81 Cal.App.3d 90, 99; *Jefferson's Evid. Benchbook*, §42.18. The attorney's legal opinions are protected even if they are not communicated to the client. ***Lohman***, 81 Cal.App.3d at 99.

(c) Facts. Any factual material included in the confidential communication. ***Costco Wholesale***, 47 Cal.4th at 736. The privilege operates only to prevent discovery of the communication as a means of obtaining the facts stated in it; the facts may still be discovered by some other means. *See id.* However, a client cannot hide factual information by using an attorney to conduct an investigation. *See* ***2,022 Ranch, L.L.C. v. Superior Ct.*** (4th Dist.2003) 113 Cal.App.4th 1377, 1398, *disapproved on other grounds*, ***Costco Wholesale Corp. v. Superior Ct.*** (2009) 47 Cal.4th 725.

2. Fact of transmission. When information is transmitted between an attorney and a client in the course of the attorney-client relationship, the fact that the information was transmitted is privileged, even if the information itself is not. Wegner, *Civil Trials & Evidence*, ¶8:2046.

(1) Transmitted legal information. The attorney-client privilege protects from discovery the transmission of legal information by the attorney to the client. ***Mitchell***, 37 Cal.3d at 600; *see* Evid. C. §952.

(2) Transmitted factual information. The attorney-client privilege protects from discovery the transmission of factual information between the attorney and the client, even if the information itself is not privileged. *See* ***Mitchell***, 37 Cal.3d at 600-01. See "Underlying factual information," §2.7.2, p. 623.

(3) Transmitted documents. The attorney-client privilege protects from discovery the transmission of documents between the attorney and the client, even if those documents are available to the public. ***Mitchell***, 37 Cal.3d at 600; ***Solin v. O'Melveny & Myers LLP*** (2d Dist.2001) 89 Cal.App.4th 451, 457. It is the fact of transmission (not the documents) that is protected because the discovery of the transmission could reveal legal strategy. ***Mitchell***, 37 Cal.3d at 600; ***Solin***, 89 Cal.App.4th at 457. *But see* ***Green & Shinee v. Superior Ct.*** (2d Dist.2001) 88 Cal.App.4th 532, 536-37 (attorney-client privilege does not cover matters that are otherwise nonprivileged merely because client has communicated those matters to attorney).

3. Attorney-client contract. The attorney-client privilege protects from discovery a written fee agreement between the attorney and the client. Bus. & Prof. C. §6149; *see* ***Hemphill v. San Diego Ass'n of Realtors, Inc.*** (S.D.Cal.2005) 225 F.R.D. 616, 624; Wegner, *Civil Trials & Evidence*, ¶8:2037.5. *But see CEB Discovery Practice*, §3.9 (fee agreement is not protected, relying on case law that predated enactment of §6149).

4. Interview to retain attorney. The attorney-client relationship covers a potential client's interviews and negotiations to determine whether to retain the attorney. *See* ***Hooser v. Superior Ct.*** (4th Dist.2000) 84 Cal.App.4th 997, 1003. See "Client," §2.4.2, p. 617.

§2.7 What attorney-client privilege does not protect.

1. Facts about attorney-client relationship. The attorney-client privilege does not prevent discovery of the fact that an attorney-client relationship was formed, that a communication took place, and the time of, date of, and participants to the communication. ***Samuels v. Mix*** (1999) 22 Cal.4th 1, 20 n.5; *see* ***Coy v. Superior Ct.*** (1962)

58 Cal.2d 210, 219-20; ***State Farm Fire & Cas. Co. v. Superior Ct.*** (2d Dist.1997) 54 Cal.App.4th 625, 640. The client's identity is not protected unless disclosure would betray confidential information or would implicate a client in unlawful activities. *See* ***Hays v. Wood*** (1979) 25 Cal.3d 772, 785; Wegner, *Civil Trials & Evidence*, ¶¶8:2034-8:2035.2; *see, e.g.*, ***People v. Stender*** (1st Dist.2012) 212 Cal.App.4th 614, 649-50 (identities of clients of immigration law firm were not protected because not all immigration clients reside in U.S. illegally).

2. Underlying factual information. The attorney-client privilege does not prevent discovery of underlying facts in the case, even if the facts are contained in or relate to privileged communications. ***State Farm Fire & Cas.***, 54 Cal.App.4th at 639-40; *see* ***Coy***, 58 Cal.2d at 219-20; ***Zurich Am. Ins. v. Superior Ct.*** (2d Dist.2007) 155 Cal.App.4th 1485, 1504; ***Benge v. Superior Ct.*** (5th Dist.1982) 131 Cal.App.3d 336, 349. A relevant fact cannot be withheld from discovery merely because it was incorporated into a communication with an attorney. ***Zurich Am.***, 155 Cal.App.4th at 1504; *see* ***Aerojet-Gen. Corp. v. Transport Indem. Ins.*** (1st Dist.1993) 18 Cal.App.4th 996, 1004. A witness's nonprivileged observations made outside the attorney-client relationship are not protected by the attorney-client privilege. *See* ***Triple A Mach. Shop, Inc. v. State*** (1st Dist.1989) 213 Cal.App.3d 131, 143; *see, e.g.*, ***State Farm Fire & Cas.***, 54 Cal.App.4th at 639 (claims specialist, who was company's contact person with attorneys, could testify about facts of case).

3. Nonprivileged client communications. The attorney-client privilege does not prevent discovery of nonprivileged client communications, which remain discoverable even if they are transmitted by the client or its agent to an attorney. *See* ***Greyhound Corp. v. Superior Ct.*** (1961) 56 Cal.2d 355, 397; *see also* ***Suezaki v. Superior Ct.*** (1962) 58 Cal.2d 166, 176-77 (transmission alone, even when parties intend for matter to be confidential, cannot create attorney-client privilege if it does not already exist). Not all communications between attorneys and their clients are confidential communications. *See* ***Greyhound Corp.***, 56 Cal.2d at 397.

(1) Documents. The attorney-client privilege does not prevent discovery of documents simply because they were created or collected by the client for transmission to the attorney. *See* ***Greyhound Corp.***, 56 Cal.2d at 397; *Jefferson's Evid. Benchbook*, §42.17; *see also* ***San Francisco Unified Sch. Dist. v. Superior Ct.*** (1961) 55 Cal.2d 451, 457 (transmission of nonprivileged records, in guise of reports, does not create privilege for contents). To be privileged, the subject of the documents transmitted by the client or its agent to the attorney must convey a confidential communication from or about the client. *See, e.g.*, ***Greyhound Corp.***, 56 Cal.2d at 397 (no attorney-client privilege for nonprivileged witness statement sent by client to attorney); *see also* ***San Diego P.A. v. Superior Ct.*** (1962) 58 Cal.2d 194, 202-03 (no attorney-client privilege for expert report when material evaluated by expert did not involve confidential communication between attorney and client).

(2) Photographs. The attorney-client privilege does not prevent discovery of photographs or films simply because they were taken by the client or its agent for transmission to the attorney. ***Suezaki***, 58 Cal.2d at 176-77. For example, the California Supreme Court has found that a film made by a defendant's agent to surreptitiously document the plaintiff's postaccident condition, and then transferred to the defendant's attorney, was not protected by the attorney-client privilege. *Id.* To be privileged, the subject of a transmitted photograph must be a "confidential communication." *See, e.g.*, *id.* (video of P was not communication because it was not graphic representation of D, his activities, his mental impressions, anything within his knowledge, or anything owned by him). See "Communication made confidentially," §2.3.3, p. 616.

(3) Facts. The attorney-client privilege does not prevent discovery of the facts of the case that the client's agent communicated to the attorney. *See* ***San Francisco Unified Sch. Dist.***, 55 Cal.2d at 456-57 (attorney-client privilege does not extend to unprivileged subject matter merely because that subject matter has been communicated to attorney).

4. Nonlegal work. The attorney-client privilege does not prevent discovery of communications with an attorney who acted only in a nonlegal capacity (e.g., as a business agent for the client). ***Costco Wholesale Corp. v. Superior Ct.*** (2009) 47 Cal.4th 725, 735; ***Aetna Cas. & Sur. Co. v. Superior Ct.*** (1st Dist.1984) 153 Cal.App.3d 467, 475. If the attorney is performing work that could be done by a nonattorney, communications about the attorney's

work are not covered by the attorney-client privilege. *See, e.g.*, ***McKnew v. Superior Ct.*** (1943) 23 Cal.2d 58, 65 (privilege did not apply because client asked attorney to witness a transaction, which is not within attorney's professional capacity); ***Chicago Title Ins. v. Superior Ct.*** (1st Dist.1985) 174 Cal.App.3d 1142, 1154 (privilege did not apply to in-house counsel communications because attorney's legal role was too intertwined with business activities); ***Montebello Rose Co. v. Agricultural Labor Relations Bd.*** (5th Dist.1981) 119 Cal.App.3d 1, 32 (privilege did not apply to attorney's communications while acting as labor negotiator). See "Dual purpose – legal & nonlegal services or advice," §2.3.1(3)(b), p. 616.

5. Nonprivileged employee communications. The attorney-client privilege does not prevent discovery of communications made by a legal entity's employee if the communication falls within one of the following categories:

(1) Employee-witness. An employee's communication to an employer's attorney in preparation for litigation is not privileged when the employee is an independent witness. ***D.I. Chadbourne, Inc. v. Superior Ct.*** (1964) 60 Cal.2d 723, 737; ***Martin v. Workers' Comp. Appeals Bd.*** (2d Dist.1997) 59 Cal.App.4th 333, 346, *disapproved on other grounds*, ***Costco Wholesale Corp. v. Superior Ct.*** (2009) 47 Cal.4th 725; ***Aerojet-Gen.***, 18 Cal.App.4th at 1004. An employee is an independent witness when the employee's only connection to an event is as a witness. ***D.I. Chadbourne, Inc.***, 60 Cal.2d at 737; ***Martin***, 59 Cal.App.4th at 346. See "Independently prepared witness statements," §3.6.1, p. 634.

(2) Unrequested report. An employee's report or statement is not privileged if the employee was not directed by the entity to make it and the employee either did not know it was sought on a confidential basis or did not intend for it to be confidential. ***D.I. Chadbourne, Inc.***, 60 Cal.2d at 737-38.

(3) Report requested by insurer. An employee's report required by the employer because it was requested by the employer's insurance carrier is not privileged if the insurance carrier does not tell the employer that the report is intended to be a confidential communication to the entity's attorney. ***D.I. Chadbourne, Inc.***, 60 Cal.2d at 738.

6. Joint clients. The attorney-client privilege cannot be asserted in litigation between joint clients. Evid. C. §962; ***Fiduciary Trust Int'l v. Superior Ct.*** (2d Dist.2013) 218 Cal.App.4th 465, 482; *see* ***American Mut. Liab. Ins. v. Superior Ct.*** (3d Dist.1974) 38 Cal.App.3d 579, 591. Joint clients are those who jointly retain or consult an attorney on a matter of common interest. Evid. C. §962.

(1) Successors. The joint-client exception applies to each client's successor in interest. Evid. C. §962.

(2) Insurer & insured. The joint-client exception can apply to an attorney hired by an insurer to represent the insured. ***Glacier Gen. Assur. Co. v. Superior Ct.*** (2d Dist.1979) 95 Cal.App.3d 836, 842. If an attorney is retained by an insurer to defend an insured under an insurance policy and there is no conflict of interest, the attorney owes a fiduciary duty to both the insurer and insured; in other words, the attorney has two clients. ***American Mut. Liab.***, 38 Cal.App.3d at 591-92. Thus, in a later suit between the insurer and the insured, neither client can claim the attorney-client privilege. *See* ***Glacier Gen. Assur. Co.***, 95 Cal.App.3d at 842.

NOTE

The Fourth District recently held that an insurer and insured can be joint clients of an attorney even if the insurer has selected the attorney under a reservation of rights as long as the issue on which coverage turns is independent of the issues in the underlying case. ***Bank of Am. v. Superior Ct.*** *(4th Dist.2013) 212 Cal.App.4th 1076, 1091-92. In other words, a reservation of rights does not automatically create a disqualifying conflict between the insurer, insured, and attorney. Id.*

---

7. Crime or fraud. The attorney-client privilege does not prevent discovery of a communication if the client sought or obtained the attorney's services to enable or aid anyone to commit or plan a crime or fraud. Evid.

C. §956; ***People v. Michaels*** (2002) 28 Cal.4th 486, 537; *CEB Trial Objections*, §34.15. The crime-fraud exception applies to communications regardless of who initiated the communication. Evid. C. §956. This exception does not apply to communications about past criminal or fraudulent activity. *See* ***State Farm Fire & Cas.***, 54 Cal.App.4th at 644.

(1) Prima facie proof. A party asserting the crime-fraud exception must make a prima facie showing that the client sought or obtained the attorney's services to enable or aid the client or another person to commit or plan a crime or fraud. ***BP Alaska Expl., Inc. v. Superior Ct.*** (5th Dist.1988) 199 Cal.App.3d 1240, 1262; Wegner, *Civil Trials & Evidence*, ¶8:2071. A prima facie showing is made by presenting evidence from which reasonable inferences can be drawn that the attorney-client communications at issue furthered a crime or fraud. ***BP Alaska Expl.***, 199 Cal.App.3d at 1262. A prima facie showing cannot be made by asking the court to conduct an in camera review of the privileged material to determine whether the exception applies. *See* Evid. C. §915; ***Southern Cal. Gas Co. v. Public Utils. Comm'n*** (1990) 50 Cal.3d 31, 45 n.19.

(2) Reasonable relationship. A prima facie showing of a crime or fraud does not result in wholesale waiver of the attorney-client privilege. ***BP Alaska Expl.***, 199 Cal.App.3d at 1269. Rather, the exception extends only to the communications reasonably related to the crime or fraud. *Id.*; Wegner, *Civil Trials & Evidence*, ¶8:2070.

(3) In camera review. Once a party makes a prima facie showing that the crime-fraud exception applies, the court may conduct an in camera review of the privileged communications to resolve whether they are reasonably related to the crime or fraud and thus discoverable. *See* ***OXY Res. Cal. LLC v. Superior Ct.*** (1st Dist.2004) 115 Cal.App.4th 874, 896; ***Geilim v. Superior Ct.*** (2d Dist.1991) 234 Cal.App.3d 166, 176; ***BP Alaska Expl.***, 199 Cal.App.3d at 1269-70; Wegner, *Civil Trials & Evidence*, ¶¶8:2070, 8:2071.2.

PRACTICE TIP

If the parties disagree on the extent to which the privilege is lost once the exception is established, the party asserting the privilege should consider requesting an in camera review of the materials at issue to avoid the disclosure of privileged communications that are not covered by the exception. See ***BP Alaska Expl.****, 199 Cal.App.3d at 1269-70.*

---

8. Prevention of injury. The attorney-client privilege does not prevent discovery of a communication if the attorney reasonably believes the communication must be disclosed to prevent a criminal act that is likely to result in death or substantial bodily harm. Evid. C. §956.5; *e.g.*, ***People v. Dang*** (2d Dist.2001) 93 Cal.App.4th 1293, 1295-96 (client told attorney he would "whack" witness if bribe was unsuccessful); *see also* Rules Prof. Conduct, rule 3-100 (allowing attorney to disclose information to prevent crime likely to result in death or substantial bodily harm).

9. Breach of duty. The attorney-client privilege does not prevent discovery of a communication relevant to a breach of duty under the attorney-client relationship. Evid. C. §958; ***Brockway v. State Bar*** (1991) 53 Cal.3d 51, 63. This exception applies only to communications between a client and an attorney charged with professional misconduct in either a malpractice suit or a disciplinary proceeding. *See* ***Brockway***, 53 Cal.3d at 63. It does not apply to a client's communications with another attorney about the alleged professional misconduct (e.g., an attorney representing a client in a malpractice suit against a former attorney). *Id.*; ***Schlumberger Ltd. v. Superior Ct.*** (2d Dist.1981) 115 Cal.App.3d 386, 392-93; *see also* ***Travelers Ins. v. Superior Ct.*** (1st Dist.1983) 143 Cal.App.3d 436, 445-46 (exception does not apply to attorney's communications with malpractice insurer and its attorneys).

NOTE

For wrongful-discharge actions brought by an in-house attorney, the attorney-client privilege does not prevent limited disclosure of relevant attorney-client privileged information to the former in-house attorney-litigant's attorney to prepare and prosecute the claim. ***Fox Searchlight Pictures v. Paladino*** *(2d Dist.2001) 89 Cal.App.4th 294, 310-11; see* ***Chubb & Son v. Superior Ct.*** *(1st Dist.2014) 228 Cal.App.4th 1094, 1110; see also* ***General Dynamics Corp. v. Superior Ct.*** *(1994) 7 Cal.4th 1164, 1190 (permitting in-house counsel to pursue wrongful-discharge actions). Courts have held such limited disclosures permissible because they provide for fundamental fairness to the former in-house attorney-litigant while avoiding "unwarranted public disclosure" of privileged information.* ***Chubb & Son****, 228 Cal.App.4th at 1106-07;* ***Fox Searchlight Pictures****, 89 Cal.App.4th at 311.*

10. Dead client. The attorney-client privilege does not prevent discovery of a dead client's communication with an attorney if the communication is relevant to any of the following:

(1) Testate succession, intestate succession, nonprobate transfer, or inter vivos transaction claims between parties who all claim through the dead client. Evid. C. §957; *see* ***Fletcher v. Superior Ct.*** (1st Dist.1996) 44 Cal.App.4th 773, 778. This exception applies only to communications between a dead client and an attorney, not to communications between an attorney and the parties making claims through the dead client. ***Fletcher***, 44 Cal.App.4th at 779.

(2) The client's intent for executing a will, deed of conveyance, or other writing affecting an interest in property. Evid. C. §960.

(3) The validity of a will, deed of conveyance, or other writing executed by a client affecting an interest in property. *Id.* §961.

11. Attesting attorney. The attorney-client privilege does not prevent discovery of a communication relevant to the client's intention or competence in executing an attested document when the attorney was acting only in the capacity of an attesting witness. Evid. C. §959; ***Estate of Kime*** (2d Dist.1983) 144 Cal.App.3d 246, 257. For example, questions about an attorney's observations of a client's mental and emotional state when the client signed a stipulation in a divorce proceeding clearly involved matters about which an attesting witness would usually testify. ***Estate of Kime***, 144 Cal.App.3d at 257 n.7. However, a client's statement while executing a deed about the conversion of the property from community to separate property is not relevant to the execution of a deed, and such a statement would be protected by the attorney-client privilege. *See id.* at 257-58.

§2.8 Waiver of attorney-client privilege.

1. Waiver of privilege. If the privilege is waived, the information is discoverable.

(1) General rules of waiver. See "Waiver of privilege," ch. 6-A, §2.2.14, p. 607.

(2) Waiver by attorney's signature on discovery response. An attorney who signs a response to interrogatories, demands for inspection, or requests for admission as an officer or agent of a public or private corporation, partnership, association, or agency waives the attorney-client and work-product privileges for the identities of the sources used for the information contained in the responses. CCP §2030.250(b) (interrogatories), §2031.250(b) (demand for inspection), §2033.240 (requests for admission); *see* ***Melendrez v. Superior Ct.*** (2d Dist.2013) 215 Cal.App.4th 1343, 1351 (if bankrupt corporation with no officers or directors no longer exists for purposes of Evid. C. §953(d), corporation's insurer could waive attorney-client privilege and authorize attorney to verify discovery responses).

(3) Waiver by party testifying as expert. A party waives the attorney-client privilege if the party is designated as an expert trial witness and discloses or testifies about privileged information, either in discovery or at trial. ***Shooker v. Superior Ct.*** (2d Dist.2003) 111 Cal.App.4th 923, 930.

2. **No waiver of privilege.** If the privilege is not waived, the information is not discoverable.

(1) **General rules of nonwaiver.** See "Privilege not waived," ch. 6-A, §3.3.2, p. 612.

(2) **Inadvertent disclosure.** A party does not waive the attorney-client privilege for confidential information that has been inadvertently disclosed. *See* Evid. C. §912(a) (holder can waive privilege by consent to disclosure), §954 (privilege can prevent anyone from testifying about privileged communication); ***State Comp. Ins. Fund v. WPS, Inc.*** (2d Dist.1999) 70 Cal.App.4th 644, 652-53 (holder's consent to disclosure is determined by examining subjective intent and relevant circumstances); *see, e.g.*, ***O'Mary v. Mitsubishi Elecs. Am., Inc.*** (4th Dist.1997) 59 Cal.App.4th 563, 577 (inadvertent disclosure of list of employees to be terminated was not consent). The privilege can be asserted to prevent anyone, even eavesdroppers and other wrongful interceptors, from testifying about a confidential communication. 7 Cal. Law Revision Comm'n Rep. (1965) p. 1167; *see* Evid. C. §954. See "Inadvertent disclosure," ch. 6-A, §3.3.2(1), p. 612.

(3) **Withdrawn designation of party as expert.** The designation of a party as an expert trial witness does not automatically waive the party's attorney-client privilege. ***Shooker***, 111 Cal.App.4th at 930. If the designation is withdrawn before the party discloses privileged information or testifies as an expert, either in discovery or at trial, the privilege is not waived. *Id.*

(4) **Common-interest doctrine.** The common-interest doctrine (also referred to as the joint-defense doctrine or pooled-information doctrine) preserves the attorney-client and work-product privileges for information shared among colitigants. Under California law, the common-interest doctrine is a nonwaiver doctrine, analyzed under the standard waiver principles applicable to attorney-client and work-product privileges. ***Seahaus La Jolla Owners Ass'n v. Superior Ct.*** (4th Dist.2014) 224 Cal.App.4th 754, 774; ***OXY Res. Cal. LLC v. Superior Ct.*** (1st Dist.2004) 115 Cal.App.4th 874, 889. To invoke the protection of the common-interest doctrine, a party must establish the following:

(a) **Protected information.** The information was initially protected from disclosure by a claim of privilege. ***OXY Res.***, 115 Cal.App.4th at 890. For example, the communication between the attorney and the client was made to obtain legal services or advice. Evid. C. §952.

(b) **Disclosed to colitigant.** The information was disclosed to a colitigant who had a common interest in obtaining legal advice relating to the same matter. ***OXY Res.***, 115 Cal.App.4th at 891; *see, e.g.*, ***Citizens for Ceres v. Superior Ct.*** (5th Dist.2013) 217 Cal.App.4th 889, 916 (communications between lead agency and project applicant under California Environmental Quality Act were not protected by common-interest doctrine because communications occurred before project approval, when interests of agency and applicant were not aligned).

(c) **Reasonably necessary.** The disclosure of the information was reasonably necessary to accomplish the purpose for which the client consulted the attorney. ***OXY Res.***, 115 Cal.App.4th at 891; *see, e.g.*, ***Seahaus La Jolla Owners Ass'n***, 224 Cal.App.4th at 776 (disclosures to individual homeowners of client association at litigation-update meetings were reasonably necessary). To decide this issue, the court can examine the documents in chambers. ***OXY Res.***, 115 Cal.App.4th at 896; *see* Evid. C. §915.

(d) **Expectation of confidentiality.** The parties had a reasonable expectation that the disclosed information would remain confidential. ***OXY Res.***, 115 Cal.App.4th at 891. *But see* ***Seahaus La Jolla Owners Ass'n***, 224 Cal.App.4th at 775-76 (presence of individuals with conflicting loyalties at litigation-update meeting did not destroy common interest).

§2.9 How to assert attorney-client privilege.

1. **Holder claims privilege.** The holder of the attorney-client privilege, or a person authorized by the holder, can claim the privilege by objecting to the discovery request on the ground that the privilege prevents disclosure of the information. See "Privileged information," ch. 7-A, §11.1.3, p. 765; "Responding party objects to discovery," ch. 7-A, §14.1.1, p. 771. Instead of serving objections, the holder can claim the privilege by filing a motion for

protective order or a motion to quash. See "Responding party moves for protective order or to quash (option 2)," ch. 7-A, §14.1.3, p. 772; "Motion for Protective Order," ch. 9-B, p. 1024; "Motion to Quash Depositions," ch. 9-C, p. 1038.

2. Discovering party moves to compel. In response to the written objection asserting the attorney-client privilege, the discovering party has the burden to enforce discovery. It must initiate the meet-and-confer procedure and, if unsuccessful, file a motion to compel discovery. See "Discovering party moves to compel (option 1)," ch. 7-A, §14.1.2, p. 772.

(1) Motion papers.

(a) Separate statement. Depending on the type of discovery request, the discovering party must include in a motion to compel a separate statement containing all the information necessary to understand each discovery request and related response. CRC 3.1345(c). See "Separate statement," ch. 9-D, §4.2.5(1)(d), p. 1054; "Separate statement," ch. 9-E, §3.2.4(4), p. 1064.

(b) Good-cause statement. Depending on the type of discovery request, the discovering party must include in a motion to compel a statement of good cause justifying the discovery. See "Good cause for production," ch. 9-D, §4.1.2(4), p. 1052; "Good cause," ch. 9-E, §3.1.2(1), p. 1061.

(2) Grounds. If, during the meet-and-confer conference, the discovering party obtained sufficient information to understand the basis of the claim of privilege, the discovering party can attempt to disprove the claim of privilege or show that the privilege was waived or that an exception to the privilege applies. See "Discovering party justifies discovery," ch. 7-A, §14.1.5, p. 773.

3. Holder serves opposition papers. In response to a motion to compel, the holder has the burden to justify its attorney-client privilege by proving the preliminary facts that support the privilege. See "Elements of attorney-client privilege," §2.3, p. 615; "Responding party satisfies burden," ch. 7-A, §14.1.4, p. 772. That is, the holder must prove there was an attorney-client privilege at the time of the communication. The holder does not need to prove the attorney-client communication was made in confidence, which is presumed. Evid. C. §917(a). See "Confidential-communication privileges," ch. 7-A, §14.1.4(1)(a)[1], p. 773.

§2.10 Court's ruling on attorney-client privilege.

1. Privilege log. The court can require the production of a privilege log. See "Privilege log," ch. 7-A, §14.1.4(2), p. 773.

2. No in camera review. The court cannot require an in camera review of documents to determine if the attorney-client privilege protects the documents from discovery. Evid. C. §915(a); ***Costco Wholesale Corp. v. Superior Ct.*** (2009) 47 Cal.4th 725, 740; *cf.* ***Regents of the Univ. of Cal. v. Workers' Comp. Appeals Bd.*** (4th Dist.2014) 226 Cal.App.4th 1530, 1535-36 (in camera review of attorney-client privilege is not available in Workers' Compensation Appeals Board proceedings). However, the privilege holder can request an in camera review if it believes the review would aid the court in making its determination. ***Costco Wholesale***, 47 Cal.4th at 740; ***Clark v. Superior Ct.*** (4th Dist.2011) 196 Cal.App.4th 37, 51.

§3. WORK-PRODUCT PRIVILEGE

NOTE

The protection provided by the work-product privilege is distinct from and broader than the protection of the attorney-client privilege. ***U.S. v. Nobles*** *(1975) 422 U.S. 225, 238 n.11. The attorney-client privilege covers only communications between the attorney and the client, while the work-product privilege protects all material generated by the attorney, including materials that are never seen by the client.* ***Aetna Cas. & Sur. Co. v. Superior Ct.*** *(1st Dist.1984) 153 Cal.App.3d 467, 478 n.4. See "Attorney-Client vs. LRS-Client vs. Work-Product Privileges," chart 6-1, p. 614.*

§3.1 General. Attorney work product is defined as the materials generated by the attorney's effort, research, and thought processes in preparing the client's case. ***Meza v. H. Muehlstein & Co.*** (2d Dist.2009) 176 Cal.App.4th 969, 977; ***BP Alaska Expl., Inc. v. Superior Ct.*** (5th Dist.1988) 199 Cal.App.3d 1240, 1253 n.4. The work-product privilege protects from discovery any writing that reflects the attorney's impressions, conclusions, opinions, or legal research or theories. ***Wellpoint Health Networks, Inc. v. Superior Ct.*** (2d Dist.1997) 59 Cal.App.4th 110, 120. Although the privilege applies explicitly to "writings," unwritten work product is also protected. ***Fireman's Fund Ins. v. Superior Ct.*** (2d Dist.2011) 196 Cal.App.4th 1263, 1277-78.

1. Purpose. The policy behind the work-product privilege is twofold. First, the privilege encourages thorough investigation of claims by protecting materials that could reveal an attorney's opinions and strategy in representing a client. *See* CCP §2018.020(a); ***Coito v. Superior Ct.*** (2012) 54 Cal.4th 480, 497-98; ***Rico v. Mitsubishi Motors Corp.*** (2007) 42 Cal.4th 807, 814. Second, the privilege prevents one attorney from taking undue advantage of another attorney's industry and effort. CCP §2018.020(b); ***Coito***, 54 Cal.4th at 497; ***Rico***, 42 Cal.4th at 814.

2. Primary authority. CCP §§2018.010-2018.080.

3. Secondary authority. The following secondary sources are cited as authority in this section:

- *California Civil Discovery Practice* (CEB Online ed. 2014) (referred to as *CEB Discovery Practice*).
- *California Trial Objections* (CEB Online ed. 2014) (referred to as *CEB Trial Objections*).
- Jefferson, *California Evidence Benchbook* (CEB Online ed. 2014) (referred to as *Jefferson's Evid. Benchbook*).
- Wegner, *California Practice Guide: Civil Trials & Evidence* (CD-ROM ed. 2014) (referred to as Wegner, *Civil Trials & Evidence*).
- Weil & Brown, *California Practice Guide: Civil Procedure Before Trial* (CD-ROM ed. 2014) (referred to as Weil, *Civil Procedure Before Trial*).

§3.2 Nature of work-product privilege.

1. Types of protection. The work-product privilege provides absolute protection against disclosure of core work product and qualified protection against discovery of noncore work product. *See Jefferson's Evid. Benchbook*, §43.12.

(1) Absolute – core work product. Writings that reflect an attorney's impressions, conclusions, opinions, or legal research or theories constitute core work product. CCP §2018.030(a); ***2,022 Ranch, L.L.C. v. Superior Ct.*** (4th Dist.2003) 113 Cal.App.4th 1377, 1390, *disapproved on other grounds*, **Costco Wholesale Corp. v. Superior Ct.** (2009) 47 Cal.4th 725; ***Wellpoint Health Networks, Inc. v. Superior Ct.*** (2d Dist.1997) 59 Cal.App.4th 110, 120. Work-product protection for core work product is absolute, which means the court can never order its disclosure. CCP §2018.030(a); *see* ***Rico v. Mitsubishi Motors Corp.*** (2007) 42 Cal.4th 807, 814. See "Core work product," §3.5.1, p. 631.

(2) Qualified – noncore work product. An attorney's writings besides what is considered core work product constitute noncore work product. *See* CCP §2018.030(b). Work-product protection for noncore work product is qualified and can be overcome by a showing of unfair prejudice or injustice. CCP §2018.030(b); ***2,022 Ranch***, 113 Cal.App.4th at 1390; ***Wellpoint Health Networks***, 59 Cal.App.4th at 120. See "Noncore work product," §3.5.2, p. 632; "Discovery of noncore work product," §3.9.2, p. 639.

2. Duration. The work-product privilege continues for as long as the attorney asserts it; the privilege does not terminate when the litigation or matter for which the work product was created comes to an end. ***Fellows v. Superior Ct.*** (2d Dist.1980) 108 Cal.App.3d 55, 62, *disapproved on other grounds*, **Coito v. Superior Ct.** (2012) 54 Cal.4th 480; Weil, *Civil Procedure Before Trial*, ¶8:271; *see Jefferson's Evid. Benchbook*, §43.4. The work-product privilege for documents or information generated during one lawsuit can be asserted to prevent discovery of the materials in a later lawsuit. ***Fellows***, 108 Cal.App.3d at 62-63; *see* ***Kizer v. Sulnick*** (2d Dist.1988) 202 Cal.App.3d 431, 440.

3. Discovery & evidentiary. All courts agree that the work-product privilege is a discovery exemption. *See* CCP §2018.030 (work product is not discoverable). The courts disagree on whether the exemption also protects work product from being introduced at trial. *CEB Trial Objections*, §35.6.

(1) Discovery & evidentiary exemption. Some courts have held that the work-product privilege is both a discovery exemption and an evidentiary exemption. *E.g.*, ***Kizer***, 202 Cal.App.3d at 440; *see, e.g.*, ***Rodriguez v. McDonnell Douglas Corp.*** (2d Dist.1978) 87 Cal.App.3d 626, 648 (work-product privilege is evidentiary privilege, relying on §2018.020(b), which prevents attorneys from taking undue advantage of adversary's industry and efforts), *disapproved on other grounds*, ***Coito v. Superior Ct.*** (2012) 54 Cal.4th 480; *see also Jefferson's Evid. Benchbook*, §43.13 (citing ***Rodriguez*** for applicability of work-product privilege at trial).

(2) Discovery exemption only. Other courts have held that the work-product privilege is a discovery exemption only and that work product can be introduced as evidence at trial. *E.g.*, ***Deluca v. State Fish Co.*** (2d Dist.2013) 217 Cal.App.4th 671, 687 (work-product "rule" is only a limitation on pretrial discovery, not a "privilege"); ***Jasper Constr., Inc. v. Foothill Junior Coll. Dist.*** (1st Dist.1979) 91 Cal.App.3d 1, 16 (work-product privilege only places limitations on pretrial discovery), *disapproved on other grounds*, ***Los Angeles Unified Sch. Dist. v. Great Am. Ins.*** (2010) 49 Cal.4th 739; ***Brokopp v. Ford Motor Co.*** (4th Dist.1977) 71 Cal.App.3d 841, 857 (dicta; protection was waived in any event because expert testified); ***Tip Top Foods, Inc. v. Lyng*** (1st Dist.1972) 28 Cal.App.3d 533, 553 (work-product privilege is a discovery privilege only and cannot be used to bar otherwise proper evidence).

§3.3 Elements of work-product privilege. To establish the work-product privilege, the person asserting the privilege must show the following:

1. Attorney & client formed relationship. The attorney and the client established an attorney-client relationship. The work-product privilege adopts the definition of "client" from the attorney-client privilege in Evid. C. §951. CCP §2018.010. See "Client," §2.4.2, p. 617.

2. Prepared by attorney. The materials were prepared by the attorney, the attorney's agents, or experts consulted by the attorney. *See* ***Citizens for Ceres v. Superior Ct.*** (5th Dist.2013) 217 Cal.App.4th 889, 911; ***Shandralina G. v. Homonchuk*** (4th Dist.2007) 147 Cal.App.4th 395, 407; ***2,022 Ranch, L.L.C. v. Superior Ct.*** (4th Dist.2003) 113 Cal.App.4th 1377, 1389-90, *disapproved on other grounds*, ***Costco Wholesale Corp. v. Superior Ct.*** (2009) 47 Cal.4th 725; ***Mack v. Superior Ct.*** (1st Dist.1968) 259 Cal.App.2d 7, 10. If a party appears pro per, the party's materials are protected by the work-product privilege. ***Dowden v. Superior Ct.*** (4th Dist.1999) 73 Cal.App.4th 126, 136. See "Unrepresented party," §3.4.1(2), p. 631.

3. Legal work. The materials are legal work. The privilege does not protect work performed in a nonlegal capacity (e.g., as a party's business agent or a claims adjuster). See "Nonlegal work," §3.6.3, p. 634.

(1) Legal & nonlegal work. The work-product privilege protects an attorney's nonlegal work if the work has both a legal and a nonlegal purpose and the dominant purpose behind creating the material was to provide a legal opinion or advice. *See* ***2,022 Ranch***, 113 Cal.App.4th at 1390-91; ***Aetna Cas. & Sur. Co. v. Superior Ct.*** (1st Dist.1984) 153 Cal.App.3d 467, 475-76.

(2) Litigation & nonlitigation materials. California's work-product privilege protects both litigation and nonlitigation materials. ***Laguna Beach Cty. Water Dist. v. Superior Ct.*** (4th Dist.2004) 124 Cal.App.4th 1453, 1461; Wegner, *Civil Trials & Evidence*, ¶8:2672.5. Unlike federal work-product protection, the protection afforded by California's work-product privilege is not limited to material prepared in anticipation of litigation. ***Laguna Beach***, 124 Cal.App.4th at 1461; *see* ***County of L.A. v. Superior Ct.*** (2d Dist.2000) 82 Cal.App.4th 819, 833. A writing prepared in a nonlitigation capacity that reflects an attorney's impressions, conclusions, opinions, or legal research or theories is protected as core work product. *See* ***Laguna Beach***, 124 Cal.App.4th at 1461; ***County of L.A.***, 82 Cal.App.4th at 833. For example, writings reflecting an attorney's thoughts about a business deal are protected as core work product. *See, e.g.*, ***Rumac, Inc. v. Bottomley*** (4th Dist.1983) 143 Cal.App.3d 810, 812 (negotiation of lease).

§3.4 Who can assert work-product privilege. The work-product privilege belongs only to the attorney, not to the client. ***Wells Fargo Bank v. Superior Ct.*** (2000) 22 Cal.4th 201, 215 n.5; ***Lasky, Haas, Cohler & Munter v. Superior Ct.*** (2d Dist.1985) 172 Cal.App.3d 264, 278; ***Fellows v. Superior Ct.*** (2d Dist.1980) 108 Cal.App.3d 55, 64,

disapproved on other grounds, ***Coito v. Superior Ct.*** (2012) 54 Cal.4th 480; ***Lohman v. Superior Ct.*** (1st Dist.1978) 81 Cal.App.3d 90, 100-01. The following people can assert the work-product privilege:

1. Holder.

(1) Attorney. The attorney is the holder of the privilege. ***Wells Fargo***, 22 Cal.4th at 215 n.5; ***Citizens for Ceres v. Superior Ct.*** (5th Dist.2013) 217 Cal.App.4th 889, 911; ***Lasky, Haas, Cohler & Munter***, 172 Cal.App.3d at 278. The attorney can assert the work-product privilege even against the client for whom the work product was prepared. ***Lasky, Haas, Cohler & Munter***, 172 Cal.App.3d at 278.

(2) Unrepresented party. A party appearing pro per can assert the work-product privilege. ***Dowden v. Superior Ct.*** (4th Dist.1999) 73 Cal.App.4th 126, 136. The work product of an unrepresented party is entitled to the same protection as the work product of an attorney. *Id.* at 135-36; *Jefferson's Evid. Benchbook*, §43.8.

2. Client. The client can assert the work-product privilege on the attorney's behalf only when the attorney is not present to assert it. ***Mylan Labs., Inc. v. Soon-Shiong*** (2d Dist.1999) 76 Cal.App.4th 71, 81 n.2; ***BP Alaska Expl., Inc. v. Superior Ct.*** (5th Dist.1988) 199 Cal.App.3d 1240, 1258; *see* ***Fellows***, 108 Cal.App.3d at 65. If the attorney is willing to waive the work-product privilege, the client does not have the power to prevent disclosure of the work product. ***Lohman***, 81 Cal.App.3d at 100-01.

§3.5 What work-product privilege protects. The work-product privilege creates two levels of protection: (1) absolute protection against discovery for core work product (i.e., documents containing the attorney's impressions, conclusions, opinions, or legal research or theories), and (2) qualified protection against discovery for noncore work product (i.e., all work product that is not core work product). CCP §2018.030; ***2,022 Ranch, L.L.C. v. Superior Ct.*** (4th Dist.2003) 113 Cal.App.4th 1377, 1390, *disapproved on other grounds*, ***Costco Wholesale Corp. v. Superior Ct.*** (2009) 47 Cal.4th 725; ***Wellpoint Health Networks, Inc. v. Superior Ct.*** (2d Dist.1997) 59 Cal.App.4th 110, 120; ***BP Alaska Expl., Inc. v. Superior Ct.*** (5th Dist.1988) 199 Cal.App.3d 1240, 1250; ***American Mut. Liab. Ins. v. Superior Ct.*** (3d Dist.1974) 38 Cal.App.3d 579, 594. Because no code provision defines "work product," the courts determine what is work product on a case-by-case basis. ***Coito v. Superior Ct.*** (2012) 54 Cal.4th 480, 489.

CAUTION

The plain language of §2018.030(a) suggests that only "writings" containing core work product are entitled to absolute protection, and thus, unwritten core work product (e.g., an attorney's thoughts), which is not mentioned, would be entitled only to qualified protection under §2018.030(b). One court of appeals has held that such a reading of the statute is not supported by its legislative history. ***Fireman's Fund Ins. v. Superior Ct.*** *(2d Dist.2011) 196 Cal.App.4th 1263, 1277-78. The court in* ***Fireman's Fund*** *found that the statute protects only writings because the Legislature assumed that unwritten core work product remained inviolate, and any other reading of the statute would lead to the absurd result of requiring attorneys to write down every thought to qualify for protection. Id. 1278-81. From the court's opinion, it does not appear that an attorney needs to invoke the statute to qualify for the protection.*

1. Core work product. Core work product (also referred to as "opinion" work product) is any writing that reflects an attorney's impressions, conclusions, opinions, or legal research or theories. CCP §2018.030(a); ***2,022 Ranch***, 113 Cal.App.4th at 1390; ***Wellpoint Health Networks***, 59 Cal.App.4th at 120. Core work product is not discoverable under any circumstances. See "Absolute – core work product," §3.2.1(1), p. 629. Examples of core work product include the following:

(1) Attorney notes. Writings that contain notes about an attorney's impressions, conclusions, or opinions are protected as core work product. CCP §2018.030(a); *see* ***Upjohn Co. v. U.S.*** (1981) 449 U.S. 383, 399 (discovery of attorney notes is particularly disfavored). Even notes about a purely factual matter can reflect the attorney's thoughts on the case; the facts included can indicate what issues the attorney thinks are important, and the facts

omitted can indicate what issues the attorney thinks are unimportant. *See* ***Upjohn Co.***, 449 U.S. at 400 n.8; ***Nacht & Lewis Architects, Inc. v. Superior Ct.*** (3d Dist.1996) 47 Cal.App.4th 214, 217.

(2) Strategy documents. Documents reflecting an attorney's strategy discussions and case evaluations are protected as core work product. *See, e.g.*, ***Laguna Beach Cty. Water Dist. v. Superior Ct.*** (4th Dist.2004) 124 Cal.App.4th 1453, 1458-59 (letters to client's auditors describing pending and threatened litigation that could affect financial condition were core work product); ***Lasky, Haas, Cohler & Munter v. Superior Ct.*** (2d Dist.1985) 172 Cal.App.3d 264, 286 (notes of attorneys' discussions about trust business were core work product).

(3) Witness statements.

(a) Lists. A list of witnesses interviewed by an attorney may be protected as core work product if the list would reveal the attorney's impressions about the case. *See* ***Coito***, 54 Cal.4th at 502. For example, in a bus accident involving 50 surviving passengers and an allegation that the bus driver fell asleep at the wheel, an attorney's list of witnesses from whom she took statements could indicate her evaluation on which witnesses were in the best position to see the cause of the accident, thus giving the defense an opportunity to "free ride" on the attorney's work. *Id.*

(b) Statements. Witness statements taken by an attorney (or an attorney's agent) are considered core work product if they were summarized to reflect the attorney's strategy, if they were edited to add the attorney's thoughts and comments, or if they include notes indicating which issues the attorney thinks are important. *See, e.g.*, ***Rico v. Mitsubishi Motors Corp.*** (2007) 42 Cal.4th 807, 815 (notes containing ideas of attorney and his legal team were absolutely protected by work-product privilege); *see also* CCP §2018.030(a) (writing is absolutely protected if it reflects attorney's impressions, conclusions, opinions, or legal research or theories). Even a verbatim transcript or recording of a witness statement can be considered core work product if (1) the line of questioning the attorney chose to pursue reveals the attorney's strategy or (2) the fact that the attorney chose to interview a particular witness discloses tactical or evaluative information. ***Coito***, 54 Cal.4th at 496.

(4) Anticipated testimony. Documents describing the testimony expected from witnesses are protected as core work product. ***Snyder v. Superior Ct.*** (2d Dist.2007) 157 Cal.App.4th 1530, 1536; ***City of Long Beach v. Superior Ct.*** (2d Dist.1976) 64 Cal.App.3d 65, 80.

(5) Compilations. Compilations of information from documents and other sources are protected as core work product if they disclose the attorney's mental impressions and thought processes. *See, e.g.*, ***Rico***, 42 Cal.4th at 814-15 (paralegal's summary of attorney's conversation with experts, made at attorney's direction and edited by attorney, was core work product).

(6) Legal research. Legal research is protected as core work product. *See* CCP §2018.030(a); ***Sav-On Drugs, Inc. v. Superior Ct.*** (1975) 15 Cal.3d 1, 5.

(7) Information about consulting experts. The identities of consulting experts and their opinions and reports are generally protected as core work product. *See* ***Schreiber v. Estate of Kiser*** (1999) 22 Cal.4th 31, 37; ***Shadow Traffic Network v. Superior Ct.*** (2d Dist.1994) 24 Cal.App.4th 1067, 1079. See "Consulting expert," ch. 7-I, §2.1, p. 898.

(8) Disclosure to client. An attorney's written opinion, delivered to the client in confidence, retains its status as core work product. ***Wells Fargo Bank v. Superior Ct.*** (2000) 22 Cal.4th 201, 214; ***BP Alaska Expl.***, 199 Cal.App.3d at 1253; ***Fellows v. Superior Ct.*** (2d Dist.1980) 108 Cal.App.3d 55, 65-66, *disapproved on other grounds*, ***Coito v. Superior Ct.*** (2012) 54 Cal.4th 480.

2. Noncore work product. Noncore work product (also referred to as "general," "conditional," "ordinary," or "qualified" work product) is defined as any material prepared by an attorney other than core work product under CCP §2018.030(a). CCP §2018.030(b); ***2,022 Ranch***, 113 Cal.App.4th at 1390; ***Wellpoint Health Networks***, 59 Cal.App.4th at 120; ***BP Alaska Expl.***, 199 Cal.App.3d at 1250; *see CEB Discovery Practice*, §3.54. Protection for noncore work product is qualified and can be overcome by a showing of unfair prejudice or injustice. See "Qualified – noncore work product," §3.2.1(2), p. 629. Examples of materials that are protected as noncore work product include the following:

(1) Demonstrative material. Charts and diagrams are protected as noncore work product. ***Dowden v. Superior Ct.*** (4th Dist.1999) 73 Cal.App.4th 126, 135; ***BP Alaska Expl.***, 199 Cal.App.3d at 1257; ***Mack v. Superior Ct.*** (1st Dist.1968) 259 Cal.App.2d 7, 10; *see* ***Rojas v. Superior Ct.*** (2004) 33 Cal.4th 407, 423 (dicta).

(2) Photographs. Photographs and recordings taken by an attorney or the attorney's agents are protected as noncore work product. *See* CCP §2016.020(c) ("writing" means writing as defined under Evid. C. §250), §2018.030 (work-product privilege protects writings); Evid. C. §250 ("writing" includes photographs and every other means of recording); ***Suezaki v. Superior Ct.*** (1962) 58 Cal.2d 166, 177-78 (film shot by attorney's investigator was work product, but work-product privilege was not recognized under California law at the time). See "Prepared by attorney," §3.3.2, p. 630.

(3) Witness lists. A list of witnesses that contains more information than required to be disclosed as part of discovery may be protected as noncore work product. *See* ***Coito***, 54 Cal.4th at 502-03; ***City of Long Beach***, 64 Cal.App.3d at 73. If a witness list contains attorney notes about a witness's statement, the notes are core work product and may be absolutely protected from discovery. See "Witness statements," §3.5.1(3), p. 632. If a witness list does not contain any attorney notes, the list may be protected as noncore work product and thus would not be discoverable without a showing of prejudice or injustice. *See* ***Snyder***, 157 Cal.App.4th at 1536.

(a) Trial witnesses. A list of nonexpert witnesses who will be called to testify at trial is protected as noncore work product. ***Snyder***, 157 Cal.App.4th at 1536; ***City of Long Beach***, 64 Cal.App.3d at 73, 79.

(b) Interviewed witnesses. A list of witnesses interviewed by an attorney may be protected as noncore work product if it could reveal the attorney's evaluation of the case's strengths and weaknesses. ***Coito***, 54 Cal.4th at 502-03; ***Nacht & Lewis Architects***, 47 Cal.App.4th at 217.

(4) Witness statements. Witness statements taken by an attorney (or the attorney's agent) are protected as noncore work product even if they do not reveal an attorney's impressions, conclusions, opinions, or legal research or theories. *See* ***Coito***, 54 Cal.4th at 497. For example, statements of all witnesses to an accident are protected as noncore work product even when they are taken without any particular foresight, strategy, selectivity, or planning. *See id.*

(5) Compilations. Compilations of information collected by the attorney and the attorney's staff are protected as noncore work product. *See* ***Rojas***, 33 Cal.4th at 423 (dicta). The protection for noncore work product applies to derivative or interpretive materials—that is, information gathered, organized, or interpreted by the attorney. *See* ***Dowden***, 73 Cal.App.4th at 135; ***BP Alaska Expl.***, 199 Cal.App.3d at 1257; ***Mack***, 259 Cal.App.2d at 10-11. A compilation that reflects an attorney's impressions, conclusions, opinions, or legal research or theories is entitled to heightened protection as core work product. See "Compilations," §3.5.1(5), p. 632.

(6) Information analysis. Documents that analyze raw data, such as audit reports and appraisals, are protected as noncore work product. ***Dowden***, 73 Cal.App.4th at 135; ***BP Alaska Expl.***, 199 Cal.App.3d at 1257; *see, e.g.*, ***San Diego P.A. v. Superior Ct.*** (1962) 58 Cal.2d 194, 202 (engineer's evaluation prepared for attorney); ***Mack***, 259 Cal.App.2d at 10 (appraiser's report).

(7) Information from consulting experts. Reports and other information from consulting experts are protected as noncore work product. *See* ***San Diego P.A.***, 58 Cal.2d at 204; ***Dowden***, 73 Cal.App.4th at 135; ***BP Alaska Expl.***, 199 Cal.App.3d at 1257; ***National Steel Prods. v. Superior Ct.*** (4th Dist.1985) 164 Cal.App.3d 476, 489-90; ***Mack***, 259 Cal.App.2d at 10. If a consulting expert's report reflects the attorney's impressions, conclusions, opinions, or legal research or theories, it is entitled to heightened protection as core work product. ***National Steel***, 164 Cal.App.3d at 489. For the definition of "consulting expert," see "Consulting expert," ch. 7-I, §2.1, p. 898. If the attorney decides to call a consulting expert as a witness, the attorney waives the work-product privilege for the expert's knowledge and opinions about the case. See "Testifying expert," §3.6.5, p. 635.

(8) Inadvertently disclosed materials. The work-product privilege is not waived by the inadvertent disclosure of confidential information. *See* CCP §2018.030; ***Regents of the Univ. of Cal. v. Superior Ct.*** (4th

Dist.2008) 165 Cal.App.4th 672, 683; ***O'Mary v. Mitsubishi Elecs. Am., Inc.*** (4th Dist.1997) 59 Cal.App.4th 563, 577; *see also* ***Rico***, 42 Cal.4th at 818-19 (discussing duty of attorney who receives inadvertently disclosed work product). See "Inadvertent disclosure," ch. 6-A, §3.3.2(1), p. 612.

§3.6 What work-product privilege does not protect.

1. Independently prepared witness statements. Witness statements that are independently prepared by witnesses are not protected by the work-product privilege. ***Coito v. Superior Ct.*** (2012) 54 Cal.4th 480, 495. A party cannot shield independently prepared witness statements by turning them over to its attorney. *Id.*

2. Independently prepared material. Materials compiled or created independently of the attorney (i.e., not requested by the attorney) are not protected by the work-product privilege. *See, e.g.*, ***Jasper Constr., Inc. v. Foothill Junior Coll. Dist.*** (1st Dist.1979) 91 Cal.App.3d 1, 16-17 (report prepared by consultant hired by party did not become work product just because it was later adopted by attorney), *disapproved on other grounds*, ***Los Angeles Unified Sch. Dist. v. Great Am. Ins.*** (2010) 49 Cal.4th 739.

3. Nonlegal work. Work performed by an attorney in a nonlegal capacity (e.g., as a party's business agent or a claims adjuster) is not protected by the work-product privilege. ***Aetna Cas. & Sur. Co. v. Superior Ct.*** (1st Dist.1984) 153 Cal.App.3d 467, 475; ***Rumac, Inc. v. Bottomley*** (4th Dist.1983) 143 Cal.App.3d 810, 817; ***Watt Indus. v. Superior Ct.*** (1st Dist.1981) 115 Cal.App.3d 802, 805. If the work can be performed by a nonattorney, it is not protected by the work-product privilege. *See, e.g.*, ***2,022 Ranch, L.L.C. v. Superior Ct.*** (4th Dist.2003) 113 Cal.App.4th 1377, 1401 (factual investigations that could be performed by nonattorney claims adjusters were not covered by work-product privilege), *disapproved on other grounds*, ***Costco Wholesale Corp. v. Superior Ct.*** (2009) 47 Cal.4th 725; ***Rumac, Inc.***, 143 Cal.App.3d at 817 (lease negotiations by attorney that required professional skill and knowledge were covered by work-product privilege); ***Watt Indus.***, 115 Cal.App.3d at 805 (acts performed by attorney acting merely as business agent were not covered by work-product privilege). When the attorney's work has both a legal and a non-legal purpose, the documents at issue are protected by the work-product privilege only if the dominant purpose behind creating the documents was to provide a legal opinion or advice. *See* ***2,022 Ranch***, 113 Cal.App.4th at 1390-91; ***Aetna Cas.***, 153 Cal.App.3d at 475-76.

4. Factual information. Purely factual information is not protected by the work-product privilege.

(1) Physical evidence. Information about the identity and location of physical evidence is not work product. ***City of Long Beach v. Superior Ct.*** (2d Dist.1976) 64 Cal.App.3d 65, 72; ***Mack v. Superior Ct.*** (1st Dist.1968) 259 Cal.App.2d 7, 10; *see* Evid. C. §911 (no privilege to refuse to produce physical evidence).

(2) Events provable at trial. Information about events provable at trial is not work product. ***City of Long Beach***, 64 Cal.App.3d at 72; ***Mack***, 259 Cal.App.2d at 10. For example, facts relied on by a plaintiff to prove its case have no work-product protection because the facts will ultimately be disclosed at trial. *See* ***Southern Pac. Co. v. Superior Ct.*** (3d Dist.1969) 3 Cal.App.3d 195, 198-99, *disapproved on other grounds*, ***Kadelbach v. Amaral*** (3d Dist.1973) 31 Cal.App.3d 814.

(3) Attorney as fact-finder. Information obtained by the attorney as a fact-finder, not as an attorney, is not work product. *See* ***2,022 Ranch***, 113 Cal.App.4th at 1401. For example, an attorney cannot refuse to disclose the names and addresses of people with knowledge of relevant facts, even if the attorney personally made an effort to acquire the information. *See* CCP §2017.010; *see, e.g.*, Judicial Council Forms, form DISC-001, interrogatory 12.1 (interrogatory asking for identities and addresses of people with knowledge of incident that is basis of suit); *cf.* ***Triple A Mach. Shop, Inc. v. State*** (1st Dist.1989) 213 Cal.App.3d 131, 143 (attorney-client privilege does not protect information about independent witness); ***City of Long Beach***, 64 Cal.App.3d at 73 (attorney-client privilege does not protect information about people with relevant knowledge).

(4) Transmitted to attorney by others. Factual information prepared by others and transmitted to the attorney is not work product. For example, independently prepared witness statements do not become privileged communications or work product merely because they are turned over to the attorney. ***Coito***, 54 Cal.4th at 495.

5. Testifying expert. Work-product protection for information provided by a testifying expert depends on the capacity in which the expert serves.

(1) Single capacity. A testifying expert's knowledge and opinion relating to the expert's role as a testifying witness is not work product. ***County of L.A. v. Superior Ct.*** (2d Dist.1990) 222 Cal.App.3d 647, 654-55.

(2) Dual capacity. If the testifying expert acted in a dual capacity as a prospective witness and as an adviser to the attorney, the information provided can be work product. ***National Steel Prods. v. Superior Ct.*** (4th Dist.1985) 164 Cal.App.3d 476, 489; ***Swartzman v. Superior Ct.*** (2d Dist.1964) 231 Cal.App.2d 195, 202-03; *see* ***DeLuca v. State Fish Co.*** (2d Dist.2013) 217 Cal.App.4th 671, 689-90 (dicta). To determine whether the information is work product, the court must conduct a three-step in camera inspection of the information:

Step 1 – Information absolutely privileged. The court must determine whether the information, in whole or in part, reflects an attorney's impressions, conclusions, opinions, or legal research or theories. ***National Steel***, 164 Cal.App.3d at 489; *see* ***DeLuca***, 217 Cal.App.4th at 690 & n.21 (dicta). If the information reflects the attorney's thoughts, it is work product protected by an absolute privilege. ***National Steel***, 164 Cal.App.3d at 489; *see* ***DeLuca***, 217 Cal.App.4th at 690 & n.21 (dicta). However, if portions of the information are easily severable from the attorney's thoughts, the court must review that information under Step 2. ***National Steel***, 164 Cal.App.3d at 489-90.

Step 2 – Information is advisory. The court must determine whether the information is advisory—that is, given by the expert to the attorney as an adviser to the client's case. ***National Steel***, 164 Cal.App.3d at 490; *see* ***DeLuca***, 217 Cal.App.4th at 690 (dicta). If portions of the information are not advisory, the information is discoverable. ***National Steel***, 164 Cal.App.3d at 490; *see* ***DeLuca***, 217 Cal.App.4th at 690 & n.21 (dicta). If portions of the information are advisory, the court must review that information under Step 3. ***National Steel***, 164 Cal.App.3d at 490; *see* ***DeLuca***, 217 Cal.App.4th at 690 (dicta).

Step 3 – Good cause for discovery. The court must determine whether there is any good cause for discovery of the advisory information. ***National Steel***, 164 Cal.App.3d at 490; *see* ***DeLuca***, 217 Cal.App.4th at 690 & n.21 (dicta). This requires the court to balance the need for disclosure against the purposes of the work-product privilege. *See* ***National Steel***, 164 Cal.App.3d at 490.

6. Breach of duty. There is no work-product privilege in an action based on an attorney's breach of duty to a client or breach of the California Rules of Professional Conduct. *See* CCP §§2018.070-2018.080.

(1) Malpractice action. When work product is relevant to the attorney's breach of duty to a client or a former client, it is not protected from discovery in the client's action for malpractice. CCP §2018.080.

(2) Disciplinary action. When work product is relevant to the attorney's breach of duty to a client or a former client, it is not protected from discovery in a disciplinary action by the State Bar if the client approves discovery of the work product. CCP §2018.070(a); *CEB Discovery Practice*, §3.55.

(a) Client approval. A client is deemed to have approved discovery of the work product if the client initiated a complaint against the attorney. CCP §2018.070(c).

(b) Protective order. A protective order can be issued to prevent disclosure of work product outside the disciplinary action. CCP §2018.070(b).

7. Crime-fraud – official investigation. There is no work-product privilege in an official investigation by a law-enforcement agency (or a proceeding brought by a public prosecutor for the State) if the services of the attorney were sought or obtained to enable or aid anyone to commit or plan a crime or fraud. CCP §2018.050. The crime-fraud exception to the work-product privilege can be asserted only by law-enforcement agencies or prosecutors; it cannot be asserted by private parties in civil cases. CCP §2018.050; ***Rico v. Mitsubishi Motors Corp.*** (2007) 42 Cal.4th 807, 820; *see* ***Wellpoint Health Networks, Inc. v. Superior Ct.*** (2d Dist.1997) 59 Cal.App.4th 110, 120; ***BP Alaska Expl., Inc. v. Superior Ct.*** (5th Dist.1988) 199 Cal.App.3d 1240, 1251.

PRACTICE TIP

Although the crime-fraud exception does not apply to work product in civil litigation between private parties, it does apply to the attorney-client privilege. See "Crime or fraud," §2.7.7, p. 624. When a party asserts and proves the crime-fraud exception to the attorney-client privilege, that same evidence can establish good cause for disclosure of noncore work product. See ***State Farm Fire & Cas. Co. v. Superior Ct.*** *(2d Dist.1997) 54 Cal.App.4th 625, 650. See "Noncore work product," §3.5.2, p. 632.*

§3.7 Waiver of work-product privilege. The work-product privilege can be waived under the same circumstances that result in waiver of the attorney-client privilege. ***Wells Fargo Bank v. Superior Ct.*** (2000) 22 Cal.4th 201, 214; ***Regents of the Univ. of Cal. v. Superior Ct.*** (4th Dist.2008) 165 Cal.App.4th 672, 678-79; ***McKesson HBOC, Inc. v. Superior Ct.*** (1st Dist.2004) 115 Cal.App.4th 1229, 1239; ***OXY Res. Cal. LLC v. Superior Ct.*** (1st Dist.2004) 115 Cal.App.4th 874, 891.

1. Waiver of privilege. The work-product privilege can be waived. *See* ***Wells Fargo***, 22 Cal.4th at 214; ***Metro Goldwyn Mayer, Inc. v. Superior Ct.*** (2d Dist.1994) 25 Cal.App.4th 242, 244.

(1) General rules of waiver. See "Waiver of privilege," ch. 6-A, §2.2.14, p. 607.

(2) Waiver by attorney's signature on discovery response. See "Waiver by attorney's signature on discovery response," §2.8.1(2), p. 626.

(3) Waiver by discovery default. See "Waiver by discovery default," ch. 6-A, §2.2.14(3), p. 609.

(4) Waiver by disclosure. The work-product privilege is waived if an attorney makes an intentional disclosure of the information that is wholly inconsistent with the purpose of the privilege (i.e., to safeguard the attorney's work and trial preparation). *E.g.*, ***Laguna Beach Cty. Water Dist. v. Superior Ct.*** (4th Dist.2004) 124 Cal.App.4th 1453, 1459 (disclosure of work-product information to auditors was not inconsistent with purpose of privilege; attorney had duty to supply information); ***OXY Res.***, 115 Cal.App.4th at 891 (disclosure of work-product information to codefendants was not inconsistent with purpose of privilege; parties had common interest in obtaining legal advice related to same matter); *see, e.g.*, ***Coito v. Superior Ct.*** (2012) 54 Cal.4th 480, 501 (use of protected witness statement during deposition waived work-product privilege for that statement). See "Waiver by disclosure," ch. 6-A, §2.2.14(1)(a), p. 607.

(5) Waiver by consent to disclosure. The work-product privilege is waived if an attorney consents to the disclosure of the information to a third person. ***Regents of the Univ. of Cal.***, 165 Cal.App.4th at 679; ***OXY Res.***, 115 Cal.App.4th at 891; *see* ***Laguna Beach***, 124 Cal.App.4th at 1459; ***Raytheon Co. v. Superior Ct.*** (6th Dist.1989) 208 Cal.App.3d 683, 689. See "Waiver by consent to disclosure," ch. 6-A, §2.2.14(1)(b), p. 607.

(a) Express consent. The work-product privilege is expressly waived by the attorney's voluntary consent to disclosure of information to a person (other than the client) who has no interest in maintaining the confidentiality of the information. ***Regents of the Univ. of Cal.***, 165 Cal.App.4th at 679; ***OXY Res.***, 115 Cal.App.4th at 891. See "Express consent," ch. 6-A, §2.2.14(1)(b)[1], p. 607.

(b) Implied consent. See "Implied consent," ch. 6-A, §2.2.14(1)(b)[2], p. 608.

[1] By conduct. The work-product privilege is impliedly waived by conduct inconsistent with claiming the privilege, including the attorney's failure to claim the privilege. ***Regents of the Univ. of Cal.***, 165 Cal.App.4th at 678-79. See "By conduct," ch. 6-A, §2.2.14(1)(b)[2][a], p. 608.

[2] By use. See "By use," ch. 6-A, §2.2.14(1)(b)[2][b], p. 608.

[3] By raising issue. The work-product privilege is impliedly waived by putting the content of the attorney's work product directly at issue in the case. ***2,022 Ranch, L.L.C. v. Superior Ct.*** (4th Dist.2003) 113 Cal.App.4th 1377, 1395, *disapproved on other grounds*, ***Costco Wholesale Corp. v. Superior Ct.*** (2009) 47 Cal.4th

725; ***Wellpoint Health Networks, Inc. v. Superior Ct.*** (2d Dist.1997) 59 Cal.App.4th 110, 128; *see* ***Steiny & Co. v. California Elec. Sup. Co.*** (2d Dist.2000) 79 Cal.App.4th 285, 292 (when privileged information goes to heart of claim, fundamental fairness requires that it be disclosed); ***Kadelbach v. Amaral*** (3d Dist.1973) 31 Cal.App.3d 814, 821-22 (dicta; work product is discoverable when used as offensive weapon for cross-examination), *disapproved on other grounds*, ***Coito v. Superior Ct.*** (2012) 54 Cal.4th 480. For example, the work-product privilege for an attorney's investigation of an employment-discrimination claim is waived when the party asserts the adequacy of its attorney's investigation as a defense. ***Wellpoint Health Networks***, 59 Cal.App.4th at 128. See "By raising issue," ch. 6-A, §2.2.14(1)(b)[2][c], p. 608.

(6) Multiple attorneys. When multiple attorneys collaborate to produce work product for the same client, all attorneys must consent to waiver of the work-product privilege. ***Armenta v. Superior Ct.*** (2d Dist.2002) 101 Cal.App.4th 525, 533. Any attorney who helped generate the work product can block its disclosure by objecting to waiver of the privilege. *See id.* at 534.

2. No waiver of privilege.

(1) General rules of nonwaiver. See "Privilege not waived," ch. 6-A, §3.3.2, p. 612.

(2) Disclosure to client. The work-product privilege is not waived by the attorney's confidential disclosure of work-product information to the client. ***Wells Fargo***, 22 Cal.4th at 214; ***BP Alaska Expl., Inc. v. Superior Ct.*** (5th Dist.1988) 199 Cal.App.3d 1240, 1253; *CEB Discovery Practice*, §3.65; *Jefferson's Evid. Benchbook*, §43.19.

(3) Disclosure to auditor. The work-product privilege is not waived by the attorney's confidential disclosure of work product to a client's auditor in response to an audit. *Jefferson's Evid. Benchbook*, §43.20; *see, e.g.*, ***Laguna Beach***, 124 Cal.App.4th at 1461 (letters to client's auditors containing work product did not waive privilege).

(4) Common-interest doctrine. The common-interest doctrine preserves the work-product privilege for information shared among colitigants. See "Common-interest doctrine," §2.8.2(4), p. 627.

§3.8 How to assert work-product privilege.

1. Holder claims privilege. The holder of the work-product privilege, or a person authorized by the holder, can claim the privilege by objecting to the discovery request on the ground that the privilege prevents disclosure of the information. See "Who can assert work-product privilege," §3.4, p. 630; "Responding party objects to discovery," ch. 7-A, §14.1.1, p. 771. Instead of serving objections, the holder can claim the privilege by filing a motion for protective order. See "Motion for Protective Order," ch. 9-B, p. 1024.

2. Discovering party moves to compel. The party seeking discovery has the burden of moving to compel it. In response to written objections asserting the work-product privilege, the discovering party must initiate the meet-and-confer procedure and, if unsuccessful, file a motion to compel to secure the discovery. See "Discovering party moves to compel (option 1)," ch. 7-A, §14.1.2, p. 772.

(1) Motion papers.

(a) Separate statement. A separate statement is necessary for a motion to compel production of work-product information. The separate statement must contain all the information necessary to understand each discovery request and related response. CRC 3.1345(c). See "Separate statement," ch. 9-D, §4.2.5(1)(d), p. 1054; "Separate statement," ch. 9-E, §3.2.4(4), p. 1064.

(b) Good cause. Once the discovering party learns what information is claimed to be core and noncore work product (usually after the meet-and-confer), the discovering party must make a good-cause statement to support a motion to compel disclosure of the noncore work product. The purpose of the good-cause statement is to show that, by balancing the need for disclosure against the purposes of the work-product privilege, the court should decide in favor of disclosure. *See* ***2,022 Ranch, L.L.C. v. Superior Ct.*** (4th Dist.2003) 113 Cal.App.4th 1377, 1390, *disapproved on other grounds*, ***Costco Wholesale Corp. v. Superior Ct.*** (2009) 47 Cal.4th 725; ***National Steel Prods.***

v. Superior Ct. (4th Dist.1985) 164 Cal.App.3d 476, 490. To compel production of noncore work product, the good-cause statement must show that denying discovery will either (1) unfairly prejudice the party in preparing its claim or defense or (2) result in an injustice. *See* CCP §2018.030(b); ***2,022 Ranch***, 113 Cal.App.4th at 1390; ***National Steel***, 164 Cal.App.3d at 490-91; *Jefferson's Evid. Benchbook*, §42.14. The court must balance the need for disclosure against the purposes of the work-product privilege. ***2,022 Ranch***, 113 Cal.App.4th at 1390; ***Hernandez v. Superior Ct.*** (2d Dist.2003) 112 Cal.App.4th 285, 297; *see* ***National Steel***, 164 Cal.App.3d at 490.

NOTE

*Although the courts use the term "good cause" to describe the burden to overcome the protection for noncore work product, the burden is heavier than good cause because the discovering party must show unfair prejudice or injustice. Weil, Civil Procedure Before Trial, ¶8:1495.3; see **Kirkland v. Superior Ct.** (2d Dist.2002) 95 Cal.App.4th 92, 98 (without claim of privilege, burden of good cause for production is met by simple fact-specific showing of relevance).*

[1] Unfair prejudice. Denial of discovery is unfairly prejudicial to the party's claim or defense when there is an overriding need for disclosure of the attorney's work product. *See* ***Armenta v. Superior Ct.*** (2d Dist.2002) 101 Cal.App.4th 525, 535; ***Lipton v. Superior Ct.*** (2d Dist.1996) 48 Cal.App.4th 1599, 1619; ***National Steel***, 164 Cal.App.3d at 491. To demonstrate an overriding need for disclosure, the discovering party must show that the privileged information sought is relevant and cannot be obtained from any other source. ***Lipton***, 48 Cal.App.4th at 1619; *see* ***Armenta***, 101 Cal.App.4th at 535. Other available sources are deemed to be adequate substitutes for the attorney's work product as long as they are comparable; the other sources do not have to provide identical information. *See* ***Armenta***, 101 Cal.App.4th at 535 (no unfair prejudice when there is equivalent opportunity to generate comparable evidence).

[2] Injustice. Denial of discovery results in an injustice when it would unfairly prejudice the party in preparing a claim or defense. *See* ***Armenta***, 101 Cal.App.4th at 532-33.

(2) Grounds. If, during the meet-and-confer conference, the discovering party obtained sufficient information to understand the basis of the claim of privilege, the discovering party can attempt to disprove the claim of privilege or show that the privilege was waived or that an exception to the privilege applies. See "Discovering party justifies discovery," ch. 7-A, §14.1.5, p. 773. If the information claimed to be privileged is noncore work product, the discovering party can also attempt to show good cause for its production. See "Good cause," §3.8.2(1)(b), p. 637.

3. Holder serves opposition papers. In response to a motion to compel, the holder has the burden to justify its work-product privilege. See "Responding party satisfies burden," ch. 7-A, §14.1.4, p. 772.

(1) Preliminary facts. The holder must support its objections to discovery by establishing the preliminary facts necessary to support the privilege. ***Citizens for Ceres v. Superior Ct.*** (5th Dist.2013) 217 Cal.App.4th 889, 911; ***Carehouse Convalescent Hosp. v. Superior Ct.*** (4th Dist.2006) 143 Cal.App.4th 1558, 1563; *see* ***Coito v. Superior Ct.*** (2012) 54 Cal.4th 480, 496-97. See "Elements of work-product privilege," §3.3, p. 630.

(2) Privilege log. The holder should itemize and describe the information sought in a privilege log and state whether each item is claimed to be protected as either core or noncore work product. See "Privilege log," ch. 7-A, §14.1.4(2), p. 773.

(3) Supporting declaration. The holder must support the preliminary facts with a declaration or affidavit. *See* ***Travelers Ins. v. Superior Ct.*** (1st Dist.1983) 143 Cal.App.3d 436, 441; Weil, *Civil Procedure Before Trial*, ¶8:192.

(4) No prejudice or injustice. The holder must attempt to demonstrate that the denial of discovery of noncore work product will not unfairly prejudice the discovering party's preparation of its claim or defense and will not result in an injustice. *See* CCP §2018.030(b).

§3.9 Court's ruling on work-product privilege.

1. In camera inspection.

(1) Core work product. The court cannot require an in camera review of documents claimed to be privileged as core work product to determine if absolute privilege applies. Evid. C. §915(a); ***Citizens for Ceres v. Superior Ct.*** (5th Dist.2013) 217 Cal.App.4th 889, 911-12; ***OXY Res. Cal. LLC v. Superior Ct.*** (1st Dist.2004) 115 Cal.App.4th 874, 895 n.16 (dicta); Weil, *Civil Procedure Before Trial*, ¶8:267. See "Core work product," §3.5.1, p. 631. Although the California Supreme Court's opinion in ***Coito v. Superior Ct.*** might be read as approving in camera review of documents to determine the applicability of absolute privilege, the Court never addressed the limitations in Evid. C. §915(a) and did not explicitly state whether the documents could be reviewed. *See* ***Coito v. Superior Ct.*** (2012) 54 Cal.4th 480, 496-97 (holding that after attorney makes foundational showing that witness statement is entitled to protection as core work product under CCP §2018.030(a), trial court should conduct in camera inspection if necessary to determine whether privilege applies).

(2) Noncore work product. The court can require an in camera review of documents claimed to be privileged as noncore work product to determine if qualified privilege applies. Evid. C. §915(b); ***Costco Wholesale Corp. v. Superior Ct.*** (2009) 47 Cal.4th 725, 736 (dicta); ***Citizens for Ceres***, 217 Cal.App.4th at 911-12; Weil, *Civil Procedure Before Trial*, ¶8:267. See "Noncore work product," §3.5.2, p. 632.

2. Discovery of noncore work product. The court can allow discovery of noncore work product only if the party seeking the material shows that denying discovery (1) will unfairly prejudice the discovering party's preparation of a claim or defense or (2) will result in an injustice. CCP §2018.030(b); ***Coito***, 54 Cal.4th at 499-500. To determine whether there is good cause for discovery of the work product, the court considers the following factors:

(1) Relevance. The relevance of the material to establishing the party's claim or defense. ***Lipton v. Superior Ct.*** (2d Dist.1996) 48 Cal.App.4th 1599, 1619; *see* ***National Steel Prods. v. Superior Ct.*** (4th Dist.1985) 164 Cal.App.3d 476, 491-92 (court must weigh impeachment value of material against benefit of protecting work product).

(2) Other available sources. Whether the party seeking discovery can obtain the same information from sources other than the attorney's work product. ***Lipton***, 48 Cal.App.4th at 1619; ***National Steel***, 164 Cal.App.3d at 491. Denial of discovery is unfairly prejudicial to the party's claim or defense when there is no adequate substitute for the attorney's work product. ***Armenta v. Superior Ct.*** (2d Dist.2002) 101 Cal.App.4th 525, 535. Other available sources are deemed to be adequate substitutes for the attorney's work product as long as they are comparable; the other sources do not have to provide identical information. *See id.* (no unfair prejudice when there is equivalent opportunity to generate comparable evidence).

(3) Attorney's privacy. The need to protect the attorney's privacy to encourage thorough case preparation and investigation of both the favorable and the unfavorable aspects of the case. CCP §2018.020(a); *e.g.*, ***Kizer v. Sulnick*** (2d Dist.1988) 202 Cal.App.3d 431, 441 (attorney's privacy was not violated when report was turned over to director of Department of Health Services because statute barred director from disclosing information).

(4) Undue advantage. The need to prevent the party seeking discovery from taking undue advantage of the attorney's industry or efforts. CCP §2018.020(b); *e.g.*, ***Kizer***, 202 Cal.App.3d at 441 (no undue advantage in turning over report to director of Department of Health Services; director was not party to case and was barred by statute from giving information to other party).

§4. LRS-CLIENT PRIVILEGE

In 2013, the California Legislature amended the Evidence Code to add a new statutory privilege for communications between a prospective client and a lawyer-referral service (LRS) in an effort to help facilitate honest and open communications between the client and the LRS. *See* Sen. Rules Comm., Off. of Sen. Floor Analyses, 3d reading analysis of Assem. Bill No. 267 (2013-2014 Reg. Sess.), as amended Apr. 9, 2013, p. 7. The purpose of the new statutory privilege is to remove any uncertainty concerning the confidentiality of such communications and whether such communications are protected from discovery in litigation. *Id.*

§4.1 General. The LRS-client privilege protects confidential communications between an LRS and its clients. Evid. C. §966(a).

§4.2 Nature of LRS-client privilege.

1. Absolute. The LRS-client privilege is most likely absolute, which means the court cannot order disclosure of information protected by the privilege. *See* Evid. C. §966(a) (client can refuse to disclose, and can prevent another from disclosing, confidential communications).

2. Duration. The LRS-client privilege lasts as long as the privilege holder, someone authorized by the privilege holder, or the LRS asserts it. *See* Evid. C. §966(a). The LRS cannot claim the privilege if the holder or someone authorized by the holder instructs the service to disclose the communication, or if no holder of the privilege exists. *Id.* §966(a)(3). The privilege does not necessarily terminate on the client's death or dissolution. *See id.* §965(c).

3. Discovery & evidentiary. The LRS-client privilege is both a discovery privilege and an evidentiary privilege because the information protected by the privilege is not subject to either discovery or disclosure at trial. *See* Evid. C. §966(a) (client can refuse to disclose, and can prevent others from disclosing, confidential communications).

§4.3 Elements of LRS-client privilege. To establish the LRS-client privilege, the person asserting the privilege must show the following:

1. LRS & client formed relationship. The LRS and the client established a relationship. *See* Evid. C. §§965(b), 966. An LRS-client relationship is established when the relationship includes (1) an LRS, (2) a client, and (3) a consultation. *See id.* §§965, 966. Once a relationship is established, it exists between not only the client and the LRS, but also between the client and any employees of the LRS who render services to the client. *Id.* §966(b).

(1) LRS. An LRS is either (1) an LRS certified under and operating in compliance with Bus. & Prof. C. §6155 or (2) a business that the client reasonably believes is certified under and operating in compliance with Bus. & Prof. C. §6155. Evid. C. §965(d).

(2) Client. A client is a person who, directly or through an authorized representative, consults an LRS to retain an attorney or to obtain professional legal services or advice from an attorney. Evid. C. §965(a).

(a) Natural person. A client can be a natural person. *See* Evid. C. §965(a). The person can be an incompetent person who consults the LRS herself or whose guardian or conservator consults the service on the client's behalf. *Id.*

(b) Legal entity. A client can be a legal entity that consults an LRS through its representative. *See* Evid. C. §966(b). This includes partnerships, corporations, limited-liability companies, and associations. *Id.*

(3) Consultation. The client must have consulted the LRS for the purpose of (1) retaining an attorney, (2) obtaining legal services from an attorney, or (3) obtaining legal advice from an attorney. Evid. C. §965(a).

2. LRS & client communicated. The LRS and client communicated (i.e., transmitted information between them) in the course of their relationship. Evid. C. §965(b); *see id.* §966(a).

3. Communication made confidentially. The LRS and client communicated confidentially. Evid. C. §965(b); *see id.* §966(a). For a communication to be confidential, the client must believe that it is confidential and that the information is not disclosed to an unnecessary third person. *Id.* §965(b). An LRS-client communication made in the presence of a third person is confidential only if (1) the third person was present to further the client's interest in the consultation or (2) the disclosure was necessary to transmit the information or accomplish the purpose for which the LRS was consulted. *Id.*; *see id.* §966(a).

§4.4 Communicants to LRS-client privilege. Communicants to the LRS-client privilege include the LRS, the client, and any necessary third persons.

1. LRS. See "LRS," §4.3.1(1), this page.

2. Client. See "Client," §4.3.1(2), this page.

3. Necessary third person. A necessary third person is any person to whom a confidential communication is disclosed in any of the following circumstances: (1) the disclosure was reasonably necessary to transmit the information between the LRS and the client, (2) the disclosure was reasonably necessary to accomplish the purpose for which the LRS was consulted, or (3) the person was present to further the client's interest in the consultation. *See* Evid. C. §965(b).

§4.5 Who can assert the LRS-client privilege. The LRS-client privilege belongs to the client. *See* Evid. C. §966(a). The following people can assert the privilege for the client:

1. Holder. A holder of the LRS-client privilege can claim the privilege. Evid. C. §966(a)(1). The following people are holders of the privilege:

(1) The client, if the client has no guardian or conservator. *Id.* §965(c)(1).

(2) A guardian or conservator of the client, if the client has a guardian or conservator. *Id.* §965(c)(2).

(3) The personal representative of the client, if the client is dead. *Id.* §965(c)(3).

(4) A successor, assign, trustee in dissolution, or a similar representative of a legal-entity client that no longer exists. *Id.* §965(c)(4).

2. Authorized person. A person who is authorized by the holder of the LRS-client privilege can claim the privilege. Evid. C. §966(a)(2).

3. LRS. The LRS or a staff person of the service can claim the privilege. Evid. C. §966(a)(3). However, the service or staff person cannot claim the privilege if no privilege holder exists or if the service or staff person is instructed by an authorized person to disclose the communication. *Id.*

§4.6 What LRS-client privilege protects. The LRS-client privilege prevents discovery or disclosure of confidential communications between the client and the LRS. Evid. C. §966(a). To be protected, the communication must be for the purpose of retaining an attorney or securing legal services or advice from an attorney. *See id.* §965(a).

§4.7 What LRS-client privilege does not protect.

1. Crime or fraud. The LRS-client privilege does not prevent discovery or disclosure of a communication if the client sought or obtained the LRS's help to enable or aid anyone to commit or plan a crime or a fraud. Evid. C. §968(a).

2. Prevention of injury. The LRS-client privilege does not prevent discovery or disclosure of a communication if a staff person of the LRS who receives a confidential communication in processing a request for legal assistance reasonably believes that disclosure of the communication is necessary to prevent a criminal act that is likely to result in death or substantial bodily harm. Evid. C. §968(b).

§4.8 Waiver of LRS-client privilege.

1. Waiver of privilege. If the privilege is waived, the information is discoverable. For the general rules of waiver, see "Waiver of privilege," ch. 6-A, §2.2.14, p. 607.

2. No waiver of privilege. If the privilege is not waived, the information is not discoverable.

(1) General rules of nonwaiver. See "Privilege not waived," ch. 6-A, §3.3.2, p. 612.

(2) Inadvertent disclosure. A party does not waive the LRS-client privilege for confidential information that has been inadvertently disclosed. *See* Evid. C. §912(a) (holder can waive privilege by consent to disclosure). See "Inadvertent disclosure," ch. 6-A, §3.3.2(1), p. 612.

§4.9 How to assert LRS-client privilege. The LRS-client privilege should be asserted in the same manner as the attorney-client privilege. See "How to assert attorney-client privilege," §2.9, p. 627.

C. BUSINESS-RELATED PRIVILEGES

This subchapter covers two business-related privileges: (1) the trade-secret privilege and (2) the private-investigator privilege.

§1. TRADE-SECRET PRIVILEGE

§1.1 General. A person has a privilege to refuse to disclose (and to prevent others from disclosing) a trade secret the person owns if the protection from disclosure will not tend to conceal fraud or work an injustice. Evid. C. §1060; ***Hypertouch, Inc. v. Superior Ct.*** (1st Dist.2005) 128 Cal.App.4th 1527, 1554-55; ***Bridgestone/Firestone, Inc. v. Superior Ct.*** (1st Dist.1992) 7 Cal.App.4th 1384, 1389.

1. Purpose. The purpose of the trade-secret privilege is to prevent disclosure of secret information that is essential to the continued operation of a business or industry. ***Bridgestone/Firestone***, 7 Cal.App.4th at 1390; 7 Cal. Law Revision Comm'n Rep. (1965) p. 1202. The privilege protects the economic value of information that has been kept secret by its owner. *See* Civ. C. §3426.1(d)(1) (defining "trade secret" under Uniform Trade Secrets Act); Evid. C. §1061(a)(1) (referring to Civ. C. §3426.1(d)(1) for definition of "trade secret").

2. Primary authority. Evid. C. §§1060, 1063; *see also* CCP §2019.210 (trade-secret misappropriation); Civ. C. §3426.1 et seq. (Uniform Trade Secrets Act).

3. Secondary authority. The following secondary sources are cited as authority in this section:

- *California Civil Discovery Practice* (CEB Online ed. 2014) (referred to as *CEB Discovery Practice*).
- *California Trial Objections* (CEB Online ed. 2014) (referred to as *CEB Trial Objections*).
- Caragozian, *Private Investigators in California: Analysis of the PIA & Case Law*, Privacy Rights Clearinghouse (2005), www.privacyrights.org/ar/PIs-Caragozian.htm (referred to as Caragozian, *Private Investigators*).
- Wegner, *California Practice Guide: Civil Trials & Evidence* (CD-ROM ed. 2014) (referred to as Wegner, *Civil Trials & Evidence*).

§1.2 Nature of trade-secret privilege.

1. Qualified. The trade-secret privilege is qualified and can be overcome by a showing of fraud or injustice. *See* Evid. C. §1060; ***State Farm Fire & Cas. Co. v. Superior Ct.*** (2d Dist.1997) 54 Cal.App.4th 625, 651; ***Bridgestone/Firestone, Inc. v. Superior Ct.*** (1st Dist.1992) 7 Cal.App.4th 1384, 1390. See "Fraud," §1.6.4, p. 644; "Injustice," §1.6.5, p. 644.

2. Continuing. The trade-secret privilege lasts as long as the information qualifies as a trade secret. *CEB Trial Objections*, §45.5; *see* ***Kewanee Oil Co. v. Bicron Corp.*** (1974) 416 U.S. 470, 494 (Marshall, J., concurring); ***Moore v. Regents of the Univ. of Cal.*** (1990) 51 Cal.3d 120, 171-72 (Mosk, J., dissenting).

3. Discovery & evidentiary. The trade-secret privilege is both a discovery privilege and an evidentiary privilege because the protected information is not subject to either discovery or disclosure at trial. *See* Evid. C. §1060 (holder has privilege to refuse to disclose and to prevent others from disclosing); *see, e.g.*, ***Citizens of Humanity, LLC v. Costco Wholesale Corp.*** (2d Dist.2009) 171 Cal.App.4th 1, 9-10 (D's sources were protected during discovery), *disapproved on other grounds*, ***Kwikset Corp. v. Superior Ct.*** (2011) 51 Cal.4th 310.

§1.3 Elements of trade-secret privilege. The elements of the trade-secret privilege are the following:

1. Ownership. The person claiming the trade-secret privilege is either the owner of the information or the owner's agent or employee. Evid. C. §1060.

2. Trade secret. The information sought to be protected qualifies as a trade secret. *See* Evid. C. §1060. Information qualifies as a trade secret if it (1) has independent actual or potential economic value, (2) is not generally known or accessible, and (3) has been kept secret by its owner. *See* Civ. C. §3426.1(d); Evid. C. §1061(a)(1); ***Citizens of Humanity, LLC v. Costco Wholesale Corp.*** (2d Dist.2009) 171 Cal.App.4th 1, 13, *disapproved on other grounds*, ***Kwikset Corp. v. Superior Ct.*** (2011) 51 Cal.4th 310; *CEB Trial Objections*, §45.2. See "What trade-secret privilege protects," §1.5, p. 643.

§1.4 Who can assert trade-secret privilege. The trade-secret privilege can be asserted by the owner of the trade secret or the owner's agents or employees. Evid. C. §1060; *CEB Trial Objections*, §45.4. This may include former employees. *CEB Trial Objections*, §45.4. The owner can assert the privilege to refuse to disclose and to prevent another person from disclosing the trade-secret information. Evid. C. §1060; ***California Sch. Empl. Ass'n v. Sunnyvale Elementary Sch. Dist.*** (1st Dist.1973) 36 Cal.App.3d 46, 66.

§1.5 What trade-secret privilege protects. The trade-secret privilege protects information that has economic value, is not generally known, and has been kept secret. "Information" includes formulas, patterns, compilations, programs, devices, methods, techniques, and processes. Civ. C. §3426.1(d).

1. Economic value. The trade-secret privilege applies to information that has independent actual or potential economic value because it is not generally known by the public or by other persons who could economically gain by knowing or using it. Civ. C. §3426.1(d)(1). In arguing that information has independent economic value, the trade-secret owner (or its agent or employee) should address (1) the value of the information to the owner and its competitors, (2) the amount of effort or money spent by the owner in developing the information, and (3) the ease or difficulty with which the information could be properly acquired or duplicated by others. *See* ***Futurecraft Corp. v. Clary Corp.*** (2d Dist.1962) 205 Cal.App.2d 279, 289.

(1) Information with economic value. Courts have found economic value in the following kinds of information:

(a) Customer lists. ***Morlife, Inc. v. Perry*** (1st Dist.1997) 56 Cal.App.4th 1514, 1522. However, for a customer list to have "economic value," the secrecy of the list must provide a business with a substantial business advantage. *Id.* In other words, the disclosure of the list would allow a competitor to direct sales to customers showing a predisposition to purchase its services. *Id.*; *see* ***American Credit Indem. Co. v. Sacks*** (2d Dist.1989) 213 Cal.App.3d 622, 630-31.

(b) Marketing strategies and plans. ***Whyte v. Schlage Lock Co.*** (4th Dist.2002) 101 Cal.App.4th 1443, 1456.

(c) Cost and pricing information. *Id.* at 1455; *cf.* ***SI Handling Sys. v. Heisley*** (3d Cir.1985) 753 F.2d 1244, 1260 (federal case).

(d) Manufacturing technologies. ***Whyte***, 101 Cal.App.4th at 1456.

(e) A customer list with billing and markup rates. ***Courtesy Temp. Serv. v. Camacho*** (2d Dist.1990) 222 Cal.App.3d 1278, 1288.

(f) Information relating to a company's bids and proposals. *See, e.g.*, ***San Jose Constr., Inc. v. S.B.C.C., Inc.*** (6th Dist.2007) 155 Cal.App.4th 1528, 1543 (fact issue whether information had economic value and was kept secret).

(g) Product plans and designs. ***Vacco Indus. v. Van Den Berg*** (2d Dist.1992) 5 Cal.App.4th 34, 50.

(h) Information relating to the identities of a company's vendors. ***Citizens of Humanity, LLC v. Costco Wholesale Corp.*** (2d Dist.2009) 171 Cal.App.4th 1, 13, *disapproved on other grounds*, ***Kwikset Corp. v. Superior Ct.*** (2011) 51 Cal.4th 310.

(2) Information without economic value. Courts have found no economic value in the following kinds of information:

(a) A customer list that included only businesses known by competitors and did not indicate which businesses would be predisposed to purchase the goods or services at issue. ***ABBA Rubber Co. v. Seaquist*** (4th Dist.1991) 235 Cal.App.3d 1, 19.

(b) Customer information that was no longer valuable because the customer had gone out of business. *See* ***Gemini Aluminum Corp. v. California Custom Shapes, Inc.*** (4th Dist.2002) 95 Cal.App.4th 1249, 1263.

2. Not generally known or accessible. The trade-secret privilege applies only when the information is not generally known or accessible. *See* Civ. C. §3426.1(d)(1). Typically, the more difficult information is to obtain, the more likely a court will find that it is not generally known or accessible. *See* ***Morlife, Inc.***, 56 Cal.App.4th at 1521-22. To be entitled to trade-secret protection, the information must be both generally unknown and not readily ascertainable; having just one of these qualities is not sufficient. *See* ***Syngenta Crop Prot., Inc. v. Helliker*** (2d Dist.2006) 138 Cal.App.4th 1135, 1172. In arguing that information is not generally known or accessible, the trade-secret owner (or its agent or employee) should address (1) the extent to which the information is known outside the owner's business and (2) the extent to which the information is known by the owner's employees and others involved in the owner's business. *See* ***Futurecraft Corp.***, 205 Cal.App.2d at 289.

3. Kept secret. The trade-secret privilege applies only when the owner of the information has made reasonable efforts to keep the information secret. Civ. C. §3426.1(d)(2); *see* ***Futurecraft Corp.***, 205 Cal.App.2d at 289 (court can consider measures taken by owner to guard secrecy of information). The owner of the information does not have to use extreme or undue measures to protect secrecy; it must only use measures that are reasonable under the circumstances. *See* Civ. C. §3426.1(d)(2). Reasonable efforts to keep information secret include the following:

(1) Advising employees that the information is a trade secret. ***Courtesy Temp.***, 222 Cal.App.3d at 1288. *But see* ***San Jose Constr.***, 155 Cal.App.4th at 1543 (merely identifying information as trade secret in employment agreement does not necessarily make it a trade secret).

(2) Requiring employees to sign confidentiality agreements. *See* ***American Credit***, 213 Cal.App.3d at 631.

(3) Limiting employee access to the information (i.e., providing the information only on a "need to know" basis). ***Courtesy Temp.***, 222 Cal.App.3d at 1288.

§1.6 What trade-secret privilege does not protect.

1. Patented or copyrighted information. The trade-secret privilege does not protect patented or copyrighted information from discovery because that information is already protected. *See* 7 Cal. Law Revision Comm'n Rep. (1965) p. 1202 (application of trade-secret privilege to patented or copyrighted information would only hinder courts).

2. Exempted information. The trade-secret privilege does not protect information from discovery that is exempt from protection by law. *See, e.g.,* ***State Farm Mut. Auto. Ins. v. Garamendi*** (2004) 32 Cal.4th 1029, 1047 (insurance data submitted to Commissioner was excluded from trade-secret privilege by Ins. C. §1861.07).

3. Disclosed by product. The trade-secret privilege does not protect information from discovery if the owner's product, sold to the public, embodies the secret and completely discloses it. ***Vacco Indus. v. Van Den Berg*** (2d Dist.1992) 5 Cal.App.4th 34, 50; ***Futurecraft Corp. v. Clary Corp.*** (2d Dist.1962) 205 Cal.App.2d 279, 289.

4. Fraud. The trade-secret privilege does not protect information from discovery if withholding the information conceals a fraud. Evid. C. §1060; 7 Cal. Law Revision Comm'n Rep. (1965) p. 1202; *see, e.g.,* ***State Farm Fire & Cas. Co. v. Superior Ct.*** (2d Dist.1997) 54 Cal.App.4th 625, 650-51 (name of software program used to identify documents was trade secret, but D's conduct justified disclosure under fraud-or-injustice exception).

5. Injustice. The trade-secret privilege does not protect information from discovery when protecting that information would work an injustice. Evid. C. §1060; ***Hypertouch, Inc. v. Superior Ct.*** (1st Dist.2005) 128 Cal.App.4th 1527, 1554-55; ***Bridgestone/Firestone, Inc. v. Superior Ct.*** (1st Dist.1992) 7 Cal.App.4th 1384, 1393. For example, the trade-secret privilege cannot be used to prevent disclosure of information to a plaintiff if the information is directly relevant to a material element of the plaintiff's cause of action and nondisclosure of the information would put the plaintiff at an unfair disadvantage in the suit. ***Bridgestone/Firestone***, 7 Cal.App.4th at 1392. The question of whether nondisclosure will work an injustice requires the court to balance the interests of the parties in light of the circumstances of the suit. *Id.* at 1393.

§1.7 Waiver of trade-secret privilege. Voluntary disclosure of trade-secret information, even if done mistakenly, constitutes a valid waiver of the trade-secret privilege. ***Masonite Corp. v. County of Mendocino Air Quality Mgmt. Dist.*** (1st Dist.1996) 42 Cal.App.4th 436, 454-55; *see* ***Vacco Indus. v. Van Den Berg*** (2d Dist.1992) 5 Cal.App.4th 34, 50. See "Waiver of privilege," ch. 6-A, §2.2.14, p. 607.

§1.8 How to assert trade-secret privilege. Asserting the trade-secret privilege is a three-step process, whether asserted first by objection or through a motion for protective order. *See* ***Raymond Handling Concepts Corp. v. Superior Ct.*** (1st Dist.1995) 39 Cal.App.4th 584, 590; ***Bridgestone/Firestone, Inc. v. Superior Ct.*** (1st Dist.1992) 7 Cal.App.4th 1384, 1393; Wegner, *Civil Trials & Evidence*, ¶¶8:2559-8.2562. Although some of the allegations and proof required by the trade-secret privilege are different from those required for other discovery disputes, the outline of the procedure is the same.

1. Option 1 – Objection & motion to compel.

(1) Owner claims privilege. The trade-secret owner (or its agent or employee) can claim the trade-secret privilege by making an objection to a discovery request. *See* Evid. C. §1060; ***Stadish v. Superior Ct.*** (2d Dist.1999) 71 Cal.App.4th 1130, 1141; *see, e.g.*, ***Bridgestone/Firestone***, 7 Cal.App.4th at 1388-89 (objection to interrogatories about tire-compound formulas based on trade secret). If the owner does not make a timely trade-secret objection to the discovery request, it waives the privilege. *See, e.g.*, ***Stadish***, 71 Cal.App.4th at 1141 (owner waived privilege by not objecting to request for production before responding and producing 40 boxes of documents). See "Responding party objects to discovery," ch. 7-A, §14.1.1, p. 771.

(2) Discovering party moves to compel. In response to an objection that the information sought is protected by the trade-secret privilege, the discovering party has the burden to enforce discovery. It must initiate the meet-and-confer procedure and, if unsuccessful, file a motion to compel discovery to secure the discovery. See "Discovering party moves to compel (option 1)," ch. 7-A, §14.1.2, p. 772.

(a) Motion papers.

[1] Separate statement. Depending on the type of discovery request, the discovering party must include in a motion to compel a separate statement containing all the information necessary to understand each discovery request and related response. *See* CRC 3.1345(a), (c). See "Separate statement," ch. 9-D, §4.2.5(1)(d), p. 1054; "Separate statement," ch. 9-E, §3.2.4(4), p. 1064.

[2] Good-cause statement. Depending on the type of discovery request, the discovering party must include in a motion to compel a statement of good cause justifying the discovery. See "Good cause for production," ch. 9-D, §4.1.2(4), p. 1052; "Good cause," ch. 9-E, §3.1.2(1), p. 1061.

(b) Grounds. If, during the meet-and-confer conference, the discovering party obtained sufficient information to understand the basis of the claim of privilege, the discovering party can attempt to disprove the claim of privilege, show that the privilege was waived or that an exception to the privilege applies, or argue that discovery should be allowed based on necessity and fairness.

[1] Disprove privilege. The discovering party can attempt to dispute the applicability of the privilege to the information sought. See "Disprove objection," ch. 7-A, §14.1.5(1), p. 774.

[2] Prove waiver or exception. The discovering party can attempt to show a waiver of the privilege or the applicability of an exception. ***Lipton v. Superior Ct.*** (2d Dist.1996) 48 Cal.App.4th 1599, 1619. See "What trade-secret privilege does not protect," §1.6, p. 644; "Waiver of privilege," ch. 6-A, §2.2.14, p. 607.

[3] Prove necessity & fairness. The discovering party can argue that the information protected by the trade-secret privilege is discoverable based on necessity and fairness. The party must make a prima facie, particularized showing that (1) the information is relevant and necessary to a material element of its cause of action or defense and (2) the information is reasonably essential to a fair resolution of the suit. ***Citizens of Humanity, LLC v. Costco Wholesale Corp.*** (2d Dist.2009) 171 Cal.App.4th 1, 13, *disapproved on other grounds*, ***Kwikset Corp. v. Superior Ct.*** (2011) 51 Cal.4th 310; ***Raymond Handling Concepts***, 39 Cal.App.4th at 590; ***Bridgestone/Firestone***, 7 Cal.App.4th at 1393.

(3) Owner opposes motion to compel. In response to a motion to compel, the trade-secret owner (or its agent or employee) must file opposition papers that address its burden.

NOTE

If the owner filed a motion for protective order before its response to discovery was due, that motion would contain the same information as set out below.

(a) Preliminary facts. The trade-secret owner must establish that the information sought by discovery qualifies as a trade secret. ***Citizens of Humanity***, 171 Cal.App.4th at 13. The owner must explain how the information fits the definition of a protectable trade secret and why protecting the information will not tend to conceal fraud or otherwise work injustice. *See* Evid. C. §1060.

[1] Proof factors. The trade-secret owner must provide preliminary facts establishing that the privilege applies to the requested information. *See* ***Bridgestone/Firestone***, 7 Cal.App.4th at 1393 (owner has burden to establish existence of privilege); 7 Cal. Law Revision Comm'n Rep. (1965) p. 1054 (objecting party has burden to show privilege applies and must submit evidence to court on preliminary issue). See "Elements of trade-secret privilege," §1.3, p. 642.

[2] Balance factors. The trade-secret owner must show why the trade secret should be protected. ***Agricultural Labor Relations Bd. v. Richard A. Glass Co.*** (4th Dist.1985) 175 Cal.App.3d 703, 715. The owner must provide the court with sufficient information to determine whether the interest involved in the trade secret's value to the owner outweighs the discovering party's need for the information. *Id.* The owner must show that protecting the trade secret would not tend to conceal a fraud or work an injustice on the discovering party. *See* Evid. C. §1060; ***Agricultural Labor Relations Bd.***, 175 Cal.App.3d at 715. To establish the value of the trade secret, the owner should show how the disclosure would harm the owner's business. *See* ***Agricultural Labor Relations Bd.***, 175 Cal.App.3d at 714-15.

(b) Supporting declaration. The motion must be supported by a declaration or affidavit, based on personal knowledge, that (1) lists the declarant's or affiant's qualifications to give an opinion about the trade secret, (2) identifies the trade secret without revealing it, and (3) presents evidence that the information qualifies as a trade secret under Civ. C. §3426.1(d). *See, e.g.*, ***Citizens of Humanity***, 171 Cal.App.4th at 13-14 (vice president's declaration stated that company's vendor information was trade secret because of intense competition in industry and because disclosure would jeopardize company's buying advantage); ***Raymond Handling Concepts***, 39 Cal.App.4th at 586 (assistant general counsel and engineering manager made declarations identifying documents and explaining basis for claims of privilege); ***Bridgestone/Firestone***, 7 Cal.App.4th at 1395-96 (employee's declaration established that tire-compound formulas qualified for protection); *cf.* Evid. C. §1061(b)(1) (requirements of affidavit for trade-secret protective order in criminal proceeding).

(c) Alternative to full disclosure. The trade-secret owner (or the discovering party) can propose (or oppose) a less intrusive alternative to disclosure of the trade secret. ***Citizens of Humanity***, 171 Cal.App.4th at 13; ***Bridgestone/Firestone***, 7 Cal.App.4th at 1393. The owner must show that the proposed alternative (1) will not unduly burden the discovering party and (2) will maintain the same fair balance in the litigation that would have been achieved by disclosure. ***Citizens of Humanity***, 171 Cal.App.4th at 13; ***Bridgestone/Firestone***, 7 Cal.App.4th at 1393.

(d) Request for protection. The trade-secret owner can request protection of its trade secrets. The owner does not need to file a separate motion for protective order when responding to a motion to compel; the owner can request a protective order in its opposition papers. *See* ***Stadish***, 71 Cal.App.4th at 1138. If the court orders disclosure because the discovering party establishes that the information should be produced for reasons of necessity and fairness, the trade-secret owner should demonstrate the disadvantages of any protective order that could be issued to protect the information. ***Citizens of Humanity***, 171 Cal.App.4th at 13; ***Bridgestone/Firestone***, 7 Cal.App.4th at 1393. See "Prove necessity & fairness," §1.8.1(2)(b)[3], p. 645.

2. Option 2 – Motion for protective order.

(1) Owner moves for protective order. The trade-secret owner (or its agent or employee) can claim the trade-secret privilege by filing a motion for protective order in response to a discovery request. *See* CCP §2025.420(a) (deposition protective order), §2033.080(a) (written-admissions protective order); *cf.* Evid. C. §1061(b)(1) (trade-secret protective order in criminal proceeding).

NOTE

When making a motion for protective order of a trade secret, the owner can look to the procedures in Evid. C. §1061(b), which governs the assertion of the trade-secret privilege in a criminal case. See ***Stadish****, 71 Cal.App.4th at 1145 (procedures under Evid. C. §1061 "have a utility" in protecting trade-secret privilege in civil cases); see, e.g.,* ***State Farm Fire & Cas. Co. v. Superior Ct.*** *(2d Dist.1997) 54 Cal.App.4th 625, 650-51 (applying Evid. C. §1061(b)(1) in civil case).*

(a) Motion papers. See "Motion," ch. 9-B, §3, p. 1028.

(b) Burden on movant. The trade-secret owner has the initial burden to establish the existence of the trade secret. ***Bridgestone/Firestone***, 7 Cal.App.4th at 1393; *cf.* Evid. C. §1061(b)(3) (movant must show by preponderance of evidence that issuance of protective order is proper in criminal proceeding). For the requirements to meet this burden, see "Preliminary facts," §1.8.1(3)(a), p. 646.

(c) Supporting declaration. The motion must be supported by a declaration or affidavit. *Cf.* Evid. C. §1061(b)(1) (requirements of affidavit in criminal proceeding). For the requirements of the declaration or affidavit, see "Supporting declaration," §1.8.1(3)(b), p. 646; "Supporting evidence," ch. 9-B, §3.3.3, p. 1034.

(d) Alternative to full disclosure. The trade-secret owner can propose an alternative to full disclosure. ***Bridgestone/Firestone***, 7 Cal.App.4th at 1393. See "Alternative to full disclosure," §1.8.1(3)(c), p. 646.

(2) Discovering party opposes motion for protective order. In response to a motion for protective order, the discovering party must file opposition papers that address its burden. *See* ***Citizens of Humanity***, 171 Cal.App.4th at 13; ***Bridgestone/Firestone***, 7 Cal.App.4th at 1393; *cf.* Evid. C. §1061(b)(2) (any party to proceeding can oppose request for protective order in criminal case).

(a) Opposition papers. See "Opposition," ch. 9-B, §4.2, p. 1035.

(b) Burden on opposition. If the trade-secret owner (or its agent or employee) meets its initial burden of establishing that the trade-secret privilege applies, the burden shifts to the discovering party to make a prima facie, particularized showing that (1) the information sought is relevant and necessary to prove or defend a material element in the case and (2) the information is reasonably essential to a fair resolution of the suit. ***Citizens of Humanity***, 171 Cal.App.4th at 13; ***Bridgestone/Firestone***, 7 Cal.App.4th at 1393.

(c) Supporting declaration. The opposition papers should include a responsive declaration or other evidence if necessary to support facts in the opposition papers or refute facts in the motion for protective order. *CEB Discovery Practice*, §15.78. See "Supporting evidence," ch. 1-D, §5.3, p. 30. If the discovering party has personal knowledge of the trade secret (e.g., the discovering party is a former employee of the trade-secret owner), the declaration may need to be filed in the court under seal. *Cf.* Evid. C. §1061(b)(2) (affidavit based on personal knowledge submitted in opposition to motion for protective order must be filed under seal in criminal case). It is not clear whether the declaration should be served on any party other than the trade-secret owner. *Cf. id.* (affidavit must be provided to trade-secret owner and to all parties in proceeding, but no person can disclose affidavit to anyone other than counsel of record without court approval).

(d) Alternative to full disclosure. The discovering party can propose an alternative to full disclosure. ***Bridgestone/Firestone***, 7 Cal.App.4th at 1393. See "Alternative to full disclosure," §1.8.1(3)(c), p. 646.

(3) **Owner replies to opposition.** In reply to an opposition to the motion for protective order, the trade-secret owner (or its agent or employee) must file reply papers that address its burden. *See* ***Citizens of Humanity***, 171 Cal.App.4th at 13; ***Bridgestone/Firestone***, 7 Cal.App.4th at 1393. See "Reply Papers," ch. 1-D, §9, p. 37. If the discovering party meets its burden of showing that the information is relevant, necessary, and essential, the trade-secret owner must respond by showing the disadvantages of a protective order that allows disclosure. *See* ***Bridgestone/Firestone***, 7 Cal.App.4th at 1393.

§1.9 Court's ruling on trade-secret privilege. See "Ruling," ch. 9-B, §8, p. 1037; "Order," ch. 9-B, §9, p. 1037.

1. In camera inspection. A court can require an in camera inspection of trade-secret information to determine the applicability of the privilege. Evid. C. §915(b).

2. Trade-secret ruling.

(1) **Not trade secret.** If the court finds that the information is not a trade secret, the information is not protected by the privilege and is discoverable.

(2) **Trade secret.** If the court finds that the information is a trade secret, it must decide whether the discovering party made a prima facie case of relevance and fairness before it can require disclosure.

(a) **Relevance.** The record must show that the trade-secret information was directly relevant to a material issue in the case. *See* ***Bridgestone/Firestone, Inc. v. Superior Ct.*** (1st Dist.1992) 7 Cal.App.4th 1384, 1392.

(b) **Fairness.** The record must show that the discovering party would be unfairly disadvantaged without the trade-secret information. *See* ***Bridgestone/Firestone***, 7 Cal.App.4th at 1392. If enforcement of the privilege would result in a fraud or injustice, the court must order disclosure. *Id.* at 1393. If enforcement of the privilege would not result in a fraud or injustice, the court must deny disclosure. *Id.*

3. Protective order. If the court orders disclosure of the trade secret, it may limit the disclosure and restrict access to the information. *See* CCP §2025.420(b)(13) (protective order can permit disclosure only to specified persons or only in specified ways); *see, e.g.*, ***Bridgestone/Firestone***, 7 Cal.App.4th at 1389 (court imposed protective order on disclosure). The court can limit the dissemination of documents for good cause, even if the owner did not assert the trade-secret privilege when it produced the documents. ***Stadish v. Superior Ct.*** (2d Dist.1999) 71 Cal.App.4th 1130, 1143-44.

(1) **To party or third party.** The court can limit the discovering party's use of the trade-secret information (e.g., who the information can be shared with), based on the need to balance the owner's interest in keeping the information secret against the need to protect the discovering party from being unfairly disadvantaged in the suit. *See* CCP §2025.420(b)(13) (protective orders for discovery), §2030.090(b)(6) (same), §2031.060(b)(5) (same), §2033.080(b)(4) (same); ***Bridgestone/Firestone***, 7 Cal.App.4th at 1393 (court must consider effectiveness of protective order and less intrusive alternatives to disclosure); *see, e.g.*, ***Raymond Handling Concepts Corp. v. Superior Ct.*** (1st Dist.1995) 39 Cal.App.4th 584, 590 (protective order allowed disclosure of trade secrets to attorneys in similar cases only if attorneys executed stipulation agreeing to be bound by protective order); *see also* ***Stadish***, 71 Cal.App.4th at 1145 (procedures under Evid. C. §1061 should be followed in civil cases); *cf.* Evid. C. §1061(b)(4) (listing examples of terms and conditions that protect trade-secret information in criminal cases). For example, if the discovering party is not a competitor, the protective order can simply bar any disclosure of the information to third parties who are competitors. ***Hypertouch, Inc. v. Superior Ct.*** (1st Dist.2005) 128 Cal.App.4th 1527, 1555 n.16; *cf.* Civ. C. §3426.5 (in action under Uniform Trade Secrets Act, court must preserve secrecy of alleged trade secret by reasonable means, which may include ordering any person involved in litigation not to disclose information without court approval).

(2) **To public.** The court can protect trade-secret information from public access by sealing the record. *See* Evid. C. §1063; ***In re Providian Credit Card Cases*** (1st Dist.2002) 96 Cal.App.4th 292, 299; *see also* CRC

2.550 (sealing trial and evidentiary records), CRC 2.551 (filing records under seal); *cf.* Civ. C. §3426.5 (in action under Uniform Trade Secrets Act, court must preserve secrecy of alleged trade secret by reasonable means, which may include sealing records). To seal the record, the court must include in its order express findings establishing the overriding interest in preventing public access to the information and the necessity of sealing the record. *See* CRC 2.550(d), (e)(1)(A); ***In re Providian***, 96 Cal.App.4th at 300 (protecting trade secrets may be "overriding interest" that requires sealing record).

§2. PRIVATE-INVESTIGATOR PRIVILEGE

Under the Private Investigator Act, a private investigator hired to investigate a matter for another person usually cannot divulge information acquired during the investigation to a third party. *See* Bus. & Prof. C. §7539(a). There is some question whether this amounts to a privilege. If there is such a privilege, it is implied from the "shall not divulge" language in Bus. & Prof. C. §7539(a).

§2.1 General. There is very little discussion in case law or legal treatises about the private investigator's duty not to divulge. *See, e.g., CEB Discovery Practice*, §3.152 (one paragraph noting duty not to divulge). Because of the uncertainty of the privilege, private investigators should look elsewhere for protection—namely, the client's constitutional right to privacy or the work-product privilege, if the investigator was hired by an attorney. *See* Caragozian, *Private Investigators*, at www.privacyrights.org/ar/PIs-Caragozian.htm; *see, e.g.*, ***Rodriguez v. McDonnell Douglas Corp.*** (2d Dist.1978) 87 Cal.App.3d 626, 647-48 (notes of investigator hired by attorney to interview witness were protected under work-product privilege), *disapproved on other grounds*, ***Coito v. Superior Ct.*** (2012) 54 Cal.4th 480. For a discussion of these privileges, see "Work-Product Privilege," ch. 6-B, §3, p. 628; "Right to Privacy," ch. 6-F, §1, p. 681. Regardless of whether there is a private-investigator privilege, an attorney should be familiar with the basic framework of the investigator's duty not to divulge communications or other information.

1. **Purpose.** The purpose of the private investigator's duty not to disclose is to prevent the investigator from disclosing information gathered on a client's behalf, except to the client or as required by law. *See* Bus. & Prof. C. §7539(a).

2. **Primary authority.** Bus. & Prof. C. §7539(a).

§2.2 Who is private investigator. A private investigator is a person (other than an insurance adjuster) who, for consideration, engages in business or accepts employment to protect a person or to make an investigation for the purpose of obtaining information about any of the following:

1. Crime or wrongs done or threatened against the United States. Bus. & Prof. C. §7521(a).

2. The identity, habits, conduct, business, occupation, honesty, integrity, credibility, knowledge, trustworthiness, efficiency, loyalty, activity, movement, whereabouts, affiliations, associations, transactions, acts, reputation, or character of a person. *Id.* §7521(b).

3. The location, disposition, or recovery of lost or stolen property. *Id.* §7521(c).

4. The cause of or responsibility for fires, libels, losses, accidents, or damage or injury to persons or to property. *Id.* §7521(d).

5. Evidence to be used before any court, board, officer, or investigating committee. *Id.* §7521(e).

15 **§2.3 Who is client.** A client is any person who employs a private investigator to obtain information. *See* Bus. & Prof. C. §7539(a); *see also id.* §§7512.10-7512.11 (defining "employer" and "employee" under Private Investigator Act). For purposes of the private investigator's duty not to divulge, a client can be an individual, firm, company, limited-liability company, association, organization, partnership, or corporation. *See* Bus. & Prof. C. §7512.3(a) (defining "person" under Private Investigator Act); *see also id.* §7512.10 (defining "employer" as a person under Private Investigator Act).

§2.4 What is private investigator's duty. The private investigator's duty prevents an investigator from divulging information acquired for a client except to the client or to another person at the client's direction. *See* Bus.

& Prof. C. §7539(a). For the duty to apply, the information must be acquired on the client's behalf while the investigator is employed by the client. ***Flynn v. Superior Ct.*** (4th Dist.1997) 57 Cal.App.4th 990, 994. This duty is not absolute, however, because the investigator may be legally required to divulge certain information. *See* Bus. & Prof. C. §7539(a).

1. To law enforcement. The private investigator may divulge to law-enforcement officers or district attorneys any information the investigator acquired about a criminal offense. Bus. & Prof. C. §7539(a).

2. To other person. The private investigator may be compelled by law to divulge information to another person. Bus. & Prof. C. §7539(a).

D. SPOUSAL PRIVILEGES

This subchapter covers privileges relating to spouses: (1) the spousal-testimonial privileges and (2) the marital-communications privilege.

6-2. COMPARISON OF SPOUSAL PRIVILEGES

		Privilege not to testify against spouse	Privilege not to be called as witness	Marital-communications privilege
		Application of privileges		
1	Evidence Code sections	§970	§971	§§980-987
2	Scope of privilege	Prevents witness spouse from being forced to testify against nonwitness spouse	Prevents witness spouse from being called by adverse party as a witness against nonwitness spouse	Prevents disclosure of confidential communications between spouses during valid marital relationship
3	What is protected	Testimony *adverse* to nonwitness spouse while the spouses are in valid marital relationship	All testimony when witness spouse is called by adverse party and nonwitness spouse is party to proceeding	Confidential communications between spouses during valid marital relationship
4	What is not protected	Testimony *in favor* of nonwitness spouse	• Testimony when nonwitness spouse is not party to proceeding • Testimony when witness spouse is called by nonwitness spouse or party who is not adverse to nonwitness spouse	• Noncommunicative conduct • Communications made before or after valid marital relationship • Communications between spouses that were not intended to be confidential • Communications made without reasonable expectation of privacy • Fact that communication was made • Factual information that does not reveal content of communication • Information previously disclosed in another proceeding
5	Who can assert	Witness spouse	Witness spouse	Either spouse
6	Who can waive	Witness spouse	Witness spouse	Must be waived by both spouses
7	Duration of privilege	As long as valid marital relationship has not been terminated by death, divorce, or annulment		As long as there is a living spouse to assert privilege

6-2. COMPARISON OF SPOUSAL PRIVILEGES (CONTINUED)				
		Privilege not to testify against spouse	Privilege not to be called as witness	Marital-communications privilege
Exceptions to privileges				
8	Action between spouses	Yes		Yes
9	Claim against surviving spouse	No		Yes
10	Commitment proceeding	Yes		Yes
11	Conservatorship or similar proceeding	Yes		Yes
12	Competency proceeding	Yes		Yes
13	Juvenile-court proceeding	Yes		Yes
14	Criminal proceeding	Exceptions for multiple types of criminal proceedings		Exceptions for multiple types of criminal proceedings
15	Support proceeding	Yes		Yes
16	Proceeding for immediate benefit of spouse	Yes		No
17	Crime-fraud exception	No		Yes
18	Abuse of confidential relationship	No		Yes

§1. SPOUSAL-TESTIMONIAL PRIVILEGES

§1.1 General. The spousal-testimonial privileges protect a witness spouse from being compelled to testify against a nonwitness spouse. Evid. C. §§970, 971; ***Jurcoane v. Superior Ct.*** (2d Dist.2001) 93 Cal.App.4th 886, 896. Under the Evidence Code, the witness spouse has two distinct spousal-testimonial privileges. Evid. C. §§970, 971; 7 Cal. Law Revision Comm'n Rep. (1965) p. 1171; Wegner, *California Practice Guide: Civil Trials & Evidence* (CD-ROM ed. 2014) ¶8:2318. The first privilege protects the witness spouse from being forced to testify against the nonwitness spouse; this is the privilege *not to testify*. Evid. C. §970; Wegner, *Civil Trials & Evidence*, ¶8.2319. The second privilege protects the witness spouse from being called to testify in a proceeding to which the nonwitness spouse is a party; this is the privilege *not to be called*. Evid. C. §971; ***Jurcoane***, 93 Cal.App.4th at 894; Wegner, *Civil Trials & Evidence*, ¶8.2320. Together, these are referred to as the "spousal-testimonial privileges."

1. Purpose. The purpose of the spousal-testimonial privileges is to (1) preserve marital harmony, (2) protect marital privacy, and (3) promote the institution of marriage. ***People v. Sinohui*** (2002) 28 Cal.4th 205, 211; *see* 7 Cal. Law Revision Comm'n Rep. (1965) p. 1172 (having to testify against spouse would seriously disturb marital relationship). The privilege not to be called has one additional purpose: to avoid prejudice to the nonwitness spouse that would result from forcing the witness spouse to assert the spousal-testimonial privilege in front of a jury. 7 Cal. Law Revision Comm'n Rep. (1965) p. 1172.

2. Primary authority. Evid. C. §§970-973.

3. Secondary authority. The following secondary sources are cited as authority in this section:

- *California Civil Discovery Practice* (CEB Online ed. 2014) (referred to as *CEB Discovery Practice*).
- Wegner, *California Practice Guide: Civil Trials & Evidence* (CD-ROM ed. 2014) (referred to as Wegner, *Civil Trials & Evidence*).
- Witkin, *California Evidence* (5th ed. 2012 & Supp.2014) (referred to as Witkin, *Cal. Evidence*).

§1.2 Nature of spousal-testimonial privileges.

1. Absolute. The spousal-testimonial privileges are absolute. *See* Evid. C. §§970-972 (listing no circumstances in which privileges apply but can be overcome). See "When spousal-testimonial privileges apply," §1.5, p. 654. However, the privileges do not apply in all proceedings. See "When spousal-testimonial privileges do not apply," §1.6, p. 655.

2. Duration. The spousal-testimonial privileges last as long as the couple is in a valid marital relationship. ***People v. Dorsey*** (2d Dist.1975) 46 Cal.App.3d 706, 716-17. See "Valid marital relationship," §1.3.2, this page.

(1) No viability requirement. The spousal-testimonial privileges continue even if the marriage is no longer viable. ***Jurcoane v. Superior Ct.*** (2d Dist.2001) 93 Cal.App.4th 886, 889. For example, a witness spouse can assert the privileges even if the spouses are separated with no chance of reconciliation. *See, e.g., id.* (privilege could be asserted even though spouses had no contact for 17 years).

(2) Immediate termination. The spousal-testimonial privileges end immediately after the marital relationship is terminated by death, divorce, or annulment. *See* Evid. C. §970 (privilege applies only to "married person"), §971 (same); Fam. C. §299 (dissolution of domestic partnership), §310 (dissolution of marriage); ***People v. Bradford*** (1969) 70 Cal.2d 333, 343 (final divorce decree terminates testimonial privilege); Wegner, *Civil Trials & Evidence*, ¶8:2315 (privileges under §§970 and 971 end with termination of marital relationship, whether by death or judgment of dissolution or nullity). For example, a witness spouse cannot assert a spousal-testimonial privilege once a final divorce is granted, even if the divorce is finalized in the middle of trial. ***Bradford***, 70 Cal.2d at 343.

3. Discovery & evidentiary. The spousal-testimonial privileges are both discovery privileges and evidentiary privileges because the spouse cannot be compelled to attend or testify in either discovery proceedings or at trial. *See* Evid. C. §§970, 971.

§1.3 Elements of spousal-testimonial privileges. The elements of the spousal-testimonial privileges are the following:

1. Asked to testify or called as witness. The witness spouse is asked to testify against the nonwitness spouse or is called as a witness in a proceeding to which the nonwitness spouse is a party. See "When spousal-testimonial privileges apply," §1.5, p. 654.

2. Valid marital relationship. The witness spouse and the nonwitness spouse are in a valid marital relationship when the witness is asked to testify or is called as a witness. *See* Evid. C. §§970, 971; ***People v. Bradford*** (1969) 70 Cal.2d 333, 343; *see also* Fam. C. §297.5 (registered domestic partners have same rights as spouses).

NOTE

*The following discussion of whether the witness spouse and nonwitness spouse are in a valid marital relationship relies on cases addressing the spousal-testimonial privileges, the marital-communications privilege, or both because all the privileges are predicated on the existence of a valid marriage. See **People v. Badgett (1995)** 10 Cal.4th 330, 363 (marital-communications privilege); **Bradford**, 70 Cal.2d at 343 (spousal-testimonial privileges); Wegner, Civil Trials & Evidence, ¶8:2312 (all privileges predicated on valid marriage).*

(1) People in marital relationship. The following people are considered to be in a valid marital relationship:

(a) Spouse in valid marriage. Spouses in a valid marriage under California law can assert the spousal-testimonial privileges. *See* Evid. C. §§970, 971; ***Bradford***, 70 Cal.2d at 343; ***Jurcoane v. Superior Ct.*** (2d Dist.2001) 93 Cal.App.4th 886, 897; *see also* Fam. C. §300 (defining "marriage").

(b) Registered domestic partner. Domestic partners registered under the California Domestic Partner Rights & Responsibilities Act (DPRRA) can assert the spousal-testimonial privileges. Wegner, *Civil Trials & Evidence*, ¶8:2310.1; *see* Fam. C. §297.5 (registered domestic partners have same rights as spouses). The DPRRA extends to registered domestic partners many of the rights and benefits of married people, including the spousal-testimonial and marital-communications privileges. *See CEB Discovery Practice*, §3.75 (marital-communications privilege "likely" applies to domestic partners); Wegner, *Civil Trials & Evidence*, ¶8:2310.1 (discussion of both privileges should be read as applying to domestic partners).

(c) Spouse under other state's law. Spouses in a valid marriage under the law of another state can assert the spousal-testimonial privileges. *See* Fam. C. §308; *cf.* ***Badgett***, 10 Cal.4th at 363 (marital-communications privilege); *CEB Discovery Practice*, §3.75 (same).

15 **NOTE**

Before 2014, a same-sex marriage contracted outside California was not recognized as a valid marriage unless the marriage was contracted before November 5, 2008. In 2014, the California Legislature amended Fam. C. §308 to eliminate this limitation, thus making valid out-of-state same-sex marriages valid in California regardless of when the marriage was contracted. Stats. 2014, ch. 82, §§1, 5, 6.

(d) Spouse in voidable marriage. Spouses in a voidable marriage can assert the spousal-testimonial privileges as long as the marriage has not been declared a nullity. *See* ***Jurcoane***, 93 Cal.App.4th at 897 (privilege can be asserted by spouses in marriage that is "legally intact" even if marriage could be characterized as "moribund," "abandoned," or "no longer viable"); Wegner, *Civil Trials & Evidence*, ¶8:2317 (voidable marriage does not defeat privileges); 2 Witkin, *Cal. Evidence*, Witnesses, §175 (privilege applies to voidable marriage until marriage is annulled); *see, e.g.*, ***People v. Livingston*** (2d Dist.1928) 88 Cal.App. 713, 714 (decision under former statute on spousal-testimonial privilege; wife should not have been allowed to testify because judgment setting aside marriage was not final when testimony was offered); *cf.* ***People v. Dorsey*** (2d Dist.1975) 46 Cal.App.3d 706, 717 (voidable marriage does not defeat marital-communications privilege). Voidable marriages are marriages that can be nullified for any of the following reasons:

[1] A spouse was unable to consent to the marriage due to minority. Fam. C. §2210(a).

[2] A spouse entered into the marriage after the absence and presumed death of a spouse from an earlier marriage that was still in force, and the spouse from the earlier marriage returned. *See id.* §2210(b).

[3] A spouse was mentally or physically incapable of marriage. *Id.* §2210(c), (f). If a spouse was physically incapable of marriage, the physical incapability must be incurable for the marriage to be voidable. *Id.* §2210(f).

[4] A spouse's consent to the marriage was obtained by fraud or force. *Id.* §2210(d), (e).

(2) People not in marital relationships. The following people are not considered spouses in a valid marital relationship:

(a) Person in invalid marriage. People whose marriage is not valid cannot assert the spousal-testimonial privileges. *See* Evid. C. §970 (privilege applies only to "married person"), §971 (same); ***Bradford***, 70 Cal.2d at 343 (valid marriage is required for assertion of testimonial privilege); ***People v. Delph*** (2d Dist.1979) 94 Cal.App.3d 411, 415 (same). The following relationships are not valid marriages for purposes of the spousal-testimonial privileges:

[1] Common-law marriage in California. A person claiming to be a common-law spouse under California law cannot assert the spousal-testimonial privileges because California has abolished common-law marriages. ***Badgett***, 10 Cal.4th at 363; *see also* ***Norman v. Norman*** (1898) 121 Cal. 620, 628-29 (concluding that

common-law marriage was abolished in California by statute). But a person can assert the spousal-testimonial privileges based on a valid common-law marriage under another state's law. See "Spouse under other state's law," §1.3.2(1)(c), p. 653.

[2] **Void marriage.** A person in a void marriage cannot assert the spousal-testimonial privileges. Wegner, *Civil Trials & Evidence*, ¶8:2317; 2 Witkin, *Cal. Evidence*, Witnesses, §175; *see* ***People v. Catlin*** (2001) 26 Cal.4th 81, 130; ***People v. Keller*** (2d Dist.1958) 165 Cal.App.2d 419, 423 (decision under former statute on spousal-testimonial privilege); *cf.* ***People v. Gallego*** (1990) 52 Cal.3d 115, 176-77 (person in void marriage cannot assert marital-communications privilege). Void marriages are marriages that are bigamous or incestuous. Fam. C. §§2200, 2201; *e.g.*, ***Catlin***, 26 Cal.4th at 130 (person in bigamous marriage could not assert marital-communications privilege).

(b) Person in invalid domestic partnership. People whose domestic partnership is not valid cannot assert the spousal-testimonial privileges. *See* Evid. C. §970 (privilege applies only to "married person"), §971 (same); Fam. C. §297.5 (registered domestic partners have same rights as spouses). The following relationships are not valid domestic partnerships for purposes of the spousal-testimonial privileges:

[1] **Unregistered domestic partnership.** A person in an unregistered domestic partnership cannot assert the spousal-testimonial privileges because the DPRRA does not give unregistered domestic partners the rights and protections of a spouse in a traditional marriage. *See* Fam. C. §297.5(a); Wegner, *Civil Trials & Evidence*, ¶8:2312. See "Registered domestic partner," §1.3.2(1)(b), p. 653.

[2] **Void domestic partnership.** A person who is not a domestic partner because the domestic partnership is void cannot assert the spousal-testimonial privileges. *See* Fam. C. §297(b)(2) & (b)(3) (prohibiting bigamous and incestuous domestic partnerships).

(c) Cohabiting person. People who are merely cohabiting without being formally married or registered as domestic partners cannot assert the spousal-testimonial privileges. *See* Evid. C. §970 (only "married person" can assert privilege), §971 (same); Fam. C. §297.5 (registered domestic partners have same rights as spouses); ***Delph***, 94 Cal.App.3d at 415 (cohabiting is insufficient for spousal-testimonial and marital-communications privileges); *see, e.g.*, ***People v. Guerra*** (2006) 37 Cal.4th 1067, 1083 n.3 (marital privilege did not apply because couple never formally married); *cf.* ***People v. Hunt*** (2d Dist.1982) 133 Cal.App.3d 543, 559 (cohabiting is insufficient for marital-communications privilege).

(d) Former spouse. People whose marital relationship was terminated by death, divorce, or annulment cannot assert the spousal-testimonial privileges. *See* ***Bradford***, 70 Cal.2d at 343.

(e) Former domestic partners. People whose domestic partnership was terminated cannot assert the spousal-testimonial privileges. *See* Evid. C. §§970, 971; Fam. C. §299.

§1.4 Who can assert spousal-testimonial privileges. The witness spouse is the only person who can assert the spousal-testimonial privileges. Evid. C. §970; ***People v. Lucas*** (1995) 12 Cal.4th 415, 490; ***People v. Resendez*** (4th Dist.1993) 12 Cal.App.4th 98, 110 n.7; 7 Cal. Law Revision Comm'n Rep. (1965) p. 1172. See "People in marital relationship," §1.3.2(1), p. 652. The nonwitness spouse cannot assert the spousal-testimonial privileges to prevent the witness spouse from being called or testifying. ***Lucas***, 12 Cal.4th at 490; ***People v. Bradford*** (1969) 70 Cal.2d 333, 343; 7 Cal. Law Revision Comm'n Rep. (1965) p. 1172.

§1.5 When spousal-testimonial privileges apply.

1. Privilege not to testify. Under Evid. C. §970, a witness spouse has a privilege not to testify against a nonwitness spouse under the following circumstances:

(1) Testimony sought. The privilege not to testify against a nonwitness spouse applies only when testimony adverse to the nonwitness spouse's interests is sought. *See* Evid. C. §970; 7 Cal. Law Revision Comm'n Rep. (1965) p. 1172. But if a witness spouse attempts to give limited testimony in favor of the nonwitness spouse,

the witness spouse opens herself up to cross-examination on matters unfavorable to the nonwitness spouse. ***People v. Lucas*** (1995) 12 Cal.4th 415, 490-91; *see* Evid. C. §973(a).

(2) Permitted proceedings. The privilege not to testify against a nonwitness spouse can be invoked in any proceeding not excepted by statute, regardless of whether the nonwitness spouse is a party to the proceeding. *See* Evid. C. §970; Wegner, *Civil Trials & Evidence*, ¶8:2321. See "Excepted proceedings," §1.6.3, p. 656. A "proceeding" includes any action, hearing, investigation, inquest, or inquiry in which testimony can be compelled. Evid. C. §901.

2. Privilege not to be called. Under Evid. C. §971, a witness spouse has a privilege not to be called as a witness under the following circumstances:

(1) Testimony sought. The privilege not to be called as a witness applies to any testimony sought by an adverse party, not just testimony that is adverse to the nonwitness spouse's interests. *See* Evid. C. §971.

(2) Permitted proceedings. The privilege not to be called as a witness can be invoked only when (1) the proceeding is not excepted by statute and (2) the nonwitness spouse is a party to the proceeding in which the witness spouse is called. Evid. C. §971; *see* Wegner, *Civil Trials & Evidence*, ¶¶8:2321, 8.2325. See "Excepted proceedings," §1.6.3, p. 656. A "proceeding" includes any action, hearing, investigation, inquest, or inquiry in which testimony can be compelled. Evid. C. §901. If the nonwitness spouse is not a party to the proceeding (e.g., a grand-jury proceeding involving the nonwitness spouse), the privilege does not apply. 7 Cal. Law Revision Comm'n Rep. (1965) p. 1172.

PRACTICE TIP

Even if the privilege not to be called cannot be invoked because the nonwitness spouse is not a party to the proceeding, the witness spouse can still assert the privilege not to testify against the nonwitness spouse. 7 Cal. Law Revision Comm'n Rep. (1965) p. 1172. *See "Privilege not to testify," §1.5.1, p. 654.*

(3) Called by adverse party. The privilege not to be called as a witness protects the witness spouse from being called to testify only by the adverse party. Evid. C. §971. The witness spouse can still be called to testify by the nonwitness spouse. *See id.*; 2 Witkin, *Cal. Evidence*, Witnesses, §180. The witness spouse can also be called to testify by a coparty whose interests are not adverse to the nonwitness spouse's interests. *See* Evid. C. §971.

NOTE

Evid. C. §971 states that the privilege not to be called to testify by an adverse party applies "unless the party calling the spouse does so in good faith without knowledge of the marital relationship." This does not mean that the privilege is lost if an adverse party who is unaware of the marriage calls a witness spouse to testify. When this happens, the witness spouse should object and assert the privilege not to be called as a witness. Once the witness spouse asserts this privilege, the court must make a preliminary factual determination of whether the privilege applies before the witness spouse can be compelled to testify. ***Hand v. Superior Ct.*** *(3d Dist.1982) 134 Cal.App.3d 436, 438.*

§1.6 When spousal-testimonial privileges do not apply.

1. Express consent. The spousal-testimonial privilege not to be called does not apply when the witness spouse has given express consent to be called as a witness by a party adverse to the nonwitness-party spouse. Evid. C. §971.

2. Waiver. The spousal-testimonial privileges cannot be invoked when the witness spouse has waived them. Evid. C. §973.

NOTE

The crime-fraud exception, which applies to confidential marital communications, does not apply to the spousal-testimonial privileges. Wegner, Civil Trials & Evidence, ¶8:2368. See "Crime-fraud exception," §2.7.6, p. 662.

(1) By testifying. A witness spouse can waive the spousal-testimonial privileges in a proceeding by testifying. Evid. C. §973(a); *see* ***People v. Petrilli*** (1st Dist.2014) 226 Cal.App.4th 814, 824; ***People v. Resendez*** (4th Dist.1993) 12 Cal.App.4th 98, 107.

(a) When testimony waives privilege. The witness spouse waives the spousal-testimonial privileges by testifying in either of the following circumstances:

[1] Spouse is party. The witness spouse waives the spousal-testimonial privileges by testifying in any proceeding to which the nonwitness spouse is a party. Evid. C. §973(a); *see, e.g.*, ***Resendez***, 12 Cal.App.4th at 109 (wife waived privilege for trial by testifying against husband at preliminary hearing); ***People v. Rice*** (5th Dist.1981) 126 Cal.App.3d 477, 485 (wife waived privilege by testifying for prosecution against husband's co-D); *see also* ***Petrilli***, 226 Cal.App.4th at 825 (husband was target of grand-jury proceeding; wife's testimony to grand jury did not waive privilege because husband was not considered party to proceeding).

[2] Testifying against spouse. The witness spouse waives the spousal-testimonial privileges by testifying against a nonwitness spouse in any proceeding (i.e., by giving testimony that is adverse to the nonwitness spouse's interests), regardless of whether the nonwitness spouse is a party to the proceeding. Evid. C. §973(a). The waiver, however, applies only in the proceeding in which the testimony is given. *Id.*; *see* ***Petrilli***, 226 Cal.App.4th at 825-26 (husband was target of grand-jury proceeding; wife's testimony to grand jury did not waive privilege in husband's later trial because grand jury and trial were different proceedings).

(b) When testimony does not waive privilege. The witness spouse does not waive spousal-testimonial privileges by testifying if the testimony was erroneously compelled. Evid. C. §973(a). There is no statute or case explaining what constitutes "erroneously compelled" testimony. ***Resendez***, 12 Cal.App.4th at 107; Wegner, *Civil Trials & Evidence*, ¶8:2338. A statement that no one advised the witness spouse of the right to assert the spousal-testimonial privileges is not enough by itself to show that the testimony was erroneously compelled. *See* ***Resendez***, 12 Cal.App.4th at 108-09. At a minimum, the witness spouse must prove the testimony was compelled—that is, it was not freely given but forced. *See* Wegner, *Civil Trials & Evidence*, ¶8:2338. This includes proving who commanded the witness to testify and why the command to testify was compelling. *Id.*; *see* ***Resendez***, 12 Cal.App.4th at 108.

(c) Entire proceeding. A witness spouse who waives the spousal-testimonial privileges by testifying at any time during a proceeding waives the privileges for the entire proceeding. *See* Evid. C. §973(a); *see, e.g.*, ***Resendez***, 12 Cal.App.4th at 109 (spouse waived privileges for criminal trial by testifying at preliminary hearing). For example, if a proceeding involves issues that are being tried separately, a witness spouse cannot testify during the trial of one issue without waiving the spousal-testimonial privileges for the trial of all other issues in that proceeding. 7 Cal. Law Revision Comm'n Rep. (1965) p. 1174.

(2) By demanding information in child-support proceeding. Any person who has an obligation to support a child who is the subject of a child-support proceeding waives the right to assert the spousal-testimonial privileges for information on income, expenses, assets, debts, and employment by demanding this information from another party. Evid. C. §972(g), ¶2.

3. Excepted proceedings. A witness spouse's privileges not to testify and not to be called as a witness cannot be invoked in the following proceedings:

(1) Spouse vs. spouse. The spousal-testimonial privileges cannot be invoked in a suit by one spouse against the other spouse. Evid. C. §972(a); *see, e.g.*, ***Estate of Gillett*** (1st Dist.1946) 73 Cal.App.2d 588, 594 (suit by husband's estate against wife).

(2) Commitment proceeding. The spousal-testimonial privileges cannot be invoked in a commitment proceeding for a spouse. Evid. C. §972(b); *see also* Welfare & Inst. C. §5358 (placement of gravely disabled conservatee in treatment facility).

(3) Conservatorship or similar proceeding. The spousal-testimonial privileges cannot be invoked in a proceeding to place the spouse or the spouse's property under the control of another person because of the spouse's mental or physical condition. Evid. C. §972(b); *see also* Prob. C. §§1800.3, 1801(a)-(c), 1802 (authorizing appointment of conservator for adult based on inability to provide for personal needs or inability to manage financial resources); Welfare & Inst. C. §§5350-5372 (conservatorship of person who is gravely disabled by mental-health disorder or chronic alcoholism).

(4) Competence proceeding. The spousal-testimonial privileges cannot be invoked in a proceeding brought by or on behalf of a spouse to establish that spouse's competence. Evid. C. §972(c).

(5) Juvenile-court proceeding. The spousal-testimonial privileges cannot be invoked in a juvenile-court proceeding. Evid. C. §972(d).

(6) Certain criminal proceedings. The spousal-testimonial privileges cannot be invoked in the following criminal proceedings:

(a) A proceeding charging a spouse with any of the following crimes, regardless of whether the crimes were committed before or after the witness spouse and nonwitness spouse were in a valid marital relationship:

[1] A crime against the person or property of the other spouse. Evid. C. §972(e)(1).

[2] A crime against the person or property of a child, parent, relative, or cohabitant of either the witness spouse or the nonwitness spouse. *Id.*; *see, e.g.*, ***People v. Siravo*** (2d Dist.1993) 17 Cal.App.4th 555, 561-63 (defining "cohabitants" as two people who live or dwell together in same household, including cotenants, regardless of nature of relationship, and finding that wife could be compelled to testify against husband in trial for rape of wife's roommate).

[3] A crime against the person or property of some other person that is committed in the course of committing a crime against the person or property of the other spouse. Evid. C. §972(e)(2). For this exception to apply, the crimes against the spouse and the other person must be part of a continuous course of criminal conduct and must bear some logical relationship to each other. ***People v. Sinohui*** (2002) 28 Cal.4th 205, 220. It applies even if no accusatory pleading charges the nonwitness spouse with a crime against the witness spouse. *Id.* at 212.

(b) Bigamy. Evid. C. §972(e)(3).

(c) Willful failure to support a child. *Id.* §972(e)(4); *see* Pen. C. §270.

(d) Willful abandonment of a spouse in a destitute condition. Evid. C. §972(e)(4); *see* Pen. C. §270a.

(e) Willful failure to support a spouse. Evid. C. §972(e)(4); *see* Pen. C. §270a.

(f) A crime that occurred before the witness spouse and nonwitness spouse were in a valid marital relationship under the following conditions:

[1] The testimony sought from the witness spouse is information the witness spouse knew before entering the valid marital relationship. Evid. C. §972(f).

[2] The witness spouse knew the nonwitness spouse had been arrested or formally charged regarding the crime at issue in the proceeding. *Id.*

[3] The witness spouse is called to testify about the crime at issue in the proceeding. *Id.*

(7) Certain family-law proceedings. The spousal-testimonial privileges cannot be invoked in the following proceedings if the witness spouse is asked to testify about the income, expenses, assets, debts, and employment of either the witness spouse or the nonwitness spouse:

(a) A proceeding brought against the witness spouse by a former spouse if the property and debts of their marriage have not been adjudicated. Evid. C. §972(g); *e.g.*, Wegner, *Civil Trials & Evidence*, ¶8:2330 (§972(g) exception applies in property-division portion of bifurcated divorce proceeding).

(b) A proceeding brought against the witness spouse by a former spouse to establish, modify, or enforce an obligation for child, family, or spousal support arising from their marriage. Evid. C. §972(g).

(c) A proceeding brought against the witness spouse by the other parent to establish, modify, or enforce a child-support obligation for a child of a nonmarital relationship of the spouse. *Id.*

(d) A proceeding brought against the witness spouse by the guardian of the spouse's child to establish, modify, or enforce a child-support obligation of the spouse. *Id.*

NOTE

Remember, the spousal-testimonial privileges apply only when the witness spouse is a "married person." See Evid. C. §§970, 971; Wegner, Civil Trials & Evidence, ¶8:2332. If the witness spouse is not in a valid marital relationship, the spousal-testimonial privileges do not apply. Section 972(g) assumes that one or both of the spouses have remarried and carves out an exception for certain testimony.

---

(8) Immediate benefit. The spousal-testimonial privileges cannot be invoked in a civil proceeding brought or defended by a spouse for the immediate benefit of the other spouse or both spouses. Evid. C. §973(b). A civil proceeding to recover damages is brought for the immediate benefit of the other spouse if the other spouse has a right to some or all of the damages as soon as they are recovered. *See* ***Waters v. Superior Ct.*** (1962) 58 Cal.2d 885, 897. The purpose of this "immediate benefit" exception is to prevent spouses from taking unfair advantage of their marital status to escape a party's duty to testify under Evid. C. §776. 7 Cal. Law Revision Comm'n Rep. (1965) p. 1174; Wegner, *Civil Trials & Evidence*, ¶8:2341; *see* Evid. C. §776.

SPLIT OF AUTHORITY

The courts are split on whether an action for damages that could result in an award benefiting or putting at risk the spouses' community property triggers the immediate-benefit exception to the spousal-testimonial privileges. ***Diepenbrock v. Brown*** *(1st Dist.2012) 208 Cal.App.4th 743, 748. Compare* ***Hand v. Superior Ct.*** *(3d Dist.1982) 134 Cal.App.3d 436, 442 (spouse's claim for personal-injury damages against third party is for immediate benefit of nonlitigating spouse, who can be forced to testify), with* ***Duggan v. Superior Ct.*** *(1st Dist.1981) 127 Cal.App.3d 267, 272 (claim for damages in action for dissolution of business partnership is not for immediate benefit of nonlitigating spouse, who cannot be forced to testify). See generally CEB Discovery Practice, §3.73; Wegner, Civil Trials & Evidence, ¶¶8:2343-8:2347. One commentator has said that the* ***Duggan*** *approach is better because it preserves the spousal-testimonial privileges by requiring more than a potential community-property interest to support a finding of immediate benefit. CEB Discovery Practice, §3.73.*

---

§1.7 How to assert spousal-testimonial privileges.

1. Witness spouse claims privilege. The witness spouse can claim a spousal-testimonial privilege by objecting to the discovery request. *See* Evid. C. §§970, 971; 7 Cal. Law Revision Comm'n Rep. (1965) p. 1171. See "Responding party objects to discovery," ch. 7-A, §14.1.1, p. 771. The nonwitness spouse cannot prevent the witness

spouse from testifying. ***Hand v. Superior Ct.*** (3d Dist.1982) 134 Cal.App.3d 436, 438; 7 Cal. Law Revision Comm'n Rep. (1965) p. 1171. Generally, the spousal-testimonial privileges are invoked in writing before a deposition or orally during the deposition. *See* ***Hand***, 134 Cal.App.3d at 438 (spousal privilege is not at issue until witness spouse is properly noticed and asserts the privilege).

2. Discovering party moves to compel. In response to the objection that the witness spouse cannot be called to appear or testify, the discovering party has the burden to enforce discovery. It must initiate the meet-and-confer procedure and, if unsuccessful, file a motion to compel discovery. See "Discovering party moves to compel (option 1)," ch. 7-A, §14.1.2, p. 772.

3. Witness spouse opposes motion. In response to a motion to compel, the witness spouse must file opposition papers that address the following:

(1) Preliminary facts. The witness spouse must establish either a valid marital relationship or a registered domestic partnership. See "Valid marital relationship," §1.3.2, p. 652; "Preliminary facts," ch. 7-A, §14.1.4(1), p. 772.

(2) Supporting declaration. The opposition papers must be supported by a declaration or affidavit, based on personal knowledge, that (1) lists the declarant's or affiant's qualifications to give an opinion about the privilege and (2) offers proof of the marital relationship or registered domestic partnership. See "Declaration," ch. 7-A, §14.1.4(1)(c), p. 773.

§2. MARITAL-COMMUNICATIONS PRIVILEGE

§2.1 General. A spouse has a privilege to prevent disclosure of confidential marital communications made to the other spouse during a valid marital relationship. Evid. C. §980.

1. Purpose. The purpose of the marital-communications privilege is to encourage free and open communication between spouses by eliminating the concern that a spouse might be called to testify about their private communications. 7 Cal. Law Revision Comm'n Rep. (1965) p. 1175. By protecting free and open communication, the marital-communications privilege promotes marital harmony. 2 Witkin, *California Evidence* (5th ed. 2012 & Supp.2014), Witnesses, §192.

2. Primary authority. Evid. C. §§980-987.

3. Secondary authority. The following secondary sources are cited as authority in this section:

- *California Civil Discovery Practice* (CEB Online ed. 2014) (referred to as *CEB Discovery Practice*).
- Jefferson, *California Evidence Benchbook* (CEB Online ed. 2014) (referred to as *Jefferson's Evid. Benchbook*).
- Wegner, *California Practice Guide: Civil Trials & Evidence* (CD-ROM ed. 2014) (referred to as Wegner, *Civil Trials & Evidence*).
- Witkin, *California Evidence* (5th ed. 2012 & Supp.2014) (referred to as Witkin, *Cal. Evidence*).

§2.2 Nature of marital-communications privilege.

1. Absolute. The marital-communications privilege is absolute. *See* Evid. C. §980 (listing no circumstances in which privilege applies but can be overcome); *cf.* ***U.S. v. Neal*** (D.Colo.1982) 532 F.Supp. 942, 948 n.5 (stating that privilege under California Evid. C. §980 is absolute), *aff'd*, (10th Cir.1984) 743 F.2d 1441. See "What marital-communications privilege protects," §2.6, p. 661. However, the privilege does not apply in all proceedings. See "What marital-communications privilege does not protect," §2.7, p. 661.

2. Duration. The marital-communications privilege lasts as long as there is a living spouse to assert it, and it can be asserted after the spousal relationship is terminated by death, divorce, or annulment. 7 Cal. Law Revision Comm'n Rep. (1965) p. 1175; *see* ***People v. Dorsey*** (2d Dist.1975) 46 Cal.App.3d 706, 717 (privilege can be asserted after divorce or annulment); Wegner, *Civil Trials & Evidence*, ¶8:2350 (privilege can be asserted after marriage is dissolved); 2 Witkin, *Cal. Evidence*, Witnesses, §194 (same).

§2.3 Elements of marital-communications privilege. The elements of the marital-communications privilege are the following:

1. Communication. A communication was made. Evid. C. §980. A "communication" is defined as a written or oral statement. *See* ***People v. Cleveland*** (2004) 32 Cal.4th 704, 743; ***Rubio v. Superior Ct.*** (4th Dist.1988) 202 Cal.App.3d 1343, 1347; *Jefferson's Evid. Benchbook*, §38.18. This includes recordings of written or oral statements. *E.g.*, ***Rubio***, 202 Cal.App.3d at 1347-48 (videotape is writing that can be covered by marital-communications privilege).

2. Between spouses. The communication was between two people who, at the time of the communication, were in a valid marriage. *See* Evid. C. §980; ***People v. Catlin*** (2001) 26 Cal.4th 81, 130; *see, e.g.*, ***Cleveland***, 32 Cal.4th at 742-43 (at time of crimes, D and witness were married); ***People v. Gallego*** (1990) 52 Cal.3d 115, 176-77 (D and witness, D's second wife, were not validly married because D did not legally dissolve first marriage). For purposes of the marital-communications privilege, the validity of the marriage is determined as of the time the communication was made. Wegner, *Civil Trials & Evidence*, ¶8:2316; *see* Evid. C. §980; ***Catlin***, 26 Cal.4th at 130; ***People v. Dorsey*** (2d Dist.1975) 46 Cal.App.3d 706, 717. See "Valid marital relationship," §1.3.2, p. 652.

3. Made in confidence. The communication was made in confidence. Evid. C. §980; ***People v. Mickey*** (1991) 54 Cal.3d 612, 654. A communication is made in confidence if (1) the spouse making the communication did not intend to disclose it to others and (2) the communication was made with a reasonable expectation of privacy. *See* ***People v. Bryant*** (2014) 60 Cal.4th 335, 420; ***Mickey***, 54 Cal.3d at 654. A communication between spouses is presumed to have been made in confidence. Evid. C. §917(a); ***Cleveland***, 32 Cal.4th at 744; ***Mickey***, 54 Cal.3d at 655; Wegner, *Civil Trials & Evidence*, ¶8:2360.

(1) Confidential intent. A spouse's intent for nondisclosure of the communication is determined by the facts surrounding the communication. *See* ***Cleveland***, 32 Cal.4th at 744. Facts the courts have considered in determining intent include the following:

(a) Spouse's conduct. A spouse's intent for nondisclosure can be demonstrated by the spouse's conduct. *See* ***People v. Von Villas*** (2d Dist.1992) 11 Cal.App.4th 175, 221. For example, if a spouse takes steps to ensure that others will not overhear or see the communication, confidential intent is likely to be present. *See* 7 Cal. Law Revision Comm'n Rep. (1965) p. 1161 (communication made in way that others could easily overhear is strong indication of no confidential intent); *see, e.g.*, ***North v. Superior Ct.*** (1972) 8 Cal.3d 301, 311 (spouses did not make communication until they were in closed room); ***Rubio***, 202 Cal.App.3d at 1347 (spouses hid videotape in closet and did not let others view it). Conversely, a lack of confidential intent is demonstrated if the spouse making the communication disclosed the same or a similar communication to others. *See, e.g.*, ***Cleveland***, 32 Cal.4th at 743-44 (husband's statement to wife that was later made in presence of others and to detective was not confidential); ***People v. Bradford*** (1969) 70 Cal.2d 333, 342 n.2 (husband's statements knowingly made in presence of third parties were not confidential); ***People v. Gomez*** (2d Dist.1982) 134 Cal.App.3d 874, 879 (husband's threats against wife made in presence of three other people were not confidential).

(b) Nature or substance of communication. A spouse's intent for nondisclosure can be demonstrated by the nature or substance of the communication. *See* ***Bryant***, 60 Cal.4th at 420; *see, e.g.*, ***Cleveland***, 32 Cal.4th at 743-44 (there was no reason why husband wanted to keep innocuous statement he made to wife two weeks before murder confidential; statement did not become incriminating until later). For example, if the nature or substance of the communication would make it reasonable to expect the spouse hearing the communication to disclose it to others, then there is likely no confidential intent. *See, e.g.*, ***Bryant***, 60 Cal.4th at 420 (husband's statement to estranged wife that he placed bomb in her lover's car and would continue to try to kill him was not confidential; it was reasonable to infer that husband intended for wife to convey threat to lover to end relationship); ***People v. Carter*** (2d Dist.1973) 34 Cal.App.3d 748, 753 (husband's threats to hurt wife's friends that were made while he was assaulting her were not confidential; husband could not expect those threats not to be divulged).

(2) Reasonable expectation of privacy. The communication must be made in a place and manner that makes it reasonable for the spouses to assume that their communication will not be overheard. *See* ***North***,

8 Cal.3d at 311. If the spouses had a reasonable expectation of privacy, the marital-communications privilege applies even if the communication is overheard. Wegner, *Civil Trials & Evidence*, ¶8:2363; *see, e.g.*, ***North***, 8 Cal.3d at 311 (spouses lulled into thinking their communication in detective's closed office would not be monitored had reasonable expectation of privacy). For the spouses to have no reasonable expectation of privacy, the circumstances of the communication that are known to the spouses must indicate a substantial risk that the communication will be overheard. *See* ***People v. Johnson*** (6th Dist.1991) 233 Cal.App.3d 425, 438 (mere possibility of being overheard does not defeat privilege).

§2.4 Communicants to marital-communications privilege. The communicants to the marital-communications privilege are the spouses in the marital relationship. *See* Evid. C. §980; ***People v. Badgett*** (1995) 10 Cal.4th 330, 363; *see also CEB Discovery Practice*, §3.75 (communication privilege "likely" applies to domestic partners); Wegner, *Civil Trials & Evidence*, ¶8:2310.1 (§980 applies to registered domestic partners). See "Valid marital relationship," §1.3.2, p. 652.

§2.5 Who can assert marital-communications privilege. The marital-communications privilege belongs to both spouses and can be asserted by either spouse (or a guardian or conservator of either spouse), regardless of whether that spouse is a party to the case. *See* Evid. C. §980; ***People v. Dorsey*** (2d Dist.1975) 46 Cal.App.3d 706, 717; 7 Cal. Law Revision Comm'n Rep. (1965) p. 1175; Wegner, *Civil Trials & Evidence*, ¶8:2351; 2 Witkin, *Cal. Evidence*, Witnesses, §193.

§2.6 What marital-communications privilege protects. The marital-communications privilege can be asserted to stop anyone, including an eavesdropper, from testifying about the content of a confidential communication between the spouses. 7 Cal. Law Revision Comm'n Rep. (1965) p. 1176; *see* Evid. C. §980; *see, e.g.*, ***North v. Superior Ct.*** (1972) 8 Cal.3d 301, 312 (tape recording of confidential communication should have been suppressed).

§2.7 What marital-communications privilege does not protect. The marital-communications privilege does not protect the following:

1. Noncommunicative conduct. The marital-communications privilege does not protect information about the nonwitness spouse's conduct or actions. Wegner, *Civil Trials & Evidence*, ¶8:2355; *see* ***People v. Cleveland*** (2004) 32 Cal.4th 704, 743; *see, e.g.*, ***People v. Bradford*** (1969) 70 Cal.2d 333, 342 n.2 (acts of placing cans in garage and giving wife the victim's jewelry were not communications within meaning of marital-communications privilege). For example, a spouse can testify about the other spouse's possession or use of an object. *See* ***People v. Dorsey*** (2d Dist.1975) 46 Cal.App.3d 706, 717 (privilege does not extend to physical facts that are observed); *see, e.g.*, ***Cleveland***, 32 Cal.4th at 743 (spouse could testify that other spouse was wearing a watch and possessed cocaine); ***Tanzola v. De Rita*** (1955) 45 Cal.2d 1, 4-5 (spouse could testify that other spouse had possession of check and left it on desk at pharmacy).

2. Nonconfidential communication. The marital-communications privilege does not protect nonconfidential communications. Evid. C. §980. A communication is nonconfidential if the spouses did not intend for it to be confidential or did not have a reasonable expectation of privacy when it was made. *See* ***People v. Mickey*** (1991) 54 Cal.3d 612, 654-55; ***North v. Superior Ct.*** (1972) 8 Cal.3d 301, 311; ***People v. Gomez*** (2d Dist.1982) 134 Cal.App.3d 874, 879. See "Made in confidence," §2.3.3, p. 660.

3. Whether communication made. The marital-communications privilege does not protect the fact that a marital communication was made; it protects only the content of the communication. ***Bradford***, 70 Cal.2d at 342 n.2; ***Rubio v. Superior Ct.*** (4th Dist.1988) 202 Cal.App.3d 1343, 1348; Wegner, *Civil Trials & Evidence*, ¶8:2356; *see* ***Tanzola***, 45 Cal.2d at 6 (decision under former marital-communications statute).

4. Factual observations. The marital-communications privilege does not protect factual matters relating to a marital communication that do not reveal the content of the communication. ***Cleveland***, 32 Cal.4th at 743. For example, a spouse can testify that a letter received from the other spouse was in the other spouse's handwriting. *See* ***People v. Saidi-Tabatabai*** (2d Dist.1970) 7 Cal.App.3d 981, 986.

5. Previously disclosed. The marital-communications privilege does not protect a marital communication that was disclosed in another proceeding. Evid. C. §912(a); ***People v. Johnson*** (6th Dist.1991) 233 Cal.App.3d 425, 437. This is true even if the exception under which the communication was previously admitted into evidence no longer applies. *See, e.g.*, ***Johnson***, 233 Cal.App.3d at 437 (communication was admitted under crime-against-spouse exception, and privilege could not be asserted after disclosure even though charge was dropped).

6. Crime-fraud exception. The marital-communications privilege does not protect a communication made, in whole or in part, to enable or aid anyone to commit or plan a crime or fraud. Evid. C. §981; *e.g.*, ***People v. Von Villas*** (2d Dist.1992) 11 Cal.App.4th 175, 222-23 (privilege did not protect husband's instructions to wife to throw away letters to obstruct justice); *see, e.g.*, ***People v. Santos*** (2d Dist.1972) 26 Cal.App.3d 397, 402-03 (privilege did not protect husband's communication with spouse to get rid of evidence of crime). This exception does not permit disclosure of a communication that merely reveals a plan to commit a crime or fraud; the communication must be made to obtain assistance in committing or planning a crime or fraud. 7 Cal. Law Revision Comm'n Rep. (1965) p. 1176; *e.g.*, ***Dorsey***, 46 Cal.App.3d at 718 (communications that merely described plan to commit crime and how crime was committed did not seek assistance and remained privileged).

7. Certain proceedings. The marital-communications privilege cannot be invoked in the following types of proceedings:

(1) Spouse vs. spouse. The marital-communications privilege cannot be invoked in a suit by or on behalf of one spouse against the other spouse. Evid. C. §984(a); *see, e.g.*, ***Estate of Gillett*** (1st Dist.1946) 73 Cal.App.2d 588, 594 (suit by husband's estate against wife).

(2) Claim against surviving spouse. The marital-communications privilege cannot be invoked in a proceeding between a surviving spouse and a person who claims through the deceased spouse, regardless of whether the claim is by testate or intestate succession or by inter vivos transaction. Evid. C. §984(b).

(3) Commitment proceeding. The marital-communications privilege cannot be invoked in a commitment proceeding for a spouse. Evid. C. §982; *see also* Welfare & Inst. C. §5358 (placement of gravely disabled conservatee in treatment facility).

(4) Conservatorship or similar proceeding. The marital-communications privilege cannot be invoked in a proceeding to place the spouse or the spouse's property under the control of another person because of the spouse's mental or physical condition. Evid. C. §982; *see also* Prob. C. §§1800.3, 1801(a)-(c), 1802 (authorizing appointment of conservator for adult based on inability to provide for personal needs or inability to manage financial resources); Welfare & Inst. C. §§5350-5372 (conservatorship of person who is gravely disabled by mental-health disorder or chronic alcoholism).

(5) Competence proceeding. The marital-communications privilege cannot be invoked in a proceeding brought by or on behalf of a spouse to establish that spouse's competence. Evid. C. §983.

(6) Juvenile-court proceeding. The marital-communications privilege cannot be invoked in a juvenile-court proceeding. Evid. C. §986.

(7) Criminal proceedings.

(a) Certain proceedings. The marital-communications privilege cannot be invoked in criminal proceedings charging a spouse with any of the following crimes:

[1] A crime against the person or property of the other spouse. Evid. C. §985(a).

[2] A crime against the person or property of a child of either spouse. *Id.*

[3] A crime against the person or property of some other person that is committed in the course of committing a crime against the person or property of the other spouse. *Id.* §985(b). For this exception to apply, the crimes against the spouse and the other person must be part of a continuous course of criminal conduct and must bear some logical relationship to each other. *Cf.* ***People v. Sinohui*** (2002) 28 Cal.4th 205, 220 (spousal-testimonial privilege).

[4] Bigamy. Evid. C. §985(c).

[5] Willful failure to support a child. *Id.* §985(d); *see* Pen. C. §270.

[6] Willful abandonment of a spouse in a destitute condition. Evid. C. §985(d); *see* Pen. C. §270a.

[7] Willful failure to support a spouse. Evid. C. §985(d); *see* Pen. C. §270a.

(b) Offered by defendant. The marital-communications privilege cannot be invoked to prevent disclosure of a communication offered into evidence by a defendant spouse in a criminal proceeding. Evid. C. §987.

8. Abuse of confidential relationship. The marital-communications privilege cannot be invoked to prevent disclosure of (1) threats of abuse in the marital relationship, such as violent threats against the other spouse, or (2) threats against third persons made by one spouse in the course of criminally victimizing the other spouse. *See* ***Johnson***, 233 Cal.App.3d at 438 (threats against spouse); ***People v. Carter*** (2d Dist.1973) 34 Cal.App.3d 748, 753 (threats against third persons). These exceptions are based on the idea that the communication is not confidential because the spouse making the threat cannot legitimately expect the threatened spouse not to reveal the communication, and the exception recognizes that the purpose of the privilege is not served by protecting communications that criminally victimize a spouse. *See* ***Johnson***, 233 Cal.App.3d at 438; ***Carter***, 34 Cal.App.3d at 753.

9. Law-enforcement administrative hearings. The marital-communications privilege cannot be invoked in law-enforcement administrative investigations or hearings. ***Riverside Cty. Sheriff's Dept. v. Zigman*** (4th Dist.2008) 169 Cal.App.4th 763, 771-72; ***Cal. Atty. Gen. Op.*** No. 05-903 (2006).

§2.8 Waiver of marital-communications privilege. The marital-communications privilege cannot be invoked if it has been waived. *See* Evid. C. §912(a), (b). For a discussion of waiver under Evid. C. §912, see "Waiver of privilege," ch. 6-A, §2.2.14, p. 607.

§2.9 How to assert marital-communications privilege.

1. Spouse claims privilege. Either spouse can claim the marital-communications privilege by making an objection to a discovery request. See "Responding party objects to discovery," ch. 7-A, §14.1.1, p. 771.

2. Discovering party moves to compel. In response to the objection that the information sought is protected by the marital-communications privilege, the discovering party has the burden to enforce discovery. It must initiate the meet-and-confer procedure and, if unsuccessful, file a motion to compel discovery. See "Discovering party moves to compel (option 1)," ch. 7-A, §14.1.2, p. 772.

3. Spouse serves opposition papers. In response to a motion to compel, the spouse who objected to the discovery request has the burden to justify the marital-communications privilege by proving the preliminary facts that support the privilege. See "Responding party satisfies burden," ch. 7-A, §14.1.4, p. 772. That is, the spouse must prove there was a valid marital relationship at the time of the communication. See "Elements of marital-communications privilege," §2.3, p. 660. It is not necessary for the spouse to prove the communication was made in confidence, which is presumed. Evid. C. §917(a).

E. MEDICAL PRIVILEGES

This subchapter covers three medical privileges: the physician-patient privilege, the psychotherapist-patient privilege, and the medical peer-review privilege.

Although the physician-patient and psychotherapist-patient privileges both involve a patient relationship, the two privileges are different in a number of respects. See chart 6-3, below.

6-3. PHYSICIAN VS. PSYCHOTHERAPIST PRIVILEGES

		Physician-patient privilege	Psychotherapist-patient privilege
Application of privileges			
1	What is covered by privilege	• Patient's diagnosis and treatment. Evid. C. §§991, 992. • Confidential communications between physician and patient to obtain medical advice in course of relationship. Evid. C. §992. • Communications with another person necessary to transmit information or accomplish goal. Evid. C. §992. • Patient's name, if it would disclose condition.	• Patient's diagnosis, treatment, and participation in research. Evid. C. §§1011, 1012. • Confidential communications between psychotherapist and patient in course of relationship. Evid. C. §1022. • Communications with another person necessary to transmit information or accomplish goal. Evid. C. §1022. • Patient's name.
2	Duration of privilege	Indefinitely, as long as someone remains to claim immunity.	
3	Who owns privilege ("holder")	Patient.	
4	Who can assert privilege	• Patient. • Physician or psychotherapist, on behalf of patient. • Person authorized by patient.	
5	Privilege available in—	Civil proceedings.	Civil and criminal proceedings.
Exceptions to privileges			
6	Injury by patient	Exception applies; information discoverable. Evid. C. §999.	No exception.
7	Dangerous patient	No exception.	Exception applies; information discoverable. Evid. C. §1024.
8	Child patient under 16 and victim of crime	No exception.	Exception applies; information discoverable. Evid. C. §1027.
9	Proceeding to put patient or property under control of another	Exception applies; information discoverable. Evid. C. §1004.	No exception.
10	Proceeding requested by D to determine sanity	No exception.	Exception applies; information discoverable. Evid. C. §1023.
11	Proceeding ordered by court to evaluate prisoner	No exception.	Exception applies; information discoverable. Evid. C. §1017.

§1. PHYSICIAN-PATIENT PRIVILEGE

§1.1 General. The physician-patient privilege protects confidential communications between physicians and their patients. Evid. C. §994. A confidential communication between a physician and a patient made during the course of the physician-patient relationship is privileged and not discoverable. *Id.* The physician-patient privilege can be asserted regardless of whether the patient is a party to the suit. *Id.*; ***Johnson v. Superior Ct.*** (2d Dist.2000) 80 Cal.App.4th 1050, 1062.

1. Purpose. The purpose of the physician-patient privilege is twofold: (1) to encourage the full disclosure of information necessary for effective diagnosis and treatment of the patient, and (2) to prevent the humiliation that might result if the patient's medical conditions were disclosed. ***Snibbe v. Superior Ct.*** (2d Dist.2014) 224 Cal.App.4th 184, 191-92; ***Board of Med. Quality Assur. v. Gherardini*** (4th Dist.1979) 93 Cal.App.3d 669, 678-79; *see* ***City & Cty. of S.F. v. Superior Ct.*** (1951) 37 Cal.2d 227, 232.

2. Primary authority. Evid. C. §§990-1007.

3. Secondary authority. The following secondary sources are cited as authority in this section:

- *California Civil Discovery Practice* (CEB Online ed. 2014) (referred to as *CEB Discovery Practice*).
- Jefferson, *California Evidence Benchbook* (CEB Online ed. 2014) (referred to as *Jefferson's Evid. Benchbook*).
- Wegner, *California Practice Guide: Civil Trials & Evidence* (CD-ROM ed. 2014) (referred to as Wegner, *Civil Trials & Evidence*).
- Weil & Brown, *California Practice Guide: Civil Procedure Before Trial* (CD-ROM ed. 2014) (referred to as Weil, *Civil Procedure Before Trial*).
- Witkin, *California Evidence* (5th ed. 2012 & Supp.2014) (referred to as Witkin, *Cal. Evidence*).

§1.2 Nature of physician-patient privilege.

1. Discovery & evidentiary. The physician-patient privilege is both a discovery privilege and an evidentiary privilege because the information protected by the privilege is not subject to either discovery or disclosure at trial. *See* Evid. C. §994 (patient has privilege to refuse to disclose and to prevent others from disclosing).

2. Absolute. Physician-patient communications are absolutely protected from discovery in civil cases because the court is not authorized to balance the need for the information against the privilege. *See* ***Rittenhouse v. Superior Ct.*** (3d Dist.1991) 235 Cal.App.3d 1584, 1590 (no balancing process for physician-patient privilege); *CEB Discovery Practice*, §3.87 (importance of information to other party is not relevant to determination of physician-patient privilege); Weil, *Civil Procedure Before Trial*, ¶8:110.1 (privileged communications are protected regardless of relevance to litigation). But the privilege is subject to statutory exceptions and can be waived. See "What physician-patient privilege does not protect," §1.7, p. 669; "Waiver of physician-patient privilege," §1.8, p. 671.

3. Duration. The physician-patient privilege survives as long as the patient or another privilege holder asserts it. *See* Evid. C. §994. See "Holder," §1.5.1, p. 667. The privilege does not terminate with the patient's death as long as there is a personal representative administering the patient's estate who claims it. *See* ***Hale v. Superior Ct.*** (4th Dist.1994) 28 Cal.App.4th 1421, 1424; ***Rittenhouse***, 235 Cal.App.3d at 1588. Once the estate is closed and the personal representative is discharged, the privilege terminates. ***Rittenhouse***, 235 Cal.App.3d at 1588 n.2.

§1.3 Elements of physician-patient privilege. The elements of the physician-patient privilege are the following:

1. Physician-patient relationship. The patient and the physician established a physician-patient relationship. *See* Evid. C. §§991, 992; 2 Witkin, *Cal. Evidence*, Witnesses, §201. See "Communicants to physician-patient privilege," §1.4, p. 666. The relationship is established when the patient consults with or is examined by the physician to obtain a diagnosis or treatment. Evid. C. §991; 2 Witkin, *Cal. Evidence*, Witnesses, §206. If the medical

consultation or examination is not for diagnosis or treatment, the privilege does not apply. *E.g.*, ***Johnson v. Superior Ct.*** (2d Dist.2000) 80 Cal.App.4th 1050, 1063 (when sperm donor consulted with sperm bank's physicians as part of donating process, physician-patient relationship was not created). See "Medical services outside privilege," §1.7.14, p. 670. The relationship's existence does not depend on proof of a contract or payment. ***Kramer v. Policy Holders Life Ins.*** (2d Dist.1935) 5 Cal.App.2d 380, 386-87; 2 Witkin, *Cal. Evidence*, Witnesses, §206.

(1) Diagnosis. The diagnosis can be for a physical, mental, or emotional condition. Evid. C. §991.

(2) Treatment. Treatment of the physical, mental, or emotional condition can be preventive, palliative, or curative. Evid. C. §991.

2. Confidential communication. The patient and physician communicated in confidence. *See* Evid. C. §§992, 994. Whether a communication is confidential is determined at the time the information was communicated to or ascertained by the physician. ***Rudnick v. Superior Ct.*** (1974) 11 Cal.3d 924, 930.

(1) Presumption of confidentiality. If the communication was made in the course of the physician-patient relationship, it is presumed to be confidential. Evid. C. §917(a); *CEB Discovery Practice*, §3.90; *Jefferson's Evid. Benchbook*, §39.10. In other words, the person claiming the privilege does not need to show that the communication was made in confidence. 7 Cal. Law Revision Comm'n Rep. (1965) pp. 1160-61. The person opposing the privilege can rebut the presumption by showing that the communication was not confidential. Evid. C. §917(a); 7 Cal. Law Revision Comm'n Rep. (1965) p. 1161.

(2) Communication shared with third persons. A physician-patient communication made in the presence of a third person is confidential only if the disclosure, as far as the patient is aware, was necessary to (1) further the patient's interest in the consultation or (2) transmit the information or accomplish the purpose for which the physician was consulted. Evid. C. §992; *e.g.*, ***Blue Cross v. Superior Ct.*** (3d Dist.1976) 61 Cal.App.3d 798, 800-01 (disclosure of patients' names and medical conditions to insurance company was necessary to accomplish purpose for which physician was consulted). See "Necessary disclosure," ch. 6-A, §3.3.2(7), p. 613. For a discussion of third persons to whom confidential communications can be disclosed, see "Third persons," §1.4.3, this page.

§1.4 Communicants to physician-patient privilege.

1. Physician. A physician is a person authorized to practice medicine in any state or nation. Evid. C. §990; *see also* ***Duronslet v. Kamps*** (1st Dist.2012) 203 Cal.App.4th 717, 731 (nurse is not "physician" under Evid. C. §990 and thus is not entitled to privilege).

(1) Medical entities. The term "physician" includes medical or podiatry corporations, partnerships, limited-liability companies, and associations, as well as the licensed physicians and surgeons employed by them to render services to patients. Evid. C. §994(c).

(2) Unlicensed physician. The term "physician" includes a person the patient reasonably believes to be authorized to practice medicine. Evid. C. §990; 2 Witkin, *Cal. Evidence*, Witnesses, §203. For example, if a patient unknowingly consults with a physician whose authorization to practice medicine has been revoked, the communication is still covered by the physician-patient privilege.

2. Patient. A patient is any person who consults or is examined by a physician for the purpose of securing a diagnosis or preventive, palliative, or curative treatment of a physical, mental, or emotional condition. Evid. C. §991; ***Johnson v. Superior Ct.*** (2d Dist.2000) 80 Cal.App.4th 1050, 1063; *see CEB Discovery Practice*, §3.85.

3. Third persons. A necessary third person is any person to whom a confidential communication is disclosed in any of the following circumstances: (1) the disclosure was reasonably necessary to transmit the information, (2) the disclosure was reasonably necessary to accomplish the purpose for which the physician was consulted, or (3) the person was present during the disclosure to further the patient's interest in the consultation. Evid. C. §992. This includes the following persons:

(1) Medical assistants. Confidential communications can be disclosed to and transmitted by nurses and other assistants to the physician. *See* Evid. C. §992 (third persons who are present to further patient's interest

during consultation); ***Shulman v. Group W Prods.*** (1998) 18 Cal.4th 200, 234 (dicta; emergency-flight nurse at scene of accident); ***Kramer v. Policy Holders Life Ins.*** (2d Dist.1935) 5 Cal.App.2d 380, 395 (stenographer who performed duties of office nurse).

(2) Pharmacist. Confidential communications can be disclosed to and transmitted by a pharmacist to whom the patient presents a prescription. ***Rudnick v. Superior Ct.*** (1974) 11 Cal.3d 924, 932 (dicta); 7 Cal. Law Revision Comm'n Rep. (1965) p. 1155.

(3) Health insurance. Confidential communications that include only a patient's name and medical condition can be disclosed to and transmitted by an insurance carrier for the purpose of paying the physician's fees. ***Blue Cross v. Superior Ct.*** (3d Dist.1976) 61 Cal.App.3d 798, 801-02.

(4) Other medical entities. Confidential communications can be disclosed to and transmitted by other medical entities if the disclosure or transmission is reasonably necessary to accomplish the purpose for which the physician was consulted. *See* Evid. C. §992; *see, e.g.*, ***Rudnick***, 11 Cal.3d at 934 (case was remanded for trial court to determine whether transmission of adverse-drug-reaction reports to drug manufacturer was reasonably necessary to accomplish purpose for which physician was consulted).

(5) Parents. Confidential communications can be disclosed to and transmitted by a minor patient's parents if the disclosure or transmission is to further the minor's interest in securing medical care. *See CEB Discovery Practice*, §3.91; *cf.* ***Grosslight v. Superior Ct.*** (2d Dist.1977) 72 Cal.App.3d 502, 506 (communications between parents and hospital to assist diagnosis were protected by psychotherapist-patient privilege).

§1.5 Who can assert physician-patient privilege. The physician-patient privilege belongs to the patient, not the physician. *See* Evid. C. §994. The following persons can claim the privilege for the patient:

1. Holder. The holder of the privilege is the principal person authorized to claim it. ***Palay v. Superior Ct.*** (2d Dist.1993) 18 Cal.App.4th 919, 927. The identity of the privilege holder depends on whether the patient is alive and has a guardian. Evid. C. §993.

(1) Live patient.

(a) Patient. The patient can assert the physician-patient privilege. *See* Evid. C. §§993(a), 994(a); ***Johnson v. Superior Ct.*** (2d Dist.2000) 80 Cal.App.4th 1050, 1063; 2 Witkin, *Cal. Evidence*, Witnesses, §204. There can be joint holders of the physician-patient privilege. For example, a mother and a child have a joint privilege to their prenatal medical records. ***Palay***, 18 Cal.App.4th at 927. When the interests of the joint holders conflict, however, one joint holder cannot invoke the privilege to prevent disclosure of confidential communications to the detriment of the other joint holder. *Id.* at 927-28.

(b) Guardian or conservator. If the patient has a guardian or conservator, the guardian or conservator must assert the physician-patient privilege. *See* Evid. C. §993(b). If a patient has separate guardians for her estate and her person, either guardian can claim the privilege. 7 Cal. Law Revision Comm'n Rep. (1965) p. 187.

(2) Dead patient. If the patient is dead, only the personal representative of the estate can assert the physician-patient privilege. *See* Evid. C. §993(c); 2 Witkin, *Cal. Evidence*, Witnesses, §204; *see also* Evid. C. §994(c) (physician cannot claim privilege if no holder exists). The privilege survives as long as the estate is open. *See* ***Rittenhouse v. Superior Ct.*** (3d Dist.1991) 235 Cal.App.3d 1584, 1588 n.2. Once the estate is closed and the personal representative is discharged, the privilege terminates. *Id.*

2. Authorized person. The physician-patient privilege can be asserted by a person who is authorized by the holder to claim the privilege. Evid. C. §994(b); ***Rudnick v. Superior Ct.*** (1974) 11 Cal.3d 924, 929; 2 Witkin, *Cal. Evidence*, Witnesses, §205. When disclosure to a third person is reasonably necessary to accomplish the purpose for which the physician was consulted, the disclosure gives that third person the right to assert the privilege on the patient's behalf. ***Rudnick***, 11 Cal.3d at 932; *see, e.g.*, ***Blue Cross v. Superior Ct.*** (3d Dist.1976) 61 Cal.App.3d 798, 800-01 (D-insurer could assert privilege in response to interrogatory request seeking names, addresses, and phone numbers of other patients who had filed claims similar to P's because information was given to D in furtherance of privilege).

3. Physician. The physician-patient privilege can be asserted on the patient's behalf by the physician with whom the patient consulted. Evid. C. §994(c); ***Rudnick***, 11 Cal.3d at 929; *see* ***Snibbe v. Superior Ct.*** (2d Dist.2014) 224 Cal.App.4th 184, 192. For purposes of asserting the privilege, "physician" can mean a partnership, corporation, limited-liability company, association, or other group or entity. See "Physician," §1.4.1, p. 666.

(1) Must assert. The physician must claim the privilege on the patient's behalf if the physician is present when disclosure of the communication is requested and is authorized to claim the privilege. Evid. C. §995; ***Binder v. Superior Ct.*** (5th Dist.1987) 196 Cal.App.3d 893, 899 (physician invoked physician-patient privilege in response to request for photographs of patients with lesions).

(2) Cannot assert. The physician cannot assert the privilege in any of the following situations:

(a) There is no holder of the privilege in existence. Evid. C. §994(c). See "Holder," §1.5.1, p. 667.

(b) The holder or authorized person instructed the physician to permit disclosure. Evid. C. §994(c).

(c) The holder waived the privilege. *See id.* §912(a) (only holder can waive privilege); *cf.* ***In re Lifschutz*** (1970) 2 Cal.3d 415, 430 (psychotherapist could not assert patient's privilege because patient waived it). See "Waiver of privilege," ch. 6-A, §2.2.14, p. 607.

4. Court. The physician-patient privilege can be asserted by the court on behalf of an absent patient if no other person is authorized to claim the privilege. *See* ***Rudnick***, 11 Cal.3d at 932-33 & n.12; *CEB Discovery Practice*, §3.97. This decision is within the court's discretion. ***Rudnick***, 11 Cal.3d at 932-33.

§1.6 What physician-patient privilege protects. The patient's medical information is protected from discovery by the physician-patient privilege. *See* Evid. C. §992 (defining "confidential information").

1. Confidential communications. The physician-patient privilege protects from discovery confidential communications between a physician and a patient, which include the following:

(1) Verbal communications. Verbal communications between the physician and the patient are protected by the physician-patient privilege. ***Blue Cross v. Superior Ct.*** (3d Dist.1976) 61 Cal.App.3d 798, 800; *see* Evid. C. §992.

(2) Nonverbal communications. Nonverbal communications secured by the physician from the patient (e.g., photographs, X-rays, lab results) are protected by the physician-patient privilege. *See* Evid. C. §992; ***Hale v. Superior Ct.*** (4th Dist.1994) 28 Cal.App.4th 1421, 1424.

(3) Diagnosis. The diagnosis of the patient's condition is protected by the physician-patient privilege. Evid. C. §992; ***Blue Cross***, 61 Cal.App.3d at 800.

(4) Medical advice. Advice given by the physician to the patient is protected by the physician-patient privilege. Evid. C. §992; ***Blue Cross***, 61 Cal.App.3d at 800.

(5) Photographs. Photographs of a patient taken by or at the request of the physician are protected by the physician-patient privilege, even if the patient cannot be identified from the photographs. *See* Wegner, *Civil Trials & Evidence*, ¶8:2125; 2 Witkin, *Cal. Evidence*, Witnesses, §207; *see, e.g.*, ***Binder v. Superior Ct.*** (5th Dist.1987) 196 Cal.App.3d 893, 897 (dermatologist's photographs of patient's lesions were protected by physician-patient privilege).

(6) Patient's name. The patient's name is protected by the physician-patient privilege only if disclosure of the name would reveal something about the patient's medical condition. ***Rudnick v. Superior Ct.*** (1974) 11 Cal.3d 924, 933 n.13 (dicta); *see* Wegner, *Civil Trials & Evidence*, ¶8:2123; *see, e.g.*, ***Akkerman v. Mecta Corp.*** (2d Dist.2007) 152 Cal.App.4th 1094, 1104 (identities of psychiatric hospitals' patients were discoverable only if there was compelling need and no less intrusive means).

(7) Other information. Any other information obtained by the physician during an examination of the patient is protected by the physician-patient privilege. Evid. C. §992; ***Hale***, 28 Cal.App.4th at 1424; ***Blue Cross***, 61 Cal.App.3d at 800.

2. Fact of transmission. The fact that certain information was transmitted between the physician and the patient is protected by the physician-patient privilege. *See* Evid. C. §992. Even if nonprivileged information is transmitted between the physician and the patient (e.g., the physician sends the patient an article about the dangers of a certain drug), the fact of transmission is protected from discovery by third persons; the nonprivileged information itself is not privileged. *Cf.* ***Mitchell v. Superior Ct.*** (1984) 37 Cal.3d 591, 600-01 (transmission of attorney-client communication).

§1.7 What physician-patient privilege does not protect.

1. Patient's name. There is no physician-patient privilege for the identity of the patient if the disclosure would not reveal anything about the patient's medical condition. *See* ***Rudnick v. Superior Ct.*** (1974) 11 Cal.3d 924, 933 n.13 (dicta); *cf.* ***County of Alameda v. Superior Ct.*** (1st Dist.1987) 194 Cal.App.3d 254, 261 (psychotherapist-patient privilege; P was able to discover name of her rapist, who was patient in same mental hospital).

2. Unidentified patient's medical condition. There is no physician-patient privilege for information about a patient's medical condition if the information does not reveal the patient's identity. *See* ***Rudnick***, 11 Cal.3d at 933 n.13 (dicta); *see, e.g.*, ***Snibbe v. Superior Ct.*** (2d Dist.2014) 224 Cal.App.4th 184, 194 (physician-patient privilege does not prevent disclosure of postoperative orders with patient-identification information redacted). *But see* ***Binder v. Superior Ct.*** (5th Dist.1987) 196 Cal.App.3d 893, 898-99 (physician-patient privilege prevents disclosure of patient photographs despite anonymity of patient identities).

3. Crime or tort. There is no physician-patient privilege if the services of the physician were sought or obtained to enable or aid anyone to commit or plan a crime or tort or to escape detection or apprehension after the commission of a crime or tort. Evid. C. §997; *see also id.* §1018 (exception to psychotherapist-patient privilege); 2 Witkin, *Cal. Evidence*, Witnesses, §212 (crime-tort exception to physician-patient privilege is broader than crime-fraud exception to attorney-client privilege).

NOTE

Unlike attorneys and psychotherapists, a physician does not have a statutory right to disclose a patient's communication that suggests she plans to commit a criminal act that is likely to result in death or substantial bodily harm. See Evid. C. §956.5 (attorney-client privilege), §§990-1007 (physician-patient privilege), §1024 (psychotherapist-patient privilege).

4. Criminal proceeding. There is no physician-patient privilege in a criminal proceeding. Evid. C. §998; ***People v. Cage*** (2007) 40 Cal.4th 965, 987 n.18; 2 Witkin, *Cal. Evidence*, Witnesses, §211.

5. Damages for patient's conduct – good cause. There is no physician-patient privilege for communications in a proceeding to recover damages on account of the patient's conduct if (1) the communications are relevant to an issue about the patient's condition and (2) there is good cause for the disclosure. Evid. C. §999; 2 Witkin, *Cal. Evidence*, Witnesses, §§213, 214; *e.g.*, ***John B. v. Superior Ct.*** (2006) 38 Cal.4th 1177, 1202 (in suit for negligently infecting P with HIV, D's extramarital affairs and more advanced infection helped establish good cause for disclosure of D's medical records); ***Slagle v. Superior Ct.*** (1st Dist.1989) 211 Cal.App.3d 1309, 1313-15 (in personal-injury suit following car accident, P's medical records describing recent vision impairment were not protected by privilege; good cause was established when D overheard P mention after accident that she had been blind six months before). When the patient's conduct is relevant to the case, the exception applies even if the patient herself is not a party. ***Slagle***, 211 Cal.App.3d at 1314; Wegner, *Civil Trials & Evidence*, ¶8:2153. For information to be discoverable, the patient's conduct must be either wrongful in some legal sense or criminal. *See* ***Jones v. Superior Ct.*** (1st Dist.1981) 119 Cal.App.3d 534, 544-45.

6. Claims through dead patient. There is no physician-patient privilege for communications relevant to an issue between parties who are all claiming through the same dead patient. Evid. C. §1000.

7. Breach of duty. There is no physician-patient privilege for communications relevant to an issue of breach, by the physician or the patient, of a duty arising from the physician-patient relationship. Evid. C. §1001; *e.g.*, ***California Consumer Health Care Council v. Kaiser Found. Health Plan, Inc.*** (1st Dist.2006) 142 Cal.App.4th 21, 32-33 (patient's medical information was not privileged in medical-malpractice suit).

8. Dead patient's writing. There is no physician-patient privilege in a dispute about a deed, will, or other writing signed by a dead patient for communications that are relevant to the dead patient's intention or the writing's validity. Evid. C. §1002 (intention), §1003 (validity).

9. Commitment proceedings. There is no physician-patient privilege for communications in a proceeding to commit the patient or to place the patient or the patient's property under the control of another because of the patient's mental or physical condition. Evid. C. §1004; *see, e.g.*, ***In re Jeannie Q.*** (2d Dist.1973) 32 Cal.App.3d 288, 304-05 (no physician-patient privilege in proceeding to declare minors dependent children of court when their physical health was in issue).

10. Competence proceedings. There is no physician-patient privilege for communications in a proceeding brought by or on behalf of the patient to establish the patient's competence. Evid. C. §1005.

11. Reports & records to public employee or office. There is no physician-patient privilege for information that the physician or patient is required to report to a public employee or to record in a public office, if the report or record is open to public inspection. Evid. C. §1006. Examples of when a physician is required to report or record include the following:

(1) Child abuse. Physicians are required to report suspected cases of child abuse to Child Protective Services. Pen. C. §§11165.7(a)(21), 11166; ***David M. v. Beverly Hosp.*** (2d Dist.2005) 131 Cal.App.4th 1272, 1278; *see* Pen. C. §11171.2(b) (requirement supersedes physician-patient privilege).

(2) Communicable diseases. Physicians are required to report cases of certain communicable diseases to the local health officer for the jurisdiction where the patient resides. Cal. Code Regs., tit. 17, §2500(b).

12. Proceedings to terminate right. There is no physician-patient privilege in proceedings brought by a public entity to determine whether a right, authority, license, or privilege (including the right or privilege to be employed by the public entity or to hold a public office) should be revoked, suspended, terminated, limited, or conditioned. Evid. C. §1007; *e.g.*, ***Board of Med. Quality Assur. v. Hazel Hawkins Mem'l Hosp.*** (1st Dist.1982) 135 Cal.App.3d 561, 566 (physician-patient privilege did not apply in investigation to determine whether physician's license should be revoked).

13. Authorized by CMIA. Under the Confidentiality of Medical Information Act (CMIA), health-care providers are authorized to disclose certain medical information in certain situations. *See* Civ. C. §56.10(c). For example, under the CMIA, a health-care provider can disclose medical information to an insurer as necessary for payment. *Id.* §56.10(c)(2).

14. Medical services outside privilege. There is no physician-patient privilege for medical services that are not provided to a patient for purposes of diagnosis or treatment. ***Johnson v. Superior Ct.*** (2d Dist.2000) 80 Cal.App.4th 1050, 1063. The following are examples:

(1) Sperm donor. A consultation by a sperm donor with a sperm bank's physician as part of the donating process does not create a physician-patient relationship. ***Johnson***, 80 Cal.App.4th at 1063.

(2) Study volunteer. City residents who participated in a medical study to determine whether the presence of a nearby waste facility was causing their health problems were not "patients" because the residents were not seeking a diagnosis. ***Kizer v. Sulnick*** (2d Dist.1988) 202 Cal.App.3d 431, 439.

(3) Medical exam for life insurance. A medical examination for purposes of obtaining life insurance is probably not covered by the physician-patient privilege. Wegner, *Civil Trials & Evidence*, ¶8:2109.

§1.8 Waiver of physician-patient privilege. There is no physician-patient privilege if the holder of the privilege, or a person authorized by the holder, waives it.

1. Waiver. If the privilege is waived, the information is discoverable.

(1) General rules of waiver. See "Waiver of privilege," ch. 6-A, §2.2.14, p. 607.

(2) Patient-litigant. There is no physician-patient privilege for communications relevant to an issue about the patient's condition if the issue was tendered by the patient or another related claimant. Evid. C. §996. See "By raising issue," ch. 6-A, §2.2.14(1)(b)[2][c], p. 608. Those persons include the following:

(a) The patient. Evid. C. §996(a); Wegner, *Civil Trials & Evidence*, ¶8:2137. A patient can tender the issue of physical health by requesting relief based on her medical condition. *E.g.*, ***Vesco v. Superior Ct.*** (2d Dist.2013) 221 Cal.App.4th 275, 279 (issue tendered by requesting trial continuance based on medical necessity); ***Slagle v. Superior Ct.*** (1st Dist.1989) 211 Cal.App.3d 1309, 1313 (issue tendered by filing personal-injury action). The patient-litigant exception prevents a person who placed her physical condition in issue from invoking the privilege on the ground that disclosure of her condition would cause her humiliation. ***Karen P. v. Superior Ct.*** (2d Dist.2011) 200 Cal.App.4th 908, 913; ***Palay v. Superior Ct.*** (2d Dist.1993) 18 Cal.App.4th 919, 928. Only information that relates to the claimed injuries becomes discoverable. ***Slagle***, 211 Cal.App.3d at 1313.

(b) A party claiming through or under the patient. Evid. C. §996(b); *see, e.g.*, ***Karen P.***, 200 Cal.App.4th at 914-15 (exception to privilege did not apply when minor patient's condition was placed in issue by DCFS, not by minor who was independent party to dependency proceeding); ***Rittenhouse v. Superior Ct.*** (3d Dist.1991) 235 Cal.App.3d 1584, 1591 (exception to privilege did not apply when patient's condition was placed in issue by adversary, not by party claiming privilege through patient); ***Jones v. Superior Ct.*** (1st Dist.1981) 119 Cal.App.3d 534, 545 (exception to privilege did not apply when nonparty patient's condition was placed in issue by patient's daughter).

(c) A party claiming as a beneficiary of the patient through a contract to which the patient is or was a party. Evid. C. §996(c).

(d) A person bringing a wrongful-death action or a parent bringing a personal-injury action on behalf of a minor child. *See id.* §996(d); 7 Cal. Law Revision Comm'n Rep. (1965) p. 1183.

2. No waiver. If the privilege is not waived, the information is not discoverable. See "Privilege not waived," ch. 6-A, §3.3.2, p. 612.

§1.9 How to assert physician-patient privilege.

1. Holder claims privilege. The holder of the physician-patient privilege, or a person authorized by the holder, can claim the privilege by serving a written objection to the discovery request on the ground that the privilege prevents disclosure of the information. In a deposition, the objection can be made orally. See "Responding party objects to discovery," ch. 7-A, §14.1.1, p. 771. Instead of serving objections, the holder can claim the privilege by filing a motion for protective order. See "Motion for Protective Order," ch. 9-B, p. 1024.

2. Discovering party moves to compel. In response to the objection that the physician-patient privilege bars discovery, the discovering party has the burden to enforce discovery. It must initiate the meet-and-confer procedure and, if unsuccessful, file a motion to compel discovery. See "Discovering party moves to compel (option 1)," ch. 7-A, §14.1.2, p. 772.

3. Holder serves opposition papers. In response to a motion to compel, the holder has the burden to justify the assertion of the privilege by proving the preliminary facts that support it. *See* ***Kizer v. Sulnick*** (2d Dist.1988) 202 Cal.App.3d 431, 439. See "Elements of physician-patient privilege," §1.3, p. 665. That is, the holder must prove there was a physician-patient privilege at the time of the communication. It is not necessary for the holder

to prove the physician-patient communication was made in confidence, which is presumed. Evid. C. §917(a). See "Responding party satisfies burden," ch. 7-A, §14.1.4, p. 772.

§2. PSYCHOTHERAPIST-PATIENT PRIVILEGE

§2.1 General. A patient's confidential communication to a psychotherapist is privileged. Evid. C. §1014.

1. Purpose. The purpose of the psychotherapist-patient privilege is to encourage the full and truthful disclosure of information for the effective treatment of mental illness. *See* ***People v. Wharton*** (1991) 53 Cal.3d 522, 555; ***Tarasoff v. Regents of the Univ. of Cal.*** (1976) 17 Cal.3d 425, 440. Psychoanalysis and psychotherapy depend on the fullest revelation of the most intimate and embarrassing details of the patient's life. ***Wharton***, 53 Cal.3d at 555; ***San Diego Trolley, Inc. v. Superior Ct.*** (4th Dist.2001) 87 Cal.App.4th 1083, 1090.

2. Primary authority. Evid. C. §§1010-1027.

3. Secondary authority. The following secondary sources are cited as authority in this section:

- *California Civil Discovery Practice* (CEB Online ed. 2014) (referred to as *CEB Discovery Practice*).
- Jefferson, *California Evidence Benchbook* (CEB Online ed. 2014) (referred to as *Jefferson's Evid. Benchbook*).
- Wegner, *California Practice Guide: Civil Trials & Evidence* (CD-ROM ed. 2014) (referred to as Wegner, *Civil Trials & Evidence*).
- Witkin, *California Evidence* (5th ed. 2012 & Supp.2014) (referred to as Witkin, *Cal. Evidence*).

§2.2 Nature of psychotherapist-patient privilege.

1. Discovery & evidentiary. The psychotherapist-patient privilege is both a discovery privilege and an evidentiary privilege because the information protected by the privilege is not subject to either discovery or disclosure at trial. *See* Evid. C. §1014 (patient has privilege to refuse to disclose and to prevent others from disclosing).

2. Qualified. The psychotherapist-patient privilege is qualified, even though it is broad and protective. *See* ***In re Lifschutz*** (1970) 2 Cal.3d 415, 438 (privilege is not absolute); ***Story v. Superior Ct.*** (6th Dist.2003) 109 Cal.App.4th 1007, 1014 (same); ***County of Alameda v. Superior Ct.*** (1st Dist.1987) 194 Cal.App.3d 254, 260 (same). Because the patient's right to privacy is not absolute, some communications are subject to disclosure when the need for disclosure outweighs the need for confidentiality. *See* ***In re Lifschutz***, 2 Cal.3d at 422-23. For example, if a patient in a psychiatric hospital rapes another patient, the identity of the rapist can be compelled. ***County of Alameda***, 194 Cal.App.3d at 263. Compare "Patient's name," §2.6.5, p. 676, with "Patient's name," §2.7.1, p. 676.

3. Duration. The psychotherapist-patient privilege survives as long as the holder of the privilege, or a person authorized by the holder, asserts it. *See* Evid. C. §1013. See "Holder," §2.5.1, p. 674. The privilege does not terminate with the patient's death as long as there is a personal representative administering the patient's estate. *Cf.* ***Rittenhouse v. Superior Ct.*** (3d Dist.1991) 235 Cal.App.3d 1584, 1588 (physician-patient privilege). The privilege presumably terminates when the patient's estate is fully distributed and the personal representative is discharged because at that point there is no holder. *Cf. id.* at 1588 n.2 (physician-patient privilege).

§2.3 Elements of psychotherapist-patient privilege. The elements of the psychotherapist-patient privilege are the following:

1. Psychotherapist-patient relationship. The patient and the psychotherapist established a psychotherapist-patient relationship. *See* Evid. C. §§1011, 1012. See "Communicants to psychotherapist-patient privilege," §2.4, p. 673. The relationship is established when the patient consults with or is examined by a psychotherapist for the following reasons:

(1) Diagnosis or treatment. The patient consulted with or was examined by a psychotherapist to obtain a diagnosis or preventive, palliative, or curative treatment for a mental or emotional condition. Evid. C. §1011.

(2) Scientific research. The patient submitted to an examination of her mental or emotional condition for scientific research on mental or emotional problems. Evid. C. §1011.

2. Confidential communication. The patient and the psychotherapist communicated in confidence. *See* Evid. C. §§1012, 1014.

(1) Presumption of confidentiality. If the communication was made in the course of the psychotherapist-patient relationship, it is presumed to be confidential. Evid. C. §917(a); *CEB Discovery Practice*, §3.90; *see Jefferson's Evid. Benchbook*, §40.14. In other words, the person claiming the privilege does not need to show that the communication was made in confidence. 7 Cal. Law Revision Comm'n Rep. (1965) pp. 1160-61. The person opposing the privilege can rebut the presumption by showing that the communication was not confidential. Evid. C. §917(a); 7 Cal. Law Revision Comm'n Rep. (1965) p. 1161; *Jefferson's Evid. Benchbook*, §40.14.

(2) Communication shared with third persons. A psychotherapist-patient communication made in the presence of a third person is confidential only if the disclosure, as far as the patient is aware, was necessary to (1) further the interest of the patient in the consultation or (2) transmit the information or accomplish the purpose for which the psychotherapist was consulted. Evid. C. §1012; *see, e.g.*, ***People v. Gomez*** (2d Dist.1982) 134 Cal.App.3d 874, 880-81 (patient's statement made to student interns with office of family-court services was not privileged). See "Necessary disclosure," ch. 6-A, §3.3.2(7), p. 613. For a discussion of third persons to whom confidential communications can be disclosed, see "Third persons," §2.4.3, p. 674.

§2.4 Communicants to psychotherapist-patient privilege.

1. Psychotherapist. The term "psychotherapist" means a person who is, or is reasonably believed by the patient to be, one of the following:

(1) A person authorized to practice medicine in any state or nation who devotes, or is reasonably believed by the patient to devote, a substantial portion of her time to the practice of psychiatry. Evid. C. §1010(a).

(2) A licensed psychologist. *Id.* §1010(b); *see* Bus. & Prof. C. §2900 et seq.

(3) A licensed clinical social worker engaged in applied, nonmedical psychotherapy. Evid. C. §1010(c); *see* Bus. & Prof. C. §4996 et seq.

(4) A state-credentialed school psychologist. Evid. C. §1010(d).

(5) A marriage and family therapist licensed under Bus. & Prof. C. §4980 et seq. Evid. C. §1010(e).

(6) A registered nurse or clinical nurse specialist involved in psychiatric mental-health nursing. *See* Bus. & Prof. C. §2700 et seq., §2838 et seq.; Evid. C. §1010(k), (*l*).

(7) An educational psychologist licensed under Bus. & Prof. C. §4989.10 et seq. Evid. C. §1010.5 (referring to former Bus. & Prof. C. §4986, now §4989.10).

(8) Certain other people who are assistants, associates, trainees, or interns working under the supervision of a psychiatrist, psychologist, or other person identified as a psychotherapist under Evid. C. §1010. *See* Evid. C. §1010(f)-(j); 2 Witkin, *Cal. Evidence*, Witnesses, §220.

(9) A person rendering mental-health treatment or counseling services as authorized by Fam. C. §6924. Evid. C. §1010(m).

(10) A licensed professional clinical counselor. *Id.* §1010(n).

(11) A registered clinical-counselor intern working under the supervision of a licensed professional clinical counselor, a licensed marriage-and-family therapist, a licensed clinical social worker, a licensed psychologist, or a licensed physician and surgeon certified in psychiatry. *Id.* §1010(o).

(12) A clinical-counselor trainee working under the supervision of a licensed psychologist, a board-certified psychiatrist, a licensed clinical social worker, a licensed marriage-and-family therapist, or a licensed professional clinical counselor. *Id.* §1010(p).

(13) A psychological, marriage and family therapy, or licensed clinical social workers corporation and psychotherapists employed by those corporations. *Id.* §1014.

2. Patient. A patient is any person who consults or is seen by a professional to receive an evaluation of, diagnosis for, or treatment for any mental or emotional condition. Evid. C. §1011; 2 Witkin, *Cal. Evidence*, Witnesses, §221.

3. Third persons. A necessary third person is any person to whom a confidential communication is disclosed in any of the following circumstances: (1) the disclosure was reasonably necessary to transmit the information, (2) the disclosure was reasonably necessary to accomplish the purpose for which the psychotherapist was consulted, or (3) the person was present during the disclosure to further the patient's interest in the consultation. Evid. C. §1012. Section 1012 does not create an exception to the psychotherapist-patient privilege, but rather ensures that the confidential nature of the communication will not be lost when the disclosure to a necessary third person occurs. *E.g.*, ***People v. Gonzales*** (2013) 56 Cal.4th 353, 373-74 (in Sexually Violent Predator Act proceeding, State did not have authority to obtain disclosure of confidential psychotherapist-patient communications made as condition of parole; disclosure was based on incorrect theory that disclosure was necessary to accomplish purpose for which psychotherapist had been consulted—namely, to determine if parolee was dangerous). Necessary third persons include the following:

(1) Staff & other therapists. Confidential communications can be disclosed to office staff or other therapists who are consulted to aid in the diagnosis and treatment of the patient. ***Gonzales***, 56 Cal.4th at 373-74.

(2) Social worker. Confidential communications can be disclosed to a clinical social worker who is supervised by a licensed psychotherapist. *See* ***Luhdorff v. Superior Ct.*** (5th Dist.1985) 166 Cal.App.3d 485, 489-90.

(3) Group therapy. Confidential communications can be disclosed to participants in group therapy. ***Farrell L. v. Superior Ct.*** (5th Dist.1988) 203 Cal.App.3d 521, 527.

(4) Superior court. Confidential communications can be disclosed to a judge of a superior court who requires testimony of a therapist to facilitate determinations about a minor's welfare. *See, e.g.*, ***In re Mark L.*** (4th Dist.2001) 94 Cal.App.4th 573, 584 ("circumscribed information" about child's therapy could be disclosed to superior and juvenile courts in dependency and child-custody cases); ***In re Pedro M.*** (2d Dist.2000) 81 Cal.App.4th 550, 554-55 (confidential communications could be disclosed to juvenile court when patient was delinquent minor who had been directed to participate in sex-offender treatment program), *disapproved on other grounds*, ***People v. Gonzales*** (2013) 56 Cal.4th 353; ***In re Edward D.*** (2d Dist.1976) 61 Cal.App.3d 10, 15 (confidential communications could be shared with court and Social Services when patient knew that purpose of examination was to provide evaluation for court and Social Services in custody case involving patient's children). Confidential communications can also be disclosed to a judge of a superior court (and other necessary personnel) if the court requires the disclosure as a condition of a minor patient's probation, the minor is directed to participate and cooperate in a rehabilitative program, and the disclosure would not jeopardize the rehabilitative process. *See* ***In re Christopher M.*** (4th Dist.2005) 127 Cal.App.4th 684, 696, *disapproved on other grounds*, ***People v. Gonzales*** (2013) 56 Cal.4th 353.

§2.5 Who can assert psychotherapist-patient privilege. The psychotherapist-patient privilege belongs to the patient, not the psychotherapist. *See* Evid. C. §1014. The following persons can claim the privilege for the patient:

1. Holder. The holder of the psychotherapist-patient privilege can assert the privilege. Evid. C. §1014(a). The identity of the privilege holder depends on whether the patient is alive and has a guardian.

(1) Live patient.

(a) Patient. The patient can assert the psychotherapist-patient privilege. *See* Evid. C. §§1013(a), 1014(a); ***In re Mark L.*** (4th Dist.2001) 94 Cal.App.4th 573, 582.

(b) Guardian or conservator. If the patient has a guardian or conservator, the guardian or conservator must assert the psychotherapist-patient privilege. *See* Evid. C. §1013(b); ***In re Mark L.***, 94 Cal.App.4th at 582.

(2) Dead patient. If the patient is dead, only the personal representative of the estate can assert the psychotherapist-patient privilege. Evid. C. §1013(c).

2. Authorized person. The psychotherapist-patient privilege can be asserted by a person who is authorized by the holder to claim the privilege. Evid. C. §1014(b). For example, when a confidential communication is disclosed to a third party because it is reasonably necessary to do so, that third party becomes authorized by the privilege holder to claim the privilege. *Cf.* ***Rudnick v. Superior Ct.*** (1974) 11 Cal.3d 924, 932 (physician-patient privilege).

3. Psychotherapist. The psychotherapist can assert the privilege on behalf of the privilege holder. Evid. C. §1014(c). The psychotherapist cannot assert the privilege to protect the therapist's own interest. *See, e.g.,* ***Reynaud v. Superior Ct.*** (1st Dist.1982) 138 Cal.App.3d 1, 10 (psychotherapist could not invoke privilege as criminal D charged with filing false Medi-Cal claims).

(1) Must assert. The psychotherapist must assert the privilege whenever the therapist is (1) present when the communication is sought to be disclosed and (2) authorized to claim the privilege under Evid. C. §1014(c). Evid. C. §1015; ***Roberts v. Superior Ct.*** (1973) 9 Cal.3d 330, 341.

(2) Cannot assert. The psychotherapist cannot assert the privilege in any of the following situations:

(a) There is no holder of the privilege in existence. Evid. C. §1014(c).

(b) The therapist is instructed by an authorized person to permit disclosure. *Id.*

(c) The therapist is asserting the privilege to protect her own interest. *See, e.g.,* ***Reynaud***, 138 Cal.App.3d at 10 (psychotherapist could not invoke privilege as criminal D charged with filing false Medi-Cal claims).

(d) The holder waived the privilege. *See* Evid. C. §912(a) (only holder can waive privilege); *see, e.g.,* ***In re Lifschutz*** (1970) 2 Cal.3d 415, 430 (psychotherapist could not assert patient's privilege because patient waived it). See "Waiver of privilege," ch. 6-A, §2.2.14, p. 607.

§2.6 What psychotherapist-patient privilege protects. The following information is protected by the psychotherapist-patient privilege:

1. Communications. Information transmitted between the psychotherapist and the patient in the course of the relationship is protected by the psychotherapist-patient privilege. Evid. C. §1012; ***Reynaud v. Superior Ct.*** (1st Dist.1982) 138 Cal.App.3d 1, 9-10; *e.g.,* ***Luhdorff v. Superior Ct.*** (5th Dist.1985) 166 Cal.App.3d 485, 489-90 (records relating to conversations between D-patient and clinical social worker who was supervised by psychotherapist were protected). Communications between a patient's family members and the therapist are also protected if they were made in the course of, or are functionally related to, the diagnosis and treatment of the patient. ***Ewing v. Goldstein*** (2d Dist.2004) 120 Cal.App.4th 807, 818; *see* ***Grosslight v. Superior Ct.*** (2d Dist.1977) 72 Cal.App.3d 502, 508. The information may not need to be transmitted verbally for the privilege to apply. *Cf.* ***Hale v. Superior Ct.*** (4th Dist.1994) 28 Cal.App.4th 1421, 1424 (physician-patient privilege).

2. Examination. Information obtained by an examination of the patient is protected by the psychotherapist-patient privilege. Evid. C. §1012.

3. Diagnosis & advice. The diagnosis made and advice given by the psychotherapist are protected by the psychotherapist-patient privilege. Evid. C. §1012.

4. Scientific research. Information obtained from an examination of the mental or emotional condition of the patient for scientific research on mental or emotional problems is protected by the psychotherapist-patient privilege. *See* Evid. C. §1011 (defining "patient" to include person who submits to examination for research); *see also* ***In re Tabatha G.*** (4th Dist.1996) 45 Cal.App.4th 1159, 1168 (bonding study of mother and daughter was not protected by psychotherapist-patient privilege because mother was not "patient"; mother was not seeking diagnosis or treatment, and no scientific research was involved).

5. Patient's name. The patient's name is protected by the psychotherapist-patient privilege because the disclosure inevitably reveals the fact that the patient suffers from mental or emotional problems. Wegner, *Civil Trials & Evidence*, ¶8:2201; 2 Witkin, *Cal. Evidence*, Witnesses, §225; *see, e.g.*, ***Pollock v. Superior Ct.*** (2d Dist.2001) 93 Cal.App.4th 817, 821 (in bad-faith action against insured for failure to pay psychiatric disability benefits, names of other insureds who had been denied benefits were not discoverable); ***Smith v. Superior Ct.*** (1st Dist.1981) 118 Cal.App.3d 136, 140-42 (in divorce proceeding, identities of husband's psychotherapy patients were not discoverable to determine husband's income; wife had less intrusive means to secure information). But in cases of extraordinary need, the name can be disclosed. See "Patient's name," §2.7.1, this page. By comparison, the physician-patient privilege protects a patient's name only in limited situations. See "Patient's name," §1.7.1, p. 669.

§2.7 What psychotherapist-patient privilege does not protect. The following psychotherapist-patient communications are discoverable:

1. Patient's name. The identity of the patient is discoverable if there is an extraordinary need for the disclosure of the patient's identity. Wegner, *Civil Trials & Evidence*, ¶8:2202; *see* 2 Witkin, *Cal. Evidence*, Witnesses, §226; *see, e.g.*, ***County of Alameda v. Superior Ct.*** (1st Dist.1987) 194 Cal.App.3d 254, 261 (P was able to discover name of her rapist, who was patient in same mental hospital).

2. Crime or tort. Psychotherapist-patient communications are discoverable if the services of the psychotherapist were sought or obtained to enable or aid anyone to commit or plan a crime or tort or to escape detection or apprehension after the commission of a crime or tort. Evid. C. §1018; Wegner, *Civil Trials & Evidence*, ¶8:2216.

3. Claims through dead patient. Psychotherapist-patient communications are discoverable if they are relevant to an issue between parties who are all claiming through the same dead patient. Evid. C. §1019; Wegner, *Civil Trials & Evidence*, ¶8:2217.

4. Breach of duty. Psychotherapist-patient communications are discoverable if the communication is relevant to an issue of breach, by the psychotherapist or the patient, of a duty arising from the psychotherapist-patient relationship. Evid. C. §1020; Wegner, *Civil Trials & Evidence*, ¶8:2218.

5. Dead patient's writings. Psychotherapist-patient communications are discoverable in a dispute about a deed, will, or other writing signed by a dead patient when the communications are relevant to the dead patient's intention or the writing's validity. Evid. C. §1021 (intention), §1022 (validity).

6. Criminal defendant's sanity. Psychotherapist-patient communications are discoverable in a proceeding initiated by the defendant in a criminal action to determine the defendant's sanity. Evid. C. §1023.

7. Dangerous patient. Psychotherapist-patient communications are discoverable if the psychotherapist has reasonable cause to believe (1) the patient has a mental or emotional condition that makes her dangerous to herself or to the person or property of another and (2) disclosure of the communication is necessary to prevent the threatened danger. Evid. C. §1024; ***People v. Gonzales*** (2013) 56 Cal.4th 353, 380; ***Menendez v. Superior Ct.*** (1992) 3 Cal.4th 435, 449; *see* 2 Witkin, *Cal. Evidence*, Witnesses, §§231-235. Even when part of a patient's communication is subject to disclosure under Evid. C. §1024, the rest of the confidential communication remains privileged. ***Gonzales***, 56 Cal.4th at 382. Section 1024 creates an exception to the psychotherapist-patient privilege, not a waiver of the privilege. ***People v. Wharton*** (1991) 53 Cal.3d 522, 560; ***San Diego Trolley, Inc. v. Superior Ct.*** (4th Dist.2001) 87 Cal.App.4th 1083, 1091-92. Once the factual predicate for the dangerous-patient exception is established, the excepted communication can be used in any proceeding, even if the dangerous patient no longer poses a threat. ***Wharton***, 53 Cal.3d at 558; ***San Diego Trolley***, 87 Cal.App.4th at 1092. The only limitation on the use of the information in later proceedings is the constitutional right to privacy. ***San Diego Trolley***, 87 Cal.App.4th at 1096; *see* ***Wharton***, 53 Cal.3d at 563. See "Right to Privacy," ch. 6-F, §1, p. 681. There is no similar exception to the physician-patient privilege.

8. Competence proceedings. Psychotherapist-patient communications are discoverable in a proceeding brought by or on behalf of the patient to establish the patient's competence. Evid. C. §1025; Wegner, *Civil Trials & Evidence*, ¶8:2227.

9. Required report. Psychotherapist-patient communications are discoverable if (1) the psychotherapist or patient is required to report the information to a public employee or to record it in a public office and (2) the report or record is open to public inspection. Evid. C. §1026; *see* ***Lemelle v. Superior Ct.*** (4th Dist.1978) 77 Cal.App.3d 148, 158 n.2 (dicta).

10. Child victim. Psychotherapist-patient communications are discoverable if (1) the patient is a child under the age of 16 and (2) the psychotherapist has reasonable cause to believe that the child has been the victim of a crime and that disclosure of the communication is in the child's best interest. Evid. C. §1027; *see, e.g.,* ***In re Courtney S.*** (1st Dist.1982) 130 Cal.App.3d 567, 574-75 (in proceeding to determine custody of child, exception applied to counseling sessions in which child discussed being molested by her stepfather).

11. Appointment by court or Board of Prison Terms. Psychotherapist-patient communications and records are discoverable if the psychotherapist was appointed by the court or the Board of Prison Terms to examine the patient. Evid. C. §1017; Wegner, *Civil Trials & Evidence*, ¶8:2215; 2 Witkin, *Cal. Evidence*, Witnesses, §236. This exception does not apply in at least two situations:

(1) D's attorney requested appointment. The psychotherapist's records are not discoverable if the court appointed the psychotherapist at the request of the defendant's attorney to provide the attorney with information needed to advise the defendant whether to enter or withdraw a plea based on insanity or to present a defense based on mental or emotional condition. Evid. C. §1017(a); ***People v. Ledesma*** (2006) 39 Cal.4th 641, 688.

(2) Records protected by attorney-client privilege. The psychotherapist's records are not discoverable if protected under the attorney-client privilege, even when not protected under §1017. *See* ***Ledesma***, 39 Cal.4th at 690.

§2.8 Waiver of psychotherapist-patient privilege. There is no psychotherapist-patient privilege if the holder of the privilege, or a person authorized by the holder, waives it.

1. Waiver. If the privilege is waived, the information is discoverable.

(1) General rules of waiver. See "Waiver of privilege," ch. 6-A, §2.2.14, p. 607.

(2) Patient-litigant. Psychotherapist-patient communications are discoverable if the issue of the patient's mental or emotional condition is raised by (1) the patient, (2) a party claiming through or under the patient, (3) a party claiming as a beneficiary of the patient through a contract to which the patient is or was a party, (4) a parent bringing a personal-injury claim on behalf of a minor child, or (5) a plaintiff bringing an action for the wrongful death of a patient. Evid. C. §1016; Wegner, *Civil Trials & Evidence*, ¶8:2212; *see* ***In re Lifschutz*** (1970) 2 Cal.3d 415, 431; *see, e.g.,* ***People v. Montiel*** (1993) 5 Cal.4th 877, 923 (by placing his mental state at issue, D waived his psychotherapist-patient privilege). The only communications that can be discovered, however, are those that are directly relevant to the specific mental conditions the patient-litigant has placed in issue. ***Britt v. Superior Ct.*** (1978) 20 Cal.3d 844, 863-64. Communications that are not directly relevant remain privileged. *Id.*; ***Roberts v. Superior Ct.*** (1973) 9 Cal.3d 330, 339; ***In re Lifschutz***, 2 Cal.3d at 435. The patient bears the burden of showing that a confidential communication is not directly relevant to her claim. ***In re Lifschutz***, 2 Cal.3d at 436.

2. No waiver. If the privilege is not waived, the information is not discoverable. See "Privilege not waived," ch. 6-A, §3.3.2, p. 612.

§2.9 How to assert psychotherapist-patient privilege. See "How to assert physician-patient privilege," §1.9, p. 671.

§3. MEDICAL PEER-REVIEW PRIVILEGE

§3.1 General. The medical peer-review privilege was enacted to improve the quality of medical care by giving peer-review committees and other similar committees the ability to confidentially review and criticize the safety and quality of patient care. *See* ***Matchett v. Superior Ct.*** (3d Dist.1974) 40 Cal.App.3d 623, 628-29.

NOTE

There are similar privileges covering (1) committees for foundations that provide nonprofit medical care, (2) committees for organizations that conduct reviews of professional standards, (3) committees established under Welfare & Inst. C. §4070 (now §14725) and §5624 (repealed) for improving mental-health care, and (4) local-government committees responsible for monitoring, evaluating, and reporting on the necessity, quality, and level of specialty health services, such as trauma care, provided by general acute-care hospitals. See Evid. C. §§1157.5-1157.7; see also Stats. 2012, ch. 34, §57 (renumbering and amending Welfare & Inst. C. §4070); Stats. 1991, ch. 89, §108 (repealing Welfare & Inst. C. §5624).

1. Purpose. The purpose of the peer-review privilege is to encourage the full and truthful disclosure of information to promote and improve the quality of medical and mental-health treatment. *See* ***People v. Superior Ct.*** (2d Dist.1991) 234 Cal.App.3d 363, 373. The rationale for the peer-review privilege is that the public's interest in improving patient care outweighs an individual plaintiff's interest in access to peer-review information, and improvement of patient care is promoted by creating an environment in which hospital staff and the peer-review committee can communicate openly without being concerned that the committee's investigations or negative appraisals could be used as evidence in a malpractice suit. *See* ***West Covina Hosp. v. Superior Ct.*** (1986) 41 Cal.3d 846, 853-54; ***Matchett***, 40 Cal.App.3d at 628-29.

2. Primary authority. Evid. C. §1157; Health & Saf. C. §1370.

3. Secondary authority. The following secondary sources are cited as authority in this section:

- Wegner, *California Practice Guide: Civil Trials & Evidence* (CD-ROM ed. 2014) (referred to as Wegner, *Civil Trials & Evidence*).
- Witkin, *California Evidence* (5th ed. 2012 & Supp.2014) (referred to as Witkin, *Cal. Evidence*).

§3.2 Nature of peer-review privilege.

1. Discovery. The peer-review privilege is a discovery privilege. *See* Evid. C. §1157(a) (peer-review information is not "subject to discovery"); Health & Saf. C. §1370 (same). "Discovery" under §1157 means the formal exchange of evidentiary information between parties to a pending case. ***Arnett v. Dal Cielo*** (1996) 14 Cal.4th 4, 24. For example, the peer-review privilege does not apply to a subpoena issued by an administrative agency for purely investigative purposes because the subpoena is not "discovery." *Id.* at 25. When the privilege applies, it prevents the discovery of committee records and the involuntary testimony of any person in attendance at a committee meeting. Evid. C. §1157(a), (b); ***Fox v. Kramer*** (2000) 22 Cal.4th 531, 544. It is not an evidentiary privilege, which means that if a party were able to secure peer-review information (e.g., if a member of the committee were to testify voluntarily), the party could introduce the information at trial. ***Fox***, 22 Cal.4th at 539; Wegner, *Civil Trials & Evidence*, ¶8:2889.

2. Absolute. The records and proceedings of peer-review committees and other committees responsible for evaluating and improving the quality of health care and related services are absolutely protected from discovery. Evid. C. §1157(a); ***Scripps Mem'l Hosp. v. Superior Ct.*** (4th Dist.1995) 37 Cal.App.4th 1720, 1724; ***Snell v. Superior Ct.*** (3d Dist.1984) 158 Cal.App.3d 44, 49.

3. Duration. The peer-review privilege lasts indefinitely. *See* Evid. C. §1157(a) (blanket exemption of peer-review records and proceedings from discovery).

§3.3 Elements of peer-review privilege. The elements of the peer-review privilege are the following:

1. Committee is protected. The committee is protected by the peer-review privilege. *See* Evid. C. §1157; ***Fox v. Kramer*** (2000) 22 Cal.4th 531, 538-39; *see, e.g.*, ***Santa Rosa Mem'l Hosp. v. Superior Ct.*** (1st Dist.1985) 174 Cal.App.3d 711, 718-19 (hospital's infection-control committee qualified for privilege). See "Committees covered by peer-review privilege," §3.4, p. 679.

2. Information is privileged. The information sought to be discovered is of a type that is protected by the peer-review privilege. *See* Evid. C. §1157; ***Arnett v. Dal Cielo*** (1996) 14 Cal.4th 4, 18. See "What peer-review privilege protects," §3.7, this page.

§3.4 Committees covered by peer-review privilege. The peer-review privilege applies to medical peer-review committees and other committees responsible for evaluating and improving the quality of health care and related services. *See* Evid. C. §1157(a).

1. Peer-review committees. A peer-review committee is a committee in a licensed hospital that is charged with the responsibility of ensuring the adequacy and quality of medical care. ***Fox v. Kramer*** (2000) 22 Cal.4th 531, 538. A peer-review committee does not have to be composed completely, or even mostly, of physicians. ***Pomona Valley Hosp. Med. Ctr. v. Superior Ct.*** (2d Dist.2012) 209 Cal.App.4th 687, 694; ***Santa Rosa Mem'l Hosp. v. Superior Ct.*** (1st Dist.1985) 174 Cal.App.3d 711, 718. Peer-review committees are responsible for reviewing such things as (1) physicians' applications for staff privileges, (2) the hospital's standards and procedures for patient care, (3) the performance of physicians with staff privileges, (4) the need for and results of surgeries performed at the hospital, (5) the patient-records system, (6) the control of infections in the hospital, and (7) the use and handling of drugs in the hospital. ***Arnett v. Dal Cielo*** (1996) 14 Cal.4th 4, 10; *see* ***Mt. Diablo Hosp. Dist. v. Superior Ct.*** (1st Dist.1986) 183 Cal.App.3d 30, 34 (privilege applies to evaluation of new treatments and drugs).

2. Other medical committees. The peer-review privilege applies to various other types of committees listed in Evid. C. §1157 that are organized to review professional treatment of patients, including peer-review bodies established under Bus. & Prof. C. §805. *See* Evid. C. §1157(a).

(1) Committee types generally. The types of committees covered under the general provisions of Evid. C. §1157(a) include dental, podiatric, dietician, social-work, professional-clinical-counseling, marriage-and-family-therapy, psychology, acupuncture, chiropractic, and veterinary committees. Evid. C. §1157(a).

(2) Peer-review bodies. Bus. & Prof. C. §805 lists the types of committees and other entities that qualify as peer-review bodies. Bus. & Prof. C. §805(a)(1).

§3.5 Committees not covered by peer-review privilege.

1. Medical-society committees – members exceed 10% of society. The peer-review privilege does not apply to certain medical-society committees listed in Evid. C. §1157(d) if the number of members on the committee exceeds ten percent of the total membership of the society. Evid. C. §1157(d).

2. Medical-society committees – party served on committee. The peer-review privilege does not apply to certain medical-society committees listed in Evid. C. §1157(d) if a party was a committee member and the committee is reviewing the party's conduct or practice. Evid. C. §1157(d); 2 Witkin, *Cal. Evidence*, Witnesses, §528.

§3.6 Who can assert peer-review privilege. A committee subject to discovery or a member subpoenaed to testify can assert the peer-review privilege. *See* Evid. C. §1157(a), (b).

§3.7 What peer-review privilege protects.

1. Records & proceedings. All records and proceedings of a peer-review committee are privileged. Evid. C. §1157; ***Fox v. Kramer*** (2000) 22 Cal.4th 531, 538-39; ***Santa Rosa Mem'l Hosp. v. Superior Ct.*** (1st Dist.1985) 174 Cal.App.3d 711, 724.

2. Compelled testimony. A person who attends a meeting of a peer-review committee cannot be forced to testify about what took place at the meeting. Evid. C. §1157(b). However, the peer-review privilege does not prevent a committee member from testifying voluntarily. *See id.*; ***West Covina Hosp. v. Superior Ct.*** (1986) 41 Cal.3d 846, 855.

3. Member identity. The identities of the members of a peer-review committee are privileged. ***Cedars-Sinai Med. Ctr. v. Superior Ct.*** (2d Dist.1993) 12 Cal.App.4th 579, 588.

§3.8 What peer-review privilege does not protect.

1. Administrative files. A party can discover administrative files that do not contain information from the peer-review committee's investigations. ***Brown v. Superior Ct.*** (2d Dist.1985) 168 Cal.App.3d 489, 501; *see* ***Matchett v. Superior Ct.*** (3d Dist.1974) 40 Cal.App.3d 623, 628. Administrative files containing both privileged and nonprivileged information must be reviewed by the court in chambers to determine which parts of the file are discoverable. *See, e.g.*, ***Schulz v. Superior Ct.*** (3d Dist.1977) 66 Cal.App.3d 440, 446-47 (court had to determine which files were not result of advisory board's investigation).

2. Medical-staff files. A party can discover medical-staff files that do not contain information from the peer-review committee's investigations. *See* ***Fox v. Kramer*** (2000) 22 Cal.4th 531, 539. Medical-staff files are subject to discovery even if they contain information that may have been considered by the peer-review committee because the information in the files is obtained independently and does not invade the confidentiality of the peer-review committee. ***Santa Rosa Mem'l Hosp. v. Superior Ct.*** (1st Dist.1985) 174 Cal.App.3d 711, 724; *see* ***Pomona Valley Hosp. Med. Ctr. v. Superior Ct.*** (2d Dist.2012) 209 Cal.App.4th 687, 696-97.

3. Whether meeting held. A party can discover whether the committee conducted meetings or reviewed a particular issue. *See, e.g.*, ***Brown***, 168 Cal.App.3d at 501 (malpractice P was entitled to discover whether hospital evaluated its physicians).

4. Party statements. A party can discover statements made by a party to a suit during a peer-review committee meeting if the subject matter of the suit was reviewed at the meeting. Evid. C. §1157(c).

5. Medical Board investigation. The peer-review privilege does not prevent the California Medical Board from subpoenaing the records of a peer-review committee during an investigation into the conduct of a physician. ***Arnett v. Dal Cielo*** (1996) 14 Cal.4th 4, 24; 2 Witkin, *Cal. Evidence*, Witnesses, §533.

6. Staff privileges. A physician whose request for hospital-staff privileges was denied or whose privileges were limited can discover peer-review committee information in a suit to obtain or broaden those privileges. Evid. C. §1157(c); ***California Eye Inst. v. Superior Ct.*** (5th Dist.1989) 215 Cal.App.3d 1477, 1486; 2 Witkin, *Cal. Evidence*, Witnesses, §528. This exception does not apply in a suit for damages based on wrongful denial of or interference with the physician's request for hospital-staff privileges. ***Joel v. Valley Surgical Ctr.*** (1st Dist.1998) 68 Cal.App.4th 360, 368.

7. Insurance bad faith. A party can discover peer-review committee information in a suit against an insurance carrier alleging that the carrier made a bad-faith refusal to accept a settlement offer within the policy limits. Evid. C. §1157(c).

8. Criminal action. The peer-review privilege does not prevent discovery or use of peer-review information in a criminal action. Evid. C. §1157(e); 2 Witkin, *Cal. Evidence*, Witnesses, §530; *e.g.*, ***People v. Superior Ct.*** (2d Dist.1991) 234 Cal.App.3d 363, 387 (prosecutor could seek discovery by search warrant even before charges were filed).

§3.9 Waiver of peer-review privilege. A member of the peer-review committee can voluntarily provide information about the committee's proceedings, even though the member cannot be forced to testify about the same matter. ***Fox v. Kramer*** (2000) 22 Cal.4th 531, 539; ***West Covina Hosp. v. Superior Ct.*** (1986) 41 Cal.3d 846, 855; Wegner, *Civil Trials & Evidence*, ¶8:2890; 2 Witkin, *Cal. Evidence*, Witnesses, §532; *see* Evid. C. §1157(b).

§3.10 How to assert peer-review privilege.

1. Committee claims privilege. The committee or committee member subject to discovery can claim the peer-review privilege by objecting to the discovery on the ground that the privilege prevents disclosure of the information. In most cases, the committee is a nonparty and discovery is by subpoena. See "Procedure to challenge subpoenas," ch. 8-E, §2.2, p. 998. Instead of serving objections, the committee can claim the privilege by filing a motion for protective order or a motion to quash. See "Motion for Protective Order," ch. 9-B, p. 1024; "Motion to Quash Depositions," ch. 9-C, p. 1038.

2. Discovering party moves to compel. In response to an objection that the peer-review privilege bars discovery, the discovering party has the burden to enforce discovery. It must initiate the meet-and-confer procedure and, if unsuccessful, file a motion to compel discovery. See "Discovering party moves to compel (option 1)," ch. 7-A, §14.1.2, p. 772.

3. Committee serves opposition papers. In response to a motion to compel, the committee has the burden to justify the assertion of the peer-review privilege by proving the preliminary facts that support it. See "Elements of peer-review privilege," §3.3, p. 678; "Responding party satisfies burden," ch. 7-A, §14.1.4, p. 772. That is, the committee must prove that the discovery seeks information from the peer-review committee's records or about the committee's proceedings, or attempts to subpoena a member of the committee. *See* Evid. C. §1157(a), (b).

F. PERSONAL PRIVILEGES

This subchapter covers the following privileges: the right to privacy, the privilege against self-incrimination, the tax-return privilege, the clergy-penitent privilege, and the voter privilege.

§1. RIGHT TO PRIVACY

§1.1 General. A person has a constitutional right to privacy, which is the right to be left alone. ***American Airlines, Inc. v. Superior Ct.*** (2d Dist.2003) 114 Cal.App.4th 881, 893; *see* Cal. Const., art. I, §1. If a party cannot claim any other privilege or immunity, it may be able to protect information from discovery by asserting the constitutional right to privacy. ***Hooser v. Superior Ct.*** (4th Dist.2000) 84 Cal.App.4th 997, 1003; *see, e.g.*, ***Valley Bank v. Superior Ct.*** (1975) 15 Cal.3d 652, 656 (there is no bank-customer privilege, but customer could protect information from discovery by asserting right to privacy). Some statutes also provide a right to privacy. *See, e.g.*, Ins. C. §§791-791.28 (Insurance Information and Privacy Protection Act).

1. Purpose. The purpose of the right to privacy is to protect against the unwarranted, compelled disclosure of private or sensitive information about someone's personal life (referred to as "informational privacy"). *See* ***Pioneer Elecs. (USA), Inc. v. Superior Ct.*** (2007) 40 Cal.4th 360, 372; ***Hill v. NCAA*** (1994) 7 Cal.4th 1, 35; ***Hooser***, 84 Cal.App.4th at 1003-04; ***Smith v. Fresno Irrigation Dist.*** (5th Dist.1999) 72 Cal.App.4th 147, 161. The right to privacy also protects a person's intimate and personal activities and decisions from unwarranted observation, intrusion, or interference (referred to as "autonomy privacy"). ***Hill***, 7 Cal.4th at 35; ***Smith***, 72 Cal.App.4th at 161.

2. Primary authority. Cal. Const., art. I, §1.

3. Secondary authority. The following secondary sources are cited as authority in this section:

- Capozzola, *Discovering Privacy*, Los Angeles Lawyer (Nov. 2003), www.lacba.org/Files/LAL/Vol26No8/1455.pdf (referred to as Capozzola, *Discovering Privacy*).
- Wegner, *California Practice Guide: Civil Trials & Evidence* (CD-ROM ed. 2014) (referred to as Wegner, *Civil Trials & Evidence*).
- Weil & Brown, *California Practice Guide: Civil Procedure Before Trial* (CD-ROM ed. 2014) (referred to as Weil, *Civil Procedure Before Trial*).

§1.2 Nature of right to privacy.

1. Constitutional. The right to privacy is based on the California Constitution. Cal. Const., art. I, §1.

2. Qualified. The right to privacy is qualified. ***Medical Bd. of Cal. v. Chiarottino*** (1st Dist.2014) 225 Cal.App.4th 623, 631; ***Ombudsman Servs. v. Superior Ct.*** (3d Dist.2007) 154 Cal.App.4th 1233, 1249; ***Hooser v. Superior Ct.*** (4th Dist.2000) 84 Cal.App.4th 997, 1004; ***Lantz v. Superior Ct.*** (5th Dist.1994) 28 Cal.App.4th 1839, 1853; ***Palay v. Superior Ct.*** (2d Dist.1993) 18 Cal.App.4th 919, 933. A person's right to privacy can be outweighed by more compelling interests. *See* Wegner, *Civil Trials & Evidence*, ¶¶8:2701, 8:2702. See "Intrusion justified," §1.7.1(3), p. 686.

§1.3 Elements of right to privacy. The elements of the right to privacy are the following:

1. Legally protected privacy interest. The holder has a legally protected privacy interest. ***County of L.A. v. Los Angeles Cty. Empl. Relations Comm'n*** (2013) 56 Cal.4th 905, 926; ***Pioneer Elecs. (USA), Inc. v. Superior Ct.*** (2007) 40 Cal.4th 360, 370; ***Heller v. Norcal Mut. Ins.*** (1994) 8 Cal.4th 30, 42-43; ***Hill v. NCAA*** (1994) 7 Cal.4th 1, 35. Whether the circumstances of the case give rise to a legally protected interest is a question of law and requires a determination that established social norms protect the claimed interest from intrusion. ***Pioneer Elecs.***, 40 Cal.4th at 370. For a list of legally protected privacy interests, see "What right to privacy protects," §1.5, p. 683.

2. Reasonable expectation of privacy. The holder has a reasonable expectation of privacy. ***County of L.A.***, 56 Cal.4th at 926; ***Pioneer Elecs.***, 40 Cal.4th at 370; ***Hill***, 7 Cal.4th at 36; *e.g.*, ***Heller***, 8 Cal.4th at 42-43 (P did not have reasonable expectation of privacy in information that would inevitably be discovered through litigation). Whether the circumstances of the case give rise to an expectation of privacy is a mixed question of law and fact and depends on an analysis of several factors, including (1) community norms (i.e., the customs of time and place, the holder's occupation, and the habits of neighbors and fellow citizens), (2) the customs, practices, and physical settings surrounding a particular activity, and (3) the holder's opportunity to consent to the activities affecting the privacy interest. ***Hill***, 7 Cal.4th at 36-37, 40; *see* ***County of L.A.***, 56 Cal.4th at 927; ***Pioneer Elecs.***, 40 Cal.4th at 370-71; ***TBG Ins. Servs. v. Superior Ct.*** (2d Dist.2002) 96 Cal.App.4th 443, 450; *see also* **Ombudsman Servs. v. Superior Ct.** (3d Dist.2007) 154 Cal.App.4th 1233, 1249 (strength of privacy interest covering worker's communications with workplace ombudsman requires analysis of several factors).

3. Serious invasion of privacy. The invasion of privacy was serious. ***County of L.A.***, 56 Cal.4th at 926; ***Pioneer Elecs.***, 40 Cal.4th at 371; ***Heller***, 8 Cal.4th at 42-43; ***Hill***, 7 Cal.4th at 37. Whether the circumstances of the case give rise to a serious invasion of privacy requires a determination that the invasion constitutes an egregious breach of the social norms underlying the particular privacy interest in question. ***Pioneer Elecs.***, 40 Cal.4th at 370-71; ***Hill***, 7 Cal.4th at 37, 40. Protective measures, safeguards, and alternative methods of discovery can alleviate the seriousness of the invasion into the privacy interest. ***Hill***, 7 Cal.4th at 38; *e.g.*, ***Pioneer Elecs.***, 40 Cal.4th at 371 (court limited disclosure of contact information by requiring written notice of proposed disclosure to affected persons and giving them opportunity to object).

§1.4 Who can assert right to privacy.

1. Holder. The holder of the right to privacy can assert it. The following can be a holder of the right to privacy:

(1) Individuals. Individuals can assert the right to privacy. *See* ***Roberts v. Gulf Oil Corp.*** (5th Dist.1983) 147 Cal.App.3d 770, 791.

(2) Business entities. Whether business entities are entitled to assert the right to privacy under the California Constitution is unsettled. ***Nativi v. Deutsche Bank Nat'l Trust Co.*** (6th Dist.2014) 223 Cal.App.4th 261, 314 n.16; ***Volkswagen v. Superior Ct.*** (1st Dist.2006) 139 Cal.App.4th 1481, 1492 n.9; ***H&M Assocs. v. City of El Centro*** (4th Dist.1980) 109 Cal.App.3d 399, 410. If business entities are entitled to assert the constitutional right to privacy, the courts will have to decide the extent of their privacy rights. *See* ***Volkswagen***, 139 Cal.App.4th at 1492 n.9.

(a) Corporations. The California Supreme Court has not decided whether corporations have a right to privacy under the California Constitution. *See* ***Connecticut Indem. Co. v. Superior Ct.*** (2000) 23 Cal.4th 807, 817 (court assumed but did not decide that corporations have constitutional privacy rights). Some courts that have addressed the issue have held that corporations do not have a constitutional right to privacy because the right was created to protect human beings. ***Roberts***, 147 Cal.App.3d at 791-92. Because corporations are not human beings, the constitutional right to privacy does not extend to them. ***Ameri-Med. Corp. v. Workers' Comp. Appeals Bd.*** (2d Dist.1996) 42 Cal.App.4th 1260, 1287; ***Roberts***, 147 Cal.App.3d at 791-93. *But see* ***H&M Assocs.***, 109 Cal.App.3d at 410-11 (dicta; constitutional protection against intrusion on right to privacy is not restricted to individuals).

(b) Unincorporated entities. As with corporations, whether unincorporated entities (e.g., partnerships, associations) have a right to privacy under the California Constitution is unclear. *See* ***Hecht, Solberg, Robinson, Goldberg & Bagley LLP v. Superior Ct.*** (4th Dist.2006) 137 Cal.App.4th 579, 594 (dicta; arguable whether business entities have constitutional right to privacy). *Compare* ***Fibreboard Corp. v. Hartford Acc. & Indem. Co.*** (1st Dist.1993) 16 Cal.App.4th 492, 516 (partnerships and unincorporated associations have no personal right to privacy), *with* ***Wilson v. California Health Facilities Comm'n*** (1st Dist.1980) 110 Cal.App.3d 317, 325 (general partners in limited-liability partnership brought suit based on right to privacy to prevent disclosure of financial records), *and* ***H&M Assocs.***, 109 Cal.App.3d at 410-11 (partnership may state cause of action for invasion of privacy).

NOTE

Even if business entities do not have a fundamental right to privacy under the California Constitution, they may be entitled to claim some right to privacy. ***Roberts****, 147 Cal.App.3d at 795; see* ***Ameri-Med.****, 42 Cal.App.4th at 1287-88. The extent of an organization's privacy rights, however, will depend on (1) the strength of the nexus between the organization and human beings and (2) the context in which the controversy arises.* ***Roberts****, 147 Cal.App.3d at 797.*

2. Person in possession. Any person (individual, public entity, or private entity) in possession of a holder's personal information or records can assert the right to privacy on the holder's behalf. *See, e.g.*, ***Pioneer Elecs. (USA), Inc. v. Superior Ct.*** (2007) 40 Cal.4th 360, 364 (electronics company asserted right to privacy on behalf of customers); ***Digital Music News LLC v. Superior Ct.*** (2d Dist.2014) 226 Cal.App.4th 216, 228 n.12 (website operator asserted right to privacy on behalf of anonymous Internet user that posted on site); ***Medical Bd. of Cal. v. Chiarottino*** (1st Dist.2014) 225 Cal.App.4th 623, 630 n.3 (physician asserted right to privacy on behalf of patients); ***Tien v. Superior Ct.*** (2d Dist.2006) 139 Cal.App.4th 528, 539 & n.7 (party asserted right to privacy on behalf of class-action class members who consulted with party's attorney); ***Doe 2 v. Superior Ct.*** (2d Dist.2005) 132 Cal.App.4th 1504, 1520 (church asserted right to privacy on behalf of third persons who communicated with pastor); ***Rancho Publ'ns v. Superior Ct.*** (4th Dist.1999) 68 Cal.App.4th 1538, 1541 (newspaper asserted right to privacy on behalf of anonymous author of advertorial). *But see* ***Matrixx Initiatives, Inc. v. Doe*** (6th Dist.2006) 138 Cal.App.4th 872, 880-81 (deponent could not assert privacy rights on behalf of anonymous Internet users because he did not have any relationship with them). A person in possession of a holder's personal information has an affirmative duty to notify the holder that the personal information may be disclosed and give the holder an opportunity to object. *See, e.g.*, ***Valley Bank v. Superior Ct.*** (1975) 15 Cal.3d 652, 658 (bank was required to notify customers of proposed disclosure in discovery proceeding and give opportunity to object); ***In re Insurance Installment Fee Cases*** (4th Dist.2012) 211 Cal.App.4th 1395, 1426-27 (insurer was required to notify policyholders of proposed disclosure in discovery proceeding and to give opportunity to object). See "Subpoenas for Personal Records," ch. 8-D, p. 977.

§1.5 What right to privacy protects.

1. Legally protected privacy interest. The right to privacy protects legally protected privacy interests. ***Pioneer Elecs. (USA), Inc. v. Superior Ct.*** (2007) 40 Cal.4th 360, 370; ***Heller v. Norcal Mut. Ins.*** (1994) 8 Cal.4th 30, 42-43; ***Hill v. NCAA*** (1994) 7 Cal.4th 1, 35. To be legally protected, the privacy interest must fall within a zone of privacy protected by the California Constitution. *See* ***Johnson v. Superior Ct.*** (2d Dist.2000) 80 Cal.App.4th 1050, 1068-69; ***Palay v. Superior Ct.*** (2d Dist.1993) 18 Cal.App.4th 919, 931-32. There are two categories of legally protected privacy interests: informational privacy and autonomy privacy.

(1) Informational privacy. Informational privacy protects a person's personal information from being disclosed or misused. ***Ruiz v. Podolsky*** (2010) 50 Cal.4th 838, 850; ***Pioneer Elecs.***, 40 Cal.4th at 372; ***Hill***, 7 Cal.4th at 35; ***Hooser v. Superior Ct.*** (4th Dist.2000) 84 Cal.App.4th 997, 1003-04; ***Smith v. Fresno Irrigation Dist.*** (5th Dist.1999) 72 Cal.App.4th 147, 161.

(2) Autonomy privacy. Autonomy privacy protects a person's intimate and personal activities and decisions from observation, intrusion, or interference. ***Ruiz***, 50 Cal.4th at 850-51; ***Hill***, 7 Cal.4th at 35; ***Smith***, 72 Cal.App.4th at 161.

2. **Zones of privacy.** Zones of privacy were first recognized under the U.S. Constitution and included matters relating to family, marriage, and sex. ***Palay***, 18 Cal.App.4th at 933; ***American G.I. Forum v. Miller*** (4th Dist.1990) 218 Cal.App.3d 859, 864; *see* ***Griswold v. Connecticut*** (1965) 381 U.S. 479, 484 (specific guarantees in Bill of Rights have created zones of privacy). These zones of privacy have been extended by the California Constitution. *See* ***American G.I. Forum***, 218 Cal.App.3d at 864 (right to privacy under California Constitution is much broader than federal right to privacy). The following are examples of protected zones of privacy under the California Constitution:

(1) **Sexual privacy.** A person has a right to prevent disclosure of personal information about sexual relationships, including information about sexual partners, extramarital affairs, and HIV status. *See* ***John B. v. Superior Ct.*** (2006) 38 Cal.4th 1177, 1199 (informational privacy in sexual history and HIV status); ***Winfred D. v. Michelin N. Am., Inc.*** (2d Dist.2008) 165 Cal.App.4th 1011, 1040 (dicta; informational privacy in extramarital affairs); Wegner, *Civil Trials & Evidence*, ¶8:2726 (person's sexual practices are protected by right to privacy).

(2) **Medical privacy.** A person has a right to prevent disclosure of the person's medical history and to prevent an intrusion into bodily autonomy. *See, e.g.*, ***Ruiz***, 50 Cal.4th at 850-51 (informational privacy in medical information; autonomy privacy in obtaining treatment); ***In re Qawi*** (2004) 32 Cal.4th 1, 14 (autonomy privacy over decisions about medical treatment); ***Medical Bd. of Cal. v. Chiarottino*** (1st Dist.2014) 225 Cal.App.4th 623, 631 & n.5 (informational privacy in patient prescription records); ***Carpenter v. Superior Ct.*** (1st Dist.2006) 141 Cal.App.4th 249, 259 (informational and autonomy privacy in compelled mental examination); ***Johnson***, 80 Cal.App.4th at 1069 (informational privacy in identity as sperm donor because identity was linked with person's medical history); ***Rains v. Belshe*** (1st Dist.1995) 32 Cal.App.4th 157, 171 (autonomy privacy over decisions about medical treatment); Wegner, *Civil Trials & Evidence*, ¶8:2719 (informational privacy in person's medical history).

(3) **Personal-finance privacy.** A person has a right to prevent disclosure of information about personal finances, including information about bank accounts, assets, and debts. *See* ***In re Insurance Installment Fee Cases*** (4th Dist.2012) 211 Cal.App.4th 1395, 1428 (informational privacy in personal financial affairs); ***Ameri-Med. Corp. v. Workers' Comp. Appeals Bd.*** (2d Dist.1996) 42 Cal.App.4th 1260, 1286-87 (limited informational privacy in corporation's financial information); ***Moskowitz v. Superior Ct.*** (2d Dist.1982) 137 Cal.App.3d 313, 315 (informational privacy in information about personal finances).

(4) **Associational privacy.** A person has a right to associate with others without observation, intrusion, or interference. *See* ***Britt v. Superior Ct.*** (1978) 20 Cal.3d 844, 848-49; ***Conejo Wellness Ctr., Inc. v. City of Agoura Hills*** (2d Dist.2013) 214 Cal.App.4th 1534, 1563. This right includes the right to marry, the right to decide whom to live with, and the right to prevent disclosure of information identifying with whom or what a person associates. *See* ***Britt***, 20 Cal.3d at 852 (informational privacy in person's associations and association activities); ***Tom v. City & Cty. of S.F.*** (1st Dist.2004) 120 Cal.App.4th 674, 680 (autonomy privacy in decision about whom to live with); ***Ortiz v. Los Angeles Police Relief Ass'n*** (2d Dist.2002) 98 Cal.App.4th 1288, 1302-03 (autonomy privacy in decision about whom to marry); Wegner, *Civil Trials & Evidence*, ¶8:2710 (informational privacy in person's associations regardless of association activities).

(5) **Personnel-records privacy.** A person has a right to prevent disclosure of confidential personnel files at her place of employment. ***Harding Lawson Assocs. v. Superior Ct.*** (1st Dist.1992) 10 Cal.App.4th 7, 10; Wegner, *Civil Trials & Evidence*, ¶8:2722; *see, e.g.*, ***Ibarra v. Superior Ct.*** (2d Dist.2013) 217 Cal.App.4th 695, 705 (peace officers' service photographs were not protected under right to privacy when officers' duties did not require anonymity); ***Alch v. Superior Ct.*** (2d Dist.2008) 165 Cal.App.4th 1412, 1432-33 (information was not protected under right to privacy because party was not seeking sensitive information ordinarily found in personnel files, such as evaluations, income information, and employment contracts).

(6) **Privacy in the home.** A person has a right to privacy in her home, which includes the right to prevent disclosure of personal addresses and phone numbers and the right to decide whom to live with or exclude

from the home. *See* ***County of L.A. v. Los Angeles Cty. Empl. Relations Comm'n*** (2013) 56 Cal.4th 905, 927 (informational privacy in personal addresses and phone numbers); ***Puerto v. Superior Ct.*** (2d Dist.2008) 158 Cal.App.4th 1242, 1252 (same); ***Tom***, 120 Cal.App.4th at 680 (autonomy privacy in decision about whom to live with or exclude from the home).

(7) Anonymous-speech privacy. A person has a right to speak anonymously. ***Digital Music News LLC v. Superior Ct.*** (2d Dist.2014) 226 Cal.App.4th 216, 228-29; ***Vogel v. Felice*** (6th Dist.2005) 127 Cal.App.4th 1006, 1024; *see* ***Rancho Publ'ns v. Superior Ct.*** (4th Dist.1999) 68 Cal.App.4th 1538, 1541; *see also* ***Huntley v. Public Utils. Comm'n*** (1968) 69 Cal.2d 67, 73-74 (right to anonymous speech on free-speech grounds); ***Krinsky v. Doe*** (6th Dist.2008) 159 Cal.App.4th 1154, 1163-64 (same).

§1.6 Waiver of right to privacy. The right to privacy does not protect privacy interests that have been waived. *See* ***Britt v. Superior Ct.*** (1978) 20 Cal.3d 844, 859; ***Heda v. Superior Ct.*** (1st Dist.1990) 225 Cal.App.3d 525, 530. See "Waiving Discovery & Objections," ch. 7-A, §15, p. 775.

1. Who can waive. Only the holder of the right to privacy can waive it; a party cannot waive a third party's privacy rights. *See* ***Boler v. Superior Ct.*** (1st Dist.1987) 201 Cal.App.3d 467, 472 n.1 (party did not waive third party's right to privacy by not timely objecting to discovery demand because third party was not notified and given opportunity to object).

2. When waived.

(1) By express consent. A holder can waive its right to privacy by expressly consenting to the waiver. *See, e.g.*, ***TBG Ins. Servs. v. Superior Ct.*** (2d Dist.2002) 96 Cal.App.4th 443, 452-53 (party waived right to privacy by signing company policy stating that information on computer was not private). The waiver must be knowing, intelligent, and voluntary. ***Kelly v. William Morrow & Co.*** (4th Dist.1986) 186 Cal.App.3d 1625, 1635.

(2) By raising claim or defense. A party can partially waive its right to privacy by raising a claim or defense in a suit that puts certain personal information at issue. *See* ***Moskowitz v. Superior Ct.*** (2d Dist.1982) 137 Cal.App.3d 313, 316-17; *see, e.g.*, ***John B. v. Superior Ct.*** (2006) 38 Cal.4th 1177, 1199 (by putting his own medical condition at issue, D substantially lowered his expectation of privacy). For example, a party who claims emotional distress from sexual harassment may waive her right to privacy as to her present mental or emotional condition. Wegner, *Civil Trials & Evidence*, ¶8:2728. The personal information should be disclosed only if (1) it is directly relevant to the party's claim or defense and (2) disclosure is essential to the fair resolution of the claim or defense. ***Moskowitz***, 137 Cal.App.3d at 317.

(3) By not objecting. See "Waiver of discovery objection," ch. 7-A, §15.2.2, p. 776.

(a) Party. A party can waive its right to privacy by (1) not objecting to a discovery request or (2) not filing a motion for protection from the request. *See, e.g.*, ***R.S. Creative, Inc. v. Creative Cotton, Ltd.*** (2d Dist.1999) 75 Cal.App.4th 486, 498 (P waived right to privacy by not seeking protective order). *But see* Capozzola, *Discovering Privacy*, at 28-32 (suggesting that failure to timely object to discovery demand does not waive right to privacy); Weil, *Civil Procedure Before Trial*, ¶¶8:319.1-8:319.3 (unclear whether complete failure to timely object waives right to privacy). However, if the party timely raises some type of objection (e.g., relevance), it may be able to assert the right to privacy later. *See* ***Heda***, 225 Cal.App.3d at 529 (D was allowed to raise privacy objection to interrogatories even though initial objection was based on relevance); ***Boler***, 201 Cal.App.3d at 472 n.1 (D was allowed to raise privacy objection in response to motion to compel deposition answer even though D raised only relevance objection during deposition).

(b) Nonparty.

[1] Request to nonparty. A nonparty can waive its right to privacy by (1) not objecting to a discovery request or (2) not filing a motion to quash a deposition notice or subpoena. *See* ***Puerto v. Superior Ct.*** (2d Dist.2008) 158 Cal.App.4th 1242, 1257 (compliance with subpoena is not optional, and witness must make motion to quash if she wants to resist). See "Objections to subpoenas," ch. 8-E, §2.1, p. 995.

[2] **Request to party in possession.** A nonparty can waive its right to privacy by not objecting to a party's disclosure of the nonparty's personal information after it was given notice of the proposed disclosure and an opportunity to object. *See, e.g.*, ***Pioneer Elecs. (USA), Inc. v. Superior Ct.*** (2007) 40 Cal.4th 360, 374-75 (customers of electronics company waived privacy interest in contact information unless they submitted written objection after receiving proper notice).

(4) By voluntary disclosure. A holder can waive its right to privacy by voluntarily disclosing personal information. *See* ***Heda***, 225 Cal.App.3d at 530 (D did not waive privacy right to medical records because he did not disclose significant portion of records).

§1.7 How to assert right to privacy.

1. Objections & motions. As with privileges, the holder or party in possession of the right to privacy can (1) object to a discovery request asserting the right to privacy, (2) file a motion for protective order based on the right to privacy, or (3) file a motion to quash a deposition notice or subpoena. *See, e.g.*, ***R.S. Creative, Inc. v. Creative Cotton, Ltd.*** (2d Dist.1999) 75 Cal.App.4th 486, 498 (P waived right to privacy by not seeking protective order); ***Davis v. Superior Ct.*** (5th Dist.1992) 7 Cal.App.4th 1008, 1013 (P filed motion to quash subpoena for P's medical records based on right to privacy); ***Fults v. Superior Ct.*** (1st Dist.1979) 88 Cal.App.3d 899, 902 (party asserted right to privacy in objection to interrogatories). Regardless of how the issue is brought to the court's attention, the holder or party in possession must prove the preliminary facts that establish the application of the right to privacy. See "Preliminary facts," ch. 7-A, §14.1.4(1), p. 772. In most discovery disputes involving the right to privacy, the discovering party challenges the holder's claim by proving one of the following:

(1) No protection. One or more of the elements of the right to privacy were not established. ***Hill v. NCAA*** (1994) 7 Cal.4th 1, 40; *see* ***Snibbe v. Superior Ct.*** (2d Dist.2014) 224 Cal.App.4th 184, 194-95 (no serious invasion of privacy). See "Elements of right to privacy," §1.3, p. 682.

(2) Waiver. The right to privacy was waived. See "Waiver of right to privacy," §1.6, p. 685.

(3) Intrusion justified. The intrusion on the right to privacy is justified. To justify the discovery request, the discovering party must show the following:

(a) Compelling need for discovery. The discovering party must show a compelling need for the discovery. ***Save Open Space Santa Monica Mountains v. Superior Ct.*** (2d Dist.2000) 84 Cal.App.4th 235, 252; *see* ***Planned Parenthood Golden Gate v. Superior Ct.*** (1st Dist.2000) 83 Cal.App.4th 347, 367. To show a compelling need, the discovering party must demonstrate that the information sought is directly relevant and essential to the fair resolution of the legal proceeding. ***Alch v. Superior Ct.*** (2d Dist.2008) 165 Cal.App.4th 1412, 1425; Wegner, *Civil Trials & Evidence*, ¶8:2748; *cf.* ***Britt v. Superior Ct.*** (1978) 20 Cal.3d 844, 859 (when party implicitly waives right to privacy by bringing suit, scope of waiver is limited to information directly relevant to claim and essential to fair resolution of suit).

(b) Compelling state interest. The discovering party must show that the disclosure of the information serves a compelling state interest. *See* ***Britt***, 20 Cal.3d at 855-56; Wegner, *Civil Trials & Evidence*, ¶8:2703. In the context of discovery disputes, the State has a compelling interest in litigation to discover the truth and obtain just results. *See* ***Britt***, 20 Cal.3d at 857; ***Tien v. Superior Ct.*** (2d Dist.2006) 139 Cal.App.4th 528, 539; ***Planned Parenthood***, 83 Cal.App.4th at 359-60; ***Johnson v. Superior Ct.*** (2d Dist.2000) 80 Cal.App.4th 1050, 1071. This interest is sufficient to allow the court to compel disclosure of material protected under a claim of privacy. ***Johnson***, 80 Cal.App.4th at 1071. However, other compelling state interests may also be implicated in the dispute. *See, e.g.*, ***Alch***, 165 Cal.App.4th at 1437 (P's request for personal information of nonparties in age-discrimination suit implicated state's interest in preventing discrimination); ***Johnson***, 80 Cal.App.4th at 1071 (P's request for name of percipient witness implicated several state interests, including interest in ensuring that persons injured by actionable conduct of others receive full redress for injuries); *see also* ***Medical Bd. of Cal. v. Chiarottino*** (1st Dist.2014) 225 Cal.App.4th 623, 636 (P's accessing controlled-substance prescription database in administrative investigation implicated state's interest in reducing illegitimate prescription drug use).

(c) **Discovery needs outweigh privacy interests.** The discovering party must show that the state interest outweighs the holder's privacy right. *See* ***Schnabel v. Superior Ct.*** (1993) 5 Cal.4th 704, 712; ***Valley Bank v. Superior Ct.*** (1975) 15 Cal.3d 652, 657; ***Alch***, 165 Cal.App.4th at 1431; Wegner, *Civil Trials & Evidence*, ¶8:2752; *see, e.g.*, ***Olympic Club v. Superior Ct.*** (1st Dist.1991) 229 Cal.App.3d 358, 364 (P's strong need for names of applicants rejected by D-club outweighed associational privacy rights of D's members). To establish that the state interest is greater than the holder's right, the discovering party should address the following:

[1] The purpose of the information sought. ***Alch***, 165 Cal.App.4th at 1425; ***Hooser v. Superior Ct.*** (4th Dist.2000) 84 Cal.App.4th 997, 1004.

[2] The nature of the information sought. ***Schnabel***, 5 Cal.4th at 714.

[3] The effect that disclosure will have on parties and nonparties. ***Hooser***, 84 Cal.App.4th at 1004; *see* ***Alch***, 165 Cal.App.4th at 1425; ***Morales v. Superior Ct.*** (5th Dist.1979) 99 Cal.App.3d 283, 291.

[4] The nature of the objection raised by the person opposing discovery. ***Alch***, 165 Cal.App.4th at 1425; ***Hooser***, 84 Cal.App.4th at 1004.

[5] The existence of any alternative, less intrusive means for obtaining the information. ***Hooser***, 84 Cal.App.4th at 1004.

[6] The ability of the court to make an alternative order that may grant partial disclosure in another form or full disclosure after the discovering party meets certain specified burdens that appear just under the circumstances. ***Alch***, 165 Cal.App.4th at 1425.

[7] Other nonprivacy interests that will be furthered if the information is obtained. *See, e.g.*, ***Department of Fair Empl. & Hous. v. Superior Ct.*** (5th Dist.2002) 99 Cal.App.4th 896, 904 (government's subpoena requesting rental information from property managers in fair-housing investigation furthered state interest in eliminating racial discrimination).

2. Court's ruling. In making the ruling, the court may need to conduct an in camera review to determine whether to exclude any information that is not essential to a fair resolution of the case. Wegner, *Civil Trials & Evidence*, ¶8:2753; *see, e.g.*, ***Harris v. Superior Ct.*** (2d Dist.1992) 3 Cal.App.4th 661, 668 (court was obliged to examine financial records in chambers to determine scope of privacy protection); *see also* ***Valley Bank***, 15 Cal.3d at 658 (court has procedural devices it can use when fashioning appropriate order, such as ordering information to be sealed and holding in camera hearings). If an in camera review would be an undue burden, the court can order the holder or her attorney to assist in conducting the review by summarizing the information under penalty of perjury. *See* ***Babcock v. Superior Ct.*** (2d Dist.1994) 29 Cal.App.4th 721, 727 (discovery of financial records in dissolution suit). If discovery is allowed, the order compelling compliance with the discovery request must be narrowly tailored to compel only what is absolutely necessary to accomplish the discovering party's needs. *See* ***Schnabel***, 5 Cal.4th at 714; ***Save Open Space***, 84 Cal.App.4th at 255; *see, e.g.*, ***Pioneer Elecs. (USA), Inc. v. Superior Ct.*** (2007) 40 Cal.4th 360, 373 (court limited disclosure of contact information by requiring written notice of proposed disclosure to affected persons and giving them opportunity to object); ***Brillantes v. Superior Ct.*** (2d Dist.1996) 51 Cal.App.4th 323, 343 (when court allowed discovery of medical records, it instructed that protective order must be enforced).

§2. PRIVILEGE AGAINST SELF-INCRIMINATION

§2.1 General. Parties and witnesses in a civil proceeding can invoke the privilege against self-incrimination. ***Segretti v. State Bar*** (1976) 15 Cal.3d 878, 886; ***Alvarez v. Sanchez*** (1st Dist.1984) 158 Cal.App.3d 709, 712; *see* Cal. Const., art. I, §15; Evid. C. §940. The privilege enables a person to refuse to testify in a civil proceeding if the evidence would tend to incriminate the person in a criminal proceeding. *See* ***Segretti***, 15 Cal.3d at 886.

1. Purpose. The privilege against self-incrimination protects the constitutional right to refuse to give testimony that may subject a person to criminal liability. Evid. C. §940; 7 Cal. Law Revision Comm'n Rep. (1965) p. 1163; Jefferson, *California Evidence Benchbook* (CEB Online ed. 2014) §46.15.

2. **Primary authority.** Cal. Const., art. I, §15; Evid. C. §§404, 911, 913, 930, 940.

3. **Secondary authority.** The following secondary sources are cited as authority in this section:

- *California Civil Discovery Practice* (CEB Online ed. 2014) (referred to as *CEB Discovery Practice*).
- *California Trial Objections* (CEB Online ed. 2014) (referred to as *CEB Trial Objections*).
- Jefferson, *California Evidence Benchbook* (CEB Online ed. 2014) (referred to as *Jefferson's Evid. Benchbook*).
- Wegner, *California Practice Guide: Civil Trials & Evidence* (CD-ROM ed. 2014) (referred to as Wegner, *Civil Trials & Evidence*).

§2.2 Nature of privilege against self-incrimination.

1. **Constitutional.** The privilege against self-incrimination in Evid. C. §940 is based on the U.S. and California Constitutions. Evid. C. §940; *see* U.S. Const. amend. 5; Cal. Const., art. I, §15.

2. **Qualified.** The privilege against self-incrimination in civil proceedings is qualified because the holder may be required to either waive the privilege or accept the civil consequences of refusing to testify. ***Oiye v. Fox*** (6th Dist.2012) 211 Cal.App.4th 1036, 1054; ***In re Marriage of Sachs*** (2d Dist.2002) 95 Cal.App.4th 1144, 1155; ***Fuller v. Superior Ct.*** (2d Dist.2001) 87 Cal.App.4th 299, 305-06; ***Alvarez v. Sanchez*** (1st Dist.1984) 158 Cal.App.3d 709, 712; Wegner, *Civil Trials & Evidence*, ¶8:2475. By comparison, the privilege against self-incrimination in criminal proceedings is absolute, meaning the holder does not have to make a choice between waiver and penalty. *See **Alvarez***, 158 Cal.App.3d at 712.

§2.3 Elements of privilege against self-incrimination. The elements of the privilege against self-incrimination are the following:

1. **Natural person.** The holder is a natural person. ***U.S. v. White*** (1944) 322 U.S. 694, 698; ***Craib v. Bulmash*** (1989) 49 Cal.3d 475, 486 n.13; *Jefferson's Evid. Benchbook*, §46.3; Wegner, *Civil Trials & Evidence*, ¶8:2481. The privilege can be claimed by parties and nonparty witnesses. ***Gonzales v. Superior Ct.*** (4th Dist.1980) 117 Cal.App.3d 57, 62. See "Who can assert privilege against self-incrimination," §2.5, p. 690; "Who cannot assert privilege against self-incrimination," §2.6, p. 690.

2. **Compelled evidence.** The holder is being compelled to give evidence. ***Verdin v. Superior Ct.*** (2008) 43 Cal.4th 1096, 1110; ***Izazaga v. Superior Ct.*** (1991) 54 Cal.3d 356, 366; ***Woods v. Superior Ct.*** (4th Dist.1994) 25 Cal.App.4th 178, 186; *Jefferson's Evid. Benchbook*, §46.24; Wegner, *Civil Trials & Evidence*, ¶8:2472; *e.g.*, ***U.S. v. Doe*** (1984) 465 U.S. 605, 610-11 (contents of subpoenaed business records that were voluntarily prepared were not privileged; they were not made under compulsion); ***Craib***, 49 Cal.3d at 486 & n.14 (privilege did not apply to subpoena for records required by law to be maintained and produced). A person can be compelled in many ways, such as by deposition, interrogatory, request for inspection or admissions, or subpoena for hearing or trial testimony. See "What privilege against self-incrimination protects," §2.7, p. 691.

3. **Testimonial evidence.** The compelled evidence is testimonial or communicative evidence, not physical evidence. ***Verdin***, 43 Cal.4th at 1111; *see **Izazaga***, 54 Cal.3d at 366; Wegner, *Civil Trials & Evidence*, ¶8:2472. Evidence is testimonial or communicative if it relates a factual assertion or reveals knowledge or information from a person's mind. ***Verdin***, 43 Cal.4th at 1110-11; *see, e.g.*, ***Craib***, 49 Cal.3d at 486 n.14 (fact that person did not keep records as required by law was not testimonial evidence); ***People v. Ellis*** (1966) 65 Cal.2d 529, 533 (results of voice-identification test were not testimonial or communicative evidence because speaker was not asked to communicate ideas or knowledge of facts); *see also Jefferson's Evid. Benchbook*, §46.18 (listing examples of nontestimonial evidence). For a discussion of physical evidence, see "Compelled production of physical evidence," §2.7.2, p. 691; "Compelled production of physical evidence," §2.8.3, p. 692.

4. **Personal evidence.** The compelled testimonial evidence is personal to the holder; that is, the compelled information must belong to the person asserting the privilege or be in her possession in a personal, rather than representative, capacity. *E.g.*, ***White***, 322 U.S. at 699 (individual cannot assert privilege on behalf of labor union);

see ***Craib***, 49 Cal.3d at 486 n.13 (person holding records on behalf of organization cannot assert privilege, even if compliance results in self-incrimination); *see, e.g.*, ***Izazaga***, 54 Cal.3d at 367 (statements of witnesses whom defense intended to call at trial were not personal to D; privilege was not implicated); *see also* ***Fielder v. Berkeley Props. Co.*** (1st Dist.1972) 23 Cal.App.3d 30, 45-46 (whether privilege extends to partnership depends on determination that partnership is so impersonal in scope of membership and activities that it does not represent purely private or personal interests of partners and embodies only common or group interests).

5. Incriminating evidence. The compelled testimonial evidence would be self-incriminating. Evid. C. §404; ***Verdin***, 43 Cal.4th at 1111; ***Izazaga***, 54 Cal.3d at 366. Evidence is self-incriminating when the following occur:

(1) Criminal liability. The evidence sought to be elicited from the holder could subject her to criminal liability. Wegner, *Civil Trials & Evidence*, ¶8:2488; *see* ***Blackburn v. Superior Ct.*** (4th Dist.1993) 21 Cal.App.4th 414, 426; *Jefferson's Evid. Benchbook*, §§46.16, 46.21. That is, the disclosure of the evidence could directly support a criminal prosecution against the holder or provide a link in the chain of evidence needed to support a criminal prosecution. ***Prudhomme v. Superior Ct.*** (1970) 2 Cal.3d 320, 326; ***Blackburn***, 21 Cal.App.4th at 428; ***Gonzales***, 117 Cal.App.3d at 63; *CEB Discovery Practice*, §3.127; *see* Wegner, *Civil Trials & Evidence*, ¶8:2491 (privilege applies only if there is possibility of criminal prosecution). Fear of prosecution is not enough to establish that the evidence would be incriminating; the fear must be reasonable considering (1) the holder's specific circumstances, (2) the content of the question, and (3) the setting in which the question is asked. ***Troy v. Superior Ct.*** (2d Dist.1986) 186 Cal.App.3d 1006, 1011; *see* ***Rogers v. U.S.*** (1951) 340 U.S. 367, 374-75 (privilege protects against "real danger," not "mere imaginary possibility").

(2) No limitations. The statute of limitations for criminal prosecution has not expired. ***Blackburn***, 21 Cal.App.4th at 428; *Jefferson's Evid. Benchbook*, §§46.17, 46.23; Wegner, *Civil Trials & Evidence*, ¶8:2492; *see* ***Pacers, Inc. v. Superior Ct.*** (4th Dist.1984) 162 Cal.App.3d 686, 690 (court stayed civil action until expiration of criminal statute of limitations).

(3) No double jeopardy. Double jeopardy does not bar the prosecution. *Jefferson's Evid. Benchbook*, §§46.17, 46.23; Wegner, *Civil Trials & Evidence*, ¶¶8:2493, 8:2494; *see* ***Blackburn***, 21 Cal.App.4th at 428 (privilege lost if witness has been tried and acquitted or, if convicted, has satisfied sentence); *see also* ***People v. Fonseca*** (2d Dist.1995) 36 Cal.App.4th 631, 634 (privilege applies while conviction is under appeal).

(4) No immunity. The holder has not been granted use immunity—that is, immunity against prosecutorial use of an answer or evidence derived from the answer in a later criminal proceeding against the holder. ***Daly v. Superior Ct.*** (1977) 19 Cal.3d 132, 142-43; *see Jefferson's Evid. Benchbook*, §§46.17, 46.23; Wegner, *Civil Trials & Evidence*, ¶8:2495; *see, e.g.*, ***People v. Superior Ct.*** (1974) 12 Cal.3d 421, 425 (P requested that court grant D use immunity to nullify D's self-incrimination objection to deposition questions). This immunity includes both direct and derivative use of the answer or evidence. ***Spielbauer v. County of Santa Clara*** (2009) 45 Cal.4th 704, 714-15. Statutory immunity provided in Welfare & Inst. C. §355.1(f) for a parent's testimony in a hearing to determine if the parent abused the child is not the equivalent of the immunity required to compel a person to testify. ***In re Brenda M.*** (4th Dist.2008) 160 Cal.App.4th 772, 774. See "Request use immunity," §2.10.4(2), p. 696.

§2.4 When privilege against self-incrimination can be asserted. The privilege against self-incrimination can be asserted in any formal or informal civil, criminal, administrative, judicial, investigatory, or adjudicatory proceeding. *See* ***Spielbauer v. County of Santa Clara*** (2009) 45 Cal.4th 704, 714; ***Segretti v. State Bar*** (1976) 15 Cal.3d 878, 886.

1. Civil litigation. The privilege against self-incrimination can be asserted in civil litigation. ***Alvarez v. Sanchez*** (1st Dist.1984) 158 Cal.App.3d 709, 712; *see, e.g.*, ***Daly v. Superior Ct.*** (1977) 19 Cal.3d 132, 151 (Ds could invoke privilege in response to deposition questions in wrongful-death action); ***Gonzales v. Superior Ct.*** (4th Dist.1980) 117 Cal.App.3d 57, 62-63 (D could invoke privilege to prevent discovery by district attorney seeking admission of paternity in civil suit for use in criminal action for nonsupport); ***Zonver v. Superior Ct.*** (2d Dist.1969)

270 Cal.App.2d 613, 624-25 (D could invoke privilege in response to interrogatories in divorce action). The person who asserts the privilege can refuse to answer a question but cannot refuse to appear as a witness. See "Compelled attendance," §2.8.1, p. 691.

2. Judgment-debtor proceeding. The privilege against self-incrimination can be asserted by a judgment debtor. ***In re Marriage of Sachs*** (2d Dist.2002) 95 Cal.App.4th 1144, 1150; ***Troy v. Superior Ct.*** (2d Dist.1986) 186 Cal.App.3d 1006, 1010; *see* ***Coleman v. Galvin*** (4th Dist.1947) 78 Cal.App.2d 313, 315; *see also* Pen. C. §154(a) (debtor-in-possession who improperly removed property is subject to fine or imprisonment or both).

3. Public-employee investigation. The privilege against self-incrimination can be asserted by a public employee during a noncriminal investigation of the employee's performance by the public employer. *See* ***Spielbauer***, 45 Cal.4th at 718.

4. State Bar disciplinary proceeding. The privilege against self-incrimination can be asserted by any attorney during a State Bar disciplinary proceeding. ***Black v. State Bar*** (1972) 7 Cal.3d 676, 688; *cf.* ***Segretti***, 15 Cal.3d at 886 (immunized testimony before Senate Watergate Committee was admissible before State Bar disciplinary proceeding because proceeding was not criminal).

5. Commission on Judicial Performance. The privilege against self-incrimination can be asserted during a judge's hearing before the Commission on Judicial Performance. ***McComb v. Superior Ct.*** (1st Dist.1977) 68 Cal.App.3d 89, 98. Because the hearing is not a criminal proceeding, the judge cannot assert the privilege against self-incrimination to avoid having to appear as a witness. *Id.*

6. Civil-commitment hearing. The privilege against self-incrimination can be asserted in a civil-commitment hearing. *See* ***Cramer v. Tyars*** (1979) 23 Cal.3d 131, 138 (commitment of mentally retarded person). Because the hearing is not a criminal proceeding, the holder cannot assert the privilege against self-incrimination to avoid having to appear as a witness. *Id.* at 137-38.

§2.5 Who can assert privilege against self-incrimination.

1. Holder. The person whose own testimony would implicate her in the incriminating matter is the holder of the privilege against self-incrimination and can assert it. ***Rogers v. U.S.*** (1951) 340 U.S. 367, 370-71; Wegner, *Civil Trials & Evidence*, ¶8:2480.

2. Attorney. The holder's attorney can assert the privilege against self-incrimination on the holder's behalf if (1) the attorney is authorized to assert the privilege and (2) the attorney asserts the privilege in response to a specific question directed to the holder. ***People v. Apodaca*** (4th Dist.1993) 16 Cal.App.4th 1706, 1714-15.

3. Sole proprietor – records. A holder who is the sole proprietor of a business can assert the privilege against self-incrimination to prevent disclosure of business records if the holder can show that the act of producing the records would amount to testimonial self-incrimination. *See* ***U.S. v. Doe*** (1984) 465 U.S. 605, 612; *see, e.g.*, ***Braswell v. U.S.*** (1988) 487 U.S. 99, 104 (privilege did not apply because business operated as corporation instead of sole proprietorship). See "Compelled production of physical evidence," §2.7.2, p. 691.

4. Custodian of records – testimony. The custodian of records of an organization can assert the privilege against self-incrimination to prevent her own oral testimony if it would incriminate her. ***Braswell***, 487 U.S. at 114; ***Curcio v. U.S.*** (1957) 354 U.S. 118, 123-24. However, the custodian has no privilege to refuse to produce the organization's documents, even if the testimonial nature of producing the documents would be incriminating. See "Entity's representative – records," §2.6.2, p. 691.

§2.6 Who cannot assert privilege against self-incrimination.

1. Artificial entity. An artificial entity, such as a corporation or partnership, cannot assert the privilege against self-incrimination. ***Braswell v. U.S.*** (1988) 487 U.S. 99, 104; ***Hale v. Henkel*** (1906) 201 U.S. 43, 74-75; ***Craib v. Bulmash*** (1989) 49 Cal.3d 475, 486 n.13; ***Fielder v. Berkeley Props. Co.*** (1st Dist.1972) 23 Cal.App.3d 30, 45; Wegner, *Civil Trials & Evidence*, ¶8:2481. The rule preventing artificial entities from asserting the privilege is called the "collective-entity rule." ***Braswell***, 487 U.S. at 104-05. The rule applies regardless of the entity's size. *See id.* at 108.

2. Entity's representative – records. A witness who is a representative of an organization cannot assert the privilege against self-incrimination to avoid producing the entity's records or documents. ***Braswell***, 487 U.S. at 105-06; ***Curcio v. U.S.*** (1957) 354 U.S. 118, 128; ***U.S. v. White*** (1944) 322 U.S. 694, 699. The records or documents are held in a representative rather than personal capacity, and the organization does not have a privilege against self-incrimination. See "Personal evidence," §2.3.4, p. 688.

(1) Representative of corporation. A representative of a corporation (e.g., officer, employee, custodian of corporate records) cannot assert the privilege against self-incrimination to avoid producing corporate records or documents, even if production of the materials could incriminate the representative. ***Braswell***, 487 U.S. at 100; ***Craib***, 49 Cal.3d at 486 n.13; Wegner, *Civil Trials & Evidence*, ¶8:2482.

(2) Representative of unincorporated entity. A representative (e.g., officer, member, custodian of records) of an unincorporated entity (e.g., sole proprietorship, partnership union) cannot assert the privilege against self-incrimination to avoid producing the entity's records or documents if the entity is the kind of organization that pursues activities for the organization's interests, not for each member's personal and individual interests. ***White***, 322 U.S. at 700-01.

§2.7 What privilege against self-incrimination protects.

1. Compelled testimony. The privilege against self-incrimination protects a witness from being compelled to testify if the testimony would be incriminating. *See* Evid. C. §940.

(1) Trial or hearing. The holder can assert the privilege against self-incrimination to refuse to testify during a trial or a pretrial hearing. *See* ***Alvarez v. Sanchez*** (1st Dist.1984) 158 Cal.App.3d 709, 715.

(2) Discovery. The holder can assert the privilege against self-incrimination to refuse to provide testimonial information during discovery. *See, e.g.*, ***James Talcott, Inc. v. Short*** (2d Dist.1979) 100 Cal.App.3d 504, 507-08 (interrogatories and request for admission), *disapproved on other grounds*, ***Morehart v. County of Santa Barbara*** (1994) 7 Cal.4th 725; ***A&M Records, Inc. v. Heilman*** (2d Dist.1977) 75 Cal.App.3d 554, 564 (deposition).

2. Compelled production of physical evidence. The holder can assert the privilege against self-incrimination to avoid producing records or documents only if the act of producing the materials would result in the disclosure of incriminating testimonial or communicative evidence about the holder. *See, e.g.*, ***U.S. v. Doe*** (1984) 465 U.S. 605, 612 (production of documents was protected by privilege; production would compel business owner to admit that documents existed, were in his possession, and were authentic); *cf.* ***Goldsmith v. Superior Ct.*** (3d Dist.1984) 152 Cal.App.3d 76, 78 (in criminal case, D could not be compelled to produce gun he was alleged to have used to commit crime). When the holder asserts the privilege to prevent disclosure of physical evidence, the evidence must be the holder's private property or be in her possession. ***U.S. v. White*** (1944) 322 U.S. 694, 699.

§2.8 What privilege against self-incrimination does not protect.

1. Compelled attendance. The privilege against self-incrimination cannot be invoked by the holder to avoid being called as a witness in a civil proceeding. Wegner, *Civil Trials & Evidence*, ¶8:2479; *e.g.*, ***In re Scott*** (2003) 29 Cal.4th 783, 815 (habeas corpus proceeding); ***Joshua D. v. Superior Ct.*** (4th Dist.2007) 157 Cal.App.4th 549, 555 (civil-commitment proceeding); *see* Evid. C. §911 (no one has privilege to refuse to be a witness, except as provided by statute). By comparison, a defendant in criminal case has the privilege not to be called as a witness. Evid. C. §930; ***Joshua D.***, 157 Cal.App.4th at 555.

2. Compelled testimony.

(1) Holder's testimony incriminates another. The privilege against self-incrimination cannot be invoked by the holder to refuse to testify because the holder's testimony would incriminate another person. ***Rogers v. U.S.*** (1951) 340 U.S. 367, 371; ***Hale v. Henkel*** (1906) 201 U.S. 43, 69-70; *CEB Trial Objections*, §46.3. One of the elements of the privilege against self-incrimination is that the evidence is personal to the holder. See "Personal evidence," §2.3.4, p. 688.

(2) **Another's testimony incriminates holder.** The privilege against self-incrimination cannot be invoked by the holder to prevent disclosure of testimonial or physical evidence sought from a third person. *See* ***U.S. v. White*** (1944) 322 U.S. 694, 699 (privilege does not protect evidence not in holder's possession); *see, e.g.*, ***People v. Superior Ct.*** (4th Dist.1991) 231 Cal.App.3d 584, 593 (D could not assert privilege to prevent her physicians from providing her medical records, although records may have been protected under another privilege). One of the elements of the privilege against self-incrimination is that the holder's testimony would incriminate the holder, not someone else. See "Criminal liability," §2.3.5(1), p. 689.

3. Compelled production of physical evidence.

(1) **Documents voluntarily prepared.** The privilege against self-incrimination does not protect from discovery documents that the holder voluntarily prepared (e.g., business records), even if the documents on their face incriminate the holder. *See* ***Fisher v. U.S.*** (1976) 425 U.S. 391, 409; Wegner, *Civil Trials & Evidence*, ¶8:2484. The contents of voluntarily prepared documents are not protected by the privilege against self-incrimination because their creation was not compelled. ***U.S. v. Doe*** (1984) 465 U.S. 605, 610-11; *CEB Discovery Practice*, §3.126. Even though a voluntarily prepared document is not privileged, its compelled disclosure might be privileged if the holder's act of producing it is testimonial and would be incriminating. ***Doe***, 465 U.S. at 612. See "Compelled production of physical evidence," §2.7.2, p. 691.

(2) **Required-records doctrine.** The privilege against self-incrimination does not protect records sought by a regulatory agency if the records were required by law to be maintained and the agency seeking the records is responsible for enforcing the law. Wegner, *Civil Trials & Evidence*, ¶8:2486; *see* ***Craib v. Bulmash*** (1989) 49 Cal.3d 475, 489-90. This is sometimes referred to as the required-records doctrine or exception. *See* ***Craib***, 49 Cal.3d at 489. The law requiring that the records be maintained must (1) be intended to promote a lawful regulatory scheme and not be directed at activities or persons that are inherently criminal and (2) require minimal disclosure of information of a kind customarily kept in the ordinary course of business. *See id.* at 487-88.

(3) **Evidence about holder.** The privilege against self-incrimination does not protect physical evidence derived from the holder. ***Schmerber v. California*** (1966) 384 U.S. 757, 764; *see* ***People v. Lopez*** (1963) 60 Cal.2d 223, 243-44. The following are examples of physical evidence not protected by the privilege:

(a) **Physical test results.** Physical test results are not protected by the privilege against self-incrimination. *E.g.*, ***Schmerber***, 384 U.S. at 765 (blood test); ***People v. Thomas*** (5th Dist.1986) 180 Cal.App.3d 47, 52 (hair and saliva tests); ***People v. Saldivar*** (1st Dist.1967) 249 Cal.App.2d 670, 672-73 (urine test).

(b) **Identification.** Visual, voice, and handwriting identifications are not protected by the privilege against self-incrimination. *E.g.*, ***People v. Ellis*** (1966) 65 Cal.2d 529, 533-34 (voice identification); ***Lopez***, 60 Cal.2d at 243-44 (police lineup); ***People v. Arnold*** (2d Dist.1966) 243 Cal.App.2d 510, 515-16 (handwriting samples).

§2.9 Waiver of privilege against self-incrimination. The privilege against self-incrimination does not protect the holder if the holder waives the privilege. *See, e.g.*, ***Black v. State Bar*** (1972) 7 Cal.3d 676, 688 (holder waived privilege against self-incrimination by testifying without objection).

1. Complete waiver. When a plaintiff files a suit, the plaintiff waives her right to assert the privilege to avoid disclosure of any factual issues raised in the complaint. *See, e.g.*, ***Hartbrodt v. Burke*** (2d Dist.1996) 42 Cal.App.4th 168, 174-75 (P could not invoke privilege to prevent compliance with discovery order after bringing contract and tort action); ***Fremont Indem. Co. v. Superior Ct.*** (4th Dist.1982) 137 Cal.App.3d 554, 560 (P could not invoke privilege to prevent deposition seeking information vitally relevant to insurance policy on which he sought to recover). The plaintiff's waiver of the privilege applies throughout the entire proceeding, including discovery and trial. ***Fremont Indem.***, 137 Cal.App.3d at 560.

2. Partial waiver. When the holder testifies in a proceeding (e.g., pretrial hearing, trial) and does not claim the privilege against self-incrimination, the holder waives the privilege only for her testimony in that proceeding. ***People v. Lopez*** (2d Dist.1980) 110 Cal.App.3d 1010, 1020; *see* Wegner, *Civil Trials & Evidence*, ¶8:2503. This rule is called the "single-proceeding rule." ***Lopez***, 110 Cal.App.3d at 1020.

(1) **Discovery proceeding.** If the holder testifies to incriminating facts during pretrial discovery proceedings without claiming the privilege, she waives the privilege for other discovery. *See, e.g.*, ***Brown v. Superior Ct.*** (2d Dist.1986) 180 Cal.App.3d 701, 712 (Ds waived privilege against self-incrimination by not objecting to interrogatories within 30-day period to respond). See "Waiver of discovery objection," ch. 7-A, §15.2.2, p. 776. However, the holder is still free to assert the privilege at trial, which is considered a different proceeding. ***Alvarez v. Sanchez*** (1st Dist.1984) 158 Cal.App.3d 709, 715. For example, when a holder files a verified answer and testifies to incriminating facts during a deposition, she cannot assert the privilege when responding to interrogatories, but she can assert it at trial. *See id.*

(2) **Trial.** If the holder testifies to incriminating facts at trial without claiming the privilege, she waives the privilege for all facts within the scope of relevant cross-examination. ***People v. Wilson*** (2008) 44 Cal.4th 758, 799; ***People v. Williams*** (2008) 43 Cal.4th 584, 615; ***People v. Apodaca*** (4th Dist.1993) 16 Cal.App.4th 1706, 1715; Wegner, *Civil Trials & Evidence*, ¶8:2502. However, the holder can assert the privilege during a different proceeding. ***People v. Maxwell*** (2d Dist.1979) 94 Cal.App.3d 562, 570-71. For example, testimony in a pretrial proceeding does not prevent the holder from asserting the privilege at trial, and presumably, testimony at trial does not prevent the holder from asserting the privilege in post-trial proceedings. *See* ***Williams***, 43 Cal.4th at 615; *see, e.g.*, ***Lopez***, 110 Cal.App.3d at 1020 (D1, who waived privilege at his own trial, could invoke privilege at D2's trial, a separate proceeding); ***Maxwell***, 94 Cal.App.3d at 570-71 (testimony during preliminary hearing did not waive privilege during trial); ***People v. Lawrence*** (1st Dist.1959) 168 Cal.App.2d 510, 517 (testimony during voir dire did not prevent holder from invoking privilege at trial).

PRACTICE TIP

If the holder testifies without objection during discovery but asserts the privilege against self-incrimination at trial, the party opposing the assertion of the privilege can ask the court to consider the holder "unavailable" and to permit introduction of her discovery testimony. Jefferson's Evid. Benchbook, §46.10; see Evid. C. §1230. *See "Admit earlier testimony," §2.11.1(2)(d), p. 697.*

§2.10 How to assert privilege against self-incrimination. The holder asserts the privilege against self-incrimination by making a specific objection to the information sought. ***Fuller v. Superior Ct.*** (2d Dist.2001) 87 Cal.App.4th 299, 305. See "Responding party objects to discovery," ch. 7-A, §14.1.1, p. 771.

1. **Objections & motions.** As with other privileges, the holder can (1) object while giving oral testimony, (2) object to a discovery request, (3) file a motion for protective order, or (4) file a motion to quash a deposition notice or subpoena. *See, e.g.*, ***In re Marriage of Sachs*** (2d Dist.2002) 95 Cal.App.4th 1144, 1149 (objection while testifying at deposition); ***People v. Superior Ct.*** (4th Dist.1991) 231 Cal.App.3d 584, 588 (motion to quash subpoena); ***Brown v. Superior Ct.*** (2d Dist.1986) 180 Cal.App.3d 701, 705 (objection to interrogatories); ***Fremont Indem. Co. v. Superior Ct.*** (4th Dist.1982) 137 Cal.App.3d 554, 556 (motion for protective order). See "How to Make Discovery Objections," ch. 7-A, §12, p. 768.

(1) **Form of objection.**

(a) **Specific objection.** The holder must assert the privilege in response to each question asked or request made; the holder cannot make a blanket objection on privilege grounds in response to all requested discovery. *See, e.g.*, ***In re Marriage of Sachs***, 95 Cal.App.4th at 1151 (deponent could not refuse to answer all questions at deposition and had to assert privilege on question-by-question basis); ***Fuller***, 87 Cal.App.4th at 308 (Ds could not invoke blanket privilege against self-incrimination for entire deposition). An objection to each specific question or request is necessary to assist the court in determining whether the privilege applies to each specific area that the discovering party seeks to explore. ***Fuller***, 87 Cal.App.4th at 305; *see* Wegner, *Civil Trials & Evidence*, ¶8:2506.

(b) **Blanket objection.** The holder can make a blanket objection on privilege grounds only if the court finds that any relevant questioning would tend to incriminate the holder. ***Warford v. Medeiros*** (1st Dist.1984) 160 Cal.App.3d 1035, 1044 n.7; Wegner, *Civil Trials & Evidence*, ¶8:2508.

(2) Incriminating evidence. Regardless of how the issue is brought to the court's attention (e.g., objection, motion to compel, motion to quash, or motion for protective order), the holder must show a reasonable belief that the answer would be incriminating. *See* ***Blackburn v. Superior Ct.*** (4th Dist.1993) 21 Cal.App.4th 414, 428-29. This showing is made under Evid. C. §404, not §405 as with other privileges. *CEB Trial Objections*, §§46.2, 46.20.

(a) Answers would incriminate. The holder must explain why and how the answers might be incriminating without disclosing the protected information. *See* Evid. C. §§404, 915(a); ***Blackburn***, 21 Cal.App.4th at 429; ***Warford***, 160 Cal.App.3d at 1045 & n.8; 7 Cal. Law Revision Comm'n Rep. (1965) p. 1053. The holder does not need to produce any evidence to meet this burden. ***Warford***, 160 Cal.App.3d at 1045 n.8; 7 Cal. Law Revision Comm'n Rep. (1965) p. 1053. See "Type of proof," §2.10.3(1)(c), p. 695. The holder's claim of privilege will be upheld unless it is clear under the circumstances that the answer to a question cannot possibly tend to incriminate her. *See* Evid. C. §404; ***Warford***, 160 Cal.App.3d at 1044.

(b) Reasonable belief. The holder must show the reasonableness of her belief that an answer to a question would be incriminating. *See* ***Warford***, 160 Cal.App.3d at 1044 (holder satisfies reasonability requirement by showing any real possibility of prosecution); ***Troy v. Superior Ct.*** (2d Dist.1986) 186 Cal.App.3d 1006, 1011 (holder's imagined fear is inadequate to establish reasonability requirement); Wegner, *Civil Trials & Evidence*, ¶8:2510 (same). To establish the reasonableness of this belief, the holder should address the following:

[1] The nature of the information sought. ***Blackburn***, 21 Cal.App.4th at 429; ***Warford***, 160 Cal.App.3d at 1045 n.8; Wegner, *Civil Trials & Evidence*, ¶8:2511.1.

[2] The implications derived from the question. Evid. C. §404, cmt. ¶1; ***Blackburn***, 21 Cal.App.4th at 429; ***Warford***, 160 Cal.App.3d at 1045 n.8; 7 Cal. Law Revision Comm'n Rep. (1965) p. 1053; Wegner, *Civil Trials & Evidence*, ¶8:2511.1.

[3] Matters disclosed by the attorneys in argument. Evid. C. §404, cmt. ¶1; ***Blackburn***, 21 Cal.App.4th at 429; ***Warford***, 160 Cal.App.3d at 1045 n.8; 7 Cal. Law Revision Comm'n Rep. (1965) p. 1053; Wegner, *Civil Trials & Evidence*, ¶8:2511.1.

[4] The nature and verifiability of any investigation or proceeding claimed to justify the fear of incrimination, or the possibility that any such investigation or proceeding might be commenced. ***Blackburn***, 21 Cal.App.4th at 429; ***Warford***, 160 Cal.App.3d at 1045 n.8; Wegner, *Civil Trials & Evidence*, ¶8:2511.1.

[5] Evidence previously admitted. ***Blackburn***, 21 Cal.App.4th at 429; ***Warford***, 160 Cal.App.3d at 1045 n.8; Wegner, *Civil Trials & Evidence*, ¶8:2511.1.

2. Responding to assertion of privilege.

(1) Dispute privilege. The discovering party can show that the holder did not prove the elements of the privilege. See "Elements of privilege against self-incrimination," §2.3, p. 688.

(2) Waiver. The discovering party can show that the holder waived the privilege. See "Waiver of privilege against self-incrimination," §2.9, p. 692.

3. Court ruling. The court must decide whether the holder can invoke the privilege. ***In re Marriage of Sachs***, 95 Cal.App.4th at 1151; ***Fisher v. Gibson*** (2d Dist.2001) 90 Cal.App.4th 275, 285; ***Warford***, 160 Cal.App.3d at 1045; Wegner, *Civil Trials & Evidence*, ¶8:2511.

(1) Hearing.

(a) Type of hearing. The court has the discretion to hold a hearing in chambers or in open court. ***Warford***, 160 Cal.App.3d at 1048; *Jefferson's Evid. Benchbook*, §46.35; *see* Wegner, *Civil Trials & Evidence*, ¶8:2513.

(b) Factors. When it is not evident from the circumstances that the questions call for incriminating information, the court must require the holder to explain why and how the answers might be incriminating. ***Blackburn***, 21 Cal.App.4th at 429; *see* Evid. C. §404; ***Warford***, 160 Cal.App.3d at 1045 & n.8; 7 Cal. Law Revision Comm'n Rep. (1965) p. 1053. For the list of factors the court must consider, see "Reasonable belief," §2.10.1(2)(b), this page.

(c) Type of proof. The holder does not need to introduce admissible evidence or to disclose the incriminating evidence itself to prove the privilege. Wegner, *Civil Trials & Evidence*, ¶8:2512; *see* Evid. C. §915(a); 7 Cal. Law Revision Comm'n Rep. (1965) p. 1053; *CEB Trial Objections*, §46.20; *Jefferson's Evid. Benchbook*, §46.32. The holder must only present information showing the danger of incrimination. 7 Cal. Law Revision Comm'n Rep. (1965) p. 1053; *see* ***Blackburn***, 21 Cal.App.4th at 428-29 (holder cannot be required to identify the precise hazard of disclosure because that would compel her to surrender the very protection the privilege is designed to guarantee).

(2) Findings. The court must make findings on the record for each claim of privilege. Wegner, *Civil Trials & Evidence*, ¶8:2514; *see* ***Warford***, 160 Cal.App.3d at 1048. The issue for each claim is whether there is any "real danger" that the answer will incriminate the holder. ***Troy***, 186 Cal.App.3d at 1011; ***Coleman v. Galvin*** (4th Dist.1947) 78 Cal.App.2d 313, 321. The court must examine each question separately and determine if its answer might incriminate the holder. ***Warford***, 160 Cal.App.3d at 1045; ***Coleman***, 78 Cal.App.2d at 322.

(a) Incriminating. If the answer to a question might tend to incriminate the person claiming the privilege, the court must sustain the privilege objection and cannot compel the holder to answer. *See* Evid. C. §404; ***In re Marriage of Sachs***, 95 Cal.App.4th at 1150-51. If the holder refuses to provide the privileged information, the court can force the holder to choose between asserting the privilege and facing civil penalties. See "Civil penalties for invoking privilege," §2.11, p. 696.

(b) Not incriminating. If it is clearly apparent to the court that the answer to a question cannot possibly tend to incriminate the person claiming the privilege, the court must overrule the privilege objection and order the holder to answer. ***People v. Cudjo*** (1993) 6 Cal.4th 585, 617; ***In re Marriage of Sachs***, 95 Cal.App.4th at 1151; 7 Cal. Law Revision Comm'n Rep. (1965) p. 1053; *CEB Trial Objections*, §46.20. If the holder refuses to provide the information, even though the court found that it was not privileged, the court can sanction the holder for violating a discovery order. See "Discovery Sanctions," ch. 9-A, p. 1003.

4. Overcoming privilege. If the court sustains the privilege objection, the discovering party can overcome the ruling by requesting the following remedies to compel testimony:

(1) Request temporary stay of civil action. To overcome the privilege, the discovering party can request that the court stay discovery in the civil action until the holder is no longer subject to criminal prosecution. See "Incriminating evidence," §2.3.5, p. 689.

(a) Grounds. The court can stay discovery in a civil action if a criminal proceeding involving the same or related transaction as in the civil action has been or could be brought. *See, e.g.*, ***Pacers, Inc. v. Superior Ct.*** (4th Dist.1984) 162 Cal.App.3d 686, 690 (proceeding stayed until statute of limitations ran); *see also CEB Discovery Practice*, §3.128 (stay of proceedings); Wegner, *Civil Trials & Evidence*, ¶8:2477.2 (same). The court is not likely to grant a stay if the criminal proceeding will not be concluded within a reasonable time. *See CEB Discovery Practice*, §3.128; *see, e.g.*, ***Bains v. Moores*** (4th Dist.2009) 172 Cal.App.4th 445, 481 (court denied P's motion for stay because date of completion of parallel criminal proceedings was speculative); ***Fuller***, 87 Cal.App.4th at 309 (court refused to stay civil action because criminal statute of limitations did not expire for another three years). To obtain a stay, the discovering party should address the following:

[1] The opposing party's interest in proceeding with the litigation without delay, including any prejudice to the opposing party if the civil action is delayed. ***Bains***, 172 Cal.App.4th at 483.

[2] The burden imposed by the civil action on the party seeking the stay. *Id.*

[3] The court's interest in management of its cases and sufficient use of judicial resources. *Id.*

[4] Any nonparty's interest in the civil action. *Id.*

[5] The public's interest in the civil and criminal litigation. *Id.*

(b) Five-year limit. To obtain a stay, the defendant may have to agree to waive the five-year time limit for a plaintiff to bring a civil action to trial. *See* CCP §§583.310, 583.330; ***Pacers, Inc.***, 162 Cal.App.3d at

690; *see, e.g.*, ***Dwyer v. Crocker Nat'l Bank*** (2d Dist.1987) 194 Cal.App.3d 1418, 1432-33 (court refused to temporarily stay civil action because five-year period for bringing D's cross-action to trial would have expired). See "No trial after action commenced," ch. 10-E, §4.3, p. 1165.

(2) Request use immunity. To overcome the privilege, the discovering party can file a motion for protective order to obtain an immunity order that limits the use of the information the discovering party seeks. *See* ***Daly v. Superior Ct.*** (1977) 19 Cal.3d 132, 147; *see, e.g.*, ***People v. Superior Ct.*** (1974) 12 Cal.3d 421, 425 (when D asserted privilege against self-incrimination, party seeking information filed motion for protective order limiting use of information sought). See "Motion for Protective Order," ch. 9-B, p. 1024. The discovering party can request two types of immunity: "use" or "derivative use." Use immunity prevents a prosecutor from using a person's answer given in a civil action against the person in a later criminal proceeding; derivative-use immunity prevents the prosecutor from using any evidence derived from the answer. *See* ***Daly***, 19 Cal.3d at 142-43. The court can grant either use or derivative-use immunity for testimony in a civil action, but only if the discovering party gives the prosecutor notice and an opportunity to object. *See id.* at 148.

(a) Notice. The discovering party must give the prosecutor in the criminal proceeding adequate notice and the opportunity to object to the requested immunity in the civil proceeding. *See* ***Daly***, 19 Cal.3d at 148. Notice is adequate if it gives the prosecutor reasonable time to prepare and submit an objection and to make any necessary investigation into possible criminal prosecution. *Id.* at 148 n.11. The notice must state the subject matter of the inquiries to which the holder's answers are to be immunized from use or derivative use. *Id.* at 148. This statement must be in a form that, when incorporated into an immunity order, will give the holder a clear guide as to what questions are within the immunity grant. *Id.*

(b) Motion. The discovering party can obtain a protective order if it shows that granting immunity will not unduly hamper any later criminal prosecutions. ***Daly***, 19 Cal.3d at 147.

[1] Prosecutor objects. If the prosecutor objects to the motion for protective order, the grant of immunity (as described in the notice) is deemed to unduly hamper the criminal prosecution of the holder, and the court is prohibited from granting the motion. ***Daly***, 19 Cal.3d at 148. To properly object, the prosecutor must file a written objection supported by a declaration stating that she (1) is familiar with the notice and (2) has reasonable grounds to believe the proposed grant of immunity might unduly hamper the prosecution of a criminal proceeding. *Id.* The prosecutor does not need to justify the declaration or assess the nature or degree of the impact the immunity grant would have on prosecutorial functions. *Id.* If the declaration is not attached, the court can disregard the objection. *Id.* If the discovering party believes the objection is unjustified, it should try to persuade the prosecutor to withdraw the objection, or it can reframe the scope of the proposed immunity order or postpone the examination of the witness. *Id.* at 149.

[2] Prosecutor does not object. If the prosecutor does not object to the motion for protective order, the grant of immunity is deemed not to unduly hamper the criminal prosecution of the holder, and the court can grant the motion. *See* ***Daly***, 19 Cal.3d at 148.

§2.11 Civil penalties for invoking privilege. The court can require the holder in a civil case who invokes the privilege against self-incrimination to either waive the privilege or accept the civil consequences of exercising the privilege. ***In re Marriage of Sachs*** (2d Dist.2002) 95 Cal.App.4th 1144, 1155; ***Alvarez v. Sanchez*** (1st Dist.1984) 158 Cal.App.3d 709, 712; *see Jefferson's Evid. Benchbook*, §46.45.

1. Permissible penalties. When the court upholds the privilege against self-incrimination in a civil suit and the party refuses to testify, the court can impose the following penalties:

(1) Case-terminating penalties. Case-terminating penalties are extremely harsh and should be imposed only after considering the relevant public and private interests at stake. ***Alvarez***, 158 Cal.App.3d at 712.

(a) Plaintiff invoked privilege. The penalty for a plaintiff who refuses to testify about factual issues in the suit based on the plaintiff's privilege against self-incrimination is generally dismissal of the case. *See* ***Alvarez***, 158 Cal.App.3d at 712; ***Fremont Indem. Co. v. Superior Ct.*** (4th Dist.1982) 137 Cal.App.3d 554, 560; *CEB*

Discovery Practice, §3.124; Wegner, *Civil Trials & Evidence*, ¶8:2476. Dismissal is required because the plaintiff, by filing the suit, waived the right to assert the privilege to prevent disclosure of facts about issues raised in the complaint. *See* ***Fremont Indem.***, 137 Cal.App.3d at 560. See "Complete waiver," §2.9.1, p. 692.

(b) Defendant invoked privilege. The penalty for a defendant who refuses to testify based on the privilege against self-incrimination can be a default judgment, but that penalty is considered too harsh in most cases. *See, e.g.*, ***Alvarez***, 158 Cal.App.3d at 713 (striking D's answer and proceeding with default was too harsh a penalty). Courts are reluctant to impose a case-terminating penalty on a defendant who invokes the privilege because the defendant, unlike the plaintiff, is not a voluntary participant in the suit. *Id.* at 712-13.

(2) Evidentiary penalties. The court can impose evidentiary penalties against a party or witness who invokes the privilege against self-incrimination. Evidentiary penalties prevent a party or witness from claiming the privilege during discovery and then waiving the privilege and testifying at trial. *See* ***A&M Records, Inc. v. Heilman*** (2d Dist.1977) 75 Cal.App.3d 554, 566. Some examples of evidentiary penalties include the following:

(a) Prevent trial testimony. The court can prevent a party or witness from testifying at trial about any matters on which the party or witness claimed the privilege against self-incrimination. *E.g.*, ***Dwyer v. Crocker Nat'l Bank*** (2d Dist.1987) 194 Cal.App.3d 1418, 1432-33 (court prevented P from introducing evidence at trial about matter he claimed privilege on during discovery); ***A&M Records***, 75 Cal.App.3d at 566 (same, but for D).

(b) Prevent introducing documents at trial. The court can prevent a party from introducing documents at a trial in which a claim of privilege has been asserted. ***A&M Records***, 75 Cal.App.3d at 565.

(c) Exclude or strike earlier testimony. The court can exclude or strike a party's or witness's earlier testimony. *See, e.g.*, ***People v. Apodaca*** (4th Dist.1993) 16 Cal.App.4th 1706, 1713-14 (court struck all of witness's testimony after witness invoked privilege against self-incrimination).

(d) Admit earlier testimony. The court can permit a party to introduce a holder's discovery testimony during trial if the holder testified during discovery without objection but refused to testify at trial and asserted the privilege, making the holder "unavailable" for the trial under the Evidence Code. *Jefferson's Evid. Benchbook*, §46.10; *see, e.g.*, ***People v. Cudjo*** (1993) 6 Cal.4th 585, 617-18 (witness's testimony at preliminary hearing was admitted at trial); ***People v. Lopez*** (2d Dist.1980) 110 Cal.App.3d 1010, 1020-21 (D1 was unavailable and his statements to girlfriend were admissible because D1 was entitled to invoke privilege at D2's trial); *see also* Evid. C. §240(a)(1) (unavailable witness), §§1291-1292 (former testimony); CCP §2025.620 (deposition testimony).

2. Prohibited penalties. When a party or witness asserts the privilege against self-incrimination in a civil suit, the following penalties are prohibited:

(1) Any comment by the court or the attorneys on the holder's exercise of the privilege. Evid. C. §913(a).

(2) Any presumption based on the holder's exercise of the privilege. *Id.*

(3) Any inference as to the holder's credibility or any other matter at issue based on the holder's exercise of the privilege. *Id.*; *see* ***People v. Holloway*** (2004) 33 Cal.4th 96, 131; *Jefferson's Evid. Benchbook*, §46.37. A party who might be adversely affected by an unfavorable inference by the jury can ask the court to instruct the jury that the exercise of the privilege does not give rise to any adverse presumption or inference. Evid. C. §913(b).

§3. TAX-RETURN PRIVILEGE

§3.1 General. The tax-return privilege protects numerous state and federal income-tax returns from forced disclosure. ***Schnabel v. Superior Ct.*** (1993) 5 Cal.4th 704, 719-20; ***Sav-On Drugs, Inc. v. Superior Ct.*** (1975) 15 Cal.3d 1, 6-7; ***Webb v. Standard Oil Co.*** (1957) 49 Cal.2d 509, 513-14. The privilege, sometimes known as the ***Webb*** rule, was originally implied from Rev. & Tax. C. §19282 (now §19542), which provides that it is a misdemeanor for a public official to disclose a taxpayer's income or other tax information. *See* ***Webb***, 49 Cal.2d at 512. The ***Webb*** court

reasoned that if a taxpayer could be forced to produce its state or federal income-tax returns in litigation, the production would effectively defeat the legislative purpose of §19282. ***Webb***, 49 Cal.2d at 513; ***King v. Mobile Home Rent Rev. Bd.*** (2d Dist.1989) 216 Cal.App.3d 1532, 1537. The ***Webb*** rule has since been extended to other statutes similar to §19542 that limit disclosure of tax-related information. *See, e.g.*, ***Sav-On Drugs***, 15 Cal.3d at 6-7 (applying ***Webb*** rule to Rev. & Tax. C. §7056 to protect sales-and-use-tax records); ***Crest Catering Co. v. Superior Ct.*** (1965) 62 Cal.2d 274, 276-77 (applying ***Webb*** rule to Unemp. Ins. C. §1094 to protect payroll-tax returns).

1. Purpose. The purpose of the tax-return privilege is to encourage voluntary filing of tax returns and truthful reporting of income, which facilitates tax collection. ***Webb***, 49 Cal.2d at 513; Wegner, *California Practice Guide: Civil Trials & Evidence* (CD-ROM ed. 2014) ¶8:2576.

2. Primary authority. ***Schnabel***, 5 Cal.4th at 720-21; ***Sav-On Drugs***, 15 Cal.3d at 7; ***Crest Catering***, 62 Cal.2d at 276-77; ***Webb***, 49 Cal.2d at 514; *see also* Rev. & Tax. C. §7056(a)(1) (sales-and-use-tax returns), §19542 (personal and business tax returns); Unemp. Ins. C. §1094(a) (payroll-tax returns).

3. Secondary authority. The following secondary sources are cited as authority in this section:

- *California Civil Discovery Practice* (CEB Online ed. 2014) (referred to as *CEB Discovery Practice*).
- Wegner, *California Practice Guide: Civil Trials & Evidence* (CD-ROM ed. 2014) (referred to as Wegner, *Civil Trials & Evidence*).

§3.2 Nature of tax-return privilege. The tax-return privilege is qualified. ***Schnabel v. Superior Ct.*** (1993) 5 Cal.4th 704, 721; *see CEB Discovery Practice*, §3.117; Wegner, *Civil Trials & Evidence*, ¶8:2584. The tax-return privilege is subject to a balancing test between the need for confidentiality and the need for discovery. See "Public-policy exception," §3.7.1, p. 699.

§3.3 Elements of tax-return privilege. To establish the tax-return privilege, a person must show that it is a taxpayer and that the information sought is a tax record. *See* ***Webb v. Standard Oil Co.*** (1957) 49 Cal.2d 509, 513.

1. Person is taxpayer. A person includes any natural person or organization that is a taxpayer. *See, e.g.*, ***Schnabel v. Superior Ct.*** (1993) 5 Cal.4th 704, 723 (***Webb*** rule protected payroll-tax returns of third parties); ***Webb***, 49 Cal.2d at 513 (personal tax returns protected); ***Rifkind v. Superior Ct.*** (2d Dist.1981) 123 Cal.App.3d 1045, 1048-49 (***Webb*** rule protected corporation's and partnership's federal and state tax returns), *disapproved on other grounds*, ***Schnabel v. Superior Ct.*** (1993) 5 Cal.4th 704.

2. Tax records. The information must be a tax return or a document related to a tax return. *See* Wegner, *Civil Trials & Evidence*, ¶¶8:2579-8:2581. See "What tax-return privilege protects," §3.5, this page.

§3.4 Who can assert tax-return privilege. The taxpayer is the holder of the privilege and has the right to refuse to disclose its tax returns. *See* Wegner, *Civil Trials & Evidence*, ¶8:2590.

§3.5 What tax-return privilege protects. The tax-return privilege protects the following information:

1. Federal and state income-tax returns. ***Webb v. Standard Oil Co.*** (1957) 49 Cal.2d 509, 513-14; *CEB Discovery Practice*, §3.116.

NOTE

Federal law does not recognize a privilege for tax returns. CEB Discovery Practice, §3.118; Wegner, Civil Trials & Evidence, ¶8:2577; see ***Stokwitz v. U.S.*** *(9th Cir.1987) 831 F.2d 893, 896.*

2. Corporate tax returns. ***Schnabel v. Superior Ct.*** (1993) 5 Cal.4th 704, 720-21.
3. Payroll-tax returns. *Id.* at 721; ***Crest Catering Co. v. Superior Ct.*** (1965) 62 Cal.2d 274, 278.
4. Sales-tax returns. ***Sav-On Drugs, Inc. v. Superior Ct.*** (1975) 15 Cal.3d 1, 3.
5. Estate-tax returns. ***Deary v. Superior Ct.*** (3d Dist.2001) 87 Cal.App.4th 1072, 1074.

6. Content of tax returns (e.g., income, deductions). ***Sav-On Drugs***, 15 Cal.3d at 7; Wegner, *Civil Trials & Evidence*, ¶8:2580.

7. Related tax documents that are an integral part of a tax return (e.g., a W-2 form). ***Brown v. Superior Ct.*** (1st Dist.1977) 71 Cal.App.3d 141, 143-44; Wegner, *Civil Trials & Evidence*, ¶8:2581. Related tax documents may include an accountant's work papers used in preparing a tax return. Wegner, *Civil Trials & Evidence*, ¶8:2583.

§3.6 What tax-return privilege does not protect.

1. Underlying records. The tax-return privilege does not protect any underlying data or records the tax return was based on (e.g., checkbooks, ledgers). Wegner, *Civil Trials & Evidence*, ¶8:2582.

2. Foreign tax returns. Foreign tax returns are not privileged. *CEB Discovery Practice*, §3.116; *e.g.*, ***Firestone v. Hoffman*** (2d Dist.2006) 140 Cal.App.4th 1408, 1419-20 (Canadian tax return).

§3.7 When tax-return privilege does not apply. The tax-return privilege does not apply in the following circumstances:

1. Public-policy exception. The tax-return privilege does not apply when a public policy greater than the confidentiality of tax returns is involved. ***Schnabel v. Superior Ct.*** (1993) 5 Cal.4th 704, 721; ***Miller v. Superior Ct.*** (1st Dist.1977) 71 Cal.App.3d 145, 149; *CEB Discovery Practice*, §3.117; Wegner, *Civil Trials & Evidence*, ¶8:2585. To establish the public-policy exception, the party seeking the tax records must show that a compelling, legislatively declared public policy warrants disclosure of the records. ***Schnabel***, 5 Cal.4th at 721; ***Fortunato v. Superior Ct.*** (2d Dist.2003) 114 Cal.App.4th 475, 483; Wegner, *Civil Trials & Evidence*, ¶8:2585.

(1) Exception applies. The public-policy exception has been applied in the following cases: • A child-support-enforcement proceeding. ***Miller***, 71 Cal.App.3d at 149; *see* Fam. C. §3552(a) (requiring submission of state and federal income-tax returns to court in proceedings involving child, family, or spousal support), §20020 (requiring production of federal and state income-tax returns in contested proceedings for temporary child or spousal support). • Marital-dissolution proceeding in which one spouse seeks corporate and payroll-tax records to determine value of corporation and parties' financial status, when other spouse is but one of two shareholders and marital community owns 30% of stock. ***Schnabel***, 5 Cal.4th at 722-23.

(2) Exception does not apply. The public-policy exception has not been applied in the following cases: • Marital-dissolution case in which one spouse seeks tax records of law corporation and partnership of which other spouse is a member. ***Rifkind v. Superior Ct.*** (2d Dist.1981) 123 Cal.App.3d 1045, 1048-49, *disapproved on other grounds*, ***Schnabel v. Superior Ct.*** (1993) 5 Cal.4th 704. • Spousal-support modification proceeding in which one former spouse seeks tax records of other former spouse. ***Sammut v. Sammut*** (1st Dist.1980) 103 Cal.App.3d 557, 562. • Child-support proceeding in which one former spouse seeks tax records of other former spouse's new spouse. ***In re Marriage of Brown*** (3d Dist.1979) 99 Cal.App.3d 702, 709. • Will contest in which decedent's daughter sought information from bank about a home loan, which included personal tax records of decedent's brother. ***Fortunato***, 114 Cal.App.4th at 483.

2. Punitive damages. The tax-return privilege does not apply to prevent compelled disclosure of tax returns sought to establish a defendant's financial worth for purposes of assessing punitive damages when the plaintiff shows all the following:

(1) The defendant has been found liable for punitive damages. ***Weingarten v. Superior Ct.*** (4th Dist.2002) 102 Cal.App.4th 268, 276.

(2) The defendant has refused to produce relevant, nonprivileged financial records or has produced only meaningless and unreliable financial information in response to punitive-damages discovery. *Id.* at 276-77.

(3) The defendant has engaged in a pattern of improperly obstructing efforts to obtain financial records through means that do not implicate the privilege, and it is reasonable to assume this pattern of conduct will continue. *Id.* at 277.

(4) Less intrusive methods to obtain the financial records have been unsuccessful. *Id.*

§3.8 Waiver of tax-return privilege. There is no tax-return privilege if the taxpayer waives it. To waive the privilege, the taxpayer must have relinquished the tax returns voluntarily. *See* ***Fortunato v. Superior Ct.*** (2d Dist.2003) 114 Cal.App.4th 475, 481-82 (tax return submitted to bank with loan application is not voluntary relinquishment and does not waive privilege); ***Thomas B. v. Superior Ct.*** (4th Dist.1985) 175 Cal.App.3d 255, 263 (tax return submitted to court as required by law is not voluntary relinquishment and does not waive privilege); Wegner, *Civil Trials & Evidence*, ¶8:2597 (same), ¶8:2598 (disclosure of tax returns to bank is not entirely voluntary). Waiver of the tax-return privilege can be either intentional or implied.

1. Intentional. The tax-return privilege is waived if the party intentionally relinquishes the privilege. ***Schnabel v. Superior Ct.***, (1993) 5 Cal.4th 704, 721; ***Crest Catering Co. v. Superior Ct.*** (1965) 62 Cal.2d 274, 278; *CEB Discovery Practice*, §3.117; *see* Wegner, *Civil Trials & Evidence*, ¶8:2591.

2. Implied. The tax-return privilege is waived if the essence of the suit is so inconsistent with the continued assertion of the taxpayer's privilege that the court can only conclude the privilege was waived. ***Schnabel***, 5 Cal.4th at 721; *CEB Discovery Practice*, §3.117; Wegner, *Civil Trials & Evidence*, ¶8:2594; *see, e.g.*, ***Wilson v. Superior Ct.*** (3d Dist.1976) 63 Cal.App.3d 825, 830 (no privilege in suit against accountant for negligently advising taxpayer).

§3.9 How to assert tax-return privilege. See "Resolving Discovery Disputes," ch. 7-A, §14, p. 771.

§4. CLERGY-PENITENT PRIVILEGE

§4.1 General. The clergy-penitent privilege (also referred to as the "priest-penitent" or "clergy-communicant" privilege) allows a person to refuse to disclose, and to prevent another from disclosing, a confidential communication made by the person (penitent) to a clergy member in her professional capacity as a spiritual adviser. *See* Evid. C. §§1032-1034; *cf.* ***In re Grand Jury Investigation*** (3d Cir.1990) 918 F.2d 374, 377 n.2, 384 (recognizing clergy-communicant privilege under federal law). The clergy-penitent privilege is actually two separate privileges covering the same communication. *See* Evid. C. §1033 (penitent's privilege), §1034 (clergy's privilege); *California Trial Objections* (CEB Online ed. 2014) §50.1 (penitent's privilege is distinct from clergy's privilege); Jefferson, *California Evidence Benchbook* (CEB Online ed. 2014) §41.2 (penitent's privilege), §41.3 (clergy's privilege). Communications between communicants and clergy members are presumed to be privileged. Evid. C. §917(a).

1. Purpose. The purpose of the clergy-penitent privilege is to protect the traditional confidentiality of communications with clergy members. *See* Evid. C. §1032. The clergy-penitent privilege recognizes the human need to disclose to a spiritual counselor, in total and absolute confidence, what are believed to be flawed acts or thoughts and to receive consolation and guidance in return. ***Trammel v. U.S.*** (1980) 445 U.S. 40, 51; ***Roman Catholic Archbishop v. Superior Ct.*** (2d Dist.2005) 131 Cal.App.4th 417, 443.

2. Primary authority. Evid. C. §§1030-1034.

3. Secondary authority. The following secondary sources are cited as authority in this section:

- *California Trial Objections* (CEB Online ed. 2014) (referred to as *CEB Trial Objections*).
- Jefferson, *California Evidence Benchbook* (CEB Online ed. 2014) (referred to as *Jefferson's Evid. Benchbook*).
- Wegner, *California Practice Guide: Civil Trials & Evidence* (CD-ROM ed. 2014) (referred to as Wegner, *Civil Trials & Evidence*).
- Witkin, *California Evidence* (5th ed. 2012 & Supp.2014) (referred to as Witkin, *Cal. Evidence*).

§4.2 Nature of clergy-penitent privilege.

1. Absolute. The clergy-penitent privilege is absolute. *See* ***In re Lifschutz*** (1970) 2 Cal.3d 415, 427. The court cannot balance the interest of confidentiality against the need for disclosure. *See id.*

2. Discovery & evidentiary.

(1) Penitent – both. For the penitent, the clergy-penitent privilege is both a discovery privilege and an evidentiary privilege because the protected information is not subject to discovery and the penitent can prevent the clergy member from disclosing it. *See* Evid. C. §1033 (penitent has privilege to refuse to disclose and to prevent another from disclosing).

(2) Clergy – discovery. For the clergy member, the clergy-penitent privilege is a discovery privilege only; the clergy member cannot prevent the penitent from disclosing the information. *See* Evid. C. §1034 (clergy has privilege to refuse to disclose).

3. Duration.

(1) Penitent. The penitent's privilege terminates on the penitent's death. *CEB Trial Objections*, §50.7. The penitent's death does not prevent the clergy member from claiming the privilege. *Id.* §§50.7, 51.7.

(2) Clergy. The clergy member's privilege terminates on the clergy member's death. *CEB Trial Objections*, §51.7. The clergy member's death does not prevent the penitent from claiming the privilege. *Id.* §§50.7, 51.7.

§4.3 Elements of clergy-penitent privilege. To establish the clergy-penitent privilege, a person must show that she made a penitential communication to a member of the clergy. *See* Evid. C. §1031.

1. Penitent. A penitent is a natural person. *See* Evid. C. §§175, 1031. In most cases, the term "penitent" includes anyone, regardless of whether the person is a member of any particular church or of the faith of the clergy member to whom the person makes the communication. ***Doe 2 v. Superior Ct.*** (2d Dist.2005) 132 Cal.App.4th 1504, 1517; *CEB Trial Objections*, §50.3; Wegner, *Civil Trials & Evidence*, ¶8:2239.1. If a church restricts the authority of its clergy to receive penitential communications to church members only, "penitent" may be limited to a member of the church. ***Doe 2***, 132 Cal.App.4th at 1517 n.13; *Jefferson's Evid. Benchbook*, §41.5.

2. Penitential communication. The communication must be a "penitential" communication. Evid. C. §1031; Wegner, *Civil Trials & Evidence*, ¶8:2236; *see* Evid. C. §§1032-1034; *CEB Trial Objections*, §50.4. A penitential communication is one that is made to the clergy member in confidence and in private. See "What clergy-penitent privilege protects," §4.6, p. 702.

NOTE

There is no requirement that the penitential communication be a confession (i.e., a revelation to a clergy member of a flawed act) to receive religious consolation and guidance in return. ***Doe 2****, 132 Cal.App.4th at 1518; see Jefferson's Evid. Benchbook, §41.6; Wegner, Civil Trials & Evidence, ¶8:2243.1. Before the 1967 revisions of the Evidence Code, the clergy-penitent privilege applied only to confessions.* ***Doe 2****, 132 Cal.App.4th at 1518; Wegner, Civil Trials & Evidence, ¶8:2243.1; see 7 Cal. Law Revision Comm'n Rep. (1965) p. 1196.*

(1) Confidential. The penitent must have intended for the communication to be confidential. ***People v. Edwards*** (1st Dist.1988) 203 Cal.App.3d 1358, 1362-63; *CEB Trial Objections*, §50.5; *Jefferson's Evid. Benchbook*, §41.1; *see* Evid. C. §1032. If the penitent knew the information would be shared with another person, there is no privilege. ***Roman Catholic Archbishop v. Superior Ct.*** (2d Dist.2005) 131 Cal.App.4th 417, 444-45.

(2) Private. The communication must have been made privately, not in the presence of any third person, as far as the penitent was aware. Evid. C. §1032. If the penitent knew the communication was made in the presence of another person, there is no privilege. ***Doe 2***, 132 Cal.App.4th at 1518; *see, e.g.*, ***U.S. v. Webb*** (9th Cir.1980) 615 F.2d 828, 828 (confession to clergy member in presence of security officer was not confidential).

3. Clergy member. A member of the clergy includes a priest, minister, religious practitioner, or similar functionary of a church, religious denomination, or religious organization. Evid. C. §1030; *CEB Trial Objections*, §51.2; *Jefferson's Evid. Benchbook*, §41.1. The penitential communication must have been made to a clergy member who (1) was authorized or accustomed to hear the type of communication and (2) had a duty to keep the type of communication secret. Evid. C. §1032.

(1) **Authorized or accustomed.** Whether the clergy member is authorized or accustomed to hear a communication depends on the discipline or practice of the clergy member's church, denomination, or organization. Evid. C. §1032; ***Doe 2***, 132 Cal.App.4th at 1516; ***Roman Catholic Archbishop***, 131 Cal.App.4th at 443-44; *see, e.g.*, ***People v. Thompson*** (4th Dist.1982) 133 Cal.App.3d 419, 426-27 (D's statements to company counselor, who was hired to help increase sales, were not privileged, in part because there was no evidence that counselor was authorized to take confidential statements); ***People v. Johnson*** (2d Dist.1969) 270 Cal.App.2d 204, 207-08 (D's statements to clergy member were not privileged because there was no evidence that clergy member was authorized or accustomed by his religion to hear penitential communications).

(2) **Duty to keep secret.** Whether the clergy member has a duty to keep the communication secret depends on the discipline or tenets of the clergy member's church, denomination, or organization. Evid. C. §1032; ***Doe 2***, 132 Cal.App.4th at 1516; ***Roman Catholic Archbishop***, 131 Cal.App.4th at 443-44; *see, e.g.*, ***Edwards***, 203 Cal.App.3d at 1363 (church's discipline did not require clergy member to keep secular confidence secret).

§4.4 Communicants to clergy-penitent privilege. The clergy-penitent privilege protects communications made by a penitent to a clergy member. *See* Evid. C. §§1033, 1034.

1. **Penitent.** A penitent is a person who makes a penitential communication to a clergy member. Evid. C. §1031. See "Penitent," §4.3.1, p. 701; "Penitential communication," §4.3.2, p. 701.

2. **Clergy member.** A clergy member is a priest, minister, religious practitioner, or similar functionary of a church, religious denomination, or religious organization. Evid. C. §1030. See "Clergy member," §4.3.3, p. 701.

§4.5 Who can assert clergy-penitent privilege. The clergy-penitent privilege can be asserted by the penitent or the clergy member, each of whom has a separate privilege to refuse to disclose the same communication. *See* Evid. C. §§1033, 1034; *Jefferson's Evid. Benchbook*, §§41.2, 41.3.

1. **Penitent.** The penitent is the holder of the privilege and has the right to refuse to disclose the communication and the right to prevent others from disclosing it. Evid. C. §1033; ***People v. Thompson*** (4th Dist.1982) 133 Cal.App.3d 419, 425; *CEB Trial Objections*, §50.6; *Jefferson's Evid. Benchbook*, §41.2. Thus, the penitent can refuse to disclose the communication and can also prevent the clergy member or an eavesdropper from disclosing it. *Jefferson's Evid. Benchbook*, §41.2; *cf.* ***San Diego Trolley, Inc. v. Superior Ct.*** (4th Dist.2001) 87 Cal.App.4th 1083, 1090-91 (psychotherapist-patient privilege).

2. **Clergy member.** The clergy member is the holder of the privilege and has the right to refuse to disclose the communication but not the right to prevent another from disclosing it. *CEB Trial Objections*, §51.6; *see* Evid. C. §1034; *Jefferson's Evid. Benchbook*, §41.3. The clergy member is under no duty to claim the privilege on the penitent's behalf. 2 Witkin, *Cal. Evidence*, Witnesses, §244.

§4.6 What clergy-penitent privilege protects. The Evidence Code does not restrict the possible subject of a privileged penitential communication. *CEB Trial Objections*, §§50.4, 51.4. As long as the communication relates to a matter that the clergy member is authorized or accustomed to hear and required to keep secret under the rules of the clergy member's religious organization, it is privileged. *Id.* §§50.4, 51.4. Because there are few examples in published opinions of rulings of California courts upholding the privilege, the following examples are provided from other jurisdictions.

1. **Communication by inmate.** The clergy-penitent privilege protects a penitential communication between a prisoner and a clergy member, even if the two are separated by glass and the communication is transmitted electronically. *Cf.* ***Card v. Dugger*** (M.D.Fla.1988) 709 F.Supp. 1098, 1105 (inmate has "privacy needs" when engaged in confidential discussion with priest), *aff'd*, (11th Cir.1989) 871 F.2d 1023.

2. **Communication with nun.** The clergy-penitent privilege protects a penitential communication between a penitent and a Catholic nun who performs priestly functions. *Cf.* ***Eckmann v. Board of Educ. of Hawthorn Sch. Dist.*** (E.D.Mo.1985) 106 F.R.D. 70, 72-73 (applying Missouri law; privilege protected penitential communication with Catholic nun who served as P's spiritual director and who performed a number of priestly functions); ***In re***

Murtha (N.J.Super.Ct.App.Div.1971) 115 N.J.Super. 380, 386-87 (applying New Jersey law; privilege did not protect penitential communication with Catholic nun because she did not perform priestly functions).

3. Grand-jury testimony by clergy. The clergy-penitent privilege protects a penitential communication between a penitent and a clergy member when the clergy member is called to testify before the grand jury. *Cf.* ***In re Grand Jury Investigation*** (3d Cir.1990) 918 F.2d 374, 386 (applying federal common law); ***People v. Reyes*** (N.Y.Sup.Ct.1989) 144 Misc.2d 805, 807 (applying New York law; communication between priest and D was privileged).

4. Counseling service by clergy. The clergy-penitent privilege protects draft-evasion counseling services rendered by a clergy member. *Cf.* ***In re Grand Jury Subpoena for Verplank*** (C.D.Cal.1971) 329 F.Supp. 433, 435-36 (protection under federal law).

§4.7 What clergy-penitent privilege does not protect.

1. Communications between clergy & superiors. The clergy-penitent privilege does not protect a communication between a priest and a bishop that the priest knew would be shared with other superiors. ***Roman Catholic Archbishop v. Superior Ct.*** (2d Dist.2005) 131 Cal.App.4th 417, 444-45. Nor is the communication protected by the constitutional right to freedom of religion. *See id.* at 431-32.

2. Letters. The clergy-penitent privilege does not protect a letter that identifies another person as receiving a copy. *See* ***Roman Catholic Archbishop***, 131 Cal.App.4th at 446; *see also* ***U.S. v. Wells*** (2d Cir.1971) 446 F.2d 2, 4 (letter to clergy member was not privileged because there was no indication it was intended to be confidential). If the letter was typed by someone other than the clergy member, the typist's knowledge would destroy the confidentiality of the letter to a penitent.

3. Religious retreats. The clergy-penitent privilege does not protect communications made at a retreat in the presence of other attendees. ***Doe 2 v. Superior Ct.*** (2d Dist.2005) 132 Cal.App.4th 1504, 1518.

4. Marriage counseling. The clergy-penitent privilege does not protect communications made during joint marriage-counseling sessions. ***Simrin v. Simrin*** (5th Dist.1965) 233 Cal.App.2d 90, 94; *CEB Trial Objections*, §50.5.

PRACTICE TIP

Although marriage counseling is not covered by the clergy-penitent privilege, if the spouses execute a confidentiality agreement covering marriage counseling with a member of the clergy, it will probably be enforceable. See ***Simrin****, 233 Cal.App.2d at 95 (because spouses' agreement did not violate public policy favoring attempts to preserve marital unit, marriage counseling with rabbi was held protected by confidentiality agreement).*

---

5. Secular communications. The clergy-penitent privilege does not protect a communication that is secular and not religious in nature. Wegner, *Civil Trials & Evidence*, ¶8:2240; *see, e.g.*, ***People v. Edwards*** (1st Dist.1988) 203 Cal.App.3d 1358, 1364-65 (embezzler's request to priest for help in stopping payment on church checks was not privileged); ***People v. Thompson*** (4th Dist.1982) 133 Cal.App.3d 419, 426 (D's statements to company counselor, who was hired to help increase sales, were not privileged); ***People v. Johnson*** (2d Dist.1969) 270 Cal.App.2d 204, 207 (robber's request for help from minister dressed in street clothes was not privileged).

§4.8 Waiver of clergy-penitent privilege. There is no clergy-penitent privilege if the holder of the privilege waives it. Evid. C. §912(a); ***Roman Catholic Archbishop v. Superior Ct.*** (2d Dist.2005) 131 Cal.App.4th 417, 445 & n.14. The right to claim the clergy-penitent privilege is waived when the holder freely discloses, or consents to the disclosure of, a significant part of the communication. Evid. C. §912(a); *see, e.g.*, ***Roman Catholic Archbishop***, 131 Cal.App.4th at 444-45 (priest in troubled-priest interventions knew communications would be shared with others). Confidentiality is not waived simply because a communication is transmitted electronically. Evid. C. §917(b). For a discussion of waiver under §912(a), see "Waiver under Evid. C. §912(a)," ch. 6-A, §2.2.14(1), p. 607.

1. Waiver by penitent. The penitent can waive the privilege by disclosing the information or by consenting to disclosure (e.g., by failing to assert the privilege). *CEB Trial Objections*, §50.8. If the penitent waives the privilege in any proceeding, it is waived for all future proceedings. Evid. C. §912(a); *CEB Trial Objections*, §50.8.

2. Waiver by clergy. The clergy member can waive the privilege by disclosing the information or by consenting to disclosure. *CEB Trial Objections*, §51.8. The penitent can prevent the clergy member from waiving the privilege. *See* Evid. C. §1033 (penitent has privilege to prevent another from disclosing); *Jefferson's Evid. Benchbook*, §41.2 (same). If the clergy member waives the privilege in any proceeding, it is waived for all future proceedings. Evid. C. §912(a); *CEB Trial Objections*, §51.8.

§4.9 How to assert clergy-penitent privilege.

1. Holder claims privilege. The penitent can claim the clergy-penitent privilege by making an objection to a discovery request made to either the penitent or the clergy member. See "Penitent," §4.5.1, p. 702. The clergy member can claim the clergy-penitent privilege by making an objection to a discovery request made to the clergy member (but not to a request made to the penitent). See "Clergy member," §4.5.2, p. 702; "Responding party objects to discovery," ch. 7-A, §14.1.1, p. 771.

2. Discovering party moves to compel. In response to the objection that the information sought is protected by the clergy-penitent privilege, the discovering party has the burden to enforce discovery. ***Roman Catholic Archbishop v. Superior Ct.*** (2d Dist.2005) 131 Cal.App.4th 417, 442. The discovering party must initiate the meet-and-confer procedure and, if unsuccessful, file a motion to compel discovery. See "Discovering party moves to compel (option 1)," ch. 7-A, §14.1.2, p. 772.

3. Holder serves opposition papers. In response to a motion to compel, the penitent or clergy member has the initial burden of proving the preliminary facts that support the privilege. ***Roman Catholic Archbishop***, 131 Cal.App.4th at 442; *see CEB Trial Objections*, §§50.10, 51.10. See "Elements of clergy-penitent privilege," §4.3, p. 701; "Responding party satisfies burden," ch. 7-A, §14.1.4, p. 772. That is, the person claiming the privilege must prove there was a clergy-penitent communication, it was made to an authorized clergy member, and it was made in private. *See CEB Trial Objections*, §§50.10, 51.10. The person claiming the privilege does not need to prove the communication was made in confidence, which is presumed. Evid. C. §917(a); *see CEB Trial Objections*, §§50.10, 51.10.

4. Discovering party justifies discovery. If the holder proved the preliminary facts that support its privilege, the discovering party has the burden to justify its discovery request, if it had not already done so in its motion to compel. *See* ***Roman Catholic Archbishop***, 131 Cal.App.4th at 442.

(1) Disprove objection. The discovering party can disprove the applicability of the privilege. For example, the discovering party can show that the holder did not prove the person to whom the communication was made was an authorized clergy member under Evid. C. §§1030 and 1032. See "Authorized or accustomed," §4.3.3(1), p. 702.

(2) Rebut confidentiality. The discovering party has the burden to rebut the presumption of confidentiality of the clergy-penitent privilege. Evid. C. §917(a); ***Roman Catholic Archbishop***, 131 Cal.App.4th at 442. See "Discovering party justifies discovery," ch. 7-A, §14.1.5, p. 773.

(3) Prove waiver. The discovering party can show that the objecting party waived the objection. See "Waiver of clergy-penitent privilege," §4.8, p. 703.

§5. VOTER PRIVILEGE

§5.1 General. A voter has a privilege to keep her vote secret. *See* Evid. C. §1050.

1. Purpose. The purpose of the voter privilege is to protect the individual's constitutional right to vote in secrecy. 7 Cal. Law Revision Comm'n Rep. (1965) p. 1202.

2. Primary authority. Cal. Const., art. II, §7; Evid. C. §1050.

3. Secondary authority. The following secondary sources are cited as authority in this section:

- *California Civil Discovery Practice* (CEB Online ed. 2014) (referred to as *CEB Discovery Practice*).
- *California Trial Objections* (CEB Online ed. 2014) (referred to as *CEB Trial Objections*).
- Wegner, *California Practice Guide: Civil Trials & Evidence* (CD-ROM ed. 2014) (referred to as Wegner, *Civil Trials & Evidence*).

§5.2 Nature of voter privilege.

1. Absolute. The voter privilege is absolute. *See* Evid. C. §1050. When the privilege is established, the court cannot weigh the need for confidentiality against the need for disclosure.

2. Scope. The scope of the voter privilege is limited. The voter cannot raise the privilege to prevent the testimony of another witness about the identity or contents of the voter's ballot. *CEB Trial Objections*, §49.4.

§5.3 Elements of voter privilege. The elements of the voter privilege are the following:

1. Public election. The vote was in a public election. Evid. C. §1050; *CEB Discovery Practice*, §3.151. For example, the election can be between candidates for public office, for ballot propositions, or a vote to incorporate a city. *See, e.g.*, ***People v. Wells*** (2d Dist.1983) 149 Cal.App.3d 721, 726 (ballot proposition).

2. Secret ballot. The voting was by secret ballot. Evid. C. §1050; *CEB Discovery Practice*, §3.151.

3. Legal voter. The voter was eligible to vote and was properly registered. *See* Evid. C. §1050; *CEB Discovery Practice*, §3.151; *CEB Trial Objections*, §49.5. There is no privilege for an illegal voter. Evid. C. §1050; ***Patterson v. Hanley*** (1902) 136 Cal. 265, 276.

4. Secret vote. The voter has not previously disclosed how she voted. Evid. C. §1050; *CEB Discovery Practice*, §3.151.

§5.4 Who can assert voter privilege. The voter is the holder of the privilege and is the only person who can assert it. *See* Evid. C. §1050; *CEB Trial Objections*, §49.4. No one else can rely on the voter's privilege. *See, e.g.*, ***People v. Ochoa*** (1998) 19 Cal.4th 353, 428 (D could not claim error when prospective juror was asked how he would vote on ballot proposition). A judge cannot invoke the privilege on behalf of an absent voter to exclude privileged information under Evid. C. §916. *CEB Trial Objections*, §49.4.

§5.5 What voter privilege protects.

1. Actual vote. The voter has a privilege to refuse to disclose how she voted. Evid. C. §1050; Wegner, *Civil Trials & Evidence*, ¶8:2570; *see* ***People v. Wells*** (2d Dist.1983) 149 Cal.App.3d 721, 726 (asking why prospective jurors voted on ballot proposition was indirect way of asking how they voted). The privilege applies to both specific questions (e.g., how she voted on a ballot measure or whether she voted for particular candidates) and general questions (e.g., whether she ever voted for candidates of a particular party). *CEB Trial Objections*, §49.3.

2. Tenor of vote. The voter has a privilege to refuse to disclose the tenor of the vote. Evid. C. §1050; *CEB Trial Objections*, §49.3; Wegner, *Civil Trials & Evidence*, ¶8:2570.

§5.6 What voter privilege does not protect.

1. Fact of voting. The voter privilege does not protect the voter from answering questions about whether, where, or when she voted. *CEB Trial Objections*, §49.3.

2. Witness's testimony. The voter privilege does not prevent a person other than the voter from testifying about the identity or contents of the voter's ballot. *CEB Trial Objections*, §49.4.

3. Illegal vote. The voter privilege does not protect a person who voted illegally from answering questions about how she voted. *CEB Trial Objections*, §49.5. A person who voted illegally forfeits the voter privilege and the secrecy of the ballot. *See* Evid. C. §1050; ***Patterson v. Hanley*** (1902) 136 Cal. 265, 275-76.

§5.7 Waiver of voter privilege. There is no voter privilege if the voter waives it. Waiver of the voter privilege can occur in two ways:

1. Express. A voter expressly waives the voter privilege by making an unprivileged disclosure of her vote. *See* Evid. C. §1050; ***Wilks v. Mouton*** (1986) 42 Cal.3d 400, 408; *CEB Trial Objections*, §49.6. For example, a military or overseas voter who faxes in her ballot expressly waives her right to a secret vote. Elec. C. §3106(a); *see* Elec. C. §300(b) (defining "military or overseas voter"); ***Bridgeman v. McPherson*** (3d Dist.2006) 141 Cal.App.4th 277, 286 (benefits of fax voting outweigh waiver of secret vote).

2. Implied. A voter can impliedly waive the voter privilege by her conduct. *See, e.g.*, Evid. C. §1050 (privilege does not apply if voter voted illegally).

§5.8 How to assert voter privilege. See "Resolving Discovery Disputes," ch. 7-A, §14, p. 771.

G. JOURNALIST PRIVILEGES & IMMUNITIES

This subchapter covers two limitations on discovery of information from journalists: the journalist's shield-law immunity and the reporter's privilege.

§1. JOURNALIST'S SHIELD-LAW IMMUNITY

§1.1 General.

1. Purpose. The purpose behind a journalist's shield-law immunity is to protect the integrity of the newsgathering process and to ensure the free flow of information to the public. ***Hammarley v. Superior Ct.*** (3d Dist.1979) 89 Cal.App.3d 388, 396, *disapproved on other grounds*, ***Delaney v. Superior Ct.*** (1990) 50 Cal.3d 785; *see* ***Shoen v. Shoen*** (9th Cir.1995) 48 F.3d 412, 416. The immunity serves this purpose by protecting journalists from being held in contempt for refusing to disclose certain kinds of information acquired while gathering news. Cal. Const., art. I, §2(b); Evid. C. §1070; ***Delaney v. Superior Ct.*** (1990) 50 Cal.3d 785, 796-97; *see* Wegner, *California Practice Guide: Civil Trials & Evidence* (CD-ROM ed. 2014) ¶8:2534. The shield law creates an immunity, not a privilege, and it does not protect against anything other than being held in contempt. ***New York Times Co. v. Superior Ct.*** (1990) 51 Cal.3d 453, 456; ***Delaney***, 50 Cal.3d at 797 n.6; *see* ***Rancho Publ'ns v. Superior Ct.*** (4th Dist.1999) 68 Cal.App.4th 1538, 1543-44.

2. Primary authority. Cal. Const., art. I, §2(b); Evid. C. §1070.

3. Secondary authority. The following secondary sources are cited as authority in this section:

- *California Civil Discovery Practice* (CEB Online ed. 2014) (referred to as *CEB Discovery Practice*).
- *California Trial Objections* (CEB Online ed. 2014) (referred to as *CEB Trial Objections*).
- Wegner, *California Practice Guide: Civil Trials & Evidence* (CD-ROM ed. 2014) (referred to as Wegner, *Civil Trials & Evidence*).
- Weil & Brown, *California Practice Guide: Civil Procedure Before Trial* (CD-ROM ed. 2014) (referred to as Weil, *Civil Procedure Before Trial*).
- Witkin, *California Evidence* (5th ed. 2012 & Supp.2014) (referred to as Witkin, *Cal. Evidence*).

§1.2 Nature of shield-law immunity.

1. Absolute. The shield law grants a journalist absolute immunity from contempt of court in civil actions. ***New York Times Co. v. Superior Ct.*** (1990) 51 Cal.3d 453, 456; ***Rancho Publ'ns v. Superior Ct.*** (4th Dist.1999) 68 Cal.App.4th 1538, 1543. By comparison, in a criminal action, the immunity is qualified by the defendant's federal constitutional right to a fair trial. ***Delaney v. Superior Ct.*** (1990) 50 Cal.3d 785, 805. The shield law prevents only the sanction of contempt, not other sanctions. ***New York Times***, 51 Cal.3d at 463. The protection afforded by the shield law for the refusal to disclose sources or information depends on whether the journalist is a party.

(1) **Party protection.** The shield law protects a party journalist who refuses to comply with discovery only from contempt, not from other sanctions such as dismissal. ***New York Times***, 51 Cal.3d at 463; *CEB Discovery Practice*, §3.130; *see, e.g.*, ***KSDO v. Superior Ct.*** (4th Dist.1982) 136 Cal.App.3d 375, 383-84 (court could strike D-reporter's defenses in libel action or award P default judgment).

(2) **Nonparty protection.** The shield law protects a nonparty journalist who refuses to comply with discovery from being held in contempt. *See* ***Mitchell v. Superior Ct.*** (1984) 37 Cal.3d 268, 274. A nonparty's protection under the shield law is virtually absolute because contempt is generally the only effective sanction against a nonparty. ***New York Times***, 51 Cal.3d at 463; *see* 2 Witkin, *Cal. Evidence*, Witnesses, §356 (monetary sanctions against nonparty newsperson under CCP §1992 are not large enough to make civil action a practical remedy).

2. Duration. The protection afforded by the shield law continues after the news story at issue is published. *See* Weil, *Civil Procedure Before Trial*, ¶8:341.13.

§1.3 Elements of shield-law immunity. The elements of shield-law immunity are the following:

1. Person is protected. The journalist is a protected person under the shield law. Cal. Const., art. I, §2(b); Evid. C. §1070(a), (b); ***Delaney v. Superior Ct.*** (1990) 50 Cal.3d 785, 805 n.17. See "Who can assert shield-law immunity," §1.4, this page.

2. Information is protected. The information sought was obtained or prepared in gathering, receiving, or processing information for communication to the public. ***Delaney***, 50 Cal.3d at 805 n.17. See "What shield-law immunity protects," §1.5, this page.

3. Information obtained while connected or employed. The journalist acquired the information while she was connected with or employed by a newspaper, magazine, other periodical publication, press association, wire service, television or radio station, or news website. Evid. C. §1070(a), (b); *see* ***O'Grady v. Superior Ct.*** (6th Dist.2006) 139 Cal.App.4th 1423, 1459 (news website).

§1.4 Who can assert shield-law immunity. Shield-law immunity can be asserted by the following people (referred to as "journalists"):

1. Traditional journalists. The shield law protects publishers, editors, reporters, and other people who are or were connected with or employed by a newspaper, magazine, other periodical publication, press association, or wire service. Cal. Const., art. I, §2(b); Evid. C. §1070(a); ***O'Grady v. Superior Ct.*** (6th Dist.2006) 139 Cal.App.4th 1423, 1459; Weil, *Civil Procedure Before Trial*, ¶8:341.1. The phrase "other periodical publication" in California Constitution article I, §2(b), and in Evid. C. §1070(a) includes websites that publish news articles. *See* ***O'Grady***, 139 Cal.App.4th at 1464-66.

2. TV & radio journalists. The shield law protects television and radio broadcasters, news reporters, and other people who are or were connected with a television or radio station. Cal. Const., art. I, §2(b); Evid. C. §1070(b).

3. Website journalists. The shield law protects publishers, editors, reporters, and other people who are or were connected with a news website. *See* ***O'Grady***, 139 Cal.App.4th at 1459; Weil, *Civil Procedure Before Trial*, ¶8:341.2. Not all people who post information on a website are protected by the shield law. *See* ***O'Grady***, 139 Cal.App.4th at 1459. Casual visitors who participate in open forums such as newsgroups, chat rooms, bulletin-board systems, or discussion groups may not be entitled to shield-law protection. *Id.*

4. Freelance journalists. The shield law protects freelance journalists. ***People v. Von Villas*** (2d Dist.1992) 10 Cal.App.4th 201, 231-32; Wegner, *Civil Trials & Evidence*, ¶8:2540.

§1.5 What shield-law immunity protects. Shield-law immunity protects a journalist from disclosing the following:

1. Sources. A journalist's sources of information are protected. *See* Cal. Const., art. I, §2(b); Evid. C. §1070(a), (b); ***McGarry v. University of San Diego*** (4th Dist.2007) 154 Cal.App.4th 97, 118; ***Playboy Enters. v. Superior Ct.*** (2d Dist.1984) 154 Cal.App.3d 14, 23; Weil, *Civil Procedure Before Trial*, ¶8:341. Even if a publication

includes verbatim transcription from the source, the source's identity is still protected by the shield law. *See, e.g.*, ***O'Grady v. Superior Ct.*** (6th Dist.2006) 139 Cal.App.4th 1423, 1457 (source was protected even though D posted on his website verbatim material obtained from source).

2. Unpublished information. Unpublished information is protected when it is obtained or prepared by a journalist while gathering, receiving, or processing information for communication to the public. Cal. Const., art. I, §2(b); Evid. C. §1070(a), (b); ***New York Times Co. v. Superior Ct.*** (1990) 51 Cal.3d 453, 458. Unpublished information is any information the journalist has not disclosed to the public, regardless of whether related information was disclosed. Evid. C. §1070(c). This includes any unpublished information that could confirm, refute, or amplify published information derived from it. ***McGarry***, 154 Cal.App.4th at 120; ***Playboy Enters.***, 154 Cal.App.3d at 23. Unpublished information is protected regardless of whether it is confidential. ***New York Times***, 51 Cal.3d at 461; ***Delaney v. Superior Ct.*** (1990) 50 Cal.3d 785, 805; Weil, *Civil Procedure Before Trial*, ¶8:341.10. Unpublished information can include the following:

(1) Notes. Cal. Const., art. I, §2(b); Evid. C. §1070(c); *e.g.*, ***Playboy Enters.***, 154 Cal.App.3d at 22-23 (editorial material related to interview from which article was published); ***Hammarley v. Superior Ct.*** (3d Dist.1979) 89 Cal.App.3d 388, 397-98 (notes from interview), *disapproved on other grounds*, ***Delaney v. Superior Ct.*** (1990) 50 Cal.3d 785.

(2) Outtakes. Cal. Const., art. I, §2(b); Evid. C. §1070(c); *cf.* ***In re Application to Quash Subpoena to NBC, Inc.*** (2d Cir.1996) 79 F.3d 346, 353 (New York shield law protected outtakes from NBC's *Dateline*).

(3) "Off the record" statements. *See CEB Trial Objections*, §48.8.

(4) Photographs. Cal. Const., art. I, §2(b); Evid. C. §1070(c); *e.g.*, ***New York Times***, 51 Cal.3d at 462 (photographs of accident scene).

(5) Tapes. Cal. Const., art. I, §2(b); Evid. C. §1070(c); *e.g.*, ***Playboy Enters.***, 154 Cal.App.3d at 22 (tapes of interviews from which article was published); ***Hammarley***, 89 Cal.App.3d at 397-98 (tapes of interview).

(6) Other data. Cal. Const., art. I, §2(b); Evid. C. §1070(c); *see, e.g.*, ***Delaney***, 50 Cal.3d at 799-800 (journalist's own eyewitness observations of nonconfidential event made while on the job).

§1.6 What shield-law immunity does not protect. Shield-law immunity does not protect a journalist from disclosing any of the following:

1. Advertisements. Sources, information, or materials related to advertisements. *See, e.g.*, ***Rancho Publ'ns v. Superior Ct.*** (4th Dist.1999) 68 Cal.App.4th 1538, 1545-46 (paid advertisements made to look like editorials).

2. Nonjournalistic materials. Sources, information, or materials obtained by a journalist outside her professional capacity. ***Delaney v. Superior Ct.*** (1990) 50 Cal.3d 785, 797 n.8; *see* Wegner, *Civil Trials & Evidence*, ¶8:2545. For example, a reporter who stops by a liquor store and happens to witness a holdup cannot refuse to testify about the holdup under the shield law. ***Delaney***, 50 Cal.3d at 797 n.8.

§1.7 Waiver of shield-law immunity.

1. Waiver. A journalist waives shield-law immunity if she does not object to discovery on that ground. *See* Evid. C. §353(a) (judgment is not reversible unless there is a record of objection).

2. No waiver.

(1) Unpublished material. A journalist does not waive shield-law immunity for unpublished information by publishing some information and attributing it to a source. ***McGarry v. University of San Diego*** (4th Dist.2007) 154 Cal.App.4th 97, 120; *e.g.*, ***Playboy Enters. v. Superior Ct.*** (2d Dist.1984) 154 Cal.App.3d 14, 23 (D-magazine did not waive immunity for unpublished tapes and interview records when it published partial transcript of interview).

(2) Testimony under subpoena. A journalist does not waive shield-law immunity by giving testimony or other evidence while under subpoena. CCP §1986.1(a); ***McGarry***, 154 Cal.App.4th at 120 n.14 (dicta).

(3) In camera review. A journalist does not waive shield-law immunity by permitting the court to review the information in chambers. ***SCI-Sacramento, Inc. v. Superior Ct.*** (3d Dist.1997) 54 Cal.App.4th 654, 663.

§1.8 How to assert shield-law immunity.

1. Discovering party serves subpoena. The procedure for asserting the shield-law immunity usually begins with the discovering party's deposition subpoena for a journalist's records. *See, e.g.*, ***New York Times Co. v. Superior Ct.*** (1990) 51 Cal.3d 453, 457 (D issued subpoena to journalist for production of unpublished photographs); ***SCI-Sacramento, Inc. v. Superior Ct.*** (3d Dist.1997) 54 Cal.App.4th 654, 658 (prosecutor issued subpoena for tape-recorded interview of D).

2. Journalist files motion to quash. The journalist usually claims shield-law immunity by filing a motion to quash the subpoena. *See, e.g.*, ***New York Times***, 51 Cal.3d at 457 (journalist filed motion to quash); ***SCI-Sacramento***, 54 Cal.App.4th at 658 (television station filed motion to quash). See "Motion to Quash Deposition Subpoena," ch. 9-C, §3, p. 1038. The journalist bears the burden of establishing all the elements of immunity to invoke the shield law's protection. ***Delaney v. Superior Ct.*** (1990) 50 Cal.3d 785, 806 n.20; *see* ***O'Grady v. Superior Ct.*** (6th Dist.2006) 139 Cal.App.4th 1423, 1456-57; ***People v. Vasco*** (4th Dist.2005) 131 Cal.App.4th 137, 151. See "Elements of shield-law immunity," §1.3, p. 707. To support her assertion of the shield law, the journalist can ask the court to review the unpublished material in chambers as long as the review would not be considered a waiver of the protection. *E.g.*, ***SCI-Sacramento***, 54 Cal.App.4th at 661-62 (television station requested in camera review without prejudice to custodian's right to review court's order and decide whether to disclose videotape or be held in contempt).

3. Discovering party serves opposition papers. If the journalist claims immunity, the discovering party should file and serve opposition papers to the motion to quash. See "Opposition," ch. 9-C, §3.2, p. 1042.

4. Court evaluates application of shield law. The court must evaluate the application of the shield law to the facts of the case. In making its decision, the court will not evaluate whether the journalist is engaged in legitimate, newsworthy journalism unless the journalist's work is clearly outside the realm of the newsgathering process. *See* ***O'Grady***, 139 Cal.App.4th at 1457; *see, e.g.*, ***Rancho Publ'ns v. Superior Ct.*** (4th Dist.1999) 68 Cal.App.4th 1538, 1546 (newspaper's published "advertorials" were not legitimate journalism because they were merely advertisements made to look like editorials). If the court denies the motion to quash, the journalist must comply with the subpoena or court order or risk contempt. *See* ***New York Times***, 51 Cal.3d at 459-60. If the journalist refuses to comply with the subpoena or court order, the court must enter a judgment of contempt before the journalist can take steps to enforce the shield-law immunity (e.g., seeking habeas corpus relief). *Id.*

5. Court adjudges contempt. If the journalist refuses to comply with the subpoena or court order, the court should find the journalist in contempt of court. If the court believes that the journalist has any colorable argument against the contempt adjudication, it can stay its judgment to allow the journalist enough time to seek writ relief. ***New York Times***, 51 Cal.3d at 460.

NOTE

Contempt is the most common and effective remedy for a nonparty journalist's disobedience of a civil subpoena, but a journalist can be subject to other types of sanctions. See ***New York Times****, 51 Cal.3d at 463. For example, a journalist can be subject to civil liability for "all damages" sustained by the discovering party as a result of the journalist's refusal to comply with the subpoena. See CCP §1992;* ***New York Times****, 51 Cal.3d at 462. If the journalist is a party to the litigation, it can also be subject to monetary and issue-preclusion sanctions.* ***Rancho Publ'ns****, 68 Cal.App.4th at 1543.*

6. Journalist seeks writ relief. Once the court finds the journalist in contempt of court, the journalist can seek review by writ. *See* ***New York Times***, 51 Cal.3d at 460.

§2. REPORTER'S PRIVILEGE

The reporter's privilege arises from state and federal constitutional guarantees of freedom of the press. ***O'Grady v. Superior Ct.*** (6th Dist.2006) 139 Cal.App.4th 1423, 1466.

§2.1 General.

1. Purpose. The purpose of the reporter's privilege is to protect the integrity of the newsgathering process and to ensure the free flow of information to the public. *See* U.S. Const. amend. 1; Cal. Const., art. I, §2(b); ***Shoen v. Shoen*** (9th Cir.1995) 48 F.3d 412, 416.

2. Primary authority. U.S. Const. amend. 1; Cal. Const., art. I, §2(b); ***Mitchell v. Superior Ct.*** (1984) 37 Cal.3d 268, 279.

3. Secondary authority. The following secondary sources are cited as authority in this section:

- Wegner, *California Practice Guide: Civil Trials & Evidence* (CD-ROM ed. 2014) (referred to as Wegner, *Civil Trials & Evidence*).
- Weil & Brown, *California Practice Guide: Civil Procedure Before Trial* (CD-ROM ed. 2014) (referred to as Weil, *Civil Procedure Before Trial*).

§2.2 Nature of reporter's privilege.

1. Qualified. The reporter's privilege is qualified. ***Mitchell v. Superior Ct.*** (1984) 37 Cal.3d 268, 279; ***O'Grady v. Superior Ct.*** (6th Dist.2006) 139 Cal.App.4th 1423, 1467; Weil, *Civil Procedure Before Trial*, ¶8:342.1. See "Apply ***Mitchell*** factors," §2.8.2(2), p. 711.

2. Duration. The reporter's privilege continues after the news story is published. *Cf.* Weil, *Civil Procedure Before Trial*, ¶8:341.13 (shield-law immunity).

§2.3 Elements of reporter's privilege. The elements of the reporter's privilege are the following:

1. Person is protected. The person is a reporter entitled to the protection of the privilege. *See* ***O'Grady v. Superior Ct.*** (6th Dist.2006) 139 Cal.App.4th 1423, 1467. See "Who can assert reporter's privilege," §2.4, this page.

2. Information is protected. The requested information is the kind entitled to protection. *See* ***O'Grady***, 139 Cal.App.4th at 1467. See "What reporter's privilege protects," §2.5, this page.

§2.4 Who can assert reporter's privilege. The reporter's privilege can be asserted by reporters, editors, and publishers who provide news to the public. ***Mitchell v. Superior Ct.*** (1984) 37 Cal.3d 268, 279; ***O'Grady v. Superior Ct.*** (6th Dist.2006) 139 Cal.App.4th 1423, 1467. The same people who can claim the protection of the shield law can claim the protection of the reporter's privilege. *See* ***O'Grady***, 139 Cal.App.4th at 1467. See "Who can assert shield-law immunity," §1.4, p. 707.

§2.5 What reporter's privilege protects. The reporter's privilege protects against disclosure of the following:

1. Confidential sources. The reporter's privilege protects the identities of the reporter's confidential sources from disclosure. ***O'Grady v. Superior Ct.*** (6th Dist.2006) 139 Cal.App.4th 1423, 1466; ***Anti-Defamation League of B'nai B'rith v. Superior Ct.*** (1st Dist.1998) 67 Cal.App.4th 1072, 1080; Wegner, *Civil Trials & Evidence*, ¶8:2521.

2. Unpublished information. The reporter's privilege protects the reporter's unpublished information obtained from confidential sources. ***Anti-Defamation League***, 67 Cal.App.4th at 1080; Wegner, *Civil Trials & Evidence*, ¶8:2521. To be protected, the reporter must have obtained and used the unpublished information for legitimate journalistic purposes. ***Anti-Defamation League***, 67 Cal.App.4th at 1077. "Legitimate journalistic purposes" means the gathering and editing of material of current significance for presentation to interested members of the public using print media, broadcast media, or the Internet. *See id.* at 1092.

§2.6 What reporter's privilege does not protect. The reporter's privilege does not protect the following:

1. A reporter's nonconfidential sources. *See* ***Anti-Defamation League of B'nai B'rith v. Superior Ct.*** (1st Dist.1998) 67 Cal.App.4th 1072, 1080.

2. Information or sources used for something other than legitimate journalistic purposes. *E.g., id.* at 1077 (privilege did not protect nonpublic information used to provide foreign government with intelligence on citizens' political activities). For the definition of "legitimate journalistic purposes," see "Unpublished information," §2.5.2, p. 710.

3. Information or sources the court decides are discoverable after considering the ***Mitchell*** factors. See "Apply ***Mitchell*** factors," §2.8.2(2), this page.

4. Editorial thought processes (e.g., the processes by which a reporter decides to include or omit information from a published story). ***Mitchell v. Superior Ct.*** (1984) 37 Cal.3d 268, 278-79; Wegner, *Civil Trials & Evidence*, ¶8:2524.

§2.7 Waiver of reporter's privilege. A reporter waives the reporter's privilege if she does not assert the privilege in response to discovery. *See* Evid. C. §353(a) (judgment is not reversible unless there is a record of objection).

§2.8 How to assert reporter's privilege.

NOTE

The procedure below assumes that the reporter is a party to the suit. If the reporter is not a party, the procedure will be similar to that for asserting shield-law immunity. See "How to assert shield-law immunity," §1.8, p. 709.

1. **Reporter claims privilege.** The reporter can claim the reporter's privilege by objecting to a discovery request based on the protection for freedom of the press provided by the U.S. and California Constitutions. *See* ***Mitchell v. Superior Ct.*** (1984) 37 Cal.3d 268, 273; *see, e.g.,* ***Anti-Defamation League of B'nai B'rith v. Superior Ct.*** (1st Dist.1998) 67 Cal.App.4th 1072, 1079 (D-journalists objected to Ps' demand for production and inspection by filing motion for protective order). See "Responding party objects to discovery," ch. 7-A, §14.1.1, p. 771.

2. **Discovering party moves to compel.** If the reporter claims the reporter's privilege, the discovering party should initiate the meet-and-confer procedure and, if unsuccessful, file a motion to compel discovery. See "Discovering party moves to compel (option 1)," ch. 7-A, §14.1.2, p. 772. The motion to compel should do the following:

(1) **Refute application of privilege.** The discovering party should challenge the reporter's assertion of the privilege. See "Discovering party justifies discovery," ch. 7-A, §14.1.5, p. 773.

(2) **Apply *Mitchell* factors.** The discovering party should show that the five factors outlined in ***Mitchell v. Superior Ct.*** weigh in favor of disclosure of the potentially privileged information. The factors are the following:

(a) **Party status.** Is the reporter a party or a nonparty? ***Mitchell***, 37 Cal.3d at 279; ***O'Grady v. Superior Ct.*** (6th Dist.2006) 139 Cal.App.4th 1423, 1468. Disclosure is more appropriate when the reporter is a party and less appropriate when the reporter is not. ***Mitchell***, 37 Cal.3d at 279; ***O'Grady***, 139 Cal.App.4th at 1468.

(b) **Enhanced relevance.** Does the information sought go to the heart of the discovering party's claim? ***Mitchell***, 37 Cal.3d at 280. Information goes to the heart of a claim if it is essential in proving a material element; ordinary relevance is not sufficient. *See, e.g., id.* at 282 (information from sources could be essential in proving Ds' actual malice in libel claim); ***O'Grady***, 139 Cal.App.4th at 1470 (identity of person who misappropriated trade secrets was crucial to P's claim).

(c) **Alternative sources.** Did the discovering party exhaust all alternative ways to obtain the information? ***Mitchell***, 37 Cal.3d at 282; ***O'Grady***, 139 Cal.App.4th at 1471. Compelled disclosure from a reporter must be a last resort and is permissible only when the discovering party has no other practical way to obtain the information. ***Mitchell***, 37 Cal.3d at 282; ***O'Grady***, 139 Cal.App.4th at 1471.

(d) Importance of confidentiality. What is the importance of preserving the confidentiality of the information? ***Mitchell***, 37 Cal.3d at 282; ***O'Grady***, 139 Cal.App.4th at 1475. When the information relates to a matter of great public importance and the risk of harm to the source is substantial, the court can refuse to require disclosure even if the plaintiff has no other way to obtain the information. ***Mitchell***, 37 Cal.3d at 283; ***O'Grady***, 139 Cal.App.4th at 1475.

(e) Strength of case. What is the demonstrated strength of the discovering party's case on the merits? ***O'Grady***, 139 Cal.App.4th at 1479; *see* ***Mitchell***, 37 Cal.3d at 283 (in defamation suit, did P make prima facie case?). The weaker the plaintiff's case, the less likely it is that the court will require disclosure. ***O'Grady***, 139 Cal.App.4th at 1479.

3. Reporter serves opposition papers. If the discovering party files a motion to compel, the reporter has the burden to justify the privilege by proving the preliminary facts that support the privilege. *See* Evid. C. §405 (determination of preliminary facts). See "Responding party satisfies burden," ch. 7-A, §14.1.4, p. 772.

(1) Elements of privilege. The reporter must prove that she is a person entitled to the protection of the reporter's privilege and that the information is the kind entitled to protection. See "Elements of reporter's privilege," §2.3, p. 710.

(2) *Mitchell* factors. The reporter should show that the ***Mitchell*** factors weigh against disclosure of the privileged information. See "Apply ***Mitchell*** factors," §2.8.2(2), p. 711.

4. Discovering party justifies discovery. If the objecting party proved the preliminary facts that support its freedom-of-the-press objection, the discovering party has the burden to justify its discovery request, if it had not already done so in its motion to compel. See "Discovering party justifies discovery," ch. 7-A, §14.1.5, p. 773.

H. GOVERNMENTAL PRIVILEGES

This subchapter covers four governmental privileges: (1) the official-information privilege, (2) the legislative privilege, (3) the informant privilege, and (4) the officer-records privilege.

§1. OFFICIAL-INFORMATION PRIVILEGE

§1.1 General. A public entity has a privilege to refuse to disclose and to prevent others from disclosing official information. Evid. C. §1040(b); ***People v. Suff*** (2014) 58 Cal.4th 1013, 1059.

1. Purpose. The purpose of the official-information privilege is to allow the government to withhold confidential information when disclosure of the information is forbidden by federal or state law or would not be in the public interest. Evid. C. §1040; 7 Cal. Law Revision Comm'n Rep. (1965) p. 1199. The official-information privilege is the exclusive means for a governmental entity to assert a claim of privilege based on the need for secrecy. ***Shepherd v. Superior Ct.*** (1976) 17 Cal.3d 107, 123, *overruled on other grounds*, ***People v. Holloway*** (2004) 33 Cal.4th 96; ***Marylander v. Superior Ct.*** (2d Dist.2000) 81 Cal.App.4th 1119, 1125; ***Rubin v. City of L.A.*** (2d Dist.1987) 190 Cal.App.3d 560, 583.

2. Primary authority. Evid. C. §1040.

3. Secondary authority. The following secondary sources are cited as authority in this section:

- *California Civil Discovery Practice* (CEB Online ed. 2014) (referred to as *CEB Discovery Practice*).
- Jefferson, *California Evidence Benchbook* (CEB Online ed. 2014) (referred to as *Jefferson's Evid. Benchbook*).
- Wegner, *California Practice Guide: Civil Trials & Evidence* (CD-ROM ed. 2014) (referred to as Wegner, *Civil Trials & Evidence*).
- Witkin, *California Evidence* (5th ed. 2012 & Supp.2014) (referred to as Witkin, *Cal. Evidence*).

§1.2 Nature of official-information privilege.

1. Absolute & qualified. Evid. C. §1040 essentially creates two different official-information privileges—an absolute privilege and a qualified privilege. ***Shepherd v. Superior Ct.*** (1976) 17 Cal.3d 107, 123, *overruled on other grounds*, ***People v. Holloway*** (2004) 33 Cal.4th 96; Wegner, *Civil Trials & Evidence*, §8:2396.

(1) Absolute privilege. The official-information privilege provides absolute protection from discovery when a federal or state statute prohibits the disclosure of the information. ***Shepherd***, 17 Cal.3d at 123; 2 Witkin, *Cal. Evidence*, Witnesses, §254; *see* Evid. C. §1040(b)(1) (disclosure is forbidden). To create an absolute privilege, the statute must do more than make the information confidential or limit disclosure to the public; the statute must show a legislative intent to bar disclosure from discovery. ***Los Angeles Unified Sch. Dist. v. Trustees of the S. Cal. IBEW-NECA Pension Plan*** (2d Dist.2010) 187 Cal.App.4th 621, 630. See "Absolute protection," §1.5.1, p. 714 (examples of statutes that created absolute privilege). Official information that is absolutely privileged cannot be compelled under any circumstances, regardless of the privilege's effect on the outcome of the case. *Jefferson's Evid. Benchbook*, §44.2; *see* ***Rittenhouse v. Superior Ct.*** (3d Dist.1991) 235 Cal.App.3d 1584, 1590 (communications that are absolutely privileged are protected from discovery regardless of relevance to issues and requesting party's interest in disclosure).

(2) Qualified privilege. The official-information privilege provides qualified (conditional) protection from discovery when there is a need to preserve the confidentiality of the official information, even though no federal or state statute prohibits the disclosure of the information. *See* Evid. C. §1040(b)(2); ***Shepherd***, 17 Cal.3d at 123; ***Marylander v. Superior Ct.*** (2d Dist.2000) 81 Cal.App.4th 1119, 1126; *Jefferson's Evid. Benchbook*, §44.3; 2 Witkin, *Cal. Evidence*, Witnesses, §254. See "Against public interest," §1.3.3(2), p. 714. The disclosure of qualified official information can be compelled if the need for disclosure outweighs the need for secrecy. *See* Evid. C. §1040(b)(2); ***Shepherd***, 17 Cal.3d at 124; ***Marylander***, 81 Cal.App.4th at 1126.

2. Duration. The duration of the official-information privilege depends on the statute or public policy that prohibits the disclosure. *See, e.g.*, ***County of Orange v. Superior Ct.*** (4th Dist.2000) 79 Cal.App.4th 759, 768 (qualified privilege for criminal investigation ends when investigation terminates).

3. Discovery & evidentiary. The official-information privilege is both a discovery privilege and an evidentiary privilege because the information protected by the privilege is not subject to either discovery or disclosure at trial. *See* Evid. C. §1040(b) (public entity has privilege to refuse to disclose and to prevent others from disclosing).

§1.3 Elements of official-information privilege. The elements of the official-information privilege are the following:

1. Public entity. The information sought is held by a public entity. See "Who can assert official-information privilege," §1.4, p. 714.

2. Official information. The information sought qualifies as "official information." *See* Evid. C. §1040(b). Official information is information that is both acquired in confidence and kept confidential. *Id.* §1040(a).

(1) Acquired in confidence. Official information must be acquired in confidence by a public employee in the course of the employee's duty. Evid. C. §1040(a); ***Shepherd v. Superior Ct.*** (1976) 17 Cal.3d 107, 124, *overruled on other grounds*, ***People v. Holloway*** (2004) 33 Cal.4th 96; ***Department of Motor Vehicles v. Superior Ct.*** (2d Dist.2002) 100 Cal.App.4th 363, 373; ***County of Orange v. Superior Ct.*** (4th Dist.2000) 79 Cal.App.4th 759, 763; *e.g.*, ***Ibarra v. Superior Ct.*** (2d Dist.2013) 217 Cal.App.4th 695, 705 (peace officer's service photograph does not contain information acquired in confidence by public employee). Even if information is not acquired "in confidence" by the public employee, the information can be deemed to have been acquired in confidence if it is by its nature confidential. *See, e.g.*, ***Department of Motor Vehicles***, 100 Cal.App.4th at 373 (medical information not acquired in confidence in accident report filed with DMV was considered confidential because medical information is intrinsically confidential); ***County of Orange***, 79 Cal.App.4th at 764 (information not acquired in confidence in police's murder-investigation file was considered confidential because evidence gathered in criminal investigation is by its nature confidential).

(2) **Kept confidential.** Official information must not be open, or officially disclosed, to the public before the claim of privilege is made. Evid. C. §1040(a); ***County of Orange***, 79 Cal.App.4th at 763. The sharing of official information between public agencies with official interest in the information does not destroy the privilege. ***Michael P. v. Superior Ct.*** (4th Dist.2001) 92 Cal.App.4th 1036, 1048.

3. **Disclosure prohibited or against public interest.** The disclosure of the information is either prohibited by law or against the public interest.

(1) **Prohibited by law.** If disclosure of the information is prohibited by law, the public entity can refuse to disclose and can prevent others from disclosing the information. Evid. C. §1040(b)(1); Wegner, *Civil Trials & Evidence*, ¶8:2394; *e.g.*, Rev. & Tax. C. §19542 (Franchise Tax Board cannot disclose tax-return information).

(2) **Against public interest.** If disclosure of the information is against the public interest, the public entity can refuse to disclose and can prevent others from disclosing the information if the need for maintaining its confidentiality outweighs the need for disclosure. Evid. C. §1040(b)(2); ***Shepherd***, 17 Cal.3d at 125-26.

§1.4 Who can assert official-information privilege. The public entity that possesses the information sought to be protected by the official-information privilege can assert the privilege, which is done through a person authorized by the public entity. *See* Evid. C. §1040(b); ***Lynna B. v. Gloradon M.*** (1st Dist.1979) 92 Cal.App.3d 682, 704. A "public entity" is a nation, state, county, city and county, city, district, public authority, public agency, or any other political subdivision or public corporation, whether domestic or foreign. Evid. C. §200.

§1.5 What official-information privilege protects. The official-information privilege provides either absolute or qualified protection for official information.

1. **Absolute protection.** The following are examples of information protected from discovery by the official-information privilege without the need to balance the interest of the party seeking the information against the public's interest in confidentiality:

(1) Personal recollections of attendees of closed sessions of a public agency. ***Kleitman v. Superior Ct.*** (6th Dist.1999) 74 Cal.App.4th 324, 335 & n.9; *see also* Gov. C. §54950 et seq. (Brown Act).

(2) Information obtained by the Department of Employment in the course of administering unemployment and disability-insurance benefits. *See* Unemp. Ins. C. §§2111, 2714; ***Richards v. Superior Ct.*** (2d Dist.1968) 258 Cal.App.2d 635, 638-39.

2. **Qualified protection.** The following are examples of information that is protected from discovery by the official-information privilege if the need for confidentiality outweighs the need for disclosure:

(1) District attorney's investigation files in closed cases. ***Shepherd v. Superior Ct.*** (1976) 17 Cal.3d 107, 125-26, *overruled on other grounds*, ***People v. Holloway*** (2004) 33 Cal.4th 96.

(2) Police investigation files in open cases. ***County of Orange v. Superior Ct.*** (4th Dist.2000) 79 Cal.App.4th 759, 765; *see* ***People v. Suff*** (2014) 58 Cal.4th 1013, 1059 (criminal case); ***People v. Jackson*** (5th Dist.2003) 110 Cal.App.4th 280, 287 (same).

(3) Medical information contained in a person's driving records at the Department of Motor Vehicles (DMV). *See* ***Department of Motor Vehicles v. Superior Ct.*** (2d Dist.2002) 100 Cal.App.4th 363, 374 (although medical information qualifies as "official information" under Evid. C. §1040, Veh. C. §1808.5 does not forbid disclosure of medical records; thus, DMV records are not entitled to absolute protection).

(4) Memorandums from state agency to Governor's office. ***Marylander v. Superior Ct.*** (2d Dist.2000) 81 Cal.App.4th 1119, 1121.

(5) Medical opinion of employee of Department of Health Services, which was based on review of privileged peer-review records. ***Fox v. Kramer*** (2000) 22 Cal.4th 531, 542.

§1.6 Waiver of official-information privilege. There is no official-information privilege when the public entity that holds the privilege consents to the release of the information in the same proceeding in which the public entity attempts to assert the privilege. *See* Evid. C. §1040(b).

§1.7 How to assert official-information privilege.

1. Public entity claims privilege. The public entity can claim the official-information privilege by objecting to the discovery request based on Evid. C. §1040. If the entity claims that the privilege is absolute, it should identify the federal or state statute that prohibits disclosure. See "Responding party objects to discovery," ch. 7-A, §14.1.1, p. 771.

2. Discovering party moves to compel. In response to the objection that the information is protected by the official-information privilege, the discovering party has the burden to enforce discovery. It must initiate the meet-and-confer procedure and, if unsuccessful, file a motion to compel discovery. See "Discovering party moves to compel (option 1)," ch. 7-A, §14.1.2, p. 772.

3. Public entity serves opposition papers. In response to a motion to compel, the public entity must serve opposition papers supported by declarations that establish the preliminary facts necessary to support the privilege. *See* ***Department of Motor Vehicles v. Superior Ct.*** (2d Dist.2002) 100 Cal.App.4th 363, 368-69. See "Responding party satisfies burden," ch. 7-A, §14.1.4, p. 772. The public entity has the burden of showing it is entitled to the privilege by establishing the elements under §1040. ***Department of Motor Vehicles***, 100 Cal.App.4th at 370; ***Marylander v. Superior Ct.*** (2d Dist.2000) 81 Cal.App.4th 1119, 1128; *CEB Discovery Practice*, §3.109. To claim the privilege, the public entity must establish the following:

(1) Official information. The public entity must show the information qualifies as official information (i.e., that it was acquired in confidence and kept confidential). *See* Evid. C. §1040(a), (b); ***Marylander***, 81 Cal.App.4th at 1128. See "Official information," §1.3.2, p. 713; "What official-information privilege protects," §1.5, p. 714.

(2) Privilege applies. The public entity must make a particularized showing that the privilege applies to each item it seeks to keep confidential. ***Shepherd v. Superior Ct.*** (1976) 17 Cal.3d 107, 125, *overruled on other grounds*, ***People v. Holloway*** (2004) 33 Cal.4th 96; ***Michael P. v. Superior Ct.*** (4th Dist.2001) 92 Cal.App.4th 1036, 1043. See "Official information," §1.3.2, p. 713.

(a) Prohibited by law. If the public entity claims absolute protection for the official information, it must identify the statute that forbids disclosure of the information. *See* ***Department of Motor Vehicles***, 100 Cal.App.4th at 374. See "Absolute privilege," §1.2.1(1), p. 713. If a statute provides that information is merely "confidential," it does not forbid disclosure under Evid. C. §1040(b)(1). ***Department of Motor Vehicles***, 100 Cal.App.4th at 374-75.

(b) Against public interest. If the public entity claims qualified protection for the official information, it must make a clear showing that the public interest in preserving the confidentiality of the information outweighs the discovering party's need for its disclosure. *See* Evid. C. §1040(b)(2); ***Shepherd***, 17 Cal.3d at 125-26; ***Marylander***, 81 Cal.App.4th at 1126; ***County of Orange v. Superior Ct.*** (4th Dist.2000) 79 Cal.App.4th 759, 765-66. See "Qualified privilege," §1.2.1(2), p. 713.

4. Discovering party justifies discovery. If the public entity proved the preliminary facts that support its assertion of privilege, the discovering party has the burden to justify its discovery request, if it had not already done so in its motion to compel.

(1) Dispute privilege. The discovering party can attempt to prove the privilege does not apply to the information sought. For example, the party can show that the information was not acquired in confidence. See "Disprove objection," ch. 7-A, §14.1.5(1), p. 774.

(2) Prove waiver. The discovering party can show that the public entity waived the official-information privilege. See "Waiver of official-information privilege," §1.6, this page; "Waiver of privilege," ch. 6-A, §2.2.14, p. 607.

(3) Prove exception. The discovering party can show that an exception to the official-information privilege applies. See "Exceptions to privilege," ch. 6-A, §2.2.13, p. 606.

(4) Prove necessity. For information subject to the qualified official-information privilege, the discovering party can show that the information is necessary to a fair resolution of the suit.

(a) Dispute need for confidentiality. The discovering party can attempt to dispute or minimize the need to preserve the confidentiality of the information. *See* ***Shepherd***, 17 Cal.3d at 126.

(b) Show need for disclosure. The discovering party should show the need for disclosure. For example, the discovering party could show the following:

[1] The information is important to the fair presentation of its case. ***Shepherd***, 17 Cal.3d at 126; *see* ***Michael P.***, 92 Cal.App.4th at 1046.

[2] The information is not available by other means. ***Shepherd***, 17 Cal.3d at 126; *see* ***Michael P.***, 92 Cal.App.4th at 1046.

[3] Obtaining the information by other means would be relatively difficult. ***Shepherd***, 17 Cal.3d at 126; *see* ***Michael P.***, 92 Cal.App.4th at 1046.

5. Court – preliminary determinations & hearing. The court should not rule on the applicability of the privilege unless the public entity shows that the information sought to be protected is covered by the privilege. ***Torres v. Superior Ct.*** (2d Dist.2000) 80 Cal.App.4th 867, 873 (criminal case). In determining whether the privilege should apply, the court must do the following:

(1) Assess privilege's applicability. The court should first assess whether the privilege's applicability can be determined without looking at the information sought to be protected. *See* ***Torres***, 80 Cal.App.4th at 873 (there are circumstances in which it is self-evident that official-information privilege applies). If the answer is yes, the court can proceed to an adversary hearing to determine the final application of the privilege. *See* ***Michael P.***, 92 Cal.App.4th at 1047 (only at conclusion of adversary hearing is court qualified to rule on claim of privilege). See "Conduct adversary hearing," §1.7.5(3), p. 717. If the answer is no, the public entity must either show in open court why the matter is privileged or declare that a showing in open court would compromise the privilege. ***Torres***, 80 Cal.App.4th at 873. If the public entity is unable to establish the privilege or show that the privilege would be compromised, the court should conduct an in camera review. *Id.*

(2) Conduct in camera review if necessary. If the court cannot determine whether the privilege applies without requiring disclosure of the information sought to be protected, the court can review the information in chambers to make a preliminary assessment of whether the claim of privilege should be upheld. *See* Evid. C. §915(b); ***Michael P.***, 92 Cal.App.4th at 1046; ***People v. Superior Ct.*** (3d Dist.1971) 19 Cal.App.3d 522, 530. During the in camera review, the court should do the following:

(a) Evaluate the requesting party's need for disclosure in the interest of justice. ***Michael P.***, 92 Cal.App.4th at 1046. This requires an assessment of the importance of the information to the fair presentation of the requesting party's case, the availability of the information to the party by other means, and the effectiveness and relative difficulty of obtaining the information by other means. ***Shepherd***, 17 Cal.3d at 126; ***Michael P.***, 92 Cal.App.4th at 1046. This may also require an evaluation of the legal sufficiency of the requesting party's case. *See* ***County of Orange***, 79 Cal.App.4th at 769-70 & n.5 (court noted that on remand, trial court will have to evaluate legal sufficiency of Ps' causes of action when weighing Ps' need for requested information).

(b) Weigh each item sought against the public interest in preserving the confidentiality of the information. ***Shepherd***, 17 Cal.3d at 125-26; ***Michael P.***, 92 Cal.App.4th at 1046.

CAUTION

Even if the court assumes it does not need to look at the requested documents to determine whether the official-information privilege applies, the requesting party may have a compelling interest at stake that requires the court to review each document in chambers. See, e.g., ***Michael P.****, 92 Cal.App.4th at 1045-46 (parents' fundamental interest in care of biological children was sufficient to require that juvenile court, which was presiding over dependency hearing for child, conduct in camera review of police investigative files sought by father accused of causing death of another child).*

(3) Conduct adversary hearing. Following the in camera review, the court should hold a hearing—and, if necessary, take testimony—to determine the following:

(a) The relevance of the information to the requesting party's case. ***Michael P.***, 92 Cal.App.4th at 1047; ***People***, 19 Cal.App.3d at 531.

(b) The reasonable alternatives to disclosure. ***Michael P.***, 92 Cal.App.4th at 1047; ***People***, 19 Cal.App.3d at 531. For example, the court could allow disclosure of the information only to the requesting party's attorney, and only subject to a protective order. *See* ***County of Orange***, 79 Cal.App.4th at 769 n.4.

§2. LEGISLATIVE PRIVILEGE

§2.1 General. The legislative privilege protects acts that occur in the regular course of the legislative process by forbidding courts from inquiring into legislators' subjective motives or mental processes in enacting legislation. *See* ***City & Cty. of S.F. v. Cooper*** (1975) 13 Cal.3d 898, 913; ***Nadler v. Schwarzenegger*** (3d Dist.2006) 137 Cal.App.4th 1327, 1336-37; ***City of Santa Cruz v. Superior Ct.*** (6th Dist.1995) 40 Cal.App.4th 1146, 1152. The legislative privilege is based on the doctrine of separation of powers as well as the practical difficulty in determining the dominant motivation behind a legislator's vote. ***City of Santa Cruz***, 40 Cal.App.4th at 1150-51; *California Civil Discovery Practice* (CEB Online ed. 2014) §3.108.

1. Purpose. The purpose of the legislative privilege is to protect the independence of the legislative branch of government under the constitutionally established separation of powers. *See* ***County of L.A. v. Superior Ct.*** (1975) 13 Cal.3d 721, 726-27 & n.5; ***Board of Supervisors v. Superior Ct.*** (2d Dist.1995) 32 Cal.App.4th 1616, 1623; *see also* Cal. Const., art. III, §3 (separation-of-powers doctrine). The legislative privilege is a corollary of the principle that the validity of a legislative act rests on the objective effect of the legislation, not on the subjective motivation of its drafters. ***County of L.A.***, 13 Cal.3d at 727.

2. Primary authority. Cal. Const., art. III, §3; ***County of L.A.***, 13 Cal.3d at 726.

3. Secondary authority. The following secondary sources are cited as authority in this section:

- *California Civil Discovery Practice* (CEB Online ed. 2014) (referred to as *CEB Discovery Practice*).
- Wegner, *California Practice Guide: Civil Trials & Evidence* (CD-ROM ed. 2014) (referred to as Wegner, *Civil Trials & Evidence*).
- Witkin, *California Evidence* (5th ed. 2012 & Supp.2014) (referred to as Witkin, *Cal. Evidence*).

§2.2 Nature of legislative privilege. The "legislative privilege" is less a privilege and more a fundamental, historically enshrined legal principle that prevents any judicially authorized inquiry into the subjective motives or mental processes of legislators. ***County of L.A. v. Superior Ct.*** (1975) 13 Cal.3d 721, 726; *see* ***Nadler v. Schwarzenegger*** (3d Dist.2006) 137 Cal.App.4th 1327, 1336.

1. Absolute. The legislative privilege is absolute. *See* ***City of Santa Cruz v. Superior Ct.*** (6th Dist.1995) 40 Cal.App.4th 1146, 1148.

2. Discovery & evidentiary. The legislative privilege is both a discovery privilege and an evidentiary privilege because the information protected by the privilege is not subject to either discovery or disclosure at trial. *See* ***County of L.A.***, 13 Cal.3d at 729 (even if legislator's motives were relevant, legislator would not be subject to

discovery); ***Nadler***, 137 Cal.App.4th at 1336-37 (even if Assembly waived privilege by submitting declaration of Assembly employee about legislators' motives, employee could not be compelled to submit to deposition testimony).

§2.3 Elements of legislative privilege. The elements of the legislative privilege are the following:

1. Legislator. The information sought is from a legislator or legislative entity. See "Who can assert legislative privilege," §2.4, this page.

2. Legislators' mental processes. The information concerns the subjective motives and thought processes of legislators in their deliberations. ***City of Santa Cruz v. Superior Ct.*** (6th Dist.1995) 40 Cal.App.4th 1146, 1153; 2 Witkin, *Cal. Evidence*, Witnesses, §322; *see* ***City of King City v. Community Bank*** (6th Dist.2005) 131 Cal.App.4th 913, 931 n.12.

3. Legislative process. The information involves the legislators' decisions in enacting legislation. *See* ***County of L.A. v. Superior Ct.*** (1975) 13 Cal.3d 721, 729; ***City of Santa Cruz***, 40 Cal.App.4th at 1150.

§2.4 Who can assert legislative privilege.

1. Legislators. The legislative privilege can be asserted by members of the State Assembly and the U.S. Congress. *See* ***County of L.A. v. Superior Ct.*** (1975) 13 Cal.3d 721, 726; ***City of Santa Cruz v. Superior Ct.*** (6th Dist.1995) 40 Cal.App.4th 1146, 1152.

2. Local legislators. The legislative privilege can be asserted by members of local governmental entities. Wegner, *Civil Trials & Evidence*, ¶8:2572.3; *e.g.*, ***Sutter's Place Inc. v. Superior Ct.*** (6th Dist.2008) 161 Cal.App.4th 1370, 1375-76 (city); ***City of Santa Cruz***, 40 Cal.App.4th at 1152 (city); ***Board of Supervisors v. Superior Ct.*** (2d Dist.1995) 32 Cal.App.4th 1616, 1619 (county board of supervisors).

3. Legislative assistants. The prohibition against questioning legislators about their motives cannot be circumvented by questioning others (e.g., legislative assistants or administrative officers) about facts that may have led to the legislators' votes. ***County of L.A.***, 13 Cal.3d at 729; Wegner, *Civil Trials & Evidence*, ¶8:2572.2; *e.g.*, ***City of Santa Cruz***, 40 Cal.App.4th at 1155 (city-planning director and commissioners); ***Board of Supervisors***, 32 Cal.App.4th at 1626 (sheriff).

§2.5 What legislative privilege protects. The following are examples of the kinds of information protected by the legislative privilege:

1. Inquiry into legislators' motives for reapportionment, even though the Assembly may have waived the privilege by submitting its employee's declaration about some of the legislators' motives. ***Nadler v. Schwarzenegger*** (3d Dist.2006) 137 Cal.App.4th 1327, 1336-37.

2. Inquiry into city council's "procedural irregularities" in passing an ordinance, which was actually an inquiry into the substance of the decision. ***City of Santa Cruz v. Superior Ct.*** (6th Dist.1995) 40 Cal.App.4th 1146, 1156.

3. Inquiry into reasons for abolishing employee positions, which resulted in the discharge of employees who were otherwise protected from discharge by civil-service provisions. *See* ***County of L.A. v. Superior Ct.*** (1975) 13 Cal.3d 721, 730-31.

§2.6 What legislative privilege does not protect. The legislative privilege does not apply to information unrelated to legislators' subjective motives and thought processes in enacting legislation. *See* ***City of King City v. Community Bank*** (6th Dist.2005) 131 Cal.App.4th 913, 931 n.12; ***City of Santa Cruz v. Superior Ct.*** (6th Dist.1995) 40 Cal.App.4th 1146, 1153. For example, the legislative privilege cannot be invoked to prevent discovery into a legislator's knowledge of objective facts and circumstances. ***City of King City***, 131 Cal.App.4th at 931 n.12; *see* ***City & Cty. of S.F. v. Superior Ct.*** (1975) 13 Cal.3d 933, 936 (legislator can refuse to answer any questions at deposition that attempt to probe her mental processes or motivation behind votes but cannot refuse to reveal otherwise discoverable information).

§2.7 How to assert legislative privilege.

1. Legislator claims privilege. The legislator can claim the legislative privilege by making an objection to a discovery request. See "Responding party objects to discovery," ch. 7-A, §14.1.1, p. 771.

2. Discovering party moves to compel. In response to the objection that the information is not subject to discovery, the discovering party has the burden to enforce discovery. It must initiate the meet-and-confer procedure and, if unsuccessful, file a motion to compel discovery. See "Discovering party moves to compel (option 1)," ch. 7-A, §14.1.2, p. 772.

3. Legislator serves opposition papers. In response to a motion to compel, the legislator must serve opposition papers supported by declarations that establish the preliminary facts necessary to support the legislative privilege. See "Responding party satisfies burden," ch. 7-A, §14.1.4, p. 772.

4. Discovering party justifies discovery. If the legislator proved the preliminary facts that support the assertion of the legislative privilege, the discovering party has the burden to justify its discovery request, if it had not already done so in its motion to compel. See "Discovering party justifies discovery," ch. 7-A, §14.1.5, p. 773.

§3. INFORMANT PRIVILEGE

§3.1 General.

A public entity has a privilege to refuse to disclose and to prevent others from disclosing the identity of an informant. Evid. C. §1041(a).

1. Purpose. The purpose of the informant privilege is to promote effective law enforcement by making citizens more willing to report their knowledge of criminal activity. *See* ***People v. Hobbs*** (1994) 7 Cal.4th 948, 958; ***People v. McShann*** (1958) 50 Cal.2d 802, 806. By protecting the anonymity of citizens who report criminal activity, the informant privilege prevents reprisals and retaliation against informants and their families. ***McCray v. Illinois*** (1967) 386 U.S. 300, 308; ***Hobbs***, 7 Cal.4th at 958.

2. Primary authority. Evid. C. §1041.

3. Secondary authority. The following secondary sources are cited as authority in this section:

- *California Civil Discovery Practice* (CEB Online ed. 2014) (referred to as *CEB Discovery Practice*).
- Witkin, *California Evidence* (5th ed. 2012 & Supp.2014) (referred to as Witkin, *Cal. Evidence*).

NOTE

Many of the civil implications of the informant privilege are covered by the reporter's privilege. See CEB Discovery Practice, §3.143; see also ***County of Riverside v. Superior Ct.*** *(2002) 27 Cal.4th 793, 804 (referring to §1041 privilege as "relating to the identity of criminal informants"). See "Reporter's Privilege," ch. 6-G, §2, p. 710.*

---

§3.2 Nature of informant privilege.

1. Absolute. The informant privilege is absolute when a federal or state statute forbids disclosure. Evid. C. §1041(a)(1); 2 Witkin, *Cal. Evidence*, Witnesses, §324. See "Disclosure forbidden," §3.3.3(1), p. 720.

2. Qualified. If disclosure of the informant's identity is not forbidden by a federal or state statute, the privilege is qualified and depends on whether the need for confidentiality outweighs the need for disclosure in the interest of justice. *See* Evid. C. §1041(a); 2 Witkin, *Cal. Evidence*, Witnesses, §324. See "Disclosure against public interest," §3.3.3(2), p. 720.

3. Discovery & evidentiary. The informant privilege is both a discovery privilege and an evidentiary privilege because the information protected by the privilege is not subject to either discovery or disclosure at trial. *See* Evid. C. §1041(a) (public entity has privilege to refuse to disclose and to prevent others from disclosing).

§3.3 Elements of informant privilege. The elements of the informant privilege are the following:

1. Informant's identity. The information sought to be disclosed is an informant's identity. Evid. C. §1041(a); 2 Witkin, *Cal. Evidence*, Witnesses, §324.

2. Informant's qualifications. The person whose identity is sought qualifies as an informant under §1041 because of all the following:

(1) Disclosed violation of law. The informant furnished information that purported to disclose a violation of a federal law, a California law, or the law of a California public entity. Evid. C. §1041(a).

(2) In confidence. The informant furnished the information in confidence. Evid. C. §1041(b).

(3) To public entity. The informant furnished the information to (1) a law-enforcement officer, (2) a representative of an administrative agency charged with the administration or enforcement of the law allegedly violated, or (3) any person for the purpose of transmitting the information to such an officer or representative. Evid. C. §1041(b). See "Who can assert informant privilege," §3.4, this page. Under Evid. C. §1041(b), a "person" includes volunteers and employees of crime-stopper organizations. Evid. C. §1041(b)(3); *see also id.* §1041(d) (defining "crime stopper organization").

3. Disclosure of identity prohibited or against public interest. The disclosure of the informant's identity is either prohibited by law or against the public interest.

(1) Disclosure forbidden. If disclosure of the informant's identity is forbidden by a federal or state statute, the public entity can refuse to disclose and to prevent others from disclosing the identity. Evid. C. §1041(a)(1).

(2) Disclosure against public interest. If disclosure of the informant's identity is against the public interest, the public entity can refuse to disclose and to prevent others from disclosing the identity. Evid. C. §1041(a)(2). Disclosure is against the public interest only if the need for preserving the informant's confidentiality outweighs the need for disclosure in the interest of justice. *Id.* When determining whether disclosure is against the public interest, the interest of the public entity as a party in the outcome of the proceeding cannot be considered. *Id.*

§3.4 Who can assert informant privilege. The public entity is the holder of the informant privilege and has the right to assert the privilege, which is done through a person authorized by the public entity to do so. Evid. C. §1041(a); 2 Witkin, *Cal. Evidence*, Witnesses, §324. A "public entity" is a nation, state, county, city and county, city, district, public authority, public agency, or any other political subdivision or public corporation, whether domestic or foreign. Evid. C. §200.

§3.5 When informant privilege does not apply.

1. Public entity's waiver. The qualified informant privilege is waived if any person who is authorized to consent to the disclosure of the informant's identity does so. Evid. C. §1041(a)(2).

2. Informant's consent. The informant privilege, whether absolute or qualified, is waived if the informant discloses her own identity. Evid. C. §1041(c).

§3.6 How to assert informant privilege.

1. Public entity claims privilege. The public entity can claim the informant privilege by making an objection to a discovery request. Evid. C. §1041(a). See "Who can assert informant privilege," §3.4, this page; "Responding party objects to discovery," ch. 7-A, §14.1.1, p. 771.

2. Discovering party moves to compel. In response to the objection that the information is not subject to discovery, the discovering party has the burden to enforce discovery. It must initiate the meet-and-confer procedure and, if unsuccessful, file a motion to compel discovery. See "Discovering party moves to compel (option 1)," ch. 7-A, §14.1.2, p. 772.

3. Public entity serves opposition papers. In response to a motion to compel, the public entity must serve opposition papers supported by declarations that establish the preliminary facts necessary to support the informant privilege. See "Responding party satisfies burden," ch. 7-A, §14.1.4, p. 772.

4. Discovering party justifies discovery. If the public entity proved the preliminary facts that support the assertion of the informant privilege, the discovering party has the burden to justify its discovery request, if it had not already done so in its motion to compel. See "Discovering party justifies discovery," ch. 7-A, §14.1.5, p. 773.

§4. OFFICER-RECORDS PRIVILEGE

§4.1 General. Peace-officer or custodial-officer personnel records and records maintained by a state or local agency under Pen. C. §832.5, as well as information obtained from those records, are confidential and cannot be disclosed in a criminal or civil proceeding except by discovery under Evid. C. §§1043 and 1046. Pen. C. §832.7(a).

1. Purpose. The purpose of the officer-records privilege is to protect the interests of peace officers in maintaining the confidentiality of their personnel information. ***Michael v. Gates*** (2d Dist.1995) 38 Cal.App.4th 737, 743.

2. Primary authority. Pen. C. §832.7; *see* Evid. C. §§1043-1047.

3. Secondary authority. The following secondary sources are cited as authority in this section:

- Jefferson, *California Evidence Benchbook* (CEB Online ed. 2014) (referred to as *Jefferson's Evid. Benchbook*).
- Weil & Brown, *California Practice Guide: Civil Procedure Before Trial* (CD-ROM ed. 2014) (referred to as Weil, *Civil Procedure Before Trial*).

§4.2 Nature of officer-records privilege.

1. Types of protection. Some officer records are protected by an absolute privilege, and some are protected by a qualified privilege. *See Jefferson's Evid. Benchbook*, §44.20.

(1) Absolute. The privilege is absolute for the records of peace officers or custodial officers who (1) were not present during the arrest of a party seeking discovery, (2) had no contact with that party from the time of the arrest until the time of booking, or (3) were not present at the time the conduct is alleged to have occurred within a jail facility. Evid. C. §1047. The absolute privilege applies regardless of whether an arrest was made. *See* ***Davis v. City of Sacramento*** (3d Dist.1994) 24 Cal.App.4th 393, 400.

(2) Qualified. The privilege is qualified except for the provisions in Evid. C. §1047. *See* Evid. C. §§1043, 1045, 1047; ***Rosales v. City of L.A.*** (2d Dist.2000) 82 Cal.App.4th 419, 426-27; ***Hackett v. Superior Ct.*** (2d Dist.1993) 13 Cal.App.4th 96, 98. Thus, there is a qualified privilege for the records of officers who (1) were present during the arrest of a party seeking discovery, (2) had some contact with that party between the arrest and booking, or (3) were present at the time the conduct is alleged to have occurred within a jail facility. Officer records that are protected by the qualified privilege can be disclosed if the party seeking disclosure shows good cause. *See* Evid. C. §1043; ***Rosales***, 82 Cal.App.4th at 425, 427. See "Discovering party makes ***Pitchess*** motion," §4.8.2, p. 724.

2. Duration. The privilege for an officer's personnel records is not terminated by the officer's retirement from service or leave from employment. ***Abatti v. Superior Ct.*** (4th Dist.2003) 112 Cal.App.4th 39, 57; ***Davis***, 24 Cal.App.4th at 400.

§4.3 Elements of officer-records privilege. The elements of the officer-records privilege are the following:

1. Covered officer. The information sought to be disclosed involves the records of a peace officer or custodial officer. Pen. C. §832.7(a).

(1) Peace officer. For lists of individuals who are defined as "peace officers," see Pen. C. §§830.1-830.65.

(2) Custodial officer. A custodial officer is a public officer (but not a peace officer) employed by a law-enforcement agency of a city or county who (1) maintains custody of prisoners and (2) operates a local detention facility used for the detention of persons pending arraignment or by court order either for their own safekeeping or for the specific purpose of serving a sentence. Pen. C. §831(a); *see id.* §831.5(a). The term "custodial officer" includes a person designated as a correctional officer, jailer, or other similar title. *Id.* §831.5(a).

2. Covered records. The information sought to be disclosed involves an officer's personnel records or complaint records. See "What officer-records privilege protects," §4.5, this page.

(1) Personnel records. The information sought to be disclosed involves personnel records, or information obtained from those records, that are protected by the officer-records privilege. Pen. C. §832.7(a). The privilege protects the officer's personnel records, regardless of whether those records could also be obtained from the officer or elsewhere. ***Hackett v. Superior Ct.*** (2d Dist.1993) 13 Cal.App.4th 96, 101. "Personnel records" means any file maintained under that individual's name by her employing agency and containing pertinent records. Pen. C. §832.8; *see, e.g.*, ***Long Beach Police Officers Ass'n v. City of Long Beach*** (2014) 59 Cal.4th 59, 71 (initial incident report involving officer is not considered personnel record; related records generated in connection with officer appraisal or discipline constitute personnel records). "Under that individual's name" does not mean that the records must be filed in an individual file with the officer's name on it. *See* ***Davis v. City of San Diego*** (4th Dist.2003) 106 Cal.App.4th 893, 900. See "Pertinent personnel records," §4.5.1, this page.

NOTE

The privilege does not protect otherwise nonconfidential information contained in a file simply because that file may also contain an officer's personnel records. ***Commission on Peace Officer Stds. & Training v. Superior Ct.*** *(2007) 42 Cal.4th 278, 293.*

(2) Complaint records. The information sought to be disclosed involves complaint records (i.e., records of complaints by members of the public against officers) maintained by any state or local agency under Pen. C. §832.5, or information obtained from those records, that are protected by the officer-records privilege. Pen. C. §832.7(a).

§4.4 Who can assert officer-records privilege. The officer-records privilege belongs to both the officer and the employing agency. *See, e.g.*, ***Michael v. Gates*** (2d Dist.1995) 38 Cal.App.4th 737, 744 (privilege held by both individual officer and police department); ***Davis v. City of Sacramento*** (3d Dist.1994) 24 Cal.App.4th 393, 401 (same). Either the officer or the employing agency can assert it. *See* ***Michael***, 38 Cal.App.4th at 744; ***Davis***, 24 Cal.App.4th at 401.

§4.5 What officer-records privilege protects. The officer-records privilege protects the following records:

1. Pertinent personnel records. Pertinent personnel records are records maintained under an officer's name by her employing agency that relate to any of the following:

(1) Personal data, including marital status, names of family members, educational and employment history, home addresses, and other similar information. Pen. C. §832.8(a); *e.g.*, ***Commission on Peace Officer Stds. & Training v. Superior Ct.*** (2007) 42 Cal.4th 278, 294 (***CPOST***) ("employment history" refers only to previous employment). "Similar information" includes items such as birth date and Social Security number. ***Garden Grove Police Dept. v. Superior Ct.*** (4th Dist.2001) 89 Cal.App.4th 430, 434. The term "personal data" does not include all information relating to an officer and is limited to the types of information listed in the statute. ***International Fed'n of Prof'l & Tech. Eng'rs v. Superior Ct.*** (2007) 42 Cal.4th 319, 341; ***Zanone v. City of Whittier*** (2d Dist.2008) 162 Cal.App.4th 174, 187-88; *see* ***CPOST***, 42 Cal.4th at 294 ("personal data" includes types of information that are commonly given to employer by employee during application process or upon employment). Whether data is personal is determined by the content of the data, not its location. *See* ***CPOST***, 42 Cal.4th at 291 (information is not confidential simply because it is located in same file as personal data specified in §832.8(a)); ***New York Times Co. v. Superior Ct.*** (2d Dist.1997) 52 Cal.App.4th 97, 103 (cannot protect otherwise unrestricted information by placing it in personnel file), *disapproved on other grounds*, ***Copley Press, Inc. v. Superior Ct.*** (2006) 39 Cal.4th 1272. The following are not "personal data" and thus are not privileged under Pen. C. §832.8(a):

(a) Officer's identity, unless the officer was the subject of a complaint or disciplinary hearing. *See* ***Long Beach Police Officers Ass'n v. City of Long Beach*** (2014) 59 Cal.4th 59, 72; ***CPOST***, 42 Cal.4th at 296.

(b) Officer's employing agency. ***CPOST***, 42 Cal.4th at 299.

(c) Officer's employment dates. *Id.*

(d) Officer's official service photograph. ***Ibarra v. Superior Ct.*** (2d Dist.2013) 217 Cal.App.4th 695, 704-05.

(e) Officer's salary. ***International Fed'n***, 42 Cal.4th at 341.

(f) Other information relating to the officer's current job status. ***CPOST***, 42 Cal.4th at 294-95.

(2) Medical history. Pen. C. §832.8(b).

(3) Election of employee benefits. *Id.* §832.8(c).

(4) Employee advancement, appraisal, or discipline. *Id.* §832.8(d); *see* ***Long Beach Police Officers Ass'n***, 59 Cal.4th at 71.

(5) Complaints, or investigations of complaints, about an event or transaction that the officer participated in or that she perceived, and about how she performed her duties. Pen. C. §832.8(e); ***Zanone***, 162 Cal.App.4th at 187-88.

(6) Any other information that would constitute an unwarranted invasion of personal privacy if disclosed. Pen. C. §832.8(f); *see, e.g.*, ***International Fed'n***, 42 Cal.4th at 345 (dicta; disclosure of payroll records, other than officer's salary, would constitute unwarranted invasion of personal privacy).

2. Complaint records. A party cannot discover complaint records about an officer if the conduct occurred more than five years before the event or transaction that is the subject of the litigation. Evid. C. §1045(b)(1). As a corollary, a public entity is not required to maintain records of complaints about peace officers for more than five years. Pen. C. §832.5(b).

§4.6 When officer-records privilege does not apply.

1. Disclosure ordered under Evid. C. §1043. The privilege does not apply when disclosure has been court-ordered following a motion under Evid. C. §1043. *See* Pen. C. §832.7(a) (information shall not be disclosed in any civil proceeding except by discovery under §1043).

2. Officer's conduct proceeding. The privilege does not apply to investigations or proceedings about the conduct of peace officers or custodial officers, or an agency or department that employs those officers, conducted by a grand jury, a district attorney's office, or the Attorney General's office. Pen. C. §832.7(a).

3. Disclosure to party. The privilege does not apply to copies of a complaining party's own statements. *See* Pen. C. §832.7(b). When a complaint is filed, the department or agency in control of the records must release to the complaining party a copy of her own statements. *Id.*

4. Data about complaints. The privilege does not apply to data about the number, type, or disposition of sustained complaints (as opposed to exonerated or unfounded complaints) made against a department's or agency's officers if that information is in a form that does not disclose the identities of the individuals involved. Pen. C. §832.7(c).

5. False statement. The privilege does not apply to factual information about a disciplinary investigation if the officer who is the subject of the investigation, or her agent or representative, publicly and knowingly makes a false statement about the investigation or the imposition of disciplinary action. Pen. C. §832.7(d). The correct factual information can be released only if the false statement was published by an established medium of communication, such as television, radio, or newspaper. *Id.* Disclosure of the information is limited to facts in the officer's personnel file about the investigation or imposition of disciplinary action that specifically refute the false statements. *Id.*

6. Marital-dissolution proceedings. The privilege does not apply in marital-dissolution proceedings. *See* ***City of L.A. v. Superior Ct.*** (4th Dist.2003) 111 Cal.App.4th 883, 894-95, *disapproved on other grounds*, ***International Fed'n of Prof'l & Tech. Eng'rs v. Superior Ct.*** (2007) 42 Cal.4th 319.

7. Internal review. The privilege does not apply when an agency, with its attorney, reviews an officer's records that it has in its custody and control. *See* ***Michael v. Gates*** (2d Dist.1995) 38 Cal.App.4th 737, 744.

§4.7 Waiver of officer-records privilege. There is no privilege for the officer's personnel records if it is waived. The privilege is waived only if both the public entity and the officer consent to the release of the information. *See* ***Davis v. City of Sacramento*** (3d Dist.1994) 24 Cal.App.4th 393, 401. Both hold the privilege, and both must waive it. *See id.*

§4.8 How to assert officer-records privilege. To obtain information in peace-officer and custodial-officer personnel records, a party seeking the information must file a motion for discovery or disclosure, which is commonly referred to as a ***Pitchess*** motion. *Jefferson's Evid. Benchbook*, §44.14; Weil, *Civil Procedure Before Trial*, ¶8:127.1. In ***Pitchess v. Superior Ct.*** (1974) 11 Cal.3d 531, the California Supreme Court held that a party alleging police misconduct had a right to discovery of records of past complaints about similar misconduct by the police officer. *Jefferson's Evid. Benchbook*, §44.14. ***Pitchess*** was partially codified in Evid. C. §1043, which sets out the procedures for seeking disclosure of peace-officer personnel and complaint records in civil or criminal cases. ***Commission on Peace Officer Stds. & Training v. Superior Ct.*** (2007) 42 Cal.4th 278, 293; *Jefferson's Evid. Benchbook*, §44.14.

1. Holder not required to object. Unlike the official-information privilege, the employing agency or the officer is not required to claim the privilege in response to a discovery request by making an objection that the privilege applies. ***County of L.A. v. Superior Ct.*** (2d Dist.1990) 219 Cal.App.3d 1605, 1611; ***City of Fresno v. Superior Ct.*** (5th Dist.1988) 205 Cal.App.3d 1459, 1473-74. The burden is instead on the discovering party to file a ***Pitchess*** motion. ***City of Fresno***, 205 Cal.App.3d at 1474. However, to avoid appearing dilatory, the agency or officer should probably bring the matter to the requesting party's attention as soon as possible. *See, e.g.*, ***County of L.A.***, 219 Cal.App.3d at 1611 (although under no technical obligation to do so, county should have raised §1043 issue at earliest opportunity).

2. Discovering party makes *Pitchess* motion. The discovering party must make a written motion for discovery or disclosure under Evid. C. §1043. Evid. C. §1043(a); *see* ***City of Fresno***, 205 Cal.App.3d at 1473-74.

(1) In writing. The ***Pitchess*** motion must be in writing. Evid. C. §1043(a).

(2) Contents.

(a) Identify proceedings, parties & date of hearing. The ***Pitchess*** motion must identify the following:

[1] The proceedings in which discovery is sought. Evid. C. §1043(b)(1).

[2] The party seeking discovery. *Id.*

[3] The peace officer or custodial officer whose records are sought. *Id.*

[4] The public entity that has custody and control of the records. *Id.*

[5] The time and place of the hearing on the motion. *Id.*

(b) Describe records. The ***Pitchess*** motion must describe the type of records or information sought. Evid. C. §1043(b)(2). The records should be identified with "adequate specificity" to avoid any characterization that the motion is a fishing expedition. ***City of Santa Cruz v. Municipal Ct.*** (1989) 49 Cal.3d 74, 85. However, the discovering party does not need to prove the existence of any particular records. *Id.* at 90-91.

(c) Show good cause. The ***Pitchess*** motion must include affidavits that establish good cause for the discovery by (1) identifying the materiality of the records or information to the pending litigation and (2) stating that, "upon reasonable belief," the employing agency has the type of records identified in §1043(b)(2) or information from those types of records. Evid. C. §1043(b)(3); ***Warrick v. Superior Ct.*** (2005) 35 Cal.4th 1011, 1019; *see*

City of Santa Cruz, 49 Cal.3d at 92 (affidavit need only identify types of records). Information is "material" if it will facilitate the ascertainment of the facts and a fair trial. ***Haggerty v. Superior Ct.*** (4th Dist.2004) 117 Cal.App.4th 1079, 1086. The affidavit can be based on reasonable inferences from the facts of the pending litigation and does not need to do the following:

[1] Allege personal knowledge of facts showing that the information sought is material to the pending litigation. ***City of Santa Cruz***, 49 Cal.3d at 89. The affidavit can be based solely on "information and belief." *Id.*

[2] Allege independent information showing that the types of records sought actually exist. *Id.* at 93 n.9. The affidavit can be based on a "reasonable belief" that the agency has these types of records. *Id.* at 92.

(3) Service. The ***Pitchess*** motion must be served on the employing agency that has custody of the records. *See* Evid. C. §1043(a). The motion papers must be filed and served at least 16 calendar days before the hearing. CCP §1005(b); *see* Evid. C. §1043(a).

3. Public entity responds.

(1) Notify officer. The public entity must notify the individual officer whose records are sought by the ***Pitchess*** motion. Evid. C. §1043(a).

(2) Serve opposition papers. In response to the motion, the employing agency must decide whether it will assert the privilege, and if so, how best to do so. ***Michael v. Gates*** (2d Dist.1995) 38 Cal.App.4th 737, 744. This will require the agency to determine whether it will oppose the ***Pitchess*** motion and either insist on the §1043 hearing or waive it. ***Michael***, 38 Cal.App.4th at 744; *see* Evid. C. §1043(c) (agency can waive hearing).

4. Court conducts hearing. The court must conduct a hearing to determine whether the discovering party has established good cause to discover the information unless any of the following occurs:

(1) The discovering party has not fully complied with the notice provisions of Evid. C. §1043. Evid. C. §1043(c).

(2) The discovering party did not show good cause for failing to comply with the notice provisions of Evid. C. §1043. *Id.* §1043(c).

(3) The employing agency waived the hearing. *Id.*

NOTE

*The California Supreme Court recently held that a **Pitchess** motion filed in an administrative proceeding may be decided by the administrative body rather than by a court. **Riverside Cty. Sheriff's Dept. v. Stiglitz** (2014) 60 Cal.4th 624, 628; see Evid. C. §§1043, 1045.*

5. Court reviews information in chambers. If the court determines the discovering party established good cause for the discovery, it must conduct an in camera review to determine the relevance and materiality of the information sought. Evid. C. §1045(b); ***Warrick***, 35 Cal.4th at 1019; ***City of Fresno***, 205 Cal.App.3d at 1472.

(1) Custodian delivers records. The custodian of records must bring to court all the documents that are potentially relevant to the discovering party's motion.

(2) Records examined. The court must examine the records for relevance. Evid. C. §1045(b). The court must review the records outside the presence and hearing of all persons except the custodian of records, the peace officer, and anyone else the custodian or officer is willing to have present. *Id.* §§915(b), 1045(b).

(3) Order disclosure. The court can order disclosure of any information that is relevant and material to the subject matter of the pending litigation. *See* ***Rosales v. City of L.A.*** (2d Dist.2000) 82 Cal.App.4th 419, 427. If the court orders disclosure of any officer records, it must order that the disclosed records cannot be used for

any purpose other than a court proceeding under applicable law. Evid. C. §1045(e). The term "applicable law" refers to Evid. C. §1043, so the discovering party can only use the records in the proceeding in which the records were sought. ***Alford v. Superior Ct.*** (2003) 29 Cal.4th 1033, 1042.

NOTE

There is a narrow exception to Evid. C. §1045(e)'s prohibition against using disclosed information in other legal proceedings. When complainant information—usually limited to name, address, and phone number—is ordered disclosed to a party's attorney and the attorney later discovers the same information under a ***Pitchess*** *motion for a different party, the attorney can refer to any derivative information (e.g., interviews of the complainant) uncovered as part of an earlier investigation conducted for the first party.* ***Chambers v. Superior Ct.*** *(2007) 42 Cal.4th 673, 681.*

(a) Records that cannot be disclosed. In determining the relevance of the requested information, the court must exclude the following from disclosure:

[1] Information consisting of complaints about conduct that occurred more than five years before the event or transaction that is the subject of the pending litigation. Evid. C. §1045(b)(1).

[2] The conclusions of any officer investigating a complaint filed under Pen. C. §832.5 if the pending litigation in which the information is sought is a criminal proceeding. Evid. C. §1045(b)(2). Although this exclusion is limited to criminal cases, that limitation cannot be interpreted to make an investigating officer's conclusions automatically discoverable in civil proceedings; the information sought must still be relevant. ***Haggerty***, 117 Cal.App.4th at 1088.

[3] Facts that are so remote as to make their disclosure of little or no practical benefit. Evid. C. §1045(b)(3).

(b) Records that can be obtained elsewhere. In determining the relevance of the requested information when the issue in the litigation concerns the employing agency's policies or pattern of conduct, the court must consider whether the information sought can be obtained from other records maintained by the agency in the regular course of its business that would not require the disclosure of individual personnel records. Evid. C. §1045(c).

6. Employing agency or officer requests protective order. The employing agency or officer whose records were sought can file a motion for protective order to protect the agency or officer from unnecessary annoyance, embarrassment, or oppression. Evid. C. §1045(d). The motion must be "seasonably" made and must establish good cause showing the necessity of the protective order. *Id.*

I. MEDIATION EXEMPTION

Information prepared for mediation and a mediator's report and findings are protected from discovery. Evid. C. §§1115-1128; *see also id.* §703.5 (arbitrators are generally not competent to testify about arbitration), §1152 (offer of compromise is inadmissible on proof of liability). The protection of mediation information is not a privilege in the traditional sense. *See* ***Eisendrath v. Superior Ct.*** (2d Dist.2003) 109 Cal.App.4th 351, 362-63 & n.7. Instead, it is a right of confidentiality that exempts mediation information from discovery. ***Wimsatt v. Superior Ct.*** (2d Dist.2007) 152 Cal.App.4th 137, 150-51 & n.4.

§1. GENERAL

§1.1 Purpose. The mediation exemption promotes a candid and informal exchange of information by protecting the confidentiality of the information. ***Simmons v. Ghaderi*** (2008) 44 Cal.4th 570, 578; ***Rojas v. Superior Ct.*** (2004) 33 Cal.4th 407, 415-16; ***Foxgate Homeowners' Ass'n v. Bramalea Cal., Inc.*** (2001) 26 Cal.4th 1, 14; *see* ***Ryan v. Garcia*** (3d Dist.1994) 27 Cal.App.4th 1006, 1011.

§1.2 Primary authority. Evid. C. §§1115-1128.

§1.3 Secondary authority. The following secondary sources are cited as authority in this subchapter:

- *California Civil Discovery Practice* (CEB Online ed. 2014) (referred to as *CEB Discovery Practice*).
- Wegner, *California Practice Guide: Civil Trials & Evidence* (CD-ROM ed. 2014) (referred to as Wegner, *Civil Trials & Evidence*).
- Weil & Brown, *California Practice Guide: Civil Procedure Before Trial* (CD-ROM ed. 2014) (referred to as Weil, *Civil Procedure Before Trial*).
- Witkin, *California Evidence* (5th ed. 2012 & Supp.2014) (referred to as Witkin, *Cal. Evidence*).
- Witkin, *California Procedure* (5th ed. 2008 & Supp.2014) (referred to as Witkin, *Cal. Procedure*).

§2. NATURE OF MEDIATION EXEMPTION

§2.1 Absolute. The mediation exemption is absolute because mediation communications are not subject to a balancing test between the need for discovery and the need for confidentiality. *See* ***Simmons v. Ghaderi*** (2008) 44 Cal.4th 570, 583 (mediation exemption does not have good-cause exception). Mediation confidentiality must be strictly enforced, except when there is an express statutory exception or when due process is implicated. *Id.* at 582; *see* ***Foxgate Homeowners' Ass'n v. Bramalea Cal., Inc.*** (2001) 26 Cal.4th 1, 15-16; ***Kurtin v. Elieff*** (4th Dist.2013) 215 Cal.App.4th 455, 477-78; ***Rinaker v. Superior Ct.*** (3d Dist.1998) 62 Cal.App.4th 155, 165-67. See "What Mediation Exemption Does Not Prevent," §6, p. 729; "When Mediation Exemption Does Not Apply," §7, p. 731.

§2.2 Duration. The mediation exemption is indefinite and protects information even after the mediation ends. Evid. C. §1126; ***Simmons v. Ghaderi*** (2008) 44 Cal.4th 570, 580.

§2.3 Discovery & evidentiary. The mediation exemption prevents the discovery of mediation communications and prevents their introduction into evidence. Evid. C. §1119; *CEB Discovery Practice*, §3.147.

§3. ELEMENTS OF MEDIATION EXEMPTION

The elements of the mediation exemption are the following:

§3.1 Noncriminal proceeding. The mediation information is sought for use in an arbitration, administrative adjudication, civil action, or other noncriminal proceeding in which testimony can be compelled. Evid. C. §1119(a), (b). A "civil action" includes civil proceedings. *Id.* §120.

§3.2 Mediation communication. The information sought was an oral or written communication made or prepared for mediation. *See* Evid. C. §1119(a), (b). See "What Mediation Exemption Prevents," §5, p. 728.

1. Oral or written. A protected mediation communication includes oral communications and writings. Evid. C. §1119(a), (b). See "Oral communications," §5.1, p. 728; "Written communications," §5.2, p. 728.

2. Related to mediation. A protected mediation communication includes communications that were made (1) for mediation, (2) during mediation, or (3) pursuant to mediation. Evid. C. §1119(a), (b). This includes statements made in open mediation sessions and private caucuses. Wegner, *Civil Trials & Evidence*, ¶8:2831.17.

§3.3 Mediation proceeding. The information sought was made or used in a mediation or a mediation consultation. *See* Evid. C. §1119(a)-(c).

1. Mediation. A mediation is a process in which a neutral person facilitates communication between disputing parties to assist them in reaching a mutually acceptable agreement. Evid. C. §1115(a); ***Saeta v. Superior Ct.*** (2d Dist.2004) 117 Cal.App.4th 261, 269; Wegner, *Civil Trials & Evidence*, ¶8:2831.16; 6 Witkin, *Cal. Procedure*, Proceedings Without Trial, §486.

2. Mediation consultation. A mediation consultation is a communication between a person and a mediator for the purpose of initiating, considering, or reconvening a mediation or retaining the mediator. Evid. C. §1115(c); Wegner, *Civil Trials & Evidence*, ¶8:2831.15; 1 Witkin, *Cal. Evidence*, Circumstantial Evidence, §157.

§4. WHO CAN ASSERT MEDIATION EXEMPTION

The participants in a mediation can assert the mediation exemption. *See* ***Rinaker v. Superior Ct.*** (3d Dist.1998) 62 Cal.App.4th 155, 163 n.2; *see also* Evid. C. §1119(c) (all communications by and between participants remain confidential). The term "participants" includes the parties, the parties' attorneys, the mediator, and any other non-party attending the mediation, including a spouse, an accountant, an insurance-company representative, a corporate employee, or an observer (e.g., a person evaluating or training the mediator). *See* ***Cassel v. Superior Ct.*** (2011) 51 Cal.4th 113, 130-31; ***Eisendrath v. Superior Ct.*** (2d Dist.2003) 109 Cal.App.4th 351, 359; 27 Cal. Law Revision Comm'n Rep. (1997) pp. 600, 603.

§4.1 Mediator. The term "mediator" means a neutral person who conducts the mediation, and includes any person designated by the mediator either to assist in the mediation or to communicate with the other participants, such as a case developer, interpreter, or secretary. Evid. C. §1115(b); 27 Cal. Law Revision Comm'n Rep. (1997) p. 597. A person can be a mediator even if she has a different title, such as "ombudsperson." 27 Cal. Law Revision Comm'n Rep. (1997) p. 597.

§4.2 Party. The term "party" means a litigant who is one of the participants in a mediation. *See* ***Cassel v. Superior Ct.*** (2011) 51 Cal.4th 113, 130.

§5. WHAT MEDIATION EXEMPTION PREVENTS

The mediation exemption prevents the admissibility or discovery of oral communications and writings that are materially related to the mediation and foster it. ***Wimsatt v. Superior Ct.*** (2d Dist.2007) 152 Cal.App.4th 137, 160. In other words, the mediation exemption limits the use or discovery of information that would not have existed but for a mediation communication, negotiation, or settlement discussion. *Id.*

§5.1 Oral communications. The mediation exemption prevents the admissibility or discovery of evidence of any oral communication made for or during the mediation process. Wegner, *Civil Trials & Evidence*, ¶8:2831.5.

1. **Oral statement.** Any oral statement made for the purpose of, in the course of, or according to a mediation or mediation consultation cannot be admitted or discovered. Evid. C. §1119(a), (c).

2. **Oral admission.** Any oral admission of liability made for the purpose of, in the course of, or according to a mediation or mediation consultation cannot be admitted or discovered. Evid. C. §1119(a), (c).

3. **Oral agreement.** An oral agreement to settle that does *not* meet all the requirements of Evid. C. §1118 cannot be admitted or discovered. *See* Evid. C. §1124; ***Simmons v. Ghaderi*** (2008) 44 Cal.4th 570, 579-81; ***Ryan v. Garcia*** (3d Dist.1994) 27 Cal.App.4th 1006, 1012-13 (discussing former §1152.5, now §1119). For the requirements of §1118, see "Oral agreement," §6.5, p. 730.

§5.2 Written communications. The mediation exemption prevents the admissibility or discovery of any writing that is prepared for the purpose of, in the course of, or according to a mediation or mediation consultation. Evid. C. §1119(b); *CEB Discovery Practice*, §3.147; Wegner, *Civil Trials & Evidence*, ¶8:2831.6. The term "writing" means any form of recording (e.g., typewriting, photographing, photocopying, e-mail) on any tangible thing, any form of communication (e.g., letters, words, pictures, sounds, or symbols, or their combinations), and any record created, regardless of how it was stored. Evid. C. §250. The following are examples of protected writings:

1. **Summaries & admissions.** Summaries of information and admissions of liability that were produced for mediation cannot be admitted or discovered. *See* Weil, *Civil Procedure Before Trial*, ¶8:190.5; *see, e.g.*, ***Doe 1 v. Superior Ct.*** (2d Dist.2005) 132 Cal.App.4th 1160, 1168 & n.9 (mediation exemption protected summaries of priests' personnel records prepared for mediation of suits against church for damages for sexual molestation).

2. **Mediation briefs.** Briefs submitted for mediation cannot be admitted or discovered. ***Wimsatt v. Superior Ct.*** (2d Dist.2007) 152 Cal.App.4th 137, 158-59; Weil, *Civil Procedure Before Trial*, ¶8:190.5.

3. **E-mails.** E-mails or other communications that quote confidential mediation information cannot be admitted or discovered. ***Wimsatt***, 152 Cal.App.4th at 159; Wegner, *Civil Trials & Evidence*, ¶8:2831.7.

4. Witness statements. Witness statements prepared for mediation cannot be admitted or discovered. ***Rojas v. Superior Ct.*** (2004) 33 Cal.4th 407, 416; Wegner, *Civil Trials & Evidence*, ¶8:2831.7. However, the facts in the statements are not exempt from discovery. ***Rojas***, 33 Cal.4th at 423 n.8; Wegner, *Civil Trials & Evidence*, ¶8:2831.8.

5. Photographs. Photographs prepared for mediation cannot be admitted or discovered. ***Rojas***, 33 Cal.4th at 416; Weil, *Civil Procedure Before Trial*, ¶8:190.5.

6. Analyses. Test-data analyses prepared for mediation cannot be admitted or discovered. ***Rojas***, 33 Cal.4th at 416-17; *see* Wegner, *Civil Trials & Evidence*, ¶8:2831.7.

§5.3 Mediator's report. The mediation exemption prevents the mediator from submitting to a court or other adjudicative body most reports, assessments, evaluations, recommendations, and findings made by the mediator about the mediation. Evid. C. §1121. For exceptions to this rule, see "Mediator's report & testimony," §6.1, this page. The purpose of §1121 is to prevent the mediator from coercing the parties to settle by threatening to report to the court on the merits of the dispute or the reasons why mediation did not resolve it. 27 Cal. Law Revision Comm'n Rep. (1997) p. 602.

§6. WHAT MEDIATION EXEMPTION DOES NOT PREVENT

§6.1 Mediator's report & testimony.

1. Disclosing report. The mediation exemption does not prevent a mediator from disclosing her report, assessment, evaluation, recommendations, and findings to a court or other adjudicative body in either of the following situations:

(1) Mandated by law. The mediator's report is mandated by court rule or other law that requires the mediator to report whether an agreement was reached. Evid. C. §1121.

(2) Agreed by parties. All the parties to the mediation expressly agree to the disclosure in writing or orally under Evid. C. §1118. Evid. C. §1121. "Parties" in §1121 may include other participants to the mediation. *E.g.*, ***Travelers Cas. & Sur. Co. v. Superior Ct.*** (2d Dist.2005) 126 Cal.App.4th 1131, 1146 n.18 (dicta; insurance-company representatives were parties to mediation); *see also* ***Doe 1 v. Superior Ct.*** (2d Dist.2005) 132 Cal.App.4th 1160, 1168-69 (parties who sat outside mediation were participants under Evid. C. §1122).

2. Compelling testimony. The mediation exemption does not prevent a mediator from testifying in a later civil proceeding about any statement, conduct, decision, or ruling that occurred at or in conjunction with a mediation in an earlier proceeding if the statement, conduct, decision, or ruling would (1) give rise to civil or criminal contempt, (2) constitute a crime, (3) be the subject of an investigation by the State Bar or the Commission on Judicial Performance, or (4) give rise to judicial-disqualification proceedings under CCP §170.1(a)(1) or (a)(6). Evid. C. §703.5; ***Wimsatt v. Superior Ct.*** (2d Dist.2007) 152 Cal.App.4th 137, 151 & n.5.

§6.2 Written materials not prepared for mediation. The mediation exemption does not prevent written materials from being admitted or disclosed when the materials were prepared for reasons other than for use at mediation, even if they were used later at a mediation. ***Rojas v. Superior Ct.*** (2004) 33 Cal.4th 407, 417. Only written materials prepared especially for mediation are protected. *Id.* A writing that was not created for the mediation and is otherwise admissible or discoverable is not protected solely because it is used in the mediation. *See* Evid. C. §1120(a).

§6.3 Agreement to mediate. The mediation exemption does not prevent an agreement to mediate a dispute from being admitted. Evid. C. §1120(b)(1).

§6.4 Written settlement agreement. The mediation exemption does not prevent a written settlement agreement from being admitted or disclosed when the agreement (1) was prepared in the course of or according to a mediation, (2) is signed by all the settling parties, and (3) satisfies any of the following conditions:

1. Agreement subject to disclosure. The agreement provides that it is admissible in court or subject to disclosure or contains words to that effect. Evid. C. §1123(a); *e.g.*, ***In re Marriage of Daly & Oyster*** (2d Dist.2014) 228 Cal.App.4th 505, 511 (written agreement expressed that stipulated judgment for dissolution of marriage was admissible); ***Provost v. Regents of the Univ. of Cal.*** (4th Dist.2011) 201 Cal.App.4th 1289, 1305 (written agreement

stated that settlement was admissible in court under Evid. C. §1123); ***Stewart v. Preston Pipeline Inc.*** (6th Dist.2005) 134 Cal.App.4th 1565, 1577-78 (written agreement stated that settlement was exempt from confidentiality provisions of Evid. C. §1152 et seq.). If the agreement is not signed by all the settling parties but rather by a combination of the settling parties and their respective counsel, the effectiveness of a confidentiality waiver may depend on whether the attorney was specifically authorized to waive confidentiality on the client's behalf. *See, e.g.*, ***Rael v. Davis*** (2d Dist.2008) 166 Cal.App.4th 1608, 1621 (confidentiality waiver was ineffective when agreement was signed only by settling party's attorney and settling party did not authorize attorney to waive confidentiality on client's behalf). *But see* ***Stewart***, 134 Cal.App.4th at 1580-83 (confidentiality waiver is effective when agreement is signed only by settling party's attorney because waiver provision affects only client's procedural, not substantive, rights, and attorney is authorized to act on procedural matters).

2. Agreement enforceable or binding. The agreement provides that it is enforceable or binding or contains words to that effect. Evid. C. §1123(b); *e.g.*, ***In re Marriage of Daly & Oyster***, 228 Cal.App.4th at 511 (written agreement expressed that stipulated judgment for dissolution of marriage was enforceable); ***Provost***, 201 Cal.App.4th at 1305 (written agreement stated that settlement was binding on the parties and enforceable by motion of any party); ***Stewart***, 134 Cal.App.4th at 1578-79 (written agreement stated that settlement was enforceable "pursuant to the provisions of Code of Civil Procedure [s]ection 664.6").

3. Express agreement. All parties to the agreement expressly agree orally or in writing to its disclosure. Evid. C. §1123(c); *see, e.g.*, ***Estate of Thottam*** (2d Dist.2008) 165 Cal.App.4th 1331, 1338-39 (mediation confidentiality agreement signed at beginning of mediation allowed party to submit mediation chart detailing property allocation in enforcement action). For an oral agreement to be binding, it must satisfy all the requirements of Evid. C. §1118. Evid. C. §1123(c).

4. Fraud, duress, or illegality. The agreement is used to show fraud, duress, or illegality that is relevant to an issue in dispute. Evid. C. §1123(d).

§6.5 Oral agreement. The mediation exemption does not prevent an oral agreement from being admitted or disclosed when the agreement (1) was made in the course of or according to mediation and (2) satisfies any of the following conditions:

1. Evid. C. §1118. The agreement is "in accordance with" Evid. C. §1118. Evid. C. §1124(a). To meet the requirements of §1118, the oral agreement must satisfy all the following conditions:

(1) The agreement must be recorded by a court reporter or a reliable means of audio recording. *Id.* §1118(a).

(2) The agreement's terms must be recited on the record in the presence of the parties and the mediator. *Id.* §1118(b). The parties must express on the record that they agree to the recited terms. *Id.*

(3) The parties must expressly state on the record that the agreement is binding or enforceable or contain words to that effect. *Id.* §1118(c).

(4) The recording of the agreement must be reduced to writing, and the writing must be signed by the parties within 72 hours after it is recorded. *Id.* §1118(d).

2. Express agreement. The agreement is in accordance with Evid. C. §1118(a), (b), and (d), and all the parties expressly agree, in writing or orally in accordance with Evid. C. §1118, to disclosure of the agreement. Evid. C. §1124(b).

3. Fraud, duress, or illegality. The agreement is in accordance with Evid. C. §1118(a), (b), and (d), and the agreement is used to show fraud, duress, or illegality that is relevant to an issue in dispute. Evid. C. §1124(c).

§6.6 Tangible things. The mediation exemption does not prevent the discoverability of physical objects, such as test samples. *See* ***Rojas v. Superior Ct.*** (2004) 33 Cal.4th 407, 416. However, the recorded analyses of samples prepared for mediation are protected. *Id.* at 416-17.

§6.7 Mediator's service. The mediation exemption does not prevent disclosure of the fact that a mediator served, is serving, will serve, or was contacted about serving as a mediator in a dispute. Evid. C. §1120(b)(3).

§6.8 Parties' conduct. The mediation exemption does not prevent one party from disclosing another party's conduct that occurred during a mediation. ***Foxgate Homeowners' Ass'n v. Bramalea Cal., Inc.*** (2001) 26 Cal.4th 1, 13-14; *see, e.g.*, ***Provost v. Regents of the Univ. of Cal.*** (4th Dist.2011) 201 Cal.App.4th 1289, 1302-03 (mediation exemption prevented P from offering into evidence allegedly coercive statements made during mediation because statements were communications and not conduct). The exemption does, however, prevent the mediator from disclosing a party's conduct except when the conduct would (1) give rise to civil or criminal contempt, (2) constitute a crime, (3) be the subject of an investigation by the State Bar or the Commission on Judicial Performance, or (4) give rise to judicial-disqualification proceedings under CCP §170.1(a)(1) or (a)(6). Evid. C. §703.5.

§6.9 Postmediation communications. The mediation exemption does not prevent disclosure of communications between the participants to a mediation that (1) occur after the mediation ends and (2) do not implicate confidential communications made before the end of the mediation. ***Eisendrath v. Superior Ct.*** (2d Dist.2003) 109 Cal.App.4th 351, 365 n.8; *see* Evid. C. §1126 (anything that is inadmissible, protected from disclosure, and confidential before mediation ends remains protected after mediation ends). To determine when a mediation ends, see Evid. C. §1125.

§7. WHEN MEDIATION EXEMPTION DOES NOT APPLY

§7.1 Arbitration. The mediation exemption does not apply to arbitration proceedings. ***Kurtin v. Elieff*** (4th Dist.2013) 215 Cal.App.4th 455, 470.

§7.2 Mediation in family-conciliation court proceeding. The mediation exemption does not apply to a mediation in a family-conciliation court proceeding. ***Rinaker v. Superior Ct.*** (3d Dist.1998) 62 Cal.App.4th 155, 164 n.3; *see* Evid. C. §1117(b)(1).

§7.3 Mediation of child custody & visitation. The mediation exemption does not apply to a mediation of child custody and visitation. ***Rinaker v. Superior Ct.*** (3d Dist.1998) 62 Cal.App.4th 155, 164 n.3; *see* Evid. C. §1117(b)(1).

§7.4 Mandatory settlement conference. The mediation exemption does not apply to a mandatory settlement conference under CRC 3.1380. Evid. C. §1117(b)(2); *see* ***Rinaker v. Superior Ct.*** (3d Dist.1998) 62 Cal.App.4th 155, 164 n.3.

§7.5 Conflicting constitutional right. The mediation exemption does not apply when it conflicts with a constitutional right. *See, e.g.*, ***Kurtin v. Elieff*** (4th Dist.2013) 215 Cal.App.4th 455, 475-76 (court considered but rejected D's argument that strictly enforcing mediation privilege violated due process); ***Rinaker v. Superior Ct.*** (3d Dist.1998) 62 Cal.App.4th 155, 165 (court compelled mediator to testify about statements that vandalism victim made during mediation because minors' due-process rights to impeach a witness in a juvenile-delinquency proceeding outweighed statutory right to mediation confidentiality).

§8. WAIVER OF MEDIATION EXEMPTION

§8.1 Mediator's report & findings. The mediation exemption does not prevent a mediator from disclosing to a court or other adjudicative body any report, assessment, evaluation, recommendation, or finding by the mediator about a mediation if all parties to the mediation expressly agree to the disclosure orally or in writing. Evid. C. §1121. An oral agreement must comply with the requirements of Evid. C. §1118. *Id.* §1121. See "Evid. C. §1118," §6.5.1, p. 730.

§8.2 Communication or writing. The mediation exemption does not prevent a communication or writing from being admitted or disclosed when (1) the communication or writing was made or prepared for the purpose of, in the course of, or according to a mediation or mediation consultation and (2) all or some of the participants consented to

the admission or disclosure. Evid. C. §1122(a); ***Simmons v. Ghaderi*** (2008) 44 Cal.4th 570, 586; ***Eisendrath v. Superior Ct.*** (2d Dist.2003) 109 Cal.App.4th 351, 364. The participants' consent must be express; it cannot be implied. ***Simmons***, 44 Cal.4th at 586.

1. All participants consent. The mediation exemption is waived if all who conducted or participated in the mediation (i.e., all participants, including parties, mediator, and nonparties) expressly agree in writing, or orally under Evid. C. §1118, to disclosure of the communication, document, or writing. Evid. C. §1122(a)(1); 27 Cal. Law Revision Comm'n Rep. (1997) p. 603. If the neutral person who conducts a mediation expressly agrees to disclosure, all other mediators and assistants (e.g., case developer, interpreter, secretary) are bound by that agreement. Evid. C. §1122(b); 27 Cal. Law Revision Comm'n Rep. (1997) p. 604. For the requirements of an oral agreement under Evid. C. §1118, see "Evid. C. §1118," §6.5.1, p. 730.

2. Some participants consent. The mediation exemption is waived if (1) a communication, document, or writing was prepared by or on behalf of fewer than all the mediation participants, (2) those participants expressly agree in writing, or orally under Evid. C. §1118, to its disclosure, and (3) the communication, document, or writing does not disclose anything said, done, or admitted in the course of the mediation. Evid. C. §1122(a)(2); *see* ***Provost v. Regents of the Univ. of Cal.*** (4th Dist.2011) 201 Cal.App.4th 1289, 1305. For the requirements of an oral agreement under Evid. C. §1118, see "Evid. C. §1118," §6.5.1, p. 730.

§9. HOW TO ASSERT MEDIATION EXEMPTION

There is no particular method for asserting, or challenging, the mediation exemption. Typically, the exemption will be raised as an objection to a party's attempt to introduce communications or writings from the mediation in support of a claim or motion. *See, e.g.*, ***Simmons v. Ghaderi*** (2008) 44 Cal.4th 570, 576-77 (Ps filed suit against D for breach of oral contract of settlement reached during mediation, and D argued in her trial brief that mediation exemption prevented Ps from proving existence of agreement). The exemption can also be raised as an objection to discovery from third parties, usually the mediator. *See, e.g.*, ***Eisendrath v. Superior Ct.*** (2d Dist.2003) 109 Cal.App.4th 351, 354 (petitioner filed motion to correct spousal-support agreement reached through mediation, respondent served mediator with deposition subpoena, and petitioner filed motion for protective order to bar discovery into mediation communications). Regardless of how the exemption is asserted, the burden is on the party seeking to prevent the use or discovery of a communication or writing to show that the information is protected by the mediation exemption. ***Wimsatt v. Superior Ct.*** (2d Dist.2007) 152 Cal.App.4th 137, 160.

CALIFORNIA CIVIL PRETRIAL

CHAPTER 7. METHODS OF DISCOVERY

TABLE OF CONTENTS

TABLE OF CONTENTS

Table of Contents

7. METHODS OF DISCOVERY

A. RULES FOR CONDUCTING DISCOVERY

§1. GENERAL

§1.1 Purpose. Discovery is the procedure used by the parties to secure admissible evidence or information that can lead to the discovery of admissible evidence. ***Arnett v. Dal Cielo*** (1996) 14 Cal.4th 4, 21; *see* ***Emerson Elec. Co. v. Superior Ct.*** (1997) 16 Cal.4th 1101, 1107-08. The purpose of discovery is to facilitate fact-finding by preventing litigation delay, preventing the litigation of false or unmeritorious claims, and clarifying the issues in the case. *See* ***Davies v. Superior Ct.*** (1984) 36 Cal.3d 291, 299; ***Greyhound Corp. v. Superior Ct.*** (1961) 56 Cal.2d 355, 376.

§1.2 Primary authority. CCP §§2016.010-2065; CRC 3.250, 3.1000, 3.1010.

§1.3 Secondary authority. The following secondary sources are cited as authority in this subchapter:

- *Action Guide: Handling Motions to Compel and Other Discovery Motions* (CEB Online ed. 2013) (referred to as *CEB Action Guide: Motions to Compel*).
- *California Civil Discovery Practice* (CEB Online ed. 2014) (referred to as *CEB Discovery Practice*).
- *California Trial Objections* (CEB Online ed. 2014) (referred to as *CEB Trial Objections*).
- *California Trial Practice: Civil Procedure During Trial* (CEB Online ed. 2014) (referred to as *CEB Procedure During Trial*).
- Jefferson, *California Evidence Benchbook* (CEB Online ed. 2014) (referred to as *Jefferson's Evid. Benchbook*).
- Thomas, *California Civil Courtroom Handbook* (2014) (referred to as Thomas, *Courtroom Handbook*).
- Wegner, *California Practice Guide: Civil Trials & Evidence* (CD-ROM ed. 2014) (referred to as Wegner, *Civil Trials & Evidence*).
- Weil & Brown, *California Practice Guide: Civil Procedure Before Trial* (CD-ROM ed. 2014) (referred to as Weil, *Civil Procedure Before Trial*).

PRACTICE TIP

Before beginning the discovery process, you should prepare a draft of the jury charge based on the pleadings. Knowing what questions the jury will be asked will help you design an effective discovery plan.

§2. TYPES OF DISCOVERY

This section provides an overview of formal and informal discovery. Formal discovery refers to discovery methods authorized by the Civil Discovery Act (CDA) and other parts of the Code of Civil Procedure. See "Formal discovery," §2.1, p. 741. Informal discovery refers to discovery methods that can be used before or instead of formal discovery. See "Informal discovery," §2.2, p. 742.

Chart 7-1, below, summarizes the procedures for discovery from parties and nonparties.

7-1. HOW TO SECURE & RESPOND TO DISCOVERY

		Need court order or subpoena?	Discovery request verified?	Discovery response signed by—	Discovery products verified?	Cross-reference
	Party discovery					
1	Oral deposition	No ❶	No	Deponent	Yes	See ch. 7-B, p. 780
2	Written deposition	No ❶	No	Deponent	Yes	See ch. 7-B, p. 780
3	Interrogatories	No	No	Party (answers); attorney (objections). CCP §2030.250(a), (c).	Yes, party's answers only	See ch. 7-C, p. 816
4	Requests for admission	No	No	Party (answers); attorney (objections). CCP §2033.240(a), (c).	Yes, party's answers only	See ch. 7-D, p. 836
5	Demand to inspect documents and things	No	No	Party (answers); attorney (objections).	Yes, party's answers only	See ch. 7-E, p. 845
6	Demand for exam of personal-injury plaintiff	No ❷	No	Attorney	No	See ch. 7-F, p. 855
7	Motion for other medical exam	Order	No	Attorney	No	See ch. 7-F, p. 855
8	Demand for exchange of expert information	No	No	Attorney	No	See ch. 7-I, p. 898
9	Motion for defendant's asset information for punitive damages	Order	Yes	Attorney or party	No	See ch. 7-G, p. 868
10	Request for statement of damages from personal-injury plaintiff	No	No	Attorney	No	See §2.1.1(8), p. 741
11	Authorization for release of medical records	No	No	Attorney or party	No	See §2.2.4, p. 743
12	Discovery pending appeal. CCP §2036.040(a).	Order	No	Attorney	Depositions only	*CEB Discovery*, §5.156
	Nonparty discovery					
13	Oral deposition	Subpoena ❶	No	Deponent	Yes	See ch. 8-B, p. 959
14	Written deposition	Subpoena ❶	No	Deponent	Yes	See ch. 8-B, p. 959
15	Deposition for business records without appearance	Subpoena	No	Custodian of records	Yes	See ch. 8-B, §5, p. 963
16	Presuit discovery	Order	Yes	Potential party	Yes	See ch. 7-J, p. 923

❶ Need court order to take deposition (1) during the plaintiff's discovery hold, (2) after discovery cutoff, or (3) of a prisoner. See "During plaintiff's discovery hold," §5.1.2(2), p. 746; "Later cutoff by court order," §5.2.3(2)(b), p. 749; "Prisoners," ch. 7-B, §7.4.2, p. 786. Can obtain court order to take deposition (1) of a person who has already been deposed, or (2) outside geographic limits. See "By motion," ch. 7-B, §9.6.2(2), p. 795; "Court order," ch. 7-B, §9.19.1, p. 804.

❷ Need court order if exam of personal-injury plaintiff is beyond scope of CCP §2032.220. See "Motion for Medical Examination," ch. 7-F, §5, p. 860.

§2.1 Formal discovery. The parties can use all the formal discovery methods authorized by the Code of Civil Procedure, most of which are found in the CDA. *See* ***Pillsbury, Madison & Sutro v. Schectman*** (1st Dist.1997) 55 Cal.App.4th 1279, 1288; ***Irvington-Moore, Inc. v. Superior Ct.*** (3d Dist.1993) 14 Cal.App.4th 733, 738-39. The Code of Civil Procedure authorizes two types of formal discovery—self-executing discovery and court-ordered discovery.

1. Self-executing discovery. Self-executing discovery operates without judicial involvement—no court order is necessary. *See* ***Volkswagenwerk A.G. v. Superior Ct.*** (3d Dist.1981) 122 Cal.App.3d 326, 331. The Code of Civil Procedure authorizes the following self-executing discovery methods:

(1) Oral deposition. An oral deposition is used to take the oral testimony of a person (party or nonparty) and can be used to secure the production of documents and things. See "Oral Deposition," ch. 7-B, §9, p. 788. Oral depositions are expensive and time-consuming and should ordinarily be used only after a party is familiar with the facts of the case. *See CEB Discovery Practice*, §5.36; Weil, *Civil Procedure Before Trial*, ¶8:418. Oral depositions are helpful to (1) probe the depth of a deponent's knowledge of the facts of the case and (2) pin down testimony by having the deponent commit to a particular version of the facts. *See* Weil, *Civil Procedure Before Trial*, ¶8:419; *CEB Discovery Practice*, §2.58. Parties and their agents are compelled to attend by deposition notice; nonparties are compelled to attend by deposition subpoena. See "How to Require Deposition Attendance," ch. 7-B, §7, p. 785.

(2) Deposition on written questions. A deposition on written questions is used to present written questions to a person (party or nonparty) whose sworn answers are transcribed by a deposition officer. Parties and their agents are compelled to attend by deposition notice; nonparties are compelled to attend by deposition subpoena. See "Deposition on Written Questions," ch. 7-B, §10, p. 804. Depositions on written questions are of limited usefulness. See "Drawbacks of written depositions," ch. 7-B, §10.1, p. 805.

(3) Deposition subpoenas. A deposition subpoena is used to require a nonparty to (1) appear at a deposition, (2) appear and produce documents and things at a deposition, or (3) produce business records without appearing at a deposition. See "Deposition Subpoenas," ch. 8-B, p. 959.

(4) Interrogatories. Interrogatories are written questions used to acquire a party's written answers under oath. They are a relatively inexpensive form of discovery normally used to narrow the issues and identify witnesses who should be deposed. See "Interrogatories," ch. 7-C, p. 816.

(5) Demand to produce. A demand to produce is used to compel a party to produce things in the party's possession, custody, or control for inspection, copying, photographing, testing, measuring, surveying, or sampling. See "Demands to Produce," ch. 7-E, p. 845.

(6) Requests for admission. Requests for admission are used to require a party to admit or deny (1) certain facts, opinions, or applications of law to facts and (2) whether specified documents are genuine. See "Requests for Admission," ch. 7-D, p. 836.

(7) Demand for exam of personal-injury P. A defendant in a personal-injury action can demand one physical examination of the plaintiff. See "Demand for Physical Examination of Personal-Injury Plaintiff," ch. 7-F, §4, p. 857.

(8) Request for statement of damages. A defendant in a personal-injury or wrongful-death action can request a statement of damages from the plaintiff. CCP §425.11(b); *CEB Discovery Practice*, §2.43; *see* Judicial Council Forms, form CIV-050 (official form for statement of damages from personal-injury P). See "Statement of Damages," ch. 3-C, §5, p. 226.

(9) Demand for exchange of expert information. A demand for the exchange of expert information is used to require the parties to simultaneously exchange information about the experts they may call as trial witnesses for expert opinions. See "Expert Discovery," ch. 7-I, p. 898.

(10) Demand for itemized account. A defendant in a suit on an account can demand an itemization of the amounts owed on the account (i.e., a bill of particulars). CCP §454; *see* Weil, *Civil Procedure Before Trial*, ¶¶8:1765-8:1787 (discussing bill of particulars).

2. **Court-ordered discovery.** A party must obtain a court order for the following discovery procedures:

(1) **Presuit discovery.** A potential litigant must obtain a court order to conduct discovery before a suit is filed. See "Petition for Presuit Discovery," ch. 7-J, §3, p. 924.

(2) **Second deposition.** A party must obtain a court order (or a written stipulation from the other parties) to take a second deposition of a witness who has already been deposed. See "Who can be redeposed," ch. 7-B, §9.19, p. 804.

(3) **Medical exams.**

(a) **Physical exam.**

[1] **Generally.** A party must obtain a court order to conduct a physical examination of a person in an action that is not a personal-injury action. CCP §2032.310(a). See "Motion for Medical Examination," ch. 7-F, §5, p. 860.

[2] **Personal-injury P.** A defendant must obtain a court order to conduct a physical examination of a personal-injury plaintiff in the following situations: (1) the examination is to be conducted more than 75 miles from the plaintiff's residence, (2) the plaintiff will have less than 30 days' notice of the examination, (3) the examination includes a diagnostic test or procedure that is painful, protracted, or intrusive, (4) the examination would be the plaintiff's second physical examination, or (5) the examination includes a mental examination of the plaintiff. See "Motion for Medical Examination," ch. 7-F, §5, p. 860.

(b) **Mental exam.** A party must obtain a court order to conduct a mental examination of a person. CCP §2032.310(a). See "Motion for Medical Examination," ch. 7-F, §5, p. 860.

(4) **Financial information for punitive damages.** A plaintiff must obtain a court order to secure information about the defendant's financial condition in a punitive-damages case. The plaintiff can get the order by making a motion supported by affidavits establishing a substantial probability that the plaintiff will prevail on the claim for punitive damages. Civ. C. §3295(c). The court may require a hearing on the motion and affidavits. *Id.*; *see CEB Discovery Practice*, §1.41. For a discussion of the motion, see "Motion to Discover Financial Information," ch. 7-G, p. 868.

(5) **Modified discovery.** A party must obtain a court order (or a written stipulation from the parties) to modify the discovery procedures in the CDA. See "Modifying Discovery Procedures," §4, p. 743.

§2.2 Informal discovery. The parties can use informal discovery methods instead of or in addition to formal discovery methods. *See* ***Pullin v. Superior Ct.*** (2d Dist.2000) 81 Cal.App.4th 1161, 1162; *CEB Discovery Practice*, §2.31; *see, e.g.*, ***Schnabel v. Superior Ct.*** (1993) 5 Cal.4th 704, 709 (dicta; wife attempted to obtain business records informally before serving deposition subpoena on custodian of records). Informal discovery can be conducted before, during, or after formal discovery. *See* ***Pullin***, 81 Cal.App.4th at 1165 n.4.

1. **Stipulate.** The parties can agree by written stipulation to less expensive and less time-consuming methods of discovery, such as voluntarily exchanging documents or conducting interviews instead of taking depositions. See "Modifying discovery by stipulation," §4.1, p. 743.

2. **Investigate.** A party can conduct its own unilateral investigation as long as it is lawful. *See, e.g.*, ***Natali v. State Bar*** (1988) 45 Cal.3d 456, 461 n.2 (attorney corresponded with potential witnesses, medical suppliers, and claims adjuster); ***Pullin***, 81 Cal.App.4th at 1164-65 (after D refused P's request to conduct tests at D's store, P sent expert into store while it was open to public to test floor).

3. **Request public records.** A party can request copies of public records under the California Public Records Act and the Freedom of Information Act. *See* 5 U.S.C. §552 (Freedom of Information Act); Gov. C. §§6250-6276.48 (California Public Records Act); ***Sierra Club v. Superior Ct.*** (2013) 57 Cal.4th 157, 164 (California Public Records Act); ***Yonemoto v. Department of Veterans Affairs*** (9th Cir.2012) 686 F.3d 681, 685 (Freedom of Information Act); *CEB Discovery Practice*, §2.48 (California Public Records Act), §2.49 (Freedom of Information Act); *see also* Cal. Const., art. I, §3(b) (right to scrutinize public meetings and writings of public officials and agencies).

4. Authorization for medical records. A party can obtain another party's medical records if the other party signs an authorization to release them. Civ. C. §56.11; *see id.* §56.10(a). A party's attorney can obtain the party's medical records from a medical provider before filing suit by presenting a signed authorization. Evid. C. §1158 ¶1.

§3. LIMITS ON NUMBER OF DISCOVERY REQUESTS

The number of discovery requests a party can make depends on whether the action is an unlimited civil case or a limited civil case. See "Procedural Classifications of Civil Cases," ch. 3-E, §4, p. 255.

7-2. LIMITS ON NUMBER OF DISCOVERY REQUESTS

	Type of discovery	Unlimited civil case		Limited civil case
		Initial discovery	Supplemental discovery	
1	Depositions. See ch. 7-B, §5.3, p. 784.	No limit on number of initial depositions; limits apply to redeposing	N/A	1 oral or written deposition
2	Deposition subpoenas duces tecum for business records. See ch. 8-B, §5, p. 963.	No limit	N/A	No limit. CCP §94(c).
3	Interrogatories, official form. See ch. 7-C, §5.2, p. 820.	No limit	2 before initial trial date set; 1 after. See ch. 7-C, §7.2, p. 825.	Combination of 35 written requests
4	Interrogatories, specially prepared. See ch. 7-C, §6.2, p. 822.	35; more than 35 with declaration		
5	Requests for admission. See ch. 7-D, §4.1, p. 837.	35; more than 35 with declaration	N/A	
6	Demands to produce. See ch. 7-E, §5.1, p. 849.	No limit	2 before initial trial date set; 1 after. See ch. 7-E, §6.2, p. 850.	
7	Demand for exam of personal-injury plaintiff. See ch. 7-F, §4.1.2, p. 858.	1 demand	N/A	N/A
8	Motions for medical exams. See ch. 7-F, §5, p. 860.	As permitted by court	N/A	As permitted by court. CCP §§94(d), 2032.310(a).

§4. MODIFYING DISCOVERY PROCEDURES

§4.1 Modifying discovery by stipulation. The parties can agree to modify the CDA's discovery procedures by stipulation. CCP §2016.030.

1. Written. The stipulation must be in writing to be enforceable. CCP §2016.030; *see, e.g., id.* §2024.060 (informal agreement to extend discovery period must be confirmed in writing). Oral agreements modifying discovery are not binding on the parties. *See id.* §§2016.030, 2024.060.

2. Who must agree. The stipulation must be agreed to by all parties affected by the modification. *See, e.g.*, CCP §2024.060 (agreement to extend discovery period). When a nonparty is affected by the modification, the nonparty must also agree. *See, e.g., id.* §2025.250(c) (nonparty organization can agree to more distant location for deposition than that provided in CDA).

3. What can be modified by stipulation. The stipulation can modify the discovery procedures for any discovery method listed in CCP §2019.010, unless the court prohibits the modification. CCP §2016.030. For example, the parties can agree to change the cutoffs or deadlines for discovery. See "Earlier cutoff by stipula-

tion," §5.2.3(1)(a), p. 748; "Later cutoff by stipulation," §5.2.3(2)(a), p. 749; "Changing discovery deadlines," §8.2, p. 755.

§4.2 Modifying discovery by court order. A party can move for a court order modifying the CDA's discovery procedures.

1. Type of motion.

(1) Noticed motion. Most requests to modify discovery procedures must be made by noticed motion. *See, e.g.*, ***St. Paul Fire & Mar. Ins. v. Superior Ct.*** (1st Dist.1984) 156 Cal.App.3d 82, 85-86 (court could not terminate or bar depositions without notice and hearing). Generally, when an order that affects the rights of an adverse party is sought, the request for the order must be made in a noticed motion. *Id.* at 85.

(2) Ex parte application. A request to modify a discovery procedure can be made in an ex parte application only if the order sought (1) is explicitly permitted by ex parte application or (2) is for an emergency or a noncontroversial issue. See "Ex Parte Practice," ch. 1-E, p. 39. The CDA explicitly permits ex parte orders under the provisions listed in chart 7-3, below.

7-3. CDA PROVISIONS FOR EX PARTE ORDERS

	Type of discovery	CDA provision for ex parte order for plaintiff to begin discovery during discovery hold	Miscellaneous CDA provisions for ex parte orders
1	Oral deposition	CCP §2025.210(b)	Order to stay deposition for decision on protective order. CCP §2025.270(d).
			Order to shorten or extend time to schedule deposition. CCP §2025.270(d).
			For out-of-state deposition, order to comply with other state's requirements for oral deposition. CCP §2026.010(f).
2	Interrogatories	CCP §2030.020(d)	Order to permit propounding and responding parties to serve copies of interrogatories and responses on fewer than all parties. CCP §§2030.080(b), 2030.260(c).
3	Demand to produce	CCP §2031.020(d)	N/A
4	Requests for admission	CCP §2033.020(d)	N/A

2. What can be modified by court order.

(1) Authorized modifications. Various provisions in the CDA authorize a court to modify discovery procedures. Examples include the following:

(a) Change discovery deadlines. The court can change the deadlines for discovery. See "Changing discovery deadlines," §8.2, p. 755.

(b) Extend discovery period. On the motion of any party, the court can extend or reopen the discovery period when a trial date is continued. CCP §2024.050(a); *see, e.g.*, ***Hernandez v. Superior Ct.*** (2d Dist.2004) 115 Cal.App.4th 1242, 1247-48 (court found that attorney's terminal illness during last weeks of discovery period was good cause to grant trial continuance and reopen discovery). See "Later cutoff by court order," §5.2.3(2)(b), p. 749.

(c) Change place for compliance. The court can change the place for compliance with a discovery request. *See* CCP §2025.420(b)(4) (change place for deposition), §2034.250(b)(4) (change place for production of expert reports). See "By motion," ch. 7-B, §9.6.2(2), p. 795; "Motion for protective order," ch. 7-I, §12.1, p. 914.

(d) Change deposition procedure. The court can change the procedures and conditions for an oral or written deposition on a motion for a protective order. CCP §§2025.420(b), 2028.070. See "Depositions," ch. 9-B, §2.2.1, p. 1025; "Relief Available Through Motion for Protective Order," chart 9-4, p. 1029.

(e) Change length of oral deposition. The court can allow oral depositions to exceed the seven-hour time limit imposed by CCP §2025.290(a). See "Length of oral deposition," ch. 7-B, §9.5, p. 793.

(f) Control sequence of discovery methods. The court can establish the sequence and timing of discovery on a party's good-cause motion for the convenience of the parties and the witnesses and in the interests of justice. CCP §2019.020(b); *e.g.*, ***Boston v. Penny Lane Ctrs., Inc.*** (2d Dist.2009) 170 Cal.App.4th 936, 952 (court can issue protective order under CCP §2034.250 requiring that all expert reports be produced by specified exchange date). However, the court cannot change a sequence or timeline established by statute unless the court is authorized by statute to do so. *See* ***Hernandez v. Superior Ct.*** (2d Dist.2003) 112 Cal.App.4th 285, 296-97; *see, e.g.*, CCP §2025.270(d) (on motion, court is authorized to shorten or extend time for scheduling deposition).

(2) Unauthorized modifications. Examples of discovery modifications the court cannot make include the following:

(a) Shorten discovery period. The court cannot shorten the discovery period. See "Not by court order," §5.2.3(1)(b), p. 748.

(b) Require unauthorized discovery. The court cannot require the parties to use a discovery method that is not specifically authorized under the CDA. Weil, *Civil Procedure Before Trial*, ¶8:12; *see CEB Discovery Practice*, §1.65 (use of "hybrid" discovery devices prohibited); *see, e.g.*, ***Hernandez***, 112 Cal.App.4th at 296-97 (court cannot order sequential disclosure of expert information because CDA requires simultaneous disclosure); ***Holm v. Superior Ct.*** (3d Dist.1986) 187 Cal.App.3d 1241, 1247 (although some statutes authorize courts to order corpses exhumed and autopsied, none of those statutes applied); ***Volkswagenwerk A.G. v. Superior Ct.*** (1st Dist.1981) 123 Cal.App.3d 840, 849 (court cannot make party require its employee to attend informal interviews), *abrogated on other grounds*, ***Societe Nationale Industrielle Aerospatiale v. U.S. Dist. Ct.*** (1987) 482 U.S. 522.

(3) Prevent unauthorized discovery. The court, on a motion for a protective order, can prevent a party from using an unauthorized discovery method that is outside the CDA. For example, in a personal-injury suit, the court granted a protective order to prevent a defendant-employer from forcing the plaintiff, its employee, to submit to extrajudicial discovery by threats of termination of employment. ***Pratt v. Union Pac. R.R.*** (3d Dist.2008) 168 Cal.App.4th 165, 181-82; *see also* CCP §2023.010(b) (sanctions can be imposed for using discovery methods in manner that does not comply with specified procedures). See "Motion for Protective Order," ch. 9-B, p. 1024.

§4.3 No modification by local rules. A court cannot modify discovery procedures by local rules. CRC 3.20(a).

§5. TIMING OF DISCOVERY

§5.1 When to initiate discovery.

1. Discovery before suit. A party can seek discovery before a suit is filed by filing a verified petition asking for permission to perpetuate testimony. See "Petition for Presuit Discovery," ch. 7-J, §3, p. 924.

2. Plaintiff's discovery.

(1) After plaintiff's discovery hold. A plaintiff cannot begin discovery until its discovery hold expires, unless it has the court's permission. *See* ***California Shellfish, Inc. v. United Shellfish Co.*** (1st Dist. 1997) 56 Cal.App.4th 16, 23 (discussing purpose of discovery hold). A "discovery hold" is the period of time the plaintiff must wait before it can make a discovery request after initiating the suit and serving the defendant. *See id.* Different types of discovery have different hold periods, and the hold periods are shorter in unlawful-detainer actions.

(a) Written discovery. The plaintiff can serve interrogatories, demands to produce, and requests for admission ten days after either the service of summons on the defendant to whom the discovery is directed or the appearance of that defendant, whichever occurs first. CCP §2030.020(b) (interrogatories), §2031.020(b) (demand to produce), §2033.020(b) (RFAs).

(b) Deposition. The plaintiff can serve a deposition notice 20 days after any defendant is served with summons or makes an appearance. CCP §2025.210(b).

(c) Unlawful-detainer action. In an unlawful-detainer action, the plaintiff can serve a written discovery request five days after either the service of the summons on the defendant to whom the discovery is directed or the appearance of that defendant, whichever occurs first. CCP §2030.020(c) (interrogatories), §2031.020(c) (demand to produce), §2033.020(c) (RFAs).

(2) During plaintiff's discovery hold. On the plaintiff's good-cause motion, with or without notice, the court can permit the plaintiff to begin discovery before the discovery hold expires.

(a) Written discovery. The plaintiff can ask the court to permit it to serve written discovery within ten days after either the service of summons on the defendant or the defendant's appearance. CCP §2030.020(d) (interrogatories), §2031.020(d) (demand to produce), §2033.020(d) (RFAs).

(b) Deposition. The plaintiff can ask the court to permit it to serve a deposition notice within 20 days after any defendant is served with summons or makes an appearance. CCP §2025.210(b).

3. Defendant's discovery.

(1) Written discovery. The defendant can serve written discovery at any time. CCP §2030.020(a) (interrogatories), §2031.020(a) (demand to produce), §2033.020(a) (RFAs).

(2) Demand for exam of personal-injury P. The defendant can serve a personal-injury plaintiff with a demand for a physical examination anytime after being served with suit or after making an appearance. CCP §2032.220(b). In other words, the defendant can demand an examination before filing pleadings and before the plaintiff's discovery hold expires. Weil, *Civil Procedure Before Trial*, ¶8:1527.

(3) Deposition. The defendant can serve a deposition notice anytime after being served with suit or after making an appearance, whichever occurs first. CCP §2025.210(a).

4. Expert discovery. The earliest a party can make a demand for the simultaneous exchange of expert-witness information is the date the court sets the initial trial date (not the initial trial date itself). CCP §2034.210; *CEB Discovery Practice*, §11.10.

§5.2 When to complete discovery. Discovery must be completed before the discovery period ends (i.e., before the discovery cutoff date). CCP §2024.020(a); *CEB Discovery Practice*, §2.20. Cutoffs for discovery requests and discovery motions can be extended by the parties' written stipulation or by court order, and the completion date for discovery is addressed at the initial case-management conference. See "Later discovery cutoff," §5.2.3(2), p. 748; "Initial Case-Management Conference," ch. 5-A, §8, p. 468. The rescheduling of the trial date does not extend or reopen the discovery period. ***Fairmont Ins. v. Superior Ct.*** (2000) 22 Cal.4th 245, 251; *see* CCP §2024.020(b) (reopen); ***Pelton-Shepherd Indus. v. Delta Packaging Prods.*** (3d Dist.2008) 165 Cal.App.4th 1568, 1587-88 (reopen). But an order granting a mistrial, new trial, or remand for a new trial following an appeal resets the discovery periods. *See* ***Fairmont Ins.***, 22 Cal.4th at 247. If a discovery cutoff falls on a weekend or a holiday, the parties have until the next day that is not a weekend or holiday to complete the discovery or to have a discovery motion heard. CCP §2016.060.

PRACTICE TIP

Do not confuse the terms "discovery cutoff" and "discovery deadline." "Discovery cutoff" (used here in §5.2) refers to the date by which all discovery in the case must be completed. "Discovery deadline" (used in "When to Respond to Discovery," §8, p. 754) refers to the date by which a particular discovery request must be answered.

1. Cutoff for discovery requests. The cutoff for discovery requests is the date by which discovery must be "completed." *See* CCP §2024.020(a). Most discovery requests are considered completed on the date the response is due, except for depositions, which are considered completed on the date the deposition begins. *Id.* §2024.010. The cutoff for discovery requests is determined by the type of discovery (e.g., interrogatories, depositions), the subject of the discovery (expert discovery or nonexpert discovery), and the initial trial date. *See id.* §§2024.020(a), 2024.030. The "initial trial date" is the first date the court assigns for the start of trial. ***Fairmont Ins.***, 22 Cal.4th at 250; ***Beverly Hosp. v. Superior Ct.*** (2d Dist.1993) 19 Cal.App.4th 1289, 1292.

(1) Cutoff for most discovery requests.

(a) Cutoff for written discovery. The cutoff for written discovery (i.e., interrogatories, requests for admission, and demands to produce) is 30 days before the initial trial date. CCP §2024.020(a). This means the discovery must be completed (request served and answered) at least 30 days before the initial trial date. *See CEB Discovery Practice*, §5.19; *see, e.g.*, ***Pelton-Shepherd Indus.***, 165 Cal.App.4th at 1573 (demand to produce was untimely because response was due three days after cutoff). Using the formula in "Calculating Cutoff for Discovery Requests," chart 7-4, p. 748, if the court sets the initial trial date for July 1, the discovery cutoff for written discovery is June 1.

(b) Cutoff for depositions. The cutoff for deposition proceedings is 30 days before the initial trial date. CCP §2024.020(a). Because a deposition is considered completed on the date the deposition begins, the deposition can start on the day before the cutoff and continue into the cutoff period. Weil, *Civil Procedure Before Trial*, ¶8:448. However, it is not a good idea to do this because there would be little time to resolve a dispute before the cutoff for discovery motions. See "Cutoff for most motions," §5.2.2(1), p. 748.

(c) Cutoff for demand for exam of personal-injury P. The cutoff to demand a physical examination of a personal-injury plaintiff is 30 days before the initial trial date. CCP §2024.020(a). Because an examination is considered complete on the day it is conducted, the examination must be scheduled before the cutoff. *See id.* §2024.010 (discovery is considered completed on day response is due or deposition begins).

(2) Cutoff for expert discovery. The cutoff for discovery proceedings regarding trial experts is 15 days before the initial trial date. CCP §2024.030.

(3) Cutoff for discovery in unlawful-detainer action. The cutoff for discovery in unlawful-detainer actions is five days before the date set for trial (which may not be the initial trial date set by the court). CCP §2024.040(b)(1) (generally), §2025.270(b) (oral depositions).

(4) Cutoff for discovery in judicial arbitration cases. The cutoff for discovery (except expert discovery) in cases that go to judicial arbitration is 15 days before the date set for the arbitration hearing. CRC 3.822(b); *CEB Discovery Practice*, §1.19; *see* CCP §2024.040(a); *CEB Discovery Practice*, §2.28. If the arbitration is vacated, discovery is automatically reopened and the new discovery cutoff depends on whether the case will be tried or arbitrated. *See* ***Roe v. Superior Ct.*** (4th Dist.1990) 224 Cal.App.3d 642, 644.

Chart 7-4, below, provides a formula for calculating the cutoff date for discovery.

PRACTICE TIP

In most cases, the parties are not required to calculate the discovery cutoffs because they are set by the trial court in the case-management order along with the initial trial date. When required to calculate them, the parties can use this formula.

7-4. CALCULATING CUTOFF FOR DISCOVERY REQUESTS		
From date in A count backward number of days in B to calculate date for C		
A	**B**	**C**
Insert initial trial date set by court. Date: ______________ ❶	Insert number of days for cutoff period for type of discovery at issue. 30 days ❷	Cutoff for discovery requests to be served and answered is: Date: ______________
❶ For an unlawful-detainer action, insert actual trial date. ❷ For discovery requests involving trial experts, substitute 15 days; for discovery requests in an unlawful-detainer action, substitute 5 days.		

2. Cutoff for discovery motions. The cutoff for discovery motions is the date by which the discovery motion must be "heard." *See* CCP §2024.020(a). If a party properly notices a discovery motion to be heard on or before the cutoff date, the party has a right to have the motion heard. ***Pelton-Shepherd Indus.***, 165 Cal.App.4th at 1586; *see* CCP §2024.020(a). If a party notices a discovery motion to be heard after the cutoff date, the court may or may not consider it. *See* ***Pelton-Shepherd Indus.***, 165 Cal.App.4th at 1586.

(1) Cutoff for most motions. The cutoff for the hearing on motions involving written discovery or depositions is 15 days before the initial trial date. CCP §2024.020(a); *CEB Procedure During Trial*, §2.10.

(2) Cutoff for expert motions. The cutoff for the hearing on discovery motions regarding designated trial experts is ten days before the initial trial date. CCP §2024.030; *CEB Procedure During Trial*, §2.10; Weil, *Civil Procedure Before Trial*, ¶8:447.

(3) Cutoff for unlawful-detainer discovery motions. The cutoff for the hearing on discovery motions in unlawful-detainer actions is five days before the date set for trial. CCP §2024.040(b)(1); *CEB Discovery Practice*, §1.71.

Chart 7-5, below, provides a formula for calculating the cutoff date for discovery motions.

7-5. CALCULATING CUTOFF FOR DISCOVERY MOTIONS		
From date in A count backward number of days in B to calculate date for C		
A	**B**	**C**
Insert initial trial date set by court. Date: ______________ ❶	Insert number of days for cutoff period for type of discovery at issue. 15 days ❷	Cutoff for discovery motions to be heard is: Date: ______________
❶ For an unlawful-detainer action, insert actual trial date. ❷ For discovery motions involving trial experts, substitute 10 days; for discovery motions in an unlawful-detainer action, substitute 5 days.		

3. Modifying discovery cutoffs.

(1) Earlier discovery cutoff.

(a) Earlier cutoff by stipulation. The parties can agree in writing to shorten the time for completing discovery. CCP §2016.030.

(b) Not by court order. The court cannot impose a cutoff that requires the parties to complete discovery more than 30 days before the initial trial date. *See* CCP §2024.020(a). But the court can extend or shorten the deadline for a particular discovery request based on a good-cause motion. See "Court order," §8.2.2, p. 756.

(2) Later discovery cutoff. When a party realizes it needs more time to serve a discovery request or discovery motion before the cutoff dates, the party must obtain either a written stipulation or a court order extending the discovery period.

(a) Later cutoff by stipulation. Parties can agree in writing to (1) extend the time to complete discovery proceedings, (2) hear a discovery motion closer to the initial trial date, or (3) reopen discovery after a new trial date has been set. CCP §2024.060. This type of stipulation will only affect the parties that consent to it. *See id.* See "Who must agree," §4.1.2, p. 743.

(b) Later cutoff by court order. The court can grant a motion to (1) extend the time to complete discovery proceedings, (2) hear a discovery motion closer to the initial trial date, or (3) reopen discovery after a new trial date has been set. CCP §2024.050(a). If a motion to extend or reopen discovery is made and set to be heard before the motion cutoff date, the party has a right to have it heard. *See* ***Pelton-Shepherd Indus.***, 165 Cal.App.4th at 1586. If the motion is not made by the motion cutoff date, the court can still hear it. *Id.*

[1] Meet-and-confer declaration. The moving party must comply with the requirements to meet and confer. CCP §2024.050(a). See "Meet-and-Confer Obligation," §10, p. 761.

[2] Good-cause factors. The moving party should address the factors that will be considered by the court in ruling on the motion, which include the following:

[a] Necessity. The necessity and reasons for the discovery. CCP §2024.050(b)(1); *see, e.g.,* ***Pelton-Shepherd Indus.***, 165 Cal.App.4th at 1589-90 (documents sought were only marginally relevant).

[b] Diligence. The moving party's diligence in seeking discovery or the hearing on a discovery motion. CCP §2024.050(b)(2); *see, e.g.,* ***Pelton-Shepherd Indus.***, 165 Cal.App.4th at 1589 (although P served answer to D's cross-complaint in 2003, P did not serve discovery demand until 2005, less than two months before initial trial date).

[c] Reasons. The reasons discovery was not completed or the discovery motion was not heard at an earlier date. CCP §2024.050(b)(2). For example, the death of a party or an attorney is considered good cause to grant a trial continuance and to reopen discovery. ***Hernandez v. Superior Ct.*** (2d Dist.2004) 115 Cal.App.4th 1242, 1247-48. However, a strategic decision to forgo discovery in favor of other trial strategies is not. *See* ***Cottini v. Enloe Med. Ctr.*** (3d Dist.2014) 226 Cal.App.4th 401, 420-21.

[d] Delay. The likelihood a later discovery cutoff will prevent the case from being tried on the date set for trial, interfere with the trial calendar, or prejudice any other party. CCP §2024.050(b)(3); *see* ***People v. Landau*** (4th Dist.2013) 214 Cal.App.4th 1, 26; *see also* ***Wagner v. Superior Ct.*** (4th Dist.1993) 12 Cal.App.4th 1314, 1320 (court should not have denied motion to extend discovery cutoff because no trial date had been set).

[e] Time. The length of time that elapsed between an earlier trial setting and the current trial date, if applicable. CCP §2024.050(b)(4); *see, e.g.,* ***Landau***, 214 Cal.App.4th at 26-27 (mental reexamination necessary after second mistrial when previous examination would have been a year old and presumably stale at third trial).

[f] Other relevant matters. The court can consider other relevant matters and is not limited to the factors listed above. *See* CCP §2024.050(b).

§6. WHEN TO SCHEDULE DISCOVERY

The time periods discussed below assume that the discovery is served by personal delivery in California. The periods are extended if the discovery is served by mail, fax, or overnight delivery or is served out of state. *See* CCP §1013 (extending response time when service is made by method other than personal delivery), §2016.050 (applying §1013 to any method of discovery under CDA). See "Add time for method of service," ch. 1-G, §6.1.4, p. 70.

NOTE

A subpoena cannot be served by mail or fax. See "Type of service," ch. 8-A, §9.1, p. 947. Any other type of discovery can be served by mail or fax. See "Methods of service," ch. 1-G, §5.1, p. 66.

§6.1 Scheduling party discovery.

1. Written discovery.

(1) Interrogatories & RFAs. The discovering party must select a date for securing answers to interrogatories and requests for admission that is at least 30 days after it serves them. *See* CCP §2030.260(a) (interrogatories), §2033.250(a) (RFAs).

(2) Demand to produce. The discovering party must select a date to produce documents and other things that is "reasonable" and at least 30 days after it serves the demand. CCP §2031.030(c)(2); *see id.* §2031.260(a).

2. Party depositions.

(1) Oral deposition. The discovering party must select a date for the oral deposition of a party (with or without documents) that is at least ten days after it serves the deposition. CCP §2025.270(a).

(2) Written deposition. The discovering party can select the date for taking a written deposition or can leave the date to be selected by the deposition officer. CCP §2028.020(b). Generally, it is not practical to select a date for a written deposition until all the questions, cross-questions, and objections have been exchanged by the parties. See "Selecting date & place for deposition," ch. 7-B, §10.8, p. 807.

3. Demand for exam of personal-injury P. The defendant must select a date for the physical examination of a personal-injury plaintiff that is at least 30 days after it serves the demand. *See* CCP §2032.220(c), (d).

4. Demand for expert information. The discovering party must select a date for the exchange of information about expert trial witnesses that is at least 50 days before the initial trial date or 20 days after it serves the demand, whichever is closer to the trial date. CCP §2034.230(b). See "Date for exchange," ch. 7-I, §6.5.3, p. 905.

5. Discovery in unlawful-detainer action. The time to comply with discovery requests in unlawful-detainer actions or other proceedings under CCP §§1159-1179a is substantially shorter than that for any other type of discovery.

(1) Interrogatories & RFAs. The discovering party must select a date for compliance with interrogatories and requests for admission that is at least five days after it serves them. *See* CCP §2030.260(b) (interrogatories), §2033.250(b) (RFAs).

(2) Demand to produce. The discovering party must select a date for compliance with a demand to produce documents and other things that is "reasonable" and at least five days after it serves the demand. CCP §2031.030(c)(2).

(3) Deposition. The discovering party must select a date for an oral deposition that is at least five days after it serves the deposition notice and no later than five days before trial. *See* CCP §2025.270(b).

§6.2 Scheduling nonparty discovery. All discovery from a nonparty must be conducted by service of a deposition subpoena. CCP §2020.010(b). Deposition subpoenas must be served personally on the nonparty; the subpoena cannot be served by mail, fax, or delivery to the nonparty's attorney, unless the nonparty agreed by written stipulation. See "Type of service," ch. 8-A, §9.1, p. 947.

1. Subpoena for oral deposition. To schedule the oral deposition of a nonparty, the discovering party must select a date for the deposition that (1) provides a reasonable time after the nonparty is personally served with the subpoena for the nonparty to locate and produce the things required by the subpoena (if production is required) and to travel to the place of the deposition (if attendance is required), and (2) is at least ten days after it serves the deposition notice on the parties. CCP §2020.220(a) (reasonable time), §2025.270(a) (ten days after service of notice). Unless the nonparty is required to produce voluminous documents or travel a considerable distance, ten days' notice is probably sufficient. *CEB Discovery Practice*, §5.65.

2. Subpoena for written deposition. To schedule the written deposition of a nonparty, the discovering party must select a date for the deposition that (1) provides a reasonable time after the nonparty is personally served with the subpoena for the nonparty to locate and produce the things required by the subpoena (if production is required) and to travel to the place of the deposition, and (2) is at least ten days after it serves the deposition notice and all questions (direct, cross, redirect, recross) on the parties. *See* CCP §2020.220(a) (reasonable time); *CEB Discovery Practice*, §5.172 (copies to all parties). Unless the nonparty is required to produce voluminous documents, ten days' notice is probably sufficient. *CEB Discovery Practice*, §5.65.

3. Subpoena for business records. To schedule the production of business records for copying from a nonparty, the discovering party must select a date for production that (1) is at least 15 days after it personally serves the nonparty with the subpoena or 20 days after the date the subpoena was issued, whichever is later, and (2) is at least ten days after it serves a copy of the subpoena (deposition notice is not necessary) on the parties. See "Deposition subpoena for business records," ch. 8-A, §7.1.3, p. 944.

4. Subpoena for personal records. To schedule discovery that requires a nonparty to produce the personal records of a consumer, see "When to set deposition for production of personal records," ch. 8-D, §8.2.1, p. 985.

§6.3 Latest date to schedule discovery. Discovery must be completed before the discovery cutoff date. See "When to complete discovery," §5.2, p. 746. To calculate the latest date to serve discovery before the cutoff, the discovering party should start with the discovery cutoff date and count backward for the total number of days the responding party has to respond to the particular type of discovery. See "Count backward," ch. 1-G, §6.2.1(2), p. 72.

PRACTICE TIP

Because the date calculated in Chart 7-6, below, allows only 15 days to resolve a discovery dispute (e.g., motion to compel) before the cutoff for discovery motions, the discovering party should count backward several more days (15 to 20) to provide additional time to resolve a discovery motion, should one be necessary.

Chart 7-6, below, provides a formula for calculating the latest date to serve a discovery request.

7-6. CALCULATING LATEST DATE TO SERVE DISCOVERY REQUESTS

From date in A count backward number of days in B and C to calculate date for D

A	B	C	D
Insert cutoff for discovery requests from column C, chart 7-4, p. 748. Date: ________	Insert number of days for responding to the discovery request. ________ days*	Insert number of days for method of service of discovery request (e.g., 0 for personal service, 5 for mail in California). ________ days	Latest date to serve discovery requests is: Date: ________

* Insert 30 days for interrogatories, demands to produce, or RFAs. For response times for other discovery, see "Deadlines to Respond to Discovery," chart 7-9, p. 754.

§6.4 Latest date to make discovery motion. The latest date to file and serve a discovery motion is 16 *court* days before the hearing, which must take place on or before the cutoff for motions (15 calendar days before the initial trial date). *See* CCP §§1005(b), 2024.020(a). For example, if the cutoff for discovery motions is October 31, 2014, the motion must be heard on or before that date. The motion must be filed and served 16 court days before October 31. Counting 16 court days before October 31 (skipping all holidays and weekends) means the discovery motion must be filed and served on October 9, 2014.

Chart 7-7, below, provides a formula for calculating the latest date to file and serve a discovery motion.

7-7. CALCULATING LATEST DATE TO MAKE DISCOVERY MOTIONS		
From date in A count backward number of days in B to calculate date for C		
A	B	C
Insert cutoff date for discovery motions from column C, chart 7-5, p. 748. Date: ____________	Calculate number of calendar days in 16 *court* days, counting backward from date in column A, and insert here.* ________ days	Latest date to file and serve discovery motion is: Date: ____________
* The number of calendar days in 16 court days varies, depending on the holidays and weekends that fall within the 16 court days. See "Court days," ch. 1-F, §5.1.3(1)(b), p. 54.		

§7. MAKING DISCOVERY REQUESTS

§7.1 Sequence for discovery. The discovery procedures provided by the CDA can be used in any sequence, except when the sequence is controlled by a Judicial Council rule, local court rule, or local uniform written policy. CCP §2019.020(a); *see* ***Sinaiko Healthcare Consulting, Inc. v. Pacific Healthcare Consultants*** (2d Dist.2007) 148 Cal.App.4th 390, 402. Based on a good-cause motion, the court can establish the sequence and timing of discovery for the convenience of the parties and witnesses and in the interests of justice. CCP §2019.020(b). For a detailed discussion of the sequence of discovery, see *CEB Discovery Practice*, §§2.56-2.65, and Weil, *Civil Procedure Before Trial*, ¶¶8:402-8:412.1. The list below divides discovery into two stages that are appropriate in many cases.

1. **First stage.** The following discovery procedures can be used to obtain background information:

- Form interrogatories. See "Official Form Interrogatories," ch. 7-C, §5, p. 820.
- Special interrogatories. See "Specially Prepared Interrogatories," ch. 7-C, §6, p. 822.
- Requests for admission. See "Requests for Admission," ch. 7-D, p. 836.
- Demand to produce and copy documents from a party. See "Demands to Produce," ch. 7-E, p. 845. Some treatises recommend serving a demand to produce before any other discovery because it allows a party to examine the physical evidence before asking questions. Weil, *Civil Procedure Before Trial*, ¶8:1434.
- Subpoena documents from a nonparty. See "Subpoenas," ch. 8, p. 929.
- Deposition on written questions. See "Deposition on Written Questions," ch. 7-B, §10, p. 804.

2. **Second stage.** Once enough background information has been obtained, the following discovery procedures can be used to commit the opposing party to specific contentions and "freeze" the testimony of witnesses. *See CEB Discovery Practice*, §2.56.

- Oral depositions. See "Oral Deposition," ch. 7-B, §9, p. 788.
- Supplemental interrogatories. See "Supplemental Interrogatories," ch. 7-C, §7, p. 825.
- Demand to exchange expert information. See "Demand for Exchange of Expert Information," ch. 7-I, §6, p. 904. The CDA restricts the discovery of retained trial experts until late in the litigation, after most of the fact issues have been subjected to discovery.

§7.2 Form of discovery requests. The form and structure for discovery requests to parties are as follows:

NOTE

The form for deposition subpoenas is controlled by the Judicial Council, not by the rules set out below. The mandatory Judicial Council forms for subpoenas can be found at the California Courts website, www.courts.ca.gov/forms.htm.

1. In writing. A request for discovery must be in writing. CCP §2025.220(a) (deposition notice), §2030.010(a) (interrogatories), §2033.010 (RFAs), §2034.230(a) (demand for exchange of expert information). Although some CDA provisions do not expressly state that the request must be in writing, it is implied. *See, e.g., id.* §2031.030(a) (each set of demands to produce must be numbered), §2032.220(e) (demand for exam of personal-injury P must be served).

2. First paragraph. In the first paragraph, immediately below the title of the case, the request must include the following:

(1) Identity of parties. The identities of the discovering party and the responding party. CCP §2030.060(b) (interrogatories), §2031.030(b) (demand to produce), §2033.060(b) (RFAs); CRC 3.1000(a)(1), (a)(2) (supplemental requests).

(2) Nature of document. The nature of the document and the set number (e.g., second set of requests for admission). *See* CCP §2030.060(b) (interrogatories), §2031.030(b) (demand to produce), §2033.060(b) (RFAs); CRC 3.1000(a)(3), (a)(4) (supplemental requests). Each set of discovery requests must be numbered consecutively. CCP §2030.060(a) (interrogatories), §2031.030(a) (demand to produce), §2033.060(a) (RFAs).

3. Deadline to comply. The request should include the deadline to comply, whether it is a specific date (e.g., deposition will be taken on September 15) or the number of days after service of the request within which the responding party must serve its response (e.g., interrogatories must be answered within 30 days after the date of service). *See CEB Discovery Practice*, §5.216 (form for deposition notice), §7.144 (form for interrogatories). See "When to Respond to Discovery," §8, p. 754.

4. Preface or instruction. Interrogatories and requests for admission can include a preface or instruction only if it has been approved under CCP §§2033.710-2033.740. *See* CCP §2030.060(d) (interrogatories), §2033.060(d) (RFAs); Judicial Council Forms, forms DISC-001–DISC-005 (forms for interrogatories), form DISC-020 (form for RFAs); *CEB Discovery Practice*, §7.9 (discussion of forms).

5. Structure of requests.

(1) Separate. Each request in each set must be stated separately. CCP §2030.060(c) (interrogatories), §2031.030(c) (demand to produce), §2033.060(c) (RFAs).

(2) Numbered or lettered. Each request in the set must be identified by number or letter (e.g., Interrogatory No. 1 or Interrogatory A). CCP §2030.060(c) (interrogatories), §2031.030(c) (demand to produce), §2033.060(c) (RFAs).

(3) Self-contained. Each interrogatory question and request for admission must be full and complete in and of itself. See "Self-contained," ch. 7-C, §6.4.3(3), p. 824; "Self-contained," ch. 7-D, §4.3.4(2), p. 837.

6. Attorney's signature. The CDA does not specifically require that all discovery requests be signed by the attorney (or pro per party) making the request. However, discovery requests drafted by the attorney are customarily signed by the attorney. *See* Thomas, *Courtroom Handbook*, §21:131 (CDA does not require demand to produce to be signed by attorney, but most are); Weil, *Civil Procedure Before Trial*, ¶8:1003 (interrogatories are customarily signed by attorney even though signature is not required by statute); *cf.* ***Elmore v. Tingley*** (3d Dist.1926) 78 Cal.App. 460, 468 (although not expressly provided for by CCP §454, demand for itemized account should be signed). One well-known collection of sample discovery forms includes signature blocks for the attorney for many types of discovery

even though the CDA does not require them. *E.g.*, *CEB Discovery Practice*, §5.216 (form for deposition notice), §7.144 (form for specially prepared interrogatories), §8.123 (form for demand to produce), §9.100 (form for RFAs), §10.79 (form for demand for exam of personal-injury P), §11.69 (form for demand to exchange expert information).

§7.3 How to describe things to be produced. A party can require things to be produced by a deposition subpoena (nonparty), a deposition notice (party), or a demand to produce (party). The standard for describing the things to be produced depends on the type of discovery method used for production. Chart 7-8, below, summarizes the different standards.

7-8. PROPER DESCRIPTION OF THINGS TO BE PRODUCED

		Each individual item must be described—	Each category of items must be described—	CCP	Cross-reference
1	Deposition subpoena	Specifically	With reasonable particularity	§2020.510(a)(2)	See ch. 8-A, §5.2.1, p. 940
2	Deposition notice	With reasonable particularity	With reasonable particularity	§2025.220(a)(4)	See ch. 7-B, §9.2.4(3), p. 791
3	Demand to produce	Specifically	With reasonable particularity	§2031.030(c)(1)	See ch. 7-E, §5.3.3(1), p. 849

§7.4 How to serve discovery. See "Serving discovery," §13.1, p. 769.

§7.5 How to compel discovery. See "Resolving Discovery Disputes," §14, p. 771.

§8. WHEN TO RESPOND TO DISCOVERY

The response deadlines outlined below assume that the discovery is served by personal delivery. The deadlines are extended if the discovery is served by mail, fax, or overnight delivery or is served out of state. *See* CCP §1013 (extending response time when service is made by method other than personal delivery), §2016.050 (applying §1013 to any method of discovery under CDA). See "Add time for method of service," ch. 1-G, §6.2.1(5), p. 72.

§8.1 Deadlines to respond to discovery. The CDA uses the term "respond to discovery" to include both the deadline for objections and the deadline to comply with the discovery request. The deadlines to object and comply are the same for interrogatories and requests for admission. For other types of discovery, the deadlines to object and comply are different, with the deadline to object being the earlier of the two. Chart 7-9, below, summarizes the deadlines to object and comply with discovery requests.

7-9. DEADLINES TO RESPOND TO DISCOVERY

		Deadline to object	Deadline to comply
1	Interrogatories	• Object and answer within 30 days after service of interrogatories on RP. CCP §2030.260(a). • In UD actions, object and answer within 5 days after service of interrogatories on RP. *Id.* §2030.260(b).	
2	Requests for admission	• Object and answer within 30 days after service of requests for admission on RP. CCP §2033.250(a). • In UD actions, object and answer within 5 days after service of requests for admission on RP. *Id.* §2033.250(b).	
3	Demand to produce	• Object within 30 days after service of demand on RP. CCP §2031.260(a). • In UD actions, object within 5 days after service of demand on RP. *Id.* §2031.260(b).	• Produce on date set by DP, which must be at least 30 days after service of demand on RP. CCP §2031.030(c)(2). • In UD actions, produce on date set by DP, which must be at least 5 days after service of demand on RP. *Id.*

7-9. DEADLINES TO RESPOND TO DISCOVERY (CONTINUED)

		Deadline to object	Deadline to comply
4	Oral deposition of RP or its related witness	• Object to defective deposition notice at least 3 days before deposition. CCP §2025.410(a). • Object to errors and irregularities and failure to answer or produce before, during, or after deposition. *Id.* §2025.460(b). • Move to quash within reasonable time before deposition. *See id.* §2025.410(c). • Move for protective order before, during, or after deposition. *Id.* §2025.420(a).	• Attend deposition on date set by DP, which must be at least 10 days after service of deposition notice. CCP §2025.270(a). • In UD actions, attend deposition on date set by DP, which must be at least 5 days after service of deposition notice but no later than 5 days before trial. *Id.* §2025.270(b).
5	Written deposition of RP or its related witness	• Object to questions within 15 days after service of notice and questions on RP. CCP §2028.040(a). • Object to defective deposition notice at least 3 days before deposition. *Id.* §2025.410(a). • Move to quash within reasonable time before deposition. *See id.* §2025.410(c). • Move for protective order before, during, or after deposition. *See id.* §2025.420(a).	Attend deposition on date set by DP or deposition officer. CCP §2028.020(b).
6	Demand for exam of personal-injury plaintiff	Object within 20 days after service of demand on plaintiff. CCP §2032.230.	Appear for exam on date set by defendant, which must be at least 30 days after service of demand on plaintiff. CCP §2032.220(d).
7	Demand for expert information	Move for protective order promptly after demand. CCP §2034.250(a).	Provide information on date set by DP, which must be at least 50 days before initial trial date or 20 days after DP serves demand on RP, whichever is closer to trial date. CCP §2034.230(b).

DP = discovering party
RP = responding party
UD = unlawful detainer
The deadlines above assume that the discovery request was personally served on the RP.

§8.2 Changing discovery deadlines. The parties can change discovery deadlines by written stipulation or by court order.

1. Stipulation. The parties can agree to change discovery deadlines by written stipulation. *See* CCP §2016.030 (parties can modify procedures for any method of discovery listed in CCP §2019.010).

(1) Written discovery. The parties can agree to extend the deadline to respond to interrogatories, demands to produce, and requests for admission (collectively, "written discovery") by informal agreement but must confirm it in writing and specify the extended date. *See* CCP §2030.270(b) (interrogatories), §2031.270(b) (demand to produce), §2033.260(b) (RFAs).

(a) Parties to stipulation. The discovering party and the responding party can stipulate to extend the response deadline for written discovery beyond the deadline provided in the CDA. CCP §2030.270(a) (interrogatories), §2031.270(a) (demand to produce), §2033.260(a) (RFAs).

(b) Some or all requests. The parties can agree to extend the response deadline for an entire set of written discovery requests or for only some of the requests in a set. CCP §2030.270(a) (interrogatories), §2031.270(a) (demand to produce), §2033.260(a) (RFAs).

(c) Type of responses. The parties can agree to limit the type of responses allowed by the extended deadline. CCP §2030.270(c) (interrogatories), §2031.270(c) (demand to produce), §2033.260(c) (RFAs). If the stipulation does not expressly limit the type of responses, the responding party has the right to make any response permitted for that type of discovery. *Id.* §2030.270(c) (interrogatories), §2031.270(c) (demand to produce), §2033.260(c) (RFAs). For example, if the stipulation provides that the responding party cannot answer any of the interrogatories at the extended deadline by identifying and producing documents instead of answering, that limitation is enforceable. *See id.* §§2030.230, 2030.270(c).

(d) Notice to other parties. For requests for admission, the responding party must serve notice of the stipulation on all other parties who were served with a copy of the request. CCP §2033.260(d).

(2) Depositions. The parties can agree to change the date and time to take a deposition. *See* CCP §2016.030.

(3) Demand for exam of personal-injury P. The parties can agree to extend or shorten the time for a personal-injury plaintiff to serve a statement of compliance with a demand for a physical examination. *See* CCP §2016.030.

(4) Demand to exchange expert-witness information. The parties can agree to change the date and time to exchange expert-witness information. *See* CCP §2016.030.

2. Court order. On a party's motion, the court can extend or shorten the deadlines for the following types of discovery:

(1) Written discovery. The court can extend or shorten the time periods for responding to written discovery. CCP §2030.260(a) (interrogatories), §2031.260(a) (demand to produce), §2033.250(a) (RFAs).

(2) Oral depositions. The court can, on the motion or ex parte application of any party or deponent, for any good cause shown, (1) shorten or extend the time for scheduling an oral deposition or (2) stay its taking until the determination of a motion for protective order. CCP §2025.270(d); *see also id.* §2025.420(b) (listing directions court can include in protective order relating to deposition). See "Motion for Protective Order," ch. 9-B, p. 1024.

(3) Written depositions. The court can extend or shorten the time periods for the exchange of cross-, redirect, and recross-questions on a showing of good cause. CCP §2028.030(e).

(4) Unlawful-detainer action. The court can extend or shorten the time for discovery in unlawful-detainer actions. CCP §2025.270(b), (d) (oral deposition), §2030.260(b) (interrogatories), §2031.260(b) (demand to produce), §2033.250(b) (RFAs). A motion to extend or shorten the time for scheduling an oral deposition requires a showing of good cause. *Id.* §2025.270(d).

(5) Demand for exam of personal-injury P. The court can shorten the time period between the service of a demand for a physical examination of a personal-injury plaintiff and the date scheduled for the examination. CCP §2032.220(d). The court can also extend or shorten the time for responding to the demand. *Id.* §2032.230(b).

(6) Demand to exchange expert-witness information. The court can extend or shorten the time for exchanging expert-witness information on a showing of good cause. CCP §2034.250(b)(2).

(7) Judicial arbitration. The court can extend the time for completing discovery in a judicial arbitration case on a showing of good cause. CRC 3.822(b).

§9. HOW TO RESPOND TO DISCOVERY REQUESTS

§9.1 Duties. A party and its attorney have certain duties in responding to discovery requests.

1. Investigate. The party has a general duty to conduct a reasonable investigation to obtain information that is responsive to discovery requests. ***Regency Health Servs. v. Superior Ct.*** (2d Dist.1998) 64 Cal.App.4th

1496, 1504; *see* CCP §2030.220(a) (interrogatory response must include information reasonably available to party), §2031.230 (demand-to-produce response must be based on diligent search and reasonable inquiry), §2033.220(a) (RFA response must be based on information reasonably available); *see, e.g.*, ***Jones v. Superior Ct.*** (1st Dist. 1981) 119 Cal.App.3d 534, 552-53 (P required to ask her mother for information to answer interrogatories); ***Chodos v. Superior Ct.*** (2d Dist.1963) 215 Cal.App.2d 318, 323 (D required to make reasonable investigation to determine whether to admit or deny RFAs). This duty requires a party to search all sources under its control for responsive information. ***Regency Health***, 64 Cal.App.4th at 1504; *see* ***Deyo v. Kilbourne*** (2d Dist.1978) 84 Cal.App.3d 771, 782.

2. Disclose & produce. The party has a general duty to disclose information and produce things known to it that are responsive to a discovery request. ***Regency Health***, 64 Cal.App.4th at 1504; *see also* ***Smith v. Superior Ct.*** (3d Dist.1961) 189 Cal.App.2d 6, 12 (information known only to party's attorney is within knowledge of party and should be disclosed).

(1) Actual possession. The party must produce things in its actual possession. "Actual possession" means direct physical control over property. *Black's Law Dictionary* 1351 (10th ed. 2014).

(2) Custody or control. The party must disclose information and produce things from all sources under its custody or control. *See, e.g.*, CCP §2031.010 (demand to produce things in party's possession, custody, or control), §2032.020 (demand to produce person in party's custody or control for medical examination); ***Smith***, 189 Cal.App.2d at 12 (D must disclose identity of witnesses even if known only by D's attorney); ***Clark v. Superior Ct.*** (1st Dist.1960) 177 Cal.App.2d 577, 579 (D must disclose information in its liability insurer's possession). A party cannot plead ignorance about information it can obtain from sources under its control. ***Gordon v. Superior Ct.*** (2d Dist.1984) 161 Cal.App.3d 157, 167; ***Deyo***, 84 Cal.App.3d at 782. Although an organization selects the person who responds to written discovery on its behalf, it has a duty to obtain information from all sources under its control, not just from the person who signs the response. ***Castaline v. City of L.A.*** (2d Dist.1975) 47 Cal.App.3d 580, 588 n.7.

§9.2 Response options. Chart 7-10, below, outlines the options for responding to the various types of discovery requests.

7-10. OPTIONS FOR RESPONDING TO DISCOVERY

	To respond to—	Written objections?	Object by motion—	Other type of responses	How to comply
1	Notice of oral deposition of party	Yes. See ch. 7-B, §9.9.1, p. 796.	For protective order. See ch. 7-B, §12.1, p. 808. To quash notice and stay deposition. See ch. 9-C, §4, p. 1042.		Attend and produce. See ch. 7-B, §9.13, p. 800.
2	Notice of deposition on written questions	Yes. See ch. 7-B, §10.6.1, p. 806.	For protective order. See ch. 7-B, §10.6.2, p. 806. To sustain objections to form of questions. See ch. 7-B, §12.7, p. 809.	Serve cross-questions. See ch. 7-B, §10.5, p. 805.	Attend and produce. See ch. 7-B, §10.10, p. 807.
3	Interrogatories	Yes. See ch. 7-C, §8.3.4, p. 829.	For protective order. See ch. 9-B, p. 1024.	Deny having sufficient knowledge to answer. Exercise option to produce documents. See ch. 7-C, §8.3, p. 826.	Serve answers. See ch. 7-C, §8.3.1, p. 826.

7-10. OPTIONS FOR RESPONDING TO DISCOVERY (CONTINUED)					
To respond to—		Written objections?	Object by motion—	Other type of responses	How to comply
4	Requests for admission	Yes. See ch. 7-D, §5.3.2, p. 839.	For protective order. See ch. 7-D, §6.1.1, p. 840.		Serve answers. See ch. 7-D, §5.3.1, p. 838.
5	Demand to produce	Yes. See ch. 7-E, §7.3.3, p. 852; ch. 7-H, §8.2.1(1)(c), p. 888.	For protective order. See ch. 7-E, §9.1, p. 853; ch. 7-H, §12.1, p. 893.	Serve statement of inability to comply. See ch. 7-E, §7.3.2, p. 851; ch. 7-H, §8.2.1(1)(b), p. 888.	Serve statement of compliance. See ch. 7-E, §7.3.1, p. 851; ch. 7-H, §8.2.1(1)(a), p. 888.
6	Demand for exam of personal-injury plaintiff	Yes. See ch. 7-F, §4.2.1(3)(c), p. 860.	For protective order. See ch. 7-F, §8.1, p. 867.	Agree to exam with modifications. See ch. 7-F, §4.2.1(3)(b), p. 859.	Serve statement of compliance. See ch. 7-F, §4.2.1(3)(a), p. 859.
7	Demand for exchange of expert information	No. See ch. 7-I, §7, p. 906.	For protective order. See ch. 7-I, §7.3, p. 909.	Serve statement that party has no experts. See ch. 7-I, §7.1, p. 907.	Produce expert information. See ch. 7-I, §7.2, p. 907.
8	Deposition subpoena for nonparty discovery	Yes. See ch. 7-H, §8.2.2(1)(b), p. 888; ch. 8-E, §2.2.3, p. 998.	For protective order. See ch. 9-B, p. 1024. To quash subpoena. See ch. 9-C, §3, p. 1038.	Oral objections at deposition. See ch. 7-H, §8.2.2(1)(d), p. 888.	Attend and produce. See ch. 7-B, §9.13, p. 800; ch. 7-H, §8.2.2(1)(a), p. 888.

§9.3 Form of response. The form for discovery responses is as follows:

1. In writing. A response to a request for discovery must be in writing. CCP §2025.410(a) (deposition notice), §2030.210(a) (interrogatories), §2032.230(a) (demand for physical examination of personal-injury P), §2033.210(a) (RFAs). Although some CDA provisions do not expressly require a discovery response to be in writing, it is implied. *See, e.g., id.* §2031.250(a) (response to demand to produce must be signed).

2. First paragraph. In the first paragraph, immediately below the title of the case, the response must include the following:

(1) Identity of parties. The identities of the discovering party and the responding party. CCP §2030.210(b) (interrogatories), §2031.210(b) (demand to produce), §2033.210(c) (RFAs); CRC 3.1000(a)(1), (a)(2) (supplemental responses).

(2) Nature of document. Each set of responses must be identified by the nature of the document and the set number (e.g., response to second set of requests for admission, supplemental response to first set of interrogatories). *See* CCP §2030.210(b) (interrogatories), §2031.210(b) (demand to produce), §2033.210(c) (RFAs); CRC 3.1000(a)(3), (a)(4) (supplemental responses).

3. Form of answers & objections.

(1) Text of request not required. The responding party is not required to reproduce the text of the request as part of the response. CCP §2030.210(c) (interrogatories), §2031.210(c) (demand to produce), §2033.210(d) (RFAs); CRC 3.1000(b) (supplemental responses).

(2) Separately stated. Each answer or objection must be stated separately. CCP §2030.210(a) (interrogatories), §2031.210(a) (demand to produce), §2033.210(a) (RFAs); *see* CRC 3.1000(b) (supplemental responses).

(3) Corresponding numbers. Each answer or objection in the response must have the same identifying number or letter and be in the same sequence as the corresponding discovery request. CCP §2030.210(c) (interrogatories), §2031.210(c) (demand to produce), §2033.210(d) (RFAs); CRC 3.1000(b) (supplemental response, amended answer, or further response).

§9.4 Signatures & verification.

1. Party's verified signature. A party can verify its discovery response with a declaration or an affidavit. See "Declaration vs. affidavit," ch. 1-B, §4.1, p. 19. The responding party's verified signature on a response to discovery is a declaration that it has disclosed all the information available to it. *See* ***Deyo v. Kilbourne*** (2d Dist.1978) 84 Cal.App.3d 771, 782 (interrogatory answers). The responding party must review the response before verifying the discovery to ensure that the answers are true. *See, e.g.*, ***Drociak v. State Bar*** (1991) 52 Cal.3d 1085, 1087, 1090 (attorney violated ethics rules when he had clients presign verifications of interrogatory answers before answers were drafted).

(1) When party's verified signature required. The CDA requires the following discovery responses that contain answers (i.e., fact-specific information) to be signed by the responding party under oath: (1) interrogatories, (2) demands to produce, and (3) requests for admission. CCP §2030.250(a) (interrogatories), §2031.250(a) (demand to produce), §2033.240(a) (RFAs). If the response contains only objections, the party is not required to sign it. *Id.* §2030.250(a) (interrogatories), §2031.250(a) (demand to produce), §2033.240(a) (RFAs).

(2) Effect of party's failure to sign or verify. When a party does not sign a response under oath as required, the answers in the response are considered no response at all or as if they were served after the deadline to respond. *See, e.g.*, ***Garber & Assocs. v. Eskandarian*** (2d Dist.2007) 150 Cal.App.4th 813, 817 n.4 (unverified answers to interrogatories); ***Food 4 Less Supermkts., Inc. v. Superior Ct.*** (2d Dist.1995) 40 Cal.App.4th 651, 657-58 (unverified response to demand to produce); ***Appleton v. Superior Ct.*** (3d Dist.1988) 206 Cal.App.3d 632, 635-36 (unverified response to RFAs). If the responding party serves answers that are not verified, the discovering party can move to compel and move for sanctions. *See* ***Food 4 Less***, 40 Cal.App.4th at 657-58; ***Appleton***, 206 Cal.App.3d at 633-34. The lack of a party's verification on a response does not affect any objections in the response, because objections do not need to be verified. *E.g.*, ***Food 4 Less***, 40 Cal.App.4th at 657-58 & n.5 (demand to produce).

(3) Who must sign for party.

(a) Natural person.

[1] Party. If the responding party is a natural person, the response must be signed under oath by the party. CCP §2030.250(a) (interrogatories), §2031.250(a) (demand to produce), §2033.240(a) (RFAs). The term "party" includes a party's guardian ad litem. *See* ***Regency Health Servs. v. Superior Ct.*** (2d Dist.1998) 64 Cal.App.4th 1496, 1504-05. A party suing under a fictitious name can verify the response by signing with the fictitious name. ***Doe v. Superior Ct.*** (2d Dist.2011) 194 Cal.App.4th 750, 754; ***Doe v. Lincoln Unified Sch. Dist.*** (1st Dist.2010) 188 Cal.App.4th 758, 767. See "Doe plaintiffs," ch. 3-C, §2.3.1(7)(a), p. 209.

[2] Not party's attorney. The party's attorney cannot sign discovery answers on the party's behalf, even if the party is unavailable (e.g., out of the country) when they are due. *See* ***Food 4 Less***, 40 Cal.App.4th at 657 (demand to produce); ***Steele v. Totah*** (1st Dist.1986) 180 Cal.App.3d 545, 550 (RFAs).

(b) Organization.

[1] Organization's officers or agents. If the responding party is a public or private corporation, partnership, association, or governmental agency, the response must be signed under oath by one of its officers or agents on its behalf. CCP §2030.250(b) (interrogatories), §2031.250(b) (demand to produce), §2033.240(b) (RFAs). The responding party, not the discovering party, selects the officer or agent to sign the response. *See* ***Mowry v. Superior Ct.*** (3d Dist.1962) 202 Cal.App.2d 229, 234-35, *disapproved on other grounds*, ***San Diego P.A.***

v. Superior Ct. (1962) 58 Cal.2d 194. The organization has the duty to collect information for its responses from all sources under its control, even if the information is not personally known to the officer or agent who signs the answer. ***Castaline v. City of L.A.*** (2d Dist.1975) 47 Cal.App.3d 580, 588 n.7.

[2] Not organization's attorney. An organization's attorney who is an officer or agent of the organization should not sign answers to interrogatories, demands for production, or requests for admission under oath on behalf of the organization. *See* CCP §2030.250(b) (interrogatories), §2031.250(b) (demand to produce), §2033.240(b) (RFAs). If she does, the organization waives any attorney-client privilege and work-product protection in later discovery from that attorney regarding the identity of the sources of the information contained in the response. ***Melendrez v. Superior Ct.*** (2d Dist.2013) 215 Cal.App.4th 1343, 1351; *see* CCP §2030.250(b) (interrogatories), §2031.250(b) (demand to produce), §2033.240(b) (RFAs).

2. Attorney's signature. The CDA requires the following discovery responses that contain objections to be signed by the party's attorney: (1) interrogatories, (2) demands to produce, and (3) requests for admission. CCP §2030.250(c) (interrogatories), §2031.250(c) (demand to produce), §2033.240(c) (RFAs). The attorney's signature is not verified. *See* ***Food 4 Less***, 40 Cal.App.4th at 657 (no reason to verify objections).

3. Signature not required. Although it is customary for attorneys to sign all discovery responses, the CDA does not require any signature on the following:

(1) Response to a demand for a physical examination of a personal-injury plaintiff. *See* CCP §2032.230. *But see CEB Discovery Practice*, §10.80 (form for response to demand for exam of personal-injury P contains signature block for attorney).

(2) Objections to a deposition notice. *See* CCP §2025.410.

§9.5 Amending & supplementing responses.

1. Amending responses.

(1) Interrogatories. Without leave of court, a party can serve an amended answer to interrogatories that includes information recently discovered, inadvertently omitted, or mistakenly stated in the initial response. CCP §2030.310(a). See "Amending answers," ch. 7-C, §8.7, p. 832.

(2) RFAs. By noticed motion, a party can move to withdraw or amend its response to requests for admission. CCP §2033.300(a). See "Motion to withdraw or amend admission," ch. 7-D, §6.1.3, p. 840.

(3) Expert-witness lists. By noticed motion, a party who timely exchanged expert information can move to augment or amend its expert-witness list. CCP §2034.610(a)(1). See "Motion to augment designation or amend declaration," ch. 7-I, §12.6, p. 918.

2. Supplementing responses.

(1) No general duty to supplement. Although there is no general duty under the CDA to supplement discovery responses, a responding party should supplement when new information is acquired. *See* ***Biles v. Exxon Mobil Corp.*** (1st Dist.2004) 124 Cal.App.4th 1315, 1328; ***Guzman v. General Motors Corp.*** (4th Dist.1984) 154 Cal.App.3d 438, 443; *CEB Discovery Practice*, §7.72. If it does not, and later it becomes known that the party had information it did not disclose, the court could construe this as an attempt to conceal facts about the case and impose sanctions. *CEB Discovery Practice*, §7.72; *see* ***Guzman***, 154 Cal.App.3d at 443 n.4. A party cannot create a duty to supplement its discovery request by stating in its request that the responding party must supplement. *See* CCP §2030.060(g); ***Smith v. Superior Ct.*** (3d Dist.1961) 189 Cal.App.2d 6, 11.

(2) Duty to supplement imposed.

(a) When imposed. A party must supplement its responses if (1) the court orders it to do so, (2) the parties agree to supplement, or (3) the other party served it with a supplemental request for discovery (interrogatory or demand to produce).

[1] Court order. A duty to supplement is created when a court orders a party to supplement its responses. *See* ***Biles***, 124 Cal.App.4th at 1327 n.8. For example, a party must supplement its discovery responses after the court sustains a motion to compel further answers to the discovery. *See id.*

[2] Stipulation. A duty to supplement is created when the parties stipulate in writing to supplement their responses. *See, e.g.*, ***Do It Urself Moving & Storage, Inc. v. Brown, Leifer, Slatkin & Berns*** (2d Dist.1992) 7 Cal.App.4th 27, 31-32 (parties stipulated that D would conduct audit and give report to P before trial). A statement in a discovery response that the party reserves its right to supplement a response at a later date is not an agreement to supplement. *See* ***Biles***, 124 Cal.App.4th at 1329.

[3] Supplemental discovery requests.

[a] Interrogatories. A duty to supplement is created when the discovering party serves supplemental interrogatories. *See* CCP §2030.070. See "Supplemental Interrogatories," ch. 7-C, §7, p. 825.

[b] Demand to produce. A duty to supplement is created when the discovering party serves supplemental demands to produce. *See* CCP §2031.050(a). See "Making Supplemental Demand to Produce," ch. 7-E, §6, p. 850.

(b) Result of not supplementing. When a responding party has a duty to supplement its responses and does not do so, the court can impose sanctions. *See* CCP §2023.010 (misuses of discovery process are subject to sanctions); ***Biles***, 124 Cal.App.4th at 1327 & n.8 (court can impose sanctions when party does not comply with court order compelling supplemental responses); *see, e.g.*, ***Do It Urself Moving***, 7 Cal.App.4th at 36 (court imposed sanctions when D did not produce discovery it had stipulated to produce).

(3) Right to supplement expert list. Without leave of court, a party who participated in an expert-witness exchange can, within 20 days after the exchange, supplement its list of expert witnesses in response to the expert list submitted by the other party, if the supplementing party has not previously retained an expert on that subject. CCP §2034.280(a). See "Adding experts," ch. 7-I, §9.1, p. 909.

§9.6 Service of response. See "Serving discovery," §13.1, p. 769.

§10. MEET-AND-CONFER OBLIGATION

§10.1 Purpose. The obligation to meet and confer requires a party to make a reasonable and good-faith attempt to resolve a discovery dispute informally. *See* CCP §2016.040; ***Obregon v. Superior Ct.*** (2d Dist.1998) 67 Cal.App.4th 424, 428. The obligation is designed to encourage the parties to resolve their differences informally to avoid the necessity for a formal order. ***Townsend v. Superior Ct.*** (2d Dist.1998) 61 Cal.App.4th 1431, 1435; ***McElhaney v. Cessna Aircraft Co.*** (2d Dist.1982) 134 Cal.App.3d 285, 289. The informal, extrajudicial resolution of discovery disputes lessens the burden on the courts, reduces costs to the parties, and shortens the time for resolving lawsuits. *See* ***Fairmont Ins. v. Superior Ct.*** (2000) 22 Cal.4th 245, 253-54; ***Townsend***, 61 Cal.App.4th at 1435.

§10.2 When meet-and-confer is required. The parties must comply with the meet-and-confer requirements at least 30 days before the initial case-management conference unless the court orders otherwise. CRC 3.724. If a discovery dispute arises after the case-management conference, the parties must meet and confer again before making a motion, unless a meet-and-confer is not required for the particular motion. *See, e.g.*, CCP §2024.050(a) (requiring meet-and-confer for motion to reopen or extend discovery), §2025.480(b) (requiring meet-and-confer for motion to compel deposition). Even when there is no statutory requirement to meet and confer, parties should attempt to resolve a discovery dispute informally before making a discovery motion. *See CEB Discovery Practice*, §7.109 (motion to compel initial answers to interrogatories). Most discovery motions must be accompanied by a meet-and-confer declaration that describes the attempts to resolve the discovery dispute

informally. *See, e.g.*, CCP §2024.050(a) (motion to reopen or extend discovery), §2025.480(b) (motion to compel deposition). For a discussion of the case-management process, see "Civil Case Management," ch. 5-A, p. 461.

7-11. MEET-AND-CONFER DECLARATIONS

	Motion	Meet & confer?	CCP
1	Protective order to limit scope of discovery	Yes	§§2017.020(a), 2019.030(b)
2	Protective order to restrict discovery	Yes	§§2017.020(a), 2019.030(b)
3	Protective order for oral deposition	Yes	§2025.420(a)
4	Protective order for written deposition	Yes	§2028.040(b)
5	Protective order for interrogatories	Yes	§2030.090(a)
6	Protective order for demand to produce	Yes	§2031.060(a)
7	Protect from abusive behavior of medical examiner	No	§2032.510(d)
8	Protect from disruptive behavior of observer of medical exam	No	§2032.510(e)
9	Protective order for requests for admission	Yes	§2033.080(a)
10	Protective order for demand to exchange expert-witness information	Yes	§2034.250(a)
11	Compel attendance at deposition	No ❶	§§1987.1, 2025.450(b)(2)
12	Compel answers or production at deposition	Yes	§§2025.450(b)(2), 2025.480(b)
13	Compel initial answers to interrogatories	No ❷	§2030.290(b)
14	Compel further answers to interrogatories	Yes	§2030.300(b)
15	Compel initial response to demand to produce	No ❷	§2031.300(b)
16	Compel further response to demand to produce	Yes	§2031.310(b)(2)
17	Compel production according to terms of statement of compliance with demand to produce	No ❷	§2031.320
18	Compel response to demand for exam of personal-injury plaintiff	No ❷	§2032.240(b)
19	Compel submission to medical exam	Yes	§§2032.250(a), 2032.310(b)
20	Compel delivery of medical-exam reports	Yes	§§2032.620(a), 2032.650(a)
21	Compel deposition of designated expert	Yes	§§2025.450(b)(2), 2034.410
22	Compel exchange of expert information	Yes	§2034.710(c)
23	Compel further responses to requests for admission	Yes	§2033.290(b)
24	Enforce subpoena for personal records	Yes	§§1985.3(g) ¶4, 1985.6(f)(4), 1987.1
25	Extend or reopen discovery	Yes	§2024.050(a)
26	Permit deposition of party at more distant location	Yes	§2025.260(a)
27	Permit augmentation or amendment of expert information	Yes	§2034.610(c)
28	Quash deposition notice to party	Yes	§2025.410(c)
29	Quash deposition subpoena to nonparty	No	§1987.1
30	Suppress deposition transcript	Yes	§§2025.520(g), 2025.530(e)

7-11. MEET-AND-CONFER DECLARATIONS (CONTINUED)

	Motion	Meet & confer?	CCP
31	Motion for ruling on privilege objection to written deposition question	Yes	§2028.050(b)
32	Deem original answers to interrogatories binding	Yes	§2030.310(b)

❶ Although a meet-and-confer declaration is not required for a motion to compel a party deponent to attend a deposition, the motion must be accompanied by a declaration showing that the moving party contacted the deponent to inquire why the deponent did not attend. See "Follow-up contact was made," ch. 9-D, §3.1.1(5), p. 1048.

❷ Although a meet-and-confer declaration is not required for this motion, the party should attempt to resolve the discovery dispute before filing the motion.

§10.3 Meet-and-confer conference.

1. Burden to initiate. The burden to initiate the meet-and-confer conference is on the party making the discovery motion. *See* CCP §2016.040; ***Volkswagenwerk A.G. v. Superior Ct.*** (3d Dist.1981) 122 Cal.App.3d 326, 330.

2. Conference.

(1) Timing. The Code of Civil Procedure does not specify when the parties must meet and confer about the discovery dispute. From a practical standpoint, the parties meet and confer after a party objects to discovery but before a discovery motion is made. *See* ***Puerto v. Superior Ct.*** (2d Dist.2008) 158 Cal.App.4th 1242, 1246-47. In the case of a deposition, the parties can sometimes satisfy the meet-and-confer requirement during the deposition because the presence of each party's attorney lends itself to an immediate discussion of the issues and attempted resolution. *See* ***Townsend v. Superior Ct.*** (2d Dist.1998) 61 Cal.App.4th 1431, 1438 (parties can satisfy meet-and-confer requirement during deposition as long as they make serious effort at negotiations and informal resolution); *see, e.g.*, ***Stewart v. Colonial W. Agency Inc.*** (2d Dist.2001) 87 Cal.App.4th 1006, 1016-17 (attorneys had opportunity to discuss objection because it was made at deposition).

(2) Type. The parties can satisfy the meet-and-confer requirement by communicating in person, by telephone, or by letter. *See* CCP §2023.010(i).

§10.4 Meet-and-confer declaration.

1. Describe attempts to resolve dispute. The declaration should describe the moving party's reasonable and good-faith attempts to resolve the discovery dispute. CCP §2016.040. The declaration should include names, dates, place of meetings, and other details.

2. Explain reasonableness & good faith. The declaration should address the factors that the court will use in determining whether the moving party's informal attempts to resolve the discovery dispute were reasonable and done in good faith. *See* ***Stewart v. Colonial W. Agency Inc.*** (2d Dist.2001) 87 Cal.App.4th 1006, 1016; ***Obregon v. Superior Ct.*** (2d Dist.1998) 67 Cal.App.4th 424, 431; Weil, *Civil Procedure Before Trial*, ¶8:1163. Some of the factors, which vary depending on the circumstances of the case, include the following:

(1) Size & complexity. The size and complexity of a case can be a factor in determining the reasonableness of the effort to resolve the dispute informally. *See* ***Stewart***, 87 Cal.App.4th at 1016. In a large, complex case, a greater effort at informal resolution may be warranted. ***Obregon***, 67 Cal.App.4th at 431. In a simple or narrowly focused case, a more modest effort may suffice. *Id.*; *e.g.*, ***Stewart***, 87 Cal.App.4th at 1016-17 (attorney's discussion of disputed issue during deposition was sufficient).

(2) History. The history of the litigation and the nature of the interaction between the attorneys can be a factor in determining the reasonableness of the effort to resolve the dispute informally. ***Stewart***, 87 Cal.App.4th at 1016.

(3) Nature of dispute. The nature of the dispute can be a factor in determining the reasonableness of the effort to resolve the dispute informally. ***Stewart***, 87 Cal.App.4th at 1016. For example, if a party notified a deposing party that it could not attend a deposition, apologized, and offered to reschedule, but the deposing party made a motion to compel, the court can deny the motion and sanction the attorney for not rescheduling or conferring with the other party. *See* ***Leko v. Cornerstone Home Inspection*** (2d Dist.2001) 86 Cal.App.4th 1109, 1123-24.

(4) Discovery requested. The type and scope of the discovery requested can be a factor in determining the reasonableness of the effort to resolve the dispute informally. ***Stewart***, 87 Cal.App.4th at 1016. An improper request (e.g., one that is overly broad), along with a perfunctory meet-and-confer letter by the discovering party, weighs against a finding that the discovering party made a good-faith effort to resolve the dispute informally. *See* ***Obregon***, 67 Cal.App.4th at 432-33.

(5) Prospects. The prospects for success can be a factor in determining the reasonableness of the effort to resolve the dispute informally. ***Stewart***, 87 Cal.App.4th at 1016; ***Obregon***, 67 Cal.App.4th at 431. *But see* ***Townsend v. Superior Ct.*** (2d Dist.1998) 61 Cal.App.4th 1431, 1438 (just because parties will probably not be able to work out their differences does not exempt them from meet-and-confer requirements).

(6) Other. Other factors can be relevant. ***Stewart***, 87 Cal.App.4th at 1016. For example, if one of the attorneys is unavailable until after the deadline to make a motion to compel, this weighs in favor of a finding that the moving party did all that was necessary to meet and confer. *See id.* at 1016-17.

3. Describe other party's response. The declaration should describe the other party's response to the attempts to meet and confer, and whether that party made a reasonable and good-faith attempt to resolve the discovery dispute. *See* CCP §2016.040. The details of the contacts should be included—for example, the names, dates, place of meetings, and other details.

4. Attachments. Any correspondence or other documents relating to the attempt to meet and confer should be attached as exhibits.

§10.5 Sanctions for failure to meet & confer. The court must impose monetary sanctions against a party or attorney who does not confer as required. CCP §2023.010(i) (failure to meet and confer is misuse of discovery process), §2023.020 (monetary sanctions for failure to confer); *see, e.g.*, ***Ellis v. Toshiba Am. Info. Sys.*** (2d Dist.2013) 218 Cal.App.4th 853, 879-80 (court imposed sanctions for party's failure to meet and confer in good faith to resolve discovery dispute). The sanctioned party or attorney must pay the reasonable expenses, including attorney fees, incurred by anyone as a result of the conduct. CCP §2023.020. Before imposing sanctions, the court must decide if the failure to meet and confer was egregious or merely inadequate.

1. Egregious. If the party or attorney made no effort to resolve the discovery dispute informally, it is considered an egregious violation of the meet-and-confer requirement, and the court can impose sanctions without any further attempts to secure an informal resolution by the parties. *See* ***Obregon v. Superior Ct.*** (2d Dist.1998) 67 Cal.App.4th 424, 433-34.

2. Inadequate. If the party or attorney made an inadequate effort to resolve the discovery dispute informally, the court should consider requiring that certain additional efforts be made before imposing discovery sanctions. ***Obregon***, 67 Cal.App.4th at 434-35; *see* ***Volkswagenwerk A.G. v. Superior Ct.*** (3d Dist.1981) 122 Cal.App.3d 326, 331-32. In making that decision, the court should consider the following factors:

(1) The history of the case. ***Obregon***, 67 Cal.App.4th at 435.

(2) The past conduct of counsel. *Id.*

(3) The nature and extent of the actual efforts made. *Id.*

(4) The nature of the discovery requested and its importance to the case. *Id.*

(5) The size and complexity of the case. *Id.*

(6) The effect of expense on litigation of the case. *Id.*

(7) Whether unfeasible levels of expense might force resolution of the case on a basis other than the merits. *Id.*

(8) The margin by which the moving party deviated from a reasonable and good-faith attempt at an informal resolution. *Id.*

(9) The likelihood any additional effort specified by the court would resolve the dispute. *Id.*; *see, e.g.*, ***Clement v. Alegre*** (1st Dist.2009) 177 Cal.App.4th 1277, 1284-85 (referee found parties were at impasse on discovery dispute).

(10) Whether supplemental responses have been served. ***Obregon***, 67 Cal.App.4th at 435.

(11) Any other factor relevant under the circumstances. *Id.*

§11. GROUNDS FOR DISCOVERY OBJECTIONS

PRACTICE TIP

Never use boilerplate objections. Even though boilerplate objections may be sufficient to avoid waiver, they can result in sanctions. ***Korea Data Sys. Co. v. Superior Ct.*** *(4th Dist.1997) 51 Cal.App.4th 1513, 1516; see CCP §2023.010(f) (sanctions available for evasive response to discovery). To avoid sanctions, make the most specific objection possible.*

§11.1 Valid objections. When a responding party objects to discovery, it must clearly state the specific ground for the objection. *See* CCP §2030.240(b) (interrogatories), §2031.240(b)(2) (demand to produce), §2033.230(a) (RFAs). A party can assert the following objections to discovery:

1. Not within scope of discovery.

(1) Not relevant to subject matter. The discovery request asks for information that is not relevant to the subject matter of the case and will not lead to the discovery of relevant information. *See* CCP §2017.010; ***Catholic Mut. Relief Soc'y v. Superior Ct.*** (2007) 42 Cal.4th 358, 366; ***Puerto v. Superior Ct.*** (2d Dist.2008) 158 Cal.App.4th 1242, 1249; *CEB Discovery Practice*, §§1.34, 9.33; *see also* CCP §2023.010(a) (sanctions available for persistent attempts to secure information outside scope of discovery); ***Coy v. Superior Ct.*** (1962) 58 Cal.2d 210, 217 (test for discovery is relevance to subject matter). A discovery request is objectionable as being outside the scope of discovery if the information requested is so unrelated to the claims and defenses raised by the parties that it will have little practical use. *See* ***CBS v. Superior Ct.*** (2d Dist.1968) 263 Cal.App.2d 12, 19 (interrogatories).

(2) Inadmissible & will not lead to admissible evidence. The discovery request asks for information that is not admissible and will not lead to the discovery of admissible evidence. *See* CCP §2017.010; ***Catholic Mut. Relief***, 42 Cal.4th at 366. There is no precise test to determine whether information is reasonably calculated to lead to the discovery of admissible evidence, but courts take a very broad approach to making that decision. *See* ***Pacific Tel. & Tel. Co. v. Superior Ct.*** (1970) 2 Cal.3d 161, 172; ***Norton v. Superior Ct.*** (2d Dist.1994) 24 Cal.App.4th 1750, 1761.

2. Unauthorized method of discovery. The discovery request asks for a type of discovery not permitted by the CDA. *See* CCP §2019.010 (lists permissible methods of discovery from parties), §2020.010 (lists permissible methods of discovery from nonparties).

3. Privileged information. The discovery request asks for information or documents that are privileged or exempt from discovery. *See* CCP §2017.010; ***Monarch Healthcare v. Superior Ct.*** (4th Dist.2000) 78 Cal.App.4th 1282, 1290. See "Privileged & exempt information," ch. 6-A, §3.3, p. 610. The objection must clearly identify the particular privilege or exemption invoked. *See* CCP §2030.240(b) (interrogatories), §2031.240(b)(2) (demand to produce).

4. Improper procedure. The discovery request was made improperly (e.g., request was made too early or too late, request should have been sought by motion and court order). *See* CCP §2023.010(b) (sanctions available for using discovery method in way that does not comply with proper procedure).

5. Cumulative or duplicative. The discovery request is unreasonably cumulative or duplicative. *See* CCP §2019.030(a)(1); ***Fairmont Ins. v. Superior Ct.*** (2000) 22 Cal.4th 245, 254; ***Sinaiko Healthcare Consulting, Inc. v. Pacific Healthcare Consultants*** (2d Dist.2007) 148 Cal.App.4th 390, 402.

6. Undue burden or expense. The discovery request imposes an undue burden or expense. *See* CCP §2017.020(a) (grounds to limit discovery), §2019.030(a)(2) (grounds to restrict discovery), §2023.010(c) (grounds for sanctions), §2025.290(c) (length of oral deposition), §2025.420(b) (taking of deposition generally), §2030.090(b) (interrogatories), §2031.060(b) (demand to produce), §2033.080(b) (RFAs); ***Deyo v. Kilbourne*** (2d Dist.1978) 84 Cal.App.3d 771, 789 (court can require financial reimbursement for unduly burdensome interrogatories). A discovery request is not objectionable merely because it would be burdensome to answer; the burden must rise to the level of injustice. ***West Pico Furniture Co. v. Superior Ct.*** (1961) 56 Cal.2d 407, 418; *see* ***Alpine Mut. Water Co. v. Superior Ct.*** (2d Dist.1968) 259 Cal.App.2d 45, 55. The objection can be raised by written objection or by a motion for a protective order. *See* CCP §§2017.020(a), 2019.030(b); *see, e.g.*, ***New Albertsons, Inc. v. Superior Ct.*** (2d Dist.2008) 168 Cal.App.4th 1403, 1427-28 (because P did not move to compel after D made burdensome objection, D had no duty to produce). When evaluating an objection based on undue burden or expense, the court should consider (1) the needs of the case, (2) the amount in controversy, (3) the importance of the issues at stake in the litigation, and (4) whether the discovery is sought from a party or nonparty. CCP §2019.030(a)(2) (elements 1-3); *see* ***Calcor Space Facility, Inc. v. Superior Ct.*** (4th Dist.1997) 53 Cal.App.4th 216, 222 (element 4). The courts should be more sensitive to a nonparty's claim that discovery is overly burdensome or expensive than to a party's claim. *See* ***Calcor Space Facility***, 53 Cal.App.4th at 222.

PRACTICE TIP

The objections of "burdensome" (above) and "oppressive" (below) are not the same. ***West Pico****, 56 Cal.2d at 417. The objection of "burdensome" must be supported by evidence of the amount of work required to comply with the discovery request, while the objection of "oppressive" must be supported by a showing of intent to create an unreasonable burden or that the ultimate effect of the burden is not commensurate with the result sought. Id.*

---

7. Oppressive. The discovery request is oppressive. *See* CCP §2023.010(c) (grounds for sanctions), §2025.290(c) (length of deposition), §2025.420(b) (taking of deposition generally), §2030.090(b) (interrogatories), §2031.060(b) (demand to produce), §2033.080(b) (RFAs); ***1880 Corp. v. Superior Ct.*** (1962) 57 Cal.2d 840, 843 (interrogatories). An objection based on oppression must show one of the following:

(1) The discovering party intended to create an unreasonable burden for the responding party. ***West Pico***, 56 Cal.2d at 417.

(2) The ultimate effect of the discovery burden is excessive compared to how useful the information will be to the discovering party. *See id.*; ***Mead Reinsurance Co. v. Superior Ct.*** (4th Dist.1986) 188 Cal.App.3d 313, 320-21; ***CBS***, 263 Cal.App.2d at 19; Weil, *Civil Procedure Before Trial*, ¶8:1096; *see, e.g.*, ***Alpine Mut.***, 259 Cal.App.2d at 52 (Ps did not have to answer interrogatories that were unrelated to their claims for relief).

8. Intrusive. The discovery request is unduly intrusive. CCP §2017.020(a); *see CEB Discovery Practice*, §7.86 (objection permitted when interrogatory results in unwarranted annoyance or embarrassment); *see also* CCP §2023.010(c) (sanctions available for use of discovery that causes unwarranted annoyance or embarrassment).

9. Obtainable from another source. The requested discovery is available from another source that is more convenient, less burdensome, or less expensive. *See* CCP §2019.030(a)(1).

10. Protected personal information.

(1) Personal records or information. The requested discovery seeks personal records or information and the discovering party has not provided a notice of privacy rights to the person whose records or information is sought. See "Subpoenas for personal records," ch. 8-E, §2.1.1(2), p. 996.

(2) Constitutional right to privacy. The discovering party seeks the disclosure of information that will violate the witness's or another person's right to privacy. *See* Cal. Const., art. I, §1; ***Heda v. Superior Ct.*** (1st Dist.1990) 225 Cal.App.3d 525, 528-29; *see, e.g.*, ***Digital Music News LLC v. Superior Ct.*** (2d Dist.2014) 226Cal.App.4th 216, 229-30 (court upheld privacy objections to subpoena seeking identity of author of anonymous comments on website); ***Planned Parenthood Golden Gate v. Superior Ct.*** (1st Dist.2000) 83 Cal.App.4th 347, 370 (court upheld privacy objections to interrogatories asking for names, home addresses, and telephone numbers of nonparty Planned Parenthood staff and volunteers). See "Right to Privacy," ch. 6-F, §1, p. 681.

(3) Sexual-harassment or sexual-assault action. The discovering party in a sexual-harassment or sexual-assault action seeks information, without having complied with CCP §2017.220, about the plaintiff's sexual conduct with a person the plaintiff contends perpetrated the harassment or assault.

(4) Free-speech action. The discovery request seeks a person's personal identifying information (e.g., name, home and e-mail address, telephone number, Social Security number, children's names) in connection with an action involving that person's exercise of free-speech rights. *See* Civ. C. §1798.79.8(b); CCP §§1987.1(b)(5), 1987.2(c); *CEB Discovery Practice*, §5.131A. If the information is sought from an Internet provider, the discovering party may have to pay certain expenses and fees if the party is unsuccessful in bringing the action. *See* CCP §1987.2(c). See "Personal information subpoenaed in free-speech case," ch. 9-C, §3.1.3(2)(d)[3], p. 1041.

11. Other objections. For other objections that are specific to the type of discovery method (e.g., objections to interrogatories), see the appropriate subchapter in this chapter.

§11.2 Invalid objections.

1. Not relevant to issues. A party cannot object to a discovery request because the information sought is not relevant to the "issues" of the case. ***Pacific Tel. & Tel. Co. v. Superior Ct.*** (1970) 2 Cal.3d 161, 174; ***Coy v. Superior Ct.*** (1962) 58 Cal.2d 210, 217; *see CEB Discovery Practice*, §9.33. The objection that the information sought is not relevant to the "issues" is too narrow; the correct objection is that the information is not relevant to the "subject matter of the case." *See* CCP §2017.010; ***Chapin v. Superior Ct.*** (5th Dist.1966) 239 Cal.App.2d 851, 855. See "Not relevant to subject matter," §11.1.1(1), p. 765.

2. Inadmissible. A party cannot object to a discovery request because the information sought will be inadmissible at trial. ***Pacific Tel.***, 2 Cal.3d at 172; ***Greyhound Corp. v. Superior Ct.*** (1961) 56 Cal.2d 355, 391. A discovery request is valid even if the information sought is not admissible, as long as the information leads to the discovery of admissible evidence. CCP §2017.010; *see* ***Shively v. Stewart*** (1966) 65 Cal.2d 475, 481. See "Inadmissible & will not lead to admissible evidence," §11.1.1(2), p. 765.

3. Unable to clearly respond. A party cannot object to a discovery request because the party is unable to clearly answer the request. ***Cembrook v. Superior Ct.*** (1961) 56 Cal.2d 423, 429. Instead, the party must explain why it cannot give a clear answer. *See, e.g., id.* at 430 (D was obligated to explain its inability to admit or deny RFAs).

4. Fishing expedition. A party cannot object to a discovery request solely on the ground that it is a "fishing expedition." *See* ***Greyhound Corp.***, 56 Cal.2d at 386; ***Irvington-Moore, Inc. v. Superior Ct.*** (3d Dist.1993) 14 Cal.App.4th 733, 739 n.4. Contrary to popular belief, fishing expeditions are allowed in some cases. ***Cruz v. Superior Ct.*** (4th Dist.2004) 121 Cal.App.4th 646, 653.

5. Information already known. A party cannot object to a discovery request because the information sought is already known to the discovering party. *See* ***Coy***, 58 Cal.2d at 217-18; ***Singer v. Superior Ct.*** (1960) 54 Cal.2d 318, 324; ***Irvington-Moore, Inc.***, 14 Cal.App.4th at 739.

6. Information pertains to pleadings. A party cannot object to a discovery request because the information sought pertains to the pleadings. *See* ***Singer***, 54 Cal.2d at 323.

7. Hearsay. A party cannot object to a discovery request because the answer would require the party to provide hearsay evidence. *See* ***Durst v. Superior Ct.*** (2d Dist.1963) 218 Cal.App.2d 460, 464; ***Smith v. Superior Ct.*** (3d Dist.1961) 189 Cal.App.2d 6, 12.

8. Existence of privileged document. A party cannot object to a discovery request because it seeks information about the existence of privileged documents. *See* ***Smith***, 189 Cal.App.2d at 12. Although the contents of privileged documents are protected from discovery, the existence of the documents is not protected. *Id.*; *see* CCP §2017.010 (discovery of existence of documents may be obtained).

9. Legal contentions – interrogatories & RFAs. A party cannot object to an interrogatory or a request for admission because the answer would require a statement of the party's legal contentions or the answer would be based on information developed in anticipation of litigation. See "Party's contentions," ch. 7-C, §3.1.5, p. 818; "What can be discovered," ch. 7-D, §3.1, p. 836.

10. Expert opinion – RFAs. A party cannot object to a request for admission because the request calls for an expert opinion and the party does not know the answer. ***Bloxham v. Saldinger*** (6th Dist.2014) 228 Cal.App.4th 729, 751. See "Assert insufficient information or knowledge," ch. 7-D, §5.3.1(3), p. 839.

§12. HOW TO MAKE DISCOVERY OBJECTIONS

There are three ways to object to discovery: (1) by serving written objections, (2) by making oral objections, and (3) by making a motion to prevent the discovery (i.e., a motion to quash or a motion for a protective order). Most discovery objections are made by serving written objections.

§12.1 Serve written objections to discovery.

1. Written objections by party.

(1) Objection to oral deposition.

(a) Deposition notice. A party can object to defects in the deposition notice by serving written objections at least three calendar days before the date of the deposition. If these objections are not made promptly, they are waived. CCP §2025.410(a). See "Objecting to deposition notice for oral deposition," ch. 7-B, §9.9, p. 796.

(b) Deposition production. A party can object to deposition production by serving written objections at least three calendar days before the date of the deposition. CCP §2025.410(a); *CEB Discovery Practice*, §5.136. Written objections can include objections to the sufficiency of the description of documents, objections based on privilege, and objections based on exemption from discovery. *See* Weil, *Civil Procedure Before Trial*, ¶¶8:529.1, 8:531. The same objections can be made in a motion to quash, in a motion for a protective order, or at the deposition. *See CEB Discovery Practice*, §5.136. See "Objecting to deposition notice for oral deposition," ch. 7-B, §9.9, p. 796.

(2) Objection to written deposition. A party can object to a written deposition by serving written objections within 15 days after service of the questions (20 days if served by mail). *See* CCP §§1013(a), 2016.050, 2028.040(a), 2028.050(a). A party objecting to the form of the questions "shall" promptly move for a hearing. *Id.* §2028.040(b). See "Objecting to written deposition," ch. 7-B, §10.6, p. 806. A discovering party whose question is objected to on the ground of privilege "may" move for a hearing. CCP §2028.050(b).

(3) Objection to interrogatories. A party can object to interrogatories in its written response to the interrogatories. See "Object," ch. 7-C, §8.3.4, p. 829.

(4) Objection to RFAs. A party can object to a request for admission in its written response to the request. See "Objection," ch. 7-D, §5.3.2, p. 839.

(5) Objection to demand to produce. A party can object to a demand to produce in its written response to the demand. CCP §2031.210(a)(3). See "Objection," ch. 7-E, §7.3.3, p. 852.

(6) Objection to exam of personal-injury P. A personal-injury plaintiff can object to a demand for a medical examination by serving written objections in its response, which must be served within 20 days after personal service of the demand (25 days if served by mail in California). *See* CCP §§1013(a), 2016.050, 2032.230; *see, e.g.*, ***Carpenter v. Superior Ct.*** (1st Dist.2006) 141 Cal.App.4th 249, 254 (P objected that description of test was not sufficiently specific). See "Written response to demand," ch. 7-F, §4.2.1, p. 859.

2. Written objections by nonparty.

(1) Objection to deposition subpoena. A nonparty deponent can serve a written objection to a deposition subpoena or make objections orally on the date the nonparty deponent is required to produce. The nonparty deponent can also make a motion to quash or a motion for a protective order. See "Challenging Subpoenas," ch. 8-E, §2, p. 995; "Motion for Protective Order," ch. 9-B, p. 1024; "Motion to Quash Depositions," ch. 9-C, p. 1038.

(2) Objection to deposition subpoena to appear & produce. A nonparty deponent can serve a written objection to a deposition subpoena to appear and produce. The nonparty deponent can also make a motion to quash, make a motion for a protective order, or object during the deposition. See "Challenging Subpoenas," ch. 8-E, §2, p. 995; "Motion for Protective Order," ch. 9-B, p. 1024; "Motion to Quash Depositions," ch. 9-C, p. 1038.

§12.2 Make oral objections to deposition discovery.

1. Oral objections by party deponent. A party deponent can object during a deposition (1) to information sought that is privileged or exempt from discovery or (2) to curable errors made during the deposition. See "Objecting during oral deposition," ch. 7-B, §9.12, p. 798.

2. Oral objections by nonparty deponent. A nonparty deponent can object during a deposition (1) to the form or content of the subpoena or (2) to the production of privileged information. Weil, *Civil Procedure Before Trial*, ¶8:606. See "Objecting during oral deposition," ch. 7-B, §9.12, p. 798. For example, a nonparty deponent can object to the production of business records on the date for production of the records. *CEB Discovery Practice*, §5.136; *see* ***Unzipped Apparel, LLC v. Bader*** (2d Dist.2007) 156 Cal.App.4th 123, 132. However, a nonparty deponent who refuses to answer or produce during a deposition risks being held in contempt. *See* CCP §2020.240 (nonparty deponent can be held in contempt for refusing to obey subpoena); *CEB Discovery Practice*, §6.69 (same).

§12.3 Make motion to prevent discovery.

1. Motion to quash. A party or nonparty can object to a deposition notice or subpoena by making a motion to quash or modify the notice or subpoena. *See* CCP §1987.1(a), (b). See "Motion to Quash Depositions," ch. 9-C, p. 1038.

2. Motion for protective order. A party or nonparty can make a motion for a protective order. See "Party or affected person," ch. 9-B, §3.1.1, p. 1028.

§13. SERVING & FILING DISCOVERY

§13.1 Serving discovery. Discovery requests and responses can be served on a party by mail, fax, personal delivery, or any other method the parties agree to. See "Methods of service," ch. 1-G, §5.1, p. 66. By comparison, deposition subpoenas must be served on a nonparty by personal delivery. See "Type of service," ch. 8-A, §9.1, p. 947.

1. **Serving discovery requests.**

(1) **Whom to serve.** The discovering party must serve its discovery requests on all parties. CCP §2025.240(a) (deposition notice), §2030.080 (interrogatories), §2031.040 (demand to produce), §2032.220(e) (demand for physical exam of personal-injury P), §2033.070 (RFAs). See "Attorney or party?," ch. 1-G, §3.1, p. 64. On motion, with or without notice, the court can relieve the discovering party from serving copies of interrogatories on all parties if the service would be unduly expensive or burdensome. CCP §2030.080(b).

(2) **What to serve.** The discovering party must serve the parties with copies of the discovery requests. CCP §2030.080 (interrogatories), §2031.040 (demand to produce), §2032.220(e) (demand for physical exam of personal-injury P), §2033.070 (RFAs). The discovering party must keep the original discovery requests. See "Custody of discovery," §16.1, p. 776.

(3) **When to serve.** See "Timing of Discovery," §5, p. 745.

2. **Serving discovery responses.**

(1) **Whom to serve.** The responding party must serve all parties who have appeared in the case. CCP §2030.260(a), (c) (interrogatories), §2031.260(a) (demand to produce), §2032.230(b) (demand for physical exam of personal-injury P), §2033.250(a) (RFAs). On motion, with or without notice, the court can relieve the responding party from serving copies of interrogatory answers on all parties if the service would be unduly expensive or burdensome. *Id.* §2030.260(c).

(2) **What to serve.** The responding party must serve the original response on the discovering party and copies on all other parties. CCP §2030.260(a), (c) (interrogatories), §2031.260(a) (demand to produce), §2032.230(b) (demand for physical exam of personal-injury P), §2033.250(a) (RFAs).

(3) **When to serve.** See "When to Respond to Discovery," §8, p. 754.

§13.2 Filing or lodging discovery.

1. **Filing discovery.**

(1) **Written discovery requests & responses.** Discovery requests and responses are not automatically filed with the court. *See* CCP §2030.280(a) (interrogatories and responses), §2031.290(a) (demand to produce and response), §2032.260(a) (demand for physical exam of personal-injury P and response), §2033.270(a) (RFAs and response), §2034.290(a) (demand for exchange of expert information); CRC 3.250(a)(1) (subpoena), CRC 3.250(a)(3) (deposition notice and response); ***Sinaiko Healthcare Consulting, Inc. v. Pacific Healthcare Consultants*** (2d Dist.2007) 148 Cal.App.4th 390, 402 (discovery demands and responses are not filed with court). Discovery requests and responses are filed with the court only when (1) they are relevant to a law-and-motion proceeding or other hearing or (2) the court orders that they be filed for good cause. CRC 3.250(a).

(2) **Deposition transcripts.** Deposition transcripts and recordings are not filed with the court unless required by the CDA, a local rule, a pretrial order, or a case-management order. See "Filing or Lodging Deposition Transcripts," ch. 7-B, §11, p. 807.

2. **Lodging discovery.** Discovery is "lodged" when it is temporarily deposited with the court but is not filed. Weil, *Civil Procedure Before Trial*, ¶8:783; *cf.* CRC 2.550(b)(3) (defining "lodged" for purposes of sealed records); *see also* CCP §2025.480(h) (lodge deposition transcript), §2034.290(c) (lodge demand for exchange of expert information). Once the matter for which the discovery is lodged is resolved, the court returns the discovery to the party who lodged it. Weil, *Civil Procedure Before Trial*, ¶8:783. To facilitate the return, a party must lodge the discovery along with a self-addressed, stamped envelope. CRC 3.1302(b).

§14. RESOLVING DISCOVERY DISPUTES

Chart 7-12, below, summarizes the procedures for objecting to discovery requests and responding to discovery objections.

7-12. PROCEDURES FOR OBJECTING TO DISCOVERY & RESPONDING TO OBJECTIONS

Discovering party serves discovery request

Option 1

Responding person makes objections
Procedure:
Object:
- in writing, for most discovery
- orally, during deposition

Discovering party opposes objections
Procedure:
1. Meet & confer
2. File motion to compel discovery with:
   - meet-and-confer declaration
   - memorandum in support
   - separate statement, if necessary
   - good-cause statement, if necessary
   - declaration of facts, if necessary
   - exhibits, if necessary
   - sanctions statement
3. Set hearing

Responding person opposes motion to compel
Procedure:
File opposition papers with:
- preliminary facts that support objections
- responsive memorandum (optional)
- responsive separate statement (optional)
- declaration of facts, if necessary
- exhibits, if necessary
- sanctions statement

Option 2

Responding person objects by motion
Procedure:
1. Meet & confer
2. File motion for protective order or motion to quash with:
   - meet-and-confer declaration
   - memorandum in support
   - preliminary facts that support objection
   - declaration of facts, if necessary
   - sanctions statement
3. Set hearing

Discovering party opposes motion
Procedure:
File opposition papers with:
- reasons to deny motion
- good-cause statement, if necessary
- sanctions statement

§14.1 Procedures. The following is an outline of the procedures for objecting to and compelling discovery.

1. Responding party objects to discovery. A party or nonparty (responding party) can object to discovery by making written objections (option 1) or by making a motion for a protective order or a motion to quash (option 2). Making written objections to discovery is easier than making a motion because written objections put the burden to enforce discovery (i.e., file motion, initiate meet-and-confer, and set hearing) on the discovering party. *See* ***Fairmont Ins. v. Superior Ct.*** (2000) 22 Cal.4th 245, 255. In either case, the responding party has the burden to prove why the information should not be disclosed, either in its own motion or in its papers opposing the discovering party's motion to compel. *See id.*; ***Coy v. Superior Ct.*** (1962) 58 Cal.2d 210, 220.

(1) Option 1. A person served with a discovery request can object by serving a written objection that identifies the specific reason the request is objectionable. See "Grounds for Discovery Objections," §11, p. 765. Oral objections can be made during a deposition. See "Make oral objections to deposition discovery," §12.2, p. 769.

(2) Option 2. A person served with a discovery request can object by serving a motion for a protective order or a motion to quash. See "Party or affected person," ch. 9-B, §3.1.1, p. 1028; "Who can make," ch. 9-C, §3.1.1, p. 1038; "Who can make," ch. 9-C, §4.1.1, p. 1042.

2. Discovering party moves to compel (option 1). If the responding party serves written objections to a discovery request, the discovering party has the burden to compel discovery.

(1) Initiate meet-and-confer. Before making most motions to compel, the discovering party must initiate a meet-and-confer conference; if that fails, the discovering party must prepare the meet-and-confer declaration as part of its motion to compel. *See* ***Fairmont Ins.***, 22 Cal.4th at 254 n.3 (parties must meet and confer); *CEB Discovery Practice*, §§15.42, 15.49 (discussing motions to compel); *see also* CCP §2030.290(b) (motion to compel initial response to interrogatories does not require meet-and-confer conference). See "Meet-and-Confer Obligation," §10, p. 761.

(2) File motion to compel. If the parties cannot reach an agreement at the meet-and-confer conference, the discovering party should file a motion to compel. If the discovering party obtained sufficient information to understand the basis of the objection during the meet-and-confer conference, the discovering party can make the allegations in its motion to compel that are included in "Discovering party justifies discovery," §14.1.5, p. 773. See "Motion to Compel Depositions," ch. 9-D, p. 1046; "Motion to Compel Written Discovery," ch. 9-E, p. 1057.

3. Responding party moves for protective order or to quash (option 2). If the responding party does not serve written objections to a discovery request, it must seek a protective order or move to quash.

(1) Initiate meet-and-confer. Before making most motions for protection or to quash, the responding party must initiate a meet-and-confer conference; if that fails, the responding party must prepare the meet-and-confer declaration as part of its motion to compel. *See, e.g.*, CCP §2019.030(b) (motion for protective order must be accompanied by meet-and-confer declaration under §2016.040), §2025.410(c) (motion to quash deposition notice must be accompanied by meet-and-confer declaration under §2016.040). See "Meet-and-Confer Obligation," §10, p. 761.

NOTE

Nonparties seeking to quash a deposition subpoena are not required to initiate a meet-and-confer conference before filing the motion. See CCP §1987.1.

---

(2) File motion for protection or to quash. If the parties cannot reach an agreement at the meet-and-confer conference, the responding party should file a motion for protection or to quash.

4. Responding party satisfies burden. Whether the discovering party files a motion to compel or the responding party moves for protection or to quash, the responding party has the burden to justify its objections to the discovery. *See* ***Fairmont Ins.***, 22 Cal.4th at 255; ***Coy***, 58 Cal.2d at 220.

(1) Preliminary facts. If the objection depends on preliminary facts, the responding party must establish the facts necessary to support the objection. *See* ***HLC Props., Ltd. v. Superior Ct.*** (2005) 35 Cal.4th 54, 59 (responding party has burden to establish privilege by evidence); ***Bank of Am. v. Superior Ct.*** (4th Dist.2013) 212 Cal.App.4th 1076, 1099 (party claiming attorney-client privilege has burden to show preliminary facts); ***Carehouse Convalescent Hosp. v. Superior Ct.*** (4th Dist.2006) 143 Cal.App.4th 1558, 1563 (party claiming work-product protection has burden to show preliminary facts). Preliminary facts are the facts that the admissibility or inadmissibility of the evidence depends on (e.g., facts that establish the existence or nonexistence of a privilege). Evid. C. §400; *see* ***Mavroudis v. Superior Ct.*** (1st Dist.1980) 102 Cal.App.3d 594, 604.

(a) Preliminary facts for privilege. Objections based on privilege must be supported by preliminary facts that support each element of the privilege. For the elements of each privilege, see the sections titled "Elements of [...] privilege," subchs. 6-B through 6-H.

[1] Confidential-communication privileges. For confidential-communication privileges, the holder of the privilege does not need to prove the communication was confidential because confidentiality is presumed once the holder establishes the preliminary facts. *See* Evid. C. §917(a); ***Bank of Am.***, 212 Cal.App.4th at 1099. For example, when asserting the psychotherapist-patient privilege, the holder must identify the psychotherapist, show that the psychotherapist is qualified under Evid. C. §1010, and show that the holder is a patient within the meaning of Evid. C. §1011. ***Mahoney v. Superior Ct.*** (1st Dist.1983) 142 Cal.App.3d 937, 940-41. See "Confidential-communication privileges," ch. 6-A, §3.3.1(1)(a), p. 611.

[2] Work-product privilege. For the work-product privilege, the holder has the burden to prove the elements of the privilege and to categorize the protected information as core or noncore work product. *See* ***Carehouse Convalescent***, 143 Cal.App.4th at 1563 (party claiming work-product protection has burden to show preliminary facts). See "Work-Product Privilege," ch. 6-B, §3, p. 628.

(b) Preliminary facts for other objections. The preliminary facts necessary to support an objection not based on privilege include whatever information provides the underlying support for the objection. *See* Evid. C. §405. For example, an objection that a discovery request seeks information that would be burdensome to produce requires the responding party to make a preliminary showing of how difficult or expensive it would be to produce the information. *See* ***West Pico Furniture Co. v. Superior Ct.*** (1961) 56 Cal.2d 407, 417.

(c) Declaration. The responding party must support any preliminary facts with a declaration (or affidavit), which can be made by the party or its attorney. *See* ***Citizens for Ceres v. Superior Ct.*** (5th Dist.2013) 217 Cal.App.4th 889, 911; Weil, *Civil Procedure Before Trial*, ¶8:192. If the objection is based on a privilege, the declaration must be made by the holder of the privilege or a person authorized by the holder.

(d) Hearing. The court can hold a hearing to resolve a discovery dispute based on disputed preliminary facts. *See* Evid. C. §§402, 405; ***Mavroudis***, 102 Cal.App.3d at 604.

(2) Privilege log. If an objection to the production of documents is based on a privilege, the court can require the responding party to produce a privilege log. Weil, *Civil Procedure Before Trial*, ¶8:192.10; *see* CCP §2031.240(c)(1); ***Best Prods. v. Superior Ct.*** (2d Dist.2004) 119 Cal.App.4th 1181, 1188-89; *see, e.g.*, ***Bank of Am.***, 212 Cal.App.4th at 1087-88 (court ordered P to submit privilege log). The purpose of a privilege log is to provide a specific factual description of documents in support of the claim of privilege, which can help the court evaluate the claim. ***Best Prods.***, 119 Cal.App.4th at 1188-89. A privilege log should identify the type of privilege or exemption claimed, the type of document withheld (e.g., letter, memo, contract, e-mail), the date of its creation or transmittal, the author, the recipients, and its number (if it was sequentially numbered for purposes of discovery). *See* ***Wells Fargo Bank v. Superior Ct.*** (2000) 22 Cal.4th 201, 205.

NOTE

The term "privilege log" is jargon used to describe the requirement in CCP §2031.240(b) that the responding party identify with particularity the document or thing it objects to and state the specific reasons for the objection. See ***Best Prods.***, *119 Cal.App.4th at 1188 & n.5 (interpreting former CCP §2031(g)(3), now §2031.240(b));* ***Hernandez v. Superior Ct.*** *(2d Dist.2003) 112 Cal.App.4th 285, 292 & n.8 (same). In 2012, the California Legislature defined the term as having the meaning given to it in California case law. CCP §2031.240(c)(2).*

5. Discovering party justifies discovery. If the responding party proves the preliminary facts that support its objection to discovery, the discovering party has the burden to justify its discovery request. For example, in response to a privilege objection, the discovering party can justify its discovery request by showing any of the following:

(1) Disprove objection. The discovering party can disprove the applicability of the objection. *See* ***Lipton v. Superior Ct.*** (2d Dist.1996) 48 Cal.App.4th 1599, 1619. For example, the discovering party can show that the responding party did not prove the necessary elements to establish a privilege. *See* Weil, *Civil Procedure Before Trial*, ¶8:192 (discovering party can disprove facts establishing claim of attorney-client privilege); *see, e.g.*, ***Johnson v. Superior Ct.*** (2d Dist.2000) 80 Cal.App.4th 1050, 1063 (physician-patient relationship was not created by sperm donor's consultation with sperm bank's physician as part of donation process).

(2) Prove waiver of privilege. The discovering party can show that the responding party waived the privilege. *See* ***Titmas v. Superior Ct.*** (4th Dist.2001) 87 Cal.App.4th 738, 745; ***Lipton***, 48 Cal.App.4th at 1619. See "Waiver of privilege," ch. 6-A, §2.2.14, p. 607.

(3) Prove exception to privilege. The discovering party can show the applicability of an exception to the privilege. *See* ***Titmas***, 87 Cal.App.4th at 745; ***Lipton***, 48 Cal.App.4th at 1619. See "Exceptions to privilege," ch. 6-A, §2.2.13, p. 606.

(4) Prove necessity & fairness. If the information is protected by a qualified privilege, the discovering party can show that the information is necessary to a fair resolution of the lawsuit. *See, e.g.*, ***Bridgestone/Firestone, Inc. v. Superior Ct.*** (1st Dist.1992) 7 Cal.App.4th 1384, 1391 (trade-secret privilege).

§14.2 In camera review of documents. The purpose of an in camera review of documents is to help the court in evaluating an objection based on privilege.

1. When permitted. The court can require an in camera review of material claimed to be protected by a discovery privilege or exemption only when it is authorized by law. *See* Evid. C. §915(b) (listing privileges that can be subject to in camera inspection); ***OXY Res. Cal. LLC v. Superior Ct.*** (1st Dist.2004) 115 Cal.App.4th 874, 895-96 (rule against in camera review is not absolute); ***Cornish v. Superior Ct.*** (4th Dist.1989) 209 Cal.App.3d 467, 480 (same).

(1) Qualified privileges. The court can conduct an in camera review of information claimed to be protected by a qualified privilege because the court must balance the need for confidentiality against the need for the information. *Jefferson's Evid. Benchbook*, §37.30; *see* ***Citizens for Ceres v. Superior Ct.*** (5th Dist.2013) 217 Cal.App.4th 889, 911-12. The following are qualified privileges:

(a) Attorney work-product privilege. *See* CCP §2018.030(b); Evid. C. §915(b); ***Wells Fargo Bank v. Superior Ct.*** (2000) 22 Cal.4th 201, 215; ***Wellpoint Health Networks, Inc. v. Superior Ct.*** (2d Dist.1997) 59 Cal.App.4th 110, 121. See "Work-Product Privilege," ch. 6-B, §3, p. 628.

(b) Official-information privilege. *See* Evid. C. §§915(b), 1040; ***In re Marcos B.*** (4th Dist.2013) 214 Cal.App.4th 299, 307; ***In re Lynna B.*** (1st Dist.1979) 92 Cal.App.3d 682, 704-05; *CEB Trial Objections*, §43.6. See "Official-Information Privilege," ch. 6-H, §1, p. 712.

(c) Identity of informers. *See* Evid. C. §§915(b), 1041. See "Informant Privilege," ch. 6-H, §3, p. 719.

(d) Trade-secret privilege. *See* Evid. C. §§915(b), 1060. See "Trade-Secret Privilege," ch. 6-C, §1, p. 642.

(e) Police or custodial officer's confidential personnel records. *See* Evid. C. §§1043, 1045; Pen. C. §832.7(a); ***Ibarra v. Superior Ct.*** (2d Dist.2013) 217 Cal.App.4th 695, 700-01. The court must conduct an in camera review if the discovering party establishes good cause. ***Rezek v. Superior Ct.*** (4th Dist.2012) 206 Cal.App.4th 633, 640; *see* Evid. C. §§1043(b)(3), 1045(b), (d). See "Officer-Records Privilege," ch. 6-H, §4, p. 721.

(2) Common-interest doctrine. The court can conduct an in camera review to determine whether the information is protected by the common-interest doctrine. ***OXY Res.***, 115 Cal.App.4th at 896; *see CEB Discovery Practice*, §3.197. The common-interest doctrine prevents waiver of the attorney-client and work-product privileges

in limited situations involving coparties. *See* ***Citizens for Ceres***, 217 Cal.App.4th at 914-15; ***OXY Res.***, 115 Cal.App.4th at 887-88. See "Common-interest doctrine," ch. 6-B, §2.8.2(4), p. 627.

(3) Exception or waiver. The court can conduct an in camera review to determine whether an exception or waiver applies that permits disclosure of privileged information. ***OXY Res.***, 115 Cal.App.4th at 896; *see CEB Trial Objections*, §34.23; *see, e.g.*, ***Mavroudis v. Superior Ct.*** (1st Dist.1980) 102 Cal.App.3d 594, 605 (dangerous-patient exception to psychotherapist privilege).

2. When prohibited. Examples of privileges not subject to an in camera review include the following:

(1) Attorney-client privilege. ***Southern Cal. Gas Co. v. Public Utils. Comm'n*** (1990) 50 Cal.3d 31, 45 n.19; *cf.* ***Regents of Univ. of Cal. v. Workers' Comp. Appeals Bd.*** (4th Dist.2014) 226 Cal.App.4th 1530, 1537 (in camera review of attorney-client privilege is not available in Workers' Compensation Appeals Board proceedings). See "Attorney-Client Privilege," ch. 6-B, §2, p. 614.

(2) Absolute attorney work-product privilege. ***Citizens for Ceres***, 217 Cal.App.4th at 911-12; *see* CCP §2018.030(a) (writing that reflects attorney's impressions, conclusions, opinions, or legal research or theories); Evid. C. §915(a) (presiding officer cannot require disclosure of work product under CCP §2018.030(a) to rule on claim of privilege); *cf.* ***Regents of Univ. of Cal.***, 226 Cal.App.4th at 1537 (in camera review of absolute work-product privilege is not available in Workers' Compensation Appeals Board proceedings). See "Work-Product Privilege," ch. 6-B, §3, p. 628.

(3) Marital-communications privilege. *See* Evid. C. §915(b) (no reference to marital-communications privilege). See "Marital-Communications Privilege," ch. 6-D, §2, p. 659.

(4) Fifth Amendment privilege. *Cf.* ***Solin v. O'Melveny & Myers LLP*** (2d Dist.2001) 89 Cal.App.4th 451, 465-66 (case involved attorney-client privilege and underlying claim of Fifth Amendment privilege).

3. Who can attend. The persons who can attend the in camera review include (1) the person authorized to claim the privilege and (2) anyone permitted to attend by the person authorized to claim the privilege. Evid. C. §915(b).

§14.3 Hearing. A hearing on a discovery motion is conducted in the same manner as civil hearings generally. If the court holds a hearing, it can be either for the taking of evidence or for the argument of counsel. See "Hearings," ch. 1-H, p. 79.

§15. WAIVING DISCOVERY & OBJECTIONS

§15.1 Waiver of right to discovery.

1. Right to discovery. A discovering party who does not serve its requests for discovery before the discovery cutoff waives the right to that discovery. See "When to complete discovery," §5.2, p. 746.

2. Right to compel.

(1) Waiver. If the CDA provides a deadline to make a motion to compel, the discovering party waives its right to compel if it does not make the motion by the deadline or by a later date stipulated to by the parties. *See* CCP §2025.480(b) (motion to compel deponent to answer or produce must be made within 60 days after deposition officer completes record), §2030.300(c) (motion to compel further response to interrogatories must be made within 45 days after service of verified response), §2031.310(c) (motion to compel further response to demand to produce must be made within 45 days after service of verified response), §2033.290(c) (motion to compel further response to RFAs must be made within 45 days after service of verified response); ***Sexton v. Superior Ct.*** (2d Dist.1997) 58 Cal.App.4th 1403, 1409-10 (court must deny late motion to compel further response to demand to produce); ***Deyo v. Kilbourne*** (2d Dist.1978) 84 Cal.App.3d 771, 788 (court must deny late motion to compel interrogatories). Once a party fails to make a timely motion to compel, it cannot obtain the information sought in the first discovery request

by asking the same question again in a second discovery request using the same method of discovery (e.g., interrogatories). *See* ***Professional Career Colls. v. Superior Ct.*** (4th Dist.1989) 207 Cal.App.3d 490, 494; *CEB Discovery Practice*, §7.111.

(2) No waiver. A discovering party's failure to make a motion to compel further responses in one type of discovery (e.g., interrogatories) does not prevent the party from seeking the same information in a different type of discovery (e.g., deposition) and making a motion to compel for that type of discovery, if necessary. *See* ***Carter v. Superior Ct.*** (1st Dist.1990) 218 Cal.App.3d 994, 997; *CEB Action Guide: Motions to Compel*, Step 37.

3. Relief from discovery deadline. If the discovering party needs more time to conduct discovery before the cutoff dates, the party must obtain either a written stipulation or a court order extending the discovery period. See "Later discovery cutoff," §5.2.3(2), p. 748.

§15.2 Waiver of objections.

1. Waiver of privilege objection. See "Waiver of privilege," ch. 6-A, §2.2.14, p. 607.

2. Waiver of discovery objection. A responding party waives its objection to a discovery request if it does not timely respond to the request or if it timely responds but does not assert the objection. *See* ***Best Prods. v. Superior Ct.*** (2d Dist.2004) 119 Cal.App.4th 1181, 1189-90 (untimely response to interrogatories waives objections); ***Stadish v. Superior Ct.*** (2d Dist.1999) 71 Cal.App.4th 1130, 1140 (untimely response to demand to produce waives objections); Weil, *Civil Procedure Before Trial*, ¶8:200 (untimely response may waive any objection). For specific time requirements, see the relevant subchapter in this book.

3. Relief from discovery waiver. If a party waives a discovery objection (e.g., serves a late response to interrogatories) but obtains relief from the waiver, the information is protected from discovery.

(1) Under CDA. The court can relieve a party from waiver if it finds both of the following:

(a) Late compliant response. The party served a late response that substantially complies with the statutory requirements. CCP §2030.290(a)(1) (response to interrogatories), §2031.300(a)(1) (response to demand to produce), §2032.240(a)(1) (response to demand for physical exam of personal-injury P), §2033.280(a)(1) (response to RFAs).

(b) Mistake or excusable neglect. The party's failure to serve a timely response was the result of mistake, inadvertence, or excusable neglect. CCP §2030.290(a)(2) (response to interrogatories), §2031.300(a)(2) (response to demand to produce), §2032.240(a)(2) (response to demand for physical exam of personal-injury P), §2033.280(a)(2) (response to RFAs); *see, e.g.*, ***Elston v. City of Turlock*** (1985) 38 Cal.3d 227, 234 (excusable neglect shown by testimony that RFA was misplaced when attorney was shorthanded and busy with other legal matters).

(2) Under CCP §473(b). A court can grant relief from mistake, inadvertence, surprise, or excusable neglect under CCP §473(b) only if the CDA does not provide similar relief. *See* ***Zellerino v. Brown*** (3d Dist.1991) 235 Cal.App.3d 1097, 1107. For example, relief from deemed admissions cannot be sought under §473(b) because the CDA already provides for it. ***St. Paul Fire & Mar. Ins. v. Superior Ct.*** (6th Dist.1992) 2 Cal.App.4th 843, 852, *disapproved on other grounds*, ***Wilcox v. Birtwhistle*** (1999) 21 Cal.4th 973.

§16. CUSTODY & DISPOSAL OF DISCOVERY

§16.1 Custody of discovery.

1. Written discovery. The discovering party must maintain custody of the original discovery request, its proof of service (POS), and the original response served by the responding party on the discovering party. CRC 3.250(a), (b); *see* CCP §2030.280(b) (interrogatories), §2031.290(b) (demand to produce), §2033.270(b) (RFAs).

2. Demand for exam of personal-injury P. The defendant must maintain custody of the original demand for a physical examination of the personal-injury plaintiff, its POS, and the original response served by the plaintiff on the defendant. CCP §2032.260(b).

3. Deposition.

(1) Deposition notice. The party who noticed the deposition must maintain custody of the deposition notice, deposition subpoena, and POS. *See* CRC 3.250(b) (custody of notice and POS).

(2) Deposition transcript. The party who noticed the deposition must maintain custody of the original transcribed deposition. See "Stenographic transcript," ch. 7-B, §9.18.6(1), p. 803.

(3) Deposition recording. The operator of electronic equipment who records the deposition must maintain custody of the electronic recording of the deposition. See "Electronic recording," ch. 7-B, §9.18.6(2), p. 803.

§16.2 Disposal of discovery. All original discovery papers can be destroyed six months after the final disposition of the case unless the court, based on a good-cause motion, orders the discovery to be preserved for a longer time. CCP §2030.280(b) (interrogatories), §2031.290(b) (demand to produce), §2032.260(b) (demand for physical exam of personal-injury P), §2033.270(b) (RFAs); CRC 3.250(b). See "Retention of deposition," ch. 7-B, §9.18.8, p. 804.

§17. REVIEW OF DISCOVERY ORDERS

NOTE

Although the CDA does not require the trial court to make written findings about the reasons for an order granting or denying discovery, findings can be helpful when the order is challenged in the appellate courts. See ***Greyhound Corp. v. Superior Ct.*** *(1961) 56 Cal.2d 355, 384. The trial court can file a memorandum opinion indicating the reasons supporting its order or include them in the order itself. Id.*

§17.1 Review by appeal. By statute, appeals in civil cases are limited to judgments and certain orders. *See* CCP §904.1 (list of appealable judgments and orders in unlimited civil cases), §904.2 (list of appealable judgments and orders in limited civil cases). Most discovery orders cannot be reviewed by the appellate court before final judgment. ***Sav-On Drugs, Inc. v. Superior Ct.*** (1975) 15 Cal.3d 1, 5; *see, e.g.*, ***Southern Pac. Co. v. Oppenheimer*** (1960) 54 Cal.2d 784, 786 (order sustaining objections to interrogatories is not reviewable before final judgment).

1. Final judgment. Most discovery orders are challenged in the appeal from the final judgment. *See* ***Sav-On Drugs***, 15 Cal.3d at 5; ***Johnson v. Superior Ct.*** (2d Dist.2000) 80 Cal.App.4th 1050, 1060; ***Brun v. Bailey*** (3d Dist.1994) 27 Cal.App.4th 641, 650; ***Barton v. Ahmanson Devs., Inc.*** (2d Dist.1993) 17 Cal.App.4th 1358, 1360-61 & n.1. For example, a terminating sanction is reviewable by appeal after entry of the final judgment resulting from the sanctions. *See* ***Sav-On Drugs***, 15 Cal.3d at 5 (discovery orders generally reviewed after final judgment); *see, e.g.*, ***Electronic Funds Solutions, LLC v. Murphy*** (4th Dist.2005) 134 Cal.App.4th 1161, 1166-67 (Ds appealed default judgment entered after trial court struck Ds' answer as discovery sanction).

2. Appealable orders.

(1) Postjudgment order. An order made after final judgment may be appealable. CCP §904.1(a)(2); *see* ***Lakin v. Watkins Associated Indus.*** (1993) 6 Cal.4th 644, 651-52 (discussing two-prong test to determine if postjudgment order is appealable); ***Macaluso v. Superior Ct.*** (4th Dist.2013) 219 Cal.App.4th 1042, 1047 (same); ***Shelton v. Rancho Mortg. & Inv.*** (4th Dist.2002) 94 Cal.App.4th 1337, 1343 (same).

(2) Order for sanctions. See "Appellate Review," ch. 9-A, §11, p. 1022.

(3) Final collateral order. An order is appealable before final judgment if it (1) is collateral to the main issue, (2) directs the payment of money or the performance of an act, and (3) is dispositive of the parties' rights in the collateral matter. ***Sjoberg v. Hastorf*** (1948) 33 Cal.2d 116, 119; ***Malek v. Koshak*** (2d Dist.2011) 200 Cal.App.4th 1540, 1545; *see* ***Steen v. Fremont Cemetery Corp.*** (6th Dist.1992) 9 Cal.App.4th 1221, 1226-27.

(a) Collateral. The order must be collateral to the subject matter of the litigation. ***Sjoberg***, 33 Cal.2d at 119; ***Marsh v. Mountain Zephyr, Inc.*** (4th Dist.1996) 43 Cal.App.4th 289, 297. A matter is collateral when it is distinct and severable from the general subject of the litigation. ***Steen***, 9 Cal.App.4th at 1227. The test is whether the order involves the merits of the issues in the main action; if the order does not affect the final determination in the main action, it is collateral. *See* ***Union Oil Co. v. Reconstruction Oil Co.*** (1935) 4 Cal.2d 541, 545. For example, an order setting the hourly rate for an expert's fee for a deposition is collateral to the subject matter of the litigation because it does not affect the outcome of the litigation. *See* ***Marsh***, 43 Cal.App.4th at 297-98; ***Brun***, 27 Cal.App.4th at 651.

(b) Payment or performance. Most courts hold that the order must require the payment of money or the performance of an act. ***Sjoberg***, 33 Cal.2d at 119; ***Malek***, 200 Cal.App.4th at 1545; *see* ***Lester v. Lennane*** (3d Dist.2000) 84 Cal.App.4th 536, 561-62; ***Conservatorship of Rich*** (1st Dist.1996) 46 Cal.App.4th 1233, 1237; ***Marsh***, 43 Cal.App.4th at 297-98. *But see* ***Meehan v. Hopps*** (1955) 45 Cal.2d 213, 216-17 (order denying disqualification of attorney was appealable); ***Muller v. Fresno Cmty. Hosp. & Med. Ctr.*** (2d Dist.2009) 172 Cal.App.4th 887, 902-03 (payment or performance is indicator that order is collateral to main action, but it is not essential; final collateral order is appealable even if no payment or performance is required). Some courts have suggested that this requirement does not apply when the order is being appealed by a nonparty. *See* ***Trimble v. Steinfeldt*** (2d Dist.1986) 178 Cal.App.3d 646, 650; *see also* ***Brun***, 27 Cal.App.4th at 649-50 (order denying expert witness's motion for protective order requiring D to pay expert-witness fee was appealable).

(c) Final. The order must be final as to the collateral matter. ***Sjoberg***, 33 Cal.2d at 119; ***Marsh***, 43 Cal.App.4th at 297. For example, an order setting the hourly rate for an expert's fee for a deposition is final as to that collateral issue. *See* ***Marsh***, 43 Cal.App.4th at 297-98; ***Brun***, 27 Cal.App.4th at 651.

§17.2 Review by writ. The review of discovery orders by writ is disfavored because the delay it causes is usually more harmful than the enforcement of an improper discovery order. ***Johnson v. Superior Ct.*** (2d Dist.2000) 80 Cal.App.4th 1050, 1060; *see* ***O'Grady v. Superior Ct.*** (6th Dist.2006) 139 Cal.App.4th 1423, 1439.

1. Discovery orders reviewable by writ. The following discovery orders can be reviewed by writ before final judgment:

(1) Order prevents proper litigation. Review of discovery orders by writ is appropriate when (1) the discovery order threatens immediate harm and (2) there is no other adequate remedy. ***Ibarra v. Superior Ct.*** (2d Dist.2013) 217 Cal.App.4th 695, 700; *see* ***Toshiba Am. Elec. Components, Inc. v. Superior Ct.*** (6th Dist.2004) 124 Cal.App.4th 762, 767; *see also* ***Fox Johns Lazar Pekin & Wexler, APC v. Superior Ct.*** (4th Dist.2013) 219 Cal.App.4th 1210, 1217-18 (treating nonappealable order as petition for writ of mandate).

(a) Privilege objection overruled. Extraordinary-writ relief is available when an order granting discovery overrules an objection based on a discovery privilege or exemption. *See* ***Roberts v. Superior Ct.*** (1973) 9 Cal.3d 330, 336. Once privileged information is disclosed, appellate review is inadequate. *See* ***O'Grady***, 139 Cal.App.4th at 1439.

(b) Fair opportunity denied. Extraordinary-writ relief is available when an order denying discovery denies a party a fair opportunity to litigate its case. ***Johnson***, 80 Cal.App.4th at 1061; ***Waicis v. Superior Ct.*** (1st Dist.1990) 226 Cal.App.3d 283, 286-87. For example, if an order denies a party a type of discovery that is essential to the preparation of its case, writ review might be appropriate. *See, e.g.,* ***Volkswagen of Am., Inc. v. Superior Ct.*** (1st Dist.2006) 139 Cal.App.4th 1481, 1487 (writ was available to review denial of demand to produce because deposition was not adequate substitute).

(2) Order presents issue of first impression. Extraordinary-writ relief is available to answer a question of first impression that is of general importance to the trial courts and the legal profession and can establish general guidelines for future cases. ***Oceanside Un. Sch. Dist. v. Superior Ct.*** (1962) 58 Cal.2d 180, 185 n.4; ***Avant! Corp. v. Superior Ct.*** (6th Dist.2000) 79 Cal.App.4th 876, 881; *see* ***O'Grady***, 139 Cal.App.4th at 1439; ***Toshiba***

Am. Elec., 124 Cal.App.4th at 767. For example, when no California court has ruled on an issue and it will likely reappear in other cases, the issue is sufficiently novel and important to justify review by extraordinary writ. *See, e.g.*, ***Toshiba Am. Elec.***, 124 Cal.App.4th at 767 (issue of who should pay to translate electronic data warranted writ review); ***Johnson***, 80 Cal.App.4th at 1061 (issue of whether parties could compel information from anonymous sperm donor warranted writ review).

(3) Order involves disclosure of public records. Extraordinary-writ relief is available when the court directs the disclosure of public records held by a public agency. *See* Gov. C. §6259(c); ***County of L.A. v. Superior Ct.*** (2d Dist.2000) 82 Cal.App.4th 819, 824.

2. Standard of review.

(1) For most orders.

(a) Abuse of discretion. Discovery orders are reviewed under the abuse-of-discretion standard. ***Bank of Am. v. Superior Ct.*** (4th Dist.2013) 212 Cal.App.4th 1076, 1089; *see* ***Greyhound Corp. v. Superior Ct.*** (1961) 56 Cal.2d 355, 380. An appellate court can reverse a trial court's decision for abuse of discretion when the trial court's exercise of discretion was not based on the law or when the court acted unreasonably. *See* ***Toshiba Am. Elec.***, 124 Cal.App.4th at 768; ***Department of Motor Vehicles v. Superior Ct.*** (2d Dist.2002) 100 Cal.App.4th 363, 369. An appellate court is likely to uphold an order allowing discovery and reverse an order denying discovery because of the liberal policy in favor of allowing discovery. ***Pacific Tel. & Tel. Co. v. Superior Ct.*** (1970) 2 Cal.3d 161, 171; ***Forthmann v. Boyer*** (2d Dist.2002) 97 Cal.App.4th 977, 987.

(b) De novo.

[1] Undisputed facts. Discovery orders are reviewed under the de novo standard when the facts are undisputed. ***Doe 2 v. Superior Ct.*** (2d Dist.2005) 132 Cal.App.4th 1504, 1515; *see* ***Toshiba Am. Elec.***, 124 Cal.App.4th at 768.

[2] Statutory interpretation. Discovery orders are reviewed under the de novo standard when the review of a discovery sanction turns on statutory interpretation. ***People v. Superior Ct.*** (4th Dist.2004) 122 Cal.App.4th 1060, 1071; ***Do v. Superior Ct.*** (4th Dist.2003) 109 Cal.App.4th 1210, 1212-13.

[3] Erroneous analysis of law. Discovery orders are reviewed under the de novo standard when a discovery motion is denied on relevancy grounds based on an erroneous analysis of the substantive law governing the case. *See* ***Children's Hosp. Cent. Cal. v. Blue Cross*** (5th Dist.2014) 226 Cal.App.4th 1260, 1277.

[4] Constitutional issue. Discovery orders are reviewed under the de novo standard when the issue is whether a discovery order violates a constitutional right. ***Maggi v. Superior Ct.*** (4th Dist.2004) 119 Cal.App.4th 1218, 1224.

(2) For orders disclosing public records.

(a) Issues of law. Issues of law in discovery orders directing the disclosure of a public agency's public records are reviewed independently. ***County of L.A.***, 82 Cal.App.4th at 824; *see* Gov. C. §6259(c) (interlocutory review of order directing or refusing to direct disclosure).

(b) Issues of fact. Issues of fact in discovery orders directing the disclosure of a public agency's public records are reviewed under a substantial-evidence standard (i.e., factual findings will be upheld if based on substantial evidence). *See* Gov. C. §6259(c); ***Times Mirror Co. v. Superior Ct.*** (1991) 53 Cal.3d 1325, 1336; ***County of L.A.***, 82 Cal.App.4th at 824.

3. Relief by writ. The appellate court can vacate a discovery order and direct the trial court to enter a new order, or it can vacate the order and remand the issue to the trial court for determination. *See* ***Doe 2***, 132 Cal.App.4th at 1517 (remanded to trial court); ***People***, 122 Cal.App.4th at 1081 (directed entry of new order).

B. DEPOSITIONS

§1. GENERAL

§1.1 Purpose. A deposition is used to secure and preserve sworn testimony for a trial or hearing. *See* CCP §2025.620. A deposition can be used to acquire information from both parties and nonparties. *See id.* §2025.010. A deposition is intended to elicit both admissible evidence and information reasonably calculated to lead to the discovery of admissible evidence. ***Kalaba v. Gray*** (2d Dist.2002) 95 Cal.App.4th 1416, 1423.

§1.2 Primary authority. CCP §§2025.010-2028.080.

§1.3 Secondary authority. The following secondary sources are cited as authority in this subchapter:

- *Action Guide: Handling Depositions* (CEB Online ed. 2013) (referred to as *CEB Action Guide: Depositions*).
- *California Civil Discovery Practice* (CEB Online ed. 2014) (referred to as *CEB Discovery Practice*).
- *California Trial Objections* (CEB Online ed. 2014) (referred to as *CEB Trial Objections*).
- *California Trial Practice: Civil Procedure During Trial* (CEB Online ed. 2014) (referred to as *CEB Procedure During Trial*).
- Jefferson, *California Evidence Benchbook* (CEB Online ed. 2014) (referred to as *Jefferson's Evid. Benchbook*).
- Sink, *California Subpoena Handbook* (2014-15) (referred to as Sink, *Subpoena Handbook*).
- State Bar of California, *Attorney Guidelines of Civility & Professionalism (Civility Toolbox)* (2009), ethics.calbar.ca.gov/Ethics/AttorneyCivilityandProfessionalism.aspx (referred to as *Cal. Attorney Guidelines*).
- Thomas, *California Civil Courtroom Handbook* (2014) (referred to as Thomas, *Courtroom Handbook*).
- Weil & Brown, *California Practice Guide: Civil Procedure Before Trial* (CD-ROM ed. 2014) (referred to as Weil, *Civil Procedure Before Trial*).
- Witkin, *California Evidence* (5th ed. 2012 & Supp.2014) (referred to as Witkin, *Cal. Evidence*).
- ***O'Connor's Federal Rules * Civil Trials*** (2015) (referred to as ***O'Connor's Federal Rules***).

§2. DEFINITIONS

§2.1 Deponent. The deponent is the person whose deposition is taken. *Black's Law Dictionary* 532 (10th ed. 2014). A deponent can be a party or nonparty. *See* CCP §2025.010; ***California Shellfish, Inc. v. United Shellfish Co.*** (1st Dist.1997) 56 Cal.App.4th 16, 23.

§2.2 Deposition officer. A deposition officer supervises and records depositions.

1. Qualifications of deposition officer.

(1) Unbiased. A deposition officer cannot be financially interested in the case and cannot be a relative or employee of any attorney or party in the case. CCP §2025.320(a); *CEB Discovery Practice*, §5.72.

(2) Authorized to administer oaths. A deposition officer must be authorized to administer oaths. CCP §2025.320; *see id.* §2028.010.

(3) Optional – authorized to record.

(a) Stenographically recorded deposition. If the deposition officer acts as the reporter for a stenographically recorded deposition (which is typical), the officer must be a certified shorthand reporter. *CEB Discovery Practice*, §5.72; *see* Bus. & Prof. C. §8016; CCP §2025.330(b).

(b) Electronically recorded deposition. The deposition officer can be the operator of the equipment for recording a deposition by videotape or audiotape if the officer is competent to record the deposition. *See* CCP §2025.340(b), (c). Generally, the deposition officer is not the operator of the audio/visual equipment. *CEB Discovery Practice*, §5.72.

NOTE

For the videotaped deposition of an expert intended for use at trial, the operator must be a person who is (1) authorized to administer oaths, (2) not financially interested in the case, and (3) not related to or employed by any of the attorneys or parties in the case. CCP §§2025.220(a)(6), 2025.340(c); see id. §2025.620(d). For all other videotape or audiotape depositions, the operator can be an employee of the attorney taking the deposition if there is another person acting as the deposition officer who can administer the oath. Id. §2025.340(b).

(4) Deposition for copying business records. A deposition for copying the business records of a nonparty is generally conducted by a deposition officer who is a registered professional photocopier. See "Deposition officer," ch. 8-B, §5.1.3(1), p. 964.

2. Duties of deposition officer.

(1) Oral deposition. The deposition officer for an oral deposition must administer the oath to the deponent and supervise the deposition. *See* CCP §§2025.320, 2025.330(a). The deposition officer will stenographically record the deposition unless the parties agree or the court orders otherwise. *See id.* §2025.330(b).

(2) Written deposition. The deposition officer for a written deposition must administer the oath to the deponent, propound each written question to the deponent, and record the deponent's answers. *CEB Discovery Practice*, §5.191; *see* CCP §§2025.330(a), 2028.010, 2028.080.

(3) Deposition for copying business records. The deposition officer at a deposition for copying a nonparty's business records must either make copies of the records at the custodian's place of business or take delivery of copies produced by the custodian. See "Complying with business-records subpoena," ch. 8-B, §6.1.4, p. 968.

§2.3 Deposition notice. A deposition notice is the statutory notice served on a party's attorney (or on a pro per party) to compel the party or its affiliated witness to appear, testify, and produce documents, electronically stored information (ESI), and other tangible things at a deposition. *See* CCP §2025.280(a). It has the same legal effect as a subpoena. See "Deposition notice for oral deposition," §9.2, p. 789.

§2.4 Deposition subpoena. A deposition subpoena is a subpoena served on a nonparty deponent to compel her to appear, testify, and produce documents and other tangible things at a deposition. See "Deposition Subpoenas," ch. 8-B, p. 959.

§2.5 Party-affiliated witness. A party-affiliated witness is a nonparty who, because of a close relationship with a party, can be required to appear, testify, and produce documents and other tangible things at a deposition by a deposition notice served on the party's attorney; it is not necessary for a deposition notice or subpoena to be served on a party-affiliated witness. *See* ***Unzipped Apparel, LLC v. Bader*** (2d Dist.2007) 156 Cal.App.4th 123, 130. Party-affiliated witnesses include the following:

1. The party's managing agent. CCP §2025.280(a). A "managing agent" of an organization is a person who can exercise her judgment and discretion in dealing with organizational matters, who can be expected to comply with the organization's directive to appear for pretrial examination, and who can be expected to identify herself with the interests of the organization. ***Waters v. Superior Ct.*** (1962) 58 Cal.2d 885, 896.

2. The party's officers and directors. CCP §2025.280(a).
3. The party's employees. *Id.*

NOTE

A party is required to produce only current managing agents, officers, directors, and employees. ***Maldonado v. Superior Ct.*** *(2d Dist.2002) 94 Cal.App.4th 1390, 1398. Former managing agents, officers, directors, and employees are not treated as party-affiliated witnesses. See* ***Haluck v. Ricoh Elecs., Inc.*** *(4th Dist.2007) 151 Cal.App.4th 994, 1005;* ***Maldonado****, 94 Cal.App.4th at 1398.*

---

4. The party's designated expert. CCP §2034.460(a). See "Expert Discovery," ch. 7-I, p. 898.

PRACTICE TIP

The list of people who are considered party-affiliated witnesses for deposition notices is different from that for trial notices. For deposition notices, party-affiliated witnesses include a party's employees, a group that is not included in the list of party-affiliated witnesses for trial notices. For trial notices, party-affiliated witnesses include people "for whose immediate benefit the suit is being prosecuted or defended," a group that is not included in the list of party-affiliated witnesses for deposition notices. See "Party-affiliated witness," ch. 8-A, §2.5, p. 933.

---

§3. COMPARING DEPOSITIONS WITH OTHER DISCOVERY

§3.1 Depositions vs. interrogatories. While both depositions and interrogatories use a question-and-answer approach to obtaining factual information from another party, they have different advantages.

1. Depositions. Depositions have some significant advantages over interrogatories. Depositions give a party the opportunity to evaluate how a deponent will perform as a witness at trial; interrogatories do not. *CEB Discovery Practice*, §7.28; *see, e.g.*, ***Hillman v. Stults*** (2d Dist.1968) 263 Cal.App.2d 848, 877 (D's testimony at deposition may have influenced her attorney to not call her as witness at trial). Depositions permit a party to obtain spontaneous answers from a witness who is under pressure to answer questions without conferring with her attorney; interrogatory answers are drafted by the responding party's attorney and give the responding party an opportunity to provide carefully worded answers that can hide potential weaknesses in her claims or defenses. *See CEB Discovery Practice*, §§7.27, 7.28. Depositions can require answers in a shorter period of time than interrogatories (10 days versus 30 days). See "Deadlines to respond to discovery," ch. 7-A, §8.1, p. 754. Depositions permit a party to immediately ask follow-up questions to answers; interrogatories do not. *CEB Discovery Practice*, §7.28. Depositions permit a party to question a witness at length, which can be useful for discovering background information; interrogatories do not. *See id.* See "Length of oral deposition," §9.5, p. 793; "Rule of 35," ch. 7-C, §6.2.1(1), p. 822. Depositions permit a party to require the production of documents and other things at the deposition; interrogatories are a less useful tool for compelling production. *See CEB Discovery Practice*, §§5.3, 7.44.

2. Interrogatories. Interrogatories have some significant advantages over depositions. Interrogatories are less expensive than depositions. *CEB Discovery Practice*, §7.28; 2 Witkin, *Cal. Evidence*, Discovery, §92. Because answers to interrogatories are not limited to the responding party's ability to quickly remember information under pressure, interrogatories are better suited for obtaining detailed, factual information. *See CEB Discovery Practice*, §7.28; Weil, *Civil Procedure Before Trial*, ¶8:901. Because a party responding to interrogatories must provide all the information that can be obtained from any person or entity under its control (as compared to depositions, during which a deponent must provide only information she knows), interrogatories are better suited for obtaining information known by more than one agent or employee of a party. *See* CCP §2030.220(c); ***Gordon v. Superior Ct.*** (2d Dist.1984) 161 Cal.App.3d 157, 167-68. Interrogatories can be used to discover a party's legal contentions in the case, which cannot be discovered through a deposition. See "Legal contentions," ch. 7-C, §3.1.5(2), p. 818.

§3.2 Depositions vs. demands to produce. While both depositions and demands to produce can require the production of documents and other tangible things, they have different advantages.

1. Depositions. Depositions can require the production of things in a shorter period of time than demands to produce (10 days versus 30 days). See "Deadlines to respond to discovery," ch. 7-A, §8.1, p. 754. Deposition notices must describe individual items to be produced with only reasonable particularity; demands to produce must describe individual items specifically. See "Proper Description of Things to Be Produced," chart 7-8, p. 754.

2. Demands to produce. Demands to produce can require the other party to provide access to real property and things located on real property; depositions cannot. See "Land," ch. 7-E, §3.1.3, p. 846. Demands to produce can require the inspection, testing, measuring, or sampling of things to be produced; a deposition notice to a party cannot. See "No testing or sampling of things to be produced," §9.2.4(5), p. 791.

§3.3 Depositions vs. requests for admission. While both depositions and requests for admission can require the production of information, they have different advantages.

1. Depositions. Depositions can require answers in a shorter period of time than requests for admission (10 days versus 30 days). See "Deadlines to respond to discovery," ch. 7-A, §8.1, p. 754.

2. RFAs. Requests for admission can produce incontrovertible evidence against the responding party; deposition questions produce mere evidence, which can be controverted. ***Murillo v. Superior Ct.*** (4th Dist.2006) 143 Cal.App.4th 730, 736. Unlike depositions, requests for admission are more than just a discovery device. *See* ***Jahn v. Brickey*** (4th Dist.1985) 168 Cal.App.3d 399, 404 (comparing RFAs to interrogatories). Requests for admission serve a function similar to the pleadings in a lawsuit in that they are aimed at resolving controverted issues; if an issue is resolved by a request for admission, the issue will not have to be tried. *Id.*; *see* ***Mardirossian v. Ersoff*** (2d Dist.2007) 153 Cal.App.4th 257, 271.

§4. TYPES OF DEPOSITIONS

§4.1 Oral deposition. An oral deposition allows a party to ask a deponent questions orally and make a record of the questions and the answers. *See Black's Law Dictionary* 534 (10th ed. 2014). The deposition is conducted under oath outside the courtroom—usually in an attorney's office—and recorded by a word-for-word stenographic transcription and, when requested, by an electronic recording device. *See id.* See "Oral Deposition," §9, p. 788.

§4.2 Deposition on written questions. A deposition on written questions (also known as a written deposition) allows a party to ask a deponent questions in writing and make a record of the questions and the answers. *See Black's Law Dictionary* 534 (10th ed. 2014). The deposition is conducted under oath outside the courtroom—usually at the deponent's place of business. *See* CCP §§2025.250, 2028.010, 2028.020(b). As with an oral deposition, a written deposition is recorded by stenographic transcription and, when requested, by an electronic recording device. *See id.* §§2025.330(b), (c), 2028.010. See "Deposition on Written Questions," §10, p. 804.

§4.3 Deposition for production of business records. A deposition for the production of a nonparty's business records (without the attendance of the nonparty) allows a party to secure business records from a nonparty. It requires a subpoena. See "Deposition Subpoena for Business Records," ch. 8-B, §5, p. 963. There is no deposition procedure to require a party to produce records without the party's attendance. The only way to secure a party's records without an appearance is with a demand to produce. See "Demands to Produce," ch. 7-E, p. 845.

§4.4 Deposition to perpetuate testimony. A deposition to perpetuate testimony allows a person to file a petition for permission to depose a witness by oral or written questions before a suit is filed. The purpose is to preserve testimony that might be lost before suit is filed. See "Presuit Discovery," ch. 7-J, p. 923.

§4.5 Deposition pending appeal. A deposition pending appeal allows a party to depose a witness by oral or written questions while the case is on appeal. The purpose is to preserve testimony that might be lost before additional postjudgment proceedings can be held. *See* CCP §§2036.010-2036.050. This book does not discuss depositions pending appeal. For more information, see *CEB Discovery Practice*, §§5.156-5.159, and Weil, *Civil Procedure Before Trial*, ¶8:431.

§5. SCOPE OF DISCOVERY BY DEPOSITIONS

§5.1 What is discoverable. At a deposition, a person can be required to answer any questions and produce anything requested that is within the scope of discovery and is not protected from discovery by a privilege or exemption. CCP §2025.010. See "Scope of Discovery," ch. 6-A, p. 603.

§5.2 What is not discoverable. A party's legal contentions are not a proper subject for deposition questions. ***Rifkind v. Superior Ct.*** (2d Dist.1994) 22 Cal.App.4th 1255, 1262-63. A deponent cannot be expected to sort through the facts during a deposition and apply the law to those facts; that is the responsibility of the attorney. *Id.* But a party's legal contentions are discoverable through interrogatories and requests for admission. *See* CCP §2030.010(b) (interrogatories), §2033.010 (RFAs). See "Legal contentions," ch. 7-C, §3.1.5(2), p. 818.

§5.3 Limit on number of depositions.

1. **Unlimited civil cases.** In unlimited civil cases, there are no restrictions on the total number of depositions a party can take, as long as the depositions are not unreasonably cumulative, burdensome, or expensive. *See* CCP §§2019.030, 2025.010. If a party considers the number of depositions sought by the other party to be excessive, the party can seek relief through a motion for a protective order. See "Motion for protective order," §12.1, p. 808. There are restrictions on the number of times a particular deponent can be deposed. *See, e.g.*, CCP §2025.610(a) (natural-person deponent can only be deposed once), §2025.610(b) (court may grant leave to take second deposition for good cause). See "Who can be redeposed," §9.19, p. 804. For a discussion of the classification of civil cases, see "Procedural Classifications of Civil Cases," ch. 3-E, §4, p. 255.

2. **Limited civil cases.**

(1) **Oral or written deposition.** In limited civil cases, a party can take only one oral or written deposition for each adverse party. CCP §94(b). For a discussion of the classification of civil cases, see "Procedural Classifications of Civil Cases," ch. 3-E, §4, p. 255.

(2) **Deposition subpoena for business records.** In limited civil cases, there is no limit on the number of deposition subpoenas for business records that a party can serve on a nonparty. *See* CCP §94(c). A subpoenaed nonparty must mail copies of the requested records to the party's attorney, along with an affidavit required by Evid. C. §1561. CCP §94(c). See "Deposition Subpoena for Business Records," ch. 8-B, §5, p. 963.

§6. WHO CAN BE DEPOSED

§6.1 Parties. Any party to the action can be deposed. CCP §2025.010. This includes opposing parties and coparties. Weil, *Civil Procedure Before Trial*, ¶8:463; *see* CCP §2025.010. A party can even depose itself. Weil, *Civil Procedure Before Trial*, ¶8:463; *see* CCP §2025.010 ("any party to the action").

§6.2 Natural persons. Any natural person can be deposed if the person can be required to attend the deposition. *See* CCP §2025.010. See "How to Require Deposition Attendance," §7, p. 785.

§6.3 Organizations. Any organization, including public and private corporations, partnerships, associations, and government agencies, can be deposed if the organization can be required to attend the deposition. *See* CCP §2025.010. See "How to Require Deposition Attendance," §7, p. 785.

§6.4 Opposing counsel. An opposing party's attorney can be deposed, but such depositions are presumptively improper and require a showing of extremely good cause. ***Melendrez v. Superior Ct.*** (2d Dist.2013) 215 Cal.App.4th 1343, 1353 n.12; ***Carehouse Convalescent Hosp. v. Superior Ct.*** (4th Dist.2006) 143 Cal.App.4th 1558, 1562. The deposition is proper only if the following conditions are satisfied:

1. The deposing party has no other practicable means to obtain the information. ***Carehouse Convalescent***, 143 Cal.App.4th at 1563; *see* ***Melendrez***, 215 Cal.App.4th at 1353 n.12 (usually information will be available by further written discovery). The deposing party has the burden of proof on this element. ***Carehouse Convalescent***, 143 Cal.App.4th at 1563.

2. The information sought is crucial to the preparation of the case. *Id.* The deposing party has the burden of proof on this element. *Id.*

3. The information is not privileged. *Id.* The opposing party has the burden of proving the information is privileged. *Id.* See "Attorney-Related Privileges," ch. 6-B, p. 613.

§7. HOW TO REQUIRE DEPOSITION ATTENDANCE

The primary ways to require a person to attend a deposition include the following:

§7.1 Agreement. The deposition of any person (party or nonparty, resident or nonresident) can be taken at any place or time if the parties and the deponent agree to it in writing. *See* CCP §2016.030; *see also CEB Discovery Practice*, §5.222 (sample form for deposition stipulation). See "Modifying discovery by stipulation," ch. 7-A, §4.1, p. 743.

§7.2 Deposition notice. A deposition notice is used to compel the party or its affiliated witnesses, whether residents or nonresidents, to appear, testify, and produce documents, ESI, and other tangible things at a deposition. *See* CCP §2025.280(a) (deposition in California), §2026.010(a), (b) (deposition outside California, but in U.S.), §2027.010(a), (b) (deposition outside U.S.); *CEB Action Guide: Depositions*, Steps 11-13; *CEB Discovery Practice*, §12.5; Thomas, *Courtroom Handbook*, §21:45; Weil, *Civil Procedure Before Trial*, ¶¶8:635, 8:643. See "Deposition notice for oral deposition," §9.2, p. 789.

PRACTICE TIP

If you are uncertain whether a witness is a party-affiliated witness that can be required to attend a deposition by a deposition notice (e.g., you do not know whether the witness is still an employee of the party), consider serving a deposition subpoena on the witness (in case the witness is not a party-affiliated witness) and a deposition notice on the other party's attorney (in case the witness is a party-affiliated witness). See "Party-affiliated witness," §2.5, p. 781.

§7.3 Deposition subpoena. A deposition subpoena is used to compel a nonparty deponent who is a California resident to appear, testify, and produce documents and other tangible things at a deposition. *See* CCP §2020.220(c). See "Deposition Subpoenas," ch. 8-B, p. 959. As a general rule, any person who can be subpoenaed can be deposed. See "Who can be subpoenaed," ch. 8-A, §4.1, p. 937.

7-13. DEPOSITION NOTICE VS. DEPOSITION SUBPOENA

		Deposition notice	Deposition subpoena
Who can be compelled by deposition notice & deposition subpoena			
1	Party	Yes. CCP §2025.280(a).	No.
2	Party's officer, director, or managing agent	Yes. CCP §2025.280(a).	No.
3	Party's employee	Yes. CCP §2025.280(a).	No.
4	Nonparty with immediate benefit in suit	No.	Yes. *See* CCP §2025.280(b).
5	Party's designated expert	Yes. CCP §2034.460(a).	No.
6	Nonretained expert (e.g., treating doctor)	No.	Yes. *See* CCP §2025.280(b).
7	Nonparty deponent	No.	Yes. *See* CCP §§2020.010(b), 2025.280(b).

7-13. DEPOSITION NOTICE VS. DEPOSITION SUBPOENA (CONTINUED)			
		Deposition notice	Deposition subpoena
Requirements for deposition notice & deposition subpoena			
8	How to describe things to be produced	All things and categories with reasonable particularity. CCP §2025.220(a)(4).	Items specifically; categories with reasonable particularity; desired form of ESI, if applicable. CCP §§2020.410(a), 2020.510(a)(2), (a)(4).
9	Attach declaration showing good cause and materiality	No. See ch. 8-A, §6.4.2, p. 943.	No. See ch. 8-A, §6.4.2, p. 943.
10	When to pay witness fees*	On service of notice or on commencement. See ch. 7-I, §11.3.2(1), p. 914.	On service of subpoena or on appearance. See ch. 8-A, §10.2.4(1)(a), p. 953.
11	Which deponents are paid fees	Expert witness but not party or party-affiliated witness. See §8, p. 788.	Subpoenaed nonparties. See ch. 8-A, §10.2.1(1), p. 952.
On whom & when to serve deposition notice & deposition subpoena			
12	For testimony only, serve—	Deposition notice on party's attorney, ten days before deposition. *See* CCP §§2025.270(a), 2025.280(a).	SUBP-015 on nonparty deponent, reasonable time before deposition. *See* CCP §2020.220(a).
13	For testimony and production, serve—	Deposition notice on party's attorney, ten days before deposition. *See* CCP §§2025.270(a), 2025.280(a).	SUBP-020 on nonparty deponent, reasonable time before deposition. *See* CCP §2020.220(a).
14	For production only, serve—	N/A	SUBP-020 on nonparty deponent, 15 days before date for production. *See* CCP §2020.410(c).
15	Serve notice of deposition on other parties—	Ten days before deposition. *See* CCP §§2025.240(a), 2025.270(a).	Ten days before deposition. *See* CCP §§2025.240(a), 2025.270(a), (c).

* Special rules apply to the payment of witness fees for public employees. See "Government witness fees," ch. 8-A, §10.4, p. 955.
SUBP-015 = Judicial Council Form SUBP-015
SUBP-020 = Judicial Council Form SUBP-020

§7.4 Court order.

1. Out-of-state parties + deposition in California. Courts are split on whether parties who are not residents of California can be required by motion and court order to travel to California for a deposition. *Compare* ***Toyota Motor Corp. v. Superior Ct.*** (2d Dist.2011) 197 Cal.App.4th 1107, 1122, 1125 (courts cannot order nonresidents to attend California depositions), *with* ***Glass v. Superior Ct.*** (4th Dist.1988) 204 Cal.App.3d 1048, 1052 (courts can order nonresident parties to attend California depositions). Such parties can be required to attend a deposition in their home state or country by service of a deposition notice. CCP §2026.010(a), (b) (party outside California, but in U.S.), §2027.010(a), (b) (party outside U.S.).

2. Prisoners.

(1) State prisoner. To take the deposition of a prisoner incarcerated in a state institution, a party must secure a court order; state prisoners are not subject to subpoenas. Sink, *Subpoena Handbook*, §2.2[A]; *see* CCP §1995 (county jail); Pen. C. §2623 (state prison). To obtain a court order, the party must make a motion accompanied by an affidavit identifying (1) the nature of the proceeding, (2) the testimony expected, and (3) the materiality of the testimony. CCP §1996; Pen. C. §2623. For more on the procedure to compel a prisoner's testimony, see Sink, *Subpoena Handbook*, §2.2[A].

(a) **Same county.** Persons incarcerated in a jail in the county where the case is pending can be produced for a deposition, trial, or hearing. *See* CCP §1997.

(b) **Different county.** Persons incarcerated in a jail in a county other than the one where the case is pending can be produced for a deposition only; they cannot be produced for a trial or hearing. *See* CCP §1997.

(2) **Federal prisoner.** To take the deposition of a federal prisoner incarcerated in California, the attorney must make arrangements with the prisoner's warden. *See* Sink, *Subpoena Handbook*, §2.2[B][2]. By comparison, to compel a trial appearance, the party must secure from a California court or federal district court a writ of habeas corpus ad testificandum that is addressed to the warden. *Id.* §2.2[B][3][a]. Persons incarcerated in federal prisons are not subject to subpoenas. *See id.* §2.2[B].

§7.5 Other states' local laws & foreign treaties. Nonparties who are not residents of California cannot be required to attend a deposition in California. *See* CCP §1989 (witness not required to attend unless she is resident of state at time of service); ***Toyota Motor Corp. v. Superior Ct.*** (2d Dist.2011) 197 Cal.App.4th 1107, 1110 (CCP §1989 applies to discovery).

1. **Out-of-state nonparties.** Nonparties who are not residents of California but are residents of a U.S. state, territory, or insular possession can be required to attend a deposition at their place of residence according to local laws. CCP §2026.010(c); Thomas, *Courtroom Handbook*, §21:42. In some states, it is easy to compel a resident to attend a deposition, while in others it is more difficult because of additional procedures.

NOTE

While the procedures for requiring a nonparty to attend a deposition out of state follow local law, questions about what is discoverable and other discovery issues are still governed by California law. ***International Ins. v. Montrose Chem. Corp.*** *(2d Dist.1991) 231 Cal.App.3d 1367, 1371; Weil, Civil Procedure Before Trial, ¶8:642.1.*

(1) **Treated like in-state case.** Some states have adopted the Uniform Interstate Depositions and Discovery Act, which allows a deposing party from one state (e.g., California) to request that the court clerk in another state (e.g., New York) issue a subpoena for the deposition of a resident of that other state. *See* ***Digital Music News LLC v. Superior Ct.*** (2d Dist.2014) 226 Cal.App.4th 216, 223; Weil, *Civil Procedure Before Trial*, ¶8:637; *see, e.g.*, CCP §§2029.100-2029.900 (Interstate and International Depositions and Discovery Act); Del. C. tit. 10, §4311 (Uniform Interstate Depositions and Discovery Act); N.Y. C.P.L.R. §3119 (same). Once served, the subpoena requires the resident to attend and produce according to local deposition procedures. *See, e.g.*, CCP §2029.500 (laws and court rules on depositions apply to discovery under Interstate and International Depositions and Discovery Act); ***Digital Music News***, 226 Cal.App.4th at 223-24 (foreign proceedings under Uniform Interstate Depositions and Discovery Act are governed by Civil Discovery Act).

(2) **California commission required.** Some states require the court clerk in California to issue a commission to a deposition officer in the state where the deposition is to be taken, authorizing the officer to conduct the deposition. *CEB Discovery Practice*, §12.8; *CEB Action Guide: Depositions*, Step 12; Weil, *Civil Procedure Before Trial*, ¶8:640. The commission will ask the other jurisdiction to issue process requiring the nonparty to attend and produce. CCP §2026.010(f). The clerk can issue the commission without a noticed motion or court order, unless the other jurisdiction requires it. *Id.*

2. **Foreign nonparties.** Nonparties who are residents of a foreign country can be required to attend a deposition in that country only under that country's laws. CCP §2027.010(c); *see CEB Action Guide: Depositions*, Step 13. If the nonparty is a resident of a country that has signed the Hague Convention on Taking of Evidence Abroad in Civil or Commercial Matters, the deposing party can use the Convention's procedures to secure the relevant testimony or other information. Weil, *Civil Procedure Before Trial*, ¶¶8:50, 8:648.

PRACTICE TIP

It is difficult, expensive, and time-consuming to take the deposition of an unwilling witness in a foreign country. See generally CCP §2027.010 (procedures for conducting deposition in foreign country). For a discussion of the procedures, see CEB Discovery Practice, ch. 13, and ***O'Connor's Federal Rules****, "In foreign country," ch. 6-F, §3.3.2, p. 595.*

§8. WITNESS FEES

§8.1 Party deponent. Witness fees are not required to be paid to compel a party served with a deposition notice to attend a deposition. Sink, *Subpoena Handbook*, §5.2[C], Rule 7; *see* ***Di Napoli v. Superior Ct.*** (5th Dist.1967) 252 Cal.App.2d 202, 204; *see also* CCP §1986.5 (any person "subpoenaed" for deposition must be paid witness fees; no mention of persons required to attend deposition by deposition notice), §2025.280(a) (party required to attend deposition by service of deposition notice; no mention of witness fees).

§8.2 Party-affiliated witness. Witness fees are not required to be paid to compel a party-affiliated witness served with a deposition notice to attend a deposition. Sink, *Subpoena Handbook*, §5.2[C], Rule 7; *see* ***Di Napoli v. Superior Ct.*** (5th Dist.1967) 252 Cal.App.2d 202, 204 (witness fees limited to persons served with deposition subpoena).

§8.3 Nonparty deponent. See "Ordinary witness fees," ch. 8-A, §10.2, p. 951.

§8.4 Custodian deponent. See "Custodian fees," ch. 8-A, §10.3, p. 953.

§8.5 Government deponent. See "Government witness fees," ch. 8-A, §10.4, p. 955.

§8.6 Expert deponent. See "Expert-Witness Fees," ch. 7-I, §11, p. 912.

§9. ORAL DEPOSITION

§9.1 Whom & what to serve. For an oral deposition, determining whom and what to serve depends on (1) whether the deponent is a party or nonparty and (2) whether personal records are sought.

1. Party deponent. For the oral deposition of a party, the deposing party must serve a deposition notice on that party's attorney and on the attorneys for all other parties who have appeared in the case. CCP §2025.240(a). See "Deposition notice for oral deposition," §9.2, p. 789. If a party is not represented by an attorney, the party can be served directly.

2. Nonparty deponent. For the oral deposition of a nonparty (with or without document production), the deposing party must serve the following documents:

(1) On nonparty deponent. The nonparty deponent must be personally served with a copy of the deposition subpoena. See "Witness," ch. 8-B, §3.4.1, p. 961 (deposition subpoena to attend); "Witness," ch. 8-B, §4.4.1, p. 963 (deposition subpoena to attend and produce).

(2) On parties. The parties who have appeared in the case must be served with copies of the deposition subpoena and the deposition notice. CCP §2025.240(c).

3. Personal records sought. Whenever a party seeks to discover personal records or information from another party or a nonparty by deposition, the request (whether by subpoena or notice) may implicate the right to privacy guaranteed in the California Constitution. *See* Cal. Const., art. I, §1; ***In re Insurance Installment Fee Cases*** (4th Dist.2012) 211 Cal.App.4th 1395, 1420 & n.15. The subpoena procedures for obtaining such information from nonparties (i.e., party-to-nonparty discovery) include specific requirements for notifying a person (whether a party or nonparty) whose records or information is sought and giving the person an opportunity to object to the request. *See* CCP §§1985.3, 1985.4, 1985.6. See "Subpoenas for Personal Records," ch. 8-D, p. 977. Strangely, no such notice and objection requirements are included in the Civil Discovery Act (CDA) procedures for obtaining personal records or information from another party (i.e., party-to-party discovery) about a different party or nonparty. *See* ***Valley Bank***

v. Superior Ct. (1975) 15 Cal.3d 652, 657 (existing discovery scheme does not protect privacy of persons whose records are sought). But the responding party may have a constitutional or statutory duty to protect the privacy of the person whose records or information is sought. *See id.* at 656; ***In re Insurance Installment Fee Cases***, 211 Cal.App.4th at 1423, 1426. See "Right to Privacy," ch. 6-F, §1, p. 681. The court can protect the privacy of the person whose information is sought by ordering the responding party to give the third person notice and an opportunity to object to the request. *See* ***Pioneer Elecs. (USA), Inc. v. Superior Ct.*** (2007) 40 Cal.4th 360, 372; ***In re Insurance Installment Fee Cases***, 211 Cal.App.4th at 1423. See "Cost of production," ch. 7-E, §8.2, p. 853; "Types of Persons & Entities Covered," ch. 8-D, §7, p. 981. At least one commentator has offered the practical recommendation that parties seeking such discovery from other parties should follow the procedures required for obtaining personal information from nonparties by subpoena. *See* Sink, *Subpoena Handbook*, §§6.2[I], 6.4. By following the procedures governing deposition subpoenas for personal-records discovery from nonparties, a deposing party may avoid both the expense of having to litigate privacy issues and possible sanctions.

NOTE

Sink's recommendation that a discovering party assume that all steps required under §1985.3, 1985.4, or 1985.6 apply to discovery under the CDA is useful only if the discovering party knows the identity of the party or nonparty whose consumer or personal records are sought. When the party's or nonparty's identity is unknown, it will be impossible for the discovering party to give advance notice of the request for records.

§9.2 Deposition notice for oral deposition. A party can be required to attend a deposition by service of a deposition notice on the party's attorney. *See* CCP §2025.280(a). It is not necessary to serve a deposition subpoena on a party to compel the party's attendance at a deposition. *See id.* The following information must be included in the deposition notice:

1. Place for deposition. The deposition notice must indicate where the deposition is to take place. CCP §2025.220(a)(1). See "Where to conduct deposition," §9.6, p. 794.

2. Date & time for deposition. The deposition notice must indicate the date and time the deposition will begin. CCP §2025.220(a)(2). See "When to schedule deposition," §9.4.1, p. 793.

3. Identity of deponent.

(1) Party deponent. The deposition notice must identify a party deponent by name. CCP §2025.220(a)(3).

(2) Nonparty deponent. The deposition notice must identify a nonparty deponent by name, address, and telephone number (if known). CCP §2025.220(a)(3).

(3) Name unknown. If the name of the deponent is not known, the deposition notice must provide a general description that is sufficient to identify either the person or the particular class to which the person belongs. CCP §2025.220(a)(3); *see also* CRC 3.768(a) (discovery from unnamed class-action members).

(4) Organization deponent. To secure the testimony of an organization (e.g., corporation, partnership, government agency), the deposing party must depose a person who is authorized to speak for the organization in a representative capacity.

(a) Representative capacity. If the deposing party wants to secure the testimony of a representative of an organization, the deposition notice must name the organization as the deponent, describe the subject matter of the questions to be asked, and require the organization to designate the persons within its organization who are most qualified to testify on its behalf about those matters. *See* CCP §2025.230; *CEB Discovery Practice*, §5.62; *see also* Evid. C. §1222 (statement by authorized person may be admissible against party).

[1] Organization's duty. The deposition notice must advise the organization that it is required to designate and produce one or more of its officers, directors, managing agents, agents, or employees to testify on its behalf about the matters described in the notice. *See* CCP §2025.230; *cf. id.* §2020.310(e) (deposition

subpoena). The organization must produce the most qualified person or persons to testify on its behalf. *Id.* §2025.230; ***Maldonado v. Superior Ct.*** (2d Dist.2002) 94 Cal.App.4th 1390, 1395; *CEB Discovery Practice*, §§5.8, 5.62. The "most qualified" person is the one who is (1) most knowledgeable about the matters described in the notice and (2) currently employed by the organization. ***Maldonado***, 94 Cal.App.4th at 1398. The organization must make sure the person it designates is given access to the organization's information and documents so as to be knowledgeable about the subjects to be covered in the deposition. *Id.*

[2] Matters for examination. The deposition notice must describe with reasonable particularity the matters on which the organization's representative will be examined. CCP §2025.230; *CEB Discovery Practice*, §5.62; Weil, *Civil Procedure Before Trial*, ¶8:471; *cf.* CCP §2020.310(e) (deposition subpoena). The description allows the organization to designate one or more persons who have knowledge about the subject of the deposition. *See* CCP §2025.230. The representative must testify to the extent of any information known or reasonably available to the organization. *Id.*

(b) Nonrepresentative capacity. If the deposing party wants to secure the testimony of a specific person in an organization, the deposing party can name that person as the deponent in the deposition notice.

[1] Named officer. If the deposing party wants to depose a specific officer, director, or managing agent of an organization, the deposing party can name that person as the deponent without naming the organization itself. *See CEB Discovery Practice*, §5.41; Weil, *Civil Procedure Before Trial*, ¶8:469. However, the deposition of a person employed by an organization is not binding on the organization unless it authorized the person to speak on its behalf. *See* Evid. C. §1222 (statement by person authorized by party is not hearsay against party). After the deposition of an unauthorized representative, the deposing party can depose an authorized representative about the unauthorized representative's testimony, or it can serve requests for admission on the organization asking it to admit or deny the unauthorized representative's testimony; if the organization adopts or admits the unauthorized representative's testimony, the testimony becomes party admissions. *See* Evid. C. §§1221, 1222; Weil, *Civil Procedure Before Trial*, ¶8:469; *see also* ***O'Mary v. Mitsubishi Elecs. Am., Inc.*** (4th Dist.1997) 59 Cal.App.4th 563, 570-74 (discussing authority of high-level employees to speak for corporation).

[2] Named employee. If the deposing party wants to depose an organization's employee not to speak for the organization but as an ordinary witness, the party can identify the employee by name as the deponent. *See* Weil, *Civil Procedure Before Trial*, ¶8:469. For example, if the party knows the name of the employee who witnessed a workplace accident, the party can notice (or subpoena) the employee by name to testify about what she saw; the employee can testify as a witness to the accident but not as the company's representative.

PRACTICE TIP

If the named deponent is a high-level officer or employee, the organization can make a motion for a protective order to prevent the deposition. See "Prevent apex deposition," §12.1.2(2), p. 808.

---

4. Production of things. The deposition notice must identify any materials or category of materials that the deponent must produce at the deposition. CCP §2025.220(a)(4). See "Tangible things," ch. 6-A, §2.2.6, p. 605.

PRACTICE TIP

Although the deposing party can secure documents during an oral deposition, it is better to secure and review documents before the deposition by serving a demand (on a party) or a subpoena (on a nonparty) to produce and copy documents. See "Demands to Produce," ch. 7-E, p. 845; "Deposition Subpoena for Testimony & Things," ch. 8-B, §4, p. 962.

---

(1) Existing things only. For the types of things a deponent can be required to produce at a deposition, see "Existing things only," ch. 8-A, §5.1, p. 939.

(2) Custody or control. The deponent can be required to produce at the deposition documents, ESI, or other tangible things under its custody or control. *See* CCP §2025.480(a) (motion to compel deponent to produce things under its control).

(3) Description of things to be produced. When a deposition notice requires the production of things by a party, the notice must identify with reasonable particularity (1) the things to be produced or (2) the category of things to be produced. CCP §2025.220(a)(4). See "Proper Description of Things to Be Produced," chart 7-8, p. 754.

NOTE

By comparison, when a deposition subpoena requires the production of things by a nonparty, the subpoena must (1) specifically describe each thing to be produced or (2) describe with reasonable particularity each category of items to be produced. CCP §2020.510(a)(2). See "Deposition subpoenas," ch. 8-A, §5.2.1, p. 940.

(4) Form of ESI. When a deposition notice requires the production of ESI, the notice must identify the form in which the ESI should be produced, if a particular form is desired. CCP §2025.220(a)(7). See "How to produce ESI," ch. 7-H, §10.2, p. 891.

(5) No testing or sampling of things to be produced. A deposition notice cannot be used to require a party to produce things at a deposition to be tested or sampled. *See* CCP §2025.220(a) (no provision in deposition notice for testing or sampling). Instead, the party should serve a demand to produce to secure things from another party to be tested or sampled. See "Other tangible things," ch. 7-E, §3.1.5, p. 847. By comparison, a deposition subpoena can require a nonparty to produce things to be tested or sampled. *See* Judicial Council Forms, form SUBP-020, Item 3. See "To attend & produce," ch. 8-A, §5.2.1(3)(a), p. 940.

5. Method of recording. The deposition notice must identify any method (or methods) by which the deposition will be recorded in addition to a stenographic recording. CCP §2025.220(a)(5).

(1) Stenographic recording. An oral deposition must be recorded stenographically. CCP §2025.330(b). The stenographic recording of a deposition can be omitted only by agreement or court order. *Id.*

(2) Audiotape recording. In addition to a stenographic recording, an oral deposition can be recorded on audiotape. CCP §2025.330(c); *CEB Discovery Practice*, §5.75; *CEB Procedure During Trial*, §12.16; *see* CCP §§2020.310(c), 2025.220(a)(5).

(3) Videotape recording. In addition to a stenographic recording, an oral deposition can be recorded on videotape. CCP §2025.330(c); *CEB Discovery Practice*, §5.75; *CEB Procedure During Trial*, §12.16; *see* CCP §§2020.310(c), 2025.220(a)(5); *CEB Discovery Practice*, §5.84. A videotaped deposition is particularly appropriate for a witness who will not be available to testify at trial because it helps the fact-finder assess the witness's credibility. *CEB Discovery Practice*, §5.77.

NOTE

If the testimony at the deposition is recorded both stenographically and by audio or video, the stenographic transcript must be the official record of that testimony for the trial and any hearing or appeal. CCP §2025.510(g); CEB Procedure During Trial, §12.18.

6. Transcripts during deposition. The deposition notice must indicate whether the deposition officer intends to provide an instant visual display or a rough-draft transcript of the testimony during the deposition. CCP §2025.220(a)(5). If one of these services will be provided, it must be offered to all parties in attendance. *Id.*

(1) Real-time display. Some deposition officers can provide an instant visual display of the testimony (often called "real time"). *See* CCP §§2020.310(d), 2025.220(a)(5); *CEB Discovery Practice*, §§5.74, 6.28. If

the deposition notice includes transcription by instant visual display as one of the methods of recording, the deposing party must send a copy of the deposition notice to the deposition officer. CCP §2025.220(a)(5).

(2) Rough draft. Some deposition officers can provide rough-draft transcriptions of the deposition (sometimes called "dailies") during the deposition. Weil, *Civil Procedure Before Trial*, ¶8:655.3; *see* CCP §2025.220(a)(5). A rough-draft transcript cannot be certified and cannot be used or relied on in any way. CCP §2025.540(b). Specifically, it cannot be used to rebut or contradict the certified transcript. *Id.*

7. Videotape of expert's deposition. The deposition notice must indicate whether the deposing party intends to use a videotaped deposition of an expert (e.g., treating physician) at trial, even though the expert is available to testify in person. CCP §§2025.220(a)(6), 2025.620(d); *CEB Procedure During Trial*, §§12.41, 12.84. Later (but before trial), the party intending to use the videotaped deposition of an expert must notify the court and the other parties in writing of its intent to use the videotaped deposition and the parts of the deposition to be offered. CCP §2025.340(m).

8. Remote attendance of deposing party. The deposition notice must indicate whether the deposing party will take the deposition from a remote location by electronic means (e.g., telephone, videoconference). CRC 3.1010(a)(1); *see* CCP §2025.310(a); *CEB Discovery Practice*, §5.30. If the deposing party intends to take the deposition from a remote location, it must do the following:

(1) Make all the arrangements necessary for taking the deposition by electronic means. *See* CRC 3.1010(a)(2).

(2) Arrange for any other party to participate in the deposition in an equivalent manner, if desired. *Id.*

(3) Pay all expenses associated with the remote attendance incurred by it or properly allocated to it. *See id.* If the deposing party is the only one to participate from a remote location, it must pay all the remote-attendance expenses. *See id.* If other parties elect to attend from remote locations, they must pay their share of the expenses. *See id.*

9. Identity of persons served. The deposition notice or its proof of service must list all attorneys and any pro per parties on whom the notice was served. *See* CCP §2025.240(a).

10. Optional things to include. The following can be included in the deposition notice, but they are not required by CCP §§2025.210-2025.280:

(1) Identity of deposition officer. The deposition notice can include the name (or descriptive title) of the deposition officer. See "Deposition officer," §2.2, p. 780.

(2) Anticipated duration of deposition. The deposition notice can include the approximate length of the deposition (e.g., three hours) or state that the deposition will continue day to day until completed. *See CEB Discovery Practice*, §5.59.

(3) Request identity of deponents. If an organization is required to designate witnesses to testify about certain subjects, the deposition notice can ask the organization to provide—before the deposition—the names of the deponents and the subject matter about which each deponent will testify.

(4) Additional attendees. The deposition notice should identify any attendees the deposing party intends to have at the deposition beyond those who would normally attend (i.e., attorneys, deponent, deposition officer, any operator of electronic equipment, and sometimes parties). If the deposing party does not give advance notice, the other parties can object, suspend the deposition, and move for a protective order. *See CEB Discovery Practice*, §6.18. See "Motion for Protective Order," ch. 9-B, p. 1024.

§9.3 Subpoena for oral deposition. To compel the oral deposition of a nonparty, the deposing party must serve a deposition subpoena on the nonparty. *See* CCP §2025.280(b). For the information that must be included in the deposition subpoena, see "Subpoena form," ch. 8-B, §3.1, p. 959 (deposition subpoena for testimony), and "Subpoena form," ch. 8-B, §4.1, p. 962 (deposition subpoena for testimony and documents or other things).

§9.4 Scheduling oral deposition.

1. When to schedule deposition.

(1) Party deposition. The oral deposition of a party (with or without documents) must be scheduled for a date that is at least ten days after the deposition notice is personally served on the parties (15 days if served by mail) and no later than 30 days before the date initially set for trial. *See* CCP §§1013(a), 2016.050, 2024.020(a), 2025.270(a).

(2) Nonparty deposition. The oral deposition of a nonparty (with or without documents) must be scheduled for a reasonable time after the subpoena is served on the deponent, at least ten days after the deposition notice is personally served on the parties (15 days if served by mail), and no later than 30 days before the date initially set for trial. *See* CCP §§1013(a), 2016.050, 2024.020(a), 2025.270(a). See "Deposition subpoena to attend," ch. 8-A, §7.1.1, p. 944.

(3) Designated expert. The deposition of a designated expert witness can be scheduled for any time after the exchange of expert information but no later than 15 days before the date initially set for trial. *See* CCP §2024.030. See "Demand for Exchange of Expert Information," ch. 7-I, §6, p. 904.

(4) Unlawful-detainer action. In an unlawful-detainer action or other proceeding under CCP §§1159-1179a, a deposition must be scheduled for a date that is at least five days after notice is personally served (ten days if served by mail) but no later than five days before trial. *See* CCP §§1013(a), 2016.050, 2025.270(b).

NOTE

When setting the date for a deposition, the deposing party should, whenever possible, accommodate the schedules of the opposing counsel and the deponent. See Super. Ct. Los Angeles Cty. Loc. R., appendix 3.A(e)(2).

---

2. Modifying schedule for deposition.

(1) By agreement. The parties can agree in writing to shorten or extend the time for scheduling a deposition or to change the time specified in a deposition notice. *See* CCP §2016.030. See "Modifying discovery by stipulation," ch. 7-A, §4.1, p. 743.

(2) By motion. On the motion or ex parte application of any party or deponent, for good cause shown, the court can shorten or extend the time for scheduling a deposition or can stay the taking of the deposition until the determination of a protective order. CCP §2025.270(d). See "Modifying discovery by court order," ch. 7-A, §4.2, p. 744.

§9.5 Length of oral deposition.

1. Generally. Generally, the deposition examination of a deponent by all counsel—other than the deponent's counsel of record—is limited to seven hours of total testimony. CCP §2025.290(a). However, this limit does not apply in the following situations:

(1) The deponent is designated as an expert. *Id.* §2025.290(b)(2).

(2) The case is designated as complex. *Id.* §2025.290(b)(3). However, if a licensed physician attests in a declaration served on the parties that the deponent suffers from a condition that raises substantial medical doubt about the deponent's survival beyond six months, the examination will be limited to two days of no more than 7 hours of total testimony each day or 14 hours of total testimony. *Id.*

(3) The case was brought by an employee or applicant for employment against an employer for acts or omissions relating to the employment relationship. *Id.* §2025.290(b)(4).

(4) The deponent is designated as the most qualified person to be deposed under CCP §2025.230. *Id.* §2025.290(b)(5). See "Representative capacity," §9.2.3(4)(a), p. 789.

(5) A new party appears in the action after the deposition concludes. CCP §2025.290(b)(6). When this happens, the new party can notice another deposition that is subject to the seven-hour limit. *Id.*

2. Modifying length of deposition.

(1) By agreement. The parties can stipulate that the seven-hour limit does not apply to a specific deposition or to any deposition. CCP §2025.290(b)(1).

(2) By court order. The court can order additional time for a deposition. CCP §2025.290(a). The court must allow additional time if it is needed to fairly examine the deponent or if the deponent or any other circumstance impedes or delays the examination. *Id.*; *see* ***Certainteed Corp. v. Superior Ct.*** (2d Dist.2014) 222 Cal.App.4th 1053, 1056 (provision requiring additional time applies to 7-hour limit in §2025.290(a) and 14-hour limit in §2025.290(b)(3)). But the court may limit the scope of a deposition or refuse additional time to protect against unwarranted annoyance, embarrassment, oppression, undue burden, or expense. CCP §2025.290(c); ***Certainteed Corp.***, 222 Cal.App.4th at 1062.

§9.6 Where to conduct deposition.

1. Choosing place for deposition. The deposing party can choose where the deposition will take place, subject to certain CDA guidelines. *See* CCP §2025.250. These guidelines vary depending on whether the deponent is (1) a resident, nonresident, or testifying expert witness, and (2) a natural person or an organization.

(1) Resident party.

(a) Natural person. A resident party or party-affiliated witness who is a natural person can be required to appear for a deposition either (1) within 75 miles of the party's residence or (2) in the county where the case is pending and within 150 miles of the party's residence. CCP §2025.250(a); *see* ***Parker v. Wolters Kluwer U.S., Inc.*** (2d Dist.2007) 149 Cal.App.4th 285, 295.

(b) Organization. The rules for selecting a location to depose a resident party organization vary depending on whether the organization has a designated principal executive or business office in California.

[1] Designated office. A resident party organization with a designated principal executive or business office in California can be required to produce its officers, directors, managing agents, employees, or agents who are most qualified to testify on its behalf for a deposition either (1) within 75 miles of the organization's designated office or (2) in the county where the case is pending and within 150 miles of the organization's designated office. *See* CCP §§2025.230, 2025.250(b).

[2] No designated office. A resident party organization that has no designated principal executive or business office in California can be required to produce its officers, directors, managing agents, employees, or agents who are most qualified to testify on its behalf for a deposition either (1) in the county where the case is pending or (2) within 75 miles of any of the organization's executive or business offices in California. *See* CCP §§2025.230, 2025.250(d).

(2) Nonresident party. A party who is not a resident of California but is a resident of a U.S. state, territory, or insular possession can be required to attend a deposition within 75 miles of the deponent's residence or business office in that state, territory, or insular possession. CCP §§2025.250(a), 2026.010(b).

(3) Expert witness. The deposition of a designated testifying expert must be taken within 75 miles of the courthouse where the case is pending. See "Place for deposition," ch. 7-I, §10.3, p. 912.

2. Modifying place for deposition.

(1) By agreement. The parties and the deponent can agree in writing to take a deposition at a place different than what is required by statute. *See* CCP §2016.030; *CEB Discovery Practice*, §12.13; *see, e.g.*, CCP §2025.250(c) (nonparty organization may consent to deposition at more distant place than permitted by statute).

(2) **By motion.** The deposing party can move for a court order to take the deposition of a party or party-affiliated witness at a more distant location than what is permitted by statute. CCP §2025.260(a); ***Parker***, 149 Cal.App.4th at 295. See "Motion to increase travel limit for party deposition," §12.6, p. 809. Although a party or party-affiliated witness can be forced by a court order to attend a deposition outside the statutory range for depositions, a nonparty cannot. Weil, *Civil Procedure Before Trial*, ¶8:626.

§9.7 Notices by nondeposing party. In the following circumstances, a nondeposing party must serve a notice of its own:

1. **Remote participation.** If a nondeposing party wants to attend and participate (i.e., ask questions and object) in the oral deposition from a remote location by telephone, videoconference, or other remote electronic means, it must (1) serve written notice of its intention on the other parties (including the deposing party) by personal delivery or fax at least three court days before the deposition and (2) make all arrangements and pay all expenses for the appearance. *See* CRC 3.1010(b).

2. **Other recording.** If a nondeposing party wants to make its own recording of the deposition using separate audio or visual equipment, it must do the following:

(1) Serve written notice of its intention at least three calendar days before the deposition date on (1) the deposing attorney, (2) all other parties or attorneys on whom the deposition notice was served, and (3) any deponent who was subpoenaed to attend. CCP §2025.330(c). If the notice is given three calendar days before the deposition date, it must be personally served. *Id.*

(2) Make all arrangements and pay all expenses for the alternative recording. *See id.*

§9.8 Who can attend deposition. The CDA does not explicitly state who can attend a deposition.

1. **Parties & attorneys.** Parties and their attorneys can attend a deposition. *CEB Discovery Practice*, §6.18; *see* CCP §§2025.310(a), 2025.420(b)(12); ***Willoughby v. Superior Ct.*** (1st Dist.1985) 172 Cal.App.3d 890, 892; *see, e.g.*, ***Jameson v. Desta*** (4th Dist.2013) 215 Cal.App.4th 1144, 1175-76 (pro per inmate should have been allowed to attend his expert's deposition by telephone). When the party is an organization, it can be represented at the deposition by a designated representative (e.g., an officer or director), but there are limits to how many people an organization can bring to a deposition. *See, e.g.*, ***Lowy Dev. Co. v. Superior Ct.*** (2d Dist.1987) 190 Cal.App.3d 317, 321-22 (number of organization's officers allowed to attend depositions was limited by court).

2. **Deponent & attorney.** The deponent must attend the deposition, and it can bring its own attorney. *See* CCP §§2025.280, 2025.310(b); *CEB Discovery Practice*, §6.18; *see, e.g.*, ***In re Marriage of Lemen*** (2d Dist.1980) 113 Cal.App.3d 769, 775-76 (attorney accompanied nonparty deponent at deposition for child-support modification proceeding).

NOTE

A nonparty deponent can use electronic means (e.g., videoconference) to "appear" for a deposition from a remote location if the court, on a motion, finds good cause and no prejudice to any party. CRC 3.1010(d); see CCP §2025.310(b). By comparison, a party deponent must appear for a deposition in person and be interrogated in the presence of the deposition officer. CCP §2025.310(b); CRC 3.1010(c). Nonparties deposed remotely must be sworn in the presence of a deposition officer or by any other means stipulated to by the parties or ordered by the court. CRC 3.1010(d).

3. **Deposition officer.** The deposition officer must attend the deposition. *See* CCP §2025.320 (deposition must be conducted under supervision of authorized deposition officer), §2025.330(a) (deposition officer must put deponent under oath).

4. **Operator of electronic equipment.** If the deposition is to be recorded by audiotape or videotape, the operator of the equipment must attend the deposition. *See* CCP §2025.340(b). See "Electronically recorded deposition," §2.2.1(3)(b), p. 781.

5. Other persons. Attendance of persons other than those listed above should be limited to persons who have a direct relationship to the case and thus have a legitimate reason for being at the deposition to hear firsthand what the deponent has to say. If persons not directly involved in the deposition attempt to attend, they can be excluded by a protective order. *See* CCP §2025.420(b)(12). See "Additional attendees," §9.2.10(4), p. 792; "Motion for Protective Order," ch. 9-B, p. 1024.

§9.9 Objecting to deposition notice for oral deposition.

1. Written objections. A party can object to errors and irregularities in the deposition notice by serving written objections on the deposing party and on any other party on whom the notice was served. CCP §2025.410(a). Written objections to the deposition notice do not stay the taking of the deposition; to do that, the party should make a motion to quash the deposition notice and stay the taking of the deposition. *See id.* §2025.410(b), (c). See "Request stay," ch. 9-C, §4.1.3(2)(b), p. 1043.

(1) Types of objections. A written objection to the deposition notice must identify the specific error or irregularity in the notice. CCP §2025.410(a). See "Deposition notice for oral deposition," §9.2, p. 789. When necessary, the party must provide evidence to support the factual allegations in the objection. *See, e.g.*, ***Parker v. Wolters Kluwer U.S., Inc.*** (2d Dist.2007) 149 Cal.App.4th 285, 295 (party did not provide evidence to support allegation that his residence was more than 2,000 miles from L.A., the place of the deposition). Some examples of errors or irregularities in a deposition notice include the following:

(a) Inadequate notice. The deposition is scheduled less than 10 days after personal service of the deposition notice or 15 days after service by mail. *See* CCP §§1013(a), 2016.050, 2025.270(a).

(b) Inadequate identification of things. The deposition notice does not properly identify the documents or other things the deponent must produce at the deposition. *CEB Discovery Practice*, §5.136; *see* CCP §2025.220(a)(4). See "Description of things to be produced," §9.2.4(3), p. 791.

(c) Location. The deposition is set at a location that does not comply with CCP §2025.250. See "Where to conduct deposition," §9.6, p. 794.

(2) Deadline to object. Objections to the deposition notice must be served at least three calendar days before the deposition date. CCP §2025.410(a); ***Parker***, 149 Cal.App.4th at 295 & n.22. If the objection is made on the last day to object (i.e., on the third calendar day before the deposition date), it must be personally served on the deposing party. CCP §2025.410(b).

(3) Waiver of objections. An objection that a deposition notice does not comply with CCP §§2025.210-2025.280 is waived if not timely made. CCP §2025.410(a). For example, a party waives an objection to the location of the deposition by not objecting in writing at least three calendar days before the deposition. *See* ***Parker***, 149 Cal.App.4th at 295.

(4) Effect of valid objection. A deposition taken after the service of a timely written objection cannot be used against the responding party if (1) the responding party did not attend the deposition and (2) the court determines that the objection was valid. CCP §2025.410(b).

2. Objections by motion. See "Motion for protective order," §12.1, p. 808; "Motion to Quash Deposition Subpoena," ch. 9-C, §3, p. 1038; "Motion to Quash Deposition Notice," ch. 9-C, §4, p. 1042.

§9.10 Objecting to subpoena for oral deposition. See "Challenging Subpoenas," ch. 8-E, §2, p. 995.

§9.11 How to take oral deposition.

1. Introductory statement. If the deposition is recorded electronically, it must begin with a statement on the record by the deposition officer or the operator of the recording equipment that includes the following:

(1) The operator's name and business address. CCP §2025.340(h).

(2) The name and business address of the operator's employer. *Id.*

(3) The date, time, and place of the deposition. *Id.*

(4) The caption of the case. *Id.*

(5) The name of the deponent. *Id.*

(6) The name of the party who noticed the deposition. *Id.*

2. Identity of attorneys. If the deposition is recorded electronically, the attorneys for the parties must identify themselves on camera or on the audio recording. CCP §2025.340(i).

3. Oath or affirmation. The deposition officer must administer the oath or affirmation to the deponent. CCP §2025.330(a). If the deposition is recorded electronically, the oath or affirmation must be administered on camera or on the audio recording. *Id.* §2025.340(j).

4. Deposition stipulations. Before the deponent is questioned, the parties should state on the record any agreements they have reached about the taking of the deposition. *See* CCP §2025.340(h). This is required if the deposition is recorded electronically. *Id.*

(1) Stipulations about objections.

(a) No agreement. If the parties do not make any stipulations about objections for the deposition, the only objections that must be made during the deposition are to (1) curable errors and (2) questions that would lead to the disclosure of privileged or protected information. See "Objections required during deposition," §9.12.1, p. 798. All other objections to the testimony can be made at trial. See "Objections not required during deposition," §9.12.2, p. 799. This is the best procedure for taking a deposition.

(b) Make all objections. If the parties stipulate that all objections must be made during the deposition, they must make all objections on the record and cannot assert any other objections at trial. Any objection not made during the deposition is waived. Agreeing to make all objections during the deposition is not recommended.

(c) Reserve all objections. If the parties stipulate that no objections are necessary during the deposition and that all objections are reserved for trial, the parties cannot make any objections during the deposition. *See* Weil, *Civil Procedure Before Trial*, ¶8:750. Agreeing to reserve all objections for trial effectively waives objections that must be made before the information is disclosed (e.g., privileged information). *See* CCP §2025.460(a), (b); Evid. C. §912(a); *CEB Discovery Practice*, §6.40. See "Objections required during deposition," §9.12.1, p. 798. Agreeing to reserve all objections until trial is not recommended. *CEB Discovery Practice*, §6.40.

PRACTICE TIP

Sometimes an attorney will ask if the other attorney wants to make the "usual stipulations" about objections to the examination. CEB Discovery Practice, §6.37; Weil, Civil Procedure Before Trial, ¶8:749.1. Do not agree to this. There are no "usual stipulations." Weil, Civil Procedure Before Trial, ¶8:749.1. If there is a dispute about which objections were required to be made during the deposition, telling the court that the attorneys agreed to the "usual stipulations" will not resolve the issue. See CEB Discovery Practice, §6.37.

---

(2) Other stipulations.

(a) Continue deposition. The parties can agree to continue the deposition until a later date. *See* ***R.S. Creative, Inc. v. Creative Cotton, Ltd.*** (2d Dist.1999) 75 Cal.App.4th 486, 489.

(b) Multiple-party objections. If there are several parties in the case, the parties can stipulate that an objection by one party preserves the objection for all other parties. *CEB Discovery Practice*, §6.41.

(c) Admissibility. The parties can stipulate to the admissibility of the deposition at a trial or hearing. *See CEB Procedure During Trial*, §12.38. See "Using Depositions in Court Proceedings," §13, p. 810.

(d) Length of deposition. The parties can agree to remove the time limit on the deposition. CCP §2025.290(b)(1). See "Length of oral deposition," §9.5, p. 793.

(e) Postdeposition procedures. The parties can stipulate to the procedure for handling the deposition transcript and recording. For example, the parties can agree that the reading, correcting, and signing of the original deposition transcript will occur after the deposition has been concluded. *See* CCP §2025.520(a).

5. Admonitions. The deposing party should admonish the witness about the nature of the deposition (e.g., recorded, under oath, can be used at trial) and tell the witness not to answer any question she does not understand. Weil, *Civil Procedure Before Trial*, ¶8:701. For sample admonitions, see *CEB Discovery Practice*, §6.141.

6. Interrogation of deponent.

(1) Questions by present parties. The parties can examine and cross-examine the deponent as permitted at trial under the Evidence Code. CCP §2025.330(d).

(2) Questions by absent parties. Instead of attending the deposition, parties can send written questions in a sealed envelope to the party taking the deposition, who will give them to the deposition officer. CCP §2025.330(e). After the oral examination has been completed, the deposition officer will unseal the envelope and ask the questions to the deponent. *Id.*

7. Beginning & end of tapes. If the deposition is recorded electronically, the operator of the recording equipment or the deposition officer must identify on the recording the end of each tape unit and the beginning of each successive unit (e.g., "This is the end of tape one"). *See* CCP §2025.340(k). Although not required by the CDA, the deposition officer should identify at the beginning of the second and later tapes the name of the deponent and the caption of the case (e.g., "This is the beginning of tape two in the deposition of John White, taken in the case of Jones v. Smith").

§9.12 Objecting during oral deposition. Objections during an oral deposition are made and recorded in the deposition transcript and reserved for a ruling by the court. Any objection during a deposition should be stated concisely in a nonargumentative and nonsuggestive manner (e.g., "Objection, question is vague"). Once the attorney states the objection on the record, the witness should be permitted to answer the question. Weil, *Civil Procedure Before Trial*, ¶8:733; *see* CCP §2025.460(b).

1. Objections required during deposition. The following objections must generally be made on the record at the deposition or else they are waived. CCP §2025.460(a), (b). For examples of valid and invalid objections, see "Grounds for Discovery Objections," ch. 7-A, §11, p. 765.

(1) Privilege. A party or deponent must object during the deposition to questions that seek disclosure of information that is privileged or protected from disclosure for some other reason. CCP §2025.460(a); *see CEB Discovery Practice*, §5.136 (parties and nonparties can object to requests for production during deposition); Weil, *Civil Procedure Before Trial*, ¶8:606 (same). See "Privileged & exempt information," ch. 6-A, §3.3, p. 610.

(2) Curable errors. A party or deponent must object to errors and irregularities of any kind during the oral examination that might be cured by a prompt objection. CCP §2025.460(b). Curable errors and irregularities include the following:

(a) Deposition procedures. Objections to the manner of taking the deposition or the administration of the oath or affirmation must be made during the deposition. CCP §2025.460(b).

(b) Qualifications of deposition officer. Objections to the qualifications of the deposition officer must be made before the deposition begins or as soon as the ground for objecting becomes known or discoverable through reasonable diligence. CCP §2025.320(e). See "Qualifications of deposition officer," §2.2.1, p. 780. Because most deposition notices do not identify the deposition officer by name, an attorney may not be able to object until the deposition starts or until the deposition ends. *CEB Discovery Practice*, §6.96. If the objection is not timely made, it is waived. CCP §2025.320(e).

(c) Conduct of attendees. Objections to the conduct of a party, attorney, deponent, or deposition officer must be made during the deposition. CCP §2025.460(b); *see id.* §2025.470. See "Conduct during oral deposition," §9.13, p. 800.

(d) Objections to form. Objections to the form of any question or answer must be made during the deposition. CCP §2025.460(b).

[1] Form of question. Objections to the form of the question include objections that the question (1) is argumentative, (2) assumes disputed facts are true, (3) assumes facts that are not in evidence, (4) misquotes the deponent, (5) calls for speculation, (6) is vague, ambiguous, confusing, or unintelligible, (7) is compound, (8) is too general, (9) calls for a narrative answer, (10) was asked and answered, (11) is harassing and oppressive, (12) is an incomplete hypothetical, or (13) is leading and the deponent is on direct or on redirect. *See* Evid. C. §§702, 765(a), 767, 800, 801; *CEB Discovery Practice*, §6.98; *CEB Trial Objections*, chs. 7-16; Thomas, *Courtroom Handbook*, §32:44; Weil, *Civil Procedure Before Trial*, ¶8:721.

[2] Form of answer. Objections to the form of the answer include objections that the deponent's answer is (1) nonresponsive or (2) evasive. *See* Evid. C. §766. An example of a nonresponsive answer is one that discusses issues not raised by the question or states more than is required by the question.

2. Objections not required during deposition. Unless the parties stipulate otherwise, the following objections are not required to be made on the record at the deposition (i.e., they can be made for the first time at trial). See "Stipulations about objections," §9.11.4(1), p. 797.

(1) Competence. Objections to the competence of the deponent can be made for the first time at trial. CCP §2025.460(c).

(2) Relevance. Objections to the relevance of the testimony or the materials produced can be made for the first time at trial. CCP §2025.460(c).

(3) Materiality. Objections to the materiality of the testimony or the materials produced can be made for the first time at trial. CCP §2025.460(c).

(4) Admissibility. Objections to the admissibility at trial of the testimony or the materials produced can be made for the first time at trial. CCP §2025.460(c).

3. Objections based on accessibility of ESI. If the deponent objects to the production of ESI on the ground that the source is not reasonably accessible because of undue burden or expense, the deponent must identify in her objection the types or categories of sources that are not reasonably accessible. CCP §2025.460(d). This will preserve any objections the deponent may have relating to the ESI. *Id.* See "Objections to Production of ESI," ch. 7-H, §9, p. 889.

PRACTICE TIP

This objection can be made orally at the deposition. See Weil, Civil Procedure Before Trial, ¶8:530. See "How to Make Discovery Objections," ch. 7-A, §12, p. 768. However, it may be better to serve a written objection or simply call opposing counsel in advance. A party deponent who raises an overbroad undue-burden objection risks sanctions and waiver of the issue. See CCP §2025.450(a), (c); Weil, Civil Procedure Before Trial, ¶¶8:1475.15, 8:1476. A nonparty deponent who refuses to produce at a deposition risks being held in contempt. See CCP §2020.240. By raising the objection before the deposition, it may be possible to resolve the issue by stipulating to certain limits on ESI production. See Weil, Civil Procedure Before Trial, ¶8:1476.

4. Instructing deponent not to answer. An attorney should not instruct a client not to answer questions during a deposition without a legal basis for doing so. *Cal. Attorney Guidelines*, §9(a)(7). If there is a legal basis, the attorney can instruct the client not to answer, and then the burden is on the deposing attorney to move to compel an answer. *CEB Discovery Practice*, §6.102; *see* CCP §2025.460(e).

(1) When proper. An attorney can instruct a client not to answer a question for the following reasons:

(a) To preserve a privilege or a right of confidentiality. *See* ***Stewart v. Colonial W. Agency Inc.*** (2d Dist.2001) 87 Cal.App.4th 1006, 1015; *CEB Discovery Practice*, §6.103; *see, e.g.*, ***I.E.S. Corp. v. Superior Ct.*** (1955) 44 Cal.2d 559, 563-64 (D refused to answer question seeking privileged communication); *see also* Super. Ct. Los Angeles Cty. Loc. R., appendix 3.A(e)(9) (attorney can direct deponent not to answer if question seeks privileged information).

(b) To protect the client from an examination conducted in bad faith or in a manner that unreasonably annoys, embarrasses, or oppresses the client. *CEB Discovery Practice*, §6.103; *see* CCP §2025.470; ***Stewart***, 87 Cal.App.4th at 1015; *see also* Super. Ct. Los Angeles Cty. Loc. R., appendix 3.A(e)(9) (attorney can direct client not to answer if question is manifestly irrelevant or calculated to harass).

(c) To prevent the client from answering a question that asks for a party's legal contentions. *CEB Discovery Practice*, §6.103; *see* ***Rifkind v. Superior Ct.*** (2d Dist.1994) 22 Cal.App.4th 1255, 1257-58. A legal-contention question asks the deponent to explain the basis for a legal contention stated in the pleadings (e.g., asking the deponent to state all facts supporting an affirmative defense). ***Rifkind***, 22 Cal.App.4th at 1258-59. Although legal-contention questions are not proper during an oral deposition, they are proper in interrogatories or requests for admission. *See* CCP §2030.010(b) (interrogatories), §2033.010 (RFAs). See "Legal contentions," ch. 7-C, §3.1.5(2), p. 818.

(d) To enforce a discovery limit imposed by the court. See "Relief Available Through Motion for Protective Order," chart 9-4, p. 1029.

PRACTICE TIP

After instructing the client not to answer a question, the attorney should state the reason for the instruction. CEB Discovery Practice, §6.104. For example, "I instruct my client not to answer that question on the ground of attorney-client privilege." See id.

---

(2) When improper.

(a) Client. An attorney cannot instruct a client not to answer a question based on an unnecessary or untenable objection. For example, because it is not necessary to object during a deposition to the relevance, materiality, or admissibility of the testimony, an attorney cannot instruct a deponent not to answer a question on any of these grounds. *See* ***Stewart***, 87 Cal.App.4th at 1014-15. Another example is when an attorney instructs a deponent not to answer based on a privilege when no privilege applies. *See, e.g.*, ***Flynn v. Superior Ct.*** (4th Dist.1997) 57 Cal.App.4th 990, 993-94 (no privilege for private investigator to refuse to disclose employer).

(b) Nonclient. In most situations, an attorney cannot instruct a nonclient not to answer a question. *CEB Discovery Practice*, §6.105. However, an attorney can instruct a nonclient not to answer if the nonclient is asked a question that will reveal privileged information belonging to the attorney's client. *Id.*

§9.13 Conduct during oral deposition.

1. Conduct of attorneys. The attorneys should (1) cooperate with and be courteous to each other and the deponent and (2) conduct the oral deposition as if the testimony were being elicited in open court. *See Cal. Attorney Guidelines*, §9(a)(3); *see, e.g.*, Super. Ct. Los Angeles Cty. Loc. R., appendix 3.A(e)(11) (attorney should not engage in conduct during deposition that would not be allowed in presence of judicial officer).

(1) No improper questions. An attorney must not ask a question solely to harass or mislead the deponent or for any other improper purpose. *See Cal. Attorney Guidelines*, §9; *see, e.g.*, Super. Ct. Los Angeles Cty. Loc. R., appendix 3.A(e)(5) (attorney should not inquire into a deponent's personal affairs or question her integrity if information is not relevant to case).

(2) No speaking objections. An attorney should not use "speaking objections" (i.e., objections intended to influence a deponent's response) or make other commentary to coach a deponent or suggest certain answers. *Cal. Attorney Guidelines*, §9(a)(6), (a)(8); Thomas, *Courtroom Handbook*, §21:76; *see* Weil, *Civil Procedure Before Trial*, ¶8:736.1; *see, e.g.*, Super. Ct. Los Angeles Cty. Loc. R., appendix 3.A(e)(8) (attorney should not coach witness through objections).

(3) Conferring with client deponent.

(a) During deposition. During the actual taking of a deposition, an attorney should not initiate a private conference with the client deponent about the testimony except to determine whether a privilege should be asserted. *See* Weil, *Civil Procedure Before Trial*, ¶8:736.2; *see, e.g.*, ***Tucker v. Pacific Bell Mobile Servs.*** (1st Dist.2010) 186 Cal.App.4th 1548, 1558-59 (writing notes to client during her deposition was improper coaching).

(b) During recess. During a deposition recess, an attorney can communicate with the client deponent, and that communication is covered by the attorney-client privilege. However, an attorney should not ask for a recess to confer with the client when a question is pending except to determine whether a privilege should be asserted. *See* Weil, *Civil Procedure Before Trial*, ¶8:736.2.

2. Conduct of deponent. The deponent should answer questions truthfully and should not be evasive or unduly delay the examination. *See, e.g.*, ***In re Marriage of Michaely*** (2d Dist.2007) 150 Cal.App.4th 802, 805-06 (husband's untruthful, evasive, and inconsistent deposition answers resulted in facts being established against him as true).

3. Conduct of deposition officer. The deposition officer is responsible for placing the deponent under oath and supervising the deposition. *See* CCP §§2025.320, 2025.330(a). If the deposition officer also acts as the reporter, the deposition officer is responsible for recording the testimony and any objections. *See id.* §2025.330(b). The deposition officer does not rule on objections; she merely records them. *See id.* §2025.330(b).

§9.14 Suspending oral deposition.

1. By deposition officer.

(1) All parties agree. The deposition officer can suspend a deposition if all the parties present agree to the suspension. CCP §2025.470.

(2) Party or deponent demands. The deposition officer can suspend a deposition on the demand of a party or deponent who wants to move for a protective order. CCP §2025.470; *CEB Discovery Practice*, §6.106; *see* CCP §§2025.420, 2025.460(b). See "Motion for Protective Order," ch. 9-B, p. 1024.

2. By deposing party. The deposing party can adjourn the deposition or complete the examination on other matters and then adjourn if the deponent refuses to answer a question or to produce a document or other tangible thing under the deponent's control that was sought by the deposition notice or subpoena. CCP §2025.460(e). The deposing party can do this without waiving its right to move for an order compelling the answer or production. *Id.* See "Motion to Compel Depositions," ch. 9-D, p. 1046.

PRACTICE TIP

Before suspending the deposition of a nonparty, ask the nonparty on the record to agree to accept service by mail at a specified address of papers supporting a motion to compel. See CRC 3.1346 (without record of agreement, nonparty deponent must be personally served with motion to compel papers).

3. By party. A party can demand that a deposition be suspended to permit the filing of a motion for a protective order under CCP §2025.420 on the ground that the deposition is being conducted in bad faith or in a manner that is unreasonably annoying, embarrassing, or oppressive. CCP §2025.470; *see id.* §2025.460(b) (party can suspend deposition for errors or irregularities during deposition if it requests motion for protective order under §§2025.420 and 2025.470). See "Motion for Protective Order," ch. 9-B, p. 1024.

4. By deponent. The deponent can demand that a deposition be suspended to permit the filing of a motion for a protective order on the same grounds as those available to a party. See "Motion for Protective Order," ch. 9-B, p. 1024.

§9.15 Terminating oral deposition. A deposition is completed when the parties indicate they have no additional questions for the deponent. *CEB Discovery Practice*, §5.15. A deposition can be continued for another session on another day without ending the deposition. *Id.* Multiple sessions with the same deponent are considered one deposition. *See id.* As a practical matter, the deposing attorney or the deposition officer should formally announce on the record that the deposition is over or is being continued. *See* CCP §2025.340(*l*); *CEB Discovery Practice*, §5.15.

§9.16 Cost of deposition.

1. Transcription costs. Generally, the deposing party must pay the cost of the deposition transcription. CCP §2025.510(b).

(1) Exception. The transcription costs must be borne or shared by another party if the court, on motion and for good cause shown, orders it. CCP §2025.510(b). Good cause for requiring the other party to pay the transcription costs may be shown if the other party unreasonably prolonged the deposition. Weil, *Civil Procedure Before Trial*, ¶8:767.2.

(2) Payment to deposition officer. The attorney or pro per party who requested the deposition must timely pay the deposition officer (or the entity providing the services of the deposition officer) for the cost of the deposition transcript and any other deposition product or service requested. CCP §2025.510(h)(1). A different person can be required to pay for the deposition if either (1) the law places responsibility for payment on a different person or (2) the deposition officer was notified before the deposition in writing that the attorney's client or another identified person would be responsible for the payment. *Id.* §2025.510(h)(2).

2. Audio & video costs. The obligation to pay for an audio or video deposition is on the attorney or the party who asked for it. *See* CCP §2025.330(c).

3. Copy costs. Any other party (including one that did not attend the deposition) or the deponent can obtain a copy of the deposition transcript at its own expense. CCP §2025.510(c); *see also id.* §2025.510(f)(2) (audio and video copies), §2025.560(b)(2) (same). The party or deponent is entitled to obtain the copies at a reasonable rate. ***Las Canoas Co. v. Kramer*** (2d Dist.2013) 216 Cal.App.4th 96, 100. If the reasonableness of the rate is disputed, the party or deponent must file a motion to set the rate in the action in which the cost dispute arises. *Id.*

4. Real-time & daily costs. The obligation to pay for the instant visual ("real-time") display of the testimony or rough-draft transcripts ("dailies") is on the party who asked for the service. CCP §2025.220(a)(5). See "Transcripts during deposition," §9.2.6, p. 791.

5. Remote-electronic-deposition costs. Each party who appears for a deposition by remote electronic means (e.g., videoconference) must pay all expenses incurred by or properly allocated to it that relate to the remote appearance. CRC 3.1010(a)(2).

6. Witness fees. See "Witness Fees," §8, p. 788.

§9.17 Request for referee. If the parties are not able to conduct depositions without serious and repeated disputes, the court can appoint a discovery referee to oversee the depositions. *See CEB Discovery Practice*, §2.68. See "Special reference," ch. 2-E, §3.2, p. 164.

§9.18 Postdeposition procedures.

1. Notice & review. After the deposition transcript or the audio or video recording (if the deposition was not stenographically recorded) is available for review, the deposition officer must send written notice to the deponent and all parties who attended the deposition that the transcript or recording is available for review. *See* CCP §§2025.520(a), 2025.530(a). If the deposition testimony was stenographically recorded, the review involves reading, correcting, and signing the deposition. *Id.* §2025.520(a). If the deposition was not stenographically recorded, the review involves listening to or watching the audio or video recording and signing an accompanying writing prepared by the deposition officer. *See id.* §2025.530(a), (c).

2. Waiver of notice & review. The deponent and the attending parties can waive notice and review of the transcript or recording by agreeing on the record to the waiver. CCP §2025.520(a) (transcript), §2025.530(a) (recording); *CEB Discovery Practice*, §6.128 (transcript). Or the deponent and the attending parties can agree to conduct the review at a later specified time. CCP §2025.520(a).

3. Deadline for changes. The deponent has 30 days after receiving the notice from the deposition officer to change the form or substance of an answer, either in person or by a signed letter to the deposition officer. CCP §§2025.520(b), (c), 2025.530(b). The deponent and the attending parties can agree on the record or in writing to a longer or shorter time period, or the court can shorten the 30-day period for good cause. *Id.* §2025.520(b) (parties and deponent can agree), §2025.520(d) (court can shorten); *CEB Discovery Practice*, §6.128 (parties and deponent can agree).

4. Refusal to approve. The deponent can refuse to approve the deposition by not signing it, either in person or by a signed letter to the deposition officer, within the 30-day review period. *See* CCP §§2025.520(b), (c), 2025.530(b), (d). After the review period ends, the deposition will be given the same effect as if the deponent had signed it, unless the court grants a timely filed motion to suppress the deposition after finding the deponent's failure or refusal to approve requires that the deposition be rejected in whole or in part. *See id.* §§2025.520(f), (g), 2025.530(d), (e). See "Motion to suppress deposition," §12.3, p. 808.

5. Certification. After the 30-day review period has passed, the deposition officer must certify on the deposition transcript or, in the case of an electronically recorded deposition, on an accompanying writing that (1) the deponent was sworn and (2) the transcript or recording is a true record of the testimony. *See* CCP §2025.540(a); Weil, *Civil Procedure Before Trial*, ¶8:778.

6. Custody of deposition. Deposition transcripts and recordings are not filed with the court. *See* CCP §§2025.550(a), 2025.560(a). The rules for custody depend on whether the deposition was transcribed or electronically recorded.

(1) Stenographic transcript. The deposition officer must securely seal the stenographic deposition transcript in a package, endorse the package with the title of the action and the identity of the deponent ("Deposition of [name of deponent]"), and send it to the attorney for the deposing party. CCP §2025.550(a). Once received, the deposing party must store the transcript in a way that will protect it against loss, destruction, or tampering. *Id.*

(2) Electronic recording. The audio or video equipment operator who recorded the deposition must retain the electronic recordings. CCP §2025.560(a). The operator must store the recordings in a way that will protect them against loss, destruction, or tampering, and preserve—to the extent that it is practical—the quality of the recordings and the integrity of the testimony and images on the recordings. *Id.*

7. Procedure for obtaining copies of transcript or recording. The nondeposing parties and the deponent are entitled to obtain copies of the deposition transcript or recording. CCP §2025.510(c) (transcript), §2025.560(b) (recording). A nonparty can obtain a copy if (1) the court has not issued an order to the contrary, (2) the deposition officer still has a copy, and (3) the deposition officer, before delivering the copy, gives notice to the deponent and to each party who attended the deposition. *Id.* §2025.570(a), (b).

(1) Stenographic transcript. The deposition officer must provide a certified copy of the deposition transcript to a nondeposing party or to the deponent upon payment of a reasonable charge set by the deposition officer. *See* CCP §§2025.510(c), 2025.570(a); ***Serrano v. Stefan Merli Plastering Co.*** (2d Dist.2008) 162 Cal.App.4th 1014, 1036-37. The deposition officer must provide the same to a nonparty if the nonparty pays the deposition officer's reasonable charge and the other conditions in CCP §2025.570(a) are satisfied. CCP §2025.570(a). If there is a dispute about the fee charged for a deposition transcript, the court has the authority to determine the reasonableness of the fee. ***Serrano***, 162 Cal.App.4th at 1038-39. But the court will not examine the reasonableness of the fee charged by the deposition officer to the deposing party because that relationship is governed by contract. *See id.* at 1035-36 & n.11.

(2) Electronic recording. The operator or a party who recorded the deposition must do the following when asked:

(a) Permit the parties or the deponent to hear or view the deposition. *See* CCP §§2025.510(f)(1), 2025.560(b)(1). An operator is entitled to payment of a reasonable fee for this service; a party is not. *See id.* §§2025.510(f)(1), 2025.560(b)(1).

(b) Make copies for the parties or the deponent upon payment of a reasonable fee for the service. *See id.* §§2025.510(f)(2), 2025.560(b)(2).

(c) Make copies for a nonparty if the nonparty pays a reasonable fee set by the deposition officer and if the other conditions in CCP §2025.570(a) are satisfied. *Id.* §2025.570(a).

8. Retention of deposition. The attorney or operator who has custody of the deposition transcript or recording must keep the transcript or recording until six months after final disposition of the case. *See* CCP §§2025.550(b), 2025.560(c). After that, it can be destroyed or erased unless the court, on the motion of any party and for good cause shown, orders that it be preserved for a longer period. *See id.* §§2025.550(b), 2025.560(c).

§9.19 Who can be redeposed. A natural person, including a party, whose deposition was completed generally cannot be redeposed by the same deposing party or any other party who was served with the deposition notice. CCP §2025.610(a); ***Fairmont Ins. v. Superior Ct.*** (2000) 22 Cal.4th 245, 254; *CEB Discovery Practice*, §5.15. A person's deposition is completed when the parties indicate they have no additional questions. See "Terminating oral deposition," §9.15, p. 802. A previously deposed person can be redeposed only in the following circumstances:

1. Court order. On a motion showing good cause, the court can grant leave for another deposition of a previously deposed person. CCP §2025.610(b).

2. Stipulation. The parties, with the consent of the previously deposed person, can stipulate to another deposition of the person. CCP §2025.610(b).

3. Party did not participate in first deposition. The previously deposed person can be deposed again if the party seeking the deposition (1) did not issue the notice for the first deposition and (2) was not served with notice for the first deposition. *See* CCP §2025.610(a).

4. Deponent was designated witness for corporation. The previously deposed person can be deposed again in an individual capacity if the person was examined in the first deposition as a designated witness for an organization under CCP §2025.230. CCP §2025.610(c)(1).

5. Deponent was witness in attachment proceeding. The previously deposed person can be deposed again if the person was originally deposed by court order under CCP §485.230 (discovery after attachment order) for the limited purpose of discovering the identity, location, and value of property in which the deponent has an interest. CCP §2025.610(c)(2). Such a person can be deposed a second time but not a third time. *Id.* §2025.610(d).

6. Deponent intends to waive previously asserted privilege. The previously deposed person can be deposed again if the person invokes a privilege at her deposition but later indicates an intent to waive that privilege at trial. *See* ***People v. Holistic Health*** (4th Dist.2013) 213 Cal.App.4th 1016, 1032 (dicta); ***Fuller v. Superior Ct.*** (2d Dist.2001) 87 Cal.App.4th 299, 310. If the person intends to waive the privilege, the court should order the person to submit to deposition questioning designed to reveal the privileged testimony. ***Holistic Health***, 213 Cal.App.4th at 1032 (dicta).

§9.20 Motion to compel. If a deponent refuses to attend, testify at, or produce documents or things at a deposition, the deposing party can make a motion to compel. See "Motion to Compel Depositions," ch. 9-D, p. 1046.

§9.21 Sanctions. For a discussion of the possible sanctions that can be imposed against deposing parties and deponents, see "Sanctions for depositions," ch. 9-A, §5.1.1, p. 1011.

§10. DEPOSITION ON WRITTEN QUESTIONS

A deposition on written questions (written deposition) is an alternative to an oral deposition. *See* CCP §2028.010. In a written deposition, the deposition officer asks the deponent questions that the parties have previously submitted

in writing. *See id.* §2028.080; Weil, *Civil Procedure Before Trial*, ¶8:381. A written deposition may be the only practical way of obtaining information from certain persons, such as an out-of-state deponent who is in the military or is incarcerated. *CEB Discovery Practice*, §12.17.

§10.1 Drawbacks of written depositions. Written depositions are seldom used because of their inherent drawbacks. *See CEB Discovery Practice*, §5.160. For example, they do not permit attorneys to assess the demeanor and credibility of the witness or ask probing follow-up questions. Written depositions are appropriate only when a party is seeking limited and specific information that can be elicited through clear and unambiguous questions. *Id.* §5.163.

NOTE

Written depositions are regularly used in other jurisdictions to secure documents and to authenticate information about the documents from their custodians. See ***O'Connor's Federal Rules****, "Deposition by Written Questions," ch. 6-F, §5, p. 604. However, these jurisdictions may not have California's procedures for obtaining records. In California, it is easier to obtain documentary evidence by using a demand to produce (for documents from a party) or a deposition subpoena for business records (for documents from a nonparty). See "Demands to Produce," ch. 7-E, p. 845; "Deposition Subpoena for Business Records," ch. 8-B, §5, p. 963.*

§10.2 Procedure for written deposition. The rules for oral depositions apply to written depositions, with the additions and exceptions noted below. *See* CCP §2028.010. See "Oral Deposition," §9, p. 788.

§10.3 Deposition notice for written deposition. The notice for a written deposition is largely the same as the notice for an oral deposition. *See* CCP §2028.020. See "Deposition notice for oral deposition," §9.2, p. 789. There are, however, the following differences:

1. Identity of deposition officer. The name or descriptive title and address of the deposition officer must be stated. CCP §2028.020(a). This is not optional, as it is for the notice for an oral deposition.

2. Direct questions. The questions to be asked of the deponent on direct must be attached to the deposition notice. CCP §2028.030(a); *CEB Discovery Practice*, §5.168.

3. Open date & place. The date, time, and place for the deposition can be left open to be determined by the deposition officer when all the questions have been collected and all objections have been resolved. *See* CCP §2028.020(b). See "Selecting date & place for deposition," §10.8, p. 807.

NOTE

Like all other discovery, written depositions must be completed no later than 30 days before the initial trial date. CCP §2024.020(a); CEB Discovery Practice, §5.161.

§10.4 Courtesy copy. The deposing party can forward to the deponent a copy of the direct questions for study before the deposition. CCP §2028.060(a). However, the deponent cannot be permitted to review the form or substance of any cross-, redirect, or recross-questions. *Id.* §2028.060(b).

§10.5 Cross-, redirect & recross-questions. After the direct questions and the deposition notice have been served, a party can serve written cross-questions on the other parties. *See* CCP §2028.030(b). The deposing party can respond to cross-questions by serving redirect questions, and the crossing party can respond to redirect questions by serving recross-questions. Thomas, *Courtroom Handbook*, §21:64; *see* CCP §2028.030(c), (d).

1. Deadlines. The deadlines for serving these types of questions are as follows:

(1) Cross-questions. A party must serve its cross-questions within 30 days after being personally served with the deposition notice and the direct questions. CCP §2028.030(b). If the deposition notice and direct

questions are served by mail, the time to serve cross-questions is extended according to the rules for service by mail. *See id.* §§1013(a), 2016.050. See "Add time for method of service," ch. 1-G, §6.2.1(5), p. 72.

(2) Redirect questions. The deposing party must serve its redirect questions within 15 days after being personally served with cross-questions. CCP §2028.030(c). If the cross-questions are served by mail, the time to serve redirect questions is extended according to the rules for service by mail. *See id.* §§1013(a), 2016.050. See "Add time for method of service," ch. 1-G, §6.2.1(5), p. 72.

(3) Recross-questions. A party must serve its recross-questions within 15 days after being personally served with redirect questions. CCP §2028.030(d). If the redirect questions are served by mail, the time to serve recross-questions is extended according to the rules for service by mail. *See id.* §§1013(a), 2016.050. See "Add time for method of service," ch. 1-G, §6.2.1(5), p. 72.

2. Changing deadlines. The court can extend or shorten the time periods for exchanging cross-, redirect, and recross-questions on a showing of good cause. CCP §2028.030(e).

§10.6 Objecting to written deposition.

1. Making objections to written deposition questions. A party can object to the written deposition questions (direct, cross, redirect, recross) in writing. Written objections must be specific, and they must be served on all parties entitled to notice of the deposition. CCP §§2028.040(a), 2028.050(a).

(1) Deadline to object. The deadline to object to written deposition questions is 15 days after the questions were personally served on the party. *See* CCP §2028.040(a) (objections to form of question), §2028.050(a) (objections based on privilege or attorney work product). If the written deposition questions were served by mail, the deadline to serve objections to the questions is extended according to the rules for service by mail. *See id.* §§1013(a), 2016.050. A party waives its objections if it does not serve them before the deadline. *Id.* §§2028.040(a), 2028.050(a).

(2) Grounds. An objection to a written deposition question can be based on the following grounds:

(a) Privilege or work product. A party can object that a specific question asks for information that is protected by a specific privilege or attorney work product. CCP §2028.050(a).

(b) Form of question. A party can object to the form of a specific question. CCP §2028.040(a).

[1] Description of things. A party can object that a written question does not properly identify the documents or other things the deponent must produce. *See* CCP §§2025.220(a)(4), 2028.010; *CEB Discovery Practice*, §5.136. See "Description of things to be produced," §9.2.4(3), p. 791.

[2] Other objections to form. See "Form of question," §9.12.1(2)(d)[1], p. 799.

2. Making objections to written-deposition procedure. A party can object to the procedure for a written deposition by making a motion for a protective order. *See* CCP §2028.070 (incorporates protective orders from CCP §2025.420).

(1) Deadline to object. There is no deadline to make a motion for a protective order. The only requirement is that the motion be made "promptly." CCP §2025.420(a).

(2) Grounds. A motion for a protective order must establish that the order is necessary to protect a party, a deponent, or a natural person from unwarranted annoyance, embarrassment or oppression or from an undue burden or expense. *See* CCP §§2025.420(b), 2028.010, 2028.070.

(3) Protective orders. Possible protective orders include the following:

(a) Change to oral deposition. The court can order that the deponent's testimony be taken by oral, instead of written, examination. CCP §2028.070(a).

(b) Permit party to attend. The court can permit one or more of the parties who received notice of the written deposition to attend and ask the deponent questions by oral examination. CCP §2028.070(b).

(c) Change deposition officer. The court can order that the deposition be taken before an officer other than the one identified in the deposition notice. CCP §2028.070(d).

3. Resolving objections to written depositions. The parties must move "promptly" for a ruling on the objections. See "Motion for ruling on objections to written deposition," §12.7, p. 809.

§10.7 Delivery to deposition officer. Once all questions have been exchanged and all objections have been resolved, the deposing party must send copies of the deposition notice and all the questions to the deposition officer. CCP §2028.080; *CEB Discovery Practice*, §5.187.

§10.8 Selecting date & place for deposition. Once the deposition officer receives copies of the deposition notice and all the questions exchanged by the parties, the deposition officer will usually set the date, time, and place for the deposition. *See* CCP §§2025.220(a)(1), (a)(2), 2028.010, 2028.020; *CEB Discovery Practice*, §5.172.

§10.9 Compelling attendance. Once the date for the written deposition has been set, the deposing party must serve the document necessary to compel the deponent's attendance. See "How to Require Deposition Attendance," §7, p. 785. To compel a nonparty deponent, a subpoena must be served personally on the nonparty a reasonable time before the deposition. See "Subpoena for written deposition," ch. 7-A, §6.2.2, p. 751.

§10.10 Taking written deposition. On the date selected for the written deposition, the deposition officer must put the deponent under oath, propound each of the questions served (direct, cross, redirect, and recross), and record the deponent's response. *CEB Discovery Practice*, §5.191; *see* CCP §2028.080.

§11. FILING OR LODGING DEPOSITION TRANSCRIPTS

Whether it is necessary to file or lodge deposition transcripts and recordings with the court depends on local rules, the pretrial order, and the case-management order. An attorney should check with the court before filing or lodging a transcript or recording. Weil, *Civil Procedure Before Trial*, ¶8:784.

§11.1 Filing deposition. Generally, deposition transcripts and recordings are not filed with the court. CCP §2025.550(a) (transcripts), §2025.560(a) (recordings); *CEB Discovery Practice*, §6.134 (transcripts); *CEB Procedure During Trial*, §12.14 (transcripts). See "Custody of deposition," §9.18.6, p. 803. However, a deposition transcript or recording can be filed with the court in the following situations:

1. For pretrial dispositive motion. A party may be required by the court to file an original deposition transcript in support of a pretrial dispositive motion (e.g., a motion for summary judgment). Weil, *Civil Procedure Before Trial*, ¶8:783.

2. For trial. A party may be required by a local rule, a pretrial order, or a case-management order to file a certified original deposition transcript or recording before trial. *See CEB Procedure During Trial*, §12.14; Weil, *Civil Procedure Before Trial*, ¶8:784.

§11.2 Lodging deposition. Deposition transcripts and recordings can be lodged with the court for temporary use by the court in the following situations. See "Lodging discovery," ch. 7-A, §13.2.2, p. 770.

1. For motion to compel. A party must lodge a certified copy of the relevant parts of a deposition transcript from a stenographically or electronically recorded deposition in support of a motion to compel a witness to answer a question or produce documents as required by a deposition notice or subpoena. CCP §2025.480(a), (h); *see* ***Unzipped Apparel, LLC v. Bader*** (2d Dist.2007) 156 Cal.App.4th 123, 135; *CEB Discovery Practice*, §6.120; Weil, *Civil Procedure Before Trial*, ¶8:802. The transcript must be lodged five days before the hearing on the motion. CCP §2025.480(h); *CEB Discovery Practice*, §§6.80, 6.120.

2. For trial or hearing. Before a party can present or offer into evidence an electronically recorded deposition at a trial or hearing, the party must lodge a transcript of the recording. CRC 2.1040(a)(1). A party may also be required by a local rule, a pretrial order, or a case-management order to lodge an original transcript of a stenographically recorded deposition before a trial or hearing. *CEB Procedure During Trial*, §12.14; *see id.* §§3.43, 12.135; Weil, *Civil Procedure Before Trial*, ¶8:784.

§12. MOTIONS RELATED TO DEPOSITIONS

§12.1 Motion for protective order. A party, deponent, or other affected natural person or organization can move for a protective order for a deposition. CCP §2025.420(a). See "Party or affected person," ch. 9-B, §3.1.1, p. 1028. The motion should ask the court to stay the taking of the deposition pending a ruling on the motion. *See* CCP §2025.270(d). See "Stay," ch. 9-B, §3.3.1(3), p. 1034.

1. Grounds. A protective order can be sought for a deposition on the following grounds:

(1) To protect from unwarranted annoyance, embarrassment, or oppression or from undue burden and expense. *See* CCP §§1987.1(a), 2025.420(b).

(2) To protect from the burden, expense, or intrusiveness of discovery when it outweighs the likelihood that the discovery will lead to admissible evidence. *Id.* §2017.020(a).

(3) To protect from discovery that is unreasonably cumulative or duplicative or when the same information is obtainable from another source that is more convenient, less burdensome, or less expensive. *Id.* §2019.030(a)(1).

(4) To protect from discovery that is unduly burdensome or expensive. *Id.* §2019.030(a)(2).

2. Relief. A party can make a motion for a protective order to ask the court for any relief listed in CCP §2025.420(b). See "Relief," ch. 9-B, §3.3.1(1)(a), p. 1029. Some examples of the relief that can be granted by a motion for a protective order include the following:

(1) Prevent excessive depositions. A party can make a motion for a protective order to prevent an excessive number of depositions. *See* CCP §2019.030(a)(1) (restricting unreasonably cumulative or duplicative discovery), §2025.420(b)(1) (protective order directing that deposition must not be taken).

(2) Prevent apex deposition. A party can make a motion for a protective order to prevent the deposition of a high-level officer or employee of an organization (called an "apex deposition"). The motion should allege that (1) the deponent does not have personal knowledge of and is not directly involved in the case and (2) the same information can be obtained by other means. *See* ***Liberty Mut. Ins. v. Superior Ct.*** (1st Dist.1992) 10 Cal.App.4th 1282, 1289; *CEB Discovery Practice*, §5.41.

(3) Stop abusive examination. A party can make a motion for a protective order to prevent the deposition examination from being conducted in bad faith or in a manner that is unreasonably annoying, embarrassing, or oppressive. CCP §§2025.420(b), 2025.470.

§12.2 Motion to quash deposition subpoena or notice. See "Motion to Quash Deposition Subpoena," ch. 9-C, §3, p. 1038; "Motion to Quash Deposition Notice," ch. 9-C, §4, p. 1042.

§12.3 Motion to suppress deposition. A party can file a motion to suppress the deposition transcript or recording if the deponent fails or refuses to approve the transcript or fails or refuses by a signature to identify the recording as the deponent's recording. *See* CCP §2025.520(g) (transcript), §2025.530(e) (recording). If the court determines that the deponent's reasons for not approving the transcript or for not identifying the recording are legitimate, it can reject the deposition in whole or in part. *See id.* §§2025.520(g), 2025.530(e); ***Chavez v. Zapata Ocean Res.*** (4th Dist.1984) 155 Cal.App.3d 115, 121-22.

1. Meet & confer. The motion must be accompanied by a meet-and-confer declaration. CCP §2025.520(g) (transcript), §2025.530(e) (recording). See "Meet-and-confer declaration," ch. 7-A, §10.4, p. 763.

2. Sanctions. The court must impose a monetary sanction against any party, person, or attorney who unsuccessfully makes or opposes a motion to suppress, unless the court finds that (1) the motion or opposition was substantially justified or (2) imposing a monetary sanction would be unjust. CCP §2025.520(h) (transcript), §2025.530(f) (recording).

§12.4 Motion to compel. See "Motion to Compel Depositions," ch. 9-D, p. 1046.

§12.5 Motion to enforce deposition subpoena for personal records. See "Motion to Enforce Deposition Subpoena for Personal Records," ch. 9-G, p. 1078.

§12.6 Motion to increase travel limit for party deposition. A deposing party can move for a court order to take the oral deposition of a party or a party-affiliated witness at a more distant location than permitted by CCP §2025.250. CCP §2025.260(a); *see* ***Parker v. Wolters Kluwer U.S., Inc.*** (2d Dist.2007) 149 Cal.App.4th 285, 295. For the distances permitted under §2025.250, see "Where to conduct deposition," §9.6, p. 794.

1. Grounds. The motion should address the factors listed in §2025.260(b) that the court must consider. See "Factors to consider," §12.6.3(1), this page. The motion should address as many of these factors as possible.

2. Meet & confer. The motion must be accompanied by a meet-and-confer declaration. CCP §2025.260(a). See "Meet-and-confer declaration," ch. 7-A, §10.4, p. 763.

3. Court's ruling & order.

(1) Factors to consider. The court must consider whether the interests of justice will be served by requiring the deponent's attendance at the more distant place, which includes, but is not limited to, the following factors:

(a) Did the deposing party select the forum? CCP §2025.260(b)(1). If not (i.e., the deposing party is the defendant), this factor would weigh in favor of permitting the deposition at a more distant location.

(b) Will the deponent be available to testify at trial? *Id.* §2025.260(b)(2). If not, this factor would weigh in favor of permitting the deposition at a more distant location.

(c) Is the more distant location convenient for the deponent? *Id.* §2025.260(b)(3). If so, this factor would weigh in favor of permitting the deposition at a more distant location.

(d) Can the deposition be taken by written questions or by using a discovery method other than a deposition? *Id.* §2025.260(b)(4). If so, this factor would weigh against permitting the deposition at a more distant location.

(e) How many depositions are to be taken at this more distant place? *Id.* §2025.260(b)(5).

(f) What expenses would the parties incur if the deposition was held within the distance permitted under CCP §2025.250? *Id.* §2025.260(b)(6).

(g) Where will the deponent be at the scheduled time for the deposition? *Id.* §2025.260(b)(7).

(2) Expenses & costs. The court can condition the order permitting the taking of the deposition at a more distant place on the advancement by the deposing party of the reasonable expenses and costs to the deponent for travel to the place of the deposition. CCP §2025.260(c).

4. Sanctions. The court must impose a monetary sanction against any party, person, or attorney who unsuccessfully makes or opposes a motion to increase travel limits, unless the court finds that (1) the motion or opposition was substantially justified or (2) imposing a monetary sanction would be unjust. CCP §2025.260(d). See "Discovery Sanctions," ch. 9-A, p. 1003.

§12.7 Motion for ruling on objections to written deposition. A party can make a motion asking the court to rule on objections to written deposition questions. For example, the motion can ask the court to sustain an objection to the form of the questions or to overrule an objection that a question asks for privileged or exempt information. CCP §2028.040(b) (motion to sustain form objection), §2028.050(b) (motion to overrule privilege objection), §2028.070(c) (court may sustain or overrule objections).

1. Deadline for motion. There is no specific deadline to make a motion to sustain or overrule an objection to a written deposition question. A motion to sustain an objection based on the form of the question must be made "promptly." CCP §2028.040(b).

2. Effect of no motion. If a responding party does not make a motion to sustain an objection to the form of the question, the question will be asked as written. *See* CCP §2028.040(b). If the deposing party does not make a motion to overrule an objection based on a privilege or exemption, the question will not be asked at the deposition. *See id.* §2028.050(b).

3. Meet & confer. The motion to sustain or overrule an objection must be accompanied by a meet-and-confer declaration. *See* CCP §§2028.040(b), 2028.050(b). See "Meet-and-confer declaration," ch. 7-A, §10.4, p. 763.

4. Request relief. The motion should ask the court to sustain or overrule the written objections to the deposition questions. CCP §2028.040(b) (sustain objections to form of question), §2028.050(c) (overrule objections based on privilege).

PRACTICE TIP

A party who objects to the written deposition questions on the ground of privilege should not move for a ruling on that objection. If neither party makes a motion to resolve the privilege objection, the objection prevents the deposition officer from asking the deponent the question. See CCP §2028.050(b).

---

5. Sanctions. The court must impose a monetary sanction against any party, person, or attorney who unsuccessfully makes or opposes a motion to sustain or overrule an objection, unless the court finds that (1) the motion or opposition was substantially justified or (2) imposing a monetary sanction would be unjust. CCP §2028.040(c) (sanctions for motion to sustain objections), §2028.050(c) (sanctions for motion to overrule objections).

§13. USING DEPOSITIONS IN COURT PROCEEDINGS

§13.1 Depositions from same case.

1. Use at trial. A party can use deposition testimony as evidence at a trial or hearing if the following conditions are met:

(1) Noticed party. The party against whom the deposition is being used either (1) was present or represented at the deposition or (2) was not present at the deposition but was notified of the deposition and did not serve valid objections to the deposition notice. CCP §2025.620; *CEB Discovery Practice*, §6.136; *CEB Procedure During Trial*, §12.32. A deposition cannot be used against a party who was added after the deposition was taken. *CEB Procedure During Trial*, §12.36; *see* CCP §2025.620. The substitution of parties, however, does not affect the use of depositions taken before the party was substituted. CCP §2025.620(f).

(2) Admissible testimony. The deponent's testimony is admissible under the rules of evidence, applied as though the testimony were given live. CCP §2025.620; *CEB Procedure During Trial*, §12.32.

(3) Proper purpose. The deponent's testimony is being offered for a proper purpose, which includes any of the following:

(a) Impeach or contradict. A party can use a deposition of a party or nonparty deponent to impeach or contradict the testimony of the deponent when the deponent appears as a witness at a trial or hearing. CCP §2025.620(a); *CEB Discovery Practice*, §6.137; *see* Evid. C. §780(h); ***Keen v. Prisinzano*** (3d Dist.1972) 23 Cal.App.3d 275, 281 n.3.

(b) Substitute or additional testimony. A party can use a deposition of the following persons as a substitute for or in addition to live, in-court testimony:

[1] Adverse party's deposition. A party can use a deposition for any purpose (e.g., to establish a material fact, make a prima facie case, or prove the whole case) if the person deposed is an adverse party or was the adverse party's officer, director, managing agent, employee, agent, or designee when the deposition was taken. CCP §2025.620(b); *CEB Discovery Practice*, §6.138; *see* ***Mayhood v. La Rosa*** (1962) 58 Cal.2d 498, 501; *see,*

e.g., ***Haluck v. Rioch Elecs., Inc.*** (4th Dist.2007) 151 Cal.App.4th 994, 1004-05 (court erred in admitting deposition testimony of witness who was not employed by party at time deposition was taken). The adverse party cannot object to the introduction of the deposition testimony on the grounds that the adverse party is available to testify, has testified, or will testify at the trial or hearing. CCP §2025.620(b); *see also* Evid. C. §1220 (admission of party).

[2] **Any person's deposition.** A party can use the deposition of any person or organization, whether a party or nonparty, for any purpose if the party can establish one of the exceptions to the requirement for live testimony. CCP §2025.620(c); *see CEB Procedure During Trial*, §12.69. The exceptions are as follows:

[a] **Distance.** The deponent resides more than 150 miles away from the place of the trial or hearing. CCP §2025.620(c)(1); *CEB Discovery Practice*, §6.138; *see CEB Procedure During Trial*, §12.69. Proof of residence beyond the 150-mile limit, without proof of unavailability, is sufficient. *See CEB Procedure During Trial*, §12.59.

[b] **Deponent unavailable.** The deponent (without any wrongdoing by the party who wants to use the deposition) is not available to testify for any of the following reasons:

- The deponent is exempt or prohibited from testifying about the relevant matter because of a privilege. CCP §2025.620(c)(2)(A).
- The deponent is disqualified from testifying. *Id.* §2025.620(c)(2)(B).
- The deponent is dead or unable to attend or testify because of a physical or mental illness or infirmity. *Id.* §2025.620(c)(2)(C); *see CEB Procedure During Trial*, §12.60.
- The deponent is not present at the trial or hearing and the court is unable to compel the deponent's attendance by its process. CCP §2025.620(c)(2)(D); *see CEB Procedure During Trial*, §12.60.
- The deponent is not present at the trial or hearing and the party who wants to use the deposition has not been able to procure the deponent's attendance by use of the court's process, despite reasonable diligence. CCP §2025.620(c)(2)(E); *see CEB Procedure During Trial*, §12.60.

[c] **Exceptional circumstances.** There are exceptional circumstances that make it desirable to allow the use of the deposition (1) in the interests of justice and (2) with due regard for the importance of presenting the testimony of witnesses orally in open court. CCP §2025.620(c)(3).

2. **Use in summary judgment.** A party can use deposition testimony as evidence to support or oppose a motion for summary judgment. See "Depositions," ch. 10-B, §9.2.3(1), p. 1133.

3. **Use of electronically recorded depositions.** An electronically recorded deposition can be used at a trial or hearing if the following conditions are met:

(1) **Noticed party.** See "Noticed party," §13.1.1(1), p. 810.

(2) **Admissible testimony.** See "Admissible testimony," §13.1.1(2), p. 810.

(3) **Notice of intent to use.** The deposing party properly notified the other parties of its intent to use the electronically recorded deposition. See "Notice of intent to use electronically recorded deposition," §13.3, p. 815.

(a) **Audio or video depositions.** A party can use the audio or video recording of a deposition at a trial or hearing if the party notified all parties and the court in writing of its intent and identified the parts of the deposition it intends to offer.

(b) **Expert's video deposition.** A party can use the video recording of an expert's deposition without showing that the expert is unavailable to testify in person if the party did the following:

[1] Reserved the right to use the deposition at trial in the deposition notice. CCP §2025.620(d); *CEB Discovery Practice*, §§6.139, 11.48; *CEB Procedure During Trial*, §§12.41, 12.84.

DEPOSITIONS

[2] Notified all parties and the court in writing of its intent to use the expert's video deposition and identified the parts of the deposition it intends to offer. CCP §§2025.340(m), 2025.620(d); *CEB Procedure During Trial*, §12.84; *see CEB Discovery Practice*, §§6.139, 11.48; *CEB Procedure During Trial*, §12.41. The notice must be given with enough time for the other parties to object and for the court to rule on the objections. CCP §2025.340(m).

4. Partial use of deposition. If a party uses only part of a deposition, any other party can introduce the other parts of it if they are relevant to the introduced part. CCP §2025.620(e); *see* Evid. C. §356.

5. Substitution of parties. The substitution of parties does not affect the right to use depositions previously taken. CCP §2025.620(f). For example, if a party transfers its interest in the litigation after being deposed, that party's deposition can still be used against the transferee by opposing parties for any purpose. Weil, *Civil Procedure Before Trial*, ¶8:878.2.

§13.2 Depositions from earlier cases. Depositions from an earlier case can be used in a later case under CCP §2025.620(g) and Evid. C. §§1291 and 1292.

NOTE

A deposition from an earlier case must be properly authenticated by the court reporter before it can be introduced as evidence in a later case. See, e.g., ***Wahlgren v. Coleco Indus.*** *(4th Dist.1984) 151 Cal.App.3d 543, 546 (notarized copy of deposition was not admissible in later case). To be admissible in a later case, a copy of a deposition from an earlier case must be a certified copy or a duplicate original. See id.*

1. Deposition under CCP §2025.620(g). A deposition from an earlier case can be used in a later case against another party as though the deposition were taken in the later case if the offering party can show the following:

(1) Same parties. The offering party must show that the offering party and the party against whom the deposition is being used either (1) were parties in the earlier case or (2) are the representatives or successors in interest of the parties in the earlier case. CCP §2025.620(g); *CEB Procedure During Trial*, §12.44.

(2) Noticed party. See "Noticed party," §13.1.1(1), p. 810.

(3) Same subject matter. The offering party must show that the earlier and later cases involve the same subject matter. CCP §2025.620(g); *CEB Procedure During Trial*, §12.44.

(4) Admissible testimony. See "Admissible testimony," §13.1.1(2), p. 810.

(5) Deposition filed. The offering party must show that the deposition was lawfully taken and "duly filed" in the earlier case. CCP §2025.620(g); *CEB Procedure During Trial*, §12.44.

(6) State or federal court. The offering party must show the earlier case was brought in a state or federal court. CCP §2025.620(g); *CEB Procedure During Trial*, §12.44.

PRACTICE TIP

If a deposition is not admissible under CCP §2025.620(g), it may be admissible under Evid. C. §1291(a)(1). For example, if a deposition from an earlier case is not admissible under §2025.620(g) because it was not "duly filed," the party can offer it under §1291(a)(1). CEB Procedure During Trial, §12.75.

2. Former testimony under Evid. C. §1291(a)(1). A deposition from an earlier case can be used in a later case against another party under Evid. C. §1291(a)(1). *CEB Procedure During Trial*, §12.75; *see* CCP §2025.620(g) (deposition can be used as permitted by Evidence Code); Evid. C. §1290(c) (former testimony includes testimony given in deposition), §1291(a)(1) (admissibility of former testimony). To do this, the offering party must show the following:

(1) Adverse party in earlier case. The offering party must show that the adverse party in the later case was a party in the earlier case or is the successor in interest to a party in the earlier case. *See* Evid. C. §1291(a)(1); ***Rufo v. Simpson*** (2d Dist.2001) 86 Cal.App.4th 573, 606-07; *CEB Trial Objections*, §19.29.

(2) Unavailable deponent. The offering party must show that the deponent in the earlier case is not available as a witness in the later case. ***Haluck v. Ricoh Elecs., Inc.*** (4th Dist.2007) 151 Cal.App.4th 994, 1004-05; ***Wahlgren***, 151 Cal.App.3d at 546; *CEB Procedure During Trial*, §12.75; *see* Evid. C. §1291(a); *CEB Trial Objections*, §19.29; *Jefferson's Evid. Benchbook*, §8.2. To establish that the witness is unable to attend, the offering party must show that the deponent is sick, dead, or otherwise beyond the court's subpoena power (e.g., introduce a certified copy of a death certificate to show that the deponent is dead). *CEB Procedure During Trial*, §12.60.

(3) Adverse party used deposition. The offering party must show that the adverse party offered the deposition in evidence in the earlier case or is the successor in interest to the party that did so. *See* Evid. C. §§1290(c), 1291(a)(1); *CEB Trial Objections*, §19.29; *Jefferson's Evid. Benchbook*, §8.2.

(4) Admissible testimony. See "Admissible testimony," §13.1.1(2), p. 810.

3. Former testimony under Evid. C. §1291(a)(2). A deposition from an earlier case can be used in a later case against another party under Evid. C. §1291(a)(2) if the offering party can show the following:

(1) Adverse party in earlier case. The offering party must show that the adverse party in the later case was a party in the earlier case. *See* Evid. C. §1291(a)(2); *CEB Trial Objections*, §19.29.

(2) Unavailable deponent. The offering party must show that the deponent in the earlier case is not available as a witness in the later case. *See* Evid. C. §§1290(c), 1291(a)(2). See "Unavailable deponent," §13.2.2(2), this page.

(3) Right & opportunity to cross-examine. The offering party must show that the adverse party had the right and opportunity to cross-examine the deponent in the earlier case. *See* Evid. C. §§1290(c), 1291(a)(2); *CEB Trial Objections*, §19.29.

(4) Similarity of interests. The offering party must show that the adverse party had an interest and motive in the earlier case that is similar to the adverse party's interest and motive in the later case. ***Wahlgren***, 151 Cal.App.3d at 546; *see* Evid. C. §1291(a)(2); *CEB Trial Objections*, §19.29; *Jefferson's Evid. Benchbook*, §8.2. The offering party must show that the similarity of interest and motive is based on practical considerations; it is not sufficient to show that the adverse party had similar positions in the two cases. *E.g.*, ***Wahlgren***, 151 Cal.App.3d at 546-47 (D's motivation to cross-examine its own officers during deposition in earlier case was not same as its motivation to cross-examine during trial in later case; parties generally avoid examining themselves at depositions, but are highly motivated to clarify their positions at trial).

PRACTICE TIP

If a deposition is not admissible under CCP §2025.620(g) or Evid. C. §1291, it may be admissible under Evid. C. §1292. For example, a deposition from an earlier case is not admissible under §2025.620(g) or §1291 if the adverse party or its predecessor in interest was not a party in the earlier case, but under §1292 this is not an impediment.

---

4. Former testimony under Evid. C. §1292. A deposition taken in an earlier case can be used in a later case against another party under Evid. C. §1292 if the offering party can show the following:

(1) Adverse party not in earlier case. The offering party must show that the adverse party was not a party in the earlier case. *See* Evid. C. §1292(a)(3) (distinguishes between party in case in which deposition was taken and party against whom deposition is being offered); ***Rufo***, 86 Cal.App.4th at 606 (Evid. C. §1292 allows admission of former testimony against party in present case who was not party in earlier case); ***Wahlgren***, 151

Cal.App.3d at 547 (same); *CEB Procedure During Trial*, §12.77 (same). *But see* ***O'Neill v. Novartis Consumer Health, Inc.*** (2d Dist.2007) 147 Cal.App.4th 1388, 1403-04 (court relied on §1292 instead of §1291, even though adverse party was party in both cases).

(2) Civil action. The offering party must show that the later case is a civil action. *See* Evid. C. §1292(a)(2); ***O'Neill***, 147 Cal.App.4th at 1403-04; ***Gatton v. A.P. Green Servs.*** (1st Dist.1998) 64 Cal.App.4th 688, 692; *CEB Procedure During Trial*, §12.77; *cf.* ***Rufo***, 86 Cal.App.4th at 605 (party attempted to introduce trial testimony from earlier criminal action at later civil action).

(3) Unavailable deponent. The offering party must show that the deponent in the earlier case is not available as a witness in the later case. *See* Evid. C. §§1290(c), 1292(a)(1); ***O'Neill***, 147 Cal.App.4th at 1403-04; ***Gatton***, 64 Cal.App.4th at 692; *CEB Procedure During Trial*, §12.77.

(4) Right & opportunity to cross-examine. The offering party must show that a party in the earlier case had the right and opportunity to cross-examine the deponent. *See* CCP §§1290(c), 1292(a)(3); ***O'Neill***, 147 Cal.App.4th at 1403-04; ***Gatton***, 64 Cal.App.4th at 692; ***Wahlgren***, 151 Cal.App.3d at 547; *CEB Procedure During Trial*, §12.77; *cf.* ***Rufo***, 86 Cal.App.4th at 607 (party could not introduce trial testimony from earlier criminal action in later civil action under §1292 because witness in earlier action was examined on direct, not cross).

(5) Similarity of interests. The offering party must show that the party in the earlier case who had the right and opportunity to cross-examine the deponent had an interest and motive that is similar to the adverse party's interest and motive in the later case. *See* Evid. C. §§1290(c), 1292(a)(3); ***O'Neill***, 147 Cal.App.4th at 1403-04; ***Gatton***, 64 Cal.App.4th at 692-93; ***Wahlgren***, 151 Cal.App.3d at 547; *CEB Procedure During Trial*, §12.77. To satisfy this element, the offering party must show that the similarity of interests and motives is based on practical considerations; the offering party cannot simply show that the parties in the two cases had similar positions. ***O'Neill***, 147 Cal.App.4th at 1404; ***Gatton***, 64 Cal.App.4th at 692; *see, e.g.*, ***Byars v. SCME Mortg. Bankers, Inc.*** (4th Dist.2003) 109 Cal.App.4th 1134, 1150 (no showing that party's interest or motive in earlier case was similar to adverse party's interest or motive in later case); ***Wahlgren***, 151 Cal.App.3d at 547 (same). For example, a defendant in an earlier asbestos case who manufactured the asbestos used in a steel plant had no interest or motive to establish the nonliability of a nonparty (the adverse party in the later case) who also manufactured asbestos used at the same steel plant. ***Gatton***, 64 Cal.App.4th at 692-93.

7-14. USING DEPOSITIONS TAKEN IN EARLIER CASES

	Party offering deposition from earlier case must show:	CCP §2025.620(g)	Evid. C. §1291(a)(1)	Evid. C. §1291(a)(2)	Evid. C. §1292
1	Adverse party was a party in earlier case	Yes	Yes	Yes	No
2	Offering party was a party in earlier case	Yes	No	No	No
3	Deposition filed in earlier case	Yes	No	No	No
4	Both cases involved same subject matter	Yes	No	No	No
5	Earlier case was brought in state or federal court	Yes	No	No	No
6	Later case is a civil action	No	No	No	Yes
7	Deponent from earlier case is unavailable to testify in later case	No	Yes	Yes	Yes
8	Adverse party used deposition in earlier case	No	Yes	No	No
9	Adverse party was present or represented at earlier deposition or had notice of it and did not object	Yes	No	No	No
10	Party in earlier case had right to cross-examine deponent	No	No	Yes	Yes

7-14. USING DEPOSITIONS TAKEN IN EARLIER CASES (CONTINUED)					
	Party offering deposition from earlier case must show:	CCP §2025.620(g)	Evid. C. §1291(a)(1)	Evid. C. §1291(a)(2)	Evid. C. §1292
11	Party in earlier case had similar interest and motive to those of party in later case	No	No	Yes	Yes
12	Deposition from earlier case is properly certified by court reporter	Yes	Yes	Yes	Yes
13	Deposition from earlier case is admissible under rules of evidence and was lawfully taken	Yes	Yes	Yes	Yes
Adverse party = party against whom deposition from earlier case is offered in later case Offering party = party who offers deposition from earlier case in later case					

§13.3 Notice of intent to use electronically recorded deposition.

1. Notice of intent. A party who intends to use an electronically recorded deposition (audio or video) during a trial or hearing must notify the court and the other parties of its intent. CCP §2025.340(m); *see id.* §2025.620(d). The notice must (1) be in writing, (2) identify the deposition recording to be offered, and (3) specify the parts of the recording to be offered. *Id.* §2025.340(m). The notice must be provided to the court and the other parties with enough time for objections to be resolved by the judge and for any necessary editing of the recording. *Id.* The party intending to offer the electronically recorded deposition must provide a stenographic transcript of the testimony if one has not already been made. *Id.*

PRACTICE TIP

To use the videotaped deposition of an expert, a party must provide two notices. First, the reservation of the right to use the expert's videotaped deposition must be included in the deposition notice or deposition subpoena. See "Videotape of expert's deposition," §9.2.7, p. 792; "Expert's video deposition," §13.1.3(3)(b), p. 811; "Expert's video deposition," ch. 8-B, §3.1.3(4), p. 960. Second, the notice of intent, described above, must be provided to the court and the other parties.

2. Object to recording. Objections to all or part of a deposition recording must be in writing. CCP §2025.340(m). A party can object to the use of an expert's videotaped deposition if the deposing party did not include the required notice in the deposition notice or deposition subpoena. See "Videotape of expert's deposition," §9.2.7, p. 792; "Expert's video deposition," ch. 8-B, §3.1.3(4), p. 960.

3. Court-ordered editing. If any parts of the recording are not designated by a party or are ruled to be objectionable, the court can require the party offering the recording to either suppress those parts or prepare an edited version of the recording for use at the trial or hearing. CCP §2025.340(m).

§13.4 How to introduce deposition testimony.

1. Trial or hearing. Before the trial or hearing, the deposition transcripts or recordings may need to be filed or lodged with the court clerk. See "Filing or Lodging Deposition Transcripts," §11, p. 807.

(1) Stenographic transcript. To introduce deposition testimony at a trial or hearing, the attorney must read the questions and answers from the transcript of the deposition into evidence. *See CEB Procedure During Trial*, §§12.48, 12.135, 13.62. The deposition transcript itself is not offered into evidence. *Id.* §13.62.

(2) Electronic recording. To offer into evidence an electronic recording of a deposition, the party offering the deposition into evidence must do the following:

(a) Before offering the evidence at a trial or hearing, the party must lodge a transcript of the deposition with the court. CRC 2.1040(a)(1). The party should lodge only the portion of the transcript being offered into evidence.

(b) At the time the recording is being played, the party must identify on the record the page and line numbers where the testimony appears in the transcript. CRC 2.1040(a)(1).

(c) If the court reporter does not take down the content of the electronic recording, the party must file and serve at the close of evidence or within five days after offering the deposition into evidence—whichever occurs later—a copy of the transcript cover showing the witness's name and a copy of the pages of the transcript where the offered testimony appeared. CRC 2.1040(a)(2), (a)(3). The transcript pages must be marked to identify the offered testimony. CRC 2.1040(a)(2).

2. **Motion papers.** See "Deposition testimony," ch. 1-D, §5.3.2, p. 31.

C. INTERROGATORIES

§1. GENERAL

§1.1 Purpose. Interrogatories are written questions served on a party that must be answered under oath. *See* CCP §§2030.010(a), 2030.250(a). Interrogatories are used for the following purposes:

1. To discover admissible evidence or obtain information that is reasonably calculated to lead to the discovery of admissible evidence. *See id.* §§2017.010, 2030.010(a); ***Kalaba v. Gray*** (2d Dist.2002) 95 Cal.App.4th 1416, 1423; *see, e.g.*, ***West Pico Furniture Co. v. Superior Ct.*** (1961) 56 Cal.2d 407, 416 (interrogatory used to identify potential deposition witnesses was reasonably calculated to lead to discovery of admissible evidence).

2. To gather information that can be used to prepare for other discovery. Weil & Brown, *California Practice Guide: Civil Procedure Before Trial* (CD-ROM ed. 2014) ¶8:901; *see* ***West Pico***, 56 Cal.2d at 416 (interrogatories can be used to identify potential deposition witnesses).

3. To ask follow-up questions about information obtained through other discovery methods. Weil & Brown, *California Practice Guide: Civil Procedure Before Trial* (CD-ROM ed. 2014) ¶8:901.

4. To detect false, fraudulent, and sham claims and defenses hidden behind evasive language in a party's pleadings. ***Deyo v. Kilbourne*** (2d Dist.1978) 84 Cal.App.3d 771, 779.

5. To compel a party to commit to or abandon particular factual or legal contentions. *See id.* at 780 (interrogatories prevent equivocation by responding party).

6. To evaluate the merit of claims and defenses. *Id.* at 779.

§1.2 Primary authority. CCP §§2030.010-2030.410; CRC 3.250, 3.1000.

§1.3 Secondary authority. The following secondary sources are cited as authority in this subchapter:

- *California Civil Discovery Practice* (CEB Online ed. 2014) (referred to as *CEB Discovery Practice*).
- *California Civil Procedure Before Trial* (CEB Online ed. 2014) (referred to as *CEB Procedure Before Trial*).
- *California Trial Practice: Civil Procedure During Trial* (CEB Online ed. 2014) (referred to as *CEB Procedure During Trial*).
- Sink, *California Subpoena Handbook* (2014-15) (referred to as Sink, *Subpoena Handbook*).
- Thomas, *California Civil Courtroom Handbook* (2014) (referred to as Thomas, *Courtroom Handbook*).
- Weil & Brown, *California Practice Guide: Civil Procedure Before Trial* (CD-ROM ed. 2014) (referred to as Weil, *Civil Procedure Before Trial*).

§1.4 Judicial Council forms. The Judicial Council has adopted official form interrogatories for optional use. See "Official Form Interrogatories," §5, p. 820.

§2. COMPARING INTERROGATORIES WITH OTHER DISCOVERY

§2.1 Interrogatories vs. depositions. See "Depositions vs. interrogatories," ch. 7-B, §3.1, p. 782.

§2.2 Interrogatories vs. RFAs. See "Comparing RFAs with Interrogatories," ch. 7-D, §2, p. 836.

§2.3 Interrogatories vs. demands to produce. See "Demands to produce vs. interrogatories," ch. 7-E, §2.2, p. 845.

§3. SCOPE OF DISCOVERY BY INTERROGATORIES

§3.1 What can be discovered. Interrogatories can ask for any information that is within the scope of discovery and is not protected by a privilege, exemption, or court order. *See* CCP §§2017.010, 2030.010(a). See "Scope of discovery," ch. 6-A, §2.1, p. 603. An interrogatory can ask for information that is itself admissible or that is likely to lead to the discovery of other information that is admissible. *See* CCP §§2017.010, 2030.010(b); ***Kalaba v. Gray*** (2d Dist.2002) 95 Cal.App.4th 1416, 1423. See "Types of discoverable information," ch. 6-A, §2.2, p. 604.

1. Identity of person answering. An interrogatory can ask the responding party to identify and provide other information about the person answering the set of interrogatories. *See, e.g.*, Judicial Council Forms, form DISC-001, interrogatories 1.0-3.0. This is useful if the responding party is an organization. *See id.* interrogatory 3.0.

2. Facts. An interrogatory can ask the responding party to provide information that is within the responding party's personal knowledge or under its control. *See* CCP §2030.220(a), (c). Information is under the responding party's control if the responding party can obtain the information with a reasonable and good-faith effort. *See id.* §2030.220(c). An interrogatory cannot require the responding party to gather information that is equally available to the discovering party. *Id.* See "Equally available," §8.3.4(2)(a)[3], p. 830.

3. Witnesses.

(1) Fact witnesses. An interrogatory can ask the responding party to identify and give the location of individuals with knowledge of relevant facts. ***Deyo v. Kilbourne*** (2d Dist.1978) 84 Cal.App.3d 771, 782; *see* CCP §2030.010(b); ***Puerto v. Superior Ct.*** (2d Dist.2008) 158 Cal.App.4th 1242, 1250; *see, e.g.*, Judicial Council Forms, form DISC-001, interrogatory 12.1 (asking for name, address, and telephone number of each person who witnessed incident or events occurring immediately before or after incident). See "Witness information," ch. 6-A, §2.2.12, p. 606.

(2) Nonretained experts. An interrogatory can ask the responding party to identify nonretained trial experts by name, address, and telephone number, describe the nature of each expert's relationship to the party (e.g., treating physician), and provide the experts' opinions. *See, e.g.*, ***Schreiber v. Estate of Kiser*** (1999) 22 Cal.4th 31, 38 (identity and opinion of treating physician was discoverable through interrogatories); Judicial Council Forms, form DISC-001, interrogatory 6.4 (asking for identity of treating health-care providers, their contact information, the date and type of consultation, examination, or treatment, and their charges). See "Experts subject to discovery," ch. 7-I, §4.1, p. 901.

4. Documents. An interrogatory can ask the responding party to provide information about the responding party's documents so that the discovering party can adequately describe them when preparing a demand to inspect (to a party) or a subpoena (to a nonparty). *See* ***Flora Crane Serv. v. Superior Ct.*** (1st Dist.1965) 234 Cal.App.2d 767, 777; *see, e.g.*, Judicial Council Forms, form DISC-001, interrogatory 15.0 (asking for identity of documents that support D's denials and defenses).

(1) Unprivileged documents. An interrogatory can ask the responding party to provide information about the existence, description, nature, custody, condition, location, and content of unprivileged documents. *See* CCP §§2017.010, 2030.010(a), 2030.230; ***Best Prods. v. Superior Ct.*** (2d Dist.2004) 119 Cal.App.4th 1181, 1190; *see, e.g.*, ***Smith v. Superior Ct.*** (3d Dist.1961) 189 Cal.App.2d 6, 12-13 (interrogatory sought information about existence of photographs of collision scene, number of photographs, dates, and photographer's name and address). See "Tangible things," ch. 6-A, §2.2.6, p. 605.

(2) Privileged documents. An interrogatory can ask the responding party to provide information about the existence, description, nature, custody, condition, and location—but not the content—of privileged documents. *See* CCP §§2017.010, 2030.010(a); ***Best Prods.***, 119 Cal.App.4th at 1190. A responding party cannot object to an interrogatory because it asks for identifying information about a privileged document. *See* ***Best Prods.***, 119 Cal.App.4th at 1190; ***Hernandez v. Superior Ct.*** (2d Dist.2003) 112 Cal.App.4th 285, 293.

5. Party's contentions. An interrogatory can ask the responding party for information about its factual and legal contentions. CCP §2030.010(b). This can help the discovering party clarify and narrow the contested issues in the case. ***Burke v. Superior Ct.*** (1969) 71 Cal.2d 276, 281. An interrogatory can ask for factual and legal contentions even if they are based on information obtained or legal theories developed in anticipation of litigation or in preparation for trial. CCP §2030.010(b); *see* ***Burke***, 71 Cal.2d at 281-82.

(1) Factual contentions.

(a) Whether party makes factual contention. A factual-contention interrogatory can ask whether a party is making a particular factual contention in the case. CCP §2030.010(b). For example, an interrogatory can ask a plaintiff in a personal-injury suit whether she contends she was physically, mentally, or emotionally injured from the defendant's actions. *See, e.g.*, Judicial Council Forms, form DISC-001, interrogatory 6.1.

(b) Basis for factual contention. A factual-contention interrogatory can ask a party to identify the specific facts relied on as support for the party's factual contentions. CCP §2030.010(b). For example, an interrogatory can ask the plaintiff in a personal-injury suit to provide facts to support the plaintiff's contention that she will lose future income as a result of the incident. *See, e.g.*, Judicial Council Forms, form DISC-001, interrogatory 8.8.

NOTE

Contention interrogatories to a defendant should not be used until the defendant has had a reasonable opportunity to investigate or conduct discovery on the plaintiff's injuries and damages. Judicial Council Forms, form DISC-001, §2(d) (instructions to discovering party), form DISC-004, §2(f) (same).

(2) Legal contentions.

(a) Whether party makes legal contention. A legal-contention interrogatory can ask whether a responding party is making particular legal contentions in the case, or it can ask the responding party to describe the legal contentions that form the basis of a particular claim or defense. *CEB Discovery Practice*, §7.39; *see* CCP §2030.010(b); ***Rifkind v. Superior Ct.*** (2d Dist.1994) 22 Cal.App.4th 1255, 1261; *CEB Discovery Practice*, §7.40. For example, an employee in a wrongful-termination suit can be asked if she contends that any adverse employment action against her was discriminatory. *See, e.g.*, Judicial Council Forms, form DISC-002, interrogatory 202.1.

(b) Basis for legal contention.

[1] Factual basis. A legal-contention interrogatory can ask a responding party to identify the specific facts relied on as support for its legal contentions. CCP §2030.010(b). For example, an interrogatory can ask the responding party to identify all the documents that support its contention that the parties were operating under a contract. *See, e.g.*, Judicial Council Forms, form DISC-002, interrogatory 200.3.

[2] Not legal basis. A legal-contention interrogatory cannot ask a responding party to describe the underlying legal reasoning or opinions for its legal contention because that would violate the attorney work-product privilege. *See* ***Sav-On Drugs, Inc. v. Superior Ct.*** (1975) 15 Cal.3d 1, 5. For example, even though a defendant could be required to disclose whether it contends an affidavit supporting a writ of attachment is defective, it could not be required to divulge the legal theory or reasoning process underlying that contention (i.e., the reasons why the affidavit is legally defective). ***Burke***, 71 Cal.2d at 285; *see also* ***Flora Crane***, 234 Cal.App.2d at 781-82 (Ds not required to divulge how P's complaint failed to state cause of action).

NOTE

The distinction between discoverable legal contentions and information protected by the work-product privilege is not clear. See "Work-Product Privilege," ch. 6-B, §3, p. 628. Ordinarily, discovery cannot be used to elicit an adverse party's legal reasoning protected by the work-product privilege. ***Burke****, 71 Cal.2d at 284; see* ***Sav-On Drugs****, 15 Cal.3d at 5 (interrogatory cannot ask party to identify laws that support its contentions because that would reveal legal reasoning). But see Judicial Council Forms, form DISC-002, interrogatory 205.1 (asking party to identify laws, regulations, and other sources of public policy that party contends were violated by D-employer for claim based on adverse employment action).*

6. Damages. An interrogatory can ask about a claimant's damages. For example, an interrogatory can ask a claimant to list the types of damages it claims it suffered and the amount of damages for each type. *See, e.g.*, Judicial Council Forms, form DISC-001, interrogatories 7.1(c), 10.3.

7. History of claims. An interrogatory can ask about a claimant's history of other suits or claims. For example, an interrogatory in a suit involving fire-insurance coverage can ask whether the claimant has made other claims under a fire-insurance policy in the past ten years. *See, e.g.*, Judicial Council Forms, form DISC-001, interrogatory 11.1.

8. Personal records. Whenever a party seeks to discover personal records or information of another party or a nonparty by interrogatory, the request may implicate the right to privacy guaranteed in the California Constitution. *See* Cal. Const., art. I, §1; ***In re Insurance Installment Fee Cases*** (4th Dist.2012) 211 Cal.App.4th 1395, 1420 & n.15. The subpoena procedures for obtaining such information from nonparties (i.e., party-to-nonparty discovery) include specific requirements for notifying a person (whether a party or nonparty) whose records or information is sought and giving the person an opportunity to object to the request. *See* CCP §§1985.3, 1985.4, 1985.6. See "Subpoenas for Personal Records," ch. 8-D, p. 977. Strangely, no such notice and objection requirements are included in the Civil Discovery Act (CDA) procedures for obtaining personal records or information from another party (i.e., party-to-party discovery) about a different party or nonparty. *See* ***Valley Bank v. Superior Ct.*** (1975) 15 Cal.3d 652, 657 (existing discovery scheme does not protect privacy of persons whose records are sought). But the responding party may have a constitutional or statutory duty to protect the privacy of the person whose records or information is sought. *See id.* at 656; ***In re Insurance Installment Fee Cases***, 211 Cal.App.4th at 1423, 1426. See "Right to Privacy," ch. 6-F, §1, p. 681. The court can protect the privacy of the person whose information is sought by ordering the responding party to give the third person notice and an opportunity to object to the request. *See* ***Pioneer Elecs. (USA), Inc. v. Superior Ct.*** (2007) 40 Cal.4th 360, 372; ***In re Insurance Installment Fee Cases***, 211 Cal.App.4th at 1423. See "Cost of production," ch. 7-E, §8.2, p. 853; "Types of Persons & Entities Covered," ch. 8-D, §7, p. 981. At least one commentator has offered the practical recommendation that parties seeking such discovery from other parties (whether by deposition, interrogatories, etc.) should follow the procedures required for obtaining personal information from nonparties by subpoena. *See* Sink, *Subpoena Handbook*, §§6:2[I], 6:4. By following the procedures governing deposition subpoenas for personal-records discovery from nonparties, a discovering party may avoid both the expense of having to litigate privacy issues and possible sanctions.

9. Sources of financial information. An interrogatory can ask a defendant to identify documents or witnesses that could help establish the defendant's financial condition. *See* Civ. C. §3295(c). While a plaintiff seeking punitive damages is not allowed to discover information about the defendant's financial condition without a court order, a plaintiff can subpoena documents or witnesses to be available at trial to introduce such evidence. *Id.* See "Motion to Discover Financial Information," ch. 7-G, p. 868.

§3.2 Who can be required to answer.

1. Any party. Interrogatories can be used to secure information from any party to the action. CCP §2030.010(a). The term "any party" in §2030.010(a) includes the initial parties to the action, any parties joined in the action, coparties (parties who are on the same side in the action), and cross-parties (parties to the main action

and parties to a cross-action). *See* ***Westrec Marina Mgmt. v. Jardine Ins. Brokers Orange Cty., Inc.*** (4th Dist.2000) 85 Cal.App.4th 1042, 1049 (dicta; interrogatory can be served on co-D); *CEB Procedure Before Trial*, §26.26 (assumes interrogatories are available against cross-parties); Weil, *Civil Procedure Before Trial*, ¶¶8:920-8:922 (for discovery purposes, parties to complaint and parties to cross-complaint should be treated as parties to same action).

2. Organizational parties. When the party served is a public or private corporation, partnership, association, or governmental agency, the discovering party cannot require a particular person to sign on the organization's behalf. ***Castaline v. City of L.A.*** (2d Dist.1975) 47 Cal.App.3d 580, 588 n.7; ***Mowry v. Superior Ct.*** (3d Dist.1962) 202 Cal.App.2d 229, 235, *disapproved on other grounds*, ***San Diego P.A. v. Superior Ct.*** (1962) 58 Cal.2d 194; *see* CCP §2030.250(b). The organization can choose the officer or agent it wants to sign for it. *See* CCP §2030.250(b). See "Organization's officers or agents," ch. 7-A, §9.4.1(3)(b)[1], p. 759.

§4. TYPES OF INTERROGATORIES

§4.1 Official form interrogatories. A party can serve official form interrogatories, which are interrogatories drafted and approved by the Judicial Council. CCP §2030.030(a)(2); *see* Judicial Council Forms, forms DISC-001–DISC-005. See "Official Form Interrogatories," §5, this page.

§4.2 Specially prepared interrogatories. A party can serve specially prepared interrogatories, which are interrogatories drafted by the party. *See* CCP §2030.030(a)(1); Thomas, *Courtroom Handbook*, §21.88. See "Specially Prepared Interrogatories," §6, p. 822.

§4.3 Supplemental interrogatories. A party can serve supplemental interrogatories, which are interrogatories that ask for updated answers to the party's earlier interrogatories. CCP §2030.070(a). Supplemental interrogatories are used to secure information that the responding party acquired after serving its original interrogatory answers. *Id.* See "Supplemental Interrogatories," §7, p. 825.

§5. OFFICIAL FORM INTERROGATORIES

§5.1 Purpose. Official form interrogatories are useful for obtaining general background information and should be used whenever possible because (1) they avoid disputes over the wording of the interrogatories and (2) they allow the discovering party to save its specially prepared interrogatories for follow-up requests or for obtaining other information. *See* Weil, *Civil Procedure Before Trial*, ¶¶8.934.1, 8.980. See "Specially Prepared Interrogatories," §6, p. 822.

§5.2 Number. The number of official form interrogatories a party can serve depends on whether the case is classified as limited or unlimited. See "Procedural Classifications of Civil Cases," ch. 3-E, §4, p. 255.

1. Unlimited civil cases. In an unlimited civil case, a party can serve an unlimited number of official form interrogatories that are relevant to the subject matter of the action. CCP §2030.030(a)(2).

2. Limited civil cases.

(1) Combination of 35. In a limited civil case, the number of official form interrogatories a party can serve is subject to a limit on written discovery. Weil, *Civil Procedure Before Trial*, ¶8:1813.3; *see* CCP §94(a). A party can serve to each adverse party a combined total of 35 of the following: (1) interrogatories (official form, specially prepared, and supplemental) with no subparts, (2) demands to produce, and (3) requests for admission with no subparts. CCP §94(a); *see* Weil, *Civil Procedure Before Trial*, ¶¶8:935, 8:1810. In a limited civil case, the Judicial Council form interrogatories count against a party's 35 total requests. Weil, *Civil Procedure Before Trial*, ¶8:1813.3; *see* CCP §94(a).

(2) More than 35. To serve more than 35 interrogatories in a limited civil case, a party must obtain either a stipulation or a court order based on a motion showing that the party is unable to prosecute or defend the action effectively without the additional discovery. CCP §95. If the party seeks a court order, the court must consider

whether the party (1) has used, in good faith, all applicable discovery methods, and (2) has attempted to secure the additional discovery by stipulation or by means other than formal discovery methods. *Id.* §95(a). See "Modifying Discovery Procedures," ch. 7-A, §4, p. 743.

§5.3 Form. The official form interrogatories served by a party must be in the form approved by the Judicial Council. *See* CRC 2.132 (party or attorney certifies that form is true copy), CRC 2.140 (CRC 2.130-2.141 apply to Judicial Council forms). To avoid disputes over form, a discovering party should use an exact duplicate of the Judicial Council form, if possible. *See* Weil, *Civil Procedure Before Trial*, ¶8:934.2; *see also* CRC 2.135 (parties can file handwritten copies of Judicial Council forms). Electronic versions of the Judicial Council form interrogatories can be found at www.courts.ca.gov/forms.htm. Different forms are available for limited and unlimited cases. See "Procedural Classifications of Civil Cases," ch. 3-E, §4, p. 255.

1. Judicial Council forms – unlimited civil cases. The official forms for interrogatories in unlimited civil cases include the following:

(1) DISC-001 (optional), general.

(2) DISC-002 (optional), interrogatories for employment-law cases.

(3) DISC-003/UD-106 (optional), interrogatories for unlawful-detainer cases.

(4) DISC-005 (optional), interrogatories for construction litigation.

(5) FL-145 (optional), interrogatories for family-law cases.

2. Judicial Council forms – limited civil cases. The official forms for interrogatories in limited civil cases include the following:

(1) DISC-004 (optional), interrogatories for limited civil cases.

(2) DISC-015 (mandatory), request for statement identifying trial witnesses and evidence to be introduced at trial.

§5.4 Contents.

1. No preface. The official form interrogatories do not contain a preface. *See* Judicial Council Forms, forms DISC-001–DISC-005. A party is not permitted to add its own preface to the official form interrogatories. *See* CCP §2030.060(d).

2. Instructions. The official form interrogatories contain instructions for the discovering and the responding parties. *See* Judicial Council Forms, forms DISC-001–DISC-005. A discovering party must use the exact instructions approved by the Judicial Council, without any additions or modifications. *See* CCP §2030.060(d); CRC 2.132, 2.140.

3. Definitions. The official form interrogatories contain definitions for use in drafting and responding to the interrogatories. *See* Judicial Council Forms, forms DISC-001–DISC-005. A discovering party must use the exact definitions approved by the Judicial Council, without any additions or modifications. *See* CRC 2.132, 2.140.

4. Questions. The official form interrogatories contain the exact language that must be used in each interrogatory. *E.g.*, Judicial Council Forms, form DISC-001, interrogatory 2.2 ("State the date and place of your birth."). A discovering party must use the exact question approved by the Judicial Council, without any additions or modifications. *See* CRC 2.132, 2.140.

5. Deadline to respond.

(1) Most cases. The official form interrogatories inform the responding party that responses are generally due within 30 days after being served with the interrogatories. *See* CCP §2030.260(a); Judicial Council Forms, form DISC-001, §3(b), form DISC-004, §3(b), form DISC-005, §3(b). The deadline to serve responses is extended if the interrogatories were served by any means other than personal service (e.g., five calendar days are added if mailed in California). *See* CCP §§1013(a), 2016.050. See "Add time for method of service," ch. 1-G, §6.1.4, p. 70.

(2) Unlawful-detainer cases. The official form interrogatories for unlawful-detainer cases inform the responding party that responses are generally due within five days after being served with the interrogatories. *See* CCP §2030.260(b); Judicial Council Forms, form DISC-003/UD-106, §3(b). The deadline to serve responses is extended if the interrogatories were served by any means other than personal service (e.g., five calendar days are added if mailed in California). *See* CCP §§1013(a), 2016.050. See "Add time for method of service," ch. 1-G, §6.1.4, p. 70.

6. No duty to supplement. An official form interrogatory cannot impose a continuing duty on the responding party to supplement its answers with later-acquired information. CCP §2030.060(g); *see* ***Biles v. Exxon Mobil Corp.*** (1st Dist.2004) 124 Cal.App.4th 1315, 1328. *But see* Gov. C. §985(c) (P served with interrogatory by public-entity D has continuing duty to disclose providers of collateral-source payments). To require interrogatory answers to be updated, the discovering party must serve supplemental interrogatories. See "Supplemental Interrogatories," §7, p. 825; "Supplementing responses," ch. 7-A, §9.5.2, p. 760.

7. Signature. There is no requirement that official form interrogatories be signed by the discovering party or its attorney. However, as a general rule, an attorney should sign all discovery requests that she drafts. See "Attorney's signature," ch. 7-A, §7.2.6, p. 753.

§5.5 When to serve. See "Timing of Discovery," ch. 7-A, §5, p. 745; "When to Schedule Discovery," ch. 7-A, §6, p. 749.

§5.6 Serving. See "Serving discovery," ch. 7-A, §13.1, p. 769.

§5.7 Custody & disposal. See "Custody & Disposal of Discovery," ch. 7-A, §16, p. 776.

§6. SPECIALLY PREPARED INTERROGATORIES

§6.1 Purpose. Specially prepared interrogatories are interrogatories drafted by the discovering party that can be used to pose questions not found in official form interrogatories.

§6.2 Number. The number of specially prepared interrogatories a party can serve depends on whether the case is classified as limited or unlimited. See "Procedural Classifications of Civil Cases," ch. 3-E, §4, p. 255.

1. Unlimited civil cases.

(1) Rule of 35. In an unlimited civil case, a party is entitled to serve 35 specially prepared interrogatories on each of the other parties. CCP §2030.030(a)(1), (b); ***Catanese v. Superior Ct.*** (2d Dist.1996) 46 Cal.App.4th 1159, 1164.

(a) Limit per party. The 35-interrogatory limit is a limit on the number of specially prepared interrogatories that can be served by one party on each of the other parties, not a limit on the total number a party can serve in the case. *See* CCP §2030.030(a)(1), (b); Weil, *Civil Procedure Before Trial*, ¶8:937. Thus, a plaintiff who sues three defendants can serve 35 specially prepared interrogatories on each defendant, for a total of 105 specially prepared interrogatories. *See* CCP §2030.030(a)(1), (b).

(b) Multiple sets. A party can serve its interrogatories to a party in multiple sets as long as the total number of interrogatories served to the party does not exceed the 35-interrogatory limit. CCP §2030.030(b).

(2) More than 35. A party can serve more than 35 specially prepared interrogatories based on either a declaration of necessity or the parties' stipulation.

(a) Declaration of necessity. A party can serve more than 35 specially prepared interrogatories if it attaches a declaration that is substantially the same as the sample provided by CCP §2030.050. CCP §2030.040(a). The declaration is often referred to as a "declaration of necessity." *CEB Discovery Practice*, §7.8. The declaration must contain the following information:

[1] Parties. The declaration must state (1) the name of the declarant (i.e., the name of the person serving additional interrogatories), (2) whether the declarant is an attorney for a party or a party appearing pro per, and (3) the name of the responding party. *See* CCP §2030.050, ¶¶1, 2.

[2] **Number of interrogatories.** The declaration must state the following:

[a] That the current set of interrogatories will cause the total number of specially prepared interrogatories served on the responding party to exceed the 35-interrogatory limit. CCP §2030.050, ¶3.

[b] The total number of interrogatories (specially prepared and official form) served on the responding party in previous sets. *Id.* ¶4.

[c] The number of specially prepared interrogatories served on the responding party in previous sets. *See id.*

[d] The number of specially prepared interrogatories included in the current set. *Id.* ¶5.

[3] **Personally examined.** The declaration must state that the declarant is familiar with the issues and previous discovery in the case and has personally examined each of the interrogatories included in the current set. CCP §2030.050, ¶¶6, 7.

[4] **No improper purpose.** The declaration must state that none of the interrogatories in the current set is being served for any improper purpose. CCP §2030.050, ¶9. Improper purposes for serving interrogatories include (1) harassing a responding party or the party's attorney, (2) causing unnecessary delay, and (3) needlessly increasing the cost of litigation. *Id.*

[5] **Grounds for additional interrogatories.** The declaration must identify one or more of the grounds listed in CCP §2030.040(a) for serving more than 35 specially prepared interrogatories and state the reasons why the grounds apply under the circumstances. CCP §2030.050, ¶8; *see, e.g.*, ***Catanese***, 46 Cal.App.4th at 1164-65 (discovering party violated "rule of 35" by serving interrogatories without supporting declaration stating grounds for additional discovery). The list of grounds for additional interrogatories in §2030.040(a) is exclusive; no other grounds can justify serving more than 35 interrogatories. *See* CCP §2030.050, ¶8. The following are the grounds in §2030.040(a):

[a] **Complexity or quantity of issues.** A party can serve more than 35 specially prepared interrogatories if the additional interrogatories are needed due to the complexity or quantity of existing and potential issues in the action. CCP §2030.040(a)(1).

[b] **Financial burden of deposition.** A party can serve more than 35 specially prepared interrogatories if the financial burden of obtaining the requested information through oral depositions would be excessive. CCP §2030.040(a)(2).

[c] **Expedience of interrogatories.** A party can serve more than 35 specially prepared interrogatories if using additional interrogatories is a more expedient method for obtaining discovery because it allows the responding party to conduct an inquiry or investigation or to search files to supply the requested information. CCP §2030.040(a)(3).

(b) Stipulation. The parties can agree by written stipulation to more than 35 specially prepared interrogatories. *See* CCP §§2016.030, 2019.010. See "Modifying discovery by stipulation," ch. 7-A, §4.1, p. 743.

2. Limited civil cases. In a limited civil case, the number of specially prepared interrogatories a party can serve is subject to the limit on written discovery. See "Limited civil cases," §5.2.2, p. 820.

§6.3 Form. See "Form of discovery requests," ch. 7-A, §7.2, p. 753.

§6.4 Contents.

1. Instructions. A set of specially prepared interrogatories can include an instruction applicable to the whole set if the instruction duplicates the exact wording of an instruction approved by the Judicial Council for official form interrogatories. *See* CCP §2030.060(d); *CEB Discovery Practice*, §7.33; Weil, *Civil Procedure Before Trial*, ¶8:967. See "Instructions," §5.4.2, p. 821.

2. Definitions. A set of specially prepared interrogatories can include definitions that apply to all interrogatories in the set. *See* CCP §2030.060(e). The specially defined words must be typed in all capital letters every time they are used in the interrogatories. *Id.*; *CEB Discovery Practice*, §7.33.

3. Questions.

(1) Separate. Each specially prepared interrogatory must be stated as a separate question. CCP §2030.060(c); *CEB Discovery Practice*, §7.34. An interrogatory is not a separate question merely because it requires multiple responses. *See, e.g.*, ***Catanese v. Superior Ct.*** (2d Dist.1996) 46 Cal.App.4th 1159, 1165 (five interrogatories asking about truthfulness of each deposition response required at least 10,000 responses). It is not necessary to provide space for answers to the interrogatories. *CEB Discovery Practice*, §7.34.

(2) Numbered or lettered. Each specially prepared interrogatory in a set must be identified by number or letter (e.g., Interrogatory No. 1 or Interrogatory A). CCP §2030.060(c).

(3) Self-contained. Each question must be full and complete in and of itself. CCP §2030.060(d). A question is not full and complete if the responding party must refer to other materials to answer the question. ***Catanese***, 46 Cal.App.4th at 1164. For example, a question is not full and complete if it asks the responding party to review deposition transcripts and state which answers the responding party contends are untruthful. *See id.*

(4) No subparts. A specially prepared interrogatory cannot contain subparts or compound, conjunctive, or disjunctive questions. CCP §2030.060(f); *CEB Discovery Practice*, §§7.35, 7.36. By comparison, many official form interrogatories have subparts. *See CEB Discovery Practice*, §7.35.

4. Deadline to respond. A set of specially prepared interrogatories can (but is not required to) state the deadline to respond to the interrogatories. If the set includes such a statement, it must conform to the language in the official form interrogatories. *See* CCP §2030.060(d); Judicial Council Forms, form DISC-001, §3(b).

(1) Most cases. In most cases, the specially prepared interrogatories can state that the responding party must serve its responses to the interrogatories on the discovering party and all other parties within 30 days after being served with the interrogatories. *See* CCP §2030.260(a). The deadline to serve responses is extended if the interrogatories were served by any means other than personal service (e.g., five calendar days are added if mailed in California). *See id.* §§1013(a), 2016.050. See "Add time for method of service," ch. 1-G, §6.1.4, p. 70.

(2) Unlawful-detainer cases. In unlawful-detainer cases, the specially prepared interrogatories can state that the responding party must serve its responses to the interrogatories on the discovering party and all other parties within five days after being served with the interrogatories. *See* CCP §2030.260(b). The deadline to serve responses is extended if the interrogatories were served by any means other than personal service (e.g., five calendar days are added if mailed in California). *See id.* §§1013(a), 2016.050. See "Add time for method of service," ch. 1-G, §6.1.4, p. 70.

5. No duty to supplement. A specially prepared interrogatory cannot impose a continuing duty on the responding party to supplement its answers with later-acquired information. CCP §2030.060(g); ***Biles v. Exxon Mobil Corp.*** (1st Dist.2004) 124 Cal.App.4th 1315, 1328. *But see* Gov. C. §985(c) (P served with interrogatory by public-entity D has continuing duty to disclose providers of collateral-source payments). To require interrogatory answers to be updated, the discovering party must serve supplemental interrogatories. See "Supplemental Interrogatories," §7, p. 825.

6. Signature. There is no requirement that specially prepared interrogatories be signed by the discovering party or its attorney. However, as a general rule, an attorney should sign all discovery requests that she drafts. See "Attorney's signature," ch. 7-A, §7.2.6, p. 753.

§6.5 When to serve. See "Timing of Discovery," ch. 7-A, §5, p. 745; "When to Schedule Discovery," ch. 7-A, §6, p. 749.

§6.6 Serving. See "Serving discovery," ch. 7-A, §13.1, p. 769.

§6.7 Custody & disposal. See "Custody & Disposal of Discovery," ch. 7-A, §16, p. 776.

§7. SUPPLEMENTAL INTERROGATORIES

§7.1 Purpose. A supplemental interrogatory asks the responding party to provide updated answers to all earlier interrogatories. *See* CCP §2030.070(a); Weil, *Civil Procedure Before Trial*, ¶8:942. Because a responding party does not have a continuing duty to supplement its earlier interrogatory answers, serving supplemental interrogatories is one way to obtain updated interrogatory answers. *See* CCP §2030.060(g). See "Supplementing responses," ch. 7-A, §9.5.2, p. 760.

§7.2 Number.

1. Unlimited civil cases. In an unlimited civil case, supplemental interrogatories are permitted in addition to the number of specially prepared interrogatories permitted. *See* CCP §2030.070(a).

(1) Before trial date set. A party in an unlimited civil case can serve a supplemental interrogatory twice before the initial setting of a trial date. *See* CCP §2030.070(b); *CEB Discovery Practice*, §§7.12, 7.15.

(2) After trial date set. A party in an unlimited civil case can serve a supplemental interrogatory once after the initial setting of a trial date. *See* CCP §2030.070(b); *CEB Discovery Practice*, §§7.12, 7.15. A supplemental interrogatory served after the initial setting is subject to the discovery cutoff for proceedings and motions. CCP §2030.070(b); *see id.* §§2024.010-2024.060. See "When to complete discovery," ch. 7-A, §5.2, p. 746.

(3) Additional supplemental interrogatories.

(a) By motion. The court can allow a party to serve additional supplemental interrogatories in an unlimited civil case based on the party's motion and a showing of good cause. *See* CCP §2030.070(c); *CEB Discovery Practice*, §§7.12, 7.15.

(b) By stipulation. The parties in an unlimited civil case can agree by written stipulation to additional supplemental interrogatories. See "Modifying discovery by stipulation," ch. 7-A, §4.1, p. 743.

2. Limited civil cases. In a limited civil case, supplemental interrogatories are counted in calculating the total limit of 35 interrogatories, demands to produce, and requests for admission. *See* CCP §§94, 2030.070(b).

(1) Before trial date set. A party in a limited civil case can serve a supplemental interrogatory twice before the initial setting of a trial date. *See* CCP §§94(a)(1), 2030.070(b).

(2) After trial date set. A party in a limited civil case can serve a supplemental interrogatory once after the initial setting of the trial date. *See* CCP §§94(a)(1), 2030.070(b).

(3) Additional interrogatories.

(a) By motion. The court can allow a party to serve additional supplemental interrogatories in a limited civil case based on a motion showing that the party is unable to prosecute or defend the case effectively without the additional discovery. CCP §95(a).

(b) By stipulation. The parties in a limited civil case can agree by written stipulation to additional supplemental interrogatories. *See* CCP §95(b). See "Modifying discovery by stipulation," ch. 7-A, §4.1, p. 743.

§7.3 Form. Supplemental interrogatories must comply with the form requirements that apply to all interrogatories. *See* CCP §2030.060. See "Form," §5.3, p. 821.

§7.4 Contents. A supplemental interrogatory asks the responding party to review its original interrogatory answers and provide updated answers that are correct and complete in light of any new or different information now known to the responding party. *See* CCP §2030.070(a); *see, e.g.*, Weil, *Civil Procedure Before Trial*, ¶8:944 ("Please review your answers to interrogatories previously served on you in this action. If, for any reason, any answer is no longer correct and complete, identify the answer and state whatever information is necessary to make it correct and complete as of this date.").

§7.5 When to serve.

1. Before trial setting. Supplemental interrogatories can be served anytime before the court sets the initial trial date. *See* CCP §2030.070(b).

2. After trial setting. Supplemental interrogatories served after the court sets the initial trial date must be served early enough to allow the responding party to comply with the deadline for completing discovery. *See* CCP §§2024.010-2024.060, 2030.070(b). See "Latest date to schedule discovery," ch. 7-A, §6.3, p. 751.

§7.6 Serving. See "Serving discovery," ch. 7-A, §13.1, p. 769.

§8. RESPONDING TO INTERROGATORIES

§8.1 Deadline to respond. In most cases, the responding party must serve its responses to the interrogatories within 30 days after being personally served with the discovery. CCP §2030.260(a). In unlawful-detainer cases, the responding party must serve its responses to the interrogatories within five days after being served with the discovery. *Id.* §2030.260(b). The deadline to serve responses is extended if the interrogatories were served by any means other than personal service (e.g., five calendar days are added if mailed in California). *See id.* §§1013(a), 2016.050. See "Add time for method of service," ch. 1-G, §6.1.4, p. 70.

§8.2 Form. See "Form of response," ch. 7-A, §9.3, p. 758.

§8.3 Contents. A party must respond to interrogatories by (1) answering, (2) denying it has sufficient knowledge to answer, (3) producing documents instead of answering, or (4) objecting.

1. Answer interrogatories. A party can respond to an interrogatory by providing an answer containing the information sought by the interrogatory. CCP §2030.210(a)(1).

(1) Based on knowledge. The responding party must answer each interrogatory based on personal knowledge or knowledge that is reasonably available to it. *See* CCP §2030.220(a), (c); *see, e.g.*, ***Marketing W., Inc. v. Sanyo Fisher Corp.*** (2d Dist.1992) 6 Cal.App.4th 603, 615 (interrogatory answers based on information and belief were inadmissible as summary-judgment evidence).

(a) Personal knowledge. The responding party must provide information that is personally known by it. *See* CCP §2030.220(c).

(b) Reasonably available information. The responding party must provide all information that is reasonably available to it. CCP §2030.220(a).

[1] From attorney. The responding party must provide information known by its attorney that is not protected from discovery by the attorney-client privilege or work-product privilege. *CEB Discovery Practice*, §7.69; *see* ***Regency Health Servs. v. Superior Ct.*** (2d Dist.1998) 64 Cal.App.4th 1496, 1504 (general duty to disclose information known by attorney when responding to discovery); ***Smith v. Superior Ct.*** (3d Dist.1961) 189 Cal.App.2d 6, 12 (responding party's attorney should disclose all witnesses she has knowledge of regardless of whether client has knowledge of witnesses).

[2] From agents or employees. The responding party must provide information available from sources under the party's control, such as its agents or employees. *See* CCP §2030.220(c); ***Castaline v. City of L.A.*** (2d Dist.1975) 47 Cal.App.3d 580, 588 n.7; ***Pantzalas v. Superior Ct.*** (2d Dist.1969) 272 Cal.App.2d 499, 503.

[3] From related nonparties. The responding party must make a reasonable and good-faith effort to obtain information needed to answer interrogatories from related persons or entities cooperating with the responding party in the lawsuit. *See, e.g.*, ***West v. Johnson & Johnson Prods.*** (6th Dist.1985) 174 Cal.App.3d 831, 874 (D-company should have produced research information from employee of sibling corporation); ***Jones v. Superior Ct.*** (1st Dist.1981) 119 Cal.App.3d 534, 553 (P should have attempted to obtain information from her mother even though mother was accessible to Ds through deposition).

[4] Not from others. The responding party is not required to search for information needed to answer interrogatories from other people or organizations not subject to the responding party's control. *CEB Discovery Practice*, §7.69; *see* CCP §2030.220(c); *see, e.g.*, ***Holguin v. Superior Ct.*** (2d Dist.1972) 22 Cal.App.3d 812, 821 (D-physicians were not required to seek information from coroner's office to answer interrogatories). The responding party should not be required to bear the burden and expense of research that should be borne by the discovering party. *See* ***Pantzalas***, 272 Cal.App.2d at 503; Weil, *Civil Procedure Before Trial*, ¶8:1062 (duty to make reasonable efforts to obtain information does not apply to information equally available to discovering party); *see, e.g.*, ***Bunnell v. Superior Ct.*** (1st Dist.1967) 254 Cal.App.2d 720, 723-24 (P was not required to search deposition transcripts for list of witnesses).

(2) Complete.

(a) Complete answer. The responding party must give an answer to each interrogatory that is as complete and straightforward as possible. CCP §2030.220(a); ***Scheiding v. Dinwiddie Constr. Co.*** (1st Dist.1999) 69 Cal.App.4th 64, 76. Each answer must be complete in itself—that is, an answer cannot simply instruct the discovering party to consult other documents for the information. *See* CCP §2030.220(a); ***Deyo v. Kilbourne*** (2d Dist.1978) 84 Cal.App.3d 771, 783-84. If the responding party must refer to other documents to answer an interrogatory, it must either (1) specifically identify the documents and summarize their contents or (2) produce the documents under CCP §2030.230. ***Deyo***, 84 Cal.App.3d at 784. See "Produce documents," §8.3.3, this page.

(b) Partial answer. If the responding party cannot answer an interrogatory completely, the party must give the most complete partial answer possible. CCP §2030.220(b); *see id.* §2030.220(a), (c). See "Deny knowledge," §8.3.2, this page.

(3) Identify documents. When an interrogatory asks for identifying information about a party's documents, the responding party must provide sufficient information to enable the discovering party to describe the documents in a demand to produce. *See* ***Flora Crane Serv. v. Superior Ct.*** (1st Dist.1965) 234 Cal.App.2d 767, 778. If an interrogatory asks for identifying information about privileged documents but does not ask for information about their content, the responding party is not required to serve a privilege log. ***Best Prods. v. Superior Ct.*** (2d Dist.2004) 119 Cal.App.4th 1181, 1190; ***Hernandez v. Superior Ct.*** (2d Dist.2003) 112 Cal.App.4th 285, 293; *see also* ***Bank of Am. v. Superior Ct.*** (4th Dist.2013) 212 Cal.App.4th 1076, 1098 (court cannot issue case-management order requiring all discovery objections based on attorney-client or work-product privilege to be accompanied by privilege log). See "Privilege log," ch. 7-A, §14.1.4(2), p. 773.

2. Deny knowledge. A party can respond to an interrogatory by stating it cannot answer the interrogatory because it does not have sufficient knowledge. CCP §2030.220(c); *see* ***Bockrath v. Aldrich Chem. Co.*** (1999) 21 Cal.4th 71, 84. A party denying the ability to answer because of a lack of knowledge must state the following:

(1) Insufficient personal knowledge. The responding party must state it does not have sufficient personal knowledge to answer the interrogatory. CCP §2030.220(c). The responding party cannot simply state that it is unable to respond to the interrogatory. ***Sinaiko Healthcare Consulting, Inc. v. Pacific Healthcare Consultants*** (2d Dist.2007) 148 Cal.App.4th 390, 406.

(2) Good faith. The responding party must state it made a reasonable and good-faith effort to obtain the requested information from other individuals and organizations. CCP §2030.220(c). The response should describe the party's good-faith attempts to obtain the information. *See* ***Deyo***, 84 Cal.App.3d at 782.

3. Produce documents. A party has the option to answer an interrogatory by identifying and producing documents containing the requested information, instead of producing the information in the answer itself. CCP §§2030.210(a)(2), 2030.230; *CEB Discovery Practice*, §7.78.

INTERROGATORIES

PRACTICE TIP

The responding party should carefully evaluate the possible consequences of giving the discovering party access to its documents. Weil, Civil Procedure Before Trial, ¶8:1070. Even if it is difficult to create a compilation or summary of the documents, it might take almost as much time to verify that the information requested by the interrogatory is contained in the documents, and producing documents carries the risk of accidentally disclosing useful information that was not requested by the discovering party. See id.

(1) When allowed. The responding party can exercise its option to identify and produce documents instead of answering an interrogatory only if the following conditions are satisfied:

(a) Compilation necessary. To answer the interrogatory, the responding party would be required to prepare a compilation, abstract, audit, or summary of documents. CCP §2030.230; *CEB Discovery Practice*, §7.79; Weil, *Civil Procedure Before Trial*, ¶8:1066. A responding party cannot exercise the option if there is a compilation, abstract, audit, or summary already in existence. *CEB Discovery Practice*, §7.79; *see* ***Deyo***, 84 Cal.App.3d at 784.

(b) Equally burdensome. The burden or expense of preparing a compilation, abstract, audit, or summary of the documents would be substantially the same for the discovering party as it would be for the responding party. CCP §2030.230.

PRACTICE TIP

The primary difference between "equally burdensome" and "equally available" (see "Equally available," §8.3.4(2)(a)[3], p. 830) is that one requires the responding party to provide documents as part of its answer. A responding party can use the "equally burdensome" answer only when it provides its own documents to the discovering party. A responding party can use the "equally available" objection when the information is accessible to the discovering party without searching through the responding party's documents. Compare CCP §2030.220(c) (equally available) with id. §2030.230 (equally burdensome).

(c) Timely response. The responding party timely serves its response to the interrogatory. *See* CCP §2030.290(a). If it does not, it waives the option to identify and provide documents. *Id.* See "Deadline to respond," §8.1, p. 826.

(2) When not allowed. The responding party cannot exercise its option to identify and produce documents if any of the following apply:

(a) Compilation available. The responding party cannot identify and produce documents if a compilation, abstract, audit, or summary of the information needed to answer the interrogatory is already available. *CEB Discovery Practice*, §7.79; *see* ***Deyo***, 84 Cal.App.3d at 784.

(b) Documents do not provide complete answer. The responding party cannot identify and produce documents if the documents do not contain enough information to provide a complete answer. *CEB Discovery Practice*, §7.79; *see, e.g.*, ***Kaiser Found. Hosps. v. Superior Ct.*** (2d Dist.1969) 275 Cal.App.2d 801, 805 (production of medical records verified as accurate and complete was complete answer); ***Fuss v. Superior Ct.*** (2d Dist.1969) 273 Cal.App.2d 807, 816 (identification and production of records with disclaimer that there may be some duplication or omission was not complete answer).

(c) Option waived. The responding party cannot identify and produce documents if it waived the right to do so by not asserting the option before the deadline to answer interrogatories. CCP §2030.290(a). See "Deadline to respond," §8.1, p. 826.

(3) Contents of response. The response must include the following:

(a) Refer to CCP §2030.230. The response must refer to CCP §2030.230—for example, "In response to this interrogatory, plaintiff exercises its option to identify and provide documents under Code of Civil Procedure §2030.230." *See* CCP §2030.230. By exercising the option to identify and produce documents, the responding party declares that the information in the identified documents provides a true, accurate, and complete answer to the interrogatory and that the responding party is providing all the information available to it. ***Deyo***, 84 Cal.App.3d at 784. See "Reasonably available information," §8.3.1(1)(b), p. 826.

(b) Identify documents. The response must specify the writings from which the answer can be obtained. CCP §2030.230; ***Deyo***, 84 Cal.App.3d at 784. This specification must identify the documents with sufficient detail to allow the discovering party to locate and identify the documents containing the requested information as readily as they could be identified and located by the responding party. CCP §2030.230. It is not sufficient to direct the discovering party to a broad group of documents that the discovering party would be required to search through to find the relevant documents. ***Deyo***, 84 Cal.App.3d at 784; *see, e.g.*, ***Fuss***, 273 Cal.App.2d at 817 (statement that information could be found in "other related records" was insufficient); *CEB Discovery Practice*, §7.80 (answer such as "see business records" is insufficient). If possible, the responding party should identify the specific paragraphs, sections, or pages of the documents that contain the requested information, although this is not required by statute. *See* CCP §2030.230; Judicial Council Forms, forms DISC-001–DISC-005.

(4) Produce documents.

(a) Provide opportunity to inspect. The responding party must give the discovering party a reasonable opportunity to inspect and make copies, compilations, abstracts, or summaries of the identified documents. CCP §2030.230; *CEB Discovery Practice*, §7.80; *see* Weil, *Civil Procedure Before Trial*, ¶8:1069.

(b) Attach as exhibits. Instead of producing the documents for inspection at a later time, the responding party can attach the identified documents as exhibits to its response. *See* Judicial Council Forms, forms DISC-001–DISC-005.

(5) Motion to compel. If the discovering party decides that the responding party's exercise of the option to produce documents under CCP §2030.230 is unwarranted or the responding party's description of the documents is inadequate, the discovering party can make a motion to compel a further response. CCP §2030.300(a)(2). See "Motion to Compel Further Response," ch. 9-E, §3, p. 1061.

4. Object. A party can respond to interrogatories with written objections. CCP §2030.210(a)(3). Alternatively, a party can respond by moving for a protective order. *Id.* §2030.090(a); *CEB Discovery Practice*, §7.122. See "Motion for Protective Order," ch. 9-B, p. 1024. In most cases, a party will serve written objections to interrogatories, which is easier than making a motion for a protective order.

(1) Form.

(a) Separately stated. Each objection must be stated separately for each interrogatory. CCP §2030.210(a)(3), (c). Blanket objections to interrogatories (e.g., a statement that the responding party "objects to Interrogatories 5 through 10 on grounds that these interrogatories are oppressive") are not allowed. *See id.* §2030.210(a)(3) (party must respond separately to each interrogatory); *cf.* ***Scottsdale Ins. v. Superior Ct.*** (2d Dist.1997) 59 Cal.App.4th 263, 275-76 (blanket objections to demands for production were improper because party must respond separately to each demand).

(b) Corresponding numbers. Each objection must be numbered or lettered in the same sequential manner used by the discovering party to identify the corresponding interrogatory. CCP §2030.210(c). For example, the responding party must make its objections to "Interrogatory No. 12" in "Response No. 12." *See id.*

(c) Specific objection. Each objection must clearly state the specific ground for the objection (e.g., the interrogatory is ambiguous). CCP §2030.240(b).

CAUTION

A responding party should assert specific objections to interrogatories, not boilerplate objections that state multiple grounds for objection without considering whether they apply to the interrogatory. See, e.g., ***Hernandez****, 112 Cal.App.4th at 291 (responding party made same objections to nearly every interrogatory). Boilerplate objections can subject the responding party to sanctions. See, e.g.,* ***Korea Data Sys. Co. v. Superior Ct.*** *(4th Dist.1997) 51 Cal.App.4th 1513, 1516 (boilerplate objections to demand for production may have been sanctionable).*

(d) Partial objection. A responding party can object to a specific part of an interrogatory instead of the whole interrogatory. *See* CCP §2030.240(a). If a party objects to only part of an interrogatory, the party must state the specific grounds for objecting to that part of the interrogatory, and then answer, deny knowledge, or identify and produce documents in response to the remaining part of the interrogatory. *See id.* §2030.240. See "Answer interrogatories," §8.3.1, p. 826; "Deny knowledge," §8.3.2, p. 827; "Produce documents," §8.3.3, p. 827.

(2) Grounds. For a list of objections, see "Valid objections," ch. 7-A, §11.1, p. 765. The following are some additional objections that can be made to interrogatories:

(a) All interrogatories. The following objections can be made to both official form interrogatories and specially prepared interrogatories:

[1] Ambiguous. The responding party can object to an interrogatory on the ground that it is ambiguous if the interrogatory is so unclear that it cannot be determined what information is sought. *See* ***Deyo***, 84 Cal.App.3d at 783. The responding party must provide an answer if the nature of the information sought is apparent despite the interrogatory being somewhat ambiguous. *Id.*

[2] Overbroad. The responding party can object to an interrogatory on the ground that it is overbroad—that is, the interrogatory asks for information that is not reasonably related to the case. *See* ***Obregon v. Superior Ct.*** (2d Dist.1998) 67 Cal.App.4th 424, 431-32; ***Perkins v. Superior Ct.*** (2d Dist.1981) 118 Cal.App.3d 761, 764.

[3] Equally available. The responding party can object to an interrogatory on the ground that it asks for information that is equally available to the discovering party. *See* CCP §2030.220(c); ***Pantzalas***, 272 Cal.App.2d at 503; *CEB Discovery Practice*, §7.88. When information is equally available to the parties, the responding party has no obligation to obtain the information for the discovering party, even if locating the information would not be burdensome for the responding party. *See* CCP §2030.220(c); ***Bunnell***, 254 Cal.App.2d at 724; Weil, *Civil Procedure Before Trial*, ¶8:1062. Examples of information that is equally available to the parties include the following:

[a] Information that is available from public records or other documents accessible to the public. ***Alpine Mut. Water Co. v. Superior Ct.*** (2d Dist.1968) 259 Cal.App.2d 45, 53-54; *see, e.g.*, ***Ryan v. Superior Ct.*** (2d Dist.1960) 186 Cal.App.2d 813, 819 (interrogatory asked for list of persons named in published book). *But see* ***Perkins***, 118 Cal.App.3d at 766 (party had to answer interrogatories asking for information on other suits involving party's product, even though party objected on ground that information was in public records).

[b] Information that is contained in documents already in the possession of the party serving the interrogatory. *See, e.g.*, ***Bunnell***, 254 Cal.App.2d at 723-24 (information about witnesses identified in previous depositions and trials).

[c] Information that is in the possession of an unrelated third party. *See* ***Pantzalas***, 272 Cal.App.2d at 505. See "Not from others," §8.3.1(1)(b)[4], p. 827.

PRACTICE TIP

*An objection to a discovery request can be based on the ground that the request asks for information that is not within the scope of discovery. See "Not within scope of discovery," ch. 7-A, §11.1.1, p. 765. But courts tend to be skeptical about this objection when it is made to an official form interrogatory because the information sought by official form interrogatories is routinely discoverable in most cases. See **Puerto v. Superior Ct.** (2d Dist.2008) 158 Cal.App.4th 1242, 1250 (form interrogatories ask for "fundamentally routine" discovery of witness contact information). To avoid any potential skepticism when making a scope-of-discovery objection to an official form interrogatory, be sure to assert that the interrogatory asks for information that is completely irrelevant to the subject matter of the case. See **CBS v. Superior Ct.** (2d Dist.1968) 263 Cal.App.2d 12, 19; see, e.g., **Thomas v. Luong** (1st Dist.1986) 187 Cal.App.3d 76, 82 (official form interrogatories would be irrelevant if court struck part of D's answer contesting liability).*

(b) Specially prepared interrogatories. The following objections can be made to specially prepared interrogatories only:

[1] More than 35 special interrogatories.

[a] Declaration not attached or defective. The responding party can object to specially prepared interrogatories that exceed the 35-interrogatory limit if (1) the interrogatories are not supported by a declaration of necessity or (2) the declaration attached by the discovering party does not include the information required by CCP §2030.050. CCP §2030.030(c). See "More than 35," §6.2.1(2), p. 822. The responding party must respond to the first 35 interrogatories served, after which the responding party can object to and not answer each additional interrogatory on the ground that it exceeds the 35-interrogatory limit. CCP §2030.030(c). The party cannot "pick and choose" which interrogatories to answer when making this objection. *See id.*; Weil, *Civil Procedure Before Trial*, ¶8:940.

[b] Supported by declaration. When a declaration that complies with §2030.050 is attached, the responding party must choose to either respond to the additional interrogatories or make a motion for a protective order. *See* CCP §§2030.030(c), 2030.040(b), 2030.090(b)(2). See "Motion for Protective Order," ch. 9-B, p. 1024.

[2] Not self-contained question. The responding party can object to a specially prepared interrogatory on the ground that it is not full and complete—that is, the interrogatory requires the responding party to refer to other materials to complete the question. *See* CCP §2030.060(d). See "Self-contained," §6.4.3(3), p. 824.

[3] Subparts. The responding party can object to a specially prepared interrogatory on the ground that it contains subparts. *See* CCP §2030.060(f). Only official form interrogatories can contain subparts. *See id.*

[4] Compound, conjunctive, or disjunctive. The responding party can object to a specially prepared interrogatory that includes a compound, conjunctive, or disjunctive question. *See* CCP §2030.060(f). Only official form interrogatories can contain compound, conjunctive, or disjunctive questions. *See id.*

(3) Invalid grounds. This section discusses invalid interrogatory objections. For a discussion of objections that are invalid against all types of discovery requests, see "Invalid objections," ch. 7-A, §11.2, p. 767.

(a) Confidential information. A responding party cannot object to an interrogatory by simply asserting that the interrogatory calls for the disclosure of confidential information. ***CBS***, 263 Cal.App.2d at 23. To protect confidential information requested by an interrogatory, the responding party must either (1) object based on a recognized privilege or (2) make a motion for a protective order based on a specific privacy right. *See id.*; *see, e.g.*,

Nacht & Lewis Architects, Inc. v. Superior Ct. (3d Dist.1996) 47 Cal.App.4th 214, 216-17 (work-product objection to official form interrogatories). See "Privileged & exempt information," ch. 6-A, §3.3, p. 610; "Protected personal information," ch. 7-A, §11.1.10, p. 767.

(b) Identity of privileged documents. A responding party cannot make a privilege objection to an interrogatory that merely asks the party to identify a privileged document. *See* ***Best Prods.***, 119 Cal.App.4th at 1190; ***Hernandez***, 112 Cal.App.4th at 293. See "Documents," §3.1.4, p. 817. The responding party is not required to produce a privilege log. *See* ***Hernandez***, 112 Cal.App.4th at 293.

(4) Waiver.

(a) Grounds for waiver. A responding party waives its objections to interrogatories if it does not timely respond to the interrogatories or if it timely responds but does not assert objections.

[1] Untimely response. A party who does not timely respond to interrogatories waives any objections to them, including objections based on privilege, and must give a full and complete answer to the interrogatories. CCP §2030.290(a); ***Sinaiko Healthcare Consulting***, 148 Cal.App.4th at 408.

[2] Untimely objection. A party who timely responds to interrogatories but does not include all its objections in the response waives the right to assert the objections not included. ***Scottsdale Ins.***, 59 Cal.App.4th at 274. *But see* ***Heda v. Superior Ct.*** (1st Dist.1990) 225 Cal.App.3d 525, 529-30 (in personal-injury action, D did not waive privacy objection to medical records by objecting to medical records on ground of relevance).

(b) Relief from waiver. The court can relieve the responding party of its waiver of objections not asserted in its original interrogatory response under certain conditions. See "Relief from discovery waiver," ch. 7-A, §15.2.3, p. 776; "Motion for Relief from Waiver of Objections," ch. 9-H, p. 1082.

(5) No privilege log. A privilege log is not necessary when responding to an interrogatory that seeks the identification of privileged documents. ***Hernandez***, 112 Cal.App.4th at 293. See "Privilege log," ch. 7-A, §14.1.4(2), p. 773.

§8.4 No duty to supplement. The responding party does not have a continuing duty to supplement its interrogatory answers with later-acquired information. See "No duty to supplement," §6.4.5, p. 824. To compel the responding party to update its original interrogatory answers, the discovering party must serve supplemental interrogatories. See "Supplemental Interrogatories," §7, p. 825.

§8.5 Signatures & verification. See "Signatures & verification," ch. 7-A, §9.4, p. 759.

§8.6 Serving responses to interrogatories. See "Serving discovery responses," ch. 7-A, §13.1.2, p. 770.

§8.7 Amending answers. The responding party can amend its original interrogatory answers. CCP §2030.310(a); *see* ***Guzman v. General Motors Corp.*** (4th Dist.1984) 154 Cal.App.3d 438, 444.

1. Voluntary. The responding party can voluntarily amend its original interrogatory answers. CCP §2030.310(a); *see CEB Discovery Practice*, §7.73.

2. Leave not required. The responding party does not need the court's permission to voluntarily amend its original interrogatory answers. CCP §2030.310(a); *CEB Discovery Practice*, §7.74.

3. Contents of amended answers. The responding party can include the following information in an amended answer:

(1) Information that was discovered after the responding party served its original interrogatory answers. CCP §2030.310(a).

(2) Information that was inadvertently omitted from the original interrogatory answers. *Id.*

(3) Information that was mistakenly stated in the original interrogatory answers. *Id.*

4. Serving amended answers to interrogatories. The responding party must serve its amended interrogatory answers on the discovering party and copies on all other parties. *See* CCP §2030.310(a); *cf. id.* §2030.260(a), (c) (serving original answers). Once amended, the responding party is not bound by its original answer to an interrogatory, even if the amended answer completely repudiates the original answer, unless the court grants a motion by the discovering party to bind the responding party to its original answer. *See id.* §2030.310(b), (c); ***Williams v. American Cas. Co.*** (1971) 6 Cal.3d 266, 275. See "Motion to deem answer binding," §9.4, this page.

§9. MOTIONS RELATED TO INTERROGATORIES

§9.1 Motion for protective order. Any party or any other affected natural person or organization can move for a protective order against interrogatories. CCP §2030.090(a); *CEB Discovery Practice*, §7.122. See "Motion for Protective Order," ch. 9-B, p. 1024. In most cases, a party will serve written objections to interrogatories rather than make a motion for a protective order.

§9.2 Motion to compel initial response. The discovering party can make a motion to compel the responding party to respond to the interrogatories. CCP §2030.290(b). See "Motion to Compel Initial Response," ch. 9-E, §2, p. 1057.

§9.3 Motion to compel further response. The discovering party can make a motion to compel the responding party to serve further responses to interrogatories. CCP §2030.300(a). See "Motion to Compel Further Response," ch. 9-E, §3, p. 1061.

§9.4 Motion to deem answer binding. On the noticed motion of a discovering party, the court can issue an order preventing the responding party from presenting evidence that contradicts an interrogatory answer that was later amended by the responding party. *See* CCP §2030.310(b), (c); *see, e.g.*, ***Thoren v. Johnston & Washer*** (2d Dist.1972) 29 Cal.App.3d 270, 273 (responding party not allowed to present testimony from fact witness that it deliberately did not identify).

1. Requirements.

(1) In writing. A motion to bind the responding party to its initial interrogatory answer must be in writing. *See* CCP §2030.310(b). See "Motion Papers," ch. 1-D, §5, p. 27.

(2) Meet & confer. The motion must be accompanied by a meet-and-confer declaration. CCP §2030.310(b). See "Meet-and-confer declaration," ch. 7-A, §10.4, p. 763.

2. Grounds. The court must grant the motion if the motion establishes all the following conditions:

(1) Incorrect answer. The responding party's initial interrogatory answer was incorrect. CCP §2030.310(c)(1).

(2) No justification. The responding party has not shown substantial justification for providing the incorrect answer. CCP §2030.310(c)(2).

(3) Substantial prejudice. The discovering party was substantially prejudiced by the initial incorrect answer. CCP §2030.310(c)(1).

(4) Not curable. The substantial prejudice to the discovering party cannot be cured by either of the following:

(a) A continuance to allow further discovery. CCP §2030.310(c)(3).

(b) The discovering party's ability to use the initial answer against the responding party. *Id.* §§2030.310(c)(3), 2030.410.

3. Impose sanctions. The court must impose a monetary sanction against any party, person, or attorney who unsuccessfully makes or opposes a motion to bind the responding party to its initial interrogatory answer, unless the person subject to sanctions acted with substantial justification or the monetary sanction would be unjust under the circumstances. CCP §2030.310(d). See "Discovery Sanctions," ch. 9-A, p. 1003.

§10. USING INTERROGATORIES IN COURT PROCEEDINGS

§10.1 How to introduce. Before the trial or hearing, the interrogatories and answers should be lodged or filed with the court clerk, depending on the local rules or the preferences of the court. *See CEB Procedure During Trial*, §12.138 (checklist for introducing interrogatories). See "Filing or lodging discovery," ch. 7-A, §13.2, p. 770.

1. Trial or hearing.

(1) Before trial or hearing. Before the trial or hearing, the discovering party must lodge or file the interrogatory questions and answers with the court and provide copies to the other parties. *See, e.g.*, Super. Ct. Alameda Cty. Loc. R., rule 3.35(c)(2) (party must provide copies of interrogatory excerpts to opposing parties three days before pretrial conference or three days before trial if no pretrial conference). Some attorneys prepare a single document, combining the questions and answers that will be used during the trial. *See* Super. Ct. Los Angeles Cty. Loc. R., rule 3.158 (requiring offering party to combine pertinent parts of interrogatories and answers into single document); *CEB Procedure During Trial*, §12.138 (local rules might require preparation of cut-and-paste extracts of interrogatories and answers for ease of reading).

(2) At trial or hearing. At the trial or hearing, the attorney must ask the court for permission to read the interrogatories and answers to the fact-finder. *See* Super. Ct. Los Angeles Cty. Loc. R., rule 3.158. If the party has not already informed the other parties and the court which interrogatories it will offer, it must identify them by number. *See id.*; *CEB Procedure During Trial*, §12.138. After reading the questions and answers, the party should formally offer the interrogatories into evidence. *CEB Procedure During Trial*, §12.138.

2. Motion papers. To use interrogatory answers to support motion papers, the party must include the text of the interrogatories and their answers in the separate statement. *CEB Discovery Practice*, §7.117. The separate statement must contain all the information necessary to understand each discovery request and related response. CRC 3.1345(c). See "Separate statement," ch. 9-E, §3.2.4(4), p. 1064. The interrogatories and answers cannot be incorporated by reference in motion papers, even if they have been lodged with the court. CRC 3.1345(c); *CEB Discovery Practice*, §7.117.

§10.2 Interrogatories in same case.

1. Use by party other than responding party.

(1) As evidence.

(a) Against responding party. Any party (other than the responding party) can use the responding party's interrogatory answers as evidence against the responding party at a trial or hearing as long as they are admissible under the rules of evidence. CCP §2030.410; *CEB Discovery Practice*, §7.6; *see CEB Procedure During Trial*, §12.107. The answers may be used to establish any material fact, to make a prima facie case, or even to prove the whole case. *See* ***Mayhood v. La Rosa*** (1962) 58 Cal.2d 498, 501. Even answers that are not admissions against interest are admissible against the responding party. ***California Sch. Empl. Ass'n v. Sunnyvale Elementary Sch. Dist.*** (1st Dist.1973) 36 Cal.App.3d 46, 69. For interrogatory answers to be admissible, it is not necessary to prove that the responding party is unavailable to testify, has testified, or will testify. *See* CCP §2030.410; ***Mayhood***, 58 Cal.2d at 501.

(b) Not against other parties. No party can use the responding party's interrogatory answers against any other party except the responding party. CCP §2030.410; ***Great Am. Ins. v. Gordon Trucking, Inc.*** (5th Dist.2008) 165 Cal.App.4th 445, 450; ***Rimmele v. Northridge Hosp. Found.*** (2d Dist.1975) 46 Cal.App.3d 123, 129; ***Petersen v. City of Vallejo*** (1st Dist.1968) 259 Cal.App.2d 757, 776.

(2) To impeach. Any party can use the responding party's interrogatory answers to impeach the responding party as a witness. ***Mayhood***, 58 Cal.2d at 501; *CEB Procedure During Trial*, §12.115. For the procedure to impeach a witness, see *CEB Procedure During Trial*, §12.116.

(3) For sanctions. Any party can use the responding party's interrogatory answers to support a motion for sanctions. ***Bunnell v. Superior Ct.*** (1st Dist.1967) 254 Cal.App.2d 720, 722.

(4) For additional discovery. If the responding party states in its interrogatory answers that a factual or legal issue is not disputed but later presents evidence that disputes that issue, the discovering party can use the interrogatory answer as grounds for a continuance to obtain additional discovery. *Cf.* ***Campain v. Safeway Stores*** (2d Dist.1972) 29 Cal.App.3d 362, 366 (new trial granted to permit additional discovery). To be entitled to additional discovery, the discovering party must demonstrate that it was surprised and unprepared to present its own evidence in response. *See id.*

(5) To exclude evidence.

(a) Unidentified witness. If the responding party willfully and falsely withholds the name of a witness when responding to an interrogatory asking for the identification of witnesses with knowledge of relevant facts, the discovering party can use the interrogatory answer as grounds to exclude the unidentified witness from testifying at trial. ***Saxena v. Goffney*** (4th Dist.2008) 159 Cal.App.4th 316, 332; *CEB Procedure During Trial*, §12.110; *see, e.g.*, ***Burdette v. Carrier Corp.*** (3d Dist.2008) 158 Cal.App.4th 1668, 1694-95 (unidentified witness properly admitted because his identity was not willfully and falsely withheld); ***Thoren v. Johnston & Washer*** (2d Dist.1972) 29 Cal.App.3d 270, 273-74 (unidentified witness properly excluded because his identity was willfully and falsely withheld).

(b) Omitted evidence. If the responding party willfully failed to provide information requested in an interrogatory, the discovering party can use the interrogatory answer as grounds to exclude the information at trial by showing that it impeded the discovering party's trial preparation. *See CEB Procedure During Trial*, §12.111; Weil, *Civil Procedure Before Trial*, ¶8:1253.

(c) Inconsistent evidence. If the responding party provided information in its interrogatory answers on certain facts but presents evidence at trial that contradicts those facts, the discovering party can use the interrogatory answer as grounds to exclude the contrary evidence if the discovering party can prove significant prejudice. *See, e.g.*, ***Phillips v. Cooper Labs.*** (1st Dist.1989) 215 Cal.App.3d 1648, 1661 (party proved later statement was inconsistent but did not prove significant prejudice); *see also CEB Procedure During Trial*, §12.112 (if court does not exclude contrary evidence, it can be used for impeachment).

2. Use by responding party.

(1) Not as evidence. A responding party cannot use its own answers to interrogatories as evidence on its own behalf or against other parties. *See* CCP §2030.410; ***Great Am. Ins.***, 165 Cal.App.4th at 450; ***Giesler v. Berman*** (2d Dist.1970) 6 Cal.App.3d 919, 929. A responding party's answers to interrogatories are hearsay against other parties. *See* ***Deyo v. Kilbourne*** (2d Dist.1978) 84 Cal.App.3d 771, 780 n.3; Weil, *Civil Procedure Before Trial*, ¶8:1246. The main reason for disallowing the use of the responding party's interrogatory answers for the benefit of the responding party or against the interests of the other parties is the lack of opportunity for cross-examination. ***Estate of Horman*** (4th Dist.1968) 265 Cal.App.2d 796, 805.

(2) In rebuttal. A responding party can use its own interrogatory answer as evidence only if (1) it served an amended answer, (2) the other party used the original answer as evidence, and (3) the responding party needs to use the amended answer to rebut the other party's use of its original answer. *See* CCP §2030.310(a).

(3) Refresh recollection. A responding party may be able to use its own interrogatory answer to refresh its recollection as a witness. *CEB Procedure During Trial*, §12.118.

§10.3 Interrogatories from earlier case. An interrogatory answer from an earlier case that is inconsistent with any part of the responding party's testimony in a later case can be used to impeach the responding party in the later case. Evid. C. §780(h); *CEB Procedure During Trial*, §12.114. This is true whether the party answered the interrogatory in an individual or representative capacity. Evid. C. §1220.

D. REQUESTS FOR ADMISSION

§1. GENERAL

§1.1 Purpose. Requests for admission (RFAs) allow a party to obtain admissions of discrete issues from another party under oath, which avoids having to prove those issues at the trial. ***Lieb v. Superior Ct.*** (4th Dist.1962) 199 Cal.App.2d 364, 367; *see* ***Smith v. Circle P Ranch Co.*** (2d Dist.1978) 87 Cal.App.3d 267, 273 (RFAs are used to put triable issues to rest in order to expedite trial). RFAs are used to narrow the issues for trial. ***Burch v. Gombos*** (6th Dist.2000) 82 Cal.App.4th 352, 359; *see* ***Cembrook v. Superior Ct.*** (1961) 56 Cal.2d 423, 429; ***Jahn v. Brickey*** (4th Dist.1985) 168 Cal.App.3d 399, 404.

§1.2 Primary authority. CCP §§2033.010-2033.740.

§1.3 Secondary authority. The following secondary sources are cited as authority in this subchapter:

- *California Civil Discovery Practice* (CEB Online ed. 2014) (referred to as *CEB Discovery Practice*).
- Weil & Brown, *California Practice Guide: Civil Procedure Before Trial* (CD-ROM ed. 2014) (referred to as Weil, *Civil Procedure Before Trial*).

§1.4 Judicial Council form.

- DISC-020 (optional), requests for admission.

§2. COMPARING RFAS WITH INTERROGATORIES

§2.1 RFAs. RFAs are used to obtain admissions by the responding party about the existence or nonexistence of factual or legal propositions and to determine the genuineness of documents. *See CEB Discovery Practice*, §9.3. A response to RFAs does not provide any information; it merely confirms or denies information or theories already known. *See id.* §9.16. RFAs can produce incontrovertible evidence against the responding party; by comparison, interrogatories produce mere evidence, which can be contradicted or explained. ***Murillo v. Superior Ct.*** (4th Dist.2006) 143 Cal.App.4th 730, 736. Unlike interrogatories, RFAs are more than just a discovery device. ***Jahn v. Brickey*** (4th Dist.1985) 168 Cal.App.3d 399, 404. RFAs have a function similar to that of a pretrial conference—they narrow the issues to save the time and expense of preparing unnecessary proof. ***Burch v. Gombos*** (6th Dist.2000) 82 Cal.App.4th 352, 359; *see also* ***Jahn***, 168 Cal.App.3d at 404 (RFAs, like pleadings, attempt to resolve disputed issues so they will not have to be tried).

§2.2 Interrogatories. Interrogatories are used to obtain detailed, factual information about the responding party's factual and legal contentions, facts known by the responding party, and the identity of witnesses with knowledge of relevant facts. See "Interrogatories," ch. 7-C, p. 816. Interrogatory answers can be contradicted or explained at trial; admissions cannot. *See, e.g.*, ***Mason v. Marriage & Family Ctr.*** (4th Dist.1991) 228 Cal.App.3d 537, 546 (date of injury given in response to interrogatory was explained as mistake).

§3. SCOPE OF DISCOVERY BY RFAS

§3.1 What can be discovered. RFAs can be used to discover any matter that is within the scope of discovery and is not protected by a privilege or other discovery exemption. CCP §2017.010. See "Scope of Discovery," ch. 6-A, p. 603. RFAs can ask the responding party to admit the following:

1. Matters of fact. The discovering party can ask the responding party to admit the truth of (1) a specific fact, (2) an opinion relating to a fact, or (3) the application of law to fact.

(1) Specific fact. The discovering party can ask the responding party to admit the truth of a specific fact. CCP §2033.010. For example, an RFA can ask the responding party to admit that it advertised its products as being safe. *See* ***Cembrook v. Superior Ct.*** (1961) 56 Cal.2d 423, 427.

(2) Opinion relating to fact. The discovering party can ask the responding party to admit the truth of the responding party's opinion relating to specific facts. CCP §2033.010. For example, an RFA can ask the responding party to admit that the discovering party's land has a greater chance of sliding than it did before the responding party dumped soil on it. *See* ***Chodos v. Superior Ct.*** (2d Dist.1963) 215 Cal.App.2d 318, 322.

(3) Application of law to fact. The discovering party can ask the responding party to admit the truth of the application of law to specific facts. CCP §2033.010. For example, an RFA can ask the responding party to admit that its negligence was the legal cause of the discovering party's injuries. *See* ***Garcia v. Hyster Co.*** (5th Dist.1994) 28 Cal.App.4th 724, 733.

2. Genuineness of document. The discovering party can ask the responding party to admit to the genuineness of a document. CCP §2033.010.

§3.2 Who can be required to respond. RFAs can be served only on a party to the case; they cannot be served on a nonparty. *See* CCP §§2033.010, 2033.020.

§4. PROPOUNDING RFAS

§4.1 Number.

1. Unlimited civil cases.

(1) Rule of 35. A party can serve up to 35 RFAs that do not relate to the genuineness of documents on each of the other parties. CCP §2033.030(a). There is no statutory limit on the number of RFAs that inquire about the genuineness of documents. *See id.* §2033.030(c). The only limit on the number of RFAs that inquire about the genuineness of documents is one imposed by a motion for protective order based on unwarranted annoyance, embarrassment, oppression, or undue burden and expense. *Id.*

(2) More than 35. A party can serve more than 35 RFAs not related to the genuineness of documents if the additional requests are necessary because of the complexity or quantity of the issues or potential issues in the case. CCP §2033.040(a). A party serving more than 35 RFAs must attach a declaration stating why the additional RFAs are necessary. *Id.* §2033.050; *see id.* §2033.040(a). The form for the declaration is included in CCP §2033.050. The responding party can object to the additional RFAs by seeking a protective order. *Id.* §2033.040(a). The procedure for serving additional RFAs is similar to that for interrogatories. See "More than 35," ch. 7-C, §6.2.1(2), p. 822.

2. Limited civil cases. In a limited civil case, a party can serve on each adverse party a combined total of 35 of the following: (1) interrogatories with no subparts, (2) demands to produce, and (3) RFAs with no subparts. CCP §94(a)(1)-(a)(3). To serve additional RFAs beyond this limit, the party must obtain either a stipulation or a court order based on a motion showing that the party is unable to prosecute or defend the action effectively without the additional discovery. *See id.* §95.

§4.2 Form. See "Form of discovery requests," ch. 7-A, §7.2, p. 753.

§4.3 Contents.

1. Instructions. RFAs should include the instructions provided in Judicial Council Form DISC-020, although the form itself is optional. No instruction or preface can be used unless it has been approved by the Judicial Council. *See* CCP §§2033.060(d), 2033.710-2033.740.

2. Deadline to respond. RFAs should state that the party to whom they are directed must respond within 30 days after the requests were personally served (or 5 days in an unlawful-detainer action). *See* CCP §2033.250; Judicial Council Forms, form DISC-020. See "When to Respond to Discovery," ch. 7-A, §8, p. 754.

3. Specially defined terms. Any term specially defined in an RFA must be typed in all capital letters whenever the term appears. CCP §2033.060(e).

4. Requests.

(1) Separate. Each request in each set must be presented as a separate RFA. CCP §2033.060(c).

(2) Self-contained. Each request must be full and complete in and of itself. CCP §2033.060(d). A request is not full and complete if the responding party must refer to other materials to respond. *Cf.* ***Catanese v. Superior Ct.*** (2d Dist.1996) 46 Cal.App.4th 1159, 1164 (interrogatory is not full and complete if it asks responding party to review deposition transcripts and state which answers responding party contends are untruthful).

(3) **No subparts.** An RFA cannot include subparts or compound, conjunctive, or disjunctive questions. CCP §2033.060(f); *e.g.*, ***People v. Ad Way Signs, Inc.*** (6th Dist.1993) 14 Cal.App.4th 187, 200 & n.13 (improper compound request asked D about D's placement of billboard and about legal effect of certain actions taken by P toward permit).

(4) **Numbered or lettered.** Each RFA must be identified by a number or letter (e.g., Request for Admission No. 1 or Request for Admission A). CCP §2033.060(c).

(5) **Not combined.** RFAs cannot be combined in a single document with any other method of discovery. CCP §2033.060(h); *see CEB Discovery Practice*, §7.38. However, RFAs can be coordinated with interrogatories. *E.g.*, *CEB Discovery Practice*, §2.53 (can use interrogatories to obtain identity of witnesses, facts, and documents supporting denial of particular RFA).

5. **Attached documents.** When an RFA asks the responding party to admit the genuineness of a document, a copy of the document must be attached to the request. CCP §2033.060(g); *CEB Discovery Practice*, §9.31. The discovering party must make the original document available for inspection, if demanded by the responding party. CCP §2033.060(g).

6. **Signature.** There is no requirement that RFAs be signed by the discovering party or its attorney. However, as a general rule, an attorney should sign all discovery requests that she drafts. See "Attorney's signature," ch. 7-A, §7.2.6, p. 753.

§4.4 When to serve. See "Timing of Discovery," ch. 7-A, §5, p. 745; "When to Schedule Discovery," ch. 7-A, §6, p. 749.

§4.5 Serving. The discovering party must serve copies of the RFAs on (1) the party to whom the requests are directed and (2) all other parties who have appeared in the case. CCP §2033.070. See "Serving discovery," ch. 7-A, §13.1, p. 769.

§4.6 Filing or lodging. See "Filing or lodging discovery," ch. 7-A, §13.2, p. 770.

§4.7 Custody & disposal. See "Custody & Disposal of Discovery," ch. 7-A, §16, p. 776.

§5. RESPONDING TO RFAS

§5.1 Deadline to respond. The responding party must serve its response within 30 days after the RFAs were served on the party. CCP §2033.250(a). The deadline is extended if the requests were served by mail, fax, or overnight delivery. *See id.* §§1013, 2016.050. See "Add time for method of service," ch. 1-G, §6.1.4, p. 70. For a discussion of how to change the deadline, see "Changing discovery deadlines," ch. 7-A, §8.2, p. 755.

§5.2 Form. See "Form of response," ch. 7-A, §9.3, p. 758.

1. **First paragraph.** The identity of the responding party, the set number, and the identity of the discovering party must appear in the first paragraph of the response, immediately below the title of the case. CCP §2033.210(c).

2. **Separately stated.** The response to each RFA must be stated separately. CCP §2033.210(a).

3. **Corresponding numbers or letters.** Each response must be numbered or lettered in the same sequential manner as the corresponding RFA. CCP §2033.210(d).

§5.3 Contents. A party can respond to RFAs by answering or objecting. CCP §2033.210(b).

1. **Answer.** A party can respond to an RFA by answering it. Each answer must be as complete and straightforward as the information reasonably available to the responding party allows. CCP §2033.220(a). A party can answer an RFA by (1) admitting the truth of the request, (2) denying the truth of the request, or (3) asserting a lack of sufficient information or knowledge about the matter involved in the request. *Id.* §2033.220(b). When answering an RFA, a party may include reasonable explanations and qualifications as long as the response is in substantial compliance with CCP §2033.220. *See* ***St. Mary v. Superior Ct.*** (6th Dist.2014) 223 Cal.App.4th 762, 780-81.

(1) Admit truth. The responding party must admit any part of the matter involved in the request that is true, either as expressed in the request itself or as reasonably and clearly qualified by the responding party. CCP §2033.220(b)(1). Any matter admitted is conclusively established against the responding party and is binding on that party for purposes of the pending case unless the court permits its withdrawal or amendment. *Id.* §2033.410; ***New Albertsons, Inc. v. Superior Ct.*** (2d Dist.2008) 168 Cal.App.4th 1403, 1418; *see, e.g.*, ***Joyce v. Ford Motor Co.*** (3d Dist.2011) 198 Cal.App.4th 1478, 1489 (D's unqualified admission was not negated by general disclaimer in preface of response that investigation was ongoing).

(2) Deny truth. The responding party must deny any part of the matter involved in the request that is untrue. CCP §2033.220(b)(2).

(3) Assert insufficient information or knowledge. The responding party can state that it lacks sufficient information or knowledge to admit or deny any part of the matter involved in the request. CCP §2033.220(b)(3). The responding party must state that it made a reasonable inquiry about the matter in the request and is unable to admit or deny based on the information known or readily obtainable by the party. *Id.* §2033.220(c). Because RFAs are not limited to things within a party's personal knowledge, the responding party must make a reasonable investigation of the facts before denying that it has sufficient knowledge to answer. ***Wimberly v. Derby Cycle Corp.*** (4th Dist.1997) 56 Cal.App.4th 618, 634; ***Brooks v. ABC*** (1st Dist.1986) 179 Cal.App.3d 500, 510; ***Smith v. Circle P Ranch Co.*** (2d Dist.1978) 87 Cal.App.3d 267, 273.

2. Objection. A party can respond to an RFA by making a written objection to it. CCP §2033.210(b).

(1) Specific objection required. The objection must clearly state the specific ground for the objection. CCP §2033.230(b).

(2) Partial objection. The responding party can object to all or part of an RFA. *See* CCP §2033.230(a). If the responding party objects to only part of a request, it must answer the rest of the request. *Id.*

(3) Grounds.

(a) More than 35 RFAs. The responding party can object to RFAs that do not relate to the genuineness of documents and that exceed the 35-request limit if the requests are not supported by a declaration under CCP §2030.050. *See* CCP §2033.030(a), (b). The responding party must respond to the first 35 RFAs that do not relate to the genuineness of documents, after which the responding party can object to and not answer the remaining requests. *Id.* §2033.030(b). See "Number," §4.1, p. 837.

(b) Improper form & content. The responding party can object to RFAs that do not comply with the form and content required under CCP §2033.060 (e.g., full and complete, no subparts). See "Contents," §4.3, p. 837.

(c) Other grounds. For a discussion of valid objections to discovery in general, see "Grounds for Discovery Objections," ch. 7-A, §11, p. 765.

(4) Waiver. If a party does not serve a timely response to an RFA, it waives all objections to the request, including objections based on privilege or work product. CCP §2033.280(a). See "Motion for Relief from Waiver of Objections," ch. 9-H, p. 1082.

§5.4 Signatures & verification. A response to RFAs containing answers (admissions, denials, or assertions of insufficient knowledge) must be signed by the responding party under oath; if the response contains objections, it must be signed by the attorney. See "Signatures & verification," ch. 7-A, §9.4, p. 759.

§5.5 Serving RFA responses. The responding party must serve its original response to the RFAs on the discovering party and copies on all other parties who have appeared in the case. CCP §2033.250(a). See "Serving discovery responses," ch. 7-A, §13.1.2, p. 770.

§5.6 Filing & lodging RFA responses. See "Filing or lodging discovery," ch. 7-A, §13.2, p. 770.

§5.7 Custody & disposal of RFA responses. See "Custody & Disposal of Discovery," ch. 7-A, §16, p. 776.

§6. MOTIONS RELATED TO RFAS

§6.1 Motions by responding party.

1. Motion for protective order. A party responding to RFAs can move for a protective order. CCP §2033.080(a). See "Motion for Protective Order," ch. 9-B, p. 1024. In most cases, a responding party will serve written objections to RFAs, which is easier than making a motion for a protective order. See "Objection," §5.3.2, p. 839.

(1) Grounds for relief. A protective order can be sought against RFAs on the following grounds:

(a) Answering the requests would cause unwarranted annoyance, embarrassment, oppression, or undue burden and expense. *See* CCP §2033.080(b).

(b) The burden, expense, or intrusiveness of the requests outweighs the likelihood they will lead to admissible evidence. *Id.* §2017.020(a).

(c) The requests seek evidence that is unreasonably cumulative or is obtainable from another source that is more convenient, less burdensome, or less expensive, or the requests are unduly burdensome or expensive in light of the needs of the case, the amount in controversy, and the importance of the issues at stake. *Id.* §2019.030(a).

(2) Relief available. The responding party can make a motion for a protective order to ask the court for various types of relief from RFAs, including the orders listed in CCP §2033.080(b). See "Relief," ch. 9-B, §3.3.1(1)(a), p. 1029.

2. Motion for relief from waiver of objections. The responding party can make a motion for relief from waiver of its objections if it failed to serve a timely response to the RFAs. See "Motion for relief from waiver," §6.2.1(2)(b), p. 842.

3. Motion to withdraw or amend admission. The responding party can make a motion to withdraw or amend its admissions. CCP §2033.300(a); *see CEB Discovery Practice*, §§9.82-9.84; Weil, *Civil Procedure Before Trial*, ¶8:1386. CCP §2033.300 eliminates undeserved windfalls obtained through the inadvertent failure to respond to RFAs and furthers the policy favoring the resolution of lawsuits on the merits. *See* ***Wilcox v. Birtwhistle*** (1999) 21 Cal.4th 973, 983 (discussing former §2033(m), now §2033.300). The responding party can ask for leave to withdraw or amend both express and deemed admissions. *See* CCP §2033.300; ***Wilcox***, 21 Cal.4th at 978-79; *CEB Discovery Practice*, §9.82. See "Motion to deem requests admitted," §6.2.1, p. 841.

(1) Motion.

(a) Deadline. There is no deadline for making a motion to withdraw or amend an admission, but the responding party should make the motion as soon as possible after learning of its mistake and before the cutoff for discovery motions. *CEB Discovery Practice*, §9.83; *see* CCP §2024.020 (cutoff for discovery motions), §2033.300 (no deadline provided for motion to withdraw or amend). See "Cutoff for discovery motions," ch. 7-A, §5.2.2, p. 748.

(b) Motion papers. The motion papers should include (1) a notice of motion and motion, (2) a memorandum of points and authorities, (3) a supporting declaration, and (4) a proposed order that identifies the admissions to be withdrawn or describes how the admissions are to be amended. *CEB Discovery Practice*, §9.83; *see id.* §9.122 (sample proposed order). See "Motion Papers," ch. 1-D, §5, p. 27.

(c) Grounds for relief. The responding party must show the following:

[1] Mistake, inadvertence, or excusable neglect. The admission was the result of the responding party's mistake, inadvertence, or excusable neglect. CCP §2033.300(b); ***New Albertsons, Inc. v. Superior Ct.*** (2d Dist.2008) 168 Cal.App.4th 1403, 1418; *cf.* ***Scottsdale Ins. v. Superior Ct.*** (2d Dist.1997) 59 Cal.App.4th 263, 270-71 (failure to assert specific objection to demand to produce because of attorney's heavy workload is not excusable neglect).

[2] **No prejudice.** The withdrawal or amendment of the admission will not substantially prejudice the discovering party's claim or defense on the merits. CCP §2033.300(b); ***New Albertsons***, 168 Cal.App.4th at 1420-21; *see* ***Gribin Von Dyl & Assocs. v. Kovalsky*** (2d Dist.1986) 185 Cal.App.3d 653, 660 (lack of prejudice alone is not sufficient for court to allow withdrawal of admission).

(2) **Response to motion.** The party who propounded the RFAs can file opposition papers contradicting the motion. The response can allege that either (1) the admission was not the result of the responding party's mistake, inadvertence, or excusable neglect or (2) the withdrawal or amendment of the admissions will substantially prejudice the discovering party's claim or defense. *See* CCP §2033.300(b).

(3) **Ruling on motion.** The court may grant the motion if it determines that the responding party established (1) mistake, inadvertence, or excusable neglect and (2) lack of prejudice to the discovering party. *See* CCP §2033.300(b); ***New Albertsons***, 168 Cal.App.4th at 1420. Any doubts in ruling on a motion to withdraw or amend an admission must be resolved in favor of the responding party. ***New Albertsons***, 168 Cal.App.4th at 1420. If the court grants the motion to withdraw or amend, it can impose conditions on the granting of the motion. *Id.* at 1421. Possible conditions include the following:

(a) **Additional discovery.** An order that the discovering party be allowed to pursue additional discovery related to the same matter. CCP §2033.300(c)(1).

(b) **Costs.** An order that the costs of any additional discovery be borne in whole or in part by the responding party. CCP §2033.300(c)(2).

§6.2 Motions by discovering party.

1. **Motion to deem requests admitted.** The discovering party can make a motion to deem as admitted any unanswered RFAs or any requests answered in a late or unverified response. *See* CCP §2033.280(b). These requests are not automatically deemed admitted; the discovering party must make the motion. *CEB Discovery Practice*, §9.46; Weil, *Civil Procedure Before Trial*, ¶8:1370; *see* CCP §2033.280(b).

(1) **Motion.**

(a) **Deadline.** There is no deadline for making a motion to deem requests admitted, but the discovering party should make the motion as soon as possible after the deadline to respond and before the cutoff for discovery motions. *See* CCP §2024.020 (cutoff for discovery motions), §2033.280(b) (no deadline provided for motion to deem RFAs admitted); ***Brigante v. Huang*** (2d Dist.1993) 20 Cal.App.4th 1569, 1584 (no time specified for bringing motion to deem RFAs admitted), *disapproved on other grounds*, ***Wilcox v. Birtwhistle*** (1999) 21 Cal.4th 973. See "Cutoff for discovery motions," ch. 7-A, §5.2.2, p. 748.

(b) **Motion papers.** The motion papers should include (1) a notice of motion and motion, (2) a memorandum of points and authorities, (3) a supporting declaration, (4) a copy of the RFAs and proof of service, and (5) the proposed order. *CEB Discovery Practice*, §9.76. It is not necessary to include a meet-and-confer declaration. See "Motion Papers," ch. 1-D, §5, p. 27. The motion should also state the following:

[1] **Requests properly served.** The motion should state that the RFAs were properly served and identify the date they were served. *See* CCP §2033.280(c) (providing for motion to deem as admitted RFAs "directed" to a party); *see also id.* §2033.070 (party seeking admissions must serve them on party to whom RFAs are "directed").

[2] **Insufficient response.** The motion should state (1) the date by which the responding party was supposed to respond and (2) the reason why the response was insufficient (i.e., no response, late response, unsworn response). *See* CCP §§2033.250, 2033.280. See "Grounds for relief," §6.2.1(1)(c), p. 842.

[3] **Waiver.** The motion should state that the responding party waived the right to make objections to the RFAs and that the requests should be deemed admitted. *See* CCP §2033.280(a) (party that does not respond to RFAs waives objections to them).

[4] Request sanctions. The motion should ask for sanctions. The court must award sanctions when a party's response is untimely and the discovering party makes a motion to deem the requests admitted. CCP §2033.280(c). Sanctions can be awarded against the responding party, the responding party's attorney, or both. *Id.* See "Discovery Sanctions," ch. 9-A, p. 1003.

(c) Grounds for relief. The discovering party can make a motion to deem requests admitted on any of the following grounds:

[1] No response. The motion can be based on the ground that the responding party served no response. CCP §2033.280(b).

[2] Late response. The motion can be based on the ground that the responding party served a late response. CCP §2033.280(b).

[3] Unsworn response. The motion can be based on the ground that the responding party served an unsworn response. *See* ***Appleton v. Superior Ct.*** (3d Dist.1988) 206 Cal.App.3d 632, 636 (unsworn response to RFAs is treated like no response).

(2) Response to motion. The responding party can (1) oppose the motion to deem requests admitted or (2) make a motion for relief from its waiver of the right to object to the requests.

(a) Opposition to motion. The responding party can serve papers opposing the motion. See "Opposition Papers," ch. 1-D, §8, p. 35. The responding party can oppose the motion on the following grounds:

[1] Timely & sufficient response. The responding party can oppose the motion on the ground that it made a timely and sufficient response to the RFAs.

[2] Response served before hearing. The responding party can oppose the motion on the ground that it served a response before the hearing on the motion that substantially complies with the requirements of CCP §2033.220. CCP §2033.280(c). Substantial compliance means each objective and purpose of CCP §2033.220 was achieved by the response; actual compliance with every specific statutory requirement is not necessary. ***St. Mary v. Superior Ct.*** (6th Dist.2014) 223 Cal.App.4th 762, 779. A successful opposition based on this ground will prevent the requests from being deemed admitted, but it will not prevent the imposition of sanctions. See "Mandatory sanctions," §6.2.1(3)(c), p. 843.

(b) Motion for relief from waiver. The responding party can make a motion asking the court for relief from its waiver of the right to object to the RFAs. See "Motion for Relief from Waiver of Objections," ch. 9-H, p. 1082. The responding party must show all of the following:

[1] The responding party has since served a response. CCP §2033.280(a)(1). The proposed response must be served before the hearing on the motion. *See id.* §2033.280(c).

[2] The response is in compliance with the statutory provisions on responses to RFAs, including verification. *Id.* §2033.280(a)(1).

[3] The responding party's failure to serve a timely response was the result of mistake, inadvertence, or excusable neglect. *Id.* §2033.280(a)(2); *CEB Discovery Practice*, §9.46.

(3) Ruling on motion.

(a) When court must grant motion. The court must grant the motion to deem requests admitted if it finds that the responding party did not serve a proposed response before the hearing on the motion that substantially complies with CCP §2033.220. CCP §2033.280(c); ***Tobin v. Oris*** (2d Dist.1992) 3 Cal.App.4th 814, 827, *disapproved on other grounds*, ***Wilcox v. Birtwhistle*** (1999) 21 Cal.4th 973. Any matter deemed admitted is conclusively established against the responding party and is binding on that party for purposes of the pending case unless the court permits its withdrawal or amendment. CCP §2033.410; ***Wilcox v. Birtwhistle*** (1999) 21 Cal.4th 973, 978-79.

(b) When court must overrule motion. The court must overrule the motion to deem requests admitted if the responding party served a proposed response before the hearing on the motion that substantially complies with CCP §2033.220. Weil, *Civil Procedure Before Trial*, ¶8:1374.2; *see* CCP §2033.280(c); *CEB Discovery Practice*, §9.72. For purposes of §2033.220, "proposed response" means the entirety of the responding party's answers. *See* ***St. Mary***, 223 Cal.App.4th at 779-80. The court cannot evaluate the answers piecemeal and determine that portions of the response are substantially compliant and others are not. *E.g.*, *id.* (trial court abused discretion in granting motion to deem RFAs admitted because 41 out of 105 responses were not substantially compliant).

NOTE

Although substantial compliance with CCP §2033.220 defeats a motion to deem RFAs admitted, the moving party may still be able to successfully move to compel further responses. See ***St. Mary****, 223 Cal.App.4th at 782 n.22. See "Motion to Compel Further Response," ch. 9-E, §3, p. 1061.*

(c) Mandatory sanctions. The court must impose monetary sanctions on the responding party or attorney (or both) whose failure to timely respond necessitated the motion to deem requests admitted. CCP §2033.280(c); *see* ***Appleton***, 206 Cal.App.3d at 635-36 (sanctions are mandatory).

2. Motion to compel. The discovering party can make a motion to compel further answers if the responding party does not respond to RFAs in an adequate manner. CCP §2033.290. See "Motion to Compel Further Response," ch. 9-E, §3, p. 1061.

3. Motion for cost-of-proof sanctions. The discovering party can make a motion to recover reasonable expenses and attorney fees incurred during trial in proving a matter denied by the responding party in its response to RFAs. CCP §2033.420; *CEB Discovery Practice*, §9.87; *see* Weil, *Civil Procedure Before Trial*, ¶8:1405.1. Cost-of-proof sanctions can be imposed only against a party, not the party's attorney. ***Estate of Manuel v. Brown*** (2d Dist.2010) 187 Cal.App.4th 400, 403-04.

(1) Motion.

(a) Deadline. There is no statutory deadline for making a motion for cost-of-proof sanctions. *See* CCP §2033.420. The motion is typically made at the conclusion of trial. *See CEB Discovery Practice*, §9.90.

(b) Motion papers. The motion papers should include (1) a memorandum of law, (2) a supporting declaration, and (3) a proposed order. *See CEB Discovery Practice*, §9.91 (memorandum of costs and declaration). See "Motion Papers," ch. 1-D, §5, p. 27. The motion should also state the following:

[1] Requests properly served. The motion should state that the RFAs were properly served. *See* CCP §2033.070 (party seeking admissions must serve them on party to whom RFAs are "directed").

[2] Denied request to admit. The motion should state that the responding party denied the truth of a matter or the genuineness of a document. *See* CCP §2033.420(a); ***Garcia v. Hyster Co.*** (5th Dist.1994) 28 Cal.App.4th 724, 734-35.

[3] Genuineness or truth proved. The motion should state that the discovering party proved the truth of the matter or the genuineness of the document. *See* CCP §2033.420(a); ***Garcia***, 28 Cal.App.4th at 735; *see, e.g.*, ***Carlsen v. Koivumaki*** (3d Dist.2014) 227 Cal.App.4th 879, 904 (D sought to prove truth of matters relating to pretrial RFAs that P had denied by showing that summary judgment had been entered in D's favor on two of P's four causes of action, but truth of matters was not established because RFA responses related to two other causes of action for which trial court found triable issues of fact). The discovering party must actually prove the truth or genuineness; it is not enough to merely offer to do so. ***Wagy v. Brown*** (3d Dist.1994) 24 Cal.App.4th 1, 6; *see* ***Stull v. Sparrow*** (4th Dist.2001) 92 Cal.App.4th 860, 865.

[4] Expenses incurred. The motion should identify the reasonable expenses and attorney fees that were incurred in proving the truth of each matter or the genuineness of each document denied. *See* CCP §2033.420(a); *CEB Discovery Practice*, §§9.87, 9.91. The requested expenses and fees should be supported by

evidence of the attorney's hourly rate and the time incurred after the responding party's denial was served. *E.g.*, ***Garcia***, 28 Cal.App.4th at 736-37 (attorney for discovering party did not provide evidence of hourly fee or accounting of time spent proving denied facts, but merely provided conclusory statement of costs and expenses incurred).

(c) Grounds for relief. The discovering party must show that (1) the responding party denied the truth of a matter or the genuineness of a document in its response to RFAs and (2) the discovering party later proved the truth of the matter or the genuineness of the document. CCP §2033.420(a).

(2) Response to motion. The responding party can serve papers opposing the motion. See "Opposition Papers," ch. 1-D, §8, p. 35. The responding party can oppose the motion on any of the following grounds:

(a) Objection sustained. The responding party can argue that the court should not award cost-of-proof sanctions because an objection to the request was sustained. *See* CCP §2033.420(b)(1).

(b) Response waived. The responding party can argue that the court should not award cost-of-proof sanctions because the discovering party waived a more complete response by failing to compel a further response under CCP §2033.290. *See* CCP §2033.420(b)(1); *see, e.g.*, ***American Fed'n of State, Cty. & Mun. Empls. v. Metropolitan Water Dist.*** (2d Dist.2005) 126 Cal.App.4th 247, 267-68 (no waiver when party did not make motion to compel because responses to requests were complete).

(c) Not substantially important. The responding party can argue that the court should not award cost-of-proof sanctions because the request sought information that was of no substantial importance. *See* CCP §2033.420(b)(2). An issue is of substantial importance if it has at least some direct relationship to one of the central issues in the case. ***Wimberly v. Derby Cycle Corp.*** (4th Dist.1997) 56 Cal.App.4th 618, 634.

(d) Belief that party would prevail. The responding party can argue that the court should not award cost-of-proof sanctions because the party had a reasonable belief that it would prevail on the matter. *See* CCP §2033.420(b)(3); *see, e.g.*, ***Carlsen***, 227 Cal.App.4th at 904 (trial court's finding that P had reasonable basis to believe he would prevail on causes of action even though court granted summary judgment in favor of D on those causes of action was not abuse of discretion); ***Miller v. American Greetings Corp.*** (2d Dist.2008) 161 Cal.App.4th 1055, 1066 (Ps' mistaken belief that they would prevail was reasonable because applicable law was unsettled); ***Wimberly***, 56 Cal.App.4th at 638 (D's misunderstanding of applicable law and hope that P would not object to testimony did not constitute "reasonable belief" that D would prevail).

(e) Other good reason. The responding party can argue that the court should not award cost-of-proof sanctions because it has some other good reason for failing to admit the request. CCP §2033.420(b)(4); *see* ***Brooks v. ABC*** (1st Dist.1986) 179 Cal.App.3d 500, 509-11 (listing factors court can use to determine "good reason" under former CCP §2034(c)); *see, e.g.*, ***Garcia***, 28 Cal.App.4th at 735 (party's argument that it denied requested admissions because they called for opinions on conclusions of fact was not "good reason").

(3) Ruling on motion. The court must grant the motion if (1) the discovering party established the grounds for the motion and (2) the responding party did not establish one of the grounds for opposition listed in CCP §2033.420(b). CCP §2033.420; *CEB Discovery Practice*, §9.87; *see* ***Garcia***, 28 Cal.App.4th at 734-35. See "Grounds for relief," §6.2.3(1)(c), this page; "Response to motion," §6.2.3(2), this page.

§7. USING ADMISSIONS IN COURT PROCEEDINGS

§7.1 How to introduce. The procedure for using RFAs and their responses at trial and hearings is the same as that for using interrogatories. See "How to introduce," ch. 7-C, §10.1, p. 834.

§7.2 What can be introduced.

1. Matters admitted or deemed admitted. Any matter admitted or deemed admitted in response to RFAs can be used as evidence that the matter has been conclusively established against the party making the admission. *See* CCP §2033.410(a). Unless a party's admission has been withdrawn or amended, no contradictory evidence can be introduced to rebut it. ***Murillo v. Superior Ct.*** (4th Dist.2006) 143 Cal.App.4th 730, 736.

2. Withdrawn or amended admission. A withdrawn or amended admission can be used for impeachment purposes. ***Jahn v. Brickey*** (4th Dist.1985) 168 Cal.App.3d 399, 405. See "Motion to withdraw or amend admission," §6.1.3, p. 840.

§7.3 What cannot be introduced. A party cannot use another party's denial of an RFA or lack of sufficient information to admit an RFA to impeach a witness, unless the other party's litigation conduct is directly at issue. ***Gonsalves v. Ran Li*** (1st Dist.2015) 232 Cal.App.4th 1406, 1417.

§7.4 Who can use admissions. Admissions can be used by any party to the case (except the responding party), including parties joined after the admissions were made. *See* CCP §2033.010; ***Swedberg v. Christiana Cmty. Builders*** (4th Dist.1985) 175 Cal.App.3d 138, 144.

§7.5 Whom admissions can be used against. Admissions can be used only against the responding party and only in the same case in which they were made. CCP §2033.410(b).

E. DEMANDS TO PRODUCE

§1. GENERAL

§1.1 Purpose. A demand to produce permits a party to secure from another party access to documents, electronically stored information (ESI), land, and other tangible things for inspecting, copying, measuring, testing, photographing, sampling, or surveying. CCP §2031.010.

§1.2 Primary authority. CCP §§2031.010-2031.510; *see also id.* §1985.8 (electronic discovery).

§1.3 Secondary authority. The following secondary sources are cited as authority in this subchapter:

- *California Civil Discovery Practice* (CEB Online ed. 2014) (referred to as *CEB Discovery Practice*).
- *California Trial Practice: Civil Procedure During Trial* (CEB Online ed. 2014) (referred to as *CEB Procedure During Trial*).
- *Sedona Principles: Best Practices Recommendations & Principles for Addressing Electronic Document Production, Second Edition* (Sedona Conference Working Group Series, 2007), www.thesedonaconference.org/publications (referred to as *Sedona Principles, Second Edition*).
- Sink, *California Subpoena Handbook* (2014-15) (referred to as Sink, *Subpoena Handbook*).
- Weil & Brown, *California Practice Guide: Civil Procedure Before Trial* (CD-ROM ed. 2014) (referred to as Weil, *Civil Procedure Before Trial*).

§2. COMPARING DEMANDS TO PRODUCE WITH OTHER DISCOVERY

§2.1 Demands to produce vs. depositions. See "Depositions vs. demands to produce," ch. 7-B, §3.2, p. 783.

§2.2 Demands to produce vs. interrogatories. Demands to produce and interrogatories serve different but complementary purposes.

1. Demands to produce. Demands to produce ask for the production of things for inspecting, copying, measuring, testing, photographing, sampling, or surveying, but they do not ask for information about the things. A demand to produce must identify what is to be produced by specifically identifying an item or by describing a category of things to be produced. See "Description of things to be produced," §5.3.3(1), p. 849. Descriptions in demands to produce often depend on descriptions provided in response to interrogatories. The number of demands to produce is generally not limited. See "Number," §5.1, p. 849.

2. Interrogatories. Interrogatories ask for information that must be provided by written response. See "Interrogatories," ch. 7-C, p. 816. One of the purposes of interrogatories is to obtain a description of documents and other things that can be made the subject of a demand to produce. See "Documents," ch. 7-C, §3.1.4, p. 817. The number of specially prepared interrogatories is generally limited to 35. See "Number," ch. 7-C, §6.2, p. 822.

§3. SCOPE OF DISCOVERY BY DEMAND TO PRODUCE

§3.1 What can be discovered. A demand to produce can be used to discover anything that is within the scope of discovery, is not protected by a privilege or other discovery exemption, and is within the possession, custody, or control of the responding party. CCP §§2017.010, 2031.010(a). See "Scope of Discovery," ch. 6-A, p. 603; "Custody or control," ch. 7-A, §9.1.2(2), p. 757. A demand to produce can ask the responding party to produce the following:

1. Documents. The discovering party can demand that the responding party permit it (or someone acting on its behalf) to inspect and copy documents in the responding party's possession, custody, or control. CCP §2031.010(b). "Document" is defined broadly and means (1) handwriting, typewriting, printing, photostating, photographing, photocopying, transmitting by electronic mail or facsimile, and every other means of recording on any tangible thing, (2) any form of communication or representation, including letters, words, pictures, sounds, or symbols, and (3) any record thereby created, regardless of how it has been stored. *See id.* §2016.020(c); Evid. C. §250; 7 Cal. Law Revision Comm'n Rep. (1965) p. 49. The following are examples of documents that can be discovered by a demand to produce:

(1) Insurance policies. *See* CCP §2016.020(c); Evid. C. §250. See "Insurance," ch. 6-A, §2.2.7, p. 605.

(2) Settlement agreements. See "Settlement agreements," ch. 6-A, §2.2.8, p. 606.

(3) Wills. *See* ***Schaff v. Superior Ct.*** (5th Dist.1983) 146 Cal.App.3d 921, 923.

(4) Drawings, charts, and graphs. Weil, *Civil Procedure Before Trial*, ¶8:1427.1; *see* ***Toshiba Am. Elec. Components, Inc. v. Superior Ct.*** (6th Dist.2004) 124 Cal.App.4th 762, 770.

(5) Photographs. *See* CCP §2016.020(c); Evid. C. §250; 7 Cal. Law Revision Comm'n Rep. (1965) p. 49.

(6) Sound recordings. *See* CCP §2016.020(c); Evid. C. §250; 7 Cal. Law Revision Comm'n Rep. (1965) p. 49.

2. ESI. The discovering party can demand that the responding party permit it (or someone acting on its behalf) to inspect, copy, test, or sample ESI in the responding party's possession, custody, or control. CCP §2031.010(e); *see also id.* §1985.8(a)(1) (by subpoena, nonparty can be required to produce ESI). See "Discovery of ESI," ch. 7-H, §7.1, p. 887.

3. Land. The discovering party can demand that the responding party permit it (or someone acting on its behalf) to enter on any land or other property in the responding party's possession, custody, or control to inspect, measure, survey, photograph, test, or sample the land, other property on the land, or any designated objects or operations located on the land. CCP §2031.010(d); *see, e.g.*, ***Volkswagenwerk A.G. v. Superior Ct.*** (1st Dist.1981) 123 Cal.App.3d 840, 847 (party requested court order allowing it to inspect and photograph opposing party's facilities), *abrogated on other grounds*, ***Societe Nationale Industrielle Aerospatiale v. U.S. Dist. Ct.*** (1987) 482 U.S. 522. For example, a demand to produce can ask the responding party to give the discovering party access to its factory so that the discovering party can inspect and photograph the scene of an accident and the equipment involved.

4. Personal records. Whenever a party seeks to discover personal records or information from another party or a nonparty by a demand to produce, the request may implicate the right to privacy guaranteed in the California Constitution. *See* Cal. Const., art. I, §1; ***In re Insurance Installment Fee Cases*** (4th Dist.2012) 211 Cal.App.4th 1395, 1420 & n.15. The subpoena procedures for obtaining such information from nonparties (i.e., party-to-nonparty discovery) include specific requirements for notifying a person (whether a party or nonparty) whose records or information is sought and giving the person an opportunity to object to the request. *See* CCP §§1985.3, 1985.4, 1985.6. See "Subpoenas for Personal Records," ch. 8-D, p. 977. Strangely, no such notice and objection requirements are included in the CDA procedures for obtaining personal records or information from another party (i.e., party-to-party discovery) about a different party or nonparty. *See* ***Valley Bank v. Superior Ct.*** (1975) 15 Cal.3d 652, 657 (existing discovery scheme does not protect privacy of persons whose records are sought). But the responding party may have a constitutional or statutory duty to protect the privacy of the person whose records or information is sought. *See id.*

at 656; ***In re Insurance Installment Fee Cases***, 211 Cal.App.4th at 1427-28. See "Right to Privacy," ch. 6-F, §1, p. 681. The court can protect the privacy of the person whose information is sought by ordering the responding party to give the third person notice and an opportunity to object to the request. *See* ***Pioneer Elecs. (USA), Inc. v. Superior Ct.*** (2007) 40 Cal.4th 360, 372; ***In re Insurance Installment Fee Cases***, 211 Cal.App.4th at 1423. See "Cost of production," §8.2, p. 853; "Types of Persons & Entities Covered," ch. 8-D, §7, p. 981. At least one commentator has offered the practical recommendation that parties seeking such discovery from other parties (whether by deposition, interrogatories, etc.) should follow the procedures required for obtaining personal information from nonparties by subpoena. *See* Sink, *Subpoena Handbook*, §§6:2[I], 6:4. By following the procedures governing deposition subpoenas for personal-records discovery from nonparties, a discovering party may avoid both the expense of having to litigate privacy issues and possible sanctions.

NOTE

Sink's recommendation that a discovering party assume that all steps required under §1985.3, 1985.4, or 1985.6 apply to discovery under the CDA is useful only if the discovering party knows the identity of the party or nonparty whose consumer or personal records are sought. When the party's or nonparty's identity is unknown, it will be impossible for the discovering party to give advance notice of the request for records.

5. Other tangible things. The discovering party can demand that the responding party permit it (or someone acting on its behalf) to inspect, photograph, test, or sample any tangible thing in the responding party's possession, custody, or control. CCP §2031.010(c). For example, in a personal-injury suit arising from a traffic accident, the plaintiff can demand the right to inspect the defendant's automobile.

§3.2 Who can be required to produce. A party can serve a demand to produce on any other party (individual or entity) in the case. CCP §2031.010(a); *CEB Discovery Practice*, §8.6; Weil, *Civil Procedure Before Trial*, ¶8:1423. By comparison, to secure documents and other things from a nonparty, a party must use a deposition subpoena. See "Deposition Subpoenas," ch. 8-B, p. 959.

§4. PRESERVING EVIDENCE FOR PRODUCTION

Sometimes there is a risk that evidence might be destroyed before a party has an opportunity to make a demand for its production (e.g., the routine deletion of company e-mails). Because there is no consensus on when the duty to preserve evidence arises, a party should consider taking steps to impose the duty on other parties (or anticipated parties). Once the duty is imposed, the party with the evidence should implement procedures and safeguards to preserve it and avoid the risk of sanctions.

NOTE

In the past, most of the cases that discussed the duty to preserve evidence involved tort liability for spoliation of evidence, which is no longer a viable cause of action. See ***Temple Cmty. Hosp. v. Superior Ct.*** *(1999) 20 Cal.4th 464, 466 (no tort for intentional spoliation by nonparty);* ***Cedars-Sinai Med. Ctr. v. Superior Ct.*** *(1998) 18 Cal.4th 1, 17-18 (no tort for intentional spoliation by party);* ***Coprich v. Superior Ct.*** *(2d Dist.2000) 80 Cal.App.4th 1081, 1091 (no tort for negligent spoliation by party). The cases below are cited for their statements about the duty to preserve evidence, not for their support of a tort cause of action for spoliation.*

§4.1 When duty to preserve evidence arises. A person has a right to destroy or alter its own property (e.g., documents and reports) unless the person has a duty to preserve it as evidence for discovery. *See* ***Willard v. Caterpillar, Inc.*** (5th Dist.1995) 40 Cal.App.4th 892, 919-20, *disapproved on other grounds*, ***Cedars-Sinai Med. Ctr. v. Superior Ct.*** (1998) 18 Cal.4th 1. When the duty to preserve evidence arises is not always clear.

1. Duty imposed by law or contract. The duty to preserve evidence can be imposed by a statute, regulation, or contract, apart from any duty imposed by the rules for discovery. *See* ***Temple Cmty. Hosp. v. Superior Ct.*** (1999) 20 Cal.4th 464, 477; *see, e.g.*, ***Johnson v. United Servs. Auto. Ass'n*** (3d Dist.1998) 67 Cal.App.4th 626, 638

(P's insurer had no contractual duty to preserve car for P's suit against other Ds). For example, the Government Code requires employers, labor organizations, and employment agencies to maintain certain records. Gov. C. §12946; *see also* Health & Saf. C. §123145 (requires health-care providers to preserve medical records for seven years); Prob. C. §710 (requires attorneys to preserve client's estate-planning documents); Welfare & Inst. C. §14124.1 (requires health-care providers to keep medical records for Medi-Cal patients for three years); 17 C.F.R. §240.17a-4 (requires certain securities-exchange members, brokers, and dealers to preserve certain records).

2. Duty imposed by notice of contemplation of suit. There is some authority that the duty to preserve evidence can arise by notice to a potential defendant of a person's injury and the person's contemplation of litigation. *See CEB Discovery Practice*, §4.8 (duty may be triggered by oral notice that complaint might be filed). *But see* Weil, *Civil Procedure Before Trial*, ¶8:19.5 (no duty under CDA to preserve evidence before lawsuit or discovery request).

3. Duty imposed by receipt of complaint. There is some authority that the duty to preserve evidence arises once the defendant is served with the complaint. *See CEB Discovery Practice*, §4.8; *see, e.g.*, ***Cedars-Sinai Med. Ctr. v. Superior Ct.*** (1998) 18 Cal.4th 1, 12 (destroying evidence in response to discovery request would be misuse of discovery process); ***Williams v. Russ*** (2d Dist.2008) 167 Cal.App.4th 1215, 1227 (P's suit dismissed as discovery sanction for destroying files before discovery requests were served). *But see* ***Dodge, Warren & Peters Ins. Servs. v. Riley*** (4th Dist.2003) 105 Cal.App.4th 1414, 1418-19 (preliminary injunction to preserve evidence upheld because CDA provides no mechanism to preserve evidence).

4. Duty imposed by party. To impose a duty to preserve evidence, a party can enter into a stipulation, send a preservation notice, get a court order, or make a discovery request. Once a duty is imposed, violating it can result in serious sanctions. *See, e.g.*, ***Karlsson v. Ford Motor Co.*** (2d Dist.2006) 140 Cal.App.4th 1202, 1211-13 (P permitted to argue to jury that D suppressed evidence in violation of court order and agreement); ***R.S. Creative, Inc. v. Creative Cotton, Ltd.*** (2d Dist.1999) 75 Cal.App.4th 486, 496-97 (P's suit dismissed because, among other things, P violated stipulation to preserve evidence); *see also* Evid. C. §413 (court can instruct jury on adverse inference for suppression of evidence).

(1) Stipulation. The party can obtain a stipulation to preserve evidence. *See, e.g.*, ***Renteria v. Juvenile Justice, Dept. of Corr. & Rehab.*** (3d Dist.2006) 135 Cal.App.4th 903, 907 (attorney general's office agreed to preserve videotape of dog-bite incident at correctional facility).

(2) Preservation notice. The party can send a letter notifying a party (actual or anticipated) who has evidence that a suit has been or will be filed and that the party must preserve evidence in its possession relevant to the suit. *See CEB Discovery Practice*, §8.17 (contents of preservation notice); Weil, *Civil Procedure Before Trial*, ¶8:19.22 ("freeze" letter to party to preserve ESI). The notice should identify the type of claim to be asserted (e.g., breach of contract) and the types of information or things to be preserved (e.g., documents relating to the contract). If the party intends to seek discovery of ESI, the notice should (1) specifically identify the ESI to be preserved and the sources of the ESI and (2) demand that no electronic file be modified or deleted unless a forensic copy of the file is made. *See CEB Discovery Practice*, §8.17; Weil, *Civil Procedure Before Trial*, ¶8:19.22. See "Forensic copy," ch. 7-H, §2.2.6, p. 876.

(3) Preservation order. The party can obtain a temporary injunction to prevent a person (party, potential party, or nonparty) from destroying or altering evidence. *See, e.g.*, ***Ameriloan v. Superior Ct.*** (2d Dist.2008) 169 Cal.App.4th 81, 88 n.5 (injunction prohibited Ds from destroying documents); ***Dodge, Warren & Peters Ins.***, 105 Cal.App.4th at 1418-19 (injunction prohibited Ds from destroying ESI). The order should specify the types of information to be preserved; if ESI is involved, the order should specifically identify what ESI should be preserved and in what form it should be preserved. *See Sedona Principles, Second Edition*, at 33-34.

§4.2 How to ensure client preserves evidence. Unless adequate steps are taken to preserve potential evidence, a party can be subject to sanctions for spoliation of evidence. See "Spoliation sanctions," ch. 9-A, §5.2.1(2)(b), p. 1018.

1. Preserving tangible things. When tangible things (e.g., documents, wrecked automobile) must be preserved as evidence, the attorney should instruct the client in writing to issue a written litigation hold to its employees that (1) identifies the scope of the litigation hold (i.e., what must be preserved), (2) identifies how the things to be preserved must be stored, and (3) instructs the employees to suspend the routine destruction of things that might be relevant to the litigation. *See Sedona Principles, Second Edition*, at 32.

2. Preserving ESI. When ESI must be preserved as evidence, the attorney should instruct the client in writing to establish a litigation hold to preserve ESI. A litigation hold for ESI is essentially the same as a litigation hold for tangible things, but it is more complicated. See "Preserve ESI," ch. 7-H, §3.2.1, p. 880.

§5. MAKING DEMAND TO PRODUCE

§5.1 Number.

1. Unlimited civil cases. In an unlimited civil case, there is no statutory limit on the number of demands to produce a party can make. *See* CCP §§2031.010-2031.060; *CEB Discovery Practice*, §8.5; Weil, *Civil Procedure Before Trial*, ¶8:1435.1. The responding party can object to excessive demands by seeking a protective order. *See* CCP §2031.060(a). See "Motion for protective order," §9.1, p. 853.

2. Limited civil cases. In a limited civil case, the number of demands to produce a party can make is subject to the general limit on written discovery—that is, the party is generally limited to a combined total of 35 interrogatories, demands to produce, and requests for admission. See "Limited civil cases," ch. 7-C, §5.2.2, p. 820.

§5.2 Form. See "Form of discovery requests," ch. 7-A, §7.2, p. 753.

§5.3 Contents.

1. Deadline to produce.

(1) Most cases. In most cases, the demand to produce must specify a reasonable date and time for the production that is at least 30 days after personal service of the demand (35 days if served by mail in California). *See* CCP §§1013(a), 2016.050, 2031.030(c)(2). The court can permit the discovering party to specify an earlier deadline on a showing of good cause. *Id.* §2031.030(c)(2).

(2) Unlawful-detainer actions. In an unlawful-detainer action, the demand to produce must specify a reasonable date and time for the production that is at least five days after personal service of the demand (ten days if served by mail). CCP §§1013(a), 2016.050, 2031.030(c)(2).

2. Place to produce. The demand to produce must specify a reasonable place for producing the things and performing any related activity (e.g., copying). CCP §2031.030(c)(3).

(1) Things easily transported. When a few documents or other things that can be easily transported are to be produced, the place for production is often the office of the discovering party's or responding party's attorney. *See CEB Discovery Practice*, §8.57.

(2) Things not easily transported. When many documents or other things that cannot be easily transported are to be produced, the place for production is often the place where the things are located. *See CEB Discovery Practice*, §8.58. Land, objects on the land, or operations on the land must be inspected on-site.

(3) Things to be copied. When documents are demanded for copying, the place for production can be the office of a copy service (unless they are too voluminous to transport). *See CEB Discovery Practice*, §§8.57, 8.58.

3. Demand.

(1) Description of things to be produced. The demand to produce must properly identify the documents, ESI, land, or other things to be produced. CCP §2031.030(c)(1). To properly identify the things, the demand must (1) specifically describe each thing to be produced or (2) describe with reasonable particularity each category of item to be produced. *Id.* This standard is the same as that for deposition subpoenas. *See* ***Calcor Space Facility, Inc. v. Superior Ct.*** (4th Dist.1997) 53 Cal.App.4th 216, 221-22. See "Deposition subpoenas," ch. 8-A, §5.2.1, p. 940.

(a) Individual items. Each thing to be produced must be described specifically. CCP §2031.030(c)(1).

(b) Category of items. Each category of things to be produced must be described with reasonable particularity. CCP §2031.030(c)(1). The request for a category of things must not be overly broad. *Cf.* ***Bearman v. Superior Ct.*** (2d Dist.2004) 117 Cal.App.4th 463, 472 (subpoena for all of patient's medical records was too broad); ***Pacific Auto. Ins. v. Superior Ct.*** (2d Dist.1969) 273 Cal.App.2d 61, 70 (subpoena for "*all* correspondence, records and documents" was too broad). Whether the description of a category is sufficiently particular is determined from the standpoint of the person who has the burden to produce. ***Calcor Space Facility***, 53 Cal.App.4th at 222.

(2) Activity to be performed.

(a) Type of activity. The demand to produce must identify the type of activity to be performed on the things produced and how the activity will be performed. CCP §2031.030(c)(4); *CEB Discovery Practice*, §8.4.

[1] Documents. A demand involving documents must state whether they are to be inspected, copied, or both. *See* CCP §2031.010(b).

[2] ESI. A demand involving ESI must state whether the ESI is to be inspected, copied, tested, or sampled. *See* CCP §2031.010(e). The right to test or sample ESI does not create a routine right of direct access to a party's ESI system. *Cf.* FRCP 34(a)(1), advisory committee's notes (2006) (discussing federal rule).

[3] Land. A demand to enter land or other property must state whether the land, other property, or designated objects on the property are to be inspected, measured, surveyed, photographed, tested, or sampled. *See* CCP §2031.010(d).

[4] Other tangible things. A demand involving tangible things must state whether they are to be inspected, photographed, tested, or sampled. *See* CCP §2031.010(c).

(b) Alteration or destruction. The demand to produce must state whether any inspection, copying, testing, sampling, or other activity will permanently alter or destroy the thing to be produced. CCP §2031.030(c)(4).

4. Not combined with RFAs. A demand to produce cannot be combined in a single document with requests for admission. CCP §2033.060(h).

§5.4 Signature. There is no requirement that a demand to produce be signed by the discovering party or its attorney. But as a general rule, an attorney should sign all discovery demands that she drafts. See "Attorney's signature," ch. 7-A, §7.2.6, p. 753.

§5.5 When to serve. See "Timing of Discovery," ch. 7-A, §5, p. 745; "When to Schedule Discovery," ch. 7-A, §6, p. 749.

§5.6 Serving. The discovering party must serve copies of the demand to produce on (1) the party to whom the demand is directed and (2) all other parties who have appeared in the case. CCP §2031.040. See "Serving discovery," ch. 7-A, §13.1, p. 769.

§5.7 Filing or lodging. See "Filing or lodging discovery," ch. 7-A, §13.2, p. 770.

§5.8 Custody & disposal. See "Custody & Disposal of Discovery," ch. 7-A, §16, p. 776.

§6. MAKING SUPPLEMENTAL DEMAND TO PRODUCE

§6.1 Purpose. The discovering party can serve a supplemental demand to produce on the responding party to inspect, copy, test, or sample any later acquired or discovered documents, ESI, land or other property, or other tangible things. CCP §2031.050(a). See "Scope of Discovery by Demand to Produce," §3, p. 846.

§6.2 Number. A party can make only three supplemental demands to produce without a court order: two before the date the court sets the initial trial date, and one after the date the court sets the initial trial date. CCP §2031.050(b). On a party's good-cause motion, the court can authorize additional supplemental demands to produce. *Id.* §2031.050(c).

§6.3 Form. See "Form of discovery requests," ch. 7-A, §7.2, p. 753.

§6.4 Contents. See "Contents," §5.3, p. 849.

§6.5 Serving. The discovering party must serve copies of the supplemental demand on (1) the party to whom the demand is directed and (2) all the other parties who have appeared in the case. See "Serving discovery," ch. 7-A, §13.1, p. 769.

§7. RESPONDING TO DEMAND TO PRODUCE

A party can respond to a demand to produce by either serving a written response or by making a motion for a protective order. For a discussion of protective orders, see "Motion for protective order," §9.1, p. 853.

§7.1 Deadline to respond.

1. Most cases. In most cases, the responding party must serve its response to a demand to produce within 30 days after the demand was personally served (35 days if served by mail in California). *See* CCP §§1013(a), 2016.050, 2031.260(a). See "When to Respond to Discovery," ch. 7-A, §8, p. 754.

2. Unlawful-detainer actions. In an unlawful-detainer action, the responding party must have at least five days after the demand was personally served to serve its response. CCP §2031.260(b).

§7.2 Form. See "Form of response," ch. 7-A, §9.3, p. 758.

§7.3 Contents. A party can respond to a demand to produce by (1) serving a statement of compliance, (2) serving a statement of inability to comply, or (3) making a written objection.

1. Statement of compliance. The responding party can respond by serving a statement of compliance—that is, a statement that it agrees to the terms of the demand to produce. CCP §2031.210(a)(1). The agreement can be a complete or partial agreement.

(1) Complete compliance. If the responding party agrees to comply with all the conditions of the demand, the response should state that (1) the party will produce the things demanded for inspection, copying, testing, sampling, or any other related activity, (2) the things demanded are in the possession, custody, or control of the party, and (3) the party makes no objection to producing the things demanded. CCP §2031.220.

(2) Partial compliance. If the responding party agrees to comply with part of the demand to produce, the response should (1) state that the party will produce in part the things demanded for inspection, copying, testing, sampling, or any other related activity, (2) identify the things the party will produce, (3) state that these things are in the possession, custody, or control of the party and that the party has no objection to producing them, (4) state that the party is unable to comply with the rest of the demand, and (5) include a statement of inability to comply for the things the party will not produce. *See* CCP §2031.220.

(3) Form for ESI. If no form is specified in a demand for ESI, the response must identify the form in which the responding party intends to produce the information. CCP §2031.280(c). See "No form specified by discovering party," ch. 7-H, §10.2.2, p. 891.

2. Statement of inability to comply. The responding party can respond by serving a statement that it is unable to comply with the demand. CCP §§2031.210(a)(2), 2031.230; *CEB Discovery Practice*, §8.70. The statement of inability to comply must contain the following:

(1) Diligent search. The statement must assert that the party made a diligent search and a reasonable inquiry in an effort to comply. CCP §2031.230.

(2) Reasons. The statement must assert that the party is unable to comply because of one of the following:

(a) The demanded item never existed. CCP §2031.230.

(b) The demanded item was destroyed. *Id.*

(c) The demanded item was lost or misplaced. *Id.*

(d) The demanded item was stolen. *Id.*

(e) The demanded item has never been or is no longer in the possession, custody, or control of the party. *Id.*; *see, e.g.*, ***People v. Superior Ct.*** (4th Dist.2004) 122 Cal.App.4th 1060, 1078 (P-State could not be required to produce things not in its control).

(3) Person in possession. The party must identify the person or organization it knows or believes has possession, custody, or control of the item and that person's or organization's address. CCP §2031.230.

3. Objection. The responding party can object to a demand to produce by making a written objection.

(1) Form.

(a) Identification of item. The response must identify with particularity the document, ESI, land, or other tangible thing being objected to. CCP §2031.240(b)(1).

(b) Specific objection. The response must identify the specific ground for the objection. CCP §2031.240(b)(2). For example, if an objection is based on a claim of privilege, the response must state the specific privilege invoked and provide sufficient factual information for other parties to evaluate the merits of the claim, including, if necessary, a privilege log. *Id.* §2031.240(b)(2), (c)(1). Similar requirements apply to an objection based on a claim that the information sought is protected work product. *Id.* §2031.240(b)(2), (c)(1). See "Privilege log," ch. 7-A, §14.1.4(2), p. 773.

(c) Extent of objection. A party can object to all or part of an item or category of items in a demand to produce. *See* CCP §2031.240(a). If a party objects to only part of an item or category of items, the response must contain a statement of compliance or inability to comply for the rest of the demand. *Id.*

(2) Grounds.

(a) Unreasonable place to produce. The responding party can object if the demand to produce does not provide a reasonable place for production. *See* CCP §2031.030(c)(3).

(b) Unreasonable date to produce. The responding party can object if the demand to produce does not provide a reasonable time for production, considering the amount or location of things required to be produced. *See* CCP §2031.030(c)(2). For example, the minimum 30-day deadline specified in CCP §2031.030(c)(2) may not give the responding party a reasonable time to produce a particularly large volume of documents.

(c) Improper demand. The responding party can object if the demand to produce does not comply with the requirements for a demand under CCP §2031.030. For example, the responding party can object if the discovering party disregards CCP §2031.030(c)(2) and sets a date for production that gives the responding party less than 30 days to produce the things demanded. See "Contents," §5.3, p. 849; "Form of discovery requests," ch. 7-A, §7.2, p. 753.

(d) Objections to production of ESI. See "ESI-specific objections," ch. 7-H, §9.2, p. 889.

(e) Other grounds for objections. See "Grounds for Discovery Objections," ch. 7-A, §11, p. 765.

(3) Waiver. If a party does not serve a timely response to a demand to produce, it waives all objections to the demand, including objections based on privilege and work product. CCP §2031.300(a). See "Waiver of objections," ch. 7-A, §15.2, p. 776; "Motion for Relief from Waiver of Objections," ch. 9-H, p. 1082.

(4) Privilege log. When a party objects to the production of documents or other records based on a privilege or exemption from discovery, it may be required to create a privilege log. See "Privilege log," ch. 7-A, §14.1.4(2), p. 773.

§7.4 Signatures & verification. The response to a demand to produce must be signed by the responding party under oath, unless it contains only objections; if the response contains objections, it must be signed by the attorney. *See* CCP §2031.250(a), (c). See "Signatures & verification," ch. 7-A, §9.4, p. 759.

§7.5 Serving response to demand. See "Serving discovery responses," ch. 7-A, §13.1.2, p. 770.

§7.6 Filing or lodging response to demand. See "Filing or lodging discovery," ch. 7-A, §13.2, p. 770.

§7.7 Custody & disposal of response to demand. See "Custody & Disposal of Discovery," ch. 7-A, §16, p. 776.

§8. PRODUCTION OF THINGS

§8.1 Deadline & place to produce. The deadline and place to produce the things demanded is the date, time, and place identified in the demand to produce. The date must be at least 30 days after the demand was personally served (35 days if served by mail in California). See "Deadline to produce," §5.3.1, p. 849; "Place to produce," §5.3.2, p. 849.

§8.2 Cost of production. Generally, the responding party bears the cost of producing documents and other things. ***Toshiba Am. Elec. Components, Inc. v. Superior Ct.*** (6th Dist.2004) 124 Cal.App.4th 762, 769; *CEB Discovery Practice*, §8.33. There are, however, cost-shifting provisions in the CDA that shift the burden to the discovering party. For example, when the responding party must translate ESI into a usable form, the discovering party pays the cost of the translation. CCP §2031.280(e); ***Toshiba Am. Elec.***, 124 Cal.App.4th at 772. Similarly, a court may order the discovering party to pay the responding party's costs of notifying other parties or nonparties whose personal records or information is sought. *See, e.g.*, ***In re Insurance Installment Fee Cases*** (4th Dist.2012) 211 Cal.App.4th 1395, 1431-32 (because policyholders were constitutionally entitled to notice, court ordered discovering party to pay responding party's costs of notification).

§8.3 How to produce things.

1. Documents. When documents are to be produced, the responding party must produce them either (1) as they are kept in the ordinary course of business or (2) organized and labeled to correspond to the categories in the demand. CCP §2031.280(a); *CEB Discovery Practice*, §8.71; *see, e.g.*, ***Kayne v. Grande Holdings Ltd.*** (2d Dist.2011) 198 Cal.App.4th 1470, 1475-76 (court did not abuse discretion in imposing sanctions when D refused to organize and label documents and did not produce evidence showing documents were found in disorderly condition).

2. ESI. When ESI is to be produced, the responding party must produce it (1) in the form agreed to by the parties, (2) in the form required by a court order, (3) in the form specified by the demand (if no objection to the form was made), or (4) in the form in which it is ordinarily maintained or that is reasonably usable (if no form was specified in the demand). CCP §2031.280(d). If no form was specified in the demand, the response must identify the form in which the ESI will be produced. *Id.* §2031.280(c). See "No form specified by discovering party," ch. 7-H, §10.2.2, p. 891.

3. Land. When land, objects on the land, or operations on the land are to be inspected, measured, surveyed, photographed, tested, or sampled, the responding party must make the land, objects, or operations available on the date and time specified in the demand. *See* CCP §2031.010(d).

4. Other tangible things. When other tangible things are to be produced, the place for production depends on the nature of the thing to be produced. For example, if a wrecked automobile is to be produced, the responding party should make it available at the place where it is stored.

§9. MOTIONS RELATED TO DEMANDS TO PRODUCE

§9.1 Motion for protective order. A party or an affected person or organization can move for a protective order from a demand to produce. CCP §2031.060(a). See "Motion for Protective Order," ch. 9-B, p. 1024. In most cases, a party will serve written objections to a demand to produce, which is easier than making a motion for a protective order. See "Objection," §7.3.3, p. 852.

1. Grounds for relief. A protective order can be sought against a demand to produce on the following grounds:

(1) Producing the things demanded would cause unwarranted annoyance, embarrassment, oppression, or undue burden and expense. CCP §2031.060(b); *see, e.g.*, ***Ibarra v. Superior Ct.*** (2d Dist.2013) 217 Cal.App.4th 695, 706 (unreasonable risk of harm was valid basis for protective order).

(2) The burden, expense, or intrusiveness of the demand outweighs the likelihood it will lead to admissible evidence. CCP §2017.020(a).

(3) The demand seeks evidence that is unreasonably cumulative or is obtainable from another source that is more convenient, less burdensome, or less expensive, or the demand is unduly burdensome or expensive in light of the needs of the case, the amount in controversy, and the importance of the issues at stake. *Id.* §2019.030(a).

2. Relief available. The responding party can make a motion for a protective order to ask the court for various types of relief from a demand to produce, including the orders listed in CCP §2031.060(b). See "Relief," ch. 9-B, §3.3.1(1)(a), p. 1029.

§9.2 Motion for earlier production date. The discovering party can move for an order that permits it to specify a date to produce that is less than 30 days after service of the demand. CCP §2031.030(c)(2). The motion must be based on good cause. *Id.*; *CEB Discovery Practice*, §8.53. For example, the discovering party can show good cause by establishing its need to obtain evidence before the deadline to respond to a motion for summary judgment. *Cf. CEB Discovery Practice*, §15.12 (motion to shorten time under CRC 3.1300(b)).

§9.3 Motion for relief from waiver of objections. The responding party can make a motion for relief from waiver of its objections if it failed to serve a timely response to the demand to produce. See "Motion for Relief from Waiver of Objections," ch. 9-H, p. 1082.

§9.4 Motion to resolve ESI claim of privilege. The discovering party can make a motion to resolve a claim by the responding party that it inadvertently produced privileged ESI in response to a demand to produce. See "Motion to resolve claim of inadvertent production of privileged ESI," ch. 7-H, §12.2, p. 895.

§9.5 Motions to compel.

1. Compel initial response to demand. The discovering party can make a motion to compel an initial response if the responding party did not serve a response to the demand to produce. CCP §2031.300(b). See "Motion to Compel Initial Response," ch. 9-E, §2, p. 1057.

2. Compel further response to demand. The discovering party can make a motion to compel a further response if the responding party did not respond to the demand to produce in an adequate manner. CCP §2031.310(a). See "Motion to compel further response to ESI demand," ch. 7-H, §12.4, p. 895; "Motion to Compel Further Response," ch. 9-E, §3, p. 1061.

3. Compel compliance with demand. The discovering party can make a motion to compel compliance with a demand to produce if the responding party did not permit the inspection, copying, testing, or sampling agreed to in its statement of compliance. CCP §2031.320(a). The discovering party can also make a motion to compel when the responding party does not produce things in the manner required by the CDA. *CEB Discovery Practice*, §8.96. For example, if a party produces documents that are not organized as required by CCP §2031.280(a), a motion to compel would be appropriate. *CEB Discovery Practice*, §8.96. See "Motion to Compel Compliance with Demand to Produce," ch. 9-E, §4, p. 1066.

§10. USING PRODUCED THINGS IN COURT PROCEEDINGS

§10.1 What can be used. Any item produced in response to a demand to produce can be used by any party if the item (1) is within the scope of discovery, (2) is not subject to exclusion based on a privilege or exemption, and

(3) is authenticated under the rules of evidence. The parties should consider stipulating before trial to the authenticity of documents produced during discovery. *See CEB Procedure During Trial*, §§13.67, 13.141. A stipulation to authenticity does not prevent objections to the documents on other grounds. *See id.* §13.67.

§10.2 Who can use. Any party can offer into evidence any item produced in response to any demand, no matter who demanded or who produced the item.

F. MEDICAL EXAMINATIONS

§1. GENERAL

§1.1 Purpose. Discovery involving medical examinations is used to secure the physical or mental examination of a person when that person's physical or mental condition is at issue in a case. CCP §2032.020(a).

§1.2 Primary authority. CCP §§2032.010-2032.650.

§1.3 Secondary authority. The following secondary sources are cited as authority in this subchapter:

- *California Civil Discovery Practice* (CEB Online ed. 2014) (referred to as *CEB Discovery Practice*).
- Weil & Brown, *California Practice Guide: Civil Procedure Before Trial* (CD-ROM ed. 2014) (referred to as Weil, *Civil Procedure Before Trial*).

§2. SCOPE OF DISCOVERY BY MEDICAL EXAMINATION

§2.1 What can be discovered.

1. Current medical condition. Medical examinations can be used to discover a person's current physical or mental condition. *See* CCP §§2032.220, 2032.310; *see, e.g.*, ***Vinson v. Superior Ct.*** (1987) 43 Cal.3d 833, 842 (P's present mental condition was relevant to her claim, but her past sexual history was not).

2. Medical history. Medical examinations can be used to discover a person's past medical or psychiatric reports. *See* CCP §2032.610(a) (examinee entitled to examination report and reports from earlier examinations of examinee), §2032.640 (party who sought examination entitled to reports from earlier examinations of examinee); Weil, *Civil Procedure Before Trial*, ¶8:1611 (P-examinee's demand for copies of examiner's report entitles D to receive, in exchange, copies of all medical reports by P's doctors and experts). See "Exchange of reports," §7.3.2, p. 866.

§2.2 Who can be examined. To be subject to a medical examination, a person must (1) be included in the statutory list of persons who can be examined, (2) have a physical or mental condition "in controversy," and (3) be alive.

1. Statutory examinees. The list of persons who can be required to submit to a medical examination under the Civil Discovery Act (CDA) is exclusive, and courts have no power to add to it. ***Cruz v. Superior Ct.*** (4th Dist.2004) 121 Cal.App.4th 646, 650. The list includes only the following persons:

(1) Party. A party can be required to submit to a medical examination. CCP §2032.020(a); Weil, *Civil Procedure Before Trial*, ¶8:1547. Generally, the party to be examined is the plaintiff, but a defendant can also be required to submit to an examination. *CEB Discovery Practice*, §10.18. For example, a plaintiff can be required to submit to a physical examination if she claims physical injuries as a result of an automobile collision with a defendant; the defendant can be required to submit to a physical examination if she admits during discovery to a physical condition that could have contributed to the collision. *See id.*; *see, e.g.*, ***Harabedian v. Superior Ct.*** (2d Dist.1961) 195 Cal.App.2d 26, 30 (during deposition, D-driver admitted to eye condition that caused blurred vision).

(2) Party's agent. A party's agent can be required to submit to a medical examination. CCP §2032.020(a); *CEB Discovery Practice*, §10.19; Weil, *Civil Procedure Before Trial*, ¶8:1547. Using the facts in the example in §2.2.1(1), above, if the driver was the defendant's employee, the plaintiff can move for an order compelling the driver to submit to an eye examination. *See CEB Discovery Practice*, §10.19.

NOTE

Whether a party's relative (e.g., parent) is considered an agent subject to examination depends on the facts of the case. See, e.g., ***Cruz****, 121 Cal.App.4th at 651-52 (guardian ad litem who was P's mother could be required to submit to examination because she could benefit from suit and her condition could determine if P's injury was inherited or caused by medical malpractice);* ***Reuter v. Superior Ct.*** *(4th Dist.1979) 93 Cal.App.3d 332, 341, 344 (guardian ad litem who was P's mother could not be required to submit to examination because her condition was not in controversy; mother's role as guardian did not justify order to submit to exam).*

(3) Person under party's control. A natural person in the custody or under the legal control of a party can be required to submit to a medical examination. CCP §2032.020(a); *CEB Discovery Practice*, §10.20; Weil, *Civil Procedure Before Trial*, ¶8:1547. For example, a minor in the custody of a party can be compelled to submit to an examination. Weil, *Civil Procedure Before Trial*, ¶8:1548.1.

2. Condition in controversy. A statutory examinee can be required to submit to a medical examination only if the person's physical or mental condition is in controversy in the case. CCP §2032.020(a). See "Statutory examinees," §2.2.1, p. 855. To be "in controversy" for purposes of compelling a physical or mental examination, the condition must be ongoing; a medical examination cannot be ordered for a past injury that has completely healed. Weil, *Civil Procedure Before Trial*, ¶8:1553; *see* ***Vinson v. Superior Ct.*** (1987) 43 Cal.3d 833, 839-40; ***Doyle v. Superior Ct.*** (6th Dist.1996) 50 Cal.App.4th 1878, 1886-87; *cf.* ***Coca-Cola Bottling Co. v. Torres*** (1st Cir.1958) 255 F.2d 149, 153 (FRCP 35 motion for physical exam denied because P had wholly recovered from physical injury). A person's physical or mental condition can be placed in controversy by the following:

(1) Pleadings. A person's physical or mental condition can be placed in controversy by the pleadings.

(a) Physical condition. A plaintiff's physical condition is usually placed in controversy by a claim for a physical injury in the complaint that the defendant challenges (by denying causation or the extent of the injury). *See* ***Vinson***, 43 Cal.3d at 839; ***Reuter***, 93 Cal.App.3d at 341; *see, e.g.*, ***Abex Corp. v. Superior Ct.*** (1st Dist.1989) 209 Cal.App.3d 755, 757 (P claimed lesions were caused by exposure to asbestos produced by Ds, which Ds denied; Ds were entitled to biopsy of lesions). A defendant can place her physical condition in controversy by asserting an affirmative defense that relies on her physical condition. *CEB Discovery Practice*, §10.8; *cf.* ***Schlagenhauf v. Holder*** (1964) 379 U.S. 104, 119 (under FRCP 35, D's assertion of physical or mental condition as defense places it in controversy).

(b) Mental condition. A plaintiff's mental condition is placed in controversy only if the plaintiff claims damages for mental or emotional distress that is severe and ongoing. *See* ***Vinson***, 43 Cal.3d at 839-40; ***Acuna v. Regents of the Univ. of Cal.*** (2d Dist.1997) 56 Cal.App.4th 639, 653; ***Reuter***, 93 Cal.App.3d at 340; Weil, *Civil Procedure Before Trial*, ¶8:1552.1. A defendant can place her mental condition in controversy by asserting an affirmative defense that relies on her mental condition. *CEB Discovery Practice*, §10.8; *cf.* ***Schlagenhauf***, 379 U.S. at 119 (under FRCP 35, D's assertion of physical or mental condition as defense places it in controversy).

(2) Discovery. A person's physical or mental condition can be placed in controversy during discovery. For example, in a personal-injury action arising from a car accident, a party's admission during a deposition that he had a congenital eye defect would put his vision in controversy. ***Harabedian***, 195 Cal.App.2d at 31-32.

3. Living person. Only living persons can be required to submit to a medical examination under the CDA because the term "person" in CCP §2032.020 does not include a corpse. *See* ***Walsh v. Caidin*** (2d Dist.1991) 232 Cal.App.3d 159, 162 (CDA does not authorize autopsies); ***Holm v. Superior Ct.*** (3d Dist.1986) 187 Cal.App.3d 1241, 1248 (exhumation and autopsy cannot be compelled under §2032).

§2.3 Who can conduct exam.

1. Who can conduct physical exam. A physical examination must be performed by a licensed physician or other appropriate licensed health-care practitioner. CCP §2032.020(b); *CEB Discovery Practice*, §10.21; *see* ***Reuter v. Superior Ct.*** (4th Dist.1979) 93 Cal.App.3d 332, 338-39. The term "other appropriate licensed health-care

practitioner" includes dentists, optometrists, podiatrists, physical therapists, chiropractors, and other similar practitioners who are required to hold a license. *See* Bus. & Prof. C. §4039; *CEB Discovery Practice*, §10.21; Weil, *Civil Procedure Before Trial*, ¶8:1533. A health-care practitioner who is not required to be licensed cannot conduct a medical examination under the CDA. *See* CCP §2032.020(b). However, an examination can be conducted by a person other than a licensed health-care practitioner if the examination is at the direction and under the supervision of a licensed health-care practitioner. Weil, *Civil Procedure Before Trial*, ¶8:1536; *see* ***Reuter***, 93 Cal.App.3d at 339-40 (under earlier version of §2032.020(b) that permitted exam only by physician, psychologist working under direction of psychiatrist could conduct testing).

2. Who can conduct mental exam. A mental examination must be performed by a licensed physician or a licensed clinical psychologist who holds a doctoral degree in psychology and has at least five years of postgraduate experience in the diagnosis of emotional and mental disorders. CCP §2032.020(c); *CEB Discovery Practice*, §10.22.

§3. HOW TO SECURE MEDICAL EXAMINATIONS

§3.1 Stipulated exam. On the parties' written stipulation, the parties can agree to any kind of medical examination. *See* CCP §§2016.030, 2032.610(a); ***Carpenter v. Superior Ct.*** (1st Dist.2006) 141 Cal.App.4th 249, 258 n.3.

§3.2 Demand for exam of personal-injury P. On the written demand of a defendant, a personal-injury plaintiff must submit to one physical examination. *See* CCP §2032.220(a). See "Demand for Physical Examination of Personal-Injury Plaintiff," §4, this page.

§3.3 Motion for exam. On a party's motion, the court can order a physical or mental examination. *See* CCP §2032.020(a). See "Motion for Medical Examination," §5, p. 860.

NOTE

The provisions for medical examinations in CCP §§2032.010-2032.650 do not prohibit discovery of medical information by other means. See ***Schreiber v. Estate of Kiser*** *(1999) 22 Cal.4th 31, 38 (dicta; medical records can be discovered by demand to produce); see, e.g.,* ***John B. v. Superior Ct.*** *(2006) 38 Cal.4th 1177, 1186 (party subpoenaed other party's medical records). See "Types of Discovery," ch. 7-A, §2, p. 739.*

§4. DEMAND FOR PHYSICAL EXAMINATION OF PERSONAL-INJURY PLAINTIFF

NOTE

In this subchapter, the phrase "personal-injury plaintiff" will be abbreviated as "PIP."

§4.1 Making demand for PIP exam.

1. Who can make demand. Any defendant in a personal-injury action can demand one physical examination of the PIP. CCP §2032.220(a); ***Carpenter v. Superior Ct.*** (1st Dist.2006) 141 Cal.App.4th 249, 258.

(1) Cross-complainants & cross-defendants. As used in the CDA provisions relating to PIP demands, "plaintiff" includes a cross-complainant and "defendant" includes a cross-defendant. CCP §2032.210.

(2) Multiple defendants. Because §2032.220(a) says "any defendant" can demand a PIP examination, it is arguable that each codefendant can demand a separate examination. *See* CCP §2032.220(a); Weil, *Civil Procedure Before Trial*, ¶8:1522. But this may be a legislative oversight because, under the former law, codefendants were required to agree to one examination before moving for an examination. Weil, *Civil Procedure Before Trial*, ¶8:1523. If multiple defendants demand separate examinations, the PIP should serve written responses refusing to submit to the examinations on the grounds that (1) they are unreasonably cumulative and (2) the burden outweighs any likely benefit. *See* CCP §§2017.020(a), 2019.030(a). This will force the defendants to make a motion to compel. See "Replying to PIP's response," §4.3, p. 860.

2. One exam. A defendant can demand only one physical examination of a PIP. CCP §2032.220(a). To obtain an additional physical examination, the defendant must move for a court order. ***Pratt v. Union Pac. R.R.*** (3d Dist.2008) 168 Cal.App.4th 165, 181; ***Shapira v. Superior Ct.*** (1st Dist.1990) 224 Cal.App.3d 1249, 1254-55; *see* CCP §2032.310(a); *CEB Discovery Practice*, §10.15. See "Motion for Medical Examination," §5, p. 860.

3. Form of demand. See "Form of discovery requests," ch. 7-A, §7.2, p. 753.

4. Contents of demand. The defendant's demand for a PIP examination must include the following information:

(1) Examinee. The demand must identify the PIP whose physical examination is demanded. *See* CCP §2032.220(a).

(2) Examiner. The demand must identify the licensed physician or other appropriate health-care practitioner who will perform the examination of the PIP and the person's specialty, if any. *See* CCP §§2032.020(b), 2032.220(c); ***Carpenter***, 141 Cal.App.4th at 261. The choice of examiner for a PIP examination belongs to the defendant. ***Pratt***, 168 Cal.App.4th at 181; *see* CCP §2032.220(c). See "Who can conduct physical exam," §2.3.1, p. 856.

(3) Exam details. The demand must specify the time, place, manner, conditions, scope, and nature of the PIP examination. CCP §2032.220(c). The defendant can only demand a physical examination of the PIP. *Id.* §2032.220(a). A mental examination is not permitted under the PIP-exam provisions; for a mental examination, the defendant must move for a court order. *Id.* §2032.310(a); ***Carpenter***, 141 Cal.App.4th at 259. See "Motion for Medical Examination," §5, p. 860.

(a) Time. The demand must specify the date and time of the PIP examination. CCP §2032.220(c). The examination must be scheduled for a date that is at least 30 days after service of the demand unless the court shortens the time on the defendant's motion. *Id.* §2032.220(d).

(b) Place. The demand must specify the place for the PIP examination. CCP §2032.220(c). The examination must be conducted within 75 miles of the PIP's residence. *Id.* §2032.220(a)(2). If the defendant wants to conduct the examination at a more distant location, the defendant must move for a court order. *See id.* §§2032.310(a), 2032.320(e). See "Motion for Medical Examination," §5, p. 860.

(c) Manner. The demand must specify how the PIP examination will be conducted. CCP §2032.220(c). For example, the demand could specify the diagnostic tests and procedures to be performed (although this is not required). *Cf.* §2032.320(d) (order granting physical or mental examination must specify diagnostic tests and procedures); ***Carpenter***, 141 Cal.App.4th at 259 (same). By specifying the tests and procedures, the defendant can show that the demand does not request tests or procedures that are painful, protracted, or intrusive. *See* CCP §2032.220(a)(1). See "Nature," §4.1.4(3)(f), this page.

(d) Conditions. The demand must specify the conditions for the PIP examination. CCP §2032.220(c). For example, the demand should specify the expected length of the examination, the schedule for the examination, who will attend, and how the examination will be recorded. *Cf.* ***Edwards v. Superior Ct.*** (1976) 16 Cal.3d 905, 913 (D's motion for mental exam sought four-hour exam).

(e) Scope. The demand must specify the scope of the PIP examination. CCP §2032.220(c). The scope of the examination must be commensurate with the scope of the injury alleged—that is, the examination must be tailored to the injuries that are in controversy. Weil, *Civil Procedure Before Trial*, ¶8:1519; *see* CCP §2032.020(a). For example, when a PIP claims general injuries from a car collision, the defendant can ask for a full physical examination, but when a PIP claims a broken arm resulting from a slip-and-fall and no other injuries, the defendant should limit the examination to the arm. See "Condition in controversy," §2.2.2, p. 856.

(f) Nature. The demand must specify the nature of the PIP examination. CCP §2032.220(c). For example, the demand should include a statement that the examination does not include any test or procedure that is painful, protracted, or intrusive. *See id.* §2032.220(a)(1). To secure a medical test or procedure that is painful, protracted, or intrusive, the defendant must move for a court order. *See id.* §§2032.220(a)(1), 2032.310(a); ***Abex Corp. v. Superior Ct.*** (1st Dist.1989) 209 Cal.App.3d 755, 758; *CEB Discovery Practice*, §10.12. See "Motion for Medical Examination," §5, p. 860.

[1] Common tests. When a demand specifies a test or procedure that is commonly known to be quick and painless (e.g., a blood test), the defendant is not required to include other information about it. *Cf. **Cruz v. Superior Ct.*** (4th Dist.2004) 121 Cal.App.4th 646, 652 (opposition to D's motion for blood test did not show it would be painful, protracted, or intrusive).

[2] Uncommon tests. When a demand specifies a test or procedure that is not commonly known to be quick and painless, the defendant should include with the demand a physician's declaration describing the examination and any pain or discomfort that could result. *Cf. **Abex Corp.***, 209 Cal.App.3d at 757-58 (Ds' motion to compel biopsy of P's warts included physician's declaration that biopsy would be conducted under local anesthetic and would involve little pain).

5. Signature. There is no requirement that the PIP demand be signed by the defendant or the defendant's attorney. But as a general rule, an attorney should sign all discovery requests that she drafts. See "Attorney's signature," ch. 7-A, §7.2.6, p. 753.

6. When to serve demand. See "Timing of Discovery," ch. 7-A, §5, p. 745; "When to Schedule Discovery," ch. 7-A, §6, p. 749.

7. Serving demand. The defendant must serve copies of the demand on the PIP and on all other parties who have appeared in the case. CCP §2032.220(e). See "Serving discovery," ch. 7-A, §13.1, p. 769.

8. Filing or lodging demand. See "Filing or lodging discovery," ch. 7-A, §13.2, p. 770.

9. Custody & disposal of demand. See "Custody & Disposal of Discovery," ch. 7-A, §16, p. 776.

§4.2 Responding to demand for PIP exam. A PIP can respond to a demand for a physical examination by (1) serving a written response or (2) making a motion for a protective order.

1. Written response to demand.

(1) Deadline for response. The PIP must serve a written response to the demand within 20 days after the PIP was personally served with the demand (25 days if mailed in California) unless the defendant has obtained a court order shortening the time for a response. *See* CCP §§1013(a), 2016.050, 2032.230. See "Add time for method of service," ch. 1-F, §5.1.4, p. 54. The failure to serve a timely written response to the demand waives any objection the PIP might have to it. CCP §2032.240(a); *CEB Discovery Practice*, §10.35. See "Waiver of objections," ch. 7-A, §15.2, p. 776; "Motion for Relief from Waiver of Objections," ch. 9-H, p. 1082. The PIP can, however, file a motion with the court to extend the time for a response. CCP §2032.230(b).

(2) Form of response. See "Form of response," ch. 7-A, §9.3, p. 758.

(3) Content of response. The written response must specify whether the PIP will fully comply with the demand, comply in a modified way, or refuse to comply.

(a) Full compliance. The written response to the demand can state that the PIP will comply with the demand as written. CCP §2032.230(a).

(b) Modified compliance. The written response to the demand can state that the PIP will comply with the demand as specifically modified by the PIP. CCP §2032.230(a). Possible modifications to the demand include the following:

[1] Limit scope. The response can limit the examination to the specific parts of the PIP's body that were injured. *See* Weil, *Civil Procedure Before Trial*, ¶8:1542.4 (P can agree to appear for exam on condition that it be limited to specific body parts).

[2] Limit exam details. The response can limit the time, place, manner, conditions, and nature of the PIP examination. See "Exam details," §4.1.4(3), p. 858.

[3] Limit X-rays. The response can provide the examining physician with access to existing X-rays. CCP §2032.520. If the PIP provides existing X-rays, no additional X-rays of that area can be taken by the physician without the PIP's consent or a court order based on good cause. *Id.*

[4] **Limit physician.** The response can include an objection to the licensed physician or health-care practitioner and request that another individual be named. *See CEB Discovery Practice*, §10.24.

(c) Refusal to comply. The written response to the demand can state that the PIP will refuse to submit to a physical examination. CCP §2032.230(a). The response must provide specific reasons for the refusal. *Id.* Possible reasons for refusal include the following:

[1] The demand specifies a date for the examination that is less than 30 days after service of the demand, or the date or time is inconvenient. *See id.* §2032.220(d). See "Time," §4.1.4(3)(a), p. 858.

[2] The demand specifies a location for the examination that is more than 75 miles from the PIP's residence. *See* CCP §2032.220(a)(2). See "Place," §4.1.4(3)(b), p. 858.

[3] The demand calls for an examination that goes beyond the scope of the injuries that are in controversy. *See* CCP §2032.020(a). See "Scope," §4.1.4(3)(e), p. 858.

[4] The demand calls for tests or procedures that are painful, protracted, or intrusive. *See* CCP §2032.220(a)(1). See "Nature," §4.1.4(3)(f), p. 858.

[5] The demand does not identify the licensed physician or health-care practitioner who will perform the examination or the physician's specialty (if any). *See* CCP §2032.220(c). See "Examiner," §4.1.4(2), p. 858.

(4) PIP's observer. If the PIP responds that it will comply with the demand (either full or modified compliance), the response can identify a person who will attend the PIP's examination as an observer (if applicable). *See* CCP §2032.510(c) (if representative of PIP's attorney is to be observer, attorney must identify representative in writing). See "Observer," §6.1.1(1), p. 865.

(5) Signature. There is no requirement that a response to a demand for a PIP examination be signed by the attorney. *See* CCP §2032.230 (no mention of attorney's signature for response to PIP demand). *But see CEB Discovery Practice*, §10.80 (form of response to demand for PIP exam contains signature block for attorney). But as a general rule, an attorney should sign all discovery responses that she drafts. See "Signatures & verification," ch. 7-A, §9.4, p. 759.

(6) How to serve response. See "Serving discovery responses," ch. 7-A, §13.1.2, p. 770.

2. Motion for protective order. A PIP can respond to a demand for a physical examination by making a motion for a protective order. See "Motion for protective order," §8.1, p. 867.

§4.3 Replying to PIP's response. If the PIP does not make any response to the examination demand, the defendant can make a motion to compel a response. CCP §2032.240(b). See "Motion to Compel Response to & Compliance with Demand for Exam of Personal-Injury P," ch. 9-F, §2, p. 1069. If the PIP makes unacceptable modifications or unfounded objections to the demand, the defendant can make a motion to compel compliance with the demand. CCP §2032.250(a). See "Motion to Compel Compliance with Demand for Exam of Personal-Injury P," ch. 9-F, §3, p. 1072.

§5. MOTION FOR MEDICAL EXAMINATION

To secure a medical examination beyond the PIP examination described in "Demand for Physical Examination of Personal-Injury Plaintiff," §4, p. 857, a party must make a motion. CCP §2032.310(a).

NOTE

For ease of reference, the following discussion refers to the party seeking the medical examination as the defendant, even though a plaintiff can seek a medical examination, and refers to the person whose medical examination is sought as the plaintiff, even though the plaintiff and the person whose medical examination is sought can be different people. See "Who can be examined," §2.2, p. 855.

§5.1 Motion.

1. Who can make motion. Any party can make a motion for a physical or mental examination. CCP §2032.310(a); *see, e.g.*, ***Doyle v. Superior Ct.*** (6th Dist.1996) 50 Cal.App.4th 1878, 1880-81 (P in defamation action made motion for mental examination of D-cross-complainant because D claimed mental anguish resulting from P's sexual harassment).

2. When motion is necessary. A defendant must make a motion for a medical examination when it cannot demand one. See "Demand for Physical Examination of Personal-Injury Plaintiff," §4, p. 857. For example, a defendant must make a motion in the following situations:

(1) Additional physical exam of PIP. The defendant in a personal-injury action must make a motion when it seeks more than one physical examination of the PIP. ***Shapira v. Superior Ct.*** (1st Dist.1990) 224 Cal.App.3d 1249, 1254-55; *see* CCP §§2032.220(a), 2032.310(a).

(2) Mental exam. The defendant must make a motion when it seeks to conduct a mental examination. CCP §2032.310(a); ***Carpenter v. Superior Ct.*** (1st Dist.2006) 141 Cal.App.4th 249, 259.

(3) Painful, protracted, or intrusive tests. The defendant must make a motion when it seeks to conduct a medical examination that will include tests or procedures that are painful, protracted, or intrusive. *See* CCP §§2032.220(a)(1), 2032.310(a); ***Abex Corp. v. Superior Ct.*** (1st Dist.1989) 209 Cal.App.3d 755, 758; *CEB Discovery Practice*, §10.12.

(4) Outside geographic limits. The defendant must make a motion when it seeks to conduct an examination at a location that is more than 75 miles from the examinee's residence. *See* CCP §§2032.220(a)(2), 2032.310(a), 2032.320(e).

3. Meet-and-confer requirement. The defendant must attempt to secure a medical examination by agreement before making a motion for the examination. *See* CCP §2032.310(b) (motion must be accompanied by meet-and-confer declaration). See "Meet-and-Confer Obligation," ch. 7-A, §10, p. 761.

4. Motion papers. A motion for a physical or mental examination should be in writing and in the same form as motions generally. See "Motion Papers," ch. 1-D, §5, p. 27. A motion for a physical or mental examination should include the following:

(1) Notice of motion & motion. The motion should include the notice of motion and motion. See "Notice of motion & motion," ch. 1-D, §5.1, p. 28.

(2) Memorandum. The motion should include a memorandum of points and authorities. See "Memorandum of points & authorities," ch. 1-D, §5.2, p. 28. The memorandum must include the following information:

(a) Examinee. The memorandum must identify the person whose physical or mental examination is required and show that the person is one of those listed in CCP §2032.020(a). See "Statutory examinees," §2.2.1, p. 855.

(b) Condition in controversy. The memorandum must show how the examinee's physical or mental condition has been placed in controversy in the case. *See* CCP §2032.020(a). See "Condition in controversy," §2.2.2, p. 856.

(c) Good cause. The memorandum must establish good cause for the physical or mental examination. CCP §2032.320(a); ***Vinson v. Superior Ct.*** (1987) 43 Cal.3d 833, 840; *CEB Discovery Practice*, §15.6; *see* CCP §2032.320(e)(1) (must show good cause for exam outside 75 miles); ***Carpenter***, 141 Cal.App.4th at 259 (must show good cause for mental exam). To show good cause, the moving party must provide specific facts justifying discovery and show that the inquiry is relevant to the subject matter of the case or is reasonably calculated to lead to the discovery of admissible evidence. ***Vinson***, 43 Cal.3d at 840 & n.6. The good-cause requirement serves as a barrier to excessive and unwarranted intrusions. *See id.* at 840; ***Greyhound Corp. v. Superior Ct.*** (1961) 56 Cal.2d 355, 388.

(d) Exam details. The memorandum must identify the type of medical examination sought (i.e., physical or mental) and provide the following information:

[1] Time. The memorandum must specify the date and time of the examination. CCP §2032.310(b).

[2] Place. The memorandum must specify the place for the examination. CCP §2032.310(b). If the place for the examination is more than 75 miles from the examinee's residence, the moving party must (1) show good cause to conduct it at that location and (2) state its willingness to advance reasonable expenses and costs to the examinee for traveling to that location. *Id.* §2032.320(e). See "Good cause," §5.1.4(2)(c), p. 861.

[3] Manner. The memorandum should specify the diagnostic tests and procedures to be performed. *See* CCP §2032.310(b). Section 2032.310 does not specifically require that the motion identify the diagnostic tests and procedures. ***Carpenter***, 141 Cal.App.4th at 259. However, only by identifying the tests and procedures in the motion will the court be able to identify them in its order granting the motion. *See* CCP §2032.320(d) (court order must identify diagnostic tests and procedures to be performed).

[4] Conditions. The memorandum must specify the conditions for the examination. CCP §2032.310(b). For example, the memorandum should specify the expected length of the examination, the schedule for the examination, who will attend, and how the examination will be recorded.

[5] Scope. The memorandum must specify the scope of the examination. CCP §2032.310(b). See "Scope," §4.1.4(3)(e), p. 858.

[6] Nature. The memorandum must specify the nature of the examination. CCP §2032.310(b). For example, the memorandum should state whether the examination includes a test or procedure that is painful, protracted, or intrusive. *See id.* §§2032.220(a)(1), 2032.310(a).

[a] Common tests. When a motion specifies a test or procedure that is commonly known to be quick and painless (e.g., a blood test), the defendant is not required to include other information about it. *See, e.g.*, ***Cruz v. Superior Ct.*** (4th Dist.2004) 121 Cal.App.4th 646, 652 (opposition to D's motion for blood test did not show it would be painful, protracted, or intrusive).

[b] Uncommon tests. When a motion specifies a test or procedure that is not commonly known to be quick and painless, the defendant should include a physician's declaration describing the examination and any pain or discomfort that could result. *Cf.* ***Abex Corp.***, 209 Cal.App.3d at 757-58 (Ds' motion to compel biopsy of P's warts included physician's declaration that biopsy would be conducted under local anesthetic and would involve little pain).

[c] Painful, protracted, or intrusive tests. When a motion specifies a test or procedure that is painful, protracted, or intrusive, the defendant should include a physician's declaration that (1) describes the examination and any pain or discomfort that could result, (2) states why the specific test or procedure is necessary, and (3) states why no other test or procedure that is less painful, protracted, or intrusive will provide the necessary information. *Cf.* ***Abex Corp.***, 209 Cal.App.3d at 757-58 (Ds' motion to compel procedure not commonly known to be painless included physician's declaration).

[7] Examiner. The memorandum must identify the person who will perform the examination and the person's specialty, if any. CCP §2032.310(b). The choice of examiner belongs to the moving party. *See id.* See "Who can conduct exam," §2.3, p. 856.

(e) Travel expenses for exam. If the motion requests a place for the examination that is more than 75 miles from the examinee's residence, the memorandum should state the moving party's willingness to pay the examinee's reasonable travel expenses and costs. *See* CCP §2032.320(e)(2).

(3) Separate statement. The motion does not need to include a separate statement. *See* CRC 3.1345(a)(6), (b).

(4) Supporting declaration. The facts in the memorandum must be supported with evidence, generally in the form of a declaration, which can be made by the party or its attorney. *See CEB Discovery Practice*, §10.46. See "Supporting evidence," ch. 1-D, §5.3, p. 30. The following information must be provided in the declaration:

(a) Motion facts. The declaration must support the motion facts included in the memorandum. *See CEB Discovery Practice*, §10.46. Copies of relevant pleadings or discovery requests and responses, if any, should be attached as exhibits.

(b) Meet-and-confer facts. The declaration must describe the efforts to resolve the issue before the motion was made. *See* CCP §§2016.040, 2032.310(b). See "Meet-and-confer declaration," ch. 7-A, §10.4, p. 763.

(5) Proposed order. See "Proposed order," ch. 1-D, §5.5, p. 32.

5. When to make motion. A motion for a physical or mental examination should be filed and served at least 16 court days before the date set for the hearing. CCP §1005(b). See "Latest date to make discovery motion," ch. 7-A, §6.4, p. 751. If the motion is served by means other than personal delivery, the plaintiff will need to add more time to the 16-day period (e.g., five calendar days are added when notice is mailed in California). CCP §1005(b). Because a motion for a physical or mental examination is a discovery motion, it must be heard at least 15 calendar days before the initial trial date. See "Scheduling Hearing," ch. 1-H, §3, p. 80; "Cutoff for discovery motions," ch. 7-A, §5.2.2, p. 748. To determine the deadline for filing and serving the motion, see chart 7-15, below.

7-15. CALCULATING DEADLINE TO FILE & SERVE DISCOVERY MOTION

	Action	Date
1	Initial trial date set by court.	
2	Count backward 15 days from date in row 1. This is the cutoff date for discovery motions.	
3	Count backward 16 *court* days from date in row 2. ❶	
4	Count backward number of days for method of service (e.g., 0 for personal delivery, 5 for mail in California) from date in row 3. ❷ This is the deadline to file and serve the discovery motion.	

❶ The number of calendar days in 16 court days varies, depending on the holidays and weekends that fall within the 16 court days. See "Court days," ch. 1-F, §5.1.3(1)(b), p. 54.

❷ If the last day falls on a Saturday, Sunday, or other judicial holiday, continue counting backward until the next day that is not a Saturday, Sunday, or judicial holiday. See "Determine last day," ch. 1-F, §5.1.5, p. 55.

6. How to serve motion. The moving party must serve copies of the motion papers on the person to be examined and on all parties who have appeared in the case. CCP §2032.310(c). See "Serving discovery requests," ch. 7-A, §13.1.1, p. 770.

§5.2 Response.

1. Opposition papers. The responding party can file an opposition to the motion for a medical examination.

(1) Form of opposition. See "Opposition Papers," ch. 1-D, §8, p. 35.

(2) Contents of opposition. The responding party can file opposition papers that negate the grounds asserted in the motion or that object to the motion for other reasons. *See, e.g.*, ***Edwards v. Superior Ct.*** (1976) 16 Cal.3d 905, 912-13 (P objected to physician identified as examiner in motion and to proposed length of examination); ***Cruz v. Superior Ct.*** (4th Dist.2004) 121 Cal.App.4th 646, 649 (P objected on grounds that requested examination would be painful, protracted, or invasive and that Ds had no right to examine nonparty examinee). For example, opposition papers can be based on the following grounds:

(a) Condition not in controversy. The responding party can show that the examinee's physical or mental condition is not in controversy. *See* ***Doyle v. Superior Ct.*** (6th Dist.1996) 50 Cal.App.4th 1878, 1882. See "Condition in controversy," §5.1.4(2)(b), p. 861.

(b) No showing of good cause. The responding party can show that there is no good cause for the examination. *See* ***Doyle***, 50 Cal.App.4th at 1882. See "Good cause," §5.1.4(2)(c), p. 861.

(c) Invasion of privacy. The responding party can show that the examination would invade the examinee's right to privacy. *See, e.g.*, ***Vinson v. Superior Ct.*** (1987) 43 Cal.3d 833, 842 (Ds in sexual-harassment suit were not allowed to examine P's sexual history based on P's privacy rights). However, a party who seeks damages for physical or mental injuries relinquishes the right to maintain the confidentiality of past medical or psychiatric records that are relevant to the claim. *See id.* See "Right to Privacy," ch. 6-F, §1, p. 681.

(d) Burden outweighs benefit. The responding party can show that the burden, expense, or intrusiveness of the discovery outweighs the likelihood the discovery will lead to admissible evidence. CCP §2017.020(a).

(e) Unreasonably cumulative or unduly burdensome. The responding party can show that (1) the discovery is unreasonably cumulative or the same information is obtainable from another source that is more convenient, less burdensome, or less expensive, or (2) the discovery is unduly burdensome or expensive. CCP §2019.030(a).

(3) Stipulation on mental injuries. The plaintiff in a personal-injury action whose mental examination is sought by the defendant can include with her opposition papers a stipulation that she disclaims any unusual mental or emotional injuries. *See* CCP §2032.320(b), (c); Weil, *Civil Procedure Before Trial*, ¶8:1567. If the stipulation is made, the court will not order a mental examination of the plaintiff except on a showing of exceptional circumstances. CCP §2032.320(b); Weil, *Civil Procedure Before Trial*, ¶8:1568. The stipulation must contain the following statements:

(a) Claim for usual mental distress only. The plaintiff stipulates that no claim is being made for mental and emotional distress beyond what is usually associated with the physical injuries claimed. CCP §2032.320(c)(1).

(b) No expert testimony. The plaintiff stipulates that no expert testimony about the usual mental and emotional distress will be presented at trial in support of the claim for damages. CCP §2032.320(c)(2).

2. Submit X-rays. If the motion seeks to secure an X-ray examination, the examinee can give the examining physician access to existing X-rays of any area of the examinee's body for the physician's inspection. CCP §2032.520. If the examinee gives the physician existing X-rays, no additional X-rays of that area can be taken by the physician without the examinee's consent or a court order based on good cause. *Id.*

3. Motion for protective order. The responding party can make a motion for a protective order. See "Motion for protective order," §8.1, p. 867. However, moving for a protective order is usually unnecessary because most objections can be raised in opposition papers.

§5.3 Order.

1. Contents of order. An order granting a motion for a physical or mental examination must contain the following information:

(1) Examiner. The order must specify the person or persons who can perform the examination. CCP §2032.320(d). See "Who can conduct exam," §2.3, p. 856.

(2) Time of exam. The order must specify the date and time of the examination. CCP §2032.320(d).

(3) Place for exam. The order must specify the place for the examination. CCP §2032.320(d). If the place is more than 75 miles from the examinee's residence, the order must be conditioned on the advancement by the moving party of the reasonable expenses and costs to the examinee for travel. *Id.* §2032.320(e)(2).

(4) Manner of exam. The order must specify the manner of the examination. CCP §2032.320(d). See "Manner," §5.1.4(2)(d)[3], p. 862.

(5) Diagnostic tests & procedures. The order must specify the diagnostic tests and procedures to be performed. CCP §2032.320(d). The court is required to identify the diagnostic tests and procedures by name, not just by category and type. *E.g.*, ***Carpenter v. Superior Ct.*** (1st Dist.2006) 141 Cal.App.4th 249, 260 ("standardized written psychological tests" was not adequate description).

(6) Conditions for exam. The order must specify the conditions for the examination. CCP §2032.320(d). For example, the order should specify the length of the examination, the schedule for the examination, who can attend, and how the examination will be recorded. See "Who can attend exam," §6.1, this page; "Recording exam," §6.2, this page.

(7) Scope of exam. The order must specify the scope of the examination. CCP §2032.320(d). See "Scope," §4.1.4(3)(e), p. 858.

(8) Nature of exam. The order must specify the nature of the examination. CCP §2032.320(d). See "Nature," §5.1.4(2)(d)[6], p. 862.

2. Number of medical exams. There is no limit to the number of physical or mental examinations a court can order. ***Shapira v. Superior Ct.*** (1st Dist.1990) 224 Cal.App.3d 1249, 1254-55. Although repetitive examinations may become unduly burdensome, they are permissible if there is a showing of good cause. ***People v. Landau*** (4th Dist.2013) 214 Cal.App.4th 1, 26; *see* ***Shapira***, 224 Cal.App.3d at 1255.

§6. CONDUCT OF MEDICAL EXAMINATION

§6.1 Who can attend exam.

1. Physical exam. The persons who can attend a physical examination (besides the examiner and the examinee) include the following:

(1) Observer. The attorney for the examinee (or for the party producing the examinee) or the attorney's representative must be allowed to attend and observe any physical examination. CCP §2032.510(a). If an attorney's representative will be an observer, the representative must be authorized to observe in a writing signed by the attorney. *Id.* §2032.510(c). An observer can monitor and record the examination but cannot participate in it or disrupt it. *See id.* §2032.510(a), (b). For a discussion of how an observer can record a physical examination, see "Physical exam," §6.2.1, this page. An observer also has the power to suspend a physical examination. See "Abusive examiner," §6.3.1, p. 866.

(2) Other persons. Unless the court orders otherwise, the parties can agree to allow other persons to attend the examination. *See* CCP §§2016.030, 2019.010(d).

2. Mental exam. A court is not required to allow anyone other than the examinee and the examiner to attend a mental examination. *See, e.g.*, ***Vinson v. Superior Ct.*** (1987) 43 Cal.3d 833, 845-46 (P's attorney was not allowed to attend); ***Edwards v. Superior Ct.*** (1976) 16 Cal.3d 905, 909-10 (same); ***Toyota Motor Sales, U.S.A. v. Superior Ct.*** (2d Dist.2010) 189 Cal.App.4th 1391, 1395-96 (same). Persons other than the examinee and the examiner can attend a mental examination only by court order or by agreement of the parties. *See* CCP §2032.530(b).

§6.2 Recording exam.

1. Physical exam. A physical examination can be recorded stenographically or by audio technology by the attorney for the examinee (or for the party producing the examinee) or by the attorney's representative. CCP §2032.510(a). A physical examination cannot be recorded by videotape. ***Edmiston v. Superior Ct.*** (1978) 22 Cal.3d 699, 704.

2. Mental exam. A mental examination can be recorded by audio technology by the examiner or the examinee. CCP §2032.530(a); ***Golfland Entm't Ctrs., Inc. v. Superior Ct.*** (3d Dist.2003) 108 Cal.App.4th 739, 750. A mental examination cannot be recorded stenographically or by videotape. *See* ***Golfland Entm't Ctrs.***, 108 Cal.App.4th at 750-51.

§6.3 Suspending physical exam. A physical examination can be suspended to stop abusive or disruptive behavior and to allow for the filing of a motion for a protective order. CCP §2032.510(d) (abusive behavior), (e) (disruptive behavior). See "Motion for protective order," §8.1, p. 867. An examination can be suspended based on the behavior of the examiner or the observer.

NOTE

The Code of Civil Procedure does not address circumstances in which a mental examination can be suspended.

1. Abusive examiner. An observer can suspend a physical examination if, in her judgment, the examiner becomes abusive to the examinee or begins to engage in unauthorized diagnostic tests or procedures. CCP §2032.510(d).

2. Disruptive observer. The examiner can suspend a physical examination if an observer begins to participate in or disrupt the examination. CCP §2032.510(e).

§7. MEDICAL-EXAMINATION REPORTS

§7.1 Demand for reports. A party who submits to or produces another person for an examination (generally the plaintiff) can make a written demand for copies of the medical reports about the examination.

1. Report of exam. The demanding party is entitled to a copy of a detailed written report setting out the history, examinations, findings (including the results of any tests), diagnoses, prognoses, and conclusions of the examiner. CCP §2032.610(a)(1). The demanding party is entitled to this report even if the examiner has not prepared one. ***Kennedy v. Superior Ct.*** (1st Dist.1998) 64 Cal.App.4th 674, 676.

2. Earlier reports. The demanding party is entitled to a copy of reports from all earlier examinations of the same condition of the examinee made by the same or any other examiner. CCP §2032.610(a)(2).

§7.2 Deadline to respond to demand. The party who sought the medical examination (generally the defendant) must deliver a copy of the demanded reports within 30 days after service of the demand (35 days if served by mail in California) or within 15 days before trial, whichever is earlier. *See* CCP §§1013(a), 2016.050, 2032.610(b).

§7.3 Effect of demand for reports.

1. Waiver. A demanding party who obtains a copy of a report of a physical or mental examination waives—in the pending action and in any later action involving the same controversy—any privilege and work-product protection that may apply to the report. *See* CCP §§2032.610(c), 2032.630. The waiver extends to the following:

(1) The reports and writings of the examiner and any other physician, psychologist, or licensed health-care practitioner who has examined the examinee or who might examine the examinee as to the same condition in the future. *See id.* §§2032.610(c), 2032.630.

(2) The testimony of the examiner and any other physician, psychologist, or licensed health-care practitioner who has examined the examinee or who might examine the examinee as to the same condition in the future. *See id.* §§2032.610(c), 2032.630.

2. Exchange of reports. The party who sought the examination and who complies with the demand for reports is entitled to receive the following from the demanding party:

(1) Existing report. A copy of any existing written report of any examination of the condition at issue by any other physician, psychologist, or licensed health-care practitioner. CCP §2032.640.

(2) Later report. A copy of any later report of an earlier or later examination of the condition at issue by any physician, psychologist, or licensed health-care practitioner. CCP §2032.640.

§8. MOTIONS RELATED TO MEDICAL EXAMINATIONS

§8.1 Motion for protective order. A party can move for a protective order from a medical examination, but doing so is generally unnecessary because most objections can be made in response to the demand or the motion. See "Motion for Protective Order," ch. 9-B, p. 1024.

1. Grounds for protective order. Possible grounds for a protective order relating to a medical examination include the following:

(1) Abusive examiner. The order can be based on the ground that the medical examiner behaved abusively or attempted to conduct unauthorized tests or procedures during the examination. CCP §2032.510(d).

(2) Disruptive observer. The order can be based on the ground that the medical observer behaved disruptively during the examination or attempted to participate in the examination. CCP §2032.510(e).

(3) Burden outweighs benefit. The order can be based on the ground that the burden, expense, or intrusiveness of the discovery outweighs the likelihood the discovery will lead to admissible evidence. CCP §2017.020(a).

(4) Unreasonably cumulative or unduly burdensome. The order can be based on the ground that (1) the discovery is unreasonably cumulative or the same information is obtainable from another source that is more convenient, less burdensome, or less expensive, or (2) the discovery is unduly burdensome or expensive. CCP §2019.030(a).

2. Relief available. See "Relief," ch. 9-B, §3.3.1(1)(a), p. 1029.

§8.2 Motion to compel response to PIP demand. If a PIP does not timely respond to a demand for a physical examination, the defendant can make a motion to compel a response and ask for sanctions. *See* CCP §2032.240(b), (c). See "Motion to Compel Response to & Compliance with Demand for Exam of Personal-Injury P," ch. 9-F, §2, p. 1069.

§8.3 Motion to compel compliance with demand for PIP exam. If a PIP refuses to submit to a physical examination or modifies the examination demand in an unwarranted manner, the defendant can make a motion to compel compliance with the demand. CCP §2032.250(a). See "Motion to Compel Compliance with Demand for Exam of Personal-Injury P," ch. 9-F, §3, p. 1072.

§8.4 Motion to compel delivery of medical records. If a party does not timely comply with an obligation to deliver medical reports and records, the other party can make a motion to compel their delivery. *See* CCP §§2032.620(a), 2032.650(a). See "Medical-Examination Reports," §7, p. 866; "Motion to Compel Delivery of Medical Reports," ch. 9-F, §4, p. 1075.

§8.5 Motion for relief from waiver of objections. If a PIP does not timely respond to a demand for a physical examination, the PIP can make a motion for relief from the waiver of her objections to the demand. See "Deadline for response," §4.2.1(1), p. 859; "Motion for Relief from Waiver of Objections," ch. 9-H, p. 1082.

G. MOTION TO DISCOVER FINANCIAL INFORMATION

In 1962, the California Supreme Court held that a plaintiff who alleges a claim for punitive damages has the right to pretrial discovery of information about the defendant's financial status. ***Coy v. Superior Ct.*** (1962) 58 Cal.2d 210, 222-23. At the time, it was thought that by allowing the discovery, the "game element" would be removed from the litigation process. ***Rawnsley v. Superior Ct.*** (2d Dist.1986) 183 Cal.App.3d 86, 90. Instead, it led to further gamesmanship because it allowed a plaintiff to pressure a defendant into settling a case by (1) exposing its financial condition and (2) putting it to the task of spending time and money compiling large amounts of information unrelated to the substantive claims and related only to a measure of damages that might not ever be awarded. *Id.* at 90-91.

In response to these perceived abuses of discovery, the California Legislature enacted Civ. C. §3295 in 1979 to codify several court decisions that had created safeguards for defendants faced with punitive-damages claims and prevent the premature disclosure of a defendant's financial condition. *See* ***Torres v. Automobile Club*** (1997) 15 Cal.4th 771, 777; ***Rawnsley***, 183 Cal.App.3d at 90-91. This subchapter discusses one of those safeguards: a motion to discover financial information. Other safeguards that are not discussed in this subchapter include (1) protective orders requiring the plaintiff to produce evidence of a prima facie case of liability for punitive damages before permitting the introduction of the defendant's profits and financial condition, (2) restrictions on disclosing the amount of punitive damages sought in a case, and (3) bifurcation of the punitive-damages portion of a trial. *See* Civ. C. §3295(a), (d), (e); ***Torres***, 15 Cal.4th at 777. See "Punitive," ch. 3-C, §3.7.1(1)(b), p. 221; "Financial information," ch. 9-B, §2.2.3(3), p. 1027.

NOTE

If the defendant's financial condition is itself an issue in the case, the plaintiff should be entitled to discovery without the need for a court order. See California Civil Discovery Practice (CEB Online ed. 2014) §1.41; see, e.g., ***Rawnsley****, 183 Cal.App.3d at 91 (P could prove claim of misappropriation only by obtaining Ds' financial documents). See "Methods of Discovery," ch. 7, p. 733.*

§1. GENERAL

§1.1 Purpose. The purpose of a motion to discover financial information is to overcome the statutory limitation on pretrial discovery of the defendant's alleged wrongful profits and financial condition. *See* Civ. C. §3295(a), (c).

NOTE

Before bringing a motion to discover financial information, consider asking the defendant to agree to (1) bringing the information to trial under seal and (2) producing the information only if the jury finds that the requirements for awarding punitive damages have been met. See ***Jabro v. Superior Ct.*** *(4th Dist.2002) 95 Cal.App.4th 754, 756 (bringing information under seal to trial is common and effective method for handling production of financial information when claim for punitive damages is alleged).*

§1.2 Primary authority. Civ. C. §§3294, 3295.

§1.3 Secondary authority. The following secondary sources are cited as authority in this subchapter:

- *Judicial Council of California Civil Jury Instructions* (2015), www.courts.ca.gov/partners/317.htm (referred to as *Civil Jury Instructions*).
- Thomas, *California Civil Courtroom Handbook* (2014) (referred to as Thomas, *Courtroom Handbook*).
- Weil & Brown, *California Practice Guide: Civil Procedure Before Trial* (CD-ROM ed. 2014) (referred to as Weil, *Civil Procedure Before Trial*).

§2. GROUNDS

To prevail on a motion to discover financial information, the plaintiff must show that (1) it is entitled to seek punitive damages and (2) there is a substantial probability it will prevail on a claim for punitive damages. *See* Civ. C. §§3294(a), 3295(c).

§2.1 Punitive damages. To be entitled to punitive damages, the plaintiff must have pleaded in its complaint (1) a cause of action that supports a claim for punitive damages and (2) ultimate facts showing that the defendant acted with malice, oppression, or fraud. *See* Civ. C. §3294(a); ***Spinks v. Equity Residential Briarwood Apts.*** (6th Dist.2009) 171 Cal.App.4th 1004, 1055. See "What to plead – ultimate facts," ch. 3-C, §3.6.3(2)(a), p. 216.

1. Cause of action supports claim. The plaintiff must have pleaded in its complaint a cause of action that supports a claim for punitive damages. These include claims either (1) based on the defendant's breach of an obligation not arising from a contract or (2) for wrongful death arising from a homicide for which the defendant has been convicted of a felony. *See* Civ. C. §3294(a), (d); *see, e.g.*, ***Crogan v. Metz*** (1956) 47 Cal.2d 398, 405 (punitive damages could not be awarded in suit based on breach of contract even though breach was fraudulent); ***Ginsberg v. Gamson*** (2d Dist.2012) 205 Cal.App.4th 873, 895-96 (punitive damages could not be awarded for breach of implied covenant of quiet enjoyment without establishing wrongful-eviction claim); ***Spinks***, 171 Cal.App.4th at 1055 (punitive damages can be awarded for wrongful eviction, trespass, invasion of privacy, and intentional infliction of emotional distress); ***Shore v. Gurnett*** (1st Dist.2004) 122 Cal.App.4th 166, 175 (D convicted of vehicular manslaughter was required to pay punitive damages in later civil suit).

2. D acted with malice, oppression, or fraud. The plaintiff must have pleaded in its complaint ultimate facts showing that the defendant acted with malice, oppression, or fraud. ***Spinks***, 171 Cal.App.4th at 1055; *see* Thomas, *Courtroom Handbook*, §9:37. Conclusory characterizations of the defendant's conduct as malicious, oppressive, fraudulent, intentional, or willful are not sufficient. *See* Thomas, *Courtroom Handbook*, §9:37; *see, e.g.*, ***Austin v. Regents of the Univ. of Cal.*** (2d Dist.1979) 89 Cal.App.3d 354, 359 (P's complaint did not state facts that supported claim for punitive damages because allegations were purely conclusory); ***Cyrus v. Haveson*** (2d Dist.1976) 65 Cal.App.3d 306, 317 (P's complaint did not state facts that supported claim for punitive damages because allegations of malice were pleaded only in conclusory terms and omitted factual allegations of wrongful motive, intent, or purpose). To be entitled to punitive damages, the plaintiff must plead facts supporting the following statutory requirements of Civ. C. §3294:

(1) Malice, oppression, or fraud.

(a) Malice. To establish malice, the plaintiff must show that the defendant (1) intended to cause injury to the plaintiff or (2) engaged in despicable conduct with a willful and conscious disregard of the rights or safety of others. *See* Civ. C. §3294(a), (c)(1).

[1] Despicable conduct. "Despicable conduct" is conduct so vile that it would be looked down on and despised by reasonable people. ***Mock v. Michigan Millers Mut. Ins.*** (2d Dist.1992) 4 Cal.App.4th 306, 331; *Civil Jury Instructions*, Damages, Series 3940, 3941, 3943-3948.

[2] Willful & conscious disregard. "Willful and conscious disregard" occurs when a defendant is aware of the dangerous and probable consequences of its conduct and deliberately fails to avoid those consequences. ***Hoch v. Allied-Signal, Inc./Bendix Safety Restraints Div.*** (1st Dist.1994) 24 Cal.App.4th 48, 61; *Civil Jury Instructions*, Damages, Series 3940, 3941, 3943-48.

(b) Oppression. To establish oppression, the plaintiff must show that the defendant engaged in despicable conduct that subjected the plaintiff to cruel and unjust hardship in conscious disregard of the plaintiff's rights. *See* Civ. C. §3294(a), (c)(2).

(c) Fraud. To establish fraud, the plaintiff must show that the defendant intentionally misrepresented or concealed a material fact known to the defendant with the intent of depriving the plaintiff of property or legal rights or causing some other injury. *See* Civ. C. §3294(a), (c)(3).

(2) D's status. The plaintiff may be required to allege additional facts depending on the defendant's status.

(a) D is natural person. When the defendant is a natural person, the defendant's conduct will support a claim for punitive damages if the defendant acted with malice, oppression, or fraud. *See* Civ. C. §3294(a); *Civil Jury Instructions*, Damages, Series 3940, 3941.

(b) D is principal or employer. When the defendant is a principal or employer of an agent or employee, the defendant's conduct will support a claim for punitive damages if the plaintiff shows both of the following:

[1] The agent or employee acted with malice, oppression, or fraud. *See* Civ. C. §3294(a), (b); *Civil Jury Instructions*, Damages, Series 3943, 3944.

[2] Any of the following conduct occurred:

[a] The agent or employee was an officer, director, or managing agent of the defendant and was acting on the defendant's behalf. *See* Civ. C. §3294(a), (b); *Civil Jury Instructions*, Damages, Series 3943, 3944; *see, e.g.*, ***Egan v. Mutual of Omaha Ins.*** (1979) 24 Cal.3d 809, 822-23 (insurance adjusters who disposed of claims with little or no supervision acted on behalf of insurance company as managing agents).

[b] An officer, director, or managing agent of the defendant had advance knowledge of the agent's or employee's unfitness and employed the agent or employee with a knowing disregard of others' rights or safety. *See* Civ. C. §3294(a), (b); *Civil Jury Instructions*, Damages, Series 3943, 3944; *see, e.g.*, ***Roby v. McKesson Corp.*** (2009) 47 Cal.4th 686, 715 (knowingly employing supervisor who was harassing employee without taking any corrective action was in conscious disregard of rights or safety of others); ***Flores v. Autozone W., Inc.*** (4th Dist.2008) 161 Cal.App.4th 373, 386 (employee's previous nonviolent misconduct with customer was insufficient to give employer notice that employee might physically assault customer); ***Weeks v. Baker & McKenzie*** (1st Dist.1998) 63 Cal.App.4th 1128, 1159-60 (D-law firm employed attorney with knowing disregard of others' rights when it did not take any real action to stop attorney from repeatedly sexually harassing staff members).

[c] An officer, director, or managing agent of the defendant authorized the agent's or employee's conduct. Civ. C. §3294(a), (b); *see Civil Jury Instructions*, Damages, Series 3943, 3944; *see, e.g.*, ***Hartman v. Shell Oil Co.*** (4th Dist.1977) 68 Cal.App.3d 240, 248 (highest officials in D-corporation's San Diego region were clearly aware of promises made to P before contract was made but later refused to honor those promises).

[d] An officer, director, or managing agent of the defendant knew of the agent's or employee's wrongful conduct and adopted or approved the conduct after it occurred. Civ. C. §3294(a), (b); *see Civil Jury Instructions*, Damages, Series 3943, 3944; *see, e.g.*, ***Streetscenes v. ITC Entm't Grp.*** (2d Dist.2002) 103 Cal.App.4th 233, 242 (P used circumstantial evidence to prove that company ratified its agent's conduct).

(c) D is corporation or other entity. When the defendant is a corporation or other entity, the defendant's conduct will support a claim for punitive damages if the plaintiff shows any of the following:

[1] One or more of the defendant's officers, directors, or managing agents acted on behalf of the defendant with malice, oppression, or fraud. Civ. C. §3294(b); ***College Hosp., Inc. v. Superior Ct.*** (1994) 8 Cal.4th 704, 723; *see Civil Jury Instructions*, Damages, Series 3945, 3946; *see, e.g.*, ***Lowe v. Yolo Cty. Consol. Water Co.*** (1910) 157 Cal. 503, 511-12 (general manager and president of company engaged in malicious and oppressive acts against P).

[2] One or more of the defendant's officers, directors, or managing agents authorized the conduct constituting malice, oppression, or fraud. Civ. C. §3294(b); ***College Hosp.***, 8 Cal.4th at 723; *e.g.*, ***Hartman***, 68 Cal.App.3d at 248 (highest officials in D-corporation's San Diego region were clearly aware of promises made to P before contract was made but later refused to honor those promises); *see Civil Jury Instructions*, Damages, Series 3945, 3946.

[3] One or more of the defendant's officers, directors, or managing agents knew of the conduct constituting malice, oppression, or fraud and adopted or approved that conduct after it occurred. Civ. C. §3294(b); ***College Hosp.***, 8 Cal.4th at 723; *see Civil Jury Instructions*, Damages, Series 3945, 3946; *see, e.g.*, ***Streetscenes***, 103 Cal.App.4th at 242-43 (D's president's attendance at meetings about fraudulent movie production showed that D ratified wrongful conduct).

§2.2 Substantial probability of prevailing. The plaintiff must show that there is a substantial probability it will prevail on its punitive-damages claim. *See* Civ. C. §§3294(a), 3295(c). To do this, the plaintiff must show that there is a "strong likelihood" it will succeed on its punitive-damages claim; showing a reasonable probability is not sufficient. *See* ***Kerner v. Superior Ct.*** (2d Dist.2012) 206 Cal.App.4th 84, 120; ***Jabro v. Superior Ct.*** (4th Dist.2002) 95 Cal.App.4th 754, 758.

§3. MOTION

§3.1 Who can file. A motion to discover financial information is made by a plaintiff. Civ. C. §3295(c).

§3.2 Deadline to file & serve. A motion to discover financial information should be filed and served at least 16 court days before the date set for the hearing. CCP §1005(b). See "Latest date to make discovery motion," ch. 7-A, §6.4, p. 751. If the motion is served by means other than personal delivery, the plaintiff will need to add more time to the 16-day period (e.g., 5 calendar days are added when notice is mailed in California). CCP §1005(b). Because a motion to discover financial information is a discovery motion, it must be heard at least 15 calendar days before the initial trial date. See "Scheduling Hearing," ch. 1-H, §3, p. 80; "Cutoff for discovery motions," ch. 7-A, §5.2.2, p. 748. To determine the deadline for filing and serving the motion, see "Calculating Deadline to File & Serve Discovery Motion," chart 7-15, p. 863.

§3.3 Contents.

1. Notice of motion & motion.

(1) Generally. The motion should be requested in writing by noticed motion. *See* Civ. C. §3295(c). See "Notice of motion & motion," ch. 1-D, §5.1, p. 28.

(2) Relief. The notice of motion and motion must state that the plaintiff seeks an order permitting pretrial discovery of the defendant's profits and financial condition under Civ. C. §3295(c). *See* CRC 3.1110(a) (notice of motion must state nature of order being sought), CRC 3.1112(d)(3) (motion must briefly state relief sought).

(3) Grounds. The notice of motion and motion must briefly state the grounds for the relief. *See* CRC 3.1110(a) (notice of motion must state grounds for issuance of order), CRC 3.1112(d)(3) (motion must briefly state basis for motion). See "Grounds," §2, p. 869.

2. Memorandum of points & authorities. The motion must include a memorandum in support of the motion. CRC 3.1112(a)(3), 3.1113(a). See "Memorandum of points & authorities," ch. 1-D, §5.2, p. 28.

3. Supporting evidence. The motion must be supported by an affidavit establishing that malice, oppression, or fraud was committed by the defendant. Civ. C. §3295(c); Weil, *Civil Procedure Before Trial*, ¶8:339.3. See "Supporting evidence," ch. 1-D, §5.3, p. 30.

4. Request for judicial notice. If the motion is based on matters the court can take judicial notice of, the plaintiff can ask the court to take judicial notice of those matters. *See* CRC 3.1113(*l*). A request for judicial notice must be made in a separate document. *Id.* See "Request for Judicial Notice," ch. 5-J, p. 547.

5. Proposed order. The plaintiff can submit a proposed order with the motion. *See* CRC 3.1113(m). If a proposed order is submitted, it must be lodged and served with the motion papers, not attached to them. *Id.*

§4. RESPONSE

§4.1 Deadline to file & serve. The opposition must be filed and served at least nine court days before the hearing. CCP §1005(b).

§4.2 Contents. For a general discussion of the contents of an opposition, see "Opposition Papers," ch. 1-D, §8, p. 35.

1. Grounds. The opposition should show that the plaintiff has not established that there is a strong likelihood it will prevail on its claim of malice, oppression, or fraud. *See* Civ. C. §3295(c); ***Jabro v. Superior Ct.*** (4th Dist.2002) 95 Cal.App.4th 754, 758.

2. Memorandum of points & authorities. See "Memorandum of points & authorities," ch. 1-D, §8.1, p. 35.

3. Supporting evidence. The opposition should be supported by an affidavit showing that the defendant did not commit malice, oppression, or fraud. *See* Civ. C. §3295(c); ***Jabro***, 95 Cal.App.4th at 758; Weil, *Civil Procedure Before Trial*, ¶8:339.3. See "Supporting evidence," ch. 1-D, §5.3, p. 30.

4. Request for judicial notice. The opposition can be accompanied by a request for judicial notice. *See* CRC 3.1113(*l*). The request must be filed and served separately from the other opposing papers and must list the specific items for which notice is requested. *Id.* See "Request for Judicial Notice," ch. 5-J, p. 547.

5. Request for protective order. The opposition should include a request for a protective order—in the event the court grants the motion—limiting the dissemination of the financial information to the plaintiff's attorney or the attorney's representative. *See* ***Richards v. Superior Ct.*** (2d Dist.1978) 86 Cal.App.3d 265, 272. See "Financial information," ch. 9-B, §2.2.3(3), p. 1027.

§5. REPLY

The plaintiff can file and serve a reply to the opposition papers. The reply must be filed and served at least five court days before the hearing. CCP §1005(b). See "Reply Papers," ch. 1-D, §9, p. 37.

§6. HEARING

If the court decides to have a hearing, it will be conducted in the same manner as civil hearings generally. *See* Civ. C. §3295(c). See "Hearings," ch. 1-H, p. 79.

§7. RULING

§7.1 Standard for granting motion. The court should grant the motion only if it finds that there is a substantial probability the plaintiff will prevail on its claim of malice, oppression, or fraud. Civ. C. §3295(c); ***Jabro v. Superior Ct.*** (4th Dist.2002) 95 Cal.App.4th 754, 758.

§7.2 Court's guidelines. The court must weigh the evidence submitted in favor of and in opposition to the motion. *E.g.*, ***Jabro v. Superior Ct.*** (4th Dist.2002) 95 Cal.App.4th 754, 758 (court erred when it granted motion without reviewing Ds' evidence and based solely on finding that P established prima facie case that he would prevail on his claim); *see* Weil, *Civil Procedure Before Trial*, ¶8:339.3 (D must be given opportunity to present opposing declarations).

§8. ORDER

§8.1 Form. The court's ruling on the motion must be recorded either in writing or by minute order. See "Record of Ruling," ch. 1-I, §4, p. 90.

§8.2 Effect of ruling.

1. No effect on merits. If the court grants the motion and enters an order permitting the discovery of financial information, the order cannot be (1) considered a determination on the merits of the claim or any defense

or (2) given in evidence or referred to at trial. Civ. C. §3295(c); *e.g.*, ***Hilton K. v. Greenbaum*** (2d Dist.2006) 144 Cal.App.4th 1406, 1413 (order allowing pretrial discovery of financial information based on substantial probability that other Ps in related case would prevail on punitive-damages claim against Ds did not prevent summary judgment dismissing suit because earlier ruling had no preclusive effect).

2. Protective order. If the court grants the motion and enters an order permitting the discovery of financial information, the defendant is presumptively entitled to a protective order limiting disclosure to the plaintiff's attorney or the attorney's representative. ***Richards v. Superior Ct.*** (2d Dist.1978) 86 Cal.App.3d 265, 272. See "Financial information," ch. 9-B, §2.2.3(3), p. 1027.

3. Application to preclude evidence. If the court grants the motion and enters an order permitting the discovery of financial information, the defendant should apply for an order precluding the admission of evidence of the defendant's financial condition at trial until the jury has returned a verdict (1) awarding actual damages and (2) finding that the defendant is guilty of malice, oppression, or fraud. *See* Civ. C. §3295(d); ***City of El Monte v. Superior Ct.*** (2d Dist.1994) 29 Cal.App.4th 272, 274-75.

§9. REVIEW

See "Review of Discovery Orders," ch. 7-A, §17, p. 777.

H. ELECTRONIC DISCOVERY

This subchapter deals with discovery issues that are unique to securing information from electronic sources. For a discussion of general discovery, see "Scope of Discovery," ch. 6-A, p. 603, and "Methods of Discovery," ch. 7, p. 733. Because the California Electronic Discovery Act (CEDA) is based on federal law, federal authorities are cited throughout. *See, e.g.*, ***Vasquez v. California Sch. of Culinary Arts, Inc.*** (2d Dist.2014) 230 Cal.App.4th 35, 42-43 (using federal case law to interpret CCP §1985.8). For a discussion of the federal electronic-discovery laws, see ***O'Connor's Federal Rules * Civil Trials*** (2015), "Electronic Discovery," ch. 6-C, p. 530.

§1. GENERAL

Although the CEDA became effective in June 2009, the California Discovery Act (CDA) has recognized electronic data as discoverable since the 1980s. Best, *California Discovery Practice Under the Electronic Discovery Act* (CEB Online Aug. 2009) 31 Cal. Litigation Rptr. 122, 123.

NOTE

For ease of reference, in this subchapter the term "discovering party" refers to the party who served either a demand to produce or a deposition subpoena, "responding party" refers to a party who received a demand to produce, and "responding person" refers to either a party who received a demand to produce or a nonparty who received a deposition subpoena.

§1.1 Purpose. Electronic discovery involves collecting, preparing, reviewing, and producing discoverable information that is stored electronically. *See Sedona Conference Glossary: E-Discovery & Digital Information Management (Fourth Edition)*, p. 15 (Sedona Conference Working Group Series, 2014), www.thesedonaconference.org/publications. The Code of Civil Procedure refers to this information as "electronically stored information" (ESI). CCP §2016.020(e). ESI is as discoverable as paper documents and tangible things. *See* Legis. Counsel's Dig., Assem. Bill No. 5, Evans, Civil Discovery: Electronic Discovery Act (2009-2010 Reg. Sess.). But unlike documents and tangible things, ESI is dynamic, which complicates its discovery. *See* Rosenthal, *A Few Thoughts on Electronic Discovery After December 1, 2006*, 116 Yale L.J. Pocket Part 167, 168 (2006).

§1.2 Primary authority. CCP §§1985.8, 2016.020, 2017.010, 2019.040, 2031.010-2031.060, 2031.210-2031.320; *see also* CRC 3.724(8) (electronic-discovery issues must be discussed during meet-and-confer conference and at first case-management conference).

§1.3 Secondary authority. The following secondary sources are cited as authority in this subchapter:

- Best et al., *AB 5's Amendments to the California Discovery Act for Electronically Stored Information*, State Bar of California CLE (2009) (referred to as Best, *AB 5's Amendments*).

- *California Civil Discovery Practice* (CEB Online ed. 2014) (referred to as *CEB Discovery Practice*).

- Diamond, *Six Critical Steps to Managing Electronically Stored Information Under FRCP* (2008), The Metropolitan Corporate Counsel, www.metrocorpcounsel.com (referred to as Diamond, *Six Critical Steps*).

- Fuchs & Wolinsky, *Understand Predictive Coding Options*, Tex. Lawyer: In-House Tex., 8 (9-3-12).

- Hedges, *Discovery of Electronically Stored Information: Surveying the Legal Landscape* (BNA Books, 2007) (referred to as Hedges, *Discovery of Electronically Stored Information*).

- Hickey & Smith, *ESI: California*, Los Angeles Daily Journal, Aug. 3, 2009 (referred to as Hickey & Smith, *ESI: California*).

- *Manual for Complex Litigation, Fourth* (2004), Federal Judicial Center, www.fjc.gov (referred to as *Manual for Complex Litigation*).

- *Navigating the Vendor Proposal Process: Best Practices for the Selection of Electronic Discovery Vendors (Second Edition)* (Sedona Conference Working Group Series, 2007), www.thesedonaconference.org/publications (referred to as *Navigating Vendor Proposal Process*).

- Peck, *Search, Forward: Will Manual Document Review & Keyword Searches Be Replaced by Computer-Assisted Coding?*, Law Technology News (2011), www.law.com/jsp/lawtechnologynews/index.jsp (referred to as Peck, *Search, Forward*).

- Rosenthal, *A Few Thoughts on Electronic Discovery After December 1, 2006*, 116 Yale L.J. Pocket Part 167 (2006) (referred to as Rosenthal, *A Few Thoughts on Electronic Discovery*).

- Rothstein et al., *Managing Discovery of Electronic Information: A Pocket Guide for Judges*, Second Edition (2012), Federal Judicial Center, www.fjc.gov (referred to as Rothstein, *Managing Discovery of Electronic Information*).

- Scheindlin, *The Ten Most FAQ's in the Post-December 1, 2006 World of E-Discovery* (2006), In Camera (Fed. Judges Ass'n), www.fjc.gov/public/pdf.nsf/lookup/FAQEDisc.pdf/$file/FAQEDisc.pdf (referred to as Scheindlin, *Ten Most FAQ's*).

- *Sedona Conference Best Practices Commentary on the Use of Search & Information Retrieval Methods in E-Discovery* (Sedona Conference Working Group Series, 2013), www.thesedonaconference.org/publications (referred to as *Sedona Conference Commentary on the Use of Search & Information Retrieval Methods*).

- *Sedona Conference Commentary on Achieving Quality in the E-Discovery Process* (Sedona Conference Working Group Series, 2013), www.thesedonaconference.org/publications (referred to as *Sedona Conference on Achieving Quality in E-Discovery*).

- *Sedona Conference Glossary: E-Discovery & Digital Information Management (Fourth Edition)* (Sedona Conference Working Group Series, 2014), www.thesedonaconference.org/publications (referred to as *Sedona Conference Glossary*).

- *Sedona Principles, Second Edition: Best Practices Recommendations & Principles for Addressing Electronic Document Production* (Sedona Conference Working Group Series, 2007), www.thesedonaconference.org/publications (referred to as *Sedona Principles, Second Edition*).

- Shah, *Use of "Predictive Coding" to Limit Cost & Improve Efficiency in Healthcare E-discovery: The Light is Green, But Proceed With Caution*, AHLA (2012), www.ebglaw.com/content/uploads/2014/06/48548_Shah-AHLA-Use-of-Predictive-Coding-1-2012.pdf (referred to as Shah, *Use of "Predictive Coding" to Limit Cost & Improve Efficiency*).

- *Summary of the Report of the Judicial Conference Committee on Rules of Practice & Procedure*, Agenda E-18, Rules App. C-42 (Sept. 2005), www.uscourts.gov/uscourts/RulesAndPolicies/rules/Reports/ST09-2005.pdf (referred to as *Summary of the Report of the Judicial Conference*).

- Weil & Brown, *California Practice Guide: Civil Procedure Before Trial* (CD-ROM ed. 2014) (referred to as Weil, *Civil Procedure Before Trial*).

§2. PREPARING FOR ELECTRONIC DISCOVERY

A party should prepare for electronic discovery before litigation begins. *See* Rothstein, *Managing Discovery of Electronic Information*, at 5 (court should encourage parties to identify potential problems with discovery of ESI in earliest stages of litigation); *Sedona Principles, Second Edition*, Principle 1, at 11 (organizations must properly preserve ESI that can reasonably be anticipated to be relevant to litigation). In preparing for electronic discovery, a party should have both a general understanding of electronic discovery and a specific understanding of its own ESI systems. *See* Hedges, *Discovery of Electronically Stored Information*, at 146.

§2.1 What is electronic discovery? Electronic discovery refers to the discovery of ESI. *Sedona Principles, Second Edition*, at 1. ESI is information stored in an electronic medium relating to technology having electrical, digital, magnetic, wireless, optical, electromagnetic, or similar capabilities. *See* CCP §2016.020(d), (e); *Sedona Principles, Second Edition*, at 1. ESI includes the following: (1) e-mail, (2) web pages, (3) audio, video, and word-processing files, (4) images, (5) computer databases, (6) servers, (7) desktops, (8) laptops, (9) cell phones, (10) hard drives and flash drives, (11) personal digital assistants, and (12) MP3 players. *Sedona Principles, Second Edition*, at 1.

§2.2 Definitions. To understand electronic discovery, a party must become familiar with the terminology. The definitions provided here are important for a basic understanding of electronic discovery, but the list is not intended to be comprehensive. For more electronic-discovery terms, see the *Sedona Conference Glossary*.

PRACTICE TIP

Understanding the terminology of electronic discovery will help in drafting precise discovery requests for ESI, dealing with electronic-discovery vendors, and communicating effectively with clients, opposing parties, and the court. See Hedges, Discovery of Electronically Stored Information, at 146.

---

1. Active data. "Active data" is data that is currently being created, received, or processed or that needs to be accessed frequently and quickly. Rothstein, *Managing Discovery of Electronic Information*, at 14. Active data is usually immediately accessible and does not have to be restored or reconstructed. *Sedona Conference Glossary*, at 1.

2. Archival data. "Archival data" is data maintained for long-term storage and record-keeping purposes. *Sedona Conference Glossary*, at 2. Archival data is not immediately accessible. *Id.*

3. Backup data. "Backup data" is a copy of active electronic data that serves as a source for the recovery of the data in the event of a system problem or other computer disaster. *Sedona Conference Glossary*, at 3; *see Manual for Complex Litigation*, §11.446 (backup data is created and maintained for short-term disaster recovery, not for retrieving particular files, data, or programs). Backup data is often stored on magnetic backup tapes or removable disk drives. Rothstein, *Managing Discovery of Electronic Information*, at 35; *see Sedona Conference Glossary*, at 3 ("backup tape"). Because backup tapes must be restored, recovery of information stored on them can involve substantial expense. *See* Rothstein, *Managing Discovery of Electronic Information*, at 4.

4. Backup-tape recycling. "Backup-tape recycling" (also called "backup-tape rotation") is the process by which backup tapes are overwritten with new data, usually on a fixed schedule. *Sedona Conference Glossary*, at 3.

5. Deleted data. "Deleted data" is data that once existed on a computer as active data but has been deleted by the computer system or a user. Rothstein, *Managing Discovery of Electronic Information*, at 36; *Sedona Conference Glossary*, at 11. Generally, deletion does not actually erase the data from the computer; rather, deletion makes the data inaccessible with normal software but leaves it on the computer. *See* Rothstein, *Managing Discovery of Electronic Information*, at 4; *Sedona Conference Glossary*, at 12. Deleted data can remain on the computer until it is overwritten or "wiped." *Sedona Conference Glossary*, at 11. Recovery of deleted data is difficult, expensive, and sometimes incomplete.

6. Forensic copy. A "forensic copy" (also known as a forensic duplicate, forensic image, mirror image, or bit-by-bit duplicate) is an exact copy of the entire physical hard storage media. *See Sedona Conference Glossary*, at 19. The imaging of a hard drive is a first step in attempting to retrieve discoverable data that has reportedly been removed or destroyed. ***Ellis v. Toshiba Am. Info. Sys.*** (2d Dist.2013) 218 Cal.App.4th 853, 879 n.18.

7. Form of production. "Form of production" is the manner in which requested ESI is produced. *See* Rothstein, *Managing Discovery of Electronic Information*, at 38. The term refers to both the file format (e.g., native format vs. static format) and the media used (i.e., paper vs. electronic). *Sedona Conference Glossary*, at 19. ESI can be produced in a variety of forms. Rothstein, *Managing Discovery of Electronic Information*, at 22. The form of production determines whether the information can be electronically searched (e.g., searchable PDF files), whether relevant information is obscured (e.g., Word document with metadata deleted or wiped), and whether confidential or privileged information can be disclosed (e.g., Word document with all metadata intact). *See id.* See "Specify form for ESI," §8.1.2, p. 887.

8. Legacy data. "Legacy data" is data that was created and is stored with software or hardware that has become obsolete. Rothstein, *Managing Discovery of Electronic Information*, at 38. Recovery of legacy data can involve substantial expense. *Id.*

9. Litigation hold. A "litigation hold" (also known as a legal hold, preservation notice, freeze notice, or hold notice) is a notice by an attorney to a client that certain information should be preserved as evidence for pending or reasonably anticipated litigation and that the normal disposition or processing of records should be suspended. *See CEB Discovery Practice*, §4.11 (uses term "legal hold"); *Sedona Conference Glossary*, at 26 (same); *cf.* ***Zubulake v. UBS Warburg LLC*** (S.D.N.Y.2003) 220 F.R.D. 212, 218 (uses term "litigation hold"). The term also refers to the notice a client must give to its employees to preserve evidence. See "Preserve ESI," §3.2.1, p. 880.

10. Metadata. "Metadata," commonly described as "data about data," is information about a particular data set that describes how, when, and by whom ESI was collected, created, accessed, or modified and how it was formatted. *See Sedona Principles, Second Edition*, at 3; *see also* Scheindlin, *Ten Most FAQ's*, at question 8 (metadata is electronic equivalent of DNA, ballistics, and fingerprint evidence). Metadata is generated automatically and is linked to the source document. *See Sedona Principles, Second Edition*, at 3. Some metadata can easily be seen by the computer user (e.g., file name, dates, size); other metadata is hidden or embedded and is unavailable to a user who is not technically adept. *See* Rothstein, *Managing Discovery of Electronic Information*, at 38-39. Metadata includes all the contextual, processing, and usage information needed to identify and certify the scope, authenticity, and integrity of active or archival electronic information or records. *See Sedona Principles, Second Edition*, at 3-4. Metadata can be important to the facts of the case or to the usability and searchability of ESI. *Id.* at 60. Examples of metadata include a file's name, a file's author, and file dates (e.g., creation date, date of last data modification, date of last data access, date of last metadata modification). *See* ***Crews v. Willows Unified Sch. Dist.*** (3d Dist.2013) 217 Cal.App.4th 1368, 1372 n.2; *Sedona Principles, Second Edition*, at 3-4. There are various types of metadata, including embedded and file-system metadata. *See Sedona Principles, Second Edition*, at 60.

(1) Embedded metadata. "Embedded metadata" (also known as application metadata) is created as a function of the application software used to create a document or file. *See Sedona Principles, Second Edition*, at 60. Embedded metadata is embedded in the file it describes and moves with the file when the file is copied or moved. *Id.* This type of metadata instructs the computer how to display the document (e.g., fonts, spacing, size) and reflects modifications such as prior edits or editorial comments. *Id.*; *see* Rothstein, *Managing Discovery of Electronic Information*, at 37.

(2) File-system metadata. "File-system metadata" (also called "system-generated metadata") includes information about the name, size, location, and usage of an electronic file. *See Sedona Conference Glossary*, at 44; *Sedona Principles, Second Edition*, at 4, 60. File-system metadata is stored apart from the ESI; it is not embedded in the file. *Sedona Principles, Second Edition*, at 60.

PRACTICE TIP

Although metadata can be used to authenticate a disputed document or to establish facts material to a dispute (e.g., when a file was accessed in a suit involving theft of trade secrets), in most cases it will have no material evidentiary value. Sedona Principles, Second Edition, at 4. There is also the real danger that information recorded by the computer as application metadata may be inaccurate. Id. For example, when a new employee uses a word-processing program to create a memorandum by using a template created by a former employee, the metadata for the new memorandum may incorrectly identify the former employee as the author. Id. However, the proper use of metadata in litigation may be able to provide substantial benefit by facilitating more effective and efficient searching and retrieval of ESI. Id.

11. Mirror imaging. "Mirror imaging" (also known as forensic duplication, forensic imaging, or bit-by-bit duplication) is the creation of an exact copy of the entire physical hard drive of a computer system. *See Sedona Conference Glossary*, at 29.

12. Native format. "Native format" is the form in which ESI is normally kept (e.g., Microsoft Excel produces native files with a .xls extension; Microsoft Word produces native files with a .doc extension). *See Sedona Conference Glossary*, at 30. Native data may include additional data or features. For example, an Excel spreadsheet may contain mathematical formulas, but an image of the spreadsheet may show only the final numbers resulting from the formulas.

13. Static format. "Static format" is ESI that has been captured as an image capable of being viewed on a standard computer system. *See Sedona Conference Glossary*, at 30 ("native format" entry). In a static format (e.g., PDF, TIFF), the ESI cannot be manipulated and metadata cannot be viewed. *Id.* PDF and TIFF files are essentially photographs of electronic documents. Rothstein, *Managing Discovery of Electronic Information*, at 22.

(1) PDF. "Portable document format" (PDF) is a file format that captures formatting information (e.g., margins, spacing, fonts) from the original software program so that the information can be viewed and printed as it was intended to be seen, regardless of whether the viewer has access to the software used to create it. Rothstein, *Managing Discovery of Electronic Discovery*, at 39; *see* ***Crews***, 217 Cal.App.4th at 1372 n.2; *Sedona Conference Glossary*, at 35.

(2) TIFF. "Tagged image file format" (TIFF) is a file format for storing images, including photographs. *See Sedona Conference Glossary*, at 46. The images can be black-and-white, grayscale, or color. *Id.*

§2.3 ESI vs. physical evidence. ESI differs from conventional paper documents and tangible things in several ways.

1. Volume. The volume of ESI is almost always much greater than the amount of paper documents. Rothstein, *Managing Discovery of Electronic Information*, at 2; *Sedona Principles, Second Edition*, at 2.

2. Location. ESI can be located in multiple places—for example, a draft of an electronic document can be located on the drafter's, reviewer's, and recipient's hard drives, on the company's and other network servers, on a laptop or home computer, and on backup tapes. Rothstein, *Managing Discovery of Electronic Information*, at 2; *see Sedona Principles, Second Edition*, at 2 & n.5. See "Backup data," §2.2.3, p. 875. By comparison, paper documents and tangible things are usually located in one place.

3. Format. ESI, unlike words on paper, may be incomprehensible when separated from the system and software that created it. Rosenthal, *A Few Thoughts on Electronic Discovery*, at 170-71; Rothstein, *Managing Discovery of Electronic Information*, at 3; *Sedona Principles, Second Edition*, at 4. The way ESI is created, maintained, stored, and accessed introduces new obstacles for parties seeking its discovery. *See* Rosenthal, *A Few Thoughts on Electronic Discovery*, at 171.

4. Form of production. The responding person must produce ESI in the form agreed to by the parties, ordered by the court, or specified by the discovering party, or if no form is agreed to or specified, in a form in which ESI is ordinarily maintained or that is reasonably usable. *See* CCP §§1985.8(d)(1), 2020.220(d)(1), 2031.280(d); *see also Sedona Principles, Second Edition*, at 66 (party should not have to produce same information electronically and in hard copies). See "Specify form for ESI," §8.1.2, p. 887. By comparison, conventional document discovery requires documents to be produced as they are kept in the ordinary course of business or organized and labeled to correspond to categories in the request. CCP §2031.280(a).

5. Indestructibility. The deletion of ESI does not necessarily get rid of the information, unlike the shredding of paper documents. Rothstein, *Managing Discovery of Electronic Information*, at 4.

6. Dimensions. ESI presents new dimensions of discovery because some types of ESI have no counterparts in documents or tangible things. *See* Rothstein, *Managing Discovery of Electronic Information*, at 3. For example, metadata is part of ESI, but it is not readily apparent on a computer screen or a printout. *See Sedona Principles, Second Edition*, at 3. See "Metadata," §2.2.10, p. 876.

7. Dynamic nature. ESI has a dynamic, mutable nature. *See* Rothstein, *Managing Discovery of Electronic Information*, at 3; *Sedona Principles, Second Edition*, at 3. A distinctive feature of ESI is that normal computer use may include the routine modification, overwriting, and deletion of documents. *See* Rosenthal, *A Few Thoughts on Electronic Discovery*, at 174. As a result, normal computer use creates a risk that a party may lose potentially discoverable information without any culpable conduct. See "Safe Harbor from Sanctions for Lost, Damaged, Altered, or Overwritten ESI," §11, p. 892.

8. Cost of production. While there is some overlap, different rules apply to the discovery of ESI and the discovery of paper documents when determining who must pay the cost of production.

(1) Responding party. A party who produces paper documents or ESI in response to a demand to produce bears the cost of production. *Sedona Principles, Second Edition*, at 67; *see* CCP §2031.060(b).

(2) Responding nonparty.

(a) Production of paper documents. A nonparty who produces paper documents in response to a subpoena must be reimbursed by the subpoenaing party for the cost of production. *See* Evid. C. §1563(b) (subpoenaing party must pay all reasonable costs incurred by nonparty for production of business records). See "Production costs for copies," ch. 8-A, §10.3.2(2), p. 953.

(b) Production of ESI. The CEDA did not adopt the cost-shifting policy from Evid. C. §1563 for the production of ESI. Instead, without specifically addressing who must bear the costs of producing ESI, CCP §1985.8 contains two provisions that assume the costs are borne by the nonparty. First, §1985.8 requires the subpoenaing party to take reasonable steps to avoid imposing an undue burden or expense on the nonparty. *See* CCP §1985.8(k). Second, when the court compels a nonparty to comply with a subpoena for ESI, the court must protect the nonparty from undue burden or expense. *Id.* §1985.8(*l*).

§3. PRESERVING ESI

In preparing a client for electronic discovery, the attorney should take steps to ensure that relevant evidence, including not only ESI but also documents and tangible things, is preserved.

§3.1 Before duty to preserve arises.

Before a duty to preserve ESI arises, the attorney should do the following:

1. Understand ESI. The attorney must acquire a general understanding of electronic discovery to communicate effectively with clients, vendors, other counsel, and the courts. Hedges, *Discovery of Electronically Stored Information*, at 146; *see Sedona Principles, Second Edition*, at 17. See "Definitions," §2.2, p. 875.

2. Understand client's ESI systems. The attorney must become familiar with its client's ESI systems so that once the duty to preserve ESI does arise, the attorney can work with the client to avoid spoliation. Hedges, *Discovery of Electronically Stored Information*, at 146; *see CEB Discovery Practice*, §4.14 (attorney should gain clear understanding of who creates or generates client's data, kind of data created or generated, purpose of data, how data is used, and where data is stored).

3. Understand when duty to preserve arises. The attorney must understand the duties that parties and nonparties have to preserve ESI and when those duties arise.

(1) Party's duty to preserve. A party or potential party has a duty to preserve ESI for use in litigation if (1) the party was served with a demand to produce the ESI, (2) the party was ordered by the court to preserve the ESI, (3) a statute requires the party to preserve the ESI, (4) the party stipulated that the ESI would be preserved, or (5) the party was served with a notice to preserve the ESI. *See, e.g.*, ***Dodge, Warren & Peters Ins. Servs. v. Riley*** (4th Dist.2003) 105 Cal.App.4th 1414, 1417 (court upheld injunction requiring Ds to preserve ESI). Some commentators contend that a party's duty to preserve evidence arises on receipt of the complaint and a potential party's duty arises on notice of contemplation of suit. See "Preserving Evidence for Production," ch. 7-E, §4, p. 847.

(2) Nonparty's duty to preserve. A nonparty has a duty to preserve ESI for use in litigation only when (1) the nonparty was served with a subpoena for the ESI, (2) the nonparty was ordered by the court to preserve the ESI, (3) a statute requires the nonparty to preserve the ESI, or (4) the nonparty has a special relationship with the party that requires it to preserve the ESI. *Cf.* ***Williams v. State*** (1983) 34 Cal.3d 18, 27-28 (duty to preserve physical evidence; special relationship arises when P detrimentally relies on nonparty's conduct or statements that induce false sense of security and thus worsen P's position). See "Duty imposed by law or contract," ch. 7-E, §4.1.1, p. 847.

4. Advise client about retention policy. Attorneys should advise their clients to formulate and implement a retention policy for ESI. *See* Best, *AB 5's Amendments*, at 12; Hickey & Smith, *ESI: California*, at 7. This ensures that, in the regular course of business, relevant ESI is retained and outdated ESI is purged. *See* Best, *AB 5's Amendments*, at 10. When designing a retention policy, a company should take into account (1) business needs, (2) information-technology needs, and (3) potential litigation needs. *See id.* After setting the retention policy, the company should follow it consistently. Although all forms of a client's ESI should be addressed in the retention policy, the policies for e-mail archives and backup data are critical. *See id.* at 12.

(1) E-mail archives. Discovery of e-mail causes many electronic-discovery disputes. Corporate entities should purge their central archive periodically to avoid having an endless source of ESI. *See* Best, *AB 5's Amendments*, at 12. Corporate policies should address the practice and ability of employees to save local copies of e-mail to their own computers. Purging a central repository does little good if copies of the same documents are kept on other computers.

(2) Backup data. Backup data can be the most expensive part of an electronic-discovery dispute, especially if the backup data is legacy data. See "Backup data," §2.2.3, p. 875; "Legacy data," §2.2.8, p. 876. Backup tapes (used to store backup data) are generally used solely for disaster recovery and not in the regular course of business. *Manual for Complex Litigation*, §11.442; *see* Rothstein, *Managing Discovery of Electronic Information*, at 14-15. If backup tapes are frequently accessed to restore data, this will negate any argument that the tapes are not reasonably accessible. *See Manual for Complex Litigation*, §11.442.

§3.2 After duty to preserve arises. Once the duty to preserve ESI arises, the attorney must take steps to ensure that the necessary ESI is preserved, whether it belongs to the client, the other parties, or nonparties. *See Sedona Conference on Achieving Quality in E-Discovery*, at 14-16. See "Understand when duty to preserve arises," §3.1.3, this page.

PRACTICE TIP

In three influential opinions, Judge Scheindlin of the Federal District Court for the Southern District of New York provides a treatise on the duties involved in preserving ESI. In ***Zubulake v. UBS Warburg LLC*** *(S.D.N.Y.2003) 220 F.R.D. 212, 216 (****Zubulake IV****), the Court discusses the client's duty to preserve ESI. In* ***Zubulake v. UBS Warburg LLC*** *(S.D.N.Y.2004) 229 F.R.D. 422, 424 (****Zubulake V****), the Court discusses the attorney's duty regarding a litigation hold. In* ***Pension Cmte. of the Univ. of Montreal Pension Plan v. Banc of Am. Secs., LLC*** *(S.D.N.Y.2010) 685 F.Supp.2d 456, 496, the Court discusses the sanctions available when parties do not implement a litigation hold. Until a California court specifically addresses the duties of parties and attorneys to preserve ESI, California attorneys should follow Judge Scheindlin's guidelines described below.*

1. Preserve ESI.

(1) Preserving client's ESI.

(a) Litigation hold. The attorney should inform the client in writing to issue a litigation hold for ESI. *See* Hickey & Smith, *ESI: California*, at 7; *see, e.g.*, ***Pension Cmte.***, 685 F.Supp.2d at 473 (attorney's e-mails, telephone calls, and memos to clients did not specifically instruct clients not to destroy records); *see also CEB Discovery Practice*, §4.11 (attorney should make sure that hold letter is also sent to client's information-technology department). See "Litigation hold," §2.2.9, p. 876.

[1] Client issues written hold. The client should issue a written litigation hold to its employees. *See* ***Pension Cmte.***, 685 F.Supp.2d at 488-89; *see also CEB Discovery Practice*, §4.38 (litigation-hold form letter). An effective litigation hold does the following:

[a] Identify scope & procedures. The litigation hold must include a description of the scope of the hold (e.g., what ESI, whose ESI, trigger date for ESI retention, forms in which to retain ESI) and the procedures necessary to implement the hold. *See Sedona Principles, Second Edition*, at 32; *see also* ***Zubulake IV***, 220 F.R.D. at 217-18 (discussing scope of and procedures for retention of ESI).

[b] Suspend routine destruction. The litigation hold should instruct the client's information-technology department to immediately suspend the backup programs and other systems that regularly delete or alter ESI that might be relevant to a claim or defense in the case. *See* ***Zubulake IV***, 220 F.R.D. at 218; *see also* ***Doe v. Norwalk Cmty. Coll.*** (D.Conn.2007) 248 F.R.D. 372, 378 (party must take steps to prevent its system from routinely destroying information). The hold should also instruct the employees not to destroy e-mails and other records on their individual computers that might be relevant to a claim or defense. *See* Scheindlin, *Ten Most FAQ's*, at question 3; *see, e.g.*, ***Zubulake IV***, 220 F.R.D. at 221 (D-employer did not notify P-employee's supervisor to preserve backup tapes containing e-mail). The duty to preserve ESI transcends any internal policy or schedule for deleting or destroying ESI. *Sedona Principles, Second Edition*, at 14. If records are destroyed after the duty to preserve arises, it is not a defense that an individual employee did not know about the need to preserve ESI. *CEB Discovery Practice*, §4.9.

[c] Identify key persons. The litigation hold should identify key persons and ensure that their e-mails and other records are preserved. *See* ***Pension Cmte.***, 685 F.Supp.2d at 471; ***Zubulake V***, 229 F.R.D. at 432.

[d] Preserve backup tapes. The litigation hold should instruct the client's information-technology department to preserve backup tapes when they are the sole source of relevant information or when they relate to key persons. *See* ***Pension Cmte.***, 685 F.Supp.2d at 471; ***Zubulake V***, 229 F.R.D. at 432; ***Zubulake IV***, 220 F.R.D. at 218. See "Backup data," §2.2.3, p. 875. As an alternative to suspending backup and other tape-recycling programs, the client can make a forensic copy of its computer system when the duty to preserve arises. *See* ***Zubulake IV***, 220 F.R.D. at 218. See "Forensic copy," §2.2.6, p. 876.

[e] Preserve records of former employees. The litigation hold should instruct the client's information-technology department to preserve the records of former employees in the client's possession that might be relevant to a claim or defense in the case. *See* ***Pension Cmte.***, 685 F.Supp.2d at 471.

[2] Attorney monitors litigation hold. Once a litigation hold is issued, some courts have held that the attorney has a duty to oversee the client's compliance with the hold and monitor the client's efforts to retain and produce relevant documents. *See* ***Zubulake V***, 229 F.R.D. at 432; *CEB Discovery Practice*, §4.12.

NOTE

Although a litigation-hold letter may be protected by the attorney-client privilege or as work product, an attorney may have to disclose the letter as evidence of compliance with a litigation hold. See CEB Discovery Practice, §4.12.

(b) Litigation hold for outsourced ESI storage. The attorney should instruct the client to notify its outside provider of electronic storage to institute a system to protect ESI that might be relevant to a claim or defense in the case. *See* Best, *AB 5's Amendments*, at 16.

(2) Preserving ESI belonging to others. The attorney should make sure that relevant ESI in the possession of the opposing party or a nonparty is preserved. This can involve sending a demand to preserve evidence, entering into a stipulation, or seeking a court order. *See* Weil, *Civil Procedure Before Trial*, ¶1:569 (demand to preserve evidence), ¶8:1801 (freeze order by court). See "How to ensure client preserves evidence," ch. 7-E, §4.2, p. 848.

2. Consider expense of electronic discovery. Before the actual litigation begins, the attorney should have the client consider the expense of electronic discovery (including the expense of preserving, retrieving, translating, reviewing, and producing ESI), the nature of the litigation, and the amount in controversy to determine whether the client should consider settling the matter. *See* Rothstein, *Managing Discovery of Electronic Information*, at 17-18; *Sedona Principles, Second Edition*, at 17. See "Cost of production," §2.3.8, p. 878.

3. Consider electronic-discovery vendor. Once it is certain that litigation involving the production of ESI is inevitable, the attorney should evaluate the need for an electronic-discovery vendor. *See Sedona Principles, Second Edition*, at 40; *see also* Hedges, *Discovery of Electronically Stored Information*, at 143 (party should hire expert when electronic-discovery issues become complicated). An electronic-discovery vendor will have experience in sampling and testing electronic information systems and knowledge about the accuracy and sufficiency of different search and retrieval methods. *See Sedona Principles, Second Edition*, at 40. For a discussion of finding an appropriate electronic-discovery vendor, see *Navigating Vendor Proposal Process*.

§4. SCOPE OF ELECTRONIC DISCOVERY

The scope of electronic discovery is largely the same as that for paper documents and tangible things—a party can discover any nonprivileged matter that is relevant to any party's claim or defense and that is either admissible in evidence or reasonably calculated to lead to admissible evidence. *See* CCP §2017.010; ***Sinaiko Healthcare Consulting, Inc. v. Pacific Healthcare Consultants*** (2d Dist.2007) 148 Cal.App.4th 390, 402; Rothstein, *Managing Discovery of Electronic Discovery*, at 13-14. See "Scope of Discovery," ch. 6-A, p. 603. However, the CEDA imposes certain limits that apply only to electronic discovery.

§4.1 ESI is not reasonably accessible. The CEDA prohibits discovery of ESI from sources that are not reasonably accessible because of undue burden or expense unless the discovering party can show good cause. *See* CCP §1985.8(e), (f) (subpoena), §2020.220(e), (f) (deposition subpoena), §2025.420(c), (d) (protective order), §2025.450(c), (d) (motion to compel party), §2025.480(d), (e) (motion to compel nonparty), §2031.060(c), (d) (motion for protective order), §2031.310(d), (e) (motion to compel party or affected person); *see also id.* §2025.460(d) (deponent can object on ground that ESI is sought from source that is not reasonably accessible), §2031.210(d) (party can object to inspection demand on ground that ESI is sought from source that is not reasonably accessible). One

corollary to this rule is that the CEDA allows discovery of ESI from sources that are reasonably accessible. *See Sedona Principles, Second Edition*, at 18. Reasonable accessibility is best understood in terms of whether the ESI is kept in an accessible or inaccessible form, which is a distinction that corresponds to the expense of the production. *See* Rothstein, *Managing Discovery of Electronic Information*, at 14-15; *Sedona Principles, Second Edition*, at 18; *cf.* ***Best Buy Stores v. Developers Diversified Rlty. Corp.*** (D.Minn.2007) 247 F.R.D. 567, 569-70; ***Zubulake v. UBS Warburg LLC*** (S.D.N.Y.2003) 217 F.R.D. 309, 318.

1. Examples of reasonably accessible sources. The primary source of reasonably accessible ESI is active data. *Sedona Principles, Second Edition*, Principle 8, at 45. Some examples of sources that are reasonably accessible include files available on or from a computer user's desktop or on a company's network in the ordinary course of operation. *Id.* at 18.

2. Examples of not reasonably accessible sources. Some examples of sources that are not reasonably accessible include the following:

(1) Backup tapes. Backup tapes intended for disaster-recovery purposes that are not indexed, organized, or susceptible to electronic searching. *Sedona Principles, Second Edition*, at 18; *Summary of the Report of the Judicial Conference*, Agenda E-18, at Rules App. C-42. See "Backup data," §2.2.3, p. 875.

(2) Legacy data. Legacy data left over from obsolete systems that cannot be retrieved on the successor systems. *Sedona Principles, Second Edition*, at 18; *Summary of the Report of the Judicial Conference*, Agenda E-18, at Rules App. C-42. See "Legacy data," §2.2.8, p. 876.

(3) Deleted data. Deleted data in fragmented form that requires some type of forensics to restore and retrieve it. *Sedona Principles, Second Edition*, at 18; *Summary of the Report of the Judicial Conference*, Agenda E-18, at Rules App. C-42. See "Deleted data," §2.2.5, p. 876.

(4) Certain databases. Databases that were designed to create information in certain ways and that cannot readily create different kinds of information. *Summary of the Report of the Judicial Conference*, Agenda E-18, at Rules App. C-42.

§4.2 Other limiting factors. The CEDA permits a court to limit the frequency or extent of electronic discovery, even from a source that is reasonably accessible, if any of the following conditions exist:

1. Other sources. The discovering party can obtain the information from some other source that is more convenient, less burdensome, or less expensive. CCP §§1985.8(i)(1), 2031.060(f)(1), 2031.310(g)(1); *cf.* ***Wells Fargo Bank v. LaSalle Bank*** (S.D.Ohio 2009) No. 3:07-cv-449 (slip op.; 7-24-09) (court found that bank's practice of making hard copies made it unlikely that more information would be obtained from ESI).

2. Cumulative or duplicative. The discovering party seeks information that is unreasonably cumulative or duplicative. CCP §§1985.8(i)(2), 2031.060(f)(2), 2031.310(g)(2).

3. Available earlier. The discovering party has already had ample opportunity to obtain the information through discovery. CCP §§1985.8(i)(3), 2031.060(f)(3), 2031.310(g)(3).

4. Burden outweighs benefit. The likely burden or expense of the proposed discovery outweighs the likely benefit, taking into account the amount in controversy, the resources of the parties, the importance of the issues in the litigation, and the importance of the discovery in resolving the issues. CCP §§1985.8(i)(4), 2031.060(f)(4), 2031.310(g)(4).

§5. ESI SEARCH TECHNIQUES

The parties should consider how to conduct searches to locate discoverable ESI within sources identified as likely to contain relevant material (e.g., an e-mail database). Aside from a traditional, manual review of ESI, the parties can consider the following search techniques.

PRACTICE TIP

If the parties intend to use a new or complex search technique, they should consider having a representative from the electronic-discovery vendor that will perform the searches attend any conferences or hearings that address the search technique. Cf. ***Da Silva Moore v. Publicis Groupe*** *(S.D.N.Y.2012) 287 F.R.D. 182, 193 (court stated that it was "very helpful" when vendors were present and spoke at hearing about ESI protocol involving predictive coding), adopted (S.D.N.Y.2012) No. 11 Civ. 1279 (ALC) (AJP) (slip op.; 4-26-12).*

§5.1 Keyword searches. The parties can consider keyword searches to locate relevant ESI. *Cf.* ***William A. Gross Constr. Assocs. v. American Mfrs. Mut. Ins.*** (S.D.N.Y.2009) 256 F.R.D. 134, 135; ***Victor Stanley, Inc. v. Creative Pipe, Inc.*** (D.Md.2008) 250 F.R.D. 251, 256-57. A keyword search involves a specified word or combination of words. *See Sedona Conference Glossary*, at 25 ("keyword"). Keyword searches are currently the most common search technique used to cull an entire set of ESI. *Sedona Conference Commentary on the Use of Search & Information Retrieval Methods*, at 15; *cf.* ***Da Silva Moore v. Publicis Groupe*** (S.D.N.Y.2012) 287 F.R.D. 182, 190, *adopted* (S.D.N.Y.2012) No. 11 Civ. 1279 (ALC) (AJP) (slip op.; 4-26-12).

1. Process. The process of using keyword searches usually includes the following steps: (1) attorneys develop a list of keywords, (2) the list of keywords is applied to all the ESI, and (3) the parties manually review only the ESI that contains the keywords. *Cf.* ***Da Silva Moore***, 287 F.R.D. at 190-91. Especially in cases involving a high volume of ESI, keyword searches may be necessary to narrow the amount of ESI because traditional manual review of all the ESI is virtually impossible. *See Sedona Conference Commentary on the Use of Search & Information Retrieval Methods*, at 15; *cf.* ***Da Silva Moore***, 287 F.R.D. at 190. To improve the effectiveness of keyword searches, the parties can consider seeking expert assistance to develop the list of keywords. *Cf.* ***Victor Stanley***, 250 F.R.D. at 259-60; ***Equity Analytics, LLC v. Lundin*** (D.D.C.2008) 248 F.R.D. 331, 333. To enhance keyword searches, the parties can use more advanced search techniques such as Boolean connectors, elimination of duplicate documents, grouping of "near duplicates," and threading e-mail chains. Peck, *Search, Forward*.

2. Limitations. Courts have become increasingly critical of keyword searches. *See Sedona Conference Commentary on the Use of Search & Information Retrieval Methods*, at 16; *cf.* ***Victor Stanley***, 250 F.R.D. at 260-62; ***Equity Analytics***, 248 F.R.D. at 333. Keyword searches are limited because the people who originally created the ESI may describe the same concept using different words, may misspell words, or may use abbreviations for certain terms. *See Sedona Conference Commentary on the Use of Search & Information Retrieval Methods*, at 16-17; Peck, *Search, Forward*. Without cooperation from all the parties, the attorneys who develop the list of keywords are essentially guessing what words will produce relevant information; thus, the list of keywords is often overinclusive, resulting in a high return of irrelevant ESI. *See* Peck, *Search, Forward*; *cf.* ***Da Silva Moore***, 287 F.R.D. at 190-91.

§5.2 Predictive coding. The parties can consider predictive coding to locate relevant ESI. *Cf.* ***Da Silva Moore v. Publicis Groupe*** (S.D.N.Y.2012) 287 F.R.D. 182, 191-92, *adopted* (S.D.N.Y.2012) No. 11 Civ. 1279 (ALC) (AJP) (slip op.; 4-26-12). Predictive coding, also referred to as computer-assisted review, is an emerging ESI search tool that requires a person (usually a senior attorney or team of attorneys) to review a small amount of ESI to "train" the predictive-coding software to identify relevant ESI; the software then applies what it learns from the human review to predict the relevance of the remaining ESI. *Sedona Conference Commentary on the Use of Search & Information Retrieval Methods*, at 26; Fuchs & Wolinsky, *Understand Predictive Coding Options*, Tex. Lawyer: In-House Tex., at 8; Shah, *Use of "Predictive Coding" to Limit Cost & Improve Efficiency*, AHLA, at 9; *cf.* ***Da Silva Moore***, 287 F.R.D. at 184.

CAUTION

Predictive coding is a relatively new technology, and only a handful of cases in the United States have addressed whether it is an appropriate way to conduct discovery. See, e.g., ***National Day Laborer Org. Network v. U.S. Immigration & Customs Enforcement Agency***

(S.D.N.Y.2012) 877 F.Supp.2d 87, 111; ***Da Silva Moore****, 287 F.R.D. at 182-83;* ***In re Actos (Pioglitazone) Prods. Liab. Litig.*** *(W.D.La.2012) No. 6:11-md-2299 (case mgmt. order; 7-27-12). Also, it is unclear to what extent predictive coding can handle privilege determinations. See Shah, Use of "Predictive Coding" to Limit Cost & Improve Efficiency, at 10.*

1. **Process.** Although the specific process for predictive coding may differ depending on the software used, the process usually includes the following steps:

(1) **Attorneys code seed set.** Attorneys review and code a small amount of the ESI—known as a "seed set"—to train the predictive-coding software. *Cf.* ***Da Silva Moore***, 287 F.R.D. at 184 (attorneys typically need to review only a few thousand documents).

(2) **Software predicts.** The software applies the principles it learned from the seed set to predict how the attorneys would code ESI outside of the seed set. *Cf.* ***Da Silva Moore***, 287 F.R.D. at 184.

(3) **Software codes all ESI.** The coding and predicting continues until the software is able to accurately predict how the attorneys would code the ESI, at which point the software codes all the ESI. *Cf.* ***Da Silva Moore***, 287 F.R.D. at 184.

(4) **Random sample selected.** When the software completes the coding, it selects a random sample of the coded ESI for quality control. Shah, *Use of "Predictive Coding" to Limit Cost & Improve Efficiency*, at 9.

(5) **Attorneys review sample.** Attorneys assess the sample of coded ESI for both the percentage of relevant ESI identified (called "completeness" or "recall") and the percentage of the identified ESI that is actually relevant (called "accuracy" or "precision"). Shah, *Use of "Predictive Coding" to Limit Cost & Improve Efficiency*, at 9; *cf.* ***Da Silva Moore***, 287 F.R.D. at 189-90.

(6) **Additional seed set may be chosen.** If the attorneys find errors, additional seed ESI is chosen, reviewed, and coded until the software reaches acceptable levels of completeness and accuracy. Shah, *Use of "Predictive Coding" to Limit Cost & Improve Efficiency*, at 9.

2. **Benefits.** The benefits of predictive coding include the following:

(1) **Minimal human review.** Predictive coding requires minimal input from human reviewers. *See* Peck, *Search, Forward*; Shah, *Use of "Predictive Coding" to Limit Cost & Improve Efficiency*, at 9.

(2) **Lower costs.** Predictive coding potentially lowers costs. *See* Peck, *Search, Forward*. Predictive coding may be less expensive because it requires fewer attorneys and fewer review hours. *See* Shah, *Use of "Predictive Coding" to Limit Cost & Improve Efficiency*, at 10.

(3) **Greater accuracy.** Predictive coding may provide greater accuracy. *See* Peck, *Search, Forward*; *cf.* ***Da Silva Moore***, 287 F.R.D. at 190 (statistics have shown that computerized searches are at least as accurate as traditional manual review, which has been considered "gold standard" in document review). Predictive coding provides greater accuracy than keyword searches because it does not rely on attorneys to develop the list of keywords and it is not based on particular keywords or Boolean operators. *See* Peck, *Search, Forward*; *cf.* ***Da Silva Moore***, 287 F.R.D. at 190-91. See "Limitations," §5.1.2, p. 883.

§5.3 Targeted searches. The parties can consider targeted searches to locate relevant ESI. Targeted searches are limited and reasonably well-defined searches in likely sources. *Cf.* ***Oracle Corp. v. SAP AG*** (N.D.Cal.2008) 566 F.Supp.2d 1010, 1014.

§5.4 Testing & sampling. The parties can consider testing or sampling to locate relevant ESI contained in sources identified as not reasonably accessible. *See* Rothstein, *Managing Discovery of Electronic Information*, at 16; *cf.* ***Hopson v. Mayor & City Council of Balt.*** (D.Md.2005) 232 F.R.D. 228, 245. Sampling can help refine the search parameters and determine the benefits and burdens associated with a more complete search. Rothstein, *Managing Discovery of Electronic Information*, at 16. See "Specify inspection & other activities," §8.1.3, p. 888.

§6. MEET & CONFER ABOUT ELECTRONIC DISCOVERY

§6.1 When to meet & confer. The parties must discuss electronic-discovery issues during the meet-and-confer conference that is required before the first case-management conference. CRC 3.724(8). See "Meet-and-Confer Requirement," ch. 5-A, §6, p. 466.

§6.2 Purpose of meet & confer. During the meet-and-confer conference, the parties (1) must consider the issues listed in CRC 3.724 and 3.727 and (2) should attempt to establish protocols for preserving and producing ESI. *See* CRC 3.724, 3.727; *Navigating Vendor Proposal Process*, at 32; *Sedona Principles, Second Edition*, at 27. The success of the meet-and-confer conference depends on the parties' candor, diligence, and reasonableness. *Sedona Principles, Second Edition*, at 20.

1. CRC 3.724 & 3.727. Under CRC 3.724 and 3.727, the parties must meet and confer about the following:

(1) General issues. The parties must meet and confer about the same general issues that apply to cases that do not involve ESI. *See* CRC 3.724(1)-(7), (9), 3.727. See "Meet-and-Confer Obligation," ch. 7-A, §10, p. 761.

(2) ESI issues. The parties must meet and confer about any issue relating to the discovery of ESI, including the following:

(a) Preservation. The parties must meet and confer about issues relating to the preservation of discoverable ESI. CRC 3.724(8)(A).

(b) Form of production. The parties must meet and confer about the form or forms in which ESI will be produced. CRC 3.724(8)(B).

(c) Time for production. The parties must meet and confer about the time within which the ESI will be produced. CRC 3.724(8)(C).

(d) Scope. The parties must meet and confer about the scope of ESI discovery. CRC 3.724(8)(D).

(e) Privilege claims. The parties must meet and confer about the method for asserting or preserving claims of privilege or attorney work product, including whether such claims can be asserted after production. CRC 3.724(8)(E).

(f) Confidentiality claims. The parties must meet and confer about the confidentiality, privacy, trade secrets, or proprietary status of ESI relating to a party or nonparty. CRC 3.724(8)(F).

(g) Cost allocation. The parties must meet and confer about how the cost of ESI production is to be allocated. CRC 3.724(8)(G).

(h) Other issues. The parties must meet and confer about any other issues relating to the discovery of ESI, including the development of a proposed plan for the discovery of ESI. CRC 3.724(8)(H).

2. Protocols. During the meet-and-confer conference, the parties should attempt to establish the following protocols. By doing so, the parties will satisfy many of the CRC 3.724 requirements described above.

(1) Protocol to preserve ESI. The parties should attempt to establish protocols for the following: (1) preserving data, including certain backup tapes, archived data, and legacy systems, (2) distributing retention notices to employees, (3) creating a limited number of forensic copies of certain computer hard drives, (4) agreeing to collect potentially relevant data, and (5) exchanging a questionnaire about each party's electronic-data systems. *See Navigating Vendor Proposal Process*, at 32; *Sedona Principles, Second Edition*, at 20-21; *cf.* ***Antioch Co. v. Scrapbook Borders, Inc.*** (D.Minn.2002) 210 F.R.D. 645, 650-51 (in motion to compel discovery and appoint neutral expert in computer forensics, P suggested protocol for duplicating computer files).

(2) Protocol for production. The parties should establish a protocol for the production of ESI. *See Sedona Principles, Second Edition*, at 20-21; *see, e.g.*, ***Ellis v. Toshiba Am. Info. Sys.*** (2d Dist.2013) 218 Cal.App.4th

853, 863-64 (court urged parties to establish protocol for examination of hard drive and to submit names for appointment of neutral computer-forensics expert). The following steps should be included in the protocol:

(a) Identify form for ESI production. The protocol should identify the form or forms in which the ESI will be produced. *See Navigating Vendor Proposal Process*, at 32. For example, the protocol can specify that the ESI will be produced in its native format with its metadata.

(b) Protect privileged ESI. The protocol can outline (and if necessary, modify) the procedures to protect inadvertently produced information that is privileged and confidential. *See Sedona Principles, Second Edition*, at 51. These agreements are often referred to as "clawback" agreements. *See id.* The procedures to protect inadvertently produced information are set out in CCP §1985.8(j) (nonparty), §2020.220(j) (nonparty), and §2031.285 (party). See "Motion to resolve claim of inadvertent production of privileged ESI," §12.2, p. 895.

(c) Minimize burden on responding party. The protocol should protect the responding party from undue burden or expense. *Cf.* ***Antioch Co.***, 210 F.R.D. at 653 (in granting motion to compel discovery and appoint neutral expert in computer forensics, federal court ordered expert to avoid unnecessarily disrupting D's normal activities); ***Simon Prop. Grp. v. mySimon, Inc.*** (S.D.Ind.2000) 194 F.R.D. 639, 641-42 (in granting motion to compel discovery, federal court intended for production procedure to minimize burden on D's business); ***Playboy Enters. v. Welles*** (S.D.Cal.1999) 60 F.Supp.2d 1050, 1053-54 (same); ***Daimler Truck N. Am. LLC v. Younessi*** (W.D.Wash.2008) No. 08-MC-5011RBL (slip op.; 6-20-08) (in granting motion for protective order, federal court ordered nonparty to search its own computers, rather than make forensic copy, to protect nonparty's privileged information and trade secrets).

(3) Protocol for forensic investigation. The parties should establish a protocol for forensic electronic discovery. *See Sedona Principles, Second Edition*, at 47. For example, if a forensic investigation is to be based on searching through a party's database, the following steps should be included in the protocol:

(a) Select expert. The protocol should identify an expert to conduct any forensic examination of the ESI or its source. *See, e.g.*, ***Simon Prop.***, 194 F.R.D. at 641 (in granting motion to compel discovery, federal court ordered P to select and pay expert to inspect D's computers and create forensic copy of hard drives); ***Playboy Enters.***, 60 F.Supp.2d at 1055 (in granting motion to compel discovery, federal court ordered appointment of electronic-discovery expert); *cf.* ***Equity Analytics, LLC v. Lundin*** (D.D.C.2008) 248 F.R.D. 331, 332. Electronic-discovery vendors can offer a variety of software and services to help with the electronic-discovery process. *Sedona Principles, Second Edition*, at 40. See "Consider electronic-discovery vendor," §3.2.3, p. 881.

(b) Select search technique. See "ESI Search Techniques," §5, p. 882.

(c) Identify scope of search. The protocol should identify the databases to be searched and outline the scope of the search. For example, the protocol can specify that the search will be conducted of all ESI depositories that contain the following: (1) e-mails to or from the plaintiff, including e-mails in which the plaintiff's name appears as a "cc" or "bcc" recipient, (2) e-mails in which the plaintiff's name is mentioned, (3) ESI created by the plaintiff, (4) ESI sent to the plaintiff, whether sent to her directly or as a "cc" or "bcc" recipient, and (5) ESI in which the plaintiff's name appears (full name, first or last name, or initials). *Cf.* ***D'Onofrio v. Sfx Sports Grp.*** (D.D.C.2008) 254 F.R.D. 129, 132.

(d) Establish search procedure. The protocol should establish the procedure for determining which documents are subject to discovery. For example, the protocol can provide that (1) the search will be conducted by the forensic expert (or the database owner), (2) the owner will conduct a privilege review of the search results, (3) the owner will withhold the documents it considers privileged, (4) the owner will file a privilege log of the withheld documents, identifying each document and its privilege, and (5) the owner will produce any nonprivileged documents to the other party. *See Sedona Conference on Achieving Quality in E-Discovery*, at 15-17; *see, e.g.*, ***Antioch Co.***, 210 F.R.D. at 650-51 (P suggested protocol for examination by forensic expert and privilege review of search results by Ds).

(e) Establish time limits. The protocol should establish the time limits for each step of the forensic investigation. For example, the protocol can provide that the on-site search by the forensic expert will be conducted on certain dates, for no more than ten hours a day, and that the database owner must complete its examination of the forensic copy and file a privilege log within three weeks after receiving the copy from the forensic expert.

§7. DISCOVERY METHODS FOR ESI

ESI can be obtained using only certain discovery methods. By comparison, information about ESI (e.g., types of storage systems used, where storage systems are kept) can be obtained using any type of discovery method.

§7.1 Discovery of ESI. The following discovery methods are the only ones that can be used to obtain ESI:

1. From party. ESI can be obtained from a party by a demand to produce. CCP §2031.010(e). A party can demand that another party produce ESI in its possession, custody, or control for inspection, copying, testing, or sampling. *Id.* A party cannot do this with a deposition notice. See "No testing or sampling of things to be produced," ch. 7-B, §9.2.4(5), p. 791. For a discussion of demands to produce, see "Demands to Produce," ch. 7-E, p. 845.

2. From nonparty. ESI can be obtained from a nonparty only by a deposition subpoena. CCP §1985.8(a)(1). A party can subpoena a nonparty to produce ESI in its possession, custody, or control for inspection, copying, testing, or sampling. *Id.* See "What Can Be Subpoenaed," ch. 8-A, §5, p. 939. For a discussion of deposition subpoenas, see "Deposition Subpoenas," ch. 8-B, p. 959.

§7.2 Discovery about ESI. Information about ESI can be obtained using any type of discovery method, including the following:

1. Oral deposition. A party can obtain information about a responding person's ESI by deposing its information-technology employee or another person who knows about the organization's ESI system. *See* CCP §2025.010; *see also* Diamond, *Six Critical Steps*, at 55 (organization should designate person in information-technology department who understands data). See "Depositions," ch. 7-B, p. 780.

2. Interrogatories. A party can obtain information about another party's ESI by serving interrogatories on the party. *See* CCP §2030.010(a). Interrogatories can be useful in determining the extent of the party's discoverable ESI (e.g., ask for identity of party's computer-network specialist, ask about policies for ESI retention and destruction) and the party's compliance with its preservation duty (e.g., ask for dates and actions taken to preserve ESI or for litigation holds). *See* 7 *Moore's Federal Practice 3d* §37A.22 (2014). See "Interrogatories," ch. 7-C, p. 816.

3. Requests for admission. A party can request that another party admit the truth of matters relating to (1) facts, the application of law to facts, or opinions about facts involving ESI, or (2) the genuineness of certain ESI. *See* CCP §2033.010. See "Requests for Admission," ch. 7-D, p. 836.

§8. INITIATING & RESPONDING TO ELECTRONIC DISCOVERY

§8.1 How to initiate discovery of ESI. To obtain ESI through discovery, a party must make a demand to produce or serve a subpoena. See "Making Demand to Produce," ch. 7-E, §5, p. 849; "How to Serve Subpoenas," ch. 8-A, §9, p. 947; "Deposition Subpoenas," ch. 8-B, p. 959.

1. Describe ESI. A demand to produce or a subpoena for ESI must describe individual items sought "specifically" and categories of items sought with "reasonable particularity." See "Description of things to be produced," ch. 7-E, §5.3.3(1), p. 849; "Deposition subpoenas," ch. 8-A, §5.2.1, p. 940.

2. Specify form for ESI. A demand to produce or a subpoena for ESI should (but is not required to) identify the form or forms in which each type of ESI should be produced (e.g., hard copy, native format, static format). CCP §1985.8(d)(1) (nonparty), §2020.220(d)(1) (nonparty), §2031.030(a)(2) (party); *see* Judicial Council Forms, form SUBP-010, Item 3. If the discovery request does not specify the form, the ESI must be produced in the form in which it is ordinarily maintained or in a form that is reasonably usable. CCP §§1985.8(d)(1), 2020.220(d)(1),

2031.280(d)(1). The request cannot require that the same ESI be produced in more than one form. *Id.* §§1985.8(d)(2), 2020.220(d)(2), 2031.280(d)(2). See "How to produce ESI," §10.2, p. 891.

3. Specify inspection & other activities. A demand to produce or a subpoena for ESI can ask to inspect, copy, test, or sample the ESI. CCP §1985.8(a)(1) (nonparty), §2031.010(e) (party). Under federal law, the right to inspect, test, or sample ESI does not mean the discovering party can routinely demand direct access to a party's ESI system. FRCP 34(a), advisory committee's notes (2006). Direct access to an ESI system probably requires a showing of some extraordinary reason (e.g., responding person is concealing or destroying ESI). *Cf. **Covad Comms. v. Revonet, Inc.*** (D.D.C.2009) 258 F.R.D. 5, 12-13 (when database itself, and not just information in it, was exhibit in case, federal court allowed forensic inspection of database servers because there was no other way to seek information and it would advance resolution of case).

§8.2 How to respond to discovery of ESI.

1. Responding to demand to produce ESI. For the general procedures for responding to a demand to produce, see "Responding to Demand to Produce," ch. 7-E, §7, p. 851.

(1) Responding party. A party can respond to a demand to produce ESI in the following ways:

(a) Statement of compliance. The party can respond to all or part of the demand by making a statement of compliance. See "Statement of compliance," ch. 7-E, §7.3.1, p. 851. If the party objects to the form of ESI specified in the demand, or if the demand does not specify a form, the party must identify in its statement of compliance the form in which it intends to produce the ESI. CCP §2031.280(c). There is no similar requirement for a responding nonparty.

(b) Statement of inability to comply. The party can respond to all or part of the demand by making a statement of inability to comply. *See* CCP §2031.230. See "Statement of inability to comply," ch. 7-E, §7.3.2, p. 851.

(c) Written objections. The party can respond to all or part of the demand by making written objections to it. See "Objections to Production of ESI," §9, p. 889.

(d) Motion for protective order. The party can respond to all or part of the demand by making a motion for a protective order. See "Motion for protective order," §12.1, p. 893.

(2) Affected person. An affected person (i.e., a person or party who is not the responding party) can respond to all or part of a demand to produce ESI by making a motion for a protective order. See "Motion for protective order," §12.1, p. 893.

2. Responding to subpoena for ESI. For the general procedures for responding to a subpoena, see "Responding to Deposition Subpoenas," ch. 8-B, §6, p. 968.

(1) Responding nonparty. A nonparty can respond to a subpoena for the production of ESI in the following ways:

(a) Compliance. The nonparty can respond to the subpoena by complying with it; no statement of compliance is necessary.

(b) Written objections. The nonparty can respond to the subpoena by making written objections to it. See "Objections to Production of ESI," §9, p. 889; "Written objections," ch. 8-E, §2.2.3, p. 998.

(c) Motion to quash. The nonparty can respond to the subpoena by making a motion to quash. See "Motion to Quash Deposition Subpoena," ch. 9-C, §3, p. 1038.

(d) Oral objections. The nonparty can respond to the subpoena by making oral objections at the deposition. See "Objections to Production of ESI," §9, p. 889.

(e) Motion for protective order. The nonparty can respond to the subpoena by making a motion for a protective order. See "Motion for protective order," §12.1, p. 893.

(2) Affected person. An affected person (i.e., a person or party who is not the responding nonparty) can respond to a subpoena for the production of ESI by making a motion for a protective order. See "Motion for protective order," §12.1, p. 893.

§8.3 How to respond to objections to ESI discovery.

1. Investigate grounds for ESI objections. The discovering party can conduct discovery to test the responding person's objections to the production of ESI (e.g., an objection that the ESI is not reasonably accessible). *See* Rothstein, *Managing Discovery of Electronic Information*, at 16. This discovery can involve (1) taking depositions of people knowledgeable about the responding person's information systems, (2) inspecting the data sources, and (3) requiring the responding person to conduct a sampling of the ESI. *Id.*

2. Make motion to compel. If the responding person objected to the demand or subpoena for ESI, the discovering party can make a motion to compel production. CCP §§2025.450(a), 2025.480(a); *see id.* §2031.310(a), (b); *see also id.* §2019.040(b) (all procedures that are available to compel production of documents or tangible things are available to compel production of ESI). See "Motion to compel initial response to ESI demand," §12.3, p. 895; "Motion to compel further response to ESI demand," §12.4, p. 895; "Motion to compel compliance with demand to produce ESI," §12.5, p. 897; "Motion to compel nonparty to produce ESI," §12.6, p. 897.

3. Oppose motion for protective order. If the responding person made a motion for a protective order, the discovering party should file opposition papers. See "Opposition papers," §12.1.2, p. 894.

§9. OBJECTIONS TO PRODUCTION OF ESI

A responding person must state a specific objection or assert an appropriate privilege or exemption from discovery for each item it does not want to produce. *See* CCP §2031.210(a)(3).

§9.1 General discovery objections. The responding person can assert the same objections to a demand to produce ESI or a subpoena for ESI that it can assert to the discovery of other types of information. See "Grounds," ch. 7-E, §7.3.3(2), p. 852; "Objections to subpoenas," ch. 8-E, §2.1, p. 995.

§9.2 ESI-specific objections. The responding person can assert the following objections that are unique to ESI demands:

1. Form of ESI. The responding person can object to the form of ESI specified for production. *See* CCP §1985.8(c) (nonparty), §2031.280(c) (party).

2. More than one form demanded. The responding person can object that the discovering party wants the same ESI produced in more than one form. *See* CCP §1985.8(d)(2) (nonparty), §2031.280(d)(2) (party). A responding person is not required to produce ESI in more than one form. *Id.* §1985.8(d)(2) (nonparty), §2031.280(d)(2) (party).

3. Other sources. The responding person can object that the same information is obtainable from another source that is more convenient, less burdensome, or less expensive than the requested form of ESI. *See* CCP §1985.8(i)(1) (nonparty), §2020.220(i)(1) (nonparty), §2025.420(f)(1) (any person), §2025.450(f)(1) (party), §2025.480(g)(1) (nonparty), §2031.060(f)(1) (party or affected person). *But see* ***Vasquez v. California Sch. of Culinary Arts, Inc.*** (2d Dist.2014) 230 Cal.App.4th 35, 43 (fact that ESI also existed in paper form did not excuse responding party from producing documents in electronic format).

4. Cumulative or duplicative. The responding person can object that the ESI is unreasonably cumulative or duplicative because the same or similar information was already provided as ESI or in another form (e.g., hard copy). *See* CCP §1985.8(i)(2) (nonparty), §2020.220(i)(2) (nonparty), §2025.420(f)(2) (any person), §2025.450(f)(2) (party), §2025.480(g)(2) (nonparty), §2031.060(f)(2) (party or affected person).

5. Available earlier. The responding person can object that the discovering party has had ample opportunity to obtain the same information through other discovery. *See* CCP §1985.8(i)(3) (nonparty), §2020.220(i)(3) (nonparty), §2025.420(f)(3) (any person), §2025.450(f)(3) (party), §2025.480(g)(3) (nonparty), §2031.060(f)(3) (party or affected person).

6. Burden outweighs benefit. The responding person can object that the likely burden or expense of producing the ESI outweighs the likely benefit, taking into account the amount in controversy, the resources of the parties, the importance of the issues in the litigation, and the importance of the requested discovery in resolving the issues. *See* CCP §1985.8(i)(4) (nonparty), §2020.220(i)(4) (nonparty), §2025.420(f)(4) (any person), §2025.450(f)(4) (party), §2025.480(g)(4) (nonparty), §2031.060(f)(4) (party); *cf.* ***Wells Fargo Bank v. LaSalle Bank*** (S.D.Ohio 2009) No. 3:07-cv-449 (slip op.; 7-24-09) (federal court found expense of restoring backup tapes was disproportionate to amount in controversy).

7. Shift expense. The responding person can object to the expense of producing the ESI and ask that it be shifted to the discovering party. *See* CCP §1985.8(g) (court can allocate expense between discovering party and responding nonparty), §1985.8(*l*) (court order must protect nonparty from undue burden or expense), §2020.220(g) (court can allocate expense between discovering party and responding nonparty), §2025.420(e) (court can allocate expense between discovering party and responding person), §2025.450(e) (court can allocate expense between discovering party and responding party), §2025.480(f) (court can allocate expense between discovering party and nonparty deponent), §2031.060(b) (court order can protect party from undue expense), §2031.060(e) (court can allocate expense of producing inaccessible ESI between discovering party and responding party). The expense of translating data into a usable form is automatically shifted to the discovering party. *Id.* §1985.8(h) (nonparty), §2020.220(h) (nonparty), §2031.280(e) (party); ***Toshiba Am. Elec. Components, Inc. v. Superior Ct.*** (6th Dist.2004) 124 Cal.App.4th 762, 772 (party).

8. ESI unavailable. The responding person can object that the ESI (1) never existed, (2) was destroyed, lost, misplaced, or stolen, or (3) has never been or is no longer in the person's custody or control. *See* CCP §2031.230; *see, e.g.*, ***Electronic Funds Solutions, LLC v. Murphy*** (4th Dist.2005) 134 Cal.App.4th 1161, 1168-69 (in response to demand to produce, D claimed virus had destroyed electronic files). See "Statement of inability to comply," §8.2.1(1)(b), p. 888. For a discussion of when a duty to preserve ESI arises, see "Understand when duty to preserve arises," §3.1.3, p. 879.

9. ESI inaccessible. The responding person can object that the discovery request seeks ESI from sources that are not reasonably accessible because of undue burden or expense. *See* CCP §1985.8(e) (nonparty), §2020.220(e) (nonparty), §2025.420(c) (any person), §2025.450(c) (party), §2025.480(d) (nonparty), §2031.210(d) (party).

(1) Contents of inaccessibility objection.

(a) No search without agreement or order. A responding person must support its objection by stating that it is not required to search the inaccessible source until an agreement is reached with the discovering party or the court orders production from the inaccessible source. *See* CCP §§2025.460(d) (deponent), 2031.210(d) (party).

(b) Undue burden or expense. A responding person has the burden to show that the ESI is not reasonably accessible because of the undue burden or expense of producing it. CCP §1985.8(e) (nonparty), §2020.220(e) (nonparty), §2025.420(c) (any person), §2025.450(c) (party), §2025.480(d) (nonparty). To establish this burden, the responding person should describe the effort and expense that would be required to comply with the discovery request. *See* ***Vasquez***, 230 Cal.App.4th at 43-44 (courts will not automatically assume that compliance with subpoena is unduly burdensome because it requests production of ESI). For example, the responding person could show that to produce the requested ESI it would be forced to restore three years of archival files that include mostly legacy data, that its own employees do not have the expertise to restore or convert the files, and that an outside expert has estimated that restoration and conversion would cost $50,000.

(c) Sources not searched. A responding person must identify, by category or type, the sources of ESI that it did not search or will not produce. *See* CCP §§2025.460(d) (deponent), 2031.210(d) (party). The identification of sources not searched should provide enough detail to enable the discovering party to evaluate the burden and expense on the responding person to produce the ESI and the likelihood of finding responsive information

in the identified sources. *See* Rosenthal, *A Few Thoughts on Electronic Discovery*, at 178. One author has suggested that the responding person should organize the information like a privilege log. *See id.* See "Privilege log," ch. 7-A, §14.1.4(2), p. 773.

(2) Other objections preserved. A responding person is not required to determine whether the inaccessible ESI sources contain relevant or privileged information. By identifying ESI that is not reasonably accessible, the responding person preserves all other objections related to the ESI. *See* CCP §§2025.460(d), 2031.210(d). The logic behind this rule is that if the ESI is inaccessible, the responding person may not know if it contains relevant or privileged information. *See* Rosenthal, *A Few Thoughts on Electronic Discovery*, at 178.

PRACTICE TIP

As soon as a responding person becomes aware that ESI is not reasonably accessible, the person should consider retaining an electronic-discovery consultant or vendor to identify the ESI by category, type, or source and to certify that the ESI is not reasonably accessible. See Sedona Principles, Second Edition, at 40. See "Consider electronic-discovery vendor," §3.2.3, p. 881.

§10. PRODUCTION OF ESI

§10.1 Who can be required to produce ESI.

1. Parties. A party can demand the production of ESI from other parties. CCP §2031.010(a).

2. Nonparties. A party can subpoena the production of ESI from nonparties. CCP §1985.8(a)(1). See "Deposition Subpoenas," ch. 8-B, p. 959. When seeking ESI from a nonparty, the CEDA requires the discovering party to take reasonable steps to avoid imposing an undue burden or expense on the nonparty. CCP §§1985.8(k), 2020.220(k); *see Sedona Principles, Second Edition*, at 43, 69.

§10.2 How to produce ESI. The responding person must produce ESI in the form agreed to by the parties, ordered by the court, or specified by the discovering party. CCP §1985.8(d)(1) (nonparty), §2020.220(d)(1) (nonparty), §2031.280(d)(1) (party). If no form was agreed to, ordered, or specified, the responding person must produce the ESI in a form in which it is ordinarily maintained or in a form that is reasonably usable. *Id.* §1985.8(d)(1) (nonparty), §2020.220(d)(1) (nonparty), §2031.280(d)(1) (party).

1. Form specified by discovering party.

(1) Party production. If a demand to produce specified a form for ESI production, and if the responding party made no objection to the specified form, the responding party must produce the ESI in that form. *See* CCP §2031.280(c), (d)(1). If the responding party objected to the form, it can produce the ESI in the form specified in its statement of compliance. *See id.* §2031.280(c). See "Form of ESI," §9.2.1, p. 889.

(2) Nonparty production. If a deposition subpoena specified a form for ESI production, and if the responding nonparty made no objection to the specified form, the responding nonparty must produce the ESI in that form. *See* CCP §§1985.8(d)(1), 2020.220(d)(1). If the responding nonparty objected to the form, it should produce the ESI in either the form in which the ESI is ordinarily maintained or in a form that is reasonably usable. *See id.* §§1985.8(d)(1), 2020.220(d)(1). See "Form of ESI," §9.2.1, p. 889.

2. No form specified by discovering party. If the discovering party did not specify the form in which the ESI is to be produced (and the form is not specified in an agreement with the discovering party or in a court order), a responding party must notify the discovering party of the form in which it intends to produce the ESI. *See* CCP §2031.280(c), (d)(1). A responding nonparty can—but does not have an obligation to—notify the discovering party of the form in which it will produce the ESI. *See id.* §1985.8(c), (d)(1). When no form was specified, a responding person can produce it in either of the following forms:

(1) Ordinarily maintained. The responding person can produce the ESI as it is ordinarily maintained. CCP §§1985.8(d)(1) (nonparty), 2020.220(d)(1) (nonparty), 2031.280(d)(1) (party). "Ordinarily maintained" is not synonymous with "native format." *Sedona Principles, Second Edition*, at 8. See "Native format,"

§2.2.12, p. 877. Because so many systems maintain and store ESI, there may be a difference between the form in which ESI is preserved and that in which it is produced for use, and the responding person can choose between those forms for production. *See Sedona Principles, Second Edition*, at 8.

(2) Reasonably usable. The responding person can produce the ESI in a reasonably usable form. CCP §§1985.8(d)(1) (nonparty), 2020.220(d)(1) (nonparty), 2031.280(d)(1) (party). Whether ESI is reasonably usable depends on the circumstances of the case and may require the responding person to ask the discovering party which form would be reasonably usable. *See Sedona Principles, Second Edition*, at 63. If necessary, the responding person may be required to convert the ESI into a reasonably usable form at the discovering party's expense. CCP §1985.8(h) (nonparty), §2020.220(h) (nonparty), §2031.280(e) (party).

§10.3 Costs of producing ESI.

1. Production cost. The responding person bears the cost of producing ESI. See "Cost of production," §2.3.8, p. 878.

2. Translation cost. If the responding person must translate data compilations into a reasonably usable form, the discovering party bears the cost. CCP §1985.8(h) (nonparty), §2020.220(h) (nonparty), §2031.280(e) (party); ***Toshiba Am. Elec. Components, Inc. v. Superior Ct.*** (6th Dist.2004) 124 Cal.App.4th 762, 772 (party).

§10.4 Inadvertent production of privileged ESI.

1. Responding person notifies parties. A responding person who inadvertently produces privileged information in response to a demand or subpoena for ESI should notify each party who received the ESI of the privilege claim and the basis for the claim. *See* CCP §1985.8(j) (nonparty), §2020.220(j) (nonparty), §2025.460(f) (any deponent), §2031.285(a) (party).

2. Receiving party sequesters & returns ESI. After receiving notice of a claim, a receiving party must do the following:

(1) Sequester & retrieve ESI. The receiving party must immediately sequester the ESI. CCP §2031.285(b). If the receiving party disclosed the ESI to another person before it was notified of the privilege claim, it must immediately take reasonable steps to retrieve the information. *Id.* §2031.285(c)(2).

(2) Return ESI. If the receiving party acknowledges that the ESI is protected, it must return all copies of the ESI containing privileged information to the responding person. CCP §2031.285(b). If the receiving party contests the responding party's claim that the ESI is protected, it should file a motion to resolve the claim. *See id.* §2031.285(d)(1). See "Motion to resolve claim of inadvertent production of privileged ESI," §12.2, p. 895.

§11. SAFE HARBOR FROM SANCTIONS FOR LOST, DAMAGED, ALTERED, OR OVERWRITTEN ESI

The CEDA contains a safe-harbor provision that can protect from sanctions responding persons and attorneys who lose, damage, alter, or overwrite ESI that should have been preserved or produced. *See* CCP §§1985.8(m)(1), 1987.2(b)(1), 2017.020(c)(1), 2020.220(m)(1), 2025.420(i)(1), 2025.450(i)(1), 2025.480(*l*)(1), 2031.060(i)(1), 2031.300(d)(1), 2031.310(j)(1), 2031.320(d)(1). This protection applies if the responding person can show that (1) the ESI was lost, damaged, altered, or overwritten because of the routine, good-faith operation of an electronic information system, and (2) no exceptional circumstances justify the imposition of sanctions. *See id.* §§1985.8(m)(1), 1987.2(b)(1), 2017.020(c)(1), 2020.220(m)(1), 2025.420(i)(1), 2025.450(i)(1), 2025.480(*l*)(1), 2031.060(i)(1), 2031.300(d)(1), 2031.310(j)(1), 2031.320(d)(1); *Sedona Principles, Second Edition*, at 72.

§11.1 Routine & good-faith operation.

1. Routine. The phrase "routine ... operation of an electronic information system" refers to the ways computer systems are designed, programmed, and implemented to meet a person's technical and business needs. *Cf.* FRCP 37, advisory committee's notes (2006) (under former FRCP 37(f), now 37(e)). The routine operation of an

electronic information system typically includes the periodic alteration and overwriting of information, often without the operator's specific direction or awareness. *See* FRCP 37, advisory committee's notes (2006). See "Backup-tape recycling," §2.2.4, p. 875.

2. Good faith. The responding person must show that it acted in good faith to prevent the destruction or alteration of relevant ESI. *Cf. **Doe v. Norwalk Cmty. Coll.*** (D.Conn.2007) 248 F.R.D. 372, 378. To show good faith, the responding person must show that it complied with its duty to preserve ESI. See "When duty to preserve evidence arises," ch. 7-E, §4.1, p. 847. To do this, the responding person must show that it suspended some or all of its backup-maintenance programs and systems as soon as the duty to preserve arose to prevent them from deleting or altering potentially relevant ESI. *See Sedona Principles, Second Edition*, at 72.

(1) In-house electronic storage. The responding person must show that it instituted a consistent and routine program to protect in-house data required for litigation. *Cf. **Doe***, 248 F.R.D. at 378 (Ds did not have consistent, routine system in place when some e-mails were retained for up to a year while others were only retained for six months or less). See "Litigation hold," §3.2.1(1)(a), p. 880.

(2) Outsourced electronic storage. The responding person should show that it notified its outside provider of electronic storage to protect data required for litigation. Best, *AB 5's Amendments*, at 16. The safe-harbor provision protects responding persons who have outsourced their electronic storage to an outside vendor.

§11.2 No exceptional circumstances. The responding person or attorney must refute any allegations by the discovering party that exceptional circumstances justify sanctions. *See* CCP §§1985.8(m)(1), 2031.060(i)(1), 2031.300(d)(1), 2031.310(j)(1), 2031.320(d)(1); Rothstein, *Managing Discovery of Electronic Information*, at 31.

NOTE

The Judicial Conference Committee on Rules of Practice and Procedure has approved an amendment to FRCP 37, the rule that the CEDA safe-harbor provision was modeled after. See Report on the Judicial Conference: Committee on Rules of Practice & Procedure, Agenda E-19, at Rules App. B-57 (Sept.2014), www.uscourts.gov/uscourts/RulesandPolicies/rules/ST09-2014-add.pdf. The proposed amendment eliminates the references to "exceptional circumstances" and "routine, good-faith operation" and specifies the actions a federal court can take when a party fails to preserve ESI. Id.If the U.S. Supreme Court approves the amendment and Congress does not take contrary action, the amendment will take effect December 1, 2015. It is unclear whether the California Legislature will make similar amendments to the CEDA.

§12. MOTIONS RELATED TO ELECTRONIC DISCOVERY

§12.1 Motion for protective order. A party, nonparty, or affected person can move for a protective order in response to a demand to produce ESI or a subpoena for ESI. *See* CCP §1987.1 (subpoenaed nonparty), §2031.060(a), (c) (party or affected person), §2031.210(d) (party); *see also id.* §2019.040(b) (all procedures that are available to limit production of documents or tangible things are available to limit production of ESI).

1. Motion papers. For the deadlines, form, and contents of a motion for a protective order, see "Motion for Protective Order," ch. 9-B, p. 1024.

(1) Grounds. A motion for a protective order can be based on the same objections as a written response to an ESI discovery request. See "Objections to Production of ESI," §9, p. 889.

(2) Burden on motion. As a general rule, the party or person moving for a protective order has the initial burden of showing good cause for the motion, regardless of the type of discovery request. See "Good cause," ch. 9-B, §2.2.1(1)(b), p. 1025 (depositions).

(3) Request relief. The motion must identify the relief requested. For a list of the types of relief available for motions for protective orders relating to subpoenas and demands to produce, see "Relief Available Through Motion for Protective Order," chart 9-4, p. 1029.

2. Opposition papers. See "Opposition," ch. 9-B, §4.2, p. 1035.

(1) Investigate grounds for ESI objections. After receiving the motion for a protective order, the discovering party can ask the court for time to conduct discovery to test the grounds for the motion (e.g., whether the ESI is truly unavailable or inaccessible). See "ESI unavailable," §9.2.8, p. 890; "ESI inaccessible," §9.2.9, p. 890.

(2) Grounds.

(a) Negate grounds in motion. The opposition papers can negate the grounds in the motion. For example, if the party or person making the motion for protective order contends that the ESI is not reasonably accessible, the opposition papers can show that the ESI is reasonably accessible.

(b) Good cause for production of inaccessible ESI. If the discovering party cannot refute allegations that the ESI is not reasonably accessible, it can still obtain the ESI if it can show good cause for its production. *See* CCP §1985.8(f) (nonparty), §2020.220(f) (nonparty), §2025.420(d) (any person), §2025.450(d) (party), §2025.480(e) (nonparty), §2031.060(d) (party); *cf.* ***Disability Rights Council v. Washington Metro. Transit Auth.*** (D.D.C.2007) 242 F.R.D. 139, 147-48 (P showed good cause for discovery when D did not stop automatic deletion of e-mails and did not impose litigation hold after suit had been filed; D was ordered to restore and produce ESI that was not reasonably accessible). To show good cause, the discovering party can allege any of the following:

[1] No other sources. The discovering party can allege that it is not possible to obtain the same information through other discovery that is more convenient, less burdensome, or less expensive. *See* CCP §1985.8(i)(1) (nonparty), §2020.220(i)(1) (nonparty), §2025.420(f)(1) (any person), §2025.450(f)(1) (party), §2025.480(g)(1) (nonparty), §2031.060(f)(1) (party).

[2] Share expenses. The discovering party can allege that it is willing to share some or bear all of the expenses of accessing the ESI. *See* CCP §1985.8(g) (court can allocate expenses between discovering party and responding nonparty), §2020.220(g) (court can allocate expenses between discovering party and responding nonparty), §2025.420(e) (court can allocate expenses between discovering party and responding person), §2025.450(e) (court can allocate expenses between discovering party and responding party), §2025.480(f) (court can allocate expenses between discovering party and nonparty deponent), §2031.060(e) (court can allocate expenses between discovering party and responding party).

[3] Benefit outweighs burden. The discovering party can allege that the likely benefit of the ESI outweighs the burden and expense of securing it. *See* CCP §1985.8(i)(4) (nonparty), §2020.220(i)(4) (nonparty), §2025.420(f)(4) (any person), §2025.450(f)(4) (party), §2025.480(g)(4) (nonparty), §2031.060(f)(4) (party). To establish this, the discovering party should show that (1) the amount in controversy justifies the expense of securing the ESI, (2) the parties have the resources to secure the ESI, (3) the issues in the litigation warrant the discovery of the ESI, and (4) the ESI is critical to the resolution of the issues in the litigation. *See id.* §1985.8(i)(4) (nonparty), §2020.220(i)(4) (nonparty), §2025.420(f)(4) (any person), §2025.450(f)(4) (party), §2025.480(g)(4) (nonparty), §2031.060(f)(4) (party). For example, the discovering party can argue that it will be unable to effectively prosecute or defend the suit without the ESI. *See id.* §2019.030(a)(2); *cf.* ***Haka v. Lincoln Cty.*** (W.D.Wis.2007) 246 F.R.D. 577, 579.

3. Ruling. See "Ruling," ch. 9-B, §8, p. 1037; "Order," ch. 9-B, §9, p. 1037.

(1) Deny protective order. The court can deny the motion for a protective order and provide terms and conditions of the production of ESI that are just. CCP §2031.060(g). For example, if the court denies a motion because it found good cause for the production of inaccessible ESI, the court can require the discovering party to pay for the discovery. *See id.* §1985.8(g) (nonparty), §2020.220(g) (nonparty), §2025.420(e) (any person), §2025.450(e) (party), §2025.480(f) (nonparty), §2031.060(e) (party).

(2) Grant protective order. The court can grant the motion for a protective order and deny the discovery. At a minimum, the court must limit the frequency or extent of ESI discovery if the court makes any of the following determinations:

(a) Other sources. The court must limit the frequency or extent of the discovery if the court determines the ESI is obtainable from another source that is more convenient, less burdensome, or less expensive. CCP §1985.8(i)(1) (nonparty), §2020.220(i)(1) (nonparty), §2025.420(f)(1) (any person), §2025.450(f)(1) (party), §2025.480(g)(1) (nonparty), §2031.060(f)(1) (party).

(b) Cumulative or duplicative. The court must limit the frequency or extent of the discovery if the court determines the ESI is unreasonably cumulative or duplicative because the same or similar information was already provided as ESI or in another form (e.g., hard copy). *See* CCP §1985.8(i)(2) (nonparty), §2020.220(i)(2) (nonparty), §2025.420(f)(2) (any person), §2025.450(f)(2) (party), §2025.480(g)(2) (nonparty), §2031.060(f)(2) (party).

(c) Available earlier. The court must limit the frequency or extent of the discovery if the court determines the discovering party had ample opportunity to obtain the same information through other discovery. CCP §1985.8(i)(3) (nonparty), §2020.220(i)(3) (nonparty), §2025.420(f)(3) (any person), §2025.450(f)(3) (party), §2025.480(g)(3) (nonparty), §2031.060(f)(3) (party).

(d) Burden outweighs benefit. The court must limit the frequency or extent of the discovery if the court determines the likely burden or expense of producing the ESI outweighs the likely benefit, taking into account the amount in controversy, the resources of the parties, the importance of the issues in the litigation, and the importance of the discovery in resolving the issues. CCP §1985.8(i)(4) (nonparty), §2020.220(i)(4) (nonparty), §2025.420(f)(4) (any person), §2025.450(f)(4) (party), §2025.480(g)(4) (nonparty), §2031.060(f)(4) (party).

§12.2 Motion to resolve claim of inadvertent production of privileged ESI. A party who obtained ESI through discovery can make a motion to resolve a claim that the production inadvertently included privileged information. See "Inadvertent disclosure," ch. 6-A, §3.3.2(1), p. 612.

1. Pre-motion procedures. See "Inadvertent production of privileged ESI," §10.4, p. 892.

2. Motion papers. If a receiving party contests the legitimacy of the privilege claim, it must make a motion to resolve the claim. CCP §2031.285(d)(1).

(1) Deadline. The receiving party must file a motion to resolve the privilege claim within 30 days after receiving the notice of the privilege claim from the responding person. CCP §2031.285(d)(1).

(2) ESI under seal. The receiving party must present the ESI to the court conditionally under seal. CCP §2031.285(b), (d)(1).

(3) Preserve confidentiality. Until the motion is resolved, the receiving party must (1) preserve the ESI, (2) maintain the ESI's confidentiality, and (3) refrain from using or disclosing the ESI. CCP §2031.285(c)(1), (d)(2).

(4) Request relief. The motion should ask the court to (1) find that the ESI is not subject to a privilege or exemption from discovery and (2) require the responding person to produce the ESI.

3. Opposition papers. Once a receiving party files a motion to determine if the privilege applies, the responding person has the burden to justify its privilege claim. If the privilege depends on proof of preliminary facts, the responding person must establish the facts necessary to support the privilege. *See* Evid. C. §400 (definition of "preliminary fact"). See "Preliminary facts for privilege," ch. 7-A, §14.1.4(1)(a), p. 773.

4. Ruling. For some privileges, the court can conduct an in camera review of the documents; for others, it cannot. See "In camera review of documents," ch. 7-A, §14.2, p. 774.

§12.3 Motion to compel initial response to ESI demand. A discovering party can file a motion to compel a party's initial response to a demand to produce ESI when the responding party does not serve a timely response to the demand. CCP §2031.300(b). See "Motion to Compel Initial Response," ch. 9-E, §2, p. 1057.

§12.4 Motion to compel further response to ESI demand. A discovering party can make a motion to compel a further response when the responding party does not adequately respond to a demand to produce ESI. CCP §2031.310(a).

1. Motion papers.

(1) Deadlines, form & contents. For the deadlines, form, and contents of a motion to compel a further response, see "Motion," ch. 9-E, §3.2, p. 1062.

(2) Grounds. The discovering party can make a motion to compel a further response based on any of the following grounds:

(a) Improper objection.

[1] Specified form objectionable. If the responding party's initial response objects to the discovering party's specified form for producing the information and indicates the form in which it intends to produce the information, the discovering party can move to compel a further response on the ground that the form specified by the responding party is neither a form in which the ESI is ordinarily maintained nor a form that is reasonably usable. *See* CCP §§2031.280(c), (d)(1), 2031.310(a)(3). See "How to produce ESI," §10.2, p. 891.

[2] ESI inaccessible. If the responding party's initial response states that the ESI is inaccessible, the discovering party can move to compel a further response on the ground that the objection is without merit because the ESI is accessible. *See* CCP §2031.310(a)(3), (d). The responding party bears the burden of demonstrating that the ESI is from a source that is not reasonably accessible. *Id.* §2031.310(d).

(b) Good cause for inaccessible ESI. If the responding party's initial response states that the ESI is inaccessible, the discovering party can move to compel a further response on the ground that there is good cause for the ESI regardless of its accessibility. *See* CCP §2031.310(b)(1), (e). The discovering party is not required to show good cause to produce inaccessible ESI until the responding party establishes that it is not reasonably accessible. *Id.* §2031.310(d), (e).

(c) Improper form of ESI. If the demand to produce did not specify a form for producing the ESI and the responding party's initial response indicates the form in which it intends to produce the ESI, the discovering party can move to compel a further response on the ground that the form specified by the responding party is neither a form in which the ESI is ordinarily maintained nor a form that is reasonably usable. *See* CCP §§2031.280(d)(1), 2031.310(a)(1). See "How to produce ESI," §10.2, p. 891.

(d) Other grounds. The discovering party can move to compel a further response on any of the general grounds described in "Compel further response to demand to produce," ch. 9-E, §3.1.2, p. 1061.

2. Opposition papers. The responding party can file opposition papers to challenge the discovering party's grounds for the motion, its good cause for production, or the sufficiency of its attempt to meet and confer. See "Opposition," ch. 9-E, §3.3.2, p. 1064. It can also file a motion for a protective order. See "Motion for protective order," §12.1, p. 893.

3. Ruling. The court has broad discretion to issue orders compelling the production of ESI. *See* CCP §2031.310(f), (g). See "Order," ch. 9-E, §3.7, p. 1065. If the court finds good cause for the production of ESI from a source that is not reasonably accessible, it can set conditions for the discovery.

(1) Limiting frequency or extent of discovery. The court must limit the frequency or extent of ESI discovery, even from a source that is reasonably accessible, if the court makes any of the following determinations:

(a) It is possible to obtain the information from some other source that is more convenient, less burdensome, or less expensive. CCP §2031.310(g)(1).

(b) The discovery is unreasonably cumulative or duplicative because the same or similar information was already provided as ESI or in another form (e.g., hard copy). *See id.* §2031.310(g)(2).

(c) The discovering party had ample opportunity to obtain the same information through other discovery. *Id.* §2031.310(g)(3).

(d) The likely burden or expense of producing the ESI outweighs the likely benefit, taking into account the amount in controversy, the resources of the parties, the importance of the issues in the litigation, and the importance of the discovery in resolving the issues. *Id.* §2031.310(g)(4).

(2) Other conditions. The court can set other conditions for electronic discovery, including allocating the cost of producing the ESI. CCP §2031.310(f).

§12.5 Motion to compel compliance with demand to produce ESI. A discovering party can file a motion to compel a party's compliance with a demand to produce when the responding party does not permit inspection, copying, testing, or sampling of ESI in accordance with the compliance statement the responding party served in response to the demand. CCP §2031.320(a). See "Motion to Compel Compliance with Demand to Produce," ch. 9-E, §4, p. 1066.

§12.6 Motion to compel nonparty to produce ESI. A discovering party can file a motion to compel a nonparty to produce ESI when the nonparty refuses to comply with a subpoena. *See* CCP §§1987.1(a), (b)(1), 2025.460(e), 2025.480(a). See "Motion to Compel Deposition Answers & Production," ch. 9-D, §4, p. 1051.

1. Motion papers.

(1) Deadlines, form & contents. For the deadlines, form, and contents of a motion to compel a nonparty to produce ESI, see "Motion," ch. 9-D, §4.2, p. 1052.

(2) Grounds. The discovering party can make a motion to compel a nonparty to comply with a deposition subpoena to produce ESI on any of the following grounds:

(a) ESI inaccessible. If the nonparty contends that the ESI is inaccessible, the discovering party can move to compel a response on the ground that the objection is without merit because the ESI is accessible. *See* CCP §§1985.8(e), 2020.220(e), 2025.480(d). The nonparty bears the burden of demonstrating that the ESI is from a source that is not reasonably accessible. *Id.* §§1985.8(e), 2020.220(e), 2025.480(d).

(b) Good cause for inaccessible ESI. If the nonparty contends that the ESI is inaccessible, the discovering party can move to compel a response on the ground that there is good cause for the ESI regardless of its accessibility. *See* CCP §§1985.8(f), 2020.220(f), 2025.480(e). The discovering party is not required to show good cause to produce inaccessible ESI until the nonparty establishes that it is not reasonably accessible. *See id.* §§1985.8(e), (f), 2020.220(e), (f), 2025.480(d), (e).

(c) Improper form of ESI.

[1] Form specified in subpoena. If the deposition subpoena specified the form for producing the ESI and the nonparty's response specifies a different form in which it intends to produce the information, the discovering party can move to compel production in the form specified in the subpoena. *See* CCP §1985.8(b). See "How to produce ESI," §10.2, p. 891.

[2] Form not specified in subpoena. If the deposition subpoena did not specify a form for producing the ESI and the nonparty's response indicates the form in which it intends to produce the ESI, the discovering party can move to compel a response on the ground that the form specified by the nonparty is neither a form in which the ESI is ordinarily maintained nor a form that is reasonably usable. *See* CCP §§1985.8(d)(1), 2020.220(d)(1). See "How to produce ESI," §10.2, p. 891.

(d) ESI production otherwise inadequate. The discovering party can move to compel on the ground that the nonparty did not permit inspection, copying, testing, or sampling according to the terms of the subpoena. *See* CCP §1985.8(a)(1).

2. Opposition papers. The responding nonparty can file opposition papers to challenge the discovering party's grounds for the motion. See "Opposition," ch. 9-D, §5.2, p. 1054. It can also file a motion for a protective order. See "Motion for protective order," §12.1, p. 893.

3. Ruling. The court has broad discretion to issue orders compelling the production of ESI. *See* CCP §§1985.8(g), (i), 1987.1(a), 2020.220(g), (i), 2025.480(f), (g). See "Order," ch. 9-D, §9, p. 1056. If the court finds good cause for the production of ESI from a source that is not reasonably accessible, it can set conditions for the discovery. CCP §§1985.8(g), (i), 1987.1(a), 2020.220(g), 2025.480(f).

(1) Limiting frequency or extent of discovery. The court must limit the frequency or extent of ESI discovery, even from a source that is reasonably accessible, if the court makes any of the following determinations:

(a) It is possible to obtain the information from some other source that is more convenient, less burdensome, or less expensive. CCP §§1985.8(i)(1), 2020.220(i)(1), 2025.480(g)(1).

(b) The discovery is unreasonably cumulative or duplicative because the same or similar information was already provided as ESI or in another form (e.g., hard copy). *See id.* §§1985.8(i)(2), 2020.220(i)(2), 2025.480(g)(2).

(c) The discovering party had ample opportunity to obtain the same information through other discovery. *Id.* §§1985.8(i)(3), 2020.220(i)(3), 2025.480(g)(3).

(d) The likely burden or expense of producing the ESI outweighs the likely benefit, taking into account the amount in controversy, the resources of the parties, the importance of the issues in the litigation, and the importance of the discovery in resolving the issues. *Id.* §§1985.8(i)(4), 2020.220(i)(4), 2025.480(g)(4).

(2) Protecting against undue burden or expense. The court must protect any person who is not a party or a party's officer from any undue burden or expense resulting from compliance with a subpoena. CCP §§1985.8(*l*), 2020.220(*l*).

(3) Other conditions. The court can set other conditions for electronic discovery, including allocating the cost of producing the ESI. CCP §§1985.8(g), 2020.220(g), 2025.480(f).

I. EXPERT DISCOVERY

§1. GENERAL

§1.1 Purpose. The purpose of the provisions of the Civil Discovery Act (CDA) on discovery of expert information is to give the parties fair notice of what the experts' testimony will be at trial. *See* ***Bonds v. Roy*** (1999) 20 Cal.4th 140, 146. Expert discovery helps the parties prepare for the cross-examination of experts and gather evidence to rebut the experts' opinions. ***Jones v. Moore*** (2d Dist.2000) 80 Cal.App.4th 557, 565.

§1.2 Primary authority. CCP §§2034.010-2034.730; *see* Evid. C. §§720-733 (expert qualification and testimony), §801 (expert's opinion testimony).

§1.3 Secondary authority. The following secondary sources are cited as authority in this subchapter:

- *California Civil Discovery Practice* (CEB Online ed. 2014) (referred to as *CEB Discovery Practice*).
- Jefferson, *California Evidence Benchbook* (CEB Online ed. 2014) (referred to as *Jefferson's Evid. Benchbook*).
- Wegner, *California Practice Guide: Civil Trials & Evidence* (CD-ROM ed. 2014) (referred to as Wegner, *Civil Trials & Evidence*).
- Weil & Brown, *California Practice Guide: Civil Procedure Before Trial* (CD-ROM ed. 2014) (referred to as Weil, *Civil Procedure Before Trial*).

§2. DEFINITIONS

§2.1 Consulting expert. A consulting expert is an expert employed by a party to serve as a litigation adviser to the party's attorney on the technical and forensic aspects of the person's specialty. ***Swartzman v. Superior Ct.*** (2d Dist.1964) 231 Cal.App.2d 195, 202. The consulting expert can assist the attorney by analyzing facts, interpreting complex or technical substantive details, and recommending persons to serve as expert witnesses on particular issues. *See id.*; *CEB Discovery Practice*, §11.5; *see also* ***DeLuca v. State Fish Co.*** (2d Dist.2013) 217 Cal.App.4th 671, 690 n.20 (expert provides advisory information that assists attorney in pleading preparation, proof presentation, and

cross-examination of opposing expert witness); ***National Steel Prods. v. Superior Ct.*** (4th Dist.1985) 164 Cal.App.3d 476, 489 (same). If a consulting expert's opinion does not support the attorney's position, the attorney can effectively "bury" the expert by not disclosing the expert's identity or opinion. ***Schreiber v. Estate of Kiser*** (1999) 22 Cal.4th 31, 37. Consulting experts do not testify at trial and are not discoverable. *See id.* See "Not subject to discovery – consulting experts," §4.1.2, p. 901.

§2.2 Expert. An expert is a person who has special knowledge, skill, experience, training, or education relating to the subject of the person's testimony. Evid. C. §720(a); *see, e.g.*, ***Miller v. Los Angeles Cty. Flood Control Dist.*** (1973) 8 Cal.3d 689, 701 (person who "observed" hundreds of houses being built was not qualified as expert on home construction). An expert's special knowledge, skill, experience, training, or education can be shown by any admissible evidence, including the expert's own testimony. Evid. C. §720(b). An expert can offer opinion testimony even if the expert does not have personal knowledge of the matter on which the opinion is based. *Id.* §801.

NOTE

Unlike an expert, a lay witness cannot offer opinion testimony based on information received from others. A lay witness can, however, offer opinion testimony if it is rationally based on the witness's perception and would help the jury understand her testimony. Evid. C. §800; Wegner, Civil Trials & Evidence, ¶8:643; see ***People v. Hamilton*** *(2009) 45 Cal.4th 863, 929. The opinion testimony of a lay witness cannot counter the opinion testimony of an expert. See* ***People v. McRoberts*** *(3d Dist.2009) 178 Cal.App.4th 1249, 1257.*

§2.3 Nonretained trial expert. A nonretained trial expert is a percipient expert (i.e., an expert who has personal knowledge of facts relevant to the subject of the litigation) who is expected to testify at trial but who is not a party, a party's employee, or a person retained by a party. *See* CCP §2034.210(a), (b); ***Schreiber v. Estate of Kiser*** (1999) 22 Cal.4th 31, 35-36; ***Kalaba v. Gray*** (2d Dist.2002) 95 Cal.App.4th 1416, 1423. See "Percipient expert," §2.5, this page. Examples of nonretained trial experts include a treating physician, a police officer, and an outside accountant. *See* ***Schreiber***, 22 Cal.4th at 33 (treating physician); ***Community Dev. Comm'n v. County of Ventura*** (5th Dist.2007) 152 Cal.App.4th 1470, 1481 (fiscal consultant); ***Alvarez v. Jacmar Pac. Pizza Corp.*** (2d Dist.2002) 100 Cal.App.4th 1190, 1216 (Epstein, J., dissenting) (police officer); *CEB Discovery Practice*, §11.4 (police officer, outside accountant, treating physician).

§2.4 Party's own trial expert. A party's own trial experts include the following:

1. **Party.** The party, if the party intends to testify at trial as an expert. *See* CCP §2034.210(b). For example, a defendant-physician can be an expert in a medical-malpractice case.

2. **Employee.** The party's employee, if the party intends to call the employee to testify at trial as an expert. *See* CCP §2034.210(b). For example, a party's employee who is an engineer can be an expert in a products-liability case.

3. **Retained trial expert.** The party's retained trial expert. See "Retained trial expert," §2.6, p. 900.

§2.5 Percipient expert. A percipient expert is an expert who acquired relevant facts independently of the party's trial preparation (e.g., treating physician). ***Schreiber v. Estate of Kiser*** (1999) 22 Cal.4th 31, 35; *see also* ***P&D Consultants, Inc. v. City of Carlsbad*** (4th Dist.2010) 190 Cal.App.4th 1332, 1347-48 (listing plumbers and electricians as possible percipient experts). A percipient expert can testify as a fact witness about matters she perceived or observed and, if properly designated, can offer opinion testimony relating to those facts. ***Schreiber***, 22 Cal.4th at 35; ***Fatica v. Superior Ct.*** (4th Dist.2002) 99 Cal.App.4th 350, 353; *see, e.g.*, ***Province v. Center for Women's Health & Family Birth*** (2d Dist.1993) 20 Cal.App.4th 1673, 1683 (undesignated pathologist could testify as fact witness but not as expert), *disapproved on other grounds*, ***Heller v. Norcal Mut. Ins.*** (1994) 8 Cal.4th 30. When a percipient expert is given additional information by a party and asked to express an opinion at trial based on that information, the expert is no longer a percipient expert but rather a retained trial expert. *See* ***Dozier v. Shapiro*** (2d Dist.2011) 199 Cal.App.4th 1509, 1521.

§2.6 Retained trial expert. A retained trial expert is an expert employed by a party to form and express an opinion in anticipation of litigation or in preparation for trial. ***Schreiber v. Estate of Kiser*** (1999) 22 Cal.4th 31, 36; *see* CCP §2034.210(b). For example, a scientist employed by a defendant to provide opinion testimony in a breast-implant case is a retained trial expert. *See, e.g.*, ***Valentine v. Baxter Healthcare Corp.*** (1st Dist.1999) 68 Cal.App.4th 1467, 1473 n.5 (immunologist testified about causal relationship between breast implants and autoimmune disease).

§3. EXPERT TESTIMONY

Before seeking or producing discovery about an expert, it is helpful to understand when an expert can give opinion testimony and when an expert is limited to fact testimony.

§3.1 Opinion testimony. As a general rule, witnesses must testify about facts known to them, not opinions, because opinion testimony might interfere with the jury's resolution of the issues. *See* Wegner, *Civil Trials & Evidence*, ¶8:625. However, an expert can testify about opinions she has formed relating to the issues in a case under the following conditions:

1. **Subject beyond common experience.** The expert's opinion must be related to a subject that is sufficiently beyond the common person's experience that the expert's opinion will be helpful to the jury. Evid. C. §801(a); ***Miller v. Los Angeles Cty. Flood Control Dist.*** (1973) 8 Cal.3d 689, 702. If an opinion offered by an expert is one that could be formed by a person of ordinary education, the expert's opinion is not admissible. *See* Evid. C. §801(a); *see, e.g.*, ***Carson v. Facilities Dev. Co.*** (1984) 36 Cal.3d 830, 845 (expert was not required for party to establish that visibility at intersection was obstructed); ***Miller***, 8 Cal.3d at 702-03 (expert was required for party to establish that contractor failed to exercise due care in constructing house).

2. **Sufficient basis for opinion.** The expert's opinion must be based on a matter that satisfies the following requirements:

(1) **Perceived or personally known.** The expert's opinion must be based on a matter (i.e., facts, data, and intangibles, such as the expert's knowledge and experience) perceived or personally known by the expert or disclosed to the expert by others. Evid. C. §801(b); ***People v. Parnell*** (2d Dist.1993) 16 Cal.App.4th 862, 868-69; ***In re Marriage of Hewitson*** (2d Dist.1983) 142 Cal.App.3d 874, 885 & n.11; 7 Cal. Law Revision Comm'n Rep. (1965) p. 1139; *see, e.g.*, ***People v. Cooper*** (2d Dist.2007) 148 Cal.App.4th 731, 747 (expert's opinion was based on videotapes of interviews of deceased victim); ***Roberti v. Andy's Termite & Pest Control, Inc.*** (2d Dist.2003) 113 Cal.App.4th 893, 901 (expert's opinion was based on studies in peer-reviewed journals and physical examination of P, using generally accepted medical techniques); ***Valentine v. Baxter Healthcare Corp.*** (1st Dist.1999) 68 Cal.App.4th 1467, 1473 n.5 (expert's opinion was based on medical studies). The matter can be made known to the expert at or before the hearing. Evid. C. §801(b).

(2) **Reasonably reliable.** The expert's opinion must be based on a reasonably reliable matter, even if the matter itself is inadmissible. Evid. C. §801(b); ***In re Marriage of Hewitson***, 142 Cal.App.3d at 885; 7 Cal. Law Revision Comm'n Rep. (1965) p. 1139; *Jefferson's Evid. Benchbook*, §30.40; Wegner, *Civil Trials & Evidence*, ¶8:742. The underlying matter must be the type of information that is reasonably relied on by others in the expert's field in formulating opinions. *See* Evid. C. §801(b); *Jefferson's Evid. Benchbook*, §30.40. An expert's opinion cannot be based on speculation or conjecture. ***Lockheed Litig. Cases*** (2d Dist.2004) 115 Cal.App.4th 558, 564.

(3) **Legally permitted.** The expert's opinion must be based on a matter that an expert is legally allowed to use to form an opinion. Evid. C. §801(b); 7 Cal. Law Revision Comm'n Rep. (1965) p. 1139; *Jefferson's Evid. Benchbook*, §30.37. The expert's opinion cannot be based on information that is considered legally unreliable by constitutional provisions, statutes, or case law. 7 Cal. Law Revision Comm'n Rep. (1965) p. 1139; *e.g.*, ***In re Marriage of Hewitson***, 142 Cal.App.3d at 885-86 (expert's valuation of closely held corporate shares was based exclusively on formula that had been declared improper in earlier case).

§3.2 Fact testimony. An expert can testify about facts within her personal knowledge, as can any witness. *See* ***Schreiber v. Estate of Kiser*** (1999) 22 Cal.4th 31, 35-36 (expert with personal knowledge can provide both opinion and fact testimony); ***Province v. Center for Women's Health & Family Birth*** (2d Dist.1993) 20 Cal.App.4th 1673,

1682-83 (undesignated expert can give fact testimony but not opinion testimony). For example, a treating physician testifying as an expert can be asked about facts learned during a medical examination. ***Schreiber***, 22 Cal.4th at 35-36. See "Percipient expert," §2.5, p. 899.

§4. SCOPE OF EXPERT DISCOVERY

§4.1 Experts subject to discovery.

1. Subject to discovery. A party can secure discovery about the experts the other party intends to call as expert witnesses at trial, including nonretained trial experts and the other party's own trial experts. CCP §2034.210(a), (b). See "Nonretained trial expert," §2.3, p. 899; "Party's own trial expert," §2.4, p. 899; "Percipient witnesses," ch. 6-A, §2.2.12(2), p. 606.

2. Not subject to discovery – consulting experts. A party cannot secure discovery about the party's consulting experts as long as their status is confidential. See "Consulting expert," §2.1, p. 898.

(1) Confidential status. The identity and opinions of consulting experts who have not been designated as trial witnesses are protected from discovery by the attorney work-product doctrine. *See* ***Schreiber v. Estate of Kiser*** (1999) 22 Cal.4th 31, 37; ***Williamson v. Superior Ct.*** (1978) 21 Cal.3d 829, 834-35; ***Hernandez v. Superior Ct.*** (2d Dist.2003) 112 Cal.App.4th 285, 297; *see also* CCP §2034.210(b) (party required to provide information only about experts expected to testify); ***San Diego P.A. v. Superior Ct.*** (1962) 58 Cal.2d 194, 204-05 (expert engineers' evaluation commissioned by attorney to prepare for trial was work product; discovery allowed under exception to work-product doctrine). Communications made by the client or the attorney to the expert so the expert can properly advise the attorney are protected from discovery by the attorney-client privilege. ***DeLuca v. State Fish Co.*** (2d Dist.2013) 217 Cal.App.4th 671, 688; *see* Evid. C. §952. See "Attorney-Related Privileges," ch. 6-B, p. 613.

(2) Loss of confidential status. Information about consulting experts (including their identities and opinions) loses its confidential status and becomes discoverable under the following circumstances:

(a) By designation. If a party designates a consulting expert as an expert witness for trial, information about the consulting expert becomes discoverable. ***Schreiber***, 22 Cal.4th at 37; ***Williamson***, 21 Cal.3d at 834-35; ***Hernandez***, 112 Cal.App.4th at 297. Discoverable information includes noncore work product and communications between the expert and the client or the attorney. *See* ***DeLuca***, 217 Cal.App.4th at 689 (work-product and attorney-client privileges no longer apply). But if the information (e.g., written report) contains both (1) information relevant to the opinion the expert will give as a testifying expert and (2) the expert's advice on trial-preparation matters, conveyed as a consulting expert, the court may be required to conduct an in camera review of the information to separate the protected work-product information provided as a consultant from the discoverable information provided as a testifying expert. *Id.* at 690; *see* ***National Steel Prods. v. Superior Ct.*** (4th Dist.1985) 164 Cal.App.3d 476, 489. For the steps the court must take to determine whether the information is protected work product, see "Dual capacity," ch. 6-B, §3.6.5(2), p. 635.

(b) Reasonable certainty of testimony. If it becomes reasonably certain that a consulting expert will testify as an expert at trial, information about the consulting expert becomes discoverable. ***DeLuca***, 217 Cal.App.4th at 689-90; ***Hernandez***, 112 Cal.App.4th at 297. If it becomes reasonably certain that the expert will act in a dual capacity as a prospective witness and as an adviser to the attorney, the court may need to conduct an in camera review of the information to determine whether it is protected work product. ***DeLuca***, 217 Cal.App.4th at 690; *see* ***National Steel***, 164 Cal.App.3d at 489. See "Dual capacity," ch. 6-B, §3.6.5(2), p. 635.

(c) Prejudice or injustice exception. Information about a consulting expert becomes discoverable if (1) the discovering party shows that denial of discovery will result in prejudice or injustice and (2) the information does not contain any core work product.

[1] Prejudice or injustice. The discovering party must show that the denial of discovery will (1) unfairly prejudice the discovering party in preparing its claim or defense or (2) result in an injustice. ***National Steel***, 164 Cal.App.3d at 487. For example, denying discovery might unfairly prejudice a party if the party

is unable to prepare its claim or defense without the information and if the information is not obtainable elsewhere. ***Hernandez***, 112 Cal.App.4th at 298; *e.g.*, ***National Steel***, 164 Cal.App.3d at 491-92 (party needed expert's report for its impeachment value). The court must balance the need for disclosure against the purposes served by the work-product doctrine. ***Hernandez***, 112 Cal.App.4th at 297. See "Discovery of noncore work product," ch. 6-B, §3.9.2, p. 639.

[2] Not core work product. The information cannot contain any core work product—that is, the information cannot reflect the attorney's impressions, conclusions, opinions, legal research, or theories. Information that includes any core work product is not discoverable under any circumstances. CCP §2018.030(a); ***DeLuca***, 217 Cal.App.4th at 690 n.21; ***National Steel***, 164 Cal.App.3d at 489. See "Core work product," ch. 6-B, §3.5.1, p. 631.

(d) Fact witness. If the consulting expert is also a percipient expert, the expert's identity and location are subject to discovery because the expert is a fact witness. *See* CCP §2017.010 (party can discover identity and location of fact witnesses); ***Puerto v. Superior Ct.*** (2d Dist.2008) 158 Cal.App.4th 1242, 1249-50 (disclosure of potential witnesses is routine and essential part of pretrial discovery); ***Huffy Corp. v. Superior Ct.*** (2d Dist.2003) 112 Cal.App.4th 97, 109 (identity and location of fact witnesses are not subject to work-product immunity); ***Huntley v. Foster*** (2d Dist.1995) 35 Cal.App.4th 753, 756 (percipient expert is a fact witness). See "Percipient witnesses," ch. 6-A, §2.2.12(2), p. 606.

§4.2 What can be discovered. A party can obtain the following information about or from discoverable experts:

1. **Identity.** The party can discover the names and addresses of the other party's own trial experts and nonretained trial experts. CCP §2034.260(b)(1); ***Schreiber v. Estate of Kiser*** (1999) 22 Cal.4th 31, 34.

2. **Qualifications.** The party can discover the qualifications of the other party's own trial experts (i.e., the party itself, its employee, or its retained trial expert) and nonretained trial experts. *See* CCP §2034.260(c)(1) (qualifications of party's own trial experts discoverable); ***Schreiber***, 22 Cal.4th at 38 (nonretained trial experts are not subject to special discovery restrictions).

3. **Expected testimony.** The party can discover what the other party's own trial experts and nonretained trial experts will testify about at trial, including their opinions. *See* CCP §2034.260(c)(2) (opinions of party's own trial experts discoverable); ***Schreiber***, 22 Cal.4th at 38 (opinions of nonretained trial experts discoverable).

4. **Fees.** The party can discover what the other party's own trial experts are charging for their testimony. *See, e.g.*, CCP §2034.260(c)(5) (expert-witness declaration must include statement of party's own trial expert's hourly and daily fee for providing deposition testimony and for consulting with retaining attorney).

5. **Reports & writings.** The party can obtain the reports and writings made by the other party's own trial experts in the course of preparing their expert opinions. *See, e.g.*, CCP §2034.210(c) (party can demand mutual and simultaneous production for inspection and copying of all discoverable reports and writings made by other party's own trial experts).

§5. COMPARING DEMANDS FOR EXPERT INFORMATION WITH OTHER DISCOVERY METHODS

There are several ways that a party can secure discovery about the other party's experts. The primary method is a demand for the exchange of expert information, but other methods can be used as well.

§5.1 Demands for exchange of expert information. Demands for the exchange of expert information are used to obtain the identity and opinions of the experts who will testify at trial. ***Kalaba v. Gray*** (2d Dist.2002) 95 Cal.App.4th 1416, 1419-20. Demands are made after nonexpert discovery has been completed so that the parties can make their final preparations for trial. *Id.* at 1423. Unlike other discovery methods, a demand creates a mutual obligation that requires both parties to simultaneously produce expert information. See "Demand for Exchange of Expert Information," §6, p. 904.

§5.2 Other methods to secure discovery about experts. Other discovery methods (e.g., depositions, interrogatories) can be used to obtain both admissible evidence about experts and information that can lead to the discovery of admissible evidence about experts. ***Kalaba v. Gray*** (2d Dist.2002) 95 Cal.App.4th 1416, 1423. See "What Is Discoverable," ch. 6-A, §2, p. 603. Determining which discovery method to use (other than a demand for exchange of expert information) depends on whether the expert is the other party's own trial expert or a nonretained trial expert.

1. Party's own trial experts. The following discovery methods can be used to obtain information about or from another party's own trial experts:

(1) Deposition notice. A party can discover information from another party's own trial expert by serving a deposition notice for the expert's deposition. See "Party's own trial experts," §10.2.1(1), p. 911.

(2) Demand to produce. A party can discover documents relating to the other party's own trial expert by serving a demand to produce the expert's file, including the expert's correspondence, related articles or other materials, models, preliminary drafts of reports, and billing records. See "Demands to Produce," ch. 7-E, p. 845.

(3) Patient's authorization. A party can discover information from an expert who is a medical provider by serving a written authorization executed by the patient for the release of the patient's medical information. *See* Civ. C. §§56.10(a), 56.11. The authorization must comply with the requirements of Civ. C. §56.11. *E.g.*, ***Colleen M. v. Fertility & Surgical Assocs.*** (2d Dist.2005) 132 Cal.App.4th 1466, 1473 (authorization was invalid because it did not comply with §56.11).

2. Nonretained trial experts. The following discovery methods can be used to obtain information about or from a party's nonretained trial experts:

(1) Deposition subpoena. A party can discover information from a nonretained trial expert by serving a deposition subpoena on the expert. See "Nonretained trial experts," §10.2.1(2), p. 911.

(2) Interrogatories. A party can discover information about a nonretained trial expert by serving interrogatories on the other party. *See* ***Schreiber v. Estate of Kiser*** (1999) 22 Cal.4th 31, 38 (identity and opinion of nonretained trial expert discoverable through interrogatories). See "Nonretained experts," ch. 7-C, §3.1.3(2), p. 817.

(3) Patient's authorization. A party can discover information from a nonretained trial expert who is a medical provider by serving a written authorization executed by the patient for the release of the patient's medical information. See "Patient's authorization," §5.2.1(3), this page.

(4) Case questionnaire. A defendant in a limited civil case involving personal injury can discover from the other party's completed case questionnaire the name, address, telephone number, and treatment information for any physician, dentist, or other health-care provider who treated or examined the plaintiff. *See* Judicial Council Forms, form DISC-010, question 2(b).

(5) Ex parte interview. A party can conduct an ex parte interview of a nonretained trial expert without the other party's authorization in the following situations:

(a) Medical malpractice. In a medical-malpractice action, a defendant's insurer can conduct an ex parte interview with the plaintiff's treating physician to assist with the defense. ***Heller v. Norcal Mut. Ins.*** (1994) 8 Cal.4th 30, 35; *see* Civ. C. §56.10(c)(4) (medical information can be released to assist with defense in medical-malpractice action).

(b) Nonprivileged information. If the nonretained trial expert has information that is not protected by a privilege, the party can conduct an ex parte interview with the expert to obtain that information. *Cf.* ***Puerto v. Superior Ct.*** (2d Dist.2008) 158 Cal.App.4th 1242, 1254 (party could obtain witness contact information from interrogatories; discovery contemplates locating witnesses so they can be contacted); ***State Farm Fire & Cas.***

Co. v. Superior Ct. (2d Dist.1997) 54 Cal.App.4th 625, 652 (P could contact managerial ex-employees of D-corporation to inquire about relevant facts but not privileged information). See "Informal discovery," ch. 7-A, §2.2, p. 742.

§6. DEMAND FOR EXCHANGE OF EXPERT INFORMATION

§6.1 Who can make demand. Any party can make a demand for the exchange of expert information in any type of case except an eminent-domain proceeding. *See* CCP §§2034.010, 2034.210, 2034.220.

§6.2 Who must exchange. A demand for the exchange of expert information compels all parties who have appeared in the case to participate in the exchange. CCP §2034.260(a).

§6.3 When to make demand. A demand for the exchange of expert information must be served within the time period specified in CCP §2034.220. If a demand is untimely, a responding party can seek a protective order under CCP §2034.250, and the demanding party can make a corresponding motion for relief under CCP §473(b). See "Motion for protective order," §12.1, p. 914; "Motion for relief from untimely demand," §12.2, p. 915.

1. Earliest date for demand. The earliest date a party can make a demand for the exchange of expert information is the date after the court sets the initial trial date (not the initial trial date itself). CCP §2034.210; *CEB Discovery Practice*, §11.10.

2. Latest date for demand. The latest date a party can make a demand for the exchange of expert information is either (1) 10 days after the court sets the initial trial date or (2) 70 days before the initial trial date, whichever is closer to the initial trial date. CCP §2034.220; ***Schreiber v. Estate of Kiser*** (1999) 22 Cal.4th 31, 37; ***Hernandez v. Superior Ct.*** (2d Dist.2003) 112 Cal.App.4th 285, 297; *CEB Discovery Practice*, §11.10. To determine which date is closer to the initial trial date, use the formula in chart 7-16, below. If the deadline to serve the demand falls on a weekend or holiday, the deadline is extended until the next court day closer to the trial date. CCP §2016.060.

7-16. CALCULATING LATEST DATE TO SERVE DEMAND FOR EXCHANGE OF EXPERT INFORMATION

Compare dates in B and D; whichever is closer to date in C = E

A	B	C	D	E
Insert date court set initial trial date (not initial trial date itself)	Add 10 days to date in column A and insert date below	Insert initial trial date	Subtract 70 days from date in column C and insert date below	Latest date to serve demand for exchange of expert information is:
Date: __________	Date: __________	Date: __________	Date: __________	Date: __________

3. Examples.

Example 1 – On April 20, the court set the initial trial date for December 1. *Step 1:* Insert April 20 in column A and insert December 1 in column C. *Step 2:* Add ten days to April 20 (April 20 + 10 days = April 30), and insert April 30 in column B. *Step 3:* Subtract 70 days from December 1 (December 1 – 70 days = September 22), and insert September 22 in column D. *Step 4:* Compare the dates in columns B and D to the date in column C. Because the date in column D (September 22) is closer to the date in column C (December 1) than the date in column B (April 30) is, the cutoff for making a demand for the exchange of expert information is September 22. To calculate the number of days the parties have to make a demand, count the days between the dates in columns A and E. In this example, the parties have 155 days (from April 20 to September 22) to make the demand.

Example 2 – On April 20, the court set the initial trial date for July 20. *Step 1:* Insert April 20 in column A and insert July 20 in column C. *Step 2:* Add 10 days to April 20 (April 20 + 10 days = April 30) and insert April 30 in column B. *Step 3:* Subtract 70 days from July 20 (July 20 – 70 days = May 11) and insert May 11 in column D. *Step 4:* Compare the dates in columns B and D to the date in column C. Because the date in column D (May 11) is closer to the date in column C (July 20) than the date in column B (April 30) is, the cutoff for making a demand for

the exchange of expert information is May 11. To calculate the number of days the parties have to make a demand, count the days between the dates in columns A and E. In this example, the parties have only 21 days (from April 20 to May 11) to make the demand.

4. Changing deadline. The parties can stipulate to a schedule for demanding expert information that deviates from the statutory guidelines. See "Modifying discovery by stipulation," ch. 7-A, §4.1, p. 743. If a stipulation cannot be obtained, a party can make a motion to change the deadline. See "Motion to change statutory deadline for demand," §12.3, p. 915.

§6.4 Form. See "Form of discovery requests," ch. 7-A, §7.2, p. 753.

§6.5 Contents. A demand for the exchange of expert information must include the following information:

1. Party. The demand must identify, below the title of the case, the party making the demand. CCP §2034.230(a).

2. Authority. The demand must state that it is being made under Chapter 18 of the CDA. CCP §2034.230(a).

3. Date for exchange. The demand must specify the date and time for the attorneys to meet and exchange the expert information in person, or if the exchange is by mail, the date for mailing the information. *See* CCP §§2034.230(b), 2034.260(a). The exchange must be made simultaneously on or before this date. *See id.* §§2034.210, 2034.260(a).

(1) Calculating date for exchange. Generally, the date selected for the exchange must be at least 50 days before the initial trial date or 20 days after service of the demand, whichever is closer to the trial date. CCP §2034.230(b); ***Hernandez v. Superior Ct.*** (2d Dist.2003) 112 Cal.App.4th 285, 297. Depending on the method of service of the demand, the deadline for the exchange may be extended. *See, e.g.*, ***Staub v. Kiley*** (3d Dist.2014) 226 Cal.App.4th 1437, 1445-46 (demand was premature because Ds failed to extend exchange date by five days under CCP §1013(a) when service was by intrastate mail). See "When to Serve," ch. 1-G, §6, p. 69. To calculate the date for the exchange, use the formula in chart 7-17, below:

7-17. CALCULATING DATE TO EXCHANGE EXPERT INFORMATION

Compare dates in B and D; whichever is closer to date in A = E				
A	**B**	**C**	**D**	**F**
Insert initial trial date Date: ________	Subtract 50 days from date in column A and insert date below Date: ________	Insert date demand was served Date: ________	Add 20* days to date in column C and insert date below Date: ________	Date to exchange expert information is: Date: ________

* This deadline is extended if the demand was served by mail, fax, or electronic means. For the number of days to add based on the method of service, see ch. 1-G, §6, p. 69.

(2) Examples.

Example 1 – The court set the initial trial date for December 1, and one of the parties served a demand for expert information by personal delivery on April 30. *Step 1:* Insert December 1 in column A and insert April 30 in column C. *Step 2:* Subtract 50 days from December 1 (December 1 – 50 days = October 12), and insert October 12 in column B. *Step 3:* Add 20 days to April 30 (April 30 + 20 days = May 20), and insert May 20 in column D. *Step 4:* Compare the dates in columns B and D to the date in column A. Because the date in column B (October 12) is closer to the date in column A (December 1) than the date in column D (May 20) is, October 12 is the deadline to exchange expert information.

Example 2 – The court set the initial trial date for July 20, and one of the parties served a demand for expert information by intrastate mail on May 11. *Step 1:* Insert July 20 in column A and insert May 11 in

column C. *Step 2:* Subtract 50 days from July 20 (July 20 – 50 days = May 31), and insert May 31 in column B. *Step 3:* Add 20 days to May 11 (May 11 + 20 days = May 31), add 5 days to May 31 because service was by intrastate mail (May 31 + 5 days = June 5), and insert June 5 in column D. *Step 4:* Compare the dates in columns B and D to the date in column A. Because the date in column D (June 5) is closer to the date in column A (July 20) than the date in column B (May 31) is, June 5 is the deadline to exchange expert information.

4. Method for exchange. The demand should specify whether the exchange will be in person or by mail. *See* CCP §2034.260(a).

5. Place for exchange. The demand should specify the place where the attorneys are supposed to meet and exchange the information, if the exchange is to be made in person. *See* CCP §2034.260(a).

6. Things demanded. The demand can be used to obtain the following:

(1) Lists of experts. The demand can require the exchange of the names and addresses of all the trial experts (i.e., party, employee, retained, and nonretained) who are expected to offer expert-opinion testimony at trial by live or deposition testimony. CCP §2034.210(a).

(2) Expert-witness declarations. The demand can require the exchange of expert-witness declarations, which contain information about a party's own trial experts. CCP §2034.210(b). See "Party's own trial expert," §2.4, p. 899; "Declaration for trial experts," §7.2.2, p. 907.

(3) Expert reports. The demand can require the exchange of all discoverable reports and writings made by any of the parties' own trial experts in the course of preparing their expert opinions. CCP §2034.210(c). See "Party's own trial expert," §2.4, p. 899; "Expert reports & writings," §7.2.3, p. 908.

7. Signature. There is no requirement that the demand be signed by the discovering party or its attorney. But as a general rule, an attorney should sign all discovery requests that she drafts. See "Attorney's signature," ch. 7-A, §7.2.6, p. 753.

§6.6 Serving. The discovering party must serve copies of the demand on all parties who have appeared in the case. CCP §2034.240. See "Serving discovery," ch. 7-A, §13.1, p. 769.

§6.7 Filing or lodging. The discovering party is not required to file the demand. CCP §2034.290(a). The demand and all the expert-witness lists and declarations exchanged in response to it must be lodged with the court only if their contents become relevant to an issue in any pending matter in the case. *Id.* §2034.290(c). See "Filing or lodging discovery," ch. 7-A, §13.2, p. 770.

§6.8 Custody & disposal. The discovering party must maintain custody of the original demand, its proof of service, and the originals of all expert-witness lists and declarations exchanged in response to the demand. CCP §2034.290(b). These documents can be destroyed six months after the final disposition of the case, unless the court, based on a good-cause motion, orders that they be preserved for a longer time. *Id.* See "Custody & Disposal of Discovery," ch. 7-A, §16, p. 776.

§6.9 Demand after new trial. Discovery is automatically reopened in a case that is retried after a mistrial, an order granting a new trial, or a reversal on appeal. *See **Fairmont Ins. v. Superior Ct.*** (2000) 22 Cal.4th 245, 250-51. An expert demand made in an initial trial is ineffective in a second trial. *See **Hirano v. Hirano*** (2d Dist.2007) 158 Cal.App.4th 1, 8. A party must make a new demand when a case is retried. If no demand is made in the second trial, it is as if no demand has been made, and no one is required to comply with the statutory exchange requirements. *See, e.g., id.* at 7-8 (P's failure to comply in first trial with demand for exchange of expert information did not prevent P from introducing undesignated expert in second trial because no demand was made in second trial). A demand for the exchange of expert information in the second trial must be made based on the new initial trial date. See "When to make demand," §6.3, p. 904.

§7. RESPONSE TO DEMAND FOR EXCHANGE

A party responding to a demand for the exchange of expert information can (1) provide a written statement that it has no experts, (2) designate experts, or (3) make a motion for a protective order.

§7.1 No experts. If the responding party does not presently intend to offer the testimony of any expert witness at trial, the responding party can serve a written statement stating so. CCP §2034.260(b)(2). But a party cannot delay its designation of experts on a disputed trial issue known to all parties, wait until the other parties designate their experts, and then name its own experts as "rebuttal" witnesses. ***Fairfax v. Lords*** (4th Dist.2006) 138 Cal.App.4th 1019, 1021; *CEB Discovery Practice*, §11.24. If a party later decides it will need to offer expert testimony, the party must make a motion to augment the designation, showing reasonable diligence or mistake. See "Motion to augment designation," §12.6.1(1)(a), p. 918.

§7.2 Designate experts. If the responding party intends to offer the testimony of expert witnesses at trial, it must produce the following information:

1. Designation of trial experts. The responding party must designate all the experts that it intends to call as witnesses at trial, either by live testimony or by deposition. CCP §2034.260(b)(1). The designation must identify each expert by name and address. *Id.*

(1) Party's own trial experts. The designation must include the responding party's own trial experts (i.e., the party itself, its employees, or its retained trial experts) that the responding party intends to call to testify as experts at trial. *See* CCP §2034.260(b)(1); ***Kalaba v. Gray*** (2d Dist.2002) 95 Cal.App.4th 1416, 1422-23. See "Party's own trial expert," §2.4, p. 899.

(2) Nonretained trial experts. The designation must include any nonretained trial experts that the responding party intends to call to testify as experts at trial. See "Nonretained trial expert," §2.3, p. 899. The responding party cannot simply state that it intends to call "all treating physicians" to testify as experts; each expert must be separately identified by name and address. *See **Gotschall v. Daley*** (3d Dist.2002) 96 Cal.App.4th 479, 481-82; ***Kalaba***, 95 Cal.App.4th at 1418.

(3) Other party's experts. The designation should include any experts of another party (e.g., a codefendant) that the responding party intends to call as experts at trial. *See **Zellerino v. Brown*** (3d Dist.1991) 235 Cal.App.3d 1097, 1116; Weil, *Civil Procedure Before Trial*, ¶8:1668.1. If a party calls an expert to testify who it did not designate but who was designated by another party, the expert will not be permitted to offer opinion testimony for the nondesignating party unless the nondesignating party can show compliance with CCP §2034.310. See "Calling undesignated experts," §13.4, p. 923.

2. Declaration for trial experts. The responding party must make an expert-witness declaration for certain experts listed in its designation.

(1) Experts covered.

(a) Party's own trial experts. If the responding party lists any of its own trial experts (i.e., the party itself, its employees, or its retained trial experts) in its designation, it must make an expert-witness declaration for those experts. CCP §§2034.210(b), 2034.260(c); ***Schreiber v. Estate of Kiser*** (1999) 22 Cal.4th 31, 34; *see **Bonds v. Roy*** (1999) 20 Cal.4th 140, 144. See "Party's own trial expert," §2.4, p. 899. The responding party is not required to include information about its nonretained trial experts (e.g., treating physicians) in the declaration. *See* CCP §§2034.210(b), 2034.260(c); ***Schreiber***, 22 Cal.4th at 34; *CEB Discovery Practice*, §11.4; *see also **Ochoa v. Dorado*** (2d Dist.2014) 228 Cal.App.4th 120, 140-41 (no expert-witness declaration is needed for treating physician testifying about value of services provided to P). See "Nonretained trial expert," §2.3, p. 899.

(b) Other party's own trial experts. If the responding party lists another party's own trial experts in its designation, the responding party must make expert-witness declarations for those experts. ***Zellerino***, 235 Cal.App.3d at 1116. By listing another party's own trial experts, the responding party assumes the burden of providing a declaration about the expert's expected testimony. *Id.*

(2) Information included. The declaration must include the following:

(a) Expert's qualifications. The declaration must provide a brief narrative statement of the qualifications of each expert. CCP §2034.260(c)(1).

(b) **Expert's testimony.**

[1] **Brief narrative.** The declaration must provide a brief narrative statement of the general substance of the expert's expected testimony. CCP §2034.260(c)(2); ***Bonds***, 20 Cal.4th at 144; ***Province v. Center for Women's Health & Family Birth*** (2d Dist.1993) 20 Cal.App.4th 1673, 1682. For example, a brief narrative of a physician's testimony in a medical-malpractice action might state that the physician-expert was hired to review the medical records and examine the plaintiff and that the physician-expert will be called to testify at trial about the standard of care, the defendant's breach of the standard of care, causation of the injury, and the plaintiff's injuries and damages.

[2] **Broad description.** The general substance of the expert's expected testimony should be described in broad terms to prevent the declaration from limiting the scope of the expert's trial testimony; an expert can be prevented from testifying at trial on a subject that was not described in the declaration. *See, e.g.*, ***Bonds***, 20 Cal.4th at 145 (physician could not testify about standard of care because it was not included in declaration); ***Jones v. Moore*** (2d Dist.2000) 80 Cal.App.4th 557, 566 (expert in family law could testify about certain legal issues because testimony was within general "ambit" of whether D breached standard of care, which was included in declaration). To expand the scope of the testimony beyond the narrative statement, the party must move to amend the declaration. ***Bonds***, 20 Cal.4th at 145. See "Motion to amend declaration," §12.6.1(1)(b), p. 918.

(c) **Expert's fee.** The declaration must provide a statement of the expert's hourly and daily fee for providing deposition testimony and for consulting with the responding party's attorney. CCP §2034.260(c)(5). To challenge the amount of the fee, a party must file a motion. See "Motion to reduce expert's fee," §12.7, p. 920.

(d) **Representations.** The declaration must make the following representations:

[1] The responding party's own trial experts have agreed to testify at trial. CCP §2034.260(c)(3); *see* ***Schreiber***, 22 Cal.4th at 38 (party is not required to state that its nonretained trial experts have agreed to testify).

[2] Each of the responding party's designated experts will be sufficiently familiar with the pending case to submit to a meaningful oral deposition concerning the specific testimony—including any opinion and its basis—that the expert is expected to provide at trial. CCP §2034.260(c)(4).

(e) **Signature & verification.** The declaration must be made under penalty of perjury and must be signed by the attorney or the responding party (if pro per). CCP §2034.260(c).

3. **Expert reports & writings.** If the demand for the exchange of expert information included a demand for the production and exchange of discoverable reports and writings made by the experts listed in CCP §2034.210(b), the responding party must produce them.

(1) **Experts covered.**

(a) **Party's own trial experts.** If the responding party lists any of its own trial experts in its designation, it must produce for inspection and copying all the discoverable reports and writings made by those experts. *See* CCP §§2034.210(b), (c), 2034.270; ***Bonds***, 20 Cal.4th at 144. See "Party's own trial expert," §2.4, p. 899. The responding party is not required to produce reports and writings made by its designated nonretained trial experts (e.g., treating physicians). *See* CCP §2034.210(c); ***Zellerino***, 235 Cal.App.3d at 1116. See "Nonretained trial expert," §2.3, p. 899.

(b) **Other party's own trial experts.** If the responding party lists another party's own trial experts in its designation, the responding party must provide discoverable reports and writings made by those experts. *See* ***Zellerino***, 235 Cal.App.3d at 1116.

(2) **What must be exchanged.** The party must produce for inspection and copying all the discoverable reports and writings of the applicable experts made in the course of preparing their expert opinions. *See* CCP §§2034.210(c), 2034.270; *CEB Discovery Practice*, §11.22. This applies to all the reports and writings that are then

in existence. *See* ***Boston v. Penny Lane Ctrs., Inc.*** (2d Dist.2009) 170 Cal.App.4th 936, 951. Reports and writings created after the exchange date should be promptly served on the opposing party. *See id.* at 953.

PRACTICE TIP

To obtain other documents from an opposing party's own trial expert beyond those created in the course of preparing the expert's opinion, a party must serve the opposing party with a demand to produce the expert's file. See "Demands to Produce," ch. 7-E, p. 845.

§7.3 Motion for protective order. The responding party can object to a demand for the exchange of expert information by making a motion for a protective order. CCP §2034.250(a); *see* ***Zellerino v. Brown*** (3d Dist.1991) 235 Cal.App.3d 1097, 1109. A motion for a protective order must be filed "promptly." CCP §2034.250(a). A party cannot merely serve an objection to a demand; instead, the party must include the objection in a motion for a protective order and comply with all the procedural requirements that encourage the informal resolution of discovery disputes. ***Zellerino***, 235 Cal.App.3d at 1110-11; *see* CCP §2034.250(a) (motion must be accompanied by meet-and-confer declaration). See "Motion for protective order," §12.1, p. 914.

§8. EXCHANGING EXPERT INFORMATION

§8.1 Procedure for exchange.

1. When to exchange. The exchange of expert information must be made on or before the date identified in the demand for the exchange. CCP §2034.260(a). See "Date for exchange," §6.5.3, p. 905.

2. Method for exchange. The exchange of expert information must be conducted either in person or by mail, as specified in the demand. *See* CCP §2034.260(a).

3. Making exchange. All parties who have appeared in the case must simultaneously exchange their expert information in writing on or before the date for the exchange specified in the demand. *See* CCP §§2034.210, 2034.260(a); ***Hernandez v. Superior Ct.*** (2d Dist.2003) 112 Cal.App.4th 285, 297. If the exchange is made by mail, the expert information can be sent on or before the date for the exchange. CCP §2034.260(a). See "Date for exchange," §6.5.3, p. 905. The court cannot require one party to provide expert information before the other parties are required to do so. ***Fairfax v. Lords*** (4th Dist.2006) 138 Cal.App.4th 1019, 1021; ***Hernandez***, 112 Cal.App.4th at 297; *see* CCP §2034.210(a).

§8.2 Changing deadline for exchange.

1. Stipulation. The parties can stipulate to a schedule for the exchange of expert information that deviates from the statutory guidelines. See "Modifying discovery by stipulation," ch. 7-A, §4.1, p. 743.

2. Motion. On a motion for a protective order showing good cause or a motion to change the statutory deadline for exchange, the court can change the date specified in the demand for the simultaneous exchange of expert information. See "Motion for protective order," §12.1, p. 914; "Motion to change statutory deadline for exchange," §12.4, p. 915.

§9. CHANGING LIST OF EXPERT WITNESSES

§9.1 Adding experts.

1. Without motion. A party can supplement its expert-witness list with additional experts without filing a motion to amend by complying with CCP §2034.280(a).

(1) Deadline. The supplemental expert list must be submitted within 20 days after the original exchange of expert information. CCP §2034.280(a).

(2) Grounds to supplement. A party is entitled to supplement its expert-witness list without a motion if (1) the supplementing party participated in the original exchange of expert information, (2) in the original

Expert Discovery

exchange, an adverse party designated an expert to cover a subject, and (3) the supplementing party had not previously retained an expert to testify on that subject. CCP §2034.280(a).

(3) What is supplemented.

(a) Witness list. The supplemental expert list must contain the name and address of each new expert. CCP §2034.280(a).

(b) Declaration. If the new experts are a party's own trial experts, the supplemental expert list must include an expert-witness declaration for each new expert. CCP §2034.280(b); *see id.* §2034.260(c). See "Party's own trial expert," §2.4, p. 899; "Declaration for trial experts," §7.2.2, p. 907.

(c) Reports. If the new experts are a party's own trial experts, the supplemental expert list must include all their discoverable reports and writings. CCP §2034.280(b); *see id.* §2034.210(c). See "Party's own trial expert," §2.4, p. 899; "Expert reports & writings," §7.2.3, p. 908.

2. With motion. If a party cannot supplement its expert-witness list under CCP §2034.280(a), it can add experts to its witness list only by filing a good-cause motion. See "Motion to augment designation or amend declaration," §12.6, p. 918.

§9.2 Withdrawing experts.

1. Procedure for withdrawal. A party can withdraw the designation of an expert from its expert-witness list by simply amending the list and omitting the expert. *See* ***Williamson v. Superior Ct.*** (1978) 21 Cal.3d 829, 835. The withdrawal of an expert can be made without advance notice and without court approval. ***County of L.A. v. Superior Ct.*** (2d Dist.1990) 222 Cal.App.3d 647, 656. A party can withdraw an expert for any reason, even if the expert reached an opinion unfavorable to the party's case. *See id.* (party can withdraw expert for "tactical reasons").

(1) Withdrawing party as expert. The designation of a party as an expert trial witness is not in itself an implied waiver of the party's attorney-client privilege. ***Shooker v. Superior Ct.*** (2d Dist.2003) 111 Cal.App.4th 923, 930. If the party provides privileged documents or testifies as an expert (e.g., giving an opinion at a deposition or in a declaration), the privilege is waived. *Id.* If the designation of a party as an expert witness is withdrawn before the party discloses a significant part of a privileged communication, or before it is known with reasonable certainty that the party will actually testify as an expert, the privileged information is not discoverable. *Id.*

(2) Withdrawing other experts. If a withdrawn retained expert has not been deposed, the party should consider employing the expert as a consulting expert. Doing so will prevent another party from hiring or even contacting the expert. ***County of L.A.***, 222 Cal.App.3d at 657-58. If an attorney for another party contacts a withdrawn expert who was retained as a consulting expert and receives confidential information from the expert, the attorney can be disqualified from the case. *See, e.g.*, ***Shandralina G. v. Homonchuk*** (4th Dist.2007) 147 Cal.App.4th 395, 417 (no attorney disqualification because no evidence consulting expert disclosed confidential information to opposing attorney); ***Collins v. State*** (3d Dist.2004) 121 Cal.App.4th 1112, 1130-31 (same); ***County of L.A.***, 222 Cal.App.3d at 657-58 (attorney disqualified for obtaining confidential information from opposing party's consulting expert).

2. Improper withdrawal. A party cannot make an agreement to withdraw the designation of an expert in exchange for indemnification or other consideration from the other party. *See, e.g.*, ***Williamson***, 21 Cal.3d at 837-38 (improper for party to withdraw designation of expert in exchange for payment from other party). Such an agreement is an illegal attempt to conceal evidence, which requires the court to invalidate the party's withdrawal of the expert and, if applicable, order full disclosure of the expert's reports and writings. *See, e.g.*, *id.* at 838-39 (court ordered disclosure of expert's report).

§10. DEPOSING EXPERTS

§10.1 Scheduling.

1. Earliest time.

(1) After designation – by right. The deposition of any designated trial expert can be taken anytime after the receipt of the other party's expert-witness list. CCP §2034.410.

(2) **Before designation – by motion.**

(a) **MSJ proceeding.** The deposition of an expert can be taken before experts are designated if there is a legitimate question about the foundation of the expert's opinion submitted in support of or in opposition to a motion for summary judgment. ***St. Mary Med. Ctr. v. Superior Ct.*** (2d Dist.1996) 50 Cal.App.4th 1531, 1540; *see* ***Sanchez v. Hillerich & Bradsby Co.*** (2d Dist.2002) 104 Cal.App.4th 703, 718 (dicta). The deposition must be limited to the foundation of the expert's opinion. *See* ***St. Mary Med. Ctr.***, 50 Cal.App.4th at 1540. To take such a deposition, the party must file a motion to compel deposition and present objective facts that create a significant question about the validity of the expert's opinion. *See id.* at 1540-41. See "Motion to Compel Depositions," ch. 9-D, p. 1046.

(b) **Anticipated nonretained trial expert.** The deposition of an anticipated nonretained trial expert (e.g., a police officer who investigated the accident) can be taken before the formal designation of experts by serving the expert with a deposition subpoena. *See* ***Schreiber v. Estate of Kiser*** (1999) 22 Cal.4th 31, 38. See "Deposition Subpoenas," ch. 8-B, p. 959.

2. **Latest time.**

(1) **Expert in original designation.** The deposition of experts identified in the original designation must be completed at least 15 days before the initial trial date. *See* CCP §2024.030.

(2) **Expert in supplemental designation.** The deposition of experts identified in a supplemental designation can be taken even though the time limit for discovery has expired. CCP §2034.280(c). The party supplementing the expert-witness list must make its additional experts available immediately for a deposition. *Id.*

§10.2 Procedure. The CDA procedures for taking oral and written depositions of nonexpert witnesses apply to a deposition of designated trial experts except as discussed below. CCP §2034.410. See "Depositions," ch. 7-B, p. 780.

1. **Deposition notice or subpoena.**

(1) **Party's own trial experts.** To take the deposition of a party's own trial expert (i.e., the party itself, its employee, or its retained trial expert), the party's attorney must be served with a notice of deposition and a tender of the expert's witness fee. *See* CCP §2034.460(a). Once a party is served with the deposition notice and fee, the party is obligated to produce its expert for a deposition. *Id.* See "Expert-Witness Fees," §11, p. 912; "Deposition notice for oral deposition," ch. 7-B, §9.2, p. 789.

(2) **Nonretained trial experts.** To take the deposition of a nonretained trial expert, a party must serve the expert with a deposition subpoena. *See* ***Hurtado v. Western Med. Ctr.*** (4th Dist.1990) 222 Cal.App.3d 1198, 1202-03 (deposition notice cannot compel production of nonretained trial expert). See "Who Is Subject to a Subpoena," ch. 8-A, §4, p. 937. A party has no obligation to produce a nonretained trial expert that it listed in its designation of experts. *See, e.g.*, ***Hurtado***, 222 Cal.App.3d at 1202-03 (P not required to produce treating physicians for deposition because they were not retained).

2. **Expert's video deposition.** If the deposition of an expert is to be recorded by videotape for use at trial, the deposition notice (for a party's own trial expert) or the deposition subpoena (for a nonretained trial expert) must reserve the right to use the video deposition at trial. For deposition notices, see "Expert's video deposition," ch. 7-B, §13.1.3(3)(b), p. 811. For deposition subpoenas, see "Expert's video deposition," ch. 8-B, §3.1.3(4), p. 960.

PRACTICE TIP

There are two notices you must provide before you can use an expert's videotaped deposition at trial. See CCP §2025.620(d). First, the deposition notice or subpoena must include the reservation of the right to use the expert's videotaped deposition at trial. See "Expert's video deposition," §10.2.2, this page. Second, the deposing party must provide a notice of intent to use the deposition to the court and the other parties before trial. See "Notice of intent to use electronically recorded deposition," ch. 7-B, §13.3, p. 815.

§10.3 Place for deposition.

1. Party's own trial expert.

(1) 75 miles from courthouse. The place for the deposition of a party's own trial expert (i.e., the party itself, its employee, or its retained trial expert) must be within 75 miles of the courthouse where the case is pending. CCP §2034.420.

(2) More distant place. The party whose own trial expert is noticed for a deposition can move for a protective order to take the deposition at a more distant location than permitted by CCP §2034.420. See "Motion for protective order," §12.1, p. 914. To justify changing the place for the deposition of the party's own trial expert, the motion must show that taking the deposition within 75 miles of the courthouse where the case is pending would result in "exceptional hardship." CCP §2034.420.

2. Nonretained trial expert. The place for the deposition of a nonretained trial expert (e.g., treating physician) must be either (1) within 75 miles of the expert's residence or (2) in the county where the case is pending and within 150 miles of the expert's residence. CCP §2025.250(a).

§11. EXPERT-WITNESS FEES

§11.1 Who is paid. Most expert witnesses are entitled to expert-witness fees.

1. Experts entitled to fees.

(1) Retained trial experts. Retained trial experts are entitled to expert-witness fees for testifying at a deposition, hearing, or trial. *See* CCP §§2034.210(b), 2034.430(a)(1), (b); Gov. C. §68092.5(a). See "Retained trial expert," §2.6, p. 900.

(2) Nonretained treating medical experts. Nonretained treating physicians, surgeons, and other health-care practitioners (collectively, "nonretained treating medical practitioners") are entitled to expert-witness fees if they are asked to provide certain types of testimony at a deposition, hearing, or trial. *See* CCP §2034.430(a)(2), (b); Gov. C. §68092.5(a); ***Baker-Hoey v. Lockheed Martin Corp.*** (4th Dist.2003) 111 Cal.App.4th 592, 602; *CEB Discovery Practice*, §11.41.

(a) Deposition testimony. When a nonretained treating medical practitioner is deposed and provides testimony that includes opinion or factual information about a past or present diagnosis or prognosis made by the practitioner or the reasons for a particular treatment decision made by the practitioner, the practitioner is entitled to an expert-witness fee. *See* CCP §2034.430(a)(2), (b). However, the practitioner is not entitled to an expert-witness fee for testimony that requires only the reading of words and symbols in a medical record or, if those words and symbols are not legible, the practitioner's approximation of the meaning of those words or symbols. *See id.* §2034.430(a)(2), (b).

(b) Hearing or trial testimony. When a nonretained treating medical practitioner provides opinion testimony at a hearing or trial, the practitioner is entitled to an expert-witness fee. Gov. C. §68092.5(a).

(3) Nonretained project experts. Nonretained architects, professional engineers, and licensed land surveyors involved with the original project design or survey at issue are entitled to expert-witness fees if they are asked to provide opinion testimony at a deposition, hearing, or trial. *See* CCP §2034.430(a)(3), (b); Gov. C. §68092.5(a); *CEB Discovery Practice*, §11.41.

(4) Governmental entity – employee is expert. A governmental entity whose employee is subpoenaed to testify at a deposition, hearing, or trial about matters perceived or investigated or expertise gained in the course of the employee's duties is entitled to be reimbursed for the employee's expenses and time, based on the employee's salary. See "Government witness fees," ch. 8-A, §10.4, p. 955.

2. Experts not entitled to fees.

(1) Party. A party who is designated as an expert is not entitled to an expert-witness fee for testifying at a deposition, hearing, or trial. *See* CCP §2034.430(a), (b); Gov. C. §68092.5(a).

(2) Party's employee. A party's employee who is designated as an expert is not entitled to an expert-witness fee for testifying at a deposition, hearing, or trial. *See* CCP §2034.430(a), (b); Gov. C. §68092.5(a).

(3) Public employee. An employee of a governmental entity is not entitled to an expert-witness fee for testifying at a deposition, hearing, or trial about matters perceived or investigated or expertise gained in the course of the employee's duties. Instead, the governmental entity is reimbursed for the employee's expenses and time, based on the employee's salary. See "Government witness fees," ch. 8-A, §10.4, p. 955.

§11.2 Amount paid.

1. Retained trial experts. A party pays its own retained trial expert the hourly or daily fee charged by the expert for providing testimony at a deposition, hearing, or trial and for consulting with the party's attorney. *See* CCP §2034.260(c)(5) (party must provide statement of expert's fee in expert-witness declaration).

2. Nonretained trial experts & opposition's retained trial experts. When a party deposes or calls as a witness at trial a nonretained treating medical expert, a nonretained project expert, or an opposing party's retained trial expert, the following rules apply:

(1) Testimony fees. The expert witness is entitled to receive from the party the expert's reasonable and customary hourly or daily fee for the expert's testimony. CCP §2034.430(b) (expert-witness fee for deposition); Gov. C. §68092.5(a) (expert-witness fee for hearing or trial).

(a) Reasonable & customary – opposing party's retained trial expert. As a general rule, an opposing party's retained trial expert should be paid a fee consistent with the fee schedule filed by the opposing party in its expert-witness declaration. *See* Gov. C. §68092.5(a) (expert's hourly or daily fee for providing testimony at hearing or trial cannot exceed fee charged to party who retained expert, unless expert donated her services to charitable or other nonprofit organization).

(b) Hourly or daily. The expert witness can charge a daily fee only if the expert is in attendance for a full day or is required to be available for a full day; otherwise, the fee must be hourly. CCP §2034.430(e); Gov. C. §68092.5(a). The expert's time is calculated according to the following rules:

[1] Deposition. Fees for a deposition are calculated based on the time the expert witness spent at the deposition, which begins at the time specified in the deposition notice or subpoena or when the expert arrives, whichever is later, and ends when the expert is dismissed from the deposition. CCP §2034.430(b).

[2] Hearing or trial. Fees for a hearing or trial are calculated based on the actual time consumed in the examination of the expert witness by any party attending the hearing or trial. Gov. C. §68092.5(a). "Actual time consumed" includes the length of time the expert is required to remain at the hearing or trial according to the notice or subpoena. *See id.* (party required to tender fee based on anticipated length of time expert will be required to remain at place under subpoena).

(2) Preparation fees. The expert witness is entitled to receive from the party the fees charged by the expert for preparing for a deposition, hearing, or trial. CCP §2034.440 (deposition); Gov. C. §68092.5(a) (hearing or trial).

(3) Travel fees. The expert witness is entitled to receive from the party the fees and expenses charged by the expert for traveling to the place of the deposition, hearing, or trial. CCP §2034.440 (deposition); Gov. C. §68092.5(a) (hearing or trial).

3. Government-employee experts. Expert-witness fees for a governmental employee are based on the employee's salary and travel expenses. See "Amount paid," ch. 8-A, §10.4.4, p. 957.

§11.3 Paying fees.

1. Amount tendered. A party seeking the attendance of an expert at a deposition, hearing, or trial must pay an amount to cover the estimated time for the expert's testimony. *See* CCP §2034.450(a); Gov. C. §68092.5(a). The estimated time for the fee is based on the anticipated time the expert will be required to attend the deposition or remain at the place where the hearing or trial is being conducted. *See* CCP §2034.450(a); Gov. C. §68092.5(a).

2. When & how tendered.

(1) Opposition's retained trial experts. A party seeking the attendance of the other party's retained trial expert at a deposition, hearing, or trial has the option to tender the estimated expert-witness fee (1) with the notice for the deposition or appearance or (2) at the commencement of the deposition or at the required time of appearance. CCP §2034.450(a) (retained expert noticed for deposition); Gov. C. §68092.5(a) (experts attending hearing or trial); *see* ***True v. Shank*** (4th Dist.2000) 81 Cal.App.4th 1250, 1256 (retained trial expert noticed for deposition). The fee must be tendered to the attorney for the other party. CCP §2034.450(b); Gov. C. §68092.5(a).

(2) Nonretained trial experts. A party seeking the attendance of a nonretained treating medical expert or a nonretained project expert at a deposition, hearing, or trial has the option to tender the estimated expert-witness fee (1) with the subpoena or (2) at the commencement of the deposition or at the required time of appearance. CCP §2020.230(a) (nonretained trial expert subpoenaed for deposition); Gov. C. §68092.5(a) (experts attending hearing or trial). The fee can be tendered directly to the nonretained trial expert. *See* CCP §2020.230(a).

(3) Government-employee experts. A party seeking the attendance of an employee of a governmental entity by subpoena to testify as an expert at a deposition, hearing, or trial must tender the estimated expert fee to the governmental entity that employs the person subpoenaed. See "Government witness fees," ch. 8-A, §10.4, p. 955.

3. Balance due. If the examination takes longer than anticipated, the examining party must pay the balance of the expert's fee within five days after receiving an itemized statement from the expert. CCP §2034.450(c); Gov. C. §68092.5(a).

§11.4 Challenging fees. If the party seeking the attendance of an expert at a deposition, hearing, or trial believes the expert's hourly or daily fee is unreasonable, the party can ask the court by noticed motion to set the expert's compensation. See "Motion to reduce expert's fee," §12.7, p. 920.

§11.5 Fees paid by tardy counsel. If an attorney representing either the expert or a party other than the deposing party is late to the expert's deposition, the tardy attorney must pay the expert's fee from the start time in the deposition notice or subpoena until the time the attorney arrived. CCP §2034.430(c). The expert's hourly or daily fee charged to the tardy attorney cannot exceed the fee charged to the party who retained the expert, unless the expert donated her services to a charitable or other nonprofit organization. *Id.* §2034.430(d).

§12. MOTIONS RELATED TO EXPERTS

§12.1 Motion for protective order. A party responding to a demand for the exchange of expert information can make a motion for a protective order. CCP §2034.250(a); *see* ***Zellerino v. Brown*** (3d Dist.1991) 235 Cal.App.3d 1097, 1109. A motion for a protective order is the only way to object to a demand for the exchange of expert information. *See* CCP §2034.250(a); ***Zellerino***, 235 Cal.App.3d at 1109. See "Motion for Protective Order," ch. 9-B, p. 1024.

1. Motion papers. For the documents to file for a motion for a protective order, see "Contents," ch. 9-B, §3.3, p. 1029.

2. Grounds for relief. A party can make a motion for a protective order in response to a demand for the exchange of expert information on the following grounds:

(1) Complying with the demand would cause unwarranted annoyance, embarrassment, oppression, or undue burden and expense. CCP §2034.250(b).

(2) The burden, expense, or intrusiveness of the demand outweighs the likelihood it will lead to admissible evidence. *Id.* §2017.020(a).

(3) The demand seeks evidence that is unreasonably cumulative or is obtainable from another source that is more convenient, less burdensome, or less expensive, or the demand is unduly burdensome or expensive in light of the needs of the case, the amount in controversy, and the importance of the issues at stake. *Id.* §2019.030(a).

3. Relief available. A party can make a motion for a protective order to ask the court for various types of relief relating to a demand, including the following orders listed in CCP §§2034.250(b) and 2034.420. See "Relief Available Through Motion for Protective Order," chart 9-4, p. 1029.

(1) Quash untimely demand. The motion can ask the court to quash an untimely demand for expert information. CCP §2034.250(b)(1); *see, e.g.*, ***Zellerino***, 235 Cal.App.3d at 1109 (P failed to file motion for protective order to attack premature demand). The motion must show that the moving party will be prejudiced by the untimely demand. *See* ***Zellerino***, 235 Cal.App.3d at 1111.

(2) Change exchange date. The motion can ask the court to change the date for the exchange of expert information to an earlier or later date than the one specified in the demand. CCP §2034.250(b)(2).

(3) Impose terms on exchange. The motion can ask the court to impose specified terms and conditions on the exchange of expert information. CCP §2034.250(b)(3).

(4) Change procedure for exchange of reports. The motion can ask the court to change the place or time specified in the demand for the production and exchange of expert reports and writings. CCP §2034.250(b)(4).

(5) Divide parties into sides. The motion can ask the court to (1) divide some or all of the parties into sides on the basis of their identity of interests in the issues in the case and (2) require the sides to designate experts who are parties, employees of parties, or retained trial experts. CCP §2034.250(b)(5).

(6) Reduce list of experts. The motion can ask the court to require a party or side to reduce the number of employed or retained trial experts designated by the party or side. CCP §2034.250(b)(6).

(7) Change place for deposition of party's own expert. The motion can ask the court to change the location for the deposition of a party's own trial expert to a place that is more than 75 miles from the courthouse where the case is pending. CCP §2034.420. See "More distant place," §10.3.1(2), p. 912.

§12.2 Motion for relief from untimely demand. A party can make a motion for relief from an untimely demand for the exchange of expert information on the grounds of mistake, inadvertence, surprise, or excusable neglect. *See* CCP §473(b); ***Zellerino v. Brown*** (3d Dist.1991) 235 Cal.App.3d 1097, 1107; *CEB Discovery Practice*, §11.12. Relief is available under §473(b) for an untimely demand because the CDA does not provide any such relief. ***Zellerino***, 235 Cal.App.3d at 1107. See "Under CCP §473(b)," ch. 7-A, §15.2.3(2), p. 776. The decision to grant or deny relief under §473(b) from an untimely demand is within the court's discretion. *See, e.g.*, ***Zellerino***, 235 Cal.App.3d at 1109 (court did not abuse discretion in granting relief under §473(b) because P's mistake was innocent and steps taken to correct mistake were reasonable).

§12.3 Motion to change statutory deadline for demand. A party can make a motion, based on good cause, to change the deadline for making a demand for the exchange of expert information to an earlier or later date than the one provided in CCP §2034.220 (i.e., 10 days after the initial trial date is set or 70 days before trial). *See* CCP §2019.020(b) (good-cause motion for changing sequence and timing of discovery). See "When to make demand," §6.3, p. 904. A party should attempt to obtain a stipulation before making this motion. See "Modifying discovery by stipulation," ch. 7-A, §4.1, p. 743.

§12.4 Motion to change statutory deadline for exchange. A party can make a motion, based on good cause, to change the deadline for exchanging expert information to an earlier or later date than the one provided in CCP §2034.230(b) (i.e., 50 days before the initial trial date or 20 days after service of the demand). CCP §2034.230(b); ***Hernandez v. Superior Ct.*** (2d Dist.2003) 112 Cal.App.4th 285, 297; *see also* CCP §2019.020(b) (good-cause motion for changing sequence and timing of discovery). See "Calculating date for exchange," §6.5.3(1), p. 905. A motion under §2034.230(b) cannot be made by a party who seeks permission to file tardy expert information. To do that, the party must file a motion under CCP §2034.710. See "Motion to submit tardy expert information," §12.5, p. 916.

1. Motion.

(1) Deadline. The party should make the motion as soon as the party discovers the need for an earlier or later date for the exchange.

(2) Motion papers. See "Motion Papers," ch. 1-D, §5, p. 27.

PRACTICE TIP

Although there is no meet-and-confer requirement in CCP §2034.230(b) (or in §2019.020(b)), an attorney should attempt to reach a consensus with the other party before filing a motion to change the date for the exchange of expert information.

(3) Grounds for relief. The moving party must provide good cause to change the date for the exchange of expert information to an earlier or later date than the one provided in CCP §2034.230(b). CCP §2034.230(b); *CEB Discovery Practice*, §§11.10, 15.9.

(a) Earlier exchange. Some examples of circumstances that may constitute good cause for the early exchange of expert information include the following:

[1] Claim or defense. A party can show that it is unable to prepare its claim or defense because it cannot obtain the information elsewhere. ***Hernandez***, 112 Cal.App.4th at 298.

[2] MSJ proceeding. A party can show there is a legitimate question about the foundation of an expert's opinion submitted in support of or in opposition to a motion for summary judgment. ***Hernandez***, 112 Cal.App.4th at 298; *cf.* ***St. Mary Med. Ctr. v. Superior Ct.*** (2d Dist.1996) 50 Cal.App.4th 1531, 1539-40 (Ds allowed to take deposition of Ps' retained expert before designation of experts for purpose of challenging foundation of expert's opinion submitted in opposition to Ds' MSJ).

PRACTICE TIP

A party can also file a motion to continue the hearing on the motion for summary judgment on the ground that expert discovery is needed to oppose the motion. See CCP §437c(h). But see **Cheviot Vista Homeowners Ass'n v. State Farm Fire & Cas. Co.** *(2d Dist.2006) 143 Cal.App.4th 1486, 1501 (P's contention that experts had not been designated or deposed did not justify continuance of MSJ). See "Motion for continuance," ch. 10-B, §7.1, p. 1126.*

[3] Numerous experts. A party can show that, because of the large number of experts expected to be designated, an early exchange is necessary to ensure the timely completion of all the experts' depositions. *See* Weil, *Civil Procedure Before Trial*, ¶8:1644. See "Cutoff for discovery requests," ch. 7-A, §5.2.1, p. 747.

(b) Later exchange. For a later exchange of expert information, a party can show the need for more time to complete other discovery. *See* ***Kalaba v. Gray*** (2d Dist.2002) 95 Cal.App.4th 1416, 1423 (expert information is exchanged after nonexpert discovery so parties can make final preparations for trial).

2. Response to motion. The responding party should serve papers opposing the motion. See "Opposition Papers," ch. 1-D, §8, p. 35.

§12.5 Motion to submit tardy expert information. If a party did not provide its expert information within the deadline identified in the demand, the party must make a motion to submit tardy expert information. See "Date for exchange," §6.5.3, p. 905.

1. Motion.

(1) Deadline. A motion to submit tardy expert information must be made early enough to allow the other parties to depose the designated experts before the cutoff for expert discovery. CCP §2034.710(b). The cutoff

for expert discovery is 15 days before the initial trial date. *Id.* §2024.030. See "Calculating Cutoff for Discovery Requests," chart 7-4, p. 748. The court can permit the motion to be made at a later time only in exceptional circumstances. CCP §2034.710(b); *e.g.*, ***Cottini v. Enloe Med. Ctr.*** (3d Dist.2014) 226 Cal.App.4th 401, 420-21 (P's argument that he did not disclose experts because D knew information anyway was not sufficient to establish exceptional circumstances).

(2) Motion papers. See "Motion Papers," ch. 1-D, §5, p. 27.

(3) Meet-and-confer declaration. The motion to submit tardy expert information must be accompanied by a meet-and-confer declaration. CCP §2034.710(c). See "Meet-and-confer declaration," ch. 7-A, §10.4, p. 763.

(4) Grounds for relief. The moving party must establish the following:

(a) Mistake. The moving party must show that it did not exchange expert information by the demand deadline because of the party's mistake, inadvertence, surprise, or excusable neglect. *See* CCP §2034.720(c)(1); *see, e.g.*, ***Cottini***, 226 Cal.App.4th at 421-22 (P's failure to disclose experts was not result of mistake, inadvertence, surprise, or excusable neglect but rather was trial strategy); *see, e.g.*, ***Barboni v. Tuomi*** (4th Dist.2012) 210 Cal.App.4th 340, 343 (Ds alleged they missed deadline for exchange of expert information because of calendaring error).

(b) Prompt action. The moving party must show that it promptly (1) sought leave to submit the information after learning of its mistake, inadvertence, surprise, or excusable neglect and (2) served a copy of its proposed expert-witness information on all other parties who have appeared in the case. *See* CCP §2034.720(c)(2), (c)(3).

(c) Exceptional circumstances. If the motion is not made with sufficient time to depose the designated experts before the cutoff for expert discovery, the moving party must show exceptional circumstances. *See* CCP §2034.710(b); ***Plunkett v. Spaulding*** (3d Dist.1997) 52 Cal.App.4th 114, 134-35, *disapproved on other grounds*, ***Schreiber v. Estate of Kiser*** (1999) 22 Cal.4th 31.

(d) No prejudice. The moving party must show that any party opposing the motion will not be prejudiced by the submission of tardy expert information. *See* CCP §2034.720(b). A party is not prejudiced simply because the expert will give testimony adverse to the party. ***Dickison v. Howen*** (3d Dist.1990) 220 Cal.App.3d 1471, 1479.

(5) Additional allegations.

(a) No reliance. The motion should address whether and to what extent the opposing party has relied on the moving party's lack of an expert-witness list. *See* CCP §2034.720(a); *see, e.g.*, ***Plunkett***, 52 Cal.App.4th at 136 (P's attorney acknowledged that D had relied on absence of expert-witness designation, but argued that D would not be prejudiced because D had anticipated and prepared for proposed testimony).

(b) Experts available for deposition. The motion should state that if the court grants the motion, the moving party will make its experts available for deposition immediately. *See* CCP §2034.720(d).

2. Response to motion. The responding party should serve papers opposing the motion. See "Opposition Papers," ch. 1-D, §8, p. 35.

3. Ruling. The court must grant the motion to submit tardy expert information if the court determines that the moving party has met its burden and that no party opposing the motion will be prejudiced in maintaining its action or defense on the merits. *See* CCP §2034.720(b). To determine whether an opposing party will be prejudiced, the court must consider the extent to which the opposing party has relied on the moving party's lack of an expert-witness list. *Id.* §2034.720(a).

4. Court's order.

(1) Conditions. If the court grants the motion to submit tardy expert information, it must require the moving party to make its experts available for deposition immediately. CCP §2034.720(d). The court can include in its order any other terms that are just, including the following:

(a) The court can grant permission for an opposing party to augment or amend its own expert-witness list or declaration. *Id.*

(b) The court can grant permission for an opposing party to elicit additional opinions from the experts previously designated. *Id.*

(c) The court can order a continuance of the trial for a reasonable period of time. *Id.*

(d) The court can award costs and expenses to an opposing party. *Id.*

(2) Monetary sanctions. The court must impose a monetary sanction against any party, person, or attorney who unsuccessfully makes or opposes a motion to submit tardy expert information, unless the court finds that the person subject to sanctions acted with substantial justification or that other circumstances make the imposition of the sanction unjust. CCP §2034.730. See "Monetary sanctions," ch. 5-K, §2.2.4(1)(b)[1][b], p. 569.

§12.6 Motion to augment designation or amend declaration. A party can make a motion to augment or amend its expert-witness information.

1. Motion.

(1) Types.

(a) Motion to augment designation. If a party determines it must offer the opinion of an expert witness who was not designated as a testifying expert, the party must make a motion to augment its expert-witness list. *See* CCP §2034.610(a)(1); *see, e.g.,* ***Province v. Center for Women's Health & Family Birth*** (2d Dist.1993) 20 Cal.App.4th 1673, 1683-84 (undesignated physician should not have been permitted to give opinion testimony); *see also* ***Richaud v. Jennings*** (5th Dist.1993) 16 Cal.App.4th 81, 90-91 (party must make motion to augment when it wants to call expert at trial who was not designated but is being substituted for a previously designated, but now unavailable, expert). If the expert to be added is the party's own trial expert (i.e., the party itself, its employee, or its retained trial expert), the party must also augment its expert-witness declaration and provide the expert's reports, if the reports were requested. *See* CCP §2034.610(a)(1). If the expert to be added is a nonretained trial expert, the party is not required to augment its expert-witness declaration or provide the expert's reports. See "Designate experts," §7.2, p. 907.

(b) Motion to amend declaration. If a party determines it must present expert testimony from its own trial expert on a subject that was not described in the expert-witness declaration, the party must make a motion to amend the declaration. *E.g.,* ***Bonds v. Roy*** (1999) 20 Cal.4th 140, 145 (physician could not testify about standard of care because it was not included in declaration); *see* CCP §2034.610(a)(2).

(2) Deadline. A motion to augment or amend must be made early enough to allow for the deposition of the expert before the cutoff for expert discovery. CCP §2034.610(b). The cutoff for expert discovery is 15 days before the initial trial date. *Id.* §2024.030. See "Calculating Cutoff for Discovery Requests," chart 7-4, p. 748. The court can permit the motion to be made at a later time only in exceptional circumstances. CCP §2034.610(b).

(3) Motion papers. See "Motion Papers," ch. 1-D, §5, p. 27.

(4) Meet-and-confer declaration. The motion to augment or amend must be accompanied by a meet-and-confer declaration. CCP §2034.610(c); *see id.* §2016.040. See "Meet-and-confer declaration," ch. 7-A, §10.4, p. 763.

(5) Grounds for relief. The moving party must establish the following:

(a) Diligence or mistake. The moving party must establish either of the following:

[1] Reasonable diligence. The moving party can show that (1) it exercised reasonable diligence in determining which experts to designate and the scope of their testimony and (2) it could not have determined to call the new expert or offer the different or additional testimony from a previously designated expert by

the exercise of that diligence. *See* CCP §2034.620(c)(1). For example, a moving party can show additional expert testimony is necessary because the opposing party's expert unexpectedly expressed an opinion at trial that differed from the opinion expressed in the expert's deposition testimony. *See* ***McLaughlin v. Sikorsky Aircraft*** (4th Dist.1983) 148 Cal.App.3d 203, 210.

[2] **Mistake.** The moving party can show that it did not call the new expert or offer different or additional testimony from a previously designated expert because of the party's mistake, inadvertence, surprise, or excusable neglect. *See* CCP §2034.620(c)(2).

(b) **Prompt action.** The moving party must show that it promptly (1) made the motion to augment or amend and (2) served the proposed augmented witness list or amended expert-witness declaration on all parties who have appeared in the case. *See* CCP §2034.620(c)(2); *CEB Discovery Practice*, §11.52.

(c) **Exceptional circumstances.** If the moving party's motion to augment or amend is not made with sufficient time to depose the expert before the cutoff for expert discovery, the moving party must show exceptional circumstances. *See* CCP §2034.610(b); *see also* ***Jones v. Moore*** (2d Dist.2000) 80 Cal.App.4th 557, 565 (party can seek to amend expert declaration as long as time remains to depose expert).

(d) **No prejudice.** The moving party must show that any party opposing the motion will not be prejudiced by the augmentation or amendment. *See* CCP §2034.620(b); *see, e.g.*, ***Jones***, 80 Cal.App.4th at 565 (when expert provides specific opinions at deposition and affirmatively states those are the only opinions to be offered at trial, allowing expert to offer additional opinions at trial would be grossly unfair and prejudicial).

(6) **Additional allegations.**

(a) **No reliance.** The motion should allege that the opposing party has not relied on the expert-witness list. *See* CCP §2034.620(a).

(b) **Experts available for deposition.** The motion should state that if the court grants the motion, the moving party will make the expert available for deposition immediately. *See* CCP §2034.620(d).

2. **Response to motion.** The responding party should serve papers opposing the motion. See "Opposition Papers," ch. 1-D, §8, p. 35.

3. **Ruling.** The court must grant the motion to augment or amend if the court determines that the moving party has met its burden and no party opposing the motion will be prejudiced in maintaining its action or defense on the merits. *See* CCP §2034.620(b). To determine whether an opposing party will be prejudiced, the court must consider the extent to which the opposing party relied on the moving party's initial expert-witness list. *Id.* §2034.620(a).

4. **Court's order.**

(1) **Conditions.** If the court grants the motion to augment or amend, it must require the moving party to make the expert available for deposition immediately. CCP §2034.620(d). The court can also include in its order any other terms that are just, including the following:

(a) The court can grant permission for an opposing party to designate additional experts. *Id.*

(b) The court can grant permission for an opposing party to elicit additional opinions from the experts previously designated. *Id.*

(c) The court can order a continuance of the trial for a reasonable period of time. *Id.*

(d) The court can award costs and expenses to an opposing party. *Id.*

(2) **Monetary sanctions.** The court must impose a monetary sanction against any party, person, or attorney who unsuccessfully makes or opposes a motion to augment or amend, unless the court finds that the person subject to sanctions acted with substantial justification or that other circumstances make the imposition of the sanction unjust. CCP §2034.630. See "Monetary sanctions," ch. 5-K, §2.2.4(1)(b)[1][b], p. 569.

§12.7 Motion to reduce expert's fee. If the party examining the expert believes the expert's hourly or daily fee for providing testimony is unreasonable, the party can ask the court by noticed motion to set the expert's compensation. CCP §2034.470(a); Gov. C. §68092.5(c).

NOTE

A motion to set an expert's fee affects only the amount the examining party must pay for the testimony of the expert; it does not limit the expert from charging or receiving more from the designating party. ***Marsh v. Mountain Zephyr, Inc.*** *(4th Dist.1996) 43 Cal.App.4th 289, 299-300.*

1. Meet-and-confer obligation. The examining party and either the expert or the designating party must make a reasonable and good-faith attempt to resolve the fee dispute before the motion can be made. *See* CCP §2034.470(b); Gov. C. §68092.5(c). See "Meet-and-Confer Obligation," ch. 7-A, §10, p. 761. In attempting to resolve the dispute, either the examining party or the expert must provide the other with the following information:

(1) Proof of the ordinary and customary fee actually charged and received by the expert for similar services provided outside the case. CCP §2034.470(b)(1); Gov. C. §68092.5(c).

(2) The total number of times the expert charged and received the demanded fee. CCP §2034.470(b)(2); Gov. C. §68092.5(c).

(3) The frequency and regularity with which the expert charged and received the demanded fee within the past two years, counting backward from the date the motion is scheduled for hearing. CCP §2034.470(b)(3); Gov. C. §68092.5(c).

2. Motion. Notice of the motion must be given to the other parties and the expert. *See* CCP §2034.470(a); Gov. C. §68092.5(c); ***Marsh***, 43 Cal.App.4th at 296.

(1) Deadline. While there is no statutory deadline, the motion should be made promptly.

(2) Motion papers. See "Motion Papers," ch. 1-D, §5, p. 27.

(3) Meet-and-confer declaration. A motion to reduce an expert's fee must be accompanied by a meet-and-confer declaration. CCP §2034.470(b); Gov. C. §68092.5(c); *see* CCP §2016.040. See "Meet-and-confer declaration," ch. 7-A, §10.4, p. 763.

(4) Grounds for relief. The motion must establish that the expert's fee is unreasonable. *See* CCP §2034.470(f). Unreasonableness can be demonstrated by the following factors:

(a) Mandatory factors. The motion must address the following factors:

[1] The ordinary and customary fee actually charged and received by the expert for similar services provided outside the case is less than the demanded fee. *See* CCP §2034.470(b)(1); Gov. C. §68092.5(c).

[2] The total number of times the expert has charged and received the demanded fee is either zero or so few that it cannot support the demanded fee. *See* CCP §2034.470(d)(1); Gov. C. §68092.5(c).

[3] The expert has not, with any frequency or regularity, charged and received the demanded fee within the past two years, counting backward from the date the motion is scheduled for hearing. *See* CCP §2034.470(d)(2); Gov. C. §68092.5(c).

(b) Discretionary factors. The motion should address the following factors:

[1] The ordinary and customary fee charged by similar experts for similar services within the relevant community is less than the demanded fee. *See* CCP §2034.470(e); Gov. C. §68092.5(c); *see, e.g.*, ***Marsh***, 43 Cal.App.4th at 294 (trial court considered customary hourly fee charged by other local architects for expert testimony in setting deponent's fee).

[2] Any other factors that establish the demanded fee is unreasonable. *See* CCP §2034.470(e); Gov. C. §68092.5(c); *see, e.g.*, ***Marsh***, 43 Cal.App.4th at 303 (court was familiar with particular expert, and local rule determined $200 per hour was ordinary and customary fee for similar expert).

3. Response to motion. The expert or the designating party can challenge the examining party's motion by filing opposition papers. *See, e.g.*, ***Marsh***, 43 Cal.App.4th at 294 (expert retained counsel and submitted declaration in opposition to motion). See "Opposition Papers," ch. 1-D, §8, p. 35. To establish the reasonableness of the expert's fee, the expert or the designating party must provide proof of the following:

(1) The ordinary and customary fee actually charged and received by the expert for similar services provided outside the present case. CCP §2034.470(c); Gov. C. §68092.5(c); *see, e.g.*, ***Marsh***, 43 Cal.App.4th at 294 (expert's declaration in opposition to motion stated he routinely charged $360 per hour for testimony).

(2) The total number of times the expert has ever charged and received the demanded fee. CCP §2034.470(d)(1); Gov. C. §68092.5(c).

(3) The frequency and regularity with which the demanded fee has been charged and received by the expert within the past two years, counting backward from the date the motion is scheduled for hearing. CCP §2034.470(d)(2); Gov. C. §68092.5(c); *see, e.g.*, ***Marsh***, 43 Cal.App.4th at 294 (expert's declaration in opposition to motion stated he charged rate on 124 separate occasions over two years).

4. Ruling. When determining whether the demanded fee is unreasonable, the court must consider the evidence presented and certain statutory factors. CCP §2034.470(f); Gov. C. §68092.5(c); *see* CCP §2034.470(c) (factors court must consider), §2034.470(d) (same), §2034.470(e) (factors court can consider). See "Grounds for relief," §12.7.2(4), p. 920.

5. Court's order.

(1) Expert's fee. If the court determines that the demanded fee is unreasonable, it must set the expert's fee. CCP §2034.470(f); Gov. C. §68092.5(c); *see, e.g.*, ***Marsh***, 43 Cal.App.4th at 294 (trial court reduced expert's demanded fee from $360 per hour to $250 per hour).

(2) Monetary sanctions. The court must impose a monetary sanction against any party, person (i.e., the expert), or attorney who unsuccessfully makes or opposes a motion to reduce the expert witness's fee for providing testimony, unless the court finds that the person subject to sanctions acted with substantial justification or that other circumstances make the imposition of the sanction unjust. CCP §2034.470(g). See "Monetary sanctions," ch. 5-K, §2.2.4(1)(b)[1][b], p. 569.

(3) Appealable order. The court's order reducing the expert's fee is a final order as to the expert and is appealable as a final collateral order. ***Marsh***, 43 Cal.App.4th at 297-98. See "Final collateral order," ch. 7-A, §17.1.2(3), p. 777. An expert who is a nonparty has standing to appeal the court's order reducing the fees because the order is binding on the expert and the order's injurious effect is immediate, pecuniary, and substantial. *See* ***Marsh***, 43 Cal.App.4th at 295-96.

§13. USING EXPERT TESTIMONY IN COURT PROCEEDINGS

§13.1 How to introduce expert's deposition testimony. See "How to introduce deposition testimony," ch. 7-B, §13.4, p. 815.

§13.2 Objecting to expert's trial testimony.

1. Mandatory exclusion. A party who made a complete and timely exchange of expert information can object to an expert offered by another party if the other party did not properly comply with the demand for the exchange of expert information. *See* CCP §2034.300; *see, e.g.*, ***Staub v. Kiley*** (3d Dist.2014) 226 Cal.App.4th 1437, 1445-46 (Ds lacked standing to seek mandatory exclusion of Ps' experts because Ds failed to make complete and timely exchange of expert information). The court must exclude the expert's opinion testimony if it finds that the other party unreasonably failed to do any of the following:

(1) Not listed. The court must exclude the expert's opinion testimony if the other party did not list the witness as an expert. CCP §2034.300(a). An undesignated expert cannot provide opinion testimony at trial. *See* ***FMC Corp. v. Plaisted & Cos.*** (6th Dist.1998) 61 Cal.App.4th 1132, 1216, *disapproved on other grounds*, ***State v. Continental Ins.*** (2012) 55 Cal.4th 186. An undesignated expert is limited to testifying about personally observed facts. *See* ***Province v. Center for Women's Health & Family Birth*** (2d Dist.1993) 20 Cal.App.4th 1673, 1683-84 (undesignated expert cannot provide opinion testimony, only factual testimony).

(2) Listed untimely. The court must exclude the expert's opinion testimony if the other party designated the expert after the exchange deadline and did not obtain leave to submit tardy expert information. *See* CCP §§2034.300(a), 2034.710. A tardy designation is subject to a motion to strike, which can prevent the party's expert from testifying. *See id.* §2034.300(a); ***Fairfax v. Lords*** (4th Dist.2006) 138 Cal.App.4th 1019, 1027. See "Motion to Strike," ch. 4-J, p. 418.

(3) No declaration. The court must exclude the expert's opinion testimony if the other party did not submit an expert-witness declaration for the expert. CCP §2034.300(b). This applies only if the expert is a party's own trial expert; a party is not required to include nonretained trial experts in its declaration. See "Declaration for trial experts," §7.2.2, p. 907.

(4) Opinion not in declaration. The court must exclude the expert's opinion testimony if the other party did not include in the expert-witness declaration the opinion to be offered at trial. *See* CCP §2034.300(b) (court must exclude expert's opinion if party did not submit declaration); ***Bonds v. Roy*** (1999) 20 Cal.4th 140, 148-49 (former §2034(j)(2), now §2034.300(b), applies when party submitted declaration that inaccurately described proposed testimony). A party cannot offer expert testimony beyond the scope of the testimony described in the declaration. *See, e.g.*, ***Bonds***, 20 Cal.4th at 145 (D's retained physician could not testify about standard of care because it was not included in declaration). See "Expert's testimony," §7.2.2(2)(b), p. 908.

(5) No reports. The court must exclude the expert's opinion testimony if the other party did not produce reports and writings for the expert (assuming they were demanded). CCP §2034.300(c); *see id.* §2034.270. This applies only if the expert is a party's own trial expert; a party is not required to produce reports and writings by nonretained trial experts. See "Expert reports & writings," §7.2.3, p. 908.

(6) No deposition. The court must exclude the expert's opinion testimony if the other party did not make the expert available for a deposition. CCP §2034.300(d); *see id.* §§2034.410-2034.470. This applies only if the expert is a party's own trial expert; a party is not required to make nonretained trial experts available for depositions. See "Deposition notice or subpoena," §10.2.1, p. 911.

(7) Opinion differs from earlier opinion. Generally, any difference between the opinion an expert gives at trial and the opinion the expert gave at a deposition goes to the expert's credibility and is not grounds for exclusion. ***Easterby v. Clark*** (2d Dist.2009) 171 Cal.App.4th 772, 781. However, the court can exclude the expert's opinion testimony if (1) the expert's opinion offered at trial will be different from the one expressed at a deposition, (2) the change in opinion is prejudicial to the party seeking to exclude the evidence, and (3) the party seeking to exclude the evidence had insufficient notice of the change in opinion. *See, e.g.*, ***McCoy v. Gustafson*** (6th Dist.2009) 180 Cal.App.4th 56, 96 (court properly excluded opinion testimony by P's expert that was not given in expert's deposition); ***Easterby***, 171 Cal.App.4th at 780 (court erred in excluding Ps' expert testimony; Ds had ample time to depose expert after receiving notice of his changed opinion).

2. Discretionary exclusion. One court has held that a party who did not make a complete and timely exchange of expert information can nevertheless object to an expert offered by another party if the other party did not properly comply with the demand for the exchange of expert information. *See* ***Cottini v. Enloe Med. Ctr.*** (3d Dist.2014) 226 Cal.App.4th 401, 428. In such a case, the court may, but is not required to, exclude the expert's opinion testimony if it finds that the other party unreasonably failed to comply with the requirements of CCP §2034.300 or a change in the expert's opinion at trial is prejudicial to the objecting party. *See* ***Cottini***, 226 Cal.App.4th at 428. See "Mandatory exclusion," §13.2.1, p. 921.

3. Request exclusion. The objecting party should ask the court to exclude the expert's opinion testimony at trial as a sanction. *See* CCP §2034.300. The exclusion of the expert's opinion testimony is the only sanction available for failure to properly disclose expert information; monetary sanctions are not authorized. ***Muller v. Fresno Cmty. Hosp. & Med. Ctr.*** (2d Dist.2009) 172 Cal.App.4th 887, 905-06.

§13.3 Objecting to expert's video deposition. A party can object to the offer of an expert's videotaped deposition if the party offering the videotape did not (1) reserve the right to use the videotape at trial by including the proper notice in the deposition notice or subpoena or (2) notify the court and the other parties of its intent to use the videotape at trial. *See* CCP §§2025.340(m), 2025.620(d). See "Expert's video deposition," §10.2.2, p. 911; "Notice of intent to use electronically recorded deposition," ch. 7-B, §13.3, p. 815.

§13.4 Calling undesignated experts. A party can call as a witness at trial an expert not designated by that party as an expert in either of the following situations:

1. Other party's expert. The party can call the expert to testify if the expert was (1) designated by another party as a trial expert and (2) deposed under the rules for deposing experts. CCP §2034.310(a); *see id.* §§2034.410-2034.470.

2. Impeachment. The party can call the expert to impeach the testimony of an expert witness offered by another party at trial. CCP §2034.310(b). The undesignated expert can contradict the other expert's testimony about facts used as the foundation for an opinion but cannot offer a contrary opinion. *Id.*; ***Fish v. Guevara*** (6th Dist.1993) 12 Cal.App.4th 142, 145; *see* ***Teroso del Valle Master Homeowners Ass'n v. Griffin*** (2d Dist.2011) 200 Cal.App.4th 619, 641 (courts strictly construe foundational-fact requirement to prevent parties from offering contrary opinions under guise of impeachment); ***Kennemur v. State*** (5th Dist.1982) 133 Cal.App.3d 907, 924 (same).

J. PRESUIT DISCOVERY

§1. GENERAL

§1.1 Purpose. The purpose of presuit discovery is to preserve evidence and perpetuate testimony in anticipation of a future lawsuit. CCP §2035.010(a); *see* ***Orr v. City of Stockton*** (3d Dist.2007) 150 Cal.App.4th 622, 631. Presuit discovery allows a potential litigant to collect and preserve evidence that may not be available by the time suit is brought. Weil & Brown, *California Practice Guide: Civil Procedure Before Trial* (CD-ROM ed. 2014) ¶8:422.

NOTE

The proceeding initiated by a presuit-discovery petition is not a "suit" because it is not an adversarial proceeding to enforce a right or redress an injury. ***Orr****, 150 Cal.App.4th at 630. Thus, filing a petition for presuit discovery does not satisfy a statute of limitations. Id. at 635.*

§1.2 Primary authority. CCP §§2035.010-2035.060.

§1.3 Secondary authority. The following secondary sources are cited as authority in this subchapter:

- *California Civil Discovery Practice* (CEB Online ed. 2014) (referred to as *CEB Discovery Practice*).
- Weil & Brown, *California Practice Guide: Civil Procedure Before Trial* (CD-ROM ed. 2014) (referred to as Weil, *Civil Procedure Before Trial*).
- Witkin, *California Evidence* (5th ed. 2012 & Supp.2014) (referred to as Witkin, *Cal. Evidence*).

§2. SCOPE OF PRESUIT DISCOVERY

The scope of presuit discovery is generally the same as that for regular discovery and is subject to the same restrictions. CCP §2035.010(a). See "Scope of Discovery," ch. 6-A, p. 603. Presuit discovery is subject to the following additional restrictions:

§2.1 No determination of action or defense. Presuit discovery cannot be used to determine the existence of a cause of action or defense. CCP §2035.010(b). This limits the usefulness of a petition for presuit discovery as a tool for prelitigation investigatory discovery. *See* ***Edwards v. Centex Real Estate Corp.*** (1st Dist.1997) 53 Cal.App.4th 15, 34 n.9 (dicta); ***Hunt-Wesson Foods, Inc. v. County of Stanislaus*** (5th Dist.1969) 273 Cal.App.2d 92, 98; ***Block v. Superior Ct.*** (2d Dist.1963) 219 Cal.App.2d 469, 477-78.

§2.2 No discovery of information that would be inadmissible. Presuit discovery cannot be used to obtain collateral information that would be inadmissible in a future court case because the purpose of preserving evidence is for its use in a probable case. *See* ***Hunt-Wesson Foods, Inc. v. County of Stanislaus*** (5th Dist.1969) 273 Cal.App.2d 92, 98.

§2.3 No identification of potential parties. Presuit discovery cannot be used to identify persons who might be made parties to an action. CCP §2035.010(b).

§3. PETITION FOR PRESUIT DISCOVERY

§3.1 Form. See "General Requirements for Papers," ch. 1-B, §2, p. 9. For a sample form, see *CEB Discovery Practice*, §5.231.

1. Name. The petition must be titled in the name of the petitioner. CCP §2035.030(b).

2. Verified. The petition must be verified. CCP §2035.030(a). See "How to verify," ch. 3-C, §3.10.2, p. 225.

§3.2 Contents.

1. Expected action. The petition must state that the petitioner expects to be a party (or expects its successor in interest to be a party) in an action that is cognizable in a California court. CCP §§2035.010(a), 2035.030(b)(1).

2. Subject matter. The petition must identify the subject matter of the expected action. CCP §2035.030(b)(3). The petition does not have to set out any factual allegations constituting a cause of action. ***Orr v. City of Stockton*** (3d Dist.2007) 150 Cal.App.4th 622, 633.

3. Petitioner's involvement. The petition must identify the petitioner's involvement in the expected action. CCP §2035.030(b)(3); ***Orr***, 150 Cal.App.4th at 633. The petitioner can be a person or entity that expects to be involved as a plaintiff, as a defendant, or in any other capacity. CCP §2035.010(a).

4. Expected adverse parties. The petition must, to the extent known, name or describe the persons the petitioner expects to be adverse parties. CCP §2035.030(b)(7).

5. Inability to bring action. The petition must show that the petitioner (or its successor in interest) is presently unable to either bring the expected action or cause it to be brought. *See* CCP §2035.030(b)(2); *see, e.g.*, ***Block v. Superior Ct.*** (2d Dist.1963) 219 Cal.App.2d 469, 470-71 (petitioner alleged he expected to be D in suit arising from car accident and thus was unable to bring suit). For example, a potential defendant cannot force a potential plaintiff to file suit. *CEB Discovery Practice*, §5.148.

6. Nature of presuit discovery sought. The petition must provide the following information about the presuit discovery sought:

(1) Proposed discovery methods. The petition must state the particular discovery methods the petitioner wants to use. CCP §2035.030(b)(4). Only the following discovery methods are available for presuit discovery:

(a) Deposition. The petition can ask to take a person's oral or written deposition. CCP §2035.020(a). A petition can seek the deposition of the petitioner, a natural person, or an organization. *Id.* §2035.010(a). See "Depositions," ch. 7-B, p. 780.

(b) Demand to produce. The petition can ask to inspect documents, things, or places. CCP §2035.020(b). See "Demands to Produce," ch. 7-E, p. 845.

(c) Medical exam. The petition can ask for the physical or mental examination of a person. CCP §2035.020(c). See "Medical Examinations," ch. 7-F, p. 855.

(2) Proposed evidence sought.

(a) Facts. The petition must state the facts that the petitioner wants to establish by the proposed discovery methods. CCP §2035.030(b)(5).

(b) Reasons. The petition must state the reasons why the petitioner wants to preserve the facts before an action is filed. CCP §2035.030(b)(6); *see, e.g.*, ***New York Cas. Co. v. Superior Ct.*** (1st Dist.1938) 30 Cal.App.2d 130, 132 (petitioner had no need to take depositions to perpetuate testimony because testimony was already preserved in earlier action).

(3) Proposed persons subject to discovery.

(a) Witnesses. The petition must identify the names and addresses of the persons from whom discovery is sought. CCP §2035.030(b)(8).

(b) Expected evidence. The petition must describe the substance of the information expected to be elicited from each person from whom discovery is sought. CCP §2035.030(b)(9).

7. Inability of successor to conduct discovery. If the petitioner expects a successor in interest to be a party to the later action, the petition should show that the successor in interest will not be able to conduct the requested discovery. *See* CCP §2035.050(a). For example, the petitioner might seek her own deposition because she is deathly ill; once dead, she will be unavailable to the successor in interest for discovery. *See* Weil, *Civil Procedure Before Trial*, ¶8:422; *see also* 34 Cal. Law Revision Comm'n Rep. (2004) p. 147 (testator might perpetuate testimony relating to her mental capacity and execution of her will).

8. Interest of justice. The petition must show that presuit discovery would prevent a failure or delay of justice. *See* CCP §2035.050(a). For example, presuit discovery might be necessary to inspect a wrecked automobile that is to be sold for scrap metal.

9. Other factors. The petition should include any other factors that would support the authorization of presuit discovery. *See* CCP §2035.050(a).

10. Request order. The petition must ask for a court order authorizing presuit discovery. CCP §2035.030(c).

11. Attachments. The petition must include a copy of any (1) written instruments relating to the subject matter of the proposed discovery and (2) written instruments whose validity or construction may be called into question. CCP §2035.030(b)(3).

§3.3 Filing & serving petition.

1. Filing petition.

(1) What to file.

(a) The petitioner must file with the court a verified petition for presuit discovery. CCP §2035.030(a); *see CEB Discovery Practice*, §5.231 (sample form).

NOTE

Although not required by statute, one commentator suggests that the petition should be accompanied by a memorandum of points and authorities, supporting declarations, and a proposed order, similar to a noticed motion. See CEB Discovery Practice, §5.150 (contents of petition), §5.231 (comment to sample form), §5.232 (comment to sample order).

(b) A proof of service (POS) for each person or entity served. See "Proving Service," ch. 1-G, §7, p. 74. For a POS form, see Judicial Council Form POS-010.

(2) Where to file. The place to file the petition depends on where the expected adverse parties reside. For a discussion of residence, see "General venue rule," ch. 3-F, §4.2, p. 273.

(a) Residents. If at least one of the expected adverse parties resides in California, the petition must be filed in the superior court of a county where at least one expected adverse party resides. CCP §2035.030(a).

(b) Nonresidents. If none of the expected adverse parties reside in California, the petition must be filed in the superior court of a county where the action or proceeding might be filed. CCP §2035.030(a). For a discussion of where an action or proceeding might be filed, see "Choosing the Court—Subject-Matter Jurisdiction," ch. 3-E, p. 248.

(3) Deadline to file. A petition for presuit discovery must be filed before the anticipated action is filed. ***Orr v. City of Stockton*** (3d Dist.2007) 150 Cal.App.4th 622, 630-31.

2. Serving notice & petition.

(1) Whom to serve. The petitioner must serve each person and organization named in the petition as an expected adverse party. CCP §2035.040(a); *see, e.g.*, ***N.N.V. v. American Ass'n of Blood Banks*** (4th Dist.1999) 75 Cal.App.4th 1358, 1396 (petition served on hospital was not effective service on nurse who was not employed by hospital).

(2) What to serve. The petitioner must serve the following:

(a) A notice of the petition stating that the petitioner will apply to the court at a specific time and place for an order for presuit discovery. CCP §2035.040(a), (b); 2 Witkin, *Cal. Evidence*, Discovery, §216; *see, e.g.*, *CEB Discovery Practice*, §5.230 (sample notice).

(b) A copy of the petition. CCP §2035.040(b); 2 Witkin, *Cal. Evidence*, Discovery, §216.

(3) How to serve. The documents must be served in the same manner as a summons. CCP §2035.040(a). See "Methods of Service," ch. 3-H, §5, p. 301. If, after the exercise of due diligence, the petitioner is unable to serve an expected adverse party, the petitioner must apply to the court for an order to serve by publication. CCP §2035.040(d). See "Service by publication," ch. 3-H, §5.1.4, p. 304; "Service by publication," ch. 3-H, §5.2.4, p. 308.

(4) Deadline to serve. A petition for presuit discovery must be served at least 20 days before the date specified in the notice for the hearing. CCP §2035.040(c).

§4. OBJECTING TO PETITION

§4.1 When to file objections. Objections to a petition for presuit discovery should be filed and served before the hearing. If that is not possible, objections should be made at the hearing. Objections can be filed until the court signs an order authorizing presuit discovery. Once the court signs the order, an expected adverse party can object only by filing a motion to vacate the order. *See* ***Tone v. Superior Ct.*** (2d Dist.1952) 111 Cal.App.2d 110, 111-12.

§4.2 Grounds.

1. Valid grounds. The following are valid grounds for objecting to a petition for presuit discovery:

(1) Procedural error. An objection can be based on the ground that the petition does not comply with CCP §§2035.010-2035.060. The objection should explain why the petition is not in compliance.

(2) Litigation unlikely. An objection can be based on the ground that it is unlikely the petitioner (or its successor in interest) will be a party in an action that is cognizable in a California court. *See* CCP §§2035.010(a), 2035.030(b)(1).

(3) Suit could be brought. An objection can be based on the ground that the petitioner (or its successor in interest) is currently able to either bring the expected action or cause it to be brought. *See* CCP §2035.030(b)(2).

(4) Successor able to conduct discovery. An objection can be based on the ground that, if the expected action is brought, the petitioner's successor in interest will be able to conduct the requested discovery in that action. *See* CCP §2035.050(a).

(5) Deny facts in petition. An objection can be based on the ground that the facts stated in the petition and the supporting declaration are not correct or true. *See* ***Block v. Superior Ct.*** (2d Dist.1963) 219 Cal.App.2d 469, 478. The objection should deny specific facts and state why they are incorrect or untrue. *See id.*

(6) Petitioner's bad faith. An objection can be based on the ground that the petitioner is using presuit discovery in bad faith and not for a legitimate purpose. *See* ***New York Cas. Co. v. Superior Ct.*** (1st Dist.1938) 30 Cal.App.2d 130, 132; *see, e.g.*, ***Tone v. Superior Ct.*** (2d Dist.1952) 111 Cal.App.2d 110, 111-12 (potential deponent argued petition was not filed in good faith and was solely for purpose of harassing and annoying her). Allegations of bad faith must be supported by facts in the supporting declarations. *See* ***Tone***, 111 Cal.App.2d at 112 (motion to vacate).

(7) No need to perpetuate evidence. An objection can be based on the ground that there is no need to perpetuate the evidence sought—that is, the evidence sought should be available if the expected action is ever filed. *See, e.g.*, ***New York Cas.***, 30 Cal.App.2d at 132 (presuit depositions were unnecessary because testimony was already on record).

(8) Beyond scope of presuit discovery. An objection can be based on the ground that the petitioner is not using presuit discovery for its intended purpose. *See* CCP §2035.010(b) (presuit discovery cannot be used to determine potential causes of actions, defenses, or parties). See "Purpose," §1.1, p. 923; "Scope of Presuit Discovery," §2, p. 923.

2. **Invalid grounds.** The following are invalid grounds for objecting to a petition for presuit discovery:

(1) Privilege. An objection cannot be based on the ground that the petition for presuit discovery seeks privileged information. *See* ***Tone***, 111 Cal.App.2d at 113. Instead, the objection must be raised when the privileged information is actually requested. *See id.* (objection to presuit deposition on privilege grounds must be made during deposition, not in motion to vacate order authorizing depositions).

(2) Cause of action. An objection cannot be based on the ground that the petition for presuit discovery does not make sufficient factual allegations to constitute a cause of action because CCP §2035.030 does not require the petitioner to set out any factual allegations in support of the petition. *See* ***Orr v. City of Stockton*** (3d Dist.2007) 150 Cal.App.4th 622, 633.

§4.3 Supporting declaration. An expected adverse party who challenges the accuracy of the facts alleged in the petition for presuit discovery should submit one or more declarations in support of the facts alleged in its objections. *See, e.g.*, ***Tone v. Superior Ct.*** (2d Dist.1952) 111 Cal.App.2d 110, 112 (motion to vacate order authorizing presuit deposition was not supported by facts).

§5. HEARING

Presuit-discovery hearings are conducted in the same manner as hearings generally. See "Hearings," ch. 1-H, p. 79.

§6. ORDER

§6.1 Interest of justice. If the court determines that all or part of the discovery requested by the petitioner may prevent a failure or delay of justice, it must make an order authorizing the discovery. CCP §2035.050(a).

§6.2 Contents of order. An order authorizing discovery must identify the following:

1. Any person or entity whose deposition can be taken. CCP §2035.050(b); *see CEB Discovery Practice*, §5.232 (form for order).

2. Any documents, things, or places that can be inspected. CCP §2035.050(b); *see CEB Discovery Practice*, §5.232 (form for order).

3. Any person whose physical or mental condition can be examined. CCP §2035.050(b).

§6.3 Appointment of attorney. If an expected adverse party served by publication does not appear at the hearing, the court must appoint an attorney to represent the expected party for the entire presuit-discovery process, including the cross-examination of persons whose testimony is taken by deposition. CCP §2035.040(e). If the court appoints an attorney, it must also order the petitioner to pay the attorney's reasonable fees and expenses. *Id.*

§7. CONDUCTING PRESUIT DISCOVERY

§7.1 Procedure. When the court issues an order authorizing presuit discovery, the discovery must be conducted in the same manner as regular pretrial discovery. CCP §2035.050(c). See "Depositions," ch. 7-B, p. 780; "Interrogatories," ch. 7-C, p. 816; "Requests for Admission," ch. 7-D, p. 836; "Demands to Produce," ch. 7-E, p. 845; "Medical Examinations," ch. 7-F, p. 855.

§7.2 Sanctions. The court can impose sanctions against a person or entity that does not comply with an order authorizing presuit discovery. *See* CCP §§2023.010(d), (g), 2023.030. See "Motion for Sanctions," ch. 5-K, p. 561.

§8. USING PRESUIT DISCOVERY AT TRIAL

§8.1 General rule – admissible. Evidence obtained in presuit discovery can generally be used at trial, just like evidence obtained in regular pretrial discovery. *See* CCP §2035.010(a) (presuit discovery is used to preserve evidence), §2035.060 (presuit deposition can be used in later actions).

§8.2 Special rule for presuit depositions. A presuit deposition can be used at trial, just like a deposition taken during regular discovery, but only if the following conditions are satisfied:

1. The action involves the same subject matter as the testimony. CCP §2035.060; ***N.N.V. v. American Ass'n of Blood Banks*** (4th Dist.1999) 75 Cal.App.4th 1358, 1396.

2. The action is brought against a party named in the petition as an expected adverse party (or its successor in interest). CCP §2035.060; *N.N.V.*, 75 Cal.App.4th at 1396.

3. The person against whom the deposition is being used was properly served with the notice of the petition and had the opportunity to participate in the deposition. *N.N.V.*, 75 Cal.App.4th at 1396. See "Depositions from same case," ch. 7-B, §13.1, p. 810.

§9. APPELLATE REVIEW

A court's decision on a petition for presuit discovery is reviewable by writ. *See* ***Superior Ins. v. Superior Ct.*** (1951) 37 Cal.2d 749, 753; *see, e.g.*, ***Block v. Superior Ct.*** (2d Dist.1963) 219 Cal.App.2d 469, 478 (court denied writ petition).

CHAPTER 8. SUBPOENAS

TABLE OF CONTENTS

TABLE OF CONTENTS

8. SUBPOENAS

This chapter covers subpoenas for depositions, trial, and hearings. For general information about subpoenas, see "General Subpoena Information," ch. 8-A, this page. For subpoenas used in the discovery process, see "Deposition Subpoenas," ch. 8-B, p. 959. For subpoenas used in the trial process, see "Trial & Hearing Subpoenas," ch. 8-C, p. 970. For subpoenas used to secure personal records, see "Subpoenas for Personal Records," ch. 8-D, p. 977. For objections and motions to quash, to enforce, and for protective orders, see "Challenging & Enforcing Subpoenas," ch. 8-E, p. 995.

A. GENERAL SUBPOENA INFORMATION

This subchapter covers general information about issuing and serving deposition and trial subpoenas.

§1. GENERAL

Chart 8-1, below, summarizes most of the information in this subchapter for an overview and comparison of subpoena procedures.

8-1. DEPOSITION SUBPOENAS VS. TRIAL SUBPOENAS

		Subpoenas for deposition				Subpoenas for trial or hearing		
		Attend only	**Attend & produce**	**Business records for copies**	**Business records for originals**	**Attend only**	**Attend & produce**	**Produce only**
1	Judicial Council forms	SUBP-015	SUBP-020, SUBP-025 ❶	SUBP-010, SUBP-025 ❶	SUBP-010, SUBP-025 ❶	SUBP-001	SUBP-002, SUBP-025 ❶	SUBP-002, SUBP-025 ❶
2	Witness	Nonparty				Party or nonparty		
3	Description of things to be produced	N/A	Individual items – describe specifically			N/A	Describe things exactly	
			Categories of things – describe with reasonable particularity					
4	Activity to be performed on things	N/A	Inspect, copy, test, or sample	Copy	Inspect and copy	N/A		
5	Good-cause and materiality affidavit?	N/A	Not required			N/A	Required	
6	Date to comply	Reasonable time		15 days after service		Reasonable time		
7	Date to produce personal records	N/A	25 days ❷ after service on consumer or employee			N/A	20 days ❷ after service on consumer or employee	
8	Type of fees paid to witness ❸	Per diem and travel	Per diem, travel, and production costs	Production costs	Compliance fee ($15) and retrieval costs	Per diem and travel	Per diem, travel, and production costs	Production costs

8-1. DEPOSITION SUBPOENAS VS. TRIAL SUBPOENAS (CONTINUED)							
		Subpoenas for deposition				**Subpoenas for trial or hearing**	
9	When to pay witness fees ❸	Service or appearance		N/A	Compliance fee payable at service	Service	
10	When to pay production costs	N/A	On delivery of copies and invoice		On delivery of originals and invoice	N/A	On delivery of copies and invoice

❶ SUBP-025 is necessary only when a consumer's personal records are sought.

❷ If the consumer is served by means other than personal delivery, add additional time. See "Add time for method of service," ch. 1-G, §6.1.4, p. 70.

❸ This chart does not cover witness fees for public employees or for expert witnesses. See "Government witness fees," §10.4, p. 955; "Expert-Witness Fees," ch. 7-I, §11, p. 912.

§1.1 Purpose. A subpoena is a legal document used to secure the attendance of a witness and the production of documents or other things. *See* CCP §1985(a). A subpoena is the only procedure authorized by the Civil Discovery Act (CDA) for obtaining discovery from a nonparty. CCP §2020.010(b); *see California Civil Discovery Practice* (CEB Online ed. 2014) §5.7.

§1.2 Primary authority. CCP §§1985-1997, 2020.010-2020.510, 2025.220(b), 2025.240(b), 2025.270(a), 2025.280(b), 2064, 2065; Evid. C. §§1560-64; Gov. C. §§68092.5-68093, 68096.1-68097.6, 68097.9.

§1.3 Secondary authority. The following secondary sources are cited as authority in this subchapter:

- *Action Guide: Handling Subpoenas* (CEB Online ed. 2014) (referred to as *CEB Action Guide: Subpoenas*).
- *California Civil Discovery Practice* (CEB Online ed. 2014) (referred to as *CEB Discovery Practice*).
- *California Trial Practice: Civil Procedure During Trial* (CEB Online ed. 2014) (referred to as *CEB Procedure During Trial*).
- Sink, *California Subpoena Handbook* (2014-15) (referred to as Sink, *Subpoena Handbook*).
- Wegner, *California Practice Guide: Civil Trials & Evidence* (CD-ROM ed. 2014) (referred to as Wegner, *Civil Trials & Evidence*).
- Weil & Brown, *California Practice Guide: Civil Procedure Before Trial* (CD-ROM ed. 2014) (referred to as Weil, *Civil Procedure Before Trial*).
- Witkin, *California Evidence* (5th ed. 2012 & Supp.2014) (referred to as Witkin, *Cal. Evidence*).
- Witkin, *California Procedure* (5th ed. 2008 & Supp.2014) (referred to as Witkin, *Cal. Procedure*).

§1.4 Judicial Council forms. The mandatory Judicial Council forms for subpoenas can be found on the California Courts website at www.courts.ca.gov/forms.htm. For other subpoena forms, see *CEB Action Guide: Subpoenas*, Appx. A-I; *CEB Discovery Practice*, §§5.217, 5.218, 5.223; *CEB Procedure During Trial*, §§4.55-4.73.

1. Deposition subpoenas. The following forms must be used to compel attendance or production at a deposition:

- SUBP-015 (mandatory), deposition subpoena for personal appearance.
- SUBP-020 (mandatory), deposition subpoena for personal appearance and production.
- SUBP-010 (mandatory), deposition subpoena for business records from custodian.
- SUBP-025 (mandatory), notice of privacy rights for consumer or employee.

GENERAL

2. Trial & hearing subpoenas. The following forms must be used to compel attendance or production at a trial or hearing:

- SUBP-001 (mandatory), trial subpoena for personal appearance.
- SUBP-002 (mandatory), trial subpoena for personal appearance and production, or for just production.
- SUBP-025 (mandatory), notice of privacy rights for consumer or employee.

§2. DEFINITIONS

§2.1 Affidavit. An affidavit is a written statement made under oath before an officer authorized to administer oaths. 6 Witkin, *Cal. Procedure*, Provisional Remedies, §2; *see* CCP §§2003, 2012; *see also* CCP §2013 (made in another state), §2014 (made in another country), §2093 (officers authorized to administer oaths). See "Affidavit," ch. 1-B, §4.1.2, p. 19.

§2.2 Declaration. A declaration is a written statement made under penalty of perjury as a substitute for an affidavit. CCP §2015.5. The form for the declaration is provided in §2015.5(a). See "Declaration," ch. 1-B, §4.1.1, p. 19.

§2.3 Nonparty. A nonparty is a person or entity that is not a litigant in the pending suit and is not a party-affiliated witness.

§2.4 Party. A party is a litigant in the pending suit. ***Poe v. Diamond*** (2d Dist.1987) 191 Cal.App.3d 1394, 1399.

§2.5 Party-affiliated witness. A party's "affiliated witnesses" are treated as parties for purposes of subpoenas because of their close relationship with the party. By treating an affiliated witness as a party, the witness can be compelled to attend or produce at a deposition, hearing, or trial by a statutory notice served on the party's attorney, rather than a subpoena personally served on the witness. See "Party-affiliated witness," ch. 7-B, §2.5, p. 781.

PRACTICE TIP

To compel a party or its affiliated witness to attend a deposition, you must use a deposition notice, not a deposition subpoena. Sink, Subpoena Handbook, §2:3[B]. By comparison, to compel a party or its affiliated witness to attend a trial or hearing, you can use either a trial notice or a trial subpoena. Id. §2:3[C].

1. Affiliated witnesses for deposition. A party's affiliated witnesses for purposes of a deposition include the following:

(1) An officer. CCP §2025.280(a).

(2) A director. *Id.*

(3) A managing agent. *Id.* A "managing agent" of an organization is a person who can exercise judgment and discretion in dealing with corporate matters, who can be expected to comply with her employer's directive to appear for pretrial examination, and who can be anticipated to identify herself with the interests of the corporation. ***Waters v. Superior Ct.*** (1962) 58 Cal.2d 885, 896.

(4) An employee. CCP §2025.280(a).

2. Affiliated witnesses for trial. A party's affiliated witnesses for purposes of a trial or hearing include the following:

(1) An officer. CCP §1987(b).

(2) A director. *Id.*

GENERAL

(3) A managing agent. *Id.* For the definition of "managing agent," see "Affiliated witnesses for deposition," §2.5.1(3), p. 933.

(4) A benefiting person. CCP §1987(b). A benefiting person is a person or entity for whose immediate benefit the suit is being prosecuted or defended. *Id.* A person who has an "immediate benefit" is a person who, when the case is resolved, has an immediate right to some recovery or has some immediate and direct liability. ***Waters***, 58 Cal.2d at 897. For example, in a personal-injury suit brought by a husband, the wife is a benefiting person because of her community-property interest in the husband's recovery. ***Hand v. Superior Ct.*** (3d Dist.1982) 134 Cal.App.3d 436, 442.

§2.6 Personal records. The term "personal records," as it relates to discovery, means the records of consumers, employees, and other persons (collectively, "consumers") that are protected from immediate disclosure by CCP §§1985.3, 1985.4, and 1985.6. See "Types of Records Covered," ch. 8-D, §6, p. 980. The protected records include those maintained by, among others, accountants, attorneys, banks, credit unions, employers, escrow agents, government agencies, insurance companies, medical providers, pharmacies, schools, and some telephone companies. See "Types of Persons & Entities Covered," ch. 8-D, §7, p. 981.

§2.7 Subpoena. A subpoena is the legal document served on a witness to compel the witness to attend and testify at a deposition, hearing, or trial and to produce documents or other things. *See* CCP §1985(a). There are two types of subpoenas:

1. Deposition subpoena. A deposition subpoena can compel a nonparty to attend or produce at a deposition. *See* CCP §§2020.010(b), 2020.020. See "Deposition Subpoenas," ch. 8-B, p. 959.

2. Trial subpoena. A trial subpoena can compel a party, a party-affiliated witness, or a nonparty to attend and produce at a trial, hearing, or any other nondeposition matter. *See* CCP §1985(a). See "Trial & Hearing Subpoenas," ch. 8-C, p. 970. A party or party-affiliated witness also can be compelled to attend a trial or hearing by a trial notice.

§2.8 Subpoena duces tecum. "Duces tecum" is Latin for "bring with you." *Black's Law Dictionary* 609 (10th ed. 2014). A subpoena duces tecum is a subpoena that is served on a nonparty witness to compel the witness to produce documents or other things at a deposition, trial, or hearing. *See* CCP §1985(b). In this book, a subpoena duces tecum is referred to as a deposition subpoena for production or a trial subpoena for production.

§2.9 Subpoenaed person. A subpoenaed person is the person to whom a subpoena is addressed and who must comply with the subpoena.

§2.10 Subpoenaing party. A subpoenaing party is the party who caused the subpoena to be issued and served.

§3. SUBPOENAS VS. STATUTORY NOTICES

It is important to discuss the procedures for subpoenas with the procedures for statutory notices because their purpose is the same: compelling a witness to attend and produce. Whether to use a subpoena or a statutory notice depends on the status of the witness (i.e., party or nonparty).

§3.1 Subpoenas. A subpoena compels a nonparty witness to do one of the following:

1. Attend. A subpoena that commands the attendance of a witness requires the subpoenaed person to attend and testify at a specified time and place, and remain until discharged or the testimony is closed. *See* CCP §§1985(a), 2020.220(c)(1), 2020.310(a), 2064.

2. Attend & produce. A subpoena that commands the attendance of a witness and the production of things requires the subpoenaed person to appear and produce books, documents, electronically stored information (ESI), or other things at a specified time and place, and remain until discharged or the testimony is closed. *See* CCP §§1985(a), 2020.220(c), 2020.510(a), 2064.

3. **Produce.** A subpoena that commands the production of things requires the subpoenaed person to produce books, documents, records, ESI, or other things at a specified time and place. *See* CCP §§1985(a), 2020.220(c)(2), (c)(3), 2020.410(a); *see also id.* §1985.3 (contents of subpoena duces tecum).

§3.2 Statutory notices. A statutory notice has two main purposes.

1. **Compel party witness.** The statutory notice compels a party or party-affiliated witness to do one of the following:

(1) **Attend.** A statutory notice that commands the attendance of a party or party-affiliated witness requires the person to appear and testify at a deposition, trial, or hearing. *See* CCP §1987(b). See "Deposition notice for oral deposition," ch. 7-B, §9.2, p. 789.

(2) **Attend & produce.** A statutory notice that commands the attendance of and production by a party or party-affiliated witness requires the person to appear, testify, and produce documents or other things under the witness's control at a deposition, trial, or hearing. *See* CCP §1987(b), (c); ***Amoco Chem. Co. v. Certain Underwriters at Lloyd's of London*** (2d Dist.1995) 34 Cal.App.4th 554, 560.

NOTE

A party or party-affiliated witness cannot be required by a statutory notice to produce things without making a personal appearance at a deposition or trial. See ***Amoco Chem.***, *34 Cal.App.4th at 560.*

2. **Notify other parties of discovery.** The subpoenaing party must serve copies of a statutory deposition notice on all parties who have appeared in the case. *See* CCP §§1987.5, 2025.240(a), (c). By comparison, the subpoenaing party does not need to serve copies of a statutory trial notice on other parties. See "Not parties," ch. 8-C, §3.3.2, p. 973.

GENERAL

8-2. SUBPOENAS VS. NOTICES

		For depositions		For trial or hearing	
		Deposition subpoena	Deposition notice	Trial subpoena	Trial notice
Who can be compelled by subpoena & by notice					
1	Party can be compelled by—		Notice. See ch. 7-B, §9.2, p. 789.	Subpoena. See ch. 8-C, §2.1, p. 970.	Notice. CCP §1987(b).
2	Party's officer, director, or managing agent can be compelled by—		Notice. CCP §2025.280(a).	Subpoena. CCP §1987(b).	Notice. CCP §1987(b).
3	Party's employee can be compelled by—		Notice. CCP §2025.280(a).	Subpoena. CCP §1987(b). ❶	
4	Person with immediate benefit in suit can be compelled by—	Subpoena. CCP §2025.280. ❷		Subpoena. CCP §1987(b).	Notice. CCP §1987(b).
5	Party's designated expert can be compelled by—		Notice. See ch. 7-I, §10.2.1(1), p. 911.	Subpoena. CCP §2064.	

8-2. SUBPOENAS VS. NOTICES (CONTINUED)					
		For depositions		For trial or hearing	
		Deposition subpoena	Deposition notice	Trial subpoena	Trial notice
Who can be compelled by subpoena & by notice (continued)					
6	Nonretained expert (e.g., treating doctor) can be compelled by—	Subpoena. See ch. 7-I, §10.2.1(2), p. 911.		Subpoena. CCP §2064.	
7	Nonparty can be compelled by—	Subpoena. CCP §§2020.010(b), 2025.280.		Subpoena. CCP §§1985(a), 1987(a).	
Requirements for subpoenas & notices					
8	Describe things to be produced—	Items specifically; categories with reasonable particularity. See §5.2.1, p. 940.	Reasonable particularity. See ch. 7-B, §9.2.4(3), p. 791.	Exactly. See §5.2.2, p. 940.	Exactly. CCP §1987(c).
9	Attach declaration showing good cause and materiality—	No. See §6.4.2, p. 943.	No. See §6.4.2, p. 943.	Yes. See ch. 8-C, §4.2, p. 974.	No. CCP §1987(b).
10	Which witnesses entitled to witness fees ❸	All subpoenaed nonparties. See §10.2.1(1), p. 952.	Not party or party-affiliated witness. See ch. 7-B, §8, p. 788.	All subpoenaed witnesses. See §10.2.1(2), p. 952.	All noticed parties and party-affiliated witnesses.
11	When to pay witness fees	On service of subpoena or on appearance. See §10.2.4(1)(a), p. 953.	On service of notice for party or party-affiliated witness. See ch. 7-B, §8, p. 788.	On service of subpoena. See §10.2.4(1)(b), p. 953.	Before testimony of party or party-affiliated witness. CCP §1987(b).
On whom & when to serve subpoena or notice					
12	For testimony only, serve—	Nonparty with SUBP-015, reasonable time before deposition. CCP §2020.220(a).	Party with deposition notice, 10 days ❹ before deposition. CCP §2025.270(a).	Witness with SUBP-001, reasonable time before appearance. CCP §1987(a).	Party's attorney with trial notice, 10 days ❹ before trial or hearing. CCP §1987(b).
13	For testimony and production (no personal records), serve—	Nonparty with SUBP-020, reasonable time before deposition. CCP §2020.220(a).	Party with deposition notice, 10 days ❹ before deposition. CCP §2025.280(a).	Witness with SUBP-002, reasonable time before appearance. CCP §1987.	Party's attorney with trial notice, 20 days ❹ before trial or hearing. CCP §1987(c).

GENERAL

8-2. SUBPOENAS VS. NOTICES (CONTINUED)

		For depositions		For trial or hearing	
		Deposition subpoena	Deposition notice	Trial subpoena	Trial notice
On whom & when to serve subpoena or notice (continued)					
14	For production of documents and other things (no personal records), serve—	Nonparty with SUBP-020 for business records, 15 days before date for production. CCP §2020.410(c).	N/A. Make demand on party for production under CCP §2031.010.	Witness with SUBP-002, reasonable time before appearance. CCP §§1985, 1987.	Party's attorney with trial notice, 20 days ❹ before trial or hearing. CCP §1987(c).
15	Serve notice of deposition on other parties—	10 days before deposition. CCP §§2025.240(a), 2025.270(a).	10 days ❹ before deposition. CCP §§2025.240(a), 2025.270(a).	Notice to other parties is not required for trial subpoena or trial notice. See §7.2.1(2), p. 946.	

❶ Although a party's employee is subject to a deposition notice under CCP §2025.280(a) (see "Deposition Notice," row 3), a party's employee is not mentioned in §1987(b) as being subject to a trial or hearing notice; thus, a party's employee who is not an officer, director, or managing agent must be served with a subpoena to appear at trial; a notice to appear is insufficient.

❷ Although a person for whose immediate benefit the action is prosecuted or defended is subject to a trial notice under CCP §1987(b) (see "Trial Notice," row 4), such a person is not mentioned in §2025.280 as being subject to a deposition notice; thus, a person for whose immediate benefit the action is prosecuted or defended must be served with a subpoena to appear for a deposition.

❸ Special rules apply to payment of witness fees for public employees. See "Government witness fees," §10.4, p. 955.

❹ If the document is served by means other than personal delivery, add additional time. See "Add time for method of service," ch. 1-G, §6.1.4, p. 70.

§4. WHO IS SUBJECT TO A SUBPOENA

§4.1 Who can be subpoenaed.

1. Residents. As a general rule, any person (including an organization) who is a resident of California can be subpoenaed to attend, testify, and produce documents or other things at a deposition, trial, or hearing. *See* CCP §§1985, 1989, 2020.220(c). "Residence" for purposes of a subpoena requires only that the witness be living in California; residence is less than "domicile" because it does not require the person to have the intention of making California her home. *See* ***In re Morelli*** (2d Dist.1970) 11 Cal.App.3d 819, 830-31; Wegner, *Civil Trials & Evidence*, ¶1:52. A person can have several residences at a time, but only one domicile. ***In re Morelli***, 11 Cal.App.3d at 831.

(1) Natural persons. A natural person who is a resident of California when the subpoena is served can be subpoenaed. *See* CCP §§1989, 2020.220(b)(1), (c).

(a) Employees.

[1] Business employees. When an organization is required by a subpoena to designate an employee to testify on its behalf, it is required to produce only employees who are themselves residents of California. *See* CCP §1989; *cf.* ***Twin Lock, Inc. v. Superior Ct.*** (1959) 52 Cal.2d 754, 759-62 (court could not sanction party for refusing to produce its N.Y. officers and directors for deposition in L.A. in response to deposition notice). The organization is required to produce only current employees, not former ones. ***Maldonado v. Superior Ct.*** (2d Dist.2002) 94 Cal.App.4th 1390, 1398.

[2] Public employees. When a public entity is required by a subpoena to designate an employee to testify on its behalf, it is required to produce its employees who are residents of California. *See* CCP §§1989, 2020.220(c). A "public employee" is an employee, officer, or agent of a public entity. Evid. C. §195. There is an exception to this rule. See "Nonresident CHP officer," §4.1.2(1), p. 938.

(b) Persons within federal enclaves. A person within a federal enclave located in California can be served with a subpoena if California expressly retained jurisdiction to serve process within the area ceded to the federal government. Sink, *Subpoena Handbook*, §3:3[C]; *see, e.g.*, Gov. C. §119 (reserving right to serve process in Kings Canyon National Park). A federal enclave is an area within a state over which the federal government exercises jurisdiction. *E.g.*, ***Taylor v. Lockheed Martin Corp.*** (2d Dist.2000) 78 Cal.App.4th 472, 478 (military base). For example, a subpoena can be served on a person within the Presidio of San Francisco because California reserved the right to execute civil process when it ceded the Presidio to the federal government. ***Consolidated Milk Producers v. Parker*** (1942) 19 Cal.2d 815, 816.

(c) Parties – trial subpoenas. A party and its affiliated witnesses can be subpoenaed to attend and produce at a trial or hearing (but not at a deposition). *See* CCP §1987(b); Sink, *Subpoena Handbook*, §§2:3[B], 11:1[D], 11:1[E]. Generally, parties and party-affiliated witnesses are compelled to attend and produce by a trial notice, not a subpoena. CCP §1987(b). However, because a trial subpoena can be served just before or even during trial, it can be used to compel a party witness after the deadline to serve a notice to attend a trial has passed, but must be served at least ten days before the time required for attendance. *See id.* By comparison, a party witness cannot be compelled to attend a deposition by a deposition subpoena. See "Parties – not by deposition subpoenas," §4.2.2, p. 939.

(2) Organizations.

(a) Business entities. California business entities (e.g., corporations, partnerships, trusts) can be subpoenaed, whether they are for-profit or not-for-profit. *See* CCP §§1989, 2020.220(b)(2), (c); Evid. C. §1270 ("business" includes for-profit and nonprofit businesses); *see also* ***Coopman v. Superior Ct.*** (1st Dist.1965) 237 Cal.App.2d 656, 660-61 (resident of California, who was president of nonresident corporation, could not be required to produce corporate records). A subpoena to a California business can be directed to the business without naming a natural person (e.g., "Acme, Inc.") and can be served on any officer, director, or custodian of records of the business or on any agent or employee authorized by the business to accept service of a subpoena. CCP §2020.220(b)(2).

(b) Public entities. California public entities can be subpoenaed. *See* ***People v. Superior Ct.*** (4th Dist.2004) 122 Cal.App.4th 1060, 1078 (nonparty state agency is subject to subpoena); *see also* Evid. C. §175 ("person" includes public entity), §1270 ("business" includes every kind of governmental activity); Sink, *Subpoena Handbook*, §1:8 (any legal entity that can be party to an action can be subpoenaed). For purposes of California subpoenas, "public entities" include the State, counties, cities, districts, public authorities, public agencies, and any other political subdivision or public corporation. Evid. C. §200. A subpoena to a public entity can be directed to the entity without naming a natural person. For example, the subpoena can be addressed to "California Department of Public Health." When the State of California is a party, it is not considered to be in possession of documents of any state agency; the state agencies and departments are considered nonparties and must be served with subpoenas. ***People***, 122 Cal.App.4th at 1078.

2. Nonresidents. Although most nonresidents cannot be compelled by a California subpoena, there are two exceptions.

(1) Nonresident CHP officer. A California Highway Patrol (CHP) officer who is not a California resident can be subpoenaed to testify about an event perceived or investigated in the course of the officer's duties in California. Gov. C. §68097.3; Sink, *Subpoena Handbook*, §3:4[A]. See "Nonresident CHP officer," §9.2.2(2), p. 948.

(2) Nonresident custodian of records. A nonresident custodian of records who is served with a deposition subpoena for business records within California may be required to produce records located in California as long as the custodian's appearance is not required. See "Business records," §5.4.2(2)(b), p. 941.

§4.2 Who cannot be subpoenaed.

1. Nonresidents. As a general rule, nonresident witnesses cannot be subpoenaed to attend a deposition, trial, or hearing in California. CCP §1989; *see* ***Toyota Motor Corp. v. Superior Ct.*** (2d Dist.2011) 197 Cal.App.4th 1107, 1118; *cf.* ***Twin Lock, Inc. v. Superior Ct.*** (1959) 52 Cal.2d 754, 761-62 (court could not sanction

nonresident party for refusing to produce nonresident employees in response to deposition notice). Generally, to compel a nonresident witness to testify and produce, the witness must be subpoenaed under the laws of the state where the witness resides. *See* CCP §2026.010(c). But there are some exceptions to this rule. See "Nonresidents," §4.1.2, p. 938.

2. Parties – not by deposition subpoenas. Parties and party-affiliated witnesses cannot be compelled by a deposition subpoena to attend and produce at a deposition. Sink, *Subpoena Handbook*, §2:3[B]; *see* CCP §2025.280 (notice to be used for compelling party's attendance and testimony; subpoena to be used for any other deponent). But party-affiliated witnesses can be compelled to attend a trial or hearing by a trial subpoena. See "Parties – trial subpoenas," §4.1.1(1)(c), p. 938.

3. Legislators during session. Members of the California Legislature cannot be subpoenaed (or subjected to other civil process) during a legislative session or for five days before and after the session. Cal. Const., art. IV, §14; ***Harmer v. Superior Ct.*** (3d Dist.1969) 275 Cal.App.2d 345, 346; Sink, *Subpoena Handbook*, §4:4. For a discussion of motions for continuance involving a legislator, see "Member of Legislature," ch. 5-I, §2.3, p. 540.

4. Diplomats. Most foreign diplomatic personnel cannot be subpoenaed. For a discussion of diplomatic immunity from subpoenas, see Sink, *Subpoena Handbook*, §4:3.

5. Federal employees. Federal employees cannot be subpoenaed to testify (or produce records) about information acquired in their official capacity when prohibited by law. *See* 5 U.S.C. §301; 44 U.S.C. §3101; *see, e.g.*, ***Civiletti v. Municipal Ct.*** (2d Dist.1981) 116 Cal.App.3d 105, 109-10 (U.S. Attorney General is not subject to California subpoena); Sink, *Subpoena Handbook*, §3:5 (some rules on production of federal records and testimony of federal employees provide criteria by which federal entity can choose to release records or provide testimony under state subpoena).

6. Prisoners. Persons incarcerated in state prisons and jails cannot be subpoenaed. To compel the appearance of a prisoner incarcerated in a state prison, the party must secure a court order. For a discussion of how to compel a prisoner's deposition testimony, see "Prisoners," ch. 7-B, §7.4.2, p. 786.

GENERAL

§5. WHAT CAN BE SUBPOENAED

Whether evidence can be required to be produced depends on four things: (1) the existence of the evidence, (2) the description of the evidence, (3) the custody or control of the evidence, and (4) the interaction of the location of the evidence, the status of the witness, and the residency of the witness.

§5.1 Existing things only. A subpoena can require the production of existing evidence only. *See* ***Flora Crane Serv. v. Superior Ct.*** (1st Dist.1965) 234 Cal.App.2d 767, 784 (subpoena presupposes existence of thing sought). A subpoena cannot require a person to create a document for production. *See, e.g.*, *id.* at 783-84 (subpoena could not require D to create list of names and addresses of employees from two-year period). Examples of things that can be subpoenaed include the following:

1. Books. CCP §1985(a); *see id.* §2020.510(a).
2. Documents. *Id.* §§1985(a), 2020.510(a).
3. Business records. *Id.* §§1987.3, 2020.410, 2020.510(a). See "Identification of business records," ch. 8-B, §5.1.4, p. 965.
4. ESI. CCP §§1985(a), 1985.8(a)(1), 2020.510(a). See "Electronic Discovery," ch. 7-H, p. 873.
5. Other tangible things. CCP §2020.510(a); *see id.* §1985(a) (things).

§5.2 Proper description. A subpoena must properly identify the documents and other things to be produced. *See* CCP §2020.510(a)(2). A trial subpoena requires a more exact description than a deposition subpoena. See "Deposition Subpoenas vs. Trial Subpoenas," chart 8-1, p. 931.

1. Deposition subpoenas. A deposition subpoena must describe the things to be produced either individually or by categories, and describe any sampling or testing that will be done to them. CCP §2020.510(a)(2), (a)(3).

(1) Individual items. If individual things are sought to be produced, each individual item must be described specifically. CCP §2020.410(a) (business records), §2020.510(a)(2) (business records, documents, ESI, and tangible things). This ensures that the subpoenaed witness can identify and locate the things sought. *See* ***Flora Crane Serv. v. Superior Ct.*** (1st Dist.1965) 234 Cal.App.2d 767, 786-87; *cf.* ***Grannis v. Board of Med. Exam'rs*** (1st Dist.1971) 19 Cal.App.3d 551, 565 (trial subpoena).

(2) Categories of items. If categories of things are sought to be produced, each category must be described with reasonable particularity. CCP §2020.410(a) (business records), §2020.510(a)(2) (business records, documents, ESI, and tangible things). The request for categories must not be too broad. *See, e.g.*, ***Bearman v. Superior Ct.*** (2d Dist.2004) 117 Cal.App.4th 463, 472 (request for all medical records of patient was too broad); ***Calcor Space Facility, Inc. v. Superior Ct.*** (4th Dist.1997) 53 Cal.App.4th 216, 219 (requested categories of materials to be produced were too broad); ***Pacific Auto. Ins. v. Superior Ct.*** (2d Dist.1969) 273 Cal.App.2d 61, 70 (request for "all correspondence, records, and documents" was too broad). Whether a category's description is particular enough must be determined from the standpoint of the person who has the burden to produce the things. ***Calcor Space Facility***, 53 Cal.App.4th at 222.

(3) Activities to be performed. The subpoena must identify the activities to be performed on each item that will be produced.

(a) To attend & produce. A deposition subpoena to attend and produce can require the nonparty to produce things for inspection, copying, testing, or sampling. *See* CCP §1985.8(a)(1) (ESI), §2020.220(c) (contents of deposition subpoena), §2020.510(a)(3) (subpoena for attendance and production).

(b) To produce only. A deposition subpoena for production of business records can require only the production of copies of the records. CCP §2020.430(a). A deposition subpoena for inspection of original business records can require that the documents be made available for inspection and copying. *Id.* §2020.430(e).

(4) Form for ESI. A subpoena that seeks the production of ESI must specify the form in which each type of information is to be produced, if a particular form is desired. CCP §§2020.410(a), 2020.510(a)(4), 2025.220(a)(7); *see id.* §§1985.8(b), (d)(1), 2020.220(d)(1); Judicial Council Forms, form SUBP-010, Item 3. Otherwise, the subpoenaed witness can produce the ESI in the form in which it is ordinarily maintained or in a form that is reasonably usable. CCP §§1985.8(d)(1), 2020.220(d)(1). See "Form specified by discovering party," ch. 7-H, §10.2.1, p. 891; "No form specified by discovering party," ch. 7-H, §10.2.2, p. 891.

2. Trial subpoenas. A trial subpoena must describe each matter or thing to be produced *exactly*. CCP §1985(b); *see* ***Grannis***, 19 Cal.App.3d at 564-65; ***Flora Crane Serv.***, 234 Cal.App.2d at 785. *Contra* Wegner, *Civil Trials & Evidence*, ¶1:129 (exact description not required; reasonable description sufficient).

§5.3 Custody or control. A subpoena can require a subpoenaed witness to produce discoverable documents or other things only if those things are within the witness's possession, custody, or control. *See* CCP §1985(a) (control), §1985(b) (possession or control), §1987(c) (possession or control), §2025.480(a) (control), §2031.010(a) (possession, custody, or control). See "Custody or control," ch. 7-A, §9.1.2(2), p. 757.

§5.4 Location, status, residence. Whether a subpoena can require the production of evidence depends on the interaction of the following: (1) the location of the evidence (inside or outside California), (2) the status of the witness (party or nonparty), and (3) the witness's residence (resident or nonresident). Chart 8-3, below, summarizes this analysis.

GENERAL

CAUTION

There is very little authority on many of these issues, and what little there is conflicts.

8-3. WHO IS REQUIRED TO PRODUCE EVIDENCE?

		Evidence located inside CA	Evidence located outside CA
Nonparty who is subpoenaed to produce is a—			
1	Resident	Yes	No
2	Nonresident	Maybe yes for business records	No
Party who is noticed to produce is a—			
3	Resident	Yes	Maybe yes
4	Nonresident	Yes	Probably no

1. Evidence in California + resident.

(1) Resident party. A resident party served with a notice to produce in California can be compelled to produce things under its control located in California. *See* CCP §§1987(c), 1989; Sink, *Subpoena Handbook*, §3:9[C][1][a]; *see also* Weil, *Civil Procedure Before Trial*, ¶8:522 (for production from party, location of documents immaterial).

(2) Resident nonparty. A resident nonparty served with a subpoena in California can be compelled to produce things under its control located in California. *See* CCP §§1985(a), 1989, 2020.220(c)(2); Sink, *Subpoena Handbook*, §3:9[C][1][a]; *see, e.g.*, ***In re Marriage of Stephens*** (2d Dist.1984) 156 Cal.App.3d 909, 912 (in California divorce proceeding, husband served subpoena on wife's California employer seeking her payroll records).

2. Evidence in California + nonresident.

(1) Nonresident party. A nonresident party served with a notice to produce can be compelled to produce things under its control located in California. *See* Sink, *Subpoena Handbook*, §3:9[C][2][a]-[c].

(2) Nonresident nonparty.

(a) Most things. A nonresident nonparty served with a subpoena cannot be compelled to produce most things under its control located in California. *See* CCP §§1987.3, 1989; Sink, *Subpoena Handbook*, §3:9[C][2][a]-[c].

(b) Business records. There may be an exception to the rule above for a subpoena for business records served on a nonresident. Sink, *Subpoena Handbook*, §3:9[C][2][c]. Sink reaches this conclusion by analyzing CCP §§1989 and 1987.3. First, §1989 states that a nonresident witness served with a subpoena "is not obliged to attend"; it does not state "is not obliged to produce." Second, Sink says the only logical way to interpret §1987.3 (which is particularly difficult to understand) is that it exempts a custodian served with a business-records subpoena from needing to be a resident when the subpoena is served. Sink, *Subpoena Handbook*, §3:9[C][2][a]. Wegner reaches the same conclusion without analysis. *See* Wegner, *Civil Trials & Evidence*, ¶1:57. But Wegner qualifies the exception by saying it probably applies to a nonresident custodian only when employed by a business subject to California jurisdiction. *Id.* ¶1:58; *see* ***Amoco Chem. Co. v. Certain Underwriters at Lloyd's of London*** (2d Dist.1995) 34 Cal.App.4th 554, 561 n.9 (quoting Wegner on this point).

3. Evidence outside California + resident.

(1) Resident party. A resident party served with a notice to produce can be compelled to produce things under its control wherever the things are located; this includes things located in another state or in a foreign

country. *See* ***Boal v. Price Waterhouse & Co.*** (2d Dist.1985) 165 Cal.App.3d 806, 810-11; Weil, *Civil Procedure Before Trial*, ¶8:522. *Contra* ***Amoco Chem.***, 34 Cal.App.4th at 561 (dicta; court disagreed with ***Boal***).

(2) Resident nonparty. A resident nonparty served with a subpoena in California cannot be compelled to produce things under its control located outside California. *See* ***Boal***, 165 Cal.App.3d at 810 (dicta as to nonparty); Sink, *Subpoena Handbook*, §3:9[C][1][b] (resident nonparty cannot be required to produce records located outside California); Wegner, *Civil Trials & Evidence*, ¶1:133 (subpoena cannot compel nonparty to produce documents located outside California). *But see* Weil, *Civil Procedure Before Trial*, ¶8:540.4 (unclear whether resident nonparty served with business-records subpoena can be compelled to produce records located outside California), ¶¶8:540.5 & 8:557.1 (resident nonparty served with subpoena to appear *and* produce can be compelled to produce records located outside California).

4. Evidence outside California + nonresident.

(1) Nonresident party. A nonresident party served with a notice to produce cannot be compelled to produce things under its control located outside California. ***Amoco Chem.***, 34 Cal.App.4th at 555. *Contra* ***Boal***, 165 Cal.App.3d at 810-11 (dicta; when court has personal jurisdiction over party, it can compel party to produce things located outside California).

(2) Nonresident nonparty. A nonresident nonparty served with a subpoena in California cannot be compelled to produce things under its control located outside California. *See* Sink, *Subpoena Handbook*, §3:9[C][2][d]; *see also* ***Coopman v. Superior Ct.*** (1st Dist.1965) 237 Cal.App.2d 656, 660-61 (corporate president, who was resident party, could not be compelled to produce business records of his nonresident, nonparty corporation because California did not have jurisdiction over corporation and only had personal, not representative, jurisdiction over president).

§6. HOW SUBPOENAS ARE PREPARED & ISSUED

§6.1 Who can issue subpoena. A subpoena is "issued" when it is signed by the person who has the authority to issue it. A pro per party cannot issue a subpoena; a pro per party must secure a court-issued subpoena. The following persons can issue subpoenas:

1. Clerk. The clerk of the court where the case is pending can issue deposition and trial subpoenas. CCP §§1985(c), 1986(a), 2020.210(a).

2. Judge. The judge of the court where the case is pending can issue trial subpoenas. CCP §1985(c). If no clerk is available, the judge can also issue deposition subpoenas. *See id.* §167 (judge can perform any act court clerk can perform), §2020.210(a) (court clerk must issue deposition subpoena).

3. Attorney of record. An attorney of record can issue deposition and trial subpoenas. CCP §§1985(c), 2020.210(b).

§6.2 How to secure issued subpoena. The party must select the correct subpoena form before having a subpoena issued. For a list of subpoena forms, see "Judicial Council forms," §1.4, p. 932.

1. Court-issued subpoena. For a court-issued subpoena, a party must ask the court clerk to issue a subpoena, which must be signed by the clerk or judge, dated, and sealed, but otherwise left blank. The party must fill in the information on the subpoena form that includes all the necessary information about who is required to attend or produce and where and when. CCP §§1985(c), 2020.210(a). A court-issued subpoena must bear the seal of the court. *Id.* §§1985(c), 2020.210(a).

2. Attorney-issued subpoena. For an attorney-issued subpoena, the attorney must fill in all the information necessary for the subpoena, including the issuing information. CCP §§1985(c), 2020.210(b). When a subpoena is issued by the attorney of record, no seal is necessary. *Id.* §§1985(c), 2020.210(b).

§6.3 Issuing information. The subpoena must include the following information about the issuance of the subpoena:

1. Printed name. The subpoena form must be filled in with the printed name of the person issuing the subpoena. *E.g.*, Judicial Council Forms, form SUBP-001, form SUBP-002, form SUBP-010, form SUBP-015, form SUBP-020, form SUBP-025; *see also* CCP §1985(c) (attorney can sign and issue deposition and trial subpoenas), §2020.210(b) (attorney can sign and issue deposition subpoenas).

2. Signature. The subpoena form must be signed by the person issuing the subpoena. CCP §1985(c) (deposition and trial subpoenas), §2020.210(b) (deposition subpoenas). That is, subpoenas must be signed by the clerk, the judge, or the attorney of record. When a subpoena is issued by the clerk or the judge, one of them will sign the subpoena form and leave the rest of it blank for the requesting party to complete it. *Id.* §§1985(c), 2020.210(a).

3. Title. The subpoena form must be filled in with the title of the person issuing the subpoena. *E.g.*, Judicial Council Forms, form SUBP-001, form SUBP-002, form SUBP-010, form SUBP-015, form SUBP-020; *see also* CCP §1985(c) (attorney can sign and issue deposition and trial subpoenas), §2020.210(b) (attorney can sign and issue deposition subpoenas).

4. Date issued. The subpoena form must include the date the subpoena was signed, which is the date the subpoena was "issued." For example, Judicial Council Form SUBP-010, which is a deposition subpoena, includes a space for "Date issued" just above the place for the name of the person issuing the subpoena.

§6.4 Attachments.

1. Subpoena POS. Each Judicial Council form for subpoenas contains its own proof of service (POS). The POS is the place on the subpoena form where the server inserts the information about how, when, and where the witness was served. *See* CCP §1987(a) (method of service); CRC 1.21(c) (defining "proof of service"); *see, e.g.*, Judicial Council Forms, form SUBP-001, form SUBP-002, form SUBP-010, form SUBP-015, form SUBP-020, form SUBP-025.

2. Good-cause declaration. A good-cause declaration (or affidavit) is a statement made by the subpoenaing party in support of a subpoena for the production of documents or other things. A good-cause declaration must (1) show good cause for the production, (2) specify the exact things to be produced, (3) establish the materiality of the things, and (4) state that the witness possesses or controls the things. CCP §1985(b). See "Good-cause declaration," ch. 8-C, §4.2, p. 974.

(1) When necessary – trial subpoena for production. A good-cause declaration must be attached to a subpoena for the production of documents or other things at a trial or hearing. CCP §1985(b); ***Terry v. SLICO*** (1st Dist.2009) 175 Cal.App.4th 352, 356; *see* Judicial Council Forms, form SUBP-002 (form for trial subpoena requires good-cause declaration); Wegner, *Civil Trials & Evidence*, ¶1:125 (subpoena for documents requires good-cause declaration).

(2) When not necessary.

(a) Trial subpoenas without production. A good-cause declaration is not necessary for a trial subpoena that does not require the witness to produce documents or other things. *See* CCP §1985(b) (good-cause declaration required when subpoena requires production of things); Judicial Council Forms, form SUBP-001 (form for trial subpoena for appearance only does not contain good-cause declaration).

(b) Deposition subpoenas. A good-cause declaration is not necessary for a deposition subpoena. CCP §1987.5 (good-cause declaration not necessary for business-records subpoena), §2020.410(c) (same), §2020.510(b) (good-cause declaration not necessary for subpoena to testify and produce); ***Terry***, 175 Cal.App.4th at 357-58 (good-cause declaration not necessary for subpoena for testimony only, business-records deposition subpoena, or subpoena for testimony and production); *see, e.g.*, Judicial Council Forms, form SUBP-010 (form for business-records subpoena does not contain good-cause declaration), form SUBP-020 (form for subpoena to testify

and produce does not contain good-cause declaration); Weil, *Civil Procedure Before Trial*, ¶8:547.5 (good-cause affidavit not required for deposition subpoena for business records), ¶8:559 (good-cause affidavit not required for deposition subpoena to attend and produce).

NOTE

There is some confusion about whether a good-cause declaration must be attached to a deposition subpoena. The second sentence of CCP §1987.5 states that a deposition subpoena for the production of things is "invalid" without a good-cause declaration. However, this was implicitly overruled by the later enactment of §2020.510(b), which states that a good-cause declaration is not necessary for a subpoena to testify and produce. ***Terry****, 175 Cal.App.4th at 358.*

(c) Statutory notices. A good-cause declaration is not necessary for a statutory notice to produce at a deposition, trial, or hearing. *See* CCP §1987(c). The discovering party must show good cause and materiality only in a motion to compel filed after objections are served to the notice. *Id.*; *see* Wegner, *Civil Trials & Evidence*, ¶1:117.

§7. WHEN TO SCHEDULE COMPLIANCE

GENERAL

The subpoenaing party must specify on the subpoena form the date by which the witness must comply. *See* Judicial Council Forms, form SUBP-001, form SUBP-002, form SUBP-010, form SUBP-015, form SUBP-020, form SUBP-025.

NOTE

In addition to the scheduling rules below, a deposition must be scheduled no earlier than the time to initiate discovery and must be completed before the discovery cutoff. See "When to Schedule Discovery," ch. 7-A, §6, p. 749.

---

§7.1 Deposition subpoenas.

1. Deposition subpoena to attend.

(1) Reasonable time to travel. The subpoenaing party must select a date for the deposition that gives the witness a reasonable time after being served to travel to the place for the deposition. CCP §2020.220(a); *CEB Discovery Practice*, §5.63; Sink, *Subpoena Handbook*, §11:4[A]. It is unclear what is a "reasonable time," but ten days' notice is probably sufficient. *CEB Discovery Practice*, §5.65; *see id.* §5.63.

(2) Serve other parties – 10 days. The other parties must be personally served with the deposition notice and the subpoena at least 10 days before the deposition (earlier if served by means other than personal delivery). *See* CCP §2025.240(a) (deposition notice must be served on parties), §2025.240(c) (subpoena must be served with deposition notice), §2025.270(a) (deposition notice must be served at least ten days before oral deposition); *CEB Discovery Practice*, §5.63 (if service is by means other than personal service, required notice period is extended).

2. Deposition subpoena to attend & produce.

(1) Reasonable time to locate things & travel. The subpoenaing party must select a date for the deposition that gives the witness a reasonable time after being served to locate and produce the designated documents or things and travel to the place for the deposition. CCP §2020.220(a). It is unclear what is a "reasonable time," but ten days' notice is probably sufficient unless the witness must produce voluminous records. *CEB Discovery Practice*, §5.65; *see id.* §5.63.

(2) Serve other parties – 10 days. See "Serve other parties – 10 days," §7.1.1(2), this page.

3. Deposition subpoena for business records. To schedule a deposition to secure business records, the subpoenaing party must select a date for production that provides enough time for serving the witness and the other parties.

(1) Serve witness – 15/20 days. The subpoenaing party must select a date for production for a business-records subpoena that is at least 15 days after the witness was personally served with the subpoena or at least 20 days after the subpoena was issued (i.e., signed), whichever is later. CCP §2020.410(c); Weil, *Civil Procedure Before Trial*, ¶8:545; *e.g.*, Judicial Council Forms, form SUBP-010, Item 2 (witness instructed not to produce records until after 15/20-day restriction). Chart 8-4, below, shows how to calculate the earliest date for the business-records deposition.

8-4. DATE TO SCHEDULE BUSINESS-RECORDS DEPOSITION

Insert dates as instructed, and select later date from A2 or B2 to calculate production date for C

	A	B	C
1	Insert date subpoena issued (i.e., signed): Date: ________	Insert date subpoena served on witness: Date: ________	Earliest date to schedule production for business-records deposition is the later date in A2 or B2.
2	Add 20 days to date in A1, above: Date: ________	Add 15 days to date in B1, above: Date: ________	Date: ________*

* If earliest date falls on a Saturday, Sunday, or judicial holiday, continue to count forward until the next day that is not a Saturday, Sunday, or judicial holiday. *See* CCP §§12, 12a. For a list of holidays, see "Determine last day," ch. 1-F, §5.1.5, p. 55.

PRACTICE TIP

To make sure you satisfy the 20-days-after-issuance requirement, compare two dates before serving Form SUBP-010: the date for production of records (see SUBP-010, Item 1), and the date the subpoena was signed (see SUBP-010, "Date issued"). There must be at least 21 days between these two dates to satisfy the 20-days-after-issuance requirement.

(2) Serve other parties – 10 days. The other parties must be personally served with a copy of the business-records subpoena at least 10 days before production (15 days if by mail). *See* CCP §2025.220(b) (business-records subpoena served on party acts as deposition notice to party), §2025.240(a) (deposition notice must be given to every party), §2025.270(a) (deposition notice must be served at least 10 days before oral deposition); ***California Shellfish, Inc. v. United Shellfish Co.*** (1st Dist.1997) 56 Cal.App.4th 16, 21 (business-records subpoena is included within general category of "oral depositions"); *CEB Action Guide: Subpoenas*, Step 6 (10-day notice required if personally served; 15-day notice required if by mail to a California address). The parties are not served with a copy of the deposition notice because the subpoena acts as a deposition notice. *See* CCP §2025.220(b).

4. Deposition subpoena for personal records. When personal records must be produced at a deposition, the procedure for calculating the date to produce is very confusing. See "Calculating date for production of personal records," ch. 8-D, §8.2, p. 985. For the list of documents to serve when a witness is subpoenaed to produce personal records, see "Documents to Serve for Production of Personal Records from Nonparty," ch. 8-D, §11, p. 991.

§7.2 Trial subpoenas.

1. Trial subpoena to appear & produce. For the list of documents to serve when a witness is subpoenaed to appear at a trial or hearing, see "Documents to serve," ch. 8-C, §3.3, p. 972. For the list of documents to serve when a witness is subpoenaed to appear and produce at a trial or hearing, see "Documents to serve," ch. 8-C, §4.4, p. 975.

(1) Serve witness.

(a) Most witnesses – reasonable time. The subpoenaing party can select any date for the appearance of a witness at a trial or hearing, as long as the date gives the witness a reasonable time to prepare and travel to the place for the appearance. CCP §1987(a); Wegner, *Civil Trials & Evidence*, ¶¶1:70, 1:130; Sink, *Subpoena*

Handbook, §2:3[C][2](1). By comparison, a statutory notice (instead of a subpoena) to appear for a trial or hearing must be served on a party at least ten days before the trial or hearing. CCP §1987(b).

(b) Journalist & nonresident CHP officer – 5 days. The subpoenaing party must select a date for the appearance of a journalist or nonresident CHP officer at a trial or hearing that is at least five days after service of the subpoena. *See* CCP §1986.1(b)(1) (journalist); Gov. C. §68097.3 (nonresident CHP officer).

(2) No notice to parties. It is not necessary to give the other parties notice that a trial subpoena was served for the attendance of a witness or production of documents at a trial or hearing. *See* CCP §1985 (no requirement for notice to other parties), §1987 (same), §1987.5 (same); Wegner, *Civil Trials & Evidence*, ¶1:132 (no notice that documents have been subpoenaed); *see, e.g.*, ***Taggart v. Super Seer Corp.*** (4th Dist.1995) 33 Cal.App.4th 1697, 1708 n.8 (because Ps subpoenaed records for trial rather than deposition, D was not entitled to notice of subpoena).

2. Trial subpoena for personal records. When personal records must be produced at a trial or hearing, the procedure for calculating the date to serve a notice of privacy rights on a consumer is very confusing. See "When to serve notice of privacy rights for production of personal records at trial," ch. 8-D, §8.2.2, p. 986. For the list of documents to serve when a witness is subpoenaed to produce personal records, see "Documents to Serve for Production of Personal Records from Nonparty," ch. 8-D, §11, p. 991.

§7.3 Relief from date for compliance. If a witness, a consumer or employee whose personal records are sought, or a party objects to the date for compliance with the subpoena, that person can take any of the following actions:

1. Agree to different date. A witness can make an agreement with the subpoenaing party to appear at another time or on certain agreed notice. *See, e.g.*, CCP §1985.1 (witness subpoenaed to attend trial); Gov. C. §68097.9 (certain public employees subpoenaed to attend deposition, trial, or hearing). If the witness does not appear as agreed, the witness can be punished for contempt of court. *See* CCP §1985.1 (witness subpoenaed to attend trial). The facts proving or disproving the agreement and the failure to appear can be established by an affidavit of any person who has personal knowledge of those facts. *See id.* (trial subpoena). See "On-call agreement," ch. 8-C, §3.3.1(1), p. 972.

2. Object to date. A nonparty consumer whose records are sought can serve written objections without having to make a motion for a court order. See "Written objections to subpoena for personal records," ch. 8-E, §2.2.3(2), p. 998.

3. Move for court order.

(1) Move to quash subpoena. The witness, consumer, employee, party, or other affected person can make a motion to quash, to modify, or to impose conditions on the subpoena. CCP §1987.1; *see id.* §1985.3(g) (party consumer), §1985.6(f)(1) (employee); ***Southern Pac. Co. v. Superior Ct.*** (1940) 15 Cal.2d 206, 209 (witness); *CEB Discovery Practice*, §5.138 (motion to quash deposition subpoena). See "Motion to Quash Depositions," ch. 9-C, p. 1038.

(2) Move for protective order. The witness, consumer, employee, party, or other affected person can make a motion for protective order seeking relief from unreasonable or oppressive demands. CCP §§1987.1, 2025.420(b); Weil, *Civil Procedure Before Trial*, ¶8:605; *see CEB Discovery Practice*, §5.139 (motion for protective order from deposition subpoena). See "Motion for Protective Order," ch. 9-B, p. 1024.

§8. WHERE TO SCHEDULE COMPLIANCE

§8.1 Place for compliance. The place for appearance or production must be stated in the subpoena. There are several rules that control where a subpoena can compel a person to appear.

1. Location of deposition. A deposition subpoena can compel a witness to appear or produce within a certain number of miles of the witness's residence or place of business or the courthouse where the case is pending, depending on whether the witness is a natural person or an organization and whether the witness is a party or a nonparty.

(1) Natural person. A natural person can be required by a subpoena to appear for a deposition at (1) a place that is within 75 miles of the witness's residence or (2) a place that is both in the county where the case is pending and within 150 miles of the witness's residence. CCP §2025.250(a).

(2) Organization. An organization can be required by a subpoena to produce an employee for deposition at either of the places listed below. The term "employees" includes officers, directors, managing agents, employees, and agents. CCP §2025.230.

(a) Designated office. An organization that has designated a principal executive or business office in California can be required by a subpoena to produce its employees for a deposition at a place within 75 miles of the organization's principal California office. CCP §2025.250(c).

(b) No designated office. An organization that has not designated a principal executive or business office in California can be required by a subpoena to produce its employees for a deposition at (1) a place within 75 miles of any of the organization's California offices or (2) a place in the county where the case is pending. CCP §2025.250(d).

(3) For business records. A deposition subpoena for business records of a nonparty can compel a witness to produce the records at either the deposition officer's address or the custodian's address. See "Place for compliance," ch. 8-B, §5.1.3(3), p. 965.

2. Location of court hearing. A trial subpoena can compel a witness to appear for a trial or hearing in any court in California, regardless of the distance from the witness's residence or principal place of business. ***Lucas v. Superior Ct.*** (4th Dist.1988) 203 Cal.App.3d 733, 736; Wegner, *Civil Trials & Evidence*, ¶1:51.

§8.2 Relief from place for compliance. If a witness, a consumer whose records are being sought, or a party objects to the place for appearance or production, that person can change the location by an agreement or a court order. See "Modifying Discovery Procedures," ch. 7-A, §4, p. 743.

§9. HOW TO SERVE SUBPOENAS

§9.1 Type of service.

1. Personal service. The subpoena must be served on the witness by personal delivery. *See* CCP §§1987(a), 2020.220(b); *CEB Discovery Practice*, §5.69; *CEB Procedure During Trial*, §4.15. Subpoenas cannot be served by mail or by delivery to the witness's attorney. CCP §1015 (subpoena cannot be served on party's attorney); *see, e.g.*, ***In re Abrams*** (4th Dist.1980) 108 Cal.App.3d 685, 687, 695 (service of subpoena on nonparty witness's attorney was ineffective).

NOTE

Two appellate divisions have held that when a party in a contested case offers the prepared testimony of an affiant in lieu of direct testimony under CCP §98, the affiant must be available for personal service at an address that is within 150 miles of the place of trial. ***CACH LLC v. Rodgers*** *(Ventura Cty. Superior Ct. Appellate Div. 2014) 229 Cal.App.4th Supp. 1, 6-7;* ***Target Nat'l Bank v. Rocha*** *(Santa Clara Cty. Superior Ct. Appellate Div. 2013) 216 Cal.App.4th Supp. 1, 8-9. In both cases, the prepared testimony was not allowed because the opposing party was unable to personally serve a subpoena on the affiant at the given address. See* ***CACH LLC****, 229 Cal.App.4th Supp. at 6-7;* ***Target Nat'l Bank****, 216 Cal.App.4th Supp. at 8-9.*

2. Exceptions to personal service. There are a few exceptions to the requirement that a subpoena be served by personal delivery:

(1) Service on proxy. The subpoena can be served on the witness's proxy (e.g., parent for minor). *See* CCP §1987(a). See "Minor," §9.2.3, p. 948.

(2) Certain public employees. It is not necessary to personally serve certain public employees with the subpoena. *See CEB Discovery Practice*, §5.69; *CEB Procedure During Trial*, §§4.15, 4.29. See "Public employee," §9.2.2, this page.

(3) By agreement. For convenience, some witnesses (e.g., treating doctors) will agree to accept service of a subpoena by mail, but the agreement must be confirmed in writing. *CEB Discovery Practice*, §5.69.

§9.2 Whom to name & serve. In most cases, the person sought as a witness is named in the subpoena and is served with the subpoena. *See* CCP §§1987(a), 2020.220(b); Wegner, *Civil Trials & Evidence*, ¶1:62. However, special rules apply when serving certain types of witnesses.

1. Organization.

(1) Deposition subpoena. An organization is subpoenaed by name, and the subpoena is served on any officer, director, custodian of records, or agent or employee authorized by the organization to accept service of a subpoena. CCP §2020.220(b)(2). Unless a particular officer, director, or employee is identified by name as the witness, the organization is responsible for designating the person who will testify on its behalf. *See id.* §2020.310(e); 2 Witkin, *Cal. Evidence*, Discovery, §43(2). See "Subject of organization's deposition," ch. 8-B, §3.1.4, p. 960.

(2) Trial subpoena.

(a) Attendance. An organization cannot be subpoenaed to testify at trial. Wegner, *Civil Trials & Evidence*, ¶1:62. Instead, a trial subpoena must be addressed to and served on a specific officer, director, or employee of the organization. *See id.* By comparison, an organization can be subpoenaed by name and be required to identify the appropriate employee to testify at a deposition. *See id.* ¶1:100.2. See "Deposition subpoena," §9.2.1(1), this page.

GENERAL

(b) Production of records. A trial subpoena to produce records of an organization can be addressed to and served on the custodian of records of the organization. Wegner, *Civil Trials & Evidence*, ¶1:63. It is not necessary to specifically identify the custodian by name. *Id.*

2. Public employee.

(1) Most employees. A public employee named in the subpoena can be subpoenaed by serving any of the following:

(a) The employee, with one copy of the subpoena. Gov. C. §68097.1(a), (b).

(b) The employee's immediate supervisor at the place of employment, with two copies of the subpoena. *Id.*

(c) An agent designated by the employee's immediate supervisor to receive service, with two copies of the subpoena. *Id.*; *see* CCP §1987; ***Nick v. Department of Motor Vehicles*** (1st Dist.1993) 12 Cal.App.4th 1407, 1412-13 (§1987 requires compliance with Gov. C. §68097.1).

(2) Nonresident CHP officer. A CHP officer named in the subpoena who lives outside California can be subpoenaed by serving any of the following:

(a) The officer personally while in California. Gov. C. §68097.3.

(b) The officer's immediate supervisor. *Id.*

(c) The CHP office where the officer filed the report, during usual business hours and at least five days before the officer's required attendance. *Id.*; *see* CCP §1987.

3. Minor. A minor is subpoenaed by naming the minor's proxy and the minor (e.g., John Smith on behalf of Joseph Smith, a minor) and by serving a copy of the subpoena on the minor's proxy (i.e., parent, guardian, conservator, or similar fiduciary). *See* CCP §1987(a). If none of these persons can be located with reasonable diligence, the subpoena must be served on all of the following:

(1) The minor, if she is at least 12 years old. *Id.*

(2) Any person having care or control of the minor, with whom the minor resides, or who employs the minor. *Id.*

(3) Regardless of the minor's age, if the minor is a ward or a dependent child of the court and is not in the custody of a parent or guardian, service must also be made on (1) the designated agent for service of process at the county child-welfare department or (2) the probation department under whose jurisdiction the minor was placed. *Id.*

4. Concealed witness. A witness who is hiding to avoid service of a subpoena can be compelled to attend a deposition, trial, or hearing by an ex parte court order giving the sheriff permission to break into the building or vessel where the witness is hiding. CCP §1988; *CEB Procedure During Trial*, §4.31. The ex parte order must be based on an affidavit stating that the party is eluding service by concealment and proving the materiality of the witness's testimony. CCP §1988.

§9.3 What to serve. The documents to serve for a subpoena vary according to whether the subpoena is for a deposition or a trial, what the subpoena commands (testimony or production of things or both), whether the subpoena is for personal records, and whether it is directed to a party or a nonparty. Chart 8-5, below, summarizes the documents to serve with the different types of subpoenas.

8-5. SERVING SUBPOENA DOCUMENTS

	Type of subpoena	On consumer	On nonparty witness	On other parties
Subpoenas – no personal records sought				
1	Deposition – attend	N/A	JCF SUBP-015, reasonable time BCD	Deposition notice, 10 days BCD
2	Deposition – attend and produce		JCF SUBP-020, reasonable time BCD	
3	Deposition – produce only		JCF SUBP-010, 15/20 days BCD. See §7.1.3(1), p. 945.	Deposition subpoena, 10 days ❶ BCD. See §7.1.3(2), p. 945.
4	Trial – attend	N/A	JCF SUBP-001, reasonable time BCD	Not necessary to give other parties notice of trial witnesses. ❷ See §7.2.1(2), p. 946.
5	Trial – attend and produce		JCF SUBP-002, reasonable time BCD	
6	Trial – produce only		JCF SUBP-002, reasonable time BCD	
Subpoenas for personal records				
7	Deposition – attend and produce	JCF SUBP-025, JCF SUBP-020, and deposition notice, 25 days ❶ BCD. See ch. 8-D, §8.2.1(1), p. 985.	JCF SUBP-025 and JCF SUBP-020, 20 days BCD. See ch. 8-D, §8.1.2(1)(a), p. 984.	Deposition notice, 10 days ❶ BCD. See §7.1.1(2), p. 944.
8	Deposition – produce only	JCF SUBP-025 and JCF SUBP-010, 20 days ❶ BCD. See ch. 8-D, §8.2.1(2), p. 986.	JCF SUBP-025 and JCF SUBP-010, 15 days BCD. See ch. 8-D, §8.1.2(1)(b), p. 984.	Deposition subpoena, 10 days ❶ BCD. See §7.1.3(2), p. 945.

8-5. SERVING SUBPOENA DOCUMENTS (CONTINUED)

	Type of subpoena	On consumer	On nonparty witness	On other parties
Subpoenas for personal records (continued)				
9	Trial – attend and produce	JCF SUBP-025 and JCF SUBP-002, 20 days ❶ BCD. See ch. 8-D, §8.2.2(1), p. 986.	JCF SUBP-025, JCF SUBP-002, and good-cause declaration, 15 days BCD. See ch. 8-D, §8.1.2(2)(a), p. 985.	Not necessary to give other parties notice of trial witnesses ❷
10	Trial – produce only	JCF SUBP-025 and JCF SUBP-002, 20 days ❶ BCD. See ch. 8-D, §8.2.2(2), p. 987.	JCF SUBP-025, JCF SUBP-002, and good-cause declaration, 15 days BCD. See ch. 8-D, §8.1.2(2)(b), p. 985.	

❶ The deadline is based on personal service of the document. If served by mail or overnight delivery, the deadline is extended. *See* CCP §1013.

❷ Notice to other parties of service of a trial subpoena or trial notice is not necessary. See "No notice to parties," §7.2.1(2), p. 946 (trial subpoenas).

BCD = before compliance date

Consumer = all persons whose personal records are sought under §1985.3, 1985.4, or 1985.6

JCF = Judicial Council Form

§9.4 When to serve. A subpoena must be served a certain time before the date for compliance. Chart 8-5, above, summarizes when to serve the subpoena before the compliance date, depending on the type of subpoena. See "When to Schedule Compliance," §7, p. 944. The server must insert on the subpoena's POS the date the subpoena was delivered to the witness. *See, e.g.*, Judicial Council Forms, form SUBP-015, p. 2.

§9.5 Where to serve. A California subpoena must be served in California. Sink, *Subpoena Handbook*, §3:3[A][1]; *see* ***Minder v. Georgia*** (1902) 183 U.S. 559, 561-62 (state subpoena cannot be served beyond state's own borders). The server must include in the subpoena's POS the address where the server delivered the subpoena, which must be a California address. *See, e.g.*, Judicial Council Forms, form SUBP-015, p. 2. If the witness lives in a gated community, once the server displays proper identification and credentials, the guard must give the server access to serve the subpoena. CCP §415.21(a); Weil, *Civil Procedure Before Trial*, ¶8:568f.

§9.6 Who can serve. A subpoena can be served by any person. CCP §1987(a). Even though the CCP does not set an age limit for persons serving subpoenas, a server should be an adult who would make a credible witness if the server's testimony is required. *CEB Action Guide: Subpoenas*, Step 19; *see* CCP §414.10 (process server must be at least 18); Judicial Council Forms, form SUBP-025 (requires server to be at least 18 and not be a party). The subpoena's POS must identify the person serving the subpoena by printed name and signature. *See, e.g.*, Judicial Council Forms, form SUBP-015, p. 2. Persons who generally serve subpoenas include the following:

1. Public officers. Public officers, including sheriffs, marshals, and constables, can serve subpoenas. *E.g.*, Gov. C. §26608 (sheriff must serve all processes), §71265 (marshal has same powers, duties, and liabilities as sheriff). Public officers are exempt from the requirements for registered process servers and professional photocopiers. Bus. & Prof. C. §§22350(b)(1), 22451(a).

2. Registered process servers. Registered process servers and their employees can serve subpoenas. *See* Bus. & Prof. C. §§22350-22360. Registered process servers must be bonded. *Id.* §§22350, 22353, 22357. When a registered process server serves the subpoena, her return of service establishes a presumption of the facts stated in the POS. Evid. C. §647; *CEB Procedure During Trial*, §4.16.

3. Registered professional photocopiers. Registered professional photocopiers (RPPs) can serve subpoenas for business records. *See* Bus. & Prof. C. §22450; *see also* CCP §2020.420 (subpoena for business records); Evid. C. §1560 et seq. (same). When an RPP serves a subpoena on a third party for the production of records to be copied by the RPP, the RPP is not governed by the Business & Professional Code chapter on process servers. Bus. & Prof. C. §22350(b)(5).

4. Licensed investigators. Licensed investigators registered in California can serve subpoenas. Licensed investigators are exempt from the requirements for registered process servers and professional photocopiers. Bus. & Prof. C. §§22350(b)(4), 22451(g).

5. Parties & attorneys of record. Parties and attorneys of record, as well as their employees, agents, and independent contractors, can serve subpoenas. *See* CCP §1987(a) ("any person"). However, it is better for the subpoena to be served by someone other than a party or an attorney to avoid disputes over the facts relating to POS. *CEB Procedure During Trial*, §4.16.

15 **§9.7 Server fee.** Once the subpoena is served, the server must include in the subpoena POS the amount charged for serving the subpoena. *See, e.g.*, Judicial Council Forms, form SUBP-015, p. 2. If a sheriff, marshal, or constable serves the subpoena, the fee is $40. Gov. C. §§26720.9, 26743; *see CEB Procedure During Trial*, §4.40.

§10. HOW TO PAY WITNESS FEES

Witness fees for subpoenas are statutory. *See* ***Fabricant v. Superior Ct.*** (2d Dist.1980) 104 Cal.App.3d 905, 911. For this reason, only witness fees provided by statute can be demanded by the witness as a condition for compliance with a subpoena. *See* ***Poe v. Diamond*** (2d Dist.1987) 191 Cal.App.3d 1394, 1399-1400.

NOTE

Not all witness fees are recoverable by the prevailing party as taxable costs. See "Witness fees as taxable costs," §10.6, p. 958.

§10.1 Types of witness fees. There are four types of witness fees for subpoenas.

1. Ordinary witness fees. See "Ordinary witness fees," §10.2, this page.
2. Custodian fees. See "Custodian fees," §10.3, p. 953.
3. Government witness fees. See "Government witness fees," §10.4, p. 955.
4. Expert-witness fees. See "Expert-Witness Fees," ch. 7-I, §11, p. 912.

§10.2 Ordinary witness fees. Ordinary witness fees are those paid to an ordinary witness (i.e., a person who is not covered by any special rule for compensation).

8-6. ORDINARY WITNESS FEES

	Type of witness	Deposition	Trial or hearing
1	Party	Deposition notice – $0	Trial notice – $0 Trial subpoena – $35 day + travel
2	Party-affiliated witness	Deposition notice – $0	Trial notice – $0 Trial subpoena – $35 day + travel
3	Nonparty witness	Deposition subpoena – $35 day + travel	Trial subpoena – $35 day + travel

1. Who is paid. As a general rule, a witness compelled to attend by a subpoena must be paid the ordinary witness fee, whether the subpoena requires attendance at a deposition, trial, or hearing. CCP §2020.230(a); Gov. C. §68093.

GENERAL

(1) Deposition. Ordinary witness fees must be paid to the following persons subpoenaed to attend a deposition:

(a) Nonparty witnesses. A nonparty witness who is subpoenaed to attend a deposition must be paid the ordinary witness fee. *See* CCP §§1986.5, 2020.230(a); *CEB Discovery Practice*, §5.70.

(b) Some public employees. A public employee who is subpoenaed to attend a deposition must be paid the ordinary witness fee when the employee's public-entity employer is not entitled to the government witness fee. See "When not required," §10.4.3, p. 956.

NOTE

Parties and their affiliated witnesses are compelled to attend a deposition by a deposition notice, not by a subpoena. For witness fees payable with deposition notices, see "Witness Fees," ch. 7-B, §8, p. 788.

(2) Trial or hearing. Ordinary witness fees must be paid to the following persons subpoenaed to attend a trial or hearing:

(a) Nonparty witnesses. A nonparty witness who is subpoenaed to attend a trial or hearing must be paid the ordinary witness fee. *See* CCP §1987(a).

(b) Some public employees. A public employee who is subpoenaed to attend a trial or hearing must be paid the ordinary witness fee when the employee's public-entity employer is not entitled to the government witness fee. See "When not required," §10.4.3, p. 956.

(c) Parties & affiliated witnesses. It is unclear whether subpoenaed parties and their affiliated witnesses must be paid witness fees for attending a trial or hearing. One treatise states that witness fees must be paid to anyone subpoenaed to attend trial—even parties and their employees. Sink, *Subpoena Handbook*, §5.2[C], Rule 3. But there is no statutory provision that clearly requires a subpoenaed party to be paid a witness fee. *See* CCP §1987(a) (subpoenaed witnesses must be given or offered witness fees if demanded). Some statutory provisions cast doubt on the proposition that parties and party-affiliated witnesses must be paid witness fees. *See id.* §1283.2 (in arbitration proceedings, subpoenaed parties and their affiliated witnesses are not entitled to witness fees), §1987(b) (when statutory notice requires party or party-affiliated witness to appear at trial, the witness is paid witness fees "[i]f entitled"). To avoid an objection for failure to pay, which could delay the trial, the subpoenaing party should pay the witness fee to parties and party-affiliated witnesses.

2. Amount paid. A subpoenaed witness is entitled to witness fees and production costs. CCP §1987(a), (b).

(1) Witness fees. Witness fees include per diem and travel costs.

(a) Per diem. A subpoenaed witness is entitled to $35 for one day of attendance. *See* CCP §1986.5 (deposition witness entitled to same fee as trial witness); Gov. C. §68093 (trial witness entitled to $35 per day); ***Poe v. Diamond*** (2d Dist.1987) 191 Cal.App.3d 1394, 1399 (deposition witness entitled to same fee as trial witness). If the witness's attendance is required for more than one day, the witness is entitled to an additional $35 for each day of actual attendance. *See* CCP §1986.5; Gov. C. §68093.

(b) Travel costs. A subpoenaed witness is entitled to 20 cents for each mile actually traveled, both ways. *See* CCP §1986.5 (deposition witness entitled to same mileage costs as trial witness); Gov. C. §68093 (trial witness entitled to 20 cents per mile, both ways); ***Poe***, 191 Cal.App.3d at 1399 (deposition witness entitled to same travel costs as trial witness).

PRACTICE TIP

Be generous when estimating the travel costs for a witness subpoenaed to attend a trial or hearing. If a witness does not appear on the date for compliance because you underestimate the mileage, you will be required to reissue and serve the subpoena, ask for a continuance, and explain the delay to your client.

GENERAL

(2) **Production costs.** If the witness is subpoenaed to produce copies of documents, the witness must be reimbursed for production costs. See "Production costs for copies," §10.3.2(2), this page.

3. **Method of payment.** The witness fee can be paid in cash or by check. CCP §2020.230(a) (deposition subpoena).

4. **When paid.**

(1) **Witness fees.**

(a) **Option of subpoenaing party.** When a deposition subpoena requires the witness to make a personal appearance, the witness fees (per diem and travel) are payable—at the option of the subpoenaing party—either when the subpoena is served or when the witness appears for the deposition. CCP §2020.230(a).

(b) **Option of witness.** When a trial subpoena requires the witness to make a personal appearance at a trial or hearing, the witness fees (per diem and travel) must be offered to the witness when the subpoena is served, and must be paid before the appearance if demanded by the witness. *See* CCP §1987(a); Gov. C. §68097. A witness who demands payment in advance cannot be compelled to attend a trial or hearing until the subpoenaing party pays the witness fees. Gov. C. §68097.

(2) **Production costs.** When a deposition or trial subpoena requires the witness to produce records but not attend a deposition, trial, or hearing, the cost for production of the records is payable when the records and an itemized statement are delivered. *See* Weil, *Civil Procedure Before Trial*, ¶8:552. See "For producing copies," §10.3.3(2), p. 954.

§10.3 Custodian fees. Custodian fees must be paid to a custodian of records (or another qualified witness) according to the following rules.

1. **Who is paid.** A nonparty custodian (not a party's custodian) must be paid custodian fees to produce or to attend and produce at a deposition, trial, or hearing. *See* Evid. C. §1560(b) (custodian cannot be party or custodian of business where action arose), §1563 (custodian fees).

2. **What is paid.**

(1) **Witness fees.**

(a) **For attendance.** When the custodian's appearance is required, the custodian must be paid the witness fee (per diem and travel). Evid. C. §1563(c). See "Ordinary witness fees," §10.2, p. 951.

(b) **No attendance.** When the custodian's appearance is not required, the custodian is not paid the witness fee (per diem and travel).

[1] **Business-records subpoena for copies.** A custodian who is required by a business-records subpoena to deliver copies of records is not entitled to the witness fee (per diem and travel). See "None for copies," ch. 8-B, §5.1.7(1)(a), p. 966.

[2] **Business-records subpoena for originals.** A custodian who is required by a business-records subpoena to produce original records for inspection is not entitled to the witness fee (per diem and travel) but is entitled to a compliance fee of no more than $15. *See* CCP §2020.230(b); Evid. C. §1563(b)(6); *CEB Discovery Practice*, §5.105; Weil, *Civil Procedure Before Trial*, ¶8:553.

(2) **Production costs for copies.** If the subpoena requires the custodian to produce copies of original documents, the custodian is entitled to the reasonable costs for reproducing the documents, which include the following:

(a) **Reproduction costs.** The custodian is entitled to the following costs for providing copies:

[1] Ten cents per page for standard reproduction of documents measuring 8½ by 14 inches or less. Evid. C. §1563(b)(1).

GENERAL

[2] Twenty cents per page for copying documents from microfilm. *Id.*

[3] Actual costs for the reproduction of oversize documents or the reproduction of documents requiring special processing that are made in response to a subpoena. *Id.*

[4] Reasonable clerical costs to locate and make documents available, at a maximum rate of $24 per hour per person, computed on the basis of $6 per quarter hour. *Id.*; *see* ***In re Marriage of Stephens*** (2d Dist.1984) 156 Cal.App.3d 909, 918.

[5] Actual postage charges. Evid. C. §1563(b)(1).

(b) Retrieval costs. The custodian is entitled to be reimbursed for the actual costs charged by a third person for retrieving and returning records from an off-site location. Evid. C. §1563(b)(1).

(c) Other reasonable costs. The custodian is entitled to any other reasonable costs of production. *See* Evid. C. §1563(b)(1) (reasonable costs not limited to items described in statute).

(3) Production costs for originals. If the subpoena requires the custodian to produce original records for inspection and copying by the subpoenaing party at the custodian's place of business, the custodian is entitled to be reimbursed for its retrieval fees (if any) paid to a third person for records held off-site. *See* CCP §2020.230(b); Evid. C. §1563(b)(6); *CEB Discovery Practice*, §5.105; Weil, *Civil Procedure Before Trial*, ¶8:553. If the retrieval was from microfilm, the custodian is entitled to the reasonable cost of retrieving it. Evid. C. §1563(b)(1), (b)(6). The custodian is not entitled to photocopying costs because the subpoenaing party incurs that cost. See "Originals at custodian's address," ch. 8-B, §5.1.3(4)(c), p. 965.

GENERAL

3. When paid.

(1) Witness fees. A custodian subpoenaed to appear with records must be paid the witness fees (per diem and travel) at the same time as other witnesses are paid. See "Witness fees," §10.2.2(1), p. 952.

(2) For producing copies. Payment for the reproduction of records depends on the custodian's delivery of the documents and an itemized statement.

(a) Delivery of copies. The custodian must be paid the reproduction costs when the copies are delivered. Evid. C. §1563(b)(2). See "Production costs for copies," §10.3.2(2), p. 953.

(b) Itemized statement. The custodian must submit an itemized statement of costs to the subpoenaing party. Evid. C. §1563(b)(3). The statement must itemize the reproduction and clerical costs incurred by the custodian. *Id.* If the itemized statement is presented before or simultaneously with the copies, the custodian can withhold the copies until payment is received. *CEB Discovery Practice*, §5.104. If the custodian refuses to produce an itemized statement, or if the costs exceed those authorized by statute, the subpoenaing party can demand that the custodian justify the costs in a written statement. Evid. C. §1563(b)(3); *see CEB Discovery Practice*, §5.104.

(3) For producing originals. A custodian subpoenaed to produce original records at the custodian's place of business for inspection and copying must be paid a witness fee ($15) when the subpoena is served. *See* CCP §2020.230(b); Evid. C. §1563(b)(6); *CEB Discovery Practice*, §5.105. If the custodian incurred retrieval costs, the custodian must be reimbursed for those costs if demanded at the time the records are presented for inspection and copying. Evid. C. §1563(b)(2), (b)(6); *see CEB Discovery Practice*, §5.105. See "Production costs for originals," §10.3.2(3), this page.

4. Disputes.

(1) Excessive production fees. If the subpoenaing party believes the custodian charged excessive fees, the party can petition the court to reduce the amount charged or to recover all or part of the amount already paid. Evid. C. §1563(b)(4). Once the party files the petition, the court will set a show-cause hearing. *Id.* If the court finds the fees were excessive, it will remit or reduce the overcharge. *Id.* If the court finds the custodian acted in bad faith, the court must remit or excuse the entire amount demanded or paid, and must award the party reasonable costs

and fees, including attorney fees. *Id.* If the court finds the fees were not excessive, the court must order the party to pay for the reasonable expenses the custodian incurred in defending the petition, including attorney fees. *Id.*

(2) Change to business-records subpoena. If a subpoena for business records is withdrawn, quashed, modified, or limited on a motion made by anyone other than the custodian, the custodian is entitled to recover from the subpoenaing party the costs incurred to comply with the subpoena up to the time the custodian was notified of the change. Evid. C. §1563(b)(5). If the subpoena was withdrawn or quashed and the fees are not paid within 30 days, the custodian can file a motion for expenses and attorney fees. *Id.*

§10.4 Government witness fees. The term "government witness fees" refers to the amount paid by the subpoenaing party to the state or local government for the testimony of certain employees who, in the course of their duties, (1) perceived or investigated certain matters or (2) acquired expertise about certain matters. Gov. C. §§68096.1, 68097.1. Government witness fees for the appearance of a public employee are calculated at actual cost to the governmental entity for the employee's time, which is much higher than the ordinary witness fee of $35 per day. See "Amount paid," §10.4.4, p. 957.

NOTE

The issue of witness fees paid to governmental entities for the attendance of public employees is very complicated. A governmental entity is only entitled to be reimbursed for the full costs of some employees' salary and travel. When a public entity is not entitled to reimbursement, it is entitled to ordinary witness fees only (i.e., $35 per diem plus travel costs). *See "Ordinary witness fees," §10.2, p. 951.*

1. Who is paid. Government witness fees are paid to the governmental entity that employs the person subpoenaed. Gov. C. §68096.1(b) (local agency employees), §68097.2(b) (state and county employees). They are not paid to the subpoenaed public employee. The governmental entity will pay the employee's salary while the employee testifies and will pay the employee's traveling expenses to attend the deposition, trial, or hearing. Gov. C. §§68096.1(a), 68097.2(a).

2. When required. Government witness fees must be paid when a statute requires the subpoenaing party to reimburse the governmental entity for the full cost of the employee's time and expenses.

(1) Deposition subpoenas. Government witness fees must be paid when certain public employees are subpoenaed to attend a deposition to testify about matters perceived or investigated during the course of their duties or about their expertise acquired on the job. *See* Gov. C. §68097.6 (list of employees whose deposition entitles government to government witness fees). To subpoena any other public employee for a deposition, the subpoenaing party need only pay ordinary witness fees. Sink, *Subpoena Handbook*, §5:4[C][4]. Government witness fees must be paid when any of the following public employees are subpoenaed to attend a deposition:

(a) Peace officers and technical analysts employed by the California Department of Justice (DOJ). *See* Gov. C. §§68097.1(a), 68097.2(a), (b), 68097.6.

(b) Peace officers and vehicle-inspection officers of the CHP. *See id.* §§68097, 68097.1(a), 68097.2(a), (b), 68097.3, 68097.6; *cf.* ***Nick v. Department of Motor Vehicles*** (1st Dist.1993) 12 Cal.App.4th 1407, 1412-13 (CHP officer subpoenaed to testify at DMV hearing).

(c) Peace-officer members of the State Fire Marshal's Office. Gov. C. §§68097.1(a), 68097.2(a), (b), 68097.6.

(d) Sheriffs and deputy sheriffs. *See id.* §§68097.1(a), 68097.2(a), (b), 68097.6.

(e) Marshals and deputy marshals. *See id.* §§68097.1(a), 68097.2(a), (b), 68097.6.

(f) City police officers. *See id.* §§68097.1(a), 68097.2(a), (b), 68097.6.

GENERAL

(g) Firefighters. *See id.* §§50925, 68097, 68097.1(a), 68097.2(a), (b), (f), 68097.6. This includes regularly employed firefighters and, in the case of volunteers, regularly enrolled firefighters. *Id.* §50925.

(2) Trial subpoenas.

(a) Matters perceived or investigated. Government witness fees must be paid when any of the following public employees are subpoenaed to attend a trial or hearing to testify about matters perceived or investigated in the course of the employee's duties:

[1] Peace officers and technical analysts employed by the California Department of Justice (DOJ). *See* Gov. C. §§68097.1(a), 68097.2(a), (b).

[2] Peace officers and vehicle-inspection officers of the CHP. *See id.* §§68097, 68097.1(a), 68097.2(a), (b), 68097.3; *see, e.g.*, ***Nick***, 12 Cal.App.4th at 1412-13 (CHP officer subpoenaed to testify at DMV hearing).

[3] Peace-officer members of the State Fire Marshal's Office. *See* Gov. C. §§68097.1(a), 68097.2(a), (b).

[4] Sheriffs and deputy sheriffs. *See id.* §§68097.1(a), 68097.2(a), (b).

[5] Marshals and deputy marshals. *See id.* §§68097.1(a), 68097.2(a), (b).

[6] City police officers. *See id.* §§68097.1(a), 68097.2(a), (b).

[7] Firefighters. *See id.* §§50925, 68097, 68097.1(a), 68097.2(a), (b), (f). This includes regularly employed firefighters and, in the case of volunteers, regularly enrolled firefighters. *Id.* §50925.

[8] Employees of local agencies. Gov. C. §68096.1(a), (b). "Local agency" is defined as any political subdivision of the State, including a city, county, special district, or redevelopment agency. *Id.* §68096.1(f).

(b) Expertise. Government witness fees must be paid when any of the following public employees are subpoenaed to attend a trial or hearing to testify about a matter, event, or transaction on which the employee has expertise gained in the course of her duties:

[1] Any state employee other than those listed in Gov. C. §68097.1(a). Gov. C. §§68097.1(b), 68097.2(b); *see, e.g.*, ***Fox v. State Pers. Bd.*** (3d Dist.1996) 49 Cal.App.4th 1034, 1041-42 (non-peace-officer employees of Department of Corrections were not entitled to government witness fee because Department's attorney stipulated that employees did not qualify as experts under §68097.1(b)).

[2] Any employee of the trial courts. Gov. C. §§68097.1(b), 68097.2(a), (b).

3. When not required. The following are some examples of when a subpoenaing party is not required to pay government witness fees for a subpoenaed public employee. Instead of paying the government witness fee, the subpoenaing party must pay the ordinary witness fee in the situations listed below. See "Ordinary witness fees," §10.2, p. 951.

(1) Government is party. Only ordinary witness fees must be paid when the employee is compelled to testify about a matter in a suit in which the government-employer is a party. *See* ***Fox***, 49 Cal.App.4th at 1042; ***Nick***, 12 Cal.App.4th at 1414; ***Patterson v. Sharp*** (2d Dist.1967) 253 Cal.App.2d 838, 841; Sink, *Subpoena Handbook*, §5:4[C][6], Rule 23.

(2) Employee not covered by statute. Only ordinary witness fees must be paid when the public employee is not covered by a statutory provision requiring payment of a government witness fee. *See, e.g.*, Gov. C. §68097.6 (only public employees listed are entitled to government witness fees for attendance and testimony at deposition); ***Fox***, 49 Cal.App.4th at 1042 (prison guards do not fit into any of the categories of employees listed in §68097.1); *see also* Sink, *Subpoena Handbook*, §5:4[C][4] (public employees not listed in §68097.6 are not covered by statutory provision requiring payment of government witness fee for employee's deposition).

PRACTICE TIP

Most treatises do not discuss the finer points of subpoenaing government witnesses, and few cover the issue of the per diem payment for depositions of public employees. Most treatises, and even governmental entities themselves, assume that the same per diem fee paid for trial testimony ($150 for local-agency employees, $275 for state, county, and trial-court employees) must be paid for the deposition testimony of all public employees. You can attempt to pay the ordinary witness fee for the deposition of a public employee not included in §68097.6, but you will have to challenge the public entity if it refuses to make its employee available. See "Ordinary witness fees," §10.2, p. 951. It is easier and cheaper to just pay the higher fee than to litigate the issue.

(3) Employee subpoenaed on personal matters. Only ordinary witness fees must be paid when the employee is compelled to testify about personal matters or matters outside the employee's course of duties (e.g., an assault the employee witnessed at a nightclub while not on duty).

4. Amount paid. Government witness fees reimburse the governmental entity for the full cost of having its employee testify. Gov. C. §68097.2(b).

(1) Full cost. "Full cost" includes reimbursement for the employee's (1) normal salary or other compensation for the time used to attend the deposition, hearing, or trial (including travel time), and (2) necessary and reasonable travel expenses. *See* Gov. C. §68096.1(b) (local-agency employees), §68097.2(b) (state, county, and trial-court employees), §68097.4 (nonresident CHP officers). If the witness is a volunteer firefighter whose employer will not pay her regular salary or other compensation for the time spent traveling and giving testimony, the normal salary or other compensation of the firefighter is deemed to be the reasonable compensation received by firefighters in jurisdictions with similar geographic and economic characteristics. *Id.* §68097.2(f).

15 **(2) Tendered fee.**

(a) Most government employees. The tendered witness fee for most government employees is $275 for each anticipated day of testimony. *See* Gov. C. §§68096.1(b), 68097.2(b).

(b) Nonresident CHP officer. The tendered witness fee for a nonresident CHP officer is the estimated amount of the officer's salary or other compensation for each anticipated day of testimony plus travel expenses. Gov. C. §68097.4.

(3) Adjusted fee. If, after the employee's appearance, the tendered fee is higher or lower than the full cost of the employee's attendance, the subpoenaing party will pay or be refunded the difference. *See* Gov. C. §68096.1(c), (d) (local-agency employees), §68097.2(c), (d) (state, county, and trial-court employees), §68097.4 (nonresident CHP officers).

5. When paid.

(1) Most employees. The government witness fee for most public employees must be tendered to the person who accepts the subpoena when the subpoena is served. Gov. C. §68096.1(b) (local agency), §68097.2(b) (state and county); *see, e.g.*, ***Nick***, 12 Cal.App.4th at 1415 (officer not required to attend DMV hearing because fee not tendered with subpoena).

(2) Nonresident CHP officer. The witness fee for the subpoena of a nonresident CHP officer is deposited with the court clerk before the subpoena is issued. Gov. C. §68097.4. It is not paid when the subpoena is served. *Id.* The clerk will remit the amount paid to the Department of the Highway Patrol. *Id.* For the amount of the fee paid for a nonresident CHP officer, see "Nonresident CHP officer," §10.4.4(2)(b), this page.

6. Fee disputes. Certain governmental entities can bring a suit to recover reimbursement fees owed by the subpoenaing party.

(1) Who can sue. The following governmental entities have standing to bring a suit to recover unpaid government witness fees: Department of Justice, Department of the California Highway Patrol, State Fire Marshal's office, and any public entity whose employee is listed in Gov. C. §68097.10. The employees listed in Gov. C. §68097.10 for whom the public entity can seek reimbursement are the same employees listed in §68097.6. For a list of those employees, see "Deposition subpoenas," §10.4.2(1), p. 955.

(2) Who cannot sue. No other government employer can bring a suit for reimbursement of government witness fees. *See* Sink, *Subpoena Handbook*, §5:4[F].

§10.5 Expert-witness fees. See "Expert-Witness Fees," ch. 7-I, §11, p. 912.

§10.6 Witness fees as taxable costs. Witness fees are recoverable as taxable costs by the prevailing party only when permitted by statute. *See* ***Hogan v. Ingold*** (1952) 38 Cal.2d 802, 814; ***Moss v. Underwriters' Report, Inc.*** (1938) 12 Cal.2d 266, 274; ***Baker-Hoey v. Lockheed Martin Corp.*** (4th Dist.2003) 111 Cal.App.4th 592, 597; ***People v. Bowman*** (2d Dist.1959) 173 Cal.App.2d 416, 417; ***McIntosh v. Crandall*** (2d Dist.1941) 47 Cal.App.2d 126, 127.

1. Ordinary witness fees. Ordinary witness fees are recoverable as taxable costs. *See* CCP §§1032(a)(4), 1033.5(a)(7); ***Baker-Hoey***, 111 Cal.App.4th at 594; ***Linforth v. San Francisco Gas & Elec. Co.*** (3d Dist.1908) 9 Cal.App. 434, 438-39; 7 Witkin, *Cal. Procedure*, Judgment, §132.

(1) When attendance voluntary. Ordinary witness fees can be recovered as taxable costs regardless of whether the witness was compelled to attend by subpoena. *See, e.g.*, ***City of Downey v. Gonzales*** (2d Dist.1968) 262 Cal.App.2d 563, 569 (witness was subpoenaed for seven days and voluntarily appeared on eighth day; prevailing party could recover ordinary witness fees as costs); ***Naylor v. Adams*** (3d Dist.1911) 15 Cal.App. 353, 357 (witnesses outside subpoena range appeared in response to request; prevailing party could recover per diem, but not travel costs); ***Linforth***, 9 Cal.App. at 437-38 (witness within subpoena range appeared in response to request; prevailing party could recover ordinary witness fees).

(2) When no testimony given. Ordinary witness fees can be recovered as taxable costs regardless of whether the witness testified. ***Prichard v. Southern Pac. Co.*** (2d Dist.1935) 9 Cal.App.2d 704, 706.

(3) When party or interest in litigation. Ordinary witness fees cannot be recovered as taxable costs when:

(a) The witness is a party to the suit. *See* ***Foothill-De Anza Cmty. Coll. Dist. v. Emerich*** (6th Dist.2007) 158 Cal.App.4th 11, 30; ***Trussell v. City of San Diego*** (4th Dist.1959) 172 Cal.App.2d 593, 617.

(b) The witness is a party-affiliated witness who has a private interest in the litigation. *See* ***Foothill-De Anza Cmty. Coll.***, 158 Cal.App.4th at 30; ***Trussell***, 172 Cal.App.2d at 617.

(4) When higher fee paid. When witnesses are paid fees that are higher than ordinary witness fees (e.g., expert-witness fees), but by law the higher fees are not taxable, the taxable fees for the witness are capped at ordinary witness fees. *See, e.g.*, ***Kinsey v. Union Pac. R.R.*** (3d Dist.2009) 178 Cal.App.4th 201, 208 (because expert-witness fees not permitted in FELA action, case was remanded to determine ordinary witness fees for experts); ***City of Downey***, 262 Cal.App.2d at 566-67 (because expert was not court-appointed, taxable fees were limited to ordinary witness fees).

2. Government witness fees. Government witness fees (i.e., fees paid by the subpoenaing party to the governmental entity) are taxable as costs by the prevailing party if the fees were paid under Gov. C. §68097.2 (for subpoena of public employee) or §68097.4 (for subpoena of nonresident CHP officer) and are not refundable. Gov. C. §68097.8.

B. DEPOSITION SUBPOENAS

§1. GENERAL

§1.1 Purpose. A deposition subpoena is a legal document that commands a nonparty to appear, to appear and produce, or to produce at a particular time and place for a deposition. *See* CCP §2020.020. A deposition subpoena for testimony is used to secure the nonparty's attendance at the deposition. *Id.* §2020.020(a). A deposition subpoena for testimony and things is used to secure the nonparty's attendance and production of documents, electronically stored information (ESI), and other tangible things at the deposition. *Id.* §2020.020(c). A deposition subpoena for business records is used to secure the nonparty's production of business records without attending a deposition. *Id.* §2020.020(b).

§1.2 Primary authority. CCP §§1985-1997, 2020.010-2020.510, 2025.220(b), 2025.240(b), 2025.270(c), 2025.280(b), 2025.440(b), 2064, 2065; Evid. C. §§1560-1564; Gov. C. §§68092.5, 68093, 68096.1-68097.6, 68097.9.

§1.3 Secondary authority. The following secondary sources are cited as authority in this subchapter:

- *California Civil Discovery Practice* (CEB Online ed. 2014) (referred to as *CEB Discovery Practice*).
- Sink, *California Subpoena Handbook* (2014-15) (referred to as Sink, *Subpoena Handbook*).
- Wegner, *California Practice Guide: Civil Trials & Evidence* (CD-ROM ed. 2014) (referred to as Wegner, *Civil Trials & Evidence*).
- Weil & Brown, *California Practice Guide: Civil Procedure Before Trial* (CD-ROM ed. 2014) (referred to as Weil, *Civil Procedure Before Trial*).

§1.4 Judicial Council forms.

- SUBP-015 (mandatory), deposition subpoena for personal appearance. See "Deposition Subpoena for Testimony," §3, this page.
- SUBP-020 (mandatory), deposition subpoena for personal appearance and production. See "Deposition Subpoena for Testimony & Things," §4, p. 962.
- SUBP-010 (mandatory), deposition subpoena for business records from a nonparty custodian without the appearance of the custodian. See "Deposition Subpoena for Business Records," §5, p. 963.
- SUBP-025 (mandatory), notice of privacy rights for consumer, employee, or other person (collectively, "consumer") whose personal records are subpoenaed. See "Subpoenas for Personal Records," ch. 8-D, p. 977.

§2. NECESSITY OF DEPOSITION SUBPOENA

§2.1 When required. A deposition subpoena is necessary to compel a witness who is not a party or party-affiliated witness to appear and give testimony or to produce things at a deposition. *See* CCP §§1985(a), 2025.280(b). See "Affiliated witnesses for deposition," ch. 8-A, §2.5.1, p. 933.

§2.2 When not required. A deposition subpoena is not used to compel a party or party-affiliated witness to appear and give testimony or to produce things at a deposition. Instead, parties and party-affiliated witnesses are compelled to attend a deposition by a deposition notice. CCP §§1987(b), 2025.280(a); Sink, *Subpoena Handbook*, §§2.3[B], 11:1[D]. See "Subpoenas vs. Notices," chart 8-2, p. 935. For a discussion of deposing parties and party-affiliated witnesses, see "Depositions," ch. 7-B, p. 780.

§3. DEPOSITION SUBPOENA FOR TESTIMONY

§3.1 Subpoena form. Judicial Council Form SUBP-015 must be used for a deposition subpoena to compel the personal appearance of a witness at a deposition when the witness is not required to produce documents or other things.

1. Heading. In the heading for SUBP-015, the subpoenaing party must identify (1) the person causing the subpoena to be issued (attorney or pro per party), that person's address, State Bar number (if applicable), telephone number, fax number (optional), and e-mail address (optional), and the name of the party represented by the attorney (if not pro per), (2) the identification of the superior court (county, address, branch name), (3) the names of the parties, and (4) the case number.

2. Witness. Below the heading for SUBP-015, the subpoenaing party must identify the person or entity to be subpoenaed. See "Who Is Subject to a Subpoena," ch. 8-A, §4, p. 937.

3. Command. Item 1 of SUBP-015 is the subpoena command.

(1) Time & place for compliance. Item 1 requires the subpoenaing party to identify the date, time, and address for the deposition. *See* CCP §2020.310(a). To calculate the date, see "Deposition subpoena to attend," ch. 8-A, §7.1.1, p. 944. To determine the place, see "Where to Schedule Compliance," ch. 8-A, §8, p. 946.

(2) Organization. The box for Item 1(a) must be checked to command a deponent that is not a natural person (e.g., a corporation) to designate and produce one or more persons to testify on the deponent's behalf about the matters described in Item 2. *See* CCP §§2020.310(e), 2025.230. See "Subject of organization's deposition," §3.1.4, this page. The organization must produce the "most qualified" person or persons to testify on its behalf. CCP §2025.230; *see id.* §2020.310(e).

NOTE

In limited civil cases, the deposition of an organization is treated as a single deposition, even when more than one person is designated or required to testify. CCP §94(b).

(3) Method of recording. The boxes for Item 1(b) must be checked to indicate (1) that the deposition will be recorded stenographically, (2) whether the recording will be made available through an instant visual ("real-time") display, and (3) whether it will be recorded by audiotape or videotape. *See* CCP §§2020.310(c), (d), 2025.330(b); *see also id.* §2025.340 (procedure for recording deposition by audio or video). See "Method of recording," ch. 7-B, §9.2.5, p. 791. All depositions must be recorded stenographically, unless the deposing party secures an agreement or court order stating otherwise. See "Stenographic recording," ch. 7-B, §9.2.5(1), p. 791.

(4) Expert's video deposition. The box for Item 1(c) must be checked if the subpoenaing party intends to use the videotaped deposition of an expert witness (including a treating or consulting physician) at trial, even though the expert may be available to testify in person at trial. *See* CCP §§2025.220(a)(6), 2025.620(d). Before trial, the subpoenaing party must notify the other parties and the court of its intention to use the videotaped deposition. *See id.* §§2025.340(m), 2025.620(d).

4. Subject of organization's deposition. The box for Item 2 of SUBP-015 must be checked if the witness is to testify as a representative of the organization being deposed. The subpoenaing party must describe on the subpoena form the matters on which the organization's representative will be questioned. CCP §§2020.310(e), 2025.230. If the subjects for the deposition are too numerous to list on the form, the subpoenaing party should type in "Continued on Attachment 2" and provide the additional areas of inquiry on a separate sheet. The organization can designate one or more persons who have knowledge about the subjects listed in the subpoena to testify as its witness, including its officers, directors, managing agents, agents, or employees. *Id.* §2025.230; *see id.* §2020.310(e). The witness designated by the organization must be able to testify about any information known or reasonably available to the organization. *Id.* §2025.230.

5. Notices for witness. SUBP-015 contains the following notices for the witness:

(1) Deposition procedure. Item 3 describes the procedure for the deposition: the witness will be asked questions while under oath; later, the witness may read the transcript and make corrections before signing the deposition. See "Notice & review," ch. 7-B, §9.18.1, p. 802.

(2) Witness fees. Item 3 provides notice that the witness is entitled to witness fees and mileage expenses (both ways), which must be paid—at the option of the subpoenaing party—either when the subpoena is served or at the deposition. *See* CCP §2020.310(b)(2) (witness must be notified of rights), §2065 (witness must be notified of rights to receive fees and mileage). See "How to Pay Witness Fees," ch. 8-A, §10, p. 951.

(3) Geographic limits for deposition. Item 3 informs the witness how far from the witness's residence the deposition can be taken without the witness's agreement or a court order. See "Location of deposition," ch. 8-A, §8.1.1, p. 946.

(4) Sanctions. A boxed paragraph under Item 3 warns the witness that if the subpoena is disobeyed, the witness can be found in contempt of court and will be liable for a fine of $500 plus damages. *See* CCP §§1992, 2020.240, 2020.310(b)(3). See "Discovery Sanctions," ch. 9-A, p. 1003.

6. Issuing information. The issuing information (i.e., the date and the identity of the person who issued the subpoena) must be provided on the bottom of SUBP-015, p. 1. See "How Subpoenas Are Prepared & Issued," ch. 8-A, §6, p. 942.

§3.2 POS. The subpoena's proof of service (POS), which is the second page of SUBP-015, must be printed on the reverse side of the subpoena or attached to it.

1. POS heading. The heading of the POS must identify the parties to the suit and the case number.

2. Identity of person served. Items 1(a) and (b) of the POS require the server to identify the person served by name and the address of the place where the person was served. See "Whom to name & serve," ch. 8-A, §9.2, p. 948. For example, if a subpoena for a corporation was served on a vice president at the corporation's office, the server would insert the name of the officer and the officer's title and insert the corporation's address.

3. Time. Items 1(c) and (d) of the POS require the server to indicate the date and time of delivery.

4. Witness fees. The boxes for Item 1(e) of the POS require the server to indicate whether the witness fees and mileage expenses were paid, not paid, or tendered to the witness's public-entity employer, if any. See "How to Pay Witness Fees," ch. 8-A, §10, p. 951.

5. Server fee. Item 1(f) of the POS requires the server to state the fee that the server received for serving the subpoena. See "Server fee," ch. 8-A, §9.7, p. 951.

6. Date server received subpoena. Item 2 of the POS requires the server to insert the date the server received the subpoena for service.

7. Identity of server. Item 3 of the POS requires the server to identify her status as a server. For a list of people who can serve subpoenas, see "Who can serve," ch. 8-A, §9.6, p. 950.

§3.3 Selecting deposition officer for oral deposition. An oral deposition must be conducted under the supervision of an officer who (1) is authorized to administer an oath, (2) does not have a financial interest in the case, and (3) is not a relative or employee of any of the parties or their attorneys. CCP §2025.320(a). See "Deposition officer," ch. 7-B, §2.2, p. 780. A stenographic transcription of the deposition must be made by a certified shorthand reporter. CCP §2025.330(b). See "Stenographically recorded deposition," ch. 7-B, §2.2.1(3)(a), p. 780.

§3.4 Documents to serve. To compel the appearance of a witness at a deposition by subpoena, certain documents must be served on the witness, other parties, and the deposition officer.

1. Witness. The witness must be personally served with the subpoena (SUBP-015). *See* CCP §§1987(a), 2020.220(c), 2025.280(b). See "Type of service," ch. 8-A, §9.1, p. 947. It is not necessary to serve the nonparty witness with a copy of the deposition notice, which must instead be served on the parties. *See* CCP §2020.220(c) (subpoena is effective to require witness to attend or produce), §2025.280(b) (same); *CEB Discovery Practice*, §5.69 (no mention of serving deposition notice on nonparty); Weil, *Civil Procedure Before Trial*, ¶8:484 (same).

2. **Parties.** When a witness is subpoenaed to appear at a deposition, the other parties who have appeared in the case must be served with copies of the subpoena and the deposition notice. *See* CCP §2025.240(a), (c).

3. **Deposition officer.** If the deposition officer is required by the deposition notice to produce an instant visual ("real-time") display of the testimony during the deposition, the deposition officer must be served with a copy of the deposition notice. CCP §2025.220(a)(5). See "Real-time display," ch. 7-B, §9.2.6(1), p. 791.

§4. DEPOSITION SUBPOENA FOR TESTIMONY & THINGS

§4.1 Subpoena form. Judicial Council Form SUBP-020 must be used for a deposition subpoena to compel oral testimony and the production of documents or other things. If the subpoena seeks the personal records of a consumer, Judicial Council Form SUBP-025 must also be used. See "Subpoenas for Personal Records," ch. 8-D, p. 977.

1. **Heading.** In the heading for SUBP-020, the subpoenaing party must identify the same information as in SUBP-015. See "Heading," §3.1.1, p. 960.

2. **Witness.** Below the heading for SUBP-020, the subpoenaing party must identify the person or entity to be subpoenaed. See "Who Is Subject to a Subpoena," ch. 8-A, §4, p. 937.

3. **Command.** Item 1 of SUBP-020 is the subpoena command.

(1) **Time for compliance.** Item 1 requires the subpoenaing party to supply a date and time for the deposition. *See* CCP §2020.510(a)(1) (subpoena for testimony and things must comply with CCP §2020.310). To calculate the date, see "Deposition subpoena to attend & produce," ch. 8-A, §7.1.2, p. 944. If personal records are sought, the subpoena must be served according to the rules for personal records. See "When to set deposition for production of personal records," ch. 8-D, §8.2.1, p. 985.

(2) **Place for compliance.** Item 1 requires the subpoenaing party to identify the place for the deposition. *See* CCP §2020.510(a)(1) (subpoena for testimony and things must comply with CCP §2020.310). See "Where to Schedule Compliance," ch. 8-A, §8, p. 946.

(3) **Organization.** The box for Item 1(a) must be checked to command a deponent that is not a natural person to designate and produce one or more persons to testify on the deponent's behalf about the matters described in Item 4. See "Subject of organization's deposition," §4.1.6, this page.

(4) **Order to produce.** The box for Item 1(b) must be checked to command the deponent to produce the items described in Item 3. See "Description of things," §4.1.5, this page.

(5) **Method of recording.** The boxes in Item 1(c) must be checked to indicate how the deposition will be recorded. See "Method of recording," §3.1.3(3), p. 960.

(6) **Expert's videotape.** The box for Item 1(d) must be checked if the subpoenaing party intends to use the videotaped deposition of an expert witness at trial. See "Expert's video deposition," §3.1.3(4), p. 960.

4. **Required to appear.** Item 2 of SUBP-020 requires the witness to appear in person with the documents or other things required by the subpoena. Item 2 warns the witness that she cannot comply with the subpoena simply by sending the documents with a custodian's declaration.

5. **Description of things.** Item 3 of SUBP-020 requires the subpoenaing party to describe the documents, records, ESI, and other tangible things to be produced. *See* CCP §2020.510(a)(2). See "Deposition subpoenas," ch. 8-A, §5.2.1, p. 940. If the things to be produced are too numerous to list on the form, the subpoenaing party must check the box "Continued on Attachment 3" and list the other items on a separate sheet.

6. **Subject of organization's deposition.** Item 4 of SUBP-020 requires a subpoena directed to an organization to describe the matters on which the organization's witness will be questioned. See "Subject of organization's deposition," §3.1.4, p. 960. If the matters are too numerous to list on the form, the subpoenaing party must check the box "Continued on Attachment 4" and list the other matters on a separate sheet.

7. Notices for witness. SUBP-020 contains the following notices for the witness:

(1) Automatic stay. Item 5 instructs a witness served with a subpoena for personal records not to produce the records if (1) the witness is served with written objections or a motion to quash and (2) no court order or agreement of the parties, the witness, and the consumer has been obtained. See "Objecting to subpoena for personal records," ch. 8-D, §12.1, p. 993.

(2) Deposition procedure. Item 6 describes the procedure for the deposition: the witness will be asked questions while under oath; later, the witness may read the transcript and make corrections before signing the deposition. See "Notice & review," ch. 7-B, §9.18.1, p. 802.

(3) Witness fees. Item 6 provides notice that the witness is entitled to witness fees and mileage expenses (both ways), which must be paid—at the option of the subpoenaing party—either when the subpoena is served or at the deposition. *See* CCP §2020.510(a)(1) (subpoena for testimony and things must comply with CCP §2020.310), §2020.310(b)(2) (witness must be notified of rights). See "How to Pay Witness Fees," ch. 8-A, §10, p. 951.

(4) Sanctions. A boxed paragraph under Item 6 warns the witness that if the subpoena is disobeyed, the witness can be found in contempt of court and will be liable for a fine of $500 plus damages. *See* CCP §§1992, 2020.240, 2020.310(b)(3). See "Forfeiture & damages," ch. 8-E, §3.3, p. 999; "Contempt," ch. 8-E, §3.4, p. 999; "Discovery Sanctions," ch. 9-A, p. 1003.

8. Issuing information. The issuing information (i.e., the date and the identity of the person who issued the subpoena) must be provided on the bottom of SUBP-020, p. 1. See "How Subpoenas Are Prepared & Issued," ch. 8-A, §6, p. 942.

§4.2 POS. The subpoena's POS, which is the second page of SUBP-020, must be printed on the reverse side of the subpoena or attached to it. The POS for SUBP-020 is similar to the POS for SUBP-015. See "POS," §3.2, p. 961.

§4.3 Selecting deposition officer. See "Selecting deposition officer for oral deposition," §3.3, p. 961.

§4.4 Documents to serve. To compel the appearance of a witness and the production of things (without personal records), the following documents must be served:

1. Witness. The witness must be personally served with the subpoena (SUBP-020). CCP §§1987(a), 2020.220(c), 2025.280(b). See "Type of service," ch. 8-A, §9.1, p. 947. It is not necessary to serve the witness with a good-cause declaration, which is served only when a subpoena commands the witness to produce things at a trial or hearing. CCP §2020.510(b). See "Good-cause declaration," ch. 8-A, §6.4.2, p. 943.

NOTE

CCP §1987.5 says a deposition subpoena for production of documents or other things must be accompanied by an affidavit. This is in direct conflict with §2020.510(b), which says an affidavit is not necessary. You can ignore §1987.5 because §2020.510(b) controls. ***Terry v. SLICO*** *(1st Dist.2009) 175 Cal.App.4th 352, 355. See "When not necessary," ch. 8-A, §6.4.2(2), p. 943.*

2. Other parties. When a witness is subpoenaed to appear at a deposition, the other parties who have appeared in the case must be served with copies of the subpoena and the deposition notice. *See* CCP §2025.240(a), (c).

3. Deposition officer. If the deposition officer is required by the deposition notice to produce an instant visual ("real-time") display of the testimony during the deposition, the deposition officer must be served with a copy of the deposition notice. CCP §2025.220(a)(5). See "Real-time display," ch. 7-B, §9.2.6(1), p. 791.

§5. DEPOSITION SUBPOENA FOR BUSINESS RECORDS

A deposition subpoena for business records ("business-records subpoena") is a streamlined procedure for obtaining business records from a nonparty without requiring the nonparty to appear at a deposition. *See* ***Unzipped Apparel, LLC v. Bader*** (2d Dist.2007) 156 Cal.App.4th 123, 130-31; ***Cooley v. Superior Ct.*** (2d Dist.2006) 140 Cal.App.4th 1039, 1044.

§5.1 Subpoena form. Judicial Council Form SUBP-010 must be used for a business-records subpoena. If the subpoena seeks the personal records of a consumer, Judicial Council Form SUBP-025 must also be used. See "Subpoenas for Personal Records," ch. 8-D, p. 977. The types of organizations that can be required to produce business records by a business-records subpoena include every kind of business, governmental activity, profession, occupation, calling, or operation of institutions, whether carried on for profit or not, if the business is not (1) a party to the suit or (2) the place where the cause of action is alleged to have arisen. *See* Evid. C. §§1270, 1560(a)(1), (b).

1. Heading. In the heading for SUBP-010, the subpoenaing party must identify the same information as in SUBP-015. See "Heading," §3.1.1, p. 960.

2. Witness. Below the heading for SUBP-010, the subpoenaing party must identify the person to be subpoenaed. The business-records subpoena must be directed to either the organization's custodian of records or another person in the organization who is qualified to certify the records. CCP §2020.410(c); ***Cooley v. Superior Ct.*** (2d Dist.2006) 140 Cal.App.4th 1039, 1044.

NOTE

A custodian of a place where the cause of action is alleged to have arisen cannot be compelled to produce records by a business-records subpoena. See Evid. C. §1560(b). Unfortunately, §1560(b) does not explain how such a custodian could determine from the subpoena whether the plaintiff's complaint alleges a cause of action that arose on the premises of the custodian's business.

3. Command. Item 1 of SUBP-010 is the subpoena command.

(1) Deposition officer. Item 1 requires the subpoenaing party to identify the deposition officer, who must be either a registered professional photocopier (RPP) or a person exempt from registration.

(a) RPP. A business-records subpoena for copying can be conducted by a professional photocopier registered under Bus. & Prof. C. §§22450-22463. CCP §2020.420. The RPP cannot have a financial interest in the case or be a relative or employee of any of the parties' attorneys. *Id.*; Weil, *Civil Procedure Before Trial*, ¶8:547.1.

(b) Exempt person. A business-records subpoena for copying can be conducted by a person who is exempt from registration under Bus. & Prof. C. §22451. CCP §2020.420. The following persons are exempt:

[1] The party's attorney, or the attorney's employees, agents, or independent contractors. Bus. & Prof. C. §22451(b); *see* Evid. C. §1560(e); Weil, *Civil Procedure Before Trial*, ¶8:547. If the attorney intends to inspect the documents before copying, the attorney can leave the box for the deposition officer's name blank. Weil, *Civil Procedure Before Trial*, ¶8:547.2.

[2] A certified shorthand reporter or official court reporter. Bus. & Prof. C. §22451(f).

[3] A public employee acting in the course of employment. *Id.* §22451(a).

(2) Time for compliance. Item 1 requires the subpoenaing party to supply a date and time for production of the business records.

(a) Production date. To calculate the compliance date, see "Deposition subpoena for business records," ch. 8-A, §7.1.3, p. 944. If personal records are sought, the business-records subpoena must be served according to the rules for personal records. See "When to set deposition for production of personal records," ch. 8-D, §8.2.1, p. 985.

(b) No early delivery. Item 1 warns a custodian not to release the records to the deposition officer before the date stated in the subpoena. CCP §2020.430(d). By prohibiting early delivery, the persons affected by the production have time to file a motion challenging production before the custodian releases the records. There are two exceptions:

[1] **Consumer agreement.** The records can be released before the compliance date if the parties (and the consumer, when personal records are sought) agree to an earlier date. CCP §2020.430(d).

[2] **Attorney inspection.** The warning does not apply if the records are made available for inspection and copying by the requesting party's attorney, the attorney's representative, or the deposition officer at the custodian's place of business under Evid. C. §1560(e). CCP §2020.430(e).

(3) Place for compliance. Item 1 requires the subpoenaing party to provide the address where the records must be produced.

(a) Deposition officer's address. The subpoenaing party must insert the deposition officer's address if the subpoena requires the custodian to mail copies of the subpoenaed records to the deposition officer. *See* CCP §2020.430(a).

(b) Custodian's address. The subpoenaing party must insert the custodian's business address if (1) the subpoena requires the custodian to deliver copies of the subpoenaed records to the deposition officer at the custodian's address, or (2) the subpoena requires the custodian to make the original records available to the attorney, the attorney's representative, or the deposition officer for inspection and copying. *See* CCP §2020.430(c); Evid. C. §1560(e).

(4) Method for compliance. Item 1 requires the subpoenaing party to state how the records must be produced.

(a) Copies to deposition officer's address. Under Item 1(a), the subpoenaing party can direct the custodian to deliver copies of the business records to the deposition officer at the deposition officer's address. See "For delivery of copies to deposition officer," §6.1.4(1), p. 969.

(b) Copies at custodian's address. Under Item 1(b), the subpoenaing party can direct the custodian to deliver copies of the business records to the deposition officer at the custodian's address, upon payment of costs. See "For pickup of copies by deposition officer," §6.1.4(2), p. 969.

(c) Originals at custodian's address. Under Item 1(c), the subpoenaing party can direct the custodian to make the original records available for inspection by the attorney, the attorney's representative, or the deposition officer and permit copying at the custodian's business address, under reasonable conditions, during normal business hours. *See* CCP §2020.430(c)(1); Evid. C. §1560(e). See "For inspection of originals," §6.1.4(3), p. 969.

4. Identification of business records. Item 3 of SUBP-010 requires the subpoenaing party to identify the business records to be produced, either individually or by categories. *See* CCP §2020.410(a). See "Deposition subpoenas," ch. 8-A, §5.2.1, p. 940. The subpoenaing party is not required, however, to include specific information identifiable only to the witness's record system (e.g., a policy number or the date when a consumer interacted with the witness). CCP §2020.410(b). If the records to be produced are too numerous to list on the form, the subpoenaing party must check the box "Continued on Attachment 3" and identify the other records on a separate sheet.

(1) Business records. "Business records" include every kind of record maintained by every kind of business, governmental activity, profession, occupation, calling, or operation of institutions, whether carried on for profit or not, about that business entity. *See* Evid. C. §§1270, 1560(a); ***Cooley***, 140 Cal.App.4th at 1044; ***Urban Pac. Equities Corp. v. Superior Ct.*** (2d Dist.1997) 59 Cal.App.4th 688, 693.

(2) Not business records. "Business records" do not include the following:

(a) Business products. A business-records subpoena cannot be used to compel the production of an organization's product. *See, e.g.*, ***Urban Pac.***, 59 Cal.App.4th at 693-94 (attorney could not use business-records subpoena to acquire less expensive copy of deposition from reporting firm because transcript was firm's business product).

(b) Private records. A business-records subpoena cannot be used to compel the production of an individual's private books and records (e.g., personal letters or memoirs), which are outside the category of business records subject to Evid. C. §1560. *See* Sink, *Subpoena Handbook*, §3:9[C][2][b].

(c) Other entity's records. A business-records subpoena cannot be used to compel the production of business records in the possession of an entity that did not prepare or generate the records. *See* ***Cooley***, 140 Cal.App.4th at 1045. The test is whether the custodian of records can make the attestation required by Evid. C. §1561(a). *See* ***Cooley***, 140 Cal.App.4th at 1044. The custodian must be able to (1) describe how the records were prepared and (2) state that the records were prepared by personnel of the business entity in the ordinary course of the business, at or near the time of the act, condition, or event. *See* Evid. C. §1561(a)(3), (a)(5); ***Cooley***, 140 Cal.App.4th at 1044-45 & n.3. A custodian cannot make those statements about records prepared by another entity. *See* ***Cooley***, 140 Cal.App.4th at 1045.

5. Notices for custodian. SUBP-010 contains the following notices for the custodian:

(1) Compliance, costs & declaration. Item 2 notifies the custodian about the following matters:

(a) No early production. The documents cannot be produced before the later of 15 days from the date the custodian was served or 20 days from the date the subpoena was issued (i.e., signed). *See* CCP §2020.410(c).

(b) Production fees. The custodian can recover the costs involved in the production under Evid. C. §1563(b). See "Custodian fees," ch. 8-A, §10.3, p. 953.

(c) Custodian's declaration. The custodian must execute a declaration authenticating the records under Evid. C. §1561. CCP §2020.430(a)(2). See "Custodian's declaration," §5.2, p. 967.

(2) Automatic stay. Item 4 instructs a witness served with a subpoena for personal records not to produce the records if (1) the witness is served with written objections or a motion to quash and (2) no court order or agreement of the parties, the witness, and the consumer has been obtained. See "Objecting to subpoena for personal records," ch. 8-D, §12.1, p. 993.

(3) Sanctions. A boxed paragraph under Item 4 warns the witness that if the subpoena is disobeyed, the witness can be found in contempt of court and will be liable for a fine of $500 plus damages. *See* CCP §§1992, 2020.240, 2020.310(b)(3). See "Forfeiture & damages," ch. 8-E, §3.3, p. 999; "Contempt," ch. 8-E, §3.4, p. 999; "Discovery Sanctions," ch. 9-A, p. 1003.

6. Issuing information. The issuing information (i.e., the date and the identity of the person who issued the subpoena) must be provided on the bottom of SUBP-010, p. 1. See "How Subpoenas Are Prepared & Issued," ch. 8-A, §6, p. 942.

7. POS. The subpoena's POS, which is the second page of SUBP-010, must be printed on the reverse side of the subpoena or attached to it. The POS for SUBP-010 is similar to the POS for SUBP-015, except SUBP-010 includes a blank for copying costs. See "POS," §3.2, p. 961.

(1) Witness fees. Item 1(e)(1) requires the server to insert the amount of the witness fee (if any) paid to the custodian when the subpoena is served.

(a) None for copies. When a business-records subpoena requires the custodian to produce copies of records, the custodian is not entitled to witness fees for per diem and travel costs. *See* Weil, *Civil Procedure Before Trial*, ¶8:551.

(b) Compliance fee for originals. When a business-records subpoena requires the custodian to produce original records for inspection and copying at the custodian's place of business, the custodian is entitled to a compliance fee of $15 when the subpoena is served. See "Business-records subpoena for originals," ch. 8-A, §10.3.2(1)(b)[2], p. 953.

(2) Copying fees. Item 1(e)(2) requires the server to insert the amount of the production fee paid when the subpoena is served. The amount entered is usually $0.00 because the custodian is entitled to production fees only when the documents (either copies or originals) and an itemized invoice are delivered to the subpoenaing

party, not when the subpoena is served. *See* CCP §2020.430(c)(2). See "Production costs for copies," ch. 8-A, §10.3.2(2), p. 953; "Production costs for originals," ch. 8-A, §10.3.2(3), p. 954.

§5.2 Custodian's declaration. The attorney should always include with a business-records subpoena a form for the custodian's declaration that authenticates the records sought by the subpoena. The attorney should not rely on the custodian to know the statements required for a custodian's declaration. *See, e.g.*, ***Taggart v. Super Seer Corp.*** (4th Dist.1995) 33 Cal.App.4th 1697, 1706 (because declaration was inadequate, business records were not admissible). By preparing the declaration, the attorney ensures that the records are properly authenticated, which will permit the records to be introduced at trial or a hearing without a sponsoring witness. For the records to be admissible without a sponsoring witness, the declaration must comply with the requirements of both Evid. C. §§1271 and 1561. *See* Evid. C. §1562; ***Taggart***, 33 Cal.App.4th at 1706-07. When the records are offered into evidence, the court must find that—had the custodian been present at trial and testified to the matters stated in the declaration—the records would be admissible. *See* Evid. C. §1562; ***Taggart***, 33 Cal.App.4th at 1705. The requirements for the declaration are as follows:

1. Authorized custodian. The declaration must state that the affiant is the authorized custodian of the records (or other qualified witness) and has the authority to certify the records. Evid. C. §1561(a)(1); ***Taggart***, 33 Cal.App.4th at 1705; *see* Evid. C. §1271(c). If more than one person has knowledge of the facts concerning the records, separate declarations can be completed. Evid. C. §1562. The declaration should identify the custodian's business and business address.

2. Describe subpoena. The declaration should identify the subpoena by the date it was served, the case in which it was served, and the court in which the case is pending.

3. Production.

(1) Copies. If the subpoena seeks copies of records, the declaration must state that the copies of the records are true copies of all the records described in the subpoena. Evid. C. §1561(a)(2); ***Taggart***, 33 Cal.App.4th at 1705.

(2) Originals. If the subpoena seeks originals for inspection and copying, the declaration must state that the original documents were made available to the subpoenaing party's attorney, the attorney's representative, or the deposition officer for inspection and copying at the custodian's place of business. Evid. C. §1561(a)(2).

4. Authentication. The declaration must state the records were prepared by the personnel of the business in the ordinary course of business at or near the time of the act, condition, or event. Evid. C. §1561(a)(3); ***Taggart***, 33 Cal.App.4th at 1705; *see* Evid. C. §1271(a), (b).

5. Method of preparation. The declaration must describe how the records were prepared. Evid. C. §1561(a)(5); *see id.* §1271(c).

6. Trustworthiness. The declaration must show that the records are trustworthy. *See* Evid. C. §§1271(d), 1562. Compliance with Evid. C. §1271(d) ensures that the records are admissible at trial under the business-records exception to the hearsay rule. *See* ***Taggart***, 33 Cal.App.4th at 1706. If the custodian's declaration does not meet the requirements of §1271(d), the records are not admissible even if the declaration meets all the requirements of Evid. C. §1561 (records affidavit). *See* ***Taggart***, 33 Cal.App.4th at 1706-07. For the records to be admissible based on the custodian's declaration, the declaration must show that the sources of the information and the method and time of the preparation of the records indicate their trustworthiness. *See* Evid. C. §§1271(d), 1562; ***Taggart***, 33 Cal.App.4th at 1706; Wegner, *Civil Trials & Evidence*, ¶8:1636. For example, a police officer's accident report is generally not admissible under the business-records exception because the report is based on information from witnesses to the event who have no business duty to make a report to the police. 7 Cal. Law Revision Comm'n Rep. (1965) pp. 1241-42.

PRACTICE TIP

Most forms for the custodian's declaration for a business-records subpoena do not include the requirements in Evid. C. §1271(d), which means the records are not admissible at trial without a sponsoring witness or the parties' stipulation to admissibility. See, e.g., CEB Discovery Practice, §5.224. If you plan to call a sponsoring witness for trial, the declaration does not need to meet the requirements for trustworthiness under §1271(d).

7. **Records produced.** The declaration must identify the records produced. Evid. C. §1561(a)(4).

8. **Records not produced.** If the organization does not have all the records described in the subpoena, the custodian must identify which records are not available. Evid. C. §1561(b).

§5.3 Documents to serve. To compel the production of business records by subpoena, the subpoena must be served on the witness and the other parties. It is not necessary to serve a deposition notice with a business-records subpoena, because the copy of the subpoena serves as the deposition notice. CCP §2025.220(b).

1. **Witness.** The witness must be personally served with a business-records subpoena (SUBP-010). *See* CCP §§1987(a), 2020.220(b), (c), 2025.280(b). In addition, the subpoenaing party should include a fill-in-the-blank form for the custodian's declaration, which the custodian can use to authenticate the records produced. *See* Evid. C. §1561. See "Custodian's declaration," §5.2, p. 967. It is not necessary to serve the witness with a good-cause declaration, which is required only when a trial subpoena commands the witness to produce documents or other things at a trial or hearing. *See* CCP §2020.410(c). See "Good-cause declaration," ch. 8-A, §6.4.2, p. 943.

2. **Other parties.** When a witness is subpoenaed to produce business records, the other parties who have appeared in the case must be served with a copy of the subpoena. *See* CCP §2025.220(b) (business-records subpoena served on party acts as deposition notice to party), §2025.240(a) (deposition notice must be given to every party); ***California Shellfish, Inc. v. United Shellfish Co.*** (1st Dist.1997) 56 Cal.App.4th 16, 21 (business-records subpoena is included within general category of "oral depositions").

§6. RESPONDING TO DEPOSITION SUBPOENAS

§6.1 Complying with deposition subpoenas.

1. **Complying with subpoena for appearance.** To comply with a subpoena that requires a witness to appear for a deposition, the witness must appear at the designated time and place as ordered. *See* CCP §§2020.220(c)(1), 2064. If the subpoena is addressed to an organization that is required to designate a person to testify about certain subjects, that person (or persons) must appear at the designated time and place. *See id.* §§2020.220(c)(1), 2025.230, 2064. For a discussion of changing the designated time and place, see "Relief from date for compliance," ch. 8-A, §7.3, p. 946.

2. **Complying with subpoena for appearance & production.** To comply with a deposition subpoena that requires the witness to appear and produce documents or other things, the witness must appear at the designated time and place with the things described in the subpoena. *See* CCP §§2020.220(c)(2), 2064. If the subpoena is addressed to an organization that is required to designate a witness to testify about certain subjects, the witness must appear at the designated time and place with the things described. *See id.* §§2020.220(c), 2025.230, 2064.

3. **Complying with subpoena for ESI.** For a discussion of how to comply with a deposition subpoena that requires the witness to produce ESI, see "Responding to subpoena for ESI," ch. 7-H, §8.2.2, p. 888; "Production of ESI," ch. 7-H, §10, p. 891.

4. **Complying with business-records subpoena.** The procedure to comply with a business-records subpoena that requires the custodian to produce records but does not require a personal appearance depends on whether the records are to be delivered or produced and whether the records are copies or originals.

(1) For delivery of copies to deposition officer. If the subpoena requires copies of the records to be delivered to the deposition officer's address, the custodian must deliver the records by personal delivery, by messenger, or by mail. CCP §2020.430(a). Although the subpoena form SUBP-010 instructs the custodian to mail the records to the deposition officer, the custodian can deliver them in person, by messenger, or by mail. *See* CCP §2020.430(a).

(a) Copy records. The custodian must copy the records subject to the subpoena. The copies must be "true, legible, and durable." CCP §2020.430(a)(1); Evid. C. §1560(b).

(b) Complete custodian's declaration. The custodian must complete the custodian's declaration. See "Custodian's declaration," §5.2, p. 967.

(c) Prepare for delivery. The custodian must assemble the documents in two envelopes, an inner envelope and an outer envelope. Evid. C. §1560(c); *see* CCP §2020.430(b).

[1] Inner envelope. The custodian must place in the inner envelope (1) copies of the subpoenaed records and (2) the original of the custodian's declaration. *See* Evid. C. §1560(c); ***In re R.R.*** (2d Dist.2010) 187 Cal.App.4th 1264, 1271. The custodian must seal the inner envelope and either attach a copy of the subpoena to the outside of the inner envelope or mark the envelope with the case name and number, the witness's name, and the date of the subpoena. *See* Evid. C. §1560(c); ***In re R.R.***, 187 Cal.App.4th at 1271.

[2] Outer envelope. The custodian must place the inner envelope in the outer envelope, seal it, and address it to the deposition officer at the address identified on the subpoena. *See* Evid. C. §1560(c).

(2) For pickup of copies by deposition officer. If the subpoena requires copies of the records to be made available to the deposition officer for pickup at the custodian's place of business, the custodian must (1) copy the records, (2) complete the custodian's declaration, (3) prepare an itemized statement of costs for preparing the copies, and (4) after receiving payment, deliver the copies of the records and the original of the custodian's declaration to the deposition officer at the custodian's business address, during regular business hours. *See* CCP §2020.430(a)(2), (c)(2). It is not necessary for copies delivered at the custodian's office to be sealed. *Id.* §2020.430(a)(2), (c)(2); *CEB Discovery Practice*, §5.101.

(3) For inspection of originals. If the subpoena requires the original records to be made available for inspection and copying, the custodian must make the records available at the custodian's business address. Evid. C. §1560(e); *see* CCP §2020.430(c)(1), (e).

(a) Make records available. The custodian must make the records available to the attorney, the attorney's representative, or the deposition officer during normal business hours and under reasonable conditions. Evid. C. §1560(e). If the subpoenaing party gives the custodian at least five business days' advance notice, the custodian must make the records available for inspection and copying for at least six continuous hours on a specified date. *Id.* To copy the records, the subpoenaing party can either bring its own copying machine or make arrangements with the custodian to use a copying machine on the premises.

(b) Complete custodian's declaration. The custodian must complete the custodian's declaration. See "Custodian's declaration," §5.2, p. 967.

(c) Complete attorney's declaration. After making copies of the records, the attorney, the attorney's representative, or the deposition officer must execute a declaration stating that the records were delivered for copying at the custodian's place of business and the copies made there are true copies of the records delivered. Evid. C. §1561(c).

§6.2 Providing copies to other parties.

1. Copies for other parties. If another party requests copies of subpoenaed business records, that party must be provided with (1) copies of the records, (2) a copy of the custodian's declaration, and (3) if the records were made available for inspection and copying at the custodian's office, a copy of the declaration executed by the attorney, the attorney's representative, or the deposition officer. *See* CCP §2020.440; Evid. C. §1561.

2. **Who must provide copies.**

(1) **Records delivered to deposition officer.** If the subpoena requires the copies of the records to be delivered to the deposition officer, the deposition officer must provide copies of the subpoenaed records to all other parties who notify the deposition officer that they want to purchase copies. CCP §2020.440. The other parties can ask for copies as late as six months after the case has settled. *Id.*

(2) **Records delivered to attorney.** If the subpoena requires the original records to be made available to the attorney, the attorney's representative, or the deposition officer for inspection and copying, that person must provide copies of the records as requested by the other parties. *CEB Discovery Practice*, §5.102.

§6.3 Challenging subpoenas. For a discussion of how to challenge a subpoena, see "Challenging Subpoenas," ch. 8-E, §2, p. 995.

§6.4 Enforcing subpoenas. For a discussion of how to enforce a subpoena, see "Enforcing Subpoenas," ch. 8-E, §3, p. 998.

C. TRIAL & HEARING SUBPOENAS

§1. GENERAL

§1.1 Purpose. A trial subpoena is a legal document that commands a person to appear at a particular time and place to testify as a witness at a trial or hearing. *See* CCP §1985(a). A trial subpoena can command the person to appear, appear and produce, or just produce documents or other things. *See id.*

NOTE

The requirements for subpoenas for hearings and for trials are the same. Thus, this book uses the term "trial subpoena" to refer to both.

§1.2 Primary authority. CCP §§1985-1997, 2064, 2065; Evid. C. §§1560-1565; Gov. C. §68097.9.

§1.3 Secondary authority. The following secondary sources are cited as authority in this subchapter:

- *Action Guide: Handling Subpoenas* (CEB Online ed. 2014) (referred to as *CEB Action Guide: Subpoenas*).
- *California Trial Practice: Civil Procedure During Trial* (CEB Online ed. 2014) (referred to as *CEB Procedure During Trial*).
- Sink, *California Subpoena Handbook* (2014-15) (referred to as Sink, *Subpoena Handbook*).
- Wegner, *California Practice Guide: Civil Trials & Evidence* (CD-ROM ed. 2014) (referred to as Wegner, *Civil Trials & Evidence*).
- Witkin, *California Evidence* (5th ed. 2012 & Supp.2014) (referred to as Witkin, *Cal. Evidence*).

§1.4 Judicial Council forms.

- SUBP-001 (mandatory), trial subpoena for personal appearance. See "Trial Subpoena for Testimony," §3, p. 971.
- SUBP-002 (mandatory), trial subpoena for personal appearance and production or just for the production of documents and things. See "Trial Subpoena for Testimony & Things," §4, p. 973.
- SUBP-025 (mandatory), notice of privacy rights for consumer, employee, or other person (collectively, "consumer") whose personal records are subpoenaed. See "Subpoenas for Personal Records," ch. 8-D, p. 977.

§2. NECESSITY OF TRIAL SUBPOENA

§2.1 When required. A trial subpoena is necessary to compel a nonparty witness to attend or produce things at a trial or hearing. CCP §1985(a). See "Nonparty," ch. 8-A, §2.3, p. 933. Although a trial subpoena can be used to compel a party or party-affiliated witness to attend or produce things at a trial or hearing, such witnesses are generally compelled to attend or produce by a "notice to attend." *See* CCP §1987(b), (c); Wegner, *Civil Trials & Evidence*, ¶¶1:97-1:106.2. See "Affiliated witnesses for trial," ch. 8-A, §2.5.2, p. 933; "Statutory notices," ch. 8-A, §3.2, p. 935.

§2.2 When not required. A trial subpoena is not necessary to compel the following persons to appear or produce at a trial or hearing:

1. Persons present at trial.

(1) In courtroom. Parties, party-affiliated witnesses, and nonparties can be compelled to testify without a subpoena if they are physically present at a trial or hearing or before a judicial officer. CCP §1990; Sink, *Subpoena Handbook*, §2:1[A][1]; Wegner, *Civil Trials & Evidence*, ¶1:107. "Judicial officer" includes justices and judges on the supreme court, courts of appeal, and superior courts. Elec. C. §327.

(2) On stand. A witness on the stand can be questioned about relevant documents or things in the witness's possession and may be required to produce them without a subpoena. *See* ***Morehouse v. Morehouse*** (1902) 136 Cal. 332, 336-37; ***Oksner v. Superior Ct.*** (2d Dist.1964) 229 Cal.App.2d 672, 682; ***McKinley v. Southern Pac. Co.*** (3d Dist.1947) 80 Cal.App.2d 301, 314-15; Sink, *Subpoena Handbook*, §2.1[B][1].

2. Things in attorney's possession. A party's attorney can be required to produce documents or things without a subpoena if the attorney has them in the courtroom. Sink, *Subpoena Handbook*, §2.1[B][1].

§2.3 When ineffective. Persons who are not residents of California (i.e., parties, party-affiliated witnesses, and nonparties) cannot be compelled to travel and attend a trial or hearing in California by subpoena, notice, or court order. See "Nonresidents," ch. 8-A, §4.2.1, p. 938.

§3. TRIAL SUBPOENA FOR TESTIMONY

§3.1 Subpoena form. Judicial Council Form SUBP-001 must be used for a trial subpoena to compel oral testimony at a trial or hearing when no documents or other things are sought.

1. Heading. In the heading for SUBP-001, the subpoenaing party must identify (1) the person causing the subpoena to be issued (attorney or pro per party), that person's address, State Bar number (if applicable), telephone number, and fax number, and the name of the party represented by the attorney (if not pro per), (2) the identification of the superior court (county, address, branch name), (3) the names of the parties, and (4) the case number.

2. Witness. Below the heading for SUBP-001, the subpoenaing party must identify the person or entity to be subpoenaed. See "Who Is Subject to a Subpoena," ch. 8-A, §4, p. 937.

3. Command. Item 1 of SUBP-001 is the subpoena command.

(1) Time for compliance. Item 1 requires the subpoenaing party to supply a date and time for the witness to appear. *See* CCP §1985.1 (parties may agree to a different time). See "Trial subpoena to appear & produce," ch. 8-A, §7.2.1, p. 945.

PRACTICE TIP

Because an attorney generally does not know when the witness will be called to testify, the attorney will require the witness to appear on the first day of trial and ask the court at the end of each day to order the witness to return. See CEB Procedure During Trial, §4.3. That requires the witness to wait in the hall until called to testify, which is inconvenient. The better practice is to serve with the subpoena a proposed on-call agreement for the witness to execute and return. See "On-call agreement," §3.3.1(1), p. 972.

---

(2) Place for compliance. Item 1 requires the subpoenaing party to identify the address for the appearance and the department, division, or room where the hearing will be conducted. A witness can be required by a trial subpoena to appear anywhere in California. See "Location of court hearing," ch. 8-A, §8.1.2, p. 947.

4. Contact information. Item 2 of SUBP-001 requires the subpoenaing attorney (or pro per party) to include contact information (name and telephone number) in case the witness has questions about the date, time, or necessity to appear. *See* CCP §1985.2.

5. Notices for witness. SUBP-001 contains the following notices for the witness:

(1) Witness fees. Item 3 provides notice that the witness is entitled to witness fees and mileage expenses (both ways), which must be paid either when the subpoena is served (if the witness asks for them at service) or before the appearance. *See* CCP §2065. See "How to Pay Witness Fees," ch. 8-A, §10, p. 951. Witness fees must be paid to any person subpoenaed to appear for a trial or hearing, including parties and nonparties. *See* 2 Witkin, *Cal. Evidence*, Witnesses, §15.

(2) Sanctions. A boxed paragraph under Item 3 warns the witness that if the subpoena is disobeyed, the witness can be found in contempt of court and will be liable for a fine of $500 plus damages. *See* CCP §§1991, 1992. See "Forfeiture & damages," ch. 8-E, §3.3, p. 999; "Contempt," ch. 8-E, §3.4, p. 999; "Discovery Sanctions," ch. 9-A, p. 1003.

(3) Witness accommodations. A boxed paragraph under the issuing information provides information about requesting assistance to hear, understand, or answer questions at trial. *See* Civ. C. §54.8.

6. Issuing information. The issuing information (i.e., who issued the subpoena and when) must be provided below the notice of sanctions. See "How Subpoenas Are Prepared & Issued," ch. 8-A, §6, p. 942.

§3.2 POS. The subpoena's proof of service (POS), which is the second page of the SUBP-001, must be printed on the reverse side of the subpoena or attached to it.

1. POS heading. The heading of the POS must identify the parties to the suit and the case number.

2. Identity of person served. Items 1(a) and (b) of the POS require the server to identify the name and address of the person served. See "Whom to name & serve," ch. 8-A, §9.2, p. 948.

3. Date & time. Items 1(c) and (d) of the POS require the server to indicate the date and time of delivery.

4. Witness fees. The boxes for Item 1(e) of the POS require the server to indicate whether the witness fees and mileage expenses were (1) offered or demanded and paid (stating the amount) or (2) not demanded or paid. See "How to Pay Witness Fees," ch. 8-A, §10, p. 951.

5. Server fee. Item 1(f) of the POS requires the server to state the fee that the server received for serving the subpoena. See "Server fee," ch. 8-A, §9.7, p. 951.

6. Date server received subpoena. Item 2 of the POS requires the server to insert the date the server received the subpoena for service.

7. Identity of server. Item 3 of the POS requires the server to identify her status as a server. For a list of people who can serve subpoenas, see "Who can serve," ch. 8-A, §9.6, p. 950.

8. Server's declaration. At the bottom of the POS, the server must sign, date, and declare or certify that the information in the POS is true and correct.

§3.3 Documents to serve. To compel the appearance of a witness at a trial or hearing by subpoena, certain documents must be served on the witness.

1. Witness. The witness must be personally served with the subpoena (SUBP-001). See "Personal service," ch. 8-A, §9.1.1, p. 947. If the witness is a government employee or a minor, additional copies are necessary. See "Public employee," ch. 8-A, §9.2.2, p. 948; "Minor," ch. 8-A, §9.2.3, p. 948.

(1) On-call agreement. If the trial is expected to take more than one day, the attorney should consider serving the witness with an on-call agreement along with the subpoena. *See* CCP §1985.1 (party and witness can agree to different time than stated in subpoena). The on-call agreement requires the witness to agree to appear at the courthouse when given a certain amount of advance notice. *See CEB Procedure During Trial*, §4.58 (form for on-call agreement); *see also CEB Action Guide: Subpoenas*, Appx. O (sample letter to witness containing on-call agreement). By executing the on-call agreement, the witness can avoid the inconvenience of waiting at the courthouse until called to testify.

(2) **No good-cause declaration.** It is not necessary to serve the witness with a copy of a good-cause declaration when the witness is not required to produce documents or other things. See "When not necessary," ch. 8-A, §6.4.2(2), p. 943.

2. **Not parties.** The parties do not have a right to be served with a copy of the trial subpoena or the right to receive notice that a witness has been subpoenaed. *See* ***Taggart v. Super Seer Corp.*** (4th Dist.1995) 33 Cal.App.4th 1697, 1708 n.8; Sink, *Subpoena Handbook*, §11:2[A][2][e][i].

§4. TRIAL SUBPOENA FOR TESTIMONY & THINGS

§4.1 Subpoena form. Judicial Council Form SUBP-002 can be used (1) to compel oral testimony of a witness and the production of documents or things at a trial or hearing, or (2) to compel the production of documents or things at a trial or hearing without the appearance of the witness. A trial subpoena for production is commonly referred to as a "subpoena duces tecum." *See, e.g.*, CCP §1985(b) (requiring good-cause declaration to accompany subpoena duces tecum). If the subpoena seeks the personal records of a consumer or employee, Judicial Council Form SUBP-025 must also be used. See "Subpoenas for Personal Records," ch. 8-D, p. 977.

1. **Heading.** In the heading for SUBP-002, the subpoenaing party must identify the same information as in SUBP-001. See "Heading," §3.1.1, p. 971.

2. **Witness.** Below the heading for SUBP-002, the subpoenaing party must identify the person or entity to be subpoenaed. See "Who Is Subject to a Subpoena," ch. 8-A, §4, p. 937.

3. **Command.** Item 1 of SUBP-002 is the subpoena command.

(1) **Time for compliance.** Item 1 requires the subpoenaing party to supply a date and time for the witness to appear and produce or to produce only. See "Trial subpoena to appear & produce," ch. 8-A, §7.2.1, p. 945.

(a) **Trial subpoena for documents & things.**

[1] **Reasonable time.** A trial subpoena that seeks production of documents or other things (but not personal records) must be scheduled to give the witness a reasonable time between the date the subpoena is served and the date for compliance. See "Most witnesses – reasonable time," ch. 8-A, §7.2.1(1)(a), p. 945. In some cases, a trial subpoena can be issued on the eve of trial or even during trial. *See* ***Boal v. Price Waterhouse & Co.*** (2d Dist.1985) 165 Cal.App.3d 806, 810 (eve of trial); Wegner, *Civil Trials & Evidence*, ¶1:130 (eve of or during trial).

NOTE

When documents or other things are subpoenaed for trial, they are not described in the subpoena but in the good-cause declaration. See "Good-cause declaration," §4.2, p. 974.

---

[2] **Five days.**

[a] **CHP officer.** A trial subpoena that seeks documents or other things from a nonresident California Highway Patrol (CHP) officer must be served at least five days before the trial or hearing date. Gov. C. §68097.3.

[b] **Journalist.** A trial subpoena that seeks documents or other things from a journalist must be served at least five days after the party issuing the subpoena provides the journalist with notice of the subpoena. CCP §1986.1(b)(2).

(b) **Trial subpoena for personal records.** A trial subpoena that seeks personal records of a consumer or employee must be scheduled to provide enough time for the consumer to be served with a notice of privacy rights and have an opportunity to object. See "When to serve notice of privacy rights for production of personal records at trial," ch. 8-D, §8.2.2, p. 986.

(2) Place for compliance. Item 1 requires the subpoenaing party to identify the address for the appearance and production or production only and the department, division, or room where the hearing will be conducted. A witness can be required by a trial subpoena to appear anywhere in California. See "Location of court hearing," ch. 8-A, §8.1.2, p. 947.

4. Necessity of appearance. Item 3 of SUBP-002 requires the subpoenaing party to designate whether the witness is required to appear in person at the trial or hearing.

(1) Appearance required. If Item 3(a) is checked, the witness is ordered to appear in person at the trial or hearing and to produce the records described.

(2) Appearance not required. If Item 3(b) is checked, the witness (i.e., custodian) must mail the documents to the court clerk according to the directions set out in the subpoena. For instructions on preparing the documents, see "Complying with subpoena for production of documents," §5.1.3, p. 976.

5. Contact information. Item 4 of SUBP-002 requires the subpoenaing attorney (or pro per party) to include contact information (name and telephone number) in case the witness has questions about the date, time, or necessity to appear. *See* CCP §1985.2.

6. Notices for witness. SUBP-002 contains the following notices for the witness:

(1) Automatic stay. Item 2 instructs a witness served with a subpoena for personal records not to produce the records if (1) the witness is served with written objections or a motion to quash and (2) no court order or agreement of the parties, the witness, and the consumer has been obtained. See "Objecting to subpoena for personal records," ch. 8-D, §12.1, p. 993.

(2) Witness fees. Item 5 provides notice that the witness is entitled to witness fees and mileage expenses (both ways), which must be paid when the subpoena is served (if the witness asks for them) or before the appearance. *See* CCP §2065. See "How to Pay Witness Fees," ch. 8-A, §10, p. 951. Witness fees must be paid to any person subpoenaed to appear for a trial or hearing, including parties and nonparties. *See* 2 Witkin, *Cal. Evidence*, Witnesses, §15.

(3) Sanctions. A boxed paragraph under Item 5 warns the witness that if the subpoena is disobeyed, the witness can be found in contempt of court and will be liable for a fine of $500 plus damages. *See* CCP §§1991, 1992. See "Forfeiture & damages," ch. 8-E, §3.3, p. 999; "Contempt," ch. 8-E, §3.4, p. 999; "Discovery Sanctions," ch. 9-A, p. 1003.

(4) Witness accommodations. A boxed paragraph under the issuing information provides information about requesting assistance to hear, understand, or answer questions at trial. *See* Civ. C. §54.8.

7. Issuing information. The issuing information (i.e., who issued the subpoena and when) must be provided below the notice of sanctions. See "How Subpoenas Are Prepared & Issued," ch. 8-A, §6, p. 942.

§4.2 Good-cause declaration. The subpoena's good-cause declaration, which is on the second page of SUBP-002, can be used for the statements necessary to support a trial subpoena for production of documents or other things. *See* CCP §1985(b); ***Flora Crane Serv. v. Superior Ct.*** (1st Dist.1965) 234 Cal.App.2d 767, 785. A separate declaration or affidavit can be used instead if it contains the required information. If the declaration is not attached to the subpoena, the subpoena is invalid. CCP §1987.5. See "Good-cause declaration," ch. 8-A, §6.4.2, p. 943. The declaration must include the following:

1. Case information. In the heading for the good-cause declaration, the subpoenaing party must identify the parties and provide the case number.

2. Option. The first statement of the good-cause declaration requires the subpoenaing party to check a box stating whether the subpoena is supported by the SUBP-002 declaration or by a separate, attached declaration.

3. Declarant. Item 1 of the good-cause declaration requires the person swearing to the truth of the declaration to identify the party's status: plaintiff, defendant, petitioner, respondent, or "other," or attorney for plaintiff, defendant, petitioner, respondent, or "other."

4. Witness possession. Item 2 of the good-cause declaration contains the statement that the witness has possession or control of the documents or other things subject to the subpoena. *See* CCP §1985(b).

5. Description of things. Item 2 of the good-cause declaration requires the subpoenaing party to describe the things to be produced. *See* CCP §1985(b). The subpoena must specify the "exact matters or things" to be produced; it cannot identify things by categories. *See id.* See "Trial subpoenas," ch. 8-A, §5.2.2, p. 940. By comparison, a deposition subpoena can identify things to be produced by category. See "Deposition subpoenas," ch. 8-A, §5.2.1, p. 940. If the things to be produced are too numerous to list on the form, the subpoenaing party must check the box "Continued on Attachment 2" and provide the other items on a separate sheet.

6. Good cause. Item 3 of the good-cause declaration requires the subpoenaing party to explain why it has good cause to compel the production of the things listed in Item 2. *See* CCP §1985(b); ***Grannis v. Board of Med. Exam'rs*** (1st Dist.1971) 19 Cal.App.3d 551, 564. The declaration must include factual allegations justifying the discovery. ***Lee v. Superior Ct.*** (4th Dist.2009) 177 Cal.App.4th 1108, 1127-28; ***Johnson v. Superior Ct.*** (2d Dist.1968) 258 Cal.App.2d 829, 836. If the factual statements are based on information and belief, the declaration must include facts supporting the information and belief. ***Grannis***, 19 Cal.App.3d at 564; *see* ***Pacific Auto. Ins. v. Superior Ct.*** (2d Dist.1969) 273 Cal.App.2d 61, 66-67; Wegner, *Civil Trials & Evidence*, ¶1:128. If the factual allegations and explanations are too numerous to list on the form, the subpoenaing party must check the box "Continued on Attachment 3" and provide the additional facts or reasons on a separate sheet.

7. Materiality. Item 4 of the good-cause declaration requires the subpoenaing party to state why the things listed in Item 2 are material to the issues in the case. The declaration must fully detail the materiality of the things. CCP §1985(b); *e.g.*, ***Johnson***, 258 Cal.App.2d at 835-36 (statement that documents were necessary to prove allegations in complaint did not show materiality). The materiality of the things must be shown by facts. ***Johnson***, 258 Cal.App.2d at 836-37; *e.g.*, ***Lee***, 177 Cal.App.4th at 1128-29 (affidavit that simply stated requested documents were material without stating facts showing materiality was ineffective). If the facts and reasons are too numerous to list on the form, the subpoenaing party must check the box "Continued on Attachment 4" and provide the additional facts or reasons on a separate sheet.

8. Oath. The good-cause declaration requires the declarant to sign it under penalty of perjury.

§4.3 POS. The subpoena's POS, which is the third page of SUBP-002, must be attached to the subpoena. See "POS," §3.2, p. 972.

§4.4 Documents to serve.

1. Witness. To compel the witness to appear and produce at a trial or hearing or to produce only, the witness must be personally served with the following:

(1) Subpoena. A copy of the subpoena. If the witness is a government employee or a minor, additional copies of the subpoena may be necessary. See "Public employee," ch. 8-A, §9.2.2, p. 948; "Minor," ch. 8-A, §9.2.3, p. 948.

(2) Good-cause declaration. A copy of the good-cause declaration. See "Good-cause declaration," §4.2, p. 974. The subpoenaing party must retain the original of the good-cause declaration until final judgment. CCP §1987.5.

(3) Optional documents.

(a) Form for custodian's declaration. If the subpoena requires the production of records but not the custodian's appearance, the subpoenaing party should serve the witness with a fill-in-the-blank form for the witness to authenticate the records produced. See "Custodian's declaration," ch. 8-B, §5.2, p. 967. For a form for the custodian's declaration, see *CEB Procedure During Trial*, §4.61.

(b) On-call agreement. If the subpoena requires the appearance of the witness and the trial is expected to last more than one day, the subpoenaing party should consider serving the witness with an on-call agreement along with the subpoena. See "On-call agreement," §3.3.1(1), p. 972.

2. **Not parties.** The parties do not have a right to be served with a copy of the trial subpoena or the right to receive notice that a witness has been subpoenaed. *See* ***Taggart v. Super Seer Corp.*** (4th Dist.1995) 33 Cal.App.4th 1697, 1708 n.8; Sink, *Subpoena Handbook*, §11:2[A][2][e][i]; Wegner, *Civil Trials & Evidence*, ¶1:132.

§5. RESPONDING TO TRIAL SUBPOENAS

§5.1 Complying with trial subpoenas.

1. **Complying with subpoena for appearance.** To comply with Judicial Council Form SUBP-001, which requires the witness to appear for a trial or hearing, the witness must appear at the designated time and place. *See* CCP §2064.

2. **Complying with subpoena for appearance & production.** To comply with Judicial Council Form SUBP-002 when it requires the witness to appear for a trial or hearing and to bring documents or other things, the witness must appear at the designated time and place with the things described in the good-cause declaration. *See* CCP §2064.

3. **Complying with subpoena for production of documents.** To comply with Judicial Council Form SUBP-002 when it requires the witness to produce documents but does not require the witness to appear, the witness must assemble and mail the documents to the court, as instructed by Item 3(b).

(1) **Deadline.** The documents must be prepared and delivered or mailed to the court clerk within 15 days after receiving the subpoena. *See* Evid. C. §1560(b)(2) (subpoena for business records). The documents must be received by the clerk within 15 days after service of the subpoena, whether they are delivered personally or by mail. *See id.* (subpoena for business records; no reference to CCP §1013(a) about extending time if document served by mail).

(2) **Prepare documents.** The documents that must be prepared include the following:

(a) **Subpoenaed documents.** The witness must copy the documents and things described in the good-cause declaration (unless originals are required).

(b) **Custodian's declaration.** The witness must prepare a custodian's declaration that complies with Evid. C. §1561(a) and (b) to authenticate the documents produced. *See* ***Taggart v. Super Seer Corp.*** (4th Dist.1995) 33 Cal.App.4th 1697, 1705 & n.5 (subpoena for business records). See "Custodian's declaration," ch. 8-B, §5.2, p. 967. If some or all of the documents cannot be produced, the declaration must identify the records that are not produced and state why they cannot be produced. *See* Evid. C. §1561(b) (subpoena for business records); *CEB Procedure During Trial*, §4.25 (same). If the documents are to be introduced into evidence without a sponsoring witness, the declaration must comply with both Evid. C. §§1271 and 1561.

PRACTICE TIP

Do not rely on the witness to know the technical statements required for a custodian's declaration. Instead, serve the witness with a form for the declaration along with the subpoena.

---

(3) **Assemble documents.**

(a) **Inner envelope.** The witness must place in an inner envelope (1) copies of the documents described in the good-cause declaration and (2) the original of the custodian's declaration. The witness must seal the inner envelope and attach a copy of the subpoena to the outside of the inner envelope or mark the envelope with the case name and number, the witness's name, and the date of the subpoena. *See* Evid. C. §1560(c) (subpoena for business records); *CEB Procedure During Trial*, §4.25 (same).

(b) **Outer envelope.** The witness must place the inner envelope in an outer envelope, seal it, and address it to the court clerk. *See* Evid. C. §1560(c)(1) (subpoena for business records); *CEB Procedure During Trial*, §4.25 (same).

(4) **Deliver documents.** The witness must deliver or mail the following documents to the following persons:

(a) **Clerk.** Mail the documents assembled in the inner and outer envelopes to the court clerk at the address identified in Item 1 of SUBP-002. *See* Evid. C. §1560(c)(1) (subpoena for business records); Judicial Council Forms, form SUBP-002, Item 3(b) (instructions for witness).

(b) **Subpoenaing party.** Mail a copy of the custodian's declaration to the attorney or pro per party listed in the heading of SUBP-002. Judicial Council Forms, form SUBP-002, Item 3(b).

§5.2 Challenging subpoenas. For a discussion of how to challenge a subpoena, see "Challenging Subpoenas," ch. 8-E, §2, p. 995.

§5.3 Enforcing subpoenas. For a discussion of how to enforce a subpoena, see "Enforcing Subpoenas," ch. 8-E, §3, p. 998.

D. SUBPOENAS FOR PERSONAL RECORDS

This subchapter covers the requirements for subpoenas to produce personal records of consumers, employees, and other persons whose records are protected from immediate disclosure by CCP §§1985.3, 1985.4, and 1985.6. These code provisions require a party who seeks personal records to notify the person whose records are sought that the party is about to serve a deposition or trial subpoena on a witness for that person's personal records.

§1. GENERAL

§1.1 Purpose. The procedure for subpoenaing personal records is designed to protect the consumer's right to privacy. ***Sasson v. Katash*** (2d Dist.1983) 146 Cal.App.3d 119, 124. *See generally* ***Pioneer Elecs. (USA), Inc. v. Superior Ct.*** (2007) 40 Cal.4th 360, 370-71 (discussing right to privacy under Cal. Const., art. I, §1). CCP §§1985.3 and 1985.6 provide a procedure that gives consumers whose personal records are being subpoenaed enough time to challenge the subpoena before the records are released. *See* ***Foothill Fed. Credit Un. v. Superior Ct.*** (2d Dist.2007) 155 Cal.App.4th 632, 638.

§1.2 Primary authority. CCP §§1985.3, 1985.4, 1985.6, 2020.410, 2020.430, 2020.510, 2025.220(b), 2025.240(b), 2025.270(c); Evid. C. §§1560-1562, 1564.

§1.3 Secondary authority. The following secondary sources are cited as authority in this subchapter:

- *California Civil Discovery Practice* (CEB Online ed. 2014) (referred to as *CEB Discovery Practice*).
- *California Trial Practice: Civil Procedure During Trial* (CEB Online ed. 2014) (referred to as *CEB Procedure During Trial*).
- Sink, *California Subpoena Handbook* (2014-15) (referred to as Sink, *Subpoena Handbook*).
- Wegner, *California Practice Guide: Civil Trials & Evidence* (CD-ROM ed. 2014) (referred to as Wegner, *Civil Trials & Evidence*).
- Weil & Brown, *California Practice Guide: Civil Procedure Before Trial* (CD-ROM ed. 2014) (referred to as Weil, *Civil Procedure Before Trial*).

§1.4 Judicial Council forms.

- SUBP-025 (mandatory), notice of privacy rights.

§2. OVERVIEW OF DISCOVERY OF PERSONAL RECORDS

To understand subpoenas for personal records, the attorney must understand the terms used when discussing personal records and the relationship between the subpoenaing party, the witness subpoenaed to produce personal records, and the person whose personal records are being subpoenaed.

§2.1 Definitions.

1. Consumer. The term "consumer" is used throughout this subchapter to refer collectively to consumers, employees, and other persons whose personal records are sought through discovery. "Consumers" are divided into "party consumers" and "nonparty consumers."

2. Notice of privacy rights. A "notice of privacy rights" is the notice a subpoenaing party must provide to a consumer when the party seeks discovery of the consumer's personal records or information. *See* CCP §§1985.3(b), (e), 1985.6(b), (e). The purpose of the notice is to inform the consumer that a subpoena will be served on a witness who is in possession of the consumer's personal records and that the consumer has the right to object to the production of those records. See "Notice of privacy rights," §9.3, p. 988.

3. Personal records. The term "personal records" refers to the personal records of consumers, employees, and other persons whose records are protected from immediate disclosure by CCP §§1985.3, 1985.4, and 1985.6. See "Records covered," §6.1, p. 980. These provisions establish a procedure that gives notice to the consumer and provides a mechanism for the consumer to object to the release of the information.

§2.2 Illustration of relationships between consumer & witness. The production of personal records is difficult to understand, primarily because of the complicated relationships between the person whose records are sought and the person who is being compelled to produce them. To illustrate the various relationships, the examples below are based on these facts: A former wife (ex-wife) sues her former husband (ex-husband) for an increase in child support; the ex-husband is living with a girlfriend.

1. Party consumer. To secure the ex-husband's financial records from his girlfriend, the ex-wife must serve a notice of privacy rights on the ex-husband (as a party consumer) and a deposition subpoena on his girlfriend (as a nonparty witness). Both the ex-husband and his girlfriend can object to the production of the personal records required by the subpoena, and the ex-wife can move to enforce the subpoena against the girlfriend.

2. Nonparty holder of nonparty's records. To secure the girlfriend's financial records from her bank, the ex-wife must serve a notice of privacy rights on the girlfriend (as a nonparty consumer) and a deposition subpoena on her bank (as a nonparty witness). Both the girlfriend and the bank can object to the subpoena, and the ex-wife can move to enforce the subpoena against the bank.

3. Nonparty holder of party's records. To secure the ex-husband's employment records, the ex-wife must serve a notice of privacy rights on him (as a party consumer) and a deposition subpoena on his employer (as a nonparty witness). Both the ex-husband and his employer can object to the production of the personal records required by the subpoena, and the ex-wife can move to enforce the subpoena against the employer.

§3. NECESSITY OF NOTICE OF PRIVACY RIGHTS

§3.1 When notice required. All persons have a constitutional right to privacy, which is classified as an "inalienable right" by the California Constitution. Cal. Const., art. I, §1. Because of this right, any person whose personal records are sought by discovery is entitled to notice of her privacy rights. A notice of privacy rights is required in the following instances:

1. Consumer's records for discovery.

(1) Nonparty consumer. When the personal records of a nonparty consumer are subpoenaed from a nonparty, the subpoenaing party must serve the consumer with Judicial Council Form SUBP-025. *See* CCP §1985.3(e) (consumer records), §1985.6(e) (employment records), §2025.240(b) (deposition subpoena for personal records); *see also id.* §1985.4 (procedures of §1985.3 apply to governmental records).

(2) Party consumer. When the personal records of a party consumer are subpoenaed from a nonparty, the subpoenaing party must give the party consumer a notice of privacy rights, either by serving SUBP-025 or by including a notice of privacy rights in the deposition notice. *See* CCP §1985.3(e) (consumer records), §1985.6(e) (employment records), §2025.240(b) (deposition subpoena for personal records); *see, e.g.*, ***Lantz v. Superior Ct.***

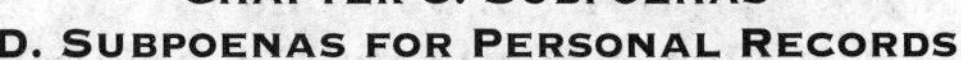

(5th Dist.1994) 28 Cal.App.4th 1839, 1852 (notice of privacy rights required for county to secure P's medical records from nonparty); ***Inabnit v. Berkson*** (5th Dist.1988) 199 Cal.App.3d 1230, 1236 (notice of privacy rights in deposition notice complied with §1985.3(e)); *see also* CCP §1985.4 (procedures of §1985.3 apply to governmental records).

2. Consumer's records for trial or hearing. When the personal records of a consumer (party or nonparty) are sought from a nonparty by a trial subpoena, the subpoenaing party must serve the consumer with SUBP-025. *See* CCP §1985.3(e) (consumer records), §1985.6(e) (employment records); *see also id.* §1985.4 (procedures of §1985.3 apply to governmental records); ***Lee v. Superior Ct.*** (4th Dist.2009) 177 Cal.App.4th 1108, 1134 (trial court erred by directing compliance with subpoenas because doing so excused P from providing notice to consumer).

§3.2 When notice not required. A notice of privacy rights is not required in the following instances:

1. Party's own records. When a party seeks her own personal records from a nonparty, the party is not required to serve SUBP-025. CCP §1985.3(*l*) (consumer), §1985.6(k) (employee). It would be pointless for a party to give herself notice that she is seeking her own records.

2. Records of certain businesses. When a subpoenaing party seeks the consumer records of an incorporated entity or partnership of over five persons, the party is not required to serve SUBP-025. See "Excluded as consumer," §5.1.2, p. 980.

3. Exempt subpoenaing party. The definition of "subpoenaing party" specifically excludes state agencies, local agencies, and entities involved in State Bar Act proceedings. CCP §1985.3(a)(3) (consumer records), §1985.6(a)(5) (employment records); *see* Weil, *Civil Procedure Before Trial*, ¶8:596; *see also* CCP §1985.4 (procedures of §1985.3 apply to governmental records).

(1) Government agencies. The exclusion of state and local agencies from the definition of "subpoenaing party" seems to exempt state and local agencies from the provisions governing notice of privacy rights when seeking any personal records. *See* CCP §1985.3(a)(3) (consumer records), §1985.6(a)(5) (employment records); Weil, *Civil Procedure Before Trial*, ¶8:596; *see also* Gov. C. §7465(e), (f) (defining "state agency" and "local agency"). However, case law has limited the government's exemption to financial records. *See* ***Lantz v. Superior Ct.*** (5th Dist.1994) 28 Cal.App.4th 1839, 1851-52; Weil, *Civil Procedure Before Trial*, ¶8:596.1. When a state or local agency seeks personal records other than financial records, the agency must comply with the provisions governing notice of privacy rights. *See* Weil, *Civil Procedure Before Trial*, ¶8:596.1; *see, e.g.*, ***Lantz***, 28 Cal.App.4th at 1852 (county was required to comply with §1985.3 when it subpoenaed medical records).

(2) State Bar Act proceeding. When a judicial entity seeks personal records in an adjudicative proceeding under the State Bar Act, it is not required to serve SUBP-025. *See* CCP §1985.3(a)(3) (consumer records), §1985.6(a)(5) (employment records); *see also id.* §1985.4 (procedures of §1985.3 apply to governmental records). *See generally* Bus. & Prof. C. §6000 et seq. (State Bar Act).

§4. WHO MUST GIVE NOTICE OF PRIVACY RIGHTS

§4.1 Notice for nonparty discovery. A party who subpoenas personal records from a nonparty for discovery must serve the person whose records are sought with a notice of privacy rights. *See* CCP §1985.3(e) (consumer records), §1985.6(e) (employment records), §2025.240(b) (deposition subpoena for personal records); *see also id.* §1985.4 (procedures of §1985.3 apply to governmental records).

§4.2 Notice for trial or hearing. A party who subpoenas personal records from a party or nonparty for production at a trial or hearing must serve the person whose records are sought with a notice of privacy rights. *See* CCP §1985.3(e) (consumer records), §1985.6(e) (employment records); *see also id.* §1985.4 (procedures of §1985.3 apply to governmental records).

§5. WHO IS ENTITLED TO NOTICE OF PRIVACY RIGHTS

The following persons are entitled to a notice of privacy rights when their personal records are subpoenaed:

§5.1 Consumer. For purposes of consumer records under CCP §1985.3, a "consumer" is defined as a person (1) that has transacted business with the subpoenaed witness, (2) that has used the services of the subpoenaed witness, or (3) for whom the subpoenaed witness acted as an agent or fiduciary. CCP §1985.3(a)(2).

1. Included as consumer. The definition of "consumer" includes individuals, partnerships of five or fewer persons, associations, and trusts. CCP §1985.3(a)(2); *see, e.g.*, ***Lantz v. Superior Ct.*** (5th Dist.1994) 28 Cal.App.4th 1839, 1849 (patient was consumer).

2. Excluded as consumer. The definition of "consumer" excludes incorporated entities and partnerships of more than five persons. *See* CCP §1985.3(a)(2). Thus, when consumer records of a corporation or a partnership of more than five persons are subpoenaed, that entity is not entitled to the protection of §1985.3.

§5.2 Natural person. For purposes of governmental records under CCP §1985.4, "consumer" is defined as (1) an employee of any state or local agency or (2) any other natural person. CCP §1985.4.

§5.3 Employee. For purposes of employment records under CCP §1985.6, an "employee" is defined as an individual who is or has been (1) employed by the subpoenaed employer or (2) represented by the subpoenaed labor organization. CCP §1985.6(a)(2).

§6. TYPES OF RECORDS COVERED

§6.1 Records covered. A notice of privacy rights must be served whenever the following types of records are sought by subpoena:

1. Consumer records. "Personal records" of a consumer include the original or any copy of books, documents, other writings, and electronically stored information (ESI) that pertain to the consumer and are maintained by any witness listed in CCP §1985.3(a)(1). CCP §1985.3(a)(1). See "Persons or entities with consumer records," §7.1, p. 981. Personal records that are "maintained" under §1985.3 include records entrusted to or preserved by the business. *See, e.g.*, ***Sasson v. Katash*** (2d Dist.1983) 146 Cal.App.3d 119, 124-25 (lease agreement belonging to consumer kept by consumer's bank was maintained under §1985.3).

2. Governmental records. "Personal information" includes records that (1) identify or describe an individual, (2) are maintained by a government agency, and (3) are otherwise exempt from public disclosure under Gov. C. §6254. *See* Civ. C. §1798.3(a); CCP §1985.4; Gov. C. §6254. See "Government agencies with records," §7.2, p. 982. The information covered by §1985.4 includes the following:

(1) An individual's name, home address, home telephone number, and Social Security number. Civ. C. §1798.3(a).

(2) An individual's education and employment history. *Id.*

(3) An individual's physical description and medical history. *Id.*

(4) An individual's financial matters. *Id.*

(5) Statements made by or attributed to the individual. *Id.*

(6) Other information that identifies or describes the individual. *See id.* (information includes but is not limited to the list in (1)-(5), above).

3. Employment records. "Employment records" include the original or any copy of books, documents, other writings, and ESI that pertain to the employment of any employee and are maintained by the current or former employer of the employee or by any labor organization that has represented or is currently representing the employee. CCP §1985.6(a)(3). See "Entities with employment records," §7.3, p. 983.

4. Other records & information. A person's right to privacy, which is classified as an "inalienable right" by the California Constitution, may protect other records or information from disclosure. *See* Cal. Const., art. I, §1.

(1) Demographic information. Demographic information (age, race, gender, income, and occupation) is protected from immediate disclosure. *See, e.g.*, ***Alch v. Superior Ct.*** (2d Dist.2008) 165 Cal.App.4th 1412, 1418 (because nonparties' privacy rights were implicated by request for nonparty demographic and personal information, parties agreed to court order providing notice of privacy rights in class action).

(2) **Names & contact information.** Names, addresses, and other contact information—though generally not considered protected information—are protected from immediate disclosure in some actions. *See* ***Puerto v. Superior Ct.*** (2d Dist.2008) 158 Cal.App.4th 1242, 1254 (only under unusual circumstances will courts restrict discovery of nonparty witnesses' residential contact information, such as when it would violate right to privacy); *see, e.g.*, ***Planned Parenthood Golden Gate v. Superior Ct.*** (1st Dist.2000) 83 Cal.App.4th 347, 359 (court refused to permit discovery sought by abortion protester for names and addresses of abortion clinic's staff and volunteers because of their right to privacy); ***Morales v. Superior Ct.*** (5th Dist.1979) 99 Cal.App.3d 283, 289-90 (in wrongful-death action, P-widower could not be required to produce names and addresses of persons with whom he had extramarital affairs).

§6.2 Records not covered. CCP §§1985.3, 1985.4, and 1985.6 do not apply to subpoenas for the production of the following records:

1. **Unidentified consumer's records.** Records of an unidentified consumer when the subpoena requires the witness to delete all information that would identify the consumer. CCP §1985.3(i) (consumer records), §1985.6(h) (employment records); *CEB Discovery Practice*, §5.114; *see also* CCP §1985.4 (procedures of §1985.3 apply to governmental records).

2. **Certain Labor Code records.**

(1) Records in proceedings involving the Department of Industrial Relations, conducted under Lab. C. §§50 through 176. *See* CCP §1985.3(j) (consumer records), §1985.6(i) (employment records); *see also id.* §1985.4 (procedures of §1985.3 apply to governmental records).

(2) Records in proceedings involving workers' compensation and insurance issues, conducted under Lab. C. §§3200 through 6002. *See* CCP §1985.3(j) (consumer records), §1985.6(i) (employment records); *see also id.* §1985.4 (procedures of §1985.3 apply to governmental records).

(3) Records in proceedings involving workers' compensation and insurance for state employees, conducted under Lab. C. §§6100 through 6149. *See* CCP §1985.3(j) (consumer records), §1985.6(i) (employment records); *see also id.* §1985.4 (procedures of §1985.3 apply to governmental records).

(4) Records in proceedings involving the retraining and rehabilitation of workers, conducted under Lab. C. §§6200 through 6208. *See* CCP §1985.3(j) (consumer records), §1985.6(i) (employment records); *see also id.* §1985.4 (procedures of §1985.3 apply to governmental records).

3. **Financial records sought by government agencies.** Financial records sought by state or local governments. See "Government agencies," §3.2.3(1), p. 979.

§7. TYPES OF PERSONS & ENTITIES COVERED

§7.1 Persons or entities with consumer records. The subpoenaing party must give a consumer a notice of privacy rights when consumer records are sought from the following persons or entities:

1. **Medical entities.**

(1) Physicians, dentists, ophthalmologists, optometrists, chiropractors, physical therapists, acupuncturists, podiatrists, and psychotherapists (e.g., psychologists, clinical workers) as defined in Evid. C. §1010. CCP §1985.3(a)(1); *e.g.*, ***Sehlmeyer v. Department of Gen. Servs.*** (2d Dist.1993) 17 Cal.App.4th 1072, 1075-76 & n.3 (psychologist subpoenaing patient's medical records from other providers for hearing before state board must comply with §1985.3).

(2) Hospitals, medical centers, clinics, radiology or MRI centers, and clinical or diagnostic laboratories. CCP §1985.3(a)(1); *see, e.g.*, ***Lee v. Superior Ct.*** (4th Dist.2009) 177 Cal.App.4th 1108, 1134 (DA subpoenaing hospital records under Sexually Violent Predator Act must comply with §1985.3).

(3) Pharmacies and pharmacists. CCP §1985.3(a)(1).

(4) Veterinarians, veterinary hospitals, and veterinary clinics. *Id.*

2. Financial entities.

(1) State or national banks, state or federal associations (as defined in Fin. C. §5102), state or federal credit unions, trust companies, anyone authorized by California to make or arrange loans that are secured by real property, security brokerage firms, and institutions of the Farm Credit System (as defined in 12 U.S.C. §2002). CCP §1985.3(a)(1); *see, e.g.*, ***Valley Bank v. Superior Ct.*** (1975) 15 Cal.3d 652, 656-57 (banks; decided before enactment of §1985.3).

(2) Insurance companies, title insurance companies, and underwritten title companies. CCP §1985.3(a)(1); *see also* ***In re Insurance Installment Fee Cases*** (4th Dist.2012) 211 Cal.App.4th 1395, 1426 (insurer has constitutional duty to protect privacy interests of policyholders).

(3) Escrow agents licensed under Fin. C. §17000 et seq. or exempt from licensure under Fin. C. §17006. CCP §1985.3(a)(1).

(4) Accountants. *Id.*

3. Attorneys. CCP §1985.3(a)(1).

4. Schools. Private or public preschools, elementary schools, secondary schools, and postsecondary schools as described in Educ. C. §76244. CCP §1985.3(a)(1).

5. Telephone corporations. Telephone corporations that are public utilities (as defined in Pub. Util. C. §216). CCP §1985.3(a)(1); *see also* Pub. Util. C. §2891 (listing telephone information protected). "Telephone corporations" include corporations owning, controlling, operating, or managing a telephone line for compensation within California. Pub. Util. C. §234(a). "Telephone corporations" do not include hospitals, hotels, or similar places of temporary accommodation that own or operate switching or billing equipment, or companies that provide one-way paging services. *Id.* §243(b).

§7.2 Government agencies with records. The subpoenaing party must give an individual a notice of privacy rights when governmental records relating to the individual are sought from the following agencies:

1. State agencies. *See* CCP §1985.4. CCP §1985.4 defines "state agency" by referring to the California Public Records Act (CPRA). *See id.*; Gov. C. §6252(f). The CPRA contains an expansive definition of "state agency" that includes the following:

(1) State offices and officers. Gov. C. §6252(f).

(2) State departments, divisions, bureaus, boards, and commissions. *Id.*

(3) Other state bodies or agencies. *Id.*

2. Local agencies. *See* CCP §1985.4. CCP §1985.4 defines "local agency" by referring to the CPRA. *See id.*; Gov. C. §6252(a). The CPRA contains an expansive definition of "local agency" that includes the following:

(1) Counties. Gov. C. §6252(a); *see, e.g.*, ***Lantz v. Superior Ct.*** (5th Dist.1994) 28 Cal.App.4th 1839, 1852 (D-county required to give P notice that it subpoenaed P's medical records from nonparty).

(2) Cities (general law or chartered). Gov. C. §6252(a).

(3) School districts. *Id.*

(4) Municipal corporations. *Id.*

(5) Districts. *Id.*

(6) Political subdivisions. *Id.*

(7) Any board, commission, or agency of a local agency. *Id.*

(8) Other local public agencies. *Id.*

(9) Entities that are legislative bodies of a local agency under Gov. C. §54952(c) and (d). *Id.* §6252(a).

§7.3 Entities with employment records. The subpoenaing party must give an employee a notice of privacy rights when employment records are sought from the following persons or entities: (1) an employer that currently employs or formerly employed the employee or (2) a labor organization that currently represents or formerly represented the employee. CCP §1985.6(a)(3).

§7.4 Other entities. When personal records are sought from entities not listed in CCP §1985.3, 1985.4, or 1985.6, those entities should not produce the records unless the person whose records are sought is given notice of the request and an opportunity to object. *See, e.g.,* ***Valley Bank v. Superior Ct.*** (1975) 15 Cal.3d 652, 658 (before enactment of §1985.3, court held bank customer entitled to notice that its records were being sought in discovery). See "Person in possession," ch. 6-F, §1.4.2, p. 683 (person in possession of holder's personal records or information can assert right to privacy on behalf of holder). Examples of other entities include the following:

1. Internet provider. An Internet provider can refuse to produce a user's personally identifying information (e.g., name, home and e-mail address, telephone number, Social Security number, children's names) when the information has been subpoenaed in connection with an action involving the user's exercise of free-speech rights. *See* Civ. C. §1798.79.8(b); CCP §§1987.1(b)(5), 1987.2(c). See "Free-speech action," ch. 7-A, §11.1.10(4), p. 767.

2. Manufacturer. A manufacturer can refuse to produce the names and addresses of its customers sought by subpoena, unless those persons are given notice of the request and an opportunity to object. *See* ***Pioneer Elecs. (USA), Inc. v. Superior Ct.*** (2007) 40 Cal.4th 360, 371-72.

3. Professional association. A professional association can refuse to produce the names and addresses of its members when sought by subpoena, unless those persons are given notice of the request and an opportunity to object. *See, e.g.,* ***Alch v. Superior Ct.*** (2d Dist.2008) 165 Cal.App.4th 1412, 1418 (because nonparties' privacy rights were implicated by subpoenas for personal information from Writers Guild, parties agreed to court order providing notice of privacy rights in class action).

4. Abortion clinic. An abortion clinic can refuse to produce the names and addresses of its staff and volunteers in an action involving the scope of a protester's right to engage in antiabortion activities, unless those persons are given notice of the request and an opportunity to object. *See, e.g.,* ***Planned Parenthood Golden Gate v. Superior Ct.*** (1st Dist.2000) 83 Cal.App.4th 347, 359 (abortion clinic's staff and volunteers had right to privacy of their names and addresses).

§8. SCHEDULING PRODUCTION OF PERSONAL RECORDS

When personal records are sought, the consumer must be served with the notice of privacy rights, along with other documents. Similarly, the witness must be served with the subpoena, along with other documents. This section uses the phrases "serve the consumer with the notice of privacy rights" and "serve the witness with the subpoena" as shorthand for all the documents that must be served on each person. For the list of all the documents that must be served, see "Documents to Serve for Production of Personal Records from Nonparty," §11, p. 991.

CAUTION

The most vexing problem with scheduling the production of personal records is CCP §§1985.3 and 1985.6, which are vague, disorganized, and difficult to understand, and which contain overlapping provisions and outright errors.

PERSONAL RECORDS

§8.1 Understanding rules for serving documents for personal records. To determine the date to schedule the production of personal records, the subpoenaing party must first understand the rules for serving the consumer, who is served with a notice of privacy rights, and the witness, who is served with a subpoena. See "Serving Documents," ch. 1-G, p. 63.

1. **Serving the consumer.** The consumer must be served as follows:

(1) **5 days before witness.** The consumer must be served with the notice of privacy rights at least five days before the witness is served with the subpoena, plus the additional time provided by CCP §1013(a) if service is by mail. CCP §1985.3(b)(3) (consumer records), §1985.6(b)(3) (employment records); *CEB Discovery Practice*, §5.66 (employment records); *see* Weil, *Civil Procedure Before Trial*, ¶¶8:590.1, 8:590.3 (consumer records); *see also* CCP §1985.4 (procedures of §1985.3 apply to governmental records).

(2) **10 days before production.**

(a) **Rule.** The consumer must be served with the notice of privacy rights at least ten days before the date for production of records, plus the additional time provided by CCP §1013(a) if service is by mail. CCP §1985.3(b)(2) (consumer records), §1985.6(b)(2) (employment records); *see also id.* §1985.4 (procedures of §1985.3 apply to governmental records).

(b) **Overlapping provision.** The provisions in CCP §§1985.3 and 1985.6 that require the consumer to be served with the notice of privacy rights at least ten days before production do not affect the date to schedule production because the time period overlaps with (and is subsumed by) the time requirements for serving the witness with the subpoena.

2. **Serving the witness.** The witness must be served as follows:

(1) **Production at deposition.**

(a) **Deposition subpoena to attend & produce.**

[1] **20 days after service.** A deposition subpoena to attend and produce personal records must be served on the witness far enough before the production date—at least 20 days—to give the witness a reasonable time to locate and produce the records. *See* CCP §1985.3(d) (consumer records, reasonable time), §1985.6(d) (employment records, reasonable time), §2025.270(c) (schedule deposition for at least 20 days after subpoena to appear and produce is served); *CEB Discovery Practice*, §5.116 (same).

[2] **Error in §2025.270(c).** We interpret CCP §2025.270(c) as requiring the deposition date to be scheduled at least 20 days after service of the subpoena. Section 2025.270(c) actually uses the phrase "after issuance" of the subpoena, not "after service." Most commentators agree that "after issuance" should read "after service." *E.g.*, *CEB Discovery Practice*, §5.67; Weil, *Civil Procedure Before Trial*, ¶8:493. Twenty days "after issuance" allows less time than 20 days "after service." For example, if a subpoena is issued on day 0, served on the consumer along with the notice of privacy rights on day 4 (assuming four days to locate and serve the consumer), and served on the witness on day 9 (allowing five days required between service on the consumer and the witness), the deposition could be scheduled as early as day 20, which gives the witness only 11 days after service of the subpoena to produce the records for the deposition. But if the 20 days in §2025.270(c) is interpreted as "after service" and if the same dates are used (day 0, subpoena issued; day 4, consumer served; day 9, witness served), the deposition could not be scheduled before day 29, which gives the witness 20 days to produce the records between service of the subpoena and production at the deposition.

(b) **Deposition subpoena to produce only.**

[1] **15 days after service.** A deposition subpoena for business records that includes personal records must be served on the witness far enough before the production date—at least 15 days—to give the

witness a reasonable time to locate and produce the records. *See* CCP §1985.3(d) (consumer records, reasonable time as provided by §2020.410), §1985.6(d) (employment records, reasonable time as provided by §2020.410), §2020.410(c) (15 days after service of subpoena); Evid. C. §1560(b)(2) (within 15 days of receipt of subpoena); Sink, *Subpoena Handbook*, §6:2[E] (15 days after service of subpoena).

[2] Overlapping provision. Section 2020.410(c) contains two time requirements for scheduling the production of records (whichever is later): (1) the date for production must be at least 15 days after service and (2) the date for production must be at least 20 days after the subpoena is issued (i.e., signed). The 20-days-after-issuance requirement is of no consequence for subpoenas for personal records because the consumer must be served at least 5 days before the witness is served, and the witness must be served at least 15 days before production, which overlaps the 20-days-after-issuance requirement. *See* Sink, *Subpoena Handbook*, §6:2[E], [F][3], [5]. The 20-days requirement may have been designed to curb abuse by pro per parties, but its actual purpose has been lost. *See id.* §6:2[E].

(2) Production of personal records at trial.

(a) Trial subpoena to attend & produce – 15 days. A trial subpoena that requires the witness to attend and produce personal records at a trial or hearing or deliver the records to the court clerk must be served on the witness (party or nonparty) far enough before the production date—at least 15 days—to give the witness a reasonable time to locate and produce the records. *See* CCP §1985.3(d) (consumer records, reasonable time as provided by §2020.410), §1985.6(d) (employment records, reasonable time as provided by §2020.410), §2020.410(c) (15 days after service of subpoena); Evid. C. §1560(b)(2) (within 15 days of receipt of subpoena); *CEB Procedure During Trial*, §4.22 (at least 15 days before production); Wegner, *Civil Trials & Evidence*, ¶1:146 (15 days after service). See "Overlapping provision," §8.1.2(1)(b)[2], this page.

(b) Trial subpoena to produce only – 15 days. A trial subpoena that requires the witness to produce personal records for a trial or hearing by mailing the records to the court clerk must be served within the same time period as for a subpoena for the witness to attend and produce. See "Trial subpoena to attend & produce – 15 days," §8.1.2(2)(a), this page. The only difference is that the records must be received by the court clerk by the date set out in the subpoena; they cannot be put in the mail on that date.

§8.2 Calculating date for production of personal records. The date to schedule the production of personal records is calculated from the date the notice of privacy rights is served on the consumer, which must be served before the subpoena is served on the witness. See "Serving Documents," ch. 1-G, p. 63.

1. When to set deposition for production of personal records. The date to select for a deposition that requires the production of personal records depends on the type of deposition (i.e., to attend and produce or to produce only).

(1) Attend & produce – 25 days. The date for the deposition of a witness served with a subpoena to attend and produce personal records must be at least 25 days after the consumer is personally served with the notice of privacy rights. This is calculated by adding the minimum notice that must be given to (1) the consumer, who must be served with the notice of privacy rights at least five days before the witness is served with the subpoena, and (2) the witness, who must be served with the deposition subpoena at least 20 days before the date of the deposition. See "5 days before witness," §8.1.1(1), p. 984; "20 days after service," §8.1.2(1)(a)[1], p. 984. Thus, the earliest date to schedule a deposition that requires a nonparty to produce personal records at an oral deposition is 25 days after the consumer is personally served with the notice of privacy rights. If the consumer is served by mail, additional time must be added. See "When to Serve," ch. 1-G, §6, p. 69. To calculate the date for the deposition, fill in the blanks in Chart 8-7, below.

8-7. DATE FOR ORAL DEPOSITION FOR PERSONAL RECORDS SUBPOENAED FROM NONPARTY				
To date in A, add number of days in B, C, and D to calculate date for E				
A	B	C	D	E
Insert date consumer served with NOPR. Date: __________	Insert number of days for type of service on consumer (e.g., 0 for personal service, 5 for service by mail). _____ days	Insert at least 5 days to satisfy requirement that consumer be served 5 days before party. _____ days	20 days inserted to satisfy requirement that deponent be served at least 20 days before E. 20 days	Insert earliest date for oral deposition for production of personal records. Date: __________*
* If earliest date falls on a Saturday, Sunday, or judicial holiday, continue to count forward until the next day that is not a Saturday, Sunday, or judicial holiday. *See* CCP §§12, 12a. For a list of holidays, see "Determine last day," ch. 1-F, §5.1.5, p. 55. NOPR = notice of privacy rights Consumer = all persons whose personal records are sought under §1985.3, 1985.4, or 1985.6				

(2) Produce only – 20 days. The date for the deposition of a witness served with a subpoena for business records must be at least 20 days after the consumer is personally served with the notice of privacy rights. This is calculated by adding the minimum notice that must be given to (1) the consumer, who must be served with the notice of privacy rights at least five days before the witness is served with the subpoena, and (2) the witness, who must be served with the subpoena at least 15 days before the date of the deposition. See "5 days before witness," §8.1.1(1), p. 984; "15 days after service," §8.1.2(1)(b)[1], p. 984. Thus, the earliest date to schedule a deposition for business records that requires a nonparty to produce personal records (but not appear at an oral deposition) is 20 days after the consumer is personally served with the notice of privacy rights. If the consumer is served by mail, additional time must be added. See "When to Serve," ch. 1-G, §6, p. 69. To calculate the date for the deposition, fill in the blanks in Chart 8-8, below.

8-8. DATE FOR BUSINESS-RECORDS DEPOSITION FOR PERSONAL RECORDS SUBPOENAED FROM NONPARTY				
To date in A, add number of days in B, C, and D to calculate date for E				
A	B	C	D	E
Insert date consumer served with NOPR. Date: __________	Insert number of days for type of service on consumer (e.g., 0 for personal service, 5 for service by mail). _____ days	Insert at least 5 days to satisfy requirement that consumer be served 5 days before party. _____ days	15 days inserted to satisfy requirement that deponent be served at least 15 days before E. 15 days	Insert earliest date for business-records deposition for production of personal records. Date: __________*
* If earliest date falls on a Saturday, Sunday, or judicial holiday, continue to count forward until the next day that is not a Saturday, Sunday, or judicial holiday. *See* CCP §§12, 12a. For a list of holidays, see "Determine last day," ch. 1-F, §5.1.5, p. 55. NOPR = notice of privacy rights Consumer = all persons whose personal records are sought under §1985.3, 1985.4, or 1985.6				

2. When to serve notice of privacy rights for production of personal records at trial. The date for production of personal records for a trial or hearing is calculated from the date set for the trial or hearing, a date not always chosen by the party. For that reason, it is calculated by starting with the date for the trial or hearing and counting backwards to determine the date to schedule service of the notice of privacy rights on the consumer.

(1) Attend & produce – 20 days. The date to serve a notice of privacy rights on a consumer when a witness is to be served with a subpoena to appear and produce personal records at a trial or hearing must be at least 20 days before the trial or hearing. *See* Evid. C. §1560(b)(2) (within 15 days of receipt of subpoena). This is

calculated by adding the minimum notice that must be given to (1) the consumer, who must be served with the notice of privacy rights at least 5 days before the witness is served with the subpoena, and (2) the witness, who must be served with the subpoena 15 days before the date for production. See "5 days before witness," §8.1.1(1), p. 984; "Trial subpoena to attend & produce – 15 days," §8.1.2(2)(a), p. 985. Thus, the latest date to serve the consumer with a notice of privacy rights when the witness will be subpoenaed to attend and produce personal records at trial is 20 days before the trial. If the consumer is served by mail, additional time must be added. See "When to Serve," ch. 1-G, §6, p. 69. To calculate the date for serving notice on the consumer, fill in the blanks in Chart 8-9, below.

8-9. DATE FOR PERSONAL RECORDS SUBPOENAED FOR TRIAL FROM PARTY OR NONPARTY

From date in A, subtract number of days in B, C, and D to calculate date for E				
A	**B**	**C**	**D**	**E**
Insert date for witness to appear at trial with personal records or deliver them to court clerk.	15 days inserted to satisfy requirement that witness be served with subpoena at least 15 days before A.	Insert at least 5 days to satisfy requirement that consumer be served 5 days before party.	Insert number of days for type of service of NOPR on consumer (e.g., 0 for personal service, 5 for service by mail).	Insert latest date to serve consumer with NOPR before trial or hearing.
Date: ________	15 days	_____ days	_____ days	Date: ________*

* If earliest date falls on a Saturday, Sunday, or judicial holiday, continue to count forward until the next day that is not a Saturday, Sunday, or judicial holiday. *See* CCP §§12, 12a. For a list of holidays, see "Determine last day," ch. 1-F, §5.1.5, p. 55.
NOPR = notice of privacy rights
Consumer = all persons whose personal records are sought under §1985.3, 1985.4, or 1985.6

(2) Produce only – 20 days. The date to serve a notice of privacy rights on the consumer when a witness is to be served with a trial subpoena that requires the witness to produce personal records for a trial or hearing by mailing the records to the court clerk must be within the same time period as for a subpoena for the witness to attend and produce. See "Attend & produce – 20 days," §8.2.2(1), p. 986.

§8.3 Shortening time for compliance. The court can shorten the time for service of a subpoena, or waive the notice-of-privacy-rights requirements of §1985.3(b) or 1985.6(b), if the subpoenaing party can establish in a motion that (1) there is good cause for the order, (2) the rights of the witness and the consumer will be preserved, and (3) the subpoenaing party exercised due diligence. CCP §1985.3(h) (consumer records), §1985.6(g) (employment records); *see also id.* §1985.4 (procedures of §1985.3 apply to governmental records). To preserve the rights of the consumer, the motion must show that the consumer will be given notice and an opportunity to object to the production of personal records. To prove the facts in the motion, the movant must provide an affidavit or declaration. *See CEB Discovery Practice*, §5.120.

§9. DOCUMENTS TO PREPARE

§9.1 Subpoena. The subpoenaing party must prepare the appropriate subpoena forms:

1. Deposition subpoena to appear & produce. Judicial Council Form SUBP-020 for a deposition subpoena for personal appearance and the production of documents and things. See "Deposition Subpoena for Testimony & Things," ch. 8-B, §4, p. 962.

2. Deposition subpoena to produce only. Judicial Council Form SUBP-010 for a deposition subpoena for production or inspection of business records from a witness without the appearance of the witness. See "Deposition Subpoena for Business Records," ch. 8-B, §5, p. 963.

3. Trial subpoena to appear & produce or produce only. Judicial Council Form SUBP-002 for a trial subpoena for personal appearance and the production of records at a trial or hearing or for the production of records only. See "Trial Subpoena for Testimony & Things," ch. 8-C, §4, p. 973. SUBP-002 includes the good-cause declaration in which the subpoenaing party lists the documents to be produced.

§9.2 Deposition notice. For a deposition subpoena to attend and produce, the subpoenaing party must prepare a deposition notice. See "Copy of deposition notice," §11.1.1(3), p. 991. A deposition notice is not necessary for a deposition for business records. *See* CCP §2025.220(b) (copy of subpoena serves as deposition notice). See "Documents to serve," ch. 8-B, §4.4, p. 963.

§9.3 Notice of privacy rights. The subpoenaing party must prepare the notice of privacy rights, using Judicial Council Form SUBP-025.

1. Notice form.

(1) Heading. In the heading for SUBP-025, the subpoenaing party must identify (1) the person causing the subpoena to be issued (attorney or pro per party), that person's address, State Bar number (if applicable), telephone number, fax number (optional), and e-mail address (optional), and the name of the party represented by the attorney (if not pro per), (2) the identification of the superior court (county, address, branch name), (3) the names of the parties, and (4) the case number.

(2) Consumer. Below the heading for SUBP-025, the subpoenaing party must identify the consumer whose records are sought. See "Who Is Entitled to Notice of Privacy Rights," §5, p. 979.

(3) Notice of request. Item 1 of SUBP-025 is the notice that the consumer's personal records are being sought.

(a) Subpoenaing party. Item 1 requires the subpoenaing party to identify itself.

(b) Date for compliance. Item 1 requires the subpoenaing party to state when the records must be produced. See "Scheduling Production of Personal Records," §8, p. 983.

(c) Witness. Item 1 requires the subpoenaing party to state the name of the person or entity subpoenaed to produce personal records. See "Types of Persons & Entities Covered," §7, p. 981.

NOTE

The records sought by the subpoenaing party are not listed in SUBP-025. For a deposition subpoena, the documents are listed in the subpoena itself; for a trial subpoena, the documents are listed in the good-cause declaration attached to the subpoena. See, e.g., Judicial Council Forms, form SUBP-002, form SUBP-010, form SUBP-020.

---

(4) Notice to consumer.

(a) Motion & objection. Item 2 of SUBP-025 instructs the consumer how to object to the subpoena.

[1] Make motion to quash or modify. If the consumer is a party to the suit, the consumer must file a motion to quash or modify the subpoena before the date set for compliance in Item 1. CCP §1985.3(g) (consumer), §1985.6(f)(1) (employee).

[2] Serve objection. If the consumer is not a party to the suit, the consumer can serve written objections to the production of the records before the date set for compliance in Item 1. See "Serve written objections," §12.1.2(1), p. 993. A nonparty consumer can also make a motion to quash or a motion for a protective order, although this is not acknowledged in SUBP-025 Item 2(b). See "Make motion to quash or for protection," §12.1.2(2), p. 994. The nonparty consumer is instructed to serve objections on the subpoenaing party and the witness, and not to file the objections with the court.

(b) Contact information. Item 3 of SUBP-025 requires the subpoenaing party to include contact information so the consumer can contact the subpoenaing party to determine if a written agreement can be reached to cancel or limit the scope of the subpoena. *See* CCP §1985.3(e) (consumer records), §1985.6(e) (employee

records). The notice advises the consumer that, if no agreement can be reached, the consumer should consult an attorney about privacy rights. *Id.* §1985.3(e) (consumer records), §1985.6(e) (employee records).

(5) Issuing information. The bottom of SUBP-025 contains the information identifying who issued the subpoena and when.

(6) Place for consumer objections. In the blank space below the issuing information on SUBP-025, p. 1, the consumer can object to the production of some or all of the records and state the reasons for the objection.

2. POS. The notice of privacy rights' proof of service (POS) must be printed on the reverse side of SUBP-025 or attached to it.

(1) POS heading. The heading of the POS must identify the parties to the suit and the case number.

(2) Server. Item 1 of the POS states the requirement that the server be at least 18 years old and not a party to the suit. See "Who can serve," ch. 8-A, §9.6, p. 950.

(3) Method of service. Below the heading for the POS, the subpoenaing party must designate whether the consumer will be served by personal delivery or by mail.

(a) Personal delivery. If the consumer is to be served by personal delivery, Item 2(a) of the POS requires the server to state the name and address of the person served, and the date and time service was completed. *See* CCP §1985.3(b), (c)(1) (consumer records), §1985.6(b), (c)(1) (employee records).

(b) Mail. If the consumer is to be served by mail, Item 2(b) of the POS requires the server to state the name and address of the person served, the date notice was mailed, and the city and state of mailing. *See* CCP §1013a (POS by mail), §1985.3(b), (c)(1) (consumer records), §1985.6(b), (c)(1) (employee records).

§9.4 Consumer's release. The subpoenaing party should always prepare a written release for the consumer to sign, even when it is optional.

1. When required.

(1) Optional. For most subpoenas for personal records, the subpoenaing party is not required to obtain the consumer's affirmative consent to the release of personal records. ***Puerto v. Superior Ct.*** (2d Dist.2008) 158 Cal.App.4th 1242, 1257. If no one with standing to challenge the subpoena (i.e., consumer, subpoenaed witness, other party) objects, all challenges to the subpoena are waived and the witness must produce the records. *See, e.g.*, ***Inabnit v. Berkson*** (5th Dist.1988) 199 Cal.App.3d 1230, 1238-39 (Ps, who sued doctor for unauthorized disclosure of medical records in another suit, had no cause of action because Ps received proper notice of subpoena under §1985.3 and did not object or claim psychotherapist-patient privilege).

(2) Mandatory. For subpoenas for telephone records, the subpoenaing party must obtain the consumer's affirmative consent to the release of the records. CCP §1985.3(f). See "Telephone corporations," §7.1.5, p. 982. If the subpoenaing party does not provide the consumer's release to the witness for the telephone corporation, the witness cannot produce the records. *See* CCP §1985.3(f). Without the signed release, a subpoena for telephone records is invalid. *Id.*

2. Form of release. The written authorization for the release of personal records must state that the consumer consents to the release of the records identified in the subpoena and must provide a signature line for the consumer (or the consumer's attorney of record). *See* CCP §1985.3(c)(2) (production of consumer records), §1985.6(c)(2) (production of employment records), §2020.410(d) (production of business records), §2020.510(c) (appearance and production of business records that are consumer records), §2020.510(d) (appearance and production of business records that are employment records); *see also id.* §1985.4 (procedures of §1985.3 apply to governmental records).

§9.5 Witness's declaration. If the records are to be produced without the appearance of the witness, the attorney should prepare a declaration for the witness to complete and execute. See "Custodian's declaration," ch. 8-B, §5.2, p. 967.

§10. HOW TO SERVE DOCUMENTS THAT COMPEL PRODUCTION OF PERSONAL RECORDS

§10.1 Whom to serve for production of personal records.

1. Nonparty witness. To compel a nonparty witness to attend and produce at a deposition, trial, or hearing, the witness must be served with a subpoena. See "Whom to name & serve," ch. 8-A, §9.2, p. 948.

2. Consumer. The consumer must be served with the notice of privacy rights.

(1) Nonparty. If the consumer is a nonparty, the notice of privacy rights must be served on the consumer. CCP §1985.3(b)(1) (consumer records), §1985.6(b)(1) (employee records); *CEB Discovery Practice*, §5.122; *CEB Procedure During Trial*, §4.22; Weil, *Civil Procedure Before Trial*, ¶8:590.

(2) Party. If the consumer is a party, the notice of privacy rights must be served on the party's attorney. CCP §1985.3(b)(1) (consumer records), §1985.6(b)(1) (employee records); *CEB Discovery Practice*, §5.122; *CEB Procedure During Trial*, §4.22; Weil, *Civil Procedure Before Trial*, ¶8:590.

(3) Minor. If the consumer is a minor, the notice of privacy rights must be served as follows:

(a) Consumer & governmental records. If the personal records sought are the minor's consumer or governmental records, the notice of privacy rights (naming the minor) must be served on the minor's parent, guardian, conservator, or similar fiduciary. CCP §1985.3(b)(1) (consumer records); *see id.* §1985.4 (governmental records). If none of these persons can be located after reasonable diligence, the notice of privacy rights can be served on the minor (if at least 12 years old) and any person (1) who has care or control of the minor, (2) with whom the minor resides, or (3) who employs the minor. *Id.* §1985.3(b)(1).

(b) Employment records. If the personal records sought are the minor's employment records, the notice of privacy rights (naming the minor) must be served on the minor's parent, guardian, conservator, or similar fiduciary. CCP §1985.6(b)(1). If none of these persons can be located after reasonable diligence, the notice of privacy rights can be served on the minor (if at least 12 years old) and any person (1) who has care or control of the minor or (2) with whom the minor resides. *Id.*

CAUTION

Although a minor's employer can be served as a proxy when the minor's consumer or governmental records are subpoenaed, the minor's employer cannot be served as a proxy when the minor's employment records are subpoenaed. See CCP §1985.6(b)(1).

---

§10.2 How to serve for production of personal records.

A subpoena can be served only by personal delivery; other documents can be served by personal delivery, mail, fax (by agreement), or electronic service (by agreement or court order). See "Methods of service," ch. 1-G, §5.1, p. 66.

1. Nonparty witness. To compel a nonparty witness to attend and produce at a deposition, trial, or hearing, the nonparty must be personally served with a subpoena. See "Type of service," ch. 8-A, §9.1, p. 947.

2. Consumer. The consumer must be served as follows:

(1) Nonparty. If the consumer is a nonparty, the notice of privacy rights can be served on the consumer personally, by mail at the consumer's last known address, or by any other authorized method of service. CCP §1985.3(b)(1) (consumer records), §1985.6(b)(1) (employee records); *CEB Discovery Practice*, §5.122; *CEB Procedure During Trial*, §4.22; Weil, *Civil Procedure Before Trial*, ¶8:590.

(2) Party's attorney. If the consumer is a party, the notice of privacy rights can be served on the party's attorney personally, by mail, or by any other authorized method of service. *See* CCP §1985.3(b)(1) (consumer records), §1985.6(b)(1) (employee records).

§10.3 When to serve for production of personal records.

1. Nonparty witness. See "Serving the witness," §8.1.2, p. 984.

2. Consumer. See "Serving the consumer," §8.1.1, p. 984.

3. Other parties. See "Serve other parties – 10 days," ch. 8-A, §7.1.1(2), p. 944; "Serve other parties – 10 days," ch. 8-A, §7.1.3(2), p. 945.

§11. DOCUMENTS TO SERVE FOR PRODUCTION OF PERSONAL RECORDS FROM NONPARTY

§11.1 Production at oral deposition.

1. Serve on consumer. When a consumer's personal records are subpoenaed for production at a deposition, the consumer must be served with the following documents:

(1) Notice of privacy rights. The consumer must be served with the notice of privacy rights and its POS. CCP §1985.3(b) (consumer records), §1985.6(b) (employee records), §2025.240(b)(2) (consumer and employee records). See "Consumer," §5.1, p. 979; "Notice of privacy rights," §9.3, p. 988.

(2) Copy of subpoena. The consumer must be served with a copy of the deposition subpoena and its POS. CCP §1985.3(b) (consumer records), §1985.6(b) (employee records); *see id.* §2025.240(b)(3). See "Subpoena," §9.1, p. 987.

(3) Copy of deposition notice. The consumer must be served with a copy of the deposition notice if the deposition subpoena requires the witness to attend and produce at the deposition. *See* CCP §1985.3(b) (consumer records), §1985.6(b) (employee records), §2025.240(b)(1) (consumer and employee records); *CEB Discovery Practice*, §5.118; Weil, *Civil Procedure Before Trial*, ¶8:486. It is not necessary to serve a deposition notice with a deposition subpoena for business records. *See* CCP §2025.220(b) (copy of subpoena serves as deposition notice).

(4) Release form. The consumer should be served with a form for the consumer or the consumer's attorney that authorizes the release of the personal records. See "Consumer's release," §9.4, p. 989. For a subpoena of telephone records, the consumer *must* be served with a release form. See "When required," §9.4.1, p. 989.

2. Serve on witness. When a consumer's personal records are subpoenaed for production at a deposition, the witness must be served with the following documents:

(1) Subpoena. The witness must be served with the deposition subpoena. See "Witness," ch. 8-B, §4.4.1, p. 963 (deposition to attend and produce); "Witness," ch. 8-B, §5.3.1, p. 968 (business-records deposition).

(2) POS. The witness must be served with a POS, attesting that the documents required to be served on the consumer were served. CCP §1985.3(c)(1) (consumer records), §1985.6(c)(1) (employee records); *see also id.* §2020.410(d) (business-records subpoena).

(3) Notice of privacy rights or release.

(a) Consumer's telephone records. When the subpoena requires the production of a consumer's records from a telephone corporation that is a public utility, the witness must be served with the consumer's signed consent to release the documents. CCP §1985.3(f). See "Telephone corporations," §7.1.5, p. 982. A telephone corporation cannot produce records when it is served only with proof that the consumer was served with the notice of privacy rights. *See* CCP §1985.3(f); Sink, *Subpoena Handbook*, §9:4[B][1][a].

(b) Other consumer records. When the subpoena requires the production of consumer records (not telephone records), the witness must be served with either (1) proof that the notice of privacy rights was served on the consumer or (2) a written authorization to release the records, signed by the consumer or the consumer's attorney. CCP §1985.3(c) (consumer records), §1985.6(c) (employee records), §2020.410(d) (deposition subpoena for production of business records), §2020.510(c) (deposition subpoena for appearance and production of business records that are consumer records), §2020.510(d) (deposition subpoena for appearance and production of

business records that are employee records); *see also id.* §1985.4 (procedures of §1985.3 apply to governmental records). If the witness is served with a written authorization signed by an attorney on a consumer's behalf, the witness can presume the release is valid. CCP §1985.3(c)(2) (consumer), §1985.6(c)(2) (employee). See "Consumer's release," §9.4, p. 989.

3. Serve on other parties. When a consumer's personal records are subpoenaed for production at a deposition, the other parties must be served with copies of all the documents served on the consumer and the witness, which should include copies of (1) the deposition notice and (2) the subpoena. *See* CCP §2025.240. Although no rule requires it, the other parties should probably be served with the notice of privacy rights and release form as well.

§11.2 Business-records subpoena. The documents to serve with a business-records subpoena that seeks production of personal records are almost the same as the documents to serve with a deposition subpoena to attend and produce. See "Production at oral deposition," §11.1, p. 991. There are two exceptions:

1. No deposition notice. The subpoenaing party is not required to serve a deposition notice with a business-records subpoena, because the copy of the subpoena acts as a deposition notice. CCP §2025.220(b).

2. Declaration for witness. The subpoenaing party should serve the witness with a form for the witness to authenticate the records to be produced. See "Custodian's declaration," ch. 8-B, §5.2, p. 967.

§11.3 Production at trial or hearing.

1. Serve on consumer. When a consumer's personal records are subpoenaed for a trial or hearing, the consumer must be served with the following documents:

(1) Notice of privacy rights. The consumer must be served with the notice of privacy rights and its POS. CCP §1985.3(b) (consumer records), §1985.6(b) (employee records); *CEB Procedure During Trial*, §4.22. See "Notice of privacy rights," §9.3, p. 988.

(2) Copy of subpoena. The consumer must be served with a copy of the subpoena and its POS. CCP §1985.3(b) (consumer records), §1985.6(b) (employee records); *CEB Procedure During Trial*, §4.22.

(3) Good-cause declaration. The consumer must be served with a copy of the good-cause declaration (which is attached to the subpoena). CCP §1985.3(b) (consumer records), §1985.6(b) (employee records); *CEB Procedure During Trial*, §4.22. See "Good-cause declaration," ch. 8-C, §4.2, p. 974.

(4) Release form. The consumer should be served with a form for the consumer or the consumer's attorney that authorizes the release of personal records. See "Consumer's release," §9.4, p. 989.

2. Serve on witness. When a consumer's personal records are subpoenaed for production at a trial or hearing, the witness must be served with the following documents:

(1) Subpoena. The witness must be served with the subpoena. CCP §1987(a). See "Subpoena form," ch. 8-C, §4.1, p. 973.

(2) Good-cause declaration. The witness must be served with a copy of the good-cause declaration (which is attached to the subpoena). See "Good-cause declaration," ch. 8-C, §4.2, p. 974.

(3) Notice of privacy rights or release. The witness must be served with (1) proof that the consumer was served with a notice of privacy rights or (2) a written authorization signed by the consumer. *CEB Procedure During Trial*, §4.22. See "Notice of privacy rights or release," §11.1.2(3), p. 991.

(4) Witness's affidavit. If the subpoena does not require the witness's attendance at the trial or hearing, the subpoenaing party should include a form for the witness to authenticate the records to be produced. See "Custodian's declaration," ch. 8-B, §5.2, p. 967.

3. Serve on other parties. When a consumer's personal records are subpoenaed for trial, the subpoenaing party does not need to serve the other parties with copies of any of the documents served on the consumer or the witness. See "Not parties," ch. 8-C, §4.4.2, p. 976.

§12. RESPONDING TO SUBPOENA FOR PERSONAL RECORDS

§12.1 Objecting to subpoena for personal records.

1. Who can object.

(1) Consumer. The consumer has the right to object to the production of her personal records. CCP §1985.3(e) (consumer records), §1985.6(e) (employee records).

(2) Witness. The witness who received a subpoena to produce a consumer's personal records has standing to object to the production of the personal records in its possession. *Cf.* ***Pioneer Elecs. (USA), Inc. v. Superior Ct.*** (2007) 40 Cal.4th 360, 368 (party deponent had standing to assert privacy rights of its customers); ***Monarch Healthcare v. Superior Ct.*** (4th Dist.2000) 78 Cal.App.4th 1282, 1285 (nonparty deponent objected to production of records of its customer). For the types of witnesses entitled to object on behalf of consumers, see "Types of Persons & Entities Covered," §7, p. 981.

(3) Parties. Any other party can object to a subpoena for personal records, based on relevance, procedure, or any other discovery objection. See "Grounds for Discovery Objections," ch. 7-A, §11, p. 765.

2. How to object.

(1) Serve written objections. A nonparty consumer or nonparty witness who objects to the production of personal records can serve written objections to the subpoena. CCP §1985.3(g) ¶2 (consumer records), §1985.6(f)(2) (employee records); *see CEB Discovery Practice*, §5.126. Written objections to a subpoena for personal records achieve the same results as a motion to quash: (1) they preserve objections to the subpoena and (2) they relieve the witness from complying with the subpoena until the court rules on the objections.

(a) Who can make written objections.

[1] Nonparty consumer. The nonparty consumer whose personal records are sought can make written objections to the subpoena. *See* CCP §1985.3(g) ¶2 (consumer records), §1985.6(f)(2) (employee records); ***Puerto v. Superior Ct.*** (2d Dist.2008) 158 Cal.App.4th 1242, 1257 (dicta); *see also* CCP §1985.4 (procedures of §1985.3 apply to governmental records). The nonparty consumer can object by using the form at the bottom of SUBP-025. *See* Judicial Council Forms, form SUBP-025. See "Place for consumer objections," §9.3.1(6), p. 989.

[2] Nonparty witness. The nonparty witness subpoenaed to produce a consumer's personal records can make written objections to the subpoena. *See* Sink, *Subpoena Handbook*, §11.5[A] (nonparty deponent not required to file motion to quash); *cf.* ***Monarch Healthcare***, 78 Cal.App.4th at 1287-88 (same).

[3] Not party. A party should not file written objections to a deposition subpoena for personal records. *See* CCP §1985.3(g) ¶2 (any other consumer that is not a party can file written objections), §1985.6(f)(2) (any nonparty employee can file written objections); *see also id.* §1985.4 (procedures of §1985.3 apply to governmental records). Objections by a party to a deposition subpoena for personal records will not stay the deposition. To challenge a subpoena for personal records, a party must file a motion to quash the subpoena or a motion for a protective order with a request for a stay. See "Make motion to quash or for protection," §12.1.2(2), p. 994.

(b) Who is served with written objections. Written objections must be served on the subpoenaing party, the subpoenaed witness, and the deposition officer (if the records were requested by a deposition subpoena). CCP §1985.3(g) ¶2 (consumer records), §1985.6(f)(2) (employee records); *CEB Procedure During Trial*, §4.23.

(c) Grounds for written objections. Written objections must cite the specific grounds on which the court should prohibit the production of personal records. CCP §1985.3(g) ¶2 (consumer records), §1985.6(f)(2) (employee records). See "Objections to subpoenas," ch. 8-E, §2.1, p. 995.

(d) Automatic stay. Service of written objections to a subpoena for personal records prevents the production of the personal records. CCP §1985.3(g) ¶3 (consumer records), §1985.6(f)(3) (employee records); *see* ***Colleen M. v. Fertility & Surgical Assocs.*** (2d Dist.2005) 132 Cal.App.4th 1466, 1479. The witness or deposition officer (for a business-records subpoena) is prohibited from producing the records until the court orders their production or the parties and the consumer reach an agreement about their production. *See* CCP §1985.3(g) ¶3 (consumer records), §1985.6(f)(3) (employee records).

(2) Make motion to quash or for protection.

(a) Motion to quash. A party, nonparty witness, or consumer who objects to the production of personal records can move to quash the subpoena. See "Motion to Quash Depositions," ch. 9-C, p. 1038. A motion to quash a deposition for personal records automatically suspends the production of the records. CCP §1985.3(g) ¶3 (consumer records), §1985.6(f)(3) (employee records).

(b) Motion for protective order. A party, nonparty witness, or consumer who objects to the production of personal records can move for a protective order. See "Motion for Protective Order," ch. 9-B, p. 1024. A motion for a protective order does not automatically suspend the production of personal records. For that reason, a motion for a protective order should include a request to stay the deposition until the court rules on the motion. *See* CCP §2025.270(d).

3. When to object.

(1) Deadline for written objections. A nonparty must serve written objections before the date set for production of the personal records. CCP §1985.3(g) ¶2 (consumer records), §1985.6(f)(2) (employee records). If the objections are not received before the date for production, the records may be produced and made available to all the parties. Judicial Council Forms, form SUBP-025, Item 2(b).

(2) Deadline for motion to quash. A party consumer must make a motion to quash a subpoena that seeks the party's personal records at least five days before the date set for production of the records. CCP §1985.3(g) ¶1 (consumer records), §1985.6(f)(1) (employee records). One court has stated that §1985.3(g) is not jurisdictional, and the trial court can consider a motion to quash filed after the date for production specified in the subpoena. ***Slagle v. Superior Ct.*** (1st Dist.1989) 211 Cal.App.3d 1309, 1312-13.

(3) Deadline for motion for protective order. A party, nonparty witness, or consumer must "promptly move" for a motion for protective order. *See* CCP §2025.420(a) (depositions). Although there is no specific deadline for seeking a protective order, the party, witness, or consumer should probably make the motion within the time allowed for a motion to quash—that is, at least five days before the date set for production of the records. *Cf. id.* §1985.3(g) ¶1 (motion to quash subpoena for consumer records), §1985.6(f)(1) (motion to quash subpoena for employee records).

4. How to respond to objections. To secure the records after being served with written objections, the subpoenaing party must make a motion to enforce the subpoena. CCP §1985.3(g) ¶4 (consumer records), §1985.6(f)(4) (employee records); *CEB Procedure During Trial*, §4.23. See "Motion to Enforce Deposition Subpoena for Personal Records," ch. 9-G, p. 1078. The motion to enforce must be made within 20 days after the subpoenaing party is served with the written objections. See "Deadline to file & serve," ch. 9-G, §4.2.2, p. 1079. If objections are raised in a motion to quash, the subpoenaing party should make its enforcement arguments in its opposition papers.

§12.2 Complying with subpoena for personal records. The procedure for complying with the subpoena depends on the type of subpoena issued.

1. Deposition subpoenas.

(1) For the procedures to comply with a deposition subpoena for appearance and production, see "Complying with subpoena for appearance & production," ch. 8-B, §6.1.2, p. 968.

(2) For the procedures to comply with a deposition subpoena for business records, see "Complying with business-records subpoena," ch. 8-B, §6.1.4, p. 968.

2. Trial subpoenas.

(1) For the procedures to comply with a trial subpoena for appearance and production, see "Complying with subpoena for appearance & production," ch. 8-C, §5.1.2, p. 976.

(2) For the procedures to comply with a trial subpoena for production only, see "Complying with subpoena for production of documents," ch. 8-C, §5.1.3, p. 976.

8-10. DEADLINES TO OBJECT & COMPLY WITH SUBPOENA FOR PERSONAL RECORDS

		Deadline to object	Deadline to comply
1	Deposition subpoena for NPD to attend and produce personal records of consumer (PC or NPC). See ch. 8-B, §4, p. 962.	• Party or NPD can object to subpoena before or during deposition. • PC can move to quash at least 5 days before deposition. • NPD or NPC can move to quash reasonable time before deposition. • Party, NPD, or NPC can move for protective order before, during, or after deposition. • NPC can serve written objections before deposition, which stays deposition.	Attend deposition on date set by DP, which must be at least 25 days after consumer served with notice of privacy rights.
2	Deposition subpoena for NPD to produce business records that include personal records of consumer (PC or NPC). See ch. 8-B, §5, p. 963.	• Party or NPD can object to subpoena before or during deposition. • Party, NPD, or NPC can move to quash reasonable time before deposition. • Party, NPD, or NPC can move for protective order before, during, or after deposition. • NPC can serve written objections before deposition, which stays deposition.	Produce records on date set by DP, which must be at least 20 days after consumer served with notice of privacy rights.

DP = discovering party
NPC = nonparty consumer
NPD = nonparty deponent
Party = includes any party in suit, even responding party
PC = party consumer
The deadlines assume that the notice of privacy rights was personally served.

CHALLENGING/ENFORCING

E. CHALLENGING & ENFORCING SUBPOENAS

§1. GENERAL

§1.1 Purpose. The purpose of challenging a subpoena is to prevent compliance with the subpoena until the court rules on the objections and to preserve the objections. The purpose of enforcing a subpoena is to obtain the discovery sought by the subpoena by asking the court to require the subpoenaed witness to attend, testify, and produce evidence.

§1.2 Primary authority. CCP §§1209-1219, 1985.3, 1985.4, 1985.6, 1987, 1987.1, 1991-1993, 2019.030, 2020.240, 2023.010-2023.030, 2025.240, 2025.410.

§1.3 Secondary authority. The following secondary sources are cited as authority in this subchapter:

- *California Civil Discovery Practice* (CEB Online ed. 2014) (referred to as *CEB Discovery Practice*).
- *California Trial Practice: Civil Procedure During Trial* (CEB Online ed. 2014) (referred to as *CEB Procedure During Trial*).
- Sink, *California Subpoena Handbook* (2014-15) (referred to as Sink, *Subpoena Handbook*).

§2. CHALLENGING SUBPOENAS

§2.1 Objections to subpoenas. There are many procedural and substantive objections that can be made to deposition and trial subpoenas. The objections outlined here can be asserted in a motion to quash, in a motion for a protective order, or in written objections (when written objections to subpoenas are permitted). See "Procedure to challenge subpoenas," §2.2, p. 998.

1. Objections to defective procedure.

(1) Subpoenas generally. Procedural defects in a deposition or trial subpoena can be challenged by any of the following objections:

(a) Time for compliance. The date and time for compliance with the subpoena do not comply with the rules in the Code of Civil Procedure. See "When to Schedule Compliance," ch. 8-A, §7, p. 944.

(b) Place for compliance. The subpoena identified a place for compliance that does not comply with the rules in the Code of Civil Procedure. See "Where to Schedule Compliance," ch. 8-A, §8, p. 946.

(c) Service. The subpoena was not properly served on the witness, as required by the Code of Civil Procedure. *See* ***Far W. S&L Ass'n v. McLaughlin*** (2d Dist.1988) 201 Cal.App.3d 67, 71. See "How to Serve Subpoenas," ch. 8-A, §9, p. 947.

(d) Witness fees. The witness fees and costs for the subpoenaed witness were not tendered or paid, as required by the Code of Civil Procedure. See "How to Pay Witness Fees," ch. 8-A, §10, p. 951.

(e) Description of things. The description of subpoenaed things was inadequate. See "Proper description," ch. 8-A, §5.2, p. 939.

(f) Unauthorized request. The subpoena requires production of something not permitted by the subpoena. For example, a business-records subpoena cannot be used to require a nonparty to produce a product of the business being subpoenaed. *E.g.*, ***Urban Pac. Equities Corp. v. Superior Ct.*** (2d Dist.1997) 59 Cal.App.4th 688, 693 (business-records subpoena could not be used to obtain deposition transcripts from court-reporting service because depositions were products, not records).

(g) Unqualified deposition officer. The deposition officer is not qualified. CCP §2020.420 (deposition officer for business-records subpoena), §2025.320(e) (deposition officer for oral deposition); *see also id.* §2028.070(d) (court can order deposition to be taken before officer other than one named in deposition notice).

(h) Defective good-cause declaration for trial subpoena. The good-cause declaration (or affidavit) for the trial subpoena does not comply with CCP §1985(b) because (1) it does not provide a sufficient description of the records sought, (2) it does not provide sufficient good cause for production, or (3) it does not show materiality of the evidence. *See* CCP §1985(b); *see, e.g.*, ***Lee v. Superior Ct.*** (4th Dist.2009) 177 Cal.App.4th 1108, 1129 (declaration in support of good cause did not show sufficient materiality). See "Good-cause declaration," ch. 8-C, §4.2, p. 974.

(2) Subpoenas for personal records. When personal records of a consumer or employee are sought by a deposition or trial subpoena, the following procedural objections are also appropriate:

(a) Notice of privacy rights. The subpoenaing party did not provide the consumer with the notice of privacy rights. CCP §1985.3(e) (consumer), §1985.4 (state or local-agency employee), §1985.6(e) (employee); *see* ***Sasson v. Katash*** (2d Dist.1983) 146 Cal.App.3d 119, 125. If the subpoenaing party did not follow the proper procedures for obtaining personal records under §1985.3 or 1985.6, that alone is a sufficient reason for the witness to refuse to produce the records. CCP §1985.3(k) (consumer), §1985.6(j) (employee).

(b) Subpoena. The subpoenaing party did not serve the consumer with a copy of the subpoena or the good-cause affidavit (for a trial subpoena). CCP §1985(b) (subpoena), §1985.3(b) (consumer), §1985.4 (state or local-agency employee), §1985.6(b) (employee).

(c) POS or release. The subpoenaing party did not serve the witness with either (1) proof that the notice of privacy rights was served on the consumer (POS) or (2) the consumer's written consent to release the records. CCP §1985.3(c) (consumer), §1985.4 (state or local-agency employee), §1985.6(c) (employee). See "When required," ch. 8-D, §9.4.1, p. 989.

(d) Telephone records. The subpoenaing party did not provide the witness of the public-utility telephone corporation with the consumer's written authorization for the release of the consumer's telephone records. CCP §1985.3(f). A telephone corporation cannot produce records when it is served with only the POS of the notice of privacy rights; the subpoenaing party must provide a written consent. *See id.* See "Telephone corporations," ch. 8-D, §7.1.5, p. 982.

2. **Objections to discovery.**

(1) Subpoenas generally. The scope of a deposition or trial subpoena can be challenged by an objection that the subpoena requests information that violates the Evidence Code or the California Discovery Act. Many of the same objections that can be asserted against discovery requests can be asserted against subpoenas, even against subpoenas for a trial or hearing. See "Grounds for Discovery Objections," ch. 7-A, §11, p. 765. For example, a subpoenaed witness can object on the following grounds:

(a) Outside scope of discovery. The subpoena seeks information outside the scope of discovery. *See, e.g.*, ***Catholic Mut. Relief Soc'y v. Superior Ct.*** (2007) 42 Cal.4th 358, 365 (motion to quash deposition subpoena because documents requested were outside scope of discovery); *cf.* ***Cadiz Land Co. v. Rail Cycle, L.P.*** (4th Dist.2000) 83 Cal.App.4th 74, 122-23 (motion to quash deposition notice because deposition would not lead to admissible evidence). See "Not within scope of discovery," ch. 7-A, §11.1.1, p. 765.

(b) Not relevant. The subpoena seeks information that is not relevant to the issues in the case. *See, e.g.*, ***Slagle v. Superior Ct.*** (1st Dist.1989) 211 Cal.App.3d 1309, 1314-15 (motion to quash trial subpoena because medical records were not relevant was properly overruled). See "Not relevant to subject matter," ch. 7-A, §11.1.1(1), p. 765.

(c) Unreasonable demands. The subpoena makes unreasonable or oppressive demands for information. *See* CCP §1987.1(a); Sink, *Subpoena Handbook*, §11.5[A]; *see, e.g.*, ***McClatchy Newspapers v. Superior Ct.*** (1945) 26 Cal.2d 386, 391 (motion to quash deposition subpoenas because they were unreasonable and oppressive). See "Oppressive," ch. 7-A, §11.1.7, p. 766.

(2) Objections based on privacy or privilege. When personal records or privileged information is sought by a deposition or trial subpoena, the following substantive objections are appropriate:

(a) Privacy rights. The disclosure of the records will violate the consumer's constitutional right to privacy. *See* Cal. Const., art. I, §1; *see, e.g.*, ***Manela v. Superior Ct.*** (2d Dist.2009) 177 Cal.App.4th 1139, 1150-51 (motion to quash subpoena to party's doctor because of privacy rights); ***Bihun v. AT&T Info. Sys.*** (2d Dist.1993) 13 Cal.App.4th 976, 991 (D objected, in bad faith, to trial subpoena on ground that production of personnel file would violate D's right to privacy), *disapproved on other grounds*, ***Lakin v. Watkins Associated Indus.*** (1993) 6 Cal.4th 644. See "Personal Privileges," ch. 6-F, p. 681; "Constitutional right to privacy," ch. 7-A, §11.1.10(2), p. 767.

(b) Privilege. The disclosure of the records will violate a privilege of the consumer, the witness, or a person with whom the witness has a relationship that requires the witness to assert the privilege on the person's behalf. *See, e.g.*, ***Monarch Healthcare v. Superior Ct.*** (4th Dist.2000) 78 Cal.App.4th 1282, 1290 (objections to subpoena for business records based on trade-secret privilege); *see also* Sink, *Subpoena Handbook*, §6:2[H][3], [4] (checklist of possible privilege objections by consumer and witness). For example, an attorney must assert the attorney-client privilege on behalf of a client. For a discussion of privileges, see "Discovery & Privileges," ch. 6, p. 599.

(c) Right of association. The disclosure will violate the witness's First Amendment right of association for members of its organization. *See* Sink, *Subpoena Handbook*, §6:2[H][4]; *see also* Cal. Const., art. I, §3(a) (right of association). For example, a political organization can object when a subpoena seeks information about the organization's members.

(d) Personal information in free-speech action. A person whose personally identifying information (e.g., name, home and e-mail address, telephone number, Social Security number, children's names) has been subpoenaed from an Internet service provider in connection with a suit involving that person's exercise of free-speech rights can make a motion to quash. CCP §1987.1(b)(5). See "Free-speech action," ch. 7-A, §11.1.10(4), p. 767; "Personal information subpoenaed in free-speech case," ch. 9-C, §3.1.3(2)(d)[3], p. 1041.

(3) Subpoenas for ESI. A number of objections can be raised to a deposition subpoena that requires the production of electronically stored information (ESI). *See* CCP §§1985.8, 2020.220. See "ESI-specific objections," ch. 7-H, §9.2, p. 889.

CHALLENGING/ENFORCING

NOTE

The Stored Communications Act (SCA), which limits the ability of Internet service providers and other electronic-communications services to disclose customer information, might give third-party websites like Facebook a basis for objecting to subpoenas seeking the contents of a party's electronically stored communications. See 18 U.S.C. §§2701-2712; ***Juror Number One v. Superior Ct.*** *(3d Dist.2012) 206 Cal.App.4th 854, 860, 864. However, the SCA does not protect a party from demands to produce its own communications that are stored by such websites. See* ***Juror Number One****, 206 Cal.App.4th at 864-65.*

§2.2 Procedure to challenge subpoenas. There are three ways to challenge subpoenas: (1) motion to quash, (2) motion for a protective order, and (3) written objections.

1. Motion to quash. See "Motion to Quash Depositions," ch. 9-C, p. 1038. The motion to quash should ask for a stay to delay production until the court rules on the motion. When a motion to quash involves personal records, the stay is automatic. See "Note," ch. 9-C, §3.1.3(2)(b), p. 1040.

2. Motion for protective order. See "Motion for Protective Order," ch. 9-B, p. 1024.

3. Written objections. Written objections to a business-records subpoena or a subpoena for personal records achieve the same results as a motion to quash: (1) they preserve objections to the subpoena and (2) they relieve the witness from complying with the subpoena until the court rules on the objections. In addition, the objections force the subpoenaing party to make a motion to compel production.

(1) Written objections to business-records subpoena. A nonparty whose business records are sought by a business-records subpoena can serve written objections to the subpoena or wait until the date scheduled for production to object on the grounds that the information sought is privileged or protected work product. *See* CCP §2025.460(a); *see, e.g.*, ***Monarch Healthcare v. Superior Ct.*** (4th Dist.2000) 78 Cal.App.4th 1282, 1290 (nonparty produced some records sought by business-records subpoena and objected at time of deposition to production of other records on trade-secret and privacy grounds). It is not clear whether the objections must be in writing or can be made orally, but the better practice is to make the objections in writing. *See, e.g.*, ***Unzipped Apparel, LLC v. Bader*** (2d Dist.2007) 156 Cal.App.4th 123, 128 (nonparties served subpoenaing party with objections at time of deposition); ***Monarch Healthcare***, 78 Cal.App.4th at 1285 (transcript of trial judge's comments suggested nonparty sent letter objecting to producing some documents). If the nonparty objects to the business-records subpoena, the subpoenaing party has 60 days after it receives the objections to file a motion to compel. *See* CCP §2025.480(b); ***Unzipped Apparel***, 156 Cal.App.4th at 136.

(2) Written objections to subpoena for personal records. A nonparty whose consumer, governmental, or employee records are sought by a subpoena can serve written objections to the subpoena. See "Serve written objections," ch. 8-D, §12.1.2(1), p. 993.

4. Oral objections. A witness subpoenaed to attend a deposition or a trial (with or without production of documents) can attend, make oral objections, and refuse to answer or produce, but risks being held in contempt of court. *See* CCP §2020.240 (nonparty can be held in contempt for refusing to obey subpoena); *CEB Discovery Practice*, §6.69 (nonparty can be held in contempt for refusing to obey deposition subpoena); *CEB Procedure During Trial*, §4.49 (witness can be held in contempt for refusing to produce at trial), §16.126 (witness can be held in contempt for refusing to answer at trial). See "Contempt," §3.4, p. 999.

§3. ENFORCING SUBPOENAS

If a witness refuses to comply with a subpoena, the subpoenaing party has several options for enforcing the subpoena.

§3.1 Motion to compel compliance. If a witness refuses to answer questions or produce documents or things in response to a deposition subpoena, the subpoenaing party can file a motion to compel. CCP §2025.480(a). The motion to compel must be made within 60 days after the transcription of the deposition record. *Id.* §2025.480(b). See "Motion to Compel Depositions," ch. 9-D, p. 1046.

§3.2 Motion to enforce subpoena for personal records. If a nonparty consumer serves written objections to a subpoena for personal records, the subpoenaing party can file a motion to enforce. CCP §1985.3(g) ¶4 (consumer), §1985.6(f)(4) (employee). See "Motion to Enforce Deposition Subpoena for Personal Records," ch. 9-G, p. 1078.

§3.3 Forfeiture & damages. If a witness does not appear as required by a subpoena, the subpoenaing party can recover $500 plus any damages sustained by that person's nonappearance. CCP §1992; *see id.* §2020.240 (deposition subpoenas). The subpoenaing party must bring a civil action to recover these amounts. *Id.* §1992; ***New York Times Co. v. Superior Ct.*** (1990) 51 Cal.3d 453, 464. Before the subpoenaing party can recover the $500 fine and damages, it must show that it has suffered some actual harm from the nonappearance. ***Church v. Payne*** (1939) 35 Cal.App.2d 752, 756. See "Misuse of discovery," ch. 9-A, §5.2.1, p. 1017.

§3.4 Contempt. A witness can be punished by contempt for disobeying a subpoena. CCP §1209(a)(10). The witness can be punished by either a fine of up to $1,000, imprisonment for up to five days, or both. *Id.* §1218(a). Generally, if the contemptuous conduct involves the failure to perform an act that is within the person's power to perform, the person can be imprisoned until she has performed it. *Id.* §1219(a); ***Morelli v. Superior Ct.*** (1969) 1 Cal.3d 328, 332 & n.3. The person can also be ordered to pay the subpoenaing party's reasonable attorney fees and costs associated with the contempt proceeding. CCP §1218(a). See "Contempt sanctions," ch. 9-A, §4.3, p. 1007.

1. Deposition subpoena. Disobeying a subpoena that requires a nonparty's attendance at a deposition is punishable by contempt under CCP §2023.030(e). CCP §1991.1; *see id.* §§2020.240, 2023.030(e); *CEB Discovery Practice*, §15.105. There is no need to show that the nonparty violated a court order; simply showing that the witness refused to comply with the subpoena is sufficient for a finding of contempt. CCP §1991.1; *CEB Discovery Practice*, §15.102.

NOTE

The contempt provisions in CCP §1991 do not apply to acts or omissions occurring during depositions. CCP §1991.2.

---

2. Trial subpoena.

(1) Appearance in court. When a subpoena requires the witness (party or nonparty) to appear in court and the witness does not appear, the court can punish the witness by contempt. CCP §1991; *see CEB Procedure During Trial*, §4.52; *see also* CCP §1211(a) (when contempt is committed in presence of court, it may be punished immediately).

(2) Appearance outside court. When a subpoena requires an appearance before an officer or commissioner outside court, contempt can be imposed as follows:

(a) Report to subpoenaing court. When a subpoena requires an appearance before an officer or commissioner outside court, that officer or commissioner has a duty to report any disobedience by the witness to the court that issued the subpoena. CCP §1991; *see also id.* §1211(a) (when contempt is not committed in presence of court, affidavit or statement describing contempt must be presented). Contempt can be imposed on a disobedient witness only after the witness violates a court order to comply with the subpoena. *Id.* §1991.

(b) Optional witness notification. The subpoenaing party can ask the officer or commissioner to notify the witness that on a certain date (not less than 5 days or more than 20 days from the date of disobedience) it will report the disobedience to the court and ask the court to issue an order requiring compliance with the subpoena and the witness's attendance at a hearing on that order. CCP §1991. If the witness does not comply with the order or does not appear at the hearing, the court can then punish the witness by contempt. *See id.*

§3.5 Arrest. Instead of contempt, the court can issue a warrant for the arrest of a witness who does not obey a subpoena. CCP §1993(a)(1). Before issuing the warrant, the court must issue a "failure to appear" notice informing the witness that a warrant can be issued for her arrest. *Id.* §1993(a)(2). This notice requirement can be omitted after a showing that the witness is material to the case and that urgency requires her immediate appearance. *Id.*

CHAPTER 9. RESOLVING DISCOVERY DISPUTES
TABLE OF CONTENTS

TABLE OF CONTENTS

9. RESOLVING DISCOVERY DISPUTES

This chapter covers the motions used to resolve discovery disputes and ensure compliance with the Civil Discovery Act. For a discussion of discovery motions specific to a particular discovery method, see "Methods of Discovery," ch. 7, p. 733.

A. DISCOVERY SANCTIONS

§1. GENERAL

§1.1 Purpose. The sanctions provisions in the Civil Discovery Act (CDA) are designed to (1) encourage parties and their attorneys to cooperate in discovery and (2) prevent unnecessary court proceedings. Donovan, *The Sanction Provision of the New California Civil Discovery Act, Section 2023: Will It Make a Difference or Is It Just Another "Paper Tiger"?*, 15 Pepp. L. Rev. 401, 410 (1988); *see* ***Ruvalcaba v. Government Empls. Ins.*** (2d Dist.1990) 222 Cal.App.3d 1579, 1581 (sanctions provisions in CDA clearly indicate preference for voluntary compliance with discovery). Sanctions are not intended as a weapon for punishment, forfeiture, or the avoidance of a trial on the merits. ***Pratt v. Union Pac. R.R.*** (3d Dist.2008) 168 Cal.App.4th 165, 183; ***Parker v. Wolters Kluwer U.S., Inc.*** (2d Dist.2007) 149 Cal.App.4th 285, 301; *see* ***Doppes v. Bentley Motors, Inc.*** (4th Dist.2009) 174 Cal.App.4th 967, 992 (court cannot impose discovery sanctions as punishment).

§1.2 Primary authority. CCP §§2023.010-2023.040.

§1.3 Secondary authority. The following secondary sources are cited as authority in this subchapter:

- *California Civil Discovery Practice* (CEB Online ed. 2014) (referred to as *CEB Discovery Practice*).
- Donovan, *The Sanction Provision of the New California Civil Discovery Act, Section 2023: Will It Make a Difference or Is It Just Another "Paper Tiger"?*, 15 Pepp. L. Rev. 401 (1988).
- Mares, *The California Civil Discovery Act of 1986: Discovery the New-Fashioned Way!*, 18 Sw. U. L. Rev. 233 (1989) (referred to as Mares, *The California Civil Discovery Act of 1986*).
- Weil & Brown, *California Practice Guide: Civil Procedure Before Trial* (CD-ROM ed. 2014) (referred to as Weil, *Civil Procedure Before Trial*).
- Witkin, *California Procedure* (5th ed. 2008 & Supp.2014) (referred to as Witkin, *Cal. Procedure*).

§2. REQUESTING SANCTIONS

Discovery sanctions can be requested as part of a discovery motion (including opposition papers to a motion) or in a separate motion for sanctions. *CEB Discovery Practice*, §15.108. For a general discussion of motion practice, see "Law & Motion Practice," ch. 1-D, p. 26.

§2.1 Discovery motion or opposition papers. A party can request discovery sanctions as part of a discovery motion or in opposition papers to a discovery motion. *See, e.g.*, CCP §2030.290(c) (court must impose sanctions against any party, person, or attorney who unsuccessfully makes or opposes motion to compel response to interrogatories). For example, sanctions can be sought in a motion to compel discovery. Weil, *Civil Procedure Before Trial*, ¶8:865. For efficiency, most requests for discovery sanctions are made as part of a discovery motion or in the opposition papers. *See id.* ¶8:865.1.

§2.2 Separate sanctions motion. A party can make a motion for discovery sanctions separately from a discovery motion. ***London v. Dri-Honing Corp.*** (3d Dist.2004) 117 Cal.App.4th 999, 1008; Weil, *Civil Procedure Before Trial*, ¶8:865. A separate motion for sanctions is appropriate when sanctions are sought without any other discovery relief. For example, a separate sanctions motion can be made against a party who noticed a deposition but did not show up for it. *See* CCP §2025.430. See "Did not attend," §5.1.1(4)(a), p. 1013. A separate sanctions motion is also appropriate when discovery misuse becomes known after the time for filing a discovery motion, such as after a verdict. *See, e.g.*, ***Sherman v. Kinetic Concepts, Inc.*** (4th Dist.1998) 67 Cal.App.4th 1152, 1163 (court had jurisdiction to

DISCOVERY SANCTIONS

consider motion for sanctions made after verdict, which was when discovery misuse was discovered). For a list of sanctions that are typically requested by a separate motion, see "Discovery Sanctions by Motions," chart 9-1, p. 1008.

§3. NOTICE REQUIREMENT

Discovery sanctions can be granted only after the person to be sanctioned is given notice and an opportunity to be heard. CCP §2023.030; ***Parker v. Wolters Kluwer U.S., Inc.*** (2d Dist.2007) 149 Cal.App.4th 285, 296; *e.g.*, ***Sole Energy Co. v. Hodges*** (4th Dist.2005) 128 Cal.App.4th 199, 207 (sanctions against D violated due process when D had no notice that sanctions might be imposed; D was not named in Ps' motion to compel requesting sanctions); *see* Mares, *The California Civil Discovery Act of 1986*, 18 Sw. U. L. Rev. at 247 (notice gives attorney one last chance to comply). A court cannot impose sanctions without notice even when it has the authority to issue an ex parte order on the underlying matter. *Cf.* ***O'Brien v. Cseh*** (2d Dist.1983) 148 Cal.App.3d 957, 961 (court could not impose sanctions requested in ex parte application to set date for arbitration). Discovery sanctions imposed ex parte violate due process. ***Sole Energy***, 128 Cal.App.4th at 208. A person can waive the right to notice, however, by voluntarily appearing at the ex parte hearing and opposing sanctions on the merits. ***Alliance Bank v. Murray*** (2d Dist.1984) 161 Cal.App.3d 1, 7.

§3.1 Required information. The party seeking sanctions must do the following:

1. **Identify person to be sanctioned.** The requesting party must identify the person against whom sanctions are sought (e.g., a party, a party's attorney, a nonparty). CCP §2023.040. This information must be included in the notice of motion or in the opposition papers. *See id.* (notice of motion must include person against whom sanctions are sought); *see, e.g.*, ***Sole Energy Co. v. Hodges*** (4th Dist.2005) 128 Cal.App.4th 199, 207 (granting terminating sanctions against co-D was error when co-D was not named in any motion to compel or discovery order).

2. **Specify type of sanctions.** The requesting party must identify the type of sanctions sought (e.g., monetary sanctions, terminating sanctions). CCP §2023.040. See "Types of Discovery Sanctions," §4, this page. This information must be included in the notice of motion or in the opposition papers. *See* CCP §2023.040 (notice of motion must specify type of sanction sought). The court cannot impose harsher sanctions than those identified in the notice. *See, e.g.*, ***Sole Energy***, 128 Cal.App.4th at 208 (Ds were given notice of monetary and unspecified sanctions but not terminating sanctions; imposition of terminating sanctions violated due process).

3. **Provide authority for sanctions.** The requesting party must support the request with a memorandum of points and authorities that identifies the legal authority for the sanctions. *See* CCP §2023.040. See "Grounds for Discovery Sanctions," §5, p. 1008. If the party is seeking monetary sanctions, the memorandum must be accompanied by a declaration stating facts supporting the amount of sanctions sought. CCP §2023.040.

§3.2 Sanctions awarded without notice. Discovery sanctions imposed without notice on the person to be sanctioned are either voidable or void, depending on whether the court had jurisdiction over the subject matter and the parties.

1. **Court had jurisdiction.** If the court had jurisdiction over the subject matter and the parties, discovery sanctions imposed without notice are valid but voidable. *E.g.*, ***Johnson v. E-Z Ins. Brokerage, Inc.*** (4th Dist.2009) 175 Cal.App.4th 86, 98 (12-year-old default judgment imposed ex parte as terminating sanction was voidable because court had fundamental jurisdiction when default judgment was entered); *cf.* ***Lee v. An*** (2d Dist.2008) 168 Cal.App.4th 558, 566 (default judgment imposed as sanctions for failure to comply with local rules was voidable because court had jurisdiction over party and questions presented). A voidable sanctions order cannot be challenged after it becomes final. *See* ***Johnson***, 175 Cal.App.4th at 98-99.

2. **Court did not have jurisdiction.** If the court did not have jurisdiction over the subject matter or the parties, discovery sanctions imposed without notice are void. *See* ***Johnson***, 175 Cal.App.4th at 98. A void sanctions order can be challenged at any time, even after it becomes final. *See id.* at 98-99.

§4. TYPES OF DISCOVERY SANCTIONS

CCP §2023.030 describes the different types of sanctions that can be imposed for misuse of the discovery process.

§4.1 Monetary sanctions. Monetary sanctions require the reimbursement of expenses incurred as a result of the conduct at issue. CCP §2023.030(a).

1. Against whom. The court can impose monetary sanctions on any person (party or nonparty) who misuses the discovery process, the attorney who advises the conduct, or both. CCP §2023.030(a).

CAUTION

If monetary sanctions are sought against an attorney, the attorney has the burden to show that she did not advise the discovery misuse. ***Ghanooni v. Super Shuttle*** *(2d Dist.1993) 20 Cal.App.4th 256, 261;* ***Corns v. Miller*** *(4th Dist.1986) 181 Cal.App.3d 195, 200-01. Interestingly, neither opinion addresses the potential conflict when sanctions are sought against both a party and the party's attorney.*

---

2. Mandatory. The court's award of monetary sanctions under the CDA—whether for specific or general misuses of the discovery process—is mandatory unless the court finds that (1) the person subject to the sanctions acted with substantial justification or (2) other circumstances make the imposition of the sanctions unjust. CCP §2023.030(a) (general misuse of discovery process); ***California Shellfish, Inc. v. United Shellfish Co.*** (1st Dist.1997) 56 Cal.App.4th 16, 25 (discussing former §2025(g), now §2025.410(d); motion to quash deposition notice); *CEB Discovery Practice*, §7.121. For a discussion of when monetary sanctions are specifically and generally authorized, see "Grounds for Discovery Sanctions," §5, p. 1008. None of the CDA provisions authorizing monetary sanctions require proof of a person's intent to misuse the discovery process. *See* ***Clement v. Alegre*** (1st Dist.2009) 177 Cal.App.4th 1277, 1286; ***Newland v. Superior Ct.*** (2d Dist.1995) 40 Cal.App.4th 608, 615; ***Kohan v. Cohan*** (2d Dist.1991) 229 Cal.App.3d 967, 971. Only when the party seeking sanctions meets its burden of proof on the underlying motion will the burden of proving substantial justification or other circumstances shift to the person seeking to avoid sanctions. ***Doe v. U.S. Swimming, Inc.*** (6th Dist.2011) 200 Cal.App.4th 1424, 1436.

(1) Substantial justification. "Substantial justification" means the person subject to sanctions had reasonably believed that her conduct (e.g., making an objection to discovery and opposing a later motion to compel) was well grounded in both law and fact. *See* ***Diepenbrock v. Brown*** (1st Dist.2012) 208 Cal.App.4th 743, 747; ***Doe***, 200 Cal.App.4th at 1434; Weil, *Civil Procedure Before Trial*, ¶8:846; *see, e.g.*, ***Clement***, 177 Cal.App.4th at 1286-87 (Ps were not substantially justified in objecting to definition of term in interrogatories when Ps clearly understood definition); ***Foothill Props. v. Lyon/Copley Corona Assocs.*** (4th Dist.1996) 46 Cal.App.4th 1542, 1558 (D's refusal to produce documents until court ruled on its pending motion for protective order was substantially justified).

(2) Other circumstances. "Other circumstances" includes anything that would make the imposition of sanctions unjust in that particular case. CCP §2023.030(a). For example, the court may determine that the imposition of monetary sanctions against an impoverished person would be unjust. Weil, *Civil Procedure Before Trial*, ¶8:847.

3. Amount. The request for monetary sanctions must state the amount sought. *See* CCP §2023.040. The amount that can be sought is limited to the reasonable expenses, including attorney fees, actually incurred as a result of the misconduct. *Id.* §2023.030(a); *see, e.g.*, ***In re Marriage of Niklas*** (2d Dist.1989) 211 Cal.App.3d 28, 37-38 (movant could not request fees and costs incurred before incident at issue). The amount sought must be supported by facts stated in a declaration. CCP §2023.040; *see, e.g.*, ***In re Marriage of Niklas***, 211 Cal.App.3d at 37-38 (entries such as "research," "review," and "letter" were insufficiently descriptive). For example, a declaration supporting a motion for monetary sanctions should identify the dates the attorney worked on the discovery dispute, the amount of time spent attempting to meet and confer about the dispute and preparing the discovery motion or opposition papers, details showing the services performed on each date and the reasons for any expenses, the attorney's hourly rate, the estimated time it will take to travel to and attend the motion hearing, and any other reasonable costs incurred.

§4.2 Case sanctions. Case sanctions are nonmonetary sanctions that affect the lawsuit. *See* CCP §2023.030(b)-(d).

1. Against whom. Case sanctions can be imposed only on parties who misuse the discovery process (not nonparties or attorneys). *See* CCP §2023.030(b)-(d).

2. Types. Case sanctions include issue sanctions, evidence sanctions, and terminating sanctions.

(1) Issue sanctions. Issue sanctions either (1) designate certain facts as established in favor of a party adversely affected by the misuse of the discovery process or (2) prohibit a party who misused the discovery process from supporting or opposing certain claims or defenses. CCP §2023.030(b); ***New Albertsons, Inc. v. Superior Ct.*** (2d Dist.2008) 168 Cal.App.4th 1403, 1422; *CEB Discovery Practice*, §15.97.

(2) Evidence sanctions. Evidence sanctions prohibit a party who misused the discovery process from introducing designated matters into evidence. CCP §2023.030(c); ***New Albertsons***, 168 Cal.App.4th at 1422; *CEB Discovery Practice*, §15.98; *see, e.g.*, CCP §2034.300 (party's expert can be excluded from testifying at trial if party did not produce proper expert information); ***In re Marriage of Falcone & Fyke*** (6th Dist.2012) 203 Cal.App.4th 964, 977 (dicta; certain evidence offered by party during trial was excluded as discovery sanction because party had willfully failed to comply with discovery).

(3) Terminating sanctions. Terminating sanctions are drastic sanctions that courts are reluctant to impose unless it is clear that the party to be sanctioned left no viable alternative. ***Mileikowsky v. Tenet Healthsystem*** (2d Dist.2005) 128 Cal.App.4th 531, 564, *disapproved on other grounds*, ***Mileikowsky v. West Hills Hosp. & Med. Ctr.*** (2009) 45 Cal.4th 1259. The court should consider the totality of the circumstances before ordering terminating sanctions, including (1) whether the conduct of the party was willful, (2) the detriment to the party propounding discovery, and (3) the number of formal and informal attempts to obtain the discovery. ***Los Defensores, Inc. v. Gomez*** (2d Dist.2014) 223 Cal.App.4th 377, 390. If terminating sanctions are warranted, the court can enter any of the following orders:

(a) An order striking all or parts of the pleadings. CCP §2023.030(d)(1); ***Doppes v. Bentley Motors, Inc.*** (4th Dist.2009) 174 Cal.App.4th 967, 992; *see, e.g.*, ***Van Sickle v. Gilbert*** (3d Dist.2011) 196 Cal.App.4th 1495, 1519 (trial court struck D's answer).

(b) An order staying proceedings until a party obeys a discovery order. CCP §2023.030(d)(2); ***Doppes***, 174 Cal.App.4th at 992.

(c) An order dismissing all or part of a party's action. CCP §2023.030(d)(3); ***Doppes***, 174 Cal.App.4th at 992.

(d) An order rendering a default judgment against a party. CCP §2023.030(d)(4); ***Los Defensores***, 223 Cal.App.4th at 390; ***Doppes***, 174 Cal.App.4th at 992; *see, e.g.*, ***Electronic Funds Solutions, LLC v. Murphy*** (4th Dist.2005) 134 Cal.App.4th 1161, 1183-84 (Ds' pervasive and consistent misuse of discovery process supported court's dismissal of answer and entry of default judgment). *But see* ***Nickell v. Matlock*** (2d Dist.2012) 206 Cal.App.4th 934, 943-44 (CCP §764.010 prohibits court from rendering judgment by default as discovery sanction in quiet-title actions). See "Default Judgment," ch. 10-A, p. 1089.

3. Discretionary. The court's imposition of case sanctions under the CDA—whether for specific or general misuses of the discovery process—is discretionary. *See, e.g.*, CCP §2025.450(h) (court may impose case sanctions when party fails to obey court order compelling deponent to attend, give testimony, and produce documents at deposition). Under the CDA, case sanctions are generally authorized only for a party's failure to obey a court order, but they have also been awarded in cases involving egregious discovery misuse unrelated to any one specific discovery method.

(1) Failure to obey court order. For a discussion of the types of court orders that must be disobeyed before case sanctions can be awarded, see the relevant discovery method under "Sanctions related to specific discovery provisions," §5.1, p. 1008.

PRACTICE TIP

Do not move for case sanctions based on a party's failure to pay monetary sanctions imposed by a court order. The failure to pay sanctions is not a ground to terminate a party's lawsuit. E.g., ***Newland v. Superior Ct.*** *(2d Dist.1995) 40 Cal.App.4th 608, 615 (party's failure to pay sanctions);* ***Midwife v. Bernal*** *(4th Dist.1988) 203 Cal.App.3d 57, 65 (same);* ***Jones v. Otero*** *(2d Dist.1984) 156 Cal.App.3d 754, 759 (attorney's failure to pay sanctions). Instead, the sanctions order should be enforced through an execution of judgment.* ***Newland****, 40 Cal.App.4th at 615. An order for monetary sanctions has the same force and effect as a money judgment. Id.*

(2) Egregious misuse. Case sanctions can be imposed for egregious misuse of the discovery process, even without the violation of a court order. ***New Albertsons***, 168 Cal.App.4th at 1426. When awarding sanctions for egregious misuse, courts have required proof of conduct that goes beyond simply failing to respond to discovery or even beyond giving evasive answers; the conduct must generally rise to the level of willfulness. *See* ***Saxena v. Goffney*** (4th Dist.2008) 159 Cal.App.4th 316, 334; ***Karlsson v. Ford Motor Co.*** (2d Dist.2006) 140 Cal.App.4th 1202, 1225; *see, e.g.*, ***Pate v. Channel Lumber Co.*** (3d Dist.1997) 51 Cal.App.4th 1447, 1454 (trial court found that D had "played games" with Ps about documents D knew or should have known were relevant to Ps' discovery request). Instead of requiring a party to show willful conduct, courts have imposed case sanctions when any attempt made by the party seeking sanctions to obtain a court order to compel discovery would have been futile. *See, e.g.*, ***Vallbona v. Springer*** (4th Dist.1996) 43 Cal.App.4th 1525, 1548 (issue sanctions were proper because order compelling production would have been futile given D's claim that requested documents had been stolen); ***Do It Urself Moving & Storage, Inc. v. Brown, Leifer, Slatkin & Berns*** (2d Dist.1992) 7 Cal.App.4th 27, 36 (evidence sanctions were proper because order to comply with discovery demand would have been futile given that Ps were unable to produce requested items). The pervasiveness of the conduct (e.g., whether there is a pattern of misuse) will usually determine the type of case sanctions imposed. *See, e.g.*, ***Doppes***, 174 Cal.App.4th at 994 (trial court was compelled to impose terminating sanctions when D's discovery abuses were willful and preceded by history of abuse and less severe sanctions would not produce compliance with discovery rules); ***R.S. Creative, Inc. v. Creative Cotton, Ltd.*** (2d Dist.1999) 75 Cal.App.4th 486, 496 (terminating sanctions against P were proper when P repeatedly violated stipulations and court orders, offered forged document as true, and deliberately destroyed evidence pertinent to exposing forgery).

§4.3 Contempt sanctions. Contempt sanctions impose a fine or imprisonment or require the payment of certain costs incurred by the party initiating the contempt proceeding. *See* CCP §1218(a).

1. Against whom. Contempt sanctions can be imposed on any person (i.e., a party, nonparty, or attorney) who misuses the discovery process. *See* CCP §§1218(a), 2023.030(e).

2. Discretionary. The court's imposition of contempt sanctions for discovery misconduct under the CDA is discretionary. *See* CCP §2023.030(e). But contempt sanctions are rarely imposed for discovery misuse. *CEB Discovery Practice*, §15.102.

3. Types. Contempt sanctions include the following:

(1) Fine. Any person who is found guilty of contempt of court can be ordered to pay the court a fine of up to $1,000. CCP §1218(a).

(2) Imprisonment. Instead of or in addition to a fine, any person who is found guilty of contempt of court can be imprisoned for up to five days. CCP §1218(a). Imposing imprisonment as a discovery sanction is considered overbearing and unnecessary in most cases. ***In re de la Parra*** (4th Dist.1986) 184 Cal.App.3d 139, 145. Imprisonment should be used as a discovery sanction only in extreme situations when the court's dignity is truly compromised and no other penalty is suitable. *Id.*

(3) Attorney fees & costs. In addition to a fine or imprisonment (or both), a party or any agent of a party (e.g., an attorney) who is found guilty of contempt of court for violating a court order can be ordered to pay the party who brought the contempt proceeding its reasonable attorney fees and costs incurred from the contempt proceeding. CCP §1218(a).

§5. GROUNDS FOR DISCOVERY SANCTIONS

To determine the proper statutory basis for sanctions, a party should first consider the sanctions authorized by the CDA for the particular discovery method at issue (e.g., depositions, interrogatories, requests for admission). *See* CCP §2023.030; ***Muller v. Fresno Cmty. Hosp. & Med. Ctr.*** (2d Dist.2009) 172 Cal.App.4th 887, 906; ***New Albertsons, Inc. v. Superior Ct.*** (2d Dist.2008) 168 Cal.App.4th 1403, 1422-23. The provisions governing particular discovery methods limit the types of sanctions a party can obtain. ***New Albertsons***, 168 Cal.App.4th at 1422; ***London v. Dri-Honing Corp.*** (3d Dist.2004) 117 Cal.App.4th 999, 1005. If the sanctions provisions for the particular discovery method do not address the misconduct, or if the sanctions authorized by the provisions would not adequately rectify the misconduct, the party should then explore the possibility of sanctions under the CDA's more general provisions. *See* ***Muller***, 172 Cal.App.4th at 906. See "General sanctions provisions," §5.2, p. 1017.

§5.1 Sanctions related to specific discovery provisions. Chart 9-1, below, lists available discovery sanctions by type of motion and discovery method.

<table>
<tr><th colspan="6">9-1. DISCOVERY SANCTIONS BY MOTIONS</th></tr>
<tr><th colspan="2">Discovery method</th><th>Conduct supporting sanctions</th><th>Who can be sanctioned?</th><th>Type of sanctions</th><th>Ch. 9-A</th></tr>
<tr><th colspan="6">Motion for protective order</th></tr>
<tr><td>1</td><td>Deposition</td><td rowspan="6">Unsuccessfully making or opposing motion for protective order</td><td rowspan="6">Any person</td><td rowspan="6">Mandatory – monetary</td><td>§5.1.1(1)(a), p. 1011</td></tr>
<tr><td>2</td><td>Interrogatories</td><td>§5.1.2(1)(a), p. 1014</td></tr>
<tr><td>3</td><td>Requests for admission</td><td>§5.1.3(1)(a), p. 1015</td></tr>
<tr><td>4</td><td>Demand to produce</td><td>§5.1.4(1)(a), p. 1015</td></tr>
<tr><td>5</td><td>Medical examination</td><td>§5.1.5(1)(a), p. 1016</td></tr>
<tr><td>6</td><td>Demand for expert-witness information</td><td>§5.1.6(1)(a), p. 1017</td></tr>
<tr><th colspan="6">Motion to quash</th></tr>
<tr><td>7</td><td>Deposition notice</td><td>Unsuccessfully making or opposing motion to quash</td><td rowspan="2">Any person</td><td>Mandatory – monetary</td><td>§5.1.1(1)(b), p. 1012</td></tr>
<tr><td rowspan="2">8</td><td rowspan="2">Deposition subpoena</td><td>Making or opposing motion to quash in bad faith or without substantial justification or serving oppressive subpoena</td><td>Discretionary – reasonable expenses</td><td>§5.1.1(2)(a), p. 1012</td></tr>
<tr><td>Improperly seeking personal information in free-speech case</td><td>Subpoenaing party</td><td>Mandatory – reasonable expenses</td><td>§5.1.1(2)(b), p. 1012</td></tr>
</table>

9-1. DISCOVERY SANCTIONS BY MOTIONS (CONTINUED)

	Discovery method	Conduct supporting sanctions	Who can be sanctioned?	Type of sanctions	Ch. 9-A
Motion to compel					
9	Deposition notice	Failing to appear or refusing to be sworn	Party deponent or party-affiliated deponent	Mandatory – monetary	§5.1.1(3)(a)[1], p. 1012
		Unsuccessfully making or opposing motion to compel testimony or production	Any person		§5.1.1(1)(c), p. 1012
10	Deposition subpoena	Unsuccessfully making or opposing motion to compel testimony or production	Any person	Mandatory – monetary	§5.1.1(1)(c), p. 1012
		Failing to appear or refusing to be sworn	Nonparty	Discretionary – contempt	§5.1.1(3)(a)[2], p. 1013
		Refusing to answer or produce			§5.1.1(3)(b), p. 1013
11	Interrogatories	Unsuccessfully making or opposing motion to compel initial response	Any person	Mandatory – monetary	§5.1.2(1)(b), p. 1014
		Unsuccessfully making or opposing motion to compel further response			§5.1.2(1)(c), p. 1014
12	Requests for admission	Unsuccessfully making or opposing motion to compel further response	Any person	Mandatory – monetary	§5.1.3(1)(b), p. 1015
13	Demand to produce	Unsuccessfully making or opposing motion to compel initial response	Any person	Mandatory – monetary	§5.1.4(1)(b), p. 1015
		Unsuccessfully making or opposing motion to compel further response			§5.1.4(1)(c), p. 1015
		Unsuccessfully making or opposing motion to compel production according to compliance statement			§5.1.4(1)(d), p. 1015
14	Medical examination	Unsuccessfully making or opposing motion to compel initial response to demand for exam of personal-injury plaintiff	Any person	Mandatory – monetary	§5.1.5(1)(b), p. 1016
		Unsuccessfully making or opposing motion to compel compliance with demand for exam of personal-injury plaintiff			§5.1.5(1)(c), p. 1016
		Unsuccessfully making or opposing motion to compel delivery of medical reports			§5.1.5(1)(d), p. 1016

9-1. DISCOVERY SANCTIONS BY MOTIONS (CONTINUED)

	Discovery method	Conduct supporting sanctions	Who can be sanctioned?	Type of sanctions	Ch. 9-A
Motion for sanctions					
15	Deposition notice	Noticing party's attorney's failure to attend deposition	Party, attorney, or both	Mandatory – monetary	§5.1.1(4)(a), p. 1013
		Disobeying order to attend, testify, or produce	Party	Discretionary – case, monetary	§5.1.1(5)(a)[1], p. 1013
		Disobeying order to testify or produce		Discretionary – case, monetary, contempt	§5.1.1(5)(a)[2], p. 1013
16	Deposition subpoena	Noticing party's attorney's failure to attend deposition	Party, attorney, or both	Mandatory – monetary	§5.1.1(4)(a), p. 1013
		Noticing party's attorney's failure to serve subpoena on nonparty deponent			§5.1.1(4)(b), p. 1013
		Disobeying order to testify or produce	Nonparty	Discretionary – contempt	§5.1.1(5)(b), p. 1014
17	Interrogatories	Disobeying order to make initial or further response	Party	Discretionary – case, monetary	§5.1.2(2), p. 1014
18	Requests for admission	Disobeying order to make further response	Party	Discretionary – monetary, matters deemed admitted	§5.1.3(3), p. 1015
		Failing to admit RFA and discovering party proved truth or genuineness		Mandatory – reasonable expenses	§5.1.3(4), p. 1015
19	Demand to produce	Disobeying order to make initial or further response or to produce	Party	Discretionary – case, monetary	§5.1.4(2), p. 1016
20	Medical examination	Disobeying order to respond to or comply with demand for exam of personal-injury plaintiff	Personal-injury plaintiff	Discretionary – case, monetary	§5.1.5(2)(a), p. 1016
		Disobeying order for party to submit to medical examination	Party		§5.1.5(2)(b), p. 1016
		Disobeying order for party to produce another person for medical examination			§5.1.5(2)(b), p. 1016
		Disobeying order for delivery of medical reports		Discretionary – case, monetary Mandatory – exclude at trial testimony of examiner whose report was not provided	§5.1.5(2)(c), p. 1016
21	All discovery methods	Misuse of discovery process	Any person	Discretionary – case, monetary, contempt	§5.2.1, p. 1017

9-1. DISCOVERY SANCTIONS BY MOTIONS (CONTINUED)

	Discovery method	Conduct supporting sanctions	Who can be sanctioned?	Type of sanctions	Ch. 9-A
Motion to deem					
22	Interrogatories	Unsuccessfully making or opposing motion to deem interrogatory answers binding	Any person	Mandatory – monetary	§5.1.2(1)(d), p. 1014
23	Requests for admission	Causing other party to make motion to deem matters admitted	Party, attorney, or both		§5.1.3(2), p. 1015
Motion to change discovery procedure					
24	Deposition	Unsuccessfully making or opposing motion to increase travel limit	Any person	Mandatory – monetary	§5.1.1(1)(e), p. 1012
25	Demand for expert-witness information	Unsuccessfully making or opposing motion to amend or augment expert-witness information			§5.1.6(1)(c), p. 1017
		Unsuccessfully making or opposing motion to submit tardy expert-witness information			§5.1.6(1)(b), p. 1017
26	All discovery methods	Unsuccessfully making or opposing motion to extend or reopen discovery			§5.2.2, p. 1019
Miscellaneous motions					
27	Deposition	Unsuccessfully making or opposing motion to suppress deposition	Any person	Mandatory – monetary	§5.1.1(1)(d), p. 1012
28	Deposition	Unsuccessfully making or opposing motion to sustain or overrule objection to written deposition			§5.1.1(1)(f), p. 1012
29	Demand for expert-witness information	Unsuccessfully making or opposing motion to reduce expert-witness fees			§5.1.6(1)(d), p. 1017
30	All discovery methods	Unsuccessfully making or opposing motion for discovery of P's sexual history			§5.2.3, p. 1019
		Making discovery motion without first satisfying meet-and-confer obligation (if meet-and-confer required)	Party or attorney		§5.2.5, p. 1019

Any person = party, nonparty, or attorney
Case sanctions = issue, evidence, and terminating sanctions

1. Sanctions for depositions. The court can (and in some cases must) award sanctions for the following conduct related to depositions:

(1) Unsuccessfully making or opposing motion. The court must impose monetary sanctions against any party, person, or attorney who unsuccessfully makes or opposes any of the motions listed below, unless the court finds that the person subject to the sanctions acted with substantial justification or other circumstances make the imposition of the sanctions unjust.

(a) A motion for a protective order. CCP §2025.420(h); *e.g.*, ***Brun v. Bailey*** (3d Dist.1994) 27 Cal.App.4th 641, 658-59 (court erred when it did not sanction nonparty expert for unsuccessfully making motion for protective order from deposition); *see* CCP §2017.020(b) (applicable to all discovery methods), §2019.030(c) (same). See "Motion for protective order," ch. 7-B, §12.1, p. 808; "Motion for Protective Order," ch. 9-B, p. 1024.

(b) A motion to quash a deposition notice. CCP §2025.410(d). See "Motion to Quash Deposition Notice," ch. 9-C, §4, p. 1042.

(c) A motion to compel a deponent (party or nonparty) to answer any question or produce any document, electronically stored information (ESI), or tangible thing under the deponent's control. CCP §2025.480(a), (j). See "Motion to Compel Deposition Answers & Production," ch. 9-D, §4, p. 1051.

(d) A motion to suppress a deposition. CCP §2025.520(h) (stenographically recorded deposition), §2025.530(f) (audio or video recording of deposition). See "Motion to suppress deposition," ch. 7-B, §12.3, p. 808.

(e) A motion to increase the travel limits for a party deponent. CCP §2025.260(d). See "Motion to increase travel limit for party deposition," ch. 7-B, §12.6, p. 809.

(f) A motion to sustain or overrule an objection to a written deposition. *See* CCP §§2028.040(c), 2028.050(c). See "Motion for ruling on objections to written deposition," ch. 7-B, §12.7, p. 809.

(2) Motion to quash deposition subpoena.

(a) Made or opposed in bad faith or without justification. The court can award reasonable expenses, including attorney fees, incurred by any person who makes or opposes a motion to quash a deposition subpoena if the court finds that the motion was made or opposed in bad faith or without substantial justification or that one or more of the requirements of the subpoena were oppressive. CCP §1987.2(a); *see also* ***Evilsizor v. Sweeney*** (1st Dist.2014) 230 Cal.App.4th 1304, 1311 (P's father failed to timely withdraw motion to quash after D cured defective subpoena; court found motion was "made" without substantial justification). See "Motion to Quash Deposition Subpoena," ch. 9-C, §3, p. 1038.

(b) Subpoena for personal information in free-speech case. The court must award reasonable expenses, including attorney fees, incurred by a person who prevails on a motion to quash a deposition subpoena if the following are shown:

[1] The subpoena was served on an Internet service provider or on the provider of another interactive computer service, as defined in 47 U.S.C. §230(f)(2). CCP §1987.2(c).

[2] The subpoena sought the production of "personally identifying information," as defined in Civ. C. §1798.79.8(b). CCP §1987.2(c).

[3] The personally identifying information was sought for use in an action pending in another state, territory, or district of the United States or in a foreign nation. *Id.*

[4] The action arose from the moving party's exercise of free-speech rights on the Internet. *Id.*

[5] The subpoenaing party did not make a prima facie showing of a cause of action against the moving party. *Id.*

NOTE

Sanctions under §1987.2(c) were designed to discourage the practice of bringing frivolous lawsuits solely to discover the identity of someone making anonymous online statements. CEB Discovery Practice, §5.131A.

(3) Deponent's misconduct.

(a) Did not appear or refused to be sworn.

[1] Monetary sanctions. The court must impose monetary sanctions against the deponent or, if the deponent is a party-affiliated witness, against the party when the deponent either did not appear for or refused to proceed with the deposition or did not produce for inspection any document, ESI, or tangible thing described in the deposition notice. CCP §2025.450(a), (g)(1), (g)(2). The party who noticed the deposition will be

awarded the sanctions only if it prevails on a motion to compel the deponent's compliance. *Id.* §2025.450(a), (g)(1). A party who attended the deposition expecting to hear the deponent's testimony can simply request sanctions. *Id.* §2025.450(g)(2).

[2] Contempt sanctions. The court can impose contempt sanctions against a nonparty who did not appear for or refused to be sworn as a witness at a deposition. CCP §1991.1; *see id.* §§2020.240, 2025.440(b). The court is not required to find that the nonparty violated an earlier court order before imposing contempt sanctions. *Id.* §§1991.1, 2020.240.

[3] Separate action for forfeiture & damages. A person subject to a subpoena or court order who does not appear for a deposition or refuses to be sworn as a witness at a deposition forfeits to the deposing party $500 and the damages sustained by the deposing party as a result of the nonappearance. *See* CCP §§1992, 2020.240, 2025.440(b). To recover these sanctions, the deposing party must file a separate action. *Id.* §1992; ***New York Times Co. v. Superior Ct.*** (1990) 51 Cal.3d 453, 464. A person could be subject to substantial damages if her nonappearance causes the deposing party to lose the case. *CEB Discovery Practice*, §15.105.

(b) Did not answer or produce. The court can impose contempt sanctions against a nonparty who refused to comply with a subpoena to answer questions or produce documents or things at a deposition. CCP §2020.240; *see id.* §2020.220(c)(1), (c)(2). The court is not required to find that the nonparty violated an earlier court order before imposing contempt sanctions. *Id.* §2020.240.

(4) Deposing party's misconduct.

(a) Did not attend. The court must impose monetary sanctions against a party, the party's attorney, or both if (1) the party gave notice of a deposition but did not attend or proceed with it and (2) the party moving for sanctions attended (in person or by attorney), unless the court finds that the person subject to the sanctions acted with substantial justification or other circumstances make the imposition of the sanctions unjust. CCP §2025.430. The sanctions must be awarded to any other party who, in person or by attorney, also attended the deposition. *Id.*

(b) Did not serve subpoena. The court must impose monetary sanctions against a party, the party's attorney, or both if (1) the party gave notice for the deposition of a nonparty but did not serve a subpoena on the nonparty, (2) the nonparty deponent did not appear, and (3) the party moving for sanctions attended (in person or by attorney) at the time and place specified in the notice expecting that the nonparty's testimony would be taken, unless the court finds that the person subject to the sanctions acted with substantial justification or other circumstances make the imposition of the sanctions unjust. CCP §2025.440(a). The sanctions must be awarded to any other party who, in person or by attorney, also attended the deposition. *Id.*

(5) Violation of court order.

(a) By party deponent.

[1] Order compelling attendance, testimony, or production. If a party deponent or party-affiliated deponent (i.e., an officer, director, managing agent, or employee of a party, or a witness designated by an organizational party) does not obey a court order compelling attendance, testimony, or production at a deposition, the court can (1) impose case sanctions (issue, evidence, or terminating sanctions), (2) impose monetary sanctions in favor of any party who, in person or by attorney, attended expecting that the deponent's testimony would be taken according to the order, and (3) make any other order that is just. CCP §2025.450(h); *see* ***Doppes v. Bentley Motors, Inc.*** (4th Dist.2009) 174 Cal.App.4th 967, 991. See "Party-affiliated witness," ch. 7-B, §2.5, p. 781. The court can impose these sanctions against the party deponent or the party with whom the deponent is affiliated. CCP §2025.450(h).

[2] Order compelling testimony or production. If a party deponent or a party-affiliated deponent (i.e., an officer, director, managing agent, or employee of a party) does not obey a court order compelling the deponent to answer questions or produce documents, ESI, or tangible things under the deponent's control at a

DISCOVERY SANCTIONS

deposition, the court can impose contempt sanctions against the deponent. CCP §2025.480(k). The court can also (1) impose case sanctions, (2) impose monetary sanctions, and (3) make any other order that is just against the party deponent or the party with whom the deponent is affiliated. *Id.*

(b) By nonparty deponent – order compelling testimony or production. If a nonparty deponent does not obey a court order compelling the deponent to answer questions or produce documents, ESI, or tangible things under the deponent's control at a deposition, the court can impose contempt sanctions. CCP §2025.480(k).

2. Sanctions for interrogatories. The court can (and in some cases must) award sanctions for the following conduct related to interrogatories:

(1) Unsuccessfully making or opposing motion. The court must impose monetary sanctions against any party, person, or attorney who unsuccessfully makes or opposes any of the motions listed below, unless the court finds that the person subject to the sanctions acted with substantial justification or other circumstances make the imposition of the sanctions unjust. *See, e.g.*, ***V&P Trading Co. v. United Charter, LLC*** (3d Dist.2012) 212 Cal.App.4th 126, 136 (necessary predicate to award of monetary sanctions against party who filed motion to compel is that motion was unsuccessful).

(a) A motion for a protective order. CCP §2030.090(d); *see id.* §2017.020(b) (applicable to all discovery methods), §2019.030(c) (same). See "Motion for protective order," ch. 7-C, §9.1, p. 833; "Motion for Protective Order," ch. 9-B, p. 1024.

(b) A motion to compel a party's initial response to interrogatories. CCP §2030.290(c). See "Motion to Compel Initial Response," ch. 9-E, §2, p. 1057.

(c) A motion to compel a party's further response to interrogatories. CCP §2030.300(d); *see, e.g.*, ***Clement v. Alegre*** (1st Dist.2009) 177 Cal.App.4th 1277, 1284-85 (court imposed $6,632 sanction on P for opposing motion to compel with "nit-picking" objections to interrogatories). See "Motion to Compel Further Response," ch. 9-E, §3, p. 1061.

(d) A motion to deem a party's initial answer to an interrogatory binding. CCP §2030.310(d). See "Motion to deem answer binding," ch. 7-C, §9.4, p. 833.

(2) Violation of court order for response. The court can do any of the following if a party does not obey a court order compelling an initial or further response to interrogatories: (1) impose case sanctions, (2) impose monetary sanctions, and (3) make any other order that is just. CCP §2030.290(c) (initial response), §2030.300(e) (further response); *see, e.g.*, ***Bell v. H.F. Cox, Inc.*** (2d Dist.2012) 209 Cal.App.4th 62, 76 (without showing that court granted order compelling D to provide further responses to interrogatories and D's later violation of that order or other egregious misconduct, Ps had no basis for motion to exclude witness testimony for misuse of discovery process); ***Mileikowsky v. Tenet Healthsystem*** (2d Dist.2005) 128 Cal.App.4th 262, 279-80 (terminating sanctions appropriate after P repeatedly refused to respond to interrogatories and demands for inspection following stipulation, which was treated as court order); ***Morgan v. Southern Cal. Rapid Transit Dist.*** (2d Dist.1987) 192 Cal.App.3d 976, 984 (D's answer was struck as terminating sanction because D did not answer interrogatory completely after two orders compelling D to do so), *disapproved on other grounds*, ***Schwab v. Rondel Homes, Inc.*** (1991) 53 Cal.3d 428.

3. Sanctions for RFAs. The court can (and in some cases must) award sanctions for the following conduct related to requests for admission (RFAs):

(1) Unsuccessfully making or opposing motion. The court must impose monetary sanctions against any party, person, or attorney who unsuccessfully makes or opposes any of the motions listed below, unless the court finds that the person subject to the sanctions acted with substantial justification or other circumstances make the imposition of the sanctions unjust.

(a) A motion for a protective order. CCP §2033.080(d); *see id.* §2017.020(b) (applicable to all discovery methods), §2019.030(c) (same). See "Motion for protective order," ch. 7-D, §6.1.1, p. 840; "Motion for Protective Order," ch. 9-B, p. 1024.

(b) A motion to compel a party's further response to RFAs. CCP §2033.290(d). See "Motion to Compel Further Response," ch. 9-E, §3, p. 1061.

(2) Motion to deem matters admitted after untimely response. The court must impose monetary sanctions against a party or attorney (or both) who does not serve a timely response to RFAs and causes the discovering party to move to deem matters admitted. CCP §2033.280(c). See "Motion to deem requests admitted," ch. 7-D, §6.2.1, p. 841.

(3) Violation of court order for further response. The court can do any of the following if a party does not obey a court order compelling the party to provide a further response to RFAs: (1) order that the matters involved in the requests be deemed admitted and (2) impose monetary sanctions. CCP §2033.290(e).

(4) Genuineness of document or truth of matter proved at trial. If a responding party does not admit to the genuineness of a document or to the truth of a matter specified in an RFA, and if the discovering party proves the genuineness of the document or the truth of the matter at trial, the discovering party can move for an order requiring the responding party to pay the discovering party's reasonable expenses (including attorney fees) incurred in making the proof. CCP §2033.420(a). See "Motion for cost-of-proof sanctions," ch. 7-D, §6.2.3, p. 843. The court must make the order unless it finds any of the following:

(a) The responding party objected to the request and the objection was sustained, or the discovering party waived a response to the request by not seeking a motion to compel a further response. CCP §2033.420(b)(1).

(b) The admission sought was of no substantial importance. *Id.* §2033.420(b)(2).

(c) The responding party had reasonable grounds to believe it would prevail on the matter. *Id.* §2033.420(b)(3).

(d) There were other good reasons for the responding party's failure to admit. *Id.* §2033.420(b)(4).

4. Sanctions for demands to produce. The court can (and in some cases must) award sanctions for the following conduct related to demands to produce:

(1) Unsuccessfully making or opposing motion. The court must impose monetary sanctions against any party, person, or attorney who unsuccessfully makes or opposes any of the motions listed below, unless the court finds that the person subject to the sanctions acted with substantial justification or other circumstances make the imposition of the sanctions unjust.

(a) A motion for a protective order. CCP §2031.060(h); *see id.* §2017.020(b) (applicable to all discovery methods), §2019.030(c) (same). See "Motion for protective order," ch. 7-E, §9.1, p. 853; "Motion for Protective Order," ch. 9-B, p. 1024.

(b) A motion to compel a party's initial response to a demand to produce. CCP §2031.300(c). See "Motion to Compel Initial Response," ch. 9-E, §2, p. 1057.

(c) A motion to compel a party's further response to a demand to produce. CCP §2031.310(h). See "Motion to Compel Further Response," ch. 9-E, §3, p. 1061.

(d) A motion to compel the production of documents or other things according to the responding party's statement of compliance. CCP §2031.320(b). See "Motion to Compel Compliance with Demand to Produce," ch. 9-E, §4, p. 1066.

(2) Violation of court order for response or production. The court can do any of the following if a party does not obey a court order compelling an initial or further response to a demand to produce or production according to a compliance statement: (1) impose case sanctions, (2) impose monetary sanctions, and (3) make any other order that is just. CCP §2031.300(c) (initial response), §2031.310(i) (further response), §2031.320(c) (production according to compliance statement); *see, e.g.*, ***Lee v. Lee*** (5th Dist.2009) 175 Cal.App.4th 1553, 1559 (court did not abuse discretion in denying evidence sanctions for failure to produce promissory notes when there was no court order and no evidence responding party willfully failed to comply with discovery request); ***New Albertsons, Inc. v. Superior Ct.*** (2d Dist.2008) 168 Cal.App.4th 1403, 1427-28 (court erred in issuing evidence sanction because P did not seek court order compelling further response to inspection demand and court did not have inherent power to issue sanction); ***Mileikowsky***, 128 Cal.App.4th at 279-80 (terminating sanctions appropriate after P repeatedly refused to respond to interrogatories and demands for inspection following stipulation, which was treated as court order); ***Sauer v. Superior Ct.*** (4th Dist.1987) 195 Cal.App.3d 213, 228-29 (issue sanction proper when P did not turn over financial records after order compelling response to inspection demand).

5. Sanctions for medical discovery. The court can (and in some cases must) award sanctions for the following conduct related to medical examinations:

(1) Unsuccessfully making or opposing motion. The court must impose monetary sanctions against any party, person, or attorney who unsuccessfully makes or opposes any of the motions listed below, unless the court finds that the person subject to the sanctions acted with substantial justification or other circumstances make the imposition of the sanctions unjust.

(a) A motion for a protective order. CCP §2032.510(f); *see id.* §2017.020(b) (applicable to all discovery methods), §2019.030(c) (same). See "Motion for protective order," ch. 7-F, §8.1, p. 867; "Motion for Protective Order," ch. 9-B, p. 1024.

(b) A motion to compel a personal-injury plaintiff to make an initial response to a demand for a physical examination. CCP §2032.240(c). See "Motion to Compel Response to & Compliance with Demand for Exam of Personal-Injury P," ch. 9-F, §2, p. 1069.

(c) A motion to compel a personal-injury plaintiff to comply with a demand for a physical examination. CCP §2032.250(b); ***Ghanooni v. Super Shuttle*** (2d Dist.1993) 20 Cal.App.4th 256, 260. See "Motion to Compel Compliance with Demand for Exam of Personal-Injury P," ch. 9-F, §3, p. 1072.

(d) A motion to compel the delivery of medical reports. CCP §§2032.620(b), 2032.650(b). See "Motion to Compel Delivery of Medical Reports," ch. 9-F, §4, p. 1075.

(2) Violation of court order.

(a) Order to respond to or comply with demand for exam of personal-injury P. The court can do any of the following if a personal-injury plaintiff does not obey a court order compelling a response to and compliance with a demand for a physical examination: (1) impose case sanctions, (2) impose monetary sanctions, and (3) make any other order that is just. CCP §2032.240(d).

(b) Order for medical exam. The court can do any of the following if a party does not obey a court order compelling the party to submit to or produce another person for a physical or mental examination: (1) impose case sanctions, (2) impose monetary sanctions, and (3) make any other order that is just. CCP §2032.410 (submit to examination), §2032.420 (produce another person for examination); *see, e.g.*, ***Conservatorship of G.H.*** (6th Dist.2014) 227 Cal.App.4th 1435, 1441 (terminating sanctions were inappropriate because court never ordered party to submit to mental examination). A party that does not produce another person for an examination can avoid sanctions if it demonstrates an inability to produce that person for examination. CCP §2032.420.

(c) Order to produce medical reports. The court can do any of the following if a party does not obey a court order compelling the party to deliver medical reports: (1) impose case sanctions, (2) impose monetary sanctions, and (3) make any other order that is just. CCP §§2032.620(c), 2032.650(c). The court must exclude at trial the testimony of any examiner or health-care practitioner whose report was not provided by the party. *Id.* §§2032.620(c), 2032.650(c).

6. Sanctions for discovery of expert information. The court can (and in some cases must) award sanctions for the following conduct related to the exchange of expert-witness information:

(1) Unsuccessfully making or opposing motion. The court must impose monetary sanctions against any party, person, or attorney who unsuccessfully makes or opposes any of the motions listed below, unless the court finds that the person subject to the sanctions acted with substantial justification or other circumstances make the imposition of the sanctions unjust.

(a) A motion for a protective order. CCP §2034.250(d); *see id.* §2017.020(b) (applicable to all discovery methods), §2019.030(c) (same). See "Motion for protective order," ch. 7-I, §12.1, p. 914; "Motion for Protective Order," ch. 9-B, p. 1024.

(b) A motion to submit tardy expert-witness information. CCP §2034.730. See "Motion to submit tardy expert information," ch. 7-I, §12.5, p. 916.

(c) A motion to augment or amend expert-witness information. CCP §2034.630. See "Motion to augment designation or amend declaration," ch. 7-I, §12.6, p. 918.

(d) A motion to reduce an expert-witness fee. CCP §2034.470(g). See "Motion to reduce expert's fee," ch. 7-I, §12.7, p. 920.

(2) Withholding expert-witness information. The court can exclude a witness's expert opinion if the party calling the witness (1) did not list the witness as an expert, (2) did not submit an expert-witness declaration for the witness, (3) did not produce the witness's reports and writings, (4) did not make the witness available for a deposition, or (5) attempts to offer an opinion not included in the expert's declaration. *See* CCP §2034.300; ***Bonds v. Roy*** (1999) 20 Cal.4th 140, 148-49; *see, e.g.*, ***McCoy v. Gustafson*** (6th Dist.2009) 180 Cal.App.4th 56, 101 (one of P's experts was prohibited from testifying because he was not designated as expert, while another expert was restricted to opinions expressed at deposition). See "Objecting to expert's trial testimony," ch. 7-I, §13.2, p. 921. Monetary sanctions are not authorized under CCP §2034.300. *See* ***Muller v. Fresno Cmty. Hosp. & Med. Ctr.*** (2d Dist.2009) 172 Cal.App.4th 887, 905-06.

§5.2 General sanctions provisions. If the sanctions for the particular discovery method at issue do not adequately address the discovery misconduct, the party should consider the CDA's more general sanctions provisions.

1. Misuse of discovery. The court can impose sanctions against anyone who misuses the discovery process. *See* CCP §§2023.010, 2023.030. Although CCP §2023.030 limits the imposition of sanctions for discovery misuse to what is authorized in other CDA provisions, courts have the inherent power to exceed that limitation in certain situations. *See* ***Stephen Slesinger, Inc. v. Walt Disney Co.*** (2d Dist.2007) 155 Cal.App.4th 736, 762. For example, courts can impose sanctions beyond what is authorized by more specific provisions in the CDA when (1) the misuse is egregious, (2) the authorized sanctions would not rectify the harm caused by the misuse, or (3) the misuse is not specifically addressed in the CDA. *See* ***Cedars-Sinai Med. Ctr. v. Superior Ct.*** (1998) 18 Cal.4th 1, 12 (although not specifically addressed in CDA, destroying evidence in response to discovery request can be sanctioned as misuse of discovery); ***New Albertsons, Inc. v. Superior Ct.*** (2d Dist.2008) 168 Cal.App.4th 1403, 1426 (egregious misconduct committed in connection with failure to produce evidence may justify imposition of nonmonetary sanctions despite lack of earlier court order); *see, e.g.*, ***Pate v. Channel Lumber Co.*** (3d Dist.1997) 51 Cal.App.4th 1447, 1455 (because discovery misuse was not revealed until after Ps had completed case-in-chief, court's only viable option was to impose evidence sanctions).

(1) Examples of misuse. Misuses of the discovery process include the following:

(a) Persisting, over objection and without substantial justification, in an attempt to obtain information or materials that are outside the scope of permissible discovery. CCP §2023.010(a).

(b) Using a discovery method in a manner that does not comply with its specified procedures. *Id.* §2023.010(b).

DISCOVERY SANCTIONS

(c) Employing a discovery method in a manner or to an extent that causes unwarranted annoyance, embarrassment, oppression, or undue burden and expense. *Id.* §2023.010(c).

(d) Failing to respond or submit to an authorized method of discovery. *Id.* §2023.010(d); *see, e.g.*, ***Vallbona v. Springer*** (4th Dist.1996) 43 Cal.App.4th 1525, 1545 (court imposed evidence sanctions when Ds misused discovery process by not responding to authorized method of discovery).

(e) Making, without substantial justification, an unmeritorious objection to discovery. CCP §2023.010(e).

(f) Making an evasive response to discovery. *Id.* §2023.010(f); *see, e.g.*, ***Puerto v. Superior Ct.*** (2d Dist.2008) 158 Cal.App.4th 1242, 1248 (naming 2,600 employees in response to interrogatory when responding party knew that employees were not percipient witnesses would likely merit sanctions for making evasive discovery response); ***R&B Auto Ctr., Inc. v. Farmers Grp.*** (4th Dist.2006) 140 Cal.App.4th 327, 357 n.15 (failure to disclose names of witnesses unknown to P before discovery cutoff could not be considered misuse of discovery process).

(g) Disobeying a court order to provide discovery. CCP §2023.010(g); *e.g.*, ***Ellis v. Toshiba Am. Info. Sys.*** (2d Dist.2013) 218 Cal.App.4th 853, 877-78 (P's attorney sanctioned for refusing to obey court-ordered inspection of computer hard drive by D's expert).

(h) Making or opposing, unsuccessfully and without substantial justification, a motion to compel or limit discovery. CCP §2023.010(h); *see, e.g.*, ***Safeco Ins. v. Parks*** (2d Dist.2004) 122 Cal.App.4th 779, 795 (attorney sanctioned for refusing to withdraw motion to compel when witness agreed to answer questions).

(i) Failing to confer with an opposing party or attorney in a reasonable and good-faith attempt to resolve a discovery dispute informally, if the statute governing the particular discovery motion at issue requires the filing of a declaration stating facts showing that an attempt at informal resolution has been made. CCP §2023.010(i).

(j) Spoliation of evidence. ***Cedars-Sinai Med. Ctr.***, 18 Cal.4th at 12; ***Williams v. Russ*** (2d Dist.2008) 167 Cal.App.4th 1215, 1223; ***R.S. Creative, Inc. v. Creative Cotton, Ltd.*** (2d Dist.1999) 75 Cal.App.4th 486, 497. *But see* ***New Albertsons***, 168 Cal.App.4th at 1430 (***Cedars-Sinai*** merely suggests that courts can impose evidence or issue sanctions for intentional spoliation of evidence without violation of court order compelling discovery; it was not part of holding). Spoliation is the destruction or significant alteration of evidence or the failure to preserve evidence for another's use in pending or future litigation. ***Williams***, 167 Cal.App.4th at 1223. Spoliation often arises as an issue in a motion to compel the production of documents when the responding party claims the information was lost, destroyed, or never existed. *See, e.g.*, ***Electronic Funds Solutions, LLC v. Murphy*** (4th Dist.2005) 134 Cal.App.4th 1161, 1183-84 (D claimed virus had destroyed electronic files, but P's expert determined D had wiped hard drive with data eraser). See "Preserving Evidence for Production," ch. 7-E, §4, p. 847.

(2) Relief available.

(a) General. The court can impose monetary sanctions, case sanctions, and contempt sanctions for misuse of the discovery process. *See* CCP §2023.030. The sanctions must be tailored to the harm caused by the discovery misuse. ***Doppes v. Bentley Motors, Inc.*** (4th Dist.2009) 174 Cal.App.4th 967, 992; *see* ***Do It Urself Moving & Storage, Inc. v. Brown, Leifer, Slatkin & Berns*** (2d Dist.1992) 7 Cal.App.4th 27, 36. The court cannot impose sanctions for misuse of the discovery process as a punishment. ***Doppes***, 174 Cal.App.4th at 992.

(b) Spoliation sanctions. The court can impose monetary sanctions, case sanctions, and contempt sanctions to rectify the effects of spoliation. *See* ***Cedars-Sinai Med. Ctr.***, 18 Cal.4th at 12. In addition, the following remedies may also be available:

[1] Evidentiary inference. The court can impose an evidentiary inference under Evid. C. §413. ***Temple Cmty. Hosp. v. Superior Ct.*** (1999) 20 Cal.4th 464, 470; *see* ***Reeves v. MV Transp.*** (1st Dist.2010) 186 Cal.App.4th 666, 681-82 (setting out test for imposing adverse inference). The inference permits the trier of fact to infer that the evidence destroyed or suppressed by a party was unfavorable to that party. ***Temple Cmty. Hosp.***, 20 Cal.4th at 470.

[2] Criminal charge. The California Supreme Court has suggested that a person found guilty of spoliation could be charged with a misdemeanor under Pen. C. §135. ***Temple Cmty. Hosp.***, 20 Cal.4th at 470.

[3] Suspension or disbarment. The California Supreme Court has suggested that an attorney found to have participated in spoliation could face disciplinary sanctions. ***Temple Cmty. Hosp.***, 20 Cal.4th at 470.

[4] Suit for contractual damages. If a person had a duty under contract or promissory estoppel to preserve evidence that it destroyed, a party can bring an action for the breach of that duty. *See* ***Cooper v. State Farm Mut. Auto. Ins.*** (4th Dist.2009) 177 Cal.App.4th 876, 894 (under promissory estoppel, P could sue its insurer who broke promise to preserve evidence); ***Coprich v. Superior Ct.*** (2d Dist.2000) 80 Cal.App.4th 1081, 1091-92 (under breach of contract, P could sue its insurer for spoliation). However, the duty to preserve cannot be based on a general tort duty of care. ***Temple Cmty. Hosp.***, 20 Cal.4th at 466 (no tort for intentional spoliation by nonparty); ***Cedars-Sinai Med. Ctr.***, 18 Cal.4th at 17-18 (no tort for intentional spoliation by party); ***Coprich***, 80 Cal.App.4th at 1090 (no tort for negligent spoliation by party or nonparty).

2. Unsuccessfully making or opposing motion to extend or reopen discovery. The court must impose monetary sanctions against any party, person, or attorney who unsuccessfully makes or opposes a motion to extend or reopen discovery, unless the court finds that the person subject to the sanctions acted with substantial justification or other circumstances make the imposition of the sanctions unjust. CCP §2024.050(c).

3. Unsuccessfully making or opposing motion for discovery of plaintiff's sexual history. In an action alleging conduct that constitutes sexual harassment, sexual assault, or sexual battery, the court must impose monetary sanctions against any party, person, or attorney who unsuccessfully makes or opposes a motion for discovery concerning the plaintiff's sexual conduct with individuals other than the alleged perpetrator, unless the court finds that the person subject to the sanctions acted with substantial justification or other circumstances make the imposition of the sanctions unjust. CCP §2017.220.

4. Necessitating motion to compel. The court can award sanctions under the CDA in favor of a party who files a motion to compel discovery even though no opposition to the motion was filed, the opposition to the motion was withdrawn, or the requested discovery was provided to the moving party after the motion was filed. CRC 3.1348(a). Thus, the court can address gamesmanship or other misconduct that forces a party to file a motion to compel. *See id.*

5. Failing to meet & confer. The court must impose monetary sanctions on any party or attorney who does not meet and confer before making a discovery motion if the CDA section governing that particular type of motion requires a meet-and-confer conference or the court otherwise ordered the parties to meet and confer. *See* CCP §§2023.010(i), 2023.020; *see, e.g.*, ***Safeco Ins.***, 122 Cal.App.4th at 795 (attorney sanctioned for failing to meet and confer in good faith before making motion to compel). See "Meet-and-Confer Obligation," ch. 7-A, §10, p. 761. For a list of the discovery motions that require a meet-and-confer declaration, see "Meet-and-Confer Declarations," chart 7-11, p. 762.

(1) Who is paid. The sanction is payable to anyone who incurred reasonable expenses, including attorney fees, as a result of the conduct. CCP §2023.020.

(2) Egregious or inadequate. Before imposing sanctions, the court must decide if the failure to meet and confer was egregious or merely inadequate. See "Sanctions for failure to meet & confer," ch. 7-A, §10.5, p. 764.

(3) Separate offense. The failure to meet and confer is a separate offense from making or opposing a discovery motion unsuccessfully. CCP §2023.020; ***Liberty Mut. Fire Ins. v. LcL Adm'rs, Inc.*** (3d Dist.2008) 163 Cal.App.4th 1093, 1104; ***Parker v. Wolters Kluwer U.S., Inc.*** (2d Dist.2007) 149 Cal.App.4th 285, 294; *CEB Discovery Practice*, §15.3. A party or attorney can be sanctioned for not meeting and conferring even if the court rules in that person's favor on the discovery motion. CCP §2023.020.

§6. SAFE HARBOR FROM SANCTIONS FOR LOST, DAMAGED, ALTERED, OR OVERWRITTEN ESI

The 2009 California Electronic Discovery Act contained a safe-harbor provision that could protect from sanctions responding persons and attorneys who lose, damage, alter, or overwrite ESI that should have been preserved or produced. See "Safe Harbor from Sanctions for Lost, Damaged, Altered, or Overwritten ESI," ch. 7-H, §11, p. 892. At the time, the provision only applied to sanctions that could be awarded in the context of discovery motions related to subpoenas and demands to produce. *See, e.g.*, CCP §1985.8(m)(1) (subpoena), §2031.060(i)(1) (motion for protection from demand to produce), §2031.300(d)(1) (motion to compel initial responses to demand to produce). In 2012, the California Legislature extended the safe-harbor protection to sanctions that could be awarded in the context of discovery motions related to any method of discovery that would require the production of ESI. *See* Sen. Bill No. 1574 (2011-2012 Reg. Sess.). For a list of all discovery motions now subject to the safe-harbor provision, see chart 9-2, below.

9-2. DISCOVERY MOTIONS SUBJECT TO SANCTIONS SAFE HARBOR			
Type of motion		Discovery method seeking ESI	Safe-harbor provision
1	Compel	Demand to produce	CCP §§2031.300(d)(1), 2031.310(j)(1)
		Deposition notice	CCP §§2025.450(i)(1), 2025.480(*l*)(1)
2	Compliance	Demand to produce	CCP §2031.320(d)(1)
		Subpoena	CCP §1985.8(m)(1)
3	Protection	Deposition notice or subpoena	CCP §2025.420(i)(1)
		Any	CCP §2017.020(c)(1)
4	Quash	Deposition notice	CCP §2025.410(e)(1)
		Subpoena generally	CCP §§1985.8(m)(1), 1987.2(b)(1)
		Business-records subpoena	*See* CCP §§2025.220(b), 2025.410(e)(1)
		Deposition subpoena	CCP §2020.220(m)(1)
5	Sanctions	Any	CCP §2023.030(f)(1)

§7. PERSONS WHO CAN BE AWARDED SANCTIONS

§7.1 Party seeking discovery. A discovering party can be awarded sanctions. For example, a discovering party is usually entitled to monetary sanctions for successfully making a motion to compel discovery or opposing a motion that seeks to prevent discovery. See "Sanctions related to specific discovery provisions," §5.1, p. 1008.

§7.2 Party resisting discovery. A party resisting discovery can be awarded sanctions. For example, a party is entitled to monetary sanctions for successfully opposing a motion to compel discovery or making a motion that opposes discovery (e.g., a motion for protective order, a motion to quash deposition). See "Sanctions related to specific discovery provisions," §5.1, p. 1008.

§7.3 Other parties. A party who neither made nor received a discovery request can sometimes be entitled to sanctions. Examples include the following:

1. **Party incurring costs.** A party who did not serve the discovery request is entitled to monetary sanctions from anyone who misused the discovery process if the party incurred costs as a result of the misuse. *See* ***Trail v. Cornwell*** (3d Dist.1984) 161 Cal.App.3d 477, 483 n.4 (sanctions can be sought by party who did not seek discovery); *see, e.g.*, CCP §2025.450(g)(2) (nonnoticing party who attended deposition of party deponent or party-affiliated deponent expecting deponent's testimony can file motion for monetary sanctions).

2. **Coparty to discovering party.** A coparty who did not serve the discovery request is entitled to sanctions against the opposing party only if (1) the coparty can show the misuse of discovery justifies sanctions, (2) the interests of the coparty and the discovering coparty are so closely aligned that it would be a useless duplication of

DISCOVERY SANCTIONS

effort for both to pursue the same discovery and invoke the same remedies against the opposing party, and (3) the coparty was prejudiced by the misuse of discovery. *See* ***Parker v. Wolters Kluwer U.S., Inc.*** (2d Dist.2007) 149 Cal.App.4th 285, 301-02.

§7.4 Nonparties. A nonparty is entitled to monetary sanctions from anyone who misused the discovery process if the nonparty incurred expenses, including attorney fees, as a result of the misuse. *See* CCP §2023.030(a) (sanctions can be imposed in favor of "anyone" who incurred expenses); *see, e.g.*, ***Sanders v. Walsh*** (4th Dist.2013) 219 Cal.App.4th 855, 874 (nonparty awarded sanctions based on denial of D's motion to compel compliance with business-records subpoena).

§7.5 Pro bono & pro per.

1. Pro bono attorney. Parties who are represented by attorneys for no charge (pro bono) are entitled to attorney fees as discovery sanctions. ***Do v. Superior Ct.*** (4th Dist.2003) 109 Cal.App.4th 1210, 1218.

2. Pro per litigants. Parties who represent themselves in litigation (i.e., pro per litigants) are not entitled to attorney fees as discovery sanctions, even if they are attorneys. ***Kravitz v. Superior Ct.*** (2d Dist.2001) 91 Cal.App.4th 1015, 1020; ***Argaman v. Ratan*** (2d Dist.1999) 73 Cal.App.4th 1173, 1180. But pro per litigants may be entitled to other reasonable expenses incurred (e.g., photocopying costs). ***Kravitz***, 91 Cal.App.4th at 1021; ***Argaman***, 73 Cal.App.4th at 1180.

§8. RULING

The court has wide discretion in ruling on a motion for sanctions. *See* ***Lee v. Lee*** (5th Dist.2009) 175 Cal.App.4th 1553, 1559. But the court cannot impose harsher sanctions than those identified in the notice of motion or the opposition papers. *See, e.g.*, ***Sole Energy Co. v. Hodges*** (4th Dist.2005) 128 Cal.App.4th 199, 208 (Ds were given notice of monetary and unspecified sanctions but not terminating sanctions; imposition of terminating sanctions violated due process).

§9. ORDER

§9.1 Form. The court's ruling on a request for discovery sanctions must be recorded either in writing or by minute order. See "Record of Ruling," ch. 1-I, §4, p. 90.

§9.2 Choosing sanctions. When the provision at issue leaves the sanctions to be imposed to the court's discretion, the following guidelines apply:

1. Incremental approach. The CDA applies an incremental approach to discovery sanctions, starting with monetary sanctions and ending with the ultimate sanction of terminating the case. ***Doppes v. Bentley Motors, Inc.*** (4th Dist.2009) 174 Cal.App.4th 967, 992; *see* ***Van Sickle v. Gilbert*** (3d Dist.2011) 196 Cal.App.4th 1495, 1516. If monetary sanctions do not curb a party's misuse of discovery, the court can impose increasingly harsher sanctions until the party's conduct is corrected or the party's case is terminated. *See* ***Van Sickle***, 196 Cal.App.4th at 1516; ***Doppes***, 174 Cal.App.4th at 992. For example, if the court imposes monetary sanctions without effect, and then imposes issue sanctions without effect, the court is justified in imposing terminating sanctions. *See* ***Doppes***, 174 Cal.App.4th at 994.

2. Tailored to harm. The sanctions must be tailored to the harm caused by the discovery misuse. ***Doppes***, 174 Cal.App.4th at 992; *see* ***Van Sickle***, 196 Cal.App.4th at 1516; ***Do It Urself Moving & Storage, Inc. v. Brown, Leifer, Slatkin & Berns*** (2d Dist.1992) 7 Cal.App.4th 27, 36. The court cannot impose sanctions for misuse of the discovery process as a punishment. ***Doppes***, 174 Cal.App.4th at 992.

3. Other factors. A variety of other factors can be relevant to the imposition of discretionary discovery sanctions. *See* ***Deyo v. Kilbourne*** (2d Dist.1978) 84 Cal.App.3d 771, 796-97 (case predates CDA, when all sanctions were discretionary). These include the difficulty in obtaining information necessary to provide discovery answers, the materiality of unanswered discovery, whether the responding party acted in good faith and with reasonable diligence, whether the responding party was unable to comply with a previous court order, and whether a sanction short

of terminating sanctions would curb the misuse of discovery. *See id.* The responding party's past conduct can also be considered as long as the court did not punish the party for that conduct earlier and the later conduct justifies the imposition of sanctions. *See* ***Van Sickle***, 196 Cal.App.4th at 1518-19.

§9.3 Findings.

1. Monetary sanctions. When monetary sanctions are awarded, the court is not required to make findings or specify with particularity the basis for awarding sanctions in the order. ***Ghanooni v. Super Shuttle*** (2d Dist.1993) 20 Cal.App.4th 256, 261; *see* ***Estate of Ruchti*** (2d Dist.1993) 12 Cal.App.4th 1593, 1603; ***Mattco Forge, Inc. v. Arthur Young & Co.*** (2d Dist.1990) 223 Cal.App.3d 1429, 1438. The rationale for this rule is that the CDA makes such sanctions "mandatory," which is a misnomer because the court can deny an award when the party to be sanctioned had reasonable grounds to believe its conduct was justified (i.e., substantial justification) or other circumstances would make an award of sanctions unjust. *See* ***Estate of Ruchti***, 12 Cal.App.4th at 1603 & n.1. When the court awards sanctions, it does not have to make a finding that the sanctioned party did not establish substantial justification or other circumstances that would warrant denying the award; the finding is implied. *See* ***Parker v. Wolters Kluwer U.S., Inc.*** (2d Dist.2007) 149 Cal.App.4th 285, 294. When the court denies sanctions, however, it must make written findings specifying the facts supporting substantial justification or other circumstances. *See* CCP §2023.030(a); ***Parker***, 149 Cal.App.4th at 294; ***California Shellfish, Inc. v. United Shellfish Co.*** (1st Dist.1997) 56 Cal.App.4th 16, 25-26; ***Estate of Ruchti***, 12 Cal.App.4th at 1603; ***Mattco Forge***, 223 Cal.App.3d at 1438.

2. Case sanctions. The court must make written findings when imposing case sanctions. *See* ***Deyo v. Kilbourne*** (2d Dist.1978) 84 Cal.App.3d 771, 787 (court must expressly find party's willful failure to provide discovery); *see, e.g.*, ***Reedy v. Bussell*** (4th Dist.2007) 148 Cal.App.4th 1272, 1292 (court expressly stated in decision denying Ps' motion to vacate default judgments that their discovery misconduct was willful).

3. Contempt sanctions. The court must specify with particularity the basis for imposing contempt sanctions, including a recitation of facts supporting the sanctions. *See* CCP §1211(a); ***In re de la Parra*** (4th Dist.1986) 184 Cal.App.3d 139, 144. For direct contempt (i.e., contempt committed in immediate view of the court), the court must state the facts supporting the contempt order, and it should incorporate those facts into the final judgment of contempt. *See* CCP §1211. For indirect contempt (i.e., contempt not committed in immediate view of the court), the court must show the basis of the contempt order by reciting the factual basis for the judgment orally on the record or in writing in the contempt judgment. ***Moss v. Superior Ct.*** (1998) 17 Cal.4th 396, 404 n.3. If contempt sanctions are imposed for violating an earlier court order, the court should state with particularity what the earlier order directed and the facts demonstrating contempt. ***In re Ringgold*** (2d Dist.2006) 142 Cal.App.4th 1001, 1014.

§10. NOTICE TO STATE BAR

Generally, when the court imposes sanctions of $1,000 or more against an attorney, both the attorney and the court must notify the State Bar. *See* Bus. & Prof. C. §§6068(o)(3), 6086.7(a)(3); CRC 10.609(a). Notice is not required if the attorney was sanctioned for failing to make discovery, but notice is required if the attorney disobeyed a court order or abused the discovery process. *See* Bus. & Prof. C. §§6068(o)(3), 6086.7(a)(3); Weil, *Civil Procedure Before Trial*, ¶9:1000. Once notified of sanctions, the State Bar must determine whether disciplinary action is appropriate. Bus. & Prof. C. §6086.7(c).

§11. APPELLATE REVIEW

For a general discussion of the review of discovery orders, see "Review of Discovery Orders," ch. 7-A, §17, p. 777.

§11.1 Limited civil cases.

1. Monetary sanctions. In limited civil cases, a party cannot directly appeal a monetary sanctions order for discovery misuse. *See* ***Drum v. Superior Ct.*** (4th Dist.2006) 139 Cal.App.4th 845, 850 & n.3 (discussing collateral-order rule and noting that, under common law, discovery sanctions were not directly appealable collateral orders); ***Hanna v. BankAmerica Bus. Credit, Inc.*** (1st Dist.1993) 16 Cal.App.4th 913, 915 (discussing differences

between sanctions orders, which are collateral and appealable, and discovery sanctions, which are not directly appealable). The award is reviewable by appeal after entry of a final judgment. *See* ***Drum***, 139 Cal.App.4th at 850-51 & n.3 (when Legislature amended CCP §904.1 in 1993 to allow for sanctions orders over $5,000 to be appealed and chose not to amend §904.2, collateral-order doctrine under common law as applied to limited civil cases remained unchanged).

NOTE

Although not covered in this subchapter, in postjudgment enforcement proceedings for a limited civil case, an order awarding monetary sanctions for discovery misuse is directly appealable to the superior court's appellate division. See CCP §904.2(b); ***General Elec. Capital Auto Fin. Servs. v. Superior Ct.*** *(2d Dist.2001) 88 Cal.App.4th 136, 144-45.*

2. Case sanctions. In limited civil cases, an order imposing case sanctions against a party is reviewable by appeal after entry of a final judgment. *See* CCP §904.2(a).

3. Contempt sanctions. In limited civil cases, an order of contempt is directly appealable. CCP §904.2(a).

§11.2 Unlimited civil cases.

1. Monetary sanctions.

(1) Direct appeal. In unlimited civil cases, the courts are split on whether a party can directly appeal a monetary sanctions order for discovery misuse under CCP §904.1(a)(11) and (a)(12), which allow a party to directly appeal an interlocutory judgment or order for monetary sanctions over $5,000.

(a) Appealable. Some courts have held that §904.1(a) makes all orders imposing monetary sanctions over $5,000 immediately appealable, including discovery sanctions. *E.g.*, ***Sinaiko Healthcare Consulting, Inc. v. Pacific Healthcare Consultants*** (2d Dist.2007) (Div. 5) 148 Cal.App.4th 390, 401; ***Guillemin v. Stein*** (3d Dist.2002) 104 Cal.App.4th 156, 161; ***Rail-Transp. Empls. Ass'n v. Union Pac. Motor Freight*** (1st Dist.1996) 46 Cal.App.4th 469, 475; *see* ***Greene v. Amante*** (4th Dist.1992) 3 Cal.App.4th 684, 690 (former version of CCP §904.1; monetary sanctions over $750 are appealable); ***Kohan v. Cohan*** (2d Dist.1991) (Div. 1) 229 Cal.App.3d 967, 970-71 (same).

NOTE

Even in courts that allow discovery sanctions orders to be directly appealed under §904.1(a), a party probably cannot appeal separate sanctions awards when each award is $5,000 or less but in the aggregate would be over $5,000. See ***Calhoun v. Vallejo City Unified Sch. Dist.*** *(1st Dist.1993) 20 Cal.App.4th 39, 43-44 (former version of CCP §904.1; party could not aggregate separate awards to reach jurisdictional threshold for appellate review); 9 Witkin, Cal. Procedure, Appeal, §105; see, e.g.,* ***Imuta v. Nakano*** *(2d Dist.1991) 233 Cal.App.3d 1570, 1585 n.20 (former version of CCP §904.1; sanctions requested by separate motions under different statutes for separate acts could not be aggregated). But see* ***Champion/L.B.S. Assocs. Dev. Co. v. E-Z Serve Pet. Mktg., Inc.*** *(4th Dist.1993) 15 Cal.App.4th 56, 59-60 (dicta; aggregating sanctions for same conduct should be allowed).*

(b) Not appealable. Some courts have held that orders imposing discovery sanctions, regardless of the amount, are not directly appealable under §904.1(a). *E.g.*, ***Green v. GTE Cal., Inc.*** (2d Dist.1994) (Div. 6) 29 Cal.App.4th 407, 409-10; ***Peterson v. General Motors Corp.*** (6th Dist.1993) 19 Cal.App.4th 1330, 1333 (former version of CCP §904.1); ***Hanna v. BankAmerica Bus. Credit, Inc.*** (1st Dist.1993) 16 Cal.App.4th 913, 918 (same); ***Russell v. General Motors Corp.*** (3d Dist.1992) 3 Cal.App.4th 1114, 1119 (same); ***Ghanooni v. Super Shuttle*** (2d Dist.1992) (Div. 7) 2 Cal.App.4th 380, 388-89 (same); ***Rao v. Campo*** (2d Dist.1991) (Div. 3) 233 Cal.App.3d 1557,

1567-68 (same). But the award is reviewable by appeal after entry of a final judgment. *See* CCP §904.1(a)(1); *see also* ***Diepenbrock v. Brown*** (1st Dist.2012) 208 Cal.App.4th 743, 746-47 (sanction against party for opposing nonparty's motion for protective order was appealable as final judgment because it finally resolved all issues between party and nonparty).

(2) Mandamus. Under CCP §904.1(b), a party can seek mandamus review of a "sanction order or judgment" of $5,000 or less. Although no court has addressed the issue, presumably the same split of authority concerning whether an order imposing discovery sanctions over $5,000 can be directly appealed under §904.1(a) would apply to petitions for mandamus to review orders imposing discovery sanctions of $5,000 or less under §904.1(b). See "Direct appeal," §11.2.1(1), p. 1023.

2. Case sanctions. In unlimited civil cases, an order imposing case sanctions against a party is reviewable by appeal after entry of a final judgment. *See* CCP §904.1(a)(1); ***NewLife Sciences, LLC v. Weinstock***, (2d Dist.2011) 197 Cal.App.4th 676, 689.

3. Contempt sanctions. In unlimited civil cases, an order of contempt is directly appealable. *See* CCP §§904.1(a)(1), 1222.

§11.3 Standard of review. An order imposing discovery sanctions is reviewed under an abuse-of-discretion standard. *See* ***Ellis v. Toshiba Am. Info. Sys.*** (2d Dist.2013) 218 Cal.App.4th 853, 878. See "Standard of review," ch. 7-A, §17.2.2, p. 779.

B. MOTION FOR PROTECTIVE ORDER

§1. GENERAL

§1.1 Purpose. A motion for a protective order is used to ask the court to modify, prohibit, or limit discovery procedures to protect a party from an excessive or unnecessary burden, expense, or intrusion. *See, e.g.*, CCP §2025.420(b) (court may make any order that justice requires to protect any person or deponent from unwarranted annoyance, embarrassment, oppression, or undue burden and expense); ***Stony Brook I Homeowners Ass'n v. Superior Ct.*** (4th Dist.2000) 84 Cal.App.4th 691, 693 (D made motion for protective order to prevent P's inquiry into how much defense work D's expert had performed in personal-injury actions). See "Modifying discovery by court order," ch. 7-A, §4.2, p. 744.

§1.2 Primary authority. CCP §1987.1(a) (subpoenas), §2017.020 (court's authority to limit discovery), §2019.030 (same), §2025.420 (depositions), §2025.460(a) (same), §2025.470 (same), §2030.090 (interrogatories), §2031.060 (demands to produce), §2032.510(d), (e) (medical examinations), §2033.080 (RFAs), §2034.250 (expert-witness discovery), §2034.420 (same).

§1.3 Secondary authority. The following secondary sources are cited as authority in this subchapter:

- *California Civil Discovery Practice* (CEB Online ed. 2014) (referred to as *CEB Discovery Practice*).
- Weil & Brown, *California Practice Guide: Civil Procedure Before Trial* (CD-ROM ed. 2014) (referred to as Weil, *Civil Procedure Before Trial*).

§2. GROUNDS

PRACTICE TIP

For many of the grounds listed below, it is unlikely that a person (party or nonparty) served with discovery would move for a protective order. It is easier for a person served with discovery to object and force the discovering party to move to compel. However, for a person who was not served with discovery, the only option is to move for a protective order.

§2.1 General grounds. A motion for a protective order can be based on a number of general objections that are not specific to any particular discovery method.

1. Not discoverable. A protective order can be issued when the discovery sought is (1) neither relevant nor reasonably calculated to lead to the discovery of admissible evidence, (2) not obtainable by the particular discovery procedure at issue, or (3) privileged or otherwise exempt from discovery. See "What Is Not Discoverable," ch. 6-A, §3, p. 610.

PRACTICE TIP

Whenever possible, a motion for a protective order should address a specific harm (e.g., undue burden or expense), as opposed to a more general attack on the "relevance" of the information sought. ***Pacific Tel. & Tel. Co. v. Superior Ct.*** *(1970) 2 Cal.3d 161, 170 n.11;* ***Norton v. Superior Ct.*** *(2d Dist.1994) 24 Cal.App.4th 1750, 1761.*

2. Obtainable from other source. A protective order can be issued when the discovery sought is obtainable from some other source that is more convenient, less burdensome, or less expensive. CCP §2019.030(a)(1), (b); *e.g., id.* §2020.220(i)(1) (protective order limiting discovery of electronically stored information by deposition subpoena), §2031.060(f)(1) (same, but by demand to produce).

3. Cumulative or duplicative. A protective order can be issued when the discovery sought is unreasonably cumulative or duplicative. CCP §2019.030(a)(1), (b); *e.g., id.* §2020.220(i)(2) (protective order limiting discovery of electronically stored information by deposition subpoena), §2031.060(f)(2) (same, but by demand to produce).

4. Unduly burdensome or expensive. A protective order can be issued when the discovery method is unduly burdensome or expensive in light of the needs of the case, the amount in controversy, and the importance of the issues at stake. CCP §2019.030(a)(2), (b); *see, e.g.,* ***Calcor Space Facility, Inc. v. Superior Ct.*** (4th Dist.1997) 53 Cal.App.4th 216, 223 (six pages of "definitions" and "instructions" was grossly excessive and made business-records subpoena unduly burdensome). See "Undue burden or expense," ch. 7-A, §11.1.6, p. 766.

5. Burden outweighs likelihood of discovering admissible evidence. A protective order can be issued when the burden, expense, or intrusiveness of the discovery clearly outweighs the likelihood that the information sought will lead to the discovery of admissible evidence. CCP §2017.020(a).

6. Discovery method unauthorized. A protective order can be issued when the party seeking discovery is using a discovery method that is not authorized by the Civil Discovery Act (CDA). See "Prevent unauthorized discovery," ch. 7-A, §4.2.2(3), p. 745.

§2.2 Specific grounds. A motion for a protective order can be based on objections that are specific to the discovery method at issue.

1. Depositions.

(1) Generally.

(a) Annoyance, oppression & undue burden. A protective order can be issued to protect any party, deponent, or other person or organization from unwarranted annoyance, embarrassment, oppression, or undue burden or expense. CCP §2025.420(b) (oral deposition); *see id.* §1987.1(a) (authorizing protective orders in response to subpoena), §2028.070 (written deposition); *see, e.g.,* ***Liberty Mut. Ins. v. Superior Ct.*** (1st Dist.1992) 10 Cal.App.4th 1282, 1285 (D sought protective order to prohibit apex deposition on grounds of annoyance and harassment); *see also* CCP §2025.570(b)(3) (deponent or party has right to seek protective order under §2025.420 if copy of deposition is requested from deposition officer). See "Undue burden or expense," ch. 7-A, §11.1.6, p. 766; "Oppressive," ch. 7-A, §11.1.7, p. 766.

(b) Good cause. To prevail on the motion, the movant must establish good cause. *See* CCP §2025.420(b) (oral deposition), §2028.070 (written deposition). To do so, the movant must show specific facts that establish the grounds for relief (e.g., annoyance, oppression, undue burden). *See* ***Goodman v. Citizens Life & Cas.***

Ins. (2d Dist.1967) 253 Cal.App.2d 807, 819 (discussing former CCP §2019); *see, e.g.*, ***Durst v. Superior Ct.*** (2d Dist.1963) 218 Cal.App.2d 460, 467-68 (trial court abused discretion in granting protective order when D made no factual showing of annoyance, expense, embarrassment, or oppression); *see also* ***Greyhound Corp. v. Superior Ct.*** (1961) 56 Cal.2d 355, 388 (good-cause showing must satisfy court that protective order can be granted without "abuse of the inherent rights of the adversary" to requested discovery).

(2) Expert beyond 75 miles. A protective order can be issued to allow the deposition of an expert retained or employed by a party beyond 75 miles from the courthouse where the action is pending. CCP §2034.420. To prevail on the motion, the movant must show "exceptional hardship," which is not defined in the statute. *See id.*

(3) Subpoena to discover consumer & employment records. A protective order can be issued to protect any person from the disclosure of consumer, employment, and certain personal identifying information sought by deposition subpoena when the discovery is prohibited, when the subpoenaing party did not comply with the statutory requirements for obtaining the records, or for other reasons, including to protect the person from unreasonable or oppressive demands. *See* CCP §§1985.3(g), (k), 1985.6(f)(1), (f)(2), (j), 1987.1(a), (b)(3)-(b)(5).

(4) ESI. For a list of objections to the production of electronically stored information (ESI), see "Objections to Production of ESI," ch. 7-H, §9, p. 889.

(a) Undue burden or expense. A protective order can be issued to set conditions for the production of ESI when the information is from a source that is not reasonably accessible because of undue burden or expense. *See* CCP §§1985.8(e)-(g), (k), (*l*), 2020.220(e)-(g), (k), (*l*), 2025.420(c)-(e), 2025.450(c)-(e), 2025.480(d)-(f).

(b) Obtainable from other source. A protective order can be issued to limit the discovery of ESI when the discovering party could obtain the information from some other source that is more convenient, less burdensome, or less expensive. *See* CCP §§1985.8(i)(1), 2020.220(i)(1), 2025.420(f)(1), 2025.450(f)(1), 2025.480(g)(1).

(c) Unreasonably cumulative or duplicative. A protective order can be issued to limit the discovery of ESI when the discovery is unreasonably cumulative or duplicative. *See* CCP §§1985.8(i)(2), 2020.220(i)(2), 2025.420(f)(2), 2025.450(f)(2), 2025.480(g)(2).

(d) Ample opportunity to discover. A protective order can be issued to limit the discovery of ESI when the discovering party had ample opportunity to obtain the information through other discovery methods. *See* CCP §§1985.8(i)(3), 2020.220(i)(3), 2025.420(f)(3), 2025.450(f)(3), 2025.480(g)(3).

(e) Burden outweighs benefit. A protective order can be issued to limit the discovery of ESI when the likely burden or expense of the proposed discovery outweighs the likely benefit, taking into account (1) the amount in controversy, (2) the resources of the parties, (3) the importance of the issues in the litigation, and (4) the importance of the requested discovery in resolving the issues. *See* CCP §§1985.8(i)(4), 2020.220(i)(4), 2025.420(f)(4), 2025.450(f)(4), 2025.480(g)(4).

2. Interrogatories.

(1) Annoyance, oppression & undue burden. A protective order can be issued to protect any party or other person or organization from unwarranted annoyance, embarrassment, oppression, or undue burden or expense. CCP §2030.090(b). See "Undue burden or expense," ch. 7-A, §11.1.6, p. 766; "Oppressive," ch. 7-A, §11.1.7, p. 766.

(2) Good cause. To prevail on the motion, the movant must establish good cause. CCP §2030.090(b). See "Good cause," §2.2.1(1)(b), p. 1025.

3. Demands to produce.

(1) Generally.

(a) Annoyance, oppression & undue burden. A protective order can be issued to protect any party or other person or organization from unwarranted annoyance, embarrassment, oppression, or undue burden

or expense. CCP §2031.060(b); *e.g.*, ***Ibarra v. Superior Ct.*** (2d Dist.2013) 217 Cal.App.4th 695, 706 (unlimited disclosure of service photographs threatened peace officers' safety). See "Undue burden or expense," ch. 7-A, §11.1.6, p. 766; "Oppressive," ch. 7-A, §11.1.7, p. 766.

(b) Good cause. To prevail on the motion, the movant must establish good cause. CCP §2031.060(b). See "Good cause," §2.2.1(1)(b), p. 1025.

(2) ESI. For a list of objections to the production of ESI, see "Objections to Production of ESI," ch. 7-H, §9, p. 889.

(a) Undue burden or expense. A protective order can be issued to set conditions for the production of ESI when the information is from a source that is not reasonably accessible because of undue burden or expense. *See* CCP §2031.060(c), (d).

(b) Obtainable from other source. A protective order can be issued to limit the discovery of ESI when the discovering party could obtain the information from some other source that is more convenient, less burdensome, or less expensive. CCP §2031.060(f)(1).

(c) Unreasonably cumulative or duplicative. A protective order can be issued to limit the discovery of ESI when the discovery is unreasonably cumulative or duplicative. CCP §2031.060(f)(2).

(d) Ample opportunity to discover. A protective order can be issued to limit the discovery of ESI when the discovering party had ample opportunity to obtain the information through other discovery methods. CCP §2031.060(f)(3).

(e) Burden outweighs benefit. A protective order can be issued to limit the discovery of ESI when the likely burden or expense of the proposed discovery outweighs the likely benefit, taking into account (1) the amount in controversy, (2) the resources of the parties, (3) the importance of the issues in the litigation, and (4) the importance of the requested discovery in resolving the issues. CCP §2031.060(f)(4).

(3) Financial information.

(a) Limiting disclosure. A protective order can be issued limiting disclosure of a defendant's financial information.

[1] Related to punitive damages. A defendant is presumptively entitled to a protective order limiting disclosure of the defendant's financial information when the court grants a plaintiff's motion to discover financial information under Civ. C. §3295(c). *See* ***Richards v. Superior Ct.*** (2d Dist.1978) 86 Cal.App.3d 265, 272. See "Motion to Discover Financial Information," ch. 7-G, p. 868. The protective order must limit disclosure of the information to the plaintiff's attorney and prohibit the information from being used for anything other than the lawsuit. ***Richards***, 86 Cal.App.3d at 272.

[2] Related to cause of action. Courts are split on whether a party is presumptively entitled to a protective order when its financial information relates to the cause of action. *Compare* ***GT, Inc. v. Superior Ct.*** (1st Dist.1984) 151 Cal.App.3d 748, 754 (when financial information sought goes to heart of cause of action, movant must meet usual burden and show good cause for protective order), *with* ***Moskowitz v. Superior Ct.*** (2d Dist.1982) 137 Cal.App.3d 313, 317-18 (even when movant puts financial condition in issue, movant is presumptively entitled to protective order limiting disclosure of financial information to discovering party's attorney and prohibiting information from being used for anything other than lawsuit).

(b) Setting conditions for use. A protective order can be issued, for good cause, prohibiting the plaintiff from introducing the following evidence before making a prima facie case of the defendant's liability for punitive damages under Civ. C. §3294:

[1] The profits the defendant gained by virtue of the wrongful course of conduct shown by the evidence. Civ. C. §3295(a)(1).

[2] The defendant's financial condition. *Id.* §3295(a)(2).

(4) Complaints about peace or custodial officer. A protective order can be issued to protect a peace or custodial officer from unnecessary annoyance, embarrassment, or oppression when a party seeks access to records of complaints, investigations of complaints, or discipline imposed as a result of investigations concerning the officer. *See* Evid. C. §1045(d).

4. Requests for admission.

(1) Annoyance, oppression & undue burden. A protective order can be issued to protect any party from unwarranted annoyance, embarrassment, oppression, or undue burden or expense. CCP §2033.080(b). See "Undue burden or expense," ch. 7-A, §11.1.6, p. 766; "Oppressive," ch. 7-A, §11.1.7, p. 766.

(2) Good cause. To prevail on the motion, the movant must establish good cause. CCP §2033.080(b). See "Good cause," §2.2.1(1)(b), p. 1025.

5. Demand to exchange expert information.

(1) Annoyance, oppression & undue burden. A protective order can be issued to protect any party from unwarranted annoyance, embarrassment, oppression, or undue burden or expense. CCP §2034.250(b). See "Undue burden or expense," ch. 7-A, §11.1.6, p. 766; "Oppressive," ch. 7-A, §11.1.7, p. 766.

(2) Good cause. To prevail on the motion, the movant must establish good cause. CCP §2034.250(b). See "Good cause," §2.2.1(1)(b), p. 1025.

6. Medical examinations.

(1) Examiner's behavior. A protective order can be issued to prevent a medical examiner's abusive behavior or performance of any unauthorized diagnostic tests and procedures at a medical examination. *See* CCP §2032.510(d). See "Suspending physical exam," ch. 7-F, §6.3, p. 866.

(2) Observer's behavior. A protective order can be issued to prevent an observer's attempted participation in or disruption of a physical examination. *See* CCP §2032.510(e). See "Suspending physical exam," ch. 7-F, §6.3, p. 866.

§3. MOTION

§3.1 Who can make.

1. Party or affected person. Any party or affected person can make a motion for a protective order. CCP §§2017.020(a), 2019.030(b); *see id.* §2025.420(a) (depositions), §2030.090(a) (interrogatories), §2031.060(a) (demands to produce), §2033.080(a) (party responding to RFA can make motion), §2034.250(a) (party served with demand for exchange of expert-witness information can make motion).

2. Court. The court can make a protective order on its own motion if a subpoena requires the attendance of a witness or the production of things at a deposition. CCP §1987.1(a).

§3.2 Deadline to file & serve. The CDA states that the movant must "promptly move" for a protective order but gives no specific deadline for making the motion. *See* CCP §2025.420(a) (depositions), §2030.090(a) (interrogatories), §2031.060(a) (demands to produce), §2033.080(a) (RFAs), §2034.250(a) (demands for exchange of expert-witness information). Thus, the motion can be made even after discovery is produced. *See id.* §2025.420(a) (motion for protective order can be made before, during, or after deposition); ***Fairmont Ins. v. Superior Ct.*** (2000) 22 Cal.4th 245, 255 (same); ***Stadish v. Superior Ct.*** (2d Dist.1999) 71 Cal.App.4th 1130, 1144 (motion for protective order can be made after producing documents). However, the motion's timeliness may depend on the type of protection sought. *See, e.g.*, ***Nativi v. Deutsche Bank Nat'l Trust Co.*** (6th Dist.2014) 223 Cal.App.4th 261, 317 (motion made after order compelling further production was timely, in part because motion sought protection against dissemination of documents, not their production). At a minimum, the motion should be filed and served at least 16 court days before the date set for the hearing. *See* CCP §1005(b) (deadline to file and serve noticed motions); Weil, *Civil Procedure Before Trial*, ¶8:687 (protective order must be made by noticed motion). If the motion is served by means other than

personal delivery, the movant will need to add more time to the 16-day period (e.g., 5 calendar days are added when notice is mailed in California). *See* CCP §1005(b). Because this is a discovery motion, it must be heard at least 15 calendar days before the initial trial date. See "Scheduling Hearing," ch. 1-H, §3, p. 80; "Cutoff for discovery motions," ch. 7-A, §5.2.2, p. 748. To determine the deadline for filing and serving the motion, see chart 9-3, below.

9-3. CALCULATING DEADLINE TO FILE & SERVE DISCOVERY MOTION

	Action	Date
1	Start with initial trial date set by court.	
2	Count backward 15 days from date in row 1. This is the cutoff date for discovery motions.	
3	Count backward 16 *court* days ❶ from date in row 2.	
4	Count backward number of days for method of service (e.g., 0 for personal service, 5 for mail in California) from date in row 3. ❷ This is the deadline to file and serve the motion.	

❶ The number of calendar days in 16 court days varies, depending on the holidays and weekends that fall within the 16 court days. See "Court days," ch. 1-F, §5.1.3(1)(b), p. 54.

❷ If the last day falls on a Saturday, Sunday, or other judicial holiday, continue counting backward until the next day that is not a Saturday, Sunday, or judicial holiday. See "Determine last day," ch. 1-F, §5.1.5, p. 55.

§3.3 Contents.

1. Notice of motion & motion. The motion should be made in writing by noticed motion. *See* CRC 3.1112; *see, e.g.*, ***St. Paul Fire & Mar. Ins. v. Superior Ct.*** (1st Dist.1984) 156 Cal.App.3d 82, 85-86 (use of term "motion" in former CCP §2019(d), now in §2025.420(a), (b), imposed notice and hearing requirements generally applicable to motions). See "Notice of motion & motion," ch. 1-D, §5.1, p. 28. The motion should contain the following information:

(1) Protective order.

(a) Relief. The notice of motion and motion should briefly state the relief sought (e.g., "Defendant asks the Court for an order restricting disclosure of trade secrets and other commercial information"). *See* CRC 3.1110(a), 3.1112(d)(3). Chart 9-4, below, outlines the types of relief that can be requested.

9-4. RELIEF AVAILABLE THROUGH MOTION FOR PROTECTIVE ORDER

	Grounds	Type of relief	Sanctions?	Authority
	All discovery			
1	Not discoverable	Deny discovery	None	See §2.1.1, p. 1025
2	Discovery unreasonably cumulative or duplicative	Any relief necessary to restrict frequency or extent of use of discovery	Monetary*	CCP §2019.030(a)(1), (c)
3	Discovery obtainable from another source	Any relief necessary to restrict frequency or extent of use of discovery	Monetary*	CCP §2019.030(a)(1), (c)
4	Discovery unduly burdensome or expensive	Any relief necessary to restrict frequency or extent of use of discovery	Monetary*	CCP §2019.030(a)(2), (c)
5	Burden of discovery outweighs chances of discovery of admissible evidence	Any relief necessary to limit scope of discovery	Monetary*	CCP §2017.020
6	Unauthorized use of discovery	Any relief necessary to protect movant	None	See ch. 7-A, §4.2.2(3), p. 745

PROTECTIVE ORDER

9-4. RELIEF AVAILABLE THROUGH MOTION FOR PROTECTIVE ORDER (CONTINUED)

	Grounds	Type of relief	Sanctions?	Authority
		Oral or written depositions by notice or subpoena		
7	Annoyance or burden	Prevent deposition	Monetary*	CCP §2025.420(b)(1), (h)
8	Annoyance or burden	Reschedule deposition	Monetary*	CCP §2025.420(b)(2), (h)
9	Annoyance or burden	Postpone expert's video deposition to allow movant to prepare for cross-examination	Monetary*	CCP §2025.420(b)(3), (h)
10	Annoyance or burden	Change location for deposition	Monetary*	CCP §2025.420(b)(4), (h)
11	Annoyance or burden	Impose terms and conditions for deposition	Monetary*	CCP §2025.420(b)(5), (h)
12	Annoyance or burden	Change oral deposition to written deposition	Monetary*	CCP §2025.420(b)(6), (h)
13	Annoyance or burden	Change oral deposition of party to interrogatories	Monetary*	CCP §2025.420(b)(7), (h)
14	Annoyance or burden	Change method of recording deposition	Monetary*	CCP §2025.420(b)(8), (h)
15	Annoyance or burden	Prohibit matters from being inquired into	Monetary*	CCP §2025.420(b)(9), (h)
16	Annoyance or burden	Limit the scope of the deposition to certain matters	Monetary*	CCP §2025.420(b)(10), (h)
17	Annoyance or burden	Prevent writings or tangible things from being produced, inspected, copied, tested, or sampled	Monetary*	CCP §2025.420(b)(11), (h)
18	Annoyance or burden	Set conditions for production of ESI	Monetary*	CCP §2025.420(b)(11), (h)
19	Annoyance or burden	Prevent certain persons other than parties and their counsel from attending the deposition	Monetary*	CCP §2025.420(b)(12), (h)
20	Annoyance or burden	Restrict disclosure of trade secrets or other commercial information	Monetary*	CCP §2025.420(b)(13), (h)
21	Annoyance or burden	Require parties to simultaneously file certain documents under seal	Monetary*	CCP §2025.420(b)(14), (h)
22	Annoyance or burden	Seal deposition transcript	Monetary*	CCP §2025.420(b)(15), (h)
23	Annoyance or burden	Terminate the deposition	Monetary*	CCP §2025.420(b)(16), (h)
24	Annoyance or burden	Any other type of relief necessary to protect movant	Monetary*	CCP §2025.420(b), (h)
25	Exceptional hardship	Allow expert deposition beyond 75-mile limit	None	CCP §2034.420
26	Undue burden or expense	Set conditions for production of ESI	Reasonable expenses**	CCP §§1985.8(e)-(g), (k), (*l*), (m)(1), 1987.1(a), 1987.2, 2020.220(e)-(g), (k), (*l*), (m)(1), 2025.420(c)-(e), 2025.450(c)-(e), 2025.480(d)-(f)
27	Discovery obtainable from another source	Limit frequency or extent of discovery of ESI	Reasonable expenses**	CCP §§1985.8(i)(1), (m)(1), 1987.1(a), 1987.2, 2020.220(i)(1), (m)(1), 2025.420(f)(1), (i)(1), 2025.450(f)(1), (i)(1), 2025.480(g)(1), (*l*)(1)

PROTECTIVE ORDER

	9-4. RELIEF AVAILABLE THROUGH MOTION FOR PROTECTIVE ORDER (CONTINUED)			
	Grounds	Type of relief	Sanctions?	Authority
	Oral or written depositions by notice or subpoena (continued)			
28	Unreasonably cumulative or duplicative	Limit frequency or extent of discovery of ESI	Reasonable expenses**	CCP §§1985.8(i)(2), (m)(1), 1987.1(a), 1987.2, 2020.220(i)(2), (m)(1), 2025.420(f)(2), (i)(1), 2025.450(f)(2), (i)(1), 2025.480(g)(2), (*l*)(1)
29	Discovering party had ample opportunity to obtain information	Limit frequency or extent of discovery of ESI	Reasonable expenses**	CCP §§1985.8(i)(3), (m)(1), 1987.1(a), 1987.2, 2020.220(i)(3), (m)(1), 2025.420(f)(3), (i)(1), 2025.450(f)(3), (i)(1), 2025.480(g)(3), (*l*)(1)
30	Burden of discovery outweighs benefit	Limit frequency or extent of discovery of ESI	Reasonable expenses**	CCP §§1985.8(i)(4), (m)(1), 1987.1(a), 1987.2, 2020.220(i)(4), (m)(1), 2025.420(f)(4), (i)(1), 2025.450(f)(4), (i)(1), 2025.480(g)(4), (*l*)(1)
	Oral depositions by subpoena			
31	Appropriate reason, including unreasonable or oppressive demand	Any type of relief necessary to protect person	Reasonable expenses*	CCP §§1987.1(a), 1987.2
32	Discovery prohibited, did not comply with statutory requirements, other appropriate reason	Protect a person from disclosure of consumer or employment records	Reasonable expenses*	CCP §§1985.3(g), (k), 1985.6(f)(2), (j), 1987.1(a), (b)(3), (b)(4), 1987.2
33	Annoyance or burden	Payment of expert-witness fees	Monetary*	CCP §2025.420(b), (h); ***Brun*** (3d Dist.1994) 27 Cal.App.4th 641, 650 (discussing former §2025(i), now §2025.420)
	Depositions by written questions			
34	Annoyance or burden	Change deposition by written questions to oral deposition	Monetary*	CCP §2028.070(a)
35	Annoyance or burden	Permit party to attend written deposition and ask oral questions	Monetary*	CCP §2028.070(b)
36	Annoyance or burden	Sustain objections based on form of question or privilege	Monetary*	CCP §2028.070(c)
37	Annoyance or burden	Require deposition to be taken before different deposition officer	Monetary*	CCP §2028.070(d)
	Interrogatories			
38	Annoyance or burden	Limit the number of interrogatories that must be answered	Monetary*	CCP §2030.090(b)(1), (d)
39	Annoyance or burden	Find that the number of interrogatories over 35 is unwarranted	Monetary*	CCP §2030.090(b)(2), (d)
40	Annoyance or burden	Extend time to respond to a set of interrogatories or a particular interrogatory	Monetary*	CCP §2030.090(b)(3), (d)

9-4. RELIEF AVAILABLE THROUGH MOTION FOR PROTECTIVE ORDER (CONTINUED)				
	Grounds	Type of relief	Sanctions?	Authority
		Interrogatories (continued)		
41	Annoyance or burden	Impose the terms and conditions for the response	Monetary*	CCP §2030.090(b)(4), (d)
42	Annoyance or burden	Change discovery method from interrogatories to oral deposition	Monetary*	CCP §2030.090(b)(5), (d)
43	Annoyance or burden	Restrict disclosure of trade secrets or other commercial information	Monetary*	CCP §2030.090(b)(6), (d)
44	Annoyance or burden	Seal answers to interrogatories	Monetary*	CCP §2030.090(b)(7), (d)
45	Annoyance or burden	Any other type of relief necessary to protect party	Monetary*	CCP §2030.090(b), (d)
		Demand to produce documents or other things		
46	Annoyance or burden	Limit or prohibit production of things demanded	Monetary*	CCP §2031.060(b)(1), (h), (i)
47	Annoyance or burden	Extend time to respond to some or all of the demands	Monetary*	CCP §2031.060(b)(2), (h), (i)
48	Annoyance or burden	Change location for production	Monetary*	CCP §2031.060(b)(3), (h), (i)
49	Annoyance or burden	Impose terms and conditions for inspection, copying, testing, or sampling	Monetary*	CCP §2031.060(b)(4), (h), (i)
50	Annoyance or burden	Restrict disclosure of trade secrets or other commercial information	Monetary*	CCP §2031.060(b)(5), (h), (i)
51	Annoyance or burden	Seal items produced	Monetary*	CCP §2031.060(b)(6), (h), (i)
52	Undue burden or expense	Set conditions for production of party's or nonparty's ESI	Monetary**	CCP §2031.060(d), (e), (h), (i)
53	Discovery obtainable from another source	Limit frequency or extent of discovery of ESI	Monetary**	CCP §2031.060(f)(1), (h), (i)
54	Unreasonably cumulative or duplicative	Limit frequency or extent of discovery of ESI	Monetary**	CCP §2031.060(f)(2), (h), (i)
55	Discovering party had ample opportunity to obtain information	Limit frequency or extent of discovery of ESI	Monetary**	CCP §2031.060(f)(3), (h), (i)
56	Burden of discovery outweighs benefit	Limit frequency or extent of discovery of ESI	Monetary**	CCP §2031.060(f)(4), (h), (i)
57	Motion to discover financial information granted	Limit disclosure of D's financial information	None	Civ. C. §3295(c); ***Richards*** (2d Dist.1978) 86 Cal.App.3d 265, 272
58	Good cause	Prohibit P from introducing evidence of D's wrongfully obtained profits or financial condition	None	Civ. C. §3295(a)
59	Annoyance, embarrassment, or oppression	Prohibit or limit disclosure of peace or custodial officer's records of complaints, investigations of complaints, or discipline imposed	None	Evid. C. §1045(d)
60	Annoyance or burden	Any other type of relief necessary to protect party	Monetary*	CCP §2031.060(b), (h)

9-4. RELIEF AVAILABLE THROUGH MOTION FOR PROTECTIVE ORDER (CONTINUED)				
Grounds		Type of relief	Sanctions?	Authority
Requests for admission				
61	Annoyance or burden	Limit the number of RFAs that must be answered	Monetary*	CCP §2033.080(b)(1), (d)
62	Annoyance or burden	Find that the number of RFAs over 35 is unwarranted	Monetary*	CCP §2033.080(b)(2), (d)
63	Annoyance or burden	Extend time to respond to some or all of the RFAs	Monetary*	CCP §2033.080(b)(3), (d)
64	Annoyance or burden	Restrict the admissions of trade secrets or other commercial information	Monetary*	CCP §2033.080(b)(4), (d)
65	Annoyance or burden	Seal answers to RFAs	Monetary*	CCP §2033.080(b)(5), (d)
66	Annoyance or burden	Any other type of relief necessary to protect party	Monetary*	CCP §2033.080(b), (d)
Demand to exchange expert-witness information				
67	Annoyance or burden	Quash untimely demand for exchange of expert information	Monetary*	CCP §2034.250(b)(1), (d)
68	Annoyance or burden	Change date for exchange of expert information to earlier or later time	Monetary*	CCP §2034.250(b)(2), (d)
69	Annoyance or burden	Impose terms or conditions on exchange of expert information	Monetary*	CCP §2034.250(b)(3), (d)
70	Annoyance or burden	Change time or place for production and exchange of expert reports	Monetary*	CCP §2034.250(b)(4), (d)
71	Annoyance or burden	Divide parties into sides and require sides to designate trial experts	Monetary*	CCP §2034.250(b)(5), (d)
72	Annoyance or burden	Reduce a party or side's list of designated experts	Monetary*	CCP §2034.250(b)(6), (d)
73	Annoyance or burden	Any other type of relief necessary to protect party	Monetary*	CCP §2034.250(b), (d)
Medical examinations				
74	Abusive behavior or unauthorized tests	Prohibit examiner's abusive behavior or unauthorized tests or procedures	Monetary*	CCP §2032.510(d), (f)
75	Disruptive behavior or participation	Prohibit observer's disruptive behavior or participation in examination	Monetary*	CCP §2032.510(e), (f)

* Sanctions are available for unsuccessfully making or opposing a motion for protective order.

** Sanctions are available for unsuccessfully making or opposing a motion for protective order, but absent exceptional circumstances, are not available when the failure to provide lost, damaged, altered, or overwritten ESI is the result of the routine, good-faith operation of an electronic information system.

ESI = electronically stored information

RFA = request for admission

(b) Grounds. The notice of motion and motion should briefly state the grounds for the motion (e.g., "The motion will be made on the grounds that Plaintiff seeks to depose John Doe, President of Defendant Corporation, who has no unique or superior personal knowledge of discoverable information"). *See* CRC 3.1110(a), 3.1112(d)(3). See "Grounds," §2, p. 1024.

(2) Sanctions. The notice of motion and motion should briefly state whether sanctions are sought. To determine whether sanctions are available, see "Discovery Sanctions by Motions," chart 9-1, p. 1008. For the information required to be in the notice when sanctions are sought, see "Required information," ch. 9-A, §3.1, p. 1004.

(3) Stay. If the motion for protective order seeks protection from a deposition notice or deposition subpoena, the notice of motion and motion should briefly state whether a stay is sought. *See* CCP §2025.270(d).

2. Memorandum of points & authorities. The motion must include a memorandum in support of the motion. CRC 3.1112(a)(3). See "Memorandum of points & authorities," ch. 1-D, §5.2, p. 28. If the movant is seeking sanctions, the memorandum must identify the legal authority for the sanctions. See "Provide authority for sanctions," ch. 9-A, §3.1.3, p. 1004.

3. Supporting evidence. The motion must include supporting evidence. *See* CRC 3.1112(b). See "Supporting evidence," ch. 1-D, §5.3, p. 30. At a minimum, the motion must be supported by a declaration stating the following facts:

(1) Grounds. The declaration must state specific facts establishing the grounds for the relief requested. For example, if the movant is seeking a protective order on the ground of oppression, the declaration should state facts showing how either the discovering party intended to create an unreasonable burden for the movant or the ultimate effect of the burden is not commensurate with the result sought. *See* ***West Pico Furniture Co. v. Superior Ct.*** (1961) 56 Cal.2d 407, 417.

(2) Meet & confer. When a meet-and-confer conference is required for a motion for a protective order, the declaration must state facts showing that the party attempted to resolve the discovery dispute informally before making the motion. See "Meet-and-confer declaration," ch. 7-A, §10.4, p. 763. Even when a meet-and-confer conference is not required, it is helpful if the declaration states that the party attempted to resolve the dispute informally and provides facts to support the statement. *Cf. CEB Discovery Practice*, §7.109 (while not required, it is advisable to make informal attempt to resolve dispute before making motion to compel answers to interrogatories). Copies of any correspondence reflecting attempts to meet and confer should be attached to the motion as exhibits. For a summary of when a meet-and-confer declaration is required, see "Meet-and-Confer Declarations," chart 7-11, p. 762. For a general discussion of the obligation to meet and confer, see "Meet-and-Confer Obligation," ch. 7-A, §10, p. 761.

(3) Sanctions. If sanctions are requested, the declaration should state facts supporting each ground for sanctions against each person identified in the notice of motion and motion as being responsible for the sanctionable conduct. *See* CCP §2023.040. For monetary sanctions, the declaration should identify the total amount sought against each person, itemized by task, fee rate, and time (including the estimated time for traveling to and attending the hearing on the motion). *See id.* See "Amount," ch. 9-A, §4.1.3, p. 1005.

(4) Stay. If a stay of a deposition is requested, the declaration should state facts supporting good cause for the stay. CCP §2025.270(d).

4. Separate statement. A separate statement must accompany a motion for a protective order that involves the content of a discovery request. CRC 3.1345(a). The separate statement must contain all the information necessary to understand each discovery request and related response at issue. CRC 3.1345(c). Specifically, the separate statement must include the following:

(1) Text of request. The separate statement must include the text of the discovery request from which the movant seeks protection. CRC 3.1345(c)(1). Discovery requests must be restated verbatim; they cannot be summarized or incorporated by reference. *Id.*

(2) Text of response. The separate statement must include the text of each response, answer, or objection to the discovery request and any further responses or answers. CRC 3.1345(c)(2).

(3) Set & number. If the motion involves interrogatories, requests for admission (RFAs), or demands to produce, the separate statement must identify their set and number. CRC 3.1345(d).

(4) Reason for order. The separate statement must set out the factual and legal reasons to protect the movant from the discovery. *See* CRC 3.1345(c)(3) (refers to motion to compel).

(5) Other information. When necessary, the separate statement must include the text of all definitions, instructions, and other matters required to understand each discovery request and its response. CRC 3.1345(c)(4). When a response to a particular discovery request depends on the response given to another discovery request, or if the reasons a further response to a particular discovery request is considered necessary are based on a response to another discovery request, the other request and its response must be included. CRC 3.1345(c)(5). When pleadings, other documents in the file, or other items of discovery are relevant to the motion, the party relying on them must summarize each relevant document. CRC 3.1345(c)(6).

5. Proof of service. The motion should include proof of service. See "Proof of service," ch. 1-D, §5.6, p. 33.

6. Proposed order. The motion can include a proposed order. *See* CRC 3.1113(m). If a proposed order is submitted, it must be lodged and served with the motion papers, not attached to them. *Id.* See "Documents lodged," ch. 1-F, §2.3, p. 47.

§4. RESPONSE

§4.1 Compliance. A party served with a motion for a protective order should consider agreeing with the motion instead of filing an opposition. An unsuccessful opposition can result in monetary sanctions. *See, e.g.*, CCP §2031.060(h) (court must impose monetary sanctions against person who unsuccessfully opposes motion for protective order relating to demand to produce unless court finds that party acted with substantial justification or that imposition of sanctions would be unjust), §2033.080(d) (court must impose monetary sanctions against person who unsuccessfully opposes motion for protective order relating to RFAs unless court finds that party acted with substantial justification or that imposition of sanctions would be unjust).

§4.2 Opposition. An opposing party can respond to a motion for a protective order by filing an opposition.

1. Deadline to file & serve. The opposition must be filed and served at least nine court days before the hearing. CCP §1005(b). See "Filing & serving opposition," ch. 1-D, §8.5, p. 36.

2. Grounds.

(1) Negate grounds in motion. A party can oppose the motion by negating the grounds relied on in the motion. *See, e.g.*, ***Brigante v. Huang*** (2d Dist.1993) 20 Cal.App.4th 1569, 1575 (when D moved for protective order on grounds of privilege, P argued waiver of privilege), *disapproved on other grounds*, ***Wilcox v. Birtwhistle*** (1999) 21 Cal.4th 973; ***Liberty Mut. Ins. v. Superior Ct.*** (1st Dist.1992) 10 Cal.App.4th 1282, 1285-86 (when D moved for protective order on ground that there was no legitimate reason to take deposition, P responded that deposition was for legitimate purpose).

(2) Meet burden. In some situations, a party opposing the motion for protective order—that is, the party seeking discovery—must satisfy a shifting burden of persuasion or proof to defeat the motion. These situations include the following:

(a) Privileged information. When a movant asks for protection to prevent the discovery of information that is privileged, and meets its burden of establishing the preliminary facts for the privilege, the discovering party has the burden to show (1) the information is not protected by a privilege, (2) there is an exception to the privilege, (3) the privilege was waived, or (4) necessity and fairness require disclosure of the privileged information. See "Preliminary facts," ch. 7-A, §14.1.4(1), p. 772; "Discovering party justifies discovery," ch. 7-A, §14.1.5, p. 773.

(b) Deposition of party's attorney. When a movant asks for protection to prevent the deposition of its attorney on the grounds of oppression or privilege, the discovering party has the burden to show "extremely good cause"; that is, the discovering party must show (1) there are no other means to obtain the information than to depose the party's attorney, (2) the information is relevant and not privileged, and (3) the information

is crucial to the preparation of the case. *See* ***Melendrez v. Superior Ct.*** (2d Dist.2013) 215 Cal.App.4th 1343, 1353 n.12; ***Carehouse Convalescent Hosp. v. Superior Ct.*** (4th Dist.2006) 143 Cal.App.4th 1558, 1563-64; ***Estate of Ruchti*** (2d Dist.1993) 12 Cal.App.4th 1593, 1600. There is a presumption against deposing opposing counsel that can be rebutted only by meeting this high standard of extremely good cause. *See* ***Carehouse Convalescent Hosp.***, 143 Cal.App.4th at 1560. *But see* ***Nemirofsky v. Kim*** (N.D.Cal.2007) 523 F.Supp.2d 998, 1000-01 (applying California law; heightened burden does not apply when proposed deposition is of former opposing counsel in different case). If the discovering party does not meet its burden, the court should grant the motion for a protective order and block the deposition. *See* ***Estate of Ruchti***, 12 Cal.App.4th at 1600-01.

(c) Apex deposition. When a movant asks for protection to prevent the deposition of an official at the highest level of management (e.g., a corporate president) on the grounds of unwarranted annoyance, embarrassment, or oppression, the discovering party has the burden to show that the official has unique or superior personal knowledge of discoverable information. ***Liberty Mut.***, 10 Cal.App.4th at 1289; *see* ***Nagle v. Superior Ct.*** (1st Dist.1994) 28 Cal.App.4th 1465, 1467-68. See "Prevent apex deposition," ch. 7-B, §12.1.2(2), p. 808.

(d) Violation of Rule of 35. When a movant asks for protection from an excessive and unwarranted number of specially prepared interrogatories or RFAs, the discovering party has the burden to justify the number of interrogatories or RFAs. CCP §2030.040(b) (special interrogatories), §2033.040(b) (RFAs). See "More than 35," ch. 7-C, §6.2.1(2), p. 822; "More than 35," ch. 7-D, §4.1.1(2), p. 837.

(e) Demand for inaccessible ESI. When a movant asks for protection from a demand or subpoena for the production of ESI that is not reasonably accessible because of the undue burden or expense required to search for, retrieve, and produce the discovery, the discovering party has the burden to show that either (1) the ESI is accessible or (2) there is good cause for the ESI's production even if it is inaccessible. See "Grounds," ch. 7-H, §12.1.2(2), p. 894.

(3) Respond to sanctions. If the motion for a protective order seeks sanctions, the opposing party should challenge the movant's request for sanctions.

(4) Request sanctions. The opposing party should include a request for sanctions if permitted by statute. See "Discovery Sanctions by Motions," chart 9-1, p. 1008. Possible grounds for sanctions include the following:

(a) Unsuccessful motion. The court must impose monetary sanctions against the movant or its attorney for making an unsuccessful motion for a protective order. See "Discovery Sanctions by Motions," chart 9-1, p. 1008. For a list of statutes authorizing monetary sanctions, see "Relief Available Through Motion for Protective Order," chart 9-4, p. 1029.

(b) No meet & confer. If the movant had a duty to meet and confer, the court must impose monetary sanctions against the movant or its attorney for not making a reasonable and good-faith attempt to resolve the discovery dispute informally before making the motion for a protective order. See "Failing to meet & confer," ch. 9-A, §5.2.5, p. 1019.

3. Contents. For a general discussion of the contents of an opposition, see "Opposition Papers," ch. 1-D, §8, p. 35.

§4.3 Motion to compel. If the motion for a protective order was filed in response to a discovery request, the opposing party should consider filing a motion to compel discovery. See "Motion to Compel Depositions," ch. 9-D, p. 1046; "Motion to Compel Written Discovery," ch. 9-E, p. 1057.

§5. REPLY

The movant can file and serve a reply to the opposition papers. The reply must be filed and served at least five court days before the hearing. CCP §1005(b). See "Reply Papers," ch. 1-D, §9, p. 37.

§6. STAY

When appropriate, the court can issue a stay of a deposition pending the hearing and ruling on the motion for a protective order. CCP §2025.270(d).

§7. HEARING

The hearing on a motion for a protective order is conducted in the same manner as civil hearings generally. See "Hearings," ch. 1-H, p. 79.

§8. RULING

In ruling on the motion for a protective order, the discovery statutes must be construed liberally in favor of disclosure when a discovery request is at issue. *See* ***Hauk v. Superior Ct.*** (1964) 61 Cal.2d 295, 298; ***Greyhound Corp. v. Superior Ct.*** (1961) 56 Cal.2d 355, 377-78. The court has wide discretion in deciding whether to grant the motion. *See* ***Hauk***, 61 Cal.2d at 298; ***Greyhound Corp.***, 56 Cal.2d at 378; ***Chronicle Publ'g v. Superior Ct.*** (1960) 54 Cal.2d 548, 575; ***Moskowitz v. Superior Ct.*** (2d Dist.1982) 137 Cal.App.3d 313, 317.

§9. ORDER

§9.1 Form. The court's ruling on a motion for a protective order must be recorded either in writing or by minute order. See "Record of Ruling," ch. 1-I, §4, p. 90.

§9.2 Contents.

1. Motion denied. If the court denies a motion for a protective order in whole or in part, it can order the objecting party to provide or permit the discovery on terms and conditions that are just. CCP §2025.420(g) (depositions), §2030.090(c) (interrogatories), §2031.060(g) (demands to produce), §2033.080(c) (RFAs), §2034.250(c) (demands for exchange of expert-witness information).

2. Motion granted. If the court grants a motion for a protective order, it can prohibit the discovery of all of what was sought, or it can permit the discovery of some of what was sought and set terms and conditions to alleviate the burden of discovery. Weil, *Civil Procedure Before Trial*, ¶8:1455; *see, e.g.*, ***Ibarra v. Superior Ct.*** (2d Dist.2013) 217 Cal.App.4th 695, 706 (protective order did not prevent discovery but merely limited disclosure to protect against unreasonable risk of harm). See "Relief Available Through Motion for Protective Order," chart 9-4, p. 1029.

3. Sanctions imposed. The court must impose sanctions against anyone (party, nonparty, or attorney) who unsuccessfully makes or opposes the motion for a protective order, unless it finds that the person to be sanctioned acted with substantial justification or other circumstances make the imposition of the sanctions unjust. CCP §§2017.020(b), 2019.030(c). See "Sanctions related to specific discovery provisions," ch. 9-A, §5.1, p. 1008. If the court imposes mandatory sanctions, the order should identify the statute the court used as authority for the sanctions and give the reasons for the sanctions. If the court refuses to impose mandatory sanctions, the order must identify the reasons for the refusal. See "Monetary sanctions," ch. 9-A, §9.3.1, p. 1022.

§10. ENFORCING ORDER

If a party does not obey a court order to provide discovery, the court can sanction the party for misuse of the discovery process. CCP §2023.010(g). See "Misuse of discovery," ch. 9-A, §5.2.1, p. 1017.

§11. REVIEW

§11.1 Generally. See "Review of Discovery Orders," ch. 7-A, §17, p. 777.

§11.2 Collateral order. An order denying a motion for a protective order compelling the payment of an expert-witness fee is appealable as a collateral order. *See* ***Brun v. Bailey*** (3d Dist.1994) 27 Cal.App.4th 641, 650-51.

C. MOTION TO QUASH DEPOSITIONS

This subchapter covers motions to quash deposition subpoenas and motions to quash deposition notices.

§1. GENERAL

§1.1 Purpose. A motion to quash a deposition subpoena or deposition notice is used to strike, modify, or impose conditions on a subpoena or notice that is procedurally or substantively defective. *See* CCP §§1987.1(a), 2025.410(c); Sink, *California Subpoena Handbook* (2014-15), §11.5[A]; *see, e.g.*, ***Catholic Mut. Relief Soc'y v. Superior Ct.*** (2007) 42 Cal.4th 358, 365 (motion was based on ground that subpoenas sought information outside scope of discovery); ***John B. v. Superior Ct.*** (2006) 38 Cal.4th 1177, 1186 (motion was based in part on ground that subpoenas violated right to privacy); ***McClatchy Newspapers v. Superior Ct.*** (1945) 26 Cal.2d 386, 391 (motion was based on ground that subpoenas were unreasonable and oppressive); ***Far W. S&L Ass'n v. McLaughlin*** (2d Dist.1988) 201 Cal.App.3d 67, 71 (motion was based on ground that subpoena was not properly served).

§1.2 Primary authority. CCP §§1987.1, 2025.410(c); *see also id.* §1985.3(g) (party consumer can move to quash subpoena for personal records under §1987.1), §1985.4 (procedures of §1985.3 apply to governmental records), §1985.6(f)(1) (employee can move to quash subpoena for personal records under §1987.1), §1987.2 (sanctions for making or opposing motion to quash subpoena).

§1.3 Secondary authority. The following secondary sources are cited as authority in this subchapter:

- *California Civil Discovery Practice* (CEB Online ed. 2014) (referred to as *CEB Discovery Practice*).
- Sink, *California Subpoena Handbook* (2014-15) (referred to as Sink, *Subpoena Handbook*).
- Weil & Brown, *California Practice Guide: Civil Procedure Before Trial* (CD-ROM ed. 2014) (referred to as Weil, *Civil Procedure Before Trial*).

§2. PERSONAL RECORDS & MOTIONS TO QUASH

Motions to quash are often made because a deposition subpoena seeks the discovery of personal records. For a discussion of the discovery of personal records, see "Subpoenas for Personal Records," ch. 8-D, p. 977.

§3. MOTION TO QUASH DEPOSITION SUBPOENA

§3.1 Motion.

1. **Who can make.** A motion to quash a deposition subpoena can be made by the following persons:

(1) **Party.** Any party to the action can make a motion to quash a subpoena. CCP §1987.1(b)(1).

(2) **Witness.** The subpoenaed witness (e.g., a custodian of another person's personal records) can make a motion to quash a subpoena. CCP §1987.1(b)(2); ***Monarch Healthcare v. Superior Ct.*** (4th Dist.2000) 78 Cal.App.4th 1282, 1287-88.

PRACTICE TIP

A nonparty consumer (whose personal records are sought) and a nonparty custodian (from whom a third party's personal records are sought) should serve written objections, not make a motion to quash. Written objections are easier to make and, when made by nonparties, are just as effective as motions to quash. See ***Monarch Healthcare****, 78 Cal.App.4th at 1288 n.2. See "Serve written objections," ch. 8-D, §12.1.2(1), p. 993.*

(3) **Consumer.** A person (party or nonparty) whose consumer, governmental, or employment records or information have been subpoenaed can make a motion to quash the subpoena. *See* CCP §1985.3(g) (party consumer), §1985.4 (state or local-agency employee or any other natural person), §1985.6(f)(1) (employee), §1987.1(b)(3) (consumer), §1987.1(b)(4) (employee). A nonparty consumer can make written objections instead of making a motion to quash. *See* CCP §§1985.3(g) ¶2, 1985.6(f)(2).

QUASH DEPOSITIONS

(4) Person in free-speech action. A person whose "personally identifying information" (as defined in Civ. C. §1798.79.8(b)) has been subpoenaed in connection with an action involving that person's exercise of free-speech rights can make a motion to quash a subpoena. CCP §1987.1(b)(5); *CEB Discovery Practice*, §5.131A.

(5) Court. The court can quash a subpoena on its own motion after giving the parties notice and the opportunity to be heard. CCP §1987.1(a).

2. Deadline to file & serve.

(1) Generally. The Code of Civil Procedure does not specify a deadline for filing a motion to quash a subpoena that does not seek the production of personal records. The only requirement in §1987.1 is that the motion be "reasonably made," but it is not clear whether this phrase refers to timeliness. *Compare* ***Unzipped Apparel, LLC v. Bader*** (2d Dist.2007) 156 Cal.App.4th 123, 135-36 (challenge to timeliness of motion to compel under §1987.1; court rejected argument that "reasonably made" means made within a reasonable time), *with* ***Lee v. Swansboro Country Prop. Owners Ass'n*** (3d Dist.2007) 151 Cal.App.4th 575, 583 (challenge to timeliness of motion to quash; court rejected argument that motion made seven days before date of hearing was not "reasonably made"). As a practical matter, the motion should be made before the date set for compliance, and it must be filed and served at least 16 court days before the date set for the hearing. CCP §1005(b). If the motion is served by means other than personal delivery, the movant will have to add more time to the 16-day period. *Id.* Because a motion to quash a deposition subpoena is a discovery motion, it must be heard at least 15 calendar days before the initial trial date. See "Scheduling Hearing," ch. 1-H, §3, p. 80; "Cutoff for discovery motions," ch. 7-A, §5.2.2, p. 748; "Calculating Deadline to File & Serve Discovery Motion," chart 9-3, p. 1029.

(2) Motion to quash deposition subpoena for personal records. A party consumer or any employee (i.e., the movant) may bring a motion to quash a subpoena that seeks either consumer or employment records before or after the date set for production. CCP §§1985.3(g) ¶1, 1985.4, 1985.6(f)(1); *see* ***Slagle v. Superior Ct.*** (1st Dist.1989) 211 Cal.App.3d 1309, 1312 (nothing in §1985.3 requires party consumer to bring motion before compliance date because statute is simply designed to guide those involved on when custodian can safely honor subpoena). As a practical matter, however, the motion should be made before the date set for compliance; otherwise, the party runs the risk that the custodian will comply with the subpoena. Thus, the motion should be made by the following dates:

(a) Before production date. The movant must give notice "of the bringing" of a motion to quash at least five days before the production date set in the subpoena. *See* CCP §1985.3(g) ¶1 (party consumer must provide notice of motion to witness and deposition officer at least five days before production), §1985.4 (procedures of §1985.3 apply to governmental records), §1985.6(f)(1) (employee must provide notice of motion to witness and deposition officer at least five days before production); *CEB Discovery Practice*, §3.195 (nonparty consumer must serve notice of motion on witness and deposition officer at least five days before date set for production), §5.125 (party consumer must serve notice of motion on witness and deposition officer at least five days before date set for production).

(b) Before hearing & cutoff. The movant must file and serve the motion at least 16 court days before the date set for the hearing and must comply with the additional deadlines for discovery motions. See "Generally," §3.1.2(1), this page.

3. Contents.

(1) Notice of motion & motion. The motion should be made in writing by noticed motion. See "Notice of motion & motion," ch. 1-D, §5.1, p. 28. The notice of motion and motion should contain the following information:

(a) Order to quash.

[1] Relief. The notice of motion and motion should briefly state the relief sought (e.g., "Plaintiff asks the Court for an order quashing service of the deposition subpoena made on the custodian of records for ABC Corp. on January 10, 2014"). *See* CRC 3.1110(a), 3.1112(d)(3). See "Request relief," §3.1.3(2)(c), p. 1040.

[2] **Grounds.** The notice of motion and motion should briefly state the grounds for the motion (e.g., "The motion is made under Code of Civil Procedure §1987.1 on the grounds that the subpoena is invalid and defective because it seeks privileged documents"). *See* CRC 3.1110(a), 3.1112(d)(3). See "Objections to subpoenas," ch. 8-E, §2.1, p. 995.

(b) Sanctions. The notice of motion and motion should briefly state whether sanctions are sought (e.g., "Plaintiff asks the Court for an order awarding reasonable attorney fees and expenses incurred in making the motion"). *See* CCP §1987.2. For the information required to be in the notice when sanctions are sought, see "Required information," ch. 9-A, §3.1, p. 1004.

(c) Stay. If the motion to quash seeks protection from a deposition subpoena, the notice of motion and motion should briefly state whether a stay is sought. *See* CCP §1987.1(a) (court may make any order to protect person from unreasonable or oppressive demands).

(2) Memorandum of points & authorities. The motion must include a memorandum in support of the motion. CRC 3.1112(a)(3). See "Memorandum of points & authorities," ch. 1-D, §5.2, p. 28.

(a) Grounds. A motion to quash a subpoena can include both procedural and substantive objections. See "Objections to subpoenas," ch. 8-E, §2.1, p. 995.

(b) Request stay. The motion can ask the court to stay the taking of the deposition pending the resolution of the motion. *See* CCP §1987.1(a) (court may make any order to protect person from unreasonable or oppressive demands).

NOTE

If a consumer makes a motion to quash to prevent the discovery of personal records, the motion results in an automatic stay that prevents the production of the records. See CCP §1985.3(g) ¶3 (consumer records), §1985.4 (governmental records), §1985.6(f)(3) (employee records). The witness cannot produce the records until a court orders their production or the parties, witnesses, and affected consumers reach an agreement about their production. See id. §1985.3(g) ¶3 (consumer records), §1985.4 (governmental records), §1985.6(f)(3) (employee records). It is unclear whether making the motion stays the deposition itself. If the consumer wants to stay the deposition (not just the production of records), the consumer should include a motion to stay with the motion to quash.

(c) Request relief.

[1] **Quash subpoena.** The motion can ask the court to quash the entire subpoena. CCP §1987.1(a).

[2] **Modify subpoena.** The motion can ask the court to modify the subpoena. CCP §1987.1(a). For example, the motion can ask the court to limit the scope of the interrogation or the number of documents the witness is required to produce. *Cf. id.* §2025.420(b)(10), (b)(11) (for good cause shown, court can issue protective order limiting scope of interrogation and things to be produced).

[3] **Condition subpoena.** The motion can ask the court to impose certain terms and conditions on the subpoena before ordering compliance with it. CCP §1987.1(a). For example, the motion can ask the court to require the subpoenaing party to pay the nonparty's costs for producing electronically stored information. See "Shift expense," ch. 7-H, §9.2.7, p. 890.

[4] **Issue protective order.** The motion can ask the court to issue a protective order. *See* CCP §1987.1(a) (court can make any other order to protect movant from unreasonable or oppressive subpoena). See "Motion for Protective Order," ch. 9-B, p. 1024; "Relief Available Through Motion for Protective Order," chart

9-4, p. 1029. If the motion seeks a protective order, the caption for the motion must also list the motion for a protective order. *See* CRC 2.111(6) (first page of each paper must state nature of paper).

(d) Request sanctions. If the motion papers include a motion for sanctions, the memorandum must identify the authority for the sanctions. See "Provide authority for sanctions," ch. 9-A, §3.1.3, p. 1004. Possible grounds for sanctions include the following:

[1] Bad-faith opposition. The court can award the movant its reasonable expenses, including attorney fees, incurred in making the motion if the court finds that the motion was opposed in bad faith or without substantial justification. CCP §1987.2(a).

[2] Oppressive subpoena requirements. The court can award the movant its reasonable expenses, including attorney fees, incurred in making the motion because one or more of the requirements of the subpoena was oppressive. CCP §1987.2(a).

[3] Personal information subpoenaed in free-speech case. The court must award the movant its reasonable expenses, including attorney fees, incurred in successfully making the motion if (1) the subpoena seeks personally identifying information from an Internet service provider for use in an action pending in an out-of-state court, (2) the underlying action arises from the movant's exercise of free-speech rights on the Internet, and (3) the subpoenaing party did not make a prima facie showing of a cause of action. CCP §1987.2(c).

(3) Supporting evidence. The motion must include supporting evidence. *See* CRC 3.1112(b). See "Supporting evidence," ch. 1-D, §5.3, p. 30.

(a) Discovery & other documents. Copies of the deposition subpoena, the proof of service (POS) of the subpoena, objections (if any), and any other necessary documents (e.g., pleadings) should be attached to the memorandum as exhibits. See "Documents," ch. 1-D, §5.3.3, p. 31.

(b) Declaration. The facts in the memorandum can be supported with evidence, and support is often provided in the form of a declaration. See "Declaration," ch. 1-B, §4.1.1, p. 19. At a minimum, the declaration should state the following facts:

[1] Grounds. The declaration must state specific facts establishing the grounds for the relief requested. *Cf. CEB Discovery Practice*, §5.229 (declaration form for motion to quash deposition notice). See "Objections to subpoenas," ch. 8-E, §2.1, p. 995.

[2] Meet & confer. Even though a meet-and-confer declaration is not required for a motion to quash a subpoena, it is helpful if the declaration states that the movant attempted to resolve the dispute informally and provides facts to support the statement. *See* CCP §1987.1 (no mention of meet-and-confer requirement).

[3] Sanctions. If sanctions are requested, the declaration should provide facts supporting each ground for sanctions against each person identified in the notice of motion and motion as being responsible for the sanctionable conduct. *See* CCP §2023.040. For monetary sanctions, the declaration should identify the total amount sought against each person, itemized by task, fee rate, and time (including the estimated time for traveling to and attending the hearing on the motion). *See id.* See "Amount," ch. 9-A, §4.1.3, p. 1005.

[4] Stay. If a stay of a deposition is requested, the declaration should provide facts supporting the request. *See* CCP §1987.1(a) (court may make any order to protect person from unreasonable or oppressive demands).

(4) Separate statement. A motion to quash a deposition subpoena that requires the production of documents or other tangible things must be accompanied by a separate statement that identifies the documents or things that are in dispute. CRC 3.1345(a)(5). The separate statement must contain all the information necessary to understand each discovery request and related response. CRC 3.1345(c). Neither the court nor any party should be required to look at any other documents to understand the nature of the dispute. *Id.* For the contents of a separate statement, see "Separate statement," ch. 9-B, §3.3.4, p. 1034.

(5) **POS.** The motion should include POS. See "Proof of service," ch. 1-D, §5.6, p. 33.

(6) **Proposed order.** The movant can submit a proposed order with the motion to quash a deposition subpoena. *See* CRC 3.1113(m). If a proposed order is submitted, it must be lodged and served with the motion papers, not attached to them. *Id.*

§3.2 Opposition. To oppose a motion to quash a deposition subpoena, the subpoenaing party can file and serve opposition papers. See "Opposition Papers," ch. 1-D, §8, p. 35.

1. Deadline to file & serve. The opposition must be filed and served at least nine court days before the hearing. CCP §1005(b). See "Filing & serving opposition," ch. 1-D, §8.5, p. 36.

2. Grounds.

(1) **Negate grounds in motion.** A party can oppose the motion by negating the grounds relied on in the motion. For example, if the motion to quash is based on a defect in the subpoena procedure, the opposition papers can refute the alleged defect.

(2) **Respond to sanctions request.** A party can oppose the motion by explaining why the court should deny the movant's request for monetary sanctions. For example, monetary sanctions under CCP §1987.2(a) can be avoided by showing that (1) the motion was not opposed in bad faith, (2) the motion was not opposed without substantial justification, and (3) the requirements of the subpoena were not oppressive. *See* CCP §1987.2(a).

(3) **Request sanctions.** A party opposing the motion should include a request for sanctions if permitted by statute. For example, the court can award the subpoenaing party its reasonable expenses, including attorney fees, incurred in opposing the motion to quash the subpoena if the motion was made in bad faith or without substantial justification. CCP §1987.2(a); *see also* ***Evilsizor v. Sweeney*** (1st Dist.2014) 230 Cal.App.4th 1304, 1311 (P's father failed to timely withdraw motion to quash after D cured defective subpoena; court found motion was "made" without substantial justification).

3. Contents. For a general discussion of the contents of an opposition, see "Opposition Papers," ch. 1-D, §8, p. 35.

§3.3 Reply. The movant can file and serve a reply to opposition papers. The reply must be filed and served at least five court days before the hearing. CCP §1005(b). See "Reply Papers," ch. 1-D, §9, p. 37.

§4. MOTION TO QUASH DEPOSITION NOTICE

§4.1 Motion.

1. Who can make.

(1) **Party.** Any party served with a deposition notice can make a motion to quash the deposition notice. CCP §2025.410(c); *CEB Discovery Practice*, §5.137.

(2) **Consumer.** A person (party or nonparty) whose consumer, governmental, or employment information or records have been requested by a deposition notice can make a motion to quash the deposition notice. See "Consumer," §3.1.1(3), p. 1038.

2. Deadline to file & serve. The Civil Discovery Act does not specify a deadline for filing a motion to quash a deposition notice regardless of whether it seeks the production of personal records. As a practical matter, however, the motion should be made before the date set for compliance, similar to a motion to quash a deposition subpoena. See "Deadline to file & serve," §3.1.2, p. 1039.

PRACTICE TIP

A nonparty consumer can object to the production of personal records by serving written objections; a motion to quash is not necessary. For nonparty consumers, serving written objections is easier and less costly than making a motion to quash and is just as effective.

3. Contents.

(1) Notice of motion & motion. The motion should be made in writing by noticed motion. *See* CCP §2025.410(c). See "Notice of motion & motion," ch. 1-D, §5.1, p. 28. The notice of motion and motion should contain the following information:

(a) Order to quash.

[1] Relief. The notice of motion and motion should briefly state the relief sought (e.g., "Plaintiff asks the Court for an order quashing service of the deposition notice made on Plaintiff on January 10, 2014"). *See* CRC 3.1110(a), 3.1112(d)(3). See "Request relief," §4.1.3(2)(c), this page.

[2] Grounds. The notice of motion and motion should briefly state the grounds for the motion (e.g., "The motion is made under Code of Civil Procedure §2025.410(c) on the grounds that the notice is invalid and defective because it seeks privileged documents"). *See* CRC 3.1110(a), 3.1112(d)(3). See "Grounds," §4.1.3(2)(a), this page.

(b) Sanctions. The notice of motion and motion should briefly state whether sanctions are sought (e.g., "Plaintiff asks the Court for an order awarding reasonable attorney fees and expenses incurred in making the motion"). *See* CCP §2025.410(d). For the information required to be in the notice when sanctions are sought, see "Required information," ch. 9-A, §3.1, p. 1004.

(c) Stay. The notice of motion and motion should briefly state whether a stay is sought. CCP §2025.410(c).

(2) Memorandum of points & authorities. The motion must include a memorandum in support of the motion. CRC 3.1112(a)(3). See "Memorandum of points & authorities," ch. 1-D, §5.2, p. 28.

(a) Grounds. A motion to quash a deposition notice can be made on the following grounds:

[1] Errors in deposition notice. The motion can be based on errors or irregularities in the deposition notice. *See* CCP §2025.410(a), (c). Errors and irregularities in a deposition notice must be addressed by written objections, but a motion to quash can be made in addition to written objections. *See id.* §2025.410(a), (c). For a discussion of written objections and examples of errors and irregularities, see "Written objections," ch. 7-B, §9.9.1, p. 796.

PRACTICE TIP

Unlike written objections, a motion to quash stays the taking of the deposition. See CCP §2025.410(b), (c). If the deposing party refuses to change the deposition notice after being served with written objections, the party who served the objections should move to quash the deposition if it wants to resolve the issue before the deposition takes place. See id. §2025.410(b), (c).

[2] Substantive objections. The motion can be based on the same substantive objections as a motion to quash a deposition subpoena. See "Objections to discovery," ch. 8-E, §2.1.2, p. 997.

(b) Request stay. The motion can ask the court to stay the taking of the deposition. CCP §2025.410(c). The filing of a motion to quash that includes a request to stay automatically stays the deposition until the motion is resolved. *Id.*; *CEB Discovery Practice*, §5.137. No court order granting the stay is required. Weil, *Civil Procedure Before Trial*, ¶8:514.

(c) Request relief.

[1] Quash deposition notice. The motion should ask the court to quash the deposition notice. CCP §2025.410(c).

[2] Modify or condition deposition notice. The motion can presumably ask the court to modify or place conditions on the deposition notice. *See* CCP §2025.410(c) (no mention of modifying or conditioning notice); *cf. id.* §1987.1(a) (motion to quash, modify, or condition deposition subpoena). See "Modify subpoena," §3.1.3(2)(c)[2], p. 1040; "Condition subpoena," §3.1.3(2)(c)[3], p. 1040.

[3] **Issue protective order.** The motion can ask the court to issue a protective order. *See* CCP §2025.420(a), (b). See "Motion for Protective Order," ch. 9-B, p. 1024; "Relief Available Through Motion for Protective Order," chart 9-4, p. 1029. If the motion seeks a protective order, the caption for the motion must also list the motion for a protective order. *See* CRC 2.111(6) (first page of each paper must state nature of paper).

(d) **Request sanctions.** If the motion papers include a motion for sanctions, the memorandum must identify the authority for the sanctions. See "Provide authority for sanctions," ch. 9-A, §3.1.3, p. 1004.

(3) **Supporting evidence.** The motion must include supporting evidence. *See* CRC 3.1112(b). See "Supporting evidence," ch. 1-D, §5.3, p. 30.

(a) **Discovery & other documents.** Copies of the deposition notice, the POS of the notice, objections (if any), and any other necessary documents (e.g., pleadings) should be attached to the memorandum as exhibits. See "Documents," ch. 1-D, §5.3.3, p. 31.

(b) **Declaration.** The facts in the memorandum can be supported with evidence, and support is often provided in the form of a declaration. See "Declaration," ch. 1-B, §4.1.1, p. 19. At a minimum, the declaration should state the following facts:

[1] **Grounds.** The declaration must state specific facts establishing the grounds for the relief requested. *See, e.g.*, *CEB Discovery Practice*, §5.229 (declaration form for motion to quash deposition notice). See "Grounds," §4.1.3(2)(a), p. 1043.

[2] **Meet & confer.** The declaration must provide facts showing that the party attempted to resolve the discovery dispute informally before making the motion. CCP §2025.410(c); *CEB Discovery Practice*, §5.137. See "Meet-and-confer declaration," ch. 7-A, §10.4, p. 763. Copies of any correspondence reflecting attempts to meet and confer should be attached to the motion as exhibits. For a discussion of the obligation to meet and confer, see "Meet-and-Confer Obligation," ch. 7-A, §10, p. 761.

[3] **Sanctions.** If sanctions are requested, the declaration should provide facts supporting each ground for sanctions against each person identified in the notice of motion and motion as being responsible for the sanctionable conduct. *See* CCP §2023.040. For monetary sanctions, the declaration should identify the total amount sought against each person, itemized by task, fee rate, and time (including the estimated time for traveling to and attending the hearing on the motion). *See id.* See "Amount," ch. 9-A, §4.1.3, p. 1005.

(4) **Separate statement.** If the motion to quash is made to prevent the production of documents or other tangible things listed in the deposition notice, the motion must include a separate statement. CRC 3.1345(a)(5). The separate statement must identify the things requested and the movant's objections to them. Weil, *Civil Procedure Before Trial*, ¶8:602.5. The separate statement must contain all the information necessary to understand each discovery request and related response at issue. CRC 3.1345(c). For the contents of a separate statement, see "Separate statement," ch. 9-B, §3.3.4, p. 1034.

(5) **POS.** The motion should include POS. See "Proof of service," ch. 1-D, §5.6, p. 33.

(6) **Proposed order.** The movant can submit a proposed order with the motion to quash. *See* CRC 3.1113(m). If a proposed order is submitted, it must be lodged and served with the motion papers, not attached to them. *Id.* See "Documents lodged," ch. 1-F, §2.3, p. 47.

§4.2 Opposition. To oppose a motion to quash a deposition notice, the party that served the deposition notice can file and serve opposition papers. See "Opposition Papers," ch. 1-D, §8, p. 35.

1. **Deadline to file & serve.** The opposition must be filed and served at least nine court days before the hearing. CCP §1005(b). See "Filing & serving opposition," ch. 1-D, §8.5, p. 36.

2. **Grounds.**

(1) **Negate grounds in motion.** A party can oppose the motion by negating the grounds relied on in the motion. For example, if the motion to quash is based on the assertion that the documents required to be produced by the deposition notice are privileged, the opposition papers can refute that the privilege applies.

(2) Respond to sanctions. If the motion to quash seeks sanctions, the opposing party should challenge the movant's request for sanctions.

(3) Request sanctions. A party opposing the motion should include a request for sanctions if permitted by statute. See "Sanctions for depositions," ch. 9-A, §5.1.1, p. 1011. Possible grounds for sanctions include the following:

(a) Unsuccessful motion. The court should impose monetary sanctions against the movant or its attorney for unsuccessfully making a motion to quash a deposition notice. CCP §2025.410(d).

(b) No meet & confer. The court should impose monetary sanctions against the movant or its attorney for not making a reasonable and good-faith attempt to resolve the discovery dispute informally before making the motion to quash a deposition notice. *See* CCP §§2023.020, 2025.410(c). See "Failing to meet & confer," ch. 9-A, §5.2.5, p. 1019.

3. Contents. For a general discussion of the contents of an opposition, see "Opposition Papers," ch. 1-D, §8, p. 35.

§4.3 Reply. The movant can file and serve a reply to opposition papers. The reply must be filed and served at least five court days before the hearing. CCP §1005(b). See "Reply Papers," ch. 1-D, §9, p. 37.

§5. HEARING

A court must hold a hearing on a motion to quash unless the parties submit the motion or application for determination without a hearing. *See* ***Titmas v. Superior Ct.*** (4th Dist.2001) 87 Cal.App.4th 738, 743 (deposition subpoena). See "Hearings," ch. 1-H, p. 79.

§6. RULING

§6.1 General. The court has wide discretion to grant or deny a motion to quash. *See* ***John B. v. Superior Ct.*** (2006) 38 Cal.4th 1177, 1186.

§6.2 Objections based on privacy. When a motion to quash seeks to prevent the discovery of personal records or information, the court must decide the following four questions:

1. Are the records sought by discovery protected from disclosure by a constitutional right to privacy? *See* ***Manela v. Superior Ct.*** (2d Dist.2009) 177 Cal.App.4th 1139, 1150.

2. Are the records within the scope of discovery? *See, e.g.*, ***John B. v. Superior Ct.*** (2006) 38 Cal.4th 1177, 1187 (in action based on P's allegation that D infected her with HIV, court held information about D's sexual history was within scope of discovery). See "Scope of Discovery," ch. 6-A, p. 603.

3. After balancing the party's right to discover relevant facts against the objecting person's right to privacy, should the court permit discovery? ***John B.***, 38 Cal.4th at 1199; ***Harris v. Superior Ct.*** (2d Dist.1992) 3 Cal.App.4th 661, 665; *see, e.g.*, ***Manela***, 177 Cal.App.4th at 1150 (in child-custody case, mother claimed father's seizures made him incapable of caring for minor child; discovery of father's medical records was permitted because father's privacy interests were outweighed by state's interest in protecting child).

4. If the records are found to be discoverable, are there limits or conditions that can be placed on the discovery? *See, e.g.*, ***John B.***, 38 Cal.4th at 1182 (court imposed time limit on discovery of D's medical records).

§7. ORDER

§7.1 Form. The court's ruling on a motion to quash must be recorded either in writing or by minute order. See "Record of Ruling," ch. 1-I, §4, p. 90.

§7.2 Contents. The court can grant or deny the motion. If the court grants the motion, it can order the following types of relief:

1. Motion to quash deposition subpoena. For the types of relief available for a motion to quash a deposition subpoena, see "Request relief," §3.1.3(2)(c), p. 1040.

2. Motion to quash deposition notice. For the types of relief available for a motion to quash a deposition notice, see "Request relief," §4.1.3(2)(c), p. 1043. For the types of sanctions available for a motion to quash a deposition subpoena, see "Request sanctions," §3.1.3(2)(d), p. 1041.

3. Sanctions. If the court imposes mandatory sanctions, the order should identify the statute the court used as authority for the sanctions and give the reasons for the sanctions (e.g., deponent did not appear for its deposition at stated time and place). If the court refuses to impose mandatory sanctions, the order must identify the reasons for the refusal. See "Monetary sanctions," ch. 9-A, §9.3.1, p. 1022.

§8. REVIEW

See "Review of Discovery Orders," ch. 7-A, §17, p. 777.

D. MOTION TO COMPEL DEPOSITIONS

§1. GENERAL

§1.1 Purpose. A motion to compel can be used to force a recalcitrant witness to attend, testify at, or produce documents, electronically stored information (ESI), or tangible things at a deposition. *See* CCP §§2025.450(a), 2025.480(a); ***Sears, Roebuck & Co. v. National Un. Fire Ins.*** (2d Dist.2005) 131 Cal.App.4th 1342, 1351. It can be used against a party deponent, a party-affiliated deponent, or a nonparty deponent. *See* CCP §2025.450(a) (motion to compel party deponent or party-affiliated deponent to attend, testify, or produce), §2025.480(a) (motion to compel party deponent or nonparty deponent to answer or produce); ***Sears, Roebuck & Co.***, 131 Cal.App.4th at 1351 (subpoenaing party can move to compel nonparty deponent to appear and produce documents). For a list of persons who are considered party-affiliated deponents, see "Party-affiliated witness," ch. 7-B, §2.5, p. 781.

NOTE

For a discussion of how to enforce a subpoena for personal records, see "Motion to Enforce Deposition Subpoena for Personal Records," ch. 9-G, p. 1078. For a discussion of how to compel a deponent to appear for a deposition at a more distant location than what is ordinarily permitted, see "Motion to increase travel limit for party deposition," ch. 7-B, §12.6, p. 809.

---

§1.2 Primary authority. CCP §§2025.450, 2025.480.

§1.3 Secondary authority. The following secondary sources are cited as authority in this subchapter:

- *California Civil Discovery Practice* (CEB Online ed. 2014) (referred to as *CEB Discovery Practice*).
- Weil & Brown, *California Practice Guide: Civil Procedure Before Trial* (CD-ROM ed. 2014) (referred to as Weil, *Civil Procedure Before Trial*).
- Younger & Bradley, *Younger on California Motions* (2014-15) (referred to as Younger, *Cal. Motions*).

§2. MAKING DEPOSITION RECORD TO SUPPORT MOTION

§2.1 Record of noncompliance. When a deponent does not attend, testify at, or produce documents or tangible things at a deposition according to the deposition notice or subpoena, the deposing party should note the deponent's noncompliance on the deposition record in order to support a motion to compel. The procedure for making a deposition record of a deponent's noncompliance varies depending on (1) the nature of the noncompliance (e.g., the deponent did not appear, the deponent appeared but refused to answer questions or produce things) and (2) whether the deponent is a party or a nonparty.

1. Deponent does not appear. When a deponent does not appear for a deposition, the deposing party should do the following:

(1) Mark notice as exhibit. The deposing party should mark the deposition notice and any other documents relating to the nonappearance as exhibits to the deposition. *See CEB Discovery Practice*, §6.71.

(2) Make record of nonappearance. The deposing party should make a record of the deponent's nonappearance. To make a record, the deposing party can do either of the following:

(a) If the deponent is a nonparty, request the deposition officer to make a report, in the form of a declaration or affidavit, certifying the deponent's nonappearance. *See* CCP §1991 ¶2; *see, e.g.*, ***In re Morelli*** (2d Dist.1970) 11 Cal.App.3d 819, 829 (reporter's certification of who was present, which did not include nonparty deponent, and deposition transcript of attorney's statement that deponent would not appear, satisfied reporting requirements of §1991).

(b) On the record, state the following:

[1] the deponent was served with a deposition notice to appear, which identified the time and place for the deposition,

[2] the deposing party, the deposition officer, and other parties appeared for the deposition,

[3] the deponent did not appear,

[4] the amount of time the deposing party and others waited for the deponent to appear,

[5] the deposing party had no advance notice that the deponent would not appear,

[6] the deposing party contacted or attempted to contact the deponent or the deponent's attorney by telephone to inquire about the nonappearance,

[7] if contact was made, that the deponent refused to appear or to reschedule the deposition, and

[8] the time the deposition was adjourned. *See CEB Discovery Practice*, §6.71.

2. Deponent does not answer or produce.

(1) No answer. When a deponent does not answer questions at a deposition, the deposing party should make sure the questions and the deponent's responses are on the record and recorded in the deposition transcript. *See* CCP §2025.480(h) (party moving to compel answers or production must lodge relevant parts of deposition transcript).

(2) No production. When a deponent appears but does not produce documents or things according to the deposition notice or subpoena, the deposing party should do the following:

(a) Mark notice as exhibit. The deposing party should mark the deposition notice or subpoena and any other documents relating to the noncompliance as exhibits to the deposition. *See CEB Discovery Practice*, §6.71.

(b) Make record of nonappearance. The deposing party should make a record of the deponent's noncompliance by doing the following:

[1] reading verbatim the production request to the deposition officer,

[2] restating the request to the deponent, and

[3] obtaining the deponent's response.

§2.2 Record of notice of motion.

1. Notice to party deponent. The deposing party can give a party deponent oral notice of a motion to compel answers or production during the deposition. CCP §2025.480(c). This procedure, referred to as "citing the witness," calls for the attorney to state on the deposition record (1) the deposing party's intention to make a motion

to compel and (2) the time and place the motion will be heard. Weil, *Civil Procedure Before Trial*, ¶8:789. The attorney should then ask the deposition officer to instruct the party deponent to appear at that time and place. *CEB Discovery Practice*, §6.79; *see* CCP §2025.480(c); *see also* ***Parker v. Wolters Kluwer U.S., Inc.*** (2d Dist.2007) 149 Cal.App.4th 285, 296 n.24 (instruction to appear made by attorney, instead of deposition officer, was harmless error). If oral notice is given, the motion to compel can be made ex parte as long as all ex parte requirements are satisfied. *See* ***Parker***, 149 Cal.App.4th at 295-96. See "Ex Parte Practice," ch. 1-E, p. 39. However, if the motion is made ex parte, the deposing party is not entitled to sanctions. ***Parker***, 149 Cal.App.4th at 296. If the deposing party intends to seek sanctions, it must make a noticed motion. See "Notice Requirement," ch. 9-A, §3, p. 1004.

2. Notice to nonparty deponent. The deposing party cannot satisfy the notice requirements for a motion to compel answers or production by giving a nonparty deponent oral notice of the motion during the deposition, even though CCP §2025.480(c) seems to apply to both parties and nonparties. The California Rules of Court specifically require a nonparty to be served with written notice of a motion to compel. CRC 3.1346; Weil, *Civil Procedure Before Trial*, ¶8:790. If a nonparty deponent is given oral notice of a motion to compel during the deposition, the movant must serve the nonparty deponent with motion papers. Weil, *Civil Procedure Before Trial*, ¶8:791.

§2.3 Record of agreement to accept service. The deposing party can ask a nonparty deponent to agree on the deposition record to accept service of a motion to compel answers or production by mail. *See* CRC 3.1346. The deposition record must reflect the nonparty deponent's agreement to accept service of the motion by mail and the mailing address provided by the nonparty deponent. *Id.*

§3. MOTION TO COMPEL DEPOSITION ATTENDANCE

§3.1 Grounds.

1. Nonappearing party deponent. A motion to compel attendance at a deposition can be made on the ground that a party deponent or party-affiliated deponent did not attend a deposition or appeared but refused to proceed. CCP §2025.450(a). To establish this ground, the movant should show the following:

(1) Deponent is party or party-affiliated witness. The movant should identify the deponent's name and state whether the deponent is a party or party-affiliated witness.

(2) Deponent was properly served. The movant should show that the deponent was properly served with a deposition notice. *See* CCP §2025.280(a). See "How to Require Deposition Attendance," ch. 7-B, §7, p. 785. The movant can make this showing by identifying who and what was served and how, when, and where service was made.

(3) Deponent was required to appear. The movant should show that the deponent was required to appear for a deposition on the date and at the time and place identified in the deposition notice, and that the date for the deposition was not rescheduled. *See* CCP §2025.280(a).

(4) Deponent did not appear or refused to proceed. The movant must show that the deponent (1) did not appear at the deposition or appeared but refused to proceed and (2) did not serve a valid written objection to defects in the deposition notice before the deposition. *See* CCP §2025.450(a); ***Robbins v. Regents of the Univ. of Cal.*** (2d Dist.2005) 127 Cal.App.4th 653, 659; *see, e.g.*, ***Parker v. Wolters Kluwer U.S., Inc.*** (2d Dist.2007) 149 Cal.App.4th 285, 292 (motion to compel appearance granted when deponent was 40 minutes late to deposition, refused to be sworn or to testify, and then left early).

(5) Follow-up contact was made. If the deponent did not appear, the movant must show that it made a follow-up contact with the deponent. *See* CCP §2025.450(b)(2); ***Leko v. Cornerstone Home Inspection*** (2d Dist.2001) 86 Cal.App.4th 1109, 1124. A follow-up contact is an informal inquiry into the reasons for a deponent's failure to appear for a deposition; it is not a formal meet-and-confer conference. *See* CCP §2025.450(b)(2). When the movant's attorney makes a follow-up contact, the attorney must listen to the reasons offered by the deponent and make a good-faith attempt to resolve the matter. ***Leko***, 86 Cal.App.4th at 1124. For example, if the deponent did not appear because of an oversight and is willing to reschedule the deposition at a mutually agreeable date, the attorney

should not file a motion to compel. *See id.* To establish that a follow-up contact was made, the movant should identify who made the contact; the person contacted; the date, time, and method of contact (e.g., by telephone); and the results of the contact (e.g., the deponent refused to reschedule the deposition). *See* CCP §2025.450(b)(2).

2. Nonappearing nonparty deponent. A motion to compel attendance at a deposition can be made on the ground that a nonparty deponent did not attend a deposition or appeared but refused to proceed with the deposition. *See* ***Sears, Roebuck & Co. v. National Un. Fire Ins.*** (2d Dist.2005) 131 Cal.App.4th 1342, 1351; *cf.* CCP §2025.450(a) (motion to compel party deponent). Although CCP §2025.450(a) does not apply to nonparties and §2025.480(a) does not address attendance, courts regularly consider and grant motions to compel nonparties to attend depositions. *See, e.g.*, ***Terry v. SLICO*** (1st Dist.2009) 175 Cal.App.4th 352, 355 (court considered motion to compel nonparty to attend deposition); ***Sears, Roebuck & Co.***, 131 Cal.App.4th at 1351 (court held that subpoenaing party can move to compel when nonparty deponent does not appear or produce documents at deposition); ***Brun v. Bailey*** (3d Dist.1994) 27 Cal.App.4th 641, 645-46 (court considered motion to compel nonparty to attend deposition); *see also* Weil, *Civil Procedure Before Trial*, ¶8:609.2 (recommending motion to compel over contempt proceedings). *Contra CEB Discovery Practice*, §6.73 (motion to compel attendance cannot be made against nonparty deponent; only remedy is contempt). To establish this ground, the movant should show the following:

(1) Deponent is nonparty. The movant should identify the deponent's name and state that the deponent is a nonparty.

(2) Deponent was properly served. The movant should show that the deponent was properly served with a deposition subpoena. *See* CCP §2025.280(b). See "How to Require Deposition Attendance," ch. 7-B, §7, p. 785. The movant can make this showing by identifying who and what was served and how, when, and where service was made.

(3) Deponent was required to appear. The movant should show that the deponent was required to appear for a deposition on the date and at the time and place identified in the deposition subpoena, and that the date for the deposition was not rescheduled. *See* CCP §2025.280(b).

(4) Deponent did not appear or refused to proceed. The movant should show that the deponent did not appear at the deposition or appeared but refused to proceed. *See* ***Sears, Roebuck & Co.***, 131 Cal.App.4th at 1351; *cf.* CCP §2025.450(a) (motion to compel party deponent).

(5) Follow-up contact was made. If the deponent did not appear, the movant should show that it made a follow-up contact with the deponent. *See* ***Sears, Roebuck & Co.***, 131 Cal.App.4th at 1351. Nothing in CCP §2025.440(b) (failure to attend by deponent) or §2025.480(a) (motion to compel answers or production) explicitly requires the movant to make a follow-up contact, but it is expected. *See* ***Sears, Roebuck & Co.***, 131 Cal.App.4th at 1351; *cf.* CCP §2025.450(b)(2) (explicitly required before motion to compel party deponent). See "Follow-up contact was made," §3.1.1(5), p. 1048.

PRACTICE TIP

If the court does not allow the discovering party to file a motion to compel the attendance of a nonparty deponent at a deposition, the party can file a motion for contempt. A motion for contempt can be made if the nonparty did not attend a deposition after being properly served with a deposition subpoena. See CCP §2020.240 (nonparty deponent who disobeys deposition subpoena can be punished by contempt); CEB Discovery Practice, §6.69 (same); see, e.g., ***In re Morelli*** *(2d Dist.1970) 11 Cal.App.3d 819, 826 (superior court found nonparty expert witness guilty of contempt for not attending deposition). See "Contempt," ch. 8-E, §3.4, p. 999. However, contempt procedures are complex and time-consuming and rarely result in actual adjudications of contempt. See Weil, Civil Procedure Before Trial, ¶¶8:609.2, 8:617.1. For a discussion of contempt procedures, see CEB Discovery Practice, §15.102, and Weil, Civil Procedure Before Trial, ¶¶8:610-8:617.1.*

§3.2 Motion.

1. Who can make. The party who served the deponent with the deposition notice or subpoena can make a motion to compel attendance at a deposition. *See* CCP §2025.450(a) (party deponents); ***Sears, Roebuck & Co. v. National Un. Fire Ins.*** (2d Dist.2005) 131 Cal.App.4th 1342, 1351 (nonparty deponents).

NOTE

Any other party who attended the scheduled deposition (in person or by attorney) of a party deponent expecting the deponent to testify can make a motion for monetary sanctions against the deponent for not attending. CCP §2025.450(g)(2); CEB Discovery Practice, §§6.74, 15.39.

2. Deadline to file & serve. A motion to compel attendance at a deposition should be filed and served at least 16 court days before the date set for the hearing. CCP §1005(b). If the motion is served by means other than personal delivery, the movant will need to add more time to the 16-day period (e.g., 5 calendar days are added when notice is mailed in California). *Id.* Because a motion to compel attendance at a deposition is a discovery motion, it must be heard at least 15 calendar days before the initial trial date. See "Scheduling Hearing," ch. 1-H, §3, p. 80; "Cut-off for discovery motions," ch. 7-A, §5.2.2, p. 748; "Calculating Deadline to File & Serve Discovery Motion," chart 9-3, p. 1029.

3. How to serve.

(1) Party deponent. The motion to compel a party deponent's attendance must be served on the party deponent's attorney by mail, fax, personal delivery, or any other method agreed to by the parties. *See* CCP §§1005(a)(13), (b), 1015. See "Whom to Serve," ch. 1-G, §3, p. 64; "Methods of service," ch. 1-G, §5.1, p. 66.

(2) Nonparty deponent. The motion to compel a nonparty deponent's attendance must be personally served on the nonparty deponent. *See* CCP §1005(a)(13) (written notice of motion is required); *cf.* CRC 3.1346 (motion to compel answers or production at deposition must be personally served on nonparty deponent); Younger, *Cal. Motions*, §29:41 (nonparty deponent entitled to personal service of deposition subpoena and motion to compel answers or production at deposition).

4. Contents.

(1) Notice of motion & motion. The motion should be made in writing by noticed motion. See "Notice of motion & motion," ch. 1-D, §5.1, p. 28. The noticed motion should contain the following information:

(a) Order compelling attendance.

[1] Relief. The notice of motion and motion should briefly state the relief sought (e.g., "Defendant asks the Court for an order compelling the deponent to attend a deposition"). CRC 3.1110(a), 3.1112(d)(3).

[2] Grounds. The notice of motion and motion should briefly state the grounds for the motion (e.g., "The motion is made on the ground that Plaintiff properly served Defendant with a deposition notice and Defendant did not attend the deposition"). CRC 3.1110(a), 3.1112(d)(3). See "Grounds," §3.1, p. 1048.

(b) Sanctions. The notice of motion and motion should briefly state whether sanctions are sought. To determine whether sanctions are available, see "Discovery Sanctions by Motions," chart 9-1, p. 1008. For the information required to be in the notice when sanctions are sought, see "Required information," ch. 9-A, §3.1, p. 1004.

(2) Memorandum of points & authorities. The motion must include a memorandum in support of the motion. CRC 3.1112(a)(3). See "Memorandum of points & authorities," ch. 1-D, §5.2, p. 28. If the movant is seeking sanctions, the memorandum must identify the legal authority for the sanctions. See "Provide authority for sanctions," ch. 9-A, §3.1.3, p. 1004.

(3) Supporting evidence. The motion must include supporting evidence. *See* CRC 3.1112(b). See "Supporting evidence," ch. 1-D, §5.3, p. 30.

(a) Declaration. At a minimum, the motion must be supported by a declaration stating the following facts:

[1] Grounds. The declaration must provide facts establishing the grounds for the relief requested. See "Grounds," §3.1, p. 1048.

[2] Follow-up contact. The declaration must provide facts supporting the statement that the movant contacted the deponent to inquire about the deponent's nonappearance. *See* CCP §2025.450(b)(2) (party deponents); ***Sears, Roebuck & Co.***, 131 Cal.App.4th at 1351 (nonparty deponents). See "Follow-up contact was made," §3.1.1(5), p. 1048.

[3] Sanctions. If sanctions are requested, the declaration should provide facts supporting each ground for sanctions against each person identified in the notice of motion and motion as being responsible for the sanctionable conduct. For monetary sanctions, the declaration should identify the total amount sought against each person, itemized by task, fee rate, and time (including the estimated time for traveling to and attending the hearing on the motion). *See* CCP §2023.040. See "Amount," ch. 9-A, §4.1.3, p. 1005.

(b) Deposition notice or subpoena. The motion should be supported by a copy of the deposition notice or subpoena with its proof of service (POS).

(c) Deposition transcript. The motion should be supported by the deposition transcript corroborating the deponent's nonappearance or refusal to proceed. See "Deponent does not appear," §2.1.1, p. 1046.

NOTE

For nonparty deponents, the movant can use the deposition officer's declaration of nonappearance instead of the deposition transcript. See "Make record of nonappearance," §2.1.1(2), p. 1047.

[1] Title page. The first page of the deposition transcript must provide the name of the deponent and the date of the deposition. CRC 3.1116(a).

[2] Relevant pages only. The deposition transcript must contain only the relevant pages. CRC 3.1116(b).

[3] Page numbers. The original page numbers of the deposition transcript must be clearly visible. CRC 3.1116(b).

[4] Highlighting of testimony. The relevant parts of the deposition testimony must be marked in a manner that calls attention to the testimony. CRC 3.1116(c). For example, the relevant text can be underlined or highlighted. Weil, *Civil Procedure Before Trial*, ¶8:804.1.

(4) POS. The motion should include POS. See "Proof of service," ch. 1-D, §5.6, p. 33.

(5) Proposed order. The motion can include a proposed order. *See* CRC 3.1113(m). If a proposed order is submitted, it must be lodged and served with the motion papers, not attached to them. *Id.* See "Documents lodged," ch. 1-F, §2.3, p. 47.

(6) No separate statement. The motion does not need to include a separate statement. *See* CRC 3.1345(b). A separate statement is required only when a discovery motion involves the content of a discovery request or response. CRC 3.1345(a).

§4. MOTION TO COMPEL DEPOSITION ANSWERS & PRODUCTION

§4.1 Grounds.

1. No answer. A motion to compel answers or production at a deposition can be made on the ground that a deponent (party or nonparty) appeared for a deposition but did not answer a question or a series of questions during the deposition. *See* CCP §2025.480(a). The deposing party can either (1) finish the deposition on other issues

before making the motion to compel (recommended procedure) or (2) adjourn the deposition and make the motion to compel. *See id.* §2025.460(e). To establish this ground, the movant should show the following:

(1) Deponent's name & status. The movant should identify the deponent by name and status (i.e., party or nonparty).

(2) Deponent was properly served. The movant should show that the deponent was properly served with a deposition notice (if the deponent is a party) or a deposition subpoena (if the deponent is a nonparty). *See* CCP §2025.280. See "How to Require Deposition Attendance," ch. 7-B, §7, p. 785. The movant can make this showing by identifying who and what was served and how, when, and where service was made.

(3) Deponent did not answer. The movant must show that the deponent appeared for a deposition but did not answer a question or a series of questions during the deposition. *See* CCP §2025.480(a).

2. No production. A motion to compel answers or production at a deposition can be made on the ground that a deponent (party or nonparty) did not produce the documents, ESI, or tangible things under the deponent's control required by the deposition notice or subpoena. *See* CCP §2025.480(a). To establish this ground, the movant should show the following:

(1) Deponent's name & status. The movant should identify the deponent by name and status (i.e., party or nonparty).

(2) Deponent was properly served. See "Deponent was properly served," §4.1.1(2), this page.

(3) Deponent did not produce. The movant must show that the deponent did not produce the documents, ESI, or tangible things under the deponent's control required by the deposition notice or subpoena. *See* CCP §2025.480(a).

(4) Good cause for production. The movant must show good cause for the production. *See* CCP §1985(b) (subpoena for production from nonparty deponent), §2025.450(b)(1) (motion to compel production from party deponent); ***Calcor Space Facility, Inc. v. Superior Ct.*** (4th Dist.1997) 53 Cal.App.4th 216, 224 (showing of good cause required when compelling production from nonparties). To do this, the movant should give a detailed statement of how the evidence sought is material to the issues in the case. *See* CCP §1985(b). The movant should also state that the documents, ESI, and tangible things sought at the deposition are subject to discovery because they are within the scope of discovery. *See id.* §2025.480(i). See "Scope of Discovery," ch. 6-A, p. 603.

§4.2 Motion.

1. Who can make. The party who served the deposition notice or subpoena can make a motion to compel the deponent to answer questions or produce things at a deposition. CCP §2025.480(a); *see id.* §2025.450(a) (party deponents); *CEB Discovery Practice*, §15.39 (general discussion of motion to compel response to discovery request).

2. Deadline to file & serve. If made by noticed motion, a motion to compel answers or production at a deposition must be filed and served by the following dates:

(1) Before hearing date & discovery cutoff. The motion must be filed and served at least 16 court days before the date set for the hearing, and it must be heard at least 15 calendar days before the initial trial date. See "Deadline to file & serve," §3.2.2, p. 1050.

(2) By 60-day deadline. The motion must be made within 60 days after the completion of the deposition record. CCP §2025.480(b); ***Unzipped Apparel, LLC v. Bader*** (2d Dist.2007) 156 Cal.App.4th 123, 127. For this reason, the movant should ask the reporter to immediately transcribe the relevant parts of the deposition as soon as it decides to make a motion to compel. The 60-day deadline applies to all depositions, including depositions for business records only. *See* ***Unzipped Apparel***, 156 Cal.App.4th at 134 (60-day deadline applies to subpoena for business records; for that type of deposition, deposition record is not complete until inspection is finished).

3. How to serve.

(1) Party deponent. A motion to compel a party deponent's answer or production can be served on the party deponent's attorney by mail, fax, personal delivery, or any other method agreed to by the parties. *See* CCP §§1005(a)(13), (b), 1015. See "Whom to Serve," ch. 1-G, §3, p. 64; "Methods of service," ch. 1-G, §5.1, p. 66.

(2) Nonparty deponent. Generally, a motion to compel a nonparty deponent's answer or production must be personally served on the nonparty deponent. CRC 3.1346; Weil, *Civil Procedure Before Trial*, ¶8:797; Younger, *Cal. Motions*, §29:41. The motion can be served on the nonparty deponent by mail only if the nonparty deponent agreed on the deposition record to accept service by mail and provided an address for service. CRC 3.1346. See "Record of agreement to accept service," §2.3, p. 1048.

4. Form. Generally, a motion to compel should be made in writing by noticed motion. *See* CCP §2025.480(c); CRC 3.1346. See "Notice of motion & motion," ch. 1-D, §5.1, p. 28. However, the motion can be made by ex parte application if the deposing party (1) gave oral notice of the motion to a party deponent and (2) does not seek sanctions against the party deponent. See "Notice to party deponent," §2.2.1, p. 1047.

5. Contents.

(1) Noticed motion.

(a) Notice of motion & motion. The noticed motion should contain the following information:

[1] Order compelling answer or production.

[a] Relief. The notice of motion and motion should briefly state the relief sought (e.g., "Defendant asks the Court for an order compelling the deponent to produce the documents and things specified in the deposition subpoena"). CRC 3.1110(a), 3.1112(d)(3).

[b] Grounds. The notice of motion and motion should briefly state the grounds for the motion (e.g., "The motion is made on the ground that Plaintiff properly served the custodian of records with a deposition subpoena and the custodian of records did not produce the documents specified in the subpoena"). CRC 3.1110(a), 3.1112(d)(3). See "Grounds," §4.1, p. 1051.

[2] Sanctions. The notice of motion and motion should briefly state whether sanctions are sought. To determine whether sanctions are available, see "Discovery Sanctions by Motions," chart 9-1, p. 1008. For the information required to be in the notice when sanctions are sought, see "Required information," ch. 9-A, §3.1, p. 1004.

(b) Memorandum of points & authorities. The motion must include a memorandum in support of the motion. CRC 3.1112(a)(3). See "Memorandum of points & authorities," ch. 1-D, §5.2, p. 28. If the movant is seeking sanctions, the memorandum must identify the legal authority for the sanctions. See "Provide authority for sanctions," ch. 9-A, §3.1.3, p. 1004.

(c) Supporting evidence. The motion must include supporting evidence. *See* CRC 3.1112(b). See "Supporting evidence," ch. 1-D, §5.3, p. 30.

[1] Declaration. At a minimum, the motion must be supported by a declaration stating the following facts:

[a] Grounds. The declaration must provide facts establishing the grounds for the relief requested. See "Grounds," §4.1, p. 1051.

[b] Meet & confer. The declaration must provide facts supporting that the meet-and-confer requirement was satisfied. CCP §2025.480(b); *see id.* §2025.450(b)(2) (party deponents). See "Meet-and-confer declaration," ch. 7-A, §10.4, p. 763. A meet-and-confer conference is required before a party can make a motion to compel a deponent to answer or produce at a deposition. CCP §2025.480(b); *see id.* §2025.450(b)(2) (party deponents). An argument between attorneys during the deposition does not satisfy the meet-and-confer requirement. *See* ***Townsend v. Superior Ct.*** (2d Dist.1998) 61 Cal.App.4th 1431, 1437-38.

[c] Sanctions. If sanctions are requested, the declaration should provide facts supporting each ground for sanctions against each person identified in the notice of motion and motion as being responsible for the sanctionable conduct. For monetary sanctions, the declaration should identify the total amount

sought against each person, itemized by task, fee rate, and time (including the estimated time for traveling to and attending the hearing on the motion). *See* CCP §2023.040. See "Amount," ch. 9-A, §4.1.3, p. 1005.

[2] Deposition notice or subpoena. The motion should be supported by a copy of the deposition notice or subpoena with its POS.

[3] Deposition transcript. The motion should be supported by the deposition transcript corroborating the deponent's refusal to answer or produce. See "Deponent does not answer or produce," §2.1.2, p. 1047; "Deposition transcript," §3.2.4(3)(c), p. 1051. At least five days before the hearing on the motion to compel, the movant must lodge a certified copy of any parts of the deposition transcript that are relevant to the deponent's refusal to answer or produce. CCP §2025.480(h); *see* ***Unzipped Apparel***, 156 Cal.App.4th at 135 (transcript does not need to be lodged when motion to compel involves failure to produce documents requested in business-records subpoena because no part of transcript will be relevant).

(d) Separate statement. A motion to compel answers or production at a deposition must be accompanied by a separate statement, unless no response was given. CRC 3.1345(a)(4), (a)(5), (b); *see CEB Discovery Practice*, §6.149 (separate-statement form). The separate statement must contain all the information necessary to understand each discovery request and related response. CRC 3.1345(c). Specifically, the separate statement must include the following:

[1] Text of request, response & objections. The separate statement must include the text of the deposition request or question and the text of the deponent's response, answer, or objection and any further responses or answers. CRC 3.1345(c)(1), (c)(2). The separate statement must restate these things verbatim; it should not summarize or incorporate them by reference. CRC 3.1345(c)(1), (c)(2); *see CEB Discovery Practice*, §15.48.

[2] Reason for order. The separate statement must set out the factual and legal reasons to compel further responses, answers, or production for each matter in dispute. CRC 3.1345(c)(3).

[3] Other information. See "Other information," ch. 9-B, §3.3.4(5), p. 1035.

(e) POS. The motion should include POS. See "Proof of service," ch. 1-D, §5.6, p. 33.

(f) Proposed order. The motion can include a proposed order. *See* CRC 3.1113(m). If a proposed order is submitted, it must be lodged and served with the motion papers, not attached to them. *Id.* See "Documents lodged," ch. 1-F, §2.3, p. 47.

(2) Ex parte application. For a discussion of the contents of ex parte applications generally, see "Application Papers," ch. 1-E, §5, p. 42. The application must be supported by the same information needed to support a noticed motion. See "Noticed motion," §4.2.5(1), p. 1053.

§5. RESPONSE

§5.1 Compliance. A deponent served with a motion to compel should consider contacting the deposing party's attorney and agreeing to comply with the discovery instead of filing an opposition. *See CEB Discovery Practice*, §15.54. An unsuccessful opposition can result in monetary sanctions unless the court finds that the opposing party acted with substantial justification or other circumstances make the imposition of sanctions unjust. CCP §2025.480(j). Once a motion to compel is filed, compliance with the discovery request does not prevent sanctions. CRC 3.1348(a). The court can award sanctions on a motion to compel even if the requested discovery is later provided, if no opposition to the motion is filed, or if opposition papers are filed and then withdrawn. *Id.*

§5.2 Opposition.

1. Opposing noticed motion. If the deposing party files a noticed motion to compel, the deponent can respond by filing an opposition.

(1) **Deadline to file & serve.** Opposition papers must be filed and served nine court days before the hearing on the motion. CCP §1005(b). See "Filing & serving opposition," ch. 1-D, §8.5, p. 36.

(2) **Grounds.** The deponent can oppose the motion to compel on the following grounds:

(a) **Negate grounds in motion.** The deponent can oppose the motion by negating the grounds relied on in the motion. *See, e.g.*, ***Leko v. Cornerstone Home Inspection*** (2d Dist.2001) 86 Cal.App.4th 1109, 1123-24 (deponents opposed motion to compel attendance at deposition on ground that movant did not conduct follow-up contact in good faith); ***Nelson v. Superior Ct.*** (4th Dist.1986) 184 Cal.App.3d 444, 454 (deponent opposed motion to compel production at deposition on ground that movant did not show good cause to compel production of documents).

(b) **Bolster objections.** The deponent can oppose the motion by elaborating on any objections made to the initial discovery demand.

(c) **Support claim of privilege.** If the motion to compel seeks information that the deponent originally objected to as privileged, the deponent should establish the preliminary facts for the privilege. *See, e.g.*, ***American Airlines, Inc. v. Superior Ct.*** (2d Dist.2003) 114 Cal.App.4th 881, 885-86 (deponent argued he was justified in not answering deposition question because of privilege; after deposing party moved to compel answer, opposition identified basis of privilege). See "Preliminary facts," ch. 7-A, §14.1.4(1), p. 772.

(d) **Respond to sanctions request.** If the motion to compel seeks sanctions, the deponent should oppose the movant's request for sanctions.

(e) **Request sanctions.** The deponent should include a request for sanctions if permitted by statute. See "Sanctions for depositions," ch. 9-A, §5.1.1, p. 1011. Possible grounds for sanctions include the following:

[1] **Unsuccessful motion.** The court must impose monetary sanctions on the movant or its attorney for making an unsuccessful motion to compel answers or production at a deposition, unless the court finds that the person subject to sanctions acted with substantial justification or other circumstances make the imposition of sanctions unjust. CCP §2025.480(j).

[2] **No meet & confer.** The court must impose monetary sanctions against the movant or its attorney for not making a reasonable and good-faith attempt to resolve the discovery dispute informally before making the motion to compel. *See* CCP §§2023.020, 2025.480(b). See "Failing to meet & confer," ch. 9-A, §5.2.5, p. 1019.

(3) **Contents.** For a general discussion of the contents of an opposition, see "Opposition Papers," ch. 1-D, §8, p. 35.

2. **Opposing ex parte application.** If the deposing party files an ex parte application to compel, the deponent can challenge the application in writing or orally at the hearing. See "Opposing Ex Parte Application," ch. 1-E, §7, p. 44. If the opposition is in writing, it should contain the same information as the opposition to a noticed motion. See "Opposing noticed motion," §5.2.1, p. 1054.

§5.3 Motion for protective order. The deponent can respond to a motion to compel by making a motion for a protective order. See "Motion for Protective Order," ch. 9-B, p. 1024.

§6. REPLY

The movant can file and serve a reply to the opposition papers. The reply must be filed and served at least five court days before the hearing. CCP §1005(b). See "Reply Papers," ch. 1-D, §9, p. 37.

§7. HEARING

The hearing on a motion to compel is conducted in the same manner as civil hearings generally. See "Hearings," ch. 1-H, p. 79.

§8. RULING

The Civil Discovery Act (CDA) gives the court wide discretion when ruling on a motion to compel attendance, answers, or production at a deposition. *See* ***John B. v. Superior Ct.*** (2006) 38 Cal.4th 1177, 1186.

§9. ORDER

§9.1 Form. The court's ruling on a motion to compel must be recorded either in writing or by minute order. See "Record of Ruling," ch. 1-I, §4, p. 90.

§9.2 Contents.

1. Motion denied. The court can deny the motion. For example, the court should deny the motion if it was untimely made. *See* ***Unzipped Apparel, LLC v. Bader*** (2d Dist.2007) 156 Cal.App.4th 123, 136.

2. Motion granted. The court can grant the motion. If the court grants the motion, it will order the deponent's attendance, answers, or production. *See* CCP §§2025.450(a), 2025.480(a).

(1) Nonverbal answers. The court can order the deponent to give a nonverbal response at the deposition, such as a demonstration or reenactment. *See* ***Emerson Elec. Co. v. Superior Ct.*** (1997) 16 Cal.4th 1101, 1111-12.

(2) No unauthorized acts. The court cannot compel the deponent to perform acts that are beyond what is authorized by the CDA. ***Stermer v. Superior Ct.*** (2d Dist.1993) 20 Cal.App.4th 777, 781, *disapproved on other grounds*, ***Emerson Elec. Co. v. Superior Ct.*** (1997) 16 Cal.4th 1101; *see, e.g.*, ***Rifkind v. Superior Ct.*** (2d Dist.1994) 22 Cal.App.4th 1255, 1263 (court cannot compel party who is represented by counsel to answer legal-contention question at deposition).

3. Sanctions. If the court imposes mandatory sanctions, the order should identify the statute the court used as authority for the sanctions and give the reasons for the sanctions (e.g., deponent did not appear for its deposition at stated time and place). If the court refuses to impose mandatory sanctions, the order must identify the reasons for the refusal. See "Monetary sanctions," ch. 9-A, §9.3.1, p. 1022.

§10. ENFORCING ORDER

If a deponent does not obey a court order compelling attendance, answers, or production, the court can sanction the deponent. See "Violation of court order," ch. 9-A, §5.1.1(5), p. 1013.

§11. REVIEW

See "Review of Discovery Orders," ch. 7-A, §17, p. 777.

E. MOTION TO COMPEL WRITTEN DISCOVERY

This subchapter covers motions to compel for interrogatories, demands to produce, and requests for admission (RFAs). It is divided into three main sections: (1) motion to compel an initial response to interrogatories and demands to produce, (2) motion to compel a further response to interrogatories, demands to produce, or RFAs, and (3) motion to compel production in accordance with the statement of compliance served in response to a demand to produce.

§1. GENERAL

§1.1 Purpose. A motion to compel discovery asks the court to order a party to respond to a discovery request. *Black's Law Dictionary* 1171 (10th ed. 2014).

§1.2 Primary authority. CCP §2030.290 (interrogatories), §2030.300 (same), §2031.300 (demand to produce), §2031.310 (same), §2031.320 (same), §2033.290 (RFAs).

§1.3 Secondary authority. The following secondary sources are cited as authority in this subchapter:

- *Action Guide: Handling Motions to Compel & Other Discovery Motions* (CEB Online ed. 2013) (referred to as *CEB Action Guide: Motions to Compel*).
- *California Civil Discovery Practice* (CEB Online ed. 2014) (referred to as *CEB Discovery Practice*).
- Capozzola, *Discovering Privacy*, Los Angeles Lawyer (Nov. 2003), www.lacba.org/Files/LAL/Vol26No8/1455.pdf (referred to as Capozzola, *Discovering Privacy*).

§2. MOTION TO COMPEL INITIAL RESPONSE

A motion to compel an initial response is used when a party does not serve a timely response to interrogatories or a demand to produce. A motion to compel an initial response should not be used to compel a response to an unanswered set of RFAs; instead, a motion to deem the answers admitted should be made. See "Motion to deem requests admitted," ch. 7-D, §6.2.1, p. 841.

§2.1 Grounds. A motion to compel an initial response can be made on the ground that a party did not serve a timely response to interrogatories or a demand to produce. CCP §2030.290(b) (interrogatories), §2031.300(b) (demand to produce); *see* ***Sinaiko Healthcare Consulting, Inc. v. Pacific Healthcare Consultants*** (2d Dist.2007) 148 Cal.App.4th 390, 404. To establish this ground, the movant must show the following:

1. **Proper service.** The movant must show that the responding party was properly served with the discovery request. *See* CCP §2030.080(a) (interrogatories), §2031.040 (demand to produce).

2. **Deadline for response has passed.** The movant must show that the deadline to respond to the discovery request has passed. *See* CCP §2030.260(a), (b) (interrogatories), §2031.260 (demand to produce). The movant should identify the date the discovery request was served, whether any extensions of time were granted, and the responding party's deadline to serve the response. *See CEB Action Guide: Motions to Compel*, Step 10. For a discussion of response deadlines, see "Deadlines to Respond to Discovery," chart 7-9, p. 754.

3. **No timely response.** The movant must show that the responding party did not timely respond to the discovery request. *See* CCP §2030.290 (interrogatories), §2031.300 (demand to produce).

NOTE

Sometimes a response is so defective or inadequate that it is considered no response at all. For example, a response to interrogatories stating that the party is unable to respond is not considered a response. ***Sinaiko Healthcare****, 148 Cal.App.4th at 406. Similarly, an unverified response is not considered a response to the extent that it contains fact-specific answers (by comparison, an unverified objection is considered a response). See "Effect of party's failure to sign or verify," ch. 7-A, §9.4.1(2), p. 759.*

4. Objections waived. The movant should show that the responding party waived any objections to the discovery request, including privilege and exemption objections, by not serving a timely response. *See* CCP §2030.290(a) (interrogatories), §2031.300(a) (demand to produce); ***Coy v. Superior Ct.*** (1962) 58 Cal.2d 210, 216-17 (interrogatories); ***Sinaiko Healthcare***, 148 Cal.App.4th at 403-04 (interrogatories and demand to produce).

§2.2 Motion.

1. Who can make. The discovering party can make a motion to compel an initial response. CCP §2030.290(b) (interrogatories), §2031.300(b) (demand to produce).

2. Deadline to file & serve. A motion to compel an initial response should be filed and served at least 16 court days before the date set for the hearing. CCP §1005(b). If the motion is served by means other than personal delivery, the movant will need to add more time to the 16-day period (e.g., 5 calendar days are added when notice is mailed in California). *Id.* Because a motion to compel an initial response is a discovery motion, it must be heard at least 15 calendar days before the initial trial date. See "Scheduling Hearing," ch. 1-H, §3, p. 80; "Cutoff for discovery motions," ch. 7-A, §5.2.2, p. 748; "Calculating Deadline to File & Serve Discovery Motion," chart 9-3, p. 1029.

3. Meet & confer not required. A meet-and-confer conference is not required for a motion to compel an initial response. ***Sinaiko Healthcare Consulting, Inc. v. Pacific Healthcare Consultants*** (2d Dist.2007) 148 Cal.App.4th 390, 404; *see* CCP §2030.290(b) (no mention of meet-and-confer requirement for motion to compel initial response to interrogatories), §2031.300(b) (no mention of meet-and-confer requirement for motion to compel initial response to demand to produce). However, to save the time and expense of making the motion, the discovering party should contact the responding party and make sure the lack of response was not just a scheduling error. *See CEB Discovery Practice*, §7.109 (interrogatories).

4. Contents.

(1) Notice of motion & motion. The motion should be made in writing by noticed motion. *See* CRC 3.1112(a). See "Notice of motion & motion," ch. 1-D, §5.1, p. 28. The notice of motion and motion should contain the following information:

(a) Order compelling response.

[1] Relief. The notice of motion and motion should briefly state the relief sought (e.g., "Plaintiff asks the Court for an order compelling Defendant to respond to its First Set of Interrogatories"). *See* CCP §2030.290(b) (interrogatories), §2031.300(b) (demand to produce); CRC 3.1110(a), 3.1112(d)(3).

[2] Grounds. The notice of motion and motion should briefly state the grounds for the motion (e.g., "The motion will be made on the ground that Defendant did not serve a timely response to a demand to produce"). *See* CRC 3.1110(a), 3.1112(d)(3). See "Grounds," §2.1, p. 1057.

(b) Sanctions. The notice of motion and motion should briefly state whether sanctions are sought. To determine whether sanctions are available, see "Discovery Sanctions by Motions," chart 9-1, p. 1008. For the information required to be in the notice when sanctions are sought, see "Required information," ch. 9-A, §3.1, p. 1004.

(2) Memorandum of points & authorities. The motion must include a memorandum in support of the motion. CRC 3.1112(a)(3), 3.1113(a). See "Memorandum of points & authorities," ch. 1-D, §5.2, p. 28. If the movant is seeking sanctions, the memorandum must identify the legal authority for the sanctions. *See* CCP §2023.040.

(3) Supporting evidence. The motion must include supporting evidence. *See* CRC 3.1112(b). See "Supporting evidence," ch. 1-D, §5.3, p. 30.

(a) Declaration. At a minimum, the motion must be supported by a declaration stating the following facts:

[1] Grounds. The declaration must provide facts supporting the grounds for the motion. *See CEB Action Guide: Motions to Compel*, Step 10. See "Grounds," §2.1, p. 1057.

[2] Meet & confer. Even though a meet-and-confer declaration is not required for a motion to compel an initial response, it is helpful if the declaration states that the party attempted to resolve the dispute informally and provides facts to support the statement. *See CEB Discovery Practice*, §7.109 (interrogatories).

[3] Sanctions. If sanctions are requested, the declaration must provide facts supporting each ground for sanctions against each person identified in the notice of motion and motion as being responsible for the sanctionable conduct. *See* CCP §2023.040. For monetary sanctions, the declaration must identify the total amount sought against each person, itemized by task, fee rate, and time (including the estimated time for traveling to and attending the hearing on the motion). *See id.* See "Amount," ch. 9-A, §4.1.3, p. 1005. If the movant is seeking sanctions for the responding party's failure to produce electronically stored information (ESI) that was lost, damaged, altered, or overwritten as the result of the routine, good-faith operation of an electronic information system, the declaration will need to state facts showing exceptional circumstances justifying a sanctions award. *See* CCP §2031.300(d)(1). See "Safe Harbor from Sanctions for Lost, Damaged, Altered, or Overwritten ESI," ch. 7-H, §11, p. 892.

(b) Discovery request. The motion should be supported by a copy of the interrogatories or the demand to produce and the proof of service (POS).

(4) No separate statement. The motion does not need to include a separate statement. CRC 3.1345(b); *see* ***Sinaiko Healthcare***, 148 Cal.App.4th at 404. A separate statement is required only when a discovery motion involves the content of a discovery request or response. CRC 3.1345(a).

(5) POS. The motion should include POS. See "Proof of service," ch. 1-D, §5.6, p. 33.

(6) Proposed order. The motion can include a proposed order. *See* CRC 3.1113(m). If a proposed order is submitted, it must be lodged and served with the motion papers, not attached to them. *Id.* See "Documents lodged," ch. 1-F, §2.3, p. 47.

§2.3 Response.

1. Compliance. A party served with a motion to compel an initial response should consider contacting the movant's attorney and agreeing to comply instead of filing opposition papers. *See CEB Discovery Practice*, §15.54. An unsuccessful opposition can result in monetary sanctions. CCP §2030.290(c) (interrogatories), §2031.300(c) (demand to produce). Once a motion to compel is filed, compliance with the discovery request does not prevent sanctions. CRC 3.1348(a). The court can award sanctions on a motion to compel an initial response even if a late response is served, if no opposition to the motion is filed, or if opposition papers are filed and then withdrawn. *Id.*; *see* ***Sinaiko Healthcare Consulting, Inc. v. Pacific Healthcare Consultants*** (2d Dist.2007) 148 Cal.App.4th 390, 396 (court can hear motion to compel even after late responses are served).

2. Opposition. A party can respond to a motion to compel an initial response by filing an opposition.

(1) Deadline to file & serve. The opposition must be filed and served at least nine court days before the hearing. CCP §1005(b). See "Filing & serving opposition," ch. 1-D, §8.5, p. 36.

(2) Grounds.

(a) Negate grounds in motion. The party can oppose the motion by negating the grounds relied on in the motion. For example, if the interrogatories were not served on the date alleged in the motion, the opposition papers should allege and prove that fact.

(b) Challenge waiver of privacy. The party may be able to oppose the motion based on a right to privacy. See "Right to Privacy," ch. 6-F, §1, p. 681. If the movant claims that the opposing party waived its right to privacy by not serving a timely response, the opposing party can argue that the right cannot be waived by a discovery default. *See* Capozzola, *Discovering Privacy* at 28. *But see* ***R.S. Creative, Inc. v. Creative Cotton, Ltd.*** (2d Dist.1999) 75 Cal.App.4th 486, 498 (P waived right to privacy by not seeking protective order).

(c) Respond to sanctions. If the motion to compel seeks sanctions, the opposing party should challenge the movant's request for sanctions.

(d) Request sanctions. A party opposing the motion should include a request for sanctions if permitted by statute. See "Discovery Sanctions by Motions," chart 9-1, p. 1008. Possible grounds for sanctions include the following:

[1] Unsuccessful motion. The court must impose monetary sanctions on the movant or its attorney for making an unsuccessful motion to compel an initial response, unless the court finds that the person subject to sanctions acted with substantial justification or other circumstances make the imposition of the sanctions unjust. CCP §2030.290(c) (interrogatories), §2031.300(c) (demand to produce).

[2] No meet & confer. The court must impose monetary sanctions on the movant or its attorney for not making a reasonable and good-faith attempt to resolve the discovery dispute informally before making the motion to compel a further response. *See* CCP §2023.020. See "Meet & confer required," §3.2.3, p. 1063; "Failing to meet & confer," ch. 9-A, §5.2.5, p. 1019.

(3) Contents. For a general discussion of the contents of an opposition, see "Opposition Papers," ch. 1-D, §8, p. 35.

3. Motion for protective order. The responding party can respond to a motion to compel an initial response by making a motion for a protective order. See "Motion for Protective Order," ch. 9-B, p. 1024.

4. Motion for relief from waiver. If the responding party cannot negate the grounds but still wants to raise objections to the interrogatories or the demand to produce, it should make a motion for relief from waiver. See "Motion for Relief from Waiver of Objections," ch. 9-H, p. 1082.

§2.4 Reply. The movant can file and serve a reply to the opposition papers. The reply must be filed and served at least five court days before the hearing. CCP §1005(b). See "Reply Papers," ch. 1-D, §9, p. 37.

§2.5 Hearing. The hearing on a motion to compel an initial response is conducted in the same manner as civil hearings generally. See "Hearings," ch. 1-H, p. 79.

§2.6 Ruling. The court has wide discretion when ruling on a motion to compel an initial response. *See* ***John B. v. Superior Ct.*** (2006) 38 Cal.4th 1177, 1186.

§2.7 Order.

1. Form. The court's ruling on a motion to compel an initial response must be recorded either in writing or by minute order. See "Record of Ruling," ch. 1-I, §4, p. 90.

2. Contents.

(1) Motion denied. The court can deny the motion. For example, the court should deny the motion if the discovery sought is outside the scope of discovery. *See* ***CBS v. Superior Ct.*** (2d Dist.1968) 263 Cal.App.2d 12, 19. See "Scope of Discovery," ch. 6-A, p. 603.

(2) Motion granted. The court can grant the motion. If the court grants the motion, it should order the responding party to respond to the interrogatories or demand to produce without objection. *See* CCP §2030.290(b) (interrogatories), §2031.300(a) & (b) (demand to produce); *see, e.g.*, ***Sinaiko Healthcare Consulting, Inc. v. Pacific Healthcare Consultants*** (2d Dist.2007) 148 Cal.App.4th 390, 399 (Ds ordered to respond to interrogatories and demand to produce without objection). The court should set the deadline for the responding party to serve its response. *See CEB Discovery Practice*, §15.119 (sample order on motion to compel); *see, e.g.*, ***Sinaiko Healthcare***, 148 Cal.App.4th at 399 (Ds ordered to respond within 20 days).

(3) Sanctions. If the court imposes mandatory sanctions, the order should identify the statute the court used as authority for the sanctions and give the reasons for the sanctions. If the court refuses to impose mandatory sanctions, the order must identify the reasons for the refusal. See "Monetary sanctions," ch. 9-A, §9.3.1, p. 1022.

(a) Sanctions for making or opposing motion. The court must impose monetary sanctions against anyone (party, nonparty, or attorney) who unsuccessfully makes or opposes the motion, unless it finds that the person to be sanctioned acted with substantial justification or other circumstances make the imposition of the sanctions unjust. CCP §2030.290(c) (interrogatories), §2031.300(c) (demand to produce); ***Sinaiko Healthcare***, 148 Cal.App.4th at 404; *see, e.g.*, ***Ellis v. Toshiba Am. Info. Sys.*** (2d Dist.2013) 218 Cal.App.4th 853, 879-80 (P's attorney could not rely on absence of inspection protocol as substantial justification for disobeying court-ordered inspection because lack of protocol was due to attorney's failure to cooperate).

(b) Sanctions for not producing ESI. The court cannot impose sanctions against a party or its attorney for failing to provide ESI that has been lost, damaged, altered, or overwritten as a result of the routine, good-faith operation of an electronic information system unless the movant established exceptional circumstances. CCP §2031.300(d)(1). See "Safe Harbor from Sanctions for Lost, Damaged, Altered, or Overwritten ESI," ch. 7-H, §11, p. 892.

§2.8 Enforcing order. If the responding party does not obey the order compelling an initial response, the court can make any order that is "just," including an order imposing case sanctions. CCP §2030.290(c) (interrogatories), §2031.300(c) (demand to produce). See "Types of Discovery Sanctions," ch. 9-A, §4, p. 1004.

§3. MOTION TO COMPEL FURTHER RESPONSE

A motion to compel a further response is used when a party gives unsatisfactory answers or makes untenable objections to interrogatories, demands to produce, or RFAs (collectively, "written discovery requests"). *See* CCP §2030.300(a) (interrogatories), §2031.310(a) (demand to produce), §2033.290(a) (RFAs); ***Sinaiko Healthcare Consulting, Inc. v. Pacific Healthcare Consultants*** (2d Dist.2007) 148 Cal.App.4th 390, 403 (interrogatories and demand to produce).

§3.1 Grounds.

1. Compel further response to interrogatories. Grounds for compelling a further response to interrogatories include the following:

(1) Evasive or incomplete answer. The movant can show that the responding party's answer to a particular interrogatory is evasive or incomplete. CCP §2030.300(a)(1); *cf.* ***Union Bank v. Superior Ct.*** (2d Dist.1995) 31 Cal.App.4th 573, 580-81 (Ps' factually devoid interrogatory answers provided basis for summary judgment). See "Complete answer," ch. 7-C, §8.3.1(2)(a), p. 827.

(2) Improper exercise of document option. The movant can show that the responding party's exercise of the option to produce documents in response to an interrogatory was unwarranted or the required specification of those documents was inadequate. CCP §2030.300(a)(2). See "Produce documents," ch. 7-C, §8.3.3, p. 827.

(3) Improper objection. The movant can show that the responding party's objection to an interrogatory is without merit or too general. CCP §2030.300(a)(3).

2. Compel further response to demand to produce. The movant must establish the following grounds to compel a further response to a demand to produce:

(1) Good cause. The movant must establish good cause for the production. CCP §2031.310(b)(1); ***Sinaiko Healthcare Consulting, Inc. v. Pacific Healthcare Consultants*** (2d Dist.2007) 148 Cal.App.4th 390, 403. The same good-cause standard is required for a motion to compel the production of documents at a deposition. See "Good cause for production," ch. 9-D, §4.1.2(4), p. 1052.

(2) Further response needed. The movant must show that a further response is needed for one of the following reasons:

(a) Incomplete statement of compliance. The movant can show that the responding party's statement of compliance with the demand to produce is incomplete. CCP §2031.310(a)(1).

(b) Inadequate statement of inability to comply. The movant can show that the responding party's representation that it is unable to comply is inadequate, incomplete, or evasive. CCP §2031.310(a)(2).

(c) Improper objection. The movant can show that the responding party's objection in the response is without merit or too general. CCP §2031.310(a)(3).

(d) ESI not inaccessible. If the responding party objected to the production of ESI on the ground that it is not reasonably accessible, the movant can show that (1) the ESI is reasonably accessible or (2) there is good cause for production of the ESI regardless of its accessibility. *See* CCP §2031.310(e). See "Motion to compel further response to ESI demand," ch. 7-H, §12.4, p. 895.

3. Compel further response to RFAs. The movant must establish one of the following grounds to compel a further response to RFAs:

(1) Evasive or incomplete response. The movant can show that the response to an RFA is evasive or incomplete. CCP §2033.290(a)(1).

(2) Improper objection. The movant can show that the objection to an RFA is without merit or too general. CCP §2033.290(a)(2).

§3.2 Motion.

1. Who can make. The discovering party can make a motion to compel a further response. CCP §2030.300(a) (interrogatories), §2031.310(a) (demand to produce), §2033.290(a) (RFAs).

2. Deadline to file & serve.

(1) Deadline. A motion to compel a further response must be filed and served by the following dates:

(a) Before hearing date & discovery cutoff. The motion must be filed and served at least 16 court days before the date set for the hearing, and it must be heard at least 15 calendar days before the initial trial date. See "Deadline to file & serve," §2.2.2, p. 1058.

(b) By 45-day deadline. The motion must be filed and served within 45 days after the initial verified response or supplemental verified response was personally served or by any specific later date that the discovering party and the responding party agreed to in writing. CCP §2030.300(c) (interrogatories), §2031.310(c) (demand to produce), §2033.290(c) (RFAs); *see* ***Sinaiko Healthcare Consulting, Inc. v. Pacific Healthcare Consultants*** (2d Dist.2007) 148 Cal.App.4th 390, 403. Extra time is added to the 45 days if the response was served by a method other than personal delivery. *See* CCP §§1013, 2016.050. See "Add time for method of service," ch. 1-G, §6.1.4, p. 70.

CAUTION

When calculating the deadline to make a motion to compel a further response to a demand to produce, do not confuse a written response to the demand with the actual production of the things sought. The 45-day deadline to make the motion is counted from the date the responding party serves the written response, not from the production date. ***Standon Co. v. Superior Ct.*** *(4th Dist.1990) 225 Cal.App.3d 898, 902-03.*

(2) Waiver of motion. If the motion to compel a further response is not timely filed, the discovering party waives the right to compel the responding party to make a further response. CCP §2030.300(c) (interrogatories), §2031.310(c) (demand to produce), §2033.290(c) (RFAs); *see* ***New Albertsons, Inc. v. Superior Ct.*** (2d Dist.2008) 168 Cal.App.4th 1403, 1427-28 (demand to produce); ***Sexton v. Superior Ct.*** (2d Dist.1997) 58 Cal.App.4th 1403, 1410 (same); *CEB Discovery Practice*, §7.111 (interrogatories). See "Deadline," §3.2.2(1), this page. The discovering party cannot avoid a waiver by serving another set of the same discovery method, asking substantially the same questions that were asked earlier. *See* ***Professional Career Colls., Magna Inst. v. Superior Ct.*** (4th Dist.1989)

207 Cal.App.3d 490, 494 (interrogatories). The discovering party can, however, seek the same information through another discovery method (e.g., in a deposition instead of by additional interrogatories). ***Carter v. Superior Ct.*** (1st Dist.1990) 218 Cal.App.3d 994, 997.

3. Meet & confer required. A meet-and-confer conference is required for a motion to compel a further response to a written discovery request. *See* CCP §2030.300(b) (interrogatories), §2031.310(b)(2) (demand to produce), §2033.290(b) (RFAs). See "Meet-and-Confer Obligation," ch. 7-A, §10, p. 761.

4. Contents.

(1) Notice of motion & motion. The motion should be made in writing by noticed motion. *See* CRC 3.1112(a). See "Notice of motion & motion," ch. 1-D, §5.1, p. 28. The notice of motion and motion should contain the following information:

(a) Order compelling response.

[1] Relief. The notice of motion and motion should briefly state the relief sought (e.g., "Defendant asks the Court for an order compelling Plaintiff to provide a further response to certain written discovery requests"). *See* CCP §2030.300(a) (interrogatories), §2031.310(a) (demand to produce), §2033.290(a) (RFAs); CRC 3.1110(a), 3.1112(d)(3).

[2] Grounds. The notice of motion and motion should briefly state the grounds for the motion (e.g., "The motion will be made on the ground that Plaintiff provided evasive and incomplete answers to certain interrogatories"). *See* CRC 3.1110(a), 3.1112(d)(3). See "Grounds," §3.1, p. 1061.

(b) Sanctions. The notice of motion and motion should briefly state whether sanctions are sought. To determine whether sanctions are available, see "Discovery Sanctions by Motions," chart 9-1, p. 1008. For the information to be contained in the notice when sanctions are sought, see "Required information," ch. 9-A, §3.1, p. 1004.

(2) Memorandum of points & authorities. The motion must include a memorandum in support of the motion. CRC 3.1112(a)(3), 3.1113(a). See "Memorandum of points & authorities," ch. 1-D, §5.2, p. 28. If the movant is seeking sanctions, the memorandum must identify the legal authority for the sanctions. *See* CCP §2023.040.

(3) Supporting evidence. The motion must include supporting evidence. *See* CRC 3.1112(b). See "Supporting evidence," ch. 1-D, §5.3, p. 30.

(a) Declaration. At a minimum, the motion should be supported by a declaration stating the following facts:

[1] Grounds. The declaration should provide facts supporting the grounds for the motion. *See CEB Action Guide: Motions to Compel*, Step 10. See "Grounds," §3.1, p. 1061. The burden is on the movant to show that the motion was timely filed. ***Sexton***, 58 Cal.App.4th at 1411.

[2] Meet & confer. The declaration must provide facts showing that the movant made a reasonable and good-faith attempt to informally resolve the dispute with the responding party before making the motion to compel. *See* CCP §2030.300(b) (interrogatories), §2031.310(b)(2) (demand to produce), §2033.290(b) (RFAs). See "Meet-and-confer declaration," ch. 7-A, §10.4, p. 763.

[3] Good cause. For a motion to compel a further response to a demand to produce, the declaration must provide specific facts showing good cause for the production. CCP §2031.310(b)(1). See "Good cause," §3.1.2(1), p. 1061.

[4] Sanctions. If sanctions are requested, the declaration should provide facts supporting each ground for sanctions against each person identified in the notice of motion and motion as being responsible for the sanctionable conduct. *See* CCP §2023.040. For monetary sanctions, the declaration should identify the

total amount sought against each person, itemized by task, fee rate, and time (including the estimated time for traveling to and attending the hearing on the motion). *See id.* See "Amount," ch. 9-A, §4.1.3, p. 1005. If the movant is seeking sanctions for the responding party's failure to produce ESI that was lost, damaged, altered, or overwritten as the result of the routine, good-faith operation of an electronic information system, the declaration will need to state facts showing exceptional circumstances justifying a sanctions award. *See* CCP §2031.310(j)(1). See "Safe Harbor from Sanctions for Lost, Damaged, Altered, or Overwritten ESI," ch. 7-H, §11, p. 892.

(b) Discovery request. The motion should be supported by a copy of the written discovery request, its POS, and the response received.

(4) Separate statement. The motion must be accompanied by a separate statement. CRC 3.1345(a)(1)-(a)(3). The separate statement must contain all the information necessary to understand each discovery request and related response at issue. CRC 3.1345(c). Specifically, the separate statement must include the following:

(a) Text of request. The separate statement must include the text of the discovery request. CRC 3.1345(c)(1). Discovery requests must be restated verbatim; they cannot be summarized or incorporated by reference. *See* CRC 3.1345(c).

(b) Text of response. The separate statement must include the text of each response, answer, or objection to the discovery request and any further responses or answers. CRC 3.1345(c)(2).

(c) Set & number. The separate statement must identify the interrogatories, demands to produce, or RFAs by their set and number. CRC 3.1345(d).

(d) Reasons for order. The separate statement must set out the factual and legal reasons to compel further responses, answers, or production for each matter in dispute. CRC 3.1345(c)(3).

(e) Other information. See "Other information," ch. 9-B, §3.3.4(5), p. 1035.

(5) POS. The motion should include POS. See "Proof of service," ch. 1-D, §5.6, p. 33.

(6) Proposed order. The motion can include a proposed order. *See* CRC 3.1113(m). If a proposed order is submitted, it must be lodged and served with the motion papers, not attached to them. *Id.* See "Documents lodged," ch. 1-F, §2.3, p. 47.

§3.3 Response.

1. Compliance. A party served with a motion to compel a further response should consider contacting the movant's attorney and agreeing to comply instead of filing opposition papers. *See CEB Discovery Practice*, §15.54. An unsuccessful opposition can result in monetary sanctions. CCP §2030.300(d) (interrogatories), §2031.310(h) (demand to produce), §2033.290(d) (RFAs).

2. Opposition.

(1) Deadline to file & serve. The opposition must be filed and served at least nine court days before the hearing. CCP §1005(b). See "Filing & serving opposition," ch. 1-D, §8.5, p. 36.

(2) Grounds.

(a) Bolster objections. The party can oppose the motion by elaborating on any timely objections to the written discovery requests. *See* ***Coy v. Superior Ct.*** (1962) 58 Cal.2d 210, 216-17 (only timely objections can be considered on motion to compel answers to interrogatories); ***Schaff v. Superior Ct.*** (5th Dist.1983) 146 Cal.App.3d 921, 923 (same). See "Grounds for Discovery Objections," ch. 7-A, §11, p. 765.

(b) Challenge motion. The party can oppose the motion by challenging the motion to compel. For example, an opposition could be based on the ground that the motion was made after the 45-day deadline and thus the movant waived the right to compel a further response. See "Waiver of motion," §3.2.2(2), p. 1062. Or an opposition could be based on the ground that the motion to compel a further response to a demand to produce did not establish good cause for production. See "Good cause," §3.1.2(1), p. 1061.

(c) Respond to sanctions. If the motion to compel seeks sanctions, the opposing party should challenge the movant's request for sanctions.

(d) Request sanctions. An opposing party should include a request for sanctions if permitted by statute. See "Discovery Sanctions by Motions," chart 9-1, p. 1008. Possible grounds for sanctions include the following:

[1] Unsuccessful motion. The court should impose monetary sanctions on the movant or its attorney for making an unsuccessful motion to compel a further response. *See* CCP §2030.300(d) (interrogatories), §2031.310(h) (demand to produce), §2033.290(d) (RFAs).

[2] No meet & confer. The court must impose monetary sanctions on the movant or its attorney for not making a reasonable and good-faith attempt to resolve the discovery dispute informally before making the motion to compel a further response. *See* CCP §2023.020. See "Meet & confer required," §3.2.3, p. 1063; "Failing to meet & confer," ch. 9-A, §5.2.5, p. 1019.

(3) Contents. For a general discussion of the contents of an opposition, see "Opposition Papers," ch. 1-D, §8, p. 35.

3. Motion for protective order. The responding party can respond to a motion to compel a further response by making a motion for a protective order. See "Motion for Protective Order," ch. 9-B, p. 1024.

§3.4 Reply. The movant can file and serve a reply to the opposition papers. The reply must be filed and served at least five court days before the hearing. CCP §1005(b). See "Reply Papers," ch. 1-D, §9, p. 37.

§3.5 Hearing. The hearing on a motion to compel a further response is conducted in the same manner as civil hearings generally. See "Hearings," ch. 1-H, p. 79.

§3.6 Ruling. The court has wide discretion when ruling on a motion to compel a further response. *See* ***John B. v. Superior Ct.*** (2006) 38 Cal.4th 1177, 1186.

§3.7 Order.

1. Form. The court's ruling on a motion to compel a further response must be recorded either in writing or by minute order. See "Record of Ruling," ch. 1-I, §4, p. 90.

2. Contents.

(1) Motion denied. The court should deny the motion to compel if the motion was untimely made or if the written discovery requests do not serve the purposes of pretrial discovery. *See* CCP §2030.300(c) (interrogatories), §2031.310(c) (demand to produce), §2033.290(c) (RFAs); ***CBS v. Superior Ct.*** (2d Dist.1968) 263 Cal.App.2d 12, 19 (interrogatories did not serve purposes of discovery); *cf.* ***Sexton v. Superior Ct.*** (2d Dist.1997) 58 Cal.App.4th 1403, 1404 (late motion to compel production of documents must be denied). See "Scope of Discovery," ch. 6-A, p. 603.

(2) Motion granted. If the court grants the motion to compel, it should order the responding party to provide further responses to the written discovery requests. *See* CCP §2030.300(a) (interrogatories), §2031.310(a) (demand to produce), §2033.290(a) (RFAs). The court should set a deadline for the responding party to serve a further response. *See CEB Discovery Practice*, §15.119 (sample order on motion to compel).

(3) Sanctions. If the court imposes mandatory sanctions, the order should identify the statute the court used as authority for the sanctions and give the reasons for the sanctions. If the court refuses to impose mandatory sanctions, the order must identify the reasons for the refusal. See "Monetary sanctions," ch. 9-A, §9.3.1, p. 1022.

(a) Sanctions for making or opposing motion. The court must impose monetary sanctions against anyone (party, nonparty, or attorney) who unsuccessfully makes or opposes the motion, unless it finds that the person to be sanctioned acted with substantial justification or other circumstances make the imposition of the sanctions unjust. CCP §2030.300(d) (interrogatories), §2031.310(h) (demand to produce), §2033.290(d) (RFAs).

(b) Sanctions for not producing ESI. The court cannot impose sanctions against a party or its attorney for failing to provide ESI that has been lost, damaged, altered, or overwritten as the result of the routine, good-faith operation of an electronic information system unless the movant established exceptional circumstances. CCP §2031.310(j)(1). See "Safe Harbor from Sanctions for Lost, Damaged, Altered, or Overwritten ESI," ch. 7-H, §11, p. 892.

§3.8 Enforcing order.

1. Interrogatories & demand to produce. If the responding party does not obey an order compelling further responses to interrogatories or a demand to produce, the court can make any order that is "just," including an order imposing case sanctions, monetary sanctions, or both. CCP §2030.300(e) (interrogatories), §2031.310(i) (demand to produce). See "Types of Discovery Sanctions," ch. 9-A, §4, p. 1004.

2. RFAs. If the responding party does not obey an order compelling further responses to RFAs, the court can impose monetary sanctions, deem admitted the matters involved in the requests, or both. CCP §2033.290(e).

§4. MOTION TO COMPEL COMPLIANCE WITH DEMAND TO PRODUCE

A discovering party should make a motion to compel compliance with a demand to produce when the responding party does not permit inspection, copying, testing, sampling, or measuring in accordance with the compliance statement the responding party served in response to the demand. CCP §2031.320(a). See "Statement of compliance," ch. 7-E, §7.3.1, p. 851.

§4.1 Grounds.

1. Compliance statement. The movant must show that the responding party served a statement of compliance in response to the demand to produce. *See* CCP §2031.320(a).

2. Noncompliance. The movant must show that the responding party did not comply with its statement of compliance. *See* CCP §2031.320(a). Examples of noncompliance include the following:

(1) Inadequate production. The responding party can violate its statement of compliance by not permitting inspection, copying, testing, sampling, or measuring in accordance with the terms of the statement. *See* CCP §2031.320(a).

(2) Disorganized mass. The responding party can violate its statement of compliance by producing an inadequately organized mass of written documents or ESI. *See CEB Discovery Practice*, §8.96. See "Documents," ch. 7-E, §8.3.1, p. 853; "How to produce ESI," ch. 7-H, §10.2, p. 891. For example, a party cannot produce a mass of ESI in response to a demand for discovery without any labeling or indexing. *Cf. **Benedict Coll. v. National Credit Sys.*** (D.S.C.2009) No. 3:08-2520-JFA (slip op.; 11-16-09) (interpreting FRCP 34); ***Espy v. Mformation Techs.*** (D.Kan.2009) No. 08-2211-EFM-DWB (slip op.; 9-9-09) (same).

(3) Wrong ESI form. The responding party can violate its statement of compliance by not producing ESI in the correct form (e.g., the form the parties agreed to, the form the demanding party specified, the form in which the ESI is ordinarily maintained). See "How to produce ESI," ch. 7-H, §10.2, p. 891.

(4) Failure to cooperate. The responding party can violate its statement of compliance by refusing to cooperate with the statutory requirements for inspecting, copying, or sampling. *CEB Discovery Practice*, §8.96; *see* CCP §2031.320(a). See "How to produce things," ch. 7-E, §8.3, p. 853.

§4.2 Motion.

1. Who can make. The discovering party can make a motion to compel compliance. CCP §2031.320(a).

2. Deadline to file & serve. The deadline for making a motion to compel compliance is calculated the same way as the deadline for making a motion to compel an initial response. See "Deadline to file & serve," §2.2.2, p. 1058.

3. Meet & confer not required. A meet-and-confer conference is not required for a motion to compel compliance with a demand to produce. *See* CCP §2031.320 (no mention of meet-and-confer requirement). However, to save the time and expense of making the motion, the discovering party should contact the responding party and make sure the noncompliance was not just a simple mistake. *See CEB Action Guide: Motions to Compel*, Steps 4, 10.

4. Contents.

(1) Notice of motion & motion. The motion should be made in writing by noticed motion. *See* CRC 3.1112(a). See "Notice of motion & motion," ch. 1-D, §5.1, p. 28. The notice of motion and motion should contain the following information:

(a) Order compelling compliance.

[1] Relief. The notice of motion and motion should briefly state the relief sought (e.g., "Plaintiff asks the Court for an order compelling Defendant to comply with its statement of compliance"). *See* CCP §2031.320(a); CRC 3.1110(a), 3.1112(d)(3).

[2] Grounds. The notice of motion and motion should briefly state the grounds for the motion (e.g., "The motion will be made on the ground that Defendant responded to Plaintiff's Demand for Inspection Set 1 with a statement of compliance and has refused to allow the inspection of documents according to that statement"). *See* CRC 3.1110(a), 3.1112(d)(3). See "Grounds," §4.1, p. 1066.

(b) Sanctions. The notice of motion and motion should briefly state whether sanctions are sought. To determine whether sanctions are available, see "Discovery Sanctions by Motions," chart 9-1, p. 1008. For the information to be contained in the notice when sanctions are sought, see "Required information," ch. 9-A, §3.1, p. 1004.

(2) Memorandum of points & authorities. The motion must include a memorandum in support of the motion. CRC 3.1112(a)(3), 3.1113(a). See "Memorandum of points & authorities," ch. 1-D, §5.2, p. 28. If the movant is seeking sanctions, the memorandum must identify the legal authority for the sanctions. *See* CCP §2023.040.

(3) Supporting evidence. The motion must include supporting evidence. *See* CRC 3.1112(b). See "Supporting evidence," ch. 1-D, §5.3, p. 30.

(a) Declaration. At a minimum, the declaration should be supported by a declaration stating the following facts:

[1] Grounds. The declaration should provide facts supporting the grounds for the motion. *CEB Discovery Practice*, §8.96; *see CEB Action Guide: Motions to Compel*, Step 10. See "Grounds," §4.1, p. 1066.

[2] Meet & confer. Even though a meet-and-confer declaration is not required for a motion to compel compliance, it is helpful if the declaration states that the party attempted to resolve the dispute informally and provides facts to support the statement. *See CEB Action Guide: Motions to Compel*, Step 10.

[3] Sanctions. If sanctions are requested, the declaration should provide facts supporting each ground for sanctions against each person identified in the notice of motion and motion as being responsible for the sanctionable conduct. *See* CCP §2023.040. For monetary sanctions, the declaration should identify the total amount sought against each person, itemized by task, fee rate, and time (including the estimated time for traveling to and attending the hearing on the motion). *See id.* See "Amount," ch. 9-A, §4.1.3, p. 1005. If the movant is seeking sanctions for the responding party's failure to produce ESI that was lost, damaged, altered, or overwritten as the result of the routine, good-faith operation of an electronic information system, the declaration will need to state facts showing exceptional circumstances justifying a sanctions award. *See* CCP §2031.320(d)(1). See "Safe Harbor from Sanctions for Lost, Damaged, Altered, or Overwritten ESI," ch. 7-H, §11, p. 892.

(b) Discovery request & compliance statement. The motion should be supported by a copy of the demand to produce, the responding party's statement of compliance, and POS.

(4) Separate statement. The motion must be accompanied by a separate statement because it involves the content of a response to a discovery request. *See* CRC 3.1345(a). See "Separate statement," §3.2.4(4), p. 1064.

(5) POS. The motion should include POS. See "Proof of service," ch. 1-D, §5.6, p. 33.

(6) Proposed order. The motion can include a proposed order. *See* CRC 3.1113(m). If a proposed order is submitted, it must be lodged and served with the motion papers, not attached to them. *Id.* See "Documents lodged," ch. 1-F, §2.3, p. 47.

§4.3 Response.

1. Compliance. A party served with a motion to compel compliance should consider contacting the movant's attorney and agreeing to comply instead of filing opposition papers. *See CEB Discovery Practice*, §15.54. An unsuccessful opposition can result in monetary sanctions. CCP §2031.320(b).

2. Opposition. A party can respond to a motion to compel compliance by filing an opposition.

(1) Deadline to file & serve. The opposition must be filed and served at least nine court days before the hearing. CCP §1005(b). See "Filing & serving opposition," ch. 1-D, §8.5, p. 36.

(2) Grounds.

(a) Negate grounds in motion. The party can oppose the motion by negating the grounds relied on in the motion. For example, the responding party can allege that it produced the documents in accordance with the terms of its statement of compliance. *See* CCP §2031.320(a). See "Grounds," §4.1, p. 1066.

(b) Respond to sanctions. If the motion to compel seeks sanctions, the opposing party should challenge the movant's request for sanctions.

(c) Request sanctions. The party opposing the motion should include a request for sanctions if permitted by statute. *See, e.g.*, CCP §2031.320(b) (monetary sanctions for unsuccessfully making motion).

(3) Contents. For a general discussion of the contents of an opposition, see "Opposition Papers," ch. 1-D, §8, p. 35.

3. Motion for protective order. The responding party can respond to a motion to compel compliance by making a motion for a protective order. See "Motion for Protective Order," ch. 9-B, p. 1024.

§4.4 Reply. The movant can file and serve a reply to the opposition papers. The reply must be filed and served at least five court days before the hearing. CCP §1005(b). See "Reply Papers," ch. 1-D, §9, p. 37.

§4.5 Hearing. The hearing on a motion to compel compliance is conducted in the same manner as civil hearings generally. See "Hearings," ch. 1-H, p. 79.

§4.6 Ruling. The court has wide discretion when ruling on a motion to compel compliance with a demand to produce. *See* ***John B. v. Superior Ct.*** (2006) 38 Cal.4th 1177, 1186. Generally, the court must construe discovery statutes liberally in favor of discovery. ***Greyhound Corp. v. Superior Ct.*** (1961) 56 Cal.2d 355, 378.

§4.7 Order.

1. Form. The court's ruling on a motion to compel compliance must be recorded either in writing or by minute order. See "Record of Ruling," ch. 1-I, §4, p. 90.

2. Contents.

(1) Motion denied. The court can deny the motion. The court should deny the motion if it finds that the responding party has complied with the statement of compliance.

(2) Motion granted. The court can grant the motion. If the court grants the motion, it should order the responding party to comply with the demand to produce. *See* CCP §2031.320(a).

(3) Sanctions. If the court imposes mandatory sanctions, the order should identify the statute the court used as authority for the sanctions and give the reasons for the sanctions. If the court refuses to impose mandatory sanctions, the order must identify the reasons for the refusal. See "Monetary sanctions," ch. 9-A, §9.3.1, p. 1022.

(a) Sanctions for making or opposing motion. The court must impose monetary sanctions against anyone (party, nonparty, or attorney) who unsuccessfully makes or opposes the motion, unless it finds that the person to be sanctioned acted with substantial justification or other circumstances make the imposition of the sanctions unjust. CCP §2031.320(b).

(b) Sanctions for not producing ESI. The court cannot impose sanctions against a party or its attorney for failing to provide ESI that has been lost, damaged, altered, or overwritten as the result of the routine, good-faith operation of an electronic information system unless the movant established exceptional circumstances. CCP §2031.320(d)(1). See "Safe Harbor from Sanctions for Lost, Damaged, Altered, or Overwritten ESI," ch. 7-H, §11, p. 892.

§4.8 Enforcing order. If the responding party does not obey the order compelling compliance, the court can make any order that is "just," including an order imposing case sanctions. CCP §2031.320(c). See "Types of Discovery Sanctions," ch. 9-A, §4, p. 1004.

§5. REVIEW

See "Review of Discovery Orders," ch. 7-A, §17, p. 777.

F. MOTION TO COMPEL DISCOVERY OF MEDICAL INFORMATION

This subchapter discusses motions to compel the discovery of medical information. It is divided into three main sections: (1) motion to compel a response to and compliance with a demand for a physical examination of a personal-injury plaintiff, (2) motion to compel compliance with a demand for a physical examination of a personal-injury plaintiff, and (3) motion to compel the delivery of medical reports.

§1. GENERAL

§1.1 Purpose. A motion to compel discovery asks the court to order a party to respond to a discovery request. *Black's Law Dictionary* 1171 (10th ed. 2014).

§1.2 Primary authority. CCP §2032.240 (motion to compel response to and compliance with demand for exam of personal-injury P), §2032.250 (motion to compel compliance with demand for exam of personal-injury P), §2032.620 (motion to compel delivery of medical reports), §2032.650 (same).

§1.3 Secondary authority. The following secondary sources are cited as authority in this subchapter:

• *Action Guide: Handling Motions to Compel & Other Discovery Motions* (CEB Online ed. 2013) (referred to as *CEB Action Guide: Motions to Compel*).

• *California Civil Discovery Practice* (CEB Online ed. 2014) (referred to as *CEB Discovery Practice*).

§2. MOTION TO COMPEL RESPONSE TO & COMPLIANCE WITH DEMAND FOR EXAM OF PERSONAL-INJURY P

§2.1 Grounds. A motion to compel a personal-injury plaintiff's response and compliance can be made on the ground that the personal-injury plaintiff did not serve a timely response to the defendant's demand for a physical examination. *See* CCP §2032.240(b). See "Demand for Physical Examination of Personal-Injury Plaintiff," ch. 7-F, §4, p. 857. To establish this ground, the defendant should show the following:

1. Proper service. The defendant should show that the personal-injury plaintiff was properly served with the demand for a physical examination. *See* CCP §2032.220(e).

2. Deadline for response has passed. The defendant should show that the deadline to respond to the demand has passed. *See* CCP §2032.240(a), (b). The defendant should state the date the demand was served, whether any extensions of time were granted, and the personal-injury plaintiff's deadline to serve the response. The personal-injury plaintiff must serve a written response within 20 days after being served with the demand. *Id.* §2032.230(b). See "Deadline for response," ch. 7-F, §4.2.1(1), p. 859.

3. No timely response. The defendant should show that the personal-injury plaintiff did not timely respond to the demand. *See* CCP §§2032.230(b), 2032.240.

4. Objections waived. The defendant should show that the personal-injury plaintiff waived any objections to the demand by not serving a timely response. *See* CCP §2032.240(a).

§2.2 Motion.

1. Who can make. The defendant who demanded the physical examination of the personal-injury plaintiff can make a motion to compel the personal-injury plaintiff's response and compliance. CCP §2032.240(b). See "Who can make demand," ch. 7-F, §4.1.1, p. 857.

2. Deadline to file & serve. A motion to compel a personal-injury plaintiff's response and compliance should be filed and served at least 16 court days before the date set for the hearing. CCP §1005(b). If the motion is served by means other than personal delivery, the movant will need to add more time to the 16-day period (e.g., 5 calendar days are added when notice is mailed in California). *Id.* Because a motion to compel a personal-injury plaintiff's response and compliance is a discovery motion, it must be heard at least 15 calendar days before the initial trial date. See "Scheduling Hearing," ch. 1-H, §3, p. 80; "Cutoff for discovery motions," ch. 7-A, §5.2.2, p. 748; "Calculating Deadline to File & Serve Discovery Motion," chart 9-3, p. 1029.

3. Contents.

(1) Notice of motion & motion. The motion should be made in writing by noticed motion. See "Notice of motion & motion," ch. 1-D, §5.1, p. 28. The notice of motion and motion should contain the following information:

(a) Order compelling response & compliance.

[1] Relief. The notice of motion and motion should briefly state the relief sought (e.g., "Defendant asks the Court for an order compelling Plaintiff to respond to and comply with Defendant's demand for a physical examination"). CRC 3.1110(a), 3.1112(d)(3).

[2] Grounds. The notice of motion and motion should briefly state the grounds for the motion (e.g., "The motion will be made on the ground that Plaintiff did not serve a timely response to Defendant's demand for a physical examination"). CRC 3.1110(a), 3.1112(d)(3). See "Grounds," §2.1, p. 1069.

(b) Sanctions. The notice of motion and motion should briefly state whether sanctions are sought. To determine whether sanctions are available, see "Discovery Sanctions by Motions," chart 9-1, p. 1008. For the information required to be in the notice when sanctions are sought, see "Required information," ch. 9-A, §3.1, p. 1004.

(2) Memorandum of points & authorities. The motion must include a memorandum in support of the motion. CRC 3.1112(a)(3). See "Memorandum of points & authorities," ch. 1-D, §5.2, p. 28. If the defendant is seeking sanctions, the memorandum must identify the legal authority for the sanctions. *See* CCP §2023.040.

(3) Supporting evidence. The motion must include supporting evidence. *See* CRC 3.1112(b). See "Supporting evidence," ch. 1-D, §5.3, p. 30.

(a) Declaration. At a minimum, the motion should be supported by a declaration stating the following facts:

[1] Grounds. The declaration should provide facts establishing the grounds for the relief requested. *See CEB Action Guide: Motions to Compel*, Step 10; *CEB Discovery Practice*, §10.82. See "Grounds," §2.1, p. 1069.

[2] **Meet & confer.** Even though a meet-and-confer declaration is not required for a motion to compel a personal-injury plaintiff's response and compliance, it is helpful if the declaration states that the defendant attempted to resolve the dispute informally and provides facts to support the statement. *See CEB Action Guide: Motions to Compel*, Step 10.

[3] **Sanctions.** If sanctions are requested, the declaration should provide facts supporting each ground for sanctions against each person identified in the notice of motion and motion as being responsible for the sanctionable conduct. For monetary sanctions, the declaration should identify the total amount sought against each person, itemized by task, fee rate, and time (including the estimated time for traveling to and attending the hearing on the motion). *See* CCP §2023.040. See "Amount," ch. 9-A, §4.1.3, p. 1005.

(b) Demand. The motion should be supported by a copy of the demand for a physical examination with its proof of service (POS).

(4) POS. The motion should include POS. See "Proof of service," ch. 1-D, §5.6, p. 33.

(5) Proposed order. The motion can include a proposed order. *See* CRC 3.1113(m). If a proposed order is submitted, it must be lodged and served with the motion papers, not attached to them. *Id.* See "Documents lodged," ch. 1-F, §2.3, p. 47.

(6) No separate statement. The motion does not need to include a separate statement. *See* CRC 3.1345(b). A separate statement is required only when a discovery motion involves the content of a discovery request or response. CRC 3.1345(a).

§2.3 Response.

1. Compliance. The personal-injury plaintiff should consider contacting the defendant's attorney and agreeing to comply instead of filing opposition papers. *See CEB Discovery Practice*, §15.54. An unsuccessful opposition can result in monetary sanctions. CCP §2032.240(c). Once a motion to compel is filed, compliance with the demand does not prevent sanctions. CRC 3.1348(a). The court can award sanctions on a motion to compel the personal-injury plaintiff's response and compliance even if a late response is served, if no opposition to the motion is filed, or if opposition papers are filed and then withdrawn. *Id.*

2. Opposition. The personal-injury plaintiff can respond to the motion by filing an opposition.

(1) Deadline to file & serve. The opposition must be served at least nine court days before the hearing. CCP §1005(b). See "Filing & serving opposition," ch. 1-D, §8.5, p. 36.

(2) Grounds. The personal-injury plaintiff can challenge the motion on the following grounds:

(a) Negate grounds in motion. The personal-injury plaintiff can oppose the motion by negating the grounds relied on in the motion. For example, if the demand was not served on the date alleged in the motion, the personal-injury plaintiff should deny that allegation.

(b) Respond to sanctions request. If the motion to compel the personal-injury plaintiff's response and compliance seeks sanctions, the personal-injury plaintiff should deny the defendant's request for sanctions.

(c) Request sanctions. The personal-injury plaintiff should include a request for sanctions if permitted by statute. *See, e.g.*, CCP §2032.240(c) (monetary sanctions for unsuccessfully making motion).

(3) Contents. For a general discussion of the contents of an opposition, see "Opposition Papers," ch. 1-D, §8, p. 35.

3. Motion for protective order. The personal-injury plaintiff can respond to the motion by making a motion for a protective order. See "Motion for Protective Order," ch. 9-B, p. 1024.

4. Motion for relief from waiver. If the personal-injury plaintiff cannot negate the grounds for the motion but still wants to raise objections to the demand, she should make a motion for relief from waiver. See "Motion for Relief from Waiver of Objections," ch. 9-H, p. 1082.

§2.4 Reply. The defendant can file and serve a reply to the opposition papers. The reply must be filed and served at least five court days before the hearing. CCP §1005(b). See "Reply Papers," ch. 1-D, §9, p. 37.

§2.5 Hearing. The hearing on a motion to compel a personal-injury plaintiff's response and compliance is conducted in the same manner as civil hearings generally. See "Hearings," ch. 1-H, p. 79.

§2.6 Ruling. The court has wide discretion when ruling on a motion to compel a personal-injury plaintiff's response and compliance. *See* ***John B. v. Superior Ct.*** (2006) 38 Cal.4th 1177, 1186.

§2.7 Order.

1. Form. The court's ruling on a motion to compel a personal-injury plaintiff's response and compliance must be recorded either in writing or by minute order. See "Record of Ruling," ch. 1-I, §4, p. 90.

2. Contents. If the court grants the motion, it should order the personal-injury plaintiff to respond to and comply with the demand. *See* CCP §2032.240(b). If the court awards mandatory sanctions, the order should identify the statute the court used as authority for the sanctions and give the reasons for the sanctions. If the court refuses to impose mandatory sanctions, the order must identify the reasons for the refusal. See "Monetary sanctions," ch. 9-A, §9.3.1, p. 1022.

§2.8 Enforcing the order. If the personal-injury plaintiff does not obey the order compelling a response and compliance, the court can make any order that is "just," including an order imposing case sanctions. CCP §2032.240(d). See "Types of Discovery Sanctions," ch. 9-A, §4, p. 1004.

§3. MOTION TO COMPEL COMPLIANCE WITH DEMAND FOR EXAM OF PERSONAL-INJURY P

§3.1 Grounds. A motion to compel a personal-injury plaintiff's compliance with a demand for a physical examination can be made on the ground that the personal-injury plaintiff's response to the demand was unwarranted. CCP §2032.250(a); *CEB Discovery Practice*, §10.37. See "Demand for Physical Examination of Personal-Injury Plaintiff," ch. 7-F, §4, p. 857. To establish this ground, the defendant should show the following:

1. Proper service. The defendant should show that the personal-injury plaintiff was properly served with the demand for a physical examination. *See* CCP §2032.220(e).

2. Unwarranted response. The defendant should show that the personal-injury plaintiff's response to the demand was unwarranted. *See* CCP §2032.250(a).

(1) Unwarranted modification. The defendant can show that the personal-injury plaintiff made an unwarranted modification to the demand. CCP §2032.250(a).

(2) Unwarranted refusal to submit to exam. The defendant can show that the personal-injury plaintiff's refusal to submit to the physical examination was unwarranted. CCP §2032.250(a). For example, if the personal-injury plaintiff raised any objections to the demand in its response, the defendant should negate the grounds for the objections. *See id.*

§3.2 Motion.

1. Who can make. The defendant who demanded the physical examination of the personal-injury plaintiff can make a motion to compel the personal-injury plaintiff's compliance with the demand. CCP §2032.250(a). See "Who can make demand," ch. 7-F, §4.1.1, p. 857.

2. Deadline to file & serve. The deadline for making a motion to compel a personal-injury plaintiff's compliance is calculated the same way as the deadline for making a motion to compel a personal-injury plaintiff's response and compliance. See "Deadline to file & serve," §2.2.2, p. 1070.

3. Contents.

(1) Notice of motion & motion. The motion should be made in writing by noticed motion. See "Notice of motion & motion," ch. 1-D, §5.1, p. 28. The notice of motion and motion should contain the following information:

(a) Order compelling compliance.

[1] Relief. The notice of motion and motion should briefly state the relief sought (e.g., "Defendant asks the Court for an order compelling Plaintiff to submit to the physical examination without any unwarranted modifications"). CRC 3.1110(a), 3.1112(d)(3).

[2] Grounds. The notice of motion and motion should briefly state the grounds for the motion (e.g., "The motion will be made on the ground that Plaintiff's response to Defendant's demand for a physical examination is unwarranted"). CRC 3.1110(a), 3.1112(d)(3). See "Grounds," §3.1, p. 1072.

(b) Sanctions. The notice of motion and motion should briefly state whether sanctions are sought. To determine whether sanctions are available, see "Discovery Sanctions by Motions," chart 9-1, p. 1008. For the information required to be in the notice when sanctions are sought, see "Required information," ch. 9-A, §3.1, p. 1004.

(2) Memorandum of points & authorities. The motion must include a memorandum in support of the motion. CRC 3.1112(a)(3). See "Memorandum of points & authorities," ch. 1-D, §5.2, p. 28. If the defendant is seeking sanctions, the memorandum must identify the legal authority for the sanctions. *See* CCP §2023.040.

(3) Supporting evidence. The motion must include supporting evidence. *See* CRC 3.1112(b). See "Supporting evidence," ch. 1-D, §5.3, p. 30.

(a) Declaration. At a minimum, the motion should be supported by a declaration stating the following facts:

[1] Grounds. The declaration should provide facts establishing the grounds for the relief requested. *See CEB Action Guide: Motions to Compel*, Step 10. See "Grounds," §3.1, p. 1072.

[2] Meet & confer. The declaration must provide facts showing that the defendant made a reasonable and good-faith attempt to informally resolve the dispute with the personal-injury plaintiff before making the motion. *See* CCP §2032.250(a). See "Meet-and-confer declaration," ch. 7-A, §10.4, p. 763.

[3] Sanctions. If sanctions are requested, the declaration should provide facts supporting each ground for sanctions against each person identified in the notice of motion and motion as being responsible for the sanctionable conduct. For monetary sanctions, the declaration should identify the total amount sought against each person, itemized by task, fee rate, and time (including the estimated time for traveling to and attending the hearing on the motion). *See* CCP §2023.040. See "Amount," ch. 9-A, §4.1.3, p. 1005.

(b) Demand. The motion should be supported by a copy of the demand for a physical examination with its POS.

(c) Response to demand. The motion should be supported by a copy of the personal-injury plaintiff's response to the demand.

(4) Separate statement. The motion must be accompanied by a separate statement. CRC 3.1345(a)(6); *CEB Discovery Practice*, §10.38. The separate statement must contain all the information necessary to understand each discovery request and related response. CRC 3.1345(c). Specifically, the separate statement must include the following:

(a) Text of request, response & objections. The separate statement must include the text of the demand for a physical examination and the text of the personal-injury plaintiff's response or objection. CRC 3.1345(c)(1), (c)(2). The separate statement must restate these things verbatim; it should not summarize or incorporate them by reference. CRC 3.1345(c)(1), (c)(2); *see CEB Discovery Practice*, §15.48.

(b) Reasons for order. The separate statement must set out the factual and legal reasons to compel compliance for each matter in dispute. CRC 3.1345(c)(3).

(c) Other information. See "Other information," ch. 9-B, §3.3.4(5), p. 1035.

(5) **POS.** The motion should include POS. See "Proof of service," ch. 1-D, §5.6, p. 33.

(6) **Proposed order.** The motion can include a proposed order. *See* CRC 3.1113(m). If a proposed order is submitted, it must be lodged and served with the motion papers, not attached to them. *Id.* See "Documents lodged," ch. 1-F, §2.3, p. 47.

§3.3 Response.

1. **Compliance.** The personal-injury plaintiff should consider contacting the defendant's attorney and agreeing to comply instead of filing opposition papers. *See CEB Discovery Practice*, §15.54. An unsuccessful opposition can result in monetary sanctions. CCP §2032.250(b). See "Compliance," §2.3.1, p. 1071.

2. **Opposition.** The personal-injury plaintiff can respond to the motion by filing an opposition.

(1) **Deadline to file & serve.** The opposition must be served at least nine court days before the hearing. CCP §1005(b). See "Filing & serving opposition," ch. 1-D, §8.5, p. 36.

(2) **Grounds.** The personal-injury plaintiff can challenge the motion on the following grounds:

(a) **Negate grounds in motion.** The personal-injury plaintiff can oppose the motion by negating the grounds relied on in the motion.

(b) **Bolster objections.** The personal-injury plaintiff can oppose the motion by elaborating on any objections made to the demand for a physical examination.

(c) **Respond to sanctions request.** If the motion to compel the personal-injury plaintiff's compliance seeks sanctions, the personal-injury plaintiff should deny the defendant's request for sanctions.

(d) **Request sanctions.** The personal-injury plaintiff should include a request for sanctions if permitted by statute. See "Sanctions for medical discovery," ch. 9-A, §5.1.5, p. 1016. Possible grounds for sanctions include the following:

[1] **Unsuccessful motion.** The court should impose monetary sanctions on the movant or its attorney for unsuccessfully making a motion to compel a personal-injury plaintiff's compliance. CCP §2032.250(b).

[2] **No meet & confer.** The court must impose monetary sanctions on the movant or its attorney for not making a reasonable and good-faith attempt to resolve the discovery dispute informally before making the motion. *See* CCP §§2023.020, 2032.250(a). See "Failing to meet & confer," ch. 9-A, §5.2.5, p. 1019.

(3) **Contents.** For a general discussion of the contents of an opposition, see "Opposition Papers," ch. 1-D, §8, p. 35.

3. **Motion for protective order.** The personal-injury plaintiff can respond to the motion by making a motion for a protective order. See "Motion for Protective Order," ch. 9-B, p. 1024.

§3.4 Reply. The defendant can file and serve a reply to the opposition papers. The reply must be filed and served at least five court days before the hearing. CCP §1005(b). See "Reply Papers," ch. 1-D, §9, p. 37.

§3.5 Hearing. The hearing on a motion to compel a personal-injury plaintiff's compliance is conducted in the same manner as civil hearings generally. See "Hearings," ch. 1-H, p. 79.

§3.6 Ruling. The court has wide discretion when ruling on a motion to compel a personal-injury plaintiff's compliance. *See* ***John B. v. Superior Ct.*** (2006) 38 Cal.4th 1177, 1186.

§3.7 Order.

1. **Form.** The court's ruling on a motion to compel a personal-injury plaintiff's compliance must be recorded either in writing or by minute order. See "Record of Ruling," ch. 1-I, §4, p. 90.

2. Contents. If the court grants the motion, it should order the personal-injury plaintiff to comply with the demand. *See* CCP §2032.250(a). If the court awards mandatory sanctions, the order should identify the statute the court used as authority for the sanctions and give the reasons for the sanctions. If the court refuses to impose mandatory sanctions, the order must identify the reasons for the refusal. See "Monetary sanctions," ch. 9-A, §9.3.1, p. 1022.

§4. MOTION TO COMPEL DELIVERY OF MEDICAL REPORTS

§4.1 Grounds.

1. Examining party does not deliver reports. A motion to compel the delivery of medical reports can be made on the ground that the examining party (i.e., the party who demanded the medical examination) did not deliver medical reports. *See* CCP §2032.620(a). To establish this ground, the movant must show the following:

(1) The examined party (i.e., the party who submitted to or produced another person for an examination) served a written demand for copies of certain medical reports relating to the medical examination. *See* CCP §2032.620(a). See "Demand for reports," ch. 7-F, §7.1, p. 866.

(2) The examining party did not deliver to the examined party the requested medical reports. *See* CCP §2032.620(a).

2. Examined party does not deliver reports. A motion to compel the delivery of medical reports can be made on the ground that the examined party did not deliver medical reports. To establish this ground, the movant must show the following:

(1) The examining party complied with the examined party's demand for medical reports relating to the medical examination. *See* CCP §2032.650(a).

(2) The examining party is entitled to receive certain medical reports from the examined party. See "Exchange of reports," ch. 7-F, §7.3.2, p. 866.

(3) The examined party did not deliver to the examining party the medical reports the examining party is entitled to receive. *See* CCP §2032.650(a).

§4.2 Motion.

1. Who can make.

(1) Examined party. The party who submitted to an examination or produced another person for an examination can make a motion to compel the delivery of medical reports. CCP §2032.620(a).

(2) Examining party. The party who demanded an examination can make a motion to compel the delivery of medical reports. CCP §2032.650(a).

2. Deadline to file & serve. The deadline for making a motion to compel the delivery of medical reports is calculated the same way as the deadline for making a motion to compel a response and compliance. See "Deadline to file & serve," §2.2.2, p. 1070.

3. Contents.

(1) Notice of motion & motion. The motion should be made in writing by noticed motion. See "Notice of motion & motion," ch. 1-D, §5.1, p. 28. The notice of motion and motion should contain the following information:

(a) Order compelling delivery of reports.

[1] Relief. The notice of motion and motion should briefly state the relief sought (e.g., "Defendant asks the Court for an order compelling Plaintiff to deliver medical reports"). CRC 3.1110(a), 3.1112(d)(3).

[2] **Grounds.** The notice of motion and motion should briefly state the grounds for the motion (e.g., "The motion will be made on the ground that Plaintiff did not deliver medical reports after Defendant complied with its own obligation to deliver medical reports"). CRC 3.1110(a), 3.1112(d)(3). See "Grounds," §4.1, p. 1075.

(b) Sanctions. The notice of motion and motion should briefly state whether sanctions are sought. To determine whether sanctions are available, see "Discovery Sanctions by Motions," chart 9-1, p. 1008. For the information to be contained in the notice when sanctions are sought, see "Required information," ch. 9-A, §3.1, p. 1004.

(2) Memorandum of points & authorities. The motion must include a memorandum in support of the motion. CRC 3.1112(a)(3). See "Memorandum of points & authorities," ch. 1-D, §5.2, p. 28. If the movant is seeking sanctions, the memorandum must identify the legal authority for the sanctions. *See* CCP §2023.040.

(3) Supporting evidence. The motion must include supporting evidence. *See* CRC 3.1112(b). See "Supporting evidence," ch. 1-D, §5.3, p. 30.

(a) Declaration. At a minimum, the motion should be supported by a declaration stating the following facts:

[1] **Grounds.** The declaration should provide facts establishing the grounds for the relief requested. *See CEB Action Guide: Motions to Compel*, Step 10. See "Grounds," §4.1, p. 1075.

[2] **Meet & confer.** The declaration must provide facts showing that the movant made a reasonable and good-faith attempt to informally resolve the dispute with the responding party before making the motion. *See* CCP §§2032.620(a), 2032.650(a). See "Meet-and-confer declaration," ch. 7-A, §10.4, p. 763.

[3] **Sanctions.** If sanctions are requested, the declaration should provide facts supporting each ground for sanctions against each person identified in the notice of motion and motion as being responsible for the sanctionable conduct. For monetary sanctions, the declaration should identify the total amount sought against each person, itemized by task, fee rate, and time (including the estimated time for traveling to and attending the hearing on the motion). *See* CCP §2023.040. See "Amount," ch. 9-A, §4.1.3, p. 1005.

(b) Demand. The motion should be supported by a copy of the demand for medical reports with its POS.

(4) Separate statement. The motion must be accompanied by a separate statement only if the motion involves the content of a discovery request or response. CRC 3.1345(a). If the other party made no response to the movant's demand for medical reports, the motion does not need to include a separate statement. CRC 3.1345(b). For the contents of a separate statement, see "Separate statement," ch. 9-B, §3.3.4, p. 1034.

(5) POS. The motion should include POS. See "Proof of service," ch. 1-D, §5.6, p. 33.

(6) Proposed order. The motion can include a proposed order. *See* CRC 3.1113(m). If a proposed order is submitted, it must be lodged and served with the motion papers, not attached to them. *Id.* See "Documents lodged," ch. 1-F, §2.3, p. 47.

§4.3 Response.

1. Compliance. The party from whom medical reports are sought should consider contacting the movant's attorney and agreeing to comply instead of filing opposition papers. *See CEB Discovery Practice*, §15.54. An unsuccessful opposition can result in monetary sanctions. CCP §2032.620(b) (motion by examined party), §2032.650(b) (motion by examining party). See "Compliance," §2.3.1, p. 1071.

2. Opposition. The opposing party can respond to the motion by filing an opposition.

(1) Deadline to file & serve. The opposition must be served at least nine court days before the hearing. CCP §1005(b). See "Filing & serving opposition," ch. 1-D, §8.5, p. 36.

(2) **Grounds.** The opposing party can challenge the motion on the following grounds:

(a) **Negate grounds in motion.** The opposing party can oppose the motion by negating the grounds relied on in the motion.

(b) **Respond to sanctions request.** If the motion to compel the delivery of medical reports requests sanctions, the opposing party should deny the movant's request for sanctions.

(c) **Request sanctions.** The opposing party should include a request for sanctions if permitted by statute.

[1] **Unsuccessful motion.** The court should impose monetary sanctions on the movant or its attorney for unsuccessfully making a motion to compel the delivery of medical reports. CCP §2032.620(b) (motion by examined party), §2032.650(b) (motion by examining party).

[2] **No meet & confer.** The court must impose monetary sanctions on the movant or its attorney for not making a reasonable and good-faith attempt to resolve the discovery dispute informally before making the motion. *See* CCP §§2023.020, 2032.620(a), 2032.650(a). See "Failing to meet & confer," ch. 9-A, §5.2.5, p. 1019.

(3) **Contents.** For a general discussion of the contents of an opposition, see "Opposition Papers," ch. 1-D, §8, p. 35.

3. **Motion for protective order.** The opposing party can respond to the motion by making a motion for a protective order. See "Motion for Protective Order," ch. 9-B, p. 1024.

§4.4 Reply. The movant can file and serve a reply to the opposition papers. The reply must be filed and served at least five court days before the hearing. CCP §1005(b). See "Reply Papers," ch. 1-D, §9, p. 37.

§4.5 Hearing. The hearing on a motion to compel the delivery of medical reports is conducted in the same manner as civil hearings generally. See "Hearings," ch. 1-H, p. 79.

§4.6 Ruling. The court has wide discretion when ruling on a motion to compel the delivery of medical reports. *See **John B. v. Superior Ct.*** (2006) 38 Cal.4th 1177, 1186.

§4.7 Order.

1. **Form.** The court's ruling on a motion to compel the delivery of medical reports must be recorded either in writing or by minute order. See "Record of Ruling," ch. 1-I, §4, p. 90.

2. **Contents.** If the court grants the motion, it should order the delivery of the medical reports. *See* CCP §§2032.620(a), 2032.650(a). If the court awards mandatory sanctions, the order should identify the statute the court used as authority for the sanctions and give the reasons for the sanctions. If the court refuses to impose mandatory sanctions, the order must identify the reasons for the refusal. See "Monetary sanctions," ch. 9-A, §9.3.1, p. 1022.

§4.8 Enforcing order. If a party does not obey the order compelling delivery of medical reports, the court can make any order that is "just," including an order imposing monetary sanctions, case sanctions, or both. CCP §§2032.620(c), 2032.650(c). See "Types of Discovery Sanctions," ch. 9-A, §4, p. 1004. The court must exclude at trial the testimony of any examiner whose report is not produced in accordance with the order. *See* CCP §§2032.620(c), 2032.650(c).

§5. REVIEW

See "Review of Discovery Orders," ch. 7-A, §17, p. 777.

DISCOVERY OF MEDICAL INFORMATION

G. MOTION TO ENFORCE DEPOSITION SUBPOENA FOR PERSONAL RECORDS

§1. GENERAL

§1.1 Purpose. A motion to enforce a deposition subpoena for personal records is used to force a nonparty deponent to produce personal records after the nonparty whose personal records are sought objects to the subpoena. *See* CCP §§1985.3(g), 1985.6(f)(2)-(f)(4).

§1.2 Primary authority. CCP §§1985.3, 1985.4, 1985.6, 1987.1, 1987.2.

§1.3 Secondary authority. The following secondary sources are cited as authority in this subchapter:

- *California Civil Discovery Practice* (CEB Online ed. 2014) (referred to as *CEB Discovery Practice*).
- Weil & Brown, *California Practice Guide: Civil Procedure Before Trial* (CD-ROM ed. 2014) (referred to as Weil, *Civil Procedure Before Trial*).

§2. DISCOVERY OF PERSONAL RECORDS

When a subpoena requests the production of documents that include personal records protected from immediate disclosure by CCP §1985.3 (consumer records), §1985.4 (governmental records), or §1985.6 (employee records), the subpoenaed deponent cannot produce the records until the person whose records are sought is given notice and the opportunity to object. For a discussion of the discovery of personal records, see "Subpoenas for Personal Records," ch. 8-D, p. 977.

§3. WHEN TO USE MOTION TO ENFORCE

A motion to enforce a deposition subpoena for personal records should be used to secure compliance with a deposition subpoena after a nonparty consumer objects to the subpoena in writing. *See* CCP §1985.3(g) (motion to enforce after nonparty consumer objects), §1985.4 (procedures of §1985.3 apply to governmental records), §1985.6(f)(2), (f)(4) (motion to enforce after nonparty employee objects); Weil, *Civil Procedure Before Trial*, ¶8:604 (motion to enforce after nonparty consumer or nonparty employee objects). The term "consumer" is used throughout this subchapter to refer collectively to consumers, employees, and other persons whose personal records are sought through discovery. For more about consumers, see "Who Is Entitled to Notice of Privacy Rights," ch. 8-D, §5, p. 979. For a discussion of written objections, see "Serve written objections," ch. 8-D, §12.1.2(1), p. 993.

PERSONAL RECORDS

§3.1 Motion to enforce vs. motion to compel. Although the Civil Discovery Act uses the term "motion to enforce," some court opinions refer to a motion to enforce as a motion to compel. *See* CCP §§1985.3(g) ¶4, 1985.6(f)(4); *see, e.g.*, ***Unzipped Apparel, LLC v. Bader*** (2d Dist.2007) 156 Cal.App.4th 123, 136 (court referred to motion under §1985.3(g) ¶¶2-4 as "motion to compel"). This is misleading—a motion to enforce and a motion to compel are two distinct motions. Important differences between the two motions include the following:

1. Different deadlines. A motion to enforce has a very short deadline (20 days after service of written objection) compared to a motion to compel the production of documents at a deposition (60 days after the deposition officer completes the record). See "Deadline to file & serve," §4.2.2, p. 1079; "Deadline to file & serve," ch. 9-D, §4.2.2, p. 1052.

2. Different sanctions. The sanctions for a motion to enforce are discretionary, while the sanctions for a motion to compel are mandatory. See "Unsuccessful motion," §4.3.1(2)(d)[1], p. 1081; "Unsuccessful motion," ch. 9-D, §5.2.1(2)(e)[1], p. 1055.

PRACTICE TIP

Regardless of which name you use for the motion—motion to enforce or motion to compel—if the motion asks the court to force a nonparty deponent to produce personal records after a nonparty consumer has objected to the production, the motion must comply with CCP §§1985.3(g) ¶4 and 1985.6(f)(4).

§3.2 Responding to party objections. If a party objects to a subpoena that requires the production of personal records, it can make a motion to quash or a motion for a protective order; parties cannot make written objections. See "Not party," ch. 8-D, §12.1.2(1)(a)[3], p. 993. If a party makes one of these motions, the subpoenaing party should make its enforcement arguments in its opposition papers, not in a separate motion to enforce. *See* CCP §1985.3(g) ¶4 (motion to enforce is made in response to written objection), §1985.6(f)(4) (same).

§4. MOTION TO ENFORCE SUBPOENA FOR PERSONAL RECORDS

§4.1 Grounds. A motion to enforce a deposition subpoena for personal records can be based on the ground that the nonparty consumer's objection is invalid. To establish this ground, the movant should show the following:

1. Proper service. The movant should show that (1) the nonparty deponent was properly served with a deposition subpoena and (2) the nonparty consumer was properly served with a notice of privacy rights. *See* CCP §§1985.3(d), (e), 1985.4, 1985.6(d), (e). See "Understanding rules for serving documents for personal records," ch. 8-D, §8.1, p. 984.

2. Timely motion. The movant should show that the motion to enforce is timely. To do this, the movant must show that the motion was filed within 20 days after the written objection was served. See "Deadline to file & serve," §4.2.2, this page.

3. Discoverable. The movant should show that the documents sought by the deposition subpoena are within the scope of discovery. See "Scope of Discovery," ch. 6-A, p. 603.

4. Good cause for production. The movant should show good cause for the production of the documents sought. *See* CCP §1985(b).

5. Invalid objection. The movant should show that the written objection to the production of the personal records is invalid. If the written objection is based on privacy, the movant should show that the need for discovery outweighs the consumer's right to privacy. *See* ***John B. v. Superior Ct.*** (2006) 38 Cal.4th 1177, 1199 (privacy objections must be balanced against party's right to fair trial). See "Right to Privacy," ch. 6-F, §1, p. 681.

§4.2 Motion.

1. Who can make. The subpoenaing party can make a motion to enforce. CCP §§1985.3(g) ¶4, 1985.6(f)(4); *see id.* §1985.4 (procedures of §1985.3 apply to governmental records).

2. Deadline to file & serve. A motion to enforce must be made within 20 days after the written objection was served. CCP §1985.3(g) ¶4 (nonparty consumer), §1985.6(f)(4) (nonparty employee); *CEB Discovery Practice*, §5.127 (nonparty consumer); *see* CCP §1985.4 (procedures of §1985.3 apply to governmental records); ***Unzipped Apparel, LLC v. Bader*** (2d Dist.2007) 156 Cal.App.4th 123, 136 (dicta). In addition, the motion must be filed and served at least 16 court days before the date set for the hearing, and it must be heard at least 15 calendar days before the initial trial date. See "Calculating Deadline to File & Serve Discovery Motion," chart 9-3, p. 1029.

3. Whom to serve.

(1) Parties. The motion must be served on the parties' attorneys. *See* CCP §1005(a)(13).

(2) Nonparty consumer. The motion must be served on the nonparty consumer personally or by mail at the nonparty consumer's last known address. *Cf.* CCP §1985.3(b)(1) (service of subpoena and notice of privacy rights on consumer), §1985.6(b)(1) (service of subpoena and notice of privacy rights on employee).

(3) Nonparty deponent. The motion must be personally served on the nonparty deponent (i.e., the custodian). *Cf.* CRC 3.1346 (motion to compel nonparty deponent must be personally served on nonparty deponent).

4. Contents.

(1) Notice of motion & motion. The motion should be made in writing by noticed motion. See "Notice of motion & motion," ch. 1-D, §5.1, p. 28. The notice of motion and motion should contain the following information:

(a) Order enforcing subpoena.

[1] Relief. The notice of motion and motion should briefly state the relief sought (e.g., "Defendant asks the Court for an order overruling the objection and enforcing the subpoena"). CRC 3.1110(a), 3.1112(d)(3).

[2] Grounds. The notice of motion and motion should briefly state the grounds for the motion (e.g., "The motion will be made on the ground that the objection to the deposition subpoena is invalid"). CRC 3.1110(a), 3.1112(d)(3). See "Grounds," §4.1, p. 1079.

(b) Sanctions. The notice of motion and motion should briefly state whether sanctions are sought. *See* CCP §1987.2.

(2) Memorandum of points & authorities. The motion must include a memorandum in support of the motion. CRC 3.1112(a)(3). See "Memorandum of points & authorities," ch. 1-D, §5.2, p. 28. If the movant is seeking sanctions, the memorandum must identify the legal authority for the sanctions. *See* CCP §2023.040.

(3) Supporting evidence. The motion should include supporting evidence. *See* CRC 3.1112(b). See "Supporting evidence," ch. 1-D, §5.3, p. 30.

(a) Declaration. At a minimum, the motion should be supported by a declaration stating the following facts:

[1] Grounds. The declaration should provide facts establishing the grounds for the relief requested. See "Grounds," §4.1, p. 1079.

[2] Meet & confer. The declaration must provide facts showing that the movant made a reasonable and good-faith attempt to informally resolve the dispute with the nonparty consumer (or the nonparty consumer's attorney). CCP §1985.3(g) ¶4 (nonparty consumer), §1985.6(f)(4) (nonparty employee); *CEB Discovery Practice*, §5.127 (nonparty consumer); *see* CCP §1985.4 (procedures of §1985.3 apply to governmental records). See "Meet-and-confer declaration," ch. 7-A, §10.4, p. 763.

[3] Sanctions. If sanctions are requested, the declaration should provide facts supporting each ground for sanctions against each person identified in the notice of motion and motion as being responsible for the sanctionable conduct. *See* CCP §2023.040. For monetary sanctions, the declaration should identify the total amount sought against each person, itemized by task, fee rate, and time (including the estimated time for traveling to and attending the hearing on the motion). *See id.* See "Amount," ch. 9-A, §4.1.3, p. 1005.

(b) Documents served. The motion should be supported by a copy of the documents served on the nonparty deponent, the nonparty consumer, and the other parties (e.g., the subpoena, the deposition notice, the notice of privacy rights, proof of service). See "Documents to Serve for Production of Personal Records from Nonparty," ch. 8-D, §11, p. 991.

(c) Objection. The motion should be supported by a copy of the nonparty's objection to the subpoena.

(4) Separate statement. A motion to enforce must be accompanied by a separate statement that identifies the discovery dispute. *See* CRC 3.1345(a). The separate statement must contain all the information necessary to understand each discovery request and related response. CRC 3.1345(c). Specifically, the separate statement must include the following:

(a) Text of request, response & objections. The separate statement must include the text of the request for personal records and the text of the nonparty consumer's response, answer, or objection and any further responses or answers. CRC 3.1345(c)(1), (c)(2). The separate statement must restate these things verbatim; it should not summarize or incorporate them by reference. *See* CRC 3.1345(c); *CEB Discovery Practice*, §15.48.

(b) Reasons for order. The separate statement must set out the factual and legal reasons to compel further responses, answers, or production for each matter in dispute. CRC 3.1345(c)(3).

(c) Other information. See "Other information," ch. 9-B, §3.3.4(5), p. 1035.

(5) Proof of service. The motion should include proof of service. See "Proof of service," ch. 1-D, §5.6, p. 33.

(6) Proposed order. The motion can include a proposed order. *See* CRC 3.1113(m). If a proposed order is submitted, it must be lodged and served with the motion papers, not attached to them. *Id.* See "Documents lodged," ch. 1-F, §2.3, p. 47.

§4.3 Response.

1. Opposition. To oppose a motion to enforce, the nonparty consumer should file and serve opposition papers. See "Opposition Papers," ch. 1-D, §8, p. 35.

(1) Deadline to file & serve. The opposition must be served at least nine court days before the hearing. CCP §1005(b). See "Filing & serving opposition," ch. 1-D, §8.5, p. 36.

(2) Grounds. The nonparty consumer can challenge the motion on the following grounds:

(a) Object to procedure. The nonparty consumer can oppose the motion based on procedural errors in the motion (e.g., no timely notice of privacy rights to consumer, errors in separate statement). *See* CCP §1985.3(k) (nonparty-consumer records), §1985.4 (governmental records), §1985.6(j) (nonparty-employee records).

(b) Bolster objections. The nonparty consumer can oppose the motion by elaborating on the objections to the production of personal records that were made in the nonparty consumer's written objection. For example, the opposition papers can explain how the records sought are not relevant.

(c) Respond to sanctions request. If the motion to enforce seeks sanctions, the nonparty consumer should deny the movant's request for sanctions.

(d) Request sanctions. The nonparty consumer should include a request for sanctions if permitted by statute.

[1] Unsuccessful motion. The court can award the nonparty consumer her reasonable expenses and attorney fees incurred in opposing the motion to enforce if the court finds that (1) the movant made the motion in bad faith, (2) the movant made the motion without substantial justification, or (3) the requirements of the subpoena were oppressive. *CEB Discovery Practice*, §5.127; *see* CCP §§1985.3(g) ¶4, 1985.4, 1985.6(f)(4), 1987.2(a).

[2] No meet & confer. The court must impose monetary sanctions against the movant or its attorney for not making a reasonable and good-faith attempt to resolve the discovery dispute informally before making the motion to enforce. *See* CCP §2023.020. See "Meet & confer," §4.2.4(3)(a)[2], p. 1080; "Failing to meet & confer," ch. 9-A, §5.2.5, p. 1019.

(3) Contents. For a general discussion of the contents of an opposition, see "Opposition Papers," ch. 1-D, §8, p. 35.

2. Motion for protective order. The nonparty consumer can respond to the motion by making a motion for a protective order. See "Motion for Protective Order," ch. 9-B, p. 1024.

§4.4 Reply. The movant can file and serve a reply to opposition papers. The reply must be filed and served at least five court days before the hearing. CCP §1005(b). See "Reply Papers," ch. 1-D, §9, p. 37.

§4.5 Hearing. The hearing on a motion to enforce is conducted in the same manner as civil hearings generally. See "Hearings," ch. 1-H, p. 79.

§4.6 Ruling. The court has wide discretion when ruling on a motion to enforce a deposition subpoena for personal records. *See* ***John B. v. Superior Ct.*** (2006) 38 Cal.4th 1177, 1186.

§4.7 Order.

1. Form. The court's ruling on a motion to enforce must be recorded either in writing or by minute order. See "Record of Ruling," ch. 1-I, §4, p. 90.

2. **Contents.**

(1) **Motion denied.** The court can deny the motion. For example, the court should deny the motion if the personal records sought are beyond the scope of discovery or if the consumer's right to privacy outweighs the need for the records. *See* ***John B. v. Superior Ct.*** (2006) 38 Cal.4th 1177, 1199 (right to privacy should be balanced against other important rights). See "Scope of Discovery," ch. 6-A, p. 603.

(2) **Motion granted.** If the court grants the motion to enforce, it should order the nonparty deponent to produce the records. *See* CCP §1985.3(g) ¶4 (nonparty-consumer records), §1985.4 (governmental records), §1985.6(f)(4) (nonparty-employee records). The court can impose terms or conditions on the production to protect the rights of the nonparty deponent and the nonparty consumer. *See id.* §1985.3(g) ¶4 (subpoenaing party can bring motion to enforce under §1987.1), §1987.1(a) (court can order compliance with subpoena on terms or conditions that court deems appropriate).

(3) **Sanctions.** If the court awards sanctions, the order should identify the statute the court used as authority for the sanctions and give the reasons for the sanctions.

§4.8 Review. See "Review of Discovery Orders," ch. 7-A, §17, p. 777.

H. MOTION FOR RELIEF FROM WAIVER OF OBJECTIONS

§1. GENERAL

§1.1 Purpose. A motion for relief from the waiver of objections to a discovery request asks the court to relieve the movant from the waiver of its objections to interrogatories, a demand to produce, a demand for a physical examination of a personal-injury plaintiff, or requests for admission (RFAs). A party waives its objections to a discovery request—including those based on privilege and attorney work product—when it does not serve a timely response to the request. CCP §2030.290(a) (interrogatories), §2031.300(a) (demand to produce), §2032.240(a) (demand for exam of personal-injury P), §2033.280(a) (RFAs).

§1.2 Primary authority. CCP §2030.290(a) (interrogatories), §2031.300(a) (demand to produce), §2032.240(a) (demand for exam of personal-injury P), §2033.280(a) (RFAs).

NOTE

When a party waives its objections to a discovery request by not making a timely response, relief from the waiver cannot be sought under CCP §473(b) because analogous (and more limited) relief is granted under the Civil Discovery Act. ***Zellerino v. Brown*** *(3d Dist.1991) 235 Cal.App.3d 1097, 1107.*

---

§1.3 Secondary authority. The following secondary sources are cited as authority in this subchapter:

- *California Civil Discovery Practice* (CEB Online ed. 2014) (referred to as *CEB Discovery Practice*).
- Weil & Brown, *California Practice Guide: Civil Procedure Before Trial* (CD-ROM ed. 2014) (referred to as Weil, *Civil Procedure Before Trial*).

§2. GROUNDS

To prevail on a motion for relief from waiver of objections, the movant must show both of the following:

§2.1 Substantial compliance. The movant must show that it has served a proposed response to the discovery request that substantially complies with the statutory requirements. CCP §2030.290(a) (interrogatories), §2031.300(a)(1) (demand to produce), §2032.240(a)(1) (demand for exam of personal-injury P), §2033.280(a)(1) (RFAs).

§2.2 Mistake, inadvertence, or excusable neglect. The movant must show that its failure to serve a timely response was the result of mistake, inadvertence, or excusable neglect. CCP §2030.290(a) (interrogatories), §2031.300(a)(2) (demand to produce), §2032.240(a)(2) (demand for exam of personal-injury P), §2033.280(a)(2) (RFAs); ***Sinaiko Healthcare Consulting, Inc. v. Pacific Healthcare Consultants*** (2d Dist.2007) 148 Cal.App.4th 390, 404 (interrogatories and demand to produce); *CEB Discovery Practice*, §7.57 (same); *e.g.*, ***Scottsdale Ins. v. Superior Ct.*** (2d Dist.1997) 59 Cal.App.4th 263, 275-76 (P was not entitled to relief from waiver of attorney-client privilege because P's attorney was inexcusably negligent when he made blanket response to demand to produce without first reviewing documents sought).

§3. MOTION

§3.1 Who can make. A party who did not serve a timely response to a discovery request can make a motion for relief from waiver. CCP §2030.290(a) (interrogatories), §2031.300(a) (demand to produce), §2032.240(a) (demand for exam of personal-injury P), §2033.280(a) (RFAs).

§3.2 Deadline to file & serve. A motion for relief from waiver should be filed and served at least 16 court days before the date set for the hearing. CCP §1005(b). If the motion is served by means other than personal delivery, the movant will need to add more time to the 16-day period (e.g., 5 calendar days are added when notice is mailed in California). *Id.* Because a motion for relief from waiver is a discovery motion, it must be heard at least 15 calendar days before the initial trial date. See "Scheduling Hearing," ch. 1-H, §3, p. 80; "Cutoff for discovery motions," ch. 7-A, §5.2.2, p. 748; "Calculating Deadline to File & Serve Discovery Motion," chart 9-3, p. 1029.

§3.3 Contents.

1. Notice of motion & motion. A motion for relief from waiver must be brought as a noticed motion. Weil, *Civil Procedure Before Trial*, ¶8:1033. *But see* ***Scottsdale Ins. v. Superior Ct.*** (2d Dist.1997) 59 Cal.App.4th 263, 275-76 (without comment, court considered ex parte application for relief from waiver). See "Notice of motion & motion," ch. 1-D, §5.1, p. 28. The notice of motion and motion should contain the following information:

(1) Relief. The notice of motion and motion should briefly state the relief sought (e.g., "Defendant asks the Court for an order granting relief from Defendant's waiver of objections to interrogatories"). CRC 3.1110(a), 3.1112(d)(3). The type of relief sought can vary depending on the type of discovery request at issue.

(a) Interrogatories. If the movant did not serve a timely response to interrogatories, the movant can ask the court for relief from the waiver of (1) its option to respond by producing writings and (2) its objections to the interrogatories. CCP §2030.290(a); *CEB Discovery Practice*, §7.57. For a discussion of the option to produce writings in response to interrogatories, see "Produce documents," ch. 7-C, §8.3.3, p. 827.

(b) Demand to produce. If the movant did not serve a timely response to a demand to produce, the movant can ask the court for relief from the waiver of its objections to the demand. CCP §2031.300(a); *see* ***Zellerino v. Brown*** (3d Dist.1991) 235 Cal.App.3d 1097, 1106 (dicta).

(c) Demand for exam of personal-injury P. If the movant did not serve a timely response to a demand for a physical examination of a personal-injury plaintiff, the movant can ask the court for relief from the waiver of its objections to the demand. CCP §2032.240(a).

(d) RFAs. If the movant did not serve a timely response to RFAs, the movant can ask the court for relief from the waiver of its objections to the requests. CCP §2033.280(a).

(2) Grounds. The notice of motion and motion should briefly state the grounds for the motion (e.g., the motion will be made on the ground that Defendant has served a proposed response that substantially complies with the statutory requirements, and the failure to serve a timely response was the result of mistake, inadvertence, or excusable neglect). CRC 3.1110(a), 3.1112(d)(3). See "Grounds," §2, p. 1082.

2. Memorandum of points & authorities. The motion must include a memorandum in support of the motion. CRC 3.1112(a)(3). See "Memorandum of points & authorities," ch. 1-D, §5.2, p. 28.

3. Supporting evidence. The motion should include supporting evidence. *See* CRC 3.1112(b). See "Supporting evidence," ch. 1-D, §5.3, p. 30.

(1) Declaration. At a minimum, the motion should be supported by a declaration stating the following facts:

(a) Grounds. The declaration should provide facts establishing the grounds for the relief requested. See "Grounds," §2, p. 1082.

(b) Meet & confer. Even though a meet-and-confer declaration is not required for a motion for relief from waiver, it is helpful if the declaration states that the party attempted to resolve the dispute informally and provides facts to support the statement.

(2) Discovery request. The motion should be supported by a copy of the discovery request.

(3) Proposed response. The motion should be supported by a copy of the proposed response to the discovery request.

4. Proof of service. The motion should include proof of service. See "Proof of service," ch. 1-D, §5.6, p. 33.

5. Proposed order. The motion can include a proposed order. *See* CRC 3.1113(m). If a proposed order is submitted, it must be lodged and served with the motion papers, not attached to them. *Id.* See "Documents lodged," ch. 1-F, §2.3, p. 47.

6. No separate statement. The motion does not need to include a separate statement. *See* CRC 3.1345(b). A separate statement is required only when a discovery motion involves the content of a discovery request or response. CRC 3.1345(a).

NOTE

In addition to a motion for relief from waiver, the movant can make a motion for a protective order to limit the dissemination of any privileged information for which an objection was waived. CEB Discovery Practice, §3.177. See "Motion for Protective Order," ch. 9-B, p. 1024.

---

§4. RESPONSE

§4.1 Stipulation. The discovering party served with a motion for relief from waiver can stipulate to relief from the waiver of objections. See "Modifying discovery by stipulation," ch. 7-A, §4.1, p. 743.

§4.2 Countermotions.

1. Motion to compel. The discovering party can make a motion to compel an initial response to interrogatories, a demand to produce, or a demand for a physical examination of a personal-injury plaintiff, even after a motion for relief from waiver is filed. See "Motion to Compel Initial Response," ch. 9-E, §2, p. 1057; "Motion to Compel Response to & Compliance with Demand for Exam of Personal-Injury P," ch. 9-F, §2, p. 1069.

2. Motion to deem RFAs admitted. The discovering party can make a motion to deem admitted the matters specified in the RFAs. CCP §2033.280(b). See "Motion to deem requests admitted," ch. 7-D, §6.2.1, p. 841.

PRACTICE TIP

The court will overrule a motion to deem requests admitted if the responding party serves a substantially compliant response before the hearing on the motion. ***Tobin v. Oris*** *(2d Dist.1992) 3 Cal.App.4th 814, 828, disapproved on other grounds,* ***Wilcox v. Birtwhistle*** *(1999) 21 Cal.4th 973; Weil, Civil Procedure Before Trial, ¶8:1374.2; see CCP §2033.280(c). Thus, the discovering party should make a motion to deem requests admitted only if the responding party either did not respond to the requests or made a late response that did not substantially comply with the statutory requirements.*

§4.3 Opposition. To oppose a motion for relief from waiver, the discovering party should file and serve opposition papers.

1. Deadline to file & serve. The opposition must be served at least nine court days before the hearing. CCP §1005(b). See "Filing & serving opposition," ch. 1-D, §8.5, p. 36.

2. Grounds. The discovering party can oppose the motion on the following grounds:

(1) Challenge motion. The discovering party can challenge the motion. For example, the discovering party can show that the late response does not substantially comply with the statutory requirements or that the response was late because of something other than mistake, inadvertence, or excusable neglect. *See, e.g.*, ***Scottsdale Ins. v. Superior Ct.*** (2d Dist.1997) 59 Cal.App.4th 263, 275-76 (P was not entitled to relief from waiver of attorney-client privilege because P's attorney was inexcusably negligent when he made blanket response to demand to produce without first reviewing documents sought).

(2) Request order on motion to deem. If there is a pending motion to deem admitted the matters in the RFAs, the discovering party should explain why the court should grant the motion. *See* CCP §2033.280(c).

3. Contents. For a general discussion of the contents of an opposition, see "Opposition Papers," ch. 1-D, §8, p. 35.

§5. REPLY

The movant can file and serve a reply to opposition papers. The reply must be filed and served at least five court days before the hearing. CCP §1005(b). See "Reply Papers," ch. 1-D, §9, p. 37.

§6. HEARING

The hearing on a motion for relief from waiver is conducted in the same manner as civil hearings generally. See "Hearings," ch. 1-H, p. 79.

§7. RULING

The ruling on a motion for relief from waiver is left within the court's discretion. *See* CCP §2030.290(a) (interrogatories), §2031.300(a) (demand to produce), §2032.240(a) (demand for exam of personal-injury P), §2033.280(a) (RFAs).

§8. ORDER

§8.1 Form. The court's ruling on a motion for relief from waiver must be recorded either in writing or by minute order. See "Record of Ruling," ch. 1-I, §4, p. 90.

§8.2 Contents.

1. Motion denied. The court can deny the motion. For example, the court can deny the motion if the late response does not substantially comply with statutory requirements or if the movant's tardiness was not the result of mistake, inadvertence, or excusable neglect. *See* CCP §2030.290(a) (interrogatories), §2031.300(a) (demand to produce), §2032.240(a) (demand for exam of personal-injury P), §2033.280(a) (RFAs).

2. Motion granted. The court can grant the motion. If the court grants the motion, the movant should be allowed to raise objections to the discovery request. *See* CCP §2030.290(a) (interrogatories), §2031.300(a) (demand to produce), §2032.240(a) (demand for exam of personal-injury P), §2033.280(a) (RFAs).

§9. REVIEW

See "Review of Discovery Orders," ch. 7-A, §17, p. 777.

CALIFORNIA CIVIL PRETRIAL

CHAPTER 10. DISPOSITION WITHOUT TRIAL
TABLE OF CONTENTS

TABLE OF CONTENTS

10. DISPOSITION WITHOUT TRIAL

A. DEFAULT JUDGMENT

This subchapter discusses how to obtain a default judgment in civil actions under CCP §§585 and 586. This subchapter does not discuss the specialized rules for obtaining a default judgment in family-law cases or collection cases. *See* Fam. C. §2336 (default for dissolution or legal separation), §17430 (default for child support); CRC 3.740(f) (default in collection cases). For a discussion of when a default judgment can be imposed as a terminating sanction for discovery abuse, see "Terminating sanctions," ch. 9-A, §4.2.2(3), p. 1006.

NOTE

The default-judgment provisions in the Code of Civil Procedure apply only to civil actions, not to special proceedings, unless the provisions are specifically made applicable (e.g., the statute governing the special proceeding explicitly permits a default judgment). ***In re Angela R.*** *(4th Dist.1989) 212 Cal.App.3d 257, 273; see, e.g., CCP §1088 (writ of mandate cannot be granted by default), §1105 (writ of prohibition cannot be granted by default); see also CCP §22 (defining "action"), §23 (defining "special proceeding").*

§1. GENERAL

§1.1 Purpose. A default judgment permits the court to render a judgment for the plaintiff on its complaint without a trial when the defendant has not timely filed an appropriate response. *See* CCP §§585, 586. A default judgment is considered a judgment on the merits and is res judicata on all issues pleaded in the complaint. ***Fitzgerald v. Herzer*** (2d Dist.1947) 78 Cal.App.2d 127, 131-32; *see* ***Murray v. Alaska Airlines, Inc.*** (2010) 50 Cal.4th 860, 871 (dicta).

NOTE

For ease of reference, this subchapter uses the term "plaintiff" throughout to refer to the party who is seeking a default from a defendant. The rules for obtaining a default, however, apply equally to cross-complainants and cross-defendants. See CCP §587.5.

§1.2 Primary authority. CCP §§585-587.5; CRC 3.110(g)-(i), 3.1800.

§1.3 Secondary authority. The following secondary sources are cited as authority in this subchapter:

- *California Civil Procedure Before Trial* (CEB Online ed. 2014) (referred to as *CEB Procedure Before Trial*).
- *California Trial Practice: Civil Procedure During Trial* (CEB Online ed. 2014) (referred to as *CEB Procedure During Trial*).
- State Bar of California, *Attorney Guidelines of Civility & Professionalism (Civility Toolbox)* (2009), ethics.calbar.ca.gov (referred to as *Cal. Attorney Guidelines*).
- Weil & Brown, *California Practice Guide: Civil Procedure Before Trial* (CD-ROM ed. 2014) (referred to as Weil, *Civil Procedure Before Trial*).
- Witkin, *California Procedure* (5th ed. 2008 & Supp.2014) (referred to as Witkin, *Cal. Procedure*).

§1.4 Judicial Council forms.

- CIV-100 (mandatory), request for entry of default and default judgment.
- CIV-130 (optional), notice of entry of judgment.
- JUD-100 (optional), judgment.
- POS-010 (mandatory), proof of service of summons.

- UD-110 (optional), judgment in unlawful detainer.
- UD-116 (optional), declaration for default judgment by court for unlawful detainer.

§2. OVERVIEW

Securing a default judgment is a three-step process involving the defendant's default, the entry of default, and the entry of a default judgment. *See* ***People v. One 1986 Toyota Pickup*** (5th Dist.1995) 31 Cal.App.4th 254, 259; *see, e.g.*, ***Gibble v. Car-Lene Research, Inc.*** (1st Dist.1998) 67 Cal.App.4th 295, 300 (D defaulted by not answering; Ps asked for entry of default, then default judgment).

Step 1 – Defendant defaults. Before the plaintiff can obtain a default judgment, the defendant must first be in default. Generally, a default occurs when the defendant does not timely file an appropriate response to the complaint. *See* CCP §§585, 586. See "Default," §3, this page. A default has no impact on the case until the plaintiff has the default entered by the court clerk. *See* ***Goddard v. Pollock*** (1st Dist.1974) 37 Cal.App.3d 137, 141; Weil, *Civil Procedure Before Trial*, ¶¶5:2, 5:4.

Step 2 – Entry of default. After the defendant defaults, the plaintiff must ask the court clerk to enter default. *See* CCP §585(a)-(c); ***Ferraro v. Camarlinghi*** (6th Dist.2008) 161 Cal.App.4th 509, 533-34. See "Application for Entry of Default," §5, p. 1096. Once default is entered, the defendant is generally considered to be out of court and is no longer permitted to conduct discovery, appear in court, or file pleadings and motions. ***One 1986 Toyota Pickup***, 31 Cal.App.4th at 259; ***Devlin v. Kearny Mesa AMC/Jeep/Renault, Inc.*** (4th Dist.1984) 155 Cal.App.3d 381, 385-86; *see* ***Garcia v. Politis*** (2d Dist.2011) 192 Cal.App.4th 1474, 1479. The only action the defendant can take after default has been entered is to attack the entry of default. Weil, *Civil Procedure Before Trial*, ¶5:116; *see* ***Todd v. Everett*** (3d Dist.1966) 247 Cal.App.2d 209, 212. See "Attacking Entry of Default & Default Judgment," §9, p. 1108.

Step 3 – Entry of default judgment. After the court clerk enters the default, the plaintiff can apply to the court (or the clerk, in certain actions) for entry of a default judgment. *See* CCP §585(a)-(c). See "Application for Default Judgment," §7, p. 1099. A default judgment is a final judgment that disposes of the action. *See* ***Peltier v. McCloud River R.R.*** (3d Dist.1995) 34 Cal.App.4th 1809, 1815.

§3. DEFAULT

A defendant defaults if it is properly served with a summons and a complaint and does not timely file an appropriate response. *See* CCP §585(a)-(c), (e); ***Lee v. An*** (2d Dist.2008) 168 Cal.App.4th 558, 564.

NOTE

The defendant is not in default if it files an answer and does not appear for trial. See ***Garamendi v. Golden Eagle Ins.*** *(1st Dist.2004) 116 Cal.App.4th 694, 705. But if the defendant does not appear for trial after receiving at least 15 days' notice of the trial date, the court can enter judgment against the defendant following an uncontested evidentiary hearing. See CCP §594(a);* ***Garamendi****, 116 Cal.App.4th at 705.*

---

§3.1 Service proper. For a default to occur, the defendant must have been properly served with a copy of the summons and a copy of the complaint. *See* CCP §585(a)-(c), (e); ***Lee v. An*** (2d Dist.2008) 168 Cal.App.4th 558, 564. Service is proper if it is accomplished by mail, personal delivery, substituted service, or publication. *See* CCP §585(a)-(c), (e). For a discussion of serving a summons and complaint, see "Joining the Defendant—Service of Process," ch. 3-H, p. 295.

CAUTION

Compliance with the statutory procedures for service of process is essential to establishing personal jurisdiction. ***American Express Centurion Bank v. Zara*** *(6th Dist.2011) 199 Cal.App.4th 383, 387;* ***Dill v. Berquist Constr. Co.*** *(4th Dist.1994) 24 Cal.App.4th 1426, 1444.*

*A default judgment entered against a defendant who was not served in the manner prescribed by statute is void. **American Express**, 199 Cal.App.4th at 387; **Lee**, 168 Cal.App.4th at 564; **Dill**, 24 Cal.App.4th at 1444.*

§3.2 No timely response. For a default to occur, the defendant must not have timely filed an appropriate response to the complaint.

1. Timeliness.

(1) Generally.

(a) Complaint served by personal delivery, mail, or substituted service. A response to a complaint served by personal delivery, mail, or substituted service is timely filed if it is made within the time stated in the summons or within any extra time allowed by statute or agreement. *See* CCP §585(a), (b), (e); ***Schwab v. Southern Cal. Gas Co.*** (4th Dist.2004) 114 Cal.App.4th 1308, 1320. Unless otherwise provided by statute, a summons typically gives a party 30 days to file a response after the summons is served. CCP §412.20(a)(3); *see, e.g., id.* §1167 (summons in unlawful-detainer action requires response in five days). The time to file a response may be extended, however, by stipulation or court order. CCP §1054; CRC 3.110(d), (e); *see, e.g.*, ***Goddard v. Pollock*** (1st Dist.1974) 37 Cal.App.3d 137, 141 (Ds were given extension to respond). See "Extending Time," ch. 5-F, p. 501.

(b) Complaint served by publication. A response to a complaint served by publication is timely filed if it is made within the time to file an answer. *See* CCP §585(c). See "Answer to complaint," ch. 4-B, §2.1.2(1)(a), p. 335. An answer to a complaint served by publication must be filed within 30 days after service is completed. *See* CCP §§412.20(a)(3), 415.50(c). Service by publication is complete once the publication period expires. *See id.* §415.50(b), (c); Gov. C. §6064.

(2) Effect of amending complaint.

(a) Before response filed. If the plaintiff amends the complaint before the defendant has filed an appropriate response, the defendant must file a response within 30 days after being served with the amended complaint. *See* CCP §471.5(a); ***Falahati v. Kondo*** (2d Dist.2005) 127 Cal.App.4th 823, 831-32 (30-day requirement applies to any amendment, substantive or nonsubstantive). *But cf.* CCP §1167.3 (five days to answer amended complaint in unlawful-detainer action).

(b) After response filed. If the plaintiff amends the complaint after the defendant has filed an appropriate response, the defendant must file a response (i.e., an answer, a demurrer, or a motion to strike) within either 30 days after the amended complaint is served or the time permitted by the court. CCP §586(a)(1); *see id.* §473(a)(1) (court may extend time to file answer or demurrer after pleading is amended). *But cf. id.* §1167.3 (five days to answer amended complaint in unlawful-detainer action).

PRACTICE TIP

*A defendant does not have to file an amended answer in response to an amended complaint if (1) the amended complaint does not change the cause of action or (2) the original answer states a defense that is sufficient for the amended complaint. See **Gray v. Hall** (1928) 203 Cal. 306, 310-11. If it is unclear whether the answer needs to be amended, ask the court for a stipulation that the answer to the original complaint can stand as an answer to the amended complaint before the time to answer has expired. See **Bristol Convalescent Hosp. v. Stone** (4th Dist.1968) 258 Cal.App.2d 848, 863.*

(c) After entry of default. If the plaintiff amends its complaint after entry of default and the amendment is considered substantive, the defendant is no longer in default on the original complaint and is free to respond to the amended complaint. ***Cole v. Roebling Constr. Co.*** (1909) 156 Cal. 443, 446; *see* ***Ostling v. Loring*** (3d Dist.1994) 27 Cal.App.4th 1731, 1744. This is true regardless of whether the amendment is accomplished by an

amended complaint or an amendment to the complaint. ***Ford v. Superior Ct.*** (4th Dist.1973) 34 Cal.App.3d 338, 343. Amendments that add a cause of action or increase the amount of damages sought are considered substantive. *See, e.g.*, ***Ostling***, 27 Cal.App.4th at 1744 (amended complaint that increased damages was substantive change); ***Ford***, 34 Cal.App.3d at 343 (amended complaint that added new cause of action was substantive change). Amendments that only correct typographical errors are considered nonsubstantive. *See, e.g.*, ***People v. Mendocino Cty. Assessor's Parcel No. 056-500-09*** (1st Dist.1997) 58 Cal.App.4th 120, 126 (amended complaint that corrected parcel number, which was correct in deed incorporated in original complaint, was not substantive change); ***Donian v. Danielian*** (2d Dist.1928) 90 Cal.App. 675, 678 (amended complaint that changed date was not substantive change).

NOTE

Although a defendant who is in default is generally not entitled to notice or service of papers, CCP §1010 requires that amendments to the pleadings or amended pleadings be served on a defendant in default.

(3) Response filed after deadline. If the defendant files an appropriate response after the deadline to respond, the late response is usually sufficient to prevent entry of default if it was filed before the plaintiff filed for entry of default. Generally, the plaintiff can request entry of default once the deadline to file the response has expired. *See* CRC 3.110(g). But if the plaintiff delays in requesting the entry of default (or improperly requests it), the court will treat the period of delay as additional time for the defendant to respond. ***Reher v. Reed*** (1913) 166 Cal. 525, 528; ***Goddard***, 37 Cal.App.3d at 141; *see, e.g.*, ***Apollo v. Gyaami*** (1st Dist.2008) 167 Cal.App.4th 1468, 1476 & n.5 (P's defective requests for entry of default permitted late answer to be effective for avoiding default). The plaintiff can move to strike the late response before entry of default, but the court has discretion to deny the motion. ***Goddard***, 37 Cal.App.3d at 141; *see, e.g.*, ***McAllister v. County of Monterey*** (6th Dist.2007) 147 Cal.App.4th 253, 281-82 (court had discretion to consider late demurrer because P did not seek entry of default). See "Motion to Strike," ch. 4-J, p. 418.

2. Appropriate response. The defendant defaults if it does not file a timely response as provided in Chart 10-1, below.

10-1. WHEN PLAINTIFF CAN MOVE FOR DEFAULT ❶

	Action	When P can seek default
1	Complaint filed and served	If no answer or responsive motion filed within 30 days after service or within time extended by agreement or court order. *See* CCP §§412.20(a)(3), 585(a), (b), 1014; CRC 3.110(d), (e). See ch. 4-B, §2.1.2(1)(a), p. 335.
2	Demurrer to complaint filed	If overruled, no answer filed within 10 days after service of ruling or within time permitted by court. *See* CCP §§472a(b), 472b, 586(a)(2); CRC 3.1320(g), (j)(1). See ch. 4-B, §2.1.1(1)(d), p. 333.
		If sustained in part without leave to amend, no answer filed to remaining part of complaint within 10 days after service of ruling or within time permitted by court. *See* CCP §472b; CRC 3.1320(g), (j)(3). See ch. 4-B, §2.1.1(2)(d)[1], p. 334.
		If sustained in part with leave to amend + P does not amend, no answer filed to remaining part of complaint within 10 days after time to amend expires or within time permitted by court. *See* CRC 3.1320(g), (j)(2); ***Carlton*** (4th Dist.2014) 228 Cal.App.4th 1200, 1209-10. See ch. 4-B, §2.1.1(2)(d)[2][b], p. 334.
		If sustained with leave to amend + P amends, no response (answer/demurrer/motion to strike) filed within 30 days after service of amended complaint or within time permitted by court. *See* CCP §§471.5(a), 586(a)(1); ***Carlton***, 228 Cal.App.4th at 1209-10. See ch. 4-B, §2.1.1(2)(d)[2][a], p. 334.

10-1. WHEN PLAINTIFF CAN MOVE FOR DEFAULT ❶ (CONTINUED)		
Action		When P can seek default
3	Motion to strike complaint filed	If overruled, no answer filed within deadline set by court. *See* CCP §§472a(d), 586(a)(2), 1054(a). See ch. 4-B, §2.1.1(1)(e), p. 334.
		If sustained in part without leave to amend, no answer filed to remaining part of complaint within deadline set by court. *See* CCP §586(a)(3). See ch. 4-B, §2.1.1(2)(e)[1], p. 334.
		If sustained in part with leave to amend + P does not amend, no answer filed to remaining part of complaint within deadline set by court. ❷ *See* CCP §§472a(d), 586(a)(3). See ch. 4-B, §2.1.1(2)(e)[2][b], p. 335.
		If sustained with leave to amend + P amends, no response (answer/demurrer/motion to strike) filed within 30 days after service of amended complaint or within time permitted by court. CCP §471.5(a); *see id.* §§472a(d), 586(a)(1). See ch. 4-B, §2.1.1(2)(e)[2][a], p. 335.
4	Motion to quash service of complaint filed	If overruled + no writ of mandate sought, no response (answer/demurrer/motion to strike) filed within 15 days after service of ruling or by extended deadline set by court for good cause. CCP §418.10(a)(1), (b); *see id.* §586(a)(4), (b). See ch. 4-B, §2.1.1(1)(a), p. 333.
		If overruled + writ of mandate sought, no response (answer/demurrer/motion to strike) filed within 10 days after service of ruling in mandate proceeding or by extended deadline set by court for good cause. CCP §418.10(a)(1), (b), (c); *see id.* §586(a)(4), (b). See ch. 4-B, §2.1.1(1)(a), p. 333.
5	Motion to stay or dismiss complaint for inconvenient forum filed	If overruled + no writ of mandate sought, no response (answer/demurrer/motion to strike) filed within 15 days after service of ruling or by extended deadline set by court for good cause. CCP §418.10(a)(2), (b). See ch. 4-B, §2.1.1(1)(b), p. 333.
		If overruled + writ of mandate sought, no response (answer/demurrer/motion to strike) filed within 10 days after service of ruling in mandate proceeding or by extended deadline set by court for good cause. CCP §418.10(a)(2), (b), (c). See ch. 4-B, §2.1.1(1)(b), p. 333.
6	Motion to dismiss complaint for delay in prosecution filed	If overruled + no writ of mandate sought, no response (answer/demurrer/motion to strike) filed within 15 days after service of ruling or by extended deadline set by court for good cause. CCP §418.10(a)(3), (b); *see id.* §586(a)(8), (b). See ch. 4-B, §2.1.1(1)(c), p. 333.
		If overruled + writ of mandate sought, no response (answer/demurrer/motion to strike) filed within 10 days after service of ruling in mandate proceeding or by extended deadline set by court for good cause. CCP §418.10(a)(3), (b), (c); *see id.* §586(a)(8), (b). See ch. 4-B, §2.1.1(1)(c), p. 333.
7	Motion to transfer venue filed	If overruled, no response (answer/demurrer/motion to strike) filed within 30 days after ruling or within time permitted by court. *See* CCP §§396b(e), 586(a)(6)(A), (a)(6)(C), (b); CRC 3.1326. See ch. 4-B, §2.1.1(1)(f), p. 334.
		If sustained, no response (answer/demurrer/motion to strike) filed within 30 days after new court mails notice of receipt and new case number. *See* CCP §586(a)(6)(B), (a)(6)(C), (b); CRC 3.1326. See ch. 4-B, §2.1.1(2)(f), p. 335.
8	Petition to compel arbitration filed	If overruled, no answer filed within 15 days after court denies petition. CCP §1281.7. See ch. 4-B, §2.1.1(1)(g), p. 334.
9	Amended complaint filed	If changes require new answer, no amended answer filed within 30 days after service of amended complaint or within time permitted by court. CCP §471.5(a); *see id.* §586(a)(1). See ch. 3-C, §6.5.1, p. 236.

DEFAULT JUDGMENT

10-1. WHEN PLAINTIFF CAN MOVE FOR DEFAULT ❶ (CONTINUED)

	Action	When P can seek default
10	Demurrer to entire answer filed	If sustained with leave to amend, no amended answer filed within 10 days after ruling or within time permitted by court. *See* CCP §586(a)(5); CRC 3.1320(g). See ch. 4-H, §9.4.2(1)(a), p. 409.
		If sustained without leave to amend. See ch. 4-H, §9.4.2(2)(b), p. 410.
11	Motion to strike entire answer filed	If sustained with leave to amend, no amended answer filed within time set by court. *See* CCP §586(a)(7). See ch. 4-J, §7.4.1(2), p. 424.
		If sustained without leave to amend. *See* CCP §586(a)(7). See ch. 4-J, §7.4.2(2), p. 424.

❶ This chart does not apply to the service of pleadings in collections cases under CRC 3.740(a), unlawful-detainer actions, proceedings under the Family Code, and other proceedings for which different service requirements are prescribed. *See* CRC 3.110(a).

❷ Usually, the court gives the defendant 10 days to answer.

§4. CONSIDERATIONS BEFORE REQUESTING ENTRY OF DEFAULT

If the defendant is in default, the plaintiff should verify certain matters before requesting entry of default.

§4.1 Is defendant proper? Before requesting entry of default, the plaintiff should verify that a default can be entered against the defendant.

1. Involuntary defendants. If the plaintiff has named a party as a defendant in the complaint because the party would not consent to being joined as a plaintiff, default cannot be entered against that defendant. ***Watkins v. Nutting*** (1941) 17 Cal.2d 490, 498-99; ***Ferraro v. Camarlinghi*** (6th Dist.2008) 161 Cal.App.4th 509, 537; *see* CCP §382. A party who is named as a defendant under CCP §382 is actually a plaintiff. ***Ferraro***, 161 Cal.App.4th at 537.

2. Misnamed defendants. If the plaintiff has erroneously named the defendant in the summons and complaint, the plaintiff may need to amend the complaint and re-serve the defendant before requesting entry of default. Generally, if the person served is aware that she is the person named as the defendant, a default judgment will be binding on the served party even though she was erroneously named. ***Brum v. Ivins*** (1908) 154 Cal. 17, 20; ***Sakaguchi v. Sakaguchi*** (2d Dist.2009) 173 Cal.App.4th 852, 857. But if the error in naming the defendant is significant enough that the served party is unaware that she is the person named as the defendant, a default judgment against the defendant will not be enforceable. *See* ***Sakaguchi***, 173 Cal.App.4th at 861 & n.8. The presumption is that different names designate different persons, and the person enforcing the judgment has the burden to prove that the person served is the same as the person designated in the judgment. ***Brum***, 154 Cal. at 20; *see, e.g.*, ***McNally v. Mott*** (1853) 3 Cal. 235, 236 (P was not permitted to amend judgment to change name of D from "George Mott" to "Gordon Mott" without proof that they were same person).

3. Doe defendants. If the plaintiff has named a Doe defendant in the complaint, the plaintiff must make sure that the requirements of CCP §474 are met before requesting entry of default. See "Doe defendants," ch. 3-C, §2.3.1(7)(b), p. 209. Before default can be entered on a Doe defendant, the summons must contain the required notice under §474, and the proof of service must state (1) the fictitious name under which the defendant was served and (2) that the summons contained the required notice. CCP §474; *see, e.g.*, ***Carol Gilbert, Inc. v. Haller*** (6th Dist.2009) 179 Cal.App.4th 852, 866 (summons was fatally defective because it did not notify D that he was being sued as Doe 1 in accompanying pleading); ***Pelayo v. J.J. Lee Mgmt. Co.*** (2d Dist.2009) 174 Cal.App.4th 484, 498 (proof of service was fatally defective because it did not contain recitals required by §474); ***Armstrong v. Superior Ct.*** (2d Dist.1956) 144 Cal.App.2d 420, 424 (summons was fatally defective because it was not properly endorsed as required by §474; trial court was ordered to quash service of summons). See "Fictitious name," ch. 3-H, §3.1.2(2)(b), p. 297. If the plaintiff discovers the Doe defendant's true name, the plaintiff must amend the complaint before requesting a default judgment (but not before entry of default). ***Jonson v. Weinstein*** (3d Dist.1967) 249 Cal.App.2d 954, 957-58; *see* CCP §474. See "Naming Doe defendant," ch. 3-C, §6.4, p. 236.

§4.2 Does complaint state cause of action? Before requesting entry of default, the plaintiff should verify that the complaint states a cause of action against the defendant. ***Kim v. Westmoore Partners*** (4th Dist.2011) 201 Cal.App.4th 267, 271. A defendant who defaults admits only facts that are well pleaded in the complaint. *Id.* at 281; ***Falahati v. Kondo*** (2d Dist.2005) 127 Cal.App.4th 823, 829. If the complaint does not state a cause action against the defendant, a default cannot be entered. ***Ferraro v. Camarlinghi*** (6th Dist.2008) 161 Cal.App.4th 509, 539; ***Falahati***, 127 Cal.App.4th at 829; *see, e.g.*, ***Kim***, 201 Cal.App.4th at 282 (P did not state cause of action when exhibits attached to his complaint contradicted allegations in complaint). For a discussion of how to plead a cause of action in the complaint, see "Body of complaint," ch. 3-C, §3.6, p. 215, and "Exhibits," ch. 3-C, §3.9, p. 223.

PRACTICE TIP

If the complaint needs to be amended to assert a new cause of action, the plaintiff should amend the complaint before seeking entry of default. If the complaint is amended after default has been entered, the amendment will open the default. ***Ford v. Superior Ct.*** *(4th Dist.1973) 34 Cal.App.3d 338, 342. See "After entry of default," §3.2.1(2)(c), p. 1091.*

§4.3 Has defendant received notice of damages? Before requesting entry of default, the plaintiff should verify that the defendant has notice of its potential liability in the action. Due process requires that the defendant receive notice of its potential liability before default can be entered. ***Schwab v. Rondel Homes, Inc.*** (1991) 53 Cal.3d 428, 435.

1. How notice must be given.

(1) By complaint.

(a) Actual damages – generally. For all actions except personal-injury actions, wrongful-death actions, or actions that require an accounting, the plaintiff must notify the defendant of its potential liability for actual damages by pleading for them in the complaint. *See* CCP §425.10(a)(2), (b). See "Either by complaint or by statement of damages – action seeking accounting," §4.3.1(3), p. 1096. Notice by any other method is ineffective to obtain a default. *See* ***Kim v. Westmoore Partners*** (4th Dist.2011) 201 Cal.App.4th 267, 286 (statement of damages is ineffective to obtain default in action not involving personal injury or wrongful death); ***Levine v. Smith*** (2d Dist.2006) 145 Cal.App.4th 1131, 1136-37 (same). For a discussion of how to plead actual damages in the complaint, see "Actual," ch. 3-C, §3.7.1(1)(a), p. 220.

(b) Attorney fees. If the plaintiff is seeking attorney fees, the plaintiff must demand the fees in the prayer of the complaint. ***Feminist Women's Health Ctr. v. Blythe*** (3d Dist.1995) 32 Cal.App.4th 1641, 1675.

(2) By statement of damages.

(a) Actual damages – personal injury & wrongful death. If the plaintiff is seeking actual damages in a personal-injury or wrongful-death action, the plaintiff must notify the defendant of its potential liability for actual damages in a statement of damages. CCP §425.11; *see id.* §425.10(b). The statement of damages must be served on the defendant before requesting entry of default. *See id.* §425.11(c) (statement of damages must be served before default can be entered); ***Hamm v. Elkin*** (1st Dist.1987) 196 Cal.App.3d 1343, 1345-46 (statement must be given before seeking entry of default, not just before seeking default judgment). For a discussion of serving a statement of damages, see "Statement of Damages," ch. 3-C, §5, p. 226.

(b) Punitive damages. If the plaintiff is seeking punitive damages in any type of action, the plaintiff must notify the defendant of its potential punitive liability by serving the defendant with a statement of punitive damages before requesting entry of default. CCP §425.115(f); *see id.* §425.10(b); *see also* Civ. C. §3295(e) (P cannot request amount of punitive damages in petition). For a discussion of serving a statement of punitive damages, see "Punitive damages," ch. 3-C, §5.2, p. 228.

PRACTICE TIP

When a statement of damages or punitive damages is required, the plaintiff should serve the defendant with the statement at the same time as the complaint. This will ensure that default can be entered as soon as the deadline to respond expires.

(3) Either by complaint or by statement of damages – action seeking accounting. If the plaintiff requests an accounting because the amount of damages is unknown, the plaintiff can give notice of damages by (1) estimating the damages in the complaint or (2) serving the defendant with a precise statement of damages after filing the complaint. *See* ***Los Defensores, Inc. v. Gomez*** (2d Dist.2014) 223 Cal.App.4th 377, 401-02; ***Finney v. Gomez*** (2d Dist.2003) 111 Cal.App.4th 527, 543-44; ***Ely v. Gray*** (3d Dist.1990) 224 Cal.App.3d 1257, 1262-63. If the plaintiff estimates the damages in the complaint, it will be bound by that amount if the defendant defaults. *See* ***Finney***, 111 Cal.App.4th at 543-44; ***Ely***, 224 Cal.App.3d at 1262. Courts are split on whether the plaintiff must give notice of damages before requesting entry of default if the plaintiff does not give an estimate in the complaint. *Compare* ***Van Sickle v. Gilbert*** (3d Dist.2011) 196 Cal.App.4th 1495, 1527 (P must give notice in statement of damages before requesting default if notice is not given in complaint), *and* ***Finney***, 111 Cal.App.4th at 543-44 (same), *with* ***Cassel v. Sullivan, Roche & Johnson*** (1st Dist.1999) 76 Cal.App.4th 1157, 1163-64 (P is not required to give notice of damages before entry of default if D has information needed to calculate amount).

2. Sets maximum award. The relief awarded to a plaintiff in a default judgment cannot exceed what is demanded in the complaint or the statement of damages. CCP §580(a); *see* ***Kim***, 201 Cal.App.4th at 286; ***Heidary v. Yadollahi*** (4th Dist.2002) 99 Cal.App.4th 857, 864. Thus, the complaint or the statement of damages must give the defendant notice of its maximum potential liability. *E.g.*, ***Electronic Funds Solutions, LLC v. Murphy*** (4th Dist.2005) 134 Cal.App.4th 1161, 1174 (default judgment on complaint that pleaded damages "in an amount in excess of $50,000" was limited to $50,000). The plaintiff does not have to specify an exact dollar amount if the defendant's maximum potential liability can be calculated from the face of the document. *See, e.g.*, ***People v. Brar*** (4th Dist.2005) 134 Cal.App.4th 659, 667-68 (default judgment on complaint that pleaded damages "in an amount of not less than $1,000,000" was affirmed for $1,787,500; complaint pleaded 1,500 violations of unfair-competition law and sought $2,500 per violation for maximum of $3.75 million).

PRACTICE TIP

If the damages pleaded in the complaint or the statement of damages are inadequate, the plaintiff should amend the complaint or statement before requesting entry of default. An amendment that increases the amount of potential liability is considered a substantive amendment. *See "After entry of default," §3.2.1(2)(c), p. 1091.* *A substantive amendment sought after entry of default will open the default. See* ***Electronic Funds Solutions****, 134 Cal.App.4th at 1177.*

§4.4 Has defendant's attorney been notified of default? Before requesting entry of default, the plaintiff's attorney has an ethical obligation to give the defendant's attorney notice of the default before having it entered if she knows the attorney's identity. *Cal. Attorney Guidelines*, §15; Weil, *Civil Procedure Before Trial*, ¶¶5:68, 5:69; *see* ***Bellm v. Bellia*** (1st Dist.1984) 150 Cal.App.3d 1036, 1038. While there is no legal obligation to give notice, the court may be more inclined to set aside a default if notice was not given. Weil, *Civil Procedure Before Trial*, ¶5:70.

§5. APPLICATION FOR ENTRY OF DEFAULT

§5.1 Who can file. Any party who has asked for affirmative relief can file an application for entry of default against the defaulting party. *See* CCP §585. In most cases, the applicant is the plaintiff, but if the defendant files a cross-complaint, the applicant can be the defendant. *See id.* §§585, 587.5.

§5.2 When to file.

1. Earliest date. The plaintiff can file an application for entry of default with the court clerk as soon as the defendant's time to file a response has expired. *See* CRC 3.110(g). See "Timeliness," §3.2.1, p. 1091.

2. Latest date. The plaintiff must file an application for entry of default no later than ten days after the time to file a response has expired unless the court grants an extension. CRC 3.110(g). If the plaintiff is late in filing its application for entry of default, the court can order the plaintiff to show cause why sanctions should not be imposed against it. *Id.* If the court orders the plaintiff to show cause, the plaintiff must file and serve responsive papers at least five calendar days before the hearing. CRC 3.110(i).

§5.3 Contents. An application for entry of default must include the following documents:

1. Request for entry of default. To request entry of default, the plaintiff must submit Judicial Council Form CIV-100.

NOTE

Judicial Council Form CIV-100 can be used to obtain entry of default, entry of a default judgment (by the court or the clerk), or both. See "Application," §7.2.3, p. 1102. Requesting entry of default and default judgment at the same time in Form CIV-100 is recommended if no prove-up hearing on the default judgment is required—that is, if (1) the defendant is in default in an action on a contract or judgment, (2) the plaintiff is seeking only money or damages, and (3) the defendant has not been served by publication. If these circumstances exist, the clerk can enter a default judgment immediately after entering default—no hearing is required. See CCP §585(a). If a prove-up hearing is required, a plaintiff may want to wait to request a default judgment until it has prepared for the hearing.

(1) Caption. The box in the caption for entry of default should be checked.

(2) Date complaint filed. Item 1(a) must state the date the complaint or cross-complaint was filed.

(3) Party seeking default. Item 1(b) must state the name of the party seeking entry of default—that is, the party who filed the complaint or cross-complaint.

(4) Defendants. Item 1(c) must list the names of the defendants against whom entry of default is sought. The defendants' names must match the names used in the summons and complaint. Weil, *Civil Procedure Before Trial*, ¶5:75. If the names are fictitious (e.g., "Doe") or incorrect, the plaintiff may need to amend the complaint before filing a request for entry of default. *See* ***Jonson v. Weinstein*** (3d Dist.1967) 249 Cal.App.2d 954, 957. See "Doe defendants," §4.1.3, p. 1094.

(5) Request default judgment. Items 1(d) and 1(e) do not have to be filled out for entry of default.

(6) Judgment entered. Item 2 does not have to be filled out for entry of default.

(7) Unlawful-detainer cases. Items 3 and 4 apply only to unlawful-detainer cases.

(8) Declaration of venue. The appropriate box in Item 5 must be checked if entry of default is sought under CCP §585(a) for the recovery of money or damages on a contract or judgment. *See* CCP §585.5(a). If any of the boxes is checked, the clerk will review the allegations in the complaint to make sure that the case is filed in the appropriate court. Weil, *Civil Procedure Before Trial*, ¶5:76.1.

(9) Declaration of mailing. The appropriate box in Item 6 must be checked for entry of default. The plaintiff must declare that either (1) no copy of the request for entry of default was mailed to the defendant because the defendant's address is unknown to the plaintiff or the plaintiff's attorney or (2) a copy of the request for entry of default was mailed to the defendant's attorney of record or, if none, to the defendant's last known address. CCP §587. If the defendant has no last known address, the plaintiff must note that in the box provided.

(10) Memorandum of costs. Item 7 does not have to be filled out for entry of default.

(11) Declaration of military status. Item 8 does not have to be filled out for entry of default. *See* ***Interinsurance Exch. of Auto. Club v. Collins*** (2d Dist.1994) 30 Cal.App.4th 1445, 1448.

PRACTICE TIP

Although a declaration of the defendant's military status is not required before entry of default, it is required before a default judgment can be entered. Because the process of verifying the defendant's military status can take some time, the plaintiff should begin the verification process as soon as possible. See "Declaration of military status," §7.1.3(1)(k), p. 1101.

2. Proof of service.

(1) Complaint. The plaintiff should file proof of service of the complaint with the request for entry of default if the original summons has not already been returned with proof of service. Weil, *Civil Procedure Before Trial*, ¶5:73; *see* CCP §585(a)-(c), (e); *see, e.g.*, Super. Ct. Sacramento Cty. Loc. R., rule 2.34(C) (request for entry of default must be accompanied by original summons and proof of service or by filed endorsed copies). See "Proof of Service," ch. 3-H, §9, p. 318. If proof of service must be filed, the plaintiff must use Judicial Council Form POS-010. *See* CCP §417.10(f). If the time to respond has been extended beyond the date of the summons, the plaintiff should submit proof of the extension. *See* Weil, *Civil Procedure Before Trial*, ¶5:73.

(2) Statement of damages. If the plaintiff was required to serve the defendant with a statement of damages, the plaintiff should file proof of service with the request for entry of default. *See* ***Scognamillo v. Herrick*** (2d Dist.2003) 106 Cal.App.4th 1139, 1147. See "By statement of damages," §4.3.1(2), p. 1095. But failure to file proof of service of the statement of damages will not prevent entry of default or render the default void. ***Scognamillo***, 106 Cal.App.4th at 1147; *see* ***Fasuyi v. Permatex, Inc.*** (1st Dist.2008) 167 Cal.App.4th 681, 692 n.6.

3. Request to fix attorney fees. The plaintiff can file a written request to have attorney fees fixed by the court. *See* CCP §585(a). Most courts, by local rule, have adopted attorney-fee schedules for default judgments. *E.g.*, Super. Ct. Los Angeles Cty. Loc. R., rules 3.207(a), 3.214(a); Super. Ct. Orange Cty. Loc. R., rule 366; Super. Ct. Sacramento Cty. Loc. R., rule 2.14(A); Super. Ct. San Diego Cty. Loc. R., rule 2.5.10; Super. Ct. San Francisco Cty. Loc. R., rule 6.5.F & Appendix A. The attorney-fee schedule permits the court clerk to enter a set amount of attorney fees in a default judgment if the plaintiff was permitted to recover a reasonable amount of attorney fees by contract or statute. CCP §585(a); *see* CRC 3.1800(b); Super. Ct. Orange Cty. Loc. R., rule 366. If the plaintiff wants to recover more attorney fees than what is permitted in the court's fee schedule, the plaintiff must file a written request when it files the application for entry of default to have attorney fees fixed by the court. *See* CCP §585(a); Super. Ct. Orange Cty. Loc. R., rule 366. If the request is filed, the plaintiff cannot have the default judgment entered by the clerk. *See* CCP §585(a). The court will have to determine the amount of attorney fees. *Id.*

§5.4 No filing fee. There is no filing fee for requesting entry of default. Gov. C. §70617(b)(8).

§6. CLERK'S ENTRY OF DEFAULT

§6.1 Procedure. After receiving an application for entry of default, the court clerk will review the application, confirm that the defendant's time to respond has passed, and determine whether a response from the defendant has been filed. *See* ***Ferraro v. Camarlinghi*** (6th Dist.2008) 161 Cal.App.4th 509, 534. If no timely response is on file, the clerk must enter a default. ***W.A. Rose Co. v. Municipal Ct.*** (1st Dist.1959) 176 Cal.App.2d 67, 71. If a response is on file, the clerk has no authority to determine the sufficiency of the response in either substance or form. ***Goddard v. Pollock*** (1st Dist.1974) 37 Cal.App.3d 137, 143; *see, e.g.*, ***Bristol Convalescent Hosp. v. Stone*** (4th Dist.1968) 258 Cal.App.2d 848, 862 (clerk has no duty or authority to determine whether answer to original complaint should stand as answer to amended complaint). The clerk must look at the caption of the form, and if the caption matches one of the responses that would prevent the entry of default, the clerk must deny entry of default. *See* ***Goddard***, 37 Cal.App.3d at 143. If the clerk enters default prematurely, a judgment based on the default is void. ***Bristol Convalescent Hosp.***, 258 Cal.App.2d at 862.

§6.2 Entering default. If the clerk determines that the defendant is in default, the clerk must check the appropriate box on Judicial Council Form CIV-100. If the statutory requirements for default are met, the clerk has a mandatory duty to enter default. *See* CCP §585(a)-(c). If the clerk does not enter default, the plaintiff can either file a petition for writ of mandate compelling the entry of default or seek a default judgment by the court. *See* ***Crouch v. H.L.***

Miller & Co. (1915) 169 Cal. 341, 345-46; ***W.A. Rose Co. v. Municipal Ct.*** (1st Dist.1959) 176 Cal.App.2d 67, 74. See "Default judgment by court," §7.2, p. 1102. A court can render a default judgment even if a clerk has not entered default. ***Crouch***, 169 Cal. at 345-46.

NOTE

A default is deemed entered when the clerk checks the appropriate box on Judicial Council Form CIV-100 and signs the form. See Weil, Civil Procedure Before Trial, ¶5:9. Generally, default is entered on the same day entry is requested. If default is not entered on the same day, most courts will backdate the entry to the filing date so that the defendant is not given additional time to file a responsive pleading. Id. ¶5:9.1.

§7. APPLICATION FOR DEFAULT JUDGMENT

Once a default has been entered, the plaintiff can file an application for default judgment. In some situations, a default judgment can be entered by the court clerk, but in most situations, it must be entered by the court.

§7.1 Default judgment by clerk.

1. When permissible. The plaintiff can file an application for default judgment by the court clerk in the following circumstances:

(1) Generally.

(a) Contract or judgment. The clerk can enter a default judgment on a contract or judgment if (1) the plaintiff is seeking the recovery of money or damages only and (2) the defendant was not served by publication. CCP §585(a). Courts have interpreted the phrase "money or damages only" to mean that the damages must be either (1) a definite sum fixed by the contract or (2) a sum that can be definitively computed in accordance with the terms of the contract. ***Landwehr v. Gillette*** (1917) 174 Cal. 654, 656-57; ***Liberty Loan Corp. v. Petersen*** (4th Dist.1972) 24 Cal.App.3d 915, 918; ***Diamond Nat'l Corp. v. Golden Empire Builders, Inc.*** (3d Dist.1963) 213 Cal.App.2d 283, 287. Whether damages are fixed or computable is determined by the allegations of the complaint and the terms of the contract, not by the prayer. ***Lynch v. Bencini*** (1941) 17 Cal.2d 521, 528. If evidence is necessary to determine the correct amount of damages or if any discretion must be exercised, the clerk cannot enter judgment. ***Norman v. Berney*** (1st Dist.1965) 235 Cal.App.2d 424, 431.

(b) Unlawful-detainer action. The clerk can enter a default judgment in an unlawful-detainer action if the plaintiff seeks only restitution of the premises. CCP §1169.

(c) Mixed actions. If the complaint pleads two or more distinct causes of action, and one cause of action would permit a clerk's default judgment (e.g., contract), the clerk can enter a judgment on that one cause of action. ***Norman***, 235 Cal.App.2d at 430; Weil, *Civil Procedure Before Trial*, ¶5:144. For the remaining causes of action, the plaintiff must file an application with the court to obtain a default judgment. Weil, *Civil Procedure Before Trial*, ¶5:144; *see* ***Norman***, 235 Cal.App.2d at 430.

(2) Exceptions.

(a) Cross-complaint. The clerk cannot enter a default judgment on a cross-complaint. *See* CCP §585(e).

(b) Multiple defendants. The clerk cannot enter a default judgment in an action involving multiple defendants unless (1) all defendants are in default and (2) the defendants are jointly liable or jointly and severally liable. ***Diamond Nat'l***, 213 Cal.App.2d at 288; *see* CCP §579 (court has discretion to render judgment against one or more Ds when a several judgment is proper); ***Lynch***, 17 Cal.2d at 529-30 (noting potential conflict between clerk's power under §585 and court's power to determine if judgment is several under §579).

(c) Attorney fees fixed by court. The clerk cannot enter a default judgment if the plaintiff has filed a request to have attorney fees fixed by the court. See "Request to fix attorney fees," §5.3.3, p. 1098.

2. When to file or obtain.

(1) Earliest date to file. The plaintiff can ask the clerk to enter a default judgment at the same time it asks for entry of default. *See* CCP §585(a).

PRACTICE TIP

The plaintiff should try to obtain a default judgment as soon as possible after entry of default. If the court grants a defendant's motion to vacate the entry of default before the plaintiff obtains a default judgment, the plaintiff will not be able to appeal the order and reinstate the default. ***Veliscescu v. Pauna*** *(2d Dist.1991) 231 Cal.App.3d 1521, 1522. Instead, the plaintiff will have to wait until a final judgment is made to challenge issues relating to the court's order to vacate. Id. at 1523 n.1.*

(2) Latest date to obtain. The plaintiff must obtain a default judgment no later than 45 days after the default was entered unless the court grants an extension. CRC 3.110(h). If the plaintiff does not obtain a default judgment or an extension within 45 days, the court can order the plaintiff to show cause why sanctions should not be imposed against it. *Id.* If the court orders the plaintiff to show cause, the plaintiff must file and serve responsive papers at least five calendar days before the hearing. CRC 3.110(i).

3. Application. An application for default judgment by the clerk must include the following documents:

(1) Request for default judgment. To request a default judgment, the plaintiff must submit Judicial Council Form CIV-100. CRC 3.1800(a). If the plaintiff did not request a default judgment at the same time it requested entry of default, Form CIV-100 will have to be submitted twice—once for entry of default and once for default judgment.

(a) Caption. The box in the caption for clerk's judgment should be checked.

(b) Date complaint filed. Item 1(a) must state the date the complaint was filed. The clerk cannot enter a default judgment on a cross-complaint. *See* CCP §585(e).

(c) Party seeking default. Item 1(b) must state the name of the party seeking default judgment—that is, the party who filed the complaint. The clerk cannot enter a default judgment on a cross-complaint. *See* CCP §585(e).

(d) Defendants. Item 1(c) does not have to be filled out if default has already been entered against the defendant. See "Defendants," §5.3.1(4), p. 1097.

CAUTION

If default was entered against multiple defendants, the clerk generally cannot enter a default judgment. See "Multiple defendants," §7.1.1(2)(b), p. 1099.

(e) Request default judgment. The box for Item 1(e) must be checked for the clerk to enter default judgment. If the plaintiff is seeking a default judgment in an unlawful-detainer action, the box for Item 1(e)(1) must also be checked. See "Unlawful-detainer action," §7.1.1(1)(b), p. 1099. If the plaintiff is seeking a default judgment on a contract or judgment, the box for Item 1(e)(2) must be checked. See "Contract or judgment," §7.1.1(1)(a), p. 1099. If default has already been entered, the box for Item 1(e)(3) must be checked and the date the default was entered must be noted.

(f) Judgment entered. Item 2 must be filled out for default judgment. Item 2(a) should state the amount demanded in the complaint. Item 2(b) is not filled out for a clerk's judgment. Item 2(c) should state the

amount of interest that is recoverable by the contract or by law. Item 2(d) should state the amount of costs recoverable as provided in Item 7. Item 2(e) should state the amount of attorney fees provided by the contract, a statute, or the court's fee schedule. If attorney fees are not fixed by a contract, statute, or fee schedule, the plaintiff must request default judgment from the court.

NOTE

For a discussion of how to calculate prejudgment interest, see CEB Procedure During Trial, §§27.122-27.127.

(g) Unlawful-detainer cases. Items 3 and 4 apply only to unlawful-detainer cases.

(h) Declaration of venue. Item 5 does not have to be filled out if default has already been entered. See "Declaration of venue," §5.3.1(8), p. 1097.

(i) Declaration of mailing. Item 6 does not have to be filled out if default has already been entered. See "Declaration of mailing," §5.3.1(9), p. 1097. Once default is entered, the defendant is not entitled to notice of the request for default judgment. CCP §1010.

(j) Memorandum of costs. Item 7 must be filled out for default judgment. The plaintiff must state the costs that were incurred under CCP §1033.5.

(k) Declaration of military status. Item 8 must be filled out for default judgment. For each defendant the plaintiff is seeking a default judgment against, the plaintiff must declare one of the following: (1) the defendant is in the military, (2) the plaintiff cannot determine if the defendant is in the military, or (3) the defendant is not in the military.

CAUTION

Any person who knowingly makes or uses a false declaration of military status is guilty of a misdemeanor punishable by up to one year of imprisonment, a $1,000 fine, or both. Mil. & Vet. C. §402(b). That person is also liable for actual damages, reasonable attorney fees, and costs incurred by the injured party. Id.

[1] Defendant is in military. If the plaintiff declares that the defendant is in the military, a default judgment can be rendered only after the court has appointed an attorney to represent the defendant. 50 U.S.C. app. §521(b)(2).

[2] Cannot determine if defendant is in military. If the plaintiff declares that it cannot determine if the defendant is in the military, the court may require the plaintiff to file a bond in a court-approved amount before the court enters a default judgment. 50 U.S.C. app. §521(b)(3).

[3] Defendant is not in military. If the plaintiff declares that the defendant is not in the military, the declaration must be supported by facts. 50 U.S.C. app. §521(b)(1)(A). It is unlikely that a court would consider the declaration in Judicial Council Form CIV-100 to meet the requirements of §521(b)(1)(A) because it only requires the declaration to be made under penalty of perjury. To comply with §521(b)(1)(A), the plaintiff should attach a declaration to Form CIV-100 specifying what steps were taken to verify the defendant's military status. *See, e.g.*, ***UMG Recordings, Inc. v. Morgan*** (W.D.Okla.2006) No. CIV-06-545-M (slip op.; 10-18-06) (affidavit was sufficient when P stated that search of available public databases indicated D was not in military); ***Fonovisa, Inc. v. Villasana*** (D.Colo.2005) No. 05-cv-539-WM-PAC (slip op.; 9-6-05) (affidavit was sufficient when P stated that search in U.S. Military Locator database of LexisNexis indicated D was not in military). One way to verify a person's military status is to submit the defendant's information to the Defense Manpower Data Center at www.dmdc.osd.mil/appj/scra/scraHome.do. If the plaintiff has the defendant's full name and either her Social Security number or date of birth, the website will produce a report, signed by the Director of the DMDC, verifying the person's military status. If the

plaintiff does not have sufficient personal information to search the database on the website, each branch of the armed forces should be contacted. Contact information for each branch can be found at www.defense.gov/faq/pis/PC09SLDR.html.

(2) Contract.

(a) Negotiable instrument. If the application for default judgment is brought on a negotiable instrument (i.e., a promissory note or other written obligation to pay money), the plaintiff should file with the clerk the original contract. Weil, *Civil Procedure Before Trial*, ¶5:163; *see* CRC 3.1806 (when judgment is rendered on written obligation to pay money, clerk must note over her official signature and across face of writing that judgment was rendered, date of judgment, and title of court and case); Super. Ct. Los Angeles Cty. Loc. R., rule 3.204 (original writing must be submitted unless otherwise ordered); ***HSBC Bank Nev. v. Aguilar*** (Los Angeles Cty. Superior Ct. Appellate Div. 2012) 205 Cal.App.4th Supp. 6, 10 (CRC 3.1806 applies only to promissory notes and other written obligations to pay money). If the original contract is not available, an authenticated copy should be filed. *See* Evid. C. §1521 (secondary-evidence rule), §1531 (attestation or certification of copies), §1550 (photocopies of business records); Weil, *Civil Procedure Before Trial*, ¶5:164; *see, e.g.*, ***Kahn v. Lasorda's Dugout, Inc.*** (2d Dist.2003) 109 Cal.App.4th 1118, 1124 (court erred when it believed it did not have discretion under former CRC 234, now CRC 3.1806, to consider copies of promissory note for default judgment).

(b) Other contract. If the application for default judgment is brought on a contract that is not a negotiable instrument, the plaintiff does not have to file with the clerk the original contract. *See, e.g.*, ***HSBC Bank***, 205 Cal.App.4th Supp. at 10-11 (P was not required to file original contract to obtain default judgment in actions for breach of contract, open book account, and account stated).

(3) Judgment. If the application for a default judgment is brought to enforce an earlier judgment, the plaintiff should file with the clerk a certified copy of the judgment. *See* Weil, *Civil Procedure Before Trial*, ¶5:165.

(4) Proposed judgment. The plaintiff should file with the clerk a proposed judgment. See "Judgment," §8, p. 1107.

(5) No filing fee. There is no filing fee for requesting a default judgment. Gov. C. §70617(b)(8).

4. No hearing. The court clerk enters a default judgment without a hearing.

§7.2 Default judgment by court.

1. When permissible. The plaintiff can file an application seeking entry of a default judgment by the court in all cases, including cases in which a court clerk can enter a default judgment. *See* CCP §167 (judge can perform any act court clerk can perform).

2. When to file. See "When to file or obtain," §7.1.2, p. 1100.

3. Application.

(1) Request for default judgment. To request a default judgment, the plaintiff must submit Judicial Council Form CIV-100. *See* CRC 3.1800(a). If the plaintiff did not request a default judgment at the same time it requested entry of default, Form CIV-100 will have to be submitted twice—once for entry of default and once for default judgment.

(a) Caption. The box in the caption for court's judgment should be checked.

(b) Date complaint filed. Item 1(a) must state the date the complaint or cross-complaint was filed.

(c) Party seeking default. Item 1(b) must state the name of the party seeking default judgment—that is, the party who filed the complaint or cross-complaint.

(d) Defendants. Item 1(c) does not have to be filled out if default has already been entered against the defendant. See "Defendants," §5.3.1(4), p. 1097.

(e) Request default judgment. The box for Item 1(d) must be checked for the court to enter default judgment. The plaintiff must also provide the names of the defendants that default judgment is being taken against and ask for a hearing date unless the court will enter judgment on declarations. See "Defendants," §5.3.1(4), p. 1097. If the court permits a default judgment to be proved up by declarations only (i.e., without a hearing), additional documentation will have to be filed with the request for default judgment. *See* CRC 3.1800(a). See "Additional documents," §7.2.3(2), this page.

NOTE

Before requesting a hearing date, check the court's local rules. Some courts require a default to be proved up by declarations only, while others require live testimony at a hearing. E.g., Super. Ct. Los Angeles Cty. Loc. R., rule 3.201 (prove-ups by declarations preferred; oral prove-ups required only by court order or when live testimony is required by law); Super. Ct. Sacramento Cty. Loc. R., rule 2.34(B) (prove-ups by declarations required if default is requested by affidavit unless, after reviewing declarations, court determines oral testimony is required); Super. Ct. San Francisco Cty. Loc. R., rule 6.5.C & 6.5.D (prove-ups by declarations required in limited-jurisdiction contract actions; oral prove-ups required in all other limited-jurisdiction cases and in unlimited-jurisdiction cases).

(f) Judgment entered. Item 2 must be filled out for default judgment. If damages were demanded in the complaint, Item 2(a) must state the amount demanded. If damages had to be asserted in a statement of damages, Item 2(b) must be filled out. Items 2(c)-(f) should be filled out as appropriate.

(g) Unlawful-detainer cases. Items 3 and 4 apply only to unlawful-detainer cases.

(h) Declaration of venue. Item 5 does not have to be filled out if default has already been entered. See "Declaration of venue," §5.3.1(8), p. 1097.

(i) Declaration of mailing. Item 6 does not have to be filled out if default has already been entered. See "Declaration of mailing," §5.3.1(9), p. 1097. Once default is entered, the defendant is not entitled to notice of the request for default judgment. CCP §1010.

CAUTION

In Los Angeles County, if the defendant was served by publication, an application for a default judgment on declarations must include a declaration about service of the application papers in compliance with CCP §587. Super. Ct. Los Angeles Cty. Loc. R., rule 3.203.

(j) Memorandum of costs. Item 7 must be filled out for default judgment. The plaintiff must state the costs that were incurred under CCP §1033.5.

(k) Declaration of military status. Item 8 must be filled out for default judgment. See "Declaration of military status," §7.1.3(1)(k), p. 1101.

(2) Additional documents. Some courts permit a default judgment to be proved up by declarations instead of live testimony. *E.g.*, Super. Ct. Los Angeles Cty. Loc. R., rule 3.201(a) (default judgment by declarations is preferred procedure); *see* CCP §585(d); CRC 3.1800(a). If the default judgment is to be proved up by declarations only, the request for default judgment should be filed with the following documents:

PRACTICE TIP

Check the local rules to determine the court's preference. Even if the court will hear live testimony, it may also want the documents described in CRC 3.1800(a) to be filed. See, e.g., Super. Ct. El Dorado Cty. Loc. R., rule 7.10.07.A(1) (all requests for default judgment must be accompanied by supporting evidence in written form).

(a) A brief summary of the case identifying the parties and the nature of the plaintiff's claim, unless the action is for unlawful detainer. CRC 3.1800(a)(1).

(b) Declarations or other admissible evidence in support of the judgment requested. CRC 3.1800(a)(2). The declaration must (1) state facts with particularity and be within the declarant's personal knowledge and (2) affirmatively show that the declarant, if sworn as a witness, can competently testify about those facts. CCP §585(d).

(c) Interest computations as necessary. CRC 3.1800(a)(3).

(d) A proposed form of judgment. CRC 3.1800(a)(6). See "Judgment," §8, p. 1107.

(e) If the case involves multiple defendants, one of the following:

[1] A dismissal of all parties against whom judgment is not sought. CRC 3.1800(a)(7).

[2] An application for a separate judgment against specified parties under CCP §579, supported by grounds for each judgment. CRC 3.1800(a)(7); *see* CCP §579 (in action against several Ds, court can render judgment against one or more Ds and continue action against any remaining Ds).

(f) Exhibits as necessary. CRC 3.1800(a)(8).

(g) A request for attorney fees if allowed by statute or agreement of the parties. CRC 3.1800(a)(9). A court can, by local rule, establish a schedule of attorney fees to be used to determine the reasonable amount of attorney fees to be allowed. CRC 3.1800(b).

NOTE

CRC 3.1800(a) also requires a memorandum of costs and a declaration of the defendant's military status to be filed with the clerk when seeking a default judgment on declarations only. CRC 3.1800(a)(4), (a)(5). This information, however, is already provided in Judicial Council Form CIV-100.

---

(3) No filing fee. There is no filing fee for requesting a default judgment. Gov. C. §70617(b)(8).

4. Court-appointed attorney. In certain situations, the court must appoint an attorney before rendering a default judgment.

(1) Military defendant. If the defendant is in the military, the court must appoint an attorney to represent the defendant before a default judgment can be rendered. 50 U.S.C. app. §521(b)(2).

(2) Indigent prisoner. If the defendant is an indigent prisoner, the court must appoint an attorney before a default judgment can be rendered if (1) the defendant plans to contest the suit, (2) an adverse judgment would affect the defendant's present or future property rights, and (3) a continuance until the defendant is released is not feasible. ***Payne v. Superior Ct.*** (1976) 17 Cal.3d 908, 924.

5. Plaintiff's burden.

(1) Proof of liability.

(a) Generally – deemed admitted. In most cases, after a default is entered, the well-pleaded allegations in the complaint are deemed admitted. ***City of L.A. v. Los Angeles Farming & Milling Co.*** (1907) 150 Cal. 647, 649; ***Kim v. Westmoore Partners*** (4th Dist.2011) 201 Cal.App.4th 267, 281; ***Vasey v. California Dance Co.*** (2d Dist.1977) 70 Cal.App.3d 742, 749. The admission, however, is limited to the factual allegations that support liability—damages are not admitted. *See* ***Kim***, 201 Cal.App.4th at 281; ***Ostling v. Loring*** (3d Dist.1994) 27 Cal.App.4th 1731, 1745. Thus, as long as the complaint states a cause of action against the defendant and the factual allegations would be considered substantial evidence supporting the judgment if admitted, the plaintiff will not need to introduce evidence supporting the admitted allegations. *See* ***City of L.A.***, 150 Cal. at 649; ***Kim***, 201 Cal.App.4th at 281. See "Does complaint state cause of action?," §4.2, p. 1095.

CAUTION

Before relying on the admitted factual allegations in the complaint to support liability, check with the clerk to determine the court's preference. Some courts may require all allegations in a complaint to be proved on default. E.g., Super. Ct. El Dorado Cty. Loc. R., rule 7.10.07.A(3) (allegations in complaint are not deemed proved on default; proof must be presented by competent evidence for all essential elements of cause of action); Super. Ct. Siskiyou Cty. Loc. R., rule 5.10.B (same).

(b) Exceptions. In certain cases, the facts alleged in the complaint must be established by proof and cannot be established by default. The claims that require proof are the following:

[1] Quiet-title actions. CCP §764.010; ***Yeung v. Soos*** (2d Dist.2004) 119 Cal.App.4th 576, 580-81; *see* CCP §585(c) (adverse possession requires proof of occupancy and ouster; claim on paper title requires evidence of equitable right to judgment); ***Nickell v. Matlock*** (2d Dist.2012) 206 Cal.App.4th 934, 947 (P not automatically entitled to judgment but must prove its case at hearing with live testimony and other admissible evidence); ***Harbour Vista, LLC v. HSBC Mortg. Servs.*** (4th Dist.2011) 201 Cal.App.4th 1496, 1502 (court must permit defaulting D to appear and present evidence at prove-up hearing).

[2] Marriage-dissolution or legal-separation proceedings. Fam. C. §2336(a).

[3] Actions to reestablish land boundaries and quiet title after an earthquake. CCP §751.59.

[4] Actions to reestablish destroyed land records. *Id.* §751.14.

[5] Small-claims actions. *See id.* §116.520(b) (if D does not appear, court must still require P to present evidence to prove claim).

(2) Proof of damages.

(a) Unliquidated damages. If damages are unliquidated, they require proof and are not considered admitted upon default. *See* ***Kim***, 201 Cal.App.4th at 287; ***Ostling***, 27 Cal.App.4th at 1745. In such cases, the court is required to render default judgment in the plaintiff's favor for that relief (not exceeding the amount pleaded) "as appears by the evidence to be just." CCP §585(b), (c). The plaintiff only has to introduce evidence establishing a prima facie case for damages; the preponderance-of-the-evidence standard does not apply. ***Johnson v. Stanhiser*** (4th Dist.1999) 72 Cal.App.4th 357, 361-62.

(b) Liquidated damages. If damages are liquidated or capable of mathematical computation, additional evidence is not required. *See* CCP §585(a); ***Kim***, 201 Cal.App.4th at 287.

6. Evidence. Evidence submitted in support of a default judgment should be admissible. *See* CRC 3.1800(a)(2). The court may disregard inadmissible evidence in a default proceeding. *See, e.g.*, Super. Ct. Los Angeles Cty. Loc. R., rule 3.205 (court has discretion to disregard hearsay or evidence lacking foundation; unauthenticated documents will not be considered unless authenticity was admitted by entry of default).

7. Hearing.

(1) Discretionary. Generally, courts have discretion to hold a prove-up hearing or permit a default judgment to be determined on declarations only. *See* CCP §585(d); CRC 3.1800(a); *see, e.g.*, Super. Ct. Los Angeles Cty. Loc. R., rule 3.201(a) (default on declarations is preferred procedure). If default is to be proved up by declarations only, the default will be determined in chambers without the presence of counsel. *CEB Procedure Before Trial*, §38.80.

(2) Mandatory.

(a) Quiet-title actions. A prove-up hearing is required in quiet-title actions. ***Yeung***, 119 Cal.App.4th at 580-81; Super. Ct. Los Angeles Cty. Loc. R., rule 3.201(b); *see* CCP §764.010.

(b) Nonresidents served by publication. If the defendant is not a California resident and was served by publication, the court must, before determining the amount of damages, require the plaintiff or the plaintiff's agent to be examined under oath about any payments toward the amount demanded in the suit that have been made to the plaintiff or to anyone for the plaintiff's use. CCP §585(c).

(3) Defendant's participation.

(a) Most cases. In most cases, the defendant is not permitted to participate in the prove-up hearing. ***Harbour Vista***, 201 Cal.App.4th at 1502; *see* ***People v. One 1986 Toyota Pickup*** (5th Dist.1995) 31 Cal.App.4th 254, 259.

(b) Quiet-title actions. Recently, two appellate courts held that a defaulting defendant has a right to appear and present evidence in a prove-up hearing for a quiet-title action. ***Harbour Vista***, 201 Cal.App.4th at 1502; *see* ***Nickell***, 206 Cal.App.4th at 943-44 (in quiet-title action, D has right to appear regardless of whether entry of default is for failure to appear or for misuse of discovery).

8. Ruling. The court has discretion to grant or deny the request for entry of default judgment. A party is not entitled to a default judgment as a matter of right, even when the defendant is technically in default. For example, a court can deny a default judgment if the plaintiff did not plead a cause of action against the defendant or present sufficient evidence to support its claim for relief. ***Kim***, 201 Cal.App.4th at 272; *see* ***Ferraro v. Camarlinghi*** (6th Dist.2008) 161 Cal.App.4th 509, 539; *see, e.g.*, ***Taliaferro v. Hoogs*** (1st Dist.1963) 219 Cal.App.2d 559, 560 (default judgment denied because P did not prove damages).

(1) Court's role.

(a) Gatekeeper. Because there is no opposing party in a default-judgment situation, the court has a duty to act as a gatekeeper to ensure that only the appropriate claims get through. ***Kim***, 201 Cal.App.4th at 272; ***Heidary v. Yadollahi*** (4th Dist.2002) 99 Cal.App.4th 857, 868. As the gatekeeper, the court must ensure that (1) the rules for default judgments are strictly followed, (2) the evidence introduced in support of the default judgment is limited to the allegations in the complaint, and (3) the judgment is not inconsistent with or in excess of the complaint. *See* ***Kim***, 201 Cal.App.4th at 272; ***Heidary***, 99 Cal.App.4th at 868; ***Lopez v. Fancelli*** (3d Dist.1990) 221 Cal.App.3d 1305, 1310. A court cannot allow a plaintiff to prove claims or damages different from those pleaded in the complaint. ***Electronic Funds Solutions, LLC v. Murphy*** (4th Dist.2005) 134 Cal.App.4th 1161, 1182; ***Heidary***, 99 Cal.App.4th at 868.

(b) May refer fact issues. The court can impanel a jury to determine a question of fact or to send a matter out for a reference if the matter involves an account (e.g., a dispute requiring the reckoning of monetary dealings) or a fact issue. CCP §585(b); *see id.* §639(a)(2). The jury's or referee's determination is not binding on the court. ***Cyrus v. Haveson*** (2d Dist.1976) 65 Cal.App.3d 306, 318. For a discussion of court-ordered references, see "Appointing Referee – Nonconsensual," ch. 2-E, §6, p. 175.

(2) Limitations on certain default judgments.

(a) Defaults against multiple defendants. The court cannot enter a default judgment against fewer than all of the defendants in an action involving multiple defendants unless the court determines that a several judgment is proper. CCP §579. A several judgment resolves the case against some defendants at one time and against other defendants at a later time. *See* ***Tinsley v. Palo Alto Unified Sch. Dist.*** (1st Dist.1979) 91 Cal.App.3d 871, 880. If a several judgment is proper, a default judgment can be entered against one or more defendants, and the action can be continued for any remaining defendants. *Id.*

(b) Defaults on cross-complaints. The court cannot enter a default judgment on a cross-complaint unless the court finds that a separate judgment can be properly awarded and would not substantially delay the final disposition of the action between the parties. CCP §585(e).

(c) Defaults against codefendants. The court cannot enter a default judgment against a defendant if (1) the defendant's liability depends on a codefendant's liability, (2) the codefendant has answered and raised a defense, and (3) the defense, if proved, would exonerate both defendants from liability. *See* ***Adams Mfg. & Eng'g v. Coast Centerless Grinding Co.*** (2d Dist.1960) 184 Cal.App.2d 649, 655-56.

§8. JUDGMENT

§8.1 Preparation. The plaintiff should prepare a proposed form of judgment and submit it when applying for entry of a default judgment. *See* CRC 3.1800(a)(6); Weil, *Civil Procedure Before Trial*, ¶5:180.2. Submitting a proposed form of judgment is mandatory if the application is supported solely by declarations. CRC 3.1800(a)(6). The plaintiff can use optional Judicial Council Form JUD-100 for judgments by the clerk or the court. For a default judgment in an unlawful-detainer action, the plaintiff can use Judicial Council Form UD-110 or UD-116.

§8.2 Contents.

1. Generally. The judgment must comply with the general rules that apply to all papers filed with the court. *See* CRC 2.3.

2. Relief. The judgment should specify the relief awarded to the plaintiff. *See* Judicial Council Forms, form JUD-100 (item 6). The relief awarded in a default judgment cannot be inconsistent with or in excess of what was requested in the complaint, the statement of damages, or the statement of punitive damages. *See* CCP §580(a); ***Heidary v. Yadollahi*** (4th Dist.2002) 99 Cal.App.4th 857, 868. See "Has defendant received notice of damages?," §4.3, p. 1095.

(1) Damages. The judgment should state the amount of monetary damages awarded to the plaintiff in dollars and cents (fractions are not allowed). CCP §577.5; *see* ***Kittle v. Lang*** (4th Dist.1951) 107 Cal.App.2d 604, 612 (judgment for money should be stated with certainty and specify amount awarded). See "Sets maximum award," §4.3.2, p. 1096.

(2) Prejudgment interest. The judgment must state the amount of any prejudgment interest awarded to the plaintiff. CRC 3.1802; *see, e.g.*, ***Taylor v. Varga*** (2d Dist.1995) 37 Cal.App.4th 750, 756 (trial court entered judgment for damages with interest). If the clerk is entering the default judgment, she can award prejudgment interest that is allowed by law or is consistent with the terms of a contract. *See* CCP §585(a).

(3) Attorney fees. The judgment should either specify the amount of attorney fees awarded to the plaintiff or leave a blank so that fees can be specified at a later time. *See* ***Bankes v. Lucas*** (2d Dist.1992) 9 Cal.App.4th 365, 369; *see also* CRC 3.1702(b)(1) (timing for serving and filing motion to claim attorney fees before judgment). If the clerk is entering the default judgment, she can award attorney fees according to the court's schedule of attorney fees if the plaintiff was permitted to recover a reasonable amount of attorney fees by contract or statute. CCP §585(a); CRC 3.1800(b); Super. Ct. Orange Cty. Loc. R., rule 366.

(4) Costs. The judgment should either specify the amount of costs awarded to the plaintiff or leave a blank so that costs can be specified at a later time. *See* ***Bankes***, 9 Cal.App.4th at 369; *see also* CRC 3.1700(a)(1) (requirements for serving and filing memorandum of costs after judgment). See "Memorandum of costs," §7.2.3(1)(j), p. 1103.

3. Date signed. The judgment should include a space for the date it was signed. *See, e.g.*, Judicial Council Forms, form JUD-100.

4. Signature line. The judgment should include a signature line for the judge or the clerk. Judicial Council Forms, form JUD-100.

§8.3 Entry of judgment. A judgment is not effective for any purpose until it is entered by the clerk. CCP §664. In most courts, a judgment is entered when the original judgment, signed by the judge, is filed with the clerk. ***Dodge v. Superior Ct.*** (4th Dist.2000) 77 Cal.App.4th 513, 518 n.5; *see* CCP §668.5. In courts that still use judgment books, a judgment is entered by the clerk when it is copied into the judgment book. ***Dodge***, 77 Cal.App.4th at 518 n.5; *see* CCP §668.

§8.4 Notice of entry. A defaulting defendant is not entitled to notice of the entry of default judgment. *See* CCP §664.5(a) (all parties who have appeared are entitled to notice), §1010 (defaulting D not entitled to any notice other than amendments to pleadings). Although serving notice of the judgment on the defendant is not required, doing so

may be advantageous. Under CCP §473.5(a), a defaulting defendant has two years after the entry of default judgment to set aside the default for lack of actual notice of the complaint. But if the defendant is served with notice of the entry of default or default judgment, the defendant has only 180 days after service to contest the default on that ground. CCP §473.5(a). The plaintiff can give notice by using optional Judicial Council Form CIV-130.

§8.5 Effect of default judgment. A default judgment operates as a final judgment and, once entered, is res judicata on all the issues in the case. *See* ***Murray v. Alaska Airlines, Inc.*** (2010) 50 Cal.4th 860, 871 (dicta); ***Martin v. General Fin. Co.*** (2d Dist.1966) 239 Cal.App.2d 438, 443.

§9. ATTACKING ENTRY OF DEFAULT & DEFAULT JUDGMENT

The entry of default and the default judgment can be attacked either directly or collaterally. *See* ***Falahati v. Kondo*** (2d Dist.2005) 127 Cal.App.4th 823, 829-30; ***Molen v. Friedman*** (3d Dist.1998) 64 Cal.App.4th 1149, 1156. A direct attack is brought for the specific purpose of setting aside the default or default judgment in the same suit the judgment was rendered in. *See* 8 Witkin, *Cal. Procedure*, Attack on Judgment in Trial Court, §1. A collateral attack occurs when a judgment is attacked in a different suit, typically in a suit brought to enforce the judgment. *See id.* §6. Chart 10-2, below, summarizes the different types of attacks that are available in the trial court and the appellate court.

10-2. METHODS FOR ATTACKING DEFAULT

	Method	Grounds for attack	Deadline to file
	Direct attacks – trial court		
1	Motion to vacate under §473(b) – discretionary. See §9.1.1(1), p. 1109.	Default was result of defendant's or attorney's excusable mistake, inadvertence, surprise, or neglect	6 months after entry of default or default judgment
2	Motion to vacate under §473(b) – mandatory. See §9.1.1(2), p. 1110.	Default was result of attorney's mistake, inadvertence, surprise, or neglect	6 months after entry of default judgment
3	Motion to vacate for lack of actual notice. See §9.1.2, p. 1111.	Defaulting defendant did not receive actual notice of suit	Earlier of (1) 2 years after entry of default judgment or (2) 180 days after service of written notice of entry of default or default judgment
4	Motion to vacate for improper venue. See §9.1.3, p. 1111.	Default in suit involving consumer transaction was not filed in proper court	60 days after receiving notice of levy under a writ of execution or other enforcement procedure
5	Motion to vacate void judgment. See §9.1.4, p. 1111.	Default judgment was void because court (1) lacked subject-matter jurisdiction, (2) lacked personal jurisdiction, or (3) granted relief with no authority	• Anytime if judgment was void on its face • 6 months after entry of default or default judgment if judgment was valid on its face but void • Earlier of (1) 2 years after entry of default judgment or (2) 180 days after service of written notice of entry of default or default judgment if judgment was void for improper service but valid on its face
6	Motion or independent action for equitable relief from judgment. See §9.1.5, p. 1113.	Defaulting defendant has a meritorious defense, extrinsic circumstances prevented defendant from answering complaint, and defendant exercised reasonable diligence in seeking relief after discovering default	Anytime as long as defendant was reasonably diligent in seeking relief once default was discovered

10-2. METHODS FOR ATTACKING DEFAULT (CONTINUED)

	Method	Grounds for attack	Deadline to file
		Direct attacks – appellate court	
7	Mandamus. See §9.2.1, p. 1115.	Trial-court clerk refused to perform ministerial act, or trial court refused to exercise its discretion	60 days after trial court's order
8	Direct appeal. See §9.2.2, p. 1116.	Motion to vacate default was denied or granted, and final judgment has been entered	Earliest of (1) 30 days after clerk or party serves order on motion to vacate or notice of entry of order, (2) 90 days after first motion to vacate is filed, or (3) 180 days after entry of judgment
		Collateral attacks	
9	Defense raised in separate suit. See §9.3, p. 1116.	Default judgment was void on its face because court (1) lacked subject-matter jurisdiction, (2) lacked personal jurisdiction, or (3) granted relief with no authority	Anytime

§9.1 Direct attacks in trial court. The defendant can directly attack the clerk's entry of default and the default judgment in the trial court by filing (1) a motion for relief under CCP §473(b) based on mistake, inadvertence, surprise, or neglect, (2) a motion to vacate for lack of actual notice, (3) a motion to vacate for improper venue, (4) a motion to vacate a void judgment, or (5) an action for equitable relief from judgment.

PRACTICE TIP

The defendant should try to vacate the entry of default before the court enters a default judgment. If the court grants the motion to vacate before entering a default judgment, the plaintiff will not be able to appeal the order and reinstate the default. ***Veliscescu v. Pauna*** *(2d Dist.1991) 231 Cal.App.3d 1521, 1522. If, however, a default judgment has already been entered, the defendant should move to set aside both the entry of default and the default judgment. A reversal of a default judgment does not vacate the default itself.* ***Electronic Funds Solutions, LLC v. Murphy*** *(4th Dist.2005) 134 Cal.App.4th 1161, 1177. Thus, if a defendant has only the default judgment set aside, the entry of default remains on the record and the plaintiff can simply seek another judgment based on that default. See* ***Howard Greer Custom Originals v. Capritti*** *(1950) 35 Cal.2d 886, 888-89; Weil, Civil Procedure Before Trial, ¶5:384.*

1. Motion to vacate under §473(b). The defendant or its legal representative (e.g., an assignee) can directly attack the entry of default or the default judgment by filing a motion for relief based on mistake, inadvertence, surprise, or neglect. *See* CCP §473(b); *see, e.g.,* ***Credit Managers Ass'n v. National Ind. Bus. Alliance*** (2d Dist.1984) 162 Cal.App.3d 1166, 1173 (surprise). Relief under §473(b) can be either discretionary or mandatory. *See* CCP §473(b).

(1) Discretionary relief.

(a) Grounds. The court may, on any just terms, vacate the entry of default and any resulting default judgment if either was the result of a party's or an attorney's mistake, inadvertence, surprise, or neglect and if that error was excusable. ***Zamora v. Clayborn Contracting Grp.*** (2002) 28 Cal.4th 249, 258; *see* CCP §473(b). An error is excusable if it might have been made by a reasonably prudent person under the same or similar circumstances. *E.g.,* ***Zamora***, 28 Cal.4th at 258 (excusable mistake or inadvertence); ***Huh v. Wang*** (6th Dist.2007) 158 Cal.App.4th 1406, 1419 (excusable neglect); ***Garcia v. Hejmadi*** (1st Dist.1997) 58 Cal.App.4th 674, 684 (excusable mistake).

(b) Deadline to file & serve. The motion must be filed and served within a reasonable time, but no later than six months after the entry of default (if challenging the entry of default) or six months after the default judgment (if challenging the judgment). *See* CCP §473(b); ***Rutan v. Summit Sports, Inc.*** (3d Dist.1985) 173 Cal.App.3d 965, 970; ***Puryear v. Stanley*** (3d Dist.1985) 172 Cal.App.3d 291, 293-94. The reasonable-time requirement compels the defendant to act with diligence in filing the motion. ***Zamora***, 28 Cal.4th at 258. If there is a significant lapse between discovering the default and filing the motion, the defendant must give a reasonable excuse for the delay even if the motion is filed within the six-month period. ***Huh***, 158 Cal.App.4th at 1422; *see* ***Benjamin v. Dalmo Mfg.*** (1948) 31 Cal.2d 523, 529 (delay of three months or more requires explanation); ***Stafford v. Mach*** (1st Dist.1998) 64 Cal.App.4th 1174, 1184 (same); *see, e.g.*, ***Smith v. Pelton Water Wheel Co.*** (1907) 151 Cal. 394, 397-98 (attorney's illness and need to attend to other pressing business was not reasonable excuse for four-month delay in filing motion after discovering default).

(c) Contents. The motion must be made by noticed motion and accompanied by a copy of the proposed responsive pleading. *See* CCP §473(b); Weil, *Civil Procedure Before Trial*, ¶¶5:382, 5:385. The proposed responsive pleading can be filed and served separately from the noticed motion as long as it is served sufficiently in advance of the hearing. ***County of Stanislaus v. Johnson*** (5th Dist.1996) 43 Cal.App.4th 832, 838. Courts disagree, however, on whether the proposed responsive pleading can be filed and served after the six-month deadline to file and serve the motion for relief has ended. *Compare id.* at 837-38 (motion for relief was not defective even though proposed answer was not served until after six-month period had ended), *and* ***Job v. Farrington*** (2d Dist.1989) 209 Cal.App.3d 338, 340-41 (same), *with* ***Puryear***, 172 Cal.App.3d at 294 (motion for relief was defective because proposed answer was not served until after six-month period had ended).

NOTE

When a default judgment affects title to or possession of real or personal property, the deadline to seek relief from that judgment under §473(b) is shortened to 90 days if the defaulting party was personally served in California with written notice of the default judgment. CCP §473(b).

(2) Mandatory relief.

(a) Grounds. The court must vacate the entry of default and any resulting default judgment if either was the result of an attorney's mistake, inadvertence, surprise, or neglect. CCP §473(b); *see* ***Lorenz v. Commercial Acceptance Ins.*** (6th Dist.1995) 40 Cal.App.4th 981, 989-90 (court can vacate clerk's or court's entry of default). The attorney's mistake, inadvertence, surprise, or neglect does not have to be reasonable; a defendant is entitled to relief even if the attorney's actions were inexcusable. *See* ***Wagner v. Wagner*** (2d Dist.2008) 162 Cal.App.4th 249, 258; ***Matera v. McLeod*** (2d Dist.2006) 145 Cal.App.4th 44, 63.

(b) Deadline to file & serve. The motion must be filed and served within six months after default judgment is entered. CCP §473(b); *see* ***Davis v. Thayer*** (2d Dist.1980) 113 Cal.App.3d 892, 903 (six months equals 182 days). Unlike requests for discretionary relief, there is no reasonable-diligence requirement for filing a motion for mandatory relief after discovering the default. ***Prieto v. Loyola Marymount Univ.*** (2d Dist.2005) (Div. 8) 132 Cal.App.4th 290, 294 n.3; *see* ***Stafford***, 64 Cal.App.4th at 1188-89; ***Metropolitan Serv. v. Casa de Palms, Ltd.*** (2d Dist.1995) (Div. 4) 31 Cal.App.4th 1481, 1487. *Contra* ***Caldwell v. Methodist Hosp.*** (2d Dist.1994) (Div. 7) 24 Cal.App.4th 1521, 1525; ***Billings v. Health Plan of Am.*** (2d Dist.1990) (Div. 1) 225 Cal.App.3d 250, 258.

(c) Contents. The motion must be made by noticed motion and accompanied by (1) the defense attorney's sworn affidavit attesting to her mistake, inadvertence, surprise, or neglect and (2) a proposed responsive pleading to the complaint. *See* CCP §473(b) (sworn affidavit); ***Carmel, Ltd. v. Tavoussi*** (4th Dist.2009) 175 Cal.App.4th 393, 402 (proposed answer must accompany application for mandatory relief); Weil, *Civil Procedure Before Trial*, ¶5:382 (noticed motion), ¶5:385 (proposed responsive pleading). For a discussion of how the proposed responsive pleading must be filed and served, see "Contents," §9.1.1(1)(c), this page.

2. Motion to vacate for lack of actual notice.

(1) Grounds. The defendant can directly attack the entry of default or the default judgment on the ground that even though service was proper, the defendant did not receive actual notice of the action. CCP §473.5(a). Actual notice means that the party had genuine knowledge of the action; it does not contemplate notice attributed to a party from an attorney's actual notice. ***Tunis v. Barrow*** (2d Dist.1986) 184 Cal.App.3d 1069, 1077. Lack of actual notice usually occurs when service is made by publication, mail, or substitution. *See, e.g.*, ***Kodiak Films, Inc. v. Jensen*** (2d Dist.1991) 230 Cal.App.3d 1260, 1261-62 (mail and substitution); ***Tunis***, 184 Cal.App.3d at 1074 (publication). If the court grants the motion to vacate, the court can set aside the entry of default or the default judgment on whatever terms it deems just and allow the defendant to defend the action. CCP §473.5(c).

NOTE

If the defendant receives actual notice from a source other than the service of summons, the court may still grant the defendant relief under CCP §473.5. ***Ellard v. Conway*** *(4th Dist.2001) 94 Cal.App.4th 540, 548;* ***Olvera v. Olvera*** *(4th Dist.1991) 232 Cal.App.3d 32, 40.*

(2) Deadline to file & serve. The motion should be filed and served within a reasonable time not exceeding the earlier of (1) two years after the default judgment is entered or (2) 180 days after the defendant is served with written notice that a default or default judgment has been entered against it. CCP §473.5(a).

(3) Contents. The motion must be made by noticed motion and accompanied by (1) a declaration that the lack of actual notice to defend the action was not caused by the defendant's inexcusable neglect or avoidance of service and (2) a responsive pleading to the action. *See* CCP §473.5(a), (b); *see, e.g.*, ***Anastos v. Lee*** (4th Dist.2004) 118 Cal.App.4th 1314, 1319 (motion to vacate denied because declaration improperly contained inadmissible hearsay and was not based on personal knowledge).

3. Motion to vacate for improper venue.

(1) Grounds. The defendant can directly attack the entry of default or the default judgment by filing a motion to vacate the judgment for improper venue in certain cases involving consumer transactions. CCP §585.5(b); *see id.* §395(b) (contracts involving goods, services, loans, or extensions of credit for personal, family, or household use); Civ. C. §1812.10 (retail installment sales), §2984.4 (motor-vehicle financings). If the plaintiff does not follow the specific venue provisions in CCP §395(b) or Civ. C. §1812.10 or §2984.4, the defendant can challenge a default or default judgment on the ground that it was not entered in the proper court. *See* CCP §585.5(b).

(2) Deadline to file & serve. The motion must be filed and served within 60 days after the defendant first receives notice of levy under a writ of execution or notice of any other procedure to enforce the judgment. CCP §585.5(b). If the court grants the motion, the court can set aside the entry of default or the default judgment on whatever terms it deems just and allow the defendant to defend the action in the proper court. *Id.* §585.5(d).

(3) Contents. The motion must be made by noticed motion and accompanied by (1) a declaration showing that the action was not filed in the proper court and (2) a proposed responsive pleading to the complaint. CCP §585.5(b), (c).

4. Motion to vacate void judgment. The defendant can directly attack the entry of default or the default judgment by filing a motion to vacate a void judgment. *See* CCP §473(d); ***Falahati v. Kondo*** (2d Dist.2005) 127 Cal.App.4th 823, 829-30; ***Heidary v. Yadollahi*** (4th Dist.2002) 99 Cal.App.4th 857, 863; ***Plotitsa v. Superior Ct.*** (2d Dist.1983) 140 Cal.App.3d 755, 758.

(1) Grounds. A default or default judgment is void in the following circumstances:

(a) No subject-matter jurisdiction. A default or default judgment is void if the court lacked subject-matter jurisdiction. ***Falahati***, 127 Cal.App.4th at 830. See "Choosing the Court—Subject-Matter Jurisdiction," ch. 3-E, p. 248.

(b) No personal jurisdiction. A default or default judgment is void if the court lacked personal jurisdiction. ***Falahati***, 127 Cal.App.4th at 830. The plaintiff has the burden to prove that personal jurisdiction over the defendant is proper. ***American Express Centurion Bank v. Zara*** (6th Dist.2011) 199 Cal.App.4th 383, 387. For a discussion of personal jurisdiction, see "Joining the Defendant—Personal Jurisdiction," ch. 3-G, p. 283.

(c) No service or improper service of process. A default or default judgment is void if the defendant was not served or was improperly served. ***American Express***, 199 Cal.App.4th at 387; ***Dill v. Berquist Constr. Co.*** (4th Dist.1994) 24 Cal.App.4th 1426, 1444. Generally, a defendant is considered properly served if the defendant had actual notice of the suit and the plaintiff substantially complied with the statutory requirements for service. *See* ***Pasadena Medi-Center Assocs. v. Superior Ct.*** (1973) 9 Cal.3d 773, 778 (if actual notice is received by D, statutory requirements should be liberally construed to effectuate service and uphold jurisdiction of court); ***Trackman v. Kenney*** (3d Dist.2010) 187 Cal.App.4th 175, 184 (minor deficiencies cannot be used to defeat service); ***Summers v. McClanahan*** (2d Dist.2006) 140 Cal.App.4th 403, 410-11 (actual notice is not enough to establish proper service if P completely failed to comply with statutory requirement). *But see* ***American Express***, 199 Cal.App.4th at 390-91 (court questioned whether substantial-compliance standard should be used to uphold default judgment); ***County of Riverside v. Superior Ct.*** (4th Dist.1997) 54 Cal.App.4th 443, 450 (court questioned whether substantial-compliance standard should be used for service by publication); ***Bishop v. Silva*** (6th Dist.1991) 234 Cal.App.3d 1317, 1323 (court declined to liberally construe statutory requirement of timely service when D had actual notice). For a discussion of service of process, including substantial compliance with statutory requirements, see "Joining the Defendant—Service of Process," ch. 3-H, p. 295.

(d) No power to grant relief. A default or default judgment is void when the clerk or court grants relief it had no power to grant. ***Falahati***, 127 Cal.App.4th at 830. This can occur in the following circumstances:

[1] The clerk enters default before the time to respond to the complaint has expired. ***Baird v. Smith*** (1932) 216 Cal. 408, 409-10.

[2] The clerk enters default judgment on an action that does not arise under a contract or judgment for the recovery of money or damages only. *See* ***Landwehr v. Gillette*** (1917) 174 Cal. 654, 655-56.

[3] The damages awarded in the default judgment exceed the amount requested in the complaint or the statement of damages. ***Yeung v. Soos*** (2d Dist.2004) 119 Cal.App.4th 576, 582.

NOTE

When the damages awarded in a default judgment exceed the amount specified in the complaint or the statement of damages, the court has the power to modify the judgment or, if requested by the plaintiff, vacate the default and allow the plaintiff to file an amended complaint. See ***Becker v. S.P.V. Constr. Co.*** *(1980) 27 Cal.3d 489, 494-95;* ***Julius Schifaugh IV Consulting Servs. v. Avaris Capital, Inc.*** *(4th Dist.2008) 164 Cal.App.4th 1393, 1397-98.*

---

[4] The evidence offered to support unliquidated damages was insufficient. ***Kim v. Westmoore Partners*** (4th Dist.2011) 201 Cal.App.4th 267, 288. See "Unliquidated damages," §7.2.5(2)(a), p. 1105.

[5] The default judgment is entered on a complaint that did not notify the defendant of its liability. *See, e.g.*, ***Matera***, 145 Cal.App.4th at 61-62 (default judgment rendered against D when D did not receive formal notice of liability until two days before entry of default was void); ***Falahati***, 127 Cal.App.4th at 830 (default judgment based on complaint that did not contain factual allegations about D was void).

[6] The default judgment was entered on a complaint that did not state a cause of action. ***Kim***, 201 Cal.App.4th at 282. See "Does complaint state cause of action?," §4.2, p. 1095.

[7] The default judgment is rendered on improper grounds. *See, e.g.*, ***Heidary***, 99 Cal.App.4th at 862 (default judgment rendered against Ds for not appearing at trial was void).

(2) **Deadline to file & serve.** The deadline to file and serve a motion under CCP §473(d) depends on whether the judgment is void or valid on its face.

(a) **Void on its face.** When the default or default judgment is void on its face, the defendant (or the court on its own) can bring a motion to vacate at any time before or after the judgment becomes final. ***People v. Davis*** (1904) 143 Cal. 673, 675-76; ***Shisler v. Sanfer Sports Cars, Inc.*** (6th Dist.2008) 167 Cal.App.4th 1, 5; ***Nagel v. P&M Distribs.*** (2d Dist.1969) 273 Cal.App.2d 176, 180; *see also* ***Falahati***, 127 Cal.App.4th at 831 (judgment void on its face was not subject to laches defense). A judgment is void on its face when the invalidity is apparent from the judgment roll. ***Davis***, 143 Cal. at 675; ***Dill***, 24 Cal.App.4th at 1441. In cases in which the defendant does not answer a complaint, the judgment roll consists of the following: (1) the summons with the affidavit or proof of service, (2) the complaint, (3) the request for entry of default with an endorsed memorandum that default was entered, and (4) a copy of the judgment. CCP §670(a). If the defendant was served by publication, the judgment roll includes the affidavit for publication of summons and the order directing publication of summons. *Id.* The following are examples of default judgments that were considered void on their face:

- A default judgment that exceeded the damages demanded in the complaint. ***David S. Karton, a Law Corp. v. Dougherty*** (2d Dist.2009) 171 Cal.App.4th 133, 151.
- A default judgment entered because the defendants did not appear at trial, even though they had answered the complaint. ***Heidary***, 99 Cal.App.4th at 862-63.
- A default judgment based on invalid service that was apparent from the proof of service. ***Dill***, 24 Cal.App.4th at 1441.
- A default judgment based on a faulty affidavit in support of service by publication. ***Olvera***, 232 Cal.App.3d at 41.

(b) **Valid on its face.**

[1] **Generally – 6 months.** When the default or default judgment is void but appears valid on its face, the defendant must bring the motion within a reasonable time not exceeding six months after entry of the default or the default judgment. *See* ***Ramos v. Homeward Residential, Inc.*** (4th Dist.2014) 223 Cal.App.4th 1434, 1440; *see, e.g.*, ***Schenkel v. Resnik*** (Los Angeles Cty. Superior Ct. Appellate Dept. 1994) 27 Cal.App.4th Supp. 1, 4 (motion to vacate was not made within reasonable time when D brought motion 20 months after learning of default). Generally, if a party must present evidence apart from the judgment roll (i.e., extrinsic evidence) to show that the judgment is void, the judgment is considered valid on its face. *See* ***Strathvale Holdings v. E.B.H.*** (2d Dist.2005) 126 Cal.App.4th 1241, 1249.

[2] **Exception – void for improper service.** When a default or default judgment that is valid on its face is void because of improper service, the defendant must bring the motion by the earlier of (1) two years after entry of the default judgment or (2) 180 days after service on the defendant of a written notice that a default or default judgment has been entered against it. *See* ***Plaza Hollister L.P. v. County of San Benito*** (6th Dist.1999) 72 Cal.App.4th 1, 19 n.11; ***Gibble v. Car-Lene Research, Inc.*** (1st Dist.1998) 67 Cal.App.4th 295, 301 n.3; ***Rogers v. Silverman*** (2d Dist.1989) 216 Cal.App.3d 1114, 1123-24; *cf.* CCP §473.5(a) (motion to vacate for lack of actual notice).

5. **Action in equity to vacate judgment.** The defendant can directly attack the entry of default and the default judgment by asking the court to vacate the default or default judgment on equitable grounds. ***Rappleyea v. Campbell*** (1994) 8 Cal.4th 975, 981; *see* ***Bennett v. Hibernia Bank*** (1956) 47 Cal.2d 540, 558 (suit in equity to vacate judgment is direct attack).

(1) **How to request.** A request for equitable relief from default or default judgment can be brought as a motion or as an independent action. ***Olivera v. Grace*** (1942) 19 Cal.2d 570, 575-76; ***In re Marriage of Baltins*** (1st Dist.1989) 212 Cal.App.3d 66, 80-81. Although filing a motion is simpler and more convenient, there are several benefits to filing an independent action. First, an independent action allows the defendant to take advantage of a

full trial (e.g., conduct discovery, subpoena witnesses, present oral testimony) to meet its burden to vacate the judgment. ***Groves v. Peterson*** (2d Dist.2002) 100 Cal.App.4th 659, 668; *see CEB Procedure Before Trial*, §38.98. Second, an independent action can be brought to challenge a judgment on the same grounds that were asserted in an earlier motion to vacate that was denied, even if the earlier motion was based on equitable relief. ***Rohrbasser v. Lederer*** (2d Dist.1986) 179 Cal.App.3d 290, 298-99; *see* ***Groves***, 100 Cal.App.4th at 668. The denial of an earlier motion to vacate has no collateral-estoppel effect on an independent action in equity unless the court conducted a hearing on the earlier motion that was the equivalent of a trial with oral testimony. ***Groves***, 100 Cal.App.4th at 668.

PRACTICE TIP

Because collateral estoppel generally does not apply to an earlier motion to vacate, the best practice is to first challenge a default or default judgment by filing a motion. ***Estudillo v. Security Loan & Trust Co.*** *(1906) 149 Cal. 556, 565;* ***Rohrbasser****, 179 Cal.App.3d at 297-98. If the motion is denied, the party can then file an independent action in equity based on the same grounds that were denied in the motion.* ***Estudillo****, 149 Cal. at 565;* ***Rohrbasser****, 179 Cal.App.3d at 297-98.*

(2) Grounds. To obtain equitable relief from a judgment, the defendant must establish that extrinsic factors prevented it from having a fair adversary trial. ***Olivera***, 19 Cal.2d at 575. Several courts have adopted a three-part test to determine if equitable relief from a judgment can be granted. Under this test, a defaulting defendant must establish (1) a meritorious defense to the plaintiff's complaint, (2) extrinsic circumstances (e.g., fraud, mistake) providing a satisfactory excuse for not answering the complaints, and (3) reasonable diligence in seeking relief once the default was discovered. ***Rappleyea***, 8 Cal.4th at 982-83; ***Lee v. An*** (2d Dist.2008) 168 Cal.App.4th 558, 566; ***Falahati***, 127 Cal.App.4th at 833. *But see* ***County of San Diego v. Gorham*** (4th Dist.2010) 186 Cal.App.4th 1215, 1233 (diligence requirement did not apply when fundamental jurisdiction was obtained through intentional fraud on court).

(a) Meritorious defense. To establish a meritorious defense, the defendant must plead facts establishing that it has a sufficient defense that would entitle it to a trial of the issue; an absolute guarantee of victory is not required. ***Olivera***, 19 Cal.2d at 579. Ordinarily, a verified answer to the complaint's allegations will be sufficient to show merit. ***Rappleyea***, 8 Cal.4th at 983; *see, e.g.*, ***Falahati***, 127 Cal.App.4th at 833 (defense that complaint did not state cause of action against D was meritorious).

(b) Extrinsic circumstances. To establish extrinsic circumstances, the defendant must show that it was prevented from timely responding to the complaint because of matters outside the issues framed by the pleadings or the issues adjudicated. ***Aldrich v. San Fernando Valley Lumber Co.*** (2d Dist.1985) 170 Cal.App.3d 725, 738. Courts have commonly referred to the extrinsic circumstances that support equitable relief as "extrinsic fraud" or "extrinsic mistake." ***In re Marriage of Park*** (1980) 27 Cal.3d 337, 342. The California Supreme Court, however, has given the phrases broader meaning to encompass almost any set of extrinsic circumstances that would deprive a party of a fair adversary hearing. *Id.*

[1] Extrinsic fraud. Extrinsic fraud generally occurs when a party is deliberately kept in ignorance of a proceeding or in some other way is fraudulently prevented from presenting its claim or defense. ***Kulchar v. Kulchar*** (1969) 1 Cal.3d 467, 471; ***Gorham***, 186 Cal.App.4th at 1228-29. Examples of extrinsic fraud include the following:

- The defendant did not receive notice of the suit because of the plaintiff's willful misstatement of the defendant's address in the affidavit of publication. ***Rivieccio v. Bothan*** (1946) 27 Cal.2d 621, 624.

- The defendant was denied an opportunity to respond to the suit when the plaintiff added the defendant's name to the complaint the same day that default was entered against the defendant. ***Falahati***, 127 Cal.App.4th at 831.

• The plaintiff entered default against the defendant after convincing the defendant not to obtain counsel by falsely promising that the suit would not proceed. ***Moghaddam v. Bone*** (4th Dist.2006) 142 Cal.App.4th 283, 290 (dicta).

• The plaintiff knowingly filed a false proof of service. ***Gorham***, 186 Cal.App.4th at 1229.

[2] Extrinsic mistake. Extrinsic mistake is defined as the doing of an act under an erroneous belief that would not have been done if not for the belief. ***Aldrich***, 170 Cal.App.3d at 738. The same definition applies to omissions. *Id.* Extrinsic mistake includes a mistake committed by a court officer. ***Baske v. Burke*** (4th Dist.1981) 125 Cal.App.3d 38, 44; *see* ***Gorham***, 186 Cal.App.4th at 1229. Examples of extrinsic mistake include the following:

• The entry of default was caused by incorrect information about filing fees given to the defendants by the court clerk. ***Rappleyea***, 8 Cal.4th at 983.

• The complaint was lost in the mail. ***Hallett v. Slaughter*** (1943) 22 Cal.2d 552, 554, 557.

• The defendant's attorney accidentally left the defendant's individual name off of the answer and named only his corporation. ***Turner v. Allen*** (2d Dist.1961) 189 Cal.App.2d 753, 756-57.

• The defendant reasonably relied on an interested third party (e.g., codefendant, insurer) to defend the action. ***Weitz v. Yankosky*** (1966) 63 Cal.2d 849, 855-56.

• The court entered a default judgment based on a false proof of service. ***Gorham***, 186 Cal.App.4th at 1229.

(c) Reasonable diligence. To establish reasonable diligence, the defendant must show that it acted the same way a person exercising ordinary care and prudence under the same circumstances would have acted to vacate the judgment once the default was discovered. ***McCreadie v. Arques*** (1st Dist.1967) 248 Cal.App.2d 39, 46. In determining whether reasonable diligence has been exercised, courts will consider the length of delay in filing the action to vacate after discovering the default, the reasons for the delay, and the prejudice to the plaintiff that might result if the judgment is vacated. *See* ***Weitz***, 63 Cal.2d at 857; ***McCreadie***, 248 Cal.App.2d at 47; *see, e.g.*, ***Falahati***, 127 Cal.App.4th at 834 (ten-month delay between default judgment and motion to set aside did not bar D from vacating default when P obtained default by violating D's due-process rights). The diligence in seeking relief after discovery of the default is intertwined with prejudice. ***Rappleyea***, 8 Cal.4th at 983-84. The longer the delay after judgment, the greater the prejudice to the plaintiff. *See* ***Falahati***, 127 Cal.App.4th at 833-34; ***McCreadie***, 248 Cal.App.2d at 47. Thus, as more time passes after entry of judgment, the burden to prove diligence is greater. *See* ***Falahati***, 127 Cal.App.4th at 833-34. Prejudice is less, however, if no default judgment has been entered and the party is seeking equitable relief only from the entry of default. ***Rappleyea***, 8 Cal.4th at 984.

(3) Deadline to file & serve. Generally, a request for equitable relief from judgment can be brought at any time as long as reasonable diligence in seeking relief has been exercised. *See* ***Rappleyea***, 8 Cal.4th at 983 (equitable defenses such as laches or estoppel may apply if prejudice is great); *see, e.g.*, ***Lee***, 168 Cal.App.4th at 566 (filing motion to vacate two years after discovering default judgment did not meet diligence requirement for equitable relief). *But see* ***Gorham***, 186 Cal.App.4th at 1233 (diligence requirement did not apply when fundamental jurisdiction was obtained through intentional fraud on court).

§9.2 Direct attacks in appellate court.

1. Writ of mandate.

(1) When applicable.

(a) Compel ministerial act. A writ of mandate is available to compel the trial-court clerk to perform the ministerial act of entering a proper default or default judgment. *See* CCP §1085(a); ***W.A. Rose Co. v. Municipal Ct.*** (1st Dist.1959) 176 Cal.App.2d 67, 68.

(b) Compel exercise of discretion. A writ of mandate is available when the trial court refuses to exercise its discretion when required to do so. *See, e.g.*, ***Gardner v. Superior Ct.*** (4th Dist.1986) 182 Cal.App.3d 335, 336-37 (mandate granted when trial court refused to exercise its discretion in ruling on motion to vacate default).

(2) Deadline to file. There is no statutory deadline for a writ of mandate, but appellate courts typically will not hear a writ of mandate more than 60 days after the challenged trial-court order. *See* 8 Witkin, *Cal. Procedure*, Extraordinary Writs, §182.

2. Direct appeal.

(1) Motion to vacate default judgment. A trial court's order on a motion to vacate the entry of a default judgment is appealable. *See* CCP §904.1(a)(2); *see, e.g.*, ***Ramos v. Homeward Residential, Inc.*** (4th Dist.2014) 223 Cal.App.4th 1434, 1440 (appeal of order granting motion to vacate). An appellate court can affirm or reverse the trial court's order in whole or in part. *See, e.g.*, ***National Diversified Servs. v. Bernstein*** (6th Dist.1985) 168 Cal.App.3d 410, 419 (court struck part of default judgment that was excessive and affirmed rest of judgment). Appellate courts are likely to affirm an order granting relief from a default because they favor a trial on the merits. ***Shamblin v. Brattain*** (1988) 44 Cal.3d 474, 478. An order denying relief will be scrutinized carefully because it deprives the defendant of the right to defend an action in court. *See* ***Lorenz v. Commercial Acceptance Ins.*** (6th Dist.1995) 40 Cal.App.4th 981, 998.

(2) Motion to vacate clerk's entry of default. A trial court's order on a motion to vacate the clerk's entry of default is not appealable but can be reviewed after the court enters a default judgment. *See* ***Rappleyea v. Campbell*** (1994) 8 Cal.4th 975, 981; *see, e.g.*, ***City of Riverside v. Horspool*** (4th Dist.2014) 223 Cal.App.4th 670, 681 (no appeal of order denying motion to vacate before default judgment was entered); ***Veliscescu v. Pauna*** (2d Dist.1991) 231 Cal.App.3d 1521, 1522 (no appeal of order granting motion to vacate before default judgment was entered). The entry of default is a ministerial act, not a final judgment, so it is not appealable until a final judgment has been entered in the action. *See* ***First Am. Title Co. v. Mirzaian*** (2d Dist.2003) 108 Cal.App.4th 956, 960.

(3) Standard of review.

(a) De novo. A trial court's order on a motion to vacate a default or a default judgment is reviewed de novo when the court has no discretion to grant or deny the motion. *See, e.g.*, ***Ramos***, 223 Cal.App.4th at 1440 (motion to vacate filed after six-month deadline); ***Matera v. McLeod*** (2d Dist.2006) 145 Cal.App.4th 44, 65-66 (motion for mandatory relief under CCP §473(b)); ***Falahati v. Kondo*** (2d Dist.2005) 127 Cal.App.4th 823, 828 (motion to vacate because statutory notice requirements were not met); ***Transamerica Title Ins. v. Hendrix*** (2d Dist.1995) 34 Cal.App.4th 740, 746 (motion to vacate for improper service).

(b) Abuse of discretion. A trial court's order on a motion to vacate a default or a default judgment is reviewed for abuse of discretion when the court can grant or deny the motion at its discretion. *See* ***Rappleyea***, 8 Cal.4th at 981; *see, e.g.*, ***Shamblin***, 44 Cal.3d at 477-78 (motion for discretionary relief under CCP §473(b)); ***Ellard v. Conway*** (4th Dist.2001) 94 Cal.App.4th 540, 547 (motion to vacate for lack of actual notice).

(4) Deadline to file. Filing a valid motion to vacate extends the time to appeal until the earliest of (1) 30 days after the clerk or a party serves an order denying the motion to vacate or a notice of entry of the order, (2) 90 days after the first motion to vacate is filed, or (3) 180 days after entry of judgment. CRC 8.108(c); *see* CRC 8.104(a) (normal time to appeal).

§9.3 Collateral attack on default judgment. A collateral attack occurs when the defendant asserts that the judgment is void as a defense to a separate action brought by a judgment creditor to enforce the judgment. *See* ***Levine v. Smith*** (2d Dist.2006) 145 Cal.App.4th 1131, 1135 & n.2; Weil, *Civil Procedure Before Trial*, ¶5:489. A party can collaterally attack a judgment only when it is void on its face because the court (1) lacked subject-matter jurisdiction, (2) lacked personal jurisdiction, or (3) granted relief it had no authority to grant. ***Becker v. S.P.V. Constr. Co.*** (1980) 27 Cal.3d 489, 493. See "Void on its face," §9.1.4(2)(a), p. 1113. Nonjurisdictional errors, such as failure

to state a cause of action, insufficiency of evidence, abuse of discretion, and mistake of law, will not support a collateral attack. ***Armstrong v. Armstrong*** (1976) 15 Cal.3d 942, 950. A judgment that is void on its face is subject to collateral attack at any time. ***Rochin v. Pat Johnson Mfg.*** (2d Dist.1998) 67 Cal.App.4th 1228, 1239; *see, e.g.*, ***Becker***, 27 Cal.3d at 492-93 (challenge to default was made by collateral attack because time to file motion to vacate under CCP §473 had passed).

NOTE

*When the damages awarded in a default judgment exceed the amount specified in the complaint or the statement of damages, the court, in a collateral attack, has the power to modify the judgment instead of vacating it. See **Becker**, 27 Cal.3d at 495 (no policy against court modifying judgment in collateral attack; fairness to Ps and judicial economy require that repetitious litigation be avoided).*

B. MOTION FOR SUMMARY JUDGMENT

This subchapter discusses how to obtain a summary judgment in civil actions and proceedings under CCP §437c. This subchapter does not discuss the special summary-judgment rules that apply to forcible-detainer and unlawful-detainer actions. For a discussion of those rules, see CCP §§437c(r) and 1170.7 and CRC 3.1351.

§1. GENERAL

§1.1 Purpose. The purpose of a motion for summary judgment (MSJ) is to determine whether there are any genuine issues of material fact for trial. ***Aguilar v. Atlantic Richfield Co.*** (2001) 25 Cal.4th 826, 843; *see* CCP §437c(c). A trial is warranted only if there is an issue of fact for the fact-finder (i.e., judge or jury) to resolve. If there are no triable issues of material fact, the moving party is entitled to a summary judgment without a trial. ***Aguilar***, 25 Cal.4th at 843. A summary judgment disposes of an entire case (i.e., action or proceeding) for one or more parties. *See* CCP §437c(k) (SJ can result in separate appealable judgments); ***24 Hour Fitness, Inc. v. Superior Ct.*** (1st Dist.1998) 66 Cal.App.4th 1199, 1208 (§437c plainly provides for circumstances in which one D is entitled to SJ even though other Ds are not); ***American Nat'l Bank v. Stanfill*** (5th Dist.1988) 205 Cal.App.3d 1089, 1095 (SJ can result in separate appealable judgments). If a party can dispose of only part of a case (i.e., a cause of action, defense, claim for damages, or issue of duty), the party must file a motion for summary adjudication instead. *See* CCP §437c(f)(1). See "Motion for Summary Adjudication," ch. 10-C, p. 1145.

§1.2 Primary authority. CCP §437c; CRC 3.1350, 3.1352, 3.1354; *see also* CCP §1038 (SJ in actions against public entities), §1170.7 (SJ in certain real-property actions).

§1.3 Secondary authority. The following secondary sources are cited as authority in this subchapter:

- *Action Guide: Making & Opposing a Summary Judgment Motion* (CEB 2005) (referred to as *CEB Action Guide: Making & Opposing a Summary Judgment Motion*).
- *California Civil Procedure Before Trial* (CEB Online ed. 2014) (referred to as *CEB Procedure Before Trial*).
- *California Trial Objections* (CEB Online ed. 2014) (referred to as *CEB Trial Objections*).
- Johnson, *California Trial Guide* (2009) (referred to as *Cal. Trial Guide*).
- Kiesel et al., *Matthew Bender Practice Guide: California Pretrial Civil Procedure* (2014) (referred to as Kiesel, *Cal. Pretrial Civil Procedure*).
- Thomas, *California Civil Courtroom Handbook* (2014) (referred to as Thomas, *Courtroom Handbook*).
- Weil & Brown, *California Practice Guide: Civil Procedure Before Trial* (CD-ROM ed. 2014) (referred to as Weil, *Civil Procedure Before Trial*).

- Witkin, *California Procedure* (5th ed. 2008 & Supp.2014) (referred to as Witkin, *Cal. Procedure*).
- Woodson, *Writing Motions for Summary Judgment*, Los Angeles Lawyer (Oct. 2002), www.lacba.org/Files/LAL/Vol25No7/1220.pdf.

§1.4 Judicial Council form.

- JUD-100 (optional), judgment.

§2. SUMMARY JUDGMENT OR DEMURRER

MSJs and demurrers are similar in that both can dispose of an entire case because a party has no viable claim or defense, but that is where the similarity ends. An MSJ is used to argue that there is no viable claim or defense based on the evidence. A demurrer is used to argue that there is no viable claim or defense based on the pleadings or matters that can be judicially noticed. *See* Weil, *Civil Procedure Before Trial*, ¶10:4. Deciding whether to file an MSJ or a demurrer can be difficult if a party is unsure whether the questions about the viability of a claim or defense are real or caused by inept pleadings. To make this decision, the party should consider the following questions.

§2.1 What is being challenged?

1. Single claim or defense. If the viability of only a single claim or defense is questionable, a party must file a demurrer. See "Demurrer," ch. 4-H, p. 396. A party cannot file an MSJ because MSJs are used only to challenge an entire action.

NOTE

A party can also challenge a single claim or defense by filing a motion for summary adjudication. For a discussion of the differences between MSJs and motions for summary adjudication, see "Summary Judgment or Summary Adjudication," §3, p. 1119.

---

2. Entire action. If the viability of all claims or defenses is questionable, a party can file an MSJ or a demurrer.

§2.2 Is extrinsic evidence required? If the party must introduce extrinsic evidence to show that the other side has no viable claim or defense, it should file an MSJ. Demurrers can only be based on matters that appear on the face of the challenged pleading or that are subject to judicial notice. Weil, *Civil Procedure Before Trial*, ¶10:4. An MSJ, on the other hand, is designed to test the other side's evidence. ***Columbia Cas. Co. v. Northwestern Nat'l Ins.*** (4th Dist.1991) 231 Cal.App.3d 457, 468.

§2.3 Is defect curable by amendment?

1. Curable. If the questions about the viability of a claim or defense can be cured with an amended pleading, the party should file a demurrer (or, if the time to file a demurrer has passed, a motion for judgment on the pleadings). *See* ***Columbia Cas. Co. v. Northwestern Nat'l Ins.*** (4th Dist.1991) 231 Cal.App.3d 457, 468 (general demurrer is equivalent to motion for judgment on the pleadings). An MSJ presupposes that the pleadings are adequate to put a claim or defense at issue. *Cal. Trial Guide*, §537.13. If the pleadings are not adequate (e.g., because the plaintiff did not allege an essential element of a claim), the MSJ proceeding, which ordinarily tests the evidence, will turn into a test of the pleadings. *See* ***American Airlines, Inc. v. County of San Mateo*** (1996) 12 Cal.4th 1110, 1117-18; ***Crouse v. Brobeck, Phleger & Harrison*** (4th Dist.1998) 67 Cal.App.4th 1509, 1532. If the court finds the pleadings to be insufficient, it will grant the opposing party leave to amend, just like it would with a demurrer or a motion for judgment on the pleadings. *See* ***Hejmadi v. AMFAC, Inc.*** (1st Dist.1988) 202 Cal.App.3d 525, 536. Thus, to arrive at the same place without the confusion or unnecessary delay, the better practice is to test curable pleadings with a demurrer (or a motion for judgment on the pleadings if the time to demur has passed). *See id.*

2. Not curable. If the questions about the viability of a claim or defense cannot be cured with an amended pleading, the party can file a demurrer or an MSJ. Some of the reasons for picking one over the other include the following:

(1) Advantages of MSJ.

- If successful, the movant is entitled to a final judgment. *See* CCP §437c(c), (m)(1).
- With a demurrer, the movant can obtain a dismissal with prejudice, but the dismissal is within the court's discretion. See "Demurrer – Without Leave to Amend," ch. 10-F, §2, p. 1180.

(2) Advantages of demurrer.

- A demurrer is less expensive and time-consuming than an MSJ. *Cal. Trial Guide*, §537.19.
- If an MSJ is denied, the opponent will have received a preview of the movant's evidence and legal theories. *Id.*

§3. SUMMARY JUDGMENT OR SUMMARY ADJUDICATION

An MSJ is nearly identical to a motion for summary adjudication (MSA) except that instead of disposing of the entire case, an MSA disposes of only part of the case. An MSA can be filed separately or as an alternative to an MSJ. CCP §437c(f)(2).

CAUTION

If a party files an MSA before filing an MSJ, the party cannot bring an MSJ on the same issues that were denied under the MSA unless the party establishes the existence of newly discovered facts or circumstances or a change in the law. CCP §437c(f)(2). A change in the law does not include a later-enacted statute unless the statute has a retroactive effect. Id. §437c(s).

§4. AVAILABILITY OF SUMMARY JUDGMENT

§4.1 Ordinary actions. Summary judgment is generally available in all ordinary actions. *See* CCP §437c(a). An ordinary action is one in which a party sues another for the declaration, enforcement, or protection of a right or for the redress or prevention of a wrong. ***Bagration v. Superior Ct.*** (2d Dist.2003) 110 Cal.App.4th 1677, 1684-85. Summary judgment is not available, however, in the following situations:

1. **Family-law actions.** Summary judgment is not available in family-law actions. CRC 5.74(b)(2).

2. **Unliquidated damages.** Summary judgment is not available when a claim for unliquidated damages is disputed. *See, e.g.*, ***Department of Indus. Relations v. UI Video Stores*** (1st Dist.1997) 55 Cal.App.4th 1084, 1097 (MSJ inappropriate despite D's liability because damages calculations were still undetermined).

PRACTICE TIP

If the only triable issue of material fact involves the calculation of damages, a party should file a motion to bifurcate and try the liability issue on undisputed facts. See ***Department of Indus. Relations****, 55 Cal.App.4th at 1097.*

3. **Motion for security deposit in medical-malpractice case.** Summary judgment is not available to a defendant in a medical-malpractice case after it moves to have the plaintiff pay a security deposit under CCP §1029.6. CCP §1029.6(e).

§4.2 Special proceedings. Summary judgment is available in a special proceeding. *See* CCP §437c(a) ("any action or proceeding"); ***In re Mark K.*** (5th Dist.1984) 159 Cal.App.3d 94, 102-03 (MSJ statutes need not be incorporated into special-proceeding statute; MSJ available whenever appropriate because (1) CCP §437c applies to "any action or proceeding" and (2) courts can disregard distinction between actions and special proceedings if necessary). "Special proceedings" are any proceedings other than ordinary actions. CCP §23. See "Ordinary actions," §4.1, this page. Special proceedings are typically statutory in origin and are not based on common law. ***Bagration v. Superior***

Ct. (2d Dist.2003) 110 Cal.App.4th 1677, 1685. Despite its apparent application to "proceedings," the summary-judgment statute is not available in the following proceedings:

1. Proceedings to terminate parental rights. ***In re Mark K.***, 159 Cal.App.3d at 103-04.
2. Class actions under the Consumer Legal Remedies Act. Civ. C. §1781(c).
3. Election contests. ***Anderson v. County of Santa Barbara*** (2d Dist.1976) 56 Cal.App.3d 780, 787.
4. Proceedings under the Sexually Violent Predators Act. ***Bagration***, 110 Cal.App.4th at 1689.

§5. MOVANT'S BURDEN

To prevail on an MSJ, the movant must prove the following:

§5.1 No triable issue of material fact. To prevail on an MSJ, the movant must prove there is no triable issue of material fact. CCP §437c(c); ***Biancalana v. T.D. Serv.*** (2013) 56 Cal.4th 807, 813; ***Coral Constr., Inc. v. City & Cty. of S.F.*** (2010) 50 Cal.4th 315, 326; ***Aguilar v. Atlantic Richfield Co.*** (2001) 25 Cal.4th 826, 850. If there is a single triable issue of material fact, the court must deny the motion. Weil, *Civil Procedure Before Trial*, ¶10:270; *see* CCP §437c(c).

1. Material fact. For a fact to be "material," it must (1) relate to some claim or defense at issue under the pleadings and (2) be essential to the judgment. ***Kelly v. First Astri Corp.*** (4th Dist.1999) 72 Cal.App.4th 462, 470.

2. Not triable. For there to be "no triable" issue of material fact, the evidence must dissuade a reasonable fact-finder from determining the contested issue in favor of the party opposing the MSJ. *See* ***Aguilar***, 25 Cal.4th at 850; ***Baughman v. Walt Disney World Co.*** (4th Dist.2013) 217 Cal.App.4th 1438, 1445.

NOTE

If both parties believe that there is no triable issue of material fact, both parties can file separate MSJs. See ***Coast Elevator Co. v. State Bd. of Equalization*** *(2d Dist.1975) 44 Cal.App.3d 576, 583-84, disapproved on other grounds,* ***Culligan Water Conditioning v. State Bd. of Equalization*** *(1976) 17 Cal.3d 86. This does not prevent the court, however, from determining that there is a triable issue. Id.*

---

§5.2 Judgment as matter of law. To prevail on an MSJ, the movant has the burden to produce evidence showing it is entitled to judgment as a matter of law. *See* CCP §437c(c); ***Coral Constr., Inc. v. City & Cty. of S.F.*** (2010) 50 Cal.4th 315, 326; ***Aguilar v. Atlantic Richfield Co.*** (2001) 25 Cal.4th 826, 850; ***Laabs v. City of Victorville*** (4th Dist.2008) 163 Cal.App.4th 1242, 1250-51.

1. Generally.

(1) Resolve entire suit. To be entitled to a judgment on an MSJ, the movant must resolve the entire suit in the MSJ (i.e., all causes of action from both claims and counterclaims). *See* Thomas, *Courtroom Handbook*, §§22:1, 22:2; *see, e.g.*, 6 Witkin, *Cal. Procedure*, Proceedings Without Trial, §238 (to be awarded SJ, D must either disprove at least one essential element of every cause of action pleaded or prove affirmative defense that would bar every cause of action). If the movant is resolving only part of the suit (e.g., one cause of action in a suit in which two causes of action are pleaded), it must file an MSA. *See* Thomas, *Courtroom Handbook*, §22:2. See "Motion for Summary Adjudication," ch. 10-C, p. 1145.

(2) Satisfy applicable evidentiary burden. The movant's evidentiary burden on an MSJ is the same burden it would have to satisfy at trial. ***Aguilar***, 25 Cal.4th at 851. For example, if a plaintiff who would have the burden of proof by a preponderance of the evidence at trial moves for summary judgment, it must produce evidence that would require the court to find the underlying material fact more likely than not. *Id.* On the other hand, if

the defendant is the movant, it must produce evidence that would require the court not to find the underlying material fact more likely than not. *Id.* See "Summary-Judgment Evidence," §9, p. 1130.

2. Plaintiff is movant. If the plaintiff moves for summary judgment, it must establish that it is entitled to judgment as a matter of law by producing admissible evidence on each element of every cause of action in its complaint. *See* CCP §437c(p)(1); ***Law Offices of Dixon R. Howell v. Valley*** (6th Dist.2005) 129 Cal.App.4th 1076, 1091-92; *see, e.g.*, ***Dawson v. Toledano*** (4th Dist.2003) 109 Cal.App.4th 387, 401 (P did not meet burden when arguments made in his motion did not apply to issues in action). Once the plaintiff has produced admissible evidence on each element of every cause of action, it has made a prima facie showing that there is no defense to the suit. *See* CCP §437c(p)(1); ***Aguilar***, 25 Cal.4th at 850-51. For example, a plaintiff makes a prima facie showing that it is entitled to summary judgment in a breach-of-contract action when its evidence establishes the existence of a contract, the defendant's breach, and the plaintiff's damages. ***City of Oakland v. Hassey*** (1st Dist.2008) 163 Cal.App.4th 1477, 1486.

3. Defendant is movant. If the defendant moves for summary judgment, it must establish that it is entitled to judgment as a matter of law by producing admissible evidence that every cause of action in the plaintiff's suit has no merit. *See* CCP §437c(p)(2); ***Slovensky v. Friedman*** (3d Dist.2006) 142 Cal.App.4th 1518, 1527; ***Bonus-Bilt, Inc. v. United Grocers, Ltd.*** (1st Dist.1982) 136 Cal.App.3d 429, 442. To establish that a cause of action has no merit, the defendant must show that (1) one or more elements of the plaintiff's cause of action cannot be established or (2) there is a complete defense to the cause of action. CCP §437c(p)(2); ***All Towing Servs. v. City of Orange*** (4th Dist.2013) 220 Cal.App.4th 946, 953; ***Mora v. Hollywood Bed & Spring*** (2d Dist.2008) 164 Cal.App.4th 1061, 1067; ***Laabs***, 163 Cal.App.4th at 1250; *see* CCP §437c(o).

(1) Plaintiff cannot establish element of cause of action. The defendant can establish that a cause of action has no merit if it proves that an element of the cause of action cannot be established. ***Nalwa v. Cedar Fair, L.P.*** (2012) 55 Cal.4th 1148, 1154; ***Aguilar***, 25 Cal.4th at 853; *see, e.g.*, ***Kids' Universe v. In2Labs*** (2d Dist.2002) 95 Cal.App.4th 870, 882 (P could not establish damage element of negligence claim). This can be accomplished either by disproving an element of the cause of action or by showing that the plaintiff lacks the evidence to prove an element of the cause of action. ***Aguilar***, 25 Cal.4th at 853-54.

(a) Disprove element. To show that the plaintiff cannot establish an element of a cause of action, the defendant can present evidence that conclusively negates an element of the cause of action. ***Aguilar***, 25 Cal.4th at 853. For example, in a wrongful-termination case, the defendant can disprove an element of the cause of action by presenting conclusive evidence that it had a legitimate, nondiscriminatory reason for firing the plaintiff. *See* ***Avila v. Continental Airlines, Inc.*** (2d Dist.2008) 165 Cal.App.4th 1237, 1247; ***King v. United Parcel Serv.*** (3d Dist.2007) 152 Cal.App.4th 426, 432-33.

(b) Show plaintiff has no evidence to establish element. To show that the plaintiff cannot establish an element of a cause of action, the defendant can present evidence that the plaintiff cannot support an element of the cause of action with evidence in the plaintiff's possession and cannot reasonably obtain the needed evidence. ***Aguilar***, 25 Cal.4th at 854; *see, e.g.*, ***Nazaretyan v. California Physicians' Serv.*** (2d Dist.2010) 182 Cal.App.4th 1601, 1614 (movant did not meet its burden because it did not introduce any evidence that P could not reasonably obtain needed evidence). To succeed on this ground, the defendant must do more than conclusively state in its MSJ that the plaintiff lacks the evidence. ***Aguilar***, 25 Cal.4th at 854. Instead, the defendant must support the MSJ with evidence from affidavits, declarations, admissions, answers to interrogatories, depositions, or matters of judicial notice. CCP §437c(b); ***Aguilar***, 25 Cal.4th at 855. For example, the defendant can show that the plaintiff cannot produce evidence to support its claim by presenting the plaintiff's factually insufficient responses to discovery as evidence in the MSJ. *See* ***Andrews v. Foster Wheeler LLC*** (1st Dist.2006) 138 Cal.App.4th 96, 106-07. See "Note," §9.2.3, p. 1133.

(2) Defendant has complete defense. The defendant can establish that a cause of action has no merit if it proves that the plaintiff is barred from recovery by a complete defense. CCP §437c(p)(2); ***Aguilar***, 25 Cal.4th

at 850. To succeed on this ground, the defendant must prove there are no disputed facts for every element of the defense. ***Anderson v. Metalclad Insulation Corp.*** (1st Dist.1999) 72 Cal.App.4th 284, 289. For example, the defendant is entitled to summary judgment if it proves every element of a statute-of-limitations defense. *See* ***Deveny v. Entropin, Inc.*** (4th Dist.2006) 139 Cal.App.4th 408, 419 (while running of statute of limitations is usually a question of fact, SJ is proper when uncontradicted facts clearly indicate time has expired); *see, e.g.*, ***County of Santa Clara v. Atlantic Richfield Co.*** (6th Dist.2006) 137 Cal.App.4th 292, 333 (MSJ was based on ground that statute of limitations in Bus. & Prof. C. §17208 had expired).

§6. MOTION

§6.1 Who can file.

1. Party. Any party—a plaintiff, defendant, cross-complainant, or cross-defendant—can file an MSJ. *See* CCP §437c(a), (p). Only a party who has filed an MSJ can be awarded a summary judgment. ***McCarthy v. CB Richard Ellis, Inc.*** (2d Dist.2009) 174 Cal.App.4th 106, 119. A summary judgment cannot be awarded to a nonmovant simply because it successfully defends against an MSJ. *See* ***Cuff v. Grossmont Un. High Sch. Dist.*** (4th Dist.2013) 221 Cal.App.4th 582, 596 & n.11 (party must make its own affirmative MSJ to obtain SJ; party cannot rely on its opposition to opponent's MSJ).

2. Court. The court cannot enter a summary judgment on its own motion. ***Certain Underwriters at Lloyd's of London v. Superior Ct.*** (2d Dist.1997) 56 Cal.App.4th 952, 958-59; *see* CCP §437c(a) ("[a]ny party may move").

§6.2 When to file & serve.

1. Filing.

(1) Generally – 60 days after appearance. Generally, an MSJ can be filed no earlier than 60 days after the nonmovant has made a general appearance. CCP §437c(a). See "General appearance," ch. 3-G, §5.1.1, p. 285. An MSJ can be filed before the defendant files an answer. *See* ***Sadlier v. Superior Ct.*** (2d Dist.1986) 184 Cal.App.3d 1050, 1056 & n.5. If a defendant files an MSJ before filing an answer, the filing of the MSJ will not extend the defendant's time to file an answer. CCP §437c(a).

(2) Exception – good cause. An MSJ can be filed earlier than 60 days after the nonmovant appears if good cause is shown. CCP §437c(a).

2. Serving.

(1) Generally. The deadline for serving an MSJ and all supporting papers depends on the method of service. *See* CCP §437c(a). See "Deadline to Serve MSJ," chart 10-3, this page. For a discussion of how to calculate the actual deadline for service, see "Retrospective deadlines," ch. 1-G, §6.2, p. 71.

10-3. DEADLINE TO SERVE MSJ

	Method of service	Deadline to serve MSJ
1	Personal delivery	75 days before hearing
2	Fax, express mail, or overnight delivery	77 days before hearing
3	Mail delivery to California address	80 days before hearing
4	Mail delivery to U.S. address outside California	85 days before hearing
5	Mail delivery to foreign address	95 days before hearing

(2) Exception. Most courts have held that the notice periods in CCP §437c(a) cannot be shortened by local rule or court order. *See, e.g.*, ***Boyle v. CertainTeed Corp.*** (1st Dist.2006) 137 Cal.App.4th 645, 655 (local rule

permitting SJ on 60 days' notice was invalid); ***Urshan v. Musicians' Credit Un.*** (2d Dist.2004) 120 Cal.App.4th 758, 768 (trial court's order shortening notice period without consent of parties was invalid); *see also* ***Robinson v. Woods*** (2d Dist.2008) 168 Cal.App.4th 1258, 1267-68 (court could not cure inadequate notice of hearing on MSJ served four days late by continuing the hearing for equal number of days). But the notice periods in §437c(a) can be shortened if the parties expressly consent to it. *See* ***Urshan***, 120 Cal.App.4th at 768 (consent to shortened notice period cannot be inferred from silence); *see also* ***Carlton v. Quint*** (2d Dist.2000) 77 Cal.App.4th 690, 697 (P waived claim of inadequate notice by filing opposition, appearing and arguing at hearing, not requesting continuance, and never claiming prejudice).

NOTE

The time extensions described in CCP §§1005(b) and 1013 do not apply to the filing and serving of MSJs. CCP §437c(b)(6).

§6.3 Contents.

1. Notice of motion & motion.

(1) Generally. An MSJ must be requested in writing by a noticed motion. For the general contents of a noticed motion, see "Notice of motion & motion," ch. 1-D, §5.1, p. 28.

(2) Relief.

(a) Generally. The motion must state the relief the movant is seeking (e.g., "ABC Corp. asks the court to enter a judgment in its favor against defendant for the relief prayed for in plaintiff's First Amended Complaint"). CRC 3.1110(a), 3.1112(d)(3).

(b) Alternative relief – summary adjudication. The motion can ask the court to grant a summary adjudication in the alternative. *See* CCP §437c(f)(2); CRC 3.1350(b). See "Motion for Summary Adjudication," ch. 10-C, p. 1145. If sought in the alternative, the cause of action, affirmative defense, claim for damages, or issue of duty that the movant seeks summary adjudication on must be stated specifically in the notice of motion and must be repeated, verbatim, in the separate statement of undisputed material facts. CRC 3.1350(b). The MSA can refer to and depend on the same evidence submitted in support of the MSJ. *Id.*

(3) Grounds. The motion must state the grounds for the relief (e.g., "The motion is made on the grounds that there is no defense to the action, there is no triable issue of material fact, and plaintiff is entitled to judgment as a matter of law."). CRC 3.1110(a), 3.1112(d)(3). Each ground the movant is relying on to support the motion should be stated with specificity. ***Juge v. County of Sacramento*** (3d Dist.1993) 12 Cal.App.4th 59, 68. The court can ignore a ground that is not cited as a basis for the motion in the notice of motion even if the party's separate statement of facts and the evidence filed in support of the motion refer to an undisputed material fact that would be dispositive of the action. *Id.*; *see* ***San Jose Constr., Inc. v. S.B.C.C., Inc.*** (6th Dist.2007) 155 Cal.App.4th 1528, 1545. The court can grant a motion on a ground that was not specifically raised by the moving party, however, if the opposing party had notice of and an opportunity to respond to that ground. ***Juge***, 12 Cal.App.4th at 70; *e.g.*, ***Bacon v. Southern Cal. Edison Co.*** (2d Dist.1997) 53 Cal.App.4th 854, 860 (opposing party had notice of ground because he addressed it in his opposition papers).

2. Memorandum of points & authorities. The MSJ must include a memorandum in support of the moving party's motion. CRC 3.1350(c)(3); *see* CRC 3.1113(a). If practical, the supporting memorandum should be attached to the notice of motion. CRC 3.1113(j); *see* CRC 3.1110(e) (method of attachment). The memorandum cannot exceed 20 pages (not including exhibits, declarations, attachments, table of contents, table of authorities, or proof of service). CRC 3.1113(d). For more on the memorandum, see "Memorandum of points & authorities," ch. 1-D, §5.2, p. 28. For a sample memorandum, see *CEB Procedure Before Trial*, §36.216.

NOTE

A party can ask the court to permit the memorandum to exceed the 20-page limit. CRC 3.1113(e). The request can be made by ex parte application with written notice to the other parties. Id. The application must be made at least 24 hours before the memorandum is due and state the reasons why the argument cannot be made within the page limit. Id.

3. Separate statement of undisputed facts. The MSJ must contain a separate statement that plainly and concisely sets out all the material facts that the movant contends are undisputed. CCP §437c(b)(1); CRC 3.1350(d). Each material fact must be followed by a reference to supporting evidence. CCP §437c(b)(1); CRC 3.1350(d).

PRACTICE TIP

Judges will often look only at the separate statement, so make sure it is properly written. See Woodson, Writing Motions for Summary Judgment, at 11; see also ***Truong v. Glasser*** *(4th Dist.2009) 181 Cal.App.4th 102, 118 (court can deny SJ if separate statement is defective).*

(1) Generally.

(a) Considered admissions. Facts recited in the separate statement are considered binding admissions. *See* ***City of San Diego v. DeLeeuw*** (4th Dist.1993) 12 Cal.App.4th 10, 12. The recited facts are considered binding admissions only for deciding the MSJ; they are not considered judicial admissions for trial. *See* ***Myers v. Trendwest Resorts, Inc.*** (3d Dist.2009) 178 Cal.App.4th 735, 748-49.

(b) Effect of omissions.

[1] Omitted facts. Facts omitted from the separate statement but included elsewhere in the papers cannot be considered by the court in ruling on the MSJ. ***Scripps Clinic v. Superior Ct.*** (4th Dist.2003) 108 Cal.App.4th 917, 929; ***North Coast Bus. Park v. Nielsen Constr. Co.*** (4th Dist.1993) 17 Cal.App.4th 22, 30-31; ***United Cmty. Ch. v. Garcin*** (2d Dist.1991) 231 Cal.App.3d 327, 337; *see* ***Parkview Villas Ass'n v. State Farm Fire & Cas. Co.*** (2d Dist.2005) 133 Cal.App.4th 1197, 1213 (explaining difference between omitted facts and omitted evidence).

[2] Omitted evidence. Evidence omitted from the separate statement may be considered by the court in its discretion. ***San Diego Watercrafts, Inc. v. Wells Fargo Bank*** (4th Dist.2002) 102 Cal.App.4th 308, 315-16; *see* ***King v. United Parcel Serv.*** (3d Dist.2007) 152 Cal.App.4th 426, 437-38. See "All evidence," §12.2.2(1), p. 1138.

(2) Format & content. The separate statement must set out each cause of action, claim, issue of duty, or affirmative defense. CRC 3.1350(d). Under each of these, there must be two columns listing certain information.

NOTE

For an example of what a separate statement looks like, see CRC 3.1350(h).

(a) Left column. The left column must state, in numerical order, (1) each supporting, undisputed material fact relating to the particular cause of action, claim, issue of duty, or affirmative defense and (2) citations to evidence that establish the undisputed fact. CRC 3.1350(d); *see* CCP §437c(b)(1). Citations to evidence must include references to the exhibit, title, page, and line numbers. CRC 3.1350(d); *see, e.g.*, CRC 3.1350(h) ("1. Plaintiff and defendant entered into written contract for the sale of widgets. Jackson declaration, 2:17-21; contract, Ex. A to Jackson declaration."). All material evidence that supports an undisputed material fact must be set out in the separate statement, regardless of whether it is favorable or unfavorable. ***Rio Linda Unified Sch. Dist. v.***

Superior Ct. (3d Dist.1997) 52 Cal.App.4th 732, 740; *see* Weil, *Civil Procedure Before Trial*, ¶10:95.10. If the evidence is inadmissible, the movant must include the evidence and state its objection in the separate statement. Weil, *Civil Procedure Before Trial*, ¶10:95.11.

CAUTION

Be careful not to recite immaterial facts in the separate statement. Weil, Civil Procedure Before Trial, ¶10:95.1. Including immaterial facts could permit the court to treat it as a concession that the facts are material and allow the opposing party to raise a triable issue on a fact that would otherwise be immaterial. Id.; see ***Nazir v. United Airlines, Inc.*** *(1st Dist.2009) 178 Cal.App.4th 243, 252.*

(b) Right column. The right column must provide a blank space for the opposing party's response and supporting evidence. *See* CRC 3.1350(f), (h).

(3) Request for electronic version. A party can ask for an electronic version of another party's separate statement. CRC 3.1350(i). The other party must deliver an electronic version within three days if it has one (if it does not, it has no duty to create one). *Id.* The electronic version can be in any form the parties agree on. *Id.* If the parties cannot agree on a form, the responding party must provide the electronic version that was used to prepare the document filed with the court. *Id.*

4. Supporting evidence. The MSJ must be supported by evidence. CRC 3.1350(c)(4). Supporting evidence can include affidavits, declarations, admissions, answers to interrogatories, depositions, and matters of judicial notice. CCP §437c(b)(1). See "Supporting evidence," ch. 1-D, §5.3, p. 30. For a discussion of the evidence that can be used to support an MSJ, see "Summary-Judgment Evidence," §9, p. 1130.

PRACTICE TIP

Sometimes relying on less evidence can be more effective than presenting the court with too much evidence. The more facts presented to the court, the more likely the MSJ will be defeated. Woodson, Writing Motions for Summary Judgment, at 11; see ***Nazir****, 178 Cal.App.4th at 253, 289-90 (dicta; courts have power to prevent movant from hiding triable issues of material fact in voluminous record);* ***Collins v. Hertz Corp.*** *(2d Dist.2006) 144 Cal.App.4th 64, 75 (court cannot be expected to address every piece of evidence presented in voluminous record).*

5. Request for judicial notice. The movant can submit a request for judicial notice with the MSJ. CRC 3.1350(c)(5); *see* CCP §437c(b)(1). The request must be made in a separate document. CRC 3.1113(*l*). See "Request for Judicial Notice," ch. 5-J, p. 547.

6. Proposed order. The movant can submit a proposed order with the MSJ. The proposed order must be served and lodged with the motion papers but not attached to them. CRC 3.1113(m). See "Documents lodged," ch. 1-F, §2.3, p. 47.

PRACTICE TIP

Because the movant does not know what argument or evidence the opposing party is going to assert against the motion, the proposed order should be filed with the movant's reply papers after the opposition has been filed. See Weil, Civil Procedure Before Trial, ¶¶10:185.2, 10:185.3.

§6.4 Filing fees. A filing fee of $500 must be paid when the MSJ is filed. Gov. C. §70617(d). For a discussion of filing fees, see "Filing Fees," ch. 1-F, §7, p. 58.

§7. RESPONSE

In response to an MSJ, the opposing party can file (1) a motion for continuance, (2) a motion to amend its pleadings, (3) opposition papers, and (4) a cross-motion for summary judgment.

§7.1 Motion for continuance. The opposing party can file a motion for continuance in response to an MSJ. A motion for continuance is used to ask the court to postpone the MSJ hearing until a later date.

1. For good cause. The opposing party can ask the court for a continuance of a summary-judgment hearing for good cause. *See* ***Oldcastle Precast, Inc. v. Lumbermens Mut. Cas. Co.*** (4th Dist.2009) 170 Cal.App.4th 554, 576 (opposing party does not have right to continuance to prepare revised separate statement; opposing party must provide reason for court to exercise discretion); *see, e.g.*, ***Lerma v. County of Orange*** (4th Dist.2004) 120 Cal.App.4th 709, 716 (attorney's hospitalization was good cause to continue SJ hearing). For a discussion of how to bring a motion for continuance for good cause, see "Continuing hearing date," ch. 5-I, §2.2.1, p. 536.

2. For additional discovery. The opposing party can ask the court for a continuance of a summary-judgment hearing because additional discovery is needed to oppose the motion. CCP §437c(h). To obtain a continuance for additional discovery, the opposing party must file a declaration stating the following: (1) the specific facts to be obtained that are essential to opposing the motion, (2) the reasons why the opposing party believes the facts may exist, (3) the reasons why the evidence was not presented earlier, and (4) the reasons why additional time is needed to obtain the evidence. ***Lerma***, 120 Cal.App.4th at 715-16; *see* CCP §437c(h); *see, e.g.*, ***Johnson v. Alameda Cty. Med. Ctr.*** (1st Dist.2012) 205 Cal.App.4th 521, 532 (P's declaration stating that discovery was reasonably necessary without specifying the facts she expected to discover or the method she would use to discover them was insufficient to support continuance).

(1) When to file. A motion for continuance under CCP §437c(h) can be filed anytime on or before the date the opposition is due. See "Deadline to file & serve," §7.3.1, p. 1127 (discussing deadline for filing opposition papers).

(2) Contents.

(a) Generally. A motion for continuance under §437c(h) can be requested in writing in the opposition papers, by noticed motion, or by ex parte application. *See* CCP §437c(h); Weil, *Civil Procedure Before Trial*, ¶10:207.10. For the general requirements for ex parte applications, see "Ex Parte Practice," ch. 1-E, p. 39.

(b) Declaration in support. A declaration that establishes each of the requirements for the continuance must be attached to the opposition papers, motion, or ex parte application. *See* CCP §437c(h). See "Declaration," ch. 1-B, §4.1.1, p. 19.

(3) Order.

(a) Mandatory. If the opposing party's declaration establishes each of the requirements for a continuance under §437c(h), then a continuance is mandatory. *See* CCP §437c(h); ***Yuzon v. Collins*** (2d Dist.2004) 116 Cal.App.4th 149, 167.

(b) Discretionary. If the opposing party does not make the requisite showing under §437c(h) or does not file a declaration in support of its application, then the court must determine whether the party has established good cause for a continuance. Weil, *Civil Procedure Before Trial*, ¶10:208; *see* ***Lerma***, 120 Cal.App.4th at 716. Whether good cause is shown is within the court's discretion. ***Lerma***, 120 Cal.App.4th at 716. For a discussion of the factors courts can consider in determining whether good cause has been established, see "Continuing hearing date," ch. 5-I, §2.2.1, p. 536.

(4) Obstructing additional discovery. If, after granting the continuance, the court determines that the party seeking summary judgment has unreasonably kept the opposing party from conducting the specified additional discovery, the court must either (1) grant a continuance allowing the discovery to go forward or (2) deny the MSJ. CCP §437c(i).

§7.2 Motion to amend pleadings. The opposing party can file a motion to amend its pleadings in response to an MSJ. The opposing party cannot challenge an MSJ based on issues that were not raised in its initial pleadings. *See* ***Laabs v. City of Victorville*** (4th Dist.2008) 163 Cal.App.4th 1242, 1253; ***Oakland Raiders v. National Football League*** (6th Dist.2005) 131 Cal.App.4th 621, 648-49. For example, if a defendant answered a plaintiff's complaint

with only a general denial, the defendant cannot assert an affirmative defense in its opposition to the plaintiff's MSJ; a general denial is only sufficient to put the material allegations of the complaint at issue. *See* ***FPI Dev., Inc. v. Nakashima*** (3d Dist.1991) 231 Cal.App.3d 367, 383-84. If the opposing party wants to challenge an MSJ based on an issue that was not in its initial pleadings, it must ask the court for leave to amend the pleadings. *See* ***Laabs***, 163 Cal.App.4th at 1258; ***Oakland Raiders***, 131 Cal.App.4th at 648. The court will usually grant leave to amend, although it is not required to do so. *See* ***Falcon v. Long Beach Genetics, Inc.*** (4th Dist.2014) 224 Cal.App.4th 1263, 1280; ***Record v. Reason*** (2d Dist.1999) 73 Cal.App.4th 472, 487. Leave might be denied if the request is not promptly made. ***Falcon***, 224 Cal.App.4th at 1280; Weil, *Civil Procedure Before Trial*, ¶10:51.11; *see* ***Record***, 73 Cal.App.4th at 486. For a discussion of filing a motion to amend pleadings, see "Amending the Complaint," ch. 3-C, §6, p. 228; "Amending the Answer," ch. 4-B, §9, p. 347.

NOTE

A motion to amend pleadings should be heard before the opposition to the MSJ because the amendment might render the MSJ moot. CEB Procedure Before Trial, §36.44; see, e.g., ***Eisenhower Med. Ctr. v. Superior Ct.*** *(4th Dist.2014) 226 Cal.App.4th 430, 433 n.2 (Ps' amended complaint did not render D's MSJ moot because Ps expressly waived issue). If there is not enough time to amend the pleadings, the opposing party can ask the court for a continuance of the MSJ hearing or an order shortening the time before the motion to amend is heard. CEB Procedure Before Trial, §36.44.*

§7.3 Opposition. The opposing party can file an opposition in response to an MSJ. An opposition is used to challenge the procedural and substantive issues in an MSJ. The opposing party is not required to file an opposition to defeat an MSJ. ***Residents of Beverly Glen, Inc. v. City of L.A.*** (2d Dist.1973) 34 Cal.App.3d 117, 127. An MSJ can be granted only if the movant's papers establish that it is entitled to a judgment as a matter of law; an MSJ cannot be granted by default. *See* ***Niederer v. Ferreira*** (2d Dist.1987) 189 Cal.App.3d 1485, 1498. If no opposition is filed, however, the movant's declarations will be treated as true. *Id.* See "Uncontroverted facts," §12.2.2(3), p. 1139. Thus, the opposing party should file an opposition if, after all the movant's declarations are accepted as true, the movant would be entitled to a judgment as a matter of law. *See* ***Niederer***, 189 Cal.App.3d at 1498; ***Residents of Beverly Glen***, 34 Cal.App.3d at 127.

1. Deadline to file & serve. The opposing party must file and serve its opposition at least 14 days before the hearing unless the court orders otherwise for good cause. CCP §437c(b)(2). The opposition papers must be served by personal delivery, fax, express mail, or other means consistent with CCP §§1010-1013. *Id.* §1005(c); *see id.* §437c(b)(6) (§1005(c) applies to opposition and reply papers). The method of service must be reasonably calculated to ensure delivery of the opposition to the other party no later than the close of the next business day after the opposition has been filed with the court clerk. *Id.* §1005(c); *see id.* §437c(b)(6) (§1005(c) applies to opposition and reply papers). See "Filing & serving opposition," ch. 1-D, §8.5, p. 36.

2. Grounds.

(1) Procedural defects. The following procedural grounds can be asserted in an opposition to an MSJ:

(a) The MSJ was not timely filed or served. *See* CRC 3.1300(d) (court has discretion to refuse to consider late papers); ***Carlton v. Quint*** (2d Dist.2000) 77 Cal.App.4th 690, 697-98.

(b) No separate statement of undisputed material fact was filed. *See* CCP §437c(b)(1) (court has discretion to deny motion if no separate statement is filed).

(c) The separate statement of undisputed material fact did not comply with statutory requirements for form or content. *See* CCP §437c(b)(1) (court has discretion to deny motion if separate statement is not in compliance).

(d) No memorandum of points and authorities was filed. *See* CRC 3.1113(a) (court can deem failure to file memorandum as admission that MSJ has no merit and deny recovery).

(e) The memorandum of points and authorities exceeded the page limit. *See* CRC 3.1113(g) (court must treat memorandum that exceeds page limits as late paper), CRC 3.1300(d) (court has discretion to refuse to consider late papers).

(2) Evidentiary objections. For a discussion of the evidentiary objections that can be raised in an opposition to an MSJ, see "Objecting to Summary-Judgment Evidence," §10, p. 1134.

(3) Substantive merits. For a discussion of the substantive arguments that can be raised in an opposition to an MSJ (i.e., there is a triable issue of material fact or the movant is not entitled to judgment as a matter of law), see "Movant's Burden," §5, p. 1120.

3. Contents. The opposition to an MSJ must include the following documents, separately stapled:

(1) Memorandum of points & authorities. The opposition must contain a memorandum opposing the motion. CRC 3.1350(e)(1). The memorandum must be titled "[Opposing party's] memorandum in opposition to [moving party's] motion for summary judgment." *Id.* The memorandum cannot exceed 20 pages (not including exhibits, declarations, attachments, table of contents, table of authorities, or proof of service). CRC 3.1113(d). See "Memorandum of points & authorities," ch. 1-D, §8.1, p. 35.

(2) Separate statement. The opposition must include a separate statement that responds to each of the material facts that the movant contends are uncontested. CCP §437c(b)(3); CRC 3.1350(e)(2); ***Sacks v. FSR Brokerage, Inc.*** (2d Dist.1992) 7 Cal.App.4th 950, 960. If the opposing party does not submit a separate statement, the court may grant the MSJ based on the lack of a separate statement or it may continue the motion or otherwise permit the filing of a proper separate statement. ***Batarse v. Service Employees Int'l Un.*** (5th Dist.2012) 209 Cal.App.4th 820, 828; *see* ***Kojababian v. Genuine Home Loans, Inc.*** (2d Dist.2009) 174 Cal.App.4th 408, 416. Generally, a court will only consider the merits of an opposition unaccompanied by a separate statement when the case involves a single, simple issue with minimal evidentiary support or when the failure to file a separate statement was not a curable defect. *See, e.g.*, ***Batarse***, 209 Cal.App.4th at 828-29 (trial court did not abuse its discretion by granting D's motion without giving P opportunity to add essential facts to P's separate statement). See "Basis for granting motion," §12.2.1(4)(a), p. 1138. For an example of a separate statement, see CRC 3.1350(h).

CAUTION

Only one opposition memorandum and separate statement can be filed. When multiple plaintiffs are opposing a single MSJ, each individual party cannot file its own memorandum and statement. See, e.g., ***Collins v. Hertz Corp.*** *(2d Dist.2006) 144 Cal.App.4th 64, 71-72 & n.4 (multiple Ps entitled to file only one 20-page memorandum as allowed by CRC 3.1113(d), subject to an extension of page length under CRC 3.1113(e)).*

(a) Title. The separate statement must be titled "[Opposing party's] separate statement of undisputed material facts in opposition to [moving party's] motion for summary judgment." CRC 3.1350(e)(2).

(b) Format & content. The separate statement must set out each cause of action, claim, issue of duty, or affirmative defense. CRC 3.1350(d); *see* CRC 3.1350(h). Under each of these, there must be two columns listing certain information. CRC 3.1350(d).

[1] Left column. The left column must look identical to the left column in the moving party's separate statement. *See* CRC 3.1350(f), (h). See "Left column," §6.3.3(2)(a), p. 1124.

[2] Right column. The right column must state the following:

[a] Whether the opposing party disputes the facts listed in the left column. CCP §437c(b)(3); CRC 3.1350(f); *see* CRC 3.1350(h). To do this, the opposing party must simply enter "disputed" or "undisputed" next to each fact. CRC 3.1350(f).

[b] For each "disputed" fact, a description of the nature of the dispute. *Id.*; *see, e.g.*, CRC 3.1350(h) (dispute over whether widgets were received).

[c] For each "disputed" fact, the evidence that supports the opposing party's claim that the fact is disputed. CCP §437c(b)(3); CRC 3.1350(f). Each reference to evidence must include the exhibit, title, page, and line numbers of the evidence. CRC 3.1350(f).

[d] Any other material facts that the opposing party contends are disputed. CCP §437c(b)(3). Each of these facts must be followed by a reference to the supporting evidence. *Id.*

NOTE

Written objections to evidence, which must be filed and served separately from the other opposing papers, cannot be restated or reargued in the separate statement. CRC 3.1354(b). But an objection to specific evidence can be referenced by its objection number in the separate statement's right column. Id.

4. Supporting evidence. The opposition must include evidence against the MSJ. CRC 3.1350(e)(3); *see* Weil, *Civil Procedure Before Trial*, ¶10:200 (insufficient to state that issue is jury question without offering evidence). The evidence must be titled "[Opposing party's] evidence in opposition to [moving party's] motion for summary judgment." CRC 3.1350(e)(3). See "Summary-Judgment Evidence," §9, p. 1130.

5. Evidentiary objections. The opposition can be accompanied by objections to the moving party's evidence. *See* CRC 3.1354(a), (b). Written objections to evidence must be filed and served separately from the other opposing papers and include a proposed order. CRC 3.1354(b), (c). See "Objecting to Summary-Judgment Evidence," §10, p. 1134.

6. Request for judicial notice. The opposition can be accompanied by a request for judicial notice. CRC 3.1350(e)(4). The request must be filed and served separately from the other opposing papers and be titled "[Opposing party's] request for judicial notice in opposition to [moving party's] motion for summary judgment." *Id.*; *see* CRC 3.1113(*l*). See "Request for Judicial Notice," ch. 5-J, p. 547.

§7.4 Cross-motion. The opposing party can file a cross-MSJ. A summary judgment can be awarded to an opposing party only if it files its own MSJ; a summary judgment cannot be awarded to a nonmovant simply because it successfully defends against an MSJ. *See* ***Cuff v. Grossmont Un. High Sch. Dist.*** (4th Dist.2013) 221 Cal.App.4th 582, 596 & n.11 (party must make its own affirmative MSJ to obtain SJ; party cannot rely on its opposition to opponent's MSJ). Cross-MSJs are subject to the same deadlines and requirements as original MSJs. *See, e.g., id.* (cross-MSJ filed 60 days before hearing was untimely). See "Motion," §6, p. 1122.

§8. REPLY

The movant can file a reply to the opposition. *See* CCP §437c(b)(4).

§8.1 Deadline to file & serve. The reply must be filed and served at least five days before the noticed or continued date of the hearing unless the court orders otherwise for good cause. CCP §437c(b)(4). The reply papers must be served by personal delivery, fax, express mail, or other means consistent with CCP §§1010-1013. *Id.* §1005(c); *see id.* §437c(b)(6) (§1005(c) applies to opposition and reply papers). The method of service must be reasonably calculated to ensure delivery of the reply to the other party no later than the close of the next business day after the reply has been filed with the court clerk. *Id.* §1005(c); *see id.* §437c(b)(6) (§1005(c) applies to opposition and reply papers). See "Filing & serving reply papers," ch. 1-D, §9.6, p. 37.

§8.2 Contents.

1. Memorandum of points & authorities. The reply memorandum cannot exceed ten pages. CRC 3.1113(d).

2. Supporting evidence. The reply can be accompanied by supporting evidence. *See* ***Weiss v. Chevron, U.S.A., Inc.*** (2d Dist.1988) 204 Cal.App.3d 1094, 1098-99. The court has discretion to consider new evidence filed with the reply—that is, evidence not originally filed with the MSJ—as long as the opposing party has notice and an

opportunity to respond to the new evidence. ***Wall St. Network, Ltd. v. New York Times Co.*** (2d Dist.2008) 164 Cal.App.4th 1171, 1183; *see* ***San Diego Watercrafts, Inc. v. Wells Fargo Bank*** (4th Dist.2002) 102 Cal.App.4th 308, 315-16. Generally, new evidence should be considered only in exceptional cases. ***Plenger v. Alza Corp.*** (4th Dist.1992) 11 Cal.App.4th 349, 362 n.8.

3. Evidentiary objections. The reply can be accompanied by objections to the opposition's evidence. *See* CRC 3.1354(a), (b). See "Objecting to Summary-Judgment Evidence," §10, p. 1134.

4. Request for judicial notice. The reply can be accompanied by a request for judicial notice. *See, e.g.*, ***Jimenez v. County of L.A.*** (2d Dist.2005) 130 Cal.App.4th 133, 138-39 (in response to new issue raised in opposition to MSJ, D's reply papers included rebuttal testimony and request for judicial notice). See "Request for Judicial Notice," ch. 5-J, p. 547.

5. Proposed order. The reply should be accompanied by a proposed order. Weil, *Civil Procedure Before Trial*, ¶10:222.6. See "Documents lodged," ch. 1-F, §2.3, p. 47.

§9. SUMMARY-JUDGMENT EVIDENCE

§9.1 Generally.

1. Must be admissible. Evidence submitted in support of or in opposition to an MSJ must be admissible. *See* CCP §437c(d); ***Hayman v. Block*** (2d Dist.1986) 176 Cal.App.3d 629, 639; ***Reid v. State Farm Mut. Auto. Ins.*** (2d Dist.1985) 173 Cal.App.3d 557, 570; *see, e.g.*, ***Great Am. Ins. v. Gordon Trucking, Inc.*** (5th Dist.2008) 165 Cal.App.4th 445, 450 (D could not use own interrogatory responses as evidence supporting statement of undisputed facts because evidence would not be admissible at trial). For example, if a party presents evidence that contains hearsay, the party has the burden to establish that an exception to the hearsay rule applies. ***Gatton v. A.P. Green Servs.*** (1st Dist.1998) 64 Cal.App.4th 688, 693.

2. Must be in admissible form.

(1) Format. Evidence exceeding 25 pages that is submitted in support of or in opposition to an MSJ must be separately bound and include a table of contents. CRC 3.1350(g). For a discussion of how exhibits should be formatted, see "Exhibits," ch. 1-B, §2.8.4, p. 17.

(2) Authenticated. Evidence submitted in support of or in opposition to an MSJ must be properly authenticated. *See* Evid. C. §1400 et seq.

(3) Secondary-evidence rule. Evidence submitted in support of or in opposition to an MSJ must comply with the secondary-evidence rule. *See* Evid. C. §1521 (secondary-evidence rule); ***People v. Hovarter*** (2008) 44 Cal.4th 983, 1013 n.13 (best-evidence rule is now called secondary-evidence rule).

§9.2 Types of evidence.

An MSJ can be supported or opposed by the following types of evidence:

1. Pleadings.

(1) Other party's pleadings. A party can use another party's pleadings as evidence to support or oppose an MSJ. *See* ***Mark Tanner Constr., Inc. v. HUB Int'l Ins. Servs.*** (3d Dist.2014) 224 Cal.App.4th 574, 586; ***Food Safety Net Servs. v. Eco Safe Sys. USA, Inc.*** (2d Dist.2012) 209 Cal.App.4th 1118, 1126-27. Statements in an opponent's pleadings are treated as judicial admissions. ***Mark Tanner Constr.***, 224 Cal.App.4th at 586. For a discussion of using pleadings as evidence, see "Using Pleadings," ch. 1-C, §8, p. 24.

(2) Not party's own pleadings. A party cannot use its own pleadings as evidence to support or oppose an MSJ. ***Aguilar v. Atlantic Richfield Co.*** (2001) 25 Cal.4th 826, 849.

CAUTION

If a defendant moves for summary judgment and does not controvert factual allegations in the complaint, the court must deem the factual allegations in the complaint as true for purposes of the summary judgment. ***Slovensky v. Friedman*** *(3d Dist.2006) 142 Cal.App.4th 1518, 1534.*

2. Declarations & affidavits. A party can use declarations and affidavits as evidence to support or oppose an MSJ. CCP §437c(b)(1), (b)(2). *But see* ***Food Safety Net***, 209 Cal.App.4th at 1129 (P cannot create triable issue through declarations that contradict factual allegations in complaint).

(1) General requirements. To be valid summary-judgment evidence, the declaration or affidavit must (1) be based on personal knowledge (or opinion if testifying as an expert), (2) present admissible evidence, and (3) affirmatively show that the witness is competent to testify. *See* CCP §437c(d); Evid. C. §§702, 801. See "General Requirements for Declarations & Affidavits," ch. 1-B, §4, p. 19.

(a) Personal knowledge.

[1] Lay witness. Declarations and affidavits from lay witnesses must be based on facts within their personal knowledge. *See* CCP §437c(d); Evid. C. §702. Facts based on "information and belief" or "best knowledge" are improper. ***Lopez v. University Partners*** (4th Dist.1997) 54 Cal.App.4th 1117, 1124 (information and belief); ***Simmons v. California Coastal Comm'n*** (4th Dist.1981) 124 Cal.App.3d 790, 798 (same); ***Bowden v. Robinson*** (4th Dist.1977) 67 Cal.App.3d 705, 719-20 (best knowledge). Facts are within the declarant's personal knowledge in the following circumstances:

[a] Fact is observed or experienced. Facts are within the declarant's personal knowledge when she observes or experiences the facts. *See, e.g.*, ***Zipusch v. LA Workout, Inc.*** (2d Dist.2007) 155 Cal.App.4th 1281, 1285 (fact that health club had not inspected exercise equipment for at least 85 minutes was within declarant's personal knowledge because she observed area); ***LaPlante v. Wellcraft Mar. Corp.*** (2d Dist.2001) 94 Cal.App.4th 282, 296 (fact that U.S. Coast Guard chose not to regulate open bow seating areas was not within declarant's personal knowledge because he had left Coast Guard before relevant time period); ***Roy Bros. Drilling Co. v. Jones*** (2d Dist.1981) 123 Cal.App.3d 175, 182 (facts surrounding disputed contract were within declarant's personal knowledge because he was in charge of negotiating contract).

[b] Fact is part of business custom or habit. Facts are within the declarant's personal knowledge—even if the declarant did not observe or experience the facts—when the facts are part of a long-continued business custom or habit the declarant has knowledge of. *E.g.*, ***Zuckerman v. Pacific Sav. Bank*** (2d Dist.1986) 187 Cal.App.3d 1394, 1404 (fact that company sent P incorrect invoice was within declarant's personal knowledge because he was familiar with company's long-standing business practices and policies); ***Kiernan v. Union Bank*** (1st Dist.1976) 55 Cal.App.3d 111, 116 (fact that bank mailed customer monthly statement listing all checks paid on account was within personal knowledge of employees because mailing was long-continued business custom).

[2] Expert witness. Declarations of expert witnesses can be based on facts within their personal knowledge or opinion. *See* CCP §437c(d); Evid. C. §§702, 801. When giving an opinion, experts can rely on matters that are not within their personal knowledge. Evid. C. §801(b).

(b) Admissible evidence. Declarations and affidavits must present admissible evidence, not hearsay, factual conclusions, legal conclusions, impermissible opinions, or other statements excluded under the rules of evidence. *See* CCP §437c(d); ***Zuckerman***, 187 Cal.App.3d at 1400; *see, e.g.*, ***Jennifer C. v. Los Angeles Unified Sch. Dist.*** (2d Dist.2008) 168 Cal.App.4th 1320, 1333 (expert's declaration was supported by reasoned explanation and was not conclusory); ***Towns v. Davidson*** (3d Dist.2007) 147 Cal.App.4th 461, 473 (expert's declaration that D was skiing recklessly was inadmissible legal conclusion; courts should be cautious of experts giving legal conclusions disguised as expert opinions); ***McGonnell v. Kaiser Gypsum Co.*** (1st Dist.2002) 98 Cal.App.4th 1098, 1106 (expert's declaration that P was exposed to asbestos while working for D, without any factual basis, explanation, or reasoning, was inadmissible); ***Guthrey v. State*** (5th Dist.1998) 63 Cal.App.4th 1108, 1120 (statements in P's declaration that he was subjected to hostile work environment, without any factual support, were inadmissible opinions and conclusions).

(c) **Competent to testify.**

[1] **Lay witness.** Declarations and affidavits from a lay witness must establish that the witness is competent to testify to the facts stated in the declaration or affidavit. *See* CCP §437c(d). Competency is established by alleging facts that are within the party's personal knowledge; it is not established by conclusory statements that the party is competent to testify. ***Roy Bros. Drilling***, 123 Cal.App.3d at 182; *see* ***Thornton v. Victor Meat Co.*** (1st Dist.1968) 260 Cal.App.2d 452, 459. See "Personal knowledge," §9.2.2(1)(a), p. 1131.

CAUTION

Courts disagree about whether a declaration or an affidavit must contain a statement that essentially says, "The following facts are within my personal knowledge and I could competently testify to them if called as a witness." Some courts have held that such a statement is not necessary as long as it can be determined that the facts in the declaration or affidavit are based on the declarant's personal knowledge. E.g., ***Wall St. Network, Ltd. v. New York Times Co.*** *(2d Dist.2008) (Div. 4) 164 Cal.App.4th 1171, 1182-83;* ***Taheri Law Grp. v. Evans*** *(2d Dist.2008) (Div. 8) 160 Cal.App.4th 482, 493;* ***Osmond v. EWAP, Inc.*** *(2d Dist.1984) (Div. 3) 153 Cal.App.3d 842, 851;* ***Thornton****, 260 Cal.App.2d at 459. Other courts have held that if the declaration or affidavit does not include such a statement, then it is improper summary-judgment evidence. E.g.,* ***Stockinger v. Feather River Cmty. Coll.*** *(3d Dist.2003) 111 Cal.App.4th 1014, 1025-26;* ***Witchell v. De Korne*** *(2d Dist.1986) (Div. 7) 179 Cal.App.3d 965, 975; see, e.g.,* ***Bowden****, 67 Cal.App.3d at 719 (declaration had to be supplemented to add required allegation that it was based on "personal knowledge").*

---

[2] **Expert witness.** Declarations and affidavits from an expert witness must establish that the witness is competent to testify to the facts or opinions stated in the declaration or affidavit. *See* CCP §437c(d). If the expert is expressing an opinion, the declaration or affidavit should include (1) the expert's qualifications, (2) the expert's opinion, (3) the matters relied on in forming the opinion, and (4) the reasoning for the opinion. *See* ***Powell v. Kleinman*** (5th Dist.2007) 151 Cal.App.4th 112, 123; ***Forensis Grp. v. Frantz, Townsend & Foldenauer*** (4th Dist.2005) 130 Cal.App.4th 14, 34; ***Kelley v. Trunk*** (2d Dist.1998) 66 Cal.App.4th 519, 524; *see also* ***Towns***, 147 Cal.App.4th at 472 (expert's testimony in declaration must meet same requirements of admissibility as if expert were testifying at trial). *But see* ***Hanson v. Grode*** (2d Dist.1999) 76 Cal.App.4th 601, 608 n.6 (disagreeing that expert's declaration on SJ must meet stringent requirements in ***Kelley v. Trunk***). If the expert relies on matters that are not within her personal knowledge to form her opinion, she must demonstrate that the matters were made known to her before the declaration or affidavit was prepared. *See* Evid. C. §801(b). For a discussion of expert opinions, see "Opinion testimony," ch. 7-I, §3.1, p. 900.

(2) **Exhibits.** Written documents that are referred to in a declaration or an affidavit should (1) be attached to the declaration or affidavit, (2) be authenticated, and (3) comply with the secondary-evidence rule. *See* Evid. C. §1521; ***Dugar v. Happy Tiger Records, Inc.*** (2d Dist.1974) 41 Cal.App.3d 811, 815-16.

(3) **Bad faith.** If the court decides at any time that a declaration or an affidavit was presented in bad faith or solely for the purpose of delay, the court must order the person presenting the offending declaration or affidavit to pay the other party's reasonable expenses incurred as a result. *See* CCP §437c(j) (affidavits); ***Cooksey v. Alexakis*** (2d Dist.2004) 123 Cal.App.4th 246, 257 (noting that §437c(j) applies to declarations). Reasonable expenses do not include attorney fees. ***Collins v. State DOT*** (3d Dist.2003) 114 Cal.App.4th 859, 862. A court cannot impose sanctions unless (1) a party or the court gives notice of the sanctions and (2) the party being sanctioned has an opportunity to be heard. CCP §437c(j).

3. **Discovery.** A party can use the following types of discovery as evidence to support or oppose an MSJ: (1) depositions, (2) interrogatories, and (3) admissions. CCP §437c(b)(1).

NOTE

A movant can use factually devoid discovery responses (e.g., "It is unknown why the truck would not start") to show that the opposing party's claim or defense has no merit. See ***Great Am. Ins. v. Gordon Trucking, Inc.*** *(5th Dist.2008) 165 Cal.App.4th 445, 451;* ***Union Bank v. Superior Ct.*** *(2d Dist.1995) 31 Cal.App.4th 573, 580-81. However, such evidence is not useful if (1) the response cannot be attributed to the opposing party or (2) the factual deficiencies arise from questions never asked. See* ***Great Am. Ins.****, 165 Cal.App.4th at 451;* ***Scheiding v. Dinwiddie Constr. Co.*** *(1st Dist.1999) 69 Cal.App.4th 64, 80. Also, objections to discovery are not equivalent to factually insufficient responses, so they cannot be used to meet the movant's burden for summary judgment. See* ***Gaggero v. Yura*** *(2d Dist.2003) 108 Cal.App.4th 884, 893.*

(1) Depositions.

(a) Use. Depositions from a party or nonparty can be used as evidence to support or oppose an MSJ. *See* CCP §2025.620; ***Leasman v. Beech Aircraft Corp.*** (1st Dist.1975) 48 Cal.App.3d 376, 380; ***Saporta v. Barbagelata*** (1st Dist.1963) 220 Cal.App.2d 463, 469; *see, e.g.*, ***Danieley v. Goldmine Ski Assocs.*** (4th Dist.1990) 218 Cal.App.3d 111, 116 (opposition contained support from depositions).

(b) Evidentiary weight. Depositions are treated like admissions against interest; they are not considered judicial admissions that conclusively establish the truth of the matter admitted. *See* ***D'Amico v. Board of Med. Exam'rs*** (1974) 11 Cal.3d 1, 21-22; ***Scalf v. D.B. Log Homes, Inc.*** (3d Dist.2005) 128 Cal.App.4th 1510, 1522. The court can disregard a party's declarations or affidavits that contradict her earlier deposition testimony unless a credible explanation is given. *See* ***D'Amico***, 11 Cal.3d at 21-22; ***Ahn v. Kumho Tire U.S.A., Inc.*** (4th Dist.2014) 223 Cal.App.4th 133, 145; ***Scalf***, 128 Cal.App.4th at 1524-25; *see, e.g.*, ***Archdale v. American Int'l Specialty Lines Ins.*** (2d Dist.2007) 154 Cal.App.4th 449, 473 (court disregarded P's declaration that contradicted his earlier deposition response); ***Niederer v. Ferreira*** (2d Dist.1987) 189 Cal.App.3d 1485, 1503 (court considered P's declaration that contradicted her earlier deposition testimony because P explained that she did not understand question asked of her at deposition). The court can, however, consider other credible evidence that contradicts or explains a party's deposition testimony. ***Ahn***, 223 Cal.App.4th at 145; ***Scalf***, 128 Cal.App.4th at 1524-25.

(2) Interrogatories.

(a) Use. Interrogatory responses can only be used as evidence against the responding party. CCP §2030.410. A party cannot use its own interrogatory responses as evidence to support or oppose an MSJ. ***Great Am. Ins.***, 165 Cal.App.4th at 450; *see* CCP §2030.410.

(b) Evidentiary weight. Interrogatory responses are treated the same as deposition testimony. *See* ***Gordon v. Superior Ct.*** (2d Dist.1984) 161 Cal.App.3d 157, 166. See "Evidentiary weight," §9.2.3(1)(b), this page.

(3) Admissions.

(a) Use. Responses to requests for admission (RFAs) can only be used as evidence against the party who made the admissions. CCP §2033.410(b). A party cannot use its own admissions as evidence to support an MSJ. *See id.*

(b) Evidentiary weight. Responses to RFAs are treated as judicial admissions. *See* CCP §2033.410(a). As a judicial admission, any matter that is admitted in response to an RFA is considered conclusively established unless the court permits the admission to be withdrawn or amended. *Id.* Responses to RFAs can be explained by parol evidence, but parol evidence cannot be used to contradict the plain meaning of an answer to an RFA. ***Monroy v. City of L.A.*** (2d Dist.2008) 164 Cal.App.4th 248, 260.

4. Matters judicially noticed. A party can use matters that have been judicially noticed, or that are capable of being judicially noticed, as evidence to support or oppose an MSJ. CCP §437c(b)(1), (b)(2). See "Request for Judicial Notice," ch. 5-J, p. 547.

5. **Stipulations.** A party can use stipulations as evidence to support or oppose an MSJ. *See, e.g.*, ***Century Sur. Co. v. United Pac. Ins.*** (2d Dist.2003) 109 Cal.App.4th 1246, 1250 n.2 (parties filed written stipulations to all material facts). Stipulations are treated as judicial admissions. *See* ***Morningred v. Golden State Co.*** (2d Dist.1961) 196 Cal.App.2d 130, 137.

6. **Testimony from another case.** Testimony given in another case can be used as evidence to support or oppose an MSJ if the testimony meets the requirements of Evid. C. §1292. *See* ***Byars v. SCME Mortg. Bankers, Inc.*** (4th Dist.2003) 109 Cal.App.4th 1134, 1150 (deposition testimony from another case); ***L&B Real Estate v. Superior Ct.*** (2d Dist.1998) (Div. 2) 67 Cal.App.4th 1342, 1348 (transcript of testimony from another case); ***Gatton v. A.P. Green Servs.*** (1st Dist.1998) 64 Cal.App.4th 688, 693-94 (deposition testimony from another case). *But see* ***Williams v. Saga Enters.*** (2d Dist.1990) (Div. 3) 225 Cal.App.3d 142, 149 & n.3 (admission of testimony from another case should not be objectionable under §1292 because testimony should be treated same as witness's declaration).

7. **Inferences from evidence.** A party can use reasonable inferences that arise from the submitted evidence to support or oppose an MSJ. *See* CCP §437c(c). See "All reasonable inferences," §12.2.2(2), p. 1139.

8. **Presumptions.** A party can use any relevant evidentiary presumptions to support or oppose an MSJ. *See* ***Security Pac. Nat'l Bank v. Associated Motor Sales*** (2d Dist.1980) 106 Cal.App.3d 171, 180 (presumptions that operate to eliminate existence of triable issue of fact when no contrary evidence is offered can support MSJ).

§9.3 Evidence in court's file. A party can incorporate a matter or document contained in the court's file. *See* CCP §437c(b)(7). To do this, the party must specifically state that it is incorporating the document by reference (which is usually done in a footnote). *See id.* The party cannot incorporate the entire file. *Id.* See "Incorporation by reference," ch. 1-B, §2.9, p. 17.

§10. OBJECTING TO SUMMARY-JUDGMENT EVIDENCE

Objecting to summary-judgment evidence is a critical component of the summary-judgment process. ***City of Long Beach v. Farmers & Merchs. Bank*** (2d Dist.2000) 81 Cal.App.4th 780, 782, *disapproved on other grounds*, ***Reid v. Google, Inc.*** (2010) 50 Cal.4th 512. When a court rules on an MSJ, it must consider all submitted evidence other than evidence that a party has objected to and that the court has sustained the objection on. CCP §437c(c). Thus, inadmissible evidence that is not objected to can be used to support an MSJ. *See id.* ("court shall consider all of the evidence"); Stats. 1980, ch. 57, §1 (1980 amendment deleted "admissible" after "consider all of the" in §437c(c)).

§10.1 All evidentiary objections waivable. All evidentiary objections to form and substance that are not properly raised are deemed waived. CCP §437c(b)(5), (d); *see* ***Reid v. Google, Inc.*** (2010) 50 Cal.4th 512, 531-32 (objections are not waived if they are made in writing before hearing or orally at hearing); Stats. 1990, ch. 1561, §1 (intent of 1990 amendment was to clarify that all objections to form and substance must be raised at trial-court level or be waived and to overrule limited-waiver rule in ***Witchell v. De Korne*** (2d Dist.1986) 179 Cal.App.3d 965, and ***Zuckerman v. Pacific Sav. Bank*** (2d Dist.1986) 187 Cal.App.3d 1394). Thus, objections based on relevancy, competency, improper opinion, privilege, hearsay, the secondary-evidence rule, and authentication can all be waived. *See, e.g.*, ***Levin v. Ligon*** (1st Dist.2006) 140 Cal.App.4th 1456, 1465 (party waived objection to authenticity by not raising it at SJ hearing); ***Aetna Cas. & Sur. Co. v. Aceves*** (4th Dist.1991) 233 Cal.App.3d 544, 558 (party waived objection to competency by not raising it at SJ hearing). A court cannot, on its own motion, object to inadmissible evidence that a party has not objected to. *See, e.g.*, ***Andrews v. Mobile Aire Estates*** (2d Dist.2005) 125 Cal.App.4th 578, 586 n.6 (court erred in raising and sustaining its own hearsay objection). For a list of possible objections to evidence, see *CEB Trial Objections*, Checklist of Objections.

NOTE

Before the 1980 amendment to CCP §437c, a party could not waive an objection to inadmissible evidence in a summary-judgment proceeding. ***Haskell v. Carli*** *(4th Dist.1987) 195 Cal.App.3d 124, 129-30; see Stats. 1980, ch. 57, §1 (1980 amendment deleted "admissible" from "consider all of the admissible evidence" in former §437c(c)).*

§10.2 When & how to object. Objections to summary-judgment evidence must be made in writing before the hearing or orally at the hearing. ***Superior Dispatch, Inc. v. Insurance Corp. of N.Y.*** (2d Dist.2010) 181 Cal.App.4th 175, 192; *see* ***Reid v. Google, Inc.*** (2010) 50 Cal.4th 512, 531-32; CRC 3.1352. If a party has filed written objections before the hearing, the party is not required to reraise the objections orally at the hearing. ***Reid***, 50 Cal.4th at 532 n.7; *see, e.g.*, ***Tilley v. CZ Master Ass'n*** (4th Dist.2005) 131 Cal.App.4th 464, 479 (party that filed written objections before hearing was not required to repeat objections out loud at hearing).

1. Objecting in writing.

(1) When to file.

(a) Opposing party's objections. The opposing party must file and serve written objections to the movant's summary-judgment evidence at the same time it files and serves its opposition. CRC 3.1354(a). See "Deadline to file & serve," §7.3.1, p. 1127. The court can permit the opposing party to file written objections at another time if good cause is shown. CRC 3.1354(a).

(b) Movant's objections. The movant must file and serve written objections to the opposing party's summary-judgment evidence at the same time it files and serves its reply. CRC 3.1354(a). See "Deadline to file & serve," §8.1, p. 1129. The court can permit the movant to file written objections at another time if good cause is shown. CRC 3.1354(a).

(2) How to file.

(a) Separately from other papers. Written objections must be filed separately from the other papers in support of or in opposition to the MSJ. CRC 3.1354(b). If objections are not filed separately, the trial court may refuse to rule on them. *See, e.g.*, ***Hodjat v. State Farm Mut. Auto. Ins.*** (2d Dist.2012) 211 Cal.App.4th 1, 9 (because P was aware of formatting requirements, trial court was not required to give P second chance to file objections separately).

(b) In approved format. Written objections must substantially comply with one of the two formats shown in CRC 3.1354(b).

(3) Contents. Written objections must be numbered consecutively and contain the following information:

(a) The name of the document being objected to. CRC 3.1354(b)(1).

(b) The exhibit, title, page, and line number of the objectionable material. CRC 3.1354(b)(2).

(c) The objectionable statement or material (either quoted or paraphrased). CRC 3.1354(b)(3).

(d) The grounds for each objection to that statement or material. CRC 3.1354(b)(4).

(4) Proposed order. Written objections must be accompanied by a proposed order that substantially complies with one of the two formats listed in CRC 3.1354(c). The proposed order must include places for the court to indicate whether it has sustained or overruled each objection and include a place for the judge's signature. CRC 3.1354(c).

2. Objecting orally at hearing. Objections to summary-judgment evidence can also be made orally at the hearing. CRC 3.1352. If a party is planning to make oral objections at the hearing, the party must make arrangements for a court reporter to be present. *Id.*; *see* ***Vineyard Springs Estates, LLC v. Superior Ct.*** (3d Dist.2004) 120 Cal.App.4th 633, 638 n.3.

§10.3 Ruling on objections. The court must expressly rule on all timely objections—that is, all objections that are made in writing before the hearing or made orally at the hearing. *See* ***Reid v. Google, Inc.*** (2010) 50 Cal.4th 512, 531-32. If the court does not expressly rule on the objections, it is presumed that they have been overruled and that the court considered the evidence in ruling on the merits of the MSJ. *Id.* at 534. Thus, timely objections that are not expressly ruled on by the court are not waived but are preserved on appeal. *Id.*

NOTE

*The California Supreme Court in **Reid** resolved two important issues related to objections in summary-judgment proceedings. First, a party is under no obligation to persuade a trial court to rule on its objections to avoid a waiver. As long as a party timely objects, the party's objections will be preserved on appeal. **Reid**, 50 Cal.4th at 531-32. Second, the trial court has a duty to expressly rule on all objections; the court cannot sidestep this responsibility by simply stating that it is considering only admissible evidence. Id. at 522, 532 & n.8. Although the Supreme Court recognized that it was placing a heavy burden on courts by requiring them to expressly rule on all objections, it did caution attorneys to be judicious in deciding what objections to assert. Id. at 532. The Supreme Court encouraged parties not to flood courts with baseless objections, but to assert only meritorious objections to items of evidence that are legitimately in dispute and pertinent to deciding the motion. Id. Otherwise, a party may face informal reprimands or formal sanctions for engaging in abusive practice. Id.*

§11. HEARING

§11.1 Generally. For a discussion of hearings generally, see "Hearings," ch. 1-H, p. 79.

§11.2 Date. The hearing on an MSJ must be conducted at least 30 days before trial unless the court orders otherwise for good cause. CCP §437c(a).

§11.3 Who can hear motion. An MSJ can be heard by a trial court or referee. A referee can hear an MSJ only if all parties consent; a court cannot appoint a referee on its own motion. ***Aetna Life Ins. v. Superior Ct.*** (4th Dist.1986) 182 Cal.App.3d 431, 435. For a discussion of how parties can request a referee, see "Stipulation or Motion for Reference," ch. 2-E, p. 163.

§11.4 Oral argument. A party has the right to present oral argument at the summary-judgment hearing. ***Brannon v. Superior Ct.*** (4th Dist.2004) 114 Cal.App.4th 1203, 1211; ***Mediterranean Constr. Co. v. State Farm Fire & Cas. Co.*** (4th Dist.1998) 66 Cal.App.4th 257, 262. Courts can impose time limits on oral argument and adopt tentative-ruling procedures, but they cannot completely deny a party the right to present oral argument. ***Brannon***, 114 Cal.App.4th at 1211; ***Mediterranean Constr.***, 66 Cal.App.4th at 265; *see also* ***Lewis v. Superior Ct.*** (1999) 19 Cal.4th 1232, 1249-53 (court's analysis of whether oral argument was required by statutes governing writ proceedings). *But see* ***Victor v. Hedges*** (2d Dist.1999) 77 Cal.App.4th 229, 245 (not reversible error when court denied request for oral argument). A party can waive the right to oral argument, however, if it does not comply with court rules governing its request. ***Brannon***, 114 Cal.App.4th at 1211.

PRACTICE TIP

Check local rules before attending the hearing. Some courts require both parties to bring proposed orders to the hearing. E.g., Super. Ct. San Francisco Cty. Loc. R., rule 8.7.B.

§12. RULING

§12.1 Standard for granting MSJ. Summary judgment must be granted if all the evidence and reasonable inferences show that there is no triable issue of material fact and that the movant is entitled to judgment as a matter of law. CCP §437c(c). See "Movant's Burden," §5, p. 1120.

§12.2 Court's determination.

1. General guidelines.

(1) Three-step analysis. In ruling on an MSJ, courts apply a three-step analysis. ***Kline v. Turner*** (4th Dist.2001) 87 Cal.App.4th 1369, 1373; *see* ***Diamond v. Superior Ct.*** (6th Dist.2013) 217 Cal.App.4th 1172, 1182 (appellate courts apply same three-step analysis when reviewing SJ).

(a) Identify issue framed by pleadings. The first step is to identify the issues framed by the pleadings. ***Kline***, 87 Cal.App.4th at 1373. The pleadings determine the scope of the issues to be resolved at summary judgment. ***Oakland Raiders v. National Football League*** (6th Dist.2005) 131 Cal.App.4th 621, 648. A party cannot use declarations, affidavits, or other summary-judgment evidence to raise issues that are not contained within the parties' pleadings. *See, e.g.*, ***Lackner v. North*** (3d Dist.2006) 135 Cal.App.4th 1188, 1201 n.5 (P could not raise facts in separate statement of undisputed facts that she did not allege in complaint). Claims, defenses, and factual allegations that are not pleaded cannot be used to support the grant or denial of an MSJ. *See* ***LaPlante v. Wellcraft Mar. Corp.*** (2d Dist.2001) 94 Cal.App.4th 282, 297; ***Distefano v. Forester*** (4th Dist.2001) 85 Cal.App.4th 1249, 1264-65.

NOTE

If it becomes clear at the hearing that there are defects in the pleadings and the defects can be cured by amending the pleadings, a party can orally ask the court for a continuance. ***Mediterranean Constr. Co. v. State Farm Fire & Cas. Co.*** *(4th Dist.1998) 66 Cal.App.4th 257, 264.*

(b) Determine if movant has met its burden. After the court has identified the issues framed by the pleadings, the court must then determine whether the movant has met its burden of proof by producing sufficient admissible evidence. *See* ***Kline***, 87 Cal.App.4th at 1373. See "Movant's Burden," §5, p. 1120. The movant has the burden to produce sufficient evidence regardless of whether a party opposes the MSJ. ***Niederer v. Ferreira*** (2d Dist.1987) 189 Cal.App.3d 1485, 1498; *see* ***AARTS Prods. v. Crocker Nat'l Bank*** (6th Dist.1986) 179 Cal.App.3d 1061, 1064 (MSJ must stand self-sufficient and cannot succeed merely because opposition is weak). If the movant does not meet its burden of production, the court must deny the MSJ. ***Garibay v. Hemmat*** (2d Dist.2008) 161 Cal.App.4th 735, 743.

(c) Determine if opposition has met its burden. If the movant meets its initial burden of production, the burden shifts to the opposing party. ***Aguilar v. Atlantic Richfield Co.*** (2001) 25 Cal.4th 826, 850; *see* ***Johnson v. Superior Ct.*** (3d Dist.2006) 143 Cal.App.4th 297, 305; ***Kline***, 87 Cal.App.4th at 1373; ***Binder v. Aetna Life Ins.*** (2d Dist.1999) 75 Cal.App.4th 832, 840. In evaluating whether the opposing party has met its burden, the court must determine whether the opposing party's evidence has raised a triable issue of fact. *See* ***Aguilar***, 25 Cal.4th at 851; ***Mamou v. Trendwest Resorts, Inc.*** (6th Dist.2008) 165 Cal.App.4th 686, 722. If the opposing party does not meet its burden, the court can enter summary judgment in favor of the movant. *See* ***Castillo v. Barrera*** (2d Dist.2007) 146 Cal.App.4th 1317, 1323.

(2) Court's role. The court's role in ruling on an MSJ is to determine whether there are issues of material fact, not to be a fact-finder. ***Molko v. Holy Spirit Ass'n for the Unification of World Christianity*** (1988) 46 Cal.3d 1092, 1107; *see* ***Binder***, 75 Cal.App.4th at 839 (court's primary function is to identify issues rather than to determine them). Because the court does not act as a fact-finder, the court cannot do the following:

(a) Cannot decide merits. The court cannot decide the merits of the issues. ***Molko***, 46 Cal.3d at 1107; *see* ***Binder***, 75 Cal.App.4th at 840 (court cannot grant SJ for D based simply on its opinion that P's claims are implausible).

(b) Cannot weigh evidence. The court cannot weigh evidence or reasonable inferences to determine which party's version is more likely to be true. ***Binder***, 75 Cal.App.4th at 840; *see* CCP §437c(c). If the evidence and inferences are indisputable on a material fact, the court can decide the issue as a matter of law. ***Binder***, 75 Cal.App.4th at 839. If conflicting evidence or inferences must be weighed to determine a material fact, the court must deny summary judgment. *See id.*

NOTE

Although the court cannot weigh the evidence as a fact-finder, the court must determine what the evidence or the inferences could show or imply to a reasonable fact-finder. ***Aguilar***, *25 Cal.4th at 856;* ***Dailey v. City of San Diego*** *(4th Dist.2013) 223 Cal.App.4th 237, 249.*

(c) Cannot assess credibility. The court cannot assess the credibility of affiants or declarants or complain that they were not cross-examined. CCP §437c(e). The court can disregard a witness's affidavit or declaration, however, if the witness made an earlier conflicting admission. *See* ***AARTS Prods.***, 179 Cal.App.3d at 1065.

(3) Doubts resolved against MSJ. Although summary judgment is no longer considered a disfavored procedure, it should be granted sparingly to avoid preempting a party's right to trial. *See* ***Skoumbas v. City of Orinda*** (1st Dist.2008) 165 Cal.App.4th 783, 790; ***Kasparian v. Avalonbay Cmty., Inc.*** (2d Dist.2007) 156 Cal.App.4th 11, 19; ***Binder***, 75 Cal.App.4th at 838. To protect a party's right to trial, the court must do the following:

(a) Strictly construe the movant's evidence and liberally construe the opponent's evidence—that is, accept as true only the portions of the movant's papers that are not contradicted by the opposition's papers and accept as true all facts stated in the opposition's papers. ***Niederer***, 189 Cal.App.3d at 1498; *see* ***Dailey***, 223 Cal.App.4th at 249; ***Minish v. Hanuman Fellowship*** (6th Dist.2013) 214 Cal.App.4th 437, 444.

(b) View reasonable inferences in the light most favorable to the opposing party. ***Minish***, 214 Cal.App.4th at 444; ***Binder***, 75 Cal.App.4th at 839.

(c) Resolve any doubts against granting summary judgment. ***Minish***, 214 Cal.App.4th at 444; ***Binder***, 75 Cal.App.4th at 839; *see* ***Dailey***, 223 Cal.App.4th at 249.

(4) Procedural error – basis for ruling.

(a) Basis for granting motion. Orders granting summary judgment based solely on a curable procedural error are viewed unfavorably. *See* ***Teselle v. McLoughlin*** (3d Dist.2009) 173 Cal.App.4th 156, 162 (abuse of discretion to grant insufficient MSJ based on opposition's procedural error); ***Kalivas v. Barry Controls Corp.*** (2d Dist.1996) 49 Cal.App.4th 1152, 1161-62 (order granting MSJ based solely on procedural error is equivalent to sanction-terminating action in favor of other party); ***Security Pac. Nat'l Bank v. Bradley*** (2d Dist.1992) 4 Cal.App.4th 89, 97 (same); *see also* ***Elkins v. Superior Ct.*** (2007) 41 Cal.4th 1337, 1364 & n.16 (noting that courts should avoid treating curable procedural error as basis for terminating litigant's right to present its case). Although courts have discretion to grant summary judgment on procedural grounds, the preferred response is to give the opposing party time to cure the procedural error. *See* CCP §437c(b)(1), (b)(3); ***Parkview Villas Ass'n v. State Farm Fire & Cas. Co.*** (2d Dist.2005) 133 Cal.App.4th 1197, 1211. Some courts have considered it an abuse of discretion to grant a summary judgment solely on procedural grounds if (1) the procedural error can be cured, (2) the movant would not suffer prejudice, and (3) the opposing party's violation of the procedural rule was not willful, the result of dilatory conduct, or an example of earlier pretrial abuse. *See, e.g.*, ***Parkview Villas***, 133 Cal.App.4th at 1215-16 (court abused its discretion by granting SJ without giving opposing party opportunity to fix separate statement of fact to comply with CRC 3.1350(f)); ***Kalivas***, 49 Cal.App.4th at 1161-62 (court abused its discretion by granting SJ without giving opposing party opportunity to file opposition); ***Security Pac.***, 4 Cal.App.4th at 98-99 (court abused its discretion by granting SJ without giving opposing party further opportunity to file separate responsive statement). Courts are not required, however, to give a party unlimited opportunities to cure a procedural error. *See, e.g.*, ***Collins v. Hertz Corp.*** (2d Dist.2006) 144 Cal.App.4th 64, 74-75 (court not required to give Ps third chance to correct statement). For a list of possible procedural errors in a summary-judgment proceeding, see "Procedural defects," §7.3.2(1), p. 1127.

(b) Basis for denying motion. Orders denying summary judgment based solely on a procedural error are viewed more favorably than orders granting summary judgment because a denial will permit the case to proceed to trial and be resolved on the merits. ***Parkview Villas***, 133 Cal.App.4th at 1213.

2. Evaluating evidence. In ruling on an MSJ, the court must consider the following:

(1) All evidence. The court must consider all the evidence presented by the parties other than evidence the court has sustained objections on. CCP §437c(c); ***Cheal v. El Camino Hosp.*** (6th Dist.2014) 223 Cal.App.4th 736, 741. The court can use one party's evidence to support another party's motion for or opposition to

summary judgment. *See* ***Laabs v. City of Victorville*** (4th Dist.2008) 163 Cal.App.4th 1242, 1267; *see, e.g.*, ***Villa v. McFerren*** (2d Dist.1995) 35 Cal.App.4th 733, 750-51 (court used deposition testimony supplied by P to determine that D met its burden of production). The court may consider evidence that was not initially included in a party's separate statement, as long as doing so would not violate the other party's due-process right to be informed of the issues it will have to oppose. *See* ***Wall St. Network, Ltd. v. New York Times Co.*** (2d Dist.2008) 164 Cal.App.4th 1171, 1189-90 & n.11; ***Laabs***, 163 Cal.App.4th at 1266; ***King v. United Parcel Serv.*** (3d Dist.2007) 152 Cal.App.4th 426, 437-38; ***Hawkins v. Wilton*** (3d Dist.2006) 144 Cal.App.4th 936, 945-46; ***San Diego Watercrafts, Inc. v. Wells Fargo Bank*** (4th Dist.2002) 102 Cal.App.4th 308, 315-16.

(2) All reasonable inferences. The court must consider all inferences that can be reasonably deduced from the evidence other than inferences that can be contradicted by other inferences or evidence. CCP §437c(c). An inference is a deduction of fact that can be logically and reasonably drawn from another fact or group of facts found or otherwise established in the action. Evid. C. §600(b). All inferences must be reasonable; they cannot derive from speculation, conjecture, imagination, or guesswork. ***O'Neil v. Dake*** (2d Dist.1985) 169 Cal.App.3d 1038, 1044; *see* ***Visueta v. General Motors Corp.*** (2d Dist.1991) 234 Cal.App.3d 1609, 1615 (court must use common sense when making inferences under §437c). The court's duty to consider all reasonable inferences is an affirmative one. ***Michael R. v. Jeffrey B.*** (2d Dist.1984) 158 Cal.App.3d 1059, 1066; ***Maxwell v. Colburn*** (5th Dist.1980) 105 Cal.App.3d 180, 185. The court is not relieved of its duty to take all reasonable inferences into account by a party's failure to ask the court to make the specific inference. ***Michael R.***, 158 Cal.App.3d at 1066; ***Maxwell***, 105 Cal.App.3d at 185. The court is under no duty, however, to search for facts on which the alleged inference can be made. ***North Coast Bus. Park v. Nielsen Constr. Co.*** (4th Dist.1993) 17 Cal.App.4th 22, 29 & n.4.

(3) Uncontroverted facts.

(a) Generally – accepted as true. Uncontroverted facts are generally accepted as true for purposes of summary judgment. *E.g.*, ***Slovensky v. Friedman*** (3d Dist.2006) 142 Cal.App.4th 1518, 1534 (uncontroverted facts in complaint were accepted as true); ***Golden W. Baseball Co. v. Talley*** (4th Dist.1991) 232 Cal.App.3d 1294, 1305 (uncontroverted facts in declaration were accepted as true).

(b) Exceptions.

[1] Sole evidence of material fact. The court may deny summary judgment when the only proof of a material fact is offered by the sole witness to that fact. CCP §437c(e).

[2] Sole evidence of individual's state of mind. The court may deny summary judgment when an individual's state of mind is a material fact and that fact is established solely by that individual's own statement. CCP §437c(e).

§13. ORDER

§13.1 Form. The court's order on an MSJ can be oral or written. CCP §437c(g). If an oral order is made, it must be recorded by a court reporter in the court's minutes. *Id.* For a discussion of preparing written orders, see "Written order," ch. 1-I, §4.2, p. 91.

NOTE

If the prevailing party is asked to prepare a written order for the court, it should ensure that the court specifies its findings—and the evidence that supports them—at the hearing. See ***Carnes v. Superior Ct.*** *(3d Dist.2005) 126 Cal.App.4th 688, 693. Although the court can delegate the duty of drafting a written order, the court cannot delegate the duty of determining the reasons for its findings. See id.*

§13.2 Contents.

1. Order granting relief. If the court grants the MSJ because there is no triable issue of material fact, the order must specify the following:

(1) The reasons for the court's determination (e.g., a complete defense to the action exists, the action has no merit, there is no defense to the action, no separate statement of disputed and undisputed facts was filed by the opposing party). *See* CCP §437c(b), (g), (o).

(2) The specific evidence indicating that there is no triable issue of material fact. *Id.* §437c(g). If the opposing party did not file a separate statement of undisputed facts, the court is not required to specify the evidence brought against the motion. *See* ***Collins v. Hertz Corp.*** (2d Dist.2006) 144 Cal.App.4th 64, 77.

(3) The reasons for any other determination (e.g., rulings on evidentiary objections). CCP §437c(g).

(4) An award for reasonable expenses if the court found that the losing party submitted declarations in bad faith or solely for delay. *Id.* §437c(j).

2. Order denying relief. If the court denies the MSJ because there is a triable issue of material fact, the order must specify the following:

(1) The material facts that present a triable controversy. CCP §437c(g).

(2) The evidence that supports the court's decision. *Id.*; *e.g.*, ***Tera Pharms. v. Superior Ct.*** (4th Dist.1985) 170 Cal.App.3d 530, 532 (order was defective when it did not detail any conflicting evidence on issues of triable fact); ***Continental Ins. v. Superior Ct.*** (1st Dist.1985) 165 Cal.App.3d 1069, 1071 (order was defective when it simply listed documents submitted as evidence without extracting facts from them and explaining why facts conflicted).

(3) The reasons for any other determination (e.g., ruling on evidentiary objections, moving party failed to meet burden of persuasion, procedural defect existed). CCP §437c(g).

(4) An award for reasonable expenses if the court found that the losing party submitted declarations in bad faith or solely for delay. *Id.* §437c(j).

§13.3 Notice of order. See "Notice of Order," ch. 1-I, §5, p. 93.

§14. MOTION FOR RECONSIDERATION

A party who is adversely affected by a court's order on an MSJ can file a motion for reconsideration. CCP §1008(a); *see* ***Le Francois v. Goel*** (2005) 35 Cal.4th 1094, 1107 (court can also reconsider its ruling on its own motion). The motion must be filed within ten days after being served with the written notice of entry of the order and must be decided before summary judgment is entered. CCP §1008(a) (filing deadline); ***Aguilar v. Atlantic Richfield Co.*** (2001) 25 Cal.4th 826, 859 n.29 (after entry of judgment, court does not have jurisdiction to decide motion for reconsideration); *see, e.g.*, ***Sole Energy Co. v. Petrominerals Corp.*** (4th Dist.2005) 128 Cal.App.4th 187, 192 (trial court treated motion for reconsideration as motion for new trial because judgment was entered on same day motion for reconsideration was filed). The motion must be based on new or different facts, circumstances, or law. *See* CCP §1008(a); ***Le Francois***, 35 Cal.4th at 1098. For a discussion of motions for reconsideration, see "Motion for Reconsideration," ch. 5-G, §3, p. 508.

§15. MOTION FOR RENEWAL

A party who was denied or conditionally granted a summary judgment can file a motion for renewal of the MSJ. CCP §1008(b). The renewal of an MSJ must (1) be based on new or different facts, circumstances, or law and (2) comply with the summary-judgment procedures in CCP §437c. *See* CCP §§437c(f)(2), 1008(b); ***Le Francois v. Goel*** (2005) 35 Cal.4th 1094, 1096; ***UAS Mgmt. v. Mater Misericordiae Hosp.*** (5th Dist.2008) 169 Cal.App.4th 357, 367-68. For a discussion of motions for renewal, see "Motion for Renewal," ch. 5-G, §4, p. 516.

§16. JUDGMENT

If the court grants an MSJ, a judgment—separate from the order—must be signed by the court and entered by the clerk. *See* CCP §664; ***Saben, Earlix & Assocs. v. Fillet*** (4th Dist.2005) 134 Cal.App.4th 1024, 1030; ***Security-First Nat'l Bank v. Hauer*** (2d Dist.1941) 47 Cal.App.2d 302, 307; *see also* CCP §577 (definition of "judgment"). *But see* ***Lieding v. Commercial Diving Ctr.*** (2d Dist.1983) 143 Cal.App.3d 72, 74 (treating order as judgment to allow appellate review).

§16.1 Preparation. The prevailing party should prepare a proposed judgment, serve it on the opposing attorney, and submit it to the court to sign and file. Weil, *Civil Procedure Before Trial*, ¶10:330; *see, e.g.*, ***Hollywood Screentest v. NBC Univ'l, Inc.*** (2d Dist.2007) 151 Cal.App.4th 631, 641 (court ordered prevailing party to prepare order and judgment). The prevailing party should submit the proposed judgment at the same time it submits the proposed order. *CEB Action Guide: Making & Opposing a Summary Judgment Motion*, Step 47, pp. 69-70.

§16.2 Contents.

1. Generally. The judgment must comply with the general rules that apply to all papers filed with the court. *See* CRC 2.3 (papers include documents offered for filing in any case), CRC 2.100 (with some exceptions, all papers offered for filing must comply with rules).

2. Date MSJ was granted. The judgment should state the date the court granted the MSJ. *See, e.g.*, Kiesel, *Cal. Pretrial Civil Procedure*, §38.65 (SJ form).

3. Relief. The judgment should specify the relief awarded to the plaintiff. *See, e.g.*, Judicial Council Forms, form JUD-100 (optional form).

(1) Damages. If the plaintiff sought monetary damages, the judgment should state one of the following:

(a) Plaintiff granted MSJ. If summary judgment is granted in favor of the plaintiff, the judgment should state the amount of monetary damages the plaintiff will recover from the defendant in dollars and cents (fractions are not allowed). *See* CCP §577.5 (judgment for money should state amount in dollars and cents, not fractions); ***Kittle v. Lang*** (4th Dist.1951) 107 Cal.App.2d 604, 612 (judgment for money should be stated with certainty and specify amount awarded); *see, e.g.*, Kiesel, *Cal. Pretrial Civil Procedure*, §38.65 (SJ form).

(b) Defendant granted MSJ. If summary judgment is granted in favor of the defendant, the judgment should state that the plaintiff take nothing. *See* Judicial Council Forms, form JUD-100 (optional form).

(2) Injunctive relief. The judgment must clearly state what a party must do or not do if an injunction has been awarded. *See* ***Comfort v. Comfort*** (1941) 17 Cal.2d 736, 741 (not an SJ case; injunction can command person to do or not do something); ***Pitchess v. Superior Ct.*** (2d Dist.1969) 2 Cal.App.3d 644, 651 (not an SJ case; injunction must be definite enough to provide standard of conduct and be enforceable); *see, e.g.*, ***Ironwood Owners Ass'n IX v. Solomon*** (4th Dist.1986) 178 Cal.App.3d 766, 768 (SJ granted injunction requiring D to remove palm trees from property).

(3) Prejudgment interest. The judgment must either specify the amount of prejudgment interest awarded or leave a blank so that interest can be specified at a later time. *See* CRC 3.1802; *see, e.g.*, Judicial Council Forms, form JUD-100 (optional form).

(4) Attorney fees. The judgment should either specify the amount of attorney fees awarded or leave a blank so that fees can be specified at a later time. *See* ***Bankes v. Lucas*** (2d Dist.1992) 9 Cal.App.4th 365, 369; *see also* CRC 3.1702(b)(1) (timing for serving and filing motion to claim attorney fees before judgment). Attorney fees are recoverable on summary judgment if they are otherwise recoverable by law (i.e., by statute, by contract, or in equity). *See, e.g.*, ***Loduca v. Polyzos*** (3d Dist.2007) 153 Cal.App.4th 334, 344-45 (D was granted SJ and awarded attorney fees based on contract).

(5) Costs. The judgment should either specify the amount of costs awarded or leave a blank so that costs can be specified at a later time. *See* ***Bankes***, 9 Cal.App.4th at 369; *see also* CRC 3.1700(a)(1) (requirements for serving and filing memorandum of costs after judgment). Costs are recoverable on summary judgment if they are otherwise recoverable by law. *See* CCP §1032(b) (prevailing party entitled to costs except as provided by statute); *see, e.g.*, ***Bustamante v. Intuit, Inc.*** (6th Dist.2006) 141 Cal.App.4th 199, 208 (court awarded costs to prevailing party on SJ); *see also* CCP §1033.5 (listing costs that are recoverable).

4. Date signed. The judgment should include the date the judgment was signed. *See, e.g.*, Judicial Council Forms, form JUD-100 (optional form); Kiesel, *Cal. Pretrial Civil Procedure*, §38.65 (SJ form).

5. Signature line. The judgment should include a signature line for the judge. *See, e.g.*, Judicial Council Forms, form JUD-100 (optional form); Kiesel, *Cal. Pretrial Civil Procedure*, §38.65 (SJ form).

§16.3 Entry of judgment. A judgment is not effective for any purpose until it is entered by the clerk. CCP §664. In most courts, a judgment is entered when the original judgment, signed by the judge, is filed with the clerk. ***Dodge v. Superior Ct.*** (4th Dist.2000) 77 Cal.App.4th 513, 518 n.5; *see* CCP §668.5. In courts that still use judgment books, a judgment is entered by the clerk when it is copied into the judgment book. ***Dodge***, 77 Cal.App.4th at 518 n.5; *see* CCP §668.

§16.4 Notice of entry. After the judgment is entered, a notice of entry of judgment must be served on all parties who appeared in the action. CCP §664.5. Failure to serve notice does not make a judgment void, but it does extend the time to file postjudgment motions. *E.g.*, ***Kimball Avenue v. Franco*** (4th Dist.2008) 162 Cal.App.4th 1224, 1228 (extending time to file notice of appeal).

1. Form of notice. There is no required form for the notice of entry; any written notice that conveys to the losing party that judgment has been entered is sufficient. ***Dodge v. Superior Ct.*** (4th Dist.2000) 77 Cal.App.4th 513, 518. Serving the losing party with a copy of the judgment showing the date of entry is sufficient for notice purposes. *Id.*

2. Who serves notice.

(1) Clerk. The court clerk must mail the notice of entry to all parties who have appeared in the action and execute a certificate that the notice was mailed if (1) the clerk was ordered to send notice or (2) the prevailing party was not represented by counsel. CCP §664.5(b), (d).

(2) Party. The party who submitted the judgment for entry must prepare and mail a copy of the notice of entry to all parties who have appeared in the action and file in the court the original notice of entry along with proof of service if (1) the clerk was not ordered to send notice and (2) the prevailing party was represented by counsel. CCP §664.5(a), (d).

§17. REVIEW

§17.1 By trial court. A party can ask the trial court to review a summary judgment by filing (1) a motion for new trial, (2) a motion to vacate under CCP §473(b), or (3) an action to vacate for equitable reasons.

1. Motion for new trial. A party who is adversely affected by a summary judgment can file a motion for new trial. *See* ***Tortorella v. Castro*** (2d Dist.2006) 140 Cal.App.4th 1, 9 (motion for new trial is appropriate following order granting SJ even if SJ determines that there is no need for trial).

2. Motion to vacate under §473(b). A party who is adversely affected by a summary judgment can file a motion to vacate the judgment under §473(b). *See* ***Kapitanski v. Von's Grocery Co.*** (4th Dist.1983) 146 Cal.App.3d 29, 32-33. Motions for relief under §473(b) can be either discretionary or mandatory. Relief under §473(b) is discretionary if a judgment is taken against a party because of the party's or the attorney's surprise or excusable mistake, inadvertence, or neglect. Relief under §473(b) is mandatory if a default, default judgment, or dismissal is taken against a party and an attorney files a sworn affidavit that this action was the result of the attorney's mistake, inadvertence, surprise, or neglect. Most courts agree that only the discretionary provision in §473(b) applies to a

summary-judgment proceeding because the granting of a summary judgment is not considered a default, default judgment, or dismissal. *E.g.*, ***Las Vegas Land & Dev. Co. v. Wilkie Way, LLC*** (2d Dist.2013) (Div. 3) 219 Cal.App.4th 1086, 1091; ***Henderson v. Pacific Gas & Elec. Co.*** (5th Dist.2010) 187 Cal.App.4th 215, 228; ***Huh v. Wang*** (6th Dist.2007) 158 Cal.App.4th 1406, 1417; ***Prieto v. Loyola Marymount Univ.*** (2d Dist.2005) (Div. 8) 132 Cal.App.4th 290, 295; ***English v. IKON Bus. Solutions, Inc.*** (3d Dist.2001) 94 Cal.App.4th 130, 149. *Contra* ***Avila v. Chua*** (2d Dist.1997) (Div. 5) 57 Cal.App.4th 860, 868. See "Motion to vacate under §473(b)," ch. 10-A, §9.1.1, p. 1109.

3. Action in equity to vacate judgment. A party who is adversely affected by a summary judgment can file an action to vacate the judgment on equitable grounds if extrinsic factors (e.g., fraud, mistake) prevented the party from presenting its case. *See, e.g.*, ***Forensis Grp. v. Frantz, Townsend & Foldenauer*** (4th Dist.2005) 130 Cal.App.4th 14, 20 (Ds' showing of extrinsic fraud was sufficient to reverse SJ); *cf.* ***In re Marriage of Park*** (1980) 27 Cal.3d 337, 342 (motion to vacate judgment of dissolution of marriage); ***Olivera v. Grace*** (1942) 19 Cal.2d 570, 575 (motion to set aside default judgment). See "Action in equity to vacate judgment," ch. 10-A, §9.1.5, p. 1113.

§17.2 By appellate court.

1. Writ of mandate.

(1) When applicable. An order denying an MSJ can be reviewed by a petition for writ of mandate. ***Diamond v. Superior Ct.*** (6th Dist.2013) 217 Cal.App.4th 1172, 1182; *see* CCP §437c(m)(1). A writ of mandate will issue when the trial court's denial of an MSJ will result in a trial on nonactionable claims. ***Diamond***, 217 Cal.App.4th at 1182.

(2) Deadline to file.

(a) Initial deadline. The initial deadline to file a petition for writ of mandate depends on how the party received written notice of the order's entry. *See* CCP §437c(m)(1).

10-4. INITIAL DEADLINE TO FILE PETITION FOR WRIT OF MANDATE

	Delivery method for notice of entry of judgment	Deadline to file petition
1	Personal delivery	20 days after service
2	Fax, express mail, or overnight delivery	22 days after service
3	Mail delivery to California address	25 days after service
4	Mail delivery to U.S. address outside California	30 days after service
5	Mail delivery to foreign address	40 days after service

(b) Extension. For good cause, the court can extend the initial deadline to file a petition for writ of mandate by up to ten days. CCP §437c(m)(1).

2. Direct appeal.

(1) When applicable.

(a) Denial of MSJ. An order denying an MSJ is not an appealable order. ***FDIC v. Dintino*** (4th Dist.2008) 167 Cal.App.4th 333, 343; ***City of Oakland v. Hassey*** (1st Dist.2008) 163 Cal.App.4th 1477, 1486; ***Sierra Craft, Inc. v. Magnum Enters.*** (4th Dist.1998) 64 Cal.App.4th 1252, 1256. An order denying an MSJ is interlocutory and can be reviewed on direct appeal only after a final judgment has been entered. ***FDIC***, 167 Cal.App.4th at 343. On direct appeal, the appellant must show that the order denying the MSJ constituted prejudicial or reversible error. *Id.* An order denying an MSJ does not constitute prejudicial error if the same question in the MSJ was decided adversely to the moving party after a trial on the merits. *Id.* But if the same question is not decided after trial, an appellant can successfully assert on appeal that the trial court prejudicially erred in denying the MSJ. *Id.*

(b) Grant of MSJ. An order granting an MSJ can be directly appealed after the summary judgment has been entered. *See* CCP §437c(m)(1).

(2) Deadline to file. See "Deadline to file," ch. 10-A, §9.2.2(4), p. 1116.

(3) Standard of review.

(a) De novo. Generally, a court's ruling on an MSJ is reviewed de novo—that is, the appellate court reviews the trial court's order independently and is not bound by the trial court's reasoning. *See* ***Biancalana v. T.D. Serv.*** (2013) 56 Cal.4th 807, 813; ***Johnson v. City of Loma Linda*** (2000) 24 Cal.4th 61, 65; ***Great Am. Ins. v. Gordon Trucking, Inc.*** (5th Dist.2008) 165 Cal.App.4th 445, 448; ***Hulett v. Farmers Ins. Exch.*** (2d Dist.1992) 10 Cal.App.4th 1051, 1057-58. In conducting its de novo review, the appellate court will apply the same three-step analysis applied by the trial court. ***Halliburton Energy Servs. v. Department of Transp.*** (5th Dist.2013) 220 Cal.App.4th 87, 93; ***Diamond***, 217 Cal.App.4th at 1182; ***Moghadam v. Regents of the Univ. of Cal.*** (2d Dist.2008) 169 Cal.App.4th 466, 474. See "Three-step analysis," §12.2.1(1), p. 1136.

(b) Abuse of discretion. While a court's ruling on an MSJ is generally reviewed de novo, when the court is required to exercise its discretion in passing on a CCP §437c MSJ and it grants or denies the motion based on a question that a court has discretion to answer, the standard of review is abuse of discretion. ***GuideOne Mut. Ins. v. Utica Nat'l Ins.*** (4th Dist.2013) 213 Cal.App.4th 1494, 1501. Some other court rulings that are reviewed for abuse of discretion include the following:

[1] Evidentiary rulings. The court's evidentiary rulings are reviewed for abuse of discretion. ***Garrett v. Howmedica Osteonics Corp.*** (2d Dist.2013) 214 Cal.App.4th 173, 181; ***Great Am. Ins.***, 165 Cal.App.4th at 449; ***Carnes v. Superior Ct.*** (3d Dist.2005) 126 Cal.App.4th 688, 694; *e.g.*, ***Dicola v. White Bros. Performance Prods.*** (4th Dist.2008) 158 Cal.App.4th 666, 679-80 (court reviewed whether evidence was hearsay using abuse-of-discretion standard).

[2] Motions for continuance. The court's ruling on a motion for continuance is reviewed for abuse of discretion. *E.g.*, ***Knapp v. Doherty*** (6th Dist.2004) 123 Cal.App.4th 76, 100-01 (applying abuse-of-discretion standard to court's ruling on continuance under §437c(h)).

[3] Motions to amend. The court's ruling on a motion to amend pleadings is reviewed for abuse of discretion. *See* ***Falcon v. Long Beach Genetics, Inc.*** (4th Dist.2014) 224 Cal.App.4th 1263, 1281.

[4] Granting MSJ on procedural error. The court's granting of a summary judgment based solely on curable procedural error is reviewed for abuse of discretion. *E.g.*, ***Parkview Villas Ass'n v. State Farm Fire & Cas. Co.*** (2d Dist.2005) 133 Cal.App.4th 1197, 1216 (court abused its discretion by granting SJ without giving opposing party opportunity to fix separate statement of fact to comply with CRC 342(f), now CRC 3.1350(f)); ***Kalivas v. Barry Controls Corp.*** (2d Dist.1996) 49 Cal.App.4th 1152, 1161 (court abused its discretion by granting SJ without giving opposing party opportunity to file opposition); *see* ***Elkins v. Superior Ct.*** (2007) 41 Cal.4th 1337, 1364 n.16.

[5] Considering evidence outside separate statement. The court's decision on whether to consider evidence not referenced in a party's separate statement is reviewed for abuse of discretion. ***San Diego Watercrafts, Inc. v. Wells Fargo Bank*** (4th Dist.2002) 102 Cal.App.4th 308, 316.

(4) Standard for affirming judgment. If the appellate court finds there is no issue of material fact, the court must affirm the summary judgment if it is correct on any legal ground applicable to the case, regardless of whether that ground was raised by the movant in the trial court or first addressed on appeal. ***Medill v. Westport Ins.*** (2d Dist.2006) 143 Cal.App.4th 819, 827-28. Before the appellate court can affirm the judgment on a ground not relied on by the trial court, the appellate court must give the parties an opportunity to present their views on the issue by submitting supplemental briefs. CCP §437c(m)(2). The supplemental briefs can include an argument that additional evidence relating to that ground exists but that the party has not had an adequate opportunity to present the

evidence or to conduct discovery on the issue. *Id.* The appellate court may reverse or remand based on the supplemental briefing to allow the parties to present additional evidence or to conduct discovery on the issue. *Id.* If the appellate court does not permit supplemental briefing, a rehearing must be ordered upon the timely petition of any party. *Id.*

C. MOTION FOR SUMMARY ADJUDICATION

This subchapter discusses a motion for summary adjudication (MSA) under CCP §437c(f)(1), which completely disposes of select causes of action, affirmative defenses, claims for damages, or issues of duty within a case. Summary adjudication is available in the same actions as summary judgment. See "Availability of Summary Judgment," ch. 10-B, §4, p. 1119.

§1. GENERAL

§1.1 Purpose. A motion for summary adjudication (MSA) under CCP §437c(f)(1) is nearly identical to a motion for summary judgment (MSJ) except that instead of disposing of the entire case, a summary adjudication disposes of only select causes of action, affirmative defenses, claims for damages, or issues of duty. *See* CCP §437c(f)(1). If a party cannot obtain summary judgment on the entire case, it can still use an MSA to dispose of one or more parts of the case. All matters that are not resolved by summary adjudication will be resolved at trial. *Id.* §437c(n)(1).

§1.2 Primary authority. CCP §437c; CRC 3.1350, 3.1352, 3.1354.

§1.3 Secondary authority. The following secondary source is cited as authority in this subchapter:

- Kiesel et al., *Matthew Bender Practice Guide: California Pretrial Civil Procedure* (2014) (referred to as Kiesel, *Cal. Pretrial Civil Procedure*).

§2. MOVANT'S BURDEN

To prevail on an MSA, the movant must prove the following:

§2.1 No triable issue of material fact. The movant has the burden to prove that there is no triable issue of material fact on the cause of action, affirmative defense, claim for damages, or issue of duty. *See* CCP §437c(c), (f); ***North Coast Women's Care Med. Grp. v. Superior Ct.*** (2008) 44 Cal.4th 1145, 1150; ***Advanced-Tech Sec. Servs. v. Superior Ct.*** (2d Dist.2008) 163 Cal.App.4th 700, 705. See "No triable issue of material fact," ch. 10-B, §5.1, p. 1120.

§2.2 Judgment as matter of law. The movant has the burden to produce evidence showing it is entitled to judgment as a matter of law on the cause of action, affirmative defense, claim for damages, or issue of duty. *See* CCP §437c(c), (f); ***North Coast Women's Care Med. Grp. v. Superior Ct.*** (2008) 44 Cal.4th 1145, 1150; ***Advanced-Tech Sec. Servs. v. Superior Ct.*** (2d Dist.2008) 163 Cal.App.4th 700, 705.

1. Generally.

(1) Dispose of entire matter. For summary adjudication to be granted under CCP §437c(f)(1), the movant must completely dispose of a distinct cause of action, affirmative defense, claim for damages, or issue of duty. CCP §437c(f)(1); ***King v. Wu*** (2d Dist.2013) 218 Cal.App.4th 1211, 1213; *see* ***Harris v. Superior Ct.*** (2011) 53 Cal.4th 170, 182; ***Catalano v. Superior Ct.*** (5th Dist.2000) 82 Cal.App.4th 91, 97-98. Whether a matter has been completely disposed of for purposes of summary adjudication has generally been an issue in cases seeking summary adjudication of a cause of action. For purposes of summary adjudication, courts have interpreted the phrase "cause of action" to mean a separate theory of liability. ***Lilienthal & Fowler v. Superior Ct.*** (1st Dist.1993) 12 Cal.App.4th 1848, 1853-54. If the plaintiff has pleaded several distinct wrongful acts that would support the same theory of liability, a defendant cannot be awarded a summary adjudication on that cause of action unless all wrongful acts are disposed of in the defendant's favor. *E.g.*, ***Hindin v. Rust*** (2d Dist.2004) 118 Cal.App.4th 1247, 1258-59 (P pleaded two wrongful acts to support claim for malicious prosecution; D could not obtain summary adjudication because it could prove only that one act lacked probable cause). But if the plaintiff mistakenly pleads several distinct wrongful acts as a single

theory of liability, the defendant can bring an MSA on each distinct wrongful act that would have supported a separate theory of liability if properly pleaded. *E.g.*, ***Edward Fineman Co. v. Superior Ct.*** (2d Dist.1998) 66 Cal.App.4th 1110, 1117-18 (P pleaded 83 acts of unauthorized payment of checks; D could obtain summary adjudication for each individual check because each check represented separate cause of action); ***Lilienthal***, 12 Cal.App.4th at 1854-55 (P pleaded two separate acts of malpractice as one single cause of action; D could obtain summary adjudication for each act separately); ***Exxon Corp. v. Superior Ct.*** (6th Dist.1997) 51 Cal.App.4th 1672, 1688 n.11 (P pleaded multiple breach-of-contract claims as single cause of action; D could obtain summary adjudication for each act separately).

NOTE

This same analysis has been applied to disposing of claims for damages. If the plaintiff has pleaded several wrongful acts under a single theory of liability that would independently support a claim for punitive damages, all wrongful acts must be resolved in favor of the defendant for summary adjudication to be granted. E.g., ***Catalano****, 82 Cal.App.4th at 97-98 (P's claim for punitive damages was based on five separate allegations of fraudulent misrepresentation; because court could only resolve four allegations in D's favor, D was not entitled to summary adjudication on claim for punitive damages).*

(2) Satisfy applicable evidentiary burden. The movant's evidentiary burden (e.g., preponderance, clear and convincing) on an MSA is the same burden it would have to satisfy at trial. See "Satisfy applicable evidentiary burden," ch. 10-B, §5.2.1(2), p. 1120.

2. Matters subject to summary adjudication.

(1) Cause of action. Either party can move for summary adjudication on a cause of action. *See* CCP §437c(f)(1); ***Paramount Pet. Corp. v. Superior Ct.*** (2d Dist.2014) 227 Cal.App.4th 226, 241.

(a) Plaintiff is movant. To prevail on an MSA on a cause of action, the plaintiff must prove each element of the claim and show that the defendant has no defense to the claim. ***Paramount Pet.***, 227 Cal.App.4th at 241; *see* CCP §437c(p)(1). For a discussion of the plaintiff's burden, see "Plaintiff is movant," ch. 10-B, §5.2.2, p. 1121.

(b) Defendant is movant. To prevail on an MSA on a cause of action, the defendant must establish that (1) one or more elements of the plaintiff's cause of action cannot be established or (2) there is a complete defense to the cause of action. CCP §437c(p)(2); ***King***, 218 Cal.App.4th at 1214. For a discussion of the defendant's burden, see "Defendant is movant," ch. 10-B, §5.2.3, p. 1121.

(2) Affirmative defense. The plaintiff can move for summary adjudication on an affirmative defense raised by the defendant. *See* CCP §437c(f)(1); ***Paramount Pet.***, 227 Cal.App.4th at 241.

(3) Claim for punitive damages. The defendant can move for summary adjudication on a claim for punitive damages brought under Civ. C. §3294. *See* CCP §437c(f)(1); ***DeCastro West Chodorow & Burns, Inc. v. Superior Ct.*** (2d Dist.1996) 47 Cal.App.4th 410, 421. To establish that a claim for punitive damages has no merit, the defendant must establish one of the following: (1) the plaintiff cannot establish an element of a cause of action that supports a claim for punitive damages, (2) the defendant's conduct does not constitute oppression, malice, or fraud, or (3) the plaintiff cannot produce clear and convincing evidence of oppression, malice, or fraud. *See* Civ. C. §3294; *see, e.g.*, ***Food Pro Int'l v. Farmers Ins. Exch.*** (6th Dist.2008) 169 Cal.App.4th 976, 994-95 (D defeated P's claim for punitive damages because P could not produce clear and convincing evidence); ***Myers v. Trendwest Resorts, Inc.*** (3d Dist.2007) 148 Cal.App.4th 1403, 1435 (D defeated P's claim for punitive damages on common-law counts that were disposed of on SJ); ***Mathieu v. Norrell Corp.*** (2d Dist.2004) 115 Cal.App.4th 1174, 1190-91 (D defeated P's claim for punitive damages because D's conduct did not constitute oppression, malice, or fraud). The clear-and-convincing evidentiary standard does not impose a duty on the plaintiff to prove a case for punitive damages at

the summary-adjudication stage. ***American Airlines, Inc. v. Sheppard, Mullin, Richter & Hampton*** (2d Dist.2002) 96 Cal.App.4th 1017, 1049. This higher standard of proof, however, must be taken into account when ruling on an MSA. *Id.* Under this standard, summary adjudication is proper only when no reasonable jury could find the plaintiff's evidence to be clear and convincing proof of oppression, malice, or fraud. *Cf.* ***Spinks v. Equity Residential Briarwood Apts.*** (6th Dist.2009) 171 Cal.App.4th 1004, 1053 (SJ).

NOTE

Courts have interpreted the phrase "claim for damages" in CCP §437c(f)(1) to be limited to claims for punitive damages under Civ. C. §3294. E.g., ***DeCastro West Chodorow & Burns****, 47 Cal.App.4th at 421. Thus, summary adjudication is not permissible under this statutory language for other types of damages. See id. But if the defendant can show that the plaintiff is unable to establish any and all damages (punitive or otherwise) for a cause of action, the defendant can move for summary adjudication on the entire cause of action. Id. at 419 n.3. See "Dispose of entire matter," §2.2.1(1), p. 1145.*

(4) Issue of duty. Either party can move for summary adjudication on the issue of whether the defendant owed a duty to the plaintiff. *See* CCP §437c(f)(1); *see, e.g.,* ***Powerine Oil Co. v. Superior Ct.*** (2005) 37 Cal.4th 377, 385 (D successfully moved for summary adjudication on P's claim that D owed a duty under insurance policies to indemnify P). Summary adjudication can resolve the existence of a duty in tort or in contract. ***Linden Partners v. Wilshire Linden Assocs.*** (2d Dist.1998) 62 Cal.App.4th 508, 518-19.

§3. MOTION

§3.1 Who can file.

1. Party. Any party—a plaintiff, defendant, cross-complainant, or cross-defendant—can file an MSA. *See* CCP §437c(f)(1), (p). Only a party who has filed an MSA can be awarded a summary adjudication. *See* ***Hawkins v. Wilton*** (3d Dist.2006) 144 Cal.App.4th 936, 949.

2. Court. The court cannot enter a summary adjudication on its own motion. *See* CCP §437c(f)(1) ("[a] party may move"); ***Rooz v. Kimmel*** (1st Dist.1997) 55 Cal.App.4th 573, 594 n.11 (dicta; noting that court's sua sponte summary adjudication raised notice and due-process concerns); *cf.* ***Certain Underwriters at Lloyd's of London v. Superior Ct.*** (2d Dist.1997) 56 Cal.App.4th 952, 958-59 (court has no power to enter SJ on its own motion).

§3.2 Deadline to file & serve. An MSA is filed and served in the same manner and according to the same deadlines as an MSJ. *See* CCP §437c(f)(2). See "When to file & serve," ch. 10-B, §6.2, p. 1122.

NOTE

In forcible-detainer and unlawful-detainer actions, filing an MSA does not extend the time for trial. See CCP §§437c(q), 1170, 1170.5.

§3.3 Contents. An MSA must include the same documents required for an MSJ. CRC 3.1350(b), (c). See "Contents," ch. 10-B, §6.3, p. 1123. The notice of motion must state the specific cause of action, affirmative defense, claim for damages, or issue of duty being challenged. CRC 3.1350(b). This information must be repeated verbatim in the separate statement of undisputed material facts. *Id.*

NOTE

An MSA under §437c(f)(1) can be filed as an alternative to an MSJ. CCP §437c(f)(2). If made in the alternative, the MSA can refer to and depend on the same evidence submitted in support of the MSJ. CRC 3.1350(b). See "Motion for Summary Judgment," ch. 10-B, p. 1117.

§3.4 Filing fee. A filing fee of $500 must be paid when the MSA is filed. Gov. C. §70617(d). For a discussion of filing fees, see "Filing Fees," ch. 1-F, §7, p. 58.

§4. RESPONSE

§4.1 Motion for continuance. The opposing party can file a motion for continuance in response to an MSA. CCP §437c(h). See "Motion for continuance," ch. 10-B, §7.1, p. 1126.

§4.2 Motion to amend pleadings. The opposing party can file a motion to amend its pleadings in response to an MSJ. See "Motion to amend pleadings," ch. 10-B, §7.2, p. 1126.

§4.3 Opposition. The opposing party can file an opposition in response to an MSA. *See* CCP §437c(h); CRC 3.1350(e). An opposition to an MSA should be filed in the same manner as an opposition to an MSJ. CRC 3.1350(e); *see* CCP §437c(f)(2). See "Opposition," ch. 10-B, §7.3, p. 1127.

§4.4 Cross-motion. An opposing party can file a cross-motion for summary adjudication. *See* ***Kaiser Found. Hosps. v. Superior Ct.*** (3d Dist.2005) 128 Cal.App.4th 85, 95-96.

§5. REPLY

The movant can file a reply to an opposition to an MSA in the same manner as a reply to an opposition to an MSJ. *See* CCP §437c(f)(2). See "Reply," ch. 10-B, §8, p. 1129.

§6. HEARING

A hearing on an MSA should be conducted in the same manner as a hearing on an MSJ. *See* CCP §437c(f)(2). See "Hearing," ch. 10-B, §11, p. 1136. Courts have held that a party has a right to present oral argument at an MSA hearing. ***Gwartz v. Superior Ct.*** (4th Dist.1999) 71 Cal.App.4th 480, 481-82.

§7. RULING

§7.1 Standard for granting MSA. Summary adjudication must be granted if there is no triable issue of fact and the movant is entitled to judgment as a matter of law on the cause of action, affirmative defense, claim for damages, or issue of duty. *See* CCP §437c(c), (f); ***North Coast Women's Care Med. Grp. v. Superior Ct.*** (2008) 44 Cal.4th 1145, 1150; ***Advanced-Tech Sec. Servs. v. Superior Ct.*** (2d Dist.2008) 163 Cal.App.4th 700, 705.

§7.2 Court's determination. Courts apply the same guidelines for ruling on an MSA as they do for an MSJ. *See* CCP §437c(p) (burden shifting in SJ procedure applies to MSA); ***Raghavan v. Boeing Co.*** (2d Dist.2005) 133 Cal.App.4th 1120, 1132 (burden of production same for MSA as MSJ); ***Oakland Raiders v. National Football League*** (6th Dist.2005) 131 Cal.App.4th 621, 630 (same three-step analysis that applies to determining MSJ applies to MSA). See "Ruling," ch. 10-B, §12, p. 1136.

§8. ORDER

§8.1 Generally. The court's order should comply with the requirements of CCP §437c(g). *See* ***Bernstein v. Consolidated Am. Ins.*** (2d Dist.1995) 37 Cal.App.4th 763, 774, *disapproved on other grounds*, ***Vandenberg v. Superior Ct.*** (1999) 21 Cal.4th 815; *see also* Kiesel, *Cal. Pretrial Civil Procedure*, §38.64 (sample order on MSA). *But see* ***Van Dyke v. S.K.I. Ltd.*** (4th Dist.1998) 67 Cal.App.4th 1310, 1319 n.12 (CCP §437c(g) does not purport to apply to MSAs). For a discussion of these requirements, see "Order," ch. 10-B, §13, p. 1139.

§8.2 Effect of order.

1. **Matter deemed established.** If the MSA is granted, the cause of action, affirmative defense, claim for damages, or issue of duty is deemed established at trial, and the action will proceed only on the remaining issues. CCP §437c(n)(1).

2. **Does not bar trial of other matters.** The granting of an MSA does not bar trial of a cause of action, an affirmative defense, a claim for damages, or an issue of duty on which summary adjudication either was not sought or was denied. CCP §437c(n)(2).

3. No comment at trial. The grant or denial of an MSA cannot be commented on to the jury at trial. CCP §437c(n)(3). This prohibition applies to the parties, their witnesses, and the court. *Id.*; *e.g.*, ***Raghavan v. Boeing Co.*** (2d Dist.2005) 133 Cal.App.4th 1120, 1137 (court committed reversible error when it instructed jury that allegation that P made misleading statements was true; allegation was resolved by summary adjudication).

§9. MOTION FOR RECONSIDERATION

A party who is adversely affected by a court's order on an MSA can file a motion for reconsideration. CCP §1008(a). See "Motion for Reconsideration," ch. 5-G, §3, p. 508.

§10. MOTION FOR RENEWAL

A party who was denied or conditionally granted a summary adjudication can file a motion for renewal of the MSA. CCP §1008(b). See "Motion for Renewal," ch. 5-G, §4, p. 516.

§11. APPELLATE REVIEW

§11.1 Writ of mandate. An order granting or denying summary adjudication is an interlocutory order that can be reviewed by a petition for writ of mandate. *See* CCP §437c(m)(1); ***Farmers Ins. Exch. v. Superior Ct.*** (2d Dist.2013) 220 Cal.App.4th 1199, 1204; ***Rehmani v. Superior Ct.*** (6th Dist.2012) 204 Cal.App.4th 945, 949. *But see* ***International Ins. v. Superior Ct.*** (2d Dist.1998) 62 Cal.App.4th 784, 788 (extraordinary writs are seldom used to review interlocutory summary-adjudication orders). For a discussion of when to file a petition for writ of mandate under §437c(m)(1), see "Deadline to file," ch. 10-B, §17.2.1(2), p. 1143.

§11.2 Direct appeal.

1. When applicable. An order granting or denying summary adjudication is not immediately appealable; it can be appealed only after a final judgment has been entered. ***Wilson v. Superior Ct.*** (2d Dist.2014) (Div. 1) 227 Cal.App.4th 579, 591 (order granting MSA); ***Gehr v. Baker Hughes Oil Field Opers., Inc.*** (2d Dist.2008) (Div. 4) 165 Cal.App.4th 660, 666 n.6 (order denying MSA); ***Jacobs-Zorne v. Superior Ct.*** (2d Dist.1996) (Div. 7) 46 Cal.App.4th 1064, 1070-71 (order granting MSA); *see also* CCP §904.1(a)(1) (listing appealable judgments). *But see* ***Belio v. Panorama Optics, Inc.*** (2d Dist.1995) (Div. 3) 33 Cal.App.4th 1096, 1101 (order granting summary adjudication on one cause of action was appealable because it effectively disposed of entire case). There is no requirement that a losing party challenge a summary adjudication by writ or by requesting reconsideration before it can be reviewed on appeal. ***Angelica Textile Servs. v. Park*** (4th Dist.2013) 220 Cal.App.4th 495, 504.

2. Standard of review. On appeal, the appellate court reviews an order of summary adjudication de novo. ***Davis v. Kiewit Pac. Co.*** (4th Dist.2013) 220 Cal.App.4th 358, 363; ***King v. Wu*** (2d Dist.2013) 218 Cal.App.4th 1211, 1213; ***Brassinga v. City of Mountain View*** (6th Dist.1998) 66 Cal.App.4th 195, 210. The court must affirm an order granting summary adjudication if it is correct on any legal ground applicable to the case, regardless of whether that ground was raised by the movant in the trial court or first addressed on appeal. *See* CCP §437c(m)(2); *cf.* ***Medill v. Westport Ins.*** (2d Dist.2006) 143 Cal.App.4th 819, 827-28 (SJ). For a discussion of affirming an order on grounds not relied on by the trial court, see "Standard for affirming judgment," ch. 10-B, §17.2.2(4), p. 1144.

NOTE

Parties can make an order on an MSA appealable by agreeing to dismiss, regardless of prejudice, the remaining issues that were not resolved by summary adjudication. See ***Kurwa v. Kislinger*** *(2013) 57 Cal.4th 1097, 1105. But if, in addition to agreeing to dismiss the remaining issues without prejudice, the parties also make an agreement that ensures the potential for future litigation (e.g., an agreement to waive or toll the statute of limitations pending an appeal), the dismissal is not final and appealable. Id. at 1105-06.*

D. VOLUNTARY DISMISSAL

This subchapter discusses voluntary dismissals in civil actions and special proceedings under CCP §581. This subchapter does not discuss involuntary dismissals for delay in prosecution or for other procedural errors. For a discussion of those topics, see "Involuntary Dismissal—Delay in Prosecution," ch. 10-E, p. 1160, and "Involuntary Dismissal—Other Grounds," ch. 10-F, p. 1180.

§1. GENERAL

§1.1 Purpose. The purpose of a voluntary dismissal is to allow a plaintiff to dispose of an action without reaching the merits. *See* ***Harris v. Billings*** (2d Dist.1993) 16 Cal.App.4th 1396, 1404. Whether a dismissal is voluntary or involuntary depends on the person seeking the dismissal. If the plaintiff or both parties consent to the dismissal, it is voluntary. ***D&J, Inc. v. Ferro Corp.*** (4th Dist.1986) 176 Cal.App.3d 1191, 1194. If the defendant or the court (on its own motion) seeks the dismissal, it is involuntary. *Id.*

NOTE

For ease of reference, this subchapter uses the term "plaintiff" throughout to refer to the party who is seeking a dismissal. The rules for obtaining a voluntary dismissal, however, apply equally to cross-complainants. CCP §581(a)(4), (a)(5).

§1.2 Primary authority. CCP §581(b), (c), (e).

§1.3 Secondary authority. The following secondary source is cited as authority in this subchapter:

- Weil & Brown, *California Practice Guide: Civil Procedure Before Trial* (CD-ROM ed. 2014) (referred to as Weil, *Civil Procedure Before Trial*).

§1.4 Judicial Council forms.

- CIV-110 (mandatory), request for dismissal.
- CIV-120 (mandatory), notice of entry of dismissal and proof of service.

§2. OVERVIEW

§2.1 Whole or partial. A voluntary dismissal can be whole or partial. CCP §581(c). A plaintiff can dismiss specific defendants or causes of action, or it can dismiss the entire complaint and all defendants. *Id.*

§2.2 With or without prejudice. A voluntary dismissal can be granted with or without prejudice. CCP §581(b), (c), (e).

1. With prejudice. A voluntary dismissal granted with prejudice is considered a judgment on the merits; it bars the plaintiff from bringing any future action on the same subject matter. ***Boeken v. Philip Morris USA, Inc.*** (2010) 48 Cal.4th 788, 793; ***Torrey Pines Bank v. Superior Ct.*** (4th Dist.1989) 216 Cal.App.3d 813, 820; *see* ***Johnson v. County of Fresno*** (5th Dist.2003) 111 Cal.App.4th 1087, 1095-96 (voluntary dismissal with prejudice is judgment on merits).

2. Without prejudice. A voluntary dismissal granted without prejudice does not bar a new action on the same allegations. ***Wells v. Marina City Props., Inc.*** (1981) 29 Cal.3d 781, 784; ***Cardiff Equities, Inc. v. Superior Ct.*** (2d Dist.2008) 166 Cal.App.4th 1541, 1550. The new action must be refiled within the applicable limitations period, however, because the dismissal is treated as if no earlier case had been filed. *See* ***Wells***, 29 Cal.3d at 784; ***Cardiff Equities***, 166 Cal.App.4th at 1550.

§2.3 Before or after trial commences. A voluntary dismissal can be requested before or after a trial commences. CCP §581(b), (c), (e).

1. Before trial. Before a trial commences, the plaintiff has an absolute right to dismiss an action without prejudice—that is, the clerk or the court cannot deny the relief if it is properly requested. *See* ***Conservatorship of Martha P.*** (4th Dist.2004) 117 Cal.App.4th 857, 866; ***O'Dell v. Freightliner Corp.*** (2d Dist.1992) 10 Cal.App.4th 645, 659. See "Voluntary Dismissal Before Trial Commences," §3, p. 1151.

2. After trial. After a trial commences, the plaintiff no longer has an absolute right to dismiss an action without prejudice. *See* CCP §581(e). Rather, the court must dismiss an action with prejudice unless both parties consent to the dismissal or the court finds good cause to dismiss without prejudice. *Id.* See "Voluntary Dismissal After Trial Commences," §4, p. 1155.

§3. VOLUNTARY DISMISSAL BEFORE TRIAL COMMENCES

§3.1 Who can request.

1. Generally. A plaintiff can request, or both parties can consent to, a voluntary dismissal before a trial commences. CCP §581(b)(1), (b)(2), (c).

2. Notice or consent of attorney required. If the request for dismissal is not made by the party's attorney (i.e., the party requests dismissal on its own), the party's attorney must give consent before the request is made, or if consent cannot be obtained, notice must be given to the attorney before dismissal can be ordered. CCP §581(j).

§3.2 When to request. A voluntary dismissal under CCP §581(b)(1) must be requested before the trial commences. CCP §581(b)(1), (c). The Legislature has defined the commencement of trial as the beginning of any party's opening statement or, if there is no opening statement, the time the oath is administered to the first witness or any evidence is introduced. *Id.* §581(a)(6). Despite this statutory directive, courts have held that the definition in §581(a)(6) is not the exclusive test for determining when a trial commences. ***Wells v. Marina City Props., Inc.*** (1981) 29 Cal.3d 781, 785-86, 788; ***Franklin Capital Corp. v. Wilson*** (4th Dist.2007) 148 Cal.App.4th 187, 194; *see* ***Mary Morgan, Inc. v. Melzark*** (1st Dist.1996) 49 Cal.App.4th 765, 769 (meaning of "trial" is not restricted to jury or court trials on merits, but includes other procedures that effectively dispose of case). To determine when a trial has commenced, one court reconciled earlier case law and developed a "mere formality" test. ***Franklin Capital***, 148 Cal.App.4th at 201-02. Under this test, when the plaintiff's case has already reached a stage where a final, adverse disposition is a mere formality, the plaintiff no longer has an absolute right to voluntarily dismiss the case. ***Zapanta v. Universal Care, Inc.*** (2d Dist.2003) 107 Cal.App.4th 1167, 1173-74. The plaintiff's case reaches this stage when (1) the court has publicly and formally expressed an adverse opinion on the legal merits of the plaintiff's case (e.g., a tentative ruling on a dispositive motion) or (2) the plaintiff has made some procedural error that makes dismissal, as opposed to voluntary dismissal, inevitable. *See* ***Franklin Capital***, 148 Cal.App.4th at 200; *see, e.g.*, ***Law Offices of Andrew L. Ellis v. Yang*** (2d Dist.2009) 178 Cal.App.4th 869, 877-78 (adopting mere-formality test); ***321 Henderson Receivables Origination LLC v. Tomahawk*** (5th Dist.2009) 172 Cal.App.4th 290, 302-03 (applying mere-formality test); ***Gogri v. Jack in the Box Inc.*** (4th Dist.2008) 166 Cal.App.4th 255, 262 (same). The following illustrates how earlier case law can be reconciled with the two prongs of the mere-formality test:

1. Public & formal expression of legal merits.

(1) Yes. The following are public and formal expressions of the court's opinion on the legal merits of the plaintiff's case that were sufficient to cut off the plaintiff's absolute right to seek a voluntary dismissal:

- Dismissal was requested after a general demurrer was sustained without leave to amend. ***Bank of Am. v. Mitchell*** (2d Dist.2012) 204 Cal.App.4th 1199, 1210.

- Dismissal was requested after a tentative ruling sustaining a demurrer without leave to amend had been announced. ***Groth Bros. Oldsmobile, Inc. v. Gallagher*** (1st Dist.2002) 97 Cal.App.4th 60, 73. For a discussion of how to dismiss an action when a demurrer without leave to amend is granted, see "Demurrer – Without Leave to Amend," ch. 10-F, §2, p. 1180.

- Dismissal was requested after the referee transmitted a written recommendation to the court after a two-day evidentiary hearing. ***Gray v. Superior Ct.*** (1st Dist.1997) 52 Cal.App.4th 165, 173.

- Dismissal was requested after a tentative ruling on a motion for summary judgment had been announced. ***Mary Morgan, Inc.***, 49 Cal.App.4th at 770.

• Dismissal was requested after a motion to dismiss for lack of prosecution was granted but not yet entered. ***M&R Props. v. Thomson*** (1st Dist.1992) 11 Cal.App.4th 899, 902.

• Dismissal was requested after an adverse result in judicial arbitration was received and a trial de novo was requested. ***Herbert Hawkins Realtors, Inc. v. Milheiser*** (4th Dist.1983) 140 Cal.App.3d 334, 339-40.

(2) No. The following are not public and formal expressions of the court's opinion on the legal merits of the plaintiff's case that were sufficient to cut off the plaintiff's absolute right to seek a voluntary dismissal:

• Dismissal was requested after a demurrer was filed to the plaintiff's amended complaint. ***Christensen v. Dewor Devs.*** (1983) 33 Cal.3d 778, 785.

• Dismissal was requested after the court issued an unfavorable tentative ruling on the plaintiff's petition under the Structured Settlement Transfer Act in a different case and ordered the plaintiff to serve the court's order on each person in all pending cases. ***321 Henderson Receivables***, 172 Cal.App.4th at 303.

• Dismissal was requested after the court ordered the case to arbitration. ***Cardiff Equities, Inc. v. Superior Ct.*** (2d Dist.2008) 166 Cal.App.4th 1541, 1550.

• Dismissal was requested after the defendant filed a motion for summary judgment but before the court ruled on it. ***Gogri***, 166 Cal.App.4th at 267.

• Dismissal was requested after a strategic-lawsuit-against-public-participation (SLAPP) motion was heard and taken under submission. ***Kyle v. Carmon*** (3d Dist.1999) 71 Cal.App.4th 901, 910.

• Dismissal was requested after a partial summary adjudication was granted disposing of some, but not all, of the issues in the action. ***Cal-Vada Aircraft, Inc. v. Superior Ct.*** (3d Dist.1986) 179 Cal.App.3d 435, 447-48.

• Dismissal was requested the day before the hearing on a demurrer and after the judge's unreported comment in chambers that the demurrer was meritorious. ***Datner v. Mann Theaters Corp.*** (2d Dist.1983) 145 Cal.App.3d 768, 771.

2. Procedural error.

(1) Yes. The following are procedural errors that cut off the plaintiff's absolute right to seek a voluntary dismissal:

• Dismissal was requested after a general demurrer was sustained with leave to amend and no amendment was filed. ***Wells***, 29 Cal.3d at 789. For a discussion of how to dismiss an action when a plaintiff has not amended the complaint after a demurrer was granted, see "Demurrer – No Amendment," ch. 10-F, §3, p. 1180.

• Dismissal was requested after no objection was filed to the defendant's motion for summary judgment. ***Cravens v. State Bd. of Equalization*** (2d Dist.1997) 52 Cal.App.4th 253, 257.

• Dismissal was requested after the time to respond to admissions had expired and all issues were deemed admitted in the defendant's favor. ***Miller v. Marina Mercy Hosp.*** (2d Dist.1984) 157 Cal.App.3d 765, 770.

(2) No. The following are not procedural errors that cut off the plaintiff's absolute right to seek a voluntary dismissal:

• Dismissal was requested after the time to respond to a motion to enforce a settlement agreement had expired under CCP §664.6. ***Lewis C. Nelson & Sons, Inc. v. Lynx Iron Corp.*** (5th Dist.2009) 174 Cal.App.4th 67, 79.

• Dismissal was requested after the plaintiff's attorney did not appear at the mandatory settlement conference. *See* ***Franklin Capital***, 148 Cal.App.4th at 209-10.

• Dismissal was requested the day before the plaintiff's opposition to the defendant's motion for summary judgment was due. ***Zapanta***, 107 Cal.App.4th at 1173-74.

• Dismissal was requested after the time to respond to admissions had expired but before they were deemed admitted. ***Harris v. Billings*** (2d Dist.1993) 16 Cal.App.4th 1396, 1403.

§3.3 How to request.

1. Generally.

(1) Orally. A voluntary dismissal before trial can be requested orally before the court. CCP §581(b)(1).

(2) In writing.

(a) Generally. In most cases, a voluntary dismissal before trial can be requested in a written motion filed with the clerk or in the court. CCP §581(b)(1). A written motion for dismissal to the clerk must be requested on mandatory Judicial Council Form CIV-110.

(b) Court approval required. In some cases, a voluntary dismissal must be approved by the court. If court approval is required to dismiss the suit, the written motion should be directed to the court. Court approval of a dismissal is required in the following cases:

[1] When the plaintiff does not obtain consent from its attorney to dismiss the suit. CCP §581(j).

[2] When dismissal of a custody or guardianship proceeding is requested. ***Ford v. Superior Ct.*** (2d Dist.1959) 171 Cal.App.2d 228, 230-31.

[3] When dismissal of a class action is requested. CCP §581(k); CRC 3.770(a); *see* Judicial Council Forms, form CIV-110 (form cannot be used to dismiss class action or any party or cause of action in class action).

[4] When dismissal of a shareholder derivative suit is requested. ***Ensher v. Ensher, Alexander & Barsoom, Inc.*** (3d Dist.1960) 187 Cal.App.2d 407, 410; *see* Judicial Council Forms, form CIV-110 (form cannot be used to dismiss derivative suit).

2. Contents. A request for a voluntary dismissal before trial must address the following:

(1) With or without prejudice. The request must state whether the dismissal is with or without prejudice. *See* Judicial Council Forms, form CIV-110. As long as the request is made before trial commences, the plaintiff has an absolute right to dismiss without prejudice. See "Before trial," §2.3.1, p. 1150.

(2) Who or what is being dismissed. The request must state who or what is being dismissed (i.e., all parties and actions or only specific defendants, pleadings, or causes of action). *See* Judicial Council Forms, form CIV-110. The plaintiff's power to dismiss may be limited depending on whether the defendant or an intervening third party has taken some action before the voluntary dismissal was requested.

(a) Defendant sought affirmative relief. If the defendant has requested affirmative relief against the plaintiff, the plaintiff cannot dismiss the whole action unless it gets consent from the defendant. *See* CCP §581(i); ***Sanabria v. Embrey*** (2d Dist.2001) 92 Cal.App.4th 422, 425; Weil, *Civil Procedure Before Trial*, ¶11:7. If consent cannot be obtained, the plaintiff can only unilaterally request a partial dismissal (i.e., dismiss only the complaint or a specific cause of action or defendant). *See* ***Sanabria***, 92 Cal.App.4th at 425.

[1] Affirmative relief defined. For relief to be considered "affirmative" under §581, the defendant must allege a new matter that entitles the defendant to relief. ***Simpson v. Superior Ct.*** (2d Dist.1945) 68 Cal.App.2d 821, 825. An allegation that only operates as a defense is not sufficient. *Id.*

[2] **Must be properly requested.** For most actions, to effectively cut off a plaintiff's right to dismiss the whole action, a defendant's request for affirmative relief must be requested in a cross-complaint; affirmative relief cannot be requested in an answer. ***Aetna Cas. & Sur. Co. v. Humboldt Loaders, Inc.*** (1st Dist.1988) 202 Cal.App.3d 921, 928-29; *see* CCP §§431.30(c), 581(i). Some actions, however, do permit affirmative relief to be requested in the answer. *See, e.g.*, ***Gray v. Superior Ct.*** (1st Dist.1997) 52 Cal.App.4th 165, 174 (affirmative relief can be requested in answer to partition suit); ***In re Marriage of Tamraz*** (2d Dist.1994) 24 Cal.App.4th 1740, 1746-47 (affirmative relief can be requested in answer to dissolution proceeding).

CAUTION

Despite the apparent clarity and unequivocal nature of CCP §§431.30(c) and 581(i), several courts have held that the substance of the pleading (i.e., whether the pleading seeks affirmative relief) rather than the form (i.e., whether it is stated in a cross-complaint) determines whether a plaintiff's unilateral right to dismiss an entire action has been cut off. ***Schwartz v. Schwartz*** *(5th Dist.2008) 167 Cal.App.4th 733, 742; see* ***Conservatorship of Martha P.*** *(4th Dist.2004) 117 Cal.App.4th 857, 869.*

(b) Defendant filed motion to transfer venue. If the defendant has filed a motion to transfer venue under CCP §396b and the motion is pending, the plaintiff cannot dismiss any part of the action. *See* CCP §581(i).

(c) Third party filed complaint in intervention. If a third party has filed a complaint in intervention that seeks affirmative relief against the plaintiff, the plaintiff cannot dismiss the whole action unless it gets consent from the intervenor. *See* ***Sanabria***, 92 Cal.App.4th at 425.

3. Service.

(1) Generally. In most cases, the plaintiff is not required to serve notice of a request for a voluntary dismissal on the defendant. *See, e.g.*, ***Associated Convalescent Enters. v. Carl Marks & Co.*** (2d Dist.1973) 33 Cal.App.3d 116, 118 (Ds were not served with request for dismissal).

(2) Class actions. Notice of a request for dismissal of a class action must be given to all members of the class if (1) the court has certified the class and (2) notice of the pendency of the action has been provided to the class members. CRC 3.770(c).

§3.4 Entry of dismissal.

1. Procedure. After receiving a request for a voluntary dismissal before trial, the clerk or court will review the request and determine whether the dismissal can be granted. *See* Judicial Council Forms, form CIV-110; *see, e.g.*, ***Boonyarit v. Payless Shoesource, Inc.*** (2d Dist.2006) 145 Cal.App.4th 1188, 1191 (clerk rejected request for dismissal because P did not indicate on form what she was dismissing). If the request for dismissal is in proper form, the clerk or court must enter the dismissal; neither the clerk nor the court has discretion to deny it. ***Conservatorship of Martha P.*** (4th Dist.2004) 117 Cal.App.4th 857, 866; ***O'Dell v. Freightliner Corp.*** (2d Dist.1992) 10 Cal.App.4th 645, 659.

2. Form.

(1) Clerk. If the clerk grants the dismissal, the clerk must check the appropriate box on mandatory Judicial Council Form CIV-110 and enter the dismissal in the clerk's register. *See* CCP §581d. A voluntary dismissal entered by the clerk does not require a formal, signed order. ***M&R Props. v. Thomson*** (1st Dist.1992) 11 Cal.App.4th 899, 902. If the clerk does not enter the dismissal in the register, the dismissal is still effective as of the date it was requested. ***Aetna Cas. & Sur. Co. v. Humboldt Loaders, Inc.*** (1st Dist.1988) 202 Cal.App.3d 921, 931; *see* ***Associated Convalescent Enters. v. Carl Marks & Co.*** (2d Dist.1973) 33 Cal.App.3d 116, 120 (if in proper form, dismissal is effective immediately).

(2) **Court order.** If the court orders the dismissal, the order must be in writing, signed by the court, and filed in the action. CCP §581d. The order must state whether the dismissal is with or without prejudice and who or what has been dismissed.

CAUTION

If an order of dismissal does not specify whether the dismissal is with or without prejudice, it will be deemed to be with prejudice. ***Tudor Ranches, Inc. v. State Comp. Ins. Fund*** *(4th Dist.1998) 65 Cal.App.4th 1422, 1430.*

---

3. **Notice of entry.** The party who requested dismissal must file and serve on all parties notice of entry of the dismissal. CRC 3.1390. The notice of entry must be filled out on mandatory Judicial Council Form CIV-120.

§4. VOLUNTARY DISMISSAL AFTER TRIAL COMMENCES

§4.1 Who can request. A plaintiff can request, or both parties can consent to, a voluntary dismissal after a trial has commenced. CCP §581(e). For a discussion of when a trial commences, see "When to request," §3.2, p. 1151.

§4.2 How to request.

1. **Motion to court.** A request to voluntarily dismiss a case after a trial has commenced must be directed to the court. CCP §581(e).

NOTE

Although CCP §581(d) seems to suggest that a court can dismiss an action (or a specific cause of action or defendant) on its own if the plaintiff abandons it before final submission of the case, some courts have required the plaintiff to unequivocally show its intent to abandon the action by filing a motion to dismiss, a stipulation of the parties, or some other form of express intent on the record. E.g., ***Kaufman & Broad Bldg. Co. v. City & Suburban Mortg. Co.*** *(2d Dist.1970) 10 Cal.App.3d 206, 212-13 (ambiguous statements about intent to abandon were not sufficient to show intent to abandon); see, e.g.,* ***Burnett v. Burnett*** *(2d Dist.1948) 88 Cal.App.2d 805, 807 (P showed intent to abandon by filing motion to dismiss).*

---

2. **Contents.**

(1) **With or without prejudice.** The motion must state whether the dismissal is with or without prejudice. Generally, a voluntary dismissal granted after a trial has commenced must be with prejudice. CCP §581(d), (e). The court can order a dismissal without prejudice, however, if either good cause is shown or the parties consent. *Id.* §581(e). See "Without prejudice," §2.2.2, p. 1150.

(2) **Who or what is being dismissed.** The request must state who or what is being dismissed (i.e., all parties and actions or only specific defendants, pleadings, or causes of action). *See* CCP §581(e).

3. **Service.** See "Service," §3.3.3, p. 1154.

§4.3 Entry of dismissal. Only a court can order a dismissal after a trial has commenced. CCP §581(e). For a discussion of the requirements of a court order of dismissal, see "Court order," §3.4.2(2), this page.

§4.4 Notice of entry. See "Notice of entry," §3.4.3, this page.

§5. EFFECT OF DISMISSAL

§5.1 Plaintiff's ability to relitigate.

1. **Dismissal without prejudice.** A dismissal without prejudice is not a final judgment on the merits and thus has no res judicata or collateral-estoppel effect. *See* ***Associated Convalescent Enters. v. Carl Marks & Co.*** (2d Dist.1973) 33 Cal.App.3d 116, 121. A party can refile an action that has been dismissed without prejudice as

long as it is filed within the applicable limitations period. ***Wells v. Marina City Props., Inc.*** (1981) 29 Cal.3d 781, 784; ***Cardiff Equities, Inc. v. Superior Ct.*** (2d Dist.2008) 166 Cal.App.4th 1541, 1550.

2. Dismissal with prejudice.

(1) Res judicata. A dismissal with prejudice constitutes a final judgment on the merits that has res judicata effect, barring the plaintiff from relitigating the same cause of action in a later suit. ***Boeken v. Philip Morris USA, Inc.*** (2010) 48 Cal.4th 788, 797-99; ***Le Parc Cmty. v. Workers' Comp. Appeals Bd.*** (2d Dist.2003) 110 Cal.App.4th 1161, 1169.

(a) Primary right. For purposes of res judicata, a "cause of action" is defined as the plaintiff's primary right. ***Le Parc Cmty.***, 110 Cal.App.4th at 1170; *see* ***Boeken***, 48 Cal.4th at 797. The violation of one primary right (e.g., the right not to be personally injured) gives rise to a single cause of action, even though there may be multiple legal theories on which recovery might be based. ***Mycogen Corp. v. Monsanto Co.*** (2002) 28 Cal.4th 888, 904. If multiple legal theories involve the same injury to the plaintiff and the same wrong by the defendant, then the same primary right is at stake even if in the second suit the plaintiff pleads different forms of relief or adds new facts to support recovery. *E.g.*, ***Le Parc Cmty.***, 110 Cal.App.4th at 1170 (dismissal of personal-injury suit did not have res judicata effect on later-filed workers' compensation action because different primary right was involved). For a discussion of the primary-right theory, see "Primary-right theory," ch. 3-C, §3.6.1(1), p. 215.

(b) No consideration required. For res judicata to take effect, the dismissal does not have to be supported by any consideration. ***Roybal v. University Ford*** (4th Dist.1989) 207 Cal.App.3d 1080, 1087. Thus, a plaintiff who inadvertently checks the wrong box on the dismissal form can be barred from relitigating the same cause of action. *See, e.g., id.* at 1085 (attorney could have sought relief from his inadvertent mistake by bringing motion to vacate under CCP §473(b)).

(2) Collateral estoppel. Courts disagree to what extent collateral estoppel applies to a voluntary dismissal with prejudice. Generally, collateral estoppel bars relitigation of issues actually litigated in an earlier proceeding. ***Le Parc Cmty.***, 110 Cal.App.4th at 1171. For collateral estoppel to apply, five requirements must be met: (1) the issue sought to be barred from relitigation must be identical to that decided in an earlier proceeding, (2) the issue must have been actually litigated in the earlier proceeding, (3) the issue must have been necessarily decided in the earlier proceeding (i.e., not be entirely unnecessary to the judgment), (4) the decision in the earlier proceeding must be final and on the merits, and (5) the party against whom collateral estoppel is sought must be the same as, or in privity with, the party in the earlier proceeding. ***Lucido v. Superior Ct.*** (1990) 51 Cal.3d 335, 341. The Fourth District has held that because a voluntary dismissal with prejudice is a final judgment on the merits, collateral estoppel applies to the issues in the dismissed case. ***Torrey Pines Bank v. Superior Ct.*** (4th Dist.1989) 216 Cal.App.3d 813, 821-22; *see* ***Alpha Mech., Heating & Air Conditioning, Inc. v. Travelers Cas. & Sur. Co.*** (4th Dist.2005) 133 Cal.App.4th 1319, 1333-34 (dicta). The Second District, on the other hand, has held that although a voluntary dismissal with prejudice constitutes a final judgment on the merits, if the dismissal occurs by settlement before trial has commenced, collateral estoppel does not apply because the issues were not actually litigated. *See* ***Rice v. Crow*** (2d Dist.2000) 81 Cal.App.4th 725, 736-37; *see, e.g.*, ***Le Parc Cmty.***, 110 Cal.App.4th at 1174-75 (because first suit was voluntarily dismissed before trial by parties' settlement agreement, P was not barred from relitigating his employment status in second suit); *see also* ***Boeken***, 48 Cal.4th at 810 (Moreno, J., dissenting) (suggesting that holding in ***Rice*** is dominant rule in state).

NOTE

If the parties enter into a settlement agreement that calls for a dismissal with prejudice, they can limit the legal effect of res judicata and collateral estoppel in their agreement. ***Alpha Mech.****, 133 Cal.App.4th at 1334.*

§5.2 Court's jurisdiction.

1. Whole dismissal.

(1) Generally – court loses jurisdiction. When the whole action is dismissed (i.e., all actions and parties), the court loses subject-matter jurisdiction over the action and personal jurisdiction over the parties. ***Gogri v. Jack in the Box Inc.*** (4th Dist.2008) 166 Cal.App.4th 255, 261.

(2) Exceptions. Although a court generally loses jurisdiction after a whole dismissal is entered, the court does retain limited jurisdiction to (1) award costs and statutory attorney fees and (2) hear a motion to vacate. *See* ***Gogri***, 166 Cal.App.4th at 273 (costs and fees); ***Gray v. Superior Ct.*** (1st Dist.1997) 52 Cal.App.4th 165, 168 (motion to vacate). See "Costs recoverable," §5.3.1, this page; "Motion to vacate," §6.1.1, p. 1158. Any other order entered by the court after a dismissal of the whole action is void for lack of jurisdiction. ***Conservatorship of Martha P.*** (4th Dist.2004) 117 Cal.App.4th 857, 866-67.

NOTE

If the parties enter into a settlement agreement that calls for a dismissal, they can ask the court to retain jurisdiction to enforce the terms of the settlement agreement. CCP §664.6; see ***City of Gardena v. Rikuo Corp.*** *(2d Dist.2011) 192 Cal.App.4th 595, 605-06 (parties themselves must formally ask for continuing jurisdiction to apply); see, e.g.,* ***Hagan Eng'g, Inc. v. Mills*** *(3d Dist.2003) 115 Cal.App.4th 1004, 1010-11 (parties not allowed to consent to continuing jurisdiction; request must be filed in court).*

2. Partial dismissal. When only part of an action is dismissed (e.g., a specific cause of action or defendant), the court retains jurisdiction over the issues and parties that remain. *See* ***Casa De Valley View Owner's Ass'n v. Stevenson*** (2d Dist.1985) 167 Cal.App.3d 1182, 1192.

§5.3 Defendant's right to recover costs. A prevailing party is entitled as a matter of right to recover costs under CCP §1033.5 in any action or proceeding unless otherwise provided by statute. CCP §§1032(b), 1033.5(a). A prevailing party includes a defendant in whose favor a dismissal is entered. *Id.* §1032(a)(4). This is true regardless of whether the dismissal is granted with or without prejudice. ***Cano v. Glover*** (2d Dist.2006) 143 Cal.App.4th 326, 331.

1. Costs recoverable.

(1) Generally. Section 1033.5 lists the costs that are typically recoverable by a prevailing party, but it is not intended to be an exhaustive list of recoverable costs. *See* CCP §1033.5(c)(4).

(2) Attorney fees. Under §1033.5(a)(10), the costs allowable to a prevailing party include attorney fees only if (1) the party is entitled to recover attorney fees based on a contract, a statute, or other law and (2) no statute expressly provides otherwise. *See* CCP §1032(b).

(a) Tort actions. Generally, if a contract, a statute, or other law permits a prevailing party to recover attorney fees in a tort action, the defendant will be permitted to recover attorney fees after a voluntary dismissal. *See* ***Santisas v. Goodin*** (1998) 17 Cal.4th 599, 619 (contractual attorney-fee provision can support recovery of attorney fees to defend tort action); *see, e.g.,* ***Gogri v. Jack in the Box Inc.*** (4th Dist.2008) 166 Cal.App.4th 255, 274 (D entitled to recover costs incurred in defense of tort claims). However, the California Supreme Court in ***Santisas*** noted that if a defendant's right to recover attorney fees in defense of a tort action is provided by contract, the defendant should not automatically recover the fees simply because a defendant is defined as a prevailing party under CCP §1032. *See* ***Santisas***, 17 Cal.4th at 621 (it would be inaccurate to characterize D as prevailing party if P dismissed action for reasons that have nothing to do with probability of success on merits). The Court in ***Santisas*** held that a court may determine whether there is a prevailing party by examining the terms of the contract, including any contractual definition of the term "prevailing party" and any provision governing payment of attorney fees

in the event of dismissal. *Id.* at 622. If the contract is silent on those issues, the court may base its decision on a pragmatic definition of the extent to which each party has realized its litigation objectives. *Id.*

(b) Contract actions. Civ. C. §1717(b)(2) expressly prohibits awarding attorney fees to a prevailing party in an action on a contract if the action has been voluntarily dismissed. ***Ford Motor Credit Co. v. Hunsberger*** (4th Dist.2008) 163 Cal.App.4th 1526, 1531. The prohibition against the recovery of attorney fees in §1717 applies even if the contract expressly provides for the recovery of attorney fees in the event of a voluntary dismissal. ***Mitchell Land & Imprv. Co. v. Ristorante Ferrantelli, Inc.*** (4th Dist.2007) 158 Cal.App.4th 479, 485.

2. Procedure for claiming costs.

(1) Generally – memorandum of costs. To recover costs, the prevailing defendant must serve and file a memorandum of costs within 15 days after being served with written notice of entry of dismissal. CRC 3.1700(a)(1); *see* ***Fries v. Rite Aid Corp.*** (1st Dist.2009) 173 Cal.App.4th 182, 187 (noting that other deadlines in CRC 3.1700 do not apply to voluntary dismissals); *see, e.g.*, ***Sanabria v. Embrey*** (2d Dist.2001) 92 Cal.App.4th 422, 426 (D not permitted to recover costs because memorandum was untimely filed).

NOTE

The entry of dismissal is a prerequisite to a motion for costs under §1032(b). ***Boonyarit v. Payless Shoesource, Inc.*** *(2d Dist.2006) 145 Cal.App.4th 1188, 1192. If the defendant is dismissed from the suit but no order is entered, the defendant should file a proposed judgment of dismissal with its memorandum of costs. See id. at 1193-94. If an order of dismissal has been entered, however, no proposed judgment of dismissal needs to be filed. See* ***Fries****, 173 Cal.App.4th at 188.*

(2) Attorney fees.

(a) Fees fixed. If the prevailing defendant is entitled to statutory or contractual attorney fees in a fixed amount without the need for a court's determination, the fees must be claimed in the memorandum of costs. CRC 3.1702(e).

(b) Fees determined by court. If the court is required to determine whether a prevailing defendant is entitled to recover attorney fees or the amount of attorney fees that are recoverable, the prevailing defendant must file and serve a notice of motion for attorney fees within the time for filing a notice of appeal. *See* CRC 3.1702(b)(1). Generally, the defendant must file and serve the motion within 60 days (30 days in a limited civil case) after being served with either notice of entry of dismissal or a file-stamped copy of the dismissal. *See* CRC 3.1702(b)(1), 8.104(a)(1), (a)(2), 8.822(a)(1), (a)(2); ***Sanabria***, 92 Cal.App.4th at 429. If neither is served on the defendant, the defendant must file the motion within 180 days (90 days in a limited civil case) after entry of dismissal. *See* CRC 3.1702(b)(1), 8.104(a)(3), 8.822(a)(3). The time for filing and serving the motion is extended, however, if the appeal period was extended. *See* CRC 3.1702(b)(1), 8.108, 8.823.

§6. REVIEW

§6.1 By trial court. A party can ask the trial court to review an order of dismissal by filing one or more of the following:

1. Motion to vacate. A party who is adversely affected by a voluntary dismissal can file a motion to vacate the dismissal. *See, e.g.*, ***Gray v. Superior Ct.*** (1st Dist.1997) 52 Cal.App.4th 165, 169 (D filed motion to vacate arguing that trial had already commenced when motion to voluntarily dismiss was filed and that D had requested affirmative relief).

2. Motion to vacate under §473(b). A party who is adversely affected by a voluntary dismissal can file a motion to vacate the dismissal under CCP §473(b). *See* CCP §473(b); *see, e.g.*, ***State Farm Fire & Cas. Co. v. Pietak*** (3d Dist.2001) 90 Cal.App.4th 600, 615 (voluntary dismissal vacated under discretionary-relief provision of §473(b)); ***Romadka v. Hoge*** (6th Dist.1991) 232 Cal.App.3d 1231, 1237 (voluntary dismissal vacated under

mandatory-relief provision of §473(b)). One court has held that the mandatory-relief provision of §473(b) does not apply to voluntary dismissals. ***Huens v. Tatum*** (3d Dist.1997) 52 Cal.App.4th 259, 264-65. The court in ***Huens*** argued that the phrase "dismissal … taken against him or her" in §473(b) means that relief under that provision is available only for involuntary dismissals. ***Huens***, 52 Cal.App.4th at 264. The California Supreme Court disapproved of the ***Huens*** interpretation of §473(b) as it applies to a claim for discretionary relief under §473(b). ***Zamora v. Clayborn Contracting Grp.*** (2002) 28 Cal.4th 249, 256. For a discussion of discretionary and mandatory relief under §473(b), see "Motion to vacate under §473(b)," ch. 10-A, §9.1.1, p. 1109.

3. Action in equity to vacate. A party who is adversely affected by a voluntary dismissal can file an action to set aside the order on equitable grounds if extrinsic factors (e.g., fraud, mistake) prevented the party from presenting its case. *See, e.g.*, ***Heyman v. Franchise Mortg. Acceptance Corp.*** (4th Dist.2003) 107 Cal.App.4th 921, 925 (voluntary dismissal can be set aside if it was obtained through extrinsic fraud); *cf.* ***Aldrich v. San Fernando Valley Lumber Co.*** (2d Dist.1985) 170 Cal.App.3d 725, 736 (court has inherent power to set aside involuntary dismissal for extrinsic fraud or mistake).

§6.2 By appellate court.

1. Writ of mandate. Because the entering of a voluntary dismissal is considered a ministerial act, a party should be able to challenge a court's or clerk's refusal to enter a voluntary dismissal by a writ of mandate. *See* CCP §1085 (mandate may be issued to compel performance of an act that law specifically enjoins); ***Conservatorship of Martha P.*** (4th Dist.2004) 117 Cal.App.4th 857, 866 (when voluntary-dismissal section applies and is properly used by P, trial court has no discretion).

2. Direct appeal. A voluntary dismissal is not appealable because a party whose total demands are granted in a judicial proceeding has no right to appeal. ***Cook v. Stewart McKee & Co.*** (2d Dist.1945) 68 Cal.App.2d 758, 762. Because the order is entered on the plaintiff's request and leaves the defendant where it wanted to be after the action was filed (assuming the defendant did not seek affirmative relief), neither party has a right to appeal. *See* ***Rosen v. Robert P. Warmington Co.*** (4th Dist.1988) 201 Cal.App.3d 939, 943; ***Cook***, 68 Cal.App.2d at 762.

PRACTICE TIP

If a party wants to appeal an adverse ruling by the trial court, the party can file a voluntary dismissal with prejudice. Courts have allowed parties to expedite an appeal of an adverse ruling by voluntarily dismissing the case with prejudice. See, e.g., ***Stewart v. Colonial W. Agency, Inc.*** *(2d Dist.2001) 87 Cal.App.4th 1006, 1012 (party could appeal sanctions order after dismissing case with prejudice);* ***Ashland Chem. Co. v. Provence*** *(4th Dist.1982) 129 Cal.App.3d 790, 793 (party could appeal court's order of demurrer without leave to amend after dismissing case with prejudice). But if the case is voluntarily dismissed without prejudice, any adverse rulings will not be subject to review.* ***Gutkin v. University of S. Cal.*** *(2d Dist.2002) 101 Cal.App.4th 967, 975.*

E. INVOLUNTARY DISMISSAL—DELAY IN PROSECUTION

This subchapter discusses motions to involuntarily dismiss an action for delay in prosecution under CCP §§583.110-583.430. For a discussion of involuntary dismissals in other situations, see "Involuntary Dismissal—Other Grounds," ch. 10-F, p. 1180.

NOTE

Generally, the statutes governing a dismissal for delay in prosecution apply only to civil actions; they do not apply to special proceedings except to the extent that dismissal statutes are expressly incorporated into the special proceeding. CCP §583.120(a); see, e.g., ***People v. Evans*** *(1st Dist.2005) 132 Cal.App.4th 950, 956 (dismissal statutes not applicable to civil-commitment proceeding). A court can apply the dismissal statutes to a special proceeding, however, if doing so would not be inconsistent with the character of the proceeding or a statute governing the proceeding. CCP §583.120(b); e.g.,* ***Oskooi v. Fountain Valley Reg'l Hosp. & Med. Ctr.*** *(4th Dist.1996) 42 Cal.App.4th 233, 238-39 (because no statute permitted or prohibited dismissal of mandamus proceeding, it would not be inconsistent to apply dismissal statutes to mandamus). For example, the dismissal statutes would not apply to a special proceeding if doing so would permit delay rather than prevent it.* ***Oskooi****, 42 Cal.App.4th at 238.*

§1. GENERAL

§1.1 Purpose. The purpose of an involuntary dismissal for delay in prosecution is to allow a defendant to dismiss an action filed against it when the plaintiff has not diligently prosecuted the action. *See* ***Sagi Plumbing v. Chartered Constr. Corp.*** (2d Dist.2004) 123 Cal.App.4th 443, 447 (purpose of dismissal statutes is to promote timely prosecution and to protect Ds from prejudice from lost or stale evidence).

§1.2 Primary authority. CCP §§583.110-583.430; CRC 3.1340, 3.1342.

§1.3 Secondary authority. The following secondary sources are cited as authority in this subchapter:

- Weil & Brown, *California Practice Guide: Civil Procedure Before Trial* (CD-ROM ed. 2014) (referred to as Weil, *Civil Procedure Before Trial*).
- Witkin, *California Procedure* (5th ed. 2008 & Supp.2014) (referred to as Witkin, *Cal. Procedure*).
- Younger & Bradley, *Younger on California Motions* (2014-15) (referred to as Younger, *Cal. Motions*).

§1.4 Judicial Council form.

- CIV-120 (mandatory), notice of entry of dismissal and proof of service.

§2. OVERVIEW

§2.1 Actions subject to dismissal. A complaint, cross-complaint, or complaint in intervention is subject to an involuntary dismissal for delay in prosecution. *See* CCP §583.110(a).

NOTE

For ease of reference, this subchapter uses the terms "plaintiff" and "complaint" throughout to refer to the party and the action subject to dismissal.

§2.2 Deadlines for prosecution. Once a complaint is filed or is subject to retrial, the plaintiff must take certain actions within a specified time or face the possibility of a dismissal for delay in prosecution. Generally, to avoid a dismissal, the plaintiff must complete the following procedures within a specified time: (1) serve the summons and complaint, (2) file proof of service, (3) bring the action to trial, and (4) retry the action. If the plaintiff does not

take the required actions in the specified time, the plaintiff's inaction may support a discretionary or mandatory motion to dismiss, depending on the length of time that has passed since the complaint was filed or was subject to retrial. Chart 10-5, below, summarizes the actions and deadlines that will support a discretionary or mandatory motion to dismiss for delay in prosecution.

10-5. GROUNDS FOR DISMISSAL

	Action	Mandatory dismissal	Discretionary dismissal
1	Serve summons and complaint	3 years after action filed. See §4.1, p. 1162.	2 years after action filed. See §5.1, p. 1171.
2	File proof of service	3 years + 60 days after action filed. See §4.2, p. 1164.	Not applicable.
3	Bring action to trial	5 years after action filed. See §4.3, p. 1165.	2 years after action filed. See §5.1, p. 1171.
4	Retry action	3 years after specified events. See §4.4, p. 1170; §4.5, p. 1170; §4.6, p. 1171.	2 years after specified events. See §5.1, p. 1171.

§2.3 Dismissal without prejudice. Dismissals for delay in prosecution—both mandatory and discretionary—are granted without prejudice. ***Franklin Capital Corp. v. Wilson*** (4th Dist.2007) 148 Cal.App.4th 187, 214-15; *see* CCP §581(b)(4), (g). *Contra* ***Black v. Lukens*** (1st Dist.2009) No. A120828 (unpub.; 2-20-09) (court has discretion to dismiss with prejudice). An action that is dismissed without prejudice can be refiled as long as the statute of limitations has not expired. See "Without prejudice," ch. 10-D, §2.2.2, p. 1150. But because the dismissal statutes require a minimum of two years to pass before a motion to dismiss can be granted, most limitations periods for actions dismissed for delay in prosecution will have already expired. *See* Younger, *Cal. Motions*, §10:3; *see, e.g.*, CCP §335.1 (two-year statute of limitations for assault, battery, and negligence actions).

§3. EFFECT OF FAST-TRACK RULES

The Trial Court Delay Reduction Act (TCDRA) has had a significant impact on dismissals for delay in prosecution. Under the TCDRA, California's Judicial Council is given the mandate to adopt rules (commonly referred to as "fast-track rules") to timely dispose of cases. Gov. C. §68603(a). These rules are to be guided by the principle that litigation, from beginning to end, should require only the time reasonably necessary for pleadings, discovery, preparation, and court events, and that any additional time is delay that should be eliminated. *Id.*

State-wide implementation of the fast-track rules did not begin until July 1, 1992—long after the deadlines in the dismissal statutes for delay in prosecution were in place. *See* 2 Witkin, *Cal. Procedure*, Courts, §257. Many of the fast-track rules that have been implemented since 1992 govern the same procedures found in the dismissal statutes (e.g., serve summons and complaint, file proof of service, bring action to trial), but they impose shorter deadlines for completion. Chart 10-6, below, summarizes the actions and deadlines that are governed by the fast-track rules.

10-6. FAST-TRACK DEADLINES

	Action	Deadline
1	Serve summons and complaint	60 days after action filed. CRC 3.110(b).
2	File proof of service	60 days after action filed. *Id.*
3	Bring action to trial	2 years after action filed (with some exceptions). CRC 3.714(b).

To enforce the fast-track rules, courts are given the authority to impose sanctions, including dismissal, for noncompliance. Gov. C. §68608(b); *see* CCP §575.1(a) (courts can implement local rules to expedite court business),

§575.2(a) (courts can impose sanctions, including dismissal, for noncompliance with local rules); *see also* CCP §583.150 (dismissal statutes do not affect court's authority to dismiss for violation of local rule or Judicial Council rule). But the court's power to dismiss an action for violation of a fast-track rule is not absolute; it is restricted by the following limitations: (1) the noncompliance must have been caused by the party, not the attorney, and (2) no less severe sanction would be effective. ***Tliche v. Van Quathem*** (2d Dist.1998) 66 Cal.App.4th 1054, 1061-62; *see* CCP §575.2(b); Gov. C. §68608(b).

Despite these limitations on the court's power to dismiss, the practical effect of the fast-track rules is that most cases today conclude before any of the deadlines in the dismissal statutes are triggered. Younger, *Cal. Motions*, §10:4; *see, e.g.*, ***Chambers v. Dane*** (6th Dist.2008) No. H031986 (unpub.; 8-29-08) (action dismissed because complaint was not served within 60 days); ***Walker v. Ryan*** (4th Dist.2006) No. D048270 (unpub.; 8-31-06) (same). Although some cases may still be subject to the dismissal statutes, attorneys should be aware that the fast-track rules could trigger an earlier dismissal for delay in prosecution. *See* Younger, *Cal. Motions*, §10:4.

§4. GROUNDS – MANDATORY DISMISSAL

A court must dismiss a complaint for delay in prosecution if any of the following grounds is established:

§4.1 No service of summons & complaint. A court must dismiss a complaint if (1) the plaintiff did not serve the summons and complaint within three years after the action commenced and (2) the defendant has not made a general appearance. *See* CCP §§583.210(a), 583.220, 583.250(a)(2), (b).

NOTE

A motion to dismiss under CCP §583.210(a) is commonly made in conjunction with a motion to quash service. See, e.g., ***Tresway Aero, Inc. v. Superior Ct.*** *(1971) 5 Cal.3d 431, 434 (after three-year deadline passed, D filed motion to quash service and dismiss action). See "Motion to Quash Service of Summons," ch. 4-G, p. 389.*

1. No service within 3 years. To obtain a mandatory dismissal under §583.210(a), the defendant must establish that the plaintiff did not serve the summons and complaint on the defendant within three years after the action commenced.

(1) No service. Service under §583.210(a) consists of serving the summons and complaint. *See* ***Biss v. Bohr*** (4th Dist.1995) 40 Cal.App.4th 1246, 1251. Service does not require proof or the return of service. *See id.* at 1250-51 (noting that serving and returning summons are now two distinct requirements with different time periods). To prevent dismissal for lack of service, the service must be valid. *See* ***Dill v. Berquist Constr. Co.*** (4th Dist.1994) 24 Cal.App.4th 1426, 1433. A defendant's actual knowledge of an action is not sufficient to prevent dismissal for lack of service. ***Kuchins v. Hawes*** (1st Dist.1990) 226 Cal.App.3d 535, 540. For the requirements of valid service, see "Joining the Defendant—Service of Process," ch. 3-H, p. 295.

NOTE

Although courts have viewed a complaint in intervention to be substantively as well as procedurally the same as a complaint, service of a complaint in intervention does not operate as effective service of the plaintiff's complaint for purposes of avoiding dismissal. See, e.g., ***Kuchins***, *226 Cal.App.3d at 539-40 (P could not rely on service of complaint in intervention to avoid dismissal of P's complaint for lack of service).*

(2) Three-year deadline. The summons and complaint must be served on the defendant within three years after the action commenced. For a discussion of how to calculate prospective deadlines, see "Prospective deadlines," ch. 1-G, §6.1, p. 70.

(a) First day. The three-year deadline begins to run from the date the action commences. CCP §583.210(a). See "Count forward," ch. 1-G, §6.1.2, p. 70.

[1] Date action commences – complaint & cross-complaint. The date an action in a complaint or cross-complaint commences is the date the complaint or cross-complaint is filed. *See* CCP §583.210(a) (complaint); ***Tomales Bay Oyster Corp. v. Superior Ct.*** (1950) 35 Cal.2d 389, 393 (cross-complaint); *see also* CCP §583.110(b) (term "complaint" includes cross-complaint).

[a] Effect of amending complaint. If the plaintiff amends the complaint, the amendment may restart the date the action commences. If the amendment relates back to the original complaint, the action is still considered to have commenced on the date the original complaint was filed. *See* ***Austin v. Massachusetts Bonding & Ins.*** (1961) 56 Cal.2d 596, 602 (amended complaint relates back when D is named as Doe D in original complaint but is later identified by true name in amended complaint); ***Hennessey's Tavern, Inc. v. American Air Filter Co.*** (2d Dist.1988) 204 Cal.App.3d 1351, 1359 (same). If the amendment does not relate back, the action commences on the date the amended complaint is filed. ***Barrington v. A.H. Robins Co.*** (1985) 39 Cal.3d 146, 150. For a discussion of the relation-back doctrine, see "Avoiding limitations – relation back," ch. 3-C, §6.3, p. 234.

[b] Effect of amending cross-complaint. Amending a cross-complaint has the same effect as amending a complaint. *See* ***Perez v. Grajales*** (6th Dist.2008) 169 Cal.App.4th 580, 585-86.

[2] Date action commences – complaint in intervention. The date an action in a complaint in intervention commences is the date the original complaint was filed—not the date the complaint in intervention was filed. ***Bright v. American Termite Control Co.*** (2d Dist.1990) 220 Cal.App.3d 1464, 1469; ***State Comp. Ins. Fund v. Selma Trailer & Mfg.*** (5th Dist.1989) 210 Cal.App.3d 740, 755.

(b) Excluded days. In calculating the three-year deadline to serve, certain days are statutorily excluded from the calculation. CCP §583.240. The statutory exceptions are exclusive; courts cannot establish additional exceptions. *See id.* §583.250(b); ***Shipley v. Sugita*** (1st Dist.1996) 50 Cal.App.4th 320, 324; *see, e.g.*, ***Dale v. ITT Life Ins.*** (4th Dist.1989) 207 Cal.App.3d 495, 499 (days excluded under CCP §583.340 do not apply to §583.240). The days that cannot be counted in calculating the deadline to serve are the following:

[1] Days defendant not amenable. Any days when the defendant was not amenable to the court's process cannot be counted. CCP §583.240(a). "Amenable" refers to whether the defendant is subject to being served (i.e., whether the court has personal jurisdiction over the defendant). ***Watts v. Crawford*** (1995) 10 Cal.4th 743, 755. See "Joining the Defendant—Personal Jurisdiction," ch. 3-G, p. 283.

[2] Days action stayed. Any days when the action was stayed and the stay affected service cannot be counted. CCP §583.240(b); *see, e.g.*, ***Highland Stucco & Lime, Inc. v. Superior Ct.*** (2d Dist.1990) 222 Cal.App.3d 637, 644 (stay that prevented service on D until it was lifted "affected service").

[3] Days validity of service challenged. Any days when the parties were involved in litigation over the validity of service cannot be counted. CCP §583.240(c). The validity of service must have been challenged within the three-year deadline for tolling to occur. *See* ***Graf v. Gaslight*** (2d Dist.1990) 225 Cal.App.3d 291, 296, *disapproved on other grounds*, ***Watts v. Crawford*** (1995) 10 Cal.4th 743; ***Dale***, 207 Cal.App.3d at 499.

[4] Days service was impossible. Any days when service, for any other reason, was impossible, impracticable, or futile due to causes beyond the plaintiff's control cannot be counted. CCP §583.240(d). For example, not discovering relevant facts or evidence is not a cause beyond the plaintiff's control. *Id.* The excuse of impossibility, impracticability, or futility should be strictly construed in light of the need to give the defendant adequate notice to preserve evidence. 17 Cal. Law Revision Comm'n Rep. (1984) p. 933. The following are some examples of how the impossibility exception has been applied:

- Service was not impossible when the plaintiff's attorney represented to him that the defendant had been properly served. ***Shipley***, 50 Cal.App.4th at 324.
- Service was impossible when the court had dismissed the action. ***Graf***, 225 Cal.App.3d at 296-97.

• Service was impossible when the court had issued an order prohibiting the plaintiff from serving the defendant. ***Highland Stucco & Lime***, 222 Cal.App.3d at 644.

• Service was not impossible when the plaintiff was incompetent and thus personally unable to serve the defendant but no reason was given for why a guardian or guardian ad litem could not serve the defendant. ***Tzolov v. International Jet Leasing, Inc.*** (6th Dist.1989) 214 Cal.App.3d 325, 328 n.5.

(c) Last day.

[1] Generally. In calculating the three-year deadline, the last day to serve the summons and complaint is generally three years from the date the complaint was filed, plus any additional days that were tolled. See "Excluded days," §4.1.1(2)(b), p. 1163; "Determine last day," ch. 1-F, §5.1.5, p. 55. The last day may be different, however, if it was extended by the parties' agreement.

[2] Effect of agreed extension. The parties can agree to extend the time to serve the summons and complaint beyond the three-year deadline. CCP §583.230. The agreement must be made either by written stipulation or by oral agreement in open court. *Id.* The stipulation or agreement does not need to be filed, but it must be brought to the court's attention. *Id.* §583.230(a). If the stipulation or agreement is made orally in open court, it must be entered in the court's minutes or recorded in a transcript. *Id.* §583.230(b).

(d) Effect of ADR.

[1] Arbitration. Submitting an action to judicial arbitration does not suspend the running of the three-year deadline. *See* CCP §1141.17; ***Hattersley v. American Nucleonics Corp.*** (2d Dist.1992) 3 Cal.App.4th 397, 400.

[2] Mediation. Submitting an action to mediation does not suspend the running of the three-year deadline. *See* CCP §1775.7.

(3) No general appearance. To obtain a mandatory dismissal under CCP §583.210(a), the defendant must establish that it has not made a general appearance in the action within the three-year period. *See* CCP §583.220; ***Brookview Condo. Owners' Ass'n v. Heltzer Enters.-Brookview*** (4th Dist.1990) 218 Cal.App.3d 502, 509. If the defendant has made a general appearance within the three-year period, a mandatory dismissal cannot be granted. ***Brookview Condo.***, 218 Cal.App.3d at 509. If the defendant makes a general appearance after the three-year period has passed, the defendant still has a mandatory right to dismiss for lack of service. *Id.* See "General appearance," ch. 3-G, §5.1.1, p. 285.

NOTE

A party who files an answer to a complaint in intervention does not make a general appearance for purposes of the plaintiff's complaint. See, e.g., ***Kuchins****, 226 Cal.App.3d at 540-41 (P could not avoid dismissal of complaint by arguing that Ds' answers to complaint in intervention amounted to general appearance);* ***Duckett v. Superior Ct.*** *(2d Dist.1989) 207 Cal.App.3d 1419, 1424 (same).*

§4.2 No proof of service filed. A court must dismiss a complaint if (1) the plaintiff did not file proof of service of summons within 60 days after the plaintiff was required to serve the defendant and (2) the defendant has not made a general appearance. *See* CCP §§583.210(b), 583.220, 583.250(a)(2), (b); ***Biss v. Bohr*** (4th Dist.1995) 40 Cal.App.4th 1246, 1249.

1. No proof of service. To obtain a mandatory dismissal under §583.210(b), the defendant must establish that the plaintiff did not file proof of service within 60 days after the plaintiff was required to serve the defendant—that is, no later than three years and 60 days after the complaint was filed. ***Biss***, 40 Cal.App.4th at 1251; *see* CCP §583.210(b). The deadline for filing proof of service is calculated in the same manner as the deadline for serving the summons and complaint. See "Three-year deadline," §4.1.1(2), p. 1162. For a discussion of filing proof of service, see "Proof of Service," ch. 3-H, §9, p. 318.

NOTE

Although CCP §583.110(f) defines "service" to include the return of summons, proving service by returning summons is no longer possible under the current procedures. Weil, Civil Procedure Before Trial, ¶11:54.

2. No general appearance. To obtain a mandatory dismissal under §583.210(b), the defendant must establish that it has not made a general appearance in the action within three years and 60 days. *See* CCP §583.220; ***Biss***, 40 Cal.App.4th at 1251; ***Wong v. Armstrong World Indus.*** (1st Dist.1991) 232 Cal.App.3d 1032, 1035. If the defendant makes a general appearance during that time period, the defendant no longer has a mandatory right to dismiss. ***Wong***, 232 Cal.App.3d at 1035; *see* ***Biss***, 40 Cal.App.4th at 1251. See "General appearance," ch. 3-G, §5.1.1, p. 285.

§4.3 No trial after action commenced. A court must grant a motion to dismiss if the plaintiff did not bring an action to trial within five years after the action commenced against the defendant. *See* CCP §§583.310, 583.360.

1. No trial. To obtain a mandatory dismissal under CCP §583.310, the defendant must establish that the action was not brought to trial.

(1) Generally. In the traditional sense, an action is brought to trial when (1) in a bench trial, the first witness is sworn in, or (2) in a jury trial, the jury is impaneled. *E.g.*, ***Hartman v. Santamarina*** (1982) 30 Cal.3d 762, 764-65 (action was brought to trial when jury was impaneled, even though it was discharged soon after). But for an action to be effectively brought to trial under §583.310, it must be contested. ***Lakkees v. Superior Ct.*** (4th Dist.1990) 222 Cal.App.3d 531, 536-37; ***Langan v. McCorkle*** (2d Dist.1969) 276 Cal.App.2d 805, 808-09, *disapproved on other grounds*, ***Brunzell Constr. Co. v. Wagner*** (1970) 2 Cal.3d 545. Thus, the swearing in of a witness at an uncontested hearing does not prevent a dismissal. *See, e.g.*, ***Lakkees***, 222 Cal.App.3d at 536 (wife's testimony at uncontested status proceeding was not sufficient to prevent dismissal); ***Langan***, 276 Cal.App.2d at 808-09 (P's testimony at hearing on entry of default was not sufficient to prevent dismissal). But a hearing held after the defendant files an answer is a trial, even if the defendant does not appear. ***Briley v. Sukoff*** (4th Dist.1979) 98 Cal.App.3d 405, 410.

NOTE

Once the trial has commenced, the statute is satisfied regardless of whether the trial proceeds immediately and continuously to a resolution. ***In re Marriage of Dunmore (3d Dist.1996) 45 Cal.App.4th 1372, 1377.***

(2) Partial trial. An action can also be brought to trial when a "partial" trial has taken place. ***In re Marriage of Macfarlane & Lang*** (1st Dist.1992) 8 Cal.App.4th 247, 254. A partial trial occurs when a determination of a contested issue of fact or law brings the action to a stage where a court can make a final disposition. *See* ***Berri v. Superior Ct.*** (1955) 43 Cal.2d 856, 859-60; ***Sagi Plumbing v. Chartered Constr. Corp.*** (2d Dist.2004) 123 Cal.App.4th 443, 448. For example, a court's order granting summary judgment or sustaining a demurrer without leave to amend constitutes a trial sufficient to prevent a dismissal. ***Berri***, 43 Cal.2d at 860-61 (demurrer); ***Southern Pac. Co. v. Seaboard Mills*** (2d Dist.1962) 207 Cal.App.2d 97, 104 (summary judgment). But an order granting a summary adjudication or sustaining a demurrer with leave to amend is not a trial for purposes of preventing a dismissal. ***King v. State*** (3d Dist.1970) 11 Cal.App.3d 307, 311 (partial summary judgment, now summary adjudication); ***Ross v. George Pepperdine Found.*** (2d Dist.1959) 174 Cal.App.2d 135, 139 (demurrer), *disapproved on other grounds*, ***Brunzell Constr. Co. v. Wagner*** (1970) 2 Cal.3d 545.

2. Five-year deadline. To obtain a mandatory dismissal under CCP §583.310, the defendant must establish that the action was not brought to trial within five years after the action commenced. For a discussion of how to calculate prospective deadlines, see "Prospective deadlines," ch. 1-F, §5.1, p. 52.

(1) First day. The five-year deadline begins to run from the date the action commences. CCP §583.310. See "Count forward," ch. 1-F, §5.1.2, p. 53. An action commences under §583.310 like an action under §583.210(a). *See* ***Brumley v. FDCC Cal., Inc.*** (1st Dist.2007) 156 Cal.App.4th 312, 318. See "First day," §4.1.1(2)(a), p. 1162.

(2) Excluded days. After the action has commenced, certain intervening days are statutorily excluded from the calculation. CCP §583.340. The excluded days are the following:

(a) Days jurisdiction suspended. Any days when the court's jurisdiction to try the action was suspended cannot be counted. CCP §583.340(a); *see, e.g.*, ***Gordon's Cabinet Shop v. State Comp. Ins. Fund*** (4th Dist.1999) 74 Cal.App.4th 33, 40-41 (court's jurisdiction not suspended when coordination petition filed); ***Bergin v. Portman*** (2d Dist.1983) 141 Cal.App.3d 23, 26 (court's jurisdiction suspended when D filed appeal); ***Herring v. Peterson*** (3d Dist.1981) 116 Cal.App.3d 608, 616 (court's jurisdiction suspended when D died). Tolling for suspended jurisdiction is automatic and not subject to a reasonable-diligence restriction. ***Ocean Servs. v. Ventura Port Dist.*** (2d Dist.1993) 15 Cal.App.4th 1762, 1775.

(b) Days action stayed. Any days when prosecution or trial of the action was stayed or enjoined cannot be counted. CCP §583.340(b); *see* ***Holland v. Dave Altman's R.V. Ctr.*** (2d Dist.1990) 222 Cal.App.3d 477, 482 ("stay" means action is indefinitely postponed pending occurrence of some designated event). For these days to be excluded, the entire action must be stayed, not just part of the action (e.g., discovery). ***Bruns v. E-Commerce Exch., Inc.*** (2011) 51 Cal.4th 717, 730. If only part of the action is stayed, a party can try to exclude those days by showing that the impossibility or impracticability exception applies (i.e., the partial stay made bringing the action to trial impossible or impracticable). *Id.* See "Days when bringing action to trial was impossible," §4.3.2(2)(c), this page.

(c) Days when bringing action to trial was impossible. Any days when bringing the action to trial was impossible, impracticable, or futile cannot be counted. CCP §583.340(c). This tolling period is generally referred to as the impossibility or impracticability exception. *See* ***Perez v. Grajales*** (6th Dist.2008) 169 Cal.App.4th 580, 590 (impossibility exception); ***De Santiago v. D&G Plumbing, Inc.*** (4th Dist.2007) 155 Cal.App.4th 365, 372 (impracticability exception). Unlike the impossibility exception under §583.240(d) (impossibility in serving the summons and complaint), the impossibility exception under §583.340(c) is to be construed liberally, consistent with the policy favoring trial on the merits. *See* ***Perez***, 169 Cal.App.4th at 590; 17 Cal. Law Revision Comm'n Rep. (1984) p. 918. In determining whether the impossibility exception applies, courts have crafted a three-part test. Under this test, the plaintiff has the burden to prove (1) a circumstance of impossibility, (2) a causal connection between that circumstance and the plaintiff's reason for not bringing the action to trial, and (3) the plaintiff's reasonable diligence in trying to bring the action to trial. ***Perez***, 169 Cal.App.4th at 594; ***De Santiago***, 155 Cal.App.4th at 372; ***Tamburina v. Combined Ins.*** (3d Dist.2007) 147 Cal.App.4th 323, 336.

[1] Circumstance of impossibility. For the impossibility exception to apply, the plaintiff must prove a circumstance of impossibility. ***De Santiago***, 155 Cal.App.4th at 372; ***Tamburina***, 147 Cal.App.4th at 329; *see* ***Perez***, 169 Cal.App.4th at 590. A circumstance of impossibility does not include delays caused by ordinary incidents like the disposition of a demurrer, an amendment of pleadings, or the normal time it takes to get a place on the court's calendar or to secure a jury trial. ***Bruns***, 51 Cal.4th at 731. The circumstance must be beyond the ordinary delays in the course of litigation and beyond the plaintiff's control. *See* ***Tamburina***, 147 Cal.App.4th at 329 (ordinary periods away from practice for illness and vacation should not be excluded); ***Sanchez v. City of L.A.*** (2d Dist.2003) 109 Cal.App.4th 1262, 1273 (P must have no control over circumstances); ***Sierra-Nev. Memorial-Miners Hosp., Inc. v. Superior Ct.*** (3d Dist.1990) 217 Cal.App.3d 464, 472 (every time period during which P does not have power to bring action should not be excluded); ***Bank of Am. Nat'l Trust & Sav. Ass'n v. Superior Ct.*** (5th Dist.1988) 200 Cal.App.3d 1000, 1014 (impossibility arises when it would be unreasonably difficult or expensive to bring action to trial because of circumstances not caused by P).

[a] Impossibility found. Courts have found that the following circumstances made it impossible to bring an action to trial:

- The death of the plaintiff. ***Dung Mahn Pham v. Wagner Litho Mach. Co.*** (4th Dist.1985) 172 Cal.App.3d 966, 972-73.

- The time during which a writ petition was pending. ***New W. Fed. S&L Ass'n v. Superior Ct.*** (5th Dist.1990) 223 Cal.App.3d 1145, 1152; *see also* ***Dowling v. Farmers Ins. Exch.*** (2d Dist.2012) 208 Cal.App.4th 685, 699 (fact that writ proceeding and current proceeding do not involve same parties does not preclude finding of impracticability).

- The time needed to assign a new judge after the original judge was challenged under CCP §170.6. ***Hartman***, 30 Cal.3d at 768.

- The time during which a default judgment was in effect. ***Howard v. Thrifty Drug & Disc. Stores*** (1995) 10 Cal.4th 424, 438.

- A reasonable amount of time between entry of default and default judgment. *Id.* at 438-39; *see, e.g.,* ***Hughes v. Kimble*** (2d Dist.1992) 5 Cal.App.4th 59, 70-71 (three-year delay between entry of default and default judgment was unreasonably long and not sufficient to toll five-year period).

- The time during which a settlement agreement was in effect between the parties. ***Brown & Bryant, Inc. v. Hartford Acc. & Indem. Co.*** (5th Dist.1994) 24 Cal.App.4th 247, 256-57; *see* ***Canal St., Ltd. v. Sorich*** (1st Dist.2000) 77 Cal.App.4th 602, 608 (settlement agreement does not have to be reduced to judgment to toll period).

- The time during which the plaintiff's attorney was ill. ***Him v. Superior Ct.*** (2d Dist.1986) 184 Cal.App.3d 35, 37-39 (statute was tolled for 42 days because of attorney's illness, which occurred within last six months before five-year deadline).

NOTE

In determining whether an attorney's illness is considered a circumstance of impossibility, courts have generally focused on the following factors: the length of the illness, whether the attorney is the sole attorney on the case, and when the illness occurred. See ***Sierra-Nev.***, *217 Cal.App.3d at 473. General illnesses that occur within the course of a proceeding are expected and are already provided for in the five-year period. Id. at 472. One court has held that the death or illness of a defendant's attorney does not impose the same impediment to bringing an action to trial as the death or illness of the plaintiff's attorney.* ***Sanchez***, *109 Cal.App.4th at 1273.*

[b] Impossibility not found. Courts have found that the following circumstances did not make it impossible to bring an action to trial:

- The time during which the plaintiff was ill. ***Singelyn v. Superior Ct.*** (2d Dist.1976) 62 Cal.App.3d 972, 974-75.

- The plaintiff's mistake in choosing a correct trial date. ***Cannon v. City of Novato*** (1st Dist.1985) 167 Cal.App.3d 216, 222.

- The court clerk's setting of a trial date beyond the five-year period. ***Central Mut. Ins. v. Executive Motor Home Sales, Inc.*** (2d Dist.1983) 143 Cal.App.3d 791, 795.

[2] Causal connection. For the impossibility exception to apply, the plaintiff must prove that the claimed circumstance was the cause of the impossibility. ***Tamburina***, 147 Cal.App.4th at 333; ***New W. Fed. S&L***, 223 Cal.App.3d at 1155-56. This can be established by showing that the claimed circumstance made it impossible, impracticable, or futile to either (1) bring the case to trial within five years or (2) move the case toward trial

(i.e., when the claimed circumstance causes the plaintiff to lose a substantial portion of the five-year period). ***Tamburina***, 147 Cal.App.4th at 335; *e.g.*, ***Sierra-Nev.***, 217 Cal.App.3d at 473-74 (attorney's illness did not cause impracticability because other attorney on case could have moved case toward trial). If a period of impossibility arises, the period must be tolled even if there is plenty of time remaining for trial after the period is over. ***New W. Fed. S&L***, 223 Cal.App.3d at 1155.

[3] Reasonable diligence. For the impossibility exception to apply, the plaintiff must prove it acted with reasonable diligence in bringing the case to trial. ***Bruns***, 51 Cal.4th at 730-31; ***De Santiago***, 155 Cal.App.4th at 372; ***Tamburina***, 147 Cal.App.4th at 336. The duty of diligence applies at all stages of the proceeding and increases as the five-year deadline approaches. ***Tamburina***, 147 Cal.App.4th at 336. The exercise of reasonable diligence includes (1) keeping track of all pertinent dates, (2) monitoring the file to prevent filing, scheduling, or calendaring errors, and (3) keeping the court aware of whether the five-year deadline is approaching. *See* ***Howard***, 10 Cal.4th at 434 (burden is on P to keep track of relevant dates and alert court to approaching deadlines); *see, e.g.*, ***De Santiago***, 155 Cal.App.4th at 374-75 (P did not keep court aware of approaching deadline); ***Sanchez***, 109 Cal.App.4th at 1270 (Ps did not keep track of court dates and did not keep court aware of approaching deadline); ***Wilcox v. Ford*** (2d Dist.1988) 206 Cal.App.3d 1170, 1175 (P did not keep track of court dates). As the five-year deadline approaches, the plaintiff has the duty to take whatever measures are available to accelerate the trial of the case before the five-year period expires, including bringing a motion to advance the trial. ***De Santiago***, 155 Cal.App.4th at 374. If the plaintiff has the means to bring a matter to trial before the deadline by filing a motion to advance but does not do so, the plaintiff cannot later claim impossibility. *Id.* at 375; ***Sanchez***, 109 Cal.App.4th at 1274.

(d) Days in ADR.

[1] Judicial arbitration. Generally, submitting an action to judicial arbitration does not suspend the running of the five-year deadline. CCP §1141.17(a). The five-year deadline may be tolled, however, if (1) the action is submitted to or remains in judicial arbitration within six months before the five-year deadline would expire or (2) a trial de novo is requested after arbitration.

[a] Six months before deadline expires. If an action is submitted to or remains in judicial arbitration within six months before the five-year deadline would expire, the deadline is tolled for the period beginning four years and six months after the plaintiff filed the action to the date a trial de novo is filed under CCP §1141.20. CCP §1141.17(b). The beginning of the tolling period—four years and six months after the complaint was filed—applies regardless of whether the case was sent to arbitration before or after that date. *See, e.g.*, ***Lazelle v. Lovelady*** (5th Dist.1985) 171 Cal.App.3d 34, 45 (tolling period began on May 27, 1983, four years and six months after complaint was filed, even though case was sent to arbitration on Nov. 22, 1983). The tolling period under §1141.17 is the exclusive means to suspend the running of the five-year period for judicial arbitration. *E.g.*, ***Dae Sung Lee v. Moo Yeol Park*** (2d Dist.1996) 43 Cal.App.4th 305, 309 (time spent selecting arbitrator that was outside statutory tolling period could not be counted); ***Drummond v. Murata*** (2d Dist.1991) 227 Cal.App.3d 44, 49 (additional six-month extension in CCP §583.350 did not apply to case submitted to judicial arbitration).

EXAMPLE

P files a complaint on January 1, 2009. The case is sent to judicial arbitration on December 1, 2012, and an arbitration award is entered on July 1, 2013 (five months before five-year deadline would expire). A trial de novo is requested on August 1, 2013. Because the case was in arbitration less than six months before the five-year deadline would expire (January 1, 2014), the deadline is tolled for 60 days for the period running from June 1, 2013 (four years and six months from date complaint was filed) until August 1, 2013 (date trial de novo was requested). After adding the tolling period to the original five-year deadline, the new deadline to bring the action to trial is March 1, 2014.

[b] Days excluded after request for trial de novo. If a trial de novo is requested after arbitration, the five-year deadline may be tolled from the date the trial de novo was requested until the date of trial if (1) the plaintiff informed the court of the date when the five-year deadline would expire and requested an earlier trial setting and (2) the court does not properly recalendar the case. ***Howard***, 10 Cal.4th at 435. This tolling period derives not from §1141.17 but from the court's duty under §1141.20 to recalendar a case, if possible, in the order of priority it held before arbitration or to give the case civil priority on the next calendar setting. ***Howard***, 10 Cal.4th at 435; *see* CCP §1141.20(b).

[2] Mediation. Generally, submitting an action to mediation does not suspend the running of the five-year deadline. CCP §1775.7(a). But if an action is submitted to or remains in mediation within six months before the five-year deadline would expire, the deadline is tolled for the period beginning four years and six months after the plaintiff filed the action and ending when a statement of nonagreement is filed under CCP §1775.9. *Id.* §1775.7(b). The beginning of the tolling period—four years and six months after the action was filed—applies regardless of whether the case was sent to mediation before or after that date. *E.g.*, ***Gonzalez v. County of L.A.*** (2d Dist.2004) 122 Cal.App.4th 1124, 1129-30 (tolling period began on Nov. 14, 2002, four years and six months after complaint was filed, even though case was sent to mediation on Feb. 26, 2003).

(3) Last day. In calculating the five-year deadline, the last day to bring an action to trial is generally five years from the date the complaint was filed plus any additional days that were tolled. See "Excluded days," §4.3.2(2), p. 1166; "Determine last day," ch. 1-F, §5.1.5, p. 55. The last day may be different, however, if it was extended by the parties' agreement or if an event that tolled or extended the period to bring the action to trial ended within the last six months of the five-year period.

(a) Effect of agreed extension. The parties can agree to extend the time for bringing an action to trial beyond the five-year deadline. CCP §583.330. The agreement must be made either by written stipulation or by oral agreement in open court. *Id.*; *see, e.g.*, ***Wright v. Groom Trucking Co.*** (1st Dist.1962) 206 Cal.App.2d 485, 492 (pretrial-conference order setting case beyond five-year deadline was not valid written stipulation extending time). See "Effect of agreed extension," §4.1.1(2)(c)[2], p. 1164. The agreement can be made before or after the five-year period has expired. *See, e.g.*, ***Estate of Thatcher*** (2d Dist.1953) 120 Cal.App.2d 811, 814 (written stipulation was made after five-year period expired). To extend the five-year deadline, the agreement must either expressly extend the time of trial to a date beyond the five-year deadline or expressly waive the right to a dismissal. ***J.C. Penney Co. v. Superior Ct.*** (1959) 52 Cal.2d 666, 669; ***Sanchez***, 109 Cal.App.4th at 1269 n.3; *see, e.g.*, ***Anderson v. Erwyn*** (2d Dist.1966) 247 Cal.App.2d 503, 506-07 (stipulation to remove matter from calendar and reset at mutually convenient time did not expressly extend deadline or waive right to dismissal). Agreements that merely extend the time for trial within the five-year period are not sufficient to extend the five-year deadline. ***J.C. Penney***, 52 Cal.2d at 669; *e.g.*, ***Sanchez***, 109 Cal.App.4th at 1269 n.3 (stipulation extending trial date for three months was not effective to extend deadline because it was not beyond original five-year period); *see* ***Brown & Bryant***, 24 Cal.App.4th at 255 n.10. The parties' agreement to extend time can be for an indefinite period or until a specific date.

[1] Indefinite extension. Extensions for an indefinite period may or may not be effective, depending on when the event that terminates the indefinite extension occurs.

[a] Before five-year deadline expires. If an event that terminates the indefinite extension occurs before the five-year deadline expires, the extension is not effective to extend the deadline. *E.g.*, ***Gentry v. Nielsen*** (3d Dist.1981) 123 Cal.App.3d 27, 33 (stipulation extending time to file answer indefinitely did not extend deadline because answer was filed two years before five-year period would expire; if answer had been filed after five-year period expired, stipulation would have been effective). But if the terminating event occurs within six months of the expiration of the five-year deadline, the party may be entitled to a six-month extension under CCP §583.350. See "Effect of tolling or extension ending within six months of deadline," §4.3.2(3)(b), p. 1170.

[b] After five-year deadline expires. If an event that terminates the indefinite extension has not occurred by the time the five-year deadline expires, the extension is effective to extend the deadline. *See, e.g.*, ***Wheeler v. Payless Super Drug Stores*** (5th Dist.1987) 193 Cal.App.3d 1292, 1302 (open-ended

extension given to D to file answer was sufficient to extend deadline to prosecute indefinitely; terminating event—notice of intent to seek default—had not occurred when D brought motion to dismiss); ***Imperial Ins. v. California Cas. Indem. Exch.*** (1st Dist.1984) 158 Cal.App.3d 540, 548 (stipulation extending deadline indefinitely was sufficient to extend deadline; terminating event—motion to advance—had not occurred when D brought motion to dismiss). *But see* ***Waxman v. Boren, Elperin, Howard & Sloan*** (2d Dist.1990) 221 Cal.App.3d 519, 526 (if open-ended extension to file answer is given to benefit P and not D, P still has to be reasonably diligent in bringing action to trial; D could bring motion to dismiss after five-year deadline expired even though no answer was filed). An indefinite extension will not be effective, however, for the entire future. *See* ***Chapin v. Superior Ct.*** (5th Dist.1965) 234 Cal.App.2d 571, 574-75. Courts will impose a reasonable time requirement on indefinite extensions that go beyond the five-year deadline. *Id.* at 575.

[2] Specific extension. An extension that states a specific date beyond the five-year deadline is effective to extend the deadline to that date. *See* ***Obergfell v. Obergfell*** (4th Dist.1955) 134 Cal.App.2d 541, 544. If the action is not brought to trial by that specific date, the action can be dismissed. *See id.*

(b) Effect of tolling or extension ending within six months of deadline.

[1] Generally. When an event that tolls or extends the five-year deadline ends and leaves the plaintiff with less than six months to bring the action to trial before the original five-year deadline (e.g., stay was lifted four years and seven months after complaint was filed), the plaintiff will generally be given six months to bring the action to trial beginning when the tolling or extension period ends (e.g., six months from the date the stay was lifted). CCP §583.350; *see, e.g.,* ***New W. Fed. S&L***, 223 Cal.App.3d at 1148-49 (six months should have started to run from day stay ended, not from day original five-year period ended). *But see* ***Him***, 184 Cal.App.3d at 38 (court added period that was tolled to end of original five-year deadline, then added six-month extension to end of that period).

[2] Exception – not applicable to judicial arbitration. The six-month extension under §583.350 does not apply when an action is tolled under §1141.17 for judicial arbitration. ***Drummond***, 227 Cal.App.3d at 49. The tolling period under §1141.17 is the exclusive means to suspend the running of the five-year period for an action submitted to judicial arbitration. ***Drummond***, 227 Cal.App.3d at 49. See "Judicial arbitration," §4.3.2(2)(d)[1], p. 1168.

§4.4 No retrial after mistrial or hung jury. A court must grant a motion to dismiss under CCP §583.320(a)(1) if the defendant establishes all of the following:

1. New trial granted. The defendant must establish that a new trial was granted because of a mistrial or hung jury. CCP §583.320(a)(1).

2. No retrial within three years. The defendant must establish that the plaintiff did not bring the action to trial within three years after the court entered its order declaring a mistrial or hung jury. CCP §583.320(a)(1).

(1) No trial. See "No trial," §4.3.1, p. 1165.

(2) Three-year deadline. The three-year deadline under §583.320(a)(1) is calculated in almost the same manner as the five-year deadline under §583.310. *See* CCP §583.330 (applies to actions brought to trial under article 3), §583.340 (same), §583.350 (same). See "Five-year deadline," §4.3.2, p. 1165. The only difference is that the three-year deadline begins to run from the date the court entered its order declaring a mistrial or hung jury, not from the date the action commenced. *Compare* CCP §583.310 (trial must be brought within five years after action commenced) *with id.* §583.320(a)(1) (retrial must be brought within three years after order declaring mistrial or hung jury is entered).

§4.5 No retrial after judgment & no appeal. A court must grant a motion to dismiss under CCP §583.320(a)(2) if the defendant establishes all of the following:

1. New trial granted. The defendant must establish that a new trial was granted after the judgment. CCP §583.320(a)(2).

2. No appeal after judgment. The defendant must establish that no appeal was taken after the judgment. CCP §583.320(a)(2).

3. No retrial within three years. The defendant must establish that the plaintiff did not bring the action to trial within three years after the court entered its order granting the new trial. CCP §583.320(a)(2).

(1) No trial. See "No trial," §4.3.1, p. 1165.

(2) Three-year deadline. The three-year deadline under §583.320(a)(2) is calculated in almost the same manner as the five-year deadline under §583.310. *See* CCP §583.330 (applies to actions brought to trial under article 3), §583.340 (same), §583.350 (same). See "Five-year deadline," §4.3.2, p. 1165. The only difference is that the three-year deadline begins to run from the date the court entered its order granting a new trial, not from the date the action commenced. *Compare* CCP §583.310 (trial must be brought within five years after action commenced) *with id.* §583.320(a)(2) (retrial must be brought within three years after order granting new trial).

§4.6 No retrial after appeal & remittitur. A court must grant a motion to dismiss under CCP §583.320(a)(3) if the defendant establishes all of the following:

1. Judgment appealed. The defendant must establish that the judgment was appealed. CCP §583.320(a)(3).

2. New trial affirmed or judgment reversed. The defendant must establish that, on appeal, a new trial was affirmed or the judgment was reversed and remanded for a new trial. CCP §583.320(a)(3).

3. No retrial within three years. The defendant must establish that the plaintiff did not bring the action to trial within three years after the remittitur was filed by the trial-court clerk. CCP §583.320(a)(3).

(1) No trial. See "No trial," §4.3.1, p. 1165.

(2) Three-year deadline. The three-year deadline under §583.320(a)(3) is calculated in almost the same manner as the five-year deadline under §583.310. *See* CCP §583.330 (applies to actions brought to trial under article 3), §583.340 (same), §583.350 (same); *see, e.g.*, ***Hattersley v. American Nucleonics Corp.*** (2d Dist.1992) 3 Cal.App.4th 397, 401 (three-year period tolled for courtroom unavailability). See "Five-year deadline," §4.3.2, p. 1165. The only difference is that the three-year deadline begins to run from the date the remittitur was filed by the trial-court clerk, not from the date the action commenced. *Compare* CCP §583.310 (trial must be brought within five years after action commenced) *with id.* §583.320(a)(2) (retrial must be brought within three years after remittitur filed).

§5. GROUNDS – DISCRETIONARY DISMISSAL

§5.1 Generally. The grounds for a discretionary dismissal are almost identical to the grounds for a mandatory dismissal. *Compare* CCP §583.210 (grounds for mandatory dismissal), §583.310 (same), *and* §583.320 (same) *with id.* §583.420 (grounds for discretionary dismissal). The only significant difference is that the deadlines that will trigger a discretionary dismissal are shorter. The deadlines themselves, including the tolling periods, are calculated like the deadlines for mandatory dismissals. *Id.* §583.420(b). Chart 10-7, below, summarizes the actions and deadlines that will trigger a discretionary dismissal.

10-7. DISCRETIONARY DISMISSAL

	Action	Deadline	Authority
1	Serve summons and complaint	2 years	CCP §583.420(a)(1). See §4.1, p. 1162.
2	Bring action to trial or conditional settlement	2 years	CCP §583.420(a)(2)(B); *see* CRC 3.1340(a) (2-year period adopted by Judicial Council under authority of §583.420(a)(2)(B)); *see also* CRC 3.1340(c) (defining "conditional settlement"). See §4.3, p. 1165.

10-7. DISCRETIONARY DISMISSAL (CONTINUED)			
	Action	Deadline	Authority
3	Retry action after mistrial or hung jury	2 years	CCP §583.420(a)(3)(A). See §4.4, p. 1170.
4	Retry action after judgment granting new trial when no appeal is taken	2 years	CCP §583.420(a)(3)(B). See §4.5, p. 1170.
5	Retry action after order granting new trial is affirmed on appeal or judgment is reversed and remanded for new trial	2 years	CCP §583.420(a)(3)(C). See §4.6, p. 1171.

§5.2 Factors favoring dismissal.

1. General factors. To obtain a discretionary dismissal, the defendant should argue that dismissal is favored in light of the following factors under CRC 3.1342(e):

(1) Availability for service. The availability of the defendant and all other essential parties for service of process. CRC 3.1342(e)(1).

(2) Diligence in serving process. The plaintiff's diligence in seeking to serve process. CRC 3.1342(e)(2); *see, e.g.*, ***Williams v. Los Angeles Unified Sch. Dist.*** (2d Dist.1994) 23 Cal.App.4th 84, 93 (first summons was not issued until 20 months after complaint was filed; when D was finally served, it was served at incorrect office).

(3) Extent of settlement discussions. The extent to which the parties engaged in any settlement negotiations or discussions. CRC 3.1342(e)(3); *see, e.g.*, ***Williams***, 23 Cal.App.4th at 93 (settlement was rejected well before two-year period to serve expired).

(4) Diligence in pursuing pretrial matters. The parties' diligence in pursuing pretrial matters, including discovery and requests for extraordinary relief. CRC 3.1342(e)(4). Pretrial matters that are pursued only after a motion to dismiss has been filed are generally viewed with disfavor. *E.g.*, ***Freedman v. Pacific Gas & Elec. Co.*** (1st Dist.1987) 196 Cal.App.3d 696, 709-10 (P's only action for four years and seven months was to file at-issue memorandum; once motion to dismiss was filed, P served discovery requests, sought leave to file amended complaint, and filed motion to advance trial); *see, e.g.*, ***Williams***, 23 Cal.App.4th at 93 (P did not file discovery until after motion to dismiss was filed).

(5) Nature & complexity of case. The nature and complexity of the case. CRC 3.1342(e)(5).

(6) Law applicable to case. The law applicable to the case, including the pendency of other litigation under a common set of facts or determinative of the legal or factual issues in the case. CRC 3.1342(e)(6).

(7) Nature of delays. The nature of any extensions of time or other delays attributable to either party. CRC 3.1342(e)(7).

(8) Condition of court's calendar. The condition of the court's calendar and the availability of an earlier trial date if the matter was ready for trial. CRC 3.1342(e)(8).

(9) Interests of justice served. Whether the interests of justice are best served by dismissal. CRC 3.1342(e)(9).

(10) Other relevant facts or circumstances. Any other facts or circumstances that are relevant to a fair determination of the issue. CRC 3.1342(e)(10). Some of the relevant facts or circumstances courts have considered include the following:

(a) Prejudice. The court can consider the prejudice suffered by the defendant for the delay in prosecution. *See* ***Fleming v. Gallegos*** (2d Dist.1994) 23 Cal.App.4th 68, 75 (actual prejudice can strengthen argument for dismissal). Prejudice is merely a factor to be considered; the defendant is not required to affirmatively show

that prejudice was incurred for a dismissal to be granted. ***Howard v. Thrifty Drug & Disc. Stores*** (1995) 10 Cal.4th 424, 443-44; ***Lopez v. State*** (4th Dist.1996) 49 Cal.App.4th 1292, 1295; ***Fleming***, 23 Cal.App.4th at 74-75; *see* ***Blank v. Kirwan*** (1985) 39 Cal.3d 311, 332. *But see* ***Yao v. Anaheim Eye Med. Grp.*** (4th Dist.1992) 10 Cal.App.4th 1024, 1032 (once P establishes excuse for delay, D has burden to prove prejudice or other factors that support dismissal). Some courts have held that prejudice can be presumed when there has been a long and unjustified delay in serving the complaint, but there is no presumption of prejudice for delay in bringing an action to trial. *See, e.g.*, ***Ladd v. Dart Equip. Corp.*** (2d Dist.1991) 230 Cal.App.3d 1088, 1106-07 (presumption of prejudice not available in all cases involving delay in service); ***Cubit v. Ridgecrest Cmty. Hosp.*** (5th Dist.1987) 194 Cal.App.3d 1552, 1572 (presumption of prejudice available only when delay in service is prolonged and unjustified); ***Luti v. Graco, Inc.*** (4th Dist.1985) 170 Cal.App.3d 228, 238 (same). *Contra* ***Wagner v. Rios*** (1st Dist.1992) 4 Cal.App.4th 608, 612 (presumption of prejudice available in cases involving delay in bringing action to trial).

(b) Excuse for delay. The court can consider the plaintiff's excuse for the delay in prosecution. The Supreme Court in ***Denham v. Superior Ct.*** disapproved of earlier cases holding that a motion to dismiss is mandatory unless the plaintiff makes an adequate showing of diligence or excusable delay. ***Denham v. Superior Ct.*** (1970) 2 Cal.3d 557, 563. A court can dismiss the action only if there is a complete absence of any showing constituting good cause. *Id.* at 564. Courts are split on whether the ruling in ***Denham*** still requires the plaintiff to present some excuse for the delay to avoid dismissal. Some courts have interpreted ***Denham*** to mean that a discretionary motion becomes mandatory if the plaintiff makes no showing of excusable delay. *E.g.*, ***Oskooi v. Fountain Valley Reg'l Hosp. & Med. Ctr.*** (4th Dist.1996) 42 Cal.App.4th 233, 241; ***Dunsmuir Masonic Temple v. Superior Ct.*** (3d Dist.1970) 12 Cal.App.3d 17, 21. Other courts have interpreted ***Denham*** to mean that a court may deny a motion to dismiss even when the plaintiff has not presented an excuse for its delay. *E.g.*, ***Williams***, 23 Cal.App.4th at 94 n.4; ***Scarzella v. DeMers*** (3d Dist.1993) 17 Cal.App.4th 1762, 1769 n.4; ***United Farm Workers Nat'l Un. v. International Bhd. of Teamsters*** (5th Dist.1978) 87 Cal.App.3d 225, 235.

2. Public-policy factors. To obtain a discretionary dismissal, the defendant should argue that dismissal is favored in light of the following public-policy factors: (1) the plaintiff's reasonable diligence in prosecuting the action, (2) the parties' cooperation in bringing the action to trial or final disposition, (3) the parties' stipulations, and (4) the policy favoring a trial or other disposition of an action on the merits over the policy of dismissing an action for delay in prosecution. CCP §583.130; CRC 3.1342(e). The policy favoring disposition on the merits prevails only if the plaintiff makes some showing of excusable delay. ***Salas v. Sears, Roebuck & Co.*** (1986) 42 Cal.3d 342, 347; ***Landry v. Berryessa Un. Sch. Dist.*** (6th Dist.1995) 39 Cal.App.4th 691, 698. See "Excuse for delay," §5.2.1(10)(b), this page.

§6. MOTION

§6.1 Who can file.

1. Defendant. The defendant can file a motion requesting a mandatory or discretionary dismissal for delay in prosecution. CCP §§583.250(a)(2), 583.360(a), 583.410(a).

2. Interested person. Any interested person in an action, whether named as a party or not, can file a motion requesting a mandatory dismissal for lack of service. CCP §583.250(a)(2). See "No service of summons & complaint," §4.1, p. 1162; "No proof of service filed," §4.2, p. 1164.

3. Court. The court on its own motion can order a mandatory or discretionary dismissal for delay in prosecution. CCP §§583.250(a)(2), 583.360(a), 583.410(a); *see, e.g.*, ***Hughes v. Kimble*** (2d Dist.1992) 5 Cal.App.4th 59, 63 (on its own motion, court dismissed action that was not brought to trial within five years).

§6.2 Deadline to file & serve.

1. Mandatory dismissal.

(1) Defendant's or interested person's motion. If the defendant or an interested person is filing a motion for mandatory dismissal, the notice of motion must be filed and served at least 16 court days before the

hearing on the motion. CCP §1005(a)(13), (b); CRC 3.1300(a); *see* CCP §583.250(a)(2) (dismissal after notice to parties), §584.360(a) (same). See "Filing & Serving Noticed Motions," ch. 1-D, §7, p. 33.

(2) Court's motion. If the court is seeking a mandatory dismissal on its own motion, the court must give notice to all parties. CCP §§583.250(a)(2), 583.360(a); *see, e.g.*, ***Hughes v. Kimble*** (2d Dist.1992) 5 Cal.App.4th 59, 63 (court served P with notice of intent to dismiss on court's own motion). The Code of Civil Procedure does not state how much notice must be given.

2. Discretionary dismissal.

(1) Defendant's motion. If the defendant is filing a motion for discretionary dismissal, the notice of motion must be filed and served at least 45 days before the hearing on the motion. CRC 3.1342(a); *see* ***Reid v. Balter*** (2d Dist.1993) 14 Cal.App.4th 1186, 1193-94 (warning Ps that their case could be dismissed if they did not appear for trial-setting conference was not sufficient notice). See "Filing & Serving Noticed Motions," ch. 1-D, §7, p. 33.

(2) Court's motion. If the court is seeking a discretionary dismissal on its own motion, the clerk must mail notice to all parties at least 20 days before the hearing on the court's motion. CRC 3.1340(b); ***Roman v. Usary Tire & Serv. Ctr.*** (2d Dist.1994) 29 Cal.App.4th 1422, 1428; *see* ***Sakhai v. Zipora*** (2d Dist.2009) 180 Cal.App.4th 593, 600 (court is not required to give parties 45 days' notice).

§6.3 Contents.

1. Notice of motion & motion.

(1) Generally. A motion to dismiss for delay in prosecution (mandatory or discretionary) must be requested in writing by noticed motion. CRC 3.1342(a); *see* CCP §583.250(a)(2) (must give notice to parties), §584.360(a) (same), §1005(a)(13) (written notice is required in any proceeding requiring notice); CRC 3.1340(b) (court must give notice); *see, e.g.*, ***Zaragoza v. Superior Ct.*** (2d Dist.1996) 49 Cal.App.4th 720, 723 (court refused to consider oral motion to dismiss petition for dissolution and ordered party to file noticed motion); ***Cohen v. Hughes Mkts., Inc.*** (2d Dist.1995) 36 Cal.App.4th 1693, 1699 (grant of dismissal on D's oral motion did not comply with court rules or due process); ***Derry v. Superior Ct.*** (2d Dist.1968) 266 Cal.App.2d 556, 561 (judgment based on oral motion violated P's due-process rights). For the general contents of a noticed motion, see "Notice of motion & motion," ch. 1-D, §5.1, p. 28.

(2) Relief. The motion must state the relief the defendant is seeking. CRC 3.1110(a), 3.1112(d)(3). In a motion to dismiss for delay in prosecution, the defendant can request only a dismissal without prejudice. ***Franklin Capital Corp. v. Wilson*** (4th Dist.2007) 148 Cal.App.4th 187, 214; *see* CCP §581(b)(4), (g). *Contra* ***Black v. Lukens*** (1st Dist.2009) No. A120828 (unpub.; 2-20-09) (court has discretion to dismiss with prejudice). For a discussion of the effect of dismissing an action without prejudice, see "Dismissal without prejudice," ch. 10-D, §5.1.1, p. 1155.

(3) Grounds. The motion must state the grounds for the relief. CRC 3.1110(a), 3.1112(d)(3). See "Grounds – Mandatory Dismissal," §4, p. 1162; "Grounds – Discretionary Dismissal," §5, p. 1171.

PRACTICE TIP

When asserting a ground for mandatory dismissal, consider requesting a discretionary dismissal in the alternative. Most of the grounds that would support a mandatory dismissal would also support a discretionary dismissal; the only difference is that a shorter deadline applies to discretionary dismissals. If you miscalculate the deadline for a mandatory dismissal and you do not request an alternative basis for dismissal, the court cannot grant the dismissal. See, e.g., ***Gonzalez v. County of L.A.*** *(2d Dist.2004) 122 Cal.App.4th 1124, 1131 (D requested mandatory dismissal because action was not brought to trial within five years; D miscalculated deadline and court could not, on its own, grant discretionary dismissal for not bringing action to trial within three years).*

2. Memorandum of points & authorities. The motion to dismiss must include a memorandum in support of the motion. CRC 3.1112(a)(3). If practical, the support memorandum should be attached to the notice of motion. CRC 3.1113(j); *see* CRC 3.1110(e) (method of attachment). The memorandum cannot exceed 15 pages (not including exhibits, declarations, attachments, table of contents, table of authorities, or proof of service). CRC 3.1113(d). For a discussion of the memorandum, see "Memorandum of points & authorities," ch. 1-D, §5.2, p. 28.

NOTE

Memorandums in support of a motion for mandatory dismissal are typically short because all they have to do is set out a chronology of events that support dismissal (e.g., the date the action commenced, any intervening events, and the deadline to act). See Younger, Cal. Motions, §§10:53, 10:54. Memorandums in support of a motion for discretionary dismissal, on the other hand, are generally more extensive because they need to address the factors that support a dismissal under CRC 3.1342(e), the public-policy considerations under CCP §583.130, and the prejudice suffered by the defendant. See Younger, Cal. Motions, §§10:54-10:56.

3. Supporting evidence. The motion to dismiss can be supported by evidence. CRC 3.1112(b). Supporting evidence can include declarations, exhibits, appendixes, and other documents and pleadings. *Id.*; *see* CRC 3.1342(a); *see, e.g.*, ***Reid v. Balter*** (2d Dist.1993) 14 Cal.App.4th 1186, 1192 (D's attorney submitted declaration in support of D's motion to dismiss). See "Supporting evidence," ch. 1-D, §5.3, p. 30.

4. Request for judicial notice. The movant can submit a request for judicial notice with the motion to dismiss. CRC 3.1113(*l*). If judicial notice is requested, it must be made in a separate document. *Id.* See "Request for Judicial Notice," ch. 5-J, p. 547.

5. Proposed order. The movant can submit a proposed order with the motion to dismiss. CRC 3.1113(m). If a proposed order is submitted, it must be lodged and served with the motion papers but not attached to them. *Id.* See "Documents lodged," ch. 1-F, §2.3, p. 47.

§7. OPPOSITION

The plaintiff can file an opposition to the motion to dismiss. *See, e.g.*, ***Denham v. Superior Ct.*** (1970) 2 Cal.3d 557, 562 (D filed motion to dismiss, and P filed opposition); ***Marra v. Mission Foods Corp.*** (1st Dist.1993) 19 Cal.App.4th 724, 726 (court gave P notice of its intent to dismiss on its own motion, and P filed opposition). If the plaintiff does not file an opposition to a motion requesting a discretionary dismissal, the court may construe that as an admission that the motion is meritorious and grant the motion without a hearing. CRC 3.1342(b).

§7.1 Deadline to file & serve.

1. Opposition to mandatory dismissal. An opposition to a motion requesting a mandatory dismissal must be filed and served at least nine court days before the hearing. *See* CCP §1005(b); CRC 3.1300(a). For a discussion of serving opposition papers, see "Filing & serving opposition," ch. 1-D, §8.5, p. 36.

2. Opposition to discretionary dismissal. An opposition to a motion requesting a discretionary dismissal must be filed and served within 15 days after service of the notice of motion. CRC 3.1342(b). For a discussion of serving opposition papers, see "Filing & serving opposition," ch. 1-D, §8.5, p. 36.

§7.2 Grounds.

1. Challenging dismissal – generally. The following grounds can be asserted in opposition to a motion requesting a mandatory or discretionary dismissal:

(1) Equitable estoppel. The plaintiff can assert the defense of equitable estoppel. *See* CCP §583.140. To prove estoppel, the plaintiff must establish the following: (1) the defendant was aware of the facts, (2) the defendant either intended that its conduct would be acted on or acted in such a way that the plaintiff was reasonable to believe it should act on the defendant's conduct, (3) the plaintiff was ignorant of the true state of facts, and (4) the

plaintiff reasonably relied on the defendant's conduct to its detriment. ***Biss v. Bohr*** (4th Dist.1995) 40 Cal.App.4th 1246, 1252; ***Evans v. City of L.A.*** (2d Dist.1983) 145 Cal.App.3d 142, 148; *see, e.g.*, ***Knapp v. Superior Ct.*** (1st Dist.1978) 79 Cal.App.3d 799, 804 (D estopped from dismissing action because parties entered into stipulation that prevented P from obtaining default judgment before deadline expired). The defense of equitable estoppel applies equally to conduct and statements made by a court. ***Greene v. State Farm Fire & Cas. Co.*** (1st Dist.1990) 224 Cal.App.3d 1583, 1592.

(2) Waiver. The plaintiff can assert the defense of waiver. *See* CCP §583.140. To prove waiver, the plaintiff must establish that the defendant voluntarily relinquished, expressly or impliedly, a known right. *E.g.*, ***Wilcox v. Ford*** (2d Dist.1988) 206 Cal.App.3d 1170, 1179 (D did not impliedly waive right to seek dismissal when it did not notify P of continued trial date and did not appear at trial); *see, e.g.*, ***Butler v. Hathcoat*** (1st Dist.1983) 146 Cal.App.3d 834, 840 (D impliedly waived right to seek dismissal when it went to trial without objecting).

(3) Voluntary dismissal entered. The plaintiff can assert the defense that the court cannot grant an involuntary dismissal because a voluntary dismissal has already been entered by the plaintiff. ***Eddings v. White*** (1st Dist.1964) 229 Cal.App.2d 579, 585. See "Effect of Dismissal," ch. 10-D, §5, p. 1155.

(4) Family-law petition. In some family-law cases, the plaintiff can assert the defense that the petition is not subject to involuntary dismissal for delay in prosecution. Under CCP §583.161, the court cannot dismiss a petition filed under Fam. C. §299, 2250, 2330, or 7600 for delay in prosecution if any of the following is true:

(a) A child-support order or an order regarding child custody or visitation has been issued in connection with the proceeding and the order has not been terminated either by the court or by operation of law. CCP §583.161(a).

(b) A spousal-support order has been issued in connection with the proceeding and the order has not been terminated by the court. *Id.* §583.161(b).

(c) A personal-conduct restraining order has been issued under the Domestic Violence Prevention Act and the order has not been terminated by operation of law or by the court. CCP §583.161(c).

(d) An issue in the case has been bifurcated and a separate trial has been conducted under either Fam. C. §2337 or the California Rules of Court. CCP §583.161(d).

(5) Class action. The plaintiff can assert the defense that the notice to dismiss was not sufficient to dismiss a class action. *See* Civ. C. §1781(f); CRC 3.770(c).

2. Challenging mandatory dismissal. In opposing a motion requesting a mandatory dismissal, the plaintiff should address any matters that would extend or toll the period to timely prosecute the action. *See* ***Hocharian v. Superior Ct.*** (1981) 28 Cal.3d 714, 721-22 & n.7 (P has burden to prove impossibility or impracticability); Younger, *Cal. Motions*, §10:60 (P must show how case falls within statutory exception).

3. Challenging discretionary dismissal. In opposing a motion requesting a discretionary dismissal, the plaintiff should address the factors under CRC 3.1342(e) and the public-policy considerations under CCP §583.130, and should assert any credible excuse for the delay. See "Factors favoring dismissal," §5.2, p. 1172.

§7.3 Contents. For a general discussion of the contents of an opposition, see "Opposition Papers," ch. 1-D, §8, p. 35.

§8. REPLY

§8.1 To mandatory dismissal. The defendant can file and serve a reply to the plaintiff's opposition to a motion requesting a mandatory dismissal. See "Reply Papers," ch. 1-D, §9, p. 37. The reply must be filed and served at least five court days before the hearing. *See* CCP §1005(b). See "Filing & serving reply papers," ch. 1-D, §9.6, p. 37.

§8.2 To discretionary dismissal.

1. Defendant's response to opposition. The defendant can file and serve a response to the plaintiff's opposition to a motion requesting a discretionary dismissal. CRC 3.1342(c). The response must be filed and served within 15 days after the plaintiff's opposition was served. *Id.*

2. Plaintiff's reply to response. The plaintiff can file and serve a reply to the defendant's response to the plaintiff's opposition to a motion requesting a discretionary dismissal. CRC 3.1342(d). The reply must be filed and served within five days after the defendant's response was served. *Id.*

§8.3 Contents. The reply memorandum cannot exceed ten pages. CRC 3.1113(d).

§9. HEARING

§9.1 Generally. For a discussion of hearings generally, see "Hearings," ch. 1-H, p. 79.

§9.2 No opposition filed. If the plaintiff does not oppose a motion requesting a discretionary dismissal, the court can interpret this as an admission that the motion is meritorious and grant the motion without a hearing on the merits. CRC 3.1342(b).

§10. RULING

§10.1 Mandatory dismissal. If the plaintiff does not perform a required action within the statutory deadlines for a mandatory dismissal, the court must dismiss the case. *See* CCP §583.250(a)(2) ("action shall be dismissed"), §583.360(a) (same). In ruling on a motion requesting a mandatory dismissal, the court cannot develop extensions, excuses, or exceptions that are not prescribed by statute. *Id.* §§583.250(b), 583.360(b).

§10.2 Discretionary dismissal.

1. Generally.

(1) Defer ruling. The court can continue or defer its ruling on a motion requesting a discretionary dismissal pending performance by either party of any conditions relating to trial or dismissal imposed by the court to carry out substantial justice. CRC 3.1342(f).

(2) Grant if no opposition filed. The court can grant a motion requesting a discretionary dismissal without considering the factors under CRC 3.1342(e) if the plaintiff does not file an opposition to the motion. *See* CRC 3.1342(b).

2. Court's determination. Courts are split on how a court should rule on a motion requesting a discretionary dismissal. Some courts have held that a court can deny a motion requesting a discretionary dismissal only if the plaintiff asserts a credible, reasonable excuse for the delay. Other courts have held that a court's decision to grant or deny a motion requesting a discretionary dismissal is always discretionary.

(1) Discretionary only after excuse. Courts holding that a motion requesting a discretionary dismissal can be denied only if the plaintiff asserts a credible, reasonable excuse generally follow these steps for ruling on the motion:

(a) Has plaintiff asserted excuse? The first step is for the court to determine whether the plaintiff has made some showing of excusable delay. ***Putnam v. Clague*** (5th Dist.1992) 3 Cal.App.4th 542, 549. If the plaintiff makes no showing of excusable delay, then the motion to dismiss must be granted. ***Oskooi v. Fountain Valley Reg'l Hosp. & Med. Ctr.*** (4th Dist.1996) 42 Cal.App.4th 233, 241; ***Dunsmuir Masonic Temple v. Superior Ct.*** (3d Dist.1970) 12 Cal.App.3d 17, 21; *see* ***Denham v. Superior Ct.*** (1970) 2 Cal.3d 557, 564 (only when there is complete absence of any showing of good cause will writ of mandate compelling dismissal issue).

(b) Is excuse credible? If the plaintiff has made some showing of excusable delay, the next step is for the court to determine if the excuse for the delay is credible. ***Yao v. Anaheim Eye Med. Grp.*** (4th Dist.1992) 10 Cal.App.4th 1024, 1029-30; ***Putnam***, 3 Cal.App.4th at 557-58. An excuse will not be considered credible if the court determines that it is merely an afterthought or pretext designed to cover up neglect. ***Putnam***, 3 Cal.App.4th at 558. If the plaintiff does not assert a credible excuse for the delay, the court may grant the motion to dismiss without considering other factors. *See id.* at 557-58.

(c) Is excuse reasonable? If the plaintiff has shown a credible excuse, the court will then determine if the excuse is reasonable. ***Yao***, 10 Cal.App.4th at 1030; ***Putnam***, 3 Cal.App.4th at 558. If the excuse is not reasonable, the court can grant the motion to dismiss without considering other factors. *See* ***American W. Banker v. Price Waterhouse*** (5th Dist.1993) 12 Cal.App.4th 39, 57 (if excuse is neither credible nor reasonable, court can grant dismissal without considering whether D was prejudiced).

[1] Delay was calculated decision. If the delay in prosecution was a calculated decision by the attorney, the question of whether the excuse was reasonable is determined by a reasonable-attorney standard—that is, whether a reasonably competent attorney would conclude that the delay was justified under the circumstances. ***American W. Banker***, 12 Cal.App.4th at 55 n.11.

[2] Delay was inadvertent. If the delay in prosecution was inadvertent, the question of whether the excuse was reasonable is determined by the court. *See* ***American W. Banker***, 12 Cal.App.4th at 55 n.11.

NOTE

Courts have uniformly held that lack of economic resources is not a reasonable excuse to delay prosecution of an action. ***Oskooi****, 42 Cal.App.4th at 241; see* ***American W. Banker****, 12 Cal.App.4th at 57.*

(d) Do remaining factors support dismissal? If the plaintiff's excuse is credible and reasonable, the burden shifts to the defendant to show that other factors support dismissal. ***Yao***, 10 Cal.App.4th at 1030; ***Putnam***, 3 Cal.App.4th at 558. In ruling on a motion requesting a discretionary dismissal, the court must consider the following:

[1] The court's file in the case and the declarations and supporting data submitted by the parties. CRC 3.1342(e)(1).

[2] All relevant matters, including the factors listed in CRC 3.3142(e)(2)-(e)(10). ***Dubois v. Corroon & Black Corp.*** (2d Dist.1993) 12 Cal.App.4th 1689, 1696; ***Wagner v. Rios*** (1st Dist.1992) 4 Cal.App.4th 608, 611-12. See "General factors," §5.2.1, p. 1172.

[3] The public-policy considerations under CCP §583.130. CRC 3.1342(e). See "Public-policy factors," §5.2.2, p. 1173.

(2) Always discretionary. Some courts have held that the court's decision to grant or deny a motion requesting a discretionary dismissal is always discretionary, regardless of whether the plaintiff asserts an excuse for delay in prosecution. ***Williams v. Los Angeles Unified Sch. Dist.*** (2d Dist.1994) 23 Cal.App.4th 84, 94 n.4; ***Scarzella v. DeMers*** (3d Dist.1993) 17 Cal.App.4th 1762, 1769 n.4; ***United Farm Workers Nat'l Un. v. International Bhd. of Teamsters*** (5th Dist.1978) 87 Cal.App.3d 225, 235; *see* ***Roach v. Lewis*** (2d Dist.1993) 14 Cal.App.4th 1179, 1184 (declining to adopt test developed in ***Putnam***). For a discussion of what the court must consider in ruling on a motion requesting a discretionary dismissal, see "Do remaining factors support dismissal?," §10.2.2(1)(d), this page.

§11. ORDER

§11.1 Form. The court's order on a motion to dismiss for delay in prosecution must be in writing. CCP §581d; *see* ***Brehm v. 21st Century Ins.*** (2d Dist.2008) 166 Cal.App.4th 1225, 1234 n.5 (courts should use separate written order of dismissal, signed by court and filed, rather than relying on signed or stamped minute order). For a discussion of preparing written orders, see "Written order," ch. 1-I, §4.2, p. 91.

§11.2 Contents.

1. Generally. An order of dismissal for delay in prosecution must state that the dismissal is without prejudice. ***Franklin Capital Corp. v. Wilson*** (4th Dist.2007) 148 Cal.App.4th 187, 215 & n.33; *see* CCP §581(b)(4), (g). *Contra* ***Black v. Lukens*** (1st Dist.2009) No. A120828 (unpub.; 2-20-09) (court has discretion to dismiss with prejudice). See "Dismissal without prejudice," ch. 10-D, §5.1.1, p. 1155.

2. Discretionary dismissal.

(1) No recitation of factors. An order granting a discretionary dismissal is not required to (1) state the basis for the court's decision, (2) recite that the court considered all relevant matters or each of the factors listed in CRC 3.1342(e), or (3) make express findings on each factor. *See* ***Howard v. Thrifty Drug & Disc. Stores*** (1995) 10 Cal.4th 424, 443; ***Wilson v. Sunshine Meat & Liquor Co.*** (1983) 34 Cal.3d 554, 562.

(2) Conditions for grant or denial. The court can impose terms on the parties as a condition of granting or denying a discretionary dismissal. CCP §583.430; *see* ***City of L.A. v. Gleneagle Dev. Co.*** (2d Dist.1976) 62 Cal.App.3d 543, 563-64. Some of the conditions the court can impose include the following: (1) requiring the defendant to waive the statute of limitations, (2) requiring the defendant to dismiss a cross-complaint, (3) requiring the completion of discovery, (4) requiring the filing of a certificate of readiness for trial, and (5) requiring preparation of a motion to advance the trial date. 17 Cal. Law Revision Comm'n Rep. (1984) p. 939.

§11.3 Notice of entry. The party who requested dismissal must file and serve on all parties notice of entry of the dismissal. CRC 3.1390. The notice of entry must be filled out on mandatory Judicial Council Form CIV-120.

§11.4 Effect of dismissal. An order granting a motion to dismiss for delay in prosecution is considered a final judgment for purposes of appeal. ***Salas v. Sears, Roebuck & Co.*** (1986) 42 Cal.3d 342, 345 n.3; *see* CCP §581d (order of dismissal is judgment). See "Effect of Dismissal," ch. 10-D, §5, p. 1155.

§12. MOTION FOR RECONSIDERATION

A party who is adversely affected by a court's order on a motion to dismiss for delay in prosecution can file a motion for reconsideration. CCP §1008(a), (e). See "Motion for Reconsideration," ch. 5-G, §3, p. 508.

§13. MOTION FOR RENEWAL

A party who was denied or conditionally granted a motion to dismiss for delay in prosecution can file a motion for renewal. CCP §1008(b). See "Motion for Renewal," ch. 5-G, §4, p. 516.

§14. REVIEW

§14.1 By trial court.

1. Motion to vacate under §473(b). A party who is adversely affected by an involuntary dismissal can file a motion to vacate the judgment under CCP §473(b). Courts have held that the mandatory-relief provision under §473(b) is not available to challenge a mandatory or discretionary dismissal if the plaintiff filed an opposition to the motion. ***Bernasconi Commercial Real Estate v. St. Joseph's Reg'l Healthcare Sys.*** (3d Dist.1997) 57 Cal.App.4th 1078, 1082; *see, e.g.*, ***Peltier v. McCloud River R.R.*** (3d Dist.1995) 34 Cal.App.4th 1809, 1817 (discretionary dismissal); ***Tustin Plaza Prtshp. v. Wehage*** (4th Dist.1994) 27 Cal.App.4th 1557, 1565-66 & n.9 (same). See "Motion to vacate under §473(b)," ch. 10-A, §9.1.1, p. 1109.

2. Motion to vacate void judgment. A party who is adversely affected by an involuntary dismissal can file a motion to vacate the judgment if it is void. *See* CCP §473(d); *see, e.g.*, ***Eddings v. White*** (1st Dist.1964) 229 Cal.App.2d 579, 585 (involuntary dismissal void because voluntary dismissal had already been granted). See "Motion to vacate void judgment," ch. 10-A, §9.1.4, p. 1111.

3. Action in equity to vacate judgment. A party who is adversely affected by an involuntary dismissal can file an action to vacate the judgment on equitable grounds. *See, e.g.*, ***Seacall Dev., Ltd. v. Santa Monica Rent Control Bd.*** (2d Dist.1999) 73 Cal.App.4th 201, 205 (court vacated discretionary dismissal on equitable grounds because attorney had abandoned P). See "Action in equity to vacate judgment," ch. 10-A, §9.1.5, p. 1113.

§14.2 By appellate court.

1. Writ of mandate.

(1) When applicable. An order denying a motion to dismiss for delay in prosecution can be reviewed by a petition for writ of mandate. ***Oskooi v. Fountain Valley Reg'l Hosp. & Med. Ctr.*** (4th Dist.1996) 42 Cal.App.4th 233, 237.

(2) Deadline to file. See "Deadline to file," ch. 10-A, §9.2.1(2), p. 1116.

2. **Direct appeal.**

(1) **When applicable.**

(a) **Denial of motion.** An order denying a motion to dismiss for delay in prosecution is not an appealable order, but it can be reviewed on direct appeal after a final judgment has been entered. ***Oskooi***, 42 Cal.App.4th at 237.

(b) **Grant of motion.** An order granting a motion to dismiss for delay in prosecution is considered a final judgment that is directly appealable. ***Salas v. Sears, Roebuck & Co.*** (1986) 42 Cal.3d 342, 345 n.3; *see* CCP §581d (order of dismissal is judgment). To be appealable, the order must be final; it cannot be preliminary to a later order of dismissal. *E.g.*, ***Eliceche v. Federal Land Bank Ass'n*** (5th Dist.2002) 103 Cal.App.4th 1349, 1359 & n.12 (unclear whether court's order granting dismissal was appealable order of dismissal).

(2) **Deadline to file.** See "Deadline to file," ch. 10-A, §9.2.2(4), p. 1116.

(3) **Standard of review.** Orders on motions to dismiss for delay in prosecution are reviewed for abuse of discretion. ***Denham v. Superior Ct.*** (1970) 2 Cal.3d 557, 563-64 (discretionary dismissal); ***Sagi Plumbing v. Chartered Constr. Corp.*** (2d Dist.2004) 123 Cal.App.4th 443, 447 (mandatory dismissal). An order granting a motion to dismiss will be given closer scrutiny than an order denying a motion to dismiss. ***Salinas v. Atchison, Topeka & Santa Fe Ry.*** (5th Dist.1992) 5 Cal.App.4th 1, 17.

F. INVOLUNTARY DISMISSAL—OTHER GROUNDS

This subchapter discusses how to involuntarily dismiss an action for reasons other than delay in prosecution. For a discussion of that topic, see "Involuntary Dismissal—Delay in Prosecution," ch. 10-E, p. 1160.

§1. GENERAL

§1.1 Purpose. See "Purpose," ch. 10-E, §1.1, p. 1160.

§1.2 Primary authority. CCP §§389(b), 399(a), 410.30, 418.10, 575.2, 581, 1030(d), 2023.010, 2023.030(d)(3); Gov. C. §68608.

§1.3 Secondary authority. The following secondary source is cited as authority in this subchapter:

- Younger & Bradley, *Younger on California Motions* (2014-15) (referred to as Younger, *Cal. Motions*).

§2. DEMURRER – WITHOUT LEAVE TO AMEND

The court can dismiss a complaint or cross-complaint if a demurrer was granted without leave to amend. CCP §581(a)(2), (f)(1). A motion to dismiss under CCP §581(f)(1) can be requested by either party or granted by the court on its own motion. *See id.* §581(f)(1) (either party); *see, e.g.*, ***Kirkpatrick v. City of Oceanside*** (4th Dist.1991) 232 Cal.App.3d 267, 272-73 (court granted dismissal on its own motion). The motion to dismiss can be made orally at the hearing after the court has granted the demurrer or, if the demurrer is taken under submission, by filing a written motion after the court has issued its order. Younger, *Cal. Motions*, §10.39; *see, e.g.*, ***Banks v. Hathaway*** (2d Dist.2002) 97 Cal.App.4th 949, 951 (written motion). An order of dismissal under §581(f)(1) is discretionary and can be granted with or without prejudice. CCP §581(f) (court may dismiss); ***Sheehan v. San Francisco 49ers, Ltd.*** (2009) 45 Cal.4th 992, 997 (with prejudice); ***Sindell v. Gibson, Dunn & Crutcher*** (2d Dist.1997) 54 Cal.App.4th 1457, 1460 (without prejudice). *Contra cf.* ***Cano v. Glover*** (2d Dist.2006) 143 Cal.App.4th 326, 329-30 (dismissal under §581(f)(2) must be with prejudice). See "Dismissal without prejudice," ch. 10-D, §5.1.1, p. 1155; "Dismissal with prejudice," ch. 10-D, §5.1.2, p. 1156. But a dismissal cannot be granted under §581(f)(1) if the defendant asks the court to proceed to trial (or the court proceeds to trial on its own) on a special defense raised by the defendant's answer under CCP §597. *See* CCP §581(f)(1).

§3. DEMURRER – NO AMENDMENT

The court can dismiss a complaint or cross-complaint if a demurrer was granted with leave to amend and the complaint or cross-complaint was not amended within the time allowed. CCP §581(a)(2), (f)(2). A motion to dismiss

under CCP §581(f)(2) can be requested by either party or granted by the court on its own motion. *See id.* §581(f)(2) (either party); *see, e.g.*, ***Ziegler v. Nickel*** (2d Dist.1998) 64 Cal.App.4th 545, 547 n.2 (court granted dismissal on its own motion). The motion to dismiss is usually made by ex parte application if no late pleading has been filed and served. *See* CRC 3.1320(h); ***Gitmed v. General Motors Corp.*** (2d Dist.1994) 26 Cal.App.4th 824, 828-29; *see also* ***Datig v. Dove Books, Inc.*** (2d Dist.1999) 73 Cal.App.4th 964, 976-77 (ex parte application must be served on all other appearing parties). See "Ex Parte Practice," ch. 1-E, p. 39. If a late pleading has been filed and served, the defendant must file a noticed motion to strike the late pleading before moving to dismiss. ***Gitmed***, 26 Cal.App.4th at 829; *see* ***Leader v. Health Indus.*** (2d Dist.2001) 89 Cal.App.4th 603, 614 (motion to strike and motion to dismiss can be requested in one noticed motion; D is not required to file separate motion to dismiss after motion to strike is granted). An order of dismissal under §581(f)(2) is discretionary and is granted with prejudice. *See* CCP §581(f); ***Cano v. Glover*** (2d Dist.2006) 143 Cal.App.4th 326, 329-30; ***Harlan v. Department of Transp.*** (5th Dist.2005) 132 Cal.App.4th 868, 873-74. See "Dismissal with prejudice," ch. 10-D, §5.1.2, p. 1156. But a dismissal cannot be granted under §581(f)(2) if the defendant asks the court to proceed to trial (or if the court proceeds to trial on its own) on a special defense raised by the defendant's answer under CCP §597. *See* CCP §581(f)(2).

§4. MOTION TO STRIKE – WITHOUT LEAVE TO AMEND

The court can dismiss a complaint or cross-complaint if a motion to strike the entire complaint or cross-complaint was granted without leave to amend. CCP §581(a)(2), (f)(3). A motion to dismiss under CCP §581(f)(3) can be requested by either party. *Id.* §581(f)(3). The motion to dismiss can be made orally at the hearing after the court has granted the motion to strike or, if the motion to strike is taken under submission, by filing a written motion after the court has issued its order. Younger, *Cal. Motions*, §10.39. An order of dismissal under §581(f)(3) is discretionary. *See* CCP §581(f).

§5. MOTION TO STRIKE – NO AMENDMENT

The court can dismiss a complaint or cross-complaint if a motion to strike the entire complaint or cross-complaint was granted with leave to amend and the complaint or cross-complaint was not amended within the time allowed. CCP §581(a)(2), (f)(4). A motion to dismiss under CCP §581(f)(4) can be requested by either party. *Id.* §581(f)(4). The motion to dismiss is usually in writing and can be made by ex parte application. *See* ***Anmaco, Inc. v. Bohlken*** (1st Dist.1993) 13 Cal.App.4th 891, 901 n.4; Younger, *Cal. Motions*, §10.39. An order of dismissal under §581(f)(4) is discretionary. *See* CCP §581(f).

§6. INCONVENIENT FORUM

The court can dismiss an action if it was brought in an inconvenient forum. CCP §§410.30(a), 418.10(a)(2). For a discussion of a motion to dismiss for inconvenient forum, see "Motion to Stay or Dismiss – Forum Non Conveniens," ch. 4-F, §2, p. 376.

§7. MISUSE OF DISCOVERY PROCESS

The court can dismiss an action if there is a misuse of the discovery process. CCP §2023.030(d)(3); *see also id.* §2023.010 (listing conduct that is misuse of discovery process). For a discussion of dismissing an action for misuse of the discovery process, see "Misuse of discovery," ch. 9-A, §5.2.1, p. 1017.

§8. NO JOINDER OF INDISPENSABLE PARTY

The court can dismiss an action if an indispensable party could not be joined. CCP §389(b). An order of dismissal under CCP §389(b) is granted without prejudice. *Id.* For a discussion of indispensable parties, see "Absent party is indispensable," ch. 3-B, §3.1.3, p. 194.

§9. NO PAYMENT OF TRANSFER FEES & COSTS

The court can dismiss an action if a party was required to pay fees and costs after an order transferring venue and did not do so within 30 days after service of the transfer order. CCP §399(a). A motion to dismiss under CCP §399(a) can be requested by either party by noticed motion. *Id.* An order of dismissal under §399(a) is discretionary and is granted without prejudice. *Id.*

§10. NO PAYMENT OF SECURITY FOR COST

The court can dismiss an action if the plaintiff was required to give a bond as a security for payment of costs and did not do so. For example, the court can dismiss an action if a nonresident, foreign, or vexatious plaintiff is required to give a bond and does not do so. *See* CCP §391.4 (vexatious litigant), §1030(d) (nonresident or foreign corporation). Dismissal for failure to give a bond as security for payment of costs is mandatory and automatic. *See* CCP §§391.4, 1030(d).

§11. VIOLATION OF FAST-TRACK RULES

The court can dismiss an action if a party has not complied with the fast-track rules adopted to implement the Trial Court Delay Reduction Act (TCDRA). *See* CCP §575.2(a); Gov. C. §68608(b); ***Garcia v. McCutchen*** (1997) 16 Cal.4th 469, 475. A motion to dismiss for violation of a fast-track rule can be requested by either party or granted by the court on its own motion after notice. *See* CCP §575.2(a). The motion to dismiss must be made by noticed motion, and the party subject to dismissal must have an opportunity to be heard. *Id.* The court can dismiss an action for noncompliance with a fast-track rule if (1) the noncompliance was caused by the party, not the attorney, and (2) no less severe sanction would be effective. ***Tliche v. Van Quathem*** (2d Dist.1998) 66 Cal.App.4th 1054, 1061-62; *see* CCP §575.2(b); Gov. C. §68606(b).

PRACTICE TIP

Consult the court's local rules to determine whether there are any additional procedural requirements for dismissing an action for noncompliance with a fast-track rule.

§12. NO APPEARANCE AT TRIAL

§12.1 Neither party appears. The court can dismiss an action if neither party appears for trial following 30 days' notice of the time and place of trial. CCP §581(b)(3). An order of dismissal under CCP §581(b)(3) is discretionary and is granted without prejudice. *Id.*

§12.2 Only one party appears. The court can dismiss an action (or the action as it relates to a particular defendant) if one party does not appear for trial and the other party appears and asks for dismissal. *See* CCP §581(b)(5), (*l*); ***Link v. Cater*** (2d Dist.1998) 60 Cal.App.4th 1315, 1320; *see, e.g.*, ***Jones v. Otero*** (2d Dist.1984) 156 Cal.App.3d 754, 757 (improper to dismiss case when P appeared but P's attorney did not appear). If the action being dismissed contains a fact issue for the court to decide, the party requesting dismissal must prove that the adverse party had 15 days' notice of trial (or 5 days' notice in an unlawful-detainer action). CCP §594(a); *see* ***In re Estate of Dean*** (1906) 149 Cal. 487, 492 (court should not dismiss action under §581 for party's nonappearance unless proof of notice of trial under §594 is provided). An order of dismissal under §§581(b)(5) and 581(*l*) is discretionary and is granted without prejudice. *See* CCP §581(b)(5), (*l*). An appearance by a party's attorney is sufficient to constitute an appearance for that party. ***Cohen v. Hughes Mkts., Inc.*** (2d Dist.1995) 36 Cal.App.4th 1693, 1700.

§13. COURT'S INHERENT POWER

Under its inherent judicial power, the court can dismiss an action for a party's misconduct that violates an established procedure or a court order. ***Stephen Slesinger, Inc. v. Walt Disney Co.*** (2d Dist.2007) 155 Cal.App.4th 736, 760; *see* CCP §581(m) (provisions of §581 are not exclusive list of reasons actions can be dismissed); *see, e.g.*, ***Del Junco v. Hufnagel*** (2d Dist.2007) 150 Cal.App.4th 789, 799-800 (dismissal proper when D disobeyed repeated court orders, made misrepresentations to court, and did not cooperate with court procedures). The court's power to dismiss under its inherent power is limited to extreme circumstances when no less severe sanction would be effective to restore fairness and when the order of dismissal would not be inconsistent with the U.S. Constitution or state law. ***Stephen Slesinger, Inc.***, 155 Cal.App.4th at 761-62; *see, e.g.*, ***People v. Lockwood*** (1st Dist.1998) 66 Cal.App.4th 222, 230 (D speaking out in court was not severe, deliberate, or extreme enough to warrant dismissal with prejudice). An order of dismissal under the court's inherent power is discretionary and can be granted with prejudice. ***Lyons v. Wickhorst*** (1986) 42 Cal.3d 911, 915.

Evidence Code

Table of Contents

Evidence Code

EVIDENCE CODE

TABLE OF CONTENTS

EVIDENCE CODE

TABLE OF CONTENTS

TABLE OF CONTENTS

TABLE OF CONTENTS

TABLE OF CONTENTS

DIVISION 1. PRELIMINARY PROVISIONS & CONSTRUCTION

§1. [TITLE]

This code shall be known as the Evidence Code.

History of Evid. C. §1: Added eff. Sept. 17, 1965, oper. Jan. 1, 1967, Stats. 1965, ch. 299, §2.

Official Comment

7 Cal. Law Revision Comm'n Rep. (1965) p. 1025.

This section is similar to comparable sections in recently enacted California codes. *E.g.*, Vehicle Code §1. *See also* Code Civ. Proc. §§1, 19.

§2. [LIBERAL CONSTRUCTION]

The rule of the common law, that statutes in derogation thereof are to be strictly construed, has no application to this code. This code establishes the law of this state respecting the subject to which it relates, and its provisions are to be liberally construed with a view to effecting its objects and promoting justice.

History of Evid. C. §2: Added eff. Sept. 17, 1965, oper. Jan. 1, 1967, Stats. 1965, ch. 299, §2.

Official Comment

7 Cal. Law Revision Comm'n Rep. (1965) p. 1025.

This section is substantially the same as Section 4 of the Code of Civil Procedure.

§3. [SEVERABLE PROVISIONS]

If any provision or clause of this code or application thereof to any person or circumstances is held invalid, such invalidity shall not affect other provisions or applications of the code which can be given effect without the invalid provision or application, and to this end the provisions of this code are declared to be severable.

History of Evid. C. §3: Added eff. Sept. 17, 1965, oper. Jan. 1, 1967, Stats. 1965, ch. 299, §2.

Official Comment

7 Cal. Law Revision Comm'n Rep. (1965) p. 1025.

Section 3 is the same as Section 1108 of the Commercial Code. *See also, e.g.*, Vehicle Code §5. This general "severability" provision permits the repeal of comparable provisions applicable to specific sections formerly compiled in the Code of Civil Procedure that are now compiled in the Evidence Code and makes it unnecessary to include similar provisions in future amendments to this code. *See* Code Civ. Proc. §1928.4 (repealed).

§4. [CODE CONSTRUCTION]

Unless the provision or context otherwise requires, these preliminary provisions and rules of construction shall govern the construction of this code.

History of Evid. C. §4: Added eff. Sept. 17, 1965, oper. Jan. 1, 1967, Stats. 1965, ch. 299, §2.

See also Civ. C. §§13, 3542; Gov. C. §9603.

Official Comment

7 Cal. Law Revision Comm'n Rep. (1965) p. 1026.

This is a standard provision in various California codes. *E.g.*, Vehicle Code §6.

§5. [HEADINGS]

Division, chapter, article, and section headings do not in any manner affect the scope, meaning, or intent of the provisions of this code.

History of Evid. C. §5: Added eff. Sept. 17, 1965, oper. Jan. 1, 1967, Stats. 1965, ch. 299, §2.

Official Comment

7 Cal. Law Revision Comm'n Rep. (1965) p. 1026.

Similar provisions appear in all the existing California codes except the Civil Code, the Commercial Code, and the Code of Civil Procedure. *E.g.*, Vehicle Code §7.

§6. [REFERENCES IN CODE]

Whenever any reference is made to any portion of this code or of any other statute, such reference shall apply to all amendments and additions heretofore or hereafter made.

History of Evid. C. §6: Added eff. Sept. 17, 1965, oper. Jan. 1, 1967, Stats. 1965, ch. 299, §2.

Official Comment

7 Cal. Law Revision Comm'n Rep. (1965) p. 1026.

This is a standard provision in various California codes. *E.g.*, Vehicle Code §10.

§7. [STRUCTURAL DEFINITIONS]

Unless otherwise expressly stated:

(a) "Division" means a division of this code.

(b) "Chapter" means a chapter of the division in which that term occurs.

(c) "Article" means an article of the chapter in which that term occurs.

(d) "Section" means a section of this code.

(e) "Subdivision" means a subdivision of the section in which that term occurs.

(f) "Paragraph" means a paragraph of the subdivision in which that term occurs.

History of Evid. C. §7: Added eff. Sept. 17, 1965, oper. Jan. 1, 1967, Stats. 1965, ch. 299, §2.

Official Comment

7 Cal. Law Revision Comm'n Rep. (1965) p. 1026.

Somewhat similar provisions appear in various California codes. *E.g.*, Vehicle Code §11. *See also* Code Civ. Proc. §17(8) [now CCP §17(b)(8)].

§8. [TENSE CONSTRUCTION]

The present tense includes the past and future tenses; and the future, the present.

History of Evid. C. §8: Added eff. Sept. 17, 1965, oper. Jan. 1, 1967, Stats. 1965, ch. 299, §2.

Official Comment

7 Cal. Law Revision Comm'n Rep. (1965) p. 1026.

This is a standard provision in various California codes. *E.g.*, Vehicle Code §12. *See also* Code Civ. Proc. §17.

§9. [GENDER]

The masculine gender includes the feminine and neuter.

History of Evid. C. §9: Added eff. Sept. 17, 1965, oper. Jan. 1, 1967, Stats. 1965, ch. 299, §2.

Official Comment

7 Cal. Law Revision Comm'n Rep. (1965) p. 1027.

This is a standard provision in various California codes. *E.g.*, Vehicle Code §13. *See also* Code Civ. Proc. §17.

§10. [NUMBER]

The singular number includes the plural; and the plural, the singular.

History of Evid. C. §10: Added eff. Sept. 17, 1965, oper. Jan. 1, 1967, Stats. 1965, ch. 299, §2.

Official Comment

7 Cal. Law Revision Comm'n Rep. (1965) p. 1027.

This is a standard provision in various California codes. *E.g.*, Vehicle Code §14. *See also* Code Civ. Proc. §17.

§11. ["SHALL" & "MAY"]

"Shall" is mandatory and "may" is permissive.

History of Evid. C. §11: Added eff. Sept. 17, 1965, oper. Jan. 1, 1967, Stats. 1965, ch. 299, §2.

Official Comment

7 Cal. Law Revision Comm'n Rep. (1965) p. 1027.

This is a standard provision in various California codes. *E.g.*, Vehicle Code §15.

§12. [OPERATIVE DATE]

(a) [Proceedings brought after.] This code shall become operative on January 1, 1967, and shall govern proceedings in actions brought on or after that date and, except as provided in subdivision (b), further proceedings in actions pending on that date.

(b) [Proceedings commenced before.] Subject to subdivision (c), a trial commenced before January 1, 1967, shall not be governed by this code. For the purpose of this subdivision:

(1) A trial is commenced when the first witness is sworn or the first exhibit is admitted into evidence and is terminated when the issue upon which such evidence is received is submitted to the trier of fact. A new trial, or a separate trial of a different issue, commenced on or after January 1, 1967, shall be governed by this code.

(2) If an appeal is taken from a ruling made at a trial commenced before January 1, 1967, the appellate court shall apply the law applicable at the time of the commencement of the trial.

(c) [Claims of privilege.] The provisions of Division 8 (commencing with Section 900) relating to privileges shall govern any claim of privilege made after December 31, 1966.

History of Evid. C. §12: Added eff. Sept. 17, 1965, oper. Jan. 1, 1967, Stats. 1965, ch. 299, §2.

Official Comment

7 Cal. Law Revision Comm'n Rep. (1965) p. 1027;
Assem. J., Apr. 6, 1965, p. 1712.

The delayed operative date provides time for California judges and attorneys to become familiar with the code before it goes into effect.

Subdivision (a) makes it clear that the Evidence Code governs all trials commenced after December 31, 1966.

Under subdivision (b), a trial that has actually commenced prior to the operative date of the code will continue to be governed by the rules of evidence (except privileges) applicable at the commencement of the trial. Thus, if the trial court makes a ruling on the admission of evidence in a trial commenced prior to January 1, 1967, such ruling (even when it is made after January 1, 1967) is not affected by the enactment of the Evidence Code; if an appeal is taken from the ruling, Section 12 requires the appellate court to apply the law applicable at the commencement of the trial. On the other hand, any ruling made by the trial court on the admission of evidence in a trial commenced after December 31, 1966, is governed by the Evidence Code, even if a previous trial in the same action was commenced prior to that date.

A hearing on a motion or a similar proceeding is to be treated the same as a trial for the purpose of applying the rules stated in subdivision (b). See subdivision (b)(1).

Under subdivision (c), all claims of privilege made after December 31, 1966, are governed by the Evidence Code in order that there might be no delay in providing protection to the important relationships and interests that are protected by the Privileges Division.

DIVISION 2. WORDS & PHRASES DEFINED

Official Comment

7 Cal. Law Revision Comm'n Rep. (1965) p. 1029.

Division 2 contains definitions of general application only. Words and phrases that have special significance only to a particular division or article are defined in the division or article in which the defined term is used. For example, Sections 900-905 define terms that are used only in Division 8 (Privileges), and Sections 950-953 define terms that are used in the article relating to the lawyer-client privilege. Some additional sections of general application that are of a definitional nature include Sections 7-11 in Division 1.

§100. [DEFINITIONS GOVERN CONSTRUCTION]

Unless the provision or context otherwise requires, these definitions govern the construction of this code.

History of Evid. C. §100: Added eff. Sept. 17, 1965, oper. Jan. 1, 1967, Stats. 1965, ch. 299, §2.

Official Comment

7 Cal. Law Revision Comm'n Rep. (1965) p. 1029.

Section 100 is a standard provision found in the definitional portion of recently enacted California codes. *See, e.g.*, Vehicle Code §100.

§105. [ACTION]

"Action" includes a civil action and a criminal action.

History of Evid. C. §105: Added eff. Sept. 17, 1965, oper. Jan. 1, 1967, Stats. 1965, ch. 299, §2.

Official Comment

7 Cal. Law Revision Comm'n Rep. (1965) p. 1029.

Defining the word "action" to include both a civil action or proceeding and a criminal action or proceeding eliminates the necessity of repeating "civil action and criminal action" in numerous code sections.

§110. [BURDEN OF PRODUCING EVIDENCE]

"Burden of producing evidence" means the obligation of a party to introduce evidence sufficient to avoid a ruling against him on the issue.

History of Evid. C. §110: Added eff. Sept. 17, 1965, oper. Jan. 1, 1967, Stats. 1965, ch. 299, §2.

Official Comment

7 Cal. Law Revision Comm'n Rep. (1965) p. 1030;
Assem. J., Apr. 6, 1965, p. 1713.

The phrases defined in Sections 110 and 115 provide a convenient means for distinguishing between the burden of proving a fact and the burden of going forward with the evidence. They recognize a distinction that is well established in California. Witkin, *California Evidence* §§53-60 (1958). The practical effect of the distinction is discussed in the Comments to Division 5 (commencing with Section 500), especially in the Comments to Sections 500 and 550.

ANNOTATIONS

California Farm Bur. Fed'n v. State Water Res. Control Bd. (2011) 51 Cal.4th 421, 436. See annotation under Evidence Code §550, p. 1231.

§115. [BURDEN OF PROOF]

"Burden of proof" means the obligation of a party to establish by evidence a requisite degree of belief concerning a fact in the mind of the trier of fact or the court. The burden of proof may require a party to raise a reasonable doubt concerning the existence or nonexistence of a fact or that he establish the existence or nonexistence of a fact by a preponderance of the evidence, by clear and convincing proof, or by proof beyond a reasonable doubt.

Except as otherwise provided by law, the burden of proof requires proof by a preponderance of the evidence.

History of Evid. C. §115: Added eff. Sept. 17, 1965, oper. Jan. 1, 1967, Stats. 1965, ch. 299, §2.

Official Comment

7 Cal. Law Revision Comm'n Rep. (1965) p. 1030;
Assem. J., Apr. 6, 1965, p. 1713.

See the Comment to Section 110.

After stating the general definition of "burden of proof," the first paragraph of Section 115 gives examples of specific burdens that may be imposed by statutory or decisional law. The list of examples is not exclusive, and in some cases the law may prescribe some other burden of proof. For example, under Penal Code Section 872, the prosecution's burden of proof at a preliminary hearing is to establish "sufficient cause"—*i.e.*, a "strong suspicion"—of the accused's guilt. *Garabedian v. Superior Court*, 59 Cal.2d 124, 28 Cal.Rptr. 318, 378 P.2d 590 (1963); *Rogers v. Superior Court*, 46 Cal.2d 3, 291 P.2d 929 (1955).

The second paragraph of Section 115 makes it clear that "burden of proof" refers to the burden of proving the fact in question by a preponderance of the evidence unless a heavier or lesser burden of proof is specifically required in a particular case by constitutional, statutory, or decisional law. See the definition of "law" in Evidence Code §160.

ANNOTATIONS

In re Estate of Ford (2004) 32 Cal.4th 160, 173. "The law providing for a higher standard of proof may include decisional law."

Cooley v. Superior Ct. (2002) 29 Cal.4th 228, 251. "'[S]ufficient cause' burden—analogous to the probable cause burden—is an example of a burden of proof prescribed by law that might be required instead of the preponderance of evidence burden."

Conservatorship of Wendland (2001) 26 Cal.4th 519, 546. "[C]ourts have applied the clear and convincing evidence standard when necessary to protect important rights. *At 552:* The clear and convincing evidence test requires a finding of high probability, based on evidence so clear as to leave no substantial doubt and sufficiently strong to command the unhesitating assent of every reasonable mind." (Internal quotes omitted.) *See also* ***Baxter Healthcare Corp. v. Denton*** (3d Dist. 2004) 120 Cal.App.4th 333, 365.

Weiner v. Fleischman (1991) 54 Cal.3d 476, 484. "While it is clear that case law may, in some instances, suggest a higher burden of proof than preponderance of the evidence is required, we have stated as a general principle that 'judicial expressions purporting to require clear and convincing [or clear and satisfactory] evidence must be read in light of the statutory provision for proof by a preponderance of the evidence....'" *See also* ***In re Marriage of Ettefagh*** (1st Dist.2007) 150 Cal.App.4th 1578, 1585.

§120. [CIVIL ACTION]

"Civil action" includes civil proceedings.

History of Evid. C. §120: Added eff. Sept. 17, 1965, oper. Jan. 1, 1967, Stats. 1965, ch. 299, §2.

Official Comment

7 Cal. Law Revision Comm'n Rep. (1965) p. 1031.

Defining "civil action" to include civil proceedings eliminates the necessity of repeating "civil action or proceeding" in numerous code sections, and, together with the definition of "criminal action" in Section 130, it assures the applicability of the Evidence Code to all actions and proceedings. *See* Evidence Code §300.

§125. [CONDUCT]

"Conduct" includes all active and passive behavior, both verbal and nonverbal.

History of Evid. C. §125: Added eff. Sept. 17, 1965, oper. Jan. 1, 1967, Stats. 1965, ch. 299, §2.

Official Comment

7 Cal. Law Revision Comm'n Rep. (1965) p. 1031.

This broad definition of "conduct" is self-explanatory.

§130. [CRIMINAL ACTION]

"Criminal action" includes criminal proceedings.

History of Evid. C. §130: Added eff. Sept. 17, 1965, oper. Jan. 1, 1967, Stats. 1965, ch. 299, §2.

Official Comment

7 Cal. Law Revision Comm'n Rep. (1965) p. 1031.

See the *Comment* to Section 120.

§135. [DECLARANT]

"Declarant" is a person who makes a statement.

History of Evid. C. §135: Added eff. Sept. 17, 1965, oper. Jan. 1, 1967, Stats. 1965, ch. 299, §2.

Official Comment

7 Cal. Law Revision Comm'n Rep. (1965) p. 1031.

Ordinarily, the word "declarant" is used in the Evidence Code to refer to a person who makes a hearsay statement as distinguished from the witness who testifies to the content of the statement. *See* Evidence Code §1200 and the *Comment* thereto.

§140. [EVIDENCE]

"Evidence" means testimony, writings, material objects, or other things presented to the senses that are offered to prove the existence or nonexistence of a fact.

History of Evid. C. §140: Added eff. Sept. 17, 1965, oper. Jan. 1, 1967, Stats. 1965, ch. 299, §2.

Official Comment

7 Cal. Law Revision Comm'n Rep. (1965) p. 1031.

"Evidence" is defined broadly to include the testimony of witnesses, tangible objects, sights (such as a jury view or the appearance of a person exhibited to a jury), sounds (such as the sound of a voice demonstrated for a jury), and any other thing that may be presented as a basis of proof. The definition includes anything offered in evidence whether or not it is technically inadmissible and whether or not it is received. For example, Division 10 (commencing with Section 1200) uses "evidence" to refer to hearsay which may be excluded as inadmissible but which may be admitted if no proper objection is made. Thus, when inadmissible hearsay or opinion testimony is admitted without objection, this definition makes it clear that it constitutes evidence that may be considered by the trier of fact.

Section 140 is a better statement of existing law than Code of Civil Procedure Section 1823, which is superseded by Section 140. Although Section 1823 by its terms restricts "judicial evidence" to that "sanctioned by law," the general principle is well established that matter which is technically inadmissible under an exclusionary rule is nonetheless evidence and may be considered in support of a judgment if it is offered and received in evidence without proper objection or motion to strike. *E.g., People v. Alexander*, 212 Cal.App.2d 84, 98, 27 Cal.Rptr. 720, 727 (1963) ("illustrations of this principle are numerous and cover a wide range of evidentiary topics such as incompetent hearsay, secondary evidence violating the best evidence rule, inadmissible opinions, lack of foundation, incompetent, privileged or unqualified witnesses, and violations of the parol evidence rule"). *See* Witkin, *California Evidence* §§723-724 (1958).

Under this definition, a presumption is not evidence. *See also* Evidence Code §600 and the *Comment* thereto.

ANNOTATIONS

Gdowski v. Gdowski (4th Dist.2009) 175 Cal.App.4th 128, 138-39. "[S]ection 140 defines evidence.... Statements and arguments by counsel are not evidence."

Denny's, Inc. v. City of Agoura Hills (2d Dist.1997) 56 Cal.App.4th 1312, 1328. "It is settled 'that a view of the scene by the trial judge is independent evidence on which a finding may be made and sustained....'"

§145. [HEARING]

"The hearing" means the hearing at which a question under this code arises, and not some earlier or later hearing.

History of Evid. C. §145: Added eff. Sept. 17, 1965, oper. Jan. 1, 1967, Stats. 1965, ch. 299, §2.

Official Comment

7 Cal. Law Revision Comm'n Rep. (1965) p. 1032.

"The hearing" is defined to mean the hearing at which the particular question under the Evidence Code arises and, unless a particular provision or its context otherwise indicates, not some earlier or later hearing. This definition is much broader than would be a reference to the trial itself; the definition includes, for example, preliminary hearings and post-trial proceedings.

§150. [HEARSAY]

"Hearsay evidence" is defined in Section 1200.

History of Evid. C. §150: Added eff. Sept. 17, 1965, oper. Jan. 1, 1967, Stats. 1965, ch. 299, §2.

Official Comment

7 Cal. Law Revision Comm'n Rep. (1965) p. 1032.

Because of its special significance to Division 10, the substantive definition of "hearsay evidence" is contained in Section 1200. *See* the *Comment* to Section 1200.

§160. [LAW]

"Law" includes constitutional, statutory, and decisional law.

History of Evid. C. §160: Added eff. Sept. 17, 1965, oper. Jan. 1, 1967, Stats. 1965, ch. 299, §2.

Official Comment

7 Cal. Law Revision Comm'n Rep. (1965) p. 1032.

This definition makes it clear that a reference to "law" includes the law established by judicial decisions as well as by constitutional and statutory provisions.

§165. [OATH]

"Oath" includes affirmation or declaration under penalty of perjury.

History of Evid. C. §165: Added eff. Sept. 17, 1965, oper. Jan. 1, 1967, Stats. 1965, ch. 299, §2.

Official Comment

7 Cal. Law Revision Comm'n Rep. (1965) p. 1032.

Similar definitions are found in other California codes. *E.g.*, Vehicle Code §16.

§170. [PERCEIVE]

"Perceive" means to acquire knowledge through one's senses.

History of Evid. C. §170: Added eff. Sept. 17, 1965, oper. Jan. 1, 1967, Stats. 1965, ch. 299, §2.

Official Comment

7 Cal. Law Revision Comm'n Rep. (1965) p. 1033.

This definition is self-explanatory.

§175. [PERSON]

"Person" includes a natural person, firm, association, organization, partnership, business trust, corporation, limited liability company, or public entity.

History of Evid. C. §175: Added eff. Sept. 17, 1965, oper. Jan. 1, 1967, Stats. 1965, ch. 299, §2. Amended eff. Jan. 1, 1995, Stats. 1994, ch. 1010, §103.

Official Comment

7 Cal. Law Revision Comm'n Rep. (1965) p. 1033.

This broad definition is similar to definitions found in other codes. *E.g.*, Gov. Code §17; Vehicle Code §470. *See also* Code Civ. Proc. §17.

§177. [DEPENDENT PERSON]

"Dependent person" means any person who has a physical or mental impairment that substantially restricts his or her ability to carry out normal activities or to protect his or her rights, including, but not limited to, persons who have physical or developmental disabilities or whose physical or mental abilities have significantly diminished because of age. "Dependent person" includes any person who is admitted as an inpatient to a 24-hour health facility, as defined in Sections 1250, 1250.2, and 1250.3 of the Health and Safety Code.

History of Evid. C. §177: Added eff. Jan. 1, 2005, Stats. 2004, ch. 823, §2.

§180. [PERSONAL PROPERTY]

"Personal property" includes money, goods, chattels, things in action, and evidences of debt.

History of Evid. C. §180: Added eff. Sept. 17, 1965, oper. Jan. 1, 1967, Stats. 1965, ch. 299, §2.

Official Comment

7 Cal. Law Revision Comm'n Rep. (1965) p. 1033.

This definition is the same as the definition of "personal property" in Section 17(3) [now CCP §17(b)(3)] of the Code of Civil Procedure.

§185. [PROPERTY]

"Property" includes both real and personal property.

History of Evid. C. §185: Added eff. Sept. 17, 1965, oper. Jan. 1, 1967, Stats. 1965, ch. 299, §2.

Official Comment

7 Cal. Law Revision Comm'n Rep. (1965) p. 1033.

This definition is the same as the definition of "property" in Section 17(1) [now CCP §17(b)(1)] of the Code of Civil Procedure.

§190. [PROOF]

"Proof" is the establishment by evidence of a requisite degree of belief concerning a fact in the mind of the trier of fact or the court.

History of Evid. C. §190: Added eff. Sept. 17, 1965, oper. Jan. 1, 1967, Stats. 1965, ch. 299, §2.

Official Comment

7 Cal. Law Revision Comm'n Rep. (1965) p. 1033.

This definition is more accurate than the definition of "proof" in Code of Civil Procedure Section 1824, which is superseded by Section 190. The disjunctive reference to "the trier of fact or the court" is needed because, even when the jury is the trier of fact, the court is required to determine preliminary questions of fact on the basis of proof.

§195. [PUBLIC EMPLOYEE]

"Public employee" means an officer, agent, or employee of a public entity.

History of Evid. C. §195: Added eff. Sept. 17, 1965, oper. Jan. 1, 1967, Stats. 1965, ch. 299, §2.

Official Comment

7 Cal. Law Revision Comm'n Rep. (1965) p. 1034.

This definition specifically includes public officers and agents, thereby eliminating any distinction between employees and officers and making it unnecessary to repeat the phrase "officer, agent, or employee" in numerous code sections.

§200. [PUBLIC ENTITY]

"Public entity" includes a nation, state, county, city and county, city, district, public authority, public agency, or any other political subdivision or public corporation, whether foreign or domestic.

History of Evid. C. §200: Added eff. Sept. 17, 1965, oper. Jan. 1, 1967, Stats. 1965, ch. 299, §2.

Official Comment

7 Cal. Law Revision Comm'n Rep. (1965) p. 1034.

The broad definition of "public entity" includes every form of public authority, both foreign and domestic. Occasionally, "public entity" is used in the Evidence Code with limiting language to refer specifically to entities within this State or the United States. *E.g.*, Evidence Code §452(b). *Cf.* Evidence Code §452(f).

ANNOTATIONS

Peterson v. City of Long Beach (1979) 24 Cal.3d 238, 244. "A city is a public entity. But so are the office of its city manager and the department that its police chief directs. Each traditionally has been regarded as an 'agency' of the city, obviously 'public.' We find it hard to believe that the Legislature would not regard city managers and police chiefs (whose power to promulgate rules is conceded) as heads of a 'form of public authority.'"

§205. [REAL PROPERTY]

"Real property" includes lands, tenements, and hereditaments.

History of Evid. C. §205: Added eff. Sept. 17, 1965, oper. Jan. 1, 1967, Stats. 1965, ch. 299, §2.

Official Comment

7 Cal. Law Revision Comm'n Rep. (1965) p. 1034.

This definition is substantially the same as the definition of "real property" in Section 17(2) [now CCP §17(b)(2)] of the Code of Civil Procedure.

§210. [RELEVANT EVIDENCE]

"Relevant evidence" means evidence, including evidence relevant to the credibility of a witness or hearsay declarant, having any tendency in reason to prove or disprove any disputed fact that is of consequence to the determination of the action.

History of Evid. C. §210: Added eff. Sept. 17, 1965, oper. Jan. 1, 1967, Stats. 1965, ch. 299, §2.

Official Comment

7 Cal. Law Revision Comm'n Rep. (1965) p. 1034.

This definition restates existing law. *E.g.*, *Larson v. Solbakken*, 221 Cal.App.2d 410, 419, 34 Cal.Rptr. 450, 455 (1963); *People v. Lint*, 182 Cal.App.2d 402, 415, 6 Cal.Rptr. 95, 102-103 (1960). Thus, under Section 210, "relevant evidence" includes not only evidence of the ultimate facts actually in dispute but also evidence of other facts from which such ultimate facts may be presumed or inferred. This retains existing law as found in subdivisions 1 and 15 of Code of Civil Procedure Section 1870, which are superseded by the Evidence Code. In addition, Section 210 makes it clear that evidence relating to the credibility of witnesses and hearsay declarants is "relevant evidence." This restates existing law. *See* Code Civ. Proc. §§1868, 1870(16) (credibility of witnesses), which are superseded by the Evidence Code, and *Tentative Recommendation and a Study Relating to the Uniform Rules of Evidence (Article VIII. Hearsay Evidence)*, 6 Cal. Law Revision Comm'n, Rep., Rec. & Studies *Appendix* at 339-340, 569-575 (1964) (credibility of hearsay declarants).

ANNOTATIONS

People v. Clark (2011) 52 Cal.4th 856, 922. "[E]vidence is relevant if it tends logically, naturally, and by reasonable inference to establish material facts such as identity, intent, or motive." (Internal quotes omitted.)

Cole v. Town of Los Gatos (6th Dist.2012) 205 Cal.App.4th 749, 764-65. "A question of relevancy involves two subsidiary inquiries: whether the *fact sought to be shown* by the evidence is 'material,' i.e., within the issues properly tendered by a party and whether the proffered evidence actually *tends to prove* that fact. … In [determining materiality], the primary considerations are 'the pleadings, the rules [of] pleading, and the substantive law relating to the particular kind of case.'" *See also* **Collins v. Navistar, Inc.** (3d Dist.2013) 214 Cal.App.4th 1486, 1513-14 (evidence is relevant if it has '*any* tendency' to prove or disprove disputed fact).

San Lorenzo Valley Cmty. Advocates for Responsible Educ. v. San Lorenzo Valley Unified Sch. Dist. (6th Dist.2006) 139 Cal.App.4th 1356, 1414. "'The trial court retains broad discretion in determining the relevance of evidence.' … Though not directly germane, a 'matter collateral to an issue in the action may nevertheless be relevant to the credibility of a witness who presents evidence on an issue….' But the admissibility of such collateral matter also lies within the trial court's discretion."

§220. [STATE]

"State" means the State of California, unless applied to the different parts of the United States. In the latter case, it includes any state, district, commonwealth, territory, or insular possession of the United States.

History of Evid. C. §220: Added eff. Sept. 17, 1965, oper. Jan. 1, 1967, Stats. 1965, ch. 299, §2.

Official Comment

7 Cal. Law Revision Comm'n Rep. (1965) p. 1035.

This definition is more precise than the comparable definition found in Section 17(7) [now CCP §17(b)(7)] of the Code of Civil Procedure. For example, Section 220 makes it clear that "state" includes Puerto Rico, even though Puerto Rico is now a "commonwealth" rather than a "territory."

ANNOTATIONS

Big Valley Band of Pomo Indians v. Superior Ct. (1st Dist.2005) 133 Cal.App.4th 1185, 1192 n.3. "'State' is defined in [§220] to include a 'territory' or 'insular possession.' While we are unaware of any reported decision treating a federally recognized tribe as a state under the Evidence Code, the characterization is appropriate for purposes of taking judicial notice of tribal laws. A federally recognized tribe is a sovereign entity and, thus, similar to a state or territory."

§225. [STATEMENT]

"Statement" means (a) oral or written verbal expression or (b) nonverbal conduct of a person intended by him as a substitute for oral or written verbal expression.

History of Evid. C. §225: Added eff. Sept. 17, 1965, oper. Jan. 1, 1967, Stats. 1965, ch. 299, §2.

Official Comment

7 Cal. Law Revision Comm'n Rep. (1965) p. 1035.

The significance of this definition is explained in the *Comment* to Evidence Code Section 1200.

§230. [STATUTE]

"Statute" includes a treaty and a constitutional provision.

History of Evid. C. §230: Added eff. Sept. 17, 1965, oper. Jan. 1, 1967, Stats. 1965, ch. 299, §2.

Official Comment

7 Cal. Law Revision Comm'n Rep. (1965) p. 1035.

In the Evidence Code, "statute" includes a constitutional provision. Thus, for example, when a particular section is subject to any exceptions "otherwise provided by statute," exceptions provided by the Constitution also are applicable.

§235. [TRIER OF FACT]

"Trier of fact" includes (a) the jury and (b) the court when the court is trying an issue of fact other than one relating to the admissibility of evidence.

History of Evid. C. §235: Added eff. Sept. 17, 1965, oper. Jan. 1, 1967, Stats. 1965, ch. 299, §2.

Official Comment

7 Cal. Law Revision Comm'n Rep. (1965) p. 1036.

"Trier of fact" is defined to include not only the jury but also the court when it is trying an issue of fact without a jury. The definition is not exclusive; a referee, court commissioner, or other officer conducting proceedings governed by the Evidence Code may be a trier of fact. *See* Evidence Code §300.

§240. [UNAVAILABLE AS WITNESS]

(a) **[Defined.]** Except as otherwise provided in subdivision (b), "unavailable as a witness" means that the declarant is any of the following:

(1) Exempted or precluded on the ground of privilege from testifying concerning the matter to which his or her statement is relevant.

(2) Disqualified from testifying to the matter.

(3) Dead or unable to attend or to testify at the hearing because of then-existing physical or mental illness or infirmity.

(4) Absent from the hearing and the court is unable to compel his or her attendance by its process.

(5) Absent from the hearing and the proponent of his or her statement has exercised reasonable diligence but has been unable to procure his or her attendance by the court's process.

(6) Persistent in refusing to testify concerning the subject matter of the declarant's statement despite having been found in contempt for refusal to testify.

(b) **[Safeguards.]** A declarant is not unavailable as a witness if the exemption, preclusion, disqualification, death, inability, or absence of the declarant was brought about by the procurement or wrongdoing of the proponent of his or her statement for the purpose of preventing the declarant from attending or testifying.

(c) **[Expert testimony.]** Expert testimony that establishes that physical or mental trauma resulting from an alleged crime has caused harm to a witness of sufficient severity that the witness is physically unable to testify or is unable to testify without suffering substantial trauma may constitute a sufficient showing of unavailability pursuant to paragraph (3) of subdivision (a). As used in this section, the term "expert" means a physician and surgeon, including a psychiatrist, or any person described by subdivision (b), (c), or (e) of Section 1010.

The introduction of evidence to establish the unavailability of a witness under this subdivision shall not be deemed procurement of unavailability, in absence of proof to the contrary.

History of Evid. C. §240: Added eff. Sept. 17, 1965, oper. Jan. 1, 1967, Stats. 1965, ch. 299, §2. Amended eff. Jan. 1, 1985, Stats. 1984, ch. 401, §1; eff. Jan. 1, 1989, Stats. 1988, ch. 485, §1; eff. Jan. 1, 2011, Stats. 2010, ch. 537, §1.

Official Comment

7 Cal. Law Revision Comm'n Rep. (1965) p. 1036; Assem. J., Apr. 6, 1965, p. 1713.

Usually, the phrase "unavailable as a witness" is used in the Evidence Code to state the condition that must be met whenever the admissibility of hearsay evidence is dependent upon the declarant's present unavailability to testify. *See, e.g.*, Evidence Code §§1230, 1251, 1291, 1292, 1310, 1311, 1323. *See also* Code Civ. Proc. §2016(d)(3) [now CCP §2025.620] and Penal Code §§1345 and 1362, relating to depositions.

"Unavailable as a witness" includes, in addition to cases where the declarant is physically unavailable (*i.e.*, dead, insane, or beyond the reach of the court's process), situations in which the declarant is legally unavailable (*i.e.*, prevented from testifying by a claim of privilege or disqualified from testifying). Of course, if the declaration made out of court is itself privileged, the fact that the declarant is unavailable to testify at the hearing on the ground of privilege does not make the declaration admissible. The exceptions to the hearsay rule that are set forth in Division 10 (commencing with Section 1200) of the Evidence Code do not declare that the evidence described is necessarily admissible. They merely declare that such evidence is not inadmissible under the hearsay rule. If there is some other rule of law—such as privilege—which makes the evidence inadmissible, the court is not authorized to admit the evidence merely because it falls within an exception to the hearsay rule. Accordingly, the hearsay exceptions permit the introduction of evidence where the declarant is unavailable because of privilege only if the declaration itself is not privileged or is not inadmissible for some other reason.

Subdivision (b) is designed to establish safeguards against sharp practices and, in the words of the Commissioners on Uniform State Laws, to assure "that unavailability is honest and not planned in order to gain an advantage." Uniform Rules of Evidence, Rule 62 *Comment*. Under this subdivision, a party may not arrange a declarant's disappearance in order to use the declarant's out-of-court statement. Moreover, if the out-of-court statement is that of the party himself, he may not create "unavailability" under this section by invoking a privilege not to testify.

Section 240 substitutes a uniform standard for the varying standards of unavailability provided by the superseded Code of Civil Procedure sections providing hearsay exceptions. *E.g.*, Code Civ. Proc. §1870 (4), (8). The conditions constituting unavailability under these superseded sections vary from exception to exception without apparent reason. Under some of these sections, the evidence is admissible if the declarant is dead; under others, the evidence is admissible if the declarant is dead or insane; under still others, the evidence is admissible if the declarant is absent from the jurisdiction. Despite the express language of these superseded sections, Section 240 may, to a considerable extent, restate existing law. *Compare People v. Spriggs*, 60 Cal.2d 868, 875, 36 Cal.Rptr. 841, 845, 389 P.2d 377, 381 (1964) (generally consistent with Section 240), *with* the older cases, some but not all of which are inconsistent with the *Spriggs* case and with Section 240. See the cases cited in *Tentative Recommendation and a Study Relating to the Uniform Rules of Evidence (Article VIII. Hearsay Evidence)*, 6 Cal. Law Revision Comm'n, Rep., Rec. & Studies *Appendix* at 411 note 7 (1964).

ANNOTATIONS

People v. Fuiava (2012) 53 Cal.4th 622, 675. "Although §240 refers to 'reasonable diligence,' this court has often described the evaluation as one involving 'due diligence.' [¶] We have said that the term 'due diligence' is incapable of a mechanical definition, but it connotes persevering application, untiring efforts in good earnest, efforts of a substantial character. Relevant considerations include whether the search was timely begun ..., the importance of the witness's testimony ..., and whether leads were competently explored...." (Internal quotes omitted.) *See also* ***People v. Thomas*** (2011) 51 Cal.4th 449, 500.

Ritter v. State Bar (1985) 40 Cal.3d 595, 601. "[T]he examiner provided the panel with a doctor's letter indicating that [witness] was suffering from [several afflictions]. The letter was dated approximately two months prior to the hearing date and stated that 'it [was] not medically advisable for [witness] to appear in court as she cannot tolerate stress of any kind.' Thereafter, over objections …, the hearing panel admitted portions of the deposition into evidence. [¶] [T]his was error. The letter was insufficient to establish unavailability under … §240. [Witness] was the individual who had initiated the disciplinary proceeding against petitioner. She was expected to be the State Bar's chief witness. Therefore, the hearing panel should have required a more reliable and timely showing of unavailability before admitting the deposition testimony."

People v. Hollinquest (1st Dist.2011) 190 Cal.App.4th 1534, 1547. "[A] witness, upon proper assertion of the privilege against self-incrimination, is unavailable as a witness at trial. … The fact that [co-D] did not assert the privilege at the preliminary hearing did not foreclose him from doing so at trial. [¶] [T]o be found unavailable on this ground, a witness must not only intend to assert the privilege, but also be entitled to assert it." (Internal quotes omitted.)

Creutz v. Superior Ct. (4th Dist.1996) 49 Cal.App.4th 822, 828. "A witness who is unable to understand the duty to tell the truth is 'disqualified,' as is one incapable of expressing himself or herself so as to be understood. It is commonplace to speak of a child witness who does not understand the duty to tell the truth either as 'incompetent to testify' or 'disqualified from testifying.' A minor who is not qualified to testify is therefore 'unavailable' under §240, subdivision (a)(2)."

§250. [WRITING]

"Writing" means handwriting, typewriting, printing, photostating, photographing, photocopying, transmitting by electronic mail or facsimile, and every other means of recording upon any tangible thing, any form of communication or representation, including letters, words, pictures, sounds, or symbols, or combinations thereof, and any record thereby created, regardless of the manner in which the record has been stored.

History of Evid. C. §250: Added eff. Sept. 17, 1965, oper. Jan. 1, 1967, Stats. 1965, ch. 299, §2. Amended eff. Jan. 1, 2003, Stats. 2002, ch. 945, §1.

Official Comment

7 Cal. Law Revision Comm'n Rep. (1965) p. 1037.

"Writing" is defined very broadly to include all forms of tangible expression, including pictures and sound recordings.

ANNOTATIONS

Ashford v. Culver City Unified Sch. Dist. (2d Dist.2005) 130 Cal.App.4th 344, 349 n.5, *disapproved on other grounds*, ***Voices of the Wetlands v. State Water Res. Control Bd.*** (2011) 52 Cal.4th 499. "Videotapes are classified as writings by [Evid. C.] §250, and [Evid. C.] §1401 … makes authentication of a writing necessary before it is used as evidence. 'Authentication of a writing means (a) the introduction of *evidence* sufficient to sustain a finding that it is the writing that the proponent of the evidence claims it is or (b) the establishment of such facts by any other means provided by law.' Thus, at [P's] administrative hearing, testimony was required from someone who had personal knowledge of the matters and circumstances depicted on the videotapes. That would be someone who saw the events depicted and could testify as to the dates and times of the events and the identification of those persons participating in them." *See also* ***People v. Archer*** (4th Dist.1989) 215 Cal.App.3d 197, 207 (videotape is properly considered a writing).

§255. [ORIGINAL]

"Original" means the writing itself or any counterpart intended to have the same effect by a person executing or issuing it. An "original" of a photograph includes the negative or any print therefrom. If data are stored in a computer or similar device, any printout or other output readable by sight, shown to reflect the data accurately, is an "original."

History of Evid. C. §255: Added eff. Jan. 1, 1978, Stats. 1977, ch. 708, §1.

§260. [DUPLICATE]

A "duplicate" is a counterpart produced by the same impression as the original, or from the same matrix, or by means of photography, including enlargements and miniatures, or by mechanical or electronic rerecording, or by chemical reproduction, or by other equivalent technique which accurately reproduces the original.

History of Evid. C. §260: Added eff. Jan. 1, 1978, Stats. 1977, ch. 708, §2.

ANNOTATIONS

People v. Bizieff (5th Dist.1991) 226 Cal.App.3d 1689, 1697. "A credit card receipt is not a duplicate of the credit card. … The credit card information imprinted on the receipt … may not 'accurately repro-

duce[] the original.' ... The ... receipts generated by the usual credit card transaction would be duplicates of the transaction but not of the credit card itself."

DIVISION 3. GENERAL PROVISIONS

CHAPTER 1. APPLICABILITY OF CODE

§300. [APPLICABILITY OF CODE]

Except as otherwise provided by statute, this code applies in every action before the Supreme Court or a court of appeal or superior court, including proceedings in such actions conducted by a referee, court commissioner, or similar officer, but does not apply in grand jury proceedings.

History of Evid. C. §300: Added eff. Sept. 17, 1965, oper. Jan. 1, 1967, Stats. 1965, ch. 299, §2. Amended eff. Nov. 8, 1967, Stats. 1967, ch. 17, §35; eff. Sept. 28, 1998, Stats. 1998, ch. 931, §141; eff. Jan. 1, 2003, Stats. 2002, ch. 784, §101.

Official Comment

7 Cal. Law Revision Comm'n Rep. (1965) p. 1038.

Section 300 makes the Evidence Code applicable to all proceedings conducted by California courts except those court proceedings to which it is made inapplicable by statute. The provisions of the code do not apply in administrative proceedings, legislative hearings, or any other proceedings unless some statute so provides or the agency concerned chooses to apply them.

Various code sections—in the Evidence Code as well as in other codes—make the provisions of the Evidence Code applicable to a certain extent in proceedings other than court proceedings. *E.g.*, Govt. Code §11513 (a finding in a proceeding conducted under the Administrative Procedure Act may not be based on hearsay evidence unless the evidence would be admissible over objection in a civil action); Penal Code §939.6 (a grand jury, in investigating a charge, may receive only evidence admissible over objection in a criminal action); Evidence Code §910 (provisions of the Evidence Code relating to privileges are applicable in all proceedings of every kind in which testimony can be compelled to be given); and Evidence Code §1566 (Sections 1560-1565 are applicable in nonjudicial proceedings).

Section 300 does not affect any other statute relaxing rules of evidence for specified purposes. *See, e.g.*, Code Civ. Proc. §117g (judge of small claims court may make informal investigation either in or out of court), §1768 (hearing of conciliation proceeding to be conducted informally), §2016(b) [now CCP §2016.020] (inadmissibility of testimony at trial is not ground for objection to testimony sought from a deponent, provided that such testimony is reasonably calculated to lead to the discovery of admissible evidence); Penal Code §1203 (judge must consider probation officer's investigative report on question of probation); Welf. & Inst. Code §706 (juvenile court must consider probation officer's social study in determining disposition to be made of ward or dependent child).

28 Cal. Law Revision Comm'n Rep. (1998) p. 254.

Section 300 is amended to reflect elimination of the justice court. Cal. Const., art. VI, §§1, 5(b).

32 Cal. Law Revision Comm'n Rep. (2002) p. 158.

Section 300 is amended to reflect unification of the municipal and superior courts pursuant to Article VI, Section 5(e), of the California Constitution.

CHAPTER 2. PROVINCE OF COURT & JURY

§310. [QUESTIONS OF LAW]

(a) [Court determination.] All questions of law (including but not limited to questions concerning the construction of statutes and other writings, the admissibility of evidence, and other rules of evidence) are to be decided by the court. Determination of issues of fact preliminary to the admission of evidence are to be decided by the court as provided in Article 2 (commencing with Section 400) of Chapter 4.

(b) [Judicial notice of foreign law.] Determination of the law of an organization of nations or of the law of a foreign nation or a public entity in a foreign nation is a question of law to be determined in the manner provided in Division 4 (commencing with Section 450).

History of Evid. C. §310: Added eff. Sept. 17, 1965, oper. Jan. 1, 1967, Stats. 1965, ch. 299, §2.

Official Comment

**7 Cal. Law Revision Comm'n Rep. (1965) p. 1039;
Assem. J., Apr. 6, 1965, p. 1714.**

Subdivision (a) of Section 310 restates the substance of and supersedes the first sentence of Section 2102 of the Code of Civil Procedure. Subdivision (b) restates the existing rule that foreign law is not a question of fact but is a question of law to be decided by the court. *See Gallegos v. Union-Tribune Publishing Co.*, 195 Cal.App.2d 791, 16 Cal.Rptr. 185 (1961).

Section 310 refers specifically to the law of organizations of nations in order to make certain that the law of supranational organizations that have lawmaking authority—such as the European Economic Community—is to be determined as other foreign law is determined. This probably does not change the law of California, for it seems likely that the law of a supranational organization would be regarded as the law in the member nations by virtue of the treaty arrangements among them. Of course, the Evidence Code does not require California courts to give the force of law to anything that does not have the force of law. The Evidence Code merely prescribes the procedure for determining the existing foreign law.

The judicial notice provisions of the Evidence Code have no effect on which party has the burden of establishing the applicable foreign law under Probate Code Section 259 [repealed] (relating to the right of nonresident aliens to inherit). The applicable foreign law is, however, to be determined in accordance with the judicial notice provisions of the Evidence Code. *Estate of Gogabashvele*, 195 Cal.App.2d 503, 16 Cal.Rptr. 77 (1961).

ANNOTATIONS

Heppler v. J.M. Peters Co. (4th Dist.1999) 73 Cal.App.4th 1265, 1285. "The interpretation of a written contract is a question of law for the trial court to determine."

Brown v. Smith (4th Dist.1997) 55 Cal.App.4th 767, 784-85. The court has a "duty to resolve statutory interpretation questions, which are not to be sent to the jury. In general, [i]nstructions in the language of a statute should only be given if the jury would have no difficulty in understanding the statute without guidance from the court. Although instructions based on code sections should follow the language of the particular section at issue, the court should give explanatory instructions where the statutory wording is confusing or couched in legal terms. It is incumbent upon the trial court to determine whether or not a code section should be explained." (Internal quotes omitted.)

§311. [INDETERMINATE FOREIGN LAW]

If the law of an organization of nations, a foreign nation or a state other than this state, or a public entity in a foreign nation or a state other than this state, is applicable and such law cannot be determined, the court may, as the ends of justice require, either:

(a) [**Apply California law.**] Apply the law of this state if the court can do so consistently with the Constitution of the United States and the Constitution of this state; or

(b) [**Dismiss.**] Dismiss the action without prejudice or, in the case of a reviewing court, remand the case to the trial court with directions to dismiss the action without prejudice.

History of Evid. C. §311: Added eff. Sept. 17, 1965, oper. Jan. 1, 1967, Stats. 1965, ch. 299, §2.

Official Comment

7 Cal. Law Revision Comm'n Rep. (1965) p. 1039; Assem. J., Apr. 6, 1965, p. 1715.

Insofar as it relates to the law of foreign nations, Section 311 restates the substance of and supersedes the last paragraph of Section 1875 of the Code of Civil Procedure. With respect to sister-state law, the result reached under existing California case law is probably the same as under Section 311. *See, e.g., Gagnon Co. v. Nevada Desert Inn*, 45 Cal.2d 448, 453-454, 289 P.2d 466, 471 (1955) ("Whether such a judgment is a bar ... is controlled by Nevada law.... We find no Nevada statute or case law covering the case we have here.... Under those circumstances we will assume the Nevada law is not out of harmony with ours and thus we look to our law for a solution of the problem.").

The last paragraph of Section 1875, which Section 311 supersedes, applies "if the court is unable to determine" the applicable foreign law. Instead, Section 311 comes into operation if the applicable out-of-state law "cannot be determined." This revised language emphasizes that every effort should be made by the court to determine the applicable law before the case is otherwise disposed of under Section 311.

The reason why the court cannot determine the applicable foreign or sister-state law may be that the parties have not provided the court with sufficient information to make such determination. In such a case, the court may, of course, grant the parties additional time within which to obtain such information and make it available to the court. If they fail to obtain such information and the court is not satisfied that they made a reasonable effort to do so, the court may dismiss the action without prejudice. On the other hand, where counsel have made a reasonable effort and when all sources of information as to the applicable foreign or sister-state law are exhausted and the court cannot determine it, the court may either apply California law, within constitutional limits, or dismiss the action without prejudice.

§312. [JURY DETERMINATION]

Except as otherwise provided by law, where the trial is by jury:

(a) All questions of fact are to be decided by the jury.

(b) Subject to the control of the court, the jury is to determine the effect and value of the evidence addressed to it, including the credibility of witnesses and hearsay declarants.

History of Evid. C. §312: Added eff. Sept. 17, 1965, oper. Jan. 1, 1967, Stats. 1965, ch. 299, §2.

Official Comment

7 Cal. Law Revision Comm'n Rep. (1965) p. 1041.

Section 312 restates the substance of and supersedes Section 2101 and the first sentence of Section 2061 of the Code of Civil Procedure. The rule stated in Section 312 is subject to such exceptions as are otherwise provided by statutory or decisional law. *See, e.g.*, Evidence Code §§310, 311, 457.

ANNOTATIONS

Heppler v. J.M. Peters Co. (4th Dist.1999) 73 Cal.App.4th 1265, 1285. "Negligence is a factual issue, which was properly placed in the hands of the jury."

Vorse v. Sarasy (1st Dist.1997) 53 Cal.App.4th 998, 1009. "It is axiomatic that questions of credibility are exclusively within the province of the jury. The court may not set itself up as a gatekeeper excluding otherwise competent and relevant evidence simply because the court finds it unbelievable."

CHAPTER 3. ORDER OF PROOF

§320. [ORDER OF PROOF]

Except as otherwise provided by law, the court in its discretion shall regulate the order of proof.

History of Evid. C. §320: Added eff. Sept. 17, 1965, oper. Jan. 1, 1967, Stats. 1965, ch. 299, §2.

Official Comment

7 Cal. Law Revision Comm'n Rep. (1965) p. 1041.

Section 320 restates the substance of and supersedes the first sentence of Section 2042 of the Code of Civil Procedure. Under Section 320, as under existing law, the trial judge has wide discretion to determine the order of proof. *See* California Civil Procedure During Trial, Parrish, *Order of Proof*, 205 (Cal.Cont. Ed. Bar 1960). Of course, the order of proof ordinarily should be as prescribed in Code of Civil Procedure Section 607 or 631.7 (added in this recommendation) or in Penal Code Sections 1093 and 1094.

Directions of the trial judge which control the order of proof should be distinguished from those which actually exclude evidence. Obviously, it is not permissible, through repeated directions of the order of proof, to prevent a party from presenting relevant evidence on a disputed fact. *Foster v. Keating*, 120 Cal.App.2d 435, 261 P.2d 529 (1953); California Civil Procedure During Trial, Parrish, *Order of Proof*, 205, 210 (Cal.Cont.Ed. Bar 1960). *See also Murry v. Manley*, 170 Cal.App.2d 364, 338 P.2d 976 (1959).

ANNOTATIONS

Rayii v. Gatica (2d Dist.2013) 218 Cal.App.4th 1402, 1413. CCP §607 "prescribes the order of proceedings at trial, 'unless the court, for special reasons otherwise directs.' [Evid. C.] §320 states that the court has the discretion to regulate the order of proof[.] Accordingly, we generally review a trial court's ruling as to the order of proof at trial for abuse of discretion. Specifically, the court exercises discretion in ruling on a request to call a witness out of order, and its ruling will not be disturbed absent a clear showing of abuse of discretion. [¶] [Here,] the trial court acted within its dis-

cretion by allowing the witnesses to testify out of order so as to avoid having to continue the trial date, force the witnesses to cancel their vacation plans or forego their testimony."

CHAPTER 4. ADMITTING & EXCLUDING EVIDENCE

ARTICLE 1. GENERAL PROVISIONS

§350. [ONLY RELEVANT EVIDENCE ADMISSIBLE]

No evidence is admissible except relevant evidence.

History of Evid. C. §350: Added eff. Sept. 17, 1965, oper. Jan. 1, 1967, Stats. 1965, ch. 299, §2.

Official Comment

7 Cal. Law Revision Comm'n Rep. (1965) p. 1041.

Section 350 restates and supersedes that portion of Code of Civil Procedure Section 1868 requiring the exclusion of irrelevant evidence.

§351. [ADMISSIBILITY OF RELEVANT EVIDENCE]

Except as otherwise provided by statute, all relevant evidence is admissible.

History of Evid. C. §351: Added eff. Sept. 17, 1965, oper. Jan. 1, 1967, Stats. 1965, ch. 299, §2.

Official Comment

7 Cal. Law Revision Comm'n Rep. (1965) p. 1042.

(technical correction—Senate J., Apr. 21, 1965)

Section 351 abolishes all limitations on the admissibility of relevant evidence except those that are based on a statute, including a constitutional provision. *See* Evidence Code §230. The Evidence Code contains a number of provisions that exclude relevant evidence either for reasons of public policy or because the evidence is too unreliable to be presented to the trier of fact. *See, e.g.*, Evidence Code §352 (cumulative, unduly prejudicial, etc. evidence), §§900-1070 (privileges), §§1100-1156 (extrinsic policies), §1200 (hearsay). Other codes also contain provisions that may in some cases result in the exclusion of relevant evidence. *See, e.g.*, Civil Code §§79.06, 79.09, 227; Code Civ. Proc. §1747; Educ. Code §14026; Fin. Code §8754; Fish & Game Code §7923; Govt. Code §§15619, 18573, 18934, 18952, 20134, 31532; Health & Saf. Code §§211.5, 410; Ins. Code §§735, 855, 10381.5; Labor Code §6319; Penal Code §§290, 938.1, 3046, 3107, 11105; Pub. Res. Code §3234; Rev. & Tax. Code §§16563, 19282-19289; Unempl. Ins. Code §§1094, 2111, 2714; Vehicle Code §§1808, 16005, 20012-20015, 40803, 40804, 40832, 40833; Water Code §12516; Welf. & Inst. Code §§118, 827.

§351.1. [POLYGRAPH EXAMINATION]

(a) [Criminal & juvenile proceedings.] Notwithstanding any other provision of law, the results of a polygraph examination, the opinion of a polygraph examiner, or any reference to an offer to take, failure to take, or taking of a polygraph examination, shall not be admitted into evidence in any criminal proceeding, including pretrial and post conviction motions and hearings, or in any trial or hearing of a juvenile for a criminal offense, whether heard in juvenile or adult court, unless all parties stipulate to the admission of such results.

(b) [Statements made during examination.] Nothing in this section is intended to exclude from evidence statements made during a polygraph examination which are otherwise admissible.

History of Evid. C. §351.1: Added eff. July 12, 1983, Stats. 1983, ch. 202, §1.

ANNOTATIONS

Arden v. State Bar (1987) 43 Cal.3d 713, 723-24. "In ***People v. Thornton*** (1974) 11 Cal.3d 738 ..., this court adopted the general rule that, because the results of polygraph examinations lack the requisite level of scientific acceptance and thus are of questionable probative value, a stipulation among the parties is required for such evidence to be admissible. A similar rule has been applied in the civil context. The substance of the ***Thornton*** rule was recently reaffirmed by the Legislature's 1983 enactment of ... §351.1, which repudiated a decision by the Court of Appeal liberalizing the rule. While §351.1 applies only to criminal proceedings specifically, its enactment by the Legislature nullifying the ***Witherspoon*** [***v. Superior Ct.*** (2d Dist. 1982) 133 Cal.App.3d 24] decision reflects a continuing doubt in the law about the reliability of polygraph examination results. [¶] In light of our concern that findings of culpability in disciplinary proceedings be based on reliable and convincing proof to a reasonable certainty ..., we conclude the ***Thornton*** rule applies to the use of polygraphic evidence in the State Bar Court. Therefore, polygraph examination evidence is inadmissible in State Bar disciplinary proceedings in the absence of a stipulation between the attorney involved and the State Bar."

§352. [GROUNDS FOR EXCLUSION OF RELEVANT EVIDENCE]

The court in its discretion may exclude evidence if its probative value is substantially outweighed by the probability that its admission will (a) necessitate undue consumption of time or (b) create substantial danger of undue prejudice, of confusing the issues, or of misleading the jury.

History of Evid. C. §352: Added eff. Sept. 17, 1965, oper. Jan. 1, 1967, Stats. 1965, ch. 299, §2.

Official Comment

7 Cal. Law Revision Comm'n Rep. (1965) p. 1042.

Section 352 expresses a rule recognized by statute and in several California decisions. Code Civ. Proc. §§1868, 2044 (repealed); *Adkins v. Brett*, 184 Cal. 252, 258, 193 Pac. 251, 254 (1920) ("the matter [of excluding prejudicial evidence] is largely one of discretion on the part of the trial judge"); *Moody v. Peirano*, 4 Cal.App. 411, 418, 88 Pac. 380, 382 (1906) ("a wide discretion is left to the trial judge in determining whether [evidence of a collateral nature] is admissible or not").

ANNOTATIONS

Generally

People v. Homick (2012) 55 Cal.4th 816, 865. "[S]ection 352 'is not limited by its terms to disputes by opposing parties; it may become applicable to parties on the same side of an action when their interests are adverse to each other.'"

Nally v. Grace Cmty. Ch. (1988) 47 Cal.3d 278, 289 n.5. "'The discretion granted the trial court by §352 is not absolute ... and must be exercised reasonably in accord with the facts before the court.' *At 304:* 'California trial judges have considerable discretion under ... §352 to exclude evidence if its probative value is substantially outweighed by its prejudicial effect.'"

People v. Holistic Health (4th Dist.2013) 213 Cal.App.4th 1016, 1029. The "primary purpose [of §352] is to pare away dross that uniquely tends to evoke an emotional bias against a party as an individual, while having only slight probative value with regard to the issues. The trial court therefore may exclude evidence that is unduly prejudicial because of the substantial likelihood the jury will use it for an illegitimate purpose. Shielding the fact finder from inflammatory material or misleading considerations, however, is not the issue at summary judgment, which consists of spotting material factual disputes, not resolving them. [¶] [P] cites no authority applying ... §352 in the summary judgment context, and our review discovered none." (Internal quotes omitted.)

Wysinger v. Automobile Club (2d Dist.2007) 157 Cal.App.4th 413, 430. "The trial court has broad discretion to exclude time-consuming evidence of limited probative value that is collateral to the issue...." *See also* ***Akers v. Miller*** (4th Dist.1998) 68 Cal.App.4th 1143, 1147.

Abuse of Discretion

People v. Merriman (2014) 60 Cal.4th 1, 74. "An appellate court reviews a court's rulings regarding relevancy and admissibility under ... §352 for abuse of discretion. We will not reverse a court's ruling on such matters unless it is shown the trial court exercised its discretion in an arbitrary, capricious, or patently absurd manner that resulted in a manifest miscarriage of justice." (Internal quotes omitted.) *See also* ***Boeken v. Philip Morris Inc.*** (2d Dist.2005) 127 Cal.App.4th 1640, 1685.

Vorse v. Sarasy (1st Dist.1997) 53 Cal.App.4th 998, 1001. "May a trial court strike a witness's live testimony under ... §352 because the court concludes the witness is lying? No. Under all but the most limited circumstances, credibility of witnesses is a question of fact to be resolved by the jury. *At 1007:* This case compels consideration of how far a trial court may go in assessing the credibility of proffered testimony during a §352 analysis without overstepping the jury's role as fact finder. Here, the court found a witness untruthful and struck his testimony for that reason. *At 1008:* The trial court erred here, because it weighed the probative value of the evidence against an inaccurate standard of prejudice and because it misconstrued its role in the factfinding process."

Rodriguez v. McDonnell Douglas Corp. (2d Dist.1978) 87 Cal.App.3d 626, 663, *disapproved on other grounds*, ***Coito v. Superior Ct.*** (2012) 54 Cal.4th 480. "Finding the photographs cumulative and calculated to inflame the jury, *with little probative value* on the issue of guilt or innocence, we concluded that the discretion conferred upon the trial court pursuant to ... §352 should have been exercised in favor of exclusion." *See also* ***Jones v. City of L.A.*** (2d Dist.1993) 20 Cal.App.4th 436, 442-43 (same considerations expressed by court in ***Rodriguez*** apply equally to question of admissibility of "Day in the Life" videos).

Ruling

Quail Lakes Owners Ass'n v. Kozina (3d Dist.2012) 204 Cal.App.4th 1132, 1140. "[I]n making [a] §352 ruling, the trial court need neither recite each factor it considered, nor detail the evidence supporting each factor. Instead, the record need only reflect that the court weighed the relevant factors." *See also* ***Burns v. 20th Century Ins.*** (2d Dist.1992) 9 Cal.App.4th 1666, 1674.

People v. Miramontes (4th Dist.2010) 189 Cal.App.4th 1085, 1097. "The weighing process under ... §352 'depends upon the trial court's consideration of the unique facts and issues of each case, rather than upon the mechanical application of automatic rules.'"

Rufo v. Simpson (2d Dist.2001) 86 Cal.App.4th 573, 598-99. "When the declarant's state of mind is relevant and the statements of threats or brutal conduct are circumstantial evidence of that state of mind, the evidence is admissible so far as a hearsay objection is concerned. ... Section 352 provides the judge with ample power to exclude evidence of this sort where its preju-

dicial effect outweighs its probative value. But, under §352, the judge must weigh the need for the evidence against the danger of its misuse in each case. ... Now that §352 codifies a safeguard for the evaluation of such evidence before it can be admitted, the trial court has a mechanism for considering the potential for misuse on the unique facts and statements in each case. Where the statement is offered as relevant circumstantial evidence of the victim's state of mind, the court may consider a variety of circumstances, *one* of which is whether the trial court believes, based on the particular facts, that the jury cannot follow the limiting instruction. The general rule is that juries are presumed to follow a trial court's limiting instruction. ... Whether it would be impossible for a jury to follow limiting instructions is determined by the circumstances of each case, primarily in the trial court's discretion under ... §352." (Internal quotes omitted.)

Norton v. Superior Ct. (2d Dist.1994) 24 Cal.App.4th 1750, 1760-61. "The possibility evidence otherwise admissible might be excluded at trial under ... §352 or some other evidentiary objection is not a relevant consideration for purposes of ruling on a discovery motion. [¶] Information which is not directly admissible in the action is nevertheless discoverable if it is reasonably calculated to lead to the discovery of admissible evidence. [¶] [T]he party seeking discovery is entitled to substantial leeway. [I]f an error is made in ruling on a discovery motion, it is better that it be made in favor of granting discovery of the nondiscoverable rather than denying discovery of information vital to preparation or presentation of the party's case or to efficacious settlement of the dispute. [W]herever possible objections to discovery should be resolved by protective orders addressing the specific harm shown by the respondent as opposed to a more general attack on the 'relevancy' of information the proponent seeks to discover."

Kessler v. Gray (2d Dist.1978) 77 Cal.App.3d 284, 291. The "balancing process [under §352] requires consideration of the relationship between the evidence and the relevant inferences to be drawn from it, whether the evidence is relevant to the main or only a collateral issue, and the necessity of the evidence to the proponent's case as well as the reasons recited in §352 for exclusion. The more substantial the probative value of the evidence, the greater the danger of the presence of one of the excluding factors that must be present to support an exercise of trial court discretion excluding the evidence."

Undue Prejudice

People v. Clark (2011) 52 Cal.4th 856, 893. "Evidence is substantially more prejudicial than probative if, broadly stated, it poses an intolerable risk to the fairness of the proceedings or the reliability of the outcome." (Internal quotes omitted.)

People v. Scott (2011) 52 Cal.4th 452, 490-91. "Prejudice as contemplated by ... §352 is not so sweeping as to include any evidence the opponent finds inconvenient. Evidence is not prejudicial ... merely because it undermines the opponent's position or shores up that of the proponent. The ability to do so is what makes evidence relevant. The code speaks in terms of *undue* prejudice. Unless the dangers of undue prejudice, confusion, or time consumption substantially outweigh the probative value of relevant evidence, a §352 objection should fail. The prejudice referred to in ... §352 applies to evidence which uniquely tends to evoke an emotional bias against the defendant as an individual and which has very little effect on the issues. [P]rejudicial is not synonymous with damaging. The prejudice that §352 is designed to avoid is not the prejudice or damage to a defense that naturally flows from relevant, highly probative evidence. Rather, the statute uses the word in its etymological sense of prejudging a person or cause on the basis of extraneous factors. In other words, evidence should be excluded as unduly prejudicial when it is of such nature as to inflame the emotions of the jury, motivating them to use the information, not to logically evaluate the point upon which it is relevant, but to reward or punish one side because of the jurors' emotional reaction. In such a circumstance, the evidence is unduly prejudicial because of the substantial likelihood the jury will use it for an illegitimate purpose." (Internal quotes omitted.) *See also* ***People v. Bryant*** (2014) 60 Cal.4th 335, 408; ***People v. Virgil*** (2011) 51 Cal.4th 1210, 1248-49; ***People v. Foster*** (2010) 50 Cal.4th 1301, 1331; ***Austin B. v. Escondido Un. Sch. Dist.*** (4th Dist.2007) 149 Cal.App.4th 860, 885.

Mize-Kurzman v. Marin Cmty. Coll. Dist. (1st Dist.2012) 202 Cal.App.4th 832, 872. "Even if relevant on another issue ..., under ... §352 the probative value of a collateral payment must be carefully weighed against the inevitable prejudicial impact such evidence

is likely to have on the jury's deliberations. Admission of evidence of collateral payments may be reversible error even if accompanied by a limiting instruction directing the jurors not to deduct the payments from their award of economic damages." (Internal quotes omitted.)

§352.1. [EXCLUSION OF VICTIM INFORMATION IN CRIMINAL PROCEEDINGS]

In any criminal proceeding under Section 261, 262, or 264.1, subdivision (d) of Section 286, or subdivision (d) of Section 288a of the Penal Code, or in any criminal proceeding under subdivision (c) of Section 286 or subdivision (c) of Section 288a of the Penal Code in which the defendant is alleged to have compelled the participation of the victim by force, violence, duress, menace, or threat of great bodily harm, the district attorney may, upon written motion with notice to the defendant or the defendant's attorney, if he or she is represented by an attorney, within a reasonable time prior to any hearing, move to exclude from evidence the current address and telephone number of any victim at the hearing. The court may order that evidence of the victim's current address and telephone number be excluded from any hearings conducted pursuant to the criminal proceeding if the court finds that the probative value of the evidence is outweighed by the creation of substantial danger to the victim. Nothing in this section shall abridge or limit the defendant's right to discover or investigate the information.

History of Evid. C. §352.1: Added eff. Jan. 1, 1986, Stats. 1985, ch. 335, §3. Amended eff. Jan. 1, 1997, Stats. 1996, ch. 1075, §5.

§353. [EFFECT OF ERRONEOUS ADMISSION]

A verdict or finding shall not be set aside, nor shall the judgment or decision based thereon be reversed, by reason of the erroneous admission of evidence unless:

(a) [Timely objection or motion.] There appears of record an objection to or a motion to exclude or to strike the evidence that was timely made and so stated as to make clear the specific ground of the objection or motion; and

(b) [Miscarriage of justice.] The court which passes upon the effect of the error or errors is of the opinion that the admitted evidence should have been excluded on the ground stated and that the error or errors complained of resulted in a miscarriage of justice.

History of Evid. C. §353: Added eff. Sept. 17, 1965, oper. Jan. 1, 1967, Stats. 1965, ch. 299, §2.

Official Comment

7 Cal. Law Revision Comm'n Rep. (1965) p. 1043; Assem. J., Apr. 6, 1965, p. 1715.

Subdivision (a) of Section 353 codifies the well-settled California rule that a failure to make a timely objection to, or motion to exclude or to strike, inadmissible evidence waives the right to complain of the erroneous admission of evidence. *See* Witkin, *California Evidence* §§700-702 (1958). Subdivision (a) also codifies the related rule that the objection or motion must specify the ground for objection, a general objection being insufficient. Witkin, *California Evidence* §§703-709 (1958).

Section 353 does not specify the form in which an objection must be made; hence, the use of a continuing objection to a line of questioning would be proper under Section 353 just as it is under existing law. *See* Witkin, *California Evidence* §708 (1958).

Subdivision (b) reiterates the requirement of Section 4½ [repealed] of Article VI of the California Constitution that a judgment may not be reversed, nor may a new trial be granted, because of an error unless the error is prejudicial.

Section 353 is, of course, subject to the constitutional requirement that a judgment must be reversed if an error has resulted in a denial of due process of law. *People v. Matteson*, 61 Cal.2d 466, 39 Cal.Rptr. 1, 393 P.2d 161 (1964).

ANNOTATIONS

People v. Partida (2005) 37 Cal.4th 428, 435. Section 353 "does not require any particular form of objection. Rather, 'the objection must be made in such a way as to alert the trial court to the nature of the anticipated evidence and the basis on which exclusion is sought, and to afford the [offering party] an opportunity to establish its admissibility.' What is important is that the objection fairly inform the trial court, as well as the party offering the evidence, of the specific reason or reasons the objecting party believes the evidence should be excluded, so the party offering the evidence can respond appropriately and the court can make a fully informed ruling. If the court overrules the objection, the objecting party may argue on appeal that the evidence should have been excluded for the reason asserted at trial, but it may not argue on appeal that the court should have excluded the evidence for a reason different from the one stated at trial. A party cannot argue the court erred in failing to conduct an analysis it was not asked to conduct." *See also* ***SCI Cal. Funeral Servs. v. Five Bridges Found.*** (1st Dist.2012) 203 Cal.App.4th 549, 564-65; ***Mosesian v. Pennwalt Corp.*** (5th Dist.1987) 191 Cal.App.3d 851, 865, *disapproved on other grounds*, ***People v. Ault*** (2004) 33 Cal.4th 1250.

People v. Morris (1991) 53 Cal.3d 152, 190, *disapproved on other grounds*, ***People v. Stansbury*** (1995) 9 Cal.4th 824. "[A] motion *in limine* to exclude evidence is a sufficient manifestation of objection to protect the record on appeal when it satisfies the basic requirements of … §353, i.e.: (1) a specific legal ground for exclusion is advanced and subsequently raised on appeal; (2) the motion is directed to a particular, identifiable body of evidence; and (3) the motion is made at a

time before or during trial when the trial judge can determine the evidentiary question in its appropriate context. When such a motion is made and denied, the issue is preserved for appeal. On the other hand, if a motion *in limine* does not satisfy each of these requirements, a proper objection satisfying … §353 must be made to preserve the evidentiary issue for appeal." *See also* ***Boston v. Penny Lane Ctrs., Inc.*** (2d Dist.2009) 170 Cal.App.4th 936, 950; ***Kelly v. New W. Fed. Sav.*** (2d Dist.1996) 49 Cal.App.4th 659, 671.

Huffman v. Interstate Brands Corp. (2d Dist. 2004) 121 Cal.App.4th 679, 692. "In civil cases, a miscarriage of justice should be declared only when the reviewing court, after an examination of the entire cause, including the evidence, is of the opinion that it is reasonably probable that a result more favorable to the appealing party would have been reached in the absence of the error." *See also* Cal. Const., art. VI, §13; ***Burton v. Sanner*** (4th Dist.2012) 207 Cal.App.4th 12, 22; ***Robertson v. Fleetwood Travel Trailers*** (5th Dist.2006) 144 Cal.App.4th 785, 815.

Alexander v. Codemasters Grp. (5th Dist.2002) 104 Cal.App.4th 129, 140. "It is well settled that the failure to object, even to otherwise inadmissible evidence, waives the defect." *See also* CCP §437c(b)(5); ***Broden v. Marin Humane Soc'y*** (1st Dist.1999) 70 Cal.App.4th 1212, 1227.

Fredrics v. Paige (2d Dist.1994) 29 Cal.App.4th 1642, 1649. "[P] did not object [to remark by D's attorney], did not request a jury admonition, and did not request a mistrial. Instead [P] proceeded with jury selection, production of evidence, and the rendition of a verdict. Only after receiving a verdict [P] considered inadequate did he belatedly complain…. [P's] complaint comes too late. '[A] claim of misconduct is entitled to no consideration on appeal unless the record shows a timely and proper objection and a request that the jury be admonished.'"

Chyten v. Lawrence & Howell Invs. (2d Dist. 1993) 23 Cal.App.4th 607, 620. "[Ds] did not object to the court's remark or ask the court to withdraw it or admonish the jury. They now assert that no objection was required because the alleged misconduct was by the court itself …, but they state this rule too broadly. Ordinarily a party complaining of improper remarks by a trial judge must object and draw the court's attention to the impropriety before the close of trial, or waive the point on appeal. This is in order to give the trial court an opportunity to cure the injury by instructing the jury or otherwise. Only when an admonition could not remove the prejudicial effect, or it is apparent that a request would be fruitless, can the complaining party dispense with objecting."

§354. [EFFECT OF ERRONEOUS EXCLUSION]

A verdict or finding shall not be set aside, nor shall the judgment or decision based thereon be reversed, by reason of the erroneous exclusion of evidence unless the court which passes upon the effect of the error or errors is of the opinion that the error or errors complained of resulted in a miscarriage of justice and it appears of record that:

(a) The substance, purpose, and relevance of the excluded evidence was made known to the court by the questions asked, an offer of proof, or by any other means;

(b) The rulings of the court made compliance with subdivision (a) futile; or

(c) The evidence was sought by questions asked during cross-examination or recross-examination.

History of Evid. C. §354: Added eff. Sept. 17, 1965, oper. Jan. 1, 1967, Stats. 1965, ch. 299, §2.

Official Comment

7 Cal. Law Revision Comm'n Rep. (1965) p. 1044.

Section 354, like Section 353, reiterates the requirement of the California Constitution that a judgment may not be reversed, nor may a new trial be granted, because of an error unless the error is prejudicial. Cal. Const., Art. VI, §4½ [repealed].

The provisions of Section 354 that require an offer of proof or other disclosure of the evidence improperly excluded reflect existing law. *See* Witkin, *California Evidence*, §713 (1958). The exceptions to this requirement that are stated in Section 354 also reflect existing law. Thus, an offer of proof is unnecessary where the judge has limited the issues so that an offer to prove matters related to excluded issues would be futile. *Lawless v. Calaway*, 24 Cal.2d 81, 91, 147 P.2d 604, 609 (1944). An offer of proof is also unnecessary when an objection is improperly sustained to a question on cross-examination. *Tossman v. Newman*, 37 Cal.2d 522, 525-526, 233 P.2d 1, 3 (1951) ("no offer of proof is necessary in order to obtain a review of rulings on cross-examination"); *People v. Jones*, 160 Cal. 358, 117 Pac. 176 (1911).

ANNOTATIONS

Clifton v. Ulis (1976) 17 Cal.3d 99, 105-06. "[A] 'miscarriage of justice' should be declared only when the court, after an examination of the entire cause, including the evidence, is of the opinion that it is reasonably probable that a result more favorable to the appealing party would have been reached in the absence of the error." (Internal quotes omitted.) *See also* ***Bell v. Mason*** (2d Dist.2011) 194 Cal.App.4th 1102, 1107.

Karlsson v. Ford Motor Co. (2d Dist.2006) 140 Cal.App.4th 1202, 1223. "In order to obtain a reversal

§353

based on the erroneous exclusion of evidence, [D] must show that a different result was probable if the evidence had been admitted. [D's] appellate brief describes the excluded evidence only in general terms and refers us to specified pages in the reporter's transcript where it sought admission of the evidence, but does not set forth the evidence it claims was erroneously admitted [and] does not acknowledge all the other evidence that was admitted on the issue of technical feasibility.... We therefore deem the issue waived."

Castaneda v. Bornstein (2d Dist.1995) 36 Cal.App.4th 1818, 1827, *disapproved on other grounds*, ***Bonds v. Roy*** (1999) 20 Cal.4th 140. "[A]s a general rule, '... any claim that evidence was wrongly excluded cannot be raised on appeal absent an offer of proof in the trial court.' There are exceptions to this rule, however. 'Where ... an entire class of evidence has been declared inadmissible or the trial court has clearly intimated that it will receive no evidence of a particular type or class, or upon a particular issue, an offer of proof is not a prerequisite to arguing on appeal the prejudicial nature of the exclusion of such evidence.' [¶] [T]he trial court declared an entire class of evidence inadmissible: expert opinion on causation by a witness not designated as a 'causation' expert. There can be no doubt such testimony was relevant and material and its exclusion prejudicial because the exclusion resulted in a nonsuit as to [D]."

In re Mark C. (4th Dist.1992) 7 Cal.App.4th 433, 444. "'The substance of evidence to be set forth in a valid offer of proof means the testimony of specific witnesses, writings, material objects, or other things presented to the senses, to be introduced to prove the existence or nonexistence of a fact in issue.' Failure to make an adequate offer of proof precludes consideration of the alleged error on appeal."

§355. [LIMITED ADMISSIBILITY]

When evidence is admissible as to one party or for one purpose and is inadmissible as to another party or for another purpose, the court upon request shall restrict the evidence to its proper scope and instruct the jury accordingly.

History of Evid. C. §355: Added eff. Sept. 17, 1965, oper. Jan. 1, 1967, Stats. 1965, ch. 299, §2.

Official Comment

7 Cal. Law Revision Comm'n Rep. (1965) p. 1044.

Section 355 codifies existing law which requires the court to instruct the jury as to the limited purpose for which evidence may be considered when such evidence is admissible for one purpose and inadmissible for another. *See Adkins v. Brett*, 184 Cal. 252, 193 Pac. 251 (1920).

Under Section 352, as under existing law, the judge is permitted to exclude such evidence if he deems it so prejudicial that a limiting instruction would not protect a party adequately and the matter in question can be proved sufficiently by other evidence. See discussion in *Adkins v. Brett*, 184 Cal. 252, 258, 193 Pac. 251, 254 (1920); *Tentative Recommendation and a Study Relating to the Uniform Rules of Evidence (Article VI. Extrinsic Policies Affecting Admissibility)*, 6 Cal. Law Revision Comm'n, Rep., Rec. & Studies 601, 612, 639-640 (1964).

ANNOTATIONS

People v. Murtishaw (2011) 51 Cal.4th 574, 590. "Absent a request, the trial court was not required to give instructions limiting the purpose for which the jury could consider the evidence. ... There is a possible narrow exception in the occasional extraordinary case in which the evidence is a dominant part of the evidence against the [defendant], and is both highly prejudicial and minimally relevant to any legitimate purpose. That exception does not apply here because the evidence in question was admitted not against [D] but in his behalf. Accordingly, the trial court had no sua sponte duty to give a limiting instruction...." (Internal quotes omitted.)

Foreman & Clark Corp. v. Fallon (1971) 3 Cal.3d 875, 887. "'It is frequently the case that evidence which is admissible to establish one issue may tend to establish another issue than that for which it is offered, and it is the rule [in the absence of a proper request for limitation] that evidence so introduced is available to establish any of the issues in the case.' *At 888:* Despite such settled law, [P] insists that to fulfill the objective of a bifurcated trial, we must imply from the proceedings below a ruling that all evidence introduced at one stage of the trial be considered only as it relates to the particular issue dealt with during that stage. We cannot agree. [¶] To assure that the trier of fact could consider all the evidence on each issue, the parties would be required to reintroduce every piece of evidence at each stage of the trial. [¶] Furthermore, the rule of limited admissibility applies properly only where the evidence is admissible for one purpose but is inadmissible for another purpose. *At 889:* [W]e find no merit in [P's] contention that the evidence could not be considered since it was introduced during a different phase of the bifurcated trial."

Dincau v. Tamayose (2d Dist.1982) 131 Cal.App.3d 780, 791. "Even if an objection is made, a limiting instruction must be requested."

§356. [WHOLE ADMISSIBLE WHEN PART RECEIVED]

Where part of an act, declaration, conversation, or writing is given in evidence by one party, the whole on the same subject may be inquired into by an adverse party; when a letter is read, the answer may be given; and when a detached act, declaration, conversation, or writing is given in evidence, any other act, declaration, conversation, or writing which is necessary to make it understood may also be given in evidence.

History of Evid. C. §356: Added eff. Sept. 17, 1965, oper. Jan. 1, 1967, Stats. 1965, ch. 299, §2.

Official Comment

7 Cal. Law Revision Comm'n Rep. (1965) p. 1045; Assem. J., Apr. 6, 1965, p. 1716.

Section 356 restates the substance of and supersedes Section 1854 of the Code of Civil Procedure.

The rule stated in Section 356, like the superseded statement of the rule in the Code of Civil Procedure, only makes admissible such parts of an act, declaration, conversation, or writing as are relevant to the part thereof previously given in evidence. *See, e.g., Witt v. Jackson*, 57 Cal.2d 57, 67, 17 Cal.Rptr. 369, 374, 366 P.2d 641, 646 (1961) (the rule "is necessarily subject to the qualification that the court may exclude those portions of the conversation not relevant to the items thereof which have been introduced"). *See also* Evidence Code §350.

§356

ANNOTATIONS

People v. Chism (2014) 58 Cal.4th 1266, 1324. "'The purpose of … §356 is to avoid creating a misleading impression. It applies only to statements that have some bearing upon, or connection with, the portion of the conversation originally introduced. Statements pertaining to other matters may be excluded.'"

People v. Riccardi (2012) 54 Cal.4th 758, 803. "Although portions of [witness's] audio-recorded statements to the detective were properly admitted to refute [D's] characterization of [witness's] testimony [as having been fabricated], this circumstance does not necessarily establish that the entire recording was admissible. To justify admission of the rest of recording, the Attorney General invokes the rule of completeness, which would allow admission of the entire recording if necessary to the understanding of the otherwise admissible portions. But it does not appear that the portions of the audio recording relevant to rehabilitate [witness] created a misleading impression requiring the playing of the entire recording to correct any such misimpression, and the prosecutor made no such argument below. … Accordingly, the trial court erred in admitting those portions of the audio-recorded interview that did more than rehabilitate [witness's] testimony."

People v. Vines (2011) 51 Cal.4th 830, 861. "'The purpose of … §356 … is to prevent the use of selected aspects of a conversation, act, declaration, or writing, so as to create a misleading impression on the subjects addressed.' *At 862:* '[S]ection 356 is not an exception to the hearsay rule that purports to assess the reliability of testimony. The statute is founded on the equitable notion that a party who elects to introduce a part of a conversation is precluded from objecting on confrontation clause grounds to introduction by the opposing party of other parts of the conversation which are necessary to make the entirety of the conversation understood.'" *See also* ***People v. Guerra*** (2006) 37 Cal.4th 1067, 1121-22.

Carson v. Facilities Dev. Co. (1984) 36 Cal.3d 830, 850-51. "Section 356 permits admission of the remainder of an otherwise inadmissible conversation where a part of the conversation has already been admitted. [¶] Here, the second statement appears to explain the first statement. … The self-serving nature of the second hearsay statement does not preclude its admission under … §356."

ARTICLE 2. PRELIMINARY DETERMINATIONS ON ADMISSIBILITY OF EVIDENCE

§400. [PRELIMINARY FACT]

As used in this article, "preliminary fact" means a fact upon the existence or nonexistence of which depends the admissibility or inadmissibility of evidence. The phrase "the admissibility or inadmissibility of evidence" includes the qualification or disqualification of a person to be a witness and the existence or nonexistence of a privilege.

History of Evid. C. §400: Added eff. Sept. 17, 1965, oper. Jan. 1, 1967, Stats. 1965, ch. 299, §2.

Official Comment

7 Cal. Law Revision Comm'n Rep. (1965) p. 1045.

"Preliminary fact" is defined to distinguish those facts upon which the admissibility of evidence depends from those facts sought to be proved by that evidence.

ANNOTATIONS

Islas v. D&G Mfg. Co. (2d Dist.2004) 120 Cal.App.4th 571, 577. "Generally, the trial court is authorized to determine preliminary facts…. *At 578:* When the factual issue resolved by the trial court overlaps with the issues subsequently submitted to the jury, the jury is not informed about the trial court's preliminary determination. Nonetheless, … '[t]he coinciding of preliminary fact and fact in issue in no way changes the rule of finality of the judge's determination of preliminary fact.'" *See also* Evidence Code §§403, 405.

§401. [PROFFERED EVIDENCE]

As used in this article, "proffered evidence" means evidence, the admissibility or inadmissibility of which is dependent upon the existence or nonexistence of a preliminary fact.

History of Evid. C. §401: Added eff. Sept. 17, 1965, oper. Jan. 1, 1967, Stats. 1965, ch. 299, §2.

Official Comment

7 Cal. Law Revision Comm'n Rep. (1965) p. 1046.

"Proffered evidence" is defined to avoid confusion between evidence whose admissibility is in question and evidence offered on the preliminary fact issue. "Proffered evidence" includes such matters as the testimony to be elicited from a witness who is claimed to be disqualified, testimony or tangible evidence claimed to be privileged, and any other evidence to which objection is made.

§402. [HEARING TO DETERMINE PRELIMINARY FACT]

(a) [Disputed preliminary fact.] When the existence of a preliminary fact is disputed, its existence or nonexistence shall be determined as provided in this article.

(b) [Court determination.] The court may hear and determine the question of the admissibility of evidence out of the presence or hearing of the jury; but in a criminal action, the court shall hear and determine the question of the admissibility of a confession or admission of the defendant out of the presence and hearing of the jury if any party so requests.

(c) [Implied findings.] A ruling on the admissibility of evidence implies whatever finding of fact is prerequisite thereto; a separate or formal finding is unnecessary unless required by statute.

History of Evid. C. §402: Added eff. Sept. 17, 1965, oper. Jan. 1, 1967, Stats. 1965, ch. 299, §2.

Official Comment

7 Cal. Law Revision Comm'n Rep. (1965) p. 1046; Assem. J., Apr. 6, 1965, p. 1716.

Under Section 310, the court must decide preliminary questions of fact upon which the admissibility of evidence depends. Section 402 prescribes certain procedures that must be observed by the court when making such preliminary determinations.

Subdivision (a). Subdivision (a) requires the judge to observe the procedures specified in Article 2 (commencing with Section 400) when he is determining disputed factual questions preliminary to the admission or exclusion of evidence. The provisions of Article 2 are designed to distinguish clearly between (1) those situations where the judge must be persuaded of the existence of the preliminary fact upon which admissibility depends and (2) those situations where the judge must admit the proffered evidence merely upon the introduction of evidence sufficient to sustain a finding of the preliminary fact. Under the Evidence Code, as under existing law, the judge determines some preliminary fact questions on the basis of all the evidence presented to him by both parties, resolving any conflicts in that evidence. Evidence Code §405. *See, e.g., People v. Glab*, 13 Cal.App.2d 528, 57 P.2d 588 (1936) (judge considered conflicting evidence and decided that a proposed witness was not married to the defendant and, therefore, was competent to testify). *See also Fairbank v. Hughson*, 58 Cal. 314 (1881) (error to permit jury to determine whether witness was an expert). On the other hand, the judge does not always resolve conflicts in the evidence submitted on preliminary fact questions; in some cases, the proffered evidence must be admitted if there is evidence sufficient to sustain a finding of the preliminary fact. Evidence Code §403. *See, e.g., Reed v. Clark*, 47 Cal. 194, 200 (1873); *Verzan v. McGregor*, 23 Cal. 339 (1863).

Subdivision (b). Subdivision (b) requires the judge, on request, to determine the admissibility of a confession or admission of a criminal defendant out of the presence and hearing of the jury. Under existing law, whether the preliminary hearing is held out of the presence of the jury is left to the judge's discretion. *People v. Gonzales*, 24 Cal.2d 870, 151 P.2d 251 (1944); *People v. Nelson*, 90 Cal.App. 27, 31, 265 Pac. 366, 367 (1928). The existing procedure permits the jury to hear evidence that may be extremely prejudicial. For example, in *People v. Black*, 73 Cal.App. 13, 238 Pac. 374 (1925), the alleged coercion consisted of threats to send the defendants to New Mexico to be prosecuted for murder. Subdivision (b) prevents this kind of prejudice. Nothing in subdivision (b) precludes a defendant from presenting to the jury evidence attacking the credibility of a confession that is admitted (Evidence Code §406), and such evidence may include some of the same matters presented to the judge during the preliminary hearing.

Subdivision (c). Subdivision (c) codifies existing law. *Wilcox v. Berry*, 32 Cal.2d 189, 195 P.2d 414 (1948) (where evidence is properly received, the ground of the court's ruling is immaterial); *City & County of San Francisco v. Western Air Lines, Inc.*, 204 Cal.App.2d 105, 22 Cal.Rptr. 216 (1962) (where evidence is excluded, the ruling will be upheld if any ground exists for the exclusion).

ANNOTATIONS

NBC Subsidiary (KNBC-TV), Inc. v. Superior Ct. (1999) 20 Cal.4th 1178, 1185. "The court considered arguments relating to an offer of proof concerning proposed reputation evidence by another of [P's] witnesses, and eventually held a hearing and heard testimony of the proposed witness pursuant to … §402, which permits a court to hold a hearing on 'foundational and other preliminary facts,' 'out of the presence or hearing of the jury.' *At 1185 n.3:* During the course of the §402 hearing, the court, in response to an evidentiary objection by [D], explained that the hearing under … §402 was 'like a preliminary hearing.'"

§403. [PROOF OF PRELIMINARY FACTS]

(a) [Burden of producing evidence.] The proponent of the proffered evidence has the burden of producing evidence as to the existence of the preliminary fact, and the proffered evidence is inadmissible unless the court finds that there is evidence sufficient to sustain a finding of the existence of the preliminary fact, when:

(1) The relevance of the proffered evidence depends on the existence of the preliminary fact;

(2) The preliminary fact is the personal knowledge of a witness concerning the subject matter of his testimony;

(3) The preliminary fact is the authenticity of a writing; or

(4) The proffered evidence is of a statement or other conduct of a particular person and the prelimi-

nary fact is whether that person made the statement or so conducted himself.

(b) [Admit conditionally.] Subject to Section 702, the court may admit conditionally the proffered evidence under this section, subject to evidence of the preliminary fact being supplied later in the course of the trial.

(c) [Jury instruction.] If the court admits the proffered evidence under this section, the court:

(1) May, and on request shall, instruct the jury to determine whether the preliminary fact exists and to disregard the proffered evidence unless the jury finds that the preliminary fact does exist.

(2) Shall instruct the jury to disregard the proffered evidence if the court subsequently determines that a jury could not reasonably find that the preliminary fact exists.

History of Evid. C. §403: Added eff. Sept. 17, 1965, oper. Jan. 1, 1967, Stats. 1965, ch. 299, §2.

Official Comment

7 Cal. Law Revision Comm'n Rep. (1965) p. 1047; Assem. J., Apr. 6, 1965, p. 1717.

As indicated in the *Comment* to Section 402, the judge does not determine in all instances whether a preliminary fact exists or does not exist. At times, the judge must admit the proffered evidence if there is evidence sufficient to sustain a finding of the preliminary fact, and the jury must finally decide whether the preliminary fact exists. *See, e.g., Verzan v. McGregor*, 23 Cal. 339 (1863). Section 403 covers those situations in which the judge is required to admit the proffered evidence upon the introduction of evidence sufficient to sustain a finding of the preliminary fact.

Subdivision (a). Some writers have attempted to distinguish the kinds of questions to be decided under the standard prescribed in Section 403 from the kinds of questions to be decided under the standard described in Section 405 on the ground that the former questions involve the *relevancy* of the proffered evidence while the latter questions involve the *competency* of evidence that is relevant. Maguire & Epstein, *Preliminary Questions of Fact in Determining the Admissibility of Evidence*, 40 Harv.L.Rev. 392 (1927); Morgan, *Functions of Judge and Jury in the Determination of Preliminary Questions of Fact*, 43 Harv.L.Rev. 165 (1929). It is difficult, however, to distinguish all preliminary fact questions upon this principle. And eminent legal authorities sometimes differ over whether a particular preliminary fact question is one of relevancy or competency. For example, Wigmore classifies admissions with questions of relevancy (4 Wigmore, *Evidence* 1 (3d ed. 1940)) while Morgan classifies admissions with questions of competency to be decided under the standard prescribed in Section 405 (Morgan, *Basic Problems of Evidence* 244 (1957)).

To eliminate uncertainties of classification, subdivision (a) lists the kinds of preliminary fact questions that are to be determined under the standard prescribed in Section 403. And to eliminate any uncertainties that are not resolved by this listing, various Evidence Code sections state specifically that admissibility depends on "evidence sufficient to sustain a finding" of certain facts. *See, e.g.*, Evidence Code §§1222, 1223, 1400.

The preliminary fact questions listed in subdivision (a), or identified elsewhere as matters to be determined under the Section 403 standard, are not finally decided by the judge because they have been traditionally regarded as jury questions. The questions involve the credibility of testimony or the probative value of evidence that is admitted on the ultimate issues. It is the jury's function to determine the effect and value of the evidence addressed to it. Evidence Code §312. Hence, the judge's function on questions of this sort is merely to determine whether there is evidence sufficient to permit a jury to decide the question. The "question of admissibility ... merges imperceptibly into the weight of the evidence, if admitted." *Di Carlo v. United States*, 6 F.2d 364, 367 (2d Cir. 1925). If the judge finally determined the existence or nonexistence of the preliminary fact, he would deprive a party of a jury decision on a question that the party has a right to have decided by the jury.

For example, if the question of *A*'s title to land is in issue, *A* may seek to prove his title by a deed from former owner *O*. Section 1401 requires that the deed be authenticated, and the judge, under Section 403, must rule on the question of authentication. If *A* introduces evidence sufficient to sustain a finding of the genuineness of the deed, the judge is required to admit it. If the rule were otherwise and the judge, on the basis of the adverse party's evidence, were permitted to decide that the deed was spurious and not admissible, the judge would be resolving the basic factual issue in the case and *A* would be deprived of a jury finding on the issue, even though he is entitled to a jury decision and even though he has introduced evidence sufficient to warrant a jury finding in his favor.

Illustrative of the preliminary fact questions that should be decided under Section 403 are the following:

Section 350—Relevancy. Under existing law, as under Section 403, if the relevancy of proffered evidence depends on the existence of some preliminary fact, the evidence is admissible if there is evidence sufficient to warrant a jury finding of the preliminary fact. *Reed v. Clark*, 47 Cal. 194, 200 (1873). Thus, for example, if *P* sues *D* upon an alleged agreement, evidence of negotiations with *A* is inadmissible because irrelevant unless *A* is shown to be *D*'s agent; but the evidence of the negotiations with *A* is admissible if there is evidence sufficient to sustain a finding of the agency. *Brown v. Spencer*, 163 Cal. 589, 126 Pac. 493 (1912). The same rule is applicable when a person is charged with criminal responsibility for the acts of another because they are conspirators. See discussion in *People v. Steccone*, 36 Cal.2d 234, 238, 223 P.2d 17, 19 (1950).

Section 702—Requirement of personal knowledge. Evidence sufficient to sustain a finding of a witness' personal knowledge seems to be sufficient under the existing California practice. *See, e.g., People v. Avery*, 35 Cal.2d 487, 492, 218 P.2d 527, 530 (1950) ("Bolton testified that he observed the incident about which he testified. His testimony, therefore, was not incompetent under section 1845 of the Code of Civil Procedure."); *People v. McCarthy*, 14 Cal.App. 148, 151, 111 Pac. 274, 275 (1910). *See also Tentative Recommendation and a Study Relating to the (Article IV. Witnesses)*, 6 Cal. Law Revision Comm'n, Rep., Rec. & Studies 701, 711-713 (1964).

Section 788—Conviction of a crime when offered to attack credibility. In this situation, the preliminary fact issue to be decided under Section 403 is whether the witness is actually the person who was convicted. This involves the relevancy of the evidence (since, obviously, the conviction of another does not affect the witness' credibility) and should be a question to be resolved by the jury. The judge should not be able to decide finally that it was the witness who was convicted and, thus, to prevent a contest on that issue before the jury. The existing law is uncertain in this regard; however, it seems likely that any evidence sufficient to identify the witness as the person convicted is sufficient to warrant admission of the conviction. *See People v. Theodore*, 121 Cal.App.2d 17, 28, 262 P.2d 630, 637 (1953) (relying on presumption of identity of person from identity of name).

Section 800—Requirement that lay opinion be based on personal perception. The requirement specified in Section 800 is merely a specific application of the personal knowledge requirement in Section 702. See the discussion of Section 702 in this *Comment, supra*.

Sections 1200-1341—Identity of hearsay declarant. For most hearsay evidence, admissibility depends upon two preliminary determinations: (1) Did the declarant actually make the statement as claimed by the proponent of the evidence? (2) Does the statement meet certain standards of trustworthiness required by some exception to the hearsay rule?

The first determination involves the relevancy of the evidence. For example, if the issue is the state of mind of *X*, a person's statement as to *his* state of mind has no tendency to prove *X*'s state of mind unless the declarant was *X*. Relevancy depends on the fact that *X* made the statement. Accordingly, if otherwise competent, a hearsay statement is admitted upon evidence sufficient to sustain a finding that the claimed declarant made the statement.

The second determination involves the competency of the evidence. Unless the evidence meets the requisite standards of an exception to the hearsay rule, it must be kept from the trier of fact despite its relevancy either because it is too unreliable or because public policy requires its suppression. For example, if an admission was in fact made by a defendant to a criminal action, the admission is relevant. But public policy requires that the admission be held inadmissible if it was not given voluntarily.

The admissibility of some hearsay declarations is dependent solely upon the determination that a particular declarant made the statement. Some of these exceptions to the hearsay rule—such as inconsistent statements of trial witnesses and admissions—are mentioned specifically below. Since the only preliminary fact to be determined in regard to these declarations involves the relevancy of the evidence, they should be admitted upon the introduction of evidence sufficient to sustain a finding of the preliminary fact.

When the admissibility of hearsay depends both upon a determination that a particular declarant made the statement and upon a determination that the requisite standards of a hearsay exception have been met, the former determination is to be made upon evidence sufficient to sustain a finding of the preliminary fact. Paragraph (4) is included in subdivision (a) to make this clear.

Section 1220—Admissions of a party. The only preliminary fact that is subject to dispute is the identity of the declarant. Under Section 403(a)(4), an admission is admissible upon the introduction of evidence sufficient to sustain a finding that the party made the statement. Existing law appears to be in accord. *Eastman v. Means*, 75 Cal.App. 537, 242 Pac. 1089 (1925).

An admission is not admissible in a criminal case unless it was given voluntarily. The voluntariness of an admission by a criminal defendant is determined under Section 405, not Section 403.

Sections 1221, 1222—Authorized and adoptive admissions. Under existing law, both authorized admissions (by an agent of a party) and adoptive admissions are admitted upon the introduction of evidence sufficient to sustain a finding of the foundational fact. *Sample v. Round Mountain Citrus Farm Co.*, 29 Cal.App. 547, 156 Pac. 983 (1916) (authorized admission); *Southers v. Savage*, 191 Cal.App.2d 100, 12 Cal.Rptr. 470 (1961) (adoptive admission).

Section 1223—Admission of co-conspirator. The admission of a co-conspirator is another form of an authorized admission. Hence, the proffered evidence is admissible upon the introduction of evidence sufficient to sustain a finding of the conspiracy. Existing law is in accord. *People v. Robinson*, 43 Cal.2d 132, 137, 271 P.2d 865, 868 (1954).

Sections 1224-1227—Admission of third person whose liability, breach of duty, or right is in issue. The only preliminary fact subject to dispute is the identity of the declarant; and the preliminary showing required in regard to this class of admissions is the same as if the declarant were being sued directly. Any evidence of the making of the statement by the claimed declarant is sufficient to warrant its admission. Existing law is in accord. *See Langley v. Zurich General Acc. & Liab. Ins. Co.*, 219 Cal. 101, 25 P.2d 418 (1933). Although Sections 1226 and 1227 are new to California law, the same principles should be applicable.

Sections 1235, 1236—Previous statements of witnesses. Prior inconsistent statements and prior consistent statements made before bias or other improper motive arose are dealt with in Sections 1235 and 1236. In each case, the evidence is relevant and probative if the witnesses to the statements are credible. The credibility of the witnesses testifying to these statements should be decided finally by the jury. Moreover, the only preliminary fact subject to dispute insofar as alleged inconsistent statements are concerned is the identity of the declarant. Hence, evidence is admitted under these sections upon the introduction of evidence sufficient to sustain a finding of the preliminary fact. The existing practice seems to be consistent with Section 403. *See Schneider v. Market Street Ry.*, 134 Cal. 482, 492, 66 Pac. 734, 738 (1901) ("Whether the [prior inconsistent] statements made to Glassman and Hubbell were made by Meley, or by some other man, was a question for the jury. Both witnesses testified that they were made by him."); *People v. Neely*, 163 Cal.App.2d 289, 312, 329 P.2d 357, 371 (1958) (two prior consistent statements held admissible because the "jury could properly infer ... the motive to fabricate did arise after the making of the two statements").

Sections 1400-1402—Authentication of writings. Under existing law, an otherwise competent writing is admissible upon the introduction of evidence sufficient to sustain a finding of the authenticity of the writing. *Verzan v. McGregor*, 23 Cal. 339 (1863). Section 403(a)(3) retains this existing law.

Sections 1410-1421—Means of authenticating writings. Sections 1410 through 1421 merely state several ways in which the requirements of Sections 1400 through 1402 may be met. Hence, to the extent that Sections 1410 through 1421 specify facts that may be shown to authenticate writings, the same principles apply: In each case, the judge must decide whether the evidence offered is sufficient to sustain a finding of the authenticity of the proffered writing and admit the writing if there is such evidence. Care should be exercised, however, to distinguish those cases where the disputed preliminary fact is the authenticity of an exemplar with which the proffered writing is to be compared (Evidence Code §§1417-1419) or the qualification of a witness to give an opinion concerning the authenticity of a writing (Evidence Code §§1416, 1418); the judge is required to determine such questions under the provisions of Section 405.

Subdivision (b). Subdivision (b) restates the apparent meaning of Section 1834 of the Code of Civil Procedure. Under this subdivision, the judge may receive evidence that is conditionally admissible under Section 403, subject to the presentation of evidence of the preliminary fact later in the course of the trial. *See Brea v. McGlashan*, 3 Cal.App.2d 454, 465, 39 P.2d 877, 882 (1934).

Subdivision (c). Subdivision (c) relates to the instructions to be given the jury when evidence is admitted whose admissibility depends on the existence of a preliminary fact determined under Section 403. When such evidence is admitted, the jury is required to make the ultimate determination of the existence of the preliminary fact. Unless the jury is persuaded that the preliminary fact exists, it is not permitted to consider the evidence.

For example, if *P* offers evidence of his negotiations with *A* in his contract action against *D*, the judge must admit the evidence if there is other evidence sufficient to sustain a finding that *A* was *D*'s agent. If the jury is not persuaded that *A* was in fact *D*'s agent, then it is not permitted to consider the evidence of the negotiations with *A* in determining *D*'s liability.

Frequently, the jury's duty to disregard conditionally admissible evidence when it is not persuaded of the existence of the preliminary fact on which relevancy is conditioned is so clear that an instruction to this effect is unnecessary. For example, if the disputed preliminary fact is the authenticity of a deed, it hardly seems necessary to instruct the jury to disregard the deed if it should find that the deed is not genuine. No rational jury could find the deed to be spurious and, yet, to be still effective to transfer title from the purported grantor.

At times, however, it is not quite so clear that conditionally admissible evidence should be disregarded unless the preliminary fact is found to exist. In such cases, the jury should be appropriately instructed. For example, the theory upon which agent's and co-conspirator's statements are admissible is that the party is vicariously responsible for the acts and statements of agents and co-conspirators within the scope of the agency or conspiracy. Yet, it is not always clear that statements made by a purported agent or co-conspirator should be disregarded if not made in furtherance of the agency or conspiracy. Hence, the jury should be instructed to disregard such statements unless it is persuaded that the statements were made within the scope of the agency or conspiracy. *People v. Geiger*, 49 Cal. 643, 649 (1875); *People v. Talbott*, 65 Cal.App.2d 654, 663, 151 P.2d 317, 322 (1944). Subdivision (c), therefore, permits the judge in any case to instruct the jury to disregard conditionally admissible evidence unless it is persuaded of the existence of the preliminary fact; further, subdivision (c) requires the judge to give such an instruction whenever he is requested by a party to do so.

ANNOTATIONS

People v. Bacon (2010) 50 Cal.4th 1082, 1102-03. "When the relevance of proffered evidence depends on the existence of a preliminary fact, the proponent of the evidence has the burden of producing evidence as to the existence of that preliminary fact. The proffered evidence is inadmissible unless the trial court finds sufficient evidence to sustain a finding of the existence of the preliminary fact. 'The decision whether the foundational evidence is sufficiently substantial is a matter within the court's discretion.'"

Islas v. D&G Mfg. Co. (2d Dist.2004) 120 Cal.App.4th 571, 577. "Under ... §403, the trial court may determine preliminary facts regarding the relevance of evidence, the personal knowledge of a witness, the authenticity of a writing, and the statements and conduct of a person. The trial court's role here is to assess whether there is sufficient evidence to present

these matters to the jury. If there is, the matter is submitted to the jury for a final determination; if not, the matter is inadmissible."

§404. [BURDEN OF PROOF ON SELF-INCRIMINATION]

Whenever the proffered evidence is claimed to be privileged under Section 940, the person claiming the privilege has the burden of showing that the proffered evidence might tend to incriminate him; and the proffered evidence is inadmissible unless it clearly appears to the court that the proffered evidence cannot possibly have a tendency to incriminate the person claiming the privilege.

History of Evid. C. §404: Added eff. Sept. 17, 1965, oper. Jan. 1, 1967, Stats. 1965, ch. 299, §2.

Official Comment

7 Cal. Law Revision Comm'n Rep. (1965) p. 1053.

Section 404 provides a special procedure to be followed by the judge when an objection is made in reliance upon the privilege against self-incrimination. Under Section 404, the objecting party has the burden of showing that the testimony sought might incriminate him. However, the party is not required to produce evidence as such. In addition to considering evidence, the judge must consider the matters disclosed in argument, the implications of the question, the setting in which it is asked, the applicable statute of limitations, and all other relevant factors. *See Cohen v. Superior Court*, 173 Cal.App.2d 61, 70, 343 P.2d 286, 291 (1959). Nonetheless, the burden is on the objector to present to the judge information of this sort sufficient to indicate that the proffered evidence might incriminate him. If he presents information of this sort, Section 404 requires the judge to sustain the claim of privilege unless it clearly appears that the proffered evidence cannot possibly have a tendency to incriminate the person claiming the privilege.

Section 404 is consistent with existing law: The party claiming the privilege "has the burden of showing that the testimony which was being required might be used in a prosecution to help establish his guilt"; the court may require testimony to be given only if it clearly appears to the court that the claim of privilege is mistaken and that any answer "'*cannot possibly*'" have a tendency to incriminate the witness. *Cohen v. Superior Court*, 173 Cal.App.2d 61, 68, 70-72, 343 P.2d 286, 290, 291-292 (1959) (italics in original).

§405. [DISPUTED PRELIMINARY FACTS]

With respect to preliminary fact determinations not governed by Section 403 or 404:

(a) [Court determination.] When the existence of a preliminary fact is disputed, the court shall indicate which party has the burden of producing evidence and the burden of proof on the issue as implied by the rule of law under which the question arises. The court shall determine the existence or nonexistence of the preliminary fact and shall admit or exclude the proffered evidence as required by the rule of law under which the question arises.

(b) [Jury determination.] If a preliminary fact is also a fact in issue in the action:

(1) The jury shall not be informed of the court's determination as to the existence or nonexistence of the preliminary fact.

(2) If the proffered evidence is admitted, the jury shall not be instructed to disregard the evidence if its determination of the fact differs from the court's determination of the preliminary fact.

History of Evid. C. §405: Added eff. Sept. 17, 1965, oper. Jan. 1, 1967, Stats. 1965, ch. 299, §2.

Official Comment

7 Cal. Law Revision Comm'n Rep. (1965) p. 1054;
Assem. J., Apr. 6, 1965, p. 1722.

Section 405 requires the judge to determine the existence or nonexistence of disputed preliminary facts except in certain situations covered by Sections 403 and 404. Section 405 deals with evidentiary rules designed to withhold evidence from the jury because it is too unreliable to be evaluated properly or because public policy requires its exclusion.

Under Section 405, the judge first indicates to the parties who has the burden of proof and the burden of producing evidence on the disputed issue as implied by the rule of law under which the question arises. For example, Section 1200 indicates that the burden of proof is usually on the proponent of the evidence to show that the proffered evidence is within a hearsay exception. Thus, if the disputed preliminary fact is whether the proffered statement was spontaneous, as required by Section 1240, the proponent would have the burden of persuading the judge as to the spontaneity of the statement. On the other hand, the privilege rules usually place the burden of proof on the objecting party to show that a privilege is applicable. Thus, if the disputed preliminary fact is whether a person is married to a party and, hence, whether their confidential communications are privileged under Section 980, the burden of proof is on the party asserting the privilege to persuade the judge of the existence of the marriage.

After the judge has indicated to the parties who has the burden of proof and the burden of producing evidence, the parties submit their evidence on the preliminary issue to the judge. If the judge is persuaded by the party with the burden of proof, he finds in favor of that party in regard to the preliminary fact and either admits or excludes the proffered evidence as required by the rule of law under which the question arises. Otherwise, he finds against that party on the preliminary fact and either admits or excludes the proffered evidence as required by such finding.

Section 405 is generally consistent with existing law. Code Civ. Proc. §2102 ("All questions of law, including the admissibility of testimony, [and] the facts preliminary to such admission, ... are to be decided by the Court") (repealed, now Evidence Code §310).

Examples of preliminary fact issues to be decided under Section 405

Illustrative of the preliminary fact questions that should be decided under Section 405 are the following:

Section 701—Disqualification of a witness for lack of mental capacity. Under existing law, as under this code, the party objecting to a proffered witness has the burden of proving the witness' lack of capacity. *People v. Craig*, 111 Cal. 460, 469, 44 Pac. 186, 188 (1896); *People v. Tyree*, 21 Cal.App. 701, 706, 132 Pac. 784, 786 (1913) (*disapproved on other grounds* in *People v. McCaughan*, 49 Cal.2d 409, 420, 317 P.2d 974, 981 (1957)).

Section 720—Qualifications of an expert witness. Under Section 720, as under existing law, the proponent must persuade the judge that his expert is qualified, and it is error for the judge to submit the qualifications of the expert to the jury. *Fairbank v. Hughson*, 58 Cal. 314 (1881); *Eble v. Peluso*, 80 Cal.App.2d 154, 181 P.2d 680 (1947).

Section 788—Conviction of a crime when offered to attack credibility. If the disputed preliminary fact is whether a pardon or some similar relief has been granted to a witness convicted of a crime, the judge's determination is made under Section 405. *Cf. Comment* to Section 403.

Section 870—Opinion evidence on sanity. Whether a witness is sufficiently acquainted with a person whose sanity is in question to be qualified to express an opinion on the matter involves, in effect, the expertise of the witness on that limited subject. The witness' qualifications to express such an

§403

opinion, therefore, are to be determined by the judge under Section 405 just as the qualifications of other experts are decided by the judge. See the discussion of Section 720 in this *Comment, supra*. Under existing law, too, determination of whether a witness is an "intimate acquaintance" is a question addressed to the court. *Estate of Budan*, 156 Cal. 230, 104 Pac. 442 (1909).

Sections 900-1070—Privileges. Under this code, as under existing law, the party claiming a privilege has the burden of proof on the preliminary facts. *San Diego Professional Ass'n v. Superior Court*, 58 Cal.2d 194, 199, 23 Cal.Rptr. 384, 387, 373 P.2d 448, 451 (1962) ("The burden of establishing that a particular matter is privileged is on the party asserting that privilege."); *Chronicle Publishing Co. v. Superior Court*, 54 Cal.2d 548, 565, 7 Cal.Rptr. 109, 117, 354 P.2d 637, 645 (1960). The proponent of the proffered evidence, however, has the burden of proof upon any preliminary fact necessary to show that an exception to the privilege is applicable. *But see Abbott v. Superior Court*, 78 Cal.App.2d 19, 21, 177 P.2d 317, 318 (1947) (suggesting that a prima facie showing by the proponent is sufficient where the issue is whether a communication between attorney and client was made in contemplation of crime).

Sections 1152, 1154—Admissions made during compromise negotiations. With respect to admissions made during compromise negotiations, the disputed preliminary fact to be decided by the judge is whether the admission occurred during compromise negotiations or at some other time. This code places the burden on the objecting party to satisfy the judge that the admission occurred during such negotiations.

Sections 1200-1341—Hearsay evidence. When hearsay evidence is offered, two preliminary fact questions may be raised. The first question relates to the authenticity of the proffered declaration—was the statement actually made by the person alleged to have made it? The second question relates to the existence of those circumstances that make the hearsay sufficiently trustworthy to be received in evidence—*e.g.*, was the declaration spontaneous, the confession voluntary, the business record trustworthy? Under this code, questions relating to the authenticity of the proffered declaration are decided under Section 403. *See* the *Comment* to Section 403. But other preliminary fact questions are decided under Section 405.

For example, the court must decide whether a statement offered as a dying declaration was made under a sense of impending death, and the proponent of the evidence has the burden of proof on this issue. *People v. Keelin*, 136 Cal.App.2d 860, 873, 289 P.2d 520, 528 (1955); *People v. Pollock*, 31 Cal.App.2d 747, 753-754, 89 P.2d 128, 131 (1939). Under this code, the proponent of a hearsay declaration has the burden of proof on the unavailability of the declarant as a witness under Section 1291 or 1310; but the party objecting to the evidence has the burden of proving that the unavailability of the declarant was procured by the proponent in order to prevent the declarant from testifying. *See* Evidence Code §240.

Section 1416—Opinion evidence on handwriting. Whether a witness is sufficiently acquainted with the handwriting of a person to give an opinion on whether a questioned writing is in that person's handwriting involves, in effect, the expertise of the witness on the limited subject of the supposed writer's handwriting. The witness' qualifications to express such an opinion, therefore, are to be determined by the judge under Section 405 just as the qualifications of other experts are decided by the judge. See the discussion of Section 720 in this *Comment, supra*.

Sections 1417-1419—Comparison of writing with exemplar. Under Sections 1417 through 1419, as under existing law, the judge must be satisfied that a writing is genuine before he may admit it for comparison with other writings whose authenticity is in dispute. *People v. Creegan*, 121 Cal. 554, 53 Pac. 1082 (1898); *Marshall v. Hancock*, 80 Cal. 82, 22 Pac. 61 (1889).

Sections 1500-1510—Best evidence rule [now Sections 1520-1522—Secondary evidence rule]. Under Section 405, as under existing law, the trial judge is required to determine the preliminary fact necessary to warrant reception of secondary evidence of a writing, and the burden of proof on the issue is on the proponent of the secondary evidence. *Cotton v. Hudson*, 42 Cal.App.2d 812, 110 P.2d 70 (1941).

Sections 1550, 1551—Photographic copy of writing. Sections 1550 and 1551 are special exceptions to the best evidence rule [now secondary evidence rule]; hence, Section 405 governs the determination of any disputed preliminary fact under these sections just as it governs the determination of disputed preliminary facts under Sections 1500 through 1510 [repealed]. See the discussion of Sections 1550-1510 [now 1520-1522] in this *Comment, supra*. [*See also* Evidence Code §§1552-1553 (admission of computer printouts, video, digital prints).]

Function of court and jury under Section 405

When preliminary fact question is also an issue involved in merits of case. In some cases, a factual issue to be decided by the judge under Section 405 will coincide with an issue involved in the merits of the case. For example, in *People v. MacDonald*, 24 Cal.App.2d 702, 76 P.2d 121 (1938), the defendant in an incest prosecution objected to the testimony of the prosecutrix on the ground that she was his wife. The judge, in ruling on the objection, had to determine whether the prosecutrix was also the defendant's daughter and, hence, whether their marriage was incestuous and void. In such a case, it would be prejudicial to the parties for the judge to inform the jury how he had decided the same factual question that it must decide in determining the merits of the case. Subdivision (b), therefore, prohibits a judge from informing the jury how he decided a question under Section 405 that the jury must ultimately resolve on the merits.

The judge is also prohibited from instructing the jury to disregard evidence that has been admitted if the jury's determination of a fact in deciding the merits differs from the judge's determination of the same fact under Section 405. The rules of admissibility being applied by the judge under Section 405 are designed to withhold evidence from the jury because it is too unreliable to be evaluated properly or because public policy requires its exclusion. The policies underlying these rules are served only by the exclusion of the evidence. No valid public or evidentiary purpose is served by submitting the admissibility question again to the jury. For example, the interspousal testimonial privilege involved in *People v. MacDonald*, 24 Cal.App.2d 702, 76 P.2d 121 (1938), exists to preclude a spouse from being involuntarily compelled to testify against the other spouse. The privilege serves its purpose only if the spouse does not testify. The harm the privilege is designed to prevent has occurred if the spouse testifies. Therefore, subdivision (b) provides for the finality of the judge's rulings on admissibility under Section 405 even in those cases where the factual questions decided by the judge coincide with the factual questions ultimately to be resolved by the jury.

Of course, Section 405 has no effect on the constitutional right of the judge to comment on the evidence and on the testimony and credibility of witnesses. *See* Cal. Const., Art. I, §13, and Art. VI, §19.

Confessions, dying declarations, and spontaneous statements. Although Section 405 is generally consistent with existing law, it will, however, substantially change the law relating to confessions, dying declarations, and spontaneous statements. Under existing law, the judge considers all of the evidence and decides whether evidence of this sort is admissible, as indicated in Section 405. But if he decides the proffered evidence is admissible, he submits the preliminary question to the jury for a final determination whether the confession was voluntary, whether the dying declaration was made in realization of impending doom, or whether the spontaneous statement was in fact spontaneous; and the jury is instructed to disregard the statement if it does not believe that the condition of admissibility has been satisfied. *People v. Baldwin*, 42 Cal.2d 858, 866-867, 270 P.2d 1028, 1033-1034 (1954) (confession—see the court's instruction, *id.* at 866, 270 P.2d at 1033); *People v. Gonzales*, 24 Cal.2d 870, 876-877, 151 P.2d 251, 254 (1944) (confession); *People v. Singh*, 182 Cal. 457, 476, 188 Pac. 987, 995 (1920) (dying declaration); *People v. Keelin*, 136 Cal.App.2d 860, 871, 289 P.2d 520, 527 (1955) (spontaneous declaration).

Under Section 405, the judge's rulings on these questions are final; the jury does not have an opportunity to redetermine the issue.

Section 405 will have no effect on the admissibility of confessions where the uncontradicted evidence shows that the confession was not voluntary. Under existing law, as under the Evidence Code, such a confession may not be admitted for consideration by the jury. *People v. Trout*, 54 Cal.2d 576, 6 Cal.Rptr. 759, 354 P.2d 231 (1960); *People v. Jones*, 24 Cal.2d 601, 150 P.2d 801 (1944). Section 405 will also have no effect on the admissibility of confessions in those instances where, despite a conflict in the evidence, the court is persuaded that the confession was not voluntary; for, under existing law (as under the Evidence Code), "if the court concludes that the confession was not free and voluntary it ... is in duty bound to withhold it from the jury's consideration." *People v. Gonzales*, 24 Cal.2d 870, 876, 151 P.2d 251, 254 (1944).

Hence, Section 405 changes the law relating to confessions only where there is a substantial conflict in the evidence over voluntariness and the court is not persuaded that the confession was involuntary. Under existing law, a court that is in doubt may "pass the buck" concerning such a confession to the jury when there is a difficult factual question to resolve; for "if there is evidence that the confession was free and voluntary, it is within the court's discretion to permit it to be read to the jury, and to submit to the jury for its determination the question whether under all the circumstances the confession was made

freely and voluntarily. *People v. Gonzales*, 24 Cal.2d 870, 876, 151 P.2d 251, 254 (1944). Under the Evidence Code, however, the court is required to withhold a confession from the jury unless the court is persuaded that the confession was made freely and voluntarily. The court has no "discretion" to avoid difficult decisions by shifting the responsibility to the jury. If the court is in doubt, if the prosecution has not persuaded it of the voluntary nature of the confession, Section 405 requires the court to exclude the confession. Thus, Section 405 makes the procedure for determining the admissibility of a confession the same as the procedure for determining the admissibility of physical evidence claimed to have been seized in violation of constitutional guarantees. *See People v. Gorg*, 45 Cal.2d 776, 291 P.2d 469 (1955); *People v. Chavez*, 208 Cal.App.2d 248, 24 Cal.Rptr. 895 (1962).

The existing law is based on the belief that a jury, in determining the defendant's guilt or innocence, can and will refuse to consider a confession that it has determined was involuntary even though it believes that the confession is true. Section 405, on the other hand, proceeds upon the belief that it is unrealistic to expect a jury to perform such a feat. Corroborating facts stated in a confession cannot but assist the jury in resolving other conflicts in the evidence. The question of voluntariness will inevitably become merged with the question of guilt and the truth of the confession; and, as a result of this merger, the admitted confession will inevitably be considered on the issue of guilt. The defendant will receive a greater degree of protection if the court is deprived of the power to shift its fact-determining responsibility to the jury and is required to exclude a confession whenever it is not persuaded that the confession was voluntary.

The foregoing discussion has focused on confessions because the case law is well developed there. But the "second crack" doctrine is equally unsatisfactory when applied to dying declarations and spontaneous statements. Hence, Section 405 requires the court to rule finally on the admissibility of these statements as well.

Of course, Section 405 does not prevent the presentation of any evidence to the jury that is relevant to the reliability of the hearsay statement. *See* Evidence Code §406. Thus, a party may present evidence of the circumstances under which a confession, dying declaration, or spontaneous statement was made where such evidence is relevant to the credibility of the statement, even though such evidence may duplicate to some degree the evidence presented to the court on the issue of admissibility. But the jury's sole concern is the truth or falsity of the facts stated, not the admissibility of the statement.

ANNOTATIONS

Islas v. D&G Mfg. Co. (2d Dist.2004) 120 Cal.App.4th 571, 578. "Under … §405, the trial court may determine preliminary facts regarding 'evidentiary rules designed to withhold evidence from the jury because it is too unreliable to be evaluated properly or because public policy requires its exclusion.'"

Brawthen v. H&R Block, Inc. (1st Dist.1975) 52 Cal.App.3d 139, 146. "Under [§405], the jury proceeds with its proper function, determining the related questions of credibility of witnesses and the parties' intent."

§406. [WEIGHT & CREDIBILITY]

This article does not limit the right of a party to introduce before the trier of fact evidence relevant to weight or credibility.

History of Evid. C. §406: Added eff. Sept. 17, 1965, oper. Jan. 1, 1967, Stats. 1965, ch. 299, §2.

Official Comment

7 Cal. Law Revision Comm'n Rep. (1965) p. 1059.

Other sections in this article provide that the judge determines whether proffered evidence is admissible, *i.e.*, whether it may be considered by the trier of fact. Section 406 simply makes it clear that the judge's decision on a question of admissibility does not preclude the parties from introducing before the trier of fact evidence relevant to weight and credibility.

CHAPTER 5. WEIGHT OF EVIDENCE GENERALLY

§410. [DIRECT EVIDENCE]

As used in this chapter, "direct evidence" means evidence that directly proves a fact, without an inference or presumption, and which in itself, if true, conclusively establishes that fact.

History of Evid. C. §410: Added eff. Sept. 17, 1965, oper. Jan. 1, 1967, Stats. 1965, ch. 299, §2.

Official Comment

7 Cal. Law Revision Comm'n Rep. (1965) p. 1060.

Section 410 restates the substance of and supersedes Section 1831 of the Code of Civil Procedure.

§411. [ONE WITNESS SUFFICIENT]

Except where additional evidence is required by statute, the direct evidence of one witness who is entitled to full credit is sufficient for proof of any fact.

History of Evid. C. §411: Added eff. Sept. 17, 1965, oper. Jan. 1, 1967, Stats. 1965, ch. 299, §2.

Official Comment

7 Cal. Law Revision Comm'n Rep. (1965) p. 1060.

Section 411 restates the substance of and supersedes Section 1844 of the Code of Civil Procedure. The phrase "except where additional evidence is required by statute" has been substituted for the phrase "except perjury and treason" in Section 1844 because the "perjury and treason" exception to Section 1844 is too limited: Corroboration is required by Section 20 of Article I of the California Constitution (treason) and by Penal Code Sections 653f (solicitation to commit felonies), 1103a (perjury), 1108 (abortion and prostitution cases), 1110 (obtaining property by oral false pretenses), and 1111 (testimony of accomplices); in addition, Civil Code Section 130 provides that divorces cannot be granted on the uncorroborated testimony of the parties.

ANNOTATIONS

Sav-on Drug Stores v. Superior Ct. (2004) 34 Cal.4th 319, 334. "Evidence of even one credible witness 'is sufficient for proof of any fact.' And 'questions as to the weight and sufficiency of the evidence, the construction to be put upon it, the inferences to be drawn therefrom, the credibility of witnesses … and the determination of [any] conflicts and inconsistency in their testimony are matters for the trial court to resolve.'"

Plastic Pipe & Fittings Ass'n v. California Bldg. Stds. Comm'n (2d Dist.2004) 124 Cal.App.4th 1390, 1407. "Evidence is substantial if a reasonable trier of fact could conclude that the evidence is reasonable, credible, and of solid value. The uncorroborated testimony of one witness can constitute substantial evidence, unless the testimony is inherently unreliable." *See also* ***DeMiglio v. Mashore*** (1st Dist.1992) 4 Cal.App.4th 1260, 1270.

Bradley v. Perrodin (2d Dist.2003) 106 Cal.App.4th 1153, 1166. "Although an appellate court will not uphold a judgment or verdict based upon evidence inherently improbable, testimony which merely discloses unusual circumstances does not come within that category. To warrant the rejection of the statements given by a witness who has been believed by a trial court, there must exist either a physical impossibility that they are true, or their falsity must be apparent without resorting to inferences or deductions. Conflicts and even testimony which is subject to justifiable suspicion do not justify the reversal of a judgment, for it is the exclusive province of the trial judge or jury to determine the credibility of a witness and the truth or falsity of the facts upon which a determination depends." (Internal quotes omitted.) *See also* ***In re Andrew I.*** (4th Dist.1991) 230 Cal.App.3d 572, 578; ***People v. Swanson*** (2d Dist.1962) 204 Cal.App.2d 169, 173.

§412. [WITHHOLDING STRONGER EVIDENCE]

If weaker and less satisfactory evidence is offered when it was within the power of the party to produce stronger and more satisfactory evidence, the evidence offered should be viewed with distrust.

History of Evid. C. §412: Added eff. Sept. 17, 1965, oper. Jan. 1, 1967, Stats. 1965, ch. 299, §2.

Official Comment

7 Cal. Law Revision Comm'n Rep. (1965) p. 1060.

Section 412 restates the substance of and supersedes subdivisions 6 and 7 of Section 2061 of the Code of Civil Procedure.

Section 413, taken together with Section 412, restates in substance the meaning that has been given to the presumptions appearing in subdivisions 5 and 6 of Code of Civil Procedure Section 1963.

Evidence Code Section 913 provides that "no presumption shall arise because of the exercise of [a] privilege, and the trier of fact may not draw any inference therefrom," and the trial judge is required to give such an instruction if he is requested to do so. However, there is no inconsistency between Section 913 and Sections 412 and 413. Section 913 deals only with the inferences that may be drawn from the exercise of a privilege; it does not purport to deal with the inferences that may be drawn from the evidence in the case. Sections 412 and 413, on the other hand, deal with the inferences to be drawn from the evidence in the case; and the fact that a privilege has been relied on is irrelevant to the application of these sections. *Cf. People v. Adamson*, 27 Cal.2d 478, 165 P.2d 3 (1946).

ANNOTATIONS

Ellis v. Toshiba Am. Info. Sys. (2d Dist.2013) 218 Cal.App.4th 853, 885. Ps' attorney "argues that the trial court abused its discretion in applying [unfavorable jury instructions] because there was no evidence that she willfully suppressed evidence. To the contrary, … the record shows that [Ps' attorney] repeatedly resisted discovery of her original time records, and we will not disturb the trial court's compliance with … §412…."

Willard v. Caterpillar, Inc. (5th Dist.1995) 40 Cal.App.4th 892, 907, *disapproved on other grounds*, ***Cedars-Sinai Med. Ctr. v. Superior Ct.*** (1998) 18 Cal.4th 1. "Spoliation is the destruction or significant alteration of evidence, or the failure to preserve property for another's use as evidence, in pending or future litigation. Spoliation occurs along a continuum of fault—ranging from innocent through the degrees of negligence to intentional conduct. [¶] The traditional remedies for spoliation of evidence include: (1) a discretionary jury inference against the spoliator …; (2) a charge of obstruction of justice …; and (3) various discovery sanctions…." *See also* ***Bihun v. AT&T Info. Sys.*** (2d Dist.1993) 13 Cal.App.4th 976, 994-95 (jury inference), *disapproved on other grounds*, ***Lakin v. Watkins Associated Indus.*** (1993) 6 Cal.4th 644; ***Puritan Ins. v. Superior Ct.*** (3d Dist.1985) 171 Cal.App.3d 877, 885-86 (discovery sanctions); ***Smith v. Superior Ct.*** (2d Dist.1984) 151 Cal.App.3d 491, 499 (obstruction of justice), *disapproved on other grounds*, ***Cedars-Sinai Med. Ctr. v. Superior Ct.*** (1998) 18 Cal.4th 1.

§413. [DETERMINATION OF INFERENCES]

In determining what inferences to draw from the evidence or facts in the case against a party, the trier of fact may consider, among other things, the party's failure to explain or to deny by his testimony such evidence or facts in the case against him, or his willful suppression of evidence relating thereto, if such be the case.

History of Evid. C. §413: Added eff. Sept. 17, 1965, oper. Jan. 1, 1967, Stats. 1965, ch. 299, §2.

Official Comment

7 Cal. Law Revision Comm'n Rep. (1965) p. 1061.

See the *Comment* to Section 412.

ANNOTATIONS

Cedars-Sinai Med. Ctr. v. Superior Ct. (1998) 18 Cal.4th 1, 17-18. "[T]here is no tort remedy for the intentional spoliation of evidence by a party to the cause of action to which the spoliated evidence is relevant, in cases in which … the spoliation victim knows or should have known of the alleged spoliation before the trial or other decision on the merits of the underlying action." *See also* ***Temple Cmty. Hosp. v. Superior Ct.*** (1999) 20 Cal.4th 464, 478 (no tort remedy for third-party intentional spoliation of evidence); ***Coprich v. Superior Ct.*** (2d Dist.2000) 80 Cal.App.4th 1081, 1090 (no tort remedy for first-party or third-party negligent spoliation of evidence).

Williamson v. Superior Ct. (1978) 21 Cal.3d 829, 835 n.2. "'The purpose of a trial is to arrive at the true facts. A trial is not a game where one counsel safely may sit back and refuse to produce evidence where in the nature of things his client is the only source from which that evidence may be secured. *A defendant is not under a duty to produce testimony adverse to himself, but if he fails to produce evidence that would naturally have been produced he must take the risk that the trier of fact will infer, and properly so, that the evidence, had it been produced, would have been adverse.*'"

Reeves v. MV Transp. (1st Dist.2010) 186 Cal.App.4th 666, 681-82. "'In order for an adverse inference to arise from the destruction of evidence, the party having control over the evidence must have had an obligation to preserve it at the time it was destroyed.' [T]he party seeking the benefit of the inference ... 'must demonstrate ... the records were destroyed with a ... culpable state of mind (i.e. ... the records were destroyed knowingly ... or negligently) [and] the destroyed records were relevant to the party's claim or defense.'"

DIVISION 4. JUDICIAL NOTICE

Official Comment

7 Cal. Law Revision Comm'n Rep. (1965) p. 1062.

The statutory scheme in Division 4 is based on Article 2 (Rules 9-12) of the Uniform Rules of Evidence. The court is required to take judicial notice of the matters listed in Section 451. It may take judicial notice of the matters listed in Section 452 even when not requested to do so; it is required to notice them, however, if a party requests it and satisfies the requirements of Section 453.

There is some overlap between the matters listed in the mandatory notice provisions of Section 451 and the matters listed in the permissive-unless-a-request-is-made provisions of Section 452. Thus, when a matter falls within Section 451, judicial notice is mandatory even though the matter would otherwise fall within Section 452. The introductory clause of Section 452 makes this clear. For example, public statutory law is required to be noticed under subdivision (a) of Section 451 even though it would also be included under official acts of the legislative department under subdivision (c) of Section 452. Certain regulations are required to be noticed under subdivision (b) of Section 451 even though they might also be included under subdivisions (b) and (c) of Section 452. And indisputable matters of universal knowledge are required to be noticed under subdivision (f) of Section 451 even though such matters might be included under subdivisions (g) and (h) of Section 452.

There is also some overlap between the various categories listed in Section 452. However, this overlap will cause no difficulty because all of the matters listed in Section 452 are treated alike.

§450. [SCOPE OF JUDICIAL NOTICE]

Judicial notice may not be taken of any matter unless authorized or required by law.

History of Evid. C. §450: Added eff. Sept. 17, 1965, oper. Jan. 1, 1967, Stats. 1965, ch. 299, §2.

Official Comment

7 Cal. Law Revision Comm'n Rep. (1965) p. 1062.

Section 450 provides that judicial notice may not be taken of any matter unless authorized or required by law. *See* Evidence Code §160, defining "law." Sections 451 and 452 state a number of matters which must or may be judicially noticed. Judicial notice of other matters is authorized or required by other statutes or by decisional law. *E.g.*, Civil Code §53; Corp. Code §6602. In this respect, the Evidence Code is consistent with existing law, for the principal judicial notice provision found in existing law—Code of Civil Procedure Section 1875 (repealed, now this division of the Evidence Code)—does not limit judicial notice to those matters specified by statute. Judicial notice has been taken of various matters not so specified, principally of those matters of common knowledge which are certain and indisputable. Witkin, *California Evidence* §§50-52 (1958).

Under the Evidence Code, as under existing law, courts may consider whatever materials are appropriate in construing statutes, determining constitutional issues, and formulating rules of law. That a court may consider legislative history, discussions by learned writers in treatises and law reviews, materials that contain controversial economic and social facts or findings or that indicate contemporary opinion, and similar materials is inherent in the requirement that it take judicial notice of the law. In many cases, the meaning and validity of statutes, the precise nature of a common law rule, or the correct interpretation of a constitutional provision can be determined only with the help of such extrinsic aids. *Cf. People v. Sterling Refining Co.*, 86 Cal.App. 558, 564, 261 Pac. 1080, 1083 (1927) (statutory authority to notice "public and private acts" of legislature held to authorize examination of legislative history of certain acts). *See also Perez v. Sharp*, 32 Cal.2d 711, 198 P.2d 17 (1948) (texts and authorities used by court in opinions determining constitutionality of statute prohibiting interracial marriages). Section 450 will neither broaden nor limit the extent to which a court may resort to extrinsic aids in determining the rules of law that it is required to notice. Nor will Section 450 broaden or limit the extent to which a court may take judicial notice of any other matter not specified in Section 451 or 452.

ANNOTATIONS

StorMedia Inc. v. Superior Ct. (1999) 20 Cal.4th 449, 456 n.9. "[A] court may consider facts of which it has taken judicial notice. This includes the existence of a document. When judicial notice is taken of a document, however, the truthfulness and proper interpretation of the document are disputable." *See also* ***Herrera v. Deutsche Bank Nat'l Trust Co.*** (3d Dist.2011) 196 Cal.App.4th 1366, 1375; ***Fremont Indem. Co. v. Fremont Gen. Corp.*** (2d Dist.2007) 148 Cal.App.4th 97, 113.

Aerojet-Gen. Corp. v. Transport Indem. Co. (1997) 17 Cal.4th 38, 56 n.8. "[A]mici curiae supporting [D's] position ... have submitted a request for judicial notice of [certain] commentaries.... We deny the request. We may take judicial notice only of matter that is 'authorized or required by law.' The indicated commentaries are not such. They may nevertheless be consulted for whatever assistance they may furnish."

Mangini v. R.J. Reynolds Tobacco Co. (1994) 7 Cal.4th 1057, 1063, *overruled on other grounds*, ***In re Tobacco Cases II*** (2007) 41 Cal.4th 1257. See annotation under Evidence Code §451, p. 1216.

Aquila, Inc. v. Superior Ct. (4th Dist.2007) 148 Cal.App.4th 556, 569. "When a trial court's judicial notice rulings are challenged, harmless error standards should apply: 'The Evidence Code declares the party's right and the trial judge's duty, but does not deal with

the problems of appellate review and reversible error. Hence, even though the matter called for compulsory notice, or was appropriate for optional notice, and the appellant fully complied with the procedural requirements, refusal to take notice is merely error. Whether it is reversible error depends on the state of the record, and also involves considerations of estoppel and waiver. Likewise, the improper taking of notice is subject to harmless error analysis.'"

Fong v. Westly (3d Dist.2004) 117 Cal.App.4th 841, 855 n.2. "[Ps] ask us to take judicial notice of certain actions allegedly taken by the Controller in response to the Legislature's recent elimination of the requirement imposed on the state to pay interest on claims made for unclaimed property. [Ps] argue the Controller's actions represent the 'decisional' law of the state of which we must take judicial notice. We disagree and deny the request."

Post v. Prati (2d Dist.1979) 90 Cal.App.3d 626, 633-34. "'The doctrine of judicial notice is an evidentiary doctrine that permits the court to consider *as established* in a case a matter of *law* or *fact* that is relevant to an issue, without the necessity of formal proof of the matter by any party. Judicial notice is a substitute for formal proof. Judicial notice may be taken of either a proposition of *law* or a proposition of *fact*. The fundamental theory of judicial notice is that the matter that is judicially noticed is one of law or fact that *cannot reasonably be disputed*.' Judicial notice may be taken by the trial court in connection with a demurrer ... and may also be considered by an appellate court in conducting review."

McGlothlen v. Department of Motor Vehicles (1st Dist.1977) 71 Cal.App.3d 1005, 1015. "It is well established that the courts may take judicial notice not only of the statutory law of this state ..., but also of the resolutions and private acts of the Legislature of this state, and, as well, the official acts of the executive departments and Legislature...." *See also* ***Auchmoody v. 911 Emerg. Servs.*** (2d Dist.1989) 214 Cal.App.3d 1510, 1518-19.

§451. [MANDATORY JUDICIAL NOTICE]

Judicial notice shall be taken of the following:

(a) [California and federal law.] The decisional, constitutional, and public statutory law of this state and of the United States and the provisions of any charter described in Section 3, 4, or 5 of Article XI of the California Constitution.

(b) [California and federal regulations.] Any matter made a subject of judicial notice by Section 11343.6, 11344.6, or 18576 of the Government Code or by Section 1507 of Title 44 of the United States Code.

(c) [Rules of professional conduct.] Rules of professional conduct for members of the bar adopted pursuant to Section 6076 of the Business and Professions Code and rules of practice and procedure for the courts of this state adopted by the Judicial Council.

(d) [Federal court rules.] Rules of pleading, practice, and procedure prescribed by the United States Supreme Court, such as the Rules of the United States Supreme Court, the Federal Rules of Civil Procedure, the Federal Rules of Criminal Procedure, the Admiralty Rules, the Rules of the Court of Claims, the Rules of the Customs Court, and the General Orders and Forms in Bankruptcy.

(e) [Words and phrases.] The true signification of all English words and phrases and of all legal expressions.

(f) [Universal knowledge.] Facts and propositions of generalized knowledge that are so universally known that they cannot reasonably be the subject of dispute.

History of Evid. C. §451: Added eff. Sept. 17, 1965, oper. Jan. 1, 1967, Stats. 1965, ch. 299, §2. Amended eff. Mar. 4, 1972, Stats. 1971, ch. 438, §88; eff. Mar. 7, 1973, Stats. 1972, ch. 764, §1; eff. Jan. 1, 1983, Stats. 1982, ch. 454, §20; eff. Jan. 1, 1986, Stats. 1985, ch. 106, §32; eff. Jan. 1, 1987, Stats. 1986, ch. 248, §43.

Official Comment

**7 Cal. Law Revision Comm'n Rep. (1965) p. 1063;
Assem. J., Apr. 6, 1965, p. 1727.**

Judicial notice of the matters specified in Section 451 is *mandatory*, whether or not the court is requested to notice them. Although the court errs if it fails to take judicial notice of the matters specified in this section, such error is not necessarily reversible error. Depending upon the circumstances, the appellate court may hold that the error was "invited" (and, hence, is not reversible error) or that points not urged in the trial court may not be advanced on appeal. These and similar principles of appellate practice are not abrogated by this section.

Section 451 includes matters both of law and of fact. The matters specified in subdivisions (a), (b), (c), and (d) are all matters that, broadly speaking, can be considered as a part of the "law" applicable to the particular case. The court can reasonably be expected to discover and apply this law even if the parties fail to provide the court with references to the pertinent cases, statutes, regulations, and rules. Other matters that also might properly be considered as a part of the law applicable to the case (such as the law of foreign nations and certain regulations and ordinances) are included under Section 452, rather than under Section 451, primarily because of the difficulty of ascertaining such matters. Subdivision (e) of Section 451 requires the court to judicially notice "the true signification of all English words and phrases and of all legal expressions." These are facts that must be judicially noticed in order to conduct meaningful proceedings. Similarly, subdivision (f) of Section 451 covers "universally known" facts.

Listed below are the matters that must be judicially noticed under Section 451.

California and federal law. The decisional, constitutional, and public statutory law of California and of the United States must be judicially noticed under subdivision (a). This requirement states existing law as found in subdivision 3 of Code of Civil Procedure Section 1875 (repealed).

Charter provisions of California cities and counties. Judicial notice must be taken under subdivision (a) of the provisions of charters adopted pursuant to Section 7½ or 8 of Article XI of the California Constitution. Notice of these provisions is mandatory under the State Constitution. Cal. Const., Art. XI, §7½ (county charter), §8 (charter of city or city and county).

Regulations of California and federal agencies. Judicial notice must be taken under subdivision (b) of the rules, regulations, orders, and standards of general application adopted by California state agencies and filed with the Secretary of State or printed in the California Administrative Code or the California Administrative Register. This is existing law as found in Government Code Sections 11383 and 11384. Under subdivision (b), judicial notice must also be taken of the rules of the State Personnel Board. This, too, is existing law under Government Code Section 18576.

Subdivision (b) also requires California courts to judicially notice documents published in the Federal Register (such as (1) presidential proclamations and executive orders having general applicability and legal effect and (2) orders, regulations, rules, certificates, codes of fair competition, licenses, notices, and similar instruments, having general applicability and legal effect, that are issued, prescribed, or promulgated by federal agencies). There is no clear holding that this is existing California law. Although Section 307 [now §1507] of Title 44 of the United States Code provides that the "contents of the Federal Register shall be judicially noticed," it is not clear that this *requires* notice by state courts. *See Broadway Fed. etc. Loan Ass'n v. Howard*, 133 Cal.App.2d 382, 386 note 4, 285 P.2d 61, 64 note 4 (1955) (referring to 44 U.S.C.A. §§301-314). *Compare* Note, 59 Harv.L.Rev. 1137, 1141 (1946) (doubt expressed that notice is required), *with* Knowlton, *Judicial Notice*, 10 Rutgers L.Rev. 501, 504 (1956) ("it would seem that this provision is binding upon the state courts"). *Livermore v. Beal*, 18 Cal.App.2d 535, 542-543, 64 P.2d 987, 992 (1937), suggests that California courts are required to judicially notice pertinent federal official action, and California courts have judicially noticed the contents of various proclamations, orders, and regulations of federal agencies. *E.g., Pacific Solvents Co. v. Superior Court*, 88 Cal.App.2d 953, 955, 199 P.2d 740, 741 (1948) (orders and regulations); *People v. Mason*, 72 Cal.App.2d 699, 706-707, 165 P.2d 481, 485 (1946) (presidential and executive proclamations) (*disapproved on other grounds* in *People v. Friend*, 50 Cal.2d 570, 578, 327 P.2d 97, 102 (1958)); *Downer v. Grizzly Livestock & Land Co.*, 6 Cal.App.2d 39, 42, 43 P.2d 843, 845 (1935) (rules and regulations). Section 451 makes the California law clear.

§451

Rules of court. Judicial notice of the California Rules of Court is required under subdivision (c). These rules, adopted by the Judicial Council, are as binding on the parties as procedural statutes. *Cantillon v. Superior Court*, 150 Cal.App.2d 184, 309 P.2d 890 (1957). *See Albermont Petroleum, Ltd. v. Cunningham*, 186 Cal.App.2d 84, 9 Cal.Rptr. 405 (1960). Likewise, the rules of pleading, practice, and procedure promulgated by the United States Supreme Court are required to be judicially noticed under subdivision (d).

The rules of the California and federal courts which are required to be judicially noticed under subdivisions (c) and (d) are, or should be, familiar to the court or easily discoverable from materials readily available to the court. However, this may not be true of the court rules of sister states or other jurisdictions nor, for example, of the rules of the various United States Courts of Appeals or local rules of a particular superior court. *See Albermont Petroleum, Ltd. v. Cunningham*, 186 Cal.App.2d 84, 9 Cal.Rptr. 405 (1960). Judicial notice of these rules is permitted under subdivision (e) of Section 452 but is not required unless there is compliance with the provisions of Section 453.

State Bar Rules of Professional Conduct. The Rules of Professional Conduct of the State Bar of California are, in effect, rules of the Supreme Court, for they must be approved by that court. *Barton v. State Bar*, 209 Cal. 677, 289 Pac. 818 (1930). Subdivision (c), therefore, requires the court to take judicial notice of these rules to the same extent that it takes notice of other rules of court.

Words, phrases, and legal expressions. Subdivision (e) requires the court to take judicial notice of "the true signification of all English words and phrases and of all legal expressions." This restates the same matter covered in subdivision 1 of Code of Civil Procedure Section 1875. Under existing law, however, it is not clear that judicial notice of these matters is mandatory.

"Universally known" facts. Subdivision (f) requires the court to take judicial notice of indisputable facts and propositions universally known. "Universally known" does not mean that every man on the street has knowledge of such facts. A fact known among persons of reasonable and average intelligence and knowledge will satisfy the "universally known" requirement. *Cf. People v. Tossetti*, 107 Cal.App. 7, 12, 289 Pac. 881, 883 (1930).

Subdivision (f) should be contrasted with subdivisions (g) and (h) of Section 452, which provide for judicial notice of indisputable facts and propositions that are matters of common knowledge or are capable of immediate and accurate determination by resort to sources of reasonably indisputable accuracy. Subdivisions (g) and (h) permit notice of facts and propositions that are indisputable but are not "universally" known.

Judicial notice does not apply to facts merely because they are known to the judge to be indisputable. The facts must fulfill the requirements of subdivision (f) of Section 451 or subdivision (g) or (h) of Section 452. If a judge happens to know a fact that is not widely enough known to be subject to judicial notice under this division, he may not "notice" it.

It is clear under existing law that the court may judicially notice the matters specified in subdivision (f); it is doubtful, however, that the court *must* notice them. *See Varcoe v. Lee*, 180 Cal. 338, 347, 181 Pac. 223, 227 (1919) (dictum). Since subdivision (f) covers universally known facts, the parties ordinarily will expect the court to take judicial notice of them; the court should not be permitted to ignore such facts merely because the parties fail to make a formal request for judicial notice.

ANNOTATIONS

Quelimane Co. v. Stewart Title Guar. Co. (1998) 19 Cal.4th 26, 45 n.9. "The court will take judicial notice of the legislative history of a statute in order to ascertain the purpose of and meaning of an ambiguous statute. This includes reports of Senate and Assembly committees. ... While the views of individual legislators as to the meaning of a statute rarely, if ever, are relevant, committee reports and analyses or digests of the Legislative Counsel are because it is reasonable to infer that all members of the Legislature considered them when voting on the proposed statute." *See also* ***Kaufman & Broad Cmty., Inc. v. Performance Plastering, Inc.*** (3d Dist.2005) 133 Cal.App.4th 26, 31-37 (listing cognizable legislative history).

In re Estate of Joseph (1998) 17 Cal.4th 203, 210 n.1. "Petitioner requests us to take judicial notice of the records of the Law Revision Commission.... We hereby grant the request. We must, of course, judicially notice California statutory law. We may also judicially notice matters underlying such law. Including, to our mind, the commission records here." *See also* ***Schmidt v. Southern Cal. Rapid Transit Dist.*** (2d Dist.1993) 14 Cal.App.4th 23, 30 n.10.

Mangini v. R.J. Reynolds Tobacco Co. (1994) 7 Cal.4th 1057, 1063, *overruled on other grounds*, ***In re Tobacco Cases II*** (2007) 41 Cal.4th 1257. "'While [Evid. C.] §451 ... provides in mandatory terms that certain matters designated therein must be judicially noticed, the provisions contained therein are subject to the qualification that the matter to be judicially noticed must be relevant ...,' as well as 'qualified by [Evid. C.]

§352....' We therefore 'decline' to judicially notice material that 'has no bearing on the limited legal question at hand.'" *See also* ***Mozzetti v. City of Brisbane*** (1st Dist.1977) 67 Cal.App.3d 565, 578.

Stockton Citizens for Sensible Planning v. City of Stockton (3d Dist.2012) 210 Cal.App.4th 1484, 1488 n.2. "While courts are permitted to take judicial notice of the *existence* of [a judicial] decision and the factual findings contained therein ..., they are not permitted to take judicial notice of the *truth* of such findings. Moreover, '[e]xcept where the sufficiency of the evidence as a matter of law is involved ..., the [law of the case] doctrine does not give any conclusive effect to determinations of questions of fact.'"

Schabarum v. California Legislature (3d Dist. 1998) 60 Cal.App.4th 1205, 1216 n.5. "Matters which are subject to mandatory judicial notice may be treated as part of the complaint and may be considered without notice to the parties. Matters which are subject to permissive judicial notice must be specified in the notice of motion, the supporting points and authorities, or as the court otherwise permits. The matters we will consider here are within the decisional, constitutional, and public statutory laws of this state and are therefore subject to mandatory judicial notice." *See also* CCP §438(d).

Scott v. County of L.A. (2d Dist.1994) 27 Cal.App.4th 125, 145. Gov. C. §11343.6 "requires judicial notice to be taken of the contents of regulations that are adopted by state agencies and filed with the Secretary of State."

§452. [PERMISSIVE JUDICIAL NOTICE]

Judicial notice may be taken of the following matters to the extent that they are not embraced within Section 451:

(a) [State law; congressional resolutions and private acts.] The decisional, constitutional, and statutory law of any state of the United States and the resolutions and private acts of the Congress of the United States and of the Legislature of this state.

(b) [Regulations & legislative enactments.] Regulations and legislative enactments issued by or under the authority of the United States or any public entity in the United States.

(c) [Official acts of government entities.] Official acts of the legislative, executive, and judicial departments of the United States and of any state of the United States.

(d) [Court records.] Records of (1) any court of this state or (2) any court of record of the United States or of any state of the United States.

(e) [Court rules.] Rules of court of (1) any court of this state or (2) any court of record of the United States or of any state of the United States.

(f) [Foreign law.] The law of an organization of nations and of foreign nations and public entities in foreign nations.

(g) [Common knowledge.] Facts and propositions that are of such common knowledge within the territorial jurisdiction of the court that they cannot reasonably be the subject of dispute.

(h) [Verifiable facts.] Facts and propositions that are not reasonably subject to dispute and are capable of immediate and accurate determination by resort to sources of reasonably indisputable accuracy.

History of Evid. C. §452: Added eff. Sept. 17, 1965, oper. Jan. 1, 1967, Stats. 1965, ch. 299, §2.

Official Comment

7 Cal. Law Revision Comm'n Rep. (1965) p. 1066; Assem. J., Apr. 6, 1965, p. 1730.

Section 452 includes matters both of law and of fact. The court *may* take judicial notice of these matters, even when not requested to do so; it is *required* to notice them if a party requests it and satisfies the requirements of Section 453.

The matters of law included under Section 452 may be neither known to the court nor easily discoverable by it because the sources of information are not readily available. However, if a party requests it and furnishes the court with "sufficient information" for it to take judicial notice, the court must do so if proper notice has been given to each adverse party. *See* Evidence Code §453. Thus, judicial notice of these matters of law is mandatory only if counsel adequately discharges his responsibility for informing the court as to the law applicable to the case. The simplified process of judicial notice can then be applied to all of the law applicable to the case, including such law as ordinances and the law of foreign nations.

Although Section 452 extends the process of judicial notice to some matters of law which the courts do not judicially notice under existing law, the wider scope of such notice is balanced by the assurance that the matter need not be judicially noticed unless adequate information to support its truth is furnished to the court. Under Section 453, this burden falls upon the party requesting that judicial notice be taken. In addition, the parties are entitled under Section 455 to a reasonable opportunity to present information to the court as to the propriety of taking judicial notice and as to the tenor of the matter to be noticed.

Listed below are the matters that may be judicially noticed under Section 452 (and must be noticed if the conditions specified in Section 453 are met).

Law of sister states. Subdivision (a) provides for judicial notice of the decisional, constitutional, and statutory law in force in sister states. California courts now take judicial notice of the law of sister states under subdivision 3 of Section 1875 of the Code of Civil Procedure. However, Section 1875 seems to preclude notice of sister-state law as interpreted by the intermediate-appellate courts of sister states, whereas Section 452 permits notice of relevant decisions of *all* sister-state courts. If this be an extension of existing law, it is a desirable one, for the courts of sister states generally can be considered as responsive to the need for properly determining the law as are equivalent courts in Califor-

nia. The existing law also is not clear as to whether a request for judicial notice of sister-state law is required and whether judicial notice is mandatory. On the necessity for a request for judicial notice, *see Comment*, 24 Cal.L.Rev. 311, 316 (1936). On whether judicial notice is mandatory, *see In re Bartges*, 44 Cal.2d 241, 282 P.2d 47 (1955), and the opinion of the Supreme Court in denying a hearing in *Estate of Moore*, 7 Cal.App.2d 722, 726, 48 P.2d 28, 29 (1935).

Law of territories and possessions of the United States. Subdivision (a) also provides for judicial notice of the decisional, constitutional, and statutory law in force in the territories and possessions of the United States. See the broad definition of "state" in Evidence Code §220. It is not clear under existing California law whether this law is treated as sister-state law or foreign law. *See* Witkin, *California Evidence* §45 (1958).

Resolutions and private acts. Subdivision (a) provides for judicial notice of resolutions and private acts of the Congress of the United States and of the legislature of any state, territory, or possession of the United States. See the broad definition of "state" in Evidence Code §220.

The California law on this matter is not clear. Our courts are authorized by subdivision 3 of Code of Civil Procedure Section 1875 to take judicial notice of private statutes of this State and the United States, and they probably would take judicial notice of resolutions of this State and the United States under the same subdivision. It is not clear whether such notice is compulsory. It may be that judicial notice of a private act pleaded in a criminal action pursuant to Penal Code Section 963 is mandatory, whereas judicial notice of the same private act may be discretionary when pleaded in a civil action pursuant to Section 459 of the Code of Civil Procedure.

Although no case in point has been found, California courts probably would not take judicial notice of a resolution or private act of a sister state or territory or possession of the United States. Although Section 1875 is not the exclusive list of the matters that will be judicially noticed, the courts did not take judicial notice of a private statute prior to the enactment of Section 1875. *Ellis v. Eastman*, 32 Cal. 447 (1867).

Regulations, ordinances, and similar legislative enactments. Subdivision (b) provides for judicial notice of regulations and legislative enactments adopted by or under the authority of the United States or of any state, territory, or possession of the United States, including public entities therein. See the broad definition of "public entity" in Evidence Code §200. The words "regulations and legislative enactments" include such matters as "ordinances" and other similar legislative enactments. Not all public entities legislate by ordinance.

This subdivision changes existing law. Under existing law, municipal courts take judicial notice of ordinances in force within their jurisdiction. *People v. Cowles*, 142 Cal.App.2d Supp. 865, 867, 298 P.2d 732, 733-734 (1956); *People v. Crittenden*, 93 Cal.App.2d Supp. 871, 877, 209 P.2d 161, 165 (1949). In addition, an ordinance pleaded in a criminal action pursuant to Penal Code Section 963 must be judicially noticed. On the other hand, neither the superior court nor a district court of appeal will take judicial notice in a civil action of municipal or county ordinances. *Thompson v. Guyer-Hays*, 207 Cal.App.2d 366, 24 Cal.Rptr. 461 (1962); *County of Los Angeles v. Bartlett*, 203 Cal.App.2d 523, 21 Cal.Rptr. 776 (1962); *Becerra v. Hochberg*, 193 Cal.App.2d 431, 14 Cal.Rptr. 101 (1961). It seems safe to assume that ordinances of sister states and of territories and possessions of the United States would not be judicially noticed under existing law.

Judicial notice of certain regulations of California and federal agencies is mandatory under subdivision (b) of Section 451. Subdivision (b) of Section 452 provides for judicial notice of California and federal regulations that are not included under subdivision (b) of Section 451 and, also, for judicial notice of regulations of other states and territories and possessions of the United States.

Both California and federal regulations have been judicially noticed under subdivision 3 of Code of Civil Procedure Section 1875. 18 Cal. Jur.2d *Evidence* §24. Although no case in point has been found, it is unlikely that regulations of other states or of territories or possessions of the United States would be judicially noticed under existing law.

Official acts of the legislative, executive, and judicial departments. Subdivision (c) provides for judicial notice of the official acts of the legislative, executive, and judicial departments of the United States and any state, territory, or possession of the United States. See the broad definition of "state" in Evidence Code §220. Subdivision (c) states existing law as found in subdivision 3 of Code of Civil Procedure Section 1875. Under this provision, the California courts have taken judicial notice of a wide variety of administrative and executive acts, such as proceedings and reports of the House Committee on Un-American Activities, records of the State Board of Education, and records of a county planning commission. *See* Witkin, *California Evidence* §49 (1958), and 1963 Supplement thereto.

Court records and rules of court. Subdivisions (d) and (e) provide for judicial notice of the court records and rules of court of (1) any court of this State or (2) any court of record of the United States or of any state, territory, or possession of the United States. See the broad definition of "state" in Evidence Code §220. So far as court records are concerned, subdivision (d) states existing law. *Flores v. Arroyo*, 56 Cal.2d 492, 15 Cal.Rptr. 87, 364 P.2d 263 (1961). While the provisions of subdivision (c) of Section 452 are broad enough to include court records, specific mention of these records in subdivision (d) is desirable in order to eliminate any uncertainty in the law on this point. *See* the *Flores* case, *supra*.

Subdivision (e) may change existing law so far as judicial notice of rules of court is concerned, but the provision is consistent with the modern philosophy of judicial notice as indicated by the holding in *Flores v. Arroyo*, *supra*. To the extent that subdivision (e) overlaps with subdivisions (c) and (d) of Section 451, notice is, of course, mandatory under Section 451.

Foreign law. Subdivision (f) provides for judicial notice of the law of organizations of nations, foreign nations, and public entities in foreign nations. See the broad definition of "public entity" in Evidence Code §200. Subdivision (f) should be read in connection with Sections 310, 311, 453, and 454. These provisions retain the substance of the existing law which was enacted in 1957 upon recommendation of the California Law Revision Commission. Code Civ. Proc. §1875. *See* 1 Cal. Law Revision Comm'n, Ref., Rec. & Studies, *Recommendation and Study Relating to Judicial Notice of the Law of Foreign Countries* at I-1 (1957).

Subdivision (f) refers to "the law" of organizations of nations, foreign nations, and public entities in foreign nations. This makes all law, in whatever form, subject to judicial notice.

Matters of "common knowledge" and verifiable facts. Subdivision (g) provides for judicial notice of matters of common knowledge within the court's territorial jurisdiction that are not subject to dispute. "Territorial jurisdiction," in this context, refers to the county in which a superior court is located or the judicial district in which a municipal or justice court is located. The fact of which notice is taken need not be something physically located within the court's territorial jurisdiction, but common knowledge of the fact must exist within the court's territorial jurisdiction. Subdivision (g) reflects existing case law. *Varcoe v. Lee*, 180 Cal. 338, 181 Pac. 223 (1919); 18 Cal. Jur.2d *Evidence* §19 at 439-440. The California courts have taken judicial notice of a wide variety of matters of common knowledge. Witkin, *California Evidence* §§50-52 (1958).

Subdivision (h) provides for judicial notice of indisputable facts immediately ascertainable by reference to sources of reasonably indisputable accuracy. In other words, the facts need not be actually known if they are readily ascertainable and indisputable. Sources of "reasonably indisputable accuracy" include not only treatises, encyclopedias, almanacs, and the like, but also persons learned in the subject matter. This would not mean that reference works would be received in evidence or sent to the jury room. Their use would be limited to consultation by the judge and the parties for the purposes of determining whether or not to take judicial notice and determining the tenor of the matter to be noticed.

Subdivisions (g) and (h) include, for example, facts which are accepted as established by experts and specialists in the natural, physical, and social sciences, if those facts are of such wide acceptance that to submit them to the jury would be to risk irrational findings. These subdivisions include such matters listed in Code of Civil Procedure Section 1875 as the "geographical divisions and political history of the world." To the extent that subdivisions (g) and (h) overlap subdivision (f) of Section 451, notice is, of course, mandatory under Section 451.

The matters covered by subdivisions (g) and (h) are included in Section 452, rather than Section 451, because it seems reasonable to put the burden on the parties to bring adequate information before the court if judicial notice of these matters is to be mandatory. *See* Evidence Code §453 and the *Comment* thereto.

Under existing law, courts take judicial notice of the matters that are included under subdivisions (g) and (h), either pursuant to Section 1875 of the Code of Civil Procedure or because such matters are matters of common knowledge which are certain and indisputable. Witkin, *California Evidence* §§50-52 (1958). Notice of these matters probably is not compulsory under existing law.

ANNOTATIONS

Subdivision (a)

Quintano v. Mercury Cas. Co. (1995) 11 Cal.4th 1049, 1062. "[D] asks that we take judicial notice [of statements made by] the author of the bill [enacting the legislation at issue]. [S]tatements of an individual legislator, including the author of a bill, are generally not considered in construing a statute, as the court's task is to ascertain the intent of the Legislature as a whole in adopting a piece of legislation."

Subdivision (b)

Trinity Park, L.P. v. City of Sunnyvale (6th Dist.2011) 193 Cal.App.4th 1014, 1027, *disapproved on other grounds*, ***Sterling Park, L.P. v. City of Palo Alto*** (2013) 57 Cal.4th 1193. "[W]e may take notice [under §452, subdivision (b)] of local ordinances … and the official resolutions, reports, and other official acts of a city…." *See also* ***City of Ontario v. Superior Ct.*** (4th Dist.1993) 12 Cal.App.4th 894, 899 n.5 (court can take judicial notice of county ordinances).

Subdivision (c)

Mangini v. R.J. Reynolds Tobacco Co. (1994) 7 Cal.4th 1057, 1063-65, *overruled on other grounds*, ***In re Tobacco Cases II*** (2007) 41 Cal.4th 1257. "While courts may notice official acts and public records, 'we do not take judicial notice of the truth of all matters stated therein.' '[T]he taking of judicial notice of the official acts of a governmental entity does not in and of itself require acceptance of the truth of factual matters which might be deduced therefrom, since in many instances what is being noticed, and thereby established, is no more than the existence of such acts and not, without supporting evidence, what might factually be associated with or flow therefrom.' [¶] Requests for judicial notice should not be used to 'circumvent[]' appellate rules and procedures, including the normal briefing process. Asking that authority be judicially noticed instead of citing and discussing it in a brief gives the parties no orderly opportunity to argue the relevance of that authority or to distinguish it." *See also* ***De Cruz v. County of L.A.*** (2d Dist.1985) 173 Cal.App.3d 1131, 1134.

Scott v. JPMorgan Chase Bank (1st Dist.2013) 214 Cal.App.4th 743, 752-53. "[P] contends that the court should not have taken judicial notice of the [agreement between FDIC and D] or the facts therein. [¶] [S]ection 452, subdivision (c) … enables courts in California to take notice of a wide variety of official acts and an expansive reading must be provided to certain of its phrases; included in 'executive' acts are those performed by administrative agencies. [T]he FDIC's official acts of seizing [bank's] assets and publishing the [a]greement are judicially noticeable. Moreover, … the FDIC's official act of transferring certain [bank] assets … to [D]—as *evinced* by the [a]greement—is an official act subject to judicial notice under §452, subdivision (c) under the circumstances of this case." (Internal quotes omitted.)

LaChance v. Valverde (4th Dist.2012) 207 Cal.App.4th 779, 783. "We reject the Attorney General's contention that e-mails exchanged between a deputy attorney general and counsel for a party to an appeal are '[o]fficial acts of the legislative, executive, and judicial departments of the U.S. and of any state of the U.S.,' of which judicial notice may be taken. We therefore deny the Attorney General's initial request to take judicial notice."

Stevens v. Superior Ct. (2d Dist.1999) 75 Cal.App.4th 594, 607-08. "Papers filed with state and federal agencies … do not fall within the ambit of subdivision (c) of §452…." *See also* ***Hughes v. Blue Cross*** (1st Dist.1989) 215 Cal.App.3d 832, 856 n.2 (materials prepared by private parties that are merely on file with state agencies may not be judicially noticed); ***California State Employees' Ass'n v. Flournoy*** (2d Dist. 1973) 32 Cal.App.3d 219, 233 n.10 (judicial notice may be taken of statistical records and other reports and records of a state agency).

Fowler v. Howell (2d Dist.1996) 42 Cal.App.4th 1746, 1750. "[S]ection 452, subdivision (c) permits the trial court to take judicial notice of the records and files of a state administrative board." *See also* ***Associated Builders & Contractors, Inc. v. San Francisco Airports Comm'n*** (1999) 21 Cal.4th 352, 374 n.4 (judicial notice of transcripts of commission hearings); ***Hogen v. Valley Hosp.*** (2d Dist.1983) 147 Cal.App.3d 119, 125 (judicial notice of records of Board of Medical Quality Assurance).

Washington v. County of Contra Costa (1st Dist.1995) 38 Cal.App.4th 890, 901. "[Ps'] complaint is not with the nature of the documents judicially noticed, but with the quality of them. As the quality of documents has no bearing on the question of whether the documents may be judicially noticed, [Ps'] arguments are irrelevant. To the extent the arguments are that the

documents do not demonstrate that the County properly performed its statutory duties, they are again irrelevant."

Edna Valley Ass'n v. San Luis Obispo Cty. & Cities Area Planning Coordinating Council (2d Dist.1977) 67 Cal.App.3d 444, 449-50. "The only authorization for judicial notice pertinent to the problem before us is ... §452, subdivision (c). [¶] Under it California courts have taken judicial notice of the records of a county commission since counties are legal subdivisions of the state ..., but have refused to take judicial notice of the records of a municipal police department since cities are not. The Council is a creature of the County of San Luis Obispo and of the incorporated cities of that county. Its acts cannot be deemed to be acts of either the State of California or of one of its subdivisions. Therefore, judicial notice may not be taken of the [environmental-impact report] at issue because such judicial notice is not authorized by either the statutory or the decisional law of this state." *See also* ***Marino v. City of L.A.*** (2d Dist.1973) 34 Cal.App.3d 461, 465.

Subdivision (d)

Mushrush v. State Bar (1976) 17 Cal.3d 487, 489 n.1. Attorney "has asked us to take judicial notice of the findings of fact, conclusions of law, and judgment in a legal malpractice action brought by [former client] against him and in which he prevailed. The court determined [attorney] had not been fully advised of the nature or terms of the transactions during their pendency by [former client] and was told nothing which would lead him to make any disclosure to the bankruptcy court or [former client's company's] creditors. ... The decision is now on appeal. We grant [attorney's] motion on the authority of ... §452, subdivision (d) and ***Yokozeki v. State Bar*** (1974) 11 Cal.3d 436 ..., with due recognition that we are not bound by the superior court's findings...."

O'Neill v. Novartis Consumer Health, Inc. (2d Dist.2007) 147 Cal.App.4th 1388, 1405. "A court may take judicial notice of a court's action, but may not use it to prove the truth of the facts found and recited." *See also* ***Taxpayers for Improving Pub. Safety v. Schwarzenegger*** (3d Dist.2009) 172 Cal.App.4th 749, 771 (court could take judicial notice of issuance of Attorney General opinions, but not substance of those opinions).

Big Valley Band of Pomo Indians v. Superior Ct. (1st Dist.2005) 133 Cal.App.4th 1185, 1191-92. "In ***Del E. Webb Corp. v. Structural Materials Co.*** [(2d Dist.1981) 123 Cal.App.3d 593], the court held it may be appropriate for a court to take judicial notice of ... affidavits and verified discovery responses to the extent they contradict allegations of the complaint. The court cautioned, however, against turning the hearing on demurrer 'into a contested evidentiary hearing through the guise of having the court take judicial notice of affidavits, declarations, depositions, and other such material which was filed on behalf of the adverse party and which purports to contradict the allegations and contentions of the plaintiff....' ***Del E. Webb Corp.*** has itself been criticized ... in ***Garcia v. Sterling*** [(2d Dist.1985) 176 Cal.App.3d 17]: 'Although the *existence* of statements contained in a deposition transcript [or declaration] filed as part of the court record can be judicially noticed, their *truth* is not subject to judicial notice.'"

Ross v. Creel Printing & Publ'g Co. (1st Dist.2002) 100 Cal.App.4th 736, 743. "Section 452, subdivision (d)(2) permits judicial notice of the records of 'any court of record of the U.S. or of any state of the U.S.' [¶] We decline to take judicial notice of the complaint because the document offered is neither certified nor provided under subpoena from the Nevada court, and we have no assurance of its authenticity. '[W]hen a party desires the appellate court to take judicial notice of a document or record on file in the court below the parties should furnish the appellate court with a copy of such document or record certified by its custodian.' It is the burden of the party seeking judicial notice to demonstrate a reason for the failure to furnish certified copies. [¶] However, even if the document were properly certified, we would take judicial notice only as to the existence of the complaint, not as to the truth of any of the allegations contained in it. *At 744:* The burden is on the party seeking judicial notice to provide sufficient information to allow the court to take judicial notice."

Sosinsky v. Grant (5th Dist.1992) 6 Cal.App.4th 1548, 1551. "This case presents the issue of whether a court may properly take judicial notice of the truth of factual findings made by a judge who sat as a trier of fact in a previous case. We hold that the court may not take judicial notice of the truth of those factual findings." *See also* ***Steed v. Department of Consumer Affairs*** (2d Dist.2012) 204 Cal.App.4th 112, 120-21; ***Kilroy v. State*** (3d Dist.2004) 119 Cal.App.4th 140,

147-48. *But see* ***Weiner v. Mitchell, Silberberg & Knupp*** (2d Dist.1980) 114 Cal.App.3d 39, 46 (proper to take judicial notice of truth of facts stated in appellate opinion).

Joslin v. H.A.S. Ins. Brokerage (4th Dist.1986) 184 Cal.App.3d 369, 374-75. "Various tests or rules have been suggested to determine whether a court which has taken judicial notice of a document may take the further step of accepting its truth or adopting a proposed interpretation of its meaning. [¶] When the court takes judicial notice of a document in its own files, or in those of another court, it has been said the court will not consider the truth of the document's contents unless it is an order, statement of decision, or judgment. Other cases have suggested the court may accept the truth of statements made by the party whose pleadings are being challenged but not statements of an opponent or third party. [¶] A third approach, which provides maximum flexibility while still insisting disputed factual issues cannot be resolved on demurrer, proposes 'judicial notice of matters upon demurrer will be dispositive only in those instances where there is not or cannot be a factual dispute concerning that which is sought to be judicially noticed.' [¶] Correct results will be reached in most cases by application of either of the first two rules, but there may be occasional cases which can only be resolved properly by using the third approach. [T]he third approach is in our opinion the most reliable in all cases."

DeYoung v. Del Mar Thoroughbred Club (4th Dist.1984) 159 Cal.App.3d 858, 863. "[S]ection 452, subdivision (d), by its terms, authorizes permissive judicial notice of records on file in the action before the trial court regardless whether they are in evidence in the proceedings and the trial judge relied upon them. However, 'as a general rule, the court should not take such notice if, upon examination of the entire record, it appears that the matter has not been presented to and considered by the trial court in the first instance.'" *See also* ***County of Orange v. Smith*** (4th Dist.2005) 132 Cal.App.4th 1434, 1450.

Carroll v. Puritan Leasing Co. (2d Dist.1978) 77 Cal.App.3d 481, 486. "[A] trial court may take notice of the prior judgment in deciding whether to sustain a demurrer based upon res judicata. In analyzing a demurrer based upon res judicata the court will take judicial notice of a prior judgment, whether or not pleaded, provided only that (1) the court has been correctly apprised of the judgment, and, (2) the plaintiff is given adequate notice and opportunity to be heard as to the effect of the judgment. *At 490:* If facts within the complaint or within the scope of judicial notice show that appellant was collaterally estopped from asserting the argument which was the basis of her claim, the complaint was subject to general demurrer because it displayed a defense upon its face."

In re Estate of Russell (1st Dist.1971) 17 Cal.App.3d 758, 765-66. "Court records are matters which *may* be judicially noticed. Such records may be judicially noticed if a party requests that such notice be taken, furnishes the court with sufficient information to enable it to take judicial notice, and gives each adverse party sufficient notice of the request to prepare to meet it. ... The court may, however, take judicial notice of such court records, even when not requested to do so, because it has the discretionary power to take such notice under §452.... However, where the matter to be noticed is one that is of *substantial consequence to the action*, the party adversely affected must be given a reasonable opportunity, before the jury is instructed or before the cause is submitted for decision by the court, to present information relevant to the propriety of taking judicial notice and as to tenor of the matter to be noticed. 'If the judge does not discover that a matter should be judicially noticed until after the cause is submitted for decision, he may, of course, order the cause to be reopened for the purpose of permitting the parties to provide him with information concerning the matter.'" *See also* ***Carroll v. State*** (4th Dist.1990) 217 Cal.App.3d 134, 144.

Subdivision (f)

In re Marriage of Nurie (1st Dist.2009) 176 Cal.App.4th 478, 509. "[D] submitted the declaration of her attorney in Pakistan for the evident purpose of proving that [an enforcement procedure similar to the UCCJEA, Cal. Fam. C. §§3441-3457] is available [in Pakistan]. The attorney did not, however, explain substantive Pakistani legal standards for enforcing foreign custody decrees; nor did [D] provide copies of Pakistani statutes or cases on this issue. While we are authorized to take judicial notice of '[t]he law of ... foreign nations and public entities in foreign nations' ..., we decline to do so here because [D] has submitted insufficient evidence to enable us to determine with confidence either the procedure or the substantive rules Pakistan would employ."

Subdivision (g)

Evans v. California Trailer Ct., Inc. (5th Dist.1994) 28 Cal.App.4th 540, 549. "On a motion for judgment on the pleadings, a court may take judicial notice of something that cannot reasonably be controverted, even if it negates an express allegation of the pleading. [¶] The court may take judicial notice of recorded deeds. [Ds] asked the court to judicially notice the recorded trustee's deed pursuant to … §452, subdivision (g). [Ps] stated they did not object to the request and the court took judicial notice of the deed. [¶] The court did not err or abuse its discretion in granting the request." *See also* ***Lockhart v. MVM, Inc.*** (2d Dist. 2009) 175 Cal.App.4th 1452, 1460-61.

Jordan v. Worthen (1st Dist.1977) 68 Cal.App.3d 310, 319. "The subject of the nature of the past use of the road to [P's ranch] is not a fact or proposition of generalized knowledge that is so universally known that it cannot reasonably be the subject of dispute. It possibly could be a fact or proposition of such common knowledge within the territorial jurisdiction of the court that it could not reasonably be the subject of dispute. … Nevertheless, in this case there was nothing to establish that the historical use of the road to [P's ranch] was a matter of common knowledge, and the declarations of others which were testified to by the witnesses were the declarants' individual observations, not common knowledge."

Comings v. State Bd. of Educ. (1st Dist.1972) 23 Cal.App.3d 94, 102. "[W]e cannot judicially notice the *truth* of the stated propositions that the use of marijuana is harmless or commonplace. [T]he accuracy of the matters asserted … is the subject of intense scientific and popular controversy; actual judicial knowledge of the relevant truths is limited; and there is no evidence, in [the] record on appeal, supporting a conclusion either way. Accordingly, it cannot be said that the 'propositions' stated in the cited authorities are of 'generalized knowledge' or 'common knowledge,' and are not reasonably subject to 'dispute,' so as to permit their being judicially noticed as true." *See also* ***Ford v. Pacific Gas & Elec. Co.*** (1st Dist.1997) 60 Cal.App.4th 696, 706.

Subdivision (h)

Boghos v. Certain Underwriters at Lloyd's of London (2005) 36 Cal.4th 495, 505 n.6. "[T]he arbitration clause expressly invokes the [American Arbitration Association's] commercial arbitration rules. The full, up-to-date text of those rules is available on the [Association's] Internet site.… Having given the parties appropriate notice before oral argument that we proposed to take judicial notice of the rules on our own motion …, we now do take judicial notice of them."

Planned Parenthood Shasta-Diablo, Inc. v. Williams (1995) 10 Cal.4th 1009, 1021 n.2. "We find the law to be well settled that trial or reviewing courts may properly notice government maps and surveys."

Ragland v. U.S. Bank (4th Dist.2012) 209 Cal.App.4th 182, 193. "While we may take judicial notice of the existence of the audit report, Web sites, and blogs, we may not accept their contents as true." *See also* ***L.B. Research & Educ. Found. v. UCLA Found.*** (2d Dist.2005) 130 Cal.App.4th 171, 180 n.2.

Fontenot v. Wells Fargo Bank (1st Dist.2011) 198 Cal.App.4th 256, 265. "[C]ourts have taken judicial notice not only of the existence and recordation of recorded documents but also of a variety of matters that can be deduced from the documents. [¶] Strictly speaking, a court takes judicial notice of facts, not documents. When a court is asked to take judicial notice of a document, the propriety of the court's action depends upon the nature of the facts of which the court takes notice from the document. [A] court may take judicial notice of the fact of a document's recordation, the date the document was recorded and executed, the parties to the transaction reflected in a recorded document, and the document's legally operative language, assuming there is no genuine dispute regarding the document's authenticity. From this, the court may deduce and rely upon the legal effect of the recorded document, when that effect is clear from its face." *See also* ***Scott v. JPMorgan Chase Bank*** (1st Dist.2013) 214 Cal.App.4th 743, 752-53.

Trinity Park, L.P. v. City of Sunnyvale (6th Dist.2011) 193 Cal.App.4th 1014, 1026-27, *disapproved on other grounds*, ***Sterling Park, L.P. v. City of Palo Alto*** (2013) 57 Cal.4th 1193. "On appeal from a judgment of dismissal after a demurrer is sustained without leave to amend, the reviewing court assumes the truth of all facts properly pleaded by the plaintiff. [¶] We also consider matters that may be judicially noticed. [Under Evid. C. §452, subdivision (h), we may] take judicial notice of an agreement where 'there is and can be no factual dispute concerning the contents of the agreements.' However, we keep in mind the general rule that

'[w]hen judicial notice is taken of a document ... the truthfulness and proper interpretation of the document are disputable.'"

Gould v. Maryland Sound Indus. (2d Dist.1995) 31 Cal.App.4th 1137, 1145. "Judicial notice under ... §452, subdivision (h) is intended to cover facts which are not reasonably subject to dispute and are easily verified. These include, for example, facts which are widely accepted as established by experts and specialists in the natural, physical, and social sciences which can be verified by reference to treatises, encyclopedias, almanacs and the like or by persons learned in the subject matter. The statute has also been used on demurrer to take judicial notice of facts commonly known in a community, such as ownership, easements and control over land ..., and the history and operation of a local museum...." *See also* ***Hughes v. Blue Cross*** (1st Dist.1989) 215 Cal.App.3d 832, 856 n.2.

Whispering Pines Mobile Home Park, Ltd. v. City of Scotts Valley (6th Dist.1986) 180 Cal.App.3d 152, 162. "The comment of the legislative committee to [§452, subdivision (h),] states that sources of 'reasonably indisputable accuracy' include not only treatises, encyclopedias, almanacs, and the like, but also persons learned in the subject matter. This would not mean that reference works would be received in evidence or sent to the jury room. Their use would be limited to consultation by the judge and the parties for the purpose of determining whether or not to take judicial notice and determining the tenor of the matter to be noticed." (Internal quotes omitted.)

§452.5. [COMPUTER RECORDS OF CRIMINAL CONVICTIONS]

(a) [Computer-generated records of conviction.] The official acts and records specified in subdivisions (c) and (d) of Section 452 include any computer-generated official court records, as specified by the Judicial Council which relate to criminal convictions, when the record is certified by a clerk of the superior court pursuant to Section 69844.5 of the Government Code at the time of computer entry.

(b) [Copy of record of conviction.]

(1) An official record of conviction certified in accordance with subdivision (a) of Section 1530, or an electronically digitized copy thereof, is admissible under Section 1280 to prove the commission, attempted commission, or solicitation of a criminal offense, prior conviction, service of a prison term, or other act, condition, or event recorded by the record.

(2) For purposes of this subdivision, "electronically digitized copy" means a copy that is made by scanning, photographing, or otherwise exactly reproducing a document, is stored or maintained in a digitized format, and bears an electronic signature or watermark unique to the entity responsible for certifying the document.

History of Evid. C. §452.5: Added eff. Jan. 1, 1997, Stats. 1996, ch. 642, §3. Amended eff. Jan. 1, 2003, Stats. 2002, ch. 784, §102; eff. Jan. 1, 2014, Stats. 2013, ch. 150, §1.

Official Comment

32 Cal. Law Revision Comm'n Rep. (2002) p. 158.

Subdivision (a) of Section 452.5 is amended to reflect unification of the municipal and superior courts pursuant to Article VI, Section 5(e), of the California Constitution. The reference to former Government Code Section 71280.5 is deleted, because that provision concerned certification and submission of municipal court records relating to criminal convictions. Government Code Section 69844.5 is the comparable superior court provision.

§453. [PROCEDURE FOR PERMISSIVE JUDICIAL NOTICE]

The trial court shall take judicial notice of any matter specified in Section 452 if a party requests it and:

(a) Gives each adverse party sufficient notice of the request, through the pleadings or otherwise, to enable such adverse party to prepare to meet the request; and

(b) Furnishes the court with sufficient information to enable it to take judicial notice of the matter.

History of Evid. C. §453: Added eff. Sept. 17, 1965, oper. Jan. 1, 1967, Stats. 1965, ch. 299, §2.

Official Comment

7 Cal. Law Revision Comm'n Rep. (1965) p. 1071.

Section 453 provides that the court must take judicial notice of any matter specified in Section 452 if a party requests that such notice be taken, furnishes the court with sufficient information to enable it to take judicial notice of the matter, and gives each adverse party sufficient notice of the request to prepare to meet it.

Section 453 is intended as a safeguard and not as a rigid limitation on the court's power to take judicial notice. The section does not affect the discretionary power of the court to take judicial notice under Section 452 where the party requesting that judicial notice be taken fails to give the requisite notice to each adverse party or fails to furnish sufficient information as to the propriety of taking judicial notice or as to the tenor of the matter to be noticed. Hence, when he considers it appropriate, the judge may take judicial notice under Section 452 and may consult and use any source of pertinent information, whether or not furnished by the parties. However, where the matter noticed under Section 452 is one that is of substantial consequence to the action—even though the court may take judicial notice under Section 452 when the requirements of Section 453 have not been satisfied—the party adversely affected must be given a reasonable opportunity to present information as to the propriety of taking judicial notice and as to the tenor of the matter to be noticed. *See* Evidence Code §455 and the *Comment* thereto.

The "notice" requirement. The party requesting the court to judicially notice a matter under Section 453 must give each adverse party sufficient notice, through the pleadings or otherwise, to enable him to prepare to meet the request. In cases where the notice given does not satisfy this requirement, the court may decline to take judicial notice. A somewhat similar notice to the adverse parties is required under subdivision 4 of Section 1875 of the Code of Civil

Procedure when a request for judicial notice of the law of a foreign country is made. Section 453 broadens this existing requirement to cover all matters specified in Section 452.

The notice requirement is an important one since judicial notice is binding on the jury under Section 457. Accordingly, the adverse parties should be given ample notice so that they will have an opportunity to prepare to oppose the taking of judicial notice and to obtain information relevant to the tenor of the matter to be noticed.

Since Section 452 relates to a wide variety of facts and law, the notice requirement should be administered with flexibility in order to insure that the policy behind the judicial notice rules is properly implemented. In many cases, it will be reasonable to expect the notice to be given at or before the time of the pretrial conference. In other cases, matters of fact or law of which the court should take judicial notice may come up at the trial. Section 453 merely requires reasonable notice, and the reasonableness of the notice given will depend upon the circumstances of the particular case.

The "sufficient information" requirement. Under Section 453, the court is not required to resort to any sources of information not provided by the parties. If the party requesting that judicial notice be taken under Section 453 fails to provide the court with "sufficient information," the judge may decline to take judicial notice. For example, if the party requests the court to take judicial notice of the specific gravity of gold, the party requesting that notice be taken must furnish the judge with definitive information as to the specific gravity of gold. The judge is not required to undertake the necessary research to determine the fact, though, of course, he is not precluded from doing such research if he so desires.

§453

Section 453 does not define "sufficient information"; this will necessarily vary from case to case. While the parties will understandably use the best evidence they can produce under the circumstances, mechanical requirements that are ill-suited to the individual case should be avoided. The court justifiably might require that the party requesting that judicial notice be taken provide expert testimony to clarify especially difficult problems.

Burden on party requesting that judicial notice be taken. Where a request is made to take judicial notice under Section 453, the court may decline to take judicial notice unless the party requesting that notice be taken persuades the judge that the matter is one that properly may be noticed under Section 452 and also persuades the judge as to the tenor of the matter to be noticed. The degree of the judge's persuasion regarding a particular matter is determined by the subdivision of Section 452 which authorizes judicial notice of the matter. For example, if the matter is claimed to be a fact of common knowledge under paragraph (g) of Section 452, the party must persuade the judge that the fact is of such common knowledge within the territorial jurisdiction of the court that it cannot reasonably be subject to dispute, *i.e.*, that no reasonable person having the same information as is available to the judge could rationally disbelieve the fact. On the other hand, if the matter to be noticed is a city ordinance under paragraph (b) of Section 452, the party must persuade the judge that a valid ordinance exists and also as to its tenor; but the judge need not believe that no reasonable person could conclude otherwise.

Without regard to the evidence supplied by the party requesting that judicial notice be taken, the judge's determination to take judicial notice of a matter specified in Section 452 will be upheld on appeal if the matter was properly noticed. The reviewing court may resort to any information, whether or not available at the trial, in order to sustain the proper taking of judicial notice. *See* Evidence Code §459. On the other hand, even though a party requested that judicial notice be taken under Section 453 and gave notice to each adverse party in compliance with subdivision (a) of Section 453, the decision of the judge not to take judicial notice will be upheld on appeal unless the reviewing court determines that the party furnished information to the judge that was so persuasive that no reasonable judge would have refused to take judicial notice of the matter.

ANNOTATIONS

Mitroff v. United Servs. Auto. Ass'n (1st Dist.1999) 72 Cal.App.4th 1230, 1243. "[W]e reject the contention that the trial court was compelled to take judicial notice of court records in two unrelated matters in which [P] argued that [D] took a different position as to coverage of similar matters. [S]ection 453, which states that the court shall take judicial notice of matters properly presented does not compel the court to admit irrelevant matters that would result in the undue consumption of time. ... The likelihood that the court would have to make a detailed inquiry into the facts and contentions of the parties in each of the other cases supports the court's denial of the request for judicial notice."

Whispering Pines Mobile Home Park, Ltd. v. City of Scotts Valley (6th Dist.1986) 180 Cal.App.3d 152, 162. "We decline to take judicial notice ... because we have not been provided with sufficient information to ensure the books cited are sources of reasonably indisputable accuracy. If there is any doubt whatever either as to a fact itself or as to its being a matter of common knowledge, evidence should be required. ... If the party requesting that judicial notice be taken under §453 fails to provide the court with sufficient information, the judge may decline to take judicial notice. The court justifiably might require that the party requesting that judicial notice be taken provide expert testimony to clarify especially difficult problems." (Internal quotes omitted.) *See also* ***Willis v. State*** (3d Dist.1994) 22 Cal.App.4th 287, 291; ***Conservatorship of Bones*** (1st Dist.1987) 189 Cal.App.3d 1010, 1014 n.2.

Stepan v. Garcia (1st Dist.1974) 43 Cal.App.3d 497, 500. "The court may take judicial notice of its own file ...: referring to the contents of the court's file by way of affidavit was a proper means of requesting the court to take such judicial notice under ... §453...."

§454. [EVIDENCE IN SUPPORT OF JUDICIAL NOTICE]

(a) [Propriety of judicial notice.] In determining the propriety of taking judicial notice of a matter, or the tenor thereof:

(1) Any source of pertinent information, including the advice of persons learned in the subject matter, may be consulted or used, whether or not furnished by a party.

(2) Exclusionary rules of evidence do not apply except for Section 352 and the rules of privilege.

(b) [Proof of foreign laws.] Where the subject of judicial notice is the law of an organization of nations, a foreign nation, or a public entity in a foreign nation and the court resorts to the advice of persons learned in the subject matter, such advice, if not received in open court, shall be in writing.

History of Evid. C. §454: Added eff. Sept. 17, 1965, oper. Jan. 1, 1967, Stats. 1965, ch. 299, §2.

Official Comment

7 Cal. Law Revision Comm'n Rep. (1965) p. 1073; Assem. J., Apr. 6, 1965, p. 1734.

Since one of the purposes of judicial notice is to simplify the process of proofmaking, the judge should be given considerable latitude in deciding what sources are trustworthy. This section permits the court to use any source of pertinent information, including the advice of persons learned in the subject matter. It probably restates existing law as found in Section 1875 of the Code of Civil Procedure. *See Estate of McNamara*, 181 Cal. 82, 89-91, 183 Pac. 552, 555 (1919); *Rogers v. Cady*, 104 Cal. 288, 290, 38 Pac. 81 (1894) (dictum); *Tentative Recommendation and a Study Relating to the Uniform Rules of Evidence (Article II. Judicial Notice)*, 6 Cal. Law Revision Comm'n, Rep., Rec. & Studies 801, 850-851 (1964).

Subdivision (b) preserves a limitation, now appearing in the next to the last paragraph of Code of Civil Procedure Section 1875, on the form in which expert advice on foreign law may be received.

§455. [OPPORTUNITY TO BE HEARD]

With respect to any matter specified in Section 452 or in subdivision (f) of Section 451 that is of substantial consequence to the determination of the action:

(a) [Opportunity to present information.] If the trial court has been requested to take or has taken or proposes to take judicial notice of such matter, the court shall afford each party reasonable opportunity, before the jury is instructed or before the cause is submitted for decision by the court, to present to the court information relevant to (1) the propriety of taking judicial notice of the matter and (2) the tenor of the matter to be noticed.

(b) [Opportunity to meet information.] If the trial court resorts to any source of information not received in open court, including the advice of persons learned in the subject matter, such information and its source shall be made a part of the record in the action and the court shall afford each party reasonable opportunity to meet such information before judicial notice of the matter may be taken.

History of Evid. C. §455: Added eff. Sept. 17, 1965, oper. Jan. 1, 1967, Stats. 1965, ch. 299, §2.

Official Comment

7 Cal. Law Revision Comm'n Rep. (1965) p. 1074.

Section 455 provides procedural safeguards designed to afford the parties reasonable opportunity to be heard both as to the propriety of taking judicial notice of a matter and as to the tenor of the matter to be noticed.

Subdivision (a). This subdivision guarantees to the parties a reasonable opportunity to present information to the court as to the propriety of taking judicial notice and as to the tenor of the matter to be noticed. In a jury case, the subdivision provides the parties with an opportunity to present their information to the judge before a jury instruction based on a matter judicially noticed is given. Where the matter subject to judicial notice relates to a cause tried by the court, the subdivision guarantees the parties an opportunity to dispute the taking of judicial notice of the matter before the cause is submitted for decision. If the judge does not discover that a matter should be judicially noticed until after the cause is submitted for decision, he may, of course, order the cause to be reopened for the purpose of permitting the parties to provide him with information concerning the matter.

Subdivision (a) is limited in its application to those matters specified in subdivision (f) of Section 451 or in Section 452 that are of substantial consequence to the determination of the action, for it would not be practicable to make the subdivision applicable to the other matters listed in Section 451 or to matters that are of inconsequential significance.

What constitutes a "reasonable opportunity" to "present ... information" will depend upon the complexity of the matter and its importance to the case. For example, in a case where there is no dispute as to the existence and validity of a city ordinance, no formal hearing would be necessary to determine the propriety of taking judicial notice of the ordinance and of its tenor. But, where there is a complex question as to the tenor of foreign law applicable to the case, the granting of a hearing under subdivision (a) would be mandatory. The New York courts have so construed their judicial notice statute, saying that an opportunity for a litigant to know what the deciding tribunal is considering and to be heard with respect to both law and fact is guaranteed by due process of law. *Arams v. Arams*, 182 Misc. 328, 182 Misc. 336, 45 N.Y.S.2d 251 (Sup. Ct. 1943).

Subdivision (b). If the court resorts to sources of information not previously known to the parties, this subdivision requires that such information and its source be made a part of the record when it relates to taking judicial notice of a matter specified in subdivision (f) of Section 451 or in Section 452 that is of substantial consequence to the determination of the action. This requirement is based on a somewhat similar requirement found in Code of Civil Procedure Section 1875 regarding the law of a foreign nation. Making the information and its source a part of the record assures its availability for examination by the parties and by a reviewing court. In addition, subdivision (b) requires the court to give the parties a reasonable opportunity to meet such additional information before judicial notice of the matter may be taken.

§456. [DENIAL OF REQUEST FOR JUDICIAL NOTICE]

If the trial court denies a request to take judicial notice of any matter, the court shall at the earliest practicable time so advise the parties and indicate for the record that it has denied the request.

History of Evid. C. §456: Added eff. Sept. 17, 1965, oper. Jan. 1, 1967, Stats. 1965, ch. 299, §2.

Official Comment

7 Cal. Law Revision Comm'n Rep. (1965) p. 1075.

Section 456 requires the judge to advise the parties and indicate for the record at the earliest practicable time any denial of a request to take judicial notice of a matter. The requirement is imposed in order to provide the parties with an adequate opportunity to submit evidence on any matter as to which judicial notice was anticipated but not taken. No comparable requirement is found in existing law. *Compare* Evidence Code §455 and the *Comment* thereto.

ANNOTATIONS

Aaronoff v. Martinez-Senftner (3d Dist.2006) 136 Cal.App.4th 910, 919. "[S]ection 456 provides the trial court must indicate for the record if it denies a request for judicial notice. The record contains no indication the request for judicial notice was denied. We conclude the trial court took judicial notice of the requested matter, particularly in light of its decision."

§457. [JURY INSTRUCTION ON MATTER NOTICED]

If a matter judicially noticed is a matter which would otherwise have been for determination by the jury, the trial court may, and upon request shall, instruct the jury to accept as a fact the matter so noticed.

History of Evid. C. §457: Added eff. Sept. 17, 1965, oper. Jan. 1, 1967, Stats. 1965, ch. 299, §2.

Official Comment

7 Cal. Law Revision Comm'n Rep. (1965) p. 1075.

Section 457 makes matters judicially noticed binding on the jury and thereby eliminates any possibility of presenting to the jury evidence disputing the fact as noticed by the court. The section is limited to instruction on a matter that would otherwise have been for determination by the jury; instruction of juries on matters of law is not a matter of evidence and is covered by the general provisions of law governing instruction of juries. The section states the substance of the existing law as found in Code of Civil Procedure Section 2102. *See People v. Mayes*, 113 Cal. 618, 625-626, 45 Pac. 860, 862 (1896); *Gallegos v. Union-Tribune Publishing Co.*, 195 Cal.App.2d 791, 797-798, 16 Cal.Rptr. 185, 189-190 (1961).

§458. [EFFECT OF FAILURE TO TAKE JUDICIAL NOTICE]

The failure or refusal of the trial court to take judicial notice of a matter, or to instruct the jury with respect to the matter, does not preclude the trial court in subsequent proceedings in the action from taking judicial notice of the matter in accordance with the procedure specified in this division.

History of Evid. C. §458: Added eff. Sept. 17, 1965, oper. Jan. 1, 1967, Stats. 1965, ch. 299, §2.

Official Comment

7 Cal. Law Revision Comm'n Rep. (1965) p. 1075.

This section provides that the failure or even the refusal of the court to take judicial notice of a matter at the trial does not bar the trial judge, or another trial judge, from taking judicial notice of that matter in a subsequent proceeding, such as a hearing on a motion for new trial or the like. Although no California case in point has been found, it seems safe to assume that the trial judge has the power to take judicial notice of a matter in subsequent proceedings, since the appellate court can properly take judicial notice of any matter that the trial court could properly notice. *See People v. Tossetti*, 107 Cal.App. 7, 12, 289 Pac. 881, 883 (1930).

ANNOTATIONS

Ponce v. Tractor Sup. (1st Dist.1972) 29 Cal.App.3d 500, 509-10. Section 458 "'provides that the failure or even the refusal of the court to take judicial notice of a matter at the trial does not bar the trial judge, or another trial judge, from taking judicial notice of that matter in a subsequent proceeding, such as a hearing on a motion for new trial or the like.' [¶] There can be no question in this case that the court below was furnished sufficient information about the prior judgment to allow it to take judicial notice. That judgment was in the same file in the same case that was before the trial court during the entire jury trial and all subsequent proceedings. We hold, therefore, that under the circumstances of this case where the court below was required to take judicial notice of the earlier judgment which was called to its attention after the entry of the later [judgment], but before that judgment became final, the appellant cannot be deemed to have waived its right to rely on the doctrine of collateral estoppel."

§459. [REVIEWING COURT DETERMINATION ON JUDICIAL NOTICE]

(a) [Scope.] The reviewing court shall take judicial notice of (1) each matter properly noticed by the trial court and (2) each matter that the trial court was required to notice under Section 451 or 453. The reviewing court may take judicial notice of any matter specified in Section 452. The reviewing court may take judicial notice of a matter in a tenor different from that noticed by the trial court.

(b) [Propriety or tenor.] In determining the propriety of taking judicial notice of a matter, or the tenor thereof, the reviewing court has the same power as the trial court under Section 454.

(c) [Opportunity to present information.] When taking judicial notice under this section of a matter specified in Section 452 or in subdivision (f) of Section 451 that is of substantial consequence to the determination of the action, the reviewing court shall comply with the provisions of subdivision (a) of Section 455 if the matter was not theretofore judicially noticed in the action.

(d) [Opportunity to meet information.] In determining the propriety of taking judicial notice of a matter specified in Section 452 or in subdivision (f) of Section 451 that is of substantial consequence to the determination of the action, or the tenor thereof, if the reviewing court resorts to any source of information not received in open court or not included in the record of the action, including the advice of persons learned in the subject matter, the reviewing court shall afford each party reasonable opportunity to meet such information before judicial notice of the matter may be taken.

History of Evid. C. §459: Added eff. Sept. 17, 1965, oper. Jan. 1, 1967, Stats. 1965, ch. 299, §2.

Official Comment

7 Cal. Law Revision Comm'n Rep. (1965) p. 1076.

Section 459 sets forth a separate set of rules for the taking of judicial notice by a reviewing court.

Subdivision (a). Subdivision (a) requires that a reviewing court take judicial notice of any matter that the trial court properly noticed or was obliged to notice. This means that the matters specified in Section 451 must be judicially noticed by the reviewing court even though the trial court failed to take judicial notice of such matters. A matter specified in Section 452 also must be judicially noticed by the reviewing court if such matter was properly noticed by the trial court in the exercise of its discretion or an appropriate request was made at the trial level and the party making the request satisfied the conditions specified in Section 453. However, if the trial court erred, the reviewing court is not bound by the tenor of the notice taken by the trial court.

Having taken judicial notice of such a matter, the reviewing court may or may not apply it in the particular case on appeal. The effect to be given to matters judicially noticed on appeal, where the question has not been raised below, depends on factors that are not evidentiary in character and are not mentioned in

this code. For example, the appellate court is required to notice the matters of law mentioned in Section 451, but it may hold that an error which the appellant has "invited" is not reversible error or that points not urged in the trial court may not be advanced on appeal, and refuse, therefore, to apply the law to the pending case. These principles do not mean that the appellate court does not take judicial notice of the applicable law; they merely mean that, for reasons of policy governing appellate review, the appellate court may refuse to apply the law to the case before it.

In addition to requiring the reviewing court to judicially notice those matters which the trial court properly noticed or was required to notice, the subdivision also provides authority for the reviewing court to exercise the same discretionary power to take judicial notice as is possessed by the trial court.

Subdivision (b). The reviewing court may consult any source of pertinent information for the purpose of determining the propriety of taking judicial notice or the tenor of the matter to be noticed. This includes, of course, the power to consult such sources for the purpose of sustaining or reversing the taking of judicial notice by the trial court. As to the rights of the parties when the reviewing court consults such materials, *see* subdivision (d) and the *Comment* thereto.

Subdivision (c). This subdivision provides the parties with the same procedural protection when judicial notice is taken by the reviewing court as is provided by Section 455(a).

Subdivision (d). This subdivision assures the parties the same procedural safeguard at the appellate level that they have in the trial court: If the appellate court resorts to sources of information not included in the record in the action or proceeding, or not received in open court at the appellate level, either to sustain the tenor of the notice taken by the trial court or to notice a matter in a tenor different from that noticed by the trial court, the parties must be given a reasonable opportunity to meet such additional information before judicial notice of the matter may be taken. *See* Evidence Code §455(b) and the *Comment* thereto.

ANNOTATIONS

Subdivision (a)

Newton-Enloe v. Horton (5th Dist.2011) 193 Cal.App.4th 1480, 1492 n.3. "[Ps] request that we take judicial notice of enrolled bills, reports, and sections of various Budget Acts. Although these materials are judicially noticeable …, we exercise our discretion to deny the request because [Ps] have not satisfactorily explained the relevance of the materials. In addition, with respect to most of the materials, [Ps] did not request judicial notice in the trial court and have not explained why they failed to provide them to the trial court."

World Fin. Grp. v. HBW Ins. & Fin. Servs. (2d Dist.2009) 172 Cal.App.4th 1561, 1569 n.7. "For the first time on appeal, [Ds] request judicial notice of several blogs, Internet articles, and Web sites purporting to demonstrate that the content of the communications at issue here involve a matter of public interest. According to [Ds], we must judicially notice those materials pursuant to … §459, subdivision (a)(2). [Ds] are incorrect. While the statute they refer to requires us to judicially notice documents *that were actually noticed in the trial court*, it does not compel us to notice matters that were not offered below."

McMahan v. City & Cty. of S.F. (1st Dist.2005) 127 Cal.App.4th 1368, 1373 n.2. "An appellate court can, but is not required to, take judicial notice of documents that were not presented to the trial court in the first instance." *See also* ***Brosterhous v. State Bar*** (1995) 12 Cal.4th 315, 325.

Evans v. Pillsbury, Madison & Sutro (1st Dist. 1998) 65 Cal.App.4th 599, 605 n.5. A declaration "is a part of the trial court's file and thus a judicial record of which permissive judicial notice could be taken. Nevertheless, the declaration is not a subject for mandatory judicial notice, and the trial court was not asked to take judicial notice of the declaration in connection with [Ps'] demurrer. The declaration is therefore not a proper subject for judicial notice."

Subdivision (c)

Deveny v. Entropin, Inc. (4th Dist.2006) 139 Cal.App.4th 408, 418. "This court may take judicial notice of court records outside the record on appeal, including unpublished orders and decisions in a related federal proceeding. However, a litigant must demonstrate that the matter as to which judicial notice is sought is both relevant to and helpful toward resolving the matters before this court." *See also* ***Jordache Enters. v. Brobeck, Phleger & Harrison*** (1998) 18 Cal.4th 739, 748 n.6.

Schneider v. Kaiser Found. Hosps. (4th Dist. 1989) 215 Cal.App.3d 1311, 1315 n.2, *disapproved on other grounds*, ***Moncharsh v. Heily & Blase*** (1992) 3 Cal.4th 1. Section 459, subdivision (c) "requires a reviewing court to notify the parties of significant material it intends to judicially notice. The rationale for this requirement … is to assure that the parties have the opportunity to present relevant argument to the court based on a fair understanding of the facts and issues which will serve as the foundation for the court's decision."

Subdivision (d)

Cuenca v. Safeway S.F. Empls. Fed. Credit Un. (1st Dist.1986) 180 Cal.App.3d 985, 997. "It is evident from the trial court's order that it took judicial notice of the trial transcript only to the extent that such evidence was called to its attention. In reviewing the trial court's order we are compelled to judicially notice any matters properly noticed by the trial court. However, we decline to take judicial notice, as [P] urges us to do, of the whole record of the prior trial. To do so would give [P] an opportunity to present evidence he elected not to bring to the attention of the trial court at the time he opposed the motion for summary judgment."

Simmons v. Southern Pac. Transp. (1st Dist. 1976) 62 Cal.App.3d 341, 366. Section "459 'merely deals with the power and duty *to take judicial notice* on appeal; the effect of matters thus noticed raises problems of appellate practice outside the scope of the Evidence Code.' Thus, although this court may take judicial notice of the proceedings of a court of this state, whether or not the matter is to be considered on review is a question which must be considered in light of the propriety of considering the matter on review."

§460. [EXPERT FOR JUDICIAL NOTICE]

Where the advice of persons learned in the subject matter is required in order to enable the court to take judicial notice of a matter, the court on its own motion or on motion of any party may appoint one or more such persons to provide such advice. If the court determines to appoint such a person, he shall be appointed and compensated in the manner provided in Article 2 (commencing with Section 730) of Chapter 3 of Division 6.

History of Evid. C. §460: Added eff. Sept. 17, 1965, oper. Jan. 1, 1967, Stats. 1965, ch. 299, §2.

Official Comment

7 Cal. Law Revision Comm'n Rep. (1965) p. 1077; Assem. J., Apr. 6, 1965, p. 1734.

Section 460 makes it clear that a court may appoint experts on matters that are subject to judicial notice when the advice of such persons is required in order to enable the court to take such notice. Such persons are to be appointed and compensated in the same manner as expert witnesses are appointed and compensated under the provisions of Evidence Code Sections 730-733. In the normal case, the parties may be expected to produce the advice of experts if it is needed. Section 460, however, enables the court to appoint experts in those cases where the advice of an expert not identified with a party seems desirable.

DIVISION 5. BURDEN OF PROOF; BURDEN OF PRODUCING EVIDENCE; PRESUMPTIONS & INFERENCES

CHAPTER 1. BURDEN OF PROOF

ARTICLE 1. GENERAL

§500. [BURDEN OF PROOF FOR ESSENTIAL FACTS]

Except as otherwise provided by law, a party has the burden of proof as to each fact the existence or nonexistence of which is essential to the claim for relief or defense that he is asserting.

History of Evid. C. §500: Added eff. Sept. 17, 1965, oper. Jan. 1, 1967, Stats. 1965, ch. 299, §2.

Official Comment

7 Cal. Law Revision Comm'n Rep. (1965) p. 1079.

As used in Section 500, the burden of proof means the obligation of a party to produce a particular state of conviction in the mind of the trier of fact as to the existence or nonexistence of a fact. *See* Evidence Code §§115, 190. If this requisite degree of conviction is not achieved as to the existence of a particular fact, the trier of fact must assume that the fact does not exist. Morgan, *Basic Problems of Evidence* 19 (1957); 9 Wigmore, *Evidence* §2485 (3d ed. 1940). Usually, the burden of proof requires a party to convince the trier of fact that the existence of a particular fact is more probable than its nonexistence—a degree of proof usually described as proof by a preponderance of the evidence. Evidence Code §115; Witkin, *California Evidence* §59 (1958). However, in some instances, the burden of proof requires a party to produce a substantially greater degree of belief in the mind of the trier of fact concerning the existence of the fact—a burden usually described by stating that the party must introduce clear and convincing proof (Witkin, *California Evidence* §60 (1958)) or, with respect to the prosecution in a criminal case, proof beyond a reasonable doubt (Penal Code §1096).

The defendant in a criminal case sometimes has the burden of proof in regard to a fact essential to negate his guilt. However, in such cases, he usually is not required to persuade the trier of fact as to the existence of such fact; he is merely required to raise a reasonable doubt in the mind of the trier of fact as to his guilt. Evidence Code §501; *People v. Bushton*, 80 Cal. 160, 22 Pac. 127 (1889). If the defendant produces no evidence concerning the fact, there is no issue on the matter to be decided by the jury; hence, the jury may be instructed that the nonexistence of the fact must be assumed. *See, e.g., People v. Harmon*, 89 Cal.App.2d 55, 58, 200 P.2d 32, 34 (1948) (prosecution for narcotics possession; jury instructed "that the burden of proof is upon the defendant that he possessed a written prescription and that in the absence of such evidence it must be assumed that he had no such prescription"). *See also People v. Boo Doo Hong*, 122 Cal. 606, 607, 55 Pac. 402, 403 (1898).

Section 1981 of the Code of Civil Procedure (repealed, now Evidence Code Section 500) provides that the party holding the affirmative of the issue must produce the evidence to prove it and that the burden of proof lies on the party who would be defeated if no evidence were given on either side. This section has been criticized as establishing a meaningless standard:

> The "affirmative of the issue" lacks any substantial objective meaning, and the allocation of the burden actually requires the application of several rules of practice and policy, not entirely consistent and not wholly reliable. [Witkin, *California Evidence* §56 at 72-73 (1958).]
>
> That the burden is on the party having the affirmative [or] that a party is not required to prove a negative ... is no more than a play on words, since practically any proposition may be stated in either affirmative or negative form. Thus a plaintiff's exercise of ordinary care equals absence of contributory negligence, in the minority of jurisdictions which place this element in plaintiff's case. In any event, the proposition seems simply not to be so. [Cleary, *Presuming and Pleading: An Essay on Juristic Immaturity*, 12 Stan.L.Rev. 5, 11 (1959).]

"The basic rule, which covers most situations, is that whatever facts a party must affirmatively plead he also has the burden of proving." Witkin, *California Evidence* §56 at 73 (1958). Section 500 follows this basic rule. However, Section 500 is broader, applying to issues not necessarily raised in the pleadings.

Under Section 500, the burden of proof as to a particular fact is normally on the party to whose case the fact is essential. "[W]hen a party seeks relief the burden is upon him to prove his case, and he cannot depend wholly upon the failure of the defendant to prove his defenses." *Cal. Employment Comm'n v. Malm*, 59 Cal.App.2d 322, 323, 138 P.2d 744, 745 (1943). And, "as a general rule, the burden is on the defendant to prove new matter alleged as a defense ..., even though it requires the proof of a negative." *Wilson v. California Cent. R.R.*, 94 Cal. 166, 172, 29 Pac. 861, 864 (1892).

Section 500 does not attempt to indicate what facts may be essential to a particular party's claim for relief or defense. The facts that must be shown to establish a cause of action or a defense are determined by the substantive law, not the law of evidence.

The general rule allocating the burden of proof applies "except as otherwise provided by law." The exception is included in recognition of the fact that the burden of proof is sometimes allocated in a manner that is at variance with the general rule. In determining whether the normal allocation of the burden of proof should be altered, the courts consider a number of factors: the knowledge of the parties concerning the particular fact, the availability of the evidence to the parties, the most desirable result in terms of public policy in the absence of proof of the particular fact, and the probability of the existence or nonexistence of the fact. In determining the incidence of the burden of proof, "the truth is that there is not and cannot be any one general solvent for all cases. It is merely a question of policy and fairness based on experience in the different situations." 9 Wigmore, *Evidence* §2486 at 275 (3d ed. 1940).

Under existing California law, certain matters have been called "presumptions" even though they do not fall within the definition contained in Code of Civil Procedure Section 1959 (repealed, now Evidence Code Section 600). Both Section 1959 and Evidence Code Section 600 define a presumption to be an assumption or conclusion of fact that the law requires to be drawn from the proof or establishment of some other fact. Despite the statutory definition, subdivisions 1 and 4 of Code of Civil Procedure Section 1963 (repealed, now Sections 520 and 521 of the Evidence Code) provide presumptions that a person is innocent of crime or wrong and that a person exercises ordinary care for his own concerns. Similarly, some cases refer to a presumption of sanity. It is apparent that these so-called presumptions do not arise from the establishment or proof of a fact in the action. In fact, they are not presumptions at all but are preliminary allocations of the burden of proof in regard to the particular issue. This preliminary allocation of the burden of proof may be satisfied in particular cases by proof of a fact giving rise to a presumption that does affect the burden of proof. For example, the initial burden of proving negligence may be satisfied in a particular case by proof that undamaged goods were delivered to a bailee and that such goods were lost or damaged while in the bailee's possession. Upon such proof, the bailee would have the burden of proof as to his lack of negligence. *George v. Bekins Van & Storage Co.*, 33 Cal.2d 834, 205 P.2d 1037 (1949). *Cf.* Com. Code §7403.

Because the assumptions referred to above do not meet the definition of a presumption contained in Section 600, they are not continued in this code as presumptions. Instead, they appear in the next article in several sections allocating the burden of proof on specific issues. *See* Article 2 (Sections 520-522).

ANNOTATIONS

California Farm Bur. Fed'n v. State Water Res. Control Bd. (2011) 51 Cal.4th 421, 436. "[A] plaintiff bears the burden of proof 'with respect to all facts essential to its claim for relief.' The plaintiff 'must present evidence sufficient to establish in the mind of the trier of fact or the court a requisite degree of belief (commonly proof by a preponderance of the evidence). The burden of proof *does not shift* ... it remains with the party who originally bears it.' *At n.17:* The terms 'burden of proof' and 'burden of persuasion' are synonymous."

Samuels v. Mix (1999) 22 Cal.4th 1, 19. "[D] points out that the ... §500 rule allocating the burden of proof applies except as otherwise provided by law and that the exception ... is included in recognition of the fact that the burden of proof is sometimes allocated in a manner that is at variance with the general rule. In determining whether the normal allocation of the burden of proof should be altered, the courts consider a number of factors: the knowledge of the parties concerning the particular fact, the availability of the evidence to the parties, the most desirable result in terms of public policy in the absence of proof of the particular fact, and the probability of the existence or nonexistence of the fact. [¶] We have not routinely found exceptions to ... §500's general rule on the basis of relative access to evidence. As [P] points out, nearly all the allegations required of plaintiffs in tort and contract actions relate to defendants' acts or omissions and so might be thought, almost by definition, to describe matters peculiarly within the defendants' knowledge or control. That circumstance, however, has not occasioned a wholesale departure in tort and contract actions from the ordinary allocation of proof burdens." (Internal quotes omitted.) *See also* ***Aydin Corp. v. First State Ins.*** (1998) 18 Cal.4th 1183, 1193; ***Lakin v. Watkins Associated Indus.*** (1993) 6 Cal.4th 644, 660-61; ***In re Marriage of Prentis-Margulis*** (4th Dist. 2011) 198 Cal.App.4th 1252, 1267-68.

Adams v. Murakami (1991) 54 Cal.3d 105, 120. "In determining the incidence of the burden of proof, the truth is that there is not and cannot be any one general solvent for all cases. *It is merely a question of policy and fairness* based on experience in the different situations." (Internal quotes omitted.)

Fisher v. City of Berkeley (1984) 37 Cal.3d 644, 697, *aff'd*, (1986) 475 U.S. 260. "The term 'law,' as used in ... §500, is defined as including 'constitutional, statutory, and decisional law.' *At 698:* [T]he question posed here [is] whether a local ordinance can be deemed a 'statute' for purposes of deviating from the established rules of evidence relating to burden of proof. [¶] [W]e cannot believe that the Legislature ... ever intended municipal ordinances to come within the exception clause of ... §500. [W]e conclude that the Legislature deliberately excluded ordinances from those sources of law that may change the traditional allocation of the burden of proof...." *See also* ***TG Oceanside, L.P. v. City of Oceanside*** (4th Dist.2007) 156 Cal.App.4th 1355, 1374-75 (***Fisher*** does not invalidate burden of producing evidence set forth in ordinance at issue in ***Oceanside***).

National Council Against Health Fraud, Inc. v. King Bio Pharms. (2d Dist.2003) 107 Cal.App.4th 1336, 1346-47. "On rare occasions, the courts have altered the normal allocation of the burden of proof. The shift in the burden of proof from the plaintiff to the defendant rests on a policy judgment that there is a substantial probability the defendant has engaged in wrongdoing and the defendant's wrongdoing makes it practically impossible for the plaintiff to prove the wrongdoing. Thus, the normal allocation of the burden of proof has been shifted in spoliation of evidence cases ..., negligence per se actions ..., and product liability cases based on design defect.... Even in these cases, however, the plaintiff has the burden of producing some evidence before the burden of proof is shifted to the defendant. ... We are aware of no cases in which

the burden of proof shifts to the defendant upon the filing of the complaint." *See also* ***Sargent Fletcher, Inc. v. Able Corp.*** (2d Dist.2003) 110 Cal.App.4th 1658, 1670.

§501. [BURDEN OF PROOF IN CRIMINAL ACTIONS]

Insofar as any statute, except Section 522, assigns the burden of proof in a criminal action, such statute is subject to Penal Code Section 1096.

History of Evid. C. §501: Added eff. Sept. 17, 1965, oper. Jan. 1, 1967, Stats. 1965, ch. 299, §2.

Official Comment

7 Cal. Law Revision Comm'n Rep. (1965) p. 1081.

A statute assigning the burden of proof may require the party to whom the burden is assigned to raise a reasonable doubt in the mind of the trier of fact or to persuade the trier of fact by a preponderance of evidence, by clear and convincing proof, or by proof beyond a reasonable doubt. *See* Evidence Code §115.

Sections 520-522 (which assign the burden of proof on specific issues) may, at times, assign the burden of proof to the defendant in a criminal action. Elsewhere in the codes are other sections that either specifically allocate the burden of proof to the defendant in a criminal action or have been construed to allocate the burden of proof to the defense. For example, Health and Safety Code Section 11721 provides specifically that, in a prosecution for the use of narcotics, it is the burden of the defense to show that the narcotics were administered by or under the direction of a person licensed to prescribe and administer narcotics. Health and Safety Code Section 11500, on the other hand, prohibits the possession of narcotics but provides an exception for narcotics possessed pursuant to a prescription. The courts have construed this section to place the burden of proof on the defense to show that the exception applies and that the narcotics were possessed pursuant to a prescription. *People v. Marschalk*, 206 Cal.App.2d 346, 23 Cal.Rptr. 743 (1962); *People v. Bill*, 140 Cal.App. 389, 392-394, 35 P.2d 645, 647-648 (1934).

Section 501 is intended to make it clear that the statutory allocations of the burden of proof appearing in this chapter and elsewhere in the codes are subject to Penal Code Section 1096, which requires that a criminal defendant be proved guilty beyond a reasonable doubt, *i.e.*, that the statutory allocations do not (except on the issue of insanity) require the defendant to persuade the trier of fact of his innocence. Under Evidence Code Section 522, as under existing law, the defendant must prove his insanity by a preponderance of the evidence. *People v. Daugherty*, 40 Cal.2d 876, 256 P.2d 911 (1953). However, where a statute allocates the burden of proof to the defendant on any other issue relating to the defendant's guilt, the defendant's burden, as under existing law, is merely to raise a reasonable doubt as to his guilt. *People v. Bushton*, 80 Cal. 160, 22 Pac. 127 (1889). Section 501 also makes it clear that, when a statute assigns the burden of proof to the prosecution in a criminal action, the prosecution must discharge that burden by proof beyond a reasonable doubt.

§502. [JURY INSTRUCTION ON BURDEN OF PROOF]

The court on all proper occasions shall instruct the jury as to which party bears the burden of proof on each issue and as to whether that burden requires that a party raise a reasonable doubt concerning the existence or nonexistence of a fact or that he establish the existence or nonexistence of a fact by a preponderance of the evidence, by clear and convincing proof, or by proof beyond a reasonable doubt.

History of Evid. C. §502: Added eff. Sept. 17, 1965, oper. Jan. 1, 1967, Stats. 1965, ch. 299, §2.

Official Comment

7 Cal. Law Revision Comm'n Rep. (1965) p. 1082.

Section 502 supersedes subdivision 5 of Code of Civil Procedure Section 2061.

ANNOTATIONS

People v. Shelmire (3d Dist.2005) 130 Cal.App.4th 1044, 1054. "A trial court has a sua sponte duty under ... §502 to instruct the jury correctly on defendant's burden of proof as to a defense."

ARTICLE 2. BURDEN OF PROOF ON SPECIFIC ISSUES

§520. [BURDEN OF PROOF ON CRIMINAL ISSUES]

The party claiming that a person is guilty of crime or wrongdoing has the burden of proof on that issue.

History of Evid. C. §520: Added eff. Sept. 17, 1965, oper. Jan. 1, 1967, Stats. 1965, ch. 299, §2.

Official Comment

7 Cal. Law Revision Comm'n Rep. (1965) p. 1082.

Section 520 restates the substance of and supersedes subdivision 1 of Code of Civil Procedure Section 1963.

ANNOTATIONS

Sargent Fletcher, Inc. v. Able Corp. (2d Dist.2003) 110 Cal.App.4th 1658, 1668. "[T]he plaintiff generally bears the burden of proof to establish its prima facie case."

FMC Corp. v. Plaisted & Cos. (6th Dist.1998) 61 Cal.App.4th 1132, 1160, *disapproved on other grounds*, ***State v. Continental Ins.*** (2012) 55 Cal.4th 186. "[P] relies on the subjective test for 'expected' damage enunciated in ***Shell*** [***Oil Co. v. Winterthur Swiss Ins.*** (1st Dist.1993) 12 Cal.App.4th 715] and applied for other purposes at the trials of this action: 'whether the insured knew or believed its conduct was substantially certain or highly likely to result in that kind of damage.' [P] asks us to conclude that conduct that met the ***Shell*** test, in the factual context of this action, would necessarily amount at least to 'wrongdoing' within the meaning of [Evid. C.] §520. [¶] We cannot so conclude. The wording, history and prior judicial application of ... §520 all support a finding that 'wrongdoing' connotes an element of moral disapprobation substantially greater than that which might be implied by the ***Shell*** test. Thus ... in ***Clemmer v. Hartford*** [***Ins.***] (1978) 22 Cal.3d 865 ..., it was deemed 'consistent with ... §520' to require an insurer to show that its insured had acted wilfully (within the meaning of [Ins. C.] §533) in shooting his employer to death, and in ***Fisher v. Supe-***

§500

rior [*Ct.*] ([2d Dist.] 1980) 103 Cal.App.3d 434 ..., the Court of Appeal referred to §520 in apparent support of its conclusion that the burden of proof as to the 'good faith' of a settlement should be upon the party who asserted the settlement was *not* made in good faith, i.e., was made in bad faith."

§521. [BURDEN OF PROOF ON NEGLIGENCE ISSUES]

The party claiming that a person did not exercise a requisite degree of care has the burden of proof on that issue.

History of Evid. C. §521: Added eff. Sept. 17, 1965, oper. Jan. 1, 1967, Stats. 1965, ch. 299, §2.

Official Comment

7 Cal. Law Revision Comm'n Rep. (1965) p. 1083.

Section 521 supersedes the presumption in subdivision 4 of Code of Civil Procedure Section 1963. Under existing law, the presumption is considered "evidence"; while under the Evidence Code, it is not. *See* Evidence Code §600 and the *Comment* thereto.

§522. [BURDEN OF PROOF ON INSANITY DEFENSE]

The party claiming that any person, including himself, is or was insane has the burden of proof on that issue.

History of Evid. C. §522: Added eff. Sept. 17, 1965, oper. Jan. 1, 1967, Stats. 1965, ch. 299, §2.

Official Comment

7 Cal. Law Revision Comm'n Rep. (1965) p. 1083.

Section 522 codifies an allocation of the burden of proof that is frequently referred to in the cases as a presumption. *See, e.g., People v. Daugherty*, 40 Cal.2d 876, 899, 256 P.2d 911, 925-926 (1953).

§523. [BURDEN OF PROOF IN LAND DISPUTES WITH STATE]

In any action where the state is a party, regardless of who is the moving party, where (a) the boundary of land patented or otherwise granted by the state is in dispute, or (b) the validity of any state patent or grant dated prior to 1950 is in dispute, the state shall have the burden of proof on all issues relating to the historic locations of rivers, streams, and other water bodies and the authority of the state in issuing the patent or grant.

This section is not intended to nor shall it be construed to supersede existing statutes governing disputes where the state is a party and regarding title to real property.

History of Evid. C. §523: Added eff. Jan. 1, 1995, Stats. 1994, ch. 128, §2.

§524. [BURDEN OF PROOF IN PROCEEDING AGAINST TAXPAYER]

(a) [Clear and convincing.] Notwithstanding any other provision of law, in a civil proceeding to which the State Board of Equalization is a party, that board shall have the burden of proof by clear and convincing evidence in sustaining its assertion of a penalty for intent to evade or fraud against a taxpayer, with respect to any factual issue relevant to ascertaining the liability of a taxpayer.

(b) [Substantiating items on return or claim filed.] Nothing in this section shall be construed to override any requirement for a taxpayer to substantiate any item on a return or claim filed with the State Board of Equalization.

(c) [No unreasonable search.] Nothing in this section shall subject a taxpayer to unreasonable search or access to records in violation of the United States Constitution, the California Constitution, or any other law.

(d) ["Taxpayer" defined.] For purposes of this section, "taxpayer" includes a person on whom fees administered by the State Board of Equalization are imposed.

History of Evid. C. §524: Added eff. Jan. 1, 2011, Stats. 2010, ch. 168, §1.

CHAPTER 2. BURDEN OF PRODUCING EVIDENCE

§550. [BURDEN OF PRODUCING EVIDENCE]

(a) [Shifting burden.] The burden of producing evidence as to a particular fact is on the party against whom a finding on that fact would be required in the absence of further evidence.

(b) [Initial burden.] The burden of producing evidence as to a particular fact is initially on the party with the burden of proof as to that fact.

History of Evid. C. §550: Added eff. Sept. 17, 1965, oper. Jan. 1, 1967, Stats. 1965, ch. 299, §2.

Official Comment

7 Cal. Law Revision Comm'n Rep. (1965) p. 1083.

Section 550 deals with the allocation of the burden of producing evidence. At the outset of the case, this burden will coincide with the burden of proof. 9 Wigmore, *Evidence* §2487 at 279 (3d ed. 1940). However, during the course of the trial, the burden may shift from one party to another, irrespective of the incidence of the burden of proof. For example, if the party with the initial burden of producing evidence establishes a fact giving rise to a presumption, the burden of producing evidence will shift to the other party, whether or not the presumption is one that affects the burden of proof. In addition, a party may introduce evidence of such overwhelming probative force that no person could reasonably disbelieve it in the absence of countervailing evidence, in which case the burden of producing evidence would shift to the opposing party to produce some evidence. These principles are in accord with well-settled California law. *See* discussion in Witkin, *California Evidence* §§53-56 (1958). *See also* 9 Wigmore, *Evidence* §2487 (3d ed. 1940).

ANNOTATIONS

California Farm Bur. Fed'n v. State Water Res. Control Bd. (2011) 51 Cal.4th 421, 436. The "burden of

persuasion is different from the 'burden of producing evidence' ..., which may shift between the parties. '[T]he burden of producing evidence as to a particular fact rests on the party with the burden of proof as to that fact. If that party fails to produce sufficient evidence to make a prima facie case, it risks nonsuit or other unfavorable determination. But once that party produces evidence sufficient to make its prima facie case, the burden of producing evidence *shifts* to the other party to refute the prima facie case.' *At n.18:* The 'burden of producing evidence' has also been referred to as the 'burden of production' and the 'burden of going forward.'" *See also* ***Sargent Fletcher, Inc. v. Able Corp.*** (2d Dist.2003) 110 Cal.App.4th 1658, 1667-68.

National Council Against Health Fraud, Inc. v. King Bio Pharms. (2d Dist.2003) 107 Cal.App.4th 1336, 1344. "As a general rule, a plaintiff has the burden of producing evidence to support the allegations of the complaint."

Smith v. Santa Rosa Police Dept. (1st Dist.2002) 97 Cal.App.4th 546, 568-69. "'Burden of producing evidence' means the obligation of a party to introduce evidence sufficient to avoid a ruling against him on the issue. Thus, if a plaintiff presents evidence to establish each element of its case, the defendant has the burden of going forward with its own evidence as to those issues. This does not alter the ultimate burden of proof, which rests with the plaintiff to prove each of the relevant facts supporting its cause of action." (Internal quotes omitted.)

CHAPTER 3. PRESUMPTIONS & INFERENCES

ARTICLE 1. GENERAL

§600. [DEFINITIONS]

(a) [Presumption.] A presumption is an assumption of fact that the law requires to be made from another fact or group of facts found or otherwise established in the action. A presumption is not evidence.

(b) [Inference.] An inference is a deduction of fact that may logically and reasonably be drawn from another fact or group of facts found or otherwise established in the action.

History of Evid. C. §600: Added eff. Sept. 17, 1965, oper. Jan. 1, 1967, Stats. 1965, ch. 299, §2.

Official Comment

7 Cal. Law Revision Comm'n Rep. (1965) p. 1084; Assem. J., Apr. 6, 1965, p. 1734.

The definition of a presumption in Section 600 is substantially the same as that contained in Code of Civil Procedure Section 1959: "A presumption is a deduction which the law expressly directs to be made from particular facts." Section 600 was derived from Rule 13 of the Uniform Rules of Evidence and supersedes Code of Civil Procedure Section 1959.

The second sentence of subdivision (a) may be unnecessary in light of the definition of "evidence" in Section 140—"testimony, writings, material objects, or other things presented to the senses that are offered to prove the existence or nonexistence of a fact." Presumptions, then, are not "evidence" but are conclusions that the law requires to be drawn (in the absence of a sufficient contrary showing) when some other fact is proved or otherwise established in the action.

Nonetheless, the second sentence has been added here to repudiate specifically the rule of *Smellie v. Southern Pac. Co.*, 212 Cal. 540, 299 Pac. 529 (1931). That case held that a presumption is evidence that must be weighed against conflicting evidence; and in *Scott v. Burke*, 39 Cal.2d 388, 247 P.2d 313 (1952), the Supreme Court held that conflicting presumptions must be weighed against each other. These decisions require the jury to perform an intellectually impossible task. The jury is required to weigh the testimony of witnesses and other evidence as to the circumstances of a particular event against the fact that the law requires an opposing conclusion in the absence of contrary evidence and to determine which "evidence" is of greater probative force. Or else, the jury is required to accept the fact that the law requires two opposing conclusions and to determine which required conclusion is of greater probative force.

Moreover, the doctrine that a presumption is evidence imposes upon the party with the burden of proof a much higher burden of proof than is warranted. For example, if a party with the burden of proof has a presumption invoked against him and if the presumption remains in the case as evidence even though the jury believes that he has produced a preponderance of the evidence, the effect is that he must produce some additional but unascertainable quantum of proof in order to dispel the effect of the presumption. *See Scott v. Burke*, 39 Cal.2d 388, 405-406, 247 P.2d 313, 323-324 (1952) (dissenting opinion). The doctrine that a presumption is evidence gives no guidance to the jury or to the parties as to the amount of this additional proof. The most that should be expected of a party in a civil case is that he prove his case by a preponderance of the evidence (unless some specific presumption or rule of law requires proof of a particular issue by clear and convincing evidence). The most that should be expected of the prosecution in a criminal case is that it establish the defendant's guilt beyond a reasonable doubt. To require some additional quantum of proof, unspecified and uncertain in amount, to dispel a presumption which persists as evidence in the case unfairly weights the scales of justice against the party with the burden of proof.

To avoid the confusion engendered by the doctrine that a presumption is evidence, this code describes "evidence" as the matters presented in judicial proceedings and uses presumptions solely as devices to aid in determining the facts from the evidence presented.

The definition of "inference" in subdivision (b) restates in substance the definition contained in Code of Civil Procedure Sections 1958 and 1960. Under the Evidence Code, an inference is not itself evidence; it is the result of reasoning from evidence.

In the sections that follow, the Evidence Code classifies presumptions and lists a number of specific presumptions. Some presumptions that have been listed in the Code of Civil Procedure have not been listed as presumptions in the Evidence Code. But the fact that a statutory presumption has been repealed will not preclude the drawing of any appropriate inferences from the facts that would have given rise to the presumption. And, in appropriate cases, the court may instruct the jury on the propriety of drawing particular inferences.

ANNOTATIONS

Presumption

Gee v. Workers' Comp. Appeals Bd. (5th Dist. 2002) 96 Cal.App.4th 1418, 1425. "'[A] presumption becomes operative at trial when the basic facts giving rise to the presumption are established by the pleadings, by stipulation, by judicial notice, or by evidence.'" *See also* ***Coso Energy Developers v. County of Inyo*** (4th Dist.2004) 122 Cal.App.4th 1512, 1536.

Shadow Traffic Network v. Superior Ct. (2d Dist.1994) 24 Cal.App.4th 1067, 1085 n.12. "The power of the higher courts to create presumptions is expressly recognized by [Evid. C. §600] (assumption that the law requires to be made) read in connection with [Evid. C. §160] ('law' includes decisional law)." (Internal quotes omitted.)

Inference

Ortega v. Kmart Corp. (2001) 26 Cal.4th 1200, 1203. "We conclude that evidence of the owner's failure to inspect the premises within a reasonable period of time is sufficient to allow an inference that the condition was on the floor long enough to give the owner the opportunity to discover and remedy it. *At 1203 n.1:* [T]he inference supports [P's] prima facie case of negligence and avoids the risk of nonsuit. It is important to distinguish an inference, which may, in the trier of fact's discretion, support [P's] negligence claim, and relieve [P] from the burden of proving how long the substance was on the floor, from a presumption…. *At 1211:* [T]he inference tends to establish a fact from which the existence of another fact in issue (that the milk was on the floor for a sufficient period of time to establish constructive knowledge) can be inferred." *See also* ***Ruiz v. Minnesota Mining & Mfg.*** (2d Dist.1971) 15 Cal.App.3d 462, 467 & n.3 (relevant evidence must have a rational tendency to prove or disprove a disputed matter).

Carlsen v. Koivumaki (3d Dist.2014) 227 Cal.App.4th 879, 891-92. "An inference must be reasonable to raise a triable issue of material fact on summary judgment. While we may not weigh [P's] evidence or inferences against [D's] evidence as though we are sitting as a trier of fact, we 'must nevertheless determine what any evidence or inference *could show or imply to a reasonable trier of fact*. … In doing so, [we do] not decide on any finding of [our] own, but simply decide[] what finding such a trier of fact could make for itself.'"

Ajaxo Inc. v. E*Trade Grp. (6th Dist.2005) 135 Cal.App.4th 21, 50-51. "A party may rely upon 'reasonable inferences' from the evidence to support a verdict. [¶] When an inference needs to be drawn from the evidence to prove a fact, we call this circumstantial evidence as opposed to direct evidence. … Circumstantial evidence, when relevant, is as admissible as direct evidence. … Circumstantial evidence is that which is applied to the principal fact, indirectly, or through the medium of other facts, from which the principal fact is inferred. The characteristics of circumstantial evidence as distinguished from that which is direct, are, first, the existence and presentation of one or more evidentiary facts; and, second, a process of inference, by which these facts are so connected with the fact sought, as to tend to produce a persuasion of its truth. [C]ircumstantial evidence, as distinguished from direct evidence, is testimony not based on actual personal knowledge or observation of the facts in controversy, but of other facts from which deductions are drawn, showing indirectly the facts sought to be proved. [¶] [T]he term 'circumstantial evidence' emphasizes the effect of the evidence—the necessity of drawing inferences from it." (Internal quotes omitted.)

Fashion 21 v. Coalition for Humane Immigrant Rights (2d Dist.2004) 117 Cal.App.4th 1138, 1149. "[A]n inference is not evidence but rather the result of reasoning from evidence. An inference of fact must be based upon substantial evidence, not conjecture. It must be such that a rational, well-constructed mind can reasonably draw from it the conclusion that the fact exists." (Internal quotes omitted.)

Cucuzza v. City of Santa Clara (6th Dist.2002) 104 Cal.App.4th 1031, 1038. "[E]ven though we may expect a plaintiff to rely on inferences rather than direct evidence to create a factual dispute on the question of motive, a material, triable controversy is not established unless the inference is reasonable. And an inference is reasonable if, and only if, it implies the unlawful motive is more likely than defendant's proffered explanation. *At 1039:* If plaintiff fails to produce substantial responsive evidence to demonstrate a material triable controversy, summary judgment is properly granted." *But see* ***McGrory v. Applied Signal Tech.***, (6th Dist.2013) 212 Cal.App.4th 1510, 1530 n.14 (to create triable issue, it should be enough to show that two conflicting inferences can be reasonably drawn from evidence, not that opposition's position is more likely).

S.C. Anderson, Inc. v. Bank of Am. (5th Dist. 1994) 24 Cal.App.4th 529, 539 n.12. "Whether the law will allow the trier of fact to draw an inference depends upon whether the court is persuaded that the proposed conclusion is a reasonable, logical, and nonspeculative deduction from the facts proved." *See also* ***Visueta v. General Motors Corp.*** (2d Dist.1991) 234 Cal.App.3d 1609, 1615; ***Dimond v. Caterpillar Tractor Co.*** (4th Dist.1976) 65 Cal.App.3d 173, 181.

Collin v. American Empire Ins. (2d Dist.1994) 21 Cal.App.4th 787, 808. "It is fundamental that one cannot make an inference from thin air: 'Where there is no evidence or not even slight evidence of an essential fact to be proved by the plaintiff, a conclusion of a trial court or jury based thereon becomes a mere conjecture and does not rise to the dignity of an inference.' The absence of critical evidence does not give rise to an inference that the missing evidence exists; rather, it indicates a failure of proof: 'If the existence of an essential fact upon which a party relies is left in doubt or uncertainty, the party upon whom the burden rests to establish that fact should suffer, and not his adversary.' A judgment cannot be based on guesses or conjectures."

§601. [CLASSIFICATION OF PRESUMPTIONS]

A presumption is either conclusive or rebuttable. Every rebuttable presumption is either (a) a presumption affecting the burden of producing evidence or (b) a presumption affecting the burden of proof.

History of Evid. C. §601: Added eff. Sept. 17, 1965, oper. Jan. 1, 1967, Stats. 1965, ch. 299, §2.

Official Comment

7 Cal. Law Revision Comm'n Rep. (1965) p. 1085.

(technical correction—Senate J., Apr. 21, 1965)

Under existing law, some presumptions are conclusive. The court or jury is required to find the existence of the presumed fact regardless of the strength of the opposing evidence. The conclusive presumptions are specified in Section 1962 of the Code of Civil Procedure (repealed, now Article 2 (Sections 620-624) of this chapter).

Under existing law, too, all presumptions that are not conclusive are rebuttable presumptions. Code Civ. Proc. §1961 (repealed, now Evidence Code §601). However, the existing statutes make no attempt to classify the rebuttable presumptions.

For several decades, courts and legal scholars have wrangled over the purpose and function of presumptions. The view espoused by Professors Thayer (Thayer, *Preliminary Treatise on Evidence* 313-352 (1898)) and Wigmore (9 Wigmore, *Evidence* §§2485-2491 (3d ed. 1940)), accepted by most courts (see Morgan, *Presumptions*, 10 Rutgers L.Rev. 512, 516 (1956)), and adopted by the American Law Institute's Model Code of Evidence, is that a presumption is a preliminary assumption of fact that disappears from the case upon the introduction of evidence sufficient to sustain a finding of the nonexistence of the presumed fact. In Professor Thayer's view, a presumption merely reflects the judicial determination that the same conclusionary fact exists so frequently when the preliminary fact exists that, once the preliminary fact is established, proof of the conclusionary fact may be dispensed with unless there is actually some contrary evidence:

> Many facts and groups of facts often recur, and when a body of men with a continuous tradition has carried on for some length of time this process of reasoning upon facts that often repeat themselves, they cut short the process and lay down a rule. To such facts they affix, by a general declaration, the character and operation which common experience has assigned to them. [Thayer, *Preliminary Treatise on Evidence* 326 (1898).]

Professors Morgan and McCormick argue that a presumption should shift the burden of proof to the adverse party. Morgan, *Some Problems of Proof* 81 (1956); McCormick, *Evidence* §317 at 671-672 (1954). They believe that presumptions are created for reasons of policy and argue that, if the policy underlying a presumption is of sufficient weight to require a finding of the presumed fact when there is no contrary evidence, it should be of sufficient weight to require a finding when the mind of the trier of fact is in equilibrium, and, *a fortiori*, it should be of sufficient weight to require a finding if the trier of fact does not believe the contrary evidence.

The classification of presumptions in the Evidence Code is based on a third view suggested by Professor Bohlen in 1920. Bohlen, *The Effect of Rebuttable Presumptions of Law Upon the Burden of Proof*, 68 U.Pa.L.Rev. 307 (1920). Underlying the presumptions provisions of the Evidence Code is the conclusion that the Thayer view is correct as to some presumptions, but that the Morgan view is right as to others. The fact is that presumptions are created for a variety of reasons, and no single theory or rationale of presumptions can deal adequately with all of them. Hence, the Evidence Code classifies all rebuttable presumptions as either (1) presumptions affecting the burden of producing evidence (essentially Thayer presumptions), or (2) presumptions affecting the burden of proof (essentially Morgan presumptions).

Sections 603 and 605 set forth the criteria by which the two classes of rebuttable presumptions may be distinguished, and Sections 604, 606, and 607 prescribe their effect. Articles 3 and 4 (Sections 630-668) classify many presumptions found in California law; but many other presumptions, both statutory and common law, must await classification by the courts in accordance with the criteria contained in Sections 603 and 605.

The classification scheme contained in the Evidence Code follows a distinction that appears in the California cases. Thus, for example, the courts have at times held that presumptions do not affect the burden of proof. *Estate of Eakle*, 33 Cal.App.2d 379, 91 P.2d 954 (1939) (presumption of undue influence); *Valentine v. Provident Mut. Life Ins. Co.*, 12 Cal.App.2d 616, 55 P.2d 1243 (1936) (presumption of death from seven years' absence). And at other times the courts have held that certain presumptions do affect the burden of proof. *Estate of Nickson*, 187 Cal. 603, 203 Pac. 106 (1921) ("clear and convincing proof" required to overcome presumption of community property); *Estate of Walker*, 180 Cal. 478, 181 Pac. 792 (1919) ("clear and satisfactory proof" required to overcome presumption of legitimacy). The cases have not, however, explicitly recognized the distinction, nor have they applied it consistently. *Compare Estate of Eakle, supra* (presumption of undue influence does not affect burden of proof), *with Estate of Witt*, 198 Cal. 407, 245 Pac. 197 (1926) (presumption of undue influence must be overcome with "the clearest and most satisfactory evidence"). The Evidence Code clarifies the law relating to presumptions by identifying the distinguishing factors, and it provides a measure of certainty by classifying a number of specific presumptions.

ANNOTATIONS

Melendrez v. D&I Inv. (6th Dist.2005) 127 Cal.App.4th 1238, 1250 n.17. "A conclusive presumption requires the trier of fact to find the existence of the presumed fact from the existence of the basic fact. An adverse party is not permitted to introduce evidence to contradict or rebut the existence of the presumed fact." (Internal quotes omitted.) *See also* ***In re Heather B.*** (3d Dist.1992) 9 Cal.App.4th 535, 560.

Griffiths v. Superior Ct. (2d Dist.2002) 96 Cal.App.4th 757, 777. "'[O]nce foundational facts upon which such a presumption is based are established, the assumed fact may not be controverted by contrary evidence.' As such[,] a conclusive presumption is a rule of substantive law. Its validity must therefore be judged under standards applicable to substantive laws. The Legislature has power to create presumptions in civil cases. Conclusive presumptions exist to further particular social policies and purposes."

§602. [REBUTTABLE PRESUMPTION]

A statute providing that a fact or group of facts is prima facie evidence of another fact establishes a rebuttable presumption.

History of Evid. C. §602: Added eff. Sept. 17, 1965, oper. Jan. 1, 1967, Stats. 1965, ch. 299, §2.

Official Comment

7 Cal. Law Revision Comm'n Rep. (1965) p. 1087.

Section 602 indicates the construction to be given to the large number of statutes scattered through the codes that state that one fact or group of facts is prima facie evidence of another fact. *See, e.g.*, Agric. Code §18, Com. Code §1202, Rev. & Tax. Code §6714. In some instances, these statutes have been enacted for reasons of public policy that require them to be treated as presumptions affecting the burden of proof. *See People v. Schwartz*, 31 Cal.2d 59, 63, 187 P.2d 12, 14 (1947); *People v. Mahoney*, 13 Cal.2d 729, 732-733, 91 P.2d 1029, 1030-1031 (1939). It seems likely, however, that in many instances such statutes are not intended to affect the burden of proof but only the burden of producing evidence. Section 602 provides that these statutes are to be regarded as rebuttable presumptions. Hence, unless some specific language applicable to the particular statute in question indicates whether it affects the burden of proof or only the burden of producing evidence, the courts will be required to classify these statutes as presumptions affecting the burden of proof or the burden of producing evidence in accordance with the criteria set forth in Sections 603 and 605.

§603. [PUBLIC POLICY OF BURDEN OF PRODUCING EVIDENCE]

A presumption affecting the burden of producing evidence is a presumption established to implement no public policy other than to facilitate the determination of the particular action in which the presumption is applied.

History of Evid. C. §603: Added eff. Sept. 17, 1965, oper. Jan. 1, 1967, Stats. 1965, ch. 299, §2.

Official Comment

7 Cal. Law Revision Comm'n Rep. (1965) p. 1088.

(technical correction—Senate J., Apr. 21, 1965)

Sections 603 and 605 set forth the criteria for determining whether a particular presumption is a presumption affecting the burden of producing evidence or a presumption affecting the burden of proof. Many presumptions are classified in Articles 3 and 4 (Sections 630-668) of this chapter. In the absence of specific statutory classification, the courts may determine whether a presumption is a presumption affecting the burden of producing evidence or a presumption affecting the burden of proof by applying the standards contained in Sections 603 and 605.

Section 603 describes those presumptions that are not based on any public policy extrinsic to the action in which they are invoked. These presumptions are designed to dispense with unnecessary proof of facts that are likely to be true if not disputed. Typically, such presumptions are based on an underlying logical inference. In some cases, the presumed fact is so likely to be true and so little likely to be disputed that the law requires it to be assumed in the absence of contrary evidence. In other cases, evidence of the nonexistence of the presumed fact, if there is any, is so much more readily available to the party against whom the presumption operates that he is not permitted to argue that the presumed fact does not exist unless he is willing to produce such evidence. In still other cases, there may be no direct evidence of the existence or nonexistence of the presumed fact; but, because the case must be decided, the law requires a determination that the presumed fact exists in light of common experience indicating that it usually exists in such cases. *Cf.* Bohlen, *Studies in the Law of Torts* 644 (1926). Typical of such presumptions are the presumption that a mailed letter was received (Section 641) and presumptions relating to the authenticity of documents (Sections 643-645).

The presumptions described in Section 603 are not expressions of policy; they are expressions of experience. They are intended solely to eliminate the need for the trier of fact to reason from the proven or established fact to the presumed fact and to forestall argument over the existence of the presumed fact when there is no evidence tending to prove the nonexistence of the presumed fact.

ANNOTATIONS

Fisher v. City of Berkeley (1984) 37 Cal.3d 644, 694-95, *aff'd*, (1986) 475 U.S. 260. "The burden of producing evidence refers to a party's obligation to introduce evidence sufficient to establish a prima facie case, or, in other words, sufficient to avoid nonsuit. [Section 603] makes clear that the purpose of such a rebuttable presumption relates solely to judicial efficiency, and does not rest on any public policy extrinsic to the action in which it is invoked. A presumption affecting the burden of producing evidence is based on an underlying logical inference that the presumed fact very likely follows from the proved fact; the presumption is designed to avoid unnecessary proof of facts likely to be true if not disputed. [S]uch a rebuttable presumption is designed to place the responsibility for establishing the nonexistence of certain facts on the party most able to do so. '[T]he presumptions described in [§603] are not expressions of policy; they are expressions of experience. They are intended solely to eliminate the need for the trier of fact to reason from the proven or established fact to the presumed fact and to forestall argument over the existence of the presumed fact when there is no evidence tending to prove the nonexistence of the presumed fact.'" *See also* ***TG Oceanside, L.P. v. City of Oceanside*** (4th Dist.2007) 156 Cal.App.4th 1355, 1375.

Rancho Santa Fe Pharm. v. Seyfert (4th Dist.1990) 219 Cal.App.3d 875, 882. "[W]hen the party against whom … a presumption [affecting the burden of producing evidence] operates produces some quantum of evidence casting doubt on the truth of the presumed fact, the other party is no longer aided by the presumption. The presumption disappears, leaving it to the party in whose favor it initially worked to prove the fact in question." *See also* ***Estate of Trikha*** (4th Dist.2013) 219 Cal.App.4th 791, 802-03.

§604. [EFFECT OF PRESUMPTION ON BURDEN OF PRODUCING EVIDENCE]

The effect of a presumption affecting the burden of producing evidence is to require the trier of fact to assume the existence of the presumed fact unless and until evidence is introduced which would support a finding of its nonexistence, in which case the trier of fact shall determine the existence or nonexistence of the presumed fact from the evidence and without regard to the presumption. Nothing in this section shall be construed to prevent the drawing of any inference that may be appropriate.

History of Evid. C. §604: Added eff. Sept. 17, 1965, oper. Jan. 1, 1967, Stats. 1965, ch. 299, §2.

Official Comment

7 Cal. Law Revision Comm'n Rep. (1965) p. 1089; Assem. J., Apr. 6, 1965, p. 1736.

Section 604 describes the manner in which a presumption affecting the burden of producing evidence operates. Such a presumption is merely a preliminary assumption in the absence of contrary evidence, *i.e.*, evidence sufficient to sustain a finding of the nonexistence of the presumed fact. If contrary evidence is introduced, the trier of fact must weigh the inferences arising from the facts that gave rise to the presumption against the contrary evidence and resolve the conflict. For example, if a party proves that a letter was mailed, the trier of fact is required to find that the letter was received in the absence of any believable contrary evidence. However, if the adverse party denies receipt, the presumption is gone from the case. The trier of fact must then weigh the denial of receipt against the inference of receipt arising from proof of mailing and decide whether or not the letter was received.

If a presumption affecting the burden of producing evidence is relied on, the judge must determine whether there is evidence sufficient to sustain a finding of the nonexistence of the presumed fact. If there is such evidence, the presumption disappears and the judge need say nothing about it in his instructions. If there is not evidence sufficient to sustain a finding of the nonexistence of the presumed fact, the judge should instruct the jury concerning the presumption. If the basic fact from which the presumption arises is established (by the pleadings, by stipulation, by judicial notice, etc.) so that the existence of the basic fact is not a question of fact for the jury, the jury should be instructed that the presumed fact is also established. If the basic fact is a question of fact for the jury, the judge should charge the jury that, if it finds the basic fact, the jury must also find the presumed fact. Morgan, *Basic Problems of Evidence* 36-38 (1957).

Of course, in a criminal case, the jury has the power to disregard the judge's instructions and find a defendant guilty of a lesser crime than that shown by the evidence or acquit a defendant despite the facts established by the undisputed evidence. *Cf. People v. Powell*, 34 Cal.2d 196, 208 P.2d 974 (1949); Pike, *What Is Second Degree Murder in California?*, 9 So. Cal.L.Rev. 112, 128-132 (1936). Nonetheless, the jury should be instructed on the rules of law applicable, including those rules of law called presumptions. The fact that the jury may choose to disregard the applicable rules of law should not affect the nature of the instructions given. *See People v. Lem You*, 97 Cal. 224, 32 Pac. 11 (1893); *People v. Macken*, 32 Cal.App.2d 31, 89 P.2d 173 (1939).

§605. [PUBLIC POLICY OF BURDEN OF PROOF]

A presumption affecting the burden of proof is a presumption established to implement some public policy other than to facilitate the determination of the particular action in which the presumption is applied, such as the policy in favor of establishment of a parent and child relationship, the validity of marriage, the stability of titles to property, or the security of those who entrust themselves or their property to the administration of others.

History of Evid. C. §605: Added eff. Sept. 17, 1965, oper. Jan. 1, 1967, Stats. 1965, ch. 299, §2. Amended eff. Jan. 1, 1976, Stats. 1975, ch. 1244, §12.

Official Comment

7 Cal. Law Revision Comm'n Rep. (1965) p. 1090.

Section 605 describes a presumption affecting the burden of proof. Such presumptions are established in order to carry out or to effectuate some public policy other than or in addition to the policy of facilitating the trial of actions.

Frequently, presumptions affecting the burden of proof are designed to facilitate determination of the action in which they are applied. Superficially, therefore, such presumptions may appear merely to be presumptions affecting the burden of producing evidence. What makes a presumption one affecting the burden of proof is the fact that there is always some further reason of policy for the establishment of the presumption. It is the existence of this further basis in policy that distinguishes a presumption affecting the burden of proof from a presumption affecting the burden of producing evidence. For example, the presumption of death from seven years' absence (Section 667) exists in part to facilitate the disposition of actions by supplying a rule of thumb to govern certain cases in which there is likely to be no direct evidence of the presumed fact. But the policy in favor of distributing estates, of settling titles, and of permitting life to proceed normally at some time prior to the expiration of the absentee's normal life expectancy (perhaps 30 or 40 years) that underlies the presumption indicates that it should be a presumption affecting the burden of proof.

Frequently, too, a presumption affecting the burden of proof will have an underlying basis in probability and logical inference. For example, the presumption of the validity of a ceremonial marriage may be based in part on the probability that most marriages are valid. However, an underlying logical inference is not essential. In fact, the lack of an underlying inference is a strong indication that the presumption affects the burden of proof. Only the needs of public policy can justify the direction of a particular assumption that is not warranted by the application of probability and common experience to the known facts. Thus, the total lack of any inference underlying the presumption of the negligence of an employer that arises from his failure to secure the payment of workmen's compensation (Labor Code §3708) is a clear indication that the presumption is based on public policy and affects the burden of proof. Similarly, the fact that the presumption of death from seven years' absence may conflict directly with the logical inference that life continues for its normal expectancy is an indication that the presumption is based on public policy and, hence, affects the burden of proof.

ANNOTATIONS

Fisher v. City of Berkeley (1984) 37 Cal.3d 644, 695, *aff'd*, (1986) 475 U.S. 260. "The burden of proof ... refers to a party's obligation to establish by evidence a requisite degree of belief concerning a fact in the mind of the trier of fact. ... '[F]requently, presumptions affecting the burden of proof are designed to facilitate determination of the action in which they are applied. Superficially, therefore, such presumptions may appear merely to be presumptions affecting the burden of producing evidence. What makes a presumption one affecting the burden of proof is the fact that there is always some further reason of policy for the establishment of the presumption. It is the existence of this further basis in policy that distinguishes a presumption affecting the burden of proof from a presumption affecting the burden of producing evidence.'" *See also* ***Estate of Trikha*** (4th Dist.2013) 219 Cal.App.4th 791, 803-04.

Pruyn v. Agricultural Ins. (2d Dist.1995) 36 Cal.App.4th 500, 529. "[P]resumptions backed by policy

concerns are justifiably given greater weight under our state's scheme. Certainly if a presumption is not based on probability, but is based solely on social policy, there may be more, and not less, reason to preserve it in the face of contrary proof. A presumption based on social policy may need an extra boost to ensure that the policy is not overlooked in the face of some explanation given by the opponent." (Internal quotes omitted.) *See also* ***Xebec Dev. Partners v. National Un. Fire Ins.*** (6th Dist.1993) 12 Cal.App.4th 501, 548, *disapproved on other grounds, **Essex Ins. v. Five Star Dye House, Inc.*** (2006) 38 Cal.4th 1252.

§606. [EFFECT OF PRESUMPTION ON BURDEN OF PROOF]

The effect of a presumption affecting the burden of proof is to impose upon the party against whom it operates the burden of proof as to the nonexistence of the presumed fact.

History of Evid. C. §606: Added eff. Sept. 17, 1965, oper. Jan. 1, 1967, Stats. 1965, ch. 299, §2.

Official Comment

7 Cal. Law Revision Comm'n Rep. (1965) p. 1091; Assem. J., Apr. 6, 1965, p. 1736.

Section 606 describes the manner in which a presumption affecting the burden of proof operates. In the ordinary case, the party against whom it is invoked will have the burden of proving the nonexistence of the presumed fact by a preponderance of the evidence. Certain presumptions affecting the burden of proof may be overcome only by clear and convincing proof. When such a presumption is relied on, the party against whom the presumption operates will have a heavier burden of proof and will be required to persuade the trier of fact of the nonexistence of the presumed fact by proof "'sufficiently strong to command the unhesitating assent of every reasonable mind.'" *Sheehan v. Sullivan*, 126 Cal. 189, 193, 58 Pac. 543, 544 (1899).

If the party against whom the presumption operates already has the same burden of proof as to the nonexistence of the presumed fact that is assigned by the presumption, the presumption can have no effect on the case and no instruction in regard to the presumption should be given. *See Speck v. Sarver*, 20 Cal.2d 585, 590, 128 P.2d 16, 19 (1942) (dissenting opinion by Traynor, J.); Morgan, *Instructing the Jury Upon Presumptions and Burden of Proof*, 47 Harv.L.Rev. 59, 69 (1933). If the evidence is not sufficient to sustain a finding of the nonexistence of the presumed fact, the judge's instructions will be the same as if the presumption were merely a presumption affecting the burden of producing evidence. *See* the *Comment* to Section 604. If there is evidence of the nonexistence of the presumed fact, the judge should instruct the jury on the manner in which the presumption affects the factfinding process. If the basic fact from which the presumption arises is so established that the existence of the basic fact is not a question of fact for the jury (as, for example, by the pleadings, by judicial notice, or by stipulation of the parties), the judge should instruct the jury that the existence of the presumed fact is to be assumed until the jury is persuaded to the contrary by the requisite degree of proof (proof by a preponderance of the evidence, clear and convincing proof, etc.). *See* McCormick, *Evidence* §317 at 672 (1954). If the basic fact is a question of fact for the jury, the judge should instruct the jury that, if it finds the basic fact, it must also find the presumed fact unless persuaded of the nonexistence of the presumed fact by the requisite degree of proof. Morgan, *Basic Problems of Evidence* 38 (1957).

In a criminal case, a presumption affecting the burden of proof may be relied upon by the prosecution *to establish an element of the crime* with which the defendant is charged. The effect of the presumption on the factfinding process and the nature of the instructions in such a case are described in Section 607 and the *Comment* thereto. On other issues, a presumption affecting the burden of proof will have the same effect in a criminal case as it does in a civil case, and the instructions will be the same.

§607. [EFFECT OF PRESUMPTION ON BURDEN OF PROOF IN CRIMINAL ACTIONS]

When a presumption affecting the burden of proof operates in a criminal action to establish presumptively any fact that is essential to the defendant's guilt, the presumption operates only if the facts that give rise to the presumption have been found or otherwise established beyond a reasonable doubt and, in such case, the defendant need only raise a reasonable doubt as to the existence of the presumed fact.

History of Evid. C. §607: Added eff. Sept. 17, 1965, oper. Jan. 1, 1967, Stats. 1965, ch. 299, §2.

Official Comment

7 Cal. Law Revision Comm'n Rep. (1965) p. 1092; Assem. J., Apr. 6, 1965, p. 1737.

If a presumption affecting the burden of proof is relied upon by the prosecution in a criminal case to establish a fact essential to the defendant's guilt, the defendant will not be required to overcome the presumption by clear and convincing evidence or even by a preponderance of the evidence; the defendant will be required merely to raise a reasonable doubt as to the existence of the presumed fact. This is the effect of a presumption in a criminal case under existing law. *People v. Hardy*, 33 Cal.2d 52, 198 P.2d 865 (1948); *People v. Scott*, 24 Cal.2d 774, 151 P.2d 517 (1944); *People v. Agnew*, 16 Cal.2d 655, 107 P.2d 601 (1940).

Instructions in criminal cases on presumptions affecting the burden of proof will be similar to the instructions given on presumptions and on issues where the defendant has the burden of proof under existing law. Where no evidence has been introduced to show the nonexistence of the presumed fact, the court should instruct the jury that, if it finds beyond a reasonable doubt the facts giving rise to the presumption, it should also find the presumed fact. Where some evidence of the nonexistence of the presumed fact has been introduced, the court should instruct the jury that, if it finds beyond a reasonable doubt the facts giving rise to the presumption, it should also find the presumed fact unless the contrary evidence has raised a reasonable doubt as to the existence of the presumed fact. *Cf. People v. Hardy*, 33 Cal.2d 52, 63-64, 198 P.2d 865, 871-872 (1948); *People v. Agnew*, 16 Cal.2d 655, 661-667, 107 P.2d 601, 603-607 (1940); *People v. Martina*, 140 Cal.App.2d 17, 25, 294 P.2d 1015, 1019 (1956). The judge must be careful to specify that a presumption is rebutted by any evidence that raises a reasonable doubt as to the presumed fact. In the absence of this qualification, the jury may be led to believe that the defendant has the burden of disproof of the presumed fact by a preponderance of the evidence and the instruction will be erroneous. *People v. Agnew*, 16 Cal.2d 655, 107 P.2d 601 (1940). *Cf. People v. Hardy*, 33 Cal.2d 52, 198 P.2d 865 (1948).

Of course, in a criminal case, the jury may choose to disregard the instructions relating to presumptions. But this should not affect the duty of the court to instruct the jury on the rules of law, including presumptions, applicable to the case. *See* the *Comment* to Section 604.

Section 607 does not apply to the "presumption" of sanity. Under the Evidence Code, the burden of proof on the issue of sanity is allocated by Section 522, and there is no "presumption" of sanity. *See* Evidence Code §522 and the *Comment* thereto. Hence, notwithstanding the provisions of Section 607, a defendant who pleads insanity has the burden of proving by a preponderance of the evidence that he was insane. *See* the *Comment* to Section 501.

ARTICLE 2. CONCLUSIVE PRESUMPTIONS

§620. [CONCLUSIVE PRESUMPTIONS]

The presumptions established by this article, and all other presumptions declared by law to be conclusive, are conclusive presumptions.

History of Evid. C. §620: Added eff. Sept. 17, 1965, oper. Jan. 1, 1967, Stats. 1965, ch. 299, §2.

Official Comment

7 Cal. Law Revision Comm'n Rep. (1965) p. 1093.

This article supersedes and continues in effect without substantive change the provisions of subdivisions 2, 3, 4, and 5 of Section 1962 of the Code of Civil Procedure. Other statutes not listed in this article also provide conclusive presumptions. *See, e.g.*, Civil Code §3440. There may also be a few nonstatutory conclusive presumptions. *See* Witkin, *California Evidence* §63 (1958).

Conclusive presumptions are not evidentiary rules so much as they are rules of substantive law. Hence, the Commission has not recommended any substantive revision of the conclusive presumptions contained in this article.

ANNOTATIONS

Grisham v. Philip Morris U.S.A., Inc. (2007) 40 Cal.4th 623, 635. "Conclusive presumptions are not evidentiary rules so much as they are rules of substantive law." (Internal quotes omitted.)

§621. REPEALED

Repealed oper. Jan. 1, 1994, Stats. 1992, ch. 162, §8.

§621.1. REPEALED

Repealed oper. Jan. 1, 1994, Stats. 1993, ch. 219, §76.

§622. [PRESUMPTION IN WRITTEN INSTRUMENTS]

The facts recited in a written instrument are conclusively presumed to be true as between the parties thereto, or their successors in interest; but this rule does not apply to the recital of a consideration.

History of Evid. C. §622: Added eff. Sept. 17, 1965, oper. Jan. 1, 1967, Stats. 1965, ch. 299, §2.

Official Comment

7 Cal. Law Revision Comm'n Rep. (1965) p. 1094.

Section 622 restates and supersedes subdivision 2 of Code of Civil Procedure Section 1962.

ANNOTATIONS

Citizens Bus. Bank v. Gevorgian (2d Dist.2013) 218 Cal.App.4th 602, 625. Section 622 "is based upon the doctrine of estoppel by contract; i.e., a party to a contract is generally estopped to deny essential facts recited therein. [T]he presumption applies as between the parties to written instruments but not to persons who are not parties to the instrument. [¶] [S]ection 622 does not bar an assertion of fraud or other grounds for rescission of a contract or to recitals in an adhesion contract." (Internal quotes omitted.)

Quintanilla v. Dunkelman (2d Dist.2005) 133 Cal.App.4th 95, 117. "While ... §622 has been applied to documents other than contracts, such as a transfer of property ... and an estoppel certificate ..., the argument that recitals in an instrument conclusively establish informed consent is inconsistent with the rationale supporting the informed consent doctrine."

§623. [ESTOPPEL BY STATEMENT OR CONDUCT]

Whenever a party has, by his own statement or conduct, intentionally and deliberately led another to believe a particular thing true and to act upon such belief, he is not, in any litigation arising out of such statement or conduct, permitted to contradict it.

History of Evid. C. §623: Added eff. Sept. 17, 1965, oper. Jan. 1, 1967, Stats. 1965, ch. 299, §2.

Official Comment

7 Cal. Law Revision Comm'n Rep. (1965) p. 1094.

Section 623 restates and supersedes subdivision 3 of Code of Civil Procedure Section 1962.

ANNOTATIONS

Lantzy v. Centex Homes (2003) 31 Cal.4th 363, 384. "[A]n estoppel may arise although there was no designed fraud on the part of the person sought to be estopped. To create an equitable estoppel, it is enough if the party has been induced to refrain from using such means or taking such action as lay in his power, by which he might have retrieved his position and saved himself from loss. Where the delay in commencing action is induced by the conduct of the defendant it cannot be availed of by him as a defense." (Internal quotes omitted.)

State Comp. Ins. Fund v. Workers' Comp. Appeals Bd. (1985) 40 Cal.3d 5, 16. "The essence of an estoppel is that the party to be estopped has by false language or conduct 'led another to do that which he would not otherwise have done and as a result thereof that he has suffered injury.' The existence of an estoppel is generally a question of fact, and the party relying on the estoppel must prove all of the elements." ***See also In re Marriage of Left*** (2d Dist.2012) 208 Cal.App.4th 1137, 1149.

Minish v. Hanuman Fellowship (6th Dist.2013) 214 Cal.App.4th 437, 459. "The elements of the doctrine [of equitable estoppel] are that (1) the party to be estopped must be apprised of the facts; (2) he must intend that his conduct shall be acted upon, or must so act that the party asserting the estoppel has a right to believe it was so intended; (3) the other party must be ignorant of the true state of facts; and (4) he must rely upon the conduct to his injury. [¶] The general rule is that estoppel must be specifically pleaded in the complaint with sufficient accuracy to disclose facts relied upon. [¶] [Ds] did not plead equitable estoppel as an affirmative defense or otherwise plead the facts necessary to establish it." (Internal quotes omitted.)

§624. [ESTOPPEL OF TENANT]

A tenant is not permitted to deny the title of his landlord at the time of the commencement of the relation.

History of Evid. C. §624: Added eff. Sept. 17, 1965, oper. Jan. 1, 1967, Stats. 1965, ch. 299, §2.

Official Comment

7 Cal. Law Revision Comm'n Rep. (1965) p. 1094.

Section 624 restates and supersedes subdivision 4 of Code of Civil Procedure Section 1962.

ARTICLE 3. PRESUMPTIONS AFFECTING THE BURDEN OF PRODUCING EVIDENCE

§630. [SCOPE]

The presumptions established by this article, and all other rebuttable presumptions established by law that fall within the criteria of Section 603, are presumptions affecting the burden of producing evidence.

History of Evid. C. §630: Added eff. Sept. 17, 1965, oper. Jan. 1, 1967, Stats. 1965, ch. 299, §2.

Official Comment

7 Cal. Law Revision Comm'n Rep. (1965) p. 1094.

Article 3 sets forth a list of presumptions, recognized in existing law, that are classified here as presumptions affecting the burden of producing evidence. The list is not exhaustive. Other presumptions affecting the burden of producing evidence may be found in other codes. Others will be found in the common law. Specific statutes will classify some of these, but some must await classification by the courts. The list here, however, will eliminate any uncertainty as to the proper classification for the presumptions in this article.

§631. [PRESUMPTION OF MONEY DUE]

Money delivered by one to another is presumed to have been due to the latter.

History of Evid. C. §631: Added eff. Sept. 17, 1965, oper. Jan. 1, 1967, Stats. 1965, ch. 299, §2.

Official Comment

7 Cal. Law Revision Comm'n Rep. (1965) p. 1095.

Section 631 restates and supersedes the presumption in subdivision 7 of Code of Civil Procedure Section 1963.

§632. [PRESUMPTION OF OWNERSHIP BY DELIVERY OF THING]

A thing delivered by one to another is presumed to have belonged to the latter.

History of Evid. C. §632: Added eff. Sept. 17, 1965, oper. Jan. 1, 1967, Stats. 1965, ch. 299, §2.

Official Comment

7 Cal. Law Revision Comm'n Rep. (1965) p. 1095.

Section 632 restates and supersedes the presumption in subdivision 8 of Code of Civil Procedure Section 1963.

§633. [PRESUMPTION OF PAYMENT OF DEBT]

An obligation delivered up to the debtor is presumed to have been paid.

History of Evid. C. §633: Added eff. Sept. 17, 1965, oper. Jan. 1, 1967, Stats. 1965, ch. 299, §2.

Official Comment

7 Cal. Law Revision Comm'n Rep. (1965) p. 1095.

Section 633 restates and supersedes the presumption in subdivision 9 of Code of Civil Procedure Section 1963.

§634. [PRESUMPTION OF ORDER FOR PAYMENT OR DELIVERY]

A person in possession of an order on himself for the payment of money, or delivery of a thing, is presumed to have paid the money or delivered the thing accordingly.

History of Evid. C. §634: Added eff. Sept. 17, 1965, oper. Jan. 1, 1967, Stats. 1965, ch. 299, §2.

Official Comment

7 Cal. Law Revision Comm'n Rep. (1965) p. 1095.

Section 634 restates and supersedes the presumption found in subdivision 13 of Code of Civil Procedure Section 1963.

§635. [PRESUMPTION OF UNPAID DEBT]

An obligation possessed by the creditor is presumed not to have been paid.

History of Evid. C. §635: Added eff. Sept. 17, 1965, oper. Jan. 1, 1967, Stats. 1965, ch. 299, §2.

Official Comment

7 Cal. Law Revision Comm'n Rep. (1965) p. 1096.

The presumption in Section 635 is a common law presumption recognized in the California cases. *E.g.*, *Light v. Stevens*, 159 Cal. 288, 113 Pac. 659 (1911).

ANNOTATIONS

Remington Invs. v. Hamedani (2d Dist.1997) 55 Cal.App.4th 1033, 1041-42. "Normally, a promissory note is given to a lender contemporaneously with the borrower's receipt of the face amount of the note. When a promissory note is paid, the note is normally cancelled. Thus when the lender holds an uncancelled promissory note, truth favors the conclusion that the borrower received the money and did not repay the note. The law thus creates a presumption in favor of this conclusion. The burden then shifts to the borrower to rebut the presumption either by proving payment, or by proving that the face amount of the note was never advanced. [¶] The presumption of nonpayment appears based to some extent on the negotiability of an unconditional promissory note, and to some extent on the simple inadvisability of repaying a note without receiving cancellation of the note. If a note is unconditional and therefore negotiable, the uncancelled note could be sold to a holder in due course, who could then enforce it against the maker of the note. Even if the note is not sold to a holder in due course, the borrower may be faced with the appearance of an outstanding debt in the hands of the lender or its successors if a promissory note is not cancelled after payment."

§636. [PRESUMPTION OF RENT PAYMENT]

The payment of earlier rent or installments is presumed from a receipt for later rent or installments.

History of Evid. C. §636: Added eff. Sept. 17, 1965, oper. Jan. 1, 1967, Stats. 1965, ch. 299, §2.

Official Comment

7 Cal. Law Revision Comm'n Rep. (1965) p. 1096.

Section 636 restates and supersedes the presumption in subdivision 10 of Code of Civil Procedure Section 1963.

§637. [PRESUMPTION OF OWNERSHIP BY POSSESSION]

The things which a person possesses are presumed to be owned by him.

History of Evid. C. §637: Added eff. Sept. 17, 1965, oper. Jan. 1, 1967, Stats. 1965, ch. 299, §2.

Official Comment

7 Cal. Law Revision Comm'n Rep. (1965) p. 1096.

Section 637 restates and supersedes the presumption found in subdivision 11 of Code of Civil Procedure Section 1963.

ANNOTATIONS

Hoffman v. Connell (1st Dist.1999) 73 Cal.App.4th 1194, 1200. "The concept of ownership refers not to a single right, but a collection of legal rights to use and enjoy property. There are several indicia of ownership. Title is one. Possession is another. The right to transfer ... and exercise control over property are also indicia of ownership."

§638. [PRESUMPTION OF OWNERSHIP BY ACTION]

A person who exercises acts of ownership over property is presumed to be the owner of it.

History of Evid. C. §638: Added eff. Sept. 17, 1965, oper. Jan. 1, 1967, Stats. 1965, ch. 299, §2.

Official Comment

7 Cal. Law Revision Comm'n Rep. (1965) p. 1096.

Section 638 restates and supersedes the presumption found in subdivision 12 of Code of Civil Procedure Section 1963. Subdivision 12 of Code of Civil Procedure Section 1963 provides that a presumption of ownership arises from common reputation of ownership. This is inaccurate, however, for common reputation is not admissible to prove private title to property. *Berniaud v. Beecher*, 76 Cal. 394, 18 Pac. 598 (1888); *Simons v. Inyo Cerro Gordo Co.*, 48 Cal. App. 524, 192 Pac. 144 (1920).

§639. [PRESUMPTION OF JUDGMENT]

A judgment, when not conclusive, is presumed to correctly determine or set forth the rights of the parties, but there is no presumption that the facts essential to the judgment have been correctly determined.

History of Evid. C. §639: Added eff. Sept. 17, 1965, oper. Jan. 1, 1967, Stats. 1965, ch. 299, §2.

Official Comment

7 Cal. Law Revision Comm'n Rep. (1965) p. 1097.

Section 639 restates and supersedes the presumption found in subdivision 17 of Code of Civil Procedure Section 1963. The presumption involved here is that the judgment correctly determines that one party owes another money, or that the parties are divorced, or their marriage has been annulled, or any similar rights of the parties. The presumption does not apply to the facts underlying the judgment. For example, a judgment of annulment is presumed to determine correctly that the marriage is void. *Clark v. City of Los Angeles*, 187 Cal.App.2d 792, 9 Cal.Rptr. 913 (1960). However, the judgment may not be used to establish presumptively that one of the parties was guilty of fraud as against some third party who is not bound by the judgment.

In a few cases, a judgment may be used as evidence of the facts necessarily determined by the judgment. *See, e.g.*, Evidence Code §§1300-1302. But, even in those cases, the judgments do not presumptively establish the facts determined; they are merely evidence.

§640. [PRESUMPTION OF DATE OF WRITING]

A writing is presumed to have been truly dated.

History of Evid. C. §640: Added eff. Sept. 17, 1965, oper. Jan. 1, 1967, Stats. 1965, ch. 299, §2.

Official Comment

7 Cal. Law Revision Comm'n Rep. (1965) p. 1097.

Section 640 restates and supersedes the presumption in subdivision 23 of Code of Civil Procedure Section 1963.

§641. [PRESUMPTION OF RECEIPT]

A letter correctly addressed and properly mailed is presumed to have been received in the ordinary course of mail.

History of Evid. C. §641: Added eff. Sept. 17, 1965, oper. Jan. 1, 1967, Stats. 1965, ch. 299, §2.

Official Comment

7 Cal. Law Revision Comm'n Rep. (1965) p. 1097.

Section 641 restates and supersedes the presumption in subdivision 24 of Code of Civil Procedure Section 1963.

ANNOTATIONS

Consumer Watchdog v. Department of Managed Health Care (2d Dist.2014) 225 Cal.App.4th 862, 884. Evid. C. §641 "has 'no application to the filing of a notice of appeal.'"

Colleen M. v. Fertility & Surgical Assocs. (2d Dist.2005) 132 Cal.App.4th 1466, 1479-80. "The proof of service of the subpoena and notice on [P's] attorney states the documents were deposited in the U.S. mail, in a sealed envelope with postage fully prepaid addressed to [P's] attorney at his office.... This declaration created a rebuttable presumption the documents were received at the attorney's office in the ordinary course of mail. [¶] The effect of this presumption is to require the trier of fact to assume the documents were received by [P's] attorney unless evidence is introduced which would support a contrary finding. The attorney's weasel worded testimony he was never 'made aware' of the subpoena and notice of right to object

would not support a finding by the trier of fact the documents were not received at the attorney's office. Without at least some evidence of the mail handling and routing procedures in the office the fact the attorney was never aware of the documents does not rebut the presumption they were received."

Bonzer v. City of Huntington Park (2d Dist.1993) 20 Cal.App.4th 1474, 1478. "The only evidence that any [D] had actually received notice of the ... hearing was a 'proof of service' declaration executed by an employee of counsel for [P]. The declarant, pursuant to [CCP] §1013a, subdivision (3), did *not* attest to actually mailing the notices or to having personal knowledge they were mailed. Rather, the declarant stated she was familiar 'with the firm's practice of collection and processing correspondence for mailing' and '[u]nder that practice it *would be* deposited with U.S. Postal service ... in the ordinary course of business.' *At 1479:* Pursuant to [Evid. C.] §641 ... this declaration created a rebuttable presumption the notice had been received in the ordinary course of mail. *At 1481:* Upon presentation of [Ds'] detailed, credible, and unimpeached evidence of no actual notice—the *presumption* of such notice ... ceased to exist. The only remaining effect of the 'Proof of Service' declaration was to enable the trial court to draw 'any inference that may be *appropriate*.' [¶] Any inference, in the face of [Ds'] declarations, that the subject notices were actually received is, as a matter of law, *inappropriate*."

§642. [PRESUMPTION OF REAL-PROPERTY CONVEYANCE]

A trustee or other person, whose duty it was to convey real property to a particular person, is presumed to have actually conveyed to him when such presumption is necessary to perfect title of such person or his successor in interest.

History of Evid. C. §642: Added eff. Sept. 17, 1965, oper. Jan. 1, 1967, Stats. 1965, ch. 299, §2.

Official Comment

7 Cal. Law Revision Comm'n Rep. (1965) p. 1097.

Section 642 restates and supersedes the presumption in subdivision 37 of Code of Civil Procedure Section 1963.

§643. [PRESUMPTION OF AUTHENTICITY OF ANCIENT DOCUMENT]

A deed or will or other writing purporting to create, terminate, or affect an interest in real or personal property is presumed to be authentic if it:

(a) Is at least 30 years old;

(b) Is in such condition as to create no suspicion concerning its authenticity;

(c) Was kept, or if found was found, in a place where such writing, if authentic, would be likely to be kept or found; and

(d) Has been generally acted upon as authentic by persons having an interest in the matter.

History of Evid. C. §643: Added eff. Sept. 17, 1965, oper. Jan. 1, 1967, Stats. 1965, ch. 299, §2.

Official Comment

7 Cal. Law Revision Comm'n Rep. (1965) p. 1098.

Section 643 restates and supersedes the presumption found in subdivision 34 of Code of Civil Procedure Section 1963. Although the statement of the ancient documents rule in Section 1963 requires the document to have been acted upon as if genuine before the presumption applies, some recent cases have not insisted upon this requirement. *Estate of Nidever*, 181 Cal.App.2d 367, 5 Cal.Rptr. 343 (1960); *Kirkpatrick v. Tapo Oil Co.*, 144 Cal.App.2d 404, 301 P.2d 274 (1956). The requirement that the document be acted upon as genuine is, in substance, a requirement of the possession of property by those persons who would be entitled to such possession under the document if it were genuine. *See* 7 Wigmore, *Evidence* §§2141, 2146 (3d ed. 1940); *Tentative Recommendation and a Study Relating to the Uniform Rules of Evidence (Article IX. Authentication and Content of Writings)*, 6 Cal. Law Revision Comm'n, Rep., Rec. & Studies 101, 135-137 (1964). Giving the ancient documents rule a presumptive effect—*i.e.*, *requiring* a finding of the authenticity of an ancient document—seems justified when it is a dispositive instrument and the persons interested in the matter have acted upon the instrument for a period of at least 30 years as if it were genuine. Evidence which is not of this strength may be sufficient in particular cases to warrant an inference of genuineness and thus justify the admission of the document into evidence, but the presumption should be confined to those cases where the evidence of genuineness is not likely to be disputed. *See* 7 Wigmore, *Evidence* §2146 (3d ed. 1940). Accordingly, Section 643 limits the presumptive application of the ancient documents rule to dispositive instruments.

§644. [PRESUMPTION OF PUBLICATION BY PUBLIC AUTHORITY]

A book, purporting to be printed or published by public authority, is presumed to have been so printed or published.

History of Evid. C. §644: Added eff. Sept. 17, 1965, oper. Jan. 1, 1967, Stats. 1965, ch. 299, §2.

Official Comment

7 Cal. Law Revision Comm'n Rep. (1965) p. 1099.

Section 644 restates and supersedes the presumption in subdivision 35 of Code of Civil Procedure Section 1963.

§645. [PRESUMPTION OF CASE REPORTERS]

A book, purporting to contain reports of cases adjudged in the tribunals of the state or nation where the book is published, is presumed to contain correct reports of such cases.

History of Evid. C. §645: Added eff. Sept. 17, 1965, oper. Jan. 1, 1967, Stats. 1965, ch. 299, §2.

Official Comment

7 Cal. Law Revision Comm'n Rep. (1965) p. 1099.

Section 645 restates and supersedes the presumption found in subdivision 36 of Code of Civil Procedure Section 1963.

§645.1. [PRESUMPTION OF NEWSPAPER]

Printed materials, purporting to be a particular newspaper or periodical, are presumed to be that newspaper or periodical if regularly issued at average intervals not exceeding three months.

History of Evid. C. §645.1: Added eff. Jan. 1, 1987, Stats. 1986, ch. 330, §1.

§646. [PRESUMPTION OF RES IPSA LOQUITUR]

(a) [Defendant.] As used in this section, "defendant" includes any party against whom the res ipsa loquitur presumption operates.

(b) [Common-law doctrine.] The judicial doctrine of res ipsa loquitur is a presumption affecting the burden of producing evidence.

(c) [Jury instruction on rebutting evidence.] If the evidence, or facts otherwise established, would support a res ipsa loquitur presumption and the defendant has introduced evidence which would support a finding that he was not negligent or that any negligence on his part was not a proximate cause of the occurrence, the court may, and upon request shall, instruct the jury to the effect that:

(1) [Inference of negligence.] If the facts which would give rise to res ipsa loquitur presumption are found or otherwise established, the jury may draw the inference from such facts that a proximate cause of the occurrence was some negligent conduct on the part of the defendant; and

(2) [More probable than not.] The jury shall not find that a proximate cause of the occurrence was some negligent conduct on the part of the defendant unless the jury believes, after weighing all the evidence in the case and drawing such inferences therefrom as the jury believes are warranted, that it is more probable than not that the occurrence was caused by some negligent conduct on the part of the defendant.

History of Evid. C. §646: Added eff. Nov. 23, 1970, Stats. 1970, ch. 69, §1.

Official Comment

8 Cal. Law Revision Comm'n Rep. (1967) p. 114.

Section 646 is designed to clarify the manner in which the doctrine of res ipsa loquitur functions under the provisions of the Evidence Code relating to presumptions.

The doctrine of res ipsa loquitur, as developed by the California courts, is applicable in an action to recover damages for negligence when the plaintiff establishes three conditions:

First, that it is the kind of [accident] [injury] which ordinarily does not occur in the absence of someone's negligence;

Second, that it was caused by an agency or instrumentality in the exclusive control of the defendant [originally, and which was not mishandled or otherwise changed after defendant relinquished control]; and

Third, that the [accident] [injury] was not due to any voluntary action or contribution on the part of the plaintiff which was the responsible cause of his injury [BAJI (5th ed. 1969) No. 4.00 (brackets in original)].

Section 646 provides that the doctrine of res ipsa loquitur is a presumption affecting the burden of producing evidence. Therefore, when the plaintiff has established the three conditions that give rise to the doctrine, the jury is required to find that the accident resulted from the defendant's negligence unless the defendant comes forward with evidence that would support a contrary finding. Evidence Code §604. If evidence is produced that would support a finding that the defendant was not negligent or that any negligence on his part was not a proximate cause of the accident, the presumptive effect of the doctrine vanishes. However, the jury may still be able to draw an inference that the accident was caused by the defendant's lack of due care from the facts that gave rise to the presumption. *See* Evidence Code §604 and the *Comment* thereto. In rare cases, the defendant may produce such conclusive evidence that the inference of negligence is dispelled as a matter of law. *See, e.g.*, *Leonard v. Watsonville Community Hosp.*, 47 Cal.2d 509, 305 P.2d 36 (1956). But, except in such a case, the facts giving rise to the doctrine will support an inference of negligence even after its presumptive effect has disappeared.

To assist the jury in the performance of its factfinding function, the court may instruct that the facts that give rise to res ipsa loquitur are themselves circumstantial evidence from which the jury can infer that the accident resulted from the defendant's failure to exercise due care. Section 646 requires the court to give such an instruction when a party so requests. Whether the jury should so find will depend on whether the jury believes that the probative force of the circumstantial and other evidence of the defendant's negligence exceeds the probative force of the contrary evidence and, therefore, that it is more probable than not that the accident resulted from the defendant's negligence.

At times the doctrine of res ipsa loquitur will coincide in a particular case with another presumption or with another rule of law that requires the defendant to discharge the burden of proof on the issue. *See* Prosser, *Res Ipsa Loquitur in California*, 37 Cal.L.Rev. 183 (1949). In such cases the defendant will have the burden of proof on issues where res ipsa loquitur appears to apply. But because of the allocation of the burden of proof to the defendant, the doctrine of res ipsa loquitur will serve no function in the disposition of the case. However, the facts that would give rise to the doctrine may nevertheless be used as circumstantial evidence tending to rebut the evidence produced by the party with the burden of proof.

For example, a bailee who has received undamaged goods and returns damaged goods has the burden of proving that the damage was not caused by his negligence unless the damage resulted from a fire. *See* discussion in *Redfoot v. J.T. Jenkins Co.*, 138 Cal.App.2d 108, 112, 291 P.2d 134 (1955). *See* Comm. Code §7403(1)(b). When the defendant has produced evidence of his exercise of care in regard to the bailed goods, the facts that would give rise to the doctrine of res ipsa loquitur may be weighed against the evidence produced by the defendant in determining whether it is more likely than not that the goods were damaged without fault on the part of the bailee. But because the bailee has both the burden of producing evidence and the burden of proving that the damage was not caused by his negligence, the presumption of negligence arising from res ipsa loquitur cannot have any effect on the proceeding.

Effect of the Failure of the Plaintiff to Establish All the Preliminary Facts That Give Rise to the Presumption

The fact that the plaintiff fails to establish all of the facts giving rise to the res ipsa presumption does not necessarily mean that he has not produced sufficient evidence of negligence to sustain a jury finding in his favor. The requirements of res ipsa loquitur are merely those that must be met to give rise to a compelled conclusion (or presumption) of negligence in the absence of contrary evidence. An inference of negligence may well be warranted from all of the evidence in the case even though the plaintiff fails to establish all the elements of res ipsa loquitur. *See* Prosser, *Res Ipsa Loquitur: A Reply to Professor Carpenter*, 10 So.Cal.L.Rev. 459 (1937). In appropriate cases, therefore, the jury may be instructed that, even though it does not find that the facts giving rise to the presumption have been proved by a preponderance of the evidence, it may nevertheless find the defendant negligent if it concludes from a consideration of all the evidence that it is more probable than not that the defendant was negligent. Such an instruction would be appropriate, for example, in a case where there was evidence of the defendant's negligence apart from the evidence going to the elements of the res ipsa loquitur doctrine.

Examples of Operation of Res Ipsa Loquitur Presumption

The doctrine of res ipsa loquitur may be applicable to a case under four varying sets of circumstances:

(1) Where the facts giving rise to the doctrine are established as a matter of law (by the pleadings, by stipulation, by pretrial order, or by some other means) and there is no evidence sufficient to sustain a finding either that the accident resulted from some cause other than the defendant's negligence or that he exercised due care in all possible respects wherein he might have been negligent.

(2) Where the facts giving rise to the doctrine are established as a matter of law, but the defendant has introduced evidence sufficient to sustain a finding either of his due care or of some cause for the accident other than his negligence.

(3) Where the defendant introduces evidence tending to show the nonexistence of the essential conditions of the doctrine but does not introduce evidence to rebut the presumption.

(4) Where the defendant introduces evidence to contest both the conditions of the doctrine and the conclusion that his negligence caused the accident.

Set forth below is an explanation of the manner in which Section 646 functions in each of these situations.

Basic facts established as a matter of law; no rebuttal evidence. If the basic facts that give rise to the presumption are established as a matter of law (*e.g.*, by the pleadings, by stipulation, by pretrial order), the presumption requires that the jury find that the defendant's negligence was the proximate cause of the accident unless evidence is introduced sufficient to sustain a finding either that the accident resulted from some cause other than the defendant's negligence or that he exercised due care in all possible respects wherein he might have been negligent. When the defendant fails to introduce such evidence, the court must simply instruct the jury that it is required to find that the accident was caused by the defendant's negligence.

For example, if a plaintiff automobile passenger sues the driver for injuries sustained in an accident, the defendant may determine not to contest the fact that the accident was of a type that ordinarily does not occur unless the driver was negligent. Moreover, the defendant may introduce no evidence that he exercised due care in the driving of the automobile. Instead, the defendant may rest his defense solely on the ground that the plaintiff was a guest and not a paying passenger. In this case, the court should instruct the jury that it must assume that the defendant was negligent. *Cf. Phillips v. Noble*, 50 Cal.2d 163, 323 P.2d 385 (1958); *Fiske v. Wilkie*, 67 Cal.App.2d 440, 154 P.2d 725 (1945).

Basic facts established as matter of law; evidence introduced to rebut presumption. Where the facts giving rise to the doctrine are established as a matter of law but the defendant has introduced evidence sufficient to sustain a finding either of his due care or of a cause for the accident other than his negligence, the presumptive effect of the doctrine vanishes. Except in those rare cases where the inference is dispelled as a matter of law, the court may instruct the jury that it may infer from the established facts that negligence on the part of the defendant was a proximate cause of the accident. The court is required to give such an instruction when requested. The instruction should make it clear, however, that the jury should not find that a proximate cause of the occurrence was some negligent conduct on the part of the defendant unless the jury believes, after weighing all the evidence in the case, that it is more probable than not that the accident was caused by the defendant's negligence.

Basic facts contested; no rebuttal evidence. The defendant may attack only the elements of the doctrine. His purpose in doing so would be to prevent the application of the doctrine. In this situation, the court cannot determine whether the doctrine is applicable or not because the basic facts that give rise to the doctrine must be determined by the jury. Therefore, the court must give an instruction on what has become known as conditional res ipsa loquitur.

Where the basic facts are contested by evidence, but there is no rebuttal evidence, the court should instruct the jury that, if it finds that the basic facts have been established by a preponderance of the evidence, then it must also find that the accident was caused by some negligent conduct on the part of the defendant.

Basic facts contested; evidence introduced to rebut presumption. The defendant may introduce evidence that both attacks the basic facts that underlie the doctrine of res ipsa loquitur and tends to show that the accident was not caused by his failure to exercise due care. Because of the evidence contesting the presumed conclusion of negligence, the presumptive effect of the doctrine vanishes, and the greatest effect the doctrine can have in the case is to support an inference that the accident resulted from the defendant's negligence.

In this situation, the court should instruct the jury that, if it finds that the basic facts have been established by a preponderance of the evidence, then it may infer from those facts that the accident was caused because the defendant was negligent. But the court shall also instruct the jury that it should not find that a proximate cause of the accident was some negligent conduct on the part of the defendant unless it believes, after weighing all of the evidence, that it is more probable than not that the defendant was negligent and that the accident resulted from his negligence.

Other Appropriate Instructions

The jury instruction referred to in Section 646 do not preclude the judge from giving the jury any additional instructions on res ipsa loquitur that are appropriate to the particular case.

ANNOTATIONS

Brown v. Poway Unified Sch. Dist. (1993) 4 Cal.4th 820, 825-26. "The [res ipsa loquitur] presumption arises when the evidence satisfies three conditions: (1) the accident must be of a kind which ordinarily does not occur in the absence of someone's negligence; (2) it must be caused by an agency or instrumentality within the exclusive control of the defendant; (3) it must not have been due to any voluntary action or contribution on the part of the plaintiff. A presumption affecting the burden of producing evidence requires the trier of fact to assume the existence of the presumed fact unless the defendant introduces evidence to the contrary. The presumed fact, in this context, is that a proximate cause of the occurrence was some negligent conduct on the part of the defendant. If the defendant introduces evidence which would support a finding that he was not negligent or that any negligence on his part was not a proximate cause of the occurrence, the trier of fact determines whether defendant was negligent without regard to the presumption, simply by weighing the evidence." (Internal quotes omitted.) *See also* ***Kerr v. Bock*** (1971) 5 Cal.3d 321, 324 (to be entitled to res ipsa loquitur instruction, P must present substantial evidence that would support inference of negligence from happening of accident itself); ***Howe v. Seven Forty Two Co.*** (2d Dist.2010) 189 Cal.App.4th 1155, 1163 (when presumptive effect vanishes, P has burden to introduce actual evidence that would show that D was negligent and D's negligence was proximate cause of accident).

Newing v. Cheatham (1975) 15 Cal.3d 351, 364-65. "Since the facts giving rise to the [res ipsa loquitur] doctrine were undisputed, the inference of negligence arose as a matter of law …; to put it another way, the conclusion is compelled that there is a balance of probabilities pointing to [pilot's] negligence. This gave rise to a presumption affecting the burden of producing evidence pursuant to … §646. It then became [D's] obli-

gation to introduce sufficient evidence to sustain a finding either that the accident resulted from some cause other than [pilot's] negligence, or, else, that [pilot] exercised due care in all possible respects wherein he might have been negligent. [D] introduced no such evidence. [D] has at most argued that the crash *could* have resulted from causes other than the negligence of [pilot]. Mere speculation of this sort is insufficient to discharge [D's] burden of explanation."

Blackwell v. Hurst (2d Dist.1996) 46 Cal.App.4th 939, 945-46. "***Brown v. Poway Unified Sch. Dist.*** [(1993) 4 Cal.4th 820] did not involve a physician-patient relationship, but rather a slip-and-fall case. The court in ***Brown*** ... held that slips and falls are not so likely to be the result of negligence as to justify a presumption to that effect. [¶] By contrast, use of the res ipsa loquitur doctrine is especially suited to a medical or dental malpractice setting in which the unwitting and often unconscious or semiconscious patient is at an evidentiary disadvantage because of his or her inability to demonstrate what occurred in the hospital or surgical room setting. [¶] As opposed to ***Brown***, in which the plaintiff was at no evidentiary disadvantage without res ipsa loquitur instructions, here, the patient is unable to testify as to the cause of the injury-producing incident, i.e., whether it could have been avoided by use of one of the precautions explained by [P's] expert, and [P] was similarly disadvantaged. The policy rationale for the use of res ipsa loquitur did not extend to the facts in ***Brown***. Here it does."

§647. [RETURN OF SERVICE OF PROCESS]

The return of a process server registered pursuant to Chapter 16 (commencing with Section 22350) of Division 8 of the Business and Professions Code upon process or notice establishes a presumption, affecting the burden of producing evidence, of the facts stated in the return.

History of Evid. C. §647: Added eff. Jan. 1, 1979, Stats. 1978, ch. 528, §1.

ANNOTATIONS

City of Riverside v. Horspool (4th Dist.2014) 223 Cal.App.4th 670, 680. "Although [D] denies being served with or receiving notice, a review of the entire record shows otherwise. [D] relies upon ... §647 providing that service by a registered process server raises a presumption that service was proper. This does not mean that other forms of service or notice are invalid. [P] served the notice of the pending proceedings in person and by mail as provided by statute. [Ds] were both properly served with all notices."

American Express Centurion Bank v. Zara (6th Dist.2011) 199 Cal.App.4th 383, 390. "[T]he proof of service filed by [P] included the declaration of a registered process server averring that he personally served [D]. Because of the statutory presumption, [D] was thus required to produce evidence that he was not served. [¶] [T]he proof of service on its face indicates that the process server did not comply with the rules governing service. It shows personal service upon [D] himself and describes [D] as an Asian with black hair, a description that does not fit [D]. The proof of service was therefore untruthful. Alternatively, the proof of service does not show personal service upon [D] by leaving a copy with someone other than [D] together with some indication that such person was authorized to accept service on [D's] behalf. The proof of service therefore cannot be construed as attesting to authorized-agent personal service. In the absence of evidence from the process server, the uncontradicted evidence is that the process server did not personally serve [D]. [P] therefore did not carry its burden of proving the facts requisite to an effective service."

ARTICLE 4. PRESUMPTIONS AFFECTING THE BURDEN OF PROOF

§660. [SCOPE]

The presumptions established by this article, and all other rebuttable presumptions established by law that fall within the criteria of Section 605, are presumptions affecting the burden of proof.

History of Evid. C. §660: Added eff. Sept. 17, 1965, oper. Jan. 1, 1967, Stats. 1965, ch. 299, §2.

Official Comment

7 Cal. Law Revision Comm'n Rep. (1965) p. 1099.

(technical correction—Senate J., Apr. 21, 1965)

In some cases it may be difficult to determine whether a particular presumption is a presumption affecting the burden of proof or a presumption affecting the burden of producing evidence. To avoid uncertainty, it is desirable to classify as many presumptions as possible. Article 4 (§§660-668), therefore, lists several presumptions that are to be regarded as presumptions affecting the burden of proof. The list is not exclusive. Other statutory and common law presumptions that affect the burden of proof must await classification by the courts.

§661. REPEALED

Repealed by Stats. 1975, ch. 1244, §14.

§662. [LEGAL TITLE TO PROPERTY]

The owner of the legal title to property is presumed to be the owner of the full beneficial title. This presumption may be rebutted only by clear and convincing proof.

History of Evid. C. §662: Added eff. Sept. 17, 1965, oper. Jan. 1, 1967, Stats. 1965, ch. 299, §2.

Official Comment

7 Cal. Law Revision Comm'n Rep. (1965) p. 1100.

Section 662 codifies a common law presumption recognized in the California cases. The presumption may be overcome only by clear and convincing proof. *Olson v. Olson*, 4 Cal.2d 434, 437, 49 P.2d 827, 828 (1935); *Rench v. McMullen*, 82 Cal.App.2d 872, 187 P.2d 111 (1947).

ANNOTATIONS

In re Marriage of Delaney (1st Dist.2003) 111 Cal.App.4th 991, 998. "In cases ... involving interspousal property transactions, the 'irreconcilable conflict' between the two presumptions established by [Fam. C.] §721 and [Evid. C.] §662 has been resolved in favor of §721, based on the intent of the Legislature in enacting fiduciary protections for interspousal transactions and general rules of statutory construction. *At 999:* [This] rationale ... applies to *any* interspousal property transaction where evidence is offered that one spouse has been disadvantaged by the other. ... Where there is undue influence, as much injustice may be effected by [a conveyance from separate property to joint tenancy as by] the reverse transaction." *See also* ***In re Marriage of Fossum*** (2d Dist.2011) 192 Cal.App.4th 336, 344-45; ***In re Marriage of Haines*** (4th Dist.1995) 33 Cal.App.4th 277, 301-02.

Murray v. Murray (5th Dist.1994) 26 Cal.App.4th 1062, 1067. "[S]ection 662 has application, by its express terms, when there is no dispute as to where *legal* title resides but there is question as to where all or part of the *beneficial* title should rest. *At 1068:* [W]e conclude that ... §662 does not apply to all quiet title actions. As its express terms state, it applies when valid legal title is undisputed and the controversy involves only beneficial title." *See also* ***In re Marriage of Weaver*** (2d Dist.1990) 224 Cal.App.3d 478, 485-86.

§663. [MARRIAGE]

A ceremonial marriage is presumed to be valid.

History of Evid. C. §663: Added eff. Sept. 17, 1965, oper. Jan. 1, 1967, Stats. 1965, ch. 299, §2.

Official Comment

7 Cal. Law Revision Comm'n Rep. (1965) p. 1100.

Section 663 codifies a common law presumption recognized in the California cases. *Estate of Hughson*, 173 Cal. 448, 160 Pac. 548 (1916); *Wilcox v. Wilcox*, 171 Cal. 770, 155 Pac. 95 (1916); *Freeman S.S. Co. v. Pillsbury*, 172 F.2d 321 (9th Cir. 1949).

ANNOTATIONS

Estate of DePasse (6th Dist.2002) 97 Cal.App.4th 92, 107. "Section 663 codifies a common law presumption recognized in California. The ... §663 presumption ... affect[s] the burden of proof. The party attacking the validity of a marriage ... has the burden of proving the marriage is illegal and void."

§664. [OFFICIAL DUTY]

It is presumed that official duty has been regularly performed. This presumption does not apply on an issue as to the lawfulness of an arrest if it is found or otherwise established that the arrest was made without a warrant.

History of Evid. C. §664: Added eff. Sept. 17, 1965, oper. Jan. 1, 1967, Stats. 1965, ch. 299, §2.

See also Evid. C. §1280.

Official Comment

7 Cal. Law Revision Comm'n Rep. (1965) p. 1101; Assem. J., Apr. 6, 1965, p. 1738.

The first sentence of Section 664 restates and supersedes subdivision 15 of Code of Civil Procedure Section 1963.

Under existing law, there is a common law presumption that an arrest made without a warrant is unlawful. *People v. Agnew*, 16 Cal.2d 655, 107 P.2d 601 (1940). Under this common law presumption, if a person arrests another without the color of legality provided by a warrant, the person making the arrest must prove the circumstances that justified the arrest without a warrant. *Badillo v. Superior Court*, 46 Cal.2d 269, 294 P.2d 23 (1956); *Dragna v. White*, 45 Cal.2d 469, 471, 289 P.2d 428, 430 (1955) ("Upon proof of [arrest without process] the burden is on the defendants to prove justification for the arrest."). The second sentence of Section 664 makes it clear that the presumption of regular performance of official duty is inapplicable whenever facts have been established that give rise to the common law presumption regarding the illegality of an arrest made without a warrant.

ANNOTATIONS

People v. Houston (2012) 54 Cal.4th 1186, 1210. "Although there is no record that all prospective jurors were administered the correct oath, [D] is not entitled to relief because under ... §664, it is presumed they were properly sworn in."

In re Hare (2d Dist.2010) 189 Cal.App.4th 1278, 1292. The §664 presumption "may be rebutted when 'irregularity is clearly shown.'"

Morgenstern v. Department of Motor Vehicles (4th Dist.2003) 111 Cal.App.4th 366, 373. "Under ... §664, '[i]t is presumed that official duty has been regularly performed....' Where it is applicable, the presumption shifts the burden of proof to the party against whom it operates to establish the nonexistence of the presumed fact." *See also* ***Bhatt v. State Dept. of Health Servs.*** (2d Dist.2005) 133 Cal.App.4th 923, 931; ***California Advocates for Nursing Home Reform v. Bonta*** (1st Dist.2003) 106 Cal.App.4th 498, 505.

Godshalk v. City of San Diego (4th Dist.1971) 16 Cal.App.3d 459, 469. "The presumption that official duty has been regularly performed cannot serve to supplement an official record seemingly complete on its face and which indicates the questioned duty has not been performed, for the reason that the same presumption

would apply to the correctness of the record." *See also* ***In re C.W.*** (1st Dist.2012) 208 Cal.App.4th 654, 660-61; ***La Costa Beach Homeowners' Ass'n v. California Coastal Comm'n*** (2d Dist.2002) 101 Cal.App.4th 804, 820.

§665. [INTENTION OF VOLUNTARY ACT]

A person is presumed to intend the ordinary consequences of his voluntary act. This presumption is inapplicable in a criminal action to establish the specific intent of the defendant where specific intent is an element of the crime charged.

History of Evid. C. §665: Added eff. Sept. 17, 1965, oper. Jan. 1, 1967, Stats. 1965, ch. 299, §2.

Official Comment

7 Cal. Law Revision Comm'n Rep. (1965) p. 1101; Assem. J., Apr. 6, 1965, p. 1738.

Section 665 restates and supersedes the presumption in subdivision 3 of Code of Civil Procedure Section 1963. The second sentence in this section also appears in Section 668 (restating the presumption in subdivision 2 of Code of Civil Procedure Section 1963). These sentences reflect the fact that it is error to rely on these presumptions when specific intent is in issue in a criminal case. *See People v. Snyder*, 15 Cal.2d 706, 104 P.2d 639 (1940); *People v. Maciel*, 71 Cal.App. 213, 234 Pac. 877 (1925).

§666. [JUDICIAL ACTS]

Any court of this state or the United States, or any court of general jurisdiction in any other state or nation, or any judge of such a court, acting as such, is presumed to have acted in the lawful exercise of its jurisdiction. This presumption applies only when the act of the court or judge is under collateral attack.

History of Evid. C. §666: Added eff. Sept. 17, 1965, oper. Jan. 1, 1967, Stats. 1965, ch. 299, §2.

Official Comment

7 Cal. Law Revision Comm'n Rep. (1965) p. 1101; Assem. J., Apr. 6, 1965, p. 1739.

Section 666 restates and supersedes the presumption in subdivision 16 of Code of Civil Procedure Section 1963. Under existing law, the presumption applies only to courts of general jurisdiction; the presumption has been held inapplicable to a superior court in California when acting in a special or limited jurisdiction. *Estate of Sharon*, 179 Cal. 447, 177 Pac. 283 (1918). The presumption also has been held inapplicable to courts of inferior jurisdiction. *Santos v. Dondero*, 11 Cal.App.2d 720, 54 P.2d 764 (1936). There is no reason to perpetuate this distinction insofar as the courts of California and of the United States are concerned. California's municipal and justice courts are served by able and conscientious judges and are no more likely to act beyond their jurisdiction than are the superior courts. Moreover, there is no reason to suppose that a superior court or a federal court is less respectful of its jurisdiction when acting in a limited capacity (for example, as a juvenile court) than it is when acting in any other capacity. Section 666, therefore, applies to any court or judge of any court of California or of the United States. So far as other states are concerned, the distinction is still applicable, and the presumption applies only to courts of general jurisdiction.

Under Section 666, as under existing law, the presumption applies only when the act of the court or judge is under collateral attack. *See City of Los Angeles v. Glassell*, 203 Cal. 44, 262 Pac. 1084 (1928).

§667. [DEATH]

A person not heard from in five years is presumed to be dead.

History of Evid. C. §667: Added eff. Sept. 17, 1965, oper. Jan. 1, 1967, Stats. 1965, ch. 299, §2. Amended eff. Jan. 1, 1984, Stats. 1983, ch. 201, §1.

See also Prob. C. §12401.

Official Comment

7 Cal. Law Rev. Comm'n Rep. (1965) p. 1102.

Section 667 restates and supersedes the presumption in subdivision 26 of Code of Civil Procedure Section 1963.

16 Cal. Law Revision Comm'n Rep. (1983) p. 113.

Section 667 is amended to adopt a five-year missing period. This period is consistent with Probate Code Section 1301 (administration of estates of persons missing five years) and Civil Code Sections 4401(2), 4425(b) (five-year absence in bigamy situations). Except for the change in the duration of the missing period from seven to five years, the amendment of Section 667 has no effect on the case law interpreting this section.

§668. [UNLAWFUL INTENT]

An unlawful intent is presumed from the doing of an unlawful act. This presumption is inapplicable in a criminal action to establish the specific intent of the defendant where specific intent is an element of the crime charged.

History of Evid. C. §668: Added eff. Sept. 17, 1965, oper. Jan. 1, 1967, Stats. 1965, ch. 299, §2.

Official Comment

7 Cal. Law Revision Comm'n Rep. (1965) p. 1102; Assem. J., Apr. 6, 1965, p. 1739.

Section 668 restates and supersedes the presumption in subdivision 2 of Code of Civil Procedure Section 1963. *See* the *Comment* to Section 665.

§669. [NEGLIGENCE PER SE]

(a) [**Presumption.**] The failure of a person to exercise due care is presumed if:

(1) He violated a statute, ordinance, or regulation of a public entity;

(2) The violation proximately caused death or injury to person or property;

(3) The death or injury resulted from an occurrence of the nature which the statute, ordinance, or regulation was designed to prevent; and

(4) The person suffering the death or the injury to his person or property was one of the class of persons for whose protection the statute, ordinance, or regulation was adopted.

(b) [**Rebutting the presumption.**] This presumption may be rebutted by proof that:

(1) The person violating the statute, ordinance, or regulation did what might reasonably be expected of a person of ordinary prudence, acting under similar circumstances, who desired to comply with the law; or

(2) The person violating the statute, ordinance, or regulation was a child and exercised the degree of care

§664

ordinarily exercised by persons of his maturity, intelligence, and capacity under similar circumstances, but the presumption may not be rebutted by such proof if the violation occurred in the course of an activity normally engaged in only by adults and requiring adult qualifications.

History of Evid. C. §669: Added eff. Nov. 8, 1967, Stats. 1967, ch. 650, §1.

Official Comment

8 Cal. Law Revision Comm'n Rep. (1967) p. 117.

Section 669 codifies a common law presumption that is frequently applied in the California cases. *See Alarid v. Vanier*, 50 Cal.2d 617, 327 P.2d 897 (1958). The presumption may be used to establish a plaintiff's contributory negligence as well as a defendant's negligence. *Nevis v. Pacific Gas & Elec. Co.*, 43 Cal.2d 626, 275 P.2d 761 (1954).

Effect of Presumption

If the conditions listed in subdivision (a) are established, a presumption of negligence arises which may be rebutted by proof of the facts specified in subdivision (b). The presumption is one of simple negligence only, not gross negligence. *Taylor v. Cockrell*, 116 Cal.App. 596, 3 P.2d 16 (1931).

Section 669 appears in Article 4 (beginning with Section 660), Chapter 3, of Division 5 of the Evidence Code and, therefore, is a presumption affecting the burden of proof. Evidence Code §660. Thus, if it is established that a person violated a statute under the conditions specified in subdivision (a), the opponent of the presumption is required to prove to the trier of fact that it is more probable than not that the violation of the statute was reasonable and justifiable under the circumstances. *See* Evidence Code §606 and *Comment* thereto. Since the ultimate question is whether the opponent of the presumption was negligent rather than whether he violated the statute, proof of justification or excuse under subdivision (b) negates the existence of negligence instead of merely establishing an excuse for negligent conduct. Therefore, if the presumption is rebutted by proof of justification or excuse under subdivision (b), the trier of fact is required to find that the violation of the statute was not negligent.

Violations by children. Section 669 applies to the violation of a statute, ordinance, or regulation by a child as well as by an adult. But in the case of a violation by a child, the presumption may be rebutted by a showing that the child, in spite of the violation, exercised the care that children of his maturity, intelligence, and capacity ordinarily exercise under similar circumstances. *Daun v. Truax*, 56 Cal.2d 647, 16 Cal.Rptr. 351, 365 P.2d 407 (1961). However, if a child engages in an activity normally engaged in only by adults and requiring adult qualifications, the "reasonable" behavior he must show to establish justification or excuse under subdivision (b) must meet the standard of conduct established primarily for adults. *Cf. Prichard v. Veterans Cab Co.*, 63 Cal.2d 727, 47 Cal.Rptr. 904, 408 P.2d 360 (1965) (minor operating a motorcycle).

Failure to establish conditions of presumption. Even though a party fails to establish that a violation occurred or that a proven violation meets all the requirements of subdivision (a), it is still possible for the party to recover by proving negligence apart from any statutory violation. *Nunneley v. Edgar Hotel*, 36 Cal.2d 493, 225 P.2d 497 (1950) (plaintiff permitted to recover even though her injury was not of the type to be prevented by statute).

Functions of Judge and Jury

If a case is tried without a jury, the judge is responsible for deciding both questions of law and questions of fact arising under Section 669. However, in a case tried by a jury, there is an allocation between the judge and jury of the responsibility for determining the existence or nonexistence of the elements underlying the presumption and the existence of excuse or justification.

Subdivision (a), paragraphs (3) and (4). Whether the death or injury involved in an action resulted from an occurrence of the nature which the statute, ordinance, or regulation was designed to prevent (paragraph (3) of subdivision (a)) and whether the plaintiff was one of the class of persons for whose protection the statute, ordinance, or regulation was adopted (paragraph (4) of subdivision (a) are questions of law. *Nunneley v. Edgar Hotel, supra* (statute requiring parapet of particular height at roofline of vent shaft designed to protect against walking into shaft, not against falling into shaft while sitting on parapet). If a party were relying solely on the violation of a statute to establish the other party's negligence or contributory negligence, his opponent would be entitled to a directed verdict on the issue if the judge failed to find either of the above elements of the presumption. *Nunneley v. Edgar Hotel, supra* (by implication).

Subdivision (a), paragraphs (1) and (2). Whether or not a party to an action has violated a statute, ordinance, or regulation (paragraph (1) of subdivision (a)) is generally a question of fact. However, if a party admits the violation or if the evidence of the violation is undisputed, it is appropriate for the judge to instruct the jury that a violation of the statute, ordinance, or regulation has been established as a matter of law. *Alarid v. Vanier*, 50 Cal.2d 617, 327 P.2d 897 (1958) (undisputed evidence of driving with faulty brakes).

The question of whether the violation has proximately caused or contributed to the plaintiff's death or injury (paragraph (2) of subdivision (a)) is normally a question for the jury. *Satterlee v. Orange Glenn Sch. Dist.*, 29 Cal.2d 581, 177 P.2d 279 (1947). However, the existence or nonexistence of proximate cause becomes a question of law to be decided by the judge if reasonable men can draw but one inference from the facts. *Satterlee v. Orange Glenn Sch. Dist.*, 29 Cal.2d 581, 177 P.2d 279 (1947). *See also Alarid v. Vanier*, 50 Cal.2d 617, 327 P.2d 897 (1958) (defendant's admission establishes proximate cause); *Moon v. Payne*, 97 Cal.App.2d 717, 218 P.2d 550 (1950) (failure to obtain permit to burn weeds not proximate cause of child's burns).

Subdivision (b). Normally, the question of justification or excuse is a jury question. *Fuentes v. Panella*, 120 Cal.App.2d 175, 260 P.2d 853 (1953). The jury should be instructed on the issue of justification or excuse whether the excuse or justification appears from the circumstances surrounding the violation itself or appears from evidence offered specifically to show justification. *Fuentes v. Panella*, 120 Cal.App.2d 175, 260 P.2d 853 (1953) (instruction on justification proper in light of conflicting testimony concerning violation itself and surrounding circumstances). However, an instruction on the issue of excuse or justification should not be given if there is no evidence that would sustain a finding by the jury that the violation was excused. *McCaughan v. Hansen Pac. Lumber Co.*, 176 Cal.App.2d 827, 833 1 Cal.Rptr. 796, 800 (1959) (evidence went to contributory negligence, not to excuse); *Fuentes v. Panella*, 120 Cal.App.2d 175, 260 P.2d 853 (1953) (dictum).

ANNOTATIONS

Cortez v. Abich (2011) 51 Cal.4th 285, 292. "Not only are Cal-OSHA violations punishable by civil and/or criminal penalties ..., but the Act specifies that '[Evid. C. §669] shall apply to this division and to occupational safety and health standards adopted under this division in the same manner as any other statute, ordinance, or regulation.' This means that 'Cal-OSHA provisions are to be treated like any other statute or regulation and may be admitted to establish a standard or duty of care in all negligence and wrongful death actions, including third party actions.'"

Stafford v. United Farm Workers (1983) 33 Cal.3d 319, 324. "[T]he relation between a statute and negligence is governed by ... §669, which codifies general judicially created doctrines. Our courts have interpreted §669 broadly, applying it to police department manuals ... and Administrative Code safety orders...."

Mark v. Pacific Gas & Elec. Co. (1972) 7 Cal.3d 170, 183. "[T]he presumption of negligence set forth in [Evid. C.] §669 did not form a proper basis for a nonsuit against decedent. First, [D] has not shown that [S.F. Police C.] §585 was intended to prevent injury or death from electrocution. ... The evident purposes of §585 are to protect public property and assure adequate

lighting of public streets. Thus, the requirement of §669, subdivision (a), subsection (3), that the death or injury resulted from an occurrence of the nature which the ordinance was designed to prevent, is not satisfied."

Bologna v. City & Cty. of S.F. (1st Dist.2011) 192 Cal.App.4th 429, 434-35. "The similarity between [Gov. C.] §815.6 and [Evid. C.] §669 is not accidental. In its practical application, the standard for determining whether a mandatory duty exists is virtually identical to the test for an implied statutory duty of care. Although there is a semantic distinction in the labels attached to each cause of action, there is no legal difference in the analytic process to determine the existence of a duty of care. [¶] Central to claims asserting both negligence per se and violation of a mandatory duty is the requirement that the harm allegedly caused is of the precise nature a statute was designed to prevent." (Internal quotes omitted.)

Millard v. Biosources, Inc. (4th Dist.2007) 156 Cal.App.4th 1338, 1353. "The presumption of negligence created by ... §669 concerns the *standard* of care, rather than the *duty* of care. In order for the presumption to be available, either the courts or the Legislature must have created a duty of care. An underlying claim of ordinary negligence must be viable before the presumption of negligence of ... §669 can be employed. It is the tort of negligence, and not the violation of the statute itself, which entitles a plaintiff to recover civil damages." (Internal quotes omitted.) *See also* ***Quiroz v. Seventh Ave. Ctr.*** (6th Dist.2006) 140 Cal.App.4th 1256, 1285-86.

California Serv. Station & Auto. Repair Ass'n v. American Home Assur. Co. (1st Dist.1998) 62 Cal.App.4th 1166, 1171 n.5. "'[N]egligence per se' implies that the violation leads automatically to negligence liability, when in fact satisfaction of the elements of subdivision (a) of ... §669 creates only a presumption of negligence that can be rebutted under the terms of subdivision (b). *At 1179:* 'Since the presumption [of negligence] arises to determine the existence of negligence, it should not apply to statutes adopted to protect people against certain types of harm where the analogous tort is not that of negligence. The analogous tort may be battery, fraud, trespass, intentional infliction of emotional distress or some other tort. A court may, of course, allow a tort action on behalf of a person injured as a result of a violation of such a statute, ... but ... §669 should not apply since the violation does not involve the tort of negligence.' *At 1180:* [W]e conclude the ... §669 presumption of negligence applies only after determining that the defendant owes the plaintiff an independent duty of care...."

Daum v. SpineCare Med. Grp. (1st Dist.1997) 52 Cal.App.4th 1285, 1304 n.5. "[W]hen negligence per se is shown, expert testimony is admissible, but not conclusive, regarding whether the statutory or regulatory violation was justified."

Traxler v. Varady (1st Dist.1993) 12 Cal.App.4th 1321, 1328. "The burden is on the proponent of a negligence per se instruction to demonstrate that these elements are met. The first and second elements of §669 [subdivision (a)], although normally questions of fact for the jury, may be resolved by the court as a matter of law where reasonable minds could not differ as to whether a violation of the regulation actually occurred or whether the violation proximately caused the plaintiff's injuries. The third and fourth elements of ... §669 [subdivision (a)] must be determined by the court as a matter of law." *See also* ***Hoff v. Vacaville Unified Sch. Dist.*** (1998) 19 Cal.4th 925, 938 (third and fourth elements); ***Reyes v. Kosha*** (4th Dist.1998) 65 Cal.App.4th 451, 463; ***Michael R. v. Jeffrey B.*** (2d Dist.1984) 158 Cal.App.3d 1059, 1066.

§669.1. [DUE CARE BY PUBLIC EMPLOYEE]

A rule, policy, manual, or guideline of state or local government setting forth standards of conduct or guidelines for its employees in the conduct of their public employment shall not be considered a statute, ordinance, or regulation of that public entity within the meaning of Section 669, unless the rule, manual, policy, or guideline has been formally adopted as a statute, as an ordinance of a local governmental entity in this state empowered to adopt ordinances, or as a regulation by an agency of the state pursuant to the Administrative Procedure Act (Chapter 3.5 (commencing with Section 11340) of Division 3 of Title 2 of the Government Code), or by an agency of the United States government pursuant to the federal Administrative Procedure Act (Chapter 5 (commencing with Section 5001) of Title 5 of the United States Code). This section affects only the presumption set forth in Section 669, and is not otherwise intended to affect the admissibility or inadmissibility of the rule, policy, manual, or guideline under other provisions of law.

History of Evid. C. §669.1: Added eff. Jan. 1, 1988, Stats. 1987, ch. 1201, §13. Amended eff. Jan. 1, 1988, Stats. 1987, ch. 1207, §2.

§669.5. [IMPACT OF ORDINANCE ON SUPPLY OF RESIDENTIAL UNITS AVAILABLE]

(a) [Limit on building permits; changing standards of development.] Any ordinance enacted by the governing body of a city, county, or city and county which (1) directly limits, by number, the building permits that may be issued for residential construction or the buildable lots which may be developed for residential purposes, or (2) changes the standards of residential development on vacant land so that the governing body's zoning is rendered in violation of Section 65913.1 of the Government Code is presumed to have an impact on the supply of residential units available in an area which includes territory outside the jurisdiction of the city, county, or city and county.

(b) [Burden of proof.] With respect to any action which challenges the validity of an ordinance specified in subdivision (a) the city, county, or city and county enacting the ordinance shall bear the burden of proof that the ordinance is necessary for the protection of the public health, safety, or welfare of the population of the city, county, or city and county.

(c) [Exclusions: building code and ordinance.] This section does not apply to state and federal building code requirements or local ordinances which (1) impose a moratorium, to protect the public health and safety, on residential construction for a specified period of time, if, under the terms of the ordinance, the moratorium will cease when the public health or safety is no longer jeopardized by the construction, (2) create agricultural preserves under Chapter 7 (commencing with Section 51200) of Part 1 of Division 1 of Title 5 of the Government Code, or (3) restrict the number of buildable parcels or designate lands within a zone for nonresidential uses in order to protect agricultural uses as defined in subdivision (b) of Section 51201 of the Government Code or open-space land as defined in subdivision (b) of Section 65560 of the Government Code.

(d) [Exclusion: voter-approved ordinance.] This section shall not apply to a voter approved ordinance adopted by referendum or initiative prior to the effective date of this section which (1) requires the city, county, or city and county to establish a population growth limit which represents its fair share of each year's statewide population growth, or (2) which sets a growth rate of no more than the average population growth rate experienced by the state as a whole. Paragraph (2) of subdivision (a) does not apply to a voter-approved ordinance adopted by referendum or initiative which exempts housing affordable to persons and families of low or moderate income, as defined in Section 50093 of the Health and Safety Code, or which otherwise provides low- and moderate-income housing sites equivalent to such an exemption.

History of Evid. C. §669.5: Added eff. Jan. 1, 1981, Stats. 1980, ch. 1144, §2. Amended eff. Jan. 1, 1989, Stats. 1988, ch. 541, §1.

ANNOTATIONS

Building Indus. Ass'n v. City of Camarillo (1986) 41 Cal.3d 810, 815. "[S]ection 669.5 applies to ordinances enacted by initiative after the effective date of that section…. *At 819:* Ambiguity *does* exist within §669.5. The language of §669.5, subdivision (a), appears to limit the provisions of subdivision (b) to ordinances 'enacted by the governing body of a city, county, or city and county….' But subdivision (d), which states that '[t]his section shall not apply to a voter approved ordinance adopted by referendum or initiative prior to the effective date of this section …' implies that §669.5 is applicable to initiative measures adopted *after* the effective date. *At 822:* Section 669.5 simply requires that, if the electorate exercises its initiative power, the local government must bear the burden of showing that the ordinance is reasonably related to the protection of the public health, safety, or welfare of the affected population."

Murphy v. City of Alameda (1st Dist.1992) 11 Cal.App.4th 906, 909. "[S]ection 669.5 requires that in any action challenging the validity of certain growth control ordinances, the city or county enacting the ordinance must bear the burden of proof that the ordinance is 'necessary for the protection of the public health, safety, or welfare' of its population. The question in this appeal is whether §669.5 is applicable in an action attacking a city charter amendment adopted by initiative and an ordinance implementing the amendment, both enacted before the effective date of the statute. We conclude that the statute applies…."

Lee v. City of Monterey Park (2d Dist.1985) 173 Cal.App.3d 798, 806-07. "Our review of the legislative history of … §669.5 leads us to conclude that its provisions apply to all ordinances whether enacted by the legislative body or the voters. [¶] [P]ursuant to … §669.5, it is [D] and not [Ps] that [has] the burden of

§669.5

proving that the ordinance in question is reasonably related to the public welfare."

§670. [CHECK PAYMENT]

(a) [Presumption of payment.] In any dispute concerning payment by means of a check, a copy of the check produced in accordance with Section 1550 of the Evidence Code, together with the original bank statement that reflects payment of the check by the bank on which it was drawn or a copy thereof produced in the same manner, creates a presumption that the check has been paid.

(b) [Definitions.] As used in this section:

(1) "Bank" means any person engaged in the business of banking and includes, in addition to a commercial bank, a savings and loan association, savings bank, or credit union.

(2) "Check" means a draft, other than a documentary draft, payable on demand and drawn on a bank, even though it is described by another term, such as "share draft" or "negotiable order of withdrawal."

History of Evid. C. §670: Added eff. Jan. 1, 1993, Stats. 1992, ch. 914, §51. Amended eff. Jan. 1, 2002, Stats. 2001, ch. 854, §3.

DIVISION 6. WITNESSES

CHAPTER 1. COMPETENCY

§700. [QUALIFICATION OF WITNESS]

Except as otherwise provided by statute, every person, irrespective of age, is qualified to be a witness and no person is disqualified to testify to any matter.

History of Evid. C. §700: Added eff. Sept. 17, 1965, oper. Jan. 1, 1967, Stats. 1965, ch. 299, §2. Amended eff. Jan. 1, 1986, Stats. 1985, ch. 884, §1.

Official Comment

7 Cal. Law Revision Comm'n Rep. (1965) p. 1103.

(technical correction—Senate J., Apr. 21, 1965)

Section 700 makes it clear that all grounds for disqualification of witnesses must be based on statute. There can be no nonstatutory grounds for disqualification. The section is similar to and supersedes Section 1879 of the Code of Civil Procedure, which provides that "all persons ... who, having organs of sense, can perceive, and perceiving, can make known their perceptions to others, may be witnesses."

Just as Code of Civil Procedure Section 1879 is limited by various statutory restrictions on the competency of witnesses, the broad rule stated in Section 700 is also substantially qualified by statutory restrictions appearing in the Evidence Code and in other California codes. *See, e.g.*, Evidence Code §701 (mental or physical capacity to be a witness), §702 (requirement of personal knowledge), §703 (judge as a witness), §704 (juror as a witness), §§900-1070 (privileges), §1150 (continuing existing law limiting use of juror's evidence concerning jury misconduct); Vehicle Code §40804 (speed trap evidence).

ANNOTATIONS

People v. Montoya (4th Dist.2007) 149 Cal.App.4th 1139, 1150. "A witness's competency to testify is determined exclusively by the judge. [T]he judge determines the preliminary facts of capacity of an ordinary witness to understand the oath and to communicate. [¶] To testify, a witness must have personal knowledge of the subject of the testimony, based on the capacity to perceive and recollect. The capacity to perceive and recollect is a condition for the admissibility of a witness's testimony on a certain matter, rather than a prerequisite for the witness's competency. If there is evidence that the witness has those capacities, the determination whether she in fact perceived and does recollect is left to the trier of fact." (Internal quotes omitted.)

Mathis v. Morrissey (3d Dist.1992) 11 Cal.App.4th 332, 348. "A pecuniary interest in litigation, even a direct and substantial one, will not disqualify a person as a witness." *See also* ***In re Estate of Parsons*** (1st Dist.1980) 103 Cal.App.3d 384, 389 (common-law disabilities to testify on account of interest have been abolished).

§701. [DISQUALIFICATION OF WITNESS FOR LACK OF MENTAL CAPACITY]

(a) [Grounds.] A person is disqualified to be a witness if he or she is:

(1) Incapable of expressing himself or herself concerning the matter so as to be understood, either directly or through interpretation by one who can understand him; or

(2) Incapable of understanding the duty of a witness to tell the truth.

(b) [Competency challenges.] In any proceeding held outside the presence of a jury, the court may reserve challenges to the competency of a witness until the conclusion of the direct examination of that witness.

History of Evid. C. §701: Added eff. Sept. 17, 1965, oper. Jan. 1, 1967, Stats. 1965, ch. 299, §2. Amended eff. Jan. 1, 1986, Stats. 1985, ch. 884, §2.

Official Comment

7 Cal. Law Revision Comm'n Rep. (1965) p. 1103.

Under existing law, the competency of a person to be a witness is a question to be determined by the court and depends upon his capacity to understand the oath and to perceive, recollect, and communicate that which he is offered to relate. "Whether he did perceive accurately, does recollect, and is communicating accurately and truthfully are questions of credibility to be resolved by the trier of fact." *People v. McCaughan*, 49 Cal.2d 409, 420, 317 P.2d 974, 981 (1957).

Under the Evidence Code, too, the competency of a person to be a witness is a question to be determined by the court. *See* Evidence Code §405 and the *Comment* thereto. However, Section 701 requires the court to determine only the prospective witness' capacity to communicate and his understanding of the duty to tell the truth. The missing qualifications—the capacity to perceive and to recollect—are determined in a different manner. Because a witness, qualified under Section 701, must have personal knowledge of the facts to which he testifies (Section 702), he must, of course, have the capacity to perceive and to

recollect those facts. But the court may exclude the testimony of a witness for lack of personal knowledge only if no jury could reasonably find that he has such knowledge. *See* Evidence Code §403 and the *Comment* thereto. Thus, the Evidence Code has made a person's capacity to perceive and to recollect a condition for the admission of his testimony concerning a particular matter instead of a condition for his competency to be a witness. And, under the Evidence Code, if there is evidence that the witness has those capacities, the determination whether he in fact perceived and does recollect is left to the trier of fact. *See* Evidence Code §§403 and 702 and the *Comments* thereto.

Although Section 701 modifies the existing law with respect to determining the competency of witnesses, it seems unlikely that the change will have much practical significance. Theoretically, Section 701 may permit children and persons suffering from mental impairment to testify in some instances where they are now disqualified from testifying; in practice, however, the California courts have permitted children of very tender years and persons with mental impairment to testify. *See* Witkin, *California Evidence* §§389, 390 (1958). *See also Bradburn v. Peacock*, 135 Cal.App.2d 161, 164-165, 286 P.2d 972, 974 (1955) (reversible error to preclude a child from testifying without conducting a *voir dire* examination to determine his competency: "We cannot say that *no* child of 3 years and 3 months is capable of receiving just impressions of the facts that a man whom he knows in a truck which he knows ran over his little sister. Nor can we say that *no* child of 3 years and 3 months would remember such facts and be able to relate them truly at the age of 5." (Emphasis in original.)); *People v. McCaughan*, 49 Cal.2d 409, 317 P.2d 974 (1957) (indicating that committed mental patients may be competent witnesses). For further discussion, *see Tentative Recommendation and a Study Relating to the Uniform Rules of Evidence (Article IV. Witnesses)*, 6 Cal. Law Revision Comm'n, Rep., Rec. & Studies 701, 709-710 (1964).

ANNOTATIONS

People v. Cudjo (1993) 6 Cal.4th 585, 622. "[T]o preserve for appeal a claim that a witness lacked testimonial competence, a party must object on this ground in the trial court." *See also* ***In re S.C.*** (3d Dist.2006) 138 Cal.App.4th 396, 420.

Adamson v. Department of Soc. Servs. (1st Dist.1988) 207 Cal.App.3d 14, 20. "The party challenging a witness's qualification has the burden of proving disqualification. Once the trial court determines the competency of a witness, this decision will not be disturbed on appeal in the absence of a clear abuse of discretion."

§702. [PERSONAL KNOWLEDGE]

(a) [Preliminary determination.] Subject to Section 801, the testimony of a witness concerning a particular matter is inadmissible unless he has personal knowledge of the matter. Against the objection of a party, such personal knowledge must be shown before the witness may testify concerning the matter.

(b) [Showing personal knowledge.] A witness' personal knowledge of a matter may be shown by any otherwise admissible evidence, including his own testimony.

History of Evid. C. §702: Added eff. Sept. 17, 1965, oper. Jan. 1, 1967, Stats. 1965, ch. 299, §2.

Official Comment

7 Cal. Law Revision Comm'n Rep. (1965) p. 1105.

Section 702 states the general requirement that a witness must have personal knowledge of the facts to which he testifies. "Personal knowledge" means a present recollection of an impression derived from the exercise of the witness' own senses. 2 Wigmore, *Evidence* §657 at 762 (3d ed. 1940). *Cf.* Evidence Code §170, defining "perceive." Section 702 restates the substance of and supersedes Code of Civil Procedure Section 1845.

Except to the extent that experts may give opinion testimony not based on personal knowledge (*see* Evidence Code §801), the requirement of Section 702 is applicable to all witnesses, whether expert or not. Certain additional qualifications that an expert witness must possess are set forth in Article 1 (commencing with Section 720) of Chapter 3.

Under existing law, as under Section 702, an objection must be made to the testimony of a witness who does not have personal knowledge; but, if there is no reasonable opportunity to object before the testimony is given, a motion to strike is appropriate after lack of knowledge has been shown. *Fildew v. Shattuck & Nimmo Warehouse Co.*, 39 Cal. App. 42, 46, 177 Pac. 866, 867 (1918) (objection to question properly sustained when foundational showing of personal knowledge was not made); *Sneed v. Marysville Gas & Elec. Co.*, 149 Cal. 704, 709, 87 Pac. 376, 378 (1906) (error to overrule motion to strike testimony after lack of knowledge shown on cross-examination); *Parker v. Smith*, 4 Cal. 105 (1854) (testimony properly stricken by court when lack of knowledge shown on cross-examination).

If a timely objection is made that a witness lacks personal knowledge, the court may not receive his testimony subject to the condition that evidence of personal knowledge be supplied later in the trial. Section 702 thus limits the ordinary power of the court with respect to the order of proof. *See* Evidence Code §403(b). *See also* Evidence Code §320.

ANNOTATIONS

People v. Rodriguez (2014) 58 Cal.4th 587, 631. "'[A]n examiner's question asking a lay witness to testify to facts that the witness has not personally observed, or to state an opinion not based on his or her own observations, calls for speculation and conjecture by the witness and is prohibited by' [Evid. C.] §§702 and 800. Here, the testimony the court permitted was based on facts the witnesses had personally observed. The court did not abuse its discretion in finding the testimony not speculative."

Tutti Mangia Italian Grill, Inc. v. American Textile Maint. Co. (2d Dist.2011) 197 Cal.App.4th 733, 742. "[W]e can locate no authority to support the evidentiary objection that declarations lacking an averment that they were made on the basis of personal knowledge must be stricken. … Personal knowledge … may be demonstrated by 'any otherwise admissible evidence, including [the witness's] own testimony.' Moreover, … §702 does not prescribe any particular method to satisfy its personal knowledge requirement."

People v. Montoya (4th Dist.2007) 149 Cal.App.4th 1139, 1150. See annotation under Evidence Code §700, p. 1250.

§703. [JUDGE AS WITNESS]

(a) [Inform parties.] Before the judge presiding at the trial of an action may be called to testify in that

trial as a witness, he shall, in proceedings held out of the presence and hearing of the jury, inform the parties of the information he has concerning any fact or matter about which he will be called to testify.

(b) [**Objection.**] Against the objection of a party, the judge presiding at the trial of an action may not testify in that trial as a witness. Upon such objection, the judge shall declare a mistrial and order the action assigned for trial before another judge.

(c) [**Mistrial.**] The calling of the judge presiding at a trial to testify in that trial as a witness shall be deemed a consent to the granting of a motion for mistrial, and an objection to such calling of a judge shall be deemed a motion for mistrial.

(d) [**No objection.**] In the absence of objection by a party, the judge presiding at the trial of an action may testify in that trial as a witness.

History of Evid. C. §703: Added eff. Sept. 17, 1965, oper. Jan. 1, 1967, Stats. 1965, ch. 299, §2.

Official Comment

7 Cal. Law Revision Comm'n Rep. (1965) p. 1106; Assem. J., Apr. 6, 1965, p. 1739.

Under existing law, a judge may be called as a witness even if a party objects, but the judge in his discretion may order the trial to be postponed or suspended and to take place before another judge. Code Civ. Proc. §1883 (repealed, now Evidence Code §§703 and 704). *But see People v. Connors*, 77 Cal.App. 438, 450-457, 246 Pac. 1072, 1076-1079 (1926) (dictum) (abuse of discretion for the presiding judge to testify to important and necessary facts).

Section 703, however, precludes the judge from testifying if a party objects. Before the judge may be called to testify in a civil or criminal action, he must disclose to the parties out of the presence and hearing of the jury the information he has concerning the case. After such disclosure, if no party objects, the judge is permitted—but not required—to testify.

Section 703 is based on the fact that examination and cross-examination of a judge-witness may be embarrassing and prejudicial to a party. By testifying as a witness for one party, a judge appears in a partisan attitude before the jury. Objections to questions and to his testimony must be ruled on by the witness himself. The extent of cross-examination and the introduction of impeaching and rebuttal evidence may be limited by the fear of appearing to attack the judge personally. For these and other reasons, Section 703 is preferable to Code of Civil Procedure Section 1883.

Subdivision (c) is designed to prevent a plea of double jeopardy by a defendant who either calls or objects to the calling of the judge to testify. Under subdivision (c), the defendant will, in effect, have consented to the mistrial and thus waived any objection to a retrial. *See* Witkin, *California Crimes* §193 (1963).

§703

§703.5. [JUDGE, ARBITRATOR, OR MEDIATOR TESTIMONY IN SUBSEQUENT CIVIL PROCEEDINGS]

No person presiding at any judicial or quasi-judicial proceeding, and no arbitrator or mediator, shall be competent to testify, in any subsequent civil proceeding, as to any statement, conduct, decision, or ruling, occurring at or in conjunction with the prior proceeding, except as to a statement or conduct that could (a) give rise to civil or criminal contempt, (b) constitute a crime, (c) be the subject of investigation by the State Bar or Commission on Judicial Performance, or (d) give rise to disqualification proceedings under paragraph (1) or (6) of subdivision (a) of Section 170.1 of the Code of Civil Procedure. However, this section does not apply to a mediator with regard to any mediation under Chapter 11 (commencing with Section 3160) of Part 2 of Division 8 of the Family Code.

History of Evid. C. §703.5: Added eff. Jan. 1, 1980, Stats. 1979, ch. 205, §1. Amended eff. Jan. 1, 1981, Stats. 1980, ch. 290, §1; eff. Jan. 1, 1989, Stats. 1988, ch. 281, §1; eff. Jan. 1, 1991, Stats. 1990, ch. 1491, §13; eff. Jan. 1, 1994, Stats. 1993, ch. 114, §1, ch. 1261, §5; eff. Jan. 1, 1995, Stats. 1994, ch. 1269, §7.

Official Comment

1994 Ann. Report, 24 Cal. Law Revision Comm'n Rep. (1994) App. 5.

Section 703.5 is amended to correct the cross-reference to former Family Code Section 3155 to reflect the reorganization of those sections in 1993 Cal. Stat. ch. 219. This is a technical, nonsubstantive change.

ANNOTATIONS

Betz v. Pankow (1st Dist.1993) 16 Cal.App.4th 919, 927. "[S]ection 703.5 limits the testimony of an arbitrator whose decision is being challenged on grounds of bias to that which addresses the charge of bias, partiality or improper conduct. The merits of the controversy, the manner in which evidence was weighed or the mental processes of the arbitrators in reaching their decision are not subject to judicial review. This rule is easier to recite than to apply, because these matters often overlap, leaving evidence that is admissible for one purpose, but not another."

§704. [JUROR AS WITNESS]

(a) [**Inform parties.**] Before a juror sworn and impaneled in the trial of an action may be called to testify before the jury in that trial as a witness, he shall, in proceedings conducted by the court out of the presence and hearing of the remaining jurors, inform the parties of the information he has concerning any fact or matter about which he will be called to testify.

(b) [**Objection.**] Against the objection of a party, a juror sworn and impaneled in the trial of an action may not testify before the jury in that trial as a witness. Upon such objection, the court shall declare a mistrial and order the action assigned for trial before another jury.

(c) [**Mistrial.**] The calling of a juror to testify before the jury as a witness shall be deemed a consent to the granting of a motion for mistrial, and an objection to such calling of a juror shall be deemed a motion for mistrial.

(d) [**No objection.**] In the absence of objection by a party, a juror sworn and impaneled in the trial of an action may be compelled to testify in that trial as a witness.

History of Evid. C. §704: Added eff. Sept. 17, 1965, oper. Jan. 1, 1967, Stats. 1965, ch. 299, §2.

Official Comment

7 Cal. Law Revision Comm'n Rep. (1965) p. 1107; Assem. J., Apr. 6, 1965, p. 1740.

Under existing law, a juror may be called as a witness even if a party objects, but the judge in his discretion may order the trial to be postponed or suspended and to take place before another jury. Code Civ. Proc. §1883 (repealed, now Evidence Code §§703 and 704). Section 704, on the other hand, prevents a juror from testifying before the jury if any party objects.

A juror-witness is in an anomalous position. He manifestly cannot weigh his own testimony impartially. A party affected adversely by the juror's testimony is placed in an embarrassing position. He cannot freely cross-examine or impeach the juror for fear of antagonizing the juror—and perhaps his fellow jurors as well. And, if he does not attack the juror's testimony, the other jurors may give his testimony undue weight. For these and other reasons, Section 704 forbids jurors to testify over the objection of any party.

Before a juror may be called to testify before the jury in a civil or criminal action, he is required to disclose to the parties out of the presence and hearing of the remaining jurors the information he has concerning the case. After such disclosure, if no party objects, the juror is required to testify. If a party objects, the objection is deemed a motion for mistrial and the judge is required to declare a mistrial and order the action assigned for trial before another jury.

Section 704 is concerned only with the problem of a juror who is called to testify before the jury. Section 704 does not deal with *voir dire* examinations of jurors, with testimony of jurors in post-verdict proceedings (such as on motions for new trial), or with the testimony of jurors on any other matter that is to be decided by the court. *Cf.* Evidence Code §1150 and the *Comment* thereto.

Subdivision (c) is designed to prevent a plea of double jeopardy by a defendant who either calls or objects to the calling of the juror to testify. Under subdivision (c), the defendant will, in effect, have consented to the mistrial and thus waived any objection to a retrial. *See* Witkin, *California Crimes* §193 (1963).

CHAPTER 2. OATH & CONFRONTATION

§710. [OATH, AFFIRMATION, OR DECLARATION]

Every witness before testifying shall take an oath or make an affirmation or declaration in the form provided by law, except that a child under the age of 10 or a dependent person with a substantial cognitive impairment, in the court's discretion, may be required only to promise to tell the truth.

History of Evid. C. §710: Added eff. Sept. 17, 1965, oper. Jan. 1, 1967, Stats. 1965, ch. 299, §2. Amended eff. Jan. 1, 1989, Stats. 1988, ch. 486, §1; eff. Jan. 1, 2005, Stats. 2004, ch. 823, §3.

Official Comment

7 Cal. Law Revision Comm'n Rep. (1965) p. 1108.

Sections 710 and 711 restate the substance of and supersede Section 1846 of the Code of Civil Procedure.

ANNOTATIONS

In re Heather H. (6th Dist.1988) 200 Cal.App.3d 91, 95. "In the absence of a waiver, such as a failure to object or a stipulation, unsworn testimony does not constitute 'evidence' within the meaning of the Evidence Code."

§711. [EXAMINATION OF WITNESS]

At the trial of an action, a witness can be heard only in the presence and subject to the examination of all the parties to the action, if they choose to attend and examine.

History of Evid. C. §711: Added eff. Sept. 17, 1965, oper. Jan. 1, 1967, Stats. 1965, ch. 299, §2.

Official Comment

7 Cal. Law Revision Comm'n Rep. (1965) p. 1108.

See the *Comment* to Section 710.

§712. [AFFIDAVIT ON BLOOD-SAMPLE TECHNIQUE IN CRIMINAL ACTION]

Notwithstanding Sections 711 and 1200, at the trial of a criminal action, evidence of the technique used in taking blood samples may be given by a registered nurse, licensed vocational nurse, or licensed clinical laboratory technologist or clinical laboratory bioanalyst, by means of an affidavit. The affidavit shall be admissible, provided the party offering the affidavit as evidence has served all other parties to the action, or their counsel, with a copy of the affidavit no less than 10 days prior to trial. Nothing in this section shall preclude any party or his counsel from objecting to the introduction of the affidavit at any time, and requiring the attendance of the affiant, or compelling attendance by subpoena.

History of Evid. C. §712: Added eff. Apr. 14, 1978, Stats. 1978, ch. 93, §1.

CHAPTER 3. EXPERT WITNESSES

ARTICLE 1. EXPERT WITNESSES GENERALLY

§720. [QUALIFICATION OF EXPERT WITNESS]

(a) A person is qualified to testify as an expert if he has special knowledge, skill, experience, training, or education sufficient to qualify him as an expert on the subject to which his testimony relates. Against the objection of a party, such special knowledge, skill, experience, training, or education must be shown before the witness may testify as an expert.

(b) A witness' special knowledge, skill, experience, training, or education may be shown by any otherwise admissible evidence, including his own testimony.

History of Evid. C. §720: Added eff. Sept. 17, 1965, oper. Jan. 1, 1967, Stats. 1965, ch. 299, §2.

Official Comment

7 Cal. Law Revision Comm'n Rep. (1965) p. 1108.

This section states existing law as declared in subdivision 9 (last clause) of Code of Civil Procedure Section 1870, which is superseded by Sections 720 and 801.

The judge must be satisfied that the proposed witness is an expert. *People v. Haeussler*, 41 Cal.2d 252, 260 P.2d 8 (1953); *Pfingsten v. Westenhaver*, 39 Cal.2d 12, 244 P.2d 395 (1952); *Bossert v. Southern Pac. Co.*, 172 Cal. 504, 157 Pac. 597 (1916); *People v. Pacific Gas & Elec. Co.*, 27 Cal.App.2d 725, 81 P.2d 584 (1938).

Against the objection of a party, the special qualifications of the proposed witness must be shown as a prerequisite to his testimony as an expert. With the consent of the parties, the judge may receive a witness' testimony conditionally, subject to the necessary foundation being supplied later in the trial. *See* Evidence Code §320. Unless the foundation is subsequently supplied, however, the judge should grant a motion to strike or should order the testimony stricken from the record on his own motion.

The judge's determination that a witness qualifies as an expert witness is binding on the trier of fact, but the trier of fact may consider the witness' qualifications as an expert in determining the weight to be given his testimony. *Pfingsten v. Westenhaver*, 39 Cal.2d 12, 244 P.2d 395 (1952); *Howland v. Oakland Consol. St. Ry.*, 110 Cal. 513, 42 Pac. 983 (1895); *Estate of Johnson*, 100 Cal.App.2d 73, 223 P.2d 105 (1950). *See* Evidence Code §§405 and 406 and the *Comments* thereto.

ANNOTATIONS

People v. Jones (2012) 54 Cal.4th 1, 57. "The trial court's determination that a witness qualifies as an expert is a matter of discretion that will not be disturbed absent a showing of manifest abuse. We will find error regarding a witness's credentials as an expert only if the evidence shows that a witness *clearly lacks* qualification as an expert." (Internal quotes omitted.) *See also* ***Miller v. Los Angeles Cty. Flood Control Dist.*** (1973) 8 Cal.3d 689, 701; ***Huffman v. Lindquist*** (1951) 37 Cal.2d 465, 476.

§720

Brown v. Colm (1974) 11 Cal.3d 639, 643. D argues "that a witness who testifies as to a particular standard of care must possess 'occupational experience' or 'practical knowledge' of the subject in order to qualify as an expert. *At 643 n.3:* [A] witness may acquire the necessary expertise by means other than occupational experience, such as by education or observation. [D] relies [on] a statement contained in Wigmore ... defining 'occupational experience' as experience 'obtained casually and incidentally, yet steadily and adequately, in the course of some occupation or livelihood.' However, Wigmore does not state that this type of experience is required in each case as a predicate to expert testimony, nor does he relate the experience to any time factor. To the contrary, he expressly recognizes in the same section that a witness may not need such experience in order to qualify as an expert. *At 644:* While a layman may not testify to a fact which he has learned only by reading a medical book, there is no question that a professional physician may rely upon medical texts as the basis for his testimony. Wigmore justifies the foregoing distinction by pointing out that a medical doctor possesses a professional experience which gives him a knowledge of the trustworthy authorities and the proper sources of information, as well as a degree of personal observation of the general subject enabling him to estimate the plausibility of the views expressed. *At 645:* The determinative issue in each case must be whether the witness has sufficient skill or experience in the field so that his testimony would be likely to assist the jury in the search for the truth, and no hard and fast rule can be laid down which would be applicable in every circumstance."

Chavez v. Glock, Inc. (2d Dist.2012) 207 Cal.App.4th 1283, 1319. "'[W]ork in a particular field is not an absolute prerequisite to qualification as an expert in that field.' For example, '[q]ualifications other than a license to practice medicine may serve to qualify a witness to give a medical opinion.' The determinative factor is whether the expert 'has sufficient skill or experience in the field so that his ... testimony would be likely to assist the jury in the search for the truth[.]' The degree of expertise goes to the weight of the expert's testimony, not its admissibility." *See also* ***In re Joy M.*** (4th Dist.2002) 99 Cal.App.4th 11, 19.

Los Altos El Granada Investors v. City of Capitola (6th Dist.2006) 139 Cal.App.4th 629, 658. "The essential questions which must be favorably answered to qualify a witness as an expert are two: Does the witness have the background to absorb and evaluate information on the subject? Does he have access to reliable sources of information about the subject? Two aspects of the witness's history are thus involved: the first, a subjective aspect, the capacity of the witness to understand and report; the second, an objective aspect, the witness's access and exposure to relevant data on the subject matter on which his opinion is sought."

§721. [CROSS-EXAMINATION OF EXPERT]

(a) [Qualifications and opinion.] Subject to subdivision (b), a witness testifying as an expert may be cross-examined to the same extent as any other witness and, in addition, may be fully cross-examined as to (1) his or her qualifications, (2) the subject to which his or her expert testimony relates, and (3) the matter upon which his or her opinion is based and the reasons for his or her opinion.

(b) [Source relied upon for opinion.] If a witness testifying as an expert testifies in the form of an opinion, he or she may not be cross-examined in regard to the content or tenor of any scientific, technical, or

professional text, treatise, journal, or similar publication unless any of the following occurs:

(1) The witness referred to, considered, or relied upon such publication in arriving at or forming his or her opinion.

(2) The publication has been admitted in evidence.

(3) The publication has been established as a reliable authority by the testimony or admission of the witness or by other expert testimony or by judicial notice. If admitted, relevant portions of the publication may be read into evidence but may not be received as exhibits.

History of Evid. C. §721: Added eff. Sept. 17, 1965, oper. Jan. 1, 1967, Stats. 1965, ch. 299, §2. Amended eff. Jan. 1, 1998, Stats. 1997, ch. 892, §11.

Official Comment

7 Cal. Law Revision Comm'n Rep. (1965) p. 1109.

Under Section 721, a witness who testifies as an expert may, of course, be cross-examined to the same extent as any other witness. See Chapter 5 (commencing with Section 760). But, under subdivision (a) of Section 721, as under existing law, the expert witness is also subject to a somewhat broader cross-examination: "Once an expert offers his opinion, however, he exposes himself to the kind of inquiry which ordinarily would have no place in the cross-examination of a factual witness. The expert invites investigation into the extent of his knowledge, the reasons for his opinion including facts and other matters upon which it is based (Code Civ. Proc. §1872), and which he took into consideration; and he may be 'subjected to the most rigid cross examination' concerning his qualifications, and his opinion and its sources [citation omitted]." *Hope v. Arrowhead & Puritas Waters, Inc.*, 174 Cal.App.2d 222, 230, 344 P.2d 428, 433 (1959). The cross-examination rule stated in subdivision (a) is based in part on the last clause of Code of Civil Procedure Section 1872.

Subdivision (b) clarifies a matter concerning which there is considerable confusion in the California decisions. It is at least clear under existing law that an expert witness may be cross-examined in regard to those books on which he relied in forming or arriving at his opinion. *Lewis v. Johnson*, 12 Cal.2d 558, 86 P.2d 99 (1939); *People v. Hooper*, 10 Cal.App.2d 332, 51 P.2d 1131 (1935). Dicta in some decisions indicate that the cross-examiner is strictly limited to the books relied on by the expert witness. *See, e.g., Baily v. Kreutzmann*, 141 Cal. 519, 75 Pac. 104 (1904). Other cases, however, suggest that an expert witness may be cross-examined in regard to any book of the same character as the books on which he relied in forming his opinion. *Griffith v. Los Angeles Pac. Co.*, 14 Cal.App. 145, 111 Pac. 107 (1910). *See Salgo v. Leland Stanford etc. Bd. Trustees*, 154 Cal.App.2d 560, 317 P.2d 170 (1957); *Gluckstein v. Lipsett*, 93 Cal.App.2d 391, 209 P.2d 98 (1949) (reviewing California authorities). (Possibly, the cross-examiner is restricted under this view to the use of such books as "are not in harmony with the testimony of the witness." *Griffith v. Los Angeles Pac. Co., supra.*) Language in several earlier cases indicated that the cross-examiner could use books to test the competency of an expert witness, whether or not the expert relied on books in forming his opinion. *Fisher v. Southern Pac. R.R.*, 89 Cal. 399, 26 Pac. 894 (1891); *People v. Hooper*, 10 Cal.App.2d 332, 51 P.2d 1131 (1935). More recent decisions indicate, however, that the opinion of an expert witness must be based either generally or specifically on books before the expert can be cross-examined concerning them. *Lewis v. Johnson*, 12 Cal.2d 558, 86 P.2d 99 (1939); *Salgo v. Leland Stanford etc. Bd. Trustees*, 154 Cal.App.2d 560, 317 P.2d 170 (1957); *Gluckstein v. Lipsett*, 93 Cal.App.2d 391, 209 P.2d 98 (1949). The conflicting California cases are gathered in Annot., 60 A.L.R.2d 77 (1958).

If an expert witness has relied on a particular publication in forming his opinion, it is necessary to permit cross-examination in regard to that publication in order to show whether the expert correctly read, interpreted, and applied the portions he relied on. Similarly, it is important to permit an expert witness to be cross-examined concerning those publications referred to or considered by him even though not specifically relied on by him in forming his opinion. An expert's reasons for not relying on particular publications that were referred to or considered by him while forming his opinion may reveal important information bearing upon the credibility of his testimony. However, a rule permitting cross-examination on technical treatises not considered by the expert witness would permit the cross-examiner to utilize this opportunity not for its ostensible purpose—to test the expert's opinion—but to bring before the trier of fact the opinions of absentee authors without the safeguard of cross-examination. Although the court would be required upon request to caution the jury that the statements read are not to be considered evidence of the truth of the propositions stated, there is a danger that at least some jurors might rely on the author's statements for this purpose. Yet, the statements in the text might be based on inadequate background research, might be subject to unexpressed qualifications that would be applicable to the case before the court, or might be unreliable for some other reason that could be revealed if the author were subject to cross-examination. Therefore, subdivision (b) does not permit cross-examination of an expert witness on scientific, technical, or professional works not referred to, considered, or relied on by him.

If a particular publication has already been admitted in evidence, however, the reason for subdivision (b)—to prevent inadmissible evidence from being brought before the jury—is inapplicable. Hence, the subdivision permits an expert witness to be examined concerning such a publication without regard to whether he referred to, considered, or relied on it in forming his opinion. *Cf. Laird v. T. W. Mather, Inc.*, 51 Cal.2d 210, 331 P.2d 617 (1958).

The rule stated in subdivision (b) thus provides a fair and workable solution to this conflict of competing interests with respect to the permissible use of scientific, technical, or professional publications by the cross-examiner.

ANNOTATIONS

Brown v. Colm (1974) 11 Cal.3d 639, 646. "[I]f the threshold test of general testimonial qualification is found to be met and the witness is permitted to testify on direct examination, he is subject to as penetrating a cross-examination as the ingenuity and intellect of opposing counsel can devise. This inquiry may challenge not only the knowledge of the witness on the specific subject at issue, but also the reasons for his opinion and his evaluation of any written material upon which he relied in preparation for his testimony. Further, a defendant is free to argue that the witness' testimony is not entitled to acceptance or credibility because he lacks personal acquaintance with the subject at the time the alleged negligent act occurred, and defendant may produce his own witnesses in rebuttal. These measures are more than adequate to protect a defendant's interests."

McGarity v. DOT (3d Dist.1992) 8 Cal.App.4th 677, 683. "[T]o counterbalance the broad scope of cross-examination of expert witnesses ..., the purpose of [§721, subdivision (b)] is 'to prevent an adverse party from getting before the trier of fact the *inadmissible hearsay* views of an *absent* expert, which may be *contrary* to the expert witness' opinion, through the device of cross-examining the expert witness regarding the absent expert's publication or report even though the testifying expert had *not* used or considered that publication or report in *any* way in arriving at or forming his opinion testimony.'"

§722. [APPOINTMENT & CREDIBILITY OF EXPERT]

(a) [Appointment.] The fact of the appointment of an expert witness by the court may be revealed to the trier of fact.

(b) [Credibility.] The compensation and expenses paid or to be paid to an expert witness by the party calling him is a proper subject of inquiry by any adverse party as relevant to the credibility of the witness and the weight of his testimony.

History of Evid. C. §722: Added eff. Sept. 17, 1965, oper. Jan. 1, 1967, Stats. 1965, ch. 299, §2.

Official Comment

7 Cal. Law Revision Comm'n Rep. (1965) p. 1111.

Subdivision (a) of Section 722 codifies a rule recognized in the California decisions. *People v. Cornell*, 203 Cal. 144, 263 Pac. 216 (1928); *People v. Strong*, 114 Cal.App. 522, 300 Pac. 84 (1931).

Subdivision (b) of Section 722 restates the substance of Section 1256.2 of the Code of Civil Procedure. Section 1256.2, however, applies only in condemnation cases, while Section 722 is not so limited. It is uncertain whether the California law in other fields of litigation is as stated in Section 722. At least one California case has held that an expert could be asked whether he was being compensated but that he could not be asked the amount of the compensation. *People v. Tomalty*, 14 Cal.App. 224, 111 Pac. 513 (1910). However, the decision may have been based on the discretionary right of the trial judge to curtail collateral inquiry.

In any event, the rule enunciated in Section 722 is a desirable rule. The tendency of some experts to become advocates for the party employing them has been recognized. 2 Wigmore, *Evidence* §563 (3d ed. 1940); Friedenthal, *Discovery and Use of an Adverse Party's Expert Information*, 14 Stan.L.Rev. 455, 485-486 (1962). The jury can better appraise the extent to which bias may have influenced an expert's opinion if it is informed of the amount of his fee—and, hence, the extent of his possible feeling of obligation to the party calling him.

ANNOTATIONS

Stony Brook I Homeowners Ass'n v. Superior Ct. (4th Dist.2000) 84 Cal.App.4th 691, 699. "In the face of an expert who is unable to provide a good faith estimate of how much of his practice is devoted to offering testimony for one side or the other in litigation and how much he has received for such work, the trial court faces a difficult task. [¶] First, a litigant's right to evidence of an expert's potential bias is not unfettered or unconditional. ... When the interest of a private litigant in discovering relevant facts conflicts with the right of others to maintain reasonable privacy regarding their financial affairs, a court must indulge in a careful balancing before ordering disclosure. It follows that a court must not generously order disclosure of the private financial affairs of nonparties without a careful scrutiny of the real needs of the litigant who seeks discovery. [¶] To show bias or prejudice, real party need not learn the details of his billing and accounting or the specifics of his prior testimony and depositions. As petitioner points out, publications which index the testimony of medical units are available to real party. Exact information as to number of cases and amounts of compensation paid to medical experts is unnecessary for the purpose of showing a bias. *At 700:* [Second,] an order requiring extensive financial disclosure may in fact operate as drastically as an order excluding an expert's testimony altogether. Given the large role expert testimony plays in modern civil litigation ... and the difficulty a litigant may have in both finding a substitute expert and obtaining leave to rely on the substitute's opinion ..., a court must act with great care before entering an order which as a practical matter excludes a designated expert from testifying." (Internal quotes omitted.)

§723. [LIMIT ON EXPERTS]

The court may, at any time before or during the trial of an action, limit the number of expert witnesses to be called by any party.

History of Evid. C. §723: Added eff. Sept. 17, 1965, oper. Jan. 1, 1967, Stats. 1965, ch. 299, §2.

Official Comment

7 Cal. Law Revision Comm'n Rep. (1965) p. 1112.

Section 723 restates the substance of and supersedes the last sentence of Section 1871 of the Code of Civil Procedure.

ANNOTATIONS

South Bay Chevrolet v. General Motors Acceptance Corp. (4th Dist.1999) 72 Cal.App.4th 861, 905. "[P] contends the trial court prejudicially erred in excluding as duplicative the testimony of [expert 2]. [P] asserts [expert 2's] testimony had independent evidentiary value in demonstrating how other lenders disclosed their use of the 365/360 method of interest calculation. However, [P] has not established error with respect to exclusion of [expert 2's] testimony. *At 906:* On this record, the trial court acted within its discretion in excluding [expert 2's] testimony as cumulative. As the court properly observed, [P's] designation of expert witnesses indicated the scope of [expert 2's] anticipated testimony was a 'duplicate' of the subject matter covered by [expert 1]. Further, [P's] counsel acknowledged that 'there's a substantial overlap' in the two experts' testimony and that [expert 2's] testimony would be covering ground already covered by [expert 1]."

ARTICLE 2. APPOINTMENT OF EXPERT WITNESS BY COURT

§730. [COURT-APPOINTED EXPERT]

When it appears to the court, at any time before or during the trial of an action, that expert evidence is or

may be required by the court or by any party to the action, the court on its own motion or on motion of any party may appoint one or more experts to investigate, to render a report as may be ordered by the court, and to testify as an expert at the trial of the action relative to the fact or matter as to which the expert evidence is or may be required. The court may fix the compensation for these services, if any, rendered by any person appointed under this section, in addition to any service as a witness, at the amount as seems reasonable to the court. Nothing in this section shall be construed to permit a person to perform any act for which a license is required unless the person holds the appropriate license to lawfully perform that act.

History of Evid. C. §730: Added eff. Jan. 1, 1980, oper. Jan. 1, 1983, Stats. 1979, ch. 746, §3. Amended eff. Jan. 1, 1991, Stats. 1990, ch. 295, §1.

History of Former Evid. C. §730: Added eff. Sept. 17, 1965, oper. Jan. 1, 1967, Stats. 1965, ch. 299, §2. Repealed eff. Jan. 1, 1980, oper. Jan. 1, 1983, Stats. 1979, ch. 746, §2.

ANNOTATIONS

In re Marriage of Laurenti (2d Dist.2007) 154 Cal.App.4th 395, 403. "When read together, we interpret [Evid. C.] §730 and [CRC] 5.220 to mean a trial court must (1) decide whether an evaluator should receive any compensation for his or her services, (2) determine a reasonable amount of compensation and (3) state which party or parties will bear what portion of the fees and costs." *See also* ***In re Marriage of Adams*** (4th Dist.2012) 209 Cal.App.4th 1543, 1568-69.

Baker-Hoey v. Lockheed Martin Corp. (4th Dist.2003) 111 Cal.App.4th 592, 601. "'[A]n expert witness ordered by the court is one who has been appointed by the court pursuant to [Evid. C.] §730 or other statutory authority. In the absence of an order of the trial court appointing an expert witness, the fees of an expert witness are not recoverable as costs under [CCP] §1032.' 'The fact that an expert is necessary to present a party's case does not mean that expert has been ordered by the court for purposes of recovery of expert witness fees as costs.' Thus, the fact that expert witness fees had to be paid under [CCP] §2034(i)(2) in order to take the depositions of the treating physicians does not mean that those fees are necessarily recoverable costs. [¶] Such fees are simply not ordinary witness fees as described in [CCP] §1033.5, subdivision (a)(7) and [D] cannot, by the verbal alchemy of its skilled attorneys, successfully transmute the phrase 'ordinary witness fees' into a higher category entitled 'ordinary witness fees of treating physicians.' Treating physicians are experts and recovery of their fees as costs are accordingly governed by §1033.5's provisions governing expert witness fees, not the provisions applicable to ordinary witnesses."

Laurie S. v. Superior Ct. (4th Dist.1994) 26 Cal.App.4th 195, 202. "The psychological evaluation is an 'information-gathering tool.' However expert witnesses are appointed only where 'expert evidence is or may be required....' Because the matter to be determined at the jurisdictional hearing is whether a child is at substantial risk of harm at the hands of a parent, due to parental acts or inaction, if that assessment can be made within ordinary experience, no expert is necessary. [¶] While a psychologist or psychiatrist may have greater insight into [petitioner's] purported illness than a layperson, whether she is a danger to her child can be evaluated by the court without an expert. This is unlike the situation where a child exhibits physical injuries or a failure to thrive and an expert medical opinion is needed to determine if the injuries were accidental or intentionally inflicted, or the child is malnourished as a result of starvation or organic problems."

§731. [COMPENSATION OF APPOINTED EXPERTS]

(a) [Criminal and juvenile proceedings.]

(1) In all criminal actions and juvenile court proceedings, the compensation fixed under Section 730 shall be a charge against the county in which the action or proceeding is pending and shall be paid out of the treasury of that county on order of the court.

(2) Notwithstanding paragraph (1), if the expert is appointed for the court's needs, the compensation shall be a charge against the court.

(b) [Medical experts in civil actions.] In any county in which the superior court so provides, the compensation fixed under Section 730 for medical experts appointed for the court's needs in civil actions shall be a charge against the court. In any county in which the board of supervisors so provides, the compensation fixed under Section 730 for medical experts appointed in civil actions, for purposes other than the court's needs, shall be a charge against and paid out of the treasury of that county on order of the court.

(c) [Civil actions.] Except as otherwise provided in this section, in all civil actions, the compensation fixed under Section 730 shall, in the first instance, be apportioned and charged to the several parties in a proportion as the court may determine and may thereafter be taxed and allowed in like manner as other costs.

History of Evid. C. §731: Added eff. Jan. 1, 1980, oper. Jan. 1, 1983, Stats. 1979, ch. 746, §5. Amended eff. Jan. 1, 2013, Stats. 2012, ch. 470, §8.

History of Former Evid. C. §731: Added eff. Sept. 17, 1965, oper. Jan. 1, 1967, Stats. 1965, ch. 299, §2. Repealed eff. Jan. 1, 1980, oper. Jan. 1, 1983, Stats. 1979, ch. 746, §2.

§732. [CALLING APPOINTED EXPERTS]

Any expert appointed by the court under Section 730 may be called and examined by the court or by any party to the action. When such witness is called and examined by the court, the parties have the same right as is expressed in Section 775 to cross-examine the witness and to object to the questions asked and the evidence adduced.

History of Evid. C. §732: Added eff. Sept. 17, 1965, oper. Jan. 1, 1967, Stats. 1965, ch. 299, §2.

Official Comment

7 Cal. Law Revision Comm'n Rep. (1965) p. 1113.

Section 732 restates the substance of and supersedes the fourth paragraph of Section 1871 of the Code of Civil Procedure. Section 732 refers to Section 775, which is based on language originally contained in Section 1871. Section 775 permits each party to the action to object to questions asked and evidence adduced and, also, to cross-examine any person called by the court as a witness to the same extent as if such person were called as a witness by an adverse party.

§733. [CALLING OTHER EXPERTS]

Nothing contained in this article shall be deemed or construed to prevent any party to any action from producing other expert evidence on the same fact or matter mentioned in Section 730; but, where other expert witnesses are called by a party to the action, their fees shall be paid by the party calling them and only ordinary witness fees shall be taxed as costs in the action.

History of Evid. C. §733: Added eff. Sept. 17, 1965, oper. Jan. 1, 1967, Stats. 1965, ch. 299, §2.

Official Comment

7 Cal. Law Revision Comm'n Rep. (1965) p. 1114.

Section 733 restates the substance of and supersedes the third paragraph of Section 1871 of the Code of Civil Procedure.

CHAPTER 4. INTERPRETERS & TRANSLATORS

§750. [WITNESS RULES APPLY]

A person who serves as an interpreter or translator in any action is subject to all the rules of law relating to witnesses.

History of Evid. C. §750: Added eff. Sept. 17, 1965, oper. Jan. 1, 1967, Stats. 1965, ch. 299, §2.

Official Comment

7 Cal. Law Revision Comm'n Rep. (1965) p. 1114.

Section 750 codifies existing law. *E.g.*, *People v. Lem Deo*, 132 Cal. 199, 201, 64 Pac. 265, 266 (1901) (interpreter); *People v. Bardin*, 148 Cal.App.2d 776, 307 P.2d 384 (1957) (translator).

§751. [TRUE INTERPRETATION OR TRANSLATION]

(a) [**Oath.**] An interpreter shall take an oath that he or she will make a true interpretation to the witness in a language that the witness understands and that he or she will make a true interpretation of the witness' answers to questions to counsel, court, or jury, in the English language, with his or her best skill and judgment.

(b) [**Testimony of deaf person.**] In any proceeding in which a deaf or hard-of-hearing person is testifying under oath, the interpreter certified pursuant to subdivision (f) of Section 754 shall advise the court whenever he or she is unable to comply with his or her oath taken pursuant to subdivision (a).

(c) [**Writings translated into English.**] A translator shall take an oath that he or she will make a true translation in the English language of any writing he or she is to decipher or translate.

(d) [**Regularly employed interpreters and translators.**] An interpreter regularly employed by the court and certified or registered in accordance with Article 4 (commencing with Section 68560) of Chapter 2 of Title 8 of the Government Code, or a translator regularly employed by the court, may file an oath as prescribed by this section with the clerk of the court. The filed oath shall serve for all subsequent court proceedings until the appointment is revoked by the court.

History of Evid. C. §751: Added eff. Sept. 17, 1965, oper. Jan. 1, 1967, Stats. 1965, ch. 299, §2. Amended eff. Mar. 7, 1984, Stats. 1984, ch. 30, §1; eff. Jan. 1, 1991, Stats. 1990, ch. 1450, §1; eff. Jan. 1, 1998, Stats. 1997, ch. 376, §1.

Official Comment

7 Cal. Law Revision Comm'n Rep. (1965) p. 1114.

Section 751 is based on language presently contained in subdivision (c) of Section 1885 of the Code of Civil Procedure.

§752. [INTERPRETER OF ENGLISH]

(a) [**Interpreter.**] When a witness is incapable of understanding the English language or is incapable of expressing himself or herself in the English language so as to be understood directly by counsel, court, and jury, an interpreter whom the witness can understand and who can understand the witness shall be sworn to interpret for the witness.

(b) [**Record.**] The record shall identify the interpreter, who may be appointed and compensated as provided in Article 2 (commencing with Section 730) of Chapter 3, with that compensation charged as follows:

(1) In all criminal actions and juvenile court proceedings, the compensation for an interpreter under this section shall be a charge against the court.

(2) In all civil actions, the compensation for an interpreter under this section shall, in the first instance, be apportioned and charged to the several parties in a proportion as the court may determine and may thereafter be taxed and allowed in a like manner as other costs.

History of Evid. C. §752: Added eff. Sept. 17, 1965, oper. Jan. 1, 1967, Stats. 1965, ch. 299, §2. Amended eff. Mar. 7, 1984, Stats. 1984, ch. 30, §2; eff. Jan. 1, 1985, Stats. 1984, ch. 768, §1; eff. Jan. 1, 2013, Stats. 2012, ch. 470, §9.

Official Comment

7 Cal. Law Revision Comm'n Rep. (1965) p. 1115.

Section 752 restates the substance of and supersedes Section 1884 of the Code of Civil Procedure. It is drawn broadly enough to authorize the use of an interpreter for a person whose inability to be understood directly stems from physical disability as well as from lack of understanding of the English language. See discussion in *People v. Walker*, 69 Cal.App. 475, 231 Pac. 572 (1924). Under Section 752, as under existing law, whether an interpreter should be appointed is largely within the discretion of the trial judge. *People v. Holtzclaw*, 76 Cal.App. 168, 243 Pac. 894 (1926).

Subdivision (b) of Section 752 substitutes for the detailed language in Code of Civil Procedure Section 1884 a reference to the general authority of a court to appoint expert witnesses, since interpreters are treated as expert witnesses and subject to the same rules of competency and examination as are experts generally. The existing procedure provided by Code of Civil Procedure Section 1884 does not insure that an interpreter who is required to testify will be paid reasonable compensation for his services. Section 752 corrects this deficiency in the existing law.

ANNOTATIONS

People v. Augustin (4th Dist.2003) 112 Cal.App.4th 444, 451. "[T]he decision on whether to appoint an interpreter falls within the trial court's discretion."

§753. [TRANSLATOR OF WRITING]

(a) [Decipher or translate.] When the written characters in a writing offered in evidence are incapable of being deciphered or understood directly, a translator who can decipher the characters or understand the language shall be sworn to decipher or translate the writing.

(b) [Record.] The record shall identify the translator, who may be appointed and compensated as provided in Article 2 (commencing with Section 730) of Chapter 3, with that compensation charged as follows:

(1) In all criminal actions and juvenile court proceedings, the compensation for a translator under this section shall be a charge against the court.

(2) In all civil actions, the compensation for a translator under this section shall, in the first instance, be apportioned and charged to the several parties in a proportion as the court may determine and may thereafter be taxed and allowed in like manner as other costs.

History of Evid. C. §753: Added eff. Sept. 17, 1965, oper. Jan. 1, 1967, Stats. 1965, ch. 299, §2. Amended eff. Mar. 7, 1984, Stats. 1984, ch. 30, §3; eff. Jan. 1, 2013, Stats. 2012, ch. 470, §10.

Official Comment

7 Cal. Law Revision Comm'n Rep. (1965) p. 1115.

Section 753 restates the substance of and supersedes Section 1863 of the Code of Civil Procedure, but the language of Section 753 is new. The same principles that require the appointment of an interpreter for a witness who is incapable of expressing himself so as to be understood directly apply with equal force to documentary evidence. *See* Evidence Code §752 and the *Comment* thereto.

§754. [HEARING-IMPAIRED PERSONS]

(a) [Deaf or hearing-impaired.] As used in this section, "individual who is deaf or hearing impaired" means an individual with a hearing loss so great as to prevent his or her understanding language spoken in a normal tone, but does not include an individual who is hearing impaired provided with, and able to fully participate in the proceedings through the use of, an assistive listening system or computer-aided transcription equipment provided pursuant to Section 54.8 of the Civil Code.

(b) [Proceedings requiring interpreter.] In any civil or criminal action, including, but not limited to, any action involving a traffic or other infraction, any small claims court proceeding, any juvenile court proceeding, any family court proceeding or service, or any proceeding to determine the mental competency of a person, in any court-ordered or court-provided alternative dispute resolution, including mediation and arbitration, or any administrative hearing, where a party or witness is an individual who is deaf or hearing impaired and the individual who is deaf or hearing impaired is present and participating, the proceedings shall be interpreted in a language that the individual who is deaf or hearing impaired understands by a qualified interpreter appointed by the court or other appointing authority, or as agreed upon.

(c) [Appointing authority.] For purposes of this section, "appointing authority" means a court, department, board, commission, agency, licensing or legislative body, or other body for proceedings requiring a qualified interpreter.

(d) [Interpreter defined.] For the purposes of this section, "interpreter" includes, but is not limited to, an oral interpreter, a sign language interpreter, or a

deaf-blind interpreter, depending upon the needs of the individual who is deaf or hearing impaired.

(e) [Intermediary interpreter defined.] For purposes of this section, "intermediary interpreter" means an individual who is deaf or hearing impaired, or a hearing individual who is able to assist in providing an accurate interpretation between spoken English and sign language or between variants of sign language or between American Sign Language and other foreign languages by acting as an intermediary between the individual who is deaf or hearing impaired and the qualified interpreter.

(f) [Qualified interpreter.] For purposes of this section, "qualified interpreter" means an interpreter who has been certified as competent to interpret court proceedings by a testing organization, agency, or educational institution approved by the Judicial Council as qualified to administer tests to court interpreters for individuals who are deaf or hearing impaired.

(g) [Appointment of intermediary interpreter.] In the event that the appointed interpreter is not familiar with the use of particular signs by the individual who is deaf or hearing impaired or his or her particular variant of sign language, the court or other appointing authority shall, in consultation with the individual who is deaf or hearing impaired or his or her representative, appoint an intermediary interpreter.

(h) [Guidelines for certifying interpreters.] Prior to July 1, 1992, the Judicial Council shall conduct a study to establish the guidelines pursuant to which it shall determine which testing organizations, agencies, or educational institutions will be approved to administer tests for certification of court interpreters for individuals who are deaf or hearing impaired. It is the intent of the Legislature that the study obtain the widest possible input from the public, including, but not limited to, educational institutions, the judiciary, linguists, members of the State Bar, court interpreters, members of professional interpreting organizations, and members of the deaf and hearing-impaired communities. After obtaining public comment and completing its study, the Judicial Council shall publish these guidelines. By January 1, 1997, the Judicial Council shall approve one or more entities to administer testing for court interpreters for individuals who are deaf or hearing impaired. Testing entities may include educational institutions, testing organizations, joint powers agencies, or public agencies.

Commencing July 1, 1997, court interpreters for individuals who are deaf or hearing impaired shall meet the qualifications specified in subdivision (f).

(i) [Compensation.] Persons appointed to serve as interpreters under this section shall be paid, in addition to actual travel costs, the prevailing rate paid to persons employed by the court to provide other interpreter services unless such service is considered to be a part of the person's regular duties as an employee of the state, county, or other political subdivision of the state. Except as provided in subdivision (j), payment of the interpreter's fee shall be a charge against the court. Payment of the interpreter's fee in administrative proceedings shall be a charge against the appointing board or authority.

(j) [Criminal matters.] Whenever a peace officer or any other person having a law enforcement or prosecutorial function in any criminal or quasi-criminal investigation or non-court proceeding questions or otherwise interviews an alleged victim or witness who demonstrates or alleges deafness or hearing impairment, a good faith effort to secure the services of an interpreter shall be made, without any unnecessary delay unless either the individual who is deaf or hearing impaired affirmatively indicates that he or she does not need or cannot use an interpreter, or an interpreter is not otherwise required by Title II of the Americans with Disabilities Act of 1990 (Public Law 101-336) and federal regulations adopted thereunder. Payment of the interpreter's fee shall be a charge against the county, or other political subdivision of the state, in which the action is pending.

(k) [Exclusion of statement in criminal matter.] No statement, written or oral, made by an individual who the court finds is deaf or hearing impaired in reply to a question of a peace officer, or any other person having a law enforcement or prosecutorial function in any criminal or quasi-criminal investigation or proceeding, may be used against that individual who is deaf or hearing impaired unless the question was accurately interpreted and the statement was made knowingly, voluntarily, and intelligently and was accurately interpreted, or the court makes special findings that either the individual could not have used an interpreter or an interpreter was not otherwise required by Title II of the Americans with Disabilities Act of 1990 (Public Law 101-336) and federal regulations adopted thereun-

der and that the statement was made knowingly, voluntarily, and intelligently.

(*l*) **[Priority in criminal matter.]** In obtaining services of an interpreter for purposes of subdivision (j) or (k), priority shall be given to first obtaining a qualified interpreter.

(m) [Qualified interpreter required in criminal matters.] Nothing in subdivision (j) or (k) shall be deemed to supersede the requirement of subdivision (b) for use of a qualified interpreter for individuals who are deaf or hearing impaired participating as parties or witnesses in a trial or hearing.

(n) [Conditions for translation.] In any action or proceeding in which an individual who is deaf or hearing impaired is a participant, the appointing authority shall not commence proceedings until the appointed interpreter is in full view of and spatially situated to assure proper communication with the participating individual who is deaf or hearing impaired.

(o) [Roster of interpreters.] Each superior court shall maintain a current roster of qualified interpreters certified pursuant to subdivision (f).

History of Evid. C. §754: Added eff. Sept. 17, 1965, oper. Jan. 1, 1967, Stats. 1965, ch. 299, §2. Amended eff. Jan. 1, 1978, Stats. 1977, ch. 1182, §1; eff. Jan. 1, 1985, Stats. 1984, ch. 768, §2; eff. Jan. 1, 1990, Stats. 1989, ch. 1002, §2; eff. Jan. 1, 1991, Stats. 1990, ch. 1450, §2; eff. Jan. 1, 1992, Stats. 1991, ch. 883, §1; eff. July 7, 1992, Stats. 1992, ch. 118, §1; eff. Jan. 1, 1993, Stats. 1992, ch. 913, §14; eff. July 18, 1995, Stats. 1995, ch. 143, §1; eff. Jan. 1, 2013, Stats. 2012, ch. 470, §11.

Official Comment

7 Cal. Law Revision Comm'n Rep. (1965) p. 1116.

Section 754 restates the substance of and supersedes Section 1885 of the Code of Civil Procedure. Subdivision (c) of Section 1885 is not continued in Section 754 but is restated in substance in Section 751.

The phrase "with or without a hearing aid" has been deleted from the definition of "deaf person" as unnecessary. The court's inquiry should be directed towards the ability of the person to hear; the court should not be concerned with the means by which he might be enabled to hear.

§754.5. [PRIVILEGE NOT WAIVED]

Whenever an otherwise valid privilege exists between an individual who is deaf or hearing impaired and another person, that privilege is not waived merely because an interpreter was used to facilitate their communication.

History of Evid. C. §754.5: Added Jan. 1, 1991, Stats. 1990, ch. 1450, §3. Amended eff. Jan. 1, 1993, Stats. 1992, ch. 913, §15.

§755. REPEALED [~~[DOMESTIC-VIOLENCE PROCEEDINGS]~~]

[~~(a)~~] [~~[Proceedings requiring interpreter.] In any action or proceeding under Division 10 (commencing with Section 6200) of the Family Code, and in any action or proceeding under the Uniform Parentage Act (Part 3 (commencing with Section 7600) of Division 12 of the Family Code) or for dissolution or nullity of marriage or legal separation of the parties in which a protective order has been granted or is being sought pursuant to Section 6221 of the Family Code, in which a party does not proficiently speak or understand the English language, and that party is present, an interpreter, as provided in this section, shall be present to interpret the proceedings in a language that the party understands, and to assist communication between the party and his or her attorney. Notwithstanding this requirement, a court may issue an ex parte order pursuant to Sections 2045 and 7710 of, and Article 1 (commencing with Section 6320) of Chapter 2 of Part 4 of Division 10 of the Family Code, without the presence of an interpreter. The interpreter selected shall be certified pursuant to Article 4 (commencing with Section 68560) of Chapter 2 of Title 8 of the Government Code, unless the court in its discretion appoints an interpreter who is not certified.~~]

[~~(b)~~] [~~[Compensation for interpreter.] The fees of interpreters utilized under this section shall be paid as provided in subdivision (b) of Section 68092 of the Government Code. However, the fees of an interpreter shall be waived for a party who needs an interpreter and appears in forma pauperis pursuant to Section 68511.3 of the Government Code. The Judicial Council shall amend subdivision (i) of California Rule of Court 985 and revise its forms accordingly by July 1, 1996.~~]

[~~(c)~~] [~~[Conditions for interpretation.] In any civil action in which an interpreter is required under this section, the court shall not commence proceedings until the appointed interpreter is present and situated near the party and his or her attorney. However, this section shall not prohibit the court from doing any of the following:~~]

[~~(1)~~] [~~Issuing an order when the necessity for the order outweighs the necessity for an interpreter.~~]

[~~(2)~~] [~~Extending the duration of a previously issued temporary order if an interpreter is not readily available.~~]

[~~(3)~~] [~~Issuing a permanent order where a party who requires an interpreter fails to make appropriate arrangements for an interpreter after receiving proper notice of the hearing with information about obtaining an interpreter.~~]

[~~(d)~~] [~~[Other assistance.]~~ ~~This section does not prohibit the presence of any other person to assist a party.~~]

[~~(e)~~] [~~[Funding.]~~ ~~A local public entity may, and the Judicial Council shall, apply to the appropriate state agency that receives federal funds authorized pursuant to the federal Violence Against Women Act (P.L. 103-322) for these federal funds or for funds from sources other than the state to implement this section. A local public entity and the Judicial Council shall comply with the requirements of this section only to the extent that any of these funds are made available.~~]

[~~(f)~~] [~~[Forms.]~~ ~~The Judicial Council shall draft rules and modify forms necessary to implement this section, including those for the petition for a temporary restraining order and related forms, to inform both parties of their right to an interpreter pursuant to this section.~~]

Repealed oper. Jan. 1, 2015, Stats. 2014, ch. 721, §1.

§755.5. [MEDICAL EXAMINATION]

(a) [Examinations requiring interpreter.] During any medical examination, requested by an insurer or by the defendant, of a person who is a party to a civil action and who does not proficiently speak or understand the English language, conducted for the purpose of determining damages in a civil action, an interpreter shall be present to interpret the examination in a language that the person understands. The interpreter shall be certified pursuant to Article 8 (commencing with Section 11435.05) of Chapter 4.5 of Part 1 of Division 3 of Title 2 of the Government Code.

(b) [Compensation.] The fees of interpreters used under subdivision (a) shall be paid by the insurer or defendant requesting the medical examination.

(c) [Exclusion of medical evidence.] The record of, or testimony concerning, any medical examination conducted in violation of subdivision (a) shall be inadmissible in the civil action for which it was conducted or any other civil action.

(d) [Other assistance.] This section does not prohibit the presence of any other person to assist a party.

(e) [Interpreter unavailable.] In the event that interpreters certified pursuant to Article 8 (commencing with Section 11435.05) of Chapter 4.5 of Part 1 of Division 3 of Title 2 of the Government Code cannot be present at the medical examination, upon stipulation of the parties the requester specified in subdivision (a) shall have the discretionary authority to provisionally qualify and use other interpreters.

History of Evid. C. §755.5: Added eff. Sept. 30, 1992, Stats. 1992, ch. 1302, §5. Amended eff. Jan. 1, 1996, oper. July 1, 1997, Stats. 1995, ch. 938, §8.

Official Comment

25 Cal. Law Revision Comm'n Rep. (1995) p. 272.

Section 755.5 is amended to correct references to the Administrative Procedure Act. The former reference in subdivision (a) to January 1, 1994, is deleted as obsolete.

ANNOTATIONS

Nazari v. Ayrapetyan (2d Dist.2009) 171 Cal.App.4th 690, 695. Section 755.5 "clearly bans the admission of medical records or medical examinations that defendants or insurance companies conduct for purposes of determining damages in a civil action without the aid of a certified interpreter when the plaintiff is not English-proficient. The statute does not appear to preclude the records or examinations conducted on behalf of the *plaintiff*, even absent a certified interpreter. *At 696:* Logically, the statute prevents the admission of evidence of a defense examination based on a miscommunication. But, not all medical examinations are language-dependent. For example, a phlebotomist can draw and evaluate a plaintiff's blood without ever speaking with the plaintiff. A doctor can silently test a patient's reflex. ... A holding that ... §755.5 precludes testimony about medical examinations that do not require any communication with the plaintiff would be absurd because no translation would be necessary. [W]e hold that ... §755.5 does not prohibit admission into evidence of the record of, or testimony concerning, evidence derived from tests or examinations that require no communication with the plaintiff."

E §756. [INTERPRETER-SERVICES FUNDING]

(a) [Eligibility.] To the extent required by other state or federal laws, the Judicial Council shall reimburse courts for court interpreter services provided in civil actions and proceedings to any party who is present in court and who does not proficiently speak or understand the English language for the purpose of interpreting the proceedings in a language the party understands, and assisting communications between the party, his or her attorney, and the court.

(b) [Priority.] If sufficient funds are not appropriated to provide an interpreter to every party that meets the standard of eligibility, court interpreter services in civil cases reimbursed by the Judicial Council, pursu-

ant to subdivision (a), shall be prioritized by case type by each court in the following order:

(1) Actions and proceedings under Division 10 (commencing with Section 6200) of the Family Code, actions or proceedings under the Uniform Parentage Act (Part 3 (commencing with Section 7600) of Division 12 of the Family Code) in which a protective order has been granted or is being sought pursuant to Section 6221 of the Family Code, and actions and proceedings for dissolution or nullity of marriage or legal separation of the parties in which a protective order has been granted or is being sought pursuant to Section 6221 of the Family Code; actions and proceedings under subdivision (w) of Section 527.6 of the Code of Civil Procedure; and actions and proceedings for physical abuse or neglect under the Elder Abuse and Dependent Adult Civil Protection Act (Chapter 11 (commencing with Section 15600) of Part 3 of Division 9 of the Welfare and Institutions Code).

(2) Actions and proceedings relating to unlawful detainer.

(3) Actions and proceedings to terminate parental rights.

(4) Actions and proceedings relating to conservatorship or guardianship, including the appointment or termination of a probate guardian or conservator.

(5) Actions and proceedings by a parent to obtain sole legal or physical custody of a child or rights to visitation.

(6) All other actions and proceedings under Section 527.6 of the Code of Civil Procedure or the Elder Abuse and Dependent Adult Civil Protection Act (Chapter 11 (commencing with Section 15600) of Part 3 of Division 9 of the Welfare and Institutions Code).

(7) All other actions and proceedings related to family law.

(8) All other civil actions or proceedings.

(c) [**Alternative priority.**]

(1) If funds are not available to provide an interpreter to every party that meets the standard of eligibility, preference shall be given for parties proceeding in forma pauperis pursuant to Section 68631 of the Government Code in any civil action or proceeding described in paragraph (3), (4), (5), (6), (7), or (8) of subdivision (b).

(2) Courts may provide an interpreter to a party outside the priority order listed in subdivision (b) when a qualified interpreter is present and available at the court location and no higher priority action that meets the standard of eligibility described in subdivision (a) is taking place at that location during the period of time for which the interpreter has already been compensated.

(d) [**Party not charged.**] A party shall not be charged a fee for the provision of a court interpreter.

(e) [**Court certification.**] In seeking reimbursement for court interpreter services, the court shall identify to the Judicial Council the case types for which the interpretation to be reimbursed was provided. Courts shall regularly certify that in providing the interpreter services, they have complied with the priorities and preferences set forth in subdivisions (b) and (c), which shall be subject to review by the Judicial Council.

(f) [**Other rights not affected.**] This section shall not be construed to alter, limit, or negate any right to an interpreter in a civil action or proceeding otherwise provided by state or federal law, or the right to an interpreter in criminal, traffic, or other infraction, juvenile, or mental competency actions or proceedings.

(g) [**No quality reduction.**] This section shall not result in a reduction in staffing or compromise the quality of interpreting services in criminal, juvenile, or other types of matters in which interpreters are provided.

History of Evid. C. §756: Added eff. Jan. 1, 2015, Stats. 2014, ch. 721, §2.

§760

E §757. [JUVENILE-IMMIGRANT PROCEEDINGS]

Pursuant to this chapter, other applicable law, and existing Judicial Council policy, including the policy adopted on January 23, 2014, existing authority to provide interpreters in civil court includes the authority to provide an interpreter in a proceeding in which a petitioner requests an order from the superior court to make the findings regarding special immigrant juvenile status pursuant to Section 1101(a)(27)(J) of Title 8 of the United States Code.

History of Evid. C. §757: Added eff. Sept. 27, 2014, Stats. 2014, ch. 685, §2.

CHAPTER 5. METHOD & SCOPE OF EXAMINATION

ARTICLE 1. DEFINITIONS

§760. [DIRECT EXAMINATION]

"Direct examination" is the first examination of a witness upon a matter that is not within the scope of a previous examination of the witness.

History of Evid. C. §760: Added eff. Sept. 17, 1965, oper. Jan. 1, 1967, Stats. 1965, ch. 299, §2.

Official Comment

7 Cal. Law Revision Comm'n Rep. (1965) p. 1117.

Section 760 restates the substance of and supersedes the first clause of Code of Civil Procedure Section 2045 and the last clause of Code of Civil Procedure Section 2048. Under Section 760, an examination of a witness called by another party is direct examination if the examination relates to a matter that is not within the scope of the previous examination of the witness.

§761. [CROSS-EXAMINATION]

"Cross-examination" is the examination of a witness by a party other than the direct examiner upon a matter that is within the scope of the direct examination of the witness.

History of Evid. C. §761: Added eff. Sept. 17, 1965, oper. Jan. 1, 1967, Stats. 1965, ch. 299, §2.

Official Comment

7 Cal. Law Revision Comm'n Rep. (1965) p. 1117.

Section 761 restates the substance of and supersedes the definition of "cross-examination" found in Section 2045 of the Code of Civil Procedure. In accordance with existing law, it limits cross-examination of a witness to the scope of the witness' direct examination. *See generally* Witkin, *California Evidence* §§622-638 (1958).

Section 761, together with Section 773, retains the cross-examination rule now applicable to a defendant in a criminal action who testifies as a witness in that action. *See People v. McCarthy*, 88 Cal.App.2d 883, 200 P.2d 69 (1948). *See also People v. Arrighini*, 122 Cal. 121, 54 Pac. 591 (1898); *People v. O'Brien*, 66 Cal. 602, 6 Pac. 695 (1885); Witkin, *California Evidence* §629 (1958). *See also* Evidence Code §772(d).

§762. [REDIRECT EXAMINATION]

"Redirect examination" is an examination of a witness by the direct examiner subsequent to the cross-examination of the witness.

History of Evid. C. §762: Added eff. Sept. 17, 1965, oper. Jan. 1, 1967, Stats. 1965, ch. 299, §2.

Official Comment

7 Cal. Law Revision Comm'n Rep. (1965) p. 1117.

"Redirect examination" and "recross-examination" are not defined in existing statutes, but the terms are recognized in practice. *See* Witkin, *California Evidence* §§697, 698 (1958). The scope of redirect and recross-examination is limited by Section 774.

The definition of "redirect examination" embraces not only the examination immediately following cross-examination of the witness but also any subsequent re-examination of the witness by the direct examiner.

§763. [RECROSS-EXAMINATION]

"Recross-examination" is an examination of a witness by a cross-examiner subsequent to a redirect examination of the witness.

History of Evid. C. §763: Added eff. Sept. 17, 1965, oper. Jan. 1, 1967, Stats. 1965, ch. 299, §2.

Official Comment

7 Cal. Law Revision Comm'n Rep. (1965) p. 1118.

See the *Comment* to Section 762. The definition of "recross-examination" embraces not only the examination immediately following the first redirect examination of the witness but also any subsequent re-examination of the witness by a cross-examiner.

§764. [LEADING QUESTION]

A "leading question" is a question that suggests to the witness the answer that the examining party desires.

History of Evid. C. §764: Added eff. Sept. 17, 1965, oper. Jan. 1, 1967, Stats. 1965, ch. 299, §2.

Official Comment

7 Cal. Law Revision Comm'n Rep. (1965) p. 1118.

Section 764 restates the substance of and supersedes the first sentence of Section 2046 of the Code of Civil Procedure. For restrictions on the use of leading questions in the examination of a witness, *see* Evidence Code §767 and the *Comment* thereto.

ANNOTATIONS

People v. Williams (2013) 56 Cal.4th 165, 192 n.17. "It is a common misconception that all questions asking for a 'yes' or 'no' answer are leading. In fact only questions that contain a direction to the witness are so. Perhaps the easiest example is a question that begins, 'Isn't it true that ...?' Some questions that begin 'Did X do [a detailed set of facts]?' may be covered. ... A question may be leading because of its form, but often the mere form of a question does not indicate whether it is leading. The question which contains a phrase like 'did he not?' is obviously and invariably leading, but almost any other type of question may be leading or not, dependent upon the content and context. The whole issue is whether an ordinary man would get the impression that the questioner desired one answer rather than another. The form of a question, or previous questioning, may indicate the desire, but the most important circumstance for consideration is the extent of the particularity of the question itself." (Internal quotes omitted.) *See also* ***People v. Abel*** (2012) 53 Cal.4th 891, 935 n.9.

ARTICLE 2. EXAMINATION OF WITNESSES

§765. [CONTROL OF INTERROGATION]

(a) [Control over mode.] The court shall exercise reasonable control over the mode of interrogation of a witness so as to make interrogation as rapid, as distinct, and as effective for the ascertainment of the truth, as may be, and to protect the witness from undue harassment or embarrassment.

(b) [Protecting youth or dependent.] With a witness under the age of 14 or a dependent person with a substantial cognitive impairment, the court shall take special care to protect him or her from undue harassment or embarrassment, and to restrict the unneces-

sary repetition of questions. The court shall also take special care to ensure that questions are stated in a form which is appropriate to the age or cognitive level of the witness. The court may, in the interests of justice, on objection by a party, forbid the asking of a question which is in a form that is not reasonably likely to be understood by a person of the age or cognitive level of the witness.

History of Evid. C. §765: Added eff. Sept. 17, 1965, oper. Jan. 1, 1967, Stats. 1965, ch. 299, §2. Amended eff. Jan. 1, 1986, Stats. 1985, ch. 884, §3; eff. Jan. 1, 1987, Stats. 1986, ch. 1051, §1; eff. Jan. 1, 2005, Stats. 2004, ch. 823, §4.

Official Comment

7 Cal. Law Revision Comm'n Rep. (1965) p. 1118.

Section 765 restates the substance of and supersedes Section 2044 of the Code of Civil Procedure. As to the latitude permitted the judge in controlling the examination of witnesses under existing law, which is continued in effect by Section 765, *see Commercial Union Assur. Co. v. Pacific Gas & Elec. Co.*, 220 Cal. 515, 31 P.2d 793 (1934). *See also People v. Davis*, 6 Cal.App. 229, 91 Pac. 810 (1907).

§766. [RESPONSIVE ANSWERS]

A witness must give responsive answers to questions, and answers that are not responsive shall be stricken on motion of any party.

History of Evid. C. §766: Added eff. Sept. 17, 1965, oper. Jan. 1, 1967, Stats. 1965, ch. 299, §2.

Official Comment

7 Cal. Law Revision Comm'n Rep. (1965) p. 1119.

Section 766 restates the substance of and supersedes Section 2056 of the Code of Civil Procedure.

ANNOTATIONS

Rayii v. Gatica (2d Dist.2013) 218 Cal.App.4th 1402, 1414. "'[A] motion to strike must be directed with precision to the matter sought to be stricken. A motion to strike out inadmissible evidence may properly be denied where it is general and embraces evidence which is admissible as well as that which is inadmissible.' If part of the answer is responsive and part is nonresponsive, the moving party must specify the nonresponsive part; and a motion to strike the entire answer as nonresponsive may properly be denied."

§767. [LEADING QUESTIONS]

(a) Except under special circumstances where the interests of justice otherwise require:

(1) A leading question may not be asked of a witness on direct or redirect examination.

(2) A leading question may be asked of a witness on cross-examination or recross-examination.

(b) The court may, in the interests of justice permit a leading question to be asked of a child under 10 years of age or a dependent person with a substantial cognitive impairment in a case involving a prosecution under Section 273a, 273d, 288.5, 368, or any of the acts described in Section 11165.1 or 11165.2 of the Penal Code.

History of Evid. C. §767: Added eff. Sept. 17, 1965, oper. Jan. 1, 1967, Stats. 1965, ch. 299, §2. Amended eff. Sept. 26, 1984, Stats. 1984, ch. 1423, §1; eff. Jan. 1, 1996, Stats. 1995, ch. 87, §1; eff. Jan. 1, 2005, Stats. 2004, ch. 823, §5.

Official Comment

**7 Cal. Law Revision Comm'n Rep. (1965) p. 1119;
Assem. J., Apr. 6, 1965, p. 1740.**

Subdivision (a) restates the substance of and supersedes the last sentence of Section 2046 of the Code of Civil Procedure. Subdivision (b) is based on and supersedes a phrase that appears in Code of Civil Procedure Section 2048.

The exception stated at the beginning of the section continues the present law that permits leading questions on direct examination where there is little danger of improper suggestion or where such questions are necessary to obtain relevant evidence. This would permit leading questions on direct examination for preliminary matters, refreshing recollection, and examining handicapped witnesses, expert witnesses, and hostile witnesses. *See* Witkin, *California Evidence* §§591, 592 (1958); 3 Wigmore, *Evidence* §769 *et seq.* (3d ed. 1940). The court may also forbid the asking of leading questions on cross-examination where the witness is biased in favor of the cross-examiner and would be unduly susceptible to the influence of questions that suggested the desired answer. *See* 3 Wigmore, *Evidence* §773 (3d ed. 1940).

§768. [WRITINGS]

(a) [Examining witness.] In examining a witness concerning a writing, it is not necessary to show, read, or disclose to him any part of the writing.

(b) [Inspection.] If a writing is shown to a witness, all parties to the action must be given an opportunity to inspect it before any question concerning it may be asked of the witness.

History of Evid. C. §768: Added eff. Sept. 17, 1965, oper. Jan. 1, 1967, Stats. 1965, ch. 299, §2.

Official Comment

**7 Cal. Law Revision Comm'n Rep. (1965) p. 1119;
Assem. J., Apr. 6, 1965, p. 1741.**

Existing law apparently does not require that a writing (other than one containing prior inconsistent statements used for impeachment purposes) be shown to a witness before he can be examined concerning it. Section 2054 of the Code of Civil Procedure, which seems to so require, actually requires only that the adverse party be given an opportunity to inspect any writing that is *actually shown* to a witness before the witness can be examined concerning the writing. *See People v. Briggs*, 58 Cal.2d 385, 413, 24 Cal.Rptr. 417, 435, 374 P.2d 257, 275 (1962); *People v. Keyes*, 103 Cal.App. 624, 284 Pac. 1096 (1930) (hearing denied); *People v. De Angelli*, 34 Cal.App. 716, 168 Pac. 699 (1917). Section 768 clarifies whatever doubt may exist in this regard by declaring that such a writing need not be shown to the witness before he can be examined concerning it. Of course, the best evidence rule may in some cases preclude eliciting testimony concerning the content of a writing. *See* Evidence Code §1500 and the *Comment* thereto.

Insofar as Section 768 relates to prior inconsistent statements that are in writing, *see* the *Comment* to Section 769.

Subdivision (b) of Section 768 preserves the right of the adverse party to inspect a writing that is *actually shown* to a witness before the witness can be examined concerning it. As indicated above, this preserves the existing requirement declared in Code of Civil Procedure Section 2054. However, the right of inspection has been extended to all parties to the action.

§769. [INCONSISTENT STATEMENT]

In examining a witness concerning a statement or other conduct by him that is inconsistent with any part of his testimony at the hearing, it is not necessary to disclose to him any information concerning the statement or other conduct.

History of Evid. C. §769: Added eff. Sept. 17, 1965, oper. Jan. 1, 1967, Stats. 1965, ch. 299, §2.

Official Comment

7 Cal. Law Revision Comm'n Rep. (1965) p. 1120; Assem. J., Apr. 6, 1965, p. 1741.

Section 769 is consistent with the existing California law regarding the examination of a witness concerning prior inconsistent *oral* statements. Under existing law, a party need not disclose to a witness any information concerning a prior inconsistent *oral* statement of the witness before asking him questions about the statement. *People v. Kidd*, 56 Cal.2d 759, 765, 16 Cal.Rptr. 793, 796-797, 366 P.2d 49, 52-53 (1961); *People v. Campos*, 10 Cal.App.2d 310, 317, 52 P.2d 251, 254 (1935). However, if a witness' prior inconsistent statements are in *writing* or, as in the case of former oral testimony, have been reduced to writing, "they must be shown to the witness before any question is put to him concerning them." Code Civ. Proc. §2052 (repealed, now Evidence Code §768); *Umemoto v. McDonald*, 6 Cal.2d 587, 592, 58 P.2d 1274, 1276 (1936).

Section 769 eliminates the distinction made in existing law between oral and written statements and permits a witness to be asked questions concerning a prior inconsistent statement, whether written or oral, even though no disclosure is made to him concerning the prior statement. (Whether a foundational showing is required before other evidence of the prior statement may be admitted is not covered in Section 769; the prerequisites for the admission of such evidence are set forth in Section 770.) The disclosure of inconsistent written statements that is required under existing law limits the effectiveness of cross-examination by removing the element of surprise. The forewarning gives the dishonest witness the opportunity to reshape his testimony in conformity with the prior statement. The existing rule is based on an English common law rule that has been abandoned in England for 100 years. *See* McCormick, *Evidence* §28 at 53 (1954).

§769

§770. [EXTRINSIC EVIDENCE OF INCONSISTENT STATEMENT]

Unless the interests of justice otherwise require, extrinsic evidence of a statement made by a witness that is inconsistent with any part of his testimony at the hearing shall be excluded unless:

(a) The witness was so examined while testifying as to give him an opportunity to explain or to deny the statement; or

(b) The witness has not been excused from giving further testimony in the action.

History of Evid. C. §770: Added eff. Sept. 17, 1965, oper. Jan. 1, 1967, Stats. 1965, ch. 299, §2.

Official Comment

7 Cal. Law Revision Comm'n Rep. (1965) p. 1121.

Under Section 2052 of the Code of Civil Procedure, extrinsic evidence of a witness' inconsistent statement may be admitted only if the witness was given the opportunity, while testifying, to explain or deny the contradictory statement. Permitting a witness to explain or deny an alleged inconsistent statement is desirable, but there is no compelling reason to provide the opportunity for explanation *before* the inconsistent statement is introduced in evidence. Accordingly, unless the interests of justice otherwise require, Section 770 permits the judge to exclude evidence of an inconsistent statement only if the witness during his examination was not given an opportunity to explain or deny the statement *and* he has been unconditionally excused and is not subject to being recalled as a witness. Among other things, Section 770 will permit more effective cross-examination and impeachment of several collusive witnesses, since there need be no disclosure of prior inconsistency before all such witnesses have been examined.

Where the interests of justice require it, the court may permit extrinsic evidence of an inconsistent statement to be admitted even though the witness has been excused and has had no opportunity to explain or deny the statement. An absolute rule forbidding introduction of such evidence where the specified conditions are not met may cause hardship in some cases. For example, the party seeking to introduce the statement may not have learned of its existence until after the witness has left the court and is no longer available to testify. For the foundational requirements for the admission of a hearsay declarant's inconsistent statement, *see* Evidence Code §1202 and the *Comment* thereto.

§771. [WRITING USED TO REFRESH MEMORY]

(a) [Production of writing.] Subject to subdivision (c), if a witness, either while testifying or prior thereto, uses a writing to refresh his memory with respect to any matter about which he testifies, such writing must be produced at the hearing at the request of an adverse party and, unless the writing is so produced, the testimony of the witness concerning such matter shall be stricken.

(b) [Inspection and cross-examination.] If the writing is produced at the hearing, the adverse party may, if he chooses, inspect the writing, cross-examine the witness concerning it, and introduce in evidence such portion of it as may be pertinent to the testimony of the witness.

(c) [Writing inaccessible.] Production of the writing is excused, and the testimony of the witness shall not be stricken, if the writing:

(1) Is not in the possession or control of the witness or the party who produced his testimony concerning the matter; and

(2) Was not reasonably procurable by such party through the use of the court's process or other available means.

History of Evid. C. §771: Added eff. Sept. 17, 1965, oper. Jan. 1, 1967, Stats. 1965, ch. 299, §2.

Official Comment

7 Cal. Law Revision Comm'n Rep. (1965) p. 1122; Assem. J., Apr. 6, 1965, p. 1742.

Section 771 grants to an adverse party the right to inspect any writing used to refresh a witness' recollection, whether the writing is used by the witness while testifying or prior thereto. The right of inspection granted by Section 771 may be broader than the similar right of inspection granted by Section 2047 of the Code of Civil Procedure, for Section 2047 has been interpreted by the courts to grant a right of inspection of only those writings used by the witness while he is testifying. *People v. Gallardo*, 41 Cal.2d 57, 257 P.2d 29 (1953); *People v. Grayson*, 172 Cal.App.2d 372, 341 P.2d 820 (1959); *Smith v. Smith*, 135 Cal.App.2d 100, 286 P.2d 1009 (1955). In a criminal case, however, the defendant can compel the prosecution to produce any written statement of a prosecution witness relating to matters covered in the witness' testimony. *People v. Estrada*, 54 Cal.2d 713, 7 Cal.Rptr. 897, 355 P.2d 641 (1960). The extent to which the public

policy reflected in criminal discovery practice overrides the restrictive interpretation of Code of Civil Procedure Section 2047 is not clear. *See* Witkin, *California Evidence* §602 (Supp. 1963). In any event, Section 771 follows the lead of the criminal cases, such as *People v. Silberstein*, 159 Cal.App.2d Supp. 848, 323 P.2d 591 (1958) (defendant entitled to inspect police report used by police officer to refresh his recollection *before* testifying), and grants a right of inspection without regard to when the writing is used to refresh recollection. If a witness' testimony depends upon the use of a writing to refresh his recollection, the adverse party's right to inspect the writing should not be made to depend upon the happenstance of when the writing is used.

Subdivision (b) gives an adverse party the right to introduce the refreshing memorandum into evidence. An adverse party has a similar right under Code of Civil Procedure Section 2047, which is superseded by this section. This right is not unlimited, however. Only those parts of the refreshing memorandum that are pertinent to the testimony given by the witness are admissible under this rule. *Cf. People v. Silberstein*, 159 Cal.App.2d Supp. 848, 851-852, 323 P.2d 591, 593 (1958) ("the right to inspect [a refreshing writing] cannot be denied although its admission in evidence may be refused if ... its contents are immaterial"); *Dragash v. Western Pac. R.R.*, 161 Cal.App.2d 233, 326 P.2d 649 (1958). *See also* Evidence Code §356 and the *Comment* thereto.

Subdivision (c) excuses the nonproduction of the memory-refreshing writing where the writing cannot be produced through no fault of the witness or the party eliciting his testimony concerning the matter. The rule is analogous to the rule announced in *People v. Parham*, 60 Cal.2d 378, 33 Cal.Rptr. 497, 384 P.2d 1001 (1963), which affirmed an order denying defendant's motion to strike certain witnesses' testimony where the witnesses' prior statements were withheld by the Federal Bureau of Investigation.

It should be noted that there is no restriction in the Evidence Code on the means that may be used to refresh recollection. Thus, the limitations on the types of writings that may be used as recorded memory under Section 1237 do not limit the types of writings that may be used to refresh recollection under Section 771.

ANNOTATIONS

In re Berman (1989) 48 Cal.3d 517, 525 n.5. "Present recollection *refreshed* should be distinguished from past recollection *recorded*, where the writing has independent evidentiary value. For past recollection recorded the witness must have insufficient present recollection to enable him or her to testify fully and accurately. If the writing meets the requirements set forth in [Evid. C.] §1237, subdivision (a), then it may be read into evidence at the instance of the party calling the witness."

People v. Lee (4th Dist.1990) 219 Cal.App.3d 829, 840. "A witness may refer to hearsay to refresh his recollection; however, before doing so the witness must testify he cannot remember the fact sought to be elicited. ... Even more fundamentally, where a writing is used to refresh recollection, *the adverse party* can introduce relevant portions of it into evidence under ... §771, but the examining party may not. 'The writing is used by the witness solely to assist him in giving his oral testimony. It has no independent evidentiary value for the party calling him, and is not admissible in evidence at his instance.'"

§772. [ORDER OF EXAMINATION]

(a) [Phases.] The examination of a witness shall proceed in the following phases: direct examination, cross-examination, redirect examination, recross-examination, and continuing thereafter by redirect and recross-examination.

(b) [Conclude each phase.] Unless for good cause the court otherwise directs, each phase of the examination of a witness must be concluded before the succeeding phase begins.

(c) [Examination beyond scope of previous examination.] Subject to subdivision (d), a party may, in the discretion of the court, interrupt his cross-examination, redirect examination, or recross-examination of a witness, in order to examine the witness upon a matter not within the scope of a previous examination of the witness.

(d) [Direct examination of criminal defendant.] If the witness is the defendant in a criminal action, the witness may not, without his consent, be examined under direct examination by another party.

History of Evid. C. §772: Added eff. Sept. 17, 1965, oper. Jan. 1, 1967, Stats. 1965, ch. 299, §2.

Official Comment

7 Cal. Law Revision Comm'n Rep. (1965) p. 1123; Assem. J., Apr. 6, 1965, p. 1743.

Subdivision (a) codifies existing but nonstatutory California law. *See* Witkin, *California Evidence* §576 at 631 (1958).

Subdivision (b) is based on and supersedes the second sentence of Section 2045 of the Code of Civil Procedure. The language of the existing section has been expanded, however, to require completion of each phase of examination of the witness, not merely the direct examination.

Under subdivision (c), as under existing law, a party examining a witness under cross-examination, redirect examination, or recross-examination may go beyond the scope of the initial direct examination if the court permits. *See* Code Civ. Proc. §§2048 (last clause), 2050; Witkin, *California Evidence* §§627, 697 (1958). Under the definition in Section 760, such an extended examination is direct examination. *Cf.* Code Civ. Proc. §2048 ("such examination is to be subject to the same rules as a direct examination"). Such direct examination may, however, be subject to the rules applicable to a cross-examination by virtue of the provisions of Section 776, 804, or 1203.

Subdivision (d) states an exception for the defendant-witness in a criminal action that reflects existing law. *See* Witkin, *California Evidence* §629 at 676 (1958).

§773. [CROSS-EXAMINATION]

(a) [Scope of direct examination.] A witness examined by one party may be cross-examined upon any matter within the scope of the direct examination by each other party to the action in such order as the court directs.

(b) [Party not adverse.] The cross-examination of a witness by any party whose interest is not adverse

to the party calling him is subject to the same rules that are applicable to the direct examination.

History of Evid. C. §773: Added eff. Sept. 17, 1965, oper. Jan. 1, 1967, Stats. 1965, ch. 299, §2.

Official Comment

7 Cal. Law Revision Comm'n Rep. (1965) p. 1124.

Subdivision (a) restates the substance of Sections 2045 (part) and 2048 of the Code of Civil Procedure and Section 1323 of the Penal Code.

Subdivision (b) is based on the holding in *Atchison, T. & S.F. Ry. v. Southern Pac. Co.*, 13 Cal.App.2d 505, 57 P.2d 575 (1936). That case held that a party not adverse to the direct examiner of a witness did not have the right to cross-examine the witness. Under subdivision (a), such a party would have the right to cross-examine the witness upon any matter within the scope of the direct examination, but he would be prohibited by Section 767 from asking leading questions during such examination. If the witness testifies on direct examination to matters that are, in fact, antagonistic to a party's position, he may be permitted to cross-examine with leading questions even though from a technical point of view the interest of the cross-examiner is not adverse to that of the direct examiner. *Cf. McCarthy v. Mobile Cranes, Inc.*, 199 Cal.App.2d 500, 18 Cal.Rptr. 750 (1962).

ANNOTATIONS

§773

Fost v. Superior Ct. (1st Dist.2000) 80 Cal.App.4th 724, 733-34. "'Cross-examination of a witness is a matter of right. [F]acts may be brought out tending to discredit the witness by showing that his testimony in chief was untrue or biased. [¶] Counsel often cannot know in advance what pertinent facts may be elicited on cross-examination. For that reason it is necessarily exploratory, and the rule that the examiner must indicate the purpose of his inquiry does not in general apply. It is the essence of a fair trial that reasonable latitude be given the cross-examiner, even though he is unable to state to the court what facts a reasonable cross-examination might develop. Prejudice ensues from a denial of the opportunity to place the witness in his proper setting and put the weight of his testimony and his credibility to a test, without which the jury cannot fairly appraise them. To say that prejudice can only be established … by showing that the cross-examination, if pursued, would necessarily have brought out facts tending to discredit the testimony in chief is to deny a substantial right and withdraw one of the safeguards essential to a fair trial.' *At 735-36:* Where a witness refuses to submit to cross-examination, or is unavailable for that purpose, the conventional remedy is to exclude the witness's testimony on direct. … This rule applies even 'where the refusal to answer is based on a valid claim of privilege.' Where a witness refuses to submit to proper cross-examination regarding material issues, the striking out or partial striking out of direct testimony is common, and has been allowed even where the result was to deprive a criminal defendant of the fundamental constitutional right to testify in his own behalf. Striking a witness' entire testimony is, of course, a 'drastic solution,' only to be employed 'after less severe means[ ] are considered.'"

§774. [REEXAMINATION]

A witness once examined cannot be reexamined as to the same matter without leave of the court, but he may be reexamined as to any new matter upon which he has been examined by another party to the action. Leave may be granted or withheld in the court's discretion.

History of Evid. C. §774: Added eff. Sept. 17, 1965, oper. Jan. 1, 1967, Stats. 1965, ch. 299, §2.

Official Comment

7 Cal. Law Revision Comm'n Rep. (1965) p. 1125.

Section 774 is based on and supersedes the first and third sentences of Section 2050 of the Code of Civil Procedure. The nature of a re-examination is to be determined in accordance with the definitions in Sections 760-763.

§775. [WITNESS CALLED BY COURT]

The court, on its own motion or on the motion of any party, may call witnesses and interrogate them the same as if they had been produced by a party to the action, and the parties may object to the questions asked and the evidence adduced the same as if such witnesses were called and examined by an adverse party. Such witnesses may be cross-examined by all parties to the action in such order as the court directs.

History of Evid. C. §775: Added eff. Sept. 17, 1965, oper. Jan. 1, 1967, Stats. 1965, ch. 299, §2.

Official Comment

7 Cal. Law Revision Comm'n Rep. (1965) p. 1125;
Assem. J., Apr. 6, 1965, p. 1743.

The power of the judge to call *expert* witnesses is well recognized by statutory and case law in California. Code Civ. Proc. §1871 (recodified as Section 723 and Article 2 (commencing with Section 730) of Chapter 3); Penal Code §1027; *Citizens State Bank v. Castro*, 105 Cal.App. 284, 287 Pac. 559 (1930). *See also* Code Civ. Proc. §§1884 and 1885 (interpreters), continued in substance by Chapter 4 (commencing with Section 750).

The power of the judge to call other witnesses is also recognized by case law. *Travis v. Southern Pac. Co.*, 210 Cal.App.2d 410, 425, 26 Cal.Rptr. 700, 707-708 (1962) ("[W]e have been cited to no case, nor has our independent research disclosed any case, dealing with a civil action in which a witness has been called to the stand by the court, over objection of a party. However, we can see no difference in this respect between a civil and a criminal case. In both, the endeavor of the court and the parties should be to get at the truth of the matter in contest. Fundamentally, there is no reason why the court in the interests of justice should not call to the stand anyone who appears to have relevant, competent and material information.").

Of course, the judge would be guilty of misconduct were he to show partiality or bias in calling and interrogating witnesses. *See* 2 Witkin, *California Procedure*, *Trial* §§14-17 (1954).

ANNOTATIONS

Travis v. Southern Pac. Co. (1st Dist.1962) 210 Cal.App.2d 410, 425-26. "[W]e have been cited to no case, nor has our independent research disclosed any case, dealing with a civil action in which a witness has

been called to the stand by the court, over objection of a party. However, we can see no difference in this respect between a civil and a criminal case. In both, the endeavor of the court and the parties should be to get at the truth of the matter in contest. Fundamentally, there is no reason why the court in the interests of justice should not call to the stand anyone who appears to have relevant, competent and material information. … The court's ruling that neither party would be bound by the witness' testimony and that both parties should have the right to cross-examine him was an eminently fair one. In all lawsuits the interests of justice should be paramount, and while the calling of a witness by the court is apparently an unusual procedure, that fact should not tie the hands of a judge who feels that it is in the interests of justice that an attempt be made to get at the truth of the matter involved."

§776. [EXAMINATION OF ADVERSE PARTY]

(a) [Examined as if under cross-examination.] A party to the record of any civil action, or a person identified with such a party, may be called and examined as if under cross-examination by any adverse party at any time during the presentation of evidence by the party calling the witness.

(b) [Cross-examination by other parties.] A witness examined by a party under this section may be cross-examined by all other parties to the action in such order as the court directs; but, subject to subdivision (e), the witness may be examined only as if under redirect examination by:

(1) In the case of a witness who is a party, his own counsel and counsel for a party who is not adverse to the witness.

(2) In the case of a witness who is not a party, counsel for the party with whom the witness is identified and counsel for a party who is not adverse to the party with whom the witness is identified.

(c) [Single party.] For the purpose of this section, parties represented by the same counsel are deemed to be a single party.

(d) [Witness identified with adverse party.] For the purpose of this section, a person is identified with a party if he is:

(1) A person for whose immediate benefit the action is prosecuted or defended by the party.

(2) A director, officer, superintendent, member, agent, employee, or managing agent of the party or of a person specified in paragraph (1), or any public employee of a public entity when such public entity is the party.

(3) A person who was in any of the relationships specified in paragraph (2) at the time of the act or omission giving rise to the cause of action.

(4) A person who was in any of the relationships specified in paragraph (2) at the time he obtained knowledge of the matter concerning which he is sought to be examined under this section.

(e) [Witness identified with both parties.] Paragraph (2) of subdivision (b) does not require counsel for the party with whom the witness is identified and counsel for a party who is not adverse to the party with whom the witness is identified to examine the witness as if under redirect examination if the party who called the witness for examination under this section:

(1) Is also a person identified with the same party with whom the witness is identified.

(2) Is the personal representative, heir, successor, or assignee of a person identified with the same party with whom the witness is identified.

History of Evid. C. §776: Added eff. Sept. 17, 1965, oper. Jan. 1, 1967, Stats. 1965, ch. 299, §2. Amended eff. Nov. 8, 1967, Stats. 1967, ch. 650, §2.

Official Comment

7 Cal. Law Revision Comm'n Rep. (1965) p. 1127.

Section 776 restates the substance of Code of Civil Procedure Section 2055 as it has been interpreted by the courts. *See* Witkin, *California Evidence* §§607-613 (1958), and pertinent cases cited and discussed therein.

Subdivision (a). Subdivision (a) restates the provisions of Section 2055 that permit a party to call and examine as if under cross-examination an adverse party and certain adverse witnesses. However, Section 776 substitutes the phrase "or a person identified with such a party" for the confusing enumeration of persons listed in the first sentence of Section 2055. This phrase is defined in subdivision (d) of Section 776 to include all of the persons presently named in Section 2055. *See* the *Comment* to subdivision (d), *infra*.

Subdivision (b). Subdivision (b) is based in part on similar provisions contained in Code of Civil Procedure Section 2055. Unlike Section 2055, however, this subdivision is drafted in recognition of the problems involved in multiple party litigation. Thus, the introductory portion of subdivision (b) states the general rule that a witness examined under this section may be cross-examined by all other parties to the action in such order as the court directs. For example, a party whose interest in the action is identical with that of the party who called the witness for examination under this section has a right to cross-examine the witness fully because he, too, has the right to call the witness for examination under this section. Similarly, a party whose interest in the action is adverse to the party who calls the witness for examination under this section has the right to cross-examine the witness fully unless he is identified with the witness as described in paragraphs (1) and (2) of this subdivision. Paragraphs (1) and (2) restrict the nature of the cross-examination permitted of a witness by a party with whom the witness is identified and by parties whose interest in the action is not adverse to the party with whom the witness is identified. These parties are limited to examination of the witness as if under redirect examination. In essence, this means that leading questions cannot be asked of the witness by these parties. *See* Evidence Code §767. Although the examination must proceed as if it were a redirect examination, under Section 761 it is in fact a cross-examination and limited to the scope of the direct. *See also* Evidence Code §§760, 773.

Subdivision (c). Subdivision (c) codifies a principle that has been recognized in the California cases even though not explicitly stated in Code of Civil Procedure Section 2055. *See Gates v. Pendleton*, 71 Cal.App. 752, 236 Pac. 365 (1925); *Goehring v. Rogers*, 67 Cal.App. 260, 227 Pac. 689 (1924).

Subdivision (d). Subdivision (d) lists the classes of persons who are "identified with a party" as that phrase and variations of it are used in subdivisions (a) and (b) of Section 776. The persons named in paragraphs (1) and (2) are those described in the first sentence of Code of Civil Procedure Section 2055 as being subject to examination pursuant to the section because of a particular relationship to a party. See the definitions of "person," "public employee," and "public entity" in Evidence Code §§175, 195, and 200, respectively. In addition, paragraph (3) of this subdivision describes persons who were in any of the requisite relationships at the time of the act or omission giving rise to the cause of action. This states existing case law. *Scott v. Del Monte Properties, Inc.*, 140 Cal.App.2d 756, 295 P.2d 947 (1956); *Wells v. Lloyd*, 35 Cal.App.2d 6, 94 P.2d 373 (1939). Similarly, paragraph (4) extends this principle to include any person who obtained relevant knowledge as a result of such a relationship but who does not fit the precise descriptions contained in paragraphs (1) through (3). For example, a person whose employment by a party began after the cause of action arose and terminated prior to the time of his examination at the trial would be included in the description contained in paragraph (4) if he obtained relevant knowledge of the incident as a result of his employment. It is not clear whether this states existing law, for no California decision has been found that decides this question. The paragraph is necessary, however, to preclude a party from preventing examination of his employee pursuant to this section by the simple expedient of discharging the employee prior to trial and reinstating him afterwards. *Cf. Wells v. Lloyd*, 35 Cal.App.2d 6, 12, 94 P.2d 373, 376-377 (1939).

8 Cal. Law Revision Comm'n Rep. (1967) p. 120.

Section 776 permits a party calling as a witness an employee of (or someone similarly identified in interest with) an adverse party to examine the witness as if under cross-examination, *i.e.*, to use leading questions in his examination. Section 776 requires the party whose employee was thus called and examined to examine the witness as if under redirect examination, *i.e.*, to refrain from the use of leading questions. If a party is able to persuade the court that the usual rule prescribed by Section 776 is not in the interest of justice in a particular case, the court may enlarge or restrict the right to use leading questions as provided in Section 767.

These rules are based on the premise that ordinarily such a witness will have a feeling of identification in the lawsuit with his employer rather than with the other party to the action.

Subdivision (b) has been amended, and subdivision (e) has been added, because the premise upon which Section 776 is based does not necessarily apply when the party calling the witness is also closely identified with the adverse party; hence, the adverse party should be entitled to the usual rights of a cross-examiner when he examines the witness. For example, when an employee sues his employer and calls a co-employee as a witness, there is no reason to assume that the witness will be adverse to the employee-party and in sympathy with the employer-party. The reverse may be the case. The amendment to Section 776 will permit an employer, as a general rule, to use leading questions in his cross-examination of an employee-witness who has been called to testify under Section 776 by a co-employee. However, if the party calling the witness can satisfy the court that the witness is in fact identified in interest with the employer or for some other reason is amenable to suggestive questioning by the employer, the court may limit the employer's use of leading questions during his examination of the witness pursuant to Section 767. *See J. & B. Motors, Inc. v. Margolis*, 75 Ariz. 392, 257 P.2d 588, 38 A.L.R. 2d 946 (1953).

ANNOTATIONS

Miller v. Los Angeles Cty. Flood Control Dist. (1973) 8 Cal.3d 689, 700 n.10. "It has long been a rule in this state that, on appeal from a nonsuit rendered against them, plaintiffs may rely on that portion of testimony given under §776 ... which is favorable to them, and disregard that which is unfavorable."

§777. [WITNESS EXCLUSION]

(a) [Not under examination.] Subject to subdivisions (b) and (c), the court may exclude from the courtroom any witness not at the time under examination so that such witness cannot hear the testimony of other witnesses.

(b) [Party not excluded.] A party to the action cannot be excluded under this section.

(c) [Corporation not excluded.] If a person other than a natural person is a party to the action, an officer or employee designated by its attorney is entitled to be present.

History of Evid. C. §777: Added eff. Sept. 17, 1965, oper. Jan. 1, 1967, Stats. 1965, ch. 299, §2.

Official Comment

7 Cal. Law Revision Comm'n Rep. (1965) p. 1128.

Section 777 is based on and supersedes Section 2043 of the Code of Civil Procedure. Under the existing law, the judge exercises broad discretion in regard to the exclusion of witnesses. *People v. Lariscy*, 14 Cal.2d 30, 92 P.2d 638 (1939); *People v. Garbutt*, 197 Cal. 200, 239 Pac. 1080 (1925). *Cf.* Penal Code §867 (power of magistrate to exclude witnesses during preliminary examination). *See also* Code Civ. Proc. §125 (general discretionary power of the court to exclude witnesses).

Under the existing law, the judge may not exclude a party to an action. If the party is a corporation, an officer designated by its attorney is entitled to be present. Section 777 permits the right of presence to be exercised by an employee as well as an officer. Also, because there is little practical distinction between corporations and other artificial entities and organizations, Section 777 extends the right of presence to all artificial parties.

§778. [WITNESS RECALL AFTER BEING EXCUSED]

After a witness has been excused from giving further testimony in the action, he cannot be recalled without leave of the court. Leave may be granted or withheld in the court's discretion.

History of Evid. C. §778: Added eff. Sept. 17, 1965, oper. Jan. 1, 1967, Stats. 1965, ch. 299, §2.

Official Comment

7 Cal. Law Revision Comm'n Rep. (1965) p. 1129.

Section 778 restates the substance of and supersedes the second and third sentences of Section 2050 of the Code of Civil Procedure.

CHAPTER 6. CREDIBILITY OF WITNESSES

ARTICLE 1. CREDIBILITY GENERALLY

§780. [DETERMINING CREDIBILITY OF WITNESS]

Except as otherwise provided by statute, the court or jury may consider in determining the credibility of a witness any matter that has any tendency in reason to prove or disprove the truthfulness of his testimony at the hearing, including but not limited to any of the following:

(a) His demeanor while testifying and the manner in which he testifies.

(b) The character of his testimony.

(c) The extent of his capacity to perceive, to recollect, or to communicate any matter about which he testifies.

(d) The extent of his opportunity to perceive any matter about which he testifies.

(e) His character for honesty or veracity or their opposites.

(f) The existence or nonexistence of a bias, interest, or other motive.

(g) A statement previously made by him that is consistent with his testimony at the hearing.

(h) A statement made by him that is inconsistent with any part of his testimony at the hearing.

(i) The existence or nonexistence of any fact testified to by him.

(j) His attitude toward the action in which he testifies or toward the giving of testimony.

(k) His admission of untruthfulness.

History of Evid. C. §780: Added eff. Sept. 17, 1965, oper. Jan. 1, 1967, Stats. 1965, ch. 299, §2.

Official Comment

7 Cal. Law Revision Comm'n Rep. (1965) p. 1130.

Section 780 is a restatement of the existing California law as declared in several sections of the Code of Civil Procedure, all of which are superseded by this section and other sections in Article 2 (commencing with Section 785) of this chapter. *See, e.g.*, Code Civ. Proc. §§1847, 2049, 2051, 2052, 2053.

Section 780 is a general catalog of those matters that have any tendency in reason to affect the credibility of a witness. So far as the admissibility of evidence relating to credibility is concerned, Section 780 is technically unnecessary because Section 351 declares that "all relevant evidence is admissible." However, this section makes it clear that matters that may not be "evidence" in a technical sense can affect the credibility of a witness, and it provides a convenient list of the most common factors that bear on the question of credibility. *See Davis v. Judson*, 159 Cal. 121, 128, 113 Pac. 147, 150 (1910); *La Jolla Casa deManana v. Hopkins*, 98 Cal.App.2d 339, 346, 219 P.2d 871, 876 (1950). *See generally* Witkin, *California Evidence* §§480-485 (1958). Limitations on the admissibility of evidence offered to attack or support the credibility of a witness are stated in Article 2 (commencing with Section 785).

There is no specific limitation in the Evidence Code on the use of impeaching evidence on the ground that it is "collateral." The so-called "collateral matter" limitation on attacking the credibility of a witness excludes evidence relevant to credibility unless such evidence is independently relevant to the issue being tried. It is based on the sensible notion that trials should be confined to settling those disputes between the parties upon which their rights in the litigation depend. Under existing law, this "collateral matter" doctrine has been treated as an inflexible rule excluding evidence relevant to the credibility of the witness. *See, e.g.*, *People v. Wells*, 33 Cal.2d 330, 340, 202 P.2d 53, 59 (1949), and cases cited therein.

The effect of Section 780 (together with Section 351) is to eliminate this inflexible rule of exclusion. This is not to say that all evidence of a collateral nature offered to attack the credibility of a witness would be admissible. Under Section 352, the court has substantial discretion to exclude collateral evidence. The effect of Section 780, therefore, is to change the present somewhat inflexible rule of exclusion to a rule of discretion to be exercised by the trial judge.

There is no limitation in the Evidence Code on the use of opinion evidence to prove the character of a witness for honesty, veracity, or the lack thereof. Hence, under Sections 780 and 1100, such evidence is admissible. This represents a change in the present law. *See People v. Methvin*, 53 Cal. 68 (1878). However, the opinion evidence that may be offered by those persons intimately familiar with the witness is likely to be of more probative value than the generally admissible evidence of reputation. *See* 7 Wigmore, *Evidence* §1986 (3d ed. 1940).

ANNOTATIONS

People v. Mendoza (2011) 52 Cal.4th 1056, 1084. "'[E]vidence that a witness is afraid to testify or fears retaliation for testifying is relevant to the credibility of that witness and is therefore admissible. An explanation of the basis for the witness's fear is likewise relevant to her credibility and is well within the discretion of the trial court.' Moreover, evidence of a 'third party' threat may bear on the credibility of the witness, whether or not the threat is directly linked to the defendant."

Calvert v. State Bar (1991) 54 Cal.3d 765, 777. "Generally, any fact or circumstance tending to show that a witness has a financial interest in the outcome of a legal proceeding is a proper ground for impeachment."

Bowman v. Wyatt (2d Dist.2010) 186 Cal.App.4th 286, 327. "Collateral and irrelevant matters may not be used for impeachment. A party cannot cross-examine his adversary's witness upon irrelevant matters, for the purpose of eliciting something to be contradicted. If a question is put to a witness on cross-examination which is collateral or irrelevant to the issue, his answer cannot be contradicted by the party who asked him the question." (Internal quotes omitted.)

Andrews v. City & Cty. of S.F. (1st Dist.1988) 205 Cal.App.3d 938, 946. "[A]lthough evidence of a specific instance of a witness' conduct is inadmissible under [Evid. C.] §787 to impeach the witness as proof of a trait of his character it may become admissible to impeach the witness pursuant to [Evid. C.] §780, subdivision (i), by proving *false* some portion of his testimony. [¶] Thus, a witness who makes a sweeping statement on direct or cross-examination may open the door to use of otherwise inadmissible evidence of prior misconduct for the purpose of contradicting such testimony." (Internal quotes omitted.)

§781. [BLANK]

§782. [SEX-OFFENSE CASES]

(a) **[Offer of proof.]** In any of the circumstances described in subdivision (c), if evidence of sexual conduct of the complaining witness is offered to attack the

credibility of the complaining witness under Section 780, the following procedure shall be followed:

(1) A written motion shall be made by the defendant to the court and prosecutor stating that the defense has an offer of proof of the relevancy of evidence of the sexual conduct of the complaining witness proposed to be presented and its relevancy in attacking the credibility of the complaining witness.

(2) The written motion shall be accompanied by an affidavit in which the offer of proof shall be stated. The affidavit shall be filed under seal and only unsealed by the court to determine if the offer of proof is sufficient to order a hearing pursuant to paragraph (3). After that determination, the affidavit shall be resealed by the court.

(3) If the court finds that the offer of proof is sufficient, the court shall order a hearing out of the presence of the jury, if any, and at the hearing allow the questioning of the complaining witness regarding the offer of proof made by the defendant.

(4) At the conclusion of the hearing, if the court finds that evidence proposed to be offered by the defendant regarding the sexual conduct of the complaining witness is relevant pursuant to Section 780, and is not inadmissible pursuant to Section 352, the court may make an order stating what evidence may be introduced by the defendant, and the nature of the questions to be permitted. The defendant may then offer evidence pursuant to the order of the court.

(5) An affidavit resealed by the court pursuant to paragraph (2) shall remain sealed, unless the defendant raises an issue on appeal or collateral review relating to the offer of proof contained in the sealed document. If the defendant raises that issue on appeal, the court shall allow the Attorney General and appellate counsel for the defendant access to the sealed affidavit. If the issue is raised on collateral review, the court shall allow the district attorney and defendant's counsel access to the sealed affidavit. The use of the information contained in the affidavit shall be limited solely to the pending proceeding.

(b) [**"Complaining witness" defined.**] As used in this section, "complaining witness" means:

(1) The alleged victim of the crime charged, the prosecution of which is subject to this section, pursuant to paragraph (1) of subdivision (c).

(2) An alleged victim offering testimony pursuant to paragraph (2) or (3) of subdivision (c).

(c) [**Applicable proceedings.**] The procedure provided by subdivision (a) shall apply in any of the following circumstances:

(1) In a prosecution under Section 261, 262, 264.1, 286, 288, 288a, 288.5, or 289 of the Penal Code, or for assault with intent to commit, attempt to commit, or conspiracy to commit any crime defined in any of those sections, except if the crime is alleged to have occurred in a local detention facility, as defined in Section 6031.4 of the Penal Code, or in the state prison, as defined in Section 4504.

(2) When an alleged victim testifies pursuant to subdivision (b) of Section 1101 as a victim of a crime listed in Section 243.4, 261, 261.5, 269, 285, 286, 288, 288a, 288.5, 289, 314, or 647.6 of the Penal Code, except if the crime is alleged to have occurred in a local detention facility, as defined in Section 6031.4 of the Penal Code, or in the state prison, as defined in Section 4504 of the Penal Code.

(3) When an alleged victim of a sexual offense testifies pursuant to Section 1108, except if the crime is alleged to have occurred in a local detention facility, as defined in Section 6031.4 of the Penal Code, or in the state prison, as defined in Section 4504 of the Penal Code.

History of Evid. C. §782: Added eff. Jan. 1, 1975, Stats. 1974, ch. 569, §1. Amended eff. Jan. 1, 1982, Stats. 1981, ch. 726, §1; eff. Jan. 1, 1988, Stats. 1987, ch. 177, §1; eff. Jan. 1, 1990, Stats. 1989, ch. 1402, §2; eff. Jan. 1, 1997, Stats. 1996, ch. 1075, §6; eff. Jan. 1, 2005, Stats. 2004, ch. 61, §1; eff. Jan. 1, 2007, Stats. 2006, ch. 225, §1; eff. Jan. 1, 2008, Stats. 2007, ch. 130, §83.

E §782.1. [POSSESSION OF CONDOMS AS EVIDENCE OF CRIME]

In any prosecution under Sections 647 and 653.22 of the Penal Code, if the possession of one or more condoms is to be introduced as evidence in support of the commission of the crime, the following procedure shall be followed:

(a) [**Motion.**] A written motion shall be made by the prosecutor to the court and to the defendant stating that the prosecution has an offer of proof of the relevancy of the possession by the defendant of one or more condoms.

(b) [**Affidavit.**] The written motion shall be accompanied by an affidavit in which the offer of proof shall be stated. The affidavit shall be filed under seal and only unsealed by the court to determine if the offer of proof is sufficient to order a hearing pursuant to subdivision (c). After that determination, the affidavit shall be resealed by the court.

§782

(c) [**Hearing.**] If the court finds that the offer of proof is sufficient, the court shall order a hearing out of the presence of the jury, if any, and at the hearing allow questioning regarding the offer of proof made by the prosecution.

(d) [**Order.**] At the conclusion of the hearing, if the court finds that evidence proposed to be offered by the prosecutor regarding the possession of condoms is relevant pursuant to Section 210, and is not inadmissible pursuant to Section 352, the court may make an order stating what evidence may be introduced by the prosecutor. The prosecutor may then offer evidence pursuant to the order of the court.

(e) [**Affidavit sealed.**] An affidavit resealed by the court pursuant to subdivision (b) shall remain sealed, unless the defendant raises an issue on appeal or collateral review relating to the offer of proof contained in the sealed document. If the defendant raises that issue on appeal, the court shall allow the Attorney General and appellate counsel for the defendant access to the sealed affidavit. If the issue is raised on collateral review, the court shall allow the district attorney and defendant's counsel access to the sealed affidavit. The use of the information contained in the affidavit shall be limited solely to the pending proceeding.

History of Evid. C. §782.1: Added eff. Jan. 1, 2015, Stats. 2014, ch. 403, §1.

§783. [SEXUAL HARASSMENT]

In any civil action alleging conduct which constitutes sexual harassment, sexual assault, or sexual battery, if evidence of sexual conduct of the plaintiff is offered to attack credibility of the plaintiff under Section 780, the following procedures shall be followed:

(a) [**Offer of proof.**] A written motion shall be made by the defendant to the court and the plaintiff's attorney stating that the defense has an offer of proof of the relevancy of evidence of the sexual conduct of the plaintiff proposed to be presented.

(b) [**Affidavit.**] The written motion shall be accompanied by an affidavit in which the offer of proof shall be stated.

(c) [**Hearing.**] If the court finds that the offer of proof is sufficient, the court shall order a hearing out of the presence of the jury, if any, and at the hearing allow the questioning of the plaintiff regarding the offer of proof made by the defendant.

(d) [**Order.**] At the conclusion of the hearing, if the court finds that evidence proposed to be offered by the defendant regarding the sexual conduct of the plaintiff is relevant pursuant to Section 780, and is not inadmissible pursuant to Section 352, the court may make an order stating what evidence may be introduced by the defendant, and the nature of the questions to be permitted. The defendant may then offer evidence pursuant to the order of the court.

History of Evid. C. §783: Added eff. Jan. 1, 1986, Stats. 1985, ch. 1328, §3.

ARTICLE 2. ATTACKING OR SUPPORTING CREDIBILITY

§785. [ATTACKING OR SUPPORTING CREDIBILITY]

The credibility of a witness may be attacked or supported by any party, including the party calling him.

History of Evid. C. §785: Added eff. Sept. 17, 1965, oper. Jan. 1, 1967, Stats. 1965, ch. 299, §2.

Official Comment

7 Cal. Law Revision Comm'n Rep. (1965) p. 1131.

Section 785 eliminates the present restriction on attacking the credibility of one's own witness. Under the existing law, a party is precluded from attacking the credibility of his own witness unless he has been surprised and damaged by the witness' testimony. Code Civ. Proc. §§2049, 2052 (repealed, now Evidence Code §§768, 769, 770, 785); *People v. LeBeau*, 39 Cal.2d 146, 148, 245 P.2d 302, 303 (1952). In large part, the present law rests upon the theory that a party producing a witness is bound by his testimony. See discussion in *Smellie v. Southern Pac. Co.*, 212 Cal. 540, 555-556, 299 Pac. 529, 535 (1931). This theory has long been abandoned in several jurisdictions where the practical exigencies of litigation have been recognized. *See* McCormick, *Evidence* §38 (1954). A party has no actual control over a person who witnesses an event and is required to testify to aid the trier of fact in its function of determining the truth. Hence, a party should not be "bound" by the testimony of a witness produced by him and should be permitted to attack the credibility of the witness without anachronistic limitations. Denial of the right to attack credibility may often work a hardship on a party where by necessity he must call a hostile witness. Expanded opportunity for testing credibility is in keeping with the interest of providing a forum for full and free disclosure. In regard to attacking the credibility of a "necessary" witness, *see generally People v. McFarlane*, 134 Cal. 618, 66 Pac. 865 (1901); *Anthony v. Hobbie*, 85 Cal.App.2d 798, 803-804, 193 P.2d 748, 751 (1948); *First Nat'l Bank v. De Moulin*, 56 Cal.App. 313, 321, 205 Pac. 92, 96 (1922).

ANNOTATIONS

People v. Osorio (4th Dist.2008) 165 Cal.App.4th 603, 615. See annotation under Evidence Code §1202, p. 1383.

§786. [CHARACTER EVIDENCE EXCLUDED]

Evidence of traits of his character other than honesty or veracity, or their opposites, is inadmissible to attack or support the credibility of a witness.

History of Evid. C. §786: Added eff. Sept. 17, 1965, oper. Jan. 1, 1967, Stats. 1965, ch. 299, §2.

Official Comment

7 Cal. Law Revision Comm'n Rep. (1965) p. 1132.

Section 786 limits evidence relating to the character of a witness to the character traits necessarily involved in a proper determination of credibility. Other character traits are not sufficiently probative of a witness' honesty or veracity to warrant their consideration on the issue of credibility.

Section 786 is substantially in accord with the present California law. Code Civ. Proc. §2051 (repealed, now Evidence Code §§780, 785-788); *People v. Yslas*, 27 Cal. 630, 633 (1865).

§787. [SPECIFIC INSTANCES OF CONDUCT]

Subject to Section 788, evidence of specific instances of his conduct relevant only as tending to prove a trait of his character is inadmissible to attack or support the credibility of a witness.

History of Evid. C. §787: Added eff. Sept. 17, 1965, oper. Jan. 1, 1967, Stats. 1965, ch. 299, §2.

Official Comment

7 Cal. Law Revision Comm'n Rep. (1965) p. 1132.

Under Section 787, as under existing law, evidence of specific instances of a witness' conduct is inadmissible to prove a trait of his character for the purpose of attacking or supporting his credibility. *See Sharon v. Sharon*, 79 Cal. 633, 673-674, 22 Pac. 26, 38 (1889); Code Civ. Proc. §2051 (repealed, now Section 787 and several other sections in Chapter 6). Section 787 is subject, however, to Section 788, which permits certain kinds of criminal convictions to be used for the purpose of attacking a witness' credibility.

§788. [CONVICTION OF FELONY WHEN OFFERED TO ATTACK CREDIBILITY]

For the purpose of attacking the credibility of a witness, it may be shown by the examination of the witness or by the record of the judgment that he has been convicted of a felony unless:

(a) A pardon based on his innocence has been granted to the witness by the jurisdiction in which he was convicted.

(b) A certificate of rehabilitation and pardon has been granted to the witness under the provisions of Chapter 3.5 (commencing with Section 4852.01) of Title 6 of Part 3 of the Penal Code.

(c) The accusatory pleading against the witness has been dismissed under the provisions of Penal Code Section 1203.4, but this exception does not apply to any criminal trial where the witness is being prosecuted for a subsequent offense.

(d) The conviction was under the laws of another jurisdiction and the witness has been relieved of the penalties and disabilities arising from the conviction pursuant to a procedure substantially equivalent to that referred to in subdivision (b) or (c).

History of Evid. C. §788: Added eff. Sept. 17, 1965, oper. Jan. 1, 1967, Stats. 1965, ch. 299, §2.

Official Comment

7 Cal. Law Revision Comm'n Rep. (1965) p. 1132; Senate J, Apr. 21, 1965.

Under Section 787, evidence of specific instances of a witness' conduct is inadmissible for the purpose of attacking or supporting his credibility. Section 788 states an exception to this general rule where the evidence of the witness' misconduct consists of his conviction of a felony. A judgment of conviction that is offered to prove that the person adjudged guilty committed the crime is hearsay. *See* Evidence Code §§1200 and 1300 and the *Comments* thereto. But the hearsay objection to the evidence specified in Section 788 is overcome by the declaration in the section that such evidence "may be shown" for the purpose of attacking a witness' credibility.

Section 788 is based on Section 2051 of the Code of Civil Procedure. Under Section 788, as under Section 2051, only the testimony of the witness himself or the record of the judgment of conviction may be used to prove the fact of conviction. As Section 788 is, in substance, a recodification of the existing law, it will have no effect on the case-developed rules limiting the circumstances under which a witness may be asked whether he was convicted of a felony. *See People v. Perez*, 58 Cal.2d 229, 23 Cal.Rptr. 569, 373 P.2d 617 (1962); *People v. Darnold*, 219 Cal.App.2d 561, 33 Cal.Rptr. 369 (1963).

Subdivision (a) prohibits the use of a conviction to attack the credibility of a witness if a pardon has been granted to the witness on the ground that he was innocent and was erroneously convicted. Subdivision (a) changes the existing California law. Under the existing law, the conviction is admissible to attack credibility, and the pardon—even though based on innocence—is admissible merely to mitigate the effect of the conviction. *People v. Hardwick*, 204 Cal. 582, 269 Pac. 427 (1928).

Subdivision (b) recodifies the provision of Section 2051 that prohibits the use of a conviction to attack credibility if a pardon has been granted upon the basis of a certificate of rehabilitation. *See also* Code Civ. Proc. §2065.

Subdivision (c) recodifies the existing law that prohibits the use of a conviction to attack the credibility of a witness if the conviction has been set aside under Penal Code Section 1203.4. *See People v. Mackey*, 58 Cal.App. 123, 208 Pac. 135 (1922). The exception that permits the use of such a conviction to attack the credibility of a criminal defendant who testifies as a witness also reflects existing law. *See People v. James*, 40 Cal.App.2d 740, 105 P.2d 947 (1940).

Subdivision (d) merely provides that a witness who has been relieved of the penalties and disabilities of a prior conviction under the laws of another jurisdiction will be subject to attacks on his credibility under the same conditions that would be applicable if such relief had been granted him under the laws of California.

ANNOTATIONS

People v. Contreras (2013) 58 Cal.4th 123, 157 n.24. "Though not mentioned by the parties on appeal, the law provides that any criminal act or other misconduct involving moral turpitude suggests a willingness to lie and is not necessarily irrelevant or inadmissible for impeachment purposes. However, to the extent such misconduct amounts to a misdemeanor or is not criminal in nature, it carries less weight in proving lax moral character and dishonesty than does either an act or conviction involving a felony. Hence, trial courts have broad discretion to exclude impeachment evidence other than felony convictions where such evidence might involve undue time, confusion, or prejudice. [¶] We further note that 'moral turpitude' refers to a general readiness to do evil even if dishonesty is not necessarily involved." (Internal quotes omitted.)

Robbins v. Wong (6th Dist.1994) 27 Cal.App.4th 261, 264. "We hold that felony impeachment evidence is admissible in civil cases under [Evid. C.] §788. *At 274:* [However,] upon proper objection to the admission of a prior felony conviction for purposes of impeachment in

a civil case, a trial court is bound to perform the weighing function prescribed by [Evid. C.] §352." *See also* ***Nguyen v. Proton Tech.*** (1st Dist.1999) 69 Cal.App.4th 140, 151 (court has discretion under Evid. C. §352 to admit evidence of prior felony conviction in civil action).

In re Ricky B. (5th Dist.1978) 82 Cal.App.3d 106, 114 n.2. "[O]nly felony convictions can be used to impeach a witness. A juvenile court adjudication is not considered a conviction and cannot be used to impeach."

§789. [WITNESS'S RELIGIOUS BELIEF]

Evidence of his religious belief or lack thereof is inadmissible to attack or support the credibility of a witness.

History of Evid. C. §789: Added eff. Sept. 17, 1965, oper. Jan. 1, 1967, Stats. 1965, ch. 299, §2.

Official Comment

7 Cal. Law Revision Comm'n Rep. (1965) p. 1134.

Section 789 codifies existing law as expressed in *People v. Copsey*, 71 Cal. 548, 12 Pac. 721 (1887), where the Supreme Court held that evidence relating to a witness' religious belief or lack thereof is incompetent on the issue of his credibility as a witness. *See* Cal. Const., Art. I, §4.

ANNOTATIONS

Drake v. Dean (3d Dist.1993) 15 Cal.App.4th 915, 933. "While one cannot be precluded from testifying because he lacks religious belief, relevant inquiry whether a witness's membership in a particular religious sect or a tenet of his faith might tend to bias him is not prohibited."

§790. [WITNESS'S GOOD CHARACTER]

Evidence of the good character of a witness is inadmissible to support his credibility unless evidence of his bad character has been admitted for the purpose of attacking his credibility.

History of Evid. C. §790: Added eff. Sept. 17, 1965, oper. Jan. 1, 1967, Stats. 1965, ch. 299, §2.

Official Comment

7 Cal. Law Revision Comm'n Rep. (1965) p. 1134.

Section 790 restates without substantive change a rule that is well recognized by statutory and case law in California. Code Civ. Proc. §2053 (repealed, now Evidence Code §§790, 1101); *People v. Bush*, 65 Cal. 129, 131, 3 Pac. 590, 591 (1884). Unless the credibility of a witness is put in issue by an attack impugning his character for honesty or veracity (*see* Section 786), evidence of the witness' good character admitted merely to support his credibility introduces collateral material that is unnecessary to a proper determination of any legitimate issue in the action. *See People v. Sweeney*, 55 Cal.2d 27, 38-39, 9 Cal.Rptr. 793, 799, 357 P.2d 1049, 1055 (1960).

§791. [WITNESS'S PRIOR CONSISTENT STATEMENT]

Evidence of a statement previously made by a witness that is consistent with his testimony at the hearing is inadmissible to support his credibility unless it is offered after:

(a) [Rebutting prior inconsistent statement.] Evidence of a statement made by him that is inconsistent with any part of his testimony at the hearing has been admitted for the purpose of attacking his credibility, and the statement was made before the alleged inconsistent statement; or

(b) [Rebutting improper motive.] An express or implied charge has been made that his testimony at the hearing is recently fabricated or is influenced by bias or other improper motive, and the statement was made before the bias, motive for fabrication, or other improper motive is alleged to have arisen.

History of Evid. C. §791: Added eff. Sept. 17, 1965, oper. Jan. 1, 1967, Stats. 1965, ch. 299, §2.

Official Comment

7 Cal. Law Revision Comm'n Rep. (1965) p. 1135.

Section 791 sets forth the conditions for admitting a witness' prior consistent statements for the purpose of supporting his credibility as a witness. For a discussion of the effect to be given to the evidence admitted under this section, *see* Evidence Code §1236 and the *Comment* thereto.

Subdivision (a). Subdivision (a) permits the introduction of a witness' prior consistent statement if evidence of an inconsistent statement of the witness has been admitted for the purpose of attacking his credibility and if the consistent statement was made *before* the alleged inconsistent statement.

Under existing California law, evidence of a prior consistent statement is admissible to rebut a charge of bias, interest, recent fabrication, or other improper motive. *See* the *Comment* to subdivision (b), *infra*. Existing law may preclude admission of a prior consistent statement to rehabilitate a witness where only a prior inconsistent statement has been admitted for the purpose of attacking his credibility. *See People v. Doyell*, 48 Cal. 85, 90-91 (1874). However, recent cases indicate that the offering of a prior inconsistent statement necessarily is an implied charge that the witness has fabricated his testimony since the time the inconsistent statement was made and justifies the admission of a consistent statement made prior to the alleged inconsistent statement. *People v. Bias*, 170 Cal.App.2d 502, 511-512, 339 P.2d 204, 210-211 (1959). Subdivision (a) makes it clear that evidence of a previous consistent statement is admissible under these circumstances to show that no such fabrication took place. Subdivision (a), thus, is no more than a logical extension of the general rule that evidence of a prior consistent statement is admissible to rehabilitate a witness following an express or implied charge of recent fabrication.

Subdivision (b). This subdivision codifies existing law. *See People v. Kynette*, 15 Cal.2d 731, 104 P.2d 794 (1940) (*overruled on other grounds* in *People v. Snyder*, 50 Cal.2d 190, 197, 324 P.2d 1, 6 (1958)). Of course, if the consistent statement was made *after* the time the improper motive is alleged to have arisen, the logical thrust of the evidence is lost and the statement is inadmissible. *See People v. Doetschman*, 69 Cal.App.2d 486, 159 P.2d 418 (1945).

ANNOTATIONS

People v. Riccardi (2012) 54 Cal.4th 758, 803. "'[R]ecent fabrication may be inferred when it is shown that a witness did not speak about an important matter at a time when it would have been natural for

§791

him to do so,' and in such a circumstance, 'it is generally proper to permit rehabilitation by a prior consistent statement.'"

CHAPTER 7. HYPNOSIS OF WITNESSES

§795. [HYPNOSIS OF WITNESSES]

(a) [Testimony admitted.] The testimony of a witness is not inadmissible in a criminal proceeding by reason of the fact that the witness has previously undergone hypnosis for the purpose of recalling events that are the subject of the witness's testimony, if all of the following conditions are met:

(1) The testimony is limited to those matters that the witness recalled and related prior to the hypnosis.

(2) The substance of the prehypnotic memory was preserved in a writing, audio recording, or video recording prior to the hypnosis.

(3) The hypnosis was conducted in accordance with all of the following procedures:

(A) A written record was made prior to hypnosis documenting the subject's description of the event, and information that was provided to the hypnotist concerning the subject matter of the hypnosis.

(B) The subject gave informed consent to the hypnosis.

(C) The hypnosis session, including the pre- and post-hypnosis interviews, was video recorded for subsequent review.

(D) The hypnosis was performed by a licensed physician and surgeon, psychologist, licensed clinical social worker, licensed marriage and family therapist, or licensed professional clinical counselor experienced in the use of hypnosis and independent of and not in the presence of law enforcement, the prosecution, or the defense.

(4) Prior to admission of the testimony, the court holds a hearing pursuant to Section 402 at which the proponent of the evidence proves by clear and convincing evidence that the hypnosis did not so affect the witness as to render the witness's prehypnosis recollection unreliable or to substantially impair the ability to cross-examine the witness concerning the witness's prehypnosis recollection. At the hearing, each side shall have the right to present expert testimony and to cross-examine witnesses.

(b) [Testimony impeachable.] Nothing in this section shall be construed to limit the ability of a party to attack the credibility of a witness who has undergone hypnosis, or to limit other legal grounds to admit or exclude the testimony of that witness.

History of Evid. C. §795: Added eff. Jan. 1, 1985, Stats. 1984, ch. 479, §1. Amended eff. Jan. 1, 1988, Stats. 1987, ch. 285, §1; eff. Jan. 1, 1997, Stats. 1996, ch. 67, §1; eff. Jan. 1, 2003, Stats. 2002, ch. 1013, §77; eff. Jan. 1, 2010, Stats. 2009, ch. 88, §34; eff. Jan. 1, 2012, Stats. 2011, ch. 381, §20.

Official Comment

37 Cal. Law Revision Comm'n Rep. (2007), p. 282.

Section 795 is amended to reflect advances in recording technology and for consistency of terminology. For a similar reform, see 2002 Cal. Stat. ch. 1068 (replacing numerous references to "audiotape" in Civil Discovery Act with either "audio technology," "audio recording," or "audio record," as context required).

DIVISION 7. OPINION TESTIMONY & SCIENTIFIC EVIDENCE

Official Comment

7 Cal. Law Revision Comm'n Rep. (1965) p. 1136.

Two matters concerning the terminology used in this division should be noted: (1) The word "opinion" is used to include all opinions, inferences, conclusions, and other subjective statements made by a witness. (2) The word "matter" is used to encompass facts, data, and such matters as a witness' knowledge, experience, and other intangibles upon which an opinion may be based. Thus, every conceivable basis for an opinion is included within this term.

CHAPTER 1. EXPERT & OTHER OPINION TESTIMONY

ARTICLE 1. EXPERT & OTHER OPINION TESTIMONY GENERALLY

§800. [LAY-WITNESS OPINION]

If a witness is not testifying as an expert, his testimony in the form of an opinion is limited to such an opinion as is permitted by law, including but not limited to an opinion that is:

(a) Rationally based on the perception of the witness; and

(b) Helpful to a clear understanding of his testimony.

History of Evid. C. §800: Added eff. Sept. 17, 1965, oper. Jan. 1, 1967, Stats. 1965, ch. 299, §2.

Official Comment

7 Cal. Law Revision Comm'n Rep. (1965) p. 1136.

This section codifies existing law. A witness who is not testifying as an expert may testify in the form of an opinion only if the opinion is based on his own perception. *Stuart v. Dotts*, 89 Cal.App.2d 683, 201 P.2d 820 (1949). See discussion in *Manney v. Housing Authority*, 79 Cal.App.2d 453, 459-460, 180 P.2d 69, 73 (1947). And, in addition, the opinion must be "helpful to a clear understanding of his testimony." *See Tentative Recommendation and a Study Relating to the Uniform Rules of Evidence (Article VII. Expert and Other Opinion Testimony)*, 6 Cal. Law Revision Comm'n, Rep., Rec. & Studies 901, 931-935 (1964).

Section 800 does not make inadmissible an opinion that is admissible under existing law, even though the requirements of subdivisions (a) and (b) are not satisfied. Thus, the section does not affect the existing rule that a nonexpert witness may give his opinion as to the value of his property or the value of his own services. *See* Witkin, *California Evidence* §179 (1958). The words "such an opinion as is permitted by law" in Section 800 make this clear.

ANNOTATIONS

People v. Rodriguez (2014) 58 Cal.4th 587, 631. See annotation under Evidence Code §702, p. 1251.

Behr v. Redmond (4th Dist.2011) 193 Cal.App.4th 517, 528. "[D] asserts that [P's] testimony of her ... herpes outbreak is not substantial evidence of an outbreak of herpes because [P] is not qualified to diagnose herself with a disease. [P] is not, as [D] points out, a doctor. We reject this argument. [¶] [L]ay witnesses are generally competent to testify as to their own knowledge of their diseases, injuries, or physical condition. There is no dispute that [P] has been diagnosed as having genital herpes. We have no doubt that a person who suffers from genital herpes is competent to testify as to when he or she had an outbreak of the disease. *At 529:* The fact that [P's] perception that the ... event was a herpes outbreak was not formed until after she was diagnosed with the disease does not necessarily invalidate the perception or render her testimony entirely without substance. It is entirely possible that symptoms of herpes might not be recognized as such by the herpes sufferer when they first appear, but can, with the benefit of hindsight and a subsequent diagnosis, be accurately perceived as an outbreak."

OCM Principal Opportunities Fund v. CIBC World Mkts. Corp. (2d Dist.2007) 157 Cal.App.4th 835, 876-77. "Under ... §800, which governs the admissibility of lay opinion, a nonexpert witness may give his opinion as to the value of his property or the value of his own services. This rule encompasses the valuation of abstract rights. [¶] The opinion of an owner of personal property is in itself competent evidence of the value of that property, and sufficient to support a judgment based on that value. The credit and weight to be given such evidence and its effect is for the trier of fact. Appellate courts accord broad deference to the trial court's decision to admit lay opinion testimony that is subject to cross-examination." (Internal quotes omitted.)

Osborn v. Mission Ready Mix (4th Dist.1990) 224 Cal.App.3d 104, 112. "The true rule as to the admissibility of lay witness opinion testimony is simple and, so far as this state is concerned, well established: to permit, or to refuse to permit, such questions is a matter resting largely in the discretion of the trial court, which discretion will not here be reviewed unless it is made plain that the court's ruling in admitting the evidence has worked an injury. Generally speaking, the admission of the answer to such a question cannot work an injury where a fair latitude upon cross-examination is allowed, for under such cross-examination the facts are certain to be adduced. [¶] [O]pinion testimony by a lay witness is admissible if it is based on the witness's perception and helpful to a clear understanding of the witness's testimony. Opinion testimony of a lay witness may be particularly helpful when the matters observed by the witness may be too complex or subtle to enable the witness accurately to convey them without resorting to the use of conclusory descriptions. *At 113:* Thus, a lay witness may express an opinion that a person was drunk ..., or that people engaged in a discussion were angry ..., or that an impact was strong enough to jar a passenger from a seat ..., or that someone appeared to be trying to break up a fight." (Internal quotes omitted.)

§801. [EXPERT-WITNESS OPINION]

If a witness is testifying as an expert, his testimony in the form of an opinion is limited to such an opinion as is:

(a) Related to a subject that is sufficiently beyond common experience that the opinion of an expert would assist the trier of fact; and

(b) Based on matter (including his special knowledge, skill, experience, training, and education) perceived by or personally known to the witness or made known to him at or before the hearing, whether or not admissible, that is of a type that reasonably may be relied upon by an expert in forming an opinion upon the subject to which his testimony relates, unless an expert is precluded by law from using such matter as a basis for his opinion.

History of Evid. C. §801: Added eff. Sept. 17, 1965, oper. Jan. 1, 1967, Stats. 1965, ch. 299, §2.

Official Comment

7 Cal. Law Revision Comm'n Rep. (1965) p. 1137.

Section 801 deals with opinion testimony of a witness testifying as an expert; it sets the standard for admissibility of such testimony.

Subdivision (a), which states *when* an expert may give his opinion upon a subject that is within the scope of his expertise, codifies the existing rule that expert opinion is limited to those subjects that are beyond the competence of persons of common experience, training, and education. *People v. Cole*, 47 Cal.2d 99, 103, 301 P.2d 854, 856 (1956). For examples of the variety of subjects upon which expert testimony is admitted, *see* Witkin, *California Evidence* §§190-195 (1958).

Subdivision (b) states a general rule in regard to the permissible bases upon which the opinion of an expert may be founded. The California courts have made it clear that the nature of the matter upon which an expert may base his opinion varies from case to case. In some fields of expert knowledge, an expert may rely on statements made by and information received from other persons; in some other fields of expert knowledge, an expert may not do so. For example, a physician may rely on statements made to him by the patient concern-

§801

ing the history of his condition. *People v. Wilson*, 25 Cal.2d 341, 153 P.2d 720 (1944). A physician may also rely on reports and opinions of other physicians. *Kelley v. Bailey*, 189 Cal.App.2d 728, 11 Cal.Rptr. 448 (1961); *Hope v. Arrowhead & Puritas Waters, Inc.*, 174 Cal.App.2d 222, 344 P.2d 428 (1959). An expert on the valuation of real or personal property, too, may rely on inquiries made of others, commercial reports, market quotations, and relevant sales known to the witness. *Betts v. Southern Cal. Fruit Exchange*, 144 Cal. 402, 77 Pac. 993 (1904); *Hammond Lumber Co. v. County of Los Angeles*, 104 Cal.App. 235, 285 Pac. 896 (1930); *Glantz v. Freedman*, 100 Cal.App. 611, 280 Pac. 704 (1929). On the other hand, an expert on automobile accidents may not rely on extrajudicial statements of others as a partial basis for an opinion as to the point of impact, whether or not the statements would be admissible evidence. *Hodges v. Severns*, 201 Cal.App.2d 99, 20 Cal.Rptr. 129 (1962); *Ribble v. Cook*, 111 Cal.App.2d 903, 245 P.2d 593 (1952). *See also Behr v. County of Santa Cruz*, 172 Cal.App.2d 697, 342 P.2d 987 (1959) (report of fire ranger as to cause of fire held inadmissible because it was based primarily upon statements made to him by other persons).

Likewise, under existing law, irrelevant or speculative matters are not a proper basis for an expert's opinion. *See Roscoe Moss Co. v. Jenkins*, 55 Cal.App.2d 369, 130 P.2d 477 (1942) (expert may not base opinion upon a comparison if the matters compared are not reasonably comparable); *People v. Luis*, 158 Cal. 185, 110 Pac. 580 (1910) (physician may not base opinion as to person's feeblemindedness merely upon the person's exterior appearance); *Long v. Cal.-Western States Life Ins. Co.*, 43 Cal.2d 871, 279 P.2d 43 (1955) (speculative or conjectural data); *Eisenmayer v. Leonardt*, 148 Cal. 596, 84 Pac. 43 (1906) (speculative or conjectural data). *Compare People v. Wochnick*, 98 Cal.App.2d 124, 219 P.2d 70 (1950) (expert may not give opinion as to the truth or falsity of certain statements on basis of lie detector test), *with People v. Jones*, 42 Cal.2d 219, 266 P.2d 38 (1954) (psychiatrist may consider an examination given under the influence of sodium pentothal—the so-called "truth serum"—in forming an opinion as to the mental state of the person examined).

The variation in the permissible bases of expert opinion is unavoidable in light of the wide variety of subjects upon which such opinion can be offered. In regard to some matters of expert opinion, an expert *must*, if he is going to give an opinion that will be helpful to the jury, rely on reports, statements, and other information that might not be admissible evidence. A physician in many instances cannot make a diagnosis without relying on the case history recited by the patient or on reports from various technicians or other physicians. Similarly, an appraiser must rely on reports of sales and other market data if he is to give an opinion that will be of value to the jury. In the usual case where a physician's or an appraiser's opinion is required, the adverse party also will have its expert who will be able to check the data relied upon by the adverse expert. On the other hand, a police officer can analyze skid marks, debris, and the condition of vehicles that have been involved in an accident without relying on the statements of bystanders; and it seems likely that the jury would be as able to evaluate the statements of others in the light of the physical facts, as interpreted by the officer, as would the officer himself. It is apparent that the extent to which an expert may base his opinion upon the statements of others is far from clear. It is at least clear, however, that it is permitted in a number of instances. *See Young v. Bates Valve Bag Corp.*, 52 Cal.App.2d 86, 96-97, 125 P.2d 840, 846 (1942), and cases therein cited. *Cf. People v. Alexander*, 212 Cal.App.2d 84, 27 Cal.Rptr. 720 (1963).

It is not practical to formulate a detailed statutory rule that lists all of the matters upon which an expert may properly base his opinion, for it would be necessary to prescribe specific rules applicable to each field of expertise. This is clearly impossible; the subjects upon which expert opinion may be received are too numerous to make statutory prescription of applicable rules a feasible venture. It is possible, however, to formulate a general rule that specifies the minimum requisites that must be met in every case, leaving to the courts the task of determining particular detail within this general framework. This standard is expressed in subdivision (b) which states a general rule that is applicable whenever expert opinion is offered on a given subject.

Under subdivision (b), the matter upon which an expert's opinion is based must meet each of three separate but related tests. *First*, the matter must be perceived by or personally known to the witness or must be made known to him at or before the hearing at which the opinion is expressed. This requirement assures the expert's acquaintance with the facts of a particular case either by his personal perception or observation or by means of assuming facts not personally known to the witness. *Second*, and without regard to the means by which an expert familiarizes himself with the matter upon which his opinion is based, the matter relied upon by the expert in forming his opinion must be of a type that reasonably may be relied upon by experts in forming an opinion upon the subject to which his testimony relates. In large measure, this assures the reliability and trustworthiness of the information used by experts in forming their opinions. *Third*, an expert may not base his opinion upon any matter that is declared by the constitutional, statutory, or decisional law of this State to be an improper basis for an opinion. For example, the statements of bystanders as to the cause of a fire may be considered reliable for some purposes by an investigator of the fire, particularly when coupled with physical evidence found at the scene, but the courts have determined this to be an improper basis for an opinion since the trier of fact is as capable as the expert of evaluating such statements in light of the physical facts as interpreted by the expert. *Behr v. County of Santa Cruz*, 172 Cal.App.2d 697, 342 P.2d 987 (1959).

The rule stated in subdivision (b) thus permits an expert to base his opinion upon reliable matter, *whether or not admissible*, of a type that may reasonably be used in forming an opinion upon the subject to which his expert testimony relates. In addition, it provides assurance that the courts and the Legislature are free to continue to develop specific rules regarding the proper bases for particular kinds of expert opinion in specific fields. *See, e.g.*, 3 Cal. Law Revision Comm'n, Rep., Rec. & Studies, *Recommendation and Study Relating to Evidence in Eminent Domain Proceedings* at A-1 (1961). Subdivision (b) thus provides a sensible standard of admissibility while, at the same time, it continues in effect the discretionary power of the courts to regulate abuses, thereby retaining in large measure the existing California law.

ANNOTATIONS

Generally

People v. McDowell (2012) 54 Cal.4th 395, 426. "The trial court has broad discretion in deciding whether to admit or exclude expert testimony ..., and its decision as to whether expert testimony meets the standard for admissibility is subject to review for abuse of discretion."

People v. Bassett (1968) 69 Cal.2d 122, 146 n.22. "Assuming the necessary minimum acquaintance with the case in which he is called to testify, 'the extent of an expert's knowledge goes to the weight of his testimony, rather than to its admissibility'...."

Amtower v. Photon Dynamics, Inc. (6th Dist. 2008) 158 Cal.App.4th 1582, 1598-99. "[T]he calling of lawyers as expert witnesses to give opinions as to the application of the law to particular facts usurps the duty of the trial court to instruct the jury on the law as applicable to the facts, and results in no more than a modern day trial by oath in which the side producing the greater number of lawyers able to opine in their favor wins." (Internal quotes omitted.)

Los Altos El Granada Investors v. City of Capitola (6th Dist.2006) 139 Cal.App.4th 629, 658. See annotation under Evidence Code §720, p. 1254.

Roberti v. Andy's Termite & Pest Control, Inc. (2d Dist.2003) 113 Cal.App.4th 893, 904. "The federal rule established in ***Daubert v. Merrell Dow*** [***Pharms.*** (1993) 509 U.S. 579] subjects *all* expert scientific and technical opinion testimony to a threshold reliability test (under [FRE] 702 ...). ***Daubert***, however, does not

alter California law with regard to admissibility of expert medical opinion testimony. *At 906:* Unless and until our Supreme Court determines that the ***Daubert*** analysis is applicable in California, we will adhere to the rule of ***People v. Kelly*** [(1976) 17 Cal.3d 24] and its progeny, and refuse to apply a more extensive preliminary admissibility test as in ***Daubert*** to expert medical opinion concerning causation." *See also* ***People v. Leahy*** (1994) 8 Cal.4th 587, 604 (***Kelly*** test survived ***Daubert***).

Subdivision (a)

People v. McDowell (2012) 54 Cal.4th 395, 426. "[T]he trial court did not abuse its discretion in concluding the jury was capable of evaluating whether [D's] childhood could have affected his adult behavior without expert opinion testimony on that issue. *At 427:* The expert opinion testimony was neither technical nor complex, and the trial court could reasonably have found that it would not assist the trier of fact because it addressed a matter readily understood by lay jurors."

People v. Jones (2012) 54 Cal.4th 1, 60. "[T]he jury need [not] be wholly ignorant of the subject matter of the expert opinion in order for it to be admissible. Rather, expert opinion testimony will be excluded only when it would add *nothing at all* to the jury's common fund of information, i.e., when the subject of inquiry is one of such common knowledge that men of ordinary education could reach a conclusion as intelligently as the witness…." (Internal quotes omitted.) *See also* ***People v. Rodriguez*** (2014) 58 Cal.4th 587, 639; ***Carson v. Facilities Dev. Co.*** (1984) 36 Cal.3d 830, 844-45; ***People v. Cole*** (1956) 47 Cal.2d 99, 103.

Soule v. General Motors Corp. (1994) 8 Cal.4th 548, 567. "[W]here the minimum safety of a product is within the common knowledge of lay jurors, expert witnesses may not be used to demonstrate what an ordinary consumer would or should expect. Use of expert testimony for that purpose would invade the jury's function … and would invite circumvention of the rule that the risks and benefits of a challenged design must be carefully balanced whenever the issue of design defect goes beyond the common experience of the product's users."

George v. Bekins Van & Storage Co. (1949) 33 Cal.2d 834, 841. "[D] contends that the trial court committed prejudicial error by admitting into evidence the opinions of [Ps'] experts that the fire was caused by careless smoking. *At 844:* The possible causes of warehouse fires are sufficiently beyond the common experience of the ordinary judge or juror to justify the admission of expert opinion testimony on that issue." *See also* ***Garbell v. Conejo Hardwoods, Inc.*** (2d Dist. 2011) 193 Cal.App.4th 1563, 1569 (expert testimony was necessary to determine origin and cause of house fire).

Sanchez v. Brooke (2d Dist.2012) 204 Cal.App.4th 126, 138. "Generally, expert testimony is required to establish the standard of care that applies to a professional. However, an exception exists where the circumstances fall within the realm of common knowledge. [¶] [No] special knowledge or skills are required to supply the common sense needed to prevent harm from everyday hazards. Given that the risk of fire posed by smoking in bed is commonly understood, no professional skills were necessary to determine an appropriate response [to the risk posed by home-healthcare patient smoking in bed] under the circumstances. Lay jurors are as capable as experts in assessing the adequacy of [home-health aide's employer's] lack of response to the obvious risk of fire in this case." (Internal quotes omitted.)

Loth v. Truck-A-Way Corp. (2d Dist.1998) 60 Cal.App.4th 757, 767. "A plaintiff's loss of enjoyment of life is not 'a subject that is sufficiently beyond common experience that the opinion of an expert would assist the trier of fact[.]' No amount of expert testimony on the value of life could possibly help a jury decide that difficult question. A life is not a stock, car, home, or other such item bought and sold in some marketplace. *At 768:* Our present system of requiring the jury to determine, without the benefit of a mathematical formula, the amount of a general damages award is not without its faults. … Just as no judge may give the jury a standard for determining pain and suffering damages …, no expert may supply a formula for computing the value of life and, by extrapolation, the value of the loss of enjoyment of life. That calculation, at present, must be left to the sound discretion of the jury."

Subdivision (b)

Sargon Enters. v. University of S. Cal. (2012) 55 Cal.4th 747, 771-72. Evid. C. §802 "expressly permits the court to examine experts concerning the matter on which they base their opinion before admitting their testimony. The *reasons* for the experts' opinions are part of the matter on which they are based just as is the *type* of matter. [Evid. C.] §801 governs judicial review

of the *type* of matter; ... §802 governs judicial review of the *reasons* for the opinion. 'The stark contrast between the wording of the two statutes strongly suggests that although under §801(b) the judge may consider only the acceptability of the generic type of information the expert relies on, the judge is not so limited under §802.' [¶] [A] court may inquire into, not only the type of material on which an expert relies, but also whether that material actually supports the expert's reasoning. 'A court may conclude that there is simply too great an analytical gap between the data and the opinion proffered.' [¶] Thus, under ... §§801, subdivision (b), and 802, the trial court acts as a gatekeeper to exclude expert opinion testimony that is (1) based on matter of a type on which an expert may not reasonably rely, (2) based on reasons unsupported by the material on which the expert relies, or (3) speculative. [¶] [But t]he court must not weigh an opinion's probative value or substitute its own opinion for the expert's opinion. Rather, the court must simply determine whether the matter relied on can provide a reasonable basis for the opinion or whether that opinion is based on a leap of logic or conjecture." *See also* ***Corenbaum v. Lampkin*** (2d Dist.2013) 215 Cal.App.4th 1308, 1331-32.

Isaacs v. Huntington Mem'l Hosp. (1985) 38 Cal.3d 112, 133-34. "[S]ection 801, subdivision (b) permits an expert to rely upon inadmissible evidence if it is 'of a type that reasonably may be relied upon by an expert in forming an opinion upon the subject to which his testimony relates....' [Ps'] expert would clearly have been entitled to testify about information that he had read in a California Department of Justice report. However, what he learned from an unidentified contact in an unidentified police department scarcely constitutes the sort of material that may be reasonably relied upon by an expert in forming his opinion."

People v. Yuksel (2d Dist.2012) 207 Cal.App.4th 850, 856. "[A]n expert's reliance on hearsay does not automatically make the hearsay evidence itself admissible. An expert may generally base his opinion on any matter known to him, including hearsay not otherwise admissible, which may reasonably be relied upon for that purpose. On direct examination, the expert may explain the reasons for his opinions, including the matters he considered in forming them. However, prejudice may arise if, under the guise of reasons, the expert's detailed explanation brings before the jury incompetent hearsay evidence." (Internal quotes omitted.) *See also* ***Korsak v. Atlas Hotels, Inc.*** (4th Dist.1992) 2 Cal.App.4th 1516, 1525.

Cole v. Town of Los Gatos (6th Dist.2012) 205 Cal.App.4th 749, 766. "An expert is entitled to base his opinion upon inadmissible matter, including factual propositions outside his personal knowledge, provided such matter is 'of a type that reasonably may be relied upon by an expert in forming an opinion upon the subject to which his testimony relates.' However, to the extent [expert] relied on facts not personally known to him, those facts were necessarily *hypothetical*.... Assertions of matter outside [expert's] personal knowledge, in ... an unconditional, unattributed form, were indeed objectionable, if only to ensure that they were not inadvertently allowed to become proof of the stated facts. [¶] But an objection on this ground goes only to the *purpose* for which the challenged statements may be received. The correct ruling is not to exclude them, but to admit them subject to appropriate limitations. In a jury trial of course the jury is instructed about these limitations; [here] the trial court need only confirm that it is not accepting the challenged statements as proof of the matters asserted, but only as a foundation for the accompanying opinions."

Scott S. v. Superior Ct. (4th Dist.2012) 204 Cal.App.4th 326, 343. "[T]he court could consider ... expert opinion on [conservatee's] capacity to consent, without having to hear only from the treating physician. *At 344:* [B]ecause the basic issue is the conservatee's capacity—his *ability* to understand and make knowing, intelligent decisions—an expert in psychiatry, psychology, or a related field may also be able to express a relevant opinion. And the expert may base his opinion on any matter 'whether or not admissible, that is of a type' that experts reasonably rely upon—including hearsay statements from the treating physician. Whether the expert was present for the treating physician's conversation with the conservatee goes to the weight of the expert's opinion, not its admissibility. Similarly, whether that expert is a medical doctor with independent knowledge of the proposed treatment's benefits and risks goes only to the opinion's weight."

Lockheed Litigation Cases (2d Dist.2004) 115 Cal.App.4th 558, 563. "'The value of opinion evidence rests not in the conclusion reached but in the factors considered and the reasoning employed. Where an expert bases his conclusion upon assumptions which are not supported by the record, upon matters which are

not reasonably relied upon by other experts, or upon factors which are speculative, remote or conjectural, then his conclusion has no evidentiary value.' *At 564:* We construe [§801, subdivision (b)] to mean that the matter relied on must provide a reasonable basis for the particular opinion offered, and that an expert opinion based on speculation or conjecture is inadmissible." *See also* ***Mitchell v. United Nat'l Ins.*** (2d Dist.2005) 127 Cal.App.4th 457, 478; ***Bushling v. Fremont Med. Ctr.*** (3d Dist.2004) 117 Cal.App.4th 493, 510.

Jennings v. Palomar Pomerado Health Sys. (4th Dist.2003) 114 Cal.App.4th 1108, 1117-18. "[E]ven when the witness qualifies as an expert, he or she does not possess a carte blanche to express any opinion within the area of expertise. For example, an expert's opinion based on assumptions of fact without evidentiary support ..., or on speculative or conjectural factors ..., has no evidentiary value ... and may be excluded from evidence. Similarly, when an expert's opinion is purely conclusory because unaccompanied by a reasoned explanation connecting the factual predicates to the ultimate conclusion, that opinion has no evidentiary value because an 'expert opinion is worth no more than the reasons upon which it rests.' [¶] Exclusion of expert opinions that rest on guess, surmise or conjecture ... is an inherent corollary to the foundational predicate for admission of the expert testimony: will the testimony assist the trier of fact to evaluate the issues it must decide? Therefore, an expert's opinion that something *could* be true if certain assumed facts are true, without any foundation for concluding those assumed facts exist in the case before the jury, does not provide assistance to the jury because the jury is charged with determining what occurred in the case before it, not hypothetical possibilities. Similarly, an expert's conclusory opinion that something did occur, when unaccompanied by a reasoned explanation illuminating how the expert employed his or her superior knowledge and training to connect the facts with the ultimate conclusion, does not assist the jury. ... An expert who gives only a conclusory opinion does not *assist* the jury to determine what occurred, but instead supplants the jury by *declaring* what occurred."

Mosesian v. Pennwalt Corp. (5th Dist.1987) 191 Cal.App.3d 851, 860, *disapproved on other grounds*, ***People v. Ault*** (2004) 33 Cal.4th 1250. "The general and well-settled rule prevents an expert from predicating an opinion upon the outside opinion of another expert. The expert should base the opinion upon facts personally observed or upon a hypothesis supported by the evidence. [¶] Experts may rely upon hearsay in forming opinions. They may not relate an out-of-court opinion by another expert as independent proof of fact. It is proper to solicit the fact that another expert was consulted to show the foundation of the testifying expert's opinion, but not to reveal the content of the hearsay opinion. *At 861-62:* The California authorities limit the introduction in testimony of hearsay material used in forming expert opinion to matters that are admissible. Whether it is reasonable for an expert to rely upon the statements of another expert affects the weight of the expert's testimony more than the admissibility of the opinion itself. The trial court has considerable latitude in qualifying an expert."

§802. [BASIS OF OPINION TESTIMONY]

A witness testifying in the form of an opinion may state on direct examination the reasons for his opinion and the matter (including, in the case of an expert, his special knowledge, skill, experience, training, and education) upon which it is based, unless he is precluded by law from using such reasons or matter as a basis for his opinion. The court in its discretion may require that a witness before testifying in the form of an opinion be first examined concerning the matter upon which his opinion is based.

§802

History of Evid. C. §802: Added eff. Sept. 17, 1965, oper. Jan. 1, 1967, Stats. 1965, ch. 299, §2.

Official Comment

7 Cal. Law Revision Comm'n Rep. (1965) p. 1140.

Section 802 restates the substance of and supersedes a portion of Section 1872 of the Code of Civil Procedure. Section 802, however, relates to all witnesses who testify in the form of opinion, while Section 1872 relates only to experts.

Although Section 802 (like its predecessor, Code of Civil Procedure Section 1872) provides that a witness *may* state the basis for his opinion on direct examination, it is clear that, in some cases, a witness is *required* to do so in order to show that his opinion is applicable to the action before the court. Under existing law, where a witness testifies in the form of opinion not based upon his personal observation, the assumed facts upon which his opinion is based must be stated in order to show that the witness has some basis for forming an intelligent opinion and to permit the trier of fact to determine the applicability of the opinion in light of the existence or nonexistence of such facts. *Eisenmayer v. Leonardt*, 148 Cal. 596, 84 Pac. 43 (1906); *Lemley v. Doak Gas Engine Co.*, 40 Cal. App. 146, 180 Pac. 671 (1919) (hearing denied). Evidence Code Section 802 will not affect the rule set forth in these cases, for it is based essentially on the requirement that all evidence must be shown to be applicable—or relevant—to the action. Evidence Code §§350, 403. But under Section 802, as under existing law, a witness testifying from his personal observation of the facts upon which his opinion is based need not be examined concerning such facts before testifying in the form of opinion; his personal observation is a sufficient basis upon which to found his opinion. *Lumbermen's Mut. Cas. Co. v. Industrial Acc. Comm'n*, 29 Cal.2d 492, 175 P.2d 823 (1946); *Hart v. Olson*, 68

Cal.App.2d 657, 157 P.2d 385 (1945); *Lemley v. Doak Gas Engine Co., supra*. However, the court may require a witness to state the facts observed before stating his opinion. In this respect, Section 802 codifies the existing rule concerning lay witnesses and, although the existing law is unclear, probably states the existing rule as to expert witnesses. *See Tentative Recommendation and a Study Relating to the Uniform Rules of Evidence (Article VII. Expert and Other Opinion Testimony)*, 6 Cal. Law Revision Comm'n, Rep., Rec. & Studies 901, 934 (lay witness), 939 (expert witness) (1964).

ANNOTATIONS

Sargon Enters. v. University of S. Cal. (2012) 55 Cal.4th 747, 771-72. See annotation under Evidence Code §801, *Subdivision (b)*, p. 1279.

Garrett v. Howmedica Osteonics Corp. (2d Dist.2013) 214 Cal.App.4th 173, 189. "Unlike ***Sargon* [*Enters. v. University of S. Cal.*** (2012) 55 Cal.4th 747], this case involves the exclusion of expert testimony presented in opposition to a summary judgment motion. The trial court here did not conduct an evidentiary hearing, and there was no examination of an expert witness pursuant to … §802. Absent more specific information on the testing methods used and the results obtained, the trial court here could not scrutinize the reasons for [expert's] opinion to the same extent as did the trial court in ***Sargon***. We do not believe, however, that the absence of such detailed information justified the exclusion of [expert's] testimony. [¶] The rule that a trial court must liberally construe the evidence submitted in opposition to a summary judgment motion applies in ruling on both the admissibility of expert testimony and its sufficiency to create a triable issue of fact. [Thus], a reasoned explanation required in an expert declaration filed in opposition to a summary judgment motion need not be as detailed or extensive as that required in expert testimony presented in support of a summary judgment motion or at trial. Liberally construing [expert's] declaration, we conclude that the explanation provided for [expert's] opinion was sufficient and that the trial court could not properly exclude the expert testimony based on [expert's] failure to identify the particular tests employed or describe the test results."

Kelley v. Trunk (2d Dist.1998) 66 Cal.App.4th 519, 523. "Expert witnesses normally testify concerning the *bases* for their opinions, and the court may *require* the expert to state the bases before giving his opinion. Standard instructions give[] juries the common sense directive that '[a]n opinion is only as good as the facts and reasons on which it is based.' An expert's opinion, even if uncontradicted, may be rejected if the reasons given for it are unsound."

People v. Odom (4th Dist.1980) 108 Cal.App.3d 100, 115. "An expert witness, … in giving the reasons for his opinion, may testify as to treatises, learned documents, textual material relied upon by him and may thereafter be *fully cross-examined* thereon by opposing counsel. However, as noted by the Supreme Court in … ***People v. La Macchia*** (1953) 41 Cal.2d 738 …: 'The general rule which permits a witness to state the reasons upon which his opinion is premised may not be used as a vehicle to bring before the jury incompetent evidence. To so open up the inquiry would create a disastrous break in the dike which stands against a flood of interminable investigation.' [¶] The basic rule of [***La Macchia***] prohibiting a witness from putting in evidence matters which are incompetent as substantive evidence for the purpose of fortifying his opinion, even though they are offered under the guise for the reasons for his opinions, and even though they might properly have been admitted on cross-examination to test *and* diminish the weight to be given to his opinion, was and is the law in this state."

§803. [IMPROPER BASIS FOR OPINION]

The court may, and upon objection shall, exclude testimony in the form of an opinion that is based in whole or in significant part on matter that is not a proper basis for such an opinion. In such case, the witness may, if there remains a proper basis for his opinion, then state his opinion after excluding from consideration the matter determined to be improper.

History of Evid. C. §803: Added eff. Sept. 17, 1965, oper. Jan. 1, 1967, Stats. 1965, ch. 299, §2.

Official Comment

7 Cal. Law Revision Comm'n Rep. (1965) p. 1141.

Under Section 803, as under existing law, an opinion may be held inadmissible or may be stricken if it is based wholly or in substantial part upon improper considerations. Whether or not the opinion should be held inadmissible or stricken will depend in a particular case on the extent to which the improper considerations have influenced the opinion. "The question is addressed to the discretion of the trial court." *People v. Lipari*, 213 Cal.App.2d 485, 493, 28 Cal.Rptr. 808, 813-814 (1963). See discussion in *City of Gilroy v. Filice*, 221 Cal.App.2d 259, 271-272, 34 Cal.Rptr. 368, 375-376 (1963), and cases cited therein. If a witness' opinion is stricken because of reliance upon improper considerations, the second sentence of Section 803 assures the witness the opportunity to express his opinion after excluding from his consideration the matter determined to be improper.

§804. [OPINION OF OTHER PERSON AS BASIS FOR OPINION]

(a) [Cross-examination of other person.] If a witness testifying as an expert testifies that his opinion is based in whole or in part upon the opinion or statement of another person, such other person may be

called and examined by any adverse party as if under cross-examination concerning the opinion or statement.

(b) [**No cross-examination of certain persons.**] This section is not applicable if the person upon whose opinion or statement the expert witness has relied is

(1) a party,

(2) a person identified with a party within the meaning of subdivision (d) of Section 776, or

(3) a witness who has testified in the action concerning the subject matter of the opinion or statement upon which the expert witness has relied.

(c) [**Inadmissible expert opinion.**] Nothing in this section makes admissible an expert opinion that is inadmissible because it is based in whole or in part on the opinion or statement of another person.

(d) [**Admissible expert opinion.**] An expert opinion otherwise admissible is not made inadmissible by this section because it is based on the opinion or statement of a person who is unavailable for examination pursuant to this section.

History of Evid. C. §804: Added eff. Sept. 17, 1965, oper. Jan. 1, 1967, Stats. 1965, ch. 299, §2.

Official Comment

7 Cal. Law Revision Comm'n Rep. (1965) p. 1141.

Section 804 is designed to provide protection to a party who is confronted with an expert witness who relies on the opinion or statement of some other person. (*See* the *Comment* to Section 801 for examples of opinions that may be based on the statements and opinions of others.) In such a situation, a party may find that cross-examination of the witness will not reveal the weakness in his opinion, for the crucial parts are based on the observations or opinions of someone else. Under existing law, if that other person is called as a witness, he is the witness of the party calling him and, therefore, that party may not subject him to cross-examination.

The existing law operates unfairly, for it unnecessarily restricts meaningful cross-examination. Hence, Section 804 permits a party to extend his cross-examination into the underlying bases of the opinion testimony introduced against him by calling the authors of opinions and statements relied on by adverse witnesses and examining them as if under cross-examination concerning the subject matter of their opinions and statements. *See* the *Comment* to Evidence Code §1203.

ANNOTATIONS

People v. Ledesma (2006) 39 Cal.4th 641, 701-02. "Section 804 does not apply if the person upon whose opinion the expert relied is 'identified with' a party, a term that includes someone who is an agent of the party. [¶] [S]ection 804 governs the manner of examination; it permits a party to cross-examine the expert even though the expert is the party's own witness. The circumstance that §804 does not apply if the expert is an agent of a party does not preclude calling the expert as a witness; that circumstance simply signifies that the examination is governed by other applicable statutes." *See also* Evidence Code §776 (rules for examination of adverse party).

§805. [OPINION ON ULTIMATE ISSUE]

Testimony in the form of an opinion that is otherwise admissible is not objectionable because it embraces the ultimate issue to be decided by the trier of fact.

History of Evid. C. §805: Added eff. Sept. 17, 1965, oper. Jan. 1, 1967, Stats. 1965, ch. 299, §2.

Official Comment

7 Cal. Law Revision Comm'n Rep. (1965) p. 1142.

Although several older cases indicated that an opinion could not be received on an ultimate issue, more recent cases have repudiated this rule. Hence, this section is declarative of existing law. *People v. Wilson*, 25 Cal.2d 341, 349-350, 153 P.2d 720, 725 (1944); *Wells Truckways, Ltd. v. Cebrian*, 122 Cal.App.2d 666, 265 P.2d 557 (1954); *People v. King*, 104 Cal.App.2d 298, 231 P.2d 156 (1951).

ANNOTATIONS

People v. Lowe (4th Dist.2012) 211 Cal.App.4th 678, 684. "[A]dmissibility depends on the nature of the issue and the circumstances of the case, there being a large element of judicial discretion involved. Oftentimes an opinion may be received on a simple ultimate issue, even when it is the sole one, as for example where the issue is the value of an article, or the sanity of a person; because it cannot be further simplified and cannot be fully tried without hearing opinions from those in better position to form them than the jury can be placed in. [¶] Nonetheless, expert opinion testimony may not invade the province of the jury to decide a case. Thus, expert opinion testimony that merely expresses a general belief as to how the jury should decide the case is not permissible." (Internal quotes omitted.) *See also* ***Summers v. A.L. Gilbert Co.*** (5th Dist. 1999) 69 Cal.App.4th 1155, 1182.

Downer v. Bramet (4th Dist.1984) 152 Cal.App.3d 837, 841. "[P] cites [§805 for] the general rule that opinion evidence which is otherwise admissible is not made inadmissible simply because it embraces the ultimate issue to be decided by the trier of fact. [Section 805] does not, however, authorize an 'expert' to testify to legal conclusions in the guise of expert opinion. Such legal conclusions do not constitute substantial evidence. 'The manner in which the law should apply to particular facts is a legal question and is not subject to expert opinion.' *At 842:* While in many cases expert opinions that are genuinely needed may happen to embrace the ultimate issue of fact (e.g., a medical opinion

whether a physician's actions constitute professional negligence), the calling of lawyers as 'expert witnesses' to give opinions as to the application of the law to particular facts usurps the duty of the trial court to instruct the jury on the law as applicable to the facts, and results in no more than a modern day 'trial by oath' in which the side producing the greater number of lawyers able to opine in their favor wins." *See also* ***WRI Opportunity Loans II, LLC v. Cooper*** (2d Dist.2007) 154 Cal.App.4th 525, 532 n.3; ***Ferreira v. Workmen's Comp. Appeals Bd.*** (5th Dist.1974) 38 Cal.App.3d 120, 125-26.

ARTICLE 2. EVIDENCE OF MARKET VALUE OF PROPERTY

Official Note

This article was not included in the Evidence Code as enacted by Chapter 299 of the Statutes of 1965; it was added to the Evidence Code by Chapter 1151 of the Statutes of 1965. Hence, there are no Comments to the sections in this article. The article is based in large part on a recommendation made by the California Law Revision Commission to the 1961 legislative session. *See* 3 Cal. Law Revision Comm'n, Rep., Rec. & Studies, *Recommendation and Study Relating to Evidence in Eminent Domain Proceedings* at A-1 (1961).

§810. [EVIDENCE OF VALUE OF PROPERTY]

(a) [Coverage.] Except where another rule is provided by statute, this article provides special rules of evidence applicable to any action in which the value of property is to be ascertained.

(b) [Exclusion.] This article does not govern ad valorem property tax assessment or equalization proceedings.

History of Evid. C. §810: Added eff. Sept. 17, 1965, oper. Jan. 1, 1967, Stats. 1965, ch. 1151, §4. Amended eff. Jan. 1, 1979, Stats. 1978, ch. 294, §3; eff. Jan. 1, 1981, Stats. 1980, ch. 381, §1.

Official Comment

14 Cal. Law Revision Comm'n Rep. App. IV (1978) p. 255.

Section 810 defines the scope of this article. This article expressly applies only to the determination of the value of property in eminent domain and inverse condemnation proceedings. However, nothing in this article precludes a court from using the rules prescribed in this article in valuation proceedings to which the article is not made applicable, where the court determines that the rules prescribed are appropriate. *See In re Marriage of Folb* (1975) 53 Cal.App.3d 862, 868-71, 126 Cal.Rptr. 306, 310-12.

15 Cal. Law Revision Comm'n Rep. (1980) p. 1459.

Section 810 is amended to remove the limitation on application of this article to eminent domain and inverse condemnation proceedings. This article does not attempt to define market value and does not apply the eminent domain definition of market value to other cases; it is limited to procedural rules for determining market value, however defined.

This article applies to any action or proceeding in which the value of real property, or real and personal property taken as a unit, is to be determined. *See* Section 811 and *Comment* thereto ("value of property" defined). *See also* Sections 105 and 120 ("action" includes action or proceeding). These cases include, but are not limited to, the following:

(1) Eminent domain proceedings. *See, e.g.*, Code Civ. Proc. §1263.310 (measure of compensation is fair market value of property taken).

(2) Inheritance taxation. *See, e.g.*, Rev. & Tax. Code §§13311 [repealed], 13951 [repealed] (property taxed on basis of market value).

(3) Breach of contract of sale. *See, e.g.*, Civil Code §§3306, 3307 (damages for breach of real property contract based on value of property).

(4) Mortgage deficiency judgments. *See, e.g.*, Code Civ. Proc. §§580a, 726 (judgments calculated on fair market value or fair value of property).

(5) Gift taxation. *See, e.g.*, Rev. & Tax. Code §15203 [repealed] (gift tax computed on market value of property).

(6) Fraud in the purchase, sale, or exchange of property. *See, e.g.*, Civil Code §3343 (measure of damages includes damages based on actual value of property).

(7) Other cases in which no statutory standard of market value or its equivalent is prescribed but in which the court is required to make a determination of market value, such as marriage dissolution. *See, e.g.*, *In re Marriage of Folb*, 53 Cal.App.3d 862, 126 Cal.Rptr. 306 (1975).

This article applies only where market value is to be determined, whether for computing damages and benefits or for any other purpose. In cases involving some other standard of value, the rules provided in this article are not made applicable by statute.

The introductory proviso of subdivision (a) ensures that, where a particular provision requires a special rule relating to value, the special rule prevails over this article. By virtue of subdivision (b), property tax assessment and equalization proceedings, whether judicial or administrative, are not subject to this article. They are governed by a well-developed and adequate set of rules that are comparable to the Evidence Code rules. *See, e.g.*, Rev. & Tax. Code §§402.1, 402.5 (valuation and assessment rules); Rev. & Tax. Code §§1606, 1609, 1609.4, 1636-1641 (equalization proceedings); Cal. Admin. Code, Title 18 (public revenues regulations).

Nothing in this section is intended to require a hearing to ascertain the value of property where a hearing is not required by statute. *See, e.g.*, Rev. & Tax. Code §§14501-14505 (Inheritance Tax Referee permitted but not required to conduct hearing to ascertain value of property).

§811. [VALUE OF PROPERTY]

As used in this article, "value of property" means market value of any of the following:

(a) Real property or any interest therein.

(b) Real property or any interest therein and tangible personal property valued as a unit.

History of Evid. C. §811: Added eff. Sept. 17, 1965, oper. Jan. 1, 1967, Stats. 1965, ch. 1151, §4. Amended eff. Jan. 1, 1976, oper. July 1, 1976, Stats. 1975, ch. 1240, §15; eff. Jan. 1, 1979, Stats. 1978, ch. 294, §4; eff. Jan. 1, 1981, Stats. 1980, ch. 381, §2.

Official Comment

12 Cal. Law Revision Comm'n Rep. (1975) p. 1901.

Section 811 is amended to conform to the numbering of the Eminent Domain Law.

Section 811 makes clear that this article as applied to eminent domain proceedings governs only evidence relating to the determination of property value and damages and benefits to the remainder. This article does not govern evidence relating to the determination of loss of goodwill (Code Civ. Proc. §1263.510).

The evidence admissible to prove loss of goodwill is governed by the general provisions of the Evidence Code. Hence, nothing in this article should be deemed a limitation on the admissibility of evidence to prove loss of goodwill if such evidence is otherwise admissible.

14 Cal. Law Revision Comm'n Rep. (1978) p. 255.

Section 811 is amended to make clear the limited application of this article. This article applies only where market value of real property, an interest in real property (*e.g.*, a leasehold), or tangible personal property is to be determined, whether for computing damages and benefits or otherwise. This article does not apply to the valuation of intangible personal property that is not an interest in real property, such as goodwill of a business; valuation of such property is governed by the rules of evidence otherwise applicable. However, nothing in this article precludes a court from using the rules prescribed in this article in valuation proceedings to which the article is not made applicable, where the court determines that the rules prescribed are appropriate. *See Comment* to Section 810.

15 Cal. Law Revision Comm'n Rep. (1980) p. 1460.

Subdivision (b) of Section 811 is amended to include personal property only when valued together with real property. The effect of this amendment is to limit the scope of the evidence of market value provisions to action[s] involving real property or real and personal property combined. *See* Section 810 (article provides rules applicable to action in which "value of property" to be ascertained). Actions involving personal property alone are governed by general law, including the general rules of evidence prescribed in this code, although where appropriate the court may look to the special rules prescribed in this article.

§812. [MARKET VALUE]

This article is not intended to alter or change the existing substantive law, whether statutory or decisional, interpreting the meaning of "market value," whether denominated "fair market value" or otherwise.

History of Evid. C. §812: Added eff. Sept. 17, 1965, oper. Jan. 1, 1967, Stats. 1965, ch. 1151, §4. Amended eff. Jan. 1, 1976, oper. July 1, 1976, Stats. 1975, ch. 1240, §16; eff. Jan. 1, 1979, Stats. 1978, ch. 294, §5.

Official Comment

2 Cal. Law Revision Comm'n Rep. (1975) p. 1902.

Section 812 is amended to conform to the numbering and terminology of the Eminent Domain Law.

14 Cal. Law Revision Comm'n Rep. (1978) p. 255.

Section 812 is amended to take into account the limited application of this article. *See* Section 811 and *Comment* thereto.

ANNOTATIONS

People v. Lynbar, Inc. (2d Dist.1967) 253 Cal.App.2d 870, 881. "[M]arket value is the highest price which the property would bring, if exposed for sale in the open market by a willing seller to a willing buyer with both parties to the transaction being fully informed of all the uses and purposes to which the property is reasonably adaptable and available."

§813. [PROVING VALUE OF PROPERTY]

(a) [Opinion testimony.] The value of property may be shown only by the opinions of any of the following:

(1) Witnesses qualified to express such opinions.

(2) The owner or the spouse of the owner of the property or property interest being valued.

(3) An officer, regular employee, or partner designated by a corporation, partnership, or unincorporated association that is the owner of the property or property interest being valued, if the designee is knowledgeable as to the value of the property or property interest.

(b) [View of property.] Nothing in this section prohibits a view of the property being valued or the admission of any other admissible evidence (including but not limited to evidence as to the nature and condition of the property and, in an eminent domain proceeding, the character of the improvement proposed to be constructed by the plaintiff) for the limited purpose of enabling the court, jury, or referee to understand and weigh the testimony given under subdivision (a); and such evidence, except evidence of the character of the improvement proposed to be constructed by the plaintiff in an eminent domain proceeding, is subject to impeachment and rebuttal.

(c) [Owner.] For the purposes of subdivision (a), "owner of the property or property interest being valued" includes, but is not limited to, the following persons:

(1) A person entitled to possession of the property.

(2) Either party in an action or proceeding to determine the ownership of the property between the parties if the court determines that it would not be in the interest of efficient administration of justice to determine the issue of ownership prior to the admission of the opinion of the party.

History of Evid. C. §813: Added eff. Sept. 17, 1965, oper. Jan. 1, 1967, Stats. 1965, ch. 1151, §4. Amended eff. Jan. 1, 1979, Stats. 1978, ch. 294, §6; eff. Jan. 1, 1981, Stats. 1980, ch. 381, §3.

Official Comment

14 Cal. Law Revision Comm'n Rep. App. IX (1977) p. 120.

Paragraph (3) is added to Section 813(a) to make clear that, where a corporation, partnership, or unincorporated association owns property being valued, a designated officer, regular employee, or partner who is knowledgeable as to the value of the property may testify to an opinion of its value as an owner, notwithstanding any contrary implication[s] in *City of Pleasant Hill v. First Baptist Church*, 1 Cal.App.3d 384, 82 Cal.Rptr. 1 (1969). The designee may be knowledgeable as to the value of the property as a result of being instrumental in its acquisition or management or as a result of being knowledgeable as to its character and use; the designee need not qualify as a general valuation expert. *Compare* Section 720 (qualification as an expert witness). Nothing in Section 813 affects the authority of the court to limit the number of expert witnesses to be called by any party (*see* Section 723) or to limit cumulative evidence (*see* Section 352).

The phrase "value of property," as used in this section, is defined in Section 811.

15 Cal. Law Revision Comm'n Rep. (1980) p. 1460.

Paragraph (2) of Section 813(a) is amended to make clear that either spouse may testify as to the value of community property since both spouses are the owners. In addition, paragraph (2) authorizes either spouse to testify as to the value of the separate property of the other spouse as well as to his or her own separate property. This authority may be useful in cases under Family Law Act where the character of the property is in dispute as well as in other cases requiring valuation where the nonowning spouse may be a more competent valuation witness than the owning spouse.

Subdivision (c) of Section 813 is amended to make clear that a person claiming to be an owner may testify as an owner in litigation over title. Such litigation may arise, for example, between a buyer and seller concerning title to and value of real property under a contract of sale, or between a landlord and tenant concerning characterization and value of property as trade fixtures.

ANNOTATIONS

County Sanitation Dist. v. Watson Land Co. (2d Dist.1993) 17 Cal.App.4th 1268, 1282. "Where an expert in a condemnation action employs a methodology not

sanctioned by California law, his opinion may be excluded. In condemnation proceedings, the trial court is vested with considerable judicial discretion in admitting or rejecting evidence of value. When the testimony of a valuation witness is based on considerations which are proper as well as those which are improper, the court, in its discretion, may strike the testimony or permit it to remain and consider the impropriety in determining the weight to be given it." (Internal quotes omitted.) *See also* ***Escondido Un. Sch. Dist. v. Casa Sueños De Oro, Inc.*** (4th Dist.2005) 129 Cal.App.4th 944, 982 (eminent-domain action).

Contra Costa Water Dist. v. Bar-C Props. (1st Dist.1992) 5 Cal.App.4th 652, 661. "The generally recognized right of an owner to testify is not absolute. In stating an opinion as to the value of property, an owner is bound by the same rules of admissibility as any other witness. To allow a witness's statement of reasons for his opinion to be used as a vehicle for bringing before the jury incompetent evidence would create a disastrous break in the dike which stands against a flood of interminable investigation. The trial court properly prevented the owners from bringing an inadmissible methodology before the jury under the guise of giving their opinion as to value." (Internal quotes omitted.)

§814. [OPINION ON PROPERTY VALUE]

The opinion of a witness as to the value of property is limited to such an opinion as is based on matter perceived by or personally known to the witness or made known to the witness at or before the hearing, whether or not admissible, that is of a type that reasonably may be relied upon by an expert in forming an opinion as to the value of property, including but not limited to the matters listed in Sections 815 to 821, inclusive, unless a witness is precluded by law from using such matter as a basis for an opinion.

History of Evid. C. §814: Added eff. Sept. 17, 1965, oper. Jan. 1, 1967, Stats. 1965, ch. 1151, §4. Amended eff. Jan. 1, 1976, oper. July 1, 1976, Stats. 1975, ch. 1240, §17; eff. Jan. 1, 1981, Stats. 1980, ch. 381, §4.

Official Comment

12 Cal. Law Revision Comm'n Rep. (1975) p. 1902.

Section 814 is amended to delete the listing of particular matters constituting fair market value that an expert may rely on in forming an opinion as to the value of property. This listing is unnecessary. *See* Code Civ. Proc. §1263.320 (fair market value).

It should be noted that the definition of fair market value contained in Section 1263.320(a) omits the phrase "in the open market" since there may be no open market for some types of special purpose properties such as schools, churches, cemeteries, parks, utilities, and similar properties. All properties, special as well as general, are valued at their fair market value. Within the limits of this article, fair market value may be determined by reference to (1) the market data (or comparable sales) approach, (2) the income (or capitalization) method, and (3) the cost analysis (or production less depreciation) formula. *See* the *Comment* to Section 12632.320.

15 Cal. Law Revision Comm'n Rep. (1980) p. 1461.

Section 814 is amended to make technical changes. While the value of property may be determined by a reference to matters listed in Sections 815 to 821 where appropriate, an opinion as to value may also be based on any other matter that satisfies the general requirements of Section 814. *See, e.g.*, *City of Los Angeles v. Retlaw Enterprises, Inc.*, 16 Cal.3d 473, 486 n.8, 546 P.2d 1380, 1388 n.8, 128 Cal.Rptr. 436, 444 n.8 (1976) (price trend data admissible); *People ex rel. Dep't of Transp. v. Southern Pac. Transp. Co.*, 84 Cal.App.3d 315, 325, 148 Cal.Rptr. 535, 541 (1978) (replacement cost of land as opposed to improvements admissible); *South Bay Irr. Dist. v. California-American Water Co.*, 61 Cal.App.3d 944, 980, 133 Cal.Rptr. 166, 191 (1976) (capitalization based on nonrental income admissible); *Redevelopment Agency v. Del-Camp Invs., Inc.*, 38 Cal.App.3d 836, 842, 113 Cal.Rptr. 762, 766-67 (1974) (capitalization based on gross rentals admissible); *People ex rel. Dep't of Pub. Works v. Home Trust Inv. Co.*, 8 Cal.App.3d 1022, 1026, 87 Cal.Rptr. 722, 724 (1970) (noncomparable sales admissible in appropriate circumstances).

ANNOTATIONS

Pacific Gas & Elec. Co. v. Zuckerman (3d Dist.1987) 189 Cal.App.3d 1113, 1135-36. "The value of opinion evidence rests not in the conclusion reached but in the factors considered and the reasoning employed. Where an expert bases his conclusion upon assumptions which are not supported by the record, upon matters which are not reasonably relied upon by other experts, or upon factors which are speculative, remote or conjectural, then his conclusion has no evidentiary value. In those circumstances the expert's opinion cannot rise to the dignity of substantial evidence. When a trial court has accepted an expert's ultimate conclusion without critical consideration of his reasoning, and it appears the conclusion was based upon improper or unwarranted matters, then the judgment must be reversed for lack of substantial evidence."

§814.5. REPEALED

Repealed oper. July 1, 1972, Stats. 1971, ch. 1574, §1.4.

§815. [SALE PRICE]

When relevant to the determination of the value of property, a witness may take into account as a basis for an opinion the price and other terms and circumstances of any sale or contract to sell and purchase which included the property or property interest being valued or any part thereof if the sale or contract was freely made in good faith within a reasonable time before or after the date of valuation, except that in an eminent domain proceeding where the sale or contract to sell and purchase includes only the property or property interest being taken or a part thereof, such sale or contract to sell and purchase may not be taken into account if it occurs after the filing of the lis pendens.

History of Evid. C. §815: Added eff. Sept. 17, 1965, oper. Jan. 1, 1967, Stats. 1965, ch. 1151, §4. Amended eff. Jan. 1, 1979, Stats. 1978, ch. 294, §7.

ANNOTATIONS

City of L.A. v. Retlaw Enters. (1976) 16 Cal.3d 473, 483. "The test for the admissibility of sales of the subject property under [Evid. C.] §815 is substantially identical to that for the admissibility of comparable properties under [Evid. C.] §816: sales are admissible when they illuminate the value of the subject property at the date of valuation. *At 483 n.3:* Sections 815 and 816 sanction the admission of sales of the subject property and comparable properties respectively '[w]hen relevant to the determination of the value of [the subject] property.' In defining comparable sales, §816 indicates that the purportedly comparable property must be sufficiently similar to the subject property that its sales price 'may fairly be considered as shedding light on the value of the property being valued.' Although the phrase 'shedding light' does not appear in §815, the standard of admissibility is the same for both sections. The transcendent requirement is that the evidence be 'relevant' to the determination of the value of the subject property; §816 simply contains a more specific statement of what renders evidence relevant, namely, a capacity to shed light on an issue."

§816. [COMPARABLE SALES]

When relevant to the determination of the value of property, a witness may take into account as a basis for his opinion the price and other terms and circumstances of any sale or contract to sell and purchase comparable property if the sale or contract was freely made in good faith within a reasonable time before or after the date of valuation. In order to be considered comparable, the sale or contract must have been made sufficiently near in time to the date of valuation, and the property sold must be located sufficiently near the property being valued, and must be sufficiently alike in respect to character, size, situation, usability, and improvements, to make it clear that the property sold and the property being valued are comparable in value and that the price realized for the property sold may fairly be considered as shedding light on the value of the property being valued.

History of Evid. C. §816: Added eff. Sept. 17, 1965, oper. Jan. 1, 1967, Stats. 1965, ch. 1151, §4.

ANNOTATIONS

City of L.A. v. Retlaw Enters. (1976) 16 Cal.3d 473, 485 n.8. "The definition of comparability in [Evid. C.] §816 ... serves a very specific purpose. That section seeks to prevent a party from representing that the value of the subject property is equal to the sales price of property with which it has very little in common. Consequently, it instructs the trial court to exclude evidence of a sale when the property sold is not sufficiently comparable to the subject property that their prices will be similar. Thus if a party plans to represent that the sales price approximates the value of the subject property, the court should first determine if it is reasonable that the price will approximate that value. The specific comparability requirement of §816 ... should not govern when the sales price is not introduced on the theory that it approximates the price for which the subject property would have sold. The relevance of evidence must be evaluated by criteria that probe the purpose for which it was introduced. If price trend data are relevant, they can be admitted into evidence without regard to §816. [Evid. C.] §814 permits a witness to base his testimony on relevant evidence, 'including but not limited to the matters listed in [Evid. C.] §§815 to 821.'"

Merced Irrigation Dist. v. Woolstenhulme (1971) 4 Cal.3d 478, 487. "[U]nder ... §816, sales are not necessarily 'non-comparable' simply because they reflect 'substantial' project enhancement, and thus a trial court, in exercising the discretion granted by the statutory provision, may properly admit such sales in evidence. *At 500:* '[N]o general rule can be laid down regarding the degree of similarity that must exist to make such evidence admissible. It must necessarily vary with the circumstances of each particular case. Whether the properties are sufficiently similar to have some bearing on the value under consideration, and to be of any aid to the jury, must necessarily rest largely in the sound discretion of the trial court, which will not be interfered with unless abused.' [¶] Section 816 ... does not establish criteria of 'substantial' or 'insubstantial' comparability, but rather requires the trial court to measure whether or not 'the property sold' is 'sufficiently alike' the property to be valued, by determining whether 'the price realized for the property sold *may be fairly considered as shedding light on the value of the property being valued.*' [¶] We recognize, of course, that in many, perhaps most, cases, a trial judge may find that sales of neighboring property which 'substantially' reflect an enhancement value not properly shared by the condemned property, will not 'shed light'

on the value of the subject property, but rather will tend to confuse the issue if admitted into evidence. In such cases the sales should properly be excluded. We can conceive of a variety of situations, however, in which a trial court may reasonably find that such sales will 'shed light' on the value of condemned land even though the sales reflect 'substantial enhancement.'"

Escondido Un. Sch. Dist. v. Casa Sueños De Oro, Inc. (4th Dist.2005) 129 Cal.App.4th 944, 983. "[I]n considering whether to admit evidence on an allegedly noncomparable sale, the trial court's task is to determine whether the sale price of one property could *shed light* upon the value of the condemned property, notwithstanding any differences that might exist between them. If it resolves that question affirmatively, it can admit the evidence. The jury then, on the basis of all the evidence, determines the extent to which any differences between the condemned property and the comparable property affect their relative values. Evidence of comparable sales is properly received if the judge, in the exercise of a wide discretion, is satisfied that the price paid was sufficiently voluntary to be a reasonable index of value." (Internal quotes omitted.) *See also* ***Redevelopment Agency of San Diego v. Attisha*** (4th Dist.2005) 128 Cal.App.4th 357, 374 (sale must only shed light on value of property being valued).

Emeryville Redev. Agency v. Harcros Pigments, Inc. (1st Dist.2002) 101 Cal.App.4th 1083, 1094. "[B]oth parties sought to establish the fair market value of the subject property through analyses, by expert appraisers, of 'comparable sales.' Under this method, the appraiser identifies sales of properties deemed to resemble the condemned property in relevant respects, and then derives a market value for the condemned property from the prices paid for these 'comparables,' typically adjusting the price to reflect such matters as material differences between the properties and differences in market forces between the time and location of the comparable sale and that of the property being valued."

§817. [LEASE]

(a) [Rent reserved.] Subject to subdivision (b), when relevant to the determination of the value of property, a witness may take into account as a basis for an opinion the rent reserved and other terms and circumstances of any lease which included the property or property interest being valued or any part thereof which was in effect within a reasonable time before or after the date of valuation, except that in an eminent domain proceeding where the lease includes only the property or property interest being taken or a part thereof, such lease may not be taken into account in the determination of the value of property if it is entered into after the filing of the lis pendens.

(b) [Rent fixed.] A witness may take into account a lease providing for a rental fixed by a percentage or other measurable portion of gross sales or gross income from a business conducted on the leased property only for the purpose of arriving at an opinion as to the reasonable net rental value attributable to the property or property interest being valued as provided in Section 819 or determining the value of a leasehold interest.

History of Evid. C. §817: Added eff. Sept. 17, 1965, oper. Jan. 1, 1967, Stats. 1965, ch. 1151, §4. Amended eff. Jan. 1, 1979, Stats. 1978, ch. 294, §8.

Official Comment

14 Cal. Law Revision Comm'n Rep. App. IX (1977) p. 121.

Subdivision (a) of Section 817 is amended to add the limitation that a lease of the subject property is not a proper basis for an opinion of value of the property after the filing of the lis pendens in an eminent domain proceeding. This is comparable to a provision of Section 815 (sale of subject property). Nothing in subdivision (a) should be construed to limit the use of leases created after filing of the lis pendens to show damages to the property, such as those authorized by *Klopping v. City of Whittier*, 8 Cal.3d 39, 500 P.2d 1345, 104 Cal.Rptr. 1 (1972).

Subdivision (b) limits the extent to which a witness may take into account a lease based on gross sales or gross income of a business conducted on the property. This limitation applies only to valuation of the real property or an interest therein, or of tangible personal property, and does not apply to the determination of loss of goodwill. *See* Section 811 and *Comment* thereto; Code Civ. Proc. §1263.510 and *Comment* thereto.

The phrase "value of property," as used in this section, is defined in Section 811.

§818. [COMPARABLE LEASE]

For the purpose of determining the capitalized value of the reasonable net rental value attributable to the property or property interest being valued as provided in Section 819 or determining the value of a leasehold interest, a witness may take into account as a basis for his opinion the rent reserved and other terms and circumstances of any lease of comparable property if the lease was freely made in good faith within a reasonable time before or after the date of valuation.

History of Evid. C. §818: Added eff. Sept. 17, 1965, oper. Jan. 1, 1967, Stats. 1965, ch. 1151, §4.

ANNOTATIONS

City of Ontario v. Kelber (4th Dist.1972) 24 Cal.App.3d 959, 969. "The safeguards defining criteria for *comparability* in [Evid. C.] §816 ... are incorporated in [Evid. C.] §818 ... by the use of the term *comparable*; thus, for a lease property to be considered comparable for purposes of forming an opinion of the fair

rental value of a subject property, it must meet the criteria specifically set forth in §816.... *At 970:* In applying §§816 and 818 ..., the trial court must, in the first instance, make its own determination as to comparability of an offered sale or lease; it must determine from the foundational testimony offered, whether the statutory criteria are satisfied; this must be an independent determination by the trial court and not merely an acquiescence in the conclusions of the witness as to comparability and, accordingly, the reasons given by the experts are persuasive only to the extent that they are based on sound premises. But, manifestly, the trial judge, in applying so vague a standard (criteria for comparability), must be granted a wide discretion. If the properties are sufficiently similar to have 'some bearing' on the value under consideration, or to 'shed light' on the proper value, the trial judge's discretion will not be interfered with on appeal. Only where it is clear that the court has abused this discretion by not adequately heeding the safeguards for determining comparability will the appellate court reverse."

§819. [NET RENTAL VALUE]

When relevant to the determination of the value of property, a witness may take into account as a basis for his opinion the capitalized value of the reasonable net rental value attributable to the land and existing improvements thereon (as distinguished from the capitalized value of the income or profits attributable to the business conducted thereon).

History of Evid. C. §819: Added eff. Sept. 17, 1965, oper. Jan. 1, 1967, Stats. 1965, ch. 1151, §4.

ANNOTATIONS

San Diego Gas & Elec. Co. v. Schmidt (4th Dist.2014) 228 Cal.App.4th 1280, 1299-1300. "We reject [P's] assertion that the discounted cashflow method violated ... §819.... [P] appears to focus on the language [in §819] regarding 'existing improvements' to argue the statute does not apply here because there were no existing improvements. This argument ignores that ... §819 allows 'the capitalized value of the reasonable net rental value attributable to the land.' [¶] [P's] reliance on [***San Diego Metro. Transit Dev. Bd. v. Cushman*** (4th Dist.1997) 53 Cal.App.4th 918] to support its position is misplaced. In ***Cushman***, the condemned property contained a retail building. The property owner's appraiser testified that the highest and best use of the property would be to expand the existing building. The appraiser then presented evidence on fair market value of the property based on capitalization of income derived from 'a nonexisting improvement.' The appellate court concluded that the evidence was improperly admitted because ... §819 did not sanction capitalization of the reasonable rental value attributable to planned or future improvements not in existence as of the date of value. We have no quarrel with the result in ***Cushman*** as we agree it is improper to capitalize income for a nonexisting improvement. Here, [expert] did not capitalize income for a nonexisting improvement; rather, he capitalized rental income attributable to the land itself—which ... §819 expressly allows." *See also* ***San Diego Metro. Transit Dev. Bd. v. Cushman*** (4th Dist.1997) 53 Cal.App.4th 918, 930 & n.5.

Millikan v. American Spectrum Real Estate Servs. Cal., Inc. (4th Dist.2004) 117 Cal.App.4th 1094, 1102. "If the property is sold, other means are available by which the tenant may prove avoidable rental loss. Most commonly, if one assumes the income producing property is sold at its fair market value, the sale price is 'the capitalized value of the reasonable net rental value attributable to the land and existing improvements.' The appropriate market capitalization rate could be established by reviewing sales of *comparable* leased premises. With an assumed capitalization rate based on the sales of comparable properties, and the known sale price for the subject building, the equivalent rental stream may be determined and compared with the rental loss resulting from the tenant's abandonment. By this means, the tenant may establish whether the landlord has recovered his lost rental, in whole or in part, by a favorable sale. While this evidence would necessarily require expert opinion testimony, it is the type of evidence often offered in other contexts where property valuations are in issue. And, of course, the tenant is also free to prove that a greater rental loss could have been avoided by retaining the building rather than selling it, or that the sale price was unreasonably low."

§820. [REPLACING IMPROVEMENTS]

When relevant to the determination of the value of property, a witness may take into account as a basis for his opinion the value of the property or property interest being valued as indicated by the value of the land together with the cost of replacing or reproducing the existing improvements thereon, if the improvements enhance the value of the property or property interest for its highest and best use, less whatever depreciation or obsolescence the improvements have suffered.

History of Evid. C. §820: Added eff. Sept. 17, 1965, oper. Jan. 1, 1967, Stats. 1965, ch. 1151, §4.

§821. [IMPROVEMENTS ON SURROUNDING PROPERTY]

When relevant to the determination of the value of property, a witness may take into account as a basis for his opinion the nature of the improvements on properties in the general vicinity of the property or property interest being valued and the character of the existing uses being made of such properties.

History of Evid. C. §821: Added eff. Sept. 17, 1965, oper. Jan. 1, 1967, Stats. 1965, ch. 1151, §4.

§822. [INADMISSIBLE EVIDENCE IN EMINENT-DOMAIN PROCEEDING]

(a) [Inadmissible evidence.] In an eminent domain or inverse condemnation proceeding, notwithstanding the provisions of Sections 814 to 821, inclusive, the following matter is inadmissible as evidence and shall not be taken into account as a basis for an opinion as to the value of property:

(1) The price or other terms and circumstances of an acquisition of property or a property interest if the acquisition was for a public use for which the property could have been taken by eminent domain. The price or other terms and circumstances shall not be excluded pursuant to this paragraph if the proceeding relates to the valuation of all or part of a water system as defined in Section 240 of the Public Utilities Code.

(2) The price at which an offer or option to purchase or lease the property or property interest being valued or any other property was made, or the price at which the property or interest was optioned, offered, or listed for sale or lease, except that an option, offer, or listing may be introduced by a party as an admission of another party to the proceeding; but nothing in this subdivision permits an admission to be used as direct evidence upon any matter that may be shown only by opinion evidence under Section 813.

(3) The value of any property or property interest as assessed for taxation purposes or the amount of taxes which may be due on the property, but nothing in this subdivision prohibits the consideration of actual or estimated taxes for the purpose of determining the reasonable net rental value attributable to the property or property interest being valued.

(4) An opinion as to the value of any property or property interest other than that being valued.

(5) The influence upon the value of the property or property interest being valued of any noncompensable items of value, damage, or injury.

(6) The capitalized value of the income or rental from any property or property interest other than that being valued.

(b) [Other proceedings.] In an action other than an eminent domain or inverse condemnation proceeding, the matters listed in subdivision (a) are not admissible as evidence, and may not be taken into account as a basis for an opinion as to the value of property, except to the extent permitted under the rules of law otherwise applicable.

History of Evid. C. §822: Added eff. Sept. 17, 1965, oper. Jan. 1, 1967, Stats. 1965, ch. 1151, §4. Amended eff. Jan. 1, 1979, Stats. 1978, ch. 294, §9; eff. Jan. 1, 1981, Stats. 1980, ch. 381, §5; eff. Jan. 1, 1987, Stats. 1986, ch. 1238, §2; eff. Jan. 1, 1988, Stats. 1987, ch. 1278, §1; eff. Jan. 1, 2001, Stats. 2000, ch. 948, §1.

Official Comment

14 Cal. Law Revision Comm'n Rep. App. IX (1977) p. 122.

Subdivision (c) of Section 822 is amended to incorporate a provision formerly found in Revenue and Taxation Code Section 4986(b). Unlike the former provision, subdivision (c) does not provide for a mistrial for mention of the amount of taxes which may be due. Whether such mention is grounds for a mistrial is governed by the general principles of court discretion to declare a mistrial when evidence has been presented which is inadmissible, highly prejudicial, and cannot be corrected by an admonition to the jury.

Subdivision (d) does not prohibit a witness from testifying to adjustments made in sales of comparable property used as a basis for an opinion. *Merced Irrigation Dist. v. Woolstenhulme*, 4 Cal.3d 478, 501-03, 483 P.2d 1, 16-17, 93 Cal.Rptr. 833, 848-49 (1971).

Section 822 does not prohibit cross-examination of a witness on any matter precluded from admission as evidence if such cross-examination is for the limited purpose of determining whether a witness based an opinion in whole or in part on matter that is not a proper basis for an opinion; such cross-examination may not, however, serve as a means of placing improper matters before the trier of fact. *See* Evid. Code §§721, 802, 803.

The phrase "value of property," as used in this section, is defined in Section 811.

15 Cal. Law Revision Comm'n Rep. (1980) p. 1461.

Section 822 is amended to limit the application of subdivision (a) to eminent domain and inverse condemnation cases despite the general expansion of this article to cover real property valuation cases generally. *See* Sections 810 and 811 and *Comments* thereto. The introductory portion of subdivision (a) is also amended to make clear that subdivision (a) regulates only the bases for an opinion of value admissible in evidence; it does not purport to prescribe rules or regulations governing the practice of the appraisal profession outside of expert testimony in a case.

Subdivision (b) is added to make clear that the exclusion of the matters listed in subdivision (a) in eminent domain and inverse condemnation cases does not imply that those matters are admissible in other cases. The rules governing admissibility in other cases of matters listed in subdivision (a) are found in Section 814 and in the general Evidence Code rules relating to relevance, prejudice, and the like.

2000-01 Ann. Report, 30 Cal. Law Revision Comm'n Rep. (2000) App. 6.

Subdivision (a)(1) of Section 822 is amended to delete the special exception relating to property appropriated to public use, in reliance on general evidentiary principles. *See, e.g.*, Section 823 ("Notwithstanding any other provision of this article, the value of property for which there is no relevant, comparable market may be determined by any method of valuation that is just and equitable."); *see also* Code Civ. Proc. §1263.320(b) (fair market value). Thus, evidence of an acquisition that is otherwise inadmissible under subdivision (a)(1) may, in an appropriate case, be admissible under Section 823 if a private

market is lacking, *e.g.*, the acquisition involves a special purpose property such as a school, church, cemetery, park, utility corridor, or similar property.

The new exception added to subdivision (a)(1) is intended to apply in an eminent domain or inverse condemnation proceeding that relates to a public agency's acquisition or taking of all or any part of a water system owned by a water company.

Subdivision (c) is deleted as obsolete.

ANNOTATIONS

City of Corona v. Liston Brick Co. (4th Dist.2012) 208 Cal.App.4th 536, 539. "[D] contends that, even assuming its evidence was otherwise inadmissible under ... §822, subdivision (a), it should have been allowed to use it in its cross-examination of [P's] valuation expert. It relies on [***State v. Stevenson*** (3d Dist.1970) 5 Cal.App.3d 60]. We conclude, however, that ***Stevenson*** does not create a 'cross-examination exception' to ... §822, subdivision (a). At most, it merely allows a party to an eminent domain proceeding to impeach an expert with a prior inconsistent valuation *by that expert*."

Escondido Un. Sch. Dist. v. Casa Sueños De Oro, Inc. (4th Dist.2005) 129 Cal.App.4th 944, 983. "[T]he fact that the comparable sales data was not verified does not render the evidence inadmissible as opinion evidence of another property under ... §822, subdivision (a)(4)."

Hurwitz v. City of Orange (4th Dist.2004) 122 Cal.App.4th 835, 856. Section 822, subdivision (a)(6) "is a protection for property owners, not condemning entities. ... 'The purpose of ... §822 is to prevent introduction into evidence of *particular acquisitions of similar properties by the condemnor itself*. The parties are to focus instead on the market value of the property at the time of condemnation.' [¶] [D's] argument, taken to its logical conclusion, is that the income method of valuation, which by its nature requires *some* capitalization rate, can never be used in condemnation proceedings, a point that quickly devolves to absurdity. [¶] As long as an expert does not rely on particular and identifiable acquisition, the statute is not offended. Any other result transforms the statute into an a priori bar to the use of the net income method, which was not intended by the Legislature." *See also* ***People v. Andresen*** (5th Dist.1987) 193 Cal.App.3d 1144, 1165.

Emeryville Redev. Agency v. Harcros Pigments, Inc. (1st Dist.2002) 101 Cal.App.4th 1083, 1095-96. "Whatever [Evid. C.] §822(a)(1) means, it does not confer a discretionary power on the trial court. It categorically excludes evidence of a specified character, subject to a stated exception [in Evid. C. §823]. [¶] We also reject any suggestion that [§822] was intended only, or primarily, for the protection of property owners, and thus should have little or no effect where ... the *condemnee* offers evidence of other acquisitions for a public use. [I]t is not competent for *either* party in a condemnation proceeding to put in evidence the amount paid by a condemning party to the owners of adjacent lands, however similar they may be to that in controversy, because the price paid under such circumstances is not a reasonable or fair test of market value. *At 1099-1100:* In adopting the 2000 amendment the Legislature confirmed that the statute does not authorize the admission of evidence of acquisitions of property privately held for private use. [¶] [S]ection 822(a)(1) has always barred evidence of acquisitions for public use of purely private property." (Internal quotes omitted.)

Ventura Cty. Flood Control Dist. v. Campbell (2d Dist.1999) 71 Cal.App.4th 211, 222. "[S]ection 822 only precludes evidence of the price paid by condemnors for acquisitions of other land for public use because 'the price paid under the circumstances of such a sale is not a reasonable or fair test of market value.' We reject [P's] contention that the open bids to remove the aggregate were inadmissible per se as reflecting enhanced value simply because removal occurred to create the flood control project. The price paid for the aggregate more likely reflects its value as building material on the open market at the time of the bids. That value has nothing to do with the fact [P] needed to create a flood control basin."

§823. [NO COMPARABLE MARKET]

Notwithstanding any other provision of this article, the value of property for which there is no relevant, comparable market may be determined by any method of valuation that is just and equitable.

History of Evid. C. §823: Added eff. Jan. 1, 1981, Stats. 1980, ch. 381, §6. Amended eff. Jan. 1, 1993, Stats. 1992, ch. 7, §4.

Official Comment

15 Cal. Law Revision Comm'n Rep. (1980) p. 1461.

Section 823 is drawn from Code of Civil Procedure Section 1263.320(b) (fair market value in eminent domain proceeding of property for which there is no relevant market). Section 823 is included because there may be no relevant market for some types of special purpose properties such as schools, churches, cemeteries, parks, utilities, and similar properties. *See* Code Civ. Proc. §1263.320(b) and *Comment* thereto.

ANNOTATIONS

County of San Diego v. Rancho Vista Del Mar, Inc. (4th Dist.1993) 16 Cal.App.4th 1046, 1062. "Cases where the property owner was allowed to show the highest and best use of property was the same use as the condemnor's proposed use must be distinguished from those cases where the government provides the only market or demand for the proposed use. *At 1063-64:* [T]he 'market' for determining 'fair market value' and just compensation is the private marketplace, i.e., what willing, knowledgeable nongovernmental buyers and sellers would pay for property to be used for a non-governmental purpose. ... To value property based on a market where the government is the only potential buyer is to engage in improperly valuing the property based on its value to the condemnor rather than based on the loss suffered by the property owner. It is the loss suffered by the property owner which provides the guide for just compensation, a loss measured by the private marketplace; the loss may not be measured by the benefit to the condemnor."

§824. [VALUE OF NONPROFIT, SPECIAL-USE PROPERTY]

(a) [No relevant, comparable market.] Notwithstanding any other provision of this article, a just and equitable method of determining the value of nonprofit, special use property, as defined by Section 1235.155 of the Code of Civil Procedure, for which there is no relevant, comparable market, is the cost of purchasing land and the reasonable cost of making it suitable for the conduct of the same nonprofit, special use, together with the cost of constructing similar improvements. The method for determining compensation for improvements shall be as set forth in subdivision (b).

(b) [Reproducing improvements.] Notwithstanding any other provision of this article, a witness providing opinion testimony on the value of nonprofit, special use property, as defined by Section 1235.155 of the Code of Civil Procedure, for which there is no relevant, comparable market, shall base his or her opinion on the value of reproducing the improvements without taking into consideration any depreciation or obsolescence of the improvements.

(c) [Public-entity acquisitions.] This section does not apply to actions or proceedings commenced by a public entity or public utility to acquire real property or any interest in real property for the use of water, sewer, electricity, telephone, natural gas, or flood control facilities or rights-of-way where those acquisitions neither require removal or destruction of existing improvements, nor render the property unfit for the owner's present or proposed use.

History of Evid. C. §824: Added eff. Jan. 1, 1993, Stats. 1992, ch. 7, §5.

ARTICLE 3. OPINION TESTIMONY ON PARTICULAR SUBJECTS

§870. [OPINION EVIDENCE ON SANITY]

A witness may state his opinion as to the sanity of a person when:

(a) [Intimate acquaintance.] The witness is an intimate acquaintance of the person whose sanity is in question;

(b) [Subscribing witness.] The witness was a subscribing witness to a writing, the validity of which is in dispute, signed by the person whose sanity is in question and the opinion relates to the sanity of such person at the time the writing was signed; or

(c) [Lay or expert witness.] The witness is qualified under Section 800 or 801 to testify in the form of an opinion.

History of Evid. C. §870: Added eff. Sept. 17, 1965, oper. Jan. 1, 1967, Stats. 1965, ch. 299, §2.

Official Comment

7 Cal. Law Revision Comm'n Rep. (1965) p. 1146.

Subdivisions (a) and (b) restate the substance of and supersede subdivision 10 of Section 1870 of the Code of Civil Procedure. Subdivision (c) merely makes it clear that a witness who meets the requirements of Section 800 or Section 801 is qualified to testify in the form of an opinion as to the sanity of a person. Section 870 does not disturb the present rule that permits a witness to testify to a person's rational or irrational appearance or conduct, even though the witness is not qualified under Section 870 to express an opinion on the person's sanity. *See Pfingst v. Goetting*, 96 Cal.App.2d 293, 215 P.2d 93 (1950).

§§890 TO 895. REPEALED

Repealed oper. Jan. 1, 1994, Stats. 1992, ch. 162, §9.

§895.5. REPEALED

Repealed oper. Jan. 1, 1994, Stats. 1993, ch. 219, §77.

§§896, 897. REPEALED

Repealed oper. Jan. 1, 1994, Stats. 1992, ch. 162, §9.

DIVISION 8. PRIVILEGES

CHAPTER 1. DEFINITIONS

§900. [SCOPE]

Unless the provision or context otherwise requires, the definitions in this chapter govern the construction of this division. They do not govern the construction of any other division.

History of Evid. C. §900: Added eff. Sept. 17, 1965, oper. Jan. 1, 1967, Stats. 1965, ch. 299, §2.

Official Comment

7 Cal. Law Revision Comm'n Rep. (1965) p. 1150.

Section 900 makes it clear that the definitions in Sections 901 through 905 apply only to Division 8 (Privileges) and that these definitions are not applicable where the context or language of a particular section in Division 8 requires that a word or phrase used in that section be given a different meaning. The definitions contained in Division 2 (commencing with Section 100) apply to the entire code, including Division 8. Definitions applicable only to a particular article are found in that article.

§901. [PROCEEDING]

"Proceeding" means any action, hearing, investigation, inquest, or inquiry (whether conducted by a court, administrative agency, hearing officer, arbitrator, legislative body, or any other person authorized by law) in which, pursuant to law, testimony can be compelled to be given.

History of Evid. C. §901: Added eff. Sept. 17, 1965, oper. Jan. 1, 1967, Stats. 1965, ch. 299, §2.

Official Comment

7 Cal. Law Revision Comm'n Rep. (1965) p. 1150.

"Proceeding" is defined to mean all proceedings of whatever kind in which testimony can be compelled by law to be given. It includes civil and criminal actions and proceedings, administrative proceedings, legislative hearings, grand jury proceedings, coroners' inquests, arbitration proceedings, and any other kind of proceeding in which a person can be compelled by law to appear and give evidence. This broad definition is necessary in order that Division 8 may be made applicable to all situations where a person can be compelled to testify. The reasons for giving this broad scope to Division 8 are stated in the *Comment* to Section 910.

§902. [CIVIL PROCEEDING]

"Civil proceeding" means any proceeding except a criminal proceeding.

History of Evid. C. §902: Added eff. Sept. 17, 1965, oper. Jan. 1, 1967, Stats. 1965, ch. 299, §2.

Official Comment

7 Cal. Law Revision Comm'n Rep. (1965) p. 1150.

"Civil proceeding" includes not only a civil action or proceeding, but also any nonjudicial proceeding in which, pursuant to law, testimony can be compelled to be given. *See* Evidence Code §§901 and 903.

§903. [CRIMINAL PROCEEDING]

"Criminal proceeding" means:

(a) A criminal action; and

(b) A proceeding pursuant to Article 3 (commencing with Section 3060) of Chapter 7 of Division 4 of Title 1 of the Government Code to determine whether a public officer should be removed from office for willful or corrupt misconduct in office.

History of Evid. C. §903: Added eff. Sept. 17, 1965, oper. Jan. 1, 1967, Stats. 1965, ch. 299, §2.

Official Comment

7 Cal. Law Revision Comm'n Rep. (1965) p. 1151.

This division treats a proceeding by accusation for the removal of a public officer under Government Code Sections 3060-3073 the same as a criminal action. Proceedings by accusation and criminal actions are so nearly alike in their basic nature that, so far as privileges are concerned, this similar treatment is justified.

§904. [BLANK]

§905. [PRESIDING OFFICER]

"Presiding officer" means the person authorized to rule on a claim of privilege in the proceeding in which the claim is made.

History of Evid. C. §905: Added eff. Sept. 17, 1965, oper. Jan. 1, 1967, Stats. 1965, ch. 299, §2.

Official Comment

7 Cal. Law Revision Comm'n Rep. (1965) p. 1151.

"Presiding officer" is defined so that reference may be made in Division 8 to the person who makes rulings on questions of privilege in nonjudicial proceedings. The term includes arbitrators, hearing officers, referees, and any other person who is authorized to make rulings on claims of privilege. It, of course, includes the judge or other person presiding in a judicial proceeding.

CHAPTER 2. APPLICABILITY OF DIVISION

§910. [APPLICABILITY OF DIVISION]

Except as otherwise provided by statute, the provisions of this division apply in all proceedings. The provisions of any statute making rules of evidence inapplicable in particular proceedings, or limiting the applicability of rules of evidence in particular proceedings, do not make this division inapplicable to such proceedings.

History of Evid. C. §910: Added eff. Sept. 17, 1965, oper. Jan. 1, 1967, Stats. 1965, ch. 299, §2.

Official Comment

7 Cal. Law Revision Comm'n Rep. (1965) p. 1151;
Senate J, Apr. 21, 1965.

Most rules of evidence are designed for use in courts. Generally, their purpose is to keep unreliable or prejudicial evidence from being presented to the trier of fact. Privileges are granted, however, for reasons of policy unrelated to the reliability of the information involved. A privilege is granted because it is considered more important to keep certain information confidential than it is to require disclosure of all the information relevant to the issues in a pending proceeding. Thus, for example, to protect the attorney-client relationship, it is necessary to prevent disclosure of confidential communications made in the course of that relationship.

If confidentiality is to be protected effectively by a privilege, the privilege must be recognized in proceedings other than judicial proceedings. The protection afforded by a privilege would be insufficient if a court were the only place where the privilege could be invoked. Every officer with power to issue subpoenas for investigative purposes, every administrative agency, every local governing board, and many more persons could pry into the protected information if the privilege rules were applicable only in judicial proceedings.

Therefore, the policy underlying the privilege rules requires their recognition in all proceedings of any nature in which testimony can be compelled by law to be given. Section 910 makes the privilege rules applicable to all such proceedings. In this respect, it follows the precedent set in New Jersey when privilege rules, based in part on the Uniform Rules of Evidence, were enacted. *See* N.J. Laws 1960, ch. 52, p. 452 (N.J. Rev. Stat. §§2A:84A-1 to 2A:84A-49).

Statutes that relax the rules of evidence in particular proceedings do not have the effect of making privileges inapplicable in such proceedings. For example, Labor Code Section 5708, which provides that the officer conducting an Industrial Accident Commission proceeding "shall not be bound by the common law or statutory rules of evidence," does not make privileges inapplicable in such proceedings. Thus, the lawyer-client privilege must be recognized in an Industrial Accident Commission proceeding. On the other hand, Division 8 and other statutes provide exceptions to particular privileges for particular types of proceedings. *E.g.*, Evidence Code §998 (physician-patient privilege inapplicable

in criminal proceeding); Labor Code §§4055, 6407, 6408 (testimony by physician and certain reports of physicians admissible as evidence in Industrial Accident Commission proceedings).

Whether Section 910 is declarative of existing law is uncertain. No California case has squarely decided whether the privileges which are recognized in judicial proceedings are also applicable in nonjudicial proceedings. By statute, however, they have been made applicable in all adjudicatory proceedings conducted under the terms of the Administrative Procedure Act. Govt. Code §11513. The reported decisions indicate that, as a general rule, privileges are assumed to be applicable in nonjudicial proceedings. *See, e.g., McKnew v. Superior Court*, 23 Cal.2d 58, 142 P.2d 1 (1943); *Ex parte McDonough*, 170 Cal. 230, 149 Pac. 566 (1915); *Board of Educ. v. Wilkinson*, 125 Cal.App.2d 100, 270 P.2d 82 (1954); *In re Bruns*, 15 Cal.App.2d 1, 58 P.2d 1318 (1936). Thus, Section 910 appears to be declarative of existing practice, but there is no authority as to whether it is declarative of existing law. Its enactment will remove the existing uncertainty concerning the right to claim a privilege in a nonjudicial proceeding. *See generally Tentative Recommendation and a Study Relating to the Uniform Rules of Evidence (Article V. Privileges)*, 6 Cal. Law Revision Comm'n, Rep., Rec. & Studies 201, 309-327 (1964).

CHAPTER 3. GENERAL PROVISIONS RELATING TO PRIVILEGES

§911. [AUTHORIZED BY STATUTE]

Except as otherwise provided by statute:

(a) [Refusal to be witness.] No person has a privilege to refuse to be a witness.

(b) [Refusal to disclose or produce.] No person has a privilege to refuse to disclose any matter or to refuse to produce any writing, object, or other thing.

(c) [Directing others.] No person has a privilege that another shall not be a witness or shall not disclose any matter or shall not produce any writing, object, or other thing.

History of Evid. C. §911: Added eff. Sept. 17, 1965, oper. Jan. 1, 1967, Stats. 1965, ch. 299, §2.

Official Comment

7 Cal. Law Revision Comm'n Rep. (1965) p. 1153.

This section codifies the existing law that privileges are not recognized in the absence of statute. *See Chronicle Pub. Co. v. Superior Court*, 54 Cal.2d 548, 565, 7 Cal.Rptr. 109, 117, 354 P.2d 637, 645 (1960); *Tatkin v. Superior Court*, 160 Cal.App.2d 745, 753, 326 P.2d 201, 205-206 (1958); *Whitlow v. Superior Court*, 87 Cal.App.2d 175, 196 P.2d 590 (1948). *See also* 8 Wigmore, *Evidence* §2286 (McNaughton rev. 1961); Witkin, *California Evidence* §396 at 446 (1958). This is one of the few instances where the Evidence Code precludes the courts from elaborating upon the statutory scheme. Even with respect to privileges, however, the courts to a limited extent are permitted to develop the details of declared principles. *See, e.g.*, Section 1060 (trade secret).

ANNOTATIONS

Roberts v. City of Palmdale (1993) 5 Cal.4th 363, 373. In §911, "the Legislature has determined that evidentiary privileges shall be available only as defined by statute. Courts may not add to the statutory privileges except as required by state or federal constitutional law ..., nor may courts imply unwritten exceptions to existing statutory privileges." *See also* ***Welfare Rights Org. v. Crisan*** (1983) 33 Cal.3d 766, 769; ***Valley Bank v. Superior Ct.*** (1975) 15 Cal.3d 652, 656-57; ***Ombudsman Servs. v. Superior Ct.*** (3d Dist.2007) 154 Cal.App.4th 1233, 1243.

§912. [WAIVER OF PRIVILEGE]

(a) [Disclosure.] Except as otherwise provided in this section, the right of any person to claim a privilege provided by Section 954 (lawyer-client privilege), 966 (lawyer referral service-client privilege), 980 (privilege for confidential marital communications), 994 (physician-patient privilege), 1014 (psychotherapist-patient privilege), 1033 (privilege of penitent), 1034 (privilege of clergy member), 1035.8 (sexual assault counselor-victim privilege), [~~or~~] 1037.5 (domestic violence counselor-victim privilege), or 1038 (human trafficking caseworker-victim privilege) is waived with respect to a communication protected by the privilege if any holder of the privilege, without coercion, has disclosed a significant part of the communication or has consented to disclosure made by anyone. Consent to disclosure is manifested by any statement or other conduct of the holder of the privilege indicating consent to the disclosure, including failure to claim the privilege in any proceeding in which the holder has [~~the~~] legal standing and the opportunity to claim the privilege.

(b) [Joint holders.] Where two or more persons are joint holders of a privilege provided by Section 954 (lawyer-client privilege), 966 (lawyer referral service-client privilege), 994 (physician-patient privilege), 1014 (psychotherapist-patient privilege), 1035.8 (sexual assault counselor-victim privilege), [~~or~~] 1037.5 (domestic violence counselor-victim privilege), or 1038 (human trafficking caseworker-victim privilege), a waiver of the right of a particular joint holder of the privilege to claim the privilege does not affect the right of another joint holder to claim the privilege. In the case of the privilege provided by Section 980 (privilege for confidential marital communications), a waiver of the right of one spouse to claim the privilege does not affect the right of the other spouse to claim the privilege.

(c) [Privileged disclosure.] A disclosure that is itself privileged is not a waiver of any privilege.

(d) [Disclosure in confidence.] A disclosure in confidence of a communication that is protected by a privilege provided by Section 954 (lawyer-client privilege), 966 (lawyer referral service-client privilege), 994 (physician-patient privilege), 1014 (psychotherapist-patient privilege), 1035.8 (sexual assault counselor-

victim privilege), [~~or~~] 1037.5 (domestic violence counselor-victim privilege), or 1038 (human trafficking caseworker-victim privilege), when disclosure is reasonably necessary for the accomplishment of the purpose for which the lawyer, lawyer referral service, physician, psychotherapist, sexual assault counselor, [~~or~~] domestic violence counselor, or human trafficking caseworker was consulted, is not a waiver of the privilege.

History of Evid. C. §912: Added eff. Sept. 17, 1965, oper. Jan. 1, 1967, Stats. 1965, ch. 299, §2. Amended eff. Jan. 1, 1981, Stats. 1980, ch. 917, §1; eff. Jan. 1, 2003, Stats. 2002, ch. 72, §1; eff. Jan. 1, 2005, Stats. 2004, ch. 405, §1; eff. Jan. 1, 2014, Stats. 2013, ch. 123, §1; eff. Jan. 1, 2015, Stats. 2014, ch. 913, §13.

Official Comment

7 Cal. Law Revision Comm'n Rep. (1965) p. 1153; Senate J, Apr. 21, 1965.

This section covers in some detail the matter of waiver of those privileges that protect confidential communications.

Subdivision (a). Subdivision (a) states the general rule with respect to the manner in which a privilege is waived. Failure to claim the privilege where the holder of the privilege has the legal standing and the opportunity to claim the privilege constitutes a waiver. This seems to be the existing law. *See City & County of San Francisco v. Superior Court*, 37 Cal.2d 227, 233, 231 P.2d 26, 29 (1951); *Lissak v. Crocker Estate Co.*, 119 Cal. 442, 51 Pac. 688 (1897). There is, however, at least one case that is out of harmony with this rule. *People v. Kor*, 129 Cal.App.2d 436, 277 P.2d 94 (1954) (defendant's failure to claim privilege to prevent a witness from testifying to a communication between the defendant and his attorney held not to waive the privilege to prevent the attorney from similarly testifying).

Subdivision (b). A waiver of the privilege by a joint holder of the privilege does not operate to waive the privilege for any of the other joint holders of the privilege. This codifies existing law. *See People v. Kor*, 129 Cal.App.2d 436, 277 P.2d 94 (1954); *People v. Abair*, 102 Cal.App.2d 765, 228 P.2d 336 (1951).

Subdivision (c). A privilege is not waived when a revelation of the privileged matter takes place in another privileged communication. Thus, for example, a person does not waive his lawyer-client privilege by telling his wife in confidence what it was that he told his attorney. Nor does a person waive the marital communication privilege by telling his attorney in confidence in the course of the attorney-client relationship what it was that he told his wife. And a person does not waive the lawyer-client privilege as to a communication by relating it to another attorney in the course of a separate relationship. A privileged communication should not cease to be privileged merely because it has been related in the course of another privileged communication. The theory underlying the concept of waiver is that the holder of the privilege has abandoned the secrecy to which he is entitled under the privilege. Where the revelation of the privileged matter takes place in another privileged communication, there has not been such an abandonment. Of course, this rule does not apply unless the revelation was within the scope of the relationship in which it was made; a client consulting his lawyer on a contract matter who blurts out that he told his doctor that he had a venereal disease has waived the privilege, even though he intended the revelation to be confidential, because the revelation was not necessary to the contract business at hand.

Subdivision (d). Subdivision (d) is designed to maintain the confidentiality of communications in certain situations where the communications are disclosed to others in the course of accomplishing the purpose for which the lawyer, physician, or psychotherapist was consulted. For example, where a confidential communication from a client is related by his attorney to a physician, appraiser, or other expert in order to obtain that person's assistance so that the attorney will better be able to advise his client, the disclosure is not a waiver of the privilege, even though the disclosure is made with the client's knowledge and consent. Nor would a physician's or psychotherapist's keeping of confidential records necessary to diagnose or treat a patient, such as confidential hospital records, be a waiver of the privilege, even though other authorized persons have access to the records. Similarly, the patient's presentation of a physician's prescription to a registered pharmacist would not constitute a waiver of the physician-patient privilege because such disclosure is reasonably necessary for the accomplishment of the purpose for which the physician is consulted. *See also* Evidence Code §992. Communications such as these, when made in confidence, should not operate to destroy the privilege even when they are made with the consent of the client or patient. Here, again, the privilege holder has not evidenced any abandonment of secrecy. Hence, he should be entitled to maintain the confidential nature of his communications to his attorney or physician despite the necessary further disclosure.

Subdivision (d) may change California law. *Green v. Superior Court*, 220 Cal.App.2d 121, 33 Cal.Rptr. 604 (1963) (hearing denied), held that the physician-patient privilege did not provide protection against disclosure by a pharmacist of information concerning the nature of drugs dispensed upon prescription. *See also Himmelfarb v. United States*, 175 F.2d 924 (9th Cir. 1949) (applying the California law of privileges and holding that a lawyer's revelation to an accountant of a client's communication to the lawyer waived the client's privilege if such revelation was authorized by the client).

31 Cal. Law Revision Comm'n Rep. (2001) p. 256.

Section 912 is amended to make clear that it applies to the privilege for confidential communications between a domestic violence victim and counselor, which did not exist when the statute was originally enacted in 1965. *See* Sections 1037-1037.7 (domestic violence victim).

ANNOTATIONS

Subdivision (a)

Calvert v. State Bar (1991) 54 Cal.3d 765, 780. Section 912, subdivision (a) "provides that a privilege is waived when a holder of a privilege fails to claim the privilege in a proceeding in which he or she has the standing and opportunity to do so. In this case, those conditions were met and the privilege must be held waived. [P] was a holder of the privilege; as a witness who was present at [D's disciplinary] hearing she had standing and opportunity to claim it; she consulted with her attorney when the issue was raised by [D]; and she evidently failed to instruct [attorney] to claim the privilege. [Attorney], as [P's] attorney, stated she was 'not sure' whether her testimony created a conflict or would jeopardize [P's] case. This equivocal statement by [P's] attorney after consultation with [P] amounts to a failure to claim the privilege when the opportunity arose. *At 780 n.5:* We note that during [D's] testimony and prior to [attorney's, P] orally waived the attorney-client privilege as to [D] only. But nothing in … §912 indicates that an assertion of a privilege at one time precludes its waiver by conduct at a later time. *At 780:* Moreover, at the next hearing session, the State Bar's attorney testified in detail as to confidential communications between [attorney] and [P] that were revealed to the State Bar; and at a later hearing date, [P] testified in detail about her confidential communications with [attorney]. These subsequent events in the same proceeding fortify our conclusion that the attorney-client privilege was waived." *See also* ***Kerner v. Superior Ct.*** (2d Dist.2012) 206 Cal.App.4th 84, 112-14.

Mitchell v. Superior Ct. (1984) 37 Cal.3d 591, 602. "Relevant case law makes it clear that mere disclosure of the fact that a communication between client and attorney had occurred does *not* amount to disclosure of the specific content of that communication, and as such does not necessarily constitute a waiver of the privilege. [¶] [P's] answers, while revealing the existence of her attorney-client relationship, *at most* affirmed that she had discussed certain warnings with her attorneys, and in no way revealed a significant part of the substance of those discussions. *At 603:* In this context, we are not persuaded that [P's] responses disclosed 'a significant part of the communication' with her attorneys, for such a conclusion would require considerably more depth and specificity than were present in [P's] answers. As such, we do not find any waiver of the attorney-client privilege under ... §912."

Roberts v. Superior Ct. (1973) 9 Cal.3d 330, 343. "[A] form consent by the patient-litigant waiving her privilege is to be strictly construed against the insurance company supplying the form so that the waiver encompasses only that which clearly appears on its face."

Los Angeles Gay & Lesbian Ctr. v. Superior Ct. (2d Dist.2011) 194 Cal.App.4th 288, 309. "The physician-patient privilege may only be waived through a clear manifestation of an intent to waive. *At 310:* When a party puts in issue a matter that is normally privileged, the privilege may be waived, and a plaintiff waives the physician-patient privilege to the extent that physical condition is an issue in the suit. However, in an opt-out class action, merely by passively consenting to membership in the class, a class member does not expressly place his or her medical condition at issue, therefore the exception of [Evid. C.] §996 or [Evid. C.] §912, subdivision (a) does not apply."

California Consumer Health Care Council, Inc. v. Department of Managed Health Care (3d Dist. 2008) 161 Cal.App.4th 684, 694. "[D] points out that the physician-patient privilege survives death and the estate's representative is the holder of the privilege. Only the holder of the privilege may waive the privilege. [P1] acknowledged in the trial court that [P2] was not the conservator of her father's estate. [D] contends that since [P2] was not the holder of the privilege, she could not waive the privilege and [D] was well within its discretion to decline to release her father's records. [¶] We agree. [P1's] argument would allow any relative to obtain records and file a complaint regardless of the wishes of the enrollee or his or her representative or designee. Such a reading basically guts the concept of confidentiality of medical records."

Shooker v. Superior Ct. (2d Dist.2003) 111 Cal.App.4th 923, 930. "The designation of a party as an expert trial witness is not in itself an implied waiver of the party's attorney-client privilege because his initial status is that of a possible expert witness. If the designation is withdrawn before the party discloses a significant part of a privileged communication ..., or before it is known with reasonable certainty that the party will actually testify as an expert, the privilege is secure; if the party provides privileged documents or testifies as an expert (such as by stating his opinion in a declaration or at a deposition) the privilege is waived."

State Comp. Ins. Fund v. WPS, Inc. (2d Dist.1999) 70 Cal.App.4th 644, 652-53. "A trial court called upon to determine whether inadvertent disclosure of privileged information constitutes waiver of the privilege must examine both the subjective intent of the holder of the privilege and the relevant surrounding circumstances for any manifestation of the holder's consent to disclose the information. *At 654:* '[W]aiver' does not include accidental, inadvertent disclosure of privileged information by the attorney. *At 657:* [W]henever a lawyer ascertains that he or she may have privileged attorney-client material that was inadvertently provided by another, that lawyer must notify the party entitled to the privilege of that fact."

Subdivision (d)

Seahaus La Jolla Owners Ass'n v. Superior Ct. (4th Dist.2014) 224 Cal.App.4th 754, 774. "The common interest doctrine is properly characterized under California law as a nonwaiver doctrine, analyzed under standard waiver principles applicable to the attorney-client privilege and the work product doctrine. For the common interest doctrine to attach, most courts seem to insist that the two parties have in common an interest in securing legal advice related to the same matter—and that the communications be made to advance their shared interest in securing legal advice on that common matter. [¶] [Ds] argue that any confidentiality of communications at the [homeowners' association] meetings was initially waived through several different sets of circumstances. First, persons employed by or affiliated with [Ds], and who were also individual homeowners, were allowed to attend, and expert consultants attended and spoke at the meetings. Second, a

few homeowners later discussed issues raised at the meetings with their relatives and friends. Third, the letters announcing the meetings stated that the letters could be shared with potential buyers or lenders. Also, [P-homeowners' association] had not kept confidential, but had made available to others, the numerous e-mails its counsel had received from individual homeowners about the defects they were experiencing in their units. *At 775:* To determine the scope of the privilege, we look to the content of the subject communications, as well as the circumstances, for indications on whether the meetings will advance the common interests in the representation by counsel. [W]e conclude that [P-homeowners' association's] duties and powers include communicating with those parties who have closely aligned common interests, and the individual homeowners at the development have such common interests in this particular context. On balance, these circumstances show that [P-homeowners' association] and its counsel, and the individual homeowners who participated in the litigation meetings, maintained a reasonable expectation that information to be disclosed about the status of the litigation was confidential in nature. Clearly, the fundamental purpose behind the privilege is to safeguard the confidential relationship between clients and their attorneys so as to promote full and open discussion of the facts and tactics surrounding individual legal matters. In the role of client, [P-homeowners' association] could properly take into account not only its own goals of protecting the common areas, but also the interests of its individual member homeowners in their units, as related to the common areas that [P-homeowners' association] was seeking to repair. The relationship of the two ... actions was close enough so that the individual homeowners had common interests in the legal status of [P-homeowners' association's] action. Moreover, the presence of some homeowners who may have had conflicting loyalties (homeowners who were affiliated with [Ds]) did not destroy all other common interests. *At 776:* We conclude that the subject litigation meetings were held to accomplish the purpose for which [P-homeowners' association's] lawyers were consulted. The common interest doctrine and its protection of confidentiality of these communications apply as a matter of law to these circumstances." (Internal quotes omitted.)

Citizens for Ceres v. Superior Ct. (5th Dist.2013) 217 Cal.App.4th 889, 914. "The common interest doctrine allows disclosure between parties, without waiver of privileges, of communications protected by the attorney-client privilege or the attorney work product doctrine where the disclosure is necessary to accomplish the purpose for which the legal advice was sought. The doctrine is not an independent privilege but a doctrine specifying circumstances under which disclosure to a third party does not waive privileges. It does *not* mean there is an expanded attorney-client relationship encompassing all parties and counsel who share a common interest. [¶] The doctrine is based on [Evid. C.] §§912 and 952.... *At 915:* Although these provisions deal specifically with the attorney-client privilege, the same considerations apply to waiver or nonwaiver of the work product doctrine. [¶] [F]or the common interest doctrine to attach, most courts seem to insist that the two parties have in common an interest in securing legal advice related to the same matter—and that the communications be made to advance their shared interest in securing legal advice on that common matter. *At 916-17:* The doctrine extends no further than this because in California there is no independent statutory joint defense or common interest *privilege*, and California courts are not authorized to establish one." (Internal quotes omitted.) *See also* ***OXY Res. Cal. LLC v. Superior Ct.*** (1st Dist.2004) 115 Cal.App.4th 874, 887-91.

§913. [EXERCISE OF PRIVILEGE]

(a) [No comment or adverse inference.] If in the instant proceeding or on a prior occasion a privilege is or was exercised not to testify with respect to any matter, or to refuse to disclose or to prevent another from disclosing any matter, neither the presiding officer nor counsel may comment thereon, no presumption shall arise because of the exercise of the privilege, and the trier of fact may not draw any inference therefrom as to the credibility of the witness or as to any matter at issue in the proceeding.

(b) [Jury instruction.] The court, at the request of a party who may be adversely affected because an unfavorable inference may be drawn by the jury because a privilege has been exercised, shall instruct the jury that no presumption arises because of the exercise of the privilege and that the jury may not draw any inference therefrom as to the credibility of the witness or as to any matter at issue in the proceeding.

History of Evid. C. §913: Added eff. Sept. 17, 1965, oper. Jan. 1, 1967, Stats. 1965, ch. 299, §2.

Official Comment

7 Cal. Law Revision Comm'n Rep. (1965) p. 1155; Assem. J., Apr. 6, 1965, p. 1744.

Section 913 prohibits any comment on the exercise of a privilege and provides that the trier of fact may not draw any inference therefrom. Except as noted below, this probably states existing law. *See People v. Wilkes*, 44 Cal.2d 679, 284 P.2d 481 (1955). In addition, the court is required, upon request of a party who may be adversely affected, to instruct the jury that no presumption arises and that no inference is to be drawn from the exercise of a privilege. If comment could be made on the exercise of a privilege and adverse inferences drawn therefrom, a litigant would be under great pressure to forgo his claim of privilege and the protection sought to be afforded by the privilege would be largely negated. Moreover, the inferences which might be drawn would, in many instances, be quite unwarranted.

It should be noted that Section 913 deals only with comment upon, and the drawing of adverse inferences from, the exercise of a privilege. Section 913 does not purport to deal with the inferences that may be drawn from, or the comment that may be made upon, the evidence in the case.

Section 13 of Article I of the California Constitution provides that, in a criminal case, the failure of the defendant to explain or to deny by his testimony the evidence in the case against him may be commented upon. The courts, in reliance on this provision, have held that the failure of a party in either a civil or criminal case to explain or to deny the evidence against him may be considered in determining what inferences should be drawn from that evidence. *People v. Adamson*, 27 Cal.2d 478, 165 P.2d 3 (1946); *Fross v. Wotton*, 3 Cal.2d 384, 44 P.2d 350 (1935). However, the cases have emphasized that this right of comment and consideration does not extend in criminal cases to the drawing of inferences from the claim of privilege itself. Inferences may be drawn only from the evidence in the case and the defendant's failure to explain or deny such evidence. *People v. Ashley*, 42 Cal.2d 246, 267 P.2d 271 (1954); *People v. Adamson, supra*, 27 Cal.2d 478, 165 P.2d 3 (1946). Section 413 of the Evidence Code expresses the principle underlying this constitutional provision; nothing in Section 913 affects the application of Section 413 in either criminal or civil cases. *See* the *Comment* to Evidence Code §413. Thus, for example, it is perfectly proper under the Evidence Code for counsel to point out that the evidence against the other party is uncontradicted.

Section 913 may modify existing California law as it applies in civil cases. In *Nelson v. Southern Pacific Co.*, 8 Cal.2d 648, 67 P.2d 682 (1937), the Supreme Court held that evidence of a person's exercise of the privilege against self-incrimination in a prior proceeding may be shown for impeachment purposes if he testifies in a self-exculpatory manner in a subsequent proceeding. The Supreme Court within recent years has overruled statements in certain criminal cases declaring a similar rule. *People v. Snyder*, 50 Cal.2d 190, 197, 324 P.2d 1, 6 (1958) (overruling or disapproving several cases there cited). *See also People v. Sharer*, 61 Cal.2d 869, 40 Cal.Rptr. 851, 395 P.2d 899 (1964). Section 913 will, in effect, overrule the holding in the *Nelson* case, for it declares that no inference may be drawn from an exercise of a privilege either on the issue of credibility or on any other issue, whether the privilege was exercised in the instant proceeding or on a prior occasion. The status of the rule in the *Nelson* case has been in doubt because of the recent holdings in criminal cases; Section 913 eliminates any remaining basis for applying a different rule in civil cases.

There is some language in *Fross v. Wotton*, 3 Cal.2d 384, 44 P.2d 350 (1935), that indicates that unfavorable inferences may be drawn in a civil case from a party's claim of the privilege against self-incrimination during the case itself. Such language was unnecessary to that decision; but, if it does indicate California law, that law is changed by Evidence Code Sections 413 and 913. Under these sections, it is clear that, in civil cases as well as criminal cases, inferences may be drawn only from the evidence in the case, not from the claim of privilege.

§914. [DETERMINING PRIVILEGE]

(a) [Presiding officer.] The presiding officer shall determine a claim of privilege in any proceeding in the same manner as a court determines such a claim under Article 2 (commencing with Section 400) of Chapter 4 of Division 3.

(b) [Contempt.] No person may be held in contempt for failure to disclose information claimed to be privileged unless he has failed to comply with an order of a court that he disclose such information. This subdivision does not apply to any governmental agency that has constitutional contempt power, nor does it apply to hearings and investigations of the Industrial Accident Commission, nor does it impliedly repeal Chapter 4 (commencing with Section 9400) of Part 1 of Division 2 of Title 2 of the Government Code. If no other statutory procedure is applicable, the procedure prescribed by Section 1991 of the Code of Civil Procedure shall be followed in seeking an order of a court that the person disclose the information claimed to be privileged.

History of Evid. C. §914: Added eff. Sept. 17, 1965, oper. Jan. 1, 1967, Stats. 1965, ch. 299, §2.

Official Comment

7 Cal. Law Revision Comm'n Rep. (1965) p. 1157; Assem. J., Apr. 6, 1965, p. 1746.

Subdivision (a) makes the general provisions concerning preliminary determinations on admissibility of evidence (Sections 400-406) applicable when a presiding officer who is not a judge is called upon to determine whether or not a privilege exists. Subdivision (a) is necessary because Sections 400-406, by their terms, apply only to determinations by a court.

Subdivision (b) is needed to protect persons claiming privileges in nonjudicial proceedings. Because such proceedings are often conducted by persons untrained in law, it is desirable to have a judicial determination of whether a person is required to disclose information claimed to be privileged before he can be held in contempt for failing to disclose such information. What is contemplated is that, if a claim of privilege is made in a nonjudicial proceeding and is overruled, application must be made to a court for an order compelling the witness to answer. Only if such order is made and is disobeyed may a witness be held in contempt. That the determination of privilege in a judicial proceeding is a question for the judge is well-established California law. *See, e.g.*, *Holm v. Superior Court*, 42 Cal.2d 500, 507, 267 P.2d 1025, 1029 (1954).

Subdivision (b), of course, does not apply to any body—such as the Public Utilities Commission—that has constitutional power to impose punishment for contempt. *See, e.g.*, Cal. Const., Art. XII, §22. Nor does this subdivision apply to witnesses before the State Legislature or its committees. *See* Gov. Code §§9400-9414. Likewise, subdivision (b) does not apply to hearings and investigations of the State Industrial Accident Commission.

§915. [NO DISCLOSURE REQUIRED TO RULE ON CLAIM]

(a) [Claim of privilege or attorney work product.] Subject to subdivision (b), the presiding officer may not require disclosure of information claimed to be privileged under this division or attorney work product under subdivision (a) of Section 2018.030 of the Code of Civil Procedure in order to rule on the claim of privilege; provided, however, that in any hearing conducted pursuant to subdivision (c) of Section 1524 of the Penal Code in which a claim of privilege is made and the court determines that there is no other feasible means to rule on the validity of the claim other than to require disclosure, the court shall proceed in accordance with subdivision (b).

(b) [Disclosure in chambers.] When a court is ruling on a claim of privilege under Article 9 (commencing with Section 1040) of Chapter 4 (official information and identity of informer) or under Section 1060 (trade secret) or under subdivision (b) of Section 2018.030 of the Code of Civil Procedure (attorney work product) and is unable to do so without requiring disclosure of the information claimed to be privileged, the court may require the person from whom disclosure is sought or the person authorized to claim the privilege, or both, to disclose the information in chambers out of the presence and hearing of all persons except the person authorized to claim the privilege and any other persons as the person authorized to claim the privilege is willing to have present. If the judge determines that the information is privileged, neither the judge nor any other person may ever disclose, without the consent of a person authorized to permit disclosure, what was disclosed in the course of the proceedings in chambers.

History of Evid. C. §915: Added eff. Sept. 17, 1965, oper. Jan. 1, 1967, Stats. 1965, ch. 299, §2. Amended eff. Jan. 1, 1980, Stats. 1979, ch. 1034, §1; eff. Jan. 1, 2002, Stats. 2001, ch. 812, §13; eff. Jan. 1, 2005, oper. July 1, 2005, Stats. 2004, ch. 182, §29.

Official Comment

7 Cal. Law Revision Comm'n Rep. (1965) p. 1158.

Subdivision (a) states the general rule that revelation of the information asserted to be privileged may not be compelled in order to determine whether or not it is privileged. This codifies existing law. *See Collette v. Sarrasin*, 184 Cal. 283, 288-289, 193 Pac. 571, 573 (1920); *People v. Glen Arms Estate, Inc.*, 230 Cal.App.2d 841, 846 note 1, 41 Cal.Rptr. 303, 305 note 1 (1964).

Subdivision (b) provides an exception to this general rule for information claimed to be privileged under Section 1040 (official information), Section 1041 (identity of an informer), or Section 1060 (trade secret). These privileges exist only if the interest in maintaining the secrecy of the information outweighs the interest in seeing that justice is done in the particular case. In at least some cases, it will be necessary for the judge to examine the information claimed to be privileged in order to balance these competing considerations intelligently. *See People v. Glen Arms Estate, Inc.*, 230 Cal.App.2d 841, 846 note 1, 41 Cal.Rptr. 303, 305 note 1 (1964), and the cases cited in 8 Wigmore, *Evidence* §2379 at 812 note 6 (McNaughton rev. 1961). And *see United States v. Reynolds*, 345 U.S. 1, 7-11 (1953), and pertinent discussion thereof in 8 Wigmore, *Evidence* §2379 (McNaughton rev. 1961). Even in these cases, Section 915 undertakes to give adequate protection to the person claiming the privilege by providing that the information be disclosed in confidence to the judge and requiring that it be kept in confidence if it is found to be privileged.

The exception in subdivision (b) applies only when a court is ruling on the claim of privilege. Thus, in view of subdivision (a), disclosure of the information cannot be required, for example, in an administrative proceeding.

Official Comment

33 Cal. Law Revision Comm'n Rep. (2004) p. 1016.

Section 915 is amended to reflect nonsubstantive reorganization of the rules governing civil discovery.

ANNOTATIONS

Costco Wholesale Corp. v. Superior Ct. (2009) 47 Cal.4th 725, 737. "[S]ection 915, while prohibiting examination of assertedly privileged information, does not prohibit disclosure or examination of *other* information to permit the court to evaluate the basis for the claim, such as whether the privilege is held by the party asserting it. [S]ection 915 also does not prevent a court from reviewing the facts asserted as the basis for the privilege to determine, for example, whether the attorney-client relationship existed at the time the communication was made, whether the client intended the communication to be confidential, or whether the communication emanated from the client. Accordingly, while the prohibition of … §915 is not absolute in the sense that a litigant may still have to reveal *some* information to permit the court to evaluate the basis for the claim of privilege …, it does not follow that courts are free to ignore the section's prohibition and demand in camera disclosure of the allegedly privileged information itself for this purpose. *At 739:* [T]he attorney-client privilege is a legislative creation, which courts have no power to limit by recognizing implied exceptions. Concern that a party may be able to prevent discovery of relevant information therefore provides no justification for inferring an exception to … §915."

Concepcion v. Amscan Holdings, Inc. (2d Dist. 2014) 223 Cal.App.4th 1309, 1326 n.11. "Under appropriate circumstances … §915, subdivision (b), authorizes the trial court to receive in camera disclosure of information to assist in deciding whether it is privileged and thus protected from disclosure. Neither … §915 nor any other statutory provision authorizes the court to use that information to decide the merits of a case if the other side has not had an opportunity to review the material and be heard."

Wellpoint Health Networks, Inc. v. Superior Ct. (2d Dist.1997) 59 Cal.App.4th 110, 121. "'[T]here is no statutory or other provision that allows for … an inspection of documents allegedly protected by the attorney-client privilege.' This means that unless the party holding the privilege allows it, there can be no in camera inspection of documents to determine whether the privilege exists. However, in camera inspection is the proper procedure to evaluate the applicability of the work product doctrine to specific documents, and categorize whether each document should be given qualified or absolute protection."

Mavroudis v. Superior Ct. (1st Dist.1980) 102 Cal.App.3d 594, 606. "[Ds] contend that the court may not require the disclosure of allegedly privileged communications when ruling on a claim of privilege, except in certain specified cases not relevant here. [Ds] cite

... §915 in support of their argument. As a general rule, their statement is correct. However, where an exception to a privilege depends upon the content of a communication, the court may require disclosure *in camera* in making its ruling. *At 606 n.4:* An *in camera* determination is authorized by ... §915, subdivision (b) when the court is ruling on a claim of privilege of official information, identity of informer or trade secret. The Supreme Court has suggested that the procedure outlined in that section also be utilized by a court when ruling upon a claim of privilege of psychotherapist-patient communications which depend upon the content of the communication."

§916. [EXCLUSION OF PRIVILEGED INFORMATION]

(a) The presiding officer, on his own motion or on the motion of any party, shall exclude information that is subject to a claim of privilege under this division if:

(1) The person from whom the information is sought is not a person authorized to claim the privilege; and

(2) There is no party to the proceeding who is a person authorized to claim the privilege.

(b) The presiding officer may not exclude information under this section if:

(1) He is otherwise instructed by a person authorized to permit disclosure; or

(2) The proponent of the evidence establishes that there is no person authorized to claim the privilege in existence.

History of Evid. C. §916: Added eff. Sept. 17, 1965, oper. Jan. 1, 1967, Stats. 1965, ch. 299, §2.

Official Comment

**7 Cal. Law Revision Comm'n Rep. (1965) p. 1159;
Assem. J., Apr. 6, 1965, p. 1746.**

Section 916 is needed to protect the holder of a privilege when he is not available to protect his own interest. For example, a third party—perhaps the lawyer's secretary—may have been present when a confidential communication to a lawyer was made. In the absence of both the holder himself and the lawyer, the secretary could be compelled to testify concerning the communication if there were no provision such as Section 916 which requires the presiding officer to recognize the privilege.

Section 916 is designed to protect only privileged information that the holder of the privilege could protect by claiming the privilege at the hearing. It is not designed to protect unprivileged information. For example, if the statement offered in evidence is a declaration against the penal interest of the declarant, Section 916 does not authorize the presiding officer to exclude the evidence on the ground of the declarant's privilege against self-incrimination. If the declarant were present, his self-incrimination privilege would merely preclude his giving self-incriminating testimony at the hearing; it could not be asserted to prevent the disclosure of previously made self-incriminating statements.

The erroneous exclusion of information pursuant to Section 916 on the ground that it is privileged might amount to prejudicial error. On the other hand, the erroneous failure to exclude information pursuant to Section 916 could *not* amount to prejudicial error. *See* Evidence Code §918.

Section 916 may be declarative of the existing law. No case in point has been found, but see the language in *People v. Atkinson*, 40 Cal. 284, 285 (1870) (attorney-client privilege).

A §917. [PRESUMPTION OF PRIVILEGE]

(a) [Burden of proof.] If a privilege is claimed on the ground that the matter sought to be disclosed is a communication made in confidence in the course of the lawyer-client, lawyer referral service-client, physician-patient, psychotherapist-patient, clergy-penitent, husband-wife, sexual assault counselor-victim, [or] domestic violence counselor-victim, or human trafficking caseworker-victim relationship, the communication is presumed to have been made in confidence and the opponent of the claim of privilege has the burden of proof to establish that the communication was not confidential.

(b) [Electronic communication.] A communication between persons in a relationship listed in subdivision (a) does not lose its privileged character for the sole reason that it is communicated by electronic means or because persons involved in the delivery, facilitation, or storage of electronic communication may have access to the content of the communication.

(c) ["Electronic" defined.] For purposes of this section, "electronic" has the same meaning provided in Section 1633.2 of the Civil Code.

History of Evid. C. §917: Added eff. Sept. 17, 1965, oper. Jan. 1, 1967, Stats. 1965, ch. 299, §2. Amended eff. Jan. 1, 2003, Stats. 2002, ch. 72, §2; eff. Jan. 1, 2004, Stats. 2003, ch. 468, §2; eff. Jan. 1, 2005, Stats. 2004, ch. 183, §93; eff. Jan. 1, 2007, Stats. 2006, ch. 689, §2; eff. Jan. 1, 2015, Stats. 2014, ch. 913, §14.

Official Comment

**7 Cal. Law Revision Comm'n Rep. (1965) p. 1160;
Assem. J., Apr. 6, 1965, p. 1747.**

A number of sections provide privileges for communications made "in confidence" in the course of certain relationships. Although there appear to have been no cases involving the question in California, the general rule elsewhere is that a communication made in the course of such a relationship is presumed to be confidential and the party objecting to the claim of privilege has the burden of showing that it was not. *See generally*, with respect to the marital communication privilege, 8 Wigmore, *Evidence* §2336 (McNaughton rev. 1961). *See also Blau v. United States*, 340 U.S. 332, 333-335 (1951) (holding that marital communications are presumed to be confidential). In adopting by statute a revised version of the privileges article of the Uniform Rules of Evidence, New Jersey included such a provision in its statement of the lawyer-client privilege. N.J. Rev. Stat. §2A:84A-20(3), added by N.J. Laws 1960, ch. 52, p. 452.

If the privilege claimant were required to show that the communication was made in confidence, he would be compelled, in many cases, to reveal the subject matter of the communication in order to establish his right to the privilege. Hence, Section 917 is included to establish a presumption of confidentiality, if this is not already the existing law in California. *See Sharon v. Sharon*, 79 Cal. 633, 678, 22 Pac. 26, 40 (1889) (attorney-client privilege); *Hager v. Shindler*, 29 Cal. 47, 63 (1865) ("*Prima facie*, all communications made by a client to his attorney or counsel [in the course of that relationship] must be regarded as confidential.").

To overcome the presumption, the proponent of the evidence must persuade the presiding officer that the communication was not made in confi-

dence. Of course, if the facts show that the communication was not intended to be kept in confidence, the communication is not privileged. *See Solon v. Lichtenstein*, 39 Cal.2d 75, 244 P.2d 907 (1952). And the fact that the communication was made under circumstances where others could easily overhear is a strong indication that the communication was not intended to be confidential and is, therefore, unprivileged. *See Sharon v. Sharon*, 79 Cal. 633, 677, 22 Pac. 26, 39 (1889); *People v. Castiel*, 153 Cal.App.2d 653, 315 P.2d 79 (1957).

31 Cal. Law Revision Comm'n Rep. (2001) p. 257.

Subdivision (a) of Section 917 is amended to make clear that it also applies to confidential communication privileges created after its original enactment in 1965. *See* Sections 1035-1036.2 (sexual assault victim), 1037-1037.7 (domestic violence victim). The presumption set forth in subdivision (a) applies regardless of how a communication is transmitted. In each instance, the opponent of the claim of privilege has the burden of proof to establish that the communication was not confidential.

Subdivision (b) is drawn from New York law (N.Y. C.P.L.R. 4548 (McKinney 2001)) and from language formerly found in Section 952 relating to confidentiality of an electronic communication between a client and a lawyer. For waiver of privileges, *see* Section 912 & *Comment*.

Under subdivision (c), the definition of "electronic" is broad, including any "intangible media which are technologically capable of storing, transmitting and reproducing information in human perceivable form." Unif. Electronic Transactions Act, §2 comment (1999) (enacted as Civ. Code §1633.2).

For discussion of ethical considerations where a lawyer communicates with a client by electronic means, *see* Bus. & Prof. Code §6068(e) (attorney has duty to "maintain inviolate the confidence, and at every peril to himself or herself to preserve the secrets, of his or her client"); ABA Standing Committee on Ethics & Professional Responsibility, Formal Op. 99-413 ("Protecting the Confidentiality of Unencrypted E-mail"); ABA Standing Committee on Ethics & Professional Responsibility, Formal Op. 92-368 ("Inadvertent Disclosure of Confidential Materials").

For examples of provisions on the admissibility of electronic communications, *see* Evid. Code §§1521 & *Comment* (Secondary Evidence Rule), 1552 (printed representation of computer information or computer program), 1553 (printed representation of images stored on video or digital medium); Civ. Code §1633.13 ("In a proceeding, evidence of a record or signature may not be excluded solely because it is in electronic form."). *See also People v. Martinez*, 22 Cal. 4th 106, 990 P.2d 563, 91 Cal.Rptr. 2d 687 (2000); *People v. Hernandez*, 55 Cal.App.4th 225, 63 Cal.Rptr. 2d 769 (1997); *Aguimatang v. California State Lottery*, 234 Cal.App.3d 769, 286 Cal.Rptr. 57 (1991); *People v. Lugashi*, 205 Cal.App.3d 632, 252 Cal.Rptr. 434 (1988).

ANNOTATIONS

Alpha Beta Co. v. Superior Ct. (5th Dist.1984) 157 Cal.App.3d 818, 824-25. "Once a party claims the attorney-client privilege, the communication sought to be suppressed is presumed confidential. A party opposing the privilege has the burden of proof to show the communication is one not made in confidence. However, the party claiming privilege has the burden to show that the communication sought to be suppressed falls within the terms of the statute." *See also* ***Nalian Truck Lines, Inc. v. Nakano Whs. & Transp.*** (2d Dist.1992) 6 Cal.App.4th 1256, 1265.

§918. [CLAIM OF ERROR BASED ON DISALLOWING PRIVILEGE]

A party may predicate error on a ruling disallowing a claim of privilege only if he is the holder of the privilege, except that a party may predicate error on a ruling disallowing a claim of privilege by his spouse under Section 970 or 971.

History of Evid. C. §918: Added eff. Sept. 17, 1965, oper. Jan. 1, 1967, Stats. 1965, ch. 299, §2.

Official Comment

7 Cal. Law Revision Comm'n Rep. (1965) p. 1161.

This section is consistent with existing law. *See People v. Gonzales*, 56 Cal. App. 330, 204 Pac. 1088 (1922), and discussion of similar cases cited in *Tentative Recommendation and a Study Relating to the Uniform Rules of Evidence (Article V. Privileges)*, 6 Cal. Law Revision Comm'n, Rep., Rec. & Studies 201, 525 note 5 (1964).

§919. [DISCLOSURE ERRONEOUSLY COMPELLED]

(a) [Inadmissible against holder.] Evidence of a statement or other disclosure of privileged information is inadmissible against a holder of the privilege if:

(1) A person authorized to claim the privilege claimed it but nevertheless disclosure erroneously was required to be made; or

(2) The presiding officer did not exclude the privileged information as required by Section 916.

(b) [Failure to oppose or appeal.] If a person authorized to claim the privilege claimed it, whether in the same or a prior proceeding, but nevertheless disclosure erroneously was required by the presiding officer to be made, neither the failure to refuse to disclose nor the failure to seek review of the order of the presiding officer requiring disclosure indicates consent to the disclosure or constitutes a waiver and, under these circumstances, the disclosure is one made under coercion.

History of Evid. C. §919: Added eff. Sept. 17, 1965, oper. Jan. 1, 1967, Stats. 1965, ch. 299, §2. Amended eff. Jan. 1, 1975, Stats. 1974, ch. 227, §1.

Official Comment

7 Cal. Law Revision Comm'n Rep. (1965) p. 1161.

Section 919 protects a holder of a privilege from the detriment he would otherwise suffer in a later proceeding when, in a prior proceeding, the presiding officer erroneously overruled a claim of privilege and compelled revelation of the privileged information. Although Section 912 provides that such a coerced disclosure does not waive a privilege, it does not provide specifically that evidence of the prior disclosure is inadmissible; Section 919 assures the inadmissibility of such evidence in the subsequent proceeding.

Section 919 probably states existing law. *See People v. Abair*, 102 Cal.App.2d 765, 228 P.2d 336 (1951) (prior disclosure by an attorney held inadmissible in a later proceeding where the holder of the privilege had first opportunity to object to attorney's testifying). *See also People v. Kor*, 129 Cal.App.2d 436, 277 P.2d 94 (1954). However, there is little case authority upon the proposition.

1973 Ann. Report, 11 Cal. Law Revision Comm'n Rep. (1973) App. III.

Subdivision (b) has been added to Section 919 to make clear that, after disclosure of privileged information has been erroneously required to be made by order of a trial court or other presiding officer, neither the failure to refuse to disclose nor the failure to challenge the order (by, for example, a petition for a writ of habeas corpus or other special writ or by an appeal from a contempt order) amounts to a waiver and the disclosure is one made under coercion for the purposes of Section 912(a) and 919(a)(1). *See* Section 905 (defining "presiding officer"). The addition of subdivision (b) will preclude any possibility of a contrary interpretation of Sections 912 and 919 based on the language found in *Markwell v. Sykes*, 173 Cal.App.2d 642, 649-650, 343 P.2d 769, 773-774 (1959). *See Recommendation Relating to Erroneously Ordered Disclosure of Privileged Information*, 11 Cal. L. Revision Comm'n Reports 1163 (1973).

The phrase "whether in the same or a prior proceeding" has been included in subdivision (b) to avoid any implication that might be drawn from the origi-

nal Law Revision Commission Comment to Section 919 that subdivision (a)(1) applies only where the privilege was claimed in a *prior* proceeding. The protection afforded by Section 919, of course, also applies where a claim of privilege is made at an earlier stage in the same proceeding and the presiding officer erroneously overruled the claim and ordered disclosure of the privileged information to be made.

ANNOTATIONS

Regents of the Univ. of Cal. v. Superior Ct. (4th Dist.2008) 165 Cal.App.4th 672, 683. "[I]t is clear that when privileged documents have been disclosed either in response to the request of a government agency or inadvertently in the course of civil discovery, no waiver of the privilege will occur if the holder of the privilege has taken reasonable steps under the circumstances to prevent disclosure. The law does not require that the holder of the privilege take 'strenuous or Herculean efforts' to resist disclosure. This standard is consistent with §919, subdivision (b), which by its terms does not require that the holder of a privilege suffer a contempt finding in order to preserve the privilege or to appeal an order directing disclosure. *At 683 n.6:* We reject [Ps'] contention that §919 sets forth the exclusive circumstances under which coercion arises. The terms of the statute are in no sense exclusive but rather exemplary." *See also* ***Schlumberger Ltd. v. Superior Ct.*** (2d Dist.1981) 115 Cal.App.3d 386, 391-92 (disclosure under court order is coerced and does not constitute waiver).

§919

§920. [STATUTES RELATING TO PRIVILEGE NOT REPEALED]

Nothing in this division shall be construed to repeal by implication any other statute relating to privileges.

History of Evid. C. §920: Added eff. Sept. 17, 1965, oper. Jan. 1, 1967, Stats. 1965, ch. 299, §2.

Official Comment

7 Cal. Law Revision Comm'n Rep. (1965) p. 1162.

Some of the statutes relating to privileges are found in other codes and are continued in force. *See, e.g.*, Penal Code §§266h and 266i (making the marital communications privilege inapplicable in prosecutions for pimping and pandering, respectively). Section 920 assures that nothing in this division makes privileged any information declared by statute to be unprivileged or makes unprivileged any information declared by statute to be privileged.

CHAPTER 4. PARTICULAR PRIVILEGES

ARTICLE 1. PRIVILEGE OF DEFENDANT IN CRIMINAL CASE

§930. [NOT TO BE CALLED OR TESTIFY]

To the extent that such privilege exists under the Constitution of the United States or the State of California, a defendant in a criminal case has a privilege not to be called as a witness and not to testify.

History of Evid. C. §930: Added eff. Sept. 17, 1965, oper. Jan. 1, 1967, Stats. 1965, ch. 299, §2.

Official Comment

7 Cal. Law Revision Comm'n Rep. (1965) p. 1162.

Section 930 recognizes that the defendant in a criminal case has a constitutional privilege not to be called as a witness and not to testify. Cal. Const., Art. I, §13. *See Killpatrick v. Superior Court*, 153 Cal.App.2d 146, 314 P.2d 164 (1957); *People v. Talle*, 111 Cal.App.2d 650, 245 P.2d 633 (1952). Section 930 also recognizes that the defendant may have a similar privilege under the United States Constitution. *See Malloy v. Hogan*, 378 U.S. 1 (1964).

ANNOTATIONS

Cramer v. Tyars (1979) 23 Cal.3d 131, 137-38. "[T]he historic purpose of the privilege against being called as a witness has been to assure that the *criminal* justice system remains accusatorial, not inquisitorial. The extension of the privilege to an area outside the criminal justice system … would contravene both the language and purpose of the privilege."

ARTICLE 2. PRIVILEGE AGAINST SELF-INCRIMINATION

§940. [PRIVILEGE AGAINST SELF-INCRIMINATION]

To the extent that such privilege exists under the Constitution of the United States or the State of California, a person has a privilege to refuse to disclose any matter that may tend to incriminate him.

History of Evid. C. §940: Added eff. Sept. 17, 1965, oper. Jan. 1, 1967, Stats. 1965, ch. 299, §2.

Official Comment

7 Cal. Law Revision Comm'n Rep. (1965) p. 1163.

Section 940 recognizes the privilege (derived from the California and United States Constitutions) of a person to refuse, when testifying, to give information that might tend to incriminate him. *See Fross v. Wotton*, 3 Cal.2d 384, 44 P.2d 350 (1935); *In re Leavitt*, 174 Cal.App.2d 535, 345 P.2d 75 (1959). This privilege should be distinguished from the privilege stated in Section 930 (privilege of defendant in a criminal case to refuse to testify at all).

Section 940 does not determine the scope of the privilege against self-incrimination; the scope of the privilege is determined by the pertinent provisions of the California and United States Constitutions as interpreted by the courts. *See* Cal. Const., Art. I, §13. *See also Malloy v. Hogan*, 378 U.S. 1 (1964). Nor does Section 940 prescribe the exceptions to the privilege or indicate when it has been waived. This, too, is determined by the cases interpreting the pertinent provisions of the California and United States Constitutions. For a statement of the scope of the constitutional privilege and some of its exceptions, *see Tentative Recommendation and a Study Relating to the Uniform Rules of Evidence (Article V. Privileges)*, 6 Cal. Law Revision Comm'n, Rep., Rec. & Studies 201, 215-218, 343-377 (1964).

ANNOTATIONS

Cramer v. Tyars (1979) 23 Cal.3d 131, 134. "May a mentally retarded person who is the subject of a petition for civil commitment … be called as a witness at the commitment hearing? *At 139:* We conclude that, while [subject of commitment petition] could not be questioned about matters that would tend to incrimi-

nate him, he was subject to call as a witness and could be required to respond to nonincriminatory questioning which may have revealed his mental condition to the jury, whose duty it was to determine whether he was mentally retarded. Reason and common sense suggest that it is appropriate under such circumstances that a jury be permitted fully to observe the person sought to be committed, and to hear him speak and respond in order that it may make an informed judgment as to the level of his mental and intellectual functioning. The receipt of such evidence may be analogized to the disclosure of physical as opposed to testimonial evidence and may in fact be the most reliable proof and probative indicator of the person's present mental condition."

In re Marriage of Sachs (2d Dist.2002) 95 Cal.App.4th 1144, 1150-52. "The privilege against self-incrimination applies in judgment debtor proceedings. But this protection must be confined to instances where the witness has reasonable cause to apprehend danger from a direct answer. To sustain the privilege, it need only be evident from the implications of the question, in the setting in which it is asked, that a responsive answer to the question or an explanation of why it cannot be answered might be dangerous because injurious disclosure could result. [¶] The trial judge in appraising the claim of privilege must be governed as much by his personal perception of the peculiarities of the case as by the facts actually in evidence. [¶] To invoke the privilege, a witness need not be guilty of any offense; rather, the privilege is properly invoked whenever the witness's answers would furnish a link in the chain of evidence needed to prosecute the witness for a criminal offense. A trial court may compel the witness to answer only if it clearly appears to the court that the proposed testimony cannot possibly have a tendency to incriminate the person claiming the privilege." (Internal quotes omitted.)

Fuller v. Superior Ct. (2d Dist.2001) 87 Cal.App.4th 299, 305-06. "[S]ection 940 excludes from discovery information which may tend to incriminate a party. This principle has been construed to allow assertion of the privilege against self-incrimination in any proceeding, civil or criminal, administrative or judicial, investigatory or adjudicatory. [¶] However, a party is not entitled to decide for himself or herself whether the privilege against self-incrimination may be invoked. Rather, this question is for the court to decide after conducting *a particularized inquiry, deciding, in connection with each specific area that the questioning party seeks to explore*, whether or not the privilege is well founded. ... Only after the party claiming the privilege objects with specificity to the information sought can the court make a determination about whether the privilege may be invoked. [¶] Consequently, a civil defendant does not have the absolute right to invoke the privilege against self-incrimination. A party or witness in a civil proceeding may be required either to waive the privilege or accept the civil consequences of silence if he or she does exercise it. Courts recognize the dilemma faced by a defendant who must choose between defending the civil litigation by providing testimony that may be incriminating on the one hand, and losing the case by asserting the constitutional right and remaining silent, on the other hand. [¶] At the same time, courts must also consider the interests of the plaintiff in civil litigation where the defendant is exposed to parallel criminal prosecution." (Internal quotes omitted.)

People v. Superior Ct. (2d Dist.1986) 181 Cal.App.3d 785, 788. "'[N]o artificial organization may utilize the personal privilege against compulsory self-incrimination.' The privilege is a purely personal one, and should be 'limited to its historic function of protecting only the natural individual from compulsory incrimination through his own testimony or personal records.'" *See also* ***Bellis v. U.S.*** (1974) 417 U.S. 85, 90.

Brown v. Superior Ct. (2d Dist.1986) 180 Cal.App.3d 701, 708. "There is no question that the privilege against self-incrimination may be asserted by civil defendants who face possible criminal prosecution based on the same facts as the civil action. *At 711:* [Evid. C.] §912 does not list the privilege against self-incrimination among the enumerated privileges which are waived by failure to claim the privilege where there is an opportunity to do so. In contrast, the Law Revision Commission's comment to the self-incrimination privilege in [Evid. C.] §940 states that §940 does not cover the question of waiver, which 'is determined by the cases interpreting the pertinent provisions of the California and U.S. Constitutions.' Even so, we find it appropriate to use the waiver provisions of §912 in the context of [§940]." *See also* ***Pacers, Inc. v. Superior Ct.*** (4th Dist.1984) 162 Cal.App.3d 686, 688-89.

ARTICLE 3. LAWYER-CLIENT PRIVILEGE

§950. [LAWYER]

As used in this article, "lawyer" means a person authorized, or reasonably believed by the client to be authorized, to practice law in any state or nation.

History of Evid. C. §950: Added eff. Sept. 17, 1965, oper. Jan. 1, 1967, Stats. 1965, ch. 299, §2.

Official Comment

7 Cal. Law Revision Comm'n Rep. (1965) p. 1163.

"Lawyer" is defined to include a person "reasonably believed by the client to be authorized" to practice law. Since the privilege is intended to encourage full disclosure, the client's reasonable belief that the person he is consulting is an attorney is sufficient to justify application of the privilege. *See* 8 Wigmore, *Evidence* §2302 (McNaughton rev. 1961), and cases there cited in note 1. *See also* McCormick, *Evidence* §92 (1954).

There is no requirement that the lawyer be licensed to practice in a jurisdiction that recognizes the lawyer-client privilege. Legal transactions frequently cross state and national boundaries and require consultation with attorneys from many different jurisdictions. When a California resident travels outside the State and has occasion to consult a lawyer during such travel, or when a lawyer from another state or nation participates in a transaction involving a California client, the client should be entitled to assume that his communications will be given as much protection as they would be if he consulted a California lawyer in California. A client should not be forced to inquire about the jurisdictions where the lawyer is authorized to practice and whether such jurisdictions recognize the lawyer-client privilege before he may safely communicate with the lawyer.

§950

§951. [CLIENT]

As used in this article, "client" means a person who, directly or through an authorized representative, consults a lawyer for the purpose of retaining the lawyer or securing legal service or advice from him in his professional capacity, and includes an incompetent (a) who himself so consults the lawyer or (b) whose guardian or conservator so consults the lawyer in behalf of the incompetent.

History of Evid. C. §951: Added eff. Sept. 17, 1965, oper. Jan. 1, 1967, Stats. 1965, ch. 299, §2.

Official Comment

7 Cal. Law Revision Comm'n Rep. (1965) p. 1164.

Under Section 951, public entities have a privilege insofar as communications made in the course of the lawyer-client relationship are concerned. This codifies existing law. *See Holm v. Superior Court*, 42 Cal.2d 500, 267 P.2d 1025 (1954). Likewise, such unincorporated organizations as labor unions, social clubs, and fraternal societies have a lawyer-client privilege when the organization (rather than its individual members) is the client. *See* Evidence Code §175 (defining "person") and §200 (defining "public entity").

ANNOTATIONS

Michelle K. v. Superior Ct. (4th Dist.2013) 221 Cal.App.4th 409, 449. Conservator "argues he may exercise [conservatee's] absolute right to replace her counsel at any time because he is [conservatee's] legal representative with the power to fix her residence, give or withhold medical consent, and contract on [her] behalf. As a general rule, a client has the right to replace his or her attorney at virtually any time with or without cause. These rules, however, do not support [conservator's] position. Although [he] is [conservatee's] legal representative and the holder of her attorney-client privilege ..., [she] remains the client.... [Conservator] does not cite any authority allowing a conservator to replace a conservatee's court-appointed independent counsel with counsel the conservator selected. [A]llowing a conservator to do so would render the right to independent appointed counsel meaningless."

Bank of Am. v. Superior Ct. (4th Dist.2013) 212 Cal.App.4th 1076, 1090. Insurer's "retention of [law firm] to represent [insured] is sufficient to establish a tripartite attorney-client relationship between [insurer, insured, and law firm]. [¶] 'In the insured-insurer relationship, the attorney characteristically is engaged and paid by the carrier to defend the insured. The insured and the insurer have certain obligations each to the other ... arising from the insurance contract. ... If the matter reaches litigation, the attorney appears of record for the insured and at all times represents him in terms measured by the extent of his employment. [¶] In such a situation, the attorney has two clients whose primary, overlapping and common interest is the speedy and successful resolution of the claim and litigation. Conceptually, each member of the trio, attorney, client-insured, and client-insurer[,] has corresponding rights and obligations founded largely on contract, and as to the attorney, by the Rules of Professional Conduct as well.'"

State Farm Fire & Cas. Co. v. Superior Ct. (2d Dist.1997) 54 Cal.App.4th 625, 639. "We have no doubt that [D's employee] was an 'authorized representative' of [D] within the meaning of ... §951 for application of the privilege. 'It is no less the client's communication to the attorney when it is given by the client to an agent for transmission to the attorney, and it is immaterial whether the agent is the agent of the attorney, the client, or both.' However, the attorney-client privilege only protects disclosure of *communications* between the attorney and the client; it does not protect disclosure of underlying facts which may be referenced within a qualifying communication. [¶] Therefore, to the extent that [D's employee] has knowledge about the practices and procedures of [D's business], or the existence of claims manuals and other documents which are normally utilized by [D] in the operation of its business, the information is not privileged. Also, it would not be a violation of the attorney-client privilege for

[D's employee] to divulge that such documents exist but were not produced in connection with the [underlying action], although to divulge a conversation to that effect or the fact that such information had been delivered to an attorney, would violate the privilege. *At 640:* Nor does the attorney-client privilege protect independent facts related to a communication; that a communication took place, and the time, date and participants in the communication. In addition, the fact that an attorney has retained one or more independent agents to aid the attorney in connection with the litigation does not automatically qualify information discovered by the agents for protection by the privilege."

§952. [CONFIDENTIAL COMMUNICATION BETWEEN CLIENT & LAWYER]

As used in this article, "confidential communication between client and lawyer" means information transmitted between a client and his or her lawyer in the course of that relationship and in confidence by a means which, so far as the client is aware, discloses the information to no third persons other than those who are present to further the interest of the client in the consultation or those to whom disclosure is reasonably necessary for the transmission of the information or the accomplishment of the purpose for which the lawyer is consulted, and includes a legal opinion formed and the advice given by the lawyer in the course of that relationship.

History of Evid. C. §952: Added eff. Sept. 17, 1965, oper. Jan. 1, 1967, Stats. 1965, ch. 299, §2. Amended eff. Nov. 8, 1967, Stats. 1967, ch. 650, §3; eff. Jan. 1, 1995, Stats. 1994, ch. 186, §1, ch. 587, §9; eff. Jan. 1, 2003, Stats. 2002, ch. 72, §3.

Official Comment

7 Cal. Law Revision Comm'n Rep. (1965) p. 1164.

The requirement that the communication be made in the course of the lawyer-client relationship and be confidential is in accord with existing law. *See City & County of San Francisco v. Superior Court*, 37 Cal.2d 227, 234-235, 231 P.2d 26, 29-30 (1951).

Confidential communications also include those made to third parties—such as the lawyer's secretary, a physician, or similar expert—for the purpose of transmitting such information to the lawyer because they are "reasonably necessary for the transmission of the information." This codifies existing law. *See, e.g., City & County of San Francisco v. Superior Court, supra* (communication to a physician); *Loftin v. Glaser*, Civil No. 789604 (L.A. Super. Ct., July 23, 1964) (communication to an accountant), as reported in Los Angeles Daily Journal Report Section, August 25, 1964 (memorandum opinion of Judge Philbrick McCoy).

A lawyer at times may desire to have a client reveal information to an expert consultant in order that the lawyer may adequately advise his client. The inclusion of the words "or the accomplishment of the purpose for which the lawyer is consulted" assures that these communications, too, are within the scope of the privilege. This part of the definition may change existing law. *Himmelfarb v. United States*, 175 F.2d 924, 938-939 (9th Cir. 1949), applying California law, held that the presence of an accountant during a lawyer-client consultation destroyed the privilege, but no California case directly in point has been found. Of course, if the expert consultant is acting merely as a conduit for communications from the client to the attorney, the doctrine of *City & County of San Francisco v. Superior Court, supra*, applies and the communication would be privileged under existing law as well as under this section. *See also* Evidence Code §912(d) and the *Comment* thereto.

The words "other than those who are present to further the interest of the client in the consultation" indicate that a communication to a lawyer is nonetheless confidential even though it is made in the presence of another person—such as a spouse, parent, business associate, or joint client—who is present to further the interest of the client in the consultation. These words refer, too, to another person and his attorney who may meet with the client and his attorney in regard to a matter of joint concern. This may change existing law, for the presence of a third person sometimes has been held to destroy the confidential character of the consultation, even where the third person was present because of his concern for the welfare of the client. *See Attorney-Client Privilege in California*, 10 Stan.L.Rev. 297, 308 (1958), and authorities there cited in notes 67-71. *See also Himmelfarb v. United States, supra.*

8 Cal. Law Revision Comm'n Rep. (1967) p. 121.

The express inclusion of "a legal opinion" in the last clause will preclude a possible construction of this section that would leave the attorney's uncommunicated legal opinion—which includes his impressions and conclusions—unprotected by the privilege. Such a construction would virtually destroy the privilege.

31 Cal. Law Revision Comm'n Rep. (2002) p. 258.

Section 952 is amended to delete the last sentence concerning confidentiality of electronic communications, because this rule is generalized in Section 917(b)-(c) applicable to all confidential communication privileges.

ANNOTATIONS

Seahaus La Jolla Owners Ass'n v. Superior Ct. (4th Dist.2014) 224 Cal.App.4th 754, 774. See annotation under Evidence Code §912, *Subdivision (d)*, p. 1296.

Citizens for Ceres v. Superior Ct. (5th Dist.2013) 217 Cal.App.4th 889, 914. See annotation under Evidence Code §912, *Subdivision (d)*, p. 1297.

Fireman's Fund Ins. v. Superior Ct. (2d Dist. 2011) 196 Cal.App.4th 1263, 1273. "[L]egal opinions formed by counsel during representation of the client are protected 'confidential communications,' even if the opinions have not been transmitted to the client. *At 1274:* [T]hird persons to whom the information ... may be conveyed without destroying confidentiality include other attorneys in the law firm representing the client. [A]ttorneys, working together and practicing law in a professional association, share each other's, and their clients', confidential information. Such sharing cannot abrogate the privilege protecting an attorney's legal opinions. [¶] [T]he legal opinions may [also] be shared with a nonattorney agent retained by the attorney to assist with the representation without losing their confidential status. [S]uch an agent would fall into the category of those to whom disclosure is reasonably necessary for the transmission of the information or the accomplishment of the purpose for which the lawyer is consulted." (Internal quotes omitted.) *See*

also ***In re Complex Asbestos Litig.*** (1st Dist.1991) 232 Cal.App.3d 572, 592 n.8.

Holmes v. Petrovich Dev. Co. (3d Dist.2011) 191 Cal.App.4th 1047, 1051-52. "[E]-mails sent by [P] to her attorney regarding possible legal action against [Ds] did not constitute confidential communication between client and lawyer within the meaning of [Evid. C.] §952 ... because [P] used [D's computer] to send the e-mails even though (1) she had been told of the company's policy that its computers were to be used only for company business and that employees were prohibited from using them to send or receive personal e-mail, (2) she had been warned that the company would monitor its computers for compliance with this company policy and thus might inspect all files and messages at any time, and (3) she had been explicitly advised that employees using company computers to create or maintain personal information or messages have no right of privacy with respect to that information or message. [¶] [Under Evid. C. §917(b),] an attorney-client communication does not lose its privileged character for the sole reason that it is communicated by electronic means or because persons involved in the delivery, facilitation, or storage of electronic communication may have access to the content of the communication. However, the e-mails [P] sent via company computer ... were akin to consulting her lawyer in her employer's conference room, in a loud voice, with the door open, so that any reasonable person would expect that their discussion of her complaints about her employer would be overheard by him. ... Consequently, the communications were not privileged." (Internal quotes omitted.)

§952

Aerojet-Gen. Corp. v. Transport Indem. Ins. (1st Dist.1993) 18 Cal.App.4th 996, 1004. "The attorney-client privilege is a shield against deliberate intrusion; it is not an insurer against inadvertent disclosure. Further, not all information that passes privately between attorney and client is entitled to remain confidential in the literal sense. The most obvious example is information that is required to be disclosed in response to discovery, such as the identification of potential witnesses. Consequently, whether the existence and identity of a witness or other nonprivileged information is revealed through formal discovery or inadvertence, the end result is the same: the opposing party is entitled to the use of that witness or information. *At 1006:* Once [an attorney acquires] the information in a manner that was not due to his own fault or wrongdoing, he cannot purge it from his mind. Indeed, his professional obligation demands that he utilize his knowledge about the case on his client's behalf."

Benge v. Superior Ct. (5th Dist.1982) 131 Cal.App.3d 336, 349. "[T]he attorney-client privilege only protects disclosure of communications; it does not protect disclosure of the underlying facts upon which the communications are based." *See also* ***Aerojet-Gen. Corp. v. Transport Indem. Ins.*** (1st Dist.1993) 18 Cal.App.4th 996, 1004.

Insurance Co. of N. Am. v. Superior Ct. (2d Dist.1980) 108 Cal.App.3d 758, 771. "[W]e construe §952 to mean that attorney-client communications in the presence of, or disclosed to, clerks, secretaries, interpreters, physicians, spouses, parents, business associates, or joint clients, when made to further the interest of the client or when reasonably necessary for transmission or accomplishment of the purpose of the consultation, remain privileged."

§953. [HOLDER OF THE PRIVILEGE]

As used in this article, "holder of the privilege" means:

(a) The client, if the client has no guardian or conservator.

(b) A guardian or conservator of the client, if the client has a guardian or conservator.

(c) The personal representative of the client if the client is dead, including a personal representative appointed pursuant to Section 12252 of the Probate Code.

(d) A successor, assign, trustee in dissolution, or any similar representative of a firm, association, organization, partnership, business trust, corporation, or public entity that is no longer in existence.

History of Evid. C. §953: Added eff. Sept. 17, 1965, oper. Jan. 1, 1967, Stats. 1965, ch. 299, §2. Amended eff. Jan. 1, 2010, Stats. 2009, ch. 8, §1.

Official Comment

7 Cal. Law Revision Comm'n Rep. (1965) p. 1166.

Under subdivisions (a) and (b), the guardian of a client is the holder of the privilege if the client has a guardian, and the client becomes the holder of the privilege when he no longer has a guardian. For example, if an underage client or his guardian consults a lawyer, the guardian is the holder of the privilege under subdivision (b) until the guardianship is terminated; thereafter, the client himself is the holder of the privilege. The present California law is uncertain. The statutes do not deal with the problem, and no appellate decision has discussed it.

Under subdivision (c), the personal representative of a client is the holder of the privilege when the client is dead. He may either claim or waive the privilege on behalf of the deceased client. This may be a change in California law. Under existing law, it seems probable that the privilege survives the death of the client and that no one can waive it after the client's death. *See Collette v. Sarrasin*, 184 Cal. 283, 289, 193 Pac. 571, 573 (1920). Hence, the privilege apparently is recognized even when it would be clearly to the interest of the estate of the deceased client to waive it. Under Section 953, however, the personal representative of a deceased client may waive the privilege. The purpose underlying the privilege—to provide a client with the assurance of confidentiality—does not require the recognition of the privilege when to do so is detrimental to his interest or to the interests of his estate.

38 Cal. Law Revision Comm'n Rep. (2009), p. 199.

Subdivision (a) of Section 953 is amended to revise a gender reference.

Subdivision (c) is amended to make clear that a personal representative holds the decedent's lawyer-client privilege at any time while the personal representative has duties as a personal representative, including, without limitation, during any subsequent estate administration. See, e.g., Prob. Code §12252 (appointment of personal representative for subsequent administration of estate); see also Prob. Code §58 (personal representative). The personal representative holds the privilege during any action asserted, commenced, continued, or defended by a personal representative. See Code Civ. Proc. §§377.30 (commencement of surviving action by personal representative), 377.31 (continuation of surviving action by personal representative), 377.40 (defense by personal representative of surviving action), 377.60 (assertion by personal representative of wrongful death action); Prob. Code §§9000-9399 (creditor claims against estate).

ANNOTATIONS

HLC Props., Ltd. v. Superior Ct. (2005) 35 Cal.4th 54, 65-66. "[T]he attorney-client privilege of a natural person transfers to the personal representative after the client's death, and the privilege thereafter terminates when there is no personal representative to claim it."

De Los Santos v. Superior Ct. (1980) 27 Cal.3d 677, 682. "In her capacity as guardian ad litem [mother] is the holder of the privilege, and she was authorized to assert it on [child's] behalf. Thus, she was entitled to refuse to answer the questions put to her by [Ds] if the information requested was subject to the privilege ... and the privilege was not waived. [¶] Since [child's] statements to his mother were made in response to questions she asked at the request of his attorney either for the purpose of preparing [child's] answers to the interrogatories or to assist the attorney in preparation for trial, the statements were clearly given in the course of a lawyer-client relationship. Nor can it be doubted that they were intended to be confidential. Under [Evid. C.] §917 ... there is a presumption that a communication between client and lawyer is in confidence, and the opponent of the claim of privilege has the burden of proving otherwise."

Chubb & Son v. Superior Ct. (1st Dist.2014) 228 Cal.App.4th 1094, 1104 n.4. D-insurance company "does not explain why it can refuse to comply with its discovery obligations based on the attorney-client privilege, when [D-insurance company] does not purport to be either the attorney or the client. On the other hand, [P] does not contend that [D-insurance company] is unable to assert the privilege, and it appears the parties proceeded upon the assumption that there is some duty—or an identity of interest between [D-insurance company] and [D-law firm], or between [D-insurance company] and its insureds—such that [D-insurance company] may or must assert the privilege on the nonparty clients' behalf. [T]he fact is that [D-insurance company] *has* invoked the privilege, thus placing at issue the narrow question before us: whether allegedly privileged or confidential material may be disclosed by the parties to their respective attorneys."

Michelle K. v. Superior Ct. (4th Dist.2013) 221 Cal.App.4th 409, 449. See annotation under Evidence Code §951, p. 1304.

Melendrez v. Superior Ct. (2d Dist.2013) 215 Cal.App.4th 1343, 1353-54. "[T]he power to assert and waive the attorney-client privilege held by a corporation belongs to corporate management and is normally exercised by the corporation's officers and directors. In considering the holder of the privilege of a corporation no longer in operation, it is important to recognize the distinction between a *dissolved* corporation, and one *no longer in existence*. If the corporation is dissolved, it continues to exist for the limited purposes of winding up. 'Because it continues in existence, ... it would appear the persons authorized to act on the dissolved corporation's behalf during the windup process—its ongoing management personnel—should be able to assert the privilege, at least until all matters involving the company have been fully resolved and no further proceedings are contemplated.' However, if the corporation 'is no longer in existence,' the privilege is held by a 'successor, assign, trustee in dissolution, or any similar representative' of the corporate entity no longer in existence."

Venture Law Grp. v. Superior Ct. (6th Dist.2004) 118 Cal.App.4th 96, 103. "After a merger, the attorney-client privilege of the corporation no longer in existence belongs to the successor corporation. This is because §953, subdivision (d), provides that the successor of a disappeared corporation becomes the holder of the attorney-client privilege. The privilege may be claimed by '[t]he person who was the lawyer at the time of the confidential communication, but such person may not claim the privilege if there is no holder of the privilege in existence or if [s]he is otherwise instructed by a person authorized to permit disclosure.' Thus, '[a]s long as there is a holder of the privilege in existence at the time disclosure is sought, the attorney

has the duty to exercise the privilege unless the holder of the privilege instructs [her] not to do so.'"

State Comp. Ins. Fund v. Superior Ct. (2d Dist.2001) 91 Cal.App.4th 1080, 1087. "A 'client' is a person who, directly or through an authorized representative, consults a lawyer for the purpose of retaining the lawyer or securing legal service or advice from him in his professional capacity. Because 'person' includes *corporations* and other *associations* ..., such unincorporated organizations as labor unions, social clubs, and fraternal societies have a lawyer-client privilege when the organization (rather than its individual members) is the client." (Internal quotes omitted.) *See also* ***Smith v. Laguna Sur Villas Cmty. Ass'n*** (4th Dist.2000) 79 Cal.App.4th 639, 643-44.

§954. [LAWYER-CLIENT PRIVILEGE]

Subject to Section 912 and except as otherwise provided in this article, the client, whether or not a party, has a privilege to refuse to disclose, and to prevent another from disclosing, a confidential communication between client and lawyer if the privilege is claimed by:

(a) [Holder.] The holder of the privilege;

(b) [Authorized person.] A person who is authorized to claim the privilege by the holder of the privilege; or

(c) [Lawyer.] The person who was the lawyer at the time of the confidential communication, but such person may not claim the privilege if there is no holder of the privilege in existence or if he is otherwise instructed by a person authorized to permit disclosure. The relationship of attorney and client shall exist between a law corporation as defined in Article 10 (commencing with Section 6160) of Chapter 4 of Division 3 of the Business and Professions Code and the persons to whom it renders professional services, as well as between such persons and members of the State Bar employed by such corporation to render services to such persons. The word "persons" as used in this subdivision includes partnerships, corporations, limited liability companies, associations and other groups and entities.

History of Evid. C. §954: Added eff. Sept. 17, 1965, oper. Jan. 1, 1967, Stats. 1965, ch. 299, §2. Amended eff. Nov. 13, 1968, Stats. 1968, ch. 1375, §2; eff. Jan. 1, 1995, Stats. 1994, ch. 1010, §104.

See also CCP §2018.030.

Official Comment

7 Cal. Law Revision Comm'n Rep. (1965) p. 1166.

Section 954 is the basic statement of the lawyer-client privilege. Exceptions to this privilege are stated in Sections 956-962.

Persons entitled to claim the privilege. The persons entitled to claim the privilege are specified in subdivisions (a), (b), and (c). *See* Evidence Code §953 for the definition of "holder of the privilege."

Eavesdroppers. Under Section 954, the lawyer-client privilege can be asserted to prevent *anyone* from testifying to a confidential communication. Thus, clients are protected against the risk of disclosure by eavesdroppers and other wrongful interceptors of confidential communications between lawyer and client. Probably no such protection was provided prior to the enactment of Penal Code Sections 653i and 653j. *See People v. Castiel*, 153 Cal.App.2d 653, 315 P.2d 79 (1957). *See also Attorney-Client Privilege in California*, 10 Stan.L.Rev. 297, 310-312 (1958), and cases there cited in note 84.

Penal Code Section 653j makes evidence obtained by *electronic* eavesdropping or recording in violation of the section inadmissible in "any judicial, administrative, legislative, or other proceeding." The section also provides a criminal penalty and contains definitions and exceptions. Penal Code Section 653i makes it a felony to eavesdrop by an electronic or other device upon a conversation between a person in custody of a public officer or on public property and that person's lawyer, religious advisor, or physician.

Section 954 is consistent with Penal Code Sections 653i and 653j but provides broader protection, for it protects against disclosure of confidential communications by anyone who obtained knowledge of the communication without the client's consent. *See also* Evidence Code §912 (when disclosure with client's consent constitutes a waiver of the privilege). The use of the privilege to prevent testimony by eavesdroppers and those to whom the communication was wrongfully disclosed does not, however, affect the rule that the making of the communication under circumstances where others could easily overhear it is evidence that the client did not intend the communication to be confidential. *See Sharon v. Sharon*, 79 Cal. 633, 677, 22 Pac. 26, 39 (1889).

Termination of privilege. The privilege may be claimed by a person listed in Section 954, or the privileged information excluded by the presiding officer under Section 916, only if there is a holder of the privilege in existence. Hence, the privilege ceases to exist when the client's estate is finally distributed and his personal representative is discharged. This is apparently a change in California law. Under the existing law, it seems likely that the privilege continues to exist indefinitely after the client's death and that no one has authority to waive the privilege. *See Collette v. Sarrasin*, 184 Cal. 283, 193 Pac. 571 (1920). *See generally Paley v. Superior Court*, 137 Cal.App.2d 450, 290 P.2d 617 (1955), and discussion of the analogous situation in connection with the physician-patient privilege in *Tentative Recommendation and a Study Relating to the Uniform Rules of Evidence (Article V. Privileges)*, 6 Cal. Law Revision Comm'n, Rep., Rec. & Studies 201, 408-410 (1964). Although there is good reason for maintaining the privilege while the estate is being administered—particularly if the estate is involved in litigation—there is little reason to preserve secrecy at the expense of excluding relevant evidence after the estate is wound up and the representative is discharged.

ANNOTATIONS

Costco Wholesale Corp. v. Superior Ct. (2009) 47 Cal.4th 725, 733. "The party claiming the privilege has the burden of establishing the preliminary facts necessary to support its exercise, i.e., a communication made in the course of an attorney-client relationship. [¶] That [attorney's] opinion letter may not have been prepared in anticipation of litigation is of no consequence; the privilege attaches to any legal advice given in the course of an attorney-client relationship. And it is settled that a corporate client ... can claim the privilege. *At 736:* [W]hen the communication is a confidential one between attorney and client, the entire communication, including its recitation or summary of factual material, is privileged. [I]f ... the factual material referred to or summarized in [attorney's] opinion letter is itself unprivileged it may be discoverable by some

§953

other means, but plaintiffs may not obtain it by compelling disclosure of the letter."

Wells Fargo Bank v. Superior Ct. (2000) 22 Cal.4th 201, 206. "[T]here is no authority in California law for requiring a trustee to produce communications protected by the attorney-client privilege, regardless of their subject matter. [¶] [Beneficiaries] contend [trustee] must produce privileged communications to fulfill its statutory and common law duties as a trustee to report to the beneficiaries about the trust and its administration. [Trustee's] duties ..., [beneficiaries] argue, take precedence over its privilege as the client of an attorney. The argument lacks merit." *See also* ***Moeller v. Superior Ct.*** (1997) 16 Cal.4th 1124, 1139 (power to assert privilege passes from predecessor trustee to successor upon successor's assumption of office).

Mitchell v. Superior Ct. (1984) 37 Cal.3d 591, 600. "In California the privilege has been held to encompass not only oral or written statements, but additionally actions, signs, or other means of communicating information. Furthermore, the privilege covers the transmission of documents which are available to the public, and not merely information in the sole possession of the attorney or client. In this regard, it is the actual fact of the transmission which merits protection, since discovery of the transmission of specific public documents might very well reveal the transmitter's intended strategy. While it is perhaps somewhat of a hyperbole to refer to the attorney-client privilege as 'sacred,' it is clearly one which our judicial system has carefully safeguarded with only a few specific exceptions."

Edwards Wildman Palmer LLP v. Superior Ct. (2d Dist.2014) 231 Cal.App.4th 1214, 1227. "[A]n attorney who consults another attorney in the same firm for the purpose of securing confidential legal advice may establish an attorney-client relationship. *At 1228:* [real party in interest] urges that a lawyer who counsels another lawyer in the same firm, regarding a current client of the firm, 'becomes a lawyer with an impermissible conflict of interest,' and when such a conflict exists, the attorney-client privilege must be subordinated to the firm's ethical duties. *At 1232:* [However, there is no] current client exception to the attorney-client privilege.... *At 1234-35:* [K]nowledge that is not otherwise privileged does not become so merely by being transmitted to an attorney. [¶] [T]he privilege will attach only when a genuine attorney-client relationship exists. ***RFF*** [***Family Prtshp. v. Burns & Levinson, LLP*** (Mass.2013) 991 N.E.2d 1066] held that four prerequisites must be present in order for the attorney-client privilege to apply to confidential communications between law firm attorneys and the firm's in-house counsel concerning a malpractice claim: (1) the law firm must have designated, either formally or informally, an attorney or attorneys within the firm to represent the firm as in-house or ethics counsel, so that there is an attorney-client relationship between in-house counsel and the firm when the consultation occurs; (2) where a current outside client has threatened litigation against the law firm, the in-house counsel must not have performed any work on the particular client matter or a substantially related matter; (3) the time spent on the in-house communications may not have been billed to the client; and (4) the communications must have been made in confidence and kept confidential. We believe these factors provide a helpful template for a court in determining whether a genuine attorney-client relationship existed between in-house counsel and a law firm's attorneys or the firm itself. [W]hile the ***RFF*** factors are not prerequisites to establishment of an attorney-client relationship under California law, they are among the factors that a trial court may analyze in determining whether an actual attorney-client relationship existed."

Chubb & Son v. Superior Ct. (1st Dist.2014) 228 Cal.App.4th 1094, 1108. "[T]he trial court (1) permitted [P, former in-house counsel for D,] and [D-insurance company] to disclose to their own attorneys documents that are subject to the attorney-client privilege or contain the confidential information of [D-insurance company's] insureds, for the purpose of consulting with their attorneys on how to proceed in the [wrongful-discharge] case.... *At 1109-10:* [D-insurance company] argues that the trial court's order created an implied exception to the attorney-client privilege, which is impermissible because only statutory exceptions to the privilege are allowed. [¶] [D-insurance company] misunderstands. ... The trial court in this case merely allowed arguably privileged information to be disclosed to the parties' own attorneys, themselves bound by ethical rules and a court order prohibiting further disclosure, for the limited purposes of ascertaining whether the information *is* privileged, invoking the privilege, and deciding how to litigate the case. [¶] [T]he prohibition against disclosure of privileged information un-

der ... §954 does not preclude a court-ordered disclosure of allegedly privileged information to a party's own attorney for purposes of preparing a wrongful discharge case or litigating the privilege, where further disclosure is expressly forbidden. While [D-insurance company] cites numerous cases for the proposition that the privilege is subject only to statutory exceptions, none of them precludes the disclosure of confidences *to the attorney for a party who already rightfully possesses them.*"

St. Croix v. Superior Ct. (1st Dist.2014) 228 Cal.App.4th 434, 443. "The [city] charter provisions, by establishing the office and responsibilities of the city attorney, establish an attorney-client relationship between the city attorney on the one hand, and City and its officers and agencies ... on the other. [S]tate law establishes that the privilege's protection of the confidentiality of written attorney-client communications is fundamental to the attorney-client relationship, in the public sector as well as in the private sector, and is vital to the effective administration of justice. We therefore conclude the charter incorporates the state law attorney-client privilege for written communications between the city attorney and his or her clients."

Bank of Am. v. Superior Ct. (4th Dist.2013) 212 Cal.App.4th 1076, 1096-97. "[D] argues [insurer] waived any right to object to production of privileged documents and information because it did not bring its own motion to quash the subpoenas or serve objections to them. [¶] We have concluded a tripartite attorney-client relationship exists among [insurer, insured, and law firm]; they are 'a unitary whole' and share a 'common purpose' lasting 'during the pendency of the claim or litigation.' As a consequence, [insured] and [insurer] are joint clients of [law firm]. 'Each of the joint clients holds the privilege protecting their confidential communications with the attorney; one client may not waive the privilege without the consent of the other.' Since [insured], one joint holder of the attorney-client privilege, did move to quash the subpoenas and serve objections to the requests for production, it was unnecessary that [insurer] do the same to prevent disclosure of privileged communications and attorney work product."

La Jolla Cove Motel & Hotel Apts., Inc. v. Superior Ct. (4th Dist.2004) 121 Cal.App.4th 773, 791. "Once a party claims the attorney-client privilege, the communication sought to be suppressed is presumed confidential. A party opposing the privilege has the burden of proof to show the communication is one not made in confidence. However, the party claiming privilege has the burden to show that the communication sought to be suppressed falls within the terms of the statute. It is also established that a communication which was not privileged to begin with may not be made so by subsequent delivery to the attorney." *See also* ***State Farm Fire & Cas. Co. v. Superior Ct.*** (2d Dist.1997) 54 Cal.App.4th 625, 639.

2,022 Ranch, L.L.C. v. Superior Ct. (4th Dist.2003) 113 Cal.App.4th 1377, 1390-91, *disapproved on other grounds*, ***Costco Wholesale Corp. v. Superior Ct.*** (2009) 47 Cal.4th 725. "In certain instances it is difficult to determine if the attorney-client privilege ... attaches to a communication, particularly where there may be more than one purpose for that communication. ... If it appears that the communication is to serve a dual purpose, one for transmittal to an attorney in the course of professional employment and one not related to that purpose, the question presented to the trial court is as to *which purpose predominates*. This 'dominant purpose' test not only looks to the dominant purpose for the communication, but also to the dominant purpose of the attorney's *work*. Thus, the attorney-client privilege would not apply without qualification where the attorney was merely acting as a negotiator for the client ..., or merely gave business advice ..., or was merely acting as a trustee for the client...." (Internal quotes omitted.)

STI Outdoor LLC v. Superior Ct. (2d Dist.2001) 91 Cal.App.4th 334, 340-41. "We are not persuaded that the attorney-client privilege is limited to litigation-related communications. Evidence Code §§912 and 952 do not use the terms 'litigation' or 'legal communications' in their description of privileged disclosures, but specifically refer to 'the accomplishment of the purpose' for which the lawyer was consulted. Attorneys are consulted for a myriad of reasons besides litigation."

Solin v. O'Melveny & Myers, LLP (2d Dist.2001) 89 Cal.App.4th 451, 457-58. "'[T]he privilege is absolute and disclosure may not be ordered, without regard to relevance, necessity or any particular circumstances peculiar to the case.' [¶] [T]here can be no balancing of the attorney-client privilege against the right to prosecute a lawsuit to redress a legal wrong. [U]nless a statutory provision removes the protection afforded by the attorney-client privilege to confidential communi-

cations between attorney and client, an attorney plaintiff may not prosecute a lawsuit if in doing so client confidences would be disclosed." *See also* ***Chubb & Son v. Superior Ct.*** (1st Dist.2014) 228 Cal.App.4th 1094, 1103.

Titmas v. Superior Ct. (4th Dist.2001) 87 Cal.App.4th 738, 740. "[W]e hold that when there is a prima facie claim of attorney-client privilege, the trial judge must accord a full hearing, *with* oral argument, before ordering the revelation of client confidences to the other side and, in effect, compelling attorney testimony against a client."

Hooser v. Superior Ct. (4th Dist.2000) 84 Cal.App.4th 997, 1003. "The attorney-client privilege applies to all confidential communications made to an attorney during preliminary discussions of the prospective professional employment, as well as those made during the course of any professional relationship resulting from such discussions. *At 1005:* Generally, the identity of an attorney's client is not considered within the protection of the attorney-client privilege. There is a recognized exception to this rule, however, where known facts concerning an attorney's representation of an anonymous client are such that the disclosure of the client's identity would implicate the client in unlawful activities, thus exposing the client to potential investigative action or criminal or civil liability. [¶] Another recognized exception arises where known facts regarding an attorney's representation are such that the disclosure of the client's identity would betray personal, confidential information regarding the client. [¶] [W]e conclude that the identity of an attorney's clients is sensitive personal information that implicates the clients' rights of privacy. *At 1006:* Upon such public disclosure of the attorney-client relationship, the client's privacy concerns regarding the fact of the consultation evaporate and there is no longer a basis for preventing the attorney from identifying the client. However, until such a public disclosure occurs, the client's identity is itself a matter of privacy, subject to the protection against involuntary disclosure through compelled discovery against the attorney." *See also* ***Tien v. Superior Ct.*** (2d Dist.2006) 139 Cal.App.4th 528, 537.

McDermott, Will & Emery v. Superior Ct. (2d Dist.2000) 83 Cal.App.4th 378, 383-84. "Generally, the filing of a legal malpractice action against one's attorney results in a waiver of the [attorney-client] privilege, thus enabling the attorney to disclose, to the extent necessary to defend against the action, information otherwise protected by the … privilege. However, because a derivative action does not result in the corporation's waiver of the privilege, such a lawsuit against the corporation's outside counsel has the dangerous potential for robbing the attorney defendant of the only means he or she may have to mount any meaningful defense. It effectively places the defendant attorney in the untenable position of having to 'preserve the attorney client privilege (the client having done nothing to waive the privilege) while trying to show that his representation of the client was not negligent.' *At 385:* California courts have refused to carve out a shareholder exception to the attorney-client privilege, even in a derivative action. We simply cannot conceive how an attorney is to mount a defense in a shareholder derivative action alleging a breach of duty to the corporate client, where, by the very nature of such an action, the attorney is foreclosed, in the absence of any waiver by the corporation, from disclosing the very communications which are alleged to constitute a breach of that duty. Thus, while we decline to view a shareholder derivative action in the same vein as an assignment, the rationale used to prohibit all assignments of legal malpractice actions, on the ground attorneys would be unable to defend such actions in the absence of a waiver of the privilege by their own client, applies with equal force here." *See also* ***Titmas v. Superior Ct.*** (4th Dist.2001) 87 Cal.App.4th 738, 741 n.1.

Mylan Labs. v. Soon-Shiong (2d Dist.1999) 76 Cal.App.4th 71, 80. "Clearly, the Evidence Code did not anticipate that the client would have to intervene and become a party as a prerequisite to asserting [the attorney-client] privilege. On the contrary, it expressly provided that the privilege could be claimed by a non-party as long as the non-party asserting the privilege was the client or other authorized person. [¶] We find that the holder of the attorney-client privilege has 'standing' to assert the privilege in a proceeding to prevent disclosure simply by virtue of the fact that they are the holder of the privilege, and that there is no need to intervene to become an actual party to the lawsuit in order to be able to assert the privilege."

National Football League Props., Inc. v. Superior Ct. (6th Dist.1998) 65 Cal.App.4th 100, 107-08. "[T]here is no shareholder exception to the corporate attorney-client privilege in California. Instead, the general rule has been stated as follows: 'An attorney repre-

senting a corporation does not become the representative of its stockholders merely because the attorney's actions on behalf of the corporation also benefit the stockholders; as attorney for the corporation, counsel's first duty is to the corporation.' [¶] Thus, '[e]ven where counsel for a closely held corporation treats the interests of majority shareholders and the corporation interchangeably, it is the attorney-client relationship with the corporation that is paramount for purposes of upholding the attorney-client privilege against a minority shareholder's challenge.' Decisions holding that corporation attorneys stand in a fiduciary relationship to individual shareholders have relied upon a finding that the attorneys stood in a confidential relationship with respect to both the corporation and the individual shareholders, and not upon a rationale for piercing the corporate attorney-client privilege. [¶] In addition to showing an independent attorney-client relationship with corporate counsel, a shareholder may also argue, as a basis for inspecting privileged corporation documents, the [Evid. C.] §956 crime-fraud exception. Under ... §956, the attorney-client privilege is nullified if the attorney's services were sought to aid anyone in the commission of a crime or fraud."

§955. [DUTY TO CLAIM PRIVILEGE]

The lawyer who received or made a communication subject to the privilege under this article shall claim the privilege whenever he is present when the communication is sought to be disclosed and is authorized to claim the privilege under subdivision (c) of Section 954.

History of Evid. C. §955: Added eff. Sept. 17, 1965, oper. Jan. 1, 1967, Stats. 1965, ch. 299, §2.

Official Comment

7 Cal. Law Revision Comm'n Rep. (1965) p. 1168.

The obligation of the lawyer to claim the privilege on behalf of the client, unless otherwise instructed by a person authorized to permit disclosure, is consistent with Section 6068(e) of the Business and Professions Code.

§956. [NO PRIVILEGE: FURTHERANCE OF CRIME OR FRAUD]

There is no privilege under this article if the services of the lawyer were sought or obtained to enable or aid anyone to commit or plan to commit a crime or a fraud.

History of Evid. C. §956: Added eff. Sept. 17, 1965, oper. Jan. 1, 1967, Stats. 1965, ch. 299, §2.

Official Comment

7 Cal. Law Revision Comm'n Rep. (1965) p. 1168.

California now recognizes this exception. *Abbott v. Superior Court*, 78 Cal.App.2d 19, 177 P.2d 317 (1947). *Cf. Nowell v. Superior Court*, 223 Cal.App.2d 652, 36 Cal.Rptr. 21 (1963).

§956.5. [NO PRIVILEGE: PREVENTION OF SUBSTANTIAL HARM]

There is no privilege under this article if the lawyer reasonably believes that disclosure of any confidential communication relating to representation of a client is necessary to prevent a criminal act that the lawyer reasonably believes is likely to result in the death of, or substantial bodily harm to, an individual.

History of Evid. C. §956.5: Added eff. Jan. 1, 1994, Stats. 1993, ch. 982, §8. Amended eff. Jan. 1, 2004, oper. July 1, 2004, Stats. 2003, ch. 765, §2; eff. Jan. 1, 2005, Stats. 2004, ch. 183, §94.

See also Bus. & Prof. C. §6068(e)(2).

§957. [NO PRIVILEGE: CLAIMANTS THROUGH SAME DECEASED CLIENT]

There is no privilege under this article as to a communication relevant to an issue between parties all of whom claim through a deceased client, regardless of whether the claims are by testate or intestate succession, nonprobate transfer, or inter vivos transaction.

History of Evid. C. §957: Added eff. Sept. 17, 1965, oper. Jan. 1, 1967, Stats. 1965, ch. 299, §2. Amended eff. Jan. 1, 2010, Stats. 2009, ch. 8, §2.

Official Comment

7 Cal. Law Revision Comm'n Rep. (1965) p. 1168.

The lawyer-client privilege does not apply to a communication relevant to an issue between parties all of whom claim through a deceased client. Under existing law, all must claim through the client by testate or intestate succession in order for this exception to be applicable; a claim by inter vivos transaction apparently is not within the exception. *Paley v. Superior Court*, 137 Cal.App.2d 450, 457-460, 290 P.2d 617, 621-623 (1955). Section 957 extends this exception to include inter vivos transactions.

The traditional exception for litigation between claimants by testate or intestate succession is based on the theory that claimants in privity with the estate claim *through* the client, not adversely, and the deceased client presumably would want his communications disclosed in litigation between such claimants so that his desires in regard to the disposition of his estate might be correctly ascertained and carried out. This rationale is equally applicable where one or more of the parties is claiming by inter vivos transaction as, for example, in an action between a party who claims under a deed (executed by a client in full possession of his faculties) and a party who claims under a will executed while the client's mental stability was dubious. See the discussion in *Tentative Recommendation and a Study Relating to the Uniform Rules of Evidence (Article V. Privileges)*, 6 Cal. Law Revision Comm'n, Rep., Rec. & Studies 201, 392-396 (1964).

38 Cal. Law Revision Comm'n Rep. (2009), p. 200.

Section 957 is amended to clarify that the exception is applicable to parties who all claim through a deceased client, including a person who claims through a nonprobate transfer.

ANNOTATIONS

Fletcher v. Superior Ct. (1st Dist.1996) 44 Cal.App.4th 773, 779. "It is evident from [the Law Revision Commission's] commentary that §957 was meant to refer only to communications between the decedent and the decedent's attorney. [¶] Section 957 does not appear to have been construed in any published California case, but virtually identical language in a Nevada statute was discussed in ***Clark v. Second Judicial***

Dist. Ct. [(Nev. 1985) 692 P.2d 512] in a manner which supports our interpretation of §957. The ***Clark*** opinion observed that an exception to the application of the *privilege on behalf of a deceased client* has long been recognized when the dispute is between various parties claiming 'through' or 'under' the client, as opposed to a dispute between the estate and a stranger. In ***Glover v. Patten*** [(1897) 165 U.S. 394], the U.S. Supreme Court held that in a suit between devisees under a will, *statements made by the deceased to counsel* respecting the execution of the will, or other similar document, are not privileged. While such communications might be privileged, if offered by third persons to establish claims against an estate, they are not within the reason of the rule requiring their exclusion, when the contest is between the heirs or next of kin. This analysis presupposes that the privilege to which the exception applies is only for communications between the decedent and the decedent's attorney." (Internal quotes omitted.)

§958. [NO PRIVILEGE: BREACH OF DUTY BY LAWYER OR CLIENT]

There is no privilege under this article as to a communication relevant to an issue of breach, by the lawyer or by the client, of a duty arising out of the lawyer-client relationship.

History of Evid. C. §958: Added eff. Sept. 17, 1965, oper. Jan. 1, 1967, Stats. 1965, ch. 299, §2.

Official Comment

7 Cal. Law Revision Comm'n Rep. (1965) p. 1169.

This exception has not been recognized by a holding in any California case, although dicta in several opinions indicate that it would be recognized if the question were presented in a proper case. *People v. Tucker*, 61 Cal.2d 828, 40 Cal.Rptr. 609, 395 P.2d 449 (1964); *Henshall v. Coburn*, 177 Cal. 50, 169 Pac. 1014 (1917); *Pacific Tel. & Tel. Co. v. Fink*, 141 Cal.App.2d 332, 335, 296 P.2d 843, 845 (1956); *Fleschler v. Strauss*, 15 Cal.App.2d 735, 60 P.2d 193 (1936). *See generally* Witkin, *California Evidence* §419 (1958).

It would be unjust to permit a client either to accuse his attorney of a breach of duty and to invoke the privilege to prevent the attorney from bringing forth evidence in defense of the charge or to refuse to pay his attorney's fee and invoke the privilege to defeat the attorney's claim. Thus, for example, if the defendant in a criminal action claims that his lawyer did not provide him with an adequate defense, communications between the lawyer and client relevant to that issue are not privileged. *See People v. Tucker*, 61 Cal.2d 828, 40 Cal.Rptr. 609, 395 P.2d 449 (1964). The duty involved must, of course, be one arising out of the lawyer-client relationship, *e.g.*, the duty of the lawyer to exercise reasonable diligence on behalf of his client, the duty of the lawyer to care faithfully and account for his client's property, or the client's duty to pay for the lawyer's services.

ANNOTATIONS

Brockway v. State Bar (1991) 53 Cal.3d 51, 63-64. Section 958 "is not a general client-litigant exception allowing disclosure of *any* privileged communication simply because it is raised in litigation. [S]ection 958 only authorizes disclosure of relevant communications between a client ... and an attorney charged with professional wrongdoing.... This approach gives the attorney a meaningful opportunity to defend against the charge, but does not deter the client from confiding in other attorneys ... about the dispute."

§959. [NO PRIVILEGE: LAWYER AS ATTESTING WITNESS]

There is no privilege under this article as to a communication relevant to an issue concerning the intention or competence of a client executing an attested document of which the lawyer is an attesting witness, or concerning the execution or attestation of such a document.

History of Evid. C. §959: Added eff. Sept. 17, 1965, oper. Jan. 1, 1967, Stats. 1965, ch. 299, §2.

Official Comment

7 Cal. Law Revision Comm'n Rep. (1965) p. 1170.

This exception relates to the type of communication about which an attesting witness would testify. The mere fact that an attorney acts as an attesting witness should not destroy the lawyer-client privilege as to all statements made concerning the document attested; but the privilege should not prohibit the lawyer from performing the duties expected of an attesting witness. Under existing law, the attesting witness exception is broader, having been used as a device to obtain information which the lawyer who is an attesting witness received in his capacity as a lawyer rather than as an attesting witness. *See In re Mullin*, 110 Cal. 252, 42 Pac. 645 (1895).

ANNOTATIONS

Estate of Kime (2d Dist.1983) 144 Cal.App.3d 246, 257. "[A] lawyer who acts as an attesting witness can divulge only information received in his capacity as an attesting witness and not in his capacity as a lawyer."

§960. [NO PRIVILEGE: DECEASED CLIENT'S INTENTION RELATING TO PROPERTY INTEREST]

There is no privilege under this article as to a communication relevant to an issue concerning the intention of a client, now deceased, with respect to a deed of conveyance, will, or other writing, executed by the client, purporting to affect an interest in property.

History of Evid. C. §960: Added eff. Sept. 17, 1965, oper. Jan. 1, 1967, Stats. 1965, ch. 299, §2.

Official Comment

7 Cal. Law Revision Comm'n Rep. (1965) p. 1170.

Although the attesting witness exception stated in Section 959 is limited to information of the kind to which one would expect an attesting witness to testify, there is merit to having an exception that applies to all dispositive instruments. A client ordinarily would desire his lawyer to communicate his true intention with regard to a dispositive instrument if the instrument itself leaves the matter in doubt and the client is deceased. Likewise, the client ordinarily would desire his attorney to testify to communications relevant to the validity of such instruments after the client dies. Accordingly, two additional exceptions—Sections 960 and 961—are provided for this purpose. These exceptions have been recognized by the California decisions only in cases where the lawyer is an attesting witness. *See* the *Comment* to Evidence Code §959.

§961. [NO PRIVILEGE: VALIDITY OF DECEASED CLIENT'S WRITING AFFECTING PROPERTY INTEREST]

There is no privilege under this article as to a communication relevant to an issue concerning the validity of a deed of conveyance, will, or other writing, executed by a client, now deceased, purporting to affect an interest in property.

History of Evid. C. §961: Added eff. Sept. 17, 1965, oper. Jan. 1, 1967, Stats. 1965, ch. 299, §2.

Official Comment

7 Cal. Law Revision Comm'n Rep. (1965) p. 1171.

See the *Comment* to Section 960.

§962. [NO PRIVILEGE: JOINT CLIENTS]

Where two or more clients have retained or consulted a lawyer upon a matter of common interest, none of them, nor the successor in interest of any of them, may claim a privilege under this article as to a communication made in the course of that relationship when such communication is offered in a civil proceeding between one of such clients (or his successor in interest) and another of such clients (or his successor in interest).

History of Evid. C. §962: Added eff. Sept. 17, 1965, oper. Jan. 1, 1967, Stats. 1965, ch. 299, §2.

Official Comment

7 Cal. Law Revision Comm'n Rep. (1965) p. 1171.

This section states existing law. *Clyne v. Brock*, 82 Cal.App.2d 958, 965, 188 P.2d 263, 267 (1947); *Croce v. Superior Court*, 21 Cal.App.2d 18, 68 P.2d 369 (1937). *See also Harris v. Harris*, 136 Cal. 379, 69 Pac. 23 (1902).

§961

ANNOTATIONS

Fiduciary Trust Int'l v. Superior Ct. (2d Dist. 2013) 218 Cal.App.4th 465, 482. "The trustees … argue that the [Rules of Prof. Conduct, rule 3-310(E)] prohibition on successive, adverse representations does not apply when the attorney jointly represented the parties in the prior matter because, under [Evid. C.] §962, any attorney-client communications made during the course of that joint representation are not privileged as between the joint clients. … The trustees contend that because the bar on successive, adverse representations is predicated on the duty of confidentiality, it does not apply where the prior representation was governed by … §962. *At 485:* [A]n attorney is forbidden to do either of two things after severing his relationship with a former client. He may not do anything which will injuriously affect his former client in any matter in which he formerly represented him nor may he at any time use against his former client knowledge or information acquired by virtue of the previous relationship. The prohibition is in the disjunctive. [¶] In this case, [law firm's] conduct falls squarely within the prohibition. Although the firm previously represented both [wife] and [husband] in the estate planning matters, it is now asserting (on behalf of [husband's] representatives) that the documents it prepared during the joint representation should be interpreted in a manner that would substantially reduce the value of [wife's] estate (or her trust), thereby harming her interests. *At 486:* [W]e do not agree that matters of disqualification should be determined solely by reference to evidentiary rules." (Internal quotes omitted.)

Roush v. Seagate Tech. (6th Dist.2007) 150 Cal.App.4th 210, 223. "There is no waiver in spite of communication to an additional person if that additional person is a joint client. The statutes do not directly define the phrase 'joint client.' It is indirectly defined in §962, which describes an exception to the attorney-client privilege…. [¶] Case law has established that joint clients are two or more persons who have retained one attorney on a matter of common interest to all of them, such as where the attorney represents both an insurer and its insureds. 'In such a situation, the attorney has two clients whose primary, overlapping and common interest is the speedy and successful resolution of the claim and litigation.' Each of the joint clients holds the privilege protecting their confidential communications with the attorney; one client may not waive the privilege without the consent of the other. [¶] In the absence of a true joint client situation, litigants may nevertheless disclose confidential information without waiving the attorney-client privilege when … information [is] disclosed to expert consultants or counsel's employees. The nonwaiver concept has also been applied to protect the sharing of information among co-litigants. In that situation the concept is referred to as the 'common interest doctrine.'"

Zador Corp. v. Kwan (6th Dist.1995) 31 Cal.App.4th 1285, 1294-95. "In California, the 'joint client' or 'common interest' exception to the attorney-client privilege applies only where two or more clients have retained or consulted a lawyer upon a matter of common interest, in which event neither may claim the privilege in an action by one against the other. [¶] Accordingly, in such circumstances, the propriety of disqualification is not dependent upon the substantial relationship test. Rather, it generally turns upon the scope

of the clients' consent. [¶] Not all conflicts of interest require disqualification. In some situations, the attorney may still represent the client if the client's consent is obtained. Giving effect to a client's consent to a conflicting representation might rest either on the ground of contract freedom or on the related ground of personal autonomy of a client to choose whatever champion the client feels is best suited to vindicate the client's legal entitlements. [¶] In some circumstances, informed client consent is required. For example, informed written consent is required before an attorney can jointly represent clients in the same matter." (Internal quotes omitted.)

ARTICLE 3.5. LAWYER REFERRAL SERVICE-CLIENT PRIVILEGE

§965. [DEFINITIONS]

For purposes of this article, the following terms have the following meanings:

(a) "Client" means a person who, directly or through an authorized representative, consults a lawyer referral service for the purpose of retaining, or securing legal services or advice from, a lawyer in his or her professional capacity, and includes an incompetent who consults the lawyer referral service himself or herself or whose guardian or conservator consults the lawyer referral service on his or her behalf.

(b) "Confidential communication between client and lawyer referral service" means information transmitted between a client and a lawyer referral service in the course of that relationship and in confidence by a means that, so far as the client is aware, does not disclose the information to third persons other than those who are present to further the interests of the client in the consultation or those to whom disclosure is reasonably necessary for the transmission of the information or the accomplishment of the purpose for which the lawyer referral service is consulted.

(c) "Holder of the privilege" means any of the following:

(1) The client, if the client has no guardian or conservator.

(2) A guardian or conservator of the client, if the client has a guardian or conservator.

(3) The personal representative of the client if the client is dead, including a personal representative appointed pursuant to Section 12252 of the Probate Code.

(4) A successor, assign, trustee in dissolution, or any similar representative of a firm, association, organization, partnership, business trust, corporation, or public entity that is no longer in existence.

(d) "Lawyer referral service" means a lawyer referral service certified under, and operating in compliance with, Section 6155 of the Business and Professions Code or an enterprise reasonably believed by the client to be a lawyer referral service certified under, and operating in compliance with, Section 6155 of the Business and Professions Code.

History of Evid. C. §965: Added eff. Jan. 1, 2014, Stats. 2013, ch. 123, §2.

§966. [LAWYER REFERRAL SERVICE-CLIENT PRIVILEGE]

(a) Subject to Section 912 and except as otherwise provided in this article, the client, whether or not a party, has a privilege to refuse to disclose, and to prevent another from disclosing, a confidential communication between client and lawyer referral service if the privilege is claimed by any of the following:

(1) [Holder.] The holder of the privilege.

(2) [Authorized person.] A person who is authorized to claim the privilege by the holder of the privilege.

(3) [Lawyer referral service or staff person.] The lawyer referral service or a staff person thereof, but the lawyer referral service or a staff person thereof may not claim the privilege if there is no holder of the privilege in existence or if the lawyer referral service or a staff person thereof is otherwise instructed by a person authorized to permit disclosure.

(b) The relationship of lawyer referral service and client shall exist between a lawyer referral service, as defined in Section 965, and the persons to whom it renders services, as well as between such persons and anyone employed by the lawyer referral service to render services to such persons. The word "persons" as used in this subdivision includes partnerships, corporations, limited liability companies, associations, and other groups and entities.

History of Evid. C. §966: Added eff. Jan. 1, 2014, Stats. 2013, ch. 123, §2.

§967. [DUTY TO CLAIM PRIVILEGE]

A lawyer referral service that has received or made a communication subject to the privilege under this article shall claim the privilege if the communication is sought to be disclosed and the client has not consented to the disclosure.

History of Evid. C. §967: Added eff. Jan. 1, 2014, Stats. 2013, ch. 123, §2.

§967

§968. [NO PRIVILEGE: CRIME OR FRAUD]

There is no privilege under this article if either of the following applies:

(a) The services of the lawyer referral service were sought or obtained to enable or aid anyone to commit or plan to commit a crime or a fraud.

(b) A staff person of the lawyer referral service who receives a confidential communication in processing a request for legal assistance reasonably believes that disclosure of the confidential communication is necessary to prevent a criminal act that the staff person of the lawyer referral service reasonably believes is likely to result in the death of, or substantial bodily harm to, an individual.

History of Evid. C. §968: Added eff. Jan. 1, 2014, Stats. 2013, ch. 123, §2.

ARTICLE 4. PRIVILEGE NOT TO TESTIFY AGAINST SPOUSE

§970. [SPOUSAL PRIVILEGE NOT TO TESTIFY]

Except as otherwise provided by statute, a married person has a privilege not to testify against his spouse in any proceeding.

History of Evid. C. §970: Added eff. Sept. 17, 1965, oper. Jan. 1, 1967, Stats. 1965, ch. 299, §2.

Official Comment

7 Cal. Law Revision Comm'n Rep. (1965) p. 1171.

Under this article, a married person has two privileges: (1) a privilege not to testify against his spouse in any proceeding (Section 970) and (2) a privilege not to be called as a witness in any proceeding to which his spouse is a party (Section 971).

The privileges under this article are not as broad as the privilege provided by existing law. Under existing law, a married person has a privilege to prevent his spouse from testifying against him, but only the witness spouse has a privilege under this article. Under the existing law, a married person may refuse to testify *for* the other spouse, but no such privilege exists under this article. For a discussion of the reasons for these changes in existing law, see the Law Revision Commission's *Comment* to Code of Civil Procedure Section 1881 (repealed).

The rationale of the privilege provided by Section 970 not to testify against one's spouse is that such testimony would seriously disturb or disrupt the marital relationship. Society stands to lose more from such disruption than it stands to gain from the testimony which would be available if the privilege did not exist. The privilege is based in part on a previous recommendation and study of the California Law Revision Commission. *See* 1 Cal. Law Revision Comm'n, Rep., Rec. & Studies, *Recommendation and Study Relating to the Marital "For and Against" Testimonial Privilege* at F-1 (1957).

ANNOTATIONS

People v. Lucas (1995) 12 Cal.4th 415, 490. "Although a person generally has no privilege to refuse to testify in *favor* of his or her spouse in a criminal proceeding, … §970 provides that a married person has a privilege not to testify *against* his or her spouse who is a party in any proceeding. The privilege belongs to the married person, not the spouse who is the party."

People v. Dorsey (2d Dist.1975) 46 Cal.App.3d 706, 716-17. "Since [Evid. C.] §§970 and 971 are each couched in the present tense, it is clear that the privilege of not being a witness against a spouse does not exist after the marital relationship is terminated by divorce."

§971. [SPOUSAL PRIVILEGE NOT TO APPEAR AS WITNESS]

Except as otherwise provided by statute, a married person whose spouse is a party to a proceeding has a privilege not to be called as a witness by an adverse party to that proceeding without the prior express consent of the spouse having the privilege under this section unless the party calling the spouse does so in good faith without knowledge of the marital relationship.

History of Evid. C. §971: Added eff. Sept. 17, 1965, oper. Jan. 1, 1967, Stats. 1965, ch. 299, §2.

Official Comment

7 Cal. Law Revision Comm'n Rep. (1965) p. 1172.

The privilege of a married person not to be called as a witness against his spouse is somewhat similar to the privilege given the defendant in a criminal case not to be called as a witness (Section 930). This privilege is necessary to avoid the prejudicial effect, for example, of the prosecution's calling the defendant's wife as a witness, thus forcing her to object before the jury. The privilege not to be called as a witness does not apply, however, in a proceeding where the other spouse is not a party. Thus, a married person may be called as a witness in a grand jury proceeding because his spouse is not a party to that proceeding, but the witness in the grand jury proceeding may claim the privilege under Section 970 to refuse to answer a question that would compel him to testify *against* his spouse.

ANNOTATIONS

People v. McWhorter (2009) 47 Cal.4th 318, 374-75. See annotation under Evidence Code §973, p. 1318.

People v. Dorsey (2d Dist.1975) 46 Cal.App.3d 706, 716-17. See annotation under Evidence Code §970, this page.

§972. [EXCEPTIONS TO SPOUSAL PRIVILEGE]

A married person does not have a privilege under this article in:

(a) [Proceedings between spouses.] A proceeding brought by or on behalf of one spouse against the other spouse.

(b) [Commitment proceedings.] A proceeding to commit or otherwise place his or her spouse or his or her spouse's property, or both, under the control of another because of the spouse's alleged mental or physical condition.

(c) [Competency proceedings.] A proceeding brought by or on behalf of a spouse to establish his or her competence.

(d) [Juvenile proceedings.] A proceeding under the Juvenile Court Law, Chapter 2 (commencing with Section 200) of Part 1 of Division 2 of the Welfare and Institutions Code.

(e) [Criminal proceedings involving spouse.] A criminal proceeding in which one spouse is charged with:

(1) A crime against the person or property of the other spouse or of a child, parent, relative, or cohabitant of either, whether committed before or during marriage.

(2) A crime against the person or property of a third person committed in the course of committing a crime against the person or property of the other spouse, whether committed before or during marriage.

(3) Bigamy.

(4) A crime defined by Section 270 or 270a of the Penal Code.

(f) [Criminal proceedings on acts occurring before marriage.] A proceeding resulting from a criminal act which occurred prior to legal marriage of the spouses to each other regarding knowledge acquired prior to that marriage if prior to the legal marriage the witness spouse was aware that his or her spouse had been arrested for or had been formally charged with the crime or crimes about which the spouse is called to testify.

(g) [Family-law proceedings.] A proceeding brought against the spouse by a former spouse so long as the property and debts of the marriage have not been adjudicated, or in order to establish, modify, or enforce a child, family or spousal support obligation arising from the marriage to the former spouse; in a proceeding brought against a spouse by the other parent in order to establish, modify, or enforce a child support obligation for a child of a nonmarital relationship of the spouse; or in a proceeding brought against a spouse by the guardian of a child of that spouse in order to establish, modify, or enforce a child support obligation of the spouse. The married person does not have a privilege under this subdivision to refuse to provide information relating to the issues of income, expenses, assets, debts, and employment of either spouse, but may assert the privilege as otherwise provided in this article if other information is requested by the former spouse, guardian, or other parent of the child. Any person demanding the otherwise privileged information made available by this subdivision, who also has an obligation to support the child for whom an order to establish, modify, or enforce child support is sought, waives his or her marital privilege to the same extent as the spouse as provided in this subdivision.

History of Evid. C. §972: Added eff. Sept. 17, 1965, oper. Jan. 1, 1967, Stats. 1965, ch. 299, §2. Amended eff. Jan. 1, 1976, Stats. 1975, ch. 71, §2; eff. Jan. 1, 1983, Stats. 1982, ch. 256, §1; eff. Jan. 1, 1984, Stats. 1983, ch. 244, §1; eff. Sept. 15, 1986, Stats. 1986, ch. 769, §1; eff. Jan. 1, 1990, Stats. 1989, ch. 1359, §9.7.

Official Comment

7 Cal. Law Revision Comm'n Rep. (1965) p. 1173.

The exceptions to the privileges under this article are similar to those contained in Code of Civil Procedure Section 1881(1) and Penal Code Section 1322, both of which are superseded by the Evidence Code. However, the exceptions in this section have been drafted so that they are consistent with those provided in Article 5 (commencing with Section 980) of this chapter (the privilege for confidential marital communications).

A discussion of comparable exceptions may be found in the *Comments* to the sections in Article 5 of this chapter.

ANNOTATIONS

People v. McWhorter (2009) 47 Cal.4th 318, 374-75. See annotation under Evidence Code §973, p. 1318.

Jurcoane v. Superior Ct. (2d Dist.2001) 93 Cal.App.4th 886, 894-95. "Section 972 expressly lists the exceptions to the privilege. Section 972 does not contain an exception for marriages where the parties have not lived together for a certain time, or where the marriage, while still legally extant, is no longer viable or intact."

§973. [WAIVER OF SPOUSAL PRIVILEGE]

(a) Unless erroneously compelled to do so, a married person who testifies in a proceeding to which his spouse is a party, or who testifies against his spouse in any proceeding, does not have a privilege under this article in the proceeding in which such testimony is given.

(b) There is no privilege under this article in a civil proceeding brought or defended by a married person for the immediate benefit of his spouse or of himself and his spouse.

History of Evid. C. §973: Added eff. Sept. 17, 1965, oper. Jan. 1, 1967, Stats. 1965, ch. 299, §2.

Official Comment

7 Cal. Law Revision Comm'n Rep. (1965) p. 1173;
Assem. J., Apr. 6, 1965, p. 1748.

Section 973 contains special waiver provisions for the privileges provided by this article.

Subdivision (a). Under subdivision (a), a married person who testifies in a proceeding to which his spouse is *a party* waives both privileges provided

for in this article. Thus, for example, a married person cannot call his spouse as a witness to give favorable testimony and have that spouse invoke the privilege provided in Section 970 to keep from testifying on cross-examination to unfavorable matters; nor can a married person testify for an adverse party as to particular matters and then invoke the privilege not to testify against his spouse as to other matters.

In any proceeding where a married person's spouse is *not a party*, the privilege not to be called as a witness is not available, and a married person may testify like any other witness without waiving the privilege provided under Section 970 so long as he does not *testify against* his spouse. However, under subdivision (a), the privilege not to testify against his spouse in that proceeding is waived as to all matters if he *testifies against* his spouse as to any matter.

The word "proceeding" is defined in Section 901 to include any action, civil or criminal. Hence, the privilege is waived for all purposes in an action if the spouse entitled to claim the privilege testifies at any time during the action. For example, if a civil action involves issues being separately tried, a wife whose husband is a party to the litigation may not testify for her husband at one trial and invoke the privilege in order to avoid testifying against him at a separate trial of a different issue. Nor may a wife testify against her husband at a preliminary hearing of a criminal action and refuse to testify against him at the trial.

Subdivision (b). This subdivision precludes married persons from taking unfair advantage of their marital status to escape their duty to give testimony under Section 776, which supersedes Code of Civil Procedure Section 2055. It recognizes a doctrine of waiver that has been developed in the California cases. Thus, for example, when suit is brought to set aside a conveyance from husband to wife allegedly in fraud of the husband's creditors, both spouses being named as defendants, it has been held that setting up the conveyance in the answer as a defense waives the privilege. *Tobias v. Adams*, 201 Cal. 689, 258 Pac. 588 (1927); *Schwartz v. Brandon*, 97 Cal.App. 30, 275 Pac. 448 (1929). *But cf. Marple v. Jackson*, 184 Cal. 411, 193 Pac. 940 (1920). Also, when husband and wife are joined as defendants in a quiet title action and assert a claim to the property, they have been held to have waived the privilege. *Hagen v. Silva*, 139 Cal.App.2d 199, 293 P.2d 143 (1956). And when both spouses joined as plaintiffs in an action to recover damages to one of them, each was held to have waived the privilege as to the testimony of the other. *In re Strand*, 123 Cal.App. 170, 11 P.2d 89 (1932). (It should be noted that, with respect to damages for personal injuries, Civil Code Section 163.5 (added by Cal. Stats. 1957, ch. 2334, §1, p. 4066) provides that all damages awarded to a married person in a civil action for personal injuries are the separate property of such married person.) This principle of waiver has seemingly been developed by the case law to prevent a spouse from refusing to testify as to matters which affect his own interest on the ground that such testimony would also be "against" his spouse. It has been held, however, that a spouse does not waive the privilege by making the other spouse his agent, even as to transactions involving the agency. *Ayres v. Wright*, 103 Cal.App. 610, 284 Pac. 1077 (1930).

ANNOTATIONS

People v. McWhorter (2009) 47 Cal.4th 318, 374-75. "The spousal privilege is personal to the spouse seeking to avoid testifying, and because [D's wife], and not [D], was the holder of the privilege, [D] does not have standing to raise the claim. ... Moreover, ... a trial court does not have a duty to advise a witness of the spousal privilege. [N]othing precluded defense counsel from directly informing [D's wife] of the privilege himself. ... Finally, counsel waited until after the prosecutor had begun his direct examination of [D's wife] to request the court to advise her of the spousal privilege. [D's wife] was the holder of the privilege, and once she decided to testify at any point in [D's] criminal proceedings, the privilege was waived for the entirety of the proceedings." *See also* ***People v. Resendez*** (4th Dist.1993) 12 Cal.App.4th 98, 108-09.

ARTICLE 5. PRIVILEGE FOR CONFIDENTIAL MARITAL COMMUNICATIONS

§980. [CONFIDENTIAL MARITAL COMMUNICATION PRIVILEGE]

Subject to Section 912 and except as otherwise provided in this article, a spouse (or his guardian or conservator when he has a guardian or conservator), whether or not a party, has a privilege during the marital relationship and afterwards to refuse to disclose, and to prevent another from disclosing, a communication if he claims the privilege and the communication was made in confidence between him and the other spouse while they were husband and wife.

History of Evid. C. §980: Added eff. Sept. 17, 1965, oper. Jan. 1, 1967, Stats. 1965, ch. 299, §2.

Official Comment

7 Cal. Law Revision Comm'n Rep. (1965) p. 1175.

Section 980 is the basic statement of the privilege for confidential marital communications. Exceptions to this privilege are stated in Sections 981-987.

Who can claim the privilege. Under Section 980, both spouses are the holders of the privilege and either spouse may claim it. Under existing law, the privilege *may* belong only to the nontestifying spouse inasmuch as Code of Civil Procedure Section 1881(1), superseded by the Evidence Code, provides: "[N]or can either ... be, *without the consent of the other*, examined as to any communication made by one to the other during the marriage." (Emphasis added.) It is likely, however, that Section 1881(1) would be construed to grant the privilege to both spouses. *See In re De Neef*, 42 Cal.App.2d 691, 109 P.2d 741 (1941). *But see People v. Keller*, 165 Cal.App.2d 419, 423-424, 332 P.2d 174, 176 (1958) (dictum).

A guardian of an incompetent spouse may claim the privilege on behalf of that spouse. However, when a spouse is dead, no one can claim the privilege for him; the privilege, if it is to be claimed at all, can be claimed only by or on behalf of the surviving spouse.

Termination of marriage. The privilege may be claimed as to confidential communications made during a marriage even though the marriage has been terminated at the time the privilege is claimed. This states existing law. Code Civ. Proc. §1881(1) (repealed); *People v. Mullings*, 83 Cal. 138, 23 Pac. 229 (1890). Free and open communication between spouses would be unduly inhibited if one of the spouses could be compelled to testify as to the nature of such communications after the termination of the marriage.

Eavesdroppers. The privilege may be asserted to prevent testimony by anyone, including eavesdroppers. To a limited extent, this constitutes a change in California law. *See* the *Comment* to Evidence Code §954. *See generally People v. Peak*, 66 Cal.App.2d 894, 153 P.2d 464 (1944); *People v. Morhar*, 78 Cal.App. 380, 248 Pac. 975 (1926); *People v. Mitchell*, 61 Cal.App. 569, 215 Pac. 117 (1923). Section 980 also changes the existing law which permits a third party, to whom one of the spouses had revealed a confidential communication, to testify concerning it. *People v. Swaile*, 12 Cal.App. 192, 195-196, 107 Pac. 134, 137 (1909); *People v. Chadwick*, 4 Cal.App. 63, 72, 87 Pac. 384, 387-388 (1906). *See also Wolfle v. United States*, 291 U.S. 7 (1934). Under Section 912, such conduct would constitute a waiver of the privilege only as to the spouse who makes the disclosure.

ANNOTATIONS

People v. Badgett (1995) 10 Cal.4th 330, 363. "The privilege [in §980] applies only in the case of a valid marriage. Although California does not recognize com-

mon law marriages …, it does recognize the validity of a marriage contracted in another state that would be valid by the laws of that state. *At 364:* The claimant of the marital privilege for confidential communications has the burden of proving, by a preponderance of the evidence, the facts necessary to sustain the claim." *See also* ***People v. Catlin*** (2001) 26 Cal.4th 81, 130 (privilege does not apply when person enters into second marriage before first marriage is legally dissolved).

People v. Dorsey (2d Dist.1975) 46 Cal.App.3d 706, 717. "The privilege not to testify at all and the privilege not to testify to privileged communications are two entirely separate and distinct privileges. That privilege against disclosure of privileged communications is vested in each spouse and consequently if a spouse is called as a witness he or she may not testify as to confidential communications without his or her consent *and* the consent of the other spouse. Either spouse may claim the privilege. The privilege survives the termination of the marriage and continues to exist even though the marriage has been terminated by divorce. The privilege exists even though the marriage is annulled for fraud since prior to the decree of annulment the marriage is voidable only. However, the privilege encompasses only communications between husband and wife during marriage. It does not extend to physical facts which are observed, which do not constitute 'communications.'"

§981. [NO PRIVILEGE: CRIME OR FRAUD]

There is no privilege under this article if the communication was made, in whole or in part, to enable or aid anyone to commit or plan to commit a crime or a fraud.

History of Evid. C. §981: Added eff. Sept. 17, 1965, oper. Jan. 1, 1967, Stats. 1965, ch. 299, §2.

Official Comment

7 Cal. Law Revision Comm'n Rep. (1965) p. 1176.

California recognizes this as an exception to the lawyer-client privilege, but it does not appear to have been recognized in the California cases dealing with the confidential marital communications privilege. Nonetheless, the exception does not seem so broad that it would impair the values that the privilege is intended to preserve; in many cases, the evidence which would be admissible under this exception will be vital in order to do justice between the parties to a lawsuit. This exception would not, of course, infringe on the privileges accorded to a married person under Sections 970 and 971.

It is important to note that the exception provided by Section 981 is quite limited. It does not permit disclosure of communications that merely reveal a plan to commit a crime or fraud; it permits disclosure only of communications made to *enable* or *aid* anyone to commit or plan to commit a crime or fraud. Thus, unless the communication is for the purpose of obtaining assistance in the commission of the crime or fraud or in furtherance thereof, it is not made admissible by the exception provided in this section. *Cf. People v. Pierce*, 61 Cal.2d 879, 40 Cal.Rptr. 845, 395 P.2d 893 (1964) (husband and wife who conspire only between themselves against others cannot claim immunity from prosecution for conspiracy on the basis of their marital status).

ANNOTATIONS

People v. Dorsey (2d Dist.1975) 46 Cal.App.3d 706, 717. Evid. C. §981 "authorizes a limited exception to [Evid. C.] §980."

§982. [NO PRIVILEGE: COMMITMENT PROCEEDING]

There is no privilege under this article in a proceeding to commit either spouse or otherwise place him or his property, or both, under the control of another because of his alleged mental or physical condition.

History of Evid. C. §982: Added eff. Sept. 17, 1965, oper. Jan. 1, 1967, Stats. 1965, ch. 299, §2.

Official Comment

7 Cal. Law Revision Comm'n Rep. (1965) p. 1177.

Sections 982 and 983 express existing law. Code Civ. Proc. §1881(1) (repealed). Commitment and competency proceedings are undertaken for the benefit of the subject person. Frequently, much or all of the evidence bearing on a spouse's competency or lack of competency will consist of communications to the other spouse. It would be undesirable to permit either spouse to invoke a privilege to prevent the presentation of this vital information inasmuch as these proceedings are of such vital importance both to society and to the spouse who is the subject of the proceedings.

§983. [NO PRIVILEGE: COMPETENCY PROCEEDING]

There is no privilege under this article in a proceeding brought by or on behalf of either spouse to establish his competence.

History of Evid. C. §983: Added eff. Sept. 17, 1965, oper. Jan. 1, 1967, Stats. 1965, ch. 299, §2.

Official Comment

7 Cal. Law Revision Comm'n Rep. (1965) p. 1177.

See the *Comment* to Section 982.

§984. [NO PRIVILEGE: PROCEEDING BETWEEN SPOUSES]

There is no privilege under this article in:

(a) A proceeding brought by or on behalf of one spouse against the other spouse.

(b) A proceeding between a surviving spouse and a person who claims through the deceased spouse, regardless of whether such claim is by testate or intestate succession or by inter vivos transaction.

History of Evid. C. §984: Added eff. Sept. 17, 1965, oper. Jan. 1, 1967, Stats. 1965, ch. 299, §2.

Official Comment

7 Cal. Law Revision Comm'n Rep. (1965) p. 1177.

The exception to the marital communications privilege for litigation between the spouses states existing law. Code Civ. Proc. §1881(1) (repealed). Section 984 extends the principle to cases where one of the spouses is dead and the litigation is between his successor and the surviving spouse. *See generally Estate of Gillett*, 73 Cal.App.2d 588, 166 P.2d 870 (1946).

§985. [NO PRIVILEGE: CRIMINAL PROCEEDING INVOLVING SPOUSE]

There is no privilege under this article in a criminal proceeding in which one spouse is charged with:

(a) A crime committed at any time against the person or property of the other spouse or of a child of either.

(b) A crime committed at any time against the person or property of a third person committed in the course of committing a crime against the person or property of the other spouse.

(c) Bigamy.

(d) A crime defined by Section 270 or 270a of the Penal Code.

History of Evid. C. §985: Added eff. Sept. 17, 1965, oper. Jan. 1, 1967, Stats. 1965, ch. 299, §2. Amended eff. Jan. 1, 1976, Stats. 1975, ch. 71, §3.

Official Comment

7 Cal. Law Revision Comm'n Rep. (1965) p. 1178.

This exception restates with minor variations an exception that is recognized under existing law. Code Civ. Proc. §1881(1) (repealed). Sections 985 and 986 together create an exception for all the proceedings mentioned in Section 1322 of the Penal Code (repealed).

§985

§986. [NO PRIVILEGE: JUVENILE COURT PROCEEDING]

There is no privilege under this article in a proceeding under the Juvenile Court Law, Chapter 2 (commencing with Section 200) of Part 1 of Division 2 of the Welfare and Institutions Code.

History of Evid. C. §986: Added eff. Sept. 17, 1965, oper. Jan. 1, 1967, Stats. 1965, ch. 299, §2. Amended eff. Jan. 1, 1983, Stats. 1982, ch. 256, §2.

Official Comment

7 Cal. Law Revision Comm'n Rep. (1965) p. 1178.

See the *Comment* to Section 985.

§987. [NO PRIVILEGE: DEFENDANT-SPOUSE IN CRIMINAL PROCEEDING]

There is no privilege under this article in a criminal proceeding in which the communication is offered in evidence by a defendant who is one of the spouses between whom the communication was made.

History of Evid. C. §987: Added eff. Sept. 17, 1965, oper. Jan. 1, 1967, Stats. 1965, ch. 299, §2.

Official Comment

7 Cal. Law Revision Comm'n Rep. (1965) p. 1178.

This exception does not appear to have been recognized in any California case. Nonetheless, it is a desirable exception. When a married person is the defendant in a criminal proceeding and seeks to introduce evidence which is material to his defense, his spouse (or his former spouse) should not be privileged to withhold the information.

ARTICLE 6. PHYSICIAN-PATIENT PRIVILEGE

§990. [PHYSICIAN]

As used in this article, "physician" means a person authorized, or reasonably believed by the patient to be authorized, to practice medicine in any state or nation.

History of Evid. C. §990: Added eff. Sept. 17, 1965, oper. Jan. 1, 1967, Stats. 1965, ch. 299, §2.

Official Comment

7 Cal. Law Revision Comm'n Rep. (1965) p. 1179.

Defining "physician" to include a person "reasonably believed by the patient to be authorized" to practice medicine changes the existing law which requires that the physician be licensed. *See* Code Civ. Proc. §1881(4) (repealed). But, if this privilege is to be recognized, it should protect the patient from reasonable mistakes as to unlicensed practitioners. The privilege also should be applicable to communications made to a physician authorized to practice in any state or nation. When a California resident travels outside the State and has occasion to visit a physician during such travel, or when a physician from another state or nation participates in the treatment of a person in California, the patient should be entitled to assume that his communications will be given as much protection as they would be if he consulted a California physician in California. A patient should not be forced to inquire about the jurisdictions where the physician is authorized to practice medicine and whether such jurisdictions recognize the physician-patient privilege before he may safely communicate with the physician.

§991. [PATIENT]

As used in this article, "patient" means a person who consults a physician or submits to an examination by a physician for the purpose of securing a diagnosis or preventive, palliative, or curative treatment of his physical or mental or emotional condition.

History of Evid. C. §991: Added eff. Sept. 17, 1965, oper. Jan. 1, 1967, Stats. 1965, ch. 299, §2.

Official Comment

7 Cal. Law Revision Comm'n Rep. (1965) p. 1179; Senate J, Apr. 21, 1965.

"Patient" means a person who consults a physician for the purpose of diagnosis *or* treatment. This definition modifies existing California law; under existing law, a person who consults a physician for diagnosis only has no physician-patient privilege. *City & County of San Francisco v. Superior Court*, 37 Cal.2d 227, 231, 231 P.2d 26, 28 (1951) (physician-patient privilege "cannot be invoked when no treatment is contemplated or given").

There seems to be little reason to perpetuate the distinction made between consultations for the purpose of diagnosis and consultations for the purpose of treatment. Persons do not ordinarily consult physicians from idle curiosity. They may be sent by their attorney to obtain a diagnosis in contemplation of some legal proceeding—in which case the attorney-client privilege will afford protection. *See, e.g., City & County of San Francisco v. Superior Court*, 37 Cal.2d 227, 231 P.2d 26 (1951). They may submit to an examination for insurance purposes—in which case the insurance contract will contain appropriate waiver provisions. They may seek diagnosis from one physician to check the diagnosis made by another. They may seek diagnosis from one physician in contemplation of seeking treatment from another. Communications made under such circumstances are as deserving of protection as are communications made to a treating physician.

§992. [CONFIDENTIAL COMMUNICATION BETWEEN PATIENT & PHYSICIAN]

As used in this article, "confidential communication between patient and physician" means information, in-

cluding information obtained by an examination of the patient, transmitted between a patient and his physician in the course of that relationship and in confidence by a means which, so far as the patient is aware, discloses the information to no third persons other than those who are present to further the interest of the patient in the consultation or those to whom disclosure is reasonably necessary for the transmission of the information or the accomplishment of the purpose for which the physician is consulted, and includes a diagnosis made and the advice given by the physician in the course of that relationship.

History of Evid. C. §992: Added eff. Sept. 17, 1965, oper. Jan. 1, 1967, Stats. 1965, ch. 299, §2. Amended eff. Nov. 8, 1967, Stats. 1967, ch. 650, §4.

Official Comment

7 Cal. Law Revision Comm'n Rep. (1965) p. 1180; Assem. J., Apr. 6, 1965, p. 1749.

This section generally restates existing law, except that it is uncertain whether a doctor's statement to a patient giving his diagnosis is presently covered by the privilege. *See* Code Civ. Proc. §1881(4) (repealed). *See also* the *Comment* to Evidence Code §952.

The definition here is sufficiently broad to include matters that are not ordinarily thought of as "communications." It is the communications that are defined here, however, to which reference is made throughout the remainder of the article. Under Section 994, the privilege applies to the communications defined here. And the exceptions in Sections 996-1007 that relate to particular communications also apply to the communications defined here. Thus, there is no information protected by the privilege in Section 994 to which the exceptions cannot be applied in an appropriate case.

8 Cal. Law Revision Comm'n Rep. (1967) p. 122.

The express inclusion of "a diagnosis" in the last clause will preclude a possible construction of this section that would leave an uncommunicated diagnosis unprotected by the privilege. Such a construction would virtually destroy the privilege.

ANNOTATIONS

Rudnick v. Superior Ct. (1974) 11 Cal.3d 924, 928. "The novel question confronting us is whether a third party recipient of confidential information from a physician may assert the physician-patient privilege. *At 933:* [Ds] may claim the physician-patient privilege on behalf of a patient to bar discovery of the adverse drug reaction report submitted by his physician if the submission of such report was in confidence and was reasonably necessary in order to accomplish the purpose for which the physician was consulted. ... The trial court on its own motion or on [Ds'] motion may, in its discretion, protect the physician-patient privilege of an absent patient who has not waived the privilege. *At 933 n.13:* [W]e note the following for the guidance of the trial court should it determine to exercise its discretion to protect an absentee holder of the privilege. 'The whole purpose of the privilege is to preclude the humiliation of the patient that might follow disclosure of his ailments.' Therefore if the disclosure of the patient's name reveals nothing of any communication concerning the patient's ailments, disclosure of the patient's name does not violate the privilege. If, however, disclosure of the patient's name inevitably in the context of such disclosure reveals the confidential information, namely the ailments, then such disclosure violates the privilege. Conversely if the disclosure reveals the ailments but not the patient's identity, then such disclosure would appear not to violate the privilege. *At 934:* [R]espondent court should determine whether [Ds] are authorized to claim that the reports are protected from disclosure by the physician-patient privilege. [¶] If the court determines that the reports are protected from disclosure by the physician-patient privilege and that [Ds] are authorized so to claim, it should further determine whether or not the patient has waived such privilege in the manner prescribed by [Evid. C.] §912...." *See also* ***Hurvitz v. Hoefflin*** (2d Dist.2000) 84 Cal.App.4th 1232, 1243 (privilege protects patient from forced disclosure during litigation, but may not be extended to dissemination of information already known outside of litigation).

Snibbe v. Superior Ct. (2d Dist.2014) 224 Cal.App.4th 184, 192-93. "Real parties in interest interpret the physician-patient privilege as excluding physician orders. This narrow interpretation is contrary to the plain language of ... §992, which defines 'confidential communication' to include not only information disclosed by the patient but also 'a diagnosis made and the advice given by the physician.' [¶] But the physician-patient privilege will not be violated by the limited production of redacted postoperative orders in this case. In ***Rudnick*** [***v. Superior Ct.*** (1974) 11 Cal.3d 924], which involved a request for production of adverse drug reaction reports, the Supreme Court explained for the guidance of the trial court that 'if the disclosure reveals the ailments but not the patient's identity, then such disclosure would appear not to violate the privilege.' Petitioner relies on ***Binder*** [***v. Superior Ct.*** (5th Dist.1987) 196 Cal.App.3d 893], where the court declined to apply what it considered to be a dictum in ***Rudnick*** ... to photographs of patients' skin lesions. The court in ***Binder*** acknowledged that the dictum in ***Rudnick*** 'may be correct under some circumstances.' It distinguished the reports in ***Rudnick*** from photographs because 'it is one thing to have a *description* of one's ailment read, but quite another to have that ailment actually *depicted* in a photograph.' The

Binder court was particularly concerned that the disclosure of patient photographs 'would discourage patients from allowing physicians to photograph their ailments or other conditions.' [¶] The postoperative orders at issue in this case do not implicate the concerns in *Binder* ... because there is no indication they contain photographs." *See also* ***Binder v. Superior Ct.*** (5th Dist.1987) 196 Cal.App.3d 893, 897-99.

§993. [HOLDER OF PRIVILEGE]

As used in this article, "holder of the privilege" means:

(a) The patient when he has no guardian or conservator.

(b) A guardian or conservator of the patient when the patient has a guardian or conservator.

(c) The personal representative of the patient if the patient is dead.

History of Evid. C. §993: Added eff. Sept. 17, 1965, oper. Jan. 1, 1967, Stats. 1965, ch. 299, §2.

Official Comment

7 Cal. Law Revision Comm'n Rep. (1965) p. 1181.

A guardian of the patient is the holder of the privilege if the patient has a guardian. If the patient has separate guardians of his estate and of his person, either guardian may claim the privilege. The provision making the personal representative of the patient the holder of the privilege when the patient is dead may change California law. The existing law may be that the privilege survives the death of the patient in some cases and that no one can waive it on behalf of the patient. See the discussion in *Tentative Recommendation and a Study Relating to the Uniform Rules of Evidence (Article V. Privileges)*, 6 Cal. Law Revision Comm'n, Rep., Rec. & Studies 201, 408-410 (1964). Sections 993 and 994 enable the personal representative to protect the interest of the patient's estate in the confidentiality of these statements and to waive the privilege when the estate would benefit by waiver. When the patient's estate has no interest in preserving confidentiality, or when the estate has been distributed and the representative discharged, the importance of providing complete access to information relevant to a particular proceeding should prevail over whatever remaining interest the decedent may have had in secrecy.

ANNOTATIONS

Los Angeles Gay & Lesbian Ctr. v. Superior Ct. (2d Dist.2011) 194 Cal.App.4th 288, 310. "[T]he named class [Ps] do not hold the [physician-patient] privilege on behalf of the unnamed class members under ... §993. Section 993 allows a representative to assert the privilege on behalf of a patient when the patient is incapacitated or deceased and thus by its terms does not apply [to] class action representation."

Rittenhouse v. Superior Ct. (3d Dist.1991) 235 Cal.App.3d 1584, 1589-90. Party opposing holographic instrument "is advocating that §993 be interpreted by virtue of the [Law Revision Commission] comment's language as meaning that there is no physician-patient privilege after the patient's death, *unless* the personal representative demonstrates an overriding interest on the part of the estate in maintaining confidentiality. ... As a general rule, privileged communications are protected regardless of their relevancy to the issues in the litigation, and despite any private or public interest in disclosure. In no other circumstance involving such a communication is the court authorized to engage in a 'balancing' process such as that advocated by [party opposing holographic instrument]."

§994. [PHYSICIAN-PATIENT PRIVILEGE]

Subject to Section 912 and except as otherwise provided in this article, the patient, whether or not a party, has a privilege to refuse to disclose, and to prevent another from disclosing, a confidential communication between patient and physician if the privilege is claimed by:

(a) [Holder.] The holder of the privilege;

(b) [Authorized person.] A person who is authorized to claim the privilege by the holder of the privilege; or

(c) [Physician.] The person who was the physician at the time of the confidential communication, but such person may not claim the privilege if there is no holder of the privilege in existence or if he or she is otherwise instructed by a person authorized to permit disclosure. The relationship of a physician and patient shall exist between a medical or podiatry corporation as defined in the Medical Practice Act and the patient to whom it renders professional services, as well as between such patients and licensed physicians and surgeons employed by such corporation to render services to such patients. The word "persons" as used in this subdivision includes partnerships, corporations, limited liability companies, associations, and other groups and entities.

History of Evid. C. §994: Added eff. Sept. 17, 1965, oper. Jan. 1, 1967, Stats. 1965, ch. 299, §2. Amended eff. Nov. 13, 1968, Stats. 1968, ch. 1375, §3; eff. Jan. 1, 1981, Stats. 1980, ch. 1313, §12; eff. Jan. 1, 1995, Stats. 1994, ch. 1010, §105.

Official Comment

7 Cal. Law Revision Comm'n Rep. (1965) p. 1182.

This section, like Section 954 (lawyer-client privilege), is based on the premise that the privilege must be claimed by a person who is authorized to claim the privilege. If there is no claim of privilege by a person with authority to make the claim, the evidence is admissible. *See* the *Comments* to Evidence Code §§993 and 954.

For the reasons indicated in the *Comment* to Section 954, an eavesdropper or other interceptor of a communication privileged under this section is not permitted to testify to the communication.

ANNOTATIONS

Rudnick v. Superior Ct. (1974) 11 Cal.3d 924, 928. See annotation under Evidence Code §992, p. 1321.

Duronslet v. Kamps (1st Dist.2012) 203 Cal.App.4th 717, 730. "[D] claimed her statements to the nurse … were protected by the physician-patient privilege set forth in [Evid. C.] §994. *At 731:* [Evid. C.] §990 defines 'physician' as 'a person authorized, or reasonably believed by the patient to be authorized, to practice medicine in any state or nation.' This definition does not encompass nurses. *At 736:* We are mindful that the physician-patient privilege is to be construed liberally in favor of the patient. … But we are prohibited from broadening the physician-patient privilege to extend it to medical personnel not explicitly mentioned in §990's definition of 'physician.' [¶] We therefore conclude [D] did not make a threshold showing that the privilege set forth in §994 extends to nurses…. [D] did not argue—or demonstrate—the nurse with whom she consulted was 'licensed to practice medicine' or that she 'reasonably believed' the nurse was authorized to practice medicine. We conclude [D] did not satisfy her initial burden to provide preliminary facts to support the existence of the physician-patient privilege."

Johnson v. Superior Ct. (2d Dist.2000) 80 Cal.App.4th 1050, 1063. "In order for a party to invoke the physician-patient privilege under … §994, there must be a 'patient.' [I]f a person does not consult a physician for diagnosis or treatment of a physical or mental ailment, the privilege does not exist. The party asserting the privilege has the burden of proof regarding the existence of the privilege."

Palay v. Superior Ct. (2d Dist.1993) 18 Cal.App.4th 919, 927-28. "The whole purpose of the physician-patient privilege is to preclude the humiliation of the patient that might follow disclosure of his ailments. When the patient himself discloses those ailments by bringing an action in which they are in issue, there is no longer any reason for the privilege." (Internal quotes omitted.)

Rittenhouse v. Superior Ct. (3d Dist.1991) 235 Cal.App.3d 1584, 1589-90. See annotation under Evidence Code §993, p. 1322.

§995. [CLAIMING THE PRIVILEGE]

The physician who received or made a communication subject to the privilege under this article shall claim the privilege whenever he is present when the communication is sought to be disclosed and is authorized to claim the privilege under subdivision (c) of Section 994.

History of Evid. C. §995: Added eff. Sept. 17, 1965, oper. Jan. 1, 1967, Stats. 1965, ch. 299, §2.

Official Comment

7 Cal. Law Revision Comm'n Rep. (1965) p. 1182.

The obligation of the physician to claim the privilege on behalf of the patient, unless otherwise instructed by a person authorized to permit disclosure, is consistent with Section 2379 of the Business and Professions Code.

§996. [NO PRIVILEGE: PATIENT-LITIGANT]

There is no privilege under this article as to a communication relevant to an issue concerning the condition of the patient if such issue has been tendered by:

(a) The patient;

(b) Any party claiming through or under the patient;

(c) Any party claiming as a beneficiary of the patient through a contract to which the patient is or was a party; or

(d) The plaintiff in an action brought under Section 376 or 377 of the Code of Civil Procedure for damages for the injury or death of the patient.

History of Evid. C. §996: Added eff. Sept. 17, 1965, oper. Jan. 1, 1967, Stats. 1965, ch. 299, §2.

Official Comment

7 Cal. Law Revision Comm'n Rep. (1965) p. 1183.

Section 996 provides that the physician-patient privilege does not exist in any proceeding in which an issue concerning the condition of the patient has been tendered by the patient. If the patient himself tenders the issue of his condition, he should not be able to withhold relevant evidence from the opposing party by the exercise of the physician-patient privilege.

A limited form of this exception is recognized by Code of Civil Procedure Section 1881(4) (repealed) which makes the privilege inapplicable in personal injury actions. This exception is also recognized in various types of administrative proceedings where the patient tenders the issue of his condition. *E.g.*, Labor Code §§4055, 5701, 5703, 6407, 6408 (proceedings before the Industrial Accident Commission). The exception provided by Section 996 applies not only to proceedings before the Industrial Accident Commission but also to any other proceeding where the patient tenders the issue of his condition. The exception in Section 996 also states existing law in applying the exception to other situations where the patient himself has raised the issue of his condition. *In re Cathey*, 55 Cal.2d 679, 690-692, 12 Cal.Rptr. 762, 768, 361 P.2d 426, 432 (1961) (prisoner in state medical facility waived physician-patient privilege by putting his mental condition in issue by application for habeas corpus); *see also City & County of San Francisco v. Superior Court*, 37 Cal.2d 227, 232, 231 P.2d 26, 28 (1951) (personal injury case).

Section 996 also provides that there is no privilege in an action brought under Section 377 of the Code of Civil Procedure (wrongful death). Under Code of Civil Procedure Section 1881(4) (repealed), a person authorized to bring the wrongful death action may consent to the testimony by the physician. As far as testimony by the physician is concerned, there is no reason why the rules of evidence should be different in a case where the patient brings the action and a case where someone else sues for the patient's wrongful death.

Section 996 also provides that there is no privilege in an action brought under Section 376 of the Code of Civil Procedure (parent's action for injury to child). In this case, as in a case under the wrongful death statute, the same rule of evidence should apply when the parent brings the action as applies when the child is the plaintiff.

ANNOTATIONS

Schreiber v. Estate of Kiser (1999) 22 Cal.4th 31, 39. "To the extent a physician is retained 'for the purpose of forming and expressing an opinion in anticipation of the litigation or in preparation for the trial of the action,' his identity and opinions are generally privileged unless he testifies. Should the physician testify, an expert witness declaration is required. On the other hand, to the extent a physician acquires personal knowledge of the relevant facts independently of the litigation, his identity and opinions based on those facts are not privileged in litigation presenting 'an issue concerning the condition of the patient.' For such a witness, no expert witness declaration is required, and he may testify as to any opinions formed on the basis of facts independently acquired and informed by his training, skill, and experience. This may well include opinions regarding causation and standard of care because such issues are inherent in a physician's work. An opposing party would therefore be prudent to ask a treating physician at his deposition whether he holds any opinions on these subjects, and if so, in what manner he obtained the factual underpinning of those opinions."

Heller v. Norcal Mut. Ins. (1994) 8 Cal.4th 30, 44 n.5. "By filing a medical malpractice action against [physician's associate], [P] was certainly aware that her medical condition would be an issue. [Ds] now claim that this awareness, *by itself*, constituted a waiver of the doctor-patient privilege under ... §996.... We reject this contention. ... The allegations in the present action are based on communications made in the first lawsuit against [physician's associate]. By suing [physician's associate] for malpractice, [P] may have waived any doctor-patient confidentiality surrounding [physician's associate's] treatment of her hand, but she did not, in that lawsuit, waive the doctor-patient privilege as to confidential information she relayed to [physician]."

Oiye v. Fox (6th Dist.2012) 211 Cal.App.4th 1036, 1068. "[T]he trial court ordered sealed ... two letters pertaining to a medical coverage dispute between [P] and her health insurer and ... a diary [P] kept ... in the course of receiving medical treatment. [¶] [D] contends that [P] has waived her right of privacy by putting her medical condition in issue. [¶] A plaintiff who puts her medical condition in issue ... waives her privilege against discovery of the medical information by the defendant. However, disclosure to an opponent in civil litigation does not necessarily waive the patient's privilege to keep the information from third parties, including the public. *At 1070:* The sealing order does not prevent [D] from either discovering any relevant information about [P's] medical condition and treatment or producing these documents in evidence at trial. It simply prevents [D] from using the court files to publicize what he recognizes to be [P's] private medical records."

Los Angeles Gay & Lesbian Ctr. v. Superior Ct. (2d Dist.2011) 194 Cal.App.4th 288, 309. See annotation under Evidence Code §912, *Subdivision (a)*, p. 1296.

Palay v. Superior Ct. (2d Dist.1993) 18 Cal.App.4th 919, 928. "Under §996, '[a] patient tenders the issue of his physical health if he files an action for personal injuries but only as to information which relates to the claimed injuries.' Disclosure is compelled in cases where the patient's own action initiates the exposure. 'The patient-litigant exception precludes one who has placed in issue his physical condition from invoking the privilege on the ground that disclosure of his condition would cause him humiliation. He cannot have his cake and eat it too.'" *See also* ***Karen P. v. Superior Ct.*** (2d Dist.2011) 200 Cal.App.4th 908, 913.

§997. [NO PRIVILEGE: CRIME OR TORT]

There is no privilege under this article if the services of the physician were sought or obtained to enable or aid anyone to commit or plan to commit a crime or a tort or to escape detection or apprehension after the commission of a crime or a tort.

History of Evid. C. §997: Added eff. Sept. 17, 1965, oper. Jan. 1, 1967, Stats. 1965, ch. 299, §2.

Official Comment

7 Cal. Law Revision Comm'n Rep. (1965) p. 1183.

This section is considerably broader in scope than Section 956 which provides that the lawyer-client privilege does not apply when the communication was made to enable anyone to commit or plan to commit a crime or a *fraud*. Section 997 creates an exception to the physician-patient privilege where the services of the physician were sought or obtained to enable or aid anyone to commit or plan to commit a crime or a *tort*, or to escape detection or apprehension after commission of a crime or a *tort*. People seldom, if ever, consult their physicians in regard to matters which might subsequently be determined to be a tort, and there is no desirable end to be served by encouraging such communications. On the other hand, people often consult lawyers about matters which may later turn out to be torts and it is desirable to encourage discussion of such matters with lawyers. Whether the exception provided by Section 997 now exists in California has not been determined in any decided case, but it probably would be recognized in an appropriate case in view of the similar court-created exception to the lawyer-client privilege. *See* the *Comment* to Evidence Code §956.

§998. [NO PRIVILEGE: CRIMINAL PROCEEDING]

There is no privilege under this article in a criminal proceeding.

History of Evid. C. §998: Added eff. Sept. 17, 1965, oper. Jan. 1, 1967, Stats. 1965, ch. 299, §2.

Official Comment

7 Cal. Law Revision Comm'n Rep. (1965) p. 1184; Assem. J., Apr. 6, 1965, p. 1749.

The physician-patient privilege is not now applicable in a criminal proceeding. Code Civ. Proc. §1881(4) (repealed). *See also People v. Griffith*, 146 Cal. 339, 80 Pac. 68 (1905).

§999. [NO PRIVILEGE: CIVIL ACTION TO RECOVER FOR CRIMINAL CONDUCT]

There is no privilege under this article as to a communication relevant to an issue concerning the condition of the patient in a proceeding to recover damages on account of the conduct of the patient if good cause for disclosure of the communication is shown.

History of Evid. C. §999: Added eff. Sept. 17, 1965, oper. Jan. 1, 1967, Stats. 1965, ch. 299, §2. Amended eff. Jan. 1, 1976, Stats. 1975, ch. 318, §1.

Official Comment

7 Cal. Law Revision Comm'n Rep. (1965) p. 1184.

Section 999 makes the physician-patient privilege inapplicable in civil actions to recover damages for any criminal conduct, whether or not felonious, on the part of the patient. Under Sections 1290-1292 (hearsay), the evidence admitted in the criminal trial would be admissible in a subsequent civil trial as former testimony. Thus, if the exception provided by Section 999 did not exist, the evidence subject to the privilege would be available in a civil trial only if a criminal trial were conducted first; it would not be available if the civil trial were conducted first. The admissibility of evidence should not depend on the order in which civil and criminal matters are tried. This exception is provided, therefore, so that the same evidence is available in the civil case without regard to when the criminal case is tried.

13 Cal. Law Revision Comm'n Rep. App. VII (1975) p. 2077.

Section 999 is amended to provide an exception to the physician-patient privilege where good cause is shown for the disclosure of a relevant communication concerning the condition of a patient in a proceeding to recover damages on account of the conduct of the patient. Section 999 permits the disclosure of communications between patient and physician (*see* Section 992 broadly defining communication) where a need for such evidence is shown while at the same time protecting from disclosure the communications of persons whose conduct is not involved in the action for damages.

Section 999 permits disclosure not only in a case where the patient is a party to the action but also in a case where a party's liability is based on the conduct of the patient. An example of the latter situation is a personal injury action brought against an employer based on the negligent conduct of his employee who was killed in the accident. On the other hand, the section does not affect the privilege of nonparty patients in malpractice actions. *See, e.g., Marcus v. Superior Court*, 18 Cal.App.3d 22, 95 Cal.Rptr. 545 (1971). However, even in such malpractice actions, it sometimes may be possible to provide the necessary information without violating the privilege. *See Rudnick v. Superior Court*, 11 Cal. 3d 924, 933 n.13, 523 P.2d 643, 650-651 n.13, 114 Cal.Rptr. 603, 610-611 n.13 (1974).

The requirement that good cause be shown for the disclosure permits the court to protect the defendant against a "fishing expedition" into his medical records. Compare Evid Code §996 (patient-litigant exception). It should be noted that the exception provided by Section 999, like the other exceptions in this article does not apply to the psychotherapist-patient privilege. That privilege is a separate and distinct privilege, and the exceptions to that privilege are much more narrowly drawn. *See* Evid Code §§1010-1028.

Formerly, Section 999 provided an exception only in a proceeding to recover damages arising out of the criminal conduct of the patient. This "criminal conduct" exception has been eliminated as unnecessary in view of the "good cause" exception now provided by section 999. Moreover, the "criminal conduct" exception was burdensome, difficult to administer, and ill designed to achieve the purpose of making needed evidence available. *See Recommendation Relating to Evidence Code Section 999—The "Criminal Conduct" Exception to the Physician-Patient Privilege*, 11 Cal. Law Revision Comm'n Reports 1147 (1973).

ANNOTATIONS

John B. v. Superior Ct. (2006) 38 Cal.4th 1177, 1202. "[D] contends that discovery must nonetheless be denied because a good cause showing should require at a minimum 'an expert declaration regarding [P's HIV-]infection status; the probable exposure period; and a description of [P's] sexual history that establishes [D] as a probable transmitter.' [¶] [D] cites no authority for his contention that a plaintiff must essentially eliminate other possible agents of infection before discovery may proceed. The statutory standard is good cause, and [P] has amply established good cause for disclosure of [D's] medical records concerning HIV and AIDS: she has recently been diagnosed as HIV positive; [D], too, has been diagnosed as HIV positive, but his viral infection has already progressed to full-blown AIDS; during the two years preceding [P's] diagnosis, she was dating [D], engaged to him, and married to him; and the couple engaged in unprotected sex during that period. [P] thus has offered far more than 'conjecture' or a 'speculative presumption' to justify the requested discovery. Moreover, [D] has not offered any evidence to suggest that an expert could pinpoint the time period for [P's] exposure to the virus. We therefore find that the superior court did not abuse its discretion in overruling [D's] objection under the physician-patient privilege."

§1000. [NO PRIVILEGE: CLAIMED THROUGH DECEASED PATIENT]

There is no privilege under this article as to a communication relevant to an issue between parties all of whom claim through a deceased patient, regardless of whether the claims are by testate or intestate succession or by inter vivos transaction.

History of Evid. C. §1000: Added eff. Sept. 17, 1965, oper. Jan. 1, 1967, Stats. 1965, ch. 299, §2.

Official Comment

7 Cal. Law Revision Comm'n Rep. (1965) p. 1185.

See the *Comment* to Section 957.

§1001. [NO PRIVILEGE: BREACH OF DUTY]

There is no privilege under this article as to a communication relevant to an issue of breach, by the

physician or by the patient, of a duty arising out of the physician-patient relationship.

History of Evid. C. §1001: Added eff. Sept. 17, 1965, oper. Jan. 1, 1967, Stats. 1965, ch. 299, §2.

Official Comment

7 Cal. Law Revision Comm'n Rep. (1965) p. 1185.

See the *Comment* to Section 958.

§1002. [NO PRIVILEGE: DECEASED PATIENT'S INTENTION RELATING TO PROPERTY INTEREST]

There is no privilege under this article as to a communication relevant to an issue concerning the intention of a patient, now deceased, with respect to a deed of conveyance, will, or other writing, executed by the patient, purporting to affect an interest in property.

History of Evid. C. §1002: Added eff. Sept. 17, 1965, oper. Jan. 1, 1967, Stats. 1965, ch. 299, §2.

Official Comment

7 Cal. Law Revision Comm'n Rep. (1965) p. 1185.

Existing law provides exceptions virtually coextensive with those provided in Sections 1002 and 1003. Code Civ. Proc. §1881(4) (repealed). *See* the *Comment* to Section 960.

§1003. [NO PRIVILEGE: VALIDITY OF DECEASED PATIENT'S WRITING AFFECTING PROPERTY INTEREST]

There is no privilege under this article as to a communication relevant to an issue concerning the validity of a deed of conveyance, will, or other writing, executed by a patient, now deceased, purporting to affect an interest in property.

History of Evid. C. §1003: Added eff. Sept. 17, 1965, oper. Jan. 1, 1967, Stats. 1965, ch. 299, §2.

Official Comment

7 Cal. Law Revision Comm'n Rep. (1965) p. 1186.

See the *Comment* to Section 1002.

§1004. [NO PRIVILEGE: COMMITMENT PROCEEDING]

There is no privilege under this article in a proceeding to commit the patient or otherwise place him or his property, or both, under the control of another because of his alleged mental or physical condition.

History of Evid. C. §1004: Added eff. Sept. 17, 1965, oper. Jan. 1, 1967, Stats. 1965, ch. 299, §2.

Official Comment

7 Cal. Law Revision Comm'n Rep. (1965) p. 1186.

This exception covers not only commitments of mentally ill persons but also such cases as the appointment of a conservator under Probate Code Section 1751. In these cases, the proceedings are being conducted for the benefit of the patient and he should not have a privilege to withhold evidence that the court needs in order to act properly for his welfare. There is no similar exception in existing law. *McClenahan v. Keyes*, 188 Cal. 574, 584, 206 Pac. 454, 458 (1922) (dictum). *But see* 35 Ops. Cal. Atty. Gen. 226 (1960), regarding the unavailability of the present physician-patient privilege where the physician acts pursuant to court appointment for the explicit purpose of giving testimony.

§1005. [NO PRIVILEGE: COMPETENCY PROCEEDING]

There is no privilege under this article in a proceeding brought by or on behalf of the patient to establish his competence.

History of Evid. C. §1005: Added eff. Sept. 17, 1965, oper. Jan. 1, 1967, Stats. 1965, ch. 299, §2.

Official Comment

7 Cal. Law Revision Comm'n Rep. (1965) p. 1186.

This exception is new to California law. When a patient has placed his mental condition in issue by instituting a proceeding to establish his competence, he should not be permitted to withhold the most vital evidence relating thereto.

§1006. [NO PRIVILEGE: REQUIRED TO REPORT]

There is no privilege under this article as to information that the physician or the patient is required to report to a public employee, or as to information required to be recorded in a public office, if such report or record is open to public inspection.

History of Evid. C. §1006: Added eff. Sept. 17, 1965, oper. Jan. 1, 1967, Stats. 1965, ch. 299, §2.

Official Comment

7 Cal. Law Revision Comm'n Rep. (1965) p. 1187.

This exception is not recognized by existing law. However, no valid purpose is served by preventing the use of relevant information when the law requiring the information to be reported to a public office does not restrict disclosure.

§1007. [NO PRIVILEGE: PUBLIC ENTITY BRINGS PROCEEDING TO LIMIT RIGHT, AUTHORITY, LICENSE, OR PRIVILEGE]

There is no privilege under this article in a proceeding brought by a public entity to determine whether a right, authority, license, or privilege (including the right or privilege to be employed by the public entity or to hold a public office) should be revoked, suspended, terminated, limited, or conditioned.

History of Evid. C. §1007: Added eff. Sept. 17, 1965, oper. Jan. 1, 1967, Stats. 1965, ch. 299, §2.

Official Comment

7 Cal. Law Revision Comm'n Rep. (1965) p. 1187; Assem. J., Apr. 6, 1965, p. 1749.

Section 998 provides that the physician-patient privilege does not apply in criminal proceedings. Section 1007 provides that the physician-patient privilege may not be claimed in those administrative proceedings that are comparable to criminal proceedings, *i.e.*, proceedings brought for the purpose of imposing discipline of some sort. Under existing law, the physician-patient privilege is available in all administrative proceedings conducted under the Administrative Procedure Act because it has been incorporated by reference in Government Code Section 11513(c); but it is not specifically made available in administrative proceedings not conducted under the Administrative Procedure Act because the statute granting the privilege in terms applies only to civil actions. The Evidence Code sweeps away this distinction, which has no basis in reason, and conditions the availability of the privilege in administrative proceedings on the nature of the proceeding in which the privilege is invoked.

ARTICLE 7. PSYCHOTHERAPIST-PATIENT PRIVILEGE

§1010. [PSYCHOTHERAPIST]

As used in this article, "psychotherapist" means a person who is, or is reasonably believed by the patient to be:

(a) A person authorized to practice medicine in any state or nation who devotes, or is reasonably believed by the patient to devote, a substantial portion of his or her time to the practice of psychiatry.

(b) A person licensed as a psychologist under Chapter 6.6 (commencing with Section 2900) of Division 2 of the Business and Professions Code.

(c) A person licensed as a clinical social worker under Article 4 (commencing with Section 4996) of Chapter 14 of Division 2 of the Business and Professions Code, when he or she is engaged in applied psychotherapy of a nonmedical nature.

(d) A person who is serving as a school psychologist and holds a credential authorizing that service issued by the state.

(e) A person licensed as a marriage and family therapist under Chapter 13 (commencing with Section 4980) of Division 2 of the Business and Professions Code.

(f) A person registered as a psychological assistant who is under the supervision of a licensed psychologist or board certified psychiatrist as required by Section 2913 of the Business and Professions Code, or a person registered as a marriage and family therapist intern who is under the supervision of a licensed marriage and family therapist, a licensed clinical social worker, a licensed psychologist, or a licensed physician and surgeon certified in psychiatry, as specified in Section 4980.44 of the Business and Professions Code.

(g) A person registered as an associate clinical social worker who is under supervision as specified in Section 4996.23 of the Business and Professions Code.

(h) A person exempt from the Psychology Licensing Law pursuant to subdivision (d) of Section 2909 of the Business and Professions Code who is under the supervision of a licensed psychologist or board certified psychiatrist.

(i) A psychological intern as defined in Section 2911 of the Business and Professions Code who is under the supervision of a licensed psychologist or board certified psychiatrist.

(j) A trainee, as defined in subdivision (c) of Section 4980.03 of the Business and Professions Code, who is fulfilling his or her supervised practicum required by subparagraph (B) of paragraph (1) of subdivision (d) of Section 4980.36 of, or subdivision (c) of Section 4980.37 of, the Business and Professions Code and is supervised by a licensed psychologist, a board certified psychiatrist, a licensed clinical social worker, a licensed marriage and family therapist, or a licensed professional clinical counselor.

(k) A person licensed as a registered nurse pursuant to Chapter 6 (commencing with Section 2700) of Division 2 of the Business and Professions Code, who possesses a master's degree in psychiatric-mental health nursing and is listed as a psychiatric-mental health nurse by the Board of Registered Nursing.

(*l*) An advanced practice registered nurse who is certified as a clinical nurse specialist pursuant to Article 9 (commencing with Section 2838) of Chapter 6 of Division 2 of the Business and Professions Code and who participates in expert clinical practice in the specialty of psychiatric-mental health nursing.

(m) A person rendering mental health treatment or counseling services as authorized pursuant to Section 6924 of the Family Code.

(n) A person licensed as a professional clinical counselor under Chapter 16 (commencing with Section 4999.10) of Division 2 of the Business and Professions Code.

(o) A person registered as a clinical counselor intern who is under the supervision of a licensed professional clinical counselor, a licensed marriage and family therapist, a licensed clinical social worker, a licensed psychologist, or a licensed physician and surgeon certified in psychiatry, as specified in Sections 4999.42 to 4999.46, inclusive, of the Business and Professions Code.

(p) A clinical counselor trainee, as defined in subdivision (g) of Section 4999.12 of the Business and Professions Code, who is fulfilling his or her supervised practicum required by paragraph (3) of subdivision (c) of Section 4999.32 of, or paragraph (3) of subdivision (c) of Section 4999.33 of, the Business and Professions Code, and is supervised by a licensed psychologist, a board-certified psychiatrist, a licensed clinical social worker, a licensed marriage and family therapist, or a licensed professional clinical counselor.

History of Evid. C. §1010: Added eff. Sept. 17, 1965, oper. Jan. 1, 1967, Stats. 1965, ch. 299, §2. Amended eff. Nov. 8, 1967, Stats. 1967, ch. 1677, §3; eff. Nov. 23, 1970, Stats. 1970, ch. 1396, §1.5, ch. 1397, §1.5; eff. Mar. 7, 1973, Stats. 1972, ch. 888, §1; eff. Jan. 1, 1975, Stats. 1974, ch. 546, §16; eff. Jan. 1, 1984, Stats. 1983, ch. 928, §8; eff. Jan. 1, 1988, Stats. 1987, ch. 724, §1; eff. Jan. 1, 1989, Stats. 1988, ch. 488, §1; eff. Jan. 1, 1990, Stats. 1989, ch. 1104, §37; eff. Jan. 1, 1991, Stats. 1990, ch. 662, §1; eff. Jan. 1, 1993, Stats. 1992, ch. 308, §2; eff. Jan. 1, 1995, Stats. 1994, ch. 1270, §1; eff. Oct. 2, 2001, Stats. 2001, ch. 420, §§1, 1.5; eff. Jan. 1, 2002, Stats. 2001, ch. 142, §1; eff. Jan. 1, 2010, Stats. 2009, ch. 26, §21; eff. Jan. 1, 2012, Stats. 2011, ch. 381, §21.

Official Comment

7 Cal. Law Revision Comm'n Rep. (1965) p. 1188.

A "psychotherapist" is defined to include only a person who is or who is reasonably believed to be a psychiatrist or who is a California certified psychologist (*see* Bus. & Prof. Code §2900 *et seq.*). *See* the *Comment* to Section 990.

9 Cal. Law Revision Comm'n Rep. (1968) p. 512.

Section 1010 is amended to include school psychologists, clinical social workers, and marriage, family, and child counselors within the definition of "psychotherapist." To be included under Section 1010, a school psychologist must hold an appropriate credential issued by the State Board of Education. *See* Educ. Code §§13187-13188 and 13196; Cal. Admin. Code, Title 5, subch. 18.1, group 7. The credential specified in subdivision (c) includes one issued under former law which is equivalent to the standard designated services credential with specialization in pupil personnel services authorizing service as a school psychologist. *See* Educ. Code §§11753 and 13187-13187.1. A clinical social worker or marriage, family, and child counselor must have the appropriate license to be included under Section 1010.

The privilege under this article covers confidential communications made in the course of diagnosis or treatment of a mental or emotional condition or an examination for purposes of psychiatric or psychological research. *See* Section 1011 and the *Comment* to that section. Thus, the privilege under this article covers individual diagnosis and treatment and such activities as marriage, family, and child counseling. *See also Recommendation Relating to the Evidence Code: Number 4—Revision of the Privileges Article* (November 1968), reprinted in 9 Cal. Law Revision Comm'n Reports 501 (1969).

§1010.5. [EDUCATIONAL PSYCHOLOGIST-PATIENT PRIVILEGE]

A communication between a patient and an educational psychologist, licensed under Article 5 (commencing with Section 4986) of Chapter 13 of Division 2 of the Business and Professions Code, shall be privileged to the same extent, and subject to the same limitations, as a communication between a patient and a psychotherapist described in subdivisions (c), (d), and (e) of Section 1010.

History of Evid. C. §1010.5: Added eff. Jan. 1, 1986, Stats. 1985, ch. 545, §1.

§1011. [PATIENT]

As used in this article, "patient" means a person who consults a psychotherapist or submits to an examination by a psychotherapist for the purpose of securing a diagnosis or preventive, palliative, or curative treatment of his mental or emotional condition or who submits to an examination of his mental or emotional condition for the purpose of scientific research on mental or emotional problems.

History of Evid. C. §1011: Added eff. Sept. 17, 1965, oper. Jan. 1, 1967, Stats. 1965, ch. 299, §2.

Official Comment

7 Cal. Law Revision Comm'n Rep. (1965) p. 1188; Assem. J., Apr. 6, 1965, p. 1749.

See the *Comment* to Section 991. Section 1011 is comparable to Section 991 (physician-patient privilege) except that the definition of "patient" in Section 1011 includes not only persons seeking diagnosis or treatment of a mental or emotional condition but also persons who submit to examination for purposes of psychiatric or psychological research. *See* the *Comment* to Section 1014.

§1012. [CONFIDENTIAL COMMUNICATION BETWEEN PATIENT & PSYCHOTHERAPIST]

As used in this article, "confidential communication between patient and psychotherapist" means information, including information obtained by an examination of the patient, transmitted between a patient and his psychotherapist in the course of that relationship and in confidence by a means which, so far as the patient is aware, discloses the information to no third persons other than those who are present to further the interest of the patient in the consultation, or those to whom disclosure is reasonably necessary for the transmission of the information or the accomplishment of the purpose for which the psychotherapist is consulted, and includes a diagnosis made and the advice given by the psychotherapist in the course of that relationship.

History of Evid. C. §1012: Added eff. Sept. 17, 1965, oper. Jan. 1, 1967, Stats. 1965, ch. 299, §2. Amended eff. Nov. 8, 1967, Stats. 1967, ch. 650, §5; eff. Nov. 23, 1970, Stats. 1970, ch. 1396, §2, ch. 1397, §2.

Official Comment

7 Cal. Law Revision Comm'n Rep. (1965) p. 1189.

See the *Comment* to Section 992.

8 Cal. Law Revision Comm'n Rep. (1967) p. 122.

The express inclusion of "a diagnosis" in the last clause will preclude a possible construction of this section that would leave an uncommunicated diagnosis unprotected by the privilege. Such a construction would virtually destroy the privilege.

9 Cal. Law Revision Comm'n Rep. (1968) p. 513.

Section 1012 is amended to add "including other patients present at joint therapy" in order to foreclose the possibility that the section would be construed not to embrace marriage counseling, family counseling, and other forms of group therapy. However, it should be noted that communications made in the course of joint therapy are within the privilege only if they are made "in confidence" and "by a means which ... discloses the information to no third persons other than those ... to whom disclosure is reasonably necessary for ... the accomplishment of the purpose for which the psychotherapist is consulted." The making of a communication that meets these two requirements in the course of joint therapy would not amount to a waiver of the privilege. *See* Evidence Code Section 912(c) and (d).

The other amendments are technical and conform the language of Section 1012 to that of Section 992, the comparable section relating to the physician-patient privilege. Deletion of the words "or examination" makes no substantive change since "consultation" is broad enough to cover an examination. *See* Section 992. Substitution of "for which the psychotherapist is consulted" for "of the consultation or examination" adopts the broader language used in subdivision (d) of Section 912 and Section 992.

ANNOTATIONS

People v. Gonzales (2013) 56 Cal.4th 353, 372-73. "The People ... argue that when psychotherapy is en-

gaged in by a parolee as a condition of parole, the disclosure of the records of such therapy to the district attorney and evaluating psychologists in [a Sexually Violent Predator Act] proceeding falls within an exception to the psychotherapist-patient privilege.... *At 374:* Contrary to the People's contention, nothing in the text, legislative history, or purpose of ... §1012 supports the proposition that the language in question was intended to give a third party ... the authority to obtain disclosure of a confidential patient-psychotherapist communication over the patient's objection or without the patient's permission on the theory that such disclosure is necessary to accomplish the purpose for which the therapist has been consulted. Whether or not it would be useful or valuable for a district attorney or an evaluating psychologist to have access to confidential communications made by a parolee in the course of therapy sessions in order to evaluate the individual's mental condition or potential danger, the usefulness or value of such information is not a valid basis to interpret §1012 to eliminate the patient's right to protect against the disclosure of such communications. *At 375:* [However, this] does not mean that when therapy is engaged in as a condition of parole the therapist cannot provide general nonintrusive information to parole authorities...."

§1013. [HOLDER OF THE PRIVILEGE]

As used in this article, "holder of the privilege" means:

(a) The patient when he has no guardian or conservator.

(b) A guardian or conservator of the patient when the patient has a guardian or conservator.

(c) The personal representative of the patient if the patient is dead.

History of Evid. C. §1013: Added eff. Sept. 17, 1965, oper. Jan. 1, 1967, Stats. 1965, ch. 299, §2.

Official Comment

7 Cal. Law Revision Comm'n Rep. (1965) p. 1189.

See the *Comment* to Section 993.

§1014. [PSYCHOTHERAPIST-PATIENT PRIVILEGE]

Subject to Section 912 and except as otherwise provided in this article, the patient, whether or not a party, has a privilege to refuse to disclose, and to prevent another from disclosing, a confidential communication between patient and psychotherapist if the privilege is claimed by:

(a) [Holder.] The holder of the privilege.

(b) [Authorized person.] A person who is authorized to claim the privilege by the holder of the privilege.

(c) [Psychotherapist.] The person who was the psychotherapist at the time of the confidential communication, but the person may not claim the privilege if there is no holder of the privilege in existence or if he or she is otherwise instructed by a person authorized to permit disclosure. The relationship of a psychotherapist and patient shall exist between a psychological corporation as defined in Article 9 (commencing with Section 2995) of Chapter 6.6 of Division 2 of the Business and Professions Code, a marriage and family therapist corporation as defined in Article 6 (commencing with Section 4987.5) of Chapter 13 of Division 2 of the Business and Professions Code, a licensed clinical social workers corporation as defined in Article 5 (commencing with Section 4998) of Chapter 14 of Division 2 of the Business and Professions Code, or a professional clinical counselor corporation as defined in Article 7 (commencing with Section 4999.123) of Chapter 16 of Division 2 of the Business and Professions Code, and the patient to whom it renders professional services, as well as between those patients and psychotherapists employed by those corporations to render services to those patients. The word "persons" as used in this subdivision includes partnerships, corporations, limited liability companies, associations, and other groups and entities.

History of Evid. C. §1014: Added eff. Sept. 17, 1965, oper. Jan. 1, 1967, Stats. 1965, ch. 299, §2. Amended eff. Nov. 10, 1969, Stats. 1969, ch. 1436, §1; eff. Mar. 7, 1973, Stats. 1972, ch. 1286, §6; eff. Jan. 1, 1990, Stats. 1989, ch. 1104, §38; eff. Jan. 1, 1991, Stats. 1990, ch. 605, §1; eff. Jan. 1, 1995, Stats. 1994, ch. 1010, §106; eff. Jan. 1, 2003, Stats. 2002, ch. 1013, §78; eff. Jan. 1, 2012, Stats. 2011, ch. 381, §22.

Official Comment

7 Cal. Law Revision Comm'n Rep. (1965) p. 1189;
Assem. J., Apr. 6, 1965, p. 1750.

This article creates a psychotherapist-patient privilege that provides much broader protection than the physician-patient privilege.

Psychiatrists now have only the physician-patient privilege which is enjoyed by physicians generally. On the other hand, persons who consult certified psychologists have a much broader privilege under Business and Professions Code Section 2904 (repealed). There is no rational basis for this distinction.

A broad privilege should apply to both psychiatrists and certified psychologists. Psychoanalysis and psychotherapy are dependent upon the fullest revelation of the most intimate and embarrassing details of the patient's life. Research on mental or emotional problems requires similar disclosure. Unless a patient or research subject is assured that such information can and will be held in utmost confidence, he will be reluctant to make the full disclosure upon which diagnosis and treatment or complete and accurate research depends.

The Law Revision Commission has received several reliable reports that persons in need of treatment sometimes refuse such treatment from psychiatrists because the confidentiality of their communications cannot be assured

under existing law. Many of these persons are seriously disturbed and constitute threats to other persons in the community. Accordingly, this article establishes a new privilege that grants to patients of psychiatrists a privilege much broader in scope than the ordinary physician-patient privilege. Although it is recognized that the granting of the privilege may operate in particular cases to withhold relevant information, the interests of society will be better served if psychiatrists are able to assure patients that their confidences will be protected.

The Commission has also been informed that adequate research cannot be carried on in this field unless persons examined in connection therewith can be guaranteed that their disclosures will be kept confidential.

The privilege also applies to psychologists and supersedes the psychologist-patient privilege provided in Section 2904 of the Business and Professions Code. The new privilege is one for psychotherapists generally.

Generally, the privilege provided by this article follows the physician-patient privilege, and the *Comments* to Sections 990 through 1007 are pertinent. The following differences, however, should be noted:

(1) The psychotherapist-patient privilege applies in all proceedings. The physician-patient privilege does not apply in criminal proceedings. This difference in the scope of the two privileges is based on the fact that the Law Revision Commission has been advised that proper psychotherapy often is denied a patient solely because he will not talk freely to a psychotherapist for fear that the latter may be compelled in a criminal proceeding to reveal what he has been told. The Commission has also been advised that research in this field will be unduly hampered unless the privilege is available in criminal proceedings.

Although the psychotherapist-patient privilege applies in a criminal proceeding, the privilege is not available to a defendant who puts his mental or emotional condition in issue, as, for example, by a plea of insanity or a claim of diminished responsibility. *See* Evidence Code §§1016 and 1023. In such a proceeding, the trier of fact should have available to it all information that can be obtained in regard to the defendant's mental or emotional condition. That evidence can often be furnished by the psychotherapist who examined or treated the patient-defendant.

(2) There is an exception in the physician-patient privilege for commitment or guardianship proceedings for the patient. Evidence Code §1004. Section 1024 provides a considerably narrower exception in the psychotherapist-patient privilege.

(3) The physician-patient privilege does not apply in civil actions for damages arising out of the patient's criminal conduct. Evidence Code §999. Nor does it apply in certain administrative proceedings. Evidence Code §1007. No similar exceptions are provided in the psychotherapist-patient privilege. These exceptions appear in the physician-patient privilege because that privilege does not apply in criminal proceedings. *See* Evidence Code §998. Therefore, an exception is also created for comparable civil and administrative cases. The psychotherapist-patient privilege, however, does apply in criminal cases; hence, there is no similar exception in administrative proceedings or civil actions involving the patient's criminal conduct.

ANNOTATIONS

Menendez v. Superior Ct. (1992) 3 Cal.4th 435, 449. ***People v. Wharton*** (1991) 53 Cal.3d 522 "bears directly on the crucial issue of the 'dangerous patient' exception. As pertinent here, ***Wharton*** holds in substance that a psychotherapist's ***Tarasoff*** warning to the patient's intended victim is not covered by the privilege even if it relates an otherwise protected communication, provided that the conditions of the exception are satisfied, [i.e.], there is reasonable cause for the psychotherapist to believe that (1) the patient is dangerous *and* (2) disclosure of the communication is necessary to prevent any harm. The reasoning that underlies the ***Wharton*** holding extends to the circumstances that present themselves here. Accordingly, a psychotherapist's warning to a possible victim of the patient is not privileged, so long as the requirements of the exception are met. *At 451:* We emphasize that the 'dangerous patient' exception requires *only* reasonable cause for belief by the psychotherapist in the dangerousness of the patient and the necessity of disclosure. Certainly, it does not demand that the patient must be dangerous to a person *other than* the psychotherapist—although here the patients were. Nor does it demand that the psychotherapist must actually disclose the relevant communication or even issue a warning. Indeed, in ***Wharton*** we made plain that the exception was 'not keyed to … disclosure' or warning, but to the 'existence of the specified factual predicate,' [i.e.], reasonable cause for belief in the dangerousness of the patient and the necessity of disclosure."

Roberts v. Superior Ct. (1973) 9 Cal.3d 330, 339. "[T]o allow discovery of past psychiatric treatment merely to ascertain whether the patient's past condition may have decreased his tolerance to pain or whether the patient may have discussed with his psychotherapist complaints similar to those to be litigated, would defeat the purpose of the privilege established by §1014.… [¶] [I]n a case such as this where there is no specific mental condition of the patient at issue, and discovery of the privileged communications is sought merely upon speculation that there may be a 'connection' between the patient's past psychiatric treatment and some 'mental component' of his present injury, those communications should remain protected by the privilege of §1014.… *At 341:* [W]e conclude that petitioner did not waive her privilege merely by stating that she received psychiatric treatment … following an overdose of pills. She has disclosed no more than we suggested in [***In re Lifschutz*** (1970) 2 Cal.3d 415] as necessary to avoid application of the patient-litigant exception to the psychotherapist-patient privilege."

Ewing v. Goldstein (2d Dist.2004) 120 Cal.App.4th 807, 818-19. "The Legislature has long recognized that information conveyed to a therapist by a patient's parent or other family member is relevant and sufficiently important to be considered and incorporated into developing the best treatment for a patient, and is worthy of protection from disclosure. Despite its privileged nature, the Legislature also has recognized that the therapist's duty to protect that information must yield once the therapist comes to believe the information must be revealed to prevent danger to his or her patient or an-

other. We discern no principled reason why equally important information in the form of an actual threat that a parent shares with his or her son's therapist about the risk of grave bodily injury the patient poses to another also should not be considered a 'patient communication' in determining whether the therapist's duty to warn is triggered under [Civ. C.] §43.92."

San Diego Trolley, Inc. v. Superior Ct. (4th Dist.2001) 87 Cal.App.4th 1083, 1090-91. "[T]he [psychotherapist-patient] privilege can cover a communication that was never, in fact, 'confidential'—so long as it was made in confidence. The communication need only comprise information transmitted between a patient and his psychotherapist in the course of that relationship and in confidence by a means which, *so far as the patient is aware*, discloses the information to no 'outside' third person. [¶] Similarly, the privilege can cover a communication that has lost its 'confidential' status. [¶] The patient has a privilege to refuse to disclose, *and to prevent another from disclosing*, a confidential communication between patient and psychotherapist. [¶] The 'privilege to prevent' disclosure to others not only prevents disclosures by a patient's psychotherapist, it also governs *any* other third person privy to a confidential communication. In this aspect, the 'privilege to prevent' effectively repudiates the old 'eavesdropper rule,' under which the privilege is defeated whenever any 'outside' third person—eavesdropper, finder or interceptor—overhears or otherwise receives the confidential communication." (Internal quotes omitted.)

Scull v. Superior Ct. (2d Dist.1988) 206 Cal.App.3d 784, 789-90. "[M]ere disclosure of the patient's identity violates the psychotherapist-patient privilege. [T]he disclosure that an individual is seeing a therapist may well serve to discourage any treatment and thereby interfere with the patient's freedom to seek and derive the benefits of psychotherapy."

§1014.5. REPEALED

Repealed oper. Jan. 1, 1995, Stats. 1994, ch. 1270, §2.

§1015. [CLAIMING THE PRIVILEGE]

The psychotherapist who received or made a communication subject to the privilege under this article shall claim the privilege whenever he is present when the communication is sought to be disclosed and is authorized to claim the privilege under subdivision (c) of Section 1014.

History of Evid. C. §1015: Added eff. Sept. 17, 1965, oper. Jan. 1, 1967, Stats. 1965, ch. 299, §2.

Official Comment

7 Cal. Law Revision Comm'n Rep. (1965) p. 1191.

See the *Comment* to Section 995.

§1016. [NO PRIVILEGE: PATIENT-LITIGANT]

There is no privilege under this article as to a communication relevant to an issue concerning the mental or emotional condition of the patient if such issue has been tendered by:

(a) The patient;

(b) Any party claiming through or under the patient;

(c) Any party claiming as a beneficiary of the patient through a contract to which the patient is or was a party; or

(d) The plaintiff in an action brought under Section 376 or 377 of the Code of Civil Procedure for damages for the injury or death of the patient.

History of Evid. C. §1016: Added eff. Sept. 17, 1965, oper. Jan. 1, 1967, Stats. 1965, ch. 299, §2.

Official Comment

7 Cal. Law Revision Comm'n Rep. (1965) p. 1192.

See the *Comment* to Section 996.

§1016

ANNOTATIONS

Jacob B. v. County of Shasta (2007) 40 Cal.4th 948, 961. "[T]he litigation privilege applies even to a constitutionally based privacy cause of action. ... The litigation privilege has existed '[f]or well over a century,' and '[a]t least since then ..., California courts have given the privilege an expansive reach.' [W]e believe the constitutional right contains within it a limitation previously based on statute. When the voters adopted [Cal. Const.], art. I, §1, they did so mindful of the preexisting litigation privilege. *At 962:* In adopting the litigation privilege, the *Legislature* has already done the balancing. The litigation privilege furthers 'the vital public policy of affording free access to the courts and facilitating the crucial functions of the finder of fact.' This policy exists even if a privacy cause of action invokes the Constitution, and not on a case-by-case basis but in all cases."

Britt v. Superior Ct. (1978) 20 Cal.3d 844, 863-64. "[W]e held in [***In re Lifschutz*** (1970) 2 Cal.3d 415] that the automatic waiver of privilege contemplated by the patient-litigant exception must be construed not as a complete waiver of the privilege but only as a limited waiver concomitant with the purposes of the exception.

Under §1016 disclosure can be compelled only with respect to *those mental conditions* the patient-litigant has disclosed by bringing an action in which *they* are in issue; communications which are not directly relevant to those specific conditions do not fall within the terms of §1016's exception and therefore remain privileged. Disclosure cannot be compelled with respect to other aspects of the patient-litigant's personality even though they may, in some sense, be relevant to the substantive issues of litigation. The patient thus is not obligated to sacrifice all privacy to seek redress for a specific mental or emotional injury; *the scope of the inquiry permitted depends upon the nature of the injuries which the patient-litigant himself has brought before the court.*" (Internal quotes omitted.) *See also* ***Roberts v. Superior Ct.*** (1973) 9 Cal.3d 330, 337-39.

Oiye v. Fox (6th Dist.2012) 211 Cal.App.4th 1036, 1068. See annotation under Evidence Code §996, p. 1324.

San Diego Trolley, Inc. v. Superior Ct. (4th Dist.2001) 87 Cal.App.4th 1083, 1093. "[A]ny waiver of the psychotherapist-patient privilege which has occurred in one proceeding must be carefully limited with respect to its later use in entirely unrelated proceedings."

§1017. [NO PRIVILEGE: APPOINTED PSYCHOTHERAPIST]

(a) [By court.] There is no privilege under this article if the psychotherapist is appointed by order of a court to examine the patient, but this exception does not apply where the psychotherapist is appointed by order of the court upon the request of the lawyer for the defendant in a criminal proceeding in order to provide the lawyer with information needed so that he or she may advise the defendant whether to enter or withdraw a plea based on insanity or to present a defense based on his or her mental or emotional condition.

(b) [By Board of Prison Terms.] There is no privilege under this article if the psychotherapist is appointed by the Board of Prison Terms to examine a patient pursuant to the provisions of Article 4 (commencing with Section 2960) of Chapter 7 of Title 1 of Part 3 of the Penal Code.

History of Evid. C. §1017: Added eff. Sept. 17, 1965, oper. Jan. 1, 1967, Stats. 1965, ch. 299, §2. Amended eff. Nov. 8, 1967, Stats. 1967, ch. 650, §6; eff. Jan. 1, 1988, Stats. 1987, ch. 687, §1.

Official Comment

7 Cal. Law Revision Comm'n Rep. (1965) p. 1192.

Section 1017 provides an exception to the psychotherapist-patient privilege if the psychotherapist is appointed by order of a court to examine the patient. Generally, where the relationship of psychotherapist and patient is created by court order, there is not a sufficiently confidential relationship to warrant extending the privilege to communications made in the course of that relationship. Moreover, when the psychotherapist is appointed by the court, it is most often for the purpose of having the psychotherapist testify concerning his conclusions as to the patient's condition. It would be inappropriate to have the privilege apply in this situation. *See generally* 35 Ops. Cal. Atty. Gen. 226 (1960), regarding the unavailability of the present physician-patient privilege under these circumstances.

On the other hand, it is essential that the privilege apply where the psychotherapist is appointed by order of the court to provide the defendant's lawyer with information needed so that he may advise the defendant whether to enter a plea based on insanity or to present a defense based on his mental or emotional condition. If the defendant determines not to tender the issue of his mental or emotional condition, the privilege will protect the confidentiality of the communication between him and his court-appointed psychotherapist. If, however, the defendant determines to tender this issue—by a plea of not guilty by reason of insanity, by presenting a defense based on his mental or emotional condition, or by raising the question of his sanity at the time of the trial—the exceptions provided in Sections 1016 and 1023 make the privilege unavailable to prevent disclosure of the communications between the defendant and the psychotherapist.

8 Cal. Law Revision Comm'n Rep. (1967) p. 123.

The words "or withdraw" are added to Section 1017 to make it clear that the psychotherapist-patient privilege applies in a case where the defendant in a criminal proceeding enters a plea based on insanity, submits to an examination by a court-appointed psychotherapist, and later withdraws the plea based on insanity prior to the trial on that issue. In such case, since the defendant does not tender an issue based on his mental or emotional condition at the trial, the privilege should remain applicable. Of course, if the defendant determines to go to trial on the plea based on insanity, the psychotherapist-patient privilege will not be applicable. *See* Section 1016.

It should be noted that violation of the constitutional right to counsel may require the exclusion of evidence that is not privileged under this article; and, even in cases where this constitutional right is not violated, the protection that this right affords may require certain procedural safeguards in the examination procedure and a limiting instruction if the psychotherapist's testimony is admitted. *See In re Spencer*, 63 Cal.2d 400, 46 Cal.Rptr. 753, 406 P.2d 33 (1965).

It is important to recognize that the attorney-client privilege may provide protection in some cases where an exception to the psychotherapist-patient privilege is applicable. *See* Section 952 and the *Comment* thereto. *See also* Sections 912(d) and 954 and the *Comments* thereto.

§1018. [NO PRIVILEGE: CRIME OR TORT]

There is no privilege under this article if the services of the psychotherapist were sought or obtained to enable or aid anyone to commit or plan to commit a crime or a tort or to escape detection or apprehension after the commission of a crime or a tort.

History of Evid. C. §1018: Added eff. Sept. 17, 1965, oper. Jan. 1, 1967, Stats. 1965, ch. 299, §2.

Official Comment

7 Cal. Law Revision Comm'n Rep. (1965) p. 1193.

See the *Comment* to Section 997.

§1019. [NO PRIVILEGE: CLAIMED THROUGH DECEASED PATIENT]

There is no privilege under this article as to a communication relevant to an issue between parties all of whom claim through a deceased patient, regardless of whether the claims are by testate or intestate succession or by inter vivos transaction.

History of Evid. C. §1019: Added eff. Sept. 17, 1965, oper. Jan. 1, 1967, Stats. 1965, ch. 299, §2.

Official Comment

7 Cal. Law Revision Comm'n Rep. (1965) p. 1193.

See the *Comment* to Section 957.

§1020. [NO PRIVILEGE: BREACH OF DUTY]

There is no privilege under this article as to a communication relevant to an issue of breach, by the psychotherapist or by the patient, of a duty arising out of the psychotherapist-patient relationship.

History of Evid. C. §1020: Added eff. Sept. 17, 1965, oper. Jan. 1, 1967, Stats. 1965, ch. 299, §2.

Official Comment

7 Cal. Law Revision Comm'n Rep. (1965) p. 1193.

See the *Comment* to Section 958.

§1021. [NO PRIVILEGE: DECEASED PATIENT'S INTENTION RELATING TO EXECUTION OF DOCUMENT]

There is no privilege under this article as to a communication relevant to an issue concerning the intention of a patient, now deceased, with respect to a deed of conveyance, will, or other writing, executed by the patient, purporting to affect an interest in property.

History of Evid. C. §1021: Added eff. Sept. 17, 1965, oper. Jan. 1, 1967, Stats. 1965, ch. 299, §2.

Official Comment

7 Cal. Law Revision Comm'n Rep. (1965) p. 1194.

See the *Comment* to Section 1002.

§1022. [NO PRIVILEGE: VALIDITY OF DOCUMENT AFFECTING PROPERTY INTEREST OF DECEASED PATIENT]

There is no privilege under this article as to a communication relevant to an issue concerning the validity of a deed of conveyance, will, or other writing, executed by a patient, now deceased, purporting to affect an interest in property.

History of Evid. C. §1022: Added eff. Sept. 17, 1965, oper. Jan. 1, 1967, Stats. 1965, ch. 299, §2.

Official Comment

7 Cal. Law Revision Comm'n Rep. (1965) p. 1194.

See the *Comment* to Section 1002.

§1023. [NO PRIVILEGE: DEFENDANT RAISES ISSUE OF SANITY]

There is no privilege under this article in a proceeding under Chapter 6 (commencing with Section 1367) of Title 10 of Part 2 of the Penal Code initiated at the request of the defendant in a criminal action to determine his sanity.

History of Evid. C. §1023: Added eff. Sept. 17, 1965, oper. Jan. 1, 1967, Stats. 1965, ch. 299, §2.

Official Comment

7 Cal. Law Revision Comm'n Rep. (1965) p. 1194.

Section 1023 is included to make it clear that the psychotherapist-patient privilege does not apply when the defendant raises the issue of his sanity at the time of trial. The section probably is unnecessary because the exception provided by Section 1016 is broad enough to cover this situation.

§1024. [NO PRIVILEGE: DANGEROUS PATIENT]

There is no privilege under this article if the psychotherapist has reasonable cause to believe that the patient is in such mental or emotional condition as to be dangerous to himself or to the person or property of another and that disclosure of the communication is necessary to prevent the threatened danger.

History of Evid. C. §1024: Added eff. Sept. 17, 1965, oper. Jan. 1, 1967, Stats. 1965, ch. 299, §2.

Official Comment

7 Cal. Law Revision Comm'n Rep. (1965) p. 1194.

This section provides a narrower exception to the psychotherapist-patient privilege than the comparable exceptions provided by Section 982 (privilege for confidential marital communications) and Section 1004 (physician-patient privilege). Although this exception might inhibit the relationship between the patient and his psychotherapist to a limited extent, it is essential that appropriate action be taken if the psychotherapist becomes convinced during the course of treatment that the patient is a menace to himself or others and the patient refuses to permit the psychotherapist to make the disclosure necessary to prevent the threatened danger.

ANNOTATIONS

People v. Gonzales (2013) 56 Cal.4th 353, 381-83. "[I]t appears that the trial court's conclusion that the dangerous patient exception was applicable was based solely on the district attorney's conclusory offer of proof that the ... records would show that [psychologist] believed [D] did present a danger. ... Although [psychologist] did express her concern that [D's] consumption of alcohol in the presence of children constituted a 'recipe for a sex offense,' that concern was not based upon any information conveyed to her by [D] during therapy and she did not testify that she believed that it was necessary to reveal any confidential communications from therapy to prevent danger to [D] or to others. [¶] [E]ven when some of a patient's statements in therapy are subject to disclosure under ... §1024, the rest of the patient's confidential communications remain privileged. Accordingly, the trial court erred in ruling that under §1024 the confidential ... therapy records could properly be disclosed to the district attorney and evaluating psychologists, and in permitting [psychologist] to testify about all of [D's] confidential communications made during their numerous therapy sessions."

Menendez v. Superior Ct. (1992) 3 Cal.4th 435, 449. ***People v. Wharton*** (1991) 53 Cal.3d 522 "holds in

substance that a psychotherapist's ***Tarasoff*** warning to the patient's intended victim is not covered by the privilege even if it relates an otherwise protected communication, provided that the conditions of the exception are satisfied, [i.e.], there is reasonable cause for the psychotherapist to believe that (1) the patient is dangerous *and* (2) disclosure of the communication is necessary to prevent any harm."

San Diego Trolley, Inc. v. Superior Ct. (4th Dist.2001) 87 Cal.App.4th 1083, 1092. Section 1024 "creates an exception to the privilege rather than anything akin to a waiver of the privilege. Hence when the factual predicate of the exception exists, an excepted communication may be used in any further proceeding, even though the threat identified by the psychotherapist no longer exists."

§1025. [NO PRIVILEGE: COMPETENCY PROCEEDING]

There is no privilege under this article in a proceeding brought by or on behalf of the patient to establish his competence.

History of Evid. C. §1025: Added eff. Sept. 17, 1965, oper. Jan. 1, 1967, Stats. 1965, ch. 299, §2.

Official Comment

7 Cal. Law Revision Comm'n Rep. (1965) p. 1195.

See the *Comment* to Section 1005.

§1026. [NO PRIVILEGE: REQUIRED TO REPORT OR RECORD]

There is no privilege under this article as to information that the psychotherapist or the patient is required to report to a public employee or as to information required to be recorded in a public office, if such report or record is open to public inspection.

History of Evid. C. §1026: Added eff. Sept. 17, 1965, oper. Jan. 1, 1967, Stats. 1965, ch. 299, §2.

Official Comment

7 Cal. Law Revision Comm'n Rep. (1965) p. 1195.

See the *Comment* to Section 1006.

§1027. [NO PRIVILEGE: VICTIM UNDER AGE OF 16]

There is no privilege under this article if all of the following circumstances exist:

(a) The patient is a child under the age of 16.

(b) The psychotherapist has reasonable cause to believe that the patient has been the victim of a crime and that disclosure of the communication is in the best interest of the child.

History of Evid. C. §1027: Added eff. Nov. 23, 1970, Stats. 1970, ch. 1397, §3.

Editor's note: The Senate bill that became Stats. 1970, ch. 1397 was an amended version based on the CLRC recommendation, but there was no Legislative Committee Comment. The original CLRC comment does not apply to the version enacted.

§1028. REPEALED

Repealed by Stats. 1985, ch. 1077, §§1, 2.

ARTICLE 8. CLERGY PENITENT PRIVILEGES

§1030. [MEMBER OF THE CLERGY]

As used in this article, a "member of the clergy" means a priest, minister, religious practitioner, or similar functionary of a church or of a religious denomination or religious organization.

History of Evid. C. §1030: Added eff. Sept. 17, 1965, oper. Jan. 1, 1967, Stats. 1965, ch. 299, §2. Amended eff. Jan. 1, 2003, Stats. 2002, ch. 806, §19.

Official Comment

7 Cal. Law Revision Comm'n Rep. (1965) p. 1195.

"Clergyman" is broadly defined in this section.

§1031. [PENITENT]

As used in this article, "penitent" means a person who has made a penitential communication to a member of the clergy.

History of Evid. C. §1031: Added eff. Sept. 17, 1965, oper. Jan. 1, 1967, Stats. 1965, ch. 299, §2. Amended eff. Jan. 1, 2003, Stats. 2002, ch. 806, §20.

Official Comment

7 Cal. Law Revision Comm'n Rep. (1965) p. 1196.

This section defines "penitent" by incorporating the definitions in Sections 1030 and 1032.

§1032. [PENITENTIAL COMMUNICATION]

As used in this article, "penitential communication" means a communication made in confidence, in the presence of no third person so far as the penitent is aware, to a member of the clergy who, in the course of the discipline or practice of the clergy member's church, denomination, or organization, is authorized or accustomed to hear those communications and, under the discipline or tenets of his or her church, denomination, or organization, has a duty to keep those communications secret.

History of Evid. C. §1032: Added eff. Sept. 17, 1965, oper. Jan. 1, 1967, Stats. 1965, ch. 299, §2. Amended eff. Jan. 1, 2003, Stats. 2002, ch. 806, §21.

Official Comment

7 Cal. Law Revision Comm'n Rep. (1965) p. 1196.

Under existing law, the communication must be a "confession." Code Civ. Proc. §1881(3) (repealed). Section 1032 extends the protection that traditionally has been provided only to those persons whose religious practice involves "confessions."

ANNOTATIONS

People v. Edwards (1st Dist.1988) 203 Cal.App.3d 1358, 1362-63. "In order for a statement to be privi-

leged, it must satisfy all of the conceptual requirements of a penitential communication: (1) it must be intended to be in confidence; (2) it must be made to a member of the clergy who in the course of his or her religious discipline or practice is authorized or accustomed to hear such communications; and (3) such member of the clergy has a duty under the discipline or tenets of the church, religious denomination or organization to keep such communications secret." *See also* ***Doe 2 v. Superior Ct.*** (2d Dist.2005) 132 Cal.App.4th 1504, 1516.

§1033. [PENITENT PRIVILEGE]

Subject to Section 912, a penitent, whether or not a party, has a privilege to refuse to disclose, and to prevent another from disclosing, a penitential communication if he or she claims the privilege.

History of Evid. C. §1033: Added eff. Sept. 17, 1965, oper. Jan. 1, 1967, Stats. 1965, ch. 299, §2. Amended eff. Jan. 1, 2003, Stats. 2002, ch. 806, §22.

Official Comment

7 Cal. Law Revision Comm'n Rep. (1965) p. 1196.

This section provides the penitent with a privilege to refuse to disclose, and to prevent another from disclosing, a penitential communication. Because of the definition of "penitential communication," Section 1033 provides a broader privilege than the existing law.

Section 1033 differs from Code of Civil Procedure Section 1881(3) (repealed) in that Section 1881(3) gives a penitent a privilege only to prevent a clergyman from disclosing the communication. Literally, Section 1881(3) does not give the penitent himself the right to refuse disclosure. However, similar privilege statutes have been held to grant a privilege both to refuse to disclose and to prevent the other communicant from disclosing the privileged statement. *See City & County of San Francisco v. Superior Court*, 37 Cal.2d 227, 236, 231 P.2d 26, 31 (1951) (attorney-client privilege); *Verdelli v. Gray's Harbor Commercial Co.*, 115 Cal. 517, 525-526, 47 Pac. 364, 366 (1897) ("a client cannot be compelled to disclose communications which his attorney cannot be permitted to disclose"). Hence, it is likely that Section 1881(3) would be similarly construed.

Section 1033 also protects against disclosure by eavesdroppers. In this respect, the section provides the same scope of protection that is provided by the other confidential communication privileges. *See* the *Comment* to Section 954.

§1034. [CLERGY PRIVILEGE]

Subject to Section 912, a member of the clergy, whether or not a party, has a privilege to refuse to disclose a penitential communication if he or she claims the privilege.

History of Evid. C. §1034: Added eff. Sept. 17, 1965, oper. Jan. 1, 1967, Stats. 1965, ch. 299, §2. Amended eff. Jan. 1, 2003, Stats. 2002, ch. 806, §23.

Official Comment

7 Cal. Law Revision Comm'n Rep. (1965) p. 1197.

This section provides the clergyman with a privilege in his own right. Moreover, he may claim this privilege even if the penitent has waived the privilege granted him by Section 1033.

There may be several reasons for granting clergymen the traditional priest-penitent privilege. At least one underlying reason seems to be that the law will not compel a clergyman to violate—nor punish him for refusing to violate—the tenets of his church which require him to maintain secrecy as to confidential statements made to him in the course of his religious duties. *See generally* 8 Wigmore, *Evidence* §§2394-2396 (McNaughton rev. 1961).

The clergyman is under no legal compulsion to claim the privilege. Hence, a penitential communication will be admitted if the clergyman fails to claim the privilege and the penitent is deceased, incompetent, absent, or fails to claim the privilege. This probably changes existing law; but, if so, the change is desirable. For example, if a murderer had confessed the crime to a clergyman, the clergyman might under some circumstances (*e.g.*, if the murderer has died) decline to claim the privilege and, instead, give the evidence on behalf of an innocent third party who had been indicted for the crime. The extent to which a clergyman should keep secret or reveal penitential communications is not an appropriate subject for legislation; the matter is better left to the discretion of the individual clergyman involved and the discipline of the religious body of which he is a member.

ARTICLE 8.5. SEXUAL ASSAULT COUNSELOR-VICTIM PRIVILEGE

§1035. [VICTIM]

As used in this article, "victim" means a person who consults a sexual assault counselor for the purpose of securing advice or assistance concerning a mental, physical, or emotional condition caused by a sexual assault.

History of Evid. C. §1035: Added eff. Jan. 1, 1981, Stats. 1980, ch. 917, §2. Amended eff. Jan. 1, 2007, Stats. 2006, ch. 689, §4.

§1035.2. [SEXUAL-ASSAULT COUNSELOR]

As used in this article, "sexual assault counselor" means any of the following:

(a) A person who is engaged in any office, hospital, institution, or center commonly known as a rape crisis center, whose primary purpose is the rendering of advice or assistance to victims of sexual assault and who has received a certificate evidencing completion of a training program in the counseling of sexual assault victims issued by a counseling center that meets the criteria for the award of a grant established pursuant to Section 13837 of the Penal Code and who meets one of the following requirements:

(1) Is a psychotherapist as defined in Section 1010; has a master's degree in counseling or a related field; or has one year of counseling experience, at least six months of which is in rape crisis counseling.

(2) Has 40 hours of training as described below and is supervised by an individual who qualifies as a counselor under paragraph (1). The training, supervised by a person qualified under paragraph (1), shall include, but not be limited to, the following areas:

(A) Law.

(B) Medicine.

(C) Societal attitudes.

(D) Crisis intervention and counseling techniques.

(E) Role playing.

(F) Referral services.

(G) Sexuality.

(b) A person who is employed by any organization providing the programs specified in Section 13835.2 of the Penal Code, whether financially compensated or not, for the purpose of counseling and assisting sexual assault victims, and who meets one of the following requirements:

(1) Is a psychotherapist as defined in Section 1010; has a master's degree in counseling or a related field; or has one year of counseling experience, at least six months of which is in rape assault counseling.

(2) Has the minimum training for sexual assault counseling required by guidelines established by the employing agency pursuant to subdivision (c) of Section 13835.10 of the Penal Code, and is supervised by an individual who qualifies as a counselor under paragraph (1). The training, supervised by a person qualified under paragraph (1), shall include, but not be limited to, the following areas:

(A) Law.

(B) Victimology.

(C) Counseling.

(D) Client and system advocacy.

(E) Referral services.

History of Evid. C. §1035.2: Added eff. Jan. 1, 1981, Stats. 1980, ch. 917, §2. Amended eff. Jan. 1, 1984, Stats. 1983, ch. 580, §1, ch. 1072, §1; eff. Jan. 1, 1991, Stats. 1990, ch. 1342, §1; eff. Jan. 1, 2007, Stats. 2006, ch. 689, §5.

§1035.4. [CONFIDENTIAL COMMUNICATION BETWEEN SEXUAL-ASSAULT COUNSELOR & VICTIM]

As used in this article, "confidential communication between the sexual assault counselor and the victim" means information transmitted between the victim and the sexual assault counselor in the course of their relationship and in confidence by a means which, so far as the victim is aware, discloses the information to no third persons other than those who are present to further the interests of the victim in the consultation or those to whom disclosures are reasonably necessary for the transmission of the information or an accomplishment of the purposes for which the sexual assault counselor is consulted. The term includes all information regarding the facts and circumstances involving the alleged sexual assault and also includes all information regarding the victim's prior or subsequent sexual conduct, and opinions regarding the victim's sexual conduct or reputation in sexual matters. The court may compel disclosure of information received by the sexual assault counselor which constitutes relevant evidence of the facts and circumstances involving an alleged sexual assault about which the victim is complaining and which is the subject of a criminal proceeding if the court determines that the probative value outweighs the effect on the victim, the treatment relationship, and the treatment services if disclosure is compelled. The court may also compel disclosure in proceedings related to child abuse if the court determines the probative value outweighs the effect on the victim, the treatment relationship, and the treatment services if disclosure is compelled. When a court is ruling on a claim of privilege under this article, the court may require the person from whom disclosure is sought or the person authorized to claim the privilege, or both, to disclose the information in chambers out of the presence and hearing of all persons except the person authorized to claim the privilege and such other persons as the person authorized to claim the privilege is willing to have present. If the judge determines that the information is privileged and must not be disclosed, neither he or she nor any other person may ever disclose, without the consent of a person authorized to permit disclosure, what was disclosed in the course of the proceedings in chambers. If the court determines certain information shall be disclosed, the court shall so order and inform the defendant. If the court finds there is a reasonable likelihood that particular information is subject to disclosure pursuant to the balancing test provided in this section, the following procedure shall be followed:

(1) The court shall inform the defendant of the nature of the information which may be subject to disclosure.

(2) The court shall order a hearing out of the presence of the jury, if any, and at the hearing allow the questioning of the sexual assault counselor regarding the information which the court has determined may be subject to disclosure.

(3) At the conclusion of the hearing, the court shall rule which items of information, if any, shall be disclosed. The court may make an order stating what evidence may be introduced by the defendant and the nature of questions to be permitted. The defendant may then offer evidence pursuant to the order of the court. Admission of evidence concerning the sexual conduct of the complaining witness is subject to Sections 352, 782, and 1103.

History of Evid. C. §1035.4: Added eff. Jan. 1, 1981, Stats. 1980, ch. 917, §2. Amended eff. Jan. 1, 1984, Stats. 1983, ch. 1072, §2.

§1035.6. [HOLDER OF PRIVILEGE]

As used in this article, "holder of the privilege" means:

(a) The victim when such person has no guardian or conservator.

(b) A guardian or conservator of the victim when the victim has a guardian or conservator.

(c) The personal representative of the victim if the victim is dead.

History of Evid. C. §1035.6: Added eff. Jan. 1, 1981, Stats. 1980, ch. 917, §2.

§1035.8. [SEXUAL ASSAULT VICTIM-COUNSELOR PRIVILEGE]

A victim of a sexual assault, whether or not a party, has a privilege to refuse to disclose, and to prevent another from disclosing, a confidential communication between the victim and a sexual assault counselor if the privilege is claimed by any of the following:

(a) [**Holder.**] The holder of the privilege;

(b) [**Authorized person.**] A person who is authorized to claim the privilege by the holder of the privilege; or

(c) [**Sexual assault counselor.**] The person who was the sexual assault counselor at the time of the confidential communication, but that person may not claim the privilege if there is no holder of the privilege in existence or if he or she is otherwise instructed by a person authorized to permit disclosure.

History of Evid. C. §1035.8: Added eff. Jan. 1, 1981, Stats. 1980, ch. 917, §2. Amended eff. Jan. 1, 2007, Stats. 2006, ch. 689, §6.

ANNOTATIONS

People v. Gilbert (6th Dist.1992) 5 Cal.App.4th 1372, 1391. "[T]he purpose of the sexual assault victim-counselor privilege is to protect the confidences of one 'who consults a sexual assault victim counselor for the purpose of securing advice or assistance concerning a mental, physical, or emotional condition caused by a sexual assault' ... and thus to encourage those who believe they have been victimized by sexual assault to come forward and to make full and frank reports so that they may be advised and assisted. ... In short the privilege is designed to protect one who considers himself or herself the victim of a sexual assault, and to avoid any disincentive to such a person to seek help from a qualified sexual assault counselor."

§1036. [CLAIMING THE PRIVILEGE]

The sexual assault counselor who received or made a communication subject to the privilege under this article shall claim the privilege if he or she is present when the communication is sought to be disclosed and is authorized to claim the privilege under subdivision (c) of Section 1035.8.

History of Evid. C. §1036: Added eff. Jan. 1, 1981, Stats. 1980, ch. 917, §2. Amended eff. Jan. 1, 2007, Stats. 2006, ch. 689, §7.

§1036.2. [SEXUAL ASSAULT]

As used in this article, "sexual assault" includes all of the following:

(a) Rape, as defined in Section 261 of the Penal Code.

(b) Unlawful sexual intercourse, as defined in Section 261.5 of the Penal Code.

(c) Rape in concert with force and violence, as defined in Section 264.1 of the Penal Code.

(d) Rape of a spouse, as defined in Section 262 of the Penal Code.

(e) Sodomy, as defined in Section 286 of the Penal Code, except a violation of subdivision (e) of that section.

(f) A violation of Section 288 of the Penal Code.

(g) Oral copulation, as defined in Section 288a of the Penal Code, except a violation of subdivision (e) of that section.

(h) Sexual penetration, as defined in Section 289 of the Penal Code.

(i) Annoying or molesting a child under 18, as defined in Section 647a of the Penal Code.

(j) Any attempt to commit any of the above acts.

History of Evid. C. §1036.2: Added eff. Jan. 1, 1981, Stats. 1980, ch. 917, §2. Amended eff. Jan. 1, 1989, Stats. 1988, ch. 102, §1; eff. Jan. 1, 2002, Stats. 2001, ch. 854, §4.

ARTICLE 8.7. DOMESTIC VIOLENCE COUNSELOR-VICTIM PRIVILEGE

§1037. [VICTIM]

As used in this article, "victim" means any person who suffers domestic violence, as defined in Section 1037.7.

History of Evid. C. §1037: Added eff. Jan. 1, 1987, Stats. 1986, ch. 854, §1.

§1037.1. [DOMESTIC-VIOLENCE COUNSELOR]

(a)(1) As used in this article, "domestic violence counselor" means a person who is employed by a domestic violence victim service organization, as defined in

this article, whether financially compensated or not, for the purpose of rendering advice or assistance to victims of domestic violence and who has at least 40 hours of training as specified in paragraph (2).

(2) The 40 hours of training shall be supervised by an individual who qualifies as a counselor under paragraph (1), and who has at least one year of experience counseling domestic violence victims for the domestic violence victim service organization. The training shall include, but need not be limited to, the following areas: history of domestic violence, civil and criminal law as it relates to domestic violence, the domestic violence victim-counselor privilege and other laws that protect the confidentiality of victim records and information, societal attitudes towards domestic violence, peer counseling techniques, housing, public assistance and other financial resources available to meet the financial needs of domestic violence victims, and referral services available to domestic violence victims.

(3) A domestic violence counselor who has been employed by the domestic violence victim service organization for a period of less than six months shall be supervised by a domestic violence counselor who has at least one year of experience counseling domestic violence victims for the domestic violence victim service organization.

(b) As used in this article, "domestic violence victim service organization" means a nongovernmental organization or entity that provides shelter, programs, or services to victims of domestic violence and their children, including, but not limited to, either of the following:

(1) Domestic violence shelter-based programs, as described in Section 18294 of the Welfare and Institutions Code.

(2) Other programs with the primary mission to provide services to victims of domestic violence whether or not that program exists in an agency that provides additional services.

History of Evid. C. §1037.1: Added eff. Jan. 1, 1987, Stats. 1986, ch. 854, §1. Amended eff. Jan. 1, 1991, Stats. 1990, ch. 1342, §2; eff. Jan. 1, 2008, Stats. 2007, ch. 206, §2.

§1037.2. [CONFIDENTIAL COMMUNICATION]

(a) As used in this article, "confidential communication" means any information, including, but not limited to, written or oral communication, transmitted between the victim and the counselor in the course of their relationship and in confidence by a means which, so far as the victim is aware, discloses the information to no third persons other than those who are present to further the interests of the victim in the consultation or those to whom disclosures are reasonably necessary for the transmission of the information or an accomplishment of the purposes for which the domestic violence counselor is consulted. The term includes all information regarding the facts and circumstances involving all incidences of domestic violence, as well as all information about the children of the victim or abuser and the relationship of the victim with the abuser.

(b) The court may compel disclosure of information received by a domestic violence counselor which constitutes relevant evidence of the facts and circumstances involving a crime allegedly perpetrated against the victim or another household member and which is the subject of a criminal proceeding, if the court determines that the probative value of the information outweighs the effect of disclosure of the information on the victim, the counseling relationship, and the counseling services. The court may compel disclosure if the victim is either dead or not the complaining witness in a criminal action against the perpetrator. The court may also compel disclosure in proceedings related to child abuse if the court determines that the probative value of the evidence outweighs the effect of the disclosure on the victim, the counseling relationship, and the counseling services.

(c) When a court rules on a claim of privilege under this article, it may require the person from whom disclosure is sought or the person authorized to claim the privilege, or both, to disclose the information in chambers out of the presence and hearing of all persons except the person authorized to claim the privilege and such other persons as the person authorized to claim the privilege consents to have present. If the judge determines that the information is privileged and shall not be disclosed, neither he nor she nor any other person may disclose, without the consent of a person authorized to permit disclosure, any information disclosed in the course of the proceedings in chambers.

(d) If the court determines that information shall be disclosed, the court shall so order and inform the defendant in the criminal action. If the court finds there is a reasonable likelihood that any information is subject to disclosure pursuant to the balancing test pro-

vided in this section, the procedure specified in subdivisions (1), (2), and (3) of Section 1035.4 shall be followed.

History of Evid. C. §1037.2: Added eff. Jan. 1, 1987, Stats. 1986, ch. 854, §1. Amended eff. Jan. 1, 2008, Stats. 2007, ch. 206, §3.

§1037.3. [No Limitation on Reporting Child Abuse]

Nothing in this article shall be construed to limit any obligation to report instances of child abuse as required by Section 11166 of the Penal Code.

History of Evid. C. §1037.3: Added eff. Jan. 1, 1987, Stats. 1986, ch. 854, §1.

§1037.4. [Holder of Privilege]

As used in this article, "holder of the privilege" means:

(a) The victim when he or she has no guardian or conservator.

(b) A guardian or conservator of the victim when the victim has a guardian or conservator, unless the guardian or conservator is accused of perpetrating domestic violence against the victim.

History of Evid. C. §1037.4: Added eff. Jan. 1, 1987, Stats. 1986, ch. 854, §1. Amended eff. Jan. 1, 2008, Stats. 2007, ch. 206, §4.

§1037.5. [Domestic Violence Counselor-Victim Privilege]

A victim of domestic violence, whether or not a party to the action, has a privilege to refuse to disclose, and to prevent another from disclosing, a confidential communication between the victim and a domestic violence counselor in any proceeding specified in Section 901 if the privilege is claimed by any of the following persons:

(a) [Holder.] The holder of the privilege.

(b) [Authorized person.] A person who is authorized to claim the privilege by the holder of the privilege.

(c) [Domestic-violence counselor.] The person who was the domestic violence counselor at the time of the confidential communication. However, that person may not claim the privilege if there is no holder of the privilege in existence or if he or she is otherwise instructed by a person authorized to permit disclosure.

History of Evid. C. §1037.5: Added eff. Jan. 1, 1987, Stats. 1986, ch. 854, §1. Amended eff. Jan. 1, 2008, Stats. 2007, ch. 206, §5.

§1037.6. [Claiming the Privilege]

The domestic violence counselor who received or made a communication subject to the privilege granted by this article shall claim the privilege whenever he or she is present when the communication is sought to be disclosed and he or she is authorized to claim the privilege under subdivision (c) of Section 1037.5.

History of Evid. C. §1037.6: Added eff. Jan. 1, 1987, Stats. 1986, ch. 854, §1.

§1037.7. [Domestic Violence]

As used in this article, "domestic violence" means "domestic violence" as defined in Section 6211 of the Family Code.

History of Evid. C. §1037.7: Added eff. Jan. 1, 1994, Stats. 1993, ch. 219, §77.4.

Official Comment

23 Cal. Law Revision Comm'n Rep. (1993) p. 825.

Section 1037.7 substitutes a reference to the Family Code provision defining "domestic violence" for the definitions of "abuse," "domestic violence," and "family or household member" in the former section. This is not a substantive change, since the Family Code definition of "domestic violence" continues the substance of the omitted definitions. *See* Fam. Code §6211 ("domestic violence" defined) & *Comment. See also* Fam. Code §§6203 ("abuse" defined), 6209 ("cohabitant" and "former cohabitant" defined).

§1037.8. [Notice of Limitations on Confidentiality]

A domestic violence counselor shall inform a domestic violence victim of any applicable limitations on confidentiality of communications between the victim and the domestic violence counselor. This information may be given orally.

History of Evid. C. §1037.8: Added eff. Jan. 1, 2003, Stats. 2002, ch. 629, §1.

Article 8.8. Human Trafficking Caseworker-Victim Privilege

§1038. [Human Trafficking Caseworker-Victim Privilege]

(a) [Generally.] A trafficking victim, whether or not a party to the action, has a privilege to refuse to disclose, and to prevent another from disclosing, a confidential communication between the victim and a human trafficking caseworker if the privilege is claimed by any of the following persons:

(1) [Holder.] The holder of the privilege.

(2) [Authorized person.] A person who is authorized to claim the privilege by the holder of the privilege.

(3) [Caseworker.] The person who was the human trafficking caseworker at the time of the confidential communication. However, that person may not claim the privilege if there is no holder of the privilege in existence or if he or she is otherwise instructed by a person authorized to permit disclosure. The human trafficking caseworker who received or made a communication subject to the privilege granted by this article shall claim the privilege whenever he or she is present

when the communication is sought to be disclosed and he or she is authorized to claim the privilege under this section.

(b) [Notice of limitations on confidentiality.] A human trafficking caseworker shall inform a trafficking victim of any applicable limitations on confidentiality of communications between the victim and the caseworker. This information may be given orally.

History of Evid. C. §1038: Added eff. Jan. 1, 2006, Stats. 2005, ch. 240, §4.

§1038.1. [COURT MAY COMPEL DISCLOSURE]

(a) [Relevant evidence involving crime.] The court may compel disclosure of information received by a human trafficking caseworker that constitutes relevant evidence of the facts and circumstances involving a crime allegedly perpetrated against the victim and that is the subject of a criminal proceeding, if the court determines that the probative value of the information outweighs the effect of disclosure of the information on the victim, the counseling relationship, and the counseling services. The court may compel disclosure if the victim is either dead or not the complaining witness in a criminal action against the perpetrator.

(b) [Disclosure in chambers.] When a court rules on a claim of privilege under this article, it may require the person from whom disclosure is sought or the person authorized to claim the privilege, or both, to disclose the information in chambers out of the presence and hearing of all persons except the person authorized to claim the privilege and those other persons that the person authorized to claim the privilege consents to have present.

(c) [Determination of privilege.] If the judge determines that the information is privileged and shall not be disclosed, neither he nor she nor any other person may disclose, without the consent of a person authorized to permit disclosure, any information disclosed in the course of the proceedings in chambers. If the court determines that information shall be disclosed, the court shall so order and inform the defendant in the criminal action. If the court finds there is a reasonable likelihood that any information is subject to disclosure pursuant to the balancing test provided in this section, the procedure specified in paragraphs (1), (2), and (3) of Section 1035.4 shall be followed.

History of Evid. C. §1038.1: Added eff. Jan. 1, 2006, Stats. 2005, ch. 240, §4.

A §1038.2. [DEFINITIONS]

(a) [Victim.] As used in this article, "victim" means any person who is a "trafficking victim" as defined in Section 236.1 of the Penal Code.

(b) [Human-trafficking caseworker.] As used in this article, "human trafficking caseworker" means any of the following:

(1) A person who is employed by any organization providing the programs specified in Section 18294 of the Welfare and Institutions Code, whether financially compensated or not, for the purpose of rendering advice or assistance to victims of human trafficking, who has received specialized training in the counseling of human trafficking victims, and who meets one of the following requirements:

(A) Has a master's degree in counseling or a related field; or has one year of counseling experience, at least six months of which is in the counseling of human trafficking victims.

(B) Has at least 40 hours of training as specified in this paragraph and is supervised by an individual who qualifies as a counselor under subparagraph (A), or is a psychotherapist, as defined in Section 1010. The training, supervised by a person qualified under subparagraph (A), shall include, but need not be limited to, the following areas: history of human trafficking, civil and criminal law as it relates to human trafficking, societal attitudes toward ~~[towards]~~ human trafficking, peer counseling techniques, housing, public assistance, and other financial resources available to meet the financial needs of human trafficking victims, and referral services available to human trafficking victims. A portion of this training must include an explanation of privileged communication.

(2) A person who is employed by any organization providing the programs specified in Section 13835.2 of the Penal Code, whether financially compensated or not, for the purpose of counseling and assisting human trafficking victims, and who meets one of the following requirements:

(A) Is a psychotherapist as defined in Section 1010, has a master's degree in counseling or a related field, or has one year of counseling experience, at least six months of which is in rape assault counseling.

(B) Has the minimum training for human trafficking counseling required by guidelines established by the employing agency pursuant to subdivision (c) of Section 13835.10 of the Penal Code, and is supervised

by an individual who qualifies as a counselor under subparagraph (A). The training, supervised by a person qualified under subparagraph (A), shall include, but not be limited to, law, victimology, counseling techniques, client and system advocacy, and referral services. A portion of this training must include an explanation of privileged communication.

(c) [Confidential communication.] As used in this article, "confidential communication" means information transmitted between the victim and the caseworker in the course of their relationship and in confidence by a means which, so far as the victim is aware, discloses the information to no third persons other than those who are present to further the interests of the victim in the consultation or those to whom disclosures are reasonably necessary for the transmission of the information or an accomplishment of the purposes for which the human trafficking counselor is consulted. It includes all information regarding the facts and circumstances involving all incidences of human trafficking.

(d) [Holder of the privilege.] As used in this article, "holder of the privilege" means the victim when he or she has no guardian or conservator, or a guardian or conservator of the victim when the victim has a guardian or conservator.

History of Evid. C. §1038.2: Added eff. Jan. 1, 2006, Stats. 2005, ch. 240, §4. Amended eff. Jan. 1, 2015, Stats. 2014, ch. 913, §15.

ARTICLE 9. OFFICIAL INFORMATION & IDENTITY OF INFORMER

§1040. [OFFICIAL-INFORMATION PRIVILEGE]

(a) [Official information.] As used in this section, "official information" means information acquired in confidence by a public employee in the course of his or her duty and not open, or officially disclosed, to the public prior to the time the claim of privilege is made.

(b) [Privilege.] A public entity has a privilege to refuse to disclose official information, and to prevent another from disclosing official information, if the privilege is claimed by a person authorized by the public entity to do so and:

(1) Disclosure is forbidden by an act of the Congress of the United States or a statute of this state; or

(2) Disclosure of the information is against the public interest because there is a necessity for preserving the confidentiality of the information that outweighs the necessity for disclosure in the interest of justice; but no privilege may be claimed under this paragraph if any person authorized to do so has consented that the information be disclosed in the proceeding. In determining whether disclosure of the information is against the public interest, the interest of the public entity as a party in the outcome of the proceeding may not be considered.

(c) [Disclosure to law enforcement.] Notwithstanding any other provision of law, the Employment Development Department shall disclose to law enforcement agencies, in accordance with the provisions of subdivision (k) of Section 1095 and subdivision (b) of Section 2714 of the Unemployment Insurance Code, information in its possession relating to any person if an arrest warrant has been issued for the person for commission of a felony.

History of Evid. C. §1040: Added eff. Sept. 17, 1965, oper. Jan. 1, 1967, Stats. 1965, ch. 299, §2. Amended eff. Jan. 1, 1985, Stats. 1984, ch. 1127, §2.

Official Comment

7 Cal. Law Revision Comm'n Rep. (1965) p. 1198; Assem. J., Apr. 6, 1965, p. 1751.

Under existing law, official information is protected either by subdivision 5 of Code of Civil Procedure Section 1881 (which, like Section 1040, prohibits disclosure when the interest of the public would suffer thereby) or by specific statutes such as the provisions of the Revenue and Taxation Code prohibiting disclosure of information reported in tax returns. *See, e.g.*, Rev. & Tax. Code §§19281-19289. Section 1881 is superseded by the Evidence Code, but the specific statutes protecting official information remain in effect. Evidence Code §1040(b)(1).

Section 1040 permits the official information privilege to be invoked by the public entity or its authorized representative. Since the privilege is granted to enable the government to protect its secrets, no reason exists for permitting the privilege to be exercised by persons who are not concerned with the public interest. It should be noted, however, that another statute may provide a person with a privilege not to disclose a report he made to the government; the Evidence Code has no effect on that privilege. *See* the *Comment* to Evidence Code §920. Where the government has received a report from an informant, the official information privilege may apply to that report. It does not apply, however, to the knowledge of the informant. The government does not acquire a privilege to prevent an informant from revealing his knowledge merely because that knowledge has been communicated to the government.

The official information privilege provided in Section 1040 does not extend to the identity of an informer. Section 1041 provides special rules for determining when the government has a privilege to keep secret the identity of an informer.

The privilege may be asserted to prevent testimony by anyone who has official information. This provides the public entity with more protection than existing law. *See* the *Comment* to Evidence Code §954 (attorney-client privilege).

Official information is absolutely privileged if its disclosure is forbidden by either a federal or state statute. Other official information is subject to a conditional privilege: The judge must determine in each instance the consequences to the public of disclosure and the consequences to the litigant of nondisclosure and then decide which outweighs the other. He should, of course, be aware that the public has an interest in seeing that justice is done in the particular cause as well as an interest in the secrecy of the information.

ANNOTATIONS

Sander v. State Bar of Cal. (2013) 58 Cal.4th 300, 304. "The question presented is whether any law re-

quires disclosure of the State Bar's admissions database on bar applicants. *At 325-26:* The State Bar asserts that [the database] is not subject to public disclosure because the information contained in it was obtained from applicants under a promise that it would remain confidential. Under longstanding common law and statutory principles, information obtained through a promise of confidentiality is not subject to the right of public access when the public interest would be furthered by maintaining confidentiality. This principle is currently reflected in … §1040, which provides a privilege to a public entity to refuse to disclose information acquired in confidence if 'there is a necessity for preserving the confidentiality of the information that outweighs the necessity for disclosure.' [¶] [H]owever, this principle has not prevented public access to otherwise confidential, private information in the possession of a public entity that is not linked to the individual to which it pertains. Because [Ps] do not seek the information in a manner that would reveal the identities of individual applicants, the State Bar's promises of confidentiality do not necessarily preclude public access to the database."

CBS, Inc. v. Block (1986) 42 Cal.3d 646, 656. "[Ds] assert that [Evid. C.] §1040 shields the sheriff from any duty to disclose. [S]ection 1040 creates a privilege for official information acquired in confidence if '[d]isclosure of the information is against the public interest because there is a necessity for preserving the confidentiality of the information that outweighs the necessity for disclosure in the interest of justice….' This privilege must be 'applied conditionally on a clear showing that disclosure is against the public's interest.' [¶] The weighing process mandated by … §1040 requires review of the same elements that must be considered under [Gov. C.] §6255. Therefore, it is consistent with the [California Public Records Act]. Under this privilege, the burden of demonstrating a need for nondisclosure is on the agency claiming the right to withhold the information. Thus, this court's rejection of the claim of exemption under §6255 on the ground that the public interest weighs in favor of disclosure similarly requires rejection of the claims of exemption under [Gov. C.] §6254, subdivision (k) and §1040." *See also* ***Humane Soc'y of the U.S. v. Superior Ct.*** (3d Dist.2013) 214 Cal.App.4th 1233, 1255 n.22 (balancing tests for catchall exemption, Gov. C. §6255, and official information privilege, Evid. C. §1040, are same).

Shepherd v. Superior Ct. (1976) 17 Cal.3d 107, 123, *overruled on other grounds*, ***People v. Holloway*** (2004) 33 Cal.4th 96. Evid. C. §1040 "establishes … a conditional privilege [that] attaches when the court determines, in accordance with precise statutory standards, that disclosure is against the public interest…. *At 125-26:* [T]his determination requires that the trial court consider, with respect to each item of material found to be discoverable under the provisions of [CCP] §1985, whether there is 'a necessity for preserving the confidentiality of the information that outweighs the necessity for disclosure in the interest of justice.' If it decides that question in the affirmative, then '[d]isclosure of the information is against the public interest' and the particular item should be deemed privileged. If it decides that question in the negative, production should be ordered. Such a weighing procedure will entail a separate assessment of the 'necessity for disclosure in the interest of justice' and the 'necessity for preserving the confidentiality [of the subject information].' [¶] Implicit in each assessment is a consideration of consequences—i.e., the consequences to the litigant of nondisclosure, and the consequences to the public of disclosure. The consideration of consequences to the litigant will involve matters similar to those in issue in the determination of materiality and good cause in the context of … §1985, including the importance of the material sought to the fair presentation of the litigant's case, the availability of the material to the litigant by other means, and the effectiveness and relative difficulty of such other means. The consideration of the consequences of disclosure to the public will involve matters relative to the effect of disclosure upon the integrity of public processes and procedures…. In this respect the court should be fully aware that … 'the public has an interest in seeing that justice is done in the particular cause as well as an interest in the secrecy of the information.'" *See also* ***Marylander v. Superior Ct.*** (2d Dist.2000) 81 Cal.App.4th 1119, 1124; ***City of Azusa v. Superior Ct.*** (2d Dist.1987) 191 Cal.App.3d 693, 695-96.

Department of Motor Vehicles v. Superior Ct. (2d Dist.2002) 100 Cal.App.4th 363, 371. "Characterizing information as confidential from public inspection is not the equivalent of establishing a privilege in a legal proceeding. [Veh. C.] §1808.5 does not use the term 'privilege' nor does it invoke the concept of privilege as that term used in the Evidence Code or discovery stat-

utes. *At 373:* Confidentiality does not equate with privilege. *At 374:* Given the broadly recognized confidentiality of medical records, we find that the medical information acquired by [public entity] constitutes 'official information' within the meaning of [Evid. C.] §1040. [¶] Because the medical information satisfies the 'official information' requirement of … §1040, our next query is whether its disclosure 'is forbidden' by statute. The same reasons that led us to conclude that §1808.5 does not establish a privilege lead to the conclusion that it is not a statute, within the meaning of … §1040, that 'forbids disclosure.'"

§1041. [IDENTITY-OF-INFORMER PRIVILEGE]

(a) [Claiming the privilege.] Except as provided in this section, a public entity has a privilege to refuse to disclose the identity of a person who has furnished information as provided in subdivision (b) purporting to disclose a violation of a law of the United States or of this state or of a public entity in this state, and to prevent another from disclosing the person's identity, if the privilege is claimed by a person authorized by the public entity to do so and either of the following apply:

(1) Disclosure is forbidden by an act of the Congress of the United States or a statute of this state.

(2) Disclosure of the identity of the informer is against the public interest because the necessity for preserving the confidentiality of his or her identity outweighs the necessity for disclosure in the interest of justice. The privilege shall not be claimed under this paragraph if a person authorized to do so has consented that the identity of the informer be disclosed in the proceeding. In determining whether disclosure of the identity of the informer is against the public interest, the interest of the public entity as a party in the outcome of the proceeding shall not be considered.

(b) [Confidential information.] The privilege described in this section applies only if the information is furnished in confidence by the informer to any of the following:

(1) A law enforcement officer.

(2) A representative of an administrative agency charged with the administration or enforcement of the law alleged to be violated.

(3) Any person for the purpose of transmittal to a person listed in paragraph (1) or (2). As used in this paragraph, "person" includes a volunteer or employee of a crime stopper organization.

(c) [Disclosure by informer.] The privilege described in this section shall not be construed to prevent the informer from disclosing his or her identity.

(d) As used in this section, "crime stopper organization" means a private, nonprofit organization that accepts and expends donations used to reward persons who report to the organization information concerning alleged criminal activity, and forwards the information to the appropriate law enforcement agency.

History of Evid. C. §1041: Added eff. Sept. 17, 1965, oper. Jan. 1, 1967, Stats. 1965, ch. 299, §2. Amended eff. Jan. 1, 2014, Stats. 2013, ch. 19, §1.

Official Comment

7 Cal. Law Revision Comm'n Rep. (1965) p. 1200.

Under existing law, the identity of an informer is protected by subdivision 5 of Code of Civil Procedure Section 1881 (which, like Section 1041, prohibits disclosure when the interest of the public would suffer thereby). Section 1881 is superseded by the Evidence Code.

This privilege may be claimed under the same conditions as the official information privilege may be claimed, except that it does not apply if a person is called as a witness and asked if he is the informer.

ANNOTATIONS

People v. Luera (2d Dist.2001) 86 Cal.App.4th 513, 525-26. "An informant is a material witness under … §1041 if it appears there is a reasonable possibility the informant could give evidence on the issue of guilt which might result in a defendant's exoneration. 'However, defendant's showing to obtain disclosure of an informant's identity must rise above the level of *sheer* or *unreasonable* speculation, and reach at least the low plateau of reasonable possibility.'"

§1042. [ADVERSE ORDERS]

(a) [Privilege sustained.] Except where disclosure is forbidden by an act of the Congress of the United States, if a claim of privilege under this article by the state or a public entity in this state is sustained in a criminal proceeding, the presiding officer shall make such order or finding of fact adverse to the public entity bringing the proceeding as is required by law upon any issue in the proceeding to which the privileged information is material.

(b) [Search pursuant to warrant.] Notwithstanding subdivision (a), where a search is made pursuant to a warrant valid on its face, the public entity bringing a criminal proceeding is not required to reveal to the defendant official information or the identity of an informer in order to establish the legality of the search or the admissibility of any evidence obtained as a result of it.

(c) [Informant is not material witness.] Notwithstanding subdivision (a), in any preliminary hear-

ing, criminal trial, or other criminal proceeding, any otherwise admissible evidence of information communicated to a peace officer by a confidential informant, who is not a material witness to the guilt or innocence of the accused of the offense charged, is admissible on the issue of reasonable cause to make an arrest or search without requiring that the name or identity of the informant be disclosed if the judge or magistrate is satisfied, based upon evidence produced in open court, out of the presence of the jury, that such information was received from a reliable informant and in his discretion does not require such disclosure.

(d) [**Informant is material witness.**] When, in any such criminal proceeding, a party demands disclosure of the identity of the informant on the ground the informant is a material witness on the issue of guilt, the court shall conduct a hearing at which all parties may present evidence on the issue of disclosure. Such hearing shall be conducted outside the presence of the jury, if any. During the hearing, if the privilege provided for in Section 1041 is claimed by a person authorized to do so or if a person who is authorized to claim such privilege refuses to answer any question on the ground that the answer would tend to disclose the identity of the informant, the prosecuting attorney may request that the court hold an in camera hearing. If such a request is made, the court shall hold such a hearing outside the presence of the defendant and his counsel. At the in camera hearing, the prosecution may offer evidence which would tend to disclose or which discloses the identity of the informant to aid the court in its determination whether there is a reasonable possibility that nondisclosure might deprive the defendant of a fair trial. A reporter shall be present at the in camera hearing. Any transcription of the proceedings at the in camera hearing, as well as any physical evidence presented at the hearing, shall be ordered sealed by the court, and only a court may have access to its contents. The court shall not order disclosure, nor strike the testimony of the witness who invokes the privilege, nor dismiss the criminal proceeding, if the party offering the witness refuses to disclose the identity of the informant, unless, based upon the evidence presented at the hearing held in the presence of the defendant and his counsel and the evidence presented at the in camera hearing, the court concludes that there is a reasonable possibility that nondisclosure might deprive the defendant of a fair trial.

History of Evid. C. §1042: Added eff. Sept. 17, 1965, oper. Jan. 1, 1967, Stats. 1965, ch. 299, §2. Amended eff. Sept. 17, 1965, oper. Jan. 1, 1967, Stats. 1965, ch. 937, §2; eff. Nov. 10, 1969, Stats. 1969, ch. 1412, §1.

Official Comment

7 Cal. Law Revision Comm'n Rep. (1965) p. 1200; Assem. J., Apr. 6, 1965, p. 1752.

Section 1042 provides special rules regarding the consequences of invocation of the privileges provided in this article by the prosecution in a criminal proceeding.

Subdivision (a). This subdivision recognizes the existing California rule in a criminal case. As was stated by the United States Supreme Court in *United States v. Reynolds*, 345 U.S. 1, 12 (1953), "since the Government which prosecutes an accused also has the duty to see that justice is done, it is unconscionable to allow it to undertake prosecution and then invoke its governmental privileges to deprive the accused of anything which might be material to his defense." This policy applies if either the official information privilege (Section 1040) or the informer privilege (Section 1041) is exercised in a criminal proceeding.

In some cases, the privileged information will be material to the issue of the defendant's guilt or innocence; in such cases, the law requires that the court dismiss the case if the public entity does not reveal the information. *People v. McShann*, 50 Cal.2d 802, 330 P.2d 33 (1958). In other cases, the privileged information will relate to narrower issues, such as the legality of a search without a warrant; in those cases, the law requires that the court strike the testimony of a particular witness or make some other order appropriate under the circumstances if the public entity insists upon its privilege. *Priestly v. Superior Court*, 50 Cal.2d 812, 330 P.2d 39 (1958).

In cases where the legality of an arrest is in issue, Section 1042 does not require disclosure of the privileged information if there was reasonable cause for the arrest aside from the privileged information, for in such a case the identity of the informer is immaterial. *Cf. People v. Hunt*, 216 Cal.App.2d 753, 756-757, 31 Cal.Rptr. 221, 223 (1963) ("The rule requiring disclosure of an informer's identity has no application in situations where reasonable cause for arrest and search exists aside from the informer's communication.").

Subdivision (a) applies only if the privilege is asserted by the State of California or a public entity in the State of California. Subdivision (a) does not require the imposition of its sanction if the privilege is invoked in an action prosecuted by the State and the information is withheld by the federal government or another state. Nor may the sanction be imposed where disclosure is forbidden by federal statute. In these respects, subdivision (a) states existing California law. *People v. Parham*, 60 Cal.2d 378, 33 Cal.Rptr. 497, 384 P.2d 1001 (1963) (prior statements of prosecution witnesses withheld by the Federal Bureau of Investigation; denial of motion to strike witnesses' testimony affirmed).

Subdivision (b). This subdivision codifies the rule declared in *People v. Keener*, 55 Cal.2d 714, 723, 12 Cal.Rptr. 859, 864, 361 P.2d 587, 592 (1961), in which the court held that "where a search is made pursuant to a warrant valid on its face, the prosecution is not required to reveal the identity of the informer in order to establish the legality of the search and the admissibility of the evidence obtained as a result of it." Subdivision (b), however, applies to all official information, not merely to the identity of an informer.

Subdivision (b) does not affect the rule that a defendant is entitled to know the identity of an informer in a case where the informer is a material witness with respect to facts directly relating to the defendant's guilt.

Editor's Note: Subdivision (c) of Section 1042 was not contained in Section 1042 as enacted by Chapter 299 of the Statutes of 1965. Subdivision (c) was added to Section 1042 by Chapter 937 of the Statutes of 1965.

See also Pen. C. §§832.5, 832.7, 832.8.

§1043. [PEACE-OFFICER PERSONNEL RECORDS]

(a) [**Procedure for disclosure.**] In any case in which discovery or disclosure is sought of peace or custodial officer personnel records or records maintained pursuant to Section 832.5 of the Penal Code or information from those records, the party seeking the discovery or disclosure shall file a written motion with the appro-

priate court or administrative body upon written notice to the governmental agency which has custody and control of the records. The written notice shall be given at the times prescribed by subdivision (b) of Section 1005 of the Code of Civil Procedure. Upon receipt of the notice the governmental agency served shall immediately notify the individual whose records are sought.

(b) [**Motion for discovery.**] The motion shall include all of the following:

(1) Identification of the proceeding in which discovery or disclosure is sought, the party seeking discovery or disclosure, the peace or custodial officer whose records are sought, the governmental agency which has custody and control of the records, and the time and place at which the motion for discovery or disclosure shall be heard.

(2) A description of the type of records or information sought.

(3) Affidavits showing good cause for the discovery or disclosure sought, setting forth the materiality thereof to the subject matter involved in the pending litigation and stating upon reasonable belief that the governmental agency identified has the records or information from the records.

(c) [**Hearing on motion.**] No hearing upon a motion for discovery or disclosure shall be held without full compliance with the notice provisions of this section except upon a showing by the moving party of good cause for noncompliance, or upon a waiver of the hearing by the governmental agency identified as having the records.

History of Evid. C. §1043: Added eff. Jan. 1, 1979, Stats. 1978, ch. 630, §1. Amended eff. Jan. 1, 1990, Stats. 1989, ch. 693, §7; eff. Jan. 1, 2003, Stats. 2002, ch. 391, §1.

ANNOTATIONS

Riverside Cty. Sheriff's Dept. v. Stiglitz (2014) 60 Cal.4th 624, 630. "In 1978, the California Legislature codified the privileges and procedures surrounding what had come to be known as ***Pitchess*** [***v. Superior Ct.*** (1974) 11 Cal.3d 531] motions through the enactment of [Pen. C.] §§832.7 and 832.8 and [Evid. C.] §§1043 through 1045. Those sections create a statutory scheme making these records confidential and subject to discovery only through the procedure set out in the Evidence Code. The sole issue here is whether, by statute, these motions may only be ruled on in the superior court, or whether they can be resolved by an administrative hearing officer. *At 631:* The expansive language of … §1043, subdivision (a) does two things. First, it makes clear that ***Pitchess*** motions may be brought in both civil and criminal cases. Second, [it] specifically states the motion should be filed in the appropriate court 'or administrative body.' [¶] [S]ection 1043 sets out the initial good cause showing an applicant must make to even begin the discovery process. If that showing is successful, … §1045 governs the conduct of the resultant hearing in camera. The materials sought must be shown relevant to the subject matter involved in the pending litigation. *At 632:* The [Sheriff's] department observes that … §1045 repeatedly refers to 'the court' as the entity that must conduct an in camera review, determine relevance, and issue appropriate protective orders. It argues that because 'the court' appears five times in … §1045, these references trump the single reference to 'administrative body' in … §1043. [¶] This argument fails for several reasons. First, it simply reads 'administrative body' out of … §1043. If the Legislature intended that only the superior court could rule on ***Pitchess*** motions, it could easily have said so. [¶] Second, the argument completely ignores the broad definition of 'proceeding' in [Evid. C.] §901, which includes administrative hearings and arbitrations. *At 633:* Further, had the Legislature intended that ***Pitchess*** motions could only be conducted in the superior court, it could have provided a mechanism to transfer a motion from an administrative proceeding to the superior courts. It did not do so. [S]ection 1043 makes no provision for the transfer of ***Pitchess*** motions from an administrative setting to the superior court. The parties agree that no other statute authorizes such a transfer. *At 636:* Accordingly, we conclude that by expressly permitting filing with an appropriate administrative body in … §1043, the Legislature intended to allow administrative hearing officers to decide such motions without court intervention." (Internal quotes omitted.)

Long Beach Police Officers Ass'n v. City of Long Beach (2014) 59 Cal.4th 59, 71. Newspaper, "citing the California Public Records Act, seeks disclosure of the names of the two Long Beach police officers involved in [a] fatal shooting … as well as the names of any … officers involved in shootings occurring [during the six years before shooting]. The [police officers'] Union and the City oppose disclosure. They rely largely on the confidentiality protections afforded peace officers under the ***Pitchess*** [***v. Superior Ct.*** (1974) 11 Cal.3d

531] statutes.... *At 72:* Significantly, the ***Pitchess*** statutes are silent as to whether the names of officers involved in shootings are protected 'personnel records.' That silence is important because, as this court observed in ***Commission on Peace Officer*** [***Stds. & Training v. Superior Ct.*** (2007) 42 Cal.4th 278], the personnel records exemption is limited to the categories of information that are expressly 'enumerated' in [Pen. C.] §832.8. That the Legislature did not intend to protect peace officers' identities can also be inferred from the Legislature's enactment of [Pen. C.] §830.10, which requires uniformed officers to display their name or identification number. That statute reflects a legislative policy that, generally, the public has a right to know the identity of an officer involved in an on-duty shooting."

Galindo v. Superior Ct. (2010) 50 Cal.4th 1, 5-6. "Although no statute prohibits a criminal defendant from filing a ***Pitchess*** [***v. Superior Ct.*** (1974) 11 Cal.3d 531] motion before a preliminary hearing is held, neither does any statute expressly grant a right to obtain ***Pitchess*** discovery for use at the preliminary hearing. Accordingly, we hold that although a defendant may file a ***Pitchess*** motion before a preliminary hearing, the pendency of that motion will not necessarily or invariably constitute good cause for postponing the preliminary hearing over the prosecution's objection. The purpose of the preliminary hearing is merely 'to establish whether there exists probable cause to believe that the defendant has committed a felony' ..., and '[b]oth the defendant and the people have the right to a preliminary examination at the earliest possible time'...."

Rezek v. Superior Ct. (4th Dist.2012) 206 Cal.App.4th 633, 639-40. "A showing of good cause exists if the defendant demonstrates both (1) a specific factual scenario that establishes a plausible factual foundation for the allegations of officer misconduct ..., and (2) that the misconduct would (if credited) be material to the defense.... [A] defendant meets the materiality element by showing (1) a logical connection between the charges and the proposed defense; (2) the requested discovery is factually specific and tailored to support the claim of officer misconduct; (3) the requested discovery supports the proposed defense or is likely to lead to information that will do so; and (4) the requested discovery is potentially admissible at trial. *At 641-42:* Unlike the typical ***Pitchess*** [***v. Superior Ct.*** (1974) 11 Cal.3d 531] motion, [D's] motion ... did not seek discovery of third party complaints of past incidents of alleged misconduct. ... The motion sought discovery of witnesses' statements pertaining to the very incident that serves as the basis for the pending charges. The trial court initially denied [D's] motion without prejudice, based upon its belief that as the internal affairs investigation contained the statements of witnesses to the charged offenses, [D] was obligated to obtain the statements from the district attorney pursuant to [Pen. C.] §1054.1. That section requires the prosecutor to disclose to the defense relevant written or recorded statements of witnesses or reports of the statements of witnesses whom the prosecutor intends to call at the trial. The prosecutor took the position that statements contained in an officer's personnel file are not subject to ... §1054.1. [¶] Although a ***Pitchess*** motion is submitted to the wide discretion of the court and we defer to the trial court absent a demonstrable abuse of discretion ..., where the court erroneously concludes the discovery cannot be obtained via a ***Pitchess*** motion based on a mistaken belief the discovery must be obtained from the prosecutor pursuant to ... §1054.1, the defendant has demonstrated an abuse of discretion.... *At 643-44:* We recognize that the information in an officer's personnel file is *conditionally* privileged by statute ..., but that privilege must be weighed against the defendant's legitimate interests in obtaining the requested information. ... When the defendant seeks the statements of witnesses to the charged incident, an officer's privacy interests are implicated less than when the information sought pertains to past incidents unconnected to the charged offense. [¶] Because of the direct relevance of the information, the courts have generally recognized that the law enforcement records of the investigation at issue may be discoverable.... [¶] Were it not for the fact the witnesses' statements are located in personnel files of police officers, there would be no question but that [D] is entitled[, under §1054.1,] to such statements. [¶] [W]e hold [D] made a sufficient showing to require an in camera review of the relevant documents and information. If disclosure of the documentation or information is not precluded by [Evid. C. §1045,] subdivision (b) or (c) ..., then disclosure is called for." (Internal quotes omitted.) *See also* ***People v. Moreno*** (4th Dist.2011) 192 Cal.App.4th 692, 700-01.

People v. White (2d Dist.2011) 191 Cal.App.4th 1333, 1335. "The procedures attendant to a ... defen-

dant's right to discover relevant evidence in confidential peace officer personnel files—through the filing of a [*Pitchess v. Superior Ct.* (1974) 11 Cal.3d 531] motion—are established by both statute and decisional law. The defining hallmark of the process is an in camera hearing in which the trial court reviews the files at issue outside the presence of the defendant and his or her counsel. The completeness of the records is established through questioning of the custodian of records who produced them. In order to protect the defendant's right to a fair trial, the custodian must be placed under oath. In this case we decide whether the trial court's failure to administer the oath in this regard compels a conditional reversal of the judgment. We conclude that it does."

Brown v. Valverde (1st Dist.2010) 183 Cal.App.4th 1531, 1535. Held: ***Pitchess v. Superior Ct.*** (1974) 11 Cal.3d 531 discovery was not available in an administrative per se hearing before the DMV to suspend the license of a person suspected of drunk driving. *See also* ***Riverside Cty. Sheriff's Dept. v. Stiglitz*** (2014) 60 Cal.4th 624, 640-41 (precedential value of ***Brown*** is limited to its facts involving driver's license suspension hearings before DMV).

Rosales v. City of L.A. (2d Dist.2000) 82 Cal.App.4th 419, 426-27. "Given the status of confidentiality conferred by the Legislature on police personnel records, the officer's right to be notified that his or her records are sought ..., and his or her right to seek a protective order from 'unnecessary annoyance, embarrassment or oppression' ..., courts have concluded that an officer has a *limited* or *conditional* 'privilege' in such records. The privilege is conditional or limited because an officer cannot prevent disclosure of his or her personnel records or information contained in those records simply because he or she does not desire disclosure. After all, the whole purpose behind the Penal and Evidence Code provisions is to provide disclosure in civil or criminal proceedings where the moving party shows the information sought is material to the subject matter involved in the pending litigation." *See also* ***Slayton v. Superior Ct.*** (3d Dist.2006) 146 Cal.App.4th 55, 59-60.

§1044. [ACCESS TO MEDICAL OR PSYCHOLOGICAL HISTORY RECORDS]

Nothing in this article shall be construed to affect the right of access to records of medical or psychological history where such access would otherwise be available under Section 996 or 1016.

History of Evid. C. §1044: Added eff. Jan. 1, 1979, Stats. 1978, ch. 630, §2.

§1045. [ACCESS TO PEACE-OFFICER RECORDS OF COMPLAINTS]

(a) [**Relevant to pending litigation.**] Nothing in this article shall be construed to affect the right of access to records of complaints, or investigations of complaints, or discipline imposed as a result of those investigations, concerning an event or transaction in which the peace officer or custodial officer, as defined in Section 831.5 of the Penal Code, participated, or which he or she perceived, and pertaining to the manner in which he or she performed his or her duties, provided that information is relevant to the subject matter involved in the pending litigation.

(b) [**In camera inspection.**] In determining relevance, the court shall examine the information in chambers in conformity with Section 915, and shall exclude from disclosure:

(1) Information consisting of complaints concerning conduct occurring more than five years before the event or transaction that is the subject of the litigation in aid of which discovery or disclosure is sought.

(2) In any criminal proceeding the conclusions of any officer investigating a complaint filed pursuant to Section 832.5 of the Penal Code.

(3) Facts sought to be disclosed that are so remote as to make disclosure of little or no practical benefit.

(c) [**Conduct of employing agency.**] In determining relevance where the issue in litigation concerns the policies or pattern of conduct of the employing agency, the court shall consider whether the information sought may be obtained from other records maintained by the employing agency in the regular course of agency business which would not necessitate the disclosure of individual personnel records.

(d) [**Protective order.**] Upon motion seasonably made by the governmental agency which has custody or control of the records to be examined or by the officer whose records are sought, and upon good cause showing the necessity thereof, the court may make any order which justice requires to protect the officer or agency from unnecessary annoyance, embarrassment or oppression.

(e) [**Use of records.**] The court shall, in any case or proceeding permitting the disclosure or discovery of

any peace or custodial officer records requested pursuant to Section 1043, order that the records disclosed or discovered may not be used for any purpose other than a court proceeding pursuant to applicable law.

History of Evid. C. §1045: Added eff. Jan. 1, 1979, Stats. 1978, ch. 630, §3. Amended eff. Jan. 1, 1983, Stats. 1982, ch. 946, §1; eff. Jan. 1, 2003, Stats. 2002, ch. 391, §2.

ANNOTATIONS

Riverside Cty. Sheriff's Dept. v. Stiglitz (2014) 60 Cal.4th 624, 630. See annotation under Evidence Code §1043, p. 1345.

Long Beach Police Officers Ass'n v. City of Long Beach (2014) 59 Cal.4th 59, 71. See annotation under Evidence Code §1043, p. 1345.

Rosales v. City of L.A. (2d Dist.2000) 82 Cal.App.4th 419, 426-27. See annotation under Evidence Code §1043, p. 1347.

§1046. [ALLEGATION OF EXCESSIVE FORCE]

In any case, otherwise authorized by law, in which the party seeking disclosure is alleging excessive force by a peace officer or custodial officer, as defined in Section 831.5 of the Penal Code, in connection with the arrest of that party, or for conduct alleged to have occurred within a jail facility, the motion shall include a copy of the police report setting forth the circumstances under which the party was stopped and arrested, or a copy of the crime report setting forth the circumstances under which the conduct is alleged to have occurred within a jail facility.

History of Evid. C. §1046: Added eff. Jan. 1, 1986, Stats. 1985, ch. 539, §1. Amended eff. Jan. 1, 2003, Stats. 2002, ch. 391, §3.

§1047. [PEACE OFFICERS NOT PRESENT]

Records of peace officers or custodial officers, as defined in Section 831.5 of the Penal Code, including supervisorial officers, who either were not present during the arrest or had no contact with the party seeking disclosure from the time of the arrest until the time of booking, or who were not present at the time the conduct is alleged to have occurred within a jail facility, shall not be subject to disclosure.

History of Evid. C. §1047: Added eff. Jan. 1, 1986, Stats. 1985, ch. 539, §2. Amended eff. Jan. 1, 2003, Stats. 2002, ch. 391, §4.

ANNOTATIONS

Riverside Cty. Sheriff's Dept. v. Stiglitz (2014) 60 Cal.4th 624, 641. Evid. C. §1047 "only applies if the discovery request relates to an incident *involving* an arrest or its equivalent. When, as here, the discovery request is unrelated to an arrest, ... §1047's limitation does not apply. [A] contrary conclusion 'would largely supplant the general discovery standards set forth in [Evid. C.] §§1043 and 1045.'" *See also* ***Alt v. Superior Ct.*** (3d Dist.1999) 74 Cal.App.4th 950, 957-58.

ARTICLE 10. POLITICAL VOTE

§1050. [SECRECY-OF-POLITICAL-VOTE PRIVILEGE]

If he claims the privilege, a person has a privilege to refuse to disclose the tenor of his vote at a public election where the voting is by secret ballot unless he voted illegally or he previously made an unprivileged disclosure of the tenor of his vote.

History of Evid. C. §1050: Added eff. Sept. 17, 1965, oper. Jan. 1, 1967, Stats. 1965, ch. 299, §2.

Official Comment

7 Cal. Law Revision Comm'n Rep. (1965) p. 1202.

Section 1050 declares existing law. The California cases declaring such a privilege have relied upon the provision of the Constitution that "secrecy in voting be preserved." Cal. Const., Art. II, §5. *See Bush v. Head*, 154 Cal. 277, 97 Pac. 512 (1908); *Smith v. Thomas*, 121 Cal. 533, 54 Pac. 71 (1898). Since the policy of ballot secrecy extends only to legally cast ballots, the California cases—as well as Section 1050—recognize that there is no privilege as to the tenor of an illegal vote. *Patterson v. Hanley*, 136 Cal. 265, 68 Pac. 821 (1902).

ARTICLE 11. TRADE SECRET

§1060. [TRADE-SECRET PRIVILEGE]

If he or his agent or employee claims the privilege, the owner of a trade secret has a privilege to refuse to disclose the secret, and to prevent another from disclosing it, if the allowance of the privilege will not tend to conceal fraud or otherwise work injustice.

History of Evid. C. §1060: Added eff. Sept. 17, 1965, oper. Jan. 1, 1967, Stats. 1965, ch. 299, §2.

Official Comment

7 Cal. Law Revision Comm'n Rep. (1965) p. 1202.

This privilege is granted so that secret information essential to the continued operation of a business or industry may be afforded some measure of protection against unnecessary disclosure. Thus, the privilege prevents the use of the witness' duty to testify as the means for injuring an otherwise profitable business where more important interests will not be jeopardized. *See generally* 8 Wigmore, *Evidence* §2212(3) (McNaughton rev. 1961). Nevertheless, there are dangers in the recognition of such a privilege. Copyright and patent laws provide adequate protection for many of the matters that might otherwise be classified as trade secrets. Recognizing the privilege as to such information would serve only to hinder the courts in determining the truth without providing the owner of the secret any needed protection. Again, disclosure of the matters protected by the privilege may be essential to disclose unfair competition or fraud or to reveal the improper use of dangerous materials by the party asserting the privilege. Recognizing the privilege in such cases would amount to a legally sanctioned license to commit the wrongs complained of, for the wrongdoer would be privileged to withhold his wrongful conduct from legal scrutiny.

Therefore, the privilege exists under this section only if its application will not tend to conceal fraud or otherwise work injustice. The limits of the privilege are necessarily uncertain and will have to be worked out through judicial decisions.

Although no California case has been found holding evidence of a trade secret to be privileged, at least one California case has recognized that such a privilege may exist unless its holder has injured another and the disclosure of the secret is indispensable to the ascertainment of the truth and the ultimate determination of the rights of the parties. *Willson v. Superior Court*, 66 Cal.App. 275, 225 Pac. 881 (1924) (trade secret held not subject to privilege because of plaintiff's need for information to establish case against the person asserting the privilege). Indirect recognition of such a privilege has also been given in Code of Civil Procedure Section 2019 [repealed, *see* CCP §§2025.010-2025.620], which provides that in discovery proceedings the court may make protective orders prohibiting inquiry into "secret processes, developments or research."

ANNOTATIONS

Hypertouch, Inc. v. Superior Ct. (1st Dist.2005) 128 Cal.App.4th 1527, 1555. "If it can be established that [D's] fax database identifies all or many individual members of the class [P] is otherwise reasonably unable to identify, the trial court may wish to consider whether, in light of [D's] conduct, it would 'work injustice' to allow [D] to maintain the secrecy of that database. [¶] If the court feels it necessary to maintain the secrecy of the fax database, and there are no means by which it can be disclosed to [P] without violating its secrecy, the court should consider whether to order [D] to provide notice by telephone facsimile to the persons whose numbers are in the fax database if that can be done without disclosure of the database to [P], and would be relatively easy and less expensive than alternative forms of notice. If so, [D] can be ordered to provide notice in this manner even if the court does not believe [D] contributed to the difficulty in identifying the class and should not bear any portion of the cost of notice. [¶] If the court concludes it would be unfair or infeasible to order [D] to notify the class, and personal notification cannot otherwise be provided, the court will then need to devise some other means of notice reasonably calculated to apprise the class members of the pendency of the action, such as that proposed by [P]."

Stadish v. Superior Ct. (2d Dist.1999) 71 Cal.App.4th 1130, 1145. "A party seeking the protective order must show by a preponderance of the evidence that the issuance of a protective order is proper. Here, [Ps] assert that the documents are relevant to public health. Where such a claim is made, the trial court is required to determine the validity of the claim. If the court decides that the documents sought to be protected are relevant to public health, the court will be required to consider the public interest in determining whether good cause exists for a protective order. Direction is found in ***Westinghouse*** [***Elec. Corp. v. Newman & Holtzinger, P.C.*** (2d Dist.1995) 39 Cal.App.4th 1194]. [¶] The ***Westinghouse*** court warned that protective orders 'impair the public's access to discovery records as well as the parties' First Amendment right to disseminate information to the public.' 'Because the judicial process is frequently the avenue by which the public and regulatory agencies learn of significant health and safety hazards, blocking this avenue may prove detrimental to the public well-being. For this reason, courts frequently consider the public interest when determining whether good cause exists for a protective order.' *At 1146:* The court emphasized that '[t]he relevancy and reliability of information obtained during discovery has not been subjected to judicial scrutiny and might never be disclosed at trial. Clearly, the release of inaccurate, unreliable or misleading information could unfairly damage the manufacturer's reputation and alarm the public unnecessarily.'"

Bridgestone/Firestone, Inc. v. Superior Ct. (1st Dist.1992) 7 Cal.App.4th 1384, 1390-91. "[S]ection 1060 may not be read in isolation. The Civil Discovery Act of 1986 ... permits any party to obtain discovery regarding any matter, *not privileged*, that is relevant to the subject matter involved in the pending action or to the determination of any motion made in that action, if the matter either is itself admissible in evidence or appears reasonably calculated to lead to the discovery of admissible evidence. ... Relevancy to the subject matter has been construed to be broader than relevancy to issues ... and may vary with the size of the case. [¶] Allowance of the trade secret privilege may not be deemed to 'work injustice' within the meaning of ... §1060 simply because it would protect information generally relevant to the subject matter of an action or helpful to preparation of a case." (Internal quotes omitted.) *See also* ***Raymond Handling Concepts Corp. v. Superior Ct.*** (1st Dist.1995) 39 Cal.App.4th 584, 590.

§1061. [ASSERTING THE PRIVILEGE]

(a) [Definitions.] For purposes of this section, and Sections 1062 and 1063:

(1) "Trade secret" means "trade secret," as defined in subdivision (d) of Section 3426.1 of the Civil Code, or paragraph (9) of subdivision (a) of Section 499c of the Penal Code.

(2) "Article" means "article," as defined in paragraph (2) of subdivision (a) of Section 499c of the Penal Code.

(b) [Procedure.] In addition to Section 1062, the following procedure shall apply whenever the owner of

a trade secret wishes to assert his or her trade secret privilege, as provided in Section 1060, during a criminal proceeding:

(1) [Motion for protective order.] The owner of the trade secret shall file a motion for a protective order, or the people may file the motion on the owner's behalf and with the owner's permission. The motion shall include an affidavit based upon personal knowledge listing the affiant's qualifications to give an opinion concerning the trade secret at issue, identifying, without revealing, the alleged trade secret and articles which disclose the secret, and presenting evidence that the secret qualifies as a trade secret under either subdivision (d) of Section 3426.1 of the Civil Code or paragraph (9) of subdivision (a) of Section 499c of the Penal Code. The motion and affidavit shall be served on all parties in the proceeding.

(2) [Opposing affidavit.] Any party in the proceeding may oppose the request for the protective order by submitting affidavits based upon the affiant's personal knowledge. The affidavits shall be filed under seal, but shall be provided to the owner of the trade secret and to all parties in the proceeding. Neither the owner of the trade secret nor any party in the proceeding may disclose the affidavit to persons other than to counsel of record without prior court approval.

(3) [Movant's burden.] The movant shall, by a preponderance of the evidence, show that the issuance of a protective order is proper. The court may rule on the request without holding an evidentiary hearing. However, in its discretion, the court may choose to hold an in camera evidentiary hearing concerning disputed articles with only the owner of the trade secret, the people's representative, the defendant, and defendant's counsel present. If the court holds such a hearing, the parties' right to examine witnesses shall not be used to obtain discovery, but shall be directed solely toward the question of whether the alleged trade secret qualifies for protection.

(4) [Protecting trade secret in criminal proceeding.] If the court finds that a trade secret may be disclosed during any criminal proceeding unless a protective order is issued and that the issuance of a protective order would not conceal a fraud or work an injustice, the court shall issue a protective order limiting the use and dissemination of the trade secret, including, but not limited to, articles disclosing that secret. The protective order may, in the court's discretion, include the following provisions:

(A) That the trade secret may be disseminated only to counsel for the parties, including their associate attorneys, paralegals, and investigators, and to law enforcement officials or clerical officials.

(B) That the defendant may view the secret only in the presence of his or her counsel, or if not in the presence of his or her counsel, at counsel's offices.

(C) That any party seeking to show the trade secret, or articles containing the trade secret, to any person not designated by the protective order shall first obtain court approval to do so:

(i) The court may require that the person receiving the trade secret do so only in the presence of counsel for the party requesting approval.

(ii) The court may require the person receiving the trade secret to sign a copy of the protective order and to agree to be bound by its terms. The order may include a provision recognizing the owner of the trade secret to be a third-party beneficiary of that agreement.

(iii) The court may require a party seeking disclosure to an expert to provide that expert's name, employment history, and any other relevant information to the court for examination. The court shall accept that information under seal, and the information shall not be disclosed by any court except upon termination of the action and upon a showing of good cause to believe the secret has been disseminated by a court-approved expert. The court shall evaluate the expert and determine whether the expert poses a discernible risk of disclosure. The court shall withhold approval if the expert's economic interests place the expert in a competitive position with the victim, unless no other experts are available. The court may interview the expert in camera in aid of its ruling. If the court rejects the expert, it shall state its reasons for doing so on the record and a transcript of those reasons shall be prepared and sealed.

(D) That no articles disclosing the trade secret shall be filed or otherwise made a part of the court record available to the public without approval of the court and prior notice to the owner of the secret. The owner of the secret may give either party permission to accept the notice on the owner's behalf.

(E) Other orders as the court deems necessary to protect the integrity of the trade secret.

(c) [Validity of trade secret.] A ruling granting or denying a motion for a protective order filed pursu-

ant to subdivision (b) shall not be construed as a determination that the alleged trade secret is or is not a trade secret as defined by subdivision (d) of Section 3426.1 of the Civil Code or paragraph (9) of subdivision (a) of Section 499c of the Penal Code. Such a ruling shall not have any effect on any civil litigation.

(d) [Prospective effect.] This section shall have prospective effect only and shall not operate to invalidate previously entered protective orders.

History of Evid. C. §1061: Added eff. Jan. 1, 1991, Stats. 1990, ch. 149, §1. Amended eff. Jan. 1, 1991, Stats. 1990, ch. 714, §1; eff. Jan. 1, 2003, Stats. 2002, ch. 784, §103.

Official Comment

32 Cal. Law Revision Comm'n Rep. (2002) p. 161.

Former subdivision (d) of Section 1061 is deleted to reflect unification of the municipal and superior courts pursuant to Article VI, Section 5(e), of the California Constitution. On unification of the municipal and superior courts in a county, preexisting records of the municipal court automatically become records of the superior court. Cal. Const., art. VI, §23(c)(3); Gov't Code §70212(c).

ANNOTATIONS

Bridgestone/Firestone, Inc. v. Superior Ct. (1st Dist.1992) 7 Cal.App.4th 1384, 1393. "[W]e believe that a court is required to order disclosure of a trade secret unless, after balancing the interests of both sides, it concludes that under the particular circumstances of the case, no fraud or injustice would result from denying disclosure. What is more, in the balancing process the court must necessarily consider the protection afforded the holder of the privilege by a protective order as well as any less intrusive alternatives to disclosure proposed by the parties. [¶] We therefore hold that the party claiming the privilege has the burden of establishing its existence. Thereafter, the party seeking discovery must make a prima facie, particularized showing that the information sought is relevant and necessary to the proof of, or defense against, a material element of one or more causes of action presented in the case, and that it is reasonable to conclude that the information sought is essential to a fair resolution of the lawsuit. It is then up to the holder of the privilege to demonstrate any claimed disadvantages of a protective order. Either party may propose or oppose less intrusive alternatives to disclosure of the trade secret, but the burden is upon the trade secret claimant to demonstrate that an alternative to disclosure will not be unduly burdensome to the opposing side and that it will maintain the same fair balance in the litigation that would have been achieved by disclosure."

§1062. [CLOSURE OF CRIMINAL PROCEEDING INVOLVING TRADE SECRET]

(a) [Motion to exclude.] Notwithstanding any other provision of law, in a criminal case, the court, upon motion of the owner of a trade secret, or upon motion by the People with the consent of the owner, may exclude the public from any portion of a criminal proceeding where the proponent of closure has demonstrated a substantial probability that the trade secret would otherwise be disclosed to the public during that proceeding and a substantial probability that the disclosure would cause serious harm to the owner of the secret, and where the court finds that there is no overriding public interest in an open proceeding. No evidence, however, shall be excluded during a criminal proceeding pursuant to this section if it would conceal a fraud, work an injustice, or deprive the People or the defendant of a fair trial.

(b) [In camera hearing.] The motion made pursuant to subdivision (a) shall identify, without revealing, the trade secrets which would otherwise be disclosed to the public. A showing made pursuant to subdivision (a) shall be made during an in camera hearing with only the owner of the trade secret, the People's representative, the defendant, and defendant's counsel present. A court reporter shall be present during the hearing. Any transcription of the proceedings at the in camera hearing, as well as any articles presented at that hearing, shall be ordered sealed by the court and only a court may allow access to its contents upon a showing of good cause. The court, in ruling upon the motion made pursuant to subdivision (a), may consider testimony presented or affidavits filed in any proceeding held in that action.

(c) [Close portion of proceeding.] If, after the in camera hearing described in subdivision (b), the court determines that exclusion of trade secret information from the public is appropriate, the court shall close only that portion of the criminal proceeding necessary to prevent disclosure of the trade secret. Before granting the motion, however, the court shall find and state for the record that the moving party has met its burden pursuant to subdivision (b), and that the closure of that portion of the proceeding will not deprive the People or the defendant of a fair trial.

(d) [Petition for extraordinary relief.] The owner of the trade secret, the People, or the defendant

may seek relief from a ruling denying or granting closure by petitioning a higher court for extraordinary relief.

(e) [Transcript of closed proceeding.] Whenever the court closes a portion of a criminal proceeding pursuant to this section, a transcript of that closed proceeding shall be made available to the public as soon as practicable. The court shall redact any information qualifying as a trade secret before making that transcript available.

(f) [Witnesses who may remain.] The court, subject to Section 867 of the Penal Code, may allow witnesses who are bound by a protective order entered in the criminal proceeding protecting trade secrets, pursuant to Section 1061, to remain within the courtroom during the closed portion of the proceeding.

History of Evid. C. §1062: Added eff. Jan. 1, 1991, Stats. 1990, ch. 149, §2. Amended eff. Jan. 1, 1991, Stats. 1990, ch. 714, §2.

§1062

§1063. [SEALING ARTICLES IN PROTECTIVE ORDER]

The following provisions shall govern requests to seal articles which are protected by a protective order entered pursuant to Evidence Code Section 1060 or 1061:

(a) [Articles filed or admitted into evidence.] The People shall request sealing of articles reasonably expected to be filed or admitted into evidence as follows:

(1) No less than 10 court days before trial, and no less than five court days before any other criminal proceeding, the People shall file with the court a list of all articles which the People reasonably expect to file with the court, or admit into evidence, under seal at that proceeding. That list shall be available to the public. The People may be relieved from providing timely notice upon showing that exigent circumstances prevent that notice.

(2) The court shall not allow the listed articles to be filed, admitted into evidence, or in any way made a part of the court record otherwise open to the public before holding a hearing to consider any objections to the People's request to seal the articles. The court at that hearing shall allow those objecting to the sealing to state their objections.

(3) After hearing any objections to sealing, the court shall conduct an in camera hearing with only the owner of the trade secret contained within those articles, the People's representative, defendant, and defendant's counsel present. The court shall review the articles sought to be sealed, evaluate objections to sealing, and determine whether the People have satisfied the constitutional standards governing public access to articles which are part of the judicial record. The court may consider testimony presented or affidavits filed in any proceeding held in that action. The People, defendant, and the owner of the trade secret may file affidavits based on the affiant's personal knowledge to be considered at that hearing. Those affidavits are to be sealed and not released to the public, but shall be made available to the parties. The court may rule on the request to seal without taking testimony. If the court takes testimony, examination of witnesses shall not be used to obtain discovery, but shall be directed solely toward whether sealing is appropriate.

(4) If the court finds that the movant has satisfied appropriate constitutional standards with respect to sealing particular articles, the court shall seal those articles if and when they are filed, admitted into evidence, or in any way made a part of the court record otherwise open to the public. The articles shall not be unsealed absent an order of a court upon a showing of good cause. Failure to examine the court file for notice of a request to seal shall not constitute good cause to consider objections to sealing.

(b) [Articles made part of record.] The following procedure shall apply to other articles made a part of the court record:

(1) Where any articles protected by a protective order entered pursuant to Section 1060 or 1061 are filed, admitted into evidence, or in any way made a part of the court record in such a way as to be otherwise open to the public, the People, a defendant, or the owner of a trade secret contained within those articles may request the court to seal those articles.

(2) The request to seal shall be made by noticed motion filed with the court. It may also be made orally in court at the time the articles are made a part of the court record. Where the request is made orally, the movant must file within 24 hours a written description of that request, including a list of the articles which are the subject of that request. These motions and lists shall be available to the public.

(3) The court shall promptly conduct hearings as provided in paragraphs (2), (3), and (4) of subdivision (a). The court shall, pending the hearings, seal those articles which are the subject of the request. Where a

request to seal is made orally, the court may conduct hearings at the time the articles are made a part of the court record, but shall reconsider its ruling in light of additional objections made by objectors within two court days after the written record of the request to seal is made available to the public.

(4) Any articles sealed pursuant to these hearings shall not be unsealed absent an order of a court upon a showing of good cause. Failure to examine the court file for notice of a request to seal shall not constitute good cause to consider objections to sealing.

History of Evid. C. §1063: Added eff. Jan. 1, 1991, Stats. 1990, ch. 714, §3.

CHAPTER 5. IMMUNITY OF NEWSMAN FROM CITATION FOR CONTEMPT

§1070. [NEWS-MEDIA PRIVILEGE]

(a) [Newspaper or magazine media.] A publisher, editor, reporter, or other person connected with or employed upon a newspaper, magazine, or other periodical publication, or by a press association or wire service, or any person who has been so connected or employed, cannot be adjudged in contempt by a judicial, legislative, administrative body, or any other body having the power to issue subpoenas, for refusing to disclose, in any proceeding as defined in Section 901, the source of any information procured while so connected or employed for publication in a newspaper, magazine or other periodical publication, or for refusing to disclose any unpublished information obtained or prepared in gathering, receiving or processing of information for communication to the public.

(b) [Radio or television media.] Nor can a radio or television news reporter or other person connected with or employed by a radio or television station, or any person who has been so connected or employed, be so adjudged in contempt for refusing to disclose the source of any information procured while so connected or employed for news or news commentary purposes on radio or television, or for refusing to disclose any unpublished information obtained or prepared in gathering, receiving or processing of information for communication to the public.

(c) [Unpublished information.] As used in this section, "unpublished information" includes information not disseminated to the public by the person from whom disclosure is sought, whether or not related information has been disseminated and includes, but is not limited to, all notes, outtakes, photographs, tapes or other data of whatever sort not itself disseminated to the public through a medium of communication, whether or not published information based upon or related to such material has been disseminated.

History of Evid. C. §1070: Added eff. Sept. 17, 1965, oper. Jan. 1, 1967, Stats. 1965, ch. 299, §2. Amended eff. Mar. 4, 1972, Stats. 1971, ch. 1717, §1; eff. Mar. 7, 1973, Stats. 1972, ch. 1431, §1; eff. Jan. 1, 1975, Stats. 1974, ch. 1323, §1, ch. 1456, §2.

See also Cal. Const., art. I, §2.

Official Comment

7 Cal. Law Revision Comm'n Rep. (1965) p. 1203; Assem. J., Apr. 6, 1965, p. 1753.

Section 1070 continues without change the provisions of subdivision 6 of Code of Civil Procedure Section 1881.

It should be noted that Section 1070, like the existing law, provides an immunity from being adjudged in contempt; it does not create a privilege. Thus, the section will not prevent the use of other sanctions for refusal of a newsman to make discovery when he is a party to a civil proceeding. *See* Code Civ. Proc. §2034; *Bramson v. Wilkerson*, Civil No. 760973 (L.A. Super.Ct., January 4, 1962), as reported in 3 Cal. Disc. Proc. 72 (Metropolitan News Review Section, January 30, 1962) (memorandum opinion by Judge Philbrick McCoy).

ANNOTATIONS

New York Times Co. v. Superior Ct. (1990) 51 Cal.3d 453, 461. "The primary issue addressed by the parties in this court is whether the shield law applies to unpublished information that was not obtained by a newsperson in confidence. [T]he shield law's protection is *not* contingent on a showing that a newsperson's unpublished information was obtained in confidence. ... There remains, however, the question of ... whether the shield law immunity is qualified rather than absolute. [¶] We find nothing in the shield law's language or history to suggest the immunity from contempt is qualified such that it can be overcome by a showing of need for unpublished information within the scope of the shield law." *See also* ***Delaney v. Superior Ct.*** (1990) 50 Cal.3d 785, 805.

Mitchell v. Superior Ct. (1984) 37 Cal.3d 268, 272. The issue "before this court for the first time [is] whether in a civil action a newsperson has a privilege to refuse to reveal confidential sources or information obtained from those sources. *At 279:* We conclude that in a civil action a reporter, editor, or publisher has a qualified privilege to withhold disclosure of the identity of confidential sources and of unpublished information supplied by such sources. The scope of that privilege in each particular case will depend upon the consideration and weighing of a number of interrelated factors."

O'Grady v. Superior Ct. (6th Dist.2006) 139 Cal.App.4th 1423, 1456. "[Ds] assert that [Cal. Const., art. I, §2, subdivision (b) and Evid. C. §1070], sometimes known as the California reporter's shield, pre-

clude compelled disclosure of their sources or any other unpublished material in their possession. [P] argues that [Ds] may not avail themselves of the shield because (1) they were not engaged in legitimate journalistic activities when they acquired the offending information; and (2) they are not among the classes of persons protected by the statute. *At 1457:* The shield law is intended to protect the gathering and dissemination of *news*, and that is what [Ds] did here. We can think of no workable test or principle that would distinguish 'legitimate' from 'illegitimate' news. Any attempt by courts to draw such a distinction would imperil a fundamental purpose of the First Amendment.... *At 1459-60:* [T]he primary and core meaning of 'to publish' is '[t]o make publicly or generally known; to declare or report openly or publicly; to announce; to tell or noise abroad; also, to propagate, disseminate (a creed or system).' Of course the term 'publisher' also possesses a somewhat narrower sense: 'One whose business is the issuing of books, newspapers, music, engravings, *or the like*, as the agent of the author or owner; one who undertakes the printing or production of copies of such works, and their distribution to the booksellers and other dealers, or to the public. ...' News-oriented Web sites like [Ds'] are surely 'like' a newspaper or magazine for these purposes." *See also* ***Rancho Publ'ns v. Superior Ct.*** (4th Dist.1999) 68 Cal.App.4th 1538, 1543-44.

§1070

DIVISION 9. EVIDENCE AFFECTED OR EXCLUDED BY EXTRINSIC POLICIES

CHAPTER 1. EVIDENCE OF CHARACTER, HABIT, OR CUSTOM

§1100. [CHARACTER ADMISSIBLE]

Except as otherwise provided by statute, any otherwise admissible evidence (including evidence in the form of an opinion, evidence of reputation, and evidence of specific instances of such person's conduct) is admissible to prove a person's character or a trait of his character.

History of Evid. C. §1100: Added eff. Sept. 17, 1965, oper. Jan. 1, 1967, Stats. 1965, ch. 299, §2.

Official Comment

7 Cal. Law Revision Comm'n Rep. (1965) p. 1204.

Section 1100 states the *kinds* of evidence that may be used to prove a person's character or a trait of his character. The section makes it clear that reputation evidence, opinion evidence, and evidence of specific instances of conduct are admissible for this purpose.

Section 1100 is technically unnecessary because Section 351 declares that all relevant evidence is admissible. Hence, all of the evidence declared to be admissible by Section 1100 would be admissible anyway under the general provisions of Section 351. Section 1100 is included in the Evidence Code, however, to forestall the argument that Section 351 does not remove all judicially created restrictions on the kinds of evidence that may be used to prove character or a trait of character.

Subject to certain statutory restrictions, the character evidence described in Section 1100 is admissible under Section 351 whenever it is relevant. Evidence of a person's character or a trait of his character is relevant in three situations: (1) when offered on the issue of his credibility as a witness, (2) when offered as circumstantial evidence of his conduct in conformity with such character or trait of character, and (3) when his character or a trait of his character is an ultimate fact in dispute in the action.

Sections 786-790 establish restrictions that are applicable when character evidence is offered to attack or to support the *credibility of a witness. See* the *Comments* to Sections 787 and 788 for a discussion of the restrictions on the kinds of evidence admissible for this purpose.

Sections 1101-1104 substantially restrict the extent to which character evidence may be used as *circumstantial evidence of conduct. See* the *Comments* to those sections for a discussion of the restrictions on the kinds of evidence admissible for this purpose.

Section 1100 applies without restriction only when character or a trait of character is an *ultimate fact in dispute* in the action. As applied to this situation, Section 1100 is generally consistent with existing law, although the existing law is uncertain in some respects. Cases involving character as an ultimate issue have admitted opinion evidence (*People v. Wade*, 118 Cal. 672, 50 Pac. 841 (1897); *People v. Samonset*, 97 Cal. 448, 450, 32 Pac. 520, 521 (1893)), reputation evidence (*Estate of Akers*, 184 Cal. 514, 519-520, 194 Pac. 706, 708-709 (1920); *People v. Samonset, supra*), and evidence of specific acts (*Guardianship of Wisdom*, 146 Cal.App.2d 635, 304 P.2d 221 (1956); *Currin v. Currin*, 125 Cal.App.2d 644, 271 P.2d 61 (1954); *Guardianship of Casad*, 106 Cal.App.2d 134, 234 P.2d 647 (1951)). However, there are cases which exclude some kinds of evidence where particular traits are involved. For example, in cases involving the unfitness or incompetency of an employee, evidence of specific acts is admissible to prove such unfitness or incompetency, while evidence of reputation is not. *E.g., Gier v. Los Angeles Consol. Elec. Ry.*, 108 Cal. 129, 41 Pac. 22 (1895). Section 1100 eliminates the uncertainties in existing law and makes admissible any evidence that is relevant to prove the character in issue.

§1101. [CHARACTER INADMISSIBLE TO PROVE CONDUCT]

(a) [Inadmissible.] Except as provided in this section and in Sections 1102, 1103, 1108, and 1109, evidence of a person's character or a trait of his or her character (whether in the form of an opinion, evidence of reputation, or evidence of specific instances of his or her conduct) is inadmissible when offered to prove his or her conduct on a specified occasion.

(b) [Admissible to prove fact other than predisposition.] Nothing in this section prohibits the admission of evidence that a person committed a crime, civil wrong, or other act when relevant to prove some fact (such as motive, opportunity, intent, preparation, plan, knowledge, identity, absence of mistake or accident, or whether a defendant in a prosecution for an unlawful sexual act or attempted unlawful sexual act did not reasonably and in good faith believe that the victim consented) other than his or her disposition to commit such an act.

(c) [Credibility.] Nothing in this section affects the admissibility of evidence offered to support or attack the credibility of a witness.

History of Evid. C. §1101: Added eff. Sept. 17, 1965, oper. Jan. 1, 1967, Stats. 1965, ch. 299, §2. Amended eff. Jan. 1, 1987, Stats. 1986, ch. 1432, §1; eff. Jan. 1, 1996, Stats. 1995, ch. 439, §1; eff. Jan. 1, 1997, Stats. 1996, ch. 261, §1.

Official Comment

7 Cal. Law Revision Comm'n Rep. (1965) p. 1205.

Section 1101 is concerned with evidence of a person's character (*i.e.*, his propensity or disposition to engage in a certain type of conduct) that is offered as a basis for an inference that he behaved in conformity with that character on a particular occasion. Section 1101 is not concerned with evidence offered to prove a person's character when that character is itself in issue; the admissibility of character evidence offered for this purpose is determined under Sections 351 and 1100. Nor is Section 1101 concerned with evidence of character offered on the issue of the credibility of a witness; the admissibility of such evidence is determined under Sections 786-790. *See* Evidence Code §1101(c).

Civil cases. Section 1101 excludes evidence of character to prove conduct in a civil case for the following reasons. *First*, character evidence is of slight probative value and may be very prejudicial. *Second*, character evidence tends to distract the trier of fact from the main question of what actually happened on the particular occasion and permits the trier of fact to reward the good man and to punish the bad man because of their respective characters. *Third*, introduction of character evidence may result in confusion of issues and require extended collateral inquiry.

Section 1101 states the general rule recognized under existing law. Code Civ. Proc. §2053 ("Evidence of the good character of a party is not admissible in a civil action...." (Section 2053 is superseded by various Evidence Code sections.)); *Deevy v. Tassi*, 21 Cal.2d 109, 130 P.2d 389 (1942) (assault; evidence of defendant's bad character for peace and quiet held inadmissible); *Vance v. Richardson*, 110 Cal. 414, 42 Pac. 909 (1895) (assault; evidence of defendant's good character for peace and quiet held inadmissible); *Van Horn v. Van Horn*, 5 Cal.App. 719, 91 Pac. 260 (1907) (divorce for adultery; evidence of defendant's and the nonparty-correspondent's good character held inadmissible). Under existing law, however, there *may* be an exception to this general rule. Existing law may permit evidence to be introduced of the unchaste character of a plaintiff to show the likelihood of her consent to an alleged rape. *Valencia v. Milliken*, 31 Cal.App. 533, 160 Pac. 1086 (1916) (civil action for rape; error, but nonprejudicial, to limit evidence of unchaste character of plaintiff to issue of damages). The Evidence Code has no such exception for civil cases. *But see* Evidence Code §1103 (criminal cases).

Criminal cases. Section 1101 states the general rule that evidence of character to prove conduct is inadmissible in a criminal case. Sections 1102 and 1103 state exceptions to this general principle. *See* the *Comment* to Section 1102.

Evidence of misconduct to show fact other than character. Section 1101 does not prohibit the admission of evidence of misconduct when it is offered as evidence of some other fact in issue, such as motive, common scheme or plan, preparation, intent, knowledge, identity, or absence of mistake or accident. Subdivision (b) of Section 1101 makes this clear. This codifies existing law. *People v. Lisenba*, 14 Cal.2d 403, 94 P.2d 569 (1939) (prior crime admissible to show general criminal plan and absence of accident); *People v. David*, 12 Cal.2d 639, 86 P.2d 811 (1939) (prior robbery admissible to show defendant's sanity and ability to devise and execute deliberate plan); *People v. Morani*, 196 Cal. 154, 236 Pac. 135 (1925) (prior abortion admissible to show that operation was not performed in ignorance of effect and, hence, to show necessary intent). See discussion in *California Criminal Law Practice* 491-498 (Cal.Cont.Ed. Bar 1964).

ANNOTATIONS

People v. Bryant (2014) 60 Cal.4th 335, 405-06, *cert. filed*, ___ S.Ct. ___ (2014) (No. 14-7386; 11-24-14). Evid. C. §1101(a) "prohibits the admission of character evidence if offered to prove conduct in conformity with that character trait, sometimes described as a propensity to act in a certain way. [Ds] argue that evidence of uncharged acts by, or connected to, a defendant is presumptively inadmissible under §1101(a). As a result, they urge the evidence must be found to fall within an 'exception' to that provision in order to be admitted at trial. That interpretation has been rejected. Section 1101(a) 'expressly prohibits the use of an uncharged offense if the *only* theory of relevance is that the accused has a propensity (or disposition) to commit the crime charged and that this propensity is circumstantial proof that the accused behaved accordingly on the occasion of the charged offense.' Section 1101(b) provides that '[n]othing in this section' prohibits the admission of uncharged acts to prove a fact 'other than [a person's] disposition to commit such an act.' Section 1101(b) is not an exception to §1101(a). Section 1101(a) prohibits the use of character to prove conduct. Section 1101(b) provides for the admission of uncharged acts when relevant to prove some other disputed fact. The true exceptions to §1101(a) are set out in [Evid. C.] §§1102, 1103, 1108, and 1109.... [¶] If an uncharged act is relevant to prove some fact other than propensity, the evidence is admissible, subject to a limiting instruction upon request."

People v. Scott (2011) 52 Cal.4th 452, 470. "When evidence is offered under ... §1101, subdivision (b), the degree of similarity required for cross-admissibility ranges along a continuum, depending on the purpose for which the evidence is received. The least degree of similarity is required to prove intent. A higher degree is required to prove common plan, and the highest degree to prove identity."

People v. Ewoldt (1994) 7 Cal.4th 380, 403. "The greatest degree of similarity is required for evidence of uncharged misconduct to be relevant to prove identity. For identity to be established, the uncharged misconduct and the charged offense must share common features that are sufficiently distinctive so as to support the inference that the same person committed both acts. 'The pattern and characteristics of the crimes must be so unusual and distinctive as to be like a signature.'" *See also* ***Hassoldt v. Patrick Media Grp.*** (2d Dist.2000) 84 Cal.App.4th 153, 165 n.11 (same evidentiary rules apply in both civil and criminal cases concerning evidence of other uncharged misconduct).

Ghadrdan v. Gorabi (2d Dist.2010) 182 Cal.App.4th 416, 423-24. "[T]he criminal conviction of [a] corporation could be admissible [against an individual defendant] under ... §1101, subdivision (b) if that conviction shows that the defendant on behalf of or in concert with the corporation 'committed a crime, civil wrong, or other act when relevant to prove some

fact (such as motive, opportunity, intent, preparation, plan, knowledge ...) other than his or her disposition to commit such an act.' Here, [Ds] sought to admit the corporate conviction not only to impeach [P] but to show he committed a crime or act that was relevant to his knowledge."

Brown v. Smith (4th Dist.1997) 55 Cal.App.4th 767, 791. "Under [Evid. C.] §1101, subdivision (b), the admissibility of prior act evidence depends upon three principal factors: (1) the *materiality* of the fact sought to be proved or disproved; (2) the *tendency* of the uncharged crime to prove or disprove the material fact; and (3) the existence of any *rule* or *policy* requiring the exclusion of relevant evidence. [¶] The policy or rule referred to [above] is primarily found in the provisions of [Evid. C.] §352 and the weighing of the prejudicial effect of such evidence against its probative value. Where such objection is raised, it is the trial court's duty to make such an evaluation before admitting the evidence. The court need not specifically articulate its weighing process, but the record must reflect the trial court has made an evaluation of the evidence. [¶] Thus, even where ... §1101 does not require exclusion of the evidence of a defendant's uncharged misconduct, such as where that evidence is relevant to prove a relevant fact other than the defendant's criminal or tortious disposition, a further inquiry under ... §352 is required...." (Internal quotes omitted.)

Bihun v. AT&T Info. Sys. (2d Dist.1993) 13 Cal.App.4th 976, 991, *disapproved on other grounds*, ***Lakin v. Watkins Associated Indus.*** (1993) 6 Cal.4th 644. "Any otherwise admissible evidence, including evidence of reputation, is admissible to prove a person's character or character trait when character or a trait of character is an ultimate fact in dispute in the action."

§1102. [CHARACTER ADMISSIBLE IF OFFERED BY DEFENDANT]

In a criminal action, evidence of the defendant's character or a trait of his character in the form of an opinion or evidence of his reputation is not made inadmissible by Section 1101 if such evidence is:

(a) Offered by the defendant to prove his conduct in conformity with such character or trait of character.

(b) Offered by the prosecution to rebut evidence adduced by the defendant under subdivision (a).

History of Evid. C. §1102: Added eff. Sept. 17, 1965, oper. Jan. 1, 1967, Stats. 1965, ch. 299, §2.

Official Comment

7 Cal. Law Revision Comm'n Rep. (1965) p. 1207.

Sections 1102 and 1103 state exceptions (applicable only in criminal cases) to the general rule of Section 1101 that character evidence is not admissible to prove conduct in conformity with that character.

Sections 1102 and 1103 generally.

Under Section 1102, the accused in a criminal case may introduce evidence of his good character to show his innocence of the alleged crime—provided that the character or trait of character to be shown is relevant to the charge made against him. This codifies existing law. *People v. Chrisman*, 135 Cal. 282, 67 Pac. 136 (1901). Sections 1101 and 1102 make it clear that the prosecution may not, on its own initiative, use character evidence to prove that the defendant had the disposition to commit the crime charged; but, if the defendant first introduces evidence of his good character to show the likelihood of innocence, the prosecution may meet his evidence by introducing evidence of the defendant's bad character to show the likelihood of guilt. This also codifies existing law. *People v. Jones*, 42 Cal.2d 219, 266 P.2d 38 (1954) (prosecution for sexual molestation of child; error to exclude expert psychiatric opinion that defendant was not a sexual psychopath); *People v. Stewart*, 28 Cal. 395 (1865) (murder prosecution; error to exclude evidence of defendant's good character for peace and quiet); *People v. Hughes*, 123 Cal.App.2d 767, 267 P.2d 376 (1954) (assault prosecution; evidence of defendant's violent nature held admissible after introduction of evidence showing his good character for peace and quiet). *See California Criminal Law Practice* 489-490 (Cal.Cont.Ed. Bar 1964).

Likewise, under Section 1103, the defendant may introduce evidence of the character of the victim of the crime where the conduct of the victim in conformity with his character would tend to exculpate the defendant; and, if the defendant introduces evidence of the bad character of the victim, the prosecution may introduce evidence of the victim's good character. This codifies existing law. *People v. Hoffman*, 195 Cal. 295, 311-312, 232 Pac. 974, 980 (1925) (murder prosecution; evidence of victim's good reputation for peace and quiet held inadmissible when defendant had not attacked reputation of victim); *People v. Lamar*, 148 Cal. 564, 83 Pac. 993 (1906) (murder prosecution; error to exclude evidence of victim's bad character for violence offered to prove victim was aggressor and defendant acted in self-defense); *People v. Shea*, 125 Cal. 151, 57 Pac. 885 (1899) (rape prosecution; error to exclude evidence of the prosecutrix's unchaste character offered to prove the likelihood of consent); *People v. Fitch*, 28 Cal.App.2d 31, 81 P.2d 1019 (1938) (murder prosecution; evidence of victim's good character for peace and quiet held admissible after defendant introduced evidence of victim's violent nature). *See also Comment*, 25 Cal.L.Rev. 459 (1937).

Thus, under Sections 1102 and 1103, the defendant in a criminal case is given the right to introduce character evidence that would be inadmissible in a civil case. However, evidence of the character of the defendant or the victim—though weak—may be enough to raise a reasonable doubt in the mind of the trier of fact concerning the defendant's guilt. And, since his life or liberty is at stake, the defendant should not be deprived of the right to introduce evidence even of such slight probative value.

Kinds of character evidence admissible to prove conduct under Sections 1102 and 1103.

The three kinds of evidence that might be offered to prove character as circumstantial evidence of conduct are: (1) evidence as to reputation, (2) opinion evidence as to character, and (3) evidence of specific acts indicating character. The admissibility of each of these kinds of evidence when character is sought to be proved as circumstantial evidence of conduct under Sections 1102 and 1103 is discussed below.

Reputation evidence. Reputation evidence is the ordinary means sanctioned by the cases for proving character as circumstantial evidence of conduct. Witkin, *California Evidence* §125 (1958). *See People v. Fair*, 43 Cal. 137 (1872). Both Sections 1102 and 1103 codify the existing law permitting character to be proved by reputation.

Opinion evidence. There is recent authority for the admission of opinion evidence to prove character as circumstantial evidence of conduct. *People v. Jones*, 42 Cal.2d 219, 266 P.2d 38 (1954) (error to exclude expert psychiatric opinion that the defendant was not a sexual psychopath and, hence, unlikely to have violated Penal Code Section 288). However, opinion evidence generally has been held inadmissible. *See People v. Spigno*, 156 Cal.App.2d 279, 319 P.2d 458 (1957) (full discussion of the *Jones* case); *California Criminal Law Practice* 489-490 (Cal.Cont.Ed. Bar 1964).

The general rule under existing law excludes the most reliable form of character evidence and admits the least reliable. The opinions of those whose personal intimacy with a person gives them firsthand knowledge of that person's character are a far more reliable indication of that character than is reputation, which is little more than accumulated hearsay. *See* 7 Wigmore, *Evidence* §1986 (3d ed. 1940). The danger of collateral issues seems no greater than that inherent in reputation evidence. Accordingly, both Section 1102 and Section 1103 permit character to be proved by opinion evidence.

Evidence of specific acts. Under existing law, the admissibility of evidence of specific acts to prove character as circumstantial evidence of conduct depends upon the nature of the conduct sought to be proved. Evidence of specific acts of the accused is excluded as a general rule in order to avoid the possibility of prejudice, undue confusion of the issues with collateral matters, unfair surprise, and the like. Thus, it is usually held that evidence of specific acts by the defendant is inadmissible to prove his guilt even though the defendant has opened the question by introducing evidence of his good character. See discussion in *People v. Gin Shue*, 58 Cal.App.2d 625, 634, 137 P.2d 742, 747-748 (1943). On the other hand, it is well settled that in a rape case the defendant may show the unchaste character of the prosecutrix by evidence of prior voluntary intercourse in order to indicate the unlikelihood of resistance on the occasion in question. *People v. Shea*, 125 Cal. 151, 57 Pac. 885 (1899); *People v. Benson*, 6 Cal. 221 (1856); *People v. Battilana*, 52 Cal.App.2d 685, 126 P.2d 923 (1942). However, in a homicide or assault case where the defense is self-defense, evidence of specific acts of violence by the victim is inadmissible to prove his violent nature (and, hence, that the victim was the aggressor) unless the prior acts were directed against the defendant himself. *People v. Yokum*, 145 Cal.App.2d 245, 302 P.2d 406 (1956); *People v. Soules*, 41 Cal.App.2d 298, 106 P.2d 639 (1940). *But see People v. Carmichael*, 198 Cal. 534, 548, 246 Pac. 62, 68 (1926) (if defendant had knowledge of victim's statement evidencing violent nature, the "statement was material and might have had an important bearing upon his plea of self-defense"); *People v. Swigart*, 80 Cal.App. 31, 251 Pac. 343 (1926). *See also Comment*, 25 Cal.L.Rev. 459, 466-469 (1937).

Section 1102 codifies the general rule under existing law which precludes evidence of specific acts of the defendant to prove character as circumstantial evidence of his innocence or of his disposition to commit the crime with which he is charged.

Section 1103 permits both the defendant and the prosecution to use evidence of specific acts of the victim of the crime to prove the victim's character as circumstantial evidence of his conduct. In this respect, the section harmonizes conflicting rules found in existing law.

§1103. [OFFER OF CHARACTER EVIDENCE OF VICTIM OR DEFENDANT]

(a) [Character of victim.] In a criminal action, evidence of the character or a trait of character (in the form of an opinion, evidence of reputation, or evidence of specific instances of conduct) of the victim of the crime for which the defendant is being prosecuted is not made inadmissible by Section 1101 if the evidence is:

(1) Offered by the defendant to prove conduct of the victim in conformity with the character or trait of character.

(2) Offered by the prosecution to rebut evidence adduced by the defendant under paragraph (1).

(b) [Character of defendant.] In a criminal action, evidence of the defendant's character for violence or trait of character for violence (in the form of an opinion, evidence of reputation, or evidence of specific instances of conduct) is not made inadmissible by Section 1101 if the evidence is offered by the prosecution to prove conduct of the defendant in conformity with the character or trait of character and is offered after evidence that the victim had a character for violence or a trait of character tending to show violence has been adduced by the defendant under paragraph (1) of subdivision (a).

(c) [Proof of consent.]

(1) Notwithstanding any other provision of this code to the contrary, and except as provided in this subdivision, in any prosecution under Section 261, 262, or 264.1 of the Penal Code, or under Section 286, 288a, or 289 of the Penal Code, or for assault with intent to commit, attempt to commit, or conspiracy to commit a crime defined in any of those sections, except where the crime is alleged to have occurred in a local detention facility, as defined in Section 6031.4, or in a state prison, as defined in Section 4504, opinion evidence, reputation evidence, and evidence of specific instances of the complaining witness' sexual conduct, or any of that evidence, is not admissible by the defendant in order to prove consent by the complaining witness.

(2) Notwithstanding paragraph (3), evidence of the manner in which the victim was dressed at the time of the commission of the offense shall not be admissible when offered by either party on the issue of consent in any prosecution for an offense specified in paragraph (1), unless the evidence is determined by the court to be relevant and admissible in the interests of justice. The proponent of the evidence shall make an offer of proof outside the hearing of the jury. The court shall then make its determination and at that time, state the reasons for its ruling on the record. For the purposes of this paragraph, "manner of dress" does not include the condition of the victim's clothing before, during, or after the commission of the offense.

(3) Paragraph (1) shall not be applicable to evidence of the complaining witness' sexual conduct with the defendant.

(4) If the prosecutor introduces evidence, including testimony of a witness, or the complaining witness as a witness gives testimony, and that evidence or testimony relates to the complaining witness' sexual conduct, the defendant may cross-examine the witness who gives the testimony and offer relevant evidence limited specifically to the rebuttal of the evidence introduced by the prosecutor or given by the complaining witness.

(5) Nothing in this subdivision shall be construed to make inadmissible any evidence offered to attack the credibility of the complaining witness as provided in Section 782.

(6) As used in this section, "complaining witness" means the alleged victim of the crime charged, the prosecution of which is subject to this subdivision.

History of Evid. C. §1103: Added eff. Sept. 17, 1965, oper. Jan. 1, 1967, Stats. 1965, ch. 299, §2. Amended eff. Jan. 1, 1975, Stats. 1974, ch. 569, §2; eff. Jan. 1, 1982, Stats. 1981, ch. 726, §2; eff. Jan. 1, 1991, Stats. 1990, ch. 268, §1; eff. Mar. 18, 1991, Stats. 1991, ch. 16, §1; eff. Jan. 1, 1997, Stats. 1996, ch. 1075, §7; eff. Jan. 1, 1999, Stats. 1998, ch. 127, §1.

Official Comment

7 Cal. Law Revision Comm'n Rep. (1965) p. 1209.

See the *Comment* to Section 1102.

§1104. [CARE OR SKILL EVIDENCE]

Except as provided in Sections 1102 and 1103, evidence of a trait of a person's character with respect to care or skill is inadmissible to prove the quality of his conduct on a specified occasion.

History of Evid. C. §1104: Added eff. Sept. 17, 1965, oper. Jan. 1, 1967, Stats. 1965, ch. 299, §2.

Official Comment

7 Cal. Law Revision Comm'n Rep. (1965) p. 1210.

Section 1104 places a further limitation on the use of character evidence. Under Section 1104, character evidence with respect to care or skill is inadmissible to prove that conduct on a specific occasion was either careless or careful, skilled or unskilled, except to the extent permitted by Sections 1102 and 1103.

Section 1104 codifies well-settled California law. *Towle v. Pacific Improvement Co.*, 98 Cal. 342, 33 Pac. 207 (1893). The purpose of the rule is to prevent collateral issues from consuming too much time and distracting the attention of the trier of fact from what was actually done on the particular occasion. Here, the slight probative value of the evidence balanced against the danger of confusion of issues, collateral inquiry, prejudice, and the like, warrants a fixed exclusionary rule.

ANNOTATIONS

Stafford v. United Farm Workers (1983) 33 Cal.3d 319, 324-25. "The argument ... is that [D's] lack of due care in omitting to publicize the contents of the TRO, is relevant on the question whether its alleged failure to tell the pickets where not to park their vehicles was negligent. In other words, the jury was invited to infer the negligent quality of the latter omission from [D's] negligence with respect to the former. That, of course, is precisely what is prohibited by §1104 [which codified ***Towle v. Pacific Imprv. Co.*** (1893) 98 Cal. 342]: '[E]vidence of a trait of a person's character with respect to care or skill is inadmissible to prove the quality of his conduct on a specified occasion.' [¶] The TRO was, therefore, not admissible on the theory that [D's] negligent failure to publicize its ban on obstruction of ingress into the fields implied negligence on the issue of lack of directions where to park."

Jeld-Wen, Inc. v. Superior Ct. (4th Dist.2005) 131 Cal.App.4th 853, 866-67. "Once the employer admittedly becomes vicariously liable for the negligent acts of the employee, there is no remaining basis at a future trial to attempt to prove the negligence of the employer itself, such as through knowledge of the employee's prior accidents, because the subject liability has already been adequately and completely established. This represents an effort to promote judicial economy by avoiding unnecessary litigation. It also represents an effort to ensure that prejudicial evidence on negligence is kept out pursuant to the principles of ... §1104, because the existence of negligence on a particular occasion should be determined from the nature of the subject act or omission, 'not by defendant's character for care [or lack thereof]....' *At 870:* Once an employer has admitted before trial to vicarious liability for its employee's negligence, if proven, the exclusionary rule of ... §1104 operates to protect the employer from being exposed to prejudicial evidence that would be used to show the employer's prior knowledge of an employee's prior accidents, for purposes of imposing direct and separate liability on the employer."

§1105. [HABIT OR CUSTOM EVIDENCE]

Any otherwise admissible evidence of habit or custom is admissible to prove conduct on a specified occasion in conformity with the habit or custom.

History of Evid. C. §1105: Added eff. Sept. 17, 1965, oper. Jan. 1, 1967, Stats. 1965, ch. 299, §2.

Official Comment

7 Cal. Law Revision Comm'n Rep. (1965) p. 1211.

Section 1105, like Section 1100, declares that certain evidence is admissible. Hence, Section 1105 is technically unnecessary because Section 351 declares that all relevant evidence is admissible. Nonetheless, Section 1105 is desirable to assure that evidence of custom or habit (a regular response to a repeated specific situation) is admissible even where evidence of a person's character (his general disposition or propensity to engage in a certain type of conduct) is inadmissible.

The admissibility of habit evidence to prove conduct in conformity with the habit has long been established in California. *Wallis v. Southern Pac. Co.*, 184 Cal. 662, 195 Pac. 408 (1921) (distinguishing cases holding character evidence as to care or skill inadmissible); *Craven v. Central Pac. R.R.*, 72 Cal. 345, 13 Pac. 878 (1887). The admissibility of evidence of the custom of a business or occupation is also well established. *Hughes v. Pacific Wharf & Storage Co.*, 188 Cal. 210, 205 Pac. 105 (1922) (mailing letter). However, under existing law, evidence of habit is admissible only if there are no eyewitnesses. *Boone v. Bank of America*, 220 Cal. 93, 29 P.2d 409 (1934). In earlier cases, the Supreme Court criticized the "no eyewitnesses" limitation:

> This limitation upon the introduction of such testimony seems rather illogical. If the fact of the existence of habits of caution in a given particular has any legitimate evidentiary weight, the party benefited ought to have the advantage of it for whatever it is worth, even against adverse eye-witnesses; and if the testimony of the eye-witnesses is in his favor, it would be at least a harmless cumulation of evidence to permit testimony of his custom or habit. [*Wallis v. Southern Pac. Co.*, 184 Cal. 662, 665, 195 Pac. 408, 409 (1921).]

The "no eyewitness" limitation is undesirable. Eyewitnesses frequently are mistaken, and some are dishonest. The trier of fact should be entitled to weigh the habit evidence against the eyewitness testimony as well as all of the other evidence in the case. Hence, Section 1105 does not contain the "no eyewitness" limitation.

ANNOTATIONS

Dincau v. Tamayose (2d Dist.1982) 131 Cal.App.3d 780, 793. "[Ps] object to admission of evidence of the habit and custom of [doctor] and his staff as to their habitual response to telephone calls about minors' conditions, including the doctor's habit and instructions and usage thereon about (a) requesting that a child be brought in if its temperature is over 100°; (b) giving of prescriptions over the telephone; and (c) contacting [doctor] if certain conditions were described by the caller. [¶] [Ps] urge that such testimony was inadmissible as falling under [Evid. C.] §1104 which makes evidence of a trait of a person's character inadmissible to prove the quality of his conduct on a specified occasion. Although the line between [Evid. C.] §1104 and §1105 may sometimes be a thin one, the nature and quality of the evidence objected to here clearly fell under §1105 which permits introduction of evidence of habit or custom to prove conduct on a specified occasion in conformity with the habit or custom."

§1106. [SEXUAL CONDUCT]

(a) **[When inadmissible.]** In any civil action alleging conduct which constitutes sexual harassment, sexual assault, or sexual battery, opinion evidence, reputation evidence, and evidence of specific instances of plaintiff's sexual conduct, or any of such evidence, is not admissible by the defendant in order to prove consent by the plaintiff or the absence of injury to the plaintiff, unless the injury alleged by the plaintiff is in the nature of loss of consortium.

(b) **[When admissible.]** Subdivision (a) shall not be applicable to evidence of the plaintiff's sexual conduct with the alleged perpetrator.

(c) **[Cross-examination.]** If the plaintiff introduces evidence, including testimony of a witness, or the plaintiff as a witness gives testimony, and the evidence or testimony relates to the plaintiff's sexual conduct, the defendant may cross-examine the witness who gives the testimony and offer relevant evidence limited specifically to the rebuttal of the evidence introduced by the plaintiff or given by the plaintiff.

(d) **[Credibility.]** Nothing in this section shall be construed to make inadmissible any evidence offered to attack the credibility of the plaintiff as provided in Section 783.

History of Evid. C. §1106: Added eff. Jan. 1, 1986, Stats. 1985, ch. 1328, §4.

ANNOTATIONS

Rieger v. Arnold (3d Dist.2002) 104 Cal.App.4th 451, 464. "We cannot accept the suggestion that we should interpret the use of perpetrator in §1106 as nothing more than a synonym for defendant. [¶] Though a case alleging a hostile work environment conceivably can name individuals as defendants, generally such actions name only the deeper-pocketed employing entity (or … the employer and individual defendants). [A]n employing entity can not only be directly liable for sexual harassment, but indirectly liable as well for the actions of its agents and supervisors or for the actions of its nonsupervisory employees if it was or should have been aware of them and did not take remedial measures. An employing entity must also take reasonable steps to prevent harassment from occurring. As a result, there could be far more actors in the harassment drama for whom a plaintiff would hold the employing entity responsible than are named as defendants. Consistent with the legislative intention to allow a defense based on genuinely probative evidence, we conclude perpetrators include not only the named defendants but also any other actor whose conduct the plaintiff seeks to ascribe to the employing entity. The employing entity would otherwise be hamstrung with imputed liability against which it could not effectively defend."

Patricia C. v. Mark D. (1st Dist.1993) 12 Cal.App.4th 1211, 1216-18. "The pivotal question is whether the present action may properly be characterized as a 'civil action alleging conduct which constitutes sexual harassment, sexual assault, or sexual battery' within the meaning of [Evid. C.] §1106. The answer turns on whether the statute was intended to apply only to cases where a plaintiff alleges a *cause of action* for sexual harassment, assault or battery, or more broadly to any case, regardless of the causes of action alleged, where the defendant's purported conduct *may be characterized* as sexual harassment, assault or battery. Section 1106 is susceptible to the broader interpretation because it specifies 'conduct which constitutes' rather than 'a cause of action' for sexual harassment, assault or battery. [P] did not allege any such

causes of action—the theory of her case was medical negligence and infliction of emotional distress—but sexual contact between [D] and [P] may be characterized as a common law *sexual battery* on the theory that any sexual contact between psychotherapist and patient is 'harmful or offensive contact.' [¶] [T]he adoption of §1106 was accompanied by a statement of intent in which the Legislature said 'it is the existing policy of the State of California to ensure that *the causes of action* for claims of sexual harassment, sexual assault, or sexual battery are given proper meaning' through protection against intrusion into plaintiffs' intimate lives. This indicates that despite the 'conduct which constitutes' language, the statute was intended to apply where the plaintiff alleges a *cause of action* for sexual harassment, assault or battery. [¶] [T]he broader construction of §1106 would create a conflict with provisions of [Civ. C.] §43.93 pertaining to admission of evidence of a plaintiff's sexual history where the plaintiff alleges a cause of action for psychotherapist-patient sexual contact. ... If §1106 is construed broadly to reach beyond causes of action for sexual harassment, assault or battery, so that it may apply to causes of action for psychotherapist-patient sexual contact, there would be an irreconcilable conflict between the two statutes. [S]ection 43.93 would permit discretionary admission of relevant sexual history evidence to prove an absence of injury, but ... §1106 would absolutely preclude it. [¶] The absolute bar of §1106 is justified in typical harassment, assault or battery cases by the need to protect victims from intrusion into their private lives. However, in actions for [psychotherapist]-patient sexual contact a countervailing consideration—the special likelihood of preexisting emotional disorder and the potential relevance of sexual history—militates against an absolute bar and in favor of discretionary admissibility as prescribed by ... §43.93 where sexual history is relevant and its probative value outweighs its prejudicial effect."

§1107. [EXPERT-WITNESS TESTIMONY ON INTIMATE-PARTNER BATTERING & ITS EFFECTS]

(a) [Expert testimony.] In a criminal action, expert testimony is admissible by either the prosecution or the defense regarding intimate partner battering and its effects, including the nature and effect of physical, emotional, or mental abuse on the beliefs, perceptions, or behavior of victims of domestic violence, except when offered against a criminal defendant to prove the occurrence of the act or acts of abuse which form the basis of the criminal charge.

(b) [Foundation for testimony.] The foundation shall be sufficient for admission of this expert testimony if the proponent of the evidence establishes its relevancy and the proper qualifications of the expert witness. Expert opinion testimony on intimate partner battering and its effects shall not be considered a new scientific technique whose reliability is unproven.

(c) [Abuse.] For purposes of this section, "abuse" is defined in Section 6203 of the Family Code, and "domestic violence" is defined in Section 6211 of the Family Code and may include acts defined in Section 242, subdivision (e) of Section 243, Section 262, 273.5, 273.6, 422, or 653m of the Penal Code.

(d) [No change to Penal Code.] This section is intended as a rule of evidence only and no substantive change affecting the Penal Code is intended.

(e) [Title.] This section shall be known, and may be cited, as the Expert Witness Testimony on Intimate Partner Battering and Its Effects Section of the Evidence Code.

(f) [Existing decisional law not affected.] The changes in this section that become effective on January 1, 2005, are not intended to impact any existing decisional law regarding this section, and that decisional law should apply equally to this section as it refers to "intimate partner battering and its effects" in place of "battered women's syndrome."

History of Evid. C. §1107: Added eff. Jan. 1, 1992, Stats. 1991, ch. 812, §1. Amended eff. Jan. 1, 1993, oper. Jan. 1, 1994, Stats. 1992, ch. 163, §72; eff. Jan. 1, 1994, Stats. 1993, ch. 219, §77.5, ch. 589, §60; eff. Jan. 1, 2001, Stats. 2000, ch. 1001, §1; eff. Jan. 1, 2005, Stats. 2004, ch. 609, §1.

Official Comment

23 Cal. Law Revision Comm'n Rep. (1993) p. 825.

Subdivision (c) of Section 1107 is amended to substitute references to the provisions of the Family Code that replaced the relevant provisions of former Code of Civil Procedure Section 542.

§1108. [ANOTHER SEXUAL OFFENSE BY DEFENDANT]

(a) [Accused of sexual offense.] In a criminal action in which the defendant is accused of a sexual offense, evidence of the defendant's commission of another sexual offense or offenses is not made inadmissible by Section 1101, if the evidence is not inadmissible pursuant to Section 352.

(b) [Disclosure of evidence.] In an action in which evidence is to be offered under this section, the people shall disclose the evidence to the defendant, including statements of witnesses or a summary of the

substance of any testimony that is expected to be offered in compliance with the provisions of Section 1054.7 of the Penal Code.

(c) [Evidence not exclusive.] This section shall not be construed to limit the admission or consideration of evidence under any other section of this code.

(d) [Definitions.] As used in this section, the following definitions shall apply:

(1) "Sexual offense" means a crime under the law of a state or of the United States that involved any of the following:

(A) Any conduct proscribed by Section 243.4, 261, 261.5, 262, 264.1, 266c, 269, 286, 288, 288a, 288.2, 288.5, or 289, or subdivision (b), (c), or (d) of Section 311.2 or Section 311.3, 311.4, 311.10, 311.11, 314, or 647.6, of the Penal Code.

(B) Any conduct proscribed by Section 220 of the Penal Code, except assault with intent to commit mayhem.

(C) Contact, without consent, between any part of the defendant's body or an object and the genitals or anus of another person.

(D) Contact, without consent, between the genitals or anus of the defendant and any part of another person's body.

(E) Deriving sexual pleasure or gratification from the infliction of death, bodily injury, or physical pain on another person.

(F) An attempt or conspiracy to engage in conduct described in this paragraph.

(2) "Consent" shall have the same meaning as provided in Section 261.6 of the Penal Code, except that it does not include consent which is legally ineffective because of the age, mental disorder, or developmental or physical disability of the victim.

History of Evid. C. §1108: Added eff. Jan. 1, 1996, Stats. 1995, ch. 439, §2. Amended eff. Jan. 1, 2002, Stats. 2001, ch. 517, §1; eff. Jan. 1, 2003, Stats. 2002, ch. 194, §1, ch. 828, §1.

§1109. [OTHER DOMESTIC VIOLENCE BY DEFENDANT]

(a) [When inadmissible.]

(1) Except as provided in subdivision (e) or (f), in a criminal action in which the defendant is accused of an offense involving domestic violence, evidence of the defendant's commission of other domestic violence is not made inadmissible by Section 1101 if the evidence is not inadmissible pursuant to Section 352.

(2) Except as provided in subdivision (e) or (f), in a criminal action in which the defendant is accused of an offense involving abuse of an elder or dependent person, evidence of the defendant's commission of other abuse of an elder or dependent person is not made inadmissible by Section 1101 if the evidence is not inadmissible pursuant to Section 352.

(3) Except as provided in subdivision (e) or (f) and subject to a hearing conducted pursuant to Section 352, which shall include consideration of any corroboration and remoteness in time, in a criminal action in which the defendant is accused of an offense involving child abuse, evidence of the defendant's commission of child abuse is not made inadmissible by Section 1101 if the evidence is not inadmissible pursuant to Section 352. Nothing in this paragraph prohibits or limits the admission of evidence pursuant to subdivision (b) of Section 1101.

(b) [Disclosure of evidence.] In an action in which evidence is to be offered under this section, the people shall disclose the evidence to the defendant, including statements of witnesses or a summary of the substance of any testimony that is expected to be offered, in compliance with the provisions of Section 1054.7 of the Penal Code.

(c) [Evidence not exclusive.] This section shall not be construed to limit or preclude the admission or consideration of evidence under any other statute or case law.

(d) [Definitions.] As used in this section:

(1) "Abuse of an elder or dependent person" means physical or sexual abuse, neglect, financial abuse, abandonment, isolation, abduction, or other treatment that results in physical harm, pain, or mental suffering, the deprivation of care by a caregiver, or other deprivation by a custodian or provider of goods or services that are necessary to avoid physical harm or mental suffering.

(2) "Child abuse" means an act proscribed by Section 273d of the Penal Code.

(3) "Domestic violence" has the meaning set forth in Section 13700 of the Penal Code. Subject to a hearing conducted pursuant to Section 352, which shall include consideration of any corroboration and remoteness in time, "domestic violence" has the further meaning as set forth in Section 6211 of the Family Code, if the act occurred no more than five years before the charged offense.

(e) [**Ten-year limitation.**] Evidence of acts occurring more than 10 years before the charged offense is inadmissible under this section, unless the court determines that the admission of this evidence is in the interest of justice.

(f) [**Agency findings.**] Evidence of the findings and determinations of administrative agencies regulating the conduct of health facilities licensed under Section 1250 of the Health and Safety Code is inadmissible under this section.

History of Evid. C. §1109: Added eff. Jan. 1, 1997, Stats. 1996, ch. 261, §2. Amended eff. Jan. 1, 1999, Stats. 1998, ch. 707, §1; eff. Jan. 1, 2001, Stats. 2000, ch. 97, §1; eff. Jan. 1, 2005, Stats. 2004, ch. 116, §1, ch. 823, §6.5; eff. Jan. 1, 2006, Stats. 2005, ch. 464, §1.

CHAPTER 2. MEDIATION

§1115. [DEFINITIONS]

For purposes of this chapter:

(a) "Mediation" means a process in which a neutral person or persons facilitate communication between the disputants to assist them in reaching a mutually acceptable agreement.

(b) "Mediator" means a neutral person who conducts a mediation. "Mediator" includes any person designated by a mediator either to assist in the mediation or to communicate with the participants in preparation for a mediation.

(c) "Mediation consultation" means a communication between a person and a mediator for the purpose of initiating, considering, or reconvening a mediation or retaining the mediator.

History of Evid. C. §1115: Added eff. Jan. 1, 1998, Stats. 1997, ch. 772, §3.

Official Comment

1997-98 Ann. Report, 27 Cal. Law Revision Comm'n Rep. (1997) App. 5.

Subdivision (a) of Section 1115 is drawn from Code of Civil Procedure Section 1775.1. To accommodate a wide range of mediation styles, the definition is broad, without specific limitations on format. For example, it would include a mediation conducted as a number of sessions, only some of which involve the mediator. The definition focuses on the nature of a proceeding, not its label. A proceeding may be a "mediation" for purposes of this chapter, even though it is denominated differently.

Under subdivision (b), a mediator must be neutral. The neutrality requirement is drawn from Code of Civil Procedure Section 1775.1. An attorney or other representative of a party is not neutral and so does not qualify as a "mediator" for purposes of this chapter.

A "mediator" may be an individual, group of individuals, or entity. *See* Section 175 ("person" defined). *See also* Section 10 (singular includes the plural). This definition of mediator encompasses not only the neutral person who takes the lead in conducting a mediation, but also any neutral who assists in the mediation, such as a case-developer, interpreter, or secretary. The definition focuses on a person's role, not the person's title. A person may be a "mediator" under this chapter even though the person has a different title, such as "ombudsperson." Any person who meets the definition of "mediator" must comply with Section 1121 (mediator reports and communications), which generally prohibits a mediator from reporting to a court or other tribunal concerning the mediated dispute.

Subdivision (c) is drawn from former Section 1152.5, which was amended in 1996 to explicitly protect mediation intake communications. *See* 1996 Cal. Stat. ch. 174, §1. Subdivision (c) is not limited to communications to retain a mediator. It also encompasses contacts concerning whether to mediate, such as where a mediator contacts a disputant because another disputant desires to mediate, and contacts concerning initiation or recommencement of mediation, such as where a case-developer meets with a disputant before mediation.

For the scope of this chapter, *see* Section 1117.

ANNOTATIONS

Saeta v. Superior Ct. (2d Dist.2004) 117 Cal.App.4th 261, 269. "Generally, mediation falls within two categories: traditional or classic mediation on the one hand, and voluntary settlement conferences on the other hand. In classic mediation, attorneys are generally not involved. The mediator meets directly with the parties to facilitate negotiation. The classic mediator is passive, expressing no judgment or opinion on the merits of either position. By contrast, in the latter form, attorneys are present; and the mediator takes a more active role, often expressing an opinion on the merits, but without authority to render a decision. *At 270:* 'Mediation involves moving parties from focusing on their individual bargaining positions to inventing options that will meet the primary needs of all parties. The concept of *self-determination*, which gives parties control over the resolution of their own dispute, is of major importance to the mediation process. It is thought that self-determination enhances commitment to the settlement terms because parties make decisions themselves instead of having a resolution imposed upon them by an authoritative third party.' The function of the mediator, therefore, is to facilitate the parties to voluntarily reach their own agreement." *See also* ***Travelers Cas. & Sur. Co. v. Superior Ct.*** (2d Dist.2005) 126 Cal.App.4th 1131, 1138-39.

§1116. [OPERATION OF CHAPTER]

(a) Nothing in this chapter expands or limits a court's authority to order participation in a dispute resolution proceeding. Nothing in this chapter authorizes or affects the enforceability of a contract clause in which parties agree to the use of mediation.

(b) Nothing in this chapter makes admissible evidence that is inadmissible under Section 1152 or any other statute.

History of Evid. C. §1116: Added eff. Jan. 1, 1998, Stats. 1997, ch. 772, §3.

Official Comment

1997-98 Ann. Report, 27 Cal. Law Revision Comm'n Rep. (1997) App. 5.

Subdivision (a) of Section 1116 establishes guiding principles for applying this chapter.

Subdivision (b) continues the first sentence of former Section 1152.5(c) without substantive change.

§1109

§1117. [SCOPE OF CHAPTER]

(a) [**Mediation.**] Except as provided in subdivision (b), this chapter applies to a mediation as defined in Section 1115.

(b) [**Exclusions.**] This chapter does not apply to either of the following:

(1) A proceeding under Part 1 (commencing with Section 1800) of Division 5 of the Family Code or Chapter 11 (commencing with Section 3160) of Part 2 of Division 8 of the Family Code.

(2) A settlement conference pursuant to Rule 3.1380 of the California Rules of Court.

History of Evid. C. §1117: Added eff. Jan. 1, 1998, Stats. 1997, ch. 772, §3. Amended eff. Jan. 1, 2008, Stats. 2007, ch. 130, §84.

Official Comment

1997-98 Ann. Report, 27 Cal. Law Revision Comm'n Rep. (1997) App. 5.

Under subdivision (a) of Section 1117, mediation confidentiality and the other safeguards of this chapter apply to a broad range of mediations. *See* Section 1115 *Comment.*

Subdivision (b) sets forth two exceptions. Section 1117(b)(1) continues without substantive change former Section 1152.5(b). Special confidentiality rules apply to a proceeding in family conciliation court or a mediation of child custody or visitation issues. *See* Section 1040; Fam. Code §§1818, 3177.

Section 1117(b)(2) establishes that a court settlement conference is not a mediation within the scope of this chapter. A settlement conference is conducted under the aura of the court and is subject to special rules.

ANNOTATIONS

Doe 1 v. Superior Ct. (2d Dist.2005) 132 Cal.App.4th 1160, 1166-67. "[T]he court used the terms 'mediation' and 'settlement' interchangeably when referring to the process taking place. We ... recognize the conceptual difficulties in distinguishing between a mediation and a settlement conference when a bench officer is presiding at those talks. [¶] If counsel wish to avoid the effect of the mediation confidentiality rules, they should make clear at the outset that something other than a mediation is intended. Except where the parties have expressly agreed otherwise, appellate courts should not seize on an occasional reference to 'settlement' as a means to frustrate the mediation confidentiality statutes."

§1118. [ORAL AGREEMENT]

An oral agreement "in accordance with Section 1118" means an oral agreement that satisfies all of the following conditions:

(a) [**Recorded.**] The oral agreement is recorded by a court reporter or reliable means of audio recording.

(b) [**Terms recited on record.**] The terms of the oral agreement are recited on the record in the presence of the parties and the mediator, and the parties express on the record that they agree to the terms recited.

(c) [**Express statement of parties.**] The parties to the oral agreement expressly state on the record that the agreement is enforceable or binding, or words to that effect.

(d) [**Reduced to writing.**] The recording is reduced to writing and the writing is signed by the parties within 72 hours after it is recorded.

History of Evid. C. §1118: Added eff. Jan. 1, 1998, Stats. 1997, ch. 772, §3. Amended eff. Jan. 1, 2010, Stats. 2009, ch. 88, §35; eff. Jan. 1, 2011, Stats. 2010, ch. 328, §64.

Official Comment

1997-98 Ann. Report, 27 Cal. Law Revision Comm'n Rep. (1997) App. 5.

Section 1118 establishes a procedure for orally memorializing an agreement, in the interest of efficiency. Provisions permitting use of that procedure for certain purposes include Sections 1121 (mediator reports and communications), 1122 (disclosure by agreement), 1123 (written settlement agreements reached through mediation), and 1124 (oral agreements reached through mediation). *See also* Section 1125 (when mediation ends). For guidance on authority to bind a litigant, *see Williams v. Saunders*, 55 Cal.App.4th 1158, 64 Cal.Rptr. 2d 571 (1997) ("The litigants' direct participation tends to ensure that the settlement is the result of their mature reflection and deliberate assent.").

37 Cal. Law Revision Comm'n Rep. (2007), p. 283.

Section 1118 is amended to reflect advances in recording technology and for consistency of terminology. For a similar reform, see 2002 Cal. Stat. ch. 1068 (replacing numerous references to "audiotape" in Civil Discovery Act with either "audio technology," "audio recording," or "audio record," as context required).

§1119. [CONFIDENTIALITY OF MEDIATION PROCEEDING]

Except as otherwise provided in this chapter:

(a) [**Statements.**] No evidence of anything said or any admission made for the purpose of, in the course of, or pursuant to, a mediation or a mediation consultation is admissible or subject to discovery, and disclosure of the evidence shall not be compelled, in any arbitration, administrative adjudication, civil action, or other noncriminal proceeding in which, pursuant to law, testimony can be compelled to be given.

(b) [**Writing.**] No writing, as defined in Section 250, that is prepared for the purpose of, in the course of, or pursuant to, a mediation or a mediation consultation, is admissible or subject to discovery, and disclosure of the writing shall not be compelled, in any arbitration, administrative adjudication, civil action, or other noncriminal proceeding in which, pursuant to law, testimony can be compelled to be given.

(c) [**Settlement discussion.**] All communications, negotiations, or settlement discussions by and between participants in the course of a mediation or a mediation consultation shall remain confidential.

History of Evid. C. §1119: Added eff. Jan. 1, 1998, Stats. 1997, ch. 772, §3.

Official Comment

1997-98 Ann. Report, 27 Cal. Law Revision Comm'n Rep. (1997) App. 5.

Subdivision (a) of Section 1119 continues without substantive change former Section 1152.5(a)(1), except that its protection explicitly applies in a subsequent arbitration or administrative adjudication, as well as in any civil action or proceeding. *See* Section 120 ("civil action" includes civil proceedings). In addition, the protection of Section 1119(a) extends to oral communications made for the purpose of or pursuant to a mediation, not just oral communications made in the course of the mediation.

Subdivision (b) continues without substantive change former Section 1152.5(a)(2), except that its protection explicitly applies in a subsequent arbitration or administrative adjudication, as well as in any civil action or proceeding. *See* Section 120 ("civil action" includes civil proceedings). In addition, subdivision (b) expressly encompasses any type of "writing" as defined in Section 250, regardless of whether the representations are on paper or on some other medium.

Subdivision (c) continues former Section 1152.5(a)(3) without substantive change. A mediation is confidential notwithstanding the presence of an observer, such as a person evaluating or training the mediator or studying the mediation process.

See Sections 1115(a) ("mediation" defined), 1115(c) ("mediation consultation" defined). *See also* Section 703.5 (testimony by a judge, arbitrator, or mediator).

For examples of specialized mediation confidentiality provisions, *see* Bus. & Prof. Code §§467.4-467.5 (community dispute resolution programs), 6200 (attorney-client fee disputes); Code Civ. Proc. §§1297.371 (international commercial disputes), 1775.10 (civil action mediation in participating courts); Fam. Code §§1818 (family conciliation court), 3177 (child custody); Food & Agric. Code §54453 (agricultural cooperative bargaining associations); Gov't Code §§11420.20-11420.30 (administrative adjudication), 12984-12985 (housing discrimination), 66032-66033 (land use); Ins. Code §10089.80 (earthquake insurance); Lab. Code §65 (labor disputes); Welf. & Inst. Code §350 (dependency mediation). *See also* Cal. Const., art. I, §1 (right to privacy); *Garstang v. Superior Court*, 39 Cal.App.4th 526, 46 Cal.Rptr. 2d 84, 88 (1995) (constitutional right of privacy protected communications made during mediation sessions before an ombudsperson).

ANNOTATIONS

Cassel v. Superior Ct. (2011) 51 Cal.4th 113, 128. "All oral or written communications are covered [under Evid. C. §1119] if they are made 'for the purpose of' or 'pursuant to' a mediation. It follows that, absent an express statutory exception, all discussions conducted in preparation for a mediation, as well as all mediation-related communications that take place during the mediation itself, are protected from disclosure. Plainly, such communications include those between a mediation disputant and his or her own counsel, even if these do not occur in the presence of the mediator or other disputants. *At 129:* This conclusion is reinforced by examination of [Evid. C.] §1122, subdivision (a)(2), which sets forth the circumstances under which fewer than all of the participants in a mediation may stipulate to the disclosure of otherwise confidential mediation-related communications. Under this statute, those mediation participants 'by or on [whose] behalf' a mediation-related communication, document, or writing was prepared may agree, under specified statutory procedures, to its disclosure, but only insofar as the communication in question 'does not [reveal] *anything said or done ... in the course of* the mediation.' Section 1122, subdivision (a)(2) thus presupposes there are mediation-related communications that (1) are prepared 'by or on behalf of fewer than all the mediation participants,' and (2) do not 'disclose anything said or done ... in the course of the mediation,' but (3) are nonetheless protected by mediation confidentiality unless the affected participants otherwise agree. Logically, these must include communications that are made or prepared outside a mediation, but are 'for the purpose of' or 'pursuant to' the mediation. Such mediation-related communications plainly encompass those between a mediation disputant and the disputant's counsel, even though these occur away from other mediation participants and reveal nothing about the mediation proceedings themselves." *See also* ***Eisendrath v. Superior Ct.*** (2d Dist.2003) 109 Cal.App.4th 351, 364.

Rojas v. Superior Ct. (2004) 33 Cal.4th 407, 421. "The Court of Appeal's conclusion that photographs and videotapes taken for purposes of mediation are not protected under §1119 is inconsistent with ... legislative history. *At 423:* The Court of Appeal also erred in holding that, although §1119's protection applies to so-called derivative material 'that is prepared for the purpose of, in the course of, or pursuant to, a mediation' ...—such as charts, diagrams, information compilations, and expert opinions and reports—such material is nevertheless discoverable 'upon a showing of good cause.' [T]he Legislature clearly knows how to establish a 'good cause' exception to a protection or privilege if it so desires. The Legislature did not enact such an exception when it passed ... §1119 and the other mediation confidentiality provisions. *At 424:* [T]here is no evidence of a legislative intent supporting the 'good cause' exception the Court of Appeal majority read into the statute. On the contrary, ... that exception 'is inconsistent with th[e] narrowly drawn exception[s]' the Legislature expressly established." *See also* ***Wimsatt v. Superior Ct.*** (2d Dist.2007) 152 Cal.App.4th 137, 154.

Foxgate Homeowners' Ass'n v. Bramalea Cal., Inc. (2001) 26 Cal.4th 1, 3-4. "The Court of Appeal held that, notwithstanding [Evid. C.] §1119 ... and §1121, which limits the content of mediators' reports, the mediator may report to the court a party's failure to comply with an order of the mediator and to participate in good faith in the mediation process. In doing so, the mediator may reveal information necessary to place sanction-

able conduct in context, including communications made during mediation. ... We granted review to consider whether §§1119 and 1121 are subject to any exceptions. [¶] We conclude that there are no exceptions to the confidentiality of mediation communications or to the statutory limits on the content of mediator's reports. Neither a mediator nor a party may reveal communications made during mediation. The judicially created exception fashioned by the Court of Appeal is inconsistent with the language and the legislative intent underlying §§1119 and 1121. We also conclude that, while a party may do so, a mediator may not report to the court about the conduct of participants in a mediation session." *See also* ***Campagnone v. Enjoyable Pools & Spa Serv. & Repairs, Inc.*** (3d Dist.2008) 163 Cal.App.4th 566, 571.

In re Marriage of Daly & Oyster (2d Dist.2014) 228 Cal.App.4th 505, 511. See annotation under Evidence Code §1123, p. 1368.

In re Marriage of Woolsey (3d Dist.2013) 220 Cal.App.4th 881, 900-01. "In the trial court, [husband] argued the marital settlement agreement is unenforceable because the mediator engaged in undue influence during the mediation. On appeal, he changes his argument to assert [wife] exerted undue influence on him during the mediation. As part of his argument, [husband] asserts [wife] gained an unfair division of property because of the mediation. In so arguing, [husband] acknowledges the confidentiality extended to mediation proceedings undermines his argument. ... We conclude [husband's] assertion of undue influence is precluded by the mediation confidentiality imposed by the Evidence Code. [¶] [Under] §1119, ... 'there are no exceptions to the confidentiality of mediation communications or to the statutory limits on the content of mediator's reports. Neither a mediator nor a party may reveal communications made during mediation.' [The] mediation confidentiality even extends to preclude complaints of deception and coercion brought by a client against his own attorney for the attorney's conduct in connection with a mediation. Accordingly, [husband] cannot establish undue influence by [wife] or any other participant in the mediation under the mediation confidentiality provisions of ... §1119."

Kurtin v. Elieff (4th Dist.2013) 215 Cal.App.4th 455, 474-75. "In ***Cassel*** [***v. Superior Ct.*** (2011) 51 Cal.4th 113], a plaintiff in a legal malpractice action claimed his attorneys had, in a pretrial mediation, pressured, harassed and otherwise coerced him into accepting a lower price than he wanted for certain licensing rights. The Supreme Court upheld a trial court order precluding the admission of evidence related *to the mediation*, including the discussions the plaintiff had with his attorneys. [¶] The application of the mediation privilege in ***Cassel*** meant, under the particular circumstances of that case, the *plaintiff's* ability to present a claim was hindered. Here, [D] argues that application of the mediation privilege supposedly hindered his ability *as defendant* to defend against a claim. And on that difference—the difference between one's status as a plaintiff or as a defendant—[D] hangs all attempts to distinguish ***Cassel***. [¶] But we cannot see any meaningful difference between plaintiffs and defendants in the mediation privilege situation. ... One need only think of the consequence of [D's] position to understand it was never intended by the Legislature. Under [D's] theory, parties to a mediation would know that if they were successful in achieving a mediated settlement in which they were the obligee, they could not enforce the settlement without running the risk of their adversaries claiming terms of the settlement were ambiguous, and forcing either (1) the disclosure of communications made in the course of the mediation or (2) the loss of the very benefit of that mediation, which was the mediated agreement itself. By contrast, obligors would have a natural advantage over obligees. They could put obligees to the Hobson's choice of giving up the benefit of the settlement or allowing the airing of privileged communications. The Legislature obviously never intended such asymmetry."

Wimsatt v. Superior Ct. (2d Dist.2007) 152 Cal.App.4th 137, 164. "In light of the harsh and inequitable results of the mediation confidentiality statutes ..., the parties and their attorneys should be warned of the unintended consequences of agreeing to mediate a dispute. If they do not intend to be bound by the mediation confidentiality statutes, then they should 'make [it] clear at the outset that something other than a mediation is intended.'"

§1120. [EVIDENCE OTHERWISE ADMISSIBLE]

(a) [Admissible evidence.] Evidence otherwise admissible or subject to discovery outside of a mediation or a mediation consultation shall not be or become

inadmissible or protected from disclosure solely by reason of its introduction or use in a mediation or a mediation consultation.

(b) [**Effect of chapter.**] This chapter does not limit any of the following:

(1) The admissibility of an agreement to mediate a dispute.

(2) The effect of an agreement not to take a default or an agreement to extend the time within which to act or refrain from acting in a pending civil action.

(3) Disclosure of the mere fact that a mediator has served, is serving, will serve, or was contacted about serving as a mediator in a dispute.

History of Evid. C. §1120: Added eff. Jan. 1, 1998, Stats. 1997, ch. 772, §3.

Official Comment

1997-98 Ann. Report, 27 Cal. Law Revision Comm'n Rep. (1997) App. 5.

Subdivision (a) of Section 1120 continues former Section 1152.5(a)(6) without change. It limits the scope of Section 1119 (mediation confidentiality), preventing parties from using a mediation as a pretext to shield materials from disclosure.

Subdivision (b)(1) makes explicit that Section 1119 does not restrict admissibility of an agreement to mediate. Subdivision (b)(2) continues former Section 1152.5(e) without substantive change, but also includes an express exception for extensions of litigation deadlines. Subdivision (b)(3) makes clear that Section 1119 does not preclude a disputant from obtaining basic information about a mediator's track record, which may be significant in selecting an impartial mediator. Similarly, mediation participants may express their views on a mediator's performance, so long as they do not disclose anything said or done at the mediation.

See Sections 1115(a) ("mediation" defined), 1115(b) ("mediator" defined), 1115(c) ("mediation consultation" defined).

ANNOTATIONS

Rojas v. Superior Ct. (2004) 33 Cal.4th 407, 417. "[U]nder [Evid. C.] §1120, a party cannot secure protection for a writing—including a photograph, a witness statement, or an analysis of a test sample—that was not 'prepared for the purpose of, in the course of, or pursuant to, a mediation' ... simply by using or introducing it in a mediation or even including it as part of a writing—such as a brief or a declaration or a consultant's report—that was 'prepared for the purpose of, in the course of, or pursuant to, a mediation.' Contrary to the Court of Appeal's conclusion, this construction does not render §1120 'surplusage' or permit parties 'to use mediation as a shield to hide evidence.' Rather, consistent with the Legislature's intent, it applies §1120 as a 'limit[]' on 'the scope of [Evid. C.] §1119' that 'prevent[s] parties from using a mediation as a pretext to shield materials from disclosure.'" *See also* ***Lappe v. Superior Ct.*** (2d Dist.2014) 232 Cal.App.4th 774, 784-85; ***Wimsatt v. Superior Ct.*** (2d Dist.2007) 152 Cal.App.4th 137, 157.

§1121. [RESTRICTION ON MEDIATOR'S REPORT]

Neither a mediator nor anyone else may submit to a court or other adjudicative body, and a court or other adjudicative body may not consider, any report, assessment, evaluation, recommendation, or finding of any kind by the mediator concerning a mediation conducted by the mediator, other than a report that is mandated by court rule or other law and that states only whether an agreement was reached, unless all parties to the mediation expressly agree otherwise in writing, or orally in accordance with Section 1118.

History of Evid. C. §1121: Added eff. Jan. 1, 1998, Stats. 1997, ch. 772, §3.

Official Comment

1997-98 Ann. Report, 27 Cal. Law Revision Comm'n Rep. (1997) App. 5.

Section 1121 continues the first sentence of former Section 1152.6 without substantive change, except to make clear that (1) the section applies to all submissions, not just filings, (2) the section is not limited to court proceedings but rather applies to all types of adjudications, including arbitrations and administrative adjudications, (3) the section applies to any report or statement of opinion, however denominated, and (4) neither a mediator nor anyone else may submit the prohibited information. The section does not prohibit a mediator from providing a mediation participant with feedback on the dispute in the course of the mediation.

Rather, the focus is on preventing coercion. As Section 1121 recognizes, a mediator should not be able to influence the result of a mediation or adjudication by reporting or threatening to report to the decisionmaker on the merits of the dispute or reasons why mediation failed to resolve it. Similarly, a mediator should not have authority to resolve or decide the mediated dispute, and should not have any function for the adjudicating tribunal with regard to the dispute, except as a nondecisionmaking neutral. *See* Section 1117 (scope of chapter), which excludes settlement conferences from this chapter.

The exception to Section 1121 (permitting submission and consideration of a mediator's report where "all parties to the mediation expressly agree" in writing) is modified to allow use of the oral procedure in Section 1118 (recorded oral agreement) and to permit [the] making of the agreement at any time, not just before the mediation. A mediator's report to a court may disclose mediation communications only if all parties to the mediation agree to the reporting and all persons who participate in the mediation agree to the disclosure. *See* Section 1122 (disclosure by agreement).

The second sentence of former Section 1152.6 is continued without substantive change in Section 1117 (scope of chapter), except that Section 1117 excludes proceedings under Part 1 (commencing with Section 1800) of Division 5 of the Family Code, as well as proceedings under Chapter 11 (commencing with Section 3160) of Part 2 of Division 8 of the Family Code.

See Sections 1115(a) ("mediation" defined), 1115(b) ("mediator" defined). *See also* Sections 703.5 (testimony by a judge, arbitrator, or mediator), 1127 (attorney's fees), 1128 (irregularity in proceedings).

§1122. [DISCLOSURE OF MEDIATION COMMUNICATION]

(a) [**Agreement to disclose.**] A communication or a writing, as defined in Section 250, that is made or prepared for the purpose of, or in the course of, or pursuant to, a mediation or a mediation consultation, is not made inadmissible, or protected from disclosure, by provisions of this chapter if either of the following conditions is satisfied:

(1) All persons who conduct or otherwise participate in the mediation expressly agree in writing, or

orally in accordance with Section 1118, to disclosure of the communication, document, or writing.

(2) The communication, document, or writing was prepared by or on behalf of fewer than all the mediation participants, those participants expressly agree in writing, or orally in accordance with Section 1118, to its disclosure, and the communication, document, or writing does not disclose anything said or done or any admission made in the course of the mediation.

(b) [Agreement by mediation.] For purposes of subdivision (a), if the neutral person who conducts a mediation expressly agrees to disclosure, that agreement also binds any other person described in subdivision (b) of Section 1115.

History of Evid. C. §1122: Added eff. Jan. 1, 1998, Stats. 1997, ch. 772, §3.

Official Comment

1997-98 Ann. Report, 27 Cal. Law Revision Comm'n Rep. (1997) App. 5.

Section 1122 supersedes former Section 1152.5(a)(4) and part of former Section 1152.5(a)(2), which were unclear regarding precisely whose agreement was required for admissibility or disclosure of mediation communications and documents.

Subdivision (a)(1) states the general rule that mediation documents and communications may be admitted or disclosed only upon agreement of all participants, including not only parties but also the mediator and other nonparties attending the mediation (*e.g.*, a disputant not involved in litigation, a spouse, an accountant, an insurance representative, or an employee of a corporate affiliate). Agreement must be express, not implied. For example, parties cannot be deemed to have agreed in advance to disclosure merely because they agreed to participate in a particular dispute resolution program.

Subdivision (a)(2) facilitates admissibility and disclosure of unilaterally prepared materials, but it only applies so long as those materials may be produced in a manner revealing nothing about the mediation discussion. Materials that necessarily disclose mediation communications may be admitted or disclosed only upon satisfying the general rule of subdivision (a)(1).

Mediation materials that satisfy the requirements of subdivisions (a)(1) or (a)(2) are not necessarily admissible or subject to disclosure. Although the provisions on mediation confidentiality do not bar admissibility or disclosure, there may be other bases for exclusion.

Subdivision (b) makes clear that if the person who takes the lead in conducting a mediation agrees to disclosure, it is unnecessary to seek out and obtain assent from each assistant to that person, such as a case developer, interpreter, or secretary.

For exceptions to Section 1122, *see* Sections 1123 (written settlement agreements reached through mediation) and 1124 (oral agreements reached through mediation) and *Comments*.

See Section 1115(a) ("mediation" defined), 1115(c) ("mediation consultation" defined). *See also* Sections 703.5 (testimony by a judge, arbitrator, or mediator), 1119 (mediation confidentiality), 1121 (mediator reports and communications).

ANNOTATIONS

Cassel v. Superior Ct. (2011) 51 Cal.4th 113, 128. See annotation under Evidence Code §1119, p. 1364.

Doe 1 v. Superior Ct. (2d Dist.2005) 132 Cal.App.4th 1160, 1168-69. "Section 1122, subdivision (a)(1), allows for the disclosure of mediation communications if all mediation participants agree to the disclosure. [Ps] contend that disclosure of the proffers is also permitted under that section because petitioners did not participate in the mediation and, as a result, all participants have agreed to their release. Because petitioners did no more than object to the disclosure of the contents of their personnel files, and did not take part in any discussions relating to liability or geared toward actually resolving the actions, [Ps] contend petitioners cannot be considered mediation participants. We disagree, because petitioners' participation was extensive enough to characterize them as mediation participants."

§1123. [ADMISSIBILITY OF WRITTEN SETTLEMENT AGREEMENT]

A written settlement agreement prepared in the course of, or pursuant to, a mediation, is not made inadmissible, or protected from disclosure, by provisions of this chapter if the agreement is signed by the settling parties and any of the following conditions are satisfied:

(a) [Admissible.] The agreement provides that it is admissible or subject to disclosure, or words to that effect.

(b) [Enforceable.] The agreement provides that it is enforceable or binding or words to that effect.

(c) [Participants.] All parties to the agreement expressly agree in writing, or orally in accordance with Section 1118, to its disclosure.

(d) [Fraud, duress, or illegality.] The agreement is used to show fraud, duress, or illegality that is relevant to an issue in dispute.

History of Evid. C. §1123: Added eff. Jan. 1, 1998, Stats. 1997, ch. 772, §3.

Official Comment

1997-98 Ann. Report, 27 Cal. Law Revision Comm'n Rep. (1997) App. 5.

Section 1123 consolidates and clarifies provisions governing written settlements reached through mediation. For guidance on binding a disputant to a written settlement agreement, *see Williams v. Saunders*, 55 Cal.App.4th 1158, 64 Cal.Rptr. 2d 571 (1997) ("The litigants direct participation tends to ensure that the settlement is the result of their mature reflection and deliberate assent.").

As to an executed written settlement agreement, subdivision (a) continues part of former Section 1152.5(a)(2). *See also Ryan v. Garcia*, 27 Cal.App.4th 1006, 1012, 33 Cal.Rptr. 2d 158, 162 (1994) (Section 1152.5 "provides a simple means by which settlement agreements executed during mediation can be made admissible in later proceedings," *i.e.*, the "parties may consent, as part of a writing, to subsequent admissibility of the agreement").

Subdivision (b) is new. It is added due to the likelihood that parties intending to be bound will use words to that effect, rather than saying their agreement is intended to be admissible or subject to disclosure.

As to fully executed written settlement agreements, subdivision (c) supersedes former Section 1152.5(a)(4). To facilitate enforceability of such agreements, disclosure pursuant to subdivision (c) requires only agreement of the parties. Agreement of the mediator and other mediation participants is not necessary. Subdivision (c) is thus an exception to the general rule governing disclosure of mediation communications by agreement. *See* Section 1122.

Subdivision (d) continues former Section 1152.5(a)(5) without substantive change.

A written settlement agreement that satisfies the requirements of subdivision (a), (b), (c), or (d) is not necessarily admissible or subject to disclosure. Although the provisions on mediation confidentiality do not bar admissibility or disclosure, there may be other bases for exclusion.

See Section 1115(a) ("mediation" defined).

ANNOTATIONS

Fair v. Bakhtiari (2006) 40 Cal.4th 189, 192. "The aim of [§1123(b)] is to allow parties in mediation to draft enforceable agreements without requiring the use of a formulaic phrase. However, the writing must make clear that it reflects an agreement and is not simply a memorandum of terms for inclusion in a future agreement. The writing need not be in finished form to be admissible under [§1123(b)], but it must be signed by the parties and include a direct statement to the effect that it is enforceable or binding. *At 199-200:* [T]o satisfy §1123(b), a settlement agreement must include a statement that it is 'enforceable' or 'binding,' or a declaration in other terms with the same meaning. The statute leaves room for various formulations. However, arbitration clauses, forum selection clauses, choice of law provisions, terms contemplating remedies for breach, and similar commonly employed enforcement provisions typically negotiated in settlement discussions do not qualify an agreement for admission under §1123(b)."

In re Marriage of Daly & Oyster (2d Dist.2014) 228 Cal.App.4th 505, 511. "To satisfy the 'words to that effect' provision of subdivision (a) or (b) of §1123, a writing must directly express the parties' agreement to disclose or be bound by the document they sign. [¶] Here, the parties characterized the stipulated judgment as a 'marital settlement agreement,' agreed it would 'be the operable court judgment with relation to the Stipulated Judgment for Dissolution,' and agreed the court would 'reserve[ ] jurisdiction to supervise the payment of any obligation ordered paid or allocated in this Stipulated Judgment; supervise the execution of any documents required or reasonably necessary to carry out the terms of this Judgment; and supervise the overall enforcement of this Judgment.' Use of such language clearly reflected the parties' agreement that the stipulated judgment be subject to disclosure and be enforceable. The parties agreed the court would enforce the document, which it could not do unless the document was disclosed to it. It was therefore admissible under ... §1123."

Estate of Thottam (2d Dist.2008) 165 Cal.App.4th 1331, 1339. "Respondents argued, and the trial court found, that the mediation and confidentiality agreement did not satisfy §1123, subdivision (c) because it was executed before the parties allegedly entered into a settlement agreement. The court's position was that the exception would only be satisfied if the disclosure agreement was executed after the parties had reached a settlement. We disagree. [¶] Subdivision (a) of §1123 requires that the settlement agreement itself provide that the agreement is admissible or subject to disclosure; §1123, subdivision (b) requires that the agreement itself provide that it is enforceable or binding. In contrast, there is nothing in §1123, subdivision (c) requiring that the express agreement in writing permitting disclosure be contained in the settlement agreement. Nor is there a requirement that the agreement regarding disclosure be made at or after the time of the settlement. The court erred in reading a timing requirement into §1123, subdivision (c)."

Stewart v. Preston Pipeline Inc. (6th Dist.2005) 134 Cal.App.4th 1565, 1583. "[T]he requirement in §1123 that the written settlement agreement be 'signed by the settling parties' does not require that an effective mediation-confidentiality waiver be signed by each of the parties litigant, so long as that written waiver is signed by each of the settling parties *or* their respective counsel."

§1124. [ADMISSIBILITY OF ORAL AGREEMENT]

An oral agreement made in the course of, or pursuant to, a mediation is not made inadmissible, or protected from disclosure, by the provisions of this chapter if any of the following conditions are satisfied:

(a) The agreement is in accordance with Section 1118.

(b) The agreement is in accordance with subdivisions (a), (b), and (d) of Section 1118, and all parties to the agreement expressly agree, in writing or orally in accordance with Section 1118, to disclosure of the agreement.

(c) The agreement is in accordance with subdivisions (a), (b), and (d) of Section 1118, and the agreement is used to show fraud, duress, or illegality that is relevant to an issue in dispute.

History of Evid. C. §1124: Added eff. Jan. 1, 1998, Stats. 1997, ch. 772, §3.

Official Comment

1997-98 Ann. Report, 27 Cal. Law Revision Comm'n Rep. (1997) App. 5.

Section 1124 sets forth specific circumstances under which mediation confidentiality is inapplicable to an oral agreement reached through mediation. Except in those circumstances, Sections 1119 (mediation confidentiality) and 1124 codify the rule of *Ryan v. Garcia*, 27 Cal.App.4th 1006, 33 Cal.Rptr. 2d 158 (1994) (mediation confidentiality applies to oral statement of settlement terms), and reject the contrary approach of *Regents of University of California v. Sumner*, 42 Cal.App.4th 1209, 50 Cal.Rptr. 2d 200 (1996) (mediation confidentiality does not protect oral statement of settlement terms).

Subdivision (a) of Section 1124 facilitates enforcement of an oral agreement that is recorded and memorialized in writing in accordance with Section 1118. For guidance in applying subdivision (a), *see* Section 1125 (when mediation ends) & *Comment*.

Subdivision (b) parallels Section 1123(c).

Subdivision (c) parallels Section 1123(d).

An oral agreement that satisfies the requirements of subdivision (a), (b), or (c) is not necessarily admissible or subject to disclosure. Although the provisions on mediation confidentiality do not bar admissibility or disclosure, there may be other bases for exclusion. For guidance on binding a disputant to a settlement agreement, *see Williams v. Saunders*, 55 Cal.App.4th 1158, 64 Cal.Rptr. 2d 571 (1997) ("The litigants' direct participation tends to ensure that the settlement is the result of their mature reflection and deliberate assent.").

See Section 1115(a) ("mediation" defined).

§1125. [WHEN A MEDIATION ENDS]

(a) [**Full resolution.**] For purposes of confidentiality under this chapter, a mediation ends when any one of the following conditions is satisfied:

(1) The parties execute a written settlement agreement that fully resolves the dispute.

(2) An oral agreement that fully resolves the dispute is reached in accordance with Section 1118.

(3) The mediator provides the mediation participants with a writing signed by the mediator that states that the mediation is terminated, or words to that effect, which shall be consistent with Section 1121.

(4) A party provides the mediator and the other mediation participants with a writing stating that the mediation is terminated, or words to that effect, which shall be consistent with Section 1121.

In a mediation involving more than two parties, the mediation may continue as to the remaining parties or be terminated in accordance with this section.

(5) For 10 calendar days, there is no communication between the mediator and any of the parties to the mediation relating to the dispute. The mediator and the parties may shorten or extend this time by agreement.

(b) [**Partial resolution.**] For purposes of confidentiality under this chapter, if a mediation partially resolves a dispute, mediation ends when either of the following conditions is satisfied:

(1) The parties execute a written settlement agreement that partially resolves the dispute.

(2) An oral agreement that partially resolves the dispute is reached in accordance with Section 1118.

(c) This section does not preclude a party from ending a mediation without reaching an agreement. This section does not otherwise affect the extent to which a party may terminate a mediation.

History of Evid. C. §1125: Added eff. Jan. 1, 1998, Stats. 1997, ch. 772, §3.

Official Comment

1997-98 Ann. Report, 27 Cal. Law Revision Comm'n Rep. (1997) App. 5.

By specifying when a mediation ends, Section 1125 provides guidance on which communications are protected by Section 1119 (mediation confidentiality).

Under subdivision (a)(1), if mediation participants reach an oral compromise and reduce it to a written settlement fully resolving their dispute, confidentiality extends until the agreement is signed by all the parties. For guidance on binding a disputant to a settlement agreement, *see Williams v. Saunders*, 55 Cal.App.4th 1158, 64 Cal.Rptr. 2d 571 (1997) ("The litigants' direct participation tends to ensure that the settlement is the result of their mature reflection and deliberate assent.").

Subdivision (a)(2) applies where mediation participants fully resolve their dispute by an oral agreement that is recorded and memorialized in writing in accordance with Section 1118. The mediation is over upon completion of that procedure, and the confidentiality protections of this chapter do not apply to any later proceedings, such as attempts to further refine the content of the agreement. *See* Section 1124 (oral agreements reached through mediation). Subdivisions (a)(3) and (a)(4) are drawn from Rule 14 of the American Arbitration Association's Commercial Mediation Rules (as amended, Jan. 1, 1992). Subdivision (a)(5) applies where an affirmative act terminating a mediation for purposes of this chapter does not occur.

Subdivision (b) applies where mediation partially resolves a dispute, such as when the disputants resolve only some of the issues (*e.g.*, contract, but not tort, liability) or when only some of the disputants settle.

Subdivision (c) limits the effect of Section 1125.

See Sections 1115(a) ("mediation" defined), 1115(b) ("mediator" defined).

§1126. [CONTINUATION OF CONFIDENTIALITY]

Anything said, any admission made, or any writing that is inadmissible, protected from disclosure, and confidential under this chapter before a mediation ends, shall remain inadmissible, protected from disclosure, and confidential to the same extent after the mediation ends.

History of Evid. C. §1126: Added eff. Jan. 1, 1998, Stats. 1997, ch. 772, §3.

Official Comment

1997-98 Ann. Report, 27 Cal. Law Revision Comm'n Rep. (1997) App. 5.

Section 1126 clarifies that mediation materials are confidential not only during a mediation, but also after the mediation ends pursuant to Section 1125 (when mediation ends).

See Section 1115(a) ("mediation" defined).

§1127. [ATTORNEY'S FEES]

If a person subpoenas or otherwise seeks to compel a mediator to testify or produce a writing, as defined in Section 250, and the court or other adjudicative body determines that the testimony or writing is inadmissible under this chapter, or protected from disclosure under this chapter, the court or adjudicative body mak-

ing the determination shall award reasonable attorney's fees and costs to the mediator against the person seeking the testimony or writing.

History of Evid. C. §1127: Added eff. Jan. 1, 1998, Stats. 1997, ch. 772, §3.

Official Comment

1997-98 Ann. Report, 27 Cal. Law Revision Comm'n Rep. (1997) App. 5.

Section 1127 continues former Section 1152.5(d) without substantive change, except to clarify that either a court or another adjudicative body (*e.g.*, an arbitrator or an administrative tribunal) may award the fees and costs. Because Section 1115 (definitions) defines "mediator" to include not only the neutral person who takes the lead in conducting a mediation, but also any neutral who assists in the mediation, fees are available regardless of the role played by the person subjected to discovery.

See Section 1115(b) ("mediator" defined).

§1128. [SUBSEQUENT CIVIL TRIAL]

Any reference to a mediation during any subsequent trial is an irregularity in the proceedings of the trial for the purposes of Section 657 of the Code of Civil Procedure. Any reference to a mediation during any other subsequent noncriminal proceeding is grounds for vacating or modifying the decision in that proceeding, in whole or in part, and granting a new or further hearing on all or part of the issues, if the reference materially affected the substantial rights of the party requesting relief.

History of Evid. C. §1128: Added eff. Jan. 1, 1998, Stats. 1997, ch. 772, §3.

Official Comment

1997-98 Ann. Report, 27 Cal. Law Revision Comm'n Rep. (1997) App. 5.

Section 1128 is drawn from Code of Civil Procedure Section 1775.12. The first sentence makes it an irregularity to refer to a mediation in a subsequent civil trial; the second sentence extends that rule to other noncriminal proceedings, such as an administrative adjudication. An appropriate situation for invoking this section is where a party urges the trier of fact to draw an adverse inference from an adversary's refusal to disclose mediation communications.

See Section 1115 ("mediation" defined).

CHAPTER 3. OTHER EVIDENCE AFFECTED OR EXCLUDED BY EXTRINSIC POLICIES

Official Comment

1997-98 Ann. Report, 27 Cal. Law Revision Comm'n Rep. (1997) App. 5.

The chapter heading is renumbered to reflect the addition of a new Chapter 2 (commencing with Section 1115) (Mediation).

§1150. [EVIDENCE TO IMPEACH A VERDICT]

(a) [Juror misconduct.] Upon an inquiry as to the validity of a verdict, any otherwise admissible evidence may be received as to statements made, or conduct, conditions, or events occurring, either within or without the jury room, of such a character as is likely to have influenced the verdict improperly. No evidence is admissible to show the effect of such statement, conduct, condition, or event upon a juror either in influencing him to assent to or dissent from the verdict or concerning the mental processes by which it was determined.

(b) [Juror testimony.] Nothing in this code affects the law relating to the competence of a juror to give evidence to impeach or support a verdict.

History of Evid. C. §1150: Added eff. Sept. 17, 1965, oper. Jan. 1, 1967, Stats. 1965, ch. 299, §2.

Official Comment

**7 Cal. Law Revision Comm'n Rep. (1965) p. 1211;
Assem. J., Apr. 6, 1965, p. 1753.**

Section 1150 codifies existing law which permits evidence of misconduct by a trial juror to be received but forbids the reception of evidence as to the effect of such misconduct on the minds of the jurors. *People v. Stokes*, 103 Cal. 193, 196-197, 37 Pac. 207, 208-209 (1894).

Section 1150 makes no change in the rules concerning when testimony or affidavits of jurors may be received to impeach or support a verdict. Under existing law, a juror is incompetent to give evidence as to matters that might impeach his verdict. *People v. Gray*, 61 Cal. 164, 183 (1882). *See also Siemsen v. Oakland, S. L., & H. Elec. Ry.*, 134 Cal. 494, 66 Pac. 672 (1901). He is competent, however, to give evidence that no misconduct was committed by the jury after independent evidence has been given that there was misconduct. *People v. Deegan*, 88 Cal. 602, 26 Pac. 500 (1891). By statute, a juror may give evidence by affidavit that a verdict was determined by chance. Code Civ. Proc. §657(2). And the courts have held that affidavits of jurors may be used to prove that a juror concealed bias or other disqualification by false answers on *voir dire* or was mentally incompetent to serve as a juror. *E.g.*, *Williams v. Bridges*, 140 Cal.App. 537, 35 P.2d 407 (1934) (false answer on *voir dire*); *Noll v. Lee*, 221 Cal.App.2d 81, 34 Cal.Rptr. 223 (1963) (hearing denied) (false answer on *voir dire*); *Church v. Capital Freight Lines*, 141 Cal.App.2d 246, 296 P.2d 563 (1956) (mental competence of juror).

Section 1150 also makes no change in the existing law concerning the *grounds* upon which a verdict may be set aside, *i.e.*, what constitutes jury misconduct. *See* Code Civ. Proc. §657 (civil case); Penal Code §1181 (criminal case).

ANNOTATIONS

Hasson v. Ford Motor Co. (1982) 32 Cal.3d 388, 413. Section 1150, subdivision (a) draws a "'distinction between proof of overt acts, objectively ascertainable, and proof of the subjective reasoning process of the individual juror, which can be neither corroborated nor disproved….' [S]ection 1150 limits impeachment evidence to 'proof of overt conduct, conditions, events, and statements…. This limitation prevents one juror from upsetting a verdict of the whole jury by impugning his own or his fellow jurors' mental processes or reasons for assent or dissent. The only improper influences that may be proved under §1150 to impeach a verdict, therefore, are those open to sight, hearing, and the other senses and thus subject to corroboration.' *At 414:* [This rule] excludes unreliable proof of jurors' thought processes and thereby preserves the stability of verdicts. It deters the harassment of jurors by losing counsel eager to discover defects in the jurors' attentive and deliberative mental processes. It reduces the risk of postverdict jury tampering. Finally, it assures the privacy of jury de-

liberations by foreclosing intrusive inquiry into the sanctity of jurors' thought processes." *See also* ***Sanchez-Corea v. Bank of Am.*** (1985) 38 Cal.3d 892, 910 (juror's declaration dealt only with jurors' mental processes and reasons for assent or dissent and was inadmissible for purposes of undermining verdict); ***Krouse v. Graham*** (1977) 19 Cal.3d 59, 80-81 (assertion that juror privately "considered" matter in arriving at verdict would seem to concern juror's mental processes, and declarations regarding them would be inadmissible under §1150); ***Bell v. Bayerische Motoren Werke A.G.*** (2d Dist.2010) 181 Cal.App.4th 1108, 1124-25 (juror declarations are inadmissible to extent they purport to describe jurors' understanding of instructions or how they arrived at verdict); ***Bandana Trading Co. v. Quality Infusion Care, Inc.*** (2d Dist.2008) 164 Cal.App.4th 1440, 1446 (juror's declaration that jurors did not vote on some issues, were discouraged from asking questions, and were rushed into deciding verdict could not be used to impeach verdict).

People v. Hutchinson (1969) 71 Cal.2d 342, 351. "[J]urors are competent witnesses to prove objective facts to impeach a verdict under §1150...." *See also* ***Wiley v. Southern Pac. Transp.*** (2d Dist.1990) 220 Cal.App.3d 177, 186.

In re Hansen (4th Dist.2014) 227 Cal.App.4th 906, 928-29. "[T]he juror declarations and questionnaires ... purport to reflect the jury's reasoning and mental impressions regarding their verdict. As such, they are inadmissible to impeach the jury's verdict, as [D] seeks to do here. [¶] The District Attorney's failure to object to these declarations and questionnaires at [D's] trial is of no moment. Evidence that violates ... §1150 is not merely inadmissible; it is irrelevant—of no jural consequence. Thus, the People did not have to object below to preserve this contention." (Internal quotes omitted.)

Grobeson v. City of L.A. (2d Dist.2010) 190 Cal.App.4th 778, 792. When a juror makes a statement indicating she has prejudged the case, "the question is whether the statement 'is likely to have influenced the *verdict* improperly' ..., not whether the jury or individual jurors were influenced by the statement. [¶] 'The guarantee is to *12* impartial jurors.... [¶] For a juror to prejudge the case is serious misconduct.'"

Enyart v. City of L.A. (2d Dist.1999) 76 Cal.App.4th 499, 507. "Juror misconduct raises a presumption of prejudice, and unless the prevailing party rebuts the presumption by showing the misconduct was harmless, a new trial should be granted. This does not mean that every insignificant infraction of the rules by a juror calls for a new trial. Where the misconduct is of such trifling nature that it could not in the nature of things have prevented either party from having a fair trial, the verdict should not be set aside."

Ford v. Bennacka (4th Dist.1990) 226 Cal.App.3d 330, 333-34. "Section 1150 does not envision a procedure whereby a trial judge, as a result of a claim of jury misconduct, reviews a 'replay' of the particular language used by various jurors as they deliberated and makes a subjective determination of its propriety. Such a procedure would be too great an extension of the court's limited authority to invade the traditionally inviolate nature of the jury proceedings. If there is one thing which is clear from the language of ... §1150 and the case law dealing with the subject, it is that the mental processes of the jurors are beyond the hindsight probing of the trial court." (Internal quotes omitted.)

§1151. [SUBSEQUENT REMEDIAL CONDUCT]

When, after the occurrence of an event, remedial or precautionary measures are taken, which, if taken previously, would have tended to make the event less likely to occur, evidence of such subsequent measures is inadmissible to prove negligence or culpable conduct in connection with the event.

History of Evid. C. §1151: Added eff. Sept. 17, 1965, oper. Jan. 1, 1967, Stats. 1965, ch. 299, §2.

Official Comment

7 Cal. Law Revision Comm'n Rep. (1965) p. 1212.

Section 1151 codifies well-settled law. *Helling v. Schindler*, 145 Cal. 303, 78 Pac. 710 (1904); *Sappenfield v. Main Street etc. R.R.*, 91 Cal. 48, 27 Pac. 590 (1891). The admission of evidence of subsequent repairs to prove negligence would substantially discourage persons from making repairs after the occurrence of an accident.

Section 1151 does not prevent the use of evidence of subsequent remedial conduct for the purpose of impeachment in appropriate cases. This is in accord with *Pierce v. J.C. Penney Co.*, 167 Cal.App.2d 3, 334 P.2d 117 (1959).

ANNOTATIONS

Fox v. Kramer (2000) 22 Cal.4th 531, 544. "[S]ection 1151 plainly refers to 'remedial or precautionary measures,' not to mere reports or investigations conducted after an accident or other event resulting in injury. By its terms, it would appear to include only *subsequent actions taken to repair or correct* a problem identified by an investigation—not the factual inquiries undertaken to determine whether such repair or correction was necessary. [S]ection 1151 also refers to

measures 'which, *if taken previously*, would have tended to make the event less likely to occur.' ... Of course, reports or investigations relating to an incident could not have been made *prior thereto*."

Ault v. International Harvester Co. (1974) 13 Cal.3d 113, 117. "[T]he language and the legislative history of §1151 demonstrate that the section is designed for cases involving negligence or culpable conduct on the part of the defendant, rather than to those circumstances in which a manufacturer is alleged to be strictly liable for placing a defective product on the market. *At 118:* Section 1151 by its own terms excludes evidence of subsequent remedial or precautionary measures only when such evidence is offered to prove negligence or culpable conduct. In an action based upon strict liability against a manufacturer, negligence or culpability is not a necessary ingredient. The plaintiff may recover if he establishes that the product was defective, and he need not show that the defendants breached a duty of due care. *At 120:* [T]he purpose of §1151 is not applicable to a strict liability case and hence its exclusionary rule should not be gratuitously extended to that field." *See also* ***Alcaraz v. Vece*** (1997) 14 Cal.4th 1149, 1168-69; ***Schelbauer v. Butler Mfg.*** (1984) 35 Cal.3d 442, 452.

§1152. [OFFER TO COMPROMISE]

(a) [Inadmissible to prove liability.] Evidence that a person has, in compromise or from humanitarian motives, furnished or offered or promised to furnish money or any other thing, act, or service to another who has sustained or will sustain or claims that he or she has sustained or will sustain loss or damage, as well as any conduct or statements made in negotiation thereof, is inadmissible to prove his or her liability for the loss or damage or any part of it.

(b) [Offers in bad-faith actions.] In the event that evidence of an offer to compromise is admitted in an action for breach of the covenant of good faith and fair dealing or violation of subdivision (h) of Section 790.03 of the Insurance Code, then at the request of the party against whom the evidence is admitted, or at the request of the party who made the offer to compromise that was admitted, evidence relating to any other offer or counteroffer to compromise the same or substantially the same claimed loss or damage shall also be admissible for the same purpose as the initial evidence regarding settlement. Other than as may be admitted in an action for breach of the covenant of good faith and fair dealing or violation of subdivision (h) of Section 790.03 of the Insurance Code, evidence of settlement offers shall not be admitted in a motion for a new trial, in any proceeding involving an additur or remittitur, or on appeal.

(c) [Effect of section.] This section does not affect the admissibility of evidence of any of the following:

(1) Partial satisfaction of an asserted claim or demand without questioning its validity when such evidence is offered to prove the validity of the claim.

(2) A debtor's payment or promise to pay all or a part of his or her preexisting debt when such evidence is offered to prove the creation of a new duty on his or her part or a revival of his or her preexisting duty.

History of Evid. C. §1152: Added eff. Sept. 17, 1965, oper. Jan. 1, 1967, Stats. 1965, ch. 299, §2. Amended eff. Nov. 8, 1967, Stats. 1967, ch. 650, §7; eff. Jan. 1, 1988, Stats. 1987, ch. 496, §1.

Official Comment

7 Cal. Law Revision Comm'n Rep. (1965) p. 1213.

Section 1152, like Section 2078 of the Code of Civil Procedure which it supersedes, declares that compromise offers are inadmissible to prove liability. Because of the particular wording of Section 2078, an offer of compromise probably may not be considered as an admission even though admitted without objection. *See Tentative Recommendation and a Study Relating to the Uniform Rules of Evidence (Article VI. Extrinsic Policies Affecting Admissibility)*, 6 Cal. Law Revision Comm'n, Rep., Rec. & Studies 601, 675-676 (1964). *See also Scott v. Wood*, 81 Cal. 398, 405-406, 22 Pac. 871, 873 (1889). Under Section 1152, however, nothing prohibits the consideration of an offer of settlement on the issue of liability if the evidence is received without objection. This modest change in the law is desirable. An offer of compromise, like other incompetent evidence, should be considered to the extent that it is relevant when it is presented to the trier of fact without objection.

The words "as well as any conduct or statements made in negotiation thereof" make it clear that statements made by parties during negotiations for the settlement of a claim may not be used as admissions in later litigation. This language will change the existing law under which certain statements made during settlement negotiations may be used as admissions. *People v. Forster*, 58 Cal.2d 257, 23 Cal.Rptr. 582, 373 P.2d 630 (1962). The rule excluding offers is based upon the public policy in favor of the settlement of disputes without litigation. The same public policy requires that admissions made during settlement negotiations also be excluded. The rule of the *Forster* case that permits such statements to be admitted places a premium on the form of the statement. The statement "Assuming, for the purposes of these negotiations, that I was negligent..." is inadmissible; but the statement "All right, I was negligent! Let's talk about damages." may be admissible. See the discussion in *People v. Glen Arms Estate, Inc.*, 230 Cal.App.2d 841, 863-864, 41 Cal.Rptr. 303, 316 (1964). The rule of the *Forster* case is changed by Section 1152 because that rule prevents the complete candor between the parties that is most conducive to settlement.

8 Cal. Law Revision Comm'n Rep. (1997) p. 123.

The amendment to Section 1152 is intended to clarify the meaning of the section without changing its substantive effect. The words "or will sustain" have been added to make it clear that the section applies to statements made in the course of negotiations concerning future loss or damage as well as past loss or damage. Such negotiations might occur as a result of an alleged anticipatory breach of contract or as an incident of an eminent domain proceeding.

ANNOTATIONS

White v. Western Title Ins. (1985) 40 Cal.3d 870, 888-89. "[D]espite their difference in wording[, Evid.

C.] §1152 and [CCP] §998 should receive a parallel construction. Section 1152 states that offers are inadmissible to prove 'liability for the loss or damage,' which we have construed to refer to liability for that loss or damage to be compromised by the offer. Section 998, subdivision (b), states that an offer cannot be 'given in evidence upon the trial.' We think that language refers to the trial upon the liability which the offer proposed to compromise. Thus both sections would serve the same purpose; to bar the introduction into evidence of an offer to compromise a claim for the purpose of proving liability for that claim, but to permit its introduction to prove some other matter at issue." *See also* ***Volkswagen of Am., Inc. v. Superior Ct.*** (1st Dist.2006) 139 Cal.App.4th 1481, 1491 (§§1152 and 1154 are not absolute bars to admissibility because settlement documents may be admissible for purposes other than proving liability).

Warner Constr. Corp. v. City of L.A. (1970) 2 Cal.3d 285, 296-97. "We cannot accept [P's] contention that the correspondence could properly have been admitted to show the contemporaneous and practical construction of the contract. [¶] The principle of 'practical construction' applies only to acts performed under the contract before any dispute has arisen. The 'construction given the contract by the acts and conduct of the parties with knowledge of its terms, *before any controversy has arisen as to its meaning*, is entitled to great weight and will, when reasonable, be adopted and enforced by the court.' By March 8, 1965, the parties had reached a stage of clear disagreement on the crucial question [of] whether [P] was entitled to a change order. Anything said in negotiations after that date could not be admitted under the rule of practical construction; it remained subject to exclusion under ... §1152. [¶] [P] argues that since the contract provides for its own modification by change orders, a dispute should not be said to arise until the parties have abandoned efforts to resolve the controversy within this contractual framework. Although the instant agreement does include an amendatory procedure, all contracts can be amended by consent of the parties; a compromise in a contract dispute, even if reached at the courthouse steps, will often take the form of a modification of the contract. We see no valid grounds for distinction between contracts which contemplate amendment and those which do not. The purpose of §1152, to promote candor in settlement negotiation ..., applies equally in both instances."

Hasler v. Howard (2d Dist.2004) 120 Cal.App.4th 1023, 1026. "[P] objected to the admission of his settlement conference statement under §1152, subdivision (a). [D] claims §1152 does not apply because here a plaintiff is not seeking to introduce statements made by a defendant to prove liability. [¶] Although [P] did not offer money, he offered another thing, to compromise his claim for a lesser amount. [D] seeks to use statements made in negotiation of that compromise to prove the return of her commission was an element of his damages claim. From this she argues she is entitled to attorney's fees. Section 1152, subdivision (a), expressly prohibits the admission of such evidence because it tends to establish liability; in this case, liability for attorney's fees."

Price v. Wells Fargo Bank (1st Dist.1989) 213 Cal.App.3d 465, 481 n.3. Ps argue that "the trial court was barred under ... §1152 from considering [certain] correspondence in the motion for summary judgment. Section 1152 codifies the rule that '[a]n offer to settle or compromise a claim by paying a sum of money or giving other consideration is *not admissible to prove liability* on the part of the offeror.' '[T]he obvious policy of the statute is to avoid deterring parties from making offers of settlement and to facilitate candid discussion which may lead to settlement of disputes.' But we find nothing in the record suggesting that there was any dispute over [Ps'] obligations under the loan agreements at the time the letters were written. Indeed, the letters affirmatively disclose that no dispute existed. Under these circumstances, ... §1152 did not apply."

§1152.5. REPEALED

Repealed oper. Jan. 1, 1998, Stats. 1997, ch. 772, §5.

§1152.6. REPEALED

Repealed oper. Jan. 1, 1998, Stats. 1997, ch. 772, §6.

§1153. [DEFENDANT'S OFFER TO PLEAD GUILTY]

Evidence of a plea of guilty, later withdrawn, or of an offer to plead guilty to the crime charged or to any other crime, made by the defendant in a criminal action is inadmissible in any action or in any proceeding of any nature, including proceedings before agencies, commissions, boards, and tribunals.

History of Evid. C. §1153: Added eff. Sept. 17, 1965, oper. Jan. 1, 1967, Stats. 1965, ch. 299, §2.

Official Comment

7 Cal. Law Revision Comm'n Rep. (1965) p. 1214.

Section 1153 is consistent with existing law. Under existing law, evidence of a rejected *offer* to plead guilty to the crime charged or to a lesser crime is in-

§1153

admissible. Penal Code §1192.4; *People v. Wilson*, 60 Cal.2d 139, 155-156, 32 Cal.Rptr. 44, 54-55, 383 P.2d 452, 462-463 (1963); *People v. Hamilton*, 60 Cal.2d 105, 113-114, 32 Cal.Rptr. 4, 8-9, 383 P.2d 412, 416-417 (1963). Likewise, a plea of guilty, later withdrawn, is inadmissible. *People v. Quinn*, 61 Cal. 2d 551, 39 Cal.Rptr. 393, 393 P.2d 705 (1964).

§1153.5. [OFFER FOR CIVIL RESOLUTION IN CRIMINAL MATTER]

Evidence of an offer for civil resolution of a criminal matter pursuant to the provisions of Section 33 of the Code of Civil Procedure, or admissions made in the course of or negotiations for the offer shall not be admissible in any action.

History of Evid. C. §1153.5: Added eff. Jan. 1, 1983, Stats. 1982, ch. 1518, §2.

§1154. [OFFER TO DISCOUNT CLAIM]

Evidence that a person has accepted or offered or promised to accept a sum of money or any other thing, act, or service in satisfaction of a claim, as well as any conduct or statements made in negotiation thereof, is inadmissible to prove the invalidity of the claim or any part of it.

History of Evid. C. §1154: Added eff. Sept. 17, 1965, oper. Jan. 1, 1967, Stats. 1965, ch. 299, §2.

Official Comment

7 Cal. Law Revision Comm'n Rep. (1965) p. 1214.

Section 1154 stems from the same policy of encouraging settlement and compromise that is reflected in Section 1152. Except for the language "as well as any conduct or statements made in negotiation thereof," this section codifies existing law. *Dennis v. Belt*, 30 Cal. 247 (1866); *Anderson v. Yousem*, 177 Cal.App.2d 135, 1 Cal.Rptr. 889 (1960); *Cramer v. Lee Wa Corp.*, 109 Cal.App.2d 691, 241 P.2d 550 (1952). The significance of the quoted language is indicated in the *Comment* to Section 1152.

§1155. [LIABILITY INSURANCE]

Evidence that a person was, at the time a harm was suffered by another, insured wholly or partially against loss arising from liability for that harm is inadmissible to prove negligence or other wrongdoing.

History of Evid. C. §1155: Added eff. Sept. 17, 1965, oper. Jan. 1, 1967, Stats. 1965, ch. 299, §2.

Official Comment

7 Cal. Law Revision Comm'n Rep. (1965) p. 1214.

Section 1155 codifies existing law. *Roche v. Llewellyn Iron Works Co.*, 140 Cal. 563, 74 Pac. 147 (1903). Evidence of liability insurance might be inadmissible in the absence of Section 1155 because it is not relevant; Section 1155 assures its inadmissibility.

ANNOTATIONS

Bell v. Bayerische Motoren Werke A.G. (2d Dist.2010) 181 Cal.App.4th 1108, 1122. "Evidence that a person was insured against liability for another person's injury is inadmissible to prove negligence or other wrongdoing. Such evidence is irrelevant to both the question of liability and the amount of damages. Evidence or statements by counsel suggesting that the defendant was insured against liability could cause the jury to find liability more readily or to inflate its award of damages in some circumstances. Although the insured's liability is not at issue if the evidence or statements by counsel relate to the plaintiff's insurance rather than the defendant's, evidence or statements suggesting that the plaintiff was insured could cause the jury to believe that the plaintiff will be compensated by insurance, which could cause the jury to find no liability more readily or to award lower damages."

§1156. [MEDICAL OR DENTAL COMMITTEE RECORDS]

(a) [Records not admissible as evidence.] In-hospital medical or medical-dental staff committees of a licensed hospital may engage in research and medical or dental study for the purpose of reducing morbidity or mortality, and may make findings and recommendations relating to such purpose. Except as provided in subdivision (b), the written records of interviews, reports, statements, or memoranda of such in-hospital medical or medical-dental staff committees relating to such medical or dental studies are subject to Title 4 (commencing with Section 2016.010) of Part 4 of the Code of Civil Procedure (relating to discovery proceedings) but, subject to subdivisions (c) and (d), shall not be admitted as evidence in any action or before any administrative body, agency, or person.

(b) [Effect of disclosure.] The disclosure, with or without the consent of the patient, of information concerning him to such in-hospital medical or medical-dental staff committee does not make unprivileged any information that would otherwise be privileged under Section 994 or 1014; but, notwithstanding Sections 994 and 1014, such information is subject to discovery under subdivision (a) except that the identity of any patient may not be discovered under subdivision (a) unless the patient consents to such disclosure.

(c) [Original records.] This section does not affect the admissibility in evidence of the original medical or dental records of any patient.

(d) [Criminal action.] This section does not exclude evidence which is relevant evidence in a criminal action.

History of Evid. C. §1156: Added eff. Sept. 17, 1965, oper. Jan. 1, 1967, Stats. 1965, ch. 299, §2. Amended eff. Jan. 1, 1976, Stats. 1975, ch. 674, §1; eff. Jan. 1, 2005, oper. July 1, 2005, Stats. 2004, ch. 182, §30.

Official Comment

7 Cal. Law Revision Comm'n Rep. (1965) p. 1215; Assem. J., Apr. 6, 1965, p. 1754.

Section 1156 supersedes Code of Civil Procedure Section 1936.1 (added by Cal. Stats. 1963, ch. 1558, §1, p. 3142). Except as noted below, Section 1156 restates the substance of the superseded section.

The phrase "Sections 2016 to 2036, inclusive," has been inserted in Section 1156 in place of the phrase "Sections 2016 and 2036," which appears in Section 1936.1, to correct an apparent inadvertence. This substitution permits use of all kinds of discovery procedures, instead of depositions only, to discover material of the type described in Section 1156. *E.g.*, Code Civ. Proc. §§2030 (written interrogatories), 2031 (motion for order for production of documents).

Section 1156 also makes it clear that the *names* of patients may not be disclosed without the consent of the patient. This limitation is necessary to preserve the physician-patient and psychotherapist-patient privileges.

33 Cal. Law Revision Comm'n Rep. (2003) p. 1017.

Subdivision (a) of Section 1156 is amended to reflect nonsubstantive reorganization of the rules governing civil discovery.

§1156.1. [MEDICAL OR PSYCHIATRIC COMMITTEE RECORDS]

(a) [Records not admissible as evidence.] A committee established in compliance with Sections 4070 and 5624 of the Welfare and Institutions Code may engage in research and medical or psychiatric study for the purpose of reducing morbidity or mortality, and may make findings and recommendations to the county and state relating to such purpose. Except as provided in subdivision (b), the written records of interviews, reports, statements, or memoranda of such committees relating to such medical or psychiatric studies are subject to Title 4 (commencing with Section 2016.010) of Part 4 of the Code of Civil Procedure but, subject to subdivisions (c) and (d), shall not be admitted as evidence in any action or before any administrative body, agency, or person.

(b) [Effect of disclosure.] The disclosure, with or without the consent of the patient, of information concerning him or her to such committee does not make unprivileged any information that would otherwise be privileged under Section 994 or 1014. However, notwithstanding Sections 994 and 1014, such information is subject to discovery under subdivision (a) except that the identity of any patient may not be discovered under subdivision (a) unless the patient consents to such disclosure.

(c) [Original records.] This section does not affect the admissibility in evidence of the original medical or psychiatric records of any patient.

(d) [Criminal action.] This section does not exclude evidence which is relevant evidence in a criminal action.

History of Evid. C. §1156.1: Added eff. June 2, 1982, Stats. 1982, ch. 234, §4. Amended eff. Jan. 1, 2005, oper. July 1, 2005, Stats. 2004, ch. 182, §31.

Official Comment

33 Cal. Law Revision Comm'n Rep. (2003) p. 1017.

Subdivision (a) of Section 1156.1 is amended to reflect nonsubstantive reorganization of the rules governing civil discovery.

§1157. [PEER-REVIEW COMMITTEE RECORDS]

(a) [Not discoverable.] Neither the proceedings nor the records of organized committees of medical, medical-dental, podiatric, registered dietitian, psychological, marriage and family therapist, licensed clinical social worker, professional clinical counselor, or veterinary staffs in hospitals, or of a peer review body, as defined in Section 805 of the Business and Professions Code, having the responsibility of evaluation and improvement of the quality of care rendered in the hospital, or for that peer review body, or medical or dental review or dental hygienist review or chiropractic review or podiatric review or registered dietitian review or veterinary review or acupuncturist review committees of local medical, dental, dental hygienist, podiatric, dietetic, veterinary, acupuncture, or chiropractic societies, marriage and family therapist, licensed clinical social worker, professional clinical counselor, or psychological review committees of state or local marriage and family therapist, state or local licensed clinical social worker, state or local licensed professional clinical counselor, or state or local psychological associations or societies having the responsibility of evaluation and improvement of the quality of care, shall be subject to discovery.

(b) [Prohibited testimony.] Except as hereinafter provided, no person in attendance at a meeting of any of those committees shall be required to testify as to what transpired at that meeting.

(c) [Exception: attendee is party.] The prohibition relating to discovery or testimony does not apply to the statements made by any person in attendance at a meeting of any of those committees who is a party to an action or proceeding the subject matter of which was reviewed at that meeting, or to any person requesting hospital staff privileges, or in any action against an insurance carrier alleging bad faith by the carrier in refusing to accept a settlement offer within the policy limits.

(d) [Exception: certain medical society committee.] The prohibitions in this section do not apply to medical, dental, dental hygienist, podiatric, dietetic, psychological, marriage and family therapist, licensed clinical social worker, professional clinical counselor,

veterinary, acupuncture, or chiropractic society committees that exceed 10 percent of the membership of the society, nor to any of those committees if any person serves upon the committee when his or her own conduct or practice is being reviewed.

(e) [Exception: criminal actions.] The amendments made to this section by Chapter 1081 of the Statutes of 1983, or at the 1985 portion of the 1985-86 Regular Session of the Legislature, at the 1990 portion of the 1989-90 Regular Session of the Legislature, at the 2000 portion of the 1999-2000 Regular Session of the Legislature, or at the 2011 portion of the 2011-12 Regular Session of the Legislature, do not exclude the discovery or use of relevant evidence in a criminal action.

History of Evid. C. §1157: Added eff. Nov. 13, 1968, Stats. 1968, ch. 1122, §1. Amended eff. Jan. 1, 1976, ch. 674, §2; eff. Feb. 10, 1978, Stats. 1978, ch. 7, §1; eff. Jan. 1, 1979, Stats. 1978, ch. 503, §2; eff. Jan. 1, 1983, Stats. 1982, ch. 705, §3; eff. Jan. 1, 1984, Stats. 1983, ch. 289, §3, ch. 422, §1, ch. 1081, §2.5; eff. Jan. 1, 1986, Stats. 1985, ch. 725, §1; eff. Jan. 1, 1991, Stats. 1990, ch. 196, §2; eff. Jan. 1, 1995, Stats. 1994, ch. 815, §3; eff. Jan. 1, 2001, Stats. 2000, ch. 136, §1; eff. Jan. 1, 2012, Stats. 2011, ch. 381, §23.

ANNOTATIONS

Fox v. Kramer (2000) 22 Cal.4th 531, 539. "The immunity described in [Evid. C. §1157, subdivision (a)] 'extends to, first, the proceedings, and second, the records of the described staff committees.' *At 544-45:* [S]ection 1157 expressly limits not only discovery but also specifies what evidence is subject to use at trial. Thus, compulsory testimony is expressly precluded under the statute.... [Section 1157, subdivision (b)] would be superfluous if the Legislature intended in every case that *all* evidence regarding hospital peer review was already inadmissible under [Evid. C.] §1151 to prove negligence. *At 545 n.2:* We do not intend to suggest that application of both ... §§1157 and 1151 to the same materials is *precluded* under all circumstances. Thus, in the appropriate case, even voluntary testimony by a participant in peer review proceedings about the implementation of subsequent remedial measures could be excluded under ... §1151 to show negligence."

Arnett v. Dal Cielo (1996) 14 Cal.4th 4, 6-7. "We address here the narrow issue whether an investigative subpoena issued by the Medical Board of California as part of its inquiry into the conduct of a physician with an apparent drug problem is 'discovery' within the meaning of [§1157]. *At 18:* The Hospital contends that as used in §1157 the word 'discovery' includes subpoenas issued by administrative agencies for investigative purposes. *At 24:* [T]he term 'discovery' in §1157 is to be given its well-established legal meaning of a formal exchange of evidentiary information between parties to a pending action, and that meaning does not include a subpoena issued ... by an administrative agency for purely investigative purposes."

Alexander v. Superior Ct. (1993) 5 Cal.4th 1218, 1223 n.4, *disapproved on other grounds*, ***Hassan v. Mercy Am. River Hosp.*** (2003) 31 Cal.4th 709. "[S]ection 1157 creates only a privilege against discovery from medical staff committees; it does not create a bar against introduction of evidence. Nor does §1157 prevent a plaintiff from otherwise discovering relevant information by, inter alia, deposing a physician and asking whether he or she was previously denied staff privileges, or by reviewing public records to determine whether the physician has suffered a malpractice judgment or disciplinary action. *At 1225:* [N]othing in [§1157, subdivision (a)] limits the privilege to records that are *generated by* a medical staff committee, and nothing in the statute supports the suggestion that materials *submitted to* a committee for review are not protected 'records' of the committee."

Pomona Valley Hosp. Med. Ctr. v. Superior Ct. (2d Dist.2012) 209 Cal.App.4th 687, 694. "Although membership on a 'medical staff' may be restricted by statute to physicians and other licensed practitioners, this statutory requirement does not preclude the medical staff from organizing a committee which includes people other than licensed practitioners. The proceedings and records of the committee are protected, even though the committee includes members who are not part of the medical staff. *At 695:* The inclusion of laypeople on [a committee] who are not affiliated with a hospital ... does not void the protection of §1157." *See also* ***Santa Rosa Mem'l Hosp. v. Superior Ct.*** (1st Dist.1985) 174 Cal.App.3d 711, 719 (fact that committee was composed of mainly hospital personnel who were not physicians did not preclude application of §1157).

Matchett v. Superior Ct. (3d Dist.1974) 40 Cal.App.3d 623, 629. Section 1157 "was enacted ... in apparent response to [***Kenney v. Superior Ct.*** (3d Dist.1967) 255 Cal.App.2d 106]. [¶] Section 1157 represents a legislative choice between competing public concerns. It embraces the goal of medical staff candor at the cost of impairing plaintiffs' access to evidence." *See also* ***Cedars-Sinai Med. Ctr. v. Superior Ct.*** (2d Dist.1993) 12 Cal.App.4th 579, 589 (immunity protects identities of evaluating committee members from discovery by medical-malpractice Ps).

§1157.5. [NONPROFIT OR MEDICAL-STANDARDS REVIEW RECORDS]

Except in actions involving a claim of a provider of health care services for payment for such services, the prohibition relating to discovery or testimony provided by Section 1157 shall be applicable to the proceedings or records of an organized committee of any nonprofit medical care foundation or professional standards review organization which is organized in a manner which makes available professional competence to review health care services with respect to medical necessity, quality of care, or economic justification of charges or level of care.

History of Evid. C. §1157.5: Added eff. Jan. 1, 1974, Stats. 1973, ch. 848, §1. Amended eff. Jan. 1, 1981, Stats. 1980, ch. 524, §1.

§1157.6. [COUNTY MENTAL HEALTH FACILITY RECORDS]

Neither the proceedings nor the records of a committee established in compliance with Sections 4070 and 5624 of the Welfare and Institutions Code having the responsibility of evaluation and improvement of the quality of mental health care rendered in county operated and contracted mental health facilities shall be subject to discovery. Except as provided in this section, no person in attendance at a meeting of any such committee shall be required to testify as to what transpired thereat. The prohibition relating to discovery or testimony shall not apply to the statements made by any person in attendance at such a meeting who is a party to an action or proceeding the subject matter of which was reviewed at such meeting, or to any person requesting facility staff privileges.

History of Evid. C. §1157.6: Added eff. June 2, 1982, Stats. 1982, ch. 234, §5.

§1157.7. [LOCAL GOVERNMENT HEALTH SERVICES COMMITTEE RECORDS]

The prohibition relating to discovery or testimony provided in Section 1157 shall be applicable to proceedings and records of any committee established by a local governmental agency to monitor, evaluate, and report on the necessity, quality, and level of specialty health services, including, but not limited to, trauma care services, provided by a general acute care hospital which has been designated or recognized by that governmental agency as qualified to render specialty health care services. The provisions of Chapter 3.5 (commencing with Section 6250) of Division 7 of Title 1 of the Government Code and Chapter 9 (commencing with Section 54950) of Division 2 of Title 5 of the Government Code shall not be applicable to the committee records and proceedings.

History of Evid. C. §1157.7: Added eff. Jan. 1, 1984, Stats. 1983, ch. 1237, §1.

§1158. [AUTHORIZATION FOR INSPECTION OF PATIENT RECORDS]

Whenever, prior to the filing of any action or the appearance of a defendant in an action, an attorney at law or his or her representative presents a written authorization therefor signed by an adult patient, by the guardian or conservator of his or her person or estate, or, in the case of a minor, by a parent or guardian of the minor, or by the personal representative or an heir of a deceased patient, or a copy thereof, a physician and surgeon, dentist, registered nurse, dispensing optician, registered physical therapist, podiatrist, licensed psychologist, osteopathic physician and surgeon, chiropractor, clinical laboratory bioanalyst, clinical laboratory technologist, or pharmacist or pharmacy, duly licensed as such under the laws of the state, or a licensed hospital, shall make all of the patient's records under his, hers or its custody or control available for inspection and copying by the attorney at law or his, or her, representative, promptly upon the presentation of the written authorization.

No copying may be performed by any medical provider or employer enumerated above, or by an agent thereof, when the requesting attorney has employed a professional photocopier or anyone identified in Section 22451 of the Business and Professions Code as his or her representative to obtain or review the records on his or her behalf. The presentation of the authorization by the agent on behalf of the attorney shall be sufficient proof that the agent is the attorney's representative.

Failure to make the records available, during business hours, within five days after the presentation of the written authorization, may subject the person or entity having custody or control of the records to liability for all reasonable expenses, including attorney's fees, incurred in any proceeding to enforce this section.

All reasonable costs incurred by any person or entity enumerated above in making patient records available pursuant to this section may be charged against the person whose written authorization required the availability of the records.

"Reasonable cost," as used in this section, shall include, but not be limited to, the following specific costs:

§1158

ten cents ($0.10) per page for standard reproduction of documents of a size 8½ by 14 inches or less; twenty cents ($0.20) per page for copying of documents from microfilm; actual costs for the reproduction of oversize documents or the reproduction of documents requiring special processing which are made in response to an authorization; reasonable clerical costs incurred in locating and making the records available to be billed at the maximum rate of sixteen dollars ($16) per hour per person, computed on the basis of four dollars ($4) per quarter hour or fraction thereof; actual postage charges; and actual costs, if any, charged to the witness by a third person for the retrieval and return of records held by that third person.

Where the records are delivered to the attorney or the attorney's representative for inspection or photocopying at the record custodian's place of business, the only fee for complying with the authorization shall not exceed fifteen dollars ($15), plus actual costs, if any, charged to the record custodian by a third person for retrieval and return of records held offsite by the third person.

History of Evid. C. §1158: Added eff. Nov. 13, 1968, Stats. 1968, ch. 1122, §2. Amended eff. Nov. 23, 1970, Stats. 1970, ch. 556, §1; eff. Jan. 1, 1975, Stats. 1974, ch. 250, §1, ch. 667, §1; eff. Jan. 1, 1976, Stats. 1975, ch. 563, §1; eff. Jan. 1, 1979, Stats. 1978, ch. 493, §1; eff. Jan. 1, 1981, Stats. 1980, ch. 697, §1; eff. Jan. 1, 1987, Stats. 1986, ch. 603, §5; eff. May 12, 1987, Stats. 1987, ch. 19, §1; eff. Jan. 1, 1994, Stats. 1993, ch. 226, §9; eff. Jan. 1, 1998, Stats. 1997, ch. 442, §15.

ANNOTATIONS

Maher v. County of Alameda (1st Dist.2014) 223 Cal.App.4th 1340, 1353. "[I]n our view, the Patient Access Law was not intended to provide redress for patients whose attorneys are seeking access to medical records in contemplation of litigation against the health care provider. Such access is instead governed by … §1158. [¶] The apparent purpose of §1158 is to permit a patient to evaluate the treatment he or she received before determining whether to bring an action against the medical provider. *At 1354:* [T]he remedy for a violation of §1158 is to bring a 'proceeding' to enforce its requirements. [P] thus would have been entitled to assert a cause of action seeking to compel [D] to provide the medical records he was seeking in contemplation of this action. If successful, he would be entitled to the attorney fees and expenses he reasonably incurred in the litigation to enforce the statute, or to any excess copying charges imposed. Section 1158 contemplates no other remedy, such as consequential damages caused by a delay in obtaining access to the records, or attorney fees other than those incurred in a proceeding to enforce its provisions. [¶] For these reasons, we conclude [D's] demurrer to [P's] medical records cause of action was properly sustained without leave to amend. [P] did not allege facts showing a violation of the Patient Access Law or compensable damages, and there is no reasonable possibility the defects could have been cured by amendment." *See also* ***Thornburg v. Superior Ct.*** (4th Dist.2006) 138 Cal.App.4th 43, 50.

Thornburg v. El Centro Reg'l Med. Ctr. (4th Dist.2006) 143 Cal.App.4th 198, 204. "Contrary to [hospital's] argument, the face of [§1158], its legislative history and the cases which have interpreted [it] all suggest that the cost limitation provisions of §1158 may be enforced directly by patients. [¶] The third paragraph [of §1158] subjects health care providers to liability for the reasonable expenses, including attorney fees, 'in any proceeding to enforce this section.'"

Thornburg v. Superior Ct. (4th Dist.2006) 138 Cal.App.4th 43, 53. "Given §1158's manifest purpose of limiting the cost of copying, we cannot construe the scope of the statute so narrowly and mechanically that the limitation is easily and effectively avoided by health care providers who attempt to contract away their responsibilities under the statute."

Person v. Farmers Ins. Grp. of Cos. (2d Dist.1997) 52 Cal.App.4th 813, 818. "In holding that a health care practitioner may not refuse inspection and copying or condition access to patient records, we refer to records which exist at the time of the discovery request. However, the health care provider may not avoid the mandate of court process by not preparing such a record when the raw data is available to do so. When billing records or 'itemized statements' are requested they should be produced if: (1) the raw data which would support such a statement exist; (2) all that is required to produce the billing statement is a compilation of existing data; and (3) preparation of the compilation would not be unduly burdensome or oppressive. Under such circumstances, we hold, the health care provider must compile and provide the itemized statement in response to a proper discovery request. The burden is upon the health care provider to establish that the compilation would be unduly burdensome or oppressive."

§1159. [ANIMAL EXPERIMENTATION IN PRODUCT-LIABILITY ACTION]

(a) [**Not admissible.**] No evidence pertaining to live animal experimentation, including, but not limited

to, injury, impact, or crash experimentation, shall be admissible in any product liability action involving a motor vehicle or vehicles.

(b) [Application of section.] This section shall apply to cases for which a trial has not actually commenced, as described in paragraph (6) of subdivision (a) of Section 581 of the Code of Civil Procedure, on January 1, 1993.

History of Evid. C. §1159: Added eff. Jan. 1, 1993, Stats. 1992, ch. 188, §1.

§1160. [WRITING EXPRESSING BENEVOLENCE]

(a) [Not admissible.] The portion of statements, writings, or benevolent gestures expressing sympathy or a general sense of benevolence relating to the pain, suffering, or death of a person involved in an accident and made to that person or to the family of that person shall be inadmissible as evidence of an admission of liability in a civil action. A statement of fault, however, which is part of, or in addition to, any of the above shall not be inadmissible pursuant to this section.

(b) [Definitions.] For purposes of this section:

(1) "Accident" means an occurrence resulting in injury or death to one or more persons which is not the result of willful action by a party.

(2) "Benevolent gestures" means actions which convey a sense of compassion or commiseration emanating from humane impulses.

(3) "Family" means the spouse, parent, grandparent, stepmother, stepfather, child, grandchild, brother, sister, half brother, half sister, adopted children of parent, or spouse's parents of an injured party.

History of Evid. C. §1160: Added eff. Jan. 1, 2001, Stats. 2000, ch. 195, §1. See also Evid. C. §1152.

§1161. [HUMAN TRAFFICKING; ADMISSIBILITY OF EVIDENCE RELATING TO VICTIM]

(a) [Evidence of commercial sexual act.] Evidence that a victim of human trafficking, as defined in Section 236.1 of the Penal Code, has engaged in any commercial sexual act as a result of being a victim of human trafficking is inadmissible to prove the victim's criminal liability for the commercial sexual act.

(b) [Evidence of sexual history.] Evidence of sexual history or history of any commercial sexual act of a victim of human trafficking, as defined in Section 236.1 of the Penal Code, is inadmissible to attack the credibility or impeach the character of the victim in any civil or criminal proceeding.

History of Evid. C. §1161: Added eff. Nov. 7, 2012 by Initiative Measure, Prop. 35, §4. Amended eff. Jan. 1, 2014, Stats. 2013, ch. 126, §1.

ANNOTATIONS

In re M.D. (1st Dist.2014) 231 Cal.App.4th 993, 999-1000. "No published authority has directly addressed which party bears the burden of proof under §1161. Typically, the party seeking to exclude otherwise relevant testimony on public policy grounds bears the burden of proof on any foundational issues of fact. [¶] In determining whether the normal allocation of the burden of proof should be altered, the courts consider a number of factors: the knowledge of the parties concerning the particular fact, the availability of the evidence to the parties, the most desirable result in terms of public policy in the absence of proof of the particular fact, and the probability of the existence or nonexistence of the fact. In determining the incidence of the burden of proof, the truth is that there is not and cannot be any one general solvent for all cases. It is merely a question of policy and fairness based on experience in the different situations. [Here, t]he minor argues that §1161 warrants reallocation of the burden of proof as a matter of both procedural fairness and public policy. [¶] The minor argues that the burden of proof should be allocated to the prosecution because the prosecution has superior access to evidence bearing on whether she was a victim of human trafficking and that whether she was such a victim is not a fact peculiarly within her personal knowledge. She argues that in a juvenile delinquency case, the government has the clear advantage in having access to the evidence of the crimes alleged against both the minor and the purported adult human trafficker. … We disagree. The facts necessary to establish that the minor was a victim of human trafficking are in fact peculiarly within *her* personal knowledge. She has the most knowledge as to the circumstances that led her to engage in prostitution, who—if anyone—induced or persuaded her to do so, and to whom—if anyone—she is reporting or delivering the proceeds of her prostitution activity. [¶] The minor's argument that public policy supports the reallocation of the burden of proof is also unpersuasive. *At 1001:* The minor asks this court to read too much into §1161. Nothing in the language of §1161 suggests an intent to create an evidentiary presumption that all minors charged with committing commercial sex acts are victims of human trafficking. Although §1161 may have the effect of exonerating a minor, the section does not

create an affirmative defense that can be asserted at trial. [S]ection 1161 does not affect the illegality of commercial sex acts prohibited by statute, and it does not negate or affect the elements of any such criminal acts which must be proved by the prosecution in a criminal prosecution. While it is certainly public policy to deter human trafficking, it is not public policy to encourage prostitution. Placing the burden of proof on the minor does not require the minor to establish the often traumatizing and debasing situations they survived, as minor argues, but simply to prove that she (or he) was induced or persuaded to engage in the activity by another. As indicated above, if true, it should not be difficult for the minor to prove this fact. [¶] Thus, we find no error in the court's decision to place the burden of proof on the minor to establish that she was a victim of human trafficking." (Internal quotes omitted.)

DIVISION 10. HEARSAY EVIDENCE

Official Comment

7 Cal. Law Revision Comm'n Rep. (1965) p. 1216.

Division 10 contains the hearsay rule and the most commonly used exceptions to the rule. Other exceptions may be found in other statutes scattered throughout the codes. Under the Evidence Code, the hearsay objection is met if the evidence offered falls within any of the exceptions to the hearsay rule. But the fact that the hearsay objection is overcome does not necessarily make the evidence admissible. All other exclusionary rules apply and may require exclusion of the evidence.

CHAPTER 1. GENERAL PROVISIONS

§1200. [THE HEARSAY RULE]

(a) [Defined.] "Hearsay evidence" is evidence of a statement that was made other than by a witness while testifying at the hearing and that is offered to prove the truth of the matter stated.

(b) [Inadmissible.] Except as provided by law, hearsay evidence is inadmissible.

(c) [Title.] This section shall be known and may be cited as the hearsay rule.

History of Evid. C. §1200: Added eff. Sept. 17, 1965, oper. Jan. 1, 1967, Stats. 1965, ch. 299, §2.

Official Comment

7 Cal. Law Revision Comm'n Rep. (1965) p. 1216; Assem. J., Apr. 6, 1965, p. 1754.

Section 1200 states the hearsay rule. It defines hearsay evidence and provides that such evidence is inadmissible unless it meets the conditions of an exception established by law. Chapter 2 (commencing with Section 1220) of this division contains a series of exceptions to the hearsay rule. Other exceptions may be found in other statutes or in decisional law. But the fact that certain evidence meets the requirements of an exception to the hearsay rule does not necessarily make such evidence admissible. The exception merely provides that such evidence is not inadmissible under the hearsay rule. If there is some other rule of law—such as privilege or the best evidence rule—that makes the evidence inadmissible, the court is not authorized to admit the evidence merely because it falls within an exception to the hearsay rule. *See also* Evidence Code §352.

Although the California courts have excluded hearsay evidence since the earliest days of the State (*see, e.g.*, *People v. Bob*, 29 Cal.2d 321, 175 P.2d 12 (1946); *Kilburn v. Ritchie*, 2 Cal. 145 (1852)), the hearsay rule has never been clearly stated in statutory form. Code of Civil Procedure Section 1845 (repealed, now Evidence Code Section 702) has at times been considered to be the statutory basis for the hearsay rule. *People v. Spriggs*, 60 Cal.2d 868, 872, 36 Cal.Rptr. 841, 844, 389 P.2d 377, 380 (1964). Analytically, however, Section 1845 does not deal with hearsay at all; it deals only with the requirement of personal knowledge. It is true that the section provides that there is an exception to the personal knowledge requirement "in those few express cases in which ... the declarations of others, are admissible"; but "this section is inaccurate, so far as it refers to [this] exception. In such case the witness testifies merely to the making of the declaration, which he must have heard in order to be a competent witness to testify to it, and hence, the fact to which he testifies is a fact within his own knowledge, derived from his own perceptions." *Sneed v. Marysville Gas etc. Co.*, 149 Cal. 704, 708, 87 Pac. 376, 378 (1906).

"Hearsay evidence" is defined in Section 1200 as "evidence of a statement that was made other than by a witness while testifying at the hearing and that is offered to prove the truth of the matter stated." Under this definition, as under existing case law, a statement that is offered for some purpose other than to prove the fact stated therein is not hearsay. *Smith v. Whittier*, 95 Cal. 279, 30 Pac. 529 (1892). *See* Witkin, *California Evidence* §§215-218 (1958).

The word "statement" used in the definition of "hearsay evidence" is defined in Section 225 as "oral or written verbal expression" or "nonverbal conduct ... intended ... as a substitute for oral or written verbal expression." Hence, evidence of a person's conduct out of court is not inadmissible under the hearsay rule expressed in Section 1200 unless that conduct is clearly assertive in character. Nonassertive conduct is not hearsay.

Some California cases have regarded evidence of nonassertive conduct as hearsay evidence if it is offered to prove the actor's belief in a particular fact as a basis for an inference that the fact believed is true. *See, e.g.*, *Estate of De Laveaga*, 165 Cal. 607, 624, 133 Pac. 307, 314 (1913) ("the manner in which a person whose sanity is in question was treated by his family is not, taken alone, competent substantive evidence tending to prove insanity, for it is a mere extra-judicial expression of opinion on the part of the family"); *People v. Mendez*, 193 Cal. 39, 52, 223 Pac. 65, 70 (1924) ("circumstances of flight [of other persons from the scene of a crime] are in the nature of confessions ... and are, therefore, in the nature of hearsay evidence") (*overruled on other grounds* in *People v. McCaughan*, 49 Cal.2d 409, 420, 317 P.2d 974, 981 (1957)).

Other California cases, however, have held that evidence of nonassertive conduct is not hearsay even though offered to prove that the belief giving rise to the conduct was based on fact. *See, e.g.*, *People v. Reifenstuhl*, 37 Cal.App.2d 402, 99 P.2d 564 (1940) (hearing denied) (incoming telephone calls made for the purpose of placing bets admissible over hearsay objection to prove that place of reception was bookmaking establishment).

Under the Evidence Code, nonassertive conduct is not regarded as hearsay for two reasons. *First*, one of the principal reasons for the hearsay rule—to exclude declarations where the veracity of the declarant cannot be tested by cross-examination—does not apply because such conduct, being nonassertive, does not involve the veracity of the declarant. *Second*, there is frequently a guarantee of the trustworthiness of the inference to be drawn from such nonassertive conduct because the actor has based his actions on the correctness of his belief, *i.e.*, his actions speak louder than words.

Of course, if the probative value of evidence of nonassertive conduct is outweighed by the probability that such evidence will be unduly prejudicial, confuse the issues, mislead the jury, or consume too much time, the judge may exclude the evidence under Section 352.

Under Section 1200, exceptions to the hearsay rule may be found either in statutes or in decisional law. Under existing law, too, the courts have recognized exceptions to the exclusionary rule in addition to those exceptions expressed in the statutes. *See People v. Spriggs*, 60 Cal.2d 868, 874, 36 Cal.Rptr. 841, 844, 389 P.2d 377, 380 (1964).

ANNOTATIONS

Elkins v. Superior Ct. (2007) 41 Cal.4th 1337, 1354. "The [local] rule and order that were applied in the present case called for the admission of declarations in lieu of direct testimony at trial. It is well estab-

lished, however, that declarations constitute hearsay [under Evid. C. §1200] and are inadmissible at trial, subject to specific statutory exceptions, unless the parties stipulate to the admission of the declarations or fail to enter a hearsay objection. *At 1355:* The law provides specific exceptions to the general rule excluding hearsay evidence …, including those governing the admission of affidavits or declarations. [¶] Another statutory exception to the hearsay rule permits courts to rely upon affidavits in certain motion matters. Although affidavits or declarations are authorized in certain *motion* matters under [CCP] §2009, this statute does not authorize their admission at a contested *trial* leading to judgment. *At 1356-57:* We conclude that respondent's [local] rule and order are inconsistent with the hearsay rule to the extent they render written declarations admissible as a basis for decision in a contested marital dissolution trial. … All relevant evidence is admissible, including evidence bearing on the issue of witness credibility …, and the oral testimony of witnesses supplies valuable evidence relevant to credibility, a critical issue in many marital dissolution trials. Permitting oral testimony rather than relying upon written declarations also is consistent with the historically and statutorily accepted practice of conducting trial by means of the oral testimony of witnesses given in the presence of the trier of fact."

Kulshrestha v. First Un. Commercial Corp. (2004) 33 Cal.4th 601, 608-09. "Largely because the declarant is absent and unavailable for cross-examination under oath, hearsay evidence is less reliable than live testimony. Hearsay evidence is generally incompetent and inadmissible without statutory or decisional authorization, or absent stipulation or waiver by the parties. [¶] Nevertheless, in limited kinds of judicial proceedings, hearsay evidence—especially written statements—may serve as the sole or primary evidence of relevant facts. Such is the case with 'motion[s]' …, including motions for summary judgment. [¶] In particular, the summary judgment statute authorizes 'affidavits' and 'declarations' to support and oppose such motions. *At 610:* [P]etitioner argues … that his declaration 'substantially complies' with [CCP] §2015.5 despite its failure to invoke 'the laws of the State of California.' A declaration is competent hearsay under this view even though it was signed in another state by someone who showed no awareness that his statements might violate California's perjury laws or trigger prosecution here. [¶] The plain statutory language [of §2015.5] defeats this claim. *At 611:* It seems clear that out-of-state declarations offend §2015.5, and are not deemed sufficiently reliable for purposes of that statute, unless they follow its literal terms."

In re Cindy L. (1997) 17 Cal.4th 15, 26. "[T]he language of [Evid. C.] §1200, read in light of [Evid. C.] §160 and the comments thereon, makes clear that one source of exceptions to the hearsay rule is from judicial decisions. *At 27:* The power of the judiciary in developing new hearsay exceptions has been little used. … But the fact that the judicial authority to create new hearsay exceptions has rarely been exercised does not thereby render it forfeit. *At 28:* Caution on the part of the judiciary is also warranted because hearsay is an area of law that is now governed by an extensive statutory scheme. Courts may not create evidentiary exceptions in conflict with statute. [¶] Despite this cautionary note, it may nonetheless be appropriate for courts to create hearsay exceptions for classes of evidence for which there is a substantial need, and which possess an intrinsic reliability that enable them to surmount constitutional and other objections that generally apply to hearsay evidence."

DiCola v. White Bros. Performance Prods. (4th Dist.2008) 158 Cal.App.4th 666, 680. "Double hearsay is admissible if each level falls within an exception to the hearsay rule. Statements that are not offered to prove the truth of the matters asserted do not constitute hearsay."

Gallagher v. Connell (2d Dist.2004) 123 Cal.App.4th 1260, 1268. "It has long been the rule an objection the evidence is 'not admissible' or 'not competent' is too general to include the objection it calls for hearsay."

Houghtaling v. Superior Ct. (4th Dist.1993) 17 Cal.App.4th 1128, 1131. "We hold that in a proceeding conducted under the Small Claims Act …, relevant hearsay evidence is admissible subject only to those limitations contained in [Evid. C.] §352 and the law of testimonial privileges. *At 1138-39:* [I]n a small claims proceeding, no party may be compelled to provide, over objection and a proper claim of the privilege, information covered by a statutory privilege, and no party may introduce such evidence absent an appropriate waiver. [¶] We also hold that the trial court retains the discretion under … §352 to exclude evidence which is cumulative, overly time-consuming, confusing or prejudicial

and also to exclude evidence not relevant pursuant to [Evid. C.] §350. [¶] Our holding places no restrictions upon the type or amount of relevant hearsay evidence which shall be received, subject to the court's power under … §352 and its duty to respect and enforce the law of privileges."

Korsak v. Atlas Hotels, Inc. (4th Dist.1992) 2 Cal.App.4th 1516, 1523. "'The chief reasons for excluding hearsay evidence are said to be: (a) The statements are not made under *oath*; (b) the adverse party has *no opportunity to cross-examine* the person who made them; and (c) the jury cannot observe his *demeanor* while making them.'"

§1201. [MULTIPLE HEARSAY STATEMENTS MEETING AN EXCEPTION]

A statement within the scope of an exception to the hearsay rule is not inadmissible on the ground that the evidence of such statement is hearsay evidence if such hearsay evidence consists of one or more statements each of which meets the requirements of an exception to the hearsay rule.

History of Evid. C. §1201: Added eff. Sept. 17, 1965, oper. Jan. 1, 1967, Stats. 1965, ch. 299, §2. Amended eff. Nov. 8, 1967, Stats. 1967, ch. 650, §8.

Official Comment

7 Cal. Law Revision Comm'n Rep. (1965) p. 1218.

Section 1201 makes it possible to use admissible hearsay to prove another statement that is also admissible hearsay. For example, under Section 1201, an official reporter's transcript of the testimony at a previous trial may be used to prove the testimony previously given (Evidence Code §1280); the former testimony may be used as evidence (Evidence Code §1291) to prove that a party made a statement; and the party's statement is admissible against him as an admission (Evidence Code §1220). Thus, under Section 1201, the evidence of the admission contained in the transcript is admissible because each of the hearsay statements involved is within an exception to the hearsay rule.

Although no California case has been found where the admissibility of "multiple hearsay" has been analyzed and discussed, the practice is apparently in accord with the rule stated in Section 1201. *See, e.g.*, *People v. Collup*, 27 Cal.2d 829, 167 P.2d 714 (1946) (transcript of former testimony used to prove admission).

Official Comment

8 Cal. Law Revision Comm'n Rep. (1967) p. 124.

This amendment is designed to clarify the meaning of Section 1201 without changing its substantive effect.

§1202. [IMPEACHMENT OF HEARSAY DECLARANT]

Evidence of a statement or other conduct by a declarant that is inconsistent with a statement by such declarant received in evidence as hearsay evidence is not inadmissible for the purpose of attacking the credibility of the declarant though he is not given and has not had an opportunity to explain or to deny such inconsistent statement or other conduct. Any other evidence offered to attack or support the credibility of the declarant is admissible if it would have been admissible had the declarant been a witness at the hearing. For the purposes of this section, the deponent of a deposition taken in the action in which it is offered shall be deemed to be a hearsay declarant.

History of Evid. C. §1202: Added eff. Sept. 17, 1965, oper. Jan. 1, 1967, Stats. 1965, ch. 299, §2.

Official Comment

7 Cal. Law Revision Comm'n Rep. (1965) p. 1219.

Section 1202 deals with the impeachment of a declarant whose hearsay statement is in evidence as distinguished from the impeachment of a witness who has testified. It clarifies two points. *First*, evidence to impeach a hearsay declarant is not to be excluded on the ground that it is collateral. *Second*, the rule applying to the impeachment of a witness—that a witness may be impeached by an inconsistent statement only if he is provided with an opportunity to explain or deny it—does not apply to a hearsay declarant.

When hearsay evidence in the form of former testimony has been admitted, the California courts have permitted a party to impeach the hearsay declarant with evidence of an inconsistent statement made by the hearsay declarant *after* the former testimony was given, even though the declarant was never given an opportunity to explain or deny the inconsistency. *People v. Collup*, 27 Cal.2d 829, 167 P.2d 714 (1946). Apparently, however, former testimony may not be impeached by evidence of an inconsistent statement made *prior* to the former testimony unless the would-be impeacher either did not know of the inconsistent statement at the time the former testimony was given or unless he had provided the declarant with an opportunity to explain or deny the inconsistent statement. *People v. Greenwell*, 20 Cal.App.2d 266, 66 P.2d 674 (1937), as limited by *People v. Collup*, 27 Cal.2d 829, 167 P.2d 714 (1946). The courts permit dying declarations to be impeached by evidence of contradictory statements by the deceased despite the lack of any foundation, for only in very rare cases would it be possible to provide the declarant with an opportunity to explain or deny the inconsistency. *People v. Lawrence*, 21 Cal. 368 (1863).

Section 1202 substitutes for this case law a uniform rule permitting a hearsay declarant to be impeached by inconsistent statements in all cases, whether or not the declarant has been given an opportunity to explain or deny the inconsistency. If the hearsay declarant is unavailable as a witness, the party against whom the evidence is admitted should not be deprived of both his right to cross-examine and his right to impeach. *Cf. People v. Lawrence*, 21 Cal. 368, 372 (1863). If the hearsay declarant is available, the party electing to use the hearsay of such a declarant should have the burden of calling him to explain or deny any alleged inconsistencies.

Of course, the trial judge may curb efforts to impeach hearsay declarants if he determines that the inquiry is becoming too remote from the issues that are actually at stake in the litigation. Evidence Code §352.

Section 1235 provides that evidence of inconsistent statements made by a trial witness may be admitted to prove the truth of the matter stated. No similar exception to the hearsay rule is applicable to a hearsay declarant's inconsistent statements that are admitted under Section 1202. Hence, the hearsay rule prohibits any such statement from being used to prove the truth of the matter stated. If the declarant is not a witness and is not subject to cross-examination upon the subject matter of his statements, there is no sufficient guarantee of the trustworthiness of the statements he has made out of court to warrant their reception as substantive evidence unless they fall within some recognized exception to the hearsay rule.

ANNOTATIONS

People v. Blacksher (2011) 52 Cal.4th 769, 808. "[T]he confrontation clause does not prohibit the prosecution from impeaching the former testimony of its own unavailable witnesses with their inconsistent statements, provided those statements are admitted only for impeachment purposes. However, under …

§1200

§1202, the prosecution may not offer for their truth the inconsistent statements of a declarant who does not testify at trial."

People v. Osorio (4th Dist.2008) 165 Cal.App.4th 603, 615. "[N]othing in the language of [Evid. C.] §1202 purports to prevent the proponent of a witness's statement from using a prior inconsistent statement to impeach a portion of that witness's statement. *At 616-17:* The general rule against impeaching one's own witness … was abrogated by the Legislature's passage of [Evid. C.] §785 in the same year it passed … §1202. [S]ection 785 provides: 'The credibility of a witness may be attacked or supported by any party, including the party calling him.' Significantly, … §§785 and 1202 were not only passed in the same year; *they were passed as part of the same bill*. [W]e may safely infer that if the Legislature had intended to make … §§785 and 1202 mutually exclusive, it would have expressly done so. Read together as a single statute, these two sections allow a prosecutor to use a prior inconsistent statement to partially impeach a hearsay statement the prosecutor had previously introduced."

People v. Corella (2d Dist.2004) 122 Cal.App.4th 461, 470. "Under §1202, when a hearsay statement by a declarant who is not a witness is admitted into evidence by the prosecution, an inconsistent hearsay statement by the same person offered by the defense is admissible to attack the declarant's credibility. [¶] The purpose of §1202 is to assure fairness to the party against whom hearsay evidence is admitted without an opportunity for cross-examination."

§1203. [CROSS-EXAMINATION OF HEARSAY DECLARANT]

(a) [Adverse party may call declarant.] The declarant of a statement that is admitted as hearsay evidence may be called and examined by any adverse party as if under cross-examination concerning the statement.

(b) [Exceptions for declarant.] This section is not applicable if the declarant is (1) a party, (2) a person identified with a party within the meaning of subdivision (d) of Section 776, or (3) a witness who has testified in the action concerning the subject matter of the statement.

(c) [Exceptions for statement.] This section is not applicable if the statement is one described in Article 1 (commencing with Section 1220), Article 3 (commencing with Section 1235), or Article 10 (commencing with Section 1300) of Chapter 2 of this division.

(d) [Declarant unavailable.] A statement that is otherwise admissible as hearsay evidence is not made inadmissible by this section because the declarant who made the statement is unavailable for examination pursuant to this section.

History of Evid. C. §1203: Added eff. Sept. 17, 1965, oper. Jan. 1, 1967, Stats. 1965, ch. 299, §2.

Official Comment

7 Cal. Law Revision Comm'n Rep. (1965) p. 1220; Assem. J., Apr. 6, 1965, p. 1756.

Hearsay evidence is generally excluded because the declarant was not in court and not subject to cross-examination before the trier of fact when he made the statement. *People v. Bob*, 29 Cal.2d 321, 325, 175 P.2d 12, 15 (1946).

In some situations, hearsay evidence is admitted because there is either some exceptional need for the evidence or some circumstantial probability of its trustworthiness, or both. *People v. Brust*, 47 Cal.2d 776, 785, 306 P.2d 480, 484 (1957); *Turney v. Sousa*, 146 Cal.App.2d 787, 791, 304 P.2d 1025, 1027-1028 (1956). Even though it may be necessary or desirable to permit certain hearsay evidence to be admitted despite the fact that the adverse party had no opportunity to cross-examine the declarant when the hearsay statement was made, there seems to be no reason to prohibit the adverse party from cross-examining the declarant concerning the statement. The policy in favor of cross-examination that underlies the hearsay rule, therefore, indicates that the adverse party should be accorded the right to call the declarant of a statement received in evidence and to cross-examine him concerning his statement.

Section 1203, therefore, reverses (insofar as a hearsay declarant is concerned) the traditional rule that a witness called by a party is a witness for that party and may not be cross-examined by him. Because a hearsay declarant is in practical effect a witness against the party against whom his hearsay statement is admitted, Section 1203 gives that party the right to call and cross-examine the hearsay declarant concerning the subject matter of the hearsay statement just as he has the right to cross-examine the witnesses who appear personally and testify against him at the trial.

Subdivisions (b) and (c) make Section 1203 inapplicable in certain situations where it would be inappropriate to permit a party to examine a hearsay declarant as if under cross-examination. Thus, for example, subdivision (b) does not permit counsel for a party to examine his own client as if under cross-examination merely because a hearsay statement of his client has been admitted; and, because a party should not have the right to cross-examine his own witness merely because the adverse party has introduced a hearsay statement of the witness, witnesses who have testified in the action concerning the subject matter of the statement are not subject to examination under Section 1203.

Subdivision (d) makes it clear that the unavailability of a hearsay declarant for examination under Section 1203 has no effect on the admissibility of his hearsay statements. The subdivision forestalls any argument that availability of the declarant for examination under Section 1203 is an additional condition of admissibility for hearsay evidence.

§1203.1. [HEARSAY OFFERED AT PRELIMINARY HEARING]

Section 1203 is not applicable if the hearsay statement is offered at a preliminary examination, as provided in Section 872 of the Penal Code.

History of Evid. C. §1203.1: Added by Initiative Measure (Prop. 115), approved June 5, 1990.

§1204. [HEARSAY AGAINST CRIMINAL DEFENDANT]

A statement that is otherwise admissible as hearsay evidence is inadmissible against the defendant in a criminal action if the statement was made, either by the defendant or by another, under such circumstances that it is inadmissible against the defendant under the Constitution of the United States or the State of California.

History of Evid. C. §1204: Added eff. Sept. 17, 1965, oper. Jan. 1, 1967, Stats. 1965, ch. 299, §2.

Official Comment

7 Cal. Law Revision Comm'n Rep. (1965) p. 1221; Assem. J., Apr. 6, 1965, p. 1757.

Section 1204 is a statutory recognition that hearsay evidence that fits within an exception to the hearsay rule may nonetheless be inadmissible under the Constitution of the United States or the Constitution of California. Thus, Section 1220, which creates an exception for the statements of a party, is subject to the constitutional rule excluding evidence of involuntary confessions against a criminal defendant.

In *People v. Underwood*, 61 Cal.2d 113, 37 Cal.Rptr. 313, 389 P.2d 937 (1964), the California Supreme Court held that a prior inconsistent statement of a witness could not be introduced to impeach him in a criminal action when the statement would have been inadmissible as an involuntary confession if the witness had been the defendant. To the extent that the *Underwood* decision is based on constitutional principles, its effect is continued by Section 1204 and its principle is made applicable to all hearsay statements.

Insofar as the Constitution of the United States is concerned, Section 1204 refers only to those rules required to be observed in state proceedings. It is not intended to make applicable in proceedings in California courts those rules the United States Constitution requires to be observed only in federal proceedings.

§1205. [NO REPEAL BY IMPLICATION]

Nothing in this division shall be construed to repeal by implication any other statute relating to hearsay evidence.

History of Evid. C. §1205: Added eff. Sept. 17, 1965, oper. Jan. 1, 1967, Stats. 1965, ch. 299, §2.

Official Comment

7 Cal. Law Revision Comm'n Rep. (1965) p. 1222.

Although some of the statutes providing for the admission of hearsay evidence will be repealed when the Evidence Code is enacted, a number of statutes will remain in the various codes. For the most part, these statutes are narrowly drawn to make a particular type of hearsay evidence admissible under specifically limited circumstances. To assure the continued validity of these provisions, Section 1205 states that they will not be impliedly repealed by the enactment of the Evidence Code.

CHAPTER 2. EXCEPTIONS TO THE HEARSAY RULE

ARTICLE 1. CONFESSIONS & ADMISSIONS

§1220. [EXCEPTION: PARTY-ADMISSION]

Evidence of a statement is not made inadmissible by the hearsay rule when offered against the declarant in an action to which he is a party in either his individual or representative capacity, regardless of whether the statement was made in his individual or representative capacity.

History of Evid. C. §1220: Added eff. Sept. 17, 1965, oper. Jan. 1, 1967, Stats. 1965, ch. 299, §2.

Official Comment

7 Cal. Law Revision Comm'n Rep. (1965) p. 1223.

Section 1220 states existing law as found in subdivision 2 of Section 1870 of the Code of Civil Procedure. The rationale underlying this exception is that the party cannot object to the lack of the right to cross-examine the declarant since the party himself made the statement. Moreover, the party can cross-examine the witness who testifies to the party's statement and can explain or deny the purported admission. The statement need not be one which would be admissible if made at the hearing. *See Shields v. Oxnard Harbor Dist.*, 46 Cal.App.2d 477, 116 P.2d 121 (1941).

In a criminal action, a defendant's statement is not admissible under this section unless it was made voluntarily. Evidence Code §1204.

ANNOTATIONS

People v. Rodriguez (2014) 58 Cal.4th 587, 637. "[S]ection 1220 makes a 'statement' of a party an exception to the general rule forbidding hearsay evidence when the statement is offered against that party. [D] argues that nothing in her deposition testimony could be considered an 'admission.' The argument is irrelevant. Although … §1220's exception to the hearsay rule is sometimes referred to as an exception for admissions, the exception is not so limited. Instead, the exception applies to all statements of the party against whom they are offered. Here, [D's] deposition testimony consisted of statements, [D] made the statements, the statements were offered against her, and she was a party to this action. Thus, the statements came within an exception to the hearsay rule. They were admissible against [D]."

People v. Russell (2010) 50 Cal.4th 1228, 1258. Section 1220 "applies only to statements offered against a party declarant, not offered by that party."

Carson v. Facilities Dev. Co. (1984) 36 Cal.3d 830, 849-50. "'[S]ection 1220 creates an exception to the hearsay rule for [an] admission of a party.... [¶] [S]ection 1220 does not define when a declarant-party's extrajudicial hearsay statement becomes *relevant* to be admissible against such party under the personal admission exception to the hearsay rule. [F]or such a statement to be admissible against a party as an admission, the statement must assert facts which would have a tendency in reason either (1) to prove some portion of the proponent's [defense], or (2) to rebut some portion of the party declarant's [cause of action].' [¶] As [D-driver] points out, [declarant's] statement constitutes an admission because it indicates that when decedent pulled into the intersection, there was insufficient time to avoid a collision with [D-driver's] vehicle. [Declarant] stated that when he looked back and saw

that his wife had pulled out into the intersection, he knew 'that she didn't have enough time to make it.' This statement implies that [D-driver] was not negligent because he could not have swerved or braked in time to prevent the accident. The statement therefore tends to rebut [P's] negligence cause of action. [Declarant's] statement was properly admitted as an exception to the hearsay rule under … §1220."

Greenspan v. LADT LLC (2d Dist.2010) 191 Cal.App.4th 486, 523-24. "Any statement, oral or written, made by [D] was admissible as to him under the hearsay exception for party admissions. That includes prior testimony, whether given in a deposition, during the arbitration hearing, in judgment debtor proceedings, or in another matter."

People v. Castille (1st Dist.2005) 129 Cal.App.4th 863, 875-76. "[A]s a general rule, if a party to a proceeding has made an out-of-court statement that is relevant and not excludable under [Evid. C.] §352 [on grounds of waste of time, prejudice, or confusion], the statement is admissible against that party declarant."

§1221. [EXCEPTION: ADOPTIVE ADMISSION]

Evidence of a statement offered against a party is not made inadmissible by the hearsay rule if the statement is one of which the party, with knowledge of the content thereof, has by words or other conduct manifested his adoption or his belief in its truth.

History of Evid. C. §1221: Added eff. Sept. 17, 1965, oper. Jan. 1, 1967, Stats. 1965, ch. 299, §2.

Official Comment

7 Cal. Law Revision Comm'n Rep. (1965) p. 1223.

Section 1221 restates an exception found in subdivision 3 of Section 1870 of the Code of Civil Procedure.

ANNOTATIONS

Bowles v. State Bar (1989) 48 Cal.3d 100, 108. "The majority of [client's] mother's testimony concerned the letter she wrote to [attorney] in which she accuses him of failing to communicate with her daughter and to perform services. She threatened to file charges of professional misconduct with the State Bar and demanded a reply. [Attorney] failed to respond, and hence the testimony is admissible as an adoptive admission."

People v. Sample (4th Dist.2011) 200 Cal.App.4th 1253, 1262. "[W]hen a person makes a statement in the presence of a party to an action under circumstances that would normally call for a response if the statement were untrue, the statement is admissible for the limited purpose of showing the party's reaction to it. His silence, evasion, or equivocation may be considered as a tacit admission of the statements made in his presence. [¶] Whether the statement constitutes an adoptive admission is determined upon the facts and circumstances therein presented. [T]here must be sufficient evidence to sustain a finding that (1) the defendant heard and understood the statement under circumstances normally calling for a response, and (2) the defendant adopted the statement as true by the defendant's words or conduct." (Internal quotes omitted.) *See also* ***Kincaid v. Kincaid*** (2d Dist.2011) 197 Cal.App.4th 75, 83 (whether D's conduct actually constituted adoptive admission is question for jury to decide).

Jazayeri v. Mao (2d Dist.2009) 174 Cal.App.4th 301, 326. "The theory of adoptive admissions expressed in §1221 is that the hearsay declaration is in effect repeated by the party; his conduct is intended by him to express the same proposition as that stated by the declarant." (Internal quotes omitted.)

§1222. [EXCEPTION: AUTHORIZED ADMISSION]

Evidence of a statement offered against a party is not made inadmissible by the hearsay rule if:

(a) The statement was made by a person authorized by the party to make a statement or statements for him concerning the subject matter of the statement; and

(b) The evidence is offered either after admission of evidence sufficient to sustain a finding of such authority or, in the court's discretion as to the order of proof, subject to the admission of such evidence.

History of Evid. C. §1222: Added eff. Sept. 17, 1965, oper. Jan. 1, 1967, Stats. 1965, ch. 299, §2.

Official Comment

7 Cal. Law Revision Comm'n Rep. (1965) p. 1224.

Section 1222 provides a hearsay exception for authorized admissions. Under this exception, if a party authorized an agent to make statements on his behalf, such statements may be introduced against the party under the same conditions as if they had been made by the party himself. The authority of the declarant to make the statement need not be express; it may be implied. It is to be determined in each case under the substantive law of agency. Section 1222 restates an exception found in the first portion of subdivision 5 of Section 1870 of the Code of Civil Procedure. *See Tentative Recommendation and a Study Relating to the Uniform Rules of Evidence (Article VIII. Hearsay Evidence)*, 6 Cal. Law Revision Comm'n, Rep., Rec. & Studies *Appendix* at 484-490 (1964).

ANNOTATIONS

Snider v. Superior Ct. (4th Dist.2003) 113 Cal.App.4th 1187, 1203. Section 1222, subdivision (a) "has been interpreted in California as only applying to high-ranking organizational agents who have actual

authority to speak on behalf of the organization." *See also* ***Thompson v. County of L.A.*** (2d Dist.2006) 142 Cal.App.4th 154, 169.

O'Mary v. Mitsubishi Elecs. Am., Inc. (4th Dist.1997) 59 Cal.App.4th 563, 570. "The authority of a declarant employee to make a statement 'for' an employer 'concerning the subject matter of the statement' can be implied, as well as express. [T]he question of an employee's authorization ... depends on the particular facts and circumstances of each case viewed in the light of the substantive law of *agency*, as distinct from evidence. [¶] In general, ... the determination requires an examination of the nature of the employee's usual and customary authority, the nature of the statement in relation to that authority, and the particular relevance or purpose of the statement. *At 572:* Place in an employer's hierarchy undoubtedly is important in determining authority to speak...." *See also* ***O'Neill v. Novartis Consumer Health, Inc.*** (2d Dist.2007) 147 Cal.App.4th 1388, 1403.

§1223. [EXCEPTION: COCONSPIRATOR]

Evidence of a statement offered against a party is not made inadmissible by the hearsay rule if:

(a) The statement was made by the declarant while participating in a conspiracy to commit a crime or civil wrong and in furtherance of the objective of that conspiracy;

(b) The statement was made prior to or during the time that the party was participating in that conspiracy; and

(c) The evidence is offered either after admission of evidence sufficient to sustain a finding of the facts specified in subdivisions (a) and (b) or, in the court's discretion as to the order of proof, subject to the admission of such evidence.

History of Evid. C. §1223: Added eff. Sept. 17, 1965, oper. Jan. 1, 1967, Stats. 1965, ch. 299, §2.

Official Comment

7 Cal. Law Revision Comm'n Rep. (1965) p. 1224.

Section 1223 is a specific example of a kind of authorized admission that is admissible under Section 1222. The statement is admitted because it is an act of the conspiracy for which the party, as a co-conspirator, is legally responsible. *People v. Lorraine*, 90 Cal.App. 317, 327, 265 Pac. 893, 897 (1928). *See California Criminal Law Practice* 471-472 (Cal.Cont.Ed. Bar 1964). Section 1223 restates an exception found in subdivision 6 of Section 1870 of the Code of Civil Procedure.

§1224. [EXCEPTION: DECLARATION AGAINST INTEREST]

When the liability, obligation, or duty of a party to a civil action is based in whole or in part upon the liability, obligation, or duty of the declarant, or when the claim or right asserted by a party to a civil action is barred or diminished by a breach of duty by the declarant, evidence of a statement made by the declarant is as admissible against the party as it would be if offered against the declarant in an action involving that liability, obligation, duty, or breach of duty.

History of Evid. C. §1224: Added eff. Sept. 17, 1965, oper. Jan. 1, 1967, Stats. 1965, ch. 299, §2.

Official Comment

7 Cal. Law Revision Comm'n Rep. (1965) p. 1225.

Section 1224 restates in substance a hearsay exception found in Code of Civil Procedure Section 1851 (repealed, now Evidence Code Sections 1224 and 1302). *See Butte County v. Morgan*, 76 Cal. 1, 18 Pac. 115 (1888); *Ingram v. Bob Jaffe Co.*, 139 Cal.App.2d 193, 293 P.2d 132 (1956); *Standard Oil Co. v. Houser*, 101 Cal.App.2d 480, 225 P.2d 539 (1950). Section 1224, however, limits this hearsay exception to civil actions. Much of the evidence within this exception is also covered by Section 1230, which makes declarations against interest admissible. However, to be admissible under Section 1230, the statement must have been against the declarant's interest when made; this requirement is not stated in Section 1224.

Code of Civil Procedure Section 1851 provides for the admission of a declarant's statements in an action where the liability of the party against whom the statements are offered is based on the declarant's breach of duty. *Butte County v. Morgan*, 76 Cal. 1, 18 Pac. 115 (1888); *Nye & Nissen v. Central etc. Ins. Corp.*, 71 Cal.App.2d 570, 163 P.2d 100 (1945). Section 1224 of the Evidence Code refers specifically to "breach of duty" in order to admit statements of a declarant whose breach of duty is in issue without regard to whether that breach gives rise to a liability of the party against whom the statements are offered or merely defeats a right being asserted by that party. For example, in *Ingram v. Bob Jaffe Co.*, 139 Cal.App.2d 193, 293 P.2d 132 (1956), a statement of a person permitted to operate a vehicle was admitted against the owner of the vehicle in an action seeking to hold the owner liable on the derivative liability of vehicle owners established by Vehicle Code Section 17150. Under Section 1224, the statement of the declarant would also be admissible against the owner in an action brought by the owner to recover for damage to his vehicle where the defense is based on the contributory negligence of the declarant.

Section 1302 supplements the rule stated in Section 1224. Section 1302 creates an exception for judgments against a third person when one of the issues between the parties is the liability, obligation, or duty of the third person and the judgment determines that liability, obligation, or duty. Together, Sections 1224 and 1302 codify the holdings of the cases applying Code of Civil Procedure Section 1851. *See Tentative Recommendation and a Study Relating to the Uniform Rules of Evidence (Article VII. Hearsay Evidence)*, 6 Cal. Law Revision Comm'n, Rep., Rec. & Studies *Appendix* at 491-496 (1964).

ANNOTATIONS

Brown v. Surety Co. of the Pac. (4th Dist.1981) 122 Cal.App.3d 614, 618. "Section 1224 contemplates situations in which the obligation or duty of a third person is an essential operative fact in establishing the cause of action or defense involved; e.g., where the party has assumed responsibility for obligations of the declarant (guarantor, *surety*)." (Internal quotes omitted.)

§1225. [EXCEPTION: DECLARATION INVOLVING PREDECESSOR'S RIGHT, TITLE, OR INTEREST]

When a right, title, or interest in any property or claim asserted by a party to a civil action requires a determination that a right, title, or interest exists or existed in the declarant, evidence of a statement made by the declarant during the time the party now claims the declarant was the holder of the right, title, or interest is as admissible against the party as it would be if offered against the declarant in an action involving that right, title, or interest.

History of Evid. C. §1225: Added eff. Sept. 17, 1965, oper. Jan. 1, 1967, Stats. 1965, ch. 299, §2.

Official Comment

7 Cal. Law Revision Comm'n Rep. (1965) p. 1226.

Section 1225 expresses a common law exception to the hearsay rule that is recognized in part in Section 1849 of the Code of Civil Procedure. Section 1849 (which is superseded by Section 1225) permits the statements of predecessors in interest of real property to be admitted against the successors; however, the California cases follow the general rule of permitting predecessors' statements to be admitted against successors of either real or personal property. *Smith v. Goethe*, 159 Cal. 628, 115 Pac. 223 (1911); 4 Wigmore, *Evidence* §1082 *et seq.* (3d ed. 1940).

It should be noted that "statements made *before title accrued in the declarant* will not be receivable. On the other hand, the time of divestiture, *after* which no statements could be treated as admissions, is the time when the party against whom they are offered has by his own hypothesis acquired the title; thus, in a suit, for example, between *A*'s heir and *A*'s grantee, *A*'s statements at any time before his death are receivable against the heir; but only his statements before the grant are receivable against the grantee." 4 Wigmore, *Evidence* §1082 at 153 (3d ed. 1940).

Despite the limitations of Section 1225, some statements of a grantor made after divestiture of title will be admissible; but another theory of admissibility must be found. For example, later statements of his state of mind may be admissible on the issue of his intent. Evidence Code §§1250 and 1251. Where it is claimed that a conveyance was in fraud of creditors, the later statements of the grantor may be admissible not as hearsay but as evidence of the fraud itself (*cf. Bush & Mallett Co. v. Helbing*, 134 Cal. 676, 66 Pac. 967 (1901)) or as declarations of a co-conspirator in the fraud (*cf. McGee v. Allen*, 7 Cal.2d 468, 60 P.2d 1026 (1936)). *See generally* 4 Wigmore, *Evidence* §1086 (3d ed. 1940).

Section 1225 supplements the rule provided in Section 1224. Under Section 1224, for example, a party suing an executor on an obligation incurred by the decedent prior to his death may introduce admissions of the decedent. Similarly, under Section 1225, a party sued by an executor on an obligation claimed to have been owed to the decedent may introduce admissions of the decedent.

ANNOTATIONS

In re Estate of Huntington (2d Dist.1976) 58 Cal.App.3d 197, 211. "Section 1225 makes admissible against a party a statement of a party's predecessor in interest which tended to impugn the interest of the predecessor at the time the predecessor held title and made the statement. The basis for reliability of this hearsay exception is that statements of a declarant, made while he has title to property and which are in disparagement of that title, are statements against the interest of the declarant."

§1226. [EXCEPTION: STATEMENT BY MINOR RELATING TO INJURY TO MINOR]

Evidence of a statement by a minor child is not made inadmissible by the hearsay rule if offered against the plaintiff in an action brought under Section 376 of the Code of Civil Procedure for injury to such minor child.

History of Evid. C. §1226: Added eff. Sept. 17, 1965, oper. Jan. 1, 1967, Stats. 1965, ch. 299, §2.

Official Comment

7 Cal. Law Revision Comm'n Rep. (1965) p. 1227.

See the *Comment* to Section 1227.

§1227. [EXCEPTION: STATEMENT BY DECEASED IN WRONGFUL-DEATH ACTION]

Evidence of a statement by the deceased is not made inadmissible by the hearsay rule if offered against the plaintiff in an action for wrongful death brought under Section 377 of the Code of Civil Procedure.

History of Evid. C. §1227: Added eff. Sept. 17, 1965, oper. Jan. 1, 1967, Stats. 1965, ch. 299, §2.

Official Comment

7 Cal. Law Revision Comm'n Rep. (1965) p. 1227.

Under existing law, an admission by a decedent is not admissible against his heirs or representatives in a wrongful death action brought by them. *Marks v. Reissinger*, 35 Cal.App. 44, 169 Pac. 243 (1917). *Cf. Hedge v. Williams*, 131 Cal. 455, 63 Pac. 721 (1901). The reason is that the action is a new action, not merely a survival of the decedent's action. This rule has been severely criticized and is contrary to the rule adopted by most American courts. *Carr v. Duncan*, 90 Cal.App.2d 282, 285, 202 P.2d 855, 856 (1949).

Under Section 1224, the admissions of a decedent are admissible to establish the liability of his executor. Similarly, when the executor brings an action for the decedent's death under Code of Civil Procedure Section 377, the defendant should be permitted to introduce the admissions of the decedent. Without Section 1227, in an action between two executors arising out of an accident which was fatal to both participants, the plaintiff executor would be able to introduce admissions of the defendant's decedent, but the defending executor would be unable to introduce admissions of the plaintiff's decedent.

Section 1227 changes the rule announced in the California cases and makes the admissions of the decedent admissible in wrongful death actions. Section 1226 provides a similar rule for the analogous cases arising under Code of Civil Procedure Section 376 (action by parent of injured child).

Section 1227 recognizes that, in an action brought under Code of Civil Procedure Section 377, the only reason for treating the admissions of a plaintiff's decedent differently from those of a defendant's decedent is a technical procedural rule. The plaintiff in a wrongful death action—and the parent of an injured child in an action under Code of Civil Procedure Section 376—stands in reality so completely on the right of the deceased or injured person that such person's admissions should be admitted against the plaintiff, even though (as a technical matter) the plaintiff is asserting an independent right.

§1228. [EXCEPTION: STATEMENT OF MINOR CHILD TO ADMIT CONFESSION OF DEFENDANT]

Notwithstanding any other provision of law, for the purpose of establishing the elements of the crime in order to admit as evidence the confession of a person ac-

cused of violating Section 261, 264.1, 285, 286, 288, 288a, 289, or 647a of the Penal Code, a court, in its discretion, may determine that a statement of the complaining witness is not made inadmissible by the hearsay rule if it finds all of the following:

(a) [**Made by minor.**] The statement was made by a minor child under the age of 12, and the contents of the statement were included in a written report of a law enforcement official or an employee of a county welfare department.

(b) [**Minor a victim of sexual abuse.**] The statement describes the minor child as a victim of sexual abuse.

(c) [**Made prior to confession.**] The statement was made prior to the defendant's confession. The court shall view with caution the testimony of a person recounting hearsay where there is evidence of personal bias or prejudice.

(d) [**Limited inconsistencies.**] There are no circumstances, such as significant inconsistencies between the confession and the statement concerning material facts establishing any element of the crime or the identification of the defendant, that would render the statement unreliable.

(e) [**Minor unavailable.**] The minor child is found to be unavailable pursuant to paragraph (2) or (3) of subdivision (a) of Section 240 or refuses to testify.

(f) [**Memorialized confession.**] The confession was memorialized in a trustworthy fashion by a law enforcement official.

If the prosecution intends to offer a statement of the complaining witness pursuant to this section, the prosecution shall serve a written notice upon the defendant at least 10 days prior to the hearing or trial at which the prosecution intends to offer the statement. If the statement is offered during trial, the court's determination shall be made out of the presence of the jury.

If the statement is found to be admissible pursuant to this section, it shall be admitted out of the presence of the jury and solely for the purpose of determining the admissibility of the confession of the defendant.

History of Evid. C. §1228: Added eff. Jan. 1, 1985, Stats. 1984, ch. 1421, §1. Amended eff. Oct. 2, 1985, Stats. 1985, ch. 1572, §1.

See also Cal. Const., art. I, §28(d).

§1228.1. [EXCEPTION: CHILD WELFARE SERVICES PLAN]

(a) [**Signature or acceptance of services.**] Except as provided in subdivision (b), neither the signature of any parent or legal guardian on a child welfare services case plan nor the acceptance of any services prescribed in the child welfare services case plan by any parent or legal guardian shall constitute an admission of guilt or be used as evidence against the parent or legal guardian in a court of law.

(b) [**Failure to cooperate.**] A parent's or guardian's failure to cooperate, except for good cause, in the provision of services specified in the child welfare services case plan may be used as evidence, if relevant, in any hearing held pursuant to Section 366.21, 366.22, or 388 of the Welfare and Institutions Code and at any jurisdictional or dispositional hearing held on a petition filed pursuant to Section 300, 342, or 387 of the Welfare and Institutions Code.

History of Evid. C. §1228.1: Added eff. Jan. 1, 1996, Stats. 1995, ch. 540, §1. Amended eff. Jan. 1, 1998, Stats. 1997, ch. 793, §1.

ARTICLE 2. DECLARATIONS AGAINST INTEREST

§1230. [EXCEPTION: DECLARATION AGAINST INTEREST OF UNAVAILABLE DECLARANT]

Evidence of a statement by a declarant having sufficient knowledge of the subject is not made inadmissible by the hearsay rule if the declarant is unavailable as a witness and the statement, when made, was so far contrary to the declarant's pecuniary or proprietary interest, or so far subjected him to the risk of civil or criminal liability, or so far tended to render invalid a claim by him against another, or created such a risk of making him an object of hatred, ridicule, or social disgrace in the community, that a reasonable man in his position would not have made the statement unless he believed it to be true.

History of Evid. C. §1230: Added eff. Sept. 17, 1965, oper. Jan. 1, 1967, Stats. 1965, ch. 299, §2.

Official Comment

7 Cal. Law Revision Comm'n Rep. (1965) p. 1228; Assem. J., Apr. 6, 1965, p. 1757.

Except for the requirement that the declarant be shown to be unavailable as a witness, Section 1230 codifies the hearsay exception for declarations against interest as that exception has been developed by the California courts (*People v. Spriggs*, 60 Cal.2d 868, 36 Cal.Rptr. 841, 389 P.2d 377 (1964)) and possibly expands the exception. It is not clear whether the existing exception for declarations against interest applies to statements that make the declarant an object of hatred, ridicule, or social disgrace in the community.

Under existing law, a declaration against interest is admissible regardless of the availability of the declarant to testify as a witness. *People v. Spriggs*, 60 Cal.2d 868, 36 Cal.Rptr. 841, 389 P.2d 377 (1964). Section 1230, however, conditions admissibility upon the unavailability of the declarant in order to require the proponent of the evidence to use the in-court testimony of the declarant if it is possible to do so. If the declarant disappoints the proponent and testifies inconsistently, the proponent may then show the prior inconsistent statement as substantive evidence of the facts stated. *See* Evidence Code §1235 and the *Comment* thereto.

Section 1230 supersedes the partial and inaccurate statements of the exception for declarations against interest found in Code of Civil Procedure Sections 1853, 1870(4), and 1946(1). *See People v. Spriggs*, 60 Cal.2d 868, 871-872, 36 Cal.Rptr. 841, 844-845, 389 P.2d 377, 380-381 (1964). The requirement that the declarant have "sufficient knowledge of the subject" continues the similar common law requirement stated in Code of Civil Procedure Section 1853 that the declarant must have had some peculiar means—such as personal observation—for obtaining accurate knowledge of the matter stated. *See* 5 Wigmore, *Evidence* §1471 (3d ed. 1940).

ANNOTATIONS

People v. McCurdy (2014) 59 Cal.4th 1063, 1108. "In determining whether a statement is truly against interest within the meaning of … §1230, and hence is sufficiently trustworthy to be admissible, the court may take into account not just the words but the circumstances under which they were uttered, the possible motivation of the declarant, and the declarant's relationship to the defendant. A trial court's decision to admit or exclude evidence is a matter committed to its discretion and will not be disturbed except on a showing the trial court exercised its discretion in an arbitrary, capricious, or patently absurd manner that resulted in a manifest miscarriage of justice." (Internal quotes omitted.)

People v. Tran (6th Dist.2013) 215 Cal.App.4th 1207, 1216. "The focus of the declaration against interest exception to the hearsay rule is the basic trustworthiness of the declaration. *At 1217:* There is no litmus test for the determination of whether a statement is trustworthy and falls within the declaration against interest exception. The trial court must look to the totality of the circumstances in which the statement was made, whether the declarant spoke from personal knowledge, the possible motivation of the declarant, what was actually said by the declarant and anything else relevant to the inquiry. [T]he most reliable circumstance is one in which the conversation occurs between friends in a noncoercive setting that fosters uninhibited disclosures. … Controversy necessarily arises when the declarant makes statements which are self-inculpatory as well as inculpatory of another. This is why … §1230 only permits an exception to the hearsay rule for statements that are specifically disserving of the declarant's penal interest. This is not to say that a statement that incriminates the declarant and also inculpates the nondeclarant cannot be specifically disserving of the declarant's penal interest. Such a determination necessarily depends upon a careful analysis of what was said and the totality of the circumstances." (Internal quotes omitted.) *See also* ***Clark v. Optical Coating Lab.*** (1st Dist.2008) 165 Cal.App.4th 150, 170-71.

Kincaid v. Kincaid (2d Dist.2011) 197 Cal.App.4th 75, 89. "In order for a statement to qualify under the exception, both the content of the statement and the fact that the statement was made must be against the declarant's social interest."

ARTICLE 2.5. SWORN STATEMENTS REGARDING GANG-RELATED CRIMES

§1231. [EXCEPTION: DECEASED DECLARANT]

Evidence of a prior statement made by a declarant is not made inadmissible by the hearsay rule if the declarant is deceased and the proponent of introducing the statement establishes each of the following:

(a) [Criminal prosecution.] The statement relates to acts or events relevant to a criminal prosecution under provisions of the California Street Terrorism Enforcement and Prevention Act (Chapter 11 (commencing with Section 186.20) of Title 7 of Part 1 of the Penal Code).

(b) [Record.] A verbatim transcript, copy, or record of the statement exists. A record may include a statement preserved by means of an audio or video recording or equivalent technology.

(c) [Personal knowledge.] The statement relates to acts or events within the personal knowledge of the declarant.

(d) [Under oath.] The statement was made under oath or affirmation in an affidavit; or was made at a deposition, preliminary hearing, grand jury hearing, or other proceeding in compliance with law, and was made under penalty of perjury.

(e) [Cause of death.] The declarant died from other than natural causes.

(f) [Trustworthy.] The statement was made under circumstances that would indicate its trustworthiness and render the declarant's statement particularly worthy of belief. For purposes of this subdivision, circumstances relevant to the issue of trustworthiness include, but are not limited to, all of the following:

(1) Whether the statement was made in contemplation of a pending or anticipated criminal or civil matter, in which the declarant had an interest, other than as a witness.

(2) Whether the declarant had a bias or motive for fabricating the statement, and the extent of any bias or motive.

(3) Whether the statement is corroborated by evidence other than statements that are admissible only pursuant to this section.

(4) Whether the statement was a statement against the declarant's interest.

History of Evid. C. §1231: Added eff. Jan. 1, 1998, Stats. 1997, ch. 499, §1.

§1231.1. [NOTICE TO ADVERSE PARTY]

A statement is admissible pursuant to Section 1231 only if the proponent of the statement makes known to the adverse party the intention to offer the statement and the particulars of the statement sufficiently in advance of the proceedings to provide the adverse party with a fair opportunity to prepare to meet the statement.

History of Evid. C. §1231.1: Added eff. Jan. 1, 1998, Stats. 1997, ch. 499, §1.

§1231.2. [OATH]

A peace officer may administer and certify oaths for purposes of this article.

History of Evid. C. §1231.2: Added eff. Jan. 1, 1998, Stats. 1997, ch. 499, §1. Amended eff. Jan. 1, 1999, Stats. 1998, ch. 606, §2.

§1231.3. [QUALIFICATIONS FOR LAW-ENFORCEMENT OFFICERS]

Any law enforcement officer testifying as to any hearsay statement pursuant to this article shall either have five years of law enforcement experience or have completed a training course certified by the Commission on Peace Officer Standards and Training which includes training in the investigation and reporting of cases and testifying at preliminary hearings and trials.

History of Evid. C. §1231.3: Added eff. Jan. 1, 1998, Stats. 1997, ch. 499, §1.

§1231.4. [DECLARANT UNAVAILABLE]

If evidence of a prior statement is introduced pursuant to this article, the jury may not be told that the declarant died from other than natural causes, but shall merely be told that the declarant is unavailable.

History of Evid. C. §1231.4: Added eff. Jan. 1, 1998, Stats. 1997, ch. 499, §1.

ARTICLE 3. PRIOR STATEMENTS OF WITNESSES

§1235. [EXCEPTION: PRIOR INCONSISTENT STATEMENT]

Evidence of a statement made by a witness is not made inadmissible by the hearsay rule if the statement is inconsistent with his testimony at the hearing and is offered in compliance with Section 770.

History of Evid. C. §1235: Added eff. Sept. 17, 1965, oper. Jan. 1, 1967, Stats. 1965, ch. 299, §2.

Official Comment

7 Cal. Law Revision Comm'n Rep. (1965) p. 1229.

Under existing law, when a prior statement of a witness that is inconsistent with his testimony at the trial is admitted in evidence, it may not be used as evidence of the truth of the matters stated. Because of the hearsay rule, a witness' prior inconsistent statement may be used only to discredit his testimony given at the trial. *Albert v. McKay & Co.*, 174 Cal. 451, 456, 163 Pac. 666, 668 (1917).

Because a witness' inconsistent statement is not substantive evidence, the courts do not permit a party—even when surprised by the testimony—to impeach his own witness with inconsistent statements if the witness' testimony at the trial has not damaged the party's case in any way. Evidence tending only to discredit the witness is irrelevant and immaterial when the witness has not given damaging testimony. *People v. Crespi*, 115 Cal. 50, 46 Pac. 863 (1896); *People v. Mitchell*, 94 Cal. 550, 29 Pac. 1106 (1892); *People v. Brown*, 81 Cal. App. 226, 253 Pac. 735 (1927).

Section 1235 permits an inconsistent statement of a witness to be used as substantive evidence if the statement is otherwise admissible under the conditions specified in Section 770—which do not include surprise on the part of the party calling the witness if he is the party offering the inconsistent statement. Because Section 1235 permits a witness' inconsistent statements to be considered as evidence of the matters stated and not merely as evidence casting discredit on the witness, it follows that a party may introduce evidence of inconsistent statements of his own witness whether or not the witness gave damaging testimony and whether or not the party was surprised by the testimony, for such evidence is no longer irrelevant (and, hence, inadmissible).

Section 1235 admits inconsistent statements of witnesses because the dangers against which the hearsay rule is designed to protect are largely nonexistent. The declarant is in court and may be examined and cross-examined in regard to his statements and their subject matter. In many cases, the inconsistent statement is more likely to be true than the testimony of the witness at the trial because it was made nearer in time to the matter to which it relates and is less likely to be influenced by the controversy that gave rise to the litigation. The trier of fact has the declarant before it and can observe his demeanor and the nature of his testimony as he denies or tries to explain away the inconsistency. Hence, it is in as good a position to determine the truth or falsity of the prior statement as it is to determine the truth or falsity of the inconsistent testimony given in court. Moreover, Section 1235 will provide a party with desirable protection against the "turncoat" witness who changes his story on the stand and deprives the party calling him of evidence essential to his case.

ANNOTATIONS

People v. Cowan (2010) 50 Cal.4th 401, 463. "[A] witness's deliberate evasion of questioning can constitute an implied denial that amounts to inconsistency, rendering a prior statement admissible under … §1235. Normally, the question of evasiveness arises when a witness claims memory loss about the subject of the questioning. Answering questions in a deliberately nonresponsive manner, however, also can rise to the level of evasion." *See also* ***People v. Homick*** (2012) 55 Cal.4th 816, 859 (witness's refusal to answer questions may be materially inconsistent with prior statements and expose witness to impeachment).

Clifton v. Ulis (1976) 17 Cal.3d 99, 105 n.2. "We assume that … §1235 reaches only that testimony which is heard by the trier of fact, inasmuch as it is the trier of fact who must weigh the inconsistency. The correctness of this assumption is implicit in the Law Revision Commission's comment to §1235, which justifies the removal of prior inconsistent statements from the pro-

tection of the hearsay rule on the ground that since the trier of fact has the declarant before it and can observe his demeanor and the nature of his testimony, the trier is in as good a position to determine the truth or falsity of the prior statement as it is to determine the truth or falsity of the inconsistent testimony given in court." (Internal quotes omitted.)

Benson v. Honda Motor Co. (2d Dist.1994) 26 Cal.App.4th 1337, 1349. Section 1235 "does not permit the wholesale admission into evidence of entire works in which a statement appears. [¶] '[T]he hearsay exception set forth in … §1235 … does *not* make admissible any prior statements of a witness that are *not* inconsistent with the witness' testimony, even though such *noninconsistent* statements are made at the same time and as a part of the same conversation in which the inconsistent statements are made.'"

§1236. [EXCEPTION: PRIOR CONSISTENT STATEMENT]

Evidence of a statement previously made by a witness is not made inadmissible by the hearsay rule if the statement is consistent with his testimony at the hearing and is offered in compliance with Section 791.

History of Evid. C. §1236: Added eff. Sept. 17, 1965, oper. Jan. 1, 1967, Stats. 1965, ch. 299, §2.

Official Comment

7 Cal. Law Revision Comm'n Rep. (1965) p. 1230.

Under existing law, a prior statement of a witness that is consistent with his testimony at the trial is admissible under certain conditions when the credibility of the witness has been attacked. The statement is admitted, however, only to rehabilitate the witness—to support his credibility—and not as evidence of the truth of the matter stated. *People v. Kynette*, 15 Cal.2d 731, 753-754, 104 P.2d 794, 805-806 (1940) (*overruled on other grounds* in *People v. Snyder*, 50 Cal.2d 190, 197, 324 P.2d 1, 6 (1958)).

Section 1236, however, permits a prior consistent statement of a witness to be used as substantive evidence if the statement is otherwise admissible under the rules relating to the rehabilitation of impeached witnesses. *See* Evidence Code §791.

There is no reason to perpetuate the subtle distinction made in the cases. It is not realistic to expect a jury to understand that it cannot believe that a witness was telling the truth on a former occasion even though it believes that the same story given at the hearing is true.

§1237. [EXCEPTION: RECORDED PAST RECOLLECTION]

(a) [Insufficient present recollection.] Evidence of a statement previously made by a witness is not made inadmissible by the hearsay rule if the statement would have been admissible if made by him while testifying, the statement concerns a matter as to which the witness has insufficient present recollection to enable him to testify fully and accurately, and the statement is contained in a writing which:

(1) Was made at a time when the fact recorded in the writing actually occurred or was fresh in the witness' memory;

(2) Was made (i) by the witness himself or under his direction or (ii) by some other person for the purpose of recording the witness' statement at the time it was made;

(3) Is offered after the witness testifies that the statement he made was a true statement of such fact; and

(4) Is offered after the writing is authenticated as an accurate record of the statement.

(b) [Read into evidence.] The writing may be read into evidence, but the writing itself may not be received in evidence unless offered by an adverse party.

History of Evid. C. §1237: Added eff. Sept. 17, 1965, oper. Jan. 1, 1967, Stats. 1965, ch. 299, §2.

Official Comment

7 Cal. Law Revision Comm'n Rep. (1965) p. 1231; Assem. J., Apr. 6, 1965, p. 1758.

Section 1237 provides a hearsay exception for what is usually referred to as "past recollection recorded." Although the provisions of Section 1237 are taken largely from the provisions of Section 2047 of the Code of Civil Procedure, there are some substantive differences between Section 1237 and existing law.

The existing law requires that a foundation be laid for the admission of such evidence by showing (1) that the writing recording the statement was made by the witness or under his direction, (2) that the writing was made at the time when the fact recorded in the writing actually occurred or at another time when the fact was fresh in the witness' memory, and (3) that the witness "knew that the same was correctly stated in the writing." Under Section 1237, however, the writing may be made not only by the witness himself or under his direction but also by some other person for the purpose of recording the witness' statement at the time it was made. In addition, Section 1237 permits testimony of the person who recorded the statement to be used to establish that the writing is a correct record of the statement. Sufficient assurance of the trustworthiness of the statement is provided if the declarant is available to testify that he made a true statement and if the person who recorded the statement is available to testify that he accurately recorded the statement.

Under subdivision (b), as under existing law, the statement is read into evidence but may not itself be introduced in evidence by its proponent. *See Anderson v. Souza*, 38 Cal.2d 825, 243 P.2d 497 (1952). The adverse party, however, may introduce the writing as evidence. *Cf. Horowitz v. Fitch*, 216 Cal.App.2d 303, 30 Cal.Rptr. 882 (1963) (dictum).

ANNOTATIONS

In re Berman (1989) 48 Cal.3d 517, 525 n.5. See annotation under Evidence Code §771, p. 1267.

§1238. [EXCEPTION: PRIOR IDENTIFICATION]

Evidence of a statement previously made by a witness is not made inadmissible by the hearsay rule if the statement would have been admissible if made by him while testifying and:

(a) [Identification.] The statement is an identification of a party or another as a person who participated in a crime or other occurrence;

(b) [Fresh in memory.] The statement was made at a time when the crime or other occurrence was fresh in the witness' memory; and

(c) [Offer of evidence.] The evidence of the statement is offered after the witness testifies that he made the identification and that it was a true reflection of his opinion at that time.

History of Evid. C. §1238: Added eff. Sept. 17, 1965, oper. Jan. 1, 1967, Stats. 1965, ch. 299, §2.

Official Comment

7 Cal. Law Revision Comm'n Rep. (1965) p. 1232.

Under Section 1235, evidence of a prior identification is admissible if the witness denies having made the prior identification or in any other way testifies inconsistently with the prior statement. Under Section 1238, evidence of a prior identification is admissible if the witness admits the prior identification and vouches for its accuracy.

Sections 1235 and 1238 codify exceptions to the hearsay rule similar to that which was recognized in *People v. Gould*, 54 Cal.2d 621, 7 Cal.Rptr. 273, 354 P.2d 865 (1960). In the *Gould* case, evidence of a prior identification made by a witness who could not repeat the identification at the trial was held admissible "because the earlier identification has greater probative value than an identification made in the courtroom after the suggestions of others and the circumstances of the trial may have intervened to create a fancied recognition in the witness' mind. [Citations omitted.] The failure of the witness to repeat the extrajudicial identification in court does not destroy its probative value, for such failure may be explained by loss of memory or other circumstances. [Moreover,] the principal danger of admitting hearsay evidence is not present since the witness is available at the trial for cross-examination." 54 Cal.2d at 626, 7 Cal.Rptr. at 275, 354 P.2d at 867.

As there was no discussion in the *Gould* opinion of the preliminary showing necessary to warrant admission of evidence of a prior identification, it cannot be determined whether Sections 1235 and 1238 modify the law as declared in that case.

Sections 1235 and 1238 deal only with the admissibility of evidence; they do not determine what constitutes evidence sufficient to sustain a verdict or finding. Hence, these sections have no effect on the holding of the *Gould* case that evidence of an extrajudicial identification that cannot be confirmed by an identification at the trial is insufficient to sustain a criminal conviction in the absence of other evidence tending to connect the defendant with the crime.

ARTICLE 4. SPONTANEOUS, CONTEMPORANEOUS, & DYING DECLARATIONS

§1240. [EXCEPTION: SPONTANEOUS STATEMENT]

Evidence of a statement is not made inadmissible by the hearsay rule if the statement:

(a) Purports to narrate, describe, or explain an act, condition, or event perceived by the declarant; and

(b) Was made spontaneously while the declarant was under the stress of excitement caused by such perception.

History of Evid. C. §1240: Added eff. Sept. 17, 1965, oper. Jan. 1, 1967, Stats. 1965, ch. 299, §2.

Official Comment

7 Cal. Law Revision Comm'n Rep. (1965) p. 1233.

Section 1240 is a codification of the existing exception to the hearsay rule for statements made spontaneously under the stress of excitement engendered by the event to which they relate. *Showalter v. Western Pacific R.R.*, 16 Cal.2d 460, 106 P.2d 895 (1940). *See Tentative Recommendation and a Study Relating to the Uniform Rules of Evidence (Article VIII. Hearsay Evidence)*, 6 Cal. Law Revision Comm'n, Rep., Rec. & Studies *Appendix* at 465-466 (1964). The rationale of this exception is that the spontaneity of such statements and the consequent lack of opportunity for reflection and deliberate fabrication provide an adequate guarantee of their trustworthiness.

ANNOTATIONS

People v. Merriman (2014) 60 Cal.4th 1, 64. The "statements in question were admitted, for the truth of the matters asserted, under the spontaneous statement exception to the hearsay rule. The admissibility requirements for such out-of-court statements are well established. (1) There must be some occurrence startling enough to produce this nervous excitement and render the utterance spontaneous and unreflecting; (2) the utterance must have been before there has been time to contrive and misrepresent, i.e., while the nervous excitement may be supposed still to dominate and the reflective powers to be yet in abeyance; and (3) the utterance must relate to the circumstance of the occurrence preceding it. A statement meeting these requirements is considered trustworthy, and admissible at trial despite its hearsay character, because in the stress of nervous excitement, the reflective faculties may be stilled and the utterance may become the instinctive and uninhibited expression of the speaker's actual impressions and belief. [¶] A number of factors may inform the court's inquiry as to whether the statement in question was made while the declarant was still under the stress and excitement of the startling event and before there was time to contrive and misrepresent. Such factors include the passage of time between the startling event and the statement, whether the declarant blurted out the statement or made it in response to questioning, the declarant's emotional state and physical condition at the time of making the statement, and whether the content of the statement suggested an opportunity for reflection and fabrication. [T]hese factors may be important, but solely as an indicator of the mental state of the declarant. For this reason, no one factor or combination of factors is dispositive. *At 65:* Whether an out-of-court statement meets the statutory requirements for admission as a spontaneous statement is generally a question of fact for the trial court, the determination of which involves an exercise of the court's discretion. We will uphold the trial court's determination of facts when they are supported by substantial evidence and review for abuse of discretion its decision to admit evidence under the spontaneous statement exception." (Internal quotes omitted.)

See also **People v. Bryant** (2014) 60 Cal.4th 335, 415-16, *cert. filed*, ___ S.Ct. ___ (2014) (No. 14-7386; 11-24-14); **People v. Clark** (2011) 52 Cal.4th 856, 925-26.

§1241. [EXCEPTION: CONTEMPORANEOUS STATEMENT]

Evidence of a statement is not made inadmissible by the hearsay rule if the statement:

(a) Is offered to explain, qualify, or make understandable conduct of the declarant; and

(b) Was made while the declarant was engaged in such conduct.

History of Evid. C. §1241: Added eff. Sept. 17, 1965, oper. Jan. 1, 1967, Stats. 1965, ch. 299, §2.

Official Comment

7 Cal. Law Revision Comm'n Rep. (1965) p. 1233; Assem. J., Apr. 6, 1965, p. 1758.

Under existing law, where a person's conduct or act is relevant but is equivocal or ambiguous, the statements accompanying it may be admitted to explain and make the conduct or act understandable. Code Civ. Proc. §1850 (repealed, now Evidence Code §1241); Witkin, *California Evidence* §216 (1958). Some writers do not regard evidence of this sort as hearsay evidence, but the definition in Section 1200 seems applicable to many of the statements received under this exception. *Cf.* 6 Wigmore, *Evidence* §1772 *et seq.* (1940). Section 1241 removes any doubt that might otherwise exist concerning the admissibility of such evidence under the hearsay rule.

§1242. [EXCEPTION: DYING DECLARATION]

Evidence of a statement made by a dying person respecting the cause and circumstances of his death is not made inadmissible by the hearsay rule if the statement was made upon his personal knowledge and under a sense of immediately impending death.

History of Evid. C. §1242: Added eff. Sept. 17, 1965, oper. Jan. 1, 1967, Stats. 1965, ch. 299, §2.

Official Comment

7 Cal. Law Revision Comm'n Rep. (1965) p. 1234.

Section 1242 is a broadened form of the well-established exception to the hearsay rule for dying declarations relating to the cause and circumstances of the declarant's death. The existing law—Code of Civil Procedure Section 1870(4) as interpreted by the courts—makes such declarations admissible only in criminal homicide actions. *People v. Hall*, 94 Cal. 595, 30 Pac. 7 (1892); *Thrasher v. Board of Medical Examiners*, 44 Cal.App. 26, 185 Pac. 1006 (1919). For the purpose of the *admissibility* of dying declarations, there is no rational basis for differentiating between civil and criminal actions or among various types of criminal actions. Hence, Section 1242 makes the exception applicable in all actions.

Under Section 1242, as under existing law, the dying declaration is admissible only if the declarant made the statement on personal knowledge. *People v. Wasson*, 65 Cal. 538, 4 Pac. 555 (1884); *People v. Taylor*, 59 Cal. 640 (1881).

ANNOTATIONS

People v. Monterroso (2004) 34 Cal.4th 743, 763. "A dying declaration constitutes an exception to the hearsay rule [under §1242] if the statement was made on personal knowledge … and under a sense of immediately impending death. This sense of impending death may be shown in any satisfactory mode, by the express language of the declarant, or be inspired from his evident danger, or the opinions of medical or other attendants stated to him, or from his conduct, or other circumstances in the case, all of which are resorted to in order to ascertain the state of the declarant's mind." (Internal quotes omitted.) *See also* **People v. Mayo** (2d Dist.2006) 140 Cal.App.4th 535, 553.

Kincaid v. Kincaid (2d Dist.2011) 197 Cal.App.4th 75, 87-88. "Although California courts have not resolved this issue, other courts have ruled that suicide declarations are not covered by their jurisdictions' respective dying declaration exceptions. Those courts have held that a statement made prior to the commission of suicide is not made in the face of impending death because the declarant controls if and when he or she is to die."

ARTICLE 5. STATEMENTS OF MENTAL OR PHYSICAL STATE

§1250. [EXCEPTION: STATE OF MIND]

(a) [Existing state of mind.] Subject to Section 1252, evidence of a statement of the declarant's then existing state of mind, emotion, or physical sensation (including a statement of intent, plan, motive, design, mental feeling, pain, or bodily health) is not made inadmissible by the hearsay rule when:

(1) The evidence is offered to prove the declarant's state of mind, emotion, or physical sensation at that time or at any other time when it is itself an issue in the action; or

(2) The evidence is offered to prove or explain acts or conduct of the declarant.

(b) [Memory or belief.] This section does not make admissible evidence of a statement of memory or belief to prove the fact remembered or believed.

History of Evid. C. §1250: Added eff. Sept. 17, 1965, oper. Jan. 1, 1967, Stats. 1965, ch. 299, §2.

Official Comment

7 Cal. Law Revision Comm'n Rep. (1965) p. 1234; Assem. J., Apr. 6, 1965, p. 1758.

Section 1250 provides an exception to the hearsay rule for statements of the declarant's *then* existing mental or physical state. Under Section 1250, as under existing law, a statement of the declarant's state of mind at the time of the statement is admissible when the then existing state of mind is itself an issue in the case. *Adkins v. Brett*, 184 Cal. 252, 193 Pac. 251 (1920). A statement of the declarant's then existing state of mind is also admissible when relevant to show the declarant's state of mind at a time prior or subsequent to the statement. *Watenpaugh v. State Teachers' Retirement System*, 51 Cal.2d 675, 336 P.2d 165 (1959); *Whitlow v. Durst*, 20 Cal.2d 523, 127 P.2d 530 (1942); *Estate of Anderson*, 185 Cal. 700, 198 Pac. 407 (1921); *Williams v. Kidd*, 170 Cal. 631, 151 Pac. 1 (1915). Section 1250 also makes a statement of then existing state of

mind admissible to "prove or explain acts or conduct of the declarant." Thus, a statement of the declarant's intent to do certain acts is admissible to prove that he did those acts. *People v. Alcalde*, 24 Cal.2d 177, 148 P.2d 627 (1944); *Benjamin v. District Grand Lodge No. 4*, 171 Cal. 260, 152 Pac. 731 (1915). Statements of then existing pain or other bodily condition also are admissible to prove the existence of such condition. *Bloomberg v. Laventhal*, 179 Cal. 616, 178 Pac. 496 (1919); *People v. Wright*, 167 Cal. 1, 138 Pac. 349 (1914).

A statement is not admissible under Section 1250 if the statement was made under circumstances indicating that the statement is not trustworthy. *See* Evidence Code §1252 and the *Comment* thereto.

In light of the definition of "hearsay evidence" in Section 1200, a distinction should be noted between the use of a declarant's statements of his then existing mental state to prove such mental state and the use of a declarant's statements of other facts as circumstantial evidence of his mental state. Under the Evidence Code, no hearsay problem is involved if the declarant's statements are not being used to prove the truth of their contents but are being used as circumstantial evidence of the declarant's mental state. *See* the *Comment* to Section 1200.

Section 1250(b) does not permit a statement of memory or belief to be used to prove the fact remembered or believed. This limitation is necessary to preserve the hearsay rule. Any statement of a past event is, of course, a statement of the declarant's then existing state of mind—his memory or belief—concerning the past event. If the evidence of that state of mind—the statement of memory—were admissible to show that the fact remembered or believed actually occurred, any statement narrating a past event would be, by a process of circuitous reasoning, admissible to prove that the event occurred.

The limitation in Section 1250(b) is generally in accord with the law developed in the California cases. Thus, in *Estate of Anderson*, 185 Cal. 700, 198 Pac. 407 (1921), a testatrix, after the execution of a will, declared, in effect, that the will had been made at an aunt's request; this statement was held to be inadmissible hearsay "because it was merely a declaration as to a past event and was not indicative of the condition of mind of the testatrix at the time she made it." 185 Cal. at 720, 198 Pac. at 415 (1921).

§1250

A major exception to the principle expressed in Section 1250(b) was created in *People v. Merkouris*, 52 Cal.2d 672, 344 P.2d 1 (1959). That case held that certain murder victims' statements relating threats by the defendant were admissible to show the victims' mental state—their fear of the defendant. Their fear was not itself an issue in the case, but the court held that the fear was relevant to show that the defendant had engaged in conduct engendering the fear, *i.e.*, that the defendant had in fact threatened them. That the defendant had threatened them was, of course, relevant to show that the threats were carried out in the homicide. Thus, in effect, the court permitted the statements to be used to prove the truth of the matters stated in them. In *People v. Purvis*, 56 Cal.2d 93, 13 Cal.Rptr. 801, 362 P.2d 713 (1961), the doctrine of the *Merkouris* case was limited to cases where identity is an issue; however, at least one subsequent decision has applied the doctrine where identity was not in issue. *See People v. Cooley*, 211 Cal.App.2d 173, 27 Cal.Rptr. 543 (1962).

The doctrine of the *Merkouris* case is repudiated in Section 1250(b) because that doctrine undermines the hearsay rule itself. Other exceptions to the hearsay rule are based on some indicia of reliability peculiar to the evidence involved. *People v. Brust*, 47 Cal.2d 776, 785, 306 P.2d 480, 484 (1957). The exception created by *Merkouris* is not based on any probability of reliability; it is based on a rationale that destroys the very foundation of the hearsay rule.

To be distinguished from the *Merkouris* decision, however, are certain other cases in which the statements of a murder victim were used to prove or explain subsequent acts of the *decedent*, and not as a basis for inferring that the defendant did the acts charged in the statements. *See, e.g.*, *People v. Atchley*, 53 Cal.2d 160, 172, 346 P.2d 764, 770 (1959); *People v. Finch*, 213 Cal.App.2d 752, 765, 29 Cal.Rptr. 420, 427 (1963). Statements of a decedent's then existing fear—*i.e.*, his state of mind—may be offered under Section 1250, as under existing law, either to prove that fear when it is itself in issue or to prove or explain the decedent's subsequent conduct. Statements of a decedent narrating threats or brutal conduct by some other person may also be used as circumstantial evidence of the decedent's fear—his state of mind—when that fear is itself in issue or when it is relevant to prove or explain the decedent's subsequent conduct; and, for that purpose, the evidence is not subject to a hearsay objection because it is not offered to prove the truth of the matter stated. *See* the *Comment* to Section 1200. *See also* the *Comment* to Section 1252. But when such evidence is used as a basis for inferring that the alleged threatener must have made threats, the evidence falls within the language of Section 1250(b) and is inadmissible hearsay evidence.

§1251. [EXCEPTION: PAST STATE OF MIND]

Subject to Section 1252, evidence of a statement of the declarant's state of mind, emotion, or physical sensation (including a statement of intent, plan, motive, design, mental feeling, pain, or bodily health) at a time prior to the statement is not made inadmissible by the hearsay rule if:

(a) [Declarant unavailable.] The declarant is unavailable as a witness; and

(b) [Issue in the action.] The evidence is offered to prove such prior state of mind, emotion, or physical sensation when it is itself an issue in the action and the evidence is not offered to prove any fact other than such state of mind, emotion, or physical sensation.

History of Evid. C. §1251: Added eff. Sept. 17, 1965, oper. Jan. 1, 1967, Stats. 1965, ch. 299, §2.

Official Comment

7 Cal. Law Revision Comm'n Rep. (1965) p. 1237.

Section 1250 forbids the use of a statement of memory or belief to prove the fact remembered or believed. Section 1251, however, permits a statement of memory or belief of a past mental or physical state to be used to prove the previous mental or physical state when the previous mental or physical state is itself an issue in the case. If the past mental or physical state is to be used merely as circumstantial evidence of some other fact, the limitation in Section 1250 still applies and the statement of the past mental state is inadmissible hearsay.

The rule stated in Section 1251 is consistent with the California case law to the extent that it permits a statement of a prior mental state to be used as evidence of that mental state. *See, e.g.*, *People v. One 1948 Chevrolet Conv. Coupe*, 45 Cal.2d 613, 290 P.2d 538 (1955) (statement of prior knowledge admitted to prove such knowledge); *Kelly v. Bank of America*, 112 Cal.App.2d 388, 246 P.2d 92 (1952) (statement of previous intent to retain title admitted to prove such intent). However, the California cases have held that statements of previous bodily conditions and symptoms are inadmissible to prove the existence of such conditions or symptoms, although they may be admitted as a basis for an expert's opinion. *People v. Brown*, 49 Cal.2d 577, 320 P.2d 5 (1958); *Willoughby v. Zylstra*, 5 Cal.App.2d 297, 42 P.2d 685 (1935). Section 1251 eliminates the distinction between statements of previous mental conditions and statements of previous physical sensations; it permits both to be admitted as evidence of the matters stated. Both kinds of statements are equally subjective, and there is no reason to believe that one kind is more unreliable than the other.

Section 1251 requires that the declarant be unavailable as a witness. Some California cases seem to indicate that the unavailability of the declarant is a necessary condition for the admission of his statements to prove a previous state of mind. *See, e.g.*, *Whitlow v. Durst*, 20 Cal.2d 523, 524, 127 P.2d 530, 531 (1942) ("declarations of a *decedent*" admissible to show previous mental state); *Kelly v. Bank of America*, 112 Cal.App.2d 388, 246 P.2d 92 (1952). But other cases have admitted such statements without insisting on the declarant's unavailability. *People v. One 1948 Chevrolet Conv. Coupe*, 45 Cal.2d 613, 290 P.2d 538 (1955). Section 1251 requires a showing of the declarant's unavailability because the statements involved are narrations of past conditions. There is, therefore, a greater opportunity for the declarant to remember inaccurately or even to fabricate. Hence, Section 1251 permits such statements to be admitted only when the declarant's unavailability necessitates reliance upon his out-of-court statements.

A statement is not admissible under Section 1251 if the statement was made under circumstances indicating that the statement is not trustworthy. *See* Evidence Code §1252 and the *Comment* thereto.

§1252. [UNTRUSTWORTHY STATE-OF-MIND STATEMENT]

Evidence of a statement is inadmissible under this article if the statement was made under circumstances such as to indicate its lack of trustworthiness.

History of Evid. C. §1252: Added eff. Sept. 17, 1965, oper. Jan. 1, 1967, Stats. 1965, ch. 299, §2.

Official Comment

7 Cal. Law Revision Comm'n Rep. (1965) p. 1238.

Section 1252 limits the admissibility of hearsay statements that would otherwise be admissible under Sections 1250 and 1251. If a statement of mental or physical state was made with a motive to misrepresent or to manufacture evidence, the statement is not sufficiently reliable to warrant its reception in evidence. The limitation expressed in Section 1252 has been held to be a condition of admissibility in some of the California cases. *See, e.g., People v. Hamilton*, 55 Cal.2d 881, 893, 895, 13 Cal.Rptr. 649, 656, 657, 362 P.2d 473, 480, 481 (1961); *People v. Alcalde*, 24 Cal.2d 177, 187, 148 P.2d 627, 632 (1944).

The *Hamilton* case mentions some additional limitations on the admissibility of statements offered in a criminal action to prove the declarant's mental state. These additional limitations do not appear in the Evidence Code. In the *Hamilton* case, the court was concerned with a murder victim's statements that she was afraid of the accused, that the accused had threatened to kill her, and that the accused had beaten her. The statements were ostensibly offered to prove that the victim feared the accused and, therefore, to cast doubt on the accused's testimony that the victim had invited him to her house on the night of the murder. As the case was tried, however, the victim's declarations were used repeatedly in argument as a basis for the prosecution's claim that the beatings actually occurred, that the threats were actually made, and that the threats were carried out in the murder.

The court said that "testimony as to the 'state of mind' of the declarant ... is admissible, but only when such testimony refers to threats as to future conduct on the part of the accused ... and when [such declarations] show primarily the then state of mind of the declarant and not the state of mind of the accused. But ... such testimony is not admissible if it refers solely to alleged past conduct on the part of the accused." 55 Cal.2d at 893-894, 13 Cal.Rptr. at 656, 362 P.2d at 480.

These additional limitations on the admissibility of state of mind evidence are not mentioned in the Evidence Code for two reasons. *First*, they are confusing and contradictory: The declarations are inadmissible if they refer to past conduct of the accused; nevertheless, they are admissible "only" when they refer to his past conduct, *i.e.*, his threats. The declarations, to be admissible, must show primarily the state of mind of the declarant and not the state of mind of the accused; nevertheless, such declarations are admissible "only" if they refer to the accused's statements of his state of mind, *i.e.*, his intent to do future harm to the victim.

Second, these additional limitations are unnecessary. Section 1200 makes it clear that statements of past events cannot be used to prove those events unless they fall within an exception to the hearsay rule; and Sections 1250 and 1251 make it clear that statements of a declarant's past state of mind may be used to prove only that state of mind and no other fact. The real problem in the *Hamilton* case was the fact that much of the evidence was offered ostensibly not as hearsay but as circumstantial evidence of the victim's fear (*see* Section 1200 and the *Comment* thereto); but the prosecution endeavored nevertheless to have the jury consider the evidence as hearsay evidence, *i.e.*, as evidence that the events related actually occurred. Evidence Code Section 352 provides the judge with ample power to exclude evidence of this sort where its prejudicial effect outweighs its probative value. But, under Section 352, the judge must weigh the need for the evidence against the danger of its misuse in each case. The Evidence Code does not freeze the courts to the arbitrary and contradictory standards mentioned in the *Hamilton* case for determining when prejudicial effect outweighs probative value.

§1253. [EXCEPTION: MEDICAL DIAGNOSIS OR TREATMENT OF CHILD-ABUSE VICTIM]

Subject to Section 1252, evidence of a statement is not made inadmissible by the hearsay rule if the statement was made for purposes of medical diagnosis or treatment and describes medical history, or past or present symptoms, pain, or sensations, or the inception or general character of the cause or external source thereof insofar as reasonably pertinent to diagnosis or treatment. This section applies only to a statement made by a victim who is a minor at the time of the proceedings, provided the statement was made when the victim was under the age of 12 describing any act, or attempted act, of child abuse or neglect. "Child abuse" and "child neglect," for purposes of this section, have the meanings provided in subdivision (c) of Section 1360. In addition, "child abuse" means any act proscribed by Chapter 5 (commencing with Section 281) of Title 9 of Part 1 of the Penal Code committed against a minor.

History of Evid. C. §1253: Added eff. Jan. 1, 1996, Stats. 1995, ch. 87, §2.

ARTICLE 6. STATEMENTS RELATING TO WILLS & TO CLAIMS AGAINST ESTATES

§1260. [STATEMENTS RELATING TO WILL]

(a) [Statements regarding will.] Except as provided in subdivision (b), evidence of any of the following statements made by a declarant who is unavailable as a witness is not made inadmissible by the hearsay rule:

(1) That the declarant has or has not made a will or established or amended a revocable trust.

(2) That the declarant has or has not revoked his or her will, revocable trust, or an amendment to a revocable trust.

(3) That identifies the declarant's will, revocable trust, or an amendment to a revocable trust.

(b) [Untrustworthy.] Evidence of a statement is inadmissible under this section if the statement was made under circumstances that indicate its lack of trustworthiness.

History of Evid. C. §1260: Added eff. Sept. 17, 1965, oper. Jan. 1, 1967, Stats. 1965, ch. 299, §2. Amended eff. Jan. 1, 2011, Stats. 2010, ch. 106, §1.

Official Comment

7 Cal. Law Revision Comm'n Rep. (1965) p. 1239.

Section 1260 codifies an exception recognized in California case law. *Estate of Morrison*, 198 Cal. 1, 242 Pac. 939 (1926); *Estate of Thompson*, 44 Cal.App.2d 774, 112 P.2d 937 (1941). The section is, of course, subject to the provisions of Probate Code Sections 350 and 351 which relate to the establishment of a lost or destroyed will.

The limitation in subdivision (b) is not mentioned in the few court decisions involving this exception. The limitation is desirable, however, to assure the reliability of the hearsay that is admissible under this section.

§1261. [EXCEPTION: ACTION AGAINST ESTATE]

(a) [Personal knowledge.] Evidence of a statement is not made inadmissible by the hearsay rule when offered in an action upon a claim or demand against the estate of the declarant if the statement was made upon the personal knowledge of the declarant at a time when the matter had been recently perceived by him and while his recollection was clear.

(b) [Untrustworthy.] Evidence of a statement is inadmissible under this section if the statement was made under circumstances such as to indicate its lack of trustworthiness.

History of Evid. C. §1261: Added eff. Sept. 17, 1965, oper. Jan. 1, 1967, Stats. 1965, ch. 299, §2.

Official Comment

7 Cal. Law Revision Comm'n Rep. (1965) p. 1240.

The dead man statute (subdivision 3 of Section 1880 of the Code of Civil Procedure) prohibits a party who sues on a claim against a decedent's estate from testifying to any fact occurring prior to the decedent's death. The theory apparently underlying the statute is that it would be unfair to permit the surviving claimant to testify to such facts when the decedent is precluded by his death from doing so. To balance the positions of the parties, the living may not speak because the dead cannot.

The dead man statute operates unsatisfactorily. It prohibits testimony concerning matters of which the decedent had no knowledge and, hence, to which he could not have testified even if he had survived. It operates unevenly since it does not prohibit testimony relating to claims *under*, as distinguished from claims *against*, the decedent's estate even though the effect of such a claim may be to frustrate the decedent's plan for the disposition of his property. See the Law Revision Commission's *Comment* to Code of Civil Procedure Section 1880 and 1 Cal. Law Revision Comm'n, Rep., Rec. & Studies, *Recommendation and Study Relating to the Dead Man Statute* at D-1 (1957). The dead man statute excludes otherwise relevant and competent evidence—even if it is the only available evidence—and frequently this forces the courts to decide cases with a minimum of information concerning the actual facts. See the Supreme Court's complaint in *Light v. Stevens*, 159 Cal. 288, 292, 113 Pac. 659, 660 (1911) ("Owing to the fact that the lips of one of the parties to the transaction are closed by death and those of the other party by the law, the evidence on this question is somewhat unsatisfactory."). Hence, the dead man statute is not continued in the Evidence Code.

Under the Evidence Code, the positions of the parties are balanced by throwing more light, not less, on the actual facts. Repeal of the dead man statute permits the claimant to testify without restriction. To balance this advantage, Section 1261 permits hearsay evidence of the decedent's statements to be admitted. Certain safeguards—*i.e.*, personal knowledge, recent perception, and circumstantial evidence of trustworthiness—are included in the section to provide some protection for the party against whom the statements are offered, for he has no opportunity to test the hearsay by cross-examination.

ANNOTATIONS

In re Estate of Luke (2d Dist.1987) 194 Cal.App.3d 1006, 1017. Declarant's "statement lacks the safeguard that it be made at a time when the matter had recently been perceived by the declarant and while his recollection was clear. [Declarant's] statement describes events which took place over a period of 40 years beginning when [declarant] sold his drug business in 1936. [Declarant's] recollection of how he handled the proceeds of the sale is not the recollection of a *recently perceived event* nor was there any evidence [declarant] had a clear recollection of these events when he wrote the affidavit. Therefore, the court erred in admitting [declarant's] affidavit."

ARTICLE 7. BUSINESS RECORDS

§1270. [BUSINESS]

As used in this article, "a business" includes every kind of business, governmental activity, profession, occupation, calling, or operation of institutions, whether carried on for profit or not.

History of Evid. C. §1270: Added eff. Sept. 17, 1965, oper. Jan. 1, 1967, Stats. 1965, ch. 299, §2.

Official Comment

7 Cal. Law Revision Comm'n Rep. (1965) p. 1241.

This article restates and supersedes the Uniform Business Records as Evidence Act appearing in Sections 1953e through 1953h of the Code of Civil Procedure. The definition of "a business" in Section 1270 is substantially the same as that appearing in Code of Civil Procedure Section 1953e. A reference to "governmental activity" has been added to the Evidence Code definition to codify the decisions in cases holding the Uniform Act applicable to governmental records. *See, e.g.*, *Nichols v. McCoy*, 38 Cal.2d 447, 240 P.2d 569 (1952); *Fox v. San Francisco Unified School Dist.*, 111 Cal.App.2d 885, 245 P.2d 603 (1952).

The definition is sufficiently broad to encompass institutions not customarily thought of as businesses. For example, the baptismal and wedding records of a church would be admissible under the section to prove the events recorded. 5 Wigmore, *Evidence* §1523 (3d ed. 1940). *Cf.* Evidence Code §1315.

§1271. [EXCEPTION: BUSINESS RECORDS]

Evidence of a writing made as a record of an act, condition, or event is not made inadmissible by the hearsay rule when offered to prove the act, condition, or event if:

(a) [Regular course.] The writing was made in the regular course of a business;

(b) [At or near time.] The writing was made at or near the time of the act, condition, or event;

(c) [Identity and preparation.] The custodian or other qualified witness testifies to its identity and the mode of its preparation; and

(d) [Trustworthy.] The sources of information and method and time of preparation were such as to indicate its trustworthiness.

History of Evid. C. §1271: Added eff. Sept. 17, 1965, oper. Jan. 1, 1967, Stats. 1965, ch. 299, §2.

Official Comment

7 Cal. Law Revision Comm'n Rep. (1965) p. 1241.

Section 1271 is the business records exception to the hearsay rule. It is stated in language taken from the Uniform Business Records as Evidence Act (Sections 1953e-1953h of the Code of Civil Procedure) and from Rule 63(13) of the Uniform Rules of Evidence.

Section 1271 requires the judge to find that the sources of information and the method and time of preparation of the record "were such as to indicate its trustworthiness." Under the language of Code of Civil Procedure Section 1953f, the judge must determine that the sources of information and method and time

of preparation "were such as to justify its admission." The language of Section 1271 is more accurate, for the cases hold that admission of a business record is not justified when there is no preliminary showing that the record is reliable or trustworthy. *E.g., People v. Grayson*, 172 Cal.App.2d 372, 341 P.2d 820 (1959) (hotel register rejected because "not shown to be true and complete").

"The chief foundation of the special reliability of business records is the requirement that they must be based upon the first-hand observation of someone whose job it is to know the facts recorded. ... But if the evidence in the particular case discloses that the record was not based upon the report of an informant having the business duty to observe and report, then the record is not admissible under this exception, to show the truth of the matter reported to the recorder." McCormick, *Evidence* §286 at 602 (1954), as quoted in *MacLean v. City & County of San Francisco*, 151 Cal.App.2d 133, 143, 311 P.2d 158, 164 (1957).

Applying this standard, the cases have rejected a variety of business records on the ground that they were not based on the personal knowledge of the recorder or of someone with a business duty to report to the recorder. Police accident and arrest reports are usually held inadmissible because they are based on the narrations of persons who have no business duty to report to the police. *MacLean v. City & County of San Francisco*, 151 Cal.App.2d 133, 311 P.2d 158 (1957); *Hoel v. City of Los Angeles*, 136 Cal.App.2d 295, 288 P.2d 989 (1955). They are admissible, however, to prove the fact of the arrest. *Harris v. Alcoholic Bev. Con. Appeals Bd.*, 212 Cal.App.2d 106, 23 Cal.Rptr. 74 (1963). Similar investigative reports on the origin of fires have been held inadmissible because they were not based on personal knowledge. *Behr v. County of Santa Cruz*, 172 Cal.App.2d 697, 342 P.2d 987 (1959); *Harrigan v. Chaperon*, 118 Cal.App.2d 167, 257 P.2d 716 (1953).

Section 1271 will continue the law developed in these cases that a business report is admissible only if the sources of information and the time and method of preparation are such as to indicate its trustworthiness.

ANNOTATIONS

Daniels v. Department of Motor Vehicles (1983) 33 Cal.3d 532, 537-38. "Two of the four requirements of ... §1271 are met in this case. The report was made shortly after the accident, and the fact that the report is made under penalty of perjury and pursuant to a legal duty tends to indicate its trustworthiness. However, [DMV] as custodian, upon receipt of the form, is in no position to testify to its identity and the mode of its preparation. Most significant, though, is the fact that the report is not made in the regular course of business. [¶] [DMV] argues that the report is made in the regular course of business because it is required by law ... and 'it is the regular course of business for [DMV] to receive such reports.' This argument, however, misconstrues the nature of the first requirement of the business records exception. Although it may be the regular course of business for [DMV] to receive the report, it undoubtedly is not in the regular course of business for the citizen author to make such a report. And, it is this aspect of the report that bears on the trustworthiness factor contemplated by this exception to the hearsay rule."

Jazayeri v. Mao (2d Dist.2009) 174 Cal.App.4th 301, 322. "The key to establishing the admissibility of a document made in the regular course of business is proof that the person who wrote the information or provided it had knowledge of the facts from personal observation. [T]he individual with personal knowledge [does not need to] testify; [§1271] permits any qualified witness to establish to the conditions of admissibility. The witness need not have been present at every transaction to establish the business records exception; he or she need only be familiar with the procedures followed...." (Internal quotes omitted.) *See also* ***People v. Sherow*** (4th Dist.2011) 196 Cal.App.4th 1296, 1302.

Garibay v. Hemmat (2d Dist.2008) 161 Cal.App.4th 735, 743. "We realize that although hospital records are hearsay, they can be used as a basis for an expert medical opinion. However, a witness's on-the-record recitation of sources relied on for an expert opinion does not transform inadmissible matter into independent proof of any fact. Although experts may properly rely on hearsay in forming their opinions, they may not relate the out-of-court statements of another as independent proof of the fact. Physicians can testify as to the basis of their opinion, but this is not intended to be a channel by which testifying physicians can place the opinion of out-of-court physicians before the trier of fact. [¶] An expert's opinion based on assumptions of fact without evidentiary support has no evidentiary value." (Internal quotes omitted.)

Aguimatang v. California State Lottery (3d Dist.1991) 234 Cal.App.3d 769, 798. "[D] complains that the computer records were not shown to qualify as business records [under §1271], because they were not made at or near the time of the event. [The computer records] are printed out only on an as needed basis because it would be too cumbersome to store hard copies of each transaction recorded for each draw. However, the information contained on the computer's magnetic tapes, from which the [record] is printed, is recorded daily as it is generated. [¶] [D] cites no authority holding that the retrieval, rather than the entry, of computer data must be made at or near the time of the event. Thus, although to qualify as a business record the 'writing' must be made at or near the time of the event, 'writing' is not limited to the commonly understood forms of writing but is defined very broadly to include all 'means of recording upon any tangible thing any form of communication or representation, including letters, words, pictures, sounds, or symbols, or combinations thereof.' Here, the 'writing' is the magnetic tape. The data entries on the magnetic tapes are made

contemporaneously with the ... transactions, hence qualify as business records."

§1272. [EXCEPTION: ABSENCE OF RECORD]

Evidence of the absence from the records of a business of a record of an asserted act, condition, or event is not made inadmissible by the hearsay rule when offered to prove the nonoccurrence of the act or event, or the nonexistence of the condition, if:

(a) [**Regular course.**] It was the regular course of that business to make records of all such acts, conditions, or events at or near the time of the act, condition, or event and to preserve them; and

(b) [**Trustworthy.**] The sources of information and method and time of preparation of the records of that business were such that the absence of a record of an act, condition, or event is a trustworthy indication that the act or event did not occur or the condition did not exist.

History of Evid. C. §1272: Added eff. Sept. 17, 1965, oper. Jan. 1, 1967, Stats. 1965, ch. 299, §2.

Official Comment

7 Cal. Law Revision Comm'n Rep. (1965) p. 1243.

Technically, evidence of the absence of a record may not be hearsay. Section 1272 removes any doubt that might otherwise exist concerning the admissibility of such evidence under the hearsay rule. It codifies existing case law. *People v. Torres*, 201 Cal.App.2d 290, 20 Cal.Rptr. 315 (1962).

ARTICLE 8. OFFICIAL RECORDS & OTHER OFFICIAL WRITINGS

§1280. [EXCEPTION: RECORD BY PUBLIC EMPLOYEE]

Evidence of a writing made as a record of an act, condition, or event is not made inadmissible by the hearsay rule when offered in any civil or criminal proceeding to prove the act, condition, or event if all of the following applies:

(a) [**Scope of duty.**] The writing was made by and within the scope of duty of a public employee.

(b) [**At or near time.**] The writing was made at or near the time of the act, condition, or event.

(c) [**Trustworthy.**] The sources of information and method and time of preparation were such as to indicate its trustworthiness.

History of Evid. C. §1280: Added eff. Sept. 17, 1965, oper. Jan. 1, 1967, Stats. 1965, ch. 299, §2. Amended eff. Jan. 1, 1997, Stats. 1996, ch. 642, §4.

Official Comment

7 Cal. Law Revision Comm'n Rep. (1965) p. 1243.

Section 1280 restates the substance of and supersedes Sections 1920 and 1926 of the Code of Civil Procedure. Although Sections 1920 and 1926 declare unequivocally that entries in public records are prima facie evidence of the facts stated, "it has been held repeatedly that those sections cannot have universal literal application." *Chandler v. Hibberd*, 165 Cal.App.2d 39, 65, 332 P.2d 133, 149 (1958). In fact, the cases require the same showing of trustworthiness in regard to an official record as is required under the business records exception. *Behr v. County of Santa Cruz*, 172 Cal.App.2d 697, 342 P.2d 987 (1959); *Hoel v. City of Los Angeles*, 136 Cal.App.2d 295, 288 P.2d 989 (1955). Section 1280 continues the law declared in these cases by explicitly requiring the same showing of trustworthiness that is required in Section 1271. *See* the *Comment* to Section 1271.

The evidence that is admissible under this section is also admissible under Section 1271, the business records exception. However, Section 1271 requires a witness to testify as to the identity of the record and its mode of preparation in every instance. In contrast, Section 1280, as does existing law, permits the court to admit an official record or report without necessarily requiring a witness to testify as to its identity and mode of preparation if the court takes judicial notice or if sufficient independent evidence shows that the record or report was prepared in such a manner as to assure its trustworthiness. *See, e.g., People v. Williams*, 64 Cal. 87, 27 Pac. 939 (1883) (census report admitted, the court judicially noticing the statutes prescribing the method of preparing the report); *Vallejo etc. R.R. v. Reed Orchard Co.*, 169 Cal. 545, 571, 147 Pac. 238, 250 (1915) (statistical report of state agency admitted, the court judicially noticing the statutory duty to prepare the report).

ANNOTATIONS

Nevarrez v. San Marino Skilled Nursing & Wellness Ctr., LLC (2d Dist.2013) 221 Cal.App.4th 102, 121. "[P] argues the citation [issued against D by the Department of Public Health (DPH)] is admissible under the official records exception. [¶] [P] argues the trustworthiness of the citation was established by the custodian of records, and the statutory presumption that official duties are properly performed ... shifted the burden to [Ds] to show the DPH investigator failed to accurately observe and record events. [Ds] argue the citation lacks trustworthiness because it was issued a year after the ... incident and was based on the investigator's review of records and statements by [D's] staff. Indeed, with the exception of the investigator's personal observation that [P's] room was 18 to 20 yards away and around a corner from the nurses' station, the citation relies on other sources of information, none of which qualifies for the official duties presumption. Because of that, the citation is not comparable to reports by public officers that are based on observations of other public employees."

Molenda v. Department of Motor Vehicles (6th Dist.2009) 172 Cal.App.4th 974, 989. "How soon a writing must be made after the act or event is a matter of degree and calls for the exercise of reasonable judgment on the part of the trial judge. The timeliness requirement is not to be judged by arbitrary or artificial time limits, measured by hours or days or even weeks. Rather, account must be taken of practical considerations, including the nature of the information recorded and the immutable reliability of the sources from which the information was drawn. Whether an en-

try made subsequent to the transaction has been made within a sufficient time to render it within the hearsay exception depends upon whether the time span between the transaction and the entry was so great as to suggest a danger of inaccuracy by lapse of memory." (Internal quotes omitted.) *See also* ***Hildebrand v. Department of Motor Vehicles*** (4th Dist.2007) 152 Cal.App.4th 1562, 1570.

Christian Research Inst. v. Alnor (4th Dist.2007) 148 Cal.App.4th 71, 83. "[Ps] contend the [Freedom of Information Act (FOIA)] letters and the [Office of the Inspector General (OIG)] report fall within the official records exception to the hearsay rule. [¶] The FOIA letters are authenticated by the declaration of ... an attorney representing [Ps]. [Attorney] declares he received the FOIA letters after submitting a written request under the FOIA for 'any and all investigative records pertaining to [Ps].' The FOIA letters each state they were prepared in response to the FOIA request, and identify the time period searched. Each of the letters is dated shortly after the requests were made, and identify the position of the sender. We conclude the official record exception to the hearsay rule has been met. [¶] The OIG report is more problematic. The report contains information which was not directly observable by the investigator who prepared the report, and the investigator identifies no independent sources. Indeed, some of the information on the report appears to have come directly from [P]. ... Because there is insufficient information to indicate the trustworthiness of the OIG report, we decline to consider it here." *See also* ***Elsworth v. Beech Aircraft Corp.*** (1984) 37 Cal.3d 540, 553.

Bhatt v. State Dept. of Health Servs. (2d Dist.2005) 133 Cal.App.4th 923, 929. "Although similar to the business records exception ..., the official records exception differs in one important respect. [Evid. C.] §1271 requires a witness to testify as to the identity of the record and its mode of preparation in every instance. In contrast, [Evid. C.] §1280 permits the court to admit an official record or report without necessarily requiring a witness to testify as to its identity and mode of preparation *if the court takes judicial notice or if sufficient independent evidence shows that the record or report was prepared in such a manner as to assure its trustworthiness*. The object of this hearsay exception is to eliminate the calling of each witness involved in preparation of the record and substitute the record of the transaction instead. Accordingly, for the exception to apply, it is not necessary that the person making the entry have personal knowledge of the transaction." (Internal quotes omitted.) *See also* ***Gananian v. Zolin*** (1st Dist.1995) (Div. 3) 33 Cal.App.4th 634, 639-40; ***People v. George*** (4th Dist.1994) 30 Cal.App.4th 262, 274. *But see* ***Rupf v. Yan***, below.

Rupf v. Yan (1st Dist.2000) (Div. 2) 85 Cal.App.4th 411, 430 n.6. "There exists ... a split of authority regarding whether hearsay statements contained in an official record are admissible where the public employee making the report ... is not the source of the information, but the information is based upon the observations made by another public employee.... Many courts, including this one, have held such evidence inadmissible. However, more recently, other courts have held that personal knowledge is not necessary so long as the source of the information is trustworthy. At least one treatise has commented that '[t]his latter view seems correct because it follows the reasoning expressed in prior Supreme Court cases.'" *See also* ***Johnson v. Alameda Cty. Med. Ctr.*** (1st Dist.2012) 205 Cal.App.4th 521, 525 n.1 (statements about condition of door lock based upon observation of public employee and party admission on same subject are admissible). *But see* ***Bhatt v. State Dept. of Health Servs.***, above.

Santos v. Department of Motor Vehicles (1st Dist.1992) 5 Cal.App.4th 537, 547-48. "Respondent urges the report does not meet the requirements of the public employee records exception to the hearsay rule because it does not indicate the time it was prepared so as to demonstrate it was made 'at or near the time of the act, condition, or event.' The presumption of duty regularly performed, however, shifts the burden to respondent to show the report was not properly prepared. In the absence of evidence the report was not properly prepared, [DMV] was entitled to rely upon it."

§1281. [EXCEPTION: VITAL RECORDS]

Evidence of a writing made as a record of a birth, fetal death, death, or marriage is not made inadmissible by the hearsay rule if the maker was required by law to file the writing in a designated public office and the writing was made and filed as required by law.

History of Evid. C. §1281: Added eff. Sept. 17, 1965, oper. Jan. 1, 1967, Stats. 1965, ch. 299, §2.

Official Comment

7 Cal. Law Revision Comm'n Rep. (1965) p. 1244.

Section 1281 provides a hearsay exception for official reports concerning birth, death, and marriage. Official reports of such events occurring within

California are now admissible under the provisions of Section 10577 of the Health and Safety Code. Section 1281 provides a broader exception which includes similar reports from other jurisdictions.

§1282. [EXCEPTION: PRESUMED DEATH]

A written finding of presumed death made by an employee of the United States authorized to make such finding pursuant to the Federal Missing Persons Act (56 Stats. 143, 1092, and P.L. 408, Ch. 371, 2d Sess. 78th Cong.; 50 U.S.C. App. 1001-1016), as enacted or as heretofore or hereafter amended, shall be received in any court, office, or other place in this state as evidence of the death of the person therein found to be dead and of the date, circumstances, and place of his disappearance.

History of Evid. C. §1282: Added eff. Sept. 17, 1965, oper. Jan. 1, 1967, Stats. 1965, ch. 299, §2.

Official Comment

7 Cal. Law Revision Comm'n Rep. (1965) p. 1245.

Section 1282 restates and supersedes the provisions of Code of Civil Procedure Section 1928.1. The evidence made admissible under Section 1282 is limited to evidence of the fact of death and of the date, circumstances, and place of disappearance.

The determination by the federal employee of the *date* of the presumed death is a determination ordinarily made for the purpose of determining whether the pay of a missing person should be stopped and his name stricken from the payroll. The date so determined should not be given any consideration in the California courts since the issues involved in the California proceedings require determination of the date of death for a different purpose. Hence, Section 1282 does not make admissible the finding of the *date* of presumed death. On the other hand, the determination of the date, circumstances, and place of *disappearance* is reliable information that will assist the trier of fact in determining the date when the person died and is admissible under this section. Often the date of death may be inferred from the circumstances of the disappearance. *See In re Thornburg's Estate*, 186 Ore. 570, 208 P.2d 349 (1949); *Lukens v. Camden Trust Co.*, 2 N.J. Super. 214, 62 A.2d 886 (Super. Ct. 1948).

Section 1282 provides a convenient and reliable method of proof of death of persons covered by the Federal Missing Persons Act. *See, e.g.*, *In re Jacobsen's Estate*, 208 Misc. 443, 143 N.Y.S.2d 432 (1955) (proof of death of 2-year-old dependent of serviceman where child was passenger on plane lost at sea).

§1283. [EXCEPTION: OFFICIAL REPORT OF MISSING PERSON OR PRISONER]

An official written report or record that a person is missing, missing in action, interned in a foreign country, captured by a hostile force, beleaguered by a hostile force, besieged by a hostile force, or detained in a foreign country against his will, or is dead or is alive, made by an employee of the United States authorized by any law of the United States to make such report or record shall be received in any court, office, or other place in this state as evidence that such person is missing, missing in action, interned in a foreign country, captured by a hostile force, beleaguered by a hostile force, besieged by a hostile force, or detained in a foreign country against his will, or is dead or is alive.

History of Evid. C. §1283: Added eff. Sept. 17, 1965, oper. Jan. 1, 1967, Stats. 1965, ch. 299, §2.

Official Comment

7 Cal. Law Revision Comm'n Rep. (1965) p. 1246.

Section 1283 restates and supersedes the provisions of Code of Civil Procedure Section 1928.2. The language of Section 1928.2 has been revised to reflect the 1953 and 1964 amendments to the Federal Missing Persons Act.

§1284. [EXCEPTION: ABSENCE OF PUBLIC RECORD]

Evidence of a writing made by the public employee who is the official custodian of the records in a public office, reciting diligent search and failure to find a record, is not made inadmissible by the hearsay rule when offered to prove the absence of a record in that office.

History of Evid. C. §1284: Added eff. Sept. 17, 1965, oper. Jan. 1, 1967, Stats. 1965, ch. 299, §2.

Official Comment

7 Cal. Law Revision Comm'n Rep. (1965) p. 1246;
Assem. J., Apr. 6, 1965, p. 1760.

Just as the existence and content of a public record may be proved under Section 1530 by a copy accompanied by the attestation or certificate of the custodian reciting that it is a copy, the absence of such a record from a particular public office may be proved under Section 1284 by a writing made by the custodian of the records in that office stating that no such record was found after a diligent search. The writing must, of course, be properly authenticated. *See* Evidence Code §§1401, 1453. *See also* Code Civ. Proc. §1893 (public official, on demand, must furnish certificate or its equivalent that he did not find a designated writing after a diligent search). The exception is justified by the likelihood that such a statement made by the custodian of the records is accurate and by the necessity for providing a simple and inexpensive method of proving the absence of a public record.

ARTICLE 9. FORMER TESTIMONY

§1290. [FORMER TESTIMONY]

As used in this article, "former testimony" means testimony given under oath in:

(a) [Another action or hearing.] Another action or in a former hearing or trial of the same action;

(b) [U.S. agency.] A proceeding to determine a controversy conducted by or under the supervision of an agency that has the power to determine such a controversy and is an agency of the United States or a public entity in the United States;

(c) [Deposition.] A deposition taken in compliance with law in another action; or

(d) [Arbitration.] An arbitration proceeding if the evidence of such former testimony is a verbatim transcript thereof.

History of Evid. C. §1290: Added eff. Sept. 17, 1965, oper. Jan. 1, 1967, Stats. 1965, ch. 299, §2.

Official Comment

7 Cal. Law Revision Comm'n Rep. (1965) p. 1247.

The purpose of Section 1290 is to provide a convenient term for use in the substantive provisions in the remainder of this article. It should be noted that

depositions taken in *another* action are considered former testimony under Section 1290, and their admissibility is determined by Sections 1291 and 1292. The use of a deposition taken in the same action, however, is not covered by this article. Code of Civil Procedure Sections 2016-2036 deal comprehensively with the conditions and circumstances under which a deposition taken in a civil action may be used at the trial of the action in which the deposition was taken, and Penal Code Sections 1345 and 1362 prescribe the conditions for admitting the deposition of a witness that has been taken, in the same criminal action. these sections will continue to govern the use of depositions in the action in which they are taken.

ANNOTATIONS

N.N.V. v. American Ass'n of Blood Banks (4th Dist.1999) 75 Cal.App.4th 1358, 1396-97. "The former testimony exception requires there must have existed at the deposition the same or similar motive and opportunity for cross-examination of the deponent. [P] argues the counsel for [hospital-Ds] who were present at the deposition had a similar motive as to [nurse-D], and [P] asserts '... it is clear that the examination of [P's father] covered matters which [nurse-D] would have covered.' We disagree. Since [nurse-D] was not an employee of any of [hospital-Ds] who were present at the deposition, none of [hospital-Ds] had any motive to question [P's father] as to the reliability and credibility of his identification of [nurse-D] as the nurse with whom he and [P's mother] spoke. If anything, [hospital-Ds] would have had an interest adverse to [nurse-D's], i.e., an interest in establishing that if any nurse failed to communicate a request for directed donation, that nurse was [nurse-D] and not one of the [nurses] employed by the hospitals. Under these circumstances, the court properly rejected admission of [P's father's] deposition in the trial against [nurse-D]."

§1291. [EXCEPTION: FORMER TESTIMONY BY PARTY IN PRIOR PROCEEDING]

(a) [**Admissibility.**] Evidence of former testimony is not made inadmissible by the hearsay rule if the declarant is unavailable as a witness and:

(1) The former testimony is offered against a person who offered it in evidence in his own behalf on the former occasion or against the successor in interest of such person; or

(2) The party against whom the former testimony is offered was a party to the action or proceeding in which the testimony was given and had the right and opportunity to cross-examine the declarant with an interest and motive similar to that which he has at the hearing.

(b) [**Objections.**] The admissibility of former testimony under this section is subject to the same limitations and objections as though the declarant were testifying at the hearing, except that former testimony offered under this section is not subject to:

(1) Objections to the form of the question which were not made at the time the former testimony was given.

(2) Objections based on competency or privilege which did not exist at the time the former testimony was given.

History of Evid. C. §1291: Added eff. Sept. 17, 1965, oper. Jan. 1, 1967, Stats. 1965, ch. 299, §2.

Official Comment

7 Cal. Law Revision Comm'n Rep. (1965) p. 1247; Assem. J., Apr. 6, 1965, p. 1760.

Section 1291 provides a hearsay exception for former testimony offered against a person who was a party to the proceeding in which the former testimony was given. For example, if a series of cases arises involving several plaintiffs and but one defendant, Section 1291 permits testimony given in the first trial to be used against the defendant in a later trial if the conditions of admissibility stated in the section are met.

Former testimony is admissible under Section 1291 only if the declarant is unavailable as a witness.

Paragraph (1) of subdivision (a) of Section 1291 provides for the admission of former testimony if it is offered against the party who offered it in the previous proceeding. Since the witness is no longer available to testify, the party's previous direct and redirect examination should be considered an adequate substitute for his present right to cross-examine the declarant.

Paragraph (2) of subdivision (a) of Section 1291 provides for the admissibility of former testimony where the party against whom it is now offered had the right and opportunity in the former proceeding to cross-examine the declarant with an interest and motive similar to that which he now has. Since the party has had his opportunity to cross-examine, the primary objection to hearsay evidence—lack of opportunity to cross-examine the declarant—is not applicable. On the other hand, paragraph (2) does not make the former testimony admissible where the party against whom it is offered did not have a similar interest and motive to cross-examine the declarant. The determination of similarity of interest and motive in cross-examination should be based on practical considerations and not merely on the similarity of the party's position in the two cases. For example, testimony contained in a deposition that was taken, but not offered in evidence at the trial, in a different action should be excluded if the judge determines that the deposition was taken for discovery purposes and that the party did not subject the witness to a thorough cross-examination because he sought to avoid a premature revelation of the weakness in the testimony of the witness or in the adverse party's case. In such a situation, the party's interest and motive for cross-examination on the previous occasion would have been substantially different from his present interest and motive.

Section 1291 supersedes Code of Civil Procedure Section 1870(8) which permits former testimony to be admitted in a civil case only if the former proceeding was an action between the same parties or their predecessors in interest, relating to the same matter, or was a former trial of the action in which the testimony is offered. Section 1291 will also permit a broader range of hearsay to be introduced against the defendant in a criminal action than has been permitted under Penal Code Section 686. Under that section, former testimony has been admissible against the defendant in a criminal action only if the former testimony was given in the same action—at the preliminary examination, in a deposition, or in a prior trial of the action. Likewise, Section 1291 will permit a broader range of hearsay to be introduced against the prosecution in a criminal action since the people of the State of California are a party to all criminal actions. *See* Penal Code §684.

Subdivision (b) of Section 1291 makes it clear that objections based on the competence of the declarant or on privilege are to be determined by reference to the time the former testimony was given. Existing California law is not clear

on this point; some California decisions indicate that competency and privilege are to be determined as of the time the former testimony was given, but others indicate that these matters are to be determined as of the time the former testimony is offered in evidence. *See Tentative Recommendation and a Study Relating to the Uniform Rules of Evidence (Article VIII. Hearsay Evidence)*, 6 Cal. Law Revision Comm'n, Rep., Rec. & Studies *Appendix* at 581-585 (1964).

Subdivision (b) also provides that objections to the form of the question may not be used to exclude the former testimony. Where the former testimony is offered under paragraph (1) of subdivision (a), the party against whom the former testimony is now offered phrased the question himself; and where the former testimony is admitted under paragraph (2) of subdivision (a), the party against whom the testimony is now offered had the opportunity to object to the form of the question when it was asked on the former occasion. Hence, the party is not permitted to raise this technical objection when the former testimony is offered against him.

ANNOTATIONS

Rufo v. Simpson (2d Dist.2001) 86 Cal.App.4th 573, 606. "[T]he official comments draw distinctions between [Evid. C.] §§1291 and 1292. According to the comments, §1291, subdivision (a)(1) allows admission against a party in the present proceeding of prior testimony that the *same party* previously offered *on its own behalf* in the prior proceeding by way of *direct and redirect* examination. Section 1292, subdivision (a) allows admission against a party in the present proceeding, who was not a party to the prior proceeding, of prior testimony that a different party having a similar interest and motive *adverse* to the testimony tested for truthfulness by *cross*-examination."

§1291

People v. King (2d Dist.1969) 269 Cal.App.2d 40, 47. Section 1291 "was intended by the Legislature to apply to criminal as well as civil cases."

§1292. [EXCEPTION: FORMER TESTIMONY IN ANOTHER CASE]

(a) [Admissibility.] Evidence of former testimony is not made inadmissible by the hearsay rule if:

(1) The declarant is unavailable as a witness;

(2) The former testimony is offered in a civil action; and

(3) The issue is such that the party to the action or proceeding in which the former testimony was given had the right and opportunity to cross-examine the declarant with an interest and motive similar to that which the party against whom the testimony is offered has at the hearing.

(b) [Objections.] The admissibility of former testimony under this section is subject to the same limitations and objections as though the declarant were testifying at the hearing, except that former testimony offered under this section is not subject to objections based on competency or privilege which did not exist at the time the former testimony was given.

History of Evid. C. §1292: Added eff. Sept. 17, 1965, oper. Jan. 1, 1967, Stats. 1965, ch. 299, §2.

Official Comment

7 Cal. Law Revision Comm'n Rep. (1965) p. 1249;
Assem. J., Apr. 6, 1965, p. 1762.

Section 1292 provides a hearsay exception for former testimony given at the former proceeding by a person who is now unavailable as a witness when such former testimony is offered against a person who was not a party to the former proceeding but whose motive for cross-examination is similar to that of a person who had the right and opportunity to cross-examine the declarant when the former testimony was given. For example, if one occurrence gives rise to a series of cases involving one defendant and several plaintiffs, Section 1292 permits testimony given against the plaintiff in the first action to be used against a different plaintiff in a subsequent action if the conditions of admissibility stated in the section are met.

Code of Civil Procedure Section 1870(8) (which is superseded by this article) authorizes the admission of former testimony only if it was given in another action between the same parties and involving the same matter. Section 1292 substitutes for these restrictive requirements what is, in effect, a more flexible "trustworthiness" approach characteristic of other hearsay exceptions. The trustworthiness of the former testimony is sufficiently guaranteed because the former adverse party had the right and opportunity to cross-examine the declarant with an interest and motive similar to that of the present adverse party. Although the party against whom the former testimony is offered did not himself have an opportunity to cross-examine the witness on the former occasion, it can be generally assumed that most prior cross-examination is adequate if the same stakes are involved. If the same stakes are not involved, the difference in interest or motivation would justify exclusion. Even where the prior cross-examination was inadequate, there is better reason here for providing a hearsay exception than there is for many of the presently recognized exceptions to the hearsay rule. As Professor McCormick states:

I suggest that if the witness *is* unavailable, then the need for the sworn, transcribed former testimony in the ascertainment of truth is so great, and its reliability so far superior to most, if not all the other types of oral hearsay coming in under the other exceptions, that the requirements of identity of parties and issues be dispensed with. This dispenses with the opportunity for cross-examination, that great characteristic weapon of our adversary system. But the other types of admissible oral hearsay, admissions, declarations against interest, statements about bodily symptoms, likewise dispense with cross-examination, for declarations having far less trustworthiness than the sworn testimony in open court, and with a far greater hazard of fabrication or mistake in the reporting of the declaration by the witness. [McCormick, Evidence §238 at 501 (1954).]

Section 1292 does not make former testimony admissible in a criminal case. This limitation preserves the right of a person accused of crime to confront and cross-examine the witnesses against him. When a person's life or liberty is at stake—as it is in a criminal action—the defendant should not be compelled to rely on the fact that another person has had an opportunity to cross-examine the witness.

Subdivision (b) of Section 1292 makes it clear that objections based on competency or privilege are to be determined by reference to the time when the former testimony was given. Existing California law is not clear on this point; some California decisions indicate that competency and privilege are to be determined as of the time the former testimony was given, but others indicate that these matters are to be determined as of the time the former testimony is offered in evidence. *See Tentative Recommendation and a Study Relating to the Uniform Rules of Evidence (Article VIII. Hearsay Evidence)*, 6 Cal. Law Revision Comm'n, Rep., Rec. & Studies *Appendix* at 581-585 (1964).

ANNOTATIONS

Byars v. SCME Mortg. Bankers, Inc. (4th Dist.2003) 109 Cal.App.4th 1134, 1150. "Former testimony from a deposition rather than a trial is problematic since depositions generally function as a discovery device where examination of one's own client is typically avoided so as not to reveal a weakness in the case or to prematurely disclose a defense. In contrast, at

trial, the parties seek to resolve issues of liability and therefore the interest and motive in cross-examination increases dramatically." (Internal quotes omitted.)

Rufo v. Simpson (2d Dist.2001) 86 Cal.App.4th 573, 606. See annotation under Evidence Code §1291, p. 1402.

L&B Real Estate v. Superior Ct. (2d Dist.1998) 67 Cal.App.4th 1342, 1348. Section 1292, subdivision (a) "requires unavailability and more before testimony can be admitted at a trial. [Ds] made no showing that the witnesses who testified during the criminal trial are unavailable, and a §1292 objection was lodged by real party [in interest].... The trial testimony submitted by [Ds] in support of its summary judgment motion was inadmissible under ... §1292, subdivision (a)." Held: Trial court properly denied Ds' motion for summary judgment. *Compare* ***Williams v. Saga Enters.*** (2d Dist.1990) 225 Cal.App.3d 142, 149 n.3 (authenticated former testimony in summary-judgment proceeding is same as declaration of witness and is admissible), *with* ***Gatton v. A.P. Green Servs.*** (1st Dist.1998) 64 Cal.App.4th 688, 692 (§1292 requires both unavailability, to ensure necessity, and similar interest and motive in prior proceeding, to ensure fairness; ***Williams*** pays no attention to similarity requirement).

§1293. [EXCEPTION: FORMER TESTIMONY BY MINOR IN PRELIMINARY EXAMINATION]

(a) [**Admissibility.**] Evidence of former testimony made at a preliminary examination by a minor child who was the complaining witness is not made inadmissible by the hearsay rule if:

(1) The former testimony is offered in a proceeding to declare the minor a dependent child of the court pursuant to Section 300 of the Welfare and Institutions Code.

(2) The issues are such that a defendant in the preliminary examination in which the former testimony was given had the right and opportunity to cross-examine the minor child with an interest and motive similar to that which the parent or guardian against whom the testimony is offered has at the proceeding to declare the minor a dependent child of the court.

(b) [**Objections.**] The admissibility of former testimony under this section is subject to the same limitations and objections as though the minor child were testifying at the proceeding to declare him or her a dependent child of the court.

(c) [**Motion.**] The attorney for the parent or guardian against whom the former testimony is offered or, if none, the parent or guardian may make a motion to challenge the admissibility of the former testimony upon a showing that new substantially different issues are present in the proceeding to declare the minor a dependent child than were present in the preliminary examination.

(d) [**Complaining witness.**] As used in this section, "complaining witness" means the alleged victim of the crime for which a preliminary examination was held.

(e) [**Effective date.**] This section shall apply only to testimony made at a preliminary examination on and after January 1, 1990.

History of Evid. C. §1293: Added eff. Jan. 1, 1990, Stats. 1989, ch. 322, §1.

§1294. [EXCEPTION: INCONSISTENT STATEMENT WITH PRELIMINARY HEARING TESTIMONY]

(a) [**Admissibility.**] The following evidence of prior inconsistent statements of a witness properly admitted in a preliminary hearing or trial of the same criminal matter pursuant to Section 1235 is not made inadmissible by the hearsay rule if the witness is unavailable and former testimony of the witness is admitted pursuant to Section 1291:

(1) A video recorded statement introduced at a preliminary hearing or prior proceeding concerning the same criminal matter.

(2) A transcript, containing the statements, of the preliminary hearing or prior proceeding concerning the same criminal matter.

(b) [**Cross-examination.**] The party against whom the prior inconsistent statements are offered, at his or her option, may examine or cross-examine any person who testified at the preliminary hearing or prior proceeding as to the prior inconsistent statements of the witness.

History of Evid. C. §1294: Added eff. Jan. 1, 1997, Stats. 1996, ch. 560, §1. Amended eff. Jan. 1, 2010, Stats. 2009, ch. 88, §36.

Official Comment

37 Cal. Law Revision Comm'n Rep. (2007), p. 284.

Section 1294 is amended to reflect advances in recording technology and for consistency of terminology. For a similar reform, see 2002 Cal. Stat. ch. 1068 (replacing numerous references to "audiotape" in Civil Discovery Act with either "audio technology," "audio recording," or "audio record," as context required).

ANNOTATIONS

People v. Martinez (4th Dist.2003) 113 Cal.App.4th 400, 409. "[S]ection 1294 appears to have been de-

§1294

signed to overcome the admissibility problems associated with out-of-court statements which are inconsistent with an unavailable witness's former testimony by requiring that the recorded statement be introduced at the prior hearing where the witness actually testified. It is well settled that the inherent unreliability typically associated with such out-of-court statements may be deemed nonexistent when the defendant has had an opportunity to question the declarant about the statements."

Article 10. Judgments

§1300. [Exception: Judgment of Felony Conviction]

Evidence of a final judgment adjudging a person guilty of a crime punishable as a felony is not made inadmissible by the hearsay rule when offered in a civil action to prove any fact essential to the judgment whether or not the judgment was based on a plea of nolo contendere.

History of Evid. C. §1300: Added eff. Sept. 17, 1965, oper. Jan. 1, 1967, Stats. 1965, ch. 299, §2. Amended eff. Jan. 1, 1983, Stats. 1982, ch. 390, §2.

Official Comment

7 Cal. Law Revision Comm'n Rep. (1965) p. 1251.

Analytically, a judgment that is offered to prove the matters determined by the judgment is hearsay evidence. Uniform Rules of Evidence, Rule 63(20) *Comment* (1953); *Tentative Recommendation and a Study Relating to the Uniform Rules of Evidence (Article VIII. Hearsay Evidence)*, 6 Cal. Law Revision Comm'n, Rep., Rec. & Studies *Appendix* at 539-541 (1964). It is in substance a statement of the court that determined the previous action ("a statement that was made other than by a witness while testifying at the hearing") that is offered "to prove the truth of the matter stated." Evidence Code §1200. Therefore, unless an exception to the hearsay rule is provided, a judgment would be inadmissible if offered in a subsequent action to prove the matters determined.

Of course, a judgment may, as a matter of substantive law, conclusively establish certain facts insofar as a party is concerned. *Teitlebaum Furs, Inc. v. Dominion Ins. Co.*, 58 Cal.2d 601, 25 Cal.Rptr. 559, 375 P.2d 439 (1962); *Bernhard v. Bank of America*, 19 Cal.2d 807, 122 P.2d 892 (1942). The sections of this article do not purport to deal with the doctrines of res judicata and estoppel by judgment. These sections deal only with the evidentiary use of judgments in those cases where the substantive law does not require that the judgments be given conclusive effect.

Section 1300 provides an exception to the hearsay rule for a final judgment adjudging a person guilty of a crime punishable as a felony. Hence, if a plaintiff sues to recover a reward offered by the defendant for the arrest and conviction of a person who committed a particular crime, Section 1300 permits the plaintiff to use a judgment of conviction as evidence that the person convicted committed the crime. The exception does not, however, apply in criminal actions. Thus, Section 1300 does not permit the judgment to be used in a criminal action as evidence of the identity of the person who committed the crime or as evidence that the crime was committed.

Section 1300 will change the California law. Under existing law, a conviction of a crime is inadmissible as evidence in a subsequent action. *Marceau v. Travelers' Ins. Co.*, 101 Cal. 338, 35 Pac. 856 (1894) (evidence of a murder conviction held inadmissible to prove the insured was intentionally killed); *Burke v. Wells, Fargo & Co.*, 34 Cal. 60 1867) (evidence of a robbery conviction held inadmissible to prove the identity of robber in an action to recover reward). The change, however, is desirable, for the evidence involved is peculiarly reliable. The seriousness of the charge assures that the facts will be thoroughly litigated, and the fact that the judgment must be based upon a determination that there was no reasonable doubt concerning the defendant's guilt assures that the question of guilt will be thoroughly considered.

Section 1300 applies to any crime punishable as a felony. The fact that a misdemeanor sentence is imposed does not affect the admissibility of the judgment of a conviction under this section. *Cf.* Penal Code §17. The exclusion of judgments based on a plea of nolo contendere from the exception in Section 1300 is a reflection of the policy expressed in Penal Code Section 1016.

Annotations

Principal Life Ins. v. Peterson (5th Dist.2007) 156 Cal.App.4th 676, 687. "[T]he ... §1300 phrase 'final judgment adjudging a person guilty of a crime punishable as a felony' includes a judgment adjudging a person guilty of a crime punishable as a felony even when an appeal from that judgment is pending. *At 691-92:* [T]he ... comment ... contains no suggestion that the commission or the Legislature intended the words 'final judgment adjudging a person guilty' ... to mean only a judgment that has been affirmed on appeal or that is no longer subject to a timely appeal. ... The comment contains no suggestion that the plaintiff must wait until the criminal conviction is affirmed on appeal before that 'judgment of conviction' may be admitted in the civil action to recover the reward."

County of L.A. v. Civil Serv. Comm'n (2d Dist.1995) 39 Cal.App.4th 620, 632. "[C]ounty relies upon ... §1300 to urge that evidence of [real party in interest's] plea should have been admitted at the disciplinary hearing. The reliance is misplaced. That provision merely creates an exception to the hearsay rule of exclusion for a judgment of conviction punishable as a felony. The exception applies even if the judgment was based upon a plea of nolo contendere. This provision of the Evidence Code is of no help to county because it only addresses the issue of overcoming a hearsay objection to the use of the judgment of conviction—it does not address the threshold issue of relevancy, the point at which precedent compels exclusion of evidence of [real party in interest's] plea."

§1301. [Exception: Final Judgment]

Evidence of a final judgment is not made inadmissible by the hearsay rule when offered by the judgment debtor to prove any fact which was essential to the judgment in an action in which he seeks to:

(a) Recover partial or total indemnity or exoneration for money paid or liability incurred because of the judgment;

(b) Enforce a warranty to protect the judgment debtor against the liability determined by the judgment; or

(c) Recover damages for breach of warranty substantially the same as the warranty determined by the judgment to have been breached.

History of Evid. C. §1301: Added eff. Sept. 17, 1965, oper. Jan. 1, 1967, Stats. 1965, ch. 299, §2.

Official Comment

7 Cal. Law Revision Comm'n Rep. (1965) p. 1252.

If a person entitled to indemnity, or if the obligee under a warranty contract, complies with certain conditions relating to notice and defense, the indemnitor or warrantor is conclusively bound by any judgment recovered. Civil Code §2778(5); Code Civ. Proc. §1912; *McCormick v. Marcy*, 165 Cal. 386, 132 Pac. 449 (1913).

Where a judgment against an indemnitee or person protected by a warranty is not made conclusive on the indemnitor or warrantor, Section 1301 permits the judgment to be used as hearsay evidence in an action to recover on the indemnity or warranty. Section 1301 reflects the existing law relating to indemnity agreements. Civil Code §2778(6). Section 1301 probably restates the law relating to warranties, too, but the law in that regard is not altogether clear. *Erie City Iron Works v. Tatum*, 1 Cal.App. 286, 82 Pac. 92 (1905). *But see Peabody v. Phelps*, 9 Cal. 213 (1858).

§1302. [EXCEPTION: JUDGMENT AGAINST THIRD PERSON]

When the liability, obligation, or duty of a third person is in issue in a civil action, evidence of a final judgment against that person is not made inadmissible by the hearsay rule when offered to prove such liability, obligation, or duty.

History of Evid. C. §1302: Added eff. Sept. 17, 1965, oper. Jan. 1, 1967, Stats. 1965, ch. 299, §2.

Official Comment

7 Cal. Law Revision Comm'n Rep. (1965) p. 1253.

Section 1302 expresses an exception contained in Code of Civil Procedure Section 1851. *Ellsworth v. Bradford*, 186 Cal. 316, 199 Pac. 335 (1921); *Nordin v. Bank of America*, 11 Cal.App.2d 98, 52 P.2d 1018 (1936). Evidence Code Sections 1302 and 1224 together restate and supersede the provisions of Code of Civil Procedure Section 1851.

Article 11. Family History

§1310. [EXCEPTION: DECLARANT'S FAMILY HISTORY]

(a) [Unavailable declarant.] Subject to subdivision (b), evidence of a statement by a declarant who is unavailable as a witness concerning his own birth, marriage, divorce, a parent and child relationship, relationship by blood or marriage, race, ancestry, or other similar fact of his family history is not made inadmissible by the hearsay rule, even though the declarant had no means of acquiring personal knowledge of the matter declared.

(b) [Untrustworthy.] Evidence of a statement is inadmissible under this section if the statement was made under circumstances such as to indicate its lack of trustworthiness.

History of Evid. C. §1310: Added eff. Sept. 17, 1965, oper. Jan. 1, 1967, Stats. 1965, ch. 299, §2. Amended eff. Jan. 1, 1976, Stats. 1975, ch. 1244, §15.

Official Comment

7 Cal. Law Revision Comm'n Rep. (1965) p. 1253.

Section 1310 provides a hearsay exception for a statement concerning the declarant's own family history. It restates in substance and supersedes Section 1870(4) of the Code of Civil Procedure. Section 1870(4), however, requires that the declarant be dead whereas unavailability of the declarant for any of the reasons specified in Section 240 makes the statement admissible under Section 1310.

The statement is not admissible if it was made under circumstances such as to indicate its lack of trustworthiness. The requirement is similar to the requirement of existing case law that the statement be made at a time when no controversy existed as to the matters stated. *See, e.g.*, *Estate of Walden*, 166 Cal. 446, 137 Pac. 35 (1913); *Estate of Nidever*, 181 Cal.App.2d 367, 5 Cal.Rptr. 343 (1960). However, the language of Section 1310 permits the judge to consider the declarant's motives to tell the truth as well as his reasons to deviate therefrom in determining whether the statement is sufficiently trustworthy to be admitted as evidence.

§1311. [EXCEPTION: ANOTHER PERSON'S FAMILY HISTORY]

(a) [Unavailable declarant.] Subject to subdivision (b), evidence of a statement concerning the birth, marriage, divorce, death, parent and child relationship, race, ancestry, relationship by blood or marriage, or other similar fact of the family history of a person other than the declarant is not made inadmissible by the hearsay rule if the declarant is unavailable as a witness and:

(1) The declarant was related to the other by blood or marriage; or

(2) The declarant was otherwise so intimately associated with the other's family as to be likely to have had accurate information concerning the matter declared and made the statement (i) upon information received from the other or from a person related by blood or marriage to the other or (ii) upon repute in the other's family.

(b) [Untrustworthy.] Evidence of a statement is inadmissible under this section if the statement was made under circumstances such as to indicate its lack of trustworthiness.

History of Evid. C. §1311: Added eff. Sept. 17, 1965, oper. Jan. 1, 1967, Stats. 1965, ch. 299, §2. Amended eff. Jan. 1, 1976, Stats. 1975, ch. 1244, §16.

Official Comment

7 Cal. Law Revision Comm'n Rep. (1965) p. 1254.

Section 1311 provides a hearsay exception for a statement concerning the family history of another. Paragraph (1) of subdivision (a) restates in substance existing law as found in Section 1870(4) of the Code of Civil Procedure which it supersedes. Paragraph (2) is new to California law, but it is a sound extension of the present law to cover a situation where the declarant was a family housekeeper or doctor or so close a friend as to be included by the family in discussions of its family history.

There are two limitations on admissibility of a statement under Section 1311. *First*, a statement is admissible only if the declarant is unavailable as a witness within the meaning of Section 240. (Section 1870(4) requires that the declarant be deceased in order for his statement to be admissible.) *Second*, a statement is not admissible if it was made under circumstances such as to indicate its lack of trustworthiness. For a discussion of this requirement, *see* the *Comment* to Evidence Code §1310.

§1312. [EXCEPTION: FAMILY-HISTORY ENTRIES]

Evidence of entries in family Bibles or other family books or charts, engravings on rings, family portraits, engravings on urns, crypts, or tombstones, and the like, is not made inadmissible by the hearsay rule when offered to prove the birth, marriage, divorce, death, parent and child relationship, race, ancestry, relationship by blood or marriage, or other similar fact of the family history of a member of the family by blood or marriage.

History of Evid. C. §1312: Added eff. Sept. 17, 1965, oper. Jan. 1, 1967, Stats. 1965, ch. 299, §2. Amended eff. Jan. 1, 1976, Stats. 1975, ch. 1244, §17.

Official Comment

7 Cal. Law Revision Comm'n Rep. (1965) p. 1255.

Section 1312 restates the substance of and supersedes the provisions of Code of Civil Procedure Section 1870(13).

§1313. [EXCEPTION: FAMILY REPUTATION]

Evidence of reputation among members of a family is not made inadmissible by the hearsay rule if the reputation concerns the birth, marriage, divorce, death, parent and child relationship, race, ancestry, relationship by blood or marriage, or other similar fact of the family history of a member of the family by blood or marriage.

History of Evid. C. §1313: Added eff. Sept. 17, 1965, oper. Jan. 1, 1967, Stats. 1965, ch. 299, §2. Amended eff. Jan. 1, 1976, Stats. 1975, ch. 1244, §18.

Official Comment

7 Cal. Law Revision Comm'n Rep. (1965) p. 1255.

Section 1313 restates the substance of and supersedes the provisions of Code of Civil Procedure Sections 1852 and 1870(11). *See Estate of Connors*, 53 Cal.App.2d 484, 128 P.2d 200 (1942); *Estate of Newman*, 34 Cal.App.2d 706, 94 P.2d 356 (1939). However, Section 1870(11) requires the family reputation in question to have existed "previous to the controversy." This qualification is not included in Section 1313 because it is unlikely that a family reputation on a matter of pedigree would be influenced by the existence of a controversy even though the declaration of an individual member of the family, covered in Sections 1310 and 1311, might be.

The family reputation admitted under Section 1313 is necessarily multiple hearsay. If, however, such reputation were inadmissible because of the hearsay rule, and if direct statements of pedigree were inadmissible because they are based on such reputation (as most of them are), the courts would be virtually helpless in determining matters of pedigree. *See Tentative Recommendation and a Study Relating to the Uniform Rules of Evidence (Article VIII. Hearsay Evidence)*, 6 Cal. Law Revision Comm'n, Rep., Rec. & Studies *Appendix* at 548 (1964).

§1314. [EXCEPTION: COMMUNITY REPUTATION]

Evidence of reputation in a community concerning the date or fact of birth, marriage, divorce, or death of a person resident in the community at the time of the reputation is not made inadmissible by the hearsay rule.

History of Evid. C. §1314: Added eff. Sept. 17, 1965, oper. Jan. 1, 1967, Stats. 1965, ch. 299, §2.

Official Comment

7 Cal. Law Revision Comm'n Rep. (1965) p. 1256.

Section 1314 restates what has been held to be existing law under Code of Civil Procedure Section 1963(30) with respect to proof of the fact of marriage. *See People v. Vogel*, 46 Cal.2d 798, 299 P.2d 850 (1956); *Estate of Baldwin*, 162 Cal. 471, 123 Pac. 267 (1912). However, Section 1314 has no counterpart in California law insofar as proof of the date or fact of birth, divorce, or death is concerned, since proof of such facts by reputation is presently limited to reputation in the family. *See Estate of Heaton*, 135 Cal. 385, 67 Pac. 321 (1902).

ANNOTATIONS

In re Marriage of Sasson (2d Dist.1982) 129 Cal.App.3d 140, 145. "While … §1314 does provide that '[e]vidence of reputation in a community concerning the date or fact of … marriage … is not made inadmissible by the hearsay rule,' it does not necessarily follow that such evidence is relevant."

§1315. [EXCEPTION: CHURCH RECORDS]

Evidence of a statement concerning a person's birth, marriage, divorce, death, parent and child relationship, race, ancestry, relationship by blood or marriage, or other similar fact of family history which is contained in a writing made as a record of a church, religious denomination, or religious society is not made inadmissible by the hearsay rule if:

(a) [Contained in record.] The statement is contained in a writing made as a record of an act, condition, or event that would be admissible as evidence of such act, condition, or event under Section 1271; and

(b) [Customarily recorded.] The statement is of a kind customarily recorded in connection with the act, condition, or event recorded in the writing.

History of Evid. C. §1315: Added eff. Sept. 17, 1965, oper. Jan. 1, 1967, Stats. 1965, ch. 299, §2. Amended eff. Jan. 1, 1976, Stats. 1975, ch. 1244, §19.

Official Comment

7 Cal. Law Revision Comm'n Rep. (1965) p. 1256.

Church records generally are admissible as business records under the provisions of Section 1271. Under Section 1271, such records would be admissible to prove the occurrence of the church activity—the baptism, confirmation, or marriage—recorded in the writing. However, it is unlikely that Section 1271 would permit such records to be used as evidence of the age or relationship of the participants, for the business records act has been held to authorize business records to be used to prove only facts known personally to the recorder of the information or to other employees of the business. *Patek & Co. v. Vineberg*, 210 Cal.App.2d 20, 23, 26 Cal.Rptr. 293, 294 (1962) (hearing denied); *People v. Williams*, 187 Cal.App.2d 355, 9 Cal.Rptr. 722 (1960); *Gough v. Security Trust & Sav. Bank*, 162 Cal.App.2d 90, 327 P.2d 555 (1958).

Section 1315 permits church records to be used to prove certain additional information. Facts of family history, such as birth dates, relationships, marital histories, etc., that are ordinarily reported to church authorities and recorded in connection with the church's baptismal, confirmation, marriage, and funeral records may be proved by such records under Section 1315.

Section 1315 continues in effect and supersedes the provisions of Code of Civil Procedure Section 1919a without, however, the special and cumbersome authentication procedure specified in Code of Civil Procedure Section 1919b. Under Section 1315, church records may be authenticated in the same manner that other business records are authenticated.

§1316. [EXCEPTION: CERTIFICATE OF CEREMONY]

Evidence of a statement concerning a person's birth, marriage, divorce, death, parent and child relationship, race, ancestry, relationship by blood or marriage, or other similar fact of family history is not made inadmissible by the hearsay rule if the statement is contained in a certificate that the maker thereof performed a marriage or other ceremony or administered a sacrament and:

(a) [**Authorized.**] The maker was a clergyman, civil officer, or other person authorized to perform the acts reported in the certificate by law or by the rules, regulations, or requirements of a church, religious denomination, or religious society; and

(b) [**Certificate.**] The certificate was issued by the maker at the time and place of the ceremony or sacrament or within a reasonable time thereafter.

History of Evid. C. §1316: Added eff. Sept. 17, 1965, oper. Jan. 1, 1967, Stats. 1965, ch. 299, §2. Amended eff. Jan. 1, 1976, Stats. 1975, ch. 1244, §20.

Official Comment

7 Cal. Law Revision Comm'n Rep. (1965) p. 1257.

Section 1316 provides a hearsay exception for marriage, baptismal, and similar certificates. This exception is somewhat broader than that found in Sections 1919a and 1919b of the Code of Civil Procedure (repealed, now Evidence Code Sections 1315 and 1316). Sections 1919a and 1919b are limited to church records and, hence, with respect to marriages, to those performed by clergymen. Moreover, they establish an elaborate and detailed authentication procedure, whereas certificates made admissible by Section 1316 need meet only the general authentication requirement of Section 1401.

ARTICLE 12. REPUTATION & STATEMENTS CONCERNING COMMUNITY HISTORY, PROPERTY INTERESTS, & CHARACTER

§1320. [EXCEPTION: REPUTATION OF EVENT]

Evidence of reputation in a community is not made inadmissible by the hearsay rule if the reputation concerns an event of general history of the community or of the state or nation of which the community is a part and the event was of importance to the community.

History of Evid. C. §1320: Added eff. Sept. 17, 1965, oper. Jan. 1, 1967, Stats. 1965, ch. 299, §2.

Official Comment

7 Cal. Law Revision Comm'n Rep. (1965) p. 1258.

Section 1320 provides a wider rule of admissibility than does Code of Civil Procedure Section 1870(11) which it supersedes in part. Section 1870 provides in relevant part that proof may be made of "common reputation existing previous to the controversy, respecting facts of a public or general interest more than thirty years old." The 30-year limitation is essentially arbitrary. The important question would seem to be whether a community reputation on the matter involved exists; its age would appear to go more to its venerability than to its truth. Nor is it necessary to include in Section 1320 the requirement that the reputation existed previous to controversy. It is unlikely that a community reputation respecting an event of general history would be influenced by the existence of a controversy.

§1321. [EXCEPTION: REPUTATION OF PUBLIC INTEREST IN PROPERTY]

Evidence of reputation in a community is not made inadmissible by the hearsay rule if the reputation concerns the interest of the public in property in the community and the reputation arose before controversy.

History of Evid. C. §1321: Added eff. Sept. 17, 1965, oper. Jan. 1, 1967, Stats. 1965, ch. 299, §2.

Official Comment

7 Cal. Law Revision Comm'n Rep. (1965) p. 1258.

Section 1321 preserves the rule in *Simons v. Inyo Cerro Gordo Co.*, 48 Cal. App. 524, 192 Pac. 144 (1920). It does not require, however, that the reputation be more than 30 years old; it requires merely that the reputation arose before there was a controversy concerning the matter. *See* the *Comment* to Section 1320.

§1322. [EXCEPTION: REPUTATION OF BOUNDARIES OF OR CUSTOM AFFECTING LAND]

Evidence of reputation in a community is not made inadmissible by the hearsay rule if the reputation concerns boundaries of, or customs affecting, land in the community and the reputation arose before controversy.

History of Evid. C. §1322: Added eff. Sept. 17, 1965, oper. Jan. 1, 1967, Stats. 1965, ch. 299, §2.

Official Comment

7 Cal. Law Revision Comm'n Rep. (1965) p. 1259.

Section 1322 restates the substance of existing law as found in Code of Civil Procedure Section 1870(11) which it supersedes in part. *See Muller v. So. Pac. Branch Ry.*, 83 Cal. 240, 23 Pac. 265 (1890); *Ferris v. Emmons*, 214 Cal. 501, 6 P.2d 950 (1931).

§1323. [EXCEPTION: UNAVAILABLE DECLARANT'S STATEMENT OF BOUNDARY]

Evidence of a statement concerning the boundary of land is not made inadmissible by the hearsay rule if the declarant is unavailable as a witness and had sufficient knowledge of the subject, but evidence of a statement is not admissible under this section if the statement was made under circumstances such as to indicate its lack of trustworthiness.

History of Evid. C. §1323: Added eff. Sept. 17, 1965, oper. Jan. 1, 1967, Stats. 1965, ch. 299, §2.

Official Comment

7 Cal. Law Revision Comm'n Rep. (1965) p. 1259.

Section 1323 codifies existing law found in such cases as *Morton v. Folger*, 15 Cal. 275 (1860), and *Morcom v. Baiersky*, 16 Cal.App. 480, 117 Pac. 560 (1911).

§1324. [EXCEPTION: REPUTATION OF CHARACTER]

Evidence of a person's general reputation with reference to his character or a trait of his character at a relevant time in the community in which he then resided or in a group with which he then habitually associated is not made inadmissible by the hearsay rule.

History of Evid. C. §1324: Added eff. Sept. 17, 1965, oper. Jan. 1, 1967, Stats. 1965, ch. 299, §2.

Official Comment

7 Cal. Law Revision Comm'n Rep. (1965) p. 1259.

Section 1324 codifies a well-settled exception to the hearsay rule. *See, e.g.*, *People v. Cobb*, 45 Cal.2d 158, 287 P.2d 752 (1955). Of course, character evidence is admissible only when the question of character is material to the matter being litigated. The only purpose of Section 1324 is to declare that reputation evidence as to character or a trait of character is not inadmissible under the hearsay rule.

ANNOTATIONS

People v. Eli (1967) 66 Cal.2d 63, 78. "When a defendant elects to initiate inquiry into his own character, presumably to establish that one with his lofty traits would be unlikely to commit the offense charged, an anomalous rule comes into effect. Opinion based upon hearsay is permitted. But the price a defendant must pay for attempting to prove his good name is to throw open a vast subject which the law has kept closed to shield him. The prosecution may pursue the inquiry with cross-examination as to the contents and extent of the hearsay upon which the opinion was based, and may disclose rumors, talk, and reports circulating in the community." *See also* ***People v. Tuggles*** (3d Dist.2009) 179 Cal.App.4th 339, 357.

ARTICLE 13. DISPOSITIVE INSTRUMENTS & ANCIENT WRITINGS

§1330. [EXCEPTION: RECITALS IN DISPOSITIVE INSTRUMENTS]

Evidence of a statement contained in a deed of conveyance or a will or other writing purporting to affect an interest in real or personal property is not made inadmissible by the hearsay rule if:

(a) [Relevant to purpose.] The matter stated was relevant to the purpose of the writing;

(b) [Relevant to issue.] The matter stated would be relevant to an issue as to an interest in the property; and

(c) [Consistent dealings.] The dealings with the property since the statement was made have not been inconsistent with the truth of the statement.

History of Evid. C. §1330: Added eff. Sept. 17, 1965, oper. Jan. 1, 1967, Stats. 1965, ch. 299, §2.

Official Comment

7 Cal. Law Revision Comm'n Rep. (1965) p. 1260.

Section 1330 restates the substance of existing California law relating to recitals in dispositive instruments. Although language in some cases appears to require that the dispositive instrument be ancient, cases may be found in which recitals in dispositive instruments have been admitted without regard to the age of the instrument. *See Russell v. Langford*, 135 Cal. 356, 67 Pac. 381 (1902) (recital in will); *Pearson v. Pearson*, 46 Cal. 609 (1873) (recital in will); *Culver v. Newhart*, 18 Cal.App. 614, 123 Pac. 975 (1912) (bill of sale). There is a sufficient likelihood that the statements made in a dispositive document, when related to the purpose of the document, will be true to warrant the admissibility of such documents without regard to their age.

§1331. [EXCEPTION: RECITALS IN ANCIENT DOCUMENTS]

Evidence of a statement is not made inadmissible by the hearsay rule if the statement is contained in a writing more than 30 years old and the statement has been since generally acted upon as true by persons having an interest in the matter.

History of Evid. C. §1331: Added eff. Sept. 17, 1965, oper. Jan. 1, 1967, Stats. 1965, ch. 299, §2.

Official Comment

7 Cal. Law Revision Comm'n Rep. (1965) p. 1260.

Section 1331 clarifies the existing law relating to the admissibility of recitals in ancient documents by providing that such recitals are admissible under an exception to the hearsay rule. Code of Civil Procedure Section 1963(34) (repealed) provides that a document more than 30 years old is presumed genuine if it has been generally acted upon as genuine by persons having an interest in the matter. The Supreme Court has held that a document meeting this section's requirements is presumed to be genuine—presumed to be what it purports to be—but that the genuineness of the document imports no verity to the recitals contained therein. *Gwin v. Calegaris*, 139 Cal. 384, 389, 73 Pac. 851, 853 (1903). Recent cases decided by district courts of appeal, however, have held that the recitals in such a document are admissible to prove the truth of the facts recited. *Estate of Nidever*, 181 Cal.App.2d 367, 5 Cal.Rptr. 343 (1960); *Kirkpatrick v. Tapo Oil Co.*, 144 Cal.App.2d 404, 301 P.2d 274 (1956). In these latter cases, the courts have not insisted that the hearsay statement itself be acted upon as true by persons with an interest in the matter; the evidence has been admitted merely upon a showing that the document containing the statement is genuine. The age of a document alone is not a sufficient guarantee of the trustworthiness of a statement contained therein to warrant the admission of the statement into evidence. Accordingly, Section 1331 makes it clear that the statement itself must have been generally acted upon as true for at least 30 years by persons having an interest in the matter.

ARTICLE 14. COMMERCIAL, SCIENTIFIC, & SIMILAR PUBLICATIONS

§1340. [EXCEPTION: COMPILATION]

Evidence of a statement, other than an opinion, contained in a tabulation, list, directory, register, or other published compilation is not made inadmissible by the hearsay rule if the compilation is generally used and relied upon as accurate in the course of a business as defined in Section 1270.

History of Evid. C. §1340: Added eff. Sept. 17, 1965, oper. Jan. 1, 1967, Stats. 1965, ch. 299, §2.

Official Comment

7 Cal. Law Revision Comm'n Rep. (1965) p. 1261.

Section 1340 codifies an exception that has been recognized by statute and by the courts in specific situations. *See, e.g.*, Com. Code §2724; *Emery v. So. Cal. Gas Co.*, 72 Cal.App.2d 821, 165 P.2d 695 (1946); *Christiansen v. Hollings*, 44 Cal.App.2d 332, 112 P.2d 723 (1941).

ANNOTATIONS

Collins v. Navistar, Inc. (3d Dist.2013) 214 Cal.App.4th 1486, 1514. Expert "testified her opinions were based upon matter reasonably relied on by other

experts. Her opinions were based upon databases[, one of which] was the most widely relied upon traffic safety database. [The other databases] were commonly used and relied upon by scientists, engineers, statisticians, and traffic safety professionals. *At 1516:* [P] contends the traffic reports that serve as the foundation of the federal databases contain multiple levels of hearsay and do not qualify as business records. While an expert may rely on inadmissible hearsay in forming an opinion and may state the matters on which he or she relied, the expert may not testify as to the details of those matters that are inadmissible hearsay. [P] contends [expert] could not testify as to the hearsay details in the reports. [¶] [P] misunderstands that [expert] testified to the databases' compilation of statistics, not the traffic reports themselves. Such compilations are admissible under ... §1340[.] [Expert] testified the databases were accurate, and commonly used and relied upon by traffic safety experts and statisticians. The trial court did not abuse its broad discretion in admitting into evidence the data from the federal databases and [expert's] testimony based on those data."

People v. Franzen (6th Dist.2012) 210 Cal.App.4th 1193, 1208. "[T]he published compilation exception is not to be broadly or uncritically applied. *At 1209:* The history, language, and rationale of §1340 suggest that the exception contemplates an organized, edited presentation of a finite quantity of information that, if not printed on paper, has been recorded and circulated in some fixed form analogous to printing. *At 1211:* To treat a database as a published compilation merely because it is accessible through a Web site would dramatically undermine the delicate balance of competing policies reflected in the hearsay rule, its exceptions, and the particular exception here under scrutiny."

§1341. [EXCEPTION: GENERAL NOTORIETY & INTEREST]

Historical works, books of science or art, and published maps or charts, made by persons indifferent between the parties, are not made inadmissible by the hearsay rule when offered to prove facts of general notoriety and interest.

History of Evid. C. §1341: Added eff. Sept. 17, 1965, oper. Jan. 1, 1967, Stats. 1965, ch. 299, §2.

Official Comment

7 Cal. Law Revision Comm'n Rep. (1965) p. 1261.

Section 1341 recodifies without substantive change Section 1936 of the Code of Civil Procedure.

ARTICLE 15. DECLARANT UNAVAILABLE AS WITNESS

§1350. [EXCEPTION: DECLARANT UNAVAILABLE]

(a) [**Admissibility.**] In a criminal proceeding charging a serious felony, evidence of a statement made by a declarant is not made inadmissible by the hearsay rule if the declarant is unavailable as a witness, and all of the following are true:

(1) There is clear and convincing evidence that the declarant's unavailability was knowingly caused by, aided by, or solicited by the party against whom the statement is offered for the purpose of preventing the arrest or prosecution of the party and is the result of the death by homicide or the kidnapping of the declarant.

(2) There is no evidence that the unavailability of the declarant was caused by, aided by, solicited by, or procured on behalf of, the party who is offering the statement.

(3) The statement has been memorialized in a tape recording made by a law enforcement official, or in a written statement prepared by a law enforcement official and signed by the declarant and notarized in the presence of the law enforcement official, prior to the death or kidnapping of the declarant.

(4) The statement was made under circumstances which indicate its trustworthiness and was not the result of promise, inducement, threat, or coercion.

(5) The statement is relevant to the issues to be tried.

(6) The statement is corroborated by other evidence which tends to connect the party against whom the statement is offered with the commission of the serious felony with which the party is charged. The corroboration is not sufficient if it merely shows the commission of the offense or the circumstances thereof.

(b) [**Notice.**] If the prosecution intends to offer a statement pursuant to this section, the prosecution shall serve a written notice upon the defendant at least 10 days prior to the hearing or trial at which the prosecution intends to offer the statement, unless the prosecution shows good cause for the failure to provide that notice. In the event that good cause is shown, the defendant shall be entitled to a reasonable continuance of the hearing or trial.

(c) [**Hearing.**] If the statement is offered during trial, the court's determination shall be made out of the

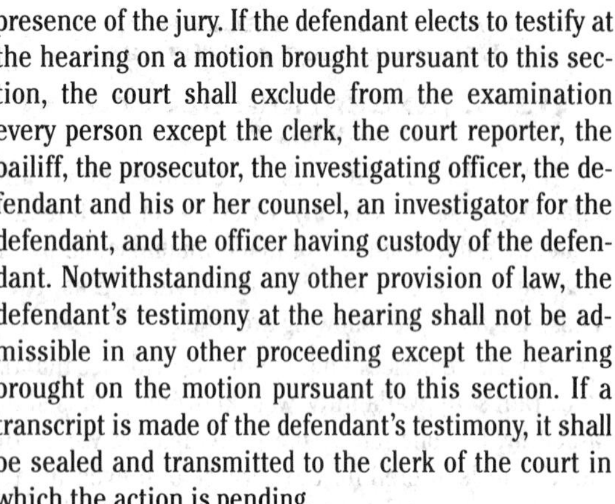
presence of the jury. If the defendant elects to testify at the hearing on a motion brought pursuant to this section, the court shall exclude from the examination every person except the clerk, the court reporter, the bailiff, the prosecutor, the investigating officer, the defendant and his or her counsel, an investigator for the defendant, and the officer having custody of the defendant. Notwithstanding any other provision of law, the defendant's testimony at the hearing shall not be admissible in any other proceeding except the hearing brought on the motion pursuant to this section. If a transcript is made of the defendant's testimony, it shall be sealed and transmitted to the clerk of the court in which the action is pending.

(d) [Serious felony.] As used in this section, "serious felony" means any of the felonies listed in subdivision (c) of Section 1192.7 of the Penal Code or any violation of Section 11351, 11352, 11378, or 11379 of the Health and Safety Code.

(e) [Statement by another.] If a statement to be admitted pursuant to this section includes hearsay statements made by anyone other than the declarant who is unavailable pursuant to subdivision (a), those hearsay statements are inadmissible unless they meet the requirements of an exception to the hearsay rule.

History of Evid. C. §1350: Added eff. Jan. 1, 1986, Stats. 1985, ch. 783, §1. Amended eff. Jan. 1, 2002, Stats. 2001, ch. 854, §5.

ARTICLE 16. STATEMENTS BY CHILDREN UNDER THE AGE OF 12 IN CHILD NEGLECT & ABUSE PROCEEDINGS

§1360. [EXCEPTION: STATEMENT OF CHILD-ABUSE VICTIM]

(a) [Admissibility.] In a criminal prosecution where the victim is a minor, a statement made by the victim when under the age of 12 describing any act of child abuse or neglect performed with or on the child by another, or describing any attempted act of child abuse or neglect with or on the child by another, is not made inadmissible by the hearsay rule if all of the following apply:

(1) The statement is not otherwise admissible by statute or court rule.

(2) The court finds, in a hearing conducted outside the presence of the jury, that the time, content, and circumstances of the statement provide sufficient indicia of reliability.

(3) The child either:

(A) Testifies at the proceedings.

(B) Is unavailable as a witness, in which case the statement may be admitted only if there is evidence of the child abuse or neglect that corroborates the statement made by the child.

(b) [Notice.] A statement may not be admitted under this section unless the proponent of the statement makes known to the adverse party the intention to offer the statement and the particulars of the statement sufficiently in advance of the proceedings in order to provide the adverse party with a fair opportunity to prepare to meet the statement.

(c) [Child abuse.] For purposes of this section, "child abuse" means an act proscribed by Section 273a, 273d, or 288.5 of the Penal Code, or any of the acts described in Section 11165.1 of the Penal Code, and "child neglect" means any of the acts described in Section 11165.2 of the Penal Code.

History of Evid. C. §1360: Added eff. Jan. 1, 1996, Stats. 1995, ch. 87, §3.

ARTICLE 17. PHYSICAL ABUSE

§1370. [EXCEPTION: INFLICTION OR THREAT OF INFLICTION OF PHYSICAL INJURY]

(a) [Admissibility.] Evidence of a statement by a declarant is not made inadmissible by the hearsay rule if all of the following conditions are met:

(1) The statement purports to narrate, describe, or explain the infliction or threat of physical injury upon the declarant.

(2) The declarant is unavailable as a witness pursuant to Section 240.

(3) The statement was made at or near the time of the infliction or threat of physical injury. Evidence of statements made more than five years before the filing of the current action or proceeding shall be inadmissible under this section.

(4) The statement was made under circumstances that would indicate its trustworthiness.

(5) The statement was made in writing, was electronically recorded, or made to a physician, nurse, paramedic, or to a law enforcement official.

(b) [Trustworthiness.] For purposes of paragraph (4) of subdivision (a), circumstances relevant to the issue of trustworthiness include, but are not limited to, the following:

(1) Whether the statement was made in contemplation of pending or anticipated litigation in which the declarant was interested.

(2) Whether the declarant has a bias or motive for fabricating the statement, and the extent of any bias or motive.

(3) Whether the statement is corroborated by evidence other than statements that are admissible only pursuant to this section.

(c) [Notice.] A statement is admissible pursuant to this section only if the proponent of the statement makes known to the adverse party the intention to offer the statement and the particulars of the statement sufficiently in advance of the proceedings in order to provide the adverse party with a fair opportunity to prepare to meet the statement.

History of Evid. C. §1370: Added eff. Sept. 4, 1996, Stats. 1996, ch. 416, §2. Amended eff. Jan. 1, 2001, Stats. 2000, ch. 1001, §2.

§1380. [VICTIM OF ELDER ABUSE]

(a) [Admissibility.] In a criminal proceeding charging a violation, or attempted violation, of Section 368 of the Penal Code, evidence of a statement made by a declarant is not made inadmissible by the hearsay rule if the declarant is unavailable as a witness, as defined in subdivisions (a) and (b) of Section 240, and all of the following are true:

(1) The party offering the statement has made a showing of particularized guarantees of trustworthiness regarding the statement, the statement was made under circumstances which indicate its trustworthiness, and the statement was not the result of promise, inducement, threat, or coercion. In making its determination, the court may consider only the circumstances that surround the making of the statement and that render the declarant particularly worthy of belief.

(2) There is no evidence that the unavailability of the declarant was caused by, aided by, solicited by, or procured on behalf of, the party who is offering the statement.

(3) The entire statement has been memorialized in a videotape recording made by a law enforcement official, prior to the death or disabling of the declarant.

(4) The statement was made by the victim of the alleged violation.

(5) The statement is supported by corroborative evidence.

(6) The victim of the alleged violation is an individual who meets both of the following requirements:

(A) Was 65 years of age or older or was a dependent adult when the alleged violation or attempted violation occurred.

(B) At the time of any criminal proceeding, including, but not limited to, a preliminary hearing or trial, regarding the alleged violation or attempted violation, is either deceased or suffers from the infirmities of aging as manifested by advanced age or organic brain damage, or other physical, mental, or emotional dysfunction, to the extent that the ability of the person to provide adequately for the person's own care or protection is impaired.

(b) [Notice.] If the prosecution intends to offer a statement pursuant to this section, the prosecution shall serve a written notice upon the defendant at least 10 days prior to the hearing or trial at which the prosecution intends to offer the statement, unless the prosecution shows good cause for the failure to provide that notice. In the event that good cause is shown, the defendant shall be entitled to a reasonable continuance of the hearing or trial.

(c) [Hearing.] If the statement is offered during trial, the court's determination as to the availability of the victim as a witness shall be made out of the presence of the jury. If the defendant elects to testify at the hearing on a motion brought pursuant to this section, the court shall exclude from the examination every person except the clerk, the court reporter, the bailiff, the prosecutor, the investigating officer, the defendant and his or her counsel, an investigator for the defendant, and the officer having custody of the defendant. Notwithstanding any other provision of law, the defendant's testimony at the hearing shall not be admissible in any other proceeding except the hearing brought on the motion pursuant to this section. If a transcript is made of the defendant's testimony, it shall be sealed and transmitted to the clerk of the court in which the action is pending.

History of Evid. C. §1380: Added eff. Jan. 1, 2000, Stats. 1999, ch. 383, §1.

§1390. [WRONGDOING PROCURING UNAVAILABILITY OF DECLARANT]

(a) [Admissibility.] Evidence of a statement is not made inadmissible by the hearsay rule if the statement is offered against a party that has engaged, or aided and abetted, in the wrongdoing that was intended to, and did, procure the unavailability of the declarant as a witness.

(b) [Hearing.]

(1) The party seeking to introduce a statement pursuant to subdivision (a) shall establish, by a prepon-

derance of the evidence, that the elements of subdivision (a) have been met at a foundational hearing.

(2) The hearsay evidence that is the subject of the foundational hearing is admissible at the foundational hearing. However, a finding that the elements of subdivision (a) have been met shall not be based solely on the unconfronted hearsay statement of the unavailable declarant, and shall be supported by independent corroborative evidence.

(3) The foundational hearing shall be conducted outside the presence of the jury. However, if the hearing is conducted after a jury trial has begun, the judge presiding at the hearing may consider evidence already presented to the jury in deciding whether the elements of subdivision (a) have been met.

(4) In deciding whether or not to admit the statement, the judge may take into account whether it is trustworthy and reliable.

(c) [Effective date.] This section shall apply to any civil, criminal, or juvenile case or proceeding initiated or pending as of January 1, 2011.

(d) [Sunset provision.] This section shall remain in effect only until January 1, 2016, and as of that date is repealed, unless a later enacted statute, that is enacted before January 1, 2016, deletes or extends that date. If this section is repealed, the fact that it is repealed, should it occur, shall not be deemed to give rise to any ground for an appeal or a postverdict challenge based on its use in a criminal or juvenile case or proceeding before January 1, 2016.

History of Evid. C. §1390: Added eff. Jan. 1, 2011, Stats. 2010, ch. 537, §2. Amended eff. Jan. 1, 2012, Stats. 2011, ch. 296, §90.

DIVISION 11. WRITINGS

CHAPTER 1. AUTHENTICATION & PROOF OF WRITINGS

ARTICLE 1. REQUIREMENT OF AUTHENTICATION

§1400. [AUTHENTICATION]

Authentication of a writing means (a) the introduction of evidence sufficient to sustain a finding that it is the writing that the proponent of the evidence claims it is or (b) the establishment of such facts by any other means provided by law.

History of Evid. C. §1400: Added eff. Sept. 17, 1965, oper. Jan. 1, 1967, Stats. 1965, ch. 299, §2.

Official Comment

7 Cal. Law Revision Comm'n Rep. (1965) p. 1263.

Before any tangible object may be admitted into evidence, the party seeking to introduce the object must make a preliminary showing that the object is in some way relevant to the issues to be decided in the action. When the object sought to be introduced is a writing, this preliminary showing of relevancy usually entails some proof that the writing is authentic—*i.e.*, that the writing was made or signed by its purported maker. Hence, this showing is normally referred to as "authentication" of the writing. But authentication, correctly understood, may involve a preliminary showing that the writing is a forgery or is a writing found in particular files regardless of its authorship. *Cf. People v. Adamson*, 118 Cal.App.2d 714, 258 P.2d 1020 (1953). When the requisite preliminary showing has been made, the judge admits the writing into evidence for consideration by the trier of fact. However, the fact that the judge permits the writing to be admitted in evidence does not necessarily establish the authenticity of the writing; all that the judge has determined is that there has been a sufficient showing of the authenticity of the writing to permit the trier of fact to find that it is authentic. The trier of fact independently determines the question of authenticity, and, if the trier of fact does not believe the evidence of authenticity, it may find that the writing is not authentic despite the fact that the judge has determined that it was "authenticated." *See* 7 Wigmore, *Evidence* §§2129-2135 (3d ed. 1940).

This chapter sets forth the rules governing this process of authentication. Sections 1400-1402 (Article 1) define and state the general requirement of authentication—either by evidence sufficient to sustain a finding of authenticity or by other means sanctioned by law. Sections 1410-1454 (Articles 2 and 3) set forth some of the means that may be used to authenticate certain kinds of writings. The operation and effect of these sections is explained in separate *Comments* relating to them.

Under Section 1400, as under existing law, a writing may be authenticated by the presentation of evidence sufficient to sustain a finding of its authenticity. *See Verzan v. McGregor*, 23 Cal. 339, 342-343 (1863). Under Section 1400, as under existing law, the authenticity of a particular writing also may be established by some means other than the introduction of evidence of authenticity. Thus, the authenticity of a writing may be established by stipulation or by the pleadings. *See, e.g.*, Code Civ. Proc. §§447 and 448. The requisite preliminary showing may also be supplied by a presumption. *See, e.g.*, Evidence Code §§1450-1454, 1530. In some instances, a presumption of authenticity may also attach to a writing authenticated in a particular manner. *See, e.g.*, Evidence Code §643 (the ancient documents rule). Where a presumption applies, the trier of fact is required to find that the writing is authentic unless the requisite contrary showing is made. Evidence Code §§600, 604, 606.

ANNOTATIONS

People v. Chism (2014) 58 Cal.4th 1226, 1303. See annotation under Evidence Code §1553, p. 1426.

Serri v. Santa Clara Univ. (6th Dist.2014) 226 Cal.App.4th 830, 855. "Unless the opposing party admits the genuineness of the document, the proponent of the evidence must present declarations or other 'evidence sufficient to sustain a finding that it is the writing that the proponent of the evidence claims it is.' [¶] [P's] evidence includes more than 20 exhibits that consist of handwritten notes.... According to [P], these are [D's] notes. However, none of the handwritten notes are signed and there is no evidence they were written by [D]. To authenticate the notes, [P] could have propounded requests for admission asking [D] to admit their authenticity and to admit that she wrote them.... [P] could also have asked [D] to authenticate the notes when she took [D's] deposition. There is no evidence in the record that [P] did either of these things. Furthermore, [Ds] did not rely on the notes in their own submission. In addition, many of the notes, to the extent we can decipher them, appear to document con-

versations with other persons and are therefore hearsay. Since [P] did not meet her burden of demonstrating the admissibility of the handwritten notes, the trial court did not err in sustaining objections to them."

People v. Valdez (4th Dist.2011) 201 Cal.App.4th 1429, 1434-35. "[D's] authentication challenge [to the admission of MySpace printouts] fails because the prosecution met its initial burden to support its claim the MySpace site belonged to [D], and that the photographs and other content at the page were not falsified but accurately depicted what they purported to show. Importantly, 'the fact that the judge permits [a] writing to be admitted in evidence does not necessarily establish the authenticity of the writing; all that the judge has determined is that there has been a sufficient showing of the authenticity of the writing to permit the trier of fact to find that it is authentic.' … The author's testimony is not required to authenticate a document …; instead, its authenticity may be established by the contents of the writing … or by other means…. 'As long as the evidence would support a finding of authenticity, the writing is admissible. The fact conflicting inferences can be drawn regarding authenticity goes to the document's weight as evidence, not its admissibility.' [¶] [The evidence] suggested the [MySpace] page belonged to [D] rather than someone else by the same name, who happened to look just like him. Although [D] was free to argue otherwise to the jury, a reasonable trier of fact could conclude from the posting of personal photographs, communications, and other details that the MySpace page belonged to him. *At 1436-37:* [Also significant here was] evidence of the password requirement for posting and deleting content[, in addition to] the pervasive consistency of the content of the page…. [¶] And unlike other authority on which [D] relies, nothing suggested he had a personal enemy with a motive to implicate [D] in future gang crimes by creating an entire site or individual postings on it. … We recognize, of course, that hacking may occur and that documents and other material on the Internet may not be what they seem. But the proponent's threshold authentication burden for admissibility is *not* to establish validity or negate falsity in a categorical fashion, but rather to make a showing on which the trier of fact reasonably could conclude the proffered writing is authentic. The prosecution met that burden here, as the trial court properly concluded. We therefore reject [D's] authentication challenge."

McGarry v. Sax (3d Dist.2008) 158 Cal.App.4th 983, 990-91. "Under … §1400, a video recording is authenticated by testimony or other evidence that it actually depicts what it purports to show. [P] fails to provide any authentication of the videotape or the stills. This failure rendered the proffered evidence inadmissible at trial. It also renders it useless on appeal because we do not know what the material actually depicts."

Ashford v. Culver City Unified Sch. Dist. (2d Dist.2005) 130 Cal.App.4th 344, 349 n.5, *disapproved on other grounds*, ***Voices of the Wetlands v. State Water Res. Control Bd.*** (2011) 52 Cal.4th 499. See annotation under Evidence Code §250, p. 1197.

Stockinger v. Feather River Cmty. Coll. (3d Dist.2003) 111 Cal.App.4th 1014, 1028. "[A]uthentication of a writing is independent of the question of whether the content of the writing is inadmissible as hearsay."

Jones v. City of L.A. (2d Dist.1993) 20 Cal.App.4th 436, 440 n.5. "Pursuant to … §1400, it is sufficient to authenticate a 'Day In The Life' videotape if the proponent makes a showing the videotape is an accurate portrayal of what it purports to be. … [I]t is well settled that the testimony of a person who was present at the time a film was made that it accurately depicts what it purports to show is legally sufficient foundation for its admission into evidence. [¶] [B]efore a 'Day in The Life' film can become evidence at trial it must first pass a two-prong test. First, a foundation must be laid, by someone having personal knowledge of the filmed object, that the film is an accurate portrayal of what it purports to show. Second, the film is only admissible if its probative value is not substantially out-weighed by the danger of unfair prejudice. [¶] [T]he reliability and accuracy of the motion picture need not necessarily rest upon the validity of the process used in its creation, but rather may be established by testimony that the motion picture accurately reproduces phenomena actually perceived by the witness. Under this theory, though the requisite foundation may, and usually will, be laid by the photographer, it may also be provided by any witness who perceived the events filmed. Of course, if the foundation testimony reveals the film to be distorted in some material particular, exclusion is the proper result." (Internal quotes omitted.)

Interinsurance Exch. v. Velji (2d Dist.1975) 44 Cal.App.3d 310, 318. "[T]he objection that a document has not been authenticated does not go to the truth of

the contents of the document, but rather to the introduction of evidence sufficient to sustain a finding that it is the writing that the proponent claims it to be." *See also* ***City of Vista v. Sutro & Co.*** (4th Dist.1997) 52 Cal.App.4th 401, 412.

§1401. [AUTHENTICATION OF WRITING]

(a) [Admissibility of writing.] Authentication of a writing is required before it may be received in evidence.

(b) [Admissibility of content.] Authentication of a writing is required before secondary evidence of its content may be received in evidence.

History of Evid. C. §1401: Added eff. Sept. 17, 1965, oper. Jan. 1, 1967, Stats. 1965, ch. 299, §2.

Official Comment

7 Cal. Law Revision Comm'n Rep. (1965) p. 1264; Assem. J., Apr. 6, 1965, p. 1763.

The requirement of authentication stated in subdivision (a) reflects existing law. *Ten Winkel v. Anglo California Sec. Co.*, 11 Cal.2d 707, 81 P.2d 958 (1938). However, the requirement has never been stated in the California statutes.

Some cases have indicated that authentication is not necessary under certain circumstances, as, for example, when the execution of the writing is not in issue. *See People v. Adamson*, 118 Cal.App.2d 714, 258 P.2d 1020 (1953). This is true, however, only if "authentication" is construed narrowly to refer only to proof of due execution. The Evidence Code defines the term more broadly and requires all writings to be authenticated. The writing involved in the *Adamson* case was a letter that a witness claimed he had received and acted upon. Under the Evidence Code, the requirement of authentication would require a showing that the letter offered in evidence was in fact the one received and acted upon; and this is the preliminary showing that was found sufficient in the *Adamson* case.

§1400

The "writing" referred to in subdivision (a) is any writing offered in evidence; although it may be either an original or a copy, it must be authenticated before it may be received in evidence.

Authentication of a writing does not in and of itself authorize the writing to be admitted in evidence. The writing, of course, must be relevant and not be made inadmissible by any exclusionary rule—*e.g.*, the hearsay rule, the best evidence rule, or the rule excluding a coerced confession. Thus, Section 1401 merely requires that an otherwise admissible writing be authenticated before it may be received in evidence.

Subdivision (b) of Section 1401 requires that a writing be authenticated even when it is not offered in evidence but is sought to be proved by a copy or by testimony as to its content under the circumstances permitted by Sections 1500-1510 (the best evidence rule). This is declarative of existing California law. *Spottiswood v. Weir*, 80 Cal. 448, 22 Pac. 289 (1889); *Smith v. Brannan*, 13 Cal. 107, 115 (1859); *Forman v. Goldberg*, 42 Cal.App.2d 308, 316-317, 108 P.2d 983, 988 (1941). Under Section 1401, therefore, if a person offers in evidence a copy of a writing, he must make a sufficient preliminary showing of the authenticity of both the copy and the original (*i.e.*, the writing sought to be proved by the copy).

In some instances, however, authentication of a copy will provide the necessary evidence to authenticate the original writing at the same time. For example: If a copy of a recorded deed is offered in evidence, Section 1401 requires that the copy be authenticated—proved to be a copy of the official record. It also requires that the official record be authenticated—proved to be the official record—because the official record is a writing of which secondary evidence of its content is being offered. Finally, Section 1401 requires the original deed itself to be authenticated—proved to have been executed by its purported maker—for it, too, is a writing of which secondary evidence of its content is being offered. The copy offered in evidence may be authenticated by the attestation or certification of the official custodian of the record as provided by Section 1530. Under Section 1530, the authenticated copy is prima facie evidence of the existence and content of the official record itself. Thus, the authenticated copy supplies the necessary authenticating evidence for the official record. Under Section 1600, the official record is prima facie evidence of the existence and content of the original deed and of its execution by its purported maker; hence, the official record is the requisite authenticating evidence for the original deed. Thus, the duly attested or certified copy of the record meets the requirement of authentication for the copy itself, for the official record, and for the original deed.

ANNOTATIONS

People v. Lucas (2014) 60 Cal.4th 153, 262. "A writing is admissible if a finding of authentication is supported by a preponderance of the evidence."

Luckman Prtshp. v. Superior Ct. (2d Dist.2010) 184 Cal.App.4th 30, 34-35. "[W]e find that the [summary-judgment] declaration of [D's] counsel sufficiently authenticated the documents. Under … §1401, '[a]uthentication of a writing is required before it may be received in evidence.' '[A] document is authenticated when sufficient evidence has been produced to sustain a finding that the document is what it purports to be….' Here, [D's] counsel in this case declared that he had personal knowledge that the documents attached to his declaration were [co-D's] verified interrogatory responses in this action, along with exhibits which [co-D] attached to its interrogatory responses. Counsel represented a party in this action, and his declaration was sufficient to show that interrogatory responses in this action were what they purported to be."

Ashford v. Culver City Unified Sch. Dist. (2d Dist.2005) 130 Cal.App.4th 344, 349 n.5, *disapproved on other grounds*, ***Voices of the Wetlands v. State Water Res. Control Bd.*** (2011) 52 Cal.4th 499. See annotation under Evidence Code §250, p. 1197.

§1402. [AUTHENTICATION OF ALTERED WRITING]

The party producing a writing as genuine which has been altered, or appears to have been altered, after its execution, in a part material to the question in dispute, must account for the alteration or appearance thereof. He may show that the alteration was made by another, without his concurrence, or was made with the consent of the parties affected by it, or otherwise properly or innocently made, or that the alteration did not change the meaning or language of the instrument. If he does that, he may give the writing in evidence, but not otherwise.

History of Evid. C. §1402: Added eff. Sept. 17, 1965, oper. Jan. 1, 1967, Stats. 1965, ch. 299, §2.

Official Comment

7 Cal. Law Revision Comm'n Rep. (1965) p. 1266.

Section 1402 restates and supersedes Code of Civil Procedure Section 1982. *See Miller v. Luco*, 80 Cal. 257, 265, 22 Pac. 195, 197 (1889); *King v. Tarabino*, 53 Cal.App. 157, 199 Pac. 890 (1921).

ANNOTATIONS

Fashion 21 v. Coalition for Humane Immigrant Rights (2d Dist.2004) 117 Cal.App.4th 1138, 1146-47. "A court's main concern in admitting a videotape as substantive evidence of an event is making sure the tape accurately depicts what occurred. Courts have recognized factors such as 'the elimination of unfavorable portions of a film' and the 'angle from which a picture is taken … may tend to create misleading impressions.' [¶] Under … §1402 the party offering an edited videotape into evidence at trial bears the burden of showing the editing did not distort the 'meaning' of the activities depicted in the tape. If, at trial, [P] failed to show the edits it made in reducing seven hours of footage to 11 minutes did not 'change the meaning' of the tape an objection under §1402 would have to be sustained. *At 1148:* Evidence made inadmissible by the hearsay rule, the parol evidence rule or a privilege could never be introduced at trial and therefore could never support a judgment for the plaintiff. But evidence that is made inadmissible only because the plaintiff failed to satisfy a precondition to its admissibility could support a judgment for the plaintiff assuming the precondition could be satisfied. Generally, authentication problems tend to be among the easiest evidentiary dilemmas to overcome once they are called to the party's attention. [¶] In most cases it would be a simple matter to have the videographer truthfully testify at trial he shot the original videotape, the tape was edited to conserve the court's time and delete the portions not relevant to this case, he compared the edited version of the tape to the original and the edited version accurately depicts the conduct on the original. Such testimony would establish a prima facie basis for admitting the tape under … §1402."

ARTICLE 2. MEANS OF AUTHENTICATING & PROVING WRITINGS

§1410. [MEANS OF AUTHENTICATION NOT EXCLUSIVE]

Nothing in this article shall be construed to limit the means by which a writing may be authenticated or proved.

History of Evid. C. §1410: Added eff. Sept. 17, 1965, oper. Jan. 1, 1967, Stats. 1965, ch. 299, §2.

Official Comment

7 Cal. Law Revision Comm'n Rep. (1965) p. 1266.

This article (Sections 1410-1421) lists many of the evidentiary means for authenticating writings and supersedes the existing statutory expressions of such means.

Section 1410 is included in this article in recognition of the fact that it would be impossible to specify all of the varieties of circumstantial evidence that may be sufficient in particular cases to sustain a finding of the authenticity of a writing. Hence, Section 1410 ensures that the means of authentication listed in this article or stated elsewhere in the codes will not be considered the exclusive means of authenticating writings. Although Section 1410 has no counterpart in previous legislation, the California courts have never considered the listing of certain means of authentication in the various California statutes as precluding reliance upon other means of authentication. *See, e.g., People v. Ramsey*, 83 Cal.App.2d 707, 189 P.2d 802 (1948) (authentication by evidence of possession); *Geary St. etc. R.R. v. Campbell*, 39 Cal.App. 496, 179 Pac. 453 (1919) (corporate stock record book authenticated by age, appropriate custody, and unsuspicious appearance). *See also* the *Comments* to Sections 1420 and 1421.

ANNOTATIONS

People v. Valdez (4th Dist.2011) 201 Cal.App.4th 1429, 1434-35. See annotation under Evidence Code §1400, p. 1413.

§1410.5. [GRAFFITI AS A WRITING]

(a) [Graffiti.] For purposes of this chapter, a writing shall include any graffiti consisting of written words, insignia, symbols, or any other markings which convey a particular meaning.

(b) [Proof of vandalism.] Any writing described in subdivision (a), or any photograph thereof, may be admitted into evidence in an action for vandalism, for the purpose of proving that the writing was made by the defendant.

(c) [Ruling on admissibility.] The admissibility of any fact offered to prove that the writing was made by the defendant shall, upon motion of the defendant, be ruled upon outside the presence of the jury, and is subject to the requirements of Sections 1416, 1417, and 1418.

History of Evid. C. §1410.5: Added eff. Jan. 1, 1990, Stats. 1989, ch. 660, §1.

§1411. [SUBSCRIBING-WITNESS TESTIMONY NOT REQUIRED]

Except as provided by statute, the testimony of a subscribing witness is not required to authenticate a writing.

History of Evid. C. §1411: Added eff. Sept. 17, 1965, oper. Jan. 1, 1967, Stats. 1965, ch. 299, §2.

Official Comment

7 Cal. Law Revision Comm'n Rep. (1965) p. 1267.

When Section 1940 of the Code of Civil Procedure was enacted in 1872, it stated the common law rule that a subscribing witness to a witnessed writing must be produced to authenticate the writing or his absence must be satisfactorily accounted for. *See Stevens v. Irwin*, 12 Cal. 306 (1859). Section 1940 was amended by the Code Amendments of 1873-74 to remove the requirement that

the subscribing witness be produced. Cal. Stats. 1873-74, ch. 383, §231 (Code Amdts., p. 386). Instead, three alternative methods of authenticating a writing were listed.

Section 1411 states directly what the 1873-74 amendment to Code of Civil Procedure Section 1940 stated indirectly—that the common law rule requiring the production of a subscribing witness to a witnessed writing is not the law in California unless a statute specifically so requires.

ANNOTATIONS

People v. Valdez (4th Dist.2011) 201 Cal.App.4th 1429, 1434-35. See annotation under Evidence Code §1400, p. 1413.

§1412. [SUBSCRIBING-WITNESS TESTIMONY REQUIRED]

If the testimony of a subscribing witness is required by statute to authenticate a writing and the subscribing witness denies or does not recollect the execution of the writing, the writing may be authenticated by other evidence.

History of Evid. C. §1412: Added eff. Sept. 17, 1965, oper. Jan. 1, 1967, Stats. 1965, ch. 299, §2.

Official Comment

7 Cal. Law Revision Comm'n Rep. (1965) p. 1267.

When enacted in 1872, Code of Civil Procedure Section 1941 stated a limitation on the common law rule requiring proof of witnessed writings by a subscribing witness. Section 1941 provided, in effect, that this rule did not prohibit the authentication of a witnessed writing by other evidence if the subscribing witness denied or did not remember the execution of the writing. Evidence Code Section 1412, which supersedes Code of Civil Procedure Section 1941, retains this limitation on the subscribing witness rule in those few cases, such as those involving wills, where a statute requires the testimony of a subscribing witness to authenticate a writing.

§1413. [WITNESS TO EXECUTION OF A WRITING]

A writing may be authenticated by anyone who saw the writing made or executed, including a subscribing witness.

History of Evid. C. §1413: Added eff. Sept. 17, 1965, oper. Jan. 1, 1967, Stats. 1965, ch. 299, §2.

Official Comment

**7 Cal. Law Revision Comm'n Rep. (1965) p. 1268;
Assem. J., Apr. 6, 1965, p. 1764.**

Section 1413 restates and supersedes the provisions of subdivisions 1 and 3 of Code of Civil Procedure Section 1940.

Section 1413 refers to writings that were "made" as well as "executed" in order to include all kinds of writings, not merely those bearing a signature. *See* Evidence Code §250, defining "writing."

§1414. [EVIDENCE THAT AUTHENTICATES A WRITING]

A writing may be authenticated by evidence that:

(a) [Adverse-party admission.] The party against whom it is offered has at any time admitted its authenticity; or

(b) [Adverse-party action.] The writing has been acted upon as authentic by the party against whom it is offered.

History of Evid. C. §1414: Added eff. Sept. 17, 1965, oper. Jan. 1, 1967, Stats. 1965, ch. 299, §2.

Official Comment

7 Cal. Law Revision Comm'n Rep. (1965) p. 1268.

Section 1414 restates and supersedes the provisions of Code of Civil Procedure Section 1942. Section 1942 is difficult to understand. It was amended in 1901 to make it more intelligible. Cal. Stats. 1901, ch. 102, §480, p. 247. However, the code revision of which the 1901 amendment was a part was held unconstitutional because of technical defects in the title of the act and because the act embraced more than one subject. *Lewis v. Dunne*, 134 Cal. 291, 66 Pac. 478 (1901). Evidence Code Section 1414 is based on the 1901 amendment of Section 1942.

§1415. [HANDWRITING OF MAKER]

A writing may be authenticated by evidence of the genuineness of the handwriting of the maker.

History of Evid. C. §1415: Added eff. Sept. 17, 1965, oper. Jan. 1, 1967, Stats. 1965, ch. 299, §2.

Official Comment

7 Cal. Law Revision Comm'n Rep. (1965) p. 1268.

Section 1415 restates and supersedes the provisions of subdivision 2 of Code of Civil Procedure Section 1940.

§1416. [OPINION EVIDENCE ON HANDWRITING]

A witness who is not otherwise qualified to testify as an expert may state his opinion whether a writing is in the handwriting of a supposed writer if the court finds that he has personal knowledge of the handwriting of the supposed writer. Such personal knowledge may be acquired from:

(a) Having seen the supposed writer write;

(b) Having seen a writing purporting to be in the handwriting of the supposed writer and upon which the supposed writer has acted or been charged;

(c) Having received letters in the due course of mail purporting to be from the supposed writer in response to letters duly addressed and mailed by him to the supposed writer; or

(d) Any other means of obtaining personal knowledge of the handwriting of the supposed writer.

History of Evid. C. §1416: Added eff. Sept. 17, 1965, oper. Jan. 1, 1967, Stats. 1965, ch. 299, §2.

Official Comment

7 Cal. Law Revision Comm'n Rep. (1965) p. 1269.

Section 1416 is based on Code of Civil Procedure Section 1943 as amended in the code revision of 1901. Cal. Stats. 1901, ch. 102, §481, p. 247. *See* the *Comment* to Section 1414.

ANNOTATIONS

People v. Lucas (2014) 60 Cal.4th 153, 266-67. Witness's "opinion [qualified] under [Evid. C.] §1416. He had sufficient personal knowledge of [D's] writing, having known and worked with [D] for several years. In that capacity, he saw various documents containing

letters and numerals written by [D], including a number of documents that he identified in court. The court reasonably held that this gave [witness] sufficient personal knowledge to opine about whether [D] authored the note. [¶] [D] asserts that ... §1416 should not apply to the handwriting on the ... note because the note contains 'handprinting' rather than 'handwriting.' He quotes the comment to [Evid. C.] §1418, the statute providing for the admissibility of expert testimony about handwriting, stating that it applies 'to any form of writing, not just handwriting.' He reasons that because 'writing' means something beyond 'handwriting' in §1418, §1416 must be intended to apply to cursive handwriting only. We disagree. [¶] First, the comment quoted by [D] is intended to clarify that expert witnesses may provide opinions comparing *typewriting* under that section. Second, [D] points to no court or other authority that has applied different standards to cursive and printed letters. Moreover, the extent to which a distinction between cursive handwriting and handprinting might affect the relevance of an opinion concerning authorship can properly be elicited through cross-examination."

§1417. [COMPARISON OF OTHER HANDWRITING BY TRIER OF FACT]

The genuineness of handwriting, or the lack thereof, may be proved by a comparison made by the trier of fact with handwriting (a) which the court finds was admitted or treated as genuine by the party against whom the evidence is offered or (b) otherwise proved to be genuine to the satisfaction of the court.

History of Evid. C. §1417: Added eff. Sept. 17, 1965, oper. Jan. 1, 1967, Stats. 1965, ch. 299, §2.

Official Comment

7 Cal. Law Revision Comm'n Rep. (1965) p. 1269.

Section 1417 is based on that portion of Code of Civil Procedure Section 1944 that permits the trier of fact to compare questioned handwriting with handwriting the court has found to be genuine.

§1418. [COMPARISON OF OTHER WRITING BY EXPERT]

The genuineness of writing, or the lack thereof, may be proved by a comparison made by an expert witness with writing (a) which the court finds was admitted or treated as genuine by the party against whom the evidence is offered or (b) otherwise proved to be genuine to the satisfaction of the court.

History of Evid. C. §1418: Added eff. Sept. 17, 1965, oper. Jan. 1, 1967, Stats. 1965, ch. 299, §2.

Official Comment

7 Cal. Law Revision Comm'n Rep. (1965) p. 1270.

Section 1418 is based on that portion of Code of Civil Procedure Section 1944 that permits a witness to compare questioned handwriting with handwriting the court has found to be genuine. However, Section 1418 applies to any form of writing, not just handwriting. This is in recognition of the fact that experts can now compare typewriting specimens and other forms of writing as accurately as they could compare handwriting specimens in 1872.

Although Code of Civil Procedure Section 1944 does not expressly require that the witness making the comparison be an expert witness (as Evidence Code Section 1418 does), the cases have nonetheless imposed this requirement. *E.g., Spottiswood v. Weir*, 80 Cal. 448, 22 Pac. 289 (1889). The witness' expertise may, of course, be derived from practical experience instead of from technical training. *In re Newell's Estate*, 75 Cal.App. 554, 243 Pac. 33 (1926) (experienced banker).

ANNOTATIONS

People v. Lucas (2014) 60 Cal.4th 153, 224. "[W]e have recognized that expert handwriting comparisons have evidentiary value and that juries should 'form their own conclusion in reference to such similarity or resemblance.' ... The Evidence Code endorses the use of expert testimony in handwriting comparison and further allows jurors to make their own comparisons of handwriting. [¶] Although our courts, to date, have not directly ruled on the applicability of [***People v. Kelly*** (1976) 17 Cal.3d 24] to expert handwriting comparison, they have frequently held that the ***Kelly*** framework does not apply to comparisons that focus on physical evidence 'whose existence, appearance, nature, and meaning are obvious to the senses of a layperson.' Under these circumstances, 'the reliability of the process in producing that result is equally apparent and need not be debated under the standards of ***Kelly***....' *At 225:* In this case, the trial court held that the method of handwriting comparison offered by the prosecution was not sufficiently 'scientific' to require a hearing under ***Kelly***. We agree.... The handwriting comparison utilized here merely isolated, and carefully compared, readily observable aspects of physical evidence through simple magnification. ... Jurors could compare the handwriting on the ... note directly with the exemplars provided by [D] and were provided enlarged versions of both that were over three times their original size. Jurors are equipped to make those evaluations and draw their own conclusions based on their independent observations of the evidence. [A] jury's competence in performing this very analysis is recognized in [Evid. C.] §1417. The magnification employed here was not a highly technical test that would hold undue sway over jurors. [¶] Additionally, the expert in this case stated that it was his 'opinion with reasonable certainty' that the author of [D's] exemplars was also the author of the handwriting on the ... note, even though he admitted that he employed no standardized number of similarities or differences in the comparison before reach-

ing that opinion. The expert further admitted that 'there is a lot of handwriting similarity in the general population' and that 'some people write alike' such that he may 'not have the ability to distinguish between them.' This testimony, therefore, was not presented as a 'definitive truth,' but rather as an informed opinion based on the witness's transparently subjective techniques. Because this method of analysis is not sufficiently 'scientific' under *Kelly*, we need not reach the other *Kelly* issues raised by [D]."

§1419. [WRITING MORE THAN 30 YEARS OLD]

Where a writing whose genuineness is sought to be proved is more than 30 years old, the comparison under Section 1417 or 1418 may be made with writing purporting to be genuine, and generally respected and acted upon as such, by persons having an interest in knowing whether it is genuine.

History of Evid. C. §1419: Added eff. Sept. 17, 1965, oper. Jan. 1, 1967, Stats. 1965, ch. 299, §2.

Official Comment

7 Cal. Law Revision Comm'n Rep. (1965) p. 1270.

Section 1419 restates and supersedes the provisions of Code of Civil Procedure Section 1945. The apparent purpose of Section 1945, continued without substantive change in Evidence Code Section 1419, is to permit the judge to be satisfied with a lesser degree of proof of the authenticity of an exemplar when the writing offered in evidence is more than 30 years old.

§1420. [WRITING RECEIVED AS A RESPONSE]

A writing may be authenticated by evidence that the writing was received in response to a communication sent to the person who is claimed by the proponent of the evidence to be the author of the writing.

History of Evid. C. §1420: Added eff. Sept. 17, 1965, oper. Jan. 1, 1967, Stats. 1965, ch. 299, §2.

Official Comment

7 Cal. Law Revision Comm'n Rep. (1965) p. 1270.

Section 1420 provides a method of authentication recognized in California case law but not previously reflected in California statutes. *House Grain Co. v. Finerman & Sons*, 116 Cal.App.2d 485, 253 P.2d 1034 (1953).

§1421. [WRITING AUTHENTICATED BY CONTENT]

A writing may be authenticated by evidence that the writing refers to or states matters that are unlikely to be known to anyone other than the person who is claimed by the proponent of the evidence to be the author of the writing.

History of Evid. C. §1421: Added eff. Sept. 17, 1965, oper. Jan. 1, 1967, Stats. 1965, ch. 299, §2.

Official Comment

7 Cal. Law Revision Comm'n Rep. (1965) p. 1271.

Section 1421 provides a method of authentication recognized in California case law but not previously reflected in California statutes. *Chaplin v. Sullivan*, 67 Cal.App.2d 728, 734, 155 P.2d 368, 372 (1945).

ANNOTATIONS

People v. Valdez (4th Dist.2011) 201 Cal.App.4th 1429, 1434-35. See annotation under Evidence Code §1400, p. 1413.

Stockinger v. Feather River Cmty. Coll. (3d Dist.2003) 111 Cal.App.4th 1014, 1028. See annotation under Evidence Code §1400, p. 1413.

Arcaro v. Silva & Silva Enters. (2d Dist.1999) 77 Cal.App.4th 152, 157 n.4. "[D] points out it verified the address, telephone number and Social Security number on the credit application belonged to [P]. However, the fact the application contains personal information about [P] is not evidence [P] actually signed the application. Furthermore, it is unfortunate but true that personal information such as a person's address, telephone number and Social Security number are *likely* to be known to a great many persons other than the person claimed to have signed the credit application."

ARTICLE 3. PRESUMPTIONS AFFECTING ACKNOWLEDGED WRITINGS & OFFICIAL WRITINGS

§1450. [PRESUMPTIONS]

The presumptions established by this article are presumptions affecting the burden of producing evidence.

History of Evid. C. §1450: Added eff. Sept. 17, 1965, oper. Jan. 1, 1967, Stats. 1965, ch. 299, §2.

Official Comment

7 Cal. Law Revision Comm'n Rep. (1965) p. 1271.

This article (Sections 1450-1454) lists several presumptions that may be used to authenticate particular kinds of writings. Section 1450 prescribes the effect of these presumptions. They require a finding of authenticity unless the adverse party produces evidence sufficient to sustain a finding that the writing in question is not authentic. *See* Evidence Code §604 and the *Comment* thereto.

ANNOTATIONS

Jacobson v. Gourley (4th Dist.2000) 83 Cal.App.4th 1331, 1334. "If the facts support the existence of a presumption, '[t]he burden is on the adverse party to introduce evidence sufficient to sustain a finding that the ... official writing is not genuine in order to dispel the presumption of authenticity or genuineness.' If the adverse party fails to come forward with evidence that disputes authenticity, the writing must be found to be authentic."

§1451. [ACKNOWLEDGED WRITING]

A certificate of the acknowledgment of a writing other than a will, or a certificate of the proof of such a writing, is prima facie evidence of the facts recited in

the certificate and the genuineness of the signature of each person by whom the writing purports to have been signed if the certificate meets the requirements of Article 3 (commencing with Section 1180) of Chapter 4, Title 4, Part 4, Division 2 of the Civil Code.

History of Evid. C. §1451: Added eff. Sept. 17, 1965, oper. Jan. 1, 1967, Stats. 1965, ch. 299, §2.

Official Comment

7 Cal. Law Revision Comm'n Rep. (1965) p. 1272.

Section 1451 continues in effect and restates a method of authenticating private writings that is contained in Code of Civil Procedure Section 1948.

§1452. [OFFICIAL SEAL]

A seal is presumed to be genuine and its use authorized if it purports to be the seal of:

(a) The United States or a department, agency, or public employee of the United States.

(b) A public entity in the United States or a department, agency, or public employee of such public entity.

(c) A nation recognized by the executive power of the United States or a department, agency, or officer of such nation.

(d) A public entity in a nation recognized by the executive power of the United States or a department, agency, or officer of such public entity.

(e) A court of admiralty or maritime jurisdiction.

(f) A notary public within any state of the United States.

History of Evid. C. §1452: Added eff. Sept. 17, 1965, oper. Jan. 1, 1967, Stats. 1965, ch. 299, §2.

Official Comment

7 Cal. Law Revision Comm'n Rep. (1965) p. 1272.

Sections 1452 and 1453 eliminate the need for formal proof of the genuineness of certain official seals and signatures when such proof would otherwise be required by the general requirement of authentication.

Under existing law, formal proof of many of the signatures and seals mentioned in Sections 1452 and 1453 is not required because such signatures and seals are the subject of judicial notice. Code Civ. Proc. §1875(5), (6), (7), (8). (Section 1875 is repealed, now Division 4 (Sections 450-460) of the Evidence Code.) The parties may not dispute a matter that has been judicially noticed. Code Civ. Proc. §2102 (repealed, now Evidence Code §457). Hence, judicial notice of facts should be confined to matters concerning which there can be no reasonable dispute. The authenticity of writings purporting to be official writings should not be determined conclusively by the judge when there is serious dispute as to such authenticity. Therefore, Sections 1452 and 1453 provide that the official seals and signatures mentioned shall be presumed genuine and authorized until evidence is introduced sufficient to sustain a finding that they are not genuine or authorized. When there is such evidence disputing the authenticity of an official seal or signature, the trier of fact is required to determine the question of authenticity without regard to any presumption created by this section. *See* Evidence Code §604 and the *Comment* thereto.

This procedure will dispense with the necessity for proof of authenticity when there is no real dispute as to such authenticity, but it will assure the parties the right to contest the authenticity of official writings when there is a real dispute as to such authenticity.

ANNOTATIONS

Jacobson v. Gourley (4th Dist.2000) 83 Cal.App.4th 1331, 1334-35. "The Evidence Code does not define 'seal,' but the [CCP] does: 'A seal is a particular sign, made to attest, in the most formal manner, the execution of an instrument.' In particular, '[a] public seal in this State is a stamp or impression made by a public officer with an instrument provided by law, to attest the execution of an official or public document, upon the paper, or upon any substance attached to the paper, which is capable of receiving a visible impression.' The execution of an instrument is its subscription and delivery. [¶] If a seal attests to the execution of a document, and if execution means subscription, then it follows that there can be no seal of a document that has not been subscribed." *See also* CCP §§1930-1933.

§1453. [OFFICIAL SIGNATURE]

A signature is presumed to be genuine and authorized if it purports to be the signature, affixed in his official capacity, of:

(a) A public employee of the United States.

(b) A public employee of any public entity in the United States.

(c) A notary public within any state of the United States.

History of Evid. C. §1453: Added eff. Sept. 17, 1965, oper. Jan. 1, 1967, Stats. 1965, ch. 299, §2.

Official Comment

7 Cal. Law Revision Comm'n Rep. (1965) p. 1273.

See the *Comment* to Section 1452.

ANNOTATIONS

Poland v. Department of Motor Vehicles (1st Dist.1995) 34 Cal.App.4th 1128, 1136. "[S]ection 1453 reflects an implicit policy decision that if a document 'purports' to be signed by a public employee acting in an official capacity, the likelihood of its authenticity is sufficiently high that in the absence of evidence to the contrary it should be found authentic. This does not 'render meaningless' the rules governing documentary evidence; it particularizes the treatment of a certain category of documents in order to accommodate the sometimes competing concerns of accurate fact-finding and adjudicatory efficiency."

§1454. [FOREIGN-OFFICIAL SIGNATURE]

A signature is presumed to be genuine and authorized if it purports to be the signature, affixed in his official capacity, of an officer, or deputy of an officer, of a nation or public entity in a nation recognized by the executive power of the United States and the writing to which the signature is affixed is accompanied by a final statement certifying the genuineness of the signature and the official position of (a) the person who executed the writing or (b) any foreign official who has certified either the genuineness of the signature and official position of the person executing the writing or the genuineness of the signature and official position of another foreign official who has executed a similar certificate in a chain of such certificates beginning with a certificate of the genuineness of the signature and official position of the person executing the writing. The final statement may be made only by a secretary of an embassy or legation, consul general, consul, vice consul, consular agent, or other officer in the foreign service of the United States stationed in the nation, authenticated by the seal of his office.

History of Evid. C. §1454: Added eff. Sept. 17, 1965, oper. Jan. 1, 1967, Stats. 1965, ch. 299, §2.

Official Comment

7 Cal. Law Revision Comm'n Rep. (1965) p. 1273.

Section 1454 supersedes the somewhat complex procedure for authenticating foreign official writings that is contained in subdivision 8 of Code of Civil Procedure Section 1918. Section 1454 is based on a proposed amendment to Rule 44 of the Federal Rules of Civil Procedure that has been prepared by the Advisory Committee on Civil Rules, the Commission and Advisory Committee on International Rules of Judicial Procedure, and the Columbia Law School Project on International Procedure. Proposed Amendments to Rules of Civil Procedure for the United States District Courts with Advisory Committee's Notes (mimeo., Feb. 25, 1964). Rule 44 and the proposed amendment, however, deal only with the question of authenticating *copies* of foreign official writings. Section 1454 relates to the authentication of *any* foreign official writing, whether it be an original or a copy.

The procedure set forth in Section 1454 is necessary for the reason that a United States foreign service officer may not be able to certify to the official position and signature of a particular foreign official. Accordingly, this section permits the original signature to be certified by a higher foreign official, whose signature can in turn be certified by a still higher official, and such certifications can be continued in a chain until a foreign official is reached as to whom the United States foreign service officer has adequate information upon which to base his final certification. *See, e.g., New York Life Ins. Co. v. Aronson*, 38 F. Supp. 687 (W.D. Pa. 1941).

See also the *Comment* to Section 1452.

CHAPTER 2. SECONDARY EVIDENCE OF WRITINGS

ARTICLE 1. PROOF OF THE CONTENT OF A WRITING

§§1500 TO 1511. REPEALED

Repealed oper. Jan. 1, 1999, Stats. 1998, ch. 100, §1.

§1520. [ADMISSIBLE ORIGINAL WRITING]

The content of a writing may be proved by an otherwise admissible original.

History of Evid. C. §1520: Added eff. Jan. 1, 1999, Stats. 1998, ch. 100, §2.

Official Comment

26 Cal. Law Revision Comm'n Rep. (1996) p. 391.

Section 1520 continues former Section 1500 insofar as it permitted proof of the content of a writing by an original of the writing. *See also* Sections 1521 (Secondary Evidence Rule), 1522 (exclusion of secondary evidence in criminal action), 1523 (oral testimony of content of writing).

§1521. [SECONDARY-EVIDENCE RULE]

(a) [Admissible secondary evidence.] The content of a writing may be proved by otherwise admissible secondary evidence. The court shall exclude secondary evidence of the content of writing if the court determines either of the following:

(1) A genuine dispute exists concerning material terms of the writing and justice requires the exclusion.

(2) Admission of the secondary evidence would be unfair.

(b) [Inadmissible oral testimony.] Nothing in this section makes admissible oral testimony to prove the content of a writing if the testimony is inadmissible under Section 1523 (oral testimony of the content of a writing).

(c) [Authentication required.] Nothing in this section excuses compliance with Section 1401 (authentication).

(d) [Title.] This section shall be known as the "Secondary Evidence Rule."

History of Evid. C. §1521: Added eff. Jan. 1, 1999, Stats. 1998, ch. 100, §2.

Official Comment

26 Cal. Law Revision Comm'n Rep. (1996) p. 392.

Sections 1520 (proof of content of writing by original), 1521 (Secondary Evidence Rule), 1522 (exclusion of secondary evidence in criminal action), and 1523 (oral testimony of content of writing) replace the *Best Evidence Rule* and its exceptions. For background, see *Best Evidence Rule*, 26 Cal. L. Revision Comm'n Reports 369 (1996). Because of the breadth of the exceptions to the *Best Evidence Rule*, this reform is not a major departure from former law, but primarily a matter of clarification and simplification. Discovery principles remain unchanged.

Subdivision (a) makes secondary evidence generally admissible to prove the content of a writing. The nature of the evidence offered affects its weight, not its admissibility. The normal motivation of parties to support their cases with convincing evidence is a deterrent to introduction of unreliable secondary evidence. *See also* Section 412 (if party offers weaker and less satisfactory evidence despite ability to produce stronger and more satisfactory evidence, the evidence offered should be viewed with distrust).

The mandatory exceptions set forth in subdivisions (a)(1) and (a)(2) provide further protection against unreliable secondary evidence. Those exceptions are modeled on the exceptions to former Section 1511 and to Rule 1003 of the Federal Rules of Evidence. Cases interpreting those statutes provide guidance in applying subdivisions (a)(1) and (a)(2). *See, e.g., United States v. Sin-*

clair, 74 F.3d 753, 760-61 (7th Cir. 1996) (admitting copies of expense account reports was not unfair); *Ruberto v. Commissioner of Internal Revenue*, 774 F.2d 61, 64 (2d Cir. 1985) (tax court did not err in excluding photocopies of canceled checks, "since problems in matching the copies of the backs of the checks with copies of the fronts made them somewhat suspect"); *Amoco Production Co. v. United States*, 619 F.2d 1383, 1391 (10th Cir. 1980) (upholding trial court's determination that "admission of the file copy would be unfair because the most critical part of the original conformed copy ... is not completely reproduced in the 'duplicate'"); *People v. Garcia*, 201 Cal.App.3d 324, 330, 247 Cal.Rptr. 94 (1988) (claim of unfairness "must be based on substance, not mere speculation that the original might contain some relevant difference"). Courts may consider a broad range of factors, for example: (1) whether the proponent attempts to use the writing in a manner that could not reasonably have been anticipated, (2) whether the original was suppressed in discovery, (3) whether discovery conducted in a reasonably diligent (as opposed to exhaustive) manner failed to result in production of the original, (4) whether there are dramatic differences between the original and the secondary evidence (*e.g.*, the original but not the secondary evidence is in color and the colors provide significant clues to interpretation), (5) whether the original is unavailable and, if so, why, and (6) whether the writing is central to the case or collateral. A classic circumstance for exclusion pursuant to subdivision (a)(2) is if the proponent destroyed the original with fraudulent intent or the doctrine of spoliation of evidence otherwise applies.

Subdivision (b) explicitly establishes that Section 1523 (oral testimony of the content of writing), not Section 1521, governs the admissibility of oral testimony to prove the content of a writing.

Subdivision (c) makes clear that like other evidence, secondary evidence is admissible only if it is properly authenticated. Under Section 1401, the proponent must not only authenticate the original writing, but must also establish that the proffered evidence is secondary evidence of the original. *See* B. Jefferson, *Jefferson's Synopsis of California Evidence Law*, §30.1, at 470-71 (1985).

ANNOTATIONS

Dart Indus. v. Commercial Un. Ins. (2002) 28 Cal.4th 1059, 1068. "The rule ... for the admission of secondary evidence of a lost paper, requires that a *bona fide* and diligent search has been unsuccessfully made for it in the place where it was most likely to be found; and further, the party is expected to show that he has in good faith exhausted in a reasonable degree all the sources of information and means of discovery which the nature of the case would naturally suggest, and which were accessible to him. *At 1069:* If any suspicion hangs over the instrument, or that it is designedly withheld, a rigid inquiry should be made into the reasons for its non-production. But where there is no such suspicion, all that ought to be required is reasonable diligence to obtain the original—in fact, courts in such cases are extremely liberal. Questions whether the search was sufficient in scope and was conducted in good faith are addressed to the discretion of the trial court, and will not be disturbed on appeal absent abuse of discretion. [¶] A corollary of the rule that the contents of lost documents may be proved by secondary evidence is that the law does not require the contents of such documents be proved verbatim." (Internal quotes omitted.)

Pajaro Valley Water Mgmt. Agency v. McGrath (6th Dist.2005) 128 Cal.App.4th 1093, 1108. "Section 1521 permits the introduction of 'otherwise admissible secondary evidence' to prove the contents of a writing. It does not excuse the proponent from complying with other rules of evidence, most notably, the hearsay rule."

Prato-Morrison v. Doe (2d Dist.2002) 103 Cal.App.4th 222, 230. "[S]econdary evidence must 'meet the threshold requirement of being trustworthy.'"

In re Kirk (1st Dist.1999) 74 Cal.App.4th 1066, 1074. "Although the secondary evidence rule may change its predecessor rule in some respects ..., the Legislature's express retention of the authentication requirements in [Evid. C.] §1521, subdivision (c) and its failure to amend the certification rules of [Evid. C.] §§1530 and 1531 point[] to the conclusion that the certification rules have not been undercut by the enactment of the secondary evidence rule."

§1522. [EXCLUSION OF SECONDARY EVIDENCE IN CRIMINAL ACTION]

(a) [Original in proponent's possession.] In addition to the grounds for exclusion authorized by Section 1521, in a criminal action the court shall exclude secondary evidence of the content of a writing if the court determines that the original is in the proponent's possession, custody, or control, and the proponent has not made the original reasonably available for inspection at or before trial. This section does not apply to any of the following:

(1) A duplicate as defined in Section 260.

(2) A writing that is not closely related to the controlling issues in the action.

(3) A copy of a writing in the custody of a public entity.

(4) A copy of a writing that is recorded in the public records, if the record or a certified copy of it is made evidence of the writing by statute.

(b) [Request to exclude secondary evidence.] In a criminal action, a request to exclude secondary evidence of the content of a writing, under this section or any other law, shall not be made in the presence of the jury.

History of Evid. C. §1522: Added eff. Jan. 1, 1999, Stats. 1998, ch. 100, §2.

Official Comment

26 Cal. Law Revision Comm'n Rep. (1996) p. 394.

Subdivision (a) of Section 1522 sets forth a mandatory exception applicable only in criminal cases, which are governed by narrower discovery rules than civil cases. *See* Section 130 ("criminal action" includes criminal proceedings). *See also* Penal Code §§1054-1054.7 (discovery in criminal cases). Section 1522 does not expand discovery obligations, it simply conditions use of secondary evidence on making the original reasonably available for inspection if

the proponent has it. In determining whether the proponent of secondary evidence has made the original "reasonably available," the court should examine specific circumstances, such as the time, place, and manner of allowing inspection. The concept is fluid, not rigid. For example, making the original available moments before using secondary evidence may in general suffice if a defendant is rebutting a surprise contention, but not if the prosecution is presenting its case in chief. Similarly, what constitutes reasonable access to computer evidence may vary from system to system.

The exceptions in subdivisions (a)(1)-(a)(4) are drawn from exceptions to the former Best Evidence Rule (former Section 1500). Subdivision (a)(1) is drawn from former Section 1511. Subdivision (a)(2) is drawn from former Section 1504. Subdivision (a)(3) is drawn from former Section 1506. Subdivision (a)(4) is drawn from former Section 1507.

Subdivision (b) continues the requirement of the second sentence of former Section 1503(a), but applies it to all requests for exclusion of secondary evidence in a criminal trial.

See also Sections 1520 (proof of content of writing by original), 1521 (Secondary Evidence Rule), and 1523 (oral testimony of content of writing).

§1523. [ORAL TESTIMONY OF CONTENT OF WRITING]

(a) [Not admissible.] Except as otherwise provided by statute, oral testimony is not admissible to prove the content of a writing.

(b) [Lost or destroyed original.] Oral testimony of the content of a writing is not made inadmissible by subdivision (a) if the proponent does not have possession or control of a copy of the writing and the original is lost or has been destroyed without fraudulent intent on the part of the proponent of the evidence.

(c) [Not procurable or related to controlling issues.] Oral testimony of the content of a writing is not made inadmissible by subdivision (a) if the proponent does not have possession or control of the original or a copy of the writing and either of the following conditions is satisfied:

(1) Neither the writing nor a copy of the writing was reasonably procurable by the proponent by use of the court's process or by other available means.

(2) The writing is not closely related to the controlling issues and it would be inexpedient to require its production.

(d) [Numerous accounts that cannot be examined in court.] Oral testimony of the content of a writing is not made inadmissible by subdivision (a) if the writing consists of numerous accounts or other writings that cannot be examined in court without great loss of time, and the evidence sought from them is only the general result of the whole.

History of Evid. C. §1523: Added eff. Jan. 1, 1999, Stats. 1998, ch. 100, §2.

Official Comment

26 Cal. Law Revision Comm'n Rep. (1996) p. 395.

Section 1523 preserves former law governing the admissibility of oral testimony to prove the content of a writing. *See* former Sections 1500, 1501-1509.

Subdivision (a) is based on an assumption that oral testimony as to the content of a writing is typically less reliable than other proof of the content of a writing. For background, *see Best Evidence Rule*, 26 Cal. L. Revision Comm'n Reports 369 (1996).

Subdivision (b) continues former Sections 1501 and 1505 without substantive change as to oral testimony of the content of a writing that is lost or has been destroyed.

Subdivision (c)(1) continues former Sections 1502 and 1505 without substantive change as to oral testimony of the content of a writing that was not reasonably procurable. In effect, subdivision (c)(1) also continues former Sections 1503 and 1505 without substantive change as to oral testimony of the content of a writing that the opponent has, but failed to produce at the hearing despite being expressly or impliedly notified that it would be needed. Under such circumstances, the writing was not reasonably procurable. Finally, subdivision (c)(1) continues former Sections 1506-1508 without substantive change as to oral testimony of the content of a writing where (1) the writing is in the custody of a public entity and the proponent could not have obtained it or a copy of it in the exercise of reasonable diligence, or (2) the writing has been recorded in the public records, the record or a certified copy of the writing is made evidence of the writing by statute, and the proponent could not have obtained it or a copy of it in the exercise of reasonable diligence. Subdivision (c)(2) continues former Sections 1504 and 1505 without substantive change as to oral testimony of the content of a collateral writing.

Subdivision (d) continues former Section 1509 without substantive change as to oral testimony of a voluminous writing.

See Sections 1520 (proof of content of writing by original), 1521 (Secondary Evidence Rule), and 1522 (exclusion of secondary evidence in criminal action).

ARTICLE 2. OFFICIAL WRITINGS & RECORDED WRITINGS

§1530. [COPY OF OFFICIAL RECORD]

(a) [Prima facie evidence.] A purported copy of a writing in the custody of a public entity, or of an entry in such a writing, is prima facie evidence of the existence and content of such writing or entry if:

(1) The copy purports to be published by the authority of the nation or state, or public entity therein in which the writing is kept;

(2) The office in which the writing is kept is within the United States or within the Panama Canal Zone, the Trust Territory of the Pacific Islands, or the Ryukyu Islands, and the copy is attested or certified as a correct copy of the writing or entry by a public employee, or a deputy of a public employee, having the legal custody of the writing; or

(3) The office in which the writing is kept is not within the United States or any other place described in paragraph (2) and the copy is attested as a correct copy of the writing or entry by a person having authority to make attestation. The attestation must be accompanied by a final statement certifying the genuineness of the signature and the official position of (i) the person who attested the copy as a correct copy or (ii) any foreign official who has certified either the genuineness of the signature and official position of the person attesting the copy or the genuineness of the signature and offi-

cial position of another foreign official who has executed a similar certificate in a chain of such certificates beginning with a certificate of the genuineness of the signature and official position of the person attesting the copy. Except as provided in the next sentence, the final statement may be made only by a secretary of an embassy or legation, consul general, consul, vice consul, or consular agent of the United States, or a diplomatic or consular official of the foreign country assigned or accredited to the United States. Prior to January 1, 1971, the final statement may also be made by a secretary of an embassy or legation, consul general, consul, vice consul, consular agent, or other officer in the foreign service of the United States stationed in the nation in which the writing is kept, authenticated by the seal of his office. If reasonable opportunity has been given to all parties to investigate the authenticity and accuracy of the documents, the court may, for good cause shown, (i) admit an attested copy without the final statement or (ii) permit the writing or entry in foreign custody to be evidenced by an attested summary with or without a final statement.

(b) [Presumptions.] The presumptions established by this section are presumptions affecting the burden of producing evidence.

History of Evid. C. §1530: Added eff. Sept. 17, 1965, oper. Jan. 1, 1967, Stats. 1965, ch. 299, §2. Amended eff. Apr. 3, 1970, Stats. 1970, ch. 41, §1.

Official Comment

7 Cal. Law Revision Comm'n Rep. (1965) p. 1281.

Section 1530 deals with three evidentiary problems. *First*, it is concerned with the problem of proving the content of an original writing by means of a copy, *i.e.*, the best evidence rule. *See* Evidence Code §1500. *Second*, it is concerned with authentication, for the copy must be authenticated as a copy of the original writing. Evidence Code §1401. *Finally*, it is concerned with the hearsay rule, for a certification or attestation of authenticity is "a statement that was made other than by a witness while testifying at the hearing and that is offered to prove the truth of the matter stated." Evidence Code §1200. Because this section is principally concerned with the use of a copy of a writing to prove the content of the original, it is located in the division relating to secondary evidence of writings.

Under existing California law, certain official records may be proved by copies purporting to have been published by official authority or by copies with attached certificates containing certain requisite seals and signatures. The rules are complex and detailed and appear for the most part in Article 2 (beginning with Section 1892) of Chapter 3, Title 2, Part IV of the Code of Civil Procedure.

Section 1530 substitutes for these rules a uniform rule that can be applied to all writings in official custody found within the United States and another rule applicable to all writings in official custody found outside the United States.

Subdivision (a)(1). Subdivision (a)(1) of Section 1530 provides that an official writing may be proved by a copy purporting to be published by official authority. Under Section 1918 of the Code of Civil Procedure, the acts and proceedings of the executive and legislature of any state, the United States, or a foreign government may be proved by documents and journals published by official authority. Subdivision (a)(1) in effect makes these provisions of Section 1918 applicable to all classes of official documents. This extension of the means of proving official documents will facilitate the proof of many official documents the authenticity of which is presumed (Evidence Code §644) and is seldom subject to question.

Subdivision (a)(2) and (a)(3) generally. Paragraphs (2) and (3) of subdivision (a) of Section 1530 set forth the rules for proving the content of writings in official custody by attested or certified copies. A person who "attests" a writing merely affirms it to be true or genuine by his signature. Black, Law Dictionary (4th ed. 1951). Existing California statutes require certain writings to be "certified." Section 1923 of the Code of Civil Procedure (repealed, now Evidence Code Section 1531) provides that the certificate affixed to a certified copy must state that the copy is a correct copy of the original, must be signed by the certifying officer, and must be under his seal of office, if he has one. Thus, the only difference between the words "attested" and "certified" is that the existing statutory definition of "certified" requires the use of a seal, if the authenticating officer has one, whereas the definition of "attested" does not. Section 1530 eliminates the requirement of the seal by the use of the word "attested." However, Section 1530 retains, in addition, the word "certified" because it is the more familiar term in California practice.

Subdivision (a)(2). Under existing law, copies of many records of the United States government and of the governments of sister states may be proved by a copy certified or attested by the custodian alone. *See, e.g.*, Code Civ. Proc. §§1901 and 1918(1), (2), (3), (9); Corp. Code §6600. Yet, other official writings must be certified or attested not only by the custodian but also by a higher official certifying the authority and signature of the custodian. In order to provide a uniform rule for the proof of all domestic official writings, subdivision (a)(2) extends the simpler and more expeditious procedure to all official writings within the United States.

Subdivision (a)(3). Under existing law, some foreign official records may be proved by a copy certified or attested by the custodian alone. *See* Code Civ. Proc. §§1901 and 1918(4). Yet, other copies of foreign official writings must be accompanied by three certificates: one executed by the custodian, another by a higher official certifying the authority and signature of the custodian, and a third by still another official certifying the signature and official position of the second official. *See* Code Civ. Proc. §§1906 and 1918(8).

For these complex rules, subdivision (a)(3) of Section 1530 substitutes a relatively simple and uniform procedure that is applicable to all classes of foreign official writings. Subdivision (a)(3) is based on a proposed amendment to Rule 44 of the Federal Rules of Civil Procedure that has been prepared by the Advisory Committee on Civil Rules, the Commission and Advisory Committee on International Rules of Judicial Procedure, and the Columbia Law School Project on Inter-national Procedure. Proposed Amendments to Rules of Civil Procedure for the United States District Courts with Advisory Committee's Notes (mimeo., Feb. 25, 1964).

Subdivision (a)(3) requires that the copy be attested as a correct copy by "a person having authority to make the attestation." In some foreign countries, the person with authority to attest a copy of an official writing is not necessarily the person with legal custody of the writing. *See* 2B Barron & Holtzoff, *Federal Practice Procedure* §992 (Wright ed. 1961). In such a case, subdivision (a)(3) requires that the attester's signature and official position be certified by another official. If this is a United States foreign service officer stationed in the country, no further certificates are required. If a United States foreign service officer is not able to certify to the signature and official position of the attester, subdivision (a)(3) permits the attester's signature and official position to be certified by a higher foreign official, whose signature can in turn be certified by a still higher official. Such certifications can be continued in a chain until a foreign official is reached as to whom the United States foreign service officer has adequate information upon which to base his final certification. *See, e.g.*, *New York Life Ins. Co. v. Aronson*, 38 F. Supp. 687 (W.D. Pa. 1941).

Subdivision (b). Where evidence is introduced that is sufficient to sustain a finding that the copy is not a correct copy, the trier of fact is required to determine whether the copy is a correct copy without regard to the presumptions created by this section. *See* Evidence Code §604 and the *Comment* thereto.

ANNOTATIONS

People v. Skiles (2011) 51 Cal.4th 1178, 1187. "[C]ertification of an official writing, under [Evid. C.] §§1530 and 1531, establishes its reliability in the absence of evidence overcoming the presumption that it

is a true and correct copy. Thus, the statutory certification process is a 'means provided by law' establishing that the official writing is the writing that the proponent of the evidence claims it is. [¶] Nevertheless, the proponent of the evidence may introduce other 'evidence sufficient to sustain a finding [of authenticity].' The means of authenticating a writing are not limited to those specified in the Evidence Code. For example, a writing can be authenticated by circumstantial evidence and by its contents."

Ambriz v. Kelegian (4th Dist.2007) 146 Cal.App.4th 1519, 1530 n.5. "[T]he Evidence Code does not require a seal in order for the presumptions of authenticity to stand."

§1531. [ATTESTATION OR CERTIFICATION OF COPY]

For the purpose of evidence, whenever a copy of a writing is attested or certified, the attestation or certificate must state in substance that the copy is a correct copy of the original, or of a specified part thereof, as the case may be.

History of Evid. C. §1531: Added eff. Sept. 17, 1965, oper. Jan. 1, 1967, Stats. 1965, ch. 299, §2.

Official Comment

7 Cal. Law Revision Comm'n Rep. (1965) p. 1283.

Section 1531 is based on the provisions of Section 1923 of the Code of Civil Procedure. The language has been modified to define the process of attestation as well as the process of certification. Since Section 1530 permits a writing to be attested or certified for purposes of evidence without the attachment of an official seal, Section 1531 omits any requirement of a seal.

§1532. [OFFICIAL RECORD OF A WRITING]

(a) [Prima facie.] The official record of a writing is prima facie evidence of the existence and content of the original recorded writing if:

(1) The record is in fact a record of an office of a public entity; and

(2) A statute authorized such a writing to be recorded in that office.

(b) [Presumption.] The presumption established by this section is a presumption affecting the burden of producing evidence.

History of Evid. C. §1532: Added eff. Sept. 17, 1965, oper. Jan. 1, 1967, Stats. 1965, ch. 299, §2.

Official Comment

7 Cal. Law Revision Comm'n Rep. (1965) p. 1284.

Section 1530 authorizes the use of a copy of a writing in official custody to prove the content of that writing. When a writing has been recorded, Section 1530 merely permits a certified copy of the record to be used to prove the record, not the original recorded writing. Section 1532 permits the official record to be used to prove the content of the original recorded writing. However, under the provisions of Section 1401, the original recorded writing must be authenticated before the copy can be introduced. If the writing was executed by a public official, or if a certificate of acknowledgment or proof was attached to the writing, the original writing is presumed to be authentic and no further evidence of authenticity is required. Evidence Code §§1450, 1451, and 1453.

Where evidence is introduced that is sufficient to sustain a finding that the original writing is not authentic, the trier of fact is required to determine the authenticity of the original writing without regard to the presumption created by this section. *See* Evidence Code §604 and the *Comment* thereto.

Code of Civil Procedure Section 1951 (repealed, now Evidence Code Section 1600) is similar to Section 1532, but the Code of Civil Procedure section relates only to writings affecting property. Section 1532 extends the principle of the Code of Civil Procedure section to all recorded writings. There is no comparable provision in existing law.

ARTICLE 3. PHOTOGRAPHIC COPIES & PRINTED REPRESENTATIONS OF WRITINGS

Official Comment

26 Cal. Law Revision Comm'n Rep. (1996) p. 396.

The article heading is amended to reflect the repeal of the Best Evidence Rule and the addition of Sections 1552 (computer printouts) and 1553 (printouts of images stored on video or digital media) to this article. *See Comments* to Section 1521 and former Sections 1500.5 and 1500.6.

§1550. [BUSINESS RECORD]

Editor's note: *This version of §1550 became effective on August 8, 2012, when the Secretary of State adopted chapter 15 of title 2 of the California Code of Regulations. Chapter 15 adopts uniform statewide standards for storing and recording permanent and nonpermanent media as required by Government Code §12168.7.*

(a) [Types of copies.] If made and preserved as a part of the records of a business, as defined in Section 1270, in the regular course of that business, the following types of evidence of a writing are as admissible as the writing itself:

(1) A nonerasable optical image reproduction or any other reproduction of a public record by a trusted system, as defined in Section 12168.7 of the Government Code, if additions, deletions, or changes to the original document are not permitted by the technology.

(2) A photostatic copy or reproduction.

(3) A microfilm, microcard, or miniature photographic copy, reprint, or enlargement.

(4) Any other photographic copy or reproduction, or an enlargement thereof.

(b) [Original admissible.] The introduction of evidence of a writing pursuant to subdivision (a) does not preclude admission of the original writing if it is still in existence. A court may require the introduction of a hard copy printout of the document.

History of Evid. C. §1550: Added eff. Sept. 17, 1965, oper. Jan. 1, 1967, Stats. 1965, ch. 299, §2. Amended eff. Jan. 1, 1993, Stats. 1992, ch. 876, §10; eff. Jan. 1, 2003, Stats. 2002, ch. 124, §1.

See also Cal. Code Regs., tit. 2, div. 7, ch. 15.

Official Comment

7 Cal. Law Revision Comm'n Rep. (1965) p. 1284.

Section 1550 continues in effect those provisions of the Uniform Photographic Copies of Business and Public Records as Evidence Act that are now found in Code of Civil Procedure Section 1953i. [**Editor's note:** CCP §1953i was repealed in 1965.]

Section 1550 omits the requirement, contained in [repealed] Section 1953i of the Code of Civil Procedure, that the original writing be a business record. As long as the original writing is admissible under any exception to the hearsay rule, its trustworthiness is sufficiently assured; and the requirement that the photographic copy be made in the regular course of business sufficiently assures the trustworthiness of the copy. If the original is admissible not as an exception to the hearsay rule but as evidence of an ultimate fact in the case (*e.g.*, a will or a contract), a photographic copy, the trustworthiness of which is sufficiently assured by the fact that it was made in the regular course of business, should be as admissible as the original.

§1550.1. [REPRODUCTION BY CRIMINAL-JUSTICE AGENCY]

Reproductions of files, records, writings, photographs, fingerprints or other instruments in the official custody of a criminal justice agency that were microphotographed or otherwise reproduced in a manner that conforms with the provisions of Section 11106.1, 11106.2, or 11106.3 of the Penal Code shall be admissible to the same extent and under the same circumstances as the original file, record, writing or other instrument would be admissible.

History of Evid. C. §1550.1: Added eff. Jan. 1, 2005, Stats. 2004, ch. 65, §1.

§1551. [DESTROYED OR LOST ORIGINAL]

A print, whether enlarged or not, from a photographic film (including a photographic plate, microphotographic film, photostatic negative, or similar reproduction) of an original writing destroyed or lost after such film was taken or a reproduction from an electronic recording of video images on magnetic surfaces is admissible as the original writing itself if, at the time of the taking of such film or electronic recording, the person under whose direction and control it was taken attached thereto, or to the sealed container in which it was placed and has been kept, or incorporated in the film or electronic recording, a certification complying with the provisions of Section 1531 and stating the date on which, and the fact that, it was so taken under his direction and control.

History of Evid. C. §1551: Added eff. Sept. 17, 1965, oper. Jan. 1, 1967, Stats. 1965, ch. 299, §2. Amended eff. Nov. 10, 1969, Stats. 1969, ch. 646, §1.

Official Comment

7 Cal. Law Revision Comm'n Rep. (1965) p. 1285.

Section 1551 restates without substantive change the provisions of Code of Civil Procedure Section 1920b.

§1552. [COMPUTER INFORMATION OR COMPUTER PROGRAM]

(a) [Presumption.] A printed representation of computer information or a computer program is presumed to be an accurate representation of the computer information or computer program that it purports to represent. This presumption is a presumption affecting the burden of producing evidence. If a party to an action introduces evidence that a printed representation of computer information or computer program is inaccurate or unreliable, the party introducing the printed representation into evidence has the burden of proving, by a preponderance of evidence, that the printed representation is an accurate representation of the existence and content of the computer information or computer program that it purports to represent.

(b) [Information stored by automated traffic-enforcement system.] Subdivision (a) applies to the printed representation of computer-generated information stored by an automated traffic enforcement system.

(c) [Official records.] Subdivision (a) shall not apply to computer-generated official records certified in accordance with Section 452.5 or 1530.

History of Evid. C. §1552: Added eff. Jan. 1, 1999, Stats. 1998, ch. 100, §4. Amended eff. Jan. 1, 2013, Stats. 2012, ch. 735, §1.

Official Comment

26 Cal. Law Revision Comm'n Rep. (1996) p. 397.

Subdivision (a) of Section 1552 continues former Section 1500.5(c) without substantive change, except that the reference to "best available evidence" is changed to "an accurate representation," due to the replacement of the Best Evidence Rule with the Secondary Evidence Rule. *See* Section 1521 *Comment. See also* Section 255 (accurate printout of computer data is an "original").

Subdivision (b) continues former Section 1500.5(d) without substantive change.

ANNOTATIONS

People v. Hawkins (6th Dist.2002) 98 Cal.App.4th 1428, 1450. The presumption in §1552 "operates to establish only that a computer's print function has worked properly. The presumption does not operate to establish the accuracy or reliability of the printed information. On that threshold issue, upon objection the proponent of the evidence must offer foundational evidence that the computer was operating properly."

Aguimatang v. California State Lottery (3d Dist.1991) 234 Cal.App.3d 769, 797. "Computer printouts are admissible and are presumed to be an accurate representation of the data in the computer. If offered for the truth, however, they must qualify under some hearsay exception, such as business records under

§1552

[Evid. C.] §1271. A trial court has wide discretion in determining whether sufficient evidence is adduced to qualify evidence as a business record."

§1553. [IMAGES ON VIDEO OR DIGITAL MEDIUM]

(a) [Presumption.] A printed representation of images stored on a video or digital medium is presumed to be an accurate representation of the images it purports to represent. This presumption is a presumption affecting the burden of producing evidence. If a party to an action introduces evidence that a printed representation of images stored on a video or digital medium is inaccurate or unreliable, the party introducing the printed representation into evidence has the burden of proving, by a preponderance of evidence, that the printed representation is an accurate representation of the existence and content of the images that it purports to represent.

(b) [Images stored by automated traffic-enforcement system.] Subdivision (a) applies to the printed representation of video or photographic images stored by an automated traffic enforcement system.

History of Evid. C. §1553: Added eff. Jan. 1, 1999, Stats. 1998, ch. 100, §5. Amended eff. Jan. 1, 2013, Stats. 2012, ch. 735, §2.

Official Comment

26 Cal. Law Revision Comm'n Rep. (1996) p. 397.

Section 1553 continues the last three sentences of the second paragraph of former Section 1500.6 without substantive change, except that the reference to "best available evidence" is changed to "an accurate representation," due to the replacement of the Best Evidence Rule with the Secondary Evidence Rule. *See* Section 1521 *Comment.*

ANNOTATIONS

People v. Chism (2014) 58 Cal.4th 1266, 1303. "'No photograph or film has any value in the absence of a proper foundation. It is necessary to know when it was taken and that it is accurate and truly represents what it purports to show. It becomes probative only upon the assumption that it is relevant and accurate.' The general rule is that a photograph is admissible upon a showing that it accurately depicts what it purportedly shows. 'This is usually shown by the testimony of the one who took the picture. However, this is not necessary and it is well settled that the showing may be made by the testimony of anyone who knows that the picture correctly depicts what it purports to represent.' [¶] [S]ection 1553, subdivision (a), establishes a rebuttable presumption that '[a] printed representation of images stored on a video or digital medium is presumed to be an accurate representation of the images it purports to represent.' The presumption affects the burden of proof and is rebutted by a showing that the 'printed representation of images stored on [the] video or digital medium is inaccurate or unreliable.' The burden then shifts to the proponent of the printed representation to prove by a preponderance of the evidence that it accurately represents the existence and content of the images on the video or digital medium. If the proponent of the evidence fails to carry his burden of showing the printed representation accurately depicts what it purportedly shows, the evidence is inadmissible for lack of adequate foundation. *At 1304:* Once properly authenticated and admitted into evidence, a photograph may be used as demonstrative evidence to support a witness's testimony or as probative evidence of what is shown. [¶] Here, the still photographs were properly authenticated and admitted into evidence. [Police officer] viewed the videotape police retrieved from the VCR at the crime scene and testified it accurately depicted [police actions] inside the store immediately after the shooting. Thus, the videotape was shown to be an accurate representation of what it purported to be, a recording of the events that occurred inside [the store] at or near the time of the shooting."

Article 4. Production of Business Records

§1560. [SUBPOENA DUCES TECUM FOR BUSINESS RECORDS]

(a) [Definitions.] As used in this article:

(1) "Business" includes every kind of business described in Section 1270.

(2) "Record" includes every kind of record maintained by a business.

(b) [Service of subpoena.] Except as provided in Section 1564, when a subpoena duces tecum is served upon the custodian of records or other qualified witness of a business in an action in which the business is neither a party nor the place where any cause of action is alleged to have arisen, and the subpoena requires the production of all or any part of the records of the business, it is sufficient compliance therewith if the custodian or other qualified witness delivers by mail or otherwise a true, legible, and durable copy of all of the records described in the subpoena to the clerk of the court or to another person described in subdivision (d) of Section 2026.010 of the Code of Civil Procedure, together with the affidavit described in Section 1561, within one of the following time periods:

§1552

(1) In any criminal action, five days after the receipt of the subpoena.

(2) In any civil action, within 15 days after the receipt of the subpoena.

(3) Within the time agreed upon by the party who served the subpoena and the custodian or other qualified witness.

(c) [Procedure for production.] The copy of the records shall be separately enclosed in an inner envelope or wrapper, sealed, with the title and number of the action, name of witness, and date of subpoena clearly inscribed thereon; the sealed envelope or wrapper shall then be enclosed in an outer envelope or wrapper, sealed, and directed as follows:

(1) If the subpoena directs attendance in court, to the clerk of the court.

(2) If the subpoena directs attendance at a deposition, to the officer before whom the deposition is to be taken, at the place designated in the subpoena for the taking of the deposition or at the officer's place of business.

(3) In other cases, to the officer, body, or tribunal conducting the hearing, at a like address.

(d) [Records sealed.] Unless the parties to the proceeding otherwise agree, or unless the sealed envelope or wrapper is returned to a witness who is to appear personally, the copy of the records shall remain sealed and shall be opened only at the time of trial, deposition, or other hearing, upon the direction of the judge, officer, body, or tribunal conducting the proceeding, in the presence of all parties who have appeared in person or by counsel at the trial, deposition, or hearing. Records that are original documents and that are not introduced in evidence or required as part of the record shall be returned to the person or entity from whom received. Records that are copies may be destroyed.

(e) [Alternative procedure.] As an alternative to the procedures described in subdivisions (b), (c), and (d), the subpoenaing party in a civil action may direct the witness to make the records available for inspection or copying by the party's attorney, the attorney's representative, or deposition officer as described in Section 2020.420 of the Code of Civil Procedure, at the witness' business address under reasonable conditions during normal business hours. Normal business hours, as used in this subdivision, means those hours that the business of the witness is normally open for business to the public. When provided with at least five business days' advance notice by the party's attorney, attorney's representative, or deposition officer, the witness shall designate a time period of not less than six continuous hours on a date certain for copying of records subject to the subpoena by the party's attorney, attorney's representative, or deposition officer. It shall be the responsibility of the attorney's representative to deliver any copy of the records as directed in the subpoena. Disobedience to the deposition subpoena issued pursuant to this subdivision is punishable as provided in Section 2020.240 of the Code of Civil Procedure.

History of Evid. C. §1560: Added eff. Sept. 17, 1965, oper. Jan. 1, 1967, Stats. 1965, ch. 299, §2. Amended eff. Nov. 10, 1969, Stats. 1969, ch. 199, §2; eff. Jan. 1, 1983, Stats. 1982, ch. 452, §2.5; eff. Jan. 1, 1985, Stats. 1984, ch. 481, §2; eff. Jan. 1, 1987, Stats. 1986, ch. 603, §6; eff. Jan. 1, 1992, Stats. 1991, ch. 1090, §14; eff. Jan. 1, 1998, Stats. 1997, ch. 442, §16; eff. Jan. 1, 2000, Stats. 1999, ch. 444, §4; eff. Jan. 1, 2001, Stats. 2000, ch. 287, §1; eff. Jan. 1, 2005, oper. July 1, 2005, Stats. 2004, ch. 182, §32; eff. Jan. 1, 2005, Stats. 2004, ch. 162, §1; eff. Jan. 1, 2006, Stats. 2005, ch. 294, §18; eff. Jan. 1, 2007, Stats. 2006, ch. 538, §155.

Official Comment

7 Cal. Law Revision Comm'n Rep. (1965) p. 1286.

Section 1560 is the same in substance as Code of Civil Procedure Section 1998, except for the clarifying definition of "hospital" added in subdivision (a).

2005-06 Ann. Report, 35 Cal. Law Revision Comm'n Rep. (2005) App. 5.

Section 1560 is amended to reflect nonsubstantive reorganization of the rules governing civil discovery. *See* 2004 Cal. Stat. ch. 182.

Section 1560 is also amended to delete language authorizing the judge to substitute for the clerk if there is no clerk. Every superior court has a clerk. *See* Gov't Code §§69840 (court clerk's powers, duties, and responsibilities), 71620 (court executive or administrative officer has authority of a court clerk). *See also* Code Civ. Proc. §167 (judge may perform any act court clerk may perform).

ANNOTATIONS

Urban Pac. Equities Corp. v. Superior Ct. (2d Dist.1997) 59 Cal.App.4th 688, 694 n.9. "'[B]usiness records' are things such as journals, account books, reports and the like, not the actual product or service the business sells or provides, for profit or otherwise."

§1561. [AFFIDAVIT ACCOMPANYING RECORDS]

(a) [Contents of affidavit.] The records shall be accompanied by the affidavit of the custodian or other qualified witness, stating in substance each of the following:

(1) The affiant is the duly authorized custodian of the records or other qualified witness and has authority to certify the records.

(2) The copy is a true copy of all the records described in the subpoena duces tecum, or pursuant to subdivision (e) of Section 1560 the records were delivered to the attorney, the attorney's representative, or deposition officer for copying at the custodian's or witness' place of business, as the case may be.

(3) The records were prepared by the personnel of the business in the ordinary course of business at or near the time of the act, condition, or event.

(4) The identity of the records.

(5) A description of the mode of preparation of the records.

(b) [Statement of inability to comply.] If the business has none of the records described, or only part thereof, the custodian or other qualified witness shall so state in the affidavit, and deliver the affidavit and those records that are available in one of the manners provided in Section 1560.

(c) [Affidavit by attorney.] Where the records described in the subpoena were delivered to the attorney or his or her representative or deposition officer for copying at the custodian's or witness' place of business, in addition to the affidavit required by subdivision (a), the records shall be accompanied by an affidavit by the attorney or his or her representative or deposition officer stating that the copy is a true copy of all the records delivered to the attorney or his or her representative or deposition officer for copying.

History of Evid. C. §1561: Added eff. Sept. 17, 1965, oper. Jan. 1, 1967, Stats. 1965, ch. 299, §2. Amended eff. Nov. 10, 1969, Stats. 1969, ch. 199, §3; eff. Jan. 1, 1987, Stats. 1986, ch. 603, §7; eff. May 12, 1987, Stats. 1987, ch. 19, §2; eff. Jan. 1, 1997, Stats. 1996, ch. 146, §1; eff. Jan. 1, 2000, Stats. 1999, ch. 444, §5.

Official Comment

7 Cal. Law Revision Comm'n Rep. (1965) p. 1287.

Section 1561 restates without substantive change the provisions of Code of Civil Procedure Section 1998.1.

ANNOTATIONS

Cooley v. Superior Ct. (2d Dist.2006) 140 Cal.App.4th 1039, 1044. "At first blush, it would seem that a person or entity that maintains records would also be the custodian of those records. Nevertheless, the custodian of records or other qualified witness contemplated by … §1561 must also be able to attest to various attributes of the records relevant to their authenticity and trustworthiness. As such, execution of a §1561 affidavit is more than simply a clerical task."

§1562. [ADMISSIBILITY OF RECORDS & AFFIDAVIT]

If the original records would be admissible in evidence if the custodian or other qualified witness had been present and testified to the matters stated in the affidavit, and if the requirements of Section 1271 have been met, the copy of the records is admissible in evidence. The affidavit is admissible as evidence of the matters stated therein pursuant to Section 1561 and the matters so stated are presumed true. When more than one person has knowledge of the facts, more than one affidavit may be made. The presumption established by this section is a presumption affecting the burden of producing evidence.

History of Evid. C. §1562: Added eff. Sept. 17, 1965, oper. Jan. 1, 1967, Stats. 1965, ch. 299, §2. Amended eff. Jan. 1, 1990, Stats. 1989, ch. 1416, §31; eff. Jan. 1, 1997, Stats. 1996, ch. 146, §2.

Official Comment

7 Cal. Law Revision Comm'n Rep. (1965) p. 1287; Assem. J., Apr. 6, 1965, p. 1764.

Section 1562 supersedes the provisions of Code of Civil Procedure Section 1998.2. Under Section 1998.2, the presumption provided in this section could be overcome only by a preponderance of the evidence. Section 1562, however, classifies the presumption as one affecting the burden of producing evidence only. *See* Evidence Code §§603 and 604 and the *Comments* thereto. Section 1562 makes it clear, too, that the presumption relates only to the truthfulness of the matters required by Section 1561 to be stated in the affidavit.

ANNOTATIONS

Taggart v. Super Seer Corp. (4th Dist.1995) 33 Cal.App.4th 1697, 1706. "'[I]n the face of a hearsay objection, the affidavit of the custodian, made pursuant to [Evid. C.] §1561, does not satisfy the requirements of the business-records exception to the hearsay rule set forth in [Evid. C.] §1271(c)-(d), and the copy of the business record, produced pursuant to [Evid. C.] §§1560-1561, is inadmissible hearsay.' [¶] Here, the custodian's declaration conformed meticulously to §1561. However, it contained no evidence as to what the [product testing] reports were, how they were prepared, or what sources of information they were based on. It offered no evidence that the [product testing] reports were trustworthy. The reports therefore failed to qualify for admission as business records under §1271. *At 1707:* [A] declaration in compliance with §§1560 and 1561 is insufficient to guarantee that the records produced will be admissible. The proponent also must comply with the additional requirements of §1271. *At 1708:* We are aware that this construction of §1560 et seq. lessens their usefulness as a low-cost way to obtain documentary evidence for use at trial. Nevertheless, our construction is compelled by the fact that the Legislature has expressly made admissibility under [Evid. C.] §1562 conditional on satisfying the business records exception of §1271. We conclude that the Legislature did so intentionally, to prevent the wholesale admission of hearsay lacking any guarantees of reliability or trustworthiness. A contrary construction would create a hole in the business records exception big enough to drive a truckload of hearsay through; the proponent

of a business record who could not show how it was prepared, or who knew that the way it was prepared would indicate that it was untrustworthy, could nevertheless introduce the record into evidence."

§1563. [FEE FOR WITNESS & MILEAGE]

(a) [One witness and mileage fee.] This article shall not be interpreted to require tender or payment of more than one witness fee and one mileage fee or other charge, to a witness or witness' business, unless there is an agreement to the contrary between the witness and the requesting party.

(b) [Nonparty production costs.] All reasonable costs incurred in a civil proceeding by any witness which is not a party with respect to the production of all or any part of business records the production of which is requested pursuant to a subpoena duces tecum may be charged against the party serving the subpoena duces tecum.

(1) "Reasonable cost," as used in this section, shall include, but not be limited to, the following specific costs: ten cents ($0.10) per page for standard reproduction of documents of a size 8½ by 14 inches or less; twenty cents ($0.20) per page for copying of documents from microfilm; actual costs for the reproduction of oversize documents or the reproduction of documents requiring special processing which are made in response to a subpoena; reasonable clerical costs incurred in locating and making the records available to be billed at the maximum rate of twenty-four dollars ($24) per hour per person, computed on the basis of six dollars ($6) per quarter hour or fraction thereof; actual postage charges; and the actual cost, if any, charged to the witness by a third person for the retrieval and return of records held offsite by that third person.

(2) The requesting party, or the requesting party's deposition officer, shall not be required to pay those costs or any estimate thereof prior to the time the records are available for delivery pursuant to the subpoena, but the witness may demand payment of costs pursuant to this section simultaneous with actual delivery of the subpoenaed records, and until payment is made, is under no obligation to deliver the records.

(3) The witness shall submit an itemized statement for the costs to the requesting party, or the requesting party's deposition officer, setting forth the reproduction and clerical costs incurred by the witness. Should the costs exceed those authorized in paragraph (1), or the witness refuses to produce an itemized statement of costs as required by paragraph (3), upon demand by the requesting party, or the requesting party's deposition officer, the witness shall furnish a statement setting forth the actions taken by the witness in justification of the costs.

(4) The requesting party may petition the court in which the action is pending to recover from the witness all or a part of the costs paid to the witness, or to reduce all or a part of the costs charged by the witness, pursuant to this subdivision, on the grounds that those costs were excessive. Upon the filing of the petition the court shall issue an order to show cause and from the time the order is served on the witness the court has jurisdiction over the witness. The court may hear testimony on the order to show cause and if it finds that the costs demanded and collected, or charged but not collected, exceed the amount authorized by this subdivision, it shall order the witness to remit to the requesting party, or reduce its charge to the requesting party by an amount equal to, the amount of the excess. In the event that the court finds the costs excessive and charged in bad faith by the witness, the court shall order the witness to remit the full amount of the costs demanded and collected, or excuse the requesting party from any payment of costs charged but not collected, and the court shall also order the witness to pay the requesting party the amount of the reasonable expenses incurred in obtaining the order including attorney's fees. If the court finds the costs were not excessive, the court shall order the requesting party to pay the witness the amount of the reasonable expenses incurred in defending the petition, including attorney's fees.

(5) If a subpoena is served to compel the production of business records and is subsequently withdrawn, or is quashed, modified or limited on a motion made other than by the witness, the witness shall be entitled to reimbursement pursuant to paragraph (1) for all costs incurred in compliance with the subpoena to the time that the requesting party has notified the witness that the subpoena has been withdrawn or quashed, modified or limited. In the event the subpoena is withdrawn or quashed, if those costs are not paid within 30 days after demand therefor, the witness may file a motion in the court in which the action is pending for an order requiring payment, and the court shall award the payment of expenses and attorney's fees in the manner set forth in paragraph (4).

(6) Where the records are delivered to the attorney, the attorney's representative, or the deposition officer for inspection or photocopying at the witness' place of business, the only fee for complying with the subpoena shall not exceed fifteen dollars ($15), plus the actual cost, if any, charged to the witness by a third person for retrieval and return of records held offsite by that third person. If the records are retrieved from microfilm, the reasonable cost, as defined in paragraph (1), shall also apply.

(c) [**Witness fee for custodian's appearance.**] When the personal attendance of the custodian of a record or other qualified witness is required pursuant to Section 1564, in a civil proceeding, he or she shall be entitled to the same witness fees and mileage permitted in a case where the subpoena requires the witness to attend and testify before a court in which the action or proceeding is pending and to any additional costs incurred as provided by subdivision (b).

History of Evid. C. §1563: Added eff. Sept. 17, 1965, oper. Jan. 1, 1967, Stats. 1965, ch. 299, §2. Amended eff. Mar. 7, 1973, Stats. 1972, ch. 396, §1; eff. Jan. 1, 1982, Stats. 1981, ch. 1014, §2; eff. Jan. 1, 1983, Stats. 1982, ch. 452, §3; eff. Jan. 1, 1987, Stats. 1986, ch. 603, §8; eff. May 12, 1987, Stats. 1987, ch. 19, §3; eff. Jan. 1, 1998, Stats. 1997, ch. 442, §17; eff. Jan. 1, 2000, Stats. 1999, ch. 444, §6.

Official Comment

7 Cal. Law Revision Comm'n Rep. (1965) p. 1287.

Section 1563 restates without substantive change the provisions of Code of Civil Procedure Section 1998.3.

§1564. [PERSONAL ATTENDANCE OF CUSTODIAN]

The personal attendance of the custodian or other qualified witness and the production of the original records is not required unless, at the discretion of the requesting party, the subpoena duces tecum contains a clause which reads: "The personal attendance of the custodian or other qualified witness and the production of the original records are required by this subpoena. The procedure authorized pursuant to subdivision (b) of Section 1560, and Sections 1561 and 1562, of the Evidence Code will not be deemed sufficient compliance with this subpoena."

History of Evid. C. §1564: Added eff. Sept. 17, 1965, oper. Jan. 1, 1967, Stats. 1965, ch. 299, §2. Amended eff. Jan. 1, 1985, Stats. 1984, ch. 603, §2; eff. Jan. 1, 1987, Stats. 1986, ch. 603, §9; eff. May 12, 1987, Stats. 1987, ch. 19, §4.

Official Comment

7 Cal. Law Revision Comm'n Rep. (1965) p. 1288.

Section 1564 restates without substantive change the provisions of Code of Civil Procedure Section 1998.4.

§1565. [MORE THAN ONE SUBPOENA DUCES TECUM SERVED]

If more than one subpoena duces tecum is served upon the custodian of records or other qualified witness and the personal attendance of the custodian or other qualified witness is required pursuant to Section 1564, the witness shall be deemed to be the witness of the party serving the first such subpoena duces tecum.

History of Evid. C. §1565: Added eff. Sept. 17, 1965, oper. Jan. 1, 1967, Stats. 1965, ch. 299, §2. Amended eff. Nov. 10, 1969, Stats. 1969, ch. 199, §4.

Official Comment

7 Cal. Law Revision Comm'n Rep. (1965) p. 1288.

Section 1565 restates without substantive change the provisions of Code of Civil Procedure Section 1998.5.

§1566. [OPERATION OF ARTICLE]

This article applies in any proceeding in which testimony can be compelled.

History of Evid. C. §1566: Added eff. Sept. 17, 1965, oper. Jan. 1, 1967, Stats. 1965, ch. 299, §2.

Official Comment

7 Cal. Law Revision Comm'n Rep. (1965) p. 1288.

This section has no counterpart in the portion of the Code of Civil Procedure from which this article is taken. Section 1566 is intended to preserve the original effect of Code of Civil Procedure Sections 1998-1998.5 by removing Sections 1560-1565 from the limiting provisions of Section 300.

§1567. [INCOME & BENEFIT INFORMATION FORM]

A completed form described in Section 3664 of the Family Code for income and benefit information provided by the employer may be admissible in a proceeding for modification or termination of an order for child, family, or spousal support if both of the following requirements are met:

(a) The completed form complies with Sections 1561 and 1562.

(b) A copy of the completed form and notice was served on the employee named therein pursuant to Section 3664 of the Family Code.

History of Evid. C. §1567: Added eff. Jan. 1, 1996, Stats. 1995, ch. 506, §1.

CHAPTER 3. OFFICIAL WRITINGS AFFECTING PROPERTY

§1600. [OFFICIAL WRITINGS AFFECTING PROPERTY]

(a) [**Prima facie evidence.**] The record of an instrument or other document purporting to establish or affect an interest in property is prima facie evidence of the existence and content of the original recorded document and its execution and delivery by each person by whom it purports to have been executed if:

(1) The record is in fact a record of an office of a public entity; and

(2) A statute authorized such a document to be recorded in that office.

(b) [**Presumption.**] The presumption established by this section is a presumption affecting the burden of proof.

History of Evid. C. §1600: Added eff. Sept. 17, 1965, oper. Jan. 1, 1967, Stats. 1965, ch. 299, §2. Amended eff. Nov. 8, 1967, Stats. 1967, ch. 650, §9.

Official Comment

7 Cal. Law Revision Comm'n Rep. (1965) p. 1288.

The sections in this chapter all relate to official writings affecting property. The provisions of some sections provide hearsay exceptions; other sections provide exceptions to the best evidence rule; still others provide authentication procedures.

Section 1600 is based on Code of Civil Procedure Section 1951, which it supersedes. It is similar to Section 1532 of the Evidence Code, which applies to all recorded writings, but it gives an added effect to the writings covered by its provisions. Under Section 1600, as under existing law, if an instrument purporting to affect an interest in property is recorded, a presumption of execution and delivery of the instrument arises. *Thomas v. Peterson*, 213 Cal. 672, 3 P.2d 306 (1931).

8 Cal. Law Revision Comm'n Rep. (1967) p. 124.

One effect of making the official record "prima facie evidence" is to create a rebuttable presumption. *See* Evidence Code §602 ("A statute providing that a fact or group of facts is prima facie evidence of another fact establishes a rebuttable presumption."). The classification of this presumption as one affecting the burden of proof is consistent with the prior case law. *See Thomas v. Peterson*, 213 Cal. 672, 3 P.2d 306 (1931); *Dubois v. Larke*, 175 Cal.App.2d 737, 346 P.2d 830 (1959); *Osterberg v. Osterberg*, 68 Cal.App.2d 254, 156 P.2d 46 (1945). Such a classification tends to support the record title to property by requiring that the record title be sustained unless the party attacking it can actually prove its invalidity. *See* Evidence Code §606 and *Comment* thereto.

The word "official," which modified "record," has been deleted as unnecessary in light of the requirements of paragraphs (1) and (2) of subdivision (a).

§1601. [LOST OR DESTROYED WRITING]

(a) [Proving contents.] Subject to subdivisions (b) and (c), when in any action it is desired to prove the contents of the official record of any writing lost or destroyed by conflagration or other public calamity, after proof of such loss or destruction, the following may, without further proof, be admitted in evidence to prove the contents of such record:

(1) Any abstract of title made and issued and certified as correct prior to such loss or destruction, and purporting to have been prepared and made in the ordinary course of business by any person engaged in the business of preparing and making abstracts of title prior to such loss or destruction; or

(2) Any abstract of title, or of any instrument affecting title, made, issued, and certified as correct by any person engaged in the business of insuring titles or issuing abstracts of title to real estate, whether the same was made, issued, or certified before or after such loss or destruction and whether the same was made from the original records or from abstract and notes, or either, taken from such records in the preparation and upkeeping of its plant in the ordinary course of its business.

(b) [Proof of loss not required.] No proof of the loss of the original writing is required other than the fact that the original is not known to the party desiring to prove its contents to be in existence.

(c) [Notice.] Any party desiring to use evidence admissible under this section shall give reasonable notice in writing to all other parties to the action who have appeared therein, of his intention to use such evidence at the trial of the action, and shall give all such other parties a reasonable opportunity to inspect the evidence, and also the abstracts, memoranda, or notes from which it was compiled, and to take copies thereof.

History of Evid. C. §1601: Added eff. Sept. 17, 1965, oper. Jan. 1, 1967, Stats. 1965, ch. 299, §2.

Official Comment

7 Cal. Law Revision Comm'n Rep. (1965) p. 1289.

Section 1601 restates without substantive change the provisions of Section 1855a of the Code of Civil Procedure.

§1602. REPEALED

Repealed by Stats. 1967, ch. 650, §10.

§1603. [DEED EXECUTED BY PROPER OFFICER]

A deed of conveyance of real property, purporting to have been executed by a proper officer in pursuance of legal process of any of the courts of record of this state, acknowledged and recorded in the office of the recorder of the county wherein the real property therein described is situated, or the record of such deed, or a certified copy of such record, is prima facie evidence that the property or interest therein described was thereby conveyed to the grantee named in such deed. The presumption established by this section is a presumption affecting the burden of proof.

History of Evid. C. §1603: Added eff. Sept. 17, 1965, oper. Jan. 1, 1967, Stats. 1965, ch. 299, §2. Amended eff. Nov. 8, 1967, Stats. 1967, ch. 650, §11.

Official Comment

7 Cal. Law Revision Comm'n Rep. (1965) p. 1290.

Section 1603 restates without substantive change the provisions of Section 1928 of the Code of Civil Procedure.

8 Cal. Law Revision Comm'n Rep. (1967) p. 125.

One effect of Section 1603 is to create a rebuttable presumption. *See* Evidence Code §602 ("A statute providing that a fact or group of facts is prima facie evidence of another fact establishes a rebuttable presumption.").

Prior to the enactment in 1911 of Code of Civil Procedure Section 1928 (upon which Section 1603 of the Evidence Code is based), the recitals in a sheriff's deed, made pursuant to legal process, could not be used as evidence of the judgment, the execution, and the sale upon which the deed was based. The existence of the prior proceedings was required to be proved with independent evidence. *Heyman v. Babcock*, 30 Cal. 367, 370 (1866); *Hihn v. Peck*, 30 Cal. 280, 287-288 (1866). The enactment of the predecessor of Evidence Code Section 1603 had two effects. First, it obviated the need for such independent proof. *See, e.g., Oakes v. Fernandez*, 108 Cal.App.2d 168, 238 P.2d 641 (1951); *Wagnor v. Blume*, 71 Cal.App.2d 94, 161 P.2d 1001 (1945). *See also* Basye, *Clearing Land Titles* §41 (1953). Second, it obviated the need for proof of a chain of title prior to the execution of the deed. *Krug v. Warden*, 57 Cal.App. 563, 207 Pac. 696 (1922).

The classification of the presumption in Section 1603 as a presumption affecting the burden of proof is consistent with the classification of the similar

and overlapping presumptions contained in Evidence Code Sections 664 (official duty regularly performed) and 1600 (official record of document affecting property). Like the presumption in Section 1600, the presumption in Section 1603 serves the purpose of supporting the record chain of title.

§1604. [CERTIFICATE OF PURCHASE OR CERTIFICATE OF LOCATION OF LAND]

A certificate of purchase, or of location, of any lands in this state, issued or made in pursuance of any law of the United States or of this state, is prima facie evidence that the holder or assignee of such certificate is the owner of the land described therein; but this evidence may be overcome by proof that, at the time of the location, or time of filing a preemption claim on which the certificate may have been issued, the land was in the adverse possession of the adverse party, or those under whom he claims, or that the adverse party is holding the land for mining purposes.

History of Evid. C. §1604: Added eff. Sept. 17, 1965, oper. Jan. 1, 1967, Stats. 1965, ch. 299, §2.

Official Comment

7 Cal. Law Revision Comm'n Rep. (1965) p. 1290.

Section 1604 restates without substantive change the provisions of Section 1925 of the Code of Civil Procedure.

§1605. [COPIES OF SPANISH TITLE PAPERS]

Duplicate copies and authenticated translations of original Spanish title papers relating to land claims in this state, derived from the Spanish or Mexican governments, prepared under the supervision of the Keeper of Archives, authenticated by the Surveyor-General or his successor and by the Keeper of Archives, and filed with a county recorder, in accordance with Chapter 281 of the Statutes of 1865-66, are admissible as evidence with like force and effect as the originals and without proving the execution of such originals.

History of Evid. C. §1605: Added eff. Sept. 17, 1965, oper. Jan. 1, 1967, Stats. 1965, ch. 299, §2. Amended eff. Nov. 8, 1967, Stats. 1967, ch. 650, §12.

Official Comment

7 Cal. Law Revision Comm'n Rep. (1965) p. 1291.

Section 1605 restates without substantive change the provisions of Section 1927.5 of the Code of Civil Procedure.

8 Cal. Law Revision Comm'n Rep. (1967) p. 126.

Chapter 281 of the Statutes of 1865-66 required the California Secretary of State to cause copies to be made of all the original Spanish title papers relating to land claims in this state derived from the Spanish and Mexican governments that were on file in the office of the United States Surveyor-General for California. These copies, authenticated by the Surveyor-General and the Keeper of Archives in his office, were then required to be recorded in the office of the county recorders of the concerned counties.

Section 5 of the 1865-66 statute, which is now codified as Section 1605 of the Evidence Code, provided that the recorded copies would be admissible "as prima facie evidence" without proving the execution of the originals. It is apparent that the original purpose of the section was to provide an exception to the best evidence rule—which would have required production of the original or an excuse for its nonproduction before the recorded copy could be admitted—and an exception to the rule, now expressed in Evidence Code Section 1401(b), requiring the authentication of the original document as a condition of the admissibility of the copy. Section 1605, therefore, has been revised to reflect this original purpose.

TABLE OF CONTENTS

1. DEFENDANT'S TIME TO ANSWER THE COMPLAINT

STEP	ACTION/FORM	DEADLINE [1]	DUE	DONE
1	P files complaint; *see* Forms PLD-C-001, PLD-PI-001	Date statute of limitations expires. CCP §§312-366.3.		
2	P serves D with complaint and summons; *see* Form SUM-100	60 days after Step 1. CRC 3.110(b).		
3	*Optional:* D obtains extension of time to answer or respond to complaint	30 days after Step 2. CRC 3.110(d), (e); *see* CCP §412.20(a)(3).		
4	*Optional:* P files and serves amended complaint	After Step 1.		
5A	*Optional:* D files preanswer motion	Original deadline: 30 days after Step 2. [2] CCP §§396b(a), 418.10(a), 430.40(a), 435(b)(1).		
		If deadline was extended by stipulation of parties: not more than 45 days after Step 2, unless court consents to later date. CRC 3.110(d). If deadline was extended by court: not more than 60 days after Step 2, unless P consents to later date. CCP §1054(a); *see id.* §473(a)(1); CRC 3.110(e).		
5B	Court rules on preanswer motion	After Step 5A.		
6	D files answer; *see* Forms PLD-C-010, PLD-PI-003	Original deadline: 30 days after Step 2. *See* CCP §412.20(a)(3).		
		If deadline was extended by stipulation of parties: not more than 45 days after Step 2, unless court consents to later date. CRC 3.110(d). If deadline was extended by court: not more than 60 days after Step 2, unless P consents to later date. CCP §1054(a); *see id.* §473(a)(1); CRC 3.110(e).		
		If P amended complaint: 30 days after Step 4. CCP §471.5(a).		
	<cont'd on next page>	If motion to quash service was denied: 15 days after service of ruling, or date set by court. CCP §418.10(b).		

[1] All deadlines for service in this chart assume the document was served by personal delivery. If served by mail or other means, the deadlines will differ. To calculate service deadlines for other types of service, see ***Commentaries***, "Add time for method of service," ch. 1-G, §6.1.4, p. 70.

[2] Some preanswer motions must be filed before or simultaneously with other preanswer motions to avoid waiver. Thus, if filing more than one preanswer motion, make sure the motions are filed not only on time but also in the correct sequence. See ***Commentaries***, "Preanswer motions & pleadings," ch. 4-A, §3.2, p. 330.

1. DEFENDANT'S TIME TO ANSWER THE COMPLAINT (CONT'D)

STEP	ACTION/FORM	DEADLINE ❶	DUE	DONE
6	***<cont'd from previous page>*** D files answer; *see* Forms PLD-C-010, PLD-PI-003	If motion to stay or dismiss for inconvenient forum was denied: 15 days after service of ruling, or date set by court. CCP §418.10(b).		
		If motion to dismiss for delay in prosecution was denied: 15 days after service of ruling, or date set by court. CCP §418.10(b).		
		If demurrer to complaint was denied: 10 days after service of ruling, or date set by court. CCP §§472a(b), 472b; CRC 3.1320(g), (j)(1). If demurrer to complaint was sustained in part without leave to amend: 10 days after service of ruling, or date set by court. CCP §§472a(c), 472b; CRC 3.1320(g), (j)(3). If demurrer to complaint was sustained in part with leave to amend, but P did not amend: 10 days after period to amend expires, or date set by court. CCP §472a(c); CRC 3.1320(g), (j)(2). If demurrer to complaint was sustained in whole with leave to amend, and P amended: 30 days after service of amended complaint, or date set by court. CCP §§471.5(a), 472a(c).		
	<cont'd on next page>	If motion to strike complaint was denied: date set by court. *See* CCP §472a(d). If motion to strike complaint was sustained in part with or without leave to amend: date set by court. CCP §472a(d). If motion to strike complaint was sustained in whole with leave to amend, and P amended: 30 days after service of amended complaint, or date set by court. CCP §§471.5(a), 472a(d).		

❶ All deadlines for service in this chart assume the document was served by personal delivery. If served by mail or other means, the deadlines will differ. To calculate service deadlines for other types of service, see ***Commentaries***, "Add time for method of service," ch. 1-G, §6.1.4, p. 70.

1. Defendant's Time to Answer the Complaint (cont'd)

STEP	ACTION/FORM	DEADLINE [1]	DUE	DONE
6	*<cont'd from previous page>* D files answer; *see* Forms PLD-C-010, PLD-PI-003	If motion to transfer venue was denied: 30 days after ruling, or date set by court. CRC 3.1326. If motion to transfer venue was granted: 30 days after new court mails notice of receipt of case and new case number. CRC 3.1326.		
		If petition to compel arbitration was denied: 15 days after ruling. CCP §1281.7.		

[1] All deadlines for service in this chart assume the document was served by personal delivery. If served by mail or other means, the deadlines will differ. To calculate service deadlines for other types of service, see ***Commentaries***, "Add time for method of service," ch. 1-G, §6.1.4, p. 70.

Legend:

CCP	California Code of Civil Procedure
CRC	California Rules of Court
D	Defendant
Form	Judicial Council Forms
P	Plaintiff

2. DEFENDANT'S DEMURRER TO THE COMPLAINT

STEP	ACTION/FORM	DEADLINE ❶	DUE	DONE
1	P files complaint; *see* Forms PLD-C-001, PLD-PI-001	Date statute of limitations expires. CCP §§312-366.3.		
2	P serves D with complaint and summons; *see* Form SUM-100	60 days after Step 1. CRC 3.110(b).		
3	D serves demurrer to complaint on P	Before Step 4. CCP §§430.40(a), 1005(b); *see* CRC 3.1320(c).		
4	D files notice of motion and proof of service with court	16 court days before Step 9, unless court permits shorter period before hearing, and Date answer is due. ❷ CCP §§430.30(c), 430.40(a), 1005(b); *see* CRC 3.1320(c).		
5	P files and serves motion to strike D's demurrer	9 court days before Step 9, unless court permits shorter period before hearing. CCP §§435(a)(2), (b)(1), (b)(3), 1005(b); CRC 3.1322(b).		
6	P files and serves opposition to demurrer	9 court days before Step 9, unless court permits shorter period before hearing. CCP §1005(b).		
7	D files and serves reply to P's opposition	5 court days before Step 9, unless court permits shorter period before hearing. CCP §1005(b).		
8	P files and serves amended complaint in response to demurrer	Before Step 9. CCP §§472, 473(a)(1).		
9	Court hears D's demurrer, P's opposition, and P's motion to strike	35 days after Step 4 or next available day thereafter, unless court permits later hearing. CCP §435(b)(3); CRC 3.1320(d), 3.1322(b).		
10	Court announces ruling	Promptly after Step 9. CCP §§472d, 1003.		
11	Clerk enters ruling in permanent minutes	Promptly after Step 10. *See* Gov. C. §69844.		
12A	If court requires written order, prevailing party prepares and serves proposed order on other parties	5 days after Step 10. CRC 3.1312(a).		
12B	Other parties serve objections to form of proposed order on prevailing party	5 days after Step 12A. CRC 3.1312(a).		

❶ All deadlines for service in this chart assume the document was served by personal delivery. If served by mail or other means, the deadlines will differ. To calculate service deadlines for other types of service, see ***Commentaries***, "Add time for method of service," ch. 1-G, §6.1.4, p. 70.

❷ The demurrer can be filed before or simultaneously with the answer. To determine when the answer is due, see Timetable 1, "Defendant's Time to Answer the Complaint," p. 1434.

2. DEFENDANT'S DEMURRER TO THE COMPLAINT (CONT'D)

STEP	ACTION/FORM	DEADLINE ❶	DUE	DONE
12C	Prevailing party forwards proposed order and other parties' responses to court	Promptly after Step 12B. CRC 3.1312(b).		
12D	Court signs written order	Promptly after Step 12C.		
13	Prevailing party serves notice of entry of order on all parties; *see* Form CIV-130	Immediately after Step 11, if written order was not required, or immediately after Step 12D, if written order was required. CCP §1019.5(a).		
14	Losing party files and serves motion to reconsider demurrer or motion to strike	10 days after Step 13. CCP §1008(a).		
15	If demurrer was overruled or motion to strike demurrer was sustained, D files and serves other responsive motions or answer to complaint (unless already filed)	10 days after Step 13, or date set by court. CCP §§472a(b), (c), 472b; CRC 3.1320(g), (j)(1).		
16A	If demurrer was sustained with leave to amend, P files and serves amended complaint	10 days after Step 13, or date set by court. CCP §§472a(c), 472b; CRC 3.1320(g).		
16B	If P amends complaint, D files and serves responsive motions or answer to amended complaint	30 days after Step 16A, or date set by court. CCP §§471.5, 472a(c).		
16C	If P does not amend complaint, D prepares and requests order of dismissal	Promptly after Step 16A deadline. CCP §581(f)(2); CRC 3.1320(h).		
17	If demurrer was sustained without leave to amend, D prepares and requests order of dismissal	Promptly after Step 11, if written order was not required, or promptly after Step 12D, if written order was required. CCP §581(f)(1).		
18	Court signs and files order of dismissal	After Step 16C or Step 17. CCP §581d.		
19	D serves notice of entry of dismissal on all parties; *see* Form CIV-130	Promptly after Step 18. CCP §664.5(a).		
20	D files original notice of entry of dismissal and proof of service by mail with court	At Step 19. CCP §664.5(a).		
21	P files MNT based on grounds in CCP §657	See Timetable 6, "Motion for New Trial," p. 1448.		

❶ All deadlines for service in this chart assume the document was served by personal delivery. If served by mail or other means, the deadlines will differ. To calculate service deadlines for other types of service, see ***Commentaries***, "Add time for method of service," ch. 1-G, §6.1.4, p. 70.

2. DEFENDANT'S DEMURRER TO THE COMPLAINT (CONT'D)

STEP	ACTION/FORM	DEADLINE ❶	DUE	DONE
22	P files motion to vacate order of dismissal for mistake, inadvertence, surprise, or excusable neglect	Reasonable time, but no later than 6 months after Step 18. CCP §473(b).		
23	Notice of appeal – see Timetable 7, "Notice of Appeal," p. 1450.			

❶ All deadlines for service in this chart assume the document was served by personal delivery. If served by mail or other means, the deadlines will differ. To calculate service deadlines for other types of service, see ***Commentaries***, "Add time for method of service," ch. 1-G, §6.1.4, p. 70.

Legend:

CCP	California Code of Civil Procedure
CRC	California Rules of Court
D	Defendant
Form	Judicial Council Forms
Gov. C.	California Government Code
MNT	Motion for new trial
P	Plaintiff

3. MOTION TO TRANSFER VENUE FROM IMPROPER COURT

STEP	ACTION/FORM	DEADLINE ❶	DUE	DONE
1	P files complaint; *see* Forms PLD-C-001, PLD-PI-001	Date statute of limitations expires. CCP §§312-366.3.		
2	P serves D with complaint and summons; *see* Form SUM-100	60 days after Step 1. CRC 3.110(b).		
3	D serves motion to transfer venue with request for expenses and attorney fees on P	Before Step 4. CCP §§396b(a), 1005(b); *see id.* §396b(b); CRC 3.1110(b).		
4	D files notice of motion and proof of service with court	16 court days before Step 7, unless court permits shorter period before hearing and Date answer is due. ❷ CCP §§396b(a), 1005(b); *see* CRC 3.1110(b).		
5	P files and serves opposition with request for expenses and attorney fees	9 court days before Step 7, unless court permits shorter period before hearing. CCP §1005(b); *see id.* §396b(d).		
6	D files and serves reply to P's opposition	5 court days before Step 7, unless court permits shorter period before hearing. CCP §1005(b).		
7	Court hears D's motion to transfer venue and P's opposition	At least 16 days after Step 4, unless court permits earlier hearing date. CCP §1005(b).		
8	Court announces ruling	Promptly after Step 7. *See* CCP §396b(a).		
9	Clerk enters ruling in permanent minutes	Promptly after Step 8. *See* Gov. C. §69844.		
10A	If court requires written order, prevailing party prepares and serves proposed order on other parties	5 days after Step 8. CRC 3.1312(a).		
10B	Other parties serve objections to form of proposed order on prevailing party	5 days after Step 10A. CRC 3.1312(a).		
10C	Prevailing party forwards proposed order and other parties' responses to court	Promptly after Step 10B. CRC 3.1312(b).		

❶ All deadlines for service in this chart assume the document was served by personal delivery. If served by mail or other means, the deadlines will differ. To calculate service deadlines for other types of service, see ***Commentaries***, "Add time for method of service," ch. 1-G, §6.1.4, p. 70.

❷ Although the motion can be filed simultaneously with the answer, the better practice is to file the motion before the answer. See ***Commentaries***, "File before or with responsive pleading," ch. 4-E, §3.4.2(5), p. 362. To determine when the answer is due, see Timetable 1, "Defendant's Time to Answer the Complaint," p. 1434.

3. MOTION TO TRANSFER VENUE FROM IMPROPER COURT (CONT'D)

STEP	ACTION/FORM	DEADLINE ❶	DUE	DONE
10D	Court signs written order	Promptly after Step 10C. *See* CCP §396b(a).		
11	Prevailing party serves notice of entry of order on all parties; *see* Form CIV-130	Immediately after Step 9, if written order was not required, or immediately after Step 10D, if written order was required. CCP §1019.5(a).		
		Motion to transfer venue denied		
12	D files other responsive motions or answer to complaint (unless already filed)	30 days after Step 9, if written order was not required, or 30 days after Step 10D, if written order was required. CRC 3.1326; *see* CCP §396b(e).		
		Motion to transfer venue granted		
12A	P pays transfer fee, uniform filing fee, and, if ordered, expenses and attorney fees	5 days after Step 11. CCP §399(a); Gov. C. §70618; *see* CCP §396b(b).		
12B	*Optional:* If P does not timely pay fees and expenses, any interested person may pay	30 days after Step 11. CCP §399(a); Gov. C. §70618; *see* CCP §396b(b).		
12C	If no one pays required fees and expenses, D files motion to dismiss	After Step 12B. CCP §399(a).		
12D	If fees and expenses are paid, clerk of original court transfers case and mails notice to parties	After Step 12A or 12B. CCP §399(b).		
13	Clerk of new court mails notice of receipt of case and new case number to parties	Promptly after Step 12D. CCP §399(b); CRC 3.1326.		
14	D files other responsive motions or answer to complaint (unless already filed)	30 days after Step 13. CRC 3.1326.		

❶ All deadlines for service in this chart assume the document was served by personal delivery. If served by mail or other means, the deadlines will differ. To calculate service deadlines for other types of service, see ***Commentaries***, "Add time for method of service," ch. 1-G, §6.1.4, p. 70.

Legend:

CCP	California Code of Civil Procedure
CRC	California Rules of Court
D	Defendant
Form	Judicial Council Forms
Gov. C.	California Government Code
P	Plaintiff

4. PLAINTIFF'S MOTION FOR NO-ANSWER DEFAULT JUDGMENT

STEP	ACTION/FORM	DEADLINE [1]	DUE	DONE
1	P files complaint; *see* Forms PLD-C-001, PLD-PI-001	Date statute of limitations expires. CCP §§312-366.3.		
2	P serves D with complaint and summons; *see* Form SUM-100	60 days after Step 1. CRC 3.110(b).		
3	D does not timely file answer or other responsive pleading	See "When Plaintiff Can Move for Default," chart 10-1, p. 1092.		
4	P files application with clerk for entry of default; *see* Form CIV-100	10 days after Step 3, unless court grants extension, and before D files late answer or responsive pleading. CCP §585(a)-(c); CRC 3.110(g).		
5	*Optional:* P files request to have attorney fees fixed by court	At Step 4. CCP §585(a).		
6	Clerk enters default	Promptly after Step 4 (generally entered on same day). CCP §585(a)-(c).		
7	*Optional:* P serves D with notice of entry of default; *see* Form CIV-130	After Step 6. *See* CCP §1010.		
8	D files motion to vacate entry of default	See "Methods for Attacking Default," chart 10-2, p. 1108.		
9	Court holds prove-up hearing (discretionary unless quiet-title action or nonresident served by publication)	After Step 6 and before Step 11. CCP §§585(a), (c), (d), 764.010; CRC 3.1800(a).		
10	P files application with clerk for entry of default-J by court or clerk	Before Step 11. [2] *See* CRC 3.110(h).		
11	Court or clerk signs default-J; *see* Form JUD-100	45 days after Step 6, unless court grants extension. CRC 3.110(h).		
12	Clerk enters default-J	45 days after Step 6, unless court grants extension. CCP §664; CRC 3.110(h).		
13	*Optional:* P serves D with notice of entry of default-J; *see* Form CIV-130	After Step 12. *See* CCP §1010.		
14	D files MNT based on grounds stated in CCP §657	See Timetable 6, "Motion for New Trial," p. 1448.		
15	D moves to vacate entry of default and default-J	See "Methods for Attacking Default," chart 10-2, p. 1108.		
16	Notice of appeal – see Timetable 7, "Notice of Appeal," p. 1450.			

[1] All deadlines for service in this chart assume the document was served by personal delivery. If served by mail or other means, the deadlines will differ. To calculate service deadlines for other types of service, see ***Commentaries***, "Add time for method of service," ch. 1-G, §6.1.4, p. 70.

[2] The application for entry of default judgment can be filed simultaneously with the application for entry of default. See ***Commentaries***, "Earliest date to file," ch. 10-A, §7.1.2(1), p. 1100.

4. PLAINTIFF'S MOTION FOR NO-ANSWER DEFAULT JUDGMENT (CONT'D)

Legend:

CCP	California Code of Civil Procedure
CRC	California Rules of Court
D	Defendant
Default-J	Default judgment
Form	Judicial Council Forms
MNT	Motion for new trial
P	Plaintiff

5. Motion & Cross-Motion for Summary Judgment or Summary Adjudication

STEP	ACTION/FORM	DEADLINE ❶	DUE	DONE
1	P files complaint; *see* Forms PLD-C-001, PLD-PI-001	Date statute of limitations expires. CCP §§312-366.3.		
2	P serves D with complaint and summons; *see* Form SUM-100	60 days after Step 1. CRC 3.110(b).		
3	D files answer; *see* Forms PLD-C-010, PLD-PI-003	See Timetable 1, "Defendant's Time to Answer the Complaint," p. 1434.		
4	M-party files and serves notice of MSJ-MSA and supporting papers ❷	If D files, at least 61 days after Step 1, unless good cause, and at least 75 days before Step 14. If P files, at least 61 days after D's general appearance, unless good cause, and at least 75 days before Step 14. ❸ CCP §437c(a).		
5	*Optional:* O-party files and serves motion to amend pleadings in response to MSJ-MSA	As soon as possible after Step 4. *See* CCP §473(a)(1); CRC 3.1324.		
6	*Optional:* O-party files and serves motion to continue MSJ-MSA hearing for additional discovery or other good cause	14 days before Step 14, unless good cause. *See* CCP §437c(b)(2), (h).		
7	O-party files and serves opposition to MSJ-MSA and objections (with proposed order) to evidence supporting MSJ-MSA ❹	14 days before Step 14 (Step 15 if hearing continued), unless good cause. CCP §437c(b)(2); CRC 3.1354(a), (c).		
8	O-party files and serves notice of XMSJ-XMSA and supporting papers ❷	If P files, at least 61 days after D's general appearance, unless good cause, and at least 75 days before Step 14 (Step 15 if hearing continued). If D files, at least 75 days before Step 14 (Step 15 if hearing continued). ❸ *Cf.* CCP §437c(a).		
9	*Optional:* M-party files and serves motion to amend pleadings in response to XMSJ-XMSA	As soon as possible after Step 8. *Cf.* CCP §473(a)(1); CRC 3.1324.		

❶ All deadlines for service in this chart assume the document was served by personal delivery. If served by mail or other means, the deadlines will differ. To calculate service deadlines for other types of service, see ***Commentaries***, "Add time for method of service," ch. 1-G, §6.1.4, p. 70; "Deadline to Serve MSJ," chart 10-3, p. 1122.

❷ An MSJ should include, as an alternative, an MSA. See ***Commentaries***, "Summary Judgment or Summary Adjudication," ch. 10-B, §3, p. 1119.

❸ The court has no authority to shorten the 75-days-before-the-hearing requirement. See ***Commentaries***, "Exception," ch. 10-B, §6.2.2(2), p. 1122.

❹ Objections to MSJ-MSA evidence can be made orally at the MSJ-MSA hearing if arrangements are made for a court reporter to be present. CRC 3.1352(2). See ***Commentaries***, "Objecting orally at hearing," ch. 10-B, §10.2.2, p. 1135.

5. MOTION & CROSS-MOTION FOR SUMMARY JUDGMENT OR SUMMARY ADJUDICATION (CONT'D)

STEP	ACTION/FORM	DEADLINE ❶	DUE	DONE
10	*Optional:* M-party files and serves motion to continue XMSJ-XMSA hearing for additional discovery or other good cause	14 days before Step 14 (Step 15 if hearing already continued), unless good cause. *See* CCP §437c(b)(2), (h).		
11	M-party files and serves opposition to XMSJ-XMSA and objections (with proposed order) to evidence supporting XMSJ-XMSA ❹	14 days before Step 14 (Step 15 if hearing continued), unless good cause. *Cf.* CCP §437c(b)(2); CRC 3.1354(a), (c).		
12	M-party files and serves reply to O-party's opposition to MSJ-MSA and objections (with proposed order) to evidence supporting opposition to MSJ-MSA ❹	5 days before Step 14 (Step 15 if hearing continued), unless good cause. CCP §437c(b)(4); CRC 3.1354(a), (c).		
13	O-party files and serves reply to M-party's opposition to XMSJ-XMSA and objections (with proposed order) to evidence supporting opposition to XMSJ-XMSA ❹	5 days before Step 14 (Step 15 if hearing continued), unless good cause. *Cf.* CCP §437c(b)(4); CRC 3.1354(a), (c).		
14	Original date for hearing on MSJ-MSA	30 days before Step 27, or later for good cause. CCP §437c(a).		
15	Continued date for hearing on MSJ-MSA	30 days before Step 27, or later for good cause. *See* CCP §437c(a), (h).		
16	Court announces ruling	Promptly after Step 14 (Step 15 if hearing continued). CCP §437c(g).		
17	Clerk enters ruling in permanent minutes	Promptly after Step 16. *See* Gov. C. §69844.		
18A	If court requires written order, prevailing party prepares and serves proposed order on other parties	5 days after Step 16. CRC 3.1312(a).		
18B	Other parties serve objections to form of proposed order on prevailing party	5 days after Step 18A. CRC 3.1312(a).		
18C	Prevailing party forwards proposed order and other parties' responses to court	Promptly after Step 18B. CRC 3.1312(b).		
18D	Court signs order on MSJ-MSA	Promptly after Step 18C. *See* CCP §437c(g).		

❶ All deadlines for service in this chart assume the document was served by personal delivery. If served by mail or other means, the deadlines will differ. To calculate service deadlines for other types of service, see ***Commentaries***, "Add time for method of service," ch. 1-G, §6.1.4, p. 70; "Deadline to Serve MSJ," chart 10-3, p. 1122.

❹ Objections to MSJ-MSA evidence can be made orally at the MSJ-MSA hearing if arrangements are made for a court reporter to be present. CRC 3.1352(2). See ***Commentaries***, "Objecting orally at hearing," ch. 10-B, §10.2.2, p. 1135.

5. MOTION & CROSS-MOTION FOR SUMMARY JUDGMENT OR SUMMARY ADJUDICATION (CONT'D)

STEP	ACTION/FORM	DEADLINE ❶	DUE	DONE
19	Prevailing party serves notice of entry of order on all parties; *see* Form CIV-130	Immediately after Step 17, if written order was not required, or immediately after Step 18D, if written order was required. CCP §1019.5(a).		
20	Losing party files and serves motion to reconsider MSJ-MSA order on new or different facts or law	10 days after Step 19 and before Step 23. CCP §1008(a).		
21	Losing party files petition for writ of mandate from order denying MSJ/XMSJ or granting or denying MSA/XMSA	20 days after Step 19 + 10 additional days for good cause. CCP §437c(m)(1).		
22	If final judgment on order can be granted, prevailing party prepares and requests entry of final summary judgment	After Step 17, if written order was not required, or after Step 18D, if written order was required. *See* CCP §437c(k); *see also id.* §§578, 579.		
23	Court signs final summary judgment	After Step 22. *See* CCP §437c(k).		
24	Clerk enters final summary judgment	Immediately after Step 23. CCP §664.		
25	Prevailing party or clerk serves notice of entry of judgment on all parties; *see* Form CIV-130	Promptly after Step 24. CCP §664.5(a), (b), (d).		
26	If serving notice of entry, prevailing party files original notice of entry of judgment and proof of service by mail with court	At Step 25. CCP §664.5(a), (b), (d).		
27	Trial date	As set by court. CRC 3.729.		
28	Losing party files MNT based on grounds stated in CCP §657	See Timetable 6, "Motion for New Trial," p. 1448.		
29	Losing party files motion to vacate judgment for mistake, inadvertence, surprise, or excusable neglect ❺	Reasonable time, but no later than 6 months after Step 23. CCP §473(b).		
30	Notice of appeal – see Timetable 7, "Notice of Appeal," p. 1450.			

❶ All deadlines for service in this chart assume the document was served by personal delivery. If served by mail or other means, the deadlines will differ. To calculate service deadlines for other types of service, see ***Commentaries***, "Add time for method of service," ch. 1-G, §6.1.4, p. 70; "Deadline to Serve MSJ," chart 10-3, p. 1122.

❺ The mandatory provision of CCP §473, which applies to defaults and dismissals, may not apply to summary judgments. *See* ***English v. IKON Bus. Solutions, Inc.*** (3d Dist.2001) 94 Cal.App.4th 130, 133.

5. MOTION & CROSS-MOTION FOR SUMMARY JUDGMENT OR SUMMARY ADJUDICATION (CONT'D)

Legend:

CCP	California Code of Civil Procedure
CRC	California Rules of Court
D	Defendant
Form	Judicial Council Forms
Gov. C.	California Government Code
MNT	Motion for new trial
M-party	Moving party
MSA	Motion for summary adjudication
MSJ	Motion for summary judgment
MSJ-MSA	Motion for summary judgment and, in the alternative, motion for summary adjudication
O-party	Opposing party
P	Plaintiff
XMSJ-XMSA	Cross-motion for summary judgment and, in the alternative, cross-motion for summary adjudication

6. MOTION FOR NEW TRIAL

STEP	ACTION/FORM	DEADLINE ❶	DUE	DONE
1	Final judgment rendered	After all issues are resolved. *See* CCP §664.		
2	Clerk enters final judgment	If trial by court, immediately after Step 1. CCP §664. If jury trial, within 24 hours after verdict. CCP §664.		
3	Prevailing party or clerk serves notice of entry of judgment on other parties; *see* Form CIV-130	Promptly after Step 2. CCP §664.5(a), (b), (d).		
4	If serving notice of entry, prevailing party files original notice of entry of judgment and proof of service by mail with court	At Step 3. CCP §664.5(a).		
5	M-party files and serves notice of MNT	After Step 1 and before Step 2 or 15 days after Step 3 or 180 days after Step 2, whichever is earlier. ❷ CCP §659(a).		
6 ⓯	M-party files and serves memorandum and affidavits	10 days after Step 5, or 20 days after Step 5 by court order on stipulation or finding of good cause. CCP §659a; CRC 3.1600(a).		
7 ⓯	O-party files and serves memorandum and counteraffidavits	10 days after Step 6, or 20 days after Step 6 by court order on stipulation or finding of good cause. CCP §659a; CRC 3.1600(a).		
8	Clerk calls MNT to attention of trial court	Immediately after Step 7 deadline expires. CCP §661.		
9	Court sets date for hearing	After Step 8. CCP §661.		
10	Clerk sends parties notice of hearing by mail	5 days before Step 11. CCP §661.		
11	Court hears MNT	As soon as possible before Step 15 and, if MNT not heard by judge who presided at trial, 10 days before Step 15. ❸ CCP §§660 ¶2, 661.		

❶ All deadlines for service in this chart assume the document was served by personal delivery. If served by mail or other means, the deadlines will differ. To calculate service deadlines for other types of service, see ***Commentaries***, "Add time for method of service," ch. 1-G, §6.1.4, p. 70.

❷ The deadline for filing the notice of MNT may not be extended by court order, stipulation of the parties, or any provision of the CCP that extends deadlines because service is achieved by means other than personal delivery. CCP §§659(b), 1010.6(a)(4)(A), 1013(a), (c), (e).

❸ The decision to hear the MNT is solely within the court's discretion. If the court does not decide the MNT before the court's power expires, the MNT will be overruled by operation of law. CCP §660 ¶3.

6. MOTION FOR NEW TRIAL (CONT'D)

STEP	ACTION/FORM	DEADLINE ❶	DUE	DONE
12	Clerk enters order on MNT in permanent minutes or court prepares, signs, and files order on MNT	As soon as possible after Step 11 and before Step 15. CCP §660 ¶¶2, 3.		
13	Court signs and files statement of reasons for granting MNT if reasons not included in order	10 days after Step 12. CCP §657 ¶4.		
14	Prevailing party or clerk serves notice of entry of order on all parties; *see* Form CIV-130	Promptly after Step 12. CCP §§664.5(a), (b), (d), 1019.5(a).		
15	Court's power to decide MNT expires; MNT overruled by operation of law	60 days after Step 3 or, if notice of entry of judgment not given, 60 days after Step 5. CCP §660 ¶3. ❸		
16	Notice of appeal – see Timetable 7, "Notice of Appeal," p. 1450.			

❶ All deadlines for service in this chart assume the document was served by personal delivery. If served by mail or other means, the deadlines will differ. To calculate service deadlines for other types of service, see ***Commentaries***, "Add time for method of service," ch. 1-G, §6.1.4, p. 70.

❸ The decision to hear the MNT is solely within the court's discretion. If the court does not decide the MNT before the court's power expires, the MNT will be overruled by operation of law. CCP §660 ¶3.

Legend:

CCP	California Code of Civil Procedure
CRC	California Rules of Court
Form	Judicial Council Forms
MNT	Motion for new trial
M-party	Moving party
O-party	Opposing party

7. NOTICE OF APPEAL

STEP	ACTION/FORM	DEADLINE ❶	DUE	DONE
1	Clerk enters appealable order or judgment	After court's ruling or decision. *See* CCP §664; Gov. C. §69844; *see, e.g.*, CCP §§904.1, 904.2.		
2	Prevailing party or clerk serves notice of entry of order or judgment on all parties and files original notice and proof of service with court; *see* Form CIV-130	Promptly after Step 1. *See* CCP §§664.5(a), (b), (d), 1019.5.		
3A	*Optional:* M-party files and serves valid postjudgment motion	If filing motion for reconsideration of appealable order, Step 2 + 10 days. CCP §1008(a). If filing notice of intention for MNT, M-JNOV, or motion to vacate judgment, before Step 1 or the earlier of Step 2 + 15 days or Step 1 + 180 days. ❷ CCP §§629(b), 659(a), 663a(a).		
3B	Court overrules postjudgment motion	After Step 3A.		
4	Prevailing party or clerk serves notice of entry of order denying motion and files original notice and proof of service with court; *see* Form CIV-130	Promptly after Step 3B. *See* CCP §§664.5(a), (b), (d), 1019.5.		

❶ All deadlines for service in this chart assume the document was served by personal delivery. If served by mail or other means, the deadlines will differ. To calculate service deadlines for other types of service, see ***Commentaries***, "Add time for method of service," ch. 1-G, §6.1.4, p. 70.

❷ The deadline for filing a notice of a motion to vacate judgment or a notice of an MNT may not be extended by court order, stipulation of the parties, or any provision of the CCP that extends deadlines because service is achieved by means other than personal delivery. CCP §§659(b), 663a(c), 1010.6(a)(4)(A), (a)(4)(B), 1013(a), (c), (e).

7. NOTICE OF APPEAL (CONT'D)

STEP	ACTION/FORM	DEADLINE ❶	DUE	DONE
5	M-party files and serves notice of appeal	If no valid postjudgment motion was filed, earlier of Step 2 + 60 days or Step 1 + 180 days. CRC 8.104(a)(1). ❸		
		If motion for reconsideration was filed, earliest of Step 4 + 30 days, Step 3A + 90 days, or Step 1 + 180 days. CRC 8.108(e). ❸		
		If MNT was filed and notice of underlying judgment was given, earliest of Step 4 + 30 days, Step 2 + 90 days, or Step 1 + 180 days. If MNT was filed but notice of underlying judgment was not given, earliest of Step 4 + 30 days, Step 3A + 90 days, or Step 1 + 180 days. ❸ CCP §660 ¶3; CRC 8.108(b)(1).		
		If M-JNOV was filed and notice of underlying judgment was given, earliest of Step 4 + 30 days, Step 2 + 90 days, or Step 1 + 180 days. If M-JNOV was filed but notice of underlying judgment was not given, earliest of Step 4 + 30 days, Step 3A + 90 days, or Step 1 + 180 days. ❸ CCP §§629(b), 660 ¶3; CRC 8.108(d).		
		If motion to vacate judgment was filed, earliest of Step 4 + 30 days, Step 3A + 90 days, or Step 1 + 180 days. ❸ CRC 8.108(c).		
6	Clerk mails all parties notice of filing of appeal	Promptly after Step 5. CRC 8.100(e)(1).		
7	O-party files and serves notice of cross-appeal	Step 6 + 20 days. CRC 8.108(g)(1).		
8	Clerk mails all parties notice of filing of cross-appeal	Promptly after Step 7. CRC 8.100(e)(1), (f).		

❶ All deadlines for service in this chart assume the document was served by personal delivery. If served by mail or other means, the deadlines will differ. To calculate service deadlines for other types of service, see ***Commentaries***, "Add time for method of service," ch. 1-G, §6.1.4, p. 70.

❸ The deadline for filing the notice of an appeal may not be extended by any provision of the CCP that extends deadlines because service is achieved by means other than personal delivery. CCP §§1010.6(a)(4)(C), 1013(a), (c), (e).

7. NOTICE OF APPEAL (CONT'D)

Legend:

CCP	California Code of Civil Procedure
CRC	California Rules of Court
Form	Judicial Council Forms
Gov. C.	California Government Code
M-JNOV	Motion for judgment notwithstanding the verdict
MNT	Motion for new trial
M-party	Moving party
O-party	Opposing party

INDEX

INDEX

Page numbers in ***boldface italic***

INDEX

Page numbers in ***boldface italic***

Page numbers in ***boldface italic***

Page numbers in ***boldface italic***

Page numbers in ***boldface italic***

Page numbers in ***boldface italic***

Page numbers in ***boldface italic***

Page numbers in ***boldface italic***

Page numbers in ***boldface italic***

Page numbers in ***boldface italic***

Page numbers in ***boldface italic***

Page numbers in ***boldface italic***

Page numbers in ***boldface italic***

Page numbers in ***boldface italic***

Page numbers in ***boldface italic***

Page numbers in ***boldface italic***

Page numbers in ***boldface italic***

INDEX

Page numbers in ***boldface italic***

INDEX

Page numbers in ***boldface italic***

Page numbers in ***boldface italic***

INDEX

Page numbers in ***boldface italic***

Page numbers in ***boldface italic***

Page numbers in ***boldface italic***

Page numbers in ***boldface italic***

Page numbers in ***boldface italic***

Page numbers in ***boldface italic***

Page numbers in ***boldface italic***

Page numbers in ***boldface italic***

Page numbers in ***boldface italic***

Page numbers in ***boldface italic***

Page numbers in ***boldface italic***

Page numbers in ***boldface italic***

INDEX

Page numbers in ***boldface italic***

INDEX

Page numbers in ***boldface italic***

Page numbers in ***boldface italic***

Page numbers in ***boldface italic***

Page numbers in ***boldface italic***

Page numbers in ***boldface italic***

Page numbers in ***boldface italic***

Page numbers in ***boldface italic***

Page numbers in ***boldface italic***

Page numbers in ***boldface italic***

Page numbers in ***boldface italic***

Page numbers in ***boldface italic***

Page numbers in ***boldface italic***

Page numbers in ***boldface italic***

Page numbers in ***boldface italic***

Notes

Notes

Notes

Notes

NOTES

Notes

Notes

Notes

Notes

Notes

NOTES

Notes

Notes

Notes

Notes

Notes

Notes